P9-DWS-252

ATHLETICS
2019
THE INTERNATIONAL
TRACK AND FIELD ANNUAL

BY PETER MATTHEWS
ASSOCIATION OF
TRACK & FIELD STATISTICIANS

**SPORTS
BOOKS**

CALGARY PUBLIC LIBRARY

JUL - 2019

Published by SportsBooks Ltd

Copyright: SportsBooks Limited and Peter Matthews 2019

SportsBooks Limited
9 St Aubyns Place
York
YO24 1EQ
United Kingdom
Tel: 01904 613475
e-mail   randall@sportsbooks.ltd.uk
Website   www.sportsbooks.ltd.uk

All rights reserved. No part of this publication may be produced or transmitted in any form or by any means, including photocopying and recording, without written permission of the publishers. Such written permission must also be obtained before any part of the publication is stored in any retrieval system of any nature.

This publication incorporates the ATFS Annual.

Front page photograph supplied by Mark Shearman, 22 Grovelands Road, Purley, Surrey, CR8 4LA. Tel: 0208 660 0156: mark@athleticsimages.com

British Library Cataloguing in Publication Data

Athletics: the international track and
field annual – 2019
1. Athletics. Track & Field events –
Serials
1. International athletics annual (London)
796.4'2'05

ISBN 9781907524585
Cover design: Kath Grimshaw

Printed arranged by Jellyfish Solutions, UK

CONTENTS

INTRODUCTION

MAINTAINING A 68-year sequence of International Athletics Annuals, this book presents a wealth of data from 2018 (and early 2019). There is no substitute for real Championship action and there was plenty of this in the past year topped by that at the World U20 Championships, European Championships and Commonwealth Games and other continental events. In the one year in the 4-year cycle without an Olympic Games or World Championships at senior level, many of the world's best competed at spectacular events brought together in the Diamond League.

In the 35 years of my editorship of this Annual the ability to gather information around the world has been transformed. We have gone from mail through to fax and then email with a wealth of information now on the Internet, and can thus compile more comprehensive statistics than before. Yet the speedy access to results does not ensure complete accuracy for these can be wrong or even, in a few cases, fraudulent. Even in such a prestigious source as the IAAF rankings there are errors or information that is missing. In order to make lists, such as those we present in this Annual, as accurate as possible it is necessary to have careful examination by experts and it is all to easy for this to be missing in the desire to provide instant data. It is very sad to see that several established reference works are no longer being published. Last year Yves Pinaud, who has done such wonderful work over the years in gathering details of athletics performances from Africa, announced that his 2018 African Annual would be his last, and Hans van Kuijen is no longer producing his Combined Events Annual in book form. I also understand that the wondrously detailed French Annual will no longer be published after this year. As with the loss of other national annuals the accurate and comprehensive chronicling of athletics could to be in severe jeopardy in future

Related to the above the IAAF's re-introduction of World Rankings might seem welcome. But quite apart from doubts as to the completeness of their data, it is disturbing to hear that the IAAF intend to use these as a basis for qualifying for global championships. The rankings are best suited to those who are full-time professionals competing regularly in the Diamond League events etc. But such events are restricted to an elite and the ranking system is simply not fit for purpose for most up-and-coming athletes. Flaws are all too obvious, such as awarding the same number of points for national championships of the major nations as to those of the tiniest. The greatest concentration of senior athletics competition in the world is the collegiate system in the USA, yet performances leading vitally to the NCAA Championships can be undervalued in the Rankings. It is reasonably straightforward to have world ranking systems in sports such as Formula One motor racing, golf or tennis where competitions are contested on a regular basis by all the best in the world, but that is not the case in the very complex sport of athletics. Athletes can and will have varying goals and differing abilities to compete regularly depending on their event. I have long been involved in national and world merit rankings and know the complicated need to weigh up factors taking into account different priorities. While devising ranking systems can be fun I do not believe that, even though the IAAF system could be improved, it is possible to have a truly satisfactory scheme across the whole range of the sport.

The leaders of our governing bodies continue to seek ways to increase the profile of athletics and to stimulate interest from younger people. New initiatives may be welcome, but some, such as the wholly misguided regulations introduced for the Continental Cup in 2018, can be a huge mistake and damaging the sport. Change for sure, but not 'Change for Change's sake'. Many sports are following similar philosophies and are alienating their core enthusiasts. We must be careful that this does not happen in our sport. Recent announcements such as compressing Diamond League events into 90 minutes and reductions in various events are worrying as is the ridiculous idea that changing race walking distances from 20 and 50km to 10 and 30km will do anything at all to increase their popularity. As with other sports, athletics is about action and TV broadcasts in such nations as Britain and the USA that go away from action to 'stories' and banal chat by ex-athletes are surely counter-productive, demonstrating the incompetence of all-too-many TV directors and editors who seem to be unable to handle the multiplicity of events that feature in our top meetings. Above all leaders in our sport should appreciate that field events that can be followed over an hour or two are often much more interesting for spectators than races that are over in a matter of seconds.

Despite my concerns at various developments I remain, as I have been for the past 60 years, a huge fan and look forward with unfailing interest to the action that we will see unfolding around the world in the months and years to come.

Peter Matthews, March 2019

ABBREVIATIONS

The following abbreviations have been used for meetings with, in parentheses, the first year that they were held.

AAU	(USA) Amateur Athletic Union Championships (1888) (later TAC)
Af-AsG	Afro-Asian Games (2003)
AfCh	African Championships (1979)
AfG	African Games (1965)
Af-J	African Junior Championships (1994)
AmCp	America's Cup (World Cup Trial) (1977)
APM	Adriaan Paulen Memorial, Hengelo
AsiC	Asian Championships (1973)
AsiG	Asian Games (1951)
Asi-J	Asian Junior Championships (1990)
ASV	Weltklasse in Köln, ASV club meeting (1934)
Athl	Athletissima, Lausanne (1976)
Balk	Balkan Games (1929), C - Championships
Barr	(Cuba) Barrientos Memorial (1946)
BGP	Budapest Grand Prix (1978)
Bisl	Bislett Games, Oslo (1965) (Bergen 2004)
Bol G	Bolivar Games (1938)
BrGP	British Grand Prix
CAC	Central American and Caribbean Championships (1967)
CAG	Central American and Caribbean Games (1926)
C.Asian	Central Asian Championships
CAU	Inter-counties, GBR (1934)
CG	Commonwealth Games (1930)
C.Cup	Continental Cup (2010)
Déca	Décanation, Paris (C) (2005)
DL	Diamond League (2010)
DNG	DN Galan, Stockholm (1966)
Drake	Drake Relays (1910)
EAF	European Athletics Festival, Bydgoszcz (2001)
EAsG	East Asian Games (1993)
EC	European Championships (1934)
ECCp	European Clubs Cup (1975)
EChall	European Challenge (10,000m 1997, Throws 2001); see ET
ECp	European Cup - track & field (1965), multi-events (1973)
EI	European Indoor Championships (1970, Games 1966-9)
EICp	European Indoor Cup (2003)
EJ	European Junior Championships (1970)
ET	European Team Championships (replaced European Cup, 2009)
EY	European Under- 18 (Youth) Championships (2016)
EU23	European Under-23 Championships (1997) and European Under-23 Cup (1992-4)
FBK	Fanny Blankers-Koen Games, Hengelo (formerly APM) (1981)
FlaR	Florida Relays (1939)
FOT	(USA) Final Olympic Trials (1920)
Franc	Francophone Games (1989)
Gaz	Gaz de France meeting, FRA (was BNP) (1968)
GGala	Golden Gala, Roma (from 1980), Verona (1988), Pescara (1989), Bologna (1990)
GL	Golden League (1998-2009)
GNR	Great North Run – Newcastle to South Shields, GBR (1981)
GP	Grand Prix
GPF	IAAF Grand Prix Final (1985)
GS	Golden Spike, Ostrava (1969)
Gugl	Zipfer Gugl Grand Prix, Linz (1988)
GWG	Goodwill Games (1986)
Gyulai	István Gyulai Memorial, Budapest (2011-13), Székesfehérvár (2014-16)
Hanz	Hanzekovic Memorial, Zagreb (1958)
Herc	Herculis, Monte Carlo, Monaco (1987)
IAAF	International Association of Athletics Federations
IAC	IAC meeting (1968), formerly Coca-Cola
IAU	International Association of Ultrarunners
IbAm	Ibero-American Championships (1983)
Is.Sol	Islamic Solidarity Games (2005)
ISTAF	Internationales Stadionfest, Berlin (1921)
Jenner	Bruce Jenner Classic, San Jose (1979)
Jerome	Harry Jerome Track Classic (1984)
Jordan	Payton Jordan U.S. Track & Field Open, Stanford (2004)
JUCO	Junior Colleges Championships, USA
KansR	Kansas Relays, Lawrence (1923)
Kuso	Janusz Kusocinski Memorial (1954)
Kuts	Vladimir Kuts Memorial (1978)
LGP	London Grand Prix, Crystal Palace
LI	Loughborough International (1958)
MAI	Malmö AI Galan, Sweden (1958)
Mast	Masters pole vault, Grenoble (1987), Donetsk
MedG	Mediterranean Games (1951)
Mill	Millrose Games, New York indoors (1908)
ModR	Modesto Relays (1942)
MSR	Mt. San Antonio College Relays (1959)
NA	Night of Athletics, Heusden (2000) formerly Hechtel
NACAC	North American, Central American & Caribbean Ch (2003)
NC	National Championships
NC-w	National Winter Championships
NCAA	National Collegiate Athletic Association Championships, USA (1921)
NCAA-r	NCAA Regional Championships (2003)
NCp	National Cup
Nebiolo	Memorial Primo Nebiolo, Torino (2000, originally 1963)
NG	National Games
Nik	Nikaïa, Nice (1976)
NM	Narodna Mladezhe, Sofia (1955)
N.Sch	National Schools
Nurmi	Paavo Nurmi Games (1957)
NYG	New York Games (1989)
OD	Olympischer Tag (Olympic Day) (1963)
Oda	Mikio Oda Memorial Meeting, Hiroshima (1967)
Odlozil	Josef Odlozil Memorial, Prague (1994)
OG	Olympic Games (1896)
OT	Olympic Trials
Owens	Jesse Owens Memorial (1981)
PAm	Pan American Games (1951)
PArab	Pan Arab Championships (1977) (G-Games 1953)
Pedro	Pedro's Cup, Poland (2005)
PennR	Pennsylvania Relays (1895)
PTS	Pravda Televízia Slovnaft, Bratislava (1957) (later GPB)

Pre	Steve Prefontaine Memorial (1976)
RdVin	Route du Vin Half Marathon, Luxembourg (1962)
RomIC	Romanian International Championships (1948)
RWC	Race Walking Challenge Final (2007)
SACh	South American Championships (1919)
SAsG	South Asian Games (1984)
SEAG	South East Asia Games (1959)
SEC	Southeastern Conference Championships
SGP	IAAF Super Grand Prix
Skol	Skolimowska Memorial (2010)
Slovn	Slovnaft, Bratislava (formerly PTS) (1990)
Spark	Sparkassen Cup, Stuttgart (indoor) (1987)
Spart	(URS) Spartakiad (1956)
Spitzen	Spitzen Leichtathletik Luzern (1987)
Stra	Stramilano Half marathon, Milan (1972)
Super	Super Meet, Japan (Tokyo, Shizuoka, Yokohama, Kawasaki)
TexR	Texas Relays (1925)
Tsik	Athens Grand Prix Tsiklitiria (1998)
USOF	US Olympic Festival (1978)
VD	Ivo Van Damme Memorial, Brussels (1977)
Veniz	Venizélia, Haniá, Crete (1936)
WAC	Western Athletic Conference Championships (1962)
WAF	World Athletics Finals (2003)
WCh	World Championships (1983)
WCM	World Challenge Meeting (2010)
WCp	World Cup - track & field (1977), marathon (1985)
	Walking – Lugano Trophy – men (1961), Eschborn Cup – women (1979)
WCT	World Championships Trial
WG	World Games, Helsinki (1961)
WI	World Indoor Championships (1987), World Indoor Games (1985)
WJ	World Junior Championships (1986)
WK	Weltklasse, Zürich (1962)
WMilG	World Military Games
WTC	World Team Championships
WRly	World Relays (2014)
WUG	World University Games (1923)
WY	World Youth Championships (1999)
Zat	Emil Zátopek Classic, Melbourne
Znam	Znamenskiy Brothers Memorial (1958)

-j, -y, -23 Junior, Youth or under-23
Dual and triangular matches are indicated by "v" (versus) followed by the name(s) of the opposition. Quadrangular and larger inter-nation matches are denoted by the number of nations and -N; viz 8-N designates an 8-nation meeting.

Events

CC	cross-country
Dec	decathlon
DT	discus
h	hurdles
Hep	heptathlon
HJ	high jump
HMar	half marathon
HT	hammer
JT	javelin
LJ	long jump
Mar	marathon
Pen	pentathlon
PV	pole vault
R	relay
SP	shot
St	steeplechase
TJ	triple jump
W	walk
Wt	weight

Miscellaneous abbreviations

+	Intermediate time in longer race
=	Tie (ex-aequo)
A	Made at an altitude of 1000m or higher
b	date of birth
D	Made in decathlon competition
dnf	did not finish
dnq	did not qualify
dns	did not start
exh	exhibition
h	heat
H	Made in heptathlon competition
hr	hour
i	indoors
kg	kilograms
km	kilometres
m	metres
M	mile
m/s	metres per second
mx	Made in mixed men's and women's race
nh	no height
O	Made in octathlon competition
P	Made in pentathlon competition
pb	personal best
Q	Made in qualifying round
qf	quarter final (or q in lists)
r	Race number in a series of races
sf	semi final (or s in lists)
w	wind assisted
WIR	world indoor record
WR	world record or best
y	yards
*	Converted time from yards to metres: For 200m: 220 yards less 0.11 second For 400m: 440 yards less 0.26 second For 110mh: 120yh plus 0.03 second

Countries

From a founding membership of 17 nations in 1912, IAAF membership now stands at 214

AFG	Afghanistan
AHO	Netherlands Antilles #
AIA	Anguilla
ALB	Albania
ALG	Algeria
AND	Andorra
ANG	Angola
ANT	Antigua & Barbuda
ARG	Argentina
ARM	Armenia
ARU	Aruba
ASA	American Samoa
AUS	Australia
AUT	Austria
AZE	Azerbaijan
BAH	Bahamas
BAN	Bangladesh
BAR	Barbados
BDI	Burundi
BEL	Belgium
BEN	Benin
BER	Bermuda
BHU	Bhutan
BIH	Bosnia Herzegovina
BIZ	Belize
BLR	Belarus
BOL	Bolivia
BOT	Botswana
BRA	Brazil
BRN	Bahrain
BRU	Brunei

Code	Country	Code	Country	Code	Country
BUL	Bulgaria	IRQ	Iraq	PNG	Papua New Guinea
BUR	Burkina Faso	ISL	Iceland	POL	Poland
CAF	Central African Republic	ISR	Israel	POR	Portugal
CAM	Cambodia	ISV	US Virgin Islands	PRK	North Korea (DPR Korea)
CAN	Canada	ITA	Italy		
CAY	Cayman Islands	IVB	British Virgin Islands	PUR	Puerto Rico
CGO	Congo	JAM	Jamaica	PYF	French Polynesia
CHA	Chad	JOR	Jordan	QAT	Qatar
CHI	Chile	JPN	Japan	ROU	Romania
CHN	People's Republic of China	KAZ	Kazakhstan	RSA	South Africa
		KEN	Kenya	RUS	Russia
CIV	Côte d'Ivoire (Ivory Coast)	KGZ	Kyrgyzstan	RWA	Rwanda
CMR	Cameroon	KIR	Kiribati	SAM	Samoa
COD	Democratic Republic of Congo	KOR	Korea	SCG	Serbia & Montenegro (to 2006)
		KOS	Kosovo		
COK	Cook Islands	KSA	Saudi Arabia	SCO	Scotland
COL	Colombia	KUW	Kuwait	SEN	Sénégal
COM	Comoros	LAO	Laos	SEY	Seychelles
CPV	Cape Verde Islands	LAT	Latvia	SGP	Singapore (SIN up to 2016)
CRC	Costa Rica	LBA	Libya	SIN	Singapore
CRO	Croatia	LBN	Lebanon (LIB up to 2016)	SKN	St Kitts & Nevis
CUB	Cuba	LBR	Liberia	SLE	Sierra Leone
CUR	Curaçao	LCA	St Lucia	SLO	Slovenia
CYP	Cyprus	LES	Lesotho	SMR	San Marino
CZE	Czech Republic	LIB	Lebanon	SOL	Solomon Islands
DEN	Denmark	LIE	Liechtenstein	SOM	Somalia
DJI	Djibouti	LTU	Lithuania	SRB	Serbia
DMA	Dominica	LUX	Luxembourg	SRI	Sri Lanka
DOM	Dominican Republic	MAC	Macao	SSD	South Sudan
		MAD	Madagascar	STP	São Tomé & Príncipe
ECU	Ecuador	MAR	Morocco	SUD	Sudan
EGY	Egypt	MAS	Malaysia	SUI	Switzerland
ENG	England	MAW	Malawi	SUR	Surinam
ERI	Eritrea	MDA	Moldova	SVK	Slovakia
ESA	El Salvador	MDV	Maldives	SWE	Sweden
ESP	Spain	MEX	Mexico	SWZ	Swaziland
EST	Estonia	MGL	Mongolia	SYR	Syria
ETH	Ethiopia	MKD	Former Yugoslav Republic of Macedonia	TAN	Tanzania
FIJ	Fiji			TCH	Czechoslovakia (to 1991)
FIN	Finland	MLI	Mali	TGA	Tonga
FRA	France	MLT	Malta	THA	Thailand
FRG	Federal Republic of Germany (1948-90)	MNE	Montenegro	TJK	Tadjikistan
		MNT	Montserrat	TKM	Turkmenistan
FSM	Micronesia	MON	Monaco	TKS	Turks & Caicos Islands
GAB	Gabon	MOZ	Mozambique	TLS	East Timor
GAM	The Gambia	MRI	Mauritius	TOG	Togo
GBR	United Kingdom of Great Britain & Northern Ireland	MSH	Marshall Islands	TPE	Taiwan (Chinese Taipei)
		MTN	Mauritania	TTO	Trinidad & Tobago
GBS	Guinea-Bissau	MYA	Myanmar	TUN	Tunisia
GDR	German Democratic Republic (1948-90)	NAM	Namibia	TUR	Turkey
		NCA	Nicaragua	TUV	Tuvalu
GEO	Georgia	NED	Netherlands	UAE	United Arab Emirates
GEQ	Equatorial Guinea	NEP	Nepal	UGA	Uganda
GER	Germany (pre 1948 and from 1991)	NFI	Norfolk Islands	UKR	Ukraine
		NGR	Nigeria	URS	Soviet Union (to 1991)
GHA	Ghana	NGU	Papua New Guinea	URU	Uruguay
GIB	Gibraltar	NI	Northern Ireland	USA	United States
GRE	Greece	NIG	Niger	UZB	Uzbekistan
GRN	Grenada	NMA	Northern Marianas Islands	VAN	Vanuatu
GUA	Guatemala			VEN	Venezuela
GUI	Guinea	NOR	Norway	VIE	Vietnam
GUM	Guam	NRU	Nauru	VIN	St Vincent & the Grenadines
GUY	Guyana	NZL	New Zealand		
HAI	Haiti	OMA	Oman	WAL	Wales
HKG	Hong Kong, China	PAK	Pakistan	YEM	Republic of Yemen
HON	Honduras	PAN	Panama	YUG	Yugoslavia (to 2002)
HUN	Hungary	PAR	Paraguay	ZAM	Zambia
INA	Indonesia	PER	Peru	ZIM	Zimbabwe
IND	India	PHI	Philippines		
IRI	Iran	PLE	Palestine		
IRL	Ireland	PLW	Palau		

ceased to exist as a separate territory in 2010, and absorbed into the Netherlands.

ACKNOWLEDGEMENTS

ONCE AGAIN I would like to thank all those who have helped me to compile this Annual – whether in a major way or just with a few items of information. The annual world lists provide the essential core of the book and I have worked up these lists from original compilations by Richard Hymans and Mirko Jalava with reference to those of many other experts. I refer all who want to follow the results of the sport closely to Mirko's superb web site www.tilastopaja.net. I am indebted to Pino Mappa for work on men's lists, Carlos Fernández for his expertise on the road lists and to Ray Herdt for the walks. I circulate draft lists to a number of ATFS experts and receive much valuable information from a worldwide circle of correspondents, most of whom have helped with information from their nations for many years. Of the great Spanish group Juan Mari Iriondo and Miguel Villaseñor checked the biographies and obituaries. Børre Lilloe provided much index data and Ken Nakamura checked distance lists. Finally the Ukrainians Ivan Kachkivskiy and Serhiy Baranov made a through check of our lists against those of the IAAF.

Both for this annual and throughout the year with *Athletics International* that I produce with Mel Watman, Winfried Kramer helps with widespread probing for results as do the area experts: *Africa*: Carole Fuchs has helped in following the terrific work for so many years by Yves Pinaud, *Asia*: Heinrich Hubbeling, *Central and South America*: Eduardo Biscayart and Luis Vinker, and specialists: *Records* György Csiki, *Road racing*: Marty Post, *Ultrarunning* Andy Milroy, *Indoors* Ed Gordon, *Multi events*: Hans van Kuijen, *Pole vault* Kenneth Lindqvist, *Sho*: Norbert Heinrich.

Australia: Paul Jenes and David Tarbotton; *Austria*: Dr Karl Graf; *Belgium*: André de Hooghe and Alain Monet; *Bulgaria*: Aleksandar Vangelov; *China*: Mirko Jalava; *Cuba*: Alfredo Sánchez; *Czech Republic*: Milan Urban; *Denmark*: Erik Laursen; *Estonia*: Erlend Teemägi and Enn Endjärv; *Finland*: Juhani Jalava, Mirko Jalava, Mikko Nieminen and Matti Hannus; *France*: Alain Bouillé, Carles Baronet and Patricia Doilin; *Greece*: Thomas Konstas; *Hungary*: György Csiki; *India*: Ram. Murali Krishnan; *Ireland*: Pierce O'Callaghan and Liam Hennessy; *Israel*: David Eiger; *Italy*: Enzo Rivis; *Japan*: Yoshimasa Noguchi, Akihiro Onishi and Ken Nakamura; *Latvia*: Andris Stagis; *Lithuania*: Stepas Misiunas; *Luxembourg*: Georges Klepper; *Malaysia*: Jad Adrian, *Montenegro*: Ivan Popovic; *New Zealand*: Murray McKinnon and Steve Hollings; *Norway*: Børre Lilloe; *Poland*: Zbigniew Jonik and Janusz Rozum; *Portugal*: Manuel Arons Carvalho; *Puerto Rico*: Pedro Anibal Diaz; *Russia*: Sergey Tikhonov; *Serbia*: Ozren Karamata and Roberto Camano; *Slovakia*: Alfons Juck; *Slovenia*: Zdravko Peternelj; *South Africa*: Riël Hauman and Clyde Kinloch; *Spain*: José Luis Hernández, Miguel Villaseñor, Carles Baronet and the AEEA team; *Sweden*: Jonas Hedman and Peter Larsson; *Switzerland*: Alberto Bordoli and Antonin Hejda; *Trinidad*: Bernard Linley, *Turkey*: Nejat Kök, *Ukraine*: Ivan Kachkivskiy; *UK*: Tony Miller and Ian Hodge; *USA*: Tom Casacky, Garry Hill, Mike Kennedy, Sieg Lindstrom, Glen McMicken, Marty Post, Jack Shepherd and *Track Newsletter*. Also various national federation lists and to those who post results or ranking lists to various web sites.

Also to Francisco Ascorbe, Marco Buccellato, Mark Butler, Stan Greenberg, Alan Lindop, Rooney Magnusson (obituaries), Bill Mallon, Pino Mappa, David Monti, Jiri Ondrácek (European U23), Bob Phillips, Zdenek Procházka (hammer) and Rob Whittingham.

My apologies to anybody whose name I may have missed or who have corresponded with other key ATFS personnel, but all help, however small is deeply appreciated.

Keep the results flowing

During the year Mel Watman and I publish marks to ATFS standards (150-200 deep on world lists) in *Athletics International*, of which there are over 35 issues per year by email. This serves as a base from which the lists in this book can be compiled, together with information from web sites, especially Mirko Jalava's *Tilastopaja*, *Track & Field News* (USA) with its email results spin-off *Track Newsletter* and newsletters, especially Alfons Juck's *EME News* and Carles Baronet's *Track in Sun*.

In order to ensure that the record of 2019 is as complete as possible I urge results contribution worldwide to AI, and then in turn our lists in *Athletics 2020* (if there is one) will be as comprehensive as we can make them.

Peter Matthews

THE ASSOCIATION OF TRACK & FIELD STATISTICIANS

The ATFS was founded in Brussels (at the European Championships) in 1950 and ever since has built upon the work of such key founding members as Roberto Quercetani, Don Potts and Fulvio Regli to produce authoritative ranking lists in the International Athletics Annual and elsewhere.
Current Executive Committee
President: Paul Jenes AUS

Vice-President: A.Lennart Julin SWE
Treasurer: Tom Casacky USA
Secretary: Michael J McLaughlin AUS
Past Presidents: Rooney Magnusson SWE, Dr Roberto Quercetani ITA
Committee: Giuseppa Mappa ITA, Peter J Matthews GBR, Yoshimasa Noguchi JPN, Yves Pinaud FRA

Website: www.atfs.org

Internet – Websites

IAAF	www.iaaf.org
IAU	www.iau-ultramarathon.org
Africa (CAA)	www.webcaa.org
Asian AA	athleticsasia.org
CAC Confederation	www.cacacathletics.org
European AA	www.european-athletics.org
NACAC	www.athleticsnacac.org
Oceania AA	www.athletics-oceania.com
South American Fed.	www.consudatle.org
WMRA	www.wmra.info
World Masters	www.world-masters-athletics.org
Marathon Majors	www.worldmarathonmajors.com
Africa	www.africathle.com
Andorra	www.faa.ad
Argentina	www.cada-atletismo.org
Australia	www.athletics.com.au
Austria	www.oelv.at
Bahamas	www.bahamastrack.com
Belarus	www.bfla.eu
Belgium	www.val.be
Bermuda	www.btfa.bm
Bosnia Hercegovina	www.asbih.org
Brazil	www.cbat.org.br
Bulgaria	www.bfla.org
Canada	www.athletics.ca
Chile	www.fedachi.cl
China	www.athletics.org.cn
Costa Rica	www.fecoa.org
Croatia	www.has.hr
Cyprus	www.koeas.org.cy
Czech Republic	www.atletika.cz
Denmark	www.dansk-atletik.dk
Dominican Republic	www.fedomatle.org
England	www.englandathletics.org
Estonia	www.ekjl.ee
Finland	www.sul.fi
France	www.athle.com
Germany	www.leichtathletik.de
Great Britain	www.britishathletics.org.uk
deep statistics	www.topsinathletics.info
	www.thepowerof10.info
Greece	www.segas.gr
Hong Kong	www.hkaaa.com
Hungary	www.masz.hu
Iceland	www.fri.is
India	www.indianathletics.org
Indonesia	www.indonesia-athletics.org
Ireland	www.athleticsireland.ie
Israel	www.iaa.co.il
Italy	www.fidal.it
Jamaica	www.trackandfieldja.com
Japan	www.jaaf.or.jp
running news	japanrunningnews.blogspot.co.uk
Kazakhstan	www.kazathletics.kz
Kenya	www.athleticskenya.or.ke
Latvia	www.lat-athletics.lv
Lithuania	www.lengvoji.lt
Luxembourg	www.fla.lu
Macedonia	www.afm.org.mk
Malaysia	www.maf.org.my
results	www.adriansprints.com
Mexico	www.fmaa.mx
Moldova	www.fam.com.md
Monaco	www.fma.mc
Montenegro	www.ascg.co.me
Morocco	www.moroccanathletics.com
Netherlands	www.atletiekunie.nl
New Zealand	www.athletics.org.nz
Northern Ireland	www.niathletics.org
Norway	www.friidrett.no
Peru	www.fedepeatle.org
Poland	www.pzla.pl
Portugal	www.fpatletismo.pt
	www.atletismo-estatistica.pt
Puerto Rico	www.atletismofapur.com
	www.pedroanibaldiaz.com
Romania	www.fra.ro
Russia	www.rusathletics.com
Scotland	www.scottishathletics.org.uk
	www.scotstats.net
Serbia	www.ass.org.rs
Singapore	www.singaporeathletics.org.sg
Slovakia	www.atletikasvk.sk
Slovenia	www.atletska-zveza.si
South Africa	www.athletics.org.za
Spain	www.rfea.es
Sweden	www.friidrott.se
Switzerland	www.swiss-athletics.ch
Taiwan	www.cttfa.org.tw
Trinidad & Tobago	www.ttnaaa.org
Turkey	www.taf.org.tr
Ukraine	www.uaf.org.ua
Uruguay	www.atlecau.org.uy
USA	www.usatf.org
collegiate results	www.ustfccca.org
Wales	www.welshathletics.org
	athleticsstatswales.webeden.co.uk

Other recommended sites for statistics and results
AIMS	www.aimsworldrunning.org
ARRS	https://arrs.run
British historical	www.gbrathletics.com
	www.athlos.co.uk
DGLD (German stats)	www.ladgld.de
French history etc.	http://cdm.athle.com
Marathons	www.marathonguide.com
Masters Track & Field	www.mastersathletics.net
Mirko Jalava	www.tilastopaja.org
NUTS/Track Stats	www.nuts.org.uk
Rankings etc	www.all-athletics.com
Runners World	www.runnersworld.com
Tracklion (NED/BEL)	sportslion.net/tracklion.html
Track & Field News	www.trackandfieldnews.com
Track in Sun results	trackinsun.blogspot.co.uk
Ultra marathon stats	statistik.d-u-v.org/index.php
World juniors	www.worldjuniorathleticsnewsnzl.co.nz
Olympic Games	www.aafla.org
	www.sports-reference.com

DIARY OF 2018
by Peter Matthews

A chronological survey of highlights in major events in the world of track and field athletics.

See Championships or National sections for more details. DL = Diamond League, WCM = World Challenge Meeting, WIT = World Indoor Tour.

January

13 **Edinburgh**, GBR. Team winners at the Great Edinburgh XCountry were Europe 138 from Britain 182 and USA 190. As in 2017 the senior winners were men: Leonard Korir 8k in 24:32, women: Yasemin Can 6k in 20:58, and Laura Muir anchored the British team to victory in the mixed 4x1k relay.

19 **Clemson**, USA. Christian Coleman, previous best 6.45, took 0.02 off the world indoor record for 60m with 6.37. There was, however, no drug testing at the meeting, so he had to drive to meet testers, and the starting blocks were not electronic as required for world records.

20 **Albuquerque** USA. Michael Saruni, a Kenyan student at the University of Texas at El Paso, set a world indoor best of 1:14.79 at 600m.

25 **Ostrava**, Czech Republic. Top mark at the EA Permit indoor meeting was 21.61 shot by Tomás Stanek.

26 **Dubai**, United Arab Emirates. 19th Standard Chartered Marathon. Mosinet Geremew won in a course record 2:04:00, with the top six finishing within 15 seconds, and a record seven under 2:05. Second was Leul Gebrselassie in 2:04:02, the second fastest debut on a standard course, and Tamirat Tola was third in 2:04:06. The women's race was equally competitive, with Roza Dereje first in a course record 2:19:17, and the top four sub-2:20, another first. Geremew and Dereje both won $200,000 for victory. Ethiopians took the first ten men's places and only 20 year-old Desi Jisa of Bahrain in 8th prevented a top ten Ethiopian women's sweep – and she was originally from Ethiopia.

27 **Eaubonne**, France. Samuel Tefera set a world junior indoor 1500m record of 3:36.05 and Fabrice Zongo set five Burundi indoor triple jump records culminating in an African record 17.23.

27 **Hustopece**, Czech Republic. The high jump winner Danil Lysenko cleared 2.37.

27 **Volgograd**, Russia Mariya Lasitskene high jumped 2.04 on her first attempt for the best mark of the year.

28 **Osaka**, Japan. 37th Women's Marathon.

Mizuki Matsuda won in 2:22:44 on her marathon debut.

31 **Cottbus**, Germany. Sam Kendricks suffered his first loss since 3 Sep 2016 when 2nd in the pole vault with 5.78 to Piotr Lisek 5.83.

February

1-3 **Asian Indoor Championships**, Tehran, Iran. Mutaz Essa Barshim won his fifth title with 2.38, but the event was very poorly attended with few top Asian athletes and representation from only 21 of the 45 Asian AA member federations, with Japan winning just one medal. *See ATHLETICS 2018 for winners.*

3 **Karlsruhe**, Germany (WIT). Genzebe Dibaba ran the third fastest indoor 1500m of all-time, 3:57.45, with Konstanze Klosterhalfen 2nd in 4:04.00. Raphael Holzdeppe recorded an indoor pb of 5.88 in the pole vault and Su Bingtian won the 60m in an Asian record 6.47.

3 **New York (Armory)**, USA. 111th Millrose Games. The capacity crowd of 5500 saw a world record of 8:05.89 for the women's 4x800m relay (Chrishuna Williams 2:05.10, Raevyn Rogers 2:00.45, Charlene Lipsey 2:01.98 and Ajee' Wilson 1:58.37) and 35.45 for women's 300m by Shaunae Miller-Uibo that tied the world best. Emmanuel Korir set a Commonwealth and African indoor 800m record with 1:44.21.

6 **Banská Bystrica**, Slovakia. A capacity crowd at the 24th high jump meeting watched Mariya Lasitskene clear 2.02 for her 33rd successive victory; she had three decent tries at 2.06. But Mutaz Essa Barshim's win streak ended at 12; he was beaten on count-back by Wang Yu, both going over 2.31, as did Donald Thomas.

6 **Düsseldorf**, Germany. 12th PSD Bank meeting (WIT). Su Bingtian improved his Asian 60m record to 6.43. Christina Manning won the women's 60mh in 7.77 from Sharika Nelvis 7.80, Tomás Stanek improved his shot best to 22.17, the best indoor throw for nearly eight years. Piotr Lisek again beat Sam Kendricks, 5.86 to 5.78 in the pole vault in which 11 men jumped 5.60 or higher. Beatrice Chepkoech won the women's 1500m in 4:04.21.

7 **Paris (Bercy)**, France: Luva Manyonga had a winning indoor debut with his 8.32 long jump.

8 **Madrid**, Spain (WIT). New star Almir dos Santos triple jumped 17.35 and,

after winning the high jump at 2.00, Mariya Lasitskene tried 2.07 unsuccessfully. Genzebe Dinbaba celebrated her 27th birthday by winning the 1500m in 4:02.43.

9   Ras Al Khaimah, United Arab Emirates. Course records were set in both races at the RAK Half Marathon. 23 year-old Fancy Chemutai, who was second in 65:36 to Joyciline Jepkosgei in her 2017 world record at Valencia, missed that by just 1 second as she won here in 64:52, three seconds ahead of Mary Keitany with Caroline Kipkirui 3rd in 65:07 and edging ahead to set a world record 49:29 at 10 miles. There were best ever times for places 2-11, all beating previous bests set in RAK races, with a record seven women under 67 minutes. Bidan Karoki, who had won in 59:10 in 2017, won again, this time in 58:42 for fifth on the world all-time list. There were the fastest ever debut half marathons for men: Jemal Yimer, 2nd 59:00, and women: Degitu Azimeraw, 6th 66:47.

9-10   Clemson, USA. Grant Holloway ran the year's best 60m hurdles time of 7.42 and Kendra Harrison tied the US women's record with 7.72. The University of Southern California team ran 3:01.98 for 4x400m, the fastest ever indoors but not eligible for a world record at US runners Zachary Shinnick, Rickey Morgan and Michael Norman were joined by Rai Benjamin, then of Antigua.

10   Tampere, Finland. On this 300m indoor track Karsten Warholm ran 34.26 the fastest ever time for 300m hurdles.

10   Boston (Roxbury), USA (WIT). After running a 3:49.44 mile (second best ever indoors) the previous night at Boston University, Edward Cheserek achieved a notable double by winning the 3000m in 7:38.74 at the New Balance Indoor Grand Prix.

10   Kingston, Jamaica. Fedrick Dacres produced the year's best discus throw – 69.83, only for this to be invalidated when the discus was found to weigh 1.998kg.

11   Metz, France. Luva Manyonga set an African indoor long jump record of 8.40.

12-14 Russian Indoor Championships, Moscow. Top mark was the 4.87 pole vault by Anzhelika Sidorova.

13   Liévin, France. Selemon Barega had a brilliant win with 7:36.64 at 3000m in the return of the big indoor meeting

15   Torun, Poland (WIT). Piotr Lisek cleared a world-leading 5.91 in the pole vault and Konrad Bukowiecki threw the shot 22.00, to become the eleventh man to reach that barrier indoors. Tomás Stanek was 2nd at 21.83 and won the World Tour title.

15-18 Australian   Championships, Gold Coast. Sally Pearson won her ninth national title at 100m hurdles in 12.73 and Lauren Wells her 11th at 400m hurdles. Cedric Dubler scored 8229

to add 115 to his pb in the decathlon with pbs in five individual events.

16-18 US Indoor Championships, Albuquerque. Taking advantage of 1513m altitude Christian Coleman set a world indoor record 6.35 for 60m with Ronnie Baker 2nd in 6.40 for world all-time third. Javianne Oliver won the women's 60m in 7.02 and Sharika Nelvis the 60m hurdles in a US record 7.70 from Kendra Harrison 7.72 and Christine Manning 7.73. In the field top marks came from Katie Nageotte 4.91 and Sandi Morris 4.86 PV, Brittney Reese 6.88 LJ and DeAnna Price 24.51 weight for women, and Will Claye 17.28 men's TJ. Erica Bougard won the pentathlon with 4760 and 1500m/3000m double victories were claimed by Paul Chelimo and Shelby Houlihan.

16-18 Italian   Indoor   Championships, Ancona. At the age of 41 Fabrizio Donato triple jumped 16.96 for his 23rd national title indoors or out.

17-18 German   Indoor   Championships, Dortmund. On her 21st birthday Konstanze Klosterhalfen won the 3000m in a national indoor record 8:38.01.

17-18 UK   Indoor   Championships, Birmingham. UK records were set in the 5000m walks. Tom Bosworth 18:28.70 and Bethan Davies 21:25.37.

18   Kobe, Japan. The Japanese Championship at 20k walk had a terrific depth of performance. The first three men Eiki Takahashi 1:17:26, Toshihazu Yamanishi 1:17:41 and Datsuke Matsunaga 1:17:46 went to 8th, 13= and 15= on the world all-time list.

18-19 Russian Winter Walks Championships, Sochi. 20k winners retained their titles: Sergey Shirobokov in 1:18:52 by 1 sec from Vasily Mizinov, and Yelena Lashmanova 1:26:23.

24-25 College   Station, USA. The South Eastern (SEC) was as usual the strongest Conference meeting and world leads for the year were set by Sydney McLaughlin, a world junior 400m record 50.52 from 50.62 by Lyna Irby who also ran 22.66 for 200m.

25   Clermont-Ferrand, France. Sam Kendricks and Renaud Lavillenie topped the world lists when they cleared 5.93 in the "All Star Perche" competition at Clermont-Ferrand, a meeting organised by Lavillenie in his hometown. Behind them five men went over 5.88, so seven at this height or more was the best ever, the previous best being four. New bests were set for places five to seven and Shawnacy Barber's 5.81 for eighth tied the best ever. Fifth-placed Armand Duplantis twice broke the world junior record – at 5.81 and 5.88. Women's winner was Katie Nageotte at 4.86.

25   Glasgow, GBR. Müller Indoor Grand Prix, the final meet of the World Indoor Tour, in which event winners earned $20,000 and a wild card for the 2018 World Indoors. Tom Bosworth achieved a world best for 3000m walk with 10:30.28. Khaddi Sagnia surprised by equalling the Swedish indoor record to win the long jump with 6.92. *See ATHLETICS 2018 for complete list of World Tour winners.*

25   **Boston (Allston)**, USA. A team of Joe McAsey 1:49.03, Kyle Merber 1:47.11, Chris Giesting 1:47.43 and Jesse Garn 1:47.33 set a world 4x800m record at 7:13.11.

25   **Tokyo Marathon**, Japan. Dickson Chumba repeated his 2014 win (and 3rd each year 2015-17) with a fine win in 2:05:30, while there was great delight that second-placed Yuta Shitara ran 2:06:11, a Japanese record. Birhane Dibaba was the women's winner (as in 2015) in 2:19:51.

March

1-4   **World Indoor Championships**, Birmingham, GBR. Championships records were set in six events: three men: Christian Coleman, 60m 6.37, Tom Walsh, shot 22.31, 4x400m Poland 4x400m 3:01.77 world indoor record; and three women: Kendra Harrison, 60mh 7.70, Sandi Morris, pole vault 4.95, USA 4x400m 3:23.85. Genzebe Dibaba won a marvellous double at 1500m and 3000m, both with long, fast drives to the finish, to take her World Indoor gold tally to five; her feat of three WI golds (at 3000m) was matched by Renaud Lavillenie, 5.90 pole vault, and Pavel Maslák, 400m 45.47. Maslák actually only finished third well behind Óscar Husillos 44.92 and Luguelín Santos 45.09, but both were disqualified for lane infractions, of which there were many. There were world indoor bests for the year in 14 events. *For report and leading results see Athletics 2018 p. 590-1.*

3   **Sir Roger Bannister** died at the age of 88. His breaking the 4-minute barrier for the mile on 6 May 1954 remains the most celebrated achievement in the history of athletics. *See obituary*

9-10   **NCAA Indoor Championships**, College Station, USA. Michael Norman set a world indoor record of 44.52 for 400m and ran the final leg in 44.52 for the University of Southern California that ran 3:00.77 for 4x400m. As that team included Rai Benjamin, then of Antigua, the time could not be recognised as a world record, and that went to runners-up Texas A&M with their all-US team of Ilolo Izu, Robert Grant, Devin Dixon and Mylik Kerley. In separate women's 400m races, Kendall Ellis ran a North American record 50.34 and Sydney McLaughlin a world junior record 50.36. Another North American indoor record was 20.02 for 200m by Elijah Hall (who also won the 60m in 6.52) and world U20 record 7.98 60m

hurdles by Tara Davis. Florida won the men's title and Georgia the women's.

10   **European Throwing Cup**, Leiria, Portugal. Top teams were Ukraine (men) and Germany (women) with the best mark 92.70 javelin by Johannes Vetter.

10   **Northridge**, USA. Dalilah Muhammad ran a world best (on automatic timing) of 25.20 for 200m hurdles.

15   **Asian Cross-Country Championships**, Guiyang, China. Japan won all four team titles but China provided the senior individual champions in Peng Jianhua and Li Dan. *For leading results see Athletics 2018 p. 592*

15-17   **South African Championships**, Pretoria (1315mA). 20-year old Clarence Munyai ran 19.69 for 200m and Chris Harmse won his 23rd South African title in the hammer, a world record for successive national titles at any event. Caster Semenya took her seventh 800m title in 1:57.80.

17   **African Cross-Country Championships**, Chlef, Algeria. Kenya won all four team titles with Alfred Barkach and Celliphine Chespol the senior champions. *For leading results see Athletics 2018 p. 592*

24   **Dudince**, Slovakia. In his first 50k race since winning the 2016 Olympic title, Matej Tóth won this annual race for the third time

24   **World Half Marathon Championships**, Valencia, Spain. Geoffrey Kamworor won his third successive title in 60:02, with a 13:01 wind-aided split from 15k to 20k so that he won by 20 sec from Abraham Cheroben (taking Bahrain's first individual medal at this event) with Aron Kifle 3rd in 60:31. Ethiopia beat Kenya to the team title with Bahrain 3rd, an order that was identical for the women after Netsanet Gudeta had won in a women's only record of 66:11 from Joyciline Jepkosgei and Pauline Kamulu. *For leading results see Athletics 2018 p. 592*

25   **Auckland (Waitakere)**, New Zealand. Tom Walsh smashed the Oceania shot record as his 22.67 was the world's best throw since 2003.

28-31 91st **Texas Relays**, Austin, USA. "Mondo" Duplantis added 2cm to his world junior pole vault record with 5.92, but was 3rd on count-back behind Renaud Lavillenie and Shawnacy Barber, the first time that three men had cleared this height or more since 1999. Blessing Okagbare ran 10.72 for 100m with a 2.7 m/s following wind.

29-31 **Florida Relays**, Gainesville, USA. Sydney McLaughlin opened her outdoor season by winning over 200m in 22.39 and 400m in 50.07 and contributing a 49.45 relay leg!

April

6-7   **Tempe**, USA. Maggie Ewen twice broke the the US collegiate hammer record with 73.61

and 74.53 and completed a great triple with shot 19.22 and discus 61.27.

7   **Prague**, Czech Republic. Joan Chelimo missed the women's half marathon world record by just 13 seconds as she went to fifth all-time in 65:03 with Caroline Kipkurui an isolated second in 66:09. Benard Kimeli 59:47 led three men under the hour in the men's race, in which the first nine finishers were Kenyan.

8   **Paris Marathon**, France. Paul Lonyangata won in 2:06:25, 15 seconds slower than when he had won in 2017, and Betsy Saina won a closely contested women's race in 2:22:55, 4 secs ahead of debutante Ruth Chepngetich. There were 42,091 finishers (31,954 men and 10,137 women).

8   **Rotterdam Marathon**, Netherlands. Winners were Kenneth Kimutai 2:05:44 and Visiline Jepkesho 2:23:47.

8-15   22nd   **Commonwealth Games**, Gold Coast, Australia. In generally excellent conditions (apart from excessive heat for the marathons) there were Games records in 13 events, including from double winner Caster Semenya at 800m 1:56.68 and 1500m 4:00.71. Joshua Cheptegei was the other individual double winner with 5000m and a Games record 27:17.62 at 10,000m, with Isaac Makwala (400m) and Janieve Russell (400mh) taking individual and relay golds. Conseslus Kipruto set a Games record 8:10.08 to head the sixth successive Kenyan clean sweep of the men's steeplechase medals, and Games records were set in five throws events: by Nick Miller with a British record 80.26 hammer, Tom Walsh with his best ever qualifying mark of 22.45 shot (he headed six men over 20m in the final at 21.41), Fedrick Dacres discus 68.20, Dani Samuels women's discus 68.26, and Kathryn Mitchell, 68.92 in the women's javelin. Major upsets included Damian Warner failing his opening height in the pole vault of the decathlon and defending champion Julius Yego failing to qualify for the javelin final. From Dane Bird-Smith's Games record 1:19:34 in the opening event, the 20k walk. Australia excelled heading the points table with 379.5 to England 238 and Jamaica 185.5.

16   122nd   **Boston Marathon**, USA. Runners faced appalling conditions of heavy rain, head-winds and 3-5°C temperature so that taking into account wind-chill was below zero throughout. The amazing Yuki Kawauchi won the men's race in 2:15:58, his 79th sub-2:20 marathon and 33rd victory, the first Japanese winner since the year of his birth, 1987. The women's winner was Desiree Linden in 2:39:54.

19-21   60th   **Mt SAC Relays**, Torrance, California, USA. Brianna McNeal (née Rollins) ran 12.43 for 100m hurdles in her third race after a year out and there were fine 100m wins from Ronnie Baker 9.97 and 19 year-old Twanisha Terry 10.99.

22   Virgin **London Marathon**, GBR. There were a record 40,273 fishers (from 41,003 starters) on the hottest race day on record (reaching 24.1°C), beating the 2017 record total by 786 runners. Eliud Kipchoge won in 2:04:17, after tearing through the first half at record pace 61:00, followed by Tola Shure Kitata 2:04:49 and Sir Mo Farah, who sealed his tenth British record with 3rd in 2:06:21. Vivian Cheruiyot was the women's winner in 2:18:31 from Brigid Kosgei 2:20:13. The favourite Mary Keitany, who led by 23secs at halfway in 67:16, faded to fifth but with Kipchoge won $250.000 as winners of the Abbott World Marathon Majors series 2017/18.

26-28   109th   **Drake Relays**, Des Moines, USA. In their continuing shot rivalry Ryan Crouser beat Tom Walsh 22.01 to 21.82. Jenny Simpson ran an American record 9:16.78 for 2 miles; Kendra Harrison ran 12.37w for 100m hurdles and Sandi Morris pole vaulted 4.88.

26-28   124th   **Penn Relays**, Philadelphia, USA. In the USA v World relays match there was a world best of 1:35.20 for the women's sprint medley relay by an American team of Destinee Brown (100m), Aaliyah Brown (100m), Kimberlyn Duncan (200m) and Raevyn Rogers (400m 50.48). In the University events there were spectacular legs in the 4x400m: 43.38 by Kahmari Montgonery to take Houston to victory over Auburn, for whom Akeem Bloomfield ran a 43.4 leg.

27-28   **Fayetteville**, USA. Sydney McLaughlin ran a world junior record time of 53.60 in her first 400m hurdles race of the year. and helped the University of Kentucky to two US national relay titles, running a 49.47 for her leg in the 4x400m at the inaugural National Relay Championships.

May

4   **Doha**, Qatar (DL). As usual this was a meeting of the very highest standard, with top performances including Abderrahman Samba, 400m hurdles 47.57, 1.51 ahead of 2nd Bershawn Jackson, Steven Gardiner, 400m 43.87, Noah Lyles 200m 19.83, Marla Josée Ta Lou, 100m 10.85, and Caroline Kipkirui, 3000m 8:29.05 from four more women under 8:31. In the field Sandra Perkovic had a record 39th DL win with a DL record 71.38 in the discus, just 3cm short of her pb, three Germans beat 90m in the javelin: Thomas Röhler 91.78, Johannes Vetter 91.56 and Andreas Hofmann 90.08 with the best ever marks for places 2nd and 3rd, Mutaz Essa Barshim 2.40 in the high jump, and Pedro Paulo Pichardo beat Christian Taylor 17.95 to 17.81 in the triple jump.

5   **Baton Rouge**, USA. Mondo Duplantis added 1cm to his world junior pole vault record with 5.93.

5-6   **World Race Walking Team Championships**, Taicang, China. China won all three women's team competitions plus the junior men, with two individual winners headed by Liang Rui, who, on her debut at the event, raced the new women's 50k in 4:04:36 and, with a $50,000 world record bonus, collected a total of $85,000 in prize money. Japanese men, however, won team and individual awards at the men's 20k (Koki Ikeda 1:21:13) and 50k (Hirooki Arai 3:44:25), including a 1-2-3 at the latter. María Guadelupe González won the women's 20k in 1:26:38 with a last 5k of 20:27.

10-13 Collegiate Conference Championships, USA. Top marks at the SEC (Southeastern Conference) in Knoxville came from Sydney McLaughlin, world junior 400mh record 52.75, and Jasmine Camacho-Quinn, 12.40 Puerto Rican record at 100mh – both world leads as was Louisiana State University's 42.05 for 100mh helped by Aleia Hobbs, who had run 10.93 and 10.92 in the individual 100m. Grant Holloway had a double of LJ 8.32w/8.17 and 110mh 13.15. Michael Norman maintained his scintillating form with a 19.88w/44.40 200m/400m double at the Pac-12 in Stanford, where Maggie Ewen had a SP/DT/HT treble with 19.22/59.81/74.38.

12   Shanghai, China (DL). Luvo Manyonga long jumped 8.56 in the final round despite heavy rain and top local successes came from Gong Lijiao 19.99 shot and Lu Huihui 66.85 javelin. Eight world leading marks were set, including Catherine Ibargüen 14.80 triple jump and 9:07.27 by Beatrice Chepkoech in the steeplechase.

12   Baie Mahault, Guadeloupe. Top marks came in the triple jumps: Almir dos Santos 17.53 ahead of Will Claye and Pedro Paulo Pichardo, both 17.40, and Tori Franklin, who improved the North American women's record to 14.81.

19   Kingston, Jamaica Invitational (WCM). DeAnna Price produced a world-leading throw in the women's hammer with 76.27.

20   Osaka, Japan. Seiko Golden GP (WCM). The Japanese 4x100m team showed their prowess with 37.85.

20   European Cup 10,000m, London (Parliament Hill). Combined for the first time with the very successful annual 10,000m races organised by Highgate Harriers, there were excellent races for men, with Richard Ringer leading seven under 28 minutes with 27:36.52 and women with Lornah Chemtai Salpeter winning in an Israeli time of 31:33.03.

24-26 NCAA Regionals, USA. The qualifying competitions for the NCAA Championships were held in Eastern and Western sections at Tampa, where Aleia Hobbs ran 10.90 for 100m, and Sacramento, where Jaylen Bacon ran 9.97 for 100m and Michael Norman a 43.06 relay leg.

25-26 Eugene, USA. 44th Prefontaine Classic (DL). Numerous world leads were set at this great meeting. Eye-catching sprint winners included Shaunae Miller-Uibo, 400m 49.52, Noah Lyles, 200m 19.69, Omar McLeod, 110mh 13.01, Marie-Josée Ta Lou, 100m 10.88 from Murielle Ahouré 10.90, and Ronnie Baker, 100m 9.78w from Christian Coleman 9.84. As usual Caster Semenya was in a different league as she took the 800m in 1:55.92 and Genzebe Dibaba was dominant in her 14:26.89 win at 5000m. Shelby Houhihan won the women's 1500m in 3:59.06 from Laura Muir 3:59.30 and Jenny Simpson 3:59.37. This was the last international meeting before renovations for the 2021 World Champs and there was a fitting climax in the Bowerman Mile won in 3:49.87 by Timothy Cheruiyot with Jakob Ingebrigtsen in a world age-18 and European U20 record 3:52.28. Jenn Suhr beat Eliza McCartney on count-back as both cleared 4.85, with the latter setting an outdoor Commonwealth pole vault record, and Ryan Crouser had a big win with 22.57 in the shot from Michal Haratyk 21.97, Darian Romani 21.95 South American record and Tom Walsh 21.84, the best ever for 4th place.

26   Halle, Germany. 44th Werfertage. Pawel Fajdek took a world lead in the hammer with 80.70 and Lu Huihui improved the Asian women's javelin record to 67.69, but Anita Wlodarczyk suffered a rare set-back as she was only 9th in the hammer with 65.71.

26-27 European Champion Clubs Cup, Birmingham, GBR. ENKA Istanbul were the men's winners and Sporting Clube de Portugal the women's.

26-27 European 24 Hours Championships, Tomisoara, Romania. Polish athletes took both individual titles and the women's team.

26-27 Götzis, Austria. 45th Hypo Meeting. Nafissatou Thiam claimed her second Götzis win in the heptathlon with a score of 6806 from Yorgelis Rodríguez CAC record 6742 and Erica Bougard 6725, and Damian Warner his fourth in the decathlon with a Canadian record 8795 well ahead of Maicel Uibo 8514. Thiam high jumped 2.01, the best ever in a heptathlon. There were 13 men over 8000 points and 15 women over 6000.

29   Bydgoszcz, Poland. 18th European Athletics Festival, Top performance was 5.85 pole vault by Piotr Lisek.

31   Rome, Italy. Golden Gala Pietro Mennea (DL). Abderrahman Samba ran 47.48 for 400m hurdles, a Diamond League and Asian record and the world's fastest for eight years while Karsten Warholm took 0.40 off his Norwegian record with 47.80. More world leading marks came from Timothy Cheruiyot, 1500m 3:31.22, Conseslus Kipruto and Hyvin Jepkemoi, 3000mSt 8:08.40 and 9:04.96, Luvo Manyonga, LJ 8.58 (from Juan Miguel Echevarría 8.53), and Mariya Lasitskene, HJ 2.02.

June

2   La Coruña, Spain. Qieyang Shenjie starred with her 20k win in 1:26:28 and Eider Arévalo won the men's race in 1:19:14.

3   Hengelo, Netherlands. 35th Fanny Blankers-Koen Games (WCM). Mariya Lasitskene, improved the world's best outdoor high jump mark to 2.03.

5   Prague, Czech Republic. Jozef Odlozil Memorial. Mike Rodgers won the 100m in 9.92, which meant that the 33 year-old has run a legal sub-10.00 time in eight years from 2009 (and ten years including windy times). Ryan Crouser had three puts over 22m (best 22.31) in his fourth shot competition (all over 22m) of 2018.

5   Turku, Finland. 56th Paavo Nurmi Games. Left-handed Magnus Kirt improved his Estonian record from 88.45 in Tartu two days earlier to 88.73 to beat the German trio, Thomas Röhler 87.51, Andreas Hofmann 85.98 and Johannes Vetter 82.50. There was a rare defeat for Pawel Fajdek at the hands of compatriot Wojciech Nowicki, who won 79.41 to 78.86.

5-8   11th South American Games, Cochabamba, Bolivia. Games records were set in 24 events, many benefitting from the very high altitude (2556m). The most notable performances included 19.93 for 200m by Alex Quiñónez, 14.59 triple jump by Nubia Soares and 4.70 pole vault by Rosbeilys Peinado.

6-9   NCAA Championships, Eugene, USA. Rai Benjamin equalled the second-fastest 400m hurdles time ever, 47.02, 25 minutes after his University of Southern California team-mate, Michael Norman, became the No. 6 performer ever in the 400m with a time of 43.61. Both were collegiate records, as was USC's 2:59.00 in the 4x400m (with legs from Benjamin 43.6 and Norman 43.62), and Houston's 38.17 for 4x100m. Lynna Irby became the fastest ever US teenager with 49.80 for 400m. After 10.91 in the semis, Aleia Hobbs had a winning margin of 0.23 to win the 100m in 11.01 despite a blinding downpour. Keturah Orji won the long and triple jumps, taking her to eight NCAA victories (including indoors), a record for field events, and Maggie Ewen became the first woman since 2000 to win a shot/discus double. Men's team winners were Georgia with 52 points from Florida 42 and Houston 35, while USC 53 were the women's winners from Georgia 52 and Stanford 51.

7   Oslo, Norway (DL). 53rd Bislett Games. Abderrahman Samba maintained his brilliant form with 47.60 for 400m hurdles from Karsten Warholm 48.22. Tatyana Kholodovich unleashed a Belarus javelin record of 67.47 to snatch victory in the final round from Lu Huihui 65.11, and another great shot clash was won by Tom Walsh 22.29 from Ryan Crouser 22.21, while Andrius Gudzius had a notable discus win with 69.10.

Murielle Ahouré won the 100m in 10.91 from Dina Asher-Smith's UK record 10.92. and Elijah Manangoi won the Dream Mile in 3:56.95.

7-10   18th Asian Junior Championships, Gifu, Japan. The host nation headed the medal table with 14 golds, 15 silver and 13 bronze from China 11-8-4.

8   Chorzów, Poland. 64th Kusocinski Memorial. World-leading performances were recorded by Genzebe Dibaba, 3:56.58 for 1500m, and Gwen Berry, regaining her North American record with 77.78 and three throws better than Anita Wlodarczyk, 2nd with 75.52. Wojciech Nowicki again beat Pawel Fajdek, 80.63 (pb, twice) to 80.04. Two days later at Glowice Nowicki won again, improving to 81.45.

8   Havana, Cuba. Jordan Díaz set a world under-18 triple jump record of 17.41.

9   Kingston, Jamaica. Zharnel Hughes 9.91 beat Noah Lyles 9.93 at 100m and Shaunae Miller-Uibo ran 22.11 for 200m.

9-10   Mediterranean U23 Championships, Jessolo, Italy.

10   Stockholm, Sweden. Bauhaus-galan meeting (DL). Juan Miguel Echavarría long jumped 8.83, the world's longest for 23 years, although the wind was 2.1m/s. Jeff Henderson was 2nd at 8.39w and Luvo Manyonga 3rd 8.25. Fedrick Dacres beat Andrius Gudzius 69.67 to 69.59 in the discus and Mondo Duplantis beat Sam Kendricks 5.86 to 5.81 in the pole vault. Mariya Lasitskene won her 42nd successive high jump competition on count-back as Mirela Demireva also cleared 2.00. Abderrahman Samba ran his fifth successive sub-48 time in the 400m hurdles and his 47.41 was an Asian and DL record; Karsten Warholm was again 2nd and improved his Norwegian record to 47.81. Brianna McNeal ran a world-leading 12.39 in the 100m hurdles from Danielle Williams pb 12.48 and more top track wins came from Selemon Barega, 5000m 13:04.05, Gudaf Tsegay, 1500m 3:57.64, Ferguson Cheruiyot, 100m 2:14.88, with Salwa Eid Naser setting her fifth Bahrain 400m record at 49.84.

12-13   Ostrava, Czech Republic. 56th Golden Spike (WCM). 19 year-old Juan Miguel Echavarría produced his best ever long jump with legal wind, 8.66, and a clear win over Luvo Manyonga 8.31, and the world's two best high jumpers had a close contest, Mutaz Essa Barshim winning with a first-attempt clearance at 2.38 after Danil Lysenko had taken the lead with 2.36. Michal Haratyk set a Polish shot record with 22.08 but was beaten by Tom Walsh 22.16. The track highlight came at 3000m in which 18 year-old Selemon Barega beat Birhanu Yemataw 7:37.53 to 7:38.25.

15-17   Guiyang, China. Gong Lijiao's 20.38 was to remain the year's best shot put by a woman. Helped by the altitude of about 1275m,

Wang Jianan set a Chinese long jump record 8.47.

16   **Marseille**, France. Caterine Ibargüen returned to the long jump for the first time for three years and twice improved the Colombian record that she had set at 6.73A in 2013 with jumps of 6.78 and 6.87 in a fine series. Jimmy Viacaut won the 100m in 9.92.

16-17 **Ratingen**, Germany. Arthur Abele achieved a third decathlon win in the annual Stadtweke Ratingen Mehrkampf-Meeting with 8481 points and Carolin Schäfer repeated her 2017 heptathlon win with 6549.

19   **Montreuil**, France. Sergey Shubenkov ran the year's first sub-13 110m hurdles time with 12.99 and Mondo Duplantis beat Renaud Lavillenie 5.91 to 5.86 in the pole vault.

21-23 **Kenyan Championships**, Nairobi. Emmanuel Korir showed his speed with a 44.21 400m win, while the 800m was won by Jonathan Kitilit in 1:43.46.

21-24 **Jamaican Championships**, Kingston. In a clash between 100m Olympic champions Elaine Thompson beat Shelly-Ann Fraser-Pryce 11.01 to 11.09. Shericka Jackson ran a pb 11.13 for 3rd, before winning the 200m easily in 22.28.

21-24 **US Championships**, Des Moines. Noah Lyles caught Ronnie Baker in the final strides of the 100m to win 9.88 to 9.90, having also set a 2018 world best of 9.89 in his semi, and Aleia Hobs ran sub-11 in all three rounds – 10.87, 10.89w and 10.91 – to become the first collegian to win the women's 100m since Carlette Guidry in 1991. DeAnna Price won the hammer with a North American record 78.12 and repeat winners included Kara Winger, with a fifth javelin title, both Evan Jager and Emma Coburn, seven at 3000m steeplechase, Sam Kendricks, 5.85 for fifth successive pole vault, Matt Centrowitz, fifth 1500m, and Molly Huddle, fourth successive 10,000m. Shelby Houlihan achieved an unprecedented double double with 1500m and 5000m here after 1500m and 3000m indoors. Reggie Jagers won the discus with 68.61, the best by a US thrower since 2011, followed by Mason Finley 67.06 and Sam Mattis 66.32, the first time since 2000 that three US throwers exceeded 66m in the same competition. There was a three-hour delay due to thunderstorms on the final day.

22   **Madrid**, Spain (WCM). Su Bingtian regained the Chinese record that he had lost just three days earlier when Xie Zhenye ran 9.97 in Montreuil with 9.91, also tying the Asian record, and Filippo Tortu was 2nd in an Italian U20 record of 9.99.

23-24 **Mannheim**, Germany, In one of the senior events accompanying the annual junior gala, Eliz McCartney set Commonwealth and Oceania pole vault records at 4.86 and 4.92.

24   **Lake Saroma 100k**, Yubetsu, Japan. Nao Kazami won in 6:09:14, but the 50% degree of separation between start and finish – way over the generally acceptable 30% – and prevailing strong assisting wind (14-20 km/h for 60% of the race) make the recognition by the IAAF of this as a world record time dubious. Mai Fujisawa was the women's winner in 7:37:56.

24   **WMRA Long Distance World Mountain Running Championships**, Karpacz, Poland.

27-30 18th **Mediterranean Games**, Tarragona, Spain. Ivana Spanovic long jumped 7.04w and 6.99 with legal wind. Morocco headed the medal table with 8 golds, 4 silver and 1 bronze from Italy 7-8-8 and France 7-1-6.

30   **Bad Langensalza**, Germany. Juan Miguel Echavarría with 8.68 won a long jump where for the first time ever four men jumped 8.40 or better with legal wind, as 2-4 were Luvo Manyonga 8.42, Ruswahl Samaii 8.40 and Zarck Visser 8.40.

30   **Paris (Charléty)**, France (DL). In hot weather (over 30°C) Abderrahman Samba produced yet another extraordinary 400m hurdles run as he became only the second man to better 47 seconds, an Asian record of 46.98 – just 0.20 off the world record Kevin Young set in winning the 1992 Olympic title. 2nd was Kyron McMaster in 47.54 and 3rd Karsten Warholm 48.06. Making his DL debut, Michael Norman won the 200m in 19.84 and Ronnie Baker equalled the year's best 100m time of 9.88 from Jimmy Vicaut and Su Bingtian, both 9.91. There were also top women's sprint wins by Shericka Jackson, 200m 22.05, and Salwa Eid Naser, Asian 400m record 49.55 and the year's fastest of year to date by Caster Semenya, who led all the way to a South African 800m record of 1:54.25, Timothy Cheruiyot, 1500m 3:29.71, and Beatrice Chepkoech, 3000m steeplechase 8:59.38. Mariya Lasitskene recorded her 45th successive high jump win with a year's best of 2.04.

30-Jul 1   **UK Championships**, Birmingham. Lorraine Ugen long jumped to the top of the world list with 7.05.

30-31 **Zhukovskiy**, Russia. 60th Znamenskiy Memorial. Timur Morgunov pole vaulted 5.92 for a Russian U23 record.

July

1   15th **European Mountain Running Championships**, Skopje, Macedonia. Italy took their 23rd men's team win in the 24 years of the event and France were the women's team winners. Bernard De Matteis had his fourth individual win.

1-2 **Székesfehérvár**, Hungary. 8th István Gyulai Memorial Meeting. Sergey Shubenkov raced to the year's best 110m hurdles time of 12.92, Mutaz Essa Barshim again high jumped

2.40 and Wojciech Nowicki had another big win with pbs at 81.81 and 81.85 to Pawel Fajdek 81.14.

5   Lausanne, Switzerland. Athletissima (DL). There were two world-leading marks: Noah Lyles beat Michael Norman at 200m, 19.69 to 19.88, and Birhanu Yemataw ran 5000m for 13:01.09 after an extraordinary incident on the final bend between the leaders. Yomif Kejelcha, who had burst into the lead at the bell, began stumbling as they approached the final straight, but as he fell he grabbed hold of Selemon Barega's shorts and dragged him out into lane three. Barega recovered for 2nd in 13:02.67 and Kejelcha was disqualified. Sergey Shubenkov, who had been disqualified for a false-start in the Paris DL, had a clear win at 110m hurdles in 12.95. Caster Semenya was only 6th in 4:00.44 in the 1500m won by Shelby Houlihan 3:57.34 from Laura Muir 3:58.18 and Sifan Hassan 3:58.39. Malaika Mihambo beat Ivana Spanovic as both had a best of 6.90 and three women cleared 4.82 in the pole vault finishing 1 Ekateríni Stefanídi, 2 Jenn Suhr and 3 Anzhelika Sidorova, and clearances at 4.72 made for the best ever marks for (5th 4= here), 6th and 7th places. Christian Taylor beat Pedro Paulo Pichardo 17.62 to 17.61.

5-8   2nd European U18 Championships, Györ, Hungary. New Championships records (i.e better than those of 2016) were set in 11 boys events (plus one equal) and in 11 girls events. A world record for the U18 specification women's heptathlon was set by María Vicente of Spain with 6221 points with pbs in six of the seven events, and there was a U18 WR for 5kg hammer, 87.82 by Myhaylo Kokhan to add 66cm to the mark set by Bence Halász in 2014. Yaroslava Mahuchikh with a high jump win at 1.94 was just 2cm short of the world U18 best. Doubles were achieved by Sarah Healy of Ireland at 1500m and 3000m and by Vicente, who also won the triple jump. Britain headed the medal table with six golds (5 by boys).

6-8   French Championships,. Ninon Guillon-Romarin set a national record 4.71 in the pole vault (1cm less than her indoor record), while Renaud Lavillenie had an easy seventh win in the men's event with 5.80. Michaël Hanany won his twelfth high jump title and Jessica Cérival her eighth successive title in the shot.

8   Bragança Paulista, Brazil. 32nd Grande Prêmio Brasil. Andressa de Morais set a South American discus record with 65.10.

8-11   West Asian Championships, Amman, Jordan. Top mark was 9.97 for 100m by Barakat Al-Harthi.

9   Luzern, Switzerland. 32nd Spitzen Leichtathletik meeting. The best marks were by sprinters including Alonso Edward 19.90 for 200m.

10-15   World U20 Championships, Tampere, Finland. There were championships records by four men: Mondo Duplantis 5.82 pole vault, Jordan Díaz 17.15 triple jump, Rhonex Kipruto, 27:21.08 10,000m, and Ashley Moloney 8190 junior decathlon, and by three women: Celliphine Chespol 9:12.78 3000m steeple to retain her title from 2016, Diribe Welteji 1:59.74 800m, and Briana Williams 22.50 200m after winning the 100m in 11.16. Two super-talented 17 year-olds met in a tactical 1500m won by George Manangoi 3:41.71 from Jakob Ingebrigtsen 3:41.89. Ingebrigtsen returned for 3rd in a European record 13:20.78 at 5000m, behind the Kenyans Edward Zakayo and Stanley Waithaka. Adrian Piperi became just the sixth junior to propel the 6kg shot beyond 22m with a US U20 record 22.06 in the fifth round, but Kyle Blignaut responded with an African record just 1cm further. Kenya headed the medal table with six golds, sweeping the men's events from 800m to 10,000m plus the women's 5000m and steeplechase, with Jamaica next on four golds.

13   Rabat, Morocco (DL). Meeting International Mohammed VI d'Athletisme. Hellen Obiri won a great 5000m in 14:21.75 from Sifan Hassan, European record 14:22.24, and the next three Letesenbet Gidey, Senbere Teferi and Agnes Tirop set pbs and ran the best ever times for places 3-5. Benjamin Kigen improved the 3000m steeplechase pb that he had set when he won in 8:09.07 at Eugene to 8:06.19, and in 2nd Chala Beyo set an Ethiopian record of 8:07.27. Yomif Kejelcha made up for his Lausanne dq by beating Birhanu Yemataw 7:32.93 to 7:34.26 at 3000m. Caterine Ibargüen's 14.96 triple jump was to remain the 2018 world best and Magnus Kirt threw his third Estonian javelin record of the year, 89.75 to beat Andreas Hofmann, Jakub Vadljech and Thomas Röhler. Mariya Lasitskene's impressive 45-meeting winning streak from June 2016 came to an end when she managed only 1.90 for 3rd equal as Mirela Demireva won with 1.94. After six weeks out, Christian Coleman returned to edge Ronnie Baker, both timed in 9.98 for 100m.

15   London (Olympic Stadium), GBR. Athletics World Cup. This new venture that reportedly cost UK Athletics a loss of $1 million pitted one athlete per event from each of the world's top nations at each discipline, with a final result of: 1. USA 219, 2. Poland 162, 3. Gt Britain & NI 155, 4. Jamaica 153, 5. France 146, 6. Germany 137, 7. South Africa 135, 8. China 81. There was prize money of $2 million, with $450,000 to be shared among the members of the winning team on a sliding scale down to $100,000 for eighth place, but clearly this was not sufficient financial reward in the eyes of all too many stars who did not participate, although many of those who did welcomed the emphasis on team competition. Much publicity was accorded the Platinum Trophy awarded to the winning team, believed to be the most valuable sporting trophy ever made, but the cost of over £300,000 might have been better spent. The outstanding performances came from Anita Wlodarczyk, 78.74 hammer, and Luvo Manyonga, with a long jump series of 8.51, 8.48, 8.50 and 8.50. As happens all too often the throws and horizontal jumps were degraded by being confined to four trials.

16-17 **Jockgrimm**, Germany. Eliza McCartney improved her Oceania pole vault record to 4.94.

19-20 **Herculis, Monaco (DL)**. On a night of sensational running at a hot and humid Stade Louis II, Beatrice Chepkoech produced the crowning performance as she took 8.46 seconds off the women's world 3000m steeplechase record, finishing alone and triumphant in 8:44.32 after going through 2k in a best ever 5:49.81. Courtney Frerichs was 2nd in a North American record 9:00.85 with Hyvin Jepkemoi 3rd in 9:04.41, and seven women beat 9:10 with the best ever times from 5th to 13th 9:25.48. Another record in depth came in the women's 800m as 11 runners finished inside 2 minutes in the race won by Caster Semenya 1:54.60 from Francine Niyonsaba 1:55.96 and Natalya Goule 1:56.15 Jamaican record. Noah Lyles, who turned 21 two days earlier, lowered his 200m pb to a world leading 19.65 (equal 8th world all-time), well ahead of Ramil Guliyev, 2nd in 19.99, and Marie Josée Ta Lou was an equally clear winner of the 100m in 10.89. Danil Lysenko cleared 2.40 in the high jump and the pole vault, won by Anzhelika Sidorova with 4.85 was a competition of unprecedented depth with bests evers for places 4th (tied), 5th to 8th and 10th (tied), four women over 4.80, eight over 4.75 (previous most four) and 10 over 4.60. There were also best place marks for 5th to 7th in the men's shot with seven men over 21m. Shaunae Miller-Uibo set a Diamond League and Bahamian record of 48.97 to hold off Salwa Eid Naser, whose 49.08 took almost half a second off her own Asian record. More world-leading times came from Soufiane El Bakkali, who ran the one sub 8-minute steeplechase of the year, 7:58.15 from Evan Jager 8:00.45, and Timothy Cheruiyot, 1500m 3:28.41. Elijah Manangoi was 2nd in 3:29.64 and in 3rd Filip Ingebrigtsen set a Norwegian record of 3:30.01, with brother Jakob finishing a place behind him in a European junior record of 3:31.18, a world age-17 best.

19-22 **Russian Championships**, Kazan. Mariya Lasitskene won the high jump with 2.00.

20-21 **Balkan Championships**, Stara Zagora, Bulgaria. Paraskévi Papahrístou triple jumped 14.74 (and 14.60) and Romania topped the medal table.

20-22 **Polish Championships**, Bialystok.

Anita Wlodarczyk won her eighth hammer title and increased her 2018 world lead to 79.59. Piotr Malachowski with 65.79 won his 11th discus title (from 2005) and Wojciech Nowicki beat Pawel Fajdek 80.26 to 80.14 in the hammer.

21 **Heusden-Zolder**, Belgium. Night of Athletics. As usual a feast of running. For instance in six 1500m races 19 men beat 3:40 and there were six men's 5000m races and 22 women bettered 16 mins in the women's 5000 (10 inside 15:16). In the last Shelby Houlihan won by nearly half a minute from Molly Huddle and broke the North American record with 14:34.45.

21-22 **London Stadium**, GBR. Müller Anniversary Games (DL). Ronnie Baker maintained his brilliant consistency with his seventh and eighth legal sub-10.00 times since April with 9.90 in both heat and final of the 100m and Akeem Bloomfield smashed his 200m best with 19.81. World-leading times were set by Emmanuel Korir, 1:42.05 for 800m, Kendra Harrison, 12.36 for 100m hurdles, and Sifan Hassan as her 4:14.71 took her to third on the world all-time mile list with Gudaf Tsegay 2nd in 4:16.14 and Hellen Obiri 3rd in a Commonwealth record 4:16.15. Mariya Lasitskene tied her best high jump of the year at 2.04 and Tom Bosworth set a world best for 3000m track walk with 10:43.84.

21-22 **Spanish Championships**, Getafe. Top mark was Bruno Hortelano's 20.04 national record in his semi of the 200m and Berta Castells won her 15th hammer title in 16 years.

22-23 **German Championships**, Nuremburg. With the big three over 87.80m, Andreas Hofmann won the javelin with 89.55 and David Storl won his eighth shot title as Christina Schwanitz was back over 20m with 20.06.

24-27 **African Youth Games**, Algiers, Algeria. Fancy Cherono had the top performance with 6:17.68 for women's 2000m steeplechase.

29- Aug 3   23rd **Central American and Caribbean Games**, Barranquilla, Colombia. There was a feast of top-class sprint performances and many national records even though the NACAC Championships were held just a week later. Games records were set in five men's and four women's events (plus two wind-assisted). Kyron McMaster won the 400m hurdles in 47.60 and Caterine Ibargüen excelled at both long (6.83w) and triple (14.92) jumps following five silvers and a gold at previous editions of this quadrennial meeting. Juan Luis Barrios won the 10,000m to take his tally of gold medals to eight (from 2002), the all-time record for these Games.

August

1-8   21st **African Championships**, Asaba, Nigeria. Organisation was chaotic throughout and some athletes were left for three days at the airport in Lagos before the event. Caster Semenya topped performances with wins at 400m 49.96 RSA record and 800m 1:56.06. Also securing a double was Marie-Josée Ta Lou, 100m 11.15 and 200m 22.50. Larbi Bouraada won a fourth title at decathlon and winning third titles were Nijel Amos 800m, Tobi Amusan 100mh and Ese Brume LJ. Ruswahl Samaai beat Luvo Manyonga 8.45 to 8.43 in the long jump and Beatrice Chepkoech won the steeplechase in 8:59.88

6-12 **European Championships**, Berlin. Another splendid event with championship records in eleven events. *See Championships section.*

10-12 **NACAC Championships**, Toronto, Canada. Levern Spencer won a third successive NACAC high jump title and equalled her own championship record with 1.91. Best marks included 1:57.52 by Ajee' Wilson to beat Natoya Goule 1:57.95 in the 800m, 48.18 400mh by Kyron McMaster, 12.68 shot by Darrell Hill, 68.47 discus by Fedrick Dacres, 12.55 100mh by Kendra Harrison, 53.32 400mh by Shamier Little, and 74.60 hammer by DeAnna Price

18 **Birmingham**, GBR (DL). Christian Coleman beat Reece Prescod by just 0.001 at 100m, 9.938 to 9.939 with Noah Lyles 3rd in 9.98. Shaunae Miller-Uibo had her third 200m win over Dina Asher-Smith 22.15 to 22.31. Top field marks included long jumps of 8.53 by Luvo Manyonga and Malaika Mihambo 6.96, and Andres Hoffman, 89.82 javelin. The 66th Emsley Carr Mile was won by Stewart McSweyn in 3:54.60.

18 **Gothenburg**, Sweden. Yomif Kejelcha ran the world's fastest 3000m since 2011 with 7:28.00.

22 **Chorzów**, Poland. Kamila Skolimowska Memorial meeting. Ronnie Baker ran 9.87 for 100m and hammer events were suitably to the fore, with Pawel Fajdek beating Wojcich Nowicki 79.44 to 77.41, and Joanna Fiodorow throwing a season's best 74.39. The women's 100m was staged in memory of Irena Szewinska, and won clearly by Caster Semenya in 50.06.

23 **Rovereto**, Italy. English Gardner made a great return as, in her first race since July 2017, she won the 100m in 11.02 at the 54th Palio della Quercia meeting.

24-26 **Eberstadt**, Germany. Brandon Starc with an Oceania record 2.36 and Airine Palsyte 1.94 were the winners at the 40th edition of the annual high jump competition.

24-26 **Swedish Championships**, Eskilstuna. Daniel Ståhl won the discus with 69.72, the world best of 2018.

24-26 **18th Ibero-American Championships**, Trujillo, Peru. Sandra Arenas produced the only new championship record, a South American

record 42:02.99 for 10,000m walk. Jennifer Dahlgren won her fourth women's hammer title at this biennial meeting.

25-30 **18th Asian Games**, Jakarta, Indonesia. There were 13 new Games records (7 men's and 6 women's) plus the new event of mixed 4x400 relay that was surely the best ever in this series. These were topped by 9.92 for 100m by Su Bingtian, 47.66 for 400m hurdles by Abderrahman Samba, 50.09 for 400m by Salwa Eid Naser (she also anchored Bahrain to gold in both relays) and 66.09 javelin by Liu Shiying, all maintaining their terrific form of 2018. Both Samba and Abdelilah Haroun, who won the 400m, won second gold medals as they combined to help the Qatar team to an Asian record 3:00.56 for 4x400m. It was very hot but that, with poor air quality, severely affected the endurance events. Ehsan Hadadi won the discus with 65.71 by a margin of 5.62m for his fourth successive title (from 2006) and winning third successive titles were high jumper Svetlana Radzivil and triple jumper Olga Rypakova.

30 **Zürich**, Switzerland. Weltklasse (DL). Half the Diamond Race titles were decided here, including a fifth title for Caterine Ibargüen at triple jump, a fourth for Conseslus Kipruto at steeplechase, and third for Caster Semenya as she won the 800m in 1:55.27 and Ekaterini Stenanidi, 4.87 pole vault. Hellen Obiri won a tough battle against Sifan Hassan 14:38.39 to 14:38.77 in the 5000m with a last 200m in 27.39. Noah Lyles beat Ramil Guiliyev in 19.67, a remarkable time in the cool conditions, 19.98 at 200m. Andreas Hofmann was again the top man in the javelin with 91.44 and Tomas Walsh set a DL shot record of 22.60 with Darrell Hill 22.40 and Ryan Crouser 22.18 over 22m and the longest ever throws for places 2-5. The men's pole vault was held the previous day and won with 5.91 by Timur Morgunov at the Hauptbahnhof.

31 **Brussels**, Belgium. 42nd Van Damme Memorial and DL final. Eight men, six of them Ethiopians, beat 13 minutes in the 5000m won by 18 year-old Selemon Barega in 12:43.02 for fourth on the world all-time list. Hagos Gebrhiwet was 2nd in 12:45.82 and Yomif Kejelcha ran 12:46.79 for the best ever third place time. There was also a world lead in the 100m, where Christian Coleman had a convincing win over Ronnie Baker 9.79 to 9.93. Beatrice Chepkoech dominated the steeplechase, her 8:55.10 the third fastest performance in history. Norah Tanui was 2nd in 8:59.62 and Hyvin Jepkemoi 3rd in 9:01.60 and there were the fastest ever 5th and 6th place times – on a cool, calm evening. Despite a pair of seven-hour flights from the Asian Games in Jakarta to Brussels earlier in the day Salwa Eid Naser won the 400m in 49.33 while Shaunae Miller-Uibo retained her unbeaten run in 2018 with 22.12 for 200m. Caterine Ibargüen added

the long jump title to the triple jump title she took in Zürich. The biggest upset came in the discus as Yaimé Pérez threw 65.00 to 64.65 by Andessa de Morais and 64.31 by Sandra Perkovic, who was thus denied a record seventh consecutive Diamond Trophy as was Christian Taylor, who was beaten 17.49 to 17.31 by Pedro Paulo Pichardo.

31-1 Sep   **Finland v Sweden**, Tampere, Finland. Finland beat Sweden 206-202 for men and Sweden won 216-194 for women in the annual Finnkampen.

September

2   **Berlin**, Germany. 77th ISTAF (WCM). Caster Semenya went to fifth on the world 1000m all-time list with 2:30.70. In the last competition of his great career Robert Harting was second with 64.95 in the discus behind his brother Christoph 65.67.

3   **Zagreb**, Croatia. 69th Boris Hanzekovic Memorial (WCM). Five of the first seven in the women's 3000m set pbs led by Kenyans Lilian Rengeruk 8:33.37 (just 0.64 off her pb) and Norah Tanui 8:33.81. Elijah Manangoi won the 1500 in 3:32.52 just from Yomif Kejelcha pb 3:32.59. Luvo Manyonga completed his brilliant year with his 13th long jump competition at 8.40 or more, and Fedrick Dacres his 11th at discus over 68m, while Marie Josée Ta Lou had her 10th win in 11 finals at 100m (adding her 11th at the Continental Cup) and Sandra Perkovic thrilled the home crowd with 67.60 to beat her main rival Yaimé Pérez by 2.82m. Ryan Crouser had his ninth competition over 22m to win the shot with 22.09 from Tom Walsh 21.78 in the city centre competition on the eve of the main meeting.

5-16 **World   Masters   Championships**, Málaga, Spain. Britain 80G-66S-57B and Spain 80G-65S-59B were close at the top of the medals table.

7-9 **Italian   Championships**, Pescara. Chiara Rosa won her 14th successive shot title.

8   **Prague**, Czech Republic. Rhonex Kipruto ran a world U20 road best 26:40 for 10k and Caroline Kipkirui was the women's winner in 30:19.

8-9   **Continental Cup**, Ostrava. With the name changed from the World Cup, the winners were the Americas with 262 points from Europe 233, Asia-Pacific 188 and Africa 142. There was plenty of exciting competition, although marred by most unfortunate innovations introduced by the IAAF such as for the horizontal field events the top four athletes from each team after three rounds had an additional attempt. The top two athletes from that fourth round went on to have one further attempt, the results of which would be used to determine the final standings; by this means some ludicrous results were produced.

Even worse was the revival of the discredited "devil take the hindmost" format in the 3000m and steeplechase – an insult to the athletes who were forced to drop out. Darian Romani won the shot with 21.89 from Ryan Crouser 21.63 and Tom Walsh 21.43, although the stupid rules gave Crouser only 5th place. Other absurdities included the second longest triple jumper (men and women) and male javelin thrower being officially placed fifth, while true winners of the women's shot (Raven Saunders) and discus (Sandra Perkovic) received second place points merely because they 'lost' in the fifth and final round. World/Continental Cup records were set by Abderrahman Samba, 400mh 47.37, Sifan Hassan, 3000m 8:27.50, Beatrice Chepkoech, 3000mSt 9:07.92, Anzhelika Sidorova, Ekateríni Stefanídi and Sandi Morris, in that order in the pole vault at 4.85, and DeAnna Price, hammer 75.46. Caster Semenya won the 800m in 1:54.77, but although she ran a 400m RSA record 49.63 was beaten by the brilliant Salwa Eid Naser 49.32, and Caterine Ibargüen won both long jump, Colombian record 6.93, and triple jump, 14.76. Christian Taylor won the triple jump with 17.59 and also led off the winning Americas team in the mixed 4x400m relay.

9   **IAU World 100km Championship.** Sveti Martin na Muri, Croatia. Hideaki Yamauchi was the men's winner in 6:28:05 and led Japan to team victory. The Japanese women packed brilliantly to take places 3rd to 6th, but the individual winner was Nikolina Sustic in a Croatian record 7:20:34.

9   36th **Great North Run, Newcastle to South Shields**, GBR. Sir Mo Farah had his fifth win in the race in 59:27 and Vivian Cheruiyot won the women's race in 67:43.

9   **New York. 5th Avenue Mile**. Jenny Simpson took the women's race for the sixth consecutive year, and seventh overall, in 4:18.8 on the slightly (8.23m) downhill course and Jake Wightman won the elite men's race in 3:53.5. There were a record 7704 finishers in numerous graded races.

14-15 **Trofeo Brasil**, Bragança Paulista, Brazil. Darian Romani set his fifth South American shot record (and his 14th Brazilian) with exactly 22m for his seventh national shot.

14-17 **Chinese   Championships**, Taiyuan. Gong Lijiao won her tenth national shot title and Li Ling her ninth at pole vault.

15-16 **Talence**, France. Kevin Mayer made up for the disappointment of his three no jumps in the long jump at the European Championships by setting a world record of 9126 points in the Decastar meeting. Remarkably he scored 4563 points on each day (the best ever second day score) and set pbs at 100m 10.55, LJ 7.80, JT 71.90 and outdoor PV 5.45. Arthur Abele was 2nd with 8301 and clinched the IAAF World

Combined Events Challenge as did Carolin Schafer, the heptathlon winner with a score of 6457.

16   45th BMW **Berlin Marathon**, Germany. Eliud Kipchoge led from the start, on his own for the final 17k, and ran a marvellous world record 2:01:39. His times for and at each kilometre are in the table. His 30k time of 1:26:45 was also a world record. Second was Amos Kipruto in 2:06:23. Gladys Cherono was the women's winner for the third time in a pb 2:18:11 (fourth all-time) from Ruti Aga 2:18:34 and Tirunesh Dibaba (who had led by 7 sec at halfway in 69:03) 2:18:55, the first time that three women had broken 2:19 in one race.

Kipchoge in Berlin

1k	2:45	2:45	22k	1:03:42	2:54
2k	5:42	2:57	23k	1:06:35	2:53
3k	8:36	2:54	24k	1:09:30	2:55
4k	11:30	2:54	25k	1:12:24	2:54
5k	14:24	2:54	26k	1:15:18	2:54
6k	17:20	2:56	27k	1:18:09	2:51
7k	20:15	2:55	28k	1:21:04	2:55
8k	23:10	2:55	29k	1:23:55	2:51
9k	26:05	2:55	30k	1:26:45	2:50
10k	29:01	2:56	31k	1:29:39	2:54
11k	31:56	2:55	32k	1:32:28	2:49
12k	34:52	2:56	33k	1:35:21	2:53
13k	37:48	2:56	34k	1:38:13	2:52
14k	40:44	2:56	35k	1:41:02	2:49
15k	43:38	2:54	36k	1:44:00	2:58
16k	46:30	2:52	37k	1:46:52	2:52
17k	49:21	2:51	38k	1:49:46	2:54
18k	52:14	2:53	39k	1:52:39	2:53
19k	55:06	2:52	40k	1:55:29	2:50
20k	57:56	2:50	41k	1:58:20	2:51
21k	1:00:48	2:52	42k	2:01:08	2:48
HM	1:01:06	—-	All	2:01:39	0:31

16   **Copenhagen**, Denmark. Sifan Hassan made a brilliant debut at half marathon to win in a European record time of 65:15 from Yeshaneh Ababel, Ethiopian record 65:46. There was excellent standard in depth with four women inside 67 minutes and eight inside 68 minutes, and also in the men's race with eight men under the hour, headed by Daniel Kipchumba who matched his pb with 59:06. He was followed by Abraham Kiptum 59:09, Jemal Yimer 59:14 and Yomif Kejelcha, who made the fourth fastest ever half marathon debut with 59:16. The 10th place time of 60:11 was a best ever by 1 second and other times were close to the best. The first 21 men and 14 women all came from Kenya or Ethiopia.

16   34th **World Mountain Running Championships**, Canillo, Andorra. As in 2017 the Ugandan men had a clean sweep of the senior men's medals, with last year's 1-2 Victor Kiplangat and Joel Ayeko third and second this time behind Robert Chemonges. Lucy Wambui Murigi retained her women's title and led Kenya

to the senior women's victory, but Uganda took both junior individual and team titles.

24-26 **Lake Taihu**, China. The final competition in the 2018 IAAF Race Walking Challenge was a three-day tour of three stages, 20k, 12k, 12k, around Lake Taihu. Eider Arévalo's win, 2:58:99 for a 2nd and two 1sts, took him to 24 points in the men's challenge, but that left him 1 point behind Andrés Chocho, who had accumulated 25 points earlier in the year. 2nd was Lebogang Shange 2:58:12. The women's winner here was Wang Yingliu in 3:13:17 from Qieyang Shenjie 3:14:31, but Qieyang was the clear women's challenge winner.

29-30 **South American U23 Championships**, Cuenca, Ecuador.

October

7   **Commonwealth Half Marathon Championships**, Cardiff, GBR. Jack Rayner, 61:01 from a previous best of 63:12, and Juliet Chekwel, 69:45, were inaugural champions.

7   41st **Chicago Marathon**, USA. Mo Farah broke the European record with 2:05:11 as he sprinted clear to win by 13 secs from Mosinet Geremew with Suguru Osako third in 2:05:50, an Asian record that earned him a 100 million yen ($879,350) for the Japanese record. Brigid Kosgei, runner-up in 2017, was the women's winner in 2:18:35 from Roza Dereje 2:21:18. There was a race record 44,600 finishers (23,946 men and 20,654 women).

11-16 **Youth Olympic Games**, Buenos Aires, Argentina. Games records were set in 15 events headed by Jordan Díaz, 17.09 triple jump, and Yaroslava Mahuchikh, 1.92 and 1.95 high jump. The competition did not have qualifying and final rounds, but two stages of equal importance: the performances from both added to determine the overall final placing. All the athletes thus competed twice in their event, except for the 1500m, 3000m, and 2000m steeplechase where the second round was a 4km cross-country race.

21   **New Delhi**, India. Winners at the 13th Airtel Delhi Half Marathon were Andamlak Belihu 59:18 and Tsehay Gemechu, in her debut at the distance, 66:50, from Joyciline Jepkosgei 66:56.

21   **Amsterdam Marathon**, Netherlands. The 2017 winners repeated as Lawrence Cherono took 1:03 off his race record with 2:04:06, while Tadelech Bekele was women's winner in 2:23:14.

28   **Valencia**, Spain. Abraham Kiptum took five seconds off the world record for half marathon with 58:18 ahead of Jemal Yimer 58:33 and Abadi Hadis 58:44 for third equal and ninth equal on the world all-time list. Kiptum's 5k splits were 13:56, 28:02, 41.37 and 55:18 world record. There were best ever times for places 1-3 and 8-13 with a record ten men under the hour.

Gelete Burka was the women's winner in 66:11 with six more women under 68 minutes.

28 **Frankfurt-am-Main**, Germany. Cool and at times extremely windy conditions held back times in the 37th Mainova Frankfurt Marathon. Yet Meskerem Assefa still broke the women's course record with a brilliant 2:20:36 and Haftamnesh Tesfay in second place also bettered the previous with 2:20:47. The men's winner was the favourite Kelkile Gezahegn in 2:06:37. In sixth place 42 year-old Mark Kiptoo broke the world M40 record with 2:07:05.

November

4 48th TCS **New York City Marathon**, USA. Mary Keitany and Lelisa Desisa won two very contrasting races. Keitany produced a breathtaking display of distance running with a 66:58 second half after 75:50 at halfway, finishing 3:14 ahead of Vivian Cheruiyot in 2:22:48, the second fastest time ever run in New York for her fourth win in the race. She ran the 5ks to 30k in 15:19 and to 35k in 15:34. Desisa, 2nd in 2014 and 3rd in 2015 and 2017, won with a powerful finish in Central Park, the Ethiopian edging his compatriot Shura Kitata to win by 2 sec in 2:05:59 with the 2017 winner Geoffrey Kamworor 3rd in 2:06:26. Both winners earned $145,000 for their race victories and time bonuses. There were a world record 52,812 finishers (30,669 men and 22,143 women).

11 **Istanbul**, Turkey. Ruth Chepngetich led all the way to women's victory in 2:18:35 for fourth equal on the world all-time list.

18 **Nijmegen**, Netherlands. Joshua Cheptegei had his fourth successive win in the NN ZevenHeuvenloop (Seven Hills) in

41:05 to take eight seconds off the world best, running 5k splits of 14:07, 13:42 and 13:16. His remarkable drive to the finish included 7:46 for the last 3k. There was also a Ugandan winner in the women's race, Stella Chesang 47:19.

December

2 **Fukuoka**, Japan. Yuma Hattori, 2:07:27 in warm weather, was the first Japanese winner of the annual Marathon since 20-04

2 **Valencia**, Spain. Both winners, Leul Gebrselassie 2:04:30, and Ashete Bekele, 2:21:14, smashed the course record. Six men ran under 2:05:30 and four women under 2:25. The second woman, 41-year-old Lydia Cheromei, broke her own women over-40 world best.

7 **Abu Dhabi**, UAE. More fast marathoning in the Gulf: Marius Kipserem 2:04:04 won from Abraham Kiptum 2:04:16 (but it seems that the first two, at least, were misdirected and ran short of the full distance) and the women's winner was Ysehaneh Ababel 2:20:16 from Eunice Chumba 2:20:54.

9 **European Cross-Country Championships**, Tilburg, Netherlands. Filip Ingebrigtsen won the senior men's race for his first cross-country success after his younger brother Jakob had won the junior (U20) race for the third successive year (to emulate Stephanie Twell, junior women's winner 2004-06). Yasemin Can was also a 3-time winner – in the women's senior race, in which the Netherlands had their first ever team at any event at the European Cross, and Jimmy Gressier retained his U23 title. Most unusually Britain did not have an individual medallist but were the one nation to take team medals in all six races.

Retired in 2018/19

Men: Leif Arrhenius SWE, Jaroslav Bába CZE, Daniel Bailey ANT, Nathan Brannen CAN, Michaël Bultheel BEL, Sam Chelanga USA, Giovanni Codrington NED, Javier Culson PUR, Jonas Fringeli SUI, Tobias Furer SUI, Vikas Gowda IND, Robbie Grabarz GBR, Robert Harting GER, Jan Hochstrasser SUI, Bershawn Jackson USA, Alexander John GER, Gerd Kanter EST, Sven Knipphals GER, Jan Felix Knobel GER, Dariusz Kuc POL, Artur Kuciapski POL, Casimir Loxsom USA, Patrick Makau KEN, Kevin Menaldo FRA, Denis Nizhegorodov RUS, Scott Rider GBR, Greg Rutherford GBR, Tobias Scherbarth GER, Sofiane Selmouni FRA, Takayuki Tanii JPN, Ncincihli Titi RSA, L J van Zyl RSA. **Women:** Abeba Aregawi SWE, Sarah Brown USA, Lashinda Demus USA, Nuria Fernández ESP, Dawn Harper-Nelson USA, Corinna Harrer GER, Kathrin Klaas GER, Lara Matheis GER, Katharina Molitor GER, Christine Ohuruogu GBR, Mary Saxer USA, Robin Schurmann SUI, Nicole Sifuentes CAN, Kerron Stewart JAM, Lena Urbaniak GER, Jennifer Wenth AUT

ATHLETICS INTERNATIONAL

Edited by Peter Matthews & Mel Watman

The newsletter has, since 1993, been keeping readers in over 60 countries informed of very detailed results (to at least world top 150-200 standards) of track and field, road and cross-country and news items from around the world. It is obtainable by email, with at least 35 issues published annually (weekly in peak season).

Annual subscription 2019: £70 or US $100 or 90 euros. Cash or cheques drawn on a UK bank, payable to Athletics International or by bank transfer (details from Mel) at:
Athletics International, 13 Garden Court, Marsh Lane, Stanmore HA7 4TE
Email: melvynwatman@gmail.com

ATHLETES OF 2018
By Peter Matthews

AFTER THERE WERE no world records in 2017 for a standard men's event we had two in 2018 and both came on the same day. First Eliud Kipchoge, who had run that amazing 2:00:25 for a marathon in irregular circumstances at Monza in 2017, took 1:18 off the 4 year-old world record with his smooth 2:01:39 in Berlin (with a world record at 30k en route) and then Kevin Mayer overcame his disappointment at having three no jumps in the long jump in the European Champs by adding 81points to the decathlon mark set by the great Ashton Eaton in 2015 with a score of 9126 in Talence.

As he had done in 2014, 2015 and 2016 Kipchoge won both the marathons that he contested during the year and now has ten wins in eleven marathons for a rating of the world's greatest ever at the event. The other unbeaten top men at their event in 2018 were Noah Lyles in his five races at 200m (all under 19.85) and best of all Abderrahman Samba, nine at 400m hurdles, all sub 48-seconds, topped by 46.98, a time bettered only by Kevin Young in 1992. In restricted competition Sergey Shirobokov won both his 20k walk races, Hirooki Arai his only race (World Team Champs) at 50k walk and contenders Rhonex Kipruto (two races) and Joshua Cheptegei (one) were unbeaten at 10,000m. Mutaz Essa Barshim won all his six

Selections for World Top Ten

	PJM	TFN	AI
* Eliud Kipchoge	1	1	1
* Abderrahman Samba	2	2	3
* Kevin Mayer	3	3	2
* Christian Coleman	4	(11)	8
Noah Lyles	5	4	4
Timothy Cheruiyot	6	9	10
Mutaz Essa Barshim	7	10	9
Sam Kendricks	8	–	–
* Armand Duplantis	9	–	6
Juan Miguel Echevarría	10	8	7
Emmanuel Korir		6	5
Tomas Walsh		5	
Sergey Shubenkov		7	

* IAAF finalists, Eliud Kipchoge was their athlete of the year.
Note that Track & Field News do not include in their criteria road running (apart from the marathon) and indoor track events. This impacted particularly on Coleman.
Armand Duplantis was IAAF Rising Star of the Year.
Mayer was the EA European Athlete of the Year.

outdoor high jump competition, but lost twice indoors.

Those who came close to perfect seasons included Emmanuel Korir with 6 wins (and a heat win) and a second in the 800m races plus 2/2 (and a heat and a semi) at 400m. Timothy Cheruiyot had 8 wins (plus two heats) at 1500m to 2 losses adding a win in his only races at 800m and 1 mile, and Juan Miguel Échevarría won 5/6 long jumps outdoors plus 2/3 indoors. Michael Norman won four of five at 200m and all seven at 400m.

Although he did not contest the final Samba was the most successful Diamond League competitor, winning at six of the seven meetings – four times breaking the DL record.

My top ten rankings are shown for each event – including indoor form (but also just on outdoor form where relevant), The rationale follows the well-developed system pioneered by Drs. Roberto Quercetani and Don Potts in *Track and Field News* from 1947. As usual the most difficult problems come from athletes with thin seasons or those who have been good for just part of the season. The Diamond League meetings (with finals at Zürich and Brussels), provided the major opportunities for many although, not all athletes get the opportunity to contest DL meetings and these are dominated by the globetrotting professionals. During the year there were major targets for athletes around the world with World Indoor Championships (WI), Continental Games and Championships – very important even if they were not generally contested by so many of the world's best at any given event as would be the case in the DL meetings and the Continental Cup.

Note that Continental Cup placings quoted here for the field events are for the order of their best marks rather than by the regulations introduced by the IAAF for the event.

100 Metres

THE YOUNGER GENERATION took over, following the retirement of Usain Bolt and with Justin Gatlin having a quiet year, although with three wins in the 10.03 to 10.06 range. Christian Coleman ran much the fastest wind-legal time of the year with 9.79 in the DL final in Brussels, well clear of Ronnie Baker 9.93 and Yohan Blake 9.94, but had only five meetings at 100m due to a hamstring injury in May. In all 21 men beat 10 seconds with legal wind and Baker was much the prolific with 12 such times (plus one wind assisted); he was 2-2 v Coleman, 9.78w to 9.84w at Eugene and 9.93 to Coleman's 4th in 10.06 at Rome, while Coleman edged ahead when both ran 9.98 in Rabat; each had three DL wins. Noah Lyles showed more at 200m, and was 3rd in his two DL 100m races – at Rabat and Birmingham, but had major wins to take the US title ahead of Baker and at the Continental Cup. The other DL winner was Reece Prescod, at Shanghai and he was also 2nd in Birmingham, 3rd in Eugene, 4th in Brussels and 5th in Rabat. His slow starting cost him, but his finish was often breath-taking although not quite enough to overtake his compatriot Zharnel Hughes in the European Champs. However he beat Hughes for the British title and also in Birmingham, when Hughes was 5th. Su Bingtian had a consistently excellent season, twice tying the Asian record of 9.91, and won at the Asian Games with 2nd in the Continental Cup, but was beaten 2-0 by Prescod. Another prolific competitor was Akani Simbine, Commonwealth Games and African champion and 3rd in the Continental Cup, and 5-2 v Blake (3rd CG) but beaten 3-0 by Hughes, who had an important win over Lyles 9.91 to 9.93 in Kingston. Mike Rodgers contested the 100m at 20 major meetings, and like Su had six legal sub-10 times. Jimmy Vicaut promised much with a 9.92 win in Marseille and 2nd to Baker in Paris in 9.91, but after 9.97 in his semi, succumbed to a hamstring injury at the Europeans; he beat Rodgers 2-0. Others in contention for ranking spots were Jak Ali Harvey, 3rd European and 4th Continental Cup, Jamaican and NACAC champion Tyquendo Tracey, Isiah Young 4th US Champs. and Japanese champion Ryota Yamagata, 3rd at the Asian Games.

Most times at 10.00/10.05 or faster: Baker 12+1w/12+1w, Rodgers 6/10, Lyles 5+2w/6+2w, Hughes 4+1w/7+1w, Simbine 4/9+1w, Vicaut 4/5, Young 4+2w/7+2w, Su 3+1w/6+1w, Coleman, Prescod 3+1w/4+1w, Tracey 2/5, Burrell, K Williams 2/4+1w, Xie Zhenye 2/4, Bacon 1+2w/2+2w, Harvey 1+1w/4+1w, Tortu 1/4, Cissé 1/3+1w, Yamagata, Erasmus 0/3, Edward 0/2+1w

1. Baker, 2. Coleman, 3. Lyles, 4. Prescod, 5. Hughes, 6. Su, 7. Simbine, 8. Blake, 9. Vicaut, 10. Rodgers

The world indoor 60m list was headed by Coleman who ran world records of 6.37 at Clemson and 6.34A to win the US title from Baker 6.40 and Rodgers 6.50. Coleman completed 4 wins in 4 indoor 60m contests with 6.37 at the World Indoors from Su, who had won his four previous races, 6.42 (his third Asian record of the year) and Baker 6.44.

200 Metres

NOAH LYLES HAS shown huge promise as a sprinter for several years and he is now unbeaten at 200m since January 2017. In 2018 he ran the distance five times, producing four of the year's five sub-19.7 times plus the ninth best: all in DL races – Doha 19.83, Eugene 19.69, Lausanne 19.69, Monaco 19.65, Zürich (final) 19.67. The 2017 World champion Ramil Guliyev improved his best to 19.76 to win the European title and was the other winner of DL races – in Oslo and Stockholm. He was, however, beaten in the Continental Cup by Alonso Edward, who had a fine return to form and had two sub-20 sec times, as did Michael Norman who beat him 2-0 and had four wins and a second place but decided not to compete in the US final. Alex Quiñónez made a big improvement at the age of 28/29 and ran a pb of 19.93A to win at the South American Games; he beat Alonso Edward 4-2 and was 3rd at four DL meets and in the Continental Cup, with 5th in the DL final in which Jereem Richards was 3rd and Aaron Brown 4th. Richards, Commonwealth champion after the disqualification of Zharnel Hughes, was 3-3 v Guliyev but beaten 2-0 by Edward, including in the straight 200m in Boston. That race was won clearly by Steven Gardiner, who also ran 19.74 around a turn, but did not run the 200m enough to earn a ranking. The same applied to Akeem Bloomfield, whose two races were 20.00 for 2nd in Luzern behind Edward and a win in London in 19.81 over Edward and Quiñónez, and Rai Benjamin, 2nd in Paris and 4th in Lausanne. Nethaneel Mitchell-Blake was 2nd and Alex Wilson (who set five Swiss records in 2018) 3rd at the Europeans. Bernardo Baloyes did not compete outside of South America but there he won the Central American & Caribbean title from Edward and Kyle Greaux, who was 6th at the Commonwealth Games and 1st at the NACAC. 20 year-old Clarence Munyai ran a South African record 19.69 at high altitude in March, but injury prevented him competing after his CG 4th place. Elijah Hall won the NCAA indoor title in 20.02, the second fastest ever indoors, but ran the event just twice outdoors. A record 14 men beat 20 seconds with legal wind.

Most times at 20.10/20.30 or better: Guliyev 6/11, Lyles 5/5, Brown 4/11, Richards 4/8, Quiñónez 4/6+1w, Norman 3+1w/3+1w, Edward 3/9, Greaux, Hortelano 2/6, Baloyes 2/4, Adams, Gardiner 2/3, Makwala 2/2, Wilson 1/6, Mitchell-Blake, Munyai 1/3, E Hall 1i/1+2i, Ewers 1w/2+2w, Oduduro 0/4+1i, Gemili 0/4, Hughes, J Thompson 0/3, Titi, K Williams, M Williams 0/2+1w.

1. Lyles, 2. Guliyev, 3. Norman, 4. Quiñónez, 5. Edward, 6. Richards, 7. Brown, 8. Mitchell-Blake, 9. Wilson, 10. Greaux

400 Metres

WAYDE VAN NIEKERK did not compete in 2018 due to injury and the 2017 no. 2 Isaac Makwala competed in just two DL Races (3rd

Doha and 2nd Stockholm) in May after winning the Commonwealth title. So the year lists were headed by younger men. Michael Norman ran the year's best time, 43.61 to win the NCAA title and was undefeated in two indoor and five outdoor competitions, but ran only in the USA. Steven Gardiner ran sub-44 to win in Doha and Shanghai, then succumbing to injury before a comeback to win at the Skolimowska Memorial in Chorzów but a non-finisher in the DL final in Zürich. Akeem Bloomfield was 2nd at the NCAAs in 43.94 and won his one DL race in Rabat, but the best record was by the world's fourth fastest (44.07 in the London DL), Abdelilah Haroun. His six wins included at the Asian Games and Continental Cup with two seconds and a third in other DL races. After three indoor wins Fred Kerley ran just five times, but all in big races, winning on the DL circuit in Rome, Birmingham and the final in Zürich. In the last he was followed by Nathan Strother (4th US, 3rd Cont. Cup), Matthew Hudson-Smith and Paul Dedewo. Dedewo was the most prolific racer of these men and his record included 2nd to Kahmari Montgomery at the US Champs and a win at the Athletics World Cup. Hudson-Smith won the European title and showed that he was capable of taking the 31 year-old European record when sauntering across the line in his Commonwealth Games heat, only to be disqualified for running inside his lane. Due to being diagnosed with Graves' Disease Kirani James had just three races with a best of 44.35 in Kingston. Faster were Nathon Allen, NCAA 3rd with 44.13 and 3-0 v Strother, and Emmanuel Korir, 44.21A to win the Kenyan title, but both had only one 400m race in Europe. Area winners were Baboloki Thebe, African, and Luguelín Santos, CAG, and these men were 2nd and 6th at the Continental Cup. 10th best of 44.35 is a new all-time record.

Most sub-45.00 times: Haroun, Dedewo 9; Hudson-Smith 7, Norman 6+1i, Allen 6, L Santos 5, Bloomfield 4+1i, F Kerley, Cherry 4, Gardiner, James, Makwala, Montgomery, Strother 3

1. Haroun, 2. Gardiner, 3. Norman, 4. Kerley,
5. Bloomfield, 6. Dedewo, 7. Makwala,
8. Hudson-Smith, 9. James, 10. Allen

800 Metres

THERE WERE THREE sub 1:43 times in 2018 – two by Emmanuel Korir, both in the DL races: 1:42.05 in London and 1:42.79 in Birmingham, and 1:42.14 by Nijel Amos in Monaco. Overall standards were well ahead of 2017: 18 times by 10 men under 1:44 compared to 8 by 5, and 10th best man at 1:43.82. although these were still below the levels of the 2014-16 years. Korir, the 2017 NCAA champion, ran an African indoor record 1:44.21 at the Millrose Games and then lost just one of his seven 800ms – to Amos in the African Champs (when there were problems at

the start), but he beat Amos 3-1 overall and was 3-0 v Wycliffe Kinyamal who won at the Commonwealth Games (Amos 8th) and was also ahead of Amos 3rd to 4th in London, but 3rd to Amos 2nd in Eugene to Korir. Kenyan champion Jonathan Kitilit had the most fast times, with ten under 1:45, but was well behind the top three on win-loss and was beaten 4-3 by Ferguson Cheruiyot. Saul Ordóñez was the fastest European with a Spanish record 1:43.65 in Monaco when he was 3rd a place behind Brandon McBride 1:43.20, but Marcin Lewandowski had a better record, including 2-0 v Adam Kszczot and 4-0 v US champion Clayton Murphy, who won at the World Cup from Kszczot. Korir won a slow race at the Continental Cup from Murphy and Amos while McBride won the NACAC title and was 2-0 v Murphy. Kszczot was the World Indoor champion and took the European title in 1:44.59, his fastest time of the year but there Ordóñez went out in the semis. Elijah Manangoi and Jake Wightman, both best known at 1500m, had good form in limited 800m action, with 3rd and 7th at Birmingham after Wightman had placed 4th at the Commonwealth Games and went on to 4th in the DL final behind Korir, Lewandowski and Cheruiyot. Due to injury David Rudisha did not run at all in 2017, but there were six Kenyans in the world list top ten (also Michael Saruni at 1:43.25 and Cornelius Tuwei 1:43.82).

Most times sub-1:45.0: Kitilit 10, Amos, Cheruiyot 5; Kinyamal, Lewandowski 4; Korir 3+1i, Kszczot, Ordóñez, Tuwei, Deng, A Kipketer 3.

1. Korir, 2, Kinyamal, 3. Amos, 4. Kitilit,
5. Cheruiyot, 6. Lewandowski, 7. McBride,
8. Murphy, 9. Kszczot, 10. Ordóñez

1500 Metres

ELIJAH MANANGOI AND Timothy Cheruiyot were the top two 1500m men in 2017, and so they were in 2018 but in reverse order as Cheruiyot had a 5-2 advantage and won five DL races to one by Manangoi. Manangoi's wins over Cheruiyot came at the Commonwealth Games and at the African Champs. Their 3:28.41 and 3:29.64 at Monaco plus Cheruiyot's 3:29.71 in Paris were the sub-3:30 times of 2018. Filip Ingebrigtsen was next fastest, 3rd in Monaco in a Norwegian record 3:30.01, but he was injured at the European Champs and his subsequent form – 5th in the DL final in Zurich and 6th in Zagreb was less good. Monaco had the best depth of times with 12 men under 3:34 and Charles Simotwo's 3:32.77 being the best ever for 11th place. Still only 17 years old Jakob Ingebrigtsen was 4th there in 3:31.18 and he followed that with his amazing 1500m/5000m double at the European Championships. He set European U20 records not only with that 1500m time but also his 3:52.28 mile for 4th in Eugene, although he was beaten by George Manangoi, younger brother of Elijah, at the World Juniors. He was also 2-0 v Ayanleh Souliman, 5th in 3:31.19 in Monaco and also sub-3:32 in Paris (2nd) and Zürich (3rd behind the big two). Although Souliman did not win a race, he was consistently well placed and was 4-0 v Abdelaati Iguider, 5-0 v Simotwo and 7-0 v Aman Wote and also 3-2 v Mediterranean Games champion Brahim Kaazouzi. Another top junior was Samuel Tefera, who after winning the World Indoor title, started well outdoors with 1st at the Ethiopian Champs, 2nd in Shanghai and Eugene and 3rd in Rome, but was then 5th in the World Juniors, 10th in the African Champs and 7th in Zürich. Manangoi, Cheruiyot and Ronald Musagala took the African Champs medals while other top men were further back: 4 Suleiman, 5 Wote, 6 Iguider, 8 Simotwo, 10 Tefera, but all could have been seriously affected by the chaotic travel arrangements to get there. Marcin Lewandowski was 2nd at the World Indoors and at the Europeans (Jake Wightman 3rd) and Continental Cup, and won at the Athletics World Cup but these were all in slow times and his best was 3:35.06 for 9th in Rabat. Iguider was 3rd and Wote 4th at the World Indoors.

Most times sub-3:35.0 or 3:52.0M: Cheruiyot 9, Souleiman 6, Manangoi, Wote; 5 Simotwo, F Ingebrigtsen 4, Tefera, Iguider, Kaazouzi, Holusa, Birgen 3

1. Cheruiyot, 2. Manangoi, 3. Souleiman,
4. J Ingebrigtsen, 5. F Ingebrigtsen, 6. Kaazouzi,
7. Iguider (8), 8. Tefera (7), 9. Wote, 10. Simotwo.
(Inc. indoors)

3000 Metres/2 Miles

YOMIF KEJELCHA RAN the year's two fastest times outdoors: 7:28.00 at Göteborg and 7:32.93 in Rabat where 2nd to 7th ran the next fastest times, headed by Birhanu Yemataw 2nd in 7:34.26. 18 year-old Selemon Barega had been fastest indoors with 7:36.64 and was runner-up to Kejelcha at the World Indoors; outdoors he won at 2 miles in Eugene in 8:20.01 and won the third fastest 3000m race – at Ostrava.

5000 Metres

THERE HAD BEEN no sub-13 minute times until suddenly eight men did so in the DL final in Brussels with four more men making it 12 of the 14 best times of the year from this one race. The winner Selemon Barega took 4.51 secs off the world junior record with 12:43.02, the sixth fastest time ever run and the best for 13 years. Second was the man whose WJR he took, Hagos Gebrhiwet then Yomif Kejelcha, Muktar Edris, Abadi Hadis, Paul Chelimo, Richard Yator and Getaneh Tamire (Molla). Sorting out a satisfactory ranking of the world men is very difficult. Barega was, however, the only man to run under 13:05 three times as when he won in Stockholm from Birhanu Yemataw, Hadis and Mohammed Ahmed, and when 2nd to Yemataw in Lausanne, a race that had the second best depth of times as 3-8 (all under 13:08) were Hadis, Tamire, Yator, Edris, Telahun Haile and Aron Kifle. Shanghai provided another fast race with Yemataw the winner in 13:09.64 from Chelimo, Edris 6th and Hadis 7th. Chelimo had wins at the US Champs and in the London DL from Edris, Yomif Kejelcha, Ahmed (9th Brussels), Yemataw. and Gebrhiwet (his only 5000m apart from Brussels). So Chelimo and Yemataw went 1-1 and both were 2-1 v Edris. The fastest non-African born runner was Ben True with 13:04.11 for 11th in Brussels. 16 year-old Edward Zakayo, after winning the Kenyan trial, was 3rd at the Commonwealth Games behind Joshua Cheptegei and Ahmed, and went on to win the World Junior and African titles. Tamire was 2nd in the Africans and Barega 4th at the Africans and at the World Juniors, where he was a place behind Jakob Ingebrigtsen, who went on to win the European title.

Most times under 13:15: Edris, Hadis 4; Barega, Chelimo, Yemataw, A Rop 3.

1. Barega, 2. Yemataw, 3. Chelimo, 4. Edris,
5. Gebrhiwet, 6. Kejelcha, 7. Hadis, 8. Tamire,
9. Yator, 10. Ahmed

10,000 Metres

SADLY, REMEMBERING THE great days of the 10,000m at the Van Damme Memorial, there was no big race to bring the top men together but until October the Commonwealth Games race dominated the world list, with five of the top six times as Joshua Cheptegei won in 27:19.62 from Mohammed Ahmed, Rodgers Chumo, Jacob Kiplimo and Jake Robertson. Next fastest was 27:21.08 by 18 year-old Rhonex Kipruto when he won the World Junior title nearly 20 seconds ahead of Kiplimo. Kipruto had also run 27:49.6 (perhaps worth under 27 minutes at low altitude) to win the Kenyan junior trial race. The top at the CG (and Robertson) had no more 10,000m races, but Chumo had won the Kenyan CG trial race and went on to win in Kobe, Gifu and Chubu. Richard Ringer had run 27:36.52 to win the European Cup race by just 0.28 from Morhad Amdouni, but while Ringer dropped out Amdouni went on to win the European title from Bashir Abdi, and Yemaneberhan Crippa was 3rd in both these races. Asian Games winner was Hassan Chani, who also had a good win in 27:38.16 in Maia. The lists were augmented considerably by many good races in Japan at the end of the year. Joel Mwaura won the Corporate Champs race in Osaka from Nicholas Kosimbei, Joseph Macharia Ndirangu and Chumo, followed by successive world leads from Richard Yator 27:14.70 in Kanagawa and Stanley Waithaka 27:13.01 in

Yokohama and fine depth at the Hachioji trials where Tulu Merga won from Bernard Kimeli and Daniel Kipkemoi with Mwaura 12th.

1. Kipruto, 2. Cheptegei, 3. Ahmed, 4. Chumo, 5. Kiplimo, 6. Amdouni, 7. Chani, 8. Crippa, 9. Waithaka, 10. Yator

Half Marathon

ABRAHAM KIPRONO TOOK five seconds off the world record with 58:18 in Valencia when he was followed by Jemal Yimer 58:33 and Abadi Hadis 58:44 for the 2nd and 5th fastest times of the year. Kiptum's other half marathon had been the previous month in Copenhagen when he ran 59:09 for 2nd in a race won by Daniel Kipchumba 59:06 with Yimer 3rd. Kipchumba had also run 59:06 to win in Verbania and was 3rd in New Delhi behind Andamlak Belihu and Amdework Walelegn, and the year's 3rd, 6th and 7th fastest times had come at Ras Al Khaimah: Bedan Karoki 58:42, Yimer 59:00 and Alex Kibet 59:06. In all 37 men bettered 1 hour during the year with Yimer, Kipchumba and Stephen Kiprop doing so three times. There was a slowish start in windy conditions at the World Championships, where Geoffrey Kamworor won in 60.02 from Abraham Cheroben, Aron Kifle and the prolific Yimer.

Marathon

ELIUD KIPCHOGE REMAINED supreme amongst world marathon runners, consolidating his status as the world's greatest of all-time with wins in London (2:04:17) and by taking 1:18 off the world record with 2:01.39 in Berlin. New standards were set with 16 men running under 2:05 in the year, seven of those times coming in Dubai where Mosinet Geremew 2:04:00, Leul Gebrselassie (on debut) 2:04:02, Tamirat Tola 2:04:06 and Asefa Mengistu 2:04:06 ran the next best times of the year, with Lawrence Cherono also running 2:04:06 when he won at Amsterdam as he had the previous year. Kenenisa Bekele, who had been 6th in London, dropped out there with hip problems. Times in London were slowed considerably by warm weather (up to 24.1°C), but the performances of 2nd Tola Shura 2:04:49 and 3rd Mo Farah, British record 2:06.21, were especially notable. Farah improved his record to 2:05:11 with a fine win in Chicago ahead of Geremew 2:05:24, and Shura was 2nd in New York in 2:06:01 two seconds behind Lelisa Desisa, with Geoffrey Kamworor 3rd and Tola 4th. Other sub-2:05 winners were Marius Kipserem, 2:04:04 in Abu Dhabi (although this may have been short) after 5th in Rotterdam, and Sisay Lemma, 2:04:58 at Ljubljana, having been 5th in Dubai and 2nd in Prague to Galen Rupp (5th Chicago). Abraham Kiptum won in Daegu in 2:06:29 and was 2nd in Abu Dhabi in 2:04:16. Cherono's other marathon was 7th

in London and Mengistu won in Seoul in November. In the December race in Valencia Leul Gebrselassie won in 2:04:30 from two new sub-2:05 men: El Hassan El Abbassi 2:04:43 and Mathew Kisorio 2:04:53 and another three under 2:05:30. Also with two sub-2:06 times was Kenneth Kipkemoi, 1st Rotterdam and 4th Chicago and another important winner was Dickson Chumba, 2:05:30 in Tokyo.

1. Kipchoge, 2. Farah, 3. Geremew, 4. Shura, 5. Gebrselassie, 6. Kipkemoi, 7. Lemma, 8. Tola, 9. Cherono, 10. Mengistu

3000 Metres Steeplechase

CONSESLUS KIPRUTO IS still looking for his first sub-8 minute time and indeed was far from that with a best of 8:08.40 in 2018, but he had five more times under 8:12 and the best overall record with 7 wins in 10 races, including at the Commonwealth Games, African Champs and Continental Cup as well as three DL races including the final in Zürich, so is top ranked for the fourth time. Soufiane El Bakkali ran a sub-8 time with 7:58.15 from Evan Jager 8:01.02 in Monaco as those were only times under 8:06 during the year. El Bakkali was 2nd in both Africans and at Zürich when Jager US champion for the seventh successive year, was 3rd. Benjamin Kigen and Chala Beyo were the next fastest men and both had good depth of performance with Kigen 3-2 up on win-loss. Then came Nicholas Bett, 4-2 v Amos Kirui, 3-2 v Hilary Bor (2nd US) and 2-2 v Abraham Kibiwot 4th and the Zürich placings are followed closely as 4th to 10th were: 4 Beyo, 5 Bett, 6 Kibiwot, 7 Bor, 8 Leonard Bett, 9 Kigen. Although 5th to 11th in Dl races, Matt Hughes was CG 4th and Continental Cup 2nd. He was quicker than Mahiedine Mekhissi-Benabbad who ran just one DL race, 5th in Rome, but took another European title with ease.

Most times under 8:15: C Kipruto 6, Kigen 5, Beyo 4, El Bakkali, Jager 3.

1. C Kipruto, 2. El Bakkali, 3. Jager, 4. Kigen, 5. Beyo, 6. Bett, 7. Kibiwot, 8. Bor, 9. Hughes, 10. Kirui

110 Metres Hurdles

SERGEY SHUBENKOV, ONE of the Russians allowed to compete internationally as an Authorised Neutral Athlete, had 11 wins in his 15 competitions and he ran the seven fastest wind-legal times of the year, four times under 13 seconds headed by 12.92 at Székesfehérvár. He returns to the top ranking he had in 2015. Next fastest was Orlando Ortega with 13.08, but this pair was beaten into 2nd and 3rd at the European Championships by the more inconsistent Pascal Martinot-Lagarde, for whom this was his one win in nine races against Shubenkov and in eight against Ortega. Omar McLeod, the top man in 2016-17, raced only four times due to injury after starting well with wins at Shanghai in 13.16 and Eugene 13.01w and so ranks as third Jamaican behind Ronald Levy and Hansle Parchment with Levy having a 4-2 advantage on win-loss. This pair were 4-3 and 2-1 against Martinot-Lagarde and 5-2 and 5-0 against Devon Allen, who won the US title from top collegian Grant Holloway. Two improving men complete the rankings: Gabriel Constantino, the Brazilian and Ibero-American champion, and Freddie Crittenden, who was 5th in the DL final in Brussels behind Shubenkov, Ortega, Parchment and Martinot-Lagarde, with Allen, Levy and Balázs Baji filling places 6-8.

Most times under 13.30: Shubenkov 14+1w, Ortega 9+1w, Levy 7+1w, Parchment. Martinot-Lagarde 5, Allen 2+1w.

1. Shubenkov, 2. Ortega, 3. Levy, 4. Parchment, 5. Martinot-Lagarde, 6. Allen, 7. Holloway, 8. McLeod, 9. Constantino, 10. Crittenden

Holloway was the year's fastest at 60m hurdles indoors with 7.42, also winning the NCAA title with 7.47, while Jarret Eaton was US champion in 7.43A from Aries Merritt 7.46. Then the 2017 fastest man Andrew Pozzi took the World title in 7.46 from Eaton, Aurel Manga, Merritt and Martinot-Lagarde.

400 Metres Hurdles

ABDERRAHMAN SAMBA, WHO had run 48.31A in his debut season of 2017, had one of the greatest ever years at this event as he was unbeaten and ran 47.90 or better in all his nine races. He set Asian records successively with 47.90A in Potchefstroom, 47.57 in Doha, 47.48 in Rome, 47.41 in Stockholm and then 46.98 in Paris, a time second only to Kevin Young's 46.78 at the 1992 Olympic Games. His nine sub-48 sec times equalled the record set by Danny Harris in 1990 and Kevin Young in 1992. Karsten Warholm was 2nd five times and 3rd once in the six DL races won by Samba and improved his Norwegian record four times – to 47.64 at the European Champs. Kyron McMaster started with a win at the Commonwealth Games and was 2-2 v Warholm, splitting the top two when second in Paris in 47.54 with Warholm running 48,06, and he also won the NACAC title from Jamaican champion Ansert Whyte, but he did not finish in Lausanne and trailed in last at the Continental Cup, won by Samba from Whyte, Warholm and Yasmani Copello. Rai Benjamin, whose ability to run for the USA rather than Antigua was confirmed at the end of the season, won the NCAA title in a CAC record 47.02, but that was the end of his racing at the event, as he ran just twice (at 200m) in Europe. Copello was the most prolific sub-49 second man, never worse than 4th in his 15 competitions. His best was 47.81 for 2nd at the Europeans when he was followed by Thomas Barr, Ludvy Vaillant. Patryk Dobek

and Rasmus Mägi, all in season's bests Kenny Selmon won the US title from T.J. Holmes and also won at the Athletics World Cup and was 2nd NCAAs. 115 men inside 50 seconds was a new record, beating the 109 of 2017.

Most times to 49.00: Copello 13, Warholm 10, Samba 9 (all under 48.00), McMaster, Holmes, Selmon 7; Whyte 6, Vaillant 5, Mägi 4, Benjamin 3

1. Samba. 2. Warholm, 3. McMaster, 4. Copello, 5. Benjamin, 6. Selmon, 7. Holmes, 8. Whyte, 9. Vaillant, 10. Barr

High Jump

MUTAZ ESSA BARSHIM cleared 2.40m at Doha and Székesfehérvár and his six successive years at this level now ties Javier Sotomayor who also had six years at 2.40 or higher. Barshim won all his six outdoor competitions, five of them at 2.36 or higher, although his season ended on July 2 due to injury, while indoors he won twice and was second twice – to Wang Yu at Banská Bystrica (both 2.31) and to Danil Lysenko at the World Indoors (2.36 to 2.33). Lysenko cleared 2.40 in Monaco and was the most prolific competitor at 2.35 or above; he won all his eight indoor competitions and outdoors had four 1sts and four 2nds (all to Barshim). After the top two the best of the year was 2.36 by Dmitriy Nabokov and Brandon Starc. Nabokov had 2.32 and 2.30 indoors but a next best outdoors of 2.28, but Starc, who had won at the Commonwealth Games with 2.32, ended the year in great form as he won at Birmingham, Eberstadt and Brussels (DL final) and was 2nd to Donald Thomas at the Continental Cup. Starc had 3-0 advantage over both the European Champs 1-2 Mateusz Przybylko and Maksim Nedosekov. Przybylko had been third at the World Indoors and was 2nd at the DL final, where his 2.33 was followed by Gianmarco Tamberi (returning to form), Andriy Protsenko, Thomas and Naoto Tobe. Jeron Robinson won the US and NACAC titles and at the Athletics World Cup, where Wang Yu was second. Wang, however, beat Robinson on the other two occasions that they met, and won at the Asian Games from Woo Sang-hyuk with Tobe and Majed El Dein third equal. Robinson beat Thomas (also CAG champion) 3-2. Ilya Ivanyuk was 3rd and Tamberi 4th at the Europeans. Ivan Ukhov was again restricted to competing in Russia, where he had bests of 2.35 indoors and 2.34 outdoors.

Most competitions over 2.35/2.30m (outdoors/in): Barshim 5+2i/5+4i, Lysenko 3+5i/7+8i, Starc 1/7, Przybylko 1/4+1i, Nabokov 1/1+2i, Ukhov 1i/2+3i, Robinson 0/4+2i, Nedosekov 4+2i, Wang Yu, Thomas 0/4+1i; Tamberi, Tobe 0/3; Ivanyuk 0/2+2i, Culver 0/3i

1. Barshim, 2. Lysenko, 3. Starc, 4. Przybylko, 5. Wang Yu, 6. Robinson, 7. Thomas, 8. Nedosekov. 9. Ghazal. 10. Tamberi.

Pole Vault

ARMAND DUPLANTIS HAD improved his world junior record indoors to 5.83 and 5.88 and outdoors to 5.92 and 5.93. Then the great story of the year came at the European Championships where the 18 year-old soared over 5.95, 6.00 and 6.05 before calling it a day. He and 21 year-old Timur Morgunov became the 23rd and 24th men over 6 metres. The 2nd (Morgunov 6.00 from a previous best of 5.92) and 3rd (Renaud Lavillenie 5.95) marks in this wonderful competition tied the best evers for these places (fifth time at 6.00 for 2nd, third time for 5.95 for 3rd), and then Piotr Lisek was 4th at 5.90 and Pawel Wojciechowski 5th at 5.80. Duplantis had a year's record of 4 wins in 6 indoor competitions and 9 in 15 outdoors and he was also World Junior champion. He was beaten 2-0 indoors by Lavillenie while these two were 4-4 outdoors, while Morgunov, who went on to big wins in Zürich and Brussels, was 4-2 v Lavillenie. However the Europeans had to yield top ranking once again to US and Continental Cup winner Sam Kendricks, who, with five DL wins, had a win-loss advantage outdoors of 5-1 v Duplantis, 6-3 v Lavillenie and 8-3 v Lisek although 2-2 v Morgunov. Indoors Kendricks and Lavillenie were 1-1 with the Frenchman winning World Indoor gold from Kendricks, Lisek and Kurtis Marschall. Lisek was the most active with 11 competitions indoors and 27 outdoors. Outdoors he was 11-5 v Wojciechowski and 10-4 v Shawnacy Barber. Marschall was 4-3 outdoors and 1-0 indoors v Wojciechowski, and won at the Commonwealth Games from Barber. Chis Nilsen did not compete in Europe but had a fine record with the NCAA title and 2nd at the US Champs. Raphael Holzdeppe and Konstadínos Filippídis were better indoors than out (bests 5.88 and 5.85 with 5= and 7th World Indoors, then 5.81 and 5.75 respectively outdoors). Holzdeppe's record was marred no several no-heights, but he was 5= at the World Indoors. Apart from a 5.90 indoors at Rouen, Thiago Braz da Silva, 12th at the World Indoors and an outdoor best of 5.70, was troubled by an injured foot.

Most competitions over 5.75m (outdoors + in): Kendricks 14+5i, Lisek 13+10i, Duplantis 11+2i, Lavillenie 11+8i, Wojciechowski 8+3i, Morgunov 7+4i, Barber 6+3i, Nilsen 6+1i, Marschall 4+2i, Holzdeppe 2+2i, Filippídis 1+2i.

1. Kendricks, 2. Duplantis, 3. Morgunov (4), 4. Lavillenie (3), 5. Lisek, 6. Marschall, 7. Wojciechowski, 8. Barber, 9. Nilsen, 10. Holzdeppe. (Including indoors).

Long Jump

LUVO MANYONGA CONFIRMED the brilliant form he had shown in 2018 by consistently jumping over 8.50 and he beat his compatriot Ruswahl Samaai 8-1, the exception being Samaii winning the African title 8.45 to 8.43. While these men had the best depth of top marks, they were headed by the brilliant young Cuban Juan Miguel Echevarría, who turned 20 in August. He beat Manyonga four times: 8.46 to 8.44 at the World Indoors, 8.83w (the world's longest since 1995), 8.50 to 8.25 (3rd) in Stockholm, 8.66 to 8.31 in Ostrava and 8.68 to 8.42 at Bad Langensalza to two wins for Manyonga, 8.40 to 8.34 indoors at Metz and 8.58 to 8.53 in Rome, before injury ended the Cuban's season in early July. Manyonga won at the Commonwealth Games from Henry Frayne, Samaii and Tajay Gayle. Wang Jianan won at the Asian Games, and Militiádis Tentóglou was European champion but beaten 4 times by Jeff Henderson to one, that when Tentóglou was 2nd in the Continental Cup behind Samaiii with Henderson 3rd, Frayne 4th and Wang 5th. Gayle was consistently good and went 2-1 v Tentóglou and 3-2 v Frayne; his best was 8.24 at the NACAC won by Marquis Dendy with 8.28, but Dendy's next best outdoors was 8.13. However, Dendy jumped 8.42 for 3rd at the World Indoors after 2nd to Jarrion Lawson at the US Indoors (8.22 to 8.38). Difficult to rank are Aleksandr Menkov, able to compete only in Russia, Shi Yuhao, whose only outdoor competition was 2nd in Shanghai with 8.43 although he had won the Asian indoor title and was 5th at the World Indoors, and Zach Bazile, who, after modest early season form in the USA, jumped 8.37 to win the NCAA title, 8.08 for second to Henderson with Dendy 3rd at the US Champs and 8.32 for 2nd to Manyonga at the World Cup. Greg Rutherford retired through persistent injury after season's bests of 7.89i/7.86 and last year's no. 3 Jarrion Lawson after 4th at the World indoors had a best of 8.25 outdoors but faced a drugs suspension. Standards are improving as shown by 10th best of 8.37 being a new record (was 8.35 in 1997).

Most competitions over 8.10m: Manyonga 15+3i, Samaai 12, Henderson 8+1w, Frayne 8, Gayle 7, Echevarría 6+3i, Tentóglou 5, Dendy 3+3i, Menkov 3+1i, Bazile, Gotch, Huang Changzhou 2+1i, Shi 1+3i

1. Echevarría, 2. Manyonga, 3. Samaai, 4. Frayne, 5. Henderson, 6. Gayle, 7. Tentóglou (8), 8. Bazile (9), 9. Menkov (-), 10. Dendy (7), - Shi (10); nr, Lawson. (Including indoors).

Triple Jump

CHRISTIAN TAYLOR IS top for the sixth time but was 2-2 against Pedro Paulo Pichardo as they shared the top eight (and three wind-assisted) performances of the year. Their best marks came in Diamond League meetings with Pichardo winning in Doha 17.95 to 17.81 and Taylor in Monaco 17.86w to 17.67w. Also Taylor's 17.62 was 1cm ahead of his rival in Lausanne, and Pichardo won the DL final in Brussels

17.49 to 17.31. Apart from his no jumps at the US Champs Taylor won all his six other competitions and Pichardo, unable yet to compete for Portugal, won twice and was 3rd once indoors and had two more wins and a 3rd outdoors. Taylor also ran all his nine 400m times under 45.8. From a best of 16.86 in 2017 Almir dos Santos burst onto the scene indoors with four competitions over 17m, headed by 17.41 when 2nd at the World Indoors, won by Will Claye 17.43 with Nelson Évora 3rd 17.40. Dos Santos, who had beaten Évora and Pichardo with 17.37 in Madrid and also had a major win in Liévin with 17.35, improved outdoors to 17.53 in Baie-Mahault from Claye and Pichardo, both 17.40, and was 3rd behind Taylor and Claye in Eugene, but injury ended his season prematurely. Claye only had four competitions (two indoors, two out) but all were excellent with 17.28A to win the US Indoor title his lowest mark; he stopped in May to concentrate on his music. Évora won the European title from Alexis Copello (4th WI) but had better marks indoors and was only 8th in Brussels and 5th at the Continental Cup, won by Taylor from Cristian Nápoles and Fabrice Zango. The 17 year-old Cuban Jordan Díaz was the most prolific competitor with 11 marks over 17m and 8 wins, including World Junior, NACAC and Youth Olympics titles, and three 2nd places, including to Nápoles at the CAG. Three more Americans were closely matched, with Omar Craddock, although only 6th at the US Champs outdoors, 3-2 v Donald Scott (1 US) and 3-1 v Chris Benard (2 US) on outdoor form (1-1 and 1-0 indoors). They were respectively 4th, 3rd and 5th in Brussels with Copello 7th. Copello was 1-0 v Nápoles and 4-3 v Évora outdoors.

Most competitions over 17.00: J Díaz 11, Taylor 7, Pichardo 7+2i, Craddock 4+2i, Scott 3+2w+1i, Carter 3+1w+2i, Évora 3+3i, Copello, Nápoles 3+1i; Benard 3, dos Santos 2+4i, Claye, Zango 2+2i

    1. Taylor, 2. Pichardo, 3. dos Santos (4), 4. Claye (3), 5. J Díaz, 6. Craddock, 7. Scott, 8. Benard (9), 9. Copello (10). 10. Nápoles (-), - Évora (8). (Including indoors).

Shot

THIS WAS ANOTHER outstanding year for shot putting as epitomised by the best ever marks for place coming for 2nd to 5th in Zürich and 6th and 7th in Monaco. There were a record 21 performances at 22m or better (18 outdoors, 3 indoors) and Ryan Crouser with 9 and Tom Walsh with 7 continued to dominate; then one each by Tomás Stanek and Konrad Bukowiecki indoors and by Darrell Hill, Michal Haratyk and Darlan Romani outdoors. Crouser won 7 of his 12 competitions, and was 6-3 v Walsh, who won 15 of 22 outdoors as well the World Indoor title with 22.31. That was his third Oceania record of

the competition and he headed the outdoor list with an Oceania record 22.67 while Crouser's best was 22.53. Romani set two South American records indoors and four outdoors to 22.00; he won the Continental Cup from Crouser, Walsh, Haratyk and Stanek, beating Haratyk 5-1 as well as at the World Indoors when they were 4th and 10th. Both men had close competition with Hill (6th WI) with whom Romani was 2-2 and 1-0 indoors and Haratyk was 4-3 and 0-1. As in 2017 Hill produced his best in the DL final where in Zürich he was 2nd at 22.40 behind Walsh 22.60, followed by Crouser 22.18, Romani 21.94, Stanek 21.87, David Storl 21.33, Haratyk 21.23 and Ryan Whiting 20.56, but Haratyk was well ahead of Hill at the World Cup. The European Champs order was Haratyk, Bukowiecki, Storl, Stanek and Aleksandr Lesnoy. Storl beat Stanek 4-2 outdoors and was also 2nd to Stanek's 3rd at the World Indoors. Curtis Jensen was the third US man over 21m and was 3rd to Hill and Crouser at the US Champs. Fourth there was Ryan Whiting, who was only 18th on the world list at 20.99 outdoors (plus 21.03 for 7th WI) but was consistent and beat Bukowiecki (8th WI) 6-2 outdoors (2-2 indoors) and was also 5-2 v O'Dayne Richards, who was 4th at the Commonwealth Games behind Walsh, Chuk Enekwechi and Tim Nedow.

Most competitions over 21.00: Walsh 22+1i, Haratyk 20+3i, Hill 12+1i, Storl 11+3i, Romani 11+1i, Crouser 11, Stanek 9+6i, Lesnoy 8+1i, Bukowiecki 6+2i, Jensen, Enekwechi 3.

    1. Crouser, 2. Walsh. 3. Romani, 4. Haratyk, 5. Hill, 6. Storl, 7. Stanek, 8. Bukowiecki, 9. Lesnoy, 10. Jensen.

Discus

THERE WAS ONLY 13 centimetres separating the top three men on the world list and they dominated the list of top 30 performances (67.82 or better): Fedrick Dacres 11, Andrius Gudzius 9 and Daniel Ståhl 6, but they could be sorted on win-loss: Dacres was 6-3 v Gudzius and 6-4 v Ståhl, and Gudzius 8-1 v Ståhl. Jamaican champion Dacres won at the World Cup, NACAC, DL final (from Gudzius, Ståhl, Mason Finley, Lukas Weisshaidinger, Christoph Harting, Robert Urbanek and Ehsan Hadadi) and the Continental Cup (from Gudzius and Ståhl). Gudzius, Ståhl and Lukas Weisshaidinger took the medals at the Europeans with Simon Pettersson 4th and Robert Harting, 6th, as Christoph Harting was a non-qualifier. Weisshaidinger had a positive win-loss against all but the top three. Reggie Jagers beat Finley 2-0 including when 1st and 2nd at the US Champs, when Jagers's 68.61 was the best ever by a left hander, but they lost 2-0 and 4-1 respectively to Asian Games champion Hadadi, who also has a 7-2 record v Ståhl from early season success. Trevor Smikle had a good year, including 2nd to Dacres at the Commonwealth Games and NACAC and 3rd at the CAG. Philip Milanov did not compete after June but beat Pettersson and Daniel Jasinski 2-1. Two great throwers ended their careers this year: Robert Harting, who had won Olympic gold, three world titles and two Europeans, and Gerd Kanter, former World and Olympic champion for whom this was his 18th successive season over 60m (with six of them over 70m).

Most competitions over 65m: Dacres 25, Gudzius 18, Ståhl 15, Weisshaidinger, Hadadi 9, C Harting 8, Jagers 6, Pettersson, Smikle 4; Finley, Milanov, Jasinski, Mattis 3.

    1. Dacres, 2. Gudzius, 3. Ståhl,
    4. Weisshaidinger, 5. Hadadi, 6. C Harting,
    7. Jagers, 8. Smikle, 9. Finley, 10. Pettersson

Hammer

FROM 2009 TO 2017 Pavel Fajdek had a 62-3 win-loss record against Wojciech Nowicki and started with three more wins against him, but then the tables were turned and Nowicki won five successive competitions before they shared honours for the last four competitions so that Fajdek now leads 67-10. These two men topped the world lists. Nowicki had the two best marks 81.85 and 81.45 and Fajdek's best was 81.14, and Nowicki was the winner at the Polish and European Champs, his only poor competition being his sixth at the Continental Cup. Fajdek won all but his seven 2nd places to his Polish rival. Nick Miller was the only other man to exceed 80m with his Commonwealth Games win at 80.26, but he dropped to 10th at the Europeans and Bence Halász, 3rd there, was clearly no. 3 in the rankings, well ahead of all but the two Poles on win-loss. Ashraf Amjad El-Seify beat Dilshod Nazarov for the Asian Games title but was 5th in the Continental Cup behind Nazarov, Diego Del Real, Halász and Mostafa Al-Gamal. The latter was also African champion but did not compete in any of the IAAF Hammer Challenge events. Pavel Boreysha, European 4th, was 2-1 against both El-Seify and Miller. Esraf Apak had some big throws in Turkey and won the Balkan title but as usual fared poorly in the major international events, and after 6th in the European Throws meeting was dq 17th at the Europeans, where further top placings were 5 Elvind Henriksen, 6 Ivan Tikhon, 7 Hlib Piskunov, 8 Serghiev Marghiev, 9 Mihaíl Anastasákis, 11 Marcel Lomnicky. Overall standards continued to decline and 10th best man at 77.37 was, as it was in 2017, the worst since 1981.

Most competitions over 79m/76m: Fajdek 10/16, Nowicki 7/14, Halász 1/13, Miller 1/4, Apak 0/7, Nazarov, Boreysha 0/5, El-Seify, Baltaci 0/4, Henriksen, Lomnicky, Bigot 0/3

    1. Nowicki, 2. Fajdek, 3. Halász, 4. Nazarov,
    5. Boreysha, 6. Miller, 7. El-Seify, 8. Henriksen,
    9. Marghiev, 10. Lomnicky

Javelin

IT WAS CLOSE at the top. Thomas Röhler was ahead in their first four meetings, Andreas Hofmann won the next three before Röhler showed ahead 89.47 to 87.60 at the Europeans, then three wins for Hofmann and finally Röhler won in Berlin, so they ended 6-6. Top, however, of the world list was Johannes Vetter at 92.70 to Hofmann 92.06 and Röhler 91.78 as the three Germans were the 90m men in 2018 with Röhler up 5-1 and Hofmann 5-2 over Vetter, who was 5th at the Europeans when Magnus Kirt was 3rd and Marcin Krukowski was 4th. Kirt had a splendid year with seven meetings ahead of his pre-season best of 86.65, headed by 89.75. He was 2-2 v Vetter and 4-2 v Jakub Vadljech, 8th Europeans and 2nd Continental Cup to Röhler. Neeraj Chopra, who had set a world junior record 86.48 to win the World Junior title in 2016, advanced with Indian records at 87.43 for 4th in Doha and 88.06 to win at the Asian Games. He was then 4th at the DL final in Zürich behind Hofmann, Kirt and Röhler and followed by Krukowski, Julian Weber and Vadlejch. Weber returned in July after a year out for a win at the World Cup and 4th in the German Champs and also had 2nd places in Birmingham and Berlin to have 3-1 advantage over Krukowski. Keshorn Walcott won the CAG title but had a fairly thin season as did Cheng Chao-Tsun, who was 5th at the Asian Games and 3rd at the Continental Cup. Of the Finns Tero Pitkämäki withdrew injured after two 82m competitions and Oliver Helander broke through with 88.02 and was the national champion but was dnq 16th at the Europeans, where Antti Ruuskanen was 6th but had a season's best of only 82.59, and Andrian Mardare was 7th.

Most competitions over 85m/83m: Röhler 14/17, Hofmann 14/15, Kirt 12/19, Vetter 8/11, Vadlejch 7/10, Chopra 7/9, Weber 2/4, Helander 2/2, Krukowski 1/6, Walcott, Strobinders 0/4, Cheng 0/3.

    1. Hofmann, 2. Röhler, 3. Kirt, 4. Vetter,
    5. Vadlejch, 6. Chopra, 7. Weber, 8. Krukowski,
    9. Walcott, 10. Cheng.

Decathlon

KEVIN MAYER HAD three no jumps, all long and only a centimetre or two into the plasticine, but that cost him the European title for which he was the clear favourite. However, he made some amends with a superb world record score of 9126 at Talence. During the year he set pbs at 6 of the 10 decathlon disciplines. The year's next best scores came at Götzis from Damien Warner (after withdrawing due to no-height in the pole vault at the Commonwealth Games) 8795 and Maicel Uibo 8514. Then came two scores by Arthur Abele: 8481 win in Ratingen and 8413 at the Europeans; 8310 for 2nd at Talence made him a very clear winner of the IAAF Challenge in which three scores are totalled. Few of the top men managed that as Pieter Braun (3 Götzis, 7 Europeans, 4 Talence) and Martin Roe (1 Florence, 12 Götzis, 6 Europeans) were 2nd and 3rd. Uibo won in Athens, GA with 8407 but did not finish at the Europeans. Five more men exceeded 8300 points: Kai Kazmirek (dnf Halle and Ratingen) and Mathias Brugger (dnf EC) when 4th and 5th at Götzis, Tim Duckworth (5th EC) NCAA winner with 8336, Ilya Shkurenyov, who was 2nd at the Europeans with 8321 ahead of 3rd Vitaliy Zhuk 8290 and Niklas Kaul 8220 (the latter two were 9th and 6th respectively at Götzis), and Lindon Victor, Commonwealth champion with 8303, but dnf Götzis, where US champion Zach Ziemek was 10th.

1. Meyer, 2. Warner, 3. Abele, 4. Uibo,
5. Shkurenyov, 6. Duckworth, 7. Braun, 8. Zhuk,
9. Kaul, 10. Kazmirek

The best indoor heptathlon scores came at the World Indoors, won by Mayer 6348 from Warner 6343, Uibo 6285 and Kazmirek 6238.

20 Kilometres Walk

SERGEY SHIROBOKOV HAD the year's fastest time, a world junior record 1:17:25, when he won the Russian title. He also won the Russian winter title with 1:18:53 with Vasiliy Mizinov 2nd, but he only competed in Russia. The world's top race was the IAAF World Team (WT) race, and this was won by Koki Ikeda from Wang Kaihua, Massimo Stano and Toshikazu Yamanishi. Of these men Ikeda also won in Lugano from Tom Bosworth (WT 14th), but he had been 4th at the Japanese Championships behind Eiki Takahashi, Yamanishi and Daisuke Matsunaga (WT 31st, but wins in Tokyo and when taking the Asian title in Nomi) with Isamu Fujisawa (WT 7th) 5th. Wang started by winning in Huangshang and later in the year won at the Asian Games with Yamanishi 2nd, Jin Xiangqin (WT 6th) 3rd and Takahashi 5th. Stano also fared well in his other 20k races, winning the Italian title and 4th at the European Champs, where the medallists were Álvaro Martín, Diego García and Mizinov, but this trio had been 8th, 23rd and 16th in the World Team race. Similarly Eider Arévalo was only World Team 12th but he had major wins at Dudince and La Coruña and won the CAG title and was the overall winner in the three-stage race around Lake Taihu. García was 2nd, Jin 5th and Martín 6th at La Coruña. Martín and García were 1-2 at Rio Maior (Jin 8th). Dane Bird-Smith did not finish in the WT but had a fine win at the Commonwealth Games in 1:19:34 from Bosworth who improved the British record to 1:19:38 and Samuel Gathimba who later won the African title. So overall form was mixed, making ranking very difficult.

1 (?). Shirobokov 2. Ikeda, 3. Wang Kaihua,
4. Yamanishi, 5. Arévalo, 6. Stano, 7. Martín,
8. García, 9. Jin, 10. Mizinov, (11) Takahashi

50 Kilometres Walk

HIROOKI ARAI WON the World Team race in 3:44:25 in his only 50k of the year and this race dominated the world list with 11 men under 3:50 and 20 under 3:55. Nonetheless the year's three fastest times were 3:39:47 for the Japanese title in October by Tomohiro Noda, 3:42:29 by Sergey Bakulin to win the Russian title and 3:42:46 by Matej Tóth in Dudince. Behind Arai at the World Team the leading finishers from 2 to 10 were Hayoto Katsuki, Satoshi Maruo (maximum team points to Japan), Maryan Zakalntskyy, Wang Win, Wang Rui, Rafal Augustyn, Perseus Karlström, Quentin Rew and Ivan Banzeruk. Zakalnytskyy won the European title from Tóth, Dmitriy Dyubin and Håvard Haukenes, and although much slower due to hot weather the Asian Games was also significant as Katsuki won from Wang Qin with Maruo 4th and Wang Rui dnf. Noda also won his other 50k race, with 3:45:56 at Wajima. Veli-Matti Partanen was fifth on the world list with 2nd at Dudince in 3:44:43 but did not finish the Europeans. Andrés Chocho had two significant wins although outside 3:50 at the IAAF Challenge race in Monterrey and at the South American Games and, with 1st at the South American Champs and 4th at Rio Maior at 20k, he won the IAAF Race Walking challenge. World champion Yohann Diniz did not compete due to a pelvic stress fracture.

1. Arai, 2, Katsuki, 3. Zakalnytskyy, 4. Tóth, 5.
Maruo, 6. Wang Qin, 7. Noda, 8. Chocho, 9.
Dyubin, 10. Augustyn. nr. Bakulin

WOMEN

WORLD RECORDS BY women in 2018 were set by Beatrice Chepkoech, 8:44.32 at 3000m steeplechase and Liang Rui at 4:04.36 for 50k walk. Chepkoech's performance, at Monaco in the Herculis Diamond League meeting, was surely the performance of the year as she flowed around the track to take 8.46 secs off the old world record and 14.83 on her own pb.

Enjoying unbeaten seasons were Shaunae Miller-Uibo, one at 150m, seven at 200m and three at 400m, Caster Semenya, all nine finals at 800m, and Caterine Ibargüen, her eight at triple jump, plus the very limited seasons of Kathryn Mitchell in the javelin, seven events but all January-April, Nafi Thiam in her two heptathlons and Liang Rui in her two 50k walks. Other top rankers who got close to perfection were Mariya Lasitskaya, all ten indoors and 14 of 15 competitions at high jump, Sandra Perkovic, 12 wins in 13 at discus, Chepkoech 7 of 8 at steeplechase. Sydney McLaughlin did not compete outside the USA, but won her four competition at 400m and for four at 400m hurdles

In the Diamond League Caterine Ibargüen won all the five competitions at triple jump and also won the long jump at the final, and Mariya Lasitskene won six of the seven DL events.

There was no clear-cut choice for world woman athlete of the year with the result that there was a wide range of selections by experts..

Selections for World Top Ten

	PJM	TFN	AI
* Beatrice Chepkoech	1	2	2
* Shaunae Miller-Uibo	2	3	1
Caster Semenya	3	1	4
Mariya Lasitskene	4	4	3
* Nafissatou Thiam	5	7	7
Sandra Perkovic	6	8	8
* Caterine Ibargüen	7	5	5
* Dina Asher-Smith	8		6
Hellen Obiri	9		9
Sifan Hassan	10		
Marie-Josée Ta Lou		10	10
Salwa Eid Naser		6	
Anita Wlodarczyk		9	

IAAF finalists, Caterine Ibargüen was their athlete of the year.

Sydney McLaughlin was IAAF Rising Star of the Year. Dina Asher-Smith was the EA European Athlete of the Year

100 Metres

THE YEAR'S FASTEST time with legal wind was 10.85 by Marie-Josée Ta Lou in Doha and by Dina Asher-Smith at the European Champs. Ta Lou ranks first after a stellar season winning 11 of her 12 100m finals, her only loss being 3rd in the DL final in Zürich behind Murielle Ahouré and Asher-Smith, but Ta Lou was 4-1 and 2-1 against these rivals and Ahouré was 3-1 v Asher-Smith. Ta Lou and Asher-Smith were the 1-2 at the Continental Cup where Jenna Prandini and Dafne Schippers were 3-4. The world no. 1 of 2016-17 Elaine Thompson had a good year, winning the Jamaican title and 2nd at the Athletics World Cup to Ashley Henderson, but did not quite get back to her best due to Achilles problems – in DL races she was 2nd at Lausanne and 3rd at Doha, Eugene and Monaco. One top women had an unbeaten record – Aleia Hobbs with a super season in the USA winning both NCAA and US titles. She had the most sub-11 second times with seven plus three wind-assisted, but is hard to rank her above the top three as she was unable to race outside the USA, needing surgery on her right knee. The situation was similar for US runner-up Henderson, apart from that World Cup win. She was, however 2-0 v Prandini, 3rd US and NACAC champion who was also 3rd in Lausanne, Luzern and Continental Cup and 4th Monaco, making her 3-0 v Dafne Schippers. Gina Lückenkemper had a thinner overall

season but was sub-11 twice at the Europeans when she was 2nd with Schippers (also 5th DL final and 4th Continental Cup) 3rd and Mujinga Kambundi 4th, as she was in the DL final. Michelle-Lee Ahye won at the Commonwealth Games and although only 6th in Zürich beat Lückenkemper 3-0. Blessing Okagbare started well with 10.72w aided by the Texas winds and 10.90 for 2nd to Ta Lou in Doha, but later her form fell away. Torie Bowie had a quiet year with two wins and 5th in Eugene, all in 11.03-11.05 before a serious leg injury.

Most times under 11.00/11.10: Hobbs 7+3w/9+3w, Ta Lou, Asher-Smith 5/7; Ahouré 4+1w/7+1w, Thompson 3/7, Prandini 2+1w/7+1w, Henderson 2+1w/5+2w, Collins 2/5+1w, Lückenkemper 2/1, Schippers 1/5, Terry 1+2w/3+2w, Bryant 1/4+1w, Kambundji, Horn 1/3; Okagbare 1+1w/2+1w, Fraser-Pryce, Wei Yongli 1/2; Brisco 1w/3+3w, Bowie 0/3, J Smith 0/2+1w

1. Ta Lou, 2. Ahouré, 3. Asher-Smith, 4. Hobbs, 5. Thompson, 6. Henderson, 7. Prandini, 8. Schippers, 9. Kambundji, 10. Ahye

Ahouré topped the indoor 60m list with 6.97 and 7.01 (semi) at the World Indoor Championships where 2-5 were Ta Lou, Kambundji, Thompson and Schippers. The second fastest in the world was Javianne Oliver who won the US title at high altitude in Albuquerque in 7.02, but she was only 4th in her World semi-final.

200 Metres

SHAUNAE MILLER-UIBO enjoyed an unbeaten season of seven 200m competitions, running six of the world's eleven fastest times, although her best of 22.06 was fourth on the world list. The only woman to beak 22 seconds with legal wind was Dina Asher-Smith, who completed her sprint double at the Europeans in 21.89. She had six 200m events, but only won twice, being 2nd to Miller-Uibo in Rabat and Birmingham, 3rd at the Commonwealth Games behind Miller-Uibo and Shericka Jackson, and 4th in London behind Jenna Prandini, Gabrielle Thomas and Jackson. However, Asher-Smith was 3-0 v Dafne Schippers, who was 2nd at the Europeans, and to Miller-Uibo in the DL final in Brussels and at the Continental Cup. Jackson had the best depth of fast times and won Jamaican and NACAC titles as well as at the Athletics World Cup but was beaten 4-1 by Schippers, with both holding a clear win-loss advantage over US champion Prandini. After winning the NCAA indoor title and 2nd outdoors to Angie Annelus with Lynna Irby 3rd, Thomas showed much promise in Europe and was 2-0 v African champion Marie-Josée Ta Lou and 2-1 v European bronze medallist Jamile Samuel. Mujinga Kambundji was well-placed in all her races including 4th at the Europeans, a place ahead of Ivet Lalova-Collio. Briana Williams, at

16, showed that she is a major prospect, taking double gold at the World Indoors in 11.16 and 22.50.

Most times under 22.70: Jackson 13, Schippers 9, Miller-Uibo, Prandini 8; Asher-Smith, Samuel 7; Ta Lou 6, Irby 5+2w+3i, Thomas 5+2w+2i, Collins 5+2w, Okagbare, T Clark, Lalova-Collio 3; Henderson 2+1w+1i, K Johnson 2+1w, Camacho-Quinn 1+2w.

1. Miller-Uibo, 2. Asher-Smith, 3. Schippers, 4. Jackson, 5. Prandini. 6. Thomas, 7. Ta Lou, 8. Samuel, 9. Kambundji, 10. Irby

400 Metres

SHAUNAE MILLER-UIBO won her three 400m races, 49.52 in Eugene, 49.53 in Székesfehérvár and the world-leading 48.97 in Monaco. Salwa Eid Naser was 2nd in that race in an Asian record 49.08 and that was her only loss in a brilliant season of ten wins including five in Diamond League to the final, plus at the Asian Games and in the Continental Cup. Second in the last was Caster Semenya in a national record 49.62, 0.3 behind Naser, and Semenya also showed prowess at this event by winning the African title in 49.96 but she did not run any DL 400m races. Phyllis Francis and US champion Shakima Wimbley had solid seasons including 2nd and 3rd in the DL final in which Jaide Stepter was 4th, Stephenie Ann McPherson 5th and Jessica Beard 6th, with Beard well ahead of those two on win-loss. McPherson, beaten 3-2 by Stepter, was Jamaican and NACAC champion and 3rd in the Continental Cup. Although racing in only three US meets outdoors, Lyna Irby ran 49.80 (fifth on the world list) to take the NCAA title; she had been 2nd in the SEC and NCAAs indoors, and Kendall Ellis was NCAA champion indoors and second outdoors with 3rd at the US champs. Amantle Montsho won at the Commonwealth Games and Justyna Swiety-Ergotic, who smashed her pb with 50.41 in Berlin, was the top European. Sydney McLaughlin was undefeated in three indoor meetings to a world junior indoor record 50.36 at the NCAAs and 50.07 in her only outdoor race. Courtney Okolo, whose outdoor best was 50.65 for US Champs 4th, won the World Indoor title from Wimbley.

Most times under 50.80: Naser 10, Beard 7, Wimbley 6, Semenya, Francis 4; Ellis, Irby 3+1i; Miller-Uibo, McPherson 3.

1. Miller-Uibo, 2. Naser, 3. Francis, 4. Wimbley, 5. Semenya, 6. Beard, 7. Stepter, 8. McPherson, 9. Irby, 10. Ellis

800 Metres

CASTER SEMENYA REMAINED, it seems, unbeatable by women at 800m, while extending her remit to 400m and 1500m. Her nine victories at 800m, including the year's four fastest times topped by a South African record (and fourth on the world all-time list) and 6 of the top 11

times, took her 800m win-streak to 29 from September 2015. Francine Niyonsaba remained the perennial runner-up although beaten by Ajee' Wilson into 3rd at Eugene and placing only 6th in the DL final in Zürich. There Semenya was followed by Wilson, Natoya Goule, Habitam Alemu and Raevyn Rogers with 7-9 Selina Büchel, Rabab Arrafi and Charlene Lipsey and that order was significant. Niyonsaba beat Wilson 3-2 for second in the ranking and these two were also 1-2 at the World Indoors. The best depth of times came in Monaco where seven women broke 1:58: Semenya, Niyonsaba, Goule, Wilson, Alemu, Arrafi and Rogers. Medallists at the Commonwealth Games were Semenya, Wambui and Goule, at the African Champs Semenya, Niyonsaba and Arrafi (with Margaret Wambui a non-finisher), and at the Europeans Nataliya Pryshchepa, Renelle Lamote and Olha Lyakhova. Wilson, Rogers and Ce'aira Brown were the 1-2-3 at the US Champs. Pryshchepa followed Semenya, Wilson and Goule with 4th at the Continental Cup. Six of the women are new to the top ten.

Most times under 1:59.5: Semenya 11, Wilson 10+1i, Goule 10, Niyonsaba 8+1i, Alemu 8, Brown 5, Wambui, Rogers, Jerotich 4; Arrafi, Lipsey, Lamote 3

1. Semenya, 2. Niyonsaba, 3. Wilson, 4. Goule, 5. Alemu, 6. Rogers, 7. Arrafi, 8. Wambui, 9. Brown, 10. Pryshchepa

1500 Metres

SHELBY HOULIHAN HAD not previously ranked in the world top ten, but burst through to top ranking in 2018 with four wins, Azusa, Eugene, US Champs and Lausanne and 2nd in Brussels (DL final) and Ostrava (Continental Cup), being beaten in the last two by Muir and by Winny Chebet. Muir had been 2nd in Eugene, Stockholm and Lausanne and 5th in London behind Sifan Hassan (year's best 4:14.71), Gudaf Tsegay, Hellen Obiri and Jenny Simpson in a 1 mile race that had the best ever times for places 2nd to 11th; Laura Weightman was 6th and Chebet 7th. Hassan also won in Birmingham and was 3rd in Lausanne and Brussels and was 4-0 v Tsegay, the 20 year-old who ran fast in all her eight races and who was 2-2 v Muir. Genzebe Dibaba had the year's fastest 1500m with 3:56.68 at the Kusocinski Memorial in Chorzów, but had only two more outdoor races: 1 mile wins in Székesfehárvár and Padua, although indoors she had won the World 1500m title (from Muir, Hassan, Houlihan and Chebet) after important wins in Karlsruhe and Madrid. Caster Semenya ran South African records in wins at the Commonwealth Games (4:00.71) and at Doha (3:59.92) before 6th at Lausanne in her only other 1500m. Simpson won in Hengelo, was 3rd in Eugene, 4th in Stockholm and 2nd at the US Champs but was only 10th in Brussels, while Chebet although placed between 5th and 10th in six DL meetings, was Kenyan and African champion (Rabab Arrafi 2nd), and Obiri only had that one race but Weightman had a good series of races, including 3rd at the Europeans, behind Muir and Sofia Ennaoui. Arrafi (8th WI), also 3rd in the Continental Cup, was 3-3 v Chebet (& 5th WI) and 2-1 v Simpson.

Most times under 4:04.0 (or 4:23.6M): Tsegay 8, Muir 6, Arrafi 5, Hassan, Semenya, Chebet, Weightman, L Hall 4; Houlihan, Simpson, Bahta, McDonald 3; Dibaba 2+2i

1. Houlihan, 2. Muir, 3. Hassan, 4. Tsegay, 5. Arrafi (6), 6. Simpson (7), 7. Semenya (8), 8. Chebet (9), 9. Dibaba (5), 10. Obiri. (Including indoors).

3000 Metres

SIFAN HASSAN RAN the year's fastest time with 8:27.50 at the Continental Cup, far ahead of Senbere Teferi 8:32.49 and Hellen Obiri 8:36.20, and the next five times came at Doha from 8:29.05 by winner Caroline Kipkuri, then Agnes Tirop, Hyvin Jepkemoi, Jenny Simpson and Letesenbet Gidey at 8:30.96. Genzebe Dibaba was fastest indoors with 8:31.23 at Sabadell and she won the World Indoor title from Hassan, Laura Muir, Obiri and Shelby Houlihan.

5000 Metres

HELLEN OBIRI RETAINS her top ranking with six wins including at the Commonwealth Games, Kenyan and African Championships. The year's five fastest times came at Rabat as Obiri 14:21.75 and Sifan Hassan 14:22.34 European record were followed by the best ever times for 3rd to 5th: Letesenbet Gidey 14:23.14, Senbere Teferi 14:23.33 and Agnes Tirop 14:24.24. Then Genzebe Dibaba won in Eugene in 14:26.89 from Gidey, Obiri (her one loss), Gudaf Tsegay (her one 5000m of the year) and Lilian Rengeruk. Shelby Houlihan won in Heusden in a near-solo run in a North American record 14:34.45 and also won the US title. Hassan won the European title easily from Eilish McColgan and Yasemin Can. Most of the above then contested the DL final in Zürich, with Obiri taking a narrow victory from Hassan, followed by Teferi, Caroline Kipkirui, Tirop, Dibaba, Gidey and Rengeruk. Margaret Kipkemboi did not break 15 minutes but was 2nd at the Commonwealth Games after winning the Kenyan trials (Kipkirui 4th) and was 6th at Eugene. Rengeruk had a busy year as she was also 3rd at the Kenyan CG trials, 2nd Kenyan Champs and 5th African Champs. Almaz Ayana, 1st or 2nd for the previous four years, did not race due to a knee injury.

Most times under 15:00: Obiri 4, Hassan, Gidey, Tirop, Dibaba 3

1. Obiri, 2. Hassan, 3. Gidey, 4. Teferi, 5. Tirop, 6. G Dibaba, 7. Kipkemboi, 8. Kipkirui, 9. Houlihan, 10. Rengeruk

10,000 Metres

This was a very poor year for women's 10,000m running and only a couple of the top women in 2017 had a race at the distance in 2018. The only woman to better 31:15 on the track was the Kenyan Pauline Kamulu, who improved from a best of 31:47.13 in 2017 to run 30:41.85 and 30:56.94 in Japanese races. 10th best woman at 31:38.4 made it the second worst since 1998. Lonah Chemtai Salpeter who had moved from Kenya in 2008 and became an Israeli citizen in 2016, started the year with a national record 31:39.63, improved that to 31:33.03 to win the European Cup race and then had a clear win in the Europeans in 31:43.29 with Susan Krumins second. The year's second fastest time came in a fast race at Yamaguchi in Japan in December, won by Minamu Yamanouchi 31:16.48 from Grace Kimanzi, Harumi Okamoto and Rina Nabeshima, all under 31:30 but without other form to establish a good claim to a ranking. Then came 31:31.17 by Stacy Ndiwa to win the African title from Alice Aprot Nawowuna, Gete Alemayehu, Stella Chesang and Mercyline Chelangat. Earlier Chesang had won at the Commonwealth Games from Nawowuna, Chelangat and Beatrice Mutai. Chelangat beat Chesang at altitude in Kampala 31:48.4 to 31:49.0 and Pauline Korikwiang won the Kenyan title in 31:51.1 from Nawowuna and also won at the Kenyan Defence Forces champs. The altitude in Nairobi for those races is such that one can deduct up to a minute to get comparability with sea-level times. Alemayehu had been 3rd in the Ethiopian Champs and was 2nd at Maia to Gloria Kite, who ran 31:41.47 in her one 10,000m race of the year. At the end of the year Hiromi Niiya made a notable return after five years out of competition to win the Zátopek race in Melbourne in 31:32.50. Molly Huddle was US champion from Marielle Hall, who won the NACAC title.

1. Kamulu, 2. Salpeter, 3. Ndiwa, 4. Chesang, 5. Aprot Nawowuna, 6. Chelangat, 7. Korikwiang, 8. Alemayehu, 9. Mutai, 10. Niiya.

Half Marathon

FANCY CHEMUTAI WON an extraordinary race in Ras Al Khaimah, as her 64:52 was just 1 second outside the world record and there were best ever times for places 2-11, all beating previous bests set in RAK races, with a record seven women under 67 minutes. 2nd was Mary Keitany in 64:55, 3rd Caroline Kipkirui 65:07 and 4th Joan Chelimo 65:37. Chelimo ran the year's third fastest time with 65:04 in Prague, with Kipkirui 2nd, and was also 3rd in 66:15 in Copenhagen behind Sifan Hassan, European record 65:15, and Yeshaneh Ababel, as well as winning in Boston and 2nd in Yangzhou. Ababel later won in Istanbul. The World Championship race was in Valencia in March with

Netsanet Gudeta (also a winner in Olomouc) winning from Joyciline Jepkosgei (5th RAK) and Pauline Kamulu (also won in Yamaguchi). There were records for standards in depth with 10th on the world list of 66:18 and 100th 69:52.

Marathon

TWO EXTRAORDINARY RUNS headed women's marathon achievements in 2018. Firstly Vivian Cheruiyot, in just her third marathon, won in London in 2:18:31 despite the race ending in very warm weather, and later Mary Keitany, who had only been 5th in London, won in New York in 2:22:41. That time does not seem especially brilliant – until one realises that she ran the second half in a stunning 66:58 including 15:19 for the 5k between 25 and 30k and 30:53 for the 10k from 30k to 35k. Overall new records were set with 11 women inside 2:20 and the 100th best woman's mark improved from the previous record of 2:28:01 to 2:26:58. Those placed 2nd to 6th behind Cheruiyot in London all went on to win major races: 2nd Brigid Kosgei 2:20:13 won in Chicago in 2:18:35, 3rd Tadelech Bekele 2:21:40 won in Amsterdam in 2:23:14, 4th Gladys Cherono won in Berlin in 2:18:11, the year's fastest time, 6th Rose Chelimo 2:26:03 won at the Asian Games As usual there were excellent times in Berlin, where Ruti Aga was 2nd in 2:18:34 after 2nd in Tokyo behind Birhane Dibaba 2:19:51, and Tirunesh Dibaba, who did not finish in London, was 3rd in 2:18:55 for the first time three women had beaten 2:19 in one marathon. The best depth of times was in Dubai in January, when Roza Dereje won in 2:19:17 from Feyse Tadesse, Yebrqual Melese, Worknesh Degefa and Haftamnesh Tesfay all under 2:20 and the best ever times run for places 4th to 7th. Dereje was also 2nd in Chicago and Tesfay in Frankfurt; Melese won in Shanghai in 2:20:36. The other winner in 2018 under 2:20 was Rose Chepngetich who led all the way in Istanbul for 2:18:35, she had also been 2nd in Paris, 3 seconds behind Betsy Saina. Meskerem Assefa had wins in Nagoya 2:21:45 and Frankfurt 2:20:36 after 2nd in Hong Kong, and Yeshaneh Ababel made a stunning marathon debut to win in Abu Dhabi in 2:20:16.

1. Cheruiyot, 2. Kosgei, 3. Cherono, 4. Keitany, 5. Aga, 6. Dereje, 7. T Bekele, 8. Assefa, 9. Chepngetich, 10. T Dibaba.

3000 Metres Steeplechase

BEATRICE CHEPKOECH, WORLD number one in 2017, had a terrific year in 2018. She started with excellent running at 1500m indoors, including a Kenyan record 4:02.21 and 7th at the World Indoors, and out with 2nd in the Commonwealth Games. Turning to steeplechasing she was only 5th in Rome at the end of May, but otherwise won all her seven races. She improved her pb to 8:59.36 in Paris and then

took a massive 8.46 secs off the world record with a stunning 8:44.32 in Monaco. In perfect conditions the best ever times for places 5 to 13 were set in that race with seven women under 9:10 and 11 under 9:20. Later in the year in the DL final in Brussels, won by Chepkoech in 8:55.10, there were best ever times for places 2-3 and 5-6. Chepkoech had four runs under 9 minutes and the only other such time was 8:59.62 by Norah Tanui for 2nd in Brussels. Tanui was, however, beaten 3-1 by Hyvin Jepkemoi, 3rd in Paris, Monaco and Brussels after wins in Rome and Oslo. US champion Emma Coburn was 2nd in Oslo and 4th in Rome, Monaco and Brussels and was 2-2 v Celliphine Chespol, who was World Junior champion and 2nd at the Commonwealth Games (won by Aisha Praught Leer) and Kenyan and African Champs (both won by Chepkoech). Courtney Frerichs had three second places in her five races: US Champs, Monaco and Continental Cup (won by Chepkoech). The World Junior Champs 2nd and 3rd, Peruth Chemutai and Winfred Yavi ,also make the top ten rankings, split by Daisy Jepkemei. all with a series of excellent times, and Roseline Chepngetich edges the final spot with a 2-1 record against Praught Colleen Quigley won in Berlin in 9:10.71 (9th on the world list) but only had one other race (10th in Monaco). The top Europeans were 13-14-15 on the world list: Russian champion Yekaterina Ivonina, Karoline Bjerkeli Grøvdal and Gesa Felicitas Krause who did well to come back from injury to win the European title. The 10th best of 9:10.71 beat the record set at 9:13.25 in 2017.

Most times under 9:25.0: Chepkoech, Jepkemei 8, Chespol 7, Tanui, Yavi 6; Jepkemoi, Coburn, Frerichs, Chemutai, Praught 5; Chepngetich 3.

1. Chepkoech, 2. Jepkemoi, 3. Tanui, 4. Coburn, 5. Chespol, 6. Frerichs, 7. Chemutai, 8. Jepkemei, 9. Yavi, 10. Chepngetich

100 Metres Hurdles

KENDRA HARRISON RANKS top for the third year, but it was close at the top as she (with 6) and the returning Brianna McNeal (with 7) had 13 of the world top 20 performances (to 12.53). The others were Alina Talay, Danielle Williams and Sharika Nelvis two each and Jasmine Camacho-Quinn one. Harrison, who won USA and NACAC titles, was 3-2 v McNeal, who won the DL final from Williams, Tobi Amusan, Nelvis and Nadine Visser. Win-loss settles the rankings third to fifth as Nelvis was 4-1 v Williams and 5-1 v Christine Manning, and Williams was 3-0 v Manning. They are followed by two women with restricted seasons: Camacho-Quinn was unbeaten and won the NCAA title but did not run outside the USA and Talay was injured, not running from June to her fall in her semi at the Europeans, where Elvira

German took the title from Pamela Dutkiewicz, Cindy Roleder and Visser. Amusan beat Williams at the Commonwealth Games and also won the African title but was down on win-loss to most of the top women. Williams won at the Continental Cup from Harrison, Dutkiewicz, German and Amusan. Queen Harrison had a solid season, including 4th at US and NACAC and was 2-0 v Amusan and Visser, to squeeze in the top in very close contention from 6th. Sally Pearson won her four competitions in January and February with bests of 12.68/12.67w but then succumbed to injury, and Dawn Harper Nelson ended her career by enjoying a final year with a best of 12.75.

Most times at 12.70 or faster: McNeal 13, K Harrison 12+2w, Williams 10, Nelvis 7, Camacho-Quinn 5+1w, Talay 5, Amusan 4+1w, Q Harrison 4, German 3+1w.

1. K Harrison, 2. McNeal, 3. Nelvis, 4. Williams,
5. Manning, 6. Talay, 7. Camacho-Quinn,
8. Dutkiewicz, 9. Q Harrison, 10. Amusan

Kendra Harrison won the World Indoor title in 7.70 from Manning, Visser, Nelvis and Roleder, and 7.70 was also run at altitude in Albuquerque by Nelvis who was followed in a close race by Harrison and Manning. This trio dominated the world lists with Harrison 8, Manning 7 and Nelvis 4 of the 21 times at 7.83 or better.

400 Metres Hurdles

SYDNEY MCLAUGHLIN IMPROVED her world junior record to 53.60 and then to 52.75 at the SEC Championships but, while that was easily the year's fastest time and she was unbeaten, she ran the event at only four meetings to the NCAAs. Determining top ranking is tricky as we have circular form on win-loss. Shamier Little was fastest with 53.32 at the NACAC, followed by Janieve Russell 53.46 behind Little 53.41 at Lausanne, and Dalilah Muhammad 53.65 at Oslo. Little beat Russell 4-2, but was 2-3 down to Muhammad, who was beaten 6-2 by Russell, who had the busiest year from winning at the Commonwealth Games ahead of Elidh Doyle, Wenda Nel, Rhonda Whyte and Sage Watson through to the Continental Cup when she won from Little and Anna Ryzhykova. Georganne Moline was fifth on the world list and 2nd to Little at the US Champs, 3rd NACAC behind Little and Russell and 4th at the DL final behind Muhammad, Little and Russell. Léa Sprunger was 6th in that race, having won the European title from Ryzhykova. There was not much between the next group, but Ashley Spencer, who did not finish the US final, was 2-0 v Sprunger and 4-1 v Leah Nugent, 2nd at the Jamaican Champs. Doyle was 4-0 v Watson and 3-1 v Nel, but 8th in the Europeans. Zuzana Hejnová, prominent for a decade, had a disappointing year with a best of 55.16, suffering from a knee injury and the 2017 no. 1 Kori Carter concentrated on 100m hurdles in 2018.

Most times under 54.0/55.0: Russell 6/15, Little 6/7, Muhammad 4/9, McLaughlin 3/6, Moline 2/8, Sprunger, Nugent 0/5; Ryzhykova, Nel 0/3.

1. Little, 2. Russell, 3. Muhammad,
4. McLaughlin, 5. Moline, 6. Sprunger,
7. Ryzhykova, 8. A Spencer, 9. Nugent,
10. Doyle,

High Jump

MARIYA LASITSKENE WAS again dominant in this event and is top for the fourth time. She won all her 11 indoor competitions, 7 of them at 2.00 or higher, and 14 of her outdoor contests, 9 at 2m plus, with just one lapse, 3= in Rabat with 1.90. Her best was 2.04 indoors in Volgograd and outdoors in London and she won six DL competitions plus World Indoor, Russian and European titles and at the Continental Cup. Mirela Demireva lost on count-back at 2m in Stockholm and at the Europeans and the only other 2m jumps were by Elena Vallortigara, who at 26 jumped 2.02 for 2nd in London having improved from a previous best of 1.91 way back in 2010, and by Nafissatou Thiam with 2.01 in the Götzis heptathlon. Yuliya Levchenko cleared 1.97 indoors and out, but fared moderately in the major championships with 5th World Indoors and 9th Europeans before 2nd in the DL final in Zürich at 1.94 when Marie-Laurence Jungfleisch and Erika Kinsey were 3-4 at 1.90. Levchenko beat Vallortigara, a non-qualifier for the European final and 5= in Zürich, 3-2 but these two had the best depth of marks after the top two – number of meetings at 1.94 or more: Levchenko 7 outdoors + 5 indoors, Vallortigara 7, Kateryna Tabashnyk 6, Vashti Cunningham 4+2i, Jungfleisch and Kinsey 3, Levern Spencer 2+2i. At the Europeans Jungfleisch was 3rd, and Airine Palsyte 4th at 1.96, with Tabashnyk 5th and Michaela Hrubá 6th. Thiam had just two HJ competitions apart from her two heptathlons, including 2nd in Paris with 1.97, and Cunningham was US titles champion indoors and out and also won at the Athletics World Cup, after 2nd at the World Indoors (where 3-6 were Alessia Trost, Morgan Lake, Levchenko and Demireva). Jungfleisch was 4-4 v Tabashnyk and while Palsyte had only four competitions, she had a good win at Eberstadt over Kinsey, Jungfleisch and Levchenko. Spencer won the Commonwealth Games title at 1.95 and cleared 1.96 in Athens. She also won CAG and NACAC titles, but was busiest with 12 events indoors; she was beaten 5-2 (and 2-1 indoors) by Kinsey. The 2017 World Youth champion Yaroslava Mahuchikh improved further as she won European Youth and Youth Olympic titles, clearing 1.95 in the latter and went over 1.96 indoors for 4th in the December competition in Minsk behind Lasitskene 2.00, Tabashnyk and Levchenko each 1.98.

Most competitions over 2.00/1.95m: Lasitskene 9+7i/13+10i, Demireva 2/3+2i, Vallortigara 1/3, Levchenko 0/2+6i, Tabashnyk 0/3+1i, Cunningham 0/2+2i, Spencer 0/2+1i.

> 1. Lasitskene, 2. Demireva, 3. Levchenko, 4. Vallortigara, 5. Jungfleisch (6), 6. Tabashnyk (7), 7. Thiam (8), 8. Cunningham (5), 9. Palsyte (10), 10. Kinsey (-). – Lake (9) (Including indoors)

Pole Vault

SANDI MORRIS TOPPED the world lists both indoors and out with 4.95 and as in 2016-17 had a great rivalry with Ekateríni Stefanídi as they went 4-4 outdoors after their only indoor clash had been at the World Indoors, won by Morris 4.95 from Anzhelika Sidorova 4.90 and Stefanídi 4.80. Stefanídi had a best of 4.87 and won 5/6 indoors and 5/11 outdoors, including at the Europeans and DL final in Zürich while Morris was 2/3 indoors and 7/15 outdoors. Morris was second with 4.86 behind Katie Nageotte at the US indoors with Jenn Suhr 3rd, and won the US outdoor title from Nageotte and Suhr, but was not quite as successful as her Greek rival in the top meetings as she was NACAC 3rd behind Nageotte and Yarisley Silva, 2nd in the DL final and 3rd in the Continental Cup behind Sidorova and Stefanídi. However, Morris had slightly the best set of marks. Suhr was 2-1 v Sidorova, who slipped a little at the Europeans for 4th place when other leading positions were 2 Nikoléta Kiriakopoúlou, 3 Holly Bradshaw, 5 Ninon Guillon-Romarin, 6 Angelica Bengtsson. Eliza McCartney was 4th at the World Indoors and 2nd to Alysha Newman at the Commonwealth Games before improving her Oceania record to 4.85, 4.86 and 4.94, but her season was cut short in August (as was Newman's in May). Nageotte (5th WI) was down on win-loss to all the top five, but was 6-3 (1 tie) v Bradshaw (4th CG, 1st World Cup ahead of Nageotte, 4= DL final) and 4-2 v Silva (1st CAG), who she beat for the NACAC title. British champion Bradshaw was 3-2 (1 tie) v Guillon-Romarin, who set French records indoors and out, and 2-2 (1 tie) v Kiriakopoúlou, who was beaten 2-1 by Silva.

Most competitions over 4.65m (outdoors + in): Morris 14+3i, Nageotte 10+5i, Suhr 10+4i, McCartney 8+1i, Silva 7, Stefanídi 6+6i, Guillon-Romarin 6+2i, Bradshaw 5, Kiriakopoúlou 4+1i, Newman 1+2i

> 1. Morris, 2. Stefanídi, 3. Suhr (4), 4. Sidorova (3), 5. McCartney. 6. Nageotte, 7. Bradshaw, 8. Silva, 9. Kiriakopoúlou, 10. Guillon-Romarin. (Including indoors)

Long Jump

CONTENDERS FOR THE top ranking on outdoor form are Malaika Mihambo and Caterine Ibargüen, who went 2-2 in their meetings. Ibargüen took with aplomb to combining long with triple jumping and improved her pb of 6.73A back in 2012 in her first go at LJ since 2015 with 6.87 in Marseille. Mihambo was 1st at 6.90 with Ibargüen 3rd 6.77 at Lausanne, 1st to 2nd at Birmingham 6.96 to 6.80, and then Ibargüen was 1st 6.80 to 4th 6.61 in the DL final in Brussels and 1st 6.93 to 2nd 6.86 in the Continental Cup. Mihambo's fuller season with 6.99 at Weinheim and gold at the Europeans (2 Marina Bekh, 3 Shara Proctor, 4 Jasmin Sawyers, 5 Anastasiya Mironchik-Ivanova) perhaps settled the issue. The best wind-legal jump of the year was 7.05 by Lorraine Ugen at the British Champs, but, although she had a good win at the World Cup, she was beaten 7-1 by compatriot Proctor and was 9th Europeans. With wind assistance Brittney Reese had 7.19w at Chula Vista and Ivana Spanovic jumped 7.04w and 6.98w (and 6.92) and was 2nd at Lausanne with 6.90 but after just four outdoor competitions she was seriously injured (Achilles) at the Europeans. However she had a good case for top ranking if we add form indoors, where she was over 6.90 twice including her win with 6.96 at the World Indoors, when Mihambo was 5th. There Reese, the 2017 No. 1, was 2nd with 6.89 and also won the US indoor title, but she competed only three times outdoors. Christabel Nettey won at the Commonwealth Games from Brooke Stratton, Proctor and Ugen, but her end-of-season form was poor and Stratton beat her 4-2 and Ugen 6-1. Ese Brume was African champion and 5th at the Continental Cup in which Stratton was 3rd, Proctor 4th and Nettey 7th. Sha'Keela Saunders won US and NACAC titles and was 2-1 v Sawyers.

Most competitions over 6.70m (outdoors + in): Proctor 10+1w, Mihambo 8+1i, Stratton 7, Nettey 6, Bradshaw 5+1w, Ugen 5, Spanovic 4+1w+4i, Saunders 3+1w, Itoya 1+3w, Reese 1+1w+2i, Moguenara 1+3w, Sagnia 1+2i

> 1. Mihambo (2), 2. Ibargüen (3), 3. Spanovic (1), 4. Proctor (5), 5. Stratton (6), 6. Ugen (7), 7. Nettey (8), 8. Reese (4), 9. Brume, 10. Saunders.

Triple Jump

YULIMAR ROJAS WAS able to have just one competition, winning the World Indoor title, before injury cost her the season. That left Caterine Ibargüen, who had an unbeaten season – of eight competitions with six of the top seven performances from 14.96 at Rabat to 14.76 and she ranks first for the fifth time. The only other mark in that range was the North American record of 14.84 by Tori Franklin at Baie-Mahault. With wind assistance Ibargüen had 14.89w at Oslo and Yekaterina Koneva 14.79w to win the Russian title. Unable to compete internationally Koneva won all her five competitions (all 14.45 or better). After Ibargüen there were several women with fairly similar performance levels with rankings determined on a mix of win-loss records and series of marks. Kimberley Williams, who won the Commonwealth Games title from Shanieka Ricketts, had a positive win-loss record against all but Ibargüen, including 3-1 v Franklin and 3-2 v Ricketts. Williams was also 2nd at the World Indoors where 3-6 were Anna Peleteiro, Elena Panturoiu, Keturah Orji and Paraskéví Papahrístou, with Franklin 8th and Ricketts 10th. Franklin was 2nd at the US Champs to Orji, NACAC to Ricketts and Continental Cup to Ibargüen, and Ricketts beat Orji at the World Cup and was 2nd in the DL final in Zürich behind Ibargüen with Williams, Franklin, Rouguy Diallo, Kristin Gierisch and Gabriela Petrova 3rd-7th. Papahrístou won the European title from Gierisch, Peleteiro, Panturoiu, Hanna Minenko and Petrova, with Diallo 8th. South American Games winner Nubia Soares and Minenko just miss a top ten ranking, and Olga Rypakova, Asian Games winner and Cont. Cup 3rd, did not have the distances of the above.

Most competitions over 14.30m: Ricketts 10, Ibargüen 8, Williams 7+1i, Franklin 6, Papahrístou 5+1w, Peleteiro 5+1i, Gierisch 5, Koneva 4+1w, Orji 4+2i, Soares 4, Petrova 3+1w, Panturoiu 3+1i, Minenko 2+1w

1. Ibargüen, 2. Williams, 3. Franklin, 4. Ricketts (5), 5. Papahrístou (6), 6. Orji (4), 7. Koneva, 8. Gierisch. 9. Peleteiro, 10. Panturoiu. (Inc. indoors)

Shot

GONG LIJIAO WAS the one 20m thrower in 2017 and she led the 2018 rankings with 20.38 and 20.31, but was joined over 20m by Cristina Schwanitz, who returned after giving birth to twins. After 3rd at the World Indoors behind Anita Márton and Danniel Thomas-Dodd, Gong lost just once in her twelve outdoor contests. That was when 3rd at the Continental Cup behind Raven Saunders and Schwanitz, with just 11cm separating these three, who rank in reverse order. Schwanitz, who had 14 wins, two 2nds and two 3rds, was surprisingly beaten for the European title by Pauline Guba but had a positive win-loss record against all but Gong, including 6-1 v Guba. Saunders was 3rd at the US Champs behind Maggie Ewen and Jessica Ramsey, but was at her best in the major late-season meets. She was 2nd to Gong with 19.67 in Monaco and with 19.64 in Brussels in the DL final when 3rd to 6th were Schwanitz, Alyona Dubitskaya (6th WI), Guba and Thomas-Dodd. Guba was 5th at the World Indoors and 2nd to Gong at the World Cup with Ewen (NCAA champion indoors and out) 3rd. Márton threw 19.62 indoors and started her outdoor season with 19.12 but was well down thereafter and did not compete after June, and Thomas-Dodd was another whose distances fell after 19.22 at the World Indoors and 19.36 to win at the

Commonwealth Games, where Valerie Adams returned to take the silver medal with 18.70, form she maintained until ending in style with 19.31 for 4th at Monaco, and Brittany Crew (10th WI) the bronze. Further top European Champs placings were 3 Dubitskaya, 4 Klaudia Kardasz, 5 Sara Gambetta and 6 Radoslava Mavrodieva. Gao Yang was 4th at the World Indoors and 2nd to Gong at the Asian Games.

Most competitions over 18.70m: Schwanitz 17, Gong, Guba 10+2i; Dubitskaya 9, Saunders 7, Ewen 6+2i, Adams 3, Thomas-Dodd 2+2i, Martón 1+3i.

1. Gong, 2. Schwanitz, 3. Saunders, 4. Guba, 5. Ewen, 6. Dubitskaya, 7. Adams (9), 8. Thomas-Dodd (8), 9. Crow (-), 10. Gambetta (-) – Márton (7), Gao Yang (10). (Including indoors).

Discus

Sandra Perkovic had another terrific season. She ranks as number one for the seventh successive year, first in 12 of her 13 competitions (counting the Continental Cup where she had the best throw even though 'losing' to Yaimé Pérez due to a foul in the final round) with the top seven performances of the year from her 71.38 in Doha to 60.44, plus performances 10-12. Her one loss came in the DL final in Brussels when 3rd behind Yaimí Pérez and Andressa de Morais. Pérez, who had a best of 67.82, won 10 of her 19 competitions and was 2nd in all the others (8 of them to Perkovic) to take second ranking and Dani Stevens, with a best of 68.26, third. Stevens won her five events in Australia up to taking Commonwealth Games gold but just had two competitions thereafter, 5th in Doha and 4th at the Continental Cup, a place behind Chen Yang, fourth on the world list at 67.03, and a place ahead of de Morais. Chen won at the Asian Games from her compatriot Feng Bin, who beat her for the Chinese title, and de Morais and Fernanda Borges were 1-2 at the South American Games,Ibero-American and Brazilian Championships. Borges did not compete in DL events but was 2-0 v the prolific Denia Cabellero, who was 4-2 v de Morais. Perkovic had started in mediocre form at the European Champs but came through with 67.62 in the fifth round for a clear win over the German trio of Nadine Müller 63.00, Shanice Craft and Claudine Vita. They and Anna Rüh were closely matched with the German Champs order being Craft, Müller, Rüh, Vita, while Vita, twice over 65m had the best marks and also won at the World Cup from Su Xinyue, 3rd at the Chinese Champs.

Most competitions over 63m: Pérez 15, Perkovic 14, Stevens 7, Chen, Caballero 6; de Morais, Borges 4; Vita, Feng 3.

1. Perkovic, 2. Pérez, 3. Chen, 4. Stevens, 5. Caballero, 6. de Morais, 7. Vita, 8. Borges, 9. Feng., 10. Su Xinyue

Hammer

SUCH HAS BEEN Anita Wlodarczyk's dominance in recent years that it was a surprise when she lost three times in 2018. She was only 9th in her first competition at Halle after a win streak of 42 from July 2014, and was 2nd to Gwen Berry in Chorzów and to DeAnna Price in the Continental Cup. Nonetheless she won seven times and is top ranked for the seventh time and had the best three performances of the year (79.59, 78.94 and 78.74). North American records were set by Price 78.12 and Berry 77.78, so they narrowed the gap and Price only lost once in nine competitions, winning US and NACAC titles but coming only 6th at the Athletics World Cup in London behind Wlodarczyk, Sophie Hitchon, Alexandra Tavernier, Luo Na and Kathleen Klaas (in her final year). Wlodarczyk had 9 and Price 6 of the world's top 20 performances. Wlodarczyk won the European title from Tavernier, Joanna Fiodorow, Malwina Kopron, Hanna Skydan, Zalina Petrovskaya and Klaas, with Hanna Malyshik 4th on the World list, having no throws. Fiodorow beat Tavernier 4-2 and was 2-2 v Berry, who was 2-1 v Tavernier. Luo Na beat Wang Zheng 5-1 and these Chinese throwers were 1st and 2nd at the Asian Games. Just missing ranking were Maggie Ewen, who threw over 74m twice but mostly competed at shot and discus and missed the NCAAs due to no throws at the West qualifying, Réka Gyurátz and Hitchon, who had no throws at the Commonwealth Games.

Most competitions over 73m: Wlodarczyk 10, Tavernier 7, Price, Fiodorow 6; Malyshik 4, Ewen 3.

1. Wlodarczyk, 2. Price, 3. Fiodorow, 4. Berry, 5. Tavernier, 6. Malyshik, 7. Luo Na, 8. Kopron, 9. Wang Zheng, 10. Skydan

Javelin

NEITHER OF THE 2017 1-2, Barbora Spotáková and Sara Kolak, competed at all. Kathryn Mitchell had the best marks of 68.92 and 68.57 and was unbeaten in her seven competitions, but did not compete after winning at the Commonwealth Games in April and that makes it very difficult to rank her. Then there were four women who had bests of 67m plus: Christin Hussong, Lu Huihui, Tatyana Kholodovich and Liu Shying. Liu beat Lu 4-3 including at the Asian Games and when 2nd to 4th at the DL final in Zürich, but Lu, the Continental Cup and Chinese champion, had better marks and a generally better record against the top Europeans including 3-0 v Hussong, who won the European title from Nikola Ogrodníková, Liveta Jasiunaite, Martina Ratej and Kholodovich, who, however, was 2-1 v Liu Shiying and Hussong, winning in Zürich with Kara Winger 3rd, Ogrodníková 5th and Ratej 6th. Winger was US champion and 3rd at the Continental Cup behind Lu and Hussong.

She beaten 2-1 by Ratej. but was 2-1 against the Commonwealth Games 2nd Kelsey-Lee Barber (née Roberts) and 3rd Sunette Viljoen. The form guide is confused with Barber 2-0 against Ratej. Just missing a ranking is Sigrid Borge, 8th Europeans and 7th Zürich, while Jasiunaité did have much with which to back up her European medal.

Most competitions over 62m: Lu Huihui 14, Hussong 11, Ogrodníková 10, Liu Shiying 7, Mitchell, Kholodovich 6; Ratej, Winger, Barber 5; Viljoen 3.

1. Mitchell, 2. Lu Huihui, 3. Hussong, 4. Kholodovich, 5. Liu Shiying, 6. Ogrodníková, 7. Ratej, 8. Winger, 9. Barber, 10. Viljoen

Heptathlon

NAFISSATOU THIAM WAS top for the third successive year; she had the year's top two scores with 6816 at Götzis and 6806 for the European title. She did not, however, have the huge victory margin of her 2017 world title as in Götzis 2nd was Yorgelis Rodríguez with a CAC record 6742 followed by Erica Bougard 6725 and Anouk Vetter 6426, and at the Europeans, which featured 8 of the year's top 20 scores, Katarina Johnson-Thomson was 2nd with 6759 followed by Carolin Schäfer 6602. Schäfer was a clear winner of the IAAF Challenge as she could add scores from her wins at Ratingen 6549 and Talence 6467, and 2-4 in the Challenge were the other three top-10 women who had three scores: Bougard (winner in Florence and US Champs), Katerina Cachová (7 Götzis, 6 EC, 3 Talence) and Verena Preiner (5 Götzis, 8 EC, 6 Talence). Rodriguez won the CAG title and further top EC placings were 4th Ivona Dadic (also 2nd at Ratingen), 5th Vetter and 7th Xénia Krizsán (4 Talence).

1. Thiam, 2. Johnson-Thompson, 3. Rodríguez, 4. Bougard, 5. Schäfer, 6. Dadic, 7. Vetter, 8. Cachová, 9. Kriszán, 10. Preiner

The best indoor pentathlon scores were 4760A by Bougard to win the US title and the World Indoor 1-2: Johnson-Thompson 4750 and Dadic 4700 (also 4692 at Vienna). Further top WI placings were 3 Rodríguez 4637, 4 Eva Klucinová 4579 (after 4662 in Prague and 4580 in Madrid), 5. Bougard 4571.

20 Kilometres Walk

YELENA LASHMANOVA IS ineligible internationally, but she won the Russian title in 1:23:39, the best ever by a woman and also had the second fastest time of the year with 1:26:23 to take the winter title from Mariya Ponomaryova and Sofiya Brodatskaya (both under 1:28), with the latter 2nd at the summer champs. The year's next best times were 1:26:28 by Qieyang Shenjie at La Coruña and 1:26:36 by María Pérez to take the European title, followed by fast times from Anezka Drahotová, Antonella Palmisano, Birgita Virbalyté-Dimsiene, Zivilé Vaiciukeviciuté, Laura García-Caro and Inna Kashyna. Their times were very similar to those by the top seven at the World Team event, where María Guadeloupe González (also an important win at Monterrey) sped away from the field in the final stages to win in 1:26:38 from Qieyang, Yang Jiayu, Erica de Sena, Eleonora Giorgio, Drahotová and Pérez, with Kashyna 9th and Dimsiené 10th. Qieyang had a busy year with seven 20k races, winning at Huangshan, Rio Maior and La Coruña with 2nd at the Asian Games to Yang who was 2nd in Huangshan. Giorgi was disqualified at the Europeans but won at Lugano and Podébrady (Dimsiené 2nd). Pérez was Spanish champion but did not finish at La Coruña, and Drahotová was 2nd at Lugano and Dudince and 5th at Podébrady. Palmisano was 2nd at Rio Maior but 17th WT. De Sena was second to Qieyang in the IAAF Challenge series; she was South American and Brazilian champion and 2nd at Monterrey but dnf Rio Maior. Further South Americans to fare well were Kimberley García, 4 Monterrey, 8 WT, 3rd S.Am Champs and winner at the South American Games, and Sandra Arenas, 15th WT after winning at Dudince. Wang Lingliu beat many top women at Suzhou after a solid year including 3rd Huangshan, 5th Rio Maior, 13th World Team. González's top ranking is pending in investigation into a positive doping test in October.

1. González, 2. Qieyang 3. Yang Jiayu, 4. Pérez, 5. Giorgi, 6. Drahotová, 7. de Sena, 8. Palmisano. 9. Virbalyté-Dimsiene, 10. García, (11. Wang Lingliu). Russians not ranked.

50 Kilometres Walk

INÊS HENRIQUES HAD set two world records in 2017, the first year that this event was recognised, and in 2018 won the European title but she did not finish at the World Team event when Liang Rui improved the world record to 4:04:36, later also winning the Chinese title. For three of the 2nd to 5th placers at the World Team it was their only 50k race: Yin Hang, Claire Tallent (later winner of the Australian title), Paola Pérez and Ma Faying, while 6th Johana Ordóñez was 2nd at the South American Champs to Magaly Bonilla (11th WT), 7th Li Macuo won in Chifeng and was 2nd at the Chinese Champs, 8th Julia Takacs was Spanish champion and 3rd at the Europeans where 2nd was Alina Tsvilly (15th WT);

1. Liang Rui, 2. Yin Hang, 3. Tallent, 4. Henriques, 5. Li Maocuo. 6. Pérez, 7. Ma, 8. Takacs, 9. Ordóñez, 10. Bonilla.

TOP JUNIORS 2018

NINE JUNIOR MEN and four junior women made the world top ten rankings on the previous pages. Four junior men topped the world lists in 2018: Seleon Barega at 5000m, Stanley Waithera at 10,000m, Mondo Duplantis at PV and Sergey Shirobakov at 20k walk. Berega and Shirobakov were also topped ranked by me as was Rhonex Kipruto at 10,000m. The one U17 athlete to make the rankings was Jordan Díaz, 5th at triple jump. Duplantis set seven world U20 records (two indoors and five outdoors) and other world U20 records came from Berega (5000m), Shirobakov, Samuel Tefera (1500m indoors), Damion Thomas (equalled 110mh with 99cm hurdles), while Kipruto twice improved the road 10k best.

Five outstanding juniors were those in the IAAF's Rising Star award for men: Barega, the Diamond League 5000m winner who clocked 12:43.02; Díaz, the world U20 and Youth Olympic Games triple jump champion who set a world U18 best of 17.41; Duplantis, who won the European title with a 6.05m pole vault; Jakob Ingebrigtsen, who won European gold at both 1500m and 5000m; and Rhonex Kipruto, the world U20 10,000m champion who also ran 26:46 for a road 10km.

The junior women in the world rankings were Sydney Mclaughlin, 4th at 400m hurdles, who improved the world U20 record to 53.60 and 52.75 and also set WJRs indoors for flat 400m at 50.52 and 50.36, and three steeplechasers: Celliphine Chespol 5th, Peruth Chemutai 7th and Winfred Yavi 9th.The only other U20 world records were 7.98 for 60m hurdles indoors by Tara Davis and 66:47 for half marathon by Degitu Azimeraw.

The five women's IAAF Rising Star candidates were: Meseret Belete, 6th World HMar Champs and 67:51 in Chicago at half marathon, Meskerem Mamo, world U20 leads at 3000m 8:33.63 & 5000m 15:05.21 and 3rd African 5000m; Celliphine Chespol, world U20 steeplechase champion and won African CC, 2nd 3000mSt CG and African Champs, Briana Williams, the 16 year-old U20 100m and 200m champion, and Sydney McLaughlin, world U20 and NCAA 400m hurdles champion with the world U20 records above.

CROSS-COUNTRY – NATIONAL CHAMPIONS 2018

	Men (long distance)	Women (long distance)
Algeria	Ali Grine	Rima Chenah
Argentina	Eulalio Muñoz	María Luján Urrutia
Austria	Peter Herzog	Sandrina Illes
Australia	Andrew Buchanan	Madeline Hills
Belarus (Nov)	Sergey Platonov	Nina Savina
Belgium	Isaac Kimeli	Imana Truyers
Bulgaria (Oct)	Mitko Tsenov	Marinela Nineva
Canada (Nov)	Lucas Bruchet	Geneviève Lalonde
Chile	Roberto Tello	Yetsemin González
Colombia	Diego Vera	Laura Cusaría
Croatia	Dino Bosnjak	Matea Parlov
Cuba	Francisco Estévez	Yudileyvis Castillo
Czech Republic (Nov)	Jirí Homolac	Moira Stewartová
England	Adam Hickey	Phoebe Law
Eritrea	Filmon Ande	Nazret Weldu
Estonia (Oct)	Olavi Allase	Kelly Nevolihhin
Ethiopia	Enyew Mekonnen	Enatnesh Alamirew
Finland	Järkko Jarvenpää	Camilla Richardsson
France	Morhad Amdouni	Sophie Duarte
Germany	Philipp Pflieger	Elena Burkard
Greece	Konstadínos Gelauózos	Koraíni-Anthí Kiriakopoúlou
Hungary	Lászlo Gregor	Zita Kácser
India	Shankar Ma Thapa	Sanjivani Jadhav
Ireland (Nov)	Kevin Dooney	Clara Mageean
Israel	Yimer Getahun	Lonah Chemtai Salpeter
Italy	Yohanes Chiappinelli	Martina Merlo
Japan	Suguru Osako	Tomoka Kimura
Kazakhstan (Oct)	Dmitriy Ivanchukov	Lyudmila Monina
Latvia (Oct)	Said Suleymanov	Diana Aidosova
Luxembourg	Janis Girgensons	Sandra Grosberga
Morocco	Christophe Kass	Isabelle Hoffmann
Netherlands	Hamza Sahli	Hajiba Hasnaoui
New Zealand	Edwin de Vries	Andrea Deelstra
Northern Ireland	Oli Chignell	Lisa Cross
Norway (Oct)	Declan Reed	Rebekah Nixon
Poland	Didrik Tønseth	Sigrid Våg
Portugal	Tomasz Grycko	Katarzyna Rutkowska
Romania (Oct)	Rui Teixeira	Catarina Ribeiro
Russia	Nicolae Soare	Ancuta Bobocel
Scotland	Aleksey Vikulov	Aleksandra Gulyayeva
Serbia (Oct)	Kris Jones	Mhairi MacLennan
Slovakia (Nov)	Nikola Raicevic	Olivera Jevtic
Slovenia	Tibir Sahajda	Veronika Zrasta
South Africa	Jan Bresan	Marusa Mismas
Spain	Precious Mashele	Glenrose Zaba
Sweden (Oct)	Ayad Lamdassem	Trihas Gebre
Switzerland	Napoleon Solomon	Meraf Bahta
Trinidad & Tobago	Jonas Raess	Nicole Egger
Turkey	Sherwin Stapleton	Samantha Shukla
UK (CAU)	Chiat Ulus	Tubay Erdal
Ukraine	Mahamed Mahamed	Phoebe Law
(Oct)	Oleksandr Matviychuk	Olesya Didovodyuk
USA	Vasyl Koval	Viktoriya Kalyuzhna
Wales	Leonard Korir	Emily Infeld
Venezuela	James Hunt	Bronwen Owen
	Whinton Palma	

Balkan (Nov)	Cihat Ulus TUR	Paula Todoran ROU
European Champion Clubs teams	David Kiplangat KEN Sporting Clube de Portugal	Katarzyna Rutkowska POL Fenerbahçe – Istanbul TUR
Lidingöloppet 30k	Napoleon Solomon SWE	Sylvia Medegu KEN
Nordic (Nov)	Amanuel Gergis SWE	Anna Emilie Møller DEN
South Asian	Pradeep Singh IND	Sanjivani Jadhav IND
World University	El Hocine Zourkane ALG	Caterina Granz GER

Short Course winners

Austria	Hans-Peter Innerhofer	
Belgium	Jeroen D'Hoedt	Renée Eykens
Denmark	Mikkel Dahl-Jessen	Alberte Pedersen
Finland	Järkko Jarvenpää	
France	Djilali Bedrani	Claire Perraux
Germany	Timo Benitz	
Norway	Erik Udø Pedersen	Sigrid Jervell Våg
Poland	Mateusz Demczyszak	
Portugal	Rui Pinto	Marianna Machado
Russia	Aleksey Popov	Marina Pospelova
South Africa	Ryan Mphalele	Lebo Phalula
Sweden (Oct)	Napoleon Solomon	Meraf Bahta
Switzerland	Jan Hochstrasser	Lisa Kurmann

Winners Major Cross-Country Races 2018

6 Jan	Antrim (IAAF)	Timothy Cheruiyot KEN	Margaret Kipkomboi KEN
6 Jan	San Georgio su Legnano	James Kibet KEN	Lilian Rengeruk KEN
7 Jan	Amorebieta	Timothy Toroitich UGA	Trihas Gebre ESP
13 Jan	Edinburgh (EA)	Leonard Korir USA	Yasemin Can TUR
14 Jan	Elgóibar	Selemon Barega ETH	Ruth Jebet BRN
21 Jan	Kerkrade (EA)	Chakib Lachgar MAR	Sylvia Medegu SUI
21 Jan	Santiponce, Seville (IAAF)	Joshua Cheptegei UGA	Agnes Tirop KEN
21 Jan	Della Lagarina, Rovereto (EA)	Telahun Bekele ETH	Norah Tanui KEN
28 Jan	San Sebastián	Aweke Ayalew BRN	Daisy Jepkemei KEN
11 Feb	San Vittore Olana (Cinque Mullina) (IAAF)	Jacob Kiplimo UGA	Letesenbet Gidey ETH
18 Feb	Albufeira (IAAF)	Soufiane El Bakkali MAR	Carla Salome Rocha POR
7 Apr	World University	El Hocine Zourkane ALG	Caterina Granz GER
23 Sep	Lidingöloppet (EA) 30k	Napoleon Solomon SWE	Sylvia Medegu SUI
11 Nov	Burgos (Atapuerca) (IAAF)	Jacob Kiplimo UGA	Senebere Teferi ETH
19 Nov	Leffinckroucke (EA)	Solomon Berihu ETH	Letesenbet Gidey ETH
18 Nov	Soria (IAAF)	Jacob Kiplimo UGA	Gloria KITE KEN
25 Nov	Alcobendas (IAAF)	Jacob Kiplimo UGA	Eva Cherono KRN
26 Nov	Tilburg (EA)	Yohanes Chiappinelli ITA	Fabienne Schlumpf SUI

IAAF – IAAF permit races, EA – European Athletics permit races

European Cross-Country Championships 2017

At Samorín-Cilistov, Slovakia, December 10

Senior Men (10.18k)
1. Kaan Kigen Özbilen TUR 29:45
2. Adel Mechaal ESP 29:54
3. Andrew Butchart GBR 30:00
4. Hassan Chahdi FRA 30:01
5. Soufiane Bouchikhi BEL 30:04
6. Ben Connor GBR 30:08
7. Aras Kaya TUR 30:14
8. Daniel Mateo ESP 30:16
9. Polat Kemboi Arikan TUR 30:17
10. Ayad Lamdassem ESP 30:18
11. Henrik Ingebrigtsen NOR 30:19
12. Richard Ringer GER 30:24
13. Lander Tijtgat BEL 30:25
14. Javier Guerra ESP 30:29
15. Seán Tobin IRL 30:43
76 of 79 finished.
Teams: 1. TUR 17, 2. ESP 20, 3. GBR 35, 4. FRA 56, 5. IRL 58, 6. DEN 80, 7. NOR 81, 8. POR 909, 9. ITA 110, 10. SWE 111, 11. AUT 138, 12. UKR 144, 13. SVK 201

Under-23 Men (8.23k)
1. Jimmy Gressier FRA 24:35
2. Hugo Hay FRA 24:37
3. Yemaneberhan Crippa ITA 24:42
4. Roudolff Lévisse FRA 24:43
5. Carlos Mayo ESP 24:46
6. Simon Debognies BEL 24:47
7. Alexis Miellet FRA 24:47
8. Topi Raitanen FIN 24:47

83 of 85 finished.
Teams: 1. FRA 7, 2. BEL 26, 3. GBR 41, 4. ESP 45, 5. ITA 49, 6. TUR 76, 7. GER 79, 8. NED 106, 9. POR 110, 10. UKR 130; 16 teams scored.
U20 Men (6.28k)
1. Jakob Ingebrigtsen NOR 18:39
2. Ramazan Barbaros TUR 18:41
3. Louis Gilavert FRA 18:45
4. Yani Khelaf FRA 18:47
5. Miguel González ESP 18:48
107 of 109 finished.
Teams: 1. ESP 20, 2. FRA 27, 3. TUR 49, 4. BEL 51, 5. NOR 51, 6. GBR 56; 20 scored.
Senior Women (8.23k)
1. Yasemin Can TUR 26:48
2. Meraf Bahta SWE 27:03
3. Karoline Bjerkeli Grøvdal NOR 27:04
4. Roxana Bârca ROU 27:21
5. Elena Burkard GER 27:21
6. Charlotte Taylor GBR 27:23
7. Fabienne Schlumpf SUI 27:24
8. Emelia Gorecka GBR 27:34
9. Gemma Steel GBR 27:41
10. Stephanie Twell GBR 27:43
11. Ancuta Bobocel ROU 27:46
12. Fionnuala McCormack IRL 27:48
13. Trihas Gebre ESP 27:53
14. Viktoriya Kalyuzhna UKR 27:54
15. Lily Partridge GBR 27:55
77 started and finished
Teams: 1. GBR 23, 2. ROU 31, 3. TUR 54, 4. POR 60,

5. ESP 60, 6. GER 70, 7. IRL 84, 8. FRA 85, 9. ITA 115, 10. DEN 131, 11. UKR 148, 12. AUT 188, 13. SVK 225.
Under-23 Women (6.28k)
1. Alina Reh GER 20:22
2. Konstanze Klosterhalfen GER 20:25
3. Jessica Judd GBR 20:45
4. Amy-Eloise Neale GBR 20:59
5. Amy Griffiths GBR 21:02
6. Isabelle Brauer SWE 21:09
7. Anna Emilie Møller DEN 21:14
8. Weronika Pyzik POL 21:18
62 of 63 finished.
Teams: 1. GBR 12, 2. GER 15, 3. TUR 46, 4. SWE 52, 5. ESP 59, 6. UKR 66, 7. DEN 77, 8. FRA 82, 9. ITA 85, 10. SUI 132, 11. POR 168.
U20 Women (4.18k)
1. Harriet Knowles-Jones GBR 13:48

2. Lili Tóth HUN 13:59
3. Miriam Dattke GER 14:03
4. Jasmijn Lau NED 14:05
5. Nadia Battocletti ITA 14:07
104 started and finished.
Teams: 1. GBR 21, 2. ITA 33, 3. ESP 47, 4. FRA 60, 5. NED 60, 6. GER 70, 20 scored.
Change this year in that Team events have three to score, previously four.
Mixed Relay (6280m): 1. GBR 18:24 (Melissa Courtney 5:39 1710m. Cameron Boyek 3:59 1500m. Sarah McDonald 4:41 1500m. Tom Marshall 4:07 1570m), 2. CZE (Vrzalová 5:35. Sasínek 4:03. Mäki 4:45. Holusa 4:04) 18:25, 3. ESP (Pereira 5:37. Ruiz 4:01. Guerrero 4:45. Gómez 4:05) 18:26, 4. SWE 19:02, 5. FRA 19:04, 6. ITA 19:10, 7. GER 19:10, 8. TUR 19:14, 9. UKR 19:26, 10. DEN 19:36, 11. SVK 20:31.

European Cross-Country Championships 2018

At Tilburg, Netherlands December 9
Senior Men (10.3k)
1. Filip Ingebrigtsen NOR 28:49
2. Isaac Kimeli BEL 28:52
3. Aras Kaya TUR 28:56
4. Kaan Kigen Özbilen TUR 29:04
5. Napoleon Solomon SWE 29:12
6. Yemaneberhan Crippa ITA 29:14
7. Polat Kemboi Arikan TUR 29:14
8. Adel Mechaal ESP 29:20
9. Marc Scott GBR 29:21
10. Seán Tobin IRL 29:22
11. Daniele Meucci ITA 29:26
12. Kristian Jones GBR 29:28
13. Dewi Griffiths GBR 29:31
14. Antonio Abadía ESP 29:35
15. Robin Hendrix BEL 29:36
85 of 88 finished.
Teams: 1. TUR 14, 2. GBR 34, 3. ITA 37, 4. BEL 38, 5. ESP 38, 6. NOR 55, 7. IRL 70, 8. SWE 78, 9. DEN 90, 10. FRA 110, 11. GER 121, 12. POR 129, 13. NED 131, 14. UKR 176, 15. EST 207, 16. SUI 238,
Under-23 Men (8.3k)
1. Jimmy Gressier FRA 23:37
2. Samuel Fitwi GER 23:45
3. Hugo Hay FRA 23:48
4. Ryan Forsyth IRL 23:49
5. Patrick Dever GBR 24:05
6. Tariku Novales ESP 24:05
7. Fabien Palcau FRA 24:06
8. Emile Cairess GBR 24:07
92 of 93 finished.
Teams: 11. FRA 11, 2. GBR 30, 3. ESP 42, 4. GER 48, 5. BEL 58, 6. IRL 69, 7. NED 78, 8. ISR 87, 9. SWE 96, 10. ITA 97; 16 scored
U20 Men (6.3k)
1. Jakob Ingebrigtsen NOR 18:00
2. Ouassim Oumaiz ESP 18:09
3. Elzan Bibic SRB 18:11
4. Jake Heyward GBR 18:16
5. Simen Halle Haugen NOR 18:18
95 of 96 finished.
Teams: 1. NOR 28, 2. GBR 30, 3. GER 38, 4. FRA 41, 5. IRL 55, 6. NED 56, 16 scored.
Senior Women (8.3k)
1. Yasemin Can TUR 26:05
2. Fabienne Schlumpf SUI 26:06
3. Karoline Bjerkeli Grøvdal NOR 26:07
4. Susan Krumins NED 26:16

5. Jip Vastenburg NED 26:45
6. Elena Burkard GER 26:53
7. Charlotte Arter GBR 26:57
8. Melissa Courtney GBR 26:59
9. Pippa Woolven GBR 27:02
10. Jessica Piasecki GBR 27:03
11. Maureen Koster NED 27:08
12. Trihas Gebre ESP 27:16
13. Charlotta Fougberg SWE 27:17
14. Anna Gosk POL 27:20
15. Kate Avery GBR 27:20
69 of 72 finished,
Teams: 1. NED 20, 2. GBR 24, 3. GER 50, 4. FRA 70, 5. SWE 80, 6. ESP 85, 7. TUR 88, 8. NOR 91, 9. ROU 106, 10. BEL 112, 11. IRL 120, 12. POR 127, 13. ITA 135, 14. UKR 137.
Under-23 Women (6.3k)
1. Anna Emilie Møller DEN 20:34
2. Anna Gehring GER 20:36
3. Weronika Pyzik POL 20:46
4. Chiara Scherrer SUI 20:48
5. Célia Antón ESP 20:57
6. Miriam Dattke GER 20:58
7. Amy Griffiths GBR 21:04
8. Carmela Cardama ESP 21:04
69 of 70 finished.
Teams: 1. GER 22, 2. ESP 25, 3. GBR 33, 4. DEN 56;5. FRA 56, 6. TUR 77, 7. ITA 78, 8. SUI 81, 9. IRL 82, 10. LTU 113, 13 scored.
U20 Women (4.3k)
1. Nadia Battocletti ITA 13:46
2. Delia Sclabas SUI 13:47
3. Inci Kalkan TUR 13:48
4. Jasmijn Lau NED 13:51
5. Amelia Quirk GBR 13:57
86 of 88 finished.
Teams: 1. GBR 23, 2. NED 28, 3. TUR 39, 4. SUI 40, 5. ITA 41, 6. IRL 42, 15 scored.
Mixed Relay (5.8k men legs 1 & 3, 1200m & 1500m; women legs 2 & 4, 1500m & 1600m): 1. ESP 16:10 (Ordóñez 3:20. Guerrero 4:29. Ruiz 3:47. Pereira 4:36), 2. FRA 16:12 (Miellet 3:17. Lamote 4:31. Mekhissi-Benabbad 3:47. Geyer-Carles 4:39), 3. BLR 16:21 (Logish 3:23. Ivanova 4:34. Platonov 3:49. Nemogai 4:36), 4. GBR 16:24 (Williamson 3:25. Bell 4:24. Sesemann 3:54. Judd 4:42), 5. UKR 16:30, 6. SWE 16:32, 7. BEL 16:34, 8. LAT 16:40, 9. IRL 16:40, 10. POR 16:44, 11. ITA 16:51, 12. DEN 17:02

2018 WORLD ROAD RACE REVIEW
By Marty Post

THERE WERE WORLD records at the half-marathon for both men and women as there were new standards of excellence for the distance in 2018. Abraham Kiptum broke the long-standing mark, 58:23 by Zersenay Tadesse at Lisbon in March 2010, as at Valencia, Spain on October 28 the 29-year-old Kenyan passed the first two 5k splits in 13:56 and 28:02 (14:06). Then he picked up the pace to reach 15k in 41:37 (13:35) and 20k in 55:18 (13:41) giving him a remarkable 27:16 between 10 and 20 kilometres. He covered the remaining distance in three minutes flat, as he stopped the clock in 58:18. Jemal Yimer Mekonen (58:33) and Abadi Hadis Embaye (58:44) recorded the best second and third place times in history. The top ten all went under one hour.

There were two other sub-59 minutes winning races. At Ras Al Khaimah, Kenyan Bedan Karoki Muchiri notched a 58:42, the same exact time countryman Erick Kiptanui would post at the Berlin Halbmarathon. Yimer Mekonen was second at RAK in 59:00 giving him an average time of 58:46.5 without winning either race. Geoffrey Kamworor defended his IAAF World title at Valencia with some splendid second half running. After a first 10k of 29:28 he reached 15k in 44:13. Bolstered by a strong tailwind, he ripped the next two kilometers in 2:30 and 2:35, blazing the last full 5k segment in 13:01 to post a 1:00:02 victory by 22 seconds.

There was much pre-race speculation that the women's-only world record would fall in Valencia and indeed it did, but not to one of more touted contenders. Netsanet Gudeta ran through fairly even 10k segments of 31:38 and 62:53 (31:15) and broke the finish tape in 66:11. On site to witness history was Lornah Kiplagat whose 2007 WOWR of 66:27 was finally surpassed.

At Ras Al Khaimah, a Fancy Chemutai/Mary Keitany stride for stride battle late into the race resulted in Chemutai missing the world record by just one second (64:52)

and Keitany becoming the first to break 65 minutes (1:04:55) without winning as she also set a world 35+ age group record. The rest of the top ten all set best-ever times for place with sixth finisher, Degitu Azimeraw of Ethiopia, claiming the world junior record of 66:47. Joan Chelimo became the fourth fastest woman in history with a 65:04 at Prague and Sifan Hassan of the Netherlands lowered the European record to 65:15 at Copenhagen.

A Haile Gebreselasie record fell by five seconds when Mark Kiptoo set a new half-marathon world age 40+ best of 61:04 at Azkoita.

There were also three men's performances in 2018 that in years past would have been world records, but the IAAF had removed these distances from its list of record events. One was the aforementioned 55:18 by Kiptum at 20k en route in the Valencia Half-Marathon. Another interim all-time world best was a 1:26:45 by Eliud Kipchoge for his 30k split at the Berlin Marathon, the first sub-87 minute time. The third was a 41:05 for 15k by Joshua Cheptegei of Uganda at Nijmegen on November 18. This had been a world record distance when Leonard Patrick Komen ran 41:13 there in 2010. And there was yet another world best at a distance the IAAF has never recognized for world records: 8k. Rhonex Kipruto, an 18-year-old Kenyan prodigy, tore through the Healthy Kidney 10k in New York's hilly Central Park in 27:08, and was timed at 21:45. Ironically Kipruto would go even faster at Prague in September lowering his world junior best and world leader to 26:46 (the number two time ever), but there was no 8k split.

Melly Chelimo had the fastest women's 10k of 2018, 30:14 en route at the Prague Half-Marathon, and later in the year Kenyans Caroline Chepkoech Kipkirui (30:19), Fancy Chemutai (30:22) and Diane Chemtai Kipyokei (30:23) had a one-two-three finish in the same city.

WINNERS OF LEADING 2018 ROAD RACES

Date	Race	Men	Women
7 Jan	Adana HMar	Felix Kibitok KEN 61:50	Diana Kipyokei KEN 68:42*
14 Jan	Egmond van Zee HMar	Edwin Kiptoo KEN 62:36	Zeyneba Yimer ETH 72:19
14 Jan	Houston HMar	Jake Robertson NZL 60:01	Ruti Aga ETH 66:39
14 Jan	Valencia 10k	Abayneh Degu ETH 28:03	Sandrafelis Tuei KEN 30:57

28 Jan	Marrakech HMar	Hicham Amghar MAR 60:23*	Hajiba Hassnaoui MAR 1:10:43
4 Feb	Marugame HMar	Edward Waweru KEN 60:31	Betsy Saina KEN 69:17
4 Feb	Napoli HMar	Asbel Kipchumba KEN 60:12*	Shitaye Eshete BRN 68:38*
9 Feb	Ras Al Khaimah HMar	Bedan Karoki KEN 58:42*	Fancy Chemutai KEN 64:52*
11 Feb	Barcelona HMar	Mule Wasihun ETH 59:44*	Tejitu Daba ETH 68:36
11 Feb	Yamaguchi HMar	Charles Ndirangyu KEN 61:55	Pauline Kamulu KEN 69:40
18 Feb	Guadalajara HMar	John Mwangangi KEN 63:49*	Diana Kipyokei KEN 70:00*
18 Feb	Verona HMar	Peter Ndorobo KEN 61:01	Vivian Kiplagat KEN 71:59
25 Feb	Casablanca 10k	Abderahmane Kachir MAR 28:39	Dorcas Kimeli KEN 31:37
25 Feb	Riyadh HMar	Getaneh Molla ETH 61:54	*no elite women*
4 Mar	London HMar	Mo Farah GBR 61:40*	Charlotte Purdue GBR 70:29*
4 Mar	Paris HMar	Evans Cheruiyot KEN 61:25	Antonia Kwambai KEN 68:07
10 Mar	Jacksonville 15k US Ch	Leonard Korir USA 43:07	Molly Huddle USA 47:50
11 Mar	Den Haag HMar	James Rungaru KEN 59:37	Maja Neuenschwander SUI 70:46
11 Mar	Lisboa HMar	Erick Kiptanui KEN 60:05	Etagegne Woldu ETH 71:27
11 Mar	Roma-Ostia HMar	Galen Rupp USA 59:47	Haftamnesh Tesfay ETH 69:02
17 Mar	Laredo 10k	Amdework Walelegn ETH 27:36	Mary Waithira KEN 31:47
18 Mar	Brunssum 10k	Joel Ayeko UGA 29:06	Maureen Koster NED 32:15
18 Mar	New York City HMar	Ben True USA 62:39*	Buze Diriba ETH 72:23*
24 Mar	Azkoita HMar	Mark Kiptoo KEN 61:04	Hawi Megersa ETH 70:24
24 Mar	Mobile 10km	Benard Ngeno KEN 27:45	Monicah Ngige KEN 32:18
25 Mar	Milano HMar	Felix Kibitok KEN 60:11	Sutume Asefa ETH 67:54
25 Mar	Venlo HMar	Stephen Kiprop KEN 59:44	Nancy Kiprop KEN 67:49*
25 Mar	Warszawa HMar	Ezrah Sang KEN 61:37	Polline Njeru KEN 70:01
31 Mar	New Orleans 10k	Jake Robertson NZL 27:28	Monicah Ngige KEN 32:05
31 Mar	Paderborn 10k	Emmanuel Kiprono KEN 27:26	Dorcas Tuitoek KEN 31:00
1 Apr	Berkane HMar	El Hassan El Abbassi BRN 61:57	Feyne Gudeto Gemecha ETH 70:39
7 Apr	Praha HMar	Benard Kimeli KEN 59:47	Joan Chelimo KEN 65:04
8 Apr	Berlin HMar	Erick Kiptanui KEN 58:42*	Melat Yisak ETH 69:04
8 Apr	Istanbul HMar	Amdework Walelegn ETH 59:50*	Ababel Yeshaneh ETH 66:20
8 Apr	Madrid HMar	Ezrah Kiprotich Sang KEN 62:37	Naomi Jebet KEN 69:56
8 Apr	Washington DC 10M	Jemal Yimer ETH 46:17	Buze Diriba ETH 53:45
14 Apr	Boston 5k	Hagos Gebrhiwet ETH 13:42	Buze Diriba ETH 15:22
15 Apr	Verbania HMar	Daniel Kipchumba KEN 59:06*	Daisy Cherotich KEN 69:44
22 Apr	Gifu HMar	Nicholas Kosimbei KEN 61:12	Degitu Azimeraw ETH 69:53
22 Apr	Yangzhou HMar	Mosinet Geremew ETH 61:31	Ababel Yeshaneh ETH 69:06
29 Apr	New York City 10k	Rhonex Kipruto KEN 27:08*	Buze Diriba ETH 32:04
29 Apr	Würzburg 10k	Emmanuel Kiprono KEN 28:17	Melat Yisak ETH 32:39
1 May	Puy-en-Velay 15k	Stephen Kiprop KEN 42:16	Dorcas Tuitoek KEN 48:53
6 May	Spokane 12k	Jemal Yimer ETH 34:18	Buze Diriba ETH 39:27
12 May	Grand Rapids 25k US Ch	Sam Chelanga USA 1:14:52	Aliphine Tuliamuk USA 1:25:35
13 May	Bucuresti HMar	Patrick Kipkorir KEN 61:05	Pauline Korikwaing KEN 70:07
19 May	Bern 10M	Kenenisa Bekele ETH 46:47	Martina Strähl SUI 53:50
19 May	Göteborg HMar	Shadrack Kimining KEN 61:31	Meseret Belete ETH 69:06
20 May	Cape Town 12k	Morris Gachaga KEN 33:42*	Jackline Chepngeno KEN 39:12*
20 May	Manchester 10k	Mo Farah GBR 28:27	Tirunesh Dibaba ETH 31:08
20 May	San Francisco 12k	Philemon Cheboi KEN 35:37	Jane Kibii KEN 40:33
20 May	Santos 10k (dist?)	Maxwell Rotich KEN 27:22	Paskalia Chekorir KEN 32:15
26 May	Ottawa 10k	Andamlak Belihu ETH 27:48	Alia M Saeed UAE 31:46
27 May	Bengaluru 10k	Geoffrey Kamworor KEN 28:18	Agnes Tirop KEN 31:19*
27 May	Lugano HMar	Cosmas Kipchoge KEN 61:30	Diana Kipyokei KEN 68:41*
28 May	Boulder (A) 10k	Getaneh Tamire Molla ETH 28:18	Mamitu Daska ETH 32:37
28 May	London 10k UK Ch	Mo Farah GBR 28:44	Stephanie Twell GBR 32:34
2 Jun	Valencia 15k	Josphat Boit KEN 42:02*	Lornah C Salpeter ISR 47:38*
3 Jun	San Diego HMar	Titus Ekiru ETH 61:02	Meseret Defar ETH 68:26
9 Jun	New York City 10k	*elite women only*	Mary Keitany KEN 30:59
9 Jun	Oelde 10k	Geoffrey Koech KEN 27:44*	Dorcas Tuitoek KEN 31:26*
10 Jun	Zwolle HMar	William Wanjiku KEN 61:31	Fancy Chemutai KEN 69:38
16 Jun	Langueux 10k	Moses Kibet KEN 28:26	Clémence Calvin FRA 31:20*
17 Jun	Duluth HMar (dh 38m)	Panuel Mkungo KEN 62:50	Monicah Ngige KEN 69:55
23 Jun	Olomouc HMar	Stephen Kiprop KEN 60:15*	Netsanet Gudeta ETH 67:30

Date	Event	Men	Women
24 Jun	Boston 10k	Gabriel Geay TAN 28:24	Mary Wacera KEN 31:55
24 Jun	Casablanca HMar	Hassan El Abbassi MAR 59:58	Kaltoum Bouaasayriya MAR 74:18
30 Jun	Appingedam 10k	Vedic Kipkoech KEN 28:19	Edith Chelimo KEN 32:13
1 Jul	Hamburg HMar	Kalipus Lomwai KEN 61:22	Gladys Kipkoech KEN 70:13*
4 Jul	Atlanta 10k (dh 34m) US Ch	Bernard Lagat USA 28:45	Stephanie Bruce USA 32:21
8 Jul	Utica 15k	Gabriel Geay TAN 43:40	Mary Wacera KEN 50:01
28 Jul	Davenport 7M	Belay Tilahun ETH 32:39	Margaret Muriuki KEN 35:57
28 Jul	Port Elizabeth HMar	Stephen Mokoka RSA 61:44*	Mamarola Tjoka LES 70:46
29 Jul	Bogotá (A) HMar	Betesfa Getahun ETH 65:10	Netsanet Gudeta ETH 71:34
4 Aug	Cape Elizabeth 10k	Jake Robertson NZL 27:37	Sandrafelis Tuei KEN 31:21
12 Aug	Sydney 14k	Ben St. Lawrence US 41:41	Ellie Pashley AUS 46:13
19 Aug	Falmouth 7M	Ben Flanagan USA 32:21	Caroline Chepkoech KEN 35:48
25 Aug	Flint 10M	Julius Kogo KEN 47:50	Brilliant Jepkorir KEN 54:05
26 Aug	Buenos Aires HMar	Mosinet Geremew ETH 59:48*	Vivian Kiplagat KEN 69:10*
1 Sep	Lille HMar	Victor Chumo KEN 60:03	Antonia Kwambai KEN 69:44
2 Sep	Tilburg 10M/10k	Rodgers Kwemoi KEN 45:23	Agnes Tirop KEN 30:50
3 Sep	New Haven 20k US Ch	Leonard Korir USA 60:17	Sara Hall USA 69:04
8 Sep	Prague 10k	Rhonex Kipruto KEN 26:46*	Caroline Kipkirui KEN 30:19
9 Sep	South Shields HMar (dh 30m)	Mo Farah GBR 59:27	Vivian Cheruiyot KEN 67:43
9 Sep	Minsk HMar	Abebe Negewo ETH 62:37*	Sheila Jerotich KEN 72:02
9 Sep	New York 5th Avenue 1M (dh)	Jake Wightman GBR 3:53.5	Jdenny Simpson USA 4:18.8
15 Sep	Ústí nad Labem HMar	Stephen Kiprop KEN 59:41	Diana Kipyokei KEN 67:17*
16 Sep	Copenhagen HMar	Daniel Kipchumba KEN 59:06	Sifan Hassan NED 65:15*
16 Sep	Philadelphia HMar	Shura Kitata ETH 59:16	Desiree Linden USA 71:48
16 Sep	Porto HMar	Mike Boit KEN 60:53	Susan Kipsang KEN 71:06
23 Sep	Krems HMar	Geoffrey Ronoh KEN 60:21	Parendis Lekapana KEN 69:23
23 Sep	Zaandam 10M	Joshua Cheptegei UGA 45:15	Lonah Chemtai Salpeter ISR 50:45
23 Sep	Udine HMar	Moses Kemei KEN 61:14	Sara Dossena ITA 70:10
24 Sep	Belfort HMar	Justus Kangogo KEN 60:56	Magdaline Masai KEN 72:48
30 Sep	Glasgow HMar	Chris Thompson GBR 62:07	Mare Dibaba ETH 69:15
6 Oct	Trento 10k	Jacob Kiplimo UGA 28:17	*elite men only*
7 Oct	Boston HMar	Daniel Chebii KEN 63:08	Joan Chelimo KEN 69:34
7 Oct	Breda HMar	Berhane Tsefay ERI 60:54	Gladys Kipkoech KEN 72:56
7 Oct	Cardiff HMar (Comm Ch)	Jack Rayner AUS 61:01	Juliet Chekwel UGA 69:45
7 Oct	Torino HMar (dh)	Charles Kamau KEN 60:47	Viola Jelagat KEN 72:00
7 Oct	Trento HMar	Abraham Akopesha KEN 62:09	Joyce Chepkemoi KEN 69:21
7 Oct	Utrecht 10k	Davis Kiplangat KEN 27:24	Eva Cherono KEN 31:17*
8 Oct	Boston 9.6k	*elite women only*	Emily Sisson USA 30:39
14 Oct	Berlin 10k	Vincent Kibet KEN 27:21	Alina Reh GER 31:23
14 Oct	Durban 10k	Joshua Cheptegei UGA 27:16*	Stella Chesang UGA 31:14*
14 Oct	Groningen 4M	Davis Kiplangat KEN 17:12	Eva Cherono KEN 19:50
14 Oct	Lisboa HMar	Mustapha El Aziz MAR 60:13	Yebrgual Melese ETH 67:14
14 Oct	Paris 20k	Samuel Tsegay ERI 58:23	Ophélie Claude-Boxberger FRA 69:48
14 Oct	Pettinengo 9.6k/4k	Jacob Kiplimo UGA 26:22*	Joan Chepkemoi KEN 12:29
21 Oct	New Delhi HMar	Andamlak Belihu ETH 59:18	Tsehay Gemechu ETH 66:50*
21 Oct	Portsmouth 10M	Chris Thompson GBR 46:56	Eilish McColgan GBR 54:43
28 Oct	Marseille-Cassis 20k	Olika Adugna ETH 00:29	Gete Alemayehu FTH 68:46
28 Oct	Valencia HMar	Abraham Kiptum KEN 58:18*	Geleta Burka ETH 66:11
3 Nov	New York City 5k US Ch	Paul Chelimo USA 13:45*	Emily Sisson USA 15:38
4 Nov	Morlaix 10k (dh 86m)	Paul Melly KEN 29:01	Chaltu Negasa ETH 32:08
4 Nov	Pittsburgh 10M	Martin Hehir USA 46:49*	Monicah Ngige KEN 52:07
11 Nov	Agadir 10k	Vincent Yegon KEN 28:11	Silenat Yismaw ETH 31:42
11 Nov	Istanbul 15k	Shadrack Korir KEN 43:03	Yasemin Can TUR 48:18
11 Nov	Las Vegas HMar	Wilkerson Given USA 62:50	Kellyn Taylor USA 70:16*
17 Nov	Bulle 6k/4k	Julien Wanders SUI 22:27.3*	Fabienne Schlumpf SUI 19:41.1
18 Nov	Addis Ababa (A) 10k	Hagos Gebrhiwet ETH 28:55	Foten Tesfaye ETH 33:44
18 Nov	Ageo HMar	Vincent Laimoi KEN 61:19*	Kaori Yoshida JPN 71:54*
18 Nov	Billancourt HMar	Taye Girma ETH 60:55	Parendis Lekapana KEN 70:48
18 Nov	Nijmegen 15k	Joshua Cheptegei UGA 41:05*	Stella Chesang UGA 47:19*
18 Nov	Philadelphia HMar	James Ngandu KEN 62:43	Vicoty Chepngeno KEN 70:18*
22 Nov	Manchester CT 4.75M	Edward Cheserek KEN 21:16*	Celliphine Chespol KEN 24:33

Date	Event	Men	Women
24 Nov	Basel 7.55/5.9 k	Julien Wanders SUI 21:23.6	Helen Bekele ETH 18:45.2
1 Dec	Ziwa (A) 10k (dh 70m)	Nicholas Kimeli KEN 28:20	Agnes Tirop KEN 31:17
2 Dec	Geneva 7.32k	Julien Wanders SUI 20:46	Helen Bekele ETH 23:52*
2 Dec	Kosa 10M	John Muritu KEN 45:56	elite men only
2 Dec	's-Heerenberg 15k	Stephen Kissa UGA 43:21	Joan Chelimo KEN 48:44
16 Dec	Kolkata 25k	Birhanu Legese ETH 75:48*	Dibaba Kuma ETH 87:34
16 Dec	Mersin 15k	Mulat Bazezew ETH 43:58	Delvine Meringor KEN 48:36*
30 Dec	Houilles 10k	Julien Wanders SUI 27:25*	Gete Alemayehu ETH 31:12*
31 Dec	Bolzano 10.05/5.05 k	Tamirat Tola ETH 28:12	Netsanet Gudeta ETH 15:46
31 Dec	Madrid 10k (dh 55m)	Jacob Kiplimo UGA 26:38*	Brigid Kosgei KEN 29:54*
31 Dec	Peuerbach 6.8/5.1 k	Davis Kiplangat KEN 18:46	Eva Cherono KEN 15:43
31 Dec	São Paulo 15k	Belay Tilahun ETH 45:03	Sandrafelis Tuei KEN 50:02\

See also World Half Marathon Chamionships
* = course record; dh = downhill course; A = altitude over 1000m

MARATHON REVIEW 2018
By Marty Post

ELIUD KIPCHOGE HAS been the headline marathoner leading off this section since 2015 and his streak continued as in 2018 he ran both the fastest time in history and won the race with the most competitive field. At the Berlin Marathon on September 16, the 33-year-old Kenyan broke the finish line tape in a world record 2 hours 1 minute and 39 seconds producing a cornucopia of statistical superlatives. His average pace was 4:38.6 per mile/2:53 per km (or 14:25 per each 5km segment). After opening with a 1:01:06 first half he accelerated to 1:00:33, the fastest second half ever. The 78 seconds reduction from the previous WR was the biggest since December 1967 while finishing 4 minutes 46 seconds ahead of the runner-up was the greatest margin in a world record race since August 1958.

Five months earlier Kipchoge won the Virgin Money London Marathon for the third time. He sped through the first half in 1:01:00 – the fastest such split in history – en route to a 2:04:17 finish. Combined with his Berlin time his one year total of 4:05:56 was another marathon best.

The long-standing British record (2:07:13, Steve Jones 1985) fell to Mo Farah in London where he finished third in 2:06:11 and then later at Chicago where he won in 2:05:11, also slicing 37 seconds off the European record. Three men lowered the Asian record: Yuta Shitara 2:06:11 and Suguru Osako 2:05:50 of Japan and ultimately El Hassan El Abbassi 2:04:43 of Bahrain.

Additional national records were set for Burundi (2:11:19, Abraham Niyonkuru and 2:09:48, Olivier Irabaruta), Canada (2:09:05, Cam Levins, bettering the former NR from December 1975), Guineau (2:16:48, Alhassane Bangoura), Israel (2:13:00, Maru Teferi and 2:12:37, Girmaw Amare), Lesotho (2:10:32, Motlokoa Nkhabutlane), Morocco (2:05:26, El Mahjoub Dazza), New Zealand (2:08:26, Jake Robertson), Paraguay (2:13:41, Derlis Ayala) Tanzania (2:07:46, Augustino Sulle) and Thailand (2:16:56, Tony Ah Thit Payne).

At the always fast Dubai Marathon the final stretch turned into an Ethiopian charge of the fleet brigade won by Mosinet Geremew 2:04:00 followed by Leul Gebrselassie 2:04:02, Tamirat Tola 2:04:06, Asefa Mengistu 2:04:06, Sisay Lemma 2:04:08 and Birhanu Legese 2:04:15 with Seifu Tura 2:04:44 a few strides behind. These were the fastest times in history for third through seventh places.

To bolster the case that 2018 was marathoning's best year ever look no further than the number of performances under almost every significant time barrier. While there was but one sub-124 minute run there were a record 16 that began with 2:04 (which would have been 18 if not for an unfortunate misdirection at Abu Dhabi). Further one-year records were set for these cutoffs: 2:06 (31), 2:07 (61), 2:08 (95), 2:09 (151) and 2:10 (223).

The year would not be complete without a tally of Yuki Kawauchi's total of barrier breaking marathon times. At year's end he held records for sub-2:12s (27), sub 2-13s (42), sub-2:14s (51), sub-2:15s (58), sub-2:16s (68), sub-2:17s (74), sub-2:18 (78), sub-2:19s (83) and sub-2:20s (84). Yet one of his slower performances was his career landmark surprise Boston Marathon victory in 2:15:58, held in arguably the most atrocious windy and heavy rain in race history, producing the slowest winning time since 1976. Mark Kiptoo, already the oldest man to break

2:07 (2:06:00 at age 39) became the oldest to break 2:08 with a world veterans record 2:07:50 at Frankfurt at the age of 42. American Gene Dykes set a 70+ age group world record of 2:54:23 at Jacksonville on December 15.

Mary Keitany, like her countryman Eliud Kipchoge, achieved the split double record with the fastest time for both the first and second half of a marathon. Already owning the opening 21.1k best of 1:06:36 from her women's only world record at London in 2017, she strolled through the first half of the New York City marathon before accelerating to a 1:06:58 and her fourth victory there. Desiree Linden was the first American winner at Boston since 1985.

The women's race at Dubai was the first in history with four sub-2:20s and Berlin was the first with three sub-2:19s For the year there were an unprecedented number of women running faster than 2:20 (11), 2:21 (17), 2:22 (29), 2:23 (46), 2:24 (64) and 2:25 (84).

There were national records set for Azerbaijan (2:42:24, Hadiyes Benafeta), the Czech Republic (2:26:31, Eva Vrabcová-Nyvltová), Eritrea (2:29:48, Nazret Weldu Gebrehiwet), Israel (2:24:17, Lonah Chemtai Salpeter), Lesotho (2:33:41, Neheng Katala), Moldova (2:28:26, Lilia Fiskovici), Morocco (2:25:35, Boulaid Kaoutar), Rwanda (2:28:02, Salomé Nyirarukundo), South Korea (2:25:41, Kim Do-yeon) and Sri Lanka (2:36:35, Hiruni Wijayaratne).

Lydia Cheromei of Kenya lowered the 40 plus world best to 2:22:11 at Valencia, demonstrating unparalled longevity for a world-class athlete; she won the IAAF World Cross County junior title in 1991 at the age of 13. Jeanne Rice (USA) set a women's 70+ age group record of 3:27:50 at Chicago.

Once again indoor world records were set at the Armory Track and Field Center in New York City. On March 25, Malcom Richards became the first sub-2:20 runner at 2:19:02 chopping 2:46 off the old standard while Lindsay Scherf shaved 1:34 from the previous women's best stopping the clock at 2:40:56. Finally Paul Zwama of the Netherlands set a new world standard for time covered to run a marathon on a treadmill. At Utrecht on August 16 the 2:18:19 marathoner (Berlin 2017) rolled to a time of 2:20:45 (55 seconds better than previous best by Eric Blake in 2006) giving new meaning to the expression "going nowhere fast."

Winners of 2018 International Marathons

Date	City				
7 Jan	Xiamen	Dejene Debela ETH	2:11:22	Fatuma Sado ETH	2:26:41
7 Jan	Tiberias	Girmaw Amare ETH	2:15:31	Ayantu Abera ETH	2:40:37
14 Jan	Houston	Bazu Worku ETH	2:08:30	Biruktayit Degefa ETH	2:24:51
21 Jan	Hong Kong	Kenneth Mungara KEN	2:13:39	Gulume Tollessa ETH	2:29:37*
21 Jan	Las Palmas	Moses Mbugua KEN	2:13:26	Betty Chepleting KEN	2:36:52
21 Jan	Mumbai	Solomon Deksisa ETH	2:09:34	Amane Gobena ETH	2:25:49
26 Jan	Dubai	Mosinet Geremew ETH	2:04:00*	Roza Dereje ETH	2:19:17*
28 Jan	Marrakech	Wycliffe Biwott KEN	2:11:04	Tinbit Gidey ETH	2:26:48*
28 Jan	Osaka	women only		Mizuki Matsuda JPN	2:22:44
4 Feb	Oita	Desmond Mokgobu RSA	2:09:31	Hiroko Yoshitomi JPN	2:33:00*
10 Feb	Lagos	Abraham Kiprotich FRA	2:15:04	Almenesh Guta ETH	2:38:25
18 Feb	Castellón	Stephen Kiplimo KEN	2:11:28	Tigist Teshome ETH	2:29:57
25 Feb	Sevilla	Dickson Tuwei KEN	2:08:22	Kaoutar Boulaïd MAR	2:25:35*
25 Feb	Tokyo	Dickson Chumba KEN	2:05:30	Birhane Dibaba ETH	2:19:51
4 Mar	Otsu	Macharia Ndirangu KEN	2:07:53	men only	
4 Mar	Rabat	Bentayehu Assefa ETH	2:11:23	Lydia Cheromei KEN	2:28:48
11 Mar	Barcelona	Anthony Maritim KEN	2:08:08	Ruth Chebitok KEN	2:25:49
11 Mar	Nagoya	women only	2:21:45	Meskerem Assefa ETH	2:21:45
18 Mar	Santa Monica (dh)	Weldon Kirui KEN	2:11:47	Sule Utura ETH	2:33:50
18 Mar	Seoul	Wilson Loyanae KEN	2:06:57	Damte Hirut ETH	2:24:08
18 Mar	Taipei City	Yuki Kawauchi JPN	2:14:12	Real Kguriatukei KEN	2:35:57
25 Mar	Chongqing	Kennedy Cheboror KEN	2:13:43	Meseret Legesse ETH	2:28:56
25 Mar	Treviso	Gilbert Chumba KEN	2:12:19	Medina Deme ETH	2:33:17
25 Mar	Wuxi	Birhanu Bekele ETH	2:12:47	Priscilla Kipruto KEN	2:33:34
25 Mar	Zhengzhou	Elias Chelimo KEN	2:13:53	Ednah Mukhwana KEN	2:30:24
1 Apr	Daegu	Abraham Kiptum KEN	2:06:29*	Janet Rono KEN	2:28:01
8 Apr	Gunsan	Robert Kwambai KEN	2:10:04	Mirriam Wangari KEN	2:34:43
8 Apr	Hannover	Seboka Nigussa ETH	2:09:44	Agnes Kiprop KEN	2:32:35
8 Apr	Milano	Abdiwak Tura ETH	2:09:04	Vivian Kiplagat KEN	2:27:08
8 Apr	Paris	Paul Lonyangata KEN	2:06:25	Betsy Saina KEN	2:22:56
8 Apr	Pyongyang	Ri Kang-bom PRK	2:12:53	Kim Hye-gyong PRK	2:27:31

8 Apr	Roma	Cosmas Kipchoge KEN	2:08:03	Rahma Tusa ETH	2:23:46
8 Apr	Rotterdam	Kenneth Kipkemoi KEN	2:05:44	Visiline Jepkesho KEN	2:23:47
8 Apr	Santiago de Chile	Kipkemei Mutai KEN	2:13:40	Aynalem Teferit ETH	2:30:29
15 Apr	Linz	Robert Kipkemboi KEN	2:10:23	Ednah Jepkosgei KEN	2:31:11
15 Apr	Nagano	Abdela Godana ETH	2:13:54	Asami Furuse JPN	2:34:09
15 Apr	Wuhan	Zakaria Boudad MAR	2:15:29	Meskerem Abera ETH	2:28:35
16 Apr	Boston (dh)	Yuki Kawauchi JPN	2:15:58	Desiree Linden USA	2:39:54
22 Apr	Eldoret (um)	Elkana Yego KEN	2:12:44	Sharon Cherop KEN	2:29:57
22 Apr	Kraków	Birhanu Bekele ETH	2:11:34	Lilia Fiscovichi MDA	2:31:27
22 Apr	London	Eliud Kipchoge KEN	2:04:17	Vivian Cheruiyot KEN	2:18:31
22 Apr	Madrid	Eliud Barngetuny KEN	2:10:15	Valentine Kipketer KEN	2:30:40
22 Apr	Padua	Mogos Shumway ERI	2:12:23	Waganesh Mekasha ETH	2:29:18*
22 Apr	Wien	Salah Bounasser MAR	2:09:29	Nancy Kiprop KEN	2:24:18
22 Apr	Warsawa	Ezekiel Omullo KEN	2:11:17	Anastasiya Ivanova BLR	2:28:03
22 Apr	Zürich	Charles Munyeki KEN	2:14:08	Maude Mathys SUI	2:31:17
29 Apr	Düsseldorf	Gilbert Yegon KEN	2:13:55	Olga Mazuronak BLR	2:25:25*
29 Apr	Hamburg	Solomon Deksisa ETH	2:06:34	Shitaye Eshete BRN	2:24:51
5 May	Dongying	Joel Kimurer KEN	2:13:28	Letebrhan Gebreslasea ETH	2:24:27*
6 May	Genève (dh)	William Yegon KEN	2:12:10	Amelework Bisho ETH	2:38:05
6 May	Pittsburgh	Fikadu Girma ETH	2:13:47	Sydney Devore USA	2:32:39
6 May	Praha	Galen Rupp USA	2:06:07	Bornes Kitur KEN	2:24:19
13 May	Købnhavn	William Morwabe KEN	2:11:15*	Shasho Insermu ETH	2:32:17
13 May	Dalian	Edwin Koech KEN	2:09:44	Mulu Seboka ETH	2:28:59
13 May	Lens	Kiprugut Letting KEN	2:11:35	Viola Chepchirchir KEN	2:48:09
20 May	Riga	Tsedat Abeje ETH	2:11:00*	Georgina Rono KEN	2:28:22*
27 May	Ottawa	Yemane Adhane ETH	2:08:52	Gelete Burka ETH	2:22:17*
4 Jun	Stockholm	Lawi Kiptanui KEN	2:13:30	Mikaela Larsson SWE	2:40:28
10 Jun	Lanzhou	Kelkile Gezahegn ETH	2:11:00	Merima Mohamed BRN	2:32:22
17 Jun	Duluth	Elisha Barno KEN	2:10:06	Kellyn Taylor USA	2:24:29*
1 Jul	Gold Coast	Kenneth Mungara KEN	2:09:49	Ruth Chebitok KEN	2:24:49*
26 Aug	Ciudas México (A)	Titus Ekiru ETH	2:10:38	Etaferahu Wodaj ETH	2:40:10
26 Aug	Sapporo	Naoki Okamoto JPN	2:11:29	Ayuko Suzuki JPN	2:28:32
8 Sep	Taiyuan	Ezekiel Omnullo KEN	2:15:36	Alice Kimutai KEN	2:31:56
9 Sep	Münster	Justus Kiprotich KEN	2:09:28	Sheila Rono KEN	2:45:46
16 Sep	Beijing	Dejene Debele ETH	2:12:08	Valary Aiyabei KEN	2:21:38
16 Sep	Berlin	Eliud Kipchoge KEN	2:01:39*	Gladys Cherono KEN	2:18:11*
16 Sep	Kassel	Edwin Yator KEN	2:12:52	Brendah Kebeya KEN	2:36:44
16 Sep	Sydney	Elijah Kemboi KEN	2:13:37	Mercy Kibarus KEN	2:31:24
23 Sep	Buenos Aires	Emmanuel Saina KEN	2:05:21*	Vivian Kiplagat KEN	2:29:03*
23 Sep	Cape Town	Stephen Mokoka RSA	2:08:31*	Helalia Johannes NAM	2:29:28*
23 Sep	Montreal	Ezekiel Mutai KEN	2:11:05	Salomé Nyirarukundo RWA	2:28:02*
29 Sep	Hengshui	Lemi Berhanu ETH	2:08:51	Waganesh Mekasha ETH	2:25:57
30 Sep	Warsawa	David Metto KEN	2:12:44	Beatrice Cherop KEN	2:35:22
7 Oct	Chicago	Mo Farah GBR	2:05:11	Brigid Kosgei KEN	2:18:35
7 Oct	Kosice	Raymond Choge KEN	2:08:11	Milliam Ebongon KEN	2:27:16*
7 Oct	St. Paul	Elisha Barno KEN	2:11:58	Sinke Biyadgilgn ETH	2:33:04
14 Oct	Bucharest	Hosea Kipkemboi KEN	2:11:31*	Almaz Gelana ETH	2:41:29
14 Oct	Eindhoven	Elisha Kipchirchir Rotich KEN	2:07:32	Nina Lauwaert BEL	2:30:24
14 Oct	Lisboa (sc)	Limenih Getachew ETH	2:07:34	Kuftu Dadiso ETH	2:24:56
14 Oct	Melbourne	Liam Adams AUS	2:15:13	Sinead Diver AUS	2:25:19*
14 Oct	Poznan	Cosmas Kyeva KEN	2:11:45*	Tesfanesh Merga ETH	2:32:31
21 Oct	Amsterdam	Lawrence Cherono KEN	2:04:06*	Tadalech Bekele ETH	2:23:14
21 Oct	Changsha	Fikadu Girma ETH	2:11:13	Bekele Beji ETH	2:32:56
21 Oct	Gyeongju	Kennedy Cheboror KEN	2:08:26	Lee Suk-jung KOR	2:36:44
21 Oct	Toronto	Benson Kipruto KEN	2:07:24	Mimi Belete BRN	2:22:29*
28 Oct	Casablanca	Erick Ndiema KEN	2:12:55	Naomi Maiyo KEN	2:35:02
28 Oct	Chunchon	Shifera Tamru ETH	2:08:50	Kim Su-na KOR	2:40:23
28 Oct	Dublin	Asefa Bekele ETH	2:13:24	Mesera Dubiso ETH	2:33:49
28 Oct	Frankfurt	Kelkile Gezahegn ETH	2:06:37	Meskerem Assefa ETH	2:20:36

Date	City	Men	Time	Women	Time
28 Oct	Ljubljana	Sisay Lemma ETH	2:04:58*	Visiline Jepkesho KEN	2:22:58*
28 Oct	Nairobi (A)	Elisha Kiprop KEN	2:14:19	Josephine Chepkoech KEN	2:33:11
28 Oct	Rennes (dh)	Lawi Kiptui KEN	2:08:30	Almaz Negede ETH	2:29:40
28 Oct	Venezia	Mekuant Ayenew ETH	2:13:23	Angela Tanui KEN	2:31:30
4 Nov	Nice to Cannes	Abrha Milaw ETH	2:07:26*	Nurit Shimels ETH	2:31:54
4 Nov	Hangzhou	Michael Kunyuga KEN	2:10:37	Hirut Tibebu ETH	2:25:10*
4 Nov	Nanjing	Felix Korir KEN	2:14;16	Kebene Chala ETH	2:30:49
4 Nov	New York City	Lelisa Desisa ETH	2:05:59	Mary Keitany KEN	2:22:48
4 Nov	Porto	Robert Chemonges UGA	2:09:05*	Abeba Tekulu ETH	2:30:13
4 Nov	Seoul	Asefa Mengistu ETH	2:08:11	Kim Seung-eun KOR	2:38:52
11 Nov	Athína	Brimin Misoi KEN	2:10:56	Shelmith Muriuki KEN	2:36:46
11 Nov	Beirut	Mohamed El Aaraby MAR	2:10:41*	Medina Deme Armino ETH	2:29:31
11 Nov	Hefei	Leonard Langat KEN	2:10:49	Magdalene Masai KEN	2:28:22*
11 Nov	Istanbul	Felix Kimutai KEN	2:09:57*	Ruth Chepngetich KEN	2:18:35*
18 Nov	Kobo	Khalil Lemoiyoh MAR	2:13:54	Susan Jerotich KEN	2:31:30*
18 Nov	Shanghai	Abdiwak Tura ETH	2:09:18	Yebrgual Melese ETH	2:20:36*
18 Nov	Suzhou	Daniel Kiptoo KEN	2:13:04	Ayantu Abera ETH	2:30:25
25 Nov	Firenze	Abdi Ali Gelechu BRN	2:11:32	Lonah Chemtai Salpeter ISR	2:24:17*
25 Nov	Osaka	Charles Munyeki KEN	2:14:11	Soud Kanbouchia MAR	2:31:19*
25 Nov	San Sebastián	David Metto KEN	2:11:10	Chaltu Negesse ETH	2:35:23
2 Dec	Fukuoka	Yuma Hattori JPN	2:07:27	*men only*	
2 Dec	Macau	Elijah Kemboi KEN	2:15:18	Mercy Kibarus KEN	2:35:16
2 Dec	Sacramento (dh)	Brogan Austin USA	2:12:39	Emma Bates USA	2:28:19
2 Dec	Valencia	Leul Gebrselassie ETH	2:04:31*	Ashete Bekele ETH	2:21:14*
7 Dec	Abu Dhabi (sc)	Marius Kipserem KEN	2:04:04	Yeshaneh Ababel ETH	2:20:16
9 Dec	Guangzhou	Mohamed Ziani MAR	2:10:44	Tigist Girma ETH	2:26:44
9 Dec	Honolulu	Titus Ekiru KEN	2:09:01	Vivian Kiplagat KEN	2:36:22
9 Dec	Málaga	Lemi Dumecha ETH	2:11:07*	Meseret Abebayehu ETH	2:32:20
9 Dec	Saitama	*women only*		Dalila Gosa BRN	2:25:35
9 Dec	Singapore	Joshua Kipkorir KEN	2:12:20	Priscah Cherono KEN	2:32:12
9 Dec	Taipei	Aredom Tiumay Degefa ETH	2:16:59	Jo Un-ok PRK	2:29:48
16 Dec	Hofu	Yuki Kawauchi JPN	2:11:29	Hisae Yoshimatsu JPN	2:38:58
16 Dec	Mersin	Kenneth Limo KEN	2:10:12*	Konjit Tilahun ETH	2:33:18
16 Dec	Shenzhen	Edwin Koech KEN	2:09:44*	Mulu Seboka ETH	2:17:12*

* course record; sc = short course; um = uncertain measurement; A = altitude over 1000m; dh = downhill course (Santa Monica 122.2m, Boston 138.3m, Geneva 46.4m, Rennes 65m, Sacramento 105m).
See also Commonwealth Games and European Championship
Original winner at Milano 8 Apr - Lucy Wangui Kabuu KEN 2:27:02 drugs dq.

World Marathon Majors

Series XI of the Abbott World Marathon Majors concluded at the April 18 London Marathon. Eliud Kipchoge (who won that race) became the first man to win the overall series a third time. Kipchoge would add another win at the first race in series XII, the Berlin Marathon in September, bringing his record total of AWMM victories to eight. Geoffrey Kirui was second and Yuki Kawauchi was third for Series XI. Mo Farah (Chicago) and Lelisa Desisa (New York City) were also winners of autumn series XII events.

Mary Keitany joined Edna Kiplagat as three-time AWMM champions. Keitany and Tirunesh Dibaba scored the same number of Series XI points, but Keitany had a better head-to-head record. Tirunesh wound up second in the standings with Brigid Kosgei third. Keitany would win New York City, her seventh career AWMM victory, with Gladys Cherono at Berlin and Kosgei at Chicago early Series XII race champions.

Edna Kiplagat finished fifth at Berlin in 2018 making her the first athlete to score at least one point in each of the six City races (Tokyo, Boston, London, Berlin, Chicago and New York City).

Prize money: 1st $250,000; 2nd $50,000; 3rd $25,000. Abbott will continue as WMM series sponsor for another four year.

REVIEW OF ULTRARUNNING 2018
by Andy Milroy

THERE WERE TWO very notable performances in 2018, one which was a major breakthrough for the sport, the other showed how the elements can have a major impact on ultra races. When the IAAF chose to amend the previously accepted standard of 30% between start and finish for record acceptable courses, this had implications for the Lake Saroma 100k course at Yubetsu in Japan. The course has a start-finish separation of greater than 30% – over 40k and it also runs parallel with the coast. It therefore can benefit from onshore winds in the morning.

The 2018 race had a tail wind for much of the race which equated to twice to three times that allowed in sprint races and, obviously over a much longer time. At one point the tail wind was 20 km per hour! A new world record of 6:09:14 was claimed and five Japanese men ran under 6:30. Five under 6:30 is unique; even in the highly competitive World Challenge events where the best 100k runners in the world are very motivated to produce their best, the most has been four and that was on the Saroma course! Elsewhere the greatest ever number is three.

Another major issue was the marked improvement by so many of that leading group. Runners are basically human machines. They run at a fixed pace for a specific distance, based on trial and error. Sudden breakthroughs, major improvements in times happen usually early in the career as runners quickly gain in experience. Nao Kazami, running 6:09:14, improved by over 24:38. Based on all the evidence – unique number of runners achieving sub 6:30, number of runners showing marked improvement, known start-finish separation, reported direction and strength of wind at the venue on the day–- the marks were wind aided. The elite women ran within the main body of male runners and therefore were shielded from the tail wind to some degree and there was not the same marked improvement so apparent among the leading men.

Elsewhere in the 100k, the event was dominated by the World Championship, held on a 5k lap at Grkavescak in Croatia and won by Hideaki Yamauchi JPN in 6:28:05. He was the existing champion, having won the race the last time it was held, in 2016, and was the only runner to break 6:30. Yamauchi had also run in the Yubetsu race and was one of the few not to set a personal best. Second was Takehiko Gyoba

JPN in 6:32:51 and third Bongmusa Mthembu RSA 6:33:47. On a flat 5k loop the other Japanese runners were not able to reproduce their times from Yubetsu. Kazami who ran 6:09:14 there, finished 5th in 6:42:30 at Grkavescak.

The women's race in Croatia was won by a runner on home soil, Nikolina Sustic in 7:20:34 from Nele Alder-Baerens GER 7:22:41 and Mei Fujisawa JPN, who had won at Yubetsu, a minute slower than in that race with 7:39:07.

Selecting the world No 1 is a little difficult with Kazami and Yamauchi each having a win over the other, but Yamauchi's win was in the greatest competition of the year. Sustic won the World title in the fastest time of the year, so was obviously women's world No 1.

The major breakthrough came in the 24 hours. Camille Herron, who has won the World 100k and has set a world road 100 miles record, aimed to break the world 24 hour track best. She improved on both the world track 100 miles (13:25) and 200k record (17:07:27). Her final distance covered in a day was 262.192k. (She was the first woman over 160 miles and 260k.) The top four female 24 hour marks of all-time have been set in the last two years and this was Heron's first 24 hour race. It will be interesting to see how the women's event develops in the next few years.

The major 24 hour competition was the European at Timisoara in Romania where the then holder of the best ever performance at 24 hours, Patrycia Bereznowska, won with 243.355k. Stine Rex DEN 241.921k, ahead of 100 miles., was second and another Pole, Malgorzata Pazda-Pozorska was third with 248.697k. Aleksandr Sorokin LTU once again tried to win the men's race with a blitz start as he had in 2016. He went through 100 miles in approximately 12:50:26 and 200k in 16:55:06, but once again he was overtaken in the closing stages by runners adopting a more prudent strategy. The eventual winner was Andrzej Radzikowski POL 265.419k with Stéphane Ruel FRA second 263.540k and Sorokin was third with 260.991k. Another advocate of the blitz start was Cavin Woodward. He too ended up being overtaken by more even paced runners until eventually his body learned to adjust. He ran a world 100k track record of 6:25:28 en route to a world record 100 miles of 11:38 in 1975. Perhaps one day Sorokin will blitz the start and just keep going!

Camille Herron's performance is substantially better than that of Bereznowska, so she is world No 1. That for men is less clear cut. Ivan Penalda López ESP ran 273.674k in a low key track race in Germany and Nobuyaki Takahashi JPN 268.783k in Tokyo on the road. Radzikowski ran 265.419k to win the European title. However López, running as an individual in the IAU Asian & Oceania 24 hour championships in Taipei, running 258.890k, beat Takahashi, so I would go with Penalda Lopez as world No 1.

Although Bereznowska had her 24 hour mark surpassed, she was to set new standards at 48 hours. Her 401.000k on the road in Athens was the absolute best mark of the year, with Sten Orsvärn SWE, the leading male runner recording 393.984k. The best 6 day mark was by the Swede Johnny Hallneby with 880.311k in Augusta in the USA with Australian Annabel Hepworth achieving 742.803k but for some such a race is perceived as a virtual sprint!

In New York on a relatively small road loop Kobi Oren ISR ran 13:15:28:24 for 1000 miles and Paula Mairer AUT ran the fastest female mark of 16:06:54:24. This was during the longest certified race in the world, the 3100 miles won by Nikolay Duzhiy RUS in 44 days 16:03:53. He went on to complete 5000k in 45 days 02:02:55.

The longest running ultra in the world, the 89k Comrades Marathon in South Africa from Pietermaritzburg to Durban was won by Bongmusz Mthembu with 5:26:34 from Joseph Mphuthi 5:35:09 and British runner Steve Way third in 5:35:37. The first woman was Ann Ashworth in 6:10:04 with Gerda Steyn second in 6:15:34 and Russian Aleksandra Morozova third 6:20:21.

The Spartathlon (Athens to Sparta), commemorating the feat of Pheidippides, was won by Yoshihiko Ishikawa JPN in 22:54:40, forty minutes ahead of Radek Brunner CZE 23:36:43 with João Pereira Oliveira POR third with 24:33:35. The leading women were more closely grouped with Zsuzsanna Maráz HUN winning in 27:04:28 from Katerina Kasparová CZE 27:46:27 and Teija Honkonen FIN 8:34:29.

The longest extended stage event was a 17-stage 1397k John of Groats-Lands End race from one end of the United Kingdom to the other. The winner was Jean-Louis Vidal FRA who had an elapsed time of 185 hours 4 minutes, from Chan Wai-Tik HKG 227 hours 24 minutes.

In such extended running events as ultramarathons weather is always likely to be a factor, sometimes it can be decisive. When a tail wind is often a reliable factor in a race, then if it is a standard event like a 100k it has global effects so that there is no longer a level playing field. The aided marks will be more than can be achieved in any other race. With onshore winds in Japan looking set to intensify in the future, this problem is not set to go away.

Olympic Legend Emil Voigt by Bob Phillips

THE IAAF IS to be commended for its enterprising choice of Emil Voigt as one the seven deceased Olympic champions honoured on 2 December as 'Heritage Legends'. Voigt was unquestionably one of the outstanding distance-runners of the early 1900s, even if it is Alfred Shrubb who is far better remembered from that era, but I wonder if the IAAF are also aware that Voigt, who led what he himself rightly described as a 'strenuous life', was an ardent anti-establishment campaigner? Before his athletics career was over in England in 1911 he had formed an 'Amateur Athletes' Union' in England in protest against officialdom, and in a letter to the widely-read *Athletic News* he lambasted the Amateur Athletic Association for continuing what

he called 'the game of spoil-sport' when its committee members unanimously rejected a petition signed by 2000 athletes.

The athletes' grievances mainly concerned the inept conduct of meetings but also focused on poor dressing-room facilities and faulty handicapping systems. Born in Manchester of German parents, Voigt was an engineer by profession and went off to Australia later in 1911, where he continued his athletics career briefly, winning the Victorian state one mile title in 1912.

He then made a highly successful career in radio broadcasting, returning to England in 1936 to work as a sports commentator for BBC Radio. He lived to the age of 90, dying in Auckland in 1973.

IAAF rule changes that have been introduced (and have been in the latest rule book in force from 1 November 2019):

1) Changeover zones in the 4x100m were 20m in length, preceded by a 10m acceleration zone. Now it is a single zone of 30m.

2) Horizontal jumpers don't need to wear bibs on their back (having been that way for HJ and PV for many years).

3) Incidental touches at the back of the circle in throws no longer result in no-throws (provided that the touch does not provide any form of leverage or propulsion).

An amendment was approved to Rule 170.10 (Substitutes for relay races) to allow for additional athletes to be used once a relay team has started the competition (applicable at all WAS events and Olympic Games).

EUROPEAN CHAMPIONSHIPS 2018

August 6-12, Berlin (GER)

IN THIS SUPER meeting with pretty much ideal conditions throughout there were championship records in eleven events. The most notable were surely in the men's pole vault when the record of 6.00 by Rodion Gataullin in 1994 was first equalled by Armand Duplantis and by Timur Morgunov and then increased to 6.05 by the amazing 18 year-old Duplantis. He set three successive world U20 records, clearing all by big margins. The even younger Jakob Ingebrigtsen emerged here as a major super-star. To win the 5000m just a day after the 1500m would be amazing for anyone, but to do so at the age of 17 as the youngest ever European male champion was simply staggering – and to see the ease with which he sped away from elder brother Henrik to the finish of the 5000m was awesome. Dina Asher-Smith tied the 2018 world lead for 100m with 10.85 and she completed a brilliant treble with a world leading time of 21.85 for 200m and a dazzling last leg for the British 4x100m team that ran 41.88. Also a world lead was Nafi Thiam's 6816 score in the heptathlon.

Sandra Perkovic won a unique fifth successive title in the discus, Anna Wlodarczyk and Mahiedine Mekhissi-Benabbad won fourth titles at hammer and steeplechase respectively, and Adam Kszczot completed three wins at 800m. There are, however, always shocks at championships, and the biggest here came from multi-event super-star Kevin Mayer, who having started with a pb in the 100m went out of the decathlon by having three narrow no-jumps in the long jump. In most events, even where the standard was below world-class standards, there was great competition but there were large margins of victory for Sifan Hassan in the women's 5000m and Christin Hussong in the women's javelin. Also Ramil Guliyev excelled to smash his Turkish record with 19.76 for 200m, winning by three metres, and later he produced a brilliant final leg in the 4x100m foa a silver medal.

Both Britain and Poland took seven gold medals and Germany six, with Germany on 19, Britain 18 and Poland 14 in total medals with Britain ahead of Germany on the points table. Excellent crowds built during the week, so that there was near capacity for the final days in this magnificent stadium.

*Dates given in brackets after the heading for each event are those of the final. * Championships record.*

100 Metres (7th) (0.0)

1. Zharnel Hughes GBR	9.95*
2. Reece Prescod GBR	9.96
3. Jak Ali Harvey TUR	10.01
4. Chijindu Ujah GBR	10.06
5. Filippo Tortu ITA	10.08
6. Churandy Martina NED	10.16
7. Emre Zafer Barnes TUR	10.29
dns. Jimmy Vicaut FRA	–

Vicaut ran a championship record 9.97 in his semi-final but withdrew from the final with pain in his right thigh. Hughes, who won his semi in 10.01, ran a controlled, relaxed race to win the final, but Prescod almost caught him with his fast finish.

200 Metres (9th) (0.7)

1. Ramil Guliyev TUR	19.76*
2. Nethaneel Mitchell-Blake GBR	20.04

Medals and Points Table

Points: 8 for 1st to 1 for 8th.

Nation	G	S	B	Total	Pts	2016
GBR	7	5	6	18	207	169.5
GER	6	7	6	19	194.5	161.2
POL	7	4	1	12	168	147.2
FRA	3	4	3	10	116	105
ESP	2	2	4	8	97	75
NED	1	3	4	8	77.5	98
UKR	2	3	2	7	76.5	52
ITA	-	-	4	4	72	67
BLR	2	1	3	6	71	45
NOR	3	1	1		58.5	39
BEL	3	2	1	6	58	44.5
SUI	1	2	1	4	50	49.5
SWE	1	2	1	4	49	40
GRE	3	2	1	6	46.5	34.7
TUR	1	2	2	5	46.5	93
CZE	-	2	1	3	42	48.5
LTU	1	-	1	2	34	11.5
POR	2	-	-	2	27	43
ISR	1	-	-	1	18	7
BUL	-	1	-	1	17	35.5
AZE	-	1	-	1	16	9
EST	-	-	1	1	16	20
AUT	-	-	1	1	13	8
IRL	-	-	1	1	13	17
SVK	-	1	-	1	12	8
ROU	-	-	-	-	11	6
CRO	1	-	-	1	10	14.7
HUN	-	-	1	1	9	26
SLO	-	-	-	-	9	13

FIN & MDA 7, ALB & DEN 5, LUX & SRB 3, CYP 1

The above counts do not include the European Marathon Cup (included in the EA table) and the EA did not want to include ANA/RUS in the table – their tally: 1G-3S-2B-62 points. Note there were no walks in 2016.

3. Alex Wilson SUI	20.04
4. Bruno Hortelano ESP	20.05
5. Adam Gemili GBR	20.10
6. Eseosa Desalu ITA	20.13
7. Leon Reid IRL	20.37
8. Solomon Bockarie NED	20.39

Hortelano and Guliyev, 1st and 2nd in 2016, met with mixed fortunes this time as the Spaniard missed a medal by 0.01 despite running 20.05 (0.01 outside his national record) while the Turk – originally from Azerbaijan – ran out the winner by a 3m margin in a brilliant national record of 19.76, 0.09 inside the 2002 championship record. Mitchell-Blake finishing strongly to take silver in his equal second fastest mark of 20.04, the same time run by former Jamaican Alex Wilson who followed up his 20.16 semifinal by breaking his own national record of 20.14.

400 Metres (10th)

1. Matthew Hudson-Smith GBR	44.78
2. Kevin Borlée BEL	45.13
3. Jonathan Borlée BEL	45.19
4. Karol Zalewski POL	45.34
5. Luka Janezic SLO	45.43
6. Óscar Husillos ESP	45.61
7. Ricardo dos Santos POR	45.78
8. Karsten Warholm NOR	46.68

Hudson-Smith looked awesome in his semi as, after building up a huge lead over Jonathan Borlée (44.87), he practically jogged over the line in 44.76 – suggesting that had he not eased off so much he could have broken Thomas Schönlebe's 1987 European record of 44.33. All the finalists ran faster in the semis than in the final, run in much cooler conditions. 12 men beat 46 secs in the qualifiying races; then, with the seeded runners added, 45.17 by Mateo Galvan in the semis was not fast enough to make the final.

800 Metres (11th)

1. Adam Kszczot POL	1:44.59
2. Andreas Kramer SWE	1:45.03
3. Pierre-Ambroise Bosse FRA	1:45.30
4. Michal Rozmys POL	1:45.32
5. Mateusz Borkowski POL	1:45.42
6. Andreas Bube DEN	1:45.92
7. Álvaro de Arriba ESP	1:46.41
8. Lukás Hodbod CZE	1:46.60

Kszczot ran the fastest times in the heats (1:46.31) and semis (1:46.11) and ran 25.53 for the last 200m to 1:44.59 in the final to take his third title. Kramer led at 200m in 25.04 before the pace slowed to 53.14 for Bosse who surged to 600m in 1:18.81.

1500 Metres (10th)

1. Jakob Ingebrigtsen NOR-J	3:38.10
2. Marcin Lewandowski POL	3:38.14
3. Jake Wightman GBR	3:38.25
4. Henrik Ingebrigtsen NOR	3:38.50
5. Charlie Da'Vall Grice GBR	3:38.65
6. Simas Bertasius LTU	3:39.04
7. Timo Benitz GER	3:39.28
8. Ismael Debjani BEL	3:39.48

Jakob Ingebrigtsen was last at 400m, but moved into the lead by 800m (2:01.12). Grice led him by 0.04 at the bell (2:44.42) and at that point Lewandowski was 12th in 2:45.08. Jakob had taken over by 1200m (2:57.76) and held on to win with a last 400m of 53.64, while Lewandowski finished fastest with 53.06 and 26.05 final 200m to take the silver while Wightman (fastest in the heats with 3:40.73) moved through from 7th to 3rd over the last 200m, but Filip Ingebrigtsen, returning from injury, fell back from 3rd to finish 12th in 3:41.66.

5000 Metres (11th)

1. Jakob Ingebrigtsen NOR-J	13:17.06
2. Henrik Ingebrigtsen NOR	13:18.75
3. Morhad Amdouni FRA	13:19.14
4. Yemaneberhan Crippa ITA	13:19.85
5. Marc Scott GBR	13:23.14
6. Polat Kemboi Arikan TUR	13:23.42
7. Rinas Akhmadiyev RUS/ANA	13:24.43
8. Julien Wanders SUI	13:24.79

Just 23 hours after his 1500m triumph, Jakob Ingebrigtsen returned to complete a unique European double and be the youngest champion (previously at this event Ian Stewart at 20 in 1969). Antonio Abadía led the big field of 24 runners at 1000m in 2:42.56 with Jakob seventh in 2:44.05, dropping to ninth in 5:25.66 as Julien Wanders reached 2000m in 5:24.73. Wanders remained in the lead at 3000m in 8:04.91 as Jakob (12th in 8:07.30) and Henrik (13th in 8:07.52) hung back before the brothers made a move to the front approaching 3800m. At 4000m Jakob was ahead in 10:48.34 and there he remained as he ticked off steadily faster 200m segments of 32.68, 31.60, 30.35, 27.49 and 26.60 – a kilometre of 2:28.72 and the European U20 record of 13:17.06. Chris Thompson (37), 9th in 13:25.11, was a competitor in the European Junior Champs before Jakob was even born!

10,000 Metres (7th)

1. Morhad Amdouni FRA	28:11.22
2. Bashir Abdi BEL	28:11.76
3. Yemaneberhan Crippa ITA	28:12.15
4. Adel Mechaal ESP	28:13.78
5. Andy Vernon GBR	28:16.90
6. Soufiane Bouchikhi BEL	28:19.04
7. Julien Wanders SUI	28:22.02
8. Florian Carvalho FRA	28:29.78

Times were ordinary in hot conditions. Halfway was reached in 14:08.93 and the second half was only a few seconds quicker. Amdouni, third at the bell when Mechaal led, sped through the last lap in 55.81. 5 of the 32 starters failed to finish, including European Cup winner Richard Ringer. Crippa and Wanders made the top eight in both 5000m and 10,000m and Chris Thompson was 9th and 12th.

Marathon *(12th)*

1. Koen Naert BEL	2:09.51
2. Tadesse Abraham SUI	2:11:24
3. Yassine Rachik ITA	2:12:09
4. Javier Guerra ESP	2:12:22
5. Eyob Ghebrehiwet ITA	2:12:43
6. Jesús España ESP	2:12:58
7. Maru Teferi ISR	2:13:00
8. Lemawork Ketema AUT	2:13:22

European Marathon Cup: 1. ITA 6:40:48, 2. ESP 6:42:43, 3. AUT 6:49:29, 4. SUI 6:51:58, 5. POL 6:52:31, 6. IRL 6:53:55, 7. GER 6:54:50, 8. UKR 6:55:04, 9. LTU 6:57:29, 10. FRA 6:59:13, 11. TUR 7:06:07, 12. GRE 7:32:58.

Naert led at halfway in 65:54 and was clear after 5k splits of 14:47 and 14:51 between 30k and 40k. His highest placing in six previous marathons was 8th and he reduced his pb by 40 secs. Abraham was second on his 36th birthday and bronze medallist Rachik led the Italian team to European Cup victory. European record holder Sondre Nordstad Moen was one of 14 non-finishers from the 72 starters.

3000 Metres Steeplechase (9th)

1. Mahiedine Mekhissi-Benabbad FRA	8:31.66
2. Fernando Carro ESP	8:34.16
3. Yohanes Chiappinelli ITA	8:35.81
4. Yoann Kowal FRA	8:36.77
5. Zak Seddon GBR	8:37.28
6. Daniel Arce ESP	8:38.12
7. Krystian Zalewski POL	8:38.59
8. Topi Raitanen FIN	8:40.11

Mekhissi-Benabbad continued his dominance of European steeplechasing as this was his fourth title, or fifth if one ignores his disqualification for removing his vest when prematurely celebrating in 2014. His finish was too good for the rest with kilometres run in 3:02.31, 2:49.32 and 2:40.03. There were 15 finalists who had run between 8:28.48 and 8:30.44 in the heats.

110 Metres Hurdles (10th) (0.0)

1. Pascal Martinot-Lagarde FRA	13.17
2. Sergey Shubenkov RUS/ANA	13.17
3. Orlando Ortega ESP	13.34
4. Damian Czykier POL	13.38
5. Gregor Traber GER	13.46
6. Andrew Pozzi GBR	13.48
7. Aurel Manga FRA	13.51
8. Balázs Baji HUN	13.55

Bidding for a third European title, Shubenkov was pipped in the closest ever finish to this event, losing to Martinot-Lagarde by just 0.002 (13.163 to 13.165). Ortega had won the fastest semi in 13.21 from Pozzi (who hit all the hurdles from number five in the final) 13.28, with the others winners being Shuben-

kov 13.24 (from Traber 13.26) and Martinot-Lagarde 13.32.

400 Metres Hurdles (9th)

1. Karsten Warholm NOR	47.64
2. Yasmani Copello TUR	47.81
3. Thomas Barr IRL	48.31
4. Ludvy Vaillant FRA	48.42
5. Patryk Dobek POL	48.59
6. Rasmus Mägi EST	48.75
7. Sergio Fernández ESP	48.98
8. Timofey Chalyy RUS/ANA	49.41

Warholm's fourth national record of the year was also a European U23 best and fourth on the European all-time list. He was given a tough race by Copello, who improved his Turkish record from 47.92 to 47.81 and Barr excelled to improve his season's best from 48.99 to 48.31. The semis were won by Warholm 48.67 and Mägi 48.80.

High Jump (11th)

1. Mateusz Przybylko GER	2.35
2. Maksim Nedosekov BLR	2.33
3. Ilya Ivanyuk RUS/ANA	2.31
4. Gianmarco Tamberi ITA	2.28
5= Alperen Acet TUR	2.24
5= Andriy Protsenko UKR	2.24
7. Sylwester Bednarek POL	2.24
8= Douwe Amels NED	2.19
8= Eike Onnen GER	2.19

The three medallists all cleared 2.31 on their first attempts, before Przybylko and Nedosekov also did so at 2.33, but the latter had two earlier failures. Przybylko settled the issue and thrilled the capacity crowd by making 2.35 first time. Nedosekov had two failures at 2.35 and one at 2.37 and Przybyklo one at 2.38. Nine of the finalists had qualified by clearing 2.25 with the other three jumping 2.21.

Pole Vault (12th)

1. Armand Duplantis SWE-J	6.05*
2. Timur Morgunov RUS/ANA	6.00
3. Renaud Lavillenie FRA	5.95
4. Piotr Lisek POL	5.90
5. Pawel Wojciechowski POL	5.80
6= Konstadínos Filippídis GRE	5.75
6= Sondre Guttormsen NOR-J	5.75
8. Axel Chappelle FRA	5.65

This was one of greatest ever pole vault competitions. Five athletes were left in at 5.95. In the lead was Duplantis, over first time for yet another world junior record and with just one earlier failure. Also clear first time was Lavillenie but with two earlier misses. Morgunov had one failure but was third as he had a clean sheet up to and including 5.90, while Lisek also had one failure at 5.95 but was fourth, also with 5.90 but with a prior failure at 5.85. Wojciechowski went out, and Lisek departed at 6.00, while Lavillenie after one miss decided to save his two remaining attempts for the next height after Duplantis and Morgunov cleared at the first attempt to equal Rodion Gataullin's 1994 championship record, becoming the 23rd and 24th men to clear 6m. Both Lavillenie and Morgunov found 6.05 beyond them ... but, incredibly, Duplantis made it first time! Only Sergey Bubka has ever gone higher outdoors. Duplantis was too tired to continue but what an exhibition he had given, and the 2nd and 3rd marks tied the best evers for these places (fifth time at 6.00 for 2nd, third time for 5.95 for 3rd).

Long Jump (8th)

1. Mitiliadís Tentóglou GRE	8.25/-0.3	
2. Fabian Heinle GER	8.13/-0.2	
3. Serhiy Nykyforov UKR	8.13/0.1	
4. Tobias Nilsson Montler SWE	8.10/0.1	
5. Tomasz Jaszczuk POL	8.08/0.2	
6. Dan Bramble GBR	7.90/0.1	
7. Michel Tornéus SWE	7.86/0.2	
8. Guillaume Victorin FRA	7.84/0.3	

Tentóglou led the qualifiers with 8.15 and won with a fifth round 8.25 in the final, although only fifth at 8.00 at that point. Heinle jumped 8.13 twice to take the silver. Overall the standard was moderate and 7.71 sufficed to make the final.

Triple Jump (12th)

1. Nelson Évora POR	17.10/-0.1	
2. Alexis Copello AZE	16.93/0.1	
3. Dimitrios Tsiámis GRE	16.78/-0.1	
4. Nazim Babayev AZE	16.76/-0.1	
5. Pablo Torrijos ESP	16.74/-0.5	
6. Nathan Douglas GBR	16.71/0.0	
7. Jean-Marc Pontvianne FRA	16.61/0.3	
8. Tomás Veszelka SVK	16.48/0.4	

The standard was very poor. The winning distance of 17.10 by Évora, ten years after his Olympic victory, was the shortest for 40 years and a mere 16.41 got through to the final, although that proved beyond two previous winners in Fabrizio Donato (20th 16.15) and Max Hess (15th 16.32) Only three men. led by Copello 16.82, made the automatic qualifying standard of 16.75.

Shot (7th)

1. Michal Haratyk POL	21.72
2. Konrad Bukowiecki POL	21.66
3. David Storl GER	21.41
4. Tomás Stanek CZE	21.16
5. Aleksandr Lesnoy RUS/ANA	21.04
6. Bob Bertemes LUX	21.00
7. Snipe Zunic CRO	20.73
8. Maksim Afonin RUS/ANA	20.68

There were men over 20m, led by Storl 20.63, in the qualifying round held on the first day of the Championships at Breitscheidplatz in central Berlin. In the final Storl led with his opening 21.41 from Haratyk 20.94, but gold and silver then went to second round throws of 21.72 from Haratyk (who also had throws of 21.50 and 21.66) and 21.66 from Bukowiecki. In sixth place Bertemes improved his Luxembourg record from 20.66 to 21.00.

Discus (8th)

1. Andrius Gudzius LTU	68.46
2. Daniel Ståhl SWE	68.23
3. Lukas Weisshaidinger AUT	65.14
4. Simon Pettersson SWE	64.55
5. Gerd Kanter EST	64.34
6. Robert Harting GER	64.33
7. Alin Firfirica ROU	63.73
8. Apostolos Parellis CYP	63.62

Five men, led by Ståhl 67.07, made the automatic qualifying standard of 64m, with 62.19 completing the twelve as Olympic champion Christoph Harting and defending European champion Piotr Malachowski failed to register a valid throw. Gudzius opened with 65.75 but with his second throw Ståhl had a throw measured at 68.02... only it was belatedly ruled a foot foul. Gudzius strengthened his lead with a third round 67.19, Ståhl took the lead in round four with 66.23, as Gudzius improved to 67.86. With his final throw of 68.46 Gudzius took the title. Robert Harting came 6th in his final major championship competition, a place behind Kanter who was in his seventh European final.

Hammer (7th)

1. Wojciech Nowicki POL	80.12
2. Pawel Fajdek POL	78.69
3. Bence Halász HUN	77.36
4. Pavel Boreysha BLR	77.02
5. Elvind Henriksen NOR	76.86
6. Ivan Tikhon BLR	75.79
7. Hlib Piskunov UKR	74.62
8. Serghei Marghiev MDA	74.47

Fajdek was top qualifier with 77.86 and took the first round lead in the final with 78.69 but could not improve on that as Nowicki (after four major championship bronze medals) threw 80.00, 80.12 and 79.00 in rounds 2-4.

Javelin (9th)

1. Thomas Röhler GER	89.47
2. Andreas Hofmann GER	87.60
3. Magnus Kirt EST	85.96
4. Marcin Krukowski POL	84.55
5. Johannes Vetter GER	83.27
6. Antti Ruuskanen FIN	81.70
7. Andrian Mardare MDA	81.54
8. Jakub Vadlejch CZE	80.64

The three Germans were the favourites and Vetter 87.39 and Röhler 85.47 were best in qualifying. In the final Kirt 85.96 and Hofmann 85.61 were best in the first round before the lead was taken in round two by Hofmann 87.60 and then Röhler 88.02. Röhler sealed gold with 89.47 followed by 87.58, p, 87.90 but there were no other changes in the leading positions, and Vetter was well below his usual form for fifth place.

Decathlon (7th/8th)

1. Arthur Abele GER		8431
2. Ilya Shkurenyov RUS/ANA		8321
3. Vitaliy Zhuk BLR		8290
4. Niklas Kaul GER		8220
5. Tim Duckworth GBR		8160
6. Martin Roe NOR		8131
7. Pieter Braun NED		8105
8. Jan Dolezal CZE		8067

World champion Kevin Mayer started with a pb 10.66 for 100m, but then shocked with three fouls in the long jump – all fine jumps, but all 1-2 cm over the line. His French teammates Ruben Gado and Romain Martin also had three fouls as did Mathias Brugger! After the first day Duckworth led with 4380 from Abele 4285 and Roe 4292, but Abele's strong second day took him to victory by 110 points over Shkurenyov, who excelled with a 5.30 pole vault.

4 x 100 Metres (12th)

1. GBR	37.80	Ujah, Hughes, Gemili. Aikines-Aryeety (ht. 4. Mitchell-Blake)
2. TUR	37.98	Barnes, Harvey, Hekimoglu, Guliyev)
3. NED	38.03	Garia, Martina, Paulina, Burnet
4. FRA	38.51	6. FIN 38.92 dns. CZE
5. UKR	38.71	7. POR 39.07

The British quartet ran a brilliant 37.84 heat and won the final in 37.80, just 0.01 outside the Championships record. They had, however, to replace their anchor leg runner Nethaneel Mitchell-Blake for the final with Harry Aikines-Aryeetey, who took over with a clear lead over the Netherlands after a particularly brilliant second leg by Zharnel Hughes. A spectacular final leg by Ramil Guliyev closed much of the gap and took Turkey to a national record 37.89. Their were also national records from Natherlands and Finland.

4 x 400 Metres (h 10th, F 11th)

1. BEL	2:59.47	D Borlée 46.1, J Borlée 44.8, J Sacoor 44.70, K Borlée 43.91 (Watrin and Vanderbemden ran in heat)
2. GBR	3:00.36	Yousif 46.1, Cowan 45.3, Hudson-Smith 44.77, Rooney 44.24 (C Chalmers ran in heat)
3. ESP	3:00.78	Husillos 45.8, Bua 44.7, S García 44.80, Hortelano 45.56 (Ujakpor and Echeverry ran in heat)
4. FRA	3:02.08	7. CZE 3:03.00
5. POL	3:02.27	8. GER 3:04.69
6. ITA	3:02.34	

History was made as three brothers won gold medals together – The Belgian Borlées of course., with Kevin's 43.91 being much the fastest of the event. Martyn Rooney showed again how good he is with baton in hand and his 44.24 leg took Britain past Spain for the silver.

20 Kilometres Walk (11th)

1. Alvaro Martín ESP	1:20:42
2. Diego García ESP	1:20:48
3. Vasiliy Mizunov RUS/ANA	1:20:50
4. Massimo Stano ITA	1:20:51
5. Nils Brembach GER	1:21:25
6. Miguel Ángel López ESP	1:21:27
7. Tom Bosworth GBR	1:21:31
8. Hagen Pohle GER	1:21:35

The race was a Spanish triumph as Martín broke away in the 19th kilometre to win by 6 sec from team-mate García with defending champion López 6th. The 5k splits were 20:42, 20:26, 20:07 and 19:27.

50 Kilometres Walk (7th)

1. Maryan Zakalnytskyy UKR	3:46:32
2. Matej Tóth SVK	3:47:27
3. Dmitriy Dyubin BLR	3:47:59
4. Håvard Haukenes NOR	3:48:35
5. Carl Dohmann GER	3:50:27
6. Rafal Augustyn POL	3:51:37
7. Rafal Sikora POL	3:52:56
8. Nathaniel Seiler GER	3:54:08

Tóth raced off from the start on a hot morning and quickly established a clear lead. Although the pack gradually hauled him in, he was always just ahead as 10k was reached in 45:57, 20k in 1:31:52 (45:55) and 30k in 2:17:17 (45:25). Tóth's next 10k was faster still at 45:07 but by 32k he had ceded the lead to the eventual winner Zakalnytskyy, who had been 47 sec behind Tóth, in 11th place, at 20k (1:32:39). At 40k (3:01:38) Zakalnytskyy (after 44:10 for the fourth 10k) led from Dyubin (3:02:10), Haukenes (3:02:11) and Tóth (3:02:24), but Tóth rallied for the silver medal.

Women

100 Metres (7th) (0.0)

1. Dina Asher-Smith GBR	10.85*
2. Gina Lückenkemper GER	10.98
3. Dafne Schippers NED	10.99
4. Mujinga Kambundji SUI	11.05
5. Jamile Samuel NED	11.14
6. Imani Lansiquot GBR	11.14
7. Carolle Zahi FRA	11.20
8. Oriann Ombissa-Dzangue FRA	11.29

In the final Asher-Smith got way to an excellent start and powered smoothly on to a British and Championship record 10.85. Both she with 10.93 and Lückenkemper 10.98 also broke 11 secs in the first semi-final, and the German's two 10.98s tied the European U23 record.

200 Metres (11th) (0.2)

1. Dina Asher-Smith GBR	21.89

2. Dafne Schippers NED	22.14
3. Jamile Samuel NED	22.37
4. Mujinga Kambundji SUI	22.45
5. Ivet Lalova-Collio BUL	22.82
6. Bianca Williams GBR	22.88
7. Beth Dobbin GBR	22.93
8. Laura Müller GER	23.08

Asher-Smith was clearly fastest in the semis at 22.33 (next Samuel 22.58) and on a cool windless evening in the final improved her British record from 22.07 to 21.89 for the fastest double in European Champs history. Schippers was two and a half metres back in a season's best of 22.14.

400 Metres *(11th)*

1. Justyna Swiety-Ersetic POL	50.41
2. María Belibasáki GRE	50.45
3. Lisanne de Witte NED	50.77
4. Laviai Nielsen GBR	51.21
5. Iga Baumgart-Witan POL	51.24
6. Agne Serksniené LTU	51.42
7. Floria Guei FRA	51.57
8. Madiea Ghafoor NED	51.57

Three of the finalists ran three rounds, with Nielsen the fastest in the qualifying round in 51.67, a pb she reduced to 51.21 for the fastest semi. She matched that in the final but was kept out of the medals by three women who all smashed their personal bests, Swiety-Ersetic improving from 51.05 to win in 50.41 followed by national records from Belibasáki (previous best 51.14) and de Witte (50.96).

800 Metres *(10th)*

1. Nataliya Pryshchepa UKR	2:00.38
2. Renelle Lamote FRA	2:00.62
3. Olha Lyakhova UKR	2:00.79
4. Adelle Tracey GBR	2:00.86
5. Anna Sabat POL	2:01.26
6. Lynsey Sharp GBR	2:01.83
7. Selina Büchel SUI	2:02.05
8. Shelayna Oskan-Clarke GBR	2:02.26
9. Lovisa Lindh SWE	2:02.36

Pryshchepa retained her title with the most effective kick after the leaders at each 200m in the final were Oskan-Clarke 27.26, Oskan-Clarke and Büchel 59.25, and Buchel 1:29.59. Lyakhova, who gained four places in the last 200m to take the bronze medal behind Lamote, had been fastest in the heats in 2:00.26 and two women broke 2 minutes in the second semi: Lamote 1:59.44 and Tracey 1:59.86 pb.

1500 Metres *(12th)*

1. Laura Muir GBR	4:02.32
2. Sofia Ennaoui POL	4:03.08
3. Laura Weightman GBR	4:03.75
4. Ciara Mageean IRL	4:04.63
5. Simona Vrzalová CZE	4:06.47
6. Marta Pen POR	4:06.54
7. Hanna Hermansson SWE	4:07.16
8. Darya Borisovich BLR	4:07.52

Muir ran a brilliant, tactically-astute race to take the title. She covered the 200m between 500m and 700m in 30.97 with only Weightman willing or able to stay close and then ran 15.30 for the next 100m to reach 800m in 2:12.74. A third lap of 61.89 meant that her time at 1200m was 3:14.20, followed by Weightman 3:15.00 and Ennaoui 3:15.48. Muir won after a last lap in 63.12 while Ennouai sped that in 61.84 to get the silver.

5000 Metres *(12th)*

1. Sifan Hassan NED	14:46.12
2. Eilish McColgan GBR	14:53.05
3. Yasemin Can TUR	14:57.63
4. Konstanze Klosterhalfen GER	15:03.73
5. Melissa Courtney GBR	15:04.75
6. Susan Krumins NED	15:09.65
7. Ancuta Bobocel ROU	15:16.13
8. Maureen Koster NED	15:21.64

McColgan, unusually, led through 1k 3:03.01 and 2k 6:01.62 and it was Can at 3k in 8:59.58 and Salpeter at 4k in 12:03.30. With two laps remaining, Hassan took the lead and leading up to the bell (13:45.57) she took off, running a spectacular last lap in 60.55 (29.72 last 200m) to win by nearly 50m over McColgan. Salpeter, after her 10k win four days earlier, finished 4th in 15:01.00 but was disqualified for cutting in too soon after the start. At the end of the penultimate lap Salpeter raced alongside Hassan in the belief that they were sprinting for the finish and raised her arms in delight believing she had won another medal. Seconds later she realised her mistake and got going again, but it was too late (she finished in 15:01.00).

10,000 Metres *(8th)*

1. Lonah Chemtai Salpeter ISR	31:43.29
2. Susan Krumins NED	31:52.55
3. Meraf Bahta SWE	32:19.34
4. Alina Reh GER	32:28.48
5. Yasemin Can TUR	32:34.34
6. Alice Wright GBR	32:36.45
7. Charlotta Fougberg SWE	32:43.04
8. Svetlana Kudzelich BLR	32:46.04

Salpeter, who had moved from Kenya in 2008, became Israel's first female European champion. She had been 0.43 behind Can (15:51.76) at 5000m, and stretched away to win, increasing her lead over Krumins from 3.90 at the bell to 9.26 at the finish, with Bahta going past Can just before 9000m. 8 of the 26 starters did not finish.

Marathon *(12th)*

1. Olga Mazuronak BLR	2:26:22
2. Clémence Calvin FRA	2:26:28
3. Eva Vrabcová-Nyvítová CZE	2:26:31
4. Marina Damantsevich BLR	2:27:44
5. Anastasiya Ivanova BLR	2:27:49
6. Sara Dossena ITA	2:27:53

7. Martina Strähl SUI   2:28:07
8. Catherine Bertone ITA   2:30:06

European Marathon Cup

(up to 5 per team, 3 to score): 1. BLR 7:21:54, 2. ITA 7:32:46, 3. ESP 7:44:06, 4. GBR 7:53:16, 5. SUI 7:54:04, 6. SWE 7:55:21: 7. UKR 8:01:10, 8. IRL 8:04:46, 9. CRO 8:08:09, 10. TUR 8:19.35

Despite a heavy nosebleed early in the race, Mazuronak justified her position as favourite, running 10k splits of 35:12, 34:58, 34:25 and 34:28, but was given a hard race by Calvin on her marathon debut and by Vrabcová-Nyvitová, who had competed at the Winter Olympics as a cross-country skier. There were 9 non-finishers from the field of 55.

3000 Metres Steeplechase (12th)

1. Gesa-Felicitas Krause GER   9:19.80
2. Fabienne Schlumpf SUI   9:22.29
3. Karoline Bjerkeli Grøvdal NOR   9:24.46
4. Luiza Gega ALB   9:24.78
5. Adva Cohen ISR   9:29.74
6. Elena Burkard GER   9:29.76
7. Anna Emilie Möller DEN   9:31.66
8. Irene Sánchez ESP   9:31.84
9. Ophélie Claude-Boxberger FRA   9:31.84

After a late start to the season defending champion Gesa-Felicitas Krause gave the crowd plenty to enthuse over as she judged her race to perfection. Schlumpf set the pace with kilometres of 3:05.79 and 3:10.53, and led until the final water jump from where Krause sprinted to victory. Cohen set Israeli records in both heat (9:36.13) and final, in which there was the best ever set of times for European Champs.

100 Metres Hurdles (9th) (-0.5)

1. Elvira German BLR   12.67
2. Pamela Dutkiewicz GER   12.72
3. Cindy Roleder GER   12.77
4. Nadine Visser NED   12.88
5. Ricarda Lobe GER   13.00
6. Karolina Koleczek POL   13.11
dq. Solène Ndama FRA   –
dq. Alina Talay BLR   fell

Ndama was fastest in the qualifying round with a 12.88 pb that she reduced to 12.77 in the semis. There the winners were Roleder 12.83, German 12.76 and Dutkiewicz 12.71 and these three took the medals in the final, the German's strong finish deciding the issue. In her first competition since June, Talay made the final but crashed out, as did Ndama.

400 Metres Hurdles (10th)

1. Léa Sprunger SUI   54.33
2. Anna Ryzhykova UKR   54.51
3. Meghan Beesley GBR   55.31
4. Hanne Claes BEL   55.75
5. Yadisleidy Pedroso ITA   55.80
6. Vera Rudakova RUS/ANA   55.89
7. Viktoriya Tkachuk UKR   56.15

8. Eilidh Doyle GBR   56.23

Ryzhykova ran a season's best 54.82 fastest in the semis where Sprunger 55.04 and Doyle 55.16 were the other winners. Sprunger and Ryzhova dominated the final with Beesley taking an unexpected bronze medal.

High Jump (10th)

1. Mariya Lasitskene RUS/ANA   2.00
2. Mirela Demireva BUL   2.00
3. Marie-Laurence Jungfleisch GER   1.96
4. Airine Palsyte LTU   1.96
5. Kateryna Tabashnyk UKR   1.94
6. Michaela Hrubá CZE   1.91
7. Morgan Lake GBR   1.91
8. Alessia Trost ITA   1.91

Despite winning, Lasitskene was very unhappy that she had not gone higher than 2.00, which she cleared on her second attempt and Demireva on her third (having daringly passed 1.96 and 1.98). Jungfleisch took the silver by clearing 1.96 on her first try while Palsyte needed two. A surprise non-qualifier was Elena Vallortigara who managed only 1.86 despite her 2.02 earlier in the year.

Pole Vault (9th)

1. Ekaterini Stefanidi GRE   4.85*
2. Nikoléta Kiriakopoúlou GRE   4.80
3. Holly Bradshaw GBR   4.75
4. Anzhelika Sidorova RUS/ANA   4.70
5. Ninon Guillon-Romarin FRA   4.65
6. Angelica Bengtsson SWE   4.65
7. Iryna Zhuk BLR   4.55
8. Maryna Kylypko UKR   4.45

Having been the only qualifier to try 4.55 that she had chosen as her opening height, Stefanidi cleared 4.55, 4.65 and 4.80 on first attempts in the final, with Kiriakopoúlou had a clear card to 4.75 and went over 4.80 on her second attempt. Stafanídi then had a third time clearance at 4.85 to add 4cm to the championships record and had three unsuccessful goes at 4.96.

Long Jump (11th

1. Malaika Mihambo GER   6.75/-0.7
2. Maryna Bekh UKR   6.73/-0.1
3. Shara Proctor GBR   6.70/-0.4
4. Jazmin Sawyers GBR   6.67/-0.4
5. Anastasiya Mironchik-Ivanova BLR   6.58/-1.1
6. Ksenija Balta EST   6.49/-1.6
7. Khaddi Sagnia SWE   6.47/-1.0
8. Evelise Veiga POR   6.47/0.6

The competition was close although the winning distance of 6.75 by Mihambo in the third round was the least since 1974. Defending champion Ivana Spanovic jumped 6.84 in qualifying (from Proctor 6.75 and Mihambo 6.71) but injured her Achilles tendon in so doing and was unable to take part in the final, in which Lorraine Ugen, world leader at 7.05, was only 9th with 6.45 after 6.70 in qualifying.

Triple Jump *(10th)*

1. Paraskeví Papahrístou GRE   14.60/-0.1
2. Kristin Gierisch GER   14.45/-0.5
3. Ana Peleteiro ESP   14.44/0.1
4. Elena Panturoiu ROU   14.38/0.4
5. Hanna Minenko ISR   14.37/0.7
6. Gabriela Petrova BUL   14.26/-0.4
7. Jeanine Assani Issouf FRA   14.12/0.2
8. Rouguy Diallo FRA   14.08/0.7

Previous champions Olha Saladukha (13th 14.04) and Patricia Mamona (16th 13.92) did not progress from the qualifying round in which nine women jumped 14.20 or better led by Papahrístou 14.49. Gierisch opened the final with 14.45 but Papahrístou won with her second round 14.60.

Shot *(8th)*

1. Paulina Guba POL   19.33
2. Christina Schwanitz GER   19.19
3. Alyona Dubitskaya BLR   18.81
4. Klaudia Kardasz POL   18.48
5. Sara Gambetta GER   18.13
6. Radoslava Mavrodieva BUL   18.03
7. Sophie McKinna GBR   17.69
8. Viktoriya Kolb BLR   17.50

In the absence of Anita Márton, Schwanitz led the qualifiers with 18.83 and was the clear favourite for the title, but although she had opening throws of 19.19 and 19.08 she was beaten by Guba, who threw 19.33 in the final round after second place had been held by round 5 throws of 18.81 by Dubitskaya and 19.02 by Guba.

Discus *(11th)*

1. Sandra Perkovic CRO   67.62
2. Nadine Müller GER   63.00
3. Shanice Craft GER   62.46
4. Claudine Vita GER   61.25
5. Daisy Osakue ITA   59.32
6. Dragana Tomasevic SRB   58.94
7. Liliana Cá POR   58.91
8. Alexandra Emilianov MDA   58.10

Perkovic was the very clear favourite. She led the qualifiers with 64.54 from Craft 61.13, but amazingly was unable to get beyond 60m in the first four rounds of the final. Then order was restored by Perkovic's 67.62 in the fifth round and she won a record fifth European title. Silver went to Müller with a season's best 63.00 in the second round and Craft took a third successive European bronze..

Hammer *(12th)*

1. Anita Wlodarczyk POL   78.94*
2. Alexandra Tavernier FRA   74.78
3. Joanna Fiodorow POL   74.00
4. Malwina Kopron POL   72.20
5. Hanna Skydan AZE   72.10
6. Zalina Petrivskaya MDA   71.80
7. Kathrin Klaas GER   71.50
8. Sophie Hitchon GBR   70.52

As has been usual in recent years Wlodarczyk dominated the event. She threw 75.10 in qualifying from Skydan 74.02, Tavernier 72.99 and Hanna Malyshik 72.39, and after a moderate 69.35 start had a series in the final of 76.50, 77.82, 78.94, 78.55, x. That put her well clear of runner-up Tavernier who set a French record of 74.78 and Fiodorow 74.00.

Javelin *(10th)*

1. Christin Hussong GER   67.90*
2. Nikola Ogrodníková CZE   61.85
3. Liveta Jasiunaite LTU   61.59
4. Martina Ratej SLO   61.41
5. Tatyana Kholodovich BLR   60.92
6. Alexie Alais FRA   60.01
7. Irena Sedivá CZE   59.76
8. Sigrid Borge NOR   59.60

Katharina Molitor was a casualty in qualifying (15th 58.00), but her compatriot Hussong threw a pb 67.29 there and even better with 67.90 on her opening throw in the final. That left her over 6m ahead of the other medallists.

Heptathlon *(9th/10th)*

1. Nafissatou Thiam BEL   6816
2. Katarina Johnson-Thompson GBR   6759
3. Carolin Schäfer GER   6602
4. Ivona Dadic AUT   6552
5. Anouk Vetter NED   6414
6. Katerina Cachová CZE   6400
7. Xénia Krizsán HUN   6367
8. Verena Preiner AUT   6337

Thiam won as expected but was pushed hard by Johnson-Thompson, the issue only being settled in the javelin. Thiam started with 46.36 and at that stage was 32 points down on KJT, but then threw 53.35 and a magnificent 57.91 for a margin of 192 points. Although KJT ran the 800m in 2:09.84 to Thiam's 2:19.35, she would have needed to have won by about 14 secs to have taken the gold. Both women had high jumped 1.91, rather below their best, but Thiam's outdoor shot best of 15.35 was far batter than 13.09 by KJT, who, however, ran a great 200m in 22.88 to her rival's 24.81. Schäfer produced a very solid set of marks for the bronze medal. The German pair of Louisa Grauvogel and Mareike Arndt, then 7th and 12th. were unable to contest the 800m as they were involved in a car accident between the stadium and hotel

4 x 100 Metres *(12th)*

1. GBR	41.88	Philip, Lansiquot, B Williams, Asher-Smith (Neita ran in heat)
2. NED	42.15	Schippers, van Hunenstijn, Samuel, Sedney
3. GER	42.23	Kwayie, Lückenkemper, Pinto, Haase
4. SUI	42.30	7. ITA	43.42
5. FRA	43.10	8. ESP	43.54
6. POL	43.34		

Dina Asher-Smith completed a perfect week by anchoring Britain to victory in the world leading time of 41.88, just 0.11 outside the British record, as she came from 4th to 1st with a brilliant leg. With Darryl Neita running instead of her, the team had run 41.29 to win their heat.

4 x 400 Metres Relay *(11th)*

1. POL	3:26.59	Holub-Kowalik 52.3, Baumgart-Witan 51.4, Wyciszkiewicz 51.20, Swiety-Ersetic 51.71 (Kaczmarek & Dabrowska ran in heat)
2. FRA	3:27.17	Diarra 52.6, Sananes 51.8, Raharolahy 51.18, Guei 51.59 (Perrossier ran in heat)
3. GBR	3:27.40	Clark 52.5, Onuora 52.0, Allcock 51.48, Doyle 51.50 (Agyapong, Abichi & Diamond ran in heat)
4. BEL	3:27.69	7. ROU 3:32.15
5. ITA	3:28.62	8. SVK 3:32.22
6. GER	3:30.33	

Unfortunately the final was held only an hour and a half after the 400m individual final. This meant that Britain was deprived of an in-form Laviai Nielsen, although the formidable relay runners Florence Guei of France and Justyna Swiety-Ersetic did run both finals and the last anchored Poland, who had led throughout, to victory for her second gold of the Championships.

20 Kilometres Walk *(11th)*

1. María Pérez ESP	1:26:36*
2. Anezka Drahotová CZE	1:27:03
3. Antonella Palmisano ITA	1:27:30
4. Brigita Virbalyté-Dimsiené LTU	1:27:59
5. Zivile Vaiciukeviciute LT	1:28:07
6. Laura García-Caro ESP	1:28:15
7. Inna Kashyna UKR	1:29:16
8. Ana Cabecinha POR	1:29:49

A delay due a suspected gas leak, meant that the women competed alongside the men for the first time in a major 20k championship. At 5k Drahatová led in 22:09, at 10k Virbalyté-Dimsiené in 43:59 and at 15k Drahatová in 1:05:33, but Pérez then produced a dynamic final 5k in 20:59 to take her from 4 sec down to a 27 sec winning margin. From 30 starters there were four non-finishers including Eleonora Giorgi, who was disqualified.

50 Kilometres Walk *(7th)*

1. Inês Henriques POR	4:09:21*
2. Alina Tsviliy UKR	4:12:44
3. Julia Takacs ESP	4:15:22
4. Khrystyna Yudkina UKR	4:20:46
5. Vasylyna Vitovshchyk UKR	4:23:15
6. Mária Czaková SVK	4:24:59
7. Ainhoa Pinedo ESP	4:27:03
8. Mar Juárez ESP	4:28:58

Just as at the 2017 Worlds, Henriques was the inaugural champion. She led all the way with 10k splits of 48:19, 48:21, 48:38, 49:58 and 54:05. Tsviliy (née Halchenko) smashed her pb of 4:28:49 to take second in a Ukrainian record 4:12:44. 19 women started the race of whom 14 finished (13 under 4:36 and last in 4:52:38).

Four athletes competed at the European Championships for a seventh time to set an all-time record:

Men: Marian Oprea ROU (TJ), Zoltán Kövágó HUN & Gerd Kanter EST (DT), David Söderberg FIN (HT), Jesús España ESP (HMar).

Women: Olha Saladukha UKR and Patricia Sarrapio ESP (TJ), Dragana Tomasevich SRB (DT), Martina Hrasnová SVK, Kathrin Klaas GER, Éva Orbán HUN (all HT) and Martina Ratej SLO (JT) competed for a sixth time to equal the women's record.

COMMONWEALTH GAMES 2018

Gold Coast, Australia April 8-14

THIS WAS THE first major international outdoor championships in April since the 1896 Olympic Games and the date certainly suited the Southern Hemisphere nations who benefitted, having had recent trials/championships as had Kenya. Other hot countries such as Jamaica and India also had outdoor competitions in preparation, but it proved a problem for those from the British countries, who lacked enough competitive preparation. Overall Australia had a terrific Games, easily heading the points table, but Jamaica had a great Games, even heading Australia in the medal table. They were weaker than usual in the sprints, but made up for this with 1-2s in the men's discus

and women's triple jump and with Danniel Thomas-Dodd winning the women's shot ahead of Dame Valerie Adams, who continued her come-back with a season's best, taking her Commonwealth Games medal tally to three golds and two silver.

Apart from the marathons, generally conditions were ideal with temperatures in the mid to high 20s helping athletes to set Games records in 13 events and provide world leading marks in 18 events. Caster Semenya heads those achievements with Games records and world leads in both 800m (1:56.68) and 1500m (4:00.71), and Joshua Cheptegei was the other individual double winner with 5000m and a Games record at 10,000m, with Isaac Makwala (400m) and Janieve Russell (400mh) taking individual and relay golds. The success of Cheptegei and his colleagues meant that Uganda headed Kenya in the men's distance races and women's 10,000m, but Kenya, even without any of their top marathoners, had the 1-2 in the men's 1500m and women's 5000m and their sixth successive clean sweep of the medals in the men's steeplechase in which Conseius Kipruto broke the Games record. Aisha Praught of Jamaica upset their plans, however, with a brilliant victory in the women's steeplechase.

There were many world-class performances by the top competitors in the field events, but often a lack of depth. Games records were set in five throws events: by Nick Miller's British record 80.26 hammer, Tom Walsh with his 22.45 shot qualifying mark, Fedrick Dacres the discus 68.20 as all his six marks were well ahead of the runner-up, Dani Samuels with similar domination in the women's event, topped by 68.26, and Kathryn Mitchell, 68.92 in the women's javelin.

There was a big shock in the decathlon when Damian Warner, heading for a top score, failed his opening height in the pole vault and in the

Medals and Points Table

Points: 8 for 1st to 1 for 8th.

	G	S	B	Total	Pts	2014	2010	2006
AUS	7	7	7	21	258	179	200	379.5
JAM	7	8	9	24	207	184	84	185.5
ENG	4	3	5	12	184	290	297	238
KEN	4	8	5	17	144	205	251	131
CAN	2	6	3	11	136	148.5	126.5	114
RSA	4	1	3	8	84	73	36	134.5
UGA	3	1	1	5	75	33	30	22
IND	1	1	1	3	57.5	31	142	39
NGR	1	2	1	4	56	70	34	54
NZL	2	3	-	5	54	55	56.5	71
TTO	2	-	-	2	48	54	37	28.5
SCO	-	1	3	4	48	55	58	20
BOT	4	1	1	5	43	16.5	21	11
BAH	1	3	-	4	35	54	41	31.5
WAL	-	-	2	2	27	25.5	53.5	35
GRN	1	-	1	2	23	14	3	14
CYP	-	-	1	1	17	26	19.5	8
NIR	-	-	1	1	16	0	0	0
IVB	1	-	-	1	14	5	4	4
NAM	1	-	-	1	14	0	7	0
DMA	-	1	1	2	13	3	2	0
CMR	-	-	1	1	11	0	17	9

Other nations to score points: SRI 9, GUY 9 (1G), LCA 8 (1G), BAR 6.5, ANT 6, GHA, LES, MRI 5; CAY, FIJ, MAS, ZAM 4; SKN, TCA 3; MRI, RWA 2; Guernsey, GUY, PAK, SAM 1.

Thus 18 nations won gold medals, 24 medals of any colour and 42 had athletes placed in the top 8 for a record spread of nations (compared to 12, 20 and 32 in 2014).

The above table does not include the various events for Paralympians that were integrated into the programme.

javelin defending champion Julius Yego failed to qualify for the final, while Sophie Hitchon had three no throws in the women's hammer final.

Dates given in brackets after the heading for each event are those of the final. * Games record.

MEN

100 Metres (9th) (0.8)

1. Akani Simbine RSA	10.03
2. Henricho Bruintjies RSA	10.17
3. Yohan Blake JAM	10.19
4. Seye Ogunlewe NGR	10.19
5. Kemar Hyman CAY	10.21
6. Jason Rogers SKN	10.24
7. Enich Adegoke NGR-J	10.35
dns. Adam Gemili ENG	–

The favourite Blake was fastest in the heats with 10.15/-0.9 and semis with 10.06/-0.3, but Simbine was totally dominant in the final as Blake never recovered from an early stumble. Gemili, the 2014 silver medallist, sustained an adductor injury despite finishing strongly in 10.11 in his semi and had to withdraw from the final.

200 Metres (12th) (0.9)

1. Jereem Richards TTO	20.12
2. Aaron Brown CAN	20.34
3. Leon Reid NIR	20.55
4. Clarence Munyai RSA	20.58
5. Sydney Siame ZAM	20.62
6. Kyle Greaux TTO	20.63
7. Warren Weir JAM	20.71
dq. Zharnel Hughes ENG	(20.12)

Hughes won his heat in a very easy looking 20.34 and his semi, equally comfortably, in 20.37. In the final he ran a storming bend and was a clear leader at halfway but Richards narrowed the gap along the finishing straight and there was little in it at the end with Hughes declared the winner (20.113 to 20.117). He ran a lap of honour believing he had won, only to be disqualified as scrutiny by the judges of the video coverage indicated that towards the end he had run on the line, his swinging left arm impeding Richards in the neighbouring lane. Brown, who had been fastest in the semis with 20.18 took the silver medal.

400 Metres (10th)

1. Isaac Makwala BOT	44.34
2. Baboloki Thebe BOT	45.09
3. Javon Francis JAM	45.11
4. Muhammed Anas IND	45.31
5. Bralon Taplin GRN	45.38
6. Demish Gaye JAM	45.56
7. Steven Solomon AUS	45.64
dnf. Rusheen McDonald JAM	

Makwala cruised through his semi in 45.00

and in the final he ran a flawless race to enter the finishing straight some 4m clear of Taplin, who faded from second to fifth in the final 30m. The one man who just might have pressed him was Matthew Hudson-Smith, who had looked fantastic when winning his heat in a heavily restrained 45.57, but he was disqualified for running on the line around the turn.

800 Metres (12th)

1. Wycliffe Kinyamal KEN	1:45.11
2. Kyle Langford ENG	1:45.16
3. Luke Mathews AUS	1:45.60
4. Jake Wightman SCO	1:45.82
5. Brad Mathas NZL	1:46.07
6. Jonathan Kitilit KEN	1:46.12
7. Joseph Deng AUS	1:47.20
8. Nijel Amos BOT	1:48.45

Defending champion Nijel Amos was much the fastest with 1:45.12 in the heats, and he led in the final for the first lap, through 200m 24.6 and 400m 52.01, and was still in contention at 700m: Kinyamal 1:30.9, Amos 1:31.3, Kitilit 1:31.4, Wightman 1:31.9 and Langford 1:31.9. but Amos cracked and practically jogged in as Kinyamal won from fast-finishing Langford.

1500 Metres (14th)

1. Elijah Manangoi KEN	3:34.78
2. Timothy Cheruiyot KEN	3:35.17
3. Jake Wightman SCO	3:35.97
4. Charlie Da'Vall Grice ENG	3:37.43
5. Jinson Johnson IND	3:37.86
6. Jordan Williamsz AUS	3:38.34
7. Kumari Taki KEN-J	3:38.74
8. Chris O'Hare SCO	3:39.04

After two slow heats, the 12-man final was run at an honest pace after a cautious opening lap of 60.95. Cheruiyot ran 59.09 for the second lap and raised the tempo considerably with a third lap of 56.06. At the bell the three Kenyans were together in the lead, but Taki faded in the closing stages of a pulsating last lap, run in 52.07 by Manangoi to win three metres ahead of Cheruiyot, with Wightman taking the bronze medal from a superbly judged race.

5000 Metres (8th)

1. Joshua Cheptegei UGA	13:50.83
2. Mohammed Ahmed CAN	13:52.78
3. Edward Zakayo KEN-Y	13:54.06
4. Thomas Ayeko UGA	13:54.78
5. Stewart McSweyn AUS	13:58.96
6. Philip Kipyeko UGA	13:59.59
7. James Sugira RWA	14:03.51
8. Morgan McDonald AUS	14:11.37

The winning time was by far the slowest in CG history, the previous slowest being Dave Moorcroft's 13:33.00 in 1982, as the leaders of the 17-man field were content to jog through the first 3000m (2:57.83, 2:57.30 and 2:51.87 for

a 3000m time of 8:47.00). It became a genuine race when Cheptegei took over at 3400m for a fourth kilometre in 2:38.31 and the fifth in a vicious 2:25.52 (56.26 last lap) with 3:42.9 for his last 1500m. Ahmed took silver and 16 year-old Zakayo the bronze.

10,000 Metres (13th)

1. Joshua Cheptegei UGA	27:19.62*
2. Mohammed Ahmed CAN	27:20.56
3. Rodgers Chumo KEN	27:28.66
4. Jacob Kiplimo UGA-J	27:30.25
5. Jake Robertson NZL	27:30.90
6. Stephen Mokoka RSA	27:44.58
7. Timothy Toroitich UGA	27:47.35
8. Jonathan Ndiku KEN	27:56.24

Cheptegei became the third man to win this distance CG double – after Cecil Matthews in 1938 and Moses Kipsiro in 2010. Kwemoi led at halfway in 13:53.42 and Cheptegei, Ahmed and Robsrton alternated in the lead until the first two contested the last couple of laps with Cheptegei (second half of 13:25.6) storming home in a Games record. Robertson broke the New Zealand record but was outkicked by 17-year old Kiplimo.

Marathon (15th)

1. Michael Shelley AUS	2:16:46
2. Solomon Mutai UGA	2:19:02
3. Robbie Simpson SCO	2:19:36
4. Kevin Seaward NIR	2:19:54
5. Liam Adams AUS	2:21:08
6. Paulus Ilyambo NAM	2:22:39
7. Alex Chesakit UGA	2:23:06
8. Lee Merrien GUERNSEY	2:24:10

17 of 24 starters finished in very hot weather and these included Callum Hawkins who had led by 1:42 at 35k. but who after 2 hours 4 minutes of superb running started to weave around the road and then stumbled and fell. He tried to carry on but at the 40k mark in 2:07:09 (2:03 ahead of Shelley) collapsed and had a long wait for help to arrive and take him to hospital, leaving Shelley to retain his title. Tsepo Mathibele LES was another to drop out, while in third place at 37k

3000 Metres Steeplechase (13th)

1. Conselus Kipruto KEN	8:10.08*
2. Abraham Kibiwott KEN	8:10.62
3. Amos Kirui KEN	8.12.24
4. Matt Hughes CAN	8:12.33
5. Albert Chemutai UGA-J	8:19.89
6. Jonathan Hopkins WAL	8:34.12
7. Ieuan Thomas WAL	8:40.02
8. Adam Kirk-Smith NIR	8:48.40

There was a Kenyan clean sweep in this event for the sixth successive CG, although Hughes was only just edged out of the bronze medal. Kipruto's gold followed those had had won at Olympic Games and World Championships.

110 Metres Hurdles (10th) (-0.3)

1. Ronald Levy JAM		13.19
2. Hansle Parchment JAM		13.22
3. Nicholas Hough AUS		13.38
4. Milan Trajkovic CYP		13.42
5. Antonio Alkana RSA		13.49
6= Andrew Pozzi ENG		13.53
6= Shane Brathwaite BAR		13.53
8. De'Jour Russell JAM-J		13.92

Heat winners were Pozzi 13.29 and Parchment 13.30, but Pozzi, the World Indoor 60mh champion, suffered a nightmare final from clobbering the first hurdle. Parchment led over the last hurdle, only to be overtaken on the run-in by the dynamic Levy for a Jamaican 1-2, ahead of Hough, who set a pb.

400 Metres Hurdles (12th)

1. Kyron McMaster IVB	48.25
2. Jeffery Gibson BAH	49.10
3. Jaheel Hyde JAM	49.16
4. Jack Green ENG	49.18
5. Rilwan Alowonle NGR	49.80
6. Haron Koech KEN	50.02
7. Andre Clarke JAM	50.08
8. Nicholas Bett KEN	51.00

McMaster won his heat in 48.78, with Clarke (49.10) the next fastest, and won the final by a margin of 0.85, the widest in the event's history. Bett vied with McMaster early in the race, but faded badly in the final straight.

High Jump (11th)

1. Brandon Starc AUS	2.32
2. Jamal Wilson BAH	2.30
3. Django Lovett CAN	2.30
4. Donald Thomas BAH	2.27
5. Allan Smith SCO	2.27
6= Michael Mason CAN	2.24
6= Tejaswin Shankar IND	2.24
8. Lee Hup Wei MAS	2.21

All the 13 men in the final qualified with 2.21. Clearing 2.30 were Wilson on first attempt, Starc on second and Lovett on third. Then Starc won by clearing 2.32 first time, adding 1 cm to his pb. In his last major championship, Robbie Grabarz ENG was a disappointing 12th at 2.18.

Pole Vault (12th)

1. Kurtis Marschall AUS	5.70
2. Shawnacy Barber CAN	5.65
3. Luke Cutts ENG	5.45
4. Adam Hague ENG	5.45
5. Angus Armstrong AUS	5.35
6. Deryk Theodore CAN	5.35
7. Nikandros Stylianou CYP	5.35
8. Iskandar Alwi MAS	5.00

The top two were a class apart. Both made 5.65 first time, and 5.70 sealed the issue, Barber going very close but Marschall clearing on his third attempt.

Long Jump (11th)

1. Luvo Manyonga RSA	8.41*/0.6
2. Henry Frayne AUS	8.33/0.8
3. Ruswahl Samaai RSA	8.22/0.2
4. Tajay Gayle JAM	8.12/-0.1
5. Dan Bramble ENG	7.94/0.1
6. Chris Mitrevski AUS	7.90/0.8
7. Janaka Wimalasari SRI	7.89/0.5
8. Damar Forbes JAM	7.88/0.9

Frayne improved his pb from 8.27 to a Games record 8.34 in qualifying and in the final took the lead from Manyonga's opening 8.24 with 8.33 in the second round. Manyonga, however, leapt to Games records 8.35 in round 4 and 8.41 in the last round.

Triple Jump (14th)

1. Troy Doris GUY	16.88/0.5
2. Yordanys Durañona DMA	16.86/-2.3
3. Marcel Mayack II CMR	16.80/-0.4
4. Arpinder Singh IND	16.46/-0.1
5. Nathan Douglas ENG	16.35/-2.1
6. Jonathan Drack MRI	16.28/-0.3
7. Clive Pullen JAM	16.25/-0.1
8. Roger Haitengi NAM	16.24/-0.4

Durañona led the qualifying with 16.75 and opened in the final with 16.86, showing consistency by following with 16.85 and 16.77. But a second-round 16.88 by Doris took him to a narrow victory. Mayack improved his pb to 16.32 in qualifying and 16.80 in the final.

Shot (9th)

1. Tom Walsh NZL	(22.45*q)	21.41
2, Chukwuebuka Enekwechi NGR		21.14
3. Tim Nedow CAN		20.91
4. O'Dayne Richards JAM		20.80
5. Damien Birkenhead AUS		20.77
6, Orazio Cremona RSA		20.51
7. Ashinia Miller JAM		19.68
8. Tejinder Pal Singh IND		19.42

Walsh produced the longest ever qualifying mark (previous best his own 22.14 in the 2017 Worlds) with a massive Games record of 22.45. He said that he tried too hard in the final when he threw 21.21 in round 2 and 21.41 in round 4. Six men over 20m exceeded the previous CG best of four.

Discus (13th)

1. Fedrick Dacres JAM	68.20*
2. Traves Smikle JAM	63.98
3. Apostolos Parellis CYP	63.61
4. Matthew Denny AUS	62.53
5. Mitchell Cooper AUS	60.40
6. Benn Harradine AUS	59.92
7. Stephen Mozia NGR	59.58
8. Alex Rose SAM	59.56

Dacres led the qualifiers with 66.20 from Denny 64.67 and dominated the final with a series of 65.55, 66.09, 68.20, 67.14, 67.51, 65.00. Smikle made it a Jamaican 1-2 with 3rd and 4th round throws of 63.83 and 63.98.

Hammer (8th)

1. Nick Miller ENG	80.26*
2. Matthew Denny AUS	74.88
3. Mark Dry SCO	73.12
4. Adam Keenan CAN	72.15
5. Taylor Campbell ENG	72.03
6. Dempsey McGuigan NIR	70.24
7. Osian Jones WAL	70.14
8. Jack Dalton AUS	68.28

Miler improved the UK record that he had set two weeks earlier in the USA with a fourth round 80.26, adding 2.73 to the Games record. He followed that with 79.25 while Denny had three throws better than the bronze medallist's best.

Javelin (14th)

1. Neeraj Chopra IND	86.47
2. Hamish Peacock AUS	82.59
3. Anderson Peters GRN	82.20
4. Phil-Mar Janse van Rensburg RSA	79.83
5. Vipin Kasana IND	77.87
6. Luke Cann AUS	76.99
7. Shakeil Waithe TTO	76.85
8. Arshad Nadeem PAK	76.02

Four men beat 80m in qualifying including a Pakistan record 80.45 by Nadeem, but defending champion Julius Yego managed only 74.55 for 13th. Chopra, the 2016 World U20 champion, started with 85.50 in the final and threw 84.78. 86.47 and 83.48 in rounds 3-5.

Decathlon (9th-10th)

1, Lindon Victor GRN	8303
2. Pierce LePage CAN	8171
3. Cedric Dubler AUS	7983
4. Kurt Felix GRN	7756
5. Kyle Cranston AUS	7734
6. John Lane ENG	7529
7. Ben Gregory WAL	7449
8. Gilbert Koech KEN	7009

After seven events Damien Warner was 223 points ahead off his closest rival but he failed three times at 4.50 in the pole vault (having cleared 4.90 at the World Indoors the previous month). Warner had achieved 10.29 100m, 7.54 LJ, 15.11 SP (a big pb), 2.04 HJ, 48.12 400m, 13.89 110mh and 46.55 DT. Victor took the lead when he threw the javelin 71.10 and had a winning margin of 132 over LaPage.

4 x 100 Metres (14th)

1. ENG	38.13	Arthur, Hughes, Kilty, Aikines-Aryeetey
2. RSA	38.24	Bruintjies. Erasmus, Jobodwana, Simbine
3. JAM	38.35	Clarke, Bailey, Weir, Blake
4. AUS	38.58	Williams, Browning, Hale, Clarke
5. BAR	39.04	7. MAS 39.37
6. SRI	39.08	dq. NGR –

Including a late substitute, Reuben Arthur for the injured Adam Gemili, England ran impressively for 38.15 in their heat and 38.13 in the final in which Akani Simbine came for fourth to almost catch Aikines-Aryettey on the final leg and help South Africa to a national record.

4 x 400 Metres (14th)

1. BOT	3:01.78	Maotoanong 46.5, Thebe 44.3, Nkobolo 46.38, Makwala 44.54
2. BAH	3:01.92	Ferguson 46.0, T Smith 46.0, Newbold 45.31, A Russell 44.52
3. JAM	3:01.97	Gayle 46.2, Gaye 44.8, Rose 46.40, Francis 44.54
4. TTO	3:02.85	Lendore 45.80, Richards 44.64, Quow 46.70, Cedenio 45.71
5. FIJ	3:15.10	dnf. IND –
6. TCA	3:16.39	dq. KEN (3:04.08)

Matt Hudson-Smith pulled up injured on the first leg for England in their heat, and two other leading teams easily ran fast enough but disqualified were Nigeria due to a lane infringement and Australia for Steven Solomon (who ran a 44.55 leg) standing in the wrong position when he lined up to take the baton. A fine 44.64 second leg by Jereem Richards gave Trinidad & Tobago a 4m lead at halfway in the final, but then Renny Quow had a poor run, and Isaac Makwala took Botswana to victory and each of the final men for the medal teams had outstanding runs.

20 Kilometres Walk (8th)

1. Dane Bird-Smith AUS	1:19:34*
2. Tom Bosworth ENG	1:19:38
3. Samuel Gathimba KEN	1:19:51
4. Benjamin Thorne CAN	1:20:49
5. Quentin Rew NZL	1:21:47
6. Manish Singh IND	1:22:22
7. Callum Wilkinson ENG	1:22:35
8. Evan Dunfee CAN	1:23:26

The first three men broke the Games record of 1:19:55, Bird-Smith went clear in the final kilometre of Bosworth, who set a British record in this the first event of the athletics programme. The winner's 2k splits were 8:10, 7:58, 7:59, 7:57 and 7:54.

WOMEN

100 Metres (9th) (1.0)

1. Michelle-Lee Ahye TTO	11.14
2. Christania Williams JAM	11.21
3. Gayon Evans JAM	11.22
4. Asha Philip ENG	11.28
5. Natasha Morrison JAM	11.31
6. Khalifa St. Fort TTO	11.37
7. Reyere Thomas TTO	11.51
8. Hor Halutie GHA-J	11.54

Philip was the fastest in the semis at 11.21, but Ahye was always in command in the final.

200 Metres (12th) (0.9)

1. Shaunae Miller-Uibo BAH	22.09*
2. Shericka Jackson JAM	22.18
3. Dina Asher-Smith ENG	22.29
4. Elaine Thompson JAM	22.30
5. Crystal Emmanuel CAN	22.70
6. Bianca Williams ENG	23.06
7. Semoy Hackett TTO	23.16
dq. Shashalee Forbes JAM	(22.59)

Emmanuel ran the fastest heat, 22.72, and Jackson the fastest semi, 22.28, but in the final Miller-Uibo ran a Games record 22.09 for a clear win over a top quality field. Thompson closed fast to nearly catch Asher-Smith who had led into the straight.

400 Metres (11th)

1. Amantle Montsho BOT	50.15
2. Anastasia Le-Roy JAM	50.57
3. Stephenie Ann McPherson JAM	50.93
4. Christine Botlogwetse BOT	51.17
5. Maximilia Imali KEN	51.32
6. Hima Das IND-J	51.32
7. Anneliese Rubie AUS	52.03
8. Yinka Ajayi NGR	52.26

The 2010 champion Montsho, who had tested positive at the 2014 Games, returned to regain her title at the age of 34, missing her Games record by just 0.05. McPherson had been fastest in the heats with 50.80 and won her semi in 51.21 but was surprisingly beaten for the silver by compatriot LeRoy, who was fastest in the semis at 51.08 and ran a pb 50.57 in the final. Das set Indian junior records at 51.53 (semi) and 51.32.

800 Metres (14th)

1. Caster Semenya RSA	1:56.68*
2. Margaret Wambui KEN	1:58.07
3. Natoya Goule JAM	1:58.82
4. Winnie Nanyondo UGA	2:00.36
5. Alexandra Bell ENG	2:00.83
6. Dorcus Ajok UGA	2:01.22
7. Emily Jerotich Tuei KEN	2:01.74
8. Eglay Nalyanya KEN	2:03.08

Semenya completed the middle distance double by leading all the way through 28.1, 58.66 and 1:38.9. She was also the one runner to beat 2 minutes with 1:59.26 in the heats from which the leading British runners, Shelayna Oskan-Clarke, Lynsey Sharp and Adelle Tracey failed to qualify.

1500 Metres (10th)

1. Caster Semenya RSA	4:00.71*
2. Beatrice Chepkoech KEN	4:03.09
3. Melissa Courtney WAL	4:03.44
4. Linden Hall AUS	4:03.67
5. Georgia Griffth AUS	4:04.17
6. Eilish McColgan SCO	4:04.30
7. Stephanie Twell SCO	4:05.56
8. Sarah McDonald ENG	4:05.77

Chepkoech led through 400m 63.82, 80m 2:10.81

and 1200m 3:16.33, before Semenya went ahead with 200m to go and powered away to a clear win. 14 women took part in the final as Zoe Buckman and Sarah McDonald were advanced as they were affected by Winny Chebet's fall in a heat.

5000 Metres (14th)

1, Hellen Obiri KEN	15:13.11
2. Margaret Kipkemboi KEN	15:15.28
3. Laura Weightman ENG	15:25.84
4. Juliet Chekwel UGA	15:30.17
5. Celia Sullohern AUS	15:34.73
6. Eilish McColgan SCO	15:34.88
7. Eva Chorono KEN	16:36.10
8. Eloise Wellings AUS	15:39.02

Obiri led the 19-woman field at 1000m reached in the very slow time of 3:22.30, then increased the tempo with kilometres of 3:00.1, 2:58.8 and 2:59.17. After a slim lead of one metre over Kipkemboi at the bell Obiri broke way to win by c.15m. Weightman took the bronze in only her second ever race at the distance.

10,000 Metres (9th)

1. Stella Chesang UGA	31:45.30
2. Stacy Ndiwa KEN	31:46.36
3. Mercyline Chelangat UGA	31:48.41
4. Beatrice Mutai KEN	31:49.81
5. Natasha Wodak CAN	31:50.18
6. Celia Sullohern AUS	31:50.75
7. Juliet Chekwel UGA	31:57.97
8. Madeline Hills AUS	32:01.04

As in the 5000m there were 19 runners and here too the pace was fairly slow, Ndiwa leading at halfway in 16:14.8. She still led with two laps to go by Chesang moved ahead to 3m at the bell and 7m at the finish. Seven runners set pbs, including a Northern Irish record 32:49.91 for Emma Mitchell in 15th place.

Marathon (15th)

1. Helalia Johannes NAM	2:32:40
2. Lisa Weightman AUS	2:33:23
3. Jessica Trengove AUS	2:34:09
4. Sheila Jerotich KEN	2:36:19
5. Sonia Samuels ENG	2:36:59
6. Alyson Dixon ENG	2:38:19
7. Lavinia Haitope NAM	2:40:54
8. Caryl Jones WAL	2:43:58

The halfway time in the hot conditions was a steady 77:31 and it wasn't until the 37th kilometre that the top four became three when Jerotich was dropped. Johannes moved away to lead by 19 secs at 40k and stretching that to 43 sec at the finish. There was only one non-finisher among the 17 starters in the race that started at 7:20am.

3000 Metres Steeplechase (11th)

1. Aisha Praught JAM	9:21.00
2. Celliphine Chespol KEN-J	9:22.61

3. Purity Kirui KEN	9:25.74
4. Rosie Clarke ENG	9:36.29
5. Genevieve LaCaze AUS	9:42.69
6. Fancy Cherono KEN-Y	9:46.27
7. Geneviève Lalonde CAN	9:46.68
8. Iona Lake ENG	9:58.92

US-born Praught switched to run for Jamaica in 2015 and here denied the Kenyans their usual steeplechase success. Chespol led at 2k in 6:17.67 and 2 seconds at the bell, but Praught's determined finish took her to an eventually clear win.

100 Metres Hurdles (13th) (0.2)

1. Tobi Amusan NGR	12.68
2. Danielle Williams JAM	12.78
3. Yanique Thompson JAM	12.97
4. Michelle Jenneke AUS	13.07
5. Brianna Beahan AUS	13.11
6. Tiffany Porter ENG	13.12
7. Megan Simmonds JAM	13.18
8. Alicia Barrett ENG	13.64

In the absence of the Games poster girl Sally Pearson, World champion Williams was fastest in the heats at 12.69, but was 0.09 slower than that in the final when she hit the first two hurdles and finished a metre behind Amusan.

400 Metres Hurdles (12th)

1. Janieve Russell JAM	54.33
2. Eilidh Doyle SCO	54.80
3. Wenda Nel RSA	54.96
4. Rhonda Whyte JAM	55.02
5. Sage Watson CAN	55.55
6. Glory Nathaniel NGR	56.39
7. Sparkle McKnight TTO	57.45
8. Ristananna Tracey JAM	57.50

The fastest time came from Russell with 54.01 in her heat and she won the final convincingly, if a little slower, from Doyle who ran 54.80 twice to gain her third CG silver medal.

High Jump (14th)

1. Lavern Spencer LCA	1.95
2. Morgan Lake ENG	1.93
3. Nicola McDermott AUS	1.91
4. Alyx Treasure CAN	1.91
5. Priscilla Frederick ANT	1.87
6. Cassie Purdon AUS	1.84
7. Nikki Manson SCO	1.84
8. Bethan Partridge ENG	1.84

After 12= in 2002, 5th in 2006, 3rd in 2010 and 2014, Spencer was at last crowned Commonwealth champion. She cleared 1.95 at her first attempt while Lake had one failure at that height and two at 1.97.

Pole Vault (13th)

1. Alysha Newman CAN	4.75*
2. Eliza McCartney NZL	4.70
3. Nina Kennedy AUS	4.60
4. Holly Bradshaw ENG	4.60
5. Molly Caudery ENG-J	4.40
6. Liz Parnov AUS	4.40
7= Lucy Bryan ENG	4.30
7= Anicka Newell CAN	4.30

Games records were set by Newman and McCartney on their first attempts at 4.65. Then McCartney went over on her second go at 4.70 while Newman failed twice but taking her final attempt at 4.75, she cleared and McCartney failed once at 4.75 and twice at 4.80 to leave the Canadian as champion. 18 year-old Caudery equalled the outdoor UK junior record.

Long Jump (12th)

1. Christabel Nettey CAN	6.84/0.2
2. Brooke Stratton AUS	6.77/0.6
3. Shara Proctor ENG	6.75/-0.1
4. Lorraine Ugen ENG	6.69/0.2
5. Chantel Malone IVB	6.48/-0.1
6. Nektaria Panagi CYP	6.44/-0.2
7. Jazmin Sawyers ENG	6.35/-0.7
8. Bianca Stuart BAH	6.30/0.2

The best jump of the event came in qualifying from Proctor's 6.89 (followed by Nettey 6.79 and Stratton 6.73) but Proctor struggled in the final, only managing 6.49 in the first three rounds before 6.75 in the fourth to take the bronze medal and passing the last two rounds due to a niggle. Nettey jumped 6.84 for her opener and that stood as the gold medal jump ahead of a good series by Stratton.

Triple Jump (10th)

1. Kimberly Williams JAM	14.64/0.7
2. Shanieka Ricketts JAM	14.52/1.0
3. Thea LaFond DMA	13.92/0.3
4. Lerato Sechele LES	13.57/0.6
5. Blessing Ibrahim NGR	13.48/0.4
6. Ayanna Alexander TTO	13.47/0.8
7. Joëlle Mbumi CMR	13.45/0.7
8. Natricia Hooper GUY	13.36/1.3

The two Jamaicans were far ahead of the best. Ricketts had four jumps over 14m, leading with her opening 14.52 from Williams 14.34 and 14.37 in rounds 2 and 4. Williams had a narrow (1cm) foul in round 5 that would have taken the lead, but she did so with her last jump of 14.64 to which Ricketts's reply was 14.51. LaFond's bronze was the first ever CG medal for Dominica and in fourth Sechele added 32cm to her Lesotho national record.

Shot (13th)

1. Danniel Thomas-Dodd JAM	19.36
2. Valerie Adams NZL	18.70
3. Brittany Crew CAN	18.32
4. Cleopatra Borel TTO	18.05
5. Sophie McKinna ENG	17.76
6. Rachel Wallader ENG	17.48
7. Jess St. John ANT	17.32
8. Taryn Suttie CAN	16.92

Adams, with three golds and a silver at previous Games, returned and was easily best in qualifying with 18.52. She started with 18.70 in the final followed by four more 18m plus throws, but Thomas-Dodd matched that 18.70 in round 2 and, when behind with an inferior second best, smashed her Jamaican record with 19.36 in the fifth round.

Discus (12th)

1. Dani Stevens AUS	68.26*	
2. Seema Punia IND	60.41	
3. Navjeet Kaur Dhillon IND	57.43	
4. Siositina Hakeai NZL	57.16	
5. Tanya Gollchewsky AUS	55.47	
6. Kimberley Mulhall AUS	54.93	
7. Jade Lally ENG	53.97	
8. Androniki Lada CYP	53.12	

The hottest of favourites Stevens showed her class with a series of 61.39, 64.51, 65.43, 68.26, 65.10, x . She retained her title while Punia won her fourth successive CG medal.

Hammer (10th)

1. Julia Ratcliffe NZL	69.94	
2. Alexandra Hulley AUS	68.20	
3. Lara Nielsen AUS	65.03	
4. Sultana Frizell CAN	63.94	
5. Queen Obisesan NGR	63.84	
6. Carys Parry WAL	61.58	
7. Tynelle Gumbs IVB	60.97	
8. Danielle McConnell AUS	59.60	

Ratcliffe took the lead with a 66.19 opener and then Hulley threw 68.20 and Ratcliffe 68.80 in the second round with Ratcliffe sealing victory with 69.94 in the fifth round. The major shock came with three no throws by both the multiple British record holder Sophie Hitchon and by the Canadian Jillian Weir (best of 72.50).

Javelin (11th)

1. Kathryn Mitchell AUS	68.92*	
2. Kelsey-Lee Roberts AUS	63.89	
3. Sunette Viljoen RSA	62.08	
4. Liz Gleadle CAN	59.85	
5. Dilhani Lekamge SRI	56.02	
6. Keichi Nwanaga NGR	53.17	
7. Jessica Rosun MRI	49.09	
8. Josephine Lalam UGA	48.92	

Mitchell was in superb form as her opening 68.92 was a Games record and was to remain the world's best of 2018. She also threw 68.14 in the fifth round. Roberts completed an Australia 1-2 and Viljoen added a bronze to her golds in 2006 and 2010 and silver in 2014.

Heptathlon (12th-13th)

1. Katarina Johnson-Thompson ENG	6255
2. Nina Schultz CAN	6133
3. Niamh Emerson ENG-J	6043
4. Celeste Mucci AUS-J	5915
5. Angela Whyte CAN	5898
6. Niki Oudenaarden CAN	5878
7. Purnima Hembram IND	5834
8. Katherine O'Connor NIR-J	5695

Johnson-Thompson recorded her first heptathlon victory since winning in Götzis in 2014. This came only six weeks after her pentathlon gold medal at the World Indoors and relatively little training during her recovery period, and she was competing injured for much of the contest, so that she was able to complete the seven events, most at well below her usual levels, was a relief. 19 year-old Schulz and 18 year-old Emerson both set pbs.

4 x 100 Metres Relay

1. ENG	42.46	Philip, Asher-Smith, B Williams, Ugen
2. JAM	42.52	C Williams, Morrison, Evans, Thompson
3. NGR	42.75	Udo-Gabriel, Okagbare, Amusan, Chukwuma
4. TTO	43.50	St. Fort, Hackett, Thomas, Selvon
5. GHA	43.64	6. CMR 45.24 dq. AUS –

Despite not having practised with the rest of the relay squad, Lorraine Ugen did well to withstand a tremendous final leg by Elaine Thompson for Jamaica to anchor England to victory.

4 x 400 Metres Relay (2nd)

1. JAM	3:24.00	Day 52.0, Le-Roy 50.9, J Russell 50.62, McPherson 50.45
2, NGR	3:25.29	P George 51.7, Nathaniel 52.0, Idamadudu 51.25, Ajayi 50.29
3. BOT	3:26.86	Moroko 53.3, Botlogetswe 50.9, Matlhaku 53.00, Montsho 49.59
4. ENG	3:27.21	Onuora 52.2, Agyapong 51.5, Shakes-Drayton 52.33, Diamond 51.07
5. AUS	3:27.43	7. IND 3:33.61
6. SCO	3:29.18	8. UGA 3:35.03

Annelise Rubie led with a 51.60 first leg for Australia, but then Anastasia LeRoy took Jamaica into a lead that they never lost. The fastest leg was 49.59 for Amantle Montsho, who passed Emily Diamond of England in the last few strides for the bronze. Eilidh Doyle took Scotland to a national record with a final leg in 51.03.

20 Kilometres Walk (8th)

1. Jemima Montag AUS	1:32:50
2. Alana Barber NZL	1:34:18
3. Bethan Davies WAL	1:36:08
4. Khushbir Kaur IND	1:39:21
5. Gemma Bridge ENG	1:39:31
6. Bekki Smith AUS	1:40:41
7. Heather Lewis WAL	1:41:45
8. Grace Njue KEN	1 42:23

Montag, in her third race at the distance, came in as a clear winner after her compatriot Claire Tallent was disqualified when leading with less than 3k to go.

CHAMPIONSHIPS 2018

28th IAAF World Race Walking Team Championships

At Taicang, China 5-6 May

Men – 20km (6 May)
1. Koki Ikeda JPN 1:21:13
2. Wang Kaihua CHN 1:21:22
3. Massimo Stano ITA 1:21:33
4. Toshikazu Yamanishi JPN 1:21:53
5. Brian Pintado ECU 1:22:21
6. Jin Xiangqian CHN 1:22:35
7. Isamu Fujisawa JPN 1:22:54
8. Álvaro Martín ESP 1:23:22
9. Francesco Furtunato JPN 1:23:31
10. Manuel Soto COL 1:23:34
11. Hagen Pohle GER 1:23:44
12. Eider Arévalo COL 1:23:46
13. Mauricio Arteaga ECU 1:23:49
14. Tom Bosworth GBR 1:23:54
15. Lebogang Shange RSA 1:23:56. **Teams**: 1. JPN 12, 2. ITA 29, 3. CHN 42, 4. ECU 47, 5. ESP 49, 6. GER 80, 7. MEX 110, 8. ГПА 124, 9. UIКЛ 125, 10. ЛOA 127, 11. РЕЛ 141, 12. POR 145, 13. AUS 172, 14. IND 184.

Men – 50km (5 May)
1. Hirooki Arai JPN 3:44:25
2. Hayato Katsuki JPN 3:44:31
3. Satoshi Maruo JPN 3:44:52
4. Maryan Zakalnytskyy UKR 3:44:59
5. Wang Qin CHN 3:45:29
6. Wang Rui CHN 3:48:01
7. Rafał Augustyn POL 3:48:22
8. Perseus Karlström SWE 3:48:54
9. Quentin Rew NZL 3:48:58
10. Ivan Banzeruk UKR 3:49:17
11. Rafal Sikora POL 3:49:54
12. Evan Dunfee CAN 3:50:18
13. Dmitriy Dyubin BLR 3:52:25
14. Michele Antonelli ITA 3:53:00
15. Valeriy Litanyuk UKR 3:53:05
49 of 59 finished
Teams: 1. JPN 6, 2. UKR 29, 3. POL 37, 4. CHN 37, 5. ESP 67, 6. GER 74, 7. ITA 76, 8. SWE 86.

Women – 20km (5 May)
1. María Guadalupe González MEX 1:26:38
2. Qieyang Shenjie CHN 1:27:06
3. Yang Jiayu CHN 1:27:22
4. Erica de Sena BRA 1:28:11
5. Eleonora Giorgi ITA 1:28:31
6. Anezka Drahotová CZE 1:28:40
7. María Pérez ESP 1:28:50
8. Kimberley García PER 1:28:56
9. Inna Kashyna UKR 1:28:58
10. Brigita Virbalyté-Dimsiené LTU 1:29:02
11. Nadiya Borovska UKR 1:29:28
12. Wang Na CHN 1:29:35
13. Wang Yingliu CHN 1:29:36
14. Laura García-Caro ESP 1:29:58
15. Sandra Lorena Arenas COL 1:30:11

79 of 84 finished
Teams: 11. CHN 17, 2. ITA 38, 3. ESP 40, 4. UKR 69, 5. COL 80, 6. LTU 85, 7. JPN 119, 8. FRA 134, 9. GER 134, 10. POR 135, 11. IND 136, 12. USA 150, 13. PER 151, 14. ROU 162, 15. KAZ 201.

Women – 50km (5 May)
1. Liang Rui CHN 4:04:36 WR
2. Yin Hang CHN 4:09:09
3. Claire Tallent AUS 4:09:33
4. Paola Pérez ECU 4:12:56
5. Ma Faying CHN 4:13:28
6. Johana Ordóñez ECU 4:14:28
7. Li Maocuo CHN 4:14:47
8. Julia Takacs ESP 4:16:37
9. Anastasiya Yatsevich BLR 4:18:00
10. Nadezhda Dorozhuk BLR 4:18:31
11. Magaly Bonilla ECU 4:19:04
12. Khrystyna Yudkina UKR 4:22:15
13. Vasylyna Vitovshchyk UKR 4:24:08
14. Mayra Carolina Herrera GUA 4:28:30
15. Alina Tsviliy UKR 4:28:49
29 of 32 finished
Teams: 1. CHN 8, 2. ECU 21, 3. UKR 40, 4. ESP 41. Prize money: Individual: 1st $30,000, 2nd $15,000, 3rd $10,000, 4th $7000, 5th $5000, 6th $3000, Team: 1st $15,000, 2nd $12,000, 3rd $9,000, 4th $7500, 5th $6000, 6th $3000, Total: $367,500.

Junior Men – 10km (6 May)
1. Zhang Yao CHN 40:07
2. Wang Zhaozhao CHN 40:12
3. José Eduardo Ortíz GUA 40:17
4. Sun Shuai CHN 40:24
5. Sho Sakazaki JPN 40:55
6. Yohanis Algaw ETH 40:56
45 of 48 finished
Teams: 1. CHN 3, 2. AUS 14, 3. JPN 24, 4. ESP 29, 5. BLR 30, 5. MEX 39, 7. ITA 39, 8. COL 40, 9. FRA 42, 10. ECU 53, 11. UKR 58, 12. TUR 69, 13. PER 73, 14. RSA 78.

Junior Women – 10km (4 May)
1. Alegna González MEX 45:08
2. Glenda Morejón ECU 45:13
3. Nanako Fujii JPN 45:29
4. Li Wenxiu CHN 45:51
5. Meryem Bekmez TUR 46:14
6. Ma Li CHN 46:49
37 of 42 finished
Teams: 1. CHN 10, 2. ECU 13, 3. TUR 15; 4, JPN 20; 5, PER 28; 6, ESP 31; 7, AUS 34; 8, POR 38; 9, UKR 57; 10, TPE 58; 11, USA 58; 12, FRA 50.

IAAF Hammer Challenge

Men: 1. Wojciech Nowicki POL 241.89, 2. Pawel Fajdek POL 240.04, 3. Bence Halász HUN 232.46, 4. Dilshod Nazarov TJK 230.55, 5. Marcel Lomnicky SVK 226.93, 6. Ashraf Amjad El Seify QAT 226.46, 7. Pavel Boreysha BLR 225.06, 8. Serghei Marghiev MDA 224.93, 9. Nick Miller GBR 221.69.
Women: 1. Anita Wlodarczyk POL (sixth successive win) 228.12, 2. Gwen Berry USA 223.31, 3. Joanna

Fiodorow POL 222.03, 4. Alexandra Tavernier 221.44,
5. Malwina Kopron POL 217.41, 6. Hanna Malyshik
BLR 216.74, 7. Wang Zheng CHN 215.37, 8. Hanna
Skydan AZE 213.46, 9. Réka Gyurátz HUN 211.82.
In 2019 there will be prize money for the top 12s.

IAAF Race Walking Challenge

*Prize money for the top eight scorers from $25,000 for
first place.*
Men: 1= Diego García ESP & Lebogang Shange RSA
27, 3. Andrés Chocho ECU 25, 4. Eider Arévalo COL
24, 5. Álvaro Martín ESP 18, 6. José Leyver Ojeda MEX
18, 7. Perseus Karlström SWE 17, 8. Mauricio Artega
ECU 17.
Women: 1. Qieyang Shenjie CHN 34, 2. Erica de Sena
BRA 23, 3. Inês Henriques POR 22, 4. Wang Lingliu
CHN 18, 5. Julia Takacs ESP 17, 6. Ana Cabecinha
POR 15, 7= Kimberley García PER & Antonella
Palmisano ITA 14.

World U20 (junior) Championships

at Tampere, Finland 10-15 July
Men
100m   1. Lalu Muhammad Zohri INA 10.18
(1.2)   2. Anthony Schwartz USA 10.22
         3. Eric Harrison USA 10.22
         4. Thembo Monareng RSA 10.23
         5. Dominic Ashwell GBR 10.25
         6. Henrik Larsson SWE 10.28
         7. Michael Stephens JAM 10.31
         8. Daisuke Miyamoto JPN 10.43
200m   1. Jona Efoloko GBR 20.48
(-0.1)   2. Charlie Dobson GBR 20.57
         3. Eric Harrison USA 20.79
         4. Pol Retamal ESP 20.85
         5. Zane Branco AUS 20.86

         6. Khance Meyers USA 20.87
         7. Milo Skupin-Alfa GER 21.07
         dnq. Henrik Larsson SWE
400m   1. Jonathan Sacoor BEL 45.03
         2. Christopher Taylor JAM 45.38
         3. Chantz Sawyers JAM 45.89
         4. Edoardo Scotti ITA 46.20
         5. Trey Fields USA 46.53
         6. Khamal Stewart-Baynes CAN 46.79
         7. Myles Misener-Daley CAN 47.03
         8. Jonathan Jones BAR 48.01
800m   1. Solomon Lekuta KEN 1:46.35
         2. Ngeno Kipngetich KEN 1:46.45
         3. Elliott Crestan BEL 1:47.27
         4. Adisu Girma ETH 1:47.58
         5. Simone Barontini ITA 1:51.08
         6. Alex Botterill GBR 1:51.64
         7. Markhim Lonsdale GBR 1:57.39
         dq (3), Oussama Cherrad ALG (1:47.10)
1500m   1. George Manangoi KEN 3:41.71
         2. Jakob Ingebrigtsen NOR 3:41.89
         3. Justus Soget KEN 3:42.14
         4. Jake Heyward GBR 3:43.76
         5. Samuel Tefera ETH 3:43.91
         6. Elzan Bibic SRB 3:44.65
         7. Oussama Cherad ALG 3:45.17
         8. Sondre Juven NOR 3:45.40
5000m   1. Edward Zakayo KEN 13:20.16
         2. Stanley Waithaka KEN 13:20.57
         3. Jakob Ingebrigtsen NOR 13:20.78
         4. Selemon Barega ETH 13:21.16
         5. Telahun Haile ETH 13:23.24
         6. Jacob Kiplimo UGA 13:23.35.
         7. Oscar Chelimo UGA-Y 14:00.68
         8. Elzan Bibic SRB 14:15.37
10,000m   1. Rhonex Kipruto KEN 27:21.08*
         2. Jacob Kiplimo UGA 27:40.36
         3. Berihu Aregawi ETH-Y 27:48.41

IAAF World Combined Events Challenge

Based on the sum of the best scores achieved in any three of the designated competitions during the year
Men Decathlon

1	Arthur Abele GER	25,222	8481 Ratingen	8431 Eur Ch	8310 Götzis
2	Pieter Braun NED	24,412	8342 Götzis	8105 Eur Ch	7965 Talence
3	Martin Roe NOR	24,374	8228 Firenze	8017 Götzis	8131 Eur Ch
4	Marcus Nilsson SWE	23.566	8120 Ratingen	7819 Eur Ch	7627 Talence
5	Vitaliy Zhuk BLR	23,470	8162 Götzis	8290 Eur Ch	7018 Talence
6	Pawel Wiesiolek POL	23,030	7650 Götzis	7696 Eur Ch	7684 Talence
7	Ilya Shkurenyov ANA/RUS	16,503	8182 Götzis	8321 Eur Ch	
8	Niklas Kaul GER	16,425	8205 Götzis	8220 Eur Ch	

Women Heptathlon

1	Carolin Schäfer GER	19,608	6549 Ratingen	6602 Eur Ch	6457 Talence
2	Erica Bougard USA	19,399	6327 Firenze	6725 Götzis	6347 USA Ch
3	Katerina Cachová CZE	19,025	6244 Götzis	6400 Eur Ch	6381 Talence
4	Verena Preiner AUT	18,778	6308 Götzis	6337 Eur Ch	6133 Talence
5	Esther Turpin FRA	18,221	6230 Götzis	6093 Eur Ch	5898 Talence
6	Alex Gochenour USA	18,177	6063 Firenze	6111 Götzis	6003 USA Ch
7	Allison Reaser USA	17,844	5799 Firenze	6144 Götzis	5901 USA Ch
8	Daryna Sloboda UKR	17,766	5804 Firenze	5999 Eurt Ch	5963 Talence

Prize Money: 1st $30,000, 2nd $20,000, 3rd $15,000, 4th $10,000, 5th $8000, 6th $7000, 7th $6000, 8th $5000.
For the first time ever in the series (initiated 1998) two athetes were in the prize money from just two
decathlons.

	4. Solomon Boit KEN 27:57.44
	5. Olika Adugna ETH 28:39.67
	6. Victor Kiplangat UGA 28:42.77
	7. Abraha Kokob ERI 28:59.32
	8. Robel Sibhatu ERI 29:44.59
3000mSt	1. Takele Nigate ETH 8:25.35
	2. Leonard Bett KEN 8:25.39
	3. Getnet Wale ETH 8:26.16
	4. Albert Chemutai UGA 8:28.63
	5. Takumi Yoshida JPN 8:50.99
	6. Giovanni Gatto ITA 8:52.09
	7. Mohamed El Rachdi MAR 8:57.21
	8. Tim Van Der Velde BEL 9:02.03
110mh	1. Damion Thomas JAM 13.16
(0.3)	2. Orlando Bennett JAM 13.33
99cm	3. Shunsuke Izumiya JPN 13.3
	4. Michael Obasuyi BEL 13.45
	5. Jason Nicholson GBR 13.62
	6. Cory Poole USA 13.74
	dnf. Anastas Eliopoulos CAN
	dnf. Enrique Llopis ESP
400mh	1. Zazini Sokwakhana RSA 49.42
	2. Bassem Hemeida QAT 49.59
	3. Alison dos Santos BRA 49.78
	4. Leonardo Ledgister JAM 49.93
	5. Malik James-King JAM 50.25
	6. Alastair Chalmers GBR 50.27
	7. Mehdi Pirjahan IRI 51.15
	8. Alessandro Sibilio ITA 52.38
HJ	1= Adónios Mérlos GRE 2.23
	1= Roberto Vilches MEX 2.23
	3= JuVaughan Blake USA 2.23
	3= Breyton Poole RSA 2.23
	5. Luca Meinke GER 2.21
	6. Nathan Ismar FRA 2.19
	7. Kyohei Tomori JPN 2.19
	8. Thomas Carmoy BEL 2.19
PV	1. Armand Duplantis SWE 5.82*
	2. Zachery Bradford USA 5.55
	3. Masiki Ejima JPN 5.55
	4. Bo Kanda Lita Baehre GER 5.50
	5. Thibaut Collet FRA 5.40
	6. Sondre Guttormsen NOR 5.40
	7. Cole Riddle USA 5.30
	8. Valco van Wyk RSA 5.30
LJ	1. Yuki Hashioka JPN 8.03/0.9
	2. Maykel Vidal CUB 7.99/0.9
	3. Wayne Pinnock JAM 7.90/-0.1
	4. Zhou Keqi CHN 7.85/1.5
	5. Yugo Sakai JPN 7.79/1.7
	6. Murali Sreeshankar IND 7.75/0.7
	7. Shakwon Cole JAM 7.73/0.8
	8. Andriy Avramenko UKR 7.63/0.1
TJ	1. Jordan Díaz CUB 17.15/-0.4*
	2. Martin Lamou FRA 16.18/-1.9
	3. Jonathan Seremes FRA 16.18/1.9
	4. Araymis Sargsyan ARM 15.89/1.1
	5. K Kamalraj IND 15.82/1.3
	6. Florin Visan ROU 15.72/1.9
	7. Lin Qinwei CHN 15.71/0.5
	8. Musyoka Mwema KEN 15.70/0.6
6kg SP	1. Kyle Blignaut RSA 22.07
	2. Adrian Piperi USA 22.06
	3. Odisséas Mouzenídis GRE 21.07
	4. Dmitriy Karpuk BLR 20.84,

	5, Oleg Tomashevich BLR 20.37
	6. Jordan West USA 19.86
	7. Aiden Harvey AUS 19.85
	8. Ryan Ballentyne NZL 19.39
1,75kg DT	1. Kai Chang JAM 62.36
	2. Yevgeniy Borgutskiy BLR 61.75
	3. Claudio Romero CHI 60.81
	4. Tim Ader GER 60.09
	5. Mouad Mohamed Ibrahim QAT 59.87
	6. Wang Yuhan CHN 59.29
	7. Georgios Koniarakis CYP 58.04
	8. Elijah Mason USA 57.96
6kg HT	1. Jake Norris GBR 80.65
	2. Mykhaylo Kokhan UKR-Y 79.68
	3. Mykhaylo Havryliuk UKR 77.71
	4. Ragnar Carlsson SWE 77.62
	5. HugoTavernier FRA 75.99
	6. Ashish Jakhar IND 74.59
	7. Donát Varga HUN 71.99
	8. Bayley Campbell GBR 71.28
JT	1. Nash Lowis AUS 75.31
	2. Tzuriel Pedigo USA 73.76
	3. Maurice Voigt GER 73.44
	4. Sahil Silwal IND 72.83
	5. Pedro Rodrigues BRA 72.44
	6. Teemu Narvi FIN 71.71
	7. Jakob Nauck GER 70.91
	8. Simon Wieland SUI 70.51
Jnr Dec	1. Ashley Moloney AUS 8190*
	2. Gary Haasbroek AUS 7798
	3. Simon Ehammer SUI 7642
	4. Manuel Wagner GER 7552
	5. Finley Gaio SUI 7455
	6. Leon Okafor AUT 7454
	7. Kyle Garland USA 7451
	8. Andrreas Bechmann GER 7333
4x100m	1. USA (Harrison, Schwartz, Kratz, M Williams) 38.88
	2. JAM (Nairne, C Taylor, Matherson, Stephens) 38.96
	3. GER (Ansah-Peprah, Schulte, Skupin-Alfa, Brandner) 39.22
	4. JPN 39.23 6. ESP 39.86
	5. CZE 39.75 7. TTO 39.8
	dnf. ITA
4x400m	1. ITA (Gjetja 47.1, Romano 45.6, Sibilio 46.06, Scotti 45.31) 3:04.05
	2. USA (Godwin 46.2, Ramey 48.6, Robinson 45.28, Fields 45.21) 3:05.26
	3. GBR (Haydock-Wilson 46.7, Brier 46.4, Chalmers 46.75, Knibbs 45.87) 3:05.64
	4. FRA (Saidy 47.4, Andant 46.1, Leblois 47.00, Mbaye 46.21) 3:05.65
	5. BEL 3:07.05 7. AUS 3:09.31
	6. GER 3:07.80 8. SRI 3:09.38
10,000W	1. Zhang Yao CHN 40:32.06
	2. David Hurtado ECU 40:32.06
	3. José Ortiz GUA 40:45.26
	4. Declan Tingay AUS 40:49.72
	5. Wang Zhaozhao CHN 41:04.22
	6. Kyle Swan AUS 41:24.12
	7. Dominic Ngingiti KEN 41:30.52
	8. Sho Sakazaki JPN 41:50.91

Women

100m
(0.0)
1. Briana Williams JAM 11.16
2. Twanisha Terry USA 11.10
3. Kristal Awuah GBR 11.37
4. Keshia Kwadwo GER 11.41
5. Magdalena Stefanowicz POL 11.47
6. Lorraine Martins BRA 11.48
7. Daija Lampkin USA 11.59
8. Gina Akpe-Moses IRL 11.64

200m
(-10.1
1. Briana Williams JAM 22.50*
2. Lauren Rain Williams USA 23.09
3. Martyna Kotwila POL 23.21
4. Polina Miller RUS/ANA 23.32
5. Sophia Junk GER 23.55
6. Corinna Schwab GER 23.55
7. Lorraine Martins BRA 23.91
dq. Jayla Kirkland USA

400m
1. Hima Das IND 51.46
2. Andrea Miklos ROU 52.07
3. Taylor Manson USA 52.28
4. Ella Connolly AUS 52.82
5. Mary Moraa KEN 52.94
6. Stacey-Ann Williams JAM 53.23
7. Elisabetta Vandi ITA 53.40
8. Ashlan Best CAN 53.59

800m
1. Diribe Welteji ETH 1:59.74*
2. Carley Thomas AUS 2:01.13
3. Delia Solubus SUI 2:01.29
4. Gabriela Gajanová SVK 2:01.90
5. Fireweyni Hailu ETH-Y 2:02.80
6. Ayaka Kawata JPN 2:03.57
7. Katy-Ann McDonald GBR 2:04.08
8. Jackline Wambui KEN 2:04.61

1500m
1. Alemaz Samuel ETH 4:09.67
2. Miriam Cherop KEN 4:10.73
3. Delia Sclabas SUI 4:11.98
4. Mariana Machado POR 4:14.93
5. Edina Jebitok KEN 4:15.17.
6. Dinke Firdisa ETH 4:17.42
7. Erin Wallace GBR 4:17.61
8. Katrina Robinson NZL 4:18.53

3000m
1. Nozomi Tanaka JPN 8:54.01
2. Meselu Kahsay ETH 8:56.39
3. Tsige Gebreselama ETH 8:59.20
4. Yuna Wada JPN 9:00.50
5. Zenah Yego KEN 9:00.76
6. Amelia Mazza-Downie AUS 9:09.19
7. Carla Gallardo ESP 9:10.07
8. Nadia Battocletti ITA 9:13.45

5000m
1. Beatrice Chebet KEN 15:30.77
2. Ejgayehu Taye ETH 15:30.87
3. Girmawit Gebrzihair ETH-Y 15:34.01
4. Sarah Chelangat KEN-Y 15:43.01
5. Helen Lobun KEN 15:45.07
6. Dolshi Tesfu ERI 15:52.84
7. Tomomi Musembi Takematsu JPN 56:55.74
8. Cailie Logue USA 15:56.00

3000mSt
1. Celliphine Chespol KEN 9:12.78*
2. Perith Chemutai UGA 9:18.87
3. Winfred Yavi BRN 9:23.47
4. Mercy Chepkurui KEN 9:43.65
5. Agrie Belachew ETH 9:44.79
6. Etalemahu Sintayehu ETH-Y 9:50.96
7. Alice Hill USA 9:57.04
8. Lisa Oed GER 9:57.45

100mh
(-1.0)
1. Tia Jones USA 13.01
2. Brittany Anderson JAM-Y 13.01
3. Cortney Jones USA 13.19
4. Sacha Alessandrini FRA 13.34
5. Sevval Ayaz TUR 13.46
6. Yu Jiaru CHN 13.58
7. Kendra Leger CAN 13.68
8. Cyrene Samba-Mayela FRA 14.11

400mh
1. Zeney van der Walt RSA 55.34
2. Shiann Salmon JAM 56.11
3. Yasmin Giger SUI 56.98
4. Sara Gallego ESP 57.11
5. Emma Zapletalová SVK 57.35
6. Natalia Wosztyl POL 58.17
7. Brooke Jaworski USA-Y 58.43
8. Xahria Santiago CAN 58.49

HJ
1. Karyna Taranda BLR 1.92
2. Sommer Lecky IRL 1.90
3. María Fernanda Murillo COL 1.90
4. Isis Guerra CUB 1.87
5. Mariya Kochanova RUS/ANA-Y 1.87
6. Urté Baikstyté LTU 1.87
7. Maja Nilsson SWE 1.87
8= Lavinja Jürgens GER 1.84
8= Martyna Lewandowska POL 1.84

PV
1. Amálie Svabíková CZE 4.51
2. Lina Gunnarsson SWE 4.35
3. Alice Moindrot FRA 4.35
4. Yelizavata Bondarenko RUS/ANA 4.35
5. Olivia McTaggart NZL 4.30
6. Niu Chunge CHN 4.25
7= Saga Andersson FIN 4.20
7= Julia Fixsen USA 4.20

LJ
1. Lea-Jasmin Riecke GER 6.51/0.4
2. Ayaka Kora JPN 6.37/1.2
3. Tara Davis USA 6.36/0.0
4. Gong Luying CHN 6.10/0.4
5. Petra Beáta Farkas HUN 6.16/0.2
6. Lucy Hadaway GBR 6.13/0.3
7. Klaudia Endrész HUN-J 6.08/0.6
8. Amanda Hansson SWE 6.03/1.1

TJ
1. Aleksandra Nacheva BUL-Y 14.18/1.6
2. Mireli Santos BRA 13.81/1.5
3. Davisleidis Velazco CUB 13.78/1.4
4. Eva Pepelnak SLO 13.68/1.0
5. Rüta Lasmane LAT 13.54/0.6
6. Georgiana Anitei ROU 13.46/1.8
7. Pan Youqi CHN 13.27/1.0
8. Esra Yilmaz TUR 13.24/-0.1

SP
1. Madison-Lee Wesche NZL 17.09
2. Zhang Linru CHN 17.05
3. Jorinde van Klinken NED 17.05
4. Selina Dantzler GER 16.16
5. Meike Strydom RSA 15.89
6. Lindsay Baker USA 15.67
7. Hanna Meinikmann GER 15.41
8. Sydney Giampietro ITA 15.19

DT
1. Alexandra Emilianova MDA 57.89
2. Helena Leveelahti FIN 56.80
3. Silinda Morales CUB 55.37
4. Amanda Ngandu-Ntumba FRA 53.22
5. Yin Yuanyuan CHN 52.21
6. Darya Harkusha UKR 50.71
7. Jorinde van Klinken NED 50.61
8. Maki Saito JPN 50.10

HT
1. Camryn Rogers CAN 64.90
2. Alyssa Wilson USA 64.45
3. Yaritza Martínez CUB 63.82
4. Huang Weilu CHN 62.63
5. Amanda Almendáris CUB 61.81
6. Jilliam Shippee USA 61.38
7. Katerina Skypalová CZE 61.37
8. Kiira Väänänen FIN 61.18

JT
1. Alina Shukh UKR 55.95
2. Tomoka Kuwazoe JPN 55.66
3. Dana Baker USA 55.04
4. Carolina Visca ITA 53.84
5. Sara Zabarino ITA 52.98
6. Dai Qianqian CHN 52.95
7. Elina Kinnunen FIN 52.50
8. Li Juei-Chun TPE 51.49

Hep
1. Niamh Emerson GBR 6253
2. Sarah Lagger AUT 6225
3. Adrianna Sulek POL 5939
4. Adriana Rodríguez CUB 5910
5. Celeste Mucci AUS 5865
6. Annik Kälin SUI 5664
7. Jade O'Dowda GBR 5660
8. Ida Eikeng NOR 5658

4x100m
1. GER (Dönicke, Schwab, Junk, Uphoff) 43.82 (ht: Kwadwo)
2. IRL (Scott, Akpe-Moses, Neville, Jumbo-Gula) 43.90 (ht: Adeleke)
3. GBR (Awuah, Rees, Adam, Carr) 44.05 (ht: M Edwards, Chinedu)
4. FRA 44.24   7. AUS 44.78
5. POL 44.61   8. ITA 44.81
6. SUI 44.65

4x400m
1. USA (Mason 51.4, Anderson 51.5, Madubuike 54.31, Manson 51.59) 3:28.74 (Ht: Ford, Minor)
2. AUS (Connolly 52.2, Jardine 53.5, Russell 54.27, Thomas 51.47) 3:31.36
3. JAM (Josephs 53.6, S-A Williams 52.9, Salmon 50.80, Taylor 54.64) 3:31.90 (ht: May)
4. CAN 3:31.93   7. DOM 3:34.09
5. GER 3:32.84   8. BRA 3:34.55
6. ITA 3:34.00

10,000W
1. Alegna González MEX 44:13.88
2. Meryem Bekmez TUR 44:17.69
3. Glenda Morejón ECU 44:19.40
4. Nanako Fujii JPN 45:08.68
5. Katie Hayward AUS 45:10.42
6. Shi Yuxia CHN 45:21.39
7. Rachelle de Orbeta PUR 45:23.05
8, Ayse Tekdal TUR 45:49.43

* *Games records. = national junior record.*

Medal table leaders

KEN	6	4	1	AUS	2	3	-
JAM	4	5	3	JPN	2	2	2
USA	3	8	7	GER	2	-	2
ETH	3	2	4	MEX	2	-	-
GBR	3	1	3	CUB	1	1	3
RSA	3	-	1				

25 nations won gold and 43 a medal of any colour.

IAAF Continental Cup

At Ostrava, Czech Republic, September 8-9
Prize Money: Individual: 1st $30,000; 2nd $15,000,

3rd $10,000, 4th $7000, 5th $5000, 6th $3000, 7th $2000, 8th $1000; Relay (for team): 1st $30,000; 2nd $20,000, 3rd $10,000, 4th $8000.
Note results here for field events are the traditional ones rather than the ones used for IAAF scoring.
TEAM: 1. Americas 262, 2. Europe 233, 3. Asia Pacific 188, 4. Africa 142

100m
(0.0)
1. Noah Lyles Am/USA 10.01
2. Su Bingtian A-P/CHN 10.03
3. Akani Simbine Afr/RSA 10.11
4. Jak Ali Harvey Eur/TUR 10.19
5. Arthur Gué Cissé Afr/CIV 10.23
6. Barakat Al Harthi A-P/OMA 10.29
7. Churandy Martina Eur/NED 10.36
8. Yohan Blake Am/JAM (injured) 11.99

200m
(-1.6)
1. Alonso Edward Am/PAN 20.19
2. Ramil Guliyev Eur/TUR 20.28
3. Alex Quinónez Am/ECU 20.36
4. Yuki Koike A-P/JPN 20.57
5. Churandy Martina Eur/NED 20.68
6. Ncincihti Titi Afr/RSA 20.78
7. Baboloki Thebe Afr/BOT 20.79
8. Joseph Millar A-P/NZL 21.68

400m
1. Abdelilah Haroun A-P/QAT 44.72
2. Baboloki Thebe Afr/BOT 45.10
3. Nathan Strother Am/USA 45.28
4. Matthew Hudson-Smith Eur/GBR 45.72
5. Y. Muhammed Anas A-P/IND 45.72
6. Luguelín Santos Am/DOM 45.81
7. Kevin Borlée Eur/BEL 46.26
dq. Thapelo Phora Afr/RSA

800m
1. Emmanuel Korir Afr/KEN 1:46.50
2. Clayton Murphy Am/USA 1:46.77
3. Nijel Amos Afr/BOT 1:46.77
4. Andreas Kramer Eur/SWE 1:47.03
5. Michal Rozmys Eur/POL 1:47.05
6. Jamal Al-Hayrani A-P/QAT 1:47.93
7. Jinson Johnson A-P/IND 1:48.44
8. Wesley Vázquez Am/PUR 1:49.60

1500m
1. Elijah Manangoi Afr/KEN 3:40.00
2. Marcin Lewandowski Eur/POL 3:40.42
3. Jakob Ingebrigtsen Eur/NOR-J 3:40.80
4. Charles Philibert-Thiboutot Am/CAN 3:40.90
5. Ryan Gregson A-P/AUS 3:40.91
6. Jinson Johnson A-P/IND 3:41.72
7. Drew Hunter Am/USA 3:43.95
8. Ronald Musagala Afr/UGA 3:43.95

3000m
1. Paul Chelimo Am/USA 7:57.13
2. Mohammed Ahmed Am/CAN 7:57.99
3. Henrik Ingebrigtsen Eur/NOR 7:58.85
4. Stewart McSweyn A-P/AUS 8:02.01
forced to abandon: Edward Zakayo Afr/KEN-Y, Marc Scott Eur/GBR, Getaneh Tamire Afr/ETH, Birhanu Yematew A-P/BRN

3000mSt
1. Conseslus Kipruto Afr/KEN 8:22.55
2. Matthew Hughes Am/CAN 8:29.70
3. Yohanes Chiappinelli Eur/ITA 8:32.89
4. Fernando Carro Eur/ESP 8:33.76
forced to abandon: Kosei Yamaguchi A-P/JPN, John Koech A-P/BRN, Soufiane El Bakkali Afr/MAR

110mh
(0.9)
1. Sergey Shubenkov Eur/RUS 13.03
2. Ronald Levy Am/JAM 13.12

Throughout this section
* indicates Championships or Games record]

        3. Pascal Martinot-Lagarde Eur/FRA 13.31
        4. Antonio Alkana Afr/RSA 13.36
        5. Devon Allen Am/USA 13.57
        6. Taio Kanai A-P/JPN 13.72
        7. Ahmad Al-Moualed A-P/KSA 13.83
        8. Oyeniyi Abejoye Afr/NGR 13.84

400mh
1. Abderrahmane Samba A-P/QAT 47.37*
2. Annsert Whyte Am/JAM 48.46
3. Karsten Warholm Eur/NOR 48.56
4. Yasmani Copello Eur/TUR 48.65
5. Abdelmalik Lahoulou Afr/ALG 49.12
6. Takatoshi Abe A-P/JPN 49.80
7. Cornel Fredericks Afr/RSA 50.54
8. Kyron McMaster Am/IVB 52.62

HJ
1. Donald Thomas Am/BAH 2.30
2. Brandon Starc A-P/AUS 2.30
3. Maksim Nedosekov Eur/BLR 2.27
4. Majed El Dein Ghazal A-P/SYR 2.24
5. Ilya Ivanyuk Eur/RUS 2.24
6. Bryan McBride Am/USA 2.20
7. Chris Moleya Afr/RSA 2.15
8. Mathew Sawe Afr/KEN 2.15

PV
1. Sam Kendricks Am/USA 5.85
2. Renaud Lavillenie Eur/FRA 5.80
3. Shawnacy Barber Am/CAN 5.65
4. Timur Morgunov Eur/RUS 5.65
5. Stephen Clough A-P/AUS 5.10
6. Valco van Wyk Afr/RSA 5.10
7. Mohamed A.H.Romdhana Afr/TUN 4.90

LJ
1. Ruswahl Samaai Afr/RSA 8.16/0.2
2. Militiádis Tentóglou Eur/GRE 8.00/-0.4
3. Jeffrey Henderson Am/USA 7.98/0.8
4. Henry Frayne A-P/AUS 7.96/-0.3
5. Wang Jianan A-P/CHN 7.95/0.2
6. Emiliano Lasa Am/URU 7.73/-0.6
7. Serhiy Nykyforov Eur/UKR 7.71/-0.9
8. Yahya Berrabah Afr/MAR 7.63/-1.0

TJ
1. Christian Taylor Am/USA 17.59/-1.9
2. Cristian Nápoles Am/CUB 17.07/0.4
3. Fabrice Zango Afr/BUR 17.02/-1.4
4. Arpinder Singh A-P/IND 16.59/1.0
5. Nelson Évora Eur/POR 16.58/-0.9
6. Ruslan Kurbanov A-P/UZB 16.34/-1.7
7. Khotso Mokoena Afr/RSA 16.25/1.5
8. Pablo Torrijos Eur/ESP 15.42/0.7

SP
1. Darian Romani Am/BRA 21.89
2. Ryan Crouser Am/USA 21.63
3. Tom Walsh A-P/NZL 21.43
4. Michal Haratyk Eur/POL 21.36
5. Tomás Stanek Eur/CZE 21.22
6. Chukwuebuka Enekwechi Afr/NGR 20.82
7. Mohamed Hamza Afr/EGY 19.45
8. Damien Birkinhead A-P/AUS 18.52

DT
1. Fedrick Dacres Am/JAM 67.97
2. Andrius Gudzius Eur/LTU 66.95
3. Daniel Ståhl Eur/SWE 64.84
4. Matt Denny A-P/AUS 63.99
5. Reggie Jagers Am/USA 63.49
6. Victor Hogan Afr/RSA 63.49
7. El Bachir Mbarki Afr/MAR 54.03
8. Joseph Millar A-P/NZL 27.15

HT
1. Dilshod Nazarov A-P/TJK 77.34
2. Diego Del Real Am/MEX 75.86
3. Bence Halász EUR/HUN 74.80
4. Mostafa Al- Gamal Afr/EGY 74.22

        5. Ashraf Amjad El-Seify A-P/QAT 74.08
        6. Wojciech Nowicki Eur/POL 71.74
        7. Tshepang Makhethe Afr/RSA 66.29
        nm. Sean Donnelly Am/USA;

JT
1. Thomas Röhler Eur/GER 87.07
2. Jakub Vadlejch Eur/CZE 84.76
3. Cheng Chao-Tsun A-P/TPE 83.28
4. Anderson Peters Am/GRN 80.86
5. Neeraj Chopra A-P/IND 80.24
6. Julius Yego AFR/KEN 78.41
7. Phil-Mar van Rensburg Afr/RSA 76.23
8. Arley Ibargüen Am/COL 71.08

4x100
1. Americas (Rodgers USA, Lyles USA, Blake JAM, Tracey JAM) 38.05
2. Europe (Barnes, Harvey, Hekimoglu, Guliyev TUR) 38.96
3. Asia-Pacific (Williams AUS, Millar NZL, Jin Su Jung AUS, Doran AUS) 39.55
dnf. Africa (Bruintjies, Magakwe, Erasmus, Simbine RSA)

Mixed
4x400m
1. Americas (C Taylor USA 46.97, L Santos DOM 44.96, McPherson JAM 50.59, Miller-Uibo BAH 50.49) 3:13.01
2. Africa (Botlogetswe BOT 52.68, Okezie NGR 46.95, Semenya RSA 49.63, Thebe BOT 46.93) 3:16.19
3. Asia-Pacific (Solomon 47.06, Goodwin 46.61, Rubie 52.71, Connolly all AUS 52.17) 3:18.55 OCE
dq. Europe (Hudson-Smith GBR 46.48, K Borlée BEL 44.93, de Witte NED 57.71, Swiety-Ersetic POL 51.16).

Seiko splits from Mark Butler

Women
100m
(-0.4)
1. Marie Joséc Ta Lou Afr/CIV 11.14
2. Dina Asher-Smith Eur/GBR 11.16
3. Jenna Prandini Am/USA 11.21
4. Dafne Schippers Eur/NED 11.23
5. Angela Tenorio Am/ECU 11.44
6. Wei Yongli A-P/CHN 11.51
7. Hajar Saad Al-Khaldi A-P/BRN 11.52
8. Janet Amponsah Afr/GHA 11.74

200m
(0.1)
1. Shaunae Miller-Uibo Am/BAH 22.16
2. Dafne Schippers Eur/NED 22.28
3. Marie Josée Ta Lou Afr/CIV 22.61
4. Shericka Jackson Am/JAM 22.62
5. Ofonime Odiong A-P/BRN 22.62
6. Ivet Lalova-Collio Eur/BUL 23.18
7. Germaine Bivina Afr/CMR 24.08
8. Viktoriya Zyabkina A-P/KAZ 24.34

400m
1. Salwa Eid Naser A-P/BRN 49.32
2. Caster Semenya Afr/RSA 49.62
3. Stephanie Ann McPherson Am/JAM 50.82
4. Lisanne de Witte Eur/NED 51.51
5. Shakima Wimbley Am/USA 51.59
6. Justyna Swiety-Ersetic Eur/POL 51.64
7. Christine Botlogetswe Afr/BOT 52.47
8. Anneliese Rubie A-P/AUS 52.50

800m
1. Caster Semenya Afr/RSA 1:54.77
2. Ajee' Wilson Am/USA 1:57.16
3. Natoya Goule Am/JAM 1:57.36
4. Nataliya Pryshchepa Eur/UKR 1:59.58
5. Angie Petty A-P/NZL 2:01.26
6. Anna Sabat Eur/POL 2:04.43

7. Besu Sado Afr/ETH 2:08.59
8. Brittany McGowan A-P/AUS 2:10.63
1500   1. Winny Chebet Afr/KEN 4:16.01
2. Shelby Houlihan Am/USA 4:16.36
3. Rabab Arrafi Afr/MAR 4:17.19
4. Unnikrishnan Chitra A-P/IND 4:18.45
5. Linden Hall A-P/AUS 4:18.82
6. Simona Vrzalová Eur/CZE 4:19.46
7. Sofia Ennaoui Eur/POL 4:22.56
8. Angelín Figueroa Am/PUR 4:33.88
3000   1. Sifan Hassan Eur/NED 8:27.50*
2. Senbere Teferi Afr/ETH 8:32.49
3. Hellen Obiri Afr/KEN 8:36.20
4. Konstanze Klosterhalfen Eur/GER
8:38.04
forced to abandon: Genevieve LaCaze A-P/AUS,
Nozomi Tanaka A-P/JPN, Lauren Paquette Am/USA,
Muriel Coneo Am/COL
3000mSt   1. Baatrice Chepkoech Afr/KEN 9:07.92*
2. Courtney Frerichs Am/USA 9:15.22
3. Winfred Yavi A-P/BRN 9:17.86
4. Anna Emilie Møller Eur/DEN 9:42.57
forced to abandon: Aisha Praught Am/JAM, Ophélie
Claude-Boxberger Eur/FRA, Sudha Singh A-P/IND,
dq. Woynshet Ansa Afr/ETH
100mh   1. Danielle Williams Am/JAM 12.49
(-0.1)   2. Kendra Harrison Am/USA 12.52
3. Pamela Dutkiewicz Eur/GER 12.82
4. Elvita German Eur/BLR 12.91
5. Tobi Amusan Afr/NGR 12.96
6. Ayako Kimura A-P/JPN 13.39
7. Marythe Koala Afr/BUR 13.42
8. Michelle Jenneke A-P/AUS 13.50
400mh   1. Janieve Russell Am/JAM 53.62
2. Shamier Little Am/USA 53.86
3. Anna Ryzhykova Eur/UKR 54.47
4. Meghan Beesley Eur/GBR 55.58
5. Aminat Odeyemi A-P/BRN 55.65
6. Wenda Nel Afr/RSA 56.54
7. Lamiae Lhabz Afr/MAR 57.35
8. Eri Utsunomiya A-P/JPN 58.92
HJ   1. Mariya Lasitskene Eur/RUS 2.00
2. Svetlana Radzivil A-P/UZB 1.95
3. Levern Spencer Am/LCA 1.93
4. Marie-Laurence Jungfleisch Eur/GER 1.91
5. Nicola McDermott A-P/AUS 1.87
6. Inika McPherson Am/USA 1.82
7. Erika Seyama Afr/SWZ 1.77
8. Hoda Hagras Afr/EGY 1.72
PV   1. Anzhelika Sidorova Eur/RUS 4.85*
2. Ekateríni Stefanídi Eur/GRE 4.85*
3. Sandi Morris Am/USA 4.85*
4. Yarisley Silva Am/CUB 4.55
5. Lisa Campbell A-P/AUS 4.00
6. Dorra Mahfoudhi Afr/TUN 4.00
7. Dina Al-Tabaa Afr/EGY 3.80
LJ   1. Caterine Ibargüen Am/COL 6.93/0.8
2. Malaika Mihambo Eur/GER 6.86/0.1
3. Brooke Stratton A-P/AUS 6.71/0.8
4. Shara Proctor Eur/GBR 6.63/-0.6
5. Ese Brume Afr/NGR 6.61/-0.9
6. Marthe Koala Afr/BUR 6.60/0.5
7. Christabel Nettey Am/CAN 6.31/1.0
8. Xu Xiaoling A-P/CHN 6.17/1.5
TJ   1. Caterine Ibargüen Am/COL 14.76/-0.9

2. Tori Franklin Am/USA 14.27/0.3
3. Olga Rypakova A-P/KAZ 14.26/0.2
4. Paraskévi Papahristóu Eur/GRE
14.22/0.0
5. Kristin Gierisch Eur/GER 13.96/-0.1
6. Parinya Chuaimaroeng A-P/THA
13.53/-0.4
7. Zinzi Chabangu Afr/RSA 12.89
8. Odile Ahouanwanou Afr/BEN 11.29/-1.3
SP   1. Raven Saunders Am/USA 19.74
2. Christina Schwanitz Eur/GER 19.73
3. Gong Lijiao A-P/CHN 19.63
4. Paulina Guba Eur/POL 18.94
5. Ischke Senekal Afr/RSA 17.10
6. Danniel Thomas-Dodd Am/JAM 16.96
7. Noora Salem Jassem A-P/BRN 16.01
8. Jessica Inchude Afr/GBS 14.51
DT   1. Sandra Perkovic Eur/CRO 68.44
2. Yaimé Pérez Am/CUB 65.30
3. Chen Yang A-P/CHN 63.34
4. Dani Stevens A-P/AUS 62.74
5. Andressa de Morais Am/BRA 58.44
6. Nadine Müller Eur/GER 58.34
7. Chioma Onyekwere Afr/NGR 56.68
8. Ischke Senekal Afr/RSA 50.21
HT   1. DeAnna Price Am/USA 75.46*
2. Anna Wlodarczyk Eur/POL 73.45
3. Alexandra Tavernier Eur/FRA 70.40
4. Jenny Dahlgren Am/ARG 68.59
5. Luo Na A-P/CHN 67.39
6. Alex Hulley A-P/AUS 62.35
7. Temi Ogunrinde Afr/NGR 59.15
8. Soukana Zakkour Afr/MAR 58.09
JT   1. Lu Huihui A-P/CHN 63.88
2. Christin Hussong Eur/GER 62.96
3. Kara Winger Am/USA 60.38
4. Laila Domingos Am/BRA 60.07
5. Kelsey-Lee Roberts A-P/AUS 59.32
6. Nikola Ogrodniková Eur/CZE 56.61
7. Jo-Ané van Dyk Afr/RSA 52.69
8. Kelechi Nwanaga Afr/NGR 51.97
4x100   1. Americas (Tenorio ECU, Miller-Uibo
BAH, Prandini USA, Rosa BRA) 42.11
2. Europe (Awuah J, Lansiquot,
B Williams, Asher-Smith all GBR) 42.55
3. Asia-Pacific (Liang Xiaojing, Wei Yongli,
Ge Manqi, Yuan Qiqi all CHN) 42.93
dq. Africa (Amponsah GHA, Okagbare
NGR, Amusan NGR, Ta Lou CIV)

Youth Olympic Games

At Buenos Aires, Arengtina 11-16 October 2018
Note, medallists were determined by combining two
results. The performance given here is the best result
of the winner.
2000m steeplechase, 1500m and 3000m races were
combined with cross country – the gold medallist is
marked with *.
Men: 100m: Luke Davids RSA 10.15w, **200m:** Abdelaziz
Mohamed QAT 20.68, **400m:** Luis Aviles MEX 46.78,
800m: Tasew Yada ETH 1:49.38, **1500m:** Melese
Nberet ETH 3:52.95, 4k **XC** : *Jean de Dieu Butoyi BDI
11:31, **3000m:** Oscar Chelimo UGA 8:08.20, 4k**XC:**
*Jackson Muema KEN   11:12, **2000mSt:** Abrham
Sime ETH 5:34.94, **110mh:** Owaab Barrow QAT 13.17,

400mh: Haruto Deguchi JPN 51.28, **HJ:** Chen Long CHN 2.22, **PV:** Baptiste Thiery FRA 5.32, **LJ:** Lester Lescay CUB 7.89w, **TJ:** Jordan Díaz CUB 17.14, 5kg**SP:** Nazareno Sasia ARG 21.94, 1.5kg**DT:** Connor Bell NZL 66.84, 5kg**HT:** Myhaylo Kokhan UKR 85.97, 700g**JT:** Topias Laine FIN 78.85, **5000mW:** Oscar Patín ECU 20:13.69. **Women: 100m:** Rosemary Chukuma NGR 11.17w, **200m:** Gudbjörg Bjarnadóttir ISL 23.47, **400m:** Barbora Malíková CZE 54.18, **800m:** Keely Small AUS 2:04.76, **1500m:** Edinah Jebitok KEN 4:16.68, **3000m/4k CC:** Sarah Chelangat KEN 9:11.63/12:32, **2000mSt:** Fancy Cherono KEN 6:26.08, **100mh:** Grace Stark USA 12.83w, **400mh:** Valeria Cabezas COL 58.39, **HJ:** Yaroslava Mahuchikh UKR 1.95, **PV:** Leni Wildgrube GER 4.17, **LJ:** Maité Beernaert BEL 6.31w, **TJ:** Aleksandra Nacheva BUL 13.86, 3kg**SP:** Li Xinhui CHN 18.42, **DT:** Melany Matheus CUB 54.95, 3kg**HT:** Valeriya Ivanenko UKR 74.90, 500g**JT:** Elina Tzénggo GRE 63.34, **5000mW:** Xi Ricuo CHN 22:23.26.

African Championships

At Asaba, Nigeria 1-5 August

100m	1. Akani Simbine RSA 10.25	
(-2.1)	2. Arthur Gue Cissé CIV 10.33	
	3. Simon Magakwe RSA 10.35	
200m	1. Ncincihli Titi RSA 20.46	
	2. Divine Oduduru NGR 20.60	
	3. Luxolo Adams RSA 20.60	
400m	1. Baboloki Thebe BOT 44.81	
	2. Thapelo Phora RSA 45.14	
	3. Chidi Okezie NGR 45.65	
800m	1. Nijel Amos BOT 1:45.20	
	2. Emmanuel Korir KEN 1:45.65	
	3. Mostafa Smaïïi MAR 1:45.90	
1500m	1. Elijah Manangoi KEN 3:35.20*	
	2. Timothy Cheruiyot KEN 3.35.94	
	3. Ronald Musagala UGA 3:36.41	
5000m	1. Edward Zakayo KEN-J 13:48.58	
	2. Getaneh Tamire ETH 13:49.06	
	3. Yemane Haileslassie ETH 13:49.58	
10,000m	1. Jemal Yimer ETH 29:08.01	
	2. Andamlak Belihu ETH 29:11.09	
	3. Timothy Toroitich UGA 29:11.88	
3000mSt	1. Conselus Kipruto KEN 8:26.38	
	2. Soufiane El Bakkali MAR 8:28.01	
	3. Getnet Wale ETH 8:30.87	
110mh	1. Antonio Alkana RSA 13.51	
(-0.9)	2. Abejoye Abejoye NGR 13.87	
	3. Wellington Zaza LBR 13.88	
400mh	1. Abdelmalik Lahoulou ALG 48.47	
	2. Cornel Fredericks RSA 49.40	
	3. Zied Azizi TUN 49.48	
HJ	1, Matthew Sawe KEN 2.30	
	2. Chris Moleya RSA 2.26	
	3. Mpho Links RSA 2.15	
PV	1. Mohamed Amine Romdhana TUN 5.20	
	2. Valco van Wyk RSA 5.10	
	3. Mejdi Chehata TUN 5.10	
LJ	1. Ruswahl Samaai RSA 8.45*/-1.2	
	2. Luvo Manyonga RSA 8.43/1.2	
	3. Yahya Berrabeh MAR 8.14w/2.3	
TJ	1. Fabrice Zango BUR 17.11/0.0	
	2. Khotso Mokoena RSA 16.83/0.8	
	3. Yasser Triki ALG 16.78/1.1	
SP	1. Chukwuebuka Enekwechi NGR 21.08*	

	2. Hamza Mohamed EGY 19.33	
	3. Kyle Blignaut RSA-J 19.05	
DT	1. Victor Hogan RSA 60.06	
	2. Werner Visser RSA 58.22	
	3. El Bachir Mbarki MAR 54.97	
HT	1. Mostafa El Gamal EGY 73.50	
	2. Islam Mohamed EGY 70.32	
	3. Hassan Mahmoud EGY 69.90	
JT	1. Julius Yego KEN 77.34	
	2. Phil-Mar van Rensburg RSA 76.57	
	3. Samuel Adams NGR 75.69	
Dec	1. Larbi Bouraada ALG 8099	
	2. Friedrich Pretorius RSA 7730	
	3. Samuel Osadolor NGR 7095	
4x100m	1. RSA (Simbine, Magakwe, Erasmus, Bruintjies) 38.25*	
	2. NGR (Ogho-Oghene, Oduduro, Arowolo, Ogunlewe) 38.74	
	3. CIV 38.92	
4x400m	1. KEN (Momanyi, Kishoyan, H Koech, E Korir) 3:00.92*	
	2. RSA 3:03.50	
	3. NGR 3:04.88	
20kmW	1. Samuel Gathimba KEN 1:25:14	
	2= Lebogang Shange RSA 1:25:25	
	2= Hassanine Sbaï TUN 1:25:25	
W 100m	1. Marie Josée Ta Lou CIV 11.15	
(-2.3)	2. Janet Amponsah GHA 11.54	
	3. Joy Udo-Gabriel NGR 11.58	
200m	1. Marie Josée Ta Lou CIV 22.50	
(0.1)	2. Germaine Bivina CMR 23.36	
	3. Janet Amponsah GHA 23.38	
400m	1. Caster Semenya RSA 49.96	
	2. Christine Botlogetswe BOT 51.19	
	3. Yinka Ajayi NGR 51.34	
800m	1. Caster Semenya RSA 1:56.06*	
	2. Francine Niyonsaba BDI 1:57.97	
	3. Habitam Alemu ETH 1:58.86	
1500m	1. Winny Chebet KEN 4:14.02	
	2. Rabab Arrafi MAR 4:14.12	
	3. Malika Akkaoui MAR 4:14.17	
5000m	1. Hellen Obiri KEN 15:47.18	
	2. Senbere Teferi ETH 15:54.48	
	3. Meskerem Mamo ETH 15:57.38	
10,000m	1. Stacy Ndiwa KEN 31:31.17	
	2. Alice Aprot Nawawuma KEN 31:36.12	
	3. Gete Alemayehu ETH 32:10.68	
3000mSt	1. Beatrice Chepkoech KEN 8:59.88*	
	2. Celliphine Chespol KEN 9:09.61	
	3. Fancy Cherono KEN-Y 9:23.92	
100mh	1. Tobi Amusan NGR 12.86	
(-1.4)	2. Rikenette Steenkamp RSA 13.18	
	3. Rosvitha Okou CIV 13.39	
400mh	1. Glory Nathaniel NGR 55.43	
	2. Lamiae Lhabze MAR 56.66	
	3. Wena Nel RSA 57.04	
HJ	1. Erika Seyama SWZ 1.80	
	2. Hoda Hagras EGY 1.80	
	3. Ariyat Dibow ETH 1.80	
PV	1. Dora Mahfoudhi TUN 4.10	
	2. Dina Ahmed Al-Tabaa EGY 4.05	
	3. Nesrine Brinsi TUN 3.90	
LJ	1. Ese Brume NGR 6.83/0.5	
	2. Marthe Koala BUR 6.54w/2.6	
	3. Linque Beneke RSA 6.38/1.7	

TJ	1. Grace Anigbata NGR 14.02/0.2
	2. Zinzi Chanbangu RSA 13.59/ 0.1
	3. Lerato Schele LES 13.31/-0.2
SP	1. Ischke Senekal RSA 17.24
	2. Jessica Inchude GBS 16.76
	3. Meike Strydom RSA 15.99
DT	1. Chioma Onyekwere NGR 58.09
	2. Chinwe Okoro NGR 57.37
	3. Ischke Senekal RSA 53.82
HT	1. Soukana Zakour MAR 68.28
	2. Temi Ogunrinde NGR 67.39
	3. Jennifer Batu CGO 66.43
JT	1. Kelechi Nwanganga NGR 56.96
	2. Jo-Ané van Dyk RSA 53.72
	3. Jospehione Lalam UGA 51.33
Hep	1. Odile Ahouanwanou BEN 5999
	2. Marthe Koala BUR 5967
	3. Hoda Hagras EGY 4646
4x100m	1. NGR (Chukwuma, Udo-Gabriel, Amusan, Okagbare) 43.77
	2. CIV 44.40
	3. KEN 45.58
4x400m	1. NGR (Okon George, Ajayi, Abugan, Egbeniyi) 3:31.17
	2. KEN 3:35.45
	3. ZAM 3:38.18
20kmW	1. Yehualeye Belelew ETH 1:31:46
	2. Grace Njue KEN 1:35:54
	3. Chahineze Nasri TUN 1:37:28

African Youth Games

At Algiers, Algeria 24-27 July
Men: 100m: Luke Davids RSA 10.34w, **200m:** Sulayman Touray GAM 20.97, **400m:** Kennedy Luchembe ZAM 46.21, **800m:** Leshoo Pesi KEN 1:50.72, **1500m:** Nickson Pariken KEN 3:49.64, **3000m:** Berihew Aregawi ERI 7:50.98, **2000mSt:** Abraham Sime ETH 5:39.05, **110mh** 91.4cm: Abderrazak Mouzdahir MAR 13.77, **400mh** 84cm: Lindokuhle Gora RSA 52.18, **HJ:** Bilel Afer ALG 2/06, **PV:** Nikolai van Huysteen RSA 4.70, **LJ:** Jason Tito RSA 7.53w, **TJ:** Meyiwa Ineh NGR 16.22, **SP** 5kg: Mohamed Salem EGY 18.39, **DT** 1.5kg: Francois Prinsloo RSA 60.55; **HT** 5kg: Mohamed Mahmoud EGY 69.49, **JT** 700g: Jano Estherhuizen RSA 72.82, **10000mW:** Saïd Khoufache ALG 49:05.11; **Women: 100m/200m:** Rosemary Chukwama NGR 11.53/23.45, **400m:** Favour Ofili NGR 53.57, **800m:** Hirut Meshesha ETH 2:04.66, **1500m:** Hailu Lemlem ETH 4:36.71. **3000m:** Aberash Minsewo ETH 9:29.02, **2000mSt:** Fancy Cherono KEN 6:17.68, **100mh** 76.2cm: Kyala van der Bergh RSA 13.48w, **400mh/TJ:** Gontse Morake RSA 60.30/12.57, **HJ:** Bianca Erasnus RSA 1.67 **PV:** Imen Rhouma TUN 3.50, **LJ:** Victory George NGR 5.62w, **SP** 3kg: Dané Roets RSA 15.97, **DT:** Rana Ahmed EGY 44.99, **HT** 3kg: Rawan Ayman Ibrahim EGY 69.16, **JT** 500g: Martha Musai KEN 54.12, **5000mW:** Marissa Swanepoel RSA 26:06.50. **Medal table leaders:** RSA 12G-11S-3B, NGR 5-3-5, ETH 5-2-2, KEN 4-3-4.

Asian Games

At Jakarta, Indonesia 25-30 August
Men

100m	1. Su Bingtian CHN 9.92*	
(0.8)	2. Tosin Ogunode QAT 10.00	
	3. Ryota Yamagata JPN 10.00	
200m	1. Yuki Koike JPN 20.23	
(0.7)	2. Yang Chun-Han TPE 20.23	
	3. Mohamed Yacoob BRN 20.55	
400m	1. Abdelilah Haroun QAT 44.89	
	2. Muhammed Anas IND 45.69	
	3. Abdulrahman Khamis Abbas BRN 45.70	
800m	1. Manjit Singh IND 1:46.15	
	2. Jinson Johnson IND 1:46.35	
	3. Abubaker Haydar Abdallah QAT 1:46.38	
1500m	1. Jinson Johnson IND 3:44.72	
	2. Amir Moradi IRI 3:45.62	
	3. Mohammed Tiouali BRN 3:45.88	
5000m	1. Birhanu Balew Yemataw BRN 13:43.17	
	2. Albert Rop BRN 13:45.76	
	3. Tariq Ahmed Al-Amri KSA 13:56.49	
10,000m	1. Hassan Chani BRN 28:35.54	
	2. Abraham Cheroben BRN 29:00.29	
	3. Zhao Changhong CHN 30:07.49	
Mar	1. Hiroto Inoue JPN 2:18:22	
	2. El Hassan El Abbassi BRN 2:18:22	
	3. Duo Buije JPN 2:18:48	
3000mSt	1. Hossein Keyhani IRI 8:22.79*	
	2. Yasser Salem Bagharab QAT 8:28.21	
	3. Kazuya Shiori JPN 8:29.42	
110mh	1. Xie Wenjun CHN 13.34	
(0.0)	2. Chen Kuei-Ru TPE 13.39	
	3. Shunya Takayama JPN 13.48	
400mh	1. Abderrahman Samba QAT 47.66*	
	2. Ayyasamy Dharun IND 48.96	
	3. Takatoshi Abe JPN 49.12	
HJ	1. Wang Yu CHN 2.30	
	2. Woo Sang-hyuk KOR 2.28	
	3= Majed El Dein SYR 2.24	
	3= Naoto Tobe JPN 2.24	
PV	1. Seito Yamamoto JPN 5.70*	
	2. Yao Jie CHN 5.50	
	3. Patsapong Umsam-Ang THA 5.50	
LJ	1. Wang Jianan CHN 8.24/0.7*	
	2. Zhang Yaoguang CHN 8.15/0.0	
	3. Sapwaturrahman INA 8.09/0.0	
TJ	1. Arpinder Singh IND 16.77/0.0	
	2. Ruslan Kurbanov UZB 16.62/0.0	
	3. Cao Shuo CHN 16.56/0.3	
SP	1. Tajinder Pal Singh IND 20.75*	
	2. Liu Yang CHN 19.52	
	3. Ivan Ivanov KAZ 19.40	
DT	1. Ehsan Hadadi IRI 65.71	
	2. Mustafa Kadhem Dagher IRQ 60.09	
	3. Essa M Al-Zankawi KUW 59.44	
HT	1. Ashraf Amjad El-Seify QAT 76.88	
	2. Dilshod Nazarov TJK 74.16	
	3. Sukhrob Khodjayev UZB 74.06	
JT	1. Neeraj Chopra IND 88.06	
	2. Liu Qizhen CHN 82.22	
	3. Arshad Nadeem PAK 80.75	
Dec	1. Keisuke Ushiro JPN 7878	
	2. Suttisak Singkhon THA 7809	
	3. Akihiko Nakamura JPN 7738	
4x100m	1. JPN (Yamagata, Tada, Kiryu, Cambridge) 38.16	
	2. INA 38.77	
	3. CHN 38.89	

4x400m	1. QAT (Samba 44.6, M Abbas 45.2, M Mohamed 46.43, Haroun 44.41) 3:00.56*
	2. IND (P K Muhammed 46.1, Dharun 45.7, Anas 45.7, Rajiv 44.4) 3:01.85
	3. JPN (Walsh 45.5, Koike 46.1, Abe 46.0, Iizuka 44.3) 3:01.94
20kW	1. Wang Kaihua CHN 1:22:04
	2. Toshikazu Yamanishi JPN 1:22:10
	3. Jin Xiangqian CHN 1:25:41
50kW	1. Hayato Katsuki JPN 4:03:30
	2. Wang Qin CHN 4:06:48
	3. Joo Hyun-myeong KOR 4:10:21
Women	
100m	1. Edidiong Odiong BRN 11.30
(0.3)	2. Dutee Chand IND 11.32
	3. Wei Yongli CHN 11.33
200m	1. Edidiong Odiong BRN 22.96
(-0.7)	2. Dutee Chand IND 23.20
	3. Wei Yongli CHN 23.27
400m	1. Salwa Naser BRN 50.09*
	2. Hima Das IND 50.79
	3. Elina Mikhina KAZ 52.63
800m	1. Wang Chunyu CHN 2:01.80
	2. Margarita Mukasheva KAZ 2:02.40
	3. Manal El Bahraoui BRN 2:02.69
1500m	1. Kalkidan Gezahegne BRN 4:07.88
	2. Tigist Gashaw BRN 4:09.12
	3. Unnikrishnan Chitra IND 4:12.56
5000m	1. Kalkidan Gezahegne BRN 15:08.08
	2. Darya Maslova KGZ 15:30.57
	3. Bontu Edao BRN 15:36.78
10,000m	1. Darya Maslova KGZ 32:07.23
	2. Eunice Chumba BRN 32:11.12
	3. Zhang Deshun CHN 32:12.78
Mar	1. Rose Chelimo BRN 2:34:51
	2. Keiko Nogami JPN 2:36:27
	3. Choi Kyung-sun KOR 2:37:49
	drugs dq (3) Kim Hye-song PRK 2:37:20
3000mSt	1. Winfred Yavi BRN-J 9:36.52
	2. Sudha Singh IND 9:40.03
	3. Nguyen Thi Qanh VIE 9:43.83
100mh	1. Jung Hye-lim KOR 13.20
(0.2)	2. Rilia Nova INA 13.33
	3. Lui Lai Yiu HKG 13.42
400mh	1. Kemi Adekoya BRN 54.48*
	2. Quach Thi Lan VIE 55.30
	3. Aminat Odeyemi BRN 55.65
HJ	1. Svetlana Radzivil UZB 1.90*
	2. Nadiya Dusanova UZB 1.94
	3. Nadezhda Dubovitskaya KAZ 1.84
PV	1. Li Ling CHN 4.60*
	2. Chayanisa Chomchuendee THA 4.30
	3. Lim Eun-ji KOR 4.20
LJ	1. Bui Thi Thu Thao VIE 6.55/0.0
	2. Narayan Neena IND 6.51/0.0
	3. Xu Xiaoling CHN 6.50/0.1
TJ	1. Olga Rypakova KAZ 14.26/0.0
	2. Parinya Chuaimaroeng THA 13.93/0.3
	3. Vu Thi Men VIE 13.93/0.0
SP	1. Gong Lijiao CHN 19.66
	2. Gao Yang CHN 17.64
	3. Noora Jassem BRN 17.11
DT	1. Chen Yang CHN 65.12
	2. Feng Bin CHN 64.25

	3. Seema Punia IND 62.26
HT	1. Luo Na CHN 71.42
	2. Wang Zheng CHN 70.86
	3. Hitomi Katsuyama JPN 62.95
JT	1. Liu Shiying CHN 66.09*
	2. Lu Huihui CHN 63.16
	3. Kim Kyeong-ae KOR 56.74
Hep	1. Swapna Barman IND 6026
	2. Wang Qingling CHN 5954
	3. Yuki Yamasaki JPN 5873
20kW	1. Yang Jiayu CHN 1:29:15*
	2. Qieyang Shijie CHN 1:29:15*
	3. Kumiko Okada JPN 1:34:02
4x100m	1. BRN (Essa Iman, E Odiong, Al-Khaldi, Naser) 42.73*
	2. CHN (Liang Xiaojing, Huang Guifen, Kong Lingwei, Yuan Qiqi) 42.84
	3. KAZ 43.82
4x400m	1. IND (Das, Poovamma, Gayakwad, Vismaya) 3:28.72
	2. BRN 3:30.61
	3. VIE 3:33.23
Mixed 4x400m	
	1. BRN (Ali Khamis, Kemi Adekoya (W), Salwa Naser (W), Abbas Abbas) 3:11.89*
	2. IND 3:15.71
	3. KAZ 3:19.52

Medal table leaders: CHN 12G-12S-9B, BRN 12-6-7, IND 7-10-2, JPN 6-2-10, QAT 4-2-1

18th Asian Junior Championships

At Gifu, Japan 7-10 June

Men: 100m: Lalu Muhammad Zohri INA 10.27, **200m:** Wei Tai-Sheng TPE 21.05, **400m:** Aruna Darshana SRI 45.79*, **800m:** Anu Kumar IND 1:54.11, **1500m/3000mSt:** Mohamed Sailfeldin QAT 3:49.30/8:51.97, **5000m:** Ajeet Kumar IND 14:15.24, **10,000m:** Suolang Cairen CHN 30:01.51, **110mh** (99cm): Lu Hao-Hua TPE 13.61, **400mh:** Yusuke Shirao JPN 50.52, **HJ:** Kyohei Tomori JPN 2.16, **PV:** Syunto Ozaki JPN 5.20, **LJ:** Yugo Sakai JPN 7.61, **TJ:** Kamalraj Kangaraj IND 15.75, 6kg **SP:** Moaaz Mohamed Ibrahim QAT 18.57, 1.75kg **DT:** Hossein Rasouli IRI 62.29*, 6kg **HT:** Ashish Jakhar IND 76.86, **JT:** Liu Zhekai CHN 70.53, **Dec** (jnr): Wang Xhen-Yu TPE 7200, **10,000mW:** Gong Hao CHN 42:47.98, **4x100m:** JPN 39.65, **4x400m:** SRI 3:08.70; **Women: 100m:** Feng Lulu CHN 11.68, **200m:** Tao Yanan CHN 24.01, **400m:** Jisna Mathew IND 53.26, **800m:** Ayaka Kawata JPN 2:04.14, **1500m:** Ririka Hironaka JPN 4:17.62, **3000m:** Nozomi Tanaka JPN 9:04.36*, **5000m:** Mikuni Yada JPN 16:31.65, **3000mSt:** Marsitela Wasanthi SRI 10:21.54, **100mh:** Yuiri Yoshida JPN 13.45*, **400mh:** Kasumi Yoshida JPN 58.43, **HJ:** Maryam Abdulelah IRQ 1.80, **PV:** Ma Li CHN 4.00, **LJ:** Ayaka Kora JPN 6.44, **TJ:** Vu Thi Ngoc Ha VIE 13.22w, **SP:** Zhang Linru CHN 16.05, **DT:** Yang Huanhuan CHN 51.53, **HT:** Zhou Mengyuan CHN 64.81, **JT:** Li Hui-Jun TPE 55.36, **Hep:** Karin Odama JPN 5133, **10,000mW:** Ma Li CHN 45:20.59*, **4x100m:** CHN 45.06, **4x400m:** JPN 3:38.20*. **Medal winners:** JPN 14G-15S-13B; CHN 11-8-4, IND 5-2-10, TPE 4-5-4, SRI 3-4-2, QAT 3-3-0, IRI 1-1-3; 15 nations won medals (10 gold).

Asian Walks Championships

At Nomi City, Japan 18 March
Men 20k: 1. Fumitaka Oikawa JPN 1:21:32, 2, Kim Hyun-sub KOR 1:21:52, 3. Georgiy Sheiko KAZ 1:21:57; **Women 20k:** 1. Duan Dandan CHN 1:35:12, 2. Jeon Yong-eun KOR 1:36:33, 3. Kaori Kazazoe JPN 1:37:47.

Balkan Championships

Walks *at Ecka, Serbia,14 April*
Men 20k: Smutro Sobchuk UKR 1:26:27; **Women 20k:** Panayióta Tsinopoúlou 1:39:01.
Team (all ages): 1, TUR 11,365; 2, ROU 8130; 3, BUL 6676
Half Marathon *at Sarejevo (BIH) 16 September*
Men: Aykut Tasdemir TUR 68:01, **Women:** Olivera Jevtic SRB 74:46

23rd Central American and Caribbean Games

At Barranquilla, Colombia 29 July-3 August
Men
100m   1. Nesta Carter JAM 10.07 (1s1 9.92w/2.1)
(1.7)   2. Jason Rogers SKN 10.15
        3. Cejhae Greene BER 10.16 (1s2 10.00 /0.5)
200m   1. Bernardo Baloyes COL 20.13
(0.0)   2. Alonso Edward PAN 20.17 (1s2 19.96*/0.4)
        3. Kyle Greaux TTO 20.26
400m   1. Luguelín Santos DOM 44.59
        2. Yoandys Lescay CUB 45.38
        3. Nery Brenes CRC 45.61
800m   1. Jesús López MEX 1:45.2h
        2. Ryan Sánchez PUR 1:46.3
        3. Wesley Vásquez PUR 1:46.6
1500m 1. Daniel Estrada MEX 3:56.57
        2. José Rodríguez MEX 3:56.70
        3. Carlos San Martín COL 3:56.78
5000m 1. José Mauricio González COL 13:53.40
        2. Mario Pacay GUA 13:56.30
        3. Victor Montañez MEX 14:05.87
10,000m 1. Juan Luis Barrios MEX 30:07.49
        2. Mario Pacay GUA 30:09.79
        3. Ivan González COL 30:15.23
Mar   1. Jeisson Suárez CO 2:29:54
        2. Daniel Vargas MEX 2:30:30
        3. Williams Julajúj GUA 2:31:42
3000mSt 1. Gerard Giraldo COL 8:44.51
        2. Ricardo Estremera PUR 8:46.24
        3. Camilo Camargo COL 8:50.66
110mh 1. Shane Brathwaite BAR 13.38
(1.4) 2. Ruebin Walters TTO 13.57
        3. Roger Iribarne CUB 13.58
400mh 1. Kyron McMaster IVB 47.60*
        2. Annsert Whyte JAM 48.50
        3. Juander Santos DOM 48.77
HJ   1. Donald Thomas BAH 2.28
        2. Eure Yáñez VEN 2.28
        3. Jermaine Francis SKN 2.28
PV   1= Lázaro Borges CUB 5.30
        1= Walter Viafara COL 5.30

LJ   3. Eduardo Nápoles CUB 5.20
        1. Ramone Bailey JAM 8.07/0.1
        2. Tyrone Smith BER 8.03/0.2
        3. Andwuelle Wright TTO 7.94/0.3
TJ   1. Cristian Nápoles CUB 17.34/1.7
        2. Jordan Díaz CUB-Y 17.29w/2.6
        3. Miguel van Assen SUR 16.96/1.3
SP   1. O'Dayne Richards JAM 21.02*
        2. Ashinia Miller JAM 20.19
        3. Eldred Henry IVB 20.18
DT   1. Mauricio Ortega COL 66.30
        2. Jorge Fernández CUB 65.27
        3. Traves Smikle JAM 64.68
HT   1. Diego Del Real MEX 74.95*
        2. Reinier Mejías CUB 73.28
        3. Roberto Janet CUB 73.11
JT   1. Keshorn Walcott TTO 84.47
        2. Anderson Peters GRN 81.80
        3. David Carreón MEX 76.27
Dec   1. Leonel Suárez CUB 8026
        2. José Lemos COL 7913
        3. Briander Rivero CUB 7858
4x100m 1. BAR (Brathwaite, Burke, Ellis, Hoyte) 38.41
        2. DOM (Valdez, Anduhar, Del Carmen, Y Martínez) 38.71
        3. JAM (Carter, R Williams, Dwyer, Tucker) 38.79
4x400m 1, CUB (Zamora, Chacón, Rojas, Lescay) 3:03.87
        2. DOM (L Santos, J Santos, Charles, Bonon) 3:03.92
        3. COL (Palomeque, R Rodríguez, Herrera, Perlaza) 3:04.35
20kW   1. Eider Arévalo COL 1:26:42
        2. Erick Barrondo GUA 1:27:17
        3. Andrés Olivas MEX 1:28:12
        dq (2). Manuel Soto COL 1:26:59
50kW   1. José Leyver Okeda MEX 4:02:45
        2. Jorge Armando Ruíz COL 4:05:28
        3. José Montaña COL 4:08:10
Women
100m   1. Jonielle Smith JAM 11.04w
(2.3) 2. Khalifa St. Fort TTO 11.15
        3. Andrea Purica VEN 11.32
200m   1. Shashalee Forbes JAM 22.80
(0.6) 2. Semoy Hackett TTO 22.95
        3. Jodean Williams JAM 22.96
400m   1. Tiffany James JAM 52.35
        2. Cofil Fiordaliiza DOM 52.72
        3. Derri-Ann Hill JAM 53.30
800m   1. Rose Mary Almanza CUB 2:01.63
        2. Alena Brooks TTO 2:02.26
        3. Sonia Gaskin BAR 2:03.13
1500m 1. Rose Mary Almanza CUB 4:22.14
        2. Angelín Figueroa PUR 4:22.52
        3. Rosibel García COL 4:23.43
5000m 1. Muriel Coneo COL 16:12.47
        2. Beverly Ramos PUR 16:14.04
        3. Brenda Flores MEX 16:16.71
10,000m 1. Patricia Sánchez MEX 33:41.48*
        2. Beverly Ramos PUR 33:46.99
        3. Vianney De La Rosa MEX 34:10.75
Mar   1. Madai Pérez MEX 2:57:55
        2. Dailín Belmonte CUB 2:59:09

	3. Anjie Orjuela COL 2:59:49
3000mSt	1. Ana Narváez MEX 10:00.01
	2. Beverly Ramos PUR 10:07.71
	3. Andrea Ferris PAN 10:18.92
100mh	1. Andrea Vargas CRC 12.90
(1.5)	2. Vanessa Clerveaux HAI 13.07
	3. Jeanine Williams JAM 13.11
400mh	1. Rhonda Whyte JAM 55.08
	2. Zudikey Rodríguez MEX 55.11
	3. Zurian Hechevarría CUB 55.13
HJ	1. Levern Spencer LCA 1.90
	2. Ximena Esquivel MEX 1.86
	3. María Fernanda Murillo COL 1.86
PV	1. Yarisley Silva CUB 4.70*
	2. Rosbeilys Peinado VEN 4.50
	3. Lisa Salomón CUB 4.10
LJ	1. Caterine Ibargüen COL 6.83w/2.9
	2. Chantel Malone IVB 6.52/1.4
	3. Alysbeth Félix PUR 6.45w/2.2
TJ	1. Caterine Ibargüen COL 14.92*/1.2
	2. Yorsiry Urrutia COL 14.48w/2.9
	3. Liadagmis Povea CUB 14.44w/2.1
SP	1. Cleopatra Borel TTO 18.14
	2. Yaniuvis López CUB 18.03
	3. María Fernanda Orozco MEX 17.88
DT	1. Yaimé Pérez CUB 66.00*
	2. Denia Caballero CUB 65.10
	3. Shanice Love JAM 58.40
HT	1. Rosa Rodríguez VEN 67.91
	2. Elianne Despaigne CUB 64.40
	3. Yaritza Martínez CUB 61.44
JT	1. María Lucelly Murillo COL 59.54
	2. Coralys Ortiz PUR 56.27
	3. Yulenmis Aguilar CUB 55.60
Hep	1. Yorgelis Rodríguez CUB 6436*
	2. Evelyn Aguilar COL 6285
	3. Luisaris Toledo VEN 5848
4x100m	1. JAM (Levy, Morrison, S Simpson, Smith) 43.41
	2. TTO (St. Fort, Denoon, R Thomas, Hackett) 43.61
	3. DOM (M Sánchez, Paulino, Medina, De Aza) 43.68
4x400m	1. CUB (Hechavarría, Almanza, Casanova, R Gómez) 3:29.48*
	2. JAM (D A Hill, James, S Walker, Bromfield) 3:30.67
	3. COL (Chávez, Escobar, M González, Padilla) 3.32.61

Medal table leaders: COL 11G-6S-9B, CUB 10-8-9, MEX 8-4-5, JAM 8-3-6, TTO 2-5-3, BAH 2-0-1, DOM 1-3-2, VEN 1-1-2, IVB 1-1-1, CRC 1-0-1, BAH & LCA 1-0-0, PUR 0-7-2; 21 nations won medals.

Commonwealth Half Marathon Championships

At Cardiff, GBR 7 October
Men: 1. Jack Rayner AUS 61:01; 2. Fred Musobo UGA 61:08, 3. Timothy Toroitich USA 61:17; Team: 1. UGA, 2. AUS, 3. ENG; **Women:** 1. Juliet Chekwel UGA 69:45, 2. Celia Sullohern AUS 71:04, 3, Doreen Chesang UGA 71:10; Team: 1. UGA, 2. AUS, 3. ENG

2nd European U18 Championships

At Györ, Hungary 5-8 August
Men: 100m: Raphael Bouju NED 10.64, **200m** Alexander Czysch GER 21.15*=, **400m:** Lorenzo Benati ITA 46.85, **800m:** Max Burgin GBR 1:47.36*, **1500m:** Kane Elliott GBR 3:55.26*, **3000m:** Thomas Keen GBR 8:27.38, **2000mSt:** Baptiste Guyon FRA 5:43.92*, 0.914m **110mh:** Sam Bennett GBR 13.19*, 0.84m **400mh:** Martin Fraysse FRA & Dániel Huller HUN 50.63*, **HJ:** Dominic Ogbechie GBR 2.16, **PV:** Pál Haugen Lillefosse NOR 5.46*, **LJ:** Nick Schmahl GER 7.60w, **TJ:** Batuhan Cakir TUR 15.62, 5kg **SP:** Aleksey Aleksandrovich BLR 20,97, 1,5kg **DT:** Yasiel Brayan Sotero ESP 64.31, 5kg **HT:** Myhaylo Kokhan UKR 87.82*, 700g **JT:** Marek Mucha POL 80.01*, Yth **Dec:** Aleksandr Komarov ANA/.RUS 7703, **MedleyR:** ITA 1:53.01, **10,000mW:** Davide Finocchieti ITA 45:01.33.
Women: 100m: Gudbjörg Bjarnadóttir ISL 11.75, **200m:** Rhasidat Adeleke IRL 23.52, **400m:** Barbora Malíková CZE 52.66*, **800m:** Keely Hodgkinson GBR 2:04.84*, **1500m/3000m:** Sarah Healy IRL 4:18.71*/9:18.05*, **2000mSt:** Lena Lebrun FRA 6:35.41, 0.76m **100mh:** Martine Hjørnevik NOR 13.25, **400mh:** Gisèle Wender GER 58.88, **HJ:** Yaroslava Mahuchikh UKR 1.94*, **PV:** Leni Wildgrube GER 4.26*, **LJ:** Tilde Johansson SWE 6.33w, **TJ/Yth Hep:** Maria Vicente ESP 13.95*/6221*, 3kg **SP:** Lizaveta Dorts BLR 17.34, **DT:** Violetta Ignatyeva RUS/ANA 54.56, 3kg **HT:** Valeriya Ivanenko UKR 73.25, 500g **JT:** Aleksandra Konyshina BLR 56.71, **5000m Walk:** Hanna Zubkova BLR 22:45.47*.
Medal table leaders: GBR 6G-2S-1B; ITA 4-4-1, ESP 4-2-1, BLR 4-0-1, FRA 3-6-3, ESP 3-2-0, IRL& UKR 3-1-0, NOR 2-1-1, TUR 1-4-2, HUN 1-3-0, NED 1-2-3; 16 nations won gold and 29 a medal of any colour.

European Cup 10,000m

At London (Parliament Hill), GBR 20 May
Men: 1. Richard Ringer GER 27:36.52, 2. Morhad Amdouni FRA 27:36.80, 3. Yemaneberhan Crippa ITA 27:44.21; Team: 1. ESP 1:24:40.66, 2. GBR 1:25:03.32, 3. FRA 1:25:13.68; **Women: 1.** Lonah Chemtai Salpeter ISR 31:33.03, 2. Ancuta Bobocel ROU 31:43.12; 3. Charlotte Arter GBR 32:15.71; **Team:** 1. GBR 1:37:28.89, 2, ROU 1:37:35.06, 3. GER 1:38:26.05.

18th Ibero-American Championships

At Trujillo, Peru 24-26 August
Men: 100m: Paulo de Oliveira BRA 10.26, **200m:** Jorge Vides BRA 20.39, **400m:** Lucas Carvalho BRA 45.92, **800m:** Thiago André BRA 1:46.73, **1500m:** Lorenc Sales ESP 3:48.27, **3000m/3000mSt:** Altobeli da Silva BRA 7:57.52/8:35.5, **5000m:** José Luis Rojas PER 13:42.38, **110mh:** Gabriel Constantino BRA 13.61, **400mh:** Marcio Teles BRA 49.64, **HJ:** Carlos Layoy ARG 2.21, **PV:** Augusto Dutra da Silva BRA 5.40, **LJ:** José Luis Mandros PER 7.87, **TJ:** Cristian Nápoles CUB 16.81, **SP:** Darlan Romani BRA 20.74, **DT:** Mauricio Ortega COL 60.49, **HT:** Javier Cienfuegos ESP 74.71, **JT:** Arley Ibargüen COL 75.50, Yth **Dec:** Román Gastaldi ARG 7634, **20,000mW:** Mauricio Arteaga ECU 1:22:18.16,

4x100m: BRA 38.78; **4x400m**: CHI 3:10.77; **Women:**
100m/200m: Vitoria Rosa BRA 11.33/22.90, **400m**:
Cátia Azevedo POR 52.26, **800m**: Esther Guerrero ESP
2:04.55, **1500m**: Solange Pereira ESP 4:18.31, **3000m**:
María Pía Fernández URU 9:16.16, **5000m**: Luz Mery
Rojas PER 16:08.77, **3000mSt**: Tatiane da Silva BRA
9:48.40, **100mh**: Andrea Vargas CRC 13.04, **400m**:
Fiorelle Chiappe ARG 56.26, **HJ**: María Fernanda
Murillo COL 1.84, **PV**: Juliana Campos BRA 4.40, **LJ**:
Juliet Itoya ESP 6.73w, **TJ**: Yorsiry Urrutia COL 14.14w,
SP: Geisa Arcanjo BRA 18.10, **DT**: Andressa de Morais
BRA 62.02, **HT**: Jenny Dahlgren ARG 68.89, **JT**: María
Lucelly Murillo COL 59.51, **Hep**: Ana Camila Pirelli
PAR 5879, **10,000mW**: Sandra Lorena Arenas COL
42:02.99, **4x100m**: PER 46.76, **4x400m**: POR 3:36.49.
Medal table leaders: BRA 18G-10S-6B, COL 6-0-2,
ESP 5-6-7, PER 4-4-8, ARG 3-4-5, POR 2-2-2, ECU
1-5-3, CRC 1-3-2, URU 2-1-3, CHI 1-2-2, PAR 1-1-1,
CUB 1-0-2; 18 nations won medals (12 gold).

18th Mediterranean Games

At Tarragona, Spain 27-30 June
Men: 100m: Jak Ali Harvey TUR 10.10*, **200m**: Ramil
Guliyev TUR 20.15*, **400m**: Davide Re ITA 45.26*,
800m: Álvaro de Arriba ESP 1:47.43, **1500m**: Brahim
Kaazouzi MAR 3:37.14, **5000m**: Younés Essalhi MAR
13:56.12, **HMar**: Mohamed El Arraby MAR 64:03*,
3000mSt: Soufiane El Bakkali MAR 8:20.97, **110mh**:
Lorenzo Perini ITA 13.49, **400mh**: Ludvy Vaillant FRA
48.76, **HJ**: Majed El Dein Ghazal SYR 2.28, **LJ**: Yahya
Berrabah MAR 8.02, **SP**: Hamza Alic BIH 20.43, **DT**:
Apostolos Parellis CYP 62.98, **JT**: Nicolás Quijera
ESP 75.13, **4x100m/4x400m**: ITA 38.49*/3:03.54.
Women: 100m: Oriann Ombissa-Dzangue FRA
11.29, **200m**: Carolle Zahi FRA 23.02, **400m**: Eleni
Artymata CYP 51.19, **800m/1500m**: Rabab Arrafi MAR
2:01.01/4:12.83, **5000m**: Kaoutar Farkoussi MAR
15:52.33, **HMar**: Sara Dossena ITA 73:48, **3000mSt**:
Luiza Gega ALB 9:27.73*, **100mh**: Andrea Ivancevic
CRO 13.19, **400mh**: Yadisleidy Pedroso ITA 55.40, **PV**:
Ninon Guillon-Romarin FRA 4.46, **LJ**: Ivana Spanovic
SRB 7.04w, **TJ**: Yanis David FRA 14.15, **DT**: Sandra
Perkovic CRO 66.46*, **HT**: Alexandra Tavernier FRA
73.67*, **4x100m**: FRA 43.29, **4x400m**: ITA 3:28.08*,
Medal Table leaders: MAR 8G-4S-1B, ITA 7-8-8, FRA
7-1-6, ESP 2-6-7, TUR 2-4-1.

NACAC Championships

At Toronto, Canada 10-12 August

100m (0.4)	1. Tyquendo Tracey JAM 10.03*	
	2. Kendal Williams USA 10.11	
	3. Cameron Burrell USA 10.12	
200m (1.7)	1. Kyle Greaux TTO 20.11	
	2. Aaron Brown CAN 20.20	
	3. Nigel Ellis JAM 20.57	
400m	1. Demish Gaye JAM 45.47	
	2. Nery Brenes CRC 45.67	
	3. Fitzroy Dunkley JAM 45.76	
800m	1. Brandon McBride CAN 1:46.14	
	2. Marco Arop CAN 1:46.82	
	3. Wesley Vásquez PUR 1:47.63	
1500m	1. Izaic Yorks USA 3:51.85	
	2. Pat Casey USA 3:51.8	
	3. Charles Philibert-Thiboutot CAN 3:52.60	

5000m	1. Hassan Mead USA 14:00.18	
	2. Riley Masters USA 14:01.04	
	3. Justyn Knight CAN 14:01.77	
10,000	1. Lopez Lomong USA 29:49.03*	
	2. Elkanah Kibet USA 29:51.37	
	3. Reed Fischer USA 29:53.63	
3000mSt	1. Andy Bayer USA 8:28.55	
	2. Travis Mahoney USA 8:29.29	
	3. Jordan Mann USA 8:45.14	
110mh (0.4)	1. Hansle Parchment JAM 13.28	
	2. Aleec Harris USA 13.49	
	3. Shane Brathwaite BER 13.52	
400mh	1. Kyron McMaster IVB 48.18*	
	2. Annsert Whyte JAM 48.91	
	3. Khallifah Rosser USA 49.13	
HJ	1. Jeron Robinson USA 2.28*	
	2. Michael Mason CAN 2.28*	
	3= Donald Thomas BAH 2.28*	
	3=Django Lovett CAN 2.28*	
PV	1. Scott Houston USA 5.45	
	2. Shaunacy Barber CAN 5.40	
LJ	1. Marquis Dendy USA 8.29/-0.4*	
	2. Tajay Gayle JAM 8.24/-0.3	
	3. Ramone Bailey JAM 8.09/-0.2	
TJ	1. Jordan Díaz CUB-J 16.83/-0.1	
	2. Chris Benard USA 16.73/-0.4	
	3. KeAndre Bates USA 16.58/-0.2	
SP	1. Darrell Hill USA 21.68*	
	2. Tom Nedow CAN 21.02	
	3. O'Dayne Richards TTO 20.89	
DT	1. Fedrick Dacres JAM 68.47*	
	2. Trevor Smikle JAM 65.46	
	3. Reggie Jagers USA 62.70	
HT	1. Roberto Sawyers CRC 72.94	
	2. Alex Young USA 72.75	
	3. Adam Keenan CAN 72.72	
JT	1. Anderson Peters GRN 79.65*	
	2. Curtis Thompson USA 76.02	
	3. Markim Felix GRN 75.14	
4x100m	1. CAN (Boateng, Blake, Ajemale, Brown) 38.56	
	2. BAR (Brathwaite, Burke, Ellis, Hoyte) 38.69	
	3. TTO (N Garonha, J Farinha, Purcell, Greaux) 38.89	
4x400m	1. USA (Strother, Igbokwe, Cherry, Montgomery) 3:00.60	
	2. BAH (Ferguson, T Smith, Mathieu, Russell) 3:03.80	
	3. CUB (Zamora, Chacón, Caballero, Lescay) 3:04.11	
20kmW	1. Evan Dunfee CAN 1:25:39	
	2. Nick Christie USA 1:30:11	
	3. John Cody Risch USA 1:36:05	
Women		
100m (0.9)	1. Jenna Prandini USA 10.96*	
	2. Jonielle Smith JAM 11.07	
	3. Crystal Emmanuel CAN 11.15	
200m (-0.3)	1. Shericka Jackson JAM 22.64	
	2. Crystal Emmanuel CAN 22.67	
	3. Phyllis Francis USA 22.91	
400	1. Stephanie-Ann McPherson JAM 51.15	
	2. Alyanna Stiverne CAN 52.00	
	3. Brionna Thomas USA 52.19	
800	1. Ajee' Wilson USA 1:57.52	

	2. Natoya Goule JAM 1:57.95
	3. Rose Mary Almanza CUB 2:00.15
1500m	1. Kate Grace USA 4:06.23*
	2. Shannon Osika USA 4:06.92
	3. Gabriela Stafford CAN 4:07.36
5000	1. Rachel Schneider USA 15:26.19*
	2. Lauren Paquette USA 15:39.40
	3. Kate Van Buskirk CAN 15:50.35
10,000	1. Marielle Hall USA 33:27.19*
	2. Rochelle Kanuho USA 33:28.33
	3. Rachel Cliff CAN 33:30.16
3000mSt	1. Mel Lawrence USA 9:45.36*
	2. Emily Oren USA 9:56.66
	3. Megan Rolland USA 9:59.85
100mh	1. Kendra Harrison USA 12.55*
(0.9)	2. Daniolle Williams JAM 12.67
	3. Andrea Vargas CRC 12.91
400mh	1. Shamier Little USA 53.32*
	2. Janieve Russell JAM 53.81
	3. Georganne Moline USA 54.26
HJ	1. Levern Spencer LCA 1.91*
	2. Liz Patterson USA 1.88
	3. Lorette Blaut USA 1.82
PV	1. Katie Nageotte USA 4.75*
	2. Yarisley Silva CUB 4.70
	3. Sandi Morris USA 4.65
LJ	1. Sha'keela Saunders 6.60/-0.2
	2. Quanesha Burks UOA 0.59/-0.1
	3. Tissanna Hickling JAM 6.38/0.5
TJ	1. Shanieka Ricketts JAM 14.25/-0.9*
	2. Tori Franklin USA 14.09/-0.4
	3. Thea LaFond DOM 14.74/-1.2
SP	1. Maggie Ewen USA 18.22
	2. Cleopatra Borel TTO 17.83
	3. Jessica Ramsey USA 17.80
DT	1. Yaimé Pérez CUB 61.97*
	2. Valarie Allman USA 59.67
	3. Maggie Ewen USA 59.00
HT	1. DeAnna Price USA 74.60*
	2. Jillian Weir CAN 71.69
	3. Brooke Anderson 70.05
JT	1. Arianna Ince USA 59.59
	2. Betrhany Drake USA 54.71
	3. Coralys Ortiz PUR 54.71
4x100m	1. USA (Parker, Collins, Bryant, Prandini) 42.50
	2. JAM (Fraser-Pryce, Levy, J Smith, C Jaslisan) 10.00
	3. CAN (Harrison, Emmanuel, Geprge, Westmey) 43.50
4x400m	1. USA (Guillory, Blocker, Horton, Okolo) 3:26.08
	2. JAM (McPherson, James, LeRoy, Day) 3:27.25
	3. CAN (Powell, Stiverne, T Jones, A Brown) 3:28.04
20kmW	1. Maria Michta-Coffey USA 1:36:34
	2. Mirna Ortiz GUA 1:38:36
	3. Katie Burnett USA 1:39:31

Medal table leaders: USA 25G-19S-17B, JAM 21-7-9, CAN 3-6-10. 14 countries won medals

Oceania Race Walking Championships

At Adelaide, Australia 11 February. **Men 20k**: 1. Quentin Rew NZL 1:21:55, 2. Dane Bird-Smith AUS 1:22:18, 3. Michael Hosking AUS 1:23:10; **Women 20k**: 1. Bekki Smith AUS 1:31:23, 2. Jemima Montag AUS 1:31:26, 3. Claire Tallent AUS 1:31:29.

11th South American Games

At Cochabamba, Bolivia (A) 5-8 June

Men

100m	1. Alonso Edward PAN 10.01*
(-0.7)	2. Alex Quiñónez ECU 10.09
	3. Vitor Hugo dos Santos BRA 10.12
200m	1. Alex Quiñónez ECU 19.93*
(-0.5)	2. Vitor Hugo dos Santos BRA 20.12
	3. Bernardo Baloyes COL 20.27
400m	1. Lucas Carvalho BRA 45.61
	2. Yilmar Andrés Herrera COL 45.64
	3. Winston George GUY 45.67
800m	1. Lucirio Garrido VEN 1:51.15
	2. Yelsin Robledo COL 1:51.50
	3. Leandro Paris ARG 1:51.94
1500m	1. Carlos Martín Díaz CHI 3:50.82
	2. Willy Canchanya PER 3:51.23
	3. Federico Bruno ARG 3:54.34
5000m	1. Bayron Piedra ECU 14:32.47
	2. Vidal Basco BOL 14:32.58
	3. José Luis Ostos PER 14:32.79
10,000m	1. Iván González COL 30:25.10
	2. Jorge César Fernández BOL 30:37.29
	3. Bayron Piedra ECU 30:51.74
3000mSt	1. Yuri Labra PER 9:01.95
	2. Gerard Giraldo COL 9:01.99
	3. Yessy Apaza BOL 9:21.81
110mh	1. Eduardo de Deus BRA 13.44*
(0.5)	2. Fanor Escobar COL 13.61
	3. Juan Carlos Moreno COL 13.68
400mh	1. Guillermo Ruggeri ARG 49.28 *
	2. Alfredo Sepúlveda CHI 49.62
	3. Marcio Teles BRA 49.78
HJ	1. Eure Yáñez VEN 2.28*
	2. Fernando Ferreira BRA 2.25
	3. Carlos Layoy ARG 2.25
PV	1. Augusto Dutra de Oliveira BRA 5.50
	2. Germán Chiaraviglio ARG 5.40
	3. Walter Viáfara COL 5.00
LJ	1. Emiliano Lasa URU 8.26*/0.7
	2. Paulo Oliveira BRA 8.12/0.7
	3. Aleksandro Melo BRA 8.09/1.1
TJ	1. Miguel van Assen SUR 16.81*/0.1
	2. Mateus de Sá BRA 16.76/0.5
	3. Leodan Torrealba VEN 16.23/0.6
SP	1. Darlan Romani BRA 21.21*
	2. Aldo González BOL 18.33
	3. Levin Moreno COL 17.60
DT	1. Mauricio Ortega COL 62.10*
	2. Juan José Caicedo ECU 57.37
	3. José Miguel Ballivian CHI 52.91
HT	1. Joaquín Gómez ARG 75.10
	2. Humberto Mansilla CHI 74.71
	3. Wágner Domingos BRA 72.53
JT	1. Arley Ibargüen COL 80.11*

2. Leslain Baird GUY 78.65
3. Braian Toledo ARG 78.57

Dec 1. Geormi Jaramillo VEN 7977*
2. José Gregorio Lemos COL 7757
3. Felipe dos Santos BRA 7739

4x100m 1. COL (Rentería, Palomeque, Chará, Baloyes) 38.97
2. VEN 39.03
3. BRA 39.54

4x400m 1. COL (Baloyes, Robledo, Palomeque, Herrera) 3:04.78
2. VEN 3:05.75
3. CHI 3:11.58

20kmW 1. Brian Pintado ECU 1:24:56
2. César Rodríguez PER 1:26:23
3. Yerko Araya CHI 1:29:37

50kmW 1. Andrés Chocho ECU 3:55:48*
2. Luis Campos PER 3:59:23
3. Ronald Rey Quispe BOL 4:05:05

Women

100m 1. Narcisa Landázuri ECU 11.12
(-0.7) 2. Ángela Tenorio ECU 11.13
3. Vitoria Rosa BRA 11.23

200m 1. Vitoria Rosa BRA 22.87*
1.0) 2. Ángela Tenorio ECU 23.07
3. Nercely Soto VEN 23.11

400m 1. Yennifer Padilla COL 52.14
2. Geisa Coutinho BRA 52.93
3. María Fernanda Mackenna CHI 53.60

800m 1. Déborah Rodríguez URU 2:16.21
2. Rosangélica Escobar COL 2:16.89
3. María Pía Fernández URU 2:17.16

1500m 1. Muriel Coneo COL 4:27.10
2. María Pía Fernández URU 4:30.56
3. Micaela Levaggi ARG 4:30.88

5000m 1. Saida Meneses PER 16:47.37
2. Luz Mery Rojas PER 17:09.59
3. Carmen Toaquiza ECU 17:16.40

10,000m 1. Inés Melchor PER 35:57.86
2. Gladys Tejeda PER 35:59.45
3. Irma Vila BOL 36:12.74

3000mSt 1. Rina Cjuro PER 10:53.83
2. Edith Mamani BOL 10:59.06
3. Jhoselyn Camargo BOL 11:18.63

100mh 1. Genesis Romero VEN 13.08*
(0.2) 2. Diana Bazalar PER 13.36
3. Jenea McCammon GUY 13.39

400mh 1. Fiorella Chiappe ARG 56.39
2. Melissa González COL 56.86
3. Gianna Woodruff PAN 57.68

HJ 1. María Fernanda Murillo COL-J 1.90*
2. Valdiléia Martins BRA 1.83
3. Amanda Vergara VEN 1.80

PV 1. Robeilys Peinado VEN 4.70 *
2. Juliana Campos BRA 4.20
3. Carmen Villanueva VEN 3.90

LJ 1. Paola Mautino PER 6.66/1.5
2. Eliane Martins BRA 6.66/1.5
3. Natalie Aranda PAN 6.60/0.8

TJ 1. Nubia Soares BRA 14.59*/0.2
2. Silvana Segura PER 13.56/0.2
3. Giselly Landázuri COL 13.46/0.3

SP 1. Natalia Ducó CHI 18.15*
2. Ahymara Espinoza VEN 18.09
3. Geisa Arcanjo BRA 17.30

DT 1. Andressa de Morais BRA 58.86
2. Fernanda Borges BRA 57.29
3. Ailén Armada ARG 48.77

HT 1. Jennifer Dahlgren ARG 70.98*
2. Rosa Rodríguez VEN 70.93
3. Valeria Chiliquinga ECU 66.77

JT 1. Laila Domingos BRA 60.25
2. María Lucelly Murillo COL 58.81
3. Eloah Scramin BRA 57.42

Hep 1. Giovana Cavaleti BRA 6081*
2. Martha Valeria Araujo COL 5719
3. Ana Camila Pirelli PAR 5503

4x100m 1. VEN (Toledo, Purica, Romero, Soto) 44.71
2. BOL 46.17
3. PER 46.43

4x400m 1. COL (Chávez, Escobar, M González, Padilla) 3:31.87*
2. CHI 3:33.42
3. ARG 3:35.96

20kmW 1. Kimberley García PER 1:33:11
2. Angela Castro BOL 1:34:25
3. Maritza Guamán ECU 1:36:23

Medal table: BRA 14G-13S-14B, COL 7-7-10, VEN 6-6-4, CHI 3-5-2, PER 3-2-3, PAN 3-2-0, URU 3-1-0, ARG 2-5-7, PAR 2-0-0. ECU 1-3-4, BOL 0-0-1.

South American Marathon Championships

At Buenos Aires, Argentina 23 September: **Men:** Christian Pacheco ECU 2:11:19; **Women:** Rosa Chacha ECU 2:35:29.

South American Walks Championships

At Sucua, Ecuador 10 Mar: **Men: 20k:** Andrés Chocho 1:22:51, **50k:** James Rendón COL 4:02:42, **Women: 20k:** Erica de Sena 21:30:22, **50k:** Magaly Bonilla ECU 4:19:43.

South American U23 Championships

At Cuenca, Ecuador (A) 29-30 September
Men: 100m: Derick Silva BRA 10.17, **200m:** Otilio Rosa ARG 21.06, **400m:** Anthony Zambrano COL 45.19, **800m:** Matheus Pessoa BRA 1:48.6, **1500m:** Carlos Hernández COL 3:59.47; **5000m:** Yuri Labra PER 14:57.61, **10,000m:** Vidal Basco BOL 31:14.72, **3000mSt:** Diego Arévalo ECU 9:24.6, **110mh:** Rafael Campos BRA 13.76, **400mh:** Alison dos Santos BRA 50.56, **HJ:** Jorge da Graca BRA 2.10, **PV:** Bruno Germano Spinelli BRA 5.20, **LJ:** Samory Bandeira BRA 7.42, **TJ:** Ulisses Costa BRA 15.87, **SP:** Welinton Morais BRA 19.85, **DT:** Cleverson Oliveira BRA 52.80, **HT:** Humberto Mansilla CHI 76.87*, **JT:** Francisco Javier Muse CHI 76.91, **Dec:** Sergio Pandiani ARG 7119, **20,000mW:** César Rodríguez PER 1:24:51.85; **4x100m/4x400m:** COL 40.08/3:09.77. **Women: 100m:** Angela Tenorio ECU 11.09, **200m:** Vitória Rosa BRA 23.04, **400m:** Martina Weil CHI 52.60, **800m:** Johana Arrieta COL 2:09.65, **1500m:** Micaela Levaggi ARG 4:31.60, **5000m:** Saida Meneses PER 17:20.54,

10,000m: Thalía Valdivia PER 36:58.03, **3000mSt:** Katherine Tisalema ECU 10:45.80, **100mh:** Micaela de Mello BRA 13.31, **400mh:** Fiorella Chiappe ARG 56.25, **HJ:** María Fernanda Murillo COL 1.80, **PV:** Juliana Campos BRA 4.40, **LJ:** Aries Sánchez VEN 6.42, **TJ:** Mirieli Santos BRA 13.34, **SP:** Amanda Scherer BRA 15.68, **DT:** Ailén Armada ARG 54.40, **HT:** Mayra Gaviria COL 62.10, **JT:** Laura Paredes PAR 55.59, **Hep:** Martha Araujo COL 5818, **20,000mW:** Leidy Guerra PER 1:32:12.42, **4x100m:** ECU 45.13, **4x400m:** COL 3:42.19. **Points (Medals):** BRA 283 (15G-12S-7B), ECU 237 (4-9-11), COL 206 (9-4-7), CHI 152 (3-5-8), PER 148 (5-8-6), ARG 132 (5-4-2), BOL 38 (1-1-2), VEN 32 (1-0-1), PAR 18 (1G), GUY 5, URU 3.

South American Youth Championships

At Cuenca, Ecuador (A) 30 June-1 July
Men: 100m: Giancarlos Mosquera COL 10.75, **200m:** Lucas Vilar BRA 21.34, **400m/** 0.84m **400mh:** Caio Teixeira BRA 48.20/52.09, **800m:** Jonathan Rodríguez COL 1:54.18, **1500m:** Lucas Leite BRA 4:11.90, **3000m:** Antony Sáez PER 9:07.75, **2000mSt:** Diego Muñoz COL 6:26.40, 0.914m **110mh:** Marcos Ferreira BRA 13.69, **HJ:** Elton Petronilho BRA 2.01, **PV:** Pablo Zaffaroni ARG 4.90, **LJ:** Adrián Vieira BRA 7.28, **TJ:** Kevin Bueno ECU 15.38, 5kg **SP:** Nazareno Sasia ARG 21.40, 1.5kg **DT:** Vítor Motin BRA 58.03, 5kg **HT:** Luis Alberto Ochoa COL 73.24, 700g **JT:** Gustavo Osorio ARG 74.47, **Dec:** Henrique Pereira Silva BRA 6716, **4x100m:** BRA 41.33, **10,000mW:** Oscar Patin ECU 46:50.5. **Women: 100m/200m:** Gabriela Suárez ECU 11.84/23.57, **400m:** Jéssica Moreira BRA 56.02, **800m/1500m:** Laura Elena Acuña CHI 2:13.01/4:44.98, **3000m:** Alejandra Sierra COL 10:29.36, **2000mSt:** Verónica Hilario PER 7:18.30, 0.76m **100mh:** Aimará Nazareno ECU 13.86, **400mh:** Valeria Cabezas COL 59.64, **HJ:** Arielly Rodrigues BRA 1.73, **PV:** Karen Bedoya COL 3.60, **LJ:** Rocío Muñoz CHI 6.04, **TJ:** Nerisnelia Sousa BRA 12.68, 3kg **SP:** Lorna Zurita ECU 15.84, **DT:** Merari Herrera ECU 44.97, 3kg **HT:** Carolina Ulloa COL 65.92, 500g **JT:** Yuleixi Angulo ECU 54.33, **Hep:** Sara Isabel García COL 5036, **5000m Walk:** María Belén Villalba ECU 24:17.79. **Medal table leaders:** BRA 14G-11S-5B, ECU 10-6-9, COL 9-8-8, ARG 3-6-6, CHI 3-0-6, PER 2-5-4.

3rd West Asian Championships

At Amman, Jordan 8-11 July
Men: 100m: Barakat Al-Harthi OMA 9.97, **200m:** Mohamed Yacoub Salem BRN 20.53w, **400m:** Abbas Abubaker BRN 46.51, **800m:** Abraham Rotich BRN 1:49.81, **1500m:** Sadik Mikhou BRN 3:41.27, **5000m:** Albert Rop BRN 13:42.94, **10,000m:** Benson Seurei BRN 30:34.79, **HMar:** Ahmad Sammpour JOR 71:37, **3000mSt:** John Koech BRN 8:46.60, **110mh:** Yaqoub Al-Yoha KUW 14.13w, **400mh:** Hamed Abdullah Saleh KUW 52.58, **HJ:** Mohamed El Beheiry JOR 2.10, **PV:** Abdullah Al-Targi KUW 4.50, **LJ:** Salem Al-Yaraibi OMA 7.29, **TJ:** Khaled Al-Subaie KUW 16.23, **SP:** Meshari Saad Suroor KUW 18.40, **DT:** Musaeb Al-Momani JOR 54.07, **HT:** Mohamed Al-Jawher KUW 61.81, **JT:** Abdullah Melhes JOR 51.25, **Dec:** Majed Al-Sayed KUW 6741, **4x100m:** OMA 40.24, **4x400m:** IRQ 3:09.96, **20kW:** Abloud Khaled Joudah

JOR 1:50:30; **Women: 100m/200m:** Hajar Saad Al-Khaldi BRN 11.17.23.09w, **400m:** Salwa Eid Naser BRN 53.03, **800m:** 16:34.40, **10,000m:** Shitaye Eshete BRN 33:37.25, **HMar:** Nahidah Al Baoat JPR 1:41:11, **3000mSt:** Hanan Al Ashosh JOR 12:55.54, **100mh/400mh:** Aminat Odeyemi BRN 14.15/56.75; **HJ:** Nourhan al Kush LBN 1.65, **PV:** Rita Abdullah JOR 2.50, **LJ:** Krystel Saneh LBN 5.73, **TJ:** Sarah Al Nsour JOR 10.44, **SP/DT:** Noora Salem Jassem BRN 16.69/47.45, **HT:** Rania Al Najo QAT 47.81, **JT:** Salsabil Al Saiar KUW 32.08, **Hep:** Zeina Abdeen JOR 3727, **10kW:** Sandy Karem LBN 63:19, **4x100m/4x400m:** BRN 44.58/3:48.89.

IAU 24 Hour European Championships

At Tomisoara, Romania 26-27 May
Men: 1, Andrzej Radzikowski POL 265.491k, 2. Stéphane Ruel FRA 263.540, 3. Aleksandr Sorokin LTU 260.991; **Team:** 1. FRA 754.625k, 2. GBR 735.155, 3. GER 725.963. **Women:** 1. Patrycja Bereznowska POL 243.355, 2. Stine Rex DEN 241.921, 3. Malgorzata Pazda-Pozorska POL 240.697; **Team:** 1. POL 720.454k, 2. GER 656.245. 3. GBR 645.069.

European Mountain Running Championships

At Skopje, Macedonia 1 July.
Men 11k: 1, Bernard De Matteis ITA 46:51; 2, Cesare Maestri ITA 47:18; 3, Martin De Matteis ITA 47:47, **Team:** 1. ITA 6, 2. GBR 28, 3. FRA 37; **Junior Men** 6k: Gabriel Bularda ROU 25:45, **Team:** GBR 17; **Women** 11k: 1. Maude Mathys SUI 52:32, 2. Anais Sabrie FRA 56:41, 3. Emma Gould GBR 57:48, **Team:** 1. FRA 18, 2, CZE 43. 3. GBR 39; **Junior Women** 6k: Angela Mattaevi ITA 29:30, **Team:** ITA 12

IAU 100Km World Championships

At Grvaveočcek - Sveti Martin na Muri, Croatia 9 September
Men: 1. Hideaki Yamauchi JPN 6:28:05, 2. Takehiko Gyoba JPN 6:32:51, 3. Bongmusa Mthembu RSA 6:33:47, 4. Koji Hayasaka JPN 6:36:05, 5. Geoff Burns USA 6:42:30, 6. Nao Kazami JPN 6:42:30. 7. Giorgio Calcaterra ITA 6:42:35, 8. Anthony Clark GBR 6:43:22, 9. Fritjof Fagerlund SWE 6:44:53, 10. Elov Olsson SWE 6:46:03; **Team:** 1. JPN 19:37:01, 2. RSA 20:33:49, 3. GER 21:02:12, 4. USA 21:05:41, 5. ESP 21:06:49. **Women** – 1. Nikolina Sustic CRO 7:20:34 rec, 2. Nele Alder-Baerens GER 7:22:41, 3. Mai Fujisawa JPN 7:39:07, 4. Mikiko Ota JPN 7:39:45, 5. Aiko Kanematsu JPN 7:44:58, 6. Yuko Kusunose JPN 7:49:33, 7. Salome Cooper RSA 7:51:13l 8. Noora Honkala FIN 7:52:04, 9. Kajsa Berg SWE 7:52:39, 10. Leonie Ton FRA 7:54:55; **Team:** 1. JPN 23:03:50, 2. RSA 23:56:44, 3. CRO 24:13:57, 4. USA 24:32:02, 5. POL 24:46:54.

World Mountain Running Championships

At Canillo, Andorra 16 September.

Men 11.933k: 1. Robert Chemonges UGA 55:37, 2. Joel Ayeko UGA 55:38, 3. Victor Kiplangat UGA 56:31, 4. Joseph Gray USA 57:08, 5. Johan Bugge NOR 58:25; Team: 1. UGA 6, 2. ITA 24, 3. NOR 42, 4. GBR 47; **Jnr 7.349k**: 1. Dan Chebet UGA 35:49, 2. Matthew Chepkurui KEN 36:05, 3. Oscar Chelimo KEN 36:42; Team: 1. UGA 6, 2. GBR 22, 3. TUR 23; **Women 11.933k**: 1. Lucy Wambui Murigi KEN 64:55, 2. Maude Mathys SUI 66:00, 3. Viola Jelagat KEN 66:26, 4. Patricia Chepkwemoi KEN 66:38, 5. Kristina Dvoráková CZE 67:20; Team: 1. USA 26, 2. ITA 32, 3. CZE 41; **Jnr W 6.5k**: 1. Risper Chebet UGA 41:19, 2. Lisa Oed GER 41:54, 3. Betty Chebet UGA 41:192; Team: 1. UGA 12, 2. ITA 18, 3. ROU 29.

DIAMOND LEAGUE
event winners

D Doha May 4, **Sh** Shanghai May 12, **E** Eugene May 26, **Ro** Rome May 31, **O** Oslo Jun 7, **St** Stockholm Jun 10, **P** Paris (Charléty) Jun 30; **L** Lausanne Jul 5, **Ra** Rabat Jul 13, **M** Monaco Jul 20, **Lo** London Jul 21-22, **Bi** Birmingham Aug 18, Finals: **Z** Zürich Aug 30, **Br** Brussels Aug 31

Men

100m: Final winner: Christian Coleman Ra 9.98, Bi 9.94, Br 9.79; Reece Prescod Sh 10.04; Ronnie Baker Ro 9.93, P 9.88, Lo 9.90.

200m: Final winner: Noel Lyles D 19.83, E 19.69, L 19.69, M 19.65, Z 19.87; Ramil Guliyev O 19.90, St 19.92.

400m: Final winner: Fred Kerley Ro 44.44, Bi 45.54, Z 44.80; Steven Gardiner D 43.87, Sh 43.99; Akeem Bloomfield Ra 44.33; Abdelilah Haroun Lo 44.07.

800m: Final winner: Emmanuel Korir D 1:45.21, Lo 1:42.05, Bi 1:42.79, Br 1:44.72; Wycliffe Kinyamal Sh 1:43.91, Ro 1:44.65; Ferguson Rotich St 1000m 2:14.88.

1500m/1M: Final winner: Timothy Cheruiyot Sh 3:31.48, Rom 3:31.22, P 3:29.71, M 3:28.41, Z 3:30.27; Elijah Manangoi O 1M 3:56.95; Brahim Kaazouzi Ra 3:33.22.

3000m/5000m: Final winner: Selemon Barega St 13:04.05, Br 12:43.02*; Birhanu Yematew L 13:01.09; Yomif Kejelcha Ra 3000m 7:32.93; Paul Chelimo Lo 13:14.01.

3000mSt: Final winner: Conselus Kipruto Bi 8:14.33, Z 8:10.15; Benjamin Kigen E 8:09.07, Ra 8:06.19; Soufiane El Bakkali Bi 8:14.33.

110mh: Final winner: Sergey Shubenkov L 12.95, M 13.07, Br 12.97; Omar McLeod Sh 13.16, E 13.01w; Ronald Levy P 13.18; Orlando Ortega Bi 13.08.

400mh: Final winner: Kevin McMaster Z 48.08; Abderrahmane Samba D 47.57*, Ro 47.48*, O 47.60, St 47.41*, P 46.98*, L 47.42.

HJ: Final winner: Brandon Starc Bi 2.33, Br 2.33; Mutaz Essa Barshim D 2.40, Sh 2.33, E 2.36, O 2.36; Danil Lysenko M 2.40.

PV: Final winner: Timur Morgunov Br 5.93; Renaud Lavillenie Sh 5.81; Sam Kendricks Ro 5.84, P 5.96, Ra 5.86, Lo 5.92; Armand Duplantis St 5.86.

LJ: Final winner: Luvo Manyonga Sh 8.56, Ro 8.58, Lo 8.58, Z 8.36; Juan Miguel Echevarría Sh 8.83w,.

TJ: Final winner: Pedro Pablo Pichardo D 17.95, Br 17.49; Christian Taylor E 17.73, P 17.29; L 17.62, M

17.86.

SP: Final winner Tom Walsh O 22.29, L 21.92, Z 22.60*; Ryan Crouser E 22.53, M 22.05.

DT: Final winner: Fedrick Dacres Ro 68.51, St 69.67, P 67.01, Br 68.67; Andrius Gudzius O 69.04.

JT: Final winner: Andreas Hofmann Lo 89.82, Z 91.44; Thomas Röhler D 91.78, E 89.88; Magnus Kirt Ra 89.75.

Women

100m: Final winner: Murielle Ahouré O 10.91, Z 11.01; Marie-Josée Ta Lou D 10.85, E 10.88, L 10.90, M 10.89; Dina Asher-Smith St 10.93.

200m: Final winner: Shaunae Miller-Uibo Sh 22.06, Ra 22.29, Bi 22.15, Br 22.12; Marie-Josée Ta Lou Ro 22.49; Shericka Jackson P 22.05; Jenna Prandini Lo 22.17.

400m: Final winner: Salwa Eid Naser O 49.98, St 49.84, P 49.55, L 49.78, Br 49.33; Shaunae Miller-Uibo E 49.52, M 48.97* .

800m: Final winner: Caster Semenya E 1:55.92, O 1:57.25, P 1:54.25*, M 1:54.60, Z 1:55.27; Francine Niyonsaba L 1:57.80, Ra 1:57.90.

1500m: Final winner: Laura Muir Br 3:58.49; Caster Semenya D 3:59.92; Shelby Houlihan E 3:59.06, L 3:57.34; Gudaf Tsegay St 3:57.64; Sifan Hassan Lo 1M 4:14.71*, Bi 4:00.60.
Sifan Hassan Bi 8:28.90.

3000m/5000m: Final winner: Hellen Obiri Ra 14:21.75, Z 14:38.39; Caroline Kipkirui D 3000m 8:29.05; Genzebe Dibaba E 14:26.89; Agnes Tirop Bi 3000m 8:32.21.

3000mSt: Final winner: Beatrice Chepkoech P 8:59.36, M 8:44.32*, Br 8:55.10; Hyvin Jepkemoi Ro 9:04.96, O 9:09.63.

100mh: Final winner: Brianna McNeal Sh 12.50, St 12.38, Ra 12.51, Br 12.61; Kendra Harrison D 12.53, Lo 12.36; Sharika Nelvis Ro 12.76.

400mh: Final winner: Dalilah Muhammad Sh 53.77, O 53.65, Z 53.88; Janieve Russell E 54.06; Shamier Little L 53.41, Lo 53.95; Léa Sprunger Br 54.86.

HJ: Final winner: Mariya Lasitskene Sh 1.97, Ro 2.02, St 2.00, P 2.04, Lo 2.04, Z 1.97; Mirela Demireva Ra 1.94.

PV: Final winner: Ekateríni Stefanídi L 4.82, Z 4.87; Sandi Morris D 4.84, O 4.81, Bi 4,62; Jenn Suhr E 4.85; Anzhelika Sidorova M 4.85.

LJ: Final winner: Caterine Ibargüen Br 6.80; Lorraine Ugen St 6.85; Malaiki Mihambo L 6.90, Bi 6.96; Shara Proctor Lo 6.91.

TJ: Final winner: Caterine Ibargüen Sh 14.80, O 14.89, P 14.83, Ra 14.96, Z 14.56

SP: Final winner: Gong Lijiao Sh 19.99, M 30.31, Br 19.83; Christina Schwanitz Ra 19.40, Bi 18.20.

DT: Final winner: Yaime Pérez Br 65.00; Sandra Perkovic D 71.38*, Ro 68.93, P 68.60, Lo 67.24.

JT: Final winner: Kholodovich O 67.47, Z 66.99; Lu Huihui Sh 66.85, Lo 65.54; Nikola Ogrodníková L 65.02.

* Diamond League record

2018 and 2019 prize money: 1st $50,000, 2nd $20,000, 3rd $10,000, 4th $6000, 5th $5000, 6th $4000, 7th $3000, 8th $2000. Prize money at the 12 qualification meetings: 1st $10,000, 2nd $6000, 3rd $4000, 4th $3000, 5th $2500, 6th $2000 7th $1500, 8th $1000.

MAJOR MEETINGS 2018–2019

Diamond League, World Challenge and European Athletics Premium Meetings

DL – Diamond League, WC – World Challenge, EAP European Premium Meeting

2018 date		Meeting	2019 date	
4 May	DL	Qatar Super Grand Prix, Doha, QAT	3 May	DL
12 May	DL	Shanghai Golden Grand Prix, CHN	18 May	DL
19 May	WC	Jamaica International, KIngston, JAM	4 May	WC
20 May	WC	Seiko Golden Grand Prix, Osaka, JPN	19 May	WC
–		Nanjing, China	21 May	WC
3 Jun	WC	Fanny Blankers-Koen Games, Hengelo, NED	9 Jun	WC
13 Jun	WC	Golden Spike, Ostrava, CZE	20 Jun	WC
25/26 May	DL	Prefontaine Classic, Eugene 2018, Stanford 2019, USA	30 Jun	DL
31 May	DL	Golden Gala, Rome, ITA	6 Jun	DL
5 Jun	EAP	Paavo Nurmi Games, Turku, Finland	11 Jun	WC
7 Jun	DL	ExxonMobil Bislett Games, Oslo, NOR	13 Jun	DL
10 Jun	DL	Bauhaus, Stockholm, SWE	2 Jun	DL
22 Jun	WC	Meeting Madrid, ESP	7 Jul	EAP
30 Jun	DL	Meeting de Paris, Paris (Charléty), FRA	24 Aug	DL
5 Jul	DL	Athletissima, Lausanne, SUI	5 Jul	DL
8 Jul		GP Brasil, Bragança Paulista	28 Apr	WC
9 Jul	EAC	Spitzen, Luzern	9 Jul	EAP
13 Jul	WC	Mohammed VI d'Athlétisme, Rabat, MAR	16 Jun	WC
19/20 Jul	DL	Herculis, Monaco, MON	12 Jul	DL
22/23 Jul	DL	Müller Anniversary Games, London (OS)	9 Jul	DL
18 Aug	DL	Müller Grand Prix, Birmingham, GBR	18 Aug	DL
23 Aug	EAP	Palio Citta della Quercia, Rovereto, ITA	27 Aug	EAP
30 Aug	DL	Weltklasse, Zürich, SUI	29 Aug	DL
31 Aug	DL	Memorial Van Damme, Brussels, BEL	6 Sep	DL
2 Sep	WC	ISTAF, Berlin, GER	1 Sep	WC
3 Sep	WC	Boris Hanzekovic Memorial, Zagreb, CRO	3 Sep	WC
		Rieti, ITA	8 Sep	EAP

INDOORS

WIT – IAAF World Indoor Tour; EAA – indoor permit meetings; US USATF series in USA.

2018 date		Meeting	2019 date	
24-26 Jan	US	Armory Track Invitational, New York, USA	26 Jan	US
25 Jan	EAA	Czech Indoor Gala, Ostrava, CZE	12 Feb	EAA
26 Jan		ISTAF, Berlin, GER	1 Feb	
3 Feb	WIT	BW-Bank Meeting, Karlsruhe, GER	2 Feb	WIT
3 Feb		Millrose Games, New York (Armory), USA	9 Feb	US
6 Feb	WIT	International PSD Bank, Düsseldorf, GER	20 Feb	WIT
8 Feb	WIT	Madrid, ESP	8 Feb	WIT
10 Feb	WIT	New Balance Indoor GP, Boston (Roxbury), USA	26 Jan	WIT/US
13 Feb		Hauts-de-France/Pas-de-Calais, FRA	10 Feb	EAA
15 Feb	EAA	Copernicus Cup, Torun, POL	6 Feb	WIT
16-18 Feb	US	USA Indoor Ch. Albuquerque 2018, Staten Island 2019	22-24 Feb	US
25 Feb	WIT	Müller Indoor GP – Glasgow/Birmingham, GBR	16 Feb	WIT
–		Folksam GP, Stockholm (Satra) , SWE	4 Feb	EAA

IAAF WORLD COMBINED EVENTS CHALLENGE 2018 & 2019

27/28 Apr	Multistars, Firenze, ITA, Lana 2019	27/28 Apr
26/27 May	Hypo-Mehrkampf Meeting, Götzis, AUT	25/26 May
2/3Jun	Arona, ESP	8/9 Jun
16/17 Jun	Stadtwerke Ratingen, GER	29/30 Jun
–	European CE Team Ch – Lutsk UKR & Ribeira Brava POR	6/7 Jul
15/16 Sep	Decastar, Talence, FRA	22/23 Sep

Plus US and World Championships

IAAF WORLD RACE WALKING CHALLENGE 2017 & 2018

11 Feb	Oceania Championships, Adelaide, AUS	10 Feb
24-25 Feb	Monterrey, MEX, Michoacan (& Pan-Am 50km Cup) 2019	20 Apr
18 Mar	Asian Champs, Nomi, JPN	17 Mar
7 Apr	Rio Maior, POR	6 Apr
23 Apr	Taicang, CHN	11-12 May
2 Jun	Gran Premio Cantones de La Coruña, ESP	8 Jun

24-26 Sep   Around Taihu, Suzhou, CHN   20-22 Oct
Plus European Race Walking Cup and World Championships
European Athletics Race Walking Permit Meetings 2018 & 2019
Dudince SVK 24/23 Mar, Podebrady CZE 7-8/6 Apr, Naumburg GER 14/13 Apr

IAAF HAMMER THROW CHALLENGE 2017

At the following meetings (above): Bragança Paulista, Osaka, Nanjing, Szczecin POL, Turku, Bydgoszcz, Székesfehérvár, Zagreb, Szombathely HUN (5 Sep). World Champs

MARATHON MAJORS 2017–2018

Tokyo 3 Mar, Boston 15 Apr, London 28 Apr, Berlin 29 Sep, Chicago 13 Oct, New York 3 Nov

ASIAN GRAND PRIX 2017

Chongqing CHN 4 Jun & 7 Jun

EUROPEAN AA CLASSIC MEETINGS 2019 (with 2018 dates of these meetings first)

Prague, CZE (Josef Odlozil Memorial) 5/3 Jun, Oslo (Clean Air Games) -/4 Jun. Haniá (Venexelia) 19 May/9 Jun, Montreuil-sous-Bois FRA 19/11 Jun, Bydgoszcz POL (European Athletics Festival) 29 May/11 Jun, Chorzów POL (Janusz Kusocinski Memorial) 8/15 Jun, Genève SUI 9/15 Jun, Samorin SVK (PTS) 29/15 Jun, København DEN 26/18 Jun, Sollentuna 28/18 Jun, Huelva ESP (Iberoamerican) 8/21 Jun, Tübingen GER 16/22 Jun, Kuortane FIN 23/22 Jun, Nancy (Tomblaine) FRA 27/22 Jun, La Chaux-de-Fonds SUI (Résisprint) 1 Jul/30 Jun, Marseille 16 Jun/2 Jul, Karlstad SWE 25/3 Jul, Székesfehérvár HUN (István Gyulai Memorial) 1-2/9 Jul, Lubin POL (Irena Szewinska Memorial) -/14 Jul, Sotteville-lès-Rouen FRA 17/16 Jul, Padova ITA 2 Sep/16 Jul, Liége (Naimette-Xhovémont, FRA 18/17 Jul. Heusden-Zolder BEL 21/20 Jul, Joensuu FIN Jul 4/24, Göteborg SWE 18/16 Aug, Bellinzona SUI 18 Jul/1 Sep, Guadalajara ESP 5 Jul.4 Sep, Andüjar ESP 1 Jun/6 Sep, 22 Aug/14 Sep Xhorzów (Kamila Skolimowska Memorial).
Special premium: Jun x/12- Athens (Filothei) GRE Women's Gala; Jun x/21 Athens street PV

USATF CHAMPIONSHIP SERIES 2018–2019

Philadelphia (Penn Relays) 26-28/27-28 Apr, Des Moines (Drake Relays) 26-28/26-27 Apr, Pasadena (USATF Distance Classic) 16 May, adidas Boost Boston Games 19 May/16 Jun, Nike Prefontaine Classic see above, US Championships Des Moines 21-24 Jun/25-28 Jul
Track Town USA Summer Series 2017: Bay Area CAL 28 Jun, Portland 2 Jul, New York 7 Jul.

NORTH AMERICA NACAC MEETINGS 2017–2018

St. George's GRN 8/21 Apr, George Town CAY -/1 Jun, Nassau BAH -/2 Jun, Kingston, JAM (Racers GP) 10/9 Jun, Guelph CAN 14/13 Jun, Vancouver (Harry Jerome Track Classic) CAN 28/27 Jun, Hamilton (Bermuda Invitational) Jul 1/11 May
2017: Baie Mahault, Guadeloupe 13 May

MAJOR INTERNATIONAL EVENTS 2019–2023

2019
European Indoor Championships – Glasgow, GBR (1-3 March)
European Throwing Cup – Samorîn, Slovakia (9-10 March)
IAAF World Cross Country Championships – Aarhus, Denmark (30 March)
African U18 and U20 Championships – Abidjan, Ivory Coast (April)
Asian Championships ~Doha, Qatar (21-24 Apr)
IAAF World Relays – Yokohama, Japan (11-12 May)
European Race Walking Cup – Alytus, Lithuania (19 May)
NACAC U23 and U18 Championships – Querétaro, Mexico (5-7 July)
European Cup 10,000m – London (Parliament Hill) (6 Jul)
European Cup Combined Events – Super League– Lutsk, Ukraine, First and Second League– Ribeira Braca, Madeira Portugal (6-7 July)
World University Games – Napoli, Italy (8-13 Jul)
European U20 Championships – Gävle, Sweden (Jul 11-14)
European U23 Championships – Borås, Sweden (Jul 18-21)
Pan-American U20 Championships – San José, Costa Rica (19-21 Jul)
Pan-American Games Lima, Peru (6- 11 Aug)
European Team Championships Super League – Bydgoszcz POL, First League – Sandnes NOR, Second League – Varazdin CRO, Third League – Skopje MKD (10-11 Aug)
All-Africa Games – RABAT, Morocco (26–30 August)
Europe v USA – Minsk, Belarus (9-10 Sep)
IAAF World Championships – Doha, Qatar (28 Sep – 6 Oct)
South East Asia Games – Manila, Philippines (1-6 Dec)
European Cross Country Championships – Lisbon, Portugal (8 Dec)

2020
IAAF World Indoor Championships – Nanjing, China (13-15 March)
European Throwing Cup Leiria, Poland (14 March)
IAAF World Half Marathon Championships – Gdynia, Poland (29 March)
IAAF World Race Walking Team Championships – Minsk, Belarus (2-3 May)
European Cup 10,000m – London (PH) (16 May)
European U18 Championships – Rieti, Italy (16-19 Jul)
IAAF World U20 Championships – Nairobi, Kenya (7-12 Jul)
European Championships – Paris (C), France (26-30 Aug)
Olympic Games – Tokyo, Japan (31 Jul – 9 Aug)
European Cross Country Championships – Fingal, Ireland (13 Dec)

2021
European Indoor Championships – Torun, Poland (5-7 March)
European Throwing Cup Leiria, Poland (13 March)
IAAF World Cross Country Championships – Bathurst, Australia (20 March)
European U23 Championships – Bergen (Fana), Norway (8-11 Jul)
European U20 Championships – Tallinn, Estonia (15-18 Jul)
Francophone Games – Moncton, Canada (23 Jul – 1 Aug)
World University Games – Chengdu, China 8-19 Aug)
IAAF World Championships – Eugene, USA (6-15 Aug)

2022
Youth Olympic Games – Daker, Sénégal (May/June)
Commonwealth Games – Birmingham, GBR (27 Jul – 7 Aug)
Asian Games – Hangzhou, China (10—25 Sep)

2023
African Games – Accra, Ghana
IAAF World Championships – Budapest, Hungary (26 Aug – 3 Sep)

Transfer of Nationality/Allegiance
Of athletes who have made world lists

Name	From	To	Noted	Eligible
Men				
Adhanom Abraha	ERI	SWE	29.4.12	2.11.18
Mohamed Ali Mohamed	SOM	NED	31.10.15	21.11.18
Amos Bartelsmeyer	USA	GER	.18	
Paraskevás Batzávalis	GRE	CYP	31.5.18	1.6.21
Rai Benjamin	ANT	USA		3.10.18
Hamid Bin Daoud	MAR	ESP	.12.18	
Nick Ekelund-Arenander	DEN	SWE		2.11.18
Mike Edwards	GBR	NGR	31.12.17	3.8.18
Ituah Enahoro	NGR	GER		
Blake Haney	USA	CAN	21.11.18	10.7.19
Patrick Ike	NGR	ESP		3.8.18
Haron Kiptoo Lagat	KEN	USA		3.10.18
Weldu Negash Gebretsadik	ETH	NOR	11.7.17	2.8.18
Sam Parsons	USA	GER	6.9.18	
Pedro Paulo Pichardo	CUB	POR	10.9.18	1.8.19
Yunier Pérez	CUB	ESP	31.12.16	.18
Leon Reid	GBR	IRL	.6.16	3.8.18
Abdelhamid Zerrifi	ALG	FRA		2.11.18
Women				
Risper Gesabwa	KEN	MEX	14.6.18	25.1.19
Kristina Knott	USA	PHI	.8.18	
Natalya Pogrebnyak	UKR	RUS		
Yanique Haye-Smith	JAM	TKS		21.11.18
Change of name and nationality				
Wilson Loyanae KEN	Oho Joo-han KOR		31.7.18	31.7.21

WORLD CHAMPIONSHIPS 2019

THE 17th IAAF World Championships will be staged in Doha, Qatar on 28 September to 6 October 20197 at the Stadium, Doha, Qatar.

Previous Championships

ATHLETICS EVENTS at the Olympic Games have had world championship status, but the first championships for athletics alone were staged in 1983. Separate World Championships were held for men's 50 kilometres walk in 1976 and for women's 3000m and 400m hurdles in 1980, as those events were not on the Olympic programme in those years.

Year	Venue	Athletes	Nations
1983	Helsinki, FIN	1572	153
1987	Rome, ITA	1741	157
1991	Tokyo, JPN	1551	164
1993	Stuttgart, GER	1624	187
1995	Göteborg, SWE	1804	191
1997	Athens, GRE	1882	198
1999	Seville, ESP	1821	201
2001	Edmonton, CAN	1677	189
2003	Saint-Denis, FRA	1679	198
2005	Helsinki, FIN	1688	189
2007	Osaka, JPN	1800	197
2009	Berlin GER	1895	200
2011	Daegu KOR	1742	199
2013	Moscow, RUS	1784	203
2015	Beijing, CHN	1761	205
2017	London GBR	1857	198

World Championship Records

Men

100m	9.58	Usain Bolt JAM	2009
200m	19.19	Usain Bolt JAM	2009
400m	43.18	Michael Johnson USA	1999
800m	1:43.06	Billy Konchellah KEN	1987
1500m	3:27.65	Hicham El Guerrouj MAR	1999
5000m	12:52.79	Eliud Kipchoge KEN	2003
10,000m	26:46.31	Kenenisa Bekele ETH	2009
Mar	2:06:54	Abel Kirui KEN	2009
3000mSt	8:00.43	Ezekiel Kemboi KEN	2009
110mh	12.91	Colin Jackson GBR	1993
400mh	47.18	Kevin Young USA	1993
HJ	2.41	Bohdan Bondarenko UKR	2013
PV	6.05	Dmitriy Markov AUS	2001
LJ	8.95	Mike Powell USA	1991
TJ	18.29	Jonathan Edwards GBR	1995
SP	22.23	Werner Günthör SUI	1987
DT	70.17	Virgilijus Alekna BLR	2005
HT	83.89	Ivan Tikhon BLR	2005
JT	92.80	Jan Zelezny CZE	2001
Dec	9045	Ashton Eaton USA	2015
4x100m	37.04	Jamaica	2011
4x400m	2:54.29	USA	1993
20kmW	1:17:21	Jefferson Pérez ECU	2003
50kmW	3:33:12	Johann Diniz FRA	2017

Women

100m	10.70	Marion Jones USA	1999
200m	21.74	Silke Gladisch GDR	1987
400m	47.99	Jarmila Kratochvílová TCH	1983
800m	1:54.68	Jarmila Kratochvílová TCH	1983
1500m	3:58.52	Tatyana Tomashova RUS	2003
3000m	8:28.71	Qu Yunxia CHN	1993
5000m	14:26.83	Almaz Ayana ETH	2016
10,000m	30:04.18	Berhane Adere ETH	2003
Mar	2:20:57	Paula Radcliffe GBR	2005
3000mSt	9:02.58	Emma Coburbn USA	2017
100mh	12.28	Sally Pearson AUS	2011
400mh	52.42	Melaine Walker JAM	2009
HJ	2.09	Stefka Kostadinova BUL	1987
PV	5.01	Yelena Isinbayeva RUS	2005
LJ	7.36	Jackie Joyner-Kersee USA	1987
TJ	15.50	Inessa Kravets UKR	1995
SP	21.24	Natalya Lisovskaya URS	1987
	21.24	Valerie Adams NZL	2011
DT	71.62	Martina Hellmann GDR	1987
HT	80.85	Anita Wlodarczyk POL	2015
JT	71,99	Mariya Abakumova RUS	2011
Hep	7128	Jackie Joyner-Kersee USA	1987
4x100m	41.07	Jamaica	2015
4x400m	3:16.71	USA	1993
20kmW	1:25:41	Olimpiada Ivanova RUS	2005
50kmW	4:05:56	Inês Henriques POR	2017

Winners of the most medals

16 Allyson Felix USA gold 200m 2005, 2007 & 2009, 400m 2015; 4x100m 2007, 2011 & 2017; 4x400m 2007, 2009, 2011, 2015; silver 400m 2011, 4x100m & 4x400m 2015; bronze 200m 2011 , 400m 2017

14 Merlene Ottey JAM gold 4x100m 1991, 200m 1993 & 1995; silver 200m 1983, 100m 1993 & 1995, 4x100m 1995; bronze 4x100m 1983, 100m & 200m 1987 & 1991, 4x100m 1993, 200m 1997

14 Usain Bolt JAM gold 100m, 200m & 4x100m 2009, 2013 & 2015; 200m & 4x100m 2011; silver 200m & 4x100m 2007, bronze 100m 2017

11 Veronica Campbell-Brown JAM gold 100m 2007, 200m 2011, 4x100m 2015; silver 100m 2005, 2011; 200m 2007, 4x100m 2005, 2007 & 2011, 200m 2009; bronze 200m 2015

11 LaShawn Merritt gold 400m 2009, 2013, 4x400m 2005, 2007, 2009, 2011, 2013, 2015; silver 400m 2007, 2011, 2015

10 Carl Lewis USA gold 100m, LJ & 4x100m 1983; 100m, LJ & 4x100m 1987, 100m & 4x100m 1991; silver LJ 1991; bronze 200m 1993

9 Jearl Miles Clark USA gold 400m 1993, 4x400m 1993, 1995 & 2003; silver 4x400m 1991, 1997, 1999; bronze 400m 1995 & 1997

9 Shelley-Ann Fraser-Pryce JAM gold 100m & 4x100m 2009 & 2015, 100m, 200m & 4x100m 2013; silver 4x100m 2007 & 2011

(8) Michael Johnson USA gold 200m 1991 & 1995, 400m 1993, 1995, 1997 & 1999, 4x400m 1993, 1995 (lost 1999 gold when team dq)

Winners of the most gold medals

11 Usain Bolt, Allyson Felix
8 Michael Johnson, Carl Lewis, LaShawn Merritt
7 Shelly-Ann Fraser-Pryce
6 Sergey Bubka PV 1983, 1987, 1991, 1993, 1995, 1997
5 Gail Devers USA 1993-9, Maurice Greene USA 1997-2001, Lars Riedel GER DT 1991-2001, Allen Johnson USA 1995-2003, Jeremy Wariner USA 2003-09, Kenenisa Bekele ETH 2005-09, Tirunesh Dibaba ETH 2003-13

Oldest world champions

Men   37y 258d Venyamin Soldatenko USSR 50kW 1976
Women 40y 268d Ellina Zvereva BLR DT 2001

Oldest medallists

Men   40y 274d Troy Douglas NED 3rd 4x1 2003
      40y 71d   John Powell USA 2nd DT 1987
Women 40y 268d Ellina Zvereva BLR 1st DT 2001

Youngest gold medallists

Women 17y 248d Merlene Frazer JAM 4x100m (ran in heat) 1991
Men   18y 177d Ismael Kirui KEN 10,000m 1993

Youngest medallists

M: 16y 305d Darrel Brown TRI 4x100m 2001
W: 15y 153d Sally Barsosio KEN 10,000m 1993

Most wins by event

Men   inc. all with 3 or more
100m   3 Carl Lewis USA 1983-87-91
         3 Maurice Greene USA 1997-99-2001
         3 Usain Bolt JAM 2011-13-15
200m   4 Usain Bolt JAM 2009-11-13-15
400m   4 Michael Johnson 1993-95-97-99
800m   3 Wilson Kipketer DEN 1995-97-99
1500m: 4 Hicham El Guerrouj MAR 1997-99-01-03
         3 Nourredine Morceli ALG 1991-93-95
5000m   3 Mo Farah GBR 2011-13-15
10,000m 4 Haile Gebrselasie ETH 1993-95-97-99
         4 Kenenisa Bekele ETH 2003-05-07-09
Mar   2 Abel Antón ESP 1997-9
         2 Jaouad Gharib MAR 2003-05
         2 Abel Kirui KEN 2009-11
3000mSt 4 Ezekiel Kemboi KEN 2009-11-13-15
         3 Moses Kiptanui KEN 1991-93-95
110mh   4 Allen Johnson USA 1995-97-2001-03
         3 Greg Foster USA 1983-87-91
400mh   2 Edwin Moses 1983-87; Félix Sánchez DOM 2001-03; Kerron Clement USA 2007-09
HJ   2 Javier Sotomayor CUB 1993-97
PV   6 Sergey Bubka UKR 1983-87-91-93-95-97
LJ   4 Iván Pedroso CUB 1995-97-99-2001
         4 Dwght Phillips USA 2003-05-09-11
TJ   3 Christian Taylor USA 2011-15-17
SP   3 Werner Günthör SUI 1987-91-93
         3 John Godina USA 1995-97-2001
DT   5 Lars Riedel GER 1991-93-95-97-2001

HT   3 Robert Harting GER 2009-11-13
         3 Pawl Fajdek POL 2013-15-17
JT   3 Jan Zelezny CZE 1993-95-2001
Dec   3 Dan O'Brien USA 1991-93-95
         3 Tomás Dvorák CZE 1997-99-2001
4x100m   7 USA 1983-87-91-93-99-2003-07
         4 Jamaica 2009-11-13-15
4x400m   9 USA 1987-93-95-2005-07-09-11-13-15
20kmW   3 Jefferson Pérez ECU 2003-05-07
50kmW   3 Rob. Korzeniowski POL 1997-2001-03
Women
100m   3 Shelly-Ann Fraser-Pryce 2009-13-15
200m   3 Allyson Felix USA 2005-07-09
400m   2 Cathy Freeman AUS 1997-99
         2 Christine Ohuruogu GBR 2009-13
800m   3 Maria Mutola MOZ 1993-2001-03
         3 Caster Semenya RSA 2009-11-17
1500m   2 Hassiba Boulmerka ALG 1991-95
         2 Tatyana Tomashova RUS 2003-05
         2 Maryam Jamal BRN 2007-09
5000m   2 Gabriela Szabo ROU 1997-99
         2 Tirunesh Dibaba ETH 2003-05
         2 Vivian Cheruiyot KEN 2009-11
         2 Meseret Defar ETH 2007-13
10,000m 3 Tirunesh Dibaba ETH 2005-07-13
Mar   2 Catherine Ndereba KEN 2003-07
         2 Edna Kiplagat KEN 2011-13
3000mSt 1 by seven women
100mh   3 Gail Devers USA 1993-95-99
400mh   2 Nezha Bidouane MAR 1997-2001
         2 Zuzana Hejnová CZE 2013-15
HJ   2 Stefka Kostadinova BUL 1987-1995
         2 Hestrie Cloete RSA 2001-03
         2 Blanka Vlasic CRO 2007-09
         2 Mariya Lasikskene RUS 2015-17
PV   3 Yelena Isinbayeva RUS 2005-07-13
LJ   4 Brittney Reese USA 2009-11-13-17
TJ   2 Tatyana Lebedeva RUS 2001-03
         2 Yargelis Savigne CUB 2007-09
         2 Caterine Ibargüen COL 2013-15
SP   4 Valerie Adams NZL 2007-09-11-13
         3 Astrid Kumbernuss GER 1995-97-99
DT   3 Franka Dietzsch GER 1999-2005-07
HT   3 Anita Wlodarczyk POL 2009-15-17
JT   2 Trine Hattestad NOR 1993-97
         2 Miréla Manjani GRE 1999-2003
         2 Osleidys Menéndez CUB 2001-05
         2 Barbora Spotáková CZE 2007-17
Hep   3 Carolina Klüft SWE 2003-05-07
         3 Jessica Ennis-Hill GBR 2009-11-15
4x100m   7 USA 1987-95-97-2001-05-07-17
         4 Jamaica 1991-2009-13-15
4x400m   7 USA 1993-95-2003-07-09-11-17
         3 Russia 1999-2005-13
         3 Germany: GDR 1983-87, GER 1997
20kmW   3 Olga Kaniskina RUS 2007-09-11
60kmW   1 Inís Henriques POR 2017

Oldest Competitor

47y 108d Merlene Ottey SLO 100m (1st round) 2007

Timetable and Qualifying Standards 2019

Days: a 27 Sep, b 28 Sep, c 29 Sep, d 30 Sep, e 1 Oct, f 2 Oct, g 3 Oct, h 4 Oct, i 5 Oct, j 6 Oct

Event	Days	Qual	No.
Men			
100m	a-a-b-b	10.10	48*
200m	c-d-e	20.40	56
400m	e-f-h	45.30	48
800m	b-c-e	1:45.80	48
1500m	g-h-j	3:36.00	45
(or 1M)		3:53.10	
5000m	a-d	13:22.50	42
10,000m	j	27:40.00	27
Mar	i/j	2:16:00	100
3000mSt	e-h	8:29.00	45
110mh	d-f-f	13.46	40
400mh	a-b-d	49.30	40
HJ	e-h	2.30	32
PV	b-e	5.71	32
LJ	a-b	8.17	32
TJ	a-c	16.95	32
SP	g-i	20.70	32
DT	b-d	65.00	32
HT	e-f	76.00	32h qual
JT	i-j	83.00	32
Dec	f-g	8200	24
4x100m	h-l		16
4x400m	i-j		16
20kmW	c/d	1:22:30	60
50kmW	b/c	3:59:00	50
Women			
100m	b-c-c	11.24	48*
200m	d-e-f	23.02	58
400m	d-e-g	51.80	48
800m	a-b-d	2:00.60	48
1500m	f-g-i	4:06.50	45
(or 1M)		4:25.20	
5000m	f-i	15:22.00	42
10,000m	b	31:50.00	27
Mar	a/b	2:37:00	100
3000mSt	a-d	9:40:00	45
100mh	i-j-j	12.98	40
400mh	e-f-h	56.00	40
HJ	a-d	1.94	32
PV	a-c	4.56	32
LJ	i-j	6.72	32
TJ	g-i	14.20	32
SP	f-g	18.00	32
DT	f-h	61.20	32
HT	a-b	71.00	32
JT	d-e	61.50	32
Hep	f-g	6300	24
4x100m	h-l		16
4x400m	i-j		16
20kmW	h/i	1:33:30	60
50kmW	b/c	4:30:00	30
Mix 4x400	b-c		16

Individual athletes can qualify by:

1. Achieving the entry standard within the qualification period with criteria decided by IAAF.

2. Finishing in designated competitions: a. Area champions (subject to approval). b. For 10,000m: top 15 in senior races at 2019 World CC Champs. c. Marathons: top 10 at IAAF Gold Label Marathons in qualification period.

3. Wild card as reigning World outdoor champion, winner of 2019 Diamond League, leaders of IAAF Challenges for Hammer. Race Walks, Combined Events. If both are from the same country, only one of the two athletes can be entered with this Wild Card. If a Member Federation has four athletes in one event as a result of this regulation, all four will be permitted to compete

4. Being amongst the best ranked athletes in the IAAF Top Performance Lists within the qualification periods (not for 10,000m, marathons, race walks).

The IAAF has established a target number of athletes for each discipline (No. as above) and extra non-qualifying athletes will be invited to fill the quotas.

Relay teams can qualify by being in the first ten (12 in mixed 4x400m) at the 2019 IAAF World Relays. or being one of the best ranked teams at the end of the qualifying period to fill the remaining places.

Qualification Period: For the 10,000m, Marathon, Race Walks, Relays and Combined Events: from 7 Mar 2018 to midnight 6 Sep 2019 (regardless of time zone).

For all other events: from 7 Sep 2018 to midnight 6 Sep 2019 (regardless of the time zone).

Age limits: athletes born in 2004 or later may not be entered; athletes born 2002-03 may compete in any event except throws, combined events, 10,000m, marathon and race walks; athletes born 2000-01 may compete in any event except marathon and 50km race walk

For full details see: media.aws.iaaf.org

Most World Champs Appearances
Men
12 Jesús Ángel García ESP 1993-2015
10 Virgilijus Alekna LTU 1995-2013
10 Kim Collins SKN 1995-2015
10 João Vieira POR 1999-2017
Women
11 Susana Feitor POR 1991-2011
10 Franka Dietzsch GER 1991-2009
10 Nicoleta Grasu ROU 1993-2013

OBITUARY 2018

Irena Szewinska (Poland) (b. 24 May 1946 Leningrad) née Kirszenstein died on 29 June in Warsaw. She was one of the greatest woman athletes of all time and a very gracious lady. Starting as a sprinter and long jumper, her long smooth strides were ideally suited to the 400m to which she progressed later in her career. Her collection of 41 medals from major championships is unrivalled and she was the only athlete, male or female, to set world records at 100, 200 and 400m. In all she set 13 world records from 1965 to 1976: 100m 11.1 in 1965 and 11.19 in 1968; 200m: four from 22.7 in 1965 to 22.0 (22.21 auto) in 1974; 400m: three from the first sub-50 second time, 49.9 in 1974 (in just her second race at the distance) to 49.28 (officially given as 49.29) in 1976; two at 440y and two at 4x100m relay.

Two of those world records were set while winning Olympic titles, 200m in 1968 and 400m in 1976. In all she won seven Olympic medals: in 1964 at 18 she took silver at 200m and long jump with gold on the Polish sprint relay team; in 1968 she also took bronze at 100m; and in 1972 a bronze at 200m. She was supreme at 400m in the mid-1970s, winning 34 consecutive finals in that period, including the 1976 Olympics when she won by some ten metres. Her Olympic career ended in anti-climax as she pulled a muscle in the semi-finals of the 400m in 1980.

At European Championships she collected a record five gold medals: 200m, LJ and 4x100m in 1966, 100m and 200m 1974, with a silver and four bronze in her four championships to 1978.

At the first World Cup in 1977 Szewinska received the trophy on behalf of the winning European team; she had won an individual double with the 200m and 400m, in which she had run a marvellous race to beat Marita Koch 49.52 to 49.76, Koch's last defeat at 400m for four years. Szewinska contested the biennial European Cup competition from 1965 to 1979 amassing a record total of points, including four 1sts, two 2nds and three 3rds in individual events. Her other honours included two golds, a silver and two bronze at European Indoors, gold and silver at European Juniors, and two golds at the World Student Games. Szewinska also set a world indoor record with 7.1 for 60m in 1974.

In all she set 38 Polish records and won 20 Polish titles at four individual events: 100m 1966-8, 1972-4, 1979; 200m 1966, 1968, 1971-5, 1979; 400m 1978, LJ 1965, 1967, 1971-2.

She married her coach Janusz Szewinski on 25 Dec 1967 and gave birth to son Andrzej in February 1970. She had many official positions in athletics and in May 1994 was elected chairwoman of the Polish Association of Women's Sports. She was president of the Polish Athletics Federation 1997-2009 and a member of the IAAF Women's Committee 1984-2007. In February 1998 she was elected a member of the International Olympic Committee and in 2005 as the third woman to the IAAF Council.

The Polish Athletics Federation will organise an **Irena Szewinska Memorial** meeting from 2019 on a date close to June 29, the day she died.

Irena KIRSZENSTEIN/SZEWINSKA – Yearly bests

	100m	200m	400m	LJ
1961	12.6	27.9		5.11
1962	11.9	25.4		5.72
1963	11.6	24.2		5.84
1964	11.5	23.1/23.13		6.60
1965	11.1	22.7		6.54
1966	11.2	23.1		6.55
1967	11.2	22.7		6.62
1968	11.19A	22.58		6.67
1969	11.3	23.0		6.56
1970	11.8	–		–
1971	11.2	22.75		6.62/6.67w
1972	11.33	22.74		6.49/6.57w
1973	11.1/11.33	22.96/22.7	52.0	6.36
1974	**11.13/10.9**	**22.21/22.0**	50.32/49.9	
1975	11.23/11.1	22.67/22.4/22.49w	50.50	
1976	11.22	22.41	49.28	
1977	11.26	22.37	49.52	
1978	11.44	22.86	50.40	
1979	11.39	22.84	50.89	
1980	11.42/11.14w	22.93/22.80w	51.00	

Also: 80mh 10.8 (1965), 100mh 14.0 (1969), 400mh 56.62 (1977), HJ 1.66 (1966), Pen 4036 (1969)

See ATHLETICS 2018 for obituaries of these men and women who died in early 2018:

Chala Adugna, Hassan Agabani, Peter Allday, Horace Ashenfelter, Guy Arbogast, Étienne Bally, Jarrod Bannister, Roger Bannister, Irina Beglyakova, Cliff Bourland, Edwin Carr, Eugene Cole, Guy Cury, Christian Fuchs, Jonathan Gray, Sergey Litvinov, David Martin, Milan Matos, Paavo Niemelä, Milica Rajkov-Ninokov, Hazel Rider, Aristístis Robánis, Clyde Scott, Jack Sinclair, Jan Smiding, Osvaldo Suárez, Basilios Syllis, Gerald Weiss, Peter Wells, Ken Young.

Erkki AHVENNIEMI (Finland) (b. 18 Dec 1932 Lappajärvi) on May 18 at Jyväskylä. A farmer and world class javelin thrower, his short career ended dramatically in Warsaw on 15 June 1958. On his first throw, in spite of rupturing a knee ligament badly, he achieved a distance of 79.33, which would remain his pb. In the weeks before the injury, he had been throwing 77-78 m regularly, and 83m on a throw that landed flat. His breakthrough season 1957 included winning the Finnish title and in four international dual matches, highlighted with a then pb 78,94 against Sweden in Stockholm. Helped by a special knee brace, he competed occasionally until the early 1970o, but never again achieving 70 m

Bernard James **'Bernie' ALLARD** (USA) (b. 26 Mar 1934 Missoula, Montana) on 28 December in San José. At high jump he had a best of 2.054 to rank 16th in the world and was 4th at 2.04 in the US Olympic Trials in 1956 when at Notre Dame University. At AAU Championships he was 3rd in 1951 (aged 17) and 2nd in 1956 and tied for 2nd at the NCAAs in 1955. Pb 110mh 14.3 (1956). He became a leading lawyer.

Lawrence **'Lol' ALLEN** (GBR) (b. 25 Apr 1921 Sheffield) on 16 December in Sheffield. A member of Sheffield United Harriers, he had a great race walk rivalry with Roland Hardy in the early 1950s. Unfortunately he was disqualified in his two 10,000m internationals – at the 1952 Olympic Games and at the 1950 Europeans (after finishing in 2nd place). He was RWA champion at both 10 miles and 20 miles 1949-51 and 1958, while at the AAAs he was 2nd at 7 miles each year 1950-52 and 3rd at 2 and 7 miles in 1949. Walks pbs: 2M 13:43.4 (1950), 5M 35:40.8 (1950), 10,000m 44:32.8 (1950), 7M 50:22.6 (1950), 10M 1:11:35 (1954), 20M 2:48:48/2:41:40 short (1954).

William David **'Bill' BAILLIE** (New Zealand) (b. 28 May 1934 Nelson) on 25 December at Cooks Beach. He was a tough and powerful, barrel-chested distance runner who excelled from half mile to the marathon. He set world records for 20,000m 59:28.6 and 1 hour 20,190m in Auckland on 24 Aug 1963. He was 6th at 5000m at the 1964 Olympic Games and competed at four Commonwealth Games: 1954- 4th 880y and 7th 1 mile, 1958- ht 1M, 9th 3M, 1962- dnf 6M, 1966- 9th 6M. NZ champion: 880y 1954-5, 1M 1958, 1961; 3M 1956, 6M 1959-60, 1963-7; 10M Rd 1965, and CC 1960 & 1963. NZ records: 3M 13:54.4 (1955), 10M 49:57.0 (1959) & 48:09.0 (1963), 15M 1:14:44.4 (1968), 25.000m 1:17:22.4 (1965), Mar 2:20:13 (1959), Other pbs: 880y 1:52.3 (1954), 1500m 3:45.1 (1965), 1M 3:59.2 (1954), 2M 8:34.8 (1964), 3M 13:15.8 (1964), 5000m 13:40.0 (1964), 6M 28:07.0 (1963), 10,000m 29:01.0 (1965). He continued with much success as a Masters athlete and was appointed a Member of the New Zealand Order of Merit in 2001.

Iain Stuart **BAIN** (b. 16 Feb 1934) on 20 April. At the hammer he was AAA junior champion in 1951-2 and a UK junior record (12 lb hammer) 52.60 in 1952. He was Scottish champion in 1956-7 and 1959, and won the UAU title when at Oxford University in 1956, with one international for Britain in 1959. Pb 56.08 (1956).

Kebede BALCHA (Ethiopia) (b. 7 Sep 1951) on 10 July in Toronto. He came to the fore by winning the Athens Marathon in 1977 and in 1979, when he also won the World Cup marathon in Montreal and was African champion. He was the only Ethiopian to earn a medal at the inaugural IAAF World Championships in 1983, with the marathon silver (2:10:27) behind Robert de Castella of Australia (2:10:03). He went on be 2nd in 1985, 3rd in 1988 and 3rd in 1989 at African Championships and was 3rd at the African Games in 1987. In all he won 7 of his 29 marathons including again in Montreal in 1981, 1983 and 1985. and he was 2nd in Tokyo 1985. In his only Olympic participation in 1980 in Moscow, he did not finish, and he was also 14th in the World Cross in 1981. He was among a group of eight Ethiopian sports people seeking asylum in Toronto in 1999.

Progression at Marathon: 1977- 2:14:41, 1979- 2:11:35, 1981- 2:11:11, 1983- 2:10:03, 1984- 2:11:40, 1985- 2:11:19, 1986- 2:14:11, 1987- 2:16:07, 1988- 2:12:04, 1990- 2:20:27.

Arthur **'Art' BARNARD** (USA) (b. 10 Mar 1929 Seattle) on 1 May in California. He was ranked in the world top ten for 110m hurdles each year 1950-3 and took the Olympic bronze medal (to complete a US medal sweep) in 1952, after 5th in the AAUs and a surprise 3rd in the US Olympic Trials. He was 3rd in the NCAAs in 1951 for the University of Southern California. Pbs: 100y 9.7 (1953), 110m/120yh 14.1/14.02w (1952), 220yh St 23.5 (1951), 440yh 54.2 (1954).

Progression at 110mh/120yh (position on world list): 1948- 14.6y (35=), 1949- 14.5 (27=), 1950- 14.2y (7=), 1951- 14.1y (6=)/14.0yw, 1952- 14.1 (7=)/14.0w, 1953- 14.1y (3=), 1954- 14.4y (18=), 1955- 14.6y (54=).

Adrienne BEAMES (Australia) (b. 7 Sep 1941) on 27 December. In the days before women's distance running was established, she claimed various world records on the track including 1500m 4:09.6, 1M 4:29.8, 5000m 15:48.5 (1972) and 10,000m 34:08.0 (all 1972), as well as 10M 57:23 and marathon 2:46:30 (1971). But none of these could be substantiated, as the only source was her coach Fred Warwick. Authenticated pbs included 1500m 4:38.5 (1969) and Marathon 3:00:50 (1978). She was 2nd in 1969 AUS cross-country.

Nicholas Kiplagat **BETT** (Kenya) (b. 27 Jan 1990 Uasin Gishu County) was killed in a car accident near Lessos in Nandi County on 8 August on his return from competing in the African Championships. Very much the peak of his career was his sensational and surprising win at 400m hurdles at the 2015 World Championships. His time of 47.79 was a Kenyan record from a previous best of 48.29A in the Kenyan Trials and pre-season best of 49.03 in 2014 when 3rd in the African Championships (also 3rd at 4x400m). He had also been 3rd in the Kenyan Champs with 50.39A in 2011, In 2016 he had a moderate start to the year and was disqualified for deliberately knocking down the last hurdle in his heat at the Olympic Games but returned to form with a 48.03 win in the Diamond League final. After a best of 49.70 in 2017 he ran a 2018 best of 48.88A in March but was last in the final at the Commonwealth Games.

Progression at 400mh: 2010- 53.11A, 2011- 50.35A, 2012- 53.2A, 2013- 49.70A, 2014- 49.03, 2015- 47.79, 2016- 48.01, 2017- 49.70, 2018- 48.88A/49.08.

Janis BOJARS (USSR/Latvia) (b. 12 May 1956 Ilukste) on 5 June in Riga. At the shot he was European Indoor champion in 1983 and 1984 and was 3rd at the World Indoors in 1985. Outdoors he was 2nd at the 1982 Europeans, 5th at the 1983 Worlds and 3rd in the European Cup in 1983. He was USSR champion outdoors in 1983 and indoors in 1981-3 and 1986, and won 18 Latvian titles indoors and out 1976-87 with a final Latvian record of 21.74 (1984).

Annual progress at shot: 1973- 14.83, 1974- 16.64, 1975- 16.63, 1976- 16.97, 1977- 17.75, 1978- 18.00, 1979- 19.42, 1980- 20.02, 1981- 20.36, 1982- 21.31, 1983- 21.40, 1984- 21.74, 1985- 21.31, 1986- 20.98, 1987- 21.14, 1988- 20.79, 1989- 19.28.

Naftali BON (Kenya) (b. 9 Oct 1945 Kapsabet) on 2 November in Kapsabet. He was a member of the silver medal-winning Kenyan 4x400m team and a quarter-finalist at 400m at the 1968 Olympic Games. He also ran in the heats of the 1970 Commonwealth Games. Pbs: 400m 46.21A (1968), 800m 1:46.5A (1989), 400mh 52.4 (1969).

Jaroslav BRABEC (Czech Republic) (b. 27 July 1949 Litomeric) on 20 May. The shot putter won the gold medal at the European Indoors in 1973 with bronze in 1972 and 1974, 4th 1975, 6th 1978 & 1979. At the Olympic Games he was 10th in

1972 and 11th in 1976 and at the Europeans: 1971- dnq 17, 1974- 7, 1978- 8. He set five Czech records from 19.73 in 1971 to 21.04 in 1973 (with discus pb 54.80 in 1971), and was Czechoslovak champion in 1971-3, 1975-6, 1979 and 1981-2, plus indoors 1971, 1973, 1975 and 1978-9. He competed for Dukla Praha, for whom he coached many top athletes from 1987.

Annual progress: 1967- 15.66, 1968- 16.45, 1969- 17.39, 1970- 18.84, 1971- 20.31, 1972- 20.97, 1973- 21.04, 1974- 20.37, 1975- 20.45, 1976- 20.58, 1977- 19.80, 1978- 20.00, 1979- 19.71, 1980- 20.05, 1981- 20.04, 1982- 19.97, 1983- 18.80, 1985- 17.39, 1987- 15.95, 1988- 16.72, 1989- 15.09.

Arthur George BRAGG (USA) (b. 3 Dec 1930 Baltimore) on 25 August in Los Angeles. He was ranked in the world's top six at 100m each year 1950-4, including 2nd in 1953 and 1954, and was 2nd in 1953 and 3rd in 1954 at 200m, He had pbs of 100y 9.4 (1954), 100m 10.3 (1953), 200m half turn 20.6 (1953), 220y turn 21.1 (1954), straight 20.8 (1951). He was 2nd at both 100m and 200m with 4x100m relay gold at the 1951 Pan-American Championships and was AAU champion at 100m/y in 1950 and 1953-4 and 220y in 1954 (2nd 1950 & 1953). For Morgan State University he won the 100y and was 2nd at 220y in the NCAAs in 1951. He won the US Olympic Trials 100m in 1952 but pulled up injured in the Olympic semi-final.

Progression at 100y/100m: 1950- 9.5/10.4, 1951- 9.6/10.6, 1952- 9.9/10.5, 1953- 9.5/10.3, 1954- 9.4.

George Henry **BROWN** Jr (USA) (b. 25 Jul 1931) on 23 July in Sacramento. Top ranked in the world in 1951, 1952 (pb 8.00) and 1953, he won 41 consecutive long jump competitions from 1950 until only 3rd at the US Olympic Trials in 1952 and then recorded no jumps in the Olympic final. He was, however, NCAA champion for UCLA in 1951 and 1952 and AAU champion each year 1951-53 with 2nd in 1954 and 1956. Other pbs 100m 10.5 (1951), 200m 21.3 (1952).

Progression at LJ (position on world list): 1948- 7.27 (50=), 1949- 7.68 (2=), 1950- 7.47 (17=), 1951- 7.95 (1), 1952- 8.00 (1), 1953- 7.90 (1), 1954 7.63 (6), 1955- 7.26 (101=), 1956- 7.75 (8), 1957- 7.49 (38=).

Andreas 'Res' BRÜGGER (Switzerland) (b. Meiringen 1927) on 27 December in Zürich. He was a coach and president of LC Zürich, and as meeting director (1973-2000) he ensured that the Weltklasse in Zürich was at the pinnacle of international one-day meetings for many years, with 19 world records set at the meeting in that era. He became the first president of Euromeetings in 1979 and in December 2018 was awarded the IAAF's President Award. In 1965 he set his shot pb of 14.55 and was Swiss champion; 7 internationals. He became a director of Swiss Re.

Garry CALVERT (Australia) (b. 15 Apr 1954) 27 July in Beijing, where he was working as coach of the Chinese javelin throwers. Australian javelin champion in 1979 and 1981-82 (and second four times), he was selected for the 1982 Commonwealth Games but unable to compete due to injury. Pb 81.21 (old spec.) (1981). He coached notable javelin throwers such as Petra Rivers, Jarrod Bannister and Neeraj Chopra (he was the Indian team coach from February 2016 to April 2017).

Delia Beatriz CAPOTOSTO (Argentina) (b. 16 May 1962 Berisso) on 20 December in Buenos Aires. At 100m hurdles she was South American Junior champion in 1977 and 1980-1 (also 100m & LJ 1978, 200mh 1980-1), South American champion in 1983 and 1985 (3rd 1979 and 1981, and 2nd 100m 1977), was 6th in 1979 and 7th in 1983 at the Pan-American Games and competed at the 1984 Olympic Games (heat). She was Argentine champion eight times: 1978, 1980-3, 1985, 1987 and 1989 and set ten national records from 13.92 (1980) to 13.45 (1984) and four hand timed to 13.2 (1983).). plus 400mh 59.86 (1984) Other pb: 60mh 8.47i (1985).

Kenneth Reginald John CARTER (GBR) (b. 7 Mar 1947) on 25 October. A member of Southend AC, he had one international for Britain at 20k walk in 1978. He was 3rd in the AAA 3000m walk in 1976 and had walks pbs of: 1M 6:37.8 (1978), 3000m 12:34.6 (1984), 5000m 22:21.0 (1974), 10,000m 45:11.0 (1984), 20k 1:32:16 (1981), 50k 4:56:05t (1972).

George CHAPLIN (GBR) (b. 18 Feb 1931) in August in Coventry. He made three international appearances for Britain at 35k/50k walks 1968-72. A member of Coventry Godiva Harriers, he was 2nd at 20M and 50k and 3rd at 1M in the RWA Champs in 1957 and won ten Midland titles. His walks pbs: 3000m 13:00.6 (1972), 2M 13:55.8 (1968), 10,000m 45:37.2 (1972), 7M 52:11.0 (1968), 20k 1:34:23 (1972), 50k 4:20:05/4:25:48t (1972), 2Hr 24,443m (1964).

Sheila CHEPNGETICH Keter (Kenya) (b. 27 Jun 1995) on 6 May in Kericho. She was 8th with team gold in the 2013 World Junior Cross-country and at 1500m was 6th in the World Youths in 2011, 3rd at the African U20 (also 2nd at 3000m) in 2013, and 3rd at the World Juniors in 2014. Pbs: 800m 2:05.4A (2013), 1500m 4:11.21 (2014), 3000m 9:33.0 (2013). She was serving a drugs ban (3 years 1 month 1 week) for a positive test on 12 December 2014.

Katherine CLAUSNITZER (Germany/GDR) (b. 6 Feb 1952 Großschönau) on 10 May in Dresden. European junior champion at 1500m in 1970, she had 7 internationals 1970-5 and ran a GDR 3000m record of 9:01.8 in 1975. Other pbs: 400m 57.5 (1976), 800m 2:05.6 (1974), 1000m 2:42.1i (1976) and 1500m 4:13.2 (1975)

Pierre COLNARD (France) (b. 18 Feb 1929 Liffol-le-Petit, Haute-Marne) on 30 March in Sermaize-les-Bains, Marne. Although he did not start his competitive career until he was 29, at the shot he was 7th in 1966 and 5th in 1969 at the European Championships, 9th at the 1968 Olympics, 4th in 1967 and 3rd in 1970 at the European Indoors, 3rd at the European Cup in 1965 and 1970, and French champion 1960-1, 1963, 1965-7 and 1969-70. He set 17 French records from 16.61 in 1961 to 19.77 in 1970, 61 internationals 1959-73, pb DT 48.82 (1966).

Paul COPPEJANS (Belgium) (b. 28 Sep 1933 Brussels) on 13 August in Ganshoren. At pole vault he had 46 internationals for Belgium and won seven national titles 1962-8, setting six national records from 4.46 (1963) to 4.73 (1966). He competed at the 1964 Olympic Games (dnq 27) and the European Championships in 1958 (21st) and 1966 (dnq 17th).

Ronald John CRAWFORD (Australia) (b. 26 Mar 1936 Randwick, New South Wales) in Sydney on 8 August. He competed at the walks at three Olympic Games: 13th in 1956, 11th in 1960 and 22nd in 1964 at 20k, and 13th in 1956, dq in 1960 and 11th in 1964 at 50k. His one national title was at 10k in 1961. Walks pbs: 3000m 13:12.4 (1961), 2M 13:50.6 (1962), 10,000m 46:31.0 (1964), 20k 1:34:08 (1964), 30k 2:33:02 (1963), 50k 4:24:19.6 (1964).

Jean DAROT (France) (b. 6 Jan 1931 Vaucresson) on 25 August in Saran. He was French discus champion 1953-5 and competed in the European Championships in 1950 (SP & DT) and 1954 (DT) without reaching a final. Pbs: SP 15.01 (1954), DT 50.95 (1959); 36 internationals 1950-62.

Aleksey DESYATCHIKOV (USSR) (b. 31 Oct 1932 Moscow) on 4 June in Moscow. He was ranked 8th in the world at 10,000m in 1958 and 8th at 5000m and 4th at 10,000m in 1960 when he was 4th in the Olympic 10,000m. In an era when the USSR was very strong in distance running, he was also 2nd to Pyotr Bolotnikov at 5000m in 1958 and at both distances in 1960 at the USSR Championships. Pbs 5000m 13:52.6, 10,000m 28:39.71 (both 1960).

Arthur R.P. EUSTACE (New Zealand) (b. 22 Apr 1926) on 24 April at his home in Kapiti Coast. An honorary life member of the IAAF from 1999, having been a Council member 1984-98 as Oceania Group Representative, he had a lifetime of service to New Zealand athletics as athlete, coach and administrator. He was elected Patron of Athletics New Zealand in 2009 and re-elected each year since. He was New Zealand champion at both 120y and 220y hurdles in 1946-8 and at 100y in 1948 and 1951. At the 1950 Commonwealth Games he won a bronze medal at 4x110y as well as being a 100y semi-finalist. He went on to run for Fiji at 4x110y at the 1954

Games, living there in 1951-4. New Zealand records: 120yh 15.0 (1947), 220yh (3) to 24.4 (1948). Pbs: 100y 9.9 (1949), 220y 21.8 (1949).

Ken FOREMAN (USA) (b. 29 Aug 1922) on 23 December. He coached for five decades at Seattle Pacific University and was head coach of US teams at the 1983 World Championships and 1986 Goodwill Games, having been appointed head women's coach of the US team that boycotted the 1980 Olympic Games. While at the University of Southern California, where he earned a doctorate, he won two national championships in gymnastics.

Ippolito 'Ito' GIANI (Italy) (b. 8 Sep 1941 Varese) on 18 September in Varese. He was 5th at 100m at the 1966 European Championships and also competed at the 1964 Olympic Games. Italian champion at 200m in 1967, when he won three medals at the World University Games (1st 4x100m, 3rd 100m and 200m) and also Mediterranean Games champion at 200m and 4x100m and medley relay silver at the 1966 European Indoor Games. 20 internationals 1963-6, pbs 100m 10.4/10.71 (1966), 200m 20.9A/21.0 (1967).

John GILMOUR (Australia) (b. 3 May 1919 Scotland) on 1 August at the age of 99. He went to Western Australia as a child and had been a promising athlete before World War II. He suffered hugely as a Japanese prisoner-of-war in Changi, Singapore, but threw himself into running after his recovery. He achieved state titles and eventually set extraordinary records as a masters athlete, including marathon records for M55 2:38:19 (1978), M60 2:41:07 (1981) and M70 3:03:04 (1989). He received the Order of Australia in 1979, the year in which he celebrated his 60th birthday in Hannover by winning every event at the World Masters Games from 800m to marathon in `a rampage unequalled in the masters' track and field,' with new world records in four of five events. His story 'All In My Stride' by Richard Harris was published in 1999.

Daeshon GORDON (Jamaica) (b. 8 Nov 1996) on 21 October in Natchitoches, Louisiana. She set a Jamaican junior 100m hurdles record with her pb 12.97 for 4th at the 2014 World Junior Championships and she was 3rd in the 2015 Pan-Am Juniors. Her sudden death came while she was studying at Northwestern State University, USA (previously she was at Louisiana State for two years). Her 2018 best was 13.14 and 13.04w. Other pbs: 60m 7.55i (2018), 60mh 8.04i (2016), 400mh 57.24 (2015).

Bo GRAHN (Finland) (b. 6 Oct 1947 Tolkkinen) on 16 July at Vantaa. The second Finn to exceed 20m in the shot, his pb 20.09 came in 1972, when he also took Finnish Champs silver, won against Sweden and competed in Munich Olympic

Games qualifying round. He worked as a sports journalist.

Joyce Alice (Hanger) **GREEN** (Australia) (b. 24 Aug 1927) on 20 May. Australian champion at 880y in 1956, her pbs were: 100y 11.2, 100m 12.4, 220y 25.6, 440y 59.6, 880y 2:26.9.

Saida GUNBA (USSR/Georgia) (b. 30 Aug 1959 Sukhumi) on 24 November in Pitsunda, Georgia At the javelin, she won the Olympic silver medal in 1980 with 67.76, close to the pb of 68.28 (7th on the world all-time list at the end of that year) that she had set three weeks earlier. She was USSR champion in 1978 and 1979, and in the latter year was 4th in the European Cup and 5th in the World Cup – also 3rd in the European Cup in 1983.

Progression at JT: 1976- 54.36, 1977- 58.28, 1978- 60.26, 1979- 63.08, 1980- 68.28, 1983- 61.52, 1984- 62.78, 1986- 61.48, 1987- 57.20, 1988- 61.50.

Jiří HEITFLEIS (Czech Republic) (b. 15 Mar 1928 Ústí nad Orlicí) on 5 July. A member of the ATFS 1966-2008 and president of the Czech Association of Athletic Statisticians 1991-2009, he was best known in the Czech Republic as an announcer at major meetings for three decades, including at the Golden Spike in Ostrava for 20 years and at the European Championships in Prague in 1978.

Jon HENDERSHOTT (USA) (b. 20 Jul 1946 Bend, Oregon) on 9 April at his home in Salem, Oregon. A great enthusiast of the sport, he joined *Track and Field News* with his first contribution in the magazine appearing in 1967. He worked for them until his retirement at the end of 2015, but continued his long association as a freelance up to the time of his death. His father was a track coach and Jon's love of the sport was such that he subscribed to T&FN from 1962. He graduated in journalism from San José State University and his principal work was "Track's Greatest Women", published by Track and Field News in 1987, with detailed profiles of 15 of the greatest female athletes in history

Lars Erik **HINDMAR** (Sweden) (b. 11 Dec 1921 Borås, né Karlsson) on 2 December in Mölndal. A race walker, he was disqualified at Olympic Games in 1952 (10,000m) and 1956 (20k) and had eight further internationals. Swedish 10,000m track champion 1949 and 1955 (2nd 1943-5). AAA champion at 2 mile 1946-7 and 7 miles 1946. Walks pbs: 1500m 5:46.2 (world best 1945), 3000m 11:58.2 (1945), 5000m 20:41.8 (1945), 10,000m 43:33.0 (1956), 20,000m 1:32:55.0 (1955), 20k 1:30:38 (1956). 50k 4:26.15 (1959).

Clarence **Darrow HOOPER** (USA) (b. 30 Jan 1932 Fort Worth) on 19 August. In 1952 he was the Olympic silver medallist in the shot when he lost to Parry O'Brien by just 2cm, 17.41 to 17.39, after beating both O'Brien and the former world record holder Jim Fuchs at the US Olympic Trials in what remained his pb of 17.40. He was ranked successively 6th, 3rd and 3rd in the world in 1951-3 but never won an AAU title, coming 3rd in 1951 and 4th in 1952. He was NCAA champion in 1951 while at Texas A&M where he also excelled at American Football. Pb discus 51.82 (1952). He worked as a civil engineer and founded his own successful company Hooper Engineering Laboratories.

Progression at SP (position on world list): 1950- 15.31 (45), 1951- 16.65 (7), 1952- 17.41 (3), 1953- 17.17 (3).

János HRENEK (Hungary) (b. 9 Sep 1954 Budapest) on 6 October in Budapest. Hungarian champion at 1500m in 1979, he was 5th at 800m at the European Juniors in 1973 and competed at 1500m at the 1977 European Indoors. Pbs: 400m 49.4 (1975), 800m 1:47.5 (1978), 1500m 3:39.5 (1977), 5000m 14:52.0 (1976). 16 internationals 1973-9.

Esko INKALA (Finland) (b. 13 Mar 1926 Jyväskylä) on 23 March in Liminka. The leading Finnish sprinter after WW II, he was an Oulu policeman who won five national titles: 100m 1949-51, 200m 1950 & 1953, losing 1952 Helsinki Olympic season to an injury. 11 international dual matches 1949-53 with 15 individual and 10 relay races. Pbs 100m 10.9 (1949) & 10.7w (1953), 200m 22.1 (1953), 400m 50.2 (1953).

Hugh Reid **JACK** (Australia) (b. 19 Dec 1929) on 19 December in Rome. At long jump he competed at the 1956 Olympic Games (dnq 24th) and was Australian champion in 1951 and 1957. Pbs: LJ 7.37/7.42w (1956), TJ 14.64 (1951).

Ivan JOKIC (Yugoslavia/Croatia) (b. 3 Feb 1945 Dicmo) on 26 July in Zadar, Croatia. Yugoslav 800m and 1500m champion 1967, he also won the Swedish 4k CC in 1970 and was 3rd at Swedish 1500m (1970) and 5000m (1975). 17 Internationals for YUG, his pbs were: 1500m 3:43.4 (1973), 3000m 7:57.0 (1973), 5000m 13:33.78 (1973), 10,000m 29:34.2 (1970) and 3000mSt 8:42.8 (1972). Later a coach of several leading Yugoslav athletes.

Wilhelmina Hendrika **'Mien' SCHOPMAN-KLAVER** (Netherlands) (b. 26 Feb 1911 Amsterdam), who was an alternate on the Dutch women's 4x100m team for the 1932 Olympics, passed away in Leiden in July at the age of 107. Pbs: 100m 12.7 (1931), LJ 5.02.

Major **Paul** Kipsilgich **KOECH** (Kenya) (b. 25 June 1969, Burnt Forest, Uasin Gishu) on 4 September in Nairobi. In 1998 he won the World half marathon title and helped Kenya to the World Road Relay title. He was in the top six at the World Cross Country Champs six times 4/4/2/6/6 1996-2000 and 5th in 2003, each time winning team gold. On the track he was African 5000m champion in 1996 and at 10,000m 6th at the 1996 Olympics and 4th at the 1997 Worlds. In the weeks following the Worlds he reduced his pbs to 12:56.29 for 5000m and 26:36.26 for 10,000m, the latter when second to Paul Tergat's world record of 26:27.85 in Brussels for third on the world all-time list. He was second in the 2003 Chicago Marathon in 2:07:07. Kenyan champion at 10,000m 1997, cross-country 1997-8. Other pbs: 2000m 5:00.8 (1997), 3000m 7:33.79 (1997), 2M 8:17.01 (1999), 10m Rd 44:45 (1997), HMar 60:01 (1998).

Progress at 5000m, 10,000m: 1995- 13:45.27, 27:50.06; 1996- 13:00.22, 26:56.78; 1997- 12:56.29, 26:36.26; 1998- 13:02.61, 26:47.89; 1999- 13:01.72, 27:10.38. At Mar: 2003- 2:07:07, 2004- 2:13:20

Dorothea KRESS (Germany) (b. 26 Aug 1924 Peude, Orlsen – now in Estonia) on 25 October in Itzehoe, Schleswig-Holstein. At the shot she was FRG champion in 1950 (2nd 1951, 3rd 1952) and was 11th at the 1952 Olympic Games. Pbs SP 13.26 (1952), DT 36.40 (1951), JT 37.66 (1950).

Walter KRÜGER (Germany/GDR) (b. 11 Apr 1930 Altenpleen) on 28 October in Prohn, Mecklenburg-Vorpommern. He was the Olympic silver medallist at javelin with 79.36 in 1960; this was his only year in the world top ten although his pb of 79.61 was set in 1959. 11 internationals 1957-71, 4th in the World University Games in 1959 and GDR champion in 1960.

Elzbieta KRYSINSKA/Niedzielska (Poland) (b. 28 Jan 1928 Brzac Kujawski) on 3 December in Warsaw. At the shot she competed at the 1952 Olympic Games (dnq 18), pb 12.85 (1952).

John Francis **LAWLOR** (Ireland) (b. 14 Mar 1931 Dublin) in Milton, Massachusetts on 20 May. At the hammer he set four Irish records: 60.94 in 1957, 62.02 and 64.59 in 1958 and 65.18 in 1960, the first and last when 3rd at the US Championships, at which he was also 3rd in 1958 and 2nd in 1959. He went to Boston University, for whom he was NCAA champion 1959 and 1960, and competed for Boston AA, becoming a leading geologist in New England. He was Irish champion with Civil Service AC in 1955, 1965 and 1966 and was 7th in 1958 and dnq 14th in 1966 at the Europeans and reached his peak with 4th in 1960 with 64.95 at the Olympic Games (also dnq 23rd in 1964).

Patrick Francis **'Pat' LEANE** (Australia) (b. 11 Jan 1930 Melbourne) on 12 October in Melbourne. He competed at the Olympic Games of 1952 – dnq HJ and LJ and withdrew injured after two events in the decathlon – and 1956 when he was 9th in the decathlon. He won the Australian decathlon title in 1960 and had a pb of 6748 (1952 tables) (6938) that year. Other pbs: HJ: 1.96 (1952), LJ 7.31 (1951).

Diane Susan **CHARLES**, née **LEATHER** (GBR) (b. 7 Jan 1933 Streetly, Staffordshire) on 5 September in Truro. She set five world bests for the mile from 5:02.6 (1953) to 4:45.0 (21 Sep

1955) including the first sub-5 minute mile by a woman, 4:59.6 on 29 May 1954. She also set world records with 880y 2:09.0 (1954), 3x880y (2, 1953-4) and 3x800m with further world bests (prior to the IAAF accepting records at these distances) at 440y 56.6 (1954), 1500m 4:30.0 and 4:29.7 (1957) and unofficial intermediate times 4:30.0 and 4:22.2 (1955). Further British records were 400m 56.3 (1955) and six at 800m from 2:08.9 (1954) to 2:06.6 (1958).

She was the silver medallist in the European 800m in 1954 and 1958, and went out in her heat when the 800m was re-introduced to the Olympic Games in 1960. WAAA champion at 880y 1954-5 and 1957, and 1 mile 1956-7, and National CC champion 1953-6. She married Peter Charles in July 1959.

Jacques LEFRAND (France) (b. 16 May 1952 Tuertheville-Bocage) in November. He was 7th in the marathon in his pb of 2:12:53 at the 1986 European Championships. Other pbs: 3000m 8:19.4 (1977), 5000m 14:01.6 (1982), 10,000m 29:02.85 (1982), 20,000m 1:01:13.8 (1982), 1Hr 19,583m (1982). 4 internationals 1981-5.

Frank LITSKY (USA) (b. 15 Aug 1926 Waterbury, Connecticut) on 30 October in Washington, New York. A graduate of the University of Connecticut, he joined *The New York Times* in 1958 after stints at United Press International in Hartford and New York City. He became a notable sports reporter, covering track and field from 1964 and was president of the New York Track Writers Association from 1969 until he retired in 2009. He also worked as a television analyst.

William Ernst 'Bill' LUCAS (GBR) (b. 16 Jan 1917 Tooting, London) on 22 March at Haywards Heath at the age of 101. He was a bomber pilot (squadron leader) in WW II, winning the Distinguished Flying Cross. That interrupted his running career with Belgrave Harriers, but after 3rd place in the AAA 3 miles he competed at 5000m at the 1948 Olympic Games in London and went on to pbs: 2M 9:30.6 (1951), 3M 14:11.6 (1950), 5000m 14:56.8 (1950), 6M 30:33.8u (1952). He was for many years an announcer at the major White City meetings.

Joachim Henrik MAARTENS (South Africa) (b. 24 May 1996) in October. In 2017 at 200m he was a semi-finalist at the 2017 World University Games and had a best of 20.40A. Other pbs: 100m 10.48A/ 10.45Aw (2016), 400m 47.18A (2017).

Richard MABUZA (Swaziland) (b. 3 Mar 1947) in 2018. At the 1972 Olympics he was 17th at the marathon and ran in a heat at the 10,000m, while at the Commonwealth Games he was 24th at 10,000m in 1970 and 3rd in 1974 and 7th in 1978 at the marathon. He was also African marathon champion in 1978 after 3rd in 1973. SWA records 10,000m 30:08.6 (1974), Mar 2:12:55 (1974).

James McALISTER (USA) (b. 5 Sep 1951) on 31 March at his home in Corona, California. A star American footballer at UCLA, he also topped the world list for long jump in 1973 with 8.24 at their home track in Westwood, Los Angeles in the annual dual meet with great rivals USC. With his football partner Kermit Johnson (they were known as the 'Blair Pair' from their High School partnership combining for 4000 yards rushing and 57 touchdowns in 1969), after setting numerous individual and team records at UCLA they signed for the fledgling World Football League but that folded after two seasons and they went to the NFL. McAlister played for the Philadelphia Eagles for two seasons and for New England for one.

Jacques MADUBOST (France) (b. 6 Jun 1944 Dangeau) on 29 June. Although he never won a French title, he was European high jump champion in 1966 and that year set French records at 2.14 and 2.15. Other pbs: LJ 7.07, JT 62.20 (both 1967). 11 internationals 1965-8. He later competed for France at shooting.

Izumi MAKI (Japan) (b. 10 Dec 1968 Namikata, Ehime) from breast cancer in Osaka on 18 October. She was 20th in 1991 and 17th in 1993 at 10,000m at the World Championships, and 12th at the Olympic Games at 10,000m in 1992 and at marathon in 1996. She received a 3-month ban for a positive test when winning the Sapporo Half Marathon on 16 Jul 1995. Pbs: 10,000m 31:40.38 (1992), 20000m 1:06:48.8 (JPN rec 1993), HMar 68:18 (1996), Mar 2:27:32 (1st Nagoya 1996).

Horst MANN (Germany/GDR) (b. 8 Jul 1927 Neustettin) on 15 October. At 400m he was GDR champion in 1955 and 1956 and ran for Germany at the 1956 Olympics (dnf heat). He set four GDR records: 47.5 twice in 1955, and 47.3 and 47.0 in 1956. Other pbs: 100m 10.9 (1954), 200m 21.6 (1956), 800m 1:57.0 (1956), 400mh 57.3 (1954).

Horst MANDL (Austria) (b. 8 Jan 1936 Graz) on 15 July in Graz. A member of the Union Leichtathletik Club Graz, at the decathlon he did not finish at the 1968 Olympic Games and was 17th in 1966 and 6th in 1969 at the European Championships. He was Austrian champion at 110mh 1967-9, HJ 1970 and 1973, LJ 1962 and 1964-6, TJ 1964-72 and decathlon 1963-5 and 1969-71. He set five Austrian decathlon records from 6962 points in 1965 to 7760 in 1969 (on 1952 tables, 7624 1984 tables). Other pbs: 100m 11.0, 200m 22.5, 400m 49.8 (all 1967), 1500m 4:38.8 (1969), 110mh 14.5 (1970), HJ 2.02 (1976), PV 4.45 (1969), LJ 7.37 (1968), TJ 15.04 (1970), SP 14.10 (1970), DT 44.06 (1968), JT 62.38 (1968). He was a successful coach and later won World Masters titles – three at M40 in 1977 and two at M50 in 1987 and set world high jump records for M40 at 2.02 in 1976, M60 with 1.76 in 1996 and M65 1.62

in 2001. His wife Doris was Austrian champion at 100mh in 1977 and their son Jürgen was a decathlete with a best of 7646 (1986).

Leopold MARIEN (Belgium) (b. 22 Mar 1934 Kontich) on 19 December at O.L.Vr.Waver. He competed at the Olympic Games in 1960 (18th decathlon) and 1964 (ht 110mh) and at the European Championships in 1962 (14th decathlon) with 41 internationals and five national titles at 200mh plus 110mh in 1961 and 1964, 400mh 1959 and decathlon 1958, 1960 and 1962. He set five national records at 110mh from 14.4 (1961) to 14.0 (1964), 200mh 23.2 (1964), 400mh 53.1 (1956) and six at Dec from 5566 (1957) to 7016 (1965). Pb 400mh 53.0 (1965).

Félix MATA (Venezuela) (b. 30 Jan 1951 Soro, Sucre) on 26 April at El Tigre. South American champion at 100m in 1971 and competed at 100m and 4x100m at the 1972 Olympic Games. Pbs: 100m 10.1 (1972), 9.9w/10.15w (1973), 200m 20.8 (1974), 20.5w (1975).

Simon MBUTHIA (Kenya) (later Saleh Bakheet Marzook BRN) (b. 1988 Nanyuki) in a car accident in Wyoming, USA on 25 September. He won the bronze medal for 3000m at the 2005 World Youth Championships. Pbs: 1500m 3:45.39 (2005), 3000m 8:03.24 (2005), 5000m 14:23.50 (2006), HMar 65:08A (2009).

Béla MÉLYKÚTI (Hungary) (b.9 Nov 1942 Szeged) in Szeged on 17 March. At 110m hurdles he competed in 16 internationals 1965-71, and at the European Championships in 1966 (heat) as well as at 50mh in the 1969 European Indoors. HUN champion each year 1965-70 with five HUN records from 14.4 (1967) to 14.1 (1968). Other pbs: 60mh 8.0i (1970), 400mh 53.3 (1962).

Omphenetse MOKGADI (Botswana) (b. 1 Jan 1986) in late November, having collapsed during training. A 400m runner with a best of 46.44A (2012) he competed at African Championships in 2008 (sf 400m, 4th 4x400m) and 2012.

Bilal Saad MUBARAK (Qatar) (b. 18 Dec 1972) on 27 October in Doha at a heart attack. At the shot he was 11th in the 1995 Worlds, 12th at the 1996 Olympics (dnq 35 2000), Arab champion in 1999 and 2nd at the Asian Games in 2002. Over 19m in nine of the ten years 1994-2003, his best was 19.65 in 1997.

Charles Nderitu **MUKORA** (Kenya) on 27 December in Nairobi. Having competed at long jump, triple jump and decathlon as well as playing football and hockey, he turned to coaching and was the national coach as Kenyan athletes came to the fore, notably at the 1968 and 1972 Olympic Games. He was head of the Kenyan athletics federation 1972-4 and in 1976 was elected to the IAAF Council. After being manager of external affairs for Coca-Cola in Kenya he became chairman of the National Olympic Committee of Kenya in 1989 and was appointed a member of the IOC in 1990, playing a huge role in the development of sport in Kenya. He was also Member of Parliament in 1992-7. He resigned from the IOC in 1999 after being implicated in the Olympic bribery scandal but strenuously denied allegations against him.

Jim NEIDHART (USA) (b. 8 Feb 1955) on 14 August in Wesley Chapel, Florida. Famed as 'The Anvil' when he wrestled in the WWE (and was a tag team champion) in the WWE after playing in the NFL for a short while. Shot pb 19.85 (1975), having set a California high school record in 1973.

Nils **Bengt NILSSON** (Sweden) (b. 17 Feb 1934 Härnösand) on 11 May in Solna. In the years leading up to the first 7-foot (2.134m) high jump, Nilsson, 1.81m tall, was the top European and was world ranked successively 8th, 2nd, 2nd and 4th by *Track & Field News* from 1953 to 1956. He was European champion in 1954 and set four Swedish records from 2.03 to 2.11 that year. His one Olympic appearance was unsuccessful, dnq 26th in 1956, due to a recurrent injury. Swedish champion 1953-5, U12 champion 1952 and 1954, 16 internationals (13 wins).

Progression at HJ (position on world list): 1949- 1.82, 1950- 1.84. 1951- 1.90, 1952- 1.95. 1953- 2.01 (15=)/2.03et, 1954- 2.11 (1), 1955- 2.10 (1), 1956- 2.09 (4), 1957- 2.04 (27=), 1958- 2.00 (72=), 1959- 1.90, 1960- 1.95.

Paola PATERNOSTER (Italy) (b. Rome 22 Dec 1935) on 27 June in San Donato Milanese. She had 21 internationals 1953-61, including 11th in the Olympic discus (dnq 1960). She was the first Italian discus thrower over 50 metres (51.33 in 1960) her fourth Italian record from 47.00 in 1956. She also set Italian records: HJ (4) 1.57 (1955) to 1.62 (1956), shot (3) 13,59 (1956) to 14.38 (1959), javelin (3) 46.06 (1955) to 47.96 (1957). Italian champion HJ 1955, SP 1955-7, 1959-60; DT 1955-7, JT 1956-7, 1959-61. She became a PE teacher.

Cristiana PELLINO (Italy) (b. 21 Sep 1970 Rome) on 23 February. She was 4th in the 1989 European Juniors at 5000m walk and had nine internationals including the 1993 World Cup and 2000 European Cup. Italian champion at 5000m walk 1999-2001 with walks pbs: 3000m 12:16.92i (2000) and 12:20.57 (1996), 5000m 20:57.96 (1998), 10,000m 43:49.5 (2000), Road: 10k 42:55 (1994), 20k 1:30:42 (2000). She was married with two sons and as a trainer discovered a young Marco De Luca.

Pedro Damián **PÉREZ** Dueñas (Cuba) (b. 23 Feb 1952 Pinar del Río) on 18 July in Havana. While still a junior (19) he set a world record for the triple jump with 17.40 with three more jumps over 17m when he won at the Pan-American Games In Calí (1046m altitude) in 1971, but his best otherwise was 16.86, also in 1971. He had previously set Cuban and World Junior records at 16.38 in 1970 and at 16.86 and 16.92A in 1971. At the Olympic Games he was dnq 24th in 1972 and 4th in 1976 and won at the CAC Games in 1970 and 1974 and CAC Championships in 1971. Pb LJ 7.44.

Progression at TJ: 1968- 15.15, 1969- 15.78, 1970- 16.38, 1971- 17.40, 1972- 16.80, 1973- 15.97, 1974- 16.83/17.01w, 1976- 16.81, 1977- 16.67, 1978- 16.47.

Milad PETRUSIC (Serbia) (b. 20 Jun 1934 Rogatica – now in BIH) on 22 October in Belgrade. At 110m hurdles he was Yugoslav champion 1963-6 and Balkan 1963 and 1966 and competed at the Olympic Games in 1960 (qf), Europeans 1958 and 1962 and European Indoor Games (at 60mh) in 1966. 36 Internationals 1956-67. Pbs: 110mh 14.2 (1965), 200mh 24.3 (1960 YUG record). He was a professor of physical education and athletics coach.

Theodorus Jacobus Leonardus 'Dick' QUAX (New Zealand) (b. 1 Jan 1948 Alkmaar, Netherlands) in Auckland on 28 May. He moved to New Zealand with his family in the 1950s and made his international debut when winning the 1500m silver medal at the 1970 Commonwealth Games, also placing 7th at 5000m. He made his Olympic debut in a heat of the 1500m in 1972 and, moving up in distance, was second to Lasse Virén at 5000m at the 1976 Olympics (also heat 10,000m). He was 9th at 10,000m at the 1978 Commonwealth Games. In 1977 he ran a world record for 5000m with 13:12.87 in Stockholm, having earlier run on New Zealand teams that set world record at 4x1 mile (16:02.8 on 3 Feb 1972 in Auckland) and an unratified 14:50.4 at 4x1500m at Oslo on 22 Aug 1973, Quax running notable anchor legs in 3:58.4 and 3:35.9 respectively. In 1979 he ran the then fastest debut marathon of 2:11:13 and improved his best to 2:10:47 in 1980 in a win at Eugene. Both were New Zealand records, and he also set six NZ records at 5000m from 13:35.0 in 1972 to that 13:12.87 and two at 10,000m: 27:46.08 (1976) and 27:41.95 (1977). Other pbs: 1500m 3:36.69 (1976), 1M 3:56.23 (1976), 2000m 5:10.0 (1972), 3000m 7:45.11 (1977), 2M 8:17.08 (1976). NZ champion at 1M 1969, 5000m 1972-4. He was a member of the NZ team that won the World Cross-country title in 1975. He went on to coach and was an Auckland City Councillor from 2011.

His son Theo (b. 27 Dec 1999) is a promising middle-distance runner (1500m 3:47.54 in 2018).

Willy Lorang **RASMUSSEN** (Norway) (b. 3 Dec 1937 Kongsberg) on 12 August in Asker. At the javelin he was 5th in 1960 and dnq 1964 at the Olympic Games, and 12th in 1958, 9th in 1962 and dnq in 1966 at the European Championships. Norwegian champion in 1958-9, 1961 and 1965, he competed in 45 international matches 1957-69 and had a pb of 84.18 (1961, then 8th world all-time), plus shot 14.53 (1961) and discus 41.05 (1958).

Laurence David George 'Laurie' REED (GBR) (b. 22 May 1936 Dulwich) on 21 May. A member of South London Harriers, he made three international appearances for Britain 1957-60, including at the Olympic Games in 1960 (heat 1500m). At 3 miles he was AAA 3rd in 1960 and at 6 miles he won CAU 1957 and Southern 1959 titles. Having run a UK junior record 9:12.6 for 2 miles in 1955. He had pbs of: 1500m 3:46.2 '60, 1M 4:01.8 '60, 2000m 5:18.8 '59, 3000m 8:11.8 '60, 2M 8:50.2 '57, 3M 13:38.84 '60, 5000m 14:05.6 '57, 6M 28:35.6 '67, 3000mSt 9:33.0 '63.

Jan 'John' Nicolaas Roousouw van REENEN (South Africa) (b. 26 Mar 1947 Bethlehem, Free State) on 21 August in Calitzdorp. After often exceeding 70m in practice, he set a world discus record of 68.48 at Stellenbosch on 14 March 1975; this was his eighth South African record from 60.49 in 1968. He also set four South African shot records from 18.86 in 1968 to 19.18 in 1970. He did not compete in international championships as his career was during the era when South Africa was banned due to its apartheid policy. However, he was NCAA champion each year 1968-70 while at Washington State University and won the AAA discus title in 1975. He was South African champion at shot 1974-8 and 1985 and discus 1966, 1973-8 and 1985-7. He was a renowned artist of figurative realism and expressionist work and lectured on the subject at Stellenbosch University.

Annual progress at DT: 1964- 45.12, 1965- 49.62, 1966- 54.87, 1967- 56.59, 1968- 60.58, 1969- 63.25, 1970- 63.65, 1971- 61.82, 1972- 65.78, 1973- 63.70, 1974- 68.04, 1975- 68.48, 1976- 66.12, 1977- 61.94, 1978- 60.98, 1980- 58.76.

Lindy John **REMIGINO** (USA) (b. 3 Jun 1931 Elmurst, Queens, New York) on 12 July in Newington, CT. He came to fame when he was the surprise 1952 Olympic gold medallist at 100m when he beat Herb McKenley by just 0.01 sec, 10.79 to 10.80 (official time 10.4), and he went on to a second gold, contributing a great third leg for the US team at the 4x100 relay. A graduate of Manhattan College and member of New York AC he was 3rd at the IC4As and 5th at the NCAAs 1952 (also 4th in a 200m heat at the AAUs) but was then 2nd in the 100m at the 1952 US Olympic Trials before that blanket finish in Helsinki when the top four finishers were all awarded the same time. He went on to three post-Olympic victories including 10.2w in Oslo. Pbs: 100y 9.5 (1954), 220y straight 21.0 (1950), turn 21.2 (1951).

After graduating from Manhattan, Remigino, who was named after aviation legend Charles Lindbergh, became a physical education teacher and track and field coach at Hartford Public

High School, his alma mater. His teams there won 31 state titles and he guided 157 athletes to individual state championships.

Mervyn RICHARDS (New Zealand)) (b. 16 Nov 1930 Oamaru) on 1 July at the age of 87. He was NZ champion at pole vault each year 1952-62 and set 11 NZ records from 3.97 (1952) to 4.34 (1962). Competing at three Empire/ Commonwealth Games he was 9th in 1950, 5th in 1954 and 3rd in 1958. He coached many athletes to national honours. His wife Winnie Garrod was NZ women's javelin champion in 1957-8 with a national record 43.36 in 1956

Donald Alexander **RITCHIE** (GBR) (b. 6 Jul 1944 Aberdeenshire) on 13 June in Lossiemouth, Scotland. One of the greatest ultra runners of modern times, in his long career he set track world bests: 50k 2:51:38.0 '77, 40M 3:48:35 '82, 50M 4:53:28 '78 & 4:51:49 '83, 100k 6:10:20 '78, 150k 10:36:42 '77, 100M 11:50:51 '77, 200k 16:32:30 '83 & 16:31:08i '90; and a road best:100k 6:18:00 '78. UK best 12Hr 161.6k '77. Other pbs: 6M 30:32.4 '68, 10M 49:54.0 '71, 1Hr 19.241m '71, Mar 2:19:35 '83, 30M/50k 2:44:36/2:50:30 '79. He also, despite physical problems, set a record for John O'Groats to Land's End of 10 days 15 hours 27 mins in 1989. He won numerous continental 100k races, the London to Brighton in 1977 and 1978, and the inaugural IAU 24 Hours Championship. He had started as a quarter-miler with Aberdeen AAC in 1962 and 23 years after his first world best in 1977 he was a member of the British team that won team bronze at Uden in 2000. Awarded the MBE in 1995. His autobiography "The Stubborn Scotsman Don Ritchie World Record Holding Ultra Distance Runner" was published in 2016

Dionne ROSE-HENLEY (Jamaica) (b. 7 Nov 1969 Kingston) on 24 December in Myrtle Beach, South Carolina, USA. At 100m hurdles was 5th at the 1996 Olympic Games (sf 1992), 5th in 1997, 6th 1999 and 2001 at the World Champs (sf 1993), 4th at the 1994 Commonwealth Games (7th long jump), 4th 1998 World Cup and was CAG champion in 1998 and 2002, and Jamaican champion at 100m hurdles in 1993 and 1995 and long jump in 1996 and 1998. . Also at 60m hurdles she was 7th at the 1999 World Indoors. She set a Jamaican 100m hurdles record at 12.86 in 1987 and set three pbs at the 1996 Olympic Games to 12.64. Other pbs: 100m 11.54 (1998), 11.38w (1995), 11.4 (1997); 50mh 6.84i (1999), 55mh 7.57i (1995), 60mh 7.96i (1997). LJ 6.72 (1995), TJ 12.73w (1990). She coached at several US universities.

Progress at 100mh: 1988- 15.18/14.9, 1989- 14.42/14.1w, 1990- 14.44/13.49w, 1991- 13.39/13.29w, 1992- 13.03, 1993- 13.03, 1994- 13.13/13.06w, 1995- 12.86/12.85w, 1996- 12.64, 1997- 12.75, 1998- 12.64, 1999- 12.79, 2000- 13.15/12.93Aw, 2001- 12.77, 2002- 12.91, 2003- 13.01, 2004- 13.04.

Rayfel Allan **ROSEMAN** (b. 19 May 1939) (GBR) in Bangkok, possibly in November. Running for South London Harriers and later for Brighton he had four internationals for Britain 1963-9. He won the Southern 1 mile in 1966 and narrowly missed running a four-minute mile for several years before finally managing 3:59.8 in 1969, Other pbs: 800m 1:50.8 (1968), 1500m 3:42.7 (1965), 3000m 8:04.6 (1969), 2M 8:52.6 (1965). 3M 13:45.4 (1968), 5000m 14:17.4 (1969), 2000mSt 5:52.4 (1966).

Mel ROSEN (USA) (b. 24 March 1928, The Bronx, New York) on 25 March in Auburn, Alabama. He was head coach for the US teams at the 1987 World Champs and 1992 Olympics. He coached at Auburn University for 36 years and was inducted into the USATF National Track & Field Hall of Fame in 1995.

Meeri SAARI (Finland) (b. 16 Sep 1925 Urjala) on 1 October in Valkeakoski. At the shot she set four Finnish records from 12.08 (1948) to 13.02 when she was 8th at the 1952 Olympic Games. She was Finnish champion each year 1948- 55 and at discus 1948. Four international dual meets 1952-5, pb DT 39.11 (1952). Her husband Leo Veisto had a javelin best of 59.94 (1932).

Franco SAR (Italy) (b. 21 Dec 1933 Abrorea, Cagliari) on 1 October at Monza. Probably Italy's best ever decathlete; he was 6th in 1960 and 13th in 1964 at the Olympic Games and 13th in 1962 and 12th in 1966 at the Europeans. He was Italian champion at PV 1973 and decathlon 1958-65 and set national records at pole vault 4.45 (1964) and nine times at decathlon from 6110 (1959) to 7368 (1965) on 1952 tables. 15 internationals 1959-66 at 110mh, PV, DT and decathlon. He was later a coach, official, organiser for many years and chairman of strong Italian athletic clubs, such as Snia Milano.

Warwick Perrins **SELVEY** (Australia) (b. 3 Dec 1939 Beecroft, New South Wales) on 16 August in Sakhon Nakhon, Thailand. He won Australian shot and discus titles in 1960 and gained selection to the Rome Olympics where he came 15th in the shot and 21st in the discus. His crowning achievement was in winning the 1962 Commonwealth Games discus in Perth 1962 and 4th shot. He also competed in the discus at the 1964 Tokyo Olympics where he did not make the final. He won 7 national titles at shot (1960-4, 1966-7) and 11 at discus (1960, 1962-7, 1970-3) and set 4 national records at shot from 16.74 in 1960 to 17.34 in 1962 and 10 at discus from 50.47 in 1960 to 58.90 in 1967. Pb decathlon 5999 points (1962 tables) in 1965.

David SHAW (GBR) (b. 19 Oct 1936 Greenock) on 4 August in Southampton. Successively a member of Leeds St. Marks H, Birchfield H and South London H, after national service in the RAF he went to Birmingham University (winning the British Universities cross-country in 1959) and then returned to the RAF as an education officer. He had one international for Britain at 3000m steeplechase, at which he set Scottish records with 9:17.0 (1957) and 8:57.0 (1958) and was 3rd in the A A As in 1958. Pb 3M 14:13.0 (1958). A congenial and much respected man, he was the first professional General Secretary of the British Amateur Athletic Board 1978-81. He was later an executive with ITN and with UK Badminton before returning to academia.

Juris **SILOVS** (USSR/Latvia) (b. 30 Aug 1950 Kraslava) on 28 September in Riga. At 4x100m he won Olympic medals: silver 1972 and bronze 1976, and was 4th at the 1974 Europeans. He was World Universities 100m champion in 1973 (1st 4x100m 1975 and 1977) and was 2nd in 1976 and 3rd in 1973-4 and 1977 at the USSR Championships. He was Latvian champion at 100m 1968, 1970-1 and 1979, 200m 1968 and 1970, 50m indoors 1971, 1973, 1977-8 and 100m indoors 1973. He equalled the European indoor records at 50m 5.5 (1970) and 60m 6.4 (1974) with other pbs 60m 6.65i (1974), 100m 10.1 (1974), 10.33 (1973); 200m 21.0 (1973).

Karl-Heinz STADTMÜLLER (Germany/ GDR) (b. 30 Jan 1953 Berlin) on 13 September in Berlin. A top race walker of the 1970s, at 20k his greatest success came at the biennial Lugano Trophy (later World Cup) with 2nd 1973, 1st 1975 and 3rd 1977 and he was ranked in the world's top three for each of those years. At the Olympic Games he was 4th in 1976 and 8th in 1980, having been 11th at 50k in 1972. He was 4th in the European Junior 10k in 1970 and disqualified in the European 20k in 1974. GDR champion at 50k 1972, 20k 1973-4 and 1980; 17 internationals 1972-80. He set world track records at 30,000m 2:14:45.6 and 2 hours 26,911m at Berlin on 16 April 1972 and a world junior record 42:39.0 for 10,000m in 1971 with GDR track records: 3000m 11:29.6 (1975), 5000m 19:26.2 (1975), 10,000m 41:12.8 (1978), 20,000m 1:24:57.1 (1977). Pbs: 10,000m 39:47.0 (1980), 1Hr 13,970m (1977). Road pbs: 20k 1:22:25 (1980), 30k 2:22:59.6 (1976), 35k 2:49:45.2 (1978), 50k 4:01:59.2 (1976).

Anthony Gordon **'Tony' STEEL** (New Zealand) (b. 31 Jul 1941 Greymouth) in Hamilton on 4 May. Best known as a wing for the All Blacks rugby team, playing in nine Tests 1966-8, he was also NZ champion at 100y and 220y in 1965. Pbs: 100y 9.7, 220y 21.7 (both 1965). He became a headmaster and national MP 1990-3 and 1996-2002.

Dragan STOJICEVIC (Serbia) (b. 21 Feb 1947 Pozarevac) in August in Belgrade. At 110m hurdles he was Yugoslav champion in 1969 and 1970 and Balkan in 1971, with the first Yugoslav auto-timed record 14.19 in 1971. He also competed at the 1971 Europeans and was 8th at the World University Games in 1970. Pb 60mh 8.14i (1976), 17 internationals 1967-76.

Lóránt STOLL (Hungary) (b. 25 Aug 1944 Lucabánya) on 31 October in Budapest. At 800m in 1966 he was Hungarian champion and ran in the heats of the European Championships. 5 internationals 1965-7; pbs: 400m 49.2 (1965), 800m 1:49.0 (1966), 1000m 2:22.6 (1966), 1500m 3:45.5 (1968), 3000m 8:14.8 (1968).

Gösta Bernhard **SVENSSON** (Sweden) (b. 21 Nov 1929 Karlshamn) on 14 October in Stockholm. At the high jump he was 5th at the 1950 European Champs and 4th at the 1952 Olympic Games. His pb was a Swedish record at 2.02 in 1952 but he did not win a Swedish title (3rd in 1951 and 1953 and 2nd in 1956); U21 champion 1949. 11 internationals, pb shot 14.24 (1953).

Aranka SZABÓ/BARTHA (Hungary) (b. 9 Oct 1926 Budapest) on 9 October in Budapest. She competed as a sprinter at the 1951 World University Championships and 1952 Olympic Games, and made 10 international appearances for Hungary. She won the Hungarian 100m in 1953 and was a member of 4x100m teams that set five HUN records 1948-54. Pbs 100m 12.1 and 200m 24.4 (both 1956).

Tamás SZÁNTHÓ (Hungary) (b. 23 May 1951 Berettyóujfalu) on 15 March in the USA. At 1500m he competed at the European Indoor Championships in 1977 (hts) and 1978 (10th), and set Hungarian indoor records with 3:46.5 (1973) and 3:40.72 (1978). 3 internationals 1973-8, other pbs: 800m 1:49.3 (1977), 1500m 3:41.1 (1977), 3000m 8:04.9 (1979).

László TÁBORI (né Talabircsuk) (Hungary) (b. 6 Jul 1931 Kosice – then TCH) in Los Angeles on 23 May. One of the great trio of Hungarian middle-distance runners of the 1950s (with Sándor Iharos and István Rózsavölgyi) he tied the world record for 1500m of 3:40.8 set by Iharos five weeks earlier when on 6 Sep 1955 at the Bislett Stadium in Oslo his fast finish just enabled him to beat Gunnar Nielsen who also ran that same time. Tábori also set world records for 4x1500m on the Honvéd Budapest (Army) teams that ran 15:21.2 in 1954 and 15:14.8 in 1955 at Budapest. On 28 July 1955 he became the third man to better 4 minutes for the mile when he won at the White City, London in 3:59.0 ahead of Chris Chataway and Brian Hewson when all three broke the 4-min barrier. After the trauma of the Hungarian revolution in 1956 Tábori did well to place 4th at 1500m and 6th at 5000m in the Olympic Games in Melbourne. He then went to live in the USA and competed until 1962 before becoming a notable coach. He was 2nd at 5000m at the 1954 World University Games and in the USA was AAU champion at 5000m in 1961 and 2nd at 5000m in 1958 and 1500m in 1960. HUN champion at 1500m in 1955, 1M record also 4:05.2 (1954); 14 internationals 1954-6. Other pbs: 800m 1:52.9, 2000m 5:03.0 (1955), 3000m 8:00.8 (1956), 2M 8:45.6 (1960), 3M 13:28.0 (1960), 5000m 13:53.2 (1955).

David Lewis **THORESON** (USA) (b. 16 May 1941 Valley City, North Dakota) on 10 October in Lynchburg, Virginia. At the decathlon he was 3rd in 1966, 2nd in 1967 and 5th in 1970 at the AAU Champs. His pb was 7392 (current tables) in 1967. He set a world best for two decathlons competed in succession (thus on four days), with 13,953 (6770 and 7183) on 5-8 Sep 1972. He was a teacher.

Finnbjörn THORVALDSSON (Iceland) (b. 25 May 1924 Hnífsdalur) on 9 July. He competed at 100m, LJ and 4x100m in the 1948 Olympic Games, and at the European Championships was 6th at 100m (sf 200m) in 1946 and also ran at 4x100m in 1950. Winner in Nordic international at 100m and 200m in 1949. His bests of 60m 6.8 and 100m 10.5 in 1949 were Icelandic records, other pbs: 200m 21.7 (1949), LJ 7.16 (1948), Dec 5967 (1950, 1934 tables). He was also a national champion at handball and basketball.

Rein TÖLP (USSR/Estonia) (b.11 Oct 1941 Tallinn) on 16 April in Tallinn. He was a semi-finalist at 800m at the 1964 Olympic Games and 1966 Europeans, competing for the USSR. He was Estonian champion at 400m 1962-5 and 1968, 800m 1961, 1964-5 and 1967-9, and 1500m 1964, 1967 and 1971. Estonian records at 800m 1:47.7 (1964) and 1000m 2:20.8 (1965), other pbs 400m 48.0 (1965), 1500m 3:47.2 (1968).

Viktor TRKAL (Czech Republic) (b. 13 Mar 1929 Prague) on 11 November. Having been a sprinter (11.2 for 100m) he became a coach, judge, organiser and technical official. From 1981 to 1999 he was a member of the IAAF technical commission and was technical delegate and ITO at numerous events such as Olympic Games and World Championships. He was a member of the working group that produced the current (from 1984) IAAF scoring tables for combined events, leading the historical research.

Michael **Bruce** Swinton **TULLOH** (GBR) (b. 29 Sep 1935 Datchet) on 28 April at his home in Marlborough. Famous for running barefoot when he emerged as a distance running star, he had 21 internationals for Britain 1959-67. His greatest moment came with his victory in the European 5000m in 1962. Although he had won the Hong Kong 5000m title in 1955 while on national service, he broke through very rapidly in 1959 to win the AAA 3 miles and make his international debut while at Southampton University and member of Portsmouth AC. In 1960 he set a British record at 3 miles of 13:17.2, a time he improved to 13:12.0

in 1961, but he did not qualify from the heats at the Olympic Games. In 1962 he ran his best ever mile (3:59.3) and a British record 8:34.0 for 2 miles in New Zealand in January before his European triumph, and was 4th at 3 miles and 9th at 1 mile at the Commonwealth Games. In 1966 he ran a British record 27:23.78 for 2nd place in the AAA 6 miles and was 6th in the Europeans in his best time for 10,000m of 28:50.4. He was also AAA 3 miles champion in 1962 and 1963 and 2nd in the National Cross-country in 1961 and 1962. CAU champion at 3M 1962, 1964-5, and 6M 1962, 1966-67. Other best times: 1500m 3:46.7 (1963), 3000m 8:02.4 (1967), 5000m 13:49.4 (1964). In 1969 he ran across the USA, 2876 miles in 65 days, writing about this in his *Four Million Footsteps (1970)*. An agricultural scientist, he remained a top-class veteran runner and coach, notably of Richard Nerurkar, World Cup marathon winner in 1993.

Otto VERHOEVEN (Germany) (b. 28 Sep 1937) on 27 February. One of the leading statisticians and athletics history researchers. He was a founder member of the DGLD, his major works included German yearbooks for 1945/46, 1947, 1948, 1949 and 1950 and compiling deep annual German lists for the past.

Roger Marcel **VERHEUEN** (Belgium) (b. 2 Feb 1927 in Nederzwalm) on 15 December in Oudenaarde. He was 6th in his 1500m heat in a Belgian record 3:43.0 at the 1958 Europeans, had 31 internationals and was Belgian 1500m champion in 1955 and 1958-9. Pbs 800m 1:49.6 (1958), 1000m 2:22.9 (1962), 1500m 3:42.4 (1961), 1M 4:08.8 (1958), 2000m 5:18.0 (1960) and 3000m 8:14.0 (1958).

Magalì VETTORAZZO (Italy) (16 Mar 1942 Preganziol, Treviso) on 18 June in Firenze. At the pentathlon she was 21st at the 1960 Olympic Games and 22nd at the 1966 Europeans (also competing at LJ 1962, 80mh 1966, 100mh 1969). Italian champion at 80mh 1965-7, 100mh 1969, LJ 1961-4, 1966-7, and 1969; Pen 1962-3,1965-7 and 1969-70; 32 internationals 1960-71, Italian records: LJ (5) 5.91 (1962) to 6.11 (1963), Pen (with 80mh) 4339 (1963), (with 100mh) 4332 (1969) & 4342 (1970).

Andrej VIPOTNIK (Slovenia) (b. 5 Nov 1933) on 3 September in Ljubljana. At 800m he competed in the 1954 Europeans and was Balkan champion in 1956 and Yugoslav champion in 1957 as well as winning the Yugoslav indoor 1000m in 1955 and 1957. 10 internationals for Yugoslavia 1954-6, pbs: 800m 1:49.2 (1957), 1500m 3:48.4 (1956).

Thomas Frederick '**Tom**' **VON RUDEN** (USA) (b. 22 Aug 1944 Coeur d'Alene, Idaho) on 17 May in Sun City West, Arizona. He won the Pan-American 1500m in 1967 and was 9th at 1500m in the Olympic Games of 1968, won three NCAA titles with Oklahoma State University: 880y indoors & 4x440y in 1965 and 4x440y in

1966 (2nd 1M), and was AAU indoor champion at 1000y in 1968 and 1971. Pbs: 800m 1:46.8 (1971), 1000m 2:19.0 (1970), 1500m 3:38.5 (1971), 1M 3:56.9 (1967), 3000mSt 8:58.6 (1971).

Miodrag VUKOMANOVIC (Serbia) (b. 23 Sep 1948 Siljevica) on 16 August in Kragujevac. At 1500m he was Yugoslav champion in 1970 and 1973 and Balkan in 1973, with a Yugoslav record 3:40.81 in 1972. 11 internationals 1970-4, other pbs: 800m 1:48.6 (1972), 5000m 13:52.6 (1973).

Raymond Henry WEINBERG (Australia) (b. 23 Oct 1929 Alexandra, Victoria) in Ballarat, Victoria on 30 May. Silver medallist at 120y hurdles at the 1950 Empire Games, he was 6th at the 1952 Olympics at 110m hurdles and also ran in the heats of the 4x100m and 4x400m (after 110mh heat in 1948). He was Australian champion at 120yh in 1948 and 1950-3 and 220yh in 1951 and 1952 and also won the AAA 120yh in England in 1952. He set national records at 120y with 14.4 (1948) and 14.0 twice in 1952 and 23.3 for 220yh. Pbs: 100y 9.8, 440yh 55.4, also set a Victorian record at decathlon (5088 on 1952 tables). He was the Australian team coach at the 1968 Olympics. He married Shirley Ogle, who was a Victorian sprint champion (100y 11.0w in 1947) and he was made a member of the Order of Australia in 2005. His son Brett was a national junior sprint champion in 1971-2.

Morice Fredrick WINTER (USA) (b. 25 Feb 1922 near Wellington, Texas) on 10 October in Manhattan, Kansas. Before he became a Hall of Fame basketball coach as 'Tex' Winter, he ranked third in the world at pole vault with his pb 4.27 in 1946. At the NCAAs he was 3rd in 1943 for Oregon State University and 4th equal in 1946 for USC.

Died in early 2019

Robert 'Bob' ADAMS (Canada) (b.20 Dec 1924 Alsask, Saskatchewan) on 23/24 February. He was 19th in the 1952 Olympic decathlon and at the Empire & Commonwealth Games was 4th at pole vault and 14th at high jump in 1954. He set three Canadian records at decathlon, all in 1952, to 5794 points on the 1952 tables (6636 previous tables) when he won the Canadian title. A founding member of the Saskatoon track club, he was head coach of the Canadian team at the 1964 Olympics.

Pierre ALARD (France) (b. 17 Sep 1937 Bordeaux) on 13 January in Luçon (Vendée). At the discus he set eight French records from 52.25 (1959) to 55.32 (1962), with a final pb of 56.26 (1969). He competed at the Olympic Games of 1956 and 1960 (dnq 18/26) and at the European Championships of 1958 and 1962 (dnq 20/21), and was French champion 11 times (1956, 1959-65, 1967-9). Other pbs: SP 16.22 (1964), HT 57.80 (1965).

Ron BENTLEY (GBR) (b. 10 Nov 1930 Gornal, Dudley) on 22 February. A member of Tipton Harriers and long-time manager of their teams, he set a world record for 24 hours with 259.603k at Walton on 3/4 November 1973, with a WR for 100k in 16:53:00 en route.

Michel BERNARD (France) (b. 31 Dec 1931 Sepmeries) on 14 February in Anzin. Ranked in the world's top ten five times at 1500m and three times at 5000m, he compiled a consistent record in a career of 67 internationals for France 1955-71. At the Olympic Games he was 7th at both 1500m and 5000m in 1960 and at 1500m in 1964, and at the European Champs was 9th in 1958, 5th in 1962 and heat 1971 at 5000m. He won 12 French titles: 1500m 1955 and 1959, 5000m 1958-60 and 1962, 10,000m 1961 and 1964-5, and cross-country 1958 and 1961-2. He ran the last leg on the French team that set the world record of 15:04.2 at Versailles on 28 Jun 1961 and set numerous French records in an era when Michel Jazy was king of French middle-distance running: 1000m 2:20.1 (1959), 1500m 3:42.2 (1958) and 3:42.0 (1960), 1M 4:05.8 (1957) and 3:58.2 (1963), 2000m 5:11.8 (1956) and 5:04.0 (1961), 3000m 8:04.6 (1957), 8:00.0 and 7:57.0 (1960), 2M 8:37.0 (1960), 3M 13:40.2 (1958), 13:29.2 (1960) and 13:26.4 (1963), 5000m 14:05.8 (1958), 13:55.6 (1960) and 13:50.2 (1963). Other pbs: 800m 1:49.2 (1959), 1500m 3:38.7 (1963), 2000m 5:03.8 (1963), 3000m 7:53.8 (1966), 5000m 13:40.0 (1971), 10,000m 29:24.6 (1963). He was president of the French Athletics Federation 1985-7.

Jean-Pierre BOCCARDO ((France) (b. 16 Mar 1942 Espéraza) on 29 January. He was French champion at 400m in 1963-4 and 1966 with three French 4x400m records 1963-6. He was a semi-finalist at the Olympic Games in 1964 and the European Champs in 1966, and at 4x400m was 8th at the 1964 and 1968 Olympics and 6th in 1962 and 4th in 1966 at the Europeans. He was 3rd at 400m and 1st at 4x400m at the 1963 Mediterranean Games. Pbs: 200m 21.5 (1968), 400m 46.34/46.3 (1964), 400mh 51.7 (1964). 30 internationals 1961-8. He became an eminent surgeon.

Donald George **BRAGG** (USA) (b. 15 May 1935 Penns Grove, New Jersey) on 16 February in California. Consistently in the world elite from 1955 to 1961, he reached a peak in 1960 when he set a world record at 4.80 (on his first attempt and not trying higher) to win at the US Olympic Trials at Stanford (the last ever to be set with a steel pole) and he went on to win the Olympic title in Rome. He had set a world indoor best of 4.81 at Philadelphia on 13 February 1959 and that year also won at the AAU Champs and Pan-American Games. He was NCAA champion in 1955 and 2nd in 1957 for Villanova University, and he was 2nd in 1957 and 1958 and 3rd equal in 1953 at the AAUs, also winning the US indoor title in 1956 and 1958 (both tied) and in 1959-61 and the IC4A title indoors and out each year 1955-7. He was known as "Tarzan" due to his wish to play the role but that never came to fruition.

Progression at PV: 1950- 2.95, 1951- 3.25, 1952- 3.55, 1953- 4.19, 1954- 4.42i, 1955- 4.60, 1956- 4.70i/4.66, 1957- 4.66i/4.65, 1958- 4.65i/4.55, 1959- 4.81i/4.70, 1960- 4.80, 1961- 4.76i/4.66, 1963- 3.96exh.

Dawn Marie **FLOCKHART** (GBR) (b. 16 May 1967 Bathgate) in Aberfeldy on 4 February. In a long career with Edinburgh Southern H/Edinburgh Woollen Mill, she had one international for Britain and although not winning a Scottish senior title was a medallist on 13 occasions. She won the WAAA girls 100m in 1981 (and that year set a Scottish U15 200m record of 24.63 that still stands) and the first WAAA intermediate indoor 200m in 1983. Pbs: 60m 7.72i (1982), 100m 11.80 (1985), 11.7w (1984); 200m 23.71 (1984), 300m 38.9 (1996), 400m 54.4 (1995), 54.70 (1996); TJ 10.90, 11.07w (1993).

Heinrich-Ludwig '**Heinz**' **FÜTTERER** (FRG/Germany) (b. 14 Oct 1931 Illingen) on 10 February in Illingen. Ranked first in the world at 100m and second at 200m in 1954 and 1955, he was European champion at both 100m and 200m in 1954 and won at 4x100m in 1958. He won Olympic bronze at 4x100m and was a quarter-finalist at 100m in 1956. He was German champion at 100m 1953-5 and 200m 1953-4, and indoors at 70m 1954 and 60m 1955. In 1954 he tied the world record for 100m with 10.2 and set European records at 100m (also 10.3 twice) and at 200m 20.9 and 20.8 twice, He also ran the third leg for the German team that tied the world record for 4x100m with 39.5 in 1958. Indoors in 1955 he tied the world best of 5.6 for 50m and ran two world records for 60m at 6.5 plus a European best of 6.2 for 60y. Other pbs: 50y 5.4i (1954), 200m half turn 20.6 (1955) 400m 49.8 (1954). 32 internationals 1951-8.

Progression at 100m/200m: 1949- 10.9/22.5, 1950- 10.9, 1951- 10.4, 1952- 10.7/22.7, 1953- 10.4/21.0, 1954- 10.2/20.8, 1955- 10.3/20.6, 1956- 10.4/21.1, 1957- 10.4/21.8, 1958- 10.2/21.4.

Klas **Göran HÖGBERG** (Sweden) (b. 20 Dec 1948 Sollefteå) on 21 January. Dnf Olympic Games marathon 1980 with 7 more internationals. Swedish champion 5000m 1973, 12k CC 1972-3 and Mar 1987. Pbs: 3000m 8:10.6 (1973), 5000m 13:49.88 (1988), 10,000m 29:00.6 (1973), Mar 2:13:59 (1987).

Henrik Hove **JØRGENSEN** (Denmark) (b. 10 Oct 1961 Copenhagen) on 26 January in Bornholm. He ran at the 1982 Europeans (heat 5000m) and at the marathon he was 19th in 1984 and 22nd in 1988 at the Olympic Games, 19th in 1983 and 9th in 1987 at the Worlds, and won in London in 1988. Danish champion at 5000m 1985 & 1991, 10,000m 1980 & 1988, HMar 1990, cross country 1988-90. He set Danish records at 5000m: 13:30.06 (1982) and 13:27.76 (1985), five at 10,000m from 29:00.3 (1980) to 27:57.98 (1985) and two at marathon (both in London) 2:10.47 (3rd 1983) and 2:09:43 (5th 1985). Other pbs: 3000m 7:55.92 (1982), HMar 62:07 (1983), 3000mSt 9:15.9 (1979). He was married to Mette Holm (Mar 2:41:42 in 1983) and their daughter Anna had a marathon best of 2:33:02 and competed at the 2016 Olympic Games.

Tapio LEHTO (Finland) (b. 8 Dec 1930 Hollola) on 5 February. A triple jumper, he was 18th at the 1956 Olympic Games, dnq 13th at the 1954 Europeans and Finnish champion in 1954-6. Pbs: LJ 7.20, TJ 15.45 (1956). He was best known in Finland as a golfer as player and teacher.

Ismail MACEV (Yugoslavia/Serbia) (b. 3 Jan 1960 Skopje, Macedonia) on 21 January in Belgrade. A member of Crvenazvezda, Belgrade, he competed at 400m or 4x400m at 1988 Olympics (heat), 1982, 1986 and 1990 Europeans and 1991 Worlds (when he helped the YUG team to finish 4th at 4x400m). He won silver medals at the Mediterranean Games for 400m 1987 and 4x400m 1991 and for 4x400m at the 1987 World University Games, 41 internationals for Yugoslavia and YUG champion at 400m 1983 and 1986-8. Pbs: 200m 21.34 (1987), 400m 45.83 (1987), 800m 1:47.46 (1988).

Nyandika MAIYORO (Kenya) (b. 1930 Kiogoro) on 24 February in Kisii. He was the first Kenyan runner to come to international prominence when he was 4th in the 3 miles in the Empire (Commonwealth) Games at Vancouver in 1954 (later 12th in 1958), and at the Olympic Games he was 7th in 1956 and 6th in 1960 at 5000m. He was also 2nd in the AAA 3 miles in 1958. He became the caretaker of Kisii Municipal Stadium, retiring in 2002. He was awarded the MBE in 1961, the Silver Star Medal in Kenya in 1987, and the Distinguished Service Award by Kenyatta University in 1995. Pbs: 1M 4:09.6 (1958), 3000m 8:09.0 (1960), 2M 8:52.8 (1956), 3M 13:34.8 (1958), 5000m 13:52.8 (1960).

John MAYAKA (Kenya) (b. 1948 Nyamira County) on 23 February in Nyamira. At the javelin he was 3rd in 1974 with his personal best and Kenyan record 77.56, and 8th in 1978 at the Commonwealth Games, and he was 2nd in 1973 and 3rd in 1978 at the All-Africa Games.

Delroy POYSER (Jamaica) (b. 5 Jan 1962) on 11 February in Lubbock, Texas. He starred at Texas Tech, where he placed 3rd in the NCAA Indoor triple jump in 1983 and 3rd in the long jump the following year. Pbs: 100m 10.30w (1984), LJ 7.90 (1982), TJ 16.58/16.69Aw (1985).

Srecko RADISIC (Serbia/Yugoslavia) (b. 26 Jul 1931 Gornji Milanovac) on 14 February in Gornji Milanovac. At 800m he was Yugoslav champion in 1955-6 and 1959 and set a YUG record at 1:49.9 in 1955. Other pbs: 400m 49.6 (1956), 1000m 2:28.0 (1956), 1500m 3:48.4 (1955). 10 internationals 1954-9. He became a strength and conditioning coach in football, among other clubs Real Madrid and Sporting Lisbon.

Volodymyr SITKIN (USSR/Ukraine) (b. 6 Dec 1934 Krasniy Liman) on 23 January in Kiev. After being a non-qualifier at the 1954 Europeans and placing 6th at the 1956 Olympic Games, he came to the fore with the advent of built-up shoes for high jump. Yuriy Styepanov jumped a world record 2.16 on 13 July 1957 and Sitkin (1.80m tall) was second on the world list with his 2.15 at Odessa on 29 September. USSR champion that year, he was world ranked 4th by *Track & Field News*. His best before the year was 2.05 in 1955 and he was 2nd in 1955 and 3rd in 1957 at the World University Games, The shoes, typically using 2-4 cm thick soles on the take-off foot were made illegal by the IAAF with maximum thicknesses fixed at 13mm in 1958, but with no retrospective measures. Sitkin's best after this was 2.09 in 1963. PBs: LJ 7.58 (1958), Dec 6711 (1963, on 1952 tables).

Mathilde Catrina 'Tilly' van der ZWAARD (Netherlands) (b. 18 Jan 1938 Leiden), (later **van der MADE**) on 6 February in Edgewater, Florida, USA. At 400m she was 3rd at the 1962 Europeans and ran at the Olympic Games in 1964 (5th) and 1968 (heat). She was Dutch champion at 200m and 400m 1962-3, and 800m 1964 with indoor titles at 500m and 800m in 1970. She set a Dutch record of 53.2A in Mexico City prior to the 1968 Games with other pbs of 100m 12.0 (1963), 200m 23.9A (1968), 500m 1:13.9i (1970) and 800m 2:04.4 (1968) and ran on her national team that set a world record 6:15.5 for 3x800m at Sittard on 20 Aug 1968.

Maura VICECONTE (Italy) (b. 3 Oct 1967 Susa, Torino) on 10 February in Chiusa di San Michele. At marathon she had eight wins in 15 races, was 3rd at the Europeans in 1998 and at the Olympic Games was 12th in 2000 after dnf 1996. She was 12th at 10,000m at the 2002 Europeans. She was Italian champion at 10,000m 2002, half marathon 2000-01 and marathon 1994-5, and set Italian records at 10,000m 31:05.57 and marathon 2:23:47 in 2000. Other pbs: 5000m 15:18.80 (2000), HMar 69:19 (2001).

Vladimír VÍŠEK (Czech Republic) (b. 18 Mar 1937) on 19 February. Statistician, editor, and issuer of the marvellous statistics bulletin START (1970-7), he was a major compiler of of all-time world and European lists. Member of the ATFS from 1966. Founding member SAS (Czech statisticians group). Editor-in-chief of *Atletika* magazine 1990-1.

Willie WILLIAMS (USA) (b. 12 Sep 1931 Gary, Indiana) on 27 February in Illinois. While at the University of Illinois he won the NCAA 100y title in 1953 (when he was world ranked no. 1 for the year) and 1954 and in 1956, after pulling up injured, 8th and last in 12.1, at the US Olympic Trials, he tied the world record of 10.1 for 100m both in heat (on Aug 3) and final (on Aug 5) of the CISM Games in Berlin when he beat Ira Murchison (10.2, who had run 10.1 in his semi-final). He was 3rd at 100m and won gold at 4x100m at the 1955 Pan-American Games. Other pbs: 100y 9.5 (1953), 9.3w (1957); 200m 21.0 (1960), 220ySt 20.5 (1960). He coached the Saudi Arabian Olympic team in 1988 and was an assistant coach at Illinois from 1982 to 2000.

Died in 2017

Suzanne ALLDAY (née Farmer) (later GOODISON) (b. 26 Nov 1934 Shoreham-by-Sea) in Chichester on 26 July 2017. She competed in 35 internationals for Britain at shot and discus 1951-64, including at the Olympic Games of 1952, 1960 and 1964, European Championships in 1958 (5th SP/10th DT) and 1962 (10th/15th), and at three Commonwealth Games 1954 (6/2, also 6th javelin), 1958 (2/1) and 1962 (3/4). She was WAAA champion at shot 1954, 1956 and 1958-61 and at discus 1952-3, 1956 and 1958-61. She set eight UK records at shot from 13.33 (1956) to 15.18 (1964) and ten at discus from 40.37 (1952) to 47.70 (1958). Formerly married to international hammer thrower Peter Allday.

Dr Hugo MAIOCCO (USA) (b. 5 Apr 1927 New York) on 9 August. He won gold (3:09.9 4x400m), silver (48.0 400m) and bronze (1:53.6 800m) at the inaugural Pan American Games in Buenos Aires in 1951 and was the AAU indoor 600y champion in 1950 and 1951 and had pbs of 47.3 for 440y (1950) and 1:53.6 for 800m (1951). He was a physician in the Los Angeles area for over 50 years. His twin brother, Dick, ran 47.1 for 440y in 1955.

Julius MÜLLER (Germany) (b. 16 Dec 1938 Delmenhorst) on 19 September in Delmenhorst. German champion at 20k walk in 1963 and 50k walk in 1962. He was disqualified in the 1968 Olympic Games 20k walk. Walks pbs: 3000m 12:39.0, 5000m 21:15.8, 10,000m 43:52.8, 1Hr 13,124m (all 1969), 20k 1:29:06.2 (1968), 50k 4:25:26 (1962)

DRUGS BANS 2018

As announced by IAAF or national governing bodies. Suspension: L - life ban, y = years, m = months, W = warning and disqualification, P = pending hearing

Leading athletes

Men

Kipyegon Bett KEN	24 Feb	4y
Marcos Chuva POR		1y
Vladislav Grinchuk RUS	14 Feb	4y
Amit Kumar IND	13 Jun	3y 6m
Samuel Kalalei KEN	8 Apr	4y
Sadif Mikhou MAR		P
Boniface Mweresa KEN	Jun	P
Krisztián Pars HUN	13 Jan	1y 6m
Luka Lobuwan Rotich KEN	28 Jan	4y
Sofiane Selmouni FRA	22 Jan	1y
Isaac Seoke BOT	27 Jan	4y
Manuel Soto COL	27 Jun	2m 1y
Vitaliy Vitovshchyk UKR	24 Dec	P
James Mwangi Wangari KEN		P

Women

Kemi Adekoya BRN	26 Nov	P
Logan Boss USA	23 Jun	6m
Natalia Ducó CHI	19 Apr	P
María Guadelupe González MEX	17 Oct	P
Lucy Kabuu KEN	8 Apr	2y
Tatyana Kachegina RUS	28 Jun	4y
Kim Hye-song PRK	8 Apr	1y
Nataliya Polyakova RUS	19 Jul	4y
Yuliya Rakhmanova KAZ	21 May	4y
Kseniya Savina RUS		P
Chaltu Shume ETH	19 Apr	4y
Ruth Wanjiru KEN	28 Jan	16m
Wu Shuijiao CHN	Jun	2y
Wu Quanming CHN	14 Jun	W

4y: Birtukan Adeba ETH (19 Jan), Toshail Alikulov KAZ (5 May), Jerromy Andreas RSA (8 Sep), Ali Arzhangnezhad IRN (11 Jan), Sarkan Baker IRQ (25 May), Veronika Broslavskaya KAZ (29 Jun), Daniel Chebolei KEN (1 Apr), Abdelaziz Guerziz ALG (6 Feb), Domen Hafner SLO 29 Jan, Viktor Khakhutskiy RUS (21 Oct), Narges Khani IRN (5 Jan), Aleksey Kiselev RUS (19 May), Viktoria Makai HUN (10 Jun), Anna Merghil MDA (3 Feb), Vasiliy Minayev RUS (4 Aug), Habib Mosbah ALG (4 Feb), Zhamalidin Musaev KGZ (26 Jul), César Antonio Pérez ESP (4 Mar), Ioan Pitigoi ROU (27 Jan), Cristina Pitonzo ITA (15 Apr), Yuliya Stupina RUS (21 Feb), Oleksandr Zobenko UKR (7 Jul); **3.5y:** Zaman Pirverdiyev AZE (27 Jan); **2y:** Yevgeniya Fondyushina KAZ (30 Jun), Igor Kondratyev KAZ (29 Jun), Alexandr Lyakh KAZ (2 Jul), Pule Maeko RSA (31 Mar), Yana Mikhaylova RUS (22 Jun), Aleksey Tolokonnikov RUS (17 Jan), Darya Tvorogova RUS (26 Jan); **1y 3m:** Federica Poletti ITA (25 Mar); **1y:** Vsevolod Krasnoshchek RUS (25 Jan); **6m:** Cao Fengying CHN (25 Mar). Léa Plumecovq FRA (4 Feb); **W:** Jeroen Gonnissen BEL (17 Feb; **Coaches: Life:** 4y: David Burrell GBR, Sergey Kotov RUS, P - Sanjeet Singh IND (20 Sep)

Add to Drugs bans in 2017

Ali Abdosh ETH	24 Dec	4y
Caio Bonfim BRA	28 May	6m
Asil Cakir Alptekin TUR	2 Feb	8y

Jordan Chipangama ZAM	17 Jun	4y
Ilias Fifa ESP		4y
Hélio Gomes POR	10 Jun	2y
Adrian Griffith BAH	22 Apr	4y
Luka Kanda KEN	29 Oct	4y
Nicholas Kiplagat Kipkoech KEN	13 May	2y
Edwin Kipyego KEN	18 May	4y
David Kirui Kiptoo KEN	5 Nov	4y
El Mahdi Lahoufi ESP		4y
Jarrion Lawson USA		P
Nigel Levine GBR	24 Nov	4y
Eliud Magut KEN	23 Apr & 7 May	4y
Ayoub Mokhtar ESP		4y
Hadout Mousaab MAR	5 Nov	4y
Moeno Nakamura JPN	26 Nov	15m
Yegor Nikolayev RUS	9 Nov	4y
Lebokeng Sesele RSA	12 Nov	4y
Suleiman Simotwo KEN	23 Apr	4y
Davinder Singh Kang IND	15 May	W

Women

Vera Barbosa POR	1 Apr	1y
Jo Blair GBR	24 Sep	4y
Natalia Ducó CHI	Apr	P
Lydia Jele BOT	14 Oct	4y
Violah Jepchumba BRN	27 Aug	4y
Liu Xiangrong CHN	20 Aug	2y
Kanga Mupupo ZAM	6 Aug	4y
Moeno Nakamura JPN	26 Nov	15m
Yekaterina Sariyeva AZE	3 Jun	1y
Simone Silva BRA	9 Jun	30y
Jemima Sumgong KEN	28 Feb	8y
Meseret Taye (Asefa) ETH	17 Sep	4y
Dépina Zapounidou GRE	11 Aug	4y
Zhang Lin CHN	5 Mar	2y

8y: Su Xueting CHN (19 Nov); **4y:** José Luis Arroyo ESP (24 Jun), Douglas Ataide BRA (7 Nov), Ahmedov Azer AZE (18 Oct), Danile Kipchirchir Bii KEN (3 Dec), Victor Manuel Castro ESP (17 Dec), Denis Chernyayev RUS (25 Nov), Absene Daba ETH (5 Nov), Antonio Farina ITA (10 Sep), Andrey Gapon RUS (25 Nov), Hou Yanmin CHN (19 Nov), Michalis Kakotas CYP (18 Jun), Baljit Kaur IND (28 Dec), Ramanpreet Kaur IND (26 Jun), Samarjit Kaur IND (30 Dec), Brendon Keenan NZL (7 Sep), Ronald Kiptai (21 Oct), Neelam Kumari KEN (20 Dec), Li Wenjie CHN (19 Nov), Prashant Malik IND (15 May), Yuliya Maluyeva RUS (2 Sep), Esther Nganga KEN (19 Nov), Lhoussaine Oukhrid MAR (15 Oct), Rani Rakhi IND (3 Sep), Lawal Rashidat NGR (9 Mar), Erick Riongu KEN (26 Jun), Jaquite Semedo POR, Jagtar Singh IND (2 Jun), Saurabh Singh (J) IND (20 Dec), Michele Stingone ITA (28 May), Su Ciai CHN (19 Nov), Maria Thom[son Omokwe NGR (7 Dec), Eliudmatu Were KEN (5 Nov), Eyob Woldegiorgis ETH (29 Oct), Wu Chunlan CHN (26 Jul); **3y:** Rosemary Katua BRN (14 Oct); **2y:** Duncan Ayiemba KEN (18 Sep), Nicholas Kiplagat KEN (13 May), Dinesh Kumar KEN (28 Sep), Nelson Mbuya KEN (26 Nov), Chegen Mekedes ETH (23 Apr), Carmen Pérez ESP (17 Jun), Remigio Queral IBáñez ESP (22 Apr), Mr Rohit IND (12 Jun); **18m:** Isaac Kipkoech Kiplagat KEN (8 Oct); **14m:** Ferdinard Omurwa KEN (9 Jun), Natasha Yaremczuk CAN (29 Oct); **1y:** Valeria Cirielli ITA (16 Jul). Silyan Georgiev BUL (3 Jun), Mohamed Safaoui

COM (6 Nov), Rohat Yadav IND (23 Apr), Joaud Zeroual MAR (29 Jul); **Coaches: Life**: 8y: Raphaël Piolanti FRA (20 Sep 17)

2016

Men

Ihab Abdelrahman EGY	17 Apr	4y
Seref Dirli TUN	19 May	8y
Inderjeet Singh IND	Jul	4y
Vasiliy Kopeykin RUS	6 Feb	4y
Arjun Kumar Singh IND	24 Apr	4y
Andrei Toader ROU	10 May	4y
Lazarus Too KEN	4 Dec	2y

Women

Silvia Danekova BUL	1 Aug	4y
Alina Fyodorova UKR	27 Jul	4y
Elena Panaet ROU	20 Feb	4y
Demi Payne USA	12 Mar	4y

8y: Birykan Adeba ETH (13 Nov), Niholai Verdehin EST (24 Jun); **4y**: Eyob Alemu ETH (30 Oct), William Barnes PUR (15 Jun), Victor Calvo ESP (13 Mar), Daniel Estrada CHI (2 Oct), Suat Karabulak TUR (4 Sep), Vincent Kipchirchir KEN (30 Apr), Philles Moriti KEN (31 Jan); **3y**: Danylo Martins Santos BRA (8 Apr); **2y**: Darah Kibet KEN (4 Dec), Micah Kiplagat Samoei KEN (4 Sep); **1y 8m**: Nelly Jepkurui KEN (19 Nov); **3m**: Miran da Silva BRA (17 Apr);

2015

Women: Sally Kipyogo KEN   27 Dec   4y
Life: Mazlum Aydemir TUR (29 Aug & 28 Nov) **8y:** Mehtap Sizmaz TUR (9 May); **3y 6m:** Sanem Eser TUR (2 Jul); **15m:** Nevin Imholz SUI (25 Oct); **W:** Suji Rani IND (17 Oct)

2014

Hakan Duvar TUR	11 Aug	4y

4y: Anouar Assila FRA (26 Oct 14 & 20 Nov 16, also banned from test on 7 Jul 12), Muratkan Karapinar (21 Jul), Mehmet Akkoyun TUR (11 Aug)
Women: Sheila Chepngetich Keter KEN   21 Dec   3y 1y 1w

2012

Natalya Ivoninskaya KAZ		P
Ineta Radevica LAT		P
Anna Titimets UKR	26 Jun	2y
Rssults annulled to 26 Jun 2014		

4y: Vedat Gunen TUR (8 Dec)

2011

Pyotr Bogatyrev RUS	12 Jul	2 y
Results annulled to 15 Oct 2015		
Women: Anisya Kiprdyaplina RUS	25 Feb	2y
Results annulled 25 Feb 2011 to 11 Oct 2013		
Yeliz Kurt TUR	3 Mar 11 & 21 Mar 17	3y
Kateryna Stetsenko UKR*	26 Aug	2y 4m
Resuts annulled 26 Aug 2011 to 26 Aug 2018		

2009

Ruslan Dmytrenko UKR	14 Aug	2y
Results annulled 14 Aug 09 to 3 Aug 12		
Women: Kseniya Agafonova RUS	15 Aug	2y
Results annulled 15 Aug 09 to 14 Aug 11		
Yelizaveta Grechishnikova RUS	18 Aug	2y
Results annulled 18 Aug 09 to 16 Oct 13		

2008

Nesta Carter JAM	12 Jul	3m
Aleksandr Pogorelov RUS	23 Aug	4y
(results annulled 23 Aug 08 to 21 Feb 10)		
Women: Mariya Abakumova RUS	21 Aug	4y
also on 2 Sep 11		
Results annulled 21 Aug 98 to 20 Aug 12		
Tatyana Lebedeva RUS	18 Aug	2y
Results annulled 18 Aug 98 to 17 Aug 12		
Yelena Slesarenko RUS	23 Aug	4y
Results annulled 23 Aug 98 to 22 Aug 122007 and 10-year ban from 20 May 2012 test. Now loses results from 1.5.2011 to 20.5.12.		
Anna Pyatykh RUS	31 Aug	4y

Further recent women's name changes

Original	Married name
Maryna Bekh UKR	Bekh-Romanchuk
Alyona Bugakova RUS	Gordeyeva
Ty Butts USA	Townsend
Carolina Carmichael USA	Moll
Sydney Clute USA	Walter
Kristin Hixson USA	Leland
Rimma Hordiyenko UKR	Buinenko
Mary Iheke GBR	Abichi
Simnita Kovala (Ozolina) LAT	Sprudzane
Ayman Kozhakhmetova KAZ	Ratova
Gunta Latiseva-Cudare LAT	Vaicule

Original	Married name
Kelsey-Lee Roberts AUS	Barber
Florentina Marincu ROU	Iusco
Yekaterina Medvedyeva RUS	Ryzhova
Megan Moye USA	Mansy
Narayanan V. Neena IND	Pinto
Marina Pandakova RUS	Novikova
Lucia Slanickova SVK	Vadlejch
Kalisse Spencer JAM	Spencer-Carter
Gabriela Stafford CAN	DeBues-Stafford
Tamara Stasyuk UKR	Havrylyuk
Hanna Suslyk UKR	Shevchuk
Natalya Vlasova RUS	Koloskova

THE BEST EVER US OLYMPIC TRIALS?
Bob Burns

AN ARGUMENT CAN be made that the 1968 US Olympic men's team boasted the greatest collection of talent in athletics history. At the very least, the Mexico City exploits of Bob Beamon, Tommie Smith, Al Oerter, Lee Evans and Dick Fosbury remain indelible, half a century later. Less remembered is the track in the forest that propelled the American men to such dizzying heights Mexico City – the final US Olympic Trials at Echo Summit, a mountain pass high above Lake Tahoe near the California-Nevada border.

This much is indisputable: There has never been, and most likely never will be, another high-level meeting conducted in such an Arcadian setting. Hundreds of ponderosa pines rose from the infield. Runners disappeared from sight on the curves and backstretch. Javelins came soaring out of the trees. The site didn't have much room for spectator seating, but fans improvised, laying down blankets on the adjacent hill or climbing atop boulders to get a good view.

'The setting, the forest in the infield, the giant boulders ... it was a mythical place,' Fosbury said. 'Mount Olympus is a mythical place, and so is Echo Summit.'

The United States Olympic Committee selected Echo Summit as the site for a high-altitude training camp and final selection meet prior to the 1968 Olympics. Its elevation of 7382 feet (2250 meters) was nearly identical to that of Mexico City, and the hotels and casinos along Lake Tahoe's South Shore picked up much of the cost of installing a Tartan track in the parking lot of what was then a beginners' ski area. The US Forest Service agreed to the track's placement at Echo Summit as long as the setting be left as undisturbed as possible.

Four world records were set in the Echo Summit Trials: Geoff Vanderstock in the 400-meter hurdles (48.8 hand time, 48.93 fully automatic), Bob Seagren in the pole vault (5.41 meters), John Carlos in the 200 meters (19.7/19.92) and Lee Evans in the 400 meters (44.0/44.06). The IAAF refused to recognize the records set by Carlos in the 200 and Evans in the 400 since they were wearing Puma's new model of 'brush' spikes, though statisticians have long regarded the marks as legitimate. Larry James, the runner-up to Evans in 44.1, received credit for a world record despite finishing a stride behind. Vince Matthews, who had lowered the 400-meter mark to 44.4 in a pre-trials meet at Echo Summit, finished fourth in the final.

Many of the Olympic contenders spent a full two months training at Echo Summit, living in trailers across the highway from the track or in motels and junior-college dormitories down the hill in South Lake Tahoe. It wasn't unusual to see an Olympic athlete standing by the side of Highway 50 in the early evening, thumbing a ride to the Tahoe casinos. 'It was sort of like Mt. Olympus,' said Bill Toomey, the 1968 Olympic decathlon champion. 'You could imagine Zeus looking down on that track, telling the gods and goddesses, `This is the way I imagined it.' Then Bacchus smiles and says, `Yeah, and they can go to Tahoe at night.''

Despite the idyllic setting, Echo Summit wasn't paradise. Black athletes were under tremendous pressure to participate in an Olympic boycott organized by San Jose State sociology instructor Harry Edwards. Only the most single-minded athletes could ignore the headlines raging across the front pages in 1968, one of the most tumultuous in US history. The assassinations of Martin Luther King Jr. and Robert Kennedy were fresh wounds, the Vietnam War was raging, and rioting at the Democratic National Convention in Chicago took place less than two weeks before the Echo Summit trials began their 10-day run on September 6.

Compounding the tension, the format by which the USOC selected the men's team in 1968 was confusing at best, duplicitous at worst. Athletes were under the impression that the winners of the semi-final Olympic Trials in Los Angeles in late June would qualify for US team, provided they demonstrated good form at Echo Summit. But the precise selection policy was unclear when athletes began arriving on the mountain. The USOC put the matter to a vote after Los Angeles, and the athletes overwhelmingly supported making Echo Summit the sole determinant of who made the Olympic team. Of course, the vast majority of voters had everything to gain from a second chance.

Fosbury, who had won the high jump in Los Angeles, was one of those who had everything to lose. 'I went to the training camp at Echo Summit thinking I was on the Olympic team,' Fosbury said. 'Lo and behold, I learned that I wasn't. Those were the days of power to the people. In this case, the people won.' Tommie Smith, the world record-holder in the 220- and 440-yard dashes, suspected something more sinister. 'I think the two trials were held to weed the blacks out,' Smith said.

As would also be the case in Mexico City, the thin air had a beneficial effect on the sprints and jumps but crippled the hopes of many distance runners. The US women weren't allowed anywhere near Echo Summit, forced to hold their trials at sea level, in Walnut, California, and do their abbreviated altitude training at a military base in Los Alamos, New Mexico. 'We were very, very disenchanted,' said Willye White, who qualified for her fourth US Olympic women's team in 1968. 'The guys got the luxury of the high-altitude training for as long as they wanted. We only had two weeks of altitude training, and we were isolated. The guys got to go to Tahoe.'

The men also got to compete in a magical setting. In the final of the 200 meters, for instance, the spectators sitting in the modest bleachers set up along the finish line had no inkling of who was winning for several interminable seconds after the gun sounded. Carlos came flying out of the trees with a big lead and held the advantage through the tape, breaking the world record and defeating Smith for the first and only time in his career.

In 2014, at a reunion held to commemorate the naming of Echo Summit as a California Historical Landmark, Smith spoke of seeing another world record being set, not from the perspective of a runner-up but as a spectator. 'I remember watching Bob Seagren jump his height in the pole vault,' Smith said. 'We were watching from the stands, and it looked like he was falling out of the trees.'

The men's high jump final, held on the final day, saw four men still in the game at 2.21 meters. John Hartfield had the fewest misses and held the lead, followed in order by 1964 Olympian Ed Caruthers, Reynaldo Brown, a 17-year-old phenom, and Fosbury, the crowd favorite due to his revolutionary style of flopping backward over the bar. Since none of the four had ever cleared 2.21, Hartfield seemed assured of a spot on the team. Conversely, Fosbury's chances seemed dim. Then, after Hartfield narrowly missed his first attempt at 2.21, the others flew over in rapid succession. A stunned Hartfield missed his final two tries and was fourth, the odd man out in the cutthroat manner of the US Trials. 'That's the one moment I remember so clearly,' said Ralph Boston, the great longer jumper who qualified for his third Olympic team at Echo Summit. 'Hartfield missing that third attempt, disappearing into the woods, his pregnant wife running after him.'

The US men went to Mexico City loaded for bear, winning 12 gold medals and setting six world records. Beamon took the long jump record into outer space. Oerter won his fourth straight gold medal in the discus. Jim Hines became the first man to break 10 seconds in the 100 meters with automatic timing, and Smith and Carlos became more famous for their raised fists on the medal stand than they did for their sprinting in the 200 meters. Fosbury introduced the flop to the world with his win at Estadio Olímpico.

Once the winter snows melted, the track at Echo Summit was uprooted and trucked down the hill, where it was reinstalled at an intermediate school in South Lake Tahoe, about 10 miles away. 'I remember going to Tahoe in 1969 for a meet the Jaycees put on,' Olympic triple jumper Norm Tate said. 'It felt different. It was the same track, but there was nothing like being on top of that mountain.'

Bob Burns, a sportswriter from Sacramento, California, is the author of *The Track in the Forest: The Creation of a Legendary US Olympic Team*. Hardback 248 pages. Published by Chicago Review Press at US$ 26.99. Available at £12.88 plus delivery from Amazon in the UK.

Some Recent Marriages

Female	Male	
Caroline Ehrhardt CAN	Taylor Stewart USA	.10.18
Viktoriya Ferents UKR	Igor Hlavan UKR	
Queen Harrison USA	Will Claye USA	13.10.18
Lauren Howarth GBR	Andrew Heyes GBR	.12.18
Genevieve LaCaze AUS	Ryan Gregson AUS	28.9.18
Nikola Lomnická SVK	Andra Haklits CRO	.18
Antonella Palmisano ITA	Lorenzo Dessi ITA	22.9.18
Emily Pidgeon GBR	Andrew Osagie GBR	.9.18
Iryna Pimenova UKR	Bohdan Bondarenko UKR	.17
Anais Poumarat FRA	Renaud Lavillenie FRA	.9.18
Lynique Prinsloo RSA	P C Beneke RSA	
Anneliese Rubie AUS	Lachlan Renshaw AUS	.11.18
Francesca Zanella ITA	Giordano Benedetti ITA	22.9.18

AMENDMENTS TO ATHLETICS 2018

p. 70-71 **European Team Champs.** Drugs dq 2. Zemlyak, so 2. Müller, 3. Iga Baumgart POL 42.18, 4x400: dq 2 UKR, 2. GER, 3. GBR (Diamond. Laviai Nielsen, McAslan, Onuora) 3:28.96

Trends (p. 106-107)
Men HT: 100th best 70.89, 112 men to 4:10:00 at 50kW.
p.180 Norway Champs 2017: delete 3000mSt: Kårbo

2017 World Lists
Men: **60m**: 6.59 Scott 24.5.94
100m: 9.92w Pérez 4th, 10.05w West 26.6.96 (also 200m 20.65), 10.08w Jefferson 25.3.96 (& 200m 20.61), 10.11w Phillips 4.4.93 (& 200m 20.53w), 10.17w DeMoss 20.5.96 (& 20.65w), 10.17w Palmer 31.8.95; drugs dq 10.13w Griffith
200m: 19.77 Makwala 24.9.85 (& 300m 31.44, 400m 43.84); wa: 20.42Aw Tsumba; **400m**: 45.54 Obi(chukwu) Igbokwe; hand 45.9 Zwane 1.12.92; **800m**: 1:45.3A Tuwei 24.5.93; 1:47.2A Rutto 30.10.95, 1:47.4A Adisu Girma 10.12.99; **1500m**: 3:32.97A Soget b. 22.10.99, 3:37.95 Mead b. 28.6.89 (also in 3000, 5000, 10000); **3000m**: drugs dq 7:51.19 Hélio Gomes; **5000m**: 13:11.83 Kibet 10.11.88, drugs dq 13:35.00 Hélio Gomes; **HMar**: 60:23 short Chani 8.10.91; **Mar**: 2:05:43 Amos Kipruto 19.9.92 (& HMar 60:24), 2:06:50 Tola Shura Kitata (HMar 60:10), Drugs dq: 2:06:15 Kanda, 2:10:36 Simotwo
3000mSt: 8:20.76 Takele Nigate 2.10.99, 8:36.55 Gay 7.11.96; **110mh**: Jnr 99cm: 13.36 Eliopoulos 4.3.99, 13.47 Hiraga 28.4.99 **400mh**: 49.91A Mogawane (& 50.28 la); 50.32 Miyako 26.8.97, 50.45 Ohara 29.7.98 (& Jnr), Jnr: 50.75 Griffith BAR-Y 5.3.00
PV: 5.70 Devin King 13.3.96, 5.65 Jeff Coover 1 Louisville 30 Jun (from 5.60i/5.51), 5.40i Pauls Pujats LAT 6.8.91 22 Jun; best out: ?? 5.75 Shawnacy Barber 1 Washington DC 24 Jun, 5.55 Deakin Volz 2 Louisville 30 Jun
TJ: 16.28w Prothro 1.1.95; **SP**: Walsh 21.83 20 Aug (5th throw 21.75), 21.31 Mustafa Amr Ahmed Hassan (20.57-15), 20.63 Geist, 19.11 Daniel McArthur, 19.03 Mahin 30.5.93, 18.98 Warning 3.2.95, 18.81i Patterson PUR, add 18.75i Christian Zimmermann GER 9.7.94 22 Dec. Jnr 18.71 McKay Johnson USA 15.4.98 1 Berkeley 4 Mar, 18.10i Jordan West USA 27.6.99 3 Bloomington 8 Dec
DT: 20th was 65.13 Williams, move all (30) to (90) down a place, (100) OK. 64.55 C Harting 10.4.90, 61.29 Ohakwe 20.7.92; Juniors: 55.67 Genethli 2 on 20 May; **HT**: 73.92 Ahmed Amjad El-Seify QAT 1.10.96 6 Szczecin 10 Jun (from 69.85); **JT**: 75.91 Matsufuji 27.9.96, 74.92 Ishizaka 2.5.97; **4x400m**: 3:08.73 Sweden; **10,000mW**: 19:29.84 Jusho 11.1.00

Women
100m: 11.24 S Jackson 16.7.94 (& 200m, 400m 50.05)
400m: drugs dq 50.60 Kabange Mupopo (best earlier 51.50 1 Ndola 11 May)'**1500m**: 4:11.15 Schlachtenhaufen 14.3.95
3000m Kamuru 30.12.94 (& 5000m 14:58.82, 10000m 31:47.13, HMar 68:04); **10k**: Jemima Sumgong ¶ 10k 31:17, HMar 66:43 (OK as pre drugs ban); drugs dq 30:25 Jepchumba 3 Praha 9 Sep; **HMar**: 70:31 Suriya Loganathan, delete 70:21+ Jepkirui; drugs dq 66:06 Jepchumba at Ústi, 2 Wien 23 Apr
400mh: 54,96 Stepter 25.9.94 (& 400m 51.12); **PV**: 4.73 Nageotte 13.6.91; **SP**: 17.93 Song 4, 17.06 Meng 6; **HT**: 62.51 Coward 26.5.96; **4x400m**: 3:30.22 UKR Stavnycha, Kachur, Melnyk, Klymiuk 3 EU23 Bydgoszcz 16 Jul; **10000mW**: 46:22.4t Baby Soumya 20.4.90
20kW: 1:29:33 Gao Ni CHN 14.9.85 5 NG Tianjin 4 Sep, 1:29:37 María Pérez, 1:33:59 C Tallent 7.7.81 (& 10kW 45:54); **50kW**: 4:54:33 le Roux 10.6.82
Index changes are reflected in this year's Annual.

Amendments to World Indoor Lists 2018
60m: 6.60 Mitchell 29.7.98; **200m**: 20.65 Zézé, 20.69 Obi Igbokwe, **400m**: delete 1st line 44.85 Kerley; 45.81 Shinnick 8.2.99; **800m**: 1:46.52 drugs dq Kipkoech; **1500m**: Kipchirchir, Bor & Erassa on 26 Jan; **PV**: 5.85 Morgunov 12.10.86, 5.78A Devin King 13.3.96; **LJ**: 8.02 Knight 18.8.96, 7.96 Downs 7.3.96; **Women – 200m**: 22.99 Chadwick 26 Jan; **PV**: 4.50 Knoroz 1 NC-j Volgograd 7 Feb, 4.40i Regina Kramer GER 5.4.93 21 Jan

Amendments to Previous World Lists
2016: DT: 59.14 drugs dq Arjun Kumar Singh; W 3000mSt: drugs dq 9:42.39 Panaet
2010: SP: delete 18.68 Wattrus; **2009**: W LJ: 6.72 +1.4 Tatyana Ter-Mesrobyan 1 Sankt-Peterburg 1 Jun
1978: SP: 18.87 not 19.87 Vancevicius

International Championships Changes.
Drugs dqs – move rest up accordingly
2008 World Athletics Final: W 3000mSt: 4. Volkova, HJ: 6= Slesarenko, LJ/TJ: 3/2 Lebedeva
2009 European Cup Comb. Events: Dec: 2. Pogorelov
2009 European Team Champs: W JT: 3. Abakumova
2009 World Champs: Dec: 3. Pogorelov; 20kW: 31 Dmytrenko; W HJ: 10 Slesarenko, LJ/TJ: 2/6 Lebedeva; JT: 3. Abakumova; World Athletics Final: W LJ/TJ: 3/3. Lebedeva JT: 1, Abakumova
2010 European Team Champs: W JT: 3. Abakumova
2010 European Champs: 20kW: 12 Dmytrenko
2010 Continental Cup: W JT: 1. Abakumova
2011 World Champs: 20kW: 4 Dmytrenko; W HJ: 4. Slesarenko, JT: 1. Abakumova
2012 World Race Walking Cup: 20kW: 4 Dmytrenko
2012 Olympics: W JT: 10. Abakumova
2013 European U23: 20kW: 1. Bogatyrev (add 3. Massimo Stano ITA 1:25:25)
2013 World University Games: W 400mh: 1. Titimets
2013 World Champs: W 400mh: 4. Titimets
2014 (not 2013 as in A 2018) European Team Champs: W HT: (3) Bulgakova
2016 World U20 Champs: SP: 2 Toader
2017 World Champs: W 400m: 7. Mupopo

Drugs disqualifications and annulled marks – IAAF Biological Passport Cases and othersd
Men – Pavel Bogatyrev RUS 20kW: 2012- 1:20:51 (& 10k 39:33), 2013- 1:19:36
Ruslan Dmytrenko UKR (14 Aug 09-3 Aug 12): 1000mW/20kW: 2010- 39:33.91/1:21:54; 2011- 40:03.08i/1:21:31, 2012- 5kW 18:44.45i
Hakan Duvar TUR 3000mSt: 2014- 8:35.66, 2016- 8:33.13; **Vasiliy Kopeykin** RUS LJ: 2016- 8.22 (best pre ban 7.91i 31 Jan)
Aleksandr Pogorelov RUS: Dec: 2009- 8528 (& 8313)
Andrei Toader ROU: 2016: SP: 20.54 (pre ban 19.80i 2 Bucuresti); 6kg SP: 22.30 & 21.47 (21.67i pre ban)
Women – Mariya Abakumova RUS (21 Aug 08-20 Aug 12): JT: 2008- 70.78 (best pre ban 67.28). 2009- 68.92, 2010- 68.89, 2011- 71.99, 2012- 66.86 (best after ban 65.80 2 Athl Lausanne 23 Aug)
Tatyana Lebedeva RUS (18 Aug 08-17 Aug 12): 2008: LJ 7.03 (best pre ban 6.88), TJ- 15.32 (best pre ban 14.92); 2009- LJ 6.97, TJ 14.72/15.01w; 2010- LJ 6.64, 2012- 14.68 (best after ban 14.39)
Demi Payne USA: PV 2016; 4.85i 12 Mar and 4.45 best out.

Yelena Slesarenko RUS: HJ: 2009- 1.96, 2010- 1,88i, 2011- 1.97; **Kateryna Stetsenko** RUS: Mar: 2012- 2:28:38, 2014- 2:30:58; **Anna Titimets** UKR (26 Jun 12 -26 Jun 14): 400mh 2013- 54.63
Yekaterina Volkova RUS: (17 Aug 08 -16 Aug 10): 3000mSt: 2009- 9:17.40 (& 1500m 4:13.19)
Zhang Lin CHN: 2017: 50kW 3:52:38

Thanks to Norbert Heinrich, Juan Mari Iriondo, Russell Stedman

In addition **12 Russian athletes** were banned after the Court of Arbitration for Sport (CAS) rejected their appeals against IAAF suspensions.
* As these are subject to appeals I have not made the changes noted here elsewhere in this Annual.
* **Lyukman Adams:** 4 year ban from Jan 31; dq of all results from 16.7.12 to 14.9.14. Loses 2014 World Ind title (17.37) & 2014 Eur silver (17.09). Last competed in 2017. Revised medals: 2014 World Ind: 1, Ernesto Revé CUB 17.33; 2, Pedro Pichardo CUB 17.24; 3, Marian Oprea ROU 17.21; 2014 Eur: 1, Benjamin Compaoré FRA 17.46; 2, Aleksey Fyodorov RUS 17.04; 3, Yoann Rapinier FRA 17.01.
Gulfiya Agafonova (née Khanafeyeva): 8 year ban from 6.1.17 (second violation); dq of all results from 15.7.12 to 6.8.14. Last competed in 2016.
Tatyana Beloborodova (née Lysenko): 8 year ban from 2.7.16 (second violation); dq of all results from 16.7.12 to 2.7.16. Loses 2012 Oly title (already dq) & 2013 World title (78.80; so pb reverts to 78.51 on 5.7.12). Last competed in 2015. Revised medals: 2013 World: 1, Anita Wlodarczyk POL 78.46; 2, Zhang Wenxiu CHN 75.58; 3, Wang Zheng CHN 74.90.
Mariya Bespalova: Currently suspended since 26.10.15; dq of all results from 17.7.12 to 26.10.15. Loses 2013 World Univ Games bronze. Last competed in 2015.
Anna Bulgakova: 4 year ban from 29.3.17 (2 years added to 2 year ban already accepted by the athlete); dq of all results from 30.6.13 to 15.8.15. Loses pb, which reverts to 74.02 in 2012, and 5th in 2013 Worlds. Last competed in 2017.
Tatyana Firova: 4 year ban from 9.6.16; dq of all results from 20.8.08 to 31.12.12. Loses 2008 Oly 4x400 silver (RUS already dq), 2009 World 4x400 bronze (RUS already dq), 2nd 2010 World Ind 400 (51.13) & 4x400, 1st 2010 Eur 400 (49.89) & 4x400 (RUS already dq), 2012 Oly 4x400 silver (RUS already dq). Her pb reverts to 50.08 in 2006. Last competed in 2015. Revised medals: 2010 World Ind 400: 1, Debbie Dunn USA 51.04; 2, Vania Stambolova BUL 51.50; 3, Amantle Montsho BOT 52.53; 4x400: 1, USA 3:27.34; 2, JAM 3:28.49; 3, CZE 3:30.05; 2010 Eur 400: 1, Kseniya Ustalova (Aksyonova) RUS 49.92; 2, Antonina Krivoshapka RUS 50.10; 3, Libania Grenot ITA 50.43.
* **Yekaterina Galitskaya**: 4 year ban from Feb 1; dq of all results from 15.7.12 to 31.12.14. Loses 2012 Oly sf placing. Ran 8.14 60mH on January 30.

Vera Ganeyeva: 2 year ban from 2.7.18 (extension of 2 year ban already served from 2.7.16 to 1.7.18); dq of all results from 25.7.12 to 2.8.14 and from 2.7.18 to 31.1.19. Last competed in 2016.
* **Yuliya Kondakova:** 4 year ban from Feb 1; dq of all results from 17.7.12 to 16.7.16. Loses 2012 Oly sf placing, 4th 2013 Eur Ind 60mH, 8th 2013 Worlds, 8th 2014 World Ind, 2014 Eur sf; pb reverts to 12.79 in 2008. Last competed in Feb 2018.
* **Svetlana Shkolina**: 4 year ban from Feb 1; dq of all results from 16.7.12 to 28.7.15. Loses 2012 Oly bronze (2.03) and 2013 World title (2.03); pb reverts to 2.01 on 4.7.12. Last competed in 2017. Revised medals: 2012 Oly: 1, Anna Chicherova RUS 2.05; 2, Brigetta Barrett USA 2.03; 3, Ruth Beitia ESP 2.00; 2013 World: 1, Barrett 2.00; 2=, Chicherova & Beitia 1.97.
* **Ivan Ukhov:** 4 year ban from Feb 1; dq of all results from 16.7.12 to 31.12.15. Loses 2012 Oly title (2.38), 4th in 2013 Worlds (2.35), 2nd in 2014 World Ind (2.38), 3rd in 2014 Eur (2.30); pb reverts to 2.40i in 2009 & 2.39 on 5.7.12. Revised medal standings: 2012 Oly: 1, Erik Kynard USA 2.33; 2=, Robbie Grabarz GBR, Derek Drouin CAN & Mutaz Essa Barshim QAT 2.29; 2014 World Ind: 1, Barshim 2.38; 2, Andriy Protsenko UKR 2.36; 3, Kynard 2.34; 2014 Eur: 1, Bohdan Bondarenko UKR 2.35; 2, Protsenko 2.33; 3, Jaroslav Bába CZE 2.30. Ukhov cleared 2.31 indoors on Jan 17 and on Jan 31 this year.
Ivan Yushkov: 4 year ban starting from 2.7.16; dq of all results from 16.7.12 to 2.7.16.

The Athletics Integrity Unit (AIU) also confirmed provisional suspension of **Ineta Radevica** from Latvia after retesting her sample from London Olympic Games 2012 (presence of prohibited substance oxandrolone). She was fourth at that Games and was also European Champion 2010 and currently President of Latvian Athletics Federation.

Russian race walker **Anisya Kirdyapkina** has received a three-year doping ban froim 27 July 2017 due to biological passport abnormalities. She has had all of her results annulled from 25 Feb 2011 to 11 Oct 2013 and will lose her World Championships silver medals from 2011 and 2013, 4th at 2012 OLympic Games and European Cup 2nd 2011 and 1st 2013. Elisa Rigaudo and Qieyang Shenjie are due to receive upgrades from the 2011 Worlds and Liu Hong and Sun Huanhuan of China from the 2013 Worlds.

CAS announced on May 31 that it had dismissed the appeal of **Nesta Carter** against his disqualification after testing positive for a banned substance. Carter was disqualified in January 2017 following re-analysis of his sample from the 2008 Olympic Games, and now Trinidad & Tobago will be officially recognised as champions with Japan second and Brazil third.

NATIONAL CHAMPIONS 2018
and BIOGRAPHIES OF LEADING ATHLETES
By Peter Matthews

THIS SECTION incorporates biographical profiles of 797 of the world's top athletes this year – 419 men and 378 women, listed by nation. Also listed are national champions at standard events in 2018 for the leading countries prominent in athletics (for which I have such details).

The athletes profiled have, as usual, changed quite considerably from the previous year. All entries have been updated, but also many newcomers have been included to replace those who have retired or faded a little from the spotlight. The choice of who to include is always invidious, but I have concentrated on those who are currently in the world's top 10-15 per event, those who have the best championship records and some up-and-coming athletes who I consider may make notable impact during the coming year.

Since this section was introduced in the 1985 Annual, biographies have been given for a total of 5078 different athletes (2867 men and 2211 women).

The high turnover in our sport is reflected in the fact that there are many newcomers to this section (117 in all, 70 men, 47 women), as well as 16 athletes (4 men, 12 women) reinstated from previous Annuals. The athletes who now have the longest continuous stretch herein are now Gerd Kanter, Zoltán Kövagó, Eliud Kipchode and Meseret Defar on 17 years, with Valerie Adams. Allyson Felix, Justin Gatlin and Bershawn Jackson on 16 years. Athletes who have retired or who have been given drugs bans have generally been omitted.

No doubt some of those dropped from this compilation will also again make their presence felt; the keen reader can look up their credentials in previous Annuals, and, of course, basic details may be in the athletes' index at the end of this book.

Athletes included in these biographies are identified in the index at the end of this Annual by * for those profiled in this section and by ^ for those who were included in previous Annuals.

The biographical information includes:
a) Name, date and place of birth, height (in metres), weight (in kilograms).
b) Previous name(s) for married women; club or university; occupation.
c) Major championships record – all placings in such events as the Olympic Games, World Championships, European Championships, Commonwealth Games, World Cup and Continental Cup; leading placings in finals of the World Indoor Championships, European or World Junior Championships, European Under-23 Championships and other Continental Championships; and first three to six in European Indoors or World University Games. European Cup/Team Champs and IAAF Grand Prix first three at each event or overall. World Athletics Final (WAF) and Diamond League series (DL) winners
d) National (outdoor) titles won or successes in other major events.
e) Records set: world, continental and national; indoor world records/bests (WIR/WIB).
f) Progression of best marks over the years at each athlete's main event(s).
g) Personal best performances at other events.
h) Other comments.
See Introduction to this Annual for lists of abbreviations used for events and championships.

Information given is as known at 30 March 2018 (to include performances at the European Indoor Championships and World Cross-Country Championships as well as some other early indoor and outdoor events of 2019.

I am most grateful to various ATFS members who have helped check these details. Additional information or corrections would be welcomed for next year's Annual.

Peter Matthews

ALBANIA

Governing body: Federata Shqiptare e Atletikes. **National Championships** first held in 1945 (women 1946).

Luiza GEGA b. 5 Nov 1988 Dibër 1.66m 56kg. At 800m: WCh: '11- h. At 1500m: WCh: '13- sf, '15- h; EC: '12- sf, '14- h; WI: '14- 6; EI: '17- 5; WUG: '13- 2. At 3000mSt: OG: '16- h; EC: '16- 2, '18- 4. Won Balkan 1500m 2011, 2015, Med G 3000mSt 2018.

Albanian records: 800m (3) 2011-14, 1500m (4) 2013-15, 3000m (2) 2012-16, 5000m 2014, 3000mSt (4) 2011-16.

Progress at 1500m, 3000mSt: 2006- 4:38.0, 2010- 4:23.20, 2011- 4:14.22, 9:54.72; 2012- 4:08.65mx/ 4:09.76. 2013- 4:05.11, 2014- 4:03.12, 2015- 4:02.63, 2016- 4:06.89i, 9:28.52; 2017- 4:06.66i/4:09.76, 9:26.05; 2018- 4:10.36i, 9:22.00. pbs: 800m 2:01.31 '14, 3000m 8:52.53i '17, 8:53.78 '16; 5000m 15:46.89 '14, 10000m 33:31.0 '17.

ALGERIA

Governing body: Fédération Algerienne d'Athlétisme. Founded 1963.

National Champions 2018: Men: 100m: Mahmoud Hamoudi 10.54, 200m: Soufiane Bouhada 21.03w, 400m: Miloud Laaredj 47.31, 800m: Mohamed Belbachir 1:48.58, 1500m: Abderrahmane Anou 3:51.43, 5000m: Kheireddine Bourouina 14:44.97, HMar: Khoudir Aggoune 64:13, Mar: Ismail Bouarouz 2:26:23; 3000mSt: Issam Zeghdane 9:12.18, 110mh: Lyès Mokdal 13.85, 400mh: Admelmalik Lahoulou 49.94, HJ: Ryad Selloum 2.15, PV: Hichem Cherabi 4.70, LJ/TJ: Yasser Triki 7.92/16.32w, DT: Abdelmoumen Bourakba 51.75, 10000mW: Mohamed Ameur 43:21.28; **Women**. 100m: Abir Barkaoui TUN 12.15w/ 24.67w, 400m: Meriem Boulahsa 56.44, 800m: Narimane Amara 2:09.26, 1500m/5000m: Rima Chenah 4:27.04/16:28.85, HMar: Malika Benderbal 74:18, Mar: Iman Momouni 3:28:00, 100mh: Marwa Selmi 14.17w, 400mh: Dihia Haddas 60.70, PV: Nesrine Brinsi TUN 3.60, LJ: Romaissa Belbiod 5.93w, TJ: Kaoutar Selmi 12.74w, DT: Nabila Bounab 43.80, HT: Zouina Bouzebra 59.72, JT: Ryma Benaissa 45.69, 10000mW: Riheb Mansouri TUN 49:42.05.

ARGENTINA

Governing body: Confederación Argentina de Atletismo (CADA). Founded 1954 (original Governing body founded 1919). **National Championships** first held in 1920 (men), 1939 (women).

2018 Champions: Men: Matías Robledo 10.67, 200m: Valentín Della Giustina 21.57, 400m: Elián Larregina 48.14, 800m: Leandro Paris 1:51.78, 1500m/5000m/3000mSt: Joaquín Arbe 3:53.10/14:34.44/8:51.63, 10000m: Javier Carriqueo 29:54.30, HMar: Marcos Molina 64:19, Mar: Miguel Guerra 2:27:25, 110mh: Agustín Carrera 14.37, 400mh: Guillermo Ruggeri 50.57, HJ: Carlos Layoy 2.23, PV: Germán Chiaraviglio 5.40, LJ: Brian López 7.08, TJ: Maximiliano Díaz 16.09, SP: Hugo Nieto 17.00, DT: Juan Ignacio Solito 52.00, HT: Joaquín Gómez 73.92, JT: Braian Toledo 75.40, Dec: Sergio Pandiani 7390. **Women**: 100m: Guillermina Cossio 11.82, 200m/400m: Noelia Martínez 23.99/54.59, 800m: Mariana Borelli 2:07.44, 1500m: Micaela Levaggi 4:23.75, 5000m: María Luz Tesuri 16:34.09, 10000m: Florencia Borelli 33:53.58, HMar: Daiana Ocampo 74:05, Mar: Dalila Dovich 2.58.36, 3000mSt: Clara Baiocchi 10:24.52, 100mh: Valentina Sánchez 14.37, 400mh: Fiorella Chiappe 58.00, HJ: Betsabé Páez 1.74, PV: Valeria Chiaraviglio 3.90, LJ: Andrea Ubiedo 5.80, TJ: Yamila Levrino 12.26, SP/DT: Ailén Armada 13.61/53.36, HT: Jennifer Dahlgren 63.65, JT: Bárbara López 48.46, Hep: Agustina Zerboni 5024.

AUSTRALIA

Governing body: Athletics Australia. Fd 1897. **National Championships** first held in 1893 (men) (Australasian until 1927), 1930 (women). **2018 Champions: Men**: 100m: Trae Williams 10.10, 200m: Alex Hartmann 20.57, 400m: Murray Goodwin 46.24, 800m: Luke Mathews 1:45.90, 1500m: Ryan Gregson 3:39.66, 1M: Matthew Ramsden 3:59.18, 5000m: Morgan McDonald 13:19.05, 10000m: Stewart McSweyn 27:50.89, HMar: Jack Rayner 64:02, Mar:, 3000mSt: James Nipperess 8:43.89, 110mh: Nicholas Hough 13.76, 400mh: Ian Dewhurst 49.80, HJ: Brandon Starc 2.28, PV: Kurtis Marschall 5.55, LJ: Chris Mitrevski 8.09w, TJ: Emmanuel Fakiye 16.08, SP: Damien Birkinhead 20.02, DT/ HT: Matthew Denny 64.03/72.78, JT: Hamish Peacock 79.38, Dec: Cedric Dubler 8229, 10,000W: Declan Tingay 41:07.88, 20kW: Dane Bird-Smith 1:22:18. **Women**: 100m/200m: Riley Day 11.56/22.93, 400m: Anneliese Rubie 51.92, 800m: Brittany McGowan 2:00.24, 1500m: Linden Hall 4:07.55, 1M: Whitney Sharpe 4:37.35, 5000m: Celia Sullohem 15:34.42, 10000m/ HMar: Sinead Diver 31:50.98/69:20, Mar:, 3000mSt: Victoria Mitchell 9:45.37, 100mh: Sally Pearson 12.73, 400mh: Lauren Wells 56.06, HJ: Cassie Purdon 1.86, PV: Nina Kennedy 4.60, LJ: Brooke Stratton 6.66, TJ: Megan O'Riley 13.44, SP: Chelsea Lenarduzzi 15.93, DT: Dani Samuels 65.30, HT: Alex Hulley 64.84, JT: Kathryn Mitchell 65.51, Hep: Celeste Mucci 5812, 10000mW/20kW: Beki Smith 45:56.09/1:31:23, 50kW: Claire Tallent 4:28:52.

Dane BIRD-SMITH b. 15 Jul 1992 Kippa-Ring 1.78m 66kg. Racewalking Queensland. Uibversity of Queensland. At 20kW: OG: '16- 3; WCh: '13- 11, '15- 8, '17- 6;

CG: '18- 1; WCp: '14- 14, '16- 4; WUG: '15- 1; OCE Champion 2016-17; At 10000mW: WJ: '10- 5; WY: '09- 8. Won AUS 5000mW 2013, 10000mW 2014-17, 20kW 2013-14, 2017-18; OCE 20kW 2017. Oceania 5000m walk record 2016.
Progress at 20kW: 2011- 1:26:38, 2012- 1:23:15, 2013- 1:22:03, 2014- 1:20:27, 2015- 1:20:05, 2016- 1:19:37, 2017- 1:19:28, 2018- 1:19:34. pbs: 3000mW 10:56.23 '14, 5000mW 18:38.97 '16, 10000mW 38:34.23 '17.

Henry FRAYNE b. 14 Apr 1990 Adelaide 1.87m 72kg. Old Melbournians. Student.
At LJ/(TJ): OG: '12- 9/dnq 17, '16- 7; WCh: '11- (9), '17- dnq 14; CG: '14- nj, '18- 2; WJ: '08- (5); CCp: '14- 7, "18- 4; WI: '12- 2. Won AUS TJ 2010. Oceania indoor long jump record 2012.
Progress at LJ, TJ: 2006- 7.01, 2007- 7.05, 15.55; 2008- 7.39, 16.58; 2009- 7.99, 16.62; 2010- 7.50w, 16.63; 2011- 7.98, 17.04; 2012- 8.27, 17.23/17.34w; 2014- 8.10, 2016- 8.16, 2017- 8.21, 2018- 8.34.
Nephew of 400m international Bruce Frayne (2nd 4x400m CG 1986). His father Geoff was a long jumper.

Ryan GREGSON b. 26 Apr 1990 Bulli, NSW 1.84m 68kg. Glenhuntly.
At 1500m: OG: '12- sf, '16- 9; WCh: '09-11-15-17: h/sf/h/h; CG: '14- h, '18- 9; WJ: '08- 5 (12 5000m); WY: '07- 5; CCp: '18- 5. AUS champion 2010, 2016-18.
Oceania 1500m record 2010.
Progress at 1500m: 2003- 4:26.00, 2004- 4:20,00, 2005- 4:06.00, 2006- 3:57.00, 2007- 3:43.84, 2008- 3:41.14, 2009- 3:37.24, 2010- 3:31.06, 2011- 3:36.64, 2012- 3:33.92, 2013- 3:35.25, 2014- 3:36.17, 2015- 3:36.51, 2016- 3:32.13, 2017- 3:34.37, 2018- 3:34.38. pbs: 800m 1:46.04 '10, 1000m 2:17.69 '10, 1M 3:52.24 '10, 3000m 7:42.19 '17, 5000m 13:56.83 '09, 10km Rd 29:09 '08.
Married Genevieve LaCaze (qv) on 29 Sep 2018.

Kurtis MARSCHALL b. 25 Apr 1997 North Adelaide 1.88m 78kg. Western District, Adelaide. Student at the University of South Australia.
At PV: OG: '16- dnq 15; WCh: '17- 7; CG: '18- 1; WJ: '14- dnq 20=, '16- 2; WI: '18- 4. AUS champion 2016-18.
Progress at PV: 2013- 4.90, 2014- 5.35, 2015- 5.42, 2016- 5.70, 2017- 5.73, 2018- 5.86i/5.80, 2019- 5.87i/5.81.

Brandon STARC b. 24 Nov 1993 Baulkham Hills, New South Wales 1.88m 73kg. Parramatta.
At HJ: OG: '16- 15; WCh: '13- dnq 25, '15- 12; CG: '18- 1; WJ: '12- 6; YOG: '10- 2; CCp: '18- 2. AUS champion 2013, 2015, 2018; DL 2018.
Equalled Oceania high jump record 2018.
Progress at HJ: 2009- 1.96, 2010- 2.19, 2011- 2.20, 2012- 2.18, 2013- 2.28, 2014- 2.25, 2015- 2.31, 2016- 2.29, 2017- 2.25, 2018- 2.36.
Brother of Australian cricketer Mitchell Starc.

Jared TALLENT b. 17 Oct 1984 Ballarat 1.78m 60kg. Ballarat YCW. Graduate of University of Canberra.
At 20kW(/50kW): OG: '08- 3/2, '12- 7/1, '16- (2); WCh: '05- 18, '07- dq, '09- 5/6, '11- 22/2, 13- (3), '15- 26/2; CG: '06- 3, '10- 1; WCp: '06-08-10-12-14-16: 14/10/(3)/(1)/(3)/(1). At 10000mW: WJ: '02- 19; WY: '01- 7. Won AUS 5000mW 2012, 20kW 2008-13; 30kW 2004, 50kW 2007, 2009, 2011.
Commonwealth 5000m walk record 2009.
Progress at 20kW, 50kW: 2002- 1:40:21, 2003- 1:31:24, 2004- 1:27:02, 2005- 1:22:53, 2006- 1:21:36, 3:55:08; 2007- 1:21:25, 3:44:45,; 2008- 1:19:41, 3:39:27; 2009- 1:19:42, 3:38:56; 2010- 1:19:15, 3:54:55; 2011- 1:19:57, 3:43:36; 2012- 1:20:02, 3:36:53; 2013- 1:20:41, 3:40:03; 2014- 1:20:55, 3:42:48; 2015- 1:24:05, 3:42.17; 2016- 1:21:50, 3:41:16; 2017- 1:32:01A. pbs: 3000mW 11:15.07 '09, 5000mW 18:41.83 '09, 10000mW 40:41.5 '06, 10kW 38:29 '10, 30kW 2:28:18 '18, 35kW 2:53:34 '18.
Won IAAF Walks Challenge 2008 and 2013.
Married Claire Woods on 30 Aug 2008. Younger sister Rachel Tallent (b. 20 Feb 1993) has 20kW pb 1:31:33 to win OCE 2016, 34 WCh '15, 40 OG '16.

Women

Kelsey BARBER b. 21 Sep 1991 East London, South Africa 1.75m 70kg. née Kelsey-Lee Roberts. South Canberra Tuggeranong.
At JT: OG: '16- dnq 28; WCh: '15- dnq 20, '17- 10; CG: '14- 3, '18- 2; CCp: '18- 5; AUS champion 2017.
Progress at JT: 2009- 46.10, 2010- 49.29, 2011- 52.01, 2013- 58.58, 2014- 63.92, 2015- 63.78, 2016- 59.02, 2017- 64.53, 2018- 64.57.

Genevieve GREGSON b. 4 Aug 1989 Benowa, Queensland 1.68m 54kg. née LaCaze. Glenhuntly. University of Florida, USA.
At 3000mSt: OG: '12- h, '16- 9 (12 5000m); WCh: '15- h, '17- 12; CG: '14- 5, '18- 5. At 1500m: WJ: '04- h. At 3000m: CCp: '18- fa. AUS champion 5000m 2016, 3000mSt 2013, 2015.
Oceania records 2000mSt 2015, 3000mSt 2016.
Progress at 3000mSt: 2009- 10:26.92, 2010- 10:30.12, 2011- 9:59.44, 2012- 9:37.90, 2013- 9:37.62, 2014- 9:33.19, 2015- 9:35.17, 2016- 9:14.28, 2017- 9:24.52, 2018- 9:23.69. pbs: 800m 2:04.05 '16, 1500m 4:10.20 '16, 1M 4:32.06 '17, 3000m 8:45.81i '17, 8:49.38 '18; 2M 9:52.21 '14, 5000m 15:06.67 '16, 10k Rd 34:51 '15, 2000mSt 6:16.86 '15.
Married Ryan Gregson (qv) on 29 Sep 2018..

Kathryn MITCHELL b. 10 Jul 1982 Hamilton, Victoria 1.68m 72kg. Eureka AC.
At JT: OG: '12- 9, '16- 6; WCh: '13- 5, '15/17- dnq 17/25; CG: '06-10-14-18: 6/5/4/1; AUS champion 2008, 2018. Three Oceania javelin records 2018.
Progress at JT: 1999- 43.17, 2000- 51.44, 2001- 54.98, 2002- 54.72, 2003- 57.11, 2004- 48.10, 2005- 54.87, 2006- 58.81, 2007- 58.61, 2008- 58.77, 2010-

59.68, 2011- 59.47, 2012- 64.34, 2013- 63.77, 2014- 66.10, 2015- 63.70, 2016- 64.37, 2017- 66.12, 2018- 68.92.

Sally PEARSON b. 19 Sep 1986 Sydney 1.66m 60kg. née McLellan. Gold Coast Victory. Griffith University.
At (100m)/100mh: OG: '08- 2, '12- 1; WCh: '03- hR, '07- sf/sf, '09-11-13-17: 5/1/2/1; CG: '06- 7/ fell/3R, '10- dq/1, '14- 1; WJ: '04- 3/4; WY: '03- 1; WCp: '06- 8/4, '10- 1. At 60mh: WI: '12- 1, '14- 2. At 200m: WY: '03- 5; won DL 2017, AUS 100m & 100mh 2005-7, 2009, 2011, 2014-15; 100mh 2017- 18, 200m 2011.
Records: Oceania 100mh (8) 2007-11, 60m 2009 & 60mh indoors (3) 2009-12; Commonwealth 100mh (2) 2011.
Progress at 100mh: 2003- 14.01, 2004- 13.30, 2005- 13.01, 2006- 12.95, 2007- 12.71, 2008- 12.53, 2009- 12.50, 2010- 12.57, 2011- 12.28, 2012- 12.35, 2013- 12.50, 2014- 12.5, 2015- 12.59, 2016- 13.14/ 12.92w, 2017- 12.48, 2018- 12.68/12.67w. pbs: 60m 7.16 '11, 100m 11.14 '07, 150m 16.86 '10, 200m 23.02/22.66w '09, 300m 38.34 '09, 400m 53.86mx '11, 200mh 27.54 '06, 60mh 7.73i '12, 200mh 26.96 '09, 400mh 62.98 '07.
Married Kieran Pearson on 3 April 2010. IAAF female Athlete of the Year 2011.

Dani STEVENS b. 26 May 1988 Fairfield, Sydney 1.82m 82kg. née Samuels. Westfields, University of Western Sydney.
At DT/(SP): OG: '08- 8, '12- 11, '16- 4; WCh: '07- 09-11-13-15-17: dnq 13/1/10/10/6/2; CG: '06- 3/12, '14- 1; WJ: '06- 1/7; WY: '05- 1/3; WCp: '06- 6; WUG: '07- 2, '09- 1; CCp: '10- 14-18: 4/2/4. AUS champion SP 2006-07, 2009, 2012; DT 2005- 12, 2014-15, 2017-18.
Commonwealth & Oceania discus record 2017.
Progress at DT: 2001- 39.17, 2002- 45.52, 2003- 47.29, 2004- 52.21, 2005- 58.52, 2006- 60.63, 2007- 60.47, 2008- 62.95, 2009- 65.44, 2010- 65.84, 2011- 62.33, 2012- 63.97, 2013- 64.46, 2014- 67.99, 2015- 66.21, 2016- 67.77, 2017- 69.64, 2018- 68.26. pbs: SP 17.05 '14, HT 45.39 '05.
Added 1.65m to her pb to win World silver in 2017. Sisters Jamie and Casey played basketball for Australia. Married Joe Stevens (SP: pb 17.34 '88; 11 WJ '06).

Brooke STRATTON b. 12 Jul 1993 Box Hill, Melbourne 1.68m 58kg. Nunawading. Was at Deakin University, Melbourne.
At LJ: OG: '16- 7; WCh: '15- dnq 14, '17- 6; CG: '18- 2; WJ: '10- 6, '12- 7; WY: '09- 10; CCp: '18- 3; WI: '16- 5. AUS champion 2014, 2018.
Oceania long jump record 2016.
Progress at LJ: 2004- 5.38, 2005- 5.40, 2006- 5.52, 2007- 5.90, 2008- 6.06, 2009- 6.13, 2010- 6.30, 2011- 6.60, 2012- 6.56, 2013- 6.53, 2014- 6.70, 2015- 6.73, 2016- 7.05, 2017- 6.79, 2018- 6.88. Pbs: 100m 11.98 '13, 11.91w '18; 200m 24.79 '16, 100mh 14.18 '10, TJ 13.34 '12.

Claire TALLENT b. 6 Jul 1981 North Adelaide 1.63m 50kg..née Woods.
At 20kW: OG: '08- 27, '12- dq; WCh: '09- 26, '11- 18, 17- 43; CG: '10- 2, '18- dq; At 50kW: WCp: '18- 3. Won AUS 5000mW 2012, 10kW 2002, 2004; 20kW 2007, 2009-12; 50kW 2018.
Commonwealth & Oceania walk records 30k, 25k & 50k 2018.
Progress at 20kW, 50kW: 2002- 1:43:56, 2003- 1:42L16, 2004- 1:35:25, 2005- 1:36:21, 2006- 1:35:18, 2007- 1:35:36, 2008- 1:33:02, 2009- 1:32:12, 2010- 1:32:02, 2011- 1:32:39, 2012- 1:28:53, 2016- 1:33:23, 2017- 1:33:59, 2018- 1:31:29, 4:09:33; 2019- 4:12:44. pbs: 3000mW 12:48,87mx '09, 5000mW 21:29.12 '12, 10000mW 46:06.59 '18, 10kW 44:19 '12, 30kW 2:10:52 '13, 35kW 2:32:37 '12.
Married Jared Tallent on 30 Aug 2008. Son Harvey born 25 May 2017.

AUSTRIA

Governing body: Österreichischer Leichtathletik Verband OLV). Founded 1902.
National Championships first held in 1911 (men), 1918 (women). **2018 Champions: Men**: 100m: Markus Fuchs 10.38, 200m: Samuel Reindl 21.39, 400m/400mh: Dominik Hufnagl 47.00/51.17, 800m: Leon Kuhn 1:54.84, 1500m/ 5000m/10000m: Andreas Vojta 3:54.35/14:41.72/ 28:59.11, HMar: Lemawork Weldearegaye 63:55, Mar Isaac Kosgei 2:20:59, 3000mSt: Jürgen Aigner 9:19.43, 110mh: Florian Domenik 14.33, HJ: Andreas Steinmetz 2.03, PV: Ricardo Klotz 5.15, LJ: Julian Kellerer 7.60, TJ: Philipp Kronsteiner 15.94, SP: Heimo Kaspar 14.63, DT: Lukas Weisshaidinger 64.53, HT: Matthias Hayek 60.48, JT: Adam Wiener 67.18, Dec: Dominik Siedlaczek 6742, 20kW: Roman Brzezowsky 1:52:49, 50kW: Dietmar Hirschmugl 5:48:16. **Women**: 100m/200: Alexandra Toth 11.51/23.65, 400m: Susanne Walli 53.68, 800m: Anna Baumgartner 2:12.05, 1500m: Nada Pauer 4:27.36, 5000m: Sandrina Illes 16:47.22, 10000m: Julia Mayer 35:37.01, HMar: Cornelia Moser 76:12, Mar: Karin Freitag 2:45:26, 3000mSt: Bettina Bachl 11:21.18, 100mh: Stephanie Dendrat 12.94, 400mh: Sigrid Fortenschlager 62.18, HJ: Sarah Zimmer 1.71, PV: Agnes Hodi 3.93, LJ: Ivona Dadic 6.28, TJ: Michaela Egger 12.58, SP: Christina Scheffauer 14.33, DT: Djeneba Touré 53.00, HT: Bettina Weber 55.21, JT: Patricia Madl 47.26, Hep: Sarah Lagger 5691, 20kW: Andrea Kovacs 1:52:37.

Lukas WEISSHAIDINGER b. 20 Feb 1992 Schärding 1.96m 136kg. ÖTB OÖ Leichtathletik.
At DT (SP): OG: '16- 6; WCh: '15- dnq 20, '17- 9; WJ: '10- dnq 16 (6); WY: '09- dnq 36 (4); EU23: '13- 7; EJ '11- 1 (5 SP). Won AUT SP 2012-15, DT 2015-16, 2018.
Three Austrian discus records 2015-18.
Progress at DT: 2008- 43.47, 2009- 45.98, 2010- 54.21, 2011- 54.85, 2012- 58.00, 2013- 59.13, 2014-

60.68, 2015- 67.24, 2016- 66.00, 2017- 66.52, 2018-
68.98. pb SP 18.90 '13.

Women

Ivona DADIC b. 29 Dec 1993 Weis 1.79m 65kg.
PSV Hornbach Weiss.
At Hep: OG: '12- 23, '16- 21; W Ch: '17- 6; EC:
'16- 3, '18- 4; WJ: '12- dnf; WY: '09- 10; EU23: '13-
5, '15- 3; EJ: 11- 10 At Pen: WI: '18- 2; EI: '17- 2,
'19- 4. Won AUT LJ 2018, SP 2017, Hep 2012.
7 Austrian heptathlon records 2012-18.
Progress at Hep: 2011- 5455, 2012- 5959, 2013-
5874, 2015- 6151, 2016- 6408, 2017- 6417, 2018-
6552. pbs: 200m 23.61 '18, 400m 56.27 '11, 800m
2:10.67 '12, 60mh 8.32i '18, 100mh 13.56 '18, HJ
1.87i/1.83 '17, LJ 6.49 '16, SP 14.86 '18, JT 52.48
'15, Pen 4767i '17.
Improved heptathlon pb by 212 points for 3rd
EC '16 and pentathlon best by 247 for 2nd EI '17.

AZERBAIJAN

Governing body: Azerbaijan Athletics
Association. Founded 1923, reorganised 1992.

Nazim BABAYEV b. 8 Oct 1997 Baku 1.85m 70kg.
At TJ: OG: '16- dnq 25; WCh: '17- dnq 14; EC: '16:
dnq 23=, '18- 4; WJ: '16- dnq 15; EU23: '17- 1; EJ:
'15- 1; YOG: '14- 3; WI. '16- 8, EI: '19- 1; WUG:
'17- 1. Won Is.Sol 2017.
Progress at TJ: 2013- 15.53, 2014- 16.18, 2015-
17.04, 2016- 16.83, 2017- 17.18, 2018- 16.89, 2019-
17.29i. pbs: 60m 7.05i '17, LJ 7.49 '16.

Alexis COPELLO Sánchez b. 12 Aug 1985
Santiago de Cuba 1.85m 80kg.
At TJ: OG: '08- dnq 13, '12- 8; WCh: '09- 3, '11- 4,
'17- 5; EC: '18- 2; WI: '12- 7, '18- 4; PAmG: '11- 1;
CAG: '06- 2; CCp: '10- 2. Won IbAm 2010, CAC
2009, Cuban 2009, 2011.
Progress at TJ: 2002- 15.38, 2003- 16.34, 2004-
16.90, 2005- 16.95/17.09w, 2006- 17.38, 2007-
16.87/17.15w, 2008- 17.50, 2009- 17.65/17.69w,
2010- 17.55, 2011- 17.68A/17.47, 2012- 17.17, 2014-
17.05, 2015- 17.15/17.24w, 2016- 16.99i/16.98,
2017- 17.16/17.17w, 2018- 17.24. pb LJ 7.35 '04.
Former Cuban, Azeri citizenship 26 Apr 2016,
cleared to compete for them from 24 Apr 2017.
Elder brother Alexander (b. 19 Feb 1978)
decathlon pb 7359 '02.

Women

Hanna SKYDAN b. 14 May 1992 Krasnyi Luch,
UKR 1.83m 114kg.
At HT: OG: '12/16- dnq 14/13; WCh: '15- dnq 23,
'17- 5; EC: '16- 3, '18- 5; WJ: '10- dnq 27; WY: '09-
12; EJ: 11- dnq; WUG: '15- 1; UKR champion
2012, Is.Sol 2017.
Eight AZE hammer records 2015-17.
Progress at HT: 2009- 56.90, 2010- 56.76, 2011-
67.56, 2012- 74.21, 2013- 68.44, 2014- 71.14, 2015-
72.31, 2016- 73.87, 2017- 75.29., 2018- 74.02 pbs: SP
13.98 '17, DT 49.50 '15.
Competed for Ukraine to 2012, AZE citizenship

15 Jan 2015 and cleared to compete for them
from 1 Jun 2015.

BAHAMAS

Governing body: Bahamas Association of
Athletics Associations. Founded 1952.
National Champions 2018: Men: 100m: Warren
Fraser 10.36, 200m: Shavez Hart 20.90w, 400m:
Alonzo Russell 45.52, 110mh: Xavier Coakley
14.27, 400mh: Andre Colebrook 50.74, HJ:
Donald Thomas 2.23, TJ: Latario Colllie 16.53,
DT: Drexel Maycock 50.65. **Women:** 100m:
Alexis Gray 11.85, 200m: Tynia Gaither 23.17w,
100mh: Devynne Charlton 13.27, 400mh:
Katrina Seymour 59.23, HJ: Shaunae Miller-
Uibo 1.70, TJ: Tamara Myers 13.67.

Steven GARDINER b. 12 Sep 1995 Moore's
Island 1.88m 75kg.
At 400m: OG: '16- sf/3R; WCh: '15- sf, '17- 2; WJ:
'14- 6R (sf 200m); BAH champion 2015-17.
Bahamas records: 200m 2018, 400m (4) 2015-18.
Progress at 200m, 400m: 2013- 47.78, 2014- 20.66,
2015- 20.69/20.51w, 44.27; 2016- 20.63/20.53w,
44.46; 2017- 43.89; 2018- 19.75, 43.87. pb 300m
32.0+ '17, 32.26i '19, St 31.28 '17.

Donald THOMAS b. 1 Jul 1984 Freeport 1.90m
75kg. Lindenwood University, USA.
At HJ: OG: '08/12- dnq 21=/30=, '16- 7= WCh:
'07-09-11-13-15-17: 1/dnq 15/11/6/6/dnq 22=;
CG: '06-10-14-18: 4/1/9=/4; PAm: '07-11-15;
2/1/3; CAG: '06- 4=, '10- 1, '18- 1; CCp: '10- 2,
'18- 1; WI: '18- 6=. Won WAF & NCAA indoors
2007, BAH 2007, 2010-11.
Progress at HJ: 2006- 2.24, 2007- 2.35, 2008-
2.28i/2.26, 2009- 2.30, 2010- 2.32, 2011- 2.32,
2012- 2.27, 2013- 2.32, 2014- 2.33i/2.25, 2015- 2.34,
2016- 2.37, 2017- 2.31i/2.29, 2018- 2.32.
A basketball player, he made a sensational start
by clearing 2.22 indoors in January 2006 with
no high jump training since he had jumped at
school five years earlier. 19 months later he was
world champion.

Women

Shaunae MILLER-UIBO b. 15 Apr 1994 Nassau
1.85m 69kg. University of Georgia, USA.
At (200m)/400m: OG: '12- ht, '16- 1; WCh: '13-
(4), '15- 2, '17- 3/4; CG: '14- 6, '18- (1); WJ: '10- 1,
'12- 4; WY: '11- 1; CCp: '18- (1)/1R/1mxR; WI:
'14- 3. Won DL 200m 2017-18, 400m 2017, BAH
200m 2017, 400m 2010-11, 2014-16;; HJ 2018
NCAA indoor 400m 2013.
Records: Tied world indoor 300m 2018, world
best 150m straight 2018, BAH 200m (4) 2015-17,
400m 2018. CAC junior 200m 2013, 400m 2013.
Progress at 200m, 400m: 2009- 55.52, 2010- 24.09,
52.45; 2011- 23.70, 51.84; 2012- 22.70, 51.25; 2013-
22.45/22.41w, 50.70; 2014- 22.87, 51.63i/51.86;
2015- 22.14, 49.67; 2016- 22.05, 49.44; 2017- 21.88,
49.46; 2018- 22.06, 48.97. Pbs: 60m 7.59i '13, 100m
11.19 '16, 150m 16.23 St '18, 300m 35.45i '18, HJ

1.70 '18, LJ 6.29 '17, SP 11.48 '18.
Married Estonian decathlete Maicel Uibo (qv) on 4 Feb 2017. Great-uncle Leslie Miller set BAH 400m record of 46.99 at 1968 Olympics.

BAHRAIN

Governing body: Bahrain Athletics Association. Founded 1974.

Abraham Naibei **CHEROBEN** b. 11 Oct 1992 1.76m 60kg.
At 10000m: OG: '16- 10; WCh: 17- 12; AsiG: '18- 2; won Is.Sol 2017. At HMar: WCh: '18- 2.
BRN records 10000m 2017, half mar (61:00) 2016.
Progress at 10000m, HMar: 2012- 63:53, 2013- 60:38, 2014- 58:48, 2015- 59:10, 2016- 27:31.86, 60:35; 2017- 27:11.08, 58:40; 2018- 60:22. Road pbs: 15k 41:55 '14, 20k 55:50 '14, 25k 1:11:47 '14.
Transferred from Kenya to Bahrain on 19 Aug 2015, with eligibility to compete for them from 1 Aug 2016.

El Hassan EL ABBASSI b. 13 Apr 1984 Morocco 1.71m 54kg.
At 10000m: OG: '16- 26, WCh: '15- 12; AsiG: '14- 1; AsiC: '15- 1; Arab, Gulf & WMilG champion 2015. HMar: WCh: '18- 21. Mar: AsiG: '18- 2. Won MAR 10000m 2012.
Asian marathon record 2018.
Progress at 10000m, HMar, Mar: 2011- 61:13, 2012- 28:12.40, 61:15; 2013- 61:09, 2014- 27:32.96, 2015- 27:25.02, 2016- 27:47.29, 62:16; 2017- 27:47.29, 61:31, 2:10:57; 2018- 59:27, 2:04:43. pbs: 1500m 3:49.2 '09, 3000m 8:15.05 '09, 5000m 13:19.36 '16.
Ex-Moroccan to Bahrain 12 Aug 2013,, eligible to compete for them from July 2014. 2nd Valencia marathon 2018.

Sadik MIKHOU b. 25 Jul 1990 Morocco 1.74 m 61kg.
At 1500m: WCh: '17- 6; won Is.Sol 2017, W.Asian 2018.
Progress at 1500m: 2013- 3:33.31, 2014- 3:33.47, 2015- 3:33.45, 2016- 3:32.30, 2017- 3:31.34, 2018- 3:34.55. pbs: 800m 1:46.55 '14, 1000m 2:16.09 '18, 1M 3:57.10 '18, 3000m 7:39.02 '16, 10k Rd 28:05 '17. Switched from Morocco to Bahrain in September 2015 with international eligibility from 17 Sep 2016.

Albert Kibichii **ROP** b. 17 Jul 1992 Kapsabet, Kenya 1.76m 55kg.
At 5000m: OG: '16- 7; WCh: '15- 11, '17- h; AsiG: '14- 3, '18- 2; AsiC: '15- 2; CCp: '14- 4; Arab champion 2013, WMilG & Gulf 2015, W.Asian 2018. World CC: '15- 11. At HMar: WCh: '18- 13. Asian CC champion 2016, Arab 2019.
Records: 1 Asian, 2 Bahrain 5000m and Bahrain 3000m 2013; Asian indoor 3000m (2) 2014 (if eligible), 5000m 2017.
Progress at 5000m: 2010- 14:15.81A, 2011- 13:03.70, 2012- 13:01.91, 2013- 12:51.96, 2014- 13:06.12, 2015- 13:06.74, 2016- 13:04.87, 2017- 13:04.82, 2018- 13:11.84. Pbs: 1500m 3:45.7A '13,

2000m 5:01.4+ '16, 3000m 7:32.02 '16, 2M 8:25.44 '18, HMar 61:21 '18.
Bahrain citizen from 2 Apr 2013, international eligibility 1 Apr 2014.

Birhanu YEMATAW Belaw b. 27 Feb 1996 Ethiopia 1.67m 54kg.
At 5000m: OG: '16- 9; WCh: '17- 12; AsiG: '18- 1; At 3000m: CCp: '18- fa; WI: '18- 10. World CC: '19- 19. Asian indoor 2000m record 2019.
Progress at 5000m: 2015- 13:39.65, 2016- 13:09.26, 2017- 13:09.93, 2018- 13:01.09. Pbs: 2000m 5:00.34i '19, 3000m 7:34.26 '18, 2M 8:21.54 '18, 10000m 31:16.51 '17, Road: 10k 29:01 '18, 15k 43:19 '16, HMar 61:45 '17.
Switched from Ethiopia as from 8 Oct 2014.

Women

Oluwakemi ADEKOYA b. 16 Jan 1993 Nigeria 1.68m 57kg. Accountancy graduate of University of Lagos.
At 400mh: WCh: '15- h (dq); AsiG: '14- 1 (1 400m), '18- 1; AsiC: '15- 1; CCp: '14- 3., won Is. Sol 2017. At 400m: OG: '16- sf; WI: '16- 1; Won Arab 400m & W.MilG 400mh 2015, Asi Ind 400m 2016.
Records: Asian indoor 400m (4) to 51.45 in 2016. Bahrain 400m (4) 2015-16, 400mh (3) 2014-15.
Progress at 400m, 400mh: 2012- 57.16H, 2013- 52.57, 55.30; 2014- 51.11, 54.59; 2015- 50.86, 54.12; 2016- 50.72, 54.87; 2017- 51.46, 54.57; 2018- 54.48. pbs: 100m 11.55 '14, 400m 50.86 '15.
Switched nationality from Nigeria to Bahrain from 11 Sep 2013, with international eligibility from 10 Sep 2014. Provisionally suspedned from a positive drugs test on 26 Nov 2018.

Mimi BELETE b. 9 Jun 1988 Addis Ababa, Ethiopia 1.69m 55kg.
At 1500m/(5000m): OG: '12- sf, '16- (h); WCh: '09-11-13-15: sf/7/sf/(11); AsiG: '10- 3/1, '14- 2/2; AsiC: '09- 6, '13- 2; CCp: '10- 4, '14- 6 (5 3000m); Asi CC: '09-14-16: 2/3/3. won W.Asian 2010, Arab 5000m 2015. Asian 2M record 2014.
Progress at 1500m, 5000m: 2007- 4:13.55, 2008- 4:06.84, 15:44.20; 2009- 4:04.36, 2010- 4:00.25, 15:15.59; 2011- 4:03.13, 2012- 4:01.72, 2013- 4:03.63, 2014- 4:00.08, 15:00.87; 2015- 4:05.37, 14:54.71; 2016- 4:12.84, 15:29.72; 2017- 15:26.49. pbs: 800m 2:04.63 '10, 2000m 5:38.0+ '14, 3000m 8:30.00 '14, 2M 9:13.85 '14, 10000m 32:46.74 '16.10MRd 53:33 '17, HMar 69:15 '17, Mar 2:22:29 '18.
From Ethiopia, has lived in Belgium from 2005; BRN from 2009. Made marathon debut with 3rd in Hamburg, then 1st in Toronto 2018. Younger sister Almensch Belete BEL pbs 1500m 4:06.87 '10, 5000m 15:03.63 '11; 5 EI 3000m 2013.

Rose CHELIMO b. 12 Jul 1989 Kenya 1.62m 45kg.
At Mar: OG: '16- 8; WCh: 17- 1; AsiG: 18- 1. World CC: '17- 9. At HMar: WCh: '18- 14.
Progress at HMar, Mar: 2010- 72:48, 2011- 69:45, 2012- 70:50, 2014- 68:40, 2015- 68:22 , 2016- 68:08,

2:24:14; 2017- 68:37, 2:22:51. Pbs: 10000m 31:37.81 '17, Road: 15k 49:08 '17, 20k 64:47 '15. Transferred from Kenya to Bahrain on 19 Aug 2015, eligible to compete for them from 1 Aug 2016. Won in Seoul on marathon debut in 2016, 2nd Boston 2017.

Violah JEPCHUMBA b. 23 Oct 1990 1.72m 52kg. Progress at HMar: 2014- 73:20, 2015- 69:30, 2016- 65:51, 2017- 65:22. pbs: Road: 10k 30:05 '17, 15k 45:40 '17, 20k 61:50 '17. BRN citizen 1 Jul 2016, international eligibilty 2 July 2017.

Salwa Eid NASER (Ebelechukwu Agbapuonwu) b. 23 May 1998 Anambra, Nigeria 1.67m 50kg. At 400m: '16- sf; WCh: '17- 2; WY: '05- 1; Yth OG: '14- 2; AsiG: '18- 1 (1 4x400, 2 4x400); CCp: '18- 1. Won Arab Jnr 200m & 400m 2014, Asi-Y & W.MilG 2015, Gulf & Isl Sol 2017, W.Asian 2018, DL 2018. 400m records: 2 Asian 2018, 7 Bahrain 2017-18. Progress at 400m: 2014- 52.74, 2015- 51.39, 2016- 50.88, 2017- 49.88, 2018- 49.08. pbs: 100m 11.70 '15, 200m 23.03 '15. Nigerian mother, Bahraini father – moved to Bahrain as a child,

Winfred Mutile **YAVI** b. 31 Dec 1999 Kenya 1.57m 48kg. At 3000mSt: WCh: '17- 8; WJ: 18- 3; AsiG: '18- 1; CCp: '18- 3. Progress at 3000mSt: 2015- 10:21.4A, 2016- 10:07.2A, 2017- 9:22.67, 2018- 9:10.74. pbs: 1500m 4:20.7A '17, 3000m 9:10.5A '16, 2000mSt 6:35.84A '15. Switched from Kenya to acquire BRN citizenship on 19 Aug 2015, and able to compete for them from 19 Aug 2016.

BARBADOS

Governing body: Athletics Association of Barbados. Founded 1947.
National Champions 2018: Men: 100m: Mario Burke 10.27, 200: Burkheart Ellis 20.67, 400m: Jonathan Jones 46.64, 800m: Anthonio Mascoll 1:48.38, 1500m/5000m: Joshua Hunte 4:07.84/16:36.84, 110mh: Shane Brathwaite 13.62, 400mh: Fabian Norgrove 50.12, HJ: Antonio Farrell 1.95. LJ: Charles Greaves 7.60, TJ: Jonathan Miller 15.21, SP: Tristan Whitehall 16.19/52.98, JT: Zion Hill 65.31. **Women**: 100m: Shemia Odaine 11.81, 200m/400m: Lisa Anne Barrow 23/DT.34/53.30, 800m: Sonia Gaskin 2:07.85, 100m: Ayanna Morgan 13.77, 400m: Shonita Brome 63.78, HJ: Jalisia Neil 1.65, LJ: Akela Jones 6.05, TJ: Aria Small 12.86, SP: Joy Squires 10.58, DT: Akelia Flemming 39.51, JT: Arianna Hayde 35.29.

BELARUS

Governing body: Belarus Athletic Federation. Founded 1991.

National Champions 2018: Men: 100m.200m: Stanislav Dorogokupets 10.47/20.96, 400m: Alekse Lazarev 47.67, 800m: Yevgeniy Yanukovich 1:50.59, 1500m/5000m: Sergey Platonov 3:43.87/14:16.07, 5000m: Artyom Logish 3:49.88/14:15.85, 10000m: Stepan Rogotsov 30:18.8, 3000mSt: Dmitriy Ivanenko 8:50.05, 110mh: Vitaliy Parakhonko 13.40, 400mh: Sergey Sergey 51.62, HJ: Dmitriy Nabokov 2.20, PV: Vladislav Chemarmazovich 5.30, LJ: Yuriy Yeremich 7.55, TJ: Andrey Churylo 16.14, SP: Aleksey Nichipor 20.37, DT: Viktor Trus 60.29, HT: Oleg Dubitskiy 74,74, JT: Aleksey Kotkovets 75.78, Dec: Eduard Mikhan 7091. **Women**: 100m/200m: Kristina Timanovskaya 11.09/23.54, 400m: Marina Mikhan 54.10, 800m/1500m: Darya Borisevich 2:05.59/4:23.01, 5000m: Yekaterina Korneyenko 15:52.46, 10000m: Anastasiya Ivanova 33:10.19, 3000mSt: Tatyana Shabanova 10:11.74, 100mh: Elvira German 12.86, 400mh: Yekaterina Belanovich 57.84, HJ: Karina Taranda 1.87, PV: Tatyana Shakhlenkova 3.60, LJ: Anastasiya Mirochik-Ivanova 6.77, TJ: Irina Vaskovskaya 13.73, SP: Alyona Dubitskaya 18.93, DT: Alena Abramchuk 53.44, HT: Hanna Malyshik 74.35, JT: Tatyana Kolodovich 64.77, Hep: Yekaterina Netsvetayeva 5304.

Pavel BOREYSHA b. 16 Feb 1991 Grodno 1.93m 120kg. Grodno State University. At HT: OG: '16- dnq 13; WCh: '15- dnq 25, '17- 9; EC: '14-16-18: 10/dnq 14/4; WJ: '10- 6; EU23: '11- dnq 17; WUG: '15- 2, '17- 2; ET: '17- 2. Won BLR 2014. Progress at HT: 2011- 69.62, 2012- 72.25, 2013- 75.62, 2014- 76.86, 2015- 77.03, 2016- 78.60, 2017- 78.04, 2018- 77.37.

Maksim NEDOSEKOV b. 21 Jan 1998 1.88m 70kg. At HJ: EC: '18- 2; WJ: '16- 8; EJ: '17- 1; CCp: '18- 3; WI: '18- 6. Won BLR 2017. Progress at HJ: 2015- 2.10, 2016- 2.20, 2017- 2.33, 2018- 2.33.

Women

Marina ARZAMASOVA b. 17 Dec 1987 Minsk 1.73m 57kg. née Kotovich. Minsk. At 800m: OG: '12- h, '16- 7; WCh: '11/13- sf, '15- 1, '17- h; EC: '12- 2, '14- 1; WJ: '06- h; CCp: '14- 3; ET: '11-3, '13- 3; WI: '14- 3; EI: '13- 3. Won W.MilG 2011, BLR 800m 2008, 2013, 2015; 1500m 2013. Progress at 800m: 2004- 2:09.37, 2005- 2:07.24, 2006- 2:06.39, 2007- 2:04.33, 2008- 2:02.67, 2009- 2:05.53i, 2011- 1:59.30, 2012- 1:59.63, 2013- 1:59.60, 2014- 1:58.15, 2015- 1:57.54, 2016- 1:58.36, 2017- 2:01.92. pbs: 400m 52.81 '12, 600m 1:27.05 '17, 1000m 2:37.93 '11, 1500m 4:15.99 '12. Married to Ilya, with daughters Sashenka born 2010 and Anastasiya in August in 2018. Parents were Aleksandr Kotovich UKR (HJ 2.35i '85, 2.33 '84; 2 EI 85) and Ravilya Agletdinova BLR

(800m 1:56.1 '82, 1500m 3:58.40 '85, 1 EC 86, 4 WCh 83).

Alyona DUBITSKAYA b. 25 Jan 1990 Grodno 1.82m 77k. née Hryshko. Grodnenskaya.
At SP: OG: '16- 8; WCh: '13- dnq 27, '15- 6, '17- dnq 14; EC: '14-16-18: 7/6/3; WJ: '08- 4; WY: '07- 1; EJ: '09- 1; WI: '16- 9, '18- 6; EI: '17- 7, '19- 4; ET: '15- 3, '17- 1. BLR champion 2009, 2014-15, 2018.
Progress at SP: 2007- 15.91, 2008- 16.55, 2009- 17.95, 2010- 18.12i/17.75, 2012- 16.63, 2013- 17.88, 2014- 19.03, 2015- 18.88, 2016- 18.78, 2017- 19.01, 2018- 19.21, 2019- 18.94i. pb DT 46.30 '14.
6-month drugs ban 2014-15.

Elvira GERMAN b. 9 Jan 1997 Pinsk 1.68m 54kg.
At 100mh: WCh: '17: sf; EC: '16- sf, '18- 1; WJ: '16- 1; EU23: '17- 2; EJ: '15- 1; CCp: '18- 4; WUG: '17- 2; Yth OG: '14- 2; won BLR 2017. At 60mh: EI: '19- 3.
European junior 100m hurdles record 2016.
Progress at 100mh: 2014- 13.50, 2015- 13.20/13.15w, 2016- 12.85, 2017- 12.96/12.95w, 2018- 12.64. pbs: 60m 7.57i '18, 200m 24.07 '81, 300m 38.99i '18, 50mh 7.18i '14, 60mh 7.97i '19.

Tatyana KHOLODOVICH b. 21 Jun 1991 Brest 1.81m 83kg.
At JT: OG: '16- 5; WCh: '15- dnq 21, '17- 6; EC: '14-16-18: 5/1/5; WJ: '08/10- dnq 16/21; EU23: '13- dnq; WUG: '15- 1; ET: '15- 2, '17- 2. BLR champion 2012-16, 2018, DL 2018.
Three Belarus javelin records 2014-16.
Progress at JT: 2007- 46.12, 2008- 53.51, 2009- 46.80, 2010- 51.17, 2011- 55.94, 2012- 59.15, 2013- 59.37, 2014- 63.61, 2015- 62.00, 2016- 66.34, 2017- 66.30, 2018- 67.47, 2019- 65.99.

Hanna MALYSHIK b. 4 Feb 1994 Drachichyn 1.75m 90kg. née Zinchuk.
At HT: OG: '16- 7; WCh: '17- 10; EC: '16- dnq 26, '18- nt; WJ: '12- dnq; WY: '11- dnq 15, EJ: '13- 1; WUG: '17- 2; ET: '17- 1. Won EY Oly 2011, BLR 2016, 2018.
Progress at HT: 2009- 50.70, 2010- 57.38, 2011- 60.11, 2012- 63.41, 2013- 66.36, 2014- 67.53, 2015- 66.50, 2016- 72.78, 2017- 74.94, 2018- 76.26, 2019- 74.95.

Olga MAZURONAK b. 14 Apr 1989 Karaganda, Kazakhstan 1.76m 56kg. née Malevich. Minsk.
At Mar: OG: '16- 5; EC: '18- 1. At 5000m: ET: '15- 2. At 10000m: EC: '14- 7; ECp: '17- 2. At 10000mW: WJ: '06- 5; EJ: '07- dq. At 5000mW: WY: '05- 4. Won BLR 5000m 2013, 10000m 2013-14.
Belarus half marathon record 2018.
Progress at Mar: 2012- 2:33:56, 2013- 2:33:33, 2014- 2:27:33, 2015- 2:25:36, 2016- 2:23:54, 2017- 2:27:14, 2018- 2:25:25. pbs: 3000m 9:11.68i '18, 5000m 15:33.06 '17, 10000m 32:13.73 '17, HMar 70:57 '18, 5000mW 22:36.55 '05, 10kW 44:30 '06.
Marathon wins: Debno & Siberia 2012, Sacramento 2014, Düsseldorf & EC 2018, Hong Kong 2019.

Anastasiya MIRONCHIK-IVANOVA b. 13 Apr 1989 Slutsk 1.71m 54kg. Minsk.
At LJ: OG: '12- dq7; WCh: '09- 10, '11- 3, '15- 9; EC: '10- 6, '18- 5; WJ: '08- 2; WY: '05- 8; EU23: '09- 2, '11- 6; WI: '12- 5; EI: '11- 6, '19- 2. BLR champion 2007, 2010-12, 2015.
Progress at LJ: 2004- 5.90, 2005- 6.10/6.13w, 2007- 6.03i/5.89, 2008- 6.71, 2009- 6.65/6.76w, 2010- 6.84, 2011- 6.85/6.92w, 2012- 7.08/7.22w, 2013- 6.60, 2015- 6.82, 2016- 6.84i, 2018- 6.77, 2019- 6.93i. pb TJ 14.29 '11.
Son born June 2014. Re-test of sample from 2012 Olympics proved positive.

Alina TALAY b. 14 May 1989 Orsha, Vitebsk 1.64m 54kg.
At 100mh: OG: '12/16- sf; WCh: '13-15-17: sf/3/6; EC: '10-12-14-16-18: sf/1/5/2/dq (fell); WJ: '08- 4; EU23: '09- 3, '11- 1; WUG: '13- 2; ET: '11-15-17: 2/1/2; won W.MilG 2011, BLR 2009-10, 2013-17 (200m 2015). At 60mh: WI: '12- 3, '16- 6; EI: '11- 13-15-17: 5/1/1/2.
Four BLR 100m hurdles records 2015-18.
Progress at 100mh: 2007- 14.38/14.01w, 2008- 13.31, 2009- 13.07, 2010- 12.87, 2011- 12.91, 2012- 12.71, 2013- 12.78, 2014- 12.89, 2015- 12.66, 2016- 12.60, 2017- 12.72, 2018- 12.41. pbs: 60m 7.31i '15, 100m 11.48 '11, 200m 23.59 '11, 50mh 6.89i '11, 60mh 7.85i '15.

BELGIUM

Governing bodies: Ligue Royale Belge d'Athlétisme (KBAB/LRBA). Vlaamse Atletiekliga (VAL); Ligue Belge Francophone d'Athlétisme (LBFA). Original Governing body founded 1889.
National Championships first held in 1889 (women 1921). **2018: Men**: 100m: Andreas Vranken 10.49, 200m: Jonathan Borlée 20.78, 400m: Kevin Borlée 45.52, 800m: Aaron Botterman 1:46.89, 1500m: Pieter Claus 3:53.94, 5000m: Jensen Mortier 14:20.11, 10000m: Nick Van Peborgh 29:46.87, Mar: Kristof Nackaerts 2:24:53, 3000mSt: Clement Deflandre 8:57.87. 110mh: Denis Hanjoul 14.11w (Dylan Caty FRA 14.11w), 400mh: Romain Nicodeme 51.49, HJ: Bram Ghuys 2.24, PV: Arnaud Art 5.40, LJ: Corentin Campener 7.66, TJ: Leopold Kapata 15.73, SP/DT: Philip Milanov 17.29/63.39, HT: Remi Malengreaux 61.86, JT: Timothy Herman 75.62, Dec: Robin Bodart 6596, 20000mW: Peter Van Hove 2:02:19.2. **Women**: 100m: Manon Depuydt 11.72, 200m: Cynthia Bolingo Mbongo 23.68; 400m: Marline De Jans 54.92, 800m: Lotte Hellinckx 2:11.22, 1500m: Sofie Van Accom 4:18.12, 5000m: Nina Lauwaert 16:14.25, 10000m: Hanne Verbruggen 35:11.55, Mar: Nina Lauwaert 2:30:24, 3000mSt: Elke Godden 10:58.59, 100mh: Eline Berings 12.98, 400mh: Hanne Claes 55.20, HJ: Claire Orcel 1.91, PV: Aurélie De Ryck 4.20, LJ: Nafissatou Thiam 6.60, TJ: Sietske Lenchant 12.63, SP: Yoika De

Pauw 13.47, DT: Katelijne Lyssens 50.71, HT: Vanessa Sterckendries 65.69, JT: Pauline Smal 46.89, Hep: Yoika De Pauw 5218, 10000mW/20kW: Annelies Sarrazin 56:16.29/1:57:45.

Jonathan BORLÉE b. 22 Feb 1988 Woluwe-Saint Lambert 1.80m 70kg. Racing Club of Brussels. Was at Florida State University.
At 400m: OG: '08- sf/5R, '12- 6, '16- h (h 200m); WCh: '11-13-15-17: 5/4/sf/sf; EC: '10- 7/3R, '12-1R, '14- dns, '16- h/1R, '18- 3/1R; WJ: '06- 4; WY: '05- 5; EJ: '07- h; WI: '10- 2R, '18- 3R; EI: '11- 3R, '15/19- 1R. Won NCAA 2009. At 200m: EC: '12- 4. Won BEL 200m 2012-13, 2018; 400m 2006, 2011, 2015.
Four Belgian 400m records 2009-12, 300m 2012.
Progress at 400m: 2005- 47.50, 2006- 46.06, 2007-47.85, 2008- 45.11, 2009- 44.78, 2010- 44.71, 2011-44.78, 2012- 44.43, 2013- 44.54, 2014- 45.37, 2015-44.67, 2016- 45.34, 2017- 45.09, 2018- 44.87. pbs: 60m 6.81i '07, 100m 10.78 '07, 200m 20.31 '12, 300m 31.87 '12, 500m 1:00.76i '15, 600m 1:18.60i '11.
Twin brother of Kevin Borlée, their sister **Olivia** (b. 10 Apr 1986) has pbs 100m 11.39 '07, 200m 22.98 '06, 3 WCh '07, 2 OG '08 at 4x100mR. Younger brother **Dylan** (b. 20 Sep 1992) pb 45.57 '15 and 2 EI '15 (the three brothers ran on BEL 4x400m team 5th WCh 2013, 1st EI 2015 & EC 2016, 4th OG 2016, 3rd WI & 1st EC 2018). Their father Jacques was an international 400m runner (45.4 '79), mother Edith Demartelaere had pbs 200m 23.89 and 400m 54.09 in 1984.

Kévin BORLÉE b. 22 Feb 1988 Woluwe-Saint Lambert 1.80m 71kg. Racing Club of Brussels. Was at Florida State University.
At 400m: OG: '08- sf/5R, '12- 5, '16- h; WCh: '09-sf/4R, '11- 3, '13/15/17- sf; EC: '10- 1/3R, '12- 1R, '14- sf, '16- 4/1R, '18- 2/1R; WJ: '06- sf; WI: '10-2R, '18- 3R; EI: '11-15-17-19: 3R/1R/2R/1R; CCp: '10- 4/2R, '18- 7/dq mxR. At 200m: WY: '05- sf. Won DL 2012, BEL 200m 2009, 2011; 400m 2007, 2013, 2017-18. BEL 400m records 2008 and 2012.
Progress at 400m: 2005- 47.86, 2006- 46.63, 2007-46.38, 2008- 44.88, 2009- 45.28, 2010- 45.01, 2011-44.74, 2012- 44.56, 2013- 44.73, 2014- 45.28, 2015-44.74, 2016- 45.17, 2017- 44.79, 2018- 45.07. pbs: 60m 6.85i '13, 100m 10.62 '07, 200m 20.72 '11, 300m 32.22 '17, 600m 1:15.65i '11.
Has run many brilliant relay legs for Belgium inc 43.6 at 2014 EC and 43.60 at 2017 WCh.

Philip MILANOV b. 6 Jul 1991 Bruges 1.91m 118kg. Vilvoorde AC, Lille Metropole, FRA.
At DT: OG: '16- 9; WCh: '15- 2, '17- dnq 14; EC: '14- dnq 20, '16- 2; EU23: '13- 5; WUG: '15- 1. Won BEL DT 2011-18, SP 2016-18.
Six Belgian discus records 2014-16.
Progress at DT: 2011- 56.00, 2012- 57.66, 2013-61.81, 2014- 66.02, 2015- 66.90, 2016- 67.26, 2017-67.05, 2018- 66.51. pb SP 18.63 '18.
His father Emil Milanov had DT pb 58.28 '82, moved from Bulgaria to Belgium in 1989.

Thomas VAN DER PLAETSEN b. 24 Dec 1990 Gent 1.85m 86kg. AC Deinze.
At Dec: OG: '16- 8; WCh: '11-13-15-17: 13/15/14/dnf; EC: '14-16-18: 10/1/dnf; EU23: '11- 1; EJ: '09-1; WUG: '13- 1, '15- 1; Won BEL PV 2011, 2013; Dec 2010. At Hep: WI: '14- 3; EI: '11- 6, '19- 6. Belgian decathlon record 2011.
Progress at Dec: 2010- 7564, 2011- 8157, 2013-8255, 2014- 8184, 2015- 8035, 2016- 8332, 2018-8007. pbs: 60m 7.13i '14, 100m 11.04 '14, 200m 22.34 '10, 400m 48.64 '11, 1000m 2:40.50i '14, 1500m 4:32.52 '11, 60mh 8.06i '14, 110mh 14.39 '16, HJ 2.17 '11, PV 5.50i '19, 5.41 '16; LJ 7.80 '13, SP 14.32i/14.12 '14, DT 44.48 '14, JT 65.31 '13, Hep 6259i '14.

Women

Nafissatou THIAM b. 19 Aug 1994 Namur 1.84m 69kg. RFCL. Student of geographical science at University of Liège.
At Hep: OG: '16- 1; WCh: '13-15-17: 14/11/1; EC: '14- 3, '18- 1; WJ: '12- 14; WY: '11- 4. At Pen: EI: '13-15-17: 6/2/1. At HJ: EC: '16- 4; EU23: '15- 2; WI: '14- 8=. Won BEL Hep 2012, LJ 2015, 2018.
Belgian records: heptathlon (4) 2013-17, javelin 2017. World junior heptathlon best 2013.
Progress at HJ, Hep: 2010- 1.74, 2011- 1.81, 2012-1.88, 5916; 2013- 1.92, 6298, 2014- 1.97, 6508; 2015-1.92, 6412; 2016- 1.98, 6810; 2017- 1.98, 7013; 2018-2.01, 6816. pbs: 60m 7.81i '13, 200m 24.40 '17, 800m 2:15.24 '17, 60mh 8.23i '17, 100mh 13.34 '17, LJ 6.62 '18, TJ 12.82 '14, SP 15.52i/15.35 '18, JT 59.32 '17, Pen 4870i '17.
Tied high jump world best in a heptathlon with 1.97 at EC 2014 and improved that to 1.98 at the Olympic Games, when she set five events pbs en route to the gold medal and adding 319 points to her pb. IAAF female Rising Star award 2016, Female Athlete of the Year 2017. Won at Götzis 2017 and in 2018, when she set a world heptathlon high jump best of 2.01.

BOSNIA & HERZEGOVINA

Governing body: Atletski savez Bosne i Hercegovine (AsBIH). Founded 1948.

Mesud PEZER b. 27 Aug 1994 Zenica 1.98m 120kg. AK Zenica
At SP: OG: '16- dnq 24; WCh: '17: dnq 21; EC: '16- 11, '18- 12; WJ: '12- 5; WY: '11- 6; EU23: '15- 4; WJ: '13- 1; WY: '17- 5; EI: '17- 7, '19- 6; Won Balkan 2017. BIH record 2017.
Progress at SP: 2012- 15.17, 2013- 18.86, 2014-19.37, 2015- 19.99, 2016- 20.58, 2017- 21.40, 2018-21.15i/20.79. Pb DT 57.08 '16.

BOTSWANA

Governing body: Botswana Athletics Association.

Nijel AMOS b. 15 Mar 1994 Marobela 1.79m 60kg.

At 800m: OG: '12- 2, '16- h; WCh: '15- sf, '17- 5; CG: '14- 1, '18- 8; WJ: '12- 1, WY: '11- 5; AfG: '15-1/2R; AfCh: '14- 1/1R, '16- 1, '18- 1; CCp: '14- 1, '18- 3; WUG: '13- 1. Won DL 2014-15, 2017.
World junior 800m and two Botswana 800m records 2012.
Progress at 800m: 2011- 1:47.28, 2012- 1:41.73, 2013- 1:44.71, 2014- 1:42.45, 2015- 1:42.66, 2016-1:44.66, 2017- 1:43.18, 2018- 1:42.14. pbs: 200m 21.34 '15, 400m 45.55 '17, 600m 1:15.0+ 12.

Isaac MAKWALA b. 24 Sep 1985 Tutume 1.83m 79kg.
At (200m)/400m: OG: '12- h, '16- sf; WCh: '09- h, '13- (h), '15- 5, '17- 6/dns; CG: '10- sf, '14- sf, '18-1/1R; AfG: '07- sf/1R, '11- 7, '15- 1/2R; AfCh: '08-10-12-14-16: 2/sf/1/1 & (2),1R/4; CCp: '14-6/2/1R. Won DL 2017.
Records: Commonwealth 400m 2015, African 400m (2) 2014-15, Botswana 100m (2) 2013-14, 200m 2013-14, 300m 2017, 400m (4) 2014-15.
Progress at 200m, 400m: 2007- 46.48, 2008-21.20, 45.64A; 2009- 20.73, 45.56; 2010- 21.33, 46.07; 2011- 21.17, 46.27; 2012- 20.87, 45.25; 2013-20.21, 45.86; 2014- 19.96/19.7A, 44.01; 2015-20.44A/20.77, 43.72; 2016- 20.42A, 44.85; 2017-19.77, 43.81; 2018 19.96, 44.23. Pbs: 100m 10.20A/10.14wA '14; 300m 31.44 '17.
Ran 43.92 & 19.77 double within two hours at Madrid 2017. Not permitted to run the 400m final at 2017 Worlds due to quarantine restriction, but allowed to compete at 200m with a solo heat after missing the first round.

Karabo SIBANDA b. 2 Jul 1998 Shashe-Mooke 1.92m 79kg.
At 400m: OG: '16- 5; WCh: '17- h; CG:'18- sf; WJ: '14- sf, 16- 3/2R; WY: '15- 5; AfCh: '16- 2/1R; Af-J: '15- 1/1R; Yth OG: '14- 2; Comm-Y: '15- 1 (1 4x100m).
Progress at 400m: 2014- 46.76, 2015- 45.83, 2016-44.25, 2017- 45.05, 2018- 45.58A. Pb 200m 21.28A '16.

Baboloki THEBE b. 18 Mar 1997 Ramonake 1.86m 77kg.
At (200m)/400m: OG: '16- sf; WCh: '17- 4; CG'18 2/1R, WJ: '11 (sf), '16 dq sf/2R, AfCh: '16- 1/1R, '18- 1; Yth OG: '14- (2); CCp: '18-7/2/2mxR. Won BOT 200m & 400m 2016.
African junior 400m record 2016.
Progress at 200m, 400m: 2014- 20.85A, 2015-20.56A, 2016- 20.21A, 44.22A/44.69; 2017- 44.02, 2018- 44.54. Pb: 100m 10.29A '15.

Women

Amantle MONTSHO b. 4 Jul 1983 Mabudutsa 1.73m 64kg.
At 400m: OG: '04- h, '08- 6, '12- 4; WCh: '05-07-09-11-13-17: h/sf/7/1/2/sf; CG: '06-10-14-18: sf/1/4dq/1&3R; AfG: '03-07-11: h/1/1; AfCh: '04-06-08-10-12: h/2/1/1/1; WI: '10- 4; CCp: '10-1/3R. Won DL 2011-13.
Botswana records 100m 2011, 200m 2001-12,

400m 2003-13; African 300m 2010.
Progress at 400m: 2003- 55.03, 2004- 53.77, 2005-52.59, 2006-52.14, 2007-50.90, 2008-49.83A/50.54, 2009- 49.89, 2010- 49.89, 2011- 49.56, 2012- 49.54, 2013- 49.33, 2014- 50.37, 2017- 51.28, 2018- 50.15.
pbs: 100m 11.60 '11, 200m 22.89 '12, 22.88w '11, 300m 36.33i '10.
First Botswana woman to win a major title. Positive test at 2014 Commonwealth Games, for which she received a two-year ban.

BRAZIL

Governing body: Confederação Brasileira de Atletismo (CBAt). Founded 1914 (Confederação 1977).
National Championships first held in 1925.
2018: Men: 100m: Paulo André de Oliveira 10.03, 200m: Aldemir Gomes da Silva 20.38, 400m: Lucas Carvalho 45.55, 800m: Matheus Pessoa 1:47.47, 1500m/5000m300mSt: Altobelli da Silva 3:44.30/14:19.90/8:39.68, 10000m: Éderson Pereira 29:09.02, 110mh: Gabriel Constantino 13.37, 400mh: Márcio Teles 48.70, HJ: Guilherme Cobbo 2.23, PV: Thiago Braz da Silva 5.55, LJ/TJ: Alexsandro de Melo 8.19/16.69, SP: Darlan Romani 22.00, DT: Douglas dos Reis 56.17, HT: Wágner Domingos 72.78, JT: Paulo Enrique da Silva 73.49, Dec: Jefferson Santos 7467, 20kW: Caio 31:25:31, 50kW: Cláudio dos Santos 4:44:20.
Women: 100m/200m: Vitória Rosa 11.18/23.06, 400m: Geisa Coutinho 52.17, 800m/1500m: July da Silva 2:05.00/4:22.62, 5000m/3000mSt: Tatiana da Silva 16:47.88/10:10.40, 10000m: Jenifer Silva 34:27.04, 100mh: Adelly Santos 13.41, 400mh: Alessandra Silva 57.55, HJ: Monique Varmeling 1.82, PV: Juliana Campos 4.35, LJ: Éliane Martins 6.68w, TJ: Mirieli Santos 13.70, SP: Geisa Arcanjo 17.74, DT: Andressa de Morais 64.75, HT: Mariana Marcelino 65.28, JT: Laila Domingo 57.90, Hep: Giovana Cavaleti 5958, 20000mW: Érica de Sena 1:45:49, 50kW: Viviane Lyra 4:41:39.

Caio Oliveira de Sena **BONFIM** b. 19 Mar 1991 Brasília 1.70m 58kg. CASO.
At 20kW: OG: '12- 38, '16- 4 (50kW 9); WCh: '11 13-15-17: 17/dq/6/3?; WCp: '12-14-16: 14/16/8; PAm: 15- 3, SACh: '13- 1; BRA champion 2012-19, IbAm 2016. At 10000mW: WJ: '08- 6, '10- 4; WY: '07- 12.
Brazil records: 20kW (2) 2016-17, 50kW 2016.
Progress at 20kW, 50kW: 2009- 1:30:17.9t, 2010-1:27:21.3t, 2011- 1:20:58.5t, 2012- 1:21:26, 2013-1:22:14, 2014- 1:20:28, 2015- 1:20:44, 4:02:20; 2016-1:19:42, 3:47:02; 2017- 1:19:04, 2018- 1:25:31, 3:55:24. Pbs: 5000mW 19:47.99 '11, 10000mW 40:00R '17, 40:40.0 '09.
National records at 20k and 50k walks at 2016 Olympics in Rio. 6-month drugs ban from 1 Mar 2018 after positive test on 28 May 2017. His mother, Gianetti de Sena Bonfim (b. 13.3.65), won the 1996 Ibero-American 10,000m walk,

and had pbs 5000m: 23:28.9 '96, 10000m: 47:42.0 '96, 20k: 1:41:07 '04.

Gabriel de Oliveira **CONSTANTINO** b. 9 Feb 1995 Rio de Janeiro 1.86m 77kg. Was at Salgado de Oliveira University.
At 110mh: WJ: '14- sf (h 200m); won S.Am U23 2016, IbAm 2018. At 60mh: WI: '18- 6. Won S. Am-Y LJ 2012.
South American records: 60m hurdles indoor and 110m hurdles 2018.
Progress at 110mh: 2014- 13.92, 2015- 13.75, 2016- 13.50, 2017- 13.52, 2018- 13.23. Pbs: 100m 10.28 '18, 200m 20.67/20.39w '18, 400m 50.42 '12, 60mh: 7.60i '18, HJ 2.01 '12, LJ 6.97 '12.

Darlan ROMANI b. 9 Apr 1991 Concórdia 1.88m 140kg.
At SP: OG: '16- 5; WCh: '15-17: dnq 15/dnq 15; WJ: '10- 7; PAm: '15- 6; SAG: '18- 1; SACh: '13-15-17: 2/2/1; CCp: '18- 1; WI: '18- 4; won IbAm 2016, 2018; BRA 2012-18.
Five South American shot records 2017-18 and 14 Brazilian records 2012-16. Two South American indoor shot records 2018.
Progress at SP: 2009- 4.60, 2010- 17.66, 2011- 18.46, 2012- 20.48, 2013- 20.08, 2014- 20.84, 2015- 20.90, 2016- 21.02, 2017- 21.82, 2018- 22.00.

Almir Cunha **dos SANTOS** b. 4 Sep 1993 Matupá 1.91m 80kg.
At TJ: WI: '18- 2. At HJ: WJ: '12; dnq 26=; won S.Am-Y 2010.
Progress at TJ: 2016- 15.89, 2017- 16.86, 2018- 17.53. Pbs: HJ 2.18 '14, LJ 7.96 '17.
Formerly a high jumper, he took up triple jumping in late 2016.

Thiago Braz da SILVA b. 16 Dec 1993 Marília 1.93m 84kg. Orcampi/Unimed.
At PV: OG: '16- 1; WCh: '13-15: dnq 14=/19; WJ: '12- 1; WI: '14- 4; PAm: '15- nh; SACh: '13- 1; Yth Oly: '10- 2, won BRA 2015-16, 2017 (=), 2018, PAm-J 2011.
Six South American pole vault records 2013-16, indoors (5) 2014-16.
Progress at PV: 2009- 4.60, 2010- 5.10, 2011- 5.31, 2012- 5.55, 2013- 5.83, 2014- 5.76i/5.73, 2015- 5.92, 2016- 6.03, 2017- 5.86i/5.60, 2018= 5.90i/5.70.
Married Ana Paula de Oliveira (HJ 1.86 '15) on 13 Dec 2014.

Women

Andressa Oliveira **de MORAIS** b. 21 Dec 1990 João Pessoa, Paraiba 1.78m 100kg. EC Pinheiros.
At DT: OG: '12/16- dnq 15/21; WCh: '11/15- dnq 17/19, '17- 11; WJ: '08- dnq 20; PAm: '15- 6; SACh: '09/11/13/15/17: 5/2/5/1/1; CCp: '18- 5. Won IbAm 2012, SAm U23 2012, SAmG 2018; BRA 2012-13, 2015, 2017-18. At HT: SAm-J: '09- 6.
Foiur South American discus records 2012-18.
Progress at DT: 2007- 42.84, 2008- 54.35, 2009- 55.52, 2010- 58.06, 2011- 59.56, 2012- 64.21, 2013- 61.04, 2014- 59.65, 2015- 64.15, 2016- 59.64, 2017- 64.68, 2018- 65.10. pbs: SP 13.87 '08, HT 58.89 '12.

Rosângela SANTOS b. 20 Dec 1990 Washington DC, USA 1.65m 55kg.
At 100m/(200m): OG: '08- 3R, '12- sf, '16- sf; WCh: '11- sf, '15- sf/sf, '17- 7/sf; WJ: '08- 4/3R; WY: '07- 2/4; PAm: '11- 1/1R, '15- 4. Won IbAm 2012, 2016, SAm U23 2008, U20 2007; BRA100m 2008, 20912, 2015-16, 200m 2012.
South American records 100m 2017, indoor 60m 2016.
Progress at 100m: 2005- 12.23, 2006- 11.82, 2007- 11.44, 2008- 11.41/11.38w, 2009- 11.90, 2010- 11.81, 2011- 11.22A/11.36, 2012- 11.17/11.07w, 2013- 11.23, 2014- 11.32, 2015- 11.04/11.01w, 2016- 11.23, 2017- 10.91, 2018- 11.23. pbs: 60m 7.17i '16, 150mSt 17.12 '13, 200m 22.77 '15.

Érica Rocha de **SENA** b. 3 May 1985 Camaragibe, Pernambuco 1.68m 55kg. Orcampi Unimed.
At 20kW: OG: '16- 7; WCh: '15- 6, '17- 4; WCp: '16- 3, '18- 4; PAm: 15- 2; BRA champion 2011-18. Won IbAm 10000mW 2016.
Walk records: S.American 10k 2017. 20k (6) 2014-17; BRA: 10000mW 2014, 20kW (5) 2012-16.
Progress at 20kW: 2006- 1:51:45.5t, 2007- 1:44:52.96t, 2008- 1:44:14.6t, 2009- 1:44:27, 2010- 1:38:59, 2011- 1:35:29.6t, 2012- 1:31:53, 2013- 1:32:59, 2014- 1:30:43, 2015- 1:29.37, 2016- 1:27:18, 2017- 1:26:59, 2018- 1:28:40. Pbs: 5000mW 23:10.59 '11, 10000mW 43:31.30 '14, 43:03 '17.
Won IAAF Walks Challenge 2017. Married to and coached by Ecuadorian Andrés Chocho (qv). Lives in Cuenca, Ecuador.

BRITISH VIRGIN ISLANDS

Kyron McMASTER b. 3 Jan 1997 Road Town 1.87m 79kg. Student at Central Arizona University.
At 400mh: WCh: '17- dq h; CG: '18- 1; CAG: '18- 1; WJ: '16- 3; CCp: '18- 8; won DL 2017-18, NACAC 2018. At 400m: WY: '13- h (h 200m).
Six IVB 400mh records 2015-18.
Progress at 400mh: 2014- 53.26, 2015- 50.16, 2016- 49.56, 2017- 47.80, 2018- 47.54. pbs: 200m 21.24 '17, 21.14w '15; HJ 1.86.

BULGARIA

Governing body: Bulgarian Athletics Federation. Founded 1924.
National Championships first held in 1926 (men), 1938 (women). **2018 Champions: Men:** 100m/200m: Denis Dimitrov 10.36/21.08, 400m: Zhivko Stoyanov 48.22, 800m: Aleks Vasilev 1:53.07, 1500m: Mitko Tsenov 3:49.20, 5000m/ 3000mSt: Ivo Balabanov 14:04.78/8:53.76, 10000m: *none*, HMar: Stoyan Vladkov 72:09, Mar: Dimcho Mitsov 2:29:41, 110mh: Stanislav Stankov 14.21, 400mh: Nikolai Nikolov 54.65, HJ: Mihail Ivanov 2.05, PV: Kamen Tsenkov 4.00, LJ: Boris Linkov 7.25, TJ: Momchil Karailiev 16.50, SP: Georgi Ivanov 18.55, DT: Rosen Karamfilov 53.45, HT: Nikola Mihov

62.36, JT: Mark Slavov 67.73, Dec: Zhulien Monev 6207, 20kW: Peter Lalov 1:57:53. **Women**: 100m/200m: Inna Eftimova 11.51/23.42, 400m/400mh: Kristina Borukova 56.01/59.86, 800m: Polina Todorova 2:12.92, (1500m/5000m: Dilyana Minkina 4:37.70/17:13.39 drugs dq), 10000m: *none*, HMar/Mar: Marinela Nineva 1:20:20/3:01:41, 3000mSt: Radosveta Simeonova 11:13.43, 100mh: Elena Miteva 14.38, HJ: Venelina Veneva-Mateeva 1.70, PV: Yoana Yordanova 3.20, LJ: Milena Mitkova 6.38, TJ: Gabriela Petrova 14.15, SP: Radoslava Mavrodieva 18.63, DT: Renata Petkova 49.04, HT: Ekaterina Dimova 47.45, JT: Mihaela Petkova 45.89, Hep: Iva Aleksandrova 4842, 20kW: Radosveta Simeonova 1:53:29.

Women

Mirela DEMIREVA b. 28 Sep 1989 Sofia 1.80m 58kg. Beroe Stara Zagora
At HJ: OG: '16- 2; WCh: '13- dnq 26, '15- 9=, '17- 7=; EC: '12-14-16-18: 8/dnq 17/2=/2; WJ: '06- dnq 16, '08- 2; EU23: '09- 7, '11- dnq 17; EJ: '07- 3; WI: '18- 6 EI: '13- 7. BUL champion 2007-08, 2011, 2013-14; Balkan 2015-16, 2018.
Progress at HJ: 2005- 1.76, 2006- 1.86, 2007- 1.88, 2000- 1.06, 2009- 1.06, 2011- 1.85l/1.84, 2012- 1.95, 2013- 1.92, 2014- 1.94, 2015- 1.94, 2016- 1.97, 2017- 1.92, 2018- 2.00.
Her mother Valia Demireva (100m 11.34) was at 4x100m 4th at the 1987 Worlds and 5th at the 1998 Olympics. and father Krasimir Demirev won the EJ 400m hurdles in 1981; pb 49.48 '88, also Bulgarian 400m record with 46.34 '83.

Ivet LALOVA-COLLIO b. 18 May 1984 Sofia 1.68m 56kg. née Lalova. IL Sprint Academy, ENKA, Turkey.
At 100m/(200m): OG: '04- 4/5, '08- sf/qf, '12- sf/ sf, '16- sf/8; WCh: '07- qf, '09- qf/h, '11- 7/sf, '13- sf/sf, '15- sf/7, '17- sf/sf; EC: '10- h, '12- 1/sf, '14- 5/sf, '16- 2/2, '18- (5); WJ: '02- sf; WY: '01- h/ sf; EJ: '03: 1/1; CCp: '18- (6); EI: '05- (1). At 60m: WI: '12- 8; EI: '13- 3. Won BUL 100m 2004-05, 200m 2004; Balkan 100m 2011, 2013, 2016.
Bulgarian 100m record 2004.
Progress at 100m, 200m: 1998- 13.0, 27.2; 1999- 12.71, 2000- 12.14, 25.24; 2001- 11.72, 24.03; 2002- 11.59, 24.4; 2003- 11.14, 22.87; 2004- 10.77, 22.51/ 22.36w; 2005- 11.03, 22.76; 2007- 11.26/11.15w, 23.00; 2008- 11.31/11.28w, 23.13; 2009- 11.48/11.24w, 23.60; 2010- 11.43, 23.71; 2011- 10.96, 22.66; 2012- 11.06/11.01w, 22.98; 2013- 11.04, 22.78; 2014- 11.10, 23.17/22.92w; 2015- 11.09, 22.32; 2016- 11.11, 22.42; 2017- 11.25, 22.82; 2018- 11.18, 22.63. pbs: 50m 6.23i+ '12, 60m 7.12i '13.
Broke her leg in a warm-up collision with two athletes on 14 Jun 2005. Married Simone Collio (Italy, 60m 6.55 ITA record 2008, 100m 10.06 in 2009) on 20 Sep 2013. Her father Miroslav Lalov had 100m best of 10.4 and won BUL 200m in 1966, mother Liliya was a pentathlete.

Radoslava MAVRODIEVA b. 13 Mar 1987 Sliven 1.78m 86k. SSCLA Silven.
At SP: OG: '12/16- dnq nh/21; WCh: '11-13-17: dnq   23/18/21;   EC: '10-12-14-16-18: dnq10/6/12/5/6; WJ: '04- 6; EJ: '05- 5; WI: '16- 6; EI: '15-17-19: 3/2/1. BUL champion 2010-11, 2013-15, 2017-18.
Progress at SP: 2003- 13.96, 2004- 17.12, 2005- 16.93i/16.40, 2006- 13.63i, 2009- 14.73, 2010- 17.42, 2011- 17.54i/16.79, 2012- 18.20, 2013- 18.67, 2014- 18.05, 2015- 18.34i/17.84, 2016- 18.27, 2017- 18.36i/17.81, 2018- 18.95, 2019- 19.12i. pb DT 44.45 '13.
Younger sister Zhenya had SP pb 14.03 '06.

Gabriela PETROVA b. 29 Jun 1992 Haskovo 1.67m 61kg. Lokomtiv Plovdiv.
At TJ: OG: '16- dnq 22; WCh: '15- 4, '17- dnq 17; EC: '14-16-18: 5/dnq 20/6; WJ: '10- dnq 17; WY: '09- dnq 18; EU23: '13- 1; EJ: '11- 5; EI: '15- 2; BUL champion LJ 2017, TJ 2010, 2013, 2016-17.
Progress at TJ: 2007- 12.43, 2008- 12.72i, 2009- 12.64, 2010- 13.35, 2011- 13.27/13.44w, 2012- 13.45, 2013- 14.14i/13.92/13.96w, 2014- 14.13, 2015- 14.66/ 14.85w, 2016- 14.32i/13.92, 2017- 14.19, 2018- 14.40/14.48w, pbs: 100m 11.85 '18, LJ 6.48 '18

BURKINA FASO

Governing body: Fédération Burkinabe d'Athlétisme.

Fabrice Hugues **ZANGO** b. 25 Jun 1993 Ouagadougou 1.80m 78kg. Atrois Athlétisme, France.
At TJ: OG: '16- dnq 34; WCh: '15- dnq; AfG: '15- 5; AfCh: '16- 2, '18- 1; CCp: '18- 3; WUG: '15- 2, 17- 2; WI: '18- 6.
African indoor triple jump record 2019.
Progress at TJ: 2011- 14.88, 2012- 15.89, 2013- 15.97, 2014- 15.83, 2015- 16.76, 2016- 16.81/16.84w, 2017- 16.79, 2018- 16.97, 2018- 17.11. pbs: 60m 6.81i'18, 100m 10.73 '17, LJ 7.35 '18.

BURUNDI

Governing body: Fédération d'Athlétisme du Burundi.

Women

Francine NIYONSABA b. 5 May 1993 Nkanda Bweru, Ruyiqi 1.61m 56kg.
At 800m: OG: '12- 5, '16- 2; WCh: '17- 2; AfCh: '12- 1, '18- 2; WI: '16- 1, '18- 1.
Seven Burundi 800m records 2012-17. 600m 2017.
Progress at 800m: 2012- 1:56.59, 2013- 1:56.72, 2015- 1:57.62, 2016- 1:56.24, 2017- 1:55.47, 2018- 1:55.86. pbs: 400m 53.48 '18, 600m 1:23.18 '16.
Won World title on her indoor debut in 2016 and first Olympic medal for a woman from Burundi. Her 1:58.31 to win 2018 World Indoor title was the world's fastest indoor time since 2011.

CANADA

Governing body: Athletics Canada. Formed as Canadian AAU in 1884.

National Championships first held in 1884 (men), 1925 (women). **2018 Champions: Men**: 100m/200m: Aaron Brown 10.16/20.17, 400m: Joshua Cunningham 46.19. 800m: Marco Arop 1:46.15, 1500m: Charles Philibert-Thiboutot 3:46.19, 5000m: Mohammed Ahmed 14:36.09, 10000m: Sergio Ráez Villanueva 30:19.19, HMar: Trevor Hofbauer 68:25, Mar: Cameron Levins 2:09:23. 3000mSt: Matt Hughes 8:54.00; 110mh: Johnathan Cabral 13.44, 400mh: Malik Metevier 51.12, HJ: Michael Mason 2.22, PV: Shawnacy Barber 5.75, LJ: Jared Kerr 7.80w, TJ: Patrick Hanna 15.97w, SP: Tim Nedow 20.94, DT: Jordan Young 57.07, HT: Adam Keenan 71.31, JT: Evan Karakolis 73.10, Dec: Christopher Robertson 7040, 20000mW: Evan Dunfee 1:27:11.67. **Women**: 100m/200m: Crystal Emmanuel 11.34/22.74, 400m: Aiyanna-Brigit Stiverne 51.86, 800m: Lindsey Bitterworth 2:00.87, 1500m: Gabriela Stafford 4:17.08, 5000m: Andrew Seccafien 16:05.60, 10000m: Rachel Cliff 33:06.53, HMar: Sasha Gollish 74:19, Mar: Kinsey Middleton 2:32:09, 3000mSt: Geneviève Lalonde 9:49.07, 100mh: Christie Moerman 13.35, 400mh: Noelle Montcalm 56.69, HJ: Alyxandria Treasure 1.85, PV: Anicka Newell 4.45, LJ: Christabel Nettey 6.21, TJ: Caroline Ehrhardt 13.44, SP: Brittany Crew 18.27, DT: Rachel Andres 56.82, HT: Gillian Weir 68.86, JT: Liz Gleadle 59.34, Hep: Niki Oudenaarden 5833.

Mohammed AHMED b. 5 Jan 1991 Mogadishu, Somalia 1.82m 56kg. Niagara Olympic Club.
At (5000m)/10000m: OG: '12- 18, '16- 4/32; WCh: '13- 9, '15- (12), 17- 6/8; CG: '14- 5/6, '18- 2/2; PAm: '15- 1; WJ: '08- 9, '10- 4; PAm-J: '09- (1). At 3000m: CCp: '18- 2; WI: '16- 9. Won CAN 5000m 2016-18, 10000m 2012.
CAN records 3000m 2017, 10000m (3) 2015-17. Progress at 5000m, 10000m: 2008- 14:26.71, 30:03.53; 2009- 14:11.84, 2010- 14:02.04, 28:57.44; 2011- 13:34.23, 29:08.29; 2012- 13:41.06, 27:34.64, 2013- 13:40.43i, 27:35.76; 2014- 13:18.88, 28:02.96; 2015- 13:10.00, 27:46.90; 2016- 13:01.74, 29:32.84; 2017- 13:04.60i/13:08.16, 27:02.35; 2018- 13:03.08, 27:20.56. pbs: 1500m 3:40.18 '15, 1M 3:56.60 '17; 3000m 7:40.11i '16, 7:40.49 '17; 2M 8:13.16i '17, 8:22.29- 18.
Moved to Canada at age 11. Younger twin brother Ibrahim 25 WJ 10000m 2012.

Shawnacy BARBER b. 27 May 1994 Las Cruces, New Mexico, USA 1.90m 82kg. Student at Akron University, USA.
At PV: OG: '16- 10; WCh: '13- dnq 27, '15- 1, '17- 8; CG: '14- 3, '18- 2; WJ: '12- 3; PAm: '15- 1; PAm-J: 13- 1; CCp: '18- 3; WI: '16- 4=; Won CAN 2013-14, 2016-17; NCAA 2015.
Pole vault records: Four Canadian 2013-15,

indoors (7) 2014-16, N.American indoor 2016.
Progress at PV: 2010- 4.42, 2011- 5.03, 2012- 5.57, 2013- 5.71, 2014- 5.75Ai/5.65, 2015- 5.93, 2016- 6.00Ai/5.91, 2017- 5.83i/5.72, 2018- 5.92.
He lost his Canadian title in 2016 following a positive test for cocaine (getting a Public Warning from the IAAF), but was cleared to compete at the Olympic Games. His father George vaulted 5.29 in 1985 and in 1983 competed for Canada at the Worlds (nh) and was Canadian champion.

Aaron BROWN b. 27 May 1992 Toronto 1.85m 79kg. Was at University of Southerrn California.
At (100m)/200m/4x100mR: OG: '12- sf, 16- h/sf/3R; WCh: '13- (sf)/3R, '15- sf/h/3R, '17- h; WJ: '10- 5/3; WY: '09- (2); CG: '14- (sf), '18- 2; PAm-J: '11- (3); Won CAN 100m 2013, 2018; 200m 2015, 2018. Canadian 200m records 2014.
Progress at 200m: 2009- 21.44/21.34w, 2010- 21.00, 2011- 21.11, 2012- 20.42, 2013- 20.44/20.26w, 2014- 20.16/20.02w, 2015- 20.30/20.11w, 2016- 20.00, 2017- 20.17/20.13w, 2018- 19.98. Pbs: 60m 6.55A/6.59 '14, 100m 9.96 '16., 400m 46.33 '19.

Andre DE GRASSE b. 10 Nov 1994 Scarborough, Ontario 1.80m 73kg. University of Southern California (sociology).
At (100m)/200m: OG: '16- 3/2/3R; WCh: '15- (3=)/3R; CG: '14- sf; PAm: '15- 1/1; PAm-J: '13- 2/3. Won NCAA 100m & 200m 2015, CAN 100m 2015-17, 200m 2017.
Four Canadian 200m records 2015-16.
Progress at 100m, 200m: 2012- 10.59, 2013- 10.25/9.96w, 20.74A/20.57w; 2014- 10.15/10.03w, 20.38; 2015- 9.92/9.75w, 19.88/19.58w; 2016- 9.91, 19.80; 2017- 10.01/9.69w, 20.01/19.96w; 2018- 10.15, 20.46. pbs: 55m 6.21i '13, 60m 6.60i '15, 400m 47.93 '14.
Father came from Barbados and mother from Trinidad. IAAF male Rising Star award 2016.

Evan DUNFEE b. 28 Sep 1990 Richmond, BC 1.86m 68kg. Was at University of British Columbia.
At (20kW)/50kW: OG: '16- 10/4; WCh: '13- 36, '15- 12/12, '17- 15; CG: '10- (6); PAm: '15- (1), WCp: '14- (11), '18- 12; won NACAC 2012. At 10000mW: WJ: '08- 10; WY: '07- 23. CAN champion 10000mW 2012, 2015, 20kW 2010-11, 2014, 2018; NACAC 20kW 2018.
N.American records: 20k & 20,000m 2014, 50kW (2) 2015-16.
Progress at 50kW: 2013- 3:59:28, 2014- 3:58:34, 2015- 3:43:45, 2016- 3:41:38, 2017- 3:46.03, 2018- 3:50:18. pbs: 5000mW 18:53.06 '14, 10000mW 39:21.30 '16, 20kW 1:20:13 '14, 30kW 2:11:54 '14; HMar 70:44 '16.

Matthew HUGHES b. 3 Aug 1989 Oshawa, Ontario 1.80m 64kg. Was at University of Louisville, USA.
At 3000mSt: OG: '16- 10, WCh: '11-13-15-17: h/6/8/6; CG: '14- 4, '18- 4; WJ: '08- h; PAm: '15- 1;

CCp: '14- 7, '18- 2; CAN champion 2013-15, 2017-18; NCAA 2010-11.
Canadian 3000m steeplechase record 2013.
Progress at 3000mSt: 2007- 9:20.61, 2008- 8:59.83, 2009- 8:47.36, 2010- 8:34.18, 2011- 8:24.87, 2012- 8:31.77, 2013- 8:11.64, 2014- 8:12.81, 2015- 8:18.63, 2016- 8:20.63, 2017- 8:21.84, 2018- 8:12.33. pbs: 1500m 3:41.49 '15, 1M 4:01.98 '16, 3000m 7:51.87i '15, 8:11.64 '13; 5000m 13:19.56 '15.

Brandon McBRIDE b. 15 Jun 1994 Windsor, Ontario 1.95m 75kg. Was at Mississippi State University, USA.
At 800m: OG: '16- sf, WCh: '17- 8; CG: '14- sf; WJ: '12- 6; WY: '11- h; NCAA champion 2014, NACAC 2018, CAN 2014, 2016-17. At 400m: PAm-J: 13- 1. Canadian 800m record 2018.
Progress at 800m: 2011- 1:48.41, 2012- 1:46.07, 2013- 1:46.38, 2014- 1:45.35, 2015- 1:45.87, 2016- 1:43.95, 2017- 1:44.41, 2018- 1:43.20. pbs: 100m 10.29w '11, 400m 45.89 '13, 500m 1:01.40i '14, 600m 1:16.2+ '18. 1500m 3:41.55 '16, 1M 4"11.96 '16, 3000m 8:27.13i '17.

Tim NEDOW b. 16 Oct 1990 Brockville 1.98m 125kg. Ottawa Lions. Was at University of Tulsa and DePaul University, USA.
At SP: OG: '16- dnq 16; WCh: '13-15-17- dnq 24/20/16; CG: '14- 3, '18- 3; WI: '16- 7, '18- 9; PAm: '15- 2 (6 DT); PAm-J: '09- 3. Won CAN SP 2013-18, DT 2012-15
Progress at SP: 2010- 17.90, 2011- 19.18i/18.84, 2012- 20.51i/20.21, 2013- 20.74, 2014- 20.98, 2015- 20.78, 2016- 21.33i/20.88, 2017- 20.73, 2018- 21.02. pb DT 61.49 '15.

Damian WARNER b. 4 Nov 1989 London, Ontario 1.85m 83kg. LWTF.
At Dec: OG: '12- 5, '16- 3; WCh: '11-13-15-17: 18/3/2/5; CG: '14- 1, '18- dnf; PAm: '15- 1. Won Canadian 110mh 2014-15, LJ 2017, Dec 2011-13.
At Hep: WI: '14- 7, '18- 2.
Two Canadian decathlon records 2015.
Progress at Dec: 2010- 7449, 2011- 8102A/7832, 2012- 8442, 2013- 8512, 2014- 8282, 2015- 8695, 2016- 8666, 2017- 8591, 2018- 8795. pbs: 60m 6.74i '10, 100m 10.15/10.09w '16, 200m 20.96 '13, 400m 46.36i '15, 46.54 '16, 1000m 2:37.12i '18, 1500m 4:24.73 '15, 60mh 7.63i '16, 110mh 13.27 '15, HJ 2.09 '13, PV 4.90 '16, LJ 8.04 '16, TJ 14.75w '08, SP 15.11 '18, DT 50.26 '16, JT 64.67 '13, Hep: 6343i '18 (CAN rec).
Made 340 points improvement on pb when 5th at 2012 Olympics, setting six pbs, and 70 more at 2013 Worlds, with three pbs. Won Götzis 2013, 2016-18, Talence 2013. Ran fastest ever in decathlons: 110mh 13.44 '15 and 100m 10.15 '16.

Women

Melissa BISHOP-NRIAGU b. 5 Aug 1988 Eganville, Ontario 1.73m 57kg. Was at University of Windsor.
At 800m: OG: '12- h, '16- 4; WCh: '13- h, '15- 2, '17- 5; CG: '14- 8; PAm: '15- 1; CAN champion

2013-14, 2016-17. At 400m: WY: '05- h.
Two Canadian 800m records 2015-16.
Progress at 800m: 2007- 2:10.51 2008- 2:10.12, 2009- 2:06.77, 2010- 2:04.12, 2011- 2:02.69, 2012- 1:59.82, 2013- 1:59.76, 2014- 1:59.70, 2015- 1:57.52, 2016- 1:57.02, 2017- 1:57.01. pbs: 400m 56.27 '10, 600m 1:27.2+ '16, 1000m 2:38.75 '14, 1500m 4:09.58 '16.
Married Osi Nriagu in October 2017, daughter Corinne born 2 July 2018.

Christabel NETTEY b. 2 Jun 1991 Brampton, Ontario 1.62m 59kg. Was at Arizona State University (justice studies).
At LJ: OG: '16- dnq 20; WCh: '13-15-17: dnq 19/4/dnq 19; CG: '14- 3, '18- 1 WY: '07- dnq 14 (8 100mh); WI: '18- 7; PAm: '15- 1; PAm-J: '09- 2; CCp: '14- 4, '18- 7. At 100mh: WY: '07- 8 (3 MedR). Won CAN LJ 2013-17, NACAC 2012
Three Canadian long jump records 2015, four indoor 2014-15.
Progress at LJ: 2006- 6.12, 2007- 6.14, 2008- 6.21, 2009- 6.05/6.10w, 2010- 6.42i/6.28, 2011- 6.49/6.55i, 2012- 6.58, 2013- 6.75, 2014- 6.73, 2015- 6.99, 2016- 6.75/6.88w, 2017- 6.92/6.94w, 2018- 6.92. pbs: 60m 7.65A '17, 100m 12.14 '06, 60mh 8.25i '13, 100mh 13.42 '13, HJ 1.66 '11, TJ 12.80 '12, 12.90w '07; SP 12.16 '11, Hep 5068 '11.
Older sister Sabrina has LJ pbs 6.32i '14, 6.26 '12.

Alysha NEWMAN b. 29 Jun 1994 London, Ontario 1.72m 67kg. Nike. Was at University of Miami
At PV: OG: '16- dnq 17; WCh: '17- 7; WJ: '12- dnq 25; WY: '11- 12; CG: '14- 3, '18- 1; WI: '18- 6; won PAm-J 2013, CAN 2016-17.
5 Canadian pole vault records 2016-18.
Progress at PV: 2010- 3.91, 2011- 4.00i/3.91, 2012- 4.06, 2013- 4.40A, 2014- 4.41, 2015- 4.40, 2016- 4.61, 2017- 4.75, 2018- 4.75. Pb 100mh 14.07 '14.

Sage WATSON b. 20 Jun 1994 Medicine Hat, Alberta 1.75m 62kg. Studied at Florida State, then University of Arizona, USA.
At 400mh: OG: '16- sf; WCh: '15- sf, '17- 6; CG: '18- 5; PAm: '15- h/3R; WJ: '12- sf; WY: '11- 8 (3 MedR). Won NCAA 2017, CAN 2011, 2017.
Progress at 400mh: 2011 59.00, 2012- 58.0 4, 2013- 56.81A/58.20, 2015- 55.97, 2016- 54.82, 2017- 54.52, 2018- 54.55. pbs: 200m 23.80 '17, 300m 37.08i '18, 400m 51.62 '18, 500m 1:08.40i '17, 600m 1:28.31 '17.

CHILE

Governing body: Federación Atlética de Chile. Founded 1914.
2018 Champions: Men: Enrique Polanco 10.43, 200m: Enzo Faulbaum 21.18, 400m: Sergio Aldea 47.15, 800m: Rafael Muñoz 1:52.33, 1500m: Carlos Martín Díaz 3:47.66, 3000m/ 5000m: Víctor Aravena 8:07.52/13:47.9, 10000m: Enzo Yáñez 30:17.14, Mar: Mauricio Flandez 2:21:27, 3000mSt: Roberto Tello 9:07.84, 110mh: Juan Pablo Gemain 14.27, 400mh: Alfredo

Sepúlveda 50.63, HJ: Cristóbal Hurtado 2.09, PV: Francisco Benavídes 4.80, LJ: Alejandro Horn 7.34, TJ: Benjamin Palazuelos 14.27, SP: Pablo Orellana 17.34, DT: Claudio Romero 55.13, HT: Hevert Álvarez 63.49, JT: Francisco Muse 73.24, Dec: César Jofre 6473, 20000mW: Moisés Beltrán 1:38:27, 35kW: Fabricio Sales 2:56:52. **Women**: 100m/200m: Isidora Jiménez 11.53/23.33, 400m: María Fernanda Mackenna 54.52, 800m/1500m: Javiera Faletto 2:11.32/ 4:33.39, 3000m/3000mSt: Margaríta Masías 10:24.61/11:32.63, 5000m: Jennifer González 18:06.88, 10000m: Giselle Álvarez 35:27.64, Mar: Clara Morales 2:59:18, 100mh: María Ignacia Eguiguren 13.92, 400mh: María José Echeverría 60.18, HJ: Victoria Rozas 1.71, PV: Fernanda Carabias 3.50, LJ: Macarena Borie 5.31, TJ: Niorka Moretic 12.10, SP: Ivana Gallardo 14.60, DT: Karen Gallardo 56.61, HT: Mariana García 60.71, JT: Carolina García 44.16, Hep: Francisca Valencia 4603, 20kW: Anastasia Sanzana 1:46:41.

CHINA

Governing body: Athletic Association of the People's Republic of China.
National Championships first held in 1910 (men), 1959 (women). **2018 Champions: Men**: 100m: Xu Zhouzheng 10.26, 200m/400m: Guo Zhongze 20.82/46.29, 800m: Li Junlin 1:51.10, 1500m: Pei Haitao 3:47.77, 5000m/10000m: Peng Jianhua 14:07.06/29:17.98, Mar: Dong Guojian 2:14:16, 3000mSt: Peng Jianqi 8:58.10, 110mh: Xie Wenjun 13.40, 400mh: Gong Debin 50.54, HJ: Chen Ji 2.24, PV: Huang Bokai 5.70, LJ: Zhang Yaoguang 8.03, TJ: Wu Ruting 16.89, SP: Liu Yang 19.06, DT: Tan Shan 57.29, HT: Wang Shizhu 70.10, JT: Liu Qizhen 81.49, Dec: Hu Yufei 7262, 20kW: Yin Jiaxing 1:21:55, 50kW: Luo Dongpo 3:57:25. **Women**: 100m: Liang Xiaojing 11.35, 200m: Kong Lingwei 23.30, 400m: Yang Huizhen 52.90, 800m: Zhang Gui 2:08.27, 1500m: Zhong Xiaoqian 4:21.46, 5000m: Jin Mingming 16:09.97, 10000m: Xia Yuyu 33:38.64, Mar: Zhang Meixia 2:33:02, 3000mSt: Xu Shuangshuang 10:05.18, 100mh: Wu Yanni 13.17, 400mh: Huang Yan 57.61, HJ: Hu Linpeng 1.84, PV: Li Ling 4.30, LJ: Chen Shuiqing 6.38, TJ: Pan Youqi 13.66, SP: Gong Lijiao 18.62, DT: Feng Bin 63.38, HT: Liu Tingting 68.41, JT: Lu Huihui 65.45, Hep: Wang Qingling 56.77, 20kW: Lu Xiuzhi 1:29:06, 50kW: Liang Rui 4:12:26.

CAI Zelin b. 11 Apr 1991 Dali, Yunnan 1.72m 55kg.
At 20kW: OG: '12- 4, '16- 2; WCh: '13- 26, '15- 5; AsiG: '14- 4; WCp: '14- 2, '16- 2. At 10000mW: WJ: '10- 2; WCp: '10- 2J. Won CHN 20kW 2012.
Progress at 20kW: 2010- 1:22:28, 2011- 1:21:07, 2012- 1:18:47, 2013- 1:18:55, 2014- 1:18:52, 2015- 1:19:45, 2016- 1:19:26, 2018- 1:20:38. Pbs: 5000mW 19:35.00 '14, 10,000mW 38:59.98 '12, 30kW 2:45:13 '09.

CAO SHUO b. 8 Oct 1991 Baoding, Hebei 1.80m 77kg.
At TJ: OG: '12- dnq 20, '16- 4; WCh: '15- dnq 15; AsiG: '10-14-18: 3/1/3; AsiC: '13- 1, '15- 2; CCp: '14- 5; WI: '14- 7. Won AsiJ 2010, CHN 2009, 2012-13, NG 2013.
World youth triple jump record 2009.
Progress at TJ: 2007- 15.82, 2008- 16.42, 2009- 17.13, 2010- 16.85, 2011- 16.86, 2012- 17.35, 2013- 17.26, 2014- 17.30, 2015- 16.77/16.98w, 2016- 17.13, 2017- 17.22, 2018- 16.80A/16.65.

DONG Bin b. 22 Nov 1988 Changshan. 1.79m 67kg.
At TJ: OG: '12- 10, '16- 3; WCh: '13- 9, '15- dnq 18; WJ: '06- dnq 14; AsiG: '14- 2; AsiC: '11- 5, '15- 4; WI: '12-16-18: 8/1/8. Won Asian indoors 2010, 2012, CHN NG 2017.
Asian indoor triple jump record 2016.
Progress at TJ: 2006- 16.22, 2007- 16.25, 2008- 16.54, 2009- 16.89i/16.65, 2010- 16.86, 2011- 17.01i/16.86, 2012- 17.38, 2013- 17.16i/16.98, 2014- 16.95, 2015- 17.12/17.21w, 2016- 17.58, 2017- 17.27, 2018- 17.22. pb LJ 7.09 '07, 7.32w '06.

GAO Xinglong b. 12 Mar 1994 Heilongjiang Prov 1.81m 65kg.
At LJ: OG: '16- dnq nj; WCh: '15- 4; AsiG: '14- 3; AsiC: '15- 1. Won CHN 2014-15.
Progress at LJ: 2012- 7.27, 2013- 8.02i/7.98, 2014- 8.18/8.21w, 2015- 8.34, 2016- 8.23, 2017- 8.22, 2018- 8.05A.

HUANG Changzhou b. 20 Aug 1994 Sichuan Prov 1.83m 64kg.
At LJ: OG: '16- 11; WCh: '17- dnq 24; AsiC: '15- dnq, '17- 1; WI: '16- 3; Won CHN NG 2017.
Progress at LJ: 2012- 7.79, 2013- 7.97, 2014- 8.12, 2015- 8.17, 2016- 8.21i/8.12, 2017- 8.26, 2018- 8.19i/8.19A/8.16, 2019- 8.21i.

SHI Yuhao b. 26 Sep 1998 Jiangsu 1.78m 61kg.
At LJ: WCh: '17- 6; WY: '15- 6 (6 TJ); WI: '18- 5. Asian indoor champion 2018.
Asian junior long jump records 2016 & 2017.
Progress at LJ: 2014- 7.39, 2015- 7.63, 2016- 8.30, 2017- 8.31, 2018- 8.43. pb TJ 15.45 '16.

SU Bingtian b. 29 Aug 1989 Zhongshan, Guangdong Prov. 1.85m 65kg. Guandong.
At 100m: OG: '12- sf, '16- sf/4R; WCh: '13- sf, '15- 9/2R, '17- 8; AsiG: '14- 2/1R, '18- 1/3R; AsiC: '11- 1, '13- 1, '15- 1R; CCp: '18- 2; WUG: '11- 3. Won Chinese 100m 2009, 2011-13; E.Asian G 2013. At 60m: WI: '14-16-18: 4/5/2; AsiG: '09- 1.
Records: Asian 100m (2) 2018, 4x100m 2016, indoor 60m (4) 2016-18, Chinese 100m (5) 2011-18 and 200m 2013.
Progress at 100m: 2006- 10.59, 2007- 10.45, 2008- 10.41, 2009- 10.28, 2010- 10.32, 2011- 10.16, 2012- 10.19/10.04w, 2013- 10.06, 2014- 10.10, 2015- 9.99, 2016- 10.08/10.04w, 2017- 10.03/9.92w, 2018- 9.91/9.90w. pbs: 60m 6.42i '18, 200m 21.23 '08.

WANG Jianan b. 27 Aug 1996 Shenyang, Liaoning prov. 1.78m 61kg.

At LJ: OG: '16- 5; WCh: '13-15-17: dnq 23/3/7; WJ: '14- 1; AsiG: '18- 1; AsiC: '13- 1; CCp: '18- 5; WI '16- 8.
Chinese long jump record 2018, Asian junior record 2015.
Progress at LJ: 2012- 8.04, 2013- 7.95, 2014- 8.10, 2015- 8.25, 2016- 8.24, 2017- 8.29, 2018- 8.47A/8.24. pbs: 60m 6.89i '12, 100m 10.88 '12, 60mh 8.46i '12, HJ 1.94 '12, PV 5.00 '12, Dec 7063 '12.
At 18 in 2015 he became the youngest ever male World Champs medallist at a field event.

WANG Kaihua b. 16 Feb 1994 Guangdong Prov. 1.80m 65kg.
At 20kW: WCh: '17- 7; AsiG: '18- 1. Won CHN NG 2017.
Progress at 20kW: 2011- 1:26:48, 2013- 1:23:35, 2014- 1:26:54, 2015- 1:19:49, 2016- 1:19:51, 2017- 1:17:54, 2018- 1:19:45. Pbs: 10000mW 41:50.75 '11, 39:50R '17 .

WANG Qin b. 8 May 1994 1.78m 65kg. Shaanxi
At 50kW: AsiG: '18- 2; WT: '18- 5.
Progress at 50kW: 2016- 13:50:16, 2017- 3:54:46, 2018- 3:45:29, 2019- 3:38:02. Pbs: 10000mW 40:00.13 '18, 20W 1:22:08 '16, 35kW: 2:33:18 '18.
6-months drugs ban 2016-17.

WANG Yu b. 18 Aug 1991 Zhuhai 1.92m 73kg. Beijing.
At HJ: OG: '16- dnq 32; WCh: '13-15-17: dnq 19/ dnq 18=/dns; AsiG: '14- 4, '18- 1; AsiC: 15- 7; WUG: '11- 4, '13- 3; WI: '18- 6. Won CHN 2015, CHN NG 2013, 2017.
Progress at HJ: 2008- 2.08, 2009- 2.17, 2010- 2.24i/2.15, 2011- 2.28, 2012- 2.28, 2013- 2.33, 2014- 2.31, 2015- 2.31, 2016- 2.33, 2017- 2.30, 2018- 2.32, 2019- 2.34i.

XIE Wenjun b. 11 Jul 1990 Shanghai 1.88m 77kg, Shanghai.
At 110mh: OG: '12- sf, '16- h; WCh: '13-15-17: h/ sf/sf; AsiG: '14- 1, '18- 1; AsiC: '15- 1; CCp: '14- 4; Won CHN 2012, 2015-16, 2018; NG 2013, 2017.
Progress at 110mh: 2007- 14.09, 2008- 13.47, 2009- 13.53, 2010- 13.47, 2011- 13.45, 2012- 13.34, 2013- 13.28, 2014- 13.23, 2015- 13.36, 2016- 13.34, 2017- 13.31, 2018- 13.34. pbs: 100m 11.04 '06, 60mh 7.60i '13.

XUE Changrui b. 31 May 1991 Shandong prov. 1.83m 60kg
At PV: OG: '16- 6; WCh: '13- 12, '17- 4; WI: '14- 5, AsiG: '14- 1; AsiC: '13- 1; CCp: '14- 2; Won CHN NG 2013, 2017.
Three Chinese pole vault records 2014-17.
Progress at PV: 2011- 5.30, 2012- 5.60, 2013- 5.75i/5.65, 2014- 5.80, 2015- 5.40, 2016- 5.81i/5.75, 2017- 5.82, 2018- 5.76i/5.71. pb LJ 7.15 '08

ZHANG Guowei b. 4 Jun 1991 Binzhon, Shandong prov. 2.00m 77kg.
At HJ: OG: '12/16- dnq 21=/25=; WCh: '11-13-15- 17: 10/9/2=/dnq 24; WI: '12-14-16: 4=/7/6, AsiG: '14- 2; AsiC: '11- 8, '17- 2; CCp: '14- 6. CHN champion 2011, 2017.

Progress at HJ: 2010- 2.23, 2011- 2.31, 2012- 2.31, 2013- 2.32i/2.29, 2014- 2.34, 2015- 2.38, 2016- 2.33, 2017- 2.31, 2018- 2.20.

Women

CHEN Yang b. 10 Jul 1991 1.80m 97kg. Hebei.
At DT: OG: '16- 7; WCh: '17- 10; AsiG: '18- 1; AsiC: '17- 1; CCp: '18- 3.
Progress at DT: 51.05- 53.79, 2011- 51.10, 2012- 53.10, 2013- 52.10, 2014- 58.53, 2015- 61.16, 2016- 63.61, 2017- 62.90, 2018- 67.03.

FENG Bin b. 3 Apr 1994 1.84m 95kg. Shandong.
At DT: OG: '16- 8; WCh: '17- 8; AsiG: '18- 2; WY: '11- 4. Won CHN 2018, W.MilG 2015.
Progress at DT: 2010- 53.77, 2011- 55.94, 2012- 55.62, 2013- 58.14, 2014- 59.73, 2015- 62.07, 2016- 65.14, 2017- 64.46, 2018- 64.58.

GAO Yang b. 1 Mar 1993. 1.78m 110kg. Army.
At SP: OG: '16- dnq 33; WCh: '15- 5, '17- 5; WJ: '12- 2; AsiG: '18- 2; AsiC: '13- 3, '15- 2; WI: '16- 8, '18- 4. Won W.MilG 2015, CHN NG 2017.
Progress at SP: 2012- 17.07, 2013- 17.76, 2014- 17.52, 2015- 19.04, 2016- 19.20, 2017- 18.34, 2018- 18.77i/18.36.

GONG Lijiao b. 24 Jan 1989 Luquan, Hebei Prov. 1.74m 110kg. Hebei.
At SP: OG: '08- 3, '12- 2, '16- 4; WCh: '07-09-11- 13-15-17: 6/3/3/3/2/1; WI: '10-14-18: 6/3/3; AsiG: '10-14-18: 2/1/1; AsiC: '09- 1; CCp: '10-14-18: 2/3/3. Won DL 2017-18, Chinese 2007-12, 2014, 2016-18; NG 2009, 2013, 2017; Asian indoor 2008.
Progress at SP: 2005- 15.41i, 2006- 17.92, 2007- 19.13, 2008- 19.46, 2009- 20.35, 2010- 20.13, 2011- 20.11, 2012- 20.22, 2013- 20.12, 2014- 19.65, 2015- 20.34, 2016- 20.43, 2017- 20.11, 2018- 20.38. pb JT 53.94 '07. Based at Neubrandenburg, Germany from 2013.

LI Ling b. 6 Jul 1989 Zhubo, Henan Province 1.80m 65kg. Zhejiang
At PV: OG: '08/12/16- dnq 27=/30/16; WCh: '09- 11-13-15: dnq 18/dnq 29/11/9; WJ: '06- nh; AsiG: '10-14-18: 2/1/1; AsiC: '11-13-15-17: 2/1/1/2; CCp: '14- 1; WUG: '15- 1. Won CHN 2008-09, 2011-13, 2015-16, 2018; NG 2013, Asian Indoors 2009, 2012, 2016.
Asian PV records: 2013 & 2015, indoor (4) 2015- 16, junior 2008.
Progress at PV: 2005- 3.90i/3.70, 2006- 4.15, 2007- 4.30, 2008- 4.45, 2009- 4.40, 2010- 4.45i/4.40, 2011- 4.40, 2012- 4.50i/4.40, 2013- 4.65, 2014- 4.61, 2015- 4.66, 2016- 4.70, 2017- 4.50, 2018- 4.60.

LI Lingwei b. 26 Jan 1989 Yantai 1.72m 75kg.
At JT: OG: '12/16- dnq 30/15; WCh: '13-15-17: 8/5/2; WJ: '06- 8, '08- 2; AsiG: '10- 3, '14- 2; AsiC: '09-13-17: 2/1/1; won Asi-J 2008, CHN 2013, 2015-17; NG 2013, 2017. Asian javelin record 2012.
Progress at JT: 2002- 49.60, 2003- 55.38, 2004- 51.19, 2005- 58.87, 2006- 58.87, 2007- 57.88, 2008- 59.25, 2009- 57.82, 2010- 60.60, 2011- 57.39, 2012-

65.11, 2013- 63.06, 2014- 62.56, 2015- 65.07, 2016-
62.89, 2017- 66.25.

LI Maocuo b. 20 Oct 1992.
At 50kW: WT: '18- 7.
Progress at 20kW, 50kW: 2010- 1:42:15, 2011-
1:35:40, 2012- 1:38:13, 2013- 1:36:06, 2014- 1:31:55,
2015- 1:33:55, 2016- 1:38:01, 4:47:28; 2017- 1:31:00,
2018- 1:30:15, 4:13:04; 2019- 4:03:51. pb 10kW
44:52 '16.

LIANG Rui b. 18 Jun 1994 Gansu Prov.
At 50kW: WCp: '18- 1; CHN champion 2018.
World record 2018 on 50k walk debut.
Progress at 20kW, 50kW: 2012- 1:37:21, 2014-
1:37:28, 2015- 1:29:22, 2016- 1:28:43, 2017- 1:28:50,
2018- 1:35:20, 4:04:36; 2019- 4:19:34. At 50kW:
2018- 4:04:36. pbs: 5000mW 22:33.10 '14, 10000,W
46:04.91 '14, 35kW 2:48:23 '18.

LIU Hong b. 12 May 1987 Anfu, Jiangxi Prov.
1.61m 48kg. Guangdong.
At 20kW: OG: '08- 4, '12- 3, '16- 1; WCh: '07-09-
11-13-15: 19/2/1/3/1; WCp: '06-14-16: 6/2/dq1;
AsiG: '06- 1, '10- 1; won CHN 2010-11, NG 2009.
At 10000mW: WJ: '06- 1; won IAAF Race
Walking Challenge 10k 2012, 2014 (2nd 2011). At
50kW: won CHN 2019.
Walk records: World 20k 2015, 50k 2019 (on
debut); Asian 5000m & 20k 2012.
Progress at 20kW, 50kW: 2004- 1:35:04, 2005-
1:29:39, 2006- 1:28:26, 2007- 1:29:41, 2008- 1:27:17,
2009- 1:28:11, 2010- 1:30:06, 2011- 1:27:17, 2012-
1:25:46, 2013- 1:27:06, 2014- 1:26:58, 2015- 1:24:38,
2016- 1:25:56, 2019- 1:30:43, 3:59:15. pbs: 3000mW
12:18.18 '05, 5000mW 20:34.76 '12, 10kW 42:30R
'10, 43:16.68t '12. Running: Mar 2:51:23 '15.
Won IAAF Race Walking Challenge 2011-12
and 2014-15. Failed drugs test when 'winning'
the World Cup 20k race in 2016 and received a
three-months ban. Baby born on 20 Nov 2017.

LIU Shiying b. 24 Sep 1993 Shandong prov.
1.79m 76kg.
At JT: OG: '16- dnq 23; WCh: '17- 8; WJ: '12- 2;
AsiG: '18- 1; AsiC: '15- 1, Asi-J '12- 1.
Asian javelin record 2017.
Progress at JT: 2010- 50.92, 2011- 55.10, 2012-
59.20, 2013- 60.23, 2014- 62.72, 2015- 62.77, 2016-
65.64, 2017- 66.47, 2018- 67.12.

LU Huihui b. 26 Jun 1989 Huwan, Henan 1.71m
68kg.
At JT: OG: '12- 5, '16- 7; WCh: '15- 2. '17- 3; AsiG:
'18- 2CCp: '18- 1. Won CHN 2018.
Four Asian javelin records 2012-18.
Progress at JT: 2005- 49.62, 2006- 49.96, 2010-
55.35, 2011- 58.72, 2012- 64.95, 2013- 64.48/
65.62dq, 2015- 66.13, 2016- 64.03, 2017- 67.59,
2018- 67.69.   One-year drugs ban for positive
test 27 Apr 2013.

LU Xiuzhi b. 26 Oct 1993 Chuzhou 1.67m 52kg.
At 20kW: OG: '12- 5, '16- 3; WCh: '15- 2, '17- dq;
AsiG: '14- 1; WCp: '12-14-16: 3/6/5, won CHN
2014, 2018; NG 2013.

Asian 20k walk record 2015, junior 2012.
Progress at 20kW: 2011- 1:29:50, 2012- 1:27:01,
2013- 1:27:53, 2014- 1:27:15, 2015- 1:25:12, 2016-
1:28:07, 2017- 1:26:28, 2018- 1:29:06. pb 10kW
43:16 '12.

LUO Na b. 8 Oct 1993 1.73m 758kg.
At HT: WCh: '17- dnq 13; WJ: '12- 6; AsiG: '18- 1;
AsiC: '15- 2, '17- 1; CCp: '18- 5; won CHN 2017.
Progress at HT: 2010- 60.43, 2011- 62.68, 2012-
63.61, 2013- 67.09, 2014- 69.81, 2015- 67.11, 2016-
62.65, 2017- 72.27, 2018- 75.02.

QIEYANG Shenjie b. 11 Nov 1990 Haiyan,
Qinghai Prov. 1.60m 50kg.
At 20kW: OG: '12- 2, '16- 5; WCh: '11- 4, '13- 15;
AsiG: '18- 2; WCp: '12-16-18: 13 2/2. CHN
champion 2015. Tied first for IAAF Race
Walking Challenge 2016.
Asian 20k walk record 2012.
Progress at 20kW: 2009- 1:35:54, 2010- 1:30:33,
2011- 1:28:04, 2012- 1:25:16, 2013- 1:28:05, 2015-
1:27:44, 2016- 1:26:49, 2017- 1:28:33, 2018- 1:27:06.
pbs: 5000mW 20:42.67 '12, 10kW 42:46 '17.
First athlete from Tibet to win an Olympic
medal. Won IAAF Race Walking Challenge
2018.

SU XInyue b. 8 Nov 1991 1.79m 70kg. Hebei
At DT: OG: '16- 5; WCh: '13- dnq 19, '15- 8, '17- 7;
AsiC: '13- 1, '15- 1; WJ: '10- dnq 13. Won CHN
NG 2017.
Progress at DT: 2007- 48.29, 2009- 52.51, 2010-
56.11, 2011- 57.57, 2012- 60.32, 2013- 61.67, 2014-
61.31, 2015- 64.27, 2016- 65.59, 2017- 64.56, 2018-
63.73.

WANG Zheng b. 14 Dec 1987 Xian, Shanxi
Province 1.74m 108kg.
At HT: OG: '08- dnq 30, '16- nt; WCh: '13- 3, '15-
5, '17- 2; WJ: '06- 9; AsiG: '10-14-18: 2/2/2; AsiC:
'13- 1; CCp: '14- 4; won Asi-J 2006, E.Asian 2009,
CHN 2014, 2016.
Asian hammer record 2014.
Progress at HT: 2004- 54.57, 2005- 55.72, 2006-
61.43, 2007- 64.04, 2008- 70.07, 2009- 67.06, 2010-
71.19, 2011- 68.75, 2012- 69.14, 2013- 74.90, 2014-
77.68, 2015- 74.92, 2016- 74.50, 2017- 76.25, 2018-
73.73.

YANG Jiayu b. 18 Feb 1996 1.63m 48kg.
At 20kW: WCh: '17- 1; WCp: '18- 3; AsiG: '18- 1;
WUG: '15- 5, won CHN NG 2017. At 10kW:
WCp: '14- 2J.
Progress at 20kW: 2013- 1:40:27, 2015- 1:36:50,
2016- 1:28:12, 2017- 1:26:18, 2018- 1:27:22. Pbs:
5000mW 22:22.47 '14, 10000mW 45:59.81 '14,
43:19R '15.

YIN Hang b. 7 Feb 1997 1.61m 50kg. Army.
At 50kW: WCh: '17- 2; WT: '18- 2.
Two Asian 50kW records 2017.
Progress at 20kW, 50kW: 2016- 1:34:25, 2017-
1:31:23, 4:08:58; 2018- 1:35:27, 4:09:09 pb 10kW
44:52 '16.

COLOMBIA

Governing body: Federación Colombiana de Atletismo. Founded 1937.
National Games Champions 2018: Men: 100m: Diego Palomeque 10.19, 200m: Bernardo Baloyes 20.40, 400m: Jhon Perlaza 46.86, 800m: Rafith Rodríguez 1:55.54, 1500m: Carlos San Martín 3:48.24, 5000m: José Mauricio González 14:18.76, 10000m: Miguel Ángel Amador 30:18.87, 3000mSt: Andrés Camargo 8:44.11, 110mh: Juan Carlos Moreno 13.71, 400mh: Yeison Rivas 51.47, HJ: Daniel Cortés 2.15, PV: Walter Viáfara 5.20, LJ: Aldair Rojas 7.56w, TJ: Juan David Campo 16.01w, SP: Willinton Aguilar 17.25, DT: Mauricio Ortega 61.59, JT: Arley Ibargüen 78.39, Dec: José Gregorio Lemus 6966, 10000mW: Alexander Casteñada 42:39.44, 20kW: José Leonardo Montaña 1:24:01. **Women**: 100m: Evelyn Rivera 11.63, 200m/400m: Yenifer Padilla 23.96/53.45, 800m: Rosangélica Escobar 2:07.44, 1500m/5000m: Muriel Coneo 4:22.50/16:28.89, 10000m: Kelly Arias 34:39.32, 3000mSt: Laura Cusaria 10:55.86, 100mh: Eliecit Palacios 13.36w, 400mh: Melisa González 58.08, HJ: Laritza Rodríguez 1.80, PV: Stefany Castillo 4.00, LJ/TJ: Yosiry Urrutia 5.91/14.35, SP: Ányela Rivas 17.08, DT: Yerlin Mesa 49.96, HT: Eli Johana Moreno 62.95, JT: María Lucelly Murillo 57.17, Hep: Evelis Aguilar 6054, 10000mW/20kW: Sandra Lorena Arenas 47:24.41/1:34:31.

Eider ARÉVALO b. 9 Mar 1993 Bogotá 1.65m 58kg.
At 20kW: OG: '12- 20, '16- 15; WCh: '13- dnf, '15-7, '17- 1; PAm: 15- 5, CAG: '18- 1; SACh: '13- 2; Won PAmCp '17, COL 2012-13. At 10000mW: WJ: '12- 1; SAmJ & PAm-J: '11- 1; WCp: '10- 1J, '12- 1J. Colombian 20k walk records 2013 & 2017.
Progress at 20kW: 2012- 1:21:49, 2013- 1:19:45, 2014- 1:21:28, 2015- 1:20:41, 2016- 1:20:47, 2017-1:18:53, 2018- 1:19:14. Pb 10000mW 39:56.01A '11. Won IAAF Walks Challenge 2017.

Women

Sandra Lorena **ARENAS** b. 17 Sep 1993 Pereira, Risaralda 1.61m 51kg
At 20kW: OG: 12- 31, '16- 32; WCh: '13-15-17: 21/19/5; WCp: '16- 10, '18- 15; PAm: 15- 4; SACh: '13- 1, '15- 1. COL champion 2012-14, 2016; SAm-J 2011, BolG 2017. At 10000mW: WJ: '12- 3; 10kW: WCp: '12- 1J; won IbAm 2018.
Walk records: S.American track 20000m 2014, 10000m 2018. Six COL 20k 2012-17.
Progress at 20kW: 2011- 1:48:36.0A, 2012- 1:32:36, 2013- 1:32:25, 2014- 1:30:18, 2015- 1:31:02.25t, 2016- 1:29:31, 2017- 1:28:10, 2018- 1:28:48. Pbs: 5000mW 23:01.4A '15, 10000mW 42:02.99 '18.

Caterine IBARGÜEN b. 12 Feb 1984 Apartadó, Antioquia 1.81m 65kg. Studying nursing.
At TJ/(LJ): OG: '12- 2, '16- 1; WCh: '11-13-15-17: 3/1/1/2; WJ: '02: dnq 17; PAm: '11- 1/3; '15- 1; SACh: '03- 3/2, '05- 3/3, '06- 2/2, '07- (3), '09- 1, '11- 1/3; CAG: '02-06-10-14-18: 2/(2)/2/1/1&1; CCp: '14- 1, '18- 1/1. At HJ: OG: '04- dnq 27=; WCh: '09- dnq 25=; PAm: '07- 4; SACh: '99-05-06-07-09: 3/1/1/1/1; CAG: '02- 2, '06- 2. Won DL 2013-16, 2018 (& LJ 2018) COL HJ 1999, 2001-03, 2005-12, 2015; LJ 2003-04, 2006-08, 2011-12, 2015; TJ 2002-05, 2007-12, 2014.
Records: South American triple jump (7) 2011-14, junior HJ 2003. Colombia HJ (7) 2002-05, LJ (10) 2004-18, TJ (15) 2004-14.
Progress at LJ, TJ: 2001- 12.90, 2002- 6.08A, 13.38A; 2003- 6.18A, 13.23A; 2004- 6.42A, 13.64A; 2005- 6.54A, 13.66A; 2006- 6.49A/6.52Aw, 13.91A/13.98Aw; 2007- 6.22A, 12.66A; 2008-6.54A, 13.79A; 2009- 6.41A, 13.96A/13.93; 2010-6.29/6.34w, 14.29; 2011- 6.63A, 14.99A/14.84; 2012- 6.73A, 6.87Aw, 14.95A/14.85; 2013- 6.54, 14.85/14.93w; 2014- 15.31, 2015- 6.63/6.66w, 14.90/15.18w; 2016- 15.17, 2017- 14.89, 2018- 6.93, 14.96. pbs: 200m 25.34 '08, 100mh 14.09 '11, HJ 1.93A '05, SP 13.79 '10, JT 44.81 '09, Hep 5742 '09.
Formerly a high jumper, concentrating fully on TJ from 2010. First Colombian woman to win a medal in world champs. Unbeaten in 9 competitions in 2013, 11 in 2014 and 9 in 2015 plus her first 4 in 2016, taking her to 34 in succession 2012-16. Unbeaten in 8 TJs in 2018. She had 77 successive competitions over 14m from April 2010 to June 2017. IAAF Female athlete of the Year 2018. Lives in Puerto Rico.

Yosiry URRUTIA b. 26 Jun 1986 Chigorodó, Antioquia 1.75m 61kg. Graduated from nursing school at Universidad Metropolitana, Puerto Rico.
At (LJ/)TJ: OG: '16- dnq 20; WCh: '15- 10; PAm: '15- 3; SACh: 13- 5/2, '17- 3; CAG: '14- 3, '18- 2. Won Ib Am 2014, 2018; BolG 2013, COL LJ 2010, 2013, 2018; TJ 2018.
Progress at TJ: 2005- 12.00, 2007- 12.43A, 2010-12.94, 2013- 14.08, 2014- 14.58, 2015- 14.22/14.36w. 2016- 14.08A/13.95, 2017- 13.59/13.64w, 2018-14.47/14.48w. pbs: 100mh 14.40 '10, LJ 6.53A/6.42 '10. Previously a long jumper, she focused fully on the triple jump from 2013,

REPUBLIC OF CONGO

Franck Dannique **ELEMBA** Owaka b. 21 Jul 1990 Brazzaville 1.98m 130kg.
At SP: OG: '16- 4; WCh: '15-17- dnq 21/24; AfG: '11- 5, '15- 1 (3 DT); AfCh: '10-12-14-16: 4/5/3/2; CCp: '10- 7, '14- 7.
Congo shot records 2010-16, DT 2016.
Progress at SP: 2009- 15.09, 2010- 15.90, 2011-16.44, 2012- 17.58, 2013- 19.02, 2014- 19.72, 2015-20.25, 2016- 21.20, 2017- 20.86i/20.72, 2018- 20.81 pb DT 54.30 '16.
Lives in Paris. His 2016 4th was the best Olympic place for an athlete from Congo.

CROATIA

Governing body: Hrvatski Atletski Savez.

Founded 1912.
National Champions 2018 Men: 100m: Marino Dotlic 11.02, 200m: Dominik Kreso 22.02, 400m/400mh: Hrvoje Cukman 46.88/50.58, 800m: Marino Bloudek 1:49.03, 1500m/3000m/5000m/10000m: Dino Bosnjak 3:56.24/8:34.53/14:52.27/30:35.15 , HMar: Petar Bratulic 69:34, Mar:, 3000mSt: Filip Svalina 9:22.17, 110mh: Trpimir Siroki 15.43, HJ: Filip Mrcic 2.14, PV: Ivan Horvat 5.71, LJ: Filip Pravdica 7.91, TJ: Ivan Dukic 15.45, SP: Stipe 820.41, DT: Roland Varga 55.63, HT: Matija Greguric 61.26, JT: Bartul Basic 68.93, Dec: Trpimir Siroki 6749, 20kW/50kW: Bruno Erent 1:44:10/4:29:44. **Women**: 100m/200m: Lucija Pokos 11.67/23.56, 400m: Kristina Dudek 54.60, 800m: Ivona Zemunik 2:11.6, 1500m: Klara Andrijasevic 4:31.31, 3000m/5000m/HMar: Bojana Bjeljac 9:38.90/16:44.17/73:40. 10000m: Matea Parlov 34:49.59, Mar:, 3000mSt: Sandra Srut 10:59.07, 100mh: Andrea Ivancevic 13.06, 400mh: Ida Simuncic 58.62, HJ: Ana Simic 1.85, PV: Elija Valentic 4.06, LJ: Neja Filipic 6.47, TJ: Paola Borvoic 13.40, SP: Marija Tolj 14.63, DT: Veronika Domjan 57.92, HT: Anamari Kozul 65.73, JT: Ludja Cvitanovic 49.11, Hep: Ivana Zeljko 4292, 10kW/20kW: Ivana Renic 52:12/1:38:33.

Filip MIHALJEVIC b. 31 Jul 1994 Livno, Bosnia & Herzegovina 2.01m 113kg. University of Virginia, USA.
At SP/(DT): OG: '16- dnq 21; WCh: '17- dnq 14; EC: '16/18: dnq 21/22; EU23: '15- 1/4; EJ: '13-2/11; WI: '16- 3. Won CRO SP 2013, DT 2015-17, NCAA SP 2016-17, DT 2017.
Progress at SP: 2012- 16.52, 2013- 17.54, 2014-19.65, 2015- 20.16, 2016- 20.87i/20.71, 2017- 21.30, 2018- 21.33. pb DT 63.76 '17.
Father Mirko Yugoslav CC champion 1987-8.

Stipe ZUNIC b. 13 Dec 1990 Zadar 1.88m 115kg. ASK Split. Sociology student at University of Florida, USA.
At SP: OG: '16- 11; WCh: '17- 3; EC: '14-16-18: 4/9/7; WY: '07- dnq 29; EI: '15- 7, '17- 5; NCAA indoor champion 2015. At JT: WJ: '08- dnq 18; WY: '07- 7; EJ: '09- 9 (11 DT); EU23: '11- 11; Croatian champion SP 2015-18, JT 2009-10.
Three Croatian shot records 2017.
Progress at SP: 2007- 15.36, 2008- 15.87, 2009-16.83, 2011- 17.39i/16.60, 2012- 17.30i, 2014- 20.68, 2015- 21.11i/20.38, 2016- 20.61i/20.60, 2017- 21.48, 2018- 21.36. pbs: DT 59.09 '15, JT 77.89 '12
Huge improvement at shot in 2014-15 after switching from javelin. Formerly world junior champion at kick-boxing.

Women

Sara KOLAK b. 22 Jun 1995 Koprivnica 1.70m 74kg. AK Kvarner Rijeka.
At JT: OG: '16- 1; WCh: '17- 4; EC: '14- dnq 21, 16- 3; WJ: '12- dnq 23, '14- 3; EU23: '17- 1EJ: '13- 3; Croatian champion 2012-14, 2016.

11 Croatian JT records 2013-17.
Progress at JT: 2008- 31.78, 2009- 43.13, 2010-55.69, 2011- 45.94, 2012- 53.98, 2013- 57.79, 2014-57.79, 2016- 66.18, 2017- 68.43.
National javelin records 63.50 for 3rd EC, and at OG 64.30 qualifying and 66.18 for gold in final.

Sandra PERKOVIC b. 21 Jun 1990 Zagreb 1.83m 80kg. Zagreb.
At DT(/SP): OG: '12- 1, '16- 1; WCh: '09-13-15-17: 9/1/2/1; EC: '10-12-14-16-18: 1/1/1/1/1; WJ: '06-dnq 21, '08- 3/dnq 13; WY: '07- 2/dnq 13; EJ: '07- 2, '09- 1/5; CCp: '10-14-18: 2/3/1. Won DL 2012-17, Med G 2013, 2018; CRO SP 2008-10, DT 2010, 2012.
9 Croatian DT records 2009-14, 2 SP 2010-11.
Progress at DT: 2004- 30.37, 2005- 36.21, 2006-50.11, 2007- 55.42, 2008- 55.89, 2009- 62.79, 2010-66.93, 2011- 67.96/69.99dq, 2012- 69.11, 2013-68.96, 2014- 71.08, 2015- 70.08, 2016- 70.88, 2017-71.41, 2018- 71.38. pb SP 16.99i/16.40 '11.
First woman to win European and Olympic gold for Croatia, now has record five European titles. Won 74 of 83 competitions 2012-18, inc. all seven competitions in 2016. Ties women's record with six Diamond League titles. Her 70.51 and 71.08 to win her third European title in 2014 and her 71.41 in 2017 were the women's world's best discus throws since 1992. Six months drugs ban 2011.

Ana SIMIC b. 5 May 1990 Gradacac, Bosnia 1.77m 58kg. Zagreb.
At HJ: OG: '12/16- dnq 29=/22=; WCh: '13/17-dnq 19/25, '15- 9=; EC: '10-12-16: dnq 22=/20/14, '14- 3, '18- 10=; WJ: '08- dnq 14=; WY: '07- dnq 21=; EU23: '11- 7; EJ: '09- dnq 18; CCp: '14- 3; EI: '17- 7; won CRO 2006-09, 2011, 2015, 2017-18.
Progress at HJ: 2003- 1.66, 2004- 1.73, 2005- 1.69, 2006- 1.78, 2007- 1.73, 2008- 1.82, 2009- 1.87, 2010-1.92, 2011- 1.92, 2012- 1.91i/1.88, 2013- 1.96, 2014-1.99, 2015- 1.95i/1.94, 2016- 1.96, 2017- 1.92i/1.90, 2018- 1.92i/1.91.

CUBA

Governing body: Federación Cubana de Atletismo. Founded 1922.
National Champions 2018: Men: HMar: Yuleidys La O 70:06, Mar: Henrry Jaen 2:33:59. **Women**: HMar: Lisandra Gómez 1:27:44, Mar: Yudileyvis Castillo 2:53:51. *Other events not held.*

Andy DÍAZ b. 25 Dec 1995 Guanabacoa, La Habana 1.91m 80kg.
At TJ: WCh: '17- 7; WJ: '14- 4. Won CUB 2017, 2019.
Progress at TJ: 2010- 13.29, 2012- 14.44, 2013-15.70, 2014- 16.38/16.43w, 2015- 16.81, 2016-16.80, 2017- 17.40, 2018- 16.52, 2019- 17.22. pb LJ 7.40 '17.

Jordan Alejandro **DÍAZ** b. 23 Feb 2001 La Habana 1.92m 73kg.
At TJ: WJ: '18- 1; WY: '17- 1; CAG: '18- 2.; YthOG:

'18- 1 Won NACAC 2018.
Three world U18 triple jump records 2017-18.
Progress at TJ: 2015- 15.02, 2016- 15.65, 2017-
17.30A/16.66, 2018- 17.41, 2019- 16.77i/17.41w.
Juan Miguel ECHEVARRÍA b. 11 Aug 1998
Camagüey 1.86m 76kg.
At LJ: WCh: '17- dnq 15; WJ: '16- 5, WY: '15- 4;
WI: '18- 1. Cuban champion 2016, 20-19.
Progress at LJ: 2012- 5.69, 2013- 6.36, 2014- 7.47,
2015- 8.05, 2016-7.96/8.15w, 2017- 8.28/8.34w,
2018- 8.68/8.83w, 8.92w. Pb TJ 14.67 '14

Lázaro MARTÍNEZ b. 3 Nov 1997 Guantánamo
1.92m 85kg.
At TJ: OG: '16- 8; WCh: '17- 12; WJ: '14- 1, '16- 1;
WY: '13- 1; CAG: '14- 2; PAm-J: '13- 1. Won CUB
2016. World youth triple jump record 2014.
Progress at TJ: 2011- 14.62, 2012- 15.38, 2013-
16.63, 2014- 17.24, 2015- 17.02, 2016- 17.06, 2017-
17.07, 2018- 17.28.

Maykel Demetrio **MASSÓ** b. 8 May 1999
Santiago de Cuba 1.78m 69kg.
At LJ: OG: '16- dnq 15; WCh: '15- dnq 23, '17- 5;
WJ: '16- 1; WY: '15- 1; CUB champion 2017.
CAC junior long jump record 2017.
Progress at LJ: 2013- 6.41, 2014- 7.59, 2015- 0.12,
2016- 8.28, 2017- 8.33, 2018- 7.92, 2019-8.22/ 8.30w.

Cristian Atanay **NÁPOLES** b. 27 Nov 1998
Marianao, La Habana 1.81m 80kg.
At TJ: WCh: '17- 4; WJ: '16- 2; WY: '15- 1; CAG:
'18- 1; CCp: '18- 2. Won IbAm 2018.
Progress at TJ: 2013- 14.41, 2014- 15.42, 2015-
16.45, 2016- 16.92, 2017- 17.27, 2018- 17.34. pb LJ
6.96 '16.

Leonel SUÁREZ b. 1 Sep 1987 Holguín 1.81m
78kg.
At Dec: OG: '08- 3, '12- 3, '16- 6; WCh: '09-11-13-
17: 2/3/10/dnf; PAm: '07-11-15: 4/1/dnf; CAG:
'18- 1. CAC champion 2009, Cuban 2009, 2015-
16. At Hep: WI: '10- 7.
Decathlon records: 4 CUB 2008-09, CAC 2009.
Progress at Dec: 2005- 7267, 2006- 7357, 2007-
8156, 2008- 8527, 2009- 8654, 2010- 8328, 2011-
8501, 2012- 8523, 2013- 8317, 2015- 8027, 2016-
8460, 2017- 8214 pb: 60m 7.11i '09, 100m 10.90
'08, 10.6w '06; 400m 47.65 '09, 1000m 2:36.12i '10,
1500m 4:16.70 '08, 60mh 7.90i '10, 110mh 14.12
'08, HJ 2.17 '08, PV 5.00 '09, LJ 7.52 '11, SP 15.20
'09, DT 47.32 '11, JT 78.29 '16, Hep 5964i '10.
Won at Talence 2010. Won IAAF Combined
Events Challenge 2011.

Women

Rose Mary ALMANZA b. 13 Jul 1992
Camagüey 1.65m 55kg.
At 800m: OG: '12- sf, '16- h; WCh: '13/15/17- sf;
WJ: '10- 4; WY: '09- 4; PAm: '11- 4, '15- 4; CAG:
'14- 1, '18- 1/1 1500m/1R; WUG: '17- 1. Won
Cuban 800m 2010-11, 2014-15, 2017, 2019; 1500m
2013, 2015, 2017, 2019.
Two CAC junior 800m records 2010-11.

Progress at 800m: 2008- 2:11.1, 2009- 2:03.61,
2010- 2:02.04, 2011- 2:00.56, 2012- 1:59.55, 2013-
1:59.4, 2014- 1:59.48, 2015- 1:57.70, 2016- 1:58.49,
2017- 1:59.11, 2018- 2:00.15. pbs: 400m 53.66 '17,
600m 1:26.33mx '14, 1:26.9 '13; 1000m 2:38.1 '14,
1500m 4:14.53 '14.

Denia CABALLERO b. 13 Jan 1990 Caibarién,
Villa Clara 1.75m 80kg. VCL.
At DT: OG: '12- dnq 25, '16- 3; WCh: '11-13-15-17:
9/8/1/5; PAm: '11- 3, '15- 1; CAG: '14- 1, '18- 2.
Won CAC 2011, Cuban 2015.
Progress at DT: 2006- 43.77, 2007- 46.08, 2008-
52.10, 2009- 57.21, 2010- 59.92, 2011- 62.94, 2012-
65.60, 2013- 63.47, 2014- 64.89, 2015- 70.65, 2016-
67.62, 2017- 67.04, 2018- 66.09.

Yaimé PÉREZ b. 29 May 1991 Santiago de Cuba
1.72m 80kg.
At DT: OG: '12- dnq 28, '16- nt; WCh: '13- 11,
'15- 4, '17- 4; WJ: '10- 1; PAm: '15- 2; CAG: '14- 2,
'18- 1; CCp: '14- 5, '18- 2. Cuban champion 2013-
14, 2016-17m 2019; NACAC 2018, DL 2018.
Progress at DT: 2007- 46.29, 2008- 51.80, 2009-
55.23, 2010- 59.30, 2011- 59.26, 2012- 62.50, 2013-
66.01, 2014- 66.03, 2015- 67.13, 2016- 68.86, 2017-
69.19, 2018- 67.82. pbs SP 13.88 '08.

Liadagmis POVEA b. 6 Feb 1996 1.65m 61kg.
Pinar del Rio.
At TJ: OG: '16- dnq 15; WCh: '17- dnq 22; PAm:
'15- 6; WJ: '14- 2. Won CUB 2016-17.
Progress at TJ: 2010- 12.09, 2011- 11.89, 2012-
12.88, 2013- 13.54, 2014- 14.02/14.07w, 2015-
14.08, 2016- 14.56, 2017- 14.45, 2018- 14.30/14.44w,
2019- 14.65/15.05w. pb LJ 6.15 '17.

Yorgelis RODRÍGUEZ b. 25 Jan 1995
Guantánamo 1.71m 65kg.
At Hep: OG: '16- 7; WCh: '13- 12, '15- 21, '17- 4;
WJ: '12- 1; '14- 2 (dnq 16= HJ); WY: '11- 2; PAm:
'15- 1; CAG: '18- 1; At Pen: WI: '18- 3; won
PAmCp 2013, 2015; CAG 2014, Cuban HJ 2017,
Hep 2013, 2016.
Heptathlon records: CAC 2017 & 2018, 2 Cuban
2016-17, 3 CAC junior 2012-14.
Progress at Hep: 2012- 5994, 2013- 6186, 2014-
6231, 2015- 6332, 2016- 6481, 2017- 6594, 2018-
6742. pbs: 200m 23.98 '18, 800m 2:10.48 '17, 60mh
8.57i '18, 100mh 13.48 '18, HJ 1.95 '17, LJ 6.41 '17,
SP 14.64 '16, JT 48.96 '18, Pen 4637i '18.
Three HJ pbs from 1.89, 1.92 & 1.95 in World
heptathlon 2017.

Yarisley SILVA b. 1 Jun 1987 Pinar del Río
1.61m 62kg.
At PV: OG: '08- dnq 27=, '12- 2, '16- 7=; WCh:
'11-13-15-17: 5/3/1/3=; WI: '12-14-18: 7/1/7; WJ:
'06- dnq; PAm: '07-11-15: 3/1/1; CAG: '14- 1, '18-
1; CCp: 18- 4; Won CAC 2009, Cuban 2004, 2006-
07, 2009, 2012-13, 2015, 2017, 2019.
Pole vault records: 19 Cuban & CAC 2007-15 (9
in 2011), 8 CAC indoor 2012 & 2013 (to 4.82).
Progress at PV: 2001- 2.50, 2002- 3.10, 2003- 3.70,
2004- 4.00, 2005- 4.10, 2006- 4.20, 2007- 4.30,

2008- 4.50, 2009- 4.50, 2010- 4.40, 2011-
4.75A/4.70, 2012- 4.75, 2013- 4.90, 2014- 4.70,
2015- 4.91, 2016- 4.84, 2017- 4.81, 2018- 4.80.

CYPRUS

Governing body: Amateur Athletic
Association of Cyprus. Founded 1983.
National Championships first held in 1896,
1952 (women). **2018 Champions**: 100m: F
Ioannou 11.00, 200m: Paisios Dimitriades 22.0,
400m: Stavros Spyrou 49.14, 800m/1500m:
Amoine Khadiri 1:57.61/3:52.91, 5000m/
3000mSt: Nikolas Frangou 14:59.45/9:10.94,
110mh: Milan Trajkovic 13.78, 400mh:
Anastasios Vasiliou 56.03, HJ: Vasilios
Constantinou 2.04, PV: Nikandros Stylianou
5.40, LJ: Georgios Kyriakou 7.45w, TJ: Andreas
Chrysanthou 15.35w, SP: Georgios Koniarskis
15.84, DT: Apostolos Parellis 60.50, HT:
Alexandros Pousanides 66.11, JT: Spyros Savva
60.67. **Women**: 100m: Olivia Fotopoulou 11.90,
200m/400m: Eleni Artymata 24.97/51.91,
800m/1500m: Natalia Evangelidou 2:11.71/
4:22.53, 5000m: Meropi Panagiotou 17:23.06,
3000mSt: Chrystalla Hadjipolydorou 10:43.08,
100mh: Natalia Christofi 13.69, 400mh:
Christiana Katsari 65.01, HJ: Despina
Charalambous 1.70, PV: Maria Aristotelous
3.70, LJ: Nektaria Panagi 6.77w, TJ: Elecytra
Papakonstantinou 12.00w, SP: Styliana
Kyrioakidou 13.88, DT: Androniki Lada 52.33,
HT: Chrytstalla Kyriakou 55.20, JT: Mariele
Rousi 42.87.

Apostolos PARELLIS b. 24 Jul 1985 Limassol
1.86m 110kg.
At DT: OG: '12- dnq 13, '16- 8; WCh: '13-15-17:
dnq 19/6/10; CG: '10-14-18: 4/2/3; EC: '10-12-14-
16: dnq 17/13/16/18, '18- 8 EU23: '07- 3. Won
CYP 2007-18, MedG 2018.
17 CYP discus records 2007-16.
Progress at DT: 2004- 48.40, 2005- 50.88, 2006-
53.77, 2007- 58.16, 2008- 56.41, 2009- 61.07, 2010-
61.92, 2011- 61.44, 2012- 65.36, 2013- 62.48, 2014-
63.89, 2015- 65.04, 2016- 65.69, 2017- 65.13, 2018-
63.62.

Milan TRAJKOVIC b. 17 Mar 1992 Surdulica,
Serbia 1.87m 72kg. GS Olympia, Limassol
At 110mh: OG: '16- 7; WCh: '17- sf; EC: '14-16-18:
h/5/sf; CG: '14- h, '18- 4; EU23: '13- 8. At 60mh:
EI: '17- 6, '19- 1. CYP champion 2012-18, Blakan
2016.
8 CYP 110m hurdles records 2013-17.
Progress at 110mh: 2011- 14.57, 2012- 14.09, 2013-
13.67, 2014- 13.65, 2015- 13.78, 2016- 13.31, 2017-
2018- 13.25, 2018- 13.36. pbs: 60m 6.78i '16, 200m
21.56 '15, 60mh 7.51i '18
Family moved to Cyrpus when he was nine.

CZECH REPUBLIC

Governing body: Cesky atleticky svaz. AAU of
Bohemia founded in 1897.

National Championships first held in 1907
(Bohemia), 1919 (Czechoslovakia), 1993 CZE.
2018 Champions: **Men**: 100m: Zdenek Stromsík
10.43, 200m: Jan Jirka 20.75, 400m: Pavel Maslák
46.09, 800m: Lukás Hodbod 1:47.36, 1500m: Jan
Fris 3:55.06, 5000m: Jakub Zemaník 14:29.69,
10000m: Lukás Olejnicek 31:30.26, HMar/Mar:
Jiri Homolac 66:15/2:20:09, 3000mSt: Jáchym
Kovár 9:01.97, 110mh: David Sklenár 14.20,
400mh: Michal Broz 50.16, HJ: Jaroslav Bába
2.14, PV: Jan Kudlicka 5.50, LJ: Radek Juska 7.92,
TJ: Jirí Vondrácek 15.49, SP: Tomás Stanek 21.52,
DT: Tomás Vonavka 57.87, HT: Miroslav
Pavlicek 69.18, JT: Petr Frydrych 83.85, Dec: Jan
Dolezal 8033, 20kW: Lukás Gdula 1:31:04, 50kW:
none. **Women**: 100m: Klára Seidlová 11.64,
200m: Janina Slaninová 23.72, 400m: Alena
Symerská 53.02, 800m: Simona Vrzalová 2:10.64,
1500m: Lucie Sekanová 4:21.54, 5000,: Kristiina
Mäki 16:34.69, 10000m: Moira Stewartová
35:52.37, HMar: Petra Kaminková 1:21:01, Mar:
Petra Pastorová 2:48:40, 3000mSt: Eva Krchová
10:11.69, 100mh: Lucie Koudelová 13.75, 400mh:
Zuzana Hejnová 56.08, HJ: Michaela Hrubá
1.88, PV: Amálie Svábíková 4.25, LJ: Adéla
Záhorová 6.29, TJ: Lucie Májková 12.93, SP:
Markéta Cervenková 16.39, DT: Eliska Stanková
56.76, HT: Katerina Skypalová 66.98, JT: Nikola
Ogrodníková 62.24, Hep: Barbora Zatloukalová
5557, 20kW: Anezka Drahotová 1:32:22.

Petr FRYDRYCH b. 13 Jan 1988 Klatovy 1.98m
99kg. Dukla Praha.
At JT: OG: '12- dnq 33, '16- 12; WCh: '09- 10, '11-
15: dnq 24/30, '17- 3; EC: '10- 10, '12/14- dnq
2/19, '18- 12; WJ: '06- dnq 16; WY: '05- 11; EU23:
'09- 2; EJ: '07- 9; ET: '09- 6, '11- 4. Won CZE 2009,
2018
Progress at JT: 2004- 57.89, 2005- 65.97, 2006-
70.91, 2007- 75.55, 2008- 74.13, 2009- 84.96, 2010-
88.23, 2011- 85.32, 2012- 81.14, 2013- 82.39, 2014-
85.07, 2015- 85.52, 2016- 84.10, 2017- 88.32, 2018-
83.85.

Jakub HOLUSA b. 20 Feb 1988 Opava 1.83m
72kg. Dukla Praha.
At 800m: OG: '08/12- h; EC: '10/12: 5/5; EU23:
'09- h; WI: '10- 5, '12- 2. At 1500m: OG: '16- sf;
WCh: '15- h, '17- 5; EC: '14-16-18: dns/dq h/h;
EU23: '09- 3; WI: '14- 5, '16- 2; EI: '11- 5, '15- 1; ET:
'14- 1 (2 3000m). At 3000m: ET: '17- 1. At
2000mSt: WY: '05- 7. At 3000mSt: EJ: '13- 1. Eur
CC: "17- 2 mxR. Won CZE 800m 2008, 5000m
2014, 2017. 3 Czech 1500m records 2015-18.
Progress at 1500m: 2003- 4:21.89, 2004- 4:04.47,
2005- 3:58.06, 2006- 3:56.23, 2007- 3:46.93, 2008-
3:41.88i/3:43.02, 2009- 3:42.15, 2010- 3:38.47, 2011-
3:38.10, 2012- 3:42.44i/3:42.79, 2013- 3:38.71, 2014-
3:35.26, 2015- 3:34.26, 2016- 3:33.36, 2017- 3:34.26,
2018- 3:32.49. pbs: 400m 47.29 '10, 800m 1:45.12
'12, 1000m 2:16.79 '14, 1M 3:53.46 '14, 3000m
7:51.39 '17, 5000m 14:06.32 '14, 2000mSt 5:43.39
'05, 3000mSt 8:50.30 '07, 400mh 54.46 '07.

Has used devastating sprint finish to good effect in major championships.

Radek JUSKA b. 8 Mar 1993 Hustopece 1.95m 82kg. PSK Olymp Praha.
At LJ: OG: '16- dnq 13; WCh: '15- 11, '17- 10; EC: '16- 4, '18- 12; WJ: '12- dnq 24; EU23: '15- 2; WI: '18- 7; EI: '15- 2, '19- 2; WUG: '17- 1; ET: '17- 3. Czech champion 2014-15, 2017-18.
Two Czech long jump records 2017.
Progress at LJ: 2009- 6.30, 2010- 6.60, 2011- 7.10/7.13w, 2012- 7.71, 2013- 7.60, 2014- 7.94, 2015- 8.15, 2016- 8.11, 2017- 8.31, 2018- 8.27. pb TJ 15.57 '18.

Pavel MASLÁK b. 21 Feb 1991 Havírov 1.76m 67kg. Dukla Praha.
At 400m: OG: '12- sf (h 200m), '16- sf; WCh: '13- 5, '15- h, '17- sf; EC: '12-16-18: 1/2.sf; WY: '07- h; WI: '12-14-16-18: 5/1/1/1; EI: '13- 1/3R, '15&17- 1/3R. At 200m: WCh: '11- sf; WJ: '10- 7; EU23: '11- 3, '13- 3; EJ: '09- 5/2R. At 100m: WJ: '08- h. Won CZE 200m 2012-13, 2015, 2017; 400m 2011, 2018. European indoor 300m & 500m bests 2014. Czech records: 200m (5) 2012-17, 300m, 400m (5) 2012-14.
Progress at 400m: 2006- 50.41, 2007- 48.30, 2008- 47.60, 2009- 47.44, 2010- 46.09, 2011- 47.05i/47.40, 2012- 44.91, 2013- 44.84, 2014- 44.79, 2015- 45.09, 2016- 45.06, 2017- 45.10, 2018- 45.47i/45.64. pbs: 60m 6.65i '14, 100m 10.35 '16, 200m 20.46 '17, 300m 31.80 '17, 500m 1:00.35 '13.
European Athletics Rising Star Award 2012. Master of indoor running.

Tomás STANEK b. 13 Jun 1991 Prague 1.90m 127kg. Dukla Praha.
At SP: OG: '16- dnq 20; WCh: '15- dnq 19, '17- 4; EC: '14: dnq 14, '18- 4; EU23: '13- 5; WI: '18- 3; EI: 17- 2, '19- 3; CCp: '18- 5; ET: '17- 1. CZE champion 2016-18. Two Czech records 2017.
Progress at SP: 2009- 15.01, 2010- 15.40, 2011- 17.16, 2012- 18.52, 2013- 19.50, 2014- 20.93, 2015- 20.94i/20.64, 2016- 21.30i/21.26, 2017- 22.01, 2018- 22.17i/21.87.

Jakub VADLEJCH b. 10 Oct 1990 Praha 1.90m 93kg. Dukla Praha.
At JT: OG: '12- dnq 24, '16- 8; WCh: '11/15- dnq 16/20, '17- 2; EC: '10-14-16-18: dnq 16/dnq 20/9/8; WJ: '08- 10; WY: '07- 12; EJ: '09- 8; CCp: '18- 2; ET: '17- 1. Won DL 2016-17, Czech 2014-15, 2017.
Progress at JT: 2006- 55.24, 2007- 66.12, 2008- 76.59, 2009- 81.95, 2010- 84.47, 2011- 84.08, 2012- 80.40A, 2013- 75.85, 2014- 82.97, 2015- 86.21, 2016- 88.02, 2017- 89.73, 2018- 89.02.
Married Lucia Slanícková (SVK records: 400mh 56.96 '14, Hep 6103 '17) in October 2017.

Vitezslav VESELY b. 27 Feb 1983 Hodonin 1.86m 94kg. Dukla Praha.
At JT: OG: '08- 12, '12- 3, '16- 7; WCh: '09-11-13-15-17: dnq 28/4/1/8/dnq 26; EC: '10-12-14-16: 9/1/2/2; WJ: '02- 9; CCp: '14- 2. Won DL 2012-13, CZE 2008, 2010-12, 20-16.

Progress at JT: 2001- 66.18, 2002- 73.22, 2003- 66.95, 2004- 72.32, 2006- 75.98, 2007- 79.45, 2008- 81.20, 2009- 80.35, 2010- 86.45, 2011- 84.11, 2012- 88.34, 2013- 87.68, 2014- 87.38, 2015- 88.18, 2016- 84.82, 2017- 82.29, 2018- 82.30.

Women

Katerina CACHOVÁ b. 26 Feb 1990 Ostrava 1.73m 63kg. USK Praha.
At Hep: OG: '16- 24; WCh: '11- 20, '17- 15; EC: '10-16-18: 16/6/6; WJ: '06- 15; WY: '05- 11, '07- 1; EU23: '11- 2; EJ: '07- dnf (dnq LJ), '09- 2; WUG: '11- 3. At Pen: WI: '16- 7, 18- 11. Won CZE 100m 2009, 100mh 2015-17, Hep 2010, 2013, 2016-17.
Progress at Hep: 205- 4212, 2006- 5481, 2007- 5292, 2008- 5706, 2009- 5776, 2010- 5911, 2011- 6123, 2012- 5600, 2013- 5899, 2016- 6328, 2017- 6337(w), 2018- 6400. pbs: 60m 7.68i '17, 100m 12.00 '15, 200m 24.10 '16, 800m 2:12.38 '17, 60mh 8.13i '15, 100mh 13.05 '16, HJ 1.85 '10, LJ 6.40 '08, 6.51w '17; SP 13.32 '18, JT 47.47 '09, Pen 4506i '16.

Anezka DRAHOTOVÁ b. 22 Jul 1995 Rumburk 1.83m 63kg. USK Praha.
At 20kW: OG: '16- 10; WCh: '13- 7, '15- 8, '17- dnf; EC: '14- 3, '18- 2; EU23: '15- 2, '17- 7; WT: '18- 6. At 10000mW: WJ: '12- 6, '14- 1; EJ: '11- 13, '13- 1 (9 3000mSt); WCp: '14- 3J; ECp: '13- 2J, '15- 4. At 5000mW: WY: '11- 6. World Mountain Running: '12- 7J. Won CZE 20kW 2014-15, 2017-18.
World junior 10000m walk record 2014. Czech records 3000mW 2015, 5000mW 2018, 10000mW 2013, 20kW (4) 2013-15.
Progress at 20kW: 2013- 1:29:05, 2014- 1:28:08. 2015- 1:26:53, 2016- 1:30:21, 2017- 1:33:18, 2018- 1:27:03. pbs: 1500m 4:24.46i '14, 4:24.89 '13, 3000m 9:26.28 '13, 5000m 16:03.18 '15, 3000mSt 10:10.45 '13, 10kmRd 33:59 '13, 3000mW 11:52.38 '15, 5000mW 20:48.75 '18, 10000mW 42:47.25 '14, HMar 74:25 '14.
19th junior women's world road race at cycling in 2013 and also a CZE champion. Twin Eliska 4/3 EJ 10000mW 2011/2013, pb 20kW 1:37:39 '14.

Zuzana HEJNOVÁ b. 19 Dec 1986 Liberec 1.70m 54kg. Dukla Praha.
At 400mh/4x400mR: OG: '08- 7, '12- 3, '16- 4; WCh: '05-07-09- sf, '11-13-15-17: 7/1/1/4; EC: '06-10-12-18: sf/4/4&3R/sf; WJ: '02- 5, '04- 2; EU23: '07- 3; EJ: '03- 3; '05- 1; WY: '03- 1; WI: '10- 3R; ET: '09- 3, '11- 1. Won DL 2013, 2015. At 400m: EI: '13- 4/3R, '17- 2. At Pen: EI: '11- 7. Won CZE 400m 2006, 2009; 400mh 2018.
12 Czech 400m records 2005-13. 3 world bests 300mh 2011 (38.91) and 2013 (38.75 & 38.16).
Progress at 400mh: 2002- 58.42, 2003- 57.54, 2004- 57.44, 2005- 55.89, 2006- 55.83, 2007- 55.04, 2008- 54.96, 2009- 54.90, 2010- 54.13, 2011- 53.29, 2012- 53.38, 2013- 52.83, 2014- 55.86, 2015- 53.50, 2016- 53.92, 2017- 53.93, 2018- 55.16. pbs: 60m 7.64i '17, 150m 17.66 '13, 200m 23.65 '13, 300m 37.49A/37.80 '13, 400m 51.90/51.27i '13, 600m 1:28.04i '15, 800m 2:03.40i '16, 60mh 8.24i '17,

100mh 13.36 '11, 13.18w '10; 200mh 26.29 '17, 300mh 38.16 '13, HJ 1.80i '11, 1.74 '04; LJ 5.96i '11, 5.76 '07, SP 12.11i '11, JT 36.11 '10, Pen 4453i '11. Unbeaten season at hurdles in 2013. Sister of Michaela Hejnová (b. 10 Apr 1980) pb Hep 6174w/6065 '04; OG: '04- 26; EC '02- 7; EU23: '01- 5; WJ: '98- 5; EJ: '97- 6/'99- 6 (100mh); WUG: '01- 5, '03- 3.

Michaela HRUBÁ b. 21 Feb 1998 Boskovice 1.91m 75kg. USK Praha.
At HJ: OG: '16- dnq 18; WCh: '17- 11; EC: '16- 12, '18- 6; WJ: '14- 2, '16- 1; WY: '15- 1; EJ: '17- 1; EI: '15-17-19: 8/6/6; YOG: '14- 3; ET: '17- 3. CZE champion 2017-18.
Progress at HJ: 2011- 1.52, 2012- 1.66, 2013- 1.83, 2014- 1.91, 2015- 1.91i/1.90, 2016- 1.95i/1.93, 2017- 1.94, 2018- 1.93i/1.91. Pbs: 100mh 15.42 '12, 200mh 29.60 '13, LJ 6.02i '18, TJ 13.19 '178

Nikola OGRODNÍKOVÁ b. 18 Aug 1990 Ostrava 1.75m 73kg. Dukla Praha.
At JT (Hep): WCh: '17- dnq 19; EC: '14- dnq 20, '18- 2; WJ: '08- 8 (22); WY: '07- (7); EU23: '11- dnq 22; EJ: '07- (3), '09- dnq 17; CCp: '18- 6; CZE champion 2018
Progress at JT: 2004- 36.49, 205- 43.06, 2006- 42.94, 2007- 50.41, 2008- 54.48, 2009- 53.58, 2010- 53.94, 2011- 54.46, 2012- 54.07, 2013- 56.20, 2014- 60.04, 2015- 56.30, 2016- 58.18, 2017- 62.24, 2018- 65.61A. Pbs: 200m 25.67 '07, 800m 2:21.92 '07, 60mh 8.44i '18, 100mh 13.75 '09, HJ 1.72 '07, LJ 5.77/5.79w '07, SP 12.82 '07, Pen 4068i '08, Hep 5607 '07.

Barbora SPOTÁKOVÁ b. 30 Jun 1981 Jablonec nad Nisou 1.82m 80kg. Dukla Praha.
At JT: OG: '04- dnq 23, '08- 1, '12- 1, '16- 3; WCh: '05-07-09-11-15-17: dnq 13/1/2/1/9/1; EC: '02-06-10-14-16: dnq 17/2/3/1/5; EU23: '03- 6; WUG: '03- 4, '05- 1; CCp: '14- 1; ET: '09-11-14-17: 2/3/1;/1 won DL 2010, 2012, 2014-15, 2017; WAF 2006-09, Czech 2003, 2005-12, 2015-17. At Hep: WJ: '00- 4.
World javelin record 2008, two European records 2008, 11 Czech records 2006-08. World heptathlon javelin best (60.90) in 2012.
Progress at JT: 1996- 31.32, 1997- 37.28, 1998- 44.56, new: 1999- 41.69, 2000- 54.15, 2001- 51.97, 2002- 56.76, 2003- 56.65, 2004- 60.95, 2005- 65.74, 2006- 66.21, 2007- 67.12, 2008- 72.28, 2009- 68.23, 2010- 68.66, 2011- 71.58, 2012- 69.55, 2013- 62.33, 2014- 67.99, 2015- 65.66, 2016- 66.87, 2017- 68.26. pbs: 200m 25.33/25.11w '00, 800m 2:18.29 '00, 60mh 8.68i '07, 100mh 13.99 '00, 400mh 62.68 '98, HJ 1.78 '00, LJ 5.65 '00, SP 14.53 '07, DT 36.80 '02, Hep 5880 '12, Dec 6749 '04.
Sons Janek born 24 May 2013 and Darek on 14 July 2018.

DENMARK
Governing body: Dansk Athletik Forbund. Founded 1907.

National Championships first held in 1894.
2018 Champions: Men: 100m: Frederick Schou 10.56, 200m/LJ: Andreas Trajkovski 21.73/7.45, 400m: Gustav Lundholm Nielsen 48.61, 800m: Andreas Bube 1:51.64, 1500m: Thijs Nijhuis 3:50.86, 5000m: Peter Glans 14:13.92, 10000m/ 3000mSt: Ole Hesselbjerg 30:13.80/8:55.57, Mar: Jesper Faurschou 2:24:30, 110mh: Andeeas Martinsen 13.87, 400mh: Jacob Aagaard Jensen 54.21, HJ: Jonas Kløjgaard Jensen 2.15, PV: Rasmus W. Jørgensen 4.75, TJ: Peder P.Nielsen 16.05, SP: Kenneth Mertz 16.65, DT: Emil Mikkelsen 54.65, HT: Brian Nielsen 59.42, JT: Mikkel Garbrecht 65.55, Dec: Christian Nielsen 6792, 5000mW: Andreas W. Nielsen 21:43.87.
Women: 100m/200m: Mathilde Kramer 11.64/23.85, 400m: Ida Karstoft 55.96, 800m/ 3000mSt: Anna Emilie Møller 2:09.67/9:34.85, 1500m: Revekka Fuglø 4:29.62, 5000m: Alberte Kjær Pedersen 16:34.62, 10000m: Laura Valgreen 35:24.83, HMar: Cecilie Mikkelsen 79:20, Mar: Sandra Hartvich Lorentzon 2:52:13, 100mh: Mathilde Heltbech 13.89, 400mh: Martha Danneskjold Rasmussen 61.99, HJ: Rikke Andersen 1.72, PV: Line Renée Jensen 3.85, LJ/ TJ: Janne Nielsen 5.86/13.32, SP: Trine Mulbjerg 15.14, DT: Lisa Brix Pedersen 53.63, HT: Lise Lotte Jepsen 58.47, JT: Liv Cantby 43.26, Hep: Sandra Böll 5082.

Sara SLOTT PETERSEN b. 9 Apr 1987 Nykøbing Falster, Sjælland 1.71m 57kg. Århus 1900 AM.
At 400mh: OG: 12- sf, '16- 2; WCh: '09/11/17- sf, '15- 4; EC: '10-12-14-16-18: h/sf/h/1/sf; WJ: '04- h; WY: '03- 4; EU23: '07- 6, '09- 6; EJ: '05- 4; WUG: '09- 3, '11-4; Won Danish 400mh 2002-09, 2011-12, 2014-15; 100m 2007, 2009; 200m 2009, 2012, 2016-17; 400m 2008-09.
12 Danish 400m records 2007-16.
Progress at 400mh: 2002- 60.67, 2003- 59.42, 2004- 60.60, 2005- 58.21, 2006- 57.65, 2007- 57.01, 2008- 57.06, 2009- 56.40, 2010- 57.28, 2011- 55.97, 2012- 55.68, 2014- 56.44, 2015- 53.99, 2016- 53.55, 2017-54.35, 2018- 55.48. pbs: 60m 7.62i '15, 100m 12.07 '07, 11.93w '09; 200m 23.59 '16. 400m 52.59i/53.55 '16, 1500m 4:27.96 '11, 60mh 8.58i '07, 100mh 14.25 '05.
Her silver was the best ever for a Danish woman at the Olympics. Partner of Thomas Cortebeeck, their son Tobias born 8 Oct 2013.

DJIBOUTI
Hassan **Ayanleh SOULEIMAN** b. 3 Dec 1992 Djibouti City 1.77m 60kg.
At (800m)/1500m: OG: '16- sf/4; WCh: '13- 3/sf, '15/17- h; WI: '12- 5; AfG: '11- 6; AfCh: '12- 2/1/4; CCp: '14- 1; WI: '14- 1, '16- 9; won DL 2013, Arab G 2011, Franc G 2013. At 3000m: WY: '09- h. Won Arab 5000m 2015.
World indoor 1000m record 2016. DJI records: 800m (5) 2012-15, 1000m (2) 2013-16, 1500m (3)

2011-14, 1M (3) 2012-14, 3000m 2012.
Progress at 800m, 1500m: 2011- 1:51.78A, 3:34.32;
2012- 1:47.45, 3:30.31; 2013- 1:43.63, 3:31.64; 2014-
1:43.69, 3:29.58; 2015- 1:42.97, 3:30.17; 2016-
1:43.52, 3:31.68; 2017- 1:45.01, 3:34.70; 2018-
3:31.19. pbs: 1000m 2:13.49 '16, 1M 3:47.32 '14,
3000m 7:39.81i '13, 7:42.22 '12, 5000m 13:17.97 '15.
Djibouti's first ever world champion 2013 and
first to set an official world record.

DOMINICAN REPUBLIC

Governing body: Federación Dominicana de
Asociaciones de Atletismo. Founded 1953.

Luguelín SANTOS b. 12 Nov 1992 Bayaguana
1.73m 61kg. Universidad Interamericana de San
Germán, Puerto Rico.
At 400m: OG: '12- 2, '16- sf; WCh: '13- 3 (h
200m), '15- 4, '17- h; WJ: '10- 6, '12- 1; PAm: '11-
2/2R, '15- 1; CAG: '18- 1/2R; CCp: '14- 5, '18-
6/1mxR; YthOG: '10- 1; WI: '18- dq (2); WUG:
'15- 1, '17- 1. Won BolG 2017.
DOM records 200m 2013, 400m (5) 2011-15. CAC
indoor 600m best 2015.
Progress at 400m: 2009- 47.88, 2010- 46.19, 2011-
44.71A, 2012- 44.45, 2013- 44.52, 2014- 44.53,
2015- 44.11, 2016- 44.71, 2017- 45.24, 2018- 44.59.
pbs: 200m 20.55A '13, 20.70 '16; 300m 32.0+, '15,
32.56 '12, 500m 59.75 '15, 600m 1:15.58 '16, 800m
1:48.67 '17.
Over-age at the 2010 Youth Olympics and 2012
World Juniors. Younger brother **Juander** (b. 7
May 1995) has pbs 400m 45.93A '14; 400mh 48.59
'17, WCh '17- 6; CAG: '18- 3/2R; WUG: '17- 1.

ECUADOR

Governing body: Federación Ecuatoriana de
Atletismo. Founded 1925.

Andrés CHOCHO b. 4 Nov 1983 Cuenca 1.67m
67kg.
At 20kW: OG: '08- 38, '16- dq; WCh: '07-09-15:
dq/36/dq; WCp: '16- 6; SACh: '11- 1, '13- 3;
WUG: '11- 2. At 50kW: OG: '12/16- dq; WCh:
'11-13-15-17: 10/dq/8/dq; PAm: '15- 1; SAG: '18-
1; won BolG 2013, 2017. Won S Am 20kW 2016,
SAm-J 10,000W 2001.
Four S.American 50k records 2011-16.
Progress at 50kW: 2010- 3:54:42, 2011- 3:49:32,
2012- 3:49:26, 2013- 3:58:50, 2014- 3:57:00, 2015-
3:46:00, 2016- 3:42:57A, 2017- 3:47:37, 2018- 3:50:27.
pbs: 10kW 40:28 '16, 41:55.50tA '15, 20kW 1:20:07
'16, 30kW 2:16:46 '14, 35kW 2:36:56 '15.
Married to Érica de Sena (Brazil) (qv).

Alex QUIÑÓNEZ b. 11 Aug 1989 Esmeraldas
1.76m 65kg. FC Barcelona.
At (100m)/200m: OG: '12- 7; WCh: '13- h/sf, '15-
h; PAm: '11- 6, '15- sf; SAG: '14- 3/2, '18- 2/1;
SACh: '11- h, '13- 1/1, '15- 2/1/1R; CCp: '18- 3.
Won IbAm 100m & 200m 2012, BolG 100m &
200m 2013. ECU records 100m 2013 & 2018,
200m (6) 2013-18.

Progress at 200m: 2008- 21.29A, 2009- 21.81w,
2011- 20.49A/21.05/20.95w, 2012- 20.28, 2013-
20.44, 2014- 20.66, 2015- 20.76/20.59w, 2016-
21.05A/21.12, 2017- 20.27, 2018- 19.93A/20.03.
pbs: 60m 6.66i '19, 100m 10.09A '13, 10.13 '17;
400m 47.26A '08

ERITREA

Governing body: Eritrean National Athletics
Federation. Founded 1992.

Ghirmay GHEBRESLASSIE b. 14 Nov 1995
Kisadeka 1.62m 52kg..
At Mar: OG: '16- 4; WCh: '15- 1. World HMar:
'14- 7; CC: '13- 7J; AfCC: '12- 9J.
Progress at Mar: 2014- 2:09:08, 2015- 2:07:47.
2016- 2:07:46, 2017- 2:09:57, 2018- dnf. pbs: 5000m
13:40.17 '12, 10000m 28:33.37 '12; Road: 10M
46:29 '12, HMar 60:09 '13, 25k 1:12:43 '16, 30k
1:28:13 '16.
Youngest ever world marathon champion at 19
in 2015 after 2nd in Hamburg Marathon. Won
New York Marathon 2016.

Aron KIFLE Teklu b. 20 Feb 1998 1.67m 523kg.
At 5000m/(10000m): OG: '16- h; WCh: '15- h,
17- 7/11; AfG: '15- 8; WJ: 16- 5/2. At HMar: WCh:
'18- 3. World CC: '17- 5, '19- 4; AfCC: 16- 3J.
Progress at 5000m, 10000m: 2015- 13:17.62,
28:18.44; 2016- 13:13.39, 27:26.20; 2017- 13:13.31,
27:09.92; 2018- 13:07.59. pbs: 3000m 7:52.19 '17,
15k Rd 45:08 '15, HMar 59:51 '18.

ESTONIA

Governing body: Eesti Kergejõustikuliit.
Founded 1920.

National Championships first held in 1917.
2018 Champions: Men: 100m: Richard Pulst
10.76. 200m: Tony Nou 21.47, 400m/400mh:
Rasmus Mägi 46.49/48.91, 800m: Rasmus Kisel
1:50.59, 1500m: Allar Lamp 3:54.89, 5000m/
HMar: Tiidrek Nurme 14:16.70/63:56, 10000m:
Mark Abner 31:25.89, Mar: Roman Fosti 2:24:05,
3000mSt: Kaur Kivistik 8:58.03, 110mh/PV:
Maicel Uibo 14.57/5.20, HJ: Karl Lumi 2.16, LJ:
Hans-Christian Hausenberg 7.64, TJ: Igor
Syunin 16.24, SP: Kristo Galeta 19.74, DT: Gerd
Kanter 63.44, HT: Toomas Tankler 61.06, JT:
Magnus Kirt 88.28, Dec: Taavi Tsernjavski 7773,
10000mW/20kW: Ruslan Sergatsjov 48:42.44/
1:41:22. **Women:** 100m: Öilme Võro 12.28, 200m:
Annika Sakkarias 25.18, 400m/400mh: Liis
Roose 54.67/60.29, 800m/1500m: Liina Tsernov
2:08.42/4:25.15, 5000m: Lily Luik 17:44.86,
10000m/Mar: Kaia Lepik 47:26.60/2:52:21, HMar:
Leilea Luik 78:34, 3000mSt: Laura Maasik
10:50.27, 100mh: Grit Sadeiko 13.63, HJ: Eleriin
Haas 1.76, PV: Reena Koll 4.30, LJ/TJ: Tähti
Alver 6.28/14.05, SP: Kätlin Piirimäe 15.23, DT:
Kätlin Töllasson 53.61, HT: Anna Maria Orel
67.25, JT: Liina Laasma 58.03, Hep: Kristella
Jurkatamm 5306, 10000mW: Jekaterina Mirotvor-
tseva 51:15.88, 20kW: Lada Rosljakova 2:03:33.

Gerd KANTER b. 6 May 1979 Tallinn 1.96m 125kg. Tallinna SS Kalev. Business management graduate.
At DT: OG: '04- dnq 19, '08- 1, '12- 3, '16- 5; WCh: '03-05-07-09-11-13-15-17:dnq25/2/1/3/2/3/4/12; EC: '02-06-10-12-14-16-18: 12/2/4/2/2/3/5; EU23: '01- 5; CCp: '14- 1; WUG: '05- 1. Won WAF 2007-08, DL 2012-13, Estonian 2004-09, 2011-15. 2018. Five Estonian discus records 2004-06.
Progress at DT: 1998- 47.37, 1999- 49.65, 2000-57.68, 2001- 60.47, 2002- 66.31, 2003- 67.13, 2004-68.50, 2005- 70.10, 2006- 73.38, 2007- 72.02, 2008-71.88, 2009- 71.64, 2010- 71.45, 2011- 67.99, 2012-68.03, 2013- 67.59, 2014- 66.28, 2015- 66.02, 2016-65.27, 2017- 65.87, 2018- 64.46. pb SP 17.31i '04, 16.11 '00.
Threw over 70m in four rounds at Helsingborg on 4 Sep 2006; a feat matched only by Virgilijus Alekna. Six successive seasons over 70m. Tied record with seven EC appearances (all finals).

Magnus KIRT b. 10 Apr 1990 Törva 1.92m 89kg. Tallinn University of Technology. Tallinna TU SK.
At JT: OG: '16- dnq 23; WCh: '15- dnq 22, '17- 11; EC: '14/16- dnq 22/26, '18- 3; EU23: '11- dnq 18; EJ: '09- dnq 22; Won EST 2015, 2017-18.
Three Estonian javelin records 2018.
Progress at JT: 2008- 54.40, 2008- 59.88, 2009-72.97, 2010- 71.41, 2011- 70.07, 2012- 76.97, 2013-79.82, 2014- 79.70, 2015- 86.65, 2016- 84.47, 2017-86.06, 2018- 89.75. Pbs: HJ 2.10 '09, LJ 6.96 '09, TJ 13.68 '09, DT 38.09 '09.

Rasmus MÄGI b. 4 May 1992 Tartu 1.88m 74kg. Tartu University ASK.
At 400mh: OG: '12- h, '16- 6; WCh: '13 & 15- sf; EC: '12-14-16-18: 5/2/sf/6; WJ: '10- h; EU23: '13-3; EJ: '11- 4; CCp: '14- 4. Won EST 400m 2012, 2016-18; 400mh 2009, 2014-15, 2018.
Seven Estonian 400mh records 2012-16
Progress at 400mh: 2010- 52.79, 2011- 50.14, 2012-49.54, 2013- 49.19, 2014- 48.54, 2015- 48.65, 2016-48.40, 2017- 48.94, 2018- 48.60. pbs: 200m 21.90 '11, 400m 46.40 '13, 600m 1:18.48i '19, 200mh 24.01 '11, LJ 7.73 '12.
His sister Maris has won 22 Estonian titles in sprints and hurdles, pbs: 400m 52.21 '11, 400mh 56.56 '13 (EST record).

Janek OIGLANE b. 25 Apr 1994 1.82m 78kg. Audentese SK.
At Dec: WCh: '15- 19, '17- 4; EC: '16- 12; EU23: '15- 3; EJ: '13- 4; ET: '17- 1. At JT: WY: '17- 11.
Progress at Dec: 2014- 7815, 2015- 7945, 2016-7762, 2017- 8371. pbs: 60m 7.07i '19, 100m 11.08 '17, 400m 49.58 '17, 1000m 2:44.37i '16, 1500m 4:34.41 '16, 60mh 8.13i '19, 110mh 14.50 '15, HJ 2.05 '17, PV 5.1§9i '19, 5.10 '17; LJ 7.42 '17, SP 15.16i '19, 15.13 '17; DT 44.62 '16, JT 71.73 '17, Hep 6085i '19.
Five pbs in 4th place 8371 at 2017 Worlds.

Maicel UIBO b. 27 Dec 1992 Pölva 1.88m 86kg. Pölva. Was at Univerity of Georgia, USA.
At Dec: OG: '16- 24; WCh: '13- 19, '15- 10, '17-dnf; EC: '16- dnf NCAA champion 2014-15. At Hep: WI: '18- 3. At HJ: WY: '09- dnq 19; EU23: '13- dnq 21. Won EST 110mh 2018. PV.
Progress at Dec: 2012- 7548, 2013- 8223, 2014-8182, 2015- 8356, 2016- 8315, 2017- 8371, 2018-8514. pbs: 60m 7.16Ai '14, 7.18 '15; 100m 10.99 '13, 400m 50.18 '18, 1000m 2:38.51i '18, 1500m 4:25.53 '15, 60mh 8.19i '18, 110mh 14.49 '18, HJ 2.18 '15, PV 5.30 '18, LJ 7.82 '13, SP 14.98 '16, DT 49.14 '15, JT 64.51 '15, Hep 6265i '18.
Married Shaunae Miller (qv) on 4 Feb 2017.

ETHIOPIA

Governing body: Ethiopian Athletic Federation. Founded 1961.
2018 National Champions: Men: 100m: Bedru Mehammed 10.1, 400m: Abdulrahman Abdu 46.3, 800m: Tolesa Bodena 1:46.4, 1500m: Samuel Tefera 3:36.1, 5000m/HMar: Getaneh Molla 13:31.5/61:25; 10000m: Taye Firma 28:26.7, 3000mSt: Getnet Wale 8:29.0, 20kW: Yohanis Algaw 1:26:16. **Women**: 400m: Frehiywot Wondie 53.4, 800m: Tola Kore 2:00.2; 1500m: Besu Sado 4:12.8, 5000m: Hawi Feysa 15:31.5, 10000m: Haftamnesh Tesfay 33:28.5, HMar: Zeyneba Yimer 70:24, 3000mSt: Weynshet Ansa 10:04.1, JT: Bizunesh Tadele 44.51, 20kW: Yehualye Beletew 1:35:14.

Guye ADOLA Idemo b. 20 Oct 1990 Adola, Oromiya region 1.74m 54kg.
At Half Marathon: WCh: '14- 3, '16- 16; AfG: '15- 5; ETH champion 2015.
Progress at 10000m, Mar: 2016- 27:09.78, 2017-28:14.19, 2:03:46; 2018- 2:32:35. pbs: HMar 59:06 '14, 25k 1:12:50 '17, 30k 1:27:24 '17.
Ran world's fastest debut marathon when 2nd in Berlin 2017.

Yenew ALAMIREW b. 27 May 1990 Tilili 1.75m 57kg.
At 5000m: OG: '12- 12; WCh: '13- 9; AfG: '11- 2; AfCh: '14- 5; won DL 2013. At 3000m: WI: '12- 9, '16- 12.
Progress at 5000m, 10000m: 2010- 13:16.53, 2011-13:00.46, 2012- 12:48.77, 2013- 12:54.95, 2014-13:00.21, 2015- 13:05.53, 2016- 13:04.29, 2017-13:06.81, 27:19.86. pbs: 1500m 3:35.09+ '11, 1M 3:50.43 '11, 3000m 7:27.26 '11, Road: 15k 42:30 '14, 10M 46:04 '15, Mar 2:08:56 '18.

Mohamed AMAN Geleto b. 10 Jan 1994 Asella 1.69m 55kg.
At 800m: OG: '12- 6, '16- sf; WCh: '11-13-15-17: 8/1/dq sf/6; WY: '11- 2; WI: '12-14-16: 1/1/4; AfCh: '14- 2; CCp: '14- 2; won DL 2012-13, Afr-J 2011, Yth OG 1000m 2010.
Records: Ethiopian 800m (6) 2011-13, 1000m 2014, world youth 800m indoors and out 2011, world junior 600m indoor 2013 (1:15.60), African

indoor 800m 2014.
Progress at 800m: 2008- 1:50.29, 2009- 1:46.34, 2010- 1:48.5A, 2011- 1:43.37, 2012- 1:42.53, 2013- 1:42.37, 2014- 1:42.83, 2015- 1:43.56, 2016- 1:44.70, 2017- 1:45.40, 2018- 1:46.74. pbs: 600m 1:15.0+ '12, 1000m 2:15.75 '14, 1500m 3:43.52 '11, 1M 3:57.14 '11.
Was disqualified from taking the African Junior 800m gold in 2009 for being under-age (at 15). Youngest ever World Indoor champion at 18 years 60 days in 2012.

Selemon BAREGA b. 20 Jan 2000 1.73m 59kg.
At 5000m: WCh: '17- 5; WJ: '16- 1; AfCh: '18- 4; Af-J: '17- 1; won DL 2018. At 3000m: WY: '17- 1; WI: '18- 2. World CC: '17- 5J, '19- 5.
World junior 5000m record 2018.
Progress at 5000m: 2015- 13:58.8A, 2016- 13:21.21, 2017- 12:55.58, 2018- 12:43.02. Pb 3000m 7:36.64i, 7:37.53 '18.

Kenenisa BEKELE b. 13 Jun 1982 near Bekoji, Arsi Province 1.62m 54kg.
At 5000m(/10000m): OG: '04- 2/1, '08- 1/1, '12- (4); WCh: '03- 3/1, '05- (1), '07- (1), '09- 1/1, '11- (dnf); WJ: '00- 2; AfG: '03- 1; AfCh: '06- 1, '08- 1. At 3000m: WY: '99- 2; WI: '06- 1; WCp: '06- 2. World CC: '99- 9J, 4k. '01- 1J/2 4k, '02-03-04-05-06: all 1/1, '08- 1. Won WAF 3000m 2003, 2009; 5000m 2006.
World records: 5000m 2004, 10000m 2004 & 2005, indoor 5000m (12:49.60) 2004, 2000m 2007, 2M 2008; World junior record 3000m 2001. ETH marathon record 2016.
Progress at 5000m, 10000m, Mar: 2000- 13:20.57, 2001- 13:13.33, 2002- 13:26.58, 2003- 12:52.26, 26:49.57; 2004- 12:37.35, 26:20.31; 2005- 12:40.18, 26:17.53; 2006- 12:48.09, 2007- 12:49.53, 26:46.19; 2008- 12:50.18, 26:25.97; 2009- 12:52.32, 26:46.31; 2011- 13:27e+, 26:43.16; 2012- 12:55.79, 27:02.59; 2013- 13:07.88, 27:12.08; 2014- 2:05:04, 2016- 2:03:03, 2017- 2:05:57, 2018- 2:08:53. pbs: 1000m 2:21.9+ '07, 1500m 3:32.35 '07, 1M 3:56.2+ '07, 2000m 4:49.99i '07, 4:58.40 '09, 3000m 7:25.79 '07, 2M 8:04.35i '08, 8:13.51 '07; Road: 15k 42:42 '01, 10M 46:06 '13, 20k 57:19 '13, HMar 60:09 '13, 25k 1:12.47 '16, 30k 1.27.25 '16.
At cross-country has a record 16 (12 individual, 4 team) world gold medals from his record winning margin of 33 seconds for the World Juniors in 2001, a day after second in senior 4km. The only man to win both World senior races in the same year, he did this five times. Unbeaten in 27 races from Dec 2001 to March 2007 when he did not finish in the Worlds. After winning all his 12 10,000m track races including five major gold medals, from a brilliant debut win over Haile Gebrselassie at Hengelo in June 2003, he had two years out through injury and then dropped out of World 10,000 in 2011 before running the year's fastest time to win at Brussels. 17 successive wins at 5000m 2006-09. Shared Golden League jackpot

in 2009. Won Great North Run on half marathon debut 2013. Won in Paris on marathon debut 2014, then 4th Chicago; 3rd London and 1st Berlin 2016, 2nd London 2017. IAAF Athlete of the Year 2004-05.
His fiancée Alem Techale (b. 13.12.87, the 2003 World Youth 1500m champion) died of a heart attack on 4 Jan 2005. He married film actress Danawit Gebregziabher on 18 Nov 2007.

Chala BEYO Techo b. 18 Jan 1996 1.74m 57kg.
At 3000mSt: OG: '16- h; AfG: '15- 5; AfCh: '14- 4, '16- 1; CCp: '14- 4.
Progress at 3000mSt: 2014- 8:25.25, 2015- 8:25.82, 2016- 8:17.84, 2017- 8:13.24, 2018- 8:07.27. Pbs: 2000m 5:15.38 '17, 3000m 7:55.01i '17, 7:59.67 '15, 5000m 14:05.43 '18.

Lelisa DESISA Benti b. 14 Jan 1990 Shewa 1.70m 52kg.
At 10000m: Af-J: '09- 1. At: HMar: WCh: '10- 7, AfG: '11- 1. At Mar: WCh: '13- 2, '15- 7.
Progress at 10000m, HMar, Mar: 2009- 28:46.74, 2010- 59:39; 2011- 59:30, 2012- 27:11.98, 62:50; 2013- 2:04:45, 2014- 59:36, 2:11:06; 2015- 2:05:52, 2016- 60:37, 2:13:32dh, 2017- 2:11:32, 2018- 59:52, 2:05:59. pbs: 5000m 13:22.91 '12, Road: 15k 42:25 '10, 10M 45:36 '11.
Brilliant marathon debut to win Dubai 2013 and then won Boston and 2nd Worlds. 1st New York 2018 (2nd 2014, 3rd 2015, 2017), 2nd Dubai 2015. Won Boston again in 2015 (2nd 2016).

Muktar EDRIS Awel b. 14 Jan 1994 Adio 1.72m 57kg.
At 5000m: OG: '16- dq; WCh: '13- 7, '17- 1; WJ: '12- 1. At 10000m: WCh: '15- 10; Af-J: '11- 4. World CC: '11-13-15-17: 7J/3J/3/6; AfCC: 12- 1J.
Progress at 5000m, 10000m: 2011- 28:44.95A, 2012- 13:04.34, 2013- 13:03.69, 2014- 12:54.83, 2015- 13:00.30, 27:17.18; 2016- 12:59.43, 2017- 12:55.23, 27:20.60; 2018- 12:55.18. pbs: 3000m 7:32.31 '17, 15k Rd 42:55 '18.
Disqualified for stepping inside kerb after finishing 4th in 2016 Olympic 5000m final.

Hagos GEBRHIWET Berhe b. 11 May 1994 Tsaedaenba, Tigray region 1.67m 55kg. Meefen Engineering
At 5000m: OG: '12- 11, '16- 3; WCh: '13- 2, '15- 3; AfCh: '14- dnf; won DL 2016. At 3000m: WY: '11- 5; WI: '14- 5, '18- 4. World CC: '13- 1J, '15- 4, AfCC: '12- 4J. World junior records 5000m 2012, indoor 3000m 2013.
Progress at 5000m: 2011- 14:10.0A, 2012- 12:47.53, 2013- 12:55.73, 2014- 13:06.88, 2015- 12:54.70, 2016- 13:00.20, 2018- 12:45.82. pbs: 3000m 7:30.36 '13, 10k Rd 27:57dh '11.

Leul GEBRSELASSIE b. 20 Sep 1993 1.70m 55kg.
At 5000m: AfG: '15- 2. At HMar: WCh: '18- 10.
Progress at 10000m, Mar: 2012- 28:10.49. 2013- 28:05.66, 2015- 27:22.89, 2016- 27:17.91, 2017- 28:10.15, 2018- 2:04:02. pbs: 3000m 7:44.50i '16,

7:53.58 '14; 5000m 13:13.88 '16, Road: 15k 42:05 '17, 10M 47:18 '14, 20k 56:17 '17, HMar 59:18 '17, 25k 1:12:57 '18, 30k 1:27:37 '18.
2nd Dubai 2018 in 2:04:02, the third fastest ever marathon debut, and 1st in Valencia in 2:04:31.

Mosinet GEREMEW Bayij b. 12 Feb 1992 1.74m 57kg.
At 10000m: WCh: '15- 11.
Progress at HMar, Mar: 2013- 62:47, 2014- 59:11, 2015- 59:21, 2016- 60:43, 2017- 60:56, 2:06:12; 2018-2:04:00, 2019- 59:37. pbs: 5000m 13:17.41 '12, 10000m 27:18.86 '15, Road: 25k 1:12:57 '18, 30k 1:27:38 '18.
Won Dubai marathon and 2nd Chicago 2018, after 2nd Xiamen and 3rd Berlin 2017.

Abadi HADIS Embaye b. 6 Nov 1997 1.70m 63kg.
At 10000m: OG: '16- 15; WCh: '17- 7; won ETH 2016. World CC: '17- 3.
Progress at 5000m, 10000m: 2015- 13:13.17, 2016-13:02.49, 26:57.88; 2017- 13:16.78, 26:59.19; 2018-12:56.27. pbs: 3000m 7:38.55 '18, 10kRd 26:54dh '18, HMar 58:44 '18.

Tsegaye KEBEDE Wordofa b. 15 Jan 1987 Gerar Ber 1.58m 50kg.
At Mar: OG: '08- 3; WCh: '09- 3, '13- 4.
Progress at Mar: 2007- 2:08:16, 2008- 2:06:10, 2009- 2:05:18, 2010- 2:05:19, 2011- 2:07:48, 2012-2:04:38, 2013- 2:06:04, 2014- 2:06:30, 2015- 2:07:58, 2016- 2:10:56, 2017- 2:08:45, 2018- 2:05:21. pbs: Road: 10k 28:10 '08, HMar 59:35 '08.
Marathon wins: Addis Ababa 2007, Paris 2008, Fukuoka 2008-09, London 2010 & 2013 (2nd 2009, 3rd 2012, 2014), Chicago 2012 (2nd 2010); 2nd New York 2013 (3rd 2011). World Marathon Majors winner 2012/13. Has record 11 sub-2:07 times and 13 sub-2:08 and 16 sub-2:09 times. Won Great Ethiopian Run 2007, Great North Run 2008.

Yomif KEJELCHA Atomsa b. 1 Aug 1997 1.86m 58kg. Nike.
At 5000m: WCh: '15- 4, '17-= 4; WJ: '14- 1; Af-J: '15- 1; won DL 2015. At 3000m: WY: '13- 1; Yth OG: '14- 1; WI: '16- 1, '18- 1. World CC: '17- 2 MxR. World junior 3000m record 2016.
Progress at 1500m, 5000m: 2014- 13:25.19, 2015-12:53.98, 2016- 13:03.29, 2017- 3:32.94; 13:01.21; 2018- 3:32.59, 12:46.79; 2019- 3:31:58i. pbs: 1000m 2:18.34i '19, 1M 3:48.46i '19, 2000m 4:57.74i '14, 3000m 7:28.00 '18, 10k Rd 28:13 '13, HMar 59:17 '18.

Abera KUMA Lema b. 31 Aug 1990 Ambo 1.60m 50kg.
At 5000m: WCh: '11- 5; Af-J: '09- 1. At 10000m: WCh: '13- 5. At 3000m: WY: '07- 5.
Tied world 30km record 2014.
Progress at 5000m, 10000m, Mar: 2009- 13:29.40, 2010- 13:07.83, 2011- 13:00.15, 27:22.54; 2012-13:09.32, 27:18.39; 2013- 26:52.85, 2014- 2:05:56, 2015- 2:06:47, 2016- 2:07:48, 2017- 2:06:44, 2018-

2:05:50. pbs: 1500m 3:48.73 '09, 3000m 7:39.09i/7:40.85 '12, Road: 15k 42:01 '10, 10M 45:28 '11, HMar 60:19 '12, 25k 1:13:08 '14, 30k 1:27:38 '14.   3rd Berlin Marathon 2014, won Rotterdam 2015 (2nd 2018).

Sisay LEMMA Kasaye b. 12 Dec 1990 1.74m 57kg.
Progress at Mar: 2012- 2:11:58, 2013- 2:09:02, 2015- 2:06:26, 2016- 2:05:16, 2017- 2:08:04, 2018-2:04:08. pbs: HMar 61:11 '16, 25k 1:12:49 '16, 30k 1:27:20 '16.
Marathon wins: Carpi 2012 (debut), Warsaw 2013, Vienna & Frankfurt 2015, Ljubljana 2018; 3rd Dubai 2017, 2nd Prague 2018.

Feyisa LILESA Gemechu b. 1 Feb 1990 Tullu Bultuma 1.58m 50kg.
At Mar: OG: '16- 2; WCh: '11- 3, '13- dnf, World CC: 2008-09-10-11-13: 14J/12/25/17/9. Won ETH CC 2013.
Progress at Mar: 2009- 2:09:12, 2010- 2:05:23, 2011- 2:10:32, 2012- 2:04:52, 2013- 2:07:46, 2014-2:08:26, 2015- 2:06:35, 2016- 2:06:56, 2017- 2:14:12, 2018- 2:07:30. pbs: 5000m 13:34.80 '08, 10000m 27:46.97 '08; Road: 15k 42:15+ '13, 20k 56:19+ '12, HMar 59:22 '12, 25k 1:13:22 '13, 30k 1:28:05 '13.
Has run 14 sub-2:10 marathons; won Dublin 2009, Xiamen 2010, Tokyo 2016. 3rd/2nd Chicago 2010/2012, 4th Rotterdam 2010 in then fastest ever by 20 year-old, 4th London 2013. Now living in the USA.

Herpasa NEGASA b. 1993.
Progress at Mar: 2013- 2:10:51, 2015- 2:10:17, 2016- 2:10:17, 2018- 2:09:14, 2019- 2:03:40. pb: 15k 43:02 '16. Improved best by 5:34 for 2nd in Dubai Marathon in 2019.

Tola SHURA Kitata b. 9 Jun 1996 1.65m 50kg.
At 10000m: AfCh: '16- 5. Won ETH 2016.
World junior marathon record 2015 (4th on debut at Dubai).
Progress at Mar: 2015- 2:08:53, 2016- 2:10:04, 2017- 2:05:50, 2018- 2:04:49. pbs: 10000m: 32:14.25 '16, 15k 42:42 '17, 20k 57:14 '17, HMar 59:17 '18, 25k 1:12:36 '18, 30k 1:27:24 '18.
Won Rome and Frankfurt marathons 2017, 2nd London & New York 2018.

Getaneh TAMIRE Molla b. 10 Jan 1994 1.71m 55kg.
At 5000m: AfCh: '16- 4, '18- 2; AfG: '15- 1. At HMar: WCh: '18- 5. Afr CC: '16- 6. Won ETH 5000m 2015-16, CC 2016-17, HMar 2018.
Progress at 5000m: 2014- 13:13.04, 2015- 13:21.88, 2016- 13:05.59, 2017- 13:18.40, 2018- 12:59.58. At Mar: 2019- 2:03:34. pbs: 1500m 3:44.91 '16, 3000m 7:46.9+'18, 10k Rd 28:18A '18, HMar 60:34 '17, 3000mSt 8:41.5A '16.
Ran fastest ever debut marathon to win in Dubai in 2019.

Samuel TEFERA b. 23 Oct 1999 1.71m 52kg.
At 1500m: WCh: '17- h; WJ: '18- 5; AfCh: '18- 10; WI: '18- 1.

World indoor 1500m record 2019, junior 2018.
Progress at 1500m: 2015- 13:58.8A, 2016- 3:43.0A, 2017- 3:33.78, 2018- 3:31.63, 2019- 3:31.04i. Pb 1M 3:51.26 '18.

Adera **Tamirat TOLA** b. 11 Aug 1991 1.81m 59kg.
At 10000m: OG: '16- 3. At HMar: WCh: '16- 5. At Mar: WCh: '17- 2. World CC: '15- 6.
Progress at 10000m, Mar: 2014- 2:06:17, 2015- 27:22.64, 2016- 26:57.33, dnf; 2017- 2:04:11, 2018- 2:04:06. pbs: 15k 42:26 '17, 20k 56:36 '17, HMar 59:37 '17, 25k 1:12:54 '17, 30k 1:27:38 '18.
Won Dubai Marathon 2017 (3rd 2018).

Mule WASIHUN Lakew b. 20 Oct 1993 1.66m 52kg.
At 10000m: AfG: '15- 7. At HMar: WCh: '16- 8.
Progress at Mar: 2015- 2:10:57, 2016- 2:05:44, 2017- 2:05:39, 2018- 2:04:37. pbs: 1500m 3:45.03 '14, 10000m: 28:23.87 '15, road: 10k 27:57 '13, 15k 43:02 '15, 20k, HMar 59:34 '19, 25k 1:13:49 '18, 30k 1:28:58 '18. Marathons include 2nd Dubai 2017, Amsterdam 2018.

Aman WOTE Fete b. 18 Apr 1984 Kabete 1.81m 64kg.
At 1500m: OG: '12- ht; WCh: 13- sf, '15- dnf; AfG: '11- 5; AfCh: '10- 7, '18- 5; WI: '12-14-16-18: 4/2/6/4. Won ETH 1500m 2014, 2016.
Ethiopian records 1500m (2) & 1M 2014.
Progress at 1500m: 2010- 3:38.89A 2011- 3:35.61, 2012- 3:35:38, 2013- 3:32.65, 2014- 3:29.91, 2015- 3:30.29, 2016- 3:34.58, 2017- 3:31.63, 2018- 3:31.90. pbs: 800m 1:44.99 '13, 1M 3:48.60 '14, 3000m 7:43.99i '13.

Jemal YIMER Mekonnen b. 11 Sep 1996 1.63m 48kg.
At 10000m: WCh: '17- 5; AfCh: 16- 4, '18- 1. At HMar: WCh: '18- 4. World CC: 17- 4.
Ethiopian half marathon record 2018.
Progress at 10000m, HMar: 2016- 28:08.92, 2017- 26:56.11, 2018- 28:30.3A, 58:33. pbs: 15k 41:14 '18, 20k 55:56 '18.

Women

Ruti AGA b. 16 Jan 1994 1.59m 45kg.
At 5000m: WJ: '12- 2; Afr J: '13- 1; World CC: '13- 5.
Progress at Mar: 2016- 2:24:41, 2017- 2:20:41, 2018- 2:18:34. pbs: 3000m 8:56.73 '13, 5000m 15:13.48 '13, 10000m 33:38.4A '13; Road: 10k 31:33 '18, 15k 47:28 '18, 20k 63:13 '18, HMar 66:39 '18, 25k 1:21:54 '18, 30k 1:38:04 '18.
Won Tokyo marathon 2019, 3rd/2nd/2nd Berlin 2016-18, 2nd Vienna 2016, Tokyo 2018.

Habitam ALEMU b. 9 Jul 1997 1.71m 52kg.
At 800m: OG: '16- sf; WCh: '15- h, '17- sf; AfG: '15- 4; AfCh: '18- 3; WI: '16- 6, '18- 4.
Ethiopian 800m records 2017 & 2018.
Progress at 800m, 1500m: 2014- 2:09.6A, 2015- 2:01.27, 4:14.67; 2016- 1:58.99, 2017- 1:57.05, 2018- 1:56.71, 4:01.41.

Meskerem ASSEFA b. 20 Sep 1985 1.55m 43kg.
At 800m: WY: '10- h. At 1500m: OG: '12- h; WCh: '09- sf, '11- h; AfG: '07- 4, '11- 4; AfCh: '08- 2, '10- 5.
Progress at Mar: 2013- 2:25:17, 2014- 2:25:59, 2015- 2:25:11, 2016- 2:30:13, 2017- 2:24:18, 2018- 2:20:36. pbs: 800m 2:02.12 '08, 1500m 4:02.12 '11, 3000m 8:46.37 '09, 5000m 15:03.49i '10, Road: 10k: 31:43 '17, 15k 47:42 '17, 20k 64:18 '17, HMar 67:42 '17, 25k 1:24:37 '18, 30k 1:41:09 '18.
Marathon wins: Houston & Rotterdam 2017, Nagoya and Frankfurt 2018.

Almaz AYANA Eba b. 21 Nov 1991 Benshangul 1.65m 50kg.
At 5000m/(10000m): OG: '16- 3/1; WCh: '13- 3, '15- 1, 17- 2/1; AfCh: '14- 1; CCp: '14- 1. At 3000mSt: WJ: '10- 5; won DL 5000m 2016, ETH 5000m 2014, 3000mSt 2013.
World record 10000m 2016, junior 3000m steeplechase 2010.
Progress at 5000m, 10000m, 3000mSt: 2009- 10:03.75, 2010- 9:22.51, 2011- 15:12.24, 9:30.23; 2012- 14:57.97, 9:38.62; 2013- 14:25.84, 9:27.49; 2014- 14:29.19, 2015- 14:14.32; 2016- 14:12.59, 29:17.45; 2017- 14:40.35, 30:16.32. pbs: 2000m 5:35.10+ '15, 3000m 8:22.22 '15, HMar 67:12 '17.
Ran 30:07.00 on 10000m track debut to win ETH trial race at Hengelo, then smashed WR in Rio. Won 2017 World 10000m by record maregin of 46.37 secs. Married to Soresa Fida (1500m 3:34.72 '11, 3 AfCh '11). IAAF female Athlete of the Year 2016.

Tadelech BEKELE Alemu b. 11 Apr 1991 Debre Birhan 1.54m 40kg.
Afr CC: 14- 5. Progress at 10000m, Mar: 2014- 2:23:02, 2015- 33:30.7A, 2:22:51; 2016- 30:54.61, 2:26:31; 2017- 2:21:54, 2018- 2:21:40. pbs: 5000m 15:28.27 '12, 10k 30:38 '13, HMar 68:38 '13, 25k 1:23:58 '18, 30k 1:40:42 '18.
Won Amsterdam marathon 2017-18, after 3rd Prague and 4th Dubai all under 2:25 in 2017. 3rd London 2018.

Gelete BURKA Bati b. 15 Feb 1986 Kofele 1.65m 45kg.
At 1500m: OG: '08- h; WCh: '05- 8, '09- 9 (fell), '11- sf, '13- h; WI: '08- 1, '10- 3; AfG: '07- 1; AfCh: '08- 1, '10- 2; CCp: '10- 6. At 3000m: WI: '12- 3. At 5000m: OG: '12- 5; WCh: '07- 9. At 10000m: OG: '16- 8; WCh: '15- 2; AfG: '15- 3. World CC: '03- 05-06-07-08-09: 3J/1J/1 4k/4/6/8. Won ETH 800m 2011, 1500m 2004-05, 2007; 5000m 2005, 4k CC 2006.
African records: 1M 2008, 200m 2009, indoor 1500m 2008, junior 1500m 2005. World youth 1M best (4:30.81) 2003.
Progress at 1500m, 5000m, 10000m, Mar: 2003- 4:10.82, 16:23.8A, 2004- 4:06.10, 2005- 3:59.60, 14:51.47; 2006- 4:02.68, 14:40.92; 2007- 4:00.48, 14:31.20; 2008- 3:59.75i/4:00.44, 14:45.84; 2009- 3:58.79, 2010- 3:59.28, 2011- 4:03.28, 2012- 14:41.43, 2013- 4:04.36, 14:42.07, 2:30:40; 2014- 2:26:03,

2015- 14:40.50, 30:49.68; 2016- 14:52.4, 30:26.66; 2017- 15:06.01, 30:40.87; 2018- 2:20:45. pbs: 800m 2:02.89 '10, 1M 4:18.23 '08, 2000m 5:30.19 '09, 3000m 8:25.92 '06; Rd: 15k 49:26 '12, HMar 66:11 '18, 25k 1:23:10 '18, 30k 1:39:42 '18.
Won Ottawa Marathon 2018. Married Taddele Gebrmehden in 2007.

Meseret DEFAR b. 19 Nov 1983 Addis Ababa 1.55m 42kg.
At 5000m(/10000m): OG: '04- 1, '08- 2, '12- 1; WCh: '03- h, '05- 2, '07- 1, '09- 3/5, '11- 3/dnf, '13- 1; WJ: '00- 2, '02- 1; AfG: '03- 1, '07- 1; AfCh: '00-06-08-10: 2/1/2/2; WCp: '06- 1. At 3000m: WJ: '02- 1; WY: '99- 2; WI: '03-04-06-08-10-12-16: 3/1/1/1/1/2/2; CCp: '10- 1. Won WAF 3000m 2004-09, 5000m 2005, 2008-09; DL 5000m 2013. World CC: '02- 13J.
Records: World 5000m 2006 & 2007, 2M 2007 (2); indoor 3000m 2007, 2M 2008 (9:10.50) & 2009 (9:06.26), 5000m 2009; African 5000m 2005, Ethiopian 3000m (2) 2006-07. World 5k road best 14:46 Carlsbad 2006.
Progress at 3000m, 5000m, 10000m: 1999- 9:02.08, 33:54.9A; 2000- 8:59.90, 15:08.36; 2001- 8:52.47, 15:08.65; 2002- 8:40.28, 15:26.45; 2003- 8:38.31, 14:40.34; 2004- 8:33.44i/8:36.46, 14:44.81; 2005- 8:30.05i/8:33.57, 14:28.98; 2006- 8:24.66, 14:24.53; 2007- 8:23.72i/8:24.51, 14:16.63; 2008- 8:27.93i/8:34.53, 14:12.88; 2009- 8:26.99i/8:30.15, 14:24.37i/14:36.38, 29:59.20; 2010- 8:24.46i/8:36.09, 14:24.79i/14:38.87; 2011- 8:36.91i/8:50.36+, 14:29.52, 31:05.05; 2012- 8:31.56i/8:46.49, 14:35.85; 2013- 8:30.29, 14:26.90, 30:08.06; 2016- 8:30.83i. pbs: 1500m 4:02.00 '10, 1M: 4:28.5ei '06, 4:33.07+ '07; 2000m 5:34.74i/5:38.0 '06, 2M 8:58.58 '07, road 15k 47:30 '13, HMar 66:09 '13, Mar 2:23:33 '19.
Married to Teodros Hailu. IAAF woman athlete of the year 2007. Record nine WAF wins. Record 45 times under 15 mins for 5000m. Daughter Gabriella born on 23 June 2014. In first race since 2013 won at 3000m indoors in 8:30.83 at Boston on 14 Feb 2016.

Worknesh DEGEFA b. 28 Oct 1990 1.59m 42kg.
At HMar: AfG: '15- 2.
Ethiopian Marathon record 2019.
Progress at HMar, Mar: 2012- 76:48, 2013- 67:49, 2014- 68:46, 2015- 67:14, 2016- 66:14, 2017- 68:10, 2:22:36; 2018- 68:10, 2:19:53; 2019- 2:17:41. pbs: 10k 31:53 '12, 25k 1:23:09 '18, 30k 1:37:16 '19.
Won at Dubai 2017 on marathon debut (4th 2018, 2nd 2019).

Shure DEMISE Ware b. 21 Jan 1996 Bore 1.59m 45kg.
At 10000m: AfCh: '16- 5. Won ETH 2016. At Mar: WCh: '17- 5. World junior marathon record 2015 (4th on debut at Dubai).
Progress at Mar: 2015- 2:20:59, 2016- 2:25:04, 2017- 2:22:57, 2018- 2:22:07. pbs: 10000m: 32:14.25 '16, 15k 49:22 '14, HMar 68:53 '14.
Won Toronto marathon 2015-16, 2nd Dubai 2017, 3rd Chicago 20198.

Roza DEREJE b. 6 May 1997 1.68m 52kg.
Progress at Mar: 2015- 2:34:02, 2016- 2:26:18, 2017- 2:22:43, 2018- 2:19:17. pbs: Road: 10k 31:43 '17, 15k 47:41 '17, 20k 63:59 '17, HMar 67:00 '18, 25k 1:23:09 '18, 30k 1:39:41 '18.
Marathon wins: Odense 2016, Shanghai 2016-17, Dubai 2018; 2nd Chicago 2018.

Birhane DIBABA b. 11 Sep 1993 Moyagajo 1.59m 44kg.
At Mar: WCh: '17- 10. Progress at Mar: 2012- 2:29:22, 2013- 2:23:01, 2014- 2:22:30, 2015- 2:23:15, 2016- 2:23:16, 2017- 2:21:19, 2018- 2:19:51. pbs: HMar 67:47 '16.
Won Valencia marathon 2012, Tokyo 2015 & 2018; 2nd São Paulo 2012, Nagoya 2013, Tokyo 2014 & 2017, Berlin 2016; 3rd Frankfurt 2013, Chicago 2014-15.

Genzebe DIBABA b. 8 Feb 1991 Bekoji. Muger Cement. 1.68m 52kg.
At 1500m: OG: '12- h, '16- 2; WCh: '13- 7, '15- 1, '17- 12; WI: '12- 1, '18- 1. At 3000m: CCp: '14- 1; WI: '14-16-18: 1/1/1. At 5000m: WCh: '09 -8, '11- 8, '15- 3; AfCh: '14- 2; WJ: '08- 2, '10- 1; Af-J: '09- 1. World CC: '07-08-09-10-11-17: 5J/1J/1J/11J/ 9/2 MxR. Won DL 5000m 2015, ETH 1500m 2010.
Records: World 1500m 2015, indoor 1500m, 3000m & 2M 2014, 5000m 2015, 1M 2016, 2000m 2017. Two African 1500m 2015. Ethiopian 1500m (3) 2012-15, 2000m 2014.
Progress at 1500m, 5000m: 2007- 15:53.46, 2008- 15:02.41, 2009- 14:55.52, 2010- 4:04.80i/4:06.10, 15:08.06; 2011- 4:05.90, 14:37.56; 2012- 3:57.77, 2013- 3:57.54, 14:37.68; 2014- 3:55.17i/4:01.00, 14:28.88; 2015- 3:50.07, 14:15.41; 2016- 3:56.46i+/ 3:57.31, 2017- 3:57.82, 14:25.22; 2018- 3:56.68, 14:26.89. pbs: 800m 1:59.37 '17, 1000m 2:33.06i '17, 2:35.6+ '15; 1M 4:13.31i/4:14.30 '16, 2000m 5:23.75i '17, 5:27.50 '14; 3000m 8:16.60i/8:26.21 '14, 2M 9:00.48i/9:14.28 '14.
Laureus World Sportswomen of the Year 2014, IAAF Woman Athlete of the Year 2015. Younger sister of Ejegayehu (2 OG 10000m 2004, 3 WCh 5000 & 10000m 2005) and Tirunesh Dibaba.

Mare DIBABA Hurssa b. 20 Oct 1989 Sululta, Oromia 1.52m 40kg.
At Mar: OG: '12- 22, '16- 3; WCh: '15- 1, '17- 8. At HMar: AfG: '11- 1. Won AZE 3000m and 5000m 2009. AZE records (as Mare Ibrahimova) at 3000m, 5000m and HMar 2009.
Progress at HMar, Mar: 2008- 70:28, 2009- 68:45, 2010- 67:13, 2:25:27, 2011- 68:39, 2:23:25; 2012- 67:44, 2:19:52; 2014- 68:56, 2:21:36/2:20:35dh; 2015- 2:19:52, 2016- 67:55, 2:24:09; 2017- 69:43, 2:28:49; 2018- 69:15, 2:25:24. pbs: 3000m 9:16.94 '09, 5000m 15:42.83 '09, Road: 10k 31:55+ '10, 15k 48:04+ '10, 10M 51:29+ '10, 20k 63:47+ '10, 30k 1:39:19 '14.
Switched to Azerbaijan in December 2008 but back to Ethiopia from 1 Feb 2010. Marathons: won at Xiamen 2014 and 2015, Chicago 2014; 2nd Boston 2014, Berlin 2015; 3rd Dubai 2012.

Tirunesh DIBABA Kenene b. 1 Oct 1985 Chefa near Bekoji, Arsi region 1.60m 47kg.
At 5000m(/10000m): OG: '04- 3, '08- 1/1, '12- 3/1, '16- (3); WCh: '03- 1, '05- 1/1, '07- (1), '13- (1), '17- (2); WJ: '02- 2; AfG: '03- 4; AfCh: '06- 2, '08- (1), '10- (1). At 3000m: WCp: '06- 1. World CC: '01-02-03-05-06-07-08-10:   5J/2J/1J/1/1/2/1/4; 4k: '03-04-05: 7/2/1. Won WAF 5000m 2006, ETH 4k CC & 5000m 2003. 8k CC 2005.
Records: World 5000m 2008, indoor 5000m 2005 (14:32.93) & 2007, junior 5000m 2003-04, indoor 3000m & 5000m 2004, world road 5k best 14:51 2005, 15k 2009. African 10000m 2008, Ethiopian Mar 2017.
Progress at 5000m, 10000m, Mar: 2002- 14:49.90, 2003- 14:39.94, 2004- 14:30.88, 2005- 14:32.42, 30:15.67; 2006- 14:30.40, 2007- 14:27.42i/14:35.67, 31:55.41; 2008- 14:11.15, 29:54.66; 2009- 14:33.65, 2010- 14:34.07, 31:51.39A; 2012- 14:50.80, 30:20.75; 2013- 14:23.68, 30:26.67; 2014- 2:20:35, 2016- 14:41.73, 29:42.56; 2017- 31:02.69, 2:17:56; 2018- 2:18:55. pbs: 2000m 5:42.7 '05, 3000m 8:29.55 '06, 2M 9:12.23i '10, road 15k 46:28 '09, 10M 51:49 '16, HMar 66:50 '17, 25k 1:20:51 '17, 30k 1:37:23 '17.
At 17 years 333 days in 2003 the youngest ever world champion at an individual event and in 2005 the first woman to win the 5000m/10000m double (with last laps of 58.19 and 58.4) at a global event after earlier in the year winning both World CC titles. Now has women's record 21 World CC medals. Married Sileshi Sihine on 26 Oct 2008; son Natan Seleshi born 26 Mar 2015. After retaining the Olympic 10,000m title she won the Great North Run on half marathon debut in 2012. Third in London on marathon debut 2014, second London and 1st Chicago in 2017. She ran eleven 10,000m track races – and won them all – before her 3rd in the 2016 Ethiopian Trial.

Dera DIDA b. 26 Oct 1996 1.55m 42kg.
At 5000m: AfCh: '16- 3. At 10000m: '17- 14. World CC: 15- 2J, '19- 2; AfCC: '16- 4. Won ETH 5000m 2016, 10000m 2017, CC 2017, 2019.
Progress at 5000m: 2014- 16:26.2A, 2015- 15:28.81, 2016- 14:42.84, 2017- 15:07.27. At Mar: 2018- 2:21:45. pbs: 1500m 4:15.41 '15, 3000m 8:48.31 '16. 10000m 30:56.48 '17; Road: 20k 66:19 '18, HMar 68:06 '17, 25k 1:22:54 '18, 30k 1:39:30 '18.

Buze DIRIBA Kejela b. 9 Feb 1994 Arsi 1.60m 43kg.
At 5000m: WCh: '13- 5; WJ: '12- 1. World CC: '11- 10J, '13- 9J
Progress at 5000m, 10000m, HMar: 2012- 14:53.06, 2013- 14:50.02, 2014- 15:16.83, 2015- 31:33.27, 72:56; 2016- 31:38.61, 71.79; 2017- 73:04, 2018- 66:50. pbs: 1500m 4:10.96 '12, 3000m 8:39.65 '12, 2M 9:29.03i '15, 9:40.01 '14; 10M Rd 51:38 '16, 15kRd 49:41 '17.

Etenesh DIRO Neda b. 10 May 1991 Jeidu, Oromiya 1.69m 47kg.

At 3000mSt: OG: '12- 5, '16- 15; WCh: '13- 5, '15-h, '17- 7; AfG: '15- 6; AfCh: '14- 4. At 3000m: AfJ: '09- 2.
Progress at 5000m, 3000mSt: 2011- 15:21.51, 9:49.18, 2012- 15:19.77, 9:14.07, 2013- 9:16.97, 2014- 9:19.71, 2015- 9:29.10, 2016- 14:33.30, 9:16.87; 2017- 14:40.29, 9:13.25. pbs: 3000m 8:38.32 '16, Road: 10k 33:32A '11, 15k 51:21 '09, HMar 71:35 '10.

Axumawit EMBAYE Abraya b. 18 Oct 1994 1.60m 50kg.
At 1500m: WJ: '12- 7; AfCh: '14- 4; WI: '14- 2, '16- 4.
Progress at 1500m: 2012- 4:12.92, 2013- 4:05.16, 2014- 4:02.35, 2015- 4:02.92i/4:03.00, 2016- 4:03.05, 2017- 4:04.95i/4:09.17, 2018- 4:02.44. pbs: 800m 2:03.27i '15, 2:05.67 '17; 1000m 2:37.43 '15, 1M 4:23.50i/4:26.84 '15, 3000m 8:43.83 '18.

Letesenbet GIDEY b. 20 Mar 1998 Endameskel, Tigray region 1.63m 48kg.
At 3000m: WY: '15- 4. At 5000m: WCh: '17- 11; World CC: '15- 1J, '17- 1J, 'q19- 3.
African junior 5000m recrd 2016.
Progress at 5000m: 2014- 16:19.3A, 2015- 15:39.83, 2016- 14:45.63, 2017- 14:33.32, 2018- 14:23.14. pbs: 1500m 4:11.11 '17, 2000m 5:43.0 '18. 3000m 8:30.96 '18.

Amane GOBENA Gemeda b. 1 Sep 1982. 1.63m 48kg.
World 4k CC: '02- 8, '04- 11.
Progress at Mar: 2009- 2:26:53, 2010- 2:24:13, 2011- 2:31:49, 2012- 2:28:38, 2013- 2:23:50, 2014- 2:27:05, 2015- 2:23:30, 2016- 2:21:51, 2017- 2:25:49, 2018- 2:25:49. pbs: 1500m 4:11.04 '04, 1M 4:41.57 '03, 3000m 9:01.46 '02, 5000m 15:19.50 '04, Road: 10km 31:44 '14, 15km 47:55 '10, HMar 68:16 '09, 30k 1:43:24 '09.
Marathon wins: Toronto 2009, Osaka and Seoul 2010, Xiamen 2011, Santa Monica 2014, Istanbul 2014-15, Mumbai 2018; 2nd Paris 2015, Tokyo 2016 (3rd 2017).

Netsanet GUDETA Kebede b. 12 Feb 1991 Bekoji 1.62m 45kg.
At 10000m: AfG: '15- dnf. At HMar: WCh: '14- 6, '16- 4, '18- 1, World CC: '15- 3,
ETH half marathon record 2015, world women only best 2018.
Progress at 10000m, HMar: 2014- 68:46, 2015- 31:06.53, 67:31; 2016- 30:36.75, 68:01; 2017- 67:26, 2018- 66:11, 2019- 65:45. pbs: 5000m 15:25.0A '17, Rd: 5k 15:22 '15, 10k 31:35 '17, 25k 47:30 '18, 20k 62:53 '18, Mar 2:29:15 '17.

Yebrqual MELESE b. 18 Apr 1990 1.64m 55kg.
Won ETH 10000m 2015.
Progress at Mar: 2014- 2:26:21, 2015- 2:23:23, 2016- 2:24:49, 2017- 2:23:13, 2018- 2:19:36. pbs: 10000m: 32:40.3A '15, 10k 31:40 '13, HMar 67:18 '18, 25k 1:23:10 '18, 30k 1:39:41 '18.
Marathon wins: Hangzhou 2014, Houston & Prague 2015, Shanghai 2018; 2nd Paris 2014, Chicago 2015; 3rd Dubai 2017-18.

Aselefech MERGIA b. 23 Jan 1985 Woliso 1.68m 51kg.
At Mar: OG: '12- 41; WCh: '09- 3, '11- dnf, '17- 12. HMar: WCh: '08- 2. World CC: '08- 16.
Ethiopian marathon record 2012.
Progress at HMar, Mar: 2006- 74:13, 2007- 74:50, 2008- 68:17, 2009- 67:48, 2:25:02; 2010- 67:22, 2:22:38; 2011- 67:21, 2:22:45; 2012- 69:42+, 2:19:31; 2014- 73:49, 2015- 71:42, 2:20:02; 2016- 2:23:57, 2017- 2:23:50. pbs: 1500m 4:14.85 '07, 3000m 8:54.42 '08; Road: 10k 31:25+ '08, 15k 47:53 '09, 20k 63:41 '09, 30k 1:41:52 '09.
2nd Paris Marathon 2009 on debut, won London 2010 (3rd 2017) and Dubai 2011-12 and 2015; 2nd New York 2015. Daughter Sena born July 2013.

Belaynesh OLJIRA Jemane b. 26 Jun 1990 Welek'a, Amhara 1.60m 47kg.
At 10000m: OG: '12- 5; WCh: '13- 3, '15- 9; AfCh: '14- 3. World CC: '11-13-15-17: 10/3/9/8; AfCC: '12- 5. Won ETH 10000m 2011.
Ethiopian 1500m record 2012.
Progress at 10000m, Mar: 2011- 31:17.80, 2012- 30:26.70, 2013- 30:31.44, 2:25:01; 2014- 32:49.39, 2:24:21dh; 2015- 30:53.69, 2016- 30:50.25, 2017- 30:44.57, 2018- 33:32.3A, 2:21:53. pbs: 1500m 4:33.14 '12, 3000m 8:38.55 '16, 2M 9:23.32 '14, 5000m 14:42.57 '16, Road: 15k 49:08 '14, 10M 52:40 '14, HMar 67:27 '11, 30k 1:39:33dh '14.

Besu SADO Beko b. 12 Jun 1996 1.72m 56kg.
At 10000m: OG: '16- 9; WCh: '15/17- sf; AfG: '15- 2; AfCh: '14- 7, '18- 4; Af-J: '15- 2; won ETH 2014, 2018. At 800m: CCp: '18- 7.
Progress at 1500m: 2014- 4:07.59, 2015- 4:00.65, 2016- 3:59.47, 2017- 4:00.98, 2018- 4:01.75. pbs: 800m 2:02.6A '14, 1000m 2:37.73 '15, 1M 4:25.99 '18.

Dawit SEYAUM Biratu b. 27 Jul 1996 Tumano 1.61m 49kg.
At 1500m: OG: '16- 8; WCh: '15- 4; WJ: '14- 1; WY: '13- 2; AfG: '15- 1; AfCh: '14- 2; Af-J: '13/15- 1; CCp: '14- 3; WI: '16- 2.
Progress at 1500m: 2013- 4:09.00, 2014- 3:59.53, 2015- 3:59.76, 2016- 3:58.09, 2017- 4:00.52, 2018- 4:02.81. pbs: 1M 4:32.13i '15, 2000m 5:35.46i '15, 3000m 8:37.65i '17.

Feysa TADESE Boru b. 19 Nov 1988 Shirka 1.67m 53kg.
At Mar: WCh: '13- dnf. World HMar: '10- 4, '12- 2; CC: '10- 7.
Progress at Mar: 2009- 2:36:57, 2011- 2:25:20, 2012- 2:23:07, 2013- 2:21:06, 2014- 2:20:27, 2016- 2:25:03, 2017- 2:26:46, 2018- 2:19:30. pbs: 10000m 32:29.07 '10, Road: 10k 32:21 '13, 15k 48:51 '12, 20k 65:41 '12, HMar 68:35 '13, 25k 1:22:58 '14, 30k 1:39:18 '14.
Marathon wins: Seoul and Shanghai 2012, Paris 2013; 2nd Berlin 2014, Dubai 2018.

Senbere TEFERI Sora b. 3 May 1995 1.59m 45kg. Oromiya.
At 1500m: WCh: '13- h; WJ: '12- 3; WY: '11- 2. At

3000m: CCp: '18- 2. At 5000m: OG: '16- 5; WCh: '15- 2, '17- 4; AfCh; '18- 2; ETH champion 2017; World CC: '15- 2, '17- 10.
Progress at 1500m, 5000m, 10000m: 2011- 16:09.0A, 2012- 15:36.74, 2013- 4:04.55, 16:21.0A, 2014- 4:08.49, 2015- 4:01.86, 14:36:44; 2016- 14:29.82, 30:40.59; 2017- 14:31.76, 30:41.68; 2018- 14:23.33. pbs: 2000m 5:34.27 '14, 3000m 8:32.49 '18, 10kRd 30:38 '17, 10M Rd 52:51 '16, HMar 65:45 '19, Mar 2:24:11 '18.
Ran fastest ever debut half marathon to win at Ras Al Khaimah in 2019.

Gudaf TSEGAY Desta b. 23 Jan 1997 1.59m 45kg.
At 1500m: WCh: '17- sf; WJ: '14- 2; WI: '16- 3. At 800m: OG: '16- h.
World junior indoor 1500m record 2016.
Progress at 1500m: 2013- 4:07.27, 2014- 4:02.83, 2015- 4:03.09, 2016- 4:00.18, 2017- 3:59.55, 2018- 3:59.09. pbs: 800m 1:59.77 '16, 1000m 2:38.05i '17, 1M 4:16.14 '18, 3000m 8:33.78 '18, 5000m 14:51.30 '18, 15k Rd 15:37 '15.

Genet YALEW b. 31 Dec 1992 1.46m 46kg. Defense.
At HMar: WCh: '14- 10, '16- 5. World CC: '10-11-13-15: 5J/2J/15/10; AfCC: '12- 8. At 3000m: WJ: '10- 6' WY: '09- 3. At 5000m: Af-J: '11- 3; AfG: '15- 5. At 10000m: AfCh: '14- 4.
Progress at 5000m, 10000m: 2009- 16:25.6A, 2010- 15:03.52, 2011- 15:10.45, 32:05.90; 2012- 14:48.43, 2013- 15:04.38, 2014- 32:45.1A, 2015- 15:43.77, 31:08.82; 2016- 14:51.04, 30:37.38. pbs: 8:49.6 '16, HMar 66:26 '16, Mar 2:27:46 '18.

FINLAND

Governing body: Suomen Urheiluliitto. Founded 1906.
National Championships first held in 1907 (men), 1913 (women). **2018 Champions: Men**: 100m: Eetu Rantala 10.58, 200m: Oskari Lehtonen 21.07, 400m/800m: Markus Teijula 47.77/1:49.38, 1500m: Joonas Rinne 3:52.55, 5000m: Arttu Vattulainen 14:02.95, 10000m: Jaakko Piesanen 30:09.87, HMar: Jarkko Järvenpää 67:02, Mar: Jaakko Nieminen 2:21:59, 3000mSt: Topi Raitanen 8:44.28, 110mh: Elmo Lakka 13.67, 400mh: Joni Vainio-Kaila 51.62, HJ: Samuli Eriksson 2.15, PV: Urho Kujanpää 5.37, LJ: Kristian Bäck 7.93, TJ: Simo Lipsanen 16.27, SP: Timo Kööpikkä 19.13, DT: Frantz Kruger 57.12, HT: Henri Liipola 72.13, JT: Oliver Helander 81.26, Dec: Juuso Hassi 7512, 20kW/30kW: Veli-Matti Partanen 1:26:45/2:07:04.
Women: 100m: Anniina Kortetmaa 11.82, 200m: Milja Thureson 23.65, 400m: Aino Pulkkinen 54.07, 800m/1500m: Sara Kuivisto 2:02.14/4:27.22, 5000m: Kristiina Mäki 16:11.72, 10000m/Mar: Alisa Vainio 33:32.77/2:34:49, HMar: Suvi Miettinen 78:56, 3000mSt: Camilla Richardsson 9:51.46, 100mh: Nooralotta Neziri 12.92, 400mh: Viivi Lehikoinen 57.26, HJ: Eleriin Haas 1.88,

PV: Wilma Murto 4.60, LJ: Kira Kytölä 6.42, TJ: Kristiina Mäkelä 14.31, SP: Senja Mäkitörmä 16.95, DT: Sanna Kämäräinen 56.96, HT: Krista Tervo 68.60, JT: Jenni Kangas 57.09, Hep: Maria Huntington 5858, 10kW/20kW: Elisa Neuvonen 47:54/1:38:32.

Tero PITKÄMÄKI b. 19 Dec 1982 Ilmajoki 1.95m 92kg. Seinäjoen Seudun Urheilijat. Electrical engineer.
At JT: OG: '04- 8, '08- 3, '12- 4, '16- dnq 21; WCh: '05-07-09-11-13-15-17: 4/1/5/dnq 17/2/3/5; EC: '06-10-12-14-16: 2/3/11/3/dnq 14; EU23: '03- 3; EJ: '01- 6; ECp: '06- 1, '15- 1. Won WAF 2005, 2007; DL 2015, Finnish 2004-07, 2013, 2016-17.
Progress at JT: 1999- 66.83, 2000- 73.75, 2001- 74.89, 2002- 77.24, 2003- 80.45, 2004- 84.64, 2005- 91.53, 2006- 91.11, 2007- 91.23, 2008- 87.70, 2009- 87.79, 2010- 86.92, 2011- 85.33, 2012- 86.98, 2013- 89.03, 2014- 86.63, 2015- 89.09, 2016- 86.13, 2017- 88.27, 2018- 82.64.
Partner is Niina Kelo (b. 26 Mar 1980) pb Hep 5956 (15 EC 2006).

Antti RUUSKANEN b. 21 Feb 1984 Kokkola 1.89m 86kg. Pielaveden Sampo.
At JT: OG: '12- 2, '16- 6; WCh: '09-11-13-15: 6/9/5/5; EC: '11- 16 10. 1/0/6, EU23: '05- 2, EJ: '03- 3; CCp: '14- 8. Won FIN 2012, 2014-15.
Progress at JT: 2002- 66.08, 2003- 72.87, 2004- 75.84, 2005- 79.75, 2006- 84.10, 2007- 82.71/ 87.88dh, 2008- 87.33, 2009- 85.39, 2010- 83.45, 2011- 82.29, 2012- 87.79, 2013- 85.70, 2014- 88.01, 2015- 88.98, 2016- 88.23, 2018- 82.59.

FRANCE

Governing body: Fédération Française d'Athlétisme. Founded 1920.
National Championships first held in 1888 (men), 1918 (women). **2018 Champions: Men**: 100m: Marvin René 10.18, 200m: Méba Mickaël Zézé 20.33w, 400m: Christophe Naliali 46.23, 800m: Pierre-Ambroise Bosse 1:46.66, 1500m: Alexis Miellet 3:43.77, 5000m: Florian Carvalho 13:41.91, 10000m: Yann Schrub 29:19.18, HMar: Azeddine Habz 65:00, Mar: Alla Hrioued MAR 2:19:25, 3000mSt: Mahiedine Mekhissi-Benabad 8:33.59, 110mh: Pascal Martinot-Lagarde 13.33w, 400mh: Ludvy Vaillant 49.04, HJ: Mickaël Hanany 2.19, PV: Renaud Lavillenie 5.80, LJ: Kafetien Gomis 8.13, TJ: Harold Corréa 17.05, SP: Fréderíc Dagée 20.01, DT: Lolasson Djouhan 59.84, HT: Quentin Bigot 74.23, JT: Albert Reynolds LCA 76.15, Dec: Ruben Gado 8128, 5000mW/20kW: Gabriel Bordier 19:38.19/1:24:03, 50kW: Florian Mayer 4:15:17. **Women**: 100m/ 200m: Carolle Zahi 11.01/22.92w, 400m: Floria Guei 51.52, 800m: Renelle Lamote 2:00.37, 1500m: Élodie Normand 4:16.20, 5000m: Liv Westphal 16:02.04, 10000m: Samira Mezegrane-Saad 33:20.01, HMar: Fadouwa Ledhem 74:32, Mar: Karine Pasquier 2:39:36, 3000mSt: Ophélie Claude-Boxberger 9.48.21, 100mh: Awa Sène

13.04w, 400mh: Aurélie Chaboudez 56.62, HJ: Prisca Duvernay 1.85, PV: Nino Guillon-Romarin 4.71, LJ: Rougui Sow 6.49, TJ: Jeanine Assani Issouf 14.43, SP: Jessica Cérival 16.70, DT: Pauline Pousse 58.09, HT: Alexandra Tavernier 73.72, JT: Alexie Alais 59.54, Hep: Esther Turpin 6100, 5000mW: Clemence Beretta 22:05.25, 20kW: Émilie Menuet 1:33:11. 50kW: Morgane Ausello 5:18:07.

Morhad AMDOUNI b. 21 Jn 1988 Porto-Vecchio, Corsica 1.75m 60kg. Val d'Europe Atlétisme.
At 5000m/(10000m): WCh: '09- h; EC: '16- 5, '18- 3/1; EJ: '07- 1; ET: '15- 1; ECp: '18- (2); At 1500m: WCh: '15- sf; EC: '16- 13; WJ: '06- h; Eur CC: '06-07-08-10-11-15: 12J/1J/8U23/5/6/9. Won FRA 1500m, 5000m 2016 2015, 2017.
European U23 3000m record 2009.
Progress at 5000m, 10000m: 2006- 14:16.55, 2007- 13:56.03, 2008- 14:04.16, 2009- 13:14.19, 2010- 13:45.49, 2015- 14:04.63, 2016- 13:22.64, 2017- 13:11.18i, 2018- 13:19.14, 27:36.80. pbs: 800m 1:47.20 '15, 1500m 3:34.05 '15, 3000m 7:37.50 '09.

Quentin BIGOT b. 1 Dec 1992 Hayange 1.78m 95kg. Athlétisme Metz Metropole..
At HT: OG: '12- dnq 24; WCh: '13- dnq 13, '17- 4; EC: '12- dnq 24, '18- dnq 16; WJ: '10- 7; WY: '09- dnq 13; EU23: '13- 3; EJ: '11- 1; ET: '13- 3. FRA champion 2017-18.
Progress at HT: 2010- 64.81, 2011- 72.71, 2012- 78.28, 2013- 76.97, 2014- 78.58, 2016- 76.10, 2017- 77.87, 2018- 76.98, 2019- 78.14.
2 years drugs ban 2014-16.

Pierre-Ambroise BOSSE b. 11 May 1992 Nantes 1.85m 68kg. UA Gujan Mestras.
At 800m: OG: '12- sf, '16- 4; WCh: '13- 7, '15- 5, '17- 1; EC: '12-14-16-18: 3/8/5/3; WJ: '10- 8; EU23: '13- 1; EJ: '11- 1; ET: 15- 2; French champion 2012, 2014-15, 2018.
French 800m and European U23 1000m records 2014; European 600m record 2016.
Progress at 800m: 2007- 2:02.81, 2008- 1:56.05, 2010- 1:48.38, 2011- 1:46.18, 2012- 1:44.97, 2013- 1:43.76, 2014- 1:42.53, 2015- 1:43.88, 2016- 1:43.41, 2017- 1:44.67, 2018- 1:44.20. pbs: 100m 17.51 '16, 600m 1:13.21 '16, 1000m 2:15.31 '14, 1500m 3:54.81 '09.

Axel CHAPELLE b. 24 Apr 1995 Colombes 1.82m 77kg. EA Cergy Pontoise Athlétisme.
At PV: WCh: '17- 6; EC: '18- 8; WJ: '12- dnq 15, '14- 1; EU23: '15- 10=, '17- 2; EJ: '13- 2; EI: '17- 6.
Progress at PV: 2009- 3.90, 2010- 4.25. 2011- 4.90i/4.75, 2012- 5.12, 2013- 5.35i/5.32, 2014- 5.55, 2015- 5.55, 2016- 5.65, 2017- 5.80i/5.72, 2018- 5.88i/5.70.

Garfield DARIEN b. 22 Dec 1987 Lyon 1.87m 76kg. EA Chambéry.
At 110mh: OG: '12- sf; WCh: '09- sf, '15- 8, '17- 4; EC: '10-12-18: 2/2/sf; WJ: '04- 7; EJ: '05- 1; CCp: '10- 4; ET: '11- 2; French champion 2012, 2015. At

60mh: WI: '14- 3; EI: '09-11-17: 6/2/4.
Progress at 110mh: 2004- 14.03/13.98w, 2005-
13.73, 2006- 13.94/13.92w, 2008- 13.50/13.43w,
2009- 13.36, 2010- 13.34, 2011- 13.37, 2012- 13.15,
2013- 14.47, 2014- 14.01, 2015- 13.17, 2017- 13.09,
2018- 13.45/13.35w. pbs: 200m 22.05 '06, 60mh
7.47i '14, HJ 1.83 '04.
Father Daniel Darien had 110mh pb 13.76 '87.

Yohann DINIZ b. 1 Jan 1978 Epernay 1.85m
69kg. EFS Reims Athlétisme.
At 20kW: ECp: '07- 1, '15- 3; At 50kW: OG: '08-
dnf, '12- dq, '16- 8; WCh: '05-07-09-11-13-17:
dq/2/11/dq/10/1; EC: '06-10-14: 1/1/1; ECp: '05-
13: 4/1. Won FRA 10000mW 2010, 2012, 2014;
20kW 2007-09, 2015; 35kW 2019; 50kW 2005,
2016.
Walks records: world track 50,000m 2011, road
50k 2014, 20k 2015. French 5000mW (3) 2006-08,
10000mW 2014, 20000mW 2014, 20kW (4) 2005-
15, 35kW 2019, 50kW 2006 & 2009, 1 Hr 2010.
Progress at 20kW, 50kW: 2001- 1:35:05.0t, 2002-
1:30:40, 2003- 1:26:54.99t, 2004- 1:24:25, 3:52:11.0t;
2005- 1:20:20, 3:45:17; 2006- 1:23:19, 3:41:39; 2007-
1:18:58, 3:44:22; 2008- 1:22:31, 2009- 1:22:50,
3:38:45; 2010- 1:20:23, 3:40:37; 2011- 3:35:27.2t,
2012- 1:17:43, 2013- 1:23:17, 3:41:07; 2014- 1:19:42.1t,
3:32:33; 2015- 1:17:02, 2016- 3:37:48, 2017- 1:27:19,
3:33:12. pbs: 3000mW 10:52.44 '08, 5000mW
18:16.76i '14, 18:18.01 '08; 10000mW 38:08.13 '14,
20000mW 1:19:42.1 '14, 1HrW 15,395m '10, 35kW
2:29:28 '19.

Renaud LAVILLENIE b. 18 Sep 1986
Barbezieux-Saint-Hilaire 1.77m 69kg. Clermont
Athl. Auvergne.
At PV: OG: '12- 1, '16- 2; WCh: '09-11-13-15-17:
3/3/2/3=/3; WI: '12-16-18- 1/1/1; EC: '10-12-14-
16-18: 1/1/1/nh/3; EU23: '07- 10; EI: '09-11-13-15:
1/1/1/1; CCp: '10- 2, '14- 1, '18- 2; ET: '09-10-13-
14-15-17: 1/1/1/1/1/1. Won DL 2010-16, French
2010, 2012-15, 2017-18.
World indoor pole vault record 2014. French
record (indoors) 2011 and outdoors 2013.
Progress at PV: 2002- 3.40, 2003- 4.30, 2004- 4.60,
2005- 4.81i/4.70, 2006- 5.25i/5.22, 2007-
5.58i/5.45, 2008- 5.81i/5.65, 2009- 6.01, 2010-
5.94, 2011- 6.03i/5.90, 2012- 5.97, 2013- 6.02, 2014-
6.16i/5.93, 2015- 6.05, 2016- 6.03i/5.98, 2017- 5.91,
2018- 5.95. pbs: 60m 7.23i '08, 100m 11.04 '11,
60mh 8.41i '08, 100m 11.04 '11, 110mh 14.51 '10,
HJ 1.89i '08, 1.87 '07; LJ 7.31 '10, Hep 5363i '08.
Broke Sergey Bubka's 21 year-old absolute
pole vault record indoors in 2014. 23
successive wins 31 Aug 2013 to EC 2014, only
man to win all seven Diamond League titles
from 2010. IAAF Male Athlete of the Year 2014.
His brother **Valentin** (b. 16 Jul 1991) has PV pb
5.80i '15, 5.71 '16; 3rd EU23 and nh WCh in 2013;
6 EI '15, dnq 14 WCh '17. Renaud married Anais
Poumarat (PV 4.26i/4.20 '14) in September 2018,

Christophe LEMAITRE b. 11 Jun 1990 Annecy
1.89m 74kg. AS Aix-les-Bains.

At 100m/(200m): OG: '12- (6)/3R, '16- sf/3; WCh:
'09- qf, '11- 4/3/2R, '13- 7, '15- sf/sf;, '17)sf) EC:
'10- 1/1/1R, '12- 1/3R, '14- 2/2/3R; WJ: '08- (1);
WY: '07- 4/5; EJ: '09- 1; CCp: '10- 1, '14- 5/4/2R;
ET: '10- 2, '11- 1/1, '13- (1), '15- 1/2R. At 60m: EI:
'11- 3. Won French 100m 2010-12, 2014, 2017;
200m 2010-15.
Records: European 4x200m 2014; French 100m
(7) 2010-11, 200m (2) 2010-11, European junior
100m 2009. U23 100m 2010-11, 200m 2011.
Progress at 100m, 200m: 2005- 11.46, 2006- 10.96,
2007- 10.53, 21.08; 2008- 10.26, 20.83; 2009-
10.04/10.03w, 20.68; 2010- 9.97, 20.16; 2011- 9.92,
19.80; 2012- 10.04/9.94w, 19.91; 2013- 10.00/9.98w,
20.07; 2014- 10.10, 20.08; 2015- 10.07, 20.21; 2016-
10.07, 20.01; 2017- 10.18, 20.21; 2018- 10.17, 20.19.
pbs: 60m 6.55i '10, 150m St 14.90 '13.
First Caucasian sub-10.00 100m runner and
first to win sprint treble at European Champs;
now has men's record eight EC medals.

Pascal MARTINOT-LAGARDE b. 22 Sep 1991
St Maur-des-Fossés 1.90m 80kg. Neuilly
Plaisance Sport.
At 110mh: OG: '16- 4; WCh: '13- h, '15- 4; EC:
'14- 3, '18- 1; WJ: '10- 1; EU23: '11- h; EJ: '09- 4;
CCp: '18- 3; ET: '13-14-15: 2/3/2; won DL 2014,
FRA 2014, 2018. At 60mh: WI: '12-14-16-18:
3/2/2/5; EI: '13-15-17-19: 3/1/2/2.
French 110m hurdles record 2014.
Progress at 110mh: 2008- 15.03, 2009- 14.13,
2010- 13.74, 2011- 13.94, 2012- 13.41/13.30w, 2013-
13.12, 2014- 12.95, 2015- 13.06, 2016- 13.12, 2018-
13.17. pbs: 60m 7.07i '10, 100m 10.94 '13, 60mh
7.45i '14.
His brother **Thomas** (b. 7 Feb 1988) has 110mh
pb 13.26, 7 WCh and French champion in 2013.

Kevin MAYER b. 10 Feb 1992 Argenteuil 1.86m
82kg. EA Tain-Tournon.
At Dec: OG: '12- 15, '16- 2; WCh: '13- 4, '17- 1; EC:
'12-14-18: dnf/2/dnf; WJ: '10- 1; EJ: '11- 1; ECp:
'13- 1. At Oct: WY: '09- 1. At Hep: WI: '18- 1; EI:
'13- 2, '17- 1.
Records: World decathlon 2018, European indoor
heptathlon 2017, French Decn 2016 & 2018.
Progress at Dec: 2011- 7992, 2012- 8447w/8415,
2013- 8446, 2014- 8521, 2015- 8469, 2016- 8834,
2017- 8768, 2018- 9126. pbs: 60m 6.85i '18, 100m
10.55 '18, 200m 21.76 '17, 400m 48.28 '16, 1000m
2:37.30i '13, 1500m 4:18.04 '12, 60mh 7.72i '19,
110mh 13.71 '18, 400mh 54.57 '17, HJ 2.10i '10,
2.09 '12; PV 5.60i/5.45 '18; LJ 7.80 '18, SP 16.51
'18, DT 52.38 '18, JT 71.90 '87, Hep 6479i '17.
Four individual event pbs when adding 313
points to his decathlon best for 2016 OG silver
and also in WR at Talence 2018. Three no jumps
in European Champs decathlon 2018..

Mahiédine MEKHISSI-BENABBAD b. 15
Mar 1985 Reims 1.90m 75kg. EFS Reims.
At 3000mSt: OG: '08- 2, '12- 2, '16- 3; WCh:
'07/09- h, '11- 3, '13- 3, '17- 4 (h 1500m); EC: '10-
12-14-16-18: 1/1,dq (1 1500m)/1/1; WJ: '04- h;

EU23: '05- h, '07- 1; CCp: '10- 3; ET: '07-08-17: 2/1/1. At 1500m: WI: '10- 8; EI: '13- 1; WCp: '06-7, '14- 3. Eur CC: '18- 2 mxR. Won FRA 1500m 2014, 3000mSt 2008, 2012-13, 2016, 2018.
Records: World best 2000m steeplechase 2010. European 3000mSt 2013, French 1M 2014
Progress at 3000mSt: 2003- 9:52.07, 2004- 9:01.01, 2005- 8:34.45, 2006- 8:28.25, 2007- 8:14.22, 2008- 8:08.95, 2009- 8:06.98, 2010- 8:02.52, 2011- 8:02.09, 2012- 8:10.90, 2013- 8:00.09, 2014- 8:03.23, 2016- 8:08.15, 2017- 8:14.67, 2018- 8:16.97. pbs: 800m 1:53.61 '04, 1000m 2:17.14 '09, 1500m 3:33.12 '13, 1M 3:51.55 '14, 2000m 4:56.85 '13, 3000m 7:43.72i '13, 7:44.98 '10; 5000m 13:20.53 '18, 2000mSt 5:10.68 '10. Disqualified after he took his vest off in the finishing straight when finishing well clear in 2014 EC steeplechase.

Teddy TAMGHO b. 15 Jun 1989 Paris 1.87m 82kg. Bordeaux
At TJ: WCh: '09- 11, '13- 1; EC: '10- 3; WI: '10- 1; WJ: '08- 1; EJ: '07- 4; EI: '11- 1 (4 LJ); ET: '10- 3, '13- 2. Won DL 2010, French 2009-10, 2013, 2016.
Four World indoor triple jump records 2010 (17.90) & 2011, four absolute French records 2009-13; three Eur U23 records 2010.
Progress at TJ: 2004- 12.56, 2005- 14.89, 2006- 15.58, 2007- 16.53i/16.35/16.42w, 2008- 17.19/ 17.33w, 2009- 17.58i/17.11, 2010- 17.98, 2011- 17.92i/17.91, 2013- 18.04, 2015- 17.24, 2016- 17.15, 2018- 16.19i. pbs: 60m 6.92i '06, 100m 10.60 '09, LJ 8.01i '11, 7.81 '13.
2011 season ended when broke ankle in warm-up for European U23s and also missed all of 2012. His 18.04 to win 2013 World title was third best ever and world's best for 17 years. Fractured his shin in November 2013 and missed all the 2014 season.

Jimmy VICAUT b. 27 Feb 1992 Bondy 1.88m 83kg. SCO Sainte-Marguerite de Marseille.
At 100m/(200m)/4x100mR: OG: '12- sf/3R, '16-7; WCh: '11- 6/2R, '13- sf/sf, '15- 8, '17- 6; EC: '10- 1R, '12- 2/3R (res), '14- sf, '16- 3/2R, '18- dns; WJ: '10- 3; WY: '09- 7; EJ: '11- 1/1R; ET: '13- 1, '14- 1. At 60m: EI: '13- 1. Won French 100m 2013, 2015-16; 200m 2016.
Equalled European 100m record 2015.
Progress at 100m: 2005- 13.0, 2006- 12.50, 2007- 11.0, 2008- 10.75/10.69w, 2009- 10.56, 2010- 10.16, 2011- 10.07, 2012- 10.02, 2013- 9.95, 2014- 9.95/9.89w, 2015- 9.86, 2016- 9.86, 2017- 9.97, 2018- 9.91. pbs: 60m 6.48i '13, 200m 20.30 '13.
His brother Willi was French U17 shot champion in 2012 and has senior pb of 17.33 '14.

Women

Floria GUEI b. 2 May 1990 Nantes 1.68m 53kg. E.Sud Lyonnais.
At 400m: OG: '16- sf; WCh: '11- hR, 13- sf/3R, '15- sf; EC: '12- 2R, '14- sf/1R, '16- 2/2R, '18-7/2R; WJ: '08- h; EU23: '11- h/3R; EI: '11- 3R, '15- 1R, '17- 1; ET: '15- 1. French champion 2013,

2015-16, 2018.
Progress at 400m: 2008- 54.08, 2009- 52.90, 2010- 53.00, 2011- 52.77, 2012- 51.96, 2013- 51.42, 2014- 51.30, 2015- 50.89, 2016- 50.84, 2017- 51.51, 2018- 51.50. Pbs: 50m 6.62i '09, 60m 7.56i '17, 100m 11.82 '09, 200m 23.00 '16, 300m 36.46i '16.
Brilliant anchor 400m legs including 49.71 at '14 EC, 49.95 at '15 WCh and 49.92 '16 EC. Expecting a baby in 2019.

Ninon GUILLON-ROMARIN b. 15 Apr 1995 Metz 1.63m 53kg. EA Cery-Pontoise.
At PV: WCh:'17- dnq 20=; EC: '18- 5; WJ: '14- 9; WY: '11- dnq 20=; EU23: '15- 7=, '17- 5; EJ: '13- 4; WI: '18- 10; EI: '19- 7; ET: '17- 3. French champion 2016, 2018, MedG 2018.
Two French PV records (& 1 indoor) 2018.
Progress at PV: 2008- 2.75i, 2009- 3.30, 2010- 3.61i, 2011- 3.81i/3,80, 2012- 4.07i/4.00, 2013- 4.16i/4.15, 2014- 4.20, 2015- 4.35, 2016- 4.40, 2017- 4.60, 2018- 4.75, 2019- 4.73i. Pbs: 60m 7.94i '13, 100m 12.44 '11.
Younger brother Gauvain 7 WY '17, pb 5.40 '18.

Rénelle LAMOTE b. 26 Dec 1993 Annecy 1.68m 57kg. Annecy Haute Savoie.
At 800m: OG: '16- h; WCh: '15- 8; EC: '14-16-18: sf/2/2; WJ: '12- sf; EU23: '13- h, 15- 1; EI: '19- 2; ET: '14- 2, '15- 1. Eur CC: '18- 2 mxR. French champion 2014, 2016, 2018.
Progress at 800m: 2009- 2:18.24, 2010- 2:14.53, 2011- 2:08.39, 2012- 2:05.23, 2013- 2:02.40, 2014- 2:00.06, 2015- 1:58.86, 2016- 1:58.01, 2018- 1:58.83. Pbs: 400m 53.92 '16, 1000m 2:34.48 '18, 1500m 4.35.93 '13, 10kRd 37:13 '14.

Solène NDAMA b. 20 Sep 1998 Bordeaux 1.75m 66kg. Bordeaux Athle.
At Hep: WY: '15- 29. At Pen: EI: '19- 3. At 100mh: EC: '18- dq; EJ: '17- 1.
Progress at 100mh, Hep: 2015- 14.43/14.15w, 2016- 13.54/13.51w, 5288; 2017- 13.15, 5657; 2018- 12.77, 5932. pbs: 60m 7.63i '18, 100m 12.19 '17, 200m 24.05 '18, 400m 57.36i '18, 800m 2:11.92i '19, 2:12.49 '18; 60mh 8.03i '19, HJ 1.78i '19, 1.74 '17; LJ 6.27i '19, 5.99/6.02w '18; SP 14.47i '19, 13.12 '18; JT 33.88 '18, Pen 4723i '18.

Mélina ROBERT-MICHON b. 18 Jul 1979 Voiron 1.80m 85kg. Lyon Athlétisme
At DT: OG: '00/04- dnq 29/30, '08- 7, '12- 5, '16- 2; WCh: '01-03-07-09-13-15-17: dnq 20/11/11/ 8/2/10/3; EC: '98-02-06-12-14-16: dnq 29/12/dnq 16/6/2/5; WJ: '98- 2; EU23: '99-12, '01- 1; WUG: '01- 3; CCp: '14- 4; ECp: '00-01-02-03-04-06-07-08-09-13-14-15-17: 5/6/8/2/4/7/5/4/2/1/1/1/1. French champion 2000-09, 2011-17; MedG 2009.
Six French discus records 2000-16.
Progress at DT: 1997- 49.10, 1998- 59.27, 1999- 60.17, 2000- 63.19/63.61dh, 2001- 63.87, 2002- 65.78, 2003- 64.27, 2004- 64.54, 2005- 58.01, 2006- 59.89, 2007- 63.48, 2008- 62.21, 2009- 63.04, 2010- 56.52, 2011- 61.07, 2012- 63.98, 2013- 66.28, 2014- 65.51, 2015- 65.04, 2016- 66.73, 2017- 66.21. pbs:

SP 15.23 '07, HT 47.92 '02.
Daughters Elyssa born in 2010 and Enora in June 2018. Broke her 11 year-old French record in winning 2013 World silver.

Alexandra TAVERNIER b. 13 Dec 1993 Annecy 1.70m 82kg. Annecy Haute Savoie.
At HT: OG: '16- 11; WCh: '15- 3, '17- 12; EC: '14-16-18: 6/dnq/2; WJ: '12- 1; EU23: '15- 1; EJ: '11- 6; CCp: '18- 3; ET: '15- 3. French champion 2014, 2016-17. French hammer record 2018.
Progress at HT: 2009- 44.96, 2010- 58.44, 2011- 62.13, 2012- 70.62, 2013- 70.79, 2014- 71.17, 2015- 74.39, 2016- 72.16, 2017- 72.69, 2018- 74.78. Pbs: SP 11.81 '14, DT 41.58 '10.
Her brother Hugo (b. 12 Dec 1999) was 5th in the 2018 World Junior hammer with a 6kg pb of 75.99; pb senior hammer 63.42 '18.

GERMANY

Governing body: Deutscher Leichtathletik Verband (DLV). Founded 1898.
National Championships first held in 1891.
2018 Champions: Men: 100m: Kevin Kranz 10.28, 200m: Robin Erewa 20.63, 400m: Johannes Trefz 45.70, 800m: Benedikt Huber 1:47.32, 1500m: Timo Benitz 3:38.77, 5000m/10000m: Sebastian Hendel 14:16.54/29:13.64, HMar: Karsten Meier 65:22, Mar: Tom Gröschel 2:15:20, 3000mSt: Martin Grau 8:33.90, 110mh: Georg Traber 13.37, 400mh: Luke Campbell 50.31, HJ: Mateusz Przybylko 2.31, PV: Bo Kanda Lita Baehre 5.50, LJ: Fabian Heinle 8.04, TJ: Felix Wenzel 16.08, SP: David Storl 21.26, DT: Christoph Harting 66.98, HT: Johannes Bichler 71.67, JT: Andreas Hofmann 89.55, Dec: Niklas Ransiek 7355, 20kW: Christopher Linke 1:20:40, 50kW: Jonathan Hilbert 3:51:22. **Women:** 100m: Gina Lückenkemper 11.15, 200m: Jessica-Bianca Wessolly 22.89, 400m: Nadine Gonska 52.07, 800m: Christina Hering 2:01.56, 1500m: Konstanze Klosterhalfen 4:06.34, 5000m: Hanna Klein 15:17.47, 10000m: Anna Ghering 33:33.96; HMar: Franziska Reng 74:14, Mar: Fabienne Amrhein 2:32:35, 3000mSt: Gesa-Felicitas Krause 9:34.58, 100mh: Pamela Dutkiewicz 12.69, 400mh: Christine Salterberg 56.97, HJ: Marie-Laurence Jungfleisch 1.87, PV: Jacqueline Otchere 4.45, LJ: Malaika Mihambo 6.72, TJ: Neele Eckhardt 14.21, SP: Christina Schwanitz 20.06, DT: Shanice Craft 62.91, HT: Kathrin Klaas 66.08, JT: Christin Hussong 63.54, Hep: Anna Maiwald 5711; 20kW: Emilia Lehmeyer 1:32:49.

Arthur ABELE b. 30 Jul 1986 Mutlangen, Baden-Württemberg 1.84m 80kg. SSV Ulm 1846.
At Dec: OG: '08- dnf, '16- 15; WCh: '07- 9; EC: '14- 5, '18- 1; WJ: '04- 7; EJ: '05- 2; ECp: '04- 4. German champion 2013. At Hep: '15- 2.
Progress at Dec: 2006- 8012, 2007- 8269, 2008- 8372, 2013- 8251, 2014- 8477, 2016- 8605, 2017-

dnf, 2018- 8481. pbs: 60m 6.93i '15, 100m 10.67 '14, 200m 22.41 '14, 400m 47.98 '08, 1000m 2:35.64i '15, 1500m 4:15.35 '08, 60mh 7.67i '15, 110mh 13.55 '14, 400mh 51.71 '04, HJ 2.04 '07, PV 5.01 '14, LJ 7.57 '16. SP 15.93 '18, DT 46.20 '16, JT 71.89 '16, Hep 6279i '15.
Five individual event absolute bests in 2015 European Indoor heptathlon, but Achilles injury cost him the summer season. Won at Ratingen 2007, 2016, 2018, IAAF Challenge 2018.

Rico FREIMUTH b. 14 Mar 1988 Potsdam 1.96m 92kg. SV Halle.
At Dec: OG: '12- 6, '16- dnf; WCh: '11-13-15-17: dnf/7/3/2; EC: '14- 7; EU23: '09- 10; EJ: '07- 3.
Progress at Dec: 2009- 7689, 2010- 7826, 2011- 8287, 2012- 8322, 2013- 8488w/8382, 2014- 8356, 2015- 8561, 2017- 8663. pbs: 60m 6.98i '12, 100m 10.40 '14, 10.36w '13; 200m 21.39 '12, 400m 47.51 '12, 1000m 2:48.22i '12, 1500m 4:34.60 '13, 60mh 7.83i '14, 110mh 13.63 '14, HJ 2.01 '17, PV 4.90 '12, LJ 7.60 '17, SP 15.62 '15, DT 51.56 '17, JT 65.04 '11, Hep 5715i '12.
Won IAAF Combined Events Challenge 2014, 2017. His father Uwe had decathlon best of 8794 (1984), and was 4th at 1983 Worlds and 1986 Europeans and twice winner at Götzis. Uwe and Rico are the highest scoring father-son combination. His uncle Jörg won the high jump bronze medal at the 1980 Olympic Games in a pb of 2.31.

Christoph HARTING b. 10 Apr 1990 Cottbus 2.07m 120kg. SCC Berlin. Police officer.
At DT: OG: '16- 1; WCh: '13- dnq 13, '15- 8; EC: '16- 4, '18- dnq; EU23: '11- 5. German champion 2015, 2018.
Progress at DT: 2008- 52.00, 2009- 50.19, 2010- 61.19, 2011- 62.12, 2012- 61.22, 2013- 64.99, 2014- 63.78, 2015- 67.93, 2016- 68.37, 2017- 64.55, 2018- 67.59. pb SP 17.75 '12.
Robert (2012) and Christoph Harting are the first siblings to win the same individual event in the history of the Summer Olympics.

Max HESS b. 13 Jul 1996 Chemnitz 1.86m 79kg. LAC Erdgas Chemnitz.
At TJ: OG: '16- dnq 15; EC: '16- 1, '18- dnq 15; WJ: '14- 2; WY: '13- 8; EU23: '17- 3; WI: '16- 2; EI: '17- 3, '19- 3; ET: 17- 1. GER champion 2016-17.
Progress at TJ: 2012- 14.58, 2013- 15.52, 2014- 16.55, 2015- 16.34i/16.07, 2016- 17.20, 2017- 17.52i/17.13/17.24w, 2018- 16.95, 2019- 17.10i. pbs: 60m 6.93i '18, LJ 8.03i '16.

Andreas HOFMANN b. 16 Dec 1991 Heidelberg 1.95m 108kg. MTG Mannheim. Sports student.
At JT: WCh: '15- 6, '17- 8; EC: '14- 9, '18- 2; EJ: '09- 1; WUG: '17- 2; ET: '14- 1. German champion 2018, DL 2018.
Progress at JT: 2008- 65.03, 2009- 77.84, 2010- 66.75, 2011- 73.98, 2012- 80.81, 2013- 75.56, 2014- 86.13, 2015- 86.14, 2016- 85.42, 2017- 92.06, 2018- 92.06. pb SP 18.59i '17.

Raphael HOLZDEPPE b. 28 Sep 1989 Kaiserslautern 1.81m 78kg. LAZ Zweibrücken. At PV: OG: 08- 7, '12- 3, '16- dnq 26; WCh: '11-13-15-17: dnq 20/1/2/nh; EC '10-12-18: 9/3/dnq; WJ: '06- 5, '08- 1; EU23: '09- 1, '11- 6; EJ: '07- dnq; ET: '15- 2; WI: '18- 5=; EI: '13- 8, '17- 5. GER champion 2015. World junior pole vault record (=) 2008 (and indoors 5.68).
Progress at PV: 2002- 3.45, 2003- 4.25, 2004- 4.50, 2005- 5.00, 2006- 5.42, 2007- 5.50, 2008- 5.80, 2009- 5.65, 2010- 5.80, 2011- 5.72, 2012- 5.91, 2013- 5.91, 2014- 5.53, 2015- 5.94, 2016- 5.84i/5.70, 2017- 5.80, 2018- 5.88i/5.81.

Daniel JASINSKI b. 5 Aug 1989 Bochum 2.07m 125kg. TV Wattenscheid.
At DT: OG: '16- 3; WCh: '15- dnq 15; EC: '14-16-18: 7/8/dnq 19; WJ: '08- dnq 24; EU23: '11- 6.
Progress at DT: 2008- 49.15, 2009- 55.01, 2010- 59.02, 2011- 61.28, 2012- 64.37, 2013- 64.69, 2014- 65.98, 2015- 65.93, 2016- 67.16, 2017- 62.20, 2018- 66.59.

Niklas KAUL b. 11 Feb 1998 Mayence 1.92m 84kg. USC Mainz.
At Dec: EC: '18- 4; WJ: '16- 1; WY: '15- 1 (2 JT); EJ: '17- 1.
World Junior record 8435 for U20 spec 2017.
Progress at Dec: 2018- 8220. pbs: 100m 11.20 '18, 400m 48.09 '18, 1500m 4:15.52 '17, 60mh 8.24i '19, 110mh 14.55 '18, HJ 2.10 '16, PV 5.00i '19, 4.80 '16; LJ 7.29 '18. SP 14.20 '18, DT 46.30 '18, JT 72.89 '17.

Kai KAZMIREK b. 28 Jan 1991 Torgau 1.89m 91kg. LG Rhein-Wied.
At Dec: OG: '16- 4; WCh: '15- 6, '17- 3; EC: '14- 6; WJ: '10- 6; EU23: '11- 6, '13- 1; EJ: '09- 3. German champion 2012. At Hep: WI: '14- 6, '18- 4.
Progress at Dec: 2011- 7802, 2012- 8130, 2013- 8366, 2014- 8471, 2015- 8462, 2016- 8580, 2017- 8488, 2018- 8329. pbs: 60m 7.01i '15, 100m 10.62 '16, 10.61w '13; 200m 21.40 '12, 400m 46.75 '11, 1000m 2:39.51i '14, 1500m 4:30.75 '18, 60mh 7.95i '18, 110mh 14.05 '14, HJ 2.15 '14, PV 5.20 '13, LJ 7.69 '16, SP 14.82 '17, DT 45.83 '15, JT 64.60 '16, Hep 6238i '18.
Won Götzis decathlon 2015. IAAF Combined Events Challenge 2016.

Christopher LINKE b. 24 Oct 1988 Potsdam 1.90m 65kg. SC Potsdam
At 20kW/(50kW): OG: '12- (21), '16- 5; WCh: '11-13-15'17: 16/9/38/5; EC: '10-14-18: (dnf)/5/13; EU23: '09- 4; WCp: '12- (3), '16- 10; ECp: '11-13-15-17: (3)/10/7/1. At 10000mW: EJ: '07- 6. Won GER 10000W 2011, 2014-16, 20kW 2012, 2014, 2016-18; 50kW 2008.
Progress at 20kW, 50kW: 2008- 1:25;25, 4:03:59; 2009- 1:24:29, 2010- 1:27:25, 3:53:24; 2011- 1:20:51, 3:52:56; 2012- 1:20:41, 3:47:33; 2013- 1:22:36, 2014- 1:21:00, 2015- 1:20:37, 2016- 1:19:19, 2017- 1:18:56; 2018- 1:20:40. pbs: 3000mW 10:49.33i '18, 11:49.10A '10, 5000mW 18:33.86i '19, 20:37.47 '08; 10000W 38:40.25 '16.

Mateusz PRZYBYLKO b. 9 Mar 1992 Bielefeld 1.95m 79kg. TSV Bayer 04 Leverkusen
At HJ: OG: '16- dnq 28; WCh: '15- dnq 28=, '17- 5; EC: '18- 1; WJ: '10- dnq; WY: '09- 11; EU23: '13- 5; EJ: '11- 7; WI: '18- 3; EI: '17- 7, '19- 8; ET: '15- 3. GER champion 2017-18.
Progress at HJ: 2009- 2.14i/2.10, 2010- 2.16, 2011- 2.20, 2012- 2.20, 2013- 2.24, 2014- 2.24i/2.22, 2015- 2.30, 2016- 2.29, 2017- 2.35, 2018- 2.35.
Clear at six heights to 2.35 for 2018 EC gold.

Thomas RÖHLER b. 30 Sep 1991 Jena 1.92m 92kg. LC Jena. Sports student.
At JT: OG: '16- 1; WCh: '13- dnq 29, '15- 4, '17- 4; EC: '12-14-16-18: dnq 13/12/5/1; WJ: '10- 9; EU23: '11- 7, '13- 3; CCp: '18- 1; ET: '13- 2, '17- 3. Won DL 2014, German champion 2012-16. German javelin record 2017.
Progress at JT: 2009- 61.26, 2010- 76.37, 2011- 78.20, 2012- 80.79, 2013- 83.95, 2014- 87.63, 2015- 89.27, 2016- 91.28, 2017- 93.90, 2018- 91.78

David STORL b. 21 Jul 1990 Rochlitz 1.98m 125kg. Leipzig SC DHfK. Federal police officer.
At SP: OG: '12- 2, '16- 7; ; WCh: '09-11-13-15-17: dnq 26/1/1/2/10; EC: '10-12-14-16-18: 4/1/1/1/3; WJ: '08- 1; WY: '07- 1; EU23: '11- 1; EJ: '09- 1; WI: '10-12-14-18: 5/2/2/2; EI: '11-15-17-19: 2/1/3/2; WCp: '14- 1; ET: '11-13-14-15-17: 1/1/1/1/2. German champion 2011-12, 2014-18.
World junior shot record and three with 6kg (to 22.73) 2009.
Progress at SP: 2008- 18.46, 2009- 20.43, 2010- 20.77, 2011- 21.78, 2012- 21.88i/21.86, 2013- 21.73, 2014- 21.97, 2015- 22.20, 2016- 21.31, 2017- 21.87, 2018- 21.62. Ten major international titles & seven second places.

Johannes VETTER b. 26 Mar 1993 Dresden 1.88m 105kg. LG Offenburg.
At JT: OG: '16- 4; WCh: '15- 7, '17- 1; EC: '16- dnq 16, '18- 5; EU23: '15- 4; EJ: '11- 12; ET: '15- 2. GER champion 2017. German javelin record 2017.
Progress at JT: 2010- 63.60, 2011- 71.60, 2012- 60.19, 2013- 76.58, 2014- 79.75, 2015- 85.40, 2016- 89.57, 2017- 94.44, 2018- 92.70.
Best ever throw in a qualifying round with 90.26 at 2017 Worlds, then 89.89 to win final.

Julian WEBER b. 29 Aug 1994 Mainz 1.90m 94kg. USC Mainz.
At JT: OG: '16- 9; EU23: '15- 5; EJ: '13- 1.
Progress at JT: 2012- 71.12, 2013- 79.68, 2014- 80.72, 2015- 81.15, 2016- 88.29, 2017- 85.85, 2018- 86.63.

Martin WIERIG b. 10 Jun 1987 Neindorf 2.02m 127kg. SC Magdeburg. Federal police officer.
At DT: OG: '12- 6; WCh: '11-/15/17 dnq 18/19/nt, '13- 4; EC: '10-12-14-16: 7/dnq 14/11/dnq 14; WJ: '04- 8, '06- 3; EU23: '07- 1, '09- 3; EJ: '05- 3 (dnq SP); ET: '15- 2.
Progress at DT: 2005- 57.44, 2006- 57.37, 2007- 61.10, 2008- 63.09, 2009- 63.90, 2010- 64.93, 2011- 67.21, 2012- 68.33, 2013- 67.46, 2014- 66.59, 2015-

65.94, 2016- 67.16, 2017- 65.56, 2018- 66.98. pb SP
17.30 '11.

Women

Shanice CRAFT b. 15 May 1993 Mannheim
1.85m 89kg. MTG Mannheim. Police officer.
At (SP)/DT: OG: '16- 11; WCh: '15- 7; EC: '14-16-
18: 3/3/3; WJ: '12- 1/2; WY: '09- 3; EU23: '13- 2/2,
'15- 2/1; EJ: '11- 1; ET: '14- 2. Won GER 2014,
2018; Yth Oly 2010,
Progress at DT: 2007- 44.86, 2008- 48.14, 2009-
50.57, 2010- 55.49, 2011- 58.65, 2012- 62.92, 2013-
60.77, 2014- 65.88, 2015- 64.79, 2016- 64.82, 2017-
63.18, 2018- 62.91. Pb SP 17.75 '14. US father.

Pamela DUTKIEWICZ b. 28 Sep 1991 Kassel
1.70m 63kgkg. TV Wattenscheid 01.
At 100mh: OG: '16- sf, WCh: '17- 3; EC: '16- dnf,
'18- 2; CCp: '18- 4; ET: '17- 1. GER champion
2017-18. At 60mh: EI: '17- 3.
Progress at 100mh: 2008- 14.13, 2009- 13.92,
2010- 13.37, 2011- 13.50/13.49w, 2012- 13.45, 2013-
13.39, 2014- 12.95, 2016- 12.85, 2017- 12.61, 2018-
12.67. pbs: 60m 7.35i '18, 100m 12.21 '13, 200m
24.17i '14, 24.65 '13;, 60mh 7.79i '17.
Polish parents, mother Brygida Bak won POL
800m in 1984, pb 2:02.39 '86.

Kristin GIERISCH b. 20 Aug 1990 Zwickau
1.78m 59kg. LAC Erdgas Chemnitz. Police.
At TJ: OG: '16- 11; WCh: '15- 7, '17- 5; EC: '14-16-
18: 9/8/2; WY: '07- 6; EU23: '11- dns; EJ: '09- 5; EI:
'15- 4, '17- 1; CCp: '18- 5; ET: '15- 2, '17- 2; WI:
'16- 2. German champion 2014-15, 2017.
Progress at TJ: 2006- 12.09, 2007- 13.00, 2008-
12.22, 2009- 14.02, 2010- 13.84, 2011- 14.10i/13.47,
2012- 14.19i/13.94, 2013- 13.91i/13.67, 2014-
14.31/14.34w, 2015- 14.46i/14.38/14.46w, 2016-
14.31, 2017- 14.40, 2018- 14.45. pbs: 60m 7.59i '12,
LJ 6.46i '15, 6.21 '14.

Julia HARTING b. 1 Apr 1990 Berlin 1.92m
95kg. née Fischer. SCC Berlin. Police officer.
At DT: OG: '12- dnq 20, '16- 9; WCh: '13- dnq 13,
'15- 5, '17- 9; EC: '12-14-16: 5/5/2; WJ: '08- 2; WY:
'07- 1; EU23: '11- 1; EJ: '09- 2; ET: '13- 2. GER
champion 2015, 2017.
Progress at DT: 2005- 45.69, 2006- 50.23, 2007-
51.39, 2008- 55.92, 2009- 56.74, 2010- 57.49, 2011-
59.60, 2012- 64.22, 2013- 66.04, 2014- 66.46, 2015-
65.98, 2016- 68.49, 2017- 63.63, 2018- 61.63.
Married Robert Harting (DT won OG 2012,
WCh 2009, 2011, 2013, EC 2012, 2014) on 17 Sep
2016. Expecting twins in 2019.

Christin HUSSONG b. 17 Apr 1994
Zweibrücken 1.87m 82kg. LAZ Zweibrücken.
Sports student.
At JT: OG: '16- 12; WCh: '15- 6, 17- dnq 17; EC:
'14-16-18: 7/dnq 17/1; WJ: '12- 7; WY: '11- 1; EU23:
'15- 1; EJ: '13- 2, YthOG: '10- 4; CCp: '18- 2. GER
champion 2016, 2018.
Progress at JT: 2009- 49.93, 2010- 55.35, 2011-
59.74, 2012- 55.74, 2013- 58.55, 2014- 63.34, 2015-
65.92, 2016- 66.41, 2017- 64.18, 2018- 67.90. Pbs: SP

15.02i '14, 14.02 '11.

Marie-Laurence JUNGFLEISCH b. 7 Oct 1990
Paris, France 1.81m 68kg. VfB Stuttgart. Soldier.
At HJ: OG: '16- 7=; WCh: '13- nh, '15- 6, '17- 4;
EC: '12-14-1-18: dnq 13=/5/5/3; EU23: '11- 8; EJ:
'09- 6; CCp: '18- 4; ET: '17- 2; WI: '14- 8. Won GER
2013-18.
Progress at HJ: 2006- 1.70, 2007- 1.75, 2008- 1.78,
2009- 1.86, 2010- 1.90, 2011- 1.93, 2012- 1.95, 2013-
1.95, 2014- 1.97, 2015- 1.99, 2016- 2.00, 2017- 2.00,
2018- 1.96.
Father from Martinique, mother German.

Konstanze KLOSTERHALFEN b. 18 Feb 1997
Königswinter 1.74m 48kg. TSV Bayer 04
Leverkusen.
At 1500m: OG: '16- sf; WCh: '17- sf; EU23: '17- 1;
EJ: '15- 3, EI: '17- 2; YthOG: '14- 4, ET: '17- 1.
German champion 2016-18. At 3000m: WJ: '16-
3; CCp: '18- 4; WI: '18- 7; EI: '19- 2. At 5000m: EC:
'18- 4. Eur CC: 14-15-16-17: 28J/1J/1J/2U23.
German 3000m record 2017.
Progress at 1500m, 5000m: 2012- 55.74, 2013-
4:26.58, 2014- 4:19.97, 2015- 4:09.58, 2016- 4:06.91,
15:16.98; 2017- 3:58.92, 14:51.38; 2018- 4:04.00i/
4:06.34, 15:03.73; 2019- 4:02.70i. Pbs: 800m 1:59.65
'17, 1000m 2:43.07i '19, 1M 4:19.98i '19, 4:24.27 '18;
3000m 8:29.89 '17, 10kRd 32:24 '16.

Gesa Felicitas KRAUSE b. 3 Aug 1992
Ehringshausen 1.67m 55kg. LG Eintracht
Frankfurt. Student.
At 3000mSt: OG: '12- 7, '16- 6; WCh: '11-13-15-17:
6/9/3/9; EC: '12-14-16-18: 3/5/1/1; WJ: '10- 4; EU23:
'13- 1; EJ: '11- 1; ET: '15- 1, '17- 1; GER
champion 2015-18 (& 5000m 2017). At 2000mSt:
WY: '09- 7. At 1500m: EI: '15- 5.
Records: European junior 3000mSt 2011,
German 2000mSt (2) 2015, 3000mSt (232016-17.
Progress at 3000mSt: 2010- 9:47.78, 2011- 9:32.74,
2012- 9:23.52, 2013- 9:37.11, 2014- 9:35.46, 2015-
9:19.25, 2016- 9:18.41, 2017- 9:11.85, 2018- 9:19.80.
pbs: 800m 2:03.09mx '17, 1000m 2:44.68 '10,
1500m 4:06.99 '16, 1M 4:29.58 '16, 3000m 8:49.43i
'16, 9:02.04 '15; 5000m 15:24.53 '17; 10k Rd 33:26
'15, HMar 72:16 '18, 2000mSt 6:04.20 '15.

Gina LÜCKENKEMPER b. 21 Nov 1996
Hamm 1.70m 57kg. TSV Bayer 04 Leverkusen.
At 100m/(200m)/4x100mR: OG: '16- (sf); WCh:
'15- h, '17- sf; EC: '16- (3)/3R, '18- 2/3R; WJ: '12-
(sf), 14- (8)/3R; WY: '12- (sf).; ET: '17- 2/1R. Won
GER 100m 2018.
Progress at 100m, 200m: 2012- 11.89, 23.98; 2013-
11.61, 23.35; 2014- 11.54/11.34w, 23.26; 2015-
11.25, 23.04/22.41w; 2016- 11.04, 22.67; 2017-
10.95, 23.04; 2018- 10.98. pbs: 60m 7.11i '18, 300m
37.11 '15.

Malaika MIHAMBO b. 3 Feb 1994 Heidelberg
1.70m 55kg. LG Kurpfalz. Studied political
science at Mannheim University.
At LJ: OG: '16- 4; WCh: '13- dnq 13, '15- 6; EC:
'14-16-18: 4/3/1; WJ: '12- dnq 14; WY: '11- 9;

EU23: '15- 1; EJ: '13- 1; WI: '18- 5; EI: '19- 4; CCp: '18- 2; ET: '14- 1. GER champion 2016, 2018.
Progress at LJ: 2008- 5.55, 2009- 5.81, 2010- 5.96, 2011- 6.40, 2012- 6.45i/6.32/6.50w, 2013- 6.70/6.80w, 2014- 6.90, 2015- 6.84, 2016- 6.95, 2017- 6.62, 2018- 6.99, 2019- 6.99i. pbs: 60m 7.34i '19, 200m 23.90 '18, HJ 1.78i/1.75 '10.
Tanzanian father, German mother.

Sosthene Taroum **MOGUENARA** b. 17 Oct 1989 Sarh, Moyen-Chari, Chad 1.82m 68kg. LG LAZ Saar 05 Saarbrücken.
At LJ: OG: '12- dnq 19, '16- 10; WCh: '11- dnq 31, '13- 11, '15- dnq 27; EC: '12-14-18: 4/9/dnq 17; EU23: '09- 4, '11- 3; ET: '15- 3; WI: '18- 3; EI: '15- 2. GER champion 2013.
Progress at LJ: 2007- 6.22, 2008- 6.37, 2009- 6.61/6.69w, 2010- 6.65, 2011- 6.83, 2012- 6.88, 2013- 7.04, 2014- 6.82, 2015- 6.94, 2016- 7.16, 2017- 6.61, 2018- 6.85i/6.84. pbs: 60m 7.66i '08, 100m 11.94 '10, 200m 24.85 '07.
Has lived in Germany from the age of nine.

Nadine MÜLLER b. 21 Nov 1985 Leipzig 1.93m 90kg. Hallesche LA-Freunde. Federal police officer.
At DT: OG: '12- 4, '16- 6; WCh: '07-09-11-13-15-17: dnq 23/6/2/4/3/6; EC: '10-12-16-18: 8/2/4/2; WJ: '04- 3; EU23: '05- 10, '07- 8; EJ: '03- 2; CCp: '18- 6; ET: '10-11-17: 1/3/2. German champion 2010-13, 2016. World indoor discus best 63.89 in 2019.
Progress at DT: 2000- 36.10, 2001- 46.27, 2002- 48.90, 2003- 53.44, 2004- 57.85, 2005- 59.35, 2006- 58.46, 2007- 62.93, 2008- 61.36, 2009- 63.46, 2010- 67.78, 2011- 66.99, 2012- 68.89, 2013- 66.89, 2014- 67.30, 2015- 65.72, 2016- 66.84, 2017- 65.76, 2018- 63.00, 2019- 63.89i.
Farher Hans-Joachim Muller was a 55m discus thrower.

Cindy ROLEDER b. 21 Aug 1989 Chemnitz 1.78m 68kg. SV Halle. Police officer.
At 100mh: OG: '12- sf, '16- 5, WCh: '11- sf, '15- 2; EC: '10-12-14-16-18: h/6/3/1/3; WJ: '08- sf; EU23: '09- sf, '11- 3; EJ: '07- 4; CCp: '14- 3; ET: '15- 3; GER champion 2011, 2015-16. At 60mh: WI: '14- 6, '18- 5; EI: '15-17-19- 4/1/2.
Progress at 100mh: 2007- 13.49, 2008- 13.72, 2009- 13.38, 2010- 12.97, 2011- 12.91, 2012- 12.91, 2013- 13.03/12.93w, 2014- 12.80, 2015- 12.59, 2016- 12.62, 2017- 12.90, 2018- 12.77. pbs: 60m 7.34i '15, 100m 11.72 '13, 150m 17.40 '15, 200m 23.35 '15, 800m 2:15.49 '15, 50mh 7.14+i '10, 60mh 7.84i '17, HJ 1.66 '15, LJ 6.32i '14, 6.17 '13, 6.18w '15; SP 13.59i '16, 13.25 '15; JT 36.33 '15, Pen 4187i '14, Hep 6055 '15.

Anna RÜH b. 17 Jun 1993 Greifswald 1.86m 78kg. SC Neubrandenburg.
At DT: OG: '12- 9; WCh: '17- dnq 14; EC: '12- 4, '14- 4; WJ: '10- dnq 21, '12- 1; EU23: '13- 1, '15- 2; EJ: '11- 2 (3 SP).
Progress at DT: 2009- 44.43, 2010- 51.67, 2011- 59.97, 2012- 63.38, 2013- 64.33, 2014- 64.17, 2015-

66.14, 2016- 64.08, 2017- 63.90, 2018- 62.66. pb SP 17.68i/17.20 '16.

Claudia SALMAN-RATH b. 25 Apr 1986 Hadamar, Hessen 1.75m 65kg. née Rath. LG Eintracht Frankfurt.
At Hep: OG: '16- 14; WCh: '11- 4, '15- 5, '17- 8 (10 LJ); EC: '10-12-14: 10/6/8. At WI Pen: '14- 5. At LJ: EI: '17- 3; ET: '17- 1. Won GER Hep 2010-11, LJ 2017.
Progress at LJ, Hep: 2003- 5.64, 5231; 2004- 5.99, 5353; 2005- 6.09, 5323; 2006- 6.13, 2007- 6.22, 5274; 2008- 6.29, 5697; 2009- 6.44, 5941; 2010- 6.50, 6107; 2011- 6.28. 6098; 2012- 6.44, 6210; 2013- 6.67, 6467; 2014- 6.46, 6314, 2015- 6.73/6.84w, 6458; 2016- 6.62, 6310; 2017- 6.94i/6.86, 6580. pbs: 200m 23.62 '17, 800m 2:05.54 '17, 60mh 8.43i '14, 100mh 13.44 '15, HJ 1.83 '13, SP 14.00 '17, JT 43.65 '16, Pen 4681i '14.

Carolin SCHÄFER b. 5 Dec 1991 Bad Wildungen 1.78m 64kg. TV Friedrichstein.
At Hep: OG: '16- 5; WCh: '15- dnf, '17- 2; EC: '12-14-18: 10/4/3; WJ: '08- 1; EU23: '11- 5, '13- 6; EJ: '09- 1. German champion 2013.
Progress at Hep: 2007- 5545, 2008- 5833, 2009- 5697, 2010- 5333, 2011- 5941, 2012- 6072, 2013- 5972, 2014- 6395, 2015- 6547, 2016- 6557, 2017- 6836, 2018- 6549. pbs: 60m 7.86i '07, 200m 23.27 '17, 800m 2:14.10 '15, 60mh 8.45i '16, 100mh 13.07 '17, HJ 1.86 '17, LJ 6.57 '17, SP 14.84 '17, JT 53.73 '18, Pen 4098i '09.
Won IAAF Combined Events Challenge 2016-18. Won Ratingen & Talence 2018. Her elder brother Sebastian had 400m best 47.10 '08 and ran at 4x100m in EJ 2005 & 2007.

Christina SCHWANITZ b. 24 Dec 1985 Dresden 1.80m 103kg. LV 90 Erzebirge. Soldier.
At SP: OG: '08- 9, '12- 9, '16- 6; WCh: '05-09-11-13-15: 7/11/10/2/1; EC: '12-14-16-18: 5/1/1/2; WJ: '04- 3; EU23: '05- 2; WI: '08- 5, '14- 2; EI: '11-13-19: 2/1/2; CCp: '14- 1, '18- 2; ET: '08-13-14-15: 1/1/1/1. Won DL 2015, GER 2011, 2013-16, 2018.
Progress at SP: 2001- 13.57, 2002- 14.26, 2003- 15.25, 2004- 16.98, 2005- 18.84, 2007- 17.06, 2008- 19.68i/19.31, 2009- 19.06, 2010- 18.28, 2011- 19.20, 2012- 19.15i/19.05, 2013- 20.41, 2014- 20.22, 2015- 20.77, 2016- 20.17, 2018- 20.06. pb DT 47.27 '03.
Gave birth to twins in 2017.

Claudine VITA b. 18 Sep 1996 Frankurt/Oder 1.79m 81kg. SC Neubrandenburg.
At (SP)/DT: EC: '18- 4; WJ: '14- 5; WY: '13- 2; EU23: '17-5/1; EJ: '15- 2/1; EI: '17- (5).
Progress at DT: 2012- 47.44, 2013- 52.59, 2014- 56.98, 2015- 62.31, 2016- 62.77, 2017- 64.45, 2018- 65.15. Pbs: LJ 5.79 '13, SP 18.09i '17, 17.90 '16.

GREECE

Governing body: Hellenic Amateur Athletic Association (SEGAS). Founded 1897.
National Championships first held in 1896 (men), 1930 (women). **2018 Champions**: 100m:

Ioánnis Nifadópoulou 10.40, 200m: Panayiótis Trivizás 21.22, 400m: Mihaíl Pappás 46.97, 800m: Erlado Oerama 1:50.44, 1500m: Andréas Dimitrákis 3:44.74, 5000m: Konstadínos Stamoúlis 14:36.29, 10000m: Yeóiryios-Mihaíl Tássis 30:09.38, HMar: Konstadínos Gelaoúzos 68:30, 3000mSt: Minos Yeóryios 9:08.75, 110mh: Konstadínos Douvalídis 13.52, 400mh: Konstadínos Nákos 51.78, HJ: Konstadínos Baniótis 2.24, PV: Konstadínos Filippídis 5.50, LJ: Miltiádis Tentóglou 8.24, TJ: Dimítrios Tsiámis 16.72, SP: Nikólaos Skarvélis 19.50, DT: Iáson Thanópoulos 55.10, HT: Mihaíl Anastasákis 73.97, JT: Konstadínos Milonás 69.31, Dec: Aléxandros Sprionídis 7273, 20kW: Aléxandros Papamihaíl 1:28:58, 50kW: Konstadínos-Aléandros Dedópoulos 4:24:57. **Women**: 100m: Rafailía Spanpudáki-Hatzucíga 11.57: 200m/ 400m: María Belibasáki 22.98/51.31, 800m: Konstadína Yiannopoúlou 2:07.58, 1500m: Viktoría-Elízabeth Tsóli 4:18.18, 5000m: Ouranía Reboúli 16:03.92, 10000m: Anasatasía Karakatsáni 34:32.00, HMar: Elefthería Petrouláki 1:20:01, 3000mSt: Yeoryía Dimitriádou 10:40.36, 100mh: Elisávet Pesirídou 13.21, 400mh: Elpída Tóka 59.27, HJ: Ioánna Zákka 1.80, PV: Nikoléta Kiriakopoúlou 4.65, LJ/TJ: Paraskevi Papahrístou 6.56/14.33, SP/HT: Stamatía Skarvéli 15.66/67.80, DT: Hrisoúla Anagnostopoúlou 58.95, JT/Hep: Sofía Ifantídou 55.49/5672 , 20kW: Antigóni Drisbióti 1:34:44, 50kW: Aggelíki Makrí 4:56:00.

Konstadínos FILIPPÍDIS b. 26 Nov 1986 Athens 1.88m 73kg. Panellínios YS Athens. Postgraduate student at Athens University of Economics and Business.
At PV: OG: '12- 6, '16- 7=; WCh: '05-09-11-13-15: dnq 14=/dnq 17/6/10/dnq 25=; EC: '06-10: dnq 26/21=, '12-14-16-18: 5/7/7=/6=; WJ: '04- 4; WY: '03- 4; EJ: '05- 2; WI: '10-12-14-16-18: 4=/7/1/7/7=; EI: '11-13-15-17: 5/4/5/2; WUG: '05- 2; ET: '09/10- 4; Won MedG 2005; Greek champion 2005, 2009-18. Ten Greek pole vault records 2005-15.
Progress at PV: 2001- 3.70, 2002- 4.80, 2003- 5.22, 2004- 5.50, 2005- 5.75, 2006- 5.55, 2007- 5.35i/5.30/5.40dq, 2009- 5.65, 2010- 5.70i/5.55, 2011- 5.75, 2012- 5.80, 2013- 5.83i/5.82, 2014- 5.80i/5.70, 2015- 5.91, 2016- 5.84i/5.72, 2017- 5.85i/5.75, 2018- 5.85i/5.75.
Two-year drugs ban (reduced to 18 months) from positive test on 16 June 2007.

Emmanouíl KARALÍS b. 20 Oct 1999 Athens 1.83m 75kg. G.S. Kifissia.
At PV: WCh: '17- dnq 21; WJ: '16- 4; WY: '15- 3; EJ: '17- dnq; WI: '18- 5; EI: '19- 4=.
World junior indoor pole vault record (5.78) 2018, world youth records 2 indoor, 1 outdoor) 2016.
Progress at PV: 2014- 4.65, 2015- 5.25, 2016- 5.55, 2017- 5.70i/5.63, 2018- 5.80i.
His father Charis decathlon pb 7392 in 1987.

Ioánnis KIRIAZÍS b. 19 Jan 1996 Athens 1.94m 98kg. Texas A&M University, USA..
At JT: WCh: '17- 6; EC: '16 - 12; WJ: '14- 7; WY: '13- dnq 16; EU23: '17- 2; EJ: '15- 4; ET: '17- 2. NCAA champion 2017.
Progress at JT: 2013- 69.30, 2014- 73.66, 2015- 78.41, 2016- 87.14, 2017- 88.01.

Mitiliadís TENTÓGLOU b. 18 Mar 1998 Grevena 1.87m 70kg. G.E. Grevena.
At LJ: OG: '16- dnq 27; WCh: '17- dnq 19; EC: '18- 1; WJ: '16- 2; WY: '15- 5; EJ: '17- 1; CCp: '18- 2; WI: '18- 9; EI: '19- 1. Greek champion 2017-18, Balkan 2018.
Progress at LJ: 2013- 6.40, 2014- 7.13, 2015- 7.73, 2016- 8.19, 2017- 8.30, 2018- 8.25, 2019- 8.38i. Pb TJ 15.61 '16.

Women

Nikoléta KIRIAKOPOÚLOU b. 21 Mar 1986 Athens 1.67m 56kg. AYES Kámiros Rhodes.
At PV: OG: '08/12- dnq 27=/19=; WCh: '09-11-13-15: dnq 19/8/dnq 13=/3; EC: '10-12-14-16-18: dnq 13/3/7=/4/2; WJ: '04- 6; EJ: '05- 7; WI: '16- 6=; EI: '11-15-19: 9/5=/3. Won DL 2015, Balkan 2008, Med G 2009, Greek 2009, 2011-14, 2018.
Nine Greek pole vault records 2010-15.
Progress at PV: 2001- 2.90, 2002- 3.10, 2003- 3.70, 2004- 4.00, 2005- 4.10, 2006- 3.60, 2007- 4.00i/3.90, 2008- 4.45, 2009- 4.50, 2010- 4.55, 2011- 4.71, 2012- 4.60, 2013- 4.65, 2014- 4.72i/4.67, 2015- 4.83, 2016- 4.81i/4.75, 2018- 4.80, 2019- 4.81i.
Married to Andreas Linardátos (400m pb 47.27 '90). Gave birth to daughter on 23 May 2017.

Paraskeví 'Voula' PAPAHRÍSTOU b. 17 Apr 1989 Athens 1.70m 53kg. AEK (Athens).
At TJ: OG: '16- 8; WCh: '09/11/17- dnq 27/16/20; EC: '12-16-18: 11/3/1; WJ: '08- 3; EU23: '09/11- 1/1; WI: '16- 3, '18- 6; EI: '17- 3, '19- 2; CCp: '18- 4; ET: '17- 1. Won Balkan TJ 2018; Greek LJ 2011-12, 2016, 2018; TJ 2009, 2011, 2015, 2017-18.
Progress at TJ: 2005- 12.75, 2006- 12.81/13.13w, 2007- 12.98i/12.92, 2008- 13.86i/13.79/13.94w, 2009- 14.47i/14.35, 2010- 13.94i/13.85, 2011- 14.72, 2012- 14.58/14.77w, 2013- 14.21, 2015- 13.99/14.20w, 2016- 14.73, 2017- 14.24, 2018- 14.60/14.74w, 2019- 14.50i. pb LJ 6.60 '12.
Daughter Konstadína born Nov 2014.

Ekateríni STEFANÍDI b. 4 Feb 1990 Athens 1.72m 63kg. Was at Stanford University, USA and then MSc in cognitive psychology at Arizona State University.
At PV: OG: '12- dnq 24, '16- 1; WCh: '15- dnq 15, '17- 1; EC: '12-14-16-18: nh/2/1/1; WJ: '08- 3; WY: '05- 1, '07- 2; EU23: '11- 2; EJ: '07- 10; WI: '16- 3, '18- 3; EI: '15-17-19: 2/1/4; WUG: '11- 3; CCp: '18- 2; ET: '17- 1. Greek champion 2015-16, NCAA 2012, DL 2016-18.
World youth pole vault best 2005. Two Greek PV records 2016-17 and indoors 2016
Progress at PV: 2001- 2.30, 2002- 3.50, 2003- 3.90, 2004- 4.14, 2005- 4.37i/4.30, 2006- 4.10, 2007-

4.25, 2008- 4.25, 2009- 4.13, 2010- 4.30, 2011- 4.45, 2012- 4.51, 2013- 4.45Ai/4.40, 2014- 4.71, 2015- 4.77Ai/4.71, 2016- 4.90i/4.86, 2017- 4.91, 2018- 4.87. Married to Mitchell Krier (PV 4.95i '16).

GRENADA

Governing body: Grenada Athletic Assocation. Founded 1924.

Kurt FELIX b. 4 Jul 1988 St George's 1.90m 88kg. Was at Boise State University.
At Dec: OG: '12- dnf, '16- 9; WCh: '13- dnf, '15- 8, '17- 7; CG: '14- 3, '18- 4; PAm: '15- 2, won NCAA 2012. At Hep: WI: '16- 6.
GRN records: decathlon (7) 2012-16, PV 2010-15.
Progress at Dec: 2008- 6946, 2009- 7091, 2010- 7412, 2012- 8062, 2013- dnf, 2014- 8070, 2015- 8302, 2016- 8323, 2017- 8509, 2018- 7756. pbs: 60m 7.00i '16, 100m 10.91 '15, 10.90w '12; 400m 48.63 '15, 1000m 2:42.91i '11, 1500m 4:30.53 '16, 60mh 8.31i '16, 110mh 14.58 '15, HJ 2.17i '11, 2.15 '09; PV 4.61i '16, 4.60 '12; LJ 7.74 '12, TJ 16.06 '09, SP 15.31 '17, DT 50.59 '15, JT 72.80 '17, Hep: 5986i '16. Half brother of Lindon Victor (qv).

Kirani JAMES b. 1 Sep 1992 St George's 1.85m 74kg. Student at University of Alabama, USA
At (200m)/400m: OG: '12- 1, '16- 2; WCh: '11- 1, '13- 7, '15- 3; CG: '14- 1; WJ: '08- 2, '10- 1; WY: '07- 2, '09- 1/1; WI: '12- 6. Won DL 2011, 2015; PAm-J 400m 2009, 200m 2011; NCAA 2010-11.
Records: CAC & Commonwealth 400m 2012 & 2014, GRN 200m 2011, 400m (2) 2011-12; Indoor 400m: CAC & Commonwealth 2010 (45.24) &. 2011, World Junior (44.80) 2011.
Progress at 400m: 2007- 46.96, 2008- 45.70, 2009- 45.24, 2010- 45.01, 2011- 44.36, 2012- 43.94, 2013- 43.96, 2014- 43.74, 2015- 43.78, 2016- 43.76, 2017- 45.44, 2018- 44.35. pbs: 200m 20.41A/20.53w '11, 20.76 '10; 300m: 31.3+ '16.
He set world age bests at 14 and 15. In 2011 he became the youngest ever World or Olympic champion at 400m and in 2012 the first Olympic medallist for Grenada at any sport. In January 2012 the 'Kirani James Boulevard' was opened in the Grenadan capital St George. IAAF Rising Star award 2011

Bralon TAPLIN b. 8 May 1992 St George's 1.80m 73kg. Was at Texas A&M University, USA
At 400m: OG: '16- 7; WCh: '15- h; CG: '14- sf, '18- 5; PAm: '15- h; WI: '16- 4.
Progress at 400m: 2008- 49.21, 2009- 47.25, 2010- 47.03, 2011- 46.79, 2012- 45.36, 2013- 46.85i/47.50, 2014- 45.18, 2015- 44.89, 2016- 44.38, 2017- 45.08, 2018- 44.67. pbs: 100m 10.53A '12, 200m 20.80i '15, 20.83 '12; 300m 31.8+ '16, 31.97i '17; 600y 1:10.14i '11.

Lindon VICTOR b. 28 Feb 1993 ST George's 1.91m 90kg. Texas A&M University, USA.
At Dec: OG: '16- 16; WCh: '17- dnf; CG: '14- 9, ''18- 1; PAm: '15- 7. Won NCAA 2016-17.
Grenada records: decathlon 2016 & 2017, pole vault (2) 2017.
Progress at Dec: 2014- 7429, 2015- 7453, 2016- 8446, 2017- 8539, 2018- 8303. pbs: 60m 6.94i '17, 100m 10.60 '16, 400m 48.24 '17, 1000m 2:51.14i '17, 1500m 4:43.81 '16, 60mh 8.24i '16, 110mh 14.45 '17, HJ 2.09 '17, PV 4.80 '18, LJ 7.37 '17, SP 16.55i/16.52 '17, DT 55.22 '17, JT 71.23 '14, Hep: 5976i '17. Half brother of Kurt Felix.

HUNGARY

Governing body: Magyar Atlétikai Szövetség. Founded 1897.

National Championships first held in 1896 (men), 1932 (women). **2018 Champions. Men**: 100m: Dániel Szabó 10.53, 200m/LJ: László Szabó 21.13/7.80w, 400m: Boldizsár Boda 47.98, 800m: Gergö Kiss 1:52.84, 1500m: Tamás Kazi 13:49.18, 5000m: László Gregor 14:25.66, 10000m: Benjamin Kovács 29:55.56, HMar/Mar: Gáspár Csere 67:14/2:20:10, 3000mSt: Balázs Juhász 9:00.49, 110mh: Balázs Baji 13.39, 400mh: Tibor Koroknai 50.80, HJ: Péter Bakosi 2.18, PV: Csanád Simonváros 4.90, TJ: Tibor Galambos 15.91, SP: Balász Detrik 17.05, DT: Róbert Szikszai 62.47, HT: Bence Halász 78.22, JT: Norbert Rivasz-Tóth 77.90, Dec: Botond Kriszt 6580, 20kW: Máté Helebrandt 1:24:02, 35kW/50kW: Bence Venyercsán 2:45:46/4:05:54. **Women**: 100m/LJ: Anasztázia Nguyen 11.58/ 6.26, 200m: Lili Furulyás 24.57, 400m: Janka Molnár 55.29, 800m: Bianka Kéri 2:04.12, 1500m/3000mSt: Viktória Gyürkés 4:16.62/ 10:04.38, 5000m: Lili Tóth 16:25.19, 10000m/HMar: Zita Kácser 33:07.64/77:47, Mar: Tünde Szabó 2:47:41, 100mh: Luca Kozák 12.86, 400mh: Sára Mátó 58.07, HJ: Györgyi Zsivoczky-Farkas 1.81, PV: Zsófia Siskó 4.10, TJ: Krisztina Hoffer 13.48w, SP/DT: Anita Márton 17.76/56.85, HT: Réka Gyurátz 67.70, JT: Angéla Moravcsik 55.12, Hep: Sára Mátó 5584, 20kW: Barbara Kovács 1:37:19

Balázs BAJI b. 9 Jun 1989 Békéscsaba 1.92m 83kg. Budapewsti Honvéd SE.
At 110mh: OG: '12- h, '16- sf; WCh: '11-13-15-17: h/sf/sf/3; WJ: '08- 7; EC: '10 12-14-16-18: h/sf/4/2/8; EU23: '09- h,'11- 2; WUG: '11- 6; won HUN 200m 2009, 110mh 2007, 2011-18. At 60mh: WI: '16- 6; EI: '13- 4, '15- 7.
Seven Hungarian 110mh records 2014-17.
Progress at 110mh: 2007- 14.48, 2008- 14.44/14.43w, 2009- 13.96/13.88w, 2010- 13.79, 2011- 13.58, 2012- 13.50, 2013- 13.36, 2014- 13.29, 2015- 13.45, 2016- 13.28, 2017- 13.15, 2018- 13.27. pbs: 60m 6.85i '13, 100m 10.60 '09, 200m 21.35 '13, 400m 49.6 '07, 60mh 7.53i '17, 400mh 56.38 '06.

Bence HALÁSZ b. 4 Aug 1997 Kiskunhalas 1.88m 86kg. Dobó SE.
At HT: WCh: '17- 11; EC: '18- 3; WJ: '14- dnq 14, '16- 1 (dnq 35 DT); WY: '13- 7; EJ: '15- 1 (dnq 15 DT); EU23: '17- 1; CCp: '18- 3; YthOG: '14- 2. Won HUN 2017-18.

Progress at HT: 2012- 51.56, 2013- 62.33, 2014-
68.55, 2015- 69.80, 2016- 73.97, 2017- 78.85, 2018-
79.57. pbs: SP 16.12 '17, DT 54.72 '18.

Zoltán KÖVÁGÓ b. 10 Apr 1979 Szolnok 2.04m
127kg. Szolnoki Honvéd SE. Army lieutenant.
At DT: OG: '00- dnq, '04- 2, '08- dnq 21, '16- 7;
WCh: '01-03-05-07-09-11-15-17: dnq 20/dnq
19/10/9/6/dnq 15/dnq 18/dnq 22; EC: '98-02-10-
12-14-16-18: dnq 22/7/dnq 21/dq (3)/dnq 14/6/
dnq 20; WJ: '96- 4, '98- 1; EJ: '97- 3; EU23: '99- 6,
'01- 1. HUN champion 2001, 2004-05, 2008-11,
2014-17; W.MilG 2015.
Progress at DT: 1995- 49.78, 1996- 59.70, 1997-
62.16, 1998- 60.27, 1999- 63.23, 2000- 66.76, 2001-
66.93, 2002- 65.98, 2003- 66.03, 2004- 68.93, 2005-
66.00, 2006- 69.95, 2007- 66.42, 2008- 68.17, 2009-
67.64, 2010- 69.69, 2011- 69.50, 2012- 68.21dq,
2014- 65.82, 2015- 67.39, 2016- 67.13, 2017- 65.67,
2018- 65.66. pb SP 15.93 '01.
2-year drugs ban 2011-13. Tied record with
seven EC appearances

Krisztián PARS b. 18 Feb 1982 Körmend 1.88m
113kg. Dobó SE.
At HT: OG: '04- 4, '08- 4, '12- 1, '16- 7; WCh: '05-
07-09-11-13-15-17: 6/5/4/2/2/4/dnq 14; EC: '06-
10-12-14: 5/3/1/1; WY: '99- 1; EJ: '01- 1; EU23:
'03- 1; CCp: '14- 1. Won HUN 2005-16; World HT
challenge 2011-12, 2014.
World junior records with 6kg hammer: 80.64
& 81.34 in 2001.
Progress at HT: 1998- 54.00, 1999- 61.92, 2000-
66.80, 2001- 73.09, 2002- 74.18, 2003- 78.81, 2004-
80.90, 2005- 80.03, 2006- 82.45, 2007- 81.40, 2008-
81.96, 2009- 81.43, 2010- 79.64, 2011- 81.89, 2012-
82.28, 2013- 82.40, 2014- 82.69, 2015- 79.91, 2016-
77.38, 2017- 76.84. pbs: SP 15.60 '05, DT 53.80 '06.
Received a 1-year, 6 month ban (to July 2019)
for a positive test for a "non-performance-
enhancing" substance on 13 Jan 2018.

Women

Xénia KRIZSÁN b. 13 Jan 1993 Budapest 1.71m
62kg. MTK Budapest.
At Hep: OG: '16- 16; WCh: '15- 9, '17- 9; EC: '14-
16-18: 9/4/7; WJ: '10- 7, '12- 2; WY: '09- 4; EU23:
'13- 7, '15- 1; EJ: 11- 7. At Pen: WI: '18- 6; EI: '17- 4,
'19- 7. Won HUN 100mh 2013,2015; LJ 2011-12,
Hep 2013.
Progress at Hep: 2010- 5594, 2011- 5794, 2012-
5957, 2013- 5896, 2014- 6317, 2015- 6322, 2016-
6266, 2017- 6390, 2018- 6367. pbs: 200m 24.72 '15,
400m 56.48 '12, 800m 2:07.17 '17, 60mh 8.30i '15,
100mh 13.51 '16, 13.50w '17; HJ 1.82 '17, LJ 6.26
'17, TJ 11.83 '10, SP 14.34 '17, JT 51.25 '17, Pen
4631i '17.

Anita MÁRTON b. 15 Jan 1989 Szeged 1.71m
84kg. Békéscsabai AC.
At SP (DT): OG: '12- dnq 22, '16- 3; WCh: '09-11-
13: dnq 23/20/19, '15- 4, '17- 2 (dnq 24); EC: '10-
12-14-16: 9/7/3/2; WJ: '06- dnq 15 (12), '08- 7 (6);
WY: '05- 11 (dnq); EU23: '09- 5, (11) '11- 5 (3); EJ:

'07- 7 (6); WUG: '13- 4; WI: '14-16-18: 5/2/1; EI:
'11-15-17-19: 5/1/1/3; won HUN SP 2006-18, DT
2008-18. Three Hungarian shot records 2014-16.
Progress at SP: 2004- 13.88, 2005- 14.12i/13.90,
2006- 15.57, 2007- 15.68, 2008- 16.90, 2009- 17.27,
2010- 18.20, 2011- 18.15, 2012- 18.48, 2013- 18.18,
2014- 19.04, 2015- 19.48, 2016- 19.87, 2017- 19.63,
2018- 19.62i/19.12. pbs: DT 60.94 '16, HT 51.12
'17.
Improved pb from 18.48/18.63i to 19.04 to take
EC bronze 2014, indoor best to 19.23i for EI gold
and outdoor pb to 19.48 for World 4th 2015 and
to 19.87 for Olympic silver 2016; HUN indoor
record 19.33 for 2nd WI 2016 and again with
19.48 and 19.62 in 2018 to become the first
Hungarian to win a World Indoor title.

ICELAND

Governing body: Frjálsíthróttasamband
Islands. Founded 1947.
National Championships first held in 1927.
2018 Champions: Men: 100/200m: Jóhann
Björn Sigurbjörnsson 10.66/21.54, 400m/400mh:
Ívar Kristinn Jasonarson 49.25/52.15, 800m:
Kristin Thór Kristinsson 1:52.50, 1500m:
Sæmundur Ólafsson 4:05.51, 5000mArnar
Pétursson 15:18.40, 3000mSt: Dagbjartur
Kristjansson 10:21.65, 110mh: Ísak Óli
Traustason 15.10, HJ: Kristján Viggó Sigfinnsson
2.02, PV: Ingi Rúnar Kristinsson 4.42, LJ:Ari
Sigthor Eiríksson 7.07w, TJ: Bjarki Rúnar
Kristinsson 14.19w, SP: Kristján Viktor
Kristinsson 14.62, DT: Jón Bjarni Bragason
43.82, HT: Hilmar Örn Jónsson 64.21, JT: Sindri
Hrafn Gudmundsson 77.01. **Women:** 100m:
Tiana ósk Whitworth 11.75, 200m: Gudbjörg
Jóna Bjarnadóttir 23.89, 400m/400mh: Thórdis
Eva Steinsdóttir 59.25/62.70, 800m: Ingibjörg
Sigurdardóttir 2:20.97, 1500m: Idunn Björg
Arnaldsdóttir 4:56.85, 3000m: Andrea
Kolbeinsdóttir 10:14.17, 100mh: María Rún
Gunnlaugsdóttir 14.40, HJ: Thóranna Ósk
Sigurjónsdóttir 1.68, LJ/TJ: Hafdís
Sigurdardóttir 6.16w/12.07, SP/ JT: Ásdis
Hjálmsdóttir 15.11/57.74, DT: Thelma Lind
Kristjánsdóttir, HT: Vigdis Jónsdóttir 58.59.

INDIA

Governing body: Athletics Federation of India.
Founded 1946.
National Championships first held as Indian
Games in 1924. **2018 Champions: Men:**
100m/200m: Sanjeet Singh 10.39/21.30, 400m:
Noah Nirmal 46.56, 800m: Mohammed Afsal
1:54.50, 1500m: Ajay Kumar 3:46.49, 5000m/
10000m: Gavit Murli Kumar 14:35.96/29:49.79,
3000mSt: Avinash Sable 8:29.80, 110mh:
Surendhar Jayakumar13.89, 400mh: Ayyasamy
Dharun 49.67, HJ: Sarvesh Anil Kushare 2.24,
PV: Subramaniam Siva 5.10, LJ: Murali
Sreeshankar 8.20, TJ: Arpinder Singh 16.62, SP:

Parveen Singh 18.76, DT: Dhram Raj Yadav 59.56, HT: Taranveer Singh 63.12, JT: Abhishek Singh 76.42, Dec: Boota Singh 6953, 20kW: Kolothum Thodi Irfan 1:21:32/Krishnan Ganapathy 1:28:35, 50kW: Sandeep Kumar 3:56:40. **Women**: 100m: Ananthan Chandralekha 11.47, 200m: Reena George 24.10, 400m: Anjali Devi 51.79, 800m: Twinkle Chaudhary 2:07.43, 1500m: P.Uunikrishnan Chitra 4:24.35, 5000m/ 10000m: Suriya Loganathan 16:10.35/34:18.62, 3000mSt: Chinta Yadav 10:10.19, 100mh: Kanimozhi Chandrasekar 13.71, 400mh: Anju Rani 57.63, HJ: Jyothi Singh 1.76, PV: Khyati Vakharia 4.00, LJ: Narayanan Neena 6.37, TJ: Renu Renu 13.63, SP: Navjeet Kaur 15.00, DT: Kamalprteet Kaur 56.11, HT: Sarita Prakash Singh 59.84, JT: Sharmila Kumari 54.85, Hep: Liksy Joseph 5271, 20kW: Baby Soumya 1:31:29/ Ravina 1:42:32.

Neeraj CHOPRA b. 24 Dec 1997 Khandra Panipat, Haryana 1.84m 80kg.
At JT: WCh: '17- dnq 15; CG: '18- 1; WJ: '16- 1; WY: '13- dnq 17, AsiG: '18- 1; AsiC: '15- 9, '17- 1; AsiJ: '16- 2; CCp: '18- 5.
Javelin records: World junior 2016, two Asian junior 2016, four Indian 2016-18.
Progress at JT: 2014- 70.19, 2015- 81.04, 2016- 86.48, 2017- 85.63, 2018- 88.06.

IRAN

Governing body: Amateur Athletic Federation of Islamic Republic of Iran. Founded 1936.

Ehsan HADADI b. 21 Jan 1985 Ahvaz 1.93m 125kg.
At DT: OG: '08- dnq 17, '12- 2, '16- dnq 24; WCh: '07-11-15-17: 7/3/dnq 24/dnq 15; WJ: '04- 1; AsiG: '06-10-14-18: 1/1/1/1; AsiC: '03-05-07-09-11-17: 8/1/1/1/1/1; AsiJ: '04- 1; WCp: '06- 2, '10- 3. Won W.Asian 2005.
Eight Asian discus records 2005-08.
Progress at DT: 2002- 53.66, 2003- 54.40, 2004- 54.96, 2005- 65.25, 2006- 63.79, 2007- 67.95, 2008- 69.32, 2009- 66.19, 2010- 68.45, 2011- 66.08, 2012- 68.20, 2013- 66.98, 2014- 65.24, 2015- 65.22, 2016- 63.61, 2017- 65.66, 2018- 68.85. pb SP 17.82i '08, 16.00 '06.
First Iranian athlete to win an Olympic medal.

IRELAND

Governing Body: The Athletic Association of Ireland (AAI). Founded in 1999. Original Irish federation (Irish Champions AC) founded 1873.
National Championships first held in 1873.
2018 Champions: Men: 100m/200m: Leon Reid 10.42/20.74, 400m: Christopher O'Donnell 46.92, 800m: Mark English 1:50.82, 1500m: John Travers 3:47.45, 5000m: Ryan Forsyth 14:30.78. 10000m: Stephen Scullion 29:25.31, HMar: David Flynn 68:51, Mar: Mick Clohisey 2:15:58, 3000mSt: Adam Kirk-Smith 9:02.09, 110mh: Gerard O'Donnell 14.05, 400mh: Thomas Barr

49.56, HJ: Ryan Carthy Walsh 2.00, PV: Michael Bowler 4.50, LJ: Adam McMullen 7.68w, TJ: Denis Finnegan 14.33w, SP: Seán Breathnach 17.53, DT: Marco Pons 53.67, HT: Owen Russell 65.91, JT: Stephen Rice 66.95, Dec Shane Aston 6776, 10000mW: Cian McManamon 42:21.92, 20kW/30kW: Brendan Boyce 1:29:34/2:14:11.
Women: 100m: Gina Akpe-Moses 11.86, 200m: Phil Healy 23.64, 400m: Claire Mooney 53.85, 800m/1500m: Ciara Mageean 2:07.93/4:22.47, 5000m: Emma Mitchell 15:59.34, HMar: Catriona Jennings 1:22:25, Mar: Lizzie Lee 2:35:05, 3000mSt: Michele Finn 9:46.19, 100mh: Sarah Lavin 13.62, 400mh: Catherine McManus 60.24, HJ: Pippa Rogan 1.80, PV: Ciara Hickey 3.40, LJ/JT: Elizabeth Morland 6.10/43.41, TJ: Sarah Buggy 12.24w, SP/HT: Michaela Walsh 14.51/60.81, DT: Niamh Fogarty 44.56, Hep: Amy McTeggart 4706, 5000mW/20kW: Kate Veale 22:19.22/1:37:54.

Thomas BARR b. 24 Jul 1992 Waterford 1.83m 73kg. Ferrybank. Engineering graduate of University of Limerick.
At 400mh: OG: '16- 4; WCh: '15/17- sf; EC: '12/14/16/18: sf/sf/sf/3, EU23: '13- 8; EJ: '11- 6, WUG: '15- 1. Irish champion 2011-18.
Five Irish 400mh records 2014-16.
Progress at 400mh: 2009- 56.53, 2010- 56.47. 2011- 50.06, 2012- 50.22, 2013- 49.78, 2014- 48.90, 2015- 48.65, 2016- 47.97, 2017- 48.95, 2018- 48.31. pbs: 200m 21.47i '16, 21.83 '17; 400m 46.87i '17, HJ 1.83 '09. Sister Jessie Barr (b. 24 Jul 1989) pb 400mh 55.93 '12, 8 EC '12.

Women

Ciara MAGEEAN b. 12 Mar 1992 Portefarry, Co. Down, Northern Ireland 1.68m 56kg. University College Dublin.
At 1500m (800m): OG: '16- sf; WCh: '17- h; EC: '16- 3, '18- 4; CG (N.Ireland): '10- 10, '18- 13 (h); WJ: '08- 10, '10- 2; WY: '09- (2); EJ: '11- 2; EI: '19- 3; Comm-Y: '08- 3 (5). Won IRL 800m 2015, 2017-18; 1500m 2011, 2014, 2016, 2018. At 3000m: ET: '13- 2. At 5000m: CG: '18- 3. Eur-J CC: '09- 9, '10- 7.
Northern Ireland records 800m & 1500m.
Progress at 1500m: 2007- 4:32.18, 2008- 4:21.2, 2009- 4:15.46, 2010- 4:09.51, 2011- 4:07.45, 2012- 4:10.74, 2014- 4:15.35, 2015- 4:06.49, 2016- 4:01.46, 2017- 4:03.57, 2018- 4:04.13. pbs: 800m 2:00.79 '16, 1000m 2:38.89 '12, 1M 4:22.40 '17, 3000m 8:55.09i '15, 9:07.47mx '16.

ISRAEL

Governing body: Israeli Athletic Association. Founded as Federation for Amateur Sport in Palestine 1931.
National Championships first held in 1935.
2018 Champions: Men: 100m: Gal Arab 10.56, 200m Imri Pressiado 21.27, 400m: Donald Blair-Sanford 45.56, 800m/1500m: Necho Tayachew

1:51.25/3:44.41, 5000m/Mar: Girmaw Amare 13:56.91/2:15:30, 10000m: Haimro Alame 28:55.89, HMar: Yimer Getahun 65:15, 3000mSt: Noam Neeman 9:17.76, 110mh: Dor Khayoun 14.67, 400mh: Adam Yaacobi 52.29, HJ: Dmitriy Kroyter 2.12, PV: Lev Skorish 5.30, LJ/TJ: Tom Yaacobov 7.13/15.93, SP: Itamir Levi 19.03, DT: Adar Sheere 56.06, HT: Viktor Zaginaiko 58.77, JT: Nikolai Gillomovitz 61.70, Dec: Konstantin Krinitzkiy 6672. **Women**: 100m/200m: Diana Vaisman 11.47/23.78, 400m: Dariya Lokshin 56.37, 800m: Rachel Martinez 2:18.70, 1500m/10000m/HMar: Lonah Chemtai Salpeter 4:11.69/31:39.63/76:55, 5000m: Irina Konovalov 17:38.92, Mar: Hagar Knaani 2:49:14, 100mh: Allina Drozdov 14.04, 400mh: Dariya Lukshin 60.69, HJ: Khanin Nassar 1.78, PV: Naama Bronstein 3.80, LJ/TJ: Hanna Minenko 6.37w/14.13, SP: Anastasia Muchkaev 13.26, DT: Estelle Valeanu 49.34, HT: Margarita Belov 57.77, JT: Margaryta Dorozhon 42.12, Hep: Jouman Joubran 4834

Women

Hanna MINENKO b. 25 Sep 1989 Periaslav-Khmelnytskyi 1.78m 61kg. née Knyazyeva. Maccabi Haifa.
At TJ: OG: '12- 4, '16- 5; WCh: '13- 6, '15- 2, '17- 4; EC: '16- 2; WJ: '08- 4; EJ: '07- 2; EU23: '11- 5; WUG: '11- 4; EI: '15- 3. Won UKR TJ 2012, ISR LJ 2014, 2018; TJ 2013-16, 2018.
Eight Israeli triple jump records 2013-15 and one long jump 2014.
Progress at TJ: 2005- 12.87, 2006- 13.28, 2007-13.85, 2009- 13.61, 2010- 13.65, 2011- 14.20, 2012-14.71, 2013- 14.58, 2014- 14.29, 2015- 14.78, 2016-14.68, 2017- 14.42, 2018- 14.41. pb LJ 6.52 '14.
Married Anatoliy Minenko (Dec 7046 '10) in November 2012 and switched from Ukraine to Israel on 12 May 2013.
Lonah Chemtai Korlima-SALPETER b. 12 Dec 1988 Kapkanyar, Kenya 1.65m 52kg. née Korlima. Maccabi Tel Aviv.
At (5000m)/10000m EC: '18- dq (4)/1; ET: '18- 1. At Mar: OG: '16- dnf. WCh: '17- 41. At HMar: WCh: '18- 12. Won ISR 1500m 2018, 5000m 2016, 10000m 2016-18, HMar 2018.
Israeli records: 1500m 2018, 3000m 2017, 5000m 2017, 10000m 2017 & 2018, HMar (4) 2017-18, Mar 2018.
Progress at 5000m, 10000m, Mar: 2011- 17:51.76, 38:16.68; 2012- 16:32.98, 35:37.59; 2013- 16:23.64, 2014- 17:00.69, 35:12.99; 2015- 16:41.30, 36:05.01; 2016- 16:27.20, 35:01.33, 2:40:16; 2017- 16:12.51, 32:43.89, 2:40:22; 2018- 15:17.81, 31:33.03. 2:24:17. pb: 800m 2:10.20 '13, 1500m 4:11.69 '18,. 1M 4:47.50 '17, 3000m 8:42.88 '18, road: 5k: 15:15 '19, 15k 47:28 '18, 10M 50:45 '18. HMar 66:40 '98, 25k 1:28:48 '17.
Moved from Kenya in 2008, married her coach Dan Salpeter and became an Israeli citizen in 2016. Won Florence Marathon 2018.

ITALY

Governing body: Federazione Italiana di Atletica Leggera (FIDA. First Governing body formed 1896.
National Championships first held in 1897 (one event)/1906 (men), 1927 (women). **2018 Champions**: **Men**: 100m: Lamont Marcell Jacobs 10.24, 200m/400m: Davide Re 21.04/45.92, 800m: Enrico Brazzale 1:49.64, 1500m: João Bussotti 3:46.41, 5000m: Marouan Razzine 14:04.31, 10000m: Stefano La Rosa 28:36.86, HMar: Ahmed El Mazoury 64:03, Mar: Alessio Terrasi 2:19:14, 3000mSt: Leonardo Feletto 8:34.17, 110mh: Lorenzo Perini 13.57, 400mh: José Bencosme 49.52, HJ: Gianmarco Tamberi 2.30, PV: Claudio Stecchi 5.50, LJ: Filippo Randazzo 7.76, TJ: Fabrizio Schembri 16.60, SP: Sebastiano Bianchetti 19.39, DT: Giovanni Faloci 61.53, HT: Marco Lingua 73.95, JT: Mauro Fraresso 76.16, Dec: Luca Di Tizio 7240, 10kW/20kW: Massimo Stano 39:19/1:21:02, 50kW: Leonardo Dei Tos 3:59:48; **Women**: 100m: Johanelis Herrera 11.59, 200m Irene Siragusa 23.25, 400m: Raphaela Lukudo 52.38, 800m: Irene Baldessari 2:02.47, 1500m: Giulia Aprile 4:15.80, 5000m: Nadia Battocletti 16:15.30, 10000m: Rosaria Console 34:56.52, HMar: Valeria Straneo 72:04, Mar: Eleonora Gardelli 2:59:19, 3000mSt: Isabel Mattuzzi 9:51.89, 100mh: Luminosa Boglioli 13.21, 400mh: Yadisleidy Pedroso 55.62, HJ: Elena Vallortigara 1.91, PV: Roberta Bruni 4.35, LJ: Laura Strati 6.41, TJ: Ottavia Cestonaro 13.53, SP: Chiara Rosa 17.08, DT: Valentina Aniballi 56.80, HT: Sara Fantini 63.72, JT: Sara Jemai 58.19, Hep: Sveva Gerevini 5322, 10kW: Antonella Palmisano 45:15, 20kW: Valentina Trapletti 1:32:15, 50kW: Beatrice Foresti 4:52:07.

Marco DE LUCA b. 12 May 1981 Rome 1.88m 69kg. Fiamme Gialle.
At 50kW: OG: '08- 19, '12- 14, '16- 21; WCh: 05-07-09-11-13-15-17: 13/dnf/7/11/15/16/9; EC: '06-10-14-18: 7/6/7/10; WCp: 06-08-10-12-16: 9/8/14/6/3; ECp: '07-09-11-15: 8/8/2/3. Won Italian 20kW 2011, 50kW 2006, 2009.
Progress at 50kW: 2002- 4:07:06, 2003- 4:13:24, 2004- 4:05:01, 2005- 3:55:30, 2006- 3:48:08, 2007- 3:47:04, 2008- 3:49:21, 2009- 3:46:31, 2010- 3:48:36, 2011- 3:49:40, 2012- 3:47:19, 2013- 3:48:05, 2014- 3:45:25, 2015- 3:46:21, 2016- 3:44:47, 2017- 3:45:02, 2018- 3:55:47. pbs: 3000mW 12:03.79 '09, 5000mW 19:29.54i '15, 20:03.6 '05, 10000mW 40:48.0 '09, 20kW 1:22:38 '10, 30kW 2:09:37 '04, 35kW 2:28:53 '10.

Massimo STANO b. 27 Feb 1992 1.79m 63kg. GS Fiamme Oro Padova.
At 20kW: WCh: '19; EC: '14- 26, '18- 4; EU23: '13- 2; WT: '18- 3. At 10000mW: WJ: '10- 13; WY: '09- 14; EJ: '11- 5; WCp: '10- 11J; ECp: '11- 14J. Won ITA 10kW 2018, 20kW 2015, 2018.

Progress at 20kW: 2011- 1:31:00, 2013- 1:25:25, 2014- 1:23:01, 2015- 1:22:16, 2016- 1:25:16, 2017- 1:22:30, 2018- 1:20:51. pbs: 5000mW 19:22.62i '15, 19:52.74 '13; 10kW 39:19 '18. 40:24.60t '17.

Gianmarco TAMBERI b. 1 Jun 1992 Civitanove Marche 1.89m 71kg. Fiamme Gialle.
At HJ: OG: '12- dnq 21=; WCh: '15- 8=, '17- dnq 13=; EC: '12-14-16-18: 5/7=/1/4; WY: '09- dnq 18; EU23: '13- dnq 13=; EJ: '11- 3; WI: '16- 1; EI: '13-17-19: 5/7/1; won ITA 2012, 2014, 2016, 2018.
Four Italian high jump records 2015-16 & three indoor 2016.
Progress at HJ: 2005- 1.52, 2006- 1.62i, 2007- 1.80, 2008- 2.01, 2009- 2.07, 2010- 2.14, 2011-2.25, 2012- 2.31, 2013- 2.30i/2.25, 2014- 2.29, 2015- 2.37, 2016- 2.39, 2017- 2.29, 2018- 2.33.
Suffered serious injury, costing him Olympic chance, just after setting Italian records at 2.37 and 2.39 in Monaco 2016. His father Marco had pb 2.28i (Italian indoor record)/2.27 '83, elder brother Gianluca 4th EJ JT 2009, pb 78.61 '10.

Women

Eleonora GIORGI b. 14 Sep 1989 Cuneo 1.63m 52kg. Fiamme Azzurre. Social-economic law graduate of University "Bocconi" of Milan.
At 20kW: OG: '12- 13, '16- dq; WCh: '13-15-17: 10/dq/14; EC: '14- 5, '18- dq; EU23: '09- 11, '11- 3; WCp: '12-14-18: 12/5/5; ECp: '13- 6, '15- 2; won MedG 2013. At 10000mW: WJ: '08- 18.
Walk records: World best 5000m 2014, 25k & 30k 2016, 35k 2019; Italian 20k (3) 2014-15.
Progress at 20kW: 2009- 1:34:27, 2010- 1:34:00, 2011- 1:33:46, 2012- 1:29:48, 2013- 1:30:01, 2014- 1:27:05, 2015- 1:26:17, 2016- 1:28:05, 2017- 1:30:34, 2018- 1:28:31. pbs: 3000mW 11:50.08i/12:05.83 '13, 5000mW 20:01.80 '14, 10kW 44:33.56t '13, 43:51R '11; 25kW 1:56:12 '16, 30kW 2:19:43 '16, 35k: 2:45:21 '19.

Antonella PALMISANO b. 6 Aug 1991 Mottola, Taranto 1.66m 49kg. Fiamme Galle.
At 20kW: OG: '16- 4; WCh: '13-15-17: 13/5/3; EC: '14- 7, '18- 3; EU23: '11- 2, '13- 2; WCp: '14- 9; ECp: 17- 1. At 10000mW: WJ: '08- 9, '10- 4; EJ: '09- 2; WCp: '10- 1J; ECp: '09- 3J. At 5000mW: WY: '07-5. Won ITA 10kW 2018.
Italian 5000m walk record 2017.
Progress at 20kW: 2009- 1:38:47, 2010- 1:36:21, 2011- 1:34:31, 2012- 1:34:27, 2013- 1:30:50, 2014- 1:27:51, 2015- 1:28:40, 2016- 1:29:03, 2017- 1:26:36, 2018- 1:27:30. pbs: 3000mW 11:55.30i '18, 10kW 41:57.29t '17.
She married Lorenzo Dessi (pbs 20kW 1:26:17 '16, 50kW 3:57:32 '11) on 22 September 2018.

Alessia TROST b. 8 Mar 1993 Pordenone 1.88m 68kg. Fiamme Gialle.
At HJ: OG: '16- 5; WCh: '13- 7=, '17- dnq 19; EC: '14-16-18: 9=/6=/8; WJ: '12- 1; WY: '09- 1; EU23: '13- 1, '15- 1; EJ: '11- 4; WI: '16- 7, '18- 3; EI: '13-4=, '15- 2; ET: '13- 2, '17- 3=; YthOly: '10- 2.
Italian champion 2013-14, 2016.

Progress at HJ: 2003- 1.37, 2004- 1.55, 2005- 1.62, 2006- 1.68, 2008- 1.81, 2009- 1.89, 2010- 1.90, 2011- 1.87, 2012- 1.92, 2013- 2.00i/1.98, 2014- 1.96i/1.91, 2015- 1.97i/1.94, 2016- 1.95i/1.94, 2017- 1.93i/1.94, 2018- 1.93i/1.91. pbs: 100mh 15.5 '11, LJ 6.01 '14, SP 10.76i '14, Pen 4035i '14.

Elena VALLORTIGARA b. 21 Sep 1991 Schio 1.84m 66kg. Carabinieri Bologna.
At HJ: EC: '18- dnq 15; WJ: '08- dnq 30=, '10- 3; WY: '07- 3; EJ: '09- 4; EYOF: '07- 1. Won ITA 2018.
Progress at HJ: 2006- 1.75, 2007- 1.86, 2008- 1.85i/1.82, 2009- 1.87, 2010- 1.91, 2011- 1.90i, 2012- 1.86, 2013- 1.85, 2014- 1.84, 2015- 1.86i/1.84, 2016- 1.82, 2017- 1 87i/1 86, 2018- 2.02. pbs: 100mh 15.62 '09, SP 10.66i '14, Pen 3626i '10.
Breakthrough from 1.96 to 2.02 at the London Diamond League 2018.

IVORY COAST

Governing body: Fédération Ivoirienne d'Athlétisme, Abidjan. Founded 1960.

Ben Youssef MEITÉ b. 11 Nov 1986 Séguéla 1.79m 70kg.
At 100m/(200m): OG: '12- sf, '16- 6; WCh: '09-11-15-17- h & qf/11- h & h/sf/sf; AfG: '07- sf/sf, '11- 2/2, '15- 1; AfCh: '06- sf, '10- 1/2, '12- h/1, '16- 1, '18- 4; CCp: '10- 5/3.
CIV records 100m (7) 2012-16, 200m 2009.
Progress at 100m: 1002- 10.95, 2004- 10.5h, 2005- 10.40, 2006- 11.07, 2007- 10.49/10.46w, 2008- 10.49, 2009- 10.21/10.15w, 2010- 10.08A/10.25/10.19w, 2011- 10.21/10.14w, 2012- 10.06, 2015- 10.04, 2016- 9.96/9.95w, 2017- 9.97/9.84w, 2018- 10.14/10.13w. pbs: 60m 6.55i '18, 200m 20.37 '09, 300m 33.68i '07.
Lives in Canada. His brother Ibrahim (b. 18 Nov 1976) had pbs of 60m 6.58i '02 (CIV rec), 100m 10.24 '00, 200m 20.64 '94 and competed at Olympic Games of 1996 and 2000. Their father Amadou had 100m pb 10.32 '80 and competed at the Olympic Games in 1972 and 1976 and won 1978 African Games 100m.

Women

Murielle AHOURÉ b. 23 Aug 1987 Abidjan 1.67m 57kg. Graduated in criminal law from the University of Miami, USA.
At 100m/200m: OG: '12- 7/6, '16- sf/sf; WCh: '13- 2/2, '15- sf/-, '17- 4; AfCh: '14- 2/1, '16- 1; won DL 2018. At 60m: WI: '12-14-18: 2/2/1. Won NCAA indoor 200m 2009.
Three African 60m indoor records 2013-18. CIV records 100m (8) 2009-16, 200m (3) 2012-13.
Progress at 100m, 200m: 2005- 11.96, 2006- 11.42, 23.33; 2007- 11.41/11.28w, 23.34; 2008- 11.45, 23.50; 2009- 11.09, 22.78; 2010- 11.41, 2011- 11.06/10.86w, 2012- 10.99, 22.42; 2013- 10.91, 22.24; 2014- 10.97, 22.36; 2015- 10.81, 22.29; 2016- 10.78, 22.52; 2017- 10.83, 22.68; 2018- 10.90, 20.60. pbs: 60m 6.97i '18, 300m 38.09i '07, 400m 54.77 '08.
Lived in Paris from age 2, then USA from age 12. Won first Ivory Coast World medals.

Marie Josée TA LOU Gonerie b. 18 Nov 1988 Bouaflé 1.59m 57kg.
At 100m/200m: OG: '16- 4/4; WCh: '15- sf/sf, '17- 2/2; AfG: '11- 7/6, 15- 1/1/3R; AfCh: '10- sf/-, '12- 4/3/3R, '14- 3/2/2R, '16- 3/1, '18- 1/1/2R; CCp: '14- 4/5, '18- 1/3/dqR. At 60m: WI: '16- 7, '18- 2. CIV 200m records 2016-17.
Progress at 100m: 2010- 12.10/11.6, 24.3; 2011- 11.56, 24.12; 2012- 11.53, 23.26; 2013- 11.58, 23.63; 2014- 11.20, 22.78; 2015- 11.02/10.95w, 22.56; 2016- 10.86, 22.21; 2017- 10.86, 22.08; 2018- 10.85/10.7mxw, 22.34/22.2mxw. pb 60m 7.02i '19.

JAMAICA

Governing body: Jamaica Athletics Administrative Association. Founded 1932.
2018 Champions: Men. 100m: Tyquendo Tracey 10.07, 200m: Jahnoy Thompson 20.21, 400m: Christopher Taylor 44.88, 800m: Jauaveney James 1:50.07, 1500m: Kemoy Campbell 3:51.04, 110mh: Ronald Levy 13.16, 400mh: Annsert Whyte 48.80, HJ: Clayton Brown 2.20, PV: Cameron Walker-Shepherd 4.70, LJ: Ramone Bailey 8.10, TJ: Jordan Scott 16.55, SP: O'Dayne Richards 20.86, DT: Fredrick Dacres 65.13, HT: Caniggia Raynor 64.72, JT: Orlando Thomas 69.27. **Women**: 100m: Elaine Thompson 11.01, 200m: Shericka Jackson 22.28, 400m: Stephanie Ann McPherson 50.74, 800m: Natolya Goule 1:58.85, 100mh: Danielle Williams 12.63, 400mh: Janieve Russell 54.18, HJ: Saniel Atkinson Grier 1.83, LJ: Tissanna Hickling 6.50, TJ: Shanieka Ricketts 14.39, SP: Lloydricia Cameron 16.73, DT: Shadae Lawrence 61.44, HT: Nayoka Clunis 57.83, JT: Kateema Rietttie 51.52.

Nathon ALLEN b. 28 Oct 1995 Bethany, St. Ann1.78m 68kg. Auburn University, USA.
At 400m/4x400mR: OG: '16- 2R; WCh: '17- 5; WJ: '14- sf/3R; WI: '16- 4R. JAM champion 2017.
Progress at 400m: 2014- 46.11, 2015- 45.30, 2016- 45.39, 2017- 44.19, 2018- 44.13. pbs: 200m 20.46/20.39w '18.; 300m 31.9+ '18.

Kemar BAILEY-COLE b. 10 Jan 1992 St Catherine 1.95m 83kg. Racers TC.
At 100m/4x100mR (200m): OG: '12- res (1)R, '16- res 1R; WCh: '13- 4/1R; CG: '14- 1/1R; WY: '09- sf/sf.
Progress at 100m: 2008- 10.85, 2009- 10.41/10.38w, 2010- 10.53, 2011- 10.28, 2012- 9.97, 2013- 9.93, 2014- 9.96/9.95w, 2015- 9.92, 2016- 10.00, 2017- 10.06, 2018- 10.12. pbs: 150mSt 15.00 '14, 200m 20.66 '15, 400m 47.20 '17.

Yohan BLAKE b. 26 Dec 1989 St James 1.81m 79kg. Racers TC.
At 100m/4x100mR: OG: '12- 2/2/1R, '16- 4/sf/1R; WCh: '11- 1/1R, '17- 4/sf; CG: '18- 3/3R; WJ: '06- 3/1R, '08- 4/2R; WY: '05- 7; PAm-J: '07- 2 (3 4x400m); CCp: '18- 8/1R; won CAC-J 100m & 200m 2006; JAM 100m & 200m 2012, 2016-17.
World record 4x100m 2012, 4x200m 2014.

Progress at 100m, 200m: 2005- 10.56, 22.10; 2006- 10.33, 20.92; 2007- 10.11, 20.62; 2008- 10.27/10.20w, 21.06; 2009- 10.07/9.93dq, 20.60; 2010- 9.89, 19.78; 2011- 9.82/9.80w, 19.26; 2012- 9.69, 19.44; 2013- 20.72, 2014- 10.02, 20.48; 2015- 10.12, 21.57; 2016- 9.93, 20.13; 2017- 9.90, 19.97; 2018- 9.94, 20.95. pbs: 60m 6.75i '08, 150mSt 14.71 '14, 400m 46.32 '13.
3-month drugs ban from positive test at Jamaican Champs 25 Jun 2009. Cut 200m pb from 20.60 to 19.78 in Monaco 2010 and then to 19.26 in Brussels 2011. Youngest ever World 100m champion at 21 in 2011.

Akeem BLOOMFIELD b. 10 Nov 1997 Kingston 1.88m 77kg. Auburn University, USA.
Progress at 200m, 400m: 2014- 21.06, 2015- 44.93, 2016- 20.66, 46.01; 2017- 20.29w, 44.74; 2018- 19.81, 43.94. pbs: 100m 10.42 '14, 300m 31.8+ '18.

Fedrick DACRES b. 28 Feb 1994 Kingston 1.94m 115kg. Irvine.
At DT: OG: '16- dnq 34; WCh: '15- 7, '17- 4; CG: '18- 1; PAm: '15- 1; WJ: '12- 1; WY '11- 1; CCp: '18- 1; won CAC-J 2012; JAM 2015-18, NACAC 2018, DL 2018.
Three Jamaican discus records 2017-18.
Progress at DT: 2011- 53.05, 2012- 55.45, 2013- 59.30, 2014- 66.75, 2015- 66.40, 2016- 68.02, 2017- 68.88, 2018- 69.67/69.83 light. pb SP 20.46 '17.

Rasheed DWYER b. 83 Jan 1989 St Mary 1.88m 80kg. G.C.Foster College.
At 200m/4x100mR: WCh: '15- res 1R, '17- sf; CG: '10- sf/2R, '14- 1, '18- sf; WJ: '08- res2R; PAm: '15- 2; CAG: '18- 4/3R; WUG: '11- 1, '13- 2; CCp: '14- 2. Won NACAC 2015.
CAC 4x200m record 2014.
Progress at 200m: 2006- 21.67, 2007- 21.81, 2008- 21.84, 2009- 21.12/20.82w, 2010- 20.49, 2011- 20.20, 2012- 20.59, 2013- 20.15, 2014- 19.98, 2015- 19.80, 2016- 20.46, 2017- 20.11, 2018- 20.19. pbs: 100m 10.10/10.08w '16, 400m 46.76 '16.

Damar FORBES b. 18 Sep 1990 Saint Ann 1.85m 77kg. Sports administration degree from Louisiana State University.
At LJ: OG: '12- dnq 19, '16- 12; WCh: '11/15- dnq 20/26, '13- 8, '17- 12; CG: '14- 9, '18- 8. Jamaican champion 2012-16, NCAA 2013.
Progress at LJ: 2009- 7.51i/7.48, 2010- 9.93, 2011- 8.23, 2012- 8.13, 2013- 8.25/8.35w, 2014- 8.10, 2015- 8.17, 2016- 8.23, 2017- 8.29, 2018- 8.07i/7.99. Pbs: 60m 6.73i '13, 100m 10.51 '13, 55mh 7.48i '09, 60mh 8.12i '09, TJ 16.11i '12, 15.85 '10.

Javon FRANCIS b. 14 Dec 1994 Bull Bay 1.83m 73kg. Akan TC.
At 400m/4x400mR: OG: '16- sf/2R; WCh: '13- sf/2R, '15- sf; CG: '18- 3/3R; WJ: '12- 9. JAM champion 2015-16.
Progress at 400m: 2012- 46.06, 2013- 45.24, 2014- 45.00, 2015- 44.50, 2016- 44.77, 2017- 45.94, 2018- 45.11. Pb 200m 20.52 '18.
Brilliant anchor relay legs at Worlds: 2013-

44.05 to move JAM from 5th to 2nd, and 43.52 in 2015, when pipped for 3rd place.

Demish GAYE b. 20 Jan 1993 Mandeville 1.88m 77kg.
At 400m/4x400mR: WCh: '17- 6; CG: '18- 6/3R; WI: '16- 4R. Won NACAC 2018.
Progress at 400m: 2015- 46.15, 2016- 45.30, 2017- 44.55. 2018- 45.08. pb 200m 20.48 '17.

Tajay GAYLE b. 2 Aug 1996 Kingston 1.83m 75kg.
At LJ: CG: '18- 4, NACAC: '18- 2.
Progress at LJ: 2016- 7.54, 2017- 8.00, 2018- 8.24.
Pbs: 60m 6.80i '17, 100m 10.50 '16, 200m 21.34 '16, HJ 2.00 '16, TJ 15.78w '16.

Jaheel HYDE b. 2 Feb 1997 1.80m 74kg. University of West Indies.
At 400mh: OG: '16- sf; WCh: '17- sf; CG: '18- 3; WJ: '14- 1/3R, '16- 1. Won JAM 2017. At 110mh: WY: '13- 1; Yth OG: '14- 1.
Progress at 400mh: 2014- 49.29, 2015- 49.01, 2016- 48.81, 2017- 48.52, 2018- 49.14. Pbs: 200m 20.78 '17, 400m 46.66 '16.
Scored a hat-trick for the Jamaican U17 football team against Bermuda in 2012. His father Lenworth played football for Jamaica.

Ronald LEVY b. 30 Oct 1992 Westmoreland 1.84m 77kg. MVP. Kingston Univ. of Technology.
At 110mh: WCh: '17- h; CG: '18- 1; CCp: '18- 2; JAM champion 2018.
Progress at 110mh: 2013- 14.42, 2015- 13.63, 2016- 13.50, 2017- 13.05, 2018- 13.12. Pbs: 60m 6.62 '16, 100m 10.17 '17, 10.10w '16; 200m 20.81 '14, 800m 1:52.47 '16, 60mh 7.49i '18, 400mh 51.77 '13.

Omar McLEOD b. 25 Apr 1994 Kingston 1.80m 73kg. Studied business management at University of Arkansas, USA.
At 110mh: OG: '16- 1; WCh: '15- 6, '17- 1; WY: '11- 4 (8 400mh). At 60mh: WI: '16- 1. Won JAM 2015-17, NCAA 110mh 2015 (& 60mh indoors 2014-15).
Commonwealth 110m hurdles record 2017.
Progress at 110mh: 2014- 13.44, 2015- 12.97, 2016- 12.98, 2017- 12.90, 2018- 13.16/13.01w. Pbs: 60m 6.61i '17, 100m 9.99 '16, 200m 20.48i '17, 20.49 '18, 400m 47.41i '15, 60mh 7.41i '16, 400mh 49.98 '13.
First man ever to run under 10 secs for 100m as well as 13 secs for 110m hurdles,

Kemar MOWATT b. 12 Mar 1995 Saint-Elizabeth 1.88m 77kg. University of Arkansas, USA.
At 400mh: WCh: '17- 4.
Progress at 400mh: 2014- 52.03, 2015- 51.13, 2016- 50.66, 2017- 48.49, 2018- 48.83. Pbs: 200m 21.07i '17, 21.34 '15; 400m 47.15i '17, 60mh 7.93i '16, 110mh 13.90 '17, 13.75w 16.

Hansle PARCHMENT b. 17 Jun 1990 Saint Thomas 1.96m 90kg. Student of psychology at University of the West Indies.
At 110mh: OG: '12- 3; WCh: '13-15-17: sf/2/8; CG: '10- 5, '18- 2; WY: '07- sf; WUG: '11- 1. Won

JAM 2012, NACAC 2018.
Three Jamaican 110mh records 2012-13.
Progress at 110mh: 2010- 13.71, 2011- 13.24, 2012- 13.12, 2013- 13.05, 2014- 12.94, 2015- 13.03, 2016- 13.10, 2017- 13.19, 2018- 13.21. Pb 400mh 53.74 '08.

O'Dayne RICHARDS b. 14 Dec 1988 St Andrew 1.77m 120kg. Data communications graduate. MVP TC.
At SP: OG: '16- 8; WCh: '13- dnq 20, '15- 3, '17- dnq 19; CG: '14- 1, '18- 4; PAm: '15- 1; WUG: '11- 1; CCp: '14- 2; won CAC 2011, 2013; JAM 2013-18.
Four CAC shot records 2014-17, indoor 2019.
Progress at SP: 2008- 16.76, 2009- 18.05, 2010- 18.74, 2011- 19.93, 2012- 20.31, 2013- 20.97, 2014- 21.61, 2015- 21.69, 2016- 20.82, 2017- 21.96, 2018- 21.02, 2-019- 20.68i. pb DT 58.31 '12.

Traves SMIKLE b. 7 May 1992 Kingston 1.93m 120kg. UWI Mona.
At DT: OG: '12- dnq 20; WCh: '17- 8; CG: '18- 2; WJ: '10- 7; WY '09- 3; won PAm-J 2011, NACAC U23 2012, JAM 2011-12.
Progress at DT: 2010- 51.54, 2011- 59.83, 2012- 67.12, 2013- 63.48, 2015- 58.96, 2016- 63.42, 2017- 65.00, 2018 67.72, 2019 67.57. pb SP 15.99 '17.
Two-year doping ban 2013-15.

Annsert WHYTE b. 10 Apr 1987 Kingston 1.88m 86kg. Racers TC.
At 400mh: OG: '16- 5; WCh: 13/15: sf; CAG: '18- 2; CCp: '18- 2; Jamaican champion 2015-16, 2018.
At 400m: PAm: '11- h.
Progress at 400mh: 2013- 49.17, 2014- 48.58, 2015- 48.90, 2016- 48.07, 2017- 50.18, 2018- 48.46. pbs: 200m 21.03 '09, 400m 46.19 '09.

Women

Christine DAY b. 23 Aug 1986 St Mary 1.68m 51kg. Cameron Blazers TC.
At 400m/4x400mR: OG: '12- sf/2R, '16- sf/res 2R; WCh: '09- sf, '15- 4/1R; CG: 14- 3/1R, '18- 1R; CCp: '14- 1R. JAM champion 2015.
Progress at 400m: 2006- 55.33, 2007- 53.91, 2008- 53.10, 2009- 51.54, 2010- 52.43, 2011- 52.08, 2012- 50.85, 2013- 50.91, 2014- 50.16, 2015- 50.14, 2016- 50.29, 2017- 51.25, 2018- 51.41. pb 200m 23.73 '13.

Simone FACEY b. 7 May 1985 Manchester 1.62m 53kg. Was at Texas A&M University.
At 200m/4x100mR: OG: '16- sf/res 2R; WCh: '07- 2R, '09- 6/1R, '17- sf/3R; PAm: '11- 2, '15- 3/2R; PAm-J: '03- 2R. At 100m: WCh: '17- sf; WJ: '02- 2/1R; WY: '01- 4. Won JAM 200m 2016, NCAA 200m 2008, CAC-J 100m & 200m 2002.
CAC junior 200m record 2004.
Progress at 200m: 2000- 24.13, 2001- 23.67. 2002- 23.22, 2004- 22.71, 2005- 23.43i, 2006- 23.36, 2007- 22.49, 2008- 22.25, 2009- 22.58, 2010- 22.90, 2011- 22.86A/23.07, 2012- 23.12, 2013- 22.95, 2014- 22.67, 2015- 22.55, 2016- 22.50, 2017- 22.74. pbs: 60m 7.14i '16, 100m 10.95A '08, 11.04/11.00w '17, 11.0 '04.

Shelly-Ann FRASER-PRYCE b. 27 Dec 1986 Kingston 1.60m 52kg. MVP. Graduate of the University of Technology. née Fraser. Married Jason Pryce on 7 Jan 2011.
At 100m/(200m)/4x100mR: OG: '08- 1, '12- 1/2/2R, '16- 3/2R; WCh: '07- res (2)R, '09- 1/1R, '11- 4/2R, '13- 1/1/1R, '15- 1/1R; CG: '14- 1R. At 60m: WI: '14- 1. Won WAF 2008, DL 100m 2012-13, 2015; 200m 2013; JAM 100m 2009, 2012, 2015; 200m 2012-13.
CAC and Commonwealth records 100m 2009 & 2012, 4x100m (4) 2011-15; CAC 4x100m 4x200m 2014.
Progress at 100m, 200m: 2002- 11.8, 2003- 11.57, 2004- 11.72, 24.08; 2005- 11.72; 2006- 11.74, 24.8; 2007- 11.31/11.21w, 23.5; 2008- 10.78, 22.15; 2009- 10.73, 22.58; 2010- 10.82dq, 22.47dq; 2011- 10.95, 22.59/22.10w; 2012- 10.70, 22.09; 2013- 10.71, 22.13; 2014- 11.01, 22.53; 2015- 10.74, 22.37; 2016- 10.86, 23.15; 2018- 10.98. pb 60m 6.98i '14, 400m 55.34 '19.
Eight global gold medals (and four silver). Huge improvement in 2008, moving to joint third on world all-time 100m list when winning 2009 world 100m title. 6-month ban for positive test for a non-performance enhancing drug on 23 May 2010. IAAF Athlete of the Year 2013. Son Zyon Pryce born 7 Aug 2017.

Natoya GOULE b. 30 Mar 1991 Manchester 1.60m 50kg. Was at Louisiana State University and then Clemson Univerity, USA.
At 800mh: OG: '16- h; WCh: '13-15-17: h; CG: '14- sf, '18- 3; WJ: '08- h; WY: '07- sf; CCp: '18- 3; WI: '14- res2R. Won CAC 2013, JAM 2013-17, NCAA 2013.
Two Jamaican 800m records 2018, CAC indoor 800m & 1000m records 2019.
Progress at 800m: 2006- 2:08.89, 2007- 2:08.37, 2008- 2:05.90, 2009- 2:04.29, 2010- 2:03.52, 2011- 2:01.45, 2012- 2:04.76, 2013- 1:59.93, 2014- 2:00.28, 2015- 1:59.63, 2016- 1:59.38, 2017- 2:00.56, 2018- 1:56.15. Pbs: 200m 24.30 '16, 400m 51.52A/52.23 '11, 600y 1:18.82i '11, 600m 1:25.35i '17, 1000m 2:37.55i '19, 2:43.03 '15,;1500m 4:17.10 '18, 1M 4:45.71i '16, 3000m 9:56.79 '06.
Won 14 gold medals at the Jamaican Schools Champs and 12 at Carifta Games.

Shericka JACKSON b. 16 Jul 1994 Saint-Anne 1.73m 60kg. UTech.
At 400m/4x400mR: OG: '16- 3/2R; WCh: '15- 3/1R, '17- 5; won JAM 2017. At 200m: CG: '18- 2; WJ: '12- 8/2R; WY: '11- 3/1 MedR; Yth OG: '10- 4; CCp: '18- 4; won NACAC 2018.
CAC & Commonwealth 4x200m record 2017
Progress at 200m, 400m: 2008- 24.56, 54.27; 2009- 23.62, 53.13; 2010- 23.94/23.64w, 53.71; 2011- 23.32, 52.94; 2012- 23.35, 53.34; 2013- 22.84, 51.60; 2014- 23.29, 51.32; 2015- 22.87, 49.99; 2016- 22.95/22.86w, 49.83; 2017- 22.46, 50.05; 2018- 22.05. pbs: 60m 7.31 '18, 100m 11.13 '18, 11.03w '19. 11 wins at Cariffta Games 2008-13.

Stephenie Ann McPHERSON b. 25 Nov 1988 Westmoreland 1.68m 55kg. MVP. Was at Kingston University of Technology.
At 400m/4x400mR: OG: '16- 6/2R; WCh: '13- 3, '15- 5/1R, '17- 6; CG: 14- 1/1R, '18- 3/1R; CCp: '14- 1R, '18- 3/1mxR; WI: 14- 2R, '16- 4. Won DL 2016, NACAC 2018, JAM 2016, 2018
Progress at 400m: 2006- 56.42, 2007- 55.77, 2008- 52.80, 2009- 51.95, 2010- 51.64, 2012- 52.98, 2013- 49.92, 2014- 50.12, 2015- 50.32, 2016- 50.04, 2017- 50.56, 2018- 50.31. pbs: 100m 11.44 '10, 11.30w '19; 200m 22.93 '14, 800m 2:15.24 '12, 400mh 57.46 '12.

Natasha MORRISON b. 17 Nov 1992 Saint-Catherine 1.70m 57kg. GGOF.
At 100m/4x100mR: WCh: '15- 7/1R, '17- sf/3R; CG: '18- 5/2R; CAG: '18- 1R.
CAC and Commonwealth 4x100m record 2015.
Progress at 100m: 2007- 12.06, 2008- 12.00, 2010- 11.98/11.47w, 2011- 11.42, 2013- 11.17/11.12w, 2014- 11.06, 2015- 10.96, 2016- 11.27, 2017- 11.09, 2018- 11.26. pbs: 60m 7.15i '16, 200m 23.08 '13.

Leah NUGENT b. 23 Nov 1992 Abington, Pennsylvania, USA 1.73m 66kg. Was at University of Kentucky.
At 400mh: OG: '16- 6; WCh: '17- sf.
Progress at 400mh: 2009- 60.72, 2010- 59.15, 2011- 57.72, 2012- 59.68, 2013- 58.47, 2014- 56.97, 2015- 55.63, 2016- 54.45, 2017- 54.54, 2018- 54.67. pbs: 60m 7.39i '16, 200m 24.03 '16, 400m 53.09i '16, 53.47 '18; 800m 2:13.07i '18, 60mh 7.96i '17, 100mh 13.11 '16, 12.83w '17.
She competed in the 2016 US Champs but then got clearance to compete for Jamaica from 22 July (her father came from Jamaica) and reduced her pb from 55.44 to 54.98 and 54.45 at the Olympic Games.

Aisha PRAUGHT LEER b. 14 Dec 1989 Moline, Illinois, USA 1.63m 50kg. Was at Illimois State University, USA.
At 3000mSt: OG: '16- 14; WCh: '15- h, '17- dq; CG: '18- 1; CCp: '18- fa. At 1500m: WI: '18- 6.
CAC 3000mSt record 2017.
Progress at 3000mSt: 2009- 10:57.05, 2010- 10:37.98, 2011- 10:23.56, 2012- 9:51.30, 2013- 9:50.06, 2014- 9:34.69, 2015- 9:36.63, 2016- 9:31.75, 2017- 9:19.39, 2018- 9:21.00. pbs: 800m 2:07.93 '12, 1500m 4:04.95i '18, 4:05.52 '15; 1M 4:27.61 '14, 2000m 5:45.51 '16, 3000m 8:41.10i '18, 8:53.43'17; 2M 9:52.21 '14, 2000mSt 6:26.72 '14.
Biological father was Jamaican, and she switched from USA, taking up Jamaican citizenship in 2015. Married **Will Leer** USA (1500m 3:34.26 & 6 WI '14, 1M 3:51.82 '14, 3000m 7:39.38 '13, 5000m 13:21.55 '13; won US indoor 1M & 3000m 2013) on 17 Oct 2016.

Shanieka RICKETTS b. 2 Feb 1992 Saint Andrew 1.82m 66kg. née Thomas.Was at San Diego State University, USA.
At TJ: OG: '16- dnq 14; WCh: '15- 11, '17- 8; CG:

'14- 4, '18- 2; PAm: '15- 9; WI: '16- 8; Won NCAA 2013-14, NACAC 2015, 2018, JAM 2018.
Progress at TJ: 2008- 11.83, 2011- 12.98i/12.90, 2012- 13.64, 2013- 14.15, 2014- 14.00, 2015- 14.23A/14.08, 2016- 14.57, 2017- 14.45, 2018- 14.61. pbs: 100m 12.24 '17, 400m 55.38 '13, HJ 1.75 '10, LJ 6.63 '15.
Married coach Kerry-Lee Ricketts in 2016.

Janeive RUSSELL b. 14 Nov 1993 Manchester 1.75m 63kg. UTech.
At 400mh/4x400mR: OG: '16- 7; WCh: '15- 5; CG: '14- 3, '18- 1/1R; WJ: '12- 1/2R; CCp: '18- 1. At 400m: WJ: '10- sf/3R. At LJ: WY: '09- 9. Won JAM Hep 2011, 400mh 2015, 2018.
Progress at 400mh: 2011- 57.71, 2012- 56.62, 2013- 56.30, 2014- 54.75, 2015- 54.64, 2016- 53.96, 2017- 54.02, 2018- 53.46. pbs: 200m 23.43 '18, 400m 51.17 '16, 800m 2:11.5 '15, 100mh 13.80 '12, HJ 1.80 '09, LJ 6.20 '10, 6.26w '11; SP 10.86 '11, JT 26.53 '11, Hep 5361 '11.

Danniel THOMAS-DODD b. 11 Nov 1992 1.68m 91kg. née Thomas. PE student at Kent State University, USA.
At SP: OG: '16- dnq 25; WCh: '15- dnq 22, '17- 4; CG: '18- 1; PAm: '15- 5; CCp: '18- 6; WI: '18- 2; won NCAA 2017. At DT. CG. '14- 0. Won JAM SP 2014-17, DT 2015.
Five Jamaican shot records 2017-18.
Progress at SP: 2012- 14.58, 2013- 16.10, 2014- 16.97i/16.82, 2015- 17.76, 2016- 17.60, 2017- 19.15, 2018- 19.36. pbs: DT 59.38 '14.
Married to Shane Dodd.

Elaine THOMPSON b. 28 Jun 1992 Manchester 1.69m 57kg. MVP. Kingston University of Technology.
At 100m: WCh: '17- 5; At 200m/4x100mR: OG: '16- 1/1/2R; WCh: '15- 2/1R; CG: '14- res 1R, '18- 4/2R Won DL 100m 2016-17, JAM 100m 2016-18, 200m 2015. At 60m: WI: '16- 3, '18- 4.
CAC and Commonwealth records 4x100m 2015, 100m 2016, 4x200m 2017.
Progress at 100m, 200m: 2008- 12.16, 25.56; 2009- 12.01, 24.35; 2010- 11.94w, 2012- 23.89, 2013- 11.41, 23.73; 2014- 11.17, 23.23; 2015- 10.84, 21.66, 2016- 11/71, 21.78; 21/2, 11/71, 21.98; 2018- 11/43, 22.30, pbs: 60m 6.98i '17, 7.02 '17; 150mSt 15.00 '14, 400m 55.98 '17.

Ristananna TRACEY b. 9 May 1992 Kingston 1.73m 68kg. Racers TC.
At 400mh: OG: '16- 5; WCh: '11/13- sf, '15- h, '17- 3; CG: '18- 8; PAm: '15- h; WJ: '10- 5; WY: '09- 8. Won CAC-J 2010, JAM 2013, 2016.
Progress at 400mh: 2009- 58.49, 2010- 57.77, 2011- 54.58, 2012- 55.64, 2013- 54.52, 2014- 55.12, 2015- 55.45, 2016- 54.15, 2017- 53.74, 2018- 55.38. pbs: 200m 23.63 '11, 400m 51.95 '11, 800m 2:03.97 '11. Sister Nikita (b. 18 Sep 1990) 400mh pb 55.18 '14, 8 WJ '08.

Christania WILLIAMS b. 17 Oct 1994 Saint Mary 1.65m 63kg. U.Tech.

At 100m/4x100mR: OG: '16- 8/2R; WCh: '17- res 3R; CG: '18- 2/2R; WJ: '12- dnf hR; WY: '11- 3 (1 MedR).
Progress at 100m: 2009- 12.01, 2011- 11.39, 2012- 11.54, 2014- 11.19, 2015- 11.11, 2016- 10.96, 2017- 11.03, 2018- 11.21. pbs: 60m 7.05 '17, 200m 23.48 '15.

Danielle WILLIAMS b. 14 Sep 1992 St.Andrew 1.68m 59kg. Johnson C.Smith University, USA.
At 100mh: WCh: '13- sf, '15- 1, '17- sf; CG: '14- 4, '18- 2; WJ: '10- 4; WUG: '13- 3, '15- 1; PAm-J: '11- 2; CCp: '18- 1. JAM champion 2013, 2015, 2017-18.
CAC and Commonwealth 4x100m record 2015.
Progress at 100mh: 2010- 13.46/13.41w, 2011- 13.32/13.13w, 2012- 14.02, 2013- 12.69, 2014- 12.99, 2015- 12.57, 2016- 12.77/12.55w, 2017- 12.56, 2018- 12.48. pbs: 60m 7.32i '14, 100m 11.24A '13, 11.25 '17; 200m 22.62A/23.43i '13, 23.48 '14; 60mh 8.02i '15.
Sister **Shermaine** (b. 4 Feb 1990) at 100mh: OG: '12/16- sf; WCh: '13- sf, '15- 7; WJ: '08- 2; WY: '05- 6, '07- 2; PAm-J: '09- 1; pb 12.78/12.65w '12.

Kimberly WILLIAMS b. 3 Nov 1988 Saint Thomas 1.69m 66kg. Florida State University, USA.
At TJ: OG: '12- 6, '16- 7; WCh: '09/11 dnq 14/14, '13-15-17: 4/5/10; CG: '14- 1, '18- 1; WJ: '06- dnq 15; WY: '05- dnq; CAG: '10- 1; PAm-J: '07- 2; CCp: '14- 4; WI: '12-14-18: 5/3/2. Won NCAA LJ & TJ 2009, JAM TJ 2010, 2012-17.
Progress at TJ: 2004- 12.53/12.65w, 2005- 12.63/13.09w, 2006- 13.18, 2007- 13.52, 2008- 13.82i/13.69/13.83w, 2009- 14.08/14.38w, 2010- 14.23, 2011- 14.25, 2012- 14.53, 2013- 14.62/14.78w, 2014- 14.59, 2015- 14.45, 2016- 14.56/14.66w, 2017- 14.54/14.60w, 2018- 14.64. pbs: 100m 11.76 '12, 200m 24.55 '11, LJ 6.55i 11, 6.42/6.66w '09.

JAPAN

Governing body: Nippon Rikujo-Kyogi Renmei. Founded 1911.
National Championships first held in 1913 (men), 1925 (women). **2018 Champions**: **Men**: 100m: Ryota Yamagata 10.05, 200m: Shota Iizuka 20.34, 400m: Julian Walsh 45.97, 800m: Sho Kawamoto 1:48.35, 1500m: Ryoji Tatezawa 3:52.62, 5000m: Hazzuma Hattori 14:21.52, 10000m: Shuho Dairokumo 28:30.66, Mar: Yuma Hattori 2:07:27, 3000mSt: Kazuya Shiojiri 8:29.14, 110mh: Taio Kanai 13.36, 400mh: Takayuki Kishimoto 49.30, HJ: Takashi Eto 2.25, PV: Seito Yamamoto 5.70, LJ: Yuki Hashioka 8.09, TJ: Kohei Yamashita 16.59, SP: Satoshi Hatase 18.36, DT: Masateru Yugami 62.16, HT: Kunihiro Sumi 70.63, JT: Ryohei Arai 77.88, Dec: Keisuke Ushiro 7944, 20kW: Eiki Takahashi 1:17:26, 50kW: Tomohiro Noda 3:39:47. **Women**: 100m: Nodoka Seko 11.64, 200m: Chisato Fukushima 23.65, 400m: Ayaka Kawata 53.75, 800m: Yume Kitamura 2:02.54, 1500m: Tomomi

Takamatsu Musembi 4:17.43, 5000m: Rina Nabeshima 15:30.93, 10000m: Mizuki Matsuda 31:52.42, Mar: Mizuki Matsuda 2:22:44, 3000mSt: Yukari Ishizawa 9:53.22, 100mh: Masumi Aoki 13.17, 400mh: Eri Utsunomiya 57.37, HJ: Haruka Nakano 1.80, PV: Jyuri Nambu 4.09, LJ: Ayaka Kora 6.22, TJ: Eri Sakamoto 13.09, SP: Nanaka Kori 15.96, DT: Maki Saito 51.42, HT: Hitomi Katsuyama 64.48, JT: Marina Saito 60.79, Hep: Yuki Yamazaki 5836, 20kW: Kumiko Okada 1:32:22, 50kW: Serena Sonoda 4:29:45.

Hirooki ARAI b. 18 May 1988 Obuse, Nagano pref. 1.80m 62kg. Japan Self-Defense Forces Physical Training School, was at Fukui University of Technology.
At 50kW: OG: '16- 3; WCh: '11-13-15-17: 9/11/4/2; WT: '18- 1; JPN champion 2015, 2017.
Progress at 50kW: 2009- 4:04:01, 2010- 3:55:56, 2011- 3:48:40, 2012- 3:47:08, 2013- 3:45:56, 2014-3:40:34, 2015- 3:40:20, 2016- 3:41:24, 2017- 3:41:17, 2018- 3:44:25. Pbs: 3000mW 12:12.73 '09, 5000mW 19:05.46 '16, 10000m 39:17.66 '14, 20kW 1:19:00 '19, 30kW 2:13:02 '16, 35kW 2:34:53 '16.

Koki IKEDA b. 3 May 1998. Toyo Univertsity
At 20kW: WT: '18- 1.
Progress at 20kW: 2017- 1:20:48, 2018- 1:19:13, 2019- 1:17:25. pbs: 5000mW 19:24.13 '18, 10000mW 38:40.04 '18.

Yuki KAWAUCHI b. 5 Mar 1987 Tokyo 1.72m 59kg. Civil servant. Was at Gakushuin University.
At Mar: WCh: '11- 17, '13- 18, 17- 9; AsiG: '14- 3.
Progress at Mar: 2009- 2:17:33, 2010- 2:12:36, 2011- 2:08:37, 2012- 2:10:29, 2013- 2:08:14, 2014-2:09:36, 2015- 2:12:13, 2016-2:09:01, 2017- 2:09:18, 2018- 2:11:46. Pbs: 1500m 3:51.99 '15, 5000m 13:58.62 '12, 10000m 29:02.33 '10, Road: 10M 47:28 '14, HMar 62:18 '12..
An astonishingly prolific marathon runner, his greatest triumph came with his win in appalling conditions at Boston 2018. This was his world record 79th sub-2:20 run and his 33rd win. His younger brother Yoshiki has marathon pb 2:17:27 '18.

Kai KOBAYASHI b. 28 Feb 1993 Odate, Akita pref. 1.64m 53kg. Bic Camera. Was at Waseda University.
At 50kW: WCh: '17- 3.
Progress at 20kW, 50kW: 2013- 1:22:47, 2014-1:21:13, 2015- 1:19:12, 2016-1:19:57, 3:42:08; 2017-1:19:13, 3:41:17; 2018- 3:46:26. Pbs: 5000mW 19:11.94 '16, 10000m 39:06.86 '17, 30kW 2:13:10 '17, 35kW 2:35:20 '17.

Satoshi MARUO b. 28 Nov 1991 Kyoto pref. 1.75m 60kg. Aichi Steel Corporation. Was at Biwako Seikei Sport College.
At 50kW: WCh: '17- 5; AsiG: '18- 4; WT: '18- 3.
Progress at 20kW, 50kW: 2010- 1:30:56, 2011-1:27:20, 2012- 1:25:09, 2013- 1:24:42, 2014- 1:24:57, 2015- 1:19:42, 2016-1:20:14, 4:02:36; 2017- 1:20:31,

3:43:03; 2018- 1:21:10, 3:44:52. Pbs: 5000mW 19:30.76 '15, 10000m 39:33.30 '15, 30kW 2:14:18 '17, 35kW 2:36:31 '18. Run: 3000m 8:53.7 '06.

Daisuke MATSUNAGA b. 24 Mar 1995 Yokohama, Kanagawa pref. 1.74m 58kg. Fujitsu, was at Iwate University.
At 20kW: OG: '16- 7; WCh: '17- 38; WUG: '15- 3.
At 10000mW: WJ: '14- 1; As-J 12- 2; WCp: '14-2J.
10000m walk records: JPN 2018, Asian junior 2013, Asian 2018.
Progress at 20kW: 2013- 1:23:56, 2014- 1:21:17, 2015- 1:19:08, 2016- 1:18:53, 2017- 1:19:40, 2018-1:17:46. pbs: 5000mW 19:28.91 '14, 10000mW 37:58.08 '18.

Tomohiro NODA b. 24 Jan 1996. 1.74m 58kg.
At 50kW: JPN champion 2018.
Progress at 20kW, 50kW: 2014- 1:22:37, 2015-1:20:08, 2016-1:22:29, 2017- 1:20:04; 2018- 1:19:49, 3:39:47. Pbs: 5000mW 19:11.94 '16, 10000m 39:06.86 '17, 30kW 2:11:06 '18, 35kW 2:32:31 '18.

Suguru OSAKO b. 23 May 1991 Machida 1.70m 53kg. Nike Oregon Project. Was at Waseda University.
At 5000m: OG: '16- h; WCh: '15- h. At 10000m: OG: '16- 17; WCh: '13- 21; WJ: '10- 8; AsiG: '14- 2; WUG: '11- 1.
Asian records: junior half marathon 61:47 '10, marathon 2018. Japanese records: 3000m 2014, 5000m 2015.
Progress at 5000m, 10000m, Mar: 2008- 13:58.66, 2009- 28:57.00, 2010- 13:47.29, 28:35.75; 2011-13:31.27, 28:42.83; 2012- 13:33.84, 27:56.94; 2013-13:20.80, 27:38.31; 2014- 13:26.15, 28:11.94; 2015-13:08.40, 27:45.24; 2016-13:31.45, 27:50.27; 2017-13:25.56, 27:46.64, 2:07:19; 2018- 13:29.11, 28:26.41, 2:05:50. Pbs: 1500m 3:40.19 '16, 3000m 7:40:09 '14, 2M 8:16.47i '15, 8:28.30 '15; 5000m 13:08.40 '15, 10000m 27:38.31 '13, HMar 61:13 '17.
Marathons: 3rd Boston and Fukuoka 2017, 3rd Chicago in 2018, when he won 100 million yen ($879,350) for setting a Japanese record.

Abdul Hakim SANI BROWN b. 6 Mar 1999 Fukuoka 1.88m 78kg. University of Florida.
At (100m)/200m: WCh: '15- sf, '17- sf/7; WY: '15-1/1. Won JPN 100m & 200m 2017.
Progress at 100m, 200m: 2010- 12.95; 2013- 10.88, 21.85; 2014- 10.45, 21.09; 2015- 10.28, 20.34; 2016-10.22, 20.54; 2017- 10.05, 20.32; 2018- 10.46/10.19w, 20.64. Ghanaian father and Japanese mother.

Eiki TAKAHASHI b. 19 Nov 1992 Hanamaki, Iwate pref. 1.75m 56kg. Fujitsu, was at Iwate University.
At 20kW: OG: '16- 42; WCh: '15- 47, '17- 14; WCp: '14- 9, '16- 12; AsiG: '14- 7.Won JPN 2015-16.
Walk records: Asian 5000m & 10000m 2015, Japanese 20k 2015, 2019.
Progress at 20kW: 2011- 1:26:16, 2012- 1:22:33, 2013- 1:20:25, 2014- 1:18:41, 2015- 1:18:03, 2016-1:18:26, 2017- 1:18:18, 2018- 1:17:26, 2019- 1:18:00. pbs: 5000mW 18:37.60 '15, 10000mW 38:01.49 '15.

Naoto TOBE b. 31 Mar 1992 Noda, Chiba pref. 1.94m 74kg.
At HJ: WCh: '15- dnq 25=; WJ: '08- 10, '10- 3; AsiG: '14- 5, '18- 3; JPN champion 2011, 2015.
Progress at HJ: 2007- 2.08, 2008- 2.16, 2009- 2.23, 2010- 2.24, 2011- 2.22, 2012- 2.22, 2013- 2.28, 2014- 2.31, 2015- 2.29, 2016- 2.25, 2017- 2.26, 2018- 2.31, 2019- 2.35i. pb :LJ 7.52 '12.

Toshikazu YAMANISHI b. 15 Feb 1996. 1.64m 53kg. Beijing University.
At 20kW: WCp: '18- 4; AsiG: '18- 2; WUG: '17- 1; Asian champion 2019, At 10000mW: WY: '13- 1.
Progress at 20kW: 2015- 1:21:20, 2016- 1:20:50, 2017- 1:19:03, 2018- 1:17:41, 2019- 1:17:15. pbs: 5000mW 19:40.48 '15, 10000mW 39:24.49 '17.

Women

Hitomi NIIYA b. 26 Feb 1988 Soja, Okayama pref. 1.64m 45kg.
At (5000m)/10000m: OG: '12- h/9; WCh: '11- (13), '13- 5; AsiC: '11- (2). At 3000m: WY: '05- 3. Won JPN 5000m 2012, 10000m 2013.
Progress at 10000m: 2012- 30:59.19, 2013- 30:56.70, 2018- 31:32.50. pbs: 3000m 9:10.34 '05, 5000m 15:10.20 '12, HMar 71:41 '08, Mar 2:30:58 '09.
Led for much of 10,000m races at OG 2012 and WCh 2013. Returned after 5-year gap in 2018.

KAZAKHSTAN

Governing body: Athletic Federation of the Republic of Kazakhstan. Founded 1959.
2018 National Champions: Men: 100m/200m: Vladislav Grigoryev 10.41/20.97, 400m: Mikhail Litvin 46.18, 800m/1500m/HMar: Aleksey Gusarov 1:52.96/3:52.12/71:52, 5000m/10000m: Mikhail Krasilov 15:13.99/32:02.01, Mar: Amir Baytukanov 2:26:33, 3000mSt: Dmitriy Ivanchukov 9:14.58, 110mh: David Efremov 14.01, 400mh: Dmitriy Koblov 52.51, HJ: Roman Loshkaryev 2.16, PV: Danil Polyanskiy 5.20, LJ: Rinat Kaysarov 7.58, TJ: Yevgeniy Ektov 16.14, SP: Ruslan Muratbai 13.05, DT: Aleksandr Mamontov 51.76, HT: Alexey Vladimirov 47.70, JT: Artur Gafner 63.34, Dec Yevgeniy Pryadkin 6242, 20000mW: Vitaliy Teryokhin 1:30:33.2; **Women**: 100m: Olga Safonova 11.64, 200m: Viktoriya Zyabkina 23.18, 400m: Lyubov Ushakova 55.41, 800m: Margarita Mukasheva 2:06.27, 1500m: Viktoriya Sergeyeva 4:29.83, 5000m/10000m/Mar: Zhanna Mamazhanova 17:43.34/37:15.18/2:38:56, 3000mSt: Olga Bogomolskaya 11:40.81, 100mh: Aygerim Shynazbekova 13.54, 400mh: Adelina Akhmetova 58.84, HJ: Alexandra Krivitskaya 1.75, PV: Polina Ivanova 3.80, LJ: Yekaterina Ektova 5.95, TJ: Irina Ektova 13.81, SP: Yekaterina Nesterova 13.19, DT: Sabina Potapova 37.00, HT: Diana Nusupbekova 60.23, JT: Varvara Nazarova 46.67, Hep: Nadezhda Kirnos 5129, 20000mW: Aiman Ratova 1:37:14.3.

Women

Olga RYPAKOVA b. 30 Nov 1984 Kamenogorsk 1.83m 62kg. née Alekseyeva.
At TJ/(LJ): OG: '08- 2 (dnq 27), '12- 1, '16- 3; WCh: '07-09-11-15-17: 9/9/2/3/3; WJ: '00- (dnq 23); AsiG: '06- (3), '10- 1/2, '14- 1, '18- 1; AsiC: '07- 1/1, '09- 1; WI: '08-10-12: 3/1/2; WUG: '07- (1); WCp: '06- (8), '10: 1/3, '18- 3; won DL TJ 2012, Asian Indoor LJ 2009, 2017; TJ 2009, 2016-17; Pen 2005-06. At Hep: WJ: '02- 2; WY: '01- 4; AsiG: '06- 1; won DL 2017, C.Asian 2003. Won KAZ LJ 2005, 2008, 2011, 2015; TJ 2008, 2011, 2015; Hep 2006.
Four Asian TJ records 2008-10, five indoors 2008-10, seven KAZ records 2007-10.
Progress at LJ, TJ: 2000- 6.23, 2001- 6.00, 2002- 6.26, 2003- 6.34i/6.14, 2004- 6.53i, 2005- 6.60, 2006- 6.63, 2007- 6.85, 14.69; 2008- 6.52/6.58w, 15.11; 2009- 6.58i/6.42, 14.53/14.69w; 2010- 6.60, 15.25; 2011- 6.56, 14.96; 2012- 14.98, 2014- 14.37, 2015- 14.77, 2016- 14.74, 2017- 14.77, 2018- 14.26.
pbs: 200m 24.83 '02, 800m 2:20.12 '02, 60mh 8.67i '06, 100mh 14.02 '06, HJ 1.92 '06, SP 13.04 '06, JT 41.60 '03, Hep 6122 '06, Pen 4582i '06 (Asian rec).
Former heptathlete, concentrated on long jump after birth of daughter. Four KAZ and three Asian TJ records with successive jumps in Olympic final 2008, three Asian indoor records when won World Indoor gold in 2010. Son Kiril born June 2013.

KENYA

Governing body: Kenya Amateur Athletic Association. Founded 1951.
2018 National Champions: Men: 100m: Mark Otieno 10.34, 200m: Peter Mwai 20.65, 400m: Emmanuel Korir 44.21, 800m: Jonathan Kitilit 1:43.46, 1500m: Timothy Cheruiyot 3:34.82, 5000m: Samuel Chebolei 13:38.27, 10000m: Vincent Rono 28:17.24, 3000mSt: Conselslus Kipruto 8:18.05, 110mh: Kiprono Kosgei 14.43, 400mh: Haron Koech 49.54, HJ: Matthew Sawe 2.26, PV: Kennedy Magut 4.10, LJ: Bethwel Lagat 7.90, TJ: Isaac Kirwa 16.39, SP: Peter Mwangi 15.56, DT: Charles Kipkemoi 48.92, HT (irreg): Dominic Abuda 62.45, JT: Julius Yego 80.91, Dec: Vincent Tarus 6636, 20kW: Samuel Gathimba 1:21:58. **Women**: 100m: Joan Cherono 11.93, 200m: Eunice Kadogo 23.93, 400m: Maximilla Imali 52.66, 800m: Emily Cherotich 1:59.52, 1500m: Winny Chebet 4:09.69; 5000m: Hellen Obiri 15:09.82, 10000m: Pauline Korikwiang 31:51.1, 3000mSt: Beatrice Chepkoech 9:23.73, 100mh: Jerotich Gathogo 14.44, 400mh: Maureen Chelagat 58.04, HJ: Priscila Tabunda 1.,66, PV: Caroline Cherotich 2.90, LJ: Vera Rorey 5.81, TJ: Gloria Mulei 12.97, SP: Patricia Isiaho 13.06, DT/HT: Rose Rakamba 47.45/53.78, JT: Damacline Nyakeruri 49.08, , Hep: Ann Kandie 4360, 20kW: Grace Wanjiru 1:33:01.

Nicholas Kiptanui **BETT** b. 20 Dec 1996 1.72m 52kg.
At 2000mSt: WY: '13- 2.
Progress at 3000mSt: 2013- 8:52.1A, 2014- 8:28.83, 2015- 8:19.26, 2016- 8:10.07, 2017- 8:12.20, 2018- 8:13.18. pbs: 5000m 14:33.6A '16, 2000mSt 5:20.92 '13.

Jairus Kipchoge **BIRECH** b. 14 Dec 1992 Uasin Gishu 1.70m 56kg.
At 3000mSt: WCh: '15- 4, '17- 12; CG: '14- 2; AfG: '11- 4; AfCh: '14- 1; Af-J: '11- 2; CCp: '14- 1. Won DL 2014-15, Kenyan 2014.
Progress at 3000mSt: 2010- 8:50.0A, 2011- 8:11.31, 2012- 8:03.43, 2013- 8:08.72, 2014- 7:58.41, 2015- 7:58.83, 2016- 8:03.90., 2017- 8:07.68, 2018- 8:18.76. pbs: 2000m 4:58.76 '11, 3000m 7:41.83 '13, 5000m 13:38.4A '15, 10000m 28:35.7A '16, 10k Rd 28:14 '17.
His elder brother Comas Birech won the Rome marathon in 2018 in a pb 2:08:03.

Bethwel Kiprotich **BIRGEN** b. 6 Aug 1988 Eldoret 1.78m 64kg.
At 1500m: WCh: '13- sf; WI: '14- 8. At 3000m: WI: '18- 3.
Progress at 1500m, 5000m: 2010- 3:35.60, 2011- 3:34.59, 2012- 3:31.00, 14:01.0A; 2013- 3:30.77, 13:50.6A; 2014- 3:31.22, 2015- 3:34.62i, 2016- 3:33.94, 13:04.66; 2017- 3:32.27, 13:17.80; 2018- 3:34.27, 13:20.08. pbs: 800m 1:48.32 '11, 1M 3:50.42 '13, 3000m 7:32.48 '16, 5000m 14:01.0A '12.

Robert Kiptoo **BIWOTT** b. 28 Jan 1996 1.80m 68kg.
At 1500m: WY: '13- 1; Af-Y: '13-1 (1 800m).
Progress at 800m, 1500m: 2011- 3:41.2A, 2012- 3:43.81, 2013- 1:46.98, 3:36.77; 2014- 1:44.69, 3:43.91A; 2015- 1:43.56, 3:30.10; 2016- 3:33.05; 2017- 1:45.05, 3:34.30. pbs: 600m 1:15.91 '15, 1000m 2:13.89 '16, 1M 3:55.62 '16.

Lawrence CHERONO b. 7 Aug 1988 1.78m 61kg.
Progress at Mar: 2014- 2:10:16, 2015- 2:09:39, 2016- 2:07:24, 2017- 2:05:09, 2018- 2:04:06. pbs: 10M 45:06 '17, HMar 61:11+ '16.
Marathon wins: Seville 2015, Prague 2016, Honolulu 2016-17, Amsterdam 2017-18.

Ferguson Rotich CHERUIYOT b. 30 Nov 1989 1.83m 73kg.
At 800m: OG: '16- 5; WCh: '13-15-17: sf/4/sf; CG: '14- 4; AfCh: '14- 4, '18- 5. Won DL 2016, Kenyan 2014.
Progress at 800m: 2013- 1:43.22, 2014- 1:42.84, 2015- 1:43.60A, 2016- 1:43.43, 2017- 1:44.37, 2018- 1:43.73. pb 1000m 2:14.88 '18, 1500m 3:33.21 '18.
Changed first name from Simon to Ferguson in honour of Manchester United manager Alex Ferguson.

Timothy CHERUIYOT b. 20 Nov 1995 1.78m 64kg.
At 1500m: WCh: '15- 7, '17- 2; CG:'18- 2; AfCh: '16- 2, '18- 2. Won DL 2017-18, KEN 2017-18.

Progress at 1500m: 2015- 3:34.86A, 2016- 3:31.34, 2017- 3:29.10, 2018- 3:28.41. pbs: 800m 1:44.74A '18, 1M 3:49.64 '17, 5000m 13:51.5A.

Edward CHESEREK b. 2 Feb 1994 Kenya 1.68m 57kg. Marakwet. Was at University of Oregon.
Won NCAA 5000m 2015-16, 10000m 2014-16, CC 2013-15, Ind 1M 2015, 3000m & 5000m 2014, 2016-17, Dist.Med R 2015-16.
Progress at 1500m (1M), 5000m: 2011- 4:03.29M, 14:02.33, 2012- 4:02.21iM, 13:57.04i; 2013- 3:48.89+, 2014- 3:36.50, 13:18.71; 2015- 3:37.08, 13:45.25; 2016- 3:41.57 (3:57.38iM), 13:25.59; 2017- 3:37.01i (3:52.01iM), 13:24.72; 2018- 3:33.76i, 3:49.44Mi. pbs: 800m 1:49.98 '12, 1M 3:49.44i '18, 4:03.29 '11; 3000m 7:38.74i '18, 7:57.26 '16; 2M 8:39.15i '13, 10000m 28:30.18 '14, 3000mSt 9:00.11 '11.
Record 17 NCAA titles. Applying for US citizenship.

Dickson Kiptolo **CHUMBA** b. 27 Oct 1986 1.67m 50kg. Nandi.
Progress at Mar: 2010- 2:09:20dh, 2011- 2:07:23, 2012- 2:05:46, 2013- 2:10:15, 2014- 2:04:32, 2015- 2:06:34, 2016- 2:07:34, 2017- 2:06:25, 2018- 2:05:30. pbs: 1500m 3:44.33 '10, 5000m 13:41.34 '10, road: 10k 28:09 '13, HMar 61:34 '12, 60:39dh '14; 30k 1:28:36 '12.
Marathon wins: Rome 2011, Eindhoven 2012, Tokyo 2014, 2018 (3rd 2015-17), Chicago 2015 (2nd 2016, 3rd 2014).

Rodgers Kwemoi **CHUMO** b. 3 Mar 1997 Mount Elgon district 1.65m 49kg.
At 10000m: CG: '18- 3; WJ: '16- 1. World CC: '15- 10J,
Progress at 10000m: 2013- 29:25.0A, 2015- 27:42.09, 2016- 27:25.23, 2017- 27:38.61, 2018- 27:28.66. pbs: 1500m 3:50.44 '15, 5000m 13:18.98 '16. 10M Rd 45:03 '17.

Geoffrey Kipsang KAMWOROR b. 22 Nov 1992 Chepkorio, Keiyo district 1.68m 54kg.
At 10000m: OG: '16- 11; WCh: '15- 2, 17- 6. World CC: '11-15-17-19: 1J/1/1/3; HMar: '14-16-18: 1/1/1. Won KEN 5000m 2015, CC 2016, 2018. Tied world 30km record 2014.
Progress at 5000m, 10000m, HMar, Mar: 2010- 13:32.01, 2011- 13:12.23, 27:06.35, 59:31; 2012- 13:28.8A, 59:26, 2:06:12; 2013- 28:17.0A, 58:54, 2:06:26; 2014- 59:08, 2:06:39; 2015- 13:13.28A, 26:52.65, 2:10:48; 2016- 12:59.98, 27:31.94, 59:10; 2017- 13:01.35, 26:57.77, 2:10:53; 2018- 60:02, 2:06:26. pbs: 1500m 3:40.7A '15, 3000m 7:51.55 '17; Road: 15k 41:41 '16, 20k 56:02 '13, 30k 1:27:37 '14.
3rd in Berlin Marathon 2012 (on debut) and 2013 (4th 2014), won New York 2017 (2nd 2015, 3rd 2018). Won RAK half marathon 2013.

Felix Kipchirchir **KANDIE** b. 10 Apr 1987 1.78m 62kg.
Progress at Mar: 2009- 2:18:31A, 2010- 2:19:06, 2012- 16:12, 2014- 2:10:37, 2015- 2:07:07, 2016- 2:06:25, 2017- 2:06:03, 2018- 2:08:30. Road pbs: 10k 28:46 '14, HMar 60:04 '16.

Marathon wins: Athens 2014, Prague 2015 (2nd 2016). 2nd Seoul 2017.

Bedan KAROKI Muchiri b. 21 Aug 1990 Nyandarua 1.69m 53kg. S&B Foods, Japan.
At 10000m: OG: 12- 5, '16- 7; WCh: '13-15-17: 6/4/4; AfG: '11- 2. World CC: '15- 2; HMar: '16- 2. Won Kenyan CC 2012.
Progress at 10000m, HMar, Mar: 2010- 27:23.62, 2011- 27:13.67, 2012- 27:05.50; 2013- 27:13.12, 2014- 26:52.36, 59:23; 2015- 27:04.77, 59:14; 2016- 27:07.30, 59:32; 2017- 26:52.12, 59:10, 2:07:41; 2018- 58:42, 2:07:59. pbs: 1500m 3:50.91 '08, 3000m 7:37.68 '13, 5000m 13:15.25 '14, 15k 41:41 '16, 10M 45:02 '14, 20k 55:55 '18, 25k 1:12:37 '18, 30k 1:27:24 '18.
Went to Japan in 2007. 3rd London 2017 on marathon debut. 2nd Tokyo 2019. Won Ra's Al-Khaymah half marathon 2018, his sixth win in eight races at the distance, seven in under 1 hour.

Vincent KIBET b. 6 May 1991 Uasin Gishu 1.73m 57kg.
At 1500m: WI: '16- 7, '18- 9.
Progress at 1500m: 2010- 3:46.7A, 2011- 3:42.7A, 2012- 3:40.51A, 2013- 3:35.62, 2014- 3:31.96, 2015- 3:34.91i/3:36.80, 2016- 3:33.56, 2017- 3:32.66, 2018- 3:36.12. pbs: 800m 1:46.71 '14, 1000m 2:19.93i '15, 1M 3:51.17 '17, 3000m 7:44.87i '16, 7:50.54 '17.

Abraham KIBIWOT b. 6 Apr 1996 1.75m 55kg.
At 3000mSt: CG: '18- 2; AfCh: '16- 3; won Af-J 2015, Kenyan 2016.
Progress at 3000mSt: 2014- 8:52.36A, 2015- 8:22.10, 2016- 8:09.25, 2017- 8:10.62, 2018- 8:10.62. pbs: 3000m 8:02.95 '16, 5000m 14:10.8A '15.

Benjamin KIGEN b. 5 Jul 1993 1.73m 57kg.
Progress at 3000mSt: 2017- 8:11:38, 2018- 8:06.19. pbs: 800m 1:52.0A '16, 1500m 3:36.36 '17, 3000m 7:44.77i '18, 5000m 14:06.2A '13, 2000mSt 5:18.67 '17.

Wycliffe KINYAMAL b. 2 Jul 1997 Trans Mara District 1.86m 75kg.
At 800m: CG: '18- 1.
Progress at 800m: 2016- 1:46.8A, 2017- 1:43.94, 2018- 1:43.12. A high jumper at school

Eliud KIPCHOGE b. 5 Nov 1984 Kapsisiywa, Nandi 1.67m 52kg.
At Mar: OG: '16- 1; At 5000m: OG: '04- 3, '08- 2; WCh: '03-05-07-09-11: 1/4/2/5/7; CG: '10- 2. At 3000m: WI: '06- 3. World CC: '02-03-04-05: 5J/1J/4/5; HMar: '12- 6. Won WAF 5000m 2003, 3000m 2004, Kenyan CC 2005.
World junior 5000m record 2003. World road best 4M 17:10 '05 and WR 30k 2016 & 2018, World marathon record 2018.
Progress at 1500m, 5000m, 10000m: 2002- 13:13.03, 2003- 3:36.17, 12:52.61; 2004- 3:33.20, 12:46.53; 2005- 3:33.80, 12:50.22; 2006- 3:36.25i, 12:54.94; 2007- 3:39.98, 12:50.38, 26:49.02; 2008- 13:02.06, 26:54.32; 2009- 12:56.46, 2010- 3:38.36,

12:51.21; 2011- 12:55.72i/12:59.01, 26:53.27; 2012- 12:55.34, 27:11.93. At HMar, Mar: 2012: 59:25, 2013- 60:04, 2:04:05, 2014- 60:52, 2:04:11; 2015- 60:50, 2:04:00; 2016- 59:44, 2:03:05; 2017- 61:29, 2:03:32/2:00:25 irreg; 2018- 2:01:39. pbs: 1M 3:50.40 '04, 2000m 4:59.?+ '04, 3000m 7:27.66 '11, 2M 8:07.39i '12, 8:07.68 '05; Road: 10k 26:55dh '06, 27:34 '05; 25k 1:12:24 '18, 30k 1:26:45 '18.
Kenyan Junior CC champion 2002-03, followed World Junior CC win by winning the World 5000m title, becoming at 18 years 298 days the second youngest world champion. Age 19 bests for 3000m & 5000m 2004. Ran 26:49.02 in 10,000m debut at Hengelo in 2007. All his seven marathons were in 2:05:30 or better until his Olympic win in 2:08:44, and now has record 10 sub 2:06 times (8 sub-2:05). He won at Hamburg on debut then 2nd Berlin in 2013, 1st Rotterdam & Chicago 2014, London & Berlin 2015, London 2016 (then second fastest of all-time), Berlin 2017 & 2018 (WR), London 2018. IAAF male athlete of the Year 2018. Won World Marathon Majors 2015/16, 2016/17 and 2018-19. Ran 2:00:25 in Nike's carefully contrived 2-hour marathon bid at Monza racetrack on 6 May 2017 after seven months of preparation.

Kenneth Kiprop **KIPKEMOI** b. 2 Aug 1984 1.65m 52kg.
At 10000m: WCh: '13- 7; AfG: '17- 7; AfCh: '12- 1. Kenyan champion 2012, 2016. At HMar: World '14-10, AfG: '11- 2.
Progress at 10000m, HMar, Mar: 2009- 62:59A, 2011- 27:48.5A, 59:47; 2012- 26:52.65, 59:11; 2013- 27:28.50, 60:45; 2014- 27:30.94, 59:01; 2015- 60:17, 2016- 27:52.1A, 60:05; 2017- 60:24, 2018- 61:44, 2:05:44. pbs: 3000m 7:49.28+ '11, 5000m 13:03.37 '12, 15k 43:22 '12, 25k 1:12:32 '14.
Won in Rotterdam on his marathon debut 2018.

Alfred KIPKETER b. 26 Dec 1996 1.69m 61kg.
At 800m: OG: '16- 7; WCh: '15- 7; WJ: '14- 1; WY: '13- 1.
Progress at 800m: 2013- 1:46.2A, 2014- 1:43.95, 2015- 1:44.07A, 2016- 1:42.87, 2017- 1:45.40, 2018- 1:44.28. pbs: 600m 1:15.60 '15, 1000m 2:17:40 '18.

Gideon Kipkemoi **KIPKETER** b. 10 Nov 1992 1.78m 57kg.
At Mar: WCh: '17- 5. World CC: '10- 8J, AfCC: '11- 4J.
Progress at Mar: 2012- 2:08:14, 2013- 2:10:41, 2014- 2:10:36, 2015- 2:09:01, 2016- 2:08:35, 2017- 2:05:51, 2018- 2:06:15. pbs: 3000m 7:52.11 '10, 5000m 13:15.77 '10, 10000m 28:25.31 '15, 10M Rd 46:36 '14, HMar 59:53 '12.
Won Mumbai marathon 2016, 2nd Tokyo 2017.

Silas KIPLAGAT b. 20 Aug 1989 Siboh village, Marakwet 1.70m 57kg.
At 1500m: OG: '12- 7; WCh: '11-13-15: 2/6/5; CG: '10- 1; AfCh: '10- 4; WI: '12- 6. Won DL 2012, 2014; Kenyan 2011.

World 4x1500m record 2014.
Progress at 1500m: 2009- 3:39.1A, 2010- 3:29.27, 2011- 3:30.47, 2012- 3:29.63, 2013- 3:30.13, 2014- 3:27.64, 2015- 3:30.12, 2016- 3:33.68, 2017- 3:32.33, 2018- 3:41.78. pbs: 800m 1:44.8A '12, 1000m 2:19.80 '16, 1M 3:47.88 '14, 3000m 7:39.94 '10, 5000m 13:54.05 '17, 10k Rd 28:00 '09.

Asbel Kipruto **KIPROP** b. 30 Jun 1989 Uasin Gishu, Eldoret. North Rift 1.86m 70kg.
At (800m)/1500m: OG: '08- 1, '12- 12, '16- 6; WCh: '07- 4, '09- sf/4, '11-13-15-17: 1/1/1/9; AfG: '07- 1; AfCh: '10- 1, '14- 2; CCp: '10- 6, '14- 2; Won DL 2010, 2015-16. At 800m: AfCh: '08- 3. World CC: '07- 1J, '17- 1 MxR. Won Kenyan 800m 2015, 1500m 2007, 2010.
World 4x1500m record 2014.
Progress at 800m, 1500m: 2007- 3:35.24, 2008- 1:44.71, 3:31.64; 2009- 1:43.17, 3:31.20; 2010- 1:43.45, 3:31.78; 2011- 1:43.15, 3:30.46; 2012- 1:45.91, 3:28.88; 2013- 1:44.8A, 3:27.72; 2014- 1:43.34, 3:28.45; 2015- 1:44.4A, 3:26.69; 2016- 1:44.6A, 3:29.33; 2017- 1:44.43, 3:33.17. pbs: 1000m 2:14.23 '16, 1M 3:48.50 '09, 3000m 7:42.32 '07, 5000m 13:48.43A '10.
Suspended for possible doping infringement.
Father David Kebenei had 1M pb 3:59.35 (1982), 4 AfG 1500m 1987.

Stephen KIPROP Kiptoo 8 Sep 1999 1.73m 52kg
Progress at HMar: 2018- 59:21, 2019- 58:42. pbs: 10000m 29:05.7A '18; Road: 10k 28:10 '19, 15k 41:49 '19, 20k 55:46 '19.
Won Ras Al Hahmah half marathon in 2019.

Amos KIPRUTO b. 19 Sep 1992. 1.65m 50kg.
Progress at Mar: 2016- 2:08:12, 2017- 2:05:43, 2018- 2:06:23. pbs: Road: 15k 44:03 '14, 25k 1:12:53 '17, 30k 1:27:39 '17; HMar 60:24 '17.
Won first completed marathon in Rome 2016. Won Seoul 2017, 3rd Tokyo and 2nd Berlin 2018.

Conseslus KIPRUTO b. 8 Dec 1994 Eldoret 1.71m 55kg.
At 3000mSt: OG: '16- 1; WCh: '13- 2, '15- 2, '17- 1; CG: '18- 1; AfCh: '18- 1; WJ: '12- 1; CCp: '18- 1; won DL 2013, 2016-18; KEN 2018 At 2000St: WY: '11- 1. World CC: '13- 5J, '19- 3 MxR.
Progress at 3000mSt: 2011- 8:27.30, 2012- 8:03.49, 2013- 8:01.16, 2014- 8:09.81, 2015- 8:05.20, 2016- 8:00.12, 2017- 8:04.63, 2018- 8:08.40. pbs: 800m 1:49.0A '15, 1000m 2:19.85 '12, 1500m 3:39.57 '13, 3000m 7:44.09 '12, 5000m 13:47.5A 16, 2000mSt 5:28.65 '11.

Rhonex KIPRUTO b. 12 Oct 1999 1.72m 57kg.
At 10000m: WJ: '18- 1; World CC: '19- 6; AfrCC: '18- 1J.
World road U20 10k bests 27:08 & 26:46 in 2018
Progress at 10000m: 2017- 28:56.5A, 2018- 27:21.08. Pbs: 5000m 7:48.08 '18, 5kRd 13:39 '18, 2000mSt 5:44.8A '15.

Wilson KIPSANG Kiprotich b. 15 Mar 1982 Keiyo district 1.78m 59kg.

At Mar: OG: '12- 3; WCh: '15- dnf; HMar: WCh: '09- 4. World marathon record 2013.
Progress at HMar, Mar: 2008- 59:16, 2009- 58:59, 2010- 60:04, 2:04:57; 2011- 60:49, 2:03:42; 2012- 59:06, 2:04:44; 2013- 61:02, 2:03:23; 2014- 60:25, 2:04:29; 2015- 61:23, 2:04:47; 2016- 61:11, 2:03:13; 2017- 61:29, 2:03:58; 2018- 2:06:48. pbs: 5000m 13:55.7A '09, 10000m 28:37.0A '07; Road: 10k 27:42 '09, 15k 41:51+ '11, 10M 44:59+ '11, 20k 56:10+ '12, 25k 1:12:47 '16, 30k 1:27:26 '16.
Third in Paris in 2:07:13 on debut and nine wins: Frankfurt in 2010 and 2011, Lake Biwa 2011, London 2012 and 2014 (2nd 2015), Honolulu 2012, Berlin 2013 (2nd 2016, 3rd 2018) and New York 2014 (2nd 2017), Tokyo 2017. Won World Marathon Majors 2013/14. Record eight marathons inside 2:05 and four inside 2:04. Won Great North Run 2012. His brother Noah Kigen HMar pb 60:25 '17.

Abraham KIPTUM b. 15 Sep 1989 Chepketei Kosirai, Nandi 1.75m 57kg
World half marathon record 2018.
Progress at HMar, Mar: 2015- 2:11:36, 2016- 59:36, 2017- 60:06, 2:05:26; 2018- 58:18, 2:04:16?/ 2:06:29. pbs: 10000m 29:18.0A '17; Road: 10k 27:44 '17, 30k 1:29:52 '17.
Won Daegu Marathon. 2nd Abu Dhabi 2018.

Abel KIRUI b. 4 Jun 1982 Bornet, Rift Valley 1.77m 62kg. Police.
At Mar: OG: '12- 2; WCh: '09- 1, '11- 1.
Progress at Mar: 2006- 2:15:22, 2007- 2:06:51, 2008- 2:07:38, 2009- 2:05:04, 2010- 2:08:04, 2011- 2:07:38, 2012- 2:07:56, 2014- 2:09:04, 2015- 2:10:55, 2016- 2:08:06, 2017- 2:07:45, 2018- 2:07:07. pbs: 1500m 3:46.10 '05, 3000m 7:55.90 '06, 5000m 13:52.71 '05, 10000m 28:16.86A '08; Road: 10k 27:59 '09, 15k 42:22 '07, 10M 46:40 '11, HMar 60:11 '07, 25k: 1:13:41 '08, 30k 1:28:25 '08.
Brilliantly retained World marathon title with halves of 65:07 and 62:31 and a fastest 5k split of 14:18. Has run 14 sub-2:10 marathons; won Vienna 2008, Chicago 2016 (2nd 2017), 2nd Berlin 2007, 3rd Rotterdam 2009. Uncle Mike Rotich had marathon pb 2:06:33 '03.

Amos KIRUI b. 9 Feb 1998 1.69m 54kg. Toyota Boshoku Corporation, Japan,.
At 3000mSt: CG: '18- 3; AfCh: '18- 4;WJ: '16- 1; At 2000mSt: 2 Yth OG '14. World CC: 7J '17.
Progress at 3000mSt: 2015- 8:51.0A, 2016- 8:20.43, 2017- 8:08.37, 2018- 8:12.24. pbs: 3000m 7:51.48 '17, 5000m 13:25.91 '16, 10000m 28:08.98 '16, 10kRd 27:48 '17, 2000mSt 5:39.23A '14.

Geoffrey Kipkorir **KIRUI** b. 16 Feb 1993 1.70m 54kg.
At Mar: WCh: '17- 1. At 10000m: WJ: '12- 3; AfG: '15- 5; Af-J: '11- 1. World CC: '13- 15
Progress at 10000m, Mar: 2011- 26:55.73, 2012- 27:08.44, 2014- 29:05.8A, 2015- 27:17.91, 2016- 29:08.6A, 2:06:27; 2017- 2:08:27, 2018- 2:06:46. Pbs: 3000m 7:42.26 13, 5000m 13:16.68 13, Road:

HMar 59:38 '15, 25k 1:14:42 '16, 30k 1:29:44 '16. Won Boston marathon 2017 (2nd 2018) after 3rd Rotterdam & 7th Amsterdam 2016.

Mathew Kipkoech **KISORIO** b. 16 May 1989 Kapchumba, Nandi North District 1.78m 62kg.
At 5000m/(10000m): WJ: '08- 2; AfCh: '10- (4); Af-J: '07- 1/1. World CC: '07-08-09-11: 3J/6J/6/4.
Progress at 5000m, 10000m, Mar: 2006- 28:50.1A, 2007- 13:28.43, 2008- 13:11.57, 29:34.96; 2009- 13:02.40, 27:15.44; 2010- 12:57.83, 27:28.13A; 2011- 26:54.25, 2:10:58; 2012- 28:05.60Adq, 2015- 29:06.2A, 2:06:13; 2017- 27:53.99A, 2:07:32; 2018- 2:04:53. pbs: 3000m 7:34.29 '09, road: 15km 42:11+ '10, 10M 44:54+ '11, 20km 55:44+ '11, 25km 1:12:13 '11, HMar 58:46 '11.
Won Daegu marathon 2017, 2nd Valencia 2015, Paris 2018. Two-year drugs ban 2012-14. His father Some Muge (1959-97) was 3rd at 1983 World Cross (Kenya's first medallist). His younger brother Peter Some was 7th in 2008 World Junior Cross and has a marathon best of 2:05:38 '13.

Jonathan Kiprotich **KITILIT** b. 24 Apr 1994 1.71m 61kg.
At 800m: CG: '18- 6; AfCh: '18- 6; Af-J: '13- 2; Won KEN 2018.
Progress at 800m: 2012- 1:47.8A, 2013- 1:48.03, 2015- 1:45.0A, 2016- 1:43.05, 2018- 1:43.95. pbs: 600m 1:15.9+ '18. 2:13.95 '16, 1500m 3:39.81 '15.

Paul Kipsiele **KOECH** b. 10 Nov 1981 Cheplanget, Buret District 1.68m 57kg.
At 3000mSt: OG: '04- 3; WCh: '05- 7, '09- 4, '13- 4; AfG: '03- 2; AfCh: '06- 1; WCp: '06- 2; won DL 2010-12, WAF 2005-08. At 3000m: WI: 08- 2.
Progress at 3000mSt: 2001- 8:15.92, 2002- 8:05.44, 2003- 7:57.42, 2004- 7:59.65, 2005- 7:56.37, 2006- 7:59.94, 2007- 7:58.80, 2008- 8:00.57, 2009- 8:01.26, 2010- 8:02.07, 2011- 7:57.32, 2012- 7:54.31, 2013- 8:02.63, 2014- 8:05.47, 2015- 8:10.24, 2016- 8:08.32, 2018- 8:23.22. pbs: 1500m 3:37.92 '07, 2000m 5:00.9+i '08, 5:01.84 '14; 3000m 7:32.78i '10, 7:33.93 '05; 2M 8:06.48i/8:13.31 '08, 5000m 13:02.69i 12, 13:05.18 '10; 15k 42:44 '17, 20k 57:52 '17, HMar 61:03 '17, Mar 2:12:02 '17.
Younger brother John Koech (b. 23 Aug 1995) transferred to BRN 2013; 3000mSt: 8:14.75 '15; OG: '16- h; WCh: '15- 5, AsiC: '15- 1, CCp: '14- 5.

Emmanuel Kipkurui **KORIR** b. 15 Jun 1995 1.77m 64kg. University of Texas El Paso.
At 800m: WCh: '17- sf; AfCh: '18- 2; CCp: '18- 1. Won DL 2018, NCAA indoors and out 2017, KEN 400m 2018.
World indoor best 600m 2017, African & Commonwealth 800m indoor record 2018.
Progress at 800m: 2016- 1:46.94A, 2017- 1:43.10, 2018- 1:42.05. Pbs: 44.21A/44.52 '18, 600m 1:14.97Ai '17.

Ronald Chebolei **KWEMOI** b. 19 Sep 1995 Mt. Elgon 1.80m 68kg.
At 1500m: OG: '16- 13; WCh: '17- sf; CG: '14- 2;

AfG: '15- 4; AfCh: '14- 3; Won KEN 1500m 2014. World CC: '13- 9J.
World junior 1500m record 2014.
Progress at 1500m: 2013- 3:45.39, 2014- 3:28.81, 2015- 3:30.43, 2016- 3:30.49, 2017- 3:30.89A. pbs: 800m 1:49.7A '17, 1M 3:49.04 '17, 3000m 7:28.73 '17, 5000m 13:16.14 '15, 10000m 27:33.94 '16. road: 15k 42:15 '18, 10M 45:23 '18.
Younger brother Samuel Chebolei won KEN 5000m 2018.

Elijah Motonei **MANANGOI** b. 5 Jan 1993 Narok 1.81m 65kg.
At 1500m: OG: '16- sf; WCh: '15- 2, '17- 1; CG: '14- 12, '18- 1; AfCh: '18- 1; CCp: '18- 1. Kenyan champion 2015. World CC: '19- 3 mxR.
Progress at 1500m: 2014- 3:35.0A, 2015- 3:29.67, 2016- 3:31.19, 2017- 3:28.80, 2018- 3:29.64. pbs: 400m 46.5A '13, 47.33A '13; 800m 1:44.15 '18, 1000m 2:17.09i '16, 1M 3:49.08 '17.
His brother **George** won the World Youth 2017 and World Junior 2018 titles in 2017-18, pbs: 800m 1:47.20A '18, 1000m 2:18.07 '18, 1500m 3:35.53 '18.

Jonathan Muia **NDIKU** b. 18 Sep 1991 Machakos 1.73m 60kg. Team Hitachi Cable, Japan.
At 3000mSt: CG: '14- 1; AfCh: '14- 2; WJ: '08- 1, '10- 1; Af-J: '09- 1. At 2000mSt: WY: '07- 4. At 10000m: CG:'18- 8.
Progress at 10,000m, 3000mSt: 2008- 28:08.28, 8:17.28; 2009- 27:37.72, 8:28.1A; 2010- 8:19.25A. 2011- 8:07.75, 2012- 8:17.88, 2013- 8:18.78, 2014- 8:10.44, 2015- 27:40.64, 8:11.64; 2016- 27:11.23, 2017- 27:39.40, 2018- 27:28.27, 8:30.75. pbs: 1500m 3:39.27 '10, 3000m 7:39.63 '14, 5000m 13:11.99 '09, HMar 62:07 '17, 2000mSt 5:37.30 '07.

David Lekuta **RUDISHA** b. 17 Dec 1988 Kilgoris 1.89m 73kg. Masai.
At 800m: OG: '12- 1, '16- 1; WCh: '09- sf, '11- 1, '15- 1; CG: '14- 2; WJ: '06- 1/4R; AfCh: '08- 1, '10- 1; Af-J: '07- 1; CCp: '10- 1. Won DL 2010-11, WAF 2009, Kenyan 2009-11.
Three world 800m records 2010-12, four African records 2009-10., Commonwealth & African 600m record 2016.
Progress at 800m: 2006- 1:46.3A, 2007- 1:44.15, 2008- 1:43.72, 2009- 1:42.01, 2010- 1:41.01, 2011- 1:41.33, 2012- 1:40.91, 2013- 1:43.87, 2014- 1:42.98, 2015- 1:43.58, 2016- 1:42.15. pbs: 400m 45.50 '10, 45.2A '13; 600m 1:13.10 '16.
IAAF Male Athlete of the Year 2010, won 26 successive 800m finals 2009-11. His father Daniel won 4x400m silver medal at 1968 Olympics with 440y pb 45.5A '67.

Michael Lotoromom **SARUNI** b. 18 Jun 1995 1.80m 78kg. University of Texas at El Paso.
At 800m: Won NCAA indoor 2018.
World best 600m indoors 2018, African & Commonwealth indoor 800m record 2019.
Progress at 800m: 2017- 1:44.61A, 2018- 1:43.25,

2019- 1:43.98i. pbs: 400m 45.42A '18, 600m
1:14.79Ai '18, 1500m 3:46.15A '17, 1M 4:03.32i '17.
Charles Cheboi **SIMOTWO** b. 6 May 1995
1.78m 60kg.
At 1500m: AfCh: '18-8.
Progress at 1500m: 2015- 3:35.86A, 2017- 3:32.59,
2018- 3:32.51. pb 800m 1:46.20 '17.
William Malel **SITONIK** b. 1 Mar 1994 1.65m
52kg. Honda, Japan.
At 3000m: WY: 11- 1. At 5000m: WJ: '12- 3.
Progress at 10000m: 2012- 29:29.3A, 2013-
27:48.55, 2014- 27:25.56, 2015- 27:22.12, 2016-
26:54.66, 2017- 27:22.79, 2018- 28:27.05. pbs:
2000m 5:07.51 '11, 3000m 7:40.10 '11 '10, 5000m
13:19.83 '13.
Edwin Cheruiyot **SOI** b. 3 Mar 1986 Kericho
1.72m 55kg.
At 5000m: OG: '08- 3, '12- h; WCh: '13- 5, '15- 10;
AfCh: '10- 1; CCp: '10- 4. At 3000m: WI: '08- 4,
'12- 3; won WAF 3000m 2007, 5000m 2007-08.
World CC: '06- 8 4k, '07- 9.
Progress at 5000m, 10000m: 2002- 29:06.5A,
2004- 13:22.57, 2005- 13:10.78, 2006- 12:52.40,
27:14.83; 2007- 13:10.21, 2008- 13:06.22, 2009-
12:55.03, 2010- 12:58.91, 2011- 12:59.15, 2012-
12:55.99, 2013- 12:51.34, 26:49.41; 2014- 12:59.82,
2015- 13:11.97, 2016- 13:03.26, 2017- 13:28.24. pbs:
1500m 3:40.52 '13, 2000m 5:01.4+ '10, 3000m
7:27.55 '11, 2M 8:14.10 '11, 10k Rd 28:13 '08.
Paul Kipngetich **TANUI** b. 22 Dec 1990
Chesubeno village, Moio district 1.72m 54kg.
Kyudenko Corporation, Japan.
At 10000m: OG: '16- 2; WCh: '11-13-15-17:
9/3/3/3. World CC: '09-10-11: 4J/8/2. Won
Kenyan CC 2010.
Progress at 5000m, 10000m: 2008- 13:59.2A,
2009- 13:37.15, 27:25.24; 2010- 13:14.87, 27:17.61;
2011- 13:04.65, 26:50.63; 2012- 13:19.18, 27:27.56;
2013- 13:16.57, 27:21.50; 2014- 13:00.53, 26:49.41;
2015- 12:58.69, 26:51.86; 2016- 13:15.22, 27:05.64;
2017- 13:14.09, 26:50.60; 2018- 13:36.97, 28:11.41.
pbs: 1500m 3:43.97 '10, 3000m 7:46.61 '16, HMar
62:48 '14.
Daniel Kinyua **WANJIRU** b. 25 May 1992
Embu county 1.74m 58kg.
At Mar: WCh: '17- 8.
Progress at Mar: 2014- 2:08:18, 2016- 2:05:21,
2017- 2:05:48, 2018- 2:10:21. pbs: 3000m 8:07.1A
10, 5000m 14:01.8A '16, 10000m 28:59.9A '16;
Road: 10k 27:43 '16, 15k 42:16 '14, 20k 56:01 '16,
HMar 59:20 '16, 30k 1:28:21 '17.
Marathon wins: Amsterdam 2016, London 2017.
Hillary Kipsang **YEGO** b. 2 Apr 1992 1.78m
60kg. At 2000mSt: WY: '09- 1.
Progress at 3000mSt: 2009- 8:46.8A, 2010-
8:19.50, 2011- 8:07.71, 2012- 8:11.83. 2013- 8:03:57,
2014- 8:09.07, 2015- 8:13.10, 2016- 8:15.10, 2017-
8:31.54, 2018- 8:25.30. pbs: 1500m 3:43.3 '10,
3000m 7:53.18 '10, 5000m 13:53.82 '16, 2000mSt
5:25.33 '09.

Julius Kiplangat **YEGO** b. 4 Jan 1989
Cheptonon, Nandi district 1.75m 90kg.
At JT: OG: '12- 11, '16- 2; WCh: '13- 4, '15- 1, '17-
13; CG: '10- 7, '14- 1, '18- dnq 13; AfG: '11- 1;
AfCh: '10-12-14-18: 3/1/1/1; CCp: '14- 4, '18- 6.
Kenyan champion 2008-14, 2018.
Javelin records: Commonwealth & two African
2015, nine Kenyan 2011-15.
Progress at JT: 2008- 72.18A, 2009- 74.00A, 2010-
75.44, 2011- 78.34A, 2012- 81.81; 2013- 85.40,
2014- 84.72, 2015- 92.72, 2016- 88.24, 2017- 87.97,
2018- 80.91A.
His winning throw at the 2015 Worlds was the
world's best javelin throw since 2001.
Edward Pingua **ZAKAYO** b. 25 Nov 2001
1.73m 59kg.
At 5000m: CG: '18- 3; WJ: '18- 1; AfCh:'18- 1. At
3000m: WY: '17- 2; CCp: '18- fa.
Progress at 5000m: 2017- 13:48.0A, 2018-
13:19.74A. Pb 3000m 7:49.17A '17.
Women
Alice APROT Nawowuna b. 2 Jan 1994 1.74m
55kg. Turkana.
At (5000m)/10000m: OG: '16- 4; WCh: '17- 4; WJ:
'10- (3); AfG: '15- 3/1; AfCh: '16- 1, '18- 2. World
CC: '10- 9J, '17- 2; AfCC: 14- 3. Won African &
Kenyan CC 2016, KEN 10000m 2016-17.
Progress at 5000m, 10000m: 2010- 15:16.74, 2011-
16:36.8A, 2014- 16:22.8A, 2015- 15:31.82, 31:24.18;
2016- 14:39.56, 29:53.51; 2017- 31:11.86, 2018-
.15:11.00, 31:36.12 pbs: 1500m 4:23.92 '14, 3000m
8:44.7 '16, 10M 51:59 '16.
Elder brother Joseph Ebuya won World CC in
2010, pb 5000m 12:51.00 '07.
Winny CHEBET b. 20 Dec 1990 1.65m 50kg.
At 800m: OG: '16- sf; WCh: '13- sf; CG: '10- 7,
'18- h (fell); AfG: '15- 5 (2- 4x400m); AfCh: '10- 5;
WJ: '06- 2, '08- 5; WY: '05- 2, '07- dq (for
obstruction after 2nd place); Af-J: '09- 2. At
1500m: WCh: '17- sf; AfCh: '18- 1; WI: '18- 5;
CCp: '18- 1; won KEN 1500m 2018.
Progress at 800m, 1500m: 2005- 2:08.15, 2006-
2:04.59, 2007- 2:04.10, 2008- 2:04.13, 2009- 2:01.36,
2010- 2:00.88A, 2011- 2:03.80A, 2012- 1:59.37,
4:16.0A; 2013- 1:59.30, 2015- 2:02.38A, 2016-
1:59.88, 4:02.66; 2017- 1:58.13, 3:59.16; 2018-
4:00.60. pbs: 1000m 2:35.73 '13, 1M 4:19.55 '17.
Fancy CHEMUTAI b. 20 Mar 1994 1.63m 48kg.
Progress at HMar: 2017- 65:36, 2018- 64:52. Road
pbs: 10k 30:09 '17, 15k 45:59 '17, 10M 49:30 '18,
20k 61:35 '18, HMar 64:52 '18.
Won Ras Al Khaimah half marathon 2018.
Beatrice CHEPKOECH Sitonik b. 6 Jul 1991
1.71m 57kg.
At 3000mSt: OG: '16- 4; WCh: '17- 4; AfCh: '18-
1; CCp: '18- 1; won DL 2018. At 1500m: CG: '18-
2; AfG: '15- 3; WI: '18- 7. World CC: '17- 1 MxR,
'19- 7. Won KEN 1500m 2017, 3000mSt 2018.
World record 3000mSt 2018.
Progress at 1500m, 3000mSt: 2011- 10:41.3A,

2013- 4:16.6A, 2014- 4:12.37A, 2015- 4:03.28, 2016-
4:18.0A, 9:10.86; 2017- 8:59.84, 2018- 8:44.32. pbs:
800m 2:05.73 '15, 1500m 4:02.21i/4:03.09 '18;
3000m 8:39.15i '18, 5000m 14:39.33 '17, 2000mSt
6:02.47 '15.
4th in 2017 Worlds despite missing the water
jump after the first lap and having to run back
to clear it and also later falling. Took 8.46 reccs
off the world record for the steeplechase in an
astonishing run at Monaco 2018.

Ruth CHEPNGETICH b. 8 Aug 1994 West
Pokot 1.68m 49kg.
World HMar: 18- 13.
Progress at Mar: 2017- 2:22:36, 2018- 2:18:351,
2019- 2:17:08. pbs: HMar 66:09 '19, 30k 1:37:16 '19.
Marathon wins: Istanbul 2017 & 2018, Dubai
2019, 2nd Paris 2018.

Lydia CHEROMEI b. 11 May 1977 Baringo
district 1.62m 47kg. Married Hosea Kogo
(5000m 13:24.22 '97) in December 1996.
At 5000m: OG: '96- h, '00- 6; WCh: '97- 5; AfG:
'95- 3; and GP 1997. At 10000m: OG: '92- h; WJ:
'90- 3, '92- 4; AfG: '91- 2; AfCh: '92- 2, '93- 2 (8
3000m). At HMar: WCh: '04- 2, '12- 4. World CC:
'91-?- 1J/3J, '97-00-01- 11/4/3. Won Kenyan
10000m 1991-2, 5000m 1997, 2000.
Records: World junior 5000m 1995, African
junior 3000m 1992, Kenyan 5000m 1995, 3000m
1997 & 2000. World W40 marathon 2017 & 2018.
Progress at 5000m, 10000m: 1990- 16:56.7,
33:20.83; 1991- 33:07.7, 1992- 15:17.31, 31:41.09;
1993- 32:54.55, 1994- 36:29.0, 1995- 14:53.44, 1996-
15:18.34, 1997- 14:46.72, 2000- 14:47.35. At Mar:
2008- 2:25:57; 2009- 2:28:09, 2011- 2:22:34, 2012-
2:21:30, 2013- 2:34:26, 2017- 2:23:31, 2018- 2:22:11.
pbs: 1500m 4:09.32 '97, 2000m 5:38.9 '97, 3000m
8:29.14 '00, road 10k 31:57 '08, 15k 47:50 '11,
HMar 67:26 '12, 30k 1:42:47 '08.
Youngest ever world junior cross-country
champion at 13 in 1991. World age bests 3000m,
5000m and 10000m at 13, 5000m at 15. Daughter
Faith born 2005. Won at Amsterdam on
marathon debut 2008, 2nd Dubai and won
Prague 2011, Yokohama 2012 and Rabat 2018;
2nd Shanghai 2017. 2-year drugs ban 2005-07.

Gladys Kiprono **CHERONO** b. 12 May 1983
Kericho 1.66m 50kg.
At 10000m: WCh: '13- 2; AfCh: '12- 1 (1 5000m).
World HMar: '14- 1. Won Kenyan 5000m 2012.
Progress at 5000m, 10000m, Mar: 2005- 16:16.8A,
2007- 16:03.8A, 2008- 15:56.0A, 2012- 15:39.5A,
32:41.40; 2013- 14:47.12, 30:29.23; 2014- 16:49.8A,
34:13.0A; 2015- 15:50.3A, 32:24.10A, 2:19:25; 2017-
2:20:23, 2018- 2:18:11; pbs: 1500m 4:25.13 '04,
3000m 8:34.05 '13, Road: 15k 47:43 '13, 20k 63:26
'13, HMar 66:07 '16, 25k 1:21:52 '18, 30k 1:38:04
'18.
Second Dubai Marathon (2:20:03, third fastest
ever debut) and won Berlin in 2015, 2017-18.
Married to Joseph Bwambok (62:25 HMar 2010).

Vivian Jepkemoi **CHERUIYOT** b. 11 Sep 1983
Keiyo 1.55m 38kg. Police.
At 5000m (/10000m): OG: '04- 14, '08- 4, '12- 2/3,
'16- 1/2; WCh: '07- 2, '09- 1, '11- 1/1, '15- (1); CG:
'10- 1; WJ: '02- 3; AfG '99- 3; AfCh: '10- 1; Af-J:
'01- 1; CCp: '10- 1; won DL 2010-12. At 3000m:
WY: '99- 3; WI: '10- 2. World CC: '98-9-00-01-02-
04-06-07-11: 5J/2J/1J/4J/3J/8 4k/8 4k/8/1. Won
KEN 1500m 2009, 5000m 2010-11, 10000m 2011-
12.
Records: African 2000m 2009, Commonwealth
5000m 2009 & 2011, 10000m 2016, indoor 3000m
(8:30.53) 2009; Kenyan 5000m 2007 & 2011,
10000m 2016.
Progress at 5000m, 10000m: 1999- 15:42.79A,
2000- 15:11.11, 2001- 15:59.4A, 2002- 15:49.7A,
2003- 15:44.8A, 2004- 15:13.26, 2006- 14:47.43,
2007- 14:22.51, 2008- 14:25.43, 2009- 14:37.01,
2010- 14:27.41, 2011- 14:20.87, 30:48.98; 2012-
14:35.62, 30:30.44; 2015- 14:46.69, 31:13.29; 2016-
14:26.17, 29:32.53. At Mar: 2017- 2:23:35, 2018-
2:18:31. pbs: 1500m 4:06.6A '12, 4:06.65 '07;
2000m 5:31.52 '09, 3000m 8:28.66 '07, 2M 9:12.35i
'10, 10M Rd 51:17 '15, HMar 66:34 '19.
Laureus Sportswomen of the Year for 2011.
Married Moses Kiplagat on 14 Apr 2012; son
Allan Kiprono Kiplagat born 19 Oct 2013. Won
Great North Run on half marathon debut 2016
and again in 2018, and 4th London on marathon
debut 2017, then 1st Frankfurt, 1st London &
2nd New York 2018.

Celliphine Chepteek **CHESPOL** b. 23 Mar
1999 1.63m 48kg.
At 3000mSt: WCh: '17- 6; CG: '18- 2; AfCh: '18- 2;
WJ: '16- 1, '18- 1; At 2000mSt: WY: '15- 1, World
CC: '17- 3J, AfCC: '18- 1.
Two World junior records 3000mSt 2017.
Progress at 3000mSt: 2015- 10:18.3A, 2016-
9:24.73, 2017- 8:58.78, 2018- 9:01.82. pbs: 800m
2:06.48A '17, 1500m 4:11.1A '17, 2000St 6:17.15 '15.

Peres JEPCHIRCHIR b. 27 Sep 1993 Usain
Gishu 1.53m 40kg.
World HMar: '16- 1.
World records 20k and half marathon 2017.
Progress at HMar: 2014- 69:12, 2015- 67:17, 2016-
66:39, 2017- 65:06. pbs: Road: 10k 30:55 '15, 15k
46:32 '17, 20k 61:40 '17, Mar 2:46:15A '18.
7 wins in 8 half marathons 2014-17, inc. RAK
2017. Married to David Ngeno. Baby born 2018.

Hyvin Kiyeng **JEPKEMOI** b. 13 Jan 1992 1.56m
45kg.
At 3000mSt: OG: '16- 2; WCh: '13- 6, '15- 1, '17- 3;
AfG: '11- 1 (4 5000m); AfCh: '12- 3. Kenyan
champion 2015. World CC: '17- 4.
African and Commonwealth 3000m
steeplechase record 2016.
Progress at 3000mSt: 2011- 10:00.50, 2012-
9:23.53, 2013- 9:22.05, 2014- 9:22.58, 2015- 9:10.15,
2016- 9:00.01, 2017- 9:02.20, 2018- 9:01.60. pbs:
1500m 4:19.4A '17, 4:19.44 '11; 3000m 8:30.51 '18,
5000m 15:40.37A '17, 10000m 35:14.0A '14.

Joyciline JEPKOSGEI b. 8 Dec 1993 Cheptil, Nandi 1.56m 52kg.
At 10000m: AfCh: '16- 3. At HMar: WCh: '18- 2. World road records in Prague Half Marathon 2017: 10k 30:04, 15k 45:37, 20k 1:01:25, HMar 1:04.52, improving at 10k to 29:43 in September and half marathon to 64:51 at Valencia in October 2017.
Progress at HMar: 2015- 74:06A, 2016- 69:07, 2017- 64:51, 2018- 66:46. pbs: 5000m 15:40.0A '16, 10000m 31:28.38 '16, Road: 10k 29:43 '17, 15k 45:37 '17, 20k 61:25 '17.
Married to Nicholas Koech (10k Rd 28:39 '07), son Brandon born 2011. Member of the RunCzech Running Team from 2014.

Nelly JEPKOSGEI Rop b. 14 Jul 1991 1.64m 53kg.
At 800m: AfG: '11- 4; At 1500m: WJ: 10- sf. Kenyan 1000m record 2018.
Progress at 1500m: 2009- 4:27.48, 2011- 4:08.10, 2013- 4:08.59, 2016- 4:04.26, 2017- 4:02.75, 2018- 4:00.99. pbs: 800m 1:59.40 '13, 1000m 2:35.30 '18, 1M 4:25.15 '17.

Pauline Kaveke **KAMULU** b. 30 Dec 1994 Machakos county 1.54m 45kg.
World HMar: '18- 3, World CC: '13- 11J; AfCC: '16- 7.
Progress at 10000m, HMar: 2010- 35:37.83A, 2011- 75:20, 2012- 68:37, 2015- 69:44, 2016- 31:56.70, 72:52; 2017- 31:47.13, 68:04; 2018- 30:41.85, 66:56. pbs: 3000m 8:48.27 '17, 5000m 14:58.82 '17, Road: 15k 47:34 '18, 20k 63:33 '18, 3000mSt 10:29.73A '11.

Mary Jepkosgei **KEITANY** b. 18 Jan 1982 Kisok, Kabarnet 1.58m 45kg.
At Mar: OG: '12- 4. World HMar: '07- 2, '09- 1. Records: World 25km 2010, 10M, 20km, half marathon 2011, 30km 2017, women's only marathon 2017. Half marathon: African and Kenyan (2) 2009, marathon: African 2012 & 2017. Commonwealth 25k 1:19:43 & 30k 1:36:05 '17. World W35 HMar 2017 & 2018, 30k & Mar 2017.
Progress at HMar, Mar: 2000- 72:53, 2002- 73:01, 2003- 73:25, 2004- 71:32, 2005- 70:18, 2006- 69:06, 2007- 66:48, 2009- 66:36, 2010- 67:14, 2:29:01; 2011- 65:50, 2:19:19; 2012- 66:49, 2:18:37; 2014- 65:39dh, 2:25:07; 2015- 66:02, 2:23:40; 2016- 68:53, 2:24:26; 2017- 65:13, 2:17:01; 2018- 64:55, 2:22:48. pbs: 1500m 4:24.33 '99, 10000m 32:18.07 '07; Road: 5k 15:25 '11, 10k 30:45 '11, 15k 46:40 '11, 10M 50:05 '11, 20k 61:34 '18, 25k 1:19:43dh '17, 30k 1:36:05 '17.
17 wins and 3 seconds in 20 half marathons 2006-18 (13 successive wins 2009-16) inc. Great North Run 2014-15 and 2017, RAK 2011-12, 2015. Marathons: won London 2011-12, 2017 (2nd 2015), New York 2014-16, 2018 (2nd 2017, 3rd 2010-11). Won World Marathon Majors 2011/12, 2015/16 & 2017/18. Married to Charles Koech (pbs 10k 27:56 & HMar 61:27 '07), son Jared Kipchumba born in June 2008 and daughter Samantha on 5 Apr 2013.

Margaret Chelimo **KIPKEMBOI** b. 9 Feb 1993 1.62m 45kg.
At 5000m: WCh: '17- 5; CG: '18- 2; AfG '15-1; AfCh '16-2. At 800m: WY: '09- h. World CC: '15- 13; AfCC: '17- 2.
Progress at 5000m, 10000m: 2014- 16:02.19A, 2015- 15:28.6A, 2016- 14:47.24, 31:16.38; 2017- 14:32.82, 2018- 15:01.98. pbs: 1500m 4:10.8A '17, 3000m 8:30.11'17.

Caroline Chepkoech **KIPKIRUI** b. 26 May 1994 1.62m 47kg.
At 5000m: WJ: '12- 5; Af-J: '11- 1; At 3000m: WY: '11- 3. World CC: '13- 4J; AfCC: 11- 1J.
World road 10 miles record 2018.
Progress at 5000m: 2010- 16:09.0A, 2011- 15:24.66A, 2012- 15:49.1A, 2013- 15:28.34, 2015- 16:17.97A, 2017- 14:27.55, 2018- 14:43.96. pbs: 1500m 4:13.21 '18, 2000m 5:43.1 '18, 3000m 8:29.05 '18, 10000m 31:16.38 '16, Road: 10k 30:19 '18, 15k 46:08 '18, 10M 49:29 '18, 20k 61:40 '18, HMar 65:07 '18, Mar 2:31:44A '12.

Edna Ngeringwony **KIPLAGAT** b. 15 Nov 1979 Eldoret 1.71m 54kg. Corporal in Kenyan Police.
At Mar: OG: '12- 19; WCh: '11-13-15-17: 1/1/5/2. At 3000m: WJ: '96- 2, '98- 3. World CC: '96-97-06: 5J/4J/13.
African record 30km 2008.
Progress at Mar: 2005- 2:50:20, 2010- 2:25:38, 2011- 2:20:46, 2012- 2:19:50, 2013- 2:21:32, 2014- 2:20:21, 2015- 2:27:16, 2016- 2:22:36, 2017- 2:21:52dh, 2018- 2:21:18. pbs: 3000m 8:53.06 '96, 5000m 15:57.3A '06, 10000m 33:27.0A '07; Road: 5k 15:20 '10, 10k 31:06 '16, 15k 47:57 '10, 10M 54:56 '09, HMar 67:41 '12, 25k 1:21:58 '18, 30k 1:38:23 '18.
Won Los Angeles and New York Marathons 2010, London 2014 (2nd 2011-13), Boston 2017; 2nd Chicago & 3rd Tokyo 2016. Won World Marathon Majors 2010/11, 2013/14, 2016/17. Married to Gilbert Koech (10000m 27:55.30 '01, 10k 27:32 '01, Mar 2:13:45 dh '05, 2:14:39 '09); two children.

Florence Jebet **KIPLAGAT** b. 27 Feb 1987 Kapkitony, Keiyo district 1.55m 42kg.
At 5000m: WJ: '06- 2. At 10000m: WCh: '09- 11; CG: '14- 2. World CC: '07- 5, '09- 1; HMar: '10- 1. Won Kenyan 1500m 2007, 10000m 2014, CC 2007 & 2009.
World records 20k and half marathon 2014 & 2015, 15k 2015.. Kenyan 10000m record 2009.
Progress at 5000m, 10000m, HMar, Mar: 2006- 15:32.34, 2007- 14:40.74, 31:06.20; 2009- 14:40.14, 30:11.53; 2010- 14:52.64, 32:46.99A, 67:40; 2011- 68:02, 2:19:44; 2012- 30:24.85, 66:38, 2:20:57; 2013- 67:13, 2:21:13; 2014- 31:48.6A, 65:12, 2:20:24; 2015- 65:09, 2:23:33; 2016- 69:19, 2:21:32; 2017- 68:15, 2:26:25; 2018- 2:26:08. pbs: 1500m 4:09.0A '07, 3000m 8:40.72 '10, Road: 15k 46:14 '15, 20k 61:54 '15, 30k 1:39:11 '14.

Won half marathon debut in Lille in 2010, followed a month later by World title. Did not finish in Boston on marathon debut in 2011; won Berlin 2011 and 2013; Chicago 2015-16 (2nd 2014), 2nd London 2014 (3rd 2016). Formerly married to Moses Mosop, daughters Faith and Aisha Chelagat (born April 2008). Niece of William Kiplagat (Mar 2:06:50 '99, 8 WCh '07).

Faith Chepngetich **KIPYEGON** b. 10 Jan 1994 Bornet 1.57m 42kg.
At 1500m: OG: '12- h, '16- 1; WCh: '13- 5, '15- 2, '17- 1; CG: '14- 1; AfCh: '14- 5; WJ: '12- 1; WY: '11- 1. Won DL 2017. World CC: '10-11-13-17: 4J/1J/1J/6; AfCC: '12- 1J, '14- 1.
Records: World 4x1500m 2014, African junior 1500m 2013, African & Commonwealth 1M 2015, Kenyan & Commonwealth 1500m (3) 2013-16.
Progress at 1500m, 5000m: 2010- 4:17.1A, 2011- 4:09.48, 2012- 4:03.82, 2013- 3:56.98, 2014- 3:58.01, 2015- 3:59.32, 14:31.95; 2016- 3:56.41, 2017- 3:57.04. pbs: 800m 1:58.02 '15, 1M 4:16.71 '15, 2000m 5:37.8+ '14, 3000m 8:23.55 '14.
Sister **Beatrice Mutai** (b. 19 Apr 1987) 11 World CC 2013, 10000m 31:49.81 '18, HMar 69:30 '14.

Purity Cherotich **KIRUI** b. 13 Aug 1991 Kericho 1.62m 47kg.
At 3000mSt: WCh: '17- 10; CG: '14- 1, '18- 3; AfG: '15- 3; AfCh: '14- 6; WJ: '10- 1; Won KEN 2014-15.
Progress at 3000mSt: 2008- 10:27.19A, 2009- 10:05.1A, 2010- 9:36.34, 2011- 9:37.85, 2012- 9:35.61, 2013- 9:19.42, 2014- 9:23.43, 2015- 9:17.74, 2016- 9:22.47, 2017- 9:20.07, 2018- 9:21.34. pbs: 800m 2:07.6A '14, 1500m 4:31.83 '08, 5000m 16:13.42 '11.
Sister of **Kipyegon Bett** (800m 1:43.76 '16, 1 WJ 2016, 3 WCh 2017, 4-year drugs ban from 24 Feb 2018).

Janet KISA b. 5 Mar 1992 near Mount Elgon 1.60m 48kg.
At 3000m: CCp: '14- 4. At 5000m: WCh: '15- 6; CG: '14- 2; AfCh: '14- 3; Af-J: '11- 2. World CC: '11-13-15: 5J/6/12; AfCC: '14- 2.
Progress at 5000m: 2010- 16:02.2A, 2011- 15:24.75, 2012- 14:57.68, 2013- 15:05.89, 2014- 14:52.59, 2015- 15.02.60, 2016- 14.58.70. pbs: 1500m 4.14.77 '11, 2000m 5:41.4+ '16, 3000m 8:28.33 '16, 10k Rd 33:55 '13, HMar 71:01 '14.

Pauline Chemning **KORIKWIANG** b. 1 Mar 1988 Kaptabuk Village, West Pokot District 1.63m 39kg.
At 3000m: WJ: '06- 2; WY: '05- 2. At 5000m: AfG: '11- 3; Af-J: '03- 4, '07- 3. At 10000m: AfG: '11- 3; AfCh: '10- 6. World CC: '05-06-09-11: 7J/1J/11/7. Won KEN 10000m 2018.
Progress at 5000m, 10000m: 2003- 16:58.26, 2004- 15:55.5A, 2005- 16:15.8A, 2006- 14:45.98, 2007- 15:59.61, 2008- 16:07.78, 2009- 14:50.08, 2010- 14:46.80, 31:06.29; 2011- 14:41.28, 31:59.5A; 2012- 32:19.32, 2015- 15:23.85, 33:32.8A; 2018- 31:51.1A. pbs: 1500m 4:12.93+ '09, 2000m 5:36.11

'09, 3000m 8:41.11 '10, HMar 66:31 '18.
Son Beblan Yego born in 2013.

Brigid Jepcheschir **KOSGEI** b. 20 Feb 1994 Kapsait 1.63m 46kg.
Progress at HMar, Mar: 2015- 2:47:59, 2016- 74:08, 2:24:45, 2017- 66:35, 2:20:22; 2018- 66:49, 2:18:35; 2019- 65:28. Pbs: Road: 10k 31:43 '17, 29:54dh '18; 15k 47:24 '17, 20k 63:17 '17.
Won Chicago Marathon 21018 (2nd 2017), 2nd London 2018, won Honolulu 2016-17, Milan 2016. Married to Mathew Mitei, daughter Faith Jepchumba born 2014.

Stacy Jepkemboi **NDIWA** b. 6 Dec 1992.
At 10000m: CG: '18- 2; AfCh: '18- 1. At 1500m: AfCh: '18- 3; WJ: '08- 12; Af-J: '11- 3; Comm-Y: '08- 1. World CC: '15- 5; AfCh CC: '18- 4. Kenyan CC champion 2018.
Progress at 10000m: 2017- 34:37.2A, 2018- 31:13.17. pbs: 1500m 4:06.10 '14, 3000m 8:30.54 '14, 5000m 15:15.14 '14, HMar 67:16 '18.

Hellen Onsando **OBIRI** b. 13 Dec 1989 Nyangusu, Kisii 1.60m 50kg.
At 1500m: OG: '12- 8; WCh: '11- 10 (fell), '13- 3; CG: '14- 6; AfCh: '14- 1; CCp: '14- 4. At 3000m: CCp: '18- 3; WI: '12-14-18: 1/2/4. At 5000m: OG: '16- 2; WCh: '17- 1; CG: '18- 1; AfCh: '18- 1; won DL 2017-18, World CC 2019. Won KEN 1500m 2011-14. Records: Two world 4x1500m 2014. African & Commonwealth 3000m 2014, Commonwealth 1M & 5000m 2017, 1M 2018.
Progress at 1500m, 5000m: 2011- 4:02.42, 2012- 3:59.68, 16:15.1A, 2013- 3:58.58, 15:49.7A; 2014- 3:57.05, 2016- 3:59.34, 14:25.78; 2017- 4:00.44, 14:18.37; 2018- 3:58.88, 14:21.75. pbs: 800m 2:00.54 '11, 1000m 2:46.00i '12, 1M 4:16.15 '18, 2000m 5:34.83 '17, 3000m 8:20.68 '14, 10k Rd 29:58dh '18. Daughter born in May 2015.

Lilian Kasait **RENGERUK** b. 3 May 1997 1.61m 44kg.
At 3000m: WJ: '14- 2; WY: '13- 1. At 5000m: AfCh: '18- 5; World CC: '17- 3, '19- 12. Won KEN 5000m 2017.
Progress at 5000m: 2015- 16:04.61A, 2017- 14:36.80, 2018- 15:01.15. pbs: 800m 2:07.6A '17, 3000m 8:32.73 '17.

Betsy SAINA b. 30 Jun 1988 Sokosik, Nandi 1.63m 48kg. Bowerman TC, USA. Graduate of Iowa State University, USA
At 10000m: OG: '16- 5; WCh: '15- 8; AfCh: '12- 3. At 3000m: WI: '16- 7. Won NCAA indoor 5000m & CC 2012, 10000m 2013.
Progress at 5000m, 10000m, Mar: 2009- 16:15.74, 36:34.94; 2010- 16:10.69, 33:13.13; 2011- 15:50.74i/ 16:06.05, 33:13.87; 2012- 15:36.09i, 31:15.97; 2013- 15:12.05, 31:37.22; 2014- 14:39.49, 30:57.30; 2015- 15:00.48, 31:51.35; 2016- 14:44.67, 30:07.78; 2018- 2:22:56. pbs: 1M 4:40.98i '13, 2000m 5:45.7 '14, 3000m 8:38.01 '14, 2M 9:16.95 '14, Rd 10k 30:46 '14, 10M 51:55 '14, HMar 69:17 '18, 67:22 short '16. Won Paris marathon 2018.

Eunice Jepkoech **SUM** b. 2 Sep 1988 Burnt Forest, Uasin Gishu 1.72m 53kg. Police.
At 800m: OG: '16- sf; WCh: '11- sf, '13- 1, '15- 3; CG: '14- 1; AfCh: '10- h,'12- 2, '14- 1; CCp: '14- 1; won DL 2013-15. At 1500m: OG: '12- h, Won Kenyan 800m 2012, 2014.
World 4x1500m record 2014, Commonwealth & African 4x800m 2014..
Progress at 800m, 1500m: 2009- 2:07.4A, 2010- 2:00.28, 2011- 1:59.66A, 4:12.41; 2012- 1:59.13, 4:04.26; 2013- 1:57.38, 4:02.05; 2014- 1:57.92, 4:01.54; 2015- 1:56.99, 4:09.7A; 2016- 1:57.47, 4:21.3A; 2017- 1:57.78, 4:13.2A; 2018- 1:59.25, 4:05.38. pb 3000m 8:53.12 '12.
Daughter Diana Cheruto born in 2008.

Norah Jeruto **TANUI** b. 2 Oct 1995 1.71m 57kg.
At 3000mSt: AfCh: '16- 1. At 2000mSt: WY: '11- 1.
Progress at 3000mSt: 2011- 9:45.1A, 2013- 10:11.4, 2014- 10:01.71A, 2015- 9:55.44, 2016- 9:25.07, 2017- 9:03.70, 2018- 8:59.62. pbs: 1500m 4:30.0A '17, 3000m 8:33.61 '18, 2000mSt 6:16.41 '11.

Agnes Jebet **TIROP** b. 23 Oct 1995 Nandi, Chesumei 1.65m 50kg.
At 5000m: WJ: '12- 3, '14- 3; At 10000m: WCh: '17- 3; AfG: '15- 5. World CC: '13-15-17: 2J/1/5; AfCC: '12- 2J, '14- 1J.
Progress at 5000m, 10000m: 2011- 16:09.0A, 2012- 15:36.74, 2013- 14:50.36, 2014- 15:00.19, 2015- 32:55.41, 2016- 15:02.67, 2017- 14:33.09, 31:03.50; 2018- 14:24.24. pbs: 1500m 4:12.68 '13, 2000m 5:48.65 '13, 3000m 8:29.09 '18, 3000mSt 10:27.4A '12, road: 10k 30:50 '18.

Mary WACERA Ngugi b. 17 Dec 1988 1.55m.
World HMar: '14- 2, '16- 3. At 5000m: WJ: '06- 3; Af-J: 07- 1.
Progress at HMar: 2012- 70:54, 2013- 70:32, 2014- 67:44, 2015- 70:21, 2016- 66:29, 2017- 68:38, 2018- 66:50. pbs: 1500m 4:24.4A '08, 3000m 8:55.89 '09, 5000m 15:20.30 '09, Road: 5k 15:07 '15, 10k 31:28 '12, 15k 48:49 '15.
Widow of Samuel Wanjiru (2008 Olympic marathon champion). Daughter born 2010.

Margaret Nyairera **WAMBUI** b. 15 Sep 1995 Endarasha 1.75m 66kg.
At 800m: OG: '16- 3; WCh: '15- h, '17- 4; CG: '18- 2; AfCh: '18- dnf; WJ: '14- 1; WI: '16- 3. At 400m: AfCh: '16- 2/3R. Won KEN 800m 2017.
Progress at 800m: 2014- 2:00.49, 2015- 2:01.32, 2016- 1:56.89, 2017- 1:56.87, 2018- 1:58.07. pbs: 200m 24.1A '17, 400m 51.39A/51.97 '16, 600m 1:27.1 '16.

KOREA

Governing body: Korea Athletics Federation. Founded 1945.
National Champions 2018: **Men**: 100m: Oh Kyung-soo 10.41, 200m: Park Tae-jun 20.40, 400m: Mo Il-hwan 47.03, 800m: Oh Jae-won 1:52.05, 1500m: Shon Dae-hyuk 3:52.15, 5000m: Shon Myung-jun 14:37.50, 10000m: Hwang Jong-pil 31:04.26, 3000mSt: Kim Young-bin 9:10.65, 110mh: Kim Byung-jun 14.16, 400mh: Han Se-hyun 50.22, HJ: Woo Sang-hyuk 2.28, PV: Jin Min-sub 5.66, LJ: Kim Duk-hyun 7.89, TJ: Won Yu-sung 15.27, SP: Jung Il-woo 18.81, DT: Lee Hyun-jae 54.54, HT: Lee Yoon-chul 72.37, JT: Bae You-il 74.02, Dec: Choe Dong-hwi 7200, 20kW: Joon Hyun-myung 1:28:36; **Women**: 100m/LJ: Kim Min-ji 11.68w/6.25, 200m: Lee Min-jung 24.38, 400m: Oh Se-ra 57.42, 800m/1500m: Kim Kak-young 2:10.75/4:35.83, 5000m: Park Ho-sun 17:03.89, 10000m: Ahn Seul-ki 35:06.43, 3000mSt: Jo Ha-rim 10:23.39, 100mh: Jung Hye-lim 13.24, 400mh: Lee Ah-reum 63.15, HJ: Suk Mi-jung 1.82, PV: Lim Eun-ji 4.00, TJ: Bae Chan-mi 13.12, SP: Lee Mi-young 16.30, DT: Kin Min 50.96, HT: Park Syeo-jin 60.94, JT: Kim Kyong-ae 56.84, Hep: Kim Chae-young 4885, 20kW: Jung Yeong-eun 1:37:58.

OH Joo-han Formerly: Wilson Erupe LOYANAE of Kenya) b. 20 Nov 1988 Lodwar, Turkana, Kenya.
Progress at Mar: 2010- ?. 2011- 2:09:23, 2012- 2:05:37, 2015- 2:06:11, 2016- 2:05:13, 2017- 2:06:27, 2018- 2:06:57. pb HMar 61:46 '12.
Marathon wins: Mombasa 2011, Gyongju 2011-12, 2015; Seoul 2012, 2015-16, 2018. Two-year drugs ban for EPO 2013-15. Granted Korean citizenship on 31 Jul 2018, andf[cleared to compete internationally for Korea from 7 March 2019.

LATVIA

Governing body: Latvian Athletic Association. Founded 1921.
National Championships first held in 1920 (men), 1922 (women). **2018 Champions**: **Men**: 100m: Janis Leitis 10.81, 200m: Ilja Petrusenko 21.55, 400m: Austris Karpinskis 48.60, 800m: Daniels Bambals 1:50.21, 1500m/3000m: Ugis Jocis 3:52.84/8:31.97, 5000m: Reinis Hartmanis 14:42.51, 10000m: Janis Girgensons 30:49.64, HMar: Janis Viskers 67:03, Mar: Valerijs Zolnerovics 2:17:06, 3000mSt: Alberts Blajs 9:22.01, 110mh: Janis Baltuss 14.53, 400mh: Maksims Sincukovs 51.66, HJ: Janis Vanags 2.05, PV: Mareks Arents 5.20, LJ: Dairis Rincs 7.18w, TJ: Elvijs Misans 16.68, SP: Maris Urtans 16.46, DT: Arnis Zvirins 49.50, HT: Igors Sokolovs 63.69, JT: Rolands Strobinders 77.28, Dec: Peteris Krauja 6540, 20kW: Ruslans Smolonskis 1:26:49. **Women**: 100m: Sindija Buksa 11.56, 200m: Evija Sefere 24.52, 400m: Gunta Latiseva-Cudare 53.74, 800m: Liga Velvere 2:08.02, 1500m/3000m: Agata Strausa 4:22.57/9:39.93, 5000m: Anita Kazemaka 18:33.29, 10000m/Mar: Karina Helmane-Sorocenkova 38:06.48/2:55:14. HMar: Jelena Prokopcuka 1:20:05, 3000mSt: Irina Stula-Pankova 11:38.79, 100mh: Ilona Dramaconoka 15.03, 400mh: Anna Sevcenko 63.27, HJ: Madara Onuzane

1.76, PV: Sonija Askinezere 3.15, LJ: Lauma Griva 6.63, TJ: Mara Griva 13.09, SP: Linda Ozola 13.85, DT: Dace Steinerte 51.18, HT: Eva Rudzite 48.66, JT: Lina Muze 63.18, Hep: Kristine Deruma 5241.

Women

Laura IKAUNIECE b. 31 May 1992 Jürmala 1.79m 60kg. Jürmalas SS.
At Hep: OG: '12- 7, '16- 4; WCh: '13- 11, '15- 3, '17- dnf; EC: '12- 2, '14- 6; WJ: '10- 6; WY: '09- 2; EJ: '11- 3; WUG: '13- 1. At Pen: EI: '19- 5; At 100mh: EC: '16- h. Won LAT 100m 2012-13, 200m 2009, 2013; 100mh & HJ 2010.
Six Latvian heptathlon records 2012-17.
Progress at Hep: 2010- 5618, 2011- 6063, 2012- 6414, 2013- 6321, 2014- 6320, 2015- 6516, 2016- 6622, 2017- 6815. Pbs: 60m 7.58i '16, 100m 11.78 '16, 200m 23.49 '17, 800m 2:09.43 '16, 60mh 8.29i '19, 100mh 13.07 '16, HJ 1.85i '12, 1.84 '14; LJ 6.64 '17, SP 14.23i '19, 14.03 '18; JT 56.32 '17, Pen 4701i '19.
Won IAAF Challenge 2015. Her mother Vineta Ikauniece set Latvian records at 100m 11.34A '87, 200m 22.49A '87 and 400m 50.71 '88, and her father Aivars Ikaunieks had 110mh bests of 13.71A '87 and 13.4 '84. Married Rolands Admidins in 2014.

Madara PALAMEIKA b. 18 Jun 1987 Valdemarpils 1.85m 76kg. Ventspils.
At JT: OG: '12- 8, '16- 10; WCh: '09-13-15-17: dnq 26/27/13/21, '11- 10; EC: '10-12-14-16-18: 7/8/4/7/9; WJ: '06- dnq 16; EU23: '07- 3, '09- 1; EJ: '05- dnq 17. Won DL 2016, LAT 2009-11, 2014- 15, 2017. Three Latvian javelin records 2009-16.
Progress at JT: 2002- 42.31, 2003- 49.11, 2004- 51.50, 2005- 51.75, 2006- 54.19, 2007- 57.98, 2008- 53.45, 2009- 64.51, 2010- 62.02, 2011- 63.46, 2012- 62.74, 2013- 62.72, 2014- 66.15, 2015- 65.01, 2016- 66.18, 2017- 63.92, 2018- 62.98.

LITHUANIA

Governing body: Athletic Federation of Lithuania. Founded 1921.
National Championships first held in 1921 (women 1922). **2018 Champions: Men** 100m: Kostas Skrabulis 10.49, 200m: Gediminas Truskauskas 20.98, 400m: Daniel Golovacki 48.92, 800m: Benediktas Mickus 1:50.46, 1500m/5000m: Simas Bertasius 3:39.78/13:57.94, 10000m: Egidijus Adomkaitis 31:58.92, HMar:, Mar:, 3000mSt: Justinas Berzanskis 8:49.32, 110mh: Rapolas Saulius 13.95w, 400mh: Arturas Janauskas 52.10, HJ: Adrijus Glebauskas 2.23, PV: Osvaldas Gedrimas 4.60, LJ: Marius Vadeikis 7.48, TJ: Paulius Svarauskas 15.76, SP: Sarunas Banevicius 19.35, DT: Andrius Gudzius 67.21, HT: Tomas Vasiliauskas 63.82, JT: Edis Matusevicius 81.70, Dec: Edgaras Benkunskas 6936, 10kW/20kW:. **Women**: 100m: Karolina Deliautaite 11.54, 200m: Eva Misiunaite 24.17,

400m: Agné Serksniené 52.03, 800m: Egle Balcunaite 2:04.22, 1500m: Monika Elenska 4:23.53, 5000m: Loreta Kancyté 16:40.87, 10000m: Monika Bytautiené 35:02.58, HMar: , Mar:, 3000mSt: Evelina Miltene 10:39.61, 100mh: Greta Pleckaityté 14.32, 400mh: Gabija Galvydyte 58.29, HJ: Airine Palsyte 1.91, PV: Judita Kazlauskaite 3.40, LJ: Auguste Regalaité 6.01, TJ: Dovilé Dzindzatelaité 13.86, SP/DT: Ieva Zarankaité 15.96/55.62, HT: Ugné Buténaité 53.68, JT: Liveta Jasiunaite 61.53, 10kW/20kW:

Andrius GUDZIUS b. 14 Feb 1991 Vilkija, Kaunas district 2.00m 130kg. COSMA.
At DT: OG: '16- 12; WCh: '15- dnq 14, '17- 1; EC: '12- 14-16-18: dnq 29/10/dnq 13/1; WJ: '08- 6, '10- 1; WY: '07- 3; EU23: '11- dnq 13, '13- 1; EJ: '09- 5; CCp: '18- 2; WUG: '15- 3. Won DL 2017, LTU 2013-14, 2017-18.
Progress at DT: 2008- 54.72, 2009- 57.17, 2010- 61.85, 2011- 58.50, 2012- 63.39, 2013- 62.40, 2014- 66.11, 2015- 65.51, 2016- 65.18/67.96dh, 2017- 69.21, 2018- 69.59.

Women

Airine PALSYTE b. 13 Jul 1992 Kaunas 1.86m 62kg. COSMA. Vilnius University
At HJ: OG: '12- 11, '16- 13=; WCh: '13- 12, '15- dnq 14=, '17- 7=; WJ: '08- dnq 23, '10- 2; WY: '09- 4; EC: '10-12-14-16-18: dnq 18/9/13/2/4; EJ: '11- 2; EU23: '13- 2; WUG: '11-15-17: 2/1/3; WI: '16- 4; EI: '15-17-19: 4/1/3; won LTU 2010, 2012-18. Three LTU high jump records 2011-14 and absolute records 2.00 & 2.01i 17.
Progress at HJ: 2003- 1.45, 2004- 1.40i, 2005- 1.60, 2006- 1.71, 2007- 1.70i/1.55, 2008- 1.80, 2009- 1.86i/1.83, 2010- 1.92, 2011- 1.96, 2012- 1.95, 2013- 1.95, 2014- 1.98, 2015- 1.98i/1.95, 2016- 1.97i/1.96, 2017- 2.01i/1.92, 2018- 1.96, 2019- 1.98i. pb 200m 24.78 '12, TJ 12.70i '12.

Birgit VIRBALYTE-DIMSIENE b. 1 Feb 1985 1.65m 50kg. née Virbalyte. Alytus-Vilnius.
At 20kW: OG: '12- 25, '16- 29; WCh: '09-11-13-15-17: 23/26/19/7/16; EC: '10-14-18- 12/18/4; EU23: 07- 8; WCp: '18- 10; ECp: 17- 8. At 10000mW: WJ: '04- 9; EJ: '03- 4; ECp: '03- 5J. At 5000mW. WY: '01- 5. Won LTU 10kW 2014-15, 2017; 20kW 2009- 11, 2013, 2016-17
Lithuanian walks records: 10k 2007, 2010, 2012, 2015, 20k 2018, 50k 2010.
Progress at 20kW: 2005- 1:39:16, 2006- 1:38:59, 2007- 1:36:38, 2008- 1:34:36, 2009- 1:32:08, 2010- 1:32>17, 2011- 1:33:24, 2012- 1:31:08, 2013- 1:30:55, 2014- 1:31:00, 2015- 1:30:20, 2016- 1:30:48, 2017- 1:30:45, 2018- 1:27:59. pbs: 3000mW 12:05.72 '18, 5000mW 21:17.8 '14, 10kW 42:43 '15, 45:18.0t '11; 50kW 4:25:22 '10.

LUXEMBOURG

Governing body: Fédération Luxembourgeoise d'Athlétisme. Founded 1928.
2018 National Champions: Men: 100m: Pol

Bidaine 11.03, 200m: Lionel Evora Delgado 22.36, 400m: Vincent Karger 49.10, 800m: Charles Grethen 1:51.32, 1500m: Christophe Bestgen 4:14.11, 5000m: Pol Mellina 15:48.62, 10000m: Christophe Kass 32:56.41, HMar: Bob Bertemes 70:08, Mar: Philippe Gillen 2:29:58, 3000mSt: Luc Scheller 10:17.19, 110mh: Pit Steinmetz 16.83, 400mh: Jacques Frisch 54.02, HJ: Charel Gaspar 2.08, PV: Joe Seil 4.80, LJ: Lex Damit 6.85, TJ: Jon Novak 13.16, SP: Bob Bertemes 20.66, DT: Sam Behler 38.94, HT: Gilles Lorang 46.18, JT: Tom Reuter 65.25; **Women**: 100m/200m: Anaïs Bauer 12.52/24.11, 400m: Charline Mathias 55.38, 800m: Vera Hoffmann 2:08.91, 1500m: Saskia Daguenet 4:56.27, 3000m/HMar: Martine Mellina 10:16.96/1:23:22, 10000m: Liz Weiler 39:45.15, Mar: Karin Schank 2:56:36, 3000mSt: Fanny Goy 11:39.82, 100mh/TJ/Hep: Lara Marx 14.44/11.52/4313, HJ: Laura Lassine 1.55, PV: Kim Hoffmann 2.80, LJ: Marie Damit 5.55, SP: Stéphanie Krumlovsky 13.80, DT/JT Noémie Pleimling 44.41/48.05, HT: Géraldine Davin 45.75.

MEXICO

Governing body: Federación Mexicana de Atletismo. Founded 1933.
National Champions 2018: Men: 100m/200m: Heber Gallegos 10.40/20.69, 400m: Luis Avilés 46.94, 800m: Jesús López 1:46.58, 1500m/5000m: Fernando Martínez 3:48.01/14:11.87, 10000m: José Uribe 29:45.37, 3000mSt: Cristopher Endoqui 8:50.44, 110mh: Genaro Rodríguez 14.05, 400mh: Sergio Esquivel 49.90, HJ: Roberto Vilches 2.25, PV: Jorge Luna 5.25, LJ: Adrián Rivera 7.33, TJ: Alberto Álvarez 16.04, SP: Uziel Muñoz 19.75, DT: Mario Cota 55.98, HT: Diego Del Real 74.10, JT: David Carreón 78.23, Dec: Felipe Ruiz 7351, 10000mW: Jesús Vega 41:47.24; **Women**: 100m/200m: Iza Flores 11.77/23.47, 400m: Gabriela Medina 53.55, 800m: Luisa Real 2:04.34, 1500m: Gabriela Eleno 4:24.20, 5000m/10000m: Úrsula Sánchez 16:53.00/34:10.41, 3000mSt: Azucena Rodríguez 10:20.75, 100mh: Gabriella Santos 14.01, 400mh: Zudikey Rodríguez 56.30, HJ: Ximena Esquivel 1.80, PV: Carmelita Correa 4.15, LJ: Jessamyn Sauceda 6.29, TJ: Ivonne Rangel 12.96, SP: Fernanda Orozco 17.04, DT: Alma Pollorena 52.98, JT: Miranda Vázquez 55.97, JT: Luz Castro 53.62, Hep: Gabriela Castañeda 4827, 10,000W: Andrea Martínez 46:11.49.

Women

María Guadalupe 'Lupita' GONZÁLEZ Romero b. 9 Jan 1989 Mexico City 1.62m 48kg.
At 20kW: OG: '16- 2; WCh: '17- 2; PAm: '15- 1; WCp: '14-16-18: 16/1/1. Won CAC 10kW 2013, PAmCp 20k 2015, 2017; MEX 20kW 2017, 10,000mW 2014. Tied first IAAF Race Walking Challenge 2016.

MEX 20k walk records 2014 & 2016 (& 20,000m track 1:33:26.8 '17), CAC 2016.
Progress at 20kW: 2013- 1:37:02, 2014- 1:28:48, 2015- 1:29:21, 2016- 1:26:17, 2017- 1:26:19, 2018- 1:26:38. pbs: 10kW 43:49 '15. Pending decision on positive drugs test on 17 Oct 2018.

MOLDOVA

Governing body: Federatia de Atletism din Republica Moldova. Founded 1991.
Serghei MARGHIEV b. 6 Nov 1992 Vladikavkaz, North Osetia, Russia 1.94m 96kg.
At HT: OG: '12- dnq 30, '16- 10; WCh: '15- dnq 23, '17- 8; EC: '14-16-18: 9/8/8; WJ: '10- dnq 14; WY: '09- dnq 28; EU23: '13- 5; EJ: '11- 2; WUG: '15- 4, '17- 3. Won Balkan 2013-14, MDA 2012-17. Four MDA hammer records 2014-15
Progress at HT: 2011- 67.54, 2012- 75.20, 2013- 74.41, 2014- 78.27, 2015- 78.72, 2016- 78.48, 2017- 77.70, 2018- 76.81.
Younger brother of Zalina (qv) and Marina.

Women

Zalina PETRIVSKAYA b. 5 Feb 1988 Vladikavkaz, North Osetia, Russia 1.74m 90kg. née Marghieva. AS-CSPLN.
At HT: OG: '08- dnq 35, '12- dq8, '16- 5; WCh: '09- dq dnq 26, '11- dq8, '15- 8, '17- dnq 19; EC: '10-12-16-18: dq5/dq8/5/6; WJ: '06- 4; WY: '05- 7; EU23: '09- 1; EJ: '07- 5; WUG: '11- dq1, '13- dq3. Won Balkan 2015-18, MDA 2016. Nine Moldovan hammer records 2005-16 (and 3 disqualified).
Progress at HT: 2005- 61.80, 2006- 65.50, 2007- 65.40, 2008- 70.22, 2009- 71.56, 2015- 73.97, 2016- 74.21, 2017- 73.80, 2018- 72.80; DQ: 2010- 71.50, 2011- 72.93, 2012- 74.47, 2013- 74.28.
Drugs ban announced in 2013 with all results annulled from 2009 Worlds to 2013. Sister **Marina** (now **Nikisenko**) (b. 28 Jun 1986) HT: 72.53 '09, seven MDA records 2007-09, OG: '08- 16: dnq/41/24; WCh: '09/11/15/17- dnq 32/17/25/27; EC: '10-12-16-18: 5, '12/16- dnq 14/14/24; received a 3-year drugs ban from 24 July 2012. Brother **Serghei** (qv).

MOROCCO

Governing body: Fédération Royale Marocaine d'Athlétisme. Founded 1957.
Soufiane EL BAKKALI b. 7 Jan 1996 Fez 1.88m 70kg.
At 3000mSt: OG: '16- 4; WCh: '17- 2; WJ: '14- 4; AfCh: '14- 10, '18- 2; CCp: 18- fa; won MedG 2018. World CC: '19- 2 mxR.
Progress at 3000mSt: 2013- 8:52.00, 2014- 8:32.66, 2015- 8:27.79, 2016- 8:14.35, 2017- 8:04.83, 2018- 7:58.15. pbs: 1500m 3:35.36 '15, 2000m 5:00.55i '19, 3000m 7:41.88i '18, 7:49.68 '16, 5000m 13:10.60i '17, 13:47.76 '14.

Abdelaati IGUIDER b. 25 Mar 1987 Errachidia 1.70m 52kg.

At 1500m(/5000m): OG: '08- 5, '12- 3/6, '16- 5; WCh: '07-09-11-13-15-17: h/11/5/sf/3/sf; WJ: '04-1, '06- 2; AfCh: '18- 6; WI: '10-12-14-18: 2/1/3/3. At 3000m: WI: '16- 4. World CC: '19- 2 mxR Progress at 1500m, 5000m: 2004- 3:35.53, 2005-3:35.63, 2006- 3:32.68, 2007-3:32.75, 2008- 3:31.88, 2009- 3:31.47, 2010- 3:34:25, 2011- 3:31.60, 2012-3:33.99, 13:09.17; 2013- 3:33.29, 2014- 3:29.83, 2015-3:28.79, 12:59.25; 2016- 3:31.40, 13:08.61; 2017-3:34.99, 2018- 3:31.59. pbs: 800m 1:46.67 '15, 1000m 2:19.14 '07, 1M 3:49.09 '14, 2000m 4:59.20 '16, 3000m 7:30.09 '16.

Brahim Al-**KAAZOUZI** b. 15 Jun 1990 Kasba Tadia 1.79m 62kg.
At 1500m: OG: '16- sf; won MedG 2018, At 5000m: WCh: '17- h.
Progress at 1500m: 2011- 3:48.92, 2012- 13:44.69, 2013- 3:46.92, 2014- 3:38.48, 2015- 3:40.14, 2016-3:35.76, 2017- 3:34.46, 2018- 3:31.62. pbs: 3000m 7:41.88 '17, 5000m 13:16.98 '17.

Women

Malika AKKAOUI b. 25 Dec 1987 Zaida, Meknès-Tafilalet 1.60m 46kg.
At 800m/(1500m): OG: '12- sf, '16- h/sf; WCh: '11- (h), '13- sf, '15- sf/12, '17- (10); AfCh: '10-12-14-16-18: 3/3/6/2/6&3; WJ: '06- h. Won MAR 400m 2014, 800m 2007-08, MedG 800m 2013, Arab 800m 2015, Is.Sol 2017.
Progress at 800m: 2004- 2:09.2, 2005- 2:08.1, 2006- 2:06.29, 2007- 2:05.04, 2008- 2:04.25, 2009-2:02.10, 2010- 2:00.6, 2011- 1:59.75, 2012- 1:59.01i/1:59.54, 2013- 1:57.64, 2014- 2:00.58, 2015- 1:59.03, 2016- 1:59.93, 2017- 2:00.71, 4:03.36; 2018- 1:59.27, 4:07.08. pbs: 400m 53.19 '13, 1000m 2:39.86 '13, 1500m 4:04.49 '15.

Rabab ARRAFI b. 12 Jan 1991 Khourigba 1.77m 64kg. ASOAK.
At (800m)/1500m: OG: '16- h/12; WCh: '13- sf, '15- 4/9, '17- 8; AfCh: 12-14-16-18: 1/3/5&2/2; CCp: 18- 3; WI: '14- dq (3rd), '18- 8; won Is.Sol 2017. MedG 800m & 1500m 2018. At 3000m: WY: '07- 12. Won FrancG 2013, 2017. World CC: '19- 2 mxR. Moroccan 1500m record 2018.
Progress at 800m, 1500m: 2006- 24:21.59, 2011- 2:09.24, 2012- 2:04.60, 4:05.80; 2013- 2:00.58, 4:05.22; 2014- 2:03.18i, 4:02.71; 2015- 1:58.55, 4:02.94; 2016- 2:01.49, 4:03.95; 2017- 4:01.75, 2018-1:57.47, 3:59.15. pbs: 1M 4:23.50 '15, 3000m 8:58.32i '13, 9:34.78 '07.

NETHERLANDS

Governing body: Koninklijke Nederlandse Atletiek Unie (KNAU). Founded 1901.
National Championships first held in 1910 (men), 1921 (women). **2018 Champions: Men**: 100m/200m: Churandy Martina 10.43/20.83, 400m: Tony van Diepen 46.91, 800m: Jurgen Wielart 1:51.26, 1500m: Richard Douna 3:58.34, 5000m/10000m: Benjamin de Haan 14:18.34/28:44.84, HMar: Bart van Nunen 63:50, Mar:

Michel Butter 2:17:18, 3000mSt: Noah Schutte 9:09.93, 110mh: Koen Smet 13.91, 400mh: Nick Smidt 51.10 , HJ: Douwe Amels 2.20, PV: Rutger Koppelaar 5.40, LJ: Ignisious Gaidah 7.64, TJ: Fabian Florant 15.24, SP: Patrick Cronie 19.01, DT: Erik Cadée 59.38, HT: Dennis Hemelaar 60.05, JT: Lars Timmerman 76.89, Dec: Rik Taam 7628. **Women**: 100m/200m: Jamile Samuel 11.49/23.04, 400m: Madiea Ghafoor 51.84, 800m: Britt Ummels 2:10.75, 1500m: Sanne Wolters-Verstegen 4:24.24, 5000m/10000m: Jip Vastenburg 15:51.55/33:03.42, HMar: Andrea Deelstra 73:58, Mar: Miranda Boonstra 2:42:07, 3000mSt: Irene van der Reijken 10:11.84, 100mh: Eefje Boons 13.27, 400mh: Anna Sjoukje Runia 58.35, HJ: Manon Schoop 1.76, PV: Killiana Heymans 4.10, LJ: Carlijn ter Laak 6.18, TJ: Patricia Krolis 12.37, SP: Melissa Boekelman 18.36, DT: Corinne Nugter 59.10, HT: Sina Mai Bolthuijsen 62.14, JT: Nadine Boersen 54.34, Hep: Myke van de Wiel 5475.

Pieter BRAUN b. 21 Jan 1993 Terheojden 1.86m 83kg. Sprint..
At Dec: OG: '16- dnf; WCh: '15- 12, '17- 16; EC: 16- 7, '18- 7; WJ: '12- 16; E23: '13- 11, '15- 1.
Progress at Dec: 2013- 7540, 2014- 7092, 2015-8197, 2016- 8058, 2017- 8334, 2018- 8342. pbs: 60m 7.23i '15. 100m 10.97 '15, 10.90w '17; 200m 22.15 '16, 400m 48.02 '15, 1000m 2:40.19i '14, 1500m 4:24.29 '18, 60mh 8.08i '16, 110mh 14.13 '15, HJ 2.05 '17, PV 5.05 '16, LJ 7.71 '17, SP 15.28 '18, DT 45.23 '17, JT 6048 '14, Hep 5837i '15.

Eelco SINTNICOLAAS b. 7 Apr 1987 Dordrecht 1.86m 81kg. AV '34 (Apeldoorn). Economics student.
At Dec: OG: '12- 11, '16- dnf; WCh: '09-11-13-15-17: dnf/5/5/dnf/dnf; EC: '10-14-16-18: 2/4/16/dnf; WJ: '06- 8; EU23: '09- 1; EJ: '05- 14; ECp: '14- 1. At Hep: WI: '14- 4, '18- 5; EI: '11-13-15: 4/1/3.
Dutch decathlon records 2012 & 2017.
Progress at Dec: 2007- 7466, 2008- 7507w, 2009-8112, 2010- 8436, 2011- 8304, 2012- 8506, 2013-8391, 2014- 8478, 2015- 8298, 2017- 8539. pbs: 60m 6.88i '13, 100m 10.57 '15, 200m 21.62 '10, 400m 47.88 '10, 1000m 2:37.42i '06, 1500m 4:22.29 '11, 60mh 7.88i '13, 110mh 13.92/13.89w '13, 400mh 51.59 '10, HJ 2.08i/2.02 '13, PV 5.52i '11, 5.45 '10; LJ 7.65i, 7.76w '09, 7.65 '12; SP 14.67 '15, DT 43.38 '14, JT 63.59 '12, Hep 6372i '13.
Set six pbs in improving pb by 277 points for European silver 2010.

Women

Nadine BROERSEN b. 29 Apr 1990 Hoorn 1.71m 62kg. AV Sprint Breda.
At Hep: OG: '12- 11, '16- 13; WCh: '13-15-17: 10/4/dnf; EC: '14- 2, '16- dnf; EU23: '11- 9; EJ: '09- 5; ECp: '14- 1. At Pen: WI: '14- 1; EI: '17- 5. Won NED HJ 2010-11, 2014; LJ 2015; JT 2013, 2018.

Four Dutch high jump records 2013-14 and indoors 2014.
Progress at Hep: 2009- 5507, 2010- 5967, 2011-5932(w)/5854, 2012- 6319, 2013- 6345, 2014- 6539, 2015- 6531, 2016- 6377, 2017- 6326. pbs: 200m 24.57 '14, 800m 2:11.11 '14, 60mh 8.32i '13, 100mh 13.39 '14, HJ 1.94 '14, LJ 6.39 '14, 6.40w '16; SP 14.93i '14, 14.82 '15; JT 54.97 '12, Pen 4830i '14.
Lost c.200 points in stumbling at last hurdle in first event of 2013 World heptathlon. Won IAAF Combined Events Challenge 2014.

Sifan HASSAN b. '1 Jan' 1993 Adama, Ethiopia 1.70m 49kg. Eindhoven Atletiek.
At 1500m/(5000m): OG: '16- 5 (h 800m); WCh: '15- 3 (sf 800m), '17- 5/3; EC: '14- 1/2, '16- 2, '18-(1); CCp: '14- 1; WI: '16- 1, '18- 3; EI: 15- 1; won DL 2015. At 3000m: WI: '14- 5, '18- 2; CCp: '18- 1; ET: '14- 1. Eur CC: '13- 1 U23, '15- 1.
Records: European 5000m & half marathon 2018, European U23 1500m (3) 2014-15, Dutch 1500m (3) 2014-15, 1M 2015 & 2018, 3000m (3) 2014-18, 5000m (3) 2014-18.
Progress at 800m, 1500m, 5000m: 2011- 4:20.13, 2012- 4:08.74, 2013- 2:00.86, 4:03.73. 2014- 1:59.95, 3:57.00, 14:59.23; 2015- 1:58.50, 3:56.05; 2016- 2:00.27, 3:57.13; 2017- 1:56.81, 3:56.14, 14:41.24; 2018- 1:59.35, 3:57.41, 14:22.34. pbs: 1000m 2:34.68 '15, 1M 4:14.71 '18, 2000m 5:46.1 '14, 3000m 8:27.50 '18, 10kRd 34:28 '12, HMar 65:15 '18 '11.
Came to the Netherlands as a refugee at age 15. Dutch eligibility from 29 Nov 2013.

Susan KRUMINS b. 8 Jul 1986 Nijmegen 1.72m 54kg. née Kuijken. Zevenheuvelen. Was at Florida State University, USA.
At 5000m/(10000m): OG: '16- 8/14; WCh: '13- 8, '15- 8/10, '17- 8/5; EC: '14- 3, '16- 4, '18- 6/2. At 1500m: WCh: '09- h; EC: '10- h; E23: '07- 4. At 3000m: WJ: '04- dnf; EJ: '05- 2; CCp: '14- 3. Eur CC: '05- 3J, '08- 1 U23, '18- 4. Won NED 1500m 2014, 5000m 2016; NCAA 1500m 2009..
Progress at 5000m, 10000m: 2003- 16:41.31, 2006- 16:20.30, 2009- 16:31.68, 2013- 15:04.36, 2014- 15:32.82, 2015- 15:07.38, 31:31.97; 2016- 15:00.69, 31:32.43; 2017- 14:51.25, 31:20.24; 2018- 15:09.65, 31:52.55. pbs: 800m 2:02.24 '09, 1000m 2:38.01 '14, 1500m 4:02.25 '17, 1M 4:34.11i '09, 2000m 5:38.37 '13, 3000m 8:34.41 '17 , 3000mSt 10:42.93 '05; Road: 10k 31:11 '19, 15k 47:41 '18, 10M 51:30 '18, HMar 70:32 '17.
In September 2016 married Andrew Krumins, who competed for Australia at the 2001 World Youth Champs, pb 800m 1:47.16 '06.

Jamile SAMUEL b. 24 Apr 1992 Amsterdam 1.68m 57kg. Phanos, Amsterdam.
At (100m)/200m/4x100mR: OG: '12- 6R, 16- h; WCh: '11/13/15 hR, '17- (h); EC: '12- 6/2R, '14-sf/6, '16- 4/1R, '18- 5/3/2R; WJ: '08- sf/6, '10-3/3/3R; EU23: '13- (h); EJ: '09- (sf)/3R, '11- 2/2. At 60m: EI: '15- 7. Won NED 100m 2009, 2017-18, 200m 2011-12, 2015, 2018.
Progress at 100m, 200m: 2007- 11.80, 24.13; 2008-

11.75, 23.57; 2009- 11.97/11.73w, 2010- 11.44, 23.21; 2011- 11.43, 23.28; 2012- 11.38, 22.93; 2013- 11.66/11.52w, 2014- 11.12, 22.72; 2015- 11.25, 22.95; 2016- 11.38, 22.83; 2017- 11.26/11.04w, 23.39; 2018- 11.10, 22.37. pbs: 60m 7.14i '16, 150m 17.18 '12, 60mh 8.42i '09, 100mh 14.44 '08, LJ 5.83 ''05.

Dafne SCHIPPERS b. 15 Jun 1992 Utrecht 1.79m 68kg. Hellas.
At (100m)/200m/4x100mR: OG: '16- 5/2; WCh: '11- sf, '15- 2/1, '17- 3/1; EC: '12- 5/2R, '14- 1/1, '16- 1/-/1R, '18- 3/2/2R; WJ: '10- 3R; EU23: '13-(1) (3 LJ); CCp: '14- 3/1, '18- 4/2; ET: '14- 1. At 60m: WI: '16- 2, '18- 5; EI: '13-15-19: 4/1/2. At Hep: OG: '12- 10; WCh: '13- 3; WJ: '10- 1; EJ: '09- 4, '11- 1. Won DL 200m 2016, NED 100m 2011-12, 2014-15; LJ 2012, 2014.
European 200m record 2015, Dutch records: 100m (5) 2014-15, 200m (5) 2011-15, LJ 2014, Hep 2013 & 2014.
Progress at 100m, 200m, Hep: 2007- 12.09/12.08w, 2008- 12.26/12.01w, 2009- 11.79, 24.21, 5507; 2010- 11.56, 23.70/23.41w, 5967; 2011- 11.19/11.13w, 22.69, 6172; 2012- 11.36, 22.70, 6360; 2013- 11.09, 22.84, 6477; 2014- 11.03, 22.03, 6545; 2015- 10.81, 21.63; 2016- 10.83, 21.88; 2017- 10.95, 22.05; 2018- 10.99, 22.14. pbs: 60m 7.00i '16, 150m 16.93 '13, 800m 2:08.59 '14, 60mh 8.18i '12, 100mh 13.13 '14, HJ 1.80 '12, LJ 6.78 '14, SP 14.66 '15, JT 42.22 '15.
Added 117 points to pb and reduced 800m best from 2:15.52 to 2:08.62 in taking 2013 World heptathlon bronze. First Dutch woman to win a medal in World Championships and emulated Fanny Blankers-Koen (1950) by winning EC sprint double 2014. European Athlete of the Year 2014-15.

Anouk VETTER b. 4 Feb 1993 Amsterdam 1.77m 62kg. Sprint.
At Hep: OG: '16- 10; WCh: '15- 12, '17- 3; EC: '14-16-18: 7/1/5; WJ: '12- dnf; EJ: '11- dnf. At Pen: EI: '15- 8. Won NED LJ 2017.
Dutch heptathlon records 2016 & 2017.
Progress at Hep: 2011- 5549, 2012- 5764, 2013-5872, 2014- 6316, 2015- 6458, 2016- 6626, 2017-6636, 2018- 6266. pbs: 60m 7.46i '16, 100m 11.61 '16, 11.44w '17, 200m 23.70 '16, 800m 2:17.71 '16, 60mh 8.25i '16, 100mh 13.29 '16, HJ 1.81 '13, LJ 6.34 '15, 6.38w '16; SP 16.00 '17, JT 58.41 '17, Pen 4548i '15.
Mother Gerda Blokziel was NED javelin champion 1987-8. pb 58.22 '86.

Nadine VISSER b. 9 Feb 1995 Hoorn 1.75m 63kg. SAV.
At Hep/(100mh): OG: '16- 19 (h); WCh: '15- 8, '17- 7/7; EC: '14 (h), '16- (sf), '18- (4); WJ: '12- 11, 14- 3 (3); EU23: '15- (3, 11 LJ), '17- (1); EJ: '13- 4; WUG: '17- (1). At 60mh: WI: '18- 3; EI: '17- 7, '19-1. Won NED heptathlon 2015.
Progress at 100mh, Hep: 2011- 13.84, 5171; 2012-13.50, 5475; 2013- 13.21, 5774; 2014- 12.99, 6110; 2015- 12.81, 6467; 2016- 12.89, 6190; 2017-

12.78/12.57w, 6370; 2018- 12.71. pbs: 60m 7.38i
'18, 100m 11.60 '14, 150m 17.69 '15, 200m 23.46,
22.83w '17, 800m 2:13.08 '15, 60mh 7.83i '18
(NED record), HJ 1.80 '14, LJ 6.48 '15, SP 13.89i,
13.64 '17, JT 44.01 '15, Pen 4428i '17.

NEW ZEALAND

Governing body: Athletics New Zealand.
Founded as the New Zealand Amateur Athletic
Association in 1887, current name from 1989.
National Championships first held in 1887
(men), 1926 (women). **2018 Champions: Men**:
100m/ 200m: Joseph Millar 10.46/21.31, 400m:
Alex Haye 47.63, 800m: Brad Mathas 1:49.49,
1500m: Hamish Carson 3:52.32, 3000m: Peter
Wheeler 8:21.66, 5000m: Oli Chignell 14:31.53,
10000m: Craig Lautenslager 29:51.97, HMar:
Sam Wreford 67:10, Mar: Blair McWhirter
2:28:59, 3000mSt: Jake Jackson-Grammer
9:56.92, 110mh: Joshua Hawkins 15.19, 400mh:
Cameron French 51.84, HJ: Hamish Kerr 2.21,
PV: Nick Southgate 5.20, LJ: Jordan Peters 7.32,
TJ: Ebuka Okpala 15.53, SP: Tom Walsh 21.58,
DT: Marshall Hall 56.46, HT: Matt Bloxham
62.52, JT: Ben Langton Burnell 73.18, Dec: Brent
Newdick 6997, 3000mW: Scott Nelson 14:44.59.
20kW: Lyndon Hohaia 1:59:47. **Women**: 100m:
Zoe Hobbs 11.66, 200m: Lucy Sheat 24.19, 400m:
Brooke Cull 54.65, 800m/1500m: Angie Petty
2:02.67/4:18.94, 3000m: Olivia Burne 9:22.83,
5000m: Olivia Burne 16:19.10, 10000m: Sally
Gibbs 36:22.10, HMar/Mar: Alice Mason
77:38/2:46:44, 3000mSt: Kelsey Forman 10:46.97,
100mh: Fiona Morrison 13.92, 400mh: Portia
Bing 57.86, HJ: Keeley O'Hagan 1.77, PV: Imogen
Ayris 4.15, LJ: Kelsey Berryman 6.17, TJ: Anna
Thomson 12.69, SP: Valerie Adams 17.83, DT:
Siositina Hakeai 57.31, HT: Julia Ratcliffe 68.39,
JT: Tori Peeters 53.56, Hep: Christina Ryan
4298, 3000mW: Roseanne Robinson 14:55.99,
20kW: Alana Barber 1:35:26 & Roseanne
Robinson 1:43:23.

Jacko GILL b. 20 Dec 1994 Auckland 1.90m
118kg. Takapuna.
At SP: OG: '16- 9; WCh: '15- 8, '17- 9; CG: '14- 11,
WJ: '10- 1, '12- 1; WY: '11- 1, YthOG: '10- 2.
Oceania champion 2014.
Five World youth shot records 5kg 23.86 '10,
24.35 and 24.45 '11; 6kg (4) 21.34 to 22.31, 7.26kg
(3) in 2011. World junior 6kg record 23.00 '13.
Three NZL records 2011.
Progress at SP: 2010- 18.57, 2011- 20.38, 2012-
20.05, 2014- 20.70, 2015- 20.75, 2016- 20.83, 2017-
21.01, 2019- 20.76.
First name actually Jackson. World age 15 and
16 bests for 5kg, 6kg and 7.26kg shot. His father
Walter was NZ champion at SP 1987 & 1989, DT
1975, pbs 16.57 '86 & 53.78 (1975); his mother
Nerida (née Morris) had discus best of 51.32
and was NZ champion in 1990. His sister Ayla
was 6th in WJ hammer 2010.

Tomas WALSH b. 1 Mar 1992 Timaru 1.86m
123kg. South Canterbury.
At SP: OG: '16- 3; WCh: '15- 4, '17- 1; CG: '14- 2,
'18- 1; WJ: '10- dnq 16; WY: '09- 6 (dnq 31 DT),
CCp: '14- 4, '18- 3; WI: '14-16-18: 3/1/1. Won DL
2016, NZ SP 2010-18, DT 2013, 2018.
Shot records: 8 Oceania 2016-18, 9 NZL 2013-18
and 9 OCE indoor 2014-18, Comm 2016 (=) &
2018.
Progress at SP: 2010- 17.57, 2011- 18.83, 2012-
19.33, 2013- 20.61, 2014- 21.26i/21.16, 2015- 21.62,
2016- 22.21, 2017- 22.14, 2018- 22.67, 2019- 21.70.
pb DT 53.58 '14.
At World Indoors: set four NZ indoor records
in 2014 and three Oceania records in both 2016
and 2018, when he beat the Championship
record set in 1995.

Nick WILLIS b. 25 Apr 1983 Lower Hutt 1.83m
68kg. Economics graduate of University of
Michigan, USA.
At 1500m: OG: '04- sf, '08- 2, '12- 9, '16- 3; WCh:
'05- 07-11-13-15-17: sf/10/12/sf/6/8; CG: '06-1,
'10- 3, '14-3 (10 5000m); WJ: '02- 4; WI: '08/14- dq,
'16- 3; WCp: '06- 3, '14- 6 (4 3000m). Won NCAA
indoor 2005, NZ 1500m 2006, 2015; 3000m 2013,
2016; 5000m 2011-12.
Records: NZ 1500m (6) 2005-15, 3000m 2014.
Oceania 1500m (3) 2012-15 and indoors 1500m
(3:35.80) 2010, 1M 2015 & 2016 (3:50.63).
Progress at 1500m: 2001- 3:43.54, 2002- 3:42.69,
2003- 3:36.58, 2004- 3:32.64, 2005- 3:32.38, 2006-
3:32.17, 2007- 3:35.85, 2008- 3:33.51, 2009- 3:38.85i,
2010- 3:35.17, 2011- 3:31.79, 2012- 3:30.35, 2013-
3:32.57, 2014- 3:29.91, 2015- 3:29.66, 2016- 3:34.29,
2017- 3:34.74, 2018- 3:35.25. pbs: 800m 1:45.54 '04,
1000m 2:16.58 '12, 1M 3:49.83 '14, 3000m 7:36.91
'14, 5000m 13:20.33 '14, HMar 67:06 '14.
His brother Steve (b. 25 Apr 1975) had pbs:
1500m 3:40.29 '99, 1M 3:59.04 '00.

Women

Valerie ADAMS b. 6 Oct 1984 Rotorua 1.93m
123kg. Auckland City.
At SP: OG: '04- 7, '08- 1, '12- 1, '16- 2; WCh: '03-
05-07-09-11-13: 5/2/1/1/1/1; CG: '02-06-10-14-18:
2/1/1/1/2; WJ: '02- 1; WY: '99- 10, '01- 1; WI:
'04-08-10-12-14-16: dnq 10/1/1/1/1/3; WCp: '02-
6, '06- 1, '10- 1. Won WAF 2005, 2007-09, DL
2010-14, 2016; NZL SP 2001-11, 2013-14, 2016,
2018; DT 2004, HT 2003.
Nine Oceania & Commonwealth shot records
2005-11, 22 NZ 2002-11, 10 OCE indoor 2004-13.
Progress at SP: 1999- 14.83, 2000- 15.72, 2001-
17.08, 2002- 18.40, 2003- 18.93, 2004- 19.29, 2005-
19.87, 2006- 20.20, 2007- 20.54, 2008- 20.56, 2009-
21.07, 2010- 20.86, 2011- 21.24, 2012- 21.11, 2013-
20.98i/20.90, 2014- 20.67i/20.59, 2015- 18.73,
2016- 20.42, 2018- 19.31. pbs: DT 58.12 '04, HT
58.75 '02.
Ten senior global shot titles. IAAF Female
Athlete of the Year 2014. Matched her age with
metres at the shot from 14 to 18 and missed that

at 19 by only two months. 28 successive shot wins from September 2007 to World Indoor silver in March 2010, and another 56 from August 2010 to July 2015. The disqualification of Nadezhda Ostapchuk meant that the win streak for Adams lengthened to 95. Her father came from England and her mother from Tonga. Married New Caledonia thrower Bertrand Vili (SP 17.81 '02, DT 63.66 '09, 4 ECp '07 for France) in November 2004 (divorced in 2010), and married Gabriel Price on 2 April 2016. She was made a Dame Companion of the New Zealand Order of Merit for services to athletics in the 2017 New Year's Honours. Daughter Kimoana born in October 2017, second child due in April 2019.

Eliza McCARTNEY b. 11 Dec 1996 Auckland 1.79m 65kg. North Harbour Bays.
At PV: OG: '16- 3; WCh: '17- 9; CG: '18- 2; WJ: '14- 3; WY: '13- 4; WUG: '15- 2; WI: '16- 5, '18- 4. NZ champion 2016.
Pole vault records: World junior 2015, Oceania & Commonwealth (6) 2016-18, 12 NZ 2014-18, Oceania indoor 2018.
Progress at PV: 2012- 3.85, 2013- 4.11, 2014- 4.45, 2015- 4.64, 2016- 4.80, 2017- 4.82, 2018- 4.94.

NIGERIA

Governing body: The Athletic Federation of Nigeria. Founded 1944.

Women

Oluwatobiloda 'Tobi' AMUSAN b. 23 Apr 1997 Ijebu Ode1.56m 57kg. University of Texas at El Paso.
At 100mh: OG: '16- sf; WCh: '17- sf; CG: '18- 1/3R; WJ: '16- 5; AfG: '15- 1; Af Ch: '18: 1; CCp: '18- 5/dqR Won Af-J 2015 (1R '13&15), NCAA 2017. At 60mh: WI: '18- 7. At 200m: WY: '13- sf.
Unratified world junior best for 100mh 2016.
Progress at 100mh: 2014- 13.89, 2015- 12.11, 2016- 12.83A/12.79w, 2017- 12.57, 2018- 12.68/12.61w.
pbs: 100m 11.50 '16, 200m 22.92A/23.35i/22.60Aw '17, 60mh 7.89Ai/7.90i '18, LJ 6.15Ai '17, 6.06 '16.

Ese BRUME b. 20 Jan 1996 Ugheli, Delta State 1.67m 58kg. Student at University of Benin.
At LJ: OG: '16- 5; WCh: '17- dnq 17; CG: '14- 1; WJ: '14- dnq 33; AfG: '15- 4; Af Ch: '14-16-18: 1/1/1; CCp: '14- 5, '18- 5. Won Af-J LJ & 4x100m 2013 & 2015, TJ 2015; NGR LJ 2014, 2016-17.
Progress at LJ: 2012- 6.02, 2013- 6.53, 2014- 6.68, 2015- 6.61, 2016- 6.83, 2017- 6.64/6.68w, 2018- 6.83. pbs: 100m 11.84 '14, 200m 24.20 '18, 400m 55.53 '16, TJ 13.16A '15.

Blessing OKAGBARE b. 9 Oct 1988 Sapele 1.80m 68kg. Married name Ighoteguonor. Was at University of Texas at El Paso.
At LJ/(100m): OG: '08- 2, '12- dnq 15/8; '16- (sf, sf 200m), WCh: '11- dnq 18/5; '13- 2/6 (3 200m), '15- (8), '17- 8/(sf); CG: '14- 1 100m & 200m/2R, '18- 3R; AfG: '07- 2 (4 TJ), '11- 1/2; AfCh: '10-

1/1/1R, '12- 1/2, '14- (1)/1R, '18- 1R; WJ: '06- dnq 17 (dnq 16 TJ); CCp: '10- 6/3/3R, '18- dqR; Won Nigerian 100m 2009-14, 2016; 200m 2013-14, 2016; LJ 2008-09, 2011-13; TJ 2008; NCAA 100m & LJ 2010.
African records 100m (2) 2013, 200m 2018, 4x200m 2015, Nigerian & African junior TJ record 2007.
Progress at 100m, 200m, LJ: 2004- 5.85 irreg, 2006- 6.16, 2007- 6.51, 2008- 23.76A, 6.91; 2009- 11.16, 6.73/6.90w; 2010- 11.00/10.98w/10.7Aw, 22.71, 6.88; 2011- 11.08/11.01w, 22.94, 6.78/6.84w; 2012- 10.92, 22.63, 6.97; 2013- 10.79/10.75w, 22.31, 7.00/7.14w; 2014- 10.85, 22.23, 6.86; 2015- 10.80, 22.67, 6.66; 2016- 11.02/10.92w, 22.58, 6.73; 2017- 10.99, 22.87, 6.77; 2018- 10.90/10.72w, 22.04. pbs: 60m 7.18i '10, 300m 37.04 '13, 400m 53.34 '15, TJ 14.13 '07.
Majestic winner of Commonwealth Games sprint double in 2014. Married football international Jude Igho Otegheri on 7 Nov 2014.

NORWAY

Governing body: Norges Friidrettsforbund. Founded 1896.
National Championships first held in 1896 (men), 1947 (women, walks 1937). **2018 Champions: Men**: 100m/200m: Jonathan Quarcoo 10.70/20.84, 400m/400mh: Karsten Warholm 47.32/49.01, 800m: Thomas Roth 1:50.63, 1500m: Jakob Ingebrigtsen 4:03.54, 5000m: Henrik Ingebrigtsen 14:13.80, 10000m/HMar: Okubamichael Fissehatsion ERI 29:34.99/67:38, Mar: Ebrahim Abdulaziz ERI 2:19:27, 3000mSt: Tom Erling Kårbo 8:58.49, 110mh: Vladimir Vukicevic 13.84, HJ: Erlend Bolstad Raa 2.00, PV: Sondre Guttormsen 5.50, LJ: Henrik Flåtnes 7.51w, TJ: Ingar Kiplesund 14.83w, SP: Marcus Thomsen 19.82, DT: Ola Stunes Isene 60.46, HT: Eivind Henriksen 74.27, JT: Gardar Johann Fridriksson 64.99, Dec: *none*, 5000mW: Håvard Haukenes 19:41.20, 10,000W: Tobias Lømo 53:01.79. **Women**: 100m: Ezinne Okparaebo 11.68, 200m/400mh: Line Kloster 24.03/58.64, 400m: Amalie Hammild Iuel 54.68, 800m: Hedda Hynne 2:06.97, 1500m/5000m: Sigrid Jervell Våg 4:31.14/16:19.14, 10000m: Pernilla Epland 34:04.98, HMar: Rune Falch 75:32, Mar: Marthe Katrine Myhre 2:46:48, 3000mSt: Delphine Poirot FRA 11:21.46, 100mh: Isabelle Pedersen 13.04, HJ: Tonje Angelsen 1.85, PV: Birgitte Kjuus 3.90, LJ/TJ: Oda Utsi Onstad 6.25w/13.33, SP: Matilde Roe 13.39, DT: Mona Ekroll Jaidi 34.96, HT: Trude Raad 63.96, JT: Sigrid Borge 60.70, Hep: Telma Eid 4169, 3000mW: Merete Helgheim 13:55.77, 5000mW: Siri Gamst Glittenberg 26:48.90.

Håvard HAUKENES b. 22 Apr 1990 Bergen 1.80m 68kg. IL Gular
At 50kW: OG: '16- 7; WCh: '13- dq, '15- 24, '17-

dq; EC: '18- 4. At 20kW: EC: '14- dq. Won NOR 5000mW 2017-18, 20kW 2014, 2016; 50kW 2012.
Progress at 50kW: 2011- 4:04:48, 2012- 3:56:38, 2015- 3:56:50, 2016- 3:46:33, 2017- 3:43:40, 2018- 3:48:35, 2019- 3:42:50. pbs: 3000mW 11:44.17 '15, 5000mW 19:19.79 '16, 10000mW 42:39.5 '16, 20kW 1:23:15 '16.

Filip Mangen **INGEBRIGTSEN** b. 20 Apr 1993 Stavanger 1.87m 75kg. Sandnes IL
At 1500m: OG: '16- h; WCh: '17- 3; EC: '14-16-18: h/1/12; WJ: '10- h, '12- 9; EU23: '13- 6. At 800m: WJ: '14- 7; EU23: '13- h; EJ: 11- h. Eur CC: '18- 1; Won NOR 800m 2016, 1500m 2013.
Norwegian 1500m record 2018.
Progress at 1500m: 2011- 3:51.70, 2012- 3:44.04, 2013- 3:38.76, 2014- 3:40.48, 2015- 3:42.32, 2016- 3:32.43, 2017- 3:32.48. 2018- 3:30.01. pbs: 800m 1:47.79 '16, 1000m 2:16.95 '16, 1M 3:53.23 '17, 3000m 7:49.70 '16, 5000m 13:30.48 '18, 10k Rd 28:47 '18, 2000mSt 5:46.15 '12.
Marrtied Astrid Mangen Cederqvist (60m 7.47i '18, 200m 23.56 '18) on 15 Sep 18,

Henrik Børkja **INGEBRIGTSEN** b. 24 Feb 1991 Stavanger 1.80m 69kg. Sandnes IL
At 1500m/(5000m): OG: '12- 5, '16- sf; WCh: '13- 8, '15- h; EC: '10 12 14 16: h/1/2/3&1/4&- 2; WJ: '10- h; EU23: '11- h, '13- (1); EJ: '09- h; CCp: '14- 4; EI: '15- 6. At 3000m: CCp: 18- 3; EI: '15-17-19: 3/2/3. Won NOR 800m 2013, 1500m 2010, 2012, 2014; 5000m 2015, 2018. Eur CC: '12- 1 U23, '17- 11. Norwegian records: 1500m (4) 2012-14, 1M (3) 2012-14.
Progress at 1500m: 2004- 4:30.63, 2005- 4:22.48, 2006- 4:04.15, 2007- 3:54.08, 2008- 3:50.63, 2009- 3:44.53, 2010- 3:38.61, 2011- 3:39.50, 2012- 3:35.43, 2013- 3:33.95, 2014- 3:31.46, 2015- 3:32.85, 2016- 3:34.57, 2017- 3:38.96, 2018- 3:35.61. pbs: 800m 1:48.09 '14, 1M 3:50.72 '14, 3000m 7:42.19 '13, 2M 8:22.31 '18, 5000m 13:16.97 '18, 10k Rd 28:41 '18, 2000mSt 5:41.03 '09, 3000mSt 8:52.56 '09.
Younger brothers: **Filip** (qv) and **Jakob** (qv)

Jakob INGEBRIGTSEN b. 19 Sep 2000 Sandnes 1.81m 65kg. Sandnes IL
At 1500m/(5000m): EC: 18- 1/1; WJ: '16- 9, '18- 2/3; EJ. 17- 8/1, EI. '19- 2 (1 3000m); CCp: 18- 3. At 3000mSt: WCh: '17- h; EJ: '17- 1. Won EU20CC 2016-18, NOR 1500m 2017-18, 5000m, 3000mSt 2017.
Records: Two world U20 indoor 1500m 2019. European U20 1500m, 1M, 5000m (2) & 3000m ind 2018 & 2019.
Progress at 1500m, 5000m: 2015- 3:48.37, 2016- 3:42.44, 14:38.67; 2017- 3:39.92, 13:35.84; 2018- 3:31.18, 13:17.06. pbs: 800m 1:49.40 '17, 1M 3:52.28 '18, 3000m 7:56.74i '18, 8:00.01 '17; 3000mSt 8:26.81 '17.
In 2017 he was the youngest ever sub-4 minute miler at 16 and in 2018 became the youngest ever male European champion, winning the 1500m at 17yr 323d and next day won the 5000m.

Sondre Nordstad MOEN b. 12 Jan 1991 Trondheim 1.78m 62kg. SK Vidar.
At Mar: OG: '16- 19; EC: '18- dnf. At 5000m: WCh: '17- h; EC: '10- h; WJ: '08- 14, EJ: '09- 5. At 10000m: EC: '10- 14, '14- 9; EU23: '11- 1; Eur CC: '07-08-09-10-11: 6J/2J/4J/5J/3 U23. Won NOR 5000m 2011, 10000 & HMar 2015, CC 2014.
European marathon record 2017, Norwegian records half marathon and marathon (2) 2017.
Progress at Mar: 2015- 2:12:43, 2016- 2:14:17, 2017- 2:05:48. Pbs: 1500m 3:48.65 '14, 3000m 7:52.55 '17, 5000m 13:20.16 '17, 10000m 28:15.12 '17, Road: 10M 47:32 '16, 10k 27:55 '17, 15k 43:52 '11, HMar 59:48 '17, 3000mSt 9:10.01 '08.
Won Fukuoka marathon 2017.

Karsten WARHOLM b. 28 Feb 1996 Volda 1.87m 78kg. Dimna IL.
At 400m: OG: '16- sf; WCh: '17- 1; EC: '16- 6, '18- 1 (8 400m); EU23: '17- 1; CCp: '18- 3. At 400m: EC: '14- h; EU23: '17- 2; EJ: '15- 2; EI: '19- 1; At Oct: WY: '13- 1; At Dec: WJ: '14- 10; EJ: '15- 2. Won NOR 400m & 400mh 2015-18, 110mh 2013-14.
Records: European indoor 400m 2019, four European U23 400mh 2018, NOR: 300m 2018, 400m (2) 2016-17, 400mh (10) 2016-18.
Progress at 400mh: 2014- 52.20, 2015- 51.09, 2016- 48.49, 2017- 48.22, 2018- 47.64. pbs: 60m 6.75i '17, 100m 10.49i '17, 10.52 '16; 200m 20.92i/21.09 '16, 21.00w '15; 300m 32.69 '18, 400m 44.87 '17, 1000m 2:45.80i '13, 1500m 4:44.73 '15, 60mh 8.10i '15, 110mh 14.30 '15, HJ 2.05 '14, PV 4.30 '15, LJ 7.66 '15, TJ 14.48i/14.33 '12, SP 9.18 '14, DT 29.40 '14, JT 45.82 '15.
Won many NOR age group titles at wide range of events. EJ silver at 400m & Dec in 2015 even though 400m was in the middle of the decathlon first day. IAAF Rising Star of the Year 2017.

Women

Karoline Bjerkeli GRØVDAL b. 14 Jun 1990 Ålesund1.67m 52kg. Sportsklubben Vidar.
At 1500m: WCh: '17- h; ET: '15- 2. At 3000m: EI: '19- 5; At 5000m/(10000m): OG: '12- h, '16- 7/9; WCh: 13- 13, '15- h, '17- dnf; (h 1500m) EC: '10- 9/dnf, '14- 12, '16- (3); EJ: '09- 1; ET: '10- 3. At 3000mSt: WCh: '09- h; EC: '18- 3; EU23; '11- h; WJ: '06- 5; EJ: '07- 1, '09- 1. At 2000mSt: WY: '07- 3. Eur CC: '06-09-13-15-16-17-18: 2J/1J/ 5/3/3/3/3. Won NOR 1500m 2013, 2015; 5000m 2008, 2010, 2012, 2014; 3000mSt 2006, 2009-10.
NOR records 1M 2016, 3000mSt 2007 & 2017, 2000mSt 2018.
Progress at 5000m, 10000m, 3000mSt: 2005- 11:07.5, 2006- 9:55.95, 2007- 15:55.62, 9:33.19; 2008- 16:08.22; 2009- 15:29.82, 9:33.34; 2010- 15:25.40, 9:39.54; 2011- 15:44.92, 9:46.07; 2012- 15:24.86, 2013- 15:16.27mx, 2014- 15:47.63, 2015- 15:15.18; 2016- 14:57.53, 31:14.07; 2017- 15:00.44. 9:13.35; 2018- 9:18.36. pbs: 800m 2:04.23 '16, 1500m 4:05.57 '18, 1M 4:26.23 '16, 2000m 5:41.04 '18, 3000m 8:37.58 '17, HMar 69:41 '12, 2000mSt 6:21.39 '08.

PANAMA

Governing body: Federación Panameña de Atletismo. Founded 1945.

Alonso EDWARD b. 8 Dec 1989 Ciudad de Panamá 1.83m 73kg. Was at Barton County CC.
At (100m)/200m: OG: '12- h, '16- 7; WCh: '09-11-13-15-17: 2/dnf/sf/4/h; WJ: '08- (h); PAm: '15- 3; SAG: '14 & '18- (1); SACh: '09- 1/1, SAm-J: '07- (1), SAm-Y: '06- 1/1; CCp: '14- 1, '18- 1. Won DL 2014-16, C.American 2012, C.AmG 100m 2010, 200m 2013; SAmG 100m 2014.
Records: S.American 200m 2009, Panama 100m (3) 2009-18, 200m (5) 2007-09; South American Junior 100m 2007.
Progress at 100m, 200m: 2006- 10.60, 21.18; 2007- 10.28/10.25w, 20.62; 2008- 10.63, 20.96; 2009- 10.09/9.97w, 19.81; 2010- 10.24/10.08w, 2011- 20.28, 2012- 21.23A, 2013- 10.13, 20.37/20.32w; 2014- 10.02, 19.84; 2015- 10.29, 19.87; 2016- 19.92, 2017- 10.00w, 20.61; 2018- 10.01A/10.02, 19.90. pbs: 300m 34.17 '17, 400m 47.40i '10.
World age-19 best 19.81 in World final 2009. Injured in April 2010; did not compete for the rest of the season, and then suffered a 10cm career-threatening hamstring tear in the 2011 World 200m final. Younger brother Mateo (b. 1 May 1993): 60m 6.73i PAN record, 100m 10.29 & 200m 21.48 '14.

PERU

Governing body: Federación Peruana de Atletismo.

Kimberley GARCÍA b. 19 Oct 1993 Huancayo 1.67m 44kg.
At 20kW: OG: '16- 14; WCh: '13/15/17: 33/dnf/7; WCp: '16- 12, '18- 8; PAm: 15- 5; SAG: '18- 1; SACh: '14- 1. At 10000mW: WJ: '12- 10. At 5000mW: WY: '09- dnf; YOG: '10- 7.
S.American walks record 10k 2017, 20k 2014. Five Peru 20kW records 2013-18, 10000mW 2018.
Progress at 20kW: 2013- 1:33:57, 2014- 1:29:44, 2015- 1:31:13, 2016- 1:29:38, 2017- 1:29:13, 2018- 1:28:56. Pbs: 5000mW 22:57.4 '11, 10000mW 42:56.97 '18.

POLAND

Governing body: Polski Zwiazek Lekkiej Atletyki (PZLA). Founded 1919.
National Championships first held in 1920 (men), 1922 (women). **2018 Champions: Men:** 100m/200m: Dominik Kopec 10.25/20.70, 400m: Karol Zalewski 45.53, 800m: Marcin Lewandowski 1:50.27, 1500m: Adam Kszczot 3:46.24, 5000m/3000mSt: Krystian Zalewski 14:15.59/8:40.45, 10000m: Tomasz Grycko 28:56.81, HMar: Szymon Kulka 65:13, Mar: Yared Shegumo 2:13:53, 110mh: Damian Czykier 13.37, 400mh: Patryk Dobek 49.17, HJ: Maciej Grynienko 2.21, PV: Pawel Wojciechowski 5.70, LJ: Tomasz Jaszczuk 8.10,

TJ: Adrian Swiderski 15.89, SP: Michal Haratyk 21.85, DT: Piotr Malachowski 65.78, HT: Wojciech Nowicki 80.26, JT: Marcin Krukowski 82.87, Dec: Pawel Wiesolek 7921, 10000mW: Dawid Tomala 40:17.62, 20kW Artur Brzozowski 1:22:19, 50kW: Jakub Jelonek 4:05:28. **Women:** 100m: Ewa Swoboda 11.12w, 200m: Martyna Kotwila 22.99, 400m: Malgorzata Holub-Kowalik 51.18, 800m: Anna Sabay 2:06.14, 1500m: Sofia Ennaoui 4:13.32, 5000m/HMar: Paulina Kaczynska 16:25.46/74:28, 10000m: Katarzyna Rutkowska 33:24.08, Mar: Karolina Pilarska 2:49:06, 3000mSt: Matylda Kowal 9:53.18, 100mh: Klaudia Siciarz 12.74w, 400mh: Joanna Linkiewicz 56.21, HJ: Michalina Kwasniewska 1.84, PV: Justyna Smietanka 4.50, LJ/TJ: Anna Jagaciak Michalska 6.47/14.24, SP: Paulina Guba 18.82, DT: Lidia Augustyniak 55.84, HT: Anna Wlodarczyk 79.59, JT: Marcelina Witek 55.97, Hep: Paulina Ligarska 5845, 5000mW/20kW: Paulina Buziak 22:50.68/ 1:35:36, 50kW: Agnieszka Ellward 4:32:47.

Rafal AUGUSTYN b. 14 May 1984 Chyki-Debiaki, near Mielec 1.78m 71kg. LKS Stal Mielec.
At 50kW: OG: '16- 22; WCh: '09- 21, '15- 28, '17- 7; EC: '14- 9, '18- 6; WCp: '12- 7, '18- 7; ECp: '11- 6. At 20kW: OG: '08- 29, '12- 29; WCh: '07-11-13: 26/19/19; EC: '10- 9; EU23: '05- 4; WCp: '10- 14; ECp: '09- 7, '13- 8. Won POL 20kW 2007, 50kW 2010-11, 2014-17.
Progress at 50kW: 2009- 3:52:16, 2010- 3:49:54, 2011- 3:46:56, 2012- 3:49:53, 2013- 3:51:33, 2014- 3:45:32, 2015- 3:43:55, 2016- 3:43:22, 2017- 3:44:18, 2018- 3:48:22. pbs: 3000mW 11:17.82 '11, 5000mW 19:16.51i '14, 19:26.55 '11; 10kW 39:47 '10, 40:37.73t '06; 20kW 1:20:53 '12, 30kW 2:13:36 '14, 35kW 2:36:55 '15.

Sylwester BEDNAREK b. 28 Apr 1989 Glówno 1.98m 75kg. RKS Lódz.
At HJ: OG: '16- dnq 30=; WCh: '09- 3, '15/17- dnq 33=/20=; EC: '10-16-18: 10=/dnq 16/7; WJ: '06- 4, '08- 2; WY: '05- 4; E23: '09- 1; EJ: '07- 6; WI: '18- 5; EI: '17- 1, '19- 6. Won POL 2014-15, 2017.
Progress at HJ: 2003- 1.76, 2004- 2.06, 2005- 2.22, 2006- 2.26, 2007- 2.22, 2008- 2.24, 2009- 2.32, 2010- 2.26, 2012- 2.20, 2013- 2.22, 2014- 2.25, 2015- 2.30, 2016- 2.30, 2017- 2.33i/2.32, 2018- 2.33i/2.27.

Konrad BUKOWIECKI b. 17 Mar 1997 Olsztyn 1.91m 140kg. KS AZS UWM Olsztyn.
At SP: OG: '16- nt; WCh: '15- dnq, '17- 8; EC: '16- 4, '18- 2; WJ: '14- 1, '16- dq1 & 5 DT; WY: '13- 5; EU23: '17- 1; EJ: '15- 1 (dnq 13 DT); Yth OG: '10- 1; WI: '16- 4, '18- 8; EI: '15- 6; WUG: '17- 2; ET: 17- 3. Polish champion 2016.
Shot records: Four world junior 7.26kg 2015-16, (6kg 23.34dq '16), indoor 6kg (4) 22.38 '15 to 22.96 '16, World youth 5kg 2 out to 22.24 & 5 indoor to 24.24 in 2014; European junior (5) 2015, indoor (3) 2016, U23 indoor 2017 & 2018.

Progress at SP: 2014- 17.29i, 2015- 20.78, 2016-21.14, 2017- 21.97i/21.59, 2018- 22.00i/21.66, 2019-21.32. Pb DT 58.42 '17.
Lost his 2016 World Junior gold with a public warning for a banned stimulant.

Patryk DOBEK b. 13 Feb 1994 Koscierzyna 1.83m 75kg. MKL Szczecin.
At 400mh: OG: '16- h; WCh: '15- 7, '17- sf; EC: '14- sf, '18- 5; EU23: '15- 1/2R; ET: '15- 2, '17- 3; Polish champion 2014-18. At 400m: WJ: '12-sf/2R; WY: '11- 3; EJ: '13- 2/2R.
Progress at 400mh: 2012- 52.00, 2013- 50.67, 2014- 49.13, 2015- 48.40, 2016- 49.01, 2017- 49.15, 2018- 48.59. pbs: 200m 21.38 '15, 300m 33.34 '13, 400m 46.15 '13, 600m 1:15.78 '14.

Pawel FAJDEK b. 4 Jun 1989 Swiebodzice 1.86m 118kg. KS Agros Zamosc.
At HT: OG: '12- dnq, '16- dnq 17; WCh: '11-13-15-17: 11/1/1/1; EC: 14-16-18: 2/1/2; WJ: '08- 4; EU23: '09- 8, '11- 1; WUG: '11-13-15-17: 1/1/1/1; CCp: '14- 3; ET: '11-13-14-15-17: 2/1/2/1/1. Won POL 2012, 2014-16; Franc G 2013, IAAF HT challenge 2013, 2015-17.
Two Polish hammer records 2014-15.
Progress at HT: 2008- 64.58, 2009- 72.36, 2010-76.07, 2011- 78.54, 2012- 81.39, 2013- 82.27, 2014-83.48, 2015- 83.93, 2016- 82.47, 2017- 83.44, 2018-81.14. pb Wt 23.22i '14.
Won 16 of 17 competitions in 2015, 13/14 in 2016 and 15/16 in 2017, with respectively the top 12 /12/10 performances of the year at hammer. The clear favourite, he failed to qualify with only 72.00 for Olympic final 2016 after 29 successive wins, all over 78m.

Michal HARATYK b. 10 Apr 1992 Cieszyn 1.94m 136kg. KS Sprint Bielsko-Biala.
At SP: OG: '16- dnq 18; WCh: '17- 5; EC: '16- 2, '18- 1; EI: '19- 1; CCp: '18- 4; POL champion 2017.
Progress at SP: 2012- 17.72, 2013- 17.24, 2014-19.95, 2015- 20.10i/19.95, 2016- 21.35i/21.23, 2017-21.88, 2018- 22.08. pb DT 53.53 '13.
Elder brother Lukasz SP 18.82 '10.

Marcin KRUKOWSKI b. 14 Jun 1992 1.82m 92kg. KS Warszawianka W-wa.
At JT. OG. '16- dnq 15, WCh. '15-15-17: dnq 24/ dnq 15/9; EC: '16- 6, '18- 4; WJ: '10- dnq 27; WY: '09- 4; EU23: '13- 9; EJ: '11- 2. Won POL 2015-18.
Progress at JT: 2009- 65.95, 2010- 72.10, 2011-79.19, 2012- 82.58, 2013- 83.04, 2014- 80.66, 2015-85.20, 2016- 84.74, 2017- 88.09, 2018- 85.32.

Adam KSZCZOT b. 2 Sep 1989 Opoczno 1.78m 64kg. RKS Lódz. Studied organisation and management.
At 800m: OG: '12/16- sf; WCh: '09/13- sf, '11-15-17: 6/2/2; EC: '10-14-16-18: 3/1/1/1; WJ: '08- 4; EU23: '09/11- 1; EJ: '07- 3; WI: '10-12-14-18: 3/4/2/1; EI: '09-11-13-17: 4/1/1/1; CCp: '14- 3; ET: '11-13-14-15: 1/1/2/3. Won POL 800m 2009-10, 2012, 2014-15; 1500m 2017-18.
Polish 1000m record 2011 and 2014.

Progress at 800m: 2005- 1:59.57, 2006- 1:51.09, 2007- 1:48.10, 2008- 1:47.16, 2009- 1:45.72, 2010-1:45.07, 2011- 1:43.30, 2012- 1:43.83, 2013- 1:44.76, 2014- 1:44.02, 2015- 1:43.45, 2016- 1:43.76, 2017-1:44.84, 2018- 1:44.59. pbs: 400m 46.51 '11, 600m 1:14.55 '10, 1000m 2:15.72 '14, 1500m 3:38.31 '17.

Marcin LEWANDOWSKI b. 13 Jun 1987 Szczecin 1.80m 64kg. CWZS Zawisza Bydgoszcz. PE student.
At 800m: OG: '08/12- sf, '16- 6; WCh: '09-11-13-15-17: 8/4/4/sf/sf; EC: '10-14-16: 1/5/2; WJ: '06-4; EU23: '07- 1, '09- 2; WI: '14- dq (3); EI: '09-11-15: 6/2/1; CCp: '10- 2; ECp: '08- 2, '10- 3; won W.MilG 2011. At 1500m: WCh: '17- 7; EC: '18- 2, EJ: '05- 7; WI: '18- 2; EI: '13-17-19: 4/1/1; CCp: 18- 2; ET: '13-14-15-17: 3/3/2/1. Won Polish 800m 2011, 2016, 2018 1500m 2008, 2010, 2014, 2016. Polish 1000m record 2011 & 2016.
Progress at 800m: 2002- 1:57.86, 2003- 1:53.31, 2004- 1:51.73, 2005- 1:48.86, 2006- 1:46.69, 2007-1:45.52, 2008- 1:45.84, 2009- 1:43.84, 2010- 1:44.10, 2011- 1:44.53, 2012- 1:44.34, 2013- 1:43.79, 2014-1:44.03, 2015- 1:43.72, 2016- 1:43.73, 2017- 1:44.77, 2018- 1:44.32. pbs: 400m 47.76 '09, 600m 1:15.17 '14, 1000m 2:14.30 '16, 1500m 3:34.04 '17, 1M 3:56.41i '19, 3000m 8:16.00i '19.
Coached by brother Tomasz (1:51.00 '03).

Piotr LISEK b. 16 Aug 1992 Duszniki, Poznan 1.94m 96kg. OSOT Szczecin.
At PV: OG: '16- 4=; WCh: '15- 3=, '17- 2; EC: '14-16-18: 6/4=/4; EU23: '13- dnq 17; ET: '15- 3; WI: 16- 3; WI: '18- 3; EI: '15-17-19: 3/1/2. Won POL 2017.
Three Polish indoor pole vault records 2015-17.
Progress at PV: 2006- 3.20, 2007- 3.30, 2008- 4.10, 2009- 4.42, 2010- 4.70, 2011- 5.10i/5.00, 2012- 5.20, 2013- 5.60, 2014- 5.82, 2015- 5.90i/5.82, 2016-5.77i/5.75, 2017- 6.00i/5.89, 2018- 5.94.
6-months drugs ban in 2012. Married to Aleksandra Wisnik (PV 4.15 '14).

Piotr MALACHOWSKI b. 7 Jun 1983 Zuromin 1.94m 135kg. WKS Slask Wroclaw. Army corporal.
At DT: OG: '08- 2, '12- 5, '16- 2; WCh: '07-09-11-13-15-17: 12/2/9/2/1/5; EC: 06-10-14-16-18: 6/1/4/1/dnq; WJ: '02- 6; EU23: '03- 9, '05- 2; EJ: '01- 5; CCp: '10- 4; ECp: '06-07-08-09-10-11-14: 1/1/3/1/2/3/2. Won DL 2010, 2014-16; POL 2005-10, 2012-15, 2018.
Nine Polish discus records 2006-13.
Progress at DT: 1999- 39.48, 2000- 52.04, 2001-54.19, 2002- 56.84, 2003- 57.83, 2004- 62.04, 2005-64.74, 2006- 66.21, 2007- 66.61, 2008- 68.65, 2009-69.15, 2010- 69.83, 2011- 68.49, 2012- 68.94, 2013-71.84, 2014- 69.28, 2015- 68.29, 2016- 68.15, 2017-67.68, 2018- 65.78.

Wojciech NOWICKI b. 22 Feb 1989 Bialystok 1.96m 112kg. KS Podlasie Bialystok.
At HT: OG: '16- 3; WCh: '15- 3, '17- 3; EC: '16- 3, '128- 1; EU23: '11- 5; CCp: 18- 6. Won POL 2017-

18, IAAF HT challenge 2018.
Progress at HT: 2008- 55.71, 2009- 64.41, 2010-
69.59, 2011- 72.72, 2012- 73.52, 2013- 75.87, 2014-
76.14, 2015- 78.71, 2016- 78.36, 2017- 80.87, 2018-
81.85. pb Wt 22.72i '14.
World number one in 2019 when his 7-5 record
against Pawel Fajdek took their career record to
67-10 in Fajdek's favour 2009-18.

Robert URBANEK b. 29 Apr 1987 Leczyca
2.00m 120kg. MKS Aleksandrów Lódzki.
At DT: OG: '12/16- dnq 32/17; WCh: '13-15-17:
6/3/7; EC: '12-14-16-18: 6/3/9/dnq 14; EU23: '09-
7; CCp: '14- 6; ET: '15- 1, 17- 2. Won POL 2017.
Progress at DT: 2004- 47.09, 2005- 47.83, 2006-
50.84, 2007- 56.18, 2008- 62.22, 2009- 60.54, 2010-
60.74, 2011- 64.37, 2012- 66.93, 2013- 65.30, 2014-
65.75, 2015- 66.31, 2016- 65.56, 2017- 66.73, 2018-
65.15. pb SP 16.21 '07.

Pawel WOJCIECHOWSKI b. 6 Jun 1989
Bydgoszcz 1.90m 81kg. CWKS Zawisza
Bydgoszcz. PE student.
At PV: OG: '12- dnq, '16- dnq 16=; WCh: '11- 1,
'15- 3=, '17- 5; EC: '14-16-18: 2/7=/5; WJ: '08- 2;
EU23: '11- 1; EJ: '07- dnq 16; EI: '11-17-19: 4/3/1;
CCp: '14- 5. Won W.MilG 2011, POL 2015-16,
2018.
Polish pole vault record 2011 and 2017.
Progress at PV: 2001- 2.50, 2002- 2.70, 2003- 3.10,
2004- 3.50, 2005- 4.10, 2006- 4.70, 2007- 5.00,
2008- 5.51, 2009- 5.40i/5.22, 2010- 5.60, 2011- 5.91,
2012- 5.62, 2014- 5.80, 2015- 5.84, 2016- 5.84i/5.71,
2017- 5.93, 2018- 5.88i/5.84, 2019- 5.90i.

Women

Sofia ENNAOUI b. 30 Aug 1995 Ben Guerir,
Morocco 1.58m 43kg. MKL Szczecin.
At 1500m: OG: '16- 10; WCh: '15/17- sf; EC: '16-
7, '18- 2; WJ: '12- 10, '14- 5; EU23: '15- 2, '17- 2; EJ:
'13- 2; CCp: '18- 7; EI: '17- 3, '19- 2. At 800m:
WCh: '15- sf; WJ: '11- h, At 3000m: WJ: '14- dnf;
ET: '15- 1, '17- 1; EI: '15- 6; Eur CC: '13- 2J, '16- 1
U23. Won POL 1500m 2015, 2017.
Progress at 1500m: 2012- 4:13.68, 2013- 4:12.05,
2014- 4:07.34, 2015- 4:04.26. 2016- 4:01.00, 2017-
4:03.35, 2018- 4:02.06. pbs: 400m 56.07 '15, 800m
2:00.11 '15, 1000m 2:35.15 '16, 1M 4:23.34 '18,
3000m 8:45.29i '17, 8:59.44 '14.
Moroccan father, she moved to Poland with her
Polish mother at the age of 2.

Joanna FIODOROW b. 4 Mar 1989 Augustów
1.69m 89kg. OS AZS Poznan.
At HT: OG: '12- 7, '16- 9; WCh: '11-15: dnq 21/17,
'17- 6; EC: '14-16-18: 3/10/3; WJ: '08- dnq 19;
EU23: '09- 4, '11- 2; ET: '14- 2; WUG: '15- 2, '17- 3.
Progress at HT: 2005- 40.96, 2006- 50.18, 2007-
55.93, 2008- 61.22, 2009- 62.80, 2010- 64.66, 2011-
70.06, 2012- 74.18, 2013- 68.92, 2014- 74.39, 2015-
72.67, 2016- 72.98, 2017- 75.09, 2018- 74.39. pbs: SP
12.87 '10, JT 35.56 '09.

Paulina GUBA b. 14 May 1991 Otwock 1.80m
90kg. AZS UMCS Lublin.

At SP: OG: '16- dnq 13; WCh: '15-11, '17- dnq 17;
EC: '12-16-18: 10/11/1; WJ: '10- 7; E23: '11- 4, '13-
5; EJ:' 09- 4; WUG: '15-2, '17- 3; CCp: '18- 4; WI:
'18- 5, EI: '15- 5, '17- 6. POL champion 2011-12,
2014-15, 2017-18.
Progress at SP: 2007- 14.01, 2008- 14.05, 2009-
15.63, 2010- 15.80i/15.70, 2011- 17.17, 2012- 17.79/
17.47, 2013- 17.17, 2014- 16.78i/16.70, 2015- 17.95,
2016- 18.63i/17.74, 2017- 18.24, 2018- 19.38.

Anna   JAGACIAK-MICHALSKA   (née
Jagaciak) b. 10 Feb 1990 Zielona Góra 1.78m
68kg. OS AZS Poznan.
At (LJ)/TJ: OG: '16- 10; WCh: '11- dnq 28, '13- 9,
'17- 6; EC: '10- 10/dnq 15, '12- (dnq 22), '14- dnq
15, '16- 4, '18- dnq 14; WJ: '08- 7/dnq 14; WY: '07-
(dnq 13); EU23: '11- 4/3; EJ: '09- 3/4; EI: '17- 4;
WUG: '13- 2, 15- 2/3. Won POL LJ 2010, 2016-17;
TJ 2013-14, 2016-17; FrancG LJ & TJ 2013.
Progress at TJ: 2007- 12.62, 2008- 13.43, 2009-
13.55, 2010- 13.93/14.16w, 2011- 14.25, 2012-
13.87/14.06w, 2013- 14.21, 2014- 14.20, 2015- 14.17,
2016- 14.33/14.40w, 2017- 14.29, 2018- 14.24. pb LJ
6.74 '10.
Married Lukasz Michalski (PV 5.85 '11, 4 WCh
& 1 WUG 2011) in July 2014.

Joanna JÓZWIK b. 30 Jan 1991 Walbrzych
1.68m 53kg. AZS-AWF Warszawa.
At 800m: OG: '16- 5; WCh: '15- 7, '17- sf; EC: '14-
3, '16- 6; WJ: '10- sf; EU23: '11- h, '13- 8; ET: '15- 2;
EI: '15- 3. Polish champion 2014-15.
Progress at 800m: 2007- 2:12.90, 2008- 2:11.55,
2009- 2:07.31, 2010- 2:05.09, 2011- 2:03.15, 2012-
2:05.87, 2013- 2:02.39, 2014- 1:59.63, 2015- 1:58.35,
2016- 1:57.37, 2017- 1:59.29i, 2:00.77. pbs: 200m
24.16 '14, 300m 39.83 '11, 400m 53.08 '14, 600m
1:25.04 '15, 1000m 2:34.93 '16.

Malwina KOPRON b. 16 Nov 1994 Pulawy
1.69m 89kg. AZS UMCS Lublin.
At HT: OG: '16- dnq 15; WCh: '15- dnq 14, '17- 3;
EC: '16- 6, '18- 4; WJ: '12- dnq nt; WY: '11- 2;
EU23: '15- 3; EJ: '13- 4; WUG: '17- 1; ET: '17- 2.
Progress at HT: 2011- 57.03, 2012- 64.88, 2013-
66.11, 2014- 69.30, 2015- 71.27, 2016- 72.74, 2017-
76.85, 2018- 72.92. pb JT 51.66 '12.

Kamila LICWINKO b. 22 Mar 1986 Bielsk
Podlaski 1.83m 66kg. née Stepaniuk. KS
Podlasie Bialystok.
At HJ: OG: '16- 9; WCh: '09-13-15-17- dnq
16/7=/4/3; EC: '14- 9=; EU23: '07- 4; EJ: '05- 7;
WI: '14- 1=,'16- 3; EI: '09- 8, '15- 3; ET: '13-14-15-
17: 2/3=/3/1; WUG: '13- 1. Won POL 2007-09,
2015-17.
Polish high jump records 2013 & 2014, three
indoor 2015.
Progress at HJ: 1999- 1.46, 2000- 1.61, 2001- 1.66,
2002- 1.75, 2003- 1.75, 2004- 1.84, 2005- 1.86,
2006- 1.85i/1.84, 2007- 1.90, 2008- 1.91, 2009- 1.93,
2010- 1.92i/1.89, 2011- 1.88i, 2012- 1.89, 2013- 1.99,
2014- 2.00i/1.97, 2015- 2.02i/1.99, 2016- 1.99, 2017-
1.99.

Married her trainer Michal Licwinko in 2013. Baby born in 2018.

Justyna SWIETY-ERSETIC b. 3 Dec 1992 Racibórz 1.67m 57kg. née Swiety. AZS-AWF Katowice.

At 400m: OG: '16- sf; WCh: '17- h; EC: '12-14-16-18: 4h/sf/6/1&1R; E23: '13- 3/1R; EJ: '11- 2R; WI: '14-16-18: 4/5&2R/4&2R; EI: '15- 3R; 17- 3/1R, '19- 6/1R; CCp: '18- 6/dq mxR. Polish champion 2013, 2016 (6 indoor titles).
Progress at 400m: 2009- 55.55, 2010- 55.30, 2011- 55.51, 2012- 52.81, 2013- 52.22, 2014- 52.22, 2015- 52.44, 2016- 51.62, 2017- 51.15, 2018- 50.41. pbs: 200m 23.81 '14, 300m 36.58 '17, 600m 1:26.68 '14, 800m 2:04.78 '12.
Brilliant relay runner. Married international wrestler Dawid Ersetic on 16 Sep 2017.

Ewa SWOBODA b. 26 Jul 1997 Zory 1.64m 55kg. AZS-AWF Katowice.
At 100m: OG: '16- sf; WCh: '17- sf; EC: '18- sf; WJ: '14- 5 (dnf h 200m), '16- 2; WY: '13- 4; EU23: '17- 1; EJ: '15- 1/2R; ET: '15- 3, '17- 2R; At 60m: EI: '15-17-19: 8/2/1. Won Polish 100m 2017.
World junior 60m indoor record 2016.
Progress at 100m, 200m: 2011- 11.97, 2012- 12.02, 2013- 11.54/11.46w, 2014- 11.30, 2015- 11.24/11.21w, 2016- 11.12/11.10w; 2017- 11.24, 2018- 11.13/11.12w. pbs: 60m 7.07i '16, 200m 23.79 '18.

Anita WLODARCZYK b. 8 Aug 1985 Rawicz 1.76m 90kg. AZS-AWF Katowice. PE student.
At HT: OG: '08- 4, '12- 1, '16- 1; WCh: '09-11-13-15-17: 1/5/1/1/1; EC: '10-12-14-16-18: 3/1/1/1/1; EU23: '07- 9; CCp: '14- 1, '18- 2; ET: '09-13-15: 1/2/1. Won POL 2009, 2011-12, 2014-18; Franc G 2013, IAAF HT challenge 2013-18.
Six world hammer records 2009-16, six Polish records 2009-14.
Progress at HT: 2002- 33.83, 2003- 43.24, 2004- 54.74, 2005- 60.51, 2006- 65.53, 2007- 69.07, 2008- 72.80, 2009- 77.96, 2010- 78.30, 2011- 75.33, 2012- 77.60, 2013- 78.46, 2014- 79.58, 2015- 81.08, 2016- 82.98, 2017- 82.87, 2018- 79.59. pbs: SP 13.25 '06, DT 52.26 '08, Wt 20.09i '14.
In 2015 she had the eight best throws of the year, including when she became first woman to throw hammer over 80m with 81.08 at Cetniewo on 1 Aug 2015, and two 80m throws (80.27 and 80.85) later that month at the World Champs. She had the top 12 performances in 2016 and the top 9 in 2017, won all her competitions in 2015- 11, 2016- 12 and 2017- 12 to take her win streak to 42 from a last loss on 16 June 2014 to a loss on 26 May 2018.

PORTUGAL

Governing body: Federação Portuguesa de Atletismo. Founded 1921.
National Championships first held in 1910 (men), 1937 (women). **2018 Champions: Men:** 100m: Carlos Nascimento 10.26, 200m: Diego

Antunes 20.94, 400m: Ricardo dos Santos 47.36, 800m: José Carlos Pinto 1:51.31, 1500m: Luís Monteiro 3:53.98, 5000m: Samuel Barata 14:04.96, 10000m: Ricardo Dias 29:26.28, Mar: Élvio Silva 2:40:46, 3000mSt: André Pereira 8:46.39, 110mh: Hélio Vaz 14.30, 400mh: Diogo Mestre 50.96, HJ: Paulo Conceiçao & Victor Korat 2.08, PV: Diogo Ferreira 5.45, LJ: Ivo Tavares 7.50, TJ: Carlos Veiga 16.03, SP: Tsanko Arnaudov 19.60, DT: Francisco Belo 58.63, HT: António Vital e Silva 71.44, JT: Tiago Aperta 72.65, Dec: Samuel Remédios 6600, 10000mW/20kW/30kW: João Vieira 41:54.2/1:25:44/2:38:18, 50kW: Pedro Isidro 4:11:25. **Women:** 100m: Lorène Bazolo 11.51, 200m: Rosalina Santos 23.89, 400m: Cátia Azevedo 52.99, 800m: Salomé Afonso 2:06.59, 1500m: Nelde Dias 4:20.21, 5000m/10000m: Sara Moreira 15:54.12/32:10.50, Mar: Rosa Madureira 2:51:23, 3000mSt: Emília Pisoeiro 10:09.87, 100mh: Olímpia Barbosa 13.83, 400mh: Andreia Crespo 59.53, HJ: Anabela Neto 1.77, PV: Marta Onofre 4.31, LJ: Evelise Veiga 6.08, TJ: Susana Costa 13.81, SP: Jessica Inchude GBS 16.66, DT: Irina Rodrigues 56.75, HT: Vânia Silva 60.42, JT: Jéssica Barreira 50.80, Hep: Dânia Furk 4284, 10000mW/35kW: Inês Henriques 43:19.3/1:30:08/2:45:51, 50kW: Sandra Silva 5:08:13.

Nelson ÉVORA b. 20 Apr 1984 Abidjan, Côte d'Ivoire 1.81m 70kg. Sporting CP.
At (LJ/)TJ: OG: '04- dnq 40, '08- 1, '16- 6; WCh: '05-07-09-11-15-17: dnq 14/1/2/5/3/3; EC: '06-14-16-18: 6&1/6/dnq 17/1; WJ: '02- dnq 18/6; EU23: '05- 3; EJ: '03- 1/1; WUG: '09- 1, '11- 1; WI: '06-08-16-18: 6/3/4/3; EI: '07-15-17-19: 5/1/1/2; CCp: '18- 5; ECp: '09- 2/1; Won WAF TJ 2008, POR LJ 2006-07, 2016; TJ 2003-04, 2006-07, 2009-11, 2013-17.
Six Portuguese triple jump records 2006-07, Cape Verde LJ & TJ records 2001-02.
Progress at TJ: 1999- 14.35, 2000- 14.93i, 2001- 16.15, 2002- 15.87, 2003- 16.43, 2004- 16.85i/16.04, 2005- 16.89, 2006- 17.23, 2007- 17.74, 2008- 17.67, 2009- 17.66/17.82w, 2010- 16.36, 2011- 17.35, 2013- 16.68, 2014- 16.97, 2015- 17.52, 2016- 17.03, 2017- 17.20i/17.19, 2018- 17.40i/17.16. pbs: LJ 2.071 '08, 1.98 '99; LJ 8.10 '07.
Portugal's first male world champion in 2007. He suffered a serious injury in right tibia (in same place where he had an operation in February 2010) in January 2012 and missed season. Father from Cape Verde, mother from Côte d'Ivoire, relocating to Portugal when he was five. Switched nationality in 2002. Sister Dorothé (b. 28 May 1991) 400m pb 53.54 '18.

Pedro Pablo PICHARDO Peralta b. 30 Jun 1993 Santiago de Cuba 1.85m 71kg. SL Benfica.
At TJ: WCh: '13- 2, '15- 2; WJ: '12- 1; PAm: '15- 1; WI: '14- 3. Won DL 2018, CAC-J 2012, CUB 2014-15.
Three CAC triple jump records 2015.
Progress at TJ: 2009- 14.55, 2010- 15.35/15.45w,

2011- 16.09, 2012- 16.79, 2013- 17.69, 2014- 17.76, 2015- 18.08, 2017- 17.60, 2018- 17.95. pb LJ 7.81 '15.
Switched from Cuba and attained Portuguese citizenship on 23 Nov 2017. The IAAF have stated that he can compete for Portugal from 1 August 2019. Injured in 2016. Father Jorge was a 2.10 high jumper.

Women

Ana CABECINHA b. 29 Apr 1984 Beja 1.68m 52kg. CO Pechão.
At 20kW: OG: '08- 8, '12- 8, '16- 6; WCh: '11-13-15-17: 6/8/4/6; EC: '10-14-18: 7/6/8; EU23: '05- 4; WCp '08-10-12-14-16: 11/8/8/8/6; ECp: '13-15-17: 5/9/2. At 5000mW: WY: '01- 10. At 10000mW: WJ: '02- 12; EJ: '03- 3; won IbAm 2006, 2010; 2nd RWC 2012; POR 10000mW 2005, 2008, 2010, 2012, 2014-17; 20kW 2012-15, 2017.
POR records 10,000m and 20km walk 2008.
Progress at 20kW: 2004- 1:37:39, 2005- 1:34:13, 2006- 1:31:02, 2007- 1:32:46, 2008- 1:27:46, 2009- 1:33:05, 2010- 1:31:14, 2011- 1:31:08, 2012- 1:28:03, 2013- 1:29:17, 2014- 1:27:49, 2015- 1:28:28, 2016- 1:28:40, 2017- 1:28:57, 2018- 1:29.41. pbs: 3000mW 12:17.50 '14, 5000mW 21:22.23 '15, 21:21R '12; 10000mW 43:08.17 '08; run: 1500m 4:31.73 '07, 3000m 9:44.81i '17, 9:46.08 '13; 5000m 17:57.34 '12.
Susana COSTA b. 22 Sep 1984 Setúbal 1.78m 65kg. Benfica.
At TJ: OG: '16- 9; WCh: '15: dnq, '17- 11; EC: '12-14-16-18: dnq 13/8/5/11; EI: '17- 7, '19- 5. POR champion 2003, 2005-06, 2018; IbAm 2012.
Nine Portuguese triple jump records 2009-16.
Progress at TJ: 2002-= 12.62, 2003- 12.68, 2004- 13.02i/13.00/13.11w, 2005- 13.07i/12.89/13.53w, 2006- 13.12/13.51w, 2007- 13.49i/12.88/13.27w, 2008- 13.77i/13.36, 2009- 12.91, 2010- 12.62/12.75w, 2011- 13.70/13.77w, 2012- 14.19, 2013- 14.16, 2014- 14.11, 2015- 14.32, 2016- 14.34, 2017- 14.35, 2018- 14.17, 2019- 14.43i. pb LJ 5.86i/5.97w '06.
Inês HENRIQUES b 1 May 1980 Santarém 1.56m 48kg. CN Rio Maior.
At 50kW: WCh: '17- 1; EC: '18- 1. At 20kW: OG: '04-12-16: 25/14/12; WCh: '01-05-07-09-11-13-15: dq/27/7/ 10/9/11/23; EC: '02-06-10-14: 15/12/8/13; EU23: '01- 10; WCp: '06-10-12-16: 13/3/9/8; ECp: '07- 7, '13- 8; Won POR 10000mW 2006, 2009, 2011, 2013, 2018; 20kW 2009, 2011, 2016, 2018; 35kW 2017-18, 50kW 2017. At 5000mW: EJ: '99- 12.
World walks records 50k (2) 2017, 35k 2018.
Progress at 20kW: Walk: 2000- 1:41:09, 2001- 1:34:49, 2002- 1:34:46.5t, 2003- 1:36:03, 2004- 1:31:23.7t, 2005- 1:33:24, 2006- 1:30:28, 2007- 1:30:24, 2008- 1:31:06, 2009- 1:30:34, 2010- 1:29:36, 2011- 1:30:29, 2012- 1:29:54, 2013- 1:29:30, 2014- 1:29:33, 2015- 1:29:52, 2016- 1:29:00, 2017- 1:30:44, 4:05:56; 2018- 1:29:15, 4:09:21. pbs: 3000mW 12:25.36i '13, 12:38.75 '07; 5000mW 21:32.08 '14, 10000mW 43:22.05 '08, 43:09R '10; 35kW 2:45:51 '18.

Inaugural women's world record holder and world champion at 50k walk.
Patrícia MAMONA b. 21 Nov 1988 Lisbon 1.68m 53kg. Sporting CP. Was at Clemson University, USA.
At TJ: OG: '12- dnq 13, '16- 6; WCh: '11-15: dnq 27/16, '17- 9; EC: '10-12-14-16-18: 8/2/dnq 13/1/ dnq 16; WJ: '06- 4; WY: '05- 7; EU23: '09- 5; EJ: '07- dnq 15; WI: '14- 4; EI: '13-15-17-19: 8/5/2/4; WUG: '11- 2. POR champion 2008-17, NCAA 2010-11.
Nine Portuguese triple jump records 2009-16.
Progress at TJ: 2004- 12.71, 2005- 12.87, 2006- 13.37/13.38w, 2007- 13.24, 2008- 13.51, 2009- 13.83, 2010- 14.12, 2011- 14.42, 2012- 14.52, 2013- 14.02/14.07w, 2014- 14.36/14.49w, 2015- 14.32i/14.19, 2016- 14.65, 2017- 14.42, 2018- 14.19, 2019- 14.43i. pbs: 200m 24.42 '10, 800m 2:19.70i '09, 60mh 8.41i '09, 100mh 13.53/13.49w '10, HJ 1.69 '04; LJ 6.34i '19, 6.16 '05; Pen 4081i '09, Hep 5293 '11.

PUERTO RICO

Governing body: Federación de Atletismo Amateur de Puerto Rico. Founded 1947.
National Champions 2018: Men: 100m: Julius Rivera 10.66, 200m: Jan Gutierrez 21.90, 400m: Alexis Ojeda 48.50, 800m: Ryan Sánchez 1:46.80, 1500m/5000m: Alfredo Santana 3:49.31/14:39.57, 3000mSt: Luis Medina 9:21.18, 110mh: Jonathan Santiago 13.92, 400mh: Javier Culson 50.33, HJ: Luis Castro 2.20, PV: Emmanuel Rivera 5.00, LJ: Michael Wiliams 7.48, TJ: Reinaldo Oyola 12.67, SP: Devon Patterson 17.73, DT: Edilberto González 50.87, HT: Jerome Vega 65.76, JT: Félix Torres 66.58, 10000mW: José Melendez 44:42.33.
Women: 100m: Genoiska Cancel 11.97, 200m: Marielis Montalvo 26.59, 400m: Priscilla Morales 54.95, 800m: Keysha Dumeng 2:11.61, 1500m: Zoe Maldonado 4:43.41, 5000m: Beverly Ramos 16:10.40, 3000mSt: Ashley Laureano 10:52.96, 100mh/HJ: Alysbeth Félix 13.8/1.75, PV: Diamara Planell 4.30, LJ: Jessica Acevedo 6.19w, TJ: Tanasia Lea 12.06, SP: Elvia Nevarez 12.45 irreg, DT: Naomi Colon 41.52, HT: Freshlian Luna 51.14, JT: Coralys Ortiz 54.90, 5000mW: Paola Sotomayor 26:30.62, 10000mW: Rachelle de Orbeta 47:56.43.

Jasmine CAMACHO-QUINN b. 21 Aug 1996 Ladson, South Carolina, USA 1.80m 73kg. University of Kentucky, USA.
At 100mh: OG: '16- dq sf. NCAA champion 2016, 2018; NACAC U23 2016
CAC 100mh record 2018, 9 PUR records 2016-18.
Progress at 100mh: 2013- 14.10, 2014- 13.37, 2016- 12.69/12.45w, 2017- 12.58, 2018- 12.40. pbs: 60m 7.59i '16, 100m 11.61 '16, 200m 22.69 '18, 300m 37.91i '17, 60mh 7.95i '18, LJ 6.15 '14.
Mother is from Puerto Rico. Her brother Robert Quinn is a defensive end for Miami Dolphins in the NFL.

QATAR

Governing body: Qatar Association of Athletics Federation. Founded 1963.

Mutaz Essa BARSHIM b. 24 Jun 1991 Doha 1.92m 70kg. Team Aspire.
At HJ: OG: '12- 3=, '16- 2; WCh: '11-13-15-17: 7/2/4/1; WJ: '10- 1; AsiG: '10- 1, '14- 1; AsiC: '11- 1, '15- 3; WI: '12-14-16-18: 9=/1/4/2; CCp: '14- 3; won DL 2014-15, 2017; Asian indoors 2010, 2012, 2014, 2016, 2018, Asi-J 2010, W.Mil G 2011, Arab 2011, 2013, 2015; Gulf 2013.
Five Asian high jump records 2012-14 and indoors (3) 2013-15, 14 Qatar records 2010-13.
Progress at HJ: 2008- 2.07, 2009- 2.14, 2010- 2.31, 2011- 2.35, 2012- 2.39, 2013- 2.40, 2014- 2.43, 2015- 2.41, 2016- 2.40, 2017- 2.40, 2018- 2.40.
IAAF Male Athlete of the Year 2017. His 2.43 at Brussels in 2014 was the world's best since 1993, second only to Javier Sotomayor. Qatari father (who was a race walker), Sudanese mother. Younger brothers Muamer Aissa Barshim (b. 3 Jan 1994) has HJ pb 2.28 '14 and was 3rd 2014 Asian Games, and Hamdi Mahamat Alamine 2.27 '18.

Ashraf Amjad EL-SEIFY (Al-Saifi) b. 20 Feb 1995 Egypt 1.83m 100kg.
At HT: OG: '16- 6; WCh: '13- dnq 25, '15- 9, '17- dnq 23; WJ: '12- 1, '14- 1; AsiG: '18- 1; CCp: '18- 5. Won Asi-J 2014.
Records: world youth 5kg 85.26 '11, world junior 6kg 85.57 '12, Asian junior 2013, three Qatar 2013-16.
Progress at HT: 2013- 76.37, 2014- 71.81, 2015- 78.04, 2016- 78.19, 2017- 76.14, 2018- 77.04.
Former Egyptian, QAT citizen from 30 Mar 2011; able to compete for them from 29 Mar 2012.

Abdelilah HAROUN b. 1 Jan 1997 Sudan 1.78m 73kg.
At 400m: OG: '16- sf; WCh: '17- 3; AsiG: '18- 1/1R; AsiC: '15- 1/1R; WJ: '16- 1; WI: '16- 2; CCp: '18-1. Won Asian indoor Champs 2016, 2018, Games 2017; Arab 2015.
Asian 400m records indoors and out 2015, 4x400m 2018; QAT 2015 & 2018. World best 500m indoors 2016.
Progress at 400m: 2014- 45.74, 2015- 44.27, 2016- 44.81, 2017- 44.48, 2018- 44.07. Pbs: 200m 21.16 '18, 500m 59.83i '16, 800m 1:56.06 '17.
Qatar citizen from 2 Feb 2015, having lived there from 2013.

Ahmed Bader MAGOUR b. 3 Mar 1996 Egypt 1.90m 90kg.
At JT: OG: '16- dnq 30; WCh: '17- 10; AsiG: '18- 6; AsiC: '17- 2. Gulf champion & Islamic Sol. 2017.
Four Qatar javelin records 2016-17.
Progress at JT: 2014-, 2015- 77.88, 2016- 84.74, 2017- 85.23, 2018- 83.71.
Formerly Egypt, eligible to compete for Qatar from 23 Apr 2016.

Abderrahmane SAMBA b. 5 Sep 1995 Saudi Arabia. 1.87m 80kg.
At 400mh: WCh: '17- 7; AsiG: '18- 1/1R; CCp: '18- 1. Three Asian and five Qatar 400mh records 2018, Asian 4x400m record 2018.
Progress at 400mh: 2017 48.31A/48.44, 2018 46.98. Pbs: 200m 21.17, '16. 20.94w '15; 400m 44.62 '18.
Ten successive wins in 400mh finals from August 2017, inc. season's record nine sub-48 times in 2018. Tranferred from Mauritania (his father is Mauritanian) to Qatar, when he has lived since 6 May 2015, citizen from 1 Oct 2015, cleared to compete from 6 May 2016.

ROMANIA

Governing body: Federatia Romana de Atletism. Founded 1912.

National Championships first held in 1914 (men), 1925 (women). **2018 Champions**: **Men**: 100m/ 200m: Ionut Neagoe 10.41/21.03, 400m: Robert Parge 46.11, 800m: Cosmin Trofin 1:47.13, 1500m: Dorin Rusu 3:49.69, 5000m/10000m/ HMar: Nicolae Soare 14:23.01/29:54.51/65:11, Mar: Sorin Mineran 2:27:29, 3000mSt: Daniel Betej 9:05.28, 110mh: Cosmin Dumitrache 14.00, 400mh: Vlad Dulcescu 52.85, HJ: Mihai Donesan 2.20, PV: Andrei Deliu 4.80, LJ: Christian Staicu 7.86, TJ: Marian Oprea 16.32, SP: Andrei Gag 19.70, DT: Alin Firfirica 63.20, HT: Mihaita Micu 64.80, JT: Alexandru Novac 81.00, Dec: Razvan Roman 6902, 20kW/ 50kW: Florin Stirbu 1:27:00/4:08:41. **Women**: 100m/ 200m: Marina Baboi 11.54/23.90, 400m: Anadrea Miklos 52.81, 800m/1500m: Claudia Bobocea 2:06.10/4:13.66, 5000m: Ancuta Bobocel 15:41.38, 10000m: Cristina Simion 35:37.83, HMar: Andreea Piscu 77:08, Mar: Adela Baltoi 2:50:05, 3000mSt: Claudia Prisecaru 10:07.77, 100mh: Anamaria Nesteriuc 13.27, 400mh: Sanda Belgyan 56.73, HJ: Daniela Stanciu 1.90, PV: Ionela Luca 3.80, LJ: Alina Rotaru 6.72, TJ: Elena Panturoiu 13.74w, SP: Andrea Huzum-Vitan 14.90, DT: Elena Asmarandei 48.45, HT: Bianca Ghelber 68.78, JT: Florina Necsoiu 53.64, Hep: Georgiana Muscalu 4747, 10kW: Andrea Arsine 49:04, 20kW: Ana Rodean 1:37:51.

Women

Elena Andreea **PANTUROIU** b. 24 Feb 1995 Ribeira 1.70m 57kg. CS Onesti.
At TJ: OG: '16- dnq 16; WCh: '15/17- dnq 18/14; EC: 16- dnq 16, '18- 4; WJ: '14- 5; WY: '11- dnq 24; E23: '15- 2, '17- 1; EJ: '13- 2; WI: '16- 5, 18- 4. Romanian champion 2016, 2018.
Progress at TJ: 2011- 12.79, 2012- 12.94i/12.67/ 13.08w, 2013- 13.26, 2014- 13.93i/13.81/14.20w, 2015- 14.13, 2016- 14.33, 2017- 14.43, 2018- 14.47. pbs: 200m 25.94 '12, 800m 2:17.41 '14, 60mh 8.51i '16, 100mh 14.65 '13, HJ 1.80i '17, 1.71 '13; LJ 6.44i/6.14 '15, SP 11.61i '17; JT 31.09 '12, Pen 4309i '17, Hep 5102 '13.

RUSSIA

Governing body: All-Russia Athletic Federation. Founded 1911.
National Championships first held 1908, USSR women from 1922. **2018 Champions: Men**: 100m: Denis Ogarkov 10.32, 200m: Aleksandr Yefimov 20.81, 400m: Mikhail Filatov 46.00, 800m: Sergey Dubrovskiy 1:46.79, 1500m/ 10000m: Vladimir Nikitin 3:35.85/28:16.43, 5000m: Yevgeniy Rybakov 13:23.57, HMar: Artyom Aplachkin 64:45, Mar: Aleksey Reunkov 2:12:20, 3000mSt: Maksim Yakushev 8:22.40, 110mh: Konstantin Shabanov 13.53, 400mh: Timofey Chalyy 49.52, HJ: Ivan Ukhov 2.32, PV: Yevgeniy Lukyanenko 5.65, LJ: Aleksandr Menkov 8.03, TJ: Aleksandr Yurchenko 16.98, SP: Aleksandr Lesnoy 21.58, DT: Aleksey Khudyakov 64.37, HT: Denis Lukyanov 74.74, JT: Dmitriy Tarabin 82.89, Dec: Artem Makarenko 7925, 20kW: Sergey Shirobokov 1:17:24, 50kW: Sergey Bakulin 3:42:19. **Women**: 100m: Kristina Sivkova 11.30, 200m: Krisztina Khorosheva 23.17; 400m: Polina Miller 51.82; 800m: Yekaterina Zavyalova 2:00.80, 1500m: Aleksandra Gulyayeva 4:05.00, 5000m: Yelena Korobkina 15:19.11, 10000m: Yelena Dedova 32:45.94, HMar: Tatyana Arkhipova 71:23, Mar: Sardana Trofimova 2:28:55, 3000mSt: Yekaterina Ivonina 9:16.68, 100mh: Yekaterina Galitskaya 13.25, 400mh: Vera Rudakova 56.03, HJ: Mariya Lasitskene 2.00, PV: Olga Mullina 4.65, LJ: Yelena Sokolova 6.68, TJ: Yekaterina Koneva 14.79w, SP: Alyona Bugakova 18.02, DT: Yelena Panova 59.17; HT: Yelizaveta Tsareva 70.72, JT: Yekaterina Starygina 60.02, Hep: Viktoriya Vaseykina 5743, 20kW: Yelena Lashmanova 1:23:39, 50kW: Klavdiya Afanasyeva 4:14:45.

Sergey BAKULIN b. 13 Nov 1986 Insar, Mordoviya. 1.69m 58kg. Mordoviya VS.
At 20kW: EC: '06- 5; EU23: '07- 3; WCp: '06- 6, '10- 7; WUG: '09- 1. At 50kW: OG: '12- dq6; WCh: '11- dq1; EC: '10- 3; WCp: '12-dq 5; ECp: '09- 4; Russian champion 2011, 2017-18.
Progress at 20kW, 50kW: 2006- 1:19:54, 2007- 1:19:14, 2008- 1:18:18, 3:52:38; 2010- 1:24:05, 3:43:26; dq: 2011- 3:38:46dq, 2012- 3:38:55dq, 2017- 1:18:51, 3:42:19; 2018- 3:42:20. pbs: 5000mW 18:26.82i '12, 10kW: 39:03 '06, 30kW: 2:05:19dq '13, 35kW 2:24:25 '09.
3 year 2 month ban announced in January 2015 for biological passport anomaly and with results annulled 25 Feb 2011 to 24 Dec 2012 lost 2011 World title and 2012 Olympic 5th place. Back competing in 2017.

Aleksandr LESNOY b. 28 Jul 1988 Krasnodar 1.94m 116kg.
At SP: WCh: '13-15-17: dnq 21/16/26; EC: '14- 10, '18- 5; WUG: '13- 1; WI: '14- 8; ET: '13-14: 3/3.

RUS champion 2014, 2017-18.
Progress at SP: 2008- 16.46, 2009- 16.80, 2010- 19.09, 2011- 19.60, 2012- 20.05, 2013- 20.60, 2014- 21.40, 2015- 20.70i/20.55, 2016- 21.03, 2017- 21.36, 2018- 21.58. pb DT 58.80 '12.

Sergey LITVINOV b. 27 Jan 1986 Rostov-on-Don 1.85m 110kg.
At HT: WCh: '09-11-13-15-17: 5/dnq 15/11/5/dnq 17; EC: '14- 3; WJ: '04- 9; EU23: '07- 11; EJ: '05- 9; WUG: '13- 3; ET: '14- 1. German champion 2009, Russian 2013, 2015-16.
Progress at HT: 2004- 60.00, 2005- 73.98, 2006- 66.46, 2007- 74.80, 2008- 75.35, 2009- 77.88, 2010- 78.98, 2011- 78.90, 2012- 80.98, 2013- 80.89, 2014- 79.35, 2015- 77.24, 2016- 77.67, 2017- 77.32, 2018- 76.13.
Switched from Belarus to Germany 15 Jul 2008 and from 1 Jan 2011 to Russia. His father Sergey Litvinov (USSR) set three world records at hammer 1980-3 with a pb of 86.04 '86; he was Olympic champion 1988 (2nd 1980) and World champion 1983 and 1987. His mother was born in Germany.

Danil LYSENKO b. 9 Oct 1986 Birsk 1.92m 73kg.
At HJ: WCh: '17- 2; WJ: '14- 6; EJ: '15- 5; YOG: '14- 1; WI: '18- 1. RUS champion 2017.
European junior indoor high jump record 2016.
Progress at HJ: 2013- 2.10, 2014- 2.24, 2015- 2.24i/2.22, 2016- 2.31i/2.30, 2017- 2.38, 2018- 2.40.
Lost ANA status and not allowed to compete at EC 2018 due to three whereabouts failurs.

Aleksandr MENKOV b. 7 Dec 1990 Minusinsk, Krasnoyarsk reg. 1.78m 74kg. Krasnoyarsk VS. Krasnoyarsk State University.
At LJ: OG: '12- 11; WCh: '09-11-13-15-17: dnq 32/6/1/6/4; EC: '14- dnq 13; WI: '12- 3, '14- 5; EU23: '11- 1; EJ: '09- 1; EI: '13- 1; WUG: '13- 2; ET: '11-13-15: 1/1/1. Won DL 2012-13, Russian 2012, 2018. Two Russian records 2013.
Progress at LJ: 2008- 6.98, 2009- 8.16, 2010- 8.10, 2011- 8.28, 2012- 8.29, 2013- 8.56, 2014- 8.30i/8.02, 2015- 8.27, 2016- 7.91, 2017- 8.32, 2018- 8.41. pbs: HJ 2.15 '10, TJ 15.20 '09.

Vasiliy MIZINOV b. 29 Dec 1997 1.67m 55kg.
At 20kW: EC: '18- 3. At 10000mW: EJ: '15- dq.
World junior 5000m walk record 2016.
Progress at 20kW: 2017- 1:21:48, 2018- 1:18:54, 2019- 1:18:32. pbs: 5000mW: 18:25.5i '19, 18:51.9 '16; 10000mW 38:58.21 '16.

Timur MORGUNOV b. 12 Oct 1996 Kopeysk 1.88m 77kg.
At PV: EC: '18- 2; EJ: '15- 5; CCp: '18- 4. Russian champion 2017, DL 2018.
Progress at PV: 2014- 5.20, 2015- 5.50, 2016- 5.80i/5.55, 2017- 5.80, 2018- 6.00. pbs: HJ 1.83 '17, LJ 7.25 '17, JT 51.68 '17. Dec 6856 '17.

Valeriy PRONKIN b. 15 Jun 1994 Nizhny Novgorod 1.95m 115kg.

At HT: WCh: '17- 2; WJ: '12- 8; WY: 11- dnq 20 (10 DT); EU23: '15- 2; EJ: '13- 1. Won RUS 2017.
Progress at HT: 2012- 64.78, 2013- 73.50, 2014- 71.34, 2015- 76.80, 2016- 75.39, 2017- 79.32.

Sergey SHIROBOKOV b. 16 Feb 1999 Malaya Ita, Sharkanskiy Dist, Udmurtia 1.68m 57kg.
At 20kW: WCh: '17- 2; ECp: '17- 12; won RUS 2018. At 10000mW: WY: '15- 1; EJ: '17- 1.
World U20 10k & 20k walks bests 2018.
Progress at 20kW: 2016- 1:22:31, 2017- 1:18:26, 2018- 1:17:25, 2019- 1:18:42. pbs: 5000mW 18:45.7i '18, 10000mW 40:58.0 '16, 38:25R '18.

Ilya SHKURENYOV b. 11 Jan 1991 Linevo, Volgograd reg. 1.91m 82kg. Volgograd Dyn.
At Dec: OG: '12- 16; WCh: '13- 8, '15- 4, '17- dnf; EC: '12-14-18: 3/3/2; WJ: '10- 2; EU23: '11- 5, '13- 2; ECp: '15- 1. Russian champion 2013, 2016-17.
At Hep: WI: '12- 4; EI: '13-15-19: 5/1/3.
Progress at Dec: 2011- 7894, 2012- 8219, 2013- 8370, 2014- 8498, 2015- 8538, 2016- 8292, 2017- 8601, 2018- 8321. pbs: 60m 6.98i '15, 100m 10.89 '17, 400m 47.88 '15, 1000m 2:41.65i '13, 1500m 4:24.98 '15, 60mh 7.86i '15, 110mh 13.95 '17, HJ 2.12 '17, PV 5.40 '13, LJ 7.78 '16, SP 14.84i '11, 14.24 '15; DT 46.04 '14, JT 63.58 '14, Hep 6353i '15. Won IAAF Challenge 2015.

Sergey SHUBENKOV b. 4 Oct 1990 Barnaul, Altay Kray 1.90m 75kg. Tyumen State University.
At 110mh: OG: '12- sf; WCh: '11-13-15-17: h/3/1/2; EC: '12-14-18: 1/1/2; EU23: '11- 1; EJ: '09- 2, WUG: '13- 3; CCp: '14- 1, '18- 1; ET: '13-14- 15: 1/1. Won DL 2017-18, WMilG 2015, Russian 2013, 20-16. At 60mh: EI: '13- 1.
Seven Russian 110mh records 2012-18.
Progress at 110mh: 2010- 13.54, 2011- 13.46, 2012- 13.09, 2013- 13.16/13.10w, 2014- 13.13, 2015- 12.98, 2016- 13.20, 2017- 13.01, 2018- 12.92. pb 60mh 7.49i '13.
Mother Natalya Shubenkova had heptathlon pb 6859 '04; 4th 1988 OG and 3rd 1986 EC.

Dmitriy TARABIN b. 29 Oct 1991 Berlin, Germany 1.76m 85kg. Student at Russian State University of Physical Education, Moscow
At JT: WCh: '11- 10, '13- 3, '15- dnq 25; EC: '14- 5; WJ: '10- 3; WY: '07- dnq 23; EU23: '11- 3; EJ: '09- dnq 13; WUG: '13- 1; ET: '13- 1, '14- 2. Won RUS 2013, 2015-18.
Progress at JT: 2007- 55.18, 2008- 67.39, 2009- 69.63, 2010- 77.65, 2011- 85.10, 2012- 82.75, 2013- 88.84, 2014- 85.92, 2015- 84.70, 2016- 81.56, 2017- 80.70, 2018- 85.38.
Switched from Moldova to Russia 9 June 2010. Married javelin thrower Mariya Abakumova on 12 Oct 2012.

Ivan UKHOV b. 29 Mar 1986 Chelyabinsk 1.92m 83kg. Sverdlovsk TU.
At HJ: OG: '12- 1; WCh: '09-11-13-15: 10/5=/4/ dnq 24; EC: '06-10-14: 12=/2/3; WJ: '04- dnq 13; EJ: '05- 1; CCp: '14- 2; WUG: '05- 4; WI: '10-12-14:

1/3/2; EI: '09- 1, '11- 1. Won DL 2010, Russian 2009, 2012-13, 2016, 2018.
Russian high jump record 2014 (& 2 indoors, inc. one European).
Progress at HJ: 2004- 2.15, 2005- 2.30, 2006- 2.37i/2.33, 2007- 2.39i/2.20, 2008- 2.36i/2.30, 2009- 2.40i/2.35, 2010- 2.38i/2.36, 2011- 2.38i/2.34, 2012- 2.39, 2013- 2.35, 2014- 2.42i/2.41, 2015- 2.32, 2016- 2.35, 2017- 2.32, 2018- 2.35i/2.34.
Pending doping case.

Women

Anna CHICHEROVA b. 22 Jul 1982 Yerevan, Armenia 1.80m 57kg. Moskva VS. Physical culture graduate.
At HJ: OG: '04- 6, '08- dq (3), '12- 1; WCh: '03-05- 07-09-11-13-15: 6/4/2=/dq2/1/3=/3; EC: '06- 7=; WJ: '00- 4; WY: '99- 1; EJ: '01- 2; WUG: '05- 1; WI: '03-04-12: 3/2/2=; EI: '05- 1, '07- 5=; ECp: '06- 3.
Won RUS 2004, 2007-08, 2011-12, 2015-16.
Progress at HJ: 1998- 1.80, 1999- 1.89, 2000- 1.90, 2001- 1.92, 2002- 2.00i/1.89, 2003- 2.04i/2.00, 2004- 2.04i/1.98, 2005- 2.01i/1.99, 2006- 1.96i/1.95, 2007- 2.03, 2008- 2.04, 2009- 2.02, 2011- 2.07, 2012- 2.06i/2.05, 2013- 2.02, 2014- 2.01, 2015- 2.01, 2016- 1.98, 2018- 1.98, 2019- 2.01i
Moved with family to Russia at the beginning of the 1990s. Married to Gennadiy Chernoval KAZ, pbs 100m 10.18, 200m 20.44 (both 2002), 2 WUG 100m & 200m 2001, 2 AsiG 2002 2002; their daughter Nika born on 7 Sep 2010. Lost her 2008 Olympic bronze medal when a re-test in 2016 showed positive; also lost her 2009 World silver with the 2-year drugs ban.

Darya KLISHINA b. 15 Jan 1991 Tver 1.80m 57kg. Moskva. Model.
At LJ: OG: '16- 9; WCh: '11-13-15-17: 6/6/10/2; EC: '14- 3; WY: '07- 1; EU23: '11- 1; EJ: '09- 1; WI: '10-12-14: 5/4/7; EI: '11-13-17: 1/1/4, WUG: '13- 1; ET: '11-13-15: 1/2/1. RUS champion 2014.
Progress at LJ: 2005- 5.83, 2006- 6.33/6.47w, 2007- 6.49, 2008- 6.52i/6.20, 2009- 6.80, 2010- 7.03, 2011- 7.05, 2012- 6.93, 2013- 7.01i/6.90/6.98w, 2014- 6.90, 2015- 6.95, 2016- 6.84, 2017- 7.00.
The one Russian athlete permitted to compete (as a neutral) at OG '16 and EI '17.

Yekaterina KONEVA b. 25 Sep 1988 Khabarovsk 1.69m 55kg. Khabarovsk.
At TJ: WCh: '13- 2, '15- 7; EC: '14- 2; WI: '14- 1; WUG: '11-13-15: 1/1/1; CCp: '14- 2; EI: '15- 1; ET: '13-14-15: 2/1/1. RUS champion 2014-15, 2018; WMilG LJ & TJ 2015.
Progress at TJ: 2010- 13.93/14.00w, 2011- 14.46, 2012- 14.60i/14.36, 2013- 14.82, 2014- 14.89, 2015- 15.04, 2016- 14.42, 2018- 14.67/14.79w. pbs: 60m 7.39i '07, 100m 11.76 '09, 200m 23.89 '09, LJ 6.82i '15, 6.70/6.80w '11.
Married Sergey Polyanskiy (LJ 8.20 '15, 8 WCh '15) in October 2016, daughter Sofiya born 17 Apr 2017. Two-year drugs ban 2007-09. Baby born Aori 2017.

Yelena LASHMANOVA b. 9 Apr 1992 Saransk 1.70m 48kg. Biology student at Mordoviya State University.
At 20kmW: OG: '12- 1; WCh: '13- 1; WCp: '12- 1; won RUS 2016-18. At 10000mW: WJ: '10- 1; EJ: '11- 1; ECp: '11- 1J. At 5000mW: WY: '09- 1.
Official world 20km walk record 2012 and world best 2018, world junior 10,000m walk record 2011.
Progress at 20kW: 2012- 1:25:02, 2013- 1:25:49, 2016- 1:24:58, 2017- 1:25:18, 2018- 1:23:39. pbs: 5000mW 20:15.6 '16, 10000mW 42:59.48 '11.
Best ever debut at 20k walk (1:26:30 in 2012) and has won all seven of her career 20k walks 2012-3. Won IAAF Walks Challenge 2013. Received two-year drugs ban from test on 4 Jan 2014.

Mariya LASITSKENE b. 14 Jan 1993 Prokhladny, Kabardino-Balkar 1.82m 66kg. née Kuchina. Moskovskaya.
At HJ: WCh: '15- 1, '17- 1; EC: '14- 2, '18- 1; WJ: '12- 3; WY: '09- 2=; EU23: '15- 12; EJ: '11- 1; WI: '14- 1=. '18- 1; EI: '15- 1, '19- 1; WUG: '13- 2; CCp: '14- 1, '18- 1; ET: '13-14-15: 1/1/1. Won DL 2014, 2017-18; Yth Oly 2010, RUS champion 2014, 2017-18; W.MilG 2015.
World junior indoor high jump record 2011.
Progress at HJ: 2009- 1.87, 2010- 1.91, 2011- 1.97i/1.95, 2012- 1.96i/1.89, 2013- 1.98i/1.96, 2014- 2.01i/2.00, 2015- 2.01, 2016- 2.00, 2017- 2.06, 2018- 2.04, 2019- 2.03i.
Married journalist Vladas Lasitskas on 17 Mar 2017. 45 successive wins from 23 June 2016 to 30 June 2018 World Indoors and had the top seven performances of 2017 and top four in 2018.

Marina PANDAKOVA 1 Mar 1989. Churvashkaya Reg.
At 20kW: WCp: '14- 10. ECp: '13- 3, '15- 5; WUG: '15- 2.
Progress at 20kW: 2008- 1:38:19, 2011- 1:33:00, 2012- 1:28:29, 2013- 1:27:39, 2014- 1:27.54, 2015- 1:25:03, 2016- 1:27:18. pbs: 3000mW: 11:50.30 '16, 5000mW 21:40.41i '13, 10kW 43:29 '12.

Marina PONOMARYOVA 18 Jun 1995.
At 20kW: EU23: '15- 1.
Progress at 20kW: 2015- 1:27:17, 2016- 1:26:46, 2017- 1:27:53, 2018- 1:27:11. pbs: 3000mW: 12:05.91 '16, 10kW: 44:07 '16.

Vira REBRIK b. 25 Feb 1989 Yalta 1.76m 65kg.
At JT: OG: '08/12- dnq 15/18; WCh: '09- 11-13-15-17: 8/dnq 15/11/dnq 24/dnq nt; EC: '10- dnq 16, '12- 1; WJ: '06- 2, '08- 1; WY: '05- 2; EU23: '09- 2, '11- 2; EJ: '07- 1; WUG: '09- 2, '11- 4; ET: '13- 3. Won UKR 2010-12, RUS 2015-17.
World junior javelin record 2008; four UKR records 2010-12.
Progress at JT: 2003- 44.94, 2004- 52.47, 2005- 57.48, 2006- 59.64, 2007- 58.48, 2008- 63.01, 2009- 62.26, 2010- 63.36, 2011- 61.60, 2012- 66.86, 2013- 64.30, 2014- 61.57, 2015- 64.93, 2016- 67.30, 2017- 62.02, 2018- 60.24.

Crimean athlete, transferred to Russia in 2015. Daughter Anna born 27 Jan 2019.

Yekaterina RYZHOVA b. 29 Mar 1994. née Medveyeva. Mordoviya.
At 10000mW: WJ: '12- 1; WCp: '12- 4J.
Progress at 20kW: 2015- 1:29:32, 2016- 1:26:40, 2017- 1:25:22, 2018- 1:29:08. pbs: 10000mW 43:50.0 '13.

Anzhelika SIDOROVA b. 28 Jun 1991 Moskva 1.70m 52kg. Moskva Youth.
At PV: WCh: '15- nh, '17- dnq nh; EC: '14- 1, '18- 4; WJ: '10- 4; EU23: '13- 2; WI: '14- 2=, '18- 2; EI: '13-15-19: 3/1/1; CCp: 18- 1; ET: '13-14-15- 2/1/2. Won RUS 2014-15.
Progress at PV: 2007- 3.80, 2008- 4.00, 2009- 4.10i/4.00, 2010- 4.30, 2011- 4.40i/4.30, 2012- 4.50, 2013- 4.62i/4.60, 2014- 4.72i/4.70, 2015- 4.80i/4.79, 2016- 4.85, 2017- 4.75, 2018- 4.90i/4.85.

Yelena SOKOLOVA b. 23 Jul 1986 Staryi Oskol, Belgorod reg. 1.70m 61kg. née Kremneva. Krasnodarsk krai.
At LJ: OG: '12- 2; WCh: '09- dnq 13, '13- 8, '15- dnq 23; WJ: '02- dnq; WY: '03- 6 (3 MedR); EU23: '07- 3; EI: '07- 5, '09- 2; WUG: '07- 2, '13- 2. Won DL 2012, RUS 2009, 2012, 2015, 2017-18.
Progress at LJ: 2002- 6.33, 2003- 6.39i?/6.31, 2006- 6.53, 2007- 6.71, 2008- 6.74, 2009- 6.92, 2010- 6.72/6.90w, 2011- 6.76, 2012- 7.07, 2013- 6.91, 2015- 6.70, 2016- 6.59, 2017- 6.85, 2018- 6.70. pbs: 60m 7.34i '12, 100m 11.61 '12, TJ 13.15i/12.93 '03.
Son born on 23 Aug 2014.

ST LUCIA
Governing body: Saint Lucia Athletics Association.

Levern SPENCER b. 23 Jun 1984 Cacao Babonneau 1.80m 54kg. Was at University of Georgia.
At HJ: OG: '08/12- dnq 24/19, '16- 6; WCh: '05-07-09-11-13-15-17: dnq 22/15=/dnq 21=/dnq 12/11/12=/dnq 13=; CG: '02-06-10-14-18: 12=/5/3/3/1; WJ: '02- 8; WY: '01- 3; PAm: '03-07-11-15: 5/3/6/1; CAG: '06-10-14-18: 3/1/1/1; WI: '14- 7, '16- 5=; CCp: '10-14-18: 3=/5/3. CAC champion 2001, 2005, 2008-09, 2011, 2013; NACAC 2007, 2015, 2018.
Nine St Lucia high jump records 2004-10.
Progress at HJ: 2000- 1.80, 2001- 1.81, 2002- 1.83, 2003- 1.86, 2004- 1.88, 2005- 1.94, 2006- 1.90, 2007- 1.94, 2008- 1.93, 2009- 1.95, 2010- 1.98, 2011- 1.94, 2012- 1.91, 2013- 1.95A, 2014- 1.96, 2015- 1.94, 2016- 1.96, 2017- 1.92, 2018- 1.96. pbs: 200m 24.22 '05, LJ 6.08 '14.

SERBIA
Governing body: Athletic Federation of Serbia. Founded in 1921 (as Yugoslav Athletic Federation).
National Championships (Yugoslav) first held in 1920 (men) and 1923 (women). **2018**

Champions: **Men**: 100m/200m: Aleksa Kijanovic 10.60/21.45w, 400m/800m: Marko Vozab 47.95/1:53.21, 1500m: Elzan Bibic 3:46.04, 3000m: Nikola Bursac 8:41.44, 5000m: Milos Pendic 15:07.44, 10000m: Milos Segedi 32:38.30, HMar: Haris Ajdarevic 69:48, Mar: Milos Dajevic 2:42:26, 3000mSt: Milos Milosavljevic 9:33.39, 110mh: Marko Miskovic 14.59w, 400mh: Emir Bekric 51.59, HJ: Miodrag Djokic 2.13, PV: Steven Antanasijevic 4.00, LJ: Strahinja Jovancevic 7.64, TJ: Dimitrije Novakovic 15.18, SP: Asmir Kolasinac 19.92, DT: Darko Radakovic 48.38, HT: Milos Covic 53.72, JT: Vedran Samac 77.03, Dec: Milan Cajic 5428, 5kW/5000mW: Jovan Delcev 22:56/23.48.91. **Women**: 100m/200m: Zorana Barjaktarovic 11.71/23.62w, 400m: Tamara Salaski 53.55, 800m/1500m: Amela Terzic 2:04.96/4:25.87, 3000m/5000m/HMar: Teodora Simovic 9:57.43/17:37.05/74:32, 10000m: Nevena Jovanovic 39:19.65, Mar: Nora Trklja 3:03:17, 3000mSt: Jasmina Pruginic 11:20.81, 100mh: Ivana Petkovic 13.87, 400mh: Jelena Grujic 62.58, HJ: Zorana Bukvic 1.78, PV: Iva Savic 3.30, LJ: Milica Gardasevic 6.21, TJ: Biljana Topic 13.36, SP: Dijana Sefcic 12.94, DT: Dragana Tomasevic 58.92, HT: Aleksandra Ivanovic 58.42, JT: Marija Vucenovic 54.63, Hep: Iva Savic 3983, 3000mW/5kW: Danica Gogov 14:38.22/24:55.

Asmir KOLASINAC b. 15 Oct 1984 Skopje, Macedonia 1.86m 137kg. AC Partizan 1945, Belgrade.
At SP: OG: '08- dnq 30, '12- 7, '16- dnq 15; WCh: '09-11-13-15: dnq 20/10/10/7; EC: '10-12-14-16-18: 7/3/5/5/dnq; EU23: '05- dnq; EI: '13- 1, '15- 2; Won Balkan 2011; SRB 2008, 2010-15, 2018.
Progress at SP: 2004- 15.50, 2005- 17.88, 2006- 17.85, 2007- 19.30, 2008- 19.99, 2009- 20.41, 2010- 20.52i/20.38, 2011- 20.50, 2012- 20.85, 2013- 20.80, 2014- 20.79, 2015- 21.58, 2016- 20.96, 2017- 20.87i/19.45, 2018- 20.48.
Older brother Almir BIH had JT best 68.32 '09.

Women

Ivana SPANOVIC b. 10 May 1990 Zrenjanin 1.76m 65kg. AC Vojvodina, Novi Sad.
At LJ: OG: '08- dnq 28, '12- 9, '16- 3; WCh: '13- 3, '15- 3, '17- 4; EC: '10-12-14-16-18: 8/dnq 14/2/1/ dns; WJ: '06- 7, '08- 1; WY: '05- dnq, '07- 2; EU23: '11- 2; EJ: '07- 5, '09- 2; WUG: '09- 1; CCp: '14- 2; WI: '14-16-18: 3/2/1; EI: '13-15-17-19: 5/1/1/1. Won DL 2016-17, Serbian 2006, 2008, 2011-13, Balkan 2011, 2013, MedG 2018
11 Serbian long jump records 2009-16 (& 11 indoor 2007-17), indoor records 60m & Pen.
Progress at LJ: 2003- 5.36, 2004- 5.91, 2005- 6.43, 2006- 6.48i/6.38, 2007- 6.53i/6.41, 2008- 6.65, 2009- 6.71, 2010- 6.78, 2011- 6.71/6.74w, 2012- 6.64, 2013- 6.82, 2014- 6.92i/6.88, 2015- 7.02, 2016- 7.10, 2017- 7.24i/6.96, 2018- 6.99/7.04w, 2019- 6.99i. pbs: 60m 7.31i '15, 100m 11.90 '13, 60mh 8.49i '13, HJ 1.78i '13, 1.65 '05, TJ 13.78 '14, SP 12.40i '13, Pen 4240i '13.
Won first medal for Serbia at World Champs and Olympic Games. Her 7.24 at EI '17 was the world's longest indoor women's LJ for 28 years. Ruptured her Achilles tendon in qualifying for 2018 European Champs final.

SLOVAKIA

Governing body: Slovak Athletic Federation. Founded 1939.
National Championships first held in 1939.
2018 Champions: **Men**: 100m/200m: Ján Volko 10.14w/20.24; 400m: Denis Danác 48.40, 800m: Matús Talán 1:54.60, 1500m: Jozef Repcík 3:56.72, 5000m: Jozef Pelikán 15:26.29, 10000m/HMar/Mar: Tibor Sahajda 30:20.93/68:11/2:15:59, 3000mSt: Jakub Valachovic 9:30.37, 110mh: Marco Adrien Drozda 14.59w, 400mh: Martin Kucera 51.51, HJ: Matús Bubeník 2.20, PV: Tomás Krajnák 5.00, LJ: Jakub Kubinec 7.26w, TJ: Ján Suba 15.15, SP: Robert Löbb 15.64, DT: Michal Holica 56.67, HT: Marcel Lomnicky 76.34, JT: Patrik Zenúch 77.09, Dec: none. 20kW: Miroslav Uradník 1:28:10, 50kW: Matej Tóth 3:42:46. **Women**: 100m/200m: Alexandra Bezeková 11.44w/23.28w, 400m: Alexandra Stuková 55.44, 800m: Iveta Putalová 2:09.56, 1500m/3000mSt: Katerina Belová 4:33.15/11:18.28, 5000m/HMar: Veronika Zrastáková 18:07.51/1:24:13, 10000m: Lubomira Maniková 37:05.31, Mar: Sylvia Sebestian 3:01:39, 100mh: Stanislava Lajcáková 13.31w, 400mh: Daniela Ledecká 59.01, HJ: Tatiana Dunajská 1.75, PV: Lujza Paliderová 4.00, LJ: Jana Veldáková 6.39w, TJ: Dana Veldáková 13.78w, SP/DT: Ivana Kristoficová 14.86/47.34, HT: Martina Hrasnová 71.11, JT: Barbora Mokrá 43.18, 20kW: María Czáková 1:41:12

Marcel LOMNICKY b. 6 Jul 1987 Nitra 1.77m 106kg. TJ Stavbár Nitra. Was at Virginia Tech University, USA.
At HT: OG: '12- dnq 14, '16- 5; WCh: '11-13-15-17: dnq 21/8/8/dnq 13; WJ: '04- dnq 17, '06- 3; EC: '10-12-14-16-18: dnq 24/11/7/5/11; EU23: '07- 3, '09- 6; EJ: '05- 8; WUG: '11- 2, '13- 2. SVK champion 2012-17, won NCAA HT 2009, indoor Wt 2012.
Progress at HT: 2005- 64.27, 2006- 69.53, 2007- 72.17, 2008- 72.66, 2009- 71.78, 2010- 74.83, 2011- 75.84, 2012- 77.43, 2013- 78.73, 2014- 79.16, 2015- 77.63, 2016- 77.48, 2017- 77.92, 2018- 77.00. pbs: SP 15.73 '07, DT 43.82 '08, Wt 23.05i '12.
Sister Nikola Lomnická (b. 16 Sep 1988) has hammer best 71.58 '14, won NCAA 2010 and was 8th EC 2014; married Andras Haklits CRO at end of 2018.

Matej TÓTH b. 10 Feb 1983 Nitra 1.85m 73kg. Dukla Banská Bystrica.
At 20kW/(50kW): OG: '04- 32, '08- 26, '12- (5), '16- (1); WCh: '05- 21, 07- 14, '09- 8/9, '11- 9/dnf, '13- (5), '15- (1); EC: '06-10-14-18: 6/6/(2)/(2);

EU23: '03- 6; WCp: '10- (1); ECp: '09-11-13-15: 9/1/3/2. At 10000mW: WJ: '02- 16, WY: '99- 8; EJ: '01- 6. Won SVK 20kW 2005-08, 2010-12, 2015, 2017; 50kW 2011, 2018.
Four SVK 50k walk records 2009-15.
Progress at 20kW, 50kW: 1999- 1:34:29, 2000- 1:30:28, 2001- 1:29:33, 2003- 1:13:17, 2004- 1:23:18, 2005- 1:21:38, 2006- 1:21:39, 2007- 1:25:10, 2008- 1:21:24, 2009- 1:20:53, 3:41:32; 2010- 1:22:04, 3:53:30; 2011- 1:20:16, 3:39:46; 2012- 1:20:25, 3:41:24; 2013- 1:20:14, 3:41:07; 2014- 1:19:48, 3:36:21; 2015- 1:20:21, 3:34:38; 2016- 1:29:04, 3:40:58; 2017- 1:24:38, 2018- 3:42:46. pbs: 3000mW 10:57.32i '11, 11:05.95 '12; 5000mW 18:34.56i '12, 18:54.39 '11; 10000W 39:45.03 '06, 39:07R '10; 30kW 2:12:44 '13, 35kW 2:34:23 '13.
First ever World and Olympic gold medallist for Slovakia. Won IAAF Race Walking Challenge 2015. Had third win at Dudince in 2018 in first 50k race since 2016 Olympics.

Women

Martina HRASNOVÁ b. 21 Mar 1983 Bratislava 1.77m 88kg. née Danisová. Dukla Banská Bystrica.
At HT: OG: '08- 6, '12/16- dnq 15/19; WCh: '01- 07-13-15: dnq 23/12/20/15, '09- 3; EC: '02 & '06- dnq 26, '12-14-16-18: 2/2/7/dnq 18; WJ: '00- 5, '02- 2; EJ: '99- 4, '01- 2; CCp: '14- 3; WUG: '07- 5, '09- 2. Won SVK SP 2003, 2006; HT 2000-01, 2006, 2008-09, 2011-15, 2018.
14 Slovakian hammer records 2001-09.
Progress at HT: 1999- 58.61, 2000- 61.62, 2001- 68.50, 2002- 68.22, 2003- 66.36, 2005- 69.24, 2006- 73.84, 2007- 69.22, 2008- 76.82, 2009- 76.90, 2011- 72.47, 2012- 73.34, 2013- 72.41, 2014- 75.27, 2015- 74.27, 2016- 72.34, 2017- 67.86, 2018- 73.25. pbs: 60m 7.96i '12, SP 15.60i '15, 15.02 '06; DT 43.15 '06, Wt 21.74i '11.
Two-year drugs ban (nandrolone) from July 2003. Daughter Rebeka born on 4 July 2010. Brother of Branislav Danis (HT 69.20 '06). Equalled EC women's record 6 appearances.

SLOVENIA

Governing body: Atletska Zveza Slovenije. Current organisation founded 1948.
2018 National Champions: Men: 100m: Luka Marolt 10.83, 200m: Gregor Grahovac 21.43w, 400m: Zan Rudolf 48.01, 800m: Tilen Simenko Lalic 1:51.23, 1500m: Jan Kokalj 3:55.00, 3000m/5000m/10000m: Jan Bresan 8:24.61/14:43.83/32:19.45, HMar: Rok Puhar 67:20, Mar: Ales Zontar 2:36:29, 3000mSt: Blaz Grad 9:56.82, 110mh/400mh: Peter Hribarsek 14.99/52.66, HJ: Axel Luxa 2.00, PV: Andrej Poljanec 5.00, LJ: Nino Celec 7.23, TJ: Ziga Vrscaj 15.40w, SP: Blaz Zupancic 18.77, DT: Tadej Hribar 55.18, HT: Nejc Plesko 75.31, JT: Matija Kranjc 70.57. **Women**: 100m: Tara Keber 12.46, 200m/400m Anita Horvat 23.64/52.32, 800m: Jerneja Smonkar 2:05.39, 1500m/3000m: Urska Arzensek 4:39.23/

10:31.38, 5000m/10000m: Klara Ljubi 18:48.49/38:44.18, HMar: Neja Krsinar 77:47, Mar: Jasmina Pitamic Vojska 2:58:27, 100mh: Joni Tomicic Prezelj 13.48, 400mh: Julija Praprotnik 61.34, HJ: Marusa Cernjul 1.85, PV: Tina Sutej 4.30, LJ: Neja Filipic 6.08, TJ: Eva Mustar 13.04, SP/DT: Veronika Domjan 13.86/54.55, HT: Claudia Stravs 65.36, JT: Martina Ratej 66.10.

Women

Martina RATEJ b. 2 Nov 1981 Celje 1.78m 69kg. AD Kladivar Celje.
At JT: OG: '08- dnq 36, '12- 7, '16- dnq 18; WCh: '09-11-13-15-17: 10/6/dnq 20/dnq 23/9; EC: '06- 10-12-14-16-18: dnq 21/6/dnq 21/6/6/4; WJ: '00- dnq 15. SLO champion 2005-14, 2016-18; MedG 2013, Balkan 2015.
Five SLO javelin records 2008-10.
Progress at JT: 1999- 48.74, 2000- 46.83, 2005- 50.86, 2006- 57.49, 2007- 58.49, 2008- 63.44, 2009- 63.42, 2010- 67.16, 2011- 65.89, 2012- 65.24, 2013- 62.60, 2014- 66.13, 2015- 65.75, 2016- 61.03, 2017- 65.64, 2018- 66.10. Mother of two. Equalled EC women's record six appearances.

SOUTH AFRICA

Governing body: Athletics South Africa. Original body founded 1894.
National Championships first held in 1894 (men), 1929 (women). **2018 Champions: Men**: 100m: Simon Magakwe 10.07, 200m: Luxolo Adams 20.08, 400m: Peter Conradie 45.55, 800m: Tshepe Tshite 1:46.04, 1500m: Nkosinathi Sibiya 3:45.08, 5000m: Jerry Motsau 14:14.07, 10000m/HMar/Mar: Stephen Mokoka 29:34.56/61:44/2:08:31, 3000mSt: Rantso Mokopane 8:51.23, 110mh: Antonio Alkana 13.48, 400mh: Lindsay Hanekom 49.17, HJ: Chris Moleya 2.23, PV: Valco van Wyke 5.40, LJ: Luvo Manyonga 8.41, TJ: Khotso Mokoena 17.09, SP: Orazio Cremona 20.71, DT: Victor Hogan 61.42, HT: Chris Harmse 70.62 (23rd successive title), JT: Phil-Mar Janse van Rensburg 76.65, Dec: Friedrich Pretorius 7764, 20kW: Wayne Snyman 1:24:58, 50kW: Mthunzi Mnisi 4:46:42. **Women**: 100m: Carina Horn 11.08, 200m/400m: Justine Palframan 22.97/51.31, 800m/1500m: Caster Semenya 1:57.80/4:10.68, 5000m: Dominique Scott Efurd 16:55.05, 10000m/3000mSt: Cherise Sims 35:55.83/10:41.14, HMar: Jenet Mbhele 73:07, Mar: Nolene Conrad 2:34:39, 100mh: Taylon Bieldt 13.71, 400mh: Wenda Nel 55.01, HJ: Julia du Plessis 1.80, PV: Jodie Sedras 3.90, LJ: Linque Beneke 6.22, TJ: Patience Ntshingila 13.78, SP/DT: Ischke Senekal 16.70/54.69, HT: Charne Coetzee 58.97, JT: Jo-ané van Dyk 53.65, Hep: Nienka du Toit 4726, 20kW: Anél Oosthuizen 1:43:56, 50kW: Natalie le Roux 4:55:20.

Anaso JOBODWANA b. 30 Jul 1992 Aberdeen, Eastern Cape 1.87m 71kg. Was at Jacksonville

State University, USA.
At (100m)/200m: OG: '12- 8, '16- h; WCh: '13-sf/6, '15- h/3; CG: '18- sf/2R; WUG: '13- 1/1. Won RSA 200m 2015.
South African 200m record 2015.
Progress at 200m: 2009- 21.68A, 2010- 20.95A, 2012- 20.27, 2013- 20.13/20.00w, 2015- 19.87, 2016-20.53, 2017- 20.62/20.10Aw, 2018- 20.07. pbs: 60m 6.60Ai '15, 6.66i '13; 100m 10.10 '13, 150m 15.08A '18.

Luvo MANYONGA b. 8 Jan 1991 Mbekweni 1.85m 65kg. Tuks, University of Pretoria.
At LJ: OG: '16- 2; WCh: '11- 5, '17- 1; CG: '18- 1; WJ: '10- 1; AfG: '11- 1, AfCh: '16- 2, '18- 2; Af-J: '09- 3; WI: '18- 2; won DL 2017-18, RSA 2018.
Two African long jump records 2017, junior 2010, two indoor 2018.
Progress at LJ: 2009- 7.65, 2010- 8.19, 2011- 8.26, 2012- 8.00, 2016- 8.48, 2017- 8.65A/8.62, 2018-8.58. pb TJ 15.71A '10.
18 months drugs ban from positive test 20 Mar 2012. Unbeaten in nine LJ competitions 2017.

Godfrey Khotso MOKOENA b. 6 Mar 1985 Heidelberg, Gauteng 1.90m 73kg. University of Johannesburg.
At LJ/(TJ). OG: '04- (dnq 29), '08- 2, '12- 8, '16-(dnq 21); WCh: '05-07-09-11-13-15: 7/5/2/dnq 15=/7/dnq 13 & 9; CG: '06- 4/2, '14- (1); WJ: '02-12, '04- 2/1; AfG: '03- 3/2, '07- 3; AfCh: '06- 2/2, '10- 1, '14- 2/1, '16- (3), '18- (2); CCp: '14- (2), '18-(7); WI: '06-08-10: 5/1/2. At HJ: WY: '01- 5. Won DL LJ 2014, RSA LJ 2005-07, 2009-11; TJ 2004-06, 2014-15, 2018.
Records: African LJ (3) 2009, RSA LJ (5) 2005-09, TJ (3) 2004-14, African junior TJ 2004.
Progress at LJ, TJ: 2001- 7.17A, 2002- 7.82A, 16.03A; 2003- 7.84A/7.83, 16.28; 2004- 8.09, 16.96A/16.77; 2005- 8.37A/8.22, 17.25; 2006-8.39/8.45w, 16.95; 2007- 8.34A/8.28/8.32w, 16.75; 2008- 8.25/8.35w, 2009- 8.50, 2010- 8.23A/8.15/8.22w, 2011- 8.25/8.31w, 2012- 8.29A/8.24, 2013-8.30, 15.68i; 2014- 8.19, 17.35; 2015- 8.16, 16.85; 2016- 16.77, 2017- 8.19, 16.55A; 2018- 7.89, 16.92/17.09Aw. pbs: 100m 10.7A '09, HJ 2.10 '01.

Clarence MUNYAI b. 20 Feb 1998 Johannesburg 1.76m 66kg. Tuks, Pretoria.
At 200m: OG: '16- h; WCh: '17- dq h; CG: '18- 4; WJ: 16- 4; AfCh: '16 sf; Af-J: 17- 1. Won RSA 200m 2016.
Records: World junior 300m 2017, African juniuor 200m 2017, South African 200m 2018.
Progress at 200m: 2014- 21.61A, 2015- 20.77A, 2016- 20.36A/20.40/20.33Aw, 2017- 20.10A/20.31, 2018- 19.69A/20.36. pbs: 100m 10.10A '18. 300m 31.61 '17.

Ruswahl SAMAAI b. 25 Sep 1991 Paarl 1.78m 73kg. Was at University of Johannesburg.
At LJ: OG: '16- 9; WCh: '15- dnq 20, '17- 3; CG: '14- 3, '18- 3; AfCh: '14-16-18: 3/1/1; CCp: '18- 1; WI: '16- 5, '18- 6; RSA champion 2015.

Progress at LJ: 2009- 6.93A, 2010- 7.41, 2011-7.75/7.80w, 2012- 7.94A/7.61w, 2013- 7.96A/7.74, 2014- 8.13A/8.08, 2015- 8.38, 2016- 8.38/8.40w, 2017- 8.49A/8.35, 2018- 8.45. pb TJ 16.10A '14.

Lebogang SHANGE b. 1 Aug 1990 Johannesburg 1.60m 56kg.
At 20kW: OG: '16- 44; WCh: '13- dnf, '15- 11, '17-4; CG: '18- 9; AfG: '15- 1, AfC: '13-14-16-18: 1/1/3/2. RSA champion 2012-16.
African 3000m walk record 2018, RSA 20k walk record 2018
Progress at 20kW: 2011- 1:27:31, 2012- 1:25:48, 2013- 1:26:06, 2014- 1:24:09, 2015- 1:21:43, 2016-1:20:06, 2017- 1:19:18, 2018- 1:23:27. Pbs: 3000mW 10:47.08 '18, 5000mW 18:55.60 '17, 10000mW 41:16.23 '17, 39:48R '17.
Won (1=) IAAF Race Walking Challenge 2018.

Akani SIMBINE b. 21 Sep 1993 Kempton Park 1.74m 67kg. Tuks, graduate of the University of Pretoria.
At 100m/(200m): OG: '16- 5; WCh: '13- h, '15- sf/sf, '17- 5/sf; CG: 14- sf/5, '18- 1/2R; AfCh: '14- 8, '16- 3, '18- 1/1R; CCp: '18- 3; WUG: '15- 1. Won RSA 100m 2015, 2017.
Three South African 100m records 2015-16.
Progress at 100m, 200m: 2010- 10.61A, 2011-10.57A, 21.27A; 2012- 10.19A, 20.68A; 2013- 10.36, 20.79A/20.78w; 2015- 9.97, 20.23; 2016- 9.89, 20.16; 2017- 9.92A/9.99, 19.95A/20.21; 2018- 9.93. pb 60m 6.60Ai '15, 6.66i '13.

Wayde van NIEKERK b. 15 Jul 1992 Cape Town 1.83m 73kg. University of the Free State, Bloemfontein.
At (200m)/400m: OG: '16- 1; WCh: '13- h, '15- 1, '17- 2/1; CG: '14- sf/2; AfCh: '14- 2, '16- (1); WJ: '10- (4); WUG: '13- 2R; CCp: '14- 4/1R. Won RSA 200m 2011, 2017, 400m 2013-15.
Records: World 400m 2016, 300m 2017, Commonwealth 400m 2015, African 300m (3) 2016-17. 400m (2) 2015, RSA 200m 2015 & 2017, 400m (2) 2015.
Progress at 200m, 400m: 2010- 21.02, 2011- 20.57, 2012- 20.91, 46.43; 2013- 20.84A, 45.09; 2014-20.19, 44.38; 2015- 19.94, 43.48; 2016- 20.02, 43.03; 2017- 19.84, 43.62. pbs: 100y 9.36 '18, 100m 9.94 '17, 300m 30.81 '17.
The only man to run under 10,0, 20.0 and 44.0, he ranks as the fourth best ever combination 100-200-400 man. Has won three successive global 400m titles.

Zarck VISSER b. 15 Sep 1989 Welkom 1.78m 70kg. University of Johannesburg.
At LJ: WCh: '13/15/17- dnq 13/19/25; CG: '14- 2; AfCh: '12- 2, '14- 1; CCp: '14- 3; won RSA 2012-14.
Progress at LJ: 2007- 7.21A, 2008- 7.62A, 2009-7.77, 2010- 7.76A/7.79Aw, 2011- 7.85, 2012- 8.15A/8.07/8.21w, 2013- 8.32, 2014- 8.31A/8.18, 2015-8.41, 2016- 7.93A/7.81, 2017- 8.22/8.23w, 2018-8.40, 2019- 8.41A pb 100m 10.68A '17, TJ 15.66A '08.

Women

Wenda NEL b. 27 May 1988 Worcester, Western Cape 1.69m 52kg. née Theron. Tuks, University of Pretoria.
At 400mh: OG: '16- sf; WCh: '11- sf, '15- 7, '17- sf; CG: '14- h, '18- 3; AfG: '11- 2; AfCh: '10-12-14-16-18: 7/5/1/1&1R/3; CCp: '14- 5, '18- 6. Won RSA 2011-2, 2014-18. At 100m/200m: WJ: '06- h/h; WY: '05: h/-.
Progress at 400mh: 2008- 60.23A, 2009- 56.45, 2010- 56.97, 2011- 56.13, 2012- 55.36A/55.79, 2013- 55.80, 2014- 54.82, 2015- 54.37, 2016- 54.47, 2017- 54.58, 2018- 54.61. pbs: 100m 11.57Aw/11.80A '15, 200m 23.39A '17, 300m 37.59A '17, 400m 52.03A/ 52.97 '17, 600m 1:28.05A 15, 100mh 14.23 '07.

Caster SEMENYA b. 7 Jan 1991 Polokwane, Limpopo Province 1.70m 64kg. NWU Pukke. Student of sports science at North West University, Potchefstroom.
At 800m (/1500m): OG: '12- 1, '16- 1; WCh: '09- 1, '11- 1, '15- sf, '17- 1/3; CG: '18- 1/1; AfG: '15- 1/8; AfCh: '16- 1/1/1R, '18- 1 (1 400m); WJ: '08- h; Afr-J: '09- 1 (1); CCp: '18- 1 (2 400m/2mxR); won DL 2016-18. RSA 400m 2016-17, 800m 2011-12, 2014-18; 1500m 2011, 2016, 2018.
World best 600m 2017. RSA records: 400m (2) 2018, 600m 2012 & 2017, 800m (6) 2009-18, 1000m (3) 2018, 1500m (2) 2018.
Progress at 400m, 800m, 1500m: 2007- 2:09.35, 2008- 2:04.23, 2009- 1:55.45, 4:08.01; 2010- 1:58.16, 2011- 52.54A/53.16, 1:56.35; 2012- 53.62, 1:57.23, 4:12.93; 2013- 1:58.92, 2014- 55.33A, 2:02.66; 2015- 53.12, 1:59.59, 4:21.63; 2016- 50.40, 50.40, 1:55.28, 4:01.99; 2017- 51.53, 1:55.16, 4:02.84; 2018- 49.62, 1:54.25, 3:59.92. pbs: 300m 37.22A '17, 600m 1:21.77 '17, 1000m 2:30.70 '18, 1500m 4:01.99 '16, 3000m 9:36.29A '17, 5000m: 16:11.59A '19.
Questions over her gender arose at the African Junior and World Champs in 2009, and she was barred from competing by Athletics South Africa until the IAAF determined whether she was free to compete again. They did so in July 2010 but saying that the medical details of her case remained confidential.

Sunette VILJOEN b. 6 Oct 1983 Johannesburg 1.70m 73kg. North West University, Potchefstroom.
At JT: OG: '04/08- dnq 35/32, '12- 4, '16- 2; WCh: '03/09- dnq 16/17, '11-13-15: 2/6/3; CG: '06-10-14-18: 1/1/2/3; AfG: '03- 3, '07- 3; AfCh: '04-06-08-10-14-16: 1/2/1/1/1/1; WUG: '07- 5, '09- 1, '11- 1; CCp: '10- 1, '14- 2. Won Afro-Asian Games 2003, RSA 2003-04, 2006, 2009-17.
Four African javelin records 2009-12, two Commonwealth 2011-12.
Progress at JT: 1999- 43.89A, 2000- 45.50A, 2001- 50.70A, 2002- 58.33A, 2003- 61.59, 2004- 61.15A, 2005- 57.31, 2006- 60.72, 2007- 58.39, 2008- 62.24A, 2009- 65.43, 2010- 66.38, 2011- 68.38, 2012- 69.35, 2013- 64.51, 2014- 65.32, 2015- 66.62,

2016- 65.14, 2017- 63.49A, 2018- 62.46A.
She played one Test and 17 ODIs for South Africa as an all-rounder at cricket 2000-02. Son Henré born in 2005.

SPAIN

Governing body: Real Federación Española de Atletismo (RFEA). Founded 1918.
National Championships first held in 1917 (men), 1931 (women). **2018 Champions: Men**: 100m: Aitor Same Ekobo 10.15, 200m: Bruno Hortelano 20.15, 400m: Oscar Husillos 45.22, 800m: Alvaro de Arriba 1:48.82, 1500m: Jesús Gómez 3:38.67, 5000m/10000m: Antonio Abadía 13:44.38/28:17.24, HMar: Houssame Benabbou 63:55, Mar: Javier Guerra 2:08:36, 3000mSt: Fernando Carro 8:29.79, 110mh: Orlando Ortega 13.32, 400mh: Sérgio Fernández 49.28, HJ: Alexis Sastre 2.18, PV Adrián Vallés 5.45, LJ: Jean Marie Okuto 8.01, TJ: Pablo Torrijos 17.23w, SP: Carlos Tobalina 19.97, DT: Lois Maikel Martínez 58,85, HT: Javier Cienfuegos 76.10, Dec: Mario Aroncón 7480, 10000mW/20kW: Álvaro Martín 39:31.72/1:21:48, 50kW: Marc Tur 3:56:05. **Women**: 100m: María Isabel Pérez 11.17w, 200m: Jaël Bestué 23.31, 400m: Laura Bueno 52.17, 800m: Zoya Naumov 2:07.84, 1500m: Marta Pérez 4:10.63, 5000m: Maitane Melero 16:09.78, 10000m: Nuria Lugueros 32:52.89, HMar: María Teresa Urbina 73:39, Mar: Marta Esteban 2:31:24, 3000mSt: Irene Sánchez-Escribano 9:57.87, 100mh: Caridad Jerez 13.41, 400mh: Sara Gallego 57.85, HJ: Raquel Álvarez 1.79. PV: Monica Clemente 4.45, LJ: Juliet Itoya 6.80, TJ: Ana Peleteiro 14.55, SP: Úrsula Ruiz 16.21, DT: Sabina Asenjo 55.99, HT: Berta Castells 68.21, JT: Lidia Parada 61.25, Hep: Patricia Ortega 5709, 10000mW: Raquel González 43:37.95, 20kW: María Pérez 1:31:46, 50kW: Julia Takacs 4:13:04.

Diego GARCÍA b. 19 Jan 1996 Madrid 1.74m 60kg. A.D.Marathon.
At 20kW: WCh: '15- 19, 17- 13; EC:'18- 2; EU23: '11- 1; ECp: '17- 7. At 10kW: WJ: '14- 2; WY: '13- 3; EJ: '15- 1; WCp: '14- 4J; ECp: '15- 1J.
Progress at 20kW: 2015- 1:21:45, 2016- 1:21:36, 2017- 1:20:34, 2018- 1:19:18. pbs: 1MW 5:36.27 '17, 3000mW 11:06.57i '18, 5000mW 19:03.16 '15, 10000mW 39:47.77 '17.
Won (1=) IAAF Race Walking Challenge 2018.

Miguel Ángel LÓPEZ b. 3 Jul 1988 Murcia 1.81m 70kg. CA Llano de Brujas-Murcia.
At 20kW: OG: '12- 5, '16- 11 (dnf 50kW); WCh: '11-13-15-17: 12/2/1/10; EC: '10-14-18: 12/1/6; EU23: '09- 1; WCp: '10- 12, '14- 5; ECp: '11-13-15-17: 5/2/1/2. At 10kW: WJ: '06- 14; WY: '05- 6; EJ: '05- 9, '07- 8; WCp: '06- 2J; ECp: '07- 2J. Won Spanish 10000mW 2010, 2012-16; 20kW 2010, 2012, 2015, 2019; 50kW 2016.
Progress at 20kW: 2008- 1:23:44, 2009- 1:22:23, 2010- 1:23:08, 2011- 1:21:41, 2012- 1:19:49, 2013-

1:21:21, 2014- 1:19:21, 2015- 1:19:14, 2016- 1:20:34, 2017- 1:19:57, 2018- 1:20:54. pbs: 3000mW 11:39.92 '13, 5000mW 18:46.95 '16, 10000mW 38:06.28 '16, 35kW 2:32:56 '15, 50kW 3:53:52 '16.

Álvaro MARTÍN b. 18 Jun 1994 Llerena 1.81m 62kg. Playas de Castellón.
At 20kW: OG: '16- 22; WCh: '13-15-17: 24/16/8; EC: '14- 6, '18- 1; EU23: '15- 2; WCp: '16- 3, '18- 8. At 10kW: WJ: '12- 5; WY: '11- 8; EJ: '13- 3; ECp: '11- 6J. Won Spanish 10000mW 2017-18, 20kW 2016-18.
Progress at 20kW: 2012- 1:22:12, 2013- 1:22:25, 2014- 1:20:39, 2015- 1:20:19, 2016- 1:19:36, 2017- 1:19:41, 2018- 1:20:42. pbs: 5000mW 18:39.65 '15, 10000mW 39:23.51 '16, 35kW 2:37:17 '14.

Saul ORDÓÑEZ b. 10 Aor 1994 Ponferrada 1.78m 63kg. New Balance.
At 800m: EC: '18- sf; EU23: '15- 2; EJ: '13- h; WI: '18- 3. Won Spanish 800m 2017. Eur CC: '18- 1 MxR. Spanish 800m record 2018.
Progress at 800m: 2010- 1:58.15, 2012- 1:58.2, 2013- 1:53.61, 2014- 1:58.96, 2015- 1:47.13, 2016- 1:47.83, 2017- 1:45.28, 2018- 1:43.65. pbs: 400m 48.74 '15, 1500m 3:39.40i '19, 3:40.39 '17; 3000m 8:07.37i '15, 2000mSt 6:03.27 '11.

Orlando ORTEGA b. 29 Jul 1991 La Habana 1.85m 70kg. Club d'Atletisme de la Vall d'Albaida.
At 110mh: OG: '12- 6, '16- 2; WCh: '13- h, '17- 7; EC: '18- 3; WJ: '10- h; PAm: '11- 3; ET: 17- 1. Won DL 2016, Cuban 2011, Spanish 2016-17. At 60mh: EI: '17- 7, '19- 4.
Two Spanish 110mh records 2016.
Progress at 110mh: 2009- 14.11, 2010- 13.99, 2011- 13.29/13.1w, 2012- 13.09, 2013- 13.08, 2014- 13.01, 2015- 12.94, 2016- 13.04, 2017- 13.15/13.09w, 2018- 13.08. pbs: 60m 6.71i '16, 100m 10.62 '11, 200m 21.08 '18, 400m 47.84 '09, 50mh 6.66+i '12, 60mh 7.45i '15, 7.48i '17 ESP record.
Left Cuba in 2013 and given Spanish citizenship on 9 Sep 2015 with eligibility confirmed from 29 Jul 2017, just before Olympic Games.

Jorge UREÑA b. 8 Oct 1993 Onil 1.78m 75kg. Playas de CFastellón.
At Dec. WCh: '15- 21, '17- 9, EC: '16- dnf, '18-16, WJ: '12- 20; EU23: '15- 2. Spanish champion 2015-16. At Hep: EI: '15-17-19: 7/2/1.
Progress at Dec: 2013- 7358, 2014- 7656, 2015- 7983, 2016- 7985, 2017- 8125, 2018- 6934. pbs: 60m 6.91i '17, 100m 10.86 '14, 400m 48.50 '18, 1000m 2:40.06i '15, 1500m 4:24.12 '17, 60mh 7.78i '17, 110mh 13.95 '16, HJ 2.10i/2.08 '17, PV 5.02i/5.00 '16, LJ 7.73i '19, 7.54 '16; SP 14.68i '19, 14.36 '17; DT 39.56 '18, JT 64.02 '15, Hep 6249i '17.

Women

Ana PELETEIRO b. 2 Dec 1995 Ribeira, La Coruña 1.71m 52kg. FC Barcelona.
At TJ: WCh: '17- 7; EC: '18-3; WJ: '12- 1, '14- 6; WY: '11- 3; E23: '17- 2; EJ: '13- 3; WI: '18- 3; EI: '17- 5, '19- 1. Spanish champion 2015, 2017-18.

Two European youth bests at triple jump 2012.
Progress at TJ: 2011- 13.17, 2012- 14.17, 2013- 13.75i/13.29/13.30w, 2014- 14.07, 2015- 14.03, 2016- 13.91i/13.55, 2017- 14.23, 2018- 14.55, 2019- 14.73i. pbs: 60m 7.56i '14, 100m 11.93 '14, LJ 5.99 '15.

María PÉREZ b. 29 Apr 1996 Orce 1.56m 48kg. VCFV.
At 20kW: WCh: '17- 10; EC: '18- 1; E23: '17- 2; WCp: '18- 7; ECp: '17- 6. Spanish champion 2019.
At 10kW: WJ: '14- 5, WCp: '14- 9J; EJ: '15- 4, ECp: '15- 3J. At 5000mW: WY: '13- 7.
Spanish walks records: 3000m & 20k 2018.
Progress at 20kW: 2015- 1:35:14, 2016- 1:33:44, 2017- 1:29:37, 2018- 1:26:36. pbs: 3000mW 12:00.87 '18, 5000mW 20:38.16 '18. 10000mW 44:13.83 '16.

Julia TAKACS b. 29 Jun 1989 Budapest, Hungary 1.71m 53kg. Playas de Castellón.
At 20kW: OG: '16- 33; WCh: '13: 9; EU23: '09- 5, '11- 1; WCp: '12- 10, '16- 13; ECp: '09- 11, '11- 10; WUG: '11- 1. At 50kW: EC: '18- 3; WT: '18- 8. At 10000mW: WJ: '08- 6. Won IbAm 10000mW 2014, Spanish 10000mW 2009, 2011, 2013-15, 2017; 20kW 2013-14, 50kW 2018.
Spanish walk records: 3000m & 5000m 2014, 10000m (2) 2013-14, 50k 2018.
Progress at 20kW, 50kW: 2006- 1:43:49, 2007- 1:38:57, 2008- 1:39:12, 2009- 1:35:04, 2010- 1:30:14, 2011- 1:31:32, 2012- 1:30:37, 2013- 1:28:44, 2014- 1:29:08, 2015- 1:31:23, 2016- 1:29:47, 2017- 1:30:14. 2018- 1:27:58, 4:13:04. pbs: 3000mW 12:11.27 '14, 5000mW 20:30.04 '14, 10000mW 42:23.37 '14, 30kW 2:31:53 '18, 35kW 2:56:59 '18.
She has lived in Spain from the age of 14 and switched from Hungary to Spain 19 June 2008.

SRI LANKA

Governing body: Athletic Association of Sri Lanka. Founded 1922.
National Champions 2018: Men: 100m: Himasha Eashan 10.41, 200m: Mohammed Safan 21.34, 400m: Aruna Darshana 46.16, 800m: G.R.Chathuranga 1:51.30, 1500m: Tharanga Fonseka 3:50.80, 5000m: A.K.Tharanga 14:36.9, 10000m: Kumar Shanmugeswaran 30:57.26, 3000mSt: R.M.S.Pushpakumara 9:09.04, 110mh: Roshan Dhammika Ranathunga 14.65, 400mh: Asanka Rathnasena 51.23, HJ: Ushan Thiwanka Perera 2.18, PV: Channa Fernando 4.50, LJ: Janaka Prasad Wimalasiri 8.14, TJ: Sanjaya Jayasinghe 16.08, SP: Samitha Jayawardhana 16.23, DT: Gayan Jayawardana 56.40, HT: Rukshan Kumarasiri 48.97, JT: Sampath Ranasinghe 78.79, Dec: Ajith Kumara Karunathilake 7356. **Women**: 100m/200m: Rumeshika Rathnayake 11.72w/24.26, 400m: Nadeesha Ramanayake 53.27, 800m: W.K.L.A. Nimali 2:04.3, 1500m: Nilani Rathnayake 4:17.52, 5000m/10000m: Anusha Lamahewage 17:15.66/36:48.4, 3000mSt: Nilani Rathnayake 9:46.76, 100mh: Lakshika Sugandi 13.92, 400mh: G.A.S.Dulani 60.11, HJ: Dulanjali Ranasinghe

1.76; PV: K.L.S. Perera, Aniththa Jegatheshwaran 3.40, LJ: Anjani Pulwansa 6.08w, TJ: Vidusha Lakshani 13.60, SP: Tharika Kumudumali Fernando 14.22, DT: Ayesha Maduwanthi 43.15, HT: Aruni Lakshika 46.18, JT: Dilhani Lekamge 54.45, Hep: Lakshika Sugandhi 4906.

SWEDEN
Governing body: Svenska Friidrottsförbundet. Founded 1895.
National Championships first held in 1896 (men), 1928 (women). 2018: Men: 100m: Henrik Larsson 10.14w, 200m: Felix Svensson 20.73, 400m: Erik Martinsson 47.26, 800m: Andreas Kramer 1:47.82, 1500m/5000m: Kalle Berglund 4:00.08/14:46.03, 10000m: Adhanom Abraha 29:35.37, HMar: Mikael Ekvall 63:52, Mar Mustafa Mohamed 2:27:39:, 3000mSt: Napoleon Solomon 8:43.29, 110mh: Fredrick Ekholm 13.78w, 400mh: Isak Andersson 50.99, HJ: Linus Thörnblad 2.11, PV: Melker Svärd Jacobsson 5.21, LJ: Thobias Nilsson Montler 8.06w, TJ: Erik Ehrlin 15.60w, SP/DT: Daniel Ståhl 18.78/69.72, HT: Mattias Lindberg 68.20, JT: Kim Amb 77.13, Dec: Andreas Gustafsson 7153, 10000mW/20kW: Perseus Karlsson 42:39.89/1:26:45, 50kW: Anders Hansson 4:13:59. Women: 100m: Fanny Runheim 11.51w, 200m: Lisa Lilja 23.66, 400m: Moa Hjelmer 53.92, 800m/1500m: Hanna Hermansson 2:04.41/4:14.22, 5000m/10000m: Linn Nilsson 16:24.30/34:33.06, HMar: Isabellah Andersson 76:11, Mar: Mikaela Larsson 2:40:28, 3000mSt: Charlotta Fougberg 9:42.14, 100mh: Elin Westerlund 13.51, 400mh: Johanna Holmén Svensson 58.74, HJ: Sofie Skoog 1.89, PV: Angelica Bengtsson 4.62, LJ: Khaddi Sagnia 6.71, TJ: Aina Griksaite LTU 13.29, SP: Fanny Roos 18.08, DT: Vanessa Kamga 55.60, HT: Grete Ahlberg 67.17, JT: Sofi Flink 58.88, Hep: Lovisa Östervall 5404, 5000mW/10kW: Monica Svensson 24:46.64/51:10.

Armand 'Mondo' DUPLANTIS b. 10 Nov 1999 Lafayette, LA, USA 1.83m 73kg. Upsala IF, Louisiana State University, USA.
At PV: WCh: '17- 9; EC: '18- 1; WJ: '16- 3, '18- 1; WY: '15- 1; EJ: '17- 1; WI: '18- 7=.
Pola vault records: World junior (4 indoor, 6 out) 2017-18; 6 Swedish 2018-19.
Progress at PV: 2007- 2.33, 2008- 2.89, 2009- 3.20, 2010- 3.86, 2011- 3.91, 2012- 3.97i, 2013- 4.44i/4.42, 2014- 4.75i/4.59, 2015- 5.30, 2016- 5.51, 2017- 5.90, 2018- 6.05. Pbs: 100m 10.73/10.57w '18, LJ 7.12, 7.15w '17.
Has dual citizenship Sweden/USA; declaration for Sweden confirmed from 9 Jun 2015. Has been setting world age records from the age of 7 in 2007. World junior records at 5.95, 6.00 and 6.05 to win EC 2018. IAAF Rising Star of the Year 2018. His father Greg (USA) had pb 5.80 '93, his mother Helena Hedlund was a Swedish heptathlete (5314 '83), and his brother Andreas

(b. 2 May 1993) had PV pb 5.43i/5.36 '13, WJ: '12- 10, EJ: '11- 9. His maternal grandfather Lars-Åke Hedlund had PV pb 3.80 '58.
Perseus KARLSTRÖM b. 2 May 1990 Eskilstuna 1.84m 75kg. né Ibáñez. Eskilstuna FI.
At 20kW: OG: '16- dnf; WCh: '13- 38, '15- dnf, '17- 37; EC: '14- 17, '18- 20; ECp: '15- 8, '17- 3. At 50kW: WT: '18- 8. At 10000mW: WJ: '08- 30; WY: '07- 24; EJ: '09- 9. Won SWE 20k 2012-16, 2018; 50kW 2013, 2016, 10000mW 2008, 2015-16, 2018.
Swedish walks records: 10000m 2017 & 2018, 20k 2016.
Progress at 20kW, 50kW: 2005- 1:53:39, 2008- 1:35:31, 2009- 1:31:22, 2010- 1:25:32, 2011- 1:26:20, 2012- 1:23:43, 2013- 1:24:55, 3:52:43; 2014- 1:21:54, 2015- 1:22:44, 2016- 1:19:11, 4:06:33; 2017- 1:20:20, 3:44:35; 2018- 1:20:30, 3:48:54. pbs: 1MW 5:38.18 '17, 5000mW 18:32.56 '19, 10000mW 38:39.28 '18.
His father Enrique Vera was 2nd in World 50kW 1976, pb 3:43:59 '79; mother Siw Gustavsson/ Ibáñez/Karlström was 3rd in European 10kW 1986. Brother Anatole Ibáñez (b. 14 Nov 1985) pbs 20kW 1:20:54 '16, 50kW 3:48:42 '14.
Simon PETTERSSON b. 3 Jan 1994 Sixarby 1.98m 106kg. Hässelby SK.
At DT: WCh: '17- 11; EC: '18- 4; EU23: '15- 5; EJ: '13- dnq 17.
Progress at DT: 2013- 49.71, 2014- 55.39, 2015- 60.25, 2016- 63.10, 2017- 64.88, 2018- 65.84. pbs: HJ 1.89 '11, PV 4.26i '12, 4.15 '11; LJ 6.82i '12, 6.67 '11; TJ: 14.32/14.39w '11, SP 17.83 '16, HT 58.43 '16, JT 61.06 '16.
Daniel STÅHL b. 27 Aug 1992 Järfälla 2.00m 155kg. Spårvägens FK.
At (SP)/DT: OG: '16- dnq 14; WCh: '15- 5, '17- 2; EC: '14-16-18: dnq 24/5/2; EU23: '13- 4; WJ: '10- (dnq 27); WY: '09- dnq 16/dnq 16; EJ: '11- (dnq 20); CCp: '18- 3. Won SWE SP 2015-16, 2018; DT 2014, 2016-18. Swedish discus record 2017.
Progress at DT: 2008- 40.36, 2009- 44.34, 2010- 50.32, 2011- 55.60, 2012- 62.16, 2013- 61.29, 2014- 66.89, 2015- 64.73, 2016- 68.72, 2017- 71.29, 2018- 69.72. pbs: SP 19.60i '17, 19.38 '16; HT 48.91 '16, JT 50.43 '16. Father Jan had pbs SP 16.80 & HT 59.14 '80, mother Taina DT 51.90 '82, sister Anneli HT 59.74 '13.
Melker SVÄRD JACOBSSON b. 8 Jan 1994 Lund 1.88m 79kg. Örgryte IS. Medical student.
At PV: EC: '14- dnq 19, 16- dns, 18-dnq nh; WJ: '12- 6; WY: '11- 2; EI: '19- 3; YOG: '10- 4. SWE champion 2017-18.
Progress at PV: 2005- 3.20i/3.10, 2006- 3.82i/3.65, 2007- 3.95i/3.93, 2008- 4.26, 2009- 4.75, 2010- 5.11, 2012- 5.48, 2013- 5.50, 2014- 5.65i/5.60, 2016- 5.70, 2017- 5.55, 2018- 5.78i/5.70, 2019- 5.82i.
Michel TORNÉUS b. 26 May 1986 Botkyrka 1.85m 75kg. Hammarby IF.
At LJ: OG: '12- 4, '16- dnq 26; WCh: '09-11-13-15-17: dnq 28/27/19/dnq/8; EC: '10-12-14-16-18:

9/3/5/2/7; EU23: '07- 10; EJ: '05- 4; WI: '14- 3; EI: '11-13-15-17: 7/2/1/2; ET: '11- 2. Won Swedish LJ 2005, 2007-10, 2012-17 (indoor 2008, 2010-17); TJ 2012, 2016.
Swedish long jump records 2012 & 2016.
Progress at LJ: 2001- 6.48, 2002- 6.74/6.86w, 2003- 7.07, 2004- 7.41, 2005- 7.94, 2006- 7.68, 2007- 7.85, 2008- 7.86, 2009- 8.11, 2010- 8.12/8.21w, 2011- 8.19, 2012- 8.22, 2013- 8.29i/8.00/8.12w, 2014- 8.21i/8.09/8.10w, 2015- 8.30i/7.83/8.07w, 2016- 8.44A/8.07/8.21w, 2017- 8.30A/8.18, 2018- 7.91. pbs: 60m 6.93i '12, 100m 10.71/10.63w '11, 400mh 55.48 '04, HJ 1.99i '05, 1.92 '04; TJ 16.10 '16, Dec 6115 '04. Father from DR of Congo.

Women

Meraf BAHTA Ogbagaber b. 24 Jun 1989 Dekishahay, Eritrea 1.76m 50kg. Hälle IF.
At 5000m: EC: '14- 1, '16- 2; ET: '14- 1. At 10000m: EC: '18- 3. At 3000m: CCp: '14- 2; EI: '17- 4. At 1500m: OG: '16- 6; WCh: '17- 9; WJ: '06- 5; EI: '17- 4. World CC: '06- 12J, '07- 6J; Eur CC: '14- 3, '17- 2. Won SWE 800m & 1500m 2017, 5000m 2011, 4k & 8k CC 2013-14, 2017.
Swedish records 2000m 2018, 3000m 2016 & 2017, 5000m 2014 & 2016, 10000m 2017.
Progress at 1500m, 5000m: 2006- 4:16.01, 2007- 4:15.12, 15:56.30; 2008- 4:12.52, 15:58.31; 2009- 4:28.93, 2010- 4:22.86, 16:28.77; 2011- 4:19.82, 16:29.08; 2012- 4:14.09, 2013- 4:05.11, 2014- 4:01.34, 14:59.49; 2015- 4:06.42i, 15:46.97; 2016- 4:02.62, 14:49.95; 2017- 4:00.49; 2018- 4:02.31, 15:08.17 pbs: 800m 2:02.45 '18, 1M 4:25.26 '16, 2000m 5:37.12 '18, 3000m 8:37.50 '17, 10000m 31:13.06 '17, 10k Rd 31:09 '19, HMar 72:08 '19.
Came from Eritrea to Sweden as a refugee in 2009; received Swedish citizenship on 23 Dec 2013 and cleared to compete for them from 14 Jan 2014.

Angelica BENGTSSON b. 8 July 1993 Väckelsång 1.64m 53kg. Hässelby SK.
At PV: OG: '12/16- dnq 19=/14=, WCh: '13- dnq 16, '15- 4=, '17- 10; EC: '12-14-16-18: 10/5/3/6; WJ: '10- 1, '12- 1; WY: '09- 1; EU23: '13- 3, '15- 1; EJ: '11- 1; YthOG: '10- 1; EI: '15- 3, '17- 3=; ET: '15- 3. SWE champion 2012, 2014-16.
Pole vault records: Two world youth 2010; four world junior indoors 2011, two world junior outdoor bests, eight Swedish 2011-18.
Progress at PV: 2004- 2.65, 2005- 3.10, 2006- 3.40, 2007- 3.90, 2008- 4.12, 2009- 4.37, 2010- 4.47, 2011- 4.63i/4.57, 2012- 4.58, 2013- 4.55, 2014- 4.62i/4.50, 2015- 4.70, 2016- 4.66i/4.65, 2017- 4.65, 2018- 4.73, 2019- 4.81i. pbs: LJ 5.66 '16, JT 35.04 '17.
Rising Star Awards: IAAF 2010, European Athletics 2012. Her father Glenn had JT pb 67.08 '82, sisters Victoria (b. 1990) PV 4.00 '09 and Maria (b. 1988) DT 43.95 '07.

Erika KINSEY b. 10 Mar 1988 Nälden 1.85m 68kg. née Wiklund. Trångsvikens IF. Was at University of Central Missouri, USA.

At HJ: OG: '16- dnq 29=; WCh: '15/17- dnq 18/21=; EC: '16- dnq 22, '18- 13; WJ: '06- 8; WY: '05- 5; EU23: '09- 8, EJ: '07- 1; WI: '16- 8, '18- 7=; EI: '19- 7.
Progress at HJ: 2002- 1.58, 2003- 1.65, 2004- 1.86, 2005- 1.84, 2006- 1.84, 2007- 1.85/1.87i, 2008- 1.91, 2009- 1.88, 2011- 1.84, 2013- 1.75, 2014- 1.88, 2015- 1.97, 2016- 1.93i/1.90, 2017- 1.94, 2018- 1.94.
Pbs: LJ 6.35i '19, 6.29 '18, 6.46w '15; TJ 13.11 '15, Pen 3935 '09.
Lives in Warrensburg, MO, USA. Married Daniel Kinsey USA (b. 25 Jul 1986, Dec: 7563 '09) in July 2014. At age 16 improved by 21 cm in one year in 2004 to 1.86. Won EJ in 2007 but lost motivation for HJ in 2012-13 and played ice hockey in Norway. Came back to athletics in 2014 with a big breakthrough in '15, improving her seven year old pb by 6 cm to 1.97.

Khaddijatou 'Khaddi' SAGNIA b. 20 Apr 1994 Helsingborg 1.73cm 63kg. Ullevi FK.
At LJ: OG: '16- dnq 27; WCh: '15- 7, '17- dnq 16; EC: '16- 6, '18- 7; WY: '11- 11; EU23: '15- 4; WI: '18- 6. At TJ: WY: '11- 9; YthOG: '10- 1. Won SWE TJ 2011, LJ 2015-18, 100m 2016.
Progress at LJ: 2007- 5.18i, 2008- 5.56, 2009- 6.00i/5.09/6.00w, 2010- 6.26, 2011- 6.92, 2014- 6.55, 2015- 6.78, 2016- 6.74, 2017- 6.72, 2018- 6.92i/6.71. Pbs: 60m 7.31i '19, 100m 11.48 '16, 200m 25.14 '14, 60mh 8.14i '18, 100mh 13.93 '15, 13.62w '14; HJ 1.78 '11, TJ 13.65/13.86w '11, JT 41.47 '14, Hep 5287 '11.

Sofie SKOOG b. 7 Jun 1990 Mora 1.81m 65kg. IF Göta Karlstad.
At HJ: OG: '16- 7; WCh: '15/17 dnq 14=/18; EC: '16- 9, '18- dnq 16; WI: '16- 5. SWE champion 2015, 2017-18.
Progress at HJ: 2004- 1.55, 2005- 1.61, 2006- 1.64, 2007- 1.70, 2008- 1.71, 2009- 1.72, 2010- 1.78, 2011- 1.75i/1.65, 2012- 1.80, 2013- 1.90, 2014- 1.88i/1.87, 2015- 1.92, 2016- 1.94, 2017- 1.94, 2018- 1.93. Pb TJ 11.05/11.29w '12.

SWITZERLAND

Governing body: Schweizerischer Leichtathletikverband (SLV) Formed 1905 as Athletischer Ausschuss des Schweizerischen Fussball-Verbandes.
National Championships first held in 1906 (men), 1934 (women). **2018: Men**: 100m/200m: Alex Wilson 10.14/20.14, 400m: Joel Burgunder 47.48, 800m: Pascal Furtwängler 1:49.92, 1500m: Julien Wanders 3:43.39, 5000m: Jonas Raess 14:20.12, 10000m: Fabian Kuert 30:16.16, HMar: Tadesse Abraham 62:16, Mar: Armin Flückiger 2:22:44, 3000mSt: Christoph Graf 9:13.78, 110mh: Jason Joseph 13.38w, 400mh: Dany Brand 51.35, HJ: Loïc Gasch 2.23, PV: Alberto Dominik 5.00, LJ: Christopher Ullmann 7.78, TJ: Nils Wicki 15.48w, SP: Stefan Wieland 16.20, DT: Stefan Grob 47.77, HT: Martin Bingisser 63.30, JT: Laurent Carron 67.58, Dec: Luca Bernaschina

7602, 10000mW: Nathan Bonzon 51:10.8, 20kW: *none*. **Women**: 100m: Mujinga Kambundji 10.95, 200m: Cornelia Halbheer 23.12, 400m: Fanette Humair 53.66, 800m: Sina Sprecher 2:08.74, 1500m: Fabienne Schlumpf 4:17.91, 5000m: Martina Tresch 16:31.01, 10000m: *none*, HMar: Susanne Rüegger 77:37, Mar: Claudia Bernmasconi 2:50:35, 3000mSt: *none*, 100mh: Kim Flattich 13.46, 400mh: Léa Springer 54.86, HJ: Nadine Odermatt 1.71, PV: Angelica Moser 4.20, LJ: Irène Pusterla 6.45w, TJ: Fatim Affesi 13.21, SP: Lea Herrsche 14.18, DT: Chantal Tanner 48.23, HT: Nicole Zihlmann 63.27, JT: Géraldine Ruckstuhl 51.85, Hep: Annina Fahr 5070, 10000mW/20kW: Corinne Henchoz 59:57.9/2:02:52.

Kariem HUSSEIN b. 1 Apr 1989 Münsterlingen 1.90m 77kg. TV Amriswil.
At 400mh: OG: '16- h; WCh: '15- sf, '17- 8; EC: '12- sf, '14- 1, '16- 3; EU23: '11- sf; CCp: '14- 2; Swiss champion 2011-15.
Swiss 300mh records 2014 & 2017.
Progress at 400mh: 2009- 52.33, 2010- 51.64, 2011- 51.09, 2012- 49.61, 2013- 49.78, 2014- 48.47, 2015- 48.45, 2016- 48.87, 2017- 48.45. pbs: 60mh 8.14i '11, 110mh 14.51 '11, 300mh 34.87 '17. Successive pbs at end of 2014 from 49.08 to 48.96 EC, 48.70 WK, 48.47 CCp. Father Ehab came from Egypt to Switzerland in the early 1980s.

Julien WANDERS b. 18 Mar 1996 Geneva 1.75m 60kg..
At 5000m: WJ: '14- 18; EC: '18- 8 (7 10000m); EJ: '15- 14. World HMar: '18- 8. Won SUI 1500m 2017, 5000m 2016.
European half marathon record 2019 (and bests at 15k, 20k), road best 10k 2018. Swiss HMar record 2018.
Progress at HMar: 2017- 61:43, 2018- 60:09, 2019- 59:13. pbs: 1500m 3:43.39 '18, 3000m 7:50.35 '18, 5000m 13:24.79 '18, 10000m 28:06.17 '17, Road: 10k 27:25 '18, 15k 41:46 '19, 10M: 45:00 '19. 20k 56:03 '19.

Alex 'Ricardo' WILSON b. 19 Sep 1990 LKingston, Jamaica 1.82m 79kg. LAS Old Boys Basel.
At 200m (100m): OG: '12- sf; WCh: '11/13- h,'17- sf (sf); EC: '10- h, 12/14- sf, '16- 7 (sf), '18- 3 (sf); EU23: '11- 7; Swiss champion 100m 2015-18, 200m 2011-12, 2014-16, 2018.
Swiss records 100m 2017, 200m (6) 2017-18.
Progress at 200m: 2007- 22.06, 2008- 22.05/21.73w, 2009- 21.63/21.34w, 2010- 20.93, 2011- 20.51, 2012- 20.52/20.43w, 2013- 20.60, 2014- 20.61, 2015- 20.58, 2016- 20.57, 2017- 20.37, 2018- 20.04. pbs: 60m 6.72i '15, 100m 10.11/10.08w '11, 150m 15.15 '16, 300m 32.83 '14.
Received Swiss citizenship in 2010.

Women

Selina BÜCHEL b. 26 Jul 1991 Mosnang 1.68m 58kg. KTV Bütschwil

At 800m: OG: '16- sf; WCh: '15/17- sf; EC: '14-16-18: sf/4/7; WJ: '10- sf; EU23: '11- 5, 13- 3; EJ: '09-7; WI: '14- 4, '18- 6; EI: '15- 1, '17- 1. Won Swiss 400m 2016, 800m 2011, 2013.
Swiss 800m record 2015.
Progress at 800m: 2008- 2:11.68, 2009- 2:06.20, 2010- 2:05.95, 2011- 2:04.25, 2012- 2:04.02, 2013- 2:01.64i/2:01.66, 2014- 2:00.93i/2:01.42, 2015- 1:57.95, 2016- 1:58.77, 2017- 1:59.46, 2018- 2:00.42. pbs: 400m 52.97 '17, 600m 1:25.45 '15, 1500m 4:08.95i '16, 4:18.57 '15.

Nicole BÜCHLER b. 17 Dec 1983 Biel 1.62m 56kg. LC Zürich.
At PV: OG: '08/12- dnq 22/25, '16- 6; WCh: '09-11-13-15: dnq 14/16/15/17=, '17- 11; EC: '14- dnq 17; EU23: '05- 12; WUG: '07- 3, '09- 2; WI: '12- 8, '16- 4. Won Swiss 400m 2016, 800m 2009, 2012-13, 2015.
12 Swiss pole vault records (and 14 indoors).
Progress at PV: 2004- 3.80, 2005- 4.15, 2006- 4.10, 2007- 4.35, 2008- 4.40, 2009- 4.50, 2010- 4.47i/4.00, 2011- 4.50, 2012- 4.60, 2013- 4.61, 2014- 4.67, 2015- 4.71, 2016- 4.80i/4.78, 2017- 4.73. pbs: 60mh 8.65i '09, 100mh 14.01 '09, LJ 5.65 '07.
She competed for Switzerland at two World and four European championships at rhythmic gymnastics, taking up pole vaulting at the age of 20. Married US pole vaulter Mitch Greeley (5.56sq '08, 5.55i '09) in 2010. Had a baby in 2018.

Mujinga KUMBUNDJI b. 17 Jun 1992 Uetendorf 1.68m 59kg. St Bern.
At 100m/(200m): OG: '16- sf/sf; WCh: '13/15/17- (h)/sf/sf; EC: '12- h, '14- 4/5, '16- 3/sf, '18- 4/4; WJ: '10- sf/sf; WY: '09- sf/6; EU23: '13- 4/5; EJ: '11- 5/5; At 60m: WI: '18- 3; EI: '15-17-19: 5/3/5. Won Swiss 100m 2009, 2011-17; 200m 2009, 2012-15, 2017.
Swiss records: 100m (10), 200m (4) 2014-18.
Progress at 100m, 200m: 2007- 12.17, 2008- 12.02, 24.30; 2009- 11.66, 23.87; 2010- 11.70/11.57w, 23.68; 2011- 11.53, 22.70/23.31w; 2012- 11.62, 23.26; 2013- 11.50, 23.24; 2014- 11.20, 22.83; 2015- 11.07, 22.64; 2016- 11.14, 22.78; 2017- 11.07, 22.42; 2018- 10.95, 22.45. pbs: 60m 7.03i '18.

Fabienne SCHLUMPF b. 17 Nov 1990 Wetzikon 1.83m 62kg. TG Hütten.
At 3000mSt: OG: '16- 18; WCh: '13/17- h; EC: '14-16-18- 13/5/2; EU23: '11- h, EJ: '09- h. World HMar: '18- 16. Eur CC: 16-17-18: 8/7/2. Won SUI 1500m 2014, 2016, 2018; 5000m 2016, 3000mSt 2009, 2012, 2017.
Swiss records HMar 2017, 2000mSt (4) 2012-17, 3000mSt (6) 2000mSt (2) 2008-09.
Progress at 3000mSt: 2008- 11:06.79, 2009- 10:57.74, 2010- 10:51.77, 2011- 10:22.07, 2012- 9:55.50, 2013- 9:46.98, 2014- 9:37.81, 2015- 9:40.63. 2016- 9:30.54, 2017- 9:21.65, 2018- 9:22.29. pbs: 800m 2:12.07 '17, 1500m 4:17.91 '18, 3000m 8:58.63 '17, 5000m 15:23.44 '18, HMar 70:17 '17, 2000mSt 6:20.33 '17.

Léa SPRUNGER b. 5 Mar 1990 Nyon 1.83m 69kg. COVA Nyon.
At 400mh: OG:'16- h; WCh: '15- sf, '17- 5; EC: '16- 3, '18- 1; At Hep: WJ: '08-10; WY: '07- 13; EU23: '11- 16; EJ: '09- 3; At 200m: OG: '12- h; EC: '12/14- sf; At 400m. EI: '17- 5, '19- 1. Won 3wiss 200m 2016-17, 400m 2014, 400mh 2018.
Swiss records: 200m 2016, 400m 2017 & 2018.
Progress at 400mh: 2015- 55.60, 2016- 54.92, 2017- 54.29, 2018- 54.33. pbs: 60m 7.37i '14, 100m 11.34 '14, 150m 17.06 '16, 200m 22.38 '16, 300m 35.70 '17, 400m 50.52 '18, 800m 2:23.94 '09, 60mh 8.65i '12, 100mh 14.31 '11, 300mh 39.29 '17, HJ 1.81 '08, LJ 6.14 '08, SP 12.77i '12, 12.63 '11; JT 38.73 '09, Pen 4047i '12, Hep 5651 '11.
Older sister Ellen Sprunger (b. 8 Aug 1986) Hep 6124 '12.

SYRIA

Majed El Dein GHAZAL b. 21 Apr 1987 Damascus 1.93m 72kg.
At HJ: OG: '08/12- dnq 24=/28=, 16- 7=; WCh: '09/11/13/15- dnq 28=/23=/21/15, '17- 3; AsiG: '10-14-18: dnq 13=/6/3=; AsiC: '11- 2, '17- 3; CCp: '18-4. Won WMilG 2015, Is.Sol & Asian Ind G 2017, Med G 2018. 13 Syrian records 2007-16.
Progress at HJ: 2006- 2.09, 2007- 2.17, 2008- 2.21i/2.20, 2009- 2.16, 2010- 2.22, 2011- 2.28, 2012- 2.326, 2013- 2.23, 2014- 2.26, 2015- 2.31, 2016- 2.36, 2017- 2.32, 2018- 2.33.

TADJIKISTAN

Governing body: Athletics Federation of Tadjikistan. Founded 1932.

Dilshod NAZAROV b. 6 May 1982 Dushanbe 1.87m 115kg.
At HT: OG: '08- 11, '12- 9, '16- 1; WCh: '05-07-09-11-13-15-17: dnq 15/dnq 21/11/10/5/2/7; WJ: '98- dnq 15, '00- 5, AsiG: '98-02-06-10-14-18: 7/9/1/1/1/2; AsiC: '03-05-07-09-13-15-17: 3/2/2/1/1/1/1; CCp: '10- 2, '14- 4, '18- 1. Won Asi-J 1999, 2001, C.Asian 2003.
Progress at HT: 1998- 63.91, 1999- 63,56, 2000- 66.50, 2001- 68.08, 2002- 69.86, 2003- 75.56, 2004- 76.58, 2005- 77.63, 2006- 74.43, 2007- 78.89, 2008- 79.05, 2009- 79.28, 2010- 80.11, 2011- 80.30, 2012- 77.70, 2013- 80.71, 2014- 80.62, 2015- 79.36, 2016- 78.87, 2017- 77.81, 2018- 78.18.
President of national federation. In 2016 he won the first Olympic gold medal at any sport for Tadjikistan.

TAIWAN

Governing body: Chinese Taipei Athletics Association.
National Championships 2018: Men: 100m: Wang Wei-Hsu 10.44, 200m: Wei Tai-Sheng 21.32, 400m: Yu Chen-Yi 47.79, 800m: Hung Yu-Chao 1:57.29, 1500m: Wen Lien-Chung 3:53.95, 5000m/10000m: Chou Ting-Yin 14:50.66/31:39.59, 3000mSt: Huang Teng-Hsian 9:37.63, 110mh: Chen Kuei-Ru 13.86. 400mh: Yu Chia-Hsuan 50.62, HJ: Fu Chao-Hsuan 2.08, PV: Yeh Hsieh Chia-Han 4.95, LJ: Lin Chia-Hsing 7.82w, TJ: Li Kuei-Lung 15.97, SP: Yang Po-En 16.74, DT: Li Tzu-Yun 52.26, HT: Huang Chieh-Ying 56.40, JT: Cheng Chao-Tsun 76.13, Dec. Wang Chien-Yu 6990, 10000mW/20kW: Chang Wei-Jui 45:19.51/1:33:15; **Women**: 100m: Liao Yen-Chun 11.64, 200m: Chen Wan-Mei 24.38, 400m: Yu Chi-Ping 57.06, 800m: Liu Yi-Hsuan 2:14.46, 1500m: Lo Pei-Tzu 4:39.94, 5000m: Hsieh Chien-Ho 16:59.98, 10000m: Yu Ya-Chun 38:36.14, 3000m St: Chen Yu-Hsuan 11:02.12, 100mh: Cheng Tang-Hsiu 13.71, 400mh: Lin Yu-Chieh 61.12, HJ: Tsai Ching-Jung 1.76, PV: Lin Ying-Tung 3.75, LJ: Huang Shih-Han 6.03, TJ: Chuang Huei-Chi 12.37, SP: Lin Chia-Ying 16.28, DT: Yang Chia-Hsiu 46.74, HT: Hsieh Hsiu-Jung 52.18, JT: Li Huei-Chun 54.21, Hep: Chu Chia-Ling 5137, 10000mW: Huang Kuan-Ling 53:19.97, 20kW: Wu Yu-Hsin 1:51:19.

CHENG Chao-Tsun b. 17 Oct 1993 Yangmei 1.82m 88kg.
At JT: OG: '16- 5; WCh: '17- dnq 22; WJ: '10- 8; WY: '09- dnq 12; AsiG: '14- 5, '18-5; AsiC: '11-15-17: 11/7/6; CCp: '18- 3; WUG: '15- 4, '17- 1. Won Asi-J 2012.
Javelin records: 4 Taiwan 2010-17, Asian 2017.
Progress at JT: 2009- 71.71, 2010- 78.68, 2011- 77.07, 2012- 77.10, 2013- 71.22, 2014- 81.61, 2015- 81.78, 2016- 71.66, 2017- 91.36, 2018- 84.60.

TRINIDAD & TOBAGO

Governing body: National Association of Athletics Administrations of Trinidad & Tobago. Founded 1945, reformed 1971.
National Championships first held in 1946 (men) and 1947 (women). **2018 Champions**: **Men**: 100m: Keston Bledman 10.20, 200m: Kyle Greaux 20.31, 400m: Deon Lendore 45.31, 800m/1500m: Nicholas Landeau 1:50.18/4:02.84, 5000m: Iley Bruce 15:38.63, 10000m: Anthony Phillips 34:28.78, 110mh: Ruebin Walters 13.63, 400mh: Jehue Gordon 50.87, HJ: Kareem Roberts 2.06, PV: Joel Andrews 3.50, LJ: Andwuelle Wright 8.23, TJ: Kyron Blaise 15.50, SP: Akeem Stewart 19.06, DT: Konnel Jacob 49.78, HT: Kesean Phillips 27.50, JT: Kashorn Walcott 84.96, Dec: Kerlon Ashby 5622. **Women**: 100m: Michelle-Lee Ahye 11.14, 200m: Semoy Hackett 22.64, 400m: Rae Serville 54.46, 800m: Alena Brooks 2:04.46, 1500m: Dawnel Collymore 4:52.44, 5000m: Samanha Shukla 18:38.42, 100mh: Akila McShine 14.07, 400mh: Sparkle McKnight 56.60, HJ: Camile Lewis 1.65, PV: Aiesha Colthurst 2.10, LJ: Tyra Gittens 6.39w, TJ: Ayanna Alexander 13.3w, SP: Cleopatra Borel 17.21 , DT: Cherisse Murray 46.24, HT: Angel Coombs 28.20, JT: Talena Murray 48.04, Hep; Safiya John 4551.

Machel CEDENIO b. 6 Sep 1995 Pt. Fortin

1.83m 70kg. Simplex.
At 400m/4x400mR: OG: '16- 4; WCh: '15- 7/2R, '17- sf/1R; CG: '18- sf; WJ: '12- 5/3R, '14- 1; WY: '11- 4; PAm: '15- 2/1R; WI: '16- res 3R. Won CAC-J 2014, TTO 2016-17.
TTO 400m record 2016.
Progress at 400m: 2010- 48.12, 2011- 46.89, 2012- 46.02, 2013- 45.93, 2014- 45.13, 2015- 44.36, 2016- 44.01, 2017- 44.90, 2018- 45.68. Pbs: 200m 21.15 '13, 300m 31.7+ '16.

Jereem RICHARDS b. 13 Jan 1994 Pt. Fortin 1.83m 66kg. University of Alabama, USA.
At 200m/4x400mR: WCh: '17- 3/1R; WJ: '12- sf/3R, WY: '11- sf; CG: '14- h, '18- 1; WI: '12- 3R. Won TTO 2017.
Progress at 200m, 400m: 2011- 21.23, 47.32; 2012- 20.82, 47.17; 2013- 20.72/20.69w, 46.20; 2014- 20.58, 46.15; 2015- 20.72, 45.91; 2016- 46.02, 2017- 19.97, 45.21; 2018- 19.99. Pbs: 300m 32.10i '18.

Keshorn WALCOTT b. 2 Apr 1993 Toco 1.88m 90kg. Rebirth.
At JT: OG: '12- 1, '16- 3; WCh: '13/15- dnq 19/26, '17- 7; CG: '14- 2; WJ: '10- dnq, '12- 1; WY: '09- dnq 13; PAm: '11- 7, '15- 1; CAG: '18- 1; CCp: '14- 3. Won CAC-J 2010, 2012; TTO 2012, 2015-16, 2018. Javelin records: CAC 2015, nine TTO 2012- 15, eight CAC junior 2011-12.
Progress at JT: 2009- 60.02, 2010- 67.01, 2011- 75.77A, 2012- 84.58, 2013- 84.39, 2014- 85.77, 2015- 90.16, 2016- 88.68, 2017- 86.61, 2018- 84.96. pb TJ 14.28 '10.
First Caribbean Olympic champion and youngest ever Olympic champion in throws. Won IAAF Rising Star Award 2012. Elder brother Elton TJ pb 16.43/16.51w '11 & 4 WY '09, aunt Anna Lee Walcott Hep pb 5224 '00.

Women

Michelle-Lee AHYE b. 10 Apr 1992 Port of Spain 1.68m 59kg. Rebirth.
At 100m/(200m): OG: '12- sf, '16- 6/6; WCh: '11- sf, '13- sf, '15- 5/3R, '17- 6; CG: '14- sf, '18- 1; WY: '07- qf; CCp: '14- 2/1R; PAm-J: '11- 1. At 60m: WI: '14-16-18: 6/4/6. TTO champion 100m & 200m 2014, 2016-17; 100m 2018.
TTO records: 100m 2017, 200m (2) 2016.
Progress at 100m, 200m: 2006- 11.94, 24.60; 2007- 11.76/11.63w, 24.30/24.23w; 2008- 11.48, 23.80; 2009- 11.69, 2010- 11.32, 24.14/23.71w; 2011- 11.20/11.15w, 22.92w; 2012- 11.19, 23.13; 2013- 11.06, 22.98; 2014- 10.85, 22.77; 2015- 10.97/10.87w, 23.19i, 22.01w; 2016- 10.90, 22.25; 2017- 10.82, 22.50; 2018- 11.06, 23.37. pbs: 50m 6.33i '13, 60m 7.09i '16, 150m St 16.57, 16.49w '18.

Kelly-Ann BAPTISTE b. 14 Oct 1986 Plymouth, Tobago 1.68m 58kg. Zenith. Studied psychology at Louisiana State University.
At 100m/(200m): OG: '08- qf, '12- 6, '16- h; WCh: '05- qf, '09: sf/sf, '11- 3, '15- 6/3R, '17- 8; WJ: '02- sf, '04- (4); WY: '03- 3; PAm: '03- h, '15- 5; CCp: '10- 1/1R. Won NCAA 100m & indoor 60m

2008, TTO 100m 2005-06, 2008-10, 2012-13, 2015; 200m 2005, 2013. TTO records: 100m (6) 2005- 14, 200m (5) 2005-13.
Progress at 100m, 200m: 2002- 11.71, 24.03; 2003- 11.48, 23.22; 2004- 11.40, 23.41/22.99w; 2005- 11.17/11.04w, 22.93; 2006- 11.08, 22.73; 2007- 11.22, 22.90i/22.95; 2008- 11.06/10.97w, 22.67; 2009- 10.94/10.91w, 22.60; 2010- 10.84, 22.78/ 22.58w; 2011- 10.90, 2012- 10.86, 22.33w; 2013- 10.83dq, 22.36bq; 2015- 10.84, 22.91w; 2016- 11.04, 22.73; 2017- 10.88, 2018- 11.23. pbs: 55m 6.73i '06, 60m 7.13i '08.
She was withdrawn from 2013 World Champs team after failing a drugs test and was given a 1y 9m ban and results annulled from 24 Mar 2013 by the IAAF.

Cleopatra BOREL b. 3 Oct 1979 Mayoro 1.68m 93kg. Rebirth. Was at University of Maryland; assistant coach at Virginia Tech University.
At SP: OG: '04- 9, '08- dnq 15, '12- dnq 11, '16- 7; WCh: '05-07-09-13: dnq 17/17/12/13, '11/15- 11/12; CG: '02-06-10-14-18: 4/3/2/2/4; PAm: '03- 07-11-15: 6/3/2/1; CAG: '06-10-14-18: 3/1/1/1; CCp: '14- 5; WI: '04-06-08-16-18: dnq 11/7/6/4/9. Won NACAC 2007, CAC 2008, 2011, 2013; TTO 2002, 2004, 2006-10, 2012, 2014-16, 2018.
Eight TTO records at shot 2004-11.
Progress at SP: 2000- 14.64i, 2001- 16.44, 2002- 17.50i/16.90, 2003- 17.95i/17.79, 2004- 19.48i/ 18.90, 2005- 18.44, 2006- 18.81, 2007- 18.91, 2008- 18.87, 2009- 18.52, 2010- 19.30, 2011- 19.42, 2012- 18.82, 2013- 17.84, 2014- 19.13, 2015- 19.26, 2016- 18.78, 2017- 17.96, 2018- 18.60. pb HT 51.28 '01.
Formerly competed under married name Borel-Brown. Her father Rayond Borel was TTO javelin champion 1973.

TUNISIA

Governing body: Fédération Tunisienne d'Athlétisme. Founded 1957.

Habiba GHRIBI b. 9 Apr 1984 Kairouan 1.70m 57kg. Entente Franconville Cesame Va, FRA.
At 3000mSt: OG: '08- 12, '12- 1, '16- 12; WCh: '05-09-11-15: h/5/1/2; AfCh: '06- 2, '14- 5 (6 1500m). At 5000m: AfCh: '02- 11. Won FRA 1500m 2014, Arab 3000mSt 2017.
African 3000mSt record 2015, Tunisian: 1500m 2014, 3000m (3) 2008-13, 3000mSt (10) 2005-15.
Progress at 3000mSt: 2005- 9:51.49, 2006- 10:14.36, 2007- 9:50.04, 2008- 9:25.50, 2009- 9:12.52, 2011- 9:11.97, 2012- 9:08.37, 2014- 9:15.23, 2015- 9:05.36, 2016- 9:18.71, 2017- 9:20.00, 2018- 9:31.36. pbs: 1500m 4:06.38 '14, 3000m 8:46.61i '15, 8:49.5+ '13; 5000m 16:12.9 '03, 10000m 35:03.83 '05, 10kRd 33:30 '04.
Missed 2010 season after toe surgery. Won first Olympic medal for a woman from Tunisia.

TURKEY

Governing body: Türkiye Atletizm Federasyonu. Founded 1922.

National Champions 2018: Men: 100m: Ertan Özkan 10.43, 200m: Yigitcan Hekimoglu 21.15, 400m: Akin Özyürek 47.86, 800m: Levent Ates 1:52.30, 1500m: Süleyman Bekmezci 3:47.97, 5000m/10000m: Ramazan Ozdemir 14:34.15/ 29:08.80, 3000mSt: Turgay Bayram 8:48.31, 110mh: Batuhan Eruygun 13.99, 400mh: Batuhan Gökgöz 53.22, HJ: Enes Talha Senses 2.12, PV: Zeki Cem Tenekebüken 4.80; LJ: Alper Kulaksiz 7.85w, TJ: Can Özüpek 16.77, SP: Osman Can Yozdeveci 19.47, DT: Yusuf Yalçinkaya 53.08, HT: Esraf Apak 78.01, JT: Ahmet Talha Kiliç 68.00, Dec: Mustafa Yilmaz 6752, 20kW: Mert Atli 1:27:13. Women: 100m: Elif Polat 11.85w, 200m/400m: Derya Yildirim 24.58/55.08, 800m/ 1500m: Damla Çelic 2:11.21/4:23.52, 5000m: Fatma Demir 16:51.22, 10000m: Nuran Satilmis 33:33.94, 3000mSt: Sümeyye Erol 10:18.17, 100m: Özge Solu 13.69, 400mh: Emel Sanli 59.21, HJ: Kadriye Aydin 1.85, PV: Buse Ankazan 4.00, LJ/TJ: Tugba Aydin 5.98/13.53w, SP: Aysel Yilmaz 15.10, DT: Nurten Mermer 47.72, HT: Kivilcim Salman-Kaya 71.66, JT: Songül Çalparmak 44.92, Hep: Ezgi Sayir 4451, 20kW: Semiha Özdemir 1:39:18.

Esref APAK b. 3 Jan 1982 Kalecik 1.85m 115kg. ENKA.
At HT: OG: '04- 2, '08/12/16- dnq 16/16/24=; WCh: '05-09-11-15-17: dnq 17/27/18/17/16, '07- 11; EC: '06-16-18 dnq 18/dnq/dnq 17; WJ: '00- 1; EU23: '03- 2; EJ: '01- 3; WUG: '05- 2; won Med G 2005, Balkan 2015-16. Turkish 2001-03, 2008-13, Is.Sol 2017. 20 Turkish hammer records 2000-05.
Progress at HT: 1997- 41.26, 1998- 49.22, 1999- 57.93, 2000- 69.97, 2001- 72.82, 2002- 73.24, 2003- 77.57, 2004- 81.27, 2005- 81.45, 2006- 79.80, 2007- 80.31, 2008- 80.36, 2009- 77.11, 2010- 75.22, 2011- 78.04, 2012- 78.28, 2013- 76.94, 2015- 76.82, 2016- 76.45, 2017- 78.00, 2018- 78.59.
2-year drugs ban from 8 Jun 2013. Married to Sema Apak (200m 23.67, 100mh 13.71 '11).

Polat Kemboi ARIKAN (ex Paul Kipkosgei KEMBOI) b. 12 Dec 1990 Cheptirte, Kenya 1.73m 62kg.
At (5000m)/10000m: OG: '12- h/9, '16- 13; WCh: '13/17- dnf; EC: '12- 3/1, '14- 4, '16- 1, '18- 6/dnf; ECp: '12-14-15: 1/1/1; won Med G 2013. At 3000m: EI: '13- 10. Eur CC: '12-13-14-16-17-18: 7/2/1/2/9/7. World HMar: 14- 16, CC: '15- 22.
Turkish records 3000m 2012, 5000m 2011, HMar 2014.
Progress at 5000m, 10000m: 2006- 14:23.4A, 2009- 13:24.25, 2010- 13:18.12, 2011- 13:05.98, 2012- 13:12.55i/13:27.21, 27:38.81; 2013- 28:17.26, 2014- 28:11.11, 2015- 13:30.76, 28:05.64; 2016- 27:35.50, 2017- 13:19.20, 27:42.55; 2018- 13:23.42, 27:56.53. pbs: 1500m 3:47.05 '12, 3000m 7:42.31 '12, HMar 61:03 '18.
Became a Turkish citizen 9 Jun 2011, originally with 2-year wait for international eligibility, but waiting period ended in February 2012.

Yasmani COPELLO Escobar. b. 15 Apr 1987 La Habana, Cuba 1.96m 86kg. Fenerbahçe.
At 400mh: OG: '16- 3; WCh: '15- 6, '17- 2; EC: '16- 1, '18- 2; CCp: '18- 4; won Ibero-American 2008, Balkan 2015, Cuban NG 2010.
Seven Turkish 400mh records 2015-18.
Progress at 400mh: 2006- 52.30, 2007- 49.99, 2008- 50.08, 2009- 49.56, 2010- 51.23, 2011- 49.76, 2012- 50.28, 2013- 49.89, 2014- 50.62, 2015- 48.46, 2016- 47.92, 2017- 48.24, 2018- 47.81. pbs: 200m 21.44 '09, 400m 46.77 '09, 110mh 14.35A '08.
Former Cuban, has lived in Turkey from 2012, acquired citizenship 21 Oct 2013, cleared to compete for them from 30 Apr 2014.

Ramil GULIYEV b. 29 May 1990 Baku, Azerbaijan 1.87m 73kg. Fenerbahçe. Student teacher
At (100m)/200m: OG: '08- qf, '16- 8; WCh: '09- 7, '15- 6, '17- 1; EC: '14- h/6, '16- 6/2, '18- 1/2E; WJ: '06- (h), '08- 5; WY: '07- 2; EJ: '09- 2/1; WUG: '09- 1, '15- 3/3; CCp: '18- 2/2R; ET: '14- 3/2. At 60m: EI: '09- 7. Won EYOF 100m & 200m 2007, Balkan 100m 2014, 2016; 200m 2014-16, TUR 100m 2012, 200m 2016; Is.Sol 100m & 200m 2017, Med G 2018.
Records: European Junior 200m 2009, AZE 100m (2) 2009, 200m (4) 2007-09; TUR 100m (2) & 200m (5) 2011-18. European sea-level 200m best 2018.
Progress at 200m: 2006- 21.74, 2007- 20.72, 2008- 20.66, 2009- 20.04, 2010- 20.73, 2011- 20.32, 2012- 20.53, 2013- 20.46, 2014- 20.38, 2015- 19.88, 2016- 20.09, 2017- 20.02/19.98w, 2018- 19.76. pbs: 60m 6.58i '12, 100m 9.97/9.9 '17, 300m 32.61 '16.
Switched from Azerbaijan to Turkey on 26 Apr 2011, and cleared to compete for Turkey from 4 Apr 2013.

Jak Ali HARVEY b. 5 Apr 1989 Hanover Parish, Jamaica 1.82m 73kg. ENKA.
At 100m/(200m): OG: '16- sf/h; WCh: '15/17- sf; EC: '16- 2, '18- 3/2R; CCp: '18- 4/2R; WUG: '11- 1; Won Med G 2018, Balkan 100m 2015, 2017, 200m 2017; TUR 2016.
Four Turkish 100m records 2015-16.
Progress at 100mh: 2007- 10.90, 2008- 10.53, 2009- 10.57/10.46w, 2010- 10.26, 2011- 10.09/10.03w, 2012- 10.08, 2013- 10.04, 2014- 10.17, 2015- 10.01, 2016- 9.92A/10.03, 2017- 10.10/10.03w, 2018- 9.99/9.91w. pb 200m 20.38 '15.
Born Jacques Montgomery Harvey. Turkey citizen from 25 Jul 2014, cleared to compete for them from 24 Jul 2015.

Kaan Kigen ÖZBILEN (Mike Kipruto KIGEN) b. 15 Jan 1986 Keiyo district, Kenya 1.70m 54kg.
At 5000m/(10000m): EC: '18- 14/10; AfCh: '06- 2/2; WCp: '06- 2. At HMar: WCh: '18- 9; EC: '16- 2. At Mar: OG: '16- 17; WCh: '17- 14. World CC: '06- 5; Eur CC: '16-17-18: 10/14. Won Kenyan 5000m 2006.
Turkish half marathon record (60:08) 2018.
Progress at 5000m, 10000m, Mar: 2005- 13:22.48,

2006- 12:58.58, 28:03.70; 2008- 13:09.84, 2009-
13:04.38, 2011- 13:11.65, 27:30.53; 2012- 13:21.55A,
27:03.49; 2013- 13:36.51, 2:08:24; 2014- 13:26.6,
2:06:59; 2015- 2:07:42, 2016- 2:06:10, 2017- 14:04.50,
27:41.99, 2:14:29; 2018- 13:35.31, 28:32.93, 2:06:24.
pbs: 3000m 7:35.87 '06, 2M 8:20.09 '05, Road:
10M 45:34 '14, HMar 59:58 '11, 25k 1:14:17 '14,
30k 1:29:15 '14.
2nd Frankfurt marathon 2014, 3rd Amsterdam
2015. Acquired Turkish citizenship as Kaan
Kigen Özbilen on 24 Jun 2015. 3rd Seoul
Marathon 2016, but his 2:06:10 not be eligible for
European record.

Women

Yasemin CAN (formerly **Vivian Jemutai** KEN)
b. 11 Dec 1996 Kenya. 1.66m 49kg. ENKA.
At 5000m/10000m: OG: 16- 6/7; WCh: '17- h/11;
EC: '16- 1/1, '18- 3/5; EU23: '17- 1/1; At 3000m:
EI: '17- 2. World CC: '17- 3 MxR; Eur CC: '16- 1,
'17- 1, '18- 1. Won Balkan 5000m & 10000m 2017;
TUR 10000m 2016, Is.Sol 2017.
European U23 records 10000m (3), 15k Rd 2016
Progress at 5000m, 10000m: 2015- 15:39.90,
32:42.31; 2016- 14:37.61, 30:26.41; 2017- 14:36.82,
31:18.20; 2018- 14:57.63, 32:34.34. pbs: 1500m
4:11.54i '17, 4:16.42- 16; 2000m 5:43.0 '18, 3000m
8:36.24 '18, 15k Rd 48:40 '16.
Became a Turkish citizen on 25 May 2015,
cleared to compete for them from 13 Mar 2016.

Eda TUGSUZ b. 27 Mar 1997 1.71m 68kg.
At JT: WCh: '17- 5; EC: '16- 11, '18- dnq 16; WJ:
'14- dnq 21, '16- 3; WY: '13- 5; EU23: '17- 4; EJ:
'15- 8. Won Isl. Sol 2017, Balkan 2016, TUR 2016
6 Turkish javelin records 2016-17, European U23
record 2017.
Progress at JT: 2013- 50.29, 2014- 52.53, 2015-
56.52, 2016- 58.95, 2017- 67.21, 2018- 65.20, 2019-
64.83.

UGANDA

Governing body: Uganda Athletics Federation.
Founded 1925.

Joshua Kiprui **CHEPTEGEI** b. 12 Sep 1996
Kapsewui 1.79m 61kg.
At (5000m)/10000m: OG: '16- 8/6; WCh: '15- 9,
'17- 2; CG: '18- 1/1; WJ: '14- 4/1; won Afr-J 2015.
Wrld CC: '19- 1; UGA champion 5000m 2014-16.
World 15k road record 2018, Ugandan 2017.
Progress at 10000m: 2013- 28:53.52A, 2014-
13:32.84, 27:56.26; 2015- 13:28.50A, 27:27.57; 2016-
13:00.60, 27:10.06; 2017- 12:59.83, 26:49.94; 2018-
27:19.62. pbs: 1500m 3:37.82 '16, 3000m 7:34.96
'17, 15k Rd 41:05 '18, 10M Rd 45:15 '18, 3000mSt
8:43.21A '13.
Had big lead at 3/4 distance in World Cross
2017, but faded badly to 30th.

Jacob KIPLIMO b. 14 Nov 2000 Bukwo, Mount
Elgon 1.70m 55kg. Casone Nosete, Italy.
At (5000m)/10000m: OG: '16-(h); WCh: '17- (h);
CG: '18- 4; WJ: '16- 3, '18- 6/2. World CC: '17- 1J,

'19- 2. Won World Mountain Running Ch 2015.
Progress at 5000m.10000m: 2015- 29:22.14A,
2016- 13:19.54, 27:26.68; 2017- 13:13.64, 2018-
13:19.66, 27:30.25. pbs: 1500m 3:50.24 '16, 3000m
7:43.73 '17, 2M 8:25.17 '18, 10kEd 26:41dh '18.

Stephen KIPROTICH b. 27 Feb 1989
Kapchorwa 1.72m 56kg.
At Mar: OG: '12- 1, '16- 14; WCh: '11- 8, '13- 1,
'15- 6. At 5000m: WCh: '07- h. At 10000m: WJ:
'08- 5, AfCh: '10- 6, World CC: '08-11-17: 12J/6/17;
AfChC: '11- 2.
Ugandan marathon records 2011 & 2015.
Progress at Mar: 2011- 2:07:20, 2012- 2:07:50,
2013- 2:08:05, 2014- 2:11:37, 2015- 2:06:33, 2016-
2:07:46, 2017- 2:07:31, 2018- 2:07:57. Pbs: 3000m
7:48.06 '07, 5000m 13:23.70 '08, 10000m 27:58.03
'10, HMar 61:15 '13, 3000mSt 8:26.66 '10.
Won Enschede marathon on debut 2011.
Became the second man ever to win Olympic
and World titles at marathon. 2nd Tokyo 2015,
Hamburg & Fukuoka 2017.

Women

Peruth CHEMUTAI b. 10 Jul 1999 Bukwo
district 1.65m 50kg.
At 3000mSt: OG: '16- h; WCh: '17- h; WJ: '16- 7,
'18- 2. World CC: '17- 7J, '19- 5. Comm-Y: '15- 2
1500m & 3000m UGA 3000mSt record 2018.
Progress at 3000mSt;, 2015- 10:19.93A, 2016-
9:31.03, 2017- 9:27.72, 2018- 9:07.94. pbs: 1500m
4:17.18 '16, 3000m 9:13.09 '17.

Stella CHESANG b. 1 Dec 1996 Namoryo,
Kween district 1.58m 42kg. Uganda Police.
At 5000m: OG: '16- h; WCh: '17- h; Af-J: '15- 3. At
10000m: CG: '18- 1; AfCh: '18- 4. At 3000m: WY:
'13- 4. Af CC: '18- 5. Won World Mountain
Running Ch 2015.
Progress at 5000m.10000m: 2012- 16:00.6A,
2013- 43:31.51A, 2014- 15:53.85, 2015- 15:25.01,
2016- 15:10.30, 2017- 15:17.91, 2018- 15:52.51A,
31:39.0A. pbs: 800m 2:08.04A '17, 1500m 4:18.80
'15, 3000m 8:52.39 '15, 10kRd 31:14 '18, 15kRd
47:19 '18.

UKRAINE

Governing body: Ukrainian Athletic
Federation (FLAU). Founded 1991.
National Champions 2018: Men: 100m/200m:
Serhiy Smelyk 10.16/20.50, 400m: Vitaliy
Butrym 46.04, 800m: Yevhen Hutsol 1:51.48,
1500m: Oley Kayafa 3:46.04, 5000m: Vasyk
Koval 14:02.04, 10000m: Mykola Nyzhnyk
29:23.46, HMar: Ihor Heletiy 66:52, Mar: Mykola
Yuhymchuk 2:17:44, 3000mSt: Vasyl Koval
8:50.78, 110mh: Artem Shamatryn 13.80, 400mh:
Denys Nechyporenko 50.34, HJ: Andriy
Protsenko 2.26, PV: Ivan Yeryomin 5.30, LJ:
Serhiy Nykyforov 8.23, TJ: Oleksandr Malosilov
16.35, SP: Viktor Samolyuk 19.12, DT: Mykyta
Nestorenko 62.56, HT: Hlib Piskunov 73.60, JT:
Yuriy Kushniruk 80.55, Dec: Vasyl Ivanytskyy

7708, 20kW: Oleksiy Kazanin 1:23:27, 50kW: Dmytro Sobchuk 3:54:57. **Women**: 100m: Hrystyna Shuy 11,20, 200m: Alina Kalistratova 23.55, 400m: Tetyana Melnyk 52.71, 800m/ 1500m: Nataliya Pryshchepa 2:01.84/4:23.21, 5000m/10000m: Olena Serdyuk 15:58.18/ 32:48.54, HMar: Tetyana Vemyhor 78:10, Mar: Oleksandra Shafar 2:40:07, 3000mSt: Nataliya Strebkova 10:05.16, 100mh: Hanna Plotitsyna 13.24, 400mh: Anna Ryzhykova 55.39, HJ: Yuliya Levchenko 1.96, PV: Maryna Kylypko 4.50, LJ: Maryna Bekh 6.86w, TJ: Olha Saladukha 14.19w, SP: Olha Holodna 16.84, DT: Viktoriya Savytska 53.52, HT: Iryna Klymets 69.96, JT: Kateryna Derun 57.09, Hep: Daryna Sloboda 6104, 20kW: Mariya Filyuk 1:34:11, 50kW: Valentyna Myrochuk 4:18:50.

Bohdan BONDARENKO b. 30 Aug 1989 Kharkiv 1.97m 80kg.
At HJ: OG: '12- 7, '16- 3; WCh: '11-13-15-17: dnq 15=/1/2=/9; EC: '12- 11, '14- 1; WJ: '06- 3, '08- 1; EU23: '11- 1; EJ: '07- 9; WUG: '11- 1, CCp: '14- 1; ET: '13- 1. Won DL 2013.
Three UKR high jump records 2013-14.
Progress at HJ: 2005- 2.15, 2006- 2.26, 2007- 2.25i/2.19, 2008- 2.26, 2009- 2.27/2.15, 2010- 2.10, 2011- 2.30, 2012- 2.31, 2013- 2.41, 2014- 2.42, 2015- 2.37, 2016- 2.37, 2017- 2.32.
Maried Iryna Pimenova (TJ 13.74 '16) in 2017. His father Viktor had decathlon pb of 7480 '87.

Oleksiy KASYANOV b. 26 Aug 1985 Stakhanov, Lugansk 1.91m 87kg. Spartak Zaporozhye.
At Dec: OG: '08- 6, '12- 7, '16- dnf; WCh: '09-11-13-15-17: 3/12/dnf/9/6; EC: '10-12-14-16: dnf/2/8/4; EU23: '07- 4; WUG: '07- 4; ECp: '09-15-17: 2/2/2. UKR champion 2008. At Hep: WI: '10-12-14-16: 6/2/5/2; EI: '09- 2.
Progress at Dec: 2006- 7599, 2007- 7964, 2008- 8238, 2009- 8479, 2010- 8381, 2011- 8251, 2012- 8312, 2014- 8231, 2015- 8262, 2016- 8077, 2017- 8281. pbs: 60m 6.83i '09, 100m 10.50 '11, 200m 21.54 '15, 400m 47.46 '08, 1000m 2:39.44i '14, 1500m 4:22.27 '08, 60mh 7.85i '13, 110mh 13.92 '15, IIJ 2.08i 14, 2.05 '09; PV 4.82 '09, LJ 8.04i/7.97 '10, SP 15.72 '09, DT 51.95 '10, JT 55.84 '07, Hep 6254i '10.
Won Talence decathlon 2009 & 2016. Married Hanna Melnychenko (qv) on 18 Oct 2014.

Andriy PROTSENKO b. 20 May 1988 Kherson 1.94m 80kg. Khersonskaya. Biotechnology graduate.
At HJ: OG: '12- 9, '16- 4=; WCh: '09-11-13-15-17: dnq 25/27/23=/17/13=; EC: '10-12: dnq 17/13=; '14-16-18: 2/9=/5=; EU23: '09- 3; EJ: '07- 2; WI: '14- 3, '16- 7; EI: '15- 6, '19- 2=; WUG: '13- 2; ET: '10- 3, '14- 1. UKR champion 2012, 2018.
Progress at HJ: 2005- 2.10, 2006- 2.18i/2.10, 2007- 2.21, 2008- 2.30, 2009- 2.25, 2010- 2.25, 2011- 2.31, 2012- 2.31, 2013- 2.32, 2014- 2.40, 2015- 2.33i/2.32, 2016- 2.33, 2017- 2.30, 2018- 2.31.

Maryan ZAKALNYTSKYY Verkhnia, Ivano-Frankivska region b. 19 Aug 1994 1.80m 65kg.
At 50kW: WCh: '17- d27 EC: '18- 1; WCp: '18- 4; ECp: '17- 6.
Progress at 50kW: 2014- 4:07:08, 2015- 3:57:18, 2016 3:56:30, 2017 3:53:50, 2018 3:44:59. pbs: 30kW: 2:13:10 '18, 35kW 2:34:48 '16.

Women

Maryna BEKH-ROMANCHUK b. 18 Jul 1995 Starokostiantyniv 1.74m 59kg. nee Bekh. Khmelnytska.
At LJ: OG: '16- nj; WCh: '13/17- dnq 24/18; EC: '16- 12, '18-2; WJ: '12- 8, '14- 9; WY: '11- 5; E23: '15- 6, '17- 3; EJ: '13- 3; WI: '18- 10; EI: '17- 7, '19- 3ET: '17- 3. Won UKR 2015-18.
Progress at LJ: 2010- 6.10, 2011- 6.47, 2012- 6.36, 2013- 6.78, 2014- 6.36, 2015- 6.63, 2016- 6.93, 2017- 6.71i/6.59/6.63w, 2018- 6.73/6.86w, 2019- 6.85i. Pbs: 60m 6.57i '19, TJ 13.07 '13.

Yuliya LEVCHENKO b. 28 Nov 1997 Bakhmut 1.79m 60kg.
At HJ: OG: '16- dnq 19; WCh: '15: dnq 24, '17- 2; EC: '18- 9; WJ: '16- 3; WY: '13- 13; EU23: '17- 1; EJ: '15- 6; YOG: '14- 1; WI: '18- 5; EI:'17- 3, '19- 2. UKR champion 2018.
Progress at HJ: 2013- 1.77, 2014- 1.89, 2015- 1.92, 2016- 1.95, 2017- 2.01, 2018- 1.98i/1.97, 2019- 1.99i.

Yarislava MAHUCHIKH b. 19 Sep 2001 Dnipro 1.65m 45kg.
At HJ: WY: '17- 1; EY: '18- 1; YOG: '18- 1.
High jump indoor records: world U18 2018, European U20 2019.
Progress at HJ: 2016- 1.76, 2017- 1.92A, 2018- 1.98i/1.95, 2019- 1.99i.

Oksana OKUNEVA b. 14 Mar 1990 Mykolaiv 1.75m 61kg. Mykolaivska.
At HJ: OG: '16- dnq 22=; WCh: '11-13-15-17: dnq 18/15/14=/dnq 20; EC: '14-16-18: 6/6=/10=; WY: '07- 6; EU23: '11- 2; EJ: '09- 6; EI: '11- 7, '17- 4; WUG: '17- 1; ET: '14- 2. UKR champion 2011, 2013-14, 2016.
Progress at HJ: 2005- 1.60, 2006- 1.75, 2007- 1.78, 2008- 1.80, 2009- 1.90, 2010- 1.92, 2011- 1.94, 2012- 1.93i/1.87, 2013- 1.92, 2014- 1.98, 2015- 1.92, 2016- 1.97, 2017- 1.97, 2018- 1.94.

Nataliya PRYSHCHEPA b. 11 Sep 1994 Kiev 1.63m 50kg. Rivnenska.
At 800m: OG: '16- sf; EC: '16- 1, '18- 1; WY: '11- sf; CCp: '18- 4. At 1500m: EC: '14- 10, '16- h; WJ: '12- h; E23: '15- 3; EJ: '13- 1; ET: '14- 3, '17- 3. Won UKR 800m 2016, 2018; 1500m 2013, 2016, 2018.
Progress at 800m, 1500m: 2011- 2:08.02, 2012- 2:04.47, 4:22.63; 2013- 2:05.52, 4:13.81; 2014- 4:08.89, 2015- 2:05.22, 4:06.29; 2016- 1:58.60, 4:10.51; 2017- 1:58.82, 4:13.51; 2018- 1:59.58, 4:23.81.

Anna RYZHYKOVA b. 24 Nov 1989 Dnipropetrovsk 1.77m 67kg. née Yaroshchuk.
At 400mh/4x400mR: OG: '12- sf/3R; WCh: '11-

sf, '13- 5, '15- sf; EC: '10- 12-14-18: sf/3/h&2R/2; WJ: '08- 6/2R; EU23: '09- 8, '11- 1/2R; WUG: '11- 1, '13- 1; CCp: '18- 3; ET: '13- 2, '14- 1. UKR champion 2009-10, 2012, 2018. At 200m: EJ: '07-h/2 4x100m.
Progress at 400mh: 2006- 57.52, 2007- 56.46, 2008- 56.09, 2009- 57.23, 2010- 55.60, 2011- 54.77, 2012- 54.35, 2013- 54.77, 2014- 55.00, 2015- 55.16, 2018- 54.47. pbs: 60m 7.74i '06, 200m 23.49 '10, 400m 52.11 '14, LJ 6.05 '13.

Olha SALADUKHA b. 4 Jun 1983 Donetsk 1.75m 55kg.
At TJ: OG: '08- 7, '12- 3, '16- dnq 18; WCh: '07-11-13-15: 5/1/3/6; EC: '06-10-12-14-16-18: 4/1/1/1/6/dnq 13; WJ: '02- 5; EU23: '05- 4; EJ: '01- 9; WI: '08- 5, '14- 2; EI: '13- 1, '19- 3 WUG: '05- 2, '07- 1; WCp: '06-10-14: 6/2/3; ECp: '06-08-10-11-13-14: 1/1/1/1/1/2. Won DL 2011, UKR 2007-08, 2017-18.
Progress at TJ: 1998- 13.32, 1999- 12.86, 2000- 13.26, 2001- 13.48, 2002- 13.66i/13.63, 2003- 13.26i/13.03, 2004- 13.22, 2005- 14.04, 2006- 14.41/14.50w, 2007- 14.79, 2008- 14.84, 2010- 14.81, 2011- 14.98/15.06w, 2012- 14.99, 2013- 14.88i/14.85, 2014- 14.73, 2015- 14.62, 2016- 14.40, 2017- 14.02i/13.97, 2018- 14.20/14.25w, 2019- 14.47i. pb LJ 6.37 '06.
Married to professional road cyclist Denys Kostyuk with a daughter Diana born 2009. Equalled EC women's record six appearances.

Alina SHUKH b. 12 Feb 1999 Izmail, Odeksa region 1.75m 60kg. BVUFK Brovary.
At Hep: WCh: '17- 14; EC: '18-15; WY: '15- 3; EJ: 17- 1; EY: '16- 1; ET: '17- 1. At Pen: WI: '18- 7. At JT: WJ: '18- 1.
World youth spec heptathlon record 6186 in 2016, world indoor U20 pentathlon record 2017.
Progress at Hep: 2016- 6099, 2017- 6381, 2018- 6177. pbs: 60m 7.9i/8.26i '18, 200m 25.88 '18, 800m 2:10.93 '18, 60mh 8.85i '17, 8.6 '18; 100mh 14.32/14.13w '17, 13.50w '17; HJ 1.92 '16, LJ 6.29 '17, TJ 12.70i '18, SP 15.08i '19, 14.43 '18; JT 56.54 '17, Pen 4581i '19.

Kateryna TABASHNYK b. 15 Jun 1994 Kharkiv 1.78m 62kg.
At HJ: EC: '18: 5; WY: '11- dnq 17=; EJ: '13-1; EI: '19- 4. At Hep: WJ: '12- dnf.
Progress at HJ: 2011- 1.80i/1.75, 2012- 1.87, 2013- 1.90, 2015- 1.83i/1.75, 2017- 1.95, 2018- 1.98i/1.96, 2019- 1.99i. Pbs: 100mh 15.21 '12. LJ 5.74 '12, Hep 5167 '12.

Alina TSVILIY b. 18 Sep 1994 Baryshivka, Kyivska region 1.56m 45kg. née Halchenko.
At 50kW: EC: '18- 2; WT: '18- 15. At 10kW: WJ: '12- 11; WCp: '12- 10. At 5000mW: WY:: '11- 4. YOG: '10- 6.
UKR 50k walk record 2018.
Progress at 50kW: 2018- 4:12:44. Pbs: 5000W 22:44.83 '16, 10000mW 46:52.33 '16, 20kW 1:33:05 '16. Pending doping case.

UNITED KINGDOM

Governing body: UK Athletics. Founded 1999 (replacing British Athletics, founded 1991, which succeeded BAAB, founded 1932). The Amateur Athletic Association was founded in 1880 and the Women's Amateur Athletic Association in 1922.
National Championships (first were English Championships 1866-79, then AAA 1880-2006, WAAA from 1922). **2018 UK Champions: Men**: 100m: Reece Prescod 10.06, 200m: Nethaneel Mitchell-Blake 20.24, 400m: Matthew Hudson-Smith 44.68, 800m: Elliot Giles 1:50.28, 1500m: Chris O'Hare 3:46.72, 5000m: Marc Scott 13:47.00, 10000m: Alex Yee 27:51.94, HMar/Mar: Mohammed Farah 61:40/2:06:21, 3000mSt: Zak Seddon 8:33.12, 110mh: Andrew Pozzi 13.61, 400mh: Dai Greene 50.06, HJ: Chris Baker 2.26, PV: Charlie Myers 5.55, LJ: Tom Duckworth 8.00, TJ: Nathan Douglas 16.83w, SP: Scott Lincoln 18.44, DT: Brett Morse 58.90, HT: Nick Miller 75.33, JT: James Whiteaker 71.29, Dec: Ben Gregory 7517, 5000mW/20kW: Tom Bosworth 18:43.28/1:23:10, 50kW: Jonathan Hobbs 4:43:45.
Women: 100m: Dina Asher-Smith 10.97, 200m: Beth Dobbin 22.59, 400m: Anyike Onuora 51.95, 800m: Laura Muir 2:01.22, 1500m: Laura Weightman 4:08.80, 5000m: Stephanie Twell 16:07.24, 10000m: Charlotte Arter 32:15.71, HMar: Charlotte Purdue 70:29, Mar: Lily Partridge 2:29:24, 3000mSt: Rosie Clarke 9:45.83, 100mh: Alicia Barrett 13.28, 400mh: Meghan Beesley 55.73, HJ: Morgan Lake 1.97, PV: Holly Bradshaw 4.60, LJ: Lorraine Ugen 7.05, TJ: Naomi Ogbeta 13.95, SP: Amelia Strickler 17.22, DT: Jade Lally 56.81, HT: Sophie Hitchon 72.02, JT: Laura Whittingham 55.55, Hep: Emma Nwofor 5559, 5000mW/20kW: Bethan Davies 22:04.98/1:36:55, 50kW: Jayne Farquhar 5:48:34.

Tom BOSWORTH b. 17 Jan 1990 Pembury, Kent 1.84m 64kg. Tonbridge, was at Leeds Metropolitan University.
At 20kW: OG: '16- 6, WCh: '15- 24, '17- dq; EC: '14- 12, '18- 7; CG: '10- 11, '18- 2; WT: '18- 14; ECp: '17- 4; won RWA 2010-11, 2016-18; UK 5000mW 2011, 2014-18; 10kW 2011.
World bests: 1MW 2017, 3000m indoor & out 2018. UK walk records: 5000m (4) 2011-17, 10k road 2015, 20k (3) 2016-18.
Progress at 20kW: 2010- 1:28:24, 2011- 1:27:18, 2012- 1:24:49, 2013- 1:24:44, 2014- 1:22:20, 2015- 1:22:33, 2016- 1:20:13, 2017- 1:20:58, 2018- 1:19:38. pbs: 1MW 5:31.08 '17, 3000mW 10:30.28i/10:43.84 '18, 11:29.54 '16; 5000mW 18:28.70i '18, 18:43.28 '17; 10kW 39:36 '15, 41:34.19t '15.

Andrew BUTCHART b. 14 Oct 1991 Dunblane 1.75m 64kg. Central.
At 5000m: OG: '16- 6; WCh: '17- 8; won UK 2016-17. At 3000m: EI: '19- 10; ET: '15- 3. Eur CC: '16- 4, '17- 3.

Progress at 5000m: 2009- 14:49.93, 2010- 15:18.33, 2013- 15:14.18, 2014- 13:58.05, 2015- 13:29.49, 2016- 13:08.61, 2017- 13:11.45. pbs: 800m 1:51.39 '14, 1500m 3:37.58i '17, 3:44.57 '15; 1M 3:54.23i '17, 4:05.40 '13; 3000m 7:37.56 '17, 2M 8:12.63i '17, 10000m 29:32.43 '15, 10k Rd 28:28 '16, HMar 70:03 '17.

Tim DUCKWORTH b. 18 Jun 1996 Clovis, California 1.85m 80kg. Liverpool H, University of Kentucky
At Dec: EC: '18- 5; EU23: '17- dnf; EJ: '15- 18. At Hep: EI: '19- 2. Won NCAA Dec & Ind Hep 2018, UK LJ 2018.
Progress at Dec: 2014- 6953, 2015- 7156, 2016- 7709, 2017- 7973, 2018- 8336. pbs: 60m 6.77i '17, 100m 10.40 '18, 200m 22.37i '15, 400m 48.78 '18, 1000m 2:49.44i '19, 1500m 4:58.28 '18, 60mh 8.03i '17, 110mh 14.30 '17, 14.19w '18; HJ 2.17 '18, PV 5.26i '17, 5.11 '18; LJ 8.03, 8.19w '18; SP 13.71 '18, DT 44.12 '18, JT 57.27 '17, Hep 6188i '18.
Parents moved to the USA two years before Tim was born, and he was educated there.

Mohamed FARAH b. 23 March 1983 Mogadishu, Somalia 1.71m 58kg. Newham & Essex Beagles.
At 5000m ('/10000m): OG: '08- 1t, '12- 1/1, '16- 1/1; WCh: '07- 6, '09- 7, '11- 1/2, '13- 1/1, '15- 1/1, '17- 2/1; EC: '06- 2, '10- 1/1, '12- 1, '14- 1/1; CG: '06- 9; WJ: '00- 10; EJ: '01- 1; EU23: '03 & '05- 2; ECp: '08-09-10-13: 1/1/1 &(1)/1. At 3000m: WY: '99- 6; WI: '08- 6, '12- 4; EI: '05-07-09-11: 6/5/1/1; ECp: '05-06: 2/2. World CC: '07- 11, '10- 20; HMar: '16- 3; Eur CC: '99-00-01-04-05-06-08-09: 5J/7J/2J/15/21/1/2/2. Won DL 5000m 2017, UK 5000m 2007, 2011; Mar 2014, 2018; HMar 201-198.
Records: World indoor 2M 2015, European 10000m 2011, indoor 5000m 2011 (u) & 2017, 1500m 2013; indoor 2M 2012, 20k and HMar 2015, 15k 2016, Mar 2018; UK 3000m 2016, 2M 2014, 5000m 2010 & 2011, HMar (3) 2011-15, Mar 2018.
Progress at 1500m, 5000m, 10000m: 1996- 4:43.9, 1997- 4:06.41, 1998- 3:57.67, 1999- 3:55.78, 2000- 3:49.60, 14:05.72; 2001- 3:46.1, 13:56.31; 2002- 3:47.78, 14:00.5; 2003-3:43.17, 13:38.41; 2004- 3:43.4, c.14:25; 2005- 3:38.62, 13:30.53; 2006- 3:38.02, 13:09.40; 2007- 3:45.2i+, 13:46.50, 13:07.00; 2008- 3:39.66, 13:08.11, 27:44.54; 2009- 3:33.98, 13:09.14; 2010- 12:57.94, 27:28.86; 2011- 12:53.11, 26:46.57; 2012- 3:34.66, 12:56.98, 27:30.42; 2013- 3:28.81, 13:05.88, 27:21.71; 2014- 13:23.42, 28:08.11; 2015- 3:28.93, 13:11.77, 26:50.97; 2016- 3:31.74, 12:59.29, 26:53.71; 2017- 13:00.70, 26:49.51. At Mar: 2014- 2:08:21, 2018- 2:05:11. pbs: 800m 1:48.69 '03, 1M 3:56.49 '05, 2000m 5:01.8i '09, 5:02.1+ '16; 3000m 7:32.62 '16, 2M 8:03.40i '15, 8:07.85 '14; 2000mSt 5:55.72 '00; road 15k 42:03+ '16, 10M 45:32+ '15, 20k 56:27 '15, HMar 59:22dh/59:32 '15, 25k 1:12:36 '18, 30k 1:27:31 '18. Joined his father in England in 1993. Sixth man to win Olympic 5000m/10,000m double at same

Games and uniquely repeated that in 2016; first British athlete to win either title and to win three/four Olympic golds. In 2013 became third man to win World 5000m/10000m double and he repeated in 2015; now has record eight global distance running titles. Won in New York on his debut in 2011 and has nine wins, including Great North Run 2014-18, and three 2nds in his 12 half marathons. He was knighted in the 2017 New Year's Honours. Having given up track running, he was 3rd in the London Marathon and 1st in Chicago in 2018.

Miguel FRANCIS b. 28 Feb 1995 Montserrat 1.86m 75kg. Team Force 2000.
At 200m: WCh: '15- sf; WJ: '14- sf; CG: '14- 7R; PAm: '15- 6.
Three Antiguan 200m records 2015-16.
Progress at 100m: 2013- 20.60/20.58w, 2014- 20.71, 2015- 20.05/19.76dt, 2016- 19.88/19.67 doubtful, 2017- 20.44, 2018- 20.38. pbs: 100m 10.28 '15, 150m 14.95 '16, 400m 46.48 '17.
Antigua to UK 24 Sep 2016. Eligible for international competition from 30 Mar 2017.

Adam GEMILI b. 6 Oct 1993 London 1.78m 73kg. Blackheath & Bromley.
At 100m/(200m)/4x100mR: OG: '12- st, '16- (4); WCh: '13- (5), '17- 1R; EC: '14- (1)/1R, '16- 1R, '18- (5)/1R; CG: '14- 2/2R, '18 dns F; WJ: '12- 1; EU23: '13- 1/4/1R; EJ: '11- 2/2R; ET: '13/14- 1R.
Won UK 200m 2016.
European 4x100m record 2017.
Progress at 100m, 200m: 2009- 11.2, 2010- 10.80/10.72w, 21.87w; 2011- 10.35/10.23w, 20.98; 2012- 10.05, 20.38; 2013- 10.06, 19.98; 2014- 10.04, 19.98; 2015- 9.97; 2016- 10.11, 19.97; 2017- 10.08/10.03w, 20.35; 2018- 10.11, 20.10. Pb 60m 6.59i '16. Sixth equal all-time junior list 10.05 to win World Junior 100m in 2012, improved 200m best from 20.30 to 20.17 and 19.98 at 2013 Worlds before 5th in final in 20.08. At football he was a member of the Chelsea youth academy before playing for Dagenham & Redbridge. Won European Athletics Rising Star award 2014.

Matthew HUDSON-SMITH b. 26 Oct 1994 Wolverhampton 1.92m 79kg. Birchfield H.
At 400m/4x400mR: OG: '16- 8; WCh: '17- sf/3R; EC: '14- 2/1R, '16- 3R, '18- 1/2R; CG: '14- 1R, '18- h; CCp: '18- 4. At 200m: EJ: '13- 3/3R. Won UK 2016-18.
Progress at 400m: 2009- 52.09, 2011- 50.61, 2013- 48.76i, 2014- 44.75, 2015- 45.09, 2016- 44.48, 2017- 44.74, 2018- 44.63. pbs: 60m 6.96i '12, 100m 10.9 '13, 10.8w '12; 200m 20.88 '13, 300m 32.3+ '16.

Zharnell HUGHES b. 13 Jul 1995 Sandy Ground, Anguilla 1.90m 79kg. Racers TC, Jamaica.
At (100m)/200m: WCh: '15- 5, '17- sf; CG: '18- dq/1R; EC: '16- h, '18- (1)/1R; WJ: '12- sf/h, '14- 5; ET: '17- 1R. Won CAC-J 2014, UK 2015, PAm-J 100m 2013.

Records: Anguilla: 100m (4), 200m (6) 2012-14. Progress at 100m, 200m: 2012- 10.42/10.41w, 20.90; 2013- 10.23A/10.39, 20.79/20.77w; 2014- 10.12, 20.32; 2015-10.15, 20.02; 2016- 10.10, 20.62; 2017- 10.12/10.08w, 20.22; 2018- 9.91, 20.23/20.12dq. pb 400m 46.95 '16.
Switched from Anguilla and cleared to compete for Britain from 19 June 2015. Disqualified after finishing first just ahead but obstructing Jereem Richards at 2018 CG.

Nick MILLER b. 1 May 1993 Carlisle 1.88m 112kg. Border H, Oklahoma State University, USA.
At HT: OG: '16- dnq 22; WCh: '15: 11, '17- 6; EC: '16- dnq 25, '18- 10; CG: '14- 2, '18- 1; WJ: '12- dnq 25; EU23: '13- 9, '15- 1; ET: '15- 2, '17- 3. UK champion 2014-15, 2017-18; NCAA 2016.
Three UK hammer records 2015-18.
Progress at HT: 2010- 49.86, 2011- 57.74, 2012- 67.56, 2013- 71.60, 2014- 74.38, 2015- 77.55, 2016- 76.93, 2017- 77.51, 2018- 80.26. Pbs: DT 45.37 '13, Wt 22.46i '15.

Nethaneel Joseph **MITCHELL-BLAKE** b. 2 Apr 1994 Newham, London 1.86m 75kg. Ilford, Louisiana State University, USA.
At 200m/4x100mR: OG: '16- sf; WCh: '17- 4/1R; EC: '16- 5, '18- 2/res(1)R; WY: '11- sf; EJ: '13- 1/5R. Won UK 2018.
European 4x100m record 2017.
Progress at 200m: 2007- 25.4, 2011- 21.54, 2012- 21.49, 2013- 20.62, 2014- 20.69, 2016- 19.95, 2017- 20.04, 2018- 20.04. Pbs: 60m 6.65i '16, 100m 9.99 '17, 400m 46.55 '16.
Moved when he was 13 with his family from London to Mandeville, Jamaica, where he went to Jamaica College, Kingston

Andrew POZZI b. 15 May 1992 Leamington Spa 1.86m 79kg. Stratford-upon-Avon. Bristol University.
At 110mh: OG: '12- h, '16- sf; WCh: '17- sf; EC: '16- dns, '18- 6; CG: '18- 6=; EJ: '11- 2. UK champion 2012, 2016, 2018. At 60mh: WI: '12-14-18: 4/4/1; EI: '17- 1, '19- 6.
Progress at 110mh: 2009- 14.8, 2011- 13.73/13.66w, 2012- 13.34, 2015- 13.62, 2016- 13.19, 2017- 13.14/13.13w, 2018- 13.28. pbs: 100m 10.44 '18, 60mh 7.43i '17, LJ 6.73 '09.

Reece PRESCOD b. 29 Feb 1996 Walthamstow, London 1.93m 75kg. Enfield & Haringey.
At 100m: WCh: '17- 7; EC: '18- 2. Won UK 2017-18.
Progress at 100m, 200m: 2010- 11.71/11.64w, 23.33/23.16w/23.1w; 2011- 22.7, 2012- 21.92, 2013- 10.73, 21.21; 2015- 20.70; 2016- 10.04, 20.38; 2017- 10.03, 20.83w; 2018- 9.94/9.88w. Pbs: 60m 6.53i '19, 150mSt: 14.87 '18.

Danny TALBOT b. 1 May 1991 Trowbridge 1.84m 73kg. Birchfield H, Bath University.
At 200m/4x100mR: OG: '12- dq hR, '16- sf; WCh: '15- sf, '17- sf/1R; EC: '12- 3, '14- sf/res 1R, '16- 3; CG: '14- 7/2R; WJ: '10- sf; E23: '11- 4/2R,

'13- 2/1R; ET: '14- 2 100m; '15- 2/1R, '17- 1R. Won UK 2014. European 4x100m record 2017.
Progress at 200m: 2005- 24.8/24.6w, 2006- 22.96, 2007- 22.03/21.8, 2008- 21.64, 2009- 21.35, 2010- 20.97, 2011- 20.54, 2012- 20.52, 2013- 20.45, 2014- 20.36, 2015- 20.25, 2016- 20.25, 2017- 20.16/19.86w.
Pbs: 60m 6.62i '14, 100m 10.14 '14, 150mSt 15/06 '16, 14.79w '15; 400m 47.84i '15.

Chijindu UJAH b. 5 Mar 1994 Enfield 1.80m 75kg. Enfield & Haringey.
At 100m: OG: '16- sf; WCh: '15- sf, '17- sf/1R; EC: '16- 1R, '18- 4/1R; WJ: '12- 6; WY: '11- 8; EJ: '13- 1; ET: '17- 1R. UK champion 2015, DL 2017.
European 4x100m record 2017.
Progress at 2009- 11.61, 2010- 10.83, 2011- 10.58/10.49w, 2012- 10.26, 2013- 10.32, 2014- 9.96, 2015- 9.96, 2016- 10.01/9.97w, 2017- 9.97/9.95w, 2018- 10.06. pbs: 60m 6.53i '15, 200m 20.39 '17.

Jake WIGHTMAN b. 11 Jul 1994 Nottingham. Edinburgh AC. 1.82m 67kg. Was at Loughborough University,
At 1500m (800m): WCh: '17- sf; CG: '14- h, '18- 3 (4); EC: '16- 7, '18- 3; EJ: '13- 1; ET: '17- 2; WI: '18- 6. Won UK 2015.
Progress at 1500m: 2009- 4:22.47, 2010- 4:13.89, 2011- 3:59.35, 2012- 3:51.74, 2013- 3:43.74, 2014- 3:35.49, 2015- 3:40.05, 2016- 3:36.64, 2017- 3:34.17, 2018- 3:33.96. pbs: 400m 48.34 '16, 800m 1:44.61 '18, 1000m 2:16.27 '18, 1M 3:54.20 '16, 3000m 8:13.6 '15, 5000m 15:37.32 '11, 5k Rd 14:18 '17, 10k Rd 30:29 '17.
Father Geoff Wightman (Mar 2:13:17 '91, 6 EC & CG '9, mother Susan Tooby (10000m 32:20.95 '88, 6 CG '86, Mar 2:31:33 & 12 OG '88).

Women

Dina ASHER-SMITH b. 4 Dec 1995 Farnborough 1.65m 55kg. Blackheath & Bromley. Was at King's College, London.
At (100m)/200m/4x100mR: OG: '16- 5/3R; WCh: '13- 3R, '15- 5, '17- 4/2R; EC: '14- dnf, '16- 1/2R, '18- 1/1/1R; CG: '18- 3/1R; WJ: '12- 7, '14- (1); EJ: '13- 1/1R; CCp: '18- (2)/2R. At 60m: WI: '16- dns; EI: '15- 2. Won UK 100m 2015, 2018.
UK records 100m (4) 2015-18, 200m (2) 2015-18, 4x100m (2) 2016.
Progress at 100m, 200m: 2009- 12.10, 24.83; 2010- 12.00/24.50; 2011- 11.96, 24.16/24.11w; 2012- 11.54, 23.49; 2013- 11.38/11.30w, 23.14; 2014- 11.14/11.93w, 22.61; 2015- 10.99, 22.07; 2016- 11.08, 22.31; 2017- 11.13, 22.22; 2018- 10.85, 21.89. pbs: 60m 7.08i '15, 150mSt 16.70 '17, 400m 53.49 '14.

Holly BRADSHAW b. 2 Nov 1991 Preston 1.75m 68kg. née Bleasdale. Blackburn Harriers.
At PV: OG: '12- 6=, '16- 5; WCh: '11- dnq, '15- 7, '17- 6; EC: '18- 3; CG: '18- 4; WI: '12- 3, '14- 9; WJ: '10- 3; EU23: '11- 1; EI: '13- 1, '19- 2. UK champion 2011-12, 2015-18.
Seven UK pole vault records 2011-17, five indoors 2011-12.
Progress at PV: 2007- 2.30, 2008- 3.10i, 2009-

4.05, 2010- 4.35, 2011- 4.71i/4.70, 2012- 4.87i/4.71, 2013- 4.77i/4.60, 2014- 4.73i, 2015- 4.70, 2016- 4.76i/4.70, 2017- 4.81, 2018- 4.80, 2019- 4.81i. pbs: SP 11.81i '17, 11.32 '11; JT 37.60 '11.
World age-19 best 2011, age-20 best 2012. Married 800m runner Paul Bradshaw (1:47.37 '09) on 25 Oct 2014.

Melissa COURTNEY b. 30 Aug 1993 1.70m 54kg. Poole, was at St Mary's & Brunel Universities.
At 1500m/(5000m): EC: '16- h, '18- (5); CG: '18- 3/9; EU23: '15- 10; WUG: '17- 5; At 3000m: EI: '19- 3. Eur CC: '17- 1mxR, '18- 8.
Progress at 1500m, 5000m: 2006- 4:52.2, 2007- 4:30.85, 2008- 4:25.40, 2009- 4:28.69, 2010- 4:25.85, 2011- 4:27.87, 2012- 4:28.67, 2013- 4:17.57i/4:17.87, 2014- 4:11.41, 2015- 4:09.74, 16:13.45; 2016- 4:07.55, 2017- 4:05.82, 15:28.95; 2018- 4:03.44, 15:04.75. pbs: 400m 59.93mx '12, 60.0 '12; 800m 2:04.03 '17, 1M 4:23.15 '17, 3000m 8:38.22i '19, 8:39.20 '18; 10kRd 33:57 '14, 33:34sh '15.
Engaged to Ashley Bryant (Dec 8163 '17, 2 CG 2014).

Eilidh DOYLE b. 20 Feb 1987 Perth 1.72m 59kg. née Child.Pitreavie. PE degree from Edinburgh University.
At 400mh/4x400mR: OG: '12- sf, '16- 8/3R; WCh: '09/11- sf, '13- 4/2R, '15- 6/3R, '17- 8/2R; EC: '10-12-14-16-18: 8/4R/1&3R/1R/8&3R; CG: '10- 2, '14- 2, '18- 2&3R; EU23: '07- 5, '09- 2; CCp: '14- 2; ET: '09-10-13-14-15-17: 3R/2/1&1R/2/1/1; UK champion 2014-17. At 400m: WI: '14- 3R, '18- 3; EI: '13- 2/1R, '17 & 19- 2R.
Progress at 400mh: 2003- 59.8mx, 2004- 59.53, 2005- 59.78, 2006- 59.7/60.05, 2007- 57.11, 2008- 56.84, 2009- 55.32, 2010- 55.16, 2011- 55.67, 2012- 54.96, 2013- 54.22, 2014- 54.39, 2015- 54.46, 2016- 54.09, 2017- 54.36, 2018- 54.80. pbs: 200m 24.51i '13, 24.56 '08; 300m 37.1i '13, 400m 51.45i/51.83 '13, 800m 2:24.2 '04, 60mh 8.89i '06, 100mh 14.51 '04, 14.38w '07, 200mhSt 25.84 '14.
Married Brian Doyle (400m 47.12 '06) Oct 2015.

Niamh EMERSON b. 22 Jan 1999 Shirland, Derbyshire 1.79m 68kg. Amber Valley & Erewash.
At Hep: CG: '18- 3; WJ: '18- 1; WY: '15- 13; EJ: '17- 4, EY: '16- 3. At Pen: EI: '19- 2. Comm-Y: '15- 1 HJ, 3 400mh.
Progress at Hep: 2017- 6013, 2018- 6253. pbs: 200m 24.40 '18, 800m 2:09.74 '18, 1500m 4:45.11mx '13, 60mh 8.54i '19, 100mh 13.76, 13.71w '18; 400mh 61.07 '15, HJ 1.89 '16, LJ 6.41 '18, SP 13.93i '19, 12.67 '17; JT 43.95 '18, Pen 4731i '19.

Sophie HITCHON b. 11 Jul 1991 Burnley 1.70m 74kg. Blackburn H.
At HT: OG: '12- 8, '16- 3; WCh: '11-13: dnq 25/17, '15- 4, '17- 7; EC: '12-14-16-18: 10/dnq 18/4/8; CG: '14- 3; WJ: '08- 7, '10- 1; WY: '07- dnq 17; EU23: '11- 3, '13- 1; EJ: '09- 3; ET: '13- 2; won Comm-Y 2008, UK 2011-12, 2014-18.

13 UK hammer records 2011-16.
Progress at HT: 2006- 40.98, 2007- 54.56, 2008- 60.73, 2009- 63.18, 2010- 66.01, 2011- 69.59, 2012- 71.98, 2013- 72.97, 2014- 71.53, 2015- 73.86, 2016- 74.54, 2017- 73.97, 2018- 73.48. pbs: 100m 12.2/12.40 '09, 200m 25.2 '08, 25.51 '09; SP 10.75 '08. Married Damien Grulick on 15 Sep 2018.

Katarina JOHNSON-THOMPSON b. 9 Jan 1993 Liverpool 1.83m 70kg. Liverpool H.
At Hep: OG: '12- 13, '16- 6; WCh: '13-15-17: 5/28 & 11 LJ/5 & 5 HJ; EC: '18- 2; CG: '18- 1; WY: '09- 1; EU23: '13- 1; EJ: '09- 8, '11- 6. At LJ: WJ: '12- 1 (sf 100mh); WI: '14- 2. At Pen: WI: '18- 1; EI: '15- 1, '19- 1. Won UK LJ 2014.
UK indoor records: high jump (2) 2014-15, long jump & pentathlon 2015.
Progress at LJ, Hep: 2006- 5.11, 2007- 5.77i/5.65, 2008- 6.11i/5.90/6.07w, 5343; 2009- 6.31, 5481; 2010- 6.25i/5.58, 2011- 6.44, 5787; 2012- 6.51/6.81w, 6267; 2013- 6449, 6.56; 2014- 6.92, 6682; 2015- 6.93i/6.79, 5039; 2016- 6.84, 6523; 2017- 6.75, 6691; 2018- 6.71i/6.70, 6759. pbs: 60m 7.50i '14, 100m 12.35 '08, 12.2 '09, 11.30w '14; 200m 22.79 '16, 300m 38.56i '08, 400m 53.7 '14, 800m 2:07.64 '13, 60mh 8.18i '15, 100mh 13.29 '18, 200mhSt 25.31 '15, 400mh 58.3 '14, HJ 1.98 '16, TJ 12.83, 13.35w '14; SP 13.15i '19. 13.14 '16; JT 42.16 '18, Pen 5000i '12.
Set pbs in the each of the last four events when adding 182 points to her pb for 5th at the 2013 Worlds and 474 points to pentathlon best to win 2015 European Indoors, including 6.89 long jump, the best ever in a pentathlon. Three no-jumps (last by 1 cm) in 2015 WCh Hep LJ. World heptathlon best HJ 1.98 at 2016 OG. Won 29 English age-group titles U15 to U23.

Morgan LAKE b. 12 May 1997 Milton Keynes 1.78m 64kg. Windsor, Slough, Eton & Honslow.
At (Hep)/HJ: OG: '16- 10=; WCh: '15- dnq 14=, '17- 6; EC: '14- dnq 17=; '16- (dnf), '18- 7; CG: '18- 2; WJ: '14- 1/1; WY: '13- (dnf); EJ: '15- 1; WI: '18- 4. At Pen: WI: '16- 6; EI: '15- 9, '17- 8) HJ. Won UK HJ 2016-18.
World youth indoor pentathlon record 2014.
Progress at HJ, Hep: 2007- 1.28, 2008- 1.50, 2009- 1.57, 2010- 1.70, 2011- 1.76, 2012- 1.80, 2013- 1.90, 2014- 1.94, 6148; 2015- 1.94, 5082; 2016- 1.94, 5951; 2017- 1.96, 1.97. pbs: 60m 7.98i '13, 200m 24.59 '14, 800m 2:18.53i '16, 2:21.06 '14; 60mh 8.63i '16, 100mh 14.25 '14, LJ 6.32 '14, TJ 12.35, 12.45w '13; SP 14.85 '14, JT 41.93 '17, Pen 4527i '15.
Record 31 English age-group titles 2010-17 (12 indoors, 19 out). Father Eldon had a TJ pb of 15.43 (1989).

Eilish McCOLGAN b. 25 Nov 1990 Dundee 1.76m 59kg. Dundee Hawkhill, was at Dundee University.
At 5000m: OG: '16- 13; WCh: '17- 10; EC: '16- 6, '18-n 2; CG: '18- 6 (6 1500m) At 3000m: EI: '17- 3,

'19- 7; At 3000mSt: OG: '12- h; WCh: '13- 10, CG: '14- 6; EU23: '11- 6; UK 2012-14.
Progress at 1500m, 5000m: 2002- 5:22.8, 2003- 4:58.14, 2004- 4:36.70, 2005- 4:37.78, 2006- 4:38.00, 2007- 4:35.56, 2008- 4:27.11, 2010- 4:21.38, 2011- 4:14.44, 15:52.69; 2012- 4:11.78mx/4:13.19, 15:44.62; 2013- 4:09.67, 2014- 4:15.23mx, 2016- 4:03.74, 15:05.00; 2017- 4:01.60, 14:48.49; 2018- 4:04.30, 14:53.05. pbs: 800m 2:12.22 '08, 1M 4:25.07 '18, 2000m 5:43.1+ '17, 3000m 8:31.00 '17, 10000m 32:10.59 '17, road: 10k 31:51 '19, 10M 54:43 '18; 2000mSt 6:42.24 '11, 3000mSt 9:35.82 '13.
Her mother Liz (10,000m OG: '88- 2, WCh: '91- 1, 30:57.07 '91), father Peter (3000mSt 8:27.93 '91).

Laura MUIR b. 9 May 1993 Milnathort, Kinross 1.62m 54kg. Dundee Hawkhill H. Was at GlAsiGow University.
At 1500m/(3000m): OG: '16- 7; WCh: '15- 5, '17- 4 (6 5000m); EC: '14- h, '18- 1; CG: '14- 11; WJ: '12- (16); EU23: '13- 3; WI: '18- 2/3; EI: '13- 6, '15- (4), '17- 1/1, 19- 1/1; won DL 2016, 2018. At 800m: WCh: '13- sf. Won UK 800m 2018, 1500m 2015- 16. Eur CC: '15- 4 U23.
Two UK 1500m records 2016, Indoor records: Commonwealth 30000m & European 1000m & 3000m 2017.
Progress at 1500m, 5000m: 2005- 5:33.16, 2006- 5:12.39, 2007- 4:48.97, 2008- 4:47.92, 2009- 4:58.77, 2010- 4:50.91. 2011- 4:38.90, 2012- 4:14.52mx/ 4:17.81, 2013- 4:07.76, 15:53.68; 2014- 4:00.07, 2015- 3:58.66. 2016- 3:55.22, 2017- 4:00.35, 14:49.12i/ 14:52.07; 2018- 3:58.18. pbs: 400m 55.36i mx '16, 55.71i '14, 56.78 '12; 800m 1:58.69 '17, 1000m 2:31.93i '17, 2:33.92 '18; 1M 4:18.03 '17, 2000m 5:41.5+i '17, 3000m 8:26.41i/8:30.64 '17, 10k Rd 38:23 '11.

Shelayna OSKAN-CLARKE b. 20 Jan 1990 London 1.67m 54kg. Windsor, Slough, Eton & Hounslow. Was at Brunel University.
At 800m: OG: '16- sf; WCh: '15- 5, '17- sf; EC: '18- 8; CG: '18- ht; WI: '18- 3; EI: '17- 2, '19- 1. Won UK 2016-17.
Progress at 800m: 2004- 2:23.1, 2005- 2:20.4, 2006- 2:21.4, 2007- 2:13.34, 2008- 2:09.20, 2009- 2:06.29, 2010- 2:08.25, 2011- 2:07.93i/2:08.02, 2012- 2:0771i/2:11.30, 2013- 2:03.52, 2014- 2:01.94. 2015- 1:58.86, 2016- 1:59.45, 2017- 1:59.82, 2018- 1:59.81i/2:00.81. pbs: 60m 7.96i '12, 200m 24.55 '11, 400m 53.20 '11, 600m 1:27.48mx '16, 1500m 4:28.29 '14.

Asha PHILIP b. 25 Oct 1990 Leytonstone, London 1.63m 54kg. Newham & Essex Beagles, was at Kingston University.
At 100m/4x100mR: OG: '16- sf/3R; WCh: '13- sf, '15- sf/4R, '17- sf/2R; EC: '14- sf/1R, '16- 4/2R, '18- 1R; CG: '14- 4/3R, '18- 4/1R; WJ: 06- 4/6R; WY: 07- 1; E23: 11- 3R; EJ: '07- 1R; ET: '15- 1. At 60m: WI: '14- 4, '16- 5; EI: '13-17-19: 5/1/3. Won UK 100m 2013-14, 2016-17.
Progress at 100m: 2004- 12.14/12.04w, 2005- 11.83, 2006- 11.45, 2007- 11.37, 2010- 12.0, 2011-

11.47, 2012- 11.53, 2013- 11.20, 2014- 11.18/11.11w, 2015- 11.10, 2016- 11.16, 2017- 11.14, 2018- 11.21. pbs: 60m 7.06i '17, 150mSt 16.69 '14, 200m 23.45, 23.07w '13.
World U17 double-mini trampoline champion in 2006, but ruptured her knee in 2007 and unable to compete until 2010.

Tiffany PORTER b. 13 Nov 1987 Ypsilanti, USA 1.72m 62kg. née Ofili. Doctorate in pharmacy from University of Michigan.
At 100mh: OG: '12- sf, '16- 7; WCh: '11-13-15-17: 4/3/5/h; EC: '14- 1, '16- 3; CG: '14- 2, '18- 6; WJ: '06- 3 (for USA); CCp: '14- 2; ET: '13- 1. At 60mh: WI: '12-14-16: 2/3/3; EI: '11- 2. Won UK 100mh 2011, 2013-16; NCAA 100mh & 60mh ind 2009.
Records: British 100mh (4) 2011-14, 50mh/55mh/60mh indoors; world best 4x100mh 2014 & 2015.
Progress at 100mh: 2005- 14.19, 2006- 13.37/ 13.15w, 2007- 12.80, 2008- 12.73, 2009- 12.77/ 12.57w, 2010- 12.85, 2011- 12.56, 2012- 12.65/12.47w, 2013- 12.55, 2014- 12.51, 2015- 12.56, 2016- 12.70, 2017- 12.75, 2018- 12.99. pbs: 60m 7.41i '11, 100m 11.70 '09, 11.63w '08; 200m 23.90 '08, 400m 61.96 '06, LJ 6.48 '09; UK records: 50mh 6.83i '12, 55mh 7.38i '12, 60mh 7.80i '11.
Opted for British nationality in September 2010; her mother being born in London (father born in Nigeria). Married US hurdler Jeff Porter (pb 13.08 '12, sf OG '12/16) in May 2011. Sister of Cindy Ofili (100mh 12.60 "15, 4 OG 2016).

Shara PROCTOR b. 16 Sep 1988 The Valley, Anguilla 1.74m 56kg. Birchfield H. Was at University of Florida, USA.
At LJ: OG: '12- 7, '16- dnq 21; WCh: '07-09-11-13- 15-17: dnq 29/5/dnq 20/5/2/dnq 13; WI: '12-14- 16: 3/4/8; EC: '18- 3; CG: '06-14-18: dnq 13/nj/3; WJ: '06- dnq 16; WY: '05- 6; EI: '13- 4; CCp: '18- 4; ET: '13- 3. Won DL 2013, CAC 2009, UK 2011-13.
Records: Anguilla: LJ 2005-09; TJ 2007-09; UK LJ (4) 2012-15.
Progress at LJ: 2003- 5.64, 2004- 5.99A, 2005- 6.24, 2006- 6.17, 2007- 6.17, 2008- 6.54A/6.52/6.61w, 2009- 6.71, 2010- 6.69, 2011- 6.81, 2012- 6.95, 2013- 6.92, 2014- 6.82, 2015- 7.07, 2016- 6.91i/6.80, 2017- 6.73, 2018- 6.91. pbs: 60m 7.36i '16, 100m 12.27 '08, 12.10w '10; TJ 13.88i '10, 13.82 '17.
Switched from Anguilla (a British Dependent Territory without a National Olympic Committee) to Britain from 16 Nov 2010. Younger sister Shinelle (b. 27 Jun 91) set Anguillan high jump records at 1.70 in 2009 and 2010 and 1.72i in 2014.

Lynsey SHARP b. 11 Jul 1990 Dumfries 1.75m 60kg. Edinburgh AC. Law graduate of Edinburgh Napier University.
At 800m: OG: '12- sf, '16- 6; WCh: '15- sf, '17- 8; EC: '12-14-18: 1/2/6; CG: '14- 2, '18- h; WJ: '08- sf; WY: '07- sf; EU23: '11- 2; CCp: '14- 5. Won UK 2012, 2014-15.

Progress at 800m: 2000- 2:38.2, 2002- 2:25.97, 2003- 2:16.57, 2004- 2:09.98, 2005- 2:10.44, 2006- 2:10.91i, 2007- 2:06.92, 2008- 2:04.44, 2011- 2:00.65, 2012- 2:00.52, 2013- 2:02.63, 2014- 1:58.80, 2015- 1:57.71, 2016- 1:57.69, 2017- 1:58.01, 2018- 1:59.34. pbs: 400m 54.43 '16, 600m 1:27.16i '17, 1:27.51 '14; 1500m 4:36.27 '11.
Father Cameron (1982: 4th 100m, 2nd 200m EC; 3rd 100m, 200m, 4x100m CG; pbs: 100m 10.20 '83, 200m 20.47 '82); mother Carol Lightfoot (800m 2:02.91 '82).

Lorraine UGEN b. 22 Aug 1991 London 1.78m 64kg. Blackheath & Bromley. Was at Texas Christian University, USA.
At LJ: OG: '16- 11; WCh: '13- dnq, '15- 5, '17- 5; EC: '16- dnq 18, '18- 9; CG: '14- 5, '18- 4/1R; WJ: '10- dnq 17; EU23: '13- dns F; EJ: '09- dnq 21; WI: '16- 3; EI: 17- 2; won UK 2017-18, NCAA 2013.
Progress at LJ: 2007- 5.55, 2008- 5.79, 2009- 6.29, 2010- 6.35/6.42w, 2011- 6.54, 2012- 6.74/6.83w, 2013- 6.77, 2014- 6.73Ai/6.59i/6.39/6.40w, 2015- 6.92/6.96w, 2016- 6.93i/6.80/6.82w, 2017- 6.97i/6.78, 2018- 7.05. pbs: 60m 7.50Ai '12, 7.51i '14; 100m 11.32 '18, 11.31w '17; 200m 23.81/23.71w '15, 100mh 15.2/15.42 '08, HJ 1.56 '08, Hep 4307 '08

Laura WEIGHTMAN b. 1 Jul 1991 Alnwick 1.72m 58kg. Morpeth H. Leeds Met University.
At 1500m: OG: '12- 7, '16- 11; WCh: '13- h, '15- sf, '17- 6; EC: '14- 3, '18- 3; CG: '14- 2; WJ: '10- 6. Won UK 2012, 2014, 2017-18. At 3000m: ET: '13- 2. At 5000m: CG: '18- 3. Eur U23 CC: '13- 8.
Progress at 1500m: 2004- 4:50.5, 2005- 4:44.0, 2006- 4:37.20, 2007- 4:26.02, 2008- 4:22.20, 2009- 4:14.9mx/4:19.9, 2010- 4:09.60mx/4:12.82, 2011- 4:07.94mx/4:15.51, 2012- 4:02.99, 2013- 4:05.36, 2014- 4:00.17, 2015- 4:04.70, 2016- 4:02.66, 2017- 4:00.71, 15:08.24; 2018- 4:01.76, 15:25.84. pbs: 400m 58.43 '09, 800m 2:01.87 '17, 1000m 2:37.56 '18, 1M 4:20.49 '18, 2000m 5:44.22 '13, 3000m 8:43.46mx '13, 9:02.62 '12, 10kRd 31:40 '19.

USA

Governing body: USA Track and Field. Founded 1979 as The Athletics Congress, when it replaced the AAU (founded 1888) as the Governing body.
National Championships first held in 1876 (men), 1923 (women). **2018 Champions: Men**: 100m: Noah Lyles 9.88, 200m: Ameer Webb 20.47; 400m: Kahmari Montgomery 44.58, 800m: Clayton Murphy 1:46.50, 1500m: Mattew Centrowitz 3:43.37, 5000m: Paul Chelimo 13:29.47, 10000m: Lopez Lomong 28:58.38, HMar: Chris Derrick 62:37, Mar: Brogan Austin 2:12:39dh, 3000mSt: Evan Jager 8:20.10, 110mh: Devon Allen 13.46, 400mh: Kenny Selmon 48.21, HJ: Jason Robinson 2.31, PV: Sam Kendricks 5.85, LJ: Jeff Henderson 8.10, TJ: Donald Scott 17.37, SP: Darrell Hill 21.57, DT: Reggie Jagers 68.61, HT: Rudy Winkler 73.76, JT: Curtis

Thompson 75.99, Dec: Trey Hardee 8225, 20000mW/50kW: Nick Christie 1:24:53.4/4:09:32.
Women: 100m: Aleia Hobbs 10.91, 200m: Jenna Prandini 22.62, 400m: Shakima Wimbley 49.52, 800m: Ajee' Wilson 1:58.18, 1500m/5000m: Shelby Houlihan 4:05.48/15:31.03, 10000m: Molly Huddle 31:52.32, HMar: Aliphine Tuliamuk 70:04, Mar: Emma Bates 2:28:19dh, 3000mSt: Emma Coburn 9:17.70, 100mh: Kendra Harrison 12.46, 400mh: Shamier Little 53.61, HJ: Vashti Cunningham 1.95, PV: Sandi Morris 4.80, LJ: Sha'keela Saunders 6.54, TJ: Keturah Orji 14.59, SP: Maggie Ewen 19.29, DT: Valarie Allman 63.55, HT: DeAnna Price 78.12, JT: Kara Winger 62.88, Hep: Erica Bougard 6347, 20000mW: Maria Michta-Coffey 1:35:21.6, 50kW: Katie Burnett 4:47:50,
NCAA Championships first held in 1921 (men), 1982 (women). **2018 Champions: Men**: 100m: Cameron Burrell 10.13, 200m: Divine Oduduru NGR 20.28, 400m: Michael Norman 43.61, 800m: Isaiah Harris 1:44.76, 1500m: Oliver Hoare AUS 3:44.77, 5000m: Sean McGorty 13:54.81, 10000m: Ben Flanagan 28:34.53, 3000mSt: Obsa Ali 8:32.23, 110mh: Grant Holloway 13.42, 400mh: Rai Benjamin ANT 47.02, HJ: Tejaswin Shankar IND 2.24, PV: Chris Nilsen 5.83, LJ: Zack Bazile 8.37, TJ: Tahar Triki ALG 16.79, SP/HT: Denzel Comenentia NED 20.61/76.41, DT: Luke Vaugn 60.41, JT: Anderson Peters GRN 82.82, Dec: Tim Duckworth GBR 8336. **Women**: 100m: Aleia Hobbs 11.01, 200m: Angie Annelus 22.76, 400m: Lynna Irby 49.80, 800m: Sammy Watson 2:04.21, 1500m: Jessica Hull AUS 4:08.75, 5000m: Karissa Schweizer 15:41.58, 10000m: Sharon Lokedi KEN 32:09.20, 3000mSt: Allie Ostrander 9:39.28, 100mh: Jasmine Camacho-Quinn PUR 12.40, 400mh: Sydney McLaughlin 54.15, HJ: Alexus Henry 1.82, PV: Olivia Gruver 4.55, LJ/TJ: Keturah Orji 6.67/14.04, SP/DT: Maggie Ewen 19.17/60.48, HT: Janeah Stewart 72.92, JT: Mackenzie Little AUS 60.36, Hep: Georgia Ellenwood 6146.

Devon ALLEN b. 12 Dec 1994 Phoenix, Arizona 1.83m 84kg. Was at at University of Oregon.
At 110mh: OG: '16- 5, WCh: '17- sf, CG: '18- 5. Won US 2014, 2016, 2018; NCAA 2014, 2016.
Progress at 110mh: 2014- 13.16, 2016- 13.03, 2017- 13.10, 2018- 13.23/13.13w. pbs: 60m 6.85Ai '14, 100m 10.26 '18, 200m 20.52 '18, 60mh 7.49Ai/7.50i '18, 400mh 51.19 '14.
On a football scholarship as a wide receiver, suffered a knee injury on the opening kickoff of the Rose Bowl at the end of 2014 and missed 2015 track season.

Ronnie BAKER b. 15 Oct 1993 Louisville, Kentucky 1.78m 73kg. Texas Christian University.
At 100m: WUG: '15- 4. At 60m: WI: '18- 3; won NCAA indoor 2015-16, US 2017.
Progress at 100m: 2011- 10.57, 2012- 10.59/10.55w,

2013- 10.58/10.33w, 2014- 10.21/10.14w, 2015- 10.05/9.94w, 2016- 10.09/9.95w, 2017- 9.98, 2018- 9.87/9.78w. pbs: 60m 6.40Ai/6.44 '18, 200m 20.55 '18, 20.06w '17; 400m 46.18 '13. Fastest in the world at indoor 60m in 2016 & 2017.

Zack BAZILE b. 7 Jan 1996 1.78m 79kg. Ohio State University.
At TJ: Won NCAA 2018.
Progress at LJ: 2014- 7.34, 2015- 7.67i/7.56, 2016- 7.58/7.69w, 2017- 7.97, 2018- 8.37. pbs: 60m 6.68i '18, 100m 10.21 '18, 200m 21.57 '18, TJ 15.69i '18, 15.42/16.21w '17

Chris BENARD b. 4 Apr 1990 1.90m 79kg. Chula Vista Elite. Was at Arizona State University.
At TJ: OG: '16- dnq 16; WCh: '17- 6.
Progress at TJ: 2008- 15.09, 2009- 15.38, 2010- 15.52/16.20w, 2011- 15.80Ai/15.75, 2012- 16.74, 2013- 16.78, 2014- 17.10, 2015- 16.95, 2016- 17.21, 2017- 17.48, 2018- 17.40. pb LJ 8.10Ai, 7.96 '14.

Rai BENJAMIN b. 27 Jul 1997 Bronx, New York 1.91m 77kg. Nike, USC.
At 400mh: WY: '13- sf; won NCAA 2018.
CAC 400m hurdles record 2018, Antiguan records: 400m (2) 2017-18, 400mh (8) 2015-18. Ran on fastest ever indoor 4x400m by USC 2018.
Progress at 400mh: 2013- 53.13, 2014- 52.12, 2015- 49.97, 2016- 49.82, 2017- 48.33, 2018- 47.02. pbs: 60m 6.72i '17, 100m 10.69 '15, 10.40w '17; 200m 20.34i '18, 20.64 '17; 3400m 32.55i '19, 400m 44.74 '18.
Parents are from Antigua, but he declined Antiguan selection for the 2016 Olympic Games and, already a US citizen; was cleared by the IAAF to compete for the USA in October 2018.

Hillary BOR b. 22 Nov 1989 Eldoret, Kenya 1.68m 57kg. Was at Iowa State University.
At 3000mSt: OG: '16- 7; WCh: '17- h.
Progress at 3000mSt: 2008- 8:36.84, 2009- 8:35.12, 2010- 8:38.05, 2011- 8:40.83, 2012- 8:36.44, 2013- 8:32.41, 2014- 8:38.42, 2015- 8:45.94, 2016- 8:13.68, 2017- 8:11.82, 2018- 8:12.20. pbs: 1500m 3:44.30 '07, 1M 4:03.43i '08, 3000m 8:10.77i '10, 5000m 13:26.81 '18, 10M Rd 48:31 '15.
US citizen from 31 December 2014 after joining the US Army with his brothers Emmanuel (1500m: 4 WUG 3:41.65 in 2007, 3000m 7:44.93i '18, 5000m 13:28.79 '17) and Julius (1500m 3:41.11 '10).

Donavan BRAZIER b. 15 Apr 1997 Grand Rapids, Michigan 1.88m 73kg. Nike. Texas A&M University.
At 800m: WCh: '17- sf; won NCAA 2016, US 2017. World and two North American indoor 800m records 2019.
Progress at 800m: 2012- 2:06, 2013- 1:54.36, 2014- 1:48.61, 2015- 1:43.55, 2016- 1:44.14, 2017- 1:43.95, 2018- 1:45.10Ai, 2019- 1:44.41i. pbs: 400m 46.91i '18, 47.02 '16; 600m 1:13.77i '19, 1000m 2:21.79i '17, 1M 3:59.30i '17.

Chris CARTER b. 11 Mar 1989 Austin 1.86m 80kg. Was at University of Houston.
At TJ: PAm: '11- 6; WI: '14- 6, '18- 5. Won US indoor 2014.
Progress at TJ: 2005- 14.43, 2006- 13.78/14.69w, 2007- 15.88, 2008- 15.41i/15.31/15.69Aw, 2009- 16.34, 2010- 15.98, 2011- 16.86, 2012- 16.61, 2013- 16.69, 2014- 17.15Ai/17.09, 2015- 16.71i/16.70, 2016- 17.18, 2017- 17.10Aidq/16.75i, 2018- 17.20Ai/17.18/17.28w. pbs: 400mh 53.90 '07, LJ 7.67 '13.

Matthew CENTROWITZ b. 18 Nov 1989 Beltsville, Maryland 1.76m 61kg. Nike Oregon Project. Studied sociology at the University of Oregon.
At 1500m: OG: '12- 4, '16- 1; WCh: '11-13-15-17: 3/2/8/h; WI: '12- 7, '16- 1. At 5000m WJ: '08- 11. Won US 2011, 2013, 2015-16, 2018; NCAA 2011, PAm-J 2007.
Progress at 1500m: 2007- 3:49.54, 2008- 3:44.98, 2009- 3:36.92, 2010- 3:40.14, 2011- 3:34.46, 2012- 3:31.96, 2013- 3:33.58, 2014- 3:31.09, 2015- 3:30.40, 2016- 3:34.09, 2017- 3:33.41, 2018- 3:31.77. pbs: 800m 1:44.62 '15, 1000m 2:16.67 '16. 1M 3:50.53 '14, 3000m 7:40.74i '16, 2M 8:21.07i '17, 8:40.55 '07; 5000m 13:20.06 '14, 10M Rd 50:39 '18.
Father Matt pbs: 1500m 3:36.60 '76, 3:54.94 '82, 5000m US record 13:12.91 '82, 10000m 28:32.7 '83; h OG 1500m 1976; 1 PAm 5000m 1979. Sister Lauren (b. 25 Sep 1986) 1500m pb 4:10.23 '09.

Paul Kipkemoi **CHELIMO** b. 27 Oct 1990 Iten, Kenya 1.71m 57kg. Nike, formerly US Army.
Went to the University of North Carolina.
At 5000m: OG: '16- 2; WCh: '17- 3; WUG: '13- 2 (1500m 6); won US 2017-18. At 3000m: CCp: '18- 1; WI: '16- 7.
Progress at 5000m: 2011- 13:53.02, 2012- 13:21.89, 2013- 13:36.27, 2015- 13:37.02, 2016- 13:03.90, 2017- 13:08.62, 2018- 12:57.55. pbs: 1500m 3:39.33 '16, 1M 3:55.96 '18, 3000m 7:31.57 '17, 2M 8:20.91 '18, 10000m 29:44.42 '11, 15k Rd 43:46 '17, 10M Rd 48:19 '15.
Came to the USA in 2010, granted US citizenship on 23 Jul 2014 and cleared to compete for the US from 15 Jun 2015. Reduced his 5000m best from 13:19.54 to 13:03.90 at the 2016 Olympic Games.

Michael CHERRY b. 23 Mar 1995 1.86m 75kg. Wsa at Louisiana State University.
At 400m/4x400mR: WCh: '17- 2R; WJ: '14- 1R; WI: '18- 2/2R; Won US indoor 2018.
Progress at 400m: 2010- 49.25, 2011- 48.57, 2012- 46.37, 2013- 46.02, 2014- 45.17, 2015- 45.43, 2016- 44.81, 2017- 44.66, 2018- 44.85. pbs: 200m 21.07 '17, 600m 1:17.17Ai '16, 1:17.19Ai '19.

Will CLAYE b. 13 Jun 1991 Phoenix 1.80m 68kg. Nike. Was at University of Oklahoma, then Florida.
At (LJ)/TJ: OG: '12- 3/2, '16- 2; WCh: '11- 9/3, '13- 3, '15- dnq 19, '17- 2; WI: '12- 4/1, '18- 1; CCp: '14- 2/3; won US 2014, 2016-17; PAm-J and NCAA 2009.

Progress at LJ, TJ: 2007- 14.91/15.19w, 2008-
7.39/7.48w, 15.97; 2009- 7.89/8.00w, 17.19/17.24w;
2010- 7.30w, 16.30; 2011- 8.29, 17.50/17.62w; 2012-
8.25, 17.70i/17.62; 2013- 8.10, 17.52; 2014-
8.19/8.29w, 17.75; 2015- 8.07/8.11w, 17.48/17.50w;
2016- 8.14/8.42w, 17.76; 2017- 7.89, 17.91; 2018-
17.44/17.46w pb 100m 10.64/10.53w '12.
Possibly youngest ever NCAA champion – he
won 2009 title on his 18th birthday with 17.24w
(and US junior record 17.19). First to win Olympic
medals at both LJ and TJ since 1936. Married
Queen Harrison (qv) on 13 October 2018.

Christian COLEMAN b. 6 Mar 1996 Atlanta
1.75m 75kg. University of Tennessee (sport
management).
At 100m: WCh: '17- 2/2R; OG: 16- resR; PAm-J:
'15- 3; won DL 2018. At 60m: WI: '18- 1. Won
NCAA 100m & 200m, indoor 60m & 200m 2017.
Two world 60m indoor records 2018.
Progress at 100m, 200m: 2013- 22.43, 2014-
10.30/10.29w, 20.94; 2015- 10.18/10.16w, 20.61;
2016- 9.95, 20.26; 2017- 9.82, 19.85; 2018- 9.79. pbs:
60m 6.34Ai/6.37i '18, LJ 7.21 '14.

Omar CRADDOCK b. 26 Apr 1991 Killeen,
Texas 1.78m 79kg. Jump Corps. Was at
University of Florida.
At TJ: WCh: '13- dnq 13, '15- 4; WJ: '10- 3; WI:
'16- 5. Won US 2015, NCAA 2012-13.
Progress at TJ: 2006- 14.67, 2007- 15.16A, 2008-
15.53, 2009- 14.87i, 2010- 16.56, 2011- 16.57i/16.46,
2012- 16.75i/16.71/16.92w, 2013- 16.92/17.15w,
2014- 16.98/17.26w, 2015- 17.53, 2016- 17.16/
17.42w, 2017- 17.08, 2018- 17.40. pb LJ 7.63i '13,
7.60 '15, 7.70w '12.

Freddie CRITTENDEN b. 3 Aug 1994 Utica,
Michigan 1.83m 73kg. Was at Syracuse
University.
Progress at 110mh: 2014- 13.73, 2015- 13.62, 2016-
13.48/13.43w, 2017- 13.42, 2018- 13.27. pb 60mh
7.53i '19.

Ryan CROUSER b. 18 Dec 1992 Boring, Oregon
2.01m 135kg. University of Texas.
At SP(/DT): OG: '16- 1; WCh: '17- 6; WY: '09-
1/2; CCp- '18- 2; won US 2016-17, NCAA 2013-
14, indoors 2014.
Progress at SP: 2011- 19.48i, 2012- 20.29i/19.32,
2013- 21.09, 2014- 21.39, 2015- 21.14i/21.11, 2016-
22.52, 2017- 22.65, 2018- 22.53. pbs: DT 63.90 '14,
JT 61.16 '09.
Set High School 1.62kg DT record 72.40 '11. His
father Mitch SP 20.04i '83, 19.94 '82, DT 67.22 '85;
uncle Dean SP 21.07 '82, DT 65.88 '83, won
NCAA SP 1982 & DT 1982-3; uncle Brian JT
83.00 '87, old JT 95.10 '85, won NCAA 1982 &
1985, dnq OG 1988 & 1992; Dean's children:
Sam SP 17.62 '13, JT 83.30 '15 (dnq 34 OG 16), US
junior & HS record '10, won NCAA 2014-15;
Haley US junior JT record 55.22 '12, 4 WY '11.

Paul DEDEWO b. 4 Jun 1991 New York 1.85m
73kg. Altis. Was at City College of New York.

At 400m/4x400mR: WI: '18- res 2R.
Progress at 400m: 2009- 51.09, 2010- 49.07, 2011-
48.15, 2012- 48.52i/48.92, 2015- 45.41, 2016- 45.67,
2017- 45.13, 2018- 44.43. pbs: 100m 10.67 '16,
200m 20.40 '17, 300m 31.92Ai '17.
Dual citizenship with Nigeria. After running
in the 2016 NGR Champs, he decided to
compete for the USA.

Marquis DENDY b. 17 Nov 1992 Middleton,
Delaware 1.92m 75kg. Nike. Was at University
of Florida.
At LJ/(TJ): WCh: '13-15-17: dnq 27/21 (13)/20;
WI: '16- 1, '18- 3. At TJ: WJ: '10- 8; won US LJ
2015; NACAC LJ 2012, 2018; NCAA LJ & TJ
2014-15, indoor LJ 2013, 2015-16; TJ 2015.
Progress at LJ, TJ: 2009- 7.20, 15.40; 2010- 7.45,
16.03; 2011- 7.47/7.56w, 15.62; 2012- 8.06i/7.81,
15.55; 2013- 8.28i/8.10/8.29w, 16.25i/16.03; 2014-
8.00, 16.52/17.05w; 2015- 8.39/8.68w, 17.50/17.71w;
2016- 8.42, 16.36; 2017- 8.18/8.39w, 2018- 8.42i/
8.29. pbs: 60m 6.88i '14, 100m 10.31 '15.

Dedric DUKES b. 4 Feb 1992 Miami 1.80m
70kg. Was at University of Florida.
At 200m: WY: '09- 4/1 MedR. Won NCAA 2014.
Progress at 200m: 2007- 21.88/21.79w, 2008-
21.19/21.12w, 2009- 20.94, 2011- 20.88w, 2012-
20.47, 2013- 20.45/20.34w, 2014- 19.97/19.91w,
2015- 19.99/19.86w, 2016- 20.41/20.14w, 2017-
20.37, 2018- 20.27. pbs: 60m 6.77i '14, 100m 10.13
'16, 10.06w '17; 400m 45.66 '14.
Football wide receiver in high school.

Johnny DUTCH b. 20 Jan 1989 Clayton NC
1.80m 82kg. Studied media arts at University of
South Carolina.
At 400mh: WCh: '09/15- sf; WJ: '08- 2; PAm-J:
'07- 1/2R. Won US 2014, NCAA 2010.
Progress at 400mh: 2005- 52.06, 2006- 51.72,
2007- 50.07, 2008- 48.52, 2009- 48.18, 2010- 47.63,
2011- 48.47, 2012- 48.90, 2013- 48.02, 2014- 48.93,
2015- 48.13, 2016- 48.10, 2017- 48.60. pbs: 400m
46.75 '13, 500m 1:03.25i '15, 55mh 7.31i '10, 60mh
7.71i '09, 110mh 13.50/13.30w '10.

Jarret EATON b. 24 Jun 1989 Philadelphia
1.83m 82kg. Was at Syracuse University
At 60mh: WI: '16- 4, '18- 2. US indoor 60m
champion 2016, 2018.
Progress at 110mh: 2008- 13.90, 2009- 14.06/
13.99w, 2010- 13.83, 2011- 13.63, 2012- 13.44, 2014-
13.71, 2015- 13.41/13.40w, 2016- 13.25, 2017-
13.34, 2018- 13.33. pbs: 55m 6.36i '16, 60m 6.83i
'16, 100m 10.96 '17, 60mh 7.43Ai/7.47i '18, 400mh
53.26 '07.

Mason FINLEY b. 7 Oct 1990 Kansas City
2.03m 150kg. Was at University of Wyoming
At DT: OG: '16- 11; WCh: '17- 3; WUG: '11- 8 (3
SP). Won US 2016-17, PAm-J SP & DT 2009.
Progress at DT: 2010- 60.18, 2011- 60.65, 2012-
61.40, 2013- 62.48A, 2014- 64.17A, 2015- 64.80A,
2016- 66.72, 2017- 68.03, 2018- 67.06. pbs: SP
20.71i '11, 19.89 '12; Wt 19.42i '14.

His father Jared DT 58.34 '79.

Eric FUTCH b. 25 Apr 1993 Darby, Pennsylvania 1.75m 70kg. Student at University of Florida.
At 400mh: WCh: '17- sf; WJ: 12- 1/1R. Won NCAA 2016-17, US 2017.
Progress at 400mh: 2011- 51.67, 2012- 50.24, 2013- 50.66, 2015- 49.45, 2016- 48.91, 2017- 48.18, 2018- 49.47. pbs: 200m 21.17 '15, 400m 46.16i/46.71 '17, 600y 1:11.10i '16.

Justin GATLIN b. 10 Feb 1982 Brooklyn, NY 1.85m 79kg. XTEP. Was at University of Tennessee.
At 100m/(200m)/4x100mR: OG: '04- 1/3/2R, '12- 3/dq2R, '16- 2/sf; WCh: '05- 1/1, '11- sf, '13- 2/2R, '15- 2/2, '17- 1/2R. At 60m: WI: '03- 1, '12- 1. Won DL 100m 2013-15, US 100m 2005-06, 2012, 2016; 200m 2005, 2015-16; (indoor 60m 2003), NCAA 100m & 200m 2001-02 (& indoor 60m/200m 2002). N.American 4x100m record 2015. World M35 100m record 2017.
Progress at 100m, 200m: 2000- 10.36, 2001- 10.08, 20.29/19.86w; 2002: under international suspension 10.05/10.00w, 19.86; 2003- 9.97, 20.04; 2004- 9.85, 20.01; 2005- 9.88/9.84w, 20.00; 2006- 9.77dq, 2010- 10.09, 20.63; 2011- 9.95, 20.20; 2012- 9.79, 20.11; 2013- 9.85, 20.21; 2014- 9.77/9.76w, 19.68; 2015- 9.74, 19.57, 2016- 9.80, 19.75; 2017- 9.92, 2018- 10.03. pbs: 60m 6.45i '03, 100y 9.10 '14, 55mh 7.39i '02, 60mh 7.86i '01, 110mh 13.41dq '02, 13.78/13.74w '01; LJ 7.34i '01, 7.21 '00.
Top hurdler in high school (110mh 13.66 and 300mh 36.74 on junior hurdles). Retained NCAA sprint titles while ineligible for international competition in 2002 after failing a drugs test in 2001 (when he won 100m, 200m and 110mh at the US Juniors) for a prescribed medication to treat Attention Deficit Disorder. Reinstated by IAAF in July 2002. Won 2005 World 100m title by biggest ever winning margin of 0.17 and all five 100ms in 2006, including the US title and tying the world record with 9.77 in Doha, but had tested positive for testosterone before these races. He received a four-year drugs ban, returning to competition in August 2010. In 2014 he was unbeaten at 100m and 200m and in Brussels on 5 Sep recorded the best-ever one-day sprint double with 9.77 and 19.71. His run of successive wins (26 finals and 7 prelims) in 2014-15 ended by Usain Bolt in World 100m in 2015.

Elijah HALL (-THOMPSON) b. 22 Aug 1994 Katy, Texas 1.74m 69kg. Student at University of Houston.
Won NCAA indoor 60m & 200m 2018.
North American indoor 200m record 2018.
Progress at 200m: 2010- 21.53, 2011- 21.12/20.76w, 2012- 20.86, 2013- 20.60, 2015- 21.16i, 2016- 20.37A/ 21.16i/20.69w; 2017- 20.21/19.96w; 2018- 20.02i/ 20.11. pbs: 60m 6.52i '18, 100m 10.10 '18, 10.00w '17.
Had to withdraw from World Champs team after 3rd in US Champs 2017.

Aleec HARRIS b. 31 Oct 1990 Lawrenceville, Georgia 1.85m 77kg. adidas. Studied sociology at University of Southern California.
At 110mh: WCh: '15/17- sf. Won US 110mh 2017, indoor 60mh 2015. World 4x110mh best 2015.
Progress at 110mh: 2010- 14.15/13.88w, 2011- 13.65/13.55w, 2013- 13.69/13.55w, 2014- 13.14, 2015- 13.11, 2016- 13.43/13.32w, 2017- 13.18, 2018- 13.37. pbs: 55mh 7.18i '11, 60mh 7.50i '15.

Mike HARTFIELD b. 29 Mar 1990 Manchester, Connecticut 1.90m 77kg. adidas. Was at Ohio State University.
At LJ: OG: '16- dnq 25; WCh: '15- nj.
Progress at LJ: 2007- 7.19w, 2008- 7.42/7.52w, 2009- 7.57, 2010- 7.61i, 2011- 7.91/7.95w, 2012- 7.96, 2013- 8.15, 2014- 8.15/8.17w, 2015- 8.27/8.42w, 2016- 8.34/8.39w, 2017- 8.21/8.22w, 2018- 8.18Ai/ 8.02 pb TJ 15.84 '13.
Broke 77 year-old Ohio State University record set by Jesse Owens.

Jeffery HENDERSON b. 19 Feb 1989 Sherwood, Arkansas 1.78m 82kg. Was at Florida Memorial University and Stillman College.
At LJ: OG: '16- 1; WCh: '15- 9, '17- dnq 17; PAm: '15- 1; CCp: '18- 3; WI: '16- 4; US champion 2014, 2016, 2018; indoors 2012.
Progress at LJ: 2006- 7.14i, 2007- 7.51i/7.41, 2008- 7.74/7.77w, 2009- 8.15u/7.88/8.19w, 2010- 7.94Ai/ 7.90i, 2011- 7.78, 2012- 7.91w, 2013- 8.22, 2014- 8.43/8.52w, 2015- 8.52/8.54w, 2016- 8.38/8.59w, 2017- 8.28, 2018- 8.44A/8.20/8.39w. pbs: 55m 6.31i '09, 60m 6.58i '16, 100m 10.18A '13, 10.25 '11, 10.19w '15; 200m 20.65A '13, TJ 14.90i '08.

Darrell HILL b. 17 Aug 1993 Darby, Pennsylvania 1.92m 150kg. Was at Penn State University.
At SP: OG: '16- dnq 23; WCh: '17- 11; PAm: '15- 4; WI: '18- 6. Won DL 2017, NACAC 2018.
Progress at SP: 2012- 17.62i/17.53, 2013- 19.13, 2014- 20.57, 2015- 20.86, 2016- 21.63, 2017- 22.44, 2018- 22.40. pbs: DT 50.20 '15, Wt 19.12i '15.

Ryan HILL b. 31 Jan 1990 Hickory, North Carolina 1.76m 60kg. Bowerman TC. Was at North Carolina State University.
At 5000m: WCh: '13- 10, '15- 7, '17- dns. At 3000m: WI: '16- 2. Won US 5000m 2015.
Progress at 5000m: 2009- 14:09.63, 2010- 13:44.36, 2011- 13:31.67, 2012- 13:26.34, 2013- 13:14.22, 2014- 13:14.31, 2015- 13:05.69, 2016- 13:15.59, 2017- 13:07.61i/13:16.99, 2018- 13:25.46. pbs: 800m 1:50.22iA '14, 1000m 2:20.26 '13, 1500m 3:35.59 '16, 1M 3:54.89i '14, 3:55.48 '18; 3000m 7:30.93 '16, 2M 8:11.56i '17, 8:22.36 '18; 10000m 29:32.28 '10.

Grant HOLLOWAY b. 19 Nov 1997 Chesapeake, Virginia 1.88m 82kg. Student at University of Florida.
Won NCAA 110mh 2017-18, 60m ind 2019, 60mh ind 2017-19.
North American indoor 60m hurdles record 2019.

Progress at 110mh, LJ: 2015- 7.84, 2016- 7.91i/7.77, 2017- 13.39, 8.05i/8.04; 2018- 13.15, 8.17/8.33w. pbs: 55m 6.22i '16, 60m 6.50i '19, 200m 20.69i '19, 21.32 '16; 300m 32.80i '17, 500m 1:03.35i '16, 60mh 7.35i '19, HJ 2.16 '14.
Wide receiver at American football Ran 43.88 anchor leg at 2017 NCAAs.

(Timothy Lamont) **T.J.HOLMES** b. 2 Jul 1995 St Petersburg, Florida 1.82m 73kg. Sports medicine student at Baylor University.
At 400mh: WCh: '17- 5; WJ: 14- 3.
Progress at 400mh: 2013- 50.61, 2014- 49.90, 2015- 51.48, 2016- 49.31, 2017- 48.44, 2018- 48.30. pbs: 400m 47.42i '17, 600y 1:10.53i '17, 800m 1:56.01 '17, 60mh 7.87i '18.

Bershawn JACKSON b. 8 May 1983 Miami 1.73m 69kg. Nike. Studied accountancy at St Augustine's University, Florida.
At 400mh/4x400mR: OG: '08- 3; WCh: '03- h (dq), '05- 1, '07- sf/res 1R, '09- 3/res 1R, '11- 6/1R, '13- sf, '15- h; WJ: '02- 3/1R; CCp: '10- 3/1R; won DL 2010, 2015; WAF 2004-05, US 2003, 2008-10, 2015. At 400m: WI: '10- 5/1R; won US indoor 2005, 2010.
Progress at 400mh: 1999- 54.53, 2000- 52.17, 2001- 50.80, 2002- 50.00, 2003- 48.23, 2004- 47.86, 2005- 47.30, 2006- 47.48, 2007- 48.13, 2008- 48.02, 2009- 47.98, 2010- 47.32, 2011- 47.93, 2012- 48.20, 2013- 48.09, 2014- 48.76, 2015- 48.09, 2016- 49.04, 2017- 48.63, 2018- 49.08. pbs: 200m 21.03/20.46w '04, 400m 45.06 '07, 500m 1:00.70i '15, 600m 1:17.85i '16, 800m 1:53.40 '11, 200mhSt 22.26 '11.

Evan JAGER b. 8 Mar 1989 Algonquin, Illinois 1.86m 66kg. Bowerman TC. Was at University of Wisconsin.
At 3000mSt: OG: '12- 6, '16- 2; WCh: '13- 5, '15- 6, '17- 3; CCp: '14- 2; US champion 2012-18. At 1500m: WJ: '08- 8. At 5000m: WCh: '09- h.
Three N.American 3000m steeplechase records 2012-15.
Progress at 5000m, 3000mSt: 2009- 13:22.18, 2012- 8:06.81, 2013- 13:02.40, 8:08.60; 2014- 13:08.63, 8:04.71; 2015- 8:00.45, 2016- 13:16.86, 8:04.01; 2017- 8:01.29, 2018- 8:01.02. pbs: 800m 1:50.10i '10, 1:51.04 '08; 1000m 2:20.29i '15, 1500m 3:32.97 '15, 1M 3:53.33 '14, 2000m 4:57.56 '14, 3000m 7:35.16 '12, 2M 8:14.95i '13.
Set US record in only his fifth steeplechase race, improving pb by 10.59 secs. In 2009 he had come 3rd in the US Champs in only his second race at 5000m.

Reggie JAGERS III b. 13 Aug 1994 Cleveland 1.88m 118kg. Chula Vista Elite. Degree in sport management from Kent State University.
At DT: CCp: '18- 5; WUG: '17- 1. Won US 2018.
Progress at DT: 2013- 55.99, 2014- 59.19, 2015- 61.00, 2016- 61.64, 2017- 62.51, 2018- 68.61. pbs: Wt 22.36i '18, HT 66.22 '17.
Best ever by a left-handed discus thrower. His brother Phillip has DT pb 62.71 '16.

Stanley Kipkoech **KEBENEI** b. 6 Nov 1989 Nakuru, Kenya 1.74m 61kg. Nike. Was at University of Arkansas.
At 3000mSt: WCh: '17- 5.
Progress at 3000mSt: 2011- 8:45.81, 2012- 8:24.45, 2014- 8:35.27, 2015- 8:23.93, 2016- 8:18.52, 2017- 8:08.30, 2018- 8:28.39. pbs: 1000m 2:46.47i '14, 1500m 3:42.8 '11, 1M 4:04.37i '13, 4:05.79 '16; 3000m 7:49.74i '15, 7:54.21 '17; 5000m 13:51.85 '14, 10000m 27:58.56 '17, 15k Rd 43:29 '17.
US citizenship 28 Aug 2014, cleared to compete for USA 5 Mar 2015.

Sam KENDRICKS b. 7 Sep 1992 Oxford, Mississippi 1.89m 79kg. Nike. Army reservist (2nd Lt.). Was at University of Mississippi.
At PV: OG: '16- 3; WCh: '15- 9=, '17- 1; CCp: '18- 1; WUG: '13- 1; WI: '16- 2, '18- 2; Won DL 2017, US 2014-18, NCAA 2013-4.
Progress at PV: 2010- 4.68, 2011- 5.18, 2012- 5.50, 2013- 5.81, 2014- 5.75, 2015- 5.86Ai/5.82, 2016- 5.92, 2017- 6.00, 2018- 5.96, 2019- 5.93i.

Fred KERLEY b. 7 May 1995 Taylor, Texas 1.905m 93kg. ALTIS. Texas A&M University.
At 400m/4x400mR: WCh: '17- 7/2R; WI: '18- 2R, Won NCAA & US 2017, DL 2018.
Progress at 400m: 2010- 52.50, 2014- 46.38, 2015- 47.15Ai/47.81, 2016- 45.10, 2017- 43.70, 2018- 44.33. pbs: 100m 10.49A '15, 200m 20.24 '17, 300m 32.10+ '17, 600y 1:11.39i '14, TJ 13.90 '13.
Brother **My'Lik** (b. 6 Jun 1996) pb 400m 44.85 '17, WIR 4x400m 2018; sister **Virginia** 400m 54.38 '17.

Leonard Essau **KORIR** b. 10 Dec 1986 Iten, Kenya 1.73m 61kg. US Army. Studied political science at Iona College.
At 10000m: OG: '16- 14; WCh: '17- 13. Won US 10kRd & HMar 2017, CC 2017-18, NCAA 10000m 2011.
Progress at 10000m: 2011- 27:29.40, 2014- 28:01.85, 2015- 28:40.46, 2016- 27:35.65, 2017- 27:20.18. pbs: 1500m 3:43.65 '11, 1M 4:03.57i '12, 3000m 7:49.98i '13, 7:51.41 '17, 2M 8:22.44i '13, 5000m 13:15.4 '13, 15k 43:07 '18, HMar 59:52 '17.
Lived in the USA from 2014, US citizenship 3 May 2016.

Joe KOVACS b. 28 Jun 1989 Bethlehem, Pennsylvania 1.81m 132kg. Nike. Was at Penn State University.
At SP: OG: '16- 2; WCh: '15- 1, '17- 2; CCp: '14- 3; Won DL 2015, US 2014-15.
Progress at SP: 2007- 16.49, 2008- 16.86i, 2009- 18.53, 2010- 19.36i/18.73, 2011- 19.84i/19.15, 2012- 21.08, 2013- 20.82, 2014- 22.03. 2015- 22.56, 2016- 22.13, 2017- 22.57, 2018- 21.02. pbs: DT 56.08 '11, HT 61.50 '11, Wt 19.07i '11.

Erik KYNARD b. 3 Feb 1991 Toledo, Ohio 1.93m 86kg. Nike Jordan. Was at Kansas State University.
At HJ: OG: '12- 2, '16- 6; WCh: '11-13-15-17: dnq 14/5/8=/dnq nh; WJ: '08- dnq 19=; CCp: '14- 5;

WI: '14-16-18: 4/3/4; Won DL 2016, US 2013-14, 2016; NCAA 2011-12.
Progress at HJ: 2007- 2.13i/2.05, 2008- 2.23i/2.15, 2009- 2.24i/2.22, 2010- 2.25, 2011- 2.33i/2.31, 2012- 2.34, 2013- 2.37, 2014- 2.37, 2015- 2.37, 2016- 2.35, 2017- 2.31i/2.30, 2018- 2.31i/2.29. pb LJ 7.15i '09.

Jarrion LAWSON b. 6 May 1994 Texarcana, Texas 1.88m 75kg. University of Arkansas.
At LJ: OG: '16- 4 (res dqR); WCh: '17- 2; WJ: '12- 3 (dnq 22 TJ); WI: '18- 4. Won US LJ 2017, NCAA 100m, 200m & LJ 2016.
Progress at LJ: 2011- 7.26/7.46w, 2012- 7.82/7.89w, 2013- 7.93, 2014- 8.39Ai/7.92/8.13w, 2015- 8.34/ 8.36w, 2016- 8.58, 2017- 8.44/8.49w, 2018- 8.38Ai/ 8.25. pbs: 60m 6.60i '16, 100m 10.03 '17, 9.9/9.90w '15; 150mSt 15.25 '17, 200m 20.17 '16, TJ 15.80 '12.
Provisionally suspended after a positive drugs test in 2018.

Wil(bert) LONDON III b. 17 Aug 1997 Waco, Texas 1.83m 68kg. Kinesiology student at Baylor University.
At 400m/4x400mR: WCh: '17- sf/2R; WJ: '16- 2/1R.
Progress at 400m: 2013- 50.54, 2014- 47.66, 2015- 45.96, 2016- 45.27, 2017- 44.47, 2018- 44.73. pb 200m 21.10 '16, 20.84w '17.

Noah LYLES b. 18 Jul 1997 Gainesville, Florida 1.80m 70kg.
At 100m: WJ: '16- 1/1R; PAm-J '15- 2 (1 200m); CCp: '18- 1/1R; won US 2018; at 200m: WY: 13- sf/2Med R; Yth OG: '14- 1, won DL 2017-18.
World indoor 300m record 2017.
Progress at 100m, 200m: 2012- 21.82, 2013- 10.86/10.73w, 21.23; 2014- 10.45, 20.71; 2015- 10.14/10.07w, 20.18; 2016- 10.16/10.08w, 20.09/ 20.04w; 2017- 9.95w, 19.90; 2018- 9.88/9.86w, 19.65. pbs: 60m 6.57i '18, 300m 31.87Ai/32.67i '17, 400m 47.04 '16, HJ: 2.03i '16.
Unbeaten in 8 finals and 1 heat at 200m Jan 17- end 2018; all his five 200m runs in 2018 were sub-19.85. His younger brother **Josephus** (b. 22 Jul 1998) 1 4x400m WJ '14, 3 200m & 2 400m WY '15; pbs 200m 20.74 '15, 20.73w '16; 400m 45.46 '15. Their father Kevin had a 400m pb 45.01 '95 and mother Keisha Caine 52.48 '94.

Tony McQUAY b. 16 Apr 1990 West Palm Beach, Florida 1.80m 70kg. adidas. Was at University of Florida.
At 400m: OG: '12- sf/2R, '16- 1R; WCh: '11- h, '13- 2/1R, '15- 1R, '17- res 2R; Won US 2011, NCAA 2012.
Progress at 400m: 2008- 48.09, 2009- 46.84, 2010- 45.37, 2011- 44.68, 2012- 44.49, 2013- 44.40, 2014- 44.92, 2015- 44.81, 2016- 44.24, 2017- 44.51. pbs: 100m 10.22 '13, 10.13w '14; 200m 20.60 '12, 300m 31.64 '16.

Aries MERRITT b. 24 Jul 1985 Marietta, Georgia 1.83m 74kg. Nike. Studied sports management at University of Tennessee.
At 110mh: OG: '12- 1; WCh: '09-11-13-15-17: h/5=/6/3/5; WJ: '04- 1. At 60mh: WI: '12-1, '18- 4, Won DL 110mh 2012, NCAA 60mh indoors & 110mh 2006, US indoor 60mh & 110mh 2012.
World 110mh record 2012.
Progress at 110mh: 2004- 13.47, 2005- 13.38/13.34w, 2006- 13.12, 2007- 13.09, 2008- 13.24, 2009- 13.15, 2010- 13.61, 2011- 13.12, 2012- 12.80, 2013- 13.09, 2014- 13.27, 2015- 13.04, 2016- 13.22, 2017- 13.09, 2018- 13.37/13.27w. pbs: 55m 6.43i '05, 60m 6.90i '10, 200m 21.31 '05, 50mh 6.54i '12, 55mh 7.02+i '12, 60mh 7.43Ai/7.44i '12, 400mh 51.94 '04.
Record 8 (and 2w) sub-13 second times in 2012. Revealed in 2015 that he had been suffering for two years from a kidney disorder and remarkably won World bronze medal just before undergoing a kidney transplant.

LaShawn MERRITT b. 27 Jun 1986 Portsmouth, Virginia 1.88m 82kg. Nike. Studied sports management at Old Dominion University, Norfolk, Virginia.
At 400m/4x400mR: OG: '08- 1/1R, '12- dnf ht, '16- 3/1R (6 200m); WCh: '05- res(1)R, '07- 2/1R, '09- 1/1R, '11- 2/1R, '13- 1/1R, '15- 2/1R, '17- sf; WJ: '04- 1/1R (1 at 4x100); WI: '06- 1R; WCp: '06- 1/1R, '14- 1/3R; won WAF 2007-09, DL 2013-14, 2016; US 2008-09, 2012-13, 2016.
World junior records 4x100m and 4x400m 2004, World indoor 400m junior best (44.93) 2005. World 4x110mh best 2015,
Progress at 200m, 400m: 2002- 21.46, 2003- 21.33, 47.69, 2004- 20.72/20.69w, 45.25; 2005- 20.38, 44.66; 2006- 20.10, 44.14; 2007- 19.98, 43.96; 2008- 20.08/19.80w, 43.75; 2009- 20.07, 44.06; 2011- 20.13, 44.63; 2012- 20.16, 44.12; 2013- 20.26, 43.74; 2014- 20.42, 43.92; 2015- 43.65, 2016- 19.74, 43.85; 2017- 20.27, 44.78; 2018- 20.48. pbs: 55m 6.33i '04, 60m 6.68i '06, 100m 10.47/10.38w '04, 300m 31.23 '16, 500m 1:01.39i '12.
World age-18 400m record with 44.66 in 2005 and world low-altitude 300m best 2006 and 2009. Two-year drugs ban for three positive tests from October 2009, reduced by three months after US arbitration panel declared that he had taken the steroid accidentally in buying a product intended for sexual enhancement; successfully challenged IOC rule preventing anyone serving 6 months or more from a drugs offence from competing in the next Games. Injured, he had to pull up in 2012 Olympic heat. Won six successive World 4x400m gold medals.

Clayton MURPHY b. 26 Feb 1995 New Madison, Ohio 1.82m 68kg. Nike. University of Akron.
At 800m: OG: '16- 3; WCh: '15- sf; PAm: '15- 1; CCp: '18- 2. Won US 800m 2016, 2018; NCAA 1500m 2016.
Progress at 800m, 1500m: 2013- 1600m 4:11.72, 2014- 1:50.03, 3:44.53; 2015- 1:45.59, 3:40.69; 2016- 1:42.93, 3:36.23; 2017- 1:43.60, 3:36.34; 2018-

1:43.12, 3:38.93. pbs: 600m 1:16.9+ '16, 1000m 2:17.17 '17, 1M 3:51.99 '17, 3000m 8:16.70i '17, 8:19.09 '16; 5000m 14:15.61 '15.

Chris NILSEN b. 13 Jan 1998 Kansas City, Missouri 1.96m 84kg. Univ. of South Dakota.
At PV: WCh: '17- dnq 13; WJ: '16- 7. Won NCAA 2018. N.American U20 pole vault record 2017.
Progress at PV: 2015- 5.18, 2016- 5.60, 2017- 5.75, 2018- 5.86.

Michael NORMAN: b. 3 Dec 1997 San Diego 1.83m 73kg. University of Southern California.
At 200m: WJ: '16- 1/1R. 400m: won NCAA 2018. World indoor 400m record (44.52) and ran on fastest ever indoor 4x400m by USC 2018.
Progress at 200m, 400m: 2013- 22.62, 49.54; 2014- 20.82, 46.94; 2015- 20.24, 45.19; 2016- 20.14/20.06w, 45.51; 2017- 20.75i, 44.60; 2018- 20.06/19.84w, 43.61. pb 100m 10.27 '16, 300m 31.9+ '18.

Vernon NORWOOD b. 10 Apr 1992 New Orleans 1.87m 77kg. New Balance. Was at Louisiana State University.
At 400m/4x400mR: WCh: '15- sf/res1R; WI: '16- 1R, '18- 2R. Won NCAA indoors and out 2015, US indoor 2016.
Progress at 400m: 2011- 47.47, 2012- 45.72A/45.98, 2013- 45.56A/45.67, 2014- 45.02, 2015- 44.44, 2016- 45.00, 2017- 44.47, 2018- 45.47. pbs: 200m 20.77 '15, 20.49w '18; 300m 32.07 '15, 500m 1:00.11i '17, 600y 1:08.80i '13, 600m 1:18.57Ai '15.

Payton OTTERDAHL b. 2 Apr 1996 Rosemount, Minnesota 1.93m 120kg. North Dakota State University.
Won NCAA indoor SP & weight 2019.
Progress at SP: 2015- 18.11, 2016- 17.88i/17.61, 2017- 18.62, 2018- 20.96, 2019- 21.81i. pbs: DT 59.96 '19, HT 60.99 '18, Wt 24.11i '19.

Gil ROBERTS b. 15 Mar 1989 Oklahoma City 1.88m 81kg. Nike. Was at Texas Tech University.
At 400m/4x400mR: OG: '16- sf/1R; WCh: '09- h, '17- sf/2R; WI: '12- 1R; US champion 2014, indoors 2012.
Progress at 400m: 2005- 47.47, 2006- 47.72A, 2007- 46.16, 2008- 46.14, 2009- 44.86, 2011- 45.22, 2012- 44.84, 2013- 45.73, 2014- 44.53, 2015- 45.29, 2016- 44.65, 2017- 44.22, 2018- 45.22. pbs: 55m 6.26i '12, 100m 10.12/9.92w '14, 200m 20.22 '14, 300m 31.81 '16.

Jeron ROBINSON b. 30 Apr 1991 Angleton, Texas 1.93m 73kg. Nike, Was at Texas A&M-Kingville University.
At HJ: WCh: '17- dnq 26; PAm: '15- 4. Won NACAC 2018.
Progress at HJ: 2008- 2.05, 2009- 2.16, 2-10- 2.18, 2011- 2.23, 2012- 2.13, 2013- 2.26, 2014- 2.30, 2015- 2.31, 2016- 2.29i/2.26, 2017- 2.30, 2018- 2.31.

Michael RODGERS b. 24 Apr 1985 Brenham, Texas 1.78m 73kg. Nike. Studied kinesiology at Oklahoma Baptist University.
At 100m/4x100mR: OG: '16- dqR; WCh: '09-13- 15-17: sf/6&2R/5/2R; CCp: '14- 2/1R, '18- 1R. At 60m: WI: '08-10-16: 4/2/6. Won US 100m 2009, 2014; indoor 60m 2008.
N.American 4x100m record 2015.
Progress at 100m: 2004- 10.55/10.31w, 2005- 10.30/10.25w, 2006- 10.29/10.18w, 2007- 10.10, 10.07w, 2008- 10.06/10.01w, 2009- 9.94/9.9/9.85w, 2010- 10.00/9.99w, 2011- 9.85, 2012- 9.94, 2013- 9.90, 2014- 9.91/9.80w, 2015- 9.86, 2016- 9.97, 20.42; 2017- 10.00/9.98w, 2018- 9.89. pbs: 60m 6.48Ai/6.50i '11, 150mSt 15.33 '14, 200m 20.24 '09.
Dropped out of US World Champs team after positive test for stimulant on 19 July 2011, for which he subsequently received a 9-month suspension. Has run 44 wind-legal and 18 wind-assisted (+ 1 dq) sub-10sec 100m times to end 2018. Younger sister Alishea Usery won US junior 400m 2009, pb 53.27 '09.

Galen RUPP b. 8 May 1986 Portland 1.80m 62kg. Nike Oregon Project. Studied business at University of Oregon.
At (5000/)10000m: OG: '08- 13, '12- 7/2, '16- 5 (3 Mar); WCh: '07- 11, '09- 8, '11- 9/7, '13- 8/4, '15- 5/5. At 5000m: WJ: '04- 9; PAm-J: '03- 1. At 3000m: WI: '10- 5, '14- 4; WY: '03- 7. Won US 5000m 2012, 10000m 2009-16, NCAA 5000m & 10000m (& indoor 3000m & 5000m) 2009, CC 2008. N.American records: 10000m 2011 & 2014, junior 5000m 2004, 10000m 2005; indoor 5000m (13:11.44) 2011 & 2014, 3000m 2013, 2M 2012, 2014.
Progress at 5000m, 10000m, Mar: 2002- 14:34.05, 2003- 14:20.29, 2004- 13:37.91, 29:09.56; 2005- 13:44.72. 28:15.52; 2006- 13:47.04, 30:42.10; 2007- 13:30.49, 27:33.48; 2008- 13:49.8+, 27:36.99; 2009- 13:18.12i/13:42.59+, 27:37.99; 2010- 13:07.35, 27:10.74; 2011- 13:06.86, 26:48.00; 2012- 12:58.90, 27:25.33; 2013- 13:01.37, 27:24.39; 2014- 13:00.99, 26:44.36; 2015- 13:08.38, 27:08.91; 2016- 13:20.69, 27:08.92, 2:10:05; 2017- 13:54.88, 28:18.29, 2:09:20; 2018- 13:34.78i, 2:06:07. pbs: 800m 1:49.87i/1:50.00 '09, 1500m 3:34.15 '14, 1M 3:50.92i/3:52.11 '13, 3000m 7:30.16i '13, 7:43.24 '10, 2M 8:07.41i '14, road: 15k 43:15 '18, 10M 46:24 '18, HMar 59:47 '18.
Won US Olympic Trials on marathon debut 2016, 2nd Boston & 1st Chicago 2017, 1st Prague 2018. Married to Keara Sammons (10000m 33:54.55 '07).

Donald SCOTT b. 23 Feb 1992 1.83m 84kg. Was at Eastern Michigan University.
At TJ: WCh: '17- dnq 13.
Progress at TJ: 2011- 15.79, 2012- 15.75, 2013- 15.58i, 2014- 16.02/16.34w, 2015- 16.84i/16.71/16.83w, 2016- 17.02, 2017- 17.25, 2018- 17.37. pb LJ 7.58 '15.

Michael STIGLER b. 5 Apr 1992 Canyon, Texas 1.78m 70kg. Studied communications at University of Kansas.
At 400mh: WCh: '17- dq h. Won NCAA 2015, 2 NACAC U23 2012, 2014.

Progress at 400mh: 2011- 52.07, 2012- 49.45, 2013-49.19, 2014- 49.34, 2015- 48.44, 2016- 49.68, 2017-48.26, 2018- 48.26. pbs: 400m 47.41i '15, 500m 1:02.11i '13, 600y 1:08.59i '14, 600m 1:18.38i '17, 800m 1:52.33 '17, 60mh 7.90i '15, 110mh 13.77 '14.

Nathan STROTHER b. 6 Sep 1995 1.83m 70kg. Was at University of Tennessee.
At 400m: CCp: '18- 3.
Progress at 400m: 2014- 47.37, 2015- 45.76, 2016-45.07, 2017- 45.07, 2018- 44.34. pbs: 200m 20.76 '18, 300m 33.16i '18.

Christian TAYLOR b. 18 Jun 1990 Fayetteville 1.90m 75kg. Li Ning. Studied at the University of Florida.
At (LJ/)TJ: OG: '12- 1, '16- 1; WCh: '11-13-15-17: 1/4/1/1; WI: '12- 2; WJ: '08- 7/8 (res 1 4x400m); WY: '07- 3/1; CCp: '18- 1/1mxR. Won DL 2012-17, NACAC 2010-11, US 2011-12, NCAA indoor 2009-10. N.American triple jump record 2015.
Progress at LJ, TJ: 2007- 7.29, 15.98; 2008-7.79i/7.68/7.77w, 16.05; 2009- 8.02i/7.72, 16.98i/16.65/16.91w; 2010- 8.19, 17.18i/17.02/17.09w; 2011- 8.00/8.07w/17.96; 2012- 8.12, 17.81; 2013-8.01/8.07w, 17.66; 2014- 8.09, 17.51; 2015- 8.18, 18.21; 2016- 7.96, 17.86; 2017- 18.11, 2018- 17.81/17.86w. pbs: 60m 6.79i '11, 200m 20.70 '13, 400m 45.07 '18.
His 18.21 in the final round of the 2015 World Champs was the second longest ever legal TJ mark; it was 18.32 from take-off to landing. Both parents came from Barbados.

Michael TINSLEY b. 21 Apr 1984 Little Rock, Arkansas 1.85m 74kg. adidas. Studied criminal justice at Jackson State University.
At 400mh: OG: '12- 2, '16- h; WCh: '13- 2, '15- 8; CCp: '14- 7; won DL 2014, NCAA 2006, US 2012-13.
Progress at 400mh: 2002- 52.5, 2004- 50.87, 2005-48.55, 2006- 48.25, 2007- 48.02, 2008- 48.84, 2009-48.53, 2010- 48.46, 2011- 48.45, 2012- 47.91, 2013-47.70, 2014- 48.25, 2015- 48.34, 2016- 48.74, 2017-49.00, 2018- 49.68 pbs: 60m 6.92i '05, 200m 20.66 '09, 20.34w '13; 400m 46.02i '06, 46.05 '07; 55mh 7.39i '04, 60mh 7.84i '06, 110mh 13.86 '04.

Ben TRUE b. 29 Dec 1985 North Yarmouth, Maine 1.83m 70kg. Saucony. Studied art history and architecture at Dartmouth College.
At 5000m: WCh: '15- 6. World CC: '13- 6.
Progress at 5000m: 2006- 14:18.61, 2007- 13:14.85, 2010- 13:43.98, 2011- 13:24.11, 2012- 13:20.53, 2013- 13:11.59, 2014- 13:02.74, 2015- 13:05.54, 2016- 13:12.67, 2017- 13:06.74i/13:10.83, 2018-13:04.11. pbs: 800m 1:50.07 '07, 1500m 3:36.05 '16, 1M 3:57.31i '17, 4:02.61 '07; 3000m 7:35.53 '17, 2M 8:11.33i '17, 8:23.76 '18; 10000m 27:41.17 '12, road: 10M 46:48 '11, 15k 43:04 '14.
Married to Sarah Groff, 4th 2012 Olympics in triathlon.

Ameer WEBB b. 19 Mar 1991 Carson, California 1.75m 75kg. Nike, Was at Texas A & M University.

At 200m: OG: '16- sf; WCh: '17- 5; won US 2017-18, NCAA 2014 (indoor 2013-13).
Progress at 100m, 200m: 2008- 10.70w, 21.81w; 2009- 10.67, 21.25/21.24w; 2010- 10.37, 20.70; 2011-10.37, 20.49; 2012- 10.17/10.05w, 20.46/20.20w; 2013- 10.14/10.07w, 20.20/20.05w; 2014- 10.37, 20.38; 2015- 10.04, 20.02; 2016- 9.94/9.90w, 19.85; 2017- 10.23, 20.01; 2018- 10.07, 20.13. pb 60m 6.60Ai/6.65i '16.

Ryan WHITING b. 24 Nov 1986 Harrisburg, Pennsylvania 1.91m 134kg. Nike. Studied civil engineering at Arizona State University.
At SP: OG: '12- 9; WCh: '11- 6, '13- 2, '17- 7; WI: '12-14-18: 1/1/7; PAm-J: '05- 1 (1 DT); Won DL 2013, US 2013, NACAC 2009, NCAA 2009-10, indoor 2008-10, DT 2010.
Progress at SP: 2006- 19.75, 2007- 20.35, 2008-21.73i/20.60, 2009- 20.99, 2010- 21.97, 2011- 21.76, 2012- 22.00i/21.66, 2013- 22.28, 2014- 22.23i/21.31, 2015- 21.80i/21.37, 2016- 21.06, 2017- 21.65, 2018-21.03i/20.99. pb DT 61.11 '08, Wt 18.94i '10.

Isiah YOUNG b. 5 Jan 1990 Junction City, Kansas 1.83m 75kg. Was at University of Mississippi.
At 200m: OG: '12- sf; WCh: '13- sf, '15- h, '17- 8.
Progress at 100m, 200m: 2008- 10.96; 2009- 10.44, 21.22; 2010- 10.32, 20.98; 2011- 10.31, 20.81; 2012-10.09/10.08w, 20.33/20.16w; 2013- 9.99/9.93w, 19.86; 2014- 10.23, 20.58/20.55w; 2015- 10.00/9.82w, 19.93/19.75w; 2016- 10.03, 20.24; 2017- 9.97/9.95w, 20.14/20.12w; 2018- 9.92, 19.93. pb 60m 6.61i '12.

Zachery ZIEMEK b. 23 Feb 1993 Itaska, Illinois 1.94m 88 kg. University of Wisconsin.
At Dec: OG: '16- 7; WCh: '15- 15, '17- dnf; won US 2018. At Hep: WI: '18- 6.
Progress at Dec: 2012- 7042, 2013- 7640, 2014-7981, 2015- 8107, 2016- 8413, 2017- 8155, 2018-8294. pbs: 60m 6.75i '16, 100m 10.57 '15, 200m 22.21 '18, 400m 48.75 '17, 1000m 2:48.25i '13, 1500m 4:41.56 '18, 60mh 8.08i '18, 110mh 14.63 '18, HJ 2.10 '14, PV 5.45 '15, LJ 7.73 '14, SP 14.77 '15, DT 49.42 '16, JT 60.92 '16, Hep 6173i '16.

Women

Morolake AKINOSUN b. 17 May 1994 Lagos, Nigeria 1.63m 61kg. University of Texas.
At 100m/200m: OG: '16- res 1R; WCh: '17- 1R; PAm: '15- sf/1R. Won US Indoor 60m 2017.
Progress at 100m, 200m: 2010- 11.94, 24.58/24.07w; 2011- 11.42, 23.49/23.44w; 2012- 11.41, 24.34; 2013- 11.45/11.29w, 23.26/23.18w; 2014-11.04/10.96w, 22.68/22.17w; 2015- 11.29/10.94w, 22.52; 2016- 10.95, 22.54; 2017- 10.98/10.94w. pbs: 60m 7.08Ai/7.17i '17.

Nia ALI b. 23 Oct 1988 Norristown 1.70m 64kg. ALTIS. Was at University of Southern California.
At 100mh: OG: '16- 2; WCh: '13- sf, '17- 8; WUG: '11- 1. Won NCAA 2011. At 60mh: WI: '14- 1, '16- 1; won US indoor 2013-14.

Progress at 100mh: 2005- 14.20, 2006- 13.63/ 13.55w, 2007- 13.25, 2008- 13.14, 2009- 13.17, 2011- 12.73/12.63w, 2012- 12.78, 2013- 12.48, 2014- 12.75, 2016- 12.55, 2017- 12.52. pbs: 60m 7.43i '14, 200m 23.90 '09, 800m 2:24.55 '07, 60mh 7.80i '14, HJ 1.86 '11, LJ 5.89 '09, SP 13.61 '09, JT 39.24 '09, Hep 5870 '16.
Son Titus born to her and Michael Tinsley in May 2015 and daughter Yuri to her and partner Andre De Grasse in June 2018.

Whitney ASHLEY b. 18 Feb 1989 Riverside, California 1.83m 93kg. Nike. Was at San Diego State University.
At DT: OG: '16- dnq nt; WCh: '13- dnq 23, '15- 9, '17- dnq 13; NCAA champion 2012.
Progress at DT: 2008- 44.86, 2009- 46.05, 2010- 47.34, 2011- 54.75, 2012- 59.99, 2013- 61.64, 2014- 63.78, 2015- 64.80, 2016- 64.62, 2017- 63.85, 2018- 61.10. pbs: SP 17.62i '16, 17.60 '17; HT 57.14 '11, Wt 19.19 '12.

Joanna ATKINS b. 31 Jan 1989 Stone Mountain, Georgia 1.80m 64kg. LifeSpeed. Was at Auburn University.
At 200m: CCp: '14- 2. At 400m: WCh: '13- res1R; WI: '14- 6/1R, '18- res 1R; Won NCAA 400m 2009.
Progress at 200m, 400m: 2004- 24.25w, 56.12; 2005- 24.02, 54.32; 2006- 23.82, 55.42; 2007- 24.35i/ 23.69w, 53.93; 2008- 23.30, 52.94; 2009- 22.89, 50.39; 2010- 23.32, 51.52; 2011- 22.68, 51.50; 2012- 23.10/22.83w, 51.12; 2013- 23.27, 50.77; 2014- 22.27/22.19w, 50.74; 2015- 23.82i, 2016- 22.40, 52.39; 2017- 22.74/22.54w, 53.26i; 2018- 22.62/ 22.31St, 51.80. pbs: 55m 6.91i '09, 600m 7.28i '09, 100m 11.02 '14, 10.99w '16; 300m 36.18Ai '17.

Tianna BARTOLETTA b. 30 Aug 1985 Elyria, Ohio 1.68m 60kg. née Madison. Nike. Studied biology at University of Central Florida, formerly at University of Tennessee.
At 100m/4x100mR: OG: '12- 4/1R, '16- sf/1R; won US 2014. At LJ: OG: '16- 1; WCh: '05- 1, '07- 10, '15- 1, '17- 3; CCp: '14- 3/1R; WI: '06- 1; PAm-J: '03- 4, won DL 2014-15, US 2015, 2017; NCAA indoors and out 2005. At 60m: WI: '12- 3, '14- 3; won US indoor 2012.
Progress at 100m, LJ: 2000 8.73, 2001 6.07, 2002 11.98/11.91w, 6.20; 2003- 11.72/11.68w, 6.28; 2004- 11.50/11.35w, 6.60; 2005- 11.41, 6.89/6.92w; 2006- 11.52/11.50w, 6.80i/6.60; 2007- 6.60/6.61w; 2008- 11.54, 6.53/6.58w; 2009- 11.05, 6.48; 2010- 11.20, 6.44; 2011- 11.29, 6.21/6.58w; 2012- 10.85, 6.48; 2013- 11.41; 2014- 10.92, 7.02; 2015- 10.94/10.90w, 7.14; 2016- 10.78, 7.17; 2017- 11.04, 7.01/7.05w; 2018- 11.43, 6.74. pbs: 55m 6.69i '09, 60m 7.02i '12, 200m 22.37/22.33w '12.
Set long jump pbs in qualifying and final of 2005 Worlds. US bobsled team in 2012/13. Married John Bartoletta in 2012, now divorced.

Jessica BEARD b. 8 Jan 1989 Euclid, Ohio 1.68m 57kg. adidas. Studied psychology at Texas A&M University.

At 400m/4x400mR: WCh: '09- sf/res (1)R, '11- sf/1R, '13- 1R, 15- res 2R; WJ: '06- 5/1R, '08- 2/1R; PAm-J: '07- 3; won NCAA 2011.
Progress at 400m: 2004- 55.22, 2005- 52.39, 2006- 51.89, 2007- 51.63, 2008- 51.09A/51.47, 2009- 50.56, 2010- 51.02, 2011- 51.06, 2012- 51.19, 2013- 51.05, 2014- 50.81, 2015- 50.68, 2016- 51.76, 2017- 50.85, 2018- 50.08. pbs: 60m 7.52i '11, 100m 11.48 '16, 200m 22.74 '18, 300m 36.65i '15.

Gwen BERRY b. 29 Jun 1989 St Louis, Missouri. 1.76m 80kg. New York AC. Was at University of Southern Illinois.
At HT: OG: '16- dnq 14; WCh: '17- dnq 14; Won US 2017, indoor weight 2013-14, 2017.
N.American hammer record 2017 & 2018. World 20lb weight indoor record record 2017.
Progress at HT: 2008- 53.70, 2009- 59.58, 2010- 62.55, 2011- 70.52, 2012- 71.95, 2013- 73.81, 2014- 72.04, 2015- 72.326, 2016- 73.09/76.12dq, 2017- 76.77, 2018- 77.78. Pbs: SP 16.99 '11, Wt 25.60i '17.
3-month ban from 29 Mar 2016 for use of a stimulant that cost her a North American 'record' of 76.31 and US indoor wight title.

Amanda BINGSON b. 20 Feb 1990 Victorville, California 1.70m 89kg. New York AC. Sports psychology graduate of University of Nevada, Las Vegas.
At HT: OG: '12- dnq 23; WCh: '13- 8, '15- 9; CCp: '14- 2; US champion 2013-14, NACAC 2012.
North American hammer record 2013.
Progress at HT: 2009- 55.19, 2010- 64.07, 2011- 69.79, 2012- 71.78, 2013- 75.73, 2014- 75.12, 2015- 72.35, 2016- 71.90, 2017- 72.06, 2018- 69.89. Pbs: DT 46.08A '11, Wt 22.42i '14. Former gymnast.

Erica BOUGARD b. 26 Jul 1993 Memphis 1.73m 57kg. Was at Mississippi State University.
At Hep: WCh: '13-15-17: 24/dnf/18; WJ: '12- 13. At Pen: WI: '18- 5.
Progress at Hep: 2011- 5270?, 2012- 5547, 2013- 5990, 2014- 6118, 2015- 6288, 2016- 6170, 2017- 6502, 2018- 6725. pbs: 100m 11.74 '18, 200m 23.28 '17, 400m 54.09 '11, 600m 1:32.78i '18, 800m 2:08.39 '15, 60mh 7.98A '18, 8.03i '15; 100mh 12.80 '18, HJ 1.92 '17, LJ 6.62 '18, TJ 12.76i '18, 12.62 '13; SP 13.02 '18, JT 44.63 '18, Pen 4760At '18.

Tori BOWIE b. 27 Aug 1990 Jackson, Mississippi 1.75m 61kg. adidas. Studied psychology at University of Southern Mississippi.
At 100m/(200m): OG: '16- 2/3/1R; WCh: '15- 3, '17- 1/1R. At 60m: WI: '16- 6. Won US 100m 2015, 200m 2016. At LJ: won NCAA 2011.
Progress at 100m, 200m, LJ: 2008- 12.21w, 6.03w; 2009- 11.82, 23.99, 6.30/6.60w; 2010- 11.76/11.72w, 24.55/23.98w, 6.43/6.50w; 2011- 6.64, 2012- 11.28, 24.06, 6.78; 2013- 11.14/11.04w, 6.91, 2014- 10.80, 22.18, 6.95i/6.82; 2015- 10.81/10.72w, 22.23; 2016- 10.78/10.74w, 21.99; 2017- 10.85/10.80w, 21.77; 2018- 11.01, 22.75. pbs: 60m 7.11i '16, 150mSt 16.30 '17 (world best), TJ 13.09i/12.65 '14.
First name actually Frentorish.

Quanesha BURKS b. 15 Mar 1995 Ozark, Alabama 1.60m 55kg. Was at University of Alabama
At LJ: WCh: '17- dnq 14; WJ: 14- 5; PAm: '15- 8; WI: '18- 4; Won NCAA 2015, NACAC 2015.
Progress at LJ: 2012- 6.13, 2013- 5.84w, 2014- 6.38, 2015- 6.93A/6.84/6.91w, 2016- 6.80i/6.77, 2017- 6.83/6.90w, 2018- 6.81i/6.59. pbs: 60m 7.20i '18, 100m 11.19 '18, 11.18w '17.

Amber CAMPBELL b. 5 Jun 1981 Indianapolis 1.70m 91kg. Mjolnar. Was at Coastal Carolina University.
At HT: OG: '08/12- dnq 19/9, '16- 6; WCh: '05-11-13: dnq 18/13/11, '09- 11, '15- nt; PAm: '11- 3, '15- 2. Won NACAC 2015, US 2012, 2015-16; indoor Wt 2007-11.
Progress at HT: 2000- 49.16, 2001- 62.08, 2002- 63.76, 2003- 64.58, 2004- 67.23, 2005- 69.52, 2006- 67.52, 2007- 70.33, 2008- 70.19, 2009- 70.61, 2010- 71.94, 2011- 72.59, 2012- 71.80, 2013- 73.03, 2014- 73.61, 2015- 72.81, 2016- 74.03, 2017- 73.58. pbs: SP 14.81i '02, 14.42 '04; 20lb Wt 24.78i '12.

Kori CARTER b. 6 Mar 1992 Pasadena, California 1.65m 57kg. Nike. Studied human biology at Stanford University.
At 400mh: WCh: '15- sf, '17- 1; WJ: '08- h; CCp: '14- 7; Won US 2014, NCAA 2013. At 100mh: WY: '09- 2.
Progress at 400mh: 2007- 62.21, 2008- 60.22, 2009- 59.89, 2010- 60.47, 2011- 57.10, 2012- 57.60, 2013- 53.21, 2014- 53.84, 2015- 54.41, 2016- 54.47, 2017- 52.95. pbs: 100m 11.57 '11, 200m 23.07 '17, 300m 39.09i '18, 60mh 8.00Ai '18, 8.11i '17; 100mh 12.76 '13.

Michelle CARTER b. 12 Oct 1985 San Jose 1.75m 110kg. Nike. Liberal arts graduate from University of Texas.
At SP: OG: '08- 13, '12- 4, '16- 1; WCh: '09-11-13-15-17: 5/8/4/3/3; WI: '12-14-16: 2/4/1; WJ: '04- 1; WY: '01- 2; PAm: '11- 3; PAm-J: '03- 1; CCp: '14- 2. Won US 2008-09, 2011, 2013-16; NCAA indoor 2006. North American shot records 2013 and 2016 and indoors (20.21) 2016.
Progress at SP: 2000- 14.76, 2001- 15.23, 2002- 16.25, 2003- 16.73, 2004- 17.55, 2005- 18.26, 2006- 17.98, 2007- 17.57, 2008- 18.85, 2009- 19.13, 2010- 18.80, 2011- 19.86, 2012- 19.60, 2013- 20.24, 2014- 19.84, 2015- 20.02, 2016- 20.63, 2017- 19.34, 2018- 18.16. pbs: DT 54.06 '07.
First US woman to win Olympic shot. Married Courtney Elder on 25 Jan 2019. Her father Mike set a world junior shot record in 1979 and won the Olympic silver in 1984, seven NCAA titles (4 in, 3 out) (a unique father-daughter double) and WUG gold in 1981 and 1983, pb 21.76 '84. Her younger sister D'Andra (b. 17 Jun 1987) won the NCAA discus in 2009, pb 57.73 '08.

Kristi CASTLIN b. 7 Jul 1988 Douglasville, Georgia 1.70m 75kg. adidas. Political science graduate of Virginia Tech University.

At 100mh: OG: '16- 3; won PAm-J 2007. At 60mh: won US indoors 2012.
World best 4x100mh 2014 & 2015.
Progress at 100mh: 2005- 13.85, 2006- 13.73, 2007- 12.91/12.82w, 2008- 12.81, 2009- 12.89, 2010- 12.83/12.59w, 2011- 12.83/12.68w, 2012- 12.56/ 12.48w, 2013- 12.61, 2014- 12.58, 2015- 12.71, 2016- 12.50, 2017- 12.61, 2018- 12.96. pbs: 55m 7.04i '08, 60m 7.47i '08, 100m 11.60 '12, 11.49w '11; 200m 23.46 '12, 50mh 6.81+i '12, 55mh 7.37i '12, 60mh 7.84Ai/7.91i '12, 400mh 60.44 '07. Married to Alonzo Nelson.

Christina CLEMONS b. 29 May 1990 Waldorf, Maryland 1.63m 54kg. adidas. née Manning. Was at Ohio State University.
At 100mh: WCh: '17- 5; WUG: '11- 3/2R. At 60mh: WI: '18- 2. Won NCAA 100mh & 60mh ind 2012.
Progress at 100mh: 2008- 13.86, 2009- 13.08, 2010- 13.10, 2011- 12.86/12.72w, 2012- 12.68/ 12.57w, 2014- 13.61, 2015- 13.04, 2016- 12.87/ 12.67w, 2017- 12.54, 2018- 12.56. pbs: 60m 7.23i '12, 100m 11.29 '11, 200m 23.27 '12, 60mh 7.73Ai/7.77i '18, LJ 5.75 '08.

Emma COBURN b. 19 Oct 1990 Boulder 1.73m 55kg. New Balance. Marketing graduate of University of Colorado.
At 3000mSt: OG: '12- 8, '16- 3; WCh: '11- 8, '15- 5, '17- 1; CCp: '14- 1; US champion 2011-12, 2014-17; NCAA 2011, 2013.
Three North American 3000m steeple records 2014 (unratified as no doping test) & 2016-17 (3).
Progress at 3000mSt: 2009- 10:06.21, 2010- 9:51.86, 2011- 9:37.16, 2012- 9:23.54, 2013- 9:28.26, 2014- 9:11.42, 2015- 9:15.59, 2016- 9:07.63, 2017- 9:02.58. 2018- 9:05.06. pbs: 800m 2:09.81 '10, 1500m 4:05.10 '15, 1M 4:29.86i '13, 4:31.08 '18; 2000m 5:41.11i '15, 3000m 8:41.16i '18, 8:48.60 '17. Married Joe Bosshard on 14 Oct 2017.

Amy CRAGG b. 21 Jan 1984 Long Beaxh 1.62m 46kg. Nike Bowerman TC. née Hastings. Was at Arizona State University.
At 5000m: WCh: '11- 14. 10000m: WCh: OG: '12- 11; WCh: '13- 14; HMar: WCh: '09- 31; Mar: OG: '16- 9; WCh: '17- 3. Won US 10000m 2012.
Progress at Mar: 2011- 2:27:03, 2012- 2:27:17, 2013- 2:42:50, 2014- 2:27:03, 2016- 2:25:04, 2017- 2:28:20, 2017- 2:27:18, 2018- 2:21:42. pbs: 1500m: 4:15.77 '09, 1M 4:47.29 '06, 3000m 8:58.21 '12, 5000m 15:09.59mx '13, 15:14.31 '11; 10000m: 31:10.69 '12, HMar 68:27 '17, 3000mSt 10:17.67 '04. Won Los Angeles marathon 2016, 3rd Tokyo 2018. Married Alistair Cragg IRL (1 EI 3000m 2005, pbs: 1M 3:55.04i '06, 3000m 7:32.49 '07, 5000m 13:03.53 '11) on 8 Nov 2014

Vashti CUNNINGHAM b. 18 Jan 1998 Las Vegas 1.85m 66kg. Nike. High school in Las Vegas, Nevada.
At HJ: OG: '16- 13=; WCh: '17- 10; WI: '16- 1, '18- 2; PAm-J: 15- 1; won US 2017-18, indoors 2016-17.

High jump records: World youth (=) 2015, World junior indoor 2016, North American junior 2017.
Progress at HJ: 2012- 1.76, 2013- 1.83, 2014- 1.90, 2015- 1.96, 2016- 1.99i/1.97, 2017- 1.99, 2018- 1.97Ai/1.95. Pb LJ 5.85w '15.
Father Randall Cunningham was a quarterback in the NFL. Her brother Randall (b. 4 Jan 1996) has HJ pbs 2.27i '17, 2.25 '16 and won PAm-J 2015 and NCAA 2016.

Kimberlyn DUNCAN b. 2 Aug 1991 Katy, Texas 1.73m 59kg. Nike. Was at Louisiana State University.
At 200m: WCh: '13- sf, '17- 6; won US 2013, NCAA 2011-13 (and indoors).
Progress at 100m, 200m: 2007- 24.54, 2008- 24.33, 2009- 23.46, 2010- 11.84, 23.08/22.96w; 2011- 11.09/11.02w, 22.24/22.18w, 2012- 10.96/10.94w, 22.19; 2013- 11.08/11.02w, 22.35/21.80w; 2014- 11.20, 22.53/22.10w; 2015- 11.13/11.08w, 22.83; 2016- 11.11, 23.01; 2017- 11.03, 22.54/22.41w; 2018- 11.41/11.34w, 22.63. pb 60m 7.16i '13.

Kendall ELLIS b. 8 Mar 1996 Pembroke Pines, Florida 1.73m 59kg. University of Southern California.
At 400m: WCh: '17- h/res1R. Won NCAA indoor 400m 2018. North American indoor 400m record 50.34 2018.
Progress at 400m: 2011- 54.83i, 2012- 53.22, 2013- 53.80, 2014- 52.95, 2015- 52.32, 2016- 51.82, 2017- 50.00, 2018- 49.99. pb 200m 22.71 '18, 300m 36.97i '19.

Maggie EWEN b. 23 Sep 1994 St Francis, Minnesota 1.78m 79kg. Arizona State University.
At HT: WCh: '17- dnq 21; won NCAA 2017. At DT: PAm-J: '13- 2. Won US SP 2018, NCAA SP & DT 2018; NACAC SP 2018.
Progress at SP, HT: 2011- 14.71, 2012- 14.78, 2013- 16.67, 2014- 15.90, 2015- 16.33, 60.54; 2016- 16.85i/16.82, 70.50; 2017- 18.12i/17.72, 74.56; 2018- 19.46, 74.53; 2019- 19.28i. pbs: DT 62.47 '18, Wt 22.26i '18.

Allyson FELIX b. 18 Nov 1985 Los Angeles 1.68m 57kg. Nike. Elementary education graduate of University of Southern California.
At 400m/(4x100mR)/4x400mR: OG: '16- 2/1R/1R; At 200m: OG: '04- 2, '08- 2/1R, '12- 1/1R/1R; WCh: '03- qf, '05- 1, '07- 1/1R/1R, '09- 1/1R, '11- 3/1R/1R (2 400m), '13- dnf, '15- 1 400m/2R/2R, '17- 3 400m/1R/1R; WJ: '02- 5; PAm: '03- 3; WI: '10- 1R. At 100m: OG: '12- 5; WY: '01- 1 (1 Medley R). Won DL 200m 2010, 2014-15; 400m 2010, WAF 200m 2005-06, 2009; US 100m 2010, 200m 2004-05, 2007-09, 2012; 400m 2011, 2015-16.
World junior record 200m 2004 after unratified mark (no doping test) at age 17 in 2003.
Progress at 100m, 200m, 400m: 2000- 12.19/11.99w, 23.90; 2001- 11.53, 23.31/23.27w; 2002- 11.40, 22.83/22.69w, 55.01; 2003- 11.29/11.12w, 22.11A/22.51, 52.26; 2004- 11.16, 22.18, 51.83A; 2005- 11.05, 22.13, 51.12; 2006- 11.04, 22.11; 2007- 11.01, 21.81, 49.70; 2008- 10.93, 21.93/21.82w, 49.83; 2009- 11.08, 21.88, 49.83; 2010- 11.27, 22.03, 50.15, 2011- 11.26+, 22.32, 49.59; 2012- 10.89, 21.69; 2013- 11.06+, 22.30, 50.19; 2014- 11.01, 22.02, 50.81; 2015- 11.09, 21.98, 49.26; 2016- 22.02, 49.51; 2017- 11.03, 22.33, 49.65; 2018- 11.30, 51.35. pbs: 50m 6.43i '02, 60m 7.10i '12, 150mSt 16.36 '13 (world best), 300m 36.33i '07.
Women's record 6 Olympic gold medals from 9 medals to equal record. First teenager to won a World sprint title. Unbeaten in ten 200m competitions 2005 and five in 2007. Has women's records of 16 medals and 11 gold at World Champs including three in 2007 when she had a record 0.53 winning margin at 200m and ran a 48.0 400m relay leg. Ran 47.72 relay leg at the 2015 Worlds. IAAF female Athlete of the Year 2012. Married to Kenneth Ferguson (400mh 48.15 '07, 2/1R WJ 2002); their daughter Camryn born 28 Nov 2018. Older brother Wes Felix won World Junior bronze at 200m and gold in WJR at 4x100m in 2002, pbs: 100m 10.23 '05, 200m 20.43 '04.

Shalane FLANAGAN b. 8 Jul 1981 Boulder 1.65m 50kg. Bowerman TC. Was at University of North Carolina.
At 5000m/(10000m): OG: '04- h, '08- 9/2; WCh: '05- h, '07- 7, '09- (13), '11- (7), '13- (8), '15- (6). At Mar: OG: '12- 9, '16- 6. World CC: '10- 12, '11-3; 4k: '04- 14, 05- 20. Won US 5000m 2005, 10000m 2008, 2011, 2013; HMar 2010, Mar 2012, CC 2008, 2010-11, 2013; 4km CC 2004-05, indoor 3000m 2007, NCAA CC 2002-03, indoor 3000m 2003.
North American records: 5000m and indoor 3000m 2007, 10000m (2) 2008, 15km & 25km road 2014.
Progress at 5000m, 10000m, Mar: 2001- 16:29.68, 2003- 15:20.54, 2004- 15:05.08, 2005- 15:10.96, 2007- 14:44.80, 2008- 14:59.69, 30:22.22; 2009- 14:47.62i/15:10.86, 31:23.43; 2010- 14:49.08, 2:28:40; 2011- 14:45.20, 30:39.57; 2012- 31:59.69, 2:25:38; 2013- 31.04.85, 2:27:08; 2014- 2:21:14, 2015- 15:10.02, 31:09.02, 2:27:47dh; 2016- 2:25:26, 2017- 14:58.99, 31:31.12, 2:26:53; 2018- 2:26:22. pbs: 800m 2:09.28 '02, 1500m 4:05.86 '07, 1M 4:33.81i '11, 4:48.47 '00; 3000m 8:33.25i/8:35.34 '07, Road: 15k 47:03 '14, 10M 51:45 '10, HMar 67:51dh '16, 68:31 '13, 25k 1:22:36 '14, 30k 1:39:15 '14.
2nd New York 2010 on marathon debut and won Olympic Trials 2012 and New York 2017; 3rd Berlin 2014. Married to Steve Edwards. Mother, Cheryl Bridges, set marathon world best with 2:49:40 in 1971 and was 4th in 1969 International CC, father Steve ran in World Cross 1976-7, 1979.

Phyllis FRANCIS b. 4 May 1992 New York 1.78m 61kg. Nike. Was at University of Oregon.
At 400m/4x400mR: OG: '16- 5/1R; WCh: '15- 7/

res2R, '17- 1/1R; PAm-J: '11- 3/1R. Won NCAA indoors 2014.
Progress at 400m: 2010- 55.82i, 2011- 52.93, 2012- 51.22, 2013- 50.86, 2014- 50.46Ai/50.59, 2015- 50.50, 2016- 49.94, 2017- 49.92, 2018- 50.07. pbs: 60m 7.30i '17, 100m 11.35 '18, 11.34w '16; 200m 22.42 '18, 300m 36.15Ai '17, 36.85i '18; 600m 1:27.38i '11, 800m 2:04.83 '08.
Younger sister Claudia pbs 400m 51.55 '16, 800m 2:02.92 '15, 400mh 55.55 '16.

Tori FRANKLIN b. 7 Oct 1992 Westmont, Illinois 1.73m 55kg. Oiselle. Was at Michigan State University.
At TJ: WCh: '17- dnq 13; CCp: '18- 2; WI: '18- 8. Won NACAC U23 2014.
North.American triple jump record 2018.
Progress at TJ: 2010- 12.53w, 2012- 13.34i/13.02, 2013- 13.36/13.56w, 2014- 13.56i/13.49, 2015- 13.38i/13.30/13.38w, 2016- 13.66i/13.54, 2017- 14.03, 2018- 14.84. pbs: 100m 11.88 '16, 200m 24.07 '16, 400m 53.47 '14, LJ 5.87i '16.

Courtney FRERICHS b. 18 Jan 1993 Barrington, Illinois 1.70m 62kg. Bowerman TC. Studied biology at University of Missouri Kansas City then University of New Mexico.
At 3000mSt: OG: '16- 11; WCh: '17- 2; CCp: '18- 2; NCAA champion 2016.
North American 3000mSt record 2018.
Progress at 3000mSt: 2009- 10:06.21, 2010- 9:51.86, 2011- 9:37.16, 2012- 10:34.48, 2013- 9:55.02, 2014- 9:43.07, 2015- 9:31.36, 2016- 9:20.92, 2017- 9:03.77, 2018- 9:00.85. pbs: 1500m 4:14.62 '18, 3000m 8:53.99 '17, 5000m 15:12.55i '19, 16:22.98 '13. Improved pb by 15.32secs to win 2017 World silver medal at 3000mSt Married to Griffin Humphreys.

Stephanie GARCIA b. 3 May 1988 Austin, Texas 1.68m 52kg. New Balance. Was at University of Virginia.
At 3000mSt: WCh: '11- h, '15- 9.
North American 3000m steeple record 2014 (unratified as no doping test), & 2000mSt best.
Progress at 3000mSt: 2007- 10:15.83, 2008- 10:17.38, 2009- 10:08.48, 2010- 10:05.05, 2011- 9:41.12, 2012- 9:47.76, 2013- 9:45.78, 2014- 9:24.28, 2015- 9:23.48, 2016- 9:19.48, 2017- 9:25.04. pbs: 800m 2:05.65i '17, 2:07.84 '18; 1500m 4:04.63 '17, 1M 4:24.68 '17, 2000m 5:48.25i '14, 3000m 8:52.74 '17, 2M 9:37.86 '18, 5000m 15:16.56 '16, 2000mSt 6:14.66 '14.

English GARDNER b. 22 Apr 1992 Philadelphia 1.62m 50kg. Nike. Was at University of Oregon.
At 100m/4x100mR: OG: '16- 7/1R; WCh: '13- 4/2R, '15- sf/2R; Won US 100m 2016, NCAA 100m 2012-13, indoor 60m 2012.
Progress at 100m, 200m: 2005- 11.99, 24.53; 2007- 11.61, 24.01; 2008- 11.82/11.49w, 24.27/24.19w; 2011- 11.03, 23.02; 2012- 11.10/11.00w, 22.82; 2013- 10.85, 22.62; 2014- 11.01, 22.81; 2015- 10.79/10.76w, 22.74; 2016- 10.74, 2017- 11.04, 22.97; 2018- 11.02. pbs: 60m 7.10i '19, 400m 53.73 '12.

Kate GRACE b. 24 Oct 1988 Sacramento 1.73m 55kg. Oiselle. Was at Yale University.
At 800m: OG: '16- 8. US champion 2016. At 1500m: WCh: '17- sf; won NACAC 2018.
Progress at 800m, 1500m: 2007- 2:10.18, 2008- 2:06.12, 4:32.29; 2009- 2:04.72i/2:05.82, 4:30.31; 2010- 2:04.22, 4:24.57; 2011- 2:03.41, 4:20.66; 2012- 2:01.63, 4:10.57; 2013- 1:59.47, 4:07.40; 2014- 2:01.22, 4:07.35; 2016- 1:58.28, 4:05.65; 2017- 1:59.30, 4:03.59; 2018- 2:00.92, 4:04.05. pbs: 400m 55.96 '06, 600m 1:27.8 '16, 1000m 2:36.97i '17, 1M 4:20.70 '18, 3000m 8:47.26i '17, 5k Rd 16:03 '16.

Kendra 'Keni' HARRISON b. 18 Sep 1992 Clayton, North Carolina 1.63m 52kg. University of Kentucky.
At 100mh: WC: '15- sf, '17- 4; CCp: '18- 2. Won DL 100mh 2016, NACAC 2018, US 2017-18, NCAA 100mh (& 60mh indoors) 2015. At 60mh: WI: '16- 8, '18- 1.
Records: World and two N.American 100m hurdles 2016, N.American 60mh (=) 2018.
Progress at 100mh, 400mh: 2010- 13.79, 59.19; 2011- 13.49, 59.13; 2012- 13.03/13.02w, 56.72; 2013- 12.88/12.87w, 55.75; 2014- 12.71/12.68w, 54.76; 2015- 12.50/12.46w, 54.09; 2016- 12.20, 2017- 12.28, 2018- 12.36. pbs: 60m 7.31i '14, 100m 11.35 '16, 200m 22.81 '18, 300m 37.84i '15, 400m 53.82i '13, 60mh 7.70i '18.

Queen HARRISON b. 10 Sep 1988 Loch Sheldrake, New York 1.70m 60kg. Studied of business marketing at Virginia Tech.
At 100mh: WCh: '13- 5; PAm: '15- 1. At 400mh: OG: '08- sf; WCh: '11- sf; PAm-J: '07- 1 (2 100mh); won NCAA 100mh, 400mh & 60mh indoors 2010. World best 4x100mh 2014 & 2015.
Progress at 100mh, 400mh: 2007- 12.98, 55.81; 2008- 12.70, 54.60; 2009- 13.14/12.98w, 56.03; 2010- 12.61/12.44w, 54.55; 2011- 12.88, 54.78; 2012- 12.62, 55.32; 2013- 12.43, 2014- 12.46, 2015- 12.52/ 12.50w, 2016- 12.57/12.54w, 2017- 12.64, 2018- 12.63. pbs: 400m 52.88 '08, 60mh 7.74Ai/7.75i 17, LJ 5.82i '06.
Married Will Claye (qv) on 13 October 2018.

Jordan HASAY b. 21 Sep 1991 Fontana, California 1.63m 45kg. Nike. Was at University of Oregon.
At 1500m: WJ: '08- 4, '10- 4 (9 3000m); Won PAm-J 2009, NACAC U23 2012. WY: '07- 2. At 10000m: WCh: '13- 12.
Progress at 10000m, Mar: 2013- 31:46.42, 2014- 31:39.67, 2015- 32:46.04, 2016- 31:58.33, 2017- 2:20:57. pbs: 800m 2:08.32 '12, 1000m 2:41.08i '15, 1500m 4:07.70 '14, 1M 4:28.27i '15, 4:42.21 '06; 3000m 8:46.89 '13, 2M 9:35.05 '14. 5000m 15:28.56 '14; road: 10k 31:39 '14, 15k 48:21 '17, 20k 64:32 '17, HMar 67:55 '17.
3rd in Boston in 2:23:00 for fastest ever US marathon debut 2017, then 3rd Chicago.

Natasha HASTINGS b. 23 Jul 1986 Brooklyn, New York 1.73m 63kg. Under Armour. Studied

exercise science at University of South Carolina. At 400m/4x400m: OG: '08- res 1R, '16- 4/1R; WCh: '07- sf/res 1R, '09/11- res 1R, '13- 4/1R, '15- sf/2R, '17- res 1R; WJ: '04- 1/1R; WY: '03- 1 (1 MedR); WI: '10/14/16- 1R, '12- 3/2R; PAm-J: '03- 1R, '05- 1/1R. Won US 2013, NCAA indoors and out 2007.
World junior 500m indoor best 2005, North American indoor 4x400m record 2014.
Progress at 400m: 2000- 54.21, 2001- 55.06, 2002- 53.42, 2003- 52.09, 2004- 52.04, 2005- 51.34, 2006- 51.45, 2007- 49.84, 2008- 50.80, 2009- 50.89, 2010- 50.53, 2011- 50.83Ai/50.97, 2012- 50.72, 2013- 49.94, 2014- 50.53, 2015- 50.24, 2016- 49.90, 2017- 50.14, 2018- 52.11Ai. pbs: 55m 7.08i '02, 60m 7.26i '13, 100m 11.24 '13, 11.08w '14; 200m 22.57 '16, 22.55w '14, 22.50St '17; 300m 35.9+ '07, 36.25i '16; 500m 1:10.05i '05.
Father from Jamaica, mother Joanne Gardner was British (ran 11.89 to win WAAA U15 100m at 14 in 1977).

Quanera HAYES b. 7 Mar 1992. Hope Mills, North Carolina 1.72m 59kg. Was at Livingstone College.
At 400m/4x400mR: WCh: '17- sf/1R; WI: '16- 0/1R, '10- 1R.
North American indoor 300m record 2017.
Progress at 400m: 2010- 56.46, 2012- 54.18A, 2013- 51.54A, 2014- 51.91, 2015- 50.84, 2016- 49.91, 2017- 49.72, 2018- 51.46Ai/53.23. pbs: 60m 7.34i '17, 100m 11.27 '16, 200m 22.55 '17, 300m 35.71i '17.

Ashley HENDERSON b. 4 Dec 1995 St Louis, Missouri 1.68m 59kg. San Diego State University.
Progress at 100m, 200m: 2009- 12.48, 25.12; 2011- 11.97, 24.47; 2012- 11.85/11.84w, 24.35A.23.89w; 2013- 11.93, 24.33; 2014- 11.86, 24.12; 2015- 11.64, 24.09Ai; 2016- 11.21/10.96w, 22.64/22.44w; 2017- 611.01, 22.54A/22.66/22.93w; 2018- 10.96/10.91w, 22.41i/22.49. pbs: 60m 7.17A/7.18i '18.

Candace HILL b. 11 Feb 1999 Conyers, Georgia. 1.75m 59kg. University of Georgia.
At 100/(200m): WJ: '16- 1/1R; WY: '15- 1/1.
World youth records 100m & 200m 2015, world indoor junior 300m record 2017.
Progress at 100m, 200m: 2013- 11.81, 23.85; 2014- 11.44/11.34w, 23.14; 2015- 10.98, 22.43A/23.05; 2016- 11.07, 22.76/22.38w; 2017- 11.23, 22.68; 2018- 11.43, 23.33. Pbs: 60m 7.30i '17, 300m 36.56Ai/36.86i '17, 400m 52.70 '17.

Daniella HILL b. 16 May 1991 Mahomet, Illinois 1.78m 95kg. née Bunch. Nike. Was at Purdue University.
At SP: WCh: '17- dnq 18.
Progress at SP: 2008- 15.10, 2009- 15.20, 2010- 15.22, 2011- 16.07i/15.72, 2012- 16.65i/16.46, 2013- 17.13, 2014- 17.39, 2015- 18.89, 2016- 18.87i/18.18, 2017- 19.64, 2018- 18.18i/18.02. pbs: DT 48.86 '13, HT 58.36 '14, Wt: 22.35i '14.

Married Zachary Hill (SP 19.25i/18.87 '12) on 7 Oct 2017,

Aleai HOBBS b. 24 Feb 1996 New Orleans 1.72m 59kg. Was at Louisiana State University.
At 100m: PAm-J: '15- 2/1R. Won US 2018, NCAA 60m ind & 100m 2018.
Progress at 100m: 2010- 11.95, 2011- 11.75, 2012- 11.77, 2013- 11.68, 2014- 11.49, 2015- 11.13, 2016- 11.34, 2017- 10.85, 2018- 10.90/10.86w. pbs: 60m 7.07i '18, 200m 22.93 '18.

Shelby HOULIHAN b. 8 Feb 1993 sioux City, Iowa 1.60m 54kg. Nike Bowerman TC. Was at Arizona State University.
At 1500m: CCp: '18- 2; WI: '18- 4 (5 3000m). At 5000m: OG: '16- 11; WCh: '17- 13. Won US 1500m & 5000m 2018, CC 2019; NCAA 1500m 2014, NACAC U23 800m 2014.
North American 5000m record 2018.
Progress at 1500m, 5000m: 2010- 4:31.21, 2011- 4:26.39, 2012- 4:22.95, 2013- 4:13.64, 16:15.85; 2014- 4:10.89, 16:11.63; 2015- 4:09.62, 15:49.72; 2016- 4:03.39, 15:06.14; 2017- 4:06.22, 15:00.37; 2018- 3:57.34, 14:34.45. pbs: 800m 2:01.12 '14, 1M 4:24.16i '17, 4:31.79 '15; 3000m 8:36.01i '18, 8:37.40 '17; 2M 9:31.38i '19.
Her mother Connie Prince Mar pb 2:35:26 '86.

Molly HUDDLE b. 31 Aug 1984 Elmira, New York 1.63m 48kg. Saucony. Was at University of Notre Dame.
At 5000m: OG: '12- 11; WCh: '11-13-17: h/6/12; CCp: '10- 3. At 10000m: OG: '16- 5; WCh: '15- 4, '17- 8. Won US 5000m 2011, 2014, 2016; 10000m 2015-18. World CC: '10- 19, '11- 17.
North American 5000m (2) records 2010-14, 10000m 2016, 10M, 20k & HMar 2018.
Progress at 5000m, 10000m: 2003- 15:36.95, 2004- 15:32.55, 2005- 16:12.17i, 2006- 15:40.41, 32:37.87; 2007- 15:17.13, 33:09.27; 2008- 15:25.47, 31:27.12; 2009- 15:53.91, 32:42.11; 2010- 14:44.76, 31:27.12; 2011- 15:10.01, 31:28.66; 2012- 15:01.32, 2013- 14:58.15, 2014- 14:42.64, 30:47.59; 2015- 14:57.23, 31:39.20; 2016- 14:48.14, 30:13:17; 2017- 15:01.64i/15:03.60, 31:24.78; 2018- 15:01.44, 31:52.32; 2019- 30:58.46 pbs. 1500m 4:08.09 '13, 1M 4:26.84 '14, 3000m 8:42.99 '13, Rd: 15k 48:52 '14, 10M 50:52 '18, 20k 63:48 '18, HMar 67:25 '18, Mar 2:26:44 '18.
Married Kurt Benninger CAN (pbs 1500m 3:38.03 '08, 1M 3:56.99 '08, 5000m 13:30.27 '09) in 2009. Won US road running titles in 2014 at a women's record four distances and now has won 27 national titles. 3rd New York 2016 on marathon debut.

Emily INFELD b. 21 Mar 1990 University Heights, Ohio 1.63m 48kg. Saucony. Was at Georgetown University.
At 10000m: OG: '16- 11; WCh: '15- 3, '17- 6. World CC: '13- 21. Won NCAA indoor 3000m 2012, US CC 2018.
Progress at 10000m: 2015- 31:38.71, 2016-

31:26.94, 2017- 31:20.45. pbs: 800m 2:06.05 '09, 1000m 2:44.56i '09, 1500m 4:07.77 '12, 1M 4:30.78 '17, 3000m 8:41.43 '13, 5000m 14:56.33 '17. Older sister Maggie (b.10 Apr 1986) has pb 1500m 4:08.31 '12.

Lynna IRBY b. 6 Dec 1998 Merrillville, Indiana 1.68m 55kg. University of Georgia.
At 400m/4x400mR: WJ: '16- 2/1R (1 4x100m); WY: '15- 2 (1 mxR). Won NCAA 2018.
Progress at 200m, 400m: 2012- 24.84, 54.62; 2013- 23.77, 54.16; 2014- 24.05, 54.38; 2015- 24.23/23.85w, 51.79; 2016- 23.53, 51.39; 2017- 23.58i, 52.83; 2018- 22.25/22.06w, 49.80. pbs: 55m 6.94i '17, 50m 7.31i '18, 100m 11.47 '15, 300m 36.73 '18.

Kyra JEFFERSON b. 23 Sep 1994 Detroit 1.65m 57kg. Student at University of Florida.
At 200m/4x400mR: PAm: '15- 2/1R. Won NACAC 2015, NCAA 2017.
North American 4x200m indoor record 2018.
Progress at 200m: 2009- 24.27, 2010- 24.24/24.07w, 2011- 23.53, 2012- 24.11i/24.27, 2013- 23.43i, 2014- 22.78, 2015- 22.24, 2016- 22.56, 2017- 22.02, 2018- 22.48. pbs: 60m 7.34i '14, 100m 11.73 '12, 11.66w '10; 300m 37.74i '18, 400m 51.50 '15.

Charlene LIPSEY b. 16 Jul 1991 Hempstead, New York 1.68m 57kg. adidas. Was at Louisiana State University.
At 800m: WCh: '17- 7; won US indoor 1000m 2017. World indoor 4x800m record 2018.
Progress at 800m: 2008- 2:07.46, 2009- 2:05.83, 2010- 2:05.34, 2011- 2:03.73, 2012- 2:01.40, 2013- 2:01.80, 2014- 2:00.91, 2015- 2;00.60, 2016- 2:00.65, 2017- 1:57.38, 2018- 1:58.05. pbs: Won 55m 55.14 '15, 600m 1:29.85i '09, 1000m 2:37.97iA '17, 2:45.39 '18; 1500m 4:04.98 '18, 1M 4:27.28 '18.

Shamier LITTLE b. 20 Mar 1995 Louisville, Kentucky 1.63m 52kg. Texas A&M University.
At 400mh: WCh: '15- 2, '17- sf; WJ: '12- dnf, '14- 1/1R; PAm: '15- 1/1R; CCp: '18- 2. Won NCAA 2014-16, NACAC 2018, US 2018.
Progress at 400mh: 2011- 57.83, 2012- 57.44, 2013- 58.80, 2014- 55.07, 2015- 53.74, 2016- 53.51, 2017- 52.75, 2018- 53.32. pbs: 60m 7.65i '17, 200m 23.17 '16, 23.01w '17; 300m 36.98i '18; 400m 50.40 '17, 800m 2:16.03i '19, 60mh 8.43i '14, 100mh 13.77 '14. Mother Tiffany Mayfield had HJ pb 1.73.

Sydney McLAUGHLIN b. 7 Aug 1999 New Brunswick, New Jersey. 1.74m 61kg. New Balance. University of Kentucky.
At 400mh: OG: '16- sf; WY: '15- 1; won NCAA 2018.
Five World junior 400mh records 2016-18, indoor 300m 2017 & 400m (3) 2018; world youth records 400mh (2) and 400m indoors 2016.
Progress at 400mh: 2014- 55.63; 2015- 55.28; 2016- 54.15, 2017- 53.82, 2018- 52.75. pbs: 200m 22.39 '18, 300m 36.12i '17, 400m 50.07 '18, 500m 1:09.46i '19, 600m 1:28.85 '18, 55mh 7.66i '15, 60mh 8.17i '15, 100mh 13.34 '14, 300mh 38.90 '17, LJ 5.89i '15. 5.81w '14.

IAAF Rising Star of the Year 2018. Her brother Taylor (b. 3 Aug 1997) was 2nd at the 2016 World Juniors; their father Willie had a 400m best of 45.30 '83.

Brianna McNEAL b. 18 Aug 1991 Miami 1.64m 55kg. née Rollins. Nike. Was at Clemson University.
At 100mh: OG: '16- 1; WCh: '13- 1, '15- 4; Won US 2013, 2016; NACAC 2012, DL 2018. At 60mh: WI: '16- 2; won US indoor 60mh 2016, NCAA 100mh 2013, indoor 60mh 2011 & 2013.
North American 100m hurdles record 2013, world best 4x100mh 2014 & 2015.
Progress at 100mh: 2007- 14.48, 2008- 13.93, 2009- 13.83, 2011- 12.99/12.88w, 2012- 12.70/12.60Aw, 2013- 12.26, 2014- 12.53, 2015- 12.56, 2016- 12.34, 2018- 12.43. pbs: 60m 7.29Ai '16, 200m 22.94 '18, 300m 37.90i '10, 400m 53.93 '13, 60mh 7.76i '16, 400mh 60.58 '09.
Undefeated in 2013: inc. heats 200m- 7, 400m- 1, 60mh- 8, 100mh- 18. Received a one-year ban due to missing three drugs test in 2016, dated from 19 Dec 2016.

Brenda MARTINEZ b. 8 Sep 1987 Upland, California 1.63m 52kg. New Balance. Studied sociology and law at University of California - Riverside.
At 800m: WCh: '13- 2, '15/17- sf. At 1500m: OG: '16- sf; WI: '16- 5.
N.American 4x800m & 4x1500m records 2014.
Progress at 800m, 1500m: 2007- 2:04.22, 4:21.18; 2008- 2:02.34, 4:17.09; 2009- 2:00.85, 4;09.52; 2010- 2:04.76, 4:18.17; 2011- 2:01.07, 4:10.77; 2012- 1:59.14, 4:06.96; 2013- 1:57.91, 4:00.94; 2014- 1:58.84, 4:01.36; 2015- 1:59.06; 2016- 1:59.64, 4:03.57; 2017- 1:58.43, 4:02.75; 2018- 2:00.74, 4:02.65. pbs: 1000m 2:38.48 '12, 1M 4:26.76 '12, 3000m 8:57.30 '18, 2M 9:32.82 '18, 5000m 15:30.89mx '13, 15:41.50 '14; 5km Rd 15:24 '14.
Married coach Carlos Handler in October 2012.

Georganne MOLINE b. 6 Mar 1990 Phoenix, Arizona 1.78m 59kg. Nike Psychology and communications student at University of Arizona.
At 400mh: OG: '12- 5; WCh: '13- h. At 4x400m: WI: '18- 1R.
Progress at 400mh: 2010- 57.88, 2011- 57.41, 2012- 53.92, 2013- 53.72, 2014- 54.00, 2015- 54.24, 2016- 53.97, 2017- 53.14, 2018- 53.90. pbs: 200m 23.23i '18, 23.37 '13; 400m 51.39i '18, 51.93 '17; 500m 1:08.84i '15, 600m 1:26.70Ai '16, 1:27.15 '15; 800m 2:08.67i '13. 2:09.58 '14.

Sandi MORRIS b. 8 Jul 1992 Downers Grove, Illinois 1.72m 65kg. Student at University of Arkansas, formerly North Carolina.
At PV: OG: '16- 2; WCh: '15- 4=, '17- 2; WI: '16- 2, '18- 1; PAm-J: 11- 2' CCp: '18- 3. Won NACAC 2014, US 2017-18.
Three North American outdoor pole vault records 2016.

Progress at PV: 2009- 3.81, 2010- 4.05, 2011- 4.30, 2012- 4.23i/4.15, 2013- 4.43i/4.02, 2014- 4.55, 2015- 4.76, 2016- 5.00, 2017- 4.87i/4.84, 2018- 4.95. Engaged to Tyrone Smith (LJ 8.34 BER record 2017).

Dalilah MUHAMMAD b. 7 Feb 1990 Jamaica, Queens, New York 1.70m 62kg. Nike, Business graduate of University of Southern Califormia. At 400mh: OG: '16- 1; WCh: '13- 2, '17-21; WY: '07- 1; PAm-J: '09- 2; US champion 2013, 2016-17, DL 2017-18. World best 200mh 2018. Progress at 400mh: 2005- 61.25, 2006- 59.82, 2007- 57.09, 2008- 57.81, 2009- 56.49, 2010- 57.14, 2011- 56.04, 2012- 56.19, 2013- 53.83, 2014- 58.02, 2015- 55.76, 2016- 52.88, 2017- 52.64, 2018- 53.65. pbs: 60m 7.64i '10, 100m 11.42 '13, 200m 23.35 '19, 400m 52.63 '19, 500m 1:09.66i '17, 600m 1:28.85 '18, 60mh 8.23i '12, 100mh 13.33 '12, 200mh 25.20 '18, HJ 1.75 '10.

Katie NAGEOTTE b. 13 Jun 1991 Olmsted Falls, Ohio 1.68m 59kg. New York AC. Was at Ashland University. At PV: WI: '18- 5; won NACAC 2018. Progress at PV: 2008- 3.76, 2009- 3.96, 2010- 3.90, 2011- 4.00i, 2012- 3.81, 2013- 4.44, 2014- 4.48, 2015- 4.55, 2016- 4.63i, 4.60, 2017- 4.73, 2018- 4.91Ai/4.80, 2019- 4.86i.

Sharika NELVIS b. 10 May 1990 Memphis 1.78m 64kg. adidas. Sociology student at Arkansas State University. At 100mh: WCh: '15- 8. At 60mh: WI: '18- 4. Won NCAA 100mh & indoor 60mh 2014. World best 4x100mh 2015. North American indoor 60mh record 2018. Progress at 100mh: 2008- 14.23, 2009- 14.03, 2011- 13.45, 2012- 13.22/12.99w, 2013- 12.84, 2014- 12.71/12.52w, 2015- 12.34, 2016- 12.60, 2017- 12.52, 2018- 12.51. pbs: 60m 7.28i '14, 100m 11.27/11.17w '14, 200m 23.19 '15, 22.70w '14, 400m 54.62 '13, 60mh 7.70Ai/7.80i '18, LJ 6.32i '13, 6.27 '14.

Courtney OKOLO b. 15 Mar 1994 Carrolltown, Texas 1.68m 54kg. Was at University of Texas. At 400m/4x400mR: OG: '16- 1R; WI: '16- 1R, '18 1/1R; PAm-J: '13- 1/1R. Won NACAC 2015, 4x400m 2018, NCAA 2014, 2016. US indoor 500m record 2017. Progress at 400m: 2009- 56.50, 2010- 54.34, 2011- 53.03, 2012- 52.40, 2013- 51.04, 2014- 50.03, 2015- 50.82A/50.99, 2016- 49.71, 2017- 50.29, 2018- 50.55i/50.65. pbs: 60m 7.52i '14, 100m 11.53 '16, 200m 22.93 '15, 22.79i '16; 300m 35.74 '16, 500m 1:07.34i '17, 600y 1:18.24i '15, 600m 1:24.00Ai/1:25.21 '17.

Keturah ORJI b. 5 Mar 1996 Mount Olive, New Jersey 1.66m 61kg. Atlanta TC. University of Georgia. At TJ: OG: '16- 4; WJ: '14- 9; WY: '13- 3 (2 LJ); WI: '16- 4, '18- 5; won US 2016-18, NCAA 2015-18 (& LJ 2018, indoor TJ 2016-18).

North American and 3 US triple jump records 2016, N.Am indoors 2017 & 2018. Progress at TJ: 2012- 12.46/12.51w, 2013- 13.69, 2014- 13.46, 2015- 14.15, 2016- 14.71, 2017- 14.32i/ 14.31, 2018- 14.62. pbs: 60m 7.53i '18, 100m 12.13/12.07w '14, LJ 6.81 '10.

Jenna PRANDINI b. 20 Nov 1992 Clovis, California 1.72m 59kg. Student of psychology at University of Oregon. At 200m/4x100mR: OG: '16- sf; WCh: '15- sf/2R. At 100m: CCp: '18- 3/1R; NACAC: '18- 1/1R. Won NCAA 100m 2015, 2018 (& 4x100); LJ 2014; US 200m 2015, 2018. Progress at 100m, 200m, LJ: 2008- 12.18/11.74w, 5.86; 2009- 11.81, 24.48/24.02w; 2010- 11.34, 24.61, 6.15/6.29w; 2011- 11.51/11.44w, 23.75/23.51w, 6.20; 2012- 24.07, 2013- 11.31/11.14w, 23.15, 6.15; 2014- 11.11, 22.60, 6.55; 2015- 10.92, 22.20/22.18w, 6.80; 2016- 10.95/10.81w, 22.39; 2017- 11.05, 22.54; 2018- 10.96/10.95w, 22.16. pbs: 60m 7.15i '15, TJ 12.73/12.98w '10.

DeAnna PRICE b. 8 Jun 1993 Moscow Mills, Missouri 1.72m 109kg. Was at Southern Illinois University. At HT: OG: '16- 8; WCh: '15- dnq 18, '17- 9; WJ: '12- dnq 11; PAm: '15- 4; CCp: '18- 1. NCAA champion 2015-16, NACAC 2018, US indoor 20lb Wt 2018. 3 North American hammer records 2013-18. Progress at HT: 2011- 55.20, 2012- 62.62, 2013- 65.18, 2015- 72.30, 2016- 73.09, 2017- 74.91, 2018- 78.12. Pbs: SP 16.30 '15, DT 53.46 '15, Wt 24.57i '19. Married coach J.C. Lambert in October 2018.

Colleen QUIGLEY b. 20 Nov 1992 St Louis, Missouri 1.73m 59kg. Nike Bowerman TC. Was at Florida State University. At 3000mSt: OG: '16- 8; WCh: '15- 12, '17- h; NCAA champion 2015. At 1500m: WI: '18- 9. Progress at 3000mSt: 2012- 10:02.53, 2013- 9:38.23, 2014- 9:56.96, 2015- 9:24.92, 2016- 9:20.00, 2017- 9:15.97, 2018- 9:10.27. pbs: 800m 2:08.69i '15, 10000m 2:36.53 '18, 1500m 4:03.02 '18, 1M 4:22.86i '19, 3000m 9:13.79i '13, 5000m 15:58.90 '13.

Brittney REESE b. 9 Sep 1986 Gulfport, Mississippi 1.73m 64kg. Nike. English graduate of University of Mississippi. At LJ: OG: '08- 4, '12- 1, '16- 2; WCh: '07-09-11-13-15-17 8/1/1/1/dnq 24/1; WI: '10-12-16: 1/1/1; won DL 2010-11, WAF 2009, US 2008-12, 2014, 2016 (& 3 indoors); NCAA 2008. North American indoor long jump record 2012. Progress at LJ: 2004- 6.31, 2006- 5.94, 2007- 6.83, 2008- 6.95, 2009- 7.10, 2010- 6.94/7.05w, 2011- 7.19, 2012- 7.23i/7.15, 2013- 7.25, 2014- 6.92, 2015- 6.97, 2016- 7.31, 2017- 7.13, 2018- 6.89i/6.87/7.19w. pbs: 50m 6.23i '12, 60m 7.24i '11, 100m 11.40 '17, 11.20w '11; HJ 1.88i/1.84 '08, TJ 13.16 '08. Concentrated on basketball at Gulf Coast

Community College in 2005-06. Has won eight global titles

Raevyn ROGERS b. 7 Sep 1996 1.71m 64kg. Nike. Was at University of Oregon.
At 800m: WJ: '08- 14; PAm–J '15- 1 (1 4x400R), NCAA 2015-17.
World indoor 4x800m record 2018.
Progress at 800m: 2008- 2:13.12, 2009- 2:06.90, 2010- 2:10.80, 2011- 2:11.09. 2012- 2:05.50, 2013- 2:03.32, 2014- 2:04.40, 2015- 1:59.71, 2016- 2:00.59, 2017- 1:59.10, 2018- 1:57.69. pbs: 200m 24.34 '10, 400m 52.06 '18, 600m 1:24.88i '09.

Shannon ROWBURY b. 19 Sep 1984 San Francisco 1.65m 52kg. Nike Oregon Project. Was at Duke University.
At 1500m: OG: '08- 7, '12- 4, '16- 4; WCh: '09- 3, '11- sf, '15- 7; CCp: '14- 2; Won US 2008-09, NCAA indoor mile 2007. At 3000m: WI: '14- 7, '16- 3; CCp: '10- 2. At 5000m: WCh: '13- 7, '17- 9. WR distance medley 2015, North American records: 2M 2014, 1500m 2015, 5000m 2016.
Progress at 1500m, 5000m: 2004- 4:17.41, 2005- 4:14.81, 2006- 4:12.31, 15:38.42; 2007- 16:59.97i, 2008- 4:00.33, 2009- 4:00.81, 15:12.95; 2010- 4:01.30, 15:00.51; 2011- 4:05.73, 2012- 4:03.15, 2013- 4:01.28, 15:06.10, 2014- 3:59.49, 14:48.68; 2015- 3:56.29, 2016- 3:57.78, 14:38.92; 2017- 4:04.56i/4:04.61, 14:57.55. pbs: 800m 1:59.97 '16, 1000m 2:40.25i '15, 1M 4:20.34 '08, 2000m 5:46.2 '14, 3000m 8:29.93 '14, 2M 9:20.25 '14, 3000mSt 9:59.4 '06.
Former ballet and Irish dancer. Married Pablo Solares (Mexican 1500m record 3:36.67 '09) on 11 April 2015, daughter Sienna born 30 June 2018.

Raven SAUNDERS b. 15 May 1996 Charleston, SC 1.65m 125kg. Student at Southern Illinois University.
At SP: OG: '16- 5; WCh: '17- 10; WJ: 14- 2; CCp: '18- 1. Won PAm-J 2015, NCAA 2016.
Progress at SP: 2014- 17.82, 2015- 18.62i/18.35, 2016- 19.35, 2017- 19.76, 2018- 19.74. pbs: DT 56.85 '16, HT 56.91 '16, Wt 21.67i '17.
4 indoor and 4 outdoor US junior records 2015.

Sha'Keela SAUNDERS b. 18 Dec 1993 Elizabeth City, North Carolina 1.68m 59kg. University of Kentucky.
At LJ: WCh: '17- dnq 21; PAm: '15- 3.Won US 2018, NACAC 2018, U23 2014, NCAA indoor2017.
Progress at LJ: 2008- 5.92w, 2011- 5.65/5.90w?, 2012- 6.00i, 2014- 6.43, 2015- 6.75, 2016- 6.89, 2017- 6.90i/6.79/6.92w, 2018- 6.77/6.88w. pbs: 55m 7.04i '09, 60m 7.49i '18, 100m 11.88 '17, 200m 23.80 '17, 300m 39.08 '09, 400m 55.47 '09, 100mh 13.99 '16, TJ 13.32i '17, 13.03/13.34w '16.

Jennifer SIMPSON b. 23 Aug 1986 Webster City, Iowa 1.65m 50kg. née Barringer. New Balance. Studied political science at University of Colorado.
At 1500m: OG: '12- sf, '16- 3; WCh: '11-13-15-17: 1/2/11/2; won DL 2014. At 3000mSt: OG: '08- 8; WCh: '07- h, '09- 4; won NCAA 2006, 2008-09. Won US 1500m 2014-17, 5000m 2013, 3000mSt 2009.
North American records: 3000m steeplechase (3) 2008-09, 2 miles indoors 2015, out 2018.
Progress at 1500m, 5000m, 3000mSt: 2006- 16:15.23, 9:53.04, 2007- 4:21.53, 15:48.24, 9:33.95; 2008- 4:11.36, 9:22.26; 2009- 3:59.90, 15:01.70i/15:05.25, 9:12.50; 2010- 4:03.63, 15:33.33; 2011- 4:03.54, 15:11.49; 2012- 4:04.07, 2013- 4:00.48, 14:56.26; 2014- 3:57.22, 2015- 3:57.30, 2016- 3:58.19, 2017- 4:00.70, 2018- 3:59.37. pbs: 800m 2:00.45 '13, 1M 4:17.30 '18, 2000m 5:45.7 '14, 3000m 8:29.58 '14, 2M 9:16.78 '18.
Married Jason Simpson on 8 Oct 2010. Won the 5th Avenue Mile seven times 2011 and 2013-18.

Emily SISSON b. 12 Oct 1991 Chesterfield, Missouri 1.65m 47kg. New Balance. Was at Providence University.
At 10000m: WCh: '17- 9. At 3000m/5000m: WJ: '10- 10/6. World CC: '10- 18J. Won NCAA 5000m indoors and out 2015.
Progress at 10000m: 2011- 35:07.35, 2013- 33:02.88, 2014- 32:31.06, 2015- 31:38.03, 2016- 32:54.06, 2017- 31:25.64, 2018- 32:06.31, 2019- 30:49.57. pbs: 1M 4:38.49i '13, 4:44.02 '10; 3000m 8:49.61 '18, 5000m 15:02.10i/15:10.90 '17, HMar 68:21 '17.

Ashley SPENCER b. 8 Jun 1993 Indianapolis 1.68m 54kg. Student at University of Texas, formerly Illinois.
At 400mh: OG: '16- 3. At 400m/4x400mR: WCh: '13- sf/1R; WJ: '12- 1/1R; WI: '16- 2/1R. Won NCAA 2012-13.
Progress at 400m, 400mh: 2012- 50.50, 59.43; 2013- 50.28, 56.32; 2014- 51.38, 59.78; 2015- 51.72, 2016- 51.09, 53.72; 2017- 52.83, 53.11; 2018- 52.67i, 54.66. pbs: 60m 7.42i '13, 100m 11.34/11.27w '14, 200m 22.92/22.69w '14, 300m 36.27i '17, 100mh 14.40/14.28w '11.

Jaide STEPTER b. 25 Sep 1994 Santa Ana, California 1.73m 64kg. Nike. Was at University of Southern California.
Progress at 400m: 2009- 58.69, 2010- 59.14, 2011- 58.04, 2013- 51.05, 2014- 53.98i, 2015- 52.89i, 2016- 50.91, 2017- 51.12, 2018- 50.63. pbs: 200m 22.80 '18, 300m 37.05i '19, 100mh 14.35 '13, 400mh 54.95 '16.
Her mother LaTanya Sheffield was NCAA champion at 400mh in 1985, 3rd PAm 1987, 8th OG 1988, pb 54.36 '88.

Deajah STEVENS b. 19 May 1995 Tarrytown, New York 1.72m 60kg. University of Oregon.
At (100m)/200m: OG: '16- 7; WCh: '17- (sf)/5. US champion 2017.
North American 4x200m indoor record 2018.
Progress at 100m, 200m: 2008- 25.54, 2009- 24.48, 2011- 12.11, 24.20; 2012- 12.10w, 24.38; 2013- 12.05, 24.15; 2015- 23.18, 2016- 11.18/11.04w,

22.25; 2017- 11.00/10.89w, 22.09; 2018- 11.18, 22.81. Pbs: 60m 7.17i '17, 300m 37.90i '13, 400m 53.63 '15. LJ 5.95 '15.

Jeneva STEVENS b. 28 Oct 1989 Dolton, Illinois 1.78m 102kg. née McCall. Was at Southern Illinois University.
At HT: WCh: '11- dnq 14, '13- 7; WUG: '13- 1. At SP: WCh: '15- 10; PAm: '15- 6; WI: '14- 7, '18- 8. Won NCAA DT 2010, HT 2012.
Progress at SP, HT: 2009- 15.22, 55.83; 2010- 17.25i/16.54, 64.17; 2011- 17.22i/16.96, 69.55; 2012- 17.97i/17.89, 69.38; 2013- 19.10i/18.47, 74.77; 2014- 18.45i/17.86, 70.78; 2015- 18.84, 72.69; 2016- 19.11, 71.10; 2017- 18.54i/18.48, 71.56; 2018- 18.55i/18.33, 70.05. Pbs: DT 59.45 '12, Wt 24.24i '18.
Daughter of 1994-5 WBC world heavyweight boxing champion Oliver McCall.

Jasmin STOWERS b. 23 Sep 1991 Pendleton, SC 1.75m 64kg. Degree in nutrition from Louisiana State University.
At 100mh: WY: '07- 4; won NCAA indoor 60mh 2013, US 2015. World best 4x100mh 2015.
Progress at 100mh: 2005- 14.27w, 2006- 14.05/13.82Aw, 2007- 13.69/13.68w, 2008- 13.66/13.46w, 2009- 13.59/13.32Aw, 2010- 14.47, 2011- 12.88/12.86w, 2012- 12.92, 2013- 13.00/12.88w, 2014- 12.71/12.54w, 2015- 12.35, 2016- 12.55, 2017- 12.47, 2018- 12.71. pbs: 60m 7.51i '12, 100m 11.82 '11, 60mh 7.82Ai '17, 7.84i '15; 400mh 61.17 '08.

Jennifer SUHR b. 5 Feb 1982 Fredonia, New York 1.80m 64kg. adidas. née Stuczynski. Graduate of Roberts Wesleyan University, now studying child psychology.
At PV: OG: '08- 2, '12- 1, '16- 7=; WCh: '07-11-13- 15-17: 10/4/2/4=/dnq nh; PAm: '15- 3; WI: '08- 14-16: 2/5=/1; WCp: '06- nh; US champion 2006- 10, 2012-16; indoors 2005, 2007-09, 2011-13.
Records: world indoors 2013 & 2016, W35 2018, four North American pole vault records 2007- 08, four indoors 2009-13.
Progress at PV: 2002- 2.75, 2004- 3.49, 2005- 4.57i/4.26, 2006- 4.68i/4.66, 2007- 4.88, 2008- 4.92, 2009- 4.83i/4.81, 2010- 4.89, 2011- 4.91, 2012- 4.88i/4.81, 2013- 5.02Ai/4.91, 2014- 4.73i/4.71, 2015- 4.82, 2016- 5.03i/4.82, 2017- 4.83, 2018- 4.93, 2019- 4.91. pbs: 55mh 8.07i '05, JT 46.82 '05.
All-time top scorer at basketball at her university, then very rapid progress at vaulting.

Cassandra TATE b. 11 Sep 1990 Hammond, Louisiana 1.74m 64kg. Management graduate of Louisiana State University.
At 400m/4x400m: WI: '14- 1R. At 400mh: WCh: '15- 3, '17- 7; won DL 2016, NCAA & NACAC 2012.
Progress at 400mh: 2010- 56.87, 2011- 55.99, 2012- 55.22, 2013- 55.45, 2014- 54.70, 2015- 54.01, 2016- 54.47, 2017- 54.59, 2018- 54.94. pbs: 60m 7.49i '11, 100m 11.79 '08, 11.47w '10; 200m 23.37i '10, 23.68 '09; 400m 52.40Ai '14, 52.51 '15; 60mh 8.61i '09,

100mh 14.21 '08, 14.08w '07; 200mhSt 26.15 '18. Engaged to David Verburg (qv).

Gabrielle THOMAS b. 7 Dec 1996 1.70m 57kg. New Balance. Was at Harvard University.
At 200m. Won NCAA indoor 2018.
Progress at 200m: 2015- 24.22, 2016- 22.47/22.37w 2017- 22.56, 2018- 22.19/22.13w. pbs: 60m 7.25i '18, 100m 11.19/10.99w '18, 150m 17.20 '16, 300m 35.98i '19, LJ 6.27 '17, 6.61w '18; TJ 12.24i '18.

Jasmine TODD b. 23 Dec 1993 San Diego 1.65m 55kg. Student of psychology at University of Oregon.
At 100m/LJ/4x100m:WCh: '15- sf/dq 19, 2R.
Progress at 100m, LJ: 2010- 11.99/11.64Aw, 6.08i/6.07; 2011- 11.80/11.73w, 6.01; 2012- 11.76, 6.13; 2013- 12.02/12.00w, 5.95; 2014- 11.25, 6.50Ai/6.06; 2015- 10.92/10.86w, 6.84; 2016- 11.20, 6.47; 2017- 11.29, 6.83/6.84w; 2018- 6.44/6.63w. pbs: 60m 7.15i '15, 200m 22.89 '15, TJ 13.10 '15.

Ariana WASHINGTON b. 4 Sep 1996 Signal Hill, California 1.75m 59kg. Student at University of Oregon.
At 100/(200m): WCh: '17- sf/res 1R; WJ: '14- 7/1R; WY: '13- 2/3. Won NCAA 100m & 200m 2016.
Progress at 100m, 200m: 2010- 12.78/12.55w, 25.176; 2011- 12.07, 24.01; 2012- 11.47, 23.41; 2013- 11.39/11.18Aw, 23.18/23.05Aw; 2014- 11.22, 22.96; 2015- 23.07i; 2016- 11.01/10.95w, 22.21; 2017- 11.06/10.97w, 22.39; 2018- 11.08, 22.54. pbs: 60m 7.20i '17, HJ 1.57 '11, LJ 5.79 '11.

Kendell WILLIAMS b. 14 Jun 1995 Marietta 1.73m 64kg. Student at University of Georgia.
At Hep: OG: '16- 17; WCh: '17- 12; WJ: '12- 8; WY: '11- 11; won US 2017, NCAA 2014, 2016-17, indoor Pen 2014-17. At Pen: WI: '16- 5, 18- 9. At 100mh: WJ: '14- 1; WY: '11- 3.
Progress at Hep: 2011- 5169, 2012- 5578, 2013- 5572A, 2014- 6018, 2015- 6223, 2016- 6402, 2017- 6564. pbs: 200m 23.50 '17, 400m 55.61Ai '18, 600m 1:34.92i '18, 800m 2:15.31 '16, 60mh 8.18i '19, 100mh 12.82 '17, 400mh 58.63 '10, HJ 1.88Ai '14, 1.84 '16; LJ 6.69/6.91w '18. SP 13.55i '16, 13.01 '17; JT 46.48 '17, Pen 4703i '16.
Her brother Devon (b. 17 Dec 1994) has decathlon pb 8345 '17, 10th WC and won NCAA indoor heptathlon with 6177 in 2017.

Ajee' WILSON b. 8 May 1994 Neptune, New Jersey 1.69m 55kg. adidas. Studied kinesiology at Temple University, Philadelphia.
At 800m: OG: '16- sf; WCh: '13- 5. '17- 3; WJ: '10- 5, '12- 1; WY: 11- 1; CCp: '14- 2, '18- 2; WI: '16- 2, '18- 2; won US 2014, 2017-18; indoor 2013-14, 2016; NACAC 2018.
Records: WR distance medley 2015, World indoor 4x800m 2018, North American 4x800m 2014, 600m 2017, Indoor 800m 1:58.60 2019, world junior 600m & North American junior 800m 2013.

Progress at 800m: 2008- 2:11.43, 2009- 2:07.08, 2010- 2:04.18, 2011- 2:02.64, 2012- 2:00.91, 2013- 1:58.21, 2014- 1:57.67, 2015- 1:57.87, 2016- 1:59.44, 2017- 1:55.61, 2018- 1:56.45. pbs: 400m 53.63 '14, 500m 1:09.63i '17, 600m 1:22.39 '17, 1000m 2:34.71i '19, 1500m 4:05.18 '18, 1M 4:33.57 '16, 3000m 10:13.41 '07.

Positive test for zeranol at the Millrose Games on 11 Feb 2017 meant that her result from then, when she had run a North American indoor 800m record of 1:58.27, was annulled, although it was announced in June she will not face a ban as it was deemed likely that the test result was due to contaminated meat. Elder sister Jade has 400mh pb 59.90 '12.

Shakima WIMBLEY b. 23 Apr 1995 Fort Lauderdale, Florida 1.87m 61kg. University of Miami.

At 400m/4x400mR: WCh: '17- 1R; WJ: '14- 1R; PAm: '15- 2/1R; CCp: '18- 5; WI: '18- 2/1R. Won US 2018.

Progress at 400m: 2012- 55.11, 2013- 53.67, 2014- 51.68, 2015- 50.84, 2016- 50.90, 2017- 50.36, 2018- 49.52. pbs: 100m 11.99 '13, 200m 22.43 '15, 300m 36.71 '17.

Kara WINGER b. 10 Apr 1986 Seattle 1.83m 84kg. née Patterson. Studied interior design at Purdue University.

At JT: OG: '08/12/16- dnq 40/30/13; WCh: '09/11/17- dnq 28/20/15, '15- 8; PAm: '15- 2; PAm-J: '05- 2; CCp: '10-14-18: 5/7/3. Won NACAC 2015, US 2008-11, 2014-15, 2017-18.

North American javelin record 2010.

Progress at JT: 2003- 44.75, 2004- 48.51, 2005- 52.09, 2006- 56.19, 2008- 61.56, 2009- 63.95, 2010- 66.67, 2011- 62.76, 2012- 60.49, 2013- 57.12, 2014- 62.90, 2015- 66.47, 2016- 61.86, 2017- 64.80, 2018- 64.75. Pb DT 35.17 '11.

Married Russ Winger (SP 21.29i '08, 21.25 '10; DT 66.04 '11, dnq 26 WCh 15) on 28 Sep 2014.

UZBEKISTAN

Governing body: Athletic Federation of Uzbekistan.

Svetlana RAZIVIL b. 17 Jan 1987 Tashkent 1.84m 61kg

At HJ: OG: '08- dnq 16, '12- 7, '16- 13=; WCh: '09- dnq 18=, '11- 7=, '15- 9=; AsiG: '06-10-14-18: 7/1/1/1; AsiC: '09-11-13-15: 3/2/2/1; WJ: '02- dnq, '04- 13, '06- 1; WY: '03- dnq; CCp: '14- 4, '18- 2; WI: '12- 8. Won Asi-J 2006, Asian indoor 2014, 2016.

Progress at HJ: 2002- 1.84, 2003- 1.78, 2004- 1.88, 2005- 1.85, 2006- 1.91, 2007- 1.91, 2008- 1.93, 2009- 1.91, 2010- 1.95, 2011- 1.95, 2012- 1.97, 2013- 1.94, 2014- 1.96, 2015- 1.94, 2016- 1.95, 2018- 1.96.

VENEZUELA

Governing body: Federación Venezolana de Atletismo. Founded 1948.

National Champions 2018: Men: 100m/200m: Rafael Vásquez 10.46/20.89, 400m: José Daniel Meléndez 46.11, 800m/1500m: Lucirio Garrido 1:49.65/3:51.24, 5000m/10000m: Marvin Blanco 15:10.38/31:45.77, Mar: Didimo Sánchez 2:26:28, 3000mSt: Frammik Semprún 9:31.02, 110mh: Adrián Almarza 15.03, 400mh: Wilson Bello 50.52, HJ: Rafael Uribe 2.00, PV: Juan Luciani 4.20, LJ: Diego Hernández 7.67, TJ: Leodán Torrealba 15.83, SP: Kendrick Rojas 12.78, DT: Cristhofer Torr 41.82, HT: Julio Gaitán 49.97, JT: Billy Julio 66.17, Dec: Geormis Jaramillo 8048, 20000mW/35kW: Wilman Vera 1:40:55.2/3:05:28.
Women: 100m/200m/100mh: Génesis Romero 11.71/23.90/13.14, 400m/800m: Pamela Milano 54.28/2:12.17, 1500m: María Garrido 4:40.76, 5000m/10000m: Nubia Arteaga 18:01.55/ 36:57.49, Mar: Arelys Rodríguez 2:53:53, 3000mSt: María Tirado 11:44.42, 400mh: Yenisquel Alfonzo 61.99, HJ: Amanda Vergara 1.84, PV: Carmen Villanueva 3.60, LJ: Tania Pollo 5.41, TJ: Williangi Mendo 11.32, SP: Ahymara Espinoza 16.44, DT: Yerilda Zapata 42.76, HT: Rosa Rodríguez 63.20, JT: Esthefany Chacón 52.60, Hep: Luisaris Toledo 5376, 20000mW: Ana Sulbarán 1:56:07.1, 20kW: Milángela Rosales 1:44:26.

Women

Robeilys PEINADO b. 26 Nov 1997 Caracas 1.68m 62kg. OSOT Szczecin, Poland.

At PV: WCh: '15- dnq 23, '17- 3=; WJ: '14- nh, '16- 2; WY: '13- 1; PAm: '15- 6; Yth OG: '14- 2; SAG: '18- 1; SACh: '15- 1, '17- 1; SAG: '14- 2. Won S.Am-U23 & -Y 2014, –J 2015.

Six Venezuelan pole vault records 2015-18, 3 SAm U20 records 2014-15.

Progress at PV: 2011- 3.90, 2012- 4.15, 2013- 4.40A, 2014- 4.31, 2015- 4.60, 2016- 4.56, 2017- 4.65, 2018- 4.70A.

Yulimar ROJAS b. 21 Oct 1995 Caracas 1.89m 75kg. FC Barcelona, Spain.

At TJ (LJ): OG: '16- 2; WCh: '17- 1; WJ: '14- dnq 17 (11); PAm: '15- 4 (11); SACh: '15- 1, '17- 2; WI: '16- 1, '18- 1. Won SAu23 LJ & TJ 2014, SAmJ HJ 2011.

Venezuelan records: LJ 2015, TJ (5) 2015-16. Five South American indoor TJ records 2016-19.

Progress at TJ: 2014- 13.65, 2015- 14.20, 2016- 15.02, 2017- 14.96, 2018- 14.63i, 2019- 14.92i. Pbs: 100m 11.94 '13, HJ 1.87 '13, LJ 6.57 '15.

Lives in Guadalajara, Spain and coached by Iván Pedroso. First woman to win an Olympic medal for Venezuela. IAAF Rising Star of the Year 2017. Missed the 2018 outdoor season through injury.

INTRODUCTION TO WORLD LISTS AND INDEX

Records
World, World U20 and U18, Olympic, Area and Continental records are listed for standard events. In running events up to and including 400 metres, only fully automatic times are shown. Marks listed are those which are considered statistically acceptable by the ATFS, and thus may differ from official records. These are followed by 'odd events', road bests and bests by over 35/40 masters.

World All-time and Year Lists
Lists are presented in the following format: Mark, Wind reading (where appropriate), Name, Nationality (abbreviated), Date of birth, Position in competition, Meeting name (if significant), Venue, Date of performance.

In standard events the best 30 or so performances are listed followed by the best marks for other athletes. Position, meet and venue details have been omitted beyond 100th in year lists.

In the all-time lists performances which have been world records (or world bests, thus including some unratified marks) are shown with WR against them (or WIR for world indoor records).

Juniors (U20) are shown with-J after date of birth, and Youths (U18) with -Y.

Indexes
These contain the names of all athletes ranked with full details in the world year lists for standard events (and others such as half marathon). The format of the index is as follows:

Family name, First name, Nationality, Birthdate, Height (cm) and Weight (kg), 2018 best mark, Lifetime best (with year) as at the end of 2017.

* indicates an athlete who is profiled in the Biographies section, and ^ one who has been profiled in previous editions.

General Notes
Altitude aid
Marks set at an altitude of 1000m or higher have been suffixed by the letter "A" in events where altitude may be of significance.

Although there are no separate world records for altitude assisted events, it is understood by experts that in all events up to 400m in length (with the possible exclusion of the 110m hurdles), and in the horizontal jumps, altitude gives a material benefit to performances. For events beyond 800m, however, the thinner air of high altitude has a detrimental effect.

Supplementary lists are included in relevant events for athletes with seasonal bests at altitude who have low altitude marks qualifying for the main list.

Some leading venues over 1000m
Addis Ababa ETH	2365m
Air Force Academy USA	2194
Albuquerque USA	1555
Antananarivo MAD	1350
Assela ETH	2430
Ávila ESP	1128
Bloemfontein RSA	1392
Bogotá COL	2644
Boulder USA	1655
Bozeman USA	1467
Calgary CAN	1045
Cali COL	1046
Ciudad de Guatemala GUA	1402
Ciudad de México MEX	2247
Cochabamba BOL	2558
Colorado Springs USA	1823
Cuenca ECU	2561
Denver USA	1609
El Paso USA	1187
Flagstaff USA	2107
Fort Collins USA	1521
Gabarone BOT	1006
Germiston RSA	1661
Guadalajara MEX	1567
Harare ZIM	1473
Johannesburg RSA	1748
Kampala UGA	1189
Krugersdorp RSA	1740
Levelland USA	1069
Logan USA	1372
Medellín COL	1541
Monachil ESP	2302
Nairobi KEN	1675
Orem USA	1455
Pietersburg RSA	1230
Pocatello USA	1361
Potchefstroom RSA	1351
Pretoria RSA	1400
Provo USA	1380
Pueblo USA	1487
Reno USA	1369
Roodepoort RSA	1623
Rustenburg RSA	1215
Salt Lake City USA	1321
San José CRC	1200
Sasolberg RSA	1488
Secunda RSA	1628
Sestriere ITA	2050
Soría ESP	1056
Windhoek NAM	1725
Xalapa MEX	1356

Some others over 500m
Albertville FRA	550
Almaty KZK	847
Ankara TUR	902
Bangalore, IND	949
Bern SUI	555
Blacksburg USA	634
Boise USA	818
Canberra AUS	581

La Chaux de Fonds SUI	997
Caracas VEN	922
Edmonton CAN	652
Jablonec CZE	598
Las Vegas USA	619
Lausanne SUI	597
Lubbock USA	981
Madrid ESP	640
Magglingen SUI	751
Malles ITA	980
Moscow, Idaho USA	787
München GER	520
Nampa, Idaho USA	760
Salamanca ESP	806
Santiago de Chile CHI	520
São Paulo BRA	725
Sofia BUL	564
Spokane USA	576
Trípoli GRE	655
Tucson USA	728
Uberlândia BRA	852
350m-500m	
Banská Bystrica SVK	362
Fayetteville USA	407
Genève SUI	385
Götzis AUT	448
Johnson City USA	499
Rieti ITA	402
Sindelfingen GER	440
Stuttgart GER	415
Tashkent UZB	477
Zürich SUI	410

Automatic timing
In the main lists for sprints and hurdles, only times recorded by fully automatic timing devices are included.

Hand timing
In the sprints and hurdles supplementary lists are included for races which are hand timed. Athletes with a hand timed best 0.01 seconds or more better than his or her automatically timed best has been included, but hand timed lists have been terminated close to the differential levels considered by the IAAF to be equivalent to automatic times, i.e. 0.24 sec. for 100m, 200m, 100mh, 110mh, and 0.14 sec. for 400m and 400mh. It should be noted that this effectively recognises bad hand timekeeping, for there should be no material difference between hand and auto times, but badly trained timekeepers anticipate the finish, having reacted to the flash at the start.

In events beyond 400m, auto times are integrated with hand timed marks, the latter identifiable by times being shown to tenths. All-time lists also include some auto times in tenths of a second, identified with '.

Indoor marks
Indoor marks are included in the main lists for field events and straightway track events, but not for other track events as track sizes vary in circumference (200m is the international standard) and banking, while outdoor tracks are standardised at 400m. Outdoor marks for athletes with indoor bests are shown in a supplemental list.

Mixed races
For record purposes athletes may not, except in road races, compete in mixed sex races. Statistically there would not appear to be any particular logic in this, and women's marks set in such races are shown in our lists – annotated with mx. In such cases the athlete's best mark in single sex competition is appended.

Field event series
Field event series are given (where known) for marks in the top 30 performances lists.

Tracks and Courses
As well as climatic conditions, the type and composition of tracks and runways will affect standards of performance, as will the variations in road race courses.

Wind assistance
Anemometer readings have been shown for sprints and horizontal jumps in metres per second to one decimal place. If the figure was given to two decimal places, it has been rounded to the next tenth upwards, e.g. a wind reading of +2.01m/s, beyond the IAAF legal limit of 2.0, is rounded to +2.1; or -1.22m/s is rounded up to -1.2.

Drugs bans
The IAAF Council may decertify an athlete's records, titles and results if he or she is found to have used a banned substance before those performances. Performances at or after such a positive finding are shown in footnotes. Such athletes are shown with ¶ after their name in year lists, and in all-time lists if at any stage of their career they have served a drugs suspension of a year or more (thus not including athletes receiving public warnings or 3 month bans for stimulants etc., which for that year only are indicated with a #). This should not be taken as implying that the athlete was using drugs at that time. Nor have those athletes who have subsequently unofficially admitted to using banned substances been indicated; the ¶ is used only for those who have been caught.

Venues
Place names occasionally change. Our policy is to use names in force at the time that the performance was set. Thus Leningrad prior to 1991, Sankt-Peterburg from its re-naming.

Amendments
Keen observers may spot errors in the lists. They are invited to send corrections as well as news and results for 2019.

Peter Matthews
Email p.matthews121@btinternet.com

WORLD & CONTINENTAL RECORDS

As at 23 March 2019. **Key**: W = World, Afr = Africa, Asi = Asia, CAC = Central America & Caribbean, Eur = Europe, NAm = North America, Oce = Oceania, SAm = South America, Com = Commonwealth, W20 = World Junior (U20), W18 = World Youth (U18, not officially ratified by IAAF). h hand timed.
A altitude over 1000m, + timing by photo-electric-cell, # awaiting ratification, § not officially ratified

100 METRES

W,CAC,Com	9.58	Usain BOLT	JAM	Berlin	16 Aug 2009
NAm	9.69	Tyson GAY	USA	Shanghai	20 Sep 2009
Afr	9.85	Olusoji FASUBA	NGR	Doha	12 May 2006
Eur	9.86	Francis OBIKWELU	POR	Athína	22 Aug 2004
	9.86	Jimmy VICAUT	FRA	Saint-Denis 4 Jul 2015 & Montreuil-sous-Bois 7 Jun 2016
Asi	9.91	Femi Seun OGUNODE	QAT	Wuhan 4 Jun 15 & Gainesville 22 Apr 2016
	9.91	SU Bingtian	CHN	Madrid 22 Jun 18 & Paris (C) 30 Jun 2018
Oce	9.93	Patrick JOHNSON	AUS	Mito	5 May 2003
SAm	10.00A	Róbson da SILVA	BRA	Ciudad de México	22 Jul 1988
W20	9.97	Trayvon BROMELL	USA	Eugene	13 Jun 2014
W18	10.15	Anthony SCHWARTZ	USA	Gainesville	31 Mar 2017

200 METRES

W,CAC,Com	19.19	Usain BOLT	JAM	Berlin	20 Aug 2009
NAm	19.32	Michael JOHNSON	USA	Atlanta	1 Aug 1996
Afr	19.68	Frank FREDERICKS	NAM	Atlanta	1 Aug 1996
Eur	19.72A	Pietro MENNEA	ITA	Ciudad de México	12 Sep 1979
SAm	19.81	Alonso EDWARD	PAN	Berlin	20 Aug 2009
Asi	19.97	Femi Seun OGUNODE	QAT	Bruxelles	11 Sep 2015
Oce	20.06A	Peter NORMAN	AUS	Ciudad de México	16 Oct 1968
W20	19.93	Usain BOLT	JAM	Hamilton, BER	11 Apr 2004
W18	20.13	Usain BOLT	JAM	Bridgetown	20 Jul 2003

400 METRES

W, Afr, Com	43.03	Wayde van NIEKERK	RSA	Rio de Janeiro	14 Aug 2016
NAm	43.18	Michael JOHNSON	USA	Sevilla	26 Aug 1999
CAC	43.74	Kirani JAMES	GRN	Lausanne	3 Jul 2014
Asi	43.93	Yousef Ahmed AL-MASRAHI	KSA	Beijing	23 Aug 2015
SAm	44.29	Sanderlei PARRELA	BRA	Sevilla	26 Aug 1999
Eur	44.33	Thomas SCHÖNLEBE	GER	Roma	3 Sep 1987
Oce	44.38	Darren CLARK	AUS	Seoul	26 Sep 1988
W20	43.87	Steve LEWIS	USA	Seoul	28 Sep 1988
W18	45.14	Obea MOORE	USA	Santiago de Chile	2 Sep 1995

800 METRES

W, Afr, Com	1:40.91	David RUDISHA	KEN	London (OS)	9 Aug 2012
Eur	1:41.11	Wilson KIPKETER	DEN	Köln	24 Aug 1997
SAm	1:41.77	Joaquim CRUZ	BRA	Köln	26 Aug 1984
NAm	1:42.60	Johnny GRAY	USA	Koblenz	28 Aug 1985
Asi	1:42.79	Youssef Saad KAMEL	BRN	Monaco	29 Jul 2008
CAC	1:42.85	Norberto TELLEZ	CUB	Atlanta	31 Jul 1996
Oce	1:44.21	Jospeh DEN	AUS	Monaco	20 Jul 2018
W20	1:41.73	Nijel AMOS	BOT	London (OS)	9 Aug 2012
W18	1:43.37	Mohamed AMAN	ETH	Rieti	10 Sep 2011

1000 METRES

W, Afr, Com	2:11.96	Noah NGENY	KEN	Rieti	5 Sep 1999
Eur	2:12.18	Sebastian COE	GBR	Oslo	11 Jul 1981
NAm	2:13.9	Rick WOHLHUTER	USA	Oslo	30 Jul 1974
SAm	2:14.09	Joaquim CRUZ	BRA	Nice	20 Aug 1984
Asi	2:14.72	Youssef Saad KAMEL	BRN	Stockholm	22 Jul 2008
Oce	2:16.09	Jeff RISELEY	AUS	Ostrava	17 Jun 2014
CAC	2:17.0	Byron DYCE	JAM	København	15 Aug 1973
W20	2:13.93 §	Abubaker KAKI	SUD	Stockholm	22 Jul 2008
W18	2:17.44	Hamza DRIOUCH	QAT	Sollentuna	9 Aug 2011

1500 METRES

W, Afr	3:26.00	Hicham EL GUERROUJ	MAR	Roma	14 Jul 1998
Com	3:26.34	Bernard LAGAT	KEN	Bruxelles	24 Aug 2001
Eur	3:28.81	Mo FARAH	GBR	Monaco	19 Jul 2013
Asi	3:29.14	Rashid RAMZI	BRN	Roma	14 Jul 2006
NAm	3:29.30	Bernard LAGAT	USA	Rieti	28 Aug 2005
Oce	3:29.66	Nick WILLIS	NZL	Monaco	17 Jul 2015

SAm	3:33.25	Hudson Santos de SOUZA	BRA	Rieti	28 Aug 2005
CAC	3:35.03	Maurys CASTILLO	CUB	Huelva	7 Jun 2012
W20	3:28.81	Ronald KWEMOI	KEN	Monaco	18 Jul 2014
W18	3:33.72	Nicholas KEMBOI	KEN	Zürich	18 Aug 2006

1 MILE

W, Afr	3:43.13	Hicham El GUERROUJ	MAR	Roma	7 Jul 1999
Com	3:43.40	Noah NGENY	KEN	Roma	7 Jul 1999
Eur	3:46.32	Steve CRAM	GBR	Oslo	27 Jul 1985
NAm	3:46.91	Alan WEBB	USA	Brasschaat	21 Jul 2007
Asi	3:47.97	Daham Najim BASHIR	QAT	Oslo	29 Jul 2005
Oce	3:48.98	Craig MOTTRAM	AUS	Oslo	29 Jul 2005
SAm	3:51.05	Hudson de SOUZA	BRA	Oslo	29 Jul 2005
CAC	3:56.13	Daniel HERRERA	MEX	Concord, MA	1 Jun 2017
W20	3:49.29	William Biwott TANUI (now ÖZBILEN)	KEN	Oslo	3 Jul 2009
W18	3:54.56	Isaac SONGOK	KEN	Linz	20 Aug 2001

2000 METRES

W, Afr	4:44.79	Hicham EL GUERROUJ	MAR	Berlin	7 Sep 1999
Com	4:48.74	John KIBOWEN	KEN	Hechtel	1 Aug 1998
Oce	4:50.76	Craig MOTTRAM	AUS	Melbourne	9 Mar 2006
Eur	4:51.39	Steve CRAM	GBR	Budapest	4 Aug 1985
NAm	4:52.44	Jim SPIVEY	USA	Lausanne	15 Sep 1987
Asi	4:55.57	Mohammed SULEIMAN	QAT	Roma	8 Jun 1995
SAm	5:03.34	Hudson Santos de SOUZA	BRA	Manaus	6 Apr 2002
CAC	5:03.4	Arturo BARRIOS	MEX	Nice	10 Jul 1989
W20	4:56.25	Tesfaye CHERU	ETH	Reims	5 Jul 2011
W18	4:56.86	Isaac SONGOK	KEN	Berlin	31 Aug 2001

3000 METRES

W, Afr, Com	7:20.67	Daniel KOMEN	KEN	Rieti	1 Sep 1996
Eur	7.20.02	Mohammed MOURHIT	BEL	Monaco	18 Aug 2000
NAm	7:29.00	Bernard LAGAT	USA	Rieti	29 Aug 2010
Asi	7:30.76	Jamal Bilal SALEM	QAT	Doha	13 May 2005
Oce	7:32.19	Craig MOTTRAM	AUS	Athína	17 Sep 2006
CAC	7:35.71	Arturo BARRIOS	MEX	Nice	10 Jul 1989
SAm	7:39.70	Hudson Santos de SOUZA	BRA	Lausanne	2 Jul 2002
W20	7:28.19	Yomif KEJELCHA	ETH	Saint-Denis	27 Aug 2016
W18	7:32.37	Abreham CHERKOS Feleke	ETH	Lausanne	11 Jul 2006

5000 METRES

W, Afr	12:37.35	Kenenisa BEKELE	ETH	Hengelo	31 May 2004
Com	12:39.74	Daniel KOMEN	KEN	Bruxelles	22 Aug 1997
Eur	12:49.71	Mohammed MOURHIT	BEL	Bruxelles	25 Aug 2000
Asi	12:51.96	Albert ROP	BRN	Monaco	19 Jul 2013
NAm	12:53.60	Bernard LAGAT	USA	Monaco	22 Jul 2011
Oce	12:55.76	Craig MOTTRAM	AUS	London	30 Jul 2004
CAC	13:07.79	Arturo BARRIOS	MEX	London (CP)	14 Jul 1989
SAm	13:19.43	Marilson dos SANTOS	BRA	Kassel	8 Jun 2006
W20	12:43.02	Selemon BAREGA	ETH	Bruxelles	31 Aug 2018
W18	12:54.19	Abreham CHERKOS Feleke	ETH	Roma	14 Jul 2006

10,000 METRES

W, Afr	26:17.53	Kenenisa BEKELE	ETH	Bruxelles	26 Aug 2005
Com	26:27.85	Paul TERGAT	KEN	Bruxelles	22 Aug 1997
Asi	26:38.76	Abdullah Ahmad HASSAN	QAT	Bruxelles	5 Sep 2003
NAm	26:44.36	Galen RUPP	USA	Eugene	30 May 2014
Eur	26:46.57	Mohamed FARAH	GBR	Eugene	3 Jun 2011
CAC	27:08.23	Arturo BARRIOS	MEX	Berlin	18 Aug 1989
Oce	27:24.95	Ben ST LAWRENCE	AUS	Stanford	1 May 2011
SAm	27:28.12	Marilson dos SANTOS	BRA	Neerpelt	2 Jun 2007
W20	26:41.75	Samuel WANJIRU	KEN	Bruxelles	26 Aug 2005
W18	27:02.81	Ibrahim JAYLAN Gashu	ETH	Bruxelles	25 Aug 2006

HALF MARATHON

W, Afr, Com	58:18	Abraham KIPTUM	KEN	Valencia	28 Oct 2018
Asi	58:40	Abraham CHEROBEN	BRN	København	17 Sep 2017
Eur	59:13	Julien WANDERS	SUI	Ras Al Khaimah	8 Feb 2019
SAm	59:33	Marilson dos SANTOS	BRA	Udine	14 Oct 2007
NAm	59:43	Ryan HALL	USA	Houston	14 Jan 2007

Oce	59:47	Zane ROBERTSON	NZL	Marugame	1 Feb 2015
CAC	60:14	Armando QUINTANILLA	MEX	Tokyo	21 Jan 1996
W20	59:16	Samuel WANJIRU	KEN	Rotterdam	11 Sep 2005
W18	60:38	Faustin BAHA Sulle	TAN	Lille	4 Sep 1999

MARATHON

W, Afr, Com	2:01:39	Eliud KIPCHOGE	KEN	Berlin	16 Sep 2018
Asi	2:04:43	El Hassan EL ABBASSI	BRN	Valencia	2 Dec 2018
Eur	2:05:11	Mohamed FARAH	GBR	Chicago	7 Oct 2018
NAm	2:05:38	Khalid KHANNOUCHI (ex MAR)	USA	London	14 Apr 2002
SAm	2:06:05	Ronaldo da COSTA	BRA	Berlin	20 Sep 1998
Oce	2:08:16	Steve MONEGHETTI	AUS	Berlin	30 Sep 1990
CAC	2:08:30	Dionicio CERÓN	MEX	London	2 Apr 1995
W20	2:04:32	Tsegaye MEKONNEN	ETH	Dubai	24 Jan 2014
W18	2:11:43	LI He	CHN	Beijing	14 Oct 2001

3000 METRES STEEPLECHASE

W, Asi	7:53.63	Saïf Saaeed SHAHEEN	QAT	Bruxelles	3 Sep 2004
Afr, Com	7:53.64	Brimin KIPRUTO	KEN	Monaco	22 Jul 2011
Eur	8:00.09	Mahiedine MEKHISSI-BENABBAD	FRA	Saint-Denis	6 Jul 2013
NAm	8:00.45	Evan JAGER	USA	Saimt-Denis	4 Jul 2015
Oce	8:14.05	Peter RENNER	NZL	Koblenz	29 Aug 1984
SAm	8:14.41	Wander MOURA	BRA	Mar del Plata	22 Mar 1995
CAC	8:25.69	Salvador MIRANDA	MEX	Barakaldo	8 Jul 2000
W20	7:58.66	Stephen CHERONO (now Shaheen)	KEN	Bruxelles	24 Aug 2001
W18	8:12.28	Getnet WALE	ETH	Hengelo	11 Jun 2017

110 METRES HURDLES

W, NAm	12.80	Aries MERRITT	USA	Bruxelles	7 Sep 2012
CAC	12.87	Dayron ROBLES	CUB	Ostrava	12 Jun 2008
Asi	12.88	LIU Xiang	CHN	Lausanne	11 Jul 2006
Com	12.90	Omar McLEOD	JAM	Kingston	24 Jun 2017
Eur	12.91	Colin JACKSON	GBR/Wal	Stuttgart	20 Aug 1993
Afr	13.11	Antonio ALKANA	RSA	Praha	5 Jun 2017
SAm	13.23	Gabriel CONSTANTINO	BRA	Montreuil	19 Jun 2018
Oce	13.29	Kyle VANDER-KUYP	AUS	Göteborg	11 Aug 1995
W20	13.12	LIU Xiang (with 3'6" hurdles)	CHN	Lausanne	2 Jul 2002
W20 99cm h	12.99	Wilhem BELOCIAN	FRA	Eugene	24 Jul 2014
	12.99	Damion THOMAS	JAM	Kingston	23 Jun 2018
W18	13.43	SHI Dongpeng	CHN	Shanghai	6 May 2001
W18 91cm h	12.96	Jaheel HYDE	JAM	Nanjing	23 Aug 2014

400 METRES HURDLES

W, NAm	46.78	Kevin YOUNG	USA	Barcelona	6 Aug 1992
Asi	46.98	Abderrahman SAMBA	QAT	Paris (C)	30 Jun 2018
CAC, Com	47.02	Rai BENJAMIN	ANT	Eugene	8 Jun 2018
Afr	47.10	Samuel MATETE	ZAM	Zürich	7 Aug 1991
Eur	47.37	Stéphane DIAGANA	FRA	Lausanne	5 Jul 1995
SAm	47.84	Bayano KAMANI	PAN	Helsinki	7 Aug 2005
Oce	48.28	Rohan ROBINSON	AUS	Atlanta	31 Jul 1996
W20	48.02	Danny HARRIS	USA	Los Angeles	17 Jun 1984
W18	48.89	L.J. VAN ZYL	RSA	Kingston	19 Jul 2002
W18 84cm	48.844	Zazini SOKWAKHANA	RSA	Pretoria	17 Mar 2017

HIGH JUMP

W, CAC	2.45	Javier SOTOMAYOR	CUB	Salamanca	27 Jul 1993
Asi	2.43	Mutaz Essa BARSHIM	QAT	Bruxelles	5 Sep 2014
Eur	2.42	Patrik SJÖBERG	SWE	Stockholm	30 Jun 1987
	2.42 i§	Carlo THRÄNHARDT	FRG	Berlin	26 Feb 1988
	2.42i	Ivan UKHOV	RUS	Praha	25 Feb 2014
	2.42	Bohdan BONDARENKO	UKR	New York	14 Jun 2014
NAm	2.40 i§	Holis CONWAY	USA	Sevilla	10 Mar 1991
	2.40	Charles AUSTIN	USA	Zürich	7 Aug 1991
NAm=, Com	2.40	Derek DROUIN	CAN	Des Moines	25 Apr 2014
Afr	2.38	Jacques FREITAG	RSA	Oudtshoorn	5 Mar 2005
Oce	2.36	Tim FORSYTH	AUS	Melbourne	2 Mar 1997
	2.36	Brandon STARC	AUS	Eberstadt	26 Aug 2018
SAm	2.33	Gilmar MAYO	COL	Pereira	17 Oct 1994
W20	2.37	Dragutin TOPIC	YUG	Plovdiv	12 Aug 1990
		Steve SMITH	GBR	Seoul	20 Sep 1992
W18	2.33	Javier SOTOMAYOR	CUB	La Habana	19 May 1984

POLE VAULT

W, Eur	6.16 i	Renaud LAVILLENIE	FRA	Donetsk	15 Feb 2014
	6.14 A	Sergey BUBKA (best outdoor mark)	UKR	Sestriere	31 Jul 1994
Oce, Com	6.06i	Steve HOOKER	AUS	Boston (R)	7 Feb 2009
	6.05	Dmitriy MARKOV	AUS	Edmonton	9 Aug 2001
NAm	6.04	Brad WALKER	USA	Eugene	8 Jun 2008
Afr	6.03	Okkert BRITS	RSA	Köln	18 Aug 1995
Asi	5.92i	Igor POTAPOVICH	KAZ	Stockholm	19 Feb 1998
	5.90	Grigoriy YEGOROV	KAZ	Stuttgart 19 Aug 1993 & London (CP)	10 Sep 1993
	5.90	Igor POTAPOVICH	KAZ	Nice	10 Jul 1996
SAm	6.03	Thiago BRAZ da SILVA	BRA	Rio de Janeiro	15 Aug 2016
CAC	5.90	Lázaro BORGES	CUB	Daegu	29 Aug 2011
W20	6.05	Armand DUPLANTIS	SWE	Berlin	12 Aug 2018
W18	5.55	Emmanouíl KARALÍS	GRE	Ostrava	20 May 2016

LONG JUMP

W, NAm	8.95	Mike POWELL	USA	Tokyo	30 Aug 1991
Eur	8.86 A	Robert EMMIYAN	ARM	Tsakhkadzor	22 May 1987
SAm	8.73	Irving SALADINO	PAN	Hengelo	24 May 2008
CAC	8.71	Iván PEDROSO	CUB	Salamanca	18 Jul 1995
Afr, Com	8.65A	Luvo MANYONGA	RSA	Potchefstroom	22 Apr 2017
Oce	8.54	Mitchell WATT	AUS	Stockholm	29 Jul 2011
Asi	8.48	Mohamed Salim AL-KHUWALIDI	KSA	Sotteville	2 Jul 2006
W20	8.35	Sergey MORGUNOV	RUS	Cheboksary	20 Jun 2012
W18	8.28	Maykel D MASSÓ	CUB	La Habana	28 May 2016

TRIPLE JUMP

W, Eur, Com	18.29	Jonathan EDWARDS	GBR/Eng	Göteborg	7 Aug 1995
NAm	18.21	Christian TAYLOR	USA	Beijing	27 Aug 2015
CAC	18.08	Pedro Pablo PICHARDO	CUB	La Habana	28 May 2015
SAm	17.90	Jadel GREGÓRIO	BRA	Belém	20 May 2007
Asi	17.59	LI Yanxi	CHN	Jinan	26 Oct 2009
Oce	17.46	Ken LORRAWAY	AUS	London (CP)	7 Aug 1982
Afr	17.37	Tareq BOUGTAÏB	MAR	Khémisset	14 Jul 2007
W20	17.50	Volker MAI	GDR	Erfurt	23 Jun 1985
W18	17.41	Jordan A. DIAZ	CUB	La Habana	8 Jun 2018

SHOT

W, NAm	23.12	Randy BARNES	USA	Los Angeles (Westwood)	20 May 1990
Eur	23.06	Ulf TIMMERMANN	GER	Haniá	22 May 1988
Oce, Com	22.67	Tom WALSH	NZL	Auckland (Waitakere)	25 Mar 2018
Com	22.21	Dylan ARMSTRONG	CAN	Calgary	25 Jun 2011
SAm	22.00	Darlan ROMANI	BRA	Bragança Paulista	15 Sep 1208
AfC	21.97	Janus ROBBERTS	RSA	Eugene	2 Jun 2001
CAC	21.96	O'Dayne RICHARDS	JAM	Rabat	16 Jul 2017
Asi	21.13	Sultan Abdulmajeed AL-HEBSHI	KSA	Doha	8 May 2009
W20	21.14	Konrad BUKOWIECKI	POL	Oslo	9 Jun 2016
W18	20.38	Jacko GILL	NZL	Auckland (North Shore)	5 Dec 2011
W20 6kg	23.34	Konrad BUKOWIECKI	POL	Bydgoszcz	19 Jul 2016
W18 5kg	24.45	Jacko GILL	NZL	Auckland (North Shore)	19 Dec 2011

DISCUS

W, Eur	74.08	Jürgen SCHULT	GDR	Neubrandenburg	6 Jun 1986
NAm	72.34 ¶	Ben PLUCKNETT	USA	Stockholm	7 Jul 1981
	71.32 §	Ben PLUCKNETT	USA	Eugene	4 Jun 1983
CAC	71.06	Luis DELIS	CUB	La Habana	21 May 1983
Afr, Com	70.32	Frantz KRUGER	RSA	Salon-de-Provence	26 May 2002
Asi	69.32	Ehsan HADADI	IRI	Tallinn	3 Jun 2008
Oce	68.20	Benn HARRADINE	AUS	Townsville	10 May 2013
SAm	66.32	Jorge BALLIENGO	ARG	Rosario	15 Apr 2006
W20	65.62 §	Werner REITERER	AUS	Melbourne	15 Dec 1987
W18/20	65.31	Mykyta NESTERENKO	UKR	Tallinn	3 Jun 2008
W20 1.75kg	70.13	Mykyta NESTERENKO	UKR	Halle	24 May 2008
W18 1.5kg	77.50	Mykyta NESTERENKO	UKR	Koncha Zaspa	19 May 2008

¶ Disallowed by the IAAF following retrospective disqualification for drug abuse, but ratified by the AAU/TAC

HAMMER

W, Eur	86.74	Yuriy SEDYKH	UKR/RUS	Stuttgart	30 Aug 1986
Asi	84.86	Koji MUROFUSHI	JPN	Praha	29 Jun 2003
NAm	82.52	Lance DEAL	USA	Milano	7 Sep 1996

Afr	81.27	Mostafa Hicham AL-GAMAL	EGY	Al-Qáhira	21 Mar 2014
Com	80.63	Chris HARMSE	RSA	Durban	15 Apr 2005
Oce	79.29	Stuart RENDELL	AUS	Varazdin	6 Jul 2002
SAm	78.63	Wagner DOMINGOS	BRA	Celje	19 Jun 2016
CAC	78.02	Roberto JANET	CUB	La Habana	28 May 2015
W20	78.33	Olli-Pekka KARJALAINEN	FIN	Seinäjoki	5 Aug 1999
W18	73.66	Vladislav PISKUNOV	UKR	Kyiv	11 Jun 1994
W20 6kg	85.57	Ashraf Amgad EL-SEIFY	QAT	Barcelona	14 Jul 2012
W18 5kg	87.82	Myhaylo KOKHAN	UKR	Györ	7 Jul 2018

JAVELIN

W, Eur	98.48	Jan ZELEZNY	CZE	Jena	25 May 1996
Afr, Com	92.72	Julius YEGO	KEN	Beijing	26 Aug 2015
Asi	91.36	CHENG Chao-Tsun	TPE	Taipei	26 Aug 2017
NAm	91.29	Breaux GREER	USA	Indianapolis	21 Jun 2007
CAC	90.16	Keshorn WALCOTT	TTO	Lausanne	9 Jul 2015
Oce	89.02	Jarrod BANNISTER	AUS	Brisbane	29 Feb 2008
SAm	84.70	Edgar BAUMANN	PAR	San Marcos	17 Oct 1999
W20	86.48	Neeraj CHOPRA	IND	Bydgoszcz	23 Jul 2016
W18 700g	89.34	Braian Ezequiel TOLEDO	ARG	Mar del Plata	6 Mar 2010

DECATHLON

W, Eur	9126	Kevin MAYER	FRA	Talence	16 Sep 2018
NAm	9045	Ashton EATON	USA	Beijing	29 Aug 2015
Com	8847	Daley THOMPSON	GBR/Eng	Los Angeles	9 Aug 1984
Asi	8725	Dmitriy KARPOV	KAZ	Athína	24 Aug 2004
CAC	8654	Leonel SUÁREZ	CUB	La Habana	4 Jul 2009
Afr	8521	Larbi BOURAADA	ALG	Rio de Janeiro	18 Aug 2016
Oce	8490	Jagan HAMES	AUS	Kuala Lumpur	18 Sep 1998
SAm	8393	Carlos Eduardo CHININ	BRA	São Paulo	8 Jun 2013
W20 Jnr spec	8435	Niklas KAUL	GER	Grosseto	20 Jul 2017
Snr spec	8397	Torsten VOSS	GDR	Erfurt	7 Jul 1982
W18	8104h	Valter KÜLVET	EST	Viimsi	23 Aug 1981
	7829	Valter KÜLVET	EST	Stockholm	13 Sep 1981

4 X 100 METRES RELAY

W, CAC, Com	36.84	JAM (Carter, M Frater, Blake, Bolt)		London (OS)	11 Aug 2012
NAm	37.38	USA (Demps, Patton, Kimmons, Gatlin)		London (OS)	10 Aug 2012
	37.38	USA (Rodgers, Gatlin, Gay, Bailey)		Nassau	2 May 2015
Eur	37.47	GBR (Ujah, Gemili, Talbot, Mitchell-Blake)		London (OS)	12 Aug 2017
Asi	37.60	JPN (Yamagata, Iizuka, Kiryu, Cambridge)		Rio de Janeiro	19 Aug 2016
SAm	37.90	BRA (V Lima, Ribeiro, A da Silva, Cl da Silva)		Sydney	30 Sep 2000
Afr	37.94	NGR (O Ezinwa, Adeniken, Obikwelu, D Ezinwa)		Athína	9 Aug 1997
Oce	38.11	AUS (Henderson, Jackson, Brimacombe, Marsh)		Göteborg	12 Aug 1995
	38.17	AUS (Alozie, Ntiamoah, McCabe, Ross)		Ldon (OS)	10 Aug 2012
W20	38.66	USA (Kimmons, Omole, Williams, Merritt)		Grosseto	18 Jul 2004
W18	39.97	JAM (Everett, Wilson, Powell, Stephens)		Willemstad	16 Apr 2017

4 X 400 METRES RELAY

W, NAm	2:54.29	USA (Valmon, Watts, Reynolds, Johnson)		Stuttgart	22 Aug 1993
Eur	2:56.60	GBR (Thomas, Baulch, Richardson, Black)		Atlanta	3 Aug 1996
CAC, Com	2:56.72	BAH (Brown, Pinder, Mathieu, Miller)		London (OS)	10 Aug 2012
SAm	2:58.56	BRA (C da Silva, A J dosSantos, de Araujo, Parrela)		Winnipeg	30 Jul 1999
Afr	2:58.68	NGR (Chukwu, Monye, Bada, Udo-Obong)		Sydney	30 Sep 2000
Oce	2:59.70	AUS (Frayne, Clark, Minihan, Mitchell)		Los Angeles	11 Aug 1984
Asi	3:00.56	QAT (Samba, Abbas, Youssef, Haroun i)		Jakarta	30 Aug 2018
W20	3:01.09	USA (Johnson, Merritt, Craig, Clement)		Grosseto	18 Jul 2004
W18	3:11.66A	TTO (Guevara, Cedenio, Walters, Lewis)		Morelia	1 Jul 2012

20 KILOMETRES WALK

W, Asi	1:16:36	Yusuke SUZUKI	JPN	Nomi	15 Mar 2015
Eur	1:17:02	Yohann DINIZ	FRA	Arles	8 Mar 2015
	1:16:43 §	Sergey MOROZOV	RUS	Saransk	8 Jun 2008
SAm	1:17:21	Jefferson PÉREZ	ECU	Saint-Denis	23 Aug 2003
CAC	1:17:25.6 t	Bernardo SEGURA	MEX	Bergen (Fana)	7 May 1994
Oce, Com	1:17:33	Nathan DEAKES	AUS	Cixi	23 Apr 2005
Afr	1:19:02	Hatem GHOULA	TUN	Eisenhüttenstadt	10 May 1997
NAm	1:19:20	Inaki GÓMEZ	CAN	Nomi	20 Mar 2016
W20	1:17:25 §	Sergey SHIROBOKOV	RUS	Cheboksary	9 Jun 2018
W18	1:18:07	LI Gaobo	CHN	Cixi	23 Apr 2005

20,000 METRES TRACK WALK

W, CAC	1:17:25.6	Bernardo SEGURA	MEX	Bergen (Fana)	7 May 1994
Asi	1:18:03.3	BU Lingtang	CHN	Beijing	7 Apr 1994
Eur	1:18:35.2	Stefan JOHANSSON	SWE	Bergen (Fana)	15 May 1992
Oce, Com	1:19:48.1	Nathan DEAKES	AUS	Brisbane	4 Sep 2001
SAm	1:20:23.8	Andrés CHOCHO	ECU	Buenos Aires	5 Jun 2011
NAm	1:21:57.0	Evan DUNFEE	CAN	Moncton	27 Jun 2014
Afr	1:22:51.84	Hatem GHOULA	TUN	Leutkirch	8 Sep 1994
W20	1:20:11.72	LI Gaobo	CHN	Wuhan	2 Nov 2007
W18	1:24:28.3	ZHU Hongjun	CHN	Xian	15 Sep 1999

50 KILOMETRES WALK

W, Eur	3:32:33	Yohann DINIZ	FRA	Zürich	15 Aug 2014
Oce, Com	3:35:47	Nathan DEAKES	AUS	Geelong	2 Dec 2006
Asi	3:36:06	YU Chaohong	CHN	Nanjing	22 Oct 2005
CAC	3:41:09	Erick BARRONDO	GUA	Dudince	23 Mar 2013
NAm	3:41:38	Evan DUNFEE	CAN	Rio de Janeiro	19 Aug 2016
SAm	3:42:57	Andrés CHOCHO	ECU	Ciudad Juárez	6 Mar 2016
Afr	3:54:12	Marc MUNDELL	RSA	Melbourne	13 Dec 2015
W20	3:41:10	ZHAO Jianguo	CHN	Wajima	16 Apr 2006
W18	3:45:46	YU Guoping	CHN	Guangzhou	23 Nov 2001

50,000 METRES TRACK WALK

W, Eur	3:35:27.2	Yoahnn DINIZ	FRA	Reims	12 Mar 2011
CAC	3:41:38.4	Raúl GONZÁLEZ	MEX	Bergen (Fana)	25 May 1979
Oce, Com	3:43:50.0	Simon BAKER	AUS	Melbourne	9 Sep 1990
Asi	3:48:13.7	ZHAO Yongshen	CHN	Bergen (Fana)	7 May 1994
NAm	3:52:21.0	Tim BERRETT	CAN	Victoria	29 Oct 2000
SAm	3:57:58.0	Claudio dos SANTOS	BRA	Blumenau	20 Sep 2008
Afr	4:21:44.5	Abdelwahab FERGUÈNE	ALG	Toulouse	25 Mar 1984

World Records at other men's events recognised by the IAAF

20,000m	56:25.98+	Haile GEBRSELASSIE	ETH	Ostrava	27 Jun 2007
1 Hour	21,285 m	Haile GEBRSELASSIE	ETH	Ostrava	27 Jun 2007
25,000m	1:12:25.4	Moses MOSOP	KEN	Eugene	3 Jun 2011
30,000m	1:26:47.4	Moses MOSOP	KEN	Eugene	3 Jun 2011
U18 Octathlon	6491	Jake STEIN	AUS	Villeneuve d'Ascq	7 Jul 2011
4 x 200m	1:18.63	National team	JAM	Nassau	24 May 2014
		(Nickel Ashmeade, Warren Weir, Jermaine Brown, Yohan Blake)			
4 x 800m	7:02.43	National Team	KEN	Bruxelles	25 Aug 2006
		(Joseph Mutua, William Yiampoy, Ismael Kombich, Wilfred Bungei)			
4 x 1500m	14:22.22	C Cheboi, A Kiplagat, Magut, A Kiprop	KEN	Nassau	25 May 2014
Distance Medley	9:15.50	Merber,Spratting,Johnson,Blankenship	USA	Nassau	3 May 2015
Walking					
2 Hours track	29,572m+	Maurizio DAMILANO	ITA	Cuneo	3 Oct 1992
30km track	2:01:44.1	Maurizio DAMILANO	ITA	Cuneo	3 Oct 1992
U20 10,000m track	38:46.4	Viktor BURAYEV	RUS	Moskva	20 May 2000
U20 10km road	37:44	WANG Zhen	CHN	Beijing	18 Sep 2010
W18 10km road	38:57	LI Tianlei	CHN	Beijing	18 Sep 2010

WOMEN

100 METRES

W, NAm	10.49	Florence GRIFFITH JOYNER	USA	Indianapolis	16 Jul 1988
CAC, Com	10.70	Shelly-Ann FRASER	JAM	Kingston	29 Jun 2012
	10.70	Elaine THOMPSON	JAM	Kingston	1 Jul 2016
Eur	10.73	Christine ARRON	FRA	Budapest	19 Aug 1998
Afr	10.78	Murielle AHOURÉ	CIV	Montverde	11 Jun 2016
Asi	10.79	LI Xuemei	CHN	Shanghai	18 Oct 1997
SAm	10.91	Rosângela SANTOS	BRA	London (OS)	6 Aug 2017
Oce	11.11	Melissa BREEN	AUS	Canberra	9 Feb 2014
W20	10.88	Marlies OELSNER/GÖHR	GDR	Dresden	1 Jul 1977
W18	10.98	Candace HILL	USA	Shoreline	20 Jun 2015

200 METRES

W, NAm	21.34	Florence GRIFFITH JOYNER	USA	Seoul	29 Sep 1988
Eur	21.63	Dafne SCHIPPERS	NED	Beijing	28 Aug 2015
CAC, Com	21.64	Merlene OTTEY	JAM	Bruxelles	13 Sep 1991
Asi	22.01	LI Xuemei	CHN	Shanghai	22 Oct 1997
Afr	22.04	Blessing OKAGBARE	NGR	Abilene	24 Mar 2018
Oce	22.23	Melinda GAINSFORD-TAYLOR	AUS	Stuttgart	13 Jul 1997

SAm	22.48	Ana Cláudia da SILVA	BRA	São Paulo	6 Aug 2011
W20	22.18	Allyson FELIX	USA	Athína	25 Aug 2004
	22.11A §	Allyson FELIX (no doping control)	USA	Ciudad de México	3 May 2003
W18	22.43A	Candace HILL	USA	Cali	19 Jul 2015

400 METRES

W, Eur	47.60	Marita KOCH	GDR	Canberra	6 Oct 1985
Oce, Com	48.63	Cathy FREEMAN	AUS	Atlanta	29 Jul 1996
NAm	48.70	Sanya RICHARDS	USA	Athína	16 Sep 2006
CAC	48.89	Ana GUEVARA	MEX	Saint-Denis	27 Aug 2003
Asi	49.08	Salwa Eid NASER	BRN	Monaco	20 Jul 2018
Afr	49.10	Falilat OGUNKOYA	NGR	Atlanta	29 Jul 1996
SAm	49.64	Ximena RESTREPO	COL	Barcelona	5 Aug 1992
W20	49.42	Grit BREUER	GER	Tokyo	27 Aug 1991
W18	50.01	LI Jing	CHN	Shanghai	18 Oct 1997

800 METRES

W, Eur	1:53.28	Jarmila KRATOCHVÍLOVÁ	CZE	München	26 Jul 1983
Afr,W20,Com	1:54.01	Pamela JELIMO	KEN	Zürich	29 Aug 2008
CAC	1:54.44	Ana Fidelia QUIROT	CUB	Barcelona	9 Sep 1989
Asi	1:55.54	LIU Dong	CHN	Beijing	9 Sep 1993
NAm	1:55.61	Ajee' WILSON	USA	Monaco	21 Jul 2017
SAm	1:56.68	Letitia VRIESDE	SUR	Göteborg	13 Aug 1995
Oce	1:58.25	Toni HODGKINSON	NZL	Atlanta	27 Jul 1996
W18	1:57.18	WANG Yuan	CHN	Beijing	8 Sep 1993

1000 METRES

W, Eur	2:28.98	Svetlana MASTERKOVA	RUS	Bruxelles	23 Aug 1996
Afr	2:29.34	Maria Lurdes MUTOLA	MOZ	Bruxelles	25 Aug 1995
Com	2:29.66	Maria Lurdes MUTOLA	MOZ	Bruxelles	23 Aug 1996
NAm	2:31.80	Regina JACOBS	USA	Brunswick	3 Jul 1999
SAm	2:32.25	Letitia VRIESDE	SUR	Berlin	10 Sep 1991
CAC	2:33.21	Ana Fidelia QUIROT	CUB	Jerez de la Frontera	13 Sep 1989
Asi	2:33.6 §	Svetlana ULMASOVA	UZB	Podolsk	5 Aug 1979
	2:40.53	ZHAO Jing	CHN	Changbaishan	2 Sep 2014
Oce	2:37.28	Angie PETTY	NZL	Chiba	15 Aug 2015
W20	2:35.4a	Irina NIKITINA	RUS	Podolsk	5 Aug 1979
	2:35.4	Katrin WÜHN	GDR	Potsdam	12 Jul 1984
W18	2:38.58	Jo WHITE	GBR	London (CP)	9 Sep 1977

1500 METRES

W, Afr	3:50.07	Genzebe DIBABA	ETH	Monaco	17 Jul 2015
Asi	3:50.46	QU Yunxia	CHN	Beijing	11 Sep 1993
Eur	3:52.47	Tatyana KAZANKINA	RUS	Zürich	13 Aug 1980
Com	3:55.22	Laura MUIR	Sco/GBR	Saint-Denis	27 Aug 2016
NAm	3:56.29	Shannon ROWBURY	USA	Monaco	17 Jul 2015
Oce	4:00.86	Linden HALL	AUS	London (OS)	22 Jul 2018
CAC	4:01.84	Yvonne GRAHAM	JAM	Monaco	25 Jul 1995
SAm	4:05.67	Letitia VRIESDE	SUR	Tokyo	31 Aug 1991
W20	3:51.34	LANG Yinglai	CHN	Shanghai	18 Oct 1997
W18	3:54.52	ZHANG Ling	CHN	Shanghai	18 Oct 1997

1 MILE

W, Eur	4:12.56	Svetlana MASTERKOVA	RUS	Zürich	14 Aug 1996
Afr	4:14.30	Genzebe DIBABA	ETH	Rovereto	6 Sep 2016
Com	4:16.15	Hellen OBIRI	KEN	London (OS)	22 Jul 2018
NAm	4:16.71	Mary SLANEY	USA	Zürich	21 Aug 1985
Asi	4:17.75	Maryam Yusuf JAMAL	BRN	Bruxelles	14 Sep 2007
Oce	4:21.40	Linden HALL	AUS	London (OS)	22 Jul 2018
CAC	4:24.64	Yvonne GRAHAM	JAM	Zürich	17 Aug 1994
SAm	4:30.05	Soraya TELLES	BRA	Praha	9 Jun 1988
W20	4:17.57	Zola BUDD	GBR	Zürich	21 Aug 1985
W18	4:30.81	Gelete BURKA	ETH	Heusden	2 Aug 2003

2000 METRES

W, Eur	5:25.36	Sonia O'SULLIVAN	IRL	Edinburgh	8 Jul 1994
Com	5:26.93	Yvonne MURRAY	GBR/Sco	Edinburgh	8 Jul 1994
Afr	5:27.50	Genzebe DIBABA	ETH	Ostrava	17 Jun 2014
Asi	5:29.43+§	WANG Junxia	CHN	Beijing	12 Sep 1993
	5:31.88	Maryam Yusuf JAMAL	BRN	Eugene	7 Jun 2009
NAm	5:32.7	Mary SLANEY	USA	Eugene	3 Aug 1984

Oce	5:37.71	Benita JOHNSON	AUS	Ostrava	12 Jun 2003
W20	5:33.15	Zola BUDD	GBR	London (CP)	13 Jul 1984
W18	5:46.5+	Sally BARSOSIO	KEN	Zürich	16 Aug 1995

3000 METRES

W, Asi	8:06.11	WANG Junxia	CHN	Beijing	13 Sep 1993
Afr, Com	8:20.68	Hellen OBIRI	KEN	Doha	9 May 2014
Eur	8:21.42	Gabriela SZABO	ROU	Monaco	19 Jul 2002
NAm	8:25.83	Mary SLANEY	USA	Roma	7 Sep 1985
Oce	8:35.31	Kimberley SMITH	NZL	Monaco	25 Jul 2007
CAC	8:37.07	Yvonne GRAHAM	JAM	Zürich	16 Aug 1995
SAm	9:02.37	Delirde BERNARDI	BRA	Linz	4 Jul 1994
W20	8:28.83	Zola BUDD	GBR	Roma	7 Sep 1985
W18	8:36.45	MA Ningning	CHN	Jinan	6 Jun 1993

5000 METRES

W, Afr	14:11.15	Tirunesh DIBABA	ETH	Oslo	6 Jun 2008
Com	14:18.37	Hellen OBIRI	KEN	Roma	8 Jun 2017
Eur	14:22.34	Sifan HASSAN	NED	Rabat	13 Jul 2018
Asi	14:28.09	JIANG Bo	CHN	Shanghai	23 Oct 1997
NAm	14:34.45	Shelby HOULIHAN	USA	Heusden-Zolder	21 Jul 2018
Oce	14:45.93	Kimberley SMITH	NZL	Roma	11 Jul 2008
CAC	15:04.32	Adriana FERNÁNDEZ	MEX	Gresham	17 May 2003
SAm	15:18.85	Simone Alves da SILVA	BRA	São Paulo	20 May 2011
W20	14:30.88	Tirunesh DIBABA	ETH	Bergen (Fana)	11 Jun 2004
W18	14:45.71	SONG Liqing	CHN	Shanghai	21 Oct 1997

10,000 METRES

W, Afr	29:17.45	Almaz AYANA	ETH	Rio de Janeiro	12 Aug 2016
Asi	29:31.78	WANG Junxia	CHN	Beijing	8 Sep 1993
Com	29:32.53	Vivian CHERUIYOT	KEN	Rio de Janeiro	12 Aug 2016
Eur	30:01.09	Paula RADCLIFFE	GBR	München	6 Aug 2002
NAm	30:13.17	Molly HUDDLE	USA	Rio de Janeiro	12 Aug 2016
Oce	30:35.54	Kimberley SMITH	NZL	Stanford	4 May 2008
CAC	31:10.12	Adriana FERNANDEZ	MEX	Brunswick	1 Jul 2000
SAm	31:47.76	Carmen de OLIVEIRA	BRA	Stuttgart	21 Aug 1993
W20	30:26.50	Linet MASAI	KEN	Beijing	15 Aug 2008
W18	31:11.26	SONG Liqing	CHN	Shanghai	19 Oct 1997

HALF MARATHON

W, Afr, Com	64:51	Joyciline JEPKOSGEI	KEN	Valencia	22 Oct 2017
Eur	65:15	Sifan HASSAN	NED	København	16 Sep 2018
Asi	65:22	Violah JEPCHUMBA	BRN	Praha	1 Apr 2017
Oce	67:11	Kimberley SMITH	NZL	Philadelphia	18 Sep 2011
NAm	67:25	Molly HUDDLE	USA	Houston	14 Jan 2018
CAC	68:34 dh	Olga APPELL	MEX	Tokyo	24 Jan 1993
	69:28	Adriana FERNÁNDEZ	MEX	Kyoto	9 Mar 2003
SAm	70:14	Gladys TEJEDA	PER	Cardiff	26 Mar 2016
W20	66:47	Degitu AZIMERAW	ETH	Ras Al Khaimah	9 Feb 2018
W18	72:31	LIU Zhuang	CHN	Yangzhou	24 Apr 2011

MARATHON

W, Eur, Com	2:15:25	Paula RADCLIFFE	GBR/Eng	London	13 Apr 2003
Wo only, Afr	2:17:01	Mary KEITANY	KEN	London	23 Apr 2017
Asi	2:19:12	Mizuki NOGUCHI	JPN	Berlin	25 Sep 2005
NAm	2:19:36	Deena KASTOR	USA	London	23 Apr 2006
Oce	2:22:36	Benita JOHNSON	AUS	Chicago	22 Oct 2006
CAC	2:22:59	Madai PÉREZ	MEX	Chicago	22 Oct 2006
SAm	2:26:48	Inés MELCHOR	PER	Berlin	28 Sep 2014
W20	2:20:59	Shure DEMISE	ETH	Dubai	23 Jan 2015

3000 METRES STEEPLECHASE

W, Afr, Com	8:44.32	Beatrice CHEPKOECH	KEN	Monaco	20 Jul 2018
Asi	8:52.78	Ruth JEBET	BRN	Sant-Denis	27 Aug 2016
Eur	8:58.81	Gulnara GALKINA	RUS	Beijing	17 Aug 2008
NAm	9:00.85	Courtney FRERICHS	USA	Monaco	20 Jul 2018
CAC	9:14.09	Aisha PRAUGHT LEER	JAM	Bruxelles	31 Aug 2018
Oce	9:14.28	Genevieve LaCAZE	AUS	Saint-Denis	27 Aug 2016
SAm	9:25.99	Belén CASETTA	ARG	London (OS)	11 Aug 2017
W20	8:58.78	Celliphine CHESPOL	KEN	Eugene	26 May 2017
W18	9:24.73	Celliphine CHESPOL	KEN	Shanghai	14 May 2016

100 METRES HURDLES

W, NAm	12.20	Kendra HARRISON	USA	London (OS)	22 Jul 2016
Eur	12.21	Yordanka DONKOVA	BUL	Stara Zagora	20 Aug 1988
Oce, Com	12.28	Sally PEARSON	AUS	Daegu	3 Sep 2011
CAC	12.40	Jasmine CAMACHO-QUINN	PUR	Knoxville	13 May 2018
Asi	12.44	Olga SHISHIGINA	KAZ	Luzern	27 Jun 1995
Afr	12.44	Glory ALOZIE NGR Monaco 8 Aug 1998, Bruxelles 28 Aug 1998, Sevilla 28 Aug 1999				
SAm	12.67	Yvette LEWIS	PAN	Lahti	17 Jul 2013
W20	12.74 §	Dior HALL	USA	Eugene	13 Jun 2015
W18	12.84	Tia JONES	USA	Clovis	25 Jun 2016

400 METRES HURDLES

Eur, W	52.34	Yuliya PECHONKINA	RUS	Tula	8 Aug 2003
CAC, Com	52.42	Melaine WALKER	JAM	Berlin	20 Aug 2009
NAm	52.47	Lashinda DEMUS	USA	Daegu	1 Sep 2011
Afr	52.90	Nezha BIDOUANE	MAR	Sevilla	25 Aug 1999
Oce	53.17	Debbie FLINTOFF-KING	AUS	Seoul	28 Sep 1988
Asi	53.96	HAN Qing	CHN	Beijing	9 Sep 1993
	53.96	SONG Yinglan	CHN	Guangzhou	22 Nov 2001
SAm	55.76	Gianna WOODRUFF	PAN	Tucson	20 May 2017
W20	52.75	Sydney McLAUGHLIN	USA	Knoxville	13 May 2018
W18	54.15	Sydney McLAUGHLIN	USA	Eugene	10 Jul 2016

HIGH JUMP

W, Eur	2.09	Stefka KOSTADINOVA	BUL	Roma	30 Aug 1987
Afr, Com	2.06	Hestrie CLOETE	RSA	Saint-Denis	31 Aug 2003
NAm	2.05	Chaunté HOWARD-LOWE	USA	Des Moines	26 Jun 2010
CAC	2.04	Silvia COSTA	CUB	Barcelona	9 Sep 1989
Asi	1.99	Marina AITOVA	KAZ	Athína	13 Jul 2009
Oce	1 98	Vanessa WARD	AUS	Perth	12 Feb 1989
	1.00	Alison INVERARITY	AUO	Ingolstadt	17 Jul 1994
SAm	1.96	Solange WITTEVEEN	ARG	Oristano	8 Sep 1997
W20	2.01	Olga TURCHAK	KAZ	Moskva	7 Jul 1986
	2.01	Heike BALCK	GDR	Chemnitz	18 Jun 1989
W18	1.96A	Charmaine GALE	RSA	Bloemfontein	4 Apr 1981
	1.96	Olga TURCHAK	UKR	Donetsk	7 Sep 1984
	1.96	Eleanor PATTERSON	AUS	Townsville	7 Dec 2013
	1.96	Vashti CUNNINGHAM	USA	Edmonton	1 Aug 2015

POLE VAULT

W, Eur	5.06	Yelena ISINBAYEVA	RUS	Zürich	28 Aug 2009
NAm	5.03i	Jennifer SUHR	USA	Brockport	30 Jan 2016
	5.00	Sandi MORRIS	USA	Bruxelles	9 Sep 2016
Com, Oce	4.94	Eliza McCARTNEY	NZL	Jockgrim	17 Jul 2018
CAC	4.91	Yarisley SILVA	CUB	Beckum	2 Aug 2015
SAm	4.87	Fabiana MURER	BRA	São Bernardo do Campo 3 Jul 2016		
Asi	4.70i	LI Ling	CHN	Doha 19 Feb 2016 & 4.66 Wuhan 6 Jun 2015		
Afr	4.42	Elmarie GERRYTS	RSA	Wesel	12 Jun 2000
W20	4.71i	Wilma MURTO	FIN	Zweibrücken	31 Jan 2016
	4.64	Eliza McCARTNEY	NZL	Auckland	19 Dec 2015
W18	4.50	Lisa GUNNARSSON	SWE	Pézenas 28 May 2016 & Angers 25 Jun 2016		

LONG JUMP

W, Eur	7.52	Galina CHISTYAKOVA	RUS	Sankt-Peterburg	11 Jun 1988
NAm	7.49	Jackie JOYNER-KERSEE	USA	New York	22 May 1994
	7.49A §	Jackie JOYNER-KERSEE	USA	Sestriere	31 Jul 1994
SAm	7.26A	Maurren MAGGI	BRA	Bogotá	26 Jun 1999
CAC, Com	7.16A	Elva GOULBOURNE	JAM	Ciudad de México	22 May 2004
Afr	7.12	Chioma AJUNWA	NGR	Atlanta	1 Aug 1996
Oce	7.05	Brooke STRATTON	AUS	Perth	12 Mar 2016
Asi	7.01	YAO Weili	CHN	Jinan	5 Jun 1993
W20	7.14	Heike DAUTE/Drechsler	GDR	Bratislava	4 Jun 1983
W18	6.91	Heike DAUTE/Drechsler	GDR	Jena	9 Aug 1981

TRIPLE JUMP

W, Eur	15.50	Inessa KRAVETS	UKR	Göteborg	10 Aug 1995
Afr, Com	15.39	Françoise MBANGO Etone	CMR	Beijing	17 Aug 2008
SAm	15.31	Caterine IBARGÜEN	COL	Monaco	18 Jul 2014
CAC	15.29	Yamilé ALDAMA	CUB	Roma	11 Jul 2003
Asi	15.25	Olga RYPAKOVA	KAZ	Split	4 Sep 2010

NAm	14.84	Tori FRANKLIN	USA	Baie Mahault	12 May 2018
Oce	14.04	Nicole MLADENIS	AUS	Hobart 9 Mar 2002 & Perth 7 Dec 2003	
W20	14.62	Tereza MARINOVA	BUL	Sydney	25 Aug 1996
W18	14.57	HUANG Qiuyan	CHN	Shanghai	19 Oct 1997

SHOT

W, Eur	22.63	Natalya LISOVSKAYA	RUS	Moskva	7 Jun 1987
Asi	21.76	LI Meisu	CHN	Shijiazhuang	23 Apr 1988
Oce, Com	21.24	Valerie ADAMS	NZL	Daegu	29 Aug 2011
CAC	20.96	Belsy LAZA	CUB	Ciudad de México	2 May 1992
NAm	20.63	Michelle CARTER	USA	Rio de Janeiro	12 Aug 2016
SAm	19.30	Elisângela ADRIANO	BRA	Tunja	14 Jul 2001
Afr	18.43	Vivian CHUKWUEMEKA	NGR	Walnut	19 Apr 2003
W20	20.54	Astrid KUMBERNUSS	GDR	Orimattila	1 Jul 1989
W18	19.08	Ilke WYLUDDA	GDR	Karl-Marx-Stadt	9 Aug 1986

DISCUS

W, Eur	76.80	Gabriele REINSCH	GDR	Neubrandenburg	9 Jul 1988
Asi	71.68	XIAO Yanling	CHN	Beijing	14 Mar 1992
CAC	70.88	Hilda RAMOS	CUB	La Habana	8 May 1992
Oce, Com	69.64	Dani STEVENS	AUS	London (OS)	13 Aug 2017
NAm	69.17	Gia LEWIS-SMALWOOD	USA	Angers	30 Aug 2014
SAm	65.10	Andressa de MORAIS	BRA	Bragança Paulista	8 Jul 2018
Afr	64.87	Elizna NAUDE	RSA	Stellenbosch	2 Mar 2007
W20	74.40	Ilke WYLUDDA	GDR	Berlin	13 Sep 1988
W18	65.86	Ilke WYLUDDA	GDR	Neubrandenburg	1 Aug 1986

HAMMER

W, Eur	82.98	Anita WLODARCZYK	POL	Warszawa	28 Aug 2016
Asi	77.68	WANG Zheng	CHN	Chengdu	29 Mar 2014
NAm	78.12	DeAnna PRICE	USA	Des Moines	23 Jun 2018
CAC	76.62	Yipsi MORENO	CUB	Zagreb	9 Sep 2008
Com	75.73	Sultana FRIZELL	CAN	Tucson	22 May 2014
SAm	73.74	Jennifer DAHLGREN	ARG	Buenos Aires	10 Apr 2010
Oce	71.12	Bronwyn EAGLES	AUS	Adelaide	6 Feb 2003
Afr	69.70	Amy SÈNE	SEN	Forbach	25 May 2014
W20	73.24	ZHANG Wenxiu	CHN	Changsha	24 Jun 2005
W18	70.60	ZHANG Wenxiu	CHN	Nanning	5 Apr 2003
W18 3kg	76.04	Réka GYURÁTZ	HUN	Zalaegerszeg	23 Jun 2013

JAVELIN

W, Eur	72.28	Barbora SPOTÁKOVÁ	CZE	Stuttgart	13 Sep 2008
CAC	71.70	Osleidys MENÉNDEZ	CUB	Helsinki	14 Aug 2005
Afr, Com	69.35	Sunette VILJOEN	RSA	New York	9 Jun 2012
Asi	67.69	LU Huihui	CHN	Halle	26 May 2018
Oce	68.57	Kathryn MITCHELL	AUS	Melbourne	3 Mar 2018
NAm	66.67	Kara PATTERSON	USA	Des Moines	25 Jun 2010
SAm	63.84A	Flor Dennis RUIZ	COL	Cali	25 Jun 2016
W20	63.86	Yulenmis AGUILAR	CUB	Edmonton	2 Aug 2015
W18	62.93	XUE Juan	CHN	Changsha	27 Oct 2003

HEPTATHLON

W, NAm	7291	Jackie JOYNER-KERSEE	USA	Seoul	24 Sep 1988
Eur	7032	Carolina KLÜFT	SWE	Osaka	26 Aug 2007
Com	6955	Jessica ENNIS	GBR/Eng	London (OS)	4 Aug 2012
Asi	6942	Ghada SHOUAA	SYR	Götzis	26 May 1996
CAC	6742	Yorgelis RODRIGUEZ	CUB	Götzis	27 May 2018
Oce	6695	Jane FLEMMING	AUS	Auckland	28 Jan 1990
Afr	6423	Margaret SIMPSON	GHA	Götzis	29 May 2005
SAm	6285	Evelis AGUILAR	COL	Barranquilla	1 Aug 2018
W20	6542	Carolina KLÜFT	SWE	München	10 Aug 2002
W18	6185	SHEN Shengfei	CHN	Shanghai	18 Oct 1997
U18 spec	6221	Maria VICENTE	ESP	Györ	6 Jul 2018

DECATHLON

W, Eur	8358	Austra SKUJYTE	LTU	Columbia, MO	15 Apr 2005
Asi	7798 §	Irina NAUMENKO	KAZ	Talence	26 Sep 2004
NAm	7577 §	Tiffany LOTT-HOGAN	USA	Lage	10 Sep 2000
CAC	7245 §	Magalys GARCÍA	CUB	Wien	29 Jun 2002
Afr, Com	6915	Margaret SIMPSON	GHA	Réduit	19 Apr 2007

| SAm | 6570 | Andrea BORDALEJO | ARG | Rosario | 28 Nov 2004 |
| Oce | 6428 | Simone CARRÉ | AUS | Melbourne | 11 Mar 2012 |

4 X 100 METRES RELAY

W, NAm	40.82	USA (Madison, Felix, Knight, Jeter)		London (OS)	10 Aug 2012
CAC, Com	41.07	JAM (Campbell-Brown, Morrison, Thompson, Fraser-Pryce)		Beijing	29 Aug 2015
Eur	41.37	GDR (Gladisch, Rieger, Auerswald, Göhr)		Canberra	6 Oct 1985
Asi	42.20	Cichuan CHIN (Xiao Lin, Li Yali, Liu Xiaomei, Li Xuemei)		Changhai	20 Oct 1997
SAm	42.29	BRA (E dos Santos, Silva, Krasucki, R Santos)		Moskva	18 Aug 2013
Afr	42.39	NGR (Utondu, Idehen, Opara-Thompson, Onyali)		Barcelona	7 Aug 1992
Oce	42.99A	AUS (Massey, Broadrick, Lambert, Gainsford-Taylor)		Pietersburg	18 Mar 2000
W20	43.27	GER (Fehm, Kwadwo, Junk, Montag)		Grosseto	23 Jul 2017
W18	44.05	GDR (Koppetsch, Oelsner, Sinzel, Brehmer)		Athína	24 Aug 1975

4 X 400 METRES RELAY

W, Eur	3:15.17	URS (Ledovskaya, Nazarova, Pinigina, Bryzgina)		Seoul	1 Oct 1988
NAm	3:15.51	USA (D.Howard, Dixon, Brisco, Griffith Joyner)		Seoul	1 Oct 1988
CAC, Com	3.18.71	JAM (Whyte, Prendergast, N Williams-Mills, 3 Williams)		Daegu	3 Sep 2011
Afr	3:21.04	NGR (Bisi Afolabi, Yusuf, Opara, Ogunkoya)		Atlanta	3 Aug 1996
Oce	3:23.81	AUS (Peris, Lewis, Gainsford-Taylor, Freeman)		Sydney	30 Sep 2000
Asi	3:24.28	Hebei CHN (An X, Bai X, Cao C, Ma Y)		Beijing	13 Sep 1993
SAm	3:26.68	BRA (Coutinho, de Oliveira, Souza, de Lima)		São Paulo	7 Aug 2011
W20	3:27.60	USA (Anderson, Kidd, Smith, Hastings)		Grosseto	18 Jul 2004
W18	3:36.98	GBR (Ravenscroft, E McMeekin, Kennedy, Pettett)		Duisburg	26 Aug 1973

10 KILOMETRES WALK

W, Eur	41:04	Yelena NIKOLAYEVA	RUS	Sochi	20 Apr 1996
Asi	41:16	WANG Yan	CHN	Eisenhüttenstadt	8 May 1999
Oce, Com	41:30	Kerry SAXBY-JUNNA	AUS	Canberra	27 Aug 1988
CAC	42:42	Graciela MENDOZA	MEX	Naumburg	25 May 1997
SAm	42:02	Erica de SENA	BRA	Suzhou	26 Sep 2017
NAm	44:09+	Maria MICHTA-COFFEY	USA	St. Louis	3 Apr 2016
Afr	45:02	Chahinez NASRI	TUN	La Coruña	28 May 2016
W20	41:52 §	Tatyana MINEYEVA	RUS	Penza	5 Sep 2009
	41:57 §	GAO Hongmiao	CHN	Beijing	8 Sep 1993
W18	43:28	Aleksandra KUDRYASHOVA	RUS	Adler	19 Feb 2006

10,000 METRES TRACK WALK

W, Asi	41:37.9 §	GAO Hongmiao	CHN	Beijing	7 Apr 1994
W, Eur	41:56.23	Nadyezhda RYASHKINA	RUS	Seattle	24 Jul 1990
Oce, Com	41:57.22	Kerry SAXBY-JUNNA	AUS	Seattle	24 Jul 1990
SAm	42:02.99	Sandra Lorena ARENAS	COL	Trujillo	25 Aug 2018
CAC	44:13.88	Alegna GONZÁLEZ	MEX	Tampere	14 Jul 2018
NAm	44:30.1 m	Alison BAKER	CAN	Bergen (Fana)	15 May 1992
	44:06 no kerb	Michelle ROHL	USA	Kenosha	2 Jun 1996
Afr	44:41.8A	Grace Njue WANJIRU	KEN	Thika	5 Mar 2016
W20	42:47.25	Anezka DRAHOTOVÁ	CZE	Eugene	23 Jul 2014
W18	42:56.09	GAO Hongmiao	CHN	Tangshan	27 Sep 1991

20,000 METRES TRACK WALK

W, Eur	1:26:52.3	Olimpiada IVANOVA	RUS	Brisbane	6 Sep 2001
Asi, W20	1:29:32.4 §	SONG Hongjuan	CHN	Changsha	24 Oct 2003
SAm	1:31:02.25	Sandra Lorena ARENAS	COL	Lima	13 Jun 2015
CAC	1:31:53.8A	Mirna ORTIZ	GUA	Ciudad de Guatemala	9 Aug 2014
NAm, Com	1:32:54.0	Rachel SEAMAN	CAN	Moncton	27 Jun 2014
Oce	1:33:40.2	Kerry SAXBY-JUNNA	AUS	Brisbane	6 Sep 2001
Afr	1:36:18.22	Nicolene CRONJE	RSA	Durban	17 Apr 2004
W18	1:34:21.56	WANG Xue	CHN	Wuhan	1 Nov 2007

20 KILOMETRES WALK

W,Eue	1:23:39 §	Yelena LASHMANOVA	RUS	Chebokjsary	9 Jun 2018
W,Asi	1:24:38	LIU Hong	CHN	La Coruna	6 Jun 2015
Eur	1:25:02	Yelena LASHMANOVA	RUS	London	11 Aug 2012
CAC	1:26:17	María Guadeloupe GONZÁLEZ	MEX	Roma	7 May 2016
SAm	1:26:59	Erica de SENA	BRA	London	13 Aug 2017
Oce, Com	1:27:44	Jane SAVILLE	AUS	Naumburg	2 May 2004
NAm	1:29:54	Rachel SEAMAN	CAN	Nomi	15 Mar 2015
Afr	1:30:43	Grace Njue WANJIRU	KEN	Nairobi	6 Jun 2016
W20	1:25:30	Anisya KIRDYAPKINA	RUS	Adler	23 Feb 2008
W18	1:30:35	ZHOU Tongmei	CHN	Cixi	23 Apr 2005

50 KILOMETRES WALK

W, Asi	3:59:15	LIU Hong	CHN	Huangshan	9 Mar 2019
Eur	4:05:56	Inês HENRIQUES	POR	London	13 Aug 2017
Oce, Com	4:09:33	Claire TALLENT	AUS	Taicang	5 May 2018
SAm	4:12:56	Paola PÉREZ	ECU	Taicang	5 May 2018
CAC	4:15:42	Mayra Carolina HERRERA	GUA	Owego	9 Sep 2017
NAm	4:21:51	Kathleen BURNETT	USA	London	13 Aug 2017
Afr	4:48:00	Natalie le ROUX	RSA	Taicang	5 May 2018

World Records at other track & field events recognised by the IAAF

1 Hour	18,517 m	Dire TUNE	ETH	Ostrava	12 Jun 2008
20,000m	1:05:26.6	Tegla LOROUPE	KEN	Borgholzhausen	3 Sep 2000
25,000m	1:27:05.84	Tegla LOROUPE	KEN	Mengerskirchen	21 Sep 2002
30,000m	1:45:50.0	Tegla LOROUPE	KEN	Warstein	6 Jun 2003
4x200m	1:27.46	L Jenkins, L Colander, N Perry, M Jones USA		Philadelphia	29 Apr 2000
4x800m	7:50.17	Olizarenko, Gurina, Borisova, Podyalovskaya USSR		Moskva	5 Aug 1984
4x1500m	16:33.58	M Cherono, Kipyegon, I Jelagat, Obiri KEN		Nassau	24 May 2014

WORLD BESTS AT NON-STANDARD EVENTS

Men

50m	5.47+e	Usain Bolt	JAM	Berlin (in 100m)	16 Aug 2009
60m	6.31+	Usain Bolt	JAM	Berlin (in 100m)	16 Aug 2009
100 yards	9.07	Asafa Powell	JAM	Ostrava	27 May 2010
150m turn	14.44+	Usain Bolt	JAM	Berlin (in 200m)	20 Aug 2009
150m straight	14.35	Usain Bolt	JAM	Manchester	17 May 2009
300m	30.81	Wayde van Niekerk	RSA	Ostrava	28 Jun 2017
500m	59.32	Orestes Rodríguez	CUB	La Habana	15 Feb 2013
600m	1:12.81	Johnny Gray	USA	Santa Monica	24 May 1986
2 miles	7:58.61	Daniel Komen	KEN	Hechtel	19 Jul 1997
2000m Steeple	5:10.68	Mahiedine Mekhissi	FRA	Reims	30 Jun 2010
200mh	22.55	Laurent Ottoz	ITA	Milano	31 May 1995
	22.55	Yoshiro Watanabe	JPN	Izumi	1 Oct 2017
200mh straight	22.10	Andrew Turner	GBR	Manchester	15 May 2011
	22.10	L.J. van Zyl	RSA	Manchester	9 May 2015
220yh straight	21.9	Don Styron	USA	Baton Rouge	2 Apr 1960
300mh	34.48	Chris Rawlinson	GBR	Sheffield	30 Jun 2002
35lb weight	25.41	Lance Deal	USA	Azusa	20 Feb 1993
Pentathlon	4282 points	Bill Toomey	USA	London (CP)	16 Aug 1969
(1985 tables)		(7.58, 66.18, 21.3, 44.52, 4:20.3)			
Double decathlon	14,571	Joe Detmer	USA	Lynchburg	24/25 Sep 2010

10.93w, 7.30, 200mh 24.25w, 12.27, 5k 18:25.32, 2:02.23, 1.98, 400m 50.43, HT 31.82, 3kSt 11:22.47
15.01, DT 40.73, 200m 22.58, 4.85, 3k 10:25.99, 400mh 53.83, 51.95, 4:26.66, TJ 13.67, 10k 40:27.26

4x110mh	52.94	USA Richardson, Harris, Merritt, Oliver Des Moines			25 Apr 2015
1 mile walk	5:31.08	Tom Bosworth	GBR	London (OS)	9 Jul 2017
3000m track walk	10:47.11	Giovanni De Benedictis	ITA	San Giovanni Valdarno	19 May 1990
5000m track walk	18:05.49	Hatem Ghoula	TUN	Tunis	1 May 1997
10,000m track walk	37:53.09	Francisco Javier Fernández	ESP	Santa Cruz de Tenerife	27 Jul 2008
10 km road walk	37:11	Roman Rasskazov	RUS	Saransk	28 May 2000
30 km road walk	2:01:13+	Vladimir Kanaykin	RUS	Adler	19 Feb 2006
35 km road walk	2:21:31	Vladimir Kanaykin	RUS	Adler	19 Feb 2006
100 km road walk	8:38:07	Viktor Ginko	BLR	Scanzorosciate	27 Oct 2002

Women

50m	5.93+	Marion Jones	USA	Sevilla (in 100m)	22 Aug 1999
60m	6.85+	Marion Jones	USA	Sevilla (in 100m)	22 Aug 1999
100 yards	9.91	Veronica-Campbell-Brown	JAM	Ostrava	31 May 2011
150m	16.10+	Florence Griffith-Joyner	USA	Seoul (in 200m)	29 Sep 1988
300m	34.1+	Marita Koch	GDR	Canberra (in 400m)	6 Oct 1985
500m	1:05.9	Tatána Kocembová	CZE	Ostrava	2 Aug 1984
600m	1:21.77	Caster Semenya	RSA	Berlin	27 Aug 2017
2 miles	8:58.58	Meseret Defar	ETH	Bruxelles	14 Sep 2007
2000m Steeple	6:02.16	Virginia Nyambura	KEN	Berlin	6 Sep 2015
200mh	24.8	Yadisleidis Pedroso	ITA	Caserta	6 Apr 2013
	25.20	Dalilah Muhammad	USA	Northridge	10 Mar 2018
300mh	38.16	Zuzana Hejnová	CZE	Cheb	2 Aug 2013
Double heptathlon	10,798	Milla Kelo	FIN	Turku	7/8 Sep 2002

100mh 14.89, HJ 1.51, 1500m 5:03.74, 400mh 62.18, SP 12.73, 200m 25.16, 100m 12.59
LJ 5.73w, 400m 56.10, JT 32.69, 800m 2:23.94, 200mh 28.72, DT 47.86, 3000m 11:48.68

4x100mh	50.50	USA Castlin, Q Harrison, Harper-Nelson, Rollins Des Moines			24 Apr 2015
3000m track walk	11:35.34i	Gillian O'Sullivan	IRL	Belfast	15 Feb 2003
	11:48.24	Ileana Salvador	ITA	Padova	29 Aug 1993

5000m track walk	20:01.80	Eleonora Giorgi	ITA	Misterbianco	18 May 2014
25 km road walk	1:56:12+	Eleonora Giorgi	ITA	Catania	31 Jan 2016
30 km road walk	2:19:43	Eleonora Giorgi	ITA	Catania	31 Jul 2016
35 km road walk	2:38:24	Klavdiya Afanasyeva	RUS	Sochi	18 Feb 2019
100 km road walk	10:04:50	Jolanta Dukure	LAT	Scanzorosciate	21 Oct 2007

LONG DISTANCE WORLD BESTS – MEN TRACK

16,000m	0:42:18.7	Haile Gebrselassie	ETH	Ostrava	27 Jun 2007
10 miles	0:45:23.8+	Haile Gebrselassie	ETH	Ostrava	27 Jun 2007
15 miles	1:11:43.1	Bill Rodgers	USA	Saratoga, Cal.	21 Feb 1979
20 miles	1:39:14.4	Jack Foster	NZL	Hamilton, NZ	15 Aug 1971
30 miles	2:40:12.6+	Tyler Andrews	USA	Santa Barbara	13 Apr 2018
50 km	2:46:06.8	Tyler Andrews	USA	Santa Barbara	13 Apr 2018
40 miles	3:48:35	Don Ritchie	GBR	London (Hendon)	16 Oct 1982
50 miles	4:51:49	Don Ritchie	GBR	London (Hendon)	12 Mar 1983
100 km	6:10:20	Don Ritchie	GBR	London (CP)	28 Oct 1978
150 km	10:34:30	Denis Zhalybin	RUS	London (CP)	20 Oct 2002
100 miles	11:28:03	Oleg Kharitonov	RUS	London (CP)	20 Oct 2002
200 km	15:10:27+	Yiannis Kouros	AUS	Adelaide	4-5 Oct 1997
200 miles	27:48:35	Yiannis Kouros	GRE	Montauban	15-16 Mar 1985
500 km	60:23.00+ ??	Yiannis Kouros	GRE	Colac, Aus	26-29 Nov 1984
500 miles	105:42:09+	Yiannis Kouros	GRE	Colac, Aus	26-30 Nov 1984
1000 km	136:17:00	Yiannis Kouros	GRE	Colac, Aus	26-31 Nov 1984
1500 km	10d 17:28:26	Petrus Silkinas	LTU	Nanango, Qld	11-21 Mar 1998
1000 mile	11d 13:54:58+	Petrus Silkinas	LTU	Nanango, Qld	11-22 Mar 1998
2 hrs	37.994 km	Jim Alder	GBR	Walton-on-Thames	17 Oct 1964
12 hrs	163,785km	Zach Bitter	USA	Phoenix	14 Dec 2013
24 hrs	303.506 km	Yiannis Kouros	AUS	Adelaide	4-5 Oct 1997
48 hrs	473.797 km	Yiannis Kouros	AUS	Surgères	3-5 May 1996
6 days	1036.8 km	Yiannis Kouros	GRE	Colac, Aus	20-26 Nov 2005

LONG DISTANCE ROAD RECORDS & BESTS – MEN

Where superior to track bests (over 10km) and run on properly measured road courses. (I) IAAF recognition.

10 km (I)	0:26:44	Leonard Patrick Komon	KEN	Utrecht	26 Sep 2010
15 km (I)	0:41:05	Jospeh Cheptegei	UGA	Nijmegen	18 Nov 2018
10 miles	0:44:24 §	Haile Gebrselassie	ETH	Tilburg	4 Sep 2005
	0:44:45	Paul Koech	KEN	Amsterdam-Zaandam	21 Sep 1997
20 km (I)	0:55:18+	Abraham Kiptum	KEB	Valencia	28 Oct 2018
25 km (I)	1:11:18	Dennis Kimetto	KEN	Berlin	6 May 2012
30 km (I)	1:26:45+	Eliud Kipchoge	KEN	Berlin	16 Sep 2018
20 miles	1:35:22+	Steve Jones	GBR	Chicago	10 Oct 1985
30 miles	2:37:31+	Thompson Magawana	RSA	Claremont-Kirstenbosch	2 Apr 1988
50 km	2:43:38+	Thompson Magawana	RSA	Claremont-Kirstenbosch	2 Apr 1988
40 miles	3:45:39	Andy Jones	CAN	Houston	23 Feb 1991
50 miles	4:50:21	Bruce Fordyce	RSA	London-Brighton	25 Sep 1983
100 km (I)	6:09:14	Nao Kazami	JPN	Yubetsu	24 Jun 2018
200 km	15:08:53+	Denis Zhalybin (at 202.5k)	RUS	Sankt-Peterburg	2-3 Sep 2006
500 km	58:00:50	Yiannis Kouros	GRE	Colac, AUS	20-23 Nov 2005
1000 miles	10d:10:30:35	Yiannis Kouros	GRE	New York	21-30 May 1988

LONG DISTANCE WORLD BESTS – WOMEN TRACK

15 km	0:48:54.91+	Dire Tune	ETH	Ostrava	12 Jun 2008
10 miles	0:54:21.8	Lorraine Moller	NZL	Auckland	9 Jan 1993
20 miles	1:59:09 !	Chantal Langlacé	FRA	Amiens	3 Sep 1983
30 miles	3:12:25+	Carolyn Hunter-Rowe	GBR	Barry, Wales	3 Mar 1996
50 km	3:18:52+	Carolyn Hunter-Rowe	GBR	Barry, Wales	3 Mar 1996
40 miles	4:26:43	Carolyn Hunter-Rowe	GBR	Barry, Wales	7 Mar 1993
50 miles	5:48:12.0+	Norimi Sakurai	JPN	San Giovanni Lupatoto	27 Sep 2003
100 km	7:14:05.8	Norimi Sakurai	JPN	San Giovanni Lupatoto	27 Sep 2003
150 km	12:49.23	Mami Kudo	JPN	Soochow	10-11 Dec 2011
100 miles	13:25	Camille Herron	USA	Phoenix	8-9 Dec 2018
200 km	17:07:27+	Camille Herron	USA	Phoenix	8-9 Dec 2018
200 miles	39:09:03	Hilary Walker	GBR	Blackpool	5-7 Nov 1988
500 km	77:53:46	Eleanor Adams	GBR	Colac, Aus.	13-16 Nov 1989
500 miles	130:59:58+	Sandra Barwick	NZL	Campbelltown, AUS	18-23 Nov 1990
1000 km	8d 00:27:06+	Eleanor Robinson	GBR	Nanango, Qld	11-19 Mar 1998
1500 km	12d 06:52:12+	Eleanor Robinson	GBR	Nanango, Qld	11-23 Mar 1998
1000 miles	13d 02:16:49	Eleanor Robinson	GBR	Nanango, Qld	11-24 Mar 1998
2 hrs	32.652 km	Chantal Langlacé	FRA	Amiens	3 Sep 1983
12 hrs	149.208 km	Camille Herron	USA	Phoenix	10 Dec 2017

24 hours	262.192 km	Camille Herron	USA	Phoenix	8-9 Dec 2018
48 hrs	385.130 km	Mami Kudo	JPN	Surgères	22-24 May 2010
6 days	883.631 km	Sandra Barwick	NZL	Campbelltown, AUS	18-24 Nov 1990

! Timed on one running watch only

LONG DISTANCE ROAD RECORDS & BESTS – WOMEN

Where superior to track bests (over 10km)

10 km (l)	0:29:43	Joyciline Jepkosgei	KEN	Praha	9 Sep 2017
15 km (l)	0:45:37	Joyciline Jepkosgei	KEN	Praha	1 Apr 2017
10 miles	0:50:05+	Mary Keitany	KEN	Ra's Al-Khaymah	18 Feb 2011
	0:50:01+ dh	Paula Radcliffe	GBR	Newcastle	21 Sep 2003
20 km (l)	1:01:25	Joyciline Jepkosgei	KEN	Praha	1 Apr 2017
25 km (l)	1:19:53	Mary Keitany	KEN	Berlin	9 May 2010
30 km (l)	1:36:05	Mary Keitany	KEN	London	23 Apr 2017
20 miles	1:43:33+	Paula Radcliffe	GBR	London	13 Apr 2003
30 miles	3:01:16+	Frith van der Merwe	RSA	Claremont-Kirstenbosch	25 Mar 1989
50 km	3:08:39	Frith van der Merwe	RSA	Claremont-Kirstenbosch	25 Mar 1989
40 miles	4:26:13+	Ann Trason	USA	Houston	23 Feb 1991
50 miles	5:40:18	Ann Trason	USA	Houston	23 Feb 1991
100 km (l)	6:33:11	Tomoe Abe	JPN	Yubetsu	25 Jun 2000
100 miles	12:42:39	Camille Herron	USA	Vienna, Illinois	10-11 Nov 2017
1000 km	7d 01:11:00+	Sandra Barwick	NZL	New York	16-23 Sep 1991
1000 miles	12d 14:38:40	Sandra Barwick	NZL	New York	16-29 Sep 1991
48 hrs	401.000k	Patrycja Bereznowska	POL	Athína	26-28 Jan 2018

100 KILOMETRES CONTINENTAL RECORDS

Men

W, Asi	6:09:14	Nao KAZAMI	JPN	Yubetsu	21 Jun 1998
Eur	6:16:41	Jean-Paul PRAET	BEL	Torhout	24 Jun 1989
SAm	6:18:09	Valmir NUNES	BRA	Winschoten	16 Sep 1995
Afr	6:24:06	Bongmusa MTHEMBU	RSA	Los Alcazares	27 Nov 2016
NAm	6:27:43	Maxwell KING	USA	Doha	21 Nov 2014
Oce	6:29:26	Tim SLOAN	AUS	Ross-Richmond	23 Apr 1995

Women

W, Asi	6:33:11	Tomoe ABE	JPN	Yubetsu	25 Jun 2000
NAm	7:00:48	Ann TRASON	USA	Winschoten	16 Sep 1995
Eur	7:10:32	Tatyana ZHYRKOVA	RUS	Winschoten	11 Sep 2004
SAm	7:20:22	Maria VENÂNCIO	BRA	Cubatão	8 Aug 1998
Afr	7:31:47	Helena JOUBERT	RSA	Winschoten	16 Sep 1995
Oce	7:34:35	Kirstin BULL	AUS	Los Alcazares	27 Nov 2016

WORLD INDOOR RECORDS

Men

50 metres	5.56A	Donovan Bailey	CAN	Reno	9 Feb 1996
60 metres	6.34A	Christian Coleman	USA	Albuquerque	18 Feb 2018
100 metres	9.98	Usain Bolt	JAM	Warszawa	23 Aug 2014
200 metres	19.92	Frank Fredericks	NAM	Liévin	18 Feb 1996
400 metres	44.52	Michael Norman	USA	College Station	10 Mar 2018
800 metres	1:42.67	Wilson Kipketer	KEN	Paris (Bercy)	9 Mar 1997
1000 metres	2:14.20	Ayanleh Souleiman	DJI	Stockholm	17 Feb 2016
1500 metres	3:31.04	Sanuel Tefera	ETH	Birmingham	16 Feb 2019
1 mile	3:47.01	Yomif Kejelcha	ETH		
2000 metres #	4:49.99	Kenenisa Bekele	ETH	Birmingham	17 Feb 2007
3000 metres	7:24.90	Daniel Komen	KEN	Budapest	6 Feb 1998
2 miles #	8:04.35	Kenenisa Bekele	ETH	Birmingham	16 Feb 2008
5000 metres	12:49.60	Kenenisa Bekele	ETH	Birmingham	20 Feb 2004
10000 metres #	27:50.29	Mark Bett	KEN	Gent	10 Feb 2002
50 m hurdles	6.25	Mark McKoy	CAN	Kobe	5 Mar 1986
60 m hurdles	7.30	Colin Jackson	GBR	Sindelfingen	6 Mar 1994
110 m hurdles	13.03	Orlando Ortega	CUB	Warszawa	23 Aug 2014
High jump	2.43	Javier Sotomayor	CUB	Budapest	4 Mar 1989
Pole vault	6.16	Renaud Lavillenie	FRA	Donetsk	15 Feb 2014
Long jump	8.79	Carl Lewis	USA	New York	27 Jan 1984
Triple jump	17.92	Teddy Tamgho	FRA	Paris (Bercy)	6 Mar 2011
Shot	22.66	Randy Barnes	USA	Los Angeles	20 Jan 1989
Javelin #	85.78	Matti Närhi	FIN	Kajaani	3 Mar 1996
35 lb weight #	25.86	Lance Deal	USA	Atlanta	4 Mar 1995
3000m walk #	10:30.28	Tom Bosworth	GBR	Glasgow	25 Feb 2018
5000m walk	18:07.08	Mikhail Shchennikov	RUS	Moskva	14 Feb 1995
10000m walk #	38:31.4	Werner Heyer	GDR	Berlin	12 Jan 1980

4 x 200m	1:22.11	United Kingdom		Glasgow	3 Mar 1991
		(Linford Christie, Darren Braithwaite, Ade Mafe, John Regis)			
4 x 400m	3:01.39 §	USA (Texas A&M University)		College Station	10 Mar 2018
		(Ilolo Izu, Robert Grant, Devin Dixon, Mylik Kerley)			
4 x 800m	7:11.30	USA (Hoka New Jersey/New York TC)		Boston (Allston)	25 Feb 2018
		(Joe McCasey, Kyle Merber, Chris Giesting, Jesse Garn)			
Distance Med	9:19.93	USA		New York (Armory)	31 Jan 2015
		(Matthew Centrowitz, Mike Berry, Erik Sowinski, Pat Casey)			
Heptathlon	6645 points	Ashton Eaton	USA	Istanbul	9/10 Mar 2012
		(6.79 60m, 8.16 LJ, 14.56 SP, 2.03 HJ, 7.68 60mh, 5.20 PV, 2:32.77 1000m)			

Women   # events not officially recognised by the IAAF

50 metres	5.96+	Irina Privalova	RUS	Madrid	9 Feb 1995
60 metres	6.92	Irina Privalova	RUS	Madrid	11 Feb 1993 & 9 Feb 1995
200 metres	21.87	Merlene Ottey	JAM	Liévin	13 Feb 1993
400 metres	49.59	Jarmila Kratochvílová	CZE	Milano	7 Mar 1982
800 metres	1:55.82	Jolanda Ceplak	SLO	Wien	3 Mar 2002
1000 metres	2:30.94	Maria Lurdes Mutola	MOZ	Stockholm	25 Feb 1999
1500 metres	3:55.17	Genzebe Dibaba	ETH	Karlsruhe	1 Feb 2014
1 mile	4:13.31	Genzebe Dibaba	ETH	Stockholm	17 Feb 2016
2000 metres #	5:23.75	Genzebe Dibaba	ETH	Sabadell	7 Feb 2017
3000 metres	8:16.60	Genzebe Dibaba	ETH	Stockholm	6 Feb 2014
2 miles #	9:00.48	Genzebe Dibaba	ETH	Birmingham	15 Feb 2014
5000 metres	14:18.86	Genzebe Dibaba	ETH	Stockholm	19 Feb 2015
50 m hurdles	6.58	Cornelia Oschkenat	GDR	Berlin	20 Feb 1988
60 m hurdles	7.68	Susanna Kallur	SWE	Karlsruhe	10 Feb 2008
100 m hurdles	12.64	Ludmila Engquist	SWE	Tampere	10 Feb 1997
High jump	2.08	Kajsa Bergqvist	SWE	Arnstadt	4 Feb 2006
Pole vault	5.03	Jenn Suhr	USA	Brockport	30 Jan 2016
Long jump	7.37	Heike Drechsler	GDR	Wien	13 Feb 1988
Triple jump	15.36	Tatyana Lebedeva	RUS	Budapest	6 Feb 2004
Shot	22.50	Helena Fibingerová	CZE	Jablonec	19 Feb 1977
Javelin #	61.29	Taina Uppa/Kolkkala	FIN	Mustasaari	28 Feb 1999
20 lb weight #	25.60	Gwen Berry	USA	Albuquerque	4 Mar 2017
3000m walk	11:35.34 un	Gillian O'Sullivan	IRL	Belfast	15 Feb 2003
	11:40.33	Claudia Iovan/Stef	ROU	Bucuresti	30 Jan 1999
5000m walk #	20:37.77	Margarita Turova	BLR	Minsk	13 Feb 2005
10000m walk	43:54.63	Yelena Ginko	BLR	Mogilyov	22 Feb 2008
4 x 200m	1:32.41	Russia		Glasgow	29 Jan 2005
		(Yekaterina Kondratyeva, Irina Khabarova, Yuliya Pechonkina, Yuliya Gushchina)			
4 x 400m	3:23.37	Russia		Glasgow	28 Jan 2006
		(Yuliya Gushchina, Olga Kotlyarova, Olga Zaytseva, Olesya Krasnomovets)			
4 x 800m	8:05.89	USA		New York (Armory)	3 Feb 2018
		(Chrishuna Williams, Raevyn Rogers, Charlene Lipsey, Ajee' Wilson)			
Distance Med	10:42.57	Newa Balance TC	USA	Boston(Roxbury)	7 Feb 2015
		(Sarah Brown, Mahogany Jones, Megan Krumpoch, Brenda Martinez)			
Pentathlon	5013 points	Nataliya Dobrynska	UKR	Istanbul	9 Mar 2012
		(8.38 60mh, 1.84 HJ, 16.51 SP, 6.57 LJ, 2:11.15 800m)			

WORLD INDOOR JUNIOR (U20) RECORDS

First approved by IAAF Council in 2011. **Men**

60 metres	6.51	Mark Lewis-Francis	GBR	Lisboa	11 Mar 2001
200 metres	20.37	Walter Dix	USA	Fayetteville	11 Mar 2005
400 metres	44.80	Kirani James	GRN	Fayetteville	27 Feb 2011
800 metres	1:44.35	Yuriy Borzakovskiy	RUS	Dortmund	30 Jan 2000
1000 metres	2:15.77	Abubaker Kaki	SUD	Stockholm	21 Feb 2008
1500 metres	3:36.02	Jakob Ingebrigtsen	NOR	Düsseldorf	20 Feb 2019
One mile	3:55.02	German Fernandez	USA	College Station	28 Feb 2009
3000 metres	7:32.87	Hagos Gebrhiwet	ETH	Boston (Roxbury)	2 Feb 2013
5000 metres	12:53.29	Isiah Koech	KEN	Düsseldorf	11 Feb 2011
60mh (99cm)	7.40	Trey Cunningham	USA	New York (Armory)	12 Mar 2017
High jump	2.35	Volodymyr Yashchenko	URS	Milano	12 Mar 1978
Pole vault	5.88	Armand Duplantis	SWE	Clermont-Ferrand	25 Feb 2018
Long jump	8.22	Viktor Kuznetsov	UKR	Brovary	22 Jan 2005
Triple jump	17.20	Melvin Raffin	FRA	Belgrade	3 Mar 2017
Shot (6kg)	22.48	Konrad Bukowiecki	POL	Torun	8 Jan 2016
Heptathlon	6022	Gunnar Nixon	USA	Fayetteville	27/28 Jan 2012
(jnr imps)		(7.10, 7.53, 13.97, 2.15, 8.21, 4.50, 2:40.15)			

Women

60 metres	7.07	Ewa Swoboda	POL	Torun	12 Feb 2016
200 metres	22.40	Bianca Knight	USA	Fayetteville	14 Mar 2008

Event	Mark	Athlete	Country	Place	Date
400 metres	50.36	Sydney McLaughlin	USA	Colleger Station	10 Mar 2018
800 metres	2:01.03	Meskerem Legesse	ETH	Fayetteville	14 Feb 2004
1000 metres	2:35.80	Mary Cain	USA	Boston (Roxbury)	8 Feb 2014
1500 metres	4:01.81	Gudaf Tsegay	ETH	Glasgow	20 Feb 2016
One mile	4:24.10	Kalkidan Gezahegne	ETH	Birmingham	20 Feb 2010
3000 metres	8:33.56	Tirunesh Dibaba	ETH	Birmingham	20 Feb 2004
5000 metres	14:53.99	Tirunesh Dibaba	ETH	Boston	31 Jan 2004
60m hurdles	7.98	Tara Davis	USA	College Station	10 Mar 2018
High jump	1.99	Vashti Cunningham	USA	Portland	12 Mar 2016
	1.99	Yaroslava Mahuchikh	UKR	Minsk	22 Dec 2018
Pole vault	4.71	Wilma Murto	FIN	Zweibrücken	31 Jan 2016
Long jump	6.88	Heike Daute	GDR	Berlin	1 Feb 1983
Triple jump	14.37	Ren Ruiping	CHN	Barcelona	11 Mar 1995
Shot	20.51	Heidi Krieger	GDR	Budapest	8 Feb 1984
Pentathlon	4635A	Kendell Williams	USA	Albuquerque	15 Mar 2014
	(8.21, 1.88, 12.05, 6.32, 2:17.31)				

WORLD VETERANS/MASTERS RECORDS

MEN – aged 35-39

Event	Mark	Athlete	Country	Place	Date
100 metres	9.92	Justin Gatlin (10.2.92)	USA	London (OS)	5 Aug 2017
200 metres	20.11	Linford Christie (2.4.60)	GBR	Villeneuve d'Ascq	25 Jun 1995
400 metres	44.54	Chris Brown (15.10.78)	BAH	Eugene	30 May 2015
800 metres	1:43.36	Johnny Gray (19.6.60)	USA	Zürich	16 Aug 1995
1000 metres	2:18.8+	William Tanui (22.2.64)	KEN	Rome	7 Jul 1999
1500 metres	3:32.45	William Tanui (22.2.64)	KEN	Athína	16 Jun 1999
1 mile	3:51.38	Bernard Lagat (12.12.74)	USA	London (CP)	6 Aug 2011
2000 metres	4:58.3+ e	William Tanui (22.2.64	KEN	Monaco	4 Aug 1999
	4:54.74i	Bernard Lagat (12.12.74)	USA	New York	15 Feb 2014
3000 metres	7:29.00	Bernard Lagat (12.12.74)	USA	Rieti	29 Aug 2010
5000 metres	12:53.60	Bernard Lagat (12.12.74)	USA	Monaco	22 Jul 2011
10000 metres	26:51.20	Haile Gebrselassie (18.4.73)	ETH	Hengelo	24 May 2008
20000 metres	57:44.4+	Gaston Roelants (5.2.37)	BEL	Bruxelles	20 Sep 1972
1 Hour	20,822m	Haile Gebrselassie (18.4.73)	ETH	Hengelo	1 Jun 2009
Half Marathon	59:10 dh	Paul Tergat (17.6.69)	KEN	Lisboa	13 Mar 2005
	59:31	Gilbert Masai (20.5.81)	KEN	København	18 Sep 2016
Marathon	2:03:59	Haile Gebrselassie (18.4.73)	ETH	Berlin	28 Sep 2008
3000m steeple	8:04.95	Simon Vroemen (11.5.69)	NED	Bruxelles	26 Aug 2005
110m hurdles	12.96	Allen Johnson (1.3.71)	USA	Athína	17 Sep 2006
400m hurdles	48.10	Felix Sánchez (30.8.77)	DOM	Moskva	13 Aug 2013
High jump	2.31	Dragutin Topic (12.3.71)	SRB	Kragujevac	28 Jul 2009
	2.31	Jamie Nieto (2.11.76)	USA	New York	9 Jun 2012
Pole vault	5.90i	Björn Otto (16.10.77)	GER	Cottbus	30 Jan 2013
	5.90i	Björn Otto		Düsseldorf	8 Feb 2013
	5.90	Björn Otto		Eugene	1 Jun 2013
Long jump	8.50	Larry Myricks (10.3.56)	USA	New York	15 Jun 1991
	8.50	Carl Lewis (1.7.61)	USA	Atlanta	29 Jul 1996
Triple jump	17.92	Jonathan Edwards (10.5.66)	GBR	Edmonton	6 Aug 2001
Shot	22.67	Kevin Toth ¶ (29.12.67)	USA	Lawrence	19 Apr 2003
Discus	71.56	Virgilijus Alekna (13.2.72)	LTU	Kaunas	25 Jul 2007
Hammer	83.62	Igor Astapkovich (4.1.63)	BLR	Staiki	20 Jun 1998
Javelin	92.80	Jan Zelezny (16.6.66)	CZE	Edmonton	12 Aug 2001
Decathlon	8241	Kip Janvrin (8.7.65)	USA	Eugene	22 Jun 2001
	(10.98, 7.01, 14.21, 1.89, 48.41, 14.72, 45.59, 5.20, 60.41, 4:14.96)				
20 km walk	1:17:02	Yohann Diniz (1.1.78)	FRA	Arles	8 Mar 2015
20000m t walk	1:19:42.1	Yohann Diniz (1.1.78)	FRA	Bogny-sur-Meuse	25 May 2014
50 km walk	3:32:33	Yohann Diniz (1.1.78)	FRA	Zürich	15 Aug 2014
50000m t walk	3:49:29.7	Alain Lemercier (11.1.57)	FRA	Franconville	3 Apr 1994

MEN – aged 40 or over

Event	Mark	Athlete	Country	Place	Date
100 metres	9.93	Kim Collins (5.4.76)	SKN	Bottrop	29 May 2016
200 metres	20.64	Troy Douglas (30.11.62)	NED	Utrecht	9 Aug 2003
400 metres	46.96	Sandro Viana (26.3.77)	BRA	São Bernardo do Campo	1 Jul 2017
800 metres	1:48.05	Anthony Whiteman (13.11.71)	GBR	Manchester (Stretford)	12 Jul 2014
1000 metres	2:24.93i	Vyacheslav Shabunin (27.9.69)	RUS	Moskva	10 Jan 2010
1500 metres	3:40.20i+	Bernard Lagat (12.12.74)	USA	New York (Armory)	14 Feb 2015
	3:41.87	Bernard Lagat		Birmingham	7 Jun 2015
1 mile	3:54.91i+	Bernard Lagat		New York (Armory)	14 Feb 2015
	3:57.91	Bernard Lagat		London (OS)	25 Jul 2015
3000 metres	7:37.92i+	Bernard Lagat (12.12.74)	USA	Metz	25 Feb 2015
	7:42.75	Bernard Lagat		Luzern	14 Jul 2015
5000 metres	13:06.78	Bernard Lagat		Rio de Janeiro	20 Aug 2016

10000 metres	27:49.35	Bernard Lagat		Stanford	1 May 2016
10 km road	27:48	Bernard Lagat (12.12.74)	USA	Manchester	10 May 2015
1 Hour	19.710k	Steve Moneghetti (26.9.62)	AUS	Geelong	17 Dec 2005
Half marathon	60:41 dh	Haile Gebrselassie (18.4.73)	ETH	South Shields	15 Sep 2013
	61:04	Mark Kiptoo (21.6.76)	KEN	Azpeitia	24 Mar 2016
Marathon	2:07:50	Mark Kiptoo (21.6.76)	KEN	Frankurt	28 Oct 2018
3000m steeple	8:38.40	Angelo Carosi (20.1.64)	ITA	Firenze	11 Jul 2004
110m hurdles	13.97	David Ashford (24.1.63)	USA	Indianapolis	3 Jul 2004
	13.79 ?	Roger Kingdom (26.8.62)	USA	Slippery Rock	23 Jun 2004
400m hurdles	49.69	Danny McFarlane (14.2.72)	JAM	Kingston	29 Jun 2012
High jump	2.28	Dragutin Topic (12.3.71)	SRB	Beograd	20 May 2012
Pole vault	5.71i	Jeff Hartwig (25.9.67)	USA	Jonesboro	31 May 2008
	5.70	Jeff Hartwig		Eugene	29 Jun 2008
Long jump	7.68A	Aaron Sampson (20.9.61)	USA	Cedar City, UT	21 Jun 2002
	7.59i	Mattias Sunneborn (27.9.70)	SWE	Sätra	3 Feb 2013
	7.57	Hans Schicker (3.10.47)	FRG	Kitzingen	16 Jul 1989
Triple jump	17.32	Fabrizio Donato (14.8.76	ITA	Pierre=Bénite	9 Jun 2017
Shot	21.41	Brian Oldfield USA (1.6.45)	USA	Innsbruck	22 Aug 1985
Discus	70.28	Virgilijus Alekna (13.2.72)	LTU	Klaipeda	23 Jun 2012
Hammer	82.23	Igor Astapkovich (4.1.63)	BLR	Minsk	10 Jul 2004
Javelin	85.92	Jan Zelezny (16.6.66)	CZE	Göteborg	9 Aug 2006
Pentathlon	3510	Werner Schallau (8.9.38)	FRG	Gelsenkirchen	24 Sep 1978
		6.74, 59.20, 23.0, 43.76, 5:05.7			
Decathlon	7525	Kip Janvrin (8.7.65)	USA	San Sebastián	24 Aug 2005
		11.56, 6.78, 14.01, 1.80, 49.46, 15.40, 42.70, 4.70, 58.43, 4:25.87			
20 km walk	1:20:20	Andriy Kovenko (25.11.73)	UKR	Alushta	28 Feb 2014
20000m t walk	1:24:46.1	Ivan Trotskiy (27.5.76)	BLR	Grodno	23 Jun 2016
50 km walk	3:40:46	Yuriy Andronov (6.11.71)	RUS	Moskva	11 Jun 2012
50000m t walk	3:51:54.5	José Marín (21.1.50)	ESP	Manresa	7 Apr 1990
4x100m	42.20	SpeedWest TC	USA	Irvine	2 May 2004
		(Frank Strong, Cornell Stephenson, Kettrell Berry, Willie Gault)			
4x400m	3:20.83	S Allah, K Morning, E Gonera, R Blackwell USA		Philadelphia	27 Apr 2001

WOMEN – aged 35-39

100 metres	10.74	Merlene Ottey (10.5.60)	JAM	Milano	7 Sep 1996
200 metres	21.93	Merlene Ottey (10.5.60)	JAM	Bruxelles	25 Aug 1995
400 metres	50.14	Novlene Williams-Mills (26.4.82)	JAM	Kingston	25 Jun 2017
800 metres	1:56.53	Lyubov Gurina (6.8.57)	RUS	Hechtel	30 Jul 1994
1000 metres	2:31.5	Maricica Puica (29.7.50)	ROU	Poiana Brasov	1 Jun 1986
1500 metres	3:57.73	Maricica Puica (29.7.50)	ROU	Bruxelles	30 Aug 1985
1 mile	4:17.33	Maricica Puica (29.7.50)	ROU	Zürich	21 Aug 1985
2000 metres	5:28.69	Maricica Puica (29.7.50)	ROU	London (CP)	11 Jul 1986
3000 metres	8:23.23	Edith Masai (4.4.67)	KEN	Monaco	19 Jul 2002
5000 metres	14:33.84	Edith Masai (4.4.67)	KEN	Oslo	2 Jun 2006
10000 metres	30:30.26	Edith Masai (4.4.67)	KEN	Helsinki	6 Aug 2005
Half Marathon	64:55	Mary Keitany (18.1.82)	KEN	Ras Al Khaimah	9 Feb 2018
Marathon	2:17:01	Mary Keitany (18.1.82)	KEN	London	23 Apr 2017
3000m steeple	9:24.26	Marta Domínguez (3.11.75)	ESP	Huelva	7 Jun 2012
100m hurdles	12.40	Gail Devers (19.11.66)	USA	Lausanne	2 Jul 2002
400m hurdles	52.94	Marina Styepanova (1.5.50)	RUS	Tashkent	17 Sep 1986
High jump	2.01	Inga Babakova (27.6.67)	UKR	Oslo	27 Jun 2003
	2.01	Ruth Beitia (1.4.79)	ESP	Zürich	17 Aug 2014
Pole vault	4.93	Jenn Suhr (5.2.82)	USA	Austin	14 Apr 2018
Long jump	6.99	Heike Drechsler (16.12.64)	GER	Sydney	29 Sep 2000
Triple jump	14.68	Tatyana Lebedeva (21.7.76)	RUS	Cheboksary	3 Jul 2012
	14.82i	Yamilé Aldama (14.8.72)	GBR	Istanbul	10 Mar 2012
Shot	21.46	Larisa Peleshenko (29.2.64)	RUS	Moskva	26 Aug 2000
	21.47i	Helena Fibingerová (13.7.49)	CZE	Jablonec	9 Feb 1985
Discus	69.60	Faina Melnik (9.6.45)	RUS	Donetsk	9 Sep 1980
Hammer	74.03	Amber Campbell (5.6.81)	USA	Eugene	6 Jul 2016
Javelin	68.92	Kathryn Mitchell (10.7.82)	AUS	Gold Coast	11 Apr 2018
Heptathlon	6533	Jane Frederick (7.4.52)	USA	Talence	27 Sep 1987
		13.60, 1.82, 15.50, 24.73; 6.29, 49.70, 2:14.88			
5000m walk	20:12.41	Elisabetta Perrone (9.7.68)	ITA	Rieti	2 Aug 2003
10km walk	41:41	Kjersti Tysse Plätzer (18.1.72)	NOR	Kraków	30 May 2009
10000m t walk	43:26.5	Elisabetta Perrone (9.7.68)	ITA	Saluzzo	4 Aug 2004
20km walk	1:25:59	Tamara Kovalenko (5.6.64)	RUS	Moskva	19 May 2000
20000m t walk	1:27:49.3	Yelena Nikolayeva (1.2.66)	RUS	Brisbane	6 Sep 2001
50km walk	4:05:56	Inês Henriques (1.5.80)	POR	London	13 Aug 2017
4x100m	47.65	Stafford, Springer, Hutchinson, Baird TTO		Lyon	16 Aug 2015
4x400m	3:50.80	Mitchell, Mathews, Beadnall, Gabriel GBR		Gateshead	8 Aug 1999

WOMEN – aged 40 or over

100 metres	10.99	Merlene Ottey (10.5.60)	JAM	Thessaloniki	30 Aug 2000
200 metres	22.72	Merlene Ottey (10.5.60)	SLO	Athína	23 Aug 2004
400 metres	53.05A	María Figueirêdo (11.11.63)	BRA	Bogotá	10 Jul 2004
	53.14	María Figueirêdo (11.11.63)	BRA	San Carlos, VEN	19 Jun 2004
800 metres	1:59.25	Yekaterina Podkopayeva (11.6.52)	RUS	Luxembourg	30 Jun 1994
1000 metres	2:36.16	Yekaterina Podkopayeva (11.6.52)	RUS	Nancy	14 Sep 1994
	2:36.08i	Yekaterina Podkopayeva	RUS	Liévin	13 Feb 1993
1500 metres	3:59.78	Yekaterina Podkopayeva (11.6.52)	RUS	Nice	18 Jul 1994
1 mile	4:23.78	Yekaterina Podkopayeva (11.6.52)	RUS	Roma	9 Jun 1993
3000 metres	9:01.1+	Jo Pavey (20.9.73)	GBR	Roma	5 Jun 2014
	8:58.20i	Nuria Fernández (16.8.76)	ESP	Beograd	3 Mar 2017
5000 metres	15:04.87	Jo Pavey (20.9.73)	GBR	Roma	5 Jun 2014
10000 metres	31:31.18	Edith Masai (4.4.67)	KEN	Alger	21 Jul 2007
1 hour	16.056k	Jackie Fairweather (10.11.67)	AUS	Canberra	24 Jan 2008
Half Marathon	68:55	Sinead Diver (17.2.77)	AUS	Marugame	3 Feb 2010
Marathon	2:22:11	Lydia Cheromei (11.5.77)	KEN	Valencia	2 Dec 2018
3000m steeple	10:00.75	Minori Hayakari (29.11.72)	JPN	Kumagaya	22 Sep 2013
100 m hurdles	13.20	Patricia Girard (8.4.68)	FRA	Paris	14 Jul 2008
400 m hurdles	58.35	Barbara Gähling (20.1.65)	GER	Erfurt	21 Jul 2007
	58.3 h	Gowry Retchakan (21.6.60)	GBR	Hoo	3 Sep 2000
High jump	1.94i	Venelina Veneva-Mateeva (13.6.74)	BUL	Dobrich 15 Feb & Praha	6 Mar 2015
	1.90	Venelina Veneva-Mateeva	BUL	Plovdiv 12 Jul & Pitesti	27 Jul 2014
Pole vault	4.10	Doris Auer (10.5.71)	AUT	Innsbruck	6 Aug 2011
	4.11 §	Doris Auer	AUT	Wien	5 Jul 2011
Long jump	6.72 (1.4)	Tatyana Ter-Mesrobian (12.5.68)	RUS	Sankt-Peterburg	1 Jun 2009
Triple jump	14.06	Yamilé Aldama (14.8.72)	GBR	Eugene	1 Jun 2013
Shot	19.05	Antonina Ivanova (25.12.32)	RUS	Oryol	28 Aug 1973
	19.16i	Antonina Ivanova	RUS	Moskva	24 Feb 1974
Discus	67.89	Iryna Yatchenko (31.10.65)	BLR	Staiki	29 Jun 2008
Hammer	67.57	Iryna Sekachyova (21.7.76)	UKR	Kyiv	14 Jun 2017
Javelin	61.96	Laverne Eve (16.6.65)	BAH	Monaco	9 Sep 2005
Heptathlon	5449	Tatyana Alisevich (22.1.69)	BLR	Staiki	3 Jun 2010
		14.80, 1.62, 13.92, 26.18, 5.55, 45.44, 2:24.39			
5000m walk	21:46.68	Kelly Ruddick (19.4.73)	AUS	Brisbane	29 Mar 2014
10000m t walk	44:50.19	Susana Feitor (28.1.75)	POR	Leiria	25 Jul 2015
20km walk	1:31:58	Susana Feitor		Rio Maior 18 Apr 2015 & Murcia	17 May 2015
20000m t walk	1:33:28.15t	Teresa Vaill (20.11.62)	USA	Carson	25 Jun 2005
50km walk	4:37:43	Lyudmyla Shelest (4.10.74)	UKR	Taicang	5 May 2018
4x100m	48.01	Mogentale, Brims, Bezuidenhout, Strong	AUS	Lahti	8 Aug 2009
4x400m	3:56.28	Roberts, Henderson, Brooker, Clark	USA	Philadelphia	25 Apr 2008

WORLD AND CONTINENTAL RECORDS SET IN 2018

OUTDOORS – MEN   § Not ratified

100	Asi =	9.91	SU Bingtian	CHN	Madrid	22 Jun 18
	Asi =	9.91	SU Bingtian	CHN	Paris (C)	30 Jun 18
800	Oce	1:44.21	Joseph DENG	AUS	Monaco	20 Jul 18
5000	W20	12:43.02	Selemon BAREGA	ETH	Bruxelles	31 Aug 18
10k	W20	27:08	Rhonex KIPRUTO	KEN	New York	29 Apr 18
	W20	26:46	Rhonex KIPRUTO	KEN	Praha	8 Sep 18
	Eur	27:32	Julien WANDERS	SUI	Durban	14 Oct 18
	Eur	27:25	Julien WANDERS	SUI	Houilles	30 Dec 18
15k	W,Afr,Com	41:05	Joshua CHEPTEGEI	UGA	Nijmegen	18 Nov 18
20k	W,Afr,Com	55:18+	Abraham KIPTUM	KEN	Valencia	28 Oct 18
HMar	W40	61:04	Mark KIPTOO	KEN	Azpeitia	24 Mar 18
	W,Afr,Com	58:18	Abraham KIPTUM	KEN	Valencia	28 Oct 18
30k	W,Afr.Com	1:26:45+	Eliud KIPCHOGE	KEN	Berlin	16 Sep 18
	Eur	1:27:31	Mo FARAH	GBR	London	22 Apr 18
Mar	W track	2:18:42.8+	Tyler ANDREWS	USA	Santa Barbara	13 Apr 18
	W,Afr,Com	2:01:39	Eliud KIPCHOGE	KEN	Berlin	16 Sep 18
	Eur	2:05:11	Mo FARAH	GBR	Chicago	7 Oct 18
	Asi	2:05:50	Shiguru OSAKO	JPN	Chicago	7 Oct 18
	W40	2:07:50	Mark KIPTOO	KEN	Frankfurt	28 Oct 18
	Asi	2:04:43	El Hassan EL ABBASSI	BRN	Valencia	2 Dec 18
30M	W track	2:40:12.6+	Tyler ANDREWS	USA	Santa Barbara	13 Apr 18
50k	W track	2:46:06.8+	Tyler ANDREWS	USA	Santa Barbara	13 Apr 18
100k	W, Asi	6:09:14	Nao KAZAMI	JPN	Yubetsu	24 Jun 18
110H/99	W20=	12.99	Damion THOMAS	JAM	Kingston	23 Jun 18
110H	SAm	13.23	Gabriel CONSTANTINO	BRA	Montreuil	19 Jun 18
400H	Asi	47.48	Abderrahman SAMBA	QAT	Roma	31 May 18

Event	Region	Mark	Athlete	Nat	Venue	Date
	CAC, Com	47.02	Rai BENJAMIN	ANT	Eugene	8 Jun 18
	Asi	47.41	Abderrahman SAMBA	QAT	Stockholm	10 Jun 18
	Asi	46.98	Abderrahman SAMBA	QAT	Paris (C)	30 Jun 18
HJ	Oce=	2.36	Brandon STARC	AUS	Eberstadt	26 Aug 18
PV	W20	5.92	Armand DUPLANTIS	SWE	Austin	31 Mar 18
	W20	5.93 §	Armand DUPLANTIS	SWE	Baton Rouge	5 May 18
	W20	5.95, 6.00 & 6.05	Armand DUPLANTIS	SWE	Berlin	12 Aug 18
T.I	W18	17.32	Jordan A. DIAZ	CUB	La Habana	17 Feb 10
	W18	17.41	Jordan A. DIAZ	CUB	La Habana	8 Jun 18
SP	Oce, Com	22.67	Tomas WALSH	NZL	Auckland (Waitakere)	25 Mar 18
	SAm	21.84 & 21.94	Darlan ROMANI	BRA	Bialystok	20 May 18
	SAm	21.95	Darlan ROMANI	BRA	Eugene	26 May 18
	SAm	22.00	Darlan ROMANI	BRA	Bragança Paulista	15 Sep 18
HT 5kg	W18	87.82	Myhaylo KOKHAN	UKR	Györ	7 Jul 18
Dec	W, Eur	9126	Kevin MAYER	FRA	Talence	16 Sep 18

(10.55, 7.80, 16.00, 2.05, 48.42 / 13.75, 50.54, 5.45, 71.90, 4:36.11)

Event	Region	Mark	Athlete	Nat	Venue	Date
4x400 R	Asi	3:00.56	Samba, Abbas, Youssef, Haroun	QAT	Jakarta	30 Aug 18
3000W	Afr	11:03.32	Lebogang SHANGE	RSA	Samorin	29 Jun 18
	W,Eur,Com	10:43.84	Tom BOSWORTH	GBR	London (OS)	21 Jul 18
	Afr	10:47.08	Lebogang SHANGE	RSA	London (OS)	21 Jul 18
10,000W	Asi	37:58.08	Daisuke MATSUNAGA	JPN	Kitami	7 Jul 18
20kW	W20	1:17:25	Sergey SHIROBOKOV	RUS	Cheboksary	9 Jun 18

OUTDOORS – WOMEN

Event	Region	Mark	Athlete	Nat	Venue	Date
150 straight	W	16.23	Shaunae MILLER-UIBO	BAH	Boston	20 May 18
200	Afr	22.04	Blessing OKAGBARE	NGR	Abilene	24 Mar 18
400	Asi	49.55	Salwa Eid NASER	BRN	Paris (C)	30 Jun 18
	Asi	49.08	Salwa Eid NASER	BRN	Monaco	20 Jul 18
1500	Oce	4:00.86	Linden HALL	AUS	Eugene	26 May 18
1M	Com	4:16.15	Hellen OBIRI	KEN	London (OS)	22 Jul 18
	Oce	4:21.40	Linden HALL	AUS	London (OS)	22 Jul 18
2M	NAm	9.10.78	Jenny SIMPSON	USA	Des Moines	27 Apr 18
5000	Eur	14:22.34	Sifan HASSAN	NED	Rabat	13 Jul 18
	NAm	14:34.45	Shelby HOULIHAN	USA	Heusden-Zolder	21 Jul 18
HMar	NAm	67:25	Molly HUDDLE	USA	Houston	14 Jan 18
	W35	64:55	Mary KEITANY	KEN	Ras Al Khaimah	9 Feb 18
	W20	66:47	Degitu AZIMERAW	ETH	Ras Al Khaimah	9 Feb 18
	W-Wo	66:11	Netsanet GUDETA	ETH	Valencia	24 Mar 18
	W40	69:20	Sinead DIVER	AUS	Gold Coast	19 Aug 18
	Eur	65:16	Sifan HASSAN	NED	København	16 Sep 18
Mar	W40	2:22:11	Lydia CHEROMEI	KEN	Valencia	2 Dec 18
200k	W	17:07:27	Camille HERRON	USA	Phoenix	9 Dec 18
24Hr (road)	W	262.192k	Camille HERRON	USA	Phoenix	9 Dec 18
48Hr (road)	W,	401.000k	Patrycja BEREZNOWSKA	POL	Athína	28 Jan 18
3000SC	W,Afr,Com	8:44.32	Beatrice CHEPKOECH	KEN	Monaco	20 Jul 18
	NAm	9:00.85	Courtney FRERICHS	USA	Monaco	20 Jul 18
	CAC	9:14.09	Aisha PRAUGHT LEER	JAM	Bruxelles	31 Aug 18
100H	CAC	12.40	Jasmine CAMACHO-QUINN	PUR	Knoxville	13 May 18
200H	W	25.20	Dalilah MUHAMMAD	USA	Northridge	10 Mar 18
400H	W20	53.60	Sydney McLAUGHLIN	USA	Fayetteville	27 Apr 18
	W20	52.75	Sydney McLAUGHLIN	USA	Knoxville	13 May 18
HJ	W/Hep	2.01	Nafissatou THIAM	BEL	Götzis	26 May 18
PV	W35	4.93	Jenn SUHR	USA	Austin	14 Apr 18
	Oce, Com	4.85	Eliza McCARTNEY	NZL	Eugene	26 May 18
	Oce, Com	4.86 & 4.92	Eliza McCARTNEY	NZL	Mannheim	23 Jun 18
	Oce, Com	4.94	Eliza McCARTNEY	NZL	Jockgrim	17 Jul 18
TJ	NAm	14.84	Tori FRANKLIN	USA	Baie Mahault	12 May 18
DT	SAm	65.10	Andressa de MORAIS	BRA	Bragança Paulista	8 Jul 18
HT	NAm	77.65	DeAnna PRICE	USA	Rathdrum	1 Jun 18
	NAm	77.78	Gwen BERRY	USA	Chorzów	8 Jun 18
	NAm	78.12	DeAnna PRICE	USA	Des Moines	23 Jun 18
JT	Oce	67.58	Kathryn MITCHELL	AUS	Melbourne	11 Feb 18
	Oce, W35	68.57	Kathryn MITCHELL	AUS	Melbourne	3 Mar 18
	Oce,W35	68.92	Kathryn MITCHELL	AUS	Gold Coast	11 Apr 18
	Asi	67.69	LU Huihui	CHN	Halle	26 May 18
HepU18	W18	6221	Maria VICENTE	ESP	Györ	6 Jul 18

(13.25, 1.72, 13.77, 23.78 / 6.37, 43.28, 2:23.29)

Event	Region	Mark	Athlete	Nat	Venue	Date
Hep	CAC	6742	Yorgelis RODRÍGUEZ	CUB	Götzis	27 May 18

(13.48, 1.86, 14.95, 23.96 / 6.58w, 48.65, 2:12.73)

Event	Region	Mark	Athlete	Nat	Venue	Date
	SAm	6285	Evelys AGUILAR	COL	Barranquilla	1 Aug 18

(13.92w, 1.77, 13.64, 23.95 / 6.47w, 43.01, 2:16.18)

4x100 R	W20	43.27	Fehm, Kwadwo, Junk, Montag	GER	Grosseto	23 Jul 18
Sprint Med R	W	1:35.20	D Brown, A Brown, Duncan, Rogers	USA	Philadelphia	28 Apr 18
10,000W	CAC	44:13.88	Alegna GONZÁLEZ	MEX	Tampere	14 Jul 18
	Sam	42:02.99	Sandra Lorena ARENAS	COL	Trujillo	25 Aug 18
20kW	Afr	1:30:40A	Grace NJUE	KEN	Nairobi	6 Jun 18
	W, Eur	1:23:39 §	Yelena LASHMANOVA	RUS	Cheboksary	9 Jun 18
35kW	W	2:45:51	Inês HENRIQUES	POR	Porto de Mos	7 Jan 18
50kW	SAm	4:19:43	Magaly BONILLA	ECU	Sucua	10 Mar 18
	W, Asi	4:04:36	LIANG Rui	CHN	Taicang	5 May 18
	Oce, Com	4:09:33	Claire TALLENT	AUS	Taicang	5 May 18
	SAm	4:12:56	Paola Bibiana PÉREZ	ECU	Taicang	5 May 18
	W40	4:37:43	Lyudmyla SHELEST	UKR	Taicang	5 May 18
	Afr	4:48:00	Natalie le ROUX	RSA	Taicang	5 May 18

WORLD AND CONTINENTAL RECORDS SET IN JAN-MAR 2019

INDOORS – MEN

60	W18	6.65	Marcellus MOORE	USA	Lexington	16 Feb 19
300	W20	32:49	Jacory PATTERSON	USA	Blacksburg	11 Jan 19
400	Eur =	45.05	Karsten WARHOLM	NOR	Glasgow	2 Mar 19
	SAm	46.07	Alejandro PERLAZA	COL	Birmingham, USA	9 Mar 19
500	SAm	1:01.35	Alejandro PERLAZA	COL	Lynchburg	26 Jan 19
600	CAC	1:15.78	Tre HINDS	BAR	Lubbock	15 Feb 19
	W	1:13.77	Donavan BRAZIER	USA	Staten Island	24 Feb 19
800	Afr, Com	1:43.98	Michael SARUNI	KEN	New York (Armory)	9 Feb 19
	NAm	1:44.41	Donavan BRAZIER	USA	New York (Armory)	9 Feb 19
	Oce	1:47.27	Joseph DENG	AUS	Birmingham	16 Feb 19
1500	W35	3:39.16+	Nick WILLIS	NZL	New York (Armory)	9 Feb 19
	W20	3:36.21	Jakob INGEBRIGTSEN	NOR	Rud	10 Feb 19
	W, Afr	3:31.04	Samuel TEFERA	ETH	Birmingham	16 Feb 19
	Oce	3:35.10	Stewart McSWEYN	AUS	Birmingham	16 Feb 19
	W20	3:36.02	Jakob INGEBRIGTSEN	NOR	Düsseldorf	20 Feb 19
1M	W35	3:54.80	Nick WILLIS	NZL	New York (Armory)	9 Feb 19
	Asi	3:56.60	Nanami ARAI	JPN	Boston (Allston)	24 Feb 19
	W, Afr	3:47.01	Yomif KEJELCHA	ETH	Boston (Allston)	3 Mar 19
2000	Asi	5:00.34	Birhanu YEMATEW	BRN	Liévin	10 Feb 19
60mh/91	W18 =	7.48	Sasha ZHOYA	FRA	Liévin	24 Feb 19
60mh	NAm	7.35	Grant HOLLOWAY	USA	Birmingham, USA	9 Mar 19
TJ	Afr	17.58	Fabrice ZANGO	BUR	Paris	27 Jan 19
SP	CAC	20.68	O'Dayne RICHARDS	JAM	Nehvizdy	1 Feb 19
Hep	Oce	5949	Gary HAASBROEK	AUS	Houston	26 Jan 19
		(7.02, 7.65, 11.52, 2.03, 8.14, 5.10, 2:46.15)				
4x400R	W	3:01.51	Lattin, Igbokwe, Holt, Montgomery	USA	Clemson	9 Feb 19

INDOORS – WOMEN

200	SAm	23.02	Brenessa THOMPSON	GUY	Lubbock	26 Jan 19
600	W20	1:26.83	Athing MU	USA	Staten Island	24 Feb 19
	W20	1:23.57	Athing MU	USA	Staten Island	24 Feb 19
800	NAm	1:58.60	Ajee' WILSON	USA	New York (Armory)	9 Feb 19
	CAC	1:59.13	Natoya GOULE	JAM	New York (Armory)	9 Feb 19
1000	CAC	2:37.55	Natoya GOULE	JAM	New York (Armory)	26 Jan 19
1500	Com	4:01.84+	Laura MUIR	GBR	Birmingham	16 Feb 19
1M	Com	4:18.75	Laura MUIR	GBR	Birmingham	16 Feb 19
HJ	W18	1.96	Yaroslava MAHUCHIKH	UKR	Minsk	22 Dec 18
	W35	1.99 & 2.01	Anna CHICHEROVA	RUS	Chelyabinsk	17 Jan 19
	W35 =	2.01	Anna CHICHEROVA	RUS	Moskva	20 Jan 19
	W20 =	1.99	Yaroslava MAHUCHIKH	UKR	Hustopece	26 Jan 19
	W35	2.02	Anna CHICHEROVA	RUS	Moskva	15 Feb 19
TJ	SAm	14.92	Yulimar ROJAS	VEN	Madrid	8 Feb 19
	NAm	14.57	Tori FRANKLIN	USA	Madrid	8 Feb 19
DT	W	63.89	Nadine MILLER	GER	Berlin	1 Feb 19
5000W	NAm	22:23.91	Miranda MELVILLE	USA	Rochester	29 Dec 18

OUTDOORS – MEN

HMar	Eur	59:13	Julien WANDERS	SUI	Ras Al Khaimah	8 Feb 19

OUTDOORS – WOMEN

5k	W	14:44	Sifan HASSAN	NED	Monaco	17 Feb 19
HMar	W40	1:08:55	Sinead DIVER	AUS	Marugame	3 Feb 19
35kW	W	2:45:21	Eleonora GIORGI	ITA	Gioiosa Marea	27 Jan 19
	W	2:38:24	Klavdiya AFANASYEVA	RUS	Sochi	18 Feb 19
50kW	W, Asi	3:59:15	LIU Hong	CHN	Huangshan	9 Mar 19

WORLD LIST TRENDS – MEN

This table shows the 10th and 100th bests in the year lists for the last eight years, with previous bests.

10th Bests	To 2009	2011	2012	2013	2014	2015	2016	2017	2018
100m	9.95- 08	**9.89**	9.94	9.97	9.96	9.91	9.93	9.95	9.93
200m	20.03- 00	20.16	20.10	20.10	20.08	19.97	**19.96**	20.01	**19.96**
400m	44.51- 90	44.78	44.77	44.82	44.71	44.36	44.46	44.48	**44.35**
800m	1:43.66- 96	1:44.07	1:43.71	1:43.87	1:43.71	1:43.72	**1:43.55**	1:44.44	1:43.82
1500m	3:31.10- 04	3:31.84	3:31.61	3:31.94	3:30.98	**3:30.29**	3:32.30	3:32.66	3:31.90
5000m	**12:54.99- 03**	12:59.15	12:55.99	13:01.64	13:03.85	13:05.30	13:03.22	13:08.16	13:03.08
10000m	**27:00.30- 07**	26:52.84	27:03.49	27:21.50	27:28.27	27:18.86	27:05.64	27:08.94	27:30.25
Half Mar	59:30- 09	59:39	**59:15**	59:54	59:21	59:28	59:31	59:22	59:17
Marathon	2:06:25- 08	2:05:45!	2:04:54	2:05:16	2:05:13	2:06:00	2:05:21	2:05:39	**2:04:40**
3000mSt	**8:08.14- 02**	8:08.43	8:10.20	8:08.83	8:11.86	8:13.37	8:10.65	8:11.82	8:13.18
110mh	13.19- 07	13.23	**13.13**	13.18	13.19	**13.13**	13.20	13.15	13.26
400mh	**48.25- 02**	48.47	48.41	48.46	48.69	48.44	48.49	48.40	48.42
HJ	**2.36- 88**	2.33	2.32	2.34	2.34	2.33	2.35	2.32	2.33
PV	**5.90- 98**	5.80	5.73	5.80	5.76	5.82	5.80	5.83	5.88
LJ	8.35- 97	8.27	8.26	8.29	8.28	8.29	8.31	8.30	**8.38**
TJ	**17.48- 85**	17.35	17.31	17.26	17.27	17.24	17.16	17.27	17.34
SP	21.63- 84	21.16	21.14	21.09	21.37	21.14	21.30	**21.82**	21.58
DT	**68.20- 82**	67.21	67.50	65.98	66.11	66.40	67.13	66.52	66.98
HT	**81.88- 88**	79.27	79.56	79.16	78.27	78.22	77.78	77.72	77.37
JT	87.12- 96/97	84.81	84.72	84.61	85.92	86.21	86.48	**87.97**	85.46
Decathlon	8526- 98	8288	8322	8390	8311	8398	8413	8345	8303
20kmW	**1:18:30- 05**	1:19:57	1:19:20	1:19:36	1:19:43	1:19:14	1:19:24	1:19:12	1:19:15
50kmW	**3:41:30- 05**	3:44:03	3:41:24	3:43:38	3:43:02	3:44:17	3:42:57	3:44:35	3:46:26

Peak years shown in bold

Men 100th Bests

	To 2009	2011	2012	2013	2014	2015	2016	2017	2018
100m	10.22- 09	10.21	10.20	10.21	10.18	10.16	**10.14**	10.17	10.16
200m	20.66- 99/00/07	20.63	20.57	20.60	20.51	20.51	**20.45**	20.49	20.47
400m	45.78- 00	45.91	45.79	45.87	45.69	**45.61**	45.71	45.65	45.70
800m	1:46.54- 99	1:46.50	1:46.56	1:46.44	1:46.60	1:46.51	1:46.44	**1:46.26**	1:46.47
1500m	3:38.42- 97	3:37.77	**3:36.84**	3:37.77	3:38.47	3:38.13	3:38.20	3:37.88	3:38.28
5000m	13:25.05- 03	13:26.29	**13:23.58**	13:27.29	13:28.60	13:27.10	13:24.13	13:26.67	13:28.03
10000m	**28:04.47- 08**	28:15.79	28:06.74	28:18.68	28:20.77	28:08.4	28:06.33	28:11.02	28:17.63
Half Mar	61:28- 09	61:31	61:19	61:25	61:17	60:58	61:21	61:04	60:52
Marathon	2:10:22- 08	2:09:19!	2:08:32	2:09:06	2:08:58	2:09:14	2:09:28	2:09:10	2:08:47
3000mSt	**8:31.06- 04**	8:35.45	8:31.2	8:34.42	8:35.05	8:33.69	8:32.63	8:32.03	8:32.23
110mh	13.67- 08	13.67	13.67	13.66	13.67	13.67	13.62	**13.61**	13.65	13.70
400mh	50.06- 00	50.28	50.15	50.16	50.21	50.06	49.89	49.88	**49.86**
HJ	**2.24- 84/88/89/92/96**	2.24	2.24	2.24	2.24	2.24	2.24	2.24	2.24
PV	**5.55- 00**	5.45	5.50	5.50	5.50	5.50	5.51	5.51	5.51
LJ	**7.96- 04**	7.94	7.93	7.92	7.89	7.90	7.94	7.93	7.95
TJ	**16.60- 88**	16.53	16.49	16.40	16.38	16.44	16.52	16.43	16.49
SP	19.48- 84	19.18	19.51	19.41	19.47	19.55	**19.56**	19.46	19.55
DT	60.96- 84	59.98	60.95	60.21	60.64	60.36	**61.36**	60.31	60.04
HT	**73.06- 84**	70.44	71.22	70.49	70.50	70.73	71.33	70.89	70.62
JT	77.14- 91	77.38	77.78	77.10	77.16	77.51	**78.29**	77.57	77.33
Decathlon	**7702- 88**	7678	7648	7586	7559	7594	7620	7634	7512
20kmW	1:22:48- 05	1:23:40	1:23:10	1:22:56	1:23:07	1:23:24	**1:22:25**	1:22:33	1:23:06
50kmW	4:03:49- 99	4:06:15	4:03:04	4:08:33	4:06:22	**4:02:23**	4:02:37	4:06:30	4:06:34

! From 2011 main marathon lists no longer include Boston or other such excessively downhill races

Number of athletes achieving base level standards for world lists:

Men		2013	2014	2015	2016	2017	2018			2013	2014	2015	2016	2017	2018
100m	10.25	132	163	168	203	187	204	HJ	2.20	197	211	216	212	213	210
200m	20.69	140	187	194	224	202	218	PV	5.40	179	178	168	192	189	172
400m	46.19	177	202	216	228	201	223	LJ	7.80	181	182	182	207	199	204
800m	1:47.59	190	202	208	226	225	202	TJ	16.30	120	124	126	154	134	139
1500m	3:39.99	184	173	171	180	179	166	SP	18.70	180	180	180	196	191	197
5000m	13:37.0	180	169	204	195	182	165	DT	58.00	166	173	171	189	168	157
10000m	28:35.0	168	155	225	202	186	202	HT	68.00	146	149	156	171	173	166
HMar	61:59	171	199	182	179	200	227	JT	74.00	190	187	199	215	213	190
Mar	2:10:59	212	207	191	169	212	206	Dec	7400	143	150	157	145	168	131
3000St	8:39.9	141	138	144	183	179	159	20kmW	1:25:00	175	151	166	192	212	183
110mh	13.89	199	208	215	220	210	200	50kmW	4:10:00	106	113	134	142	112	112
400mh	50.79	177	191	200	224	237	243								
								TOTAL		3854	3992	4173	4448	4372	4276

The 2018 numbers compared to those of 2017: for 10th best 13-10, 100th best 8-13 (2 tie), base level 9-13 (1 tie)

WORLD LIST TRENDS - WOMEN

This table shows the 10th and 100th bests in the year lists for the last eight years, with previous bests.

10th Bests	To 2009	2011	2012	2013	2014	2015	2016	2017	2018
100m	10.92- 88	11.01	10.99	10.93	11.01	10.92	**10.90**	10.94	10.98
200m	22.24- 88	22.55	22.37	22.40	22.46	22.23	**22.16**	22.39	22.34
400m	**49.74- 84**	50.67	50.06	50.19	50.74	50.32	50.25	50.14	50.16
800m	**1:56.91- 88**	1:58.21	1:57.77	1:58.92	1:58.84	1:58.34	1:58.28	1:58.01	1:58.05
1500m	**3:58.07- 97**	4:01.73	3:59.71	4:01.48	4:00.17	4:01.26	4:00.18	4:00.52	4:00.60
5000m	**14:38.64- 10**	14:39.44	14:50.80	14:47.12	14:52.67	14:47.75	14:38.92	14:39.33	14:52.83
10000m	30:39.86- 08	31:10.02	30:59.19	31:04.85	31:48.6	31:13.29	**30:37.38**	31:11.86	31:38.4
Half Mar	68:23- 00	68:07	67:42	67:39	68:13	68:18	67:16	66:35	**66:18**
Marathon	2:23:22- 06	2:22:43!	2:20:57	2:23:00	2:22:30	2:22:51	2:22:40	2:20:59	**2:19:51**
3000mSt	9:18.54-09	9:25.96	9:23.52	9:27.49	9:23.43	9:20.64	9:18.85	9:13.35	**9:10.71**
100mh	**12.58- 08**	12.73	12.62	12.81	12.71	12.59	12.63	12.61	12.65
400mh	**53.99- 04**	54.69	54.21	54.38	54.74	54.37	54.15	54.29	54.61
HJ	**2.01- 03**	1.96	1.96	1.97	1.97	1.97	1.98	1.96	1.96
PV	4.70- 07/08	4.71	4.70	4.71	4.71	4.72	**4.81**	4.73	4.75
LJ	**7.07- 88**	6.88	6.97	6.91	6.90	6.93	6.93	6.83	6.88
TJ	**14.84- 08**	14.57	14.60	14.50	14.40	14.32	14.56	14.42	14.55
SP	**20.85- 87**	19.26	19.60	18.81	19.03	18.89	19.11	18.83	19.21
DT	**70.34- 88**	63.91	64.45	64.46	65.51	64.79	65.14	64.56	63.92
HT	74.40- 08	72.65	**75.59**	75.02	74.20	73.66	73.09	74.56	74.02
JT	64.89- 00	63.50	64.91	63.55	64.50	65.01	65.14	**65.37**	64.75
Heptathlon	**6540- 88**	6338	6466	6345	6395	6458	6458	6421	6367
20kmW	1:27:18- 08	1:28:41	**1:27:08**	1:27:53	1:27:54	1:27:09	1:27:18	1:27:53	1:27:58

Peak years shown in bold

Women 100th Bests

100m	11.36- 00/08	11.36	11.34	11.35	11.32	11.31	11.27	11.29	**11.25**
200m	23.17- 08	23.21	23.10	23.19	23.17	23.08	**23.00**	23.03	**23.00**
400m	**52.08- 08**	52.33	52.16	52.25	52.36	52.25	52.13	52.15	52.12
800m	2:01.50- 84	2:01.86	2:01.48	2:02.05	2:02.05	2:02.06	2:01.80	2:02.14	2:01.82
1500m	4:10.22- 84	4:09.88	**4:09.06**	4:09.98	4:10.09	4:10.24	4:09.28	4:09.17	4:09.52
5000m	15:27.20- 04	15:31.67	15:32.88	15:35.74	15:33.42	15:32.67	**15:26.28**	15:30.28	15:31.21
10000m	32:30.10- 08	32:53.44	32:38.95	32:48.60	32:43.90	32:29.06	**32:21.98**	32:37.21	32:34.37
Half Mar	70:57- 09	71:06	70:48	70:44	70:45	70:43	70:35	70:15	**69:52**
Marathon	2:29:53- 08	2:28:32	2:28:01	2:29:10	2:29:17	2:28:24	2:28:49	2:28:15	**2:26:56**
3000mSt	9:56.48- 08	9:59.44	9:53.79	9:56.50	9:53.19	9:52.62	**9:46.86**	9:52.89	9:50.94
100mh	13.22- 00/08	13.16	13.11	13.19	13.14	13.14	**13.07**	13.14	13.14
400mh	57.21- 07	57.26	57.14	57.40	57.34	57.08	**56.85**	57.03	57.22
HJ	**1.88- 86/87/88/92/93**	1.86	1.87	1.87	1.86	1.86	1.87	1.86	1.86
PV	4.25- 08	4.30	4.31	4.30	4.30	4.32	**4.35**	4.33	4.34
LJ	6.53- 88	6.50	**6.55**	6.49	6.45	6.49	6.51	6.48	6.47
TJ	**13.75- 08**	13.70	13.71	13.69	13.60	13.62	13.60	13.56	13.61
SP	**17.19- 87**	16.60	16.82	16.65	16.60	16.84	16.96	16.92	16.95
DT	**58.50- 92**	56.12	56.94	55.70	56.27	56.26	56.83	55.99	55.88
HT	64.81- 08	64.79	**65.78**	64.65	64.79	65.67	65.75	64.86	65.35
JT	55.55- 00	55.34	55.97	55.10	55.78	55.95	56.19	**56.20**	55.66
Heptathlon	**5741- 88**	5591	5702	5560	5668	5715	5735	5703	5719
20kmW	1:34:11- 05	1:34:52	1:33:43	1:33:48	1:35:20	1:34:16	1:33:41	**1:33:32**	1:34:13

All-time record levels indicated in bold.

! From 2011 main marathon lists no longer include Boston or other such excessively downhill races.

Number of athletes achieving base level standards for world lists:

Women		2013	2014	2015	2016	2017	2018			2013	2014	2015	2016	2017	2018
100m	11.44	151	169	179	215	196	216	400mh	57.99	143	152	166	192	159	167
200m	23.29	140	138	174	198	183	189	HJ	1.85	155	148	142	170	143	131
400m	52.99	196	190	213	236	230	234	PV	4.25	123	133	143	169	140	170
800m	2:03.50	166	184	191	211	188	189	LJ	6.35	171	168	186	189	175	172
1500m	4:13.5	167	169	164	195	202	189	TJ	13.30	184	171	169	189	158	169
5000m	15:45.0	167	172	192	224	187	184	SP	15.85	177	189	194	216	200	220
10000m	33:00.0	131	133	169	176	154	163	DT	53.65	159	152	165	180	174	168
HMar	72:00	204	193	200	212	237	251	HT	61.00	190	193	205	227	224	236
Mar	2:32:00	170	171	195	196	230	259	JT	53.00	159	172	176	188	202	187
3000mSt	10:05.0	144	161	166	195	164	178	Hep	5450	140	156	155	189	140	174
100mh	13.39	175	195	191	228	212	229	20kmW	1:38:00	194	148	176	198	192	186
								TOTAL		3463	3505	3745	4201	4107	4261

The 2018 numbers compared to those of 2017: for 10th best 8-13 (1T), 100th best 14-6 (2T), base level 15-7
In 2018 there was an interesting increase in standards in depth for women as against a decline for men.

Mark	Wind	Name		Nat	Born	Pos	Meet	Venue	Date

WORLD MEN'S ALL-TIME LISTS

100 METRES

Mark	Wind	Name		Nat	Born	Pos	Meet	Venue	Date
9.58 WR	0.9	Usain	Bolt	JAM	21.8.86	1	WCh	Berlin	16 Aug 09
9.63	1.5		Bolt			1	OG	London (OS)	5 Aug 12
9.69 WR	0.0		Bolt			1	OG	Beijing	16 Aug 08
9.69	2.0	Tyson	Gay ¶	USA	9.8.82	1		Shanghai	20 Sep 09
9.69	-0.1	Yohan	Blake	JAM	26.12.89	1	Athl	Lausanne	23 Aug 12
9.71	0.9		Gay			2	WCh	Berlin	16 Aug 09
9.72 WR	1.7		Bolt			1	Reebok	New York (RI)	31 May 08
9.72	0.2	Asafa	Powell	JAM	23.11.82	1rA	Athl	Lausanne	2 Sep 08
9.74 WR	1.7		Powell			1h2	GP	Rieti	9 Sep 07
9.74	0.9	Justin	Gatlin ¶	USA	10.2.82	1	DL	Doha	15 May 15
9.75	1.1		Blake			1	NC	Kingston	29 Jun 12
9.75	1.5		Blake			2	OG	London (OS)	5 Aug 12
9.75	0.9		Gatlin			1	GGala	Roma	4 Jun 15
9.75	1.4		Gatlin			1	Athl	Lausanne	9 Jul 15
9.76	1.8		Bolt			1		Kingston	3 May 08
9.76	1.3		Bolt			1	VD	Bruxelles	16 Sep 11
9.76	-0.1		Bolt			1	GGala	Roma	31 May 12
9.76	1.4		Blake			1	WK	Zürich	30 Aug 12
9.77 WR	1.6		Powell			1	Tsik	Athína	14 Jun 05
9.77 WR	1.5		Powell			1	BrGP	Gateshead	11 Jun 06
9.77 WR	1.0		Powell			1rA	WK	Zürich	18 Aug 06
9.77	1.6		Gay			1q1	NC/OT	Eugene	28 Jun 08
9.77	-1.3		Bolt			1	VD	Bruxelles	5 Sep 08
9.77	0.9		Powell			1h1	GP	Rieti	7 Sep 08
9.77	0.4		Gay			1	GGala	Roma	10 Jul 09
9.77	-0.3		Bolt			1	WCh	Moskva	11 Aug 13
9.77	0.6		Gatlin			1	VD	Bruxelles	5 Sep 14
9.77	0.9		Gatlin			1s2	WCh	Beijing	23 Aug 15
9.78	0.0		Powell			1	GP	Rieti	9 Sep 07
9.78	-0.4		Gay			1	LGP	London (CP)	13 Aug 10
9.78	0.9	Nesta	Carter ¶	JAM	10.11.85	1		Rieti	29 Aug 10
9.78	1.0		Powell			1	Athl	Lausanne	30 Jun 11
9.78	-0.3		Gatlin			1	Herc	Monaco	17 Jul 15
		(34 performances by 6 athletes)							
9.79 WR	0.1	Maurice	Greene	USA	23.7.74	1rA	Tsik	Athína	16 Jun 99
9.79	-0.3	Christian	Coleman	USA	6.3.96	1	VD	Bruxelles	31 Aug 18
9.80	0.4	Steve	Mullings ¶	JAM	29.11.82	1	Pre	Eugene	4 Jun 11
9.82	1.7	Richard	Thompson	TTO	7.6.85	1	NC	Port of Spain	21 Jun 14
		(10)							
9.84 WR	0.7	Donovan	Bailey	CAN	16.12.67	1	OG	Atlanta	27 Jul 96
9.84	0.2	Bruny	Surin	CAN	12.7.67	2	WCh	Sevilla	22 Aug 99
9.84	1.3	Trayvon	Bromell	USA	10.7.95	1h4	NC	Eugene	25 Jun 15
9.85 WR	1.2	Leroy	Burrell	USA	21.2.67	1rA	Athl	Lausanne	6 Jul 94
9.85	1.7	Olusoji	Fasuba	NGR	9.7.84	2	SGP	Doha	12 May 06
9.85	1.3	Michael	Rodgers	USA	24.4.85	2	Pre	Eugene	4 Jun 11
9.86 WR	1.2	Carl	Lewis	USA	1.7.61	1	WCh	Tokyo	25 Aug 91
9.86	-0.4	Frank	Fredericks	NAM	2.10.67	1rA	Athl	Lausanne	3 Jul 96
9.86	1.8	Ato	Boldon	TTO	30.12.73	1rA	MSR	Walnut	19 Apr 98
9.86	0.0	Francis	Obikwelu	NGR/POR	22.11.78	2	OG	Athína	22 Aug 04
		(20)							
9.86	1.4	Keston	Bledman	TTO	8.3.88	1	NC	Port of Spain	23 Jun 12
9.86	1.3	Jimmy	Vicaut	FRA	27.2.92	2	DL	Saint-Denis	4 Jul 15
9.87	0.3	Linford	Christie ¶	GBR	2.4.60	1	WCh	Stuttgart	15 Aug 93
9.87A	-0.2	Obadele	Thompson	BAR	30.3.76	1	WCp	Johannesburg	11 Sep 98
9.87	-0.1	Ronnie	Baker	USA	15.10.93	1	Skol	Chorzów	22 Aug 18
9.88	1.8	Shawn	Crawford ¶	USA	14.1.78	1	Pre	Eugene	19 Jun 04
9.88	0.6	Walter	Dix	USA	31.1.86	2		Nottwil	8 Aug 10
9.88	0.9	Ryan	Bailey	USA	13.4.89	2		Rieti	29 Aug 10
9.88	1.0	Michael	Frater	JAM	6.10.82	2	Athl	Lausanne	30 Jun 11
9.88	1.1	Noah	Lyles	USA	18.7.97	1	NC	Des Moines	22 Jun 18
		(30)							
9.89	1.6	Travis	Padgett	USA	13.12.86	1q2	NC/OT	Eugene	28 Jun 08
9.89	1.6	Darvis	Patton	USA	4.12.77	1q3	NC/OT	Eugene	28 Jun 08
9.89	1.3	Ngonidzashe	Makusha	ZIM	11.3.87	1	NCAA	Des Moines	10 Jun 11
9.89	1.9	Akani	Simbine	RSA	21.9.93	1	Gyulai	Székesfehérvár	18 Jul 16
9.90	0.4	Nickel	Ashmeade	JAM	7.4.90	1s2	WCh	Moskva	11 Aug 13
9.91	1.2	Dennis	Mitchell ¶	USA	20.2.66	3	WCh	Tokyo	25 Aug 91

Mark	Wind	Name		Nat	Born	Pos	Meet	Venue	Date
9.91	0.9	Leonard	Scott	USA	19.1.80	2	WAF	Stuttgart	9 Sep 06
9.91	-0.5	Derrick	Atkins	BAH	5.1.84	2	WCh	Osaka	26 Aug 07
9.91	-0.2	Daniel	Bailey	ANT	9.9.86	2	GL	Saint-Denis	17 Jul 09
9.91	0.7	Churandy	Martina	NED	3.7.84	2s1	OG	London (OS)	5 Aug 12
		(40)							
9.91	1.1	James	Dasaolu	GBR	5.9.87	1s2	NC	Birmingham	13 Jul 13
9.91	1.8	Femi Seun	Ogunode ¶	QAT	15.5.91	1	AsiC	Wuhan	4 Jun 15
9.91	0.2	Andre	De Grasse	CAN	10.11.94	3	OG	Rio de Janeiro	14 Aug 16
9.91	1.0	Julian	Forte	JAM	7.1.93	1	ISTAF	Berlin	27 Aug 17
9.91	0.4	Zharnel	Hughes	GBR	13.7.95	1rA		Kingston	9 Jun 18
9.91	0.2		Su Bingtian	CHN	29.8.89	1		Madrid	22 Jun 18
9.92	0.3	Andre	Cason	USA	20.1.69	2	WCh	Stuttgart	15 Aug 93
9.92	0.8	Jon	Drummond	USA	9.9.68	1h3	NC	Indianapolis	12 Jun 97
9.92	0.2	Tim	Montgomery ¶	USA	28.1.75	2	NC	Indianapolis	13 Jun 97
9.92A	-0.2	Seun	Ogunkoya	NGR	28.12.77	2	WCp	Johannesburg	11 Sep 98
9.92	1.0	Tim	Harden	USA	27.1.74	1	Spitzen	Luzern	5 Jul 99
9.92	2.0	Christophe	Lemaitre	FRA	11.6.90	1	NC	Albi	29 Jul 11
9.92	-0.8	Kemar	Bailey-Cole	JAM	10.1.92	3	DL	London (OS)	24 Jul 15
9.92A	0.9	Jak Ali	Harvey	JAM/TUR	5.4.89	1		Erzurum	12 Jun 16
9.92	0.7	Isiah	Young	USA	5.1.90	1r2		Montverde	9 Jun 18
		(55)							

100th man 9.97, 200th 10.04, 300th 10.08, 400th 10.11, 500th 10.14

Doubtful timing: 9.88A 0.2 Sydney Siame   ZAM 7.10.97 1   Lusaka   8 Apr 17

Doubtful wind reading: 9.91 -2.3 Davidso Ezinwa NGR 22.11.71 1   Azusa   11 Apr 92

Wind-assisted – performances to 9.76, performers listed to 9.88W

Mark	Wind	Name		Nat	Born	Pos	Meet	Venue	Date
9.68	4.1	Tyson	Gay ¶	USA	9.8.82	1	NC/OT	Eugene	29 Jun 08
9.69A	5+	Obadele	Thompson	BAR	30.3.76	1		El Paso	13 Apr 96
9.69	4.8	Andre	De Grasse	CAN	10.11.94	1	DL	Stockholm	18 Jun 17
9.72	2.1		Powell			1	Bisl	Oslo	4 Jun 10
9.74	w	Richard	Thompson	TTO	7.6.85	1		Clermont	31 May 14
9.75	3.4		Gay			1h1	NC	Eugene	25 Jun 09
9.75	2.6		Powell			1h2	DL	Doha	14 May 10
9.75	4.3	Darvis	Patton	USA	4.12.77	1rA	TexR	Austin	30 Mar 13
9.75	2.7		De Grasse			1	NCAA	Eugene	12 Jun 15
9.76A	6.1	Churandy	Martina	AHO	3.7.84	1		El Paso	13 May 06
9.76	2.2		Gay			1	GP	New York	2 Jun 07
9.76	2.7		Gatlin			1	Pre	Eugene	31 May 14
9.76	3.7	Trayvon	Bromell	USA	10.7.95	1s1	NC	Eugene	26 Jun 15
9.78	5.2	Carl	Lewis	USA	1.7.61	1	NC/OT	Indianapolis	16 Jul 88
9.78	3.7	Maurice	Greene	USA	23.7.74	1	GP II	Stanford	31 May 04
9.78	2.4	Ronnie	Baker	USA	15.10.93	1	Pre	Eugene	26 May 18
9.79	5.3	Andre	Cason	USA	20.1.69	1h4	NC	Eugene	16 Jun 93
9.80	4.1	Walter	Dix	USA	31.1.86	2	NC/OT	Eugene	29 Jun 08
9.80	2.7	Michael	Rodgers	USA	24.4.85	2	Pre	Eugene	31 May 14
9.82	3.0	Isiah	Young	USA	5.1.90	1		Clermont	16 May 15
9.82	4.9	Remontay	McClain	USA	21.9.92	1h3	NC	Eugene	25 Jun 15
9.83	7.1	Leonard	Scott	USA	19.1.80	1r1	Sea Ray	Knoxville	9 Apr 99
9.83	2.2	Derrick	Atkins	BAH	5.1.84	2	GP	New York	2 Jun 07
9.84	5.4	Francis	Obikwelu	NGR/POR	22.11.78	1		Zaragoza	3 Jun 06
9.84	4.8	Ben Youssef	Meité	CIV	11.11.86	2	DL	Stockholm	18 Jun 17
9.85	4.8	Dennis	Mitchell ¶	USA	20.2.66	2	NC	Eugene	17 Jun 93
9.85A	3.0	Frank	Fredericks	NAM	2.10.67	1		Nairobi	18 May 02
9.85	4.1	Travis	Padgett	USA	13.12.86	4	NC/OT	Eugene	29 Jun 08
9.85	3.6	Keston	Bledman	TTO	8.3.88	1rA		Clermont	2 Jun 12
9.85	3.2	Charles	Silmon	USA	4.7.91	1s1	NC	Des Moines	21 Jun 13
9.85A	3.0	Kemar	Hyman	CAY	11.10.89	1s2	NACAC	San José, CRC	7 Aug 15
9.86	2.6	Shawn	Crawford ¶	USA	14.1.78	1	GP	Doha	14 May 04
9.86	3.6	Michael	Frater	JAM	6.10.82	2h4	NC	Kingston	23 Jun 11
9.86	3.2	Rakieem "Mookie"	Salaam	USA	5.4.90	2s1	NC	Des Moines	21 Jun 13
9.86	3.7	Diondre	Batson	USA	13.7.92	2s1	NC	Eugene	26 Jun 15
9.86	4.1	Noah	Lyles	USA	18.7.97	1rF		Gainesville	13 Apr 18
9.87	11.2	William	Snoddy	USA	6.12.57	1		Dallas	1 Apr 78
9.87	4.9	Calvin	Smith	USA	8.1.61	1s2	NC/OT	Indianapolis	16 Jul 88
9.87	2.4	Michael	Marsh	USA	4.8.67	1rA		Walnut	20 Apr 97
9.87	3.3	Yoshihide	Kiryu	JPN	15.12.95	1r1	TexR	Austin	28 Mar 15
9.87	2.1	Tevin	Hester	USA	10.1.94	1	ACC	Tallahassee	16 May 15
9.88	2.3	James	Sanford	USA	27.12.57	1		Los Angeles (Ww)	3 May 80
9.88	5.2	Albert	Robinson	USA	28.11.64	4	NC/OT	Indianapolis	16 Jul 88
9.88	4.9	Tim	Harden	USA	27.1.74	1	NC	New Orleans	20 Jun 98
9.88	4.5	Coby	Miller	USA	19.10.76	1		Auburn	1 Apr 00
9.88	3.6	Patrick	Johnson	AUS	26.9.72	1		Perth	8 Feb 03

Mark	Wind	Name		Nat	Born	Pos	Meet	Venue	Date
9.88	3.0	Darrel	Brown	TTO	11.10.84	1	NC	Port of Spain	23 Jun 07
9.88	3.7	Ivory	Williams #	USA	2.5.85	1	TexR	Austin	3 Apr 10
9.88	2.4	Reece	Prescod	GBR	29.2.96	3	Pre	Eugene	26 May 18
Drugs disqualification									
9.75	1.1		Gay ¶			(1)	NC	Des Moines	21 Jun 13
9.77	1.7		Gatlin ¶	USA	10.2.82	(1)	SGP	Doha	12 May 06
9.78	2.0	Tim	Montgomery ¶	USA	28.1.75	(1)	GPF	Paris (C)	14 Sep 02
9.79	1.1	Ben	Johnson ¶	CAN	30.12.61	(1)	OG	Seoul	24 Sep 88
9.87	2.0	Dwain	Chambers ¶	GBR	5.4.78	(2)	GPF	Paris (C)	14 Sep 02
9.75w	2.4		Gay			(1s2)	NC	Des Moines	21 Jun 13

200 METRES

Mark	Wind	Name		Nat	Born	Pos	Meet	Venue	Date
19.19	wr-0.3	Usain	Bolt	JAM	21.8.86	1	WCh	Berlin	20 Aug 09
19.26	0.7	Yohan	Blake	JAM	26.12.89	1	VD	Bruxelles	16 Sep 11
19.30	wr-0.9		Bolt			1	OG	Beijing	20 Aug 08
19.32	wr0.4	Michael	Johnson	USA	13.9.67	1	OG	Atlanta	1 Aug 96
19.32	0.4		Bolt			1	OG	London (OS)	9 Aug 12
19.40	0.8		Bolt			1	WCh	Daegu	3 Sep 11
19.44	0.4		Blake			2	OG	London (OS)	9 Aug 12
19.53	0.7	Walter	Dix	USA	31.1.86	2	VD	Bruxelles	16 Sep 11
19.54	0.0		Blake			1	VD	Bruxelles	7 Sep 12
19.55	-0.1		Bolt			1	WCh	Beijing	27 Aug 15
19.56	-0.8		Bolt			1		Kingston	1 May 10
19.57	0.0		Bolt			1	VD	Bruxelles	4 Sep 09
19.57	0.4	Justin	Gatlin ¶	USA	10.2.82	1	NC	Eugene	28 Jun 15
19.58	1.3	Tyson	Gay ¶	USA	9.8.82	1	Reebok	New York	30 May 09
19.58	1.4		Bolt			1	Athl	Lausanne	23 Aug 12
19.59	-0.9		Bolt			1	Athl	Lausanne	7 Jul 09
19.62	-0.3		Gay			1	NC	Indianapolis	24 Jun 07
19.63	0.4	Xavier	Carter	USA	8.12.85	1	Athl	Lausanne	11 Jul 06
19.63	-0.9		Bolt			1	Athl	Lausanne	2 Sep 08
19.65	0.0	Wallace	Spearmon	USA	24.12.84	1		Daegu	28 Sep 06
19.65	0.9	Noah	Lyles	USA	18.7.97	1	Herc	Monaco	20 Jul 18
19.66	wr1.7		M Johnson			1	NC	Atlanta	23 Jun 96
19.66	0.0		Bolt			1	WK	Zürich	30 Aug 12
19.66	0.0		Bolt			1	WCh	Moskva	17 Aug 13
19.67	-0.5		Bolt			1	GP	Athína	13 Jul 08
19.68	0.4	Frank	Fredericks (10)	NAM	2.10.67	2	OG	Atlanta	1 Aug 96
19.68	-0.1		Gay			1	WAF	Stuttgart	10 Sep 06
19.68	-0.1		Bolt			1	WAF	Thessaloníki	13 Sep 09
19.68	-0.5		Gatlin			1	Herc	Monaco	18 Jul 14
19.68	0.9		Gatlin			1	Pre	Eugene	30 May 15
19.69	0.9		Dix			1	NCAA-r	Gainesville	26 May 07
19.69A	-0.5	Clarence	Munyai	RSA	20.2.98	1s1	NC	Pretoria	16 Mar 18
		(32/11)							
19.72A	wr 1.8	Pietro	Mennea	ITA	28.6.52	1	WUG	Ciudad de México	12 Sep 79
19.73	-0.2	Michael	Marsh	USA	4.8.67	1s1	OG	Barcelona	5 Aug 92
19.75	1.5	Carl	Lewis	USA	1.7.61	1	NC	Indianapolis	19 Jun 83
19.74	1.4	LaShawn	Merritt ¶	USA	27.6.86	1s3	NC/OT	Eugene	8 Jul 16
19.75	1.7	Joe	DeLoach	USA	5.6.67	1	OG	Seoul	28 Sep 88
19.75	0.3	Steven	Gardiner	BAH	12.9.95	1	Coral Gables		7 Apr 18
19.76	0.7	Ramil	Guliyev	AZE/TUR	29.5.90	1	EC	Berlin	9 Aug 18
19.77	0.7	Ato	Boldon	TTO	30.12.73	1rA		Stuttgart	13 Jul 97
19.77	0.0	Isaac	Makwala	BOT	29.9.86	1		Madrid	14 Jul 17
19.79	1.2	Shawn	Crawford ¶	USA	14.1.78	1	OG	Athína	26 Aug 04
		(20)							
19.79	0.9	Warren	Weir	JAM	31.10.89	1	NC	Kingston	23 Jun 13
19.80	0.8	Christophe	Lemaitre	FRA	11.6.90	3	WCh	Daegu	3 Sep 11
19.80	2.0	Rasheed	Dwyer	JAM	29.1.89	1s1	PAm	Toronto	23 Jul 15
19.80	-0.3	Andre	De Grasse	CAN	10.11.94	2s2	OG	Rio de Janeiro	17 Aug 16
19.81	-0.3	Alonso	Edward	PAN	8.12.89	2	WCh	Berlin	20 Aug 09
19.81	0.4	Churandy	Martina	NED	3.7.84	1	Athl	Lausanne	25 Aug 16
19.81	0.1	Akeem	Bloomfield	JAM	10.11.97	1	DL	London (OS)	22 Jul 18
19.83A	wr 0.9	Tommie	Smith	USA	6.6.44	1	OG	Ciudad de México	16 Oct 68
19.84	1.7	Francis	Obikwelu	NGR/POR	22.11.78	1s2	WCh	Sevilla	25 Aug 99
19.84	1.2	Wayde	van Niekerk	RSA	15.7.92	1		Kingston	10 Jun 17
		(30)							
19.84	-0.6	Michael	Norman	USA	3.12.97	1	DL	Paris (C)	30 Jun 18
19.85	-0.3	John	Capel ¶	USA	27.10.78	1	NC	Sacramento	23 Jul 00
19.85	-0.5	Konstadínos	Kedéris ¶	GRE	11.7.73	1	EC	München	9 Aug 02

Mark	Wind	Name		Nat	Born	Pos	Meet	Venue	Date
19.85	0.0	Nickel	Ashmeade	JAM	4.7.90	2	WK	Zürich	30 Aug 12
19.85	1.9	Ameer	Webb	USA	19.3.91	1	DL	Doha	6 May 16
19.85	-0.5	Christian	Coleman	USA	6.3.96	1q1	NCAA-E	Lexington	27 May 17
19.86A	1.0	Don	Quarrie	JAM	25.2.51	1	PAm	Cali	3 Aug 71
19.86	1.6	Maurice	Greene	USA	23.7.74	2rA	DNG	Stockholm	7 Jul 97
19.86	1.5	Jason	Young	JAM	21.3.91	1	Spitzen	Luzern	17 Jul 12
19.86	1.6	Isiah	Young	USA	5.1.90	1	NC	Des Moines	23 Jun 13
		(40)							
19.87	0.8	Lorenzo	Daniel	USA	23.3.66	1	NCAA	Eugene	3 Jun 88
19.87A	1.8	John	Regis	GBR	13.10.66	1		Sestriere	31 Jul 94
19.87	1.2	Jeff	Williams	USA	31.12.65	1		Fresno	13 Apr 96
19.87	-0.1	Anaso	Jobodwana	RSA	30.7.92	3	WCh	Beijing	27 Aug 15
19.88	-0.3	Floyd	Heard	USA	24.3.66	2	NC	Sacramento	23 Jul 00
19.88	0.1	Joshua 'J.J'	Johnson	USA	10.5.76	1	VD	Bruxelles	24 Aug 01
19.88	1.2	Miguel	Francis	ANT/GBR	28.2.95	1		Kingston	11 Jun 16
19.89	-0.8	Claudinei	da Silva	BRA	19.11.70	1	GPF	München	11 Sep 99
19.89	1.3	Jaysuma	Saidy Ndure	NOR	1.1.84	1	WAF	Stuttgart	23 Sep 07
19.90	1.3	Asafa	Powell	JAM	23.11.82	1	NC	Kingston	25 Jun 06
		(50)							

100th man 20.08, 200th 20.21, 300th 20.29, 400th 20.35, 500th 20.39

Wind-assisted 2 performances to 19.69, performers listed to 19.87

Mark	Wind	Name		Nat	Born	Pos	Meet	Venue	Date
19.58	2.4	Andre	De Grasse	CAN	10.11.94	1	NCAA	Eugene	12 Jun 15
19.61	>4.0	Leroy	Burrell	USA	21.2.67	1	SWC	College Station	19 May 90
19.73	3.3	Shawn	Crawford ¶	USA	14.1.78	1	NC	Eugene	28 Jun 09
19.75	4.1	Isiah	Young	USA	5.1.90	1rA		Clermont	16 May 15
19.83	9.2	Bobby	Cruse	USA	20.3.78	1r2	Sea Ray	Knoxville	9 Apr 99
19.86	4.6	Roy	Martin	USA	25.12.66	1	SWC	Houston	18 May 86
19.86	2.4	Dedric	Dukes	USA	2.4.92	2	NCAA	Eugene	12 Jun 15
19.86	2.4	Trayvon	Bromell	USA	10.7.95	3	NCAA	Eugene	12 Jun 15
19.86	2.9	Danny	Talbot	GBR	1.5.91	1r2		Clermont	15 Apr 17
19.87	5.7	Malik	Moffett	USA	11.4.94	1	Big 10	University Park	14 May 17

300 METRES

In 300m races only, not including intermediate times in 400m races

Mark		Name		Nat	Born	Pos	Meet	Venue	Date
30.81		Wayde	van Niekerk	RSA	15.7.92	1	GS	Ostrava	28 Jun 17
30.85A		Michael	Johnson	USA	13.9.67	1		Pretoria	24 Mar 00
30.97		Usain	Bolt	JAM	21.8.86	1	GS	Ostrava	27 May 10
31.23		LaShawn	Merritt ¶	USA	27.6.86	2		Kingston	11 Jun 16
31.44		Isaac	Makwala	BOT	29.9.86	2	GS	Ostrava	28 Jun 17
31.48		Danny	Everett	USA	1.11.66	1		Jerez de la Frontera	3 Sep 90
31.48		Roberto	Hernández	CUB	6.3.67	2		Jerez de la Frontera	3 Sep 90
31.56		Doug	Walker ¶	GBR	28.7.73	1		Gateshead	19 Jul 98
31.61		Anthuan	Maybank	USA	30.12.69	1		Durham	13 Jul 96
31.61		Clarence	Munyai	RSA	20.2.98	3	GS	Ostrava	28 Jun 17
31.64		Tony	McQuay	USA	16.4.90	3		Kingston	11 Jun 16
31.67		John	Regis	GBR	13.10.66	1	Vaux	Gateshead	17 Jul 92

400 METRES

Mark		Name		Nat	Born	Pos	Meet	Venue	Date
43.03 WR		Wayde	van Niekerk	RSA	15.7.92	1	OG	Rio de Janeiro	14 Aug 16
43.18 WR		Michael	Johnson	USA	13.9.67	1	WCh	Sevilla	26 Aug 99
43.29 WR		Butch	Reynolds ¶	USA	8.6.64	1	WK	Zürich	17 Aug 88
43.39			Johnson			1	WCh	Göteborg	9 Aug 95
43.44			Johnson			1	NC	Atlanta	19 Jun 96
43.45		Jeremy	Wariner	USA	31.1.84	1	WCh	Osaka	31 Aug 07
43.48			van Niekerk			1	WCh	Beijing	26 Aug 15
43.49			Johnson			1	OG	Atlanta	29 Jul 96
43.50		Quincy	Watts	USA	19.6.70	1	OG	Barcelona	5 Aug 92
43.50			Wariner			1	DNG	Stockholm	7 Aug 07
43.61		Michael	Norman	USA	3.12.97	1	NCAA	Eugene	8 Jun 18
43.62			Wariner			1rA	GGala	Roma	14 Jul 06
43.62			van Niekerk			1	Athl	Lausanne	6 Jul 17
43.65			Johnson			1	WCh	Stuttgart	17 Aug 93
43.65		LaShawn	Merritt ¶	USA	27.6.86	2	WCh	Beijing	26 Aug 15
43.66			Johnson			1	NC	Sacramento	16 Jun 95
43.66			Johnson			1rA	Athl	Lausanne	3 Jul 96
43.68			Johnson			1	WK	Zürich	12 Aug 98
43.68			Johnson			1	NC	Sacramento	16 Jul 00
43.70		Fred	Kerley	USA	7.5.95	1q1	NCAA-W	Austin	26 May 17
43.71			Watts			1s2	OG	Barcelona	3 Aug 92
43.72		Isaac	Makwala	BOT	29.9.86	1		La Chaux-de-Fonds	5 Jul 15
43.73			van Niekerk			1	Herc	Monaco	21 Jul 17
43.74			Johnson			1	NC	Eugene	19 Jun 93
43.74			Merritt			1	WCh	Moskva	13 Aug 13

Mark	Wind	Name		Nat	Born	Pos	Meet	Venue	Date
43.74		Kirani	James	GRN	1.9.92	1	Athl	Lausanne	3 Jul 14
43.75			Johnson			1		Waco	19 Apr 97
43.75			Merritt			1	OG	Beijing	21 Aug 08
43.76			Johnson			1	GWG	Uniondale, NY	22 Jul 98
43.76			James			2	OG	Rio de Janeiro	14 Aug 16
	(30/10)								
43.81		Danny	Everett	USA	1.11.66	1	NC/OT	New Orleans	26 Jun 92
43.86A WR		Lee	Evans	USA	25.2.47	1	OG	Ciudad de México	18 Oct 68
43.87		Steve	Lewis	USA	16.5.69	1	OG	Seoul	28 Sep 88
43.87		Steven	Gardiner	BAH	12.9.95	1	DL	Doha	4 May 18
43.93		Youssef	Al-Masrahi	KSA	31.12.87	1h2	WCh	Beijing	23 Aug 15
43.93		Rusheen	McDonald	JAM	17.8.92	2h2	WCh	Beijing	23 Aug 15
43.94		Akeem	Bloomfield	JAM	10.11.97	2	NCAA	Eugene	8 Jun 18
43.97A		Larry	James	USA	6.11.47	2	OG	Ciudad de México	18 Oct 68
44.01		Machel	Cedenio	TTO	6.9.95	4	OG	Rio de Janeiro	14 Aug 16
44.02		Baboloki	Thebe	BOT	18.3.97	2	Athl	Lausanne	6 Jul 17
	(20)								
44.05		Angelo	Taylor	USA	29.12.78	1	NC	Indianapolis	23 Jun 07
44.07		Abdelilah	Haroun	QAT	.97	1	DL	London (OS)	21 Jul 18
44.09		Alvin	Harrison ¶	USA/DOM	20.1.74	3	NC	Atlanta	19 Jun 96
44.09		Jerome	Young ¶	USA	14.8.76	1	NC	New Orleans	21 Jun 98
44.10		Gary	Kikaya	COD	4.2.78	2	WAF	Stuttgart	9 Sep 06
44.11		Luguelín	Santos	DOM	12.11.92	4	WCh	Beijing	26 Aug 15
44.13		Derek	Mills	USA	9.7.72	1	Pre	Eugene	4 Jun 95
44.13		Nathon	Allen	JAM	28.10.95	3	NCAA	Eugene	8 Jun 18
44.14		Roberto	Hernández	CUB	6.3.67	2		Sevilla	30 May 90
44.15		Anthuan	Maybank	USA	30.12.69	1rB	Athl	Lausanne	3 Jul 96
	(30)								
44.16		Otis	Harris	USA	30.6.82	2	OG	Athína	23 Aug 04
44.17		Innocent	Egbunike	NGR	30.11.61	1rA	WK	Zürich	19 Aug 87
44.18		Samson	Kitur	KEN	25.2.66	2s2	OG	Barcelona	3 Aug 92
44.20A		Charles	Gitonga	KEN	5.10.71	1	NC	Nairobi	29 Jun 96
44.21		Ian	Morris	TTO	30.11.61	3s2	OG	Barcelona	3 Aug 92
44.21A		Emmanuel	Korir	KEN	15.6.95	1	NC	Nairobi	23 Jun 18
44.22		Gil	Roberts	USA	15.3.89	2	NC	Sacramento	24 Jun 17
44.24		Tony	McQuay	USA	16.4.90	1s1	NC/OT	Eugene	2 Jul 16
44.25		Karabo	Sibanda	BOT	2.7.98	5	OG	Rio de Janeiro	14 Aug 16
44.26		Alberto	Juantorena	CUB	21.11.50	1	OG	Montreal	29 Jul 76
	(40)								
44.27		Alonzo	Babers	USA	31.10.61	1	OG	Los Angeles	8 Aug 84
44.27		Antonio	Pettigrew ¶	USA	3.11.67	1	NC	Houston	17 Jun 89
44.27		Darold	Williamson	USA	19.2.83	1s1	NCAA	Sacramento	10 Jun 05
44.28		Andrew	Valmon	USA	1.1.65	4	NC	Eugene	19 Jun 93
44.28		Tyree	Washington	USA	28.8.76	1		Los Angeles (ER)	12 May 01
44.29		Derrick	Brew	USA	28.12.77	1	SEC	Athens, GA	16 May 99
44.29		Sanderlei	Parrela	BRA	7.10.74	2	WCh	Sevilla	26 Aug 99
44.30		Gabriel	Tiacoh	CIV	10.9.63	1	NCAA	Indianapolis	7 Jun 86
44.30		Lamont	Smith	USA	11.12.72	4	NC	Atlanta	19 Jun 96
44.31		Alejandro	Cárdenas	MEX	4.10.74	3	WCh	Sevilla	26 Aug 99
	(50)	100th man 44.56, 200th 44.80, 300th 45.00, 400th 45.15, 500th 45.27							
Drugs disqualification									
44.21		Antonio	Pettigrew ¶	USA	3.11.67	1		Nassau	26 May 99
Hand timing		*440 yards time less 0.3 secs							
44.1		Wayne	Collett	USA	20.10.49	1	OT	Eugene	9 Jul 72
44.2*		John	Smith	USA	5.8.50	1	AAU	Eugene	26 Jun 71
44.2		Fred	Newhouse	USA	8.11.48	1s1	OT	Eugene	7 Jul 72

600 METRES

Mark	Wind	Name		Nat	Born	Pos	Meet	Venue	Date
1:12.81		Johnny	Gray	USA	19.6.60	1		Santa Monica	24 May 86
1:13.10		David	Rudisha	KEN	17.12.88	1	DL	Birmingham	5 Jun 16
1:13.2 + ?		John	Kipkurgat	KEN	16.3.44	1		Pointe-à-Pierre	23 Mar 74
1:13.21		Pierre-Ambroise	Bosse	FRA	11.5.92	2	DL	Birmingham	5 Jun 16
1:13.28		Duane	Solomon	USA	28.12.84	1		Burnaby	1 Jul 13
1:13.49		Joseph	Mutua	KEN	10.12.78	1		Liège (NX)	27 Aug 02

800 METRES

Mark	Wind	Name		Nat	Born	Pos	Meet	Venue	Date
1:40.91 WR		David	Rudisha	KEN	17.12.88	1	OG	London (OS)	9 Aug 12
1:41.01 WR			Rudisha			1rA		Rieti	29 Aug 10
1:41.09 WR			Rudisha			1	ISTAF	Berlin	22 Aug 10
1:41.11 WR		Wilson	Kipketer	DEN	12.12.70	1	ASV	Köln	24 Aug 97
1:41.24 WR			Kipketer			1rA	WK	Zürich	13 Aug 97

Mark	Wind	Name		Nat	Born	Pos	Meet	Venue	Date
1:41.33			Rudisha			1		Rieti	10 Sep 11
1:41.51			Rudisha			1	NA	Heusden-Zolder	10 Jul 10
1:41.54			Rudisha			1	DL	Saint-Denis	6 Jul 12
1:41.73!WR		Sebastian	Coe	GBR	29.9.56	1		Firenze	10 Jun 81
1:41.73 WR			Kipketer			1rA	DNG	Stockholm	7 Jul 97
1:41.73		Nijel	Amos	BOT	15.3.94	2	OG	London (OS)	9 Aug 12
1:41.74			Rudisha			1	adidas	New York	9 Jun 12
1:41.77		Joaquim	Cruz	BRA	12.3.63	1	ASV	Köln	26 Aug 84
1:41.83			Kipketer			1	GP II	Rieti	1 Sep 96
1:42.01			Rudisha			1	GP	Rieti	6 Sep 09
1:42.04			Rudisha			1	Bisl	Oslo	4 Jun 10
1:42.05		Emmanuel	Korir	KEN	15.6.95	1	DL	London (OS)	22 Jul 18
1:42.12A			Rudisha			1	OT	Nairobi	23 Jun 12
1:42.14			Amos			1	Herc	Monaco	20 Jul 18
1:42.15			Rudisha			1	OG	Rio de Janeiro	15 Aug 16
1:42.17			Kipketer			1	TOTO	Tokyo	16 Sep 96
1:42.20			Kipketer			1	VD	Bruxelles	22 Aug 97
1:42.23		Abubaker	Kaki	SUD	21.6.89	2	Bisl	Oslo	4 Jun 10
1:42.27			Kipketer			1	VD	Bruxelles	3 Sep 99
1:42.28		Sammy	Koskei	KEN	14.5.61	2	ASV	Köln	26 Aug 84
1:42.32			Kipketer			1	GP II	Rieti	8 Sep 02
1:42.33 WR			Coe			1	Bisl	Oslo	5 Jul 79
1:42.34			Cruz			1r1	WK	Zürich	22 Aug 84
1:42.34		Wilfred	Bungei	KEN	24.7.80	2	GP II	Rieti	8 Sep 02
1:42.37		Mohammed	Aman	ETH	10.1.94	1	VD	Bruxelles	6 Sep 13
		(31/10)							
				! photo-electric cell time					
1:42.47		Yuriy	Borzakovskiy	RUS	12.4.81	1	VD	Bruxelles	24 Aug 01
1:42.51		Amel	Tuka	BIH	9.1.91	1	Herc	Monaco	17 Jul 15
1:42.53		Timothy	Kitum	KEN	20.11.94	3	OG	London (OS)	9 Aug 12
1:42.53		Pierre-Ambroise	Bosse	FRA	11.5.92	2	Herc	Monaco	18 Jul 14
1:42.55		André	Bucher	SUI	19.10.76	1rA	WK	Zürich	17 Aug 01
1:42.58		Vebjørn	Rodal	NOR	16.9.72	1	OG	Atlanta	31 Jul 96
1:42.60		Johnny	Gray	USA	19.6.60	2r1		Koblenz	28 Aug 85
1:42.61		Taoufik	Makhloufi	ALG	29.4.88	2	OG	Rio de Janeiro	15 Aug 16
1:42.62		Patrick	Ndururu	KEN	12.1.69	2rA	WK	Zürich	13 Aug 97
1:42.67		Alfred	Kirwa Yego	KEN	28.11.86	2	GP	Rieti	6 Sep 09
		(20)							
1:42.69		Hezekiél	Sepeng ¶	RSA	30.6.74	2	VD	Bruxelles	3 Sep 99
1:42.69		Japheth	Kimutai	KEN	20.12.78	3	VD	Bruxelles	3 Sep 99
1:42.79		Fred	Onyancha	KEN	25.12.69	3	OG	Atlanta	31 Jul 96
1:42.79		Youssef Saad	Kamel	KEN/BRN	29.3.83	2	Herc	Monaco	29 Jul 08
1:42.81		Jean-Patrick	Nduwimana	BDI	9.5.78	2rA	WK	Zürich	17 Aug 01
1:42.82		Duane	Solomon	USA	28.12.84	4	OG	London (OS)	9 Aug 12
1:42.84		Ferguson	Cheruiyot	KEN	30.11.89	4	Herc	Monaco	18 Jul 14
1:42.85		Norberto	Téllez	CUB	22.1.72	4	OG	Atlanta	31 Jul 96
1:42.86		Mbulaeni	Mulaudzi	RSA	8.9.80	3	GP	Rieti	6 Sep 09
1:42.87		Alfred	Kipketer	KEN	26.12.96	1	DL	Saint-Denis	27 Aug 16
		(30)							
1:42.88		Steve	Cram	GBR	14.10.60	1rA	WK	Zürich	21 Aug 85
1:42.91		William	Yiampoy	KEN	17.5.74	3	GP II	Rieti	8 Sep 02
1:42.93		Clayton	Murphy	USA	26.2.95	3	OG	Rio de Janeiro	15 Aug 16
1:42.95		Boaz	Lalang	KEN	8.2.89	2rA		Rieti	29 Aug 10
1:42.95		Nick	Symmonds	USA	30.12.83	5	OG	London (OS)	9 Aug 12
1:42.97		Peter	Elliott	GBR	9.10.62	1		Sevilla	30 May 90
1:42.97		Ayanleh	Souleiman	DJI	3.12.92	3	Herc	Monaco	17 Jul 15
1:42.98		Patrick	Konchellah	KEN	20.4.68	2	ASV	Köln	24 Aug 97
1:43.03		Kennedy/Kenneth	Kimwetich	KEN	1.1.73	2		Stuttgart	19 Jul 98
1:43.05		Jonathan	Kitilit	KEN	24.4.94	3	DL	Saint-Denis	27 Aug 16
		(40)							
1:43.06		Billy	Konchellah	KEN	20.10.62	1	WCh	Roma	1 Sep 87
1:43.07		Yeimer	López	CUB	20.8.82	1		Jerez de la Frontera	24 Jun 08
1:43.08		José Luiz	Barbosa	BRA	27.5.61	1		Rieti	6 Sep 91
1:43.09		Djabir	Saïd-Guerni	ALG	29.3.77	5	VD	Bruxelles	3 Sep 99
1:43.12		Wycliffe	Kinyamal	KEN	2.7.97	3	DL	London (OS)	22 Jul 18
1:43.13		Abraham Kipchirchir	Rotich	KEN	26.6.93	1	Herc	Monaco	20 Jul 12
1:43.15		Mehdi	Baala	FRA	17.8.78	5	GP II	Rieti	8 Sep 02
1:43.15		Asbel	Kiprop	KEN	30.6.89	2	Herc	Monaco	22 Jul 11
1:43.16		Paul	Ereng	KEN	22.8.67	1	WK	Zürich	16 Aug 89
		(50)							

100th man 1:43.76, 200th 1:44.54, 300th 1:44.92, 400th 1:45.24, 500th 1:45.52

Mark	Wind	Name		Nat	Born	Pos	Meet	Venue	Date
1000 METRES									
2:11.96	WR	Noah	Ngeny	KEN	2.11.78	1	GP II	Rieti	5 Sep 99
2:12.18	WR	Sebastian	Coe	GBR	29.9.56	1	OsloG	Oslo	11 Jul 81
2:12.66			Ngeny			1	Nik	Nice	17 Jul 99
2:12.88		Steve	Cram	GBR	14.10.60	1		Gateshead	9 Aug 85
2:13.08		Taoufik	Makhloufi	ALG	20.4.88	1		Tomblaine	1 Jul 15
2:13.40	WR		Coe			1	Bisl	Oslo	1 Jul 80
2:13.49		Ayanleh	Souleiman	DJI	3.12.92	1	Athl	Lausanne	25 Aug 16
2:13.56		Kennedy/Kenneth	Kimwetich	KEN	1.1.73	2	Nik	Nice	17 Jul 99
2:13.62		Abubaker	Kaki	SUD	21.6.89	1	Pre	Eugene	3 Jul 10
2:13.73		Noureddine	Morceli	ALG	28.2.70	1	BNP	Villeneuve d'Ascq	2 Jul 93
2:13.89		Robert	Biwott	KEN	28.1.96	2	Athl	Lausanne	25 Aug 16
2:13.9	WR	Rick	Wohlhuter	USA	23.12.48	1	King	Oslo	30 Jul 74
2:13.95		Jonathan	Kitilit	KEN	24.4.94	3	Athl	Lausanne	25 Aug 16
2:13.96		Mehdi	Baala	FRA	17.8.78	1		Strasbourg	26 Jun 03
		(12)	50th man 2:15.72, 100th 2:16.56, 200th 2:17.46						
1500 METRES									
3:26.00	WR	Hicham	El Guerrouj	MAR	14.9.74	1	GGala	Roma	14 Jul 98
3:26.12			El Guerrouj			1	VD	Bruxelles	24 Aug 01
3:26.34		Bernard	Lagat	KEN/USA	12.12.74	2	VD	Bruxelles	24 Aug 01
3:26.45			El Guerrouj			1 rA	WK	Zürich	12 Aug 98
3:26.69		Asbel	Kiprop	KEN	30.6.89	1	Herc	Monaco	17 Jul 15
3:26.89			El Guerrouj			1	WK	Zürich	16 Aug 02
3:26.96			El Guerrouj			1	GP II	Rieti	8 Sep 02
3:27.21			El Guerrouj			1	WK	Zürich	11 Aug 00
3:27.34			El Guerrouj			1	Herc	Monaco	19 Jul 02
3:27.37	WR	Noureddine	Morceli	ALG	28.2.70	1	Nik	Nice	12 Jul 95
3:27.40			Lagat			1rA	WK	Zürich	6 Aug 04
3:27.52			Morceli			1	Herc	Monaco	25 Jul 95
3:27.64			El Guerrouj			2rA	WK	Zürich	6 Aug 04
3:27.64		Silas	Kiplagat	KEN	20.8.89	1	Herc	Monaco	18 Jul 14
3:27.65			El Guerrouj			1	WCh	Sevilla	24 Aug 99
3:27.72			Kiprop			1	Herc	Monaco	19 Jul 13
3:27.91			Lagat			2	Herc	Monaco	19 Jul 02
3:28.12		Noah	Ngeny	KEN	2.11.78	2	WK	Zürich	11 Aug 00
3:28.21+			El Guerrouj			1	in 1M	Roma	7 Jul 99
3:28.37			Morceli			1	GPF	Monaco	9 Sep 95
3:28.37			El Guerrouj			1	Herc	Monaco	8 Aug 98
3:28.38			El Guerrouj			1	GP	Saint-Denis	6 Jul 01
3:28.40			El Guerrouj			1	VD	Bruxelles	5 Sep 03
3:28.41		Timothy	Cheruiyot	KEN	20.11.95	1	Herc	Monaco	20 Jul 18
3:28.45			Kiprop			2	Herc	Monaco	18 Jul 14
3:28.51			Lagat			3	WK	Zürich	11 Aug 00
3:28.57			El Guerrouj			1rA	WK	Zürich	11 Aug 99
3:28.6+			Ngeny			2	in 1M	Roma	7 Jul 99
3:28.73			Ngeny			2	WCh	Sevilla	24 Aug 99
3:28.75		Taoufik	Makhloufi	ALG	29.4.88	2	Herc	Monaco	17 Jul 15
		(30/8)							
3:28.79		Abdelaati	Iguider	MAR	25.3.87	3	Herc	Monaco	17 Jul 15
3:28.80		Elijah	Manangoi (10)	KEN	5.1.93	1	Herc	Monaco	21 Jul 17
3:28.81		Mohamed	Farah	GBR	23.3.83	2	Herc	Monaco	19 Jul 13
3:28.81		Ronald	Kwemoi	KEN	19.9.95	3	Herc	Monaco	18 Jul 14
3:28.95		Fermín	Cacho	ESP	16.2.69	2rA	WK	Zürich	13 Aug 97
3:28.98		Mehdi	Baala	FRA	17.8.78	2	VD	Bruxelles	5 Sep 03
3:29.02		Daniel Kipchirchir	Komen	KEN	27.11.84	1	GGala	Roma	14 Jul 06
3:29.14		Rashid	Ramzi ¶	MAR/BRN	17.7.80	2	GGala	Roma	14 Jul 06
3:29.18		Vénuste	Niyongabo	BDI	9.12.73	2	VD	Bruxelles	22 Aug 97
3:29.29		William	Chirchir	KEN	6.2.79	3	VD	Bruxelles	24 Aug 01
3:29.46	WR	Saïd	Aouita	MAR	2.11.59	1	ISTAF	Berlin	23 Aug 85
3:29.46		Daniel	Komen	KEN	17.5.76	1	Herc	Monaco	16 Aug 97
		(20)							
3:29.47		Augustine	Choge	KEN	21.1.87	1	ISTAF	Berlin	14 Jun 09
3:29.50		Caleb	Ndiku	KEN	9.10.92	3	Herc	Monaco	19 Jul 13
3:29.51		Ali	Saïdi-Sief ¶	ALG	15.3.78	1	Athl	Lausanne	4 Jul 01
3:29.53		Amine	Laâlou ¶	MAR	13.5.82	2	Herc	Monaco	22 Jul 10
3:29.58		Ayanleh	Souleiman	DJI	3.12.92	4	Herc	Monaco	18 Jul 14
3:29.66		Nick	Willis	NZL	25.4.83	5	Herc	Monaco	17 Jul 15
3:29.67	WR	Steve	Cram	GBR	14.10.60	1	Nik	Nice	16 Jul 85
3:29.77		Sydney	Maree	USA	9.9.56	1	ASV	Köln	25 Aug 85

Mark	Wind	Name		Nat	Born	Pos	Meet	Venue	Date
3:29.77		Sebastian	Coe	GBR	29.9.56	1		Rieti	7 Sep 86
3:29.77		Nixon	Chepseba	KEN	12.12.90	2	Herc	Monaco	20 Jul 12
		(30)							
3:29.91		Laban	Rotich	KEN	20.1.69	2rA	WK	Zürich	12 Aug 98
3:29.91		Aman	Wote	ETH	18.4.84	6	Herc	Monaco	14 Jul 14
3:30.01		Filip	Ingebrigtsen	NOR	20.4.93	3	Herc	Monaco	20 Jul 18
3:30.04		Timothy	Kiptanui	KEN	5.1.80	2	GP	Saint-Denis	23 Jul 04
3:30.07		Rui	Silva	POR	3.8.77	3	Herc	Monaco	19 Jul 02
3:30.10		Robert	Biwott	KEN	28.1.96	7	Herc	Monaco	17 Jul 15
3:30.18		John	Kibowen	KEN	21.4.69	3rA	WK	Zürich	12 Aug 98
3:30.20		Haron	Keitany	KEN	17.12.83	2	ISTAF	Berlin	14 Jun 09
3:30.24		Cornelius	Chirchir	KEN	5.6.83	4	Herc	Monaco	19 Jul 02
3:30.33		Ivan	Heshko	UKR	19.8.79	2	VD	Bruxelles	3 Sep 04
		(40)							
3:30.34		Collins	Cheboi	KEN	25.9.87	9	Herc	Monaco	17 Jul 15
3:30.40		Matthew	Centrowitz	USA	18.10.89	10	Herc	Monaco	17 Jul 15
3:30.46		Alex	Kipchirchir	KEN	26.11.84	3	VD	Bruxelles	3 Sep 04
3:30.54		Alan	Webb	USA	13.1.83	1	Gaz	Saint-Denis	6 Jul 07
3:30.55		Abdi	Bile	SOM	28.12.62	1		Rieti	3 Sep 89
3:30.57		Reyes	Estévez	ESP	2.8.76	3	WCh	Sevilla	24 Aug 99
3:30.58		William	Tanui	KEN	22.2.64	3	Herc	Monaco	16 Aug 97
3:30.61		James	Magut	KEN	20.7.90	5	DL	Doha	9 May 14
3:30.67		Benjamin	Kipkurui	KEN	28.12.80	2	Herc	Monaco	20 Jul 01
3:30.72		Paul	Korir	KEN	15.7.77	3	VD	Bruxelles	5 Sep 03
		(50)	100th man 3:31.89, 200th 3:33.71, 300th 3:34.60, 400th 3:35.53, 500th 3:36.09						

1 MILE

Mark	Wind	Name		Nat	Born	Pos	Meet	Venue	Date
3:43.13	WR	Hicham	El Guerrouj	MAR	14.9.74	1	GGala	Roma	7 Jul 99
3:43.40		Noah	Ngeny	KEN	2.11.78	2	GGala	Roma	7 Jul 99
3:44.39	WR	Noureddine	Morceli	ALG	28.2.70	1		Rieti	5 Sep 93
3:44.60			El Guerrouj			1	Nik	Nice	16 Jul 00
3:44.90			El Guerrouj			1	Bisl	Oslo	4 Jul 97
3:44.95			El Guerrouj			1	GGala	Roma	29 Jun 01
3:45.19			Morceli			1	WK	Zürich	16 Aug 95
3:45.64			El Guerrouj			1	ISTAF	Berlin	26 Aug 97
3:45.96			El Guerrouj			1	BrGP	London (CP)	5 Aug 00
3:46.24			El Guerrouj			1	Bisl	Oslo	28 Jul 00
3:46.32	WR	Steve	Cram	GBR	14.10.60	1	Bisl	Oslo	27 Jul 85
3:46.38		Daniel	Komen	KEN	17.5.76	2	ISTAF	Berlin	26 Aug 97
3:46.70		Vénuste	Niyongabo	BDI	9.12.73	3	ISTAF	Berlin	26 Aug 97
3:46.76		Saïd	Aouita	MAR	2.11.59	1	WG	Helsinki	2 Jul 87
3:46.78			Morceli			1	ISTAF	Berlin	27 Aug 93
3:46.91		Alan	Webb	USA	13.1.83	1		Brasschaat	21 Jul 07
3:46.92			Aouita			1	WK	Zürich	21 Aug 85
3:47.10			El Guerrouj			1	BrGP	London (CP)	7 Aug 99
3:47.28		Bernard	Lagat	KEN/USA	12.12.74	2	GGala	Roma	29 Jun 01
3:47.30			Morceli			1	VD	Bruxelles	3 Sep 93
3:47.32		Ayanleh	Souleiman (10)	DJI	3.12.92	1	Pre	Eugene	31 May 14
3:47.33	WR	Sebastian	Coe	GBR	29.9.56	1	VD	Bruxelles	28 Aug 81
		(22/11)							
3:47.65		Laban	Rotich	KEN	20.1.69	2	Bisl	Oslo	4 Jul 97
3:47.69		Steve	Scott	USA	5.5.56	1	OsloG	Oslo	7 Jul 82
3:47.79		José Luis	González	ESP	8.12.57	2	Bisl	Oslo	27 Jul 85
3:47.88		John	Kibowen	KEN	21.4.69	3	Bisl	Oslo	4 Jul 97
3:47.88		Silas	Kiplagat	KEN	20.8.89	2	Pre	Eugene	31 May 14
3:47.94		William	Chirchir	KEN	6.2.79	2	Bisl	Oslo	28 Jul 00
3:47.97		Daham Najim	Bashir	KEN/QAT	8.11.78	1	Bisl	Oslo	29 Jul 05
3:48.17		Paul	Korir	KEN	15.7.77	1	GP	London (CP)	8 Aug 03
3:48.23		Ali	Saïdi-Sief ¶	ALG	15.3.78	1	Bisl	Oslo	13 Jul 01
		(20)							
3:48.28		Daniel Kipchirchir	Komen	KEN	27.11.84	1	Pre	Eugene	10 Jun 07
3:48.38		Andrés Manuel	Díaz	ESP	12.7.69	3	GGala	Roma	29 Jun 01
3:48.40	WR	Steve	Ovett	GBR	9.10.55	1	R-W	Koblenz	26 Aug 81
3:48.50		Asbel	Kiprop	KEN	30.6.89	1	Pre	Eugene	7 Jun 09
3:48.60		Aman	Wote	ETH	18.4.84	3	Pre	Eugene	31 May 14
3:48.78		Haron	Keitany	KEN	17.12.83	2	Pre	Eugene	7 Jun 09
3:48.80		William	Kemei	KEN	22.2.69	1	ISTAF	Berlin	21 Aug 92
3:48.83		Sydney	Maree	USA	9.9.56	1		Rieti	9 Sep 81
3:48.95		Deresse	Mekonnen	ETH	20.10.87	1	Bisl	Oslo	3 Jul 09
3:48.98		Craig	Mottram	AUS	18.6.80	5	Bisl	Oslo	29 Jul 05
		(30)							

MEN All-time

Mark	Wind	Name		Nat	Born	Pos	Meet	Venue	Date
3:49.04		Ronald	Kwemoi	KEN	19.9.95	1	Pre	Eugene	27 May 17
3:49.08		John	Walker	NZL	12.1.52	2	OsloG	Oslo	7 Jul 82
3:49.08		Elijah	Manangoi	KEN	5.1.93	2	Pre	Eugene	27 May 17
3:49.09		Abdelaati	Iguider	MAR	25.3.87	4	Pre	Eugene	31 May 14
3:49.20		Peter	Elliott	GBR	9.10.62	2	Bisl	Oslo	2 Jul 88
3:49.22		Jens Peter	Herold	GDR	2.6.65	3	Bisl	Oslo	2 Jul 88
3:49.29		William	Biwott/Özbilen	KEN/TUR	5.3.90	2	Bisl	Oslo	3 Jul 09
3:49.31		Joe	Falcon	USA	23.6.66	1	Bisl	Oslo	14 Jul 90
3:49.34		David	Moorcroft	GBR	10.4.53	3	Bisl	Oslo	26 Jun 82
3:49.34		Benjamin	Kipkurui	KEN	28.12.80	3	VD	Bruxelles	25 Aug 00
		(40)							
3:49.38		Andrew	Baddeley	GBR	20.6.82	1	Bisl	Oslo	6 Jun 08
3:49.40		Abdi	Bile	SOM	28.12.62	4	Bisl	Oslo	2 Jul 88
3:49.43		James	Magut	KEN	20.7.90	5	Pre	Eugene	31 May 14
3:49.45		Mike	Boit	KEN	6.1.49	2	VD	Bruxelles	28 Aug 81
3:49.50		Rui	Silva	POR	3.8.77	3	GGala	Roma	12 Jul 02
3:49.56		Fermín	Cacho	ESP	16.2.69	2	Bisl	Oslo	5 Jul 96
3:49.56		Collins	Cheboi	KEN	25.9.87	6	Pre	Eugene	31 May 14
3:49.60		José Antonio	Redolat	ESP	17.2.76	4	GGala	Roma	29 Jun 01
3:49.64		Timothy	Cheruiyot	KEN	20.11.95	3	Pre	Eugene	27 May 17
3:49.70		Mekonnen	Gebremedhin	ETH	11.10.88	4	Pre	Eugene	4 Jun 11
		(50)							
			100th 3:50.98, 200th 3:53.05, 300th 3:54.68, 400th 3:55.79						
Indoors: 3:49.44		Edward	Cheserek	KEN	2.2.94	1		Boston (A)	9 Feb 18

2000 METRES

Mark	Wind	Name		Nat	Born	Pos	Meet	Venue	Date
4:44.79 WR		Hicham	El Guerrouj	MAR	14.9.74	1	ISTAF	Berlin	7 Sep 99
4:46.88		Ali	Saïdi-Sief ¶	ALG	15.3.78	1		Strasbourg	19 Jun 01
4:47.88 WR		Noureddine	Morceli	ALG	28.2.70	1		Paris (JB)	3 Jul 95
4:48.36			El Guerrouj			1		Gateshead	19 Jul 98
4:48.69		Vénuste	Niyongabo	BDI	9.12.73	1	Nik	Nice	12 Jul 95
4:48.74		John	Kibowen	KEN	21.4.69	1		Hechtel	1 Aug 98
4:49.00			Niyongabo			1		Rieti	3 Sep 97
4:49.55			Morceli			1	Nik	Nice	10 Jul 96
4:50.08		Noah	Ngeny	KEN	2.11.78	1	DNG	Stockholm	30 Jul 99
4:50.76		Craig	Mottram	AUS	18.6.80	1		Melbourne (OP)	9 Mar 06
4:50.81 WR			Saïd Aouita	MAR	2.11.59	1	BNP	Paris (JB)	16 Jul 87
4:51.30		Daniel	Komen	KEN	17.5.76	1		Milano	5 Jun 98
4:51.39 WR		Steve	Cram (10)	GBR	14.10.60	1	BGP	Budapest	4 Aug 85
Indoors									
4:49.99		Kenenisa	Bekele	ETH	13.6.82	1		Birmingham	17 Feb 07

3000 METRES

Mark	Wind	Name		Nat	Born	Pos	Meet	Venue	Date
7:20.67 WR		Daniel	Komen	KEN	17.5.76	1		Rieti	1 Sep 96
7:23.09		Hicham	El Guerrouj	MAR	14.9.74	1	VD	Bruxelles	3 Sep 99
7:25.02		Ali	Saïdi-Sief ¶	ALG	15.3.78	1	Herc	Monaco	18 Aug 00
7:25.09		Haile	Gebrselassie	ETH	18.4.73	1	VD	Bruxelles	28 Aug 98
7:25.11 WR		Noureddine	Morceli	ALG	28.2.70	1	Herc	Monaco	2 Aug 94
7:25.16			Komen			1	Herc	Monaco	10 Aug 96
7:25.54			Gebrselassie			1	Herc	Monaco	8 Aug 98
7:25.79		Kenenisa	Bekele	ETH	13.6.82	1	DNG	Stockholm	7 Aug 07
7:25.87			Komen			1	VD	Bruxelles	23 Aug 96
7:26.02			Gebrselassie			1	VD	Bruxelles	22 Aug 97
7:26.03			Gebrselassie			1	GP II	Helsinki	10 Jun 99
7:26.5 e			Komen			1	in 2M	Sydney	28 Feb 98
7:26.62		Mohammed	Mourhit ¶	BEL	10.10.70	2	Herc	Monaco	18 Aug 00
7:26.69			K Bekele			1	BrGP	Sheffield	15 Jul 07
7:27.18		Moses	Kiptanui	KEN	1.10.70	1	Herc	Monaco	25 Jul 95
7:27.26		Yenew	Alamirew	ETH	27.5.90	1	DL	Doha	6 May 11
7:27.3+			Komen			1	in 2M	Hechtel	19 Jul 97
7:27.42			Gebrselassie			1	Bisl	Oslo	9 Jul 98
7:27.50			Morceli			1	VD	Bruxelles	25 Aug 95
7:27.55		Edwin	Soi (10)	KEN	3.3.86	2	DL	Doha	6 May 11
7:27.59		Luke	Kipkosgei	KEN	27.11.75	2	Herc	Monaco	8 Aug 98
7:27.66		Eliud	Kipchoge	KEN	5.11.84	3	DL	Doha	6 May 11
7:27.67			Saïdi-Sief			1	Gaz	Saint-Denis	23 Jun 00
7:27.72			Kipchoge			1	VD	Bruxelles	3 Sep 04
7:27.75		Thomas	Nyariki	KEN	27.9.71	2	Herc	Monaco	10 Aug 96
7:28.00		Yomif	Kejelcha	ETH	1.8.97	1		Göteborg	18 Aug 18
7:28.04			Kiptanui			1	ASV	Köln	18 Aug 95
7:28.19			Kejelcha			1	DL	Saint-Denis	27 Aug 16

Mark	Wind	Name		Nat	Born	Pos	Meet	Venue	Date
7:28.28			Kipkosgei			2	Bisl	Oslo	9 Jul 98
7:28.28		James	Kwalia	KEN/QAT	12.6.84	2	VD	Bruxelles	3 Sep 04
	(30/15)								
7:28.41		Paul	Bitok	KEN	26.6.70	3	Herc	Monaco	10 Aug 96
7:28.45		Assefa	Mezegebu	ETH	19.6.78	3	Herc	Monaco	8 Aug 98
7:28.67		Benjamin	Limo	KEN	23.8.74	1	Herc	Monaco	4 Aug 99
7:28.70		Paul	Tergat	KEN	17.6.69	4	Herc	Monaco	10 Aug 96
7:28.70		Tariku	Bekele	ETH	21.1.87	1		Rieti	29 Aug 10
	(20)								
7:28.72		Isaac K.	Songok	KEN	25.4.84	1	GP	Rieti	27 Aug 06
7:28.73		Ronald	Kwemoi	KEN	19.9.95	1	DL	Doha	5 May 17
7:28.76		Augustine	Choge	KEN	21.1.87	4	DL	Doha	6 May 11
7:28.93		Salah	Hissou	MAR	16.1.72	2	Herc	Monaco	4 Aug 99
7:28.94		Brahim	Lahlafi	FRA/MAR	15.4.68	3	Herc	Monaco	4 Aug 99
7:29.00		Bernard	Lagat	USA	12.12.74	2		Rieti	29 Aug 10
7:29.09		John	Kibowen	KEN	21.4.69	3	Bisl	Oslo	9 Jul 98
7:29.34		Isaac	Viciosa	ESP	26.12.69	4	Bisl	Oslo	9 Jul 98
7:29.45	WR	Saïd	Aouita	MAR	2.11.59	1	ASV	Köln	20 Aug 89
7:29.92		Sileshi	Sihine	ETH	29.1.83	1	GP	Rieti	28 Aug 05
	(30)								
7:30.09		Ismaïl	Sghyr	MAR/FRA	16.3.72	2	Herc	Monaco	25 Jul 95
7:30.09		Thomas	Longosiwa	KEN	14.1.82	2	SGP	Doha	8 May 09
7:30.09		Abdelaati	Iguider	MAR	25.3.87	2	DL	Saint-Denis	27 Aug 16
7:30.15		Vincent	Chepkok	KEN	5.7.88	5	DL	Doha	6 May 11
7:30.36		Mark	Carroll	IRL	15.1.72	5	Herc	Monaco	4 Aug 99
7:30.36		Hagos	Gebrhiwet	ETH	11.5.94	1	DL	Doha	10 May 13
7:30.43		Isiah	Koech	KEN	19.12.93	1	DNG	Stockholm	17 Aug 12
7:30.50		Dieter	Baumann ¶	GER	9.2.65	6	Herc	Monaco	8 Aug 98
7:30.53		El Hassan	Lahssini	MAR/FRA	1.1.75	6	Herc	Monaco	10 Aug 96
7:30.53		Hailu	Mekonnen	ETH	4.4.80	1	VD	Bruxelles	24 Aug 01
	(40)								
7:30.62		Boniface	Songok	KEN	25.12.80	3	VD	Bruxelles	3 Sep 04
7:30.76		Jamal Bilal	Salem	KEN/QAT	12.9.78	4	SGP	Doha	13 May 05
7:30.78		Mustapha	Essaïd	FRA	20.1.70	7	Herc	Monaco	8 Aug 98
7:30.84		Bob	Kennedy	USA	18.8.70	8	Herc	Monaco	8 Aug 98
7:30.93		Ryan	Hill	USA	31.1.90	4	DL	Saint-Denis	27 Aug 16
7:30.95		Moses	Kipsiro	UGA	2.9.86	1	Herc	Monaco	28 Jul 09
7:30.99		Khalid	Boulami	MAR	7.8.69	1	Nik	Nice	16 Jul 97
7:30.99		Caleb	Ndiku	KEN	9.10.92	2	DNG	Stockholm	17 Aug 12
7:31.13		Julius	Gitahi	KEN	29.4.78	6	Bisl	Oslo	9 Jul 98
7:31.14		William	Kalya	KEN	4.8.74	3	Herc	Monaco	16 Aug 97
	(50)	100th man 7:34.67, 200th man 7:38.78, 300th man 7:41.33, 400th 7:43.21, 500th 7:447							

Indoors

Mark	Wind	Name		Nat	Born	Pos	Meet	Venue	Date
7:24.90	WIR		Komen			1		Budapest	6 Feb 98
7:26.15	WIR		Gebrselassie			1		Karlsruhe	25 Jan 98
7:26.80			Gebrselassie			1		Karlsruhe	24 Jan 99
7:27.80			Alamirew			1	Spark	Stuttgart	5 Feb 11
7:27.93			Komen			1	Spark	Stuttgart	1 Feb 98
7:28.00		Augustine	Choge	KEN	21.1.87	2	Spark	Stuttgart	5 Feb 11
7:30.16		Galen	Rupp	USA	8.5.86	1		Stockholm	21 Feb 13

2 MILES

Mark	Wind	Name		Nat	Born	Pos	Meet	Venue	Date
7:58.61	WR	Daniel	Komen	KEN	17.5.76	1		Hechtel	19 Jul 97
7:58.91			Komen			1		Sydney	28 Feb 98
8:01.08	WR	Haile	Gebrselassie	ETH	18.4.73	1	APM	Hengelo	31 May 97
8:01.72			Gebrselassie			1	BrGP	London (CP)	7 Aug 99
8:01.86			Gebrselassie			1	APM	Hengelo	30 May 99
8:03.50		Craig	Mottram	AUS	18.6.80	1	Pre	Eugene	10 Jun 07
8:03.54	WR		Komen			1		Lappeenranta	14 Jul 96

Indoors

Mark	Wind	Name		Nat	Born	Pos	Meet	Venue	Date
8:03.40		Mohamed	Farah	GBR	23.3.83	1	GP	Birmingham	21 Feb 15
8:04.35		Kenenisa	Bekele	ETH	13.6.82	1	GP	Birmingham	16 Feb 08

5000 METRES

Mark	Wind	Name		Nat	Born	Pos	Meet	Venue	Date
12:37.35	WR	Kenenisa	Bekele	ETH	13.6.82	1	FBK	Hengelo	31 May 04
12:39.36	WR	Haile	Gebrselassie	ETH	18.4.73	1	GP II	Helsinki	13 Jun 98
12:39.74	WR	Daniel	Komen	KEN	17.5.76	1	VD	Bruxelles	22 Aug 97
12:40.18			K Bekele			1	Gaz	Saint-Denis	1 Jul 05
12:41.86	WR		Gebrselassie			1	WK	Zürich	13 Aug 97

A – mark made at an altitude of 1000m or higher, i – indoors, Q – in qualifying competition, WR - world record

MEN All-time

Mark	Wind	Name		Nat	Born	Pos	Meet	Venue	Date
12:43.02		Selemon	Barega	ETH	20.1.00	1	VD	Bruxelles	31 Aug 18
12:44.39	WR		Gebrselassie			1	WK	Zürich	16 Aug 95
12:44.90			Komen			2	WK	Zürich	13 Aug 97
12:45.09			Komen			1	WK	Zürich	14 Aug 96
12:45.82		Hagos	Gebrhiwet	ETH	11.5.94	2	VD	Bruxelles	31 Aug 18
12:46.53		Eliud	Kipchoge	KEN	5.11.84	1	GGala	Roma	2 Jul 04
12:46.79		Yomif	Kejelcha	ETH	1.8.97	3	VD	Bruxelles	31 Aug 18
12:46.81		Dejen	Gebremeskel	ETH	24.11.89	1	DL	Saint-Denis	6 Jul 12
12:47.04		Sileshi	Sihine	ETH	29.9.83	2	GGala	Roma	2 Jul 04
12:47.53			Gebrhiwet			2	DL	Saint-Denis	6 Jul 12
12:48.09			K Bekele			1	VD	Bruxelles	25 Aug 06
12:48.25			K Bekele			1	WK	Zürich	18 Aug 06
12:48.64		Isiah	Koech	KEN	19.12.93	3	DL	Saint-Denis	6 Jul 12
12:48.66		Isaac K.	Songok (10)	KEN	25.4.84	2	WK	Zürich	18 Aug 06
12:48.77		Yenew	Alamirew	ETH	27.5.90	4	DL	Saint-Denis	6 Jul 12
12:48.81		Stephen	Cherono/Shaheen	KEN/QAT	15.10.82	1	GS	Ostrava	12 Jun 03
12:48.98			Komen			1	GGala	Roma	5 Jun 97
12:49.04		Thomas	Longosiwa	KEN	14.1.82	5	DL	Saint-Denis	6 Jul 12
12:49.28		Brahim	Lahlafi	MAR	15.4.68	1	VD	Bruxelles	25 Aug 00
12:49.50		John	Kipkoech	KEN	29.12.91	6	DL	Saint-Denis	6 Jul 12
12:49.53			K Bekele			1	Aragón	Zaragoza	28 Jul 07
12:49.64			Gebrselassie			1	WK	Zürich	11 Aug 99
12:49.71		Mohammed	Mourhit ¶	BEL	10.10.70	2	VD	Bruxelles	25 Aug 00
12:49.87		Paul	Tergat	KEN	17.6.69	3	WK	Zürich	13 Aug 97
12:50.16			Sihine			1	VD	Bruxelles	14 Sep 07
		(30/17)							
12:50.24		Hicham	El Guerrouj	MAR	14.9.74	2	GS	Ostrava	12 Jun 03
12:50.25		Abderrahim	Goumri ¶	MAR	21.5.76	2	VD	Bruxelles	26 Aug 05
12:50.55		Moses	Mosop	KEN	1.6.86	1	ISTAF	Berlin	1 Jun 08
		(20)							
12:50.72		Moses	Kipsiro	UGA	2.9.86	3	VD	Bruxelles	14 Sep 07
12:50.80		Salah	Hissou	MAR	16.1.72	1	GGala	Roma	5 Jun 96
12:50.86		Ali	Saïdi-Sief ¶	ALG	15.3.78	1	GGala	Roma	30 Jun 00
12:51.00		Joseph	Ebuya	KEN	20.6.87	4	VD	Bruxelles	14 Sep 07
12:51.34		Edwin	Soi	KEN	3.3.86	1	Herc	Monaco	19 Jul 13
12:51.45		Vincent	Chepkok	KEN	5.7.88	2	DL	Doha	14 May 10
12:51.96		Albert	Rop	KEN/BRN	17.7.92	2	Herc	Monaco	19 Jul 13
12:52.33		Sammy	Kipketer	KEN	29.9.81	2	Bisl	Oslo	27 Jun 03
12:52.45		Tariku	Bekele	ETH	21.1.87	2	ISTAF	Berlin	1 Jun 08
12:52.80		Gebre-egziabher	Gebremariam	ETH	10.9.84	3	GGala	Roma	8 Jul 05
		(30)							
12:52.99		Abraham	Chebii	KEN	23.12.79	4	Bisl	Oslo	27 Jun 03
12:53.11		Mohamed	Farah	GBR	23.3.83	1	Herc	Monaco	22 Jul 11
12:53.41		Khalid	Boulami	MAR	7.8.69	4	WK	Zürich	13 Aug 97
12:53.46		Mark	Kiptoo	KEN	21.6.76	1	DNG	Stockholm	6 Aug 10
12:53.58		Imane	Merga	ETH	15.10.88	3	DNG	Stockholm	6 Aug 10
12:53.60		Bernard	Lagat	USA	12.12.74	2	Herc	Monaco	22 Jul 11
12:53.66		Augustine	Choge	KEN	21.1.87	4	GGala	Roma	8 Jul 05
12:53.72		Philip	Mosima	KEN	2.1.77	2	GGala	Roma	5 Jun 96
12:53.84		Assefa	Mezegebu	ETH	19.6.78	1	VD	Bruxelles	28 Aug 98
12:54.07		John	Kibowen	KEN	21.4.69	4	WCh	Saint-Denis	31 Aug 03
		(40)							
12:54.15		Dejene	Berhanu	ETH	12.12.80	3	GGala	Roma	2 Jul 04
12:54.19		Abreham	Cherkos	ETH	23.9.89	5	GGala	Roma	14 Jul 06
12:54.46		Moses	Mosop	KEN	17.7.85	3	Gaz	Saint-Denis	8 Jul 06
12:54.58		James	Kwalia	KEN/QAT	12.6.84	5	Bisl	Oslo	27 Jun 03
12:54.70		Dieter	Baumann ¶	GER	9.2.65	5	WK	Zürich	13 Aug 97
12:54.83		Muktar	Edris	ETH	14.1.94	1	DNG	Stockholm	21 Aug 14
12:54.85		Moses	Kiptanui	KEN	1.10.70	3	GGala	Roma	5 Jun 96
12:54.99		Benjamin	Limo	KEN	23.8.74	3	Gaz	Saint-Denis	4 Jul 03
12:55.06		Lucas	Rotich	KEN	16.4.90	4	Bisl	Oslo	4 Jun 10
12:55.52		Hicham	Bellani	MAR	15.9.79	7	GGala	Roma	14 Jul 06
		(50)	100th man 13:00.25, 200th 13:07.59, 300th 13:11.99, 400th 13:15.0, 500th 13:1775						
Indoors: 12:49.60			K Bekele			1		Birmingham	20 Feb 04

10,000 METRES

26:17.53	WR	Kenenisa	Bekele	ETH	13.6.82	1	VD	Bruxelles	26 Aug 05
26:20.31	WR		K Bekele			1	GS	Ostrava	8 Jun 04
26:22.75	WR	Haile	Gebrselassie	ETH	18.4.73	1	APM	Hengelo	1 Jun 98
26:25.97			K Bekele			1	Pre	Eugene	8 Jun 08

Mark	Wind	Name		Nat	Born	Pos	Meet	Venue	Date
26:27.85	WR	Paul	Tergat	KEN	17.6.69	1	VD	Bruxelles	22 Aug 97
26:28.72			K Bekele			1	FBK	Hengelo	29 May 05
26:29.22			Gebrselassie			1	VD	Bruxelles	5 Sep 03
26:30.03		Nicholas	Kemboi	KEN/QAT	25.11.83	2	VD	Bruxelles	5 Sep 03
26:30.74		Abebe	Dinkesa	ETH	6.3.84	2	FBK	Hengelo	29 May 05
26:31.32	WR		Gebrselassie			1	Bisl	Oslo	4 Jul 97
26:35.63		Micah	Kogo	KEN	3.6.86	1	VD	Bruxelles	25 Aug 06
26:36.26		Paul	Koech	KEN	25.6.69	2	VD	Bruxelles	22 Aug 97
26:37.25		Zersenay	Tadese	ERI	8.2.82	2	VD	Bruxelles	25 Aug 06
26:38.08	WR	Salah	Hissou	MAR	16.1.72	1	VD	Bruxelles	23 Aug 96
26:38.76		Abdullah Ahmad	Hassan (10)	QAT	4.4.81	3	VD	Bruxelles	5 Sep 03
		(Formerly Albert Chepkurui KEN)							
26:39.69		Sileshi	Sihine	ETH	29.9.83	1	FBK	Hengelo	31 May 04
26:39.77		Boniface	Kiprop	UGA	12.10.85	2	VD	Bruxelles	26 Aug 05
26:41.58			Gebrselassie			2	FBK	Hengelo	31 May 04
26:41.75		Samuel	Wanjiru	KEN	10.11.86	3	VD	Bruxelles	26 Aug 05
26:41.95			Kiprop			3	VD	Bruxelles	25 Aug 06
26:43.16			K Bekele			1	VD	Bruxelles	16 Sep 11
26:43.53	WR		Gebrselassie			1	APM	Hengelo	5 Jun 95
26:43.98		Lucas	Rotich	KEN	16.4.90	2	VD	Bruxelles	16 Sep 11
26:44.36		Galen	Rupp	USA	8.5.86	1	Pre	Eugene	30 May 14
26:46.19			K Bekele			1	VD	Bruxelles	14 Sep 07
26:46.31			K Bekele			1	WCh	Berlin	17 Aug 09
26:46.44			Tergat			1	VD	Bruxelles	28 Aug 98
26:46.57		Mohamed	Farah	GBR	23.3.83	1	Pre	Eugene	3 Jun 11
26:47.89			Koech			2	VD	Bruxelles	28 Aug 98
26:48.00			Rupp			3	VD	Bruxelles	16 Sep 11
		(30/16)							
26:48.35		Imane	Merga	ETH	15.10.88	2	Pre	Eugene	3 Jun 11
26:48.99		Josphat	Bett	KEN	12.6.90	3	Pre	Eugene	3 Jun 11
26:49.02		Eliud	Kipchoge	KEN	5.11.84	2	FBK	Hengelo	26 May 07
26:49.20		Moses	Masai	KEN	1.6.86	2	VD	Bruxelles	14 Sep 07
		(20)							
26:49.38		Sammy	Kipketer	KEN	29.9.81	1	VD	Bruxelles	30 Aug 02
26:49.41		Paul	Tanui	KEN	22.12.90	2	Pre	Eugene	30 May 14
26:49.55		Moses	Mosop	KEN	17.7.85	3	FBK	Hengelo	26 May 07
26:49.90		Assefa	Mezegebu	ETH	19.6.78	2	VD	Bruxelles	30 Aug 02
26:49.94		Joshua	Cheptegei	UGA	12.9.96	2	WCh	London (OS)	4 Aug 17
26:50.20		Richard	Limo	KEN	18.11.80	3	VD	Bruxelles	30 Aug 02
26:51.02		Dejen	Gebremeskel	ETH	24.11.89	1		Sollentuna	27 Jun 13
26:51.11		Yigrem	Demelash	ETH	28.1.94	1	OT	Hengelo	29 Jun 16
26:51.16		Emmanuel	Bett	KEN	30.3.83	1	VD	Bruxelles	7 Sep 12
26:51.49		Charles	Kamathi	KEN	18.5.78	1	VD	Bruxelles	3 Sep 99
		(30)							
26:51.68		Vincent	Chepkok	KEN	5.7.88	2	VD	Bruxelles	7 Sep 12
26:52.12		Bedan	Karoki	KEN	21.8.90	4	WCh	London (OS)	4 Aug 17
26:52.23	WR	William	Sigei	KEN	14.10.69	1	Bisl	Oslo	22 Jul 94
26:52.30		Mohammed	Mourhit ¶	BEL	10.10.70	2	VD	Bruxelles	3 Sep 99
26:52.33		Gebre-egziabher	Gebremariam	ETH	10.9.84	4	FBK	Hengelo	26 May 07
26:52.65		Kenneth	Kipkemoi	KEN	2.8.84	3	VD	Bruxelles	7 Sep 12
26:52.65		Geoffrey	Kamworor	KEN	28.11.92	3	Pre	Eugene	29 May 15
26:52.85		Abera	Kuma	ETH	31.8.90	2		Sollentuna	27 Jun 13
26:52.87		John Cheruiyot	Korir	KEN	13.12.81	5	VD	Bruxelles	30 Aug 02
26:52.93		Mark	Bett	KEN	22.12.76	6	VD	Bruxelles	26 Aug 05
		(40)							
26:54.25		Mathew	Kisorio ¶	KEN	16.5.89	7	Pre	Eugene	3 Jun 11
26:54.61		Stephen	Sambu	KEN	3.7.88	4	Pre	Eugene	30 May 14
26:54.64		Mark	Kiptoo	KEN	21.6.76	8	Pre	Eugene	3 Jun 11
26:54.66		William Malel	Sitonik	KEN	1.3.94	2	Pre	Eugene	27 May 16
26:55.29		Leonard Patrick	Komon	KEN	10.1.88	9	Pre	Eugene	3 Jun 11
26:55.73		Geoffrey	Kirui	KEN	16.2.93	6	VD	Bruxelles	16 Sep 11
26:56.11		Jemal	Yimer	ETH	11.9.96	5	WCh	London(OS)	4 Aug 17
26:56.74		Josphat	Menjo	KEN	20.8.79	1		Turku	29 Aug 10
26:57.33		Tamirat	Tola	ETH	11.8.91	3	Pre	Eugene	27 May 16
26:57.36		Josphat	Muchiri Ndambiri	KEN	12.2.85	1		Fukuroi	3 May 09
		(50)							

100th man 27:12.39, 200th 27:26.93, 300th 27:35.72, 400th 27:41.94, 500th 27:46.97

20,000 METRES & 1 HOUR

Mark	Wind		Name		Nat	Born	Pos	Meet	Venue	Date
56:25.98+	21 285m		Haile	Gebrselassie	ETH	18.4.73	1	GS	Ostrava	27 Jun 07
56:55.6+	21 101	Arturo		Barrios	MEX	12.12.63	1		La Flèche	30 Mar 91

Mark	Wind		Name	Nat	Born	Pos	Meet	Venue	Date
57:24.19+	20 944	Jos	Hermens	NED	8.1.50	1		Papendal	1 May 76
57:18.4+	20 943	Dionísio	Castro	POR	22.11.63	1		La Flèche	31 Mar 90

HALF MARATHON

Included are the slightly downhill courses: Newcastle to South Shields 30.5m, Tokyo 33m, Lisboa (Spring to 2008) 69m

Mark	Wind		Name	Nat	Born	Pos	Meet	Venue	Date
58.18	WR	Abraham	Kiptum	KEN	15.9.00	1		Valencia	28 Oct 18
58:23	WR	Zersenay	Tadese	ERI	8.2.82	1		Lisboa	21 Mar 10
58:30			Z Tadese			1		Lisboa	20 Mar 11
58:33	WR	Samuel	Wanjiru	KEN	10.11.86	1		Den Haag	17 Mar 07
58:33		Jemal	Yimer	ETH	11.9.96	2		Valencia	28 Oct 18
58:40		Abraham	Cheroben	KEN/BRN	11.10.92	1		København	17 Sep 17
58:42		Bedan	Karoki	KEN	21.8.90	1		Ras Al Khaimah	9 Feb 18
58:42		Erick	Kiptanui	KEN	19.4.90	1		Berlin	8 Apr 18
58:44		Solomon	Yego	KEN	10.5.87	1		Ostia	13 Mar 16
58:44		Abadi	Hadis	ETH	6.11.97	3		Valencia	28 Oct 18
58:46		Mathew	Kisorio ¶ (10)	KEN	16.5.89	1		Philadelphia	18 Sep 11
58:47		Atsedu	Tsegay	ETH	17.12.91	1		Praha	31 Mar 12
58:48		Sammy	Kitwara	KEN	26.11.86	2		Philadelphia	18 Sep 11
58:48			Cheroben			1		Valencia	19 Oct 14
58:48		Jorum	Okumbo	KEN	10.12.97	2		København	17 Sep 17
58:51		Alex	Oloitiptip Korio	KEN	20.12.90	3		København	17 Sep 17
58:52		Patrick	Makau	KEN	2.3.85	1		Ras Al Khaimah	20 Feb 09
58:53	WR		Wanjiru			1		Ras Al Khaimah	9 Feb 07
58:54		Stephen	Kibet	KEN	9.11.86	1		Den Haag	11 Mar 12
58:54		Geoffrey	Kamworor	KEN	28.11.92	1		Ras Al Khaimah	15 Feb 13
58:55	WR	Haile	Gebrselassie	ETH	18.4.73	1		Tempe	15 Jan 06
58:56			Makau			1		Berlin	1 Apr 07
58:56	dh	Martin	Mathathi	KEN	25.12.85	1	GNR	South Shields	18 Sep 11
58:56		Stanley	Biwott (20)	KEN	21.4.86	2		Ras Al Khaimah	15 Feb 13
58:58			Kitwara			1		Rotterdam	13 Sep 09
58:58		Geoffrey	Mutai	KEN	7.10.81	3		Ras Al Khaimah	15 Feb 13
58:59			Z Tadese			1	WCh	Udine	14 Oct 07
58:59		Wilson	Kipsang	KEN	15.3.82	2		Ras Al Khaimah	20 Feb 09
59:00			Yimer			2		Ras Al Khaimah	9 Feb 18
59:01		Kenneth	Kipkemoi	KEN	2.8.84	2		Valencia	19 Oct 14
		(30/23)							
59:02		Jonathan	Maiyo	KEN	5.5.88	2		Den Haag	11 Mar 12
59:05		Evans	Cheruiyot	KEN	10.5.82	3	WCh	Udine	14 Oct 07
59:05		Ezekiel	Chebii	KEN	3.1.91	1		Lille	1 Sep 12
59:06	dh	Paul	Tergat	KEN	17.6.69	1		Lisboa	26 Mar 00
59:06		Guye	Adola	ETH	20.10.90	1		New Delhi	23 Nov 14
59:06		Alex	Kibet	KEN	20.10.90	3		Ras Al Khaimah	9 Feb 18
59:06		Daniel	Kipchumba	KEN	12.12.97	1		Verbania	15 Apr 18
		(30)							
59:07		Paul	Kosgei	KEN	22.4.78	1		Berlin	2 Apr 06
59:07	dh	Micah	Kogo	KEN	3.6.86	2	GNR	South Shields	16 Sep 12
59:07		James	Wangari	KEN	23.3.94	1		København	18 Sep 16
59:07		Mang'ata	Ndiwa	KEN	12.12.87	2		Verbania	15 Apr 18
59:09		James Kipsang	Kwambai	KEN	28.2.83	3		Rotterdam	13 Sep 09
59:10		Bernard	Kipyego	KEN	16.7.86	4		Rotterdam	13 Sep 09
59.10		Bernard	Koech	KEN	01.1.00	2		Lille	1 Sep 12
59:11		Mosinet	Geremew	ETH	12.2.92	3		New Delhi	23 Nov 14
59:12		Cyprian	Kotut	KEN	.92	4		New Delhi	23 Nov 14
59:14		Dennis	Kimetto	KEN	22.1.84	1		Berlin	1 Apr 12
		(40)							
59:14		Leonard Patrick	Komon	KEN	10.1.88	1		Berlin	30 Mar 14
59:14		Barselius	Kipyego	KEN	23.7.93	1		Ústí nad Labem	16 Sep 17
59:15		Deriba	Merga	ETH	26.10.80	1		New Delhi	9 Nov 08
59:15		Wilson	Chebet	KEN	12.7.85	5		Rotterdam	13 Sep 09
59:15		Wilson	Kiprop	KEN	14.4.87	2		Berlin	1 Apr 12
59:17		Tola	Shura Kitata	ETH	9.6.96	1		Philadelphia	16 Sep 18
59:17		Yomif	Kejelcha	ETH	1.8.97	4		København	16 Sep 18
59:18		Leonard	Langat	KEN	7.8.90	2		Ostia	13 Mar 16
59:18		Leul	Gebrselassie	ETH	20.9.93	2		Valencia	22 Oct 17
59:18		Andamlak	Belihu	ETH	20.11.98	1		New Delhi	21 Oct 18
		(50)		100th man 59:35, 200th man 60:03, 300th 60:24, 400th 60:42, 500th 60:56						

Short course:		58:51	Paul Tergat	KEN	17.6.69	1	Stra	Milano 49m sh	30 Mar 96
Excessively downhill:	58:42	Bernard Koech		KEN	31.1.88	1		San Diego (dh 86m)	2 Jun 13

MARATHON

MEN All-time

Mark	Wind	Name		Nat	Born	Pos	Meet	Venue	Date
2:01:39	WR	Eliud	Kipchoge	KEN	5.11.84	1		Berlin	16 Sep 18
2:02:57	WR	Dennis	Kimetto	KEN	22.1.84	1		Berlin	28 Sep 14
2:03:03		Kenenisa	Bekele	ETH	13.6.82	1		Berlin	25 Sep 16
2:03:05			Kipchoge			1		London	24 Apr 16
2:03:13		Emmanuel	Mutai	KEN	12.10.84	2		Berlin	28 Sep 14
2:03:13		Wilson	Kipsang	KEN	15.3.82	2		Berlin	25 Sep 16
2:03:23	WR		W Kipsang			1		Berlin	29 Sep 13
2:03:32			Kipchoge			1		Berlin	24 Sep 17
2:03:38	WR	Patrick	Makau	KEN	2.3.85	1		Berlin	25 Sep 11
2:03:42			W Kipsang			1		Frankfurt	30 Oct 11
2:03:45			Kimetto			1		Chicago	13 Oct 13
2:03:46		Guye	Adola	ETH	20.10.90	2		Berlin	24 Sep 17
2:03:51		Stanley	Biwott	KEN	21.4.86	2		London	24 Apr 16
2:03:52			Mutai			2		Chicago	13 Oct 13
2:03:58			W Kipsang			1		Tokyo	26 Feb 17
2:03:59	WR	Haile	Gebrselassie	ETH	18.4.73	1		Berlin	28 Sep 08
2:04:00			Kipchoge			1		Berlin	27 Sep 15
2:04:00		Mosinet	Geremew (10)	ETH	12.2.92	1		Dubai	26 Jan 18
2:04:02		Leul	Gebrselassie	ETH	20.9.93	2		Dubai	26 Jan 18
2:04:05			Kipchoge			2		Berlin	29 Sep 13
2:04:06		Tamirat	Tola	ETH	11.8.91	3		Dubai	26 Jan 18
2:04:06		Asefa	Mengistu	ETH	18.1.85	4		Dubai	26 Jan 18
2:04:06		Lawrence	Cherono	KEN	7.8.88	1		Amsterdam	21 Oct 18
2:04:08		Sisay	Lemma	ETH	12.12.90	5		Dubai	26 Jan 18
2:04:11			Kipchoge			1		Chicago	12 Oct 14
2:04:11			Tam. Tola	ETH	11.8.91	1		Dubai	20 Jan 17
2:04:15		Geoffrey	Mutai	KEN	7.10.81	1		Berlin	30 Sep 12
2:04:15		Berhanu	Legesse	ETH	11.9.94	6		Dubai	26 Jan 18
2:04:16			Kimetto			2		Berlin	30 Sep 12
2:04:17			Kipchoge			1		London	22 Apr 18
2:04:23		Ayele	Abshero	ETH	28.12.90	1		Dubai	27 Jan 12
2:04:24		Tesfaye	Abera	ETH	31.3.92	1		Dubai	22 Jan 16
		(32/20)							
2:04:27		Duncan	Kibet	KEN	25.4.78	1		Rotterdam	5 Apr 09
2:04:27		James Kipsang	Kwambai	KEN	28.2.83	2		Rotterdam	5 Apr 09
2:04:28		Sammy	Kitwara	KEN	26.11.86	2		Chicago	12 Oct 14
2:04:32		Tsegaye	Mekonnen	ETH	15.6.95	1		Dubai	24 Jan 14
2:04:32		Dickson	Chumba	KEN	27.10.86	3		Chicago	12 Oct 14
2:04:33		Hayle	Lemi Berhanu	ETH	13.9.94	2		Dubai	22 Jan 16
2:04:37		Mule	Wasihun	ETH	20.10.93	2		Amsterdam	21 Oct 18
2:04:38		Tsegaye	Kebede	ETH	15.1.87	1		Chicago	7 Oct 12
2:04:40		Solomon	Deksisa	ETH	11.3.94	3		Amsterdam	21 Oct 18
2:04:43		El Hassan	El Abbassi	BRN	13.4.84	1		Valencia	2 Dec 18
		(30)							
2:04:44		Abdiwak	Tura	ETH	.95	7		Dubai	26 Jan 18
2:04:45		Lelisa	Desisa	ETH	14.1.90	1		Dubai	25 Jan 13
2:04:48		Yemane	Tsegay Adhane	ETH	8.4.85	1		Rotterdam	15 Apr 12
2:04:48		Berhanu	Shiferaw	ETH	31.5.93	2		Dubai	25 Jan 13
2:04:49		Tadesse	Tola	ETH	31.10.87	3		Dubai	25 Jan 13
2:04:49		Tola	Shura Kitata	ETH	9.6.96	2		London	22 Apr 18
2:04:50		Dino	Sefir	ETH	28.5.88	2		Dubai	27 Jan 12
2:04:50		Getu	Feleke	ETH	28.11.86	2		Rotterdam	15 Apr 12
2:04:52		Feyisa	Lilesa	ETH	1.2.90	2		Chicago	7 Oct 12
2:04:52		Endeshaw	Negesse	ETH	13.3.88	4		Dubai	25 Jan 13
		(40)							
2:04:53		Bernard	Koech	KEN	31.1.88	5		Dubai	25 Jan 13
2:04:53		Mathew	Kisorio ¶	KEN	16.5.89	3		Valencia	2 Dec 18
2:04:54		Markos	Geneti	ETH	30.5.84	3		Dubai	27 Jan 12
2:04:55	WR	Paul	Tergat	KEN	17.6.69	1		Berlin	28 Sep 03
2:04:56		Sammy	Korir	KEN	12.12.71	2		Berlin	28 Sep 03
2:04:56		Jonathan	Maiyo	KEN	5.5.88	4		Dubai	27 Jan 12
2:05:03		Moses	Mosop	KEN	17.7.85	3		Rotterdam	15 Apr 12
2:05:04		Abel	Kirui	KEN	4.6.82	3		Rotterdam	5 Apr 09
2:05:10		Samuel	Wanjiru	KEN	10.11.86	1		London	26 Apr 09
2:05:11		Mohamed	Farah	GBR	23.3.83	1		Chicago	7 Oct 18
		(5o)							

100th man 2:06:11, 200th 2:07:04, 300th 2:07:42, 400th 2:08:17, 500th 2:08:36

Downhill point-to-point course – Boston marathon is downhill overall (139m) and sometimes strongly wind-aided.

Mark	Wind	Name		Nat	Born	Pos	Meet	Venue	Date
2:03:02		Geoffrey	Mutai	KEN	7.10.81	1		Boston	18 Apr 11
2:03:06		Moses	Mosop	KEN	17.7.85	2		Boston	18 Apr 11

Mark	Wind	Name		Nat	Born	Pos	Meet	Venue	Date
2:04:53		Gebre-egziabher	Gebremariam	ETH	10.9.84	3		Boston	18 Apr 11
2:04:58		Ryan	Hall	USA	14.10.82	4		Boston	18 Apr 11
Uncertain distance									
2:04:04		Marius	Kipserem	KEN	17.5.88	1		Abu Dhabi	7 Dec 18
2:04:16		Abraham	Kiptum	KEN	5.9.89	2		Abu Dhabi	7 Dec 18
Illegally paced									
2:00:25		Eliud	Kipchoge	KEN	5.11.84	1		Monza	6 May 17

2000 METRES STEEPLECHASE

Mark	Wind	Name		Nat	Born	Pos	Meet	Venue	Date
5:10.68		Mahiedine	Mekhissi-Benabbad	FRA	15.3.85	1		Reims	30 Jun 10
5:13.47		Bouabdellah	Tahri	FRA	20.12.78	1		Tomblaine	25 Jun 10
5:14.43		Julius	Kariuki	KEN	12.6.61	1		Rovereto	21 Aug 90
5:14.53		Saïf Saaeed	Shaheen	QAT	15.10.82	1	SGP	Doha	13 May 05
5:16.22		Phillip	Barkutwo	KEN	6.10.66	2		Rovereto	21 Aug 90
5:16.46		Wesley	Kiprotich	KEN	31.7.79	2	SGP	Doha	13 May 05
5:16.85		Eliud	Barngetuny	KEN	20.5.73	1		Parma	13 Jun 95

3000 METRES STEEPLECHASE

Mark	Wind	Name		Nat	Born	Pos	Meet	Venue	Date
7:53.63 WR		Saïf Saaeed	Shaheen	KEN/QAT	15.10.82	1	VD	Bruxelles	3 Sep 04
7:53.64		Brimin	Kipruto	KEN	31.7.85	1	Herc	Monaco	22 Jul 11
7:54.31		Paul Kipsiele	Koech	KEN	10.11.81	1	GGala	Roma	31 May 12
7:55.28 WR		Brahim	Boulami ¶	MAR	20.4.72	1	VD	Bruxelles	24 Aug 01
7:55.51			Shaheen			1	VD	Bruxelles	26 Aug 05
7:55.72 WR		Bernard	Barmasai	KEN	6.5.74	1	ASV	Köln	24 Aug 97
7:55.76		Ezekiel	Kemboi	KEN	25.5.82	2	Herc	Monaco	22 Jul 11
7:56.16		Moses	Kiptanui	KEN	1.10.70	2	ASV	Köln	24 Aug 97
7:56.32			Shaheen			1	Tsik	Athína	3 Jul 06
7:56.34			Shaheen			1	GGala	Roma	8 Jul 05
7:56.07			P K Koech			2	GGala	Roma	8 Jul 05
7:56.54			Shaheen			1	WK	Zürich	18 Aug 06
7:56.58			P K Koech			1	DL	Doha	11 May 12
7:56.81		Richard	Mateelong	KEN	14.10.83	2	DL	Doha	11 May 12
7:56.94			Shaheen			1	WAF	Monaco	19 Sep 04
7:57.28			Shaheen			1	Tsik	Athína	14 Jun 05
7:57.29		Reuben	Kosgei	KEN	2.8.79	2	VD	Bruxelles	24 Aug 01
7:57.32			P K Koech			3	Herc	Monaco	22 Jul 11
7:57.38			Shaheen			1	WAF	Monaco	14 Sep 03
7:57.42			P K Koech			2	WAF	Monaco	14 Sep 03
7:58.09			Boulami			1	Herc	Monaco	19 Jul 02
7:58.10			S Cherono			2	Herc	Monaco	19 Jul 02
7:58.15		Soufiane	El Bakkali (10)	MAR	7.1.96	1	Herc	Monaco	20 Jul 18
7:58.41		Jairus	Birech	KEN	14.12.92	1	VD	Bruxelles	5 Sep 14
7:58.50			Boulami			1	WK	Zürich	17 Aug 01
7:58.66			S Cherono			3	VD	Bruxelles	24 Aug 01
7:58.80			P K Koech			1	VD	Bruxelles	14 Sep 07
7:58.83			Birech			1	DL	Saint-Denis	4 Jul 15
7:58.85			Kemboi			1	SGP	Doha	8 May 09
7:58.98			Barmasai			1	Herc	Monaco	4 Aug 99
		(30/11)							
7:59.08 WR		Wilson	Boit Kipketer	KEN	6.10.73	1	WK	Zürich	13 Aug 97
8:00.09		Mahiedine	Mekhissi-Benabbad	FRA	15.3.85	2	DL	Saint-Denis	6 Jul 13
8:00.12		Conseslus	Kipruto	KEN	8.12.94	1	DL	Birmingham	5 Jun 16
8:00.45		Evan	Jager	USA	8.3.89	2	DL	Saint-Denis	4 Jul 15
8:01.18		Bouabdellah	Tahri	FRA	20.12.78	3	WCh	Berlin	18 Aug 09
8:01.67		Abel	Mutai	KEN	2.10.88	2	GGala	Roma	31 May 12
8:01.69		Kipkirui	Misoi	KEN	23.12.78	4	VD	Bruxelles	24 Aug 01
8:03.41		Patrick	Sang	KEN	11.4.64	3	ASV	Köln	24 Aug 97
8:03.57		Ali	Ezzine	MAR	3.9.78	1	Gaz	Saint-Denis	23 Jun 00
		(20)							
8:03.57		Hillary	Yego	KEN	2.4.92	3	DL	Shanghai	18 May 13
8:03.74		Raymond	Yator	KEN	7.4.81	3	Herc	Monaco	18 Aug 00
8:03.81		Benjamin	Kiplagat	UGA	4.3.89	2	Athl	Lausanne	8 Jul 10
8:03.89		John	Kosgei	KEN	13.7.73	3	Herc	Monaco	16 Aug 97
8:04.95		Simon	Vroemen ¶	NED	11.5.69	2	VD	Bruxelles	26 Aug 05
8:05.01		Eliud	Barngetuny	KEN	20.5.73	1	Herc	Monaco	25 Jul 95
8:05.35 WR		Peter	Koech	KEN	18.2.58	1	DNG	Stockholm	3 Jul 89
8:05.37		Philip	Barkutwo	KEN	6.10.66	2		Rieti	6 Sep 92
8:05.4 WR		Henry	Rono	KEN	12.2.52	1		Seattle	13 May 78
8:05.43		Christopher	Kosgei	KEN	14.8.74	2	WK	Zürich	11 Aug 99
		(30)							

Mark	Wind	Name		Nat	Born	Pos	Meet	Venue	Date
8:05.51		Julius	Kariuki	KEN	12.6.61	1	OG	Seoul	30 Sep 88
8:05.68		Wesley	Kiprotich	KEN	1.8.79	4	VD	Bruxelles	3 Sep 04
8:05.75		Mustafa	Mohamed	SWE	1.3.79	1	NA	Heusden-Zolder	28 Jul 07
8:05.88		Bernard	Mbugua Nganga	KEN	17.1.85	2	ISTAF	Berlin	11 Sep 11
8:05.99		Joseph	Keter	KEN	13.6.69	1	Herc	Monaco	10 Aug 96
8:06.13		Tareq Mubarak	Taher	BRN	24.3.84	3	Tsik	Athína	13 Jul 09
8:06.16		Roba	Gari	ETH	12.4.82	3	DL	Doha	11 May 12
8:06.19		Benjamin	Kigen	KEN	5.7.93	1	DL	Rabat	13 Jul 18
8:06.77		Gideon	Chirchir	KEN	24.2.66	2	WK	Zürich	16 Aug 95
8:06.88		Richard	Kosgei	KEN	29.12.70	2	GPF	Monaco	9 Sep 95
		(40)							
8:06.96		Gilbert	Kirui	KEN	22.1.94	2	DL	London (OS)	27 Jul 13
8:07.02		Brahim	Taleb	MAR	16.2.85	2	NA	Heusden-Zolder	28 Jul 07
8:07.13		Paul	Kosgei	KEN	22.4.78	2	GP II	Saint-Denis	3 Jul 99
8:07.18		Obaid Moussa	Amer ¶	KEN/QAT	18.4.85	4	OG	Athína	24 Aug 04
8:07.27		Chala	Beyo	ETH	18.1.96	2	DL	Rabat	13 Jul 18
8:07.44		Luis Miguel	Martín	ESP	11.1.72	2	VD	Bruxelles	30 Aug 02
8:07.59		Julius	Nyamu	KEN	1.12.77	5	VD	Bruxelles	24 Aug 01
8:07.62		Joseph	Mahmoud	FRA	13.12.55	1	VD	Bruxelles	24 Aug 84
8:07.75		Jonathan	Ndiku Muia	KEN	18.9.91	6	Herc	Monaco	22 Jul 11
8:07.96		Mark	Rowland	GBR	7.3.63	3	OG	Seoul	30 Sep 88
		(50)							

100th man 8:11.80, 200th 8:16.92, 300th 8:20.58, 400th 8:22.9, 500th 8:25.33
7:53.63 Shaheen formerly Stephen Cherono KEN
Drugs disqualification: 7:53.17 Brahim Boulami ¶ MAR 20.4.72 1 WK Zürich 16 Aug 02

110 METRES HURDLES

Mark	Wind	Name		Nat	Born	Pos	Meet	Venue	Date
12.80	WR 0.3	Aries	Merritt	USA	24.7.85	1	VD	Bruxelles	7 Sep 12
12.87	WR 0.9	Dayron	Robles	CUB	19.11.86	1	GS	Ostrava	12 Jun 08
12.88	WR 1.1		Liu Xiang	CHN	13.7.83	1rA	Athl	Lausanne	11 Jul 06
12.88	0.5		Robles			1	Gaz	Saint-Denis	18 Jul 08
12.89	0.5	David	Oliver	USA	24.4.82	1	DL	Saint-Denis	16 Jul 10
12.90	1.1	Dominique	Arnold	USA	14.9.73	2rA	Athl	Lausanne	11 Jul 06
12.90	1.6		Oliver			1	Pre	Eugene	3 Jul 10
12.90	0.7	Omar	McLeod	JAM	25.4.94	1	NC	Kingston	24 Jun 17
12.91	WR 0.5	Colin	Jackson	GBR	18.2.67	1	WCh	Stuttgart	20 Aug 93
12.91	WR 0.3		Liu Xiang			1	OG	Athína	27 Aug 04
12.91	0.2		Robles			1	DNG	Stockholm	22 Jul 08
12.92	WR -0.1	Roger	Kingdom	USA	26.8.62	1	WK	Zürich	16 Aug 89
12.92	0.9	Allen	Johnson	USA	1.3.71	1	NC	Atlanta	23 Jun 96
12.92	0.2		Johnson			1	VD	Bruxelles	23 Aug 96
12.92	1.5		Liu Xiang			1	GP	New York	2 Jun 07
12.92	0.0		Robles			1	WAF	Stuttgart	23 Sep 07
12.92	-0.3		Merritt			1	OG	London (OS)	8 Aug 12
12.92	0.6	Sergey	Shubenkov (10)	RUS	4.10.90	1	Gyulai	Székesfehérvár	2 Jul 18
12.93	WR -0.2	Renaldo	Nehemiah	USA	24.3.59	1	WK	Zürich	19 Aug 81
12.93	0.0		Johnson			1	WCh	Athína	7 Aug 97
12.93	-0.6		Liu Xiang			1	WAF	Stuttgart	9 Sep 06
12.93	0.1		Robles			1	OG	Beijing	21 Aug 08
12.93	1.7		Oliver			1	NC	Des Moines	27 Jun 10
12.93	-0.3		Oliver			1	WK	Zürich	19 Aug 10
12.93	1.2		Merritt			1	NC/OT	Eugene	30 Jun 12
12.93	0.6		Merritt			1	LGP	London (CP)	13 Jul 12
12.93	0.0		Merritt			1	Herc	Monaco	20 Jul 12
12.94	1.6	Jack	Pierce	USA	23.9.62	1s2	NC	Atlanta	22 Jun 96
12.94	1.8		Oliver			1	Pre	Eugene	4 Jun 11
12.94	0.1		Merritt			1s2	OG	London (OS)	8 Aug 12
12.94	0.8	Hansle	Parchment	JAM	17.6.90	1	DL	Saint-Denis	5 Jul 14
12.94	0.5	Orlando	Ortega	CUB/ESP	29.7.91	1	DL	Saint-Denis	4 Jul 15
		(32/14)							
12.95	1.5	Terrence	Trammell	USA	23.11.78	2	GP	New York	2 Jun 07
12.95	0.2	Pascal	Martinot-Lagarde	FRA	22.9.91	1	Herc	Monaco	18 Jul 14
12.97	1.0	Ladji	Doucouré	FRA	28.3.83	1	NC	Angers	15 Jul 05
12.98	0.6	Mark	Crear	USA	2.10.68	1		Zagreb	5 Jul 99
12.98	1.5	Jason	Richardson	USA	4.4.86	1s3	NC/OT	Eugene	30 Jun 12
12.99	1.2	Ronnie	Ash	USA	2.7.88	1s1	NC	Sacramento	29 Jun 14
		(20)							
13.00	0.5	Anthony	Jarrett	GBR	13.8.68	2	WCh	Stuttgart	20 Aug 93
13.00	0.6	Anier	García	CUB	9.3.76	1	OG	Sydney	25 Sep 00
13.01	0.3	Larry	Wade ¶	USA	22.11.74	1rA	Athl	Lausanne	2 Jul 99
13.02	1.5	Ryan	Wilson	USA	19.12.80	3	GP	New York	2 Jun 07

MEN All-time

Mark	Wind	Name		Nat	Born	Pos	Meet	Venue	Date
13.02	1.7	David	Payne	USA	24.7.82	3	WCh	Osaka	31 Aug 07
13.03	-0.2	Greg	Foster	USA	4.8.58	2	WK	Zürich	19 Aug 81
13.03	1.0	Reggie	Torian	USA	22.4.75	1	NC	New Orleans	21 Jun 98
13.03	1.0	Devon	Allen	USA	12.12.94	1	NC/OT	Eugene	9 Jul 16
13.05	1.4	Tony	Dees ¶	USA	6.8.63	1		Vigo	23 Jul 91
13.05	-0.8	Florian	Schwarthoff	GER	7.5.68	1	NC	Bremen	2 Jul 95
		(30)							
13.05	-0.1	Ronald	Levy	JAM	30.10.92	1	DL	Paris (C)	1 Jul 17
13.08	1.2	Mark	McKoy	CAN	10.12.61	1	BNP	Villeneuve-d'Ascq	2 Jul 93
13.08	0.0	Stanislav	Olijar	LAT	22.3.79	2	Athl	Lausanne	1 Jul 03
13.08	1.2	Jeff	Porter	USA	27.11.85	3	NC/OT	Eugene	30 Jun 12
13.09	2.0	Antwon	Hicks	USA	12.3.83	2s2	NC/OT	Eugene	6 Jul 08
13.09	0.6	Garfield	Darien	FRA	22.12.87	1	GS	Ostrava	28 Jun 17
13.11	0.5	Aleec	Harris	USA	31.10.90	4	DL	Saint-Denis	4 Jul 15
13.11	1.8	Antonio	Alkana	RSA	12.4.90	1	Odlozil	Praha	5 Jun 17
13.12	1.5	Falk	Balzer ¶	GER	14.12.73	2	EC	Budapest	22 Aug 98
13.12	1.0	Duane	Ross ¶	USA	5.12.72	3	WCh	Sevilla	25 Aug 99
		(40)							
13.12	1.9	Anwar	Moore	USA	5.3.79	1	ModR	Modesto	5 May 07
13.12	0.0	Dimitri	Bascou	FRA	20.7.87	2	Herc	Monaco	15 Jul 16
13.13	1.6	Igor	Kovác	SVK	12.5.69	1	DNG	Stockholm	7 Jul 97
13.13	2.0	Dexter	Faulk	USA	14.4.84	2	GS	Ostrava	17 Jun 09
13.14	0.1	Ryan	Brathwaite	BAR	6.6.88	1	WCh	Berlin	20 Aug 09
13.14	0.0	Andrew	Riley	JAM	6.9.88	4	DL	Saint-Denis	6 Jul 13
13.14	-0.1	Andrew	Pozzi	GBR	15.5.92	2	DL	Paris (C)	1 Jul 17
13.15	0.3	Robin	Korving	NED	29.7.74	5rA	Athl	Lausanne	2 Jul 99
13.15	0.1	Dwight	Thomas	JAM	23.9.80	2	Bisl	Oslo	9 Jun 11
13.15	0.3	Balázs	Baji	HUN	9.6.89	4	Gyulai	Székesfehérvár	4 Jul 17
13.15	0.9	Grant	Holloway	USA	19.11.97	1	SEC	Knoxville	13 May 18
		(51)		100th man 10.06, 200th 13.08, 300th 13.16, 400th 13.53, 500th 13.58					

Rolling start but accepted by race officials

| 13.10A | 2.0 | Falk | Balzer ¶ | GER | 14.12.73 | 1 | WCp | Johannesburg | 13 Sep 98 |

Doubtful timing: Scheessel 4 Jun 95 +1.3 1. Mike Fenner GER 24.4.71 13.06, 2. Eric Kaiser ¶ GER 7.3.71 13.08

Wind-assisted marks   *Performances to 12.94, performers to 13.14*

12.87	2.6	Roger	Kingdom	USA	26.8.62	1	WCp	Barcelona	10 Sep 89
12.87	2.4		Liu Xiang	CHN	13.7.83	1	Pre	Eugene	2 Jun 12
12.89	3.2	David	Oliver	USA	24.4.82	1s1	NC/OT	Eugene	6 Jul 08
12.91	3.5	Renaldo	Nehemiah	USA	24.3.59	1	NCAA	Champaign	1 Jun 79
12.94A	2.8		Jackson			1rA		Sestriere	31 Jul 94
12.98	3.1	Ronnie	Ash	USA	2.7.88	1	NACAC	Miramar	9 Jul 10
13.00	2.6	Anwar	Moore	USA	5.3.79	1	DrakeR	Des Moines	28 Apr 07
13.05	3.6	Ryan	Brathwaite	BAR	6.6.88	1		Austin	2 May 09
13.05	2.1	Dimitri	Bascou	FRA	20.7.87	1	NC	Angers	26 Jun 16
13.06	2.1	Mark	McKoy	CAN	10.12.61	1	Gugl	Linz	13 Aug 92
13.12	2.4	Dexter	Faulk	USA	14.4.84	4	Pre	Eugene	2 Jun 12
13.13	5.8	Andrew	Pozzi	GBR	15.5.92	1		Clermont	15 Apr 17
13.14	2.9	Igor	Kazanov	LAT	24.9.63	1r1	Znam	Leningrad	8 Jun 86
13.14	4.7	Lawrence	Clarke	GBR	12.3.90	1h1		Madrid	7 Jul 12
13.14	3.8	Wayne	Davis	TTO	22.8.91	1	NCAA	Eugene	8 Jun 13

Hand timing

12.7		Sergey	Shubenkov	RUS	4.10.90	1		Barnaul	2 Jul 16
12.8	1.0	Renaldo	Nehemiah	USA	24.3.59	1		Kingston	11 May 79
12.9	0.0	Yordan	O'Farrill	CUB	9.2.93	1	Barr	La Habana	23 May 14

Wind-assisted

12.8	2.4	Colin	Jackson	GBR	18.2.67	1		Sydney	10 Jan 90
12.9	4.1	Mark	Crear	USA	2.10.68	1rA	S&W	Modesto	8 May 93
12.9	3.1	William	Sharman	GBR	12.9.84	1r2		Madrid	2 Jul 10

400 METRES HURDLES

46.78 WR		Kevin	Young	USA	16.9.66	1	OG	Barcelona	6 Aug 92
46.98		Abderrahman	Samba	QAT	5.9.95	1	DL	Paris (C)	30 Jun 18
47.02 WR		Edwin	Moses	USA	31.8.55	1		Koblenz	31 Aug 83
47.02		Rai	Benjamin	ANT/USA	27.7.97	1	NCAA	Eugene	8 Jun 18
47.03		Bryan	Bronson ¶	USA	9.9.72	1	NC	New Orleans	21 Jun 98
47.10		Samuel	Matete	ZAM	27.7.68	1rA	WK	Zürich	7 Aug 91
47.13 WR			Moses			1		Milano	3 Jul 80
47.14			Moses			1	Athl	Lausanne	14 Jul 81
47.17			Moses			1	ISTAF	Berlin	8 Aug 80
47.18			Young			1	WCh	Stuttgart	19 Aug 93
47.19		Andre	Phillips	USA	5.9.59	1	OG	Seoul	25 Sep 88

Mark	Wind	Name		Nat	Born	Pos	Meet	Venue	Date
47.23		Amadou	Dia Bâ	SEN	22.9.58	2	OG	Seoul	25 Sep 88
47.24		Kerron	Clement	USA	31.10.85	1	NC	Carson	26 Jun 05
47.25		Félix	Sánchez (10)	DOM	30.8.77	1	WCh	Saint-Denis	29 Aug 03
47.25		Angelo	Taylor	USA	29.12.78	1	OG	Beijing	18 Aug 08
47.27			Moses			1	ISTAF	Berlin	21 Aug 81
47.30		Bershawn	Jackson	USA	8.5.83	1	WCh	Helsinki	9 Aug 05
47.32			Moses			1		Koblenz	29 Aug 84
47.32			Jackson			1	NC	Des Moines	26 Jun 10
47.35			Sánchez			1rA	WK	Zürich	16 Aug 02
47.37			Moses			1	WCp	Roma	4 Sep 81
47.37			Moses			1	WK	Zürich	24 Aug 83
47.37			Moses			1	NC/OT	Indianapolis	17 Jul 88
47.37			Young			1	Athl	Lausanne	7 Jul 93
47.37		Stéphane	Diagana	FRA	23.7.69	1	Athl	Lausanne	5 Jul 95
47.37			Samba			1	C.Cup	Ostrava	8 Sep 18
47.38			Moses			1	Athl	Lausanne	2 Sep 86
47.38		Danny	Harris ¶	USA	7.9.65	1	Athl	Lausanne	10 Jul 91
47.38			Sánchez			1rA	WK	Zürich	17 Aug 01
47.39			Clement			1	NC	Indianapolis	24 Jun 06
		(30/14)							
47.43		James	Carter	USA	7.5.78	2	WCh	Helsinki	9 Aug 05
47.48		Harald	Schmid	FRG	29.9.57	1	EC	Athína	8 Sep 82
47.53		Hadi Soua'an	Al-Somaily	KSA	21.8.76	2	OG	Sydney	27 Sep 00
47.54		Derrick	Adkins	USA	2.7.70	2	Athl	Lausanne	5 Jul 95
47.54		Fabrizio	Mori	ITA	28.6.69	2	WCh	Edmonton	10 Aug 01
47.54		Kyron	McMaster	IVB	3.1.97	3	DL	Paris (C)	30 Jun 18
		(20)							
47.60		Winthrop	Graham	JAM	17.11.65	1	WK	Zürich	4 Aug 93
47.63		Johnny	Dutch	USA	20.1.89	2	NC	Des Moines	26 Jun 10
47.64		Karsten	Warholm	NOR	28.2.96	1	EC	Berlin	9 Aug 18
47.66A		L.J. 'Louis'	van Zyl	RSA	20.7.85	1		Pretoria	25 Feb 11
47.67		Bennie	Brazell	USA	2.6.82	2	NCAA	Sacramento	11 Jun 05
47.69		Jehue	Gordon	TTO	15.12.91	1	WCh	Moskva	15 Aug 13
47.70		Michael	Tinsley	USA	21.4.84	2	WCh	Moskva	15 Aug 13
47.72		Javier	Culson	PUR	25.7.84	1		Ponce	8 May 10
47.75		David	Patrick	USA	12.6.60	4	NC/OT	Indianapolis	17 Jul 88
47.78		Boniface Mucheru	Tumuti	KEN	2.5.92	2	OG	Rio de Janeiro	18 Aug 16
		(30)							
47.79		Nicholas	Bett	KEN	14.6.92	1	WCh	Beijing	25 Aug 15
47.81		Llewellyn	Herbert	RSA	21.7.77	3	OG	Sydney	27 Sep 00
47.81		Yasmani	Copello	CUB/TUR	15.4.87	2	EC	Berlin	9 Aug 18
47.82 WR		John	Akii-Bua	UGA	3.12.49	1	OG	München	2 Sep 72
47.82		Kriss	Akabusi	GBR	28.11.58	3	OG	Barcelona	6 Aug 92
47.82		Periklis	Iakovákis	GRE	24.3.79	2	GP	Osaka	6 May 06
47.84		Bayano	Kamani	PAN	17.4.80	2s1	WCh	Helsinki	7 Aug 05
47.84		David	Greene	GBR	11.4.86	2	DL	Saint-Denis	6 Jul 12
47.89		Dai	Tamesue	JPN	3.5.78	3	WCh	Edmonton	10 Aug 01
47.91		Calvin	Davis	USA	2.4.72	1s2	OG	Atlanta	31 Jul 96
		(40)							
47.92		Aleksandr	Vasilyev	BLR	26.7.61	2	ECp	Moskva	17 Aug 85
47.93		Kenji	Narisako	JPN	25.7.84	3	GP	Osaka	6 May 06
47.93		Jeshua	Anderson	USA	22.6.89	1	NC	Eugene	26 Jun 11
47.93		Omar	Cisneros	CUB	19.11.89	1s3	WCh	Moskva	13 Aug 13
47.94		Eric	Thomas	USA	1.12.73	1	GGala	Roma	30 Jun 00
47.97		Maurice	Mitchell	USA	14.5.71	2rA	WK	Zürich	14 Aug 96
47.97		Joey	Woody	USA	22.5.73	3	NC	New Orleans	21 Jun 98
47.97		Thomas	Barr	IRL	24.7.92	4	OG	Rio de Janeiro	18 Aug 16
47.98		Sven	Nylander	SWE	1.1.62	4	OG	Atlanta	1 Aug 96
48.00		Danny	McFarlane	JAM	14.2.72	1s2	OG	Athína	24 Aug 04
		(50)							

100th man 48.40, 200th man 4888, 300th man 49.13, 400th 49.34, 500th 49.51

Best at low altitude: 47.66 van Zyl   1   GS   Ostrava   31 May 11
Drugs disqualification   47.15 Bronson ¶ 1   GWG   Uniondale, NY   19 Jul 98

HIGH JUMP

2.45 WR		Javier	Sotomayor ¶	CUB	13.10.67	1		Salamanca	27 Jul 93
2.44 WR			Sotomayor			1	CAC	San Juan	29 Jul 89
2.43 WR			Sotomayor			1		Salamanca	8 Sep 88
2.43i			Sotomayor			1	WI	Budapest	4 Mar 89
2.43		Mutaz Essa	Barshim	QAT	24.6.91	1	VD	Bruxelles	5 Sep 14
2.42 WR		Patrik	Sjöberg	SWE	5.1.65	1	DNG	Stockholm	30 Jun 87

Mark	Wind	Name		Nat	Born	Pos	Meet	Venue	Date
2.42i	WR	Carlo	Thränhardt	FRG	5.7.57	1		Berlin	26 Feb 88
2.42			Sotomayor			1		Sevilla	5 Jun 94
2.42i		Ivan	Ukhov	RUS	29.3.86	1		Praha	25 Feb 14
2.42		Bohdan	Bondarenko	UKR	30.8.89	1	adidas	New York	14 Jun 14
2.42			Barshim			2	adidas	New York	14 Jun 14
2.41	WR	Igor	Paklin	KGZ	15.6.63	1	WUG	Kobe	4 Sep 85
2.41i			Sjöberg			1		Pireás	1 Feb 87
2.41i			Sotomayor			1	WI	Toronto	14 Mar 93
2.41			Sotomayor			1	NC	La Habana	25 Jun 94
2.41			Sotomayor			1	TSB	London (CP)	15 Jul 94
2.41			Bondarenko			1	Athl	Lausanne	4 Jul 13
2.41			Bondarenko			1	WCh	Moskva	15 Aug 13
2.41i			Ukhov			1		Chelyabinsk	16 Jan 14
2.41			Ukhov			1	DL	Doha	9 May 14
2.41			Barshim			1	GGala	Roma	5 Jun 14
2.41			Barshim			1		Eberstadt	22 Aug 14
2.41i			Barshim			1		Athlone	18 Feb 15
2.41			Barshim			1	Pre	Eugene	30 May 15
2.40	WR	Rudolf	Povarnitsyn	UKR	13.6.62	1		Donetsk	11 Aug 85
2.40		Sorin	Matei	ROU	6.7.63	1	PTS	Bratislava	20 Jun 90
2.40i		Hollis	Conway (10)	USA	8.1.67	1	WI	Sevilla	10 Mar 91
2.40		Charles	Austin	USA	19.12.67	1	WK	Zürich	7 Aug 91
2.40		Vyacheslav	Voronin	RUS	5.4.74	1	BrGP	London (CP)	5 Aug 00
2.40i		Stefan	Holm	SWE	25.5.76	1	EI	Madrid	6 Mar 05
2.40i		Aleksey	Dmitrik	RUS	12.4.84	1		Arnstadt	8 Feb 14
2.40		Derek	Drouin	CAN	6.3.90	1	DrakeR	Des Moines	25 Apr 14
2.40		Andriy	Protsenko	UKR	20.5.88	2	Athl	Lausanne	3 Jul 14
2.40		Danil	Lysenko	RUS	19.5.97	1	Herc	Monaco	20 Jul 18

To 2.40   Most performances: Sotomayor 21, Barshim 13, Bondarenko 7, Ukhov 5, Sjöberg 4, Thränhardt 2 for 63/7

Mark	Wind	Name		Nat	Born	Pos	Meet	Venue	Date
2.39	WR		Zhu Jianhua	CHN	29.5.63	1		Eberstadt	10 Jun 84
2.39i		Dietmar	Mögenburg	FRG	15.8.61	1		Köln	24 Feb 85
2.39i		Ralf (20)	Sonn	GER	17.1.67	1		Berlin	1 Mar 91
2.39		Gianmarco	Tamberi	ITA	1.6.92	1	Herc	Monaco	15 Jul 16
2.38i		Gennadiy	Avdeyenko	UKR	4.11.63	2	WI	Indianapolis	7 Mar 87
2.38		Sergey	Malchenko	RUS	2.11.63	1		Banská Bystrica	4 Sep 88
2.38		Dragutin	Topic ¶	YUG	12.3.71	1		Beograd	1 Aug 93
2.38i		Steve	Smith	GBR	29.3.73	2		Wuppertal	4 Feb 94
2.38i		Wolf-Hendrik	Beyer	GER	14.2.72	1		Weinheim	18 Mar 94
2.38		Troy	Kemp	BAH	18.6.66	1	Nik	Nice	12 Jul 95
2.38		Artur	Partyka	POL	25.7.69	1		Eberstadt	18 Aug 96
2.38i		Matt	Hemingway	USA	24.10.72	1	NC	Atlanta	4 Mar 00
2.38		Yaroslav (30)	Rybakov	RUS	22.11.80	1		Stockholm	15 Feb 05
2.38		Jacques	Freitag	RSA	11.6.82	1		Oudtshoorn	5 Mar 05
2.38		Andriy	Sokolovskyy	UKR	16.7.78	1	GGala	Roma	8 Jul 05
2.38i		Linus	Thörnblad	SWE	6.3.85	2	NC	Göteborg	25 Feb 07
2.38		Andrey	Silnov	RUS	9.9.84	1	LGP	London (CP)	25 Jul 08
2.38			Zhang Guowei	CHN	4.6.91	2	Pre	Eugene	30 May 15
2.37		Valeriy	Sereda	RUS	30.6.59	1		Rieti	2 Sep 84
2.37		Tom	McCants	USA	27.11.62	1	Owens	Columbus	8 May 88
2.37		Jerome	Carter	USA	25.3.63	2	Owens	Columbus	8 May 88
2.37		Sergey	Dymchenko	UKR	23.8.67	1		Kyiv	10 Sep 90
2.37i		Dalton (40)	Grant	GBR	8.4.66	1	EI	Paris	13 Mar 94
2.37i		Jaroslav	Bába	CZE	2.9.84	2		Arnstadt	5 Feb 05
2.37		Jesse	Williams	USA	27.12.83	1	NC	Eugene	26 Jun 11
2.37		Robbie	Grabarz	GBR	3.10.87	3	Athl	Lausanne	23 Aug 12
2.37		Eric	Kynard	USA	3.2.91	2	Athl	Lausanne	4 Jul 13
2.37		Donald	Thomas	BAH	1.7.84	1	Gyulai	Székesfehérvár	18 Jul 16
2.36	WR	Gerd	Wessig	GDR	16.7.59	1	OG	Moskva	1 Aug 80

and 23 more men at 2.36   (45 to 2.37)   100th man 2.34, 200th 2.31, 300th 2.30, 400th 2.28, 500th 2.27

Best outdoor marks for athletes with indoor bests

Mark	Name	Pos	Meet	Venue	Date		Mark	Name	Pos	Meet	Venue	Date
2.41	Ukhov	1	DL	Doha	9 May 14		2.36	Mögenburg	3		Eberstadt	10 Jun 84
2.39	Conway	1	USOF	Norman	30 Jul 89		2.36	Howard	1		Rehlingen	8 Jun 87
2.38	Avdeyenko	2=	WCh	Roma	6 Sep 87		2.36	Zvara	1		Praha	23 Aug 87
2.37	Thränhardt	2		Rieti	2 Sep 84		2.36	Grant	4	WCh	Tokyo	1 Sep 91
2.37	Smith	1	WJ	Seoul	20 Sep 92		2.36	Hoen	1		Oslo	1 Jul 97
2.37	Holm	1		Athína	13 Jul 08		2.36	Bába	2=	GGala	Roma	8 Jul 05
							2.36	Dmitrik	1	NC	Chelyabinsk	23 Jul 11

Mark	Wind		Name	Nat	Born	Pos	Meet	Venue	Date

Ancillary jumps – en route to final marks

Mark		Name			Born			Venue	Date
2.40	Sotomayor		8 Sep 88	2.40	Sotomayor	5 Jun 94	2.40	Barshim	14 Jun 14
2.40	Sotomayor		29 Jul 89	2.40	Bondarenko	14 Jun 14	2.40	Barshim	5 Sep 14

POLE VAULT

Mark	Wind	Name		Nat	Born	Pos	Meet	Venue	Date
6.16i	WR	Renaud	Lavillenie	FRA	18.9.86	1		Donetsk	15 Feb 14
6.15i	WR	Sergey	Bubka	UKR	4.12.63	1		Donetsk	21 Feb 93
6.14i	WIR		Bubka			1		Liévin	13 Feb 93
6.14A	WIR		Bubka			1		Sestriere	31 Jul 94
6.13i	WIR		Bubka			1		Berlin	21 Feb 92
6.13	WR		Bubka			1	TOTO	Tokyo	19 Sep 92
6.12i	WIR		Bubka			1	Mast	Grenoble	23 Mar 91
6.12	WR		Bubka			1		Padova	30 Aug 92
6.11i	WIR		Bubka			1		Donetsk	19 Mar 91
6.11	WR		Bubka			1		Dijon	13 Jun 92
6.10i	WIR		Bubka			1		San Sebastián	15 Mar 91
6.10	WR		Bubka			1	MAI	Malmö	5 Aug 91
6.09	WR		Bubka			1		Formia	8 Jul 91
6.08i	WIR		Bubka			1	NC	Volgograd	9 Feb 91
6.08	WR		Bubka			1	Znam	Moskva	9 Jun 91
6.08i			Lavillenie			1		Bydgoszcz	31 Jan 14
6.07	WR		Bubka			1	Super	Shizuoka	6 May 91
6.06	WR		Bubka			1	Nik	Nice	10 Jul 88
6.06i		Steve	Hooker	AUS	16.7.82	1		Boston (R)	7 Feb 09
6.05	WR		Bubka			1	PTS	Bratislava	9 Jun 88
6.05i			Bubka			1		Donetsk	17 Mar 90
6.05i			Bubka			1		Berlin	5 Mar 93
6.05			Bubka			1	GPF	London (CP)	10 Sep 93
6.05i			Bubka			1	Mast	Grenoble	6 Feb 94
6.05			Bubka			1	ISTAF	Berlin	30 Aug 94
6.05			Bubka			1	GPF	Fukuoka	13 Sep 97
6.05		Maksim	Tarasov	RUS	2.12.70	1	GP II	Athína	16 Jun 99
6.05		Dmitriy	Markov	BLR/AUS	14.3.75	1	WCh	Edmonton	9 Aug 01
6.05			Lavillenie			1	Pre	Eugene	30 May 15
6.05		Armand	Duplantis	SWE	10.11.99	1	EC	Berlin	12 Aug 18
		(30/6)							
6.04		Brad	Walker	USA	21.6.81	1	Pre	Eugene	8 Jun 08
6.03		Okkert	Brits	RSA	22.8.73	1	ASV	Köln	18 Aug 95
6.03		Jeff	Hartwig	USA	25.9.67	1		Jonesboro	14 Jun 00
6.03		Thiago	Braz da Silva	BRA	16.12.93	1	OG	Rio de Janeiro	15 Aug 16
		(10)							
6.02i		Rodion	Gataullin	RUS	23.11.65	1	NC	Gomel	4 Feb 89
6.01		Igor	Trandenkov	RUS	17.8.66	1	NC	Sankt Peterburg	4 Jul 96
		Hit bar hard, but kept it on with his hand illegally. Next best 5.95 1						Dijon	26 May 96
6.01		Tim	Mack	USA	15.9.72	1	WAF	Monaco	18 Sep 04
6.01		Yevgeniy	Lukyanenko	RUS	23.1.85	1	EAF	Bydgoszcz	1 Jul 08
6.01	sq	Björn	Otto	GER	16.10.77	1		Aachen	5 Sep 12
6.00		Tim	Lobinger	GER	3.9.72	1	ASV	Köln	24 Aug 97
6.00i		Jean	Galfione	FRA	9.6.71	1	WI	Maebashi	6 Mar 99
6.00i		Danny	Ecker	GER	21.7.77	1		Dortmund	11 Feb 01
6.00		Toby	Stevenson	USA	19.11.76	1eA	CalR	Modesto	8 May 04
6.00		Paul	Burgess	AUS	14.8.79	1		Perth	25 Feb 05
		(20)							
6.00Ai		Shawnacy	Barber	CAN	27.5.94	1		Reno	15 Jan 16
6.00i		Piotr	Lisek	POL	16.8.92	1		Potsdam	4 Feb 17
6.00		Sam	Kendricks	USA	7.9.92	1	NC	Sacramento	24 Jun 17
6.00		Timur	Morgunov	RUS	12.10.96	2	EC	Berlin	12 Aug 18
5.98		Lawrence	Johnson	USA	7.5.74	1		Knoxville	25 May 96
5.97		Scott	Huffman	USA	30.11.64	1	NC	Knoxville	18 Jun 94
5.96		Joe	Dial	USA	26.10.62	1		Norman	18 Jun 87
5.95		Andrei	Tivontchik	GER	13.7.70	1	ASV	Köln	16 Aug 96
5.95		Michael	Stolle	GER	17.12.74	1	Herc	Monaco	18 Aug 00
5.95		Romain	Mesnil	FRA	13.6.77	1		Castres	6 Aug 03
		(30)							
5.94i		Philippe	Collet	FRA	13.12.63	1	Mast	Grenoble	10 Mar 90
5.94		Raphael	Holzdeppe	GER	28.9.89	1	NC	Nürnberg	26 Jul 15
5.93i	WIR	Billy	Olson	USA	19.7.58	1		East Rutherford	8 Feb 86
5.93i		Tye	Harvey	USA	25.9.74	2	NC	Atlanta	3 Mar 01
5.93		Alex	Averbukh	ISR	1.10.74	1	GP	Madrid (C)	19 Jul 03
5.93		Pawel	Wojciechowski	POL	6.6.89	2	Athl	Lausanne	6 Jul 17
5.92		István	Bagyula	HUN	2.1.69	1	Gugl	Linz	5 Jul 91

MEN All-time

Mark	Wind	Name		Nat	Born	Pos	Meet	Venue	Date
5.92		Igor	Potapovich	KAZ	6.9.67	2		Dijon	13 Jun 92
5.92		Dean	Starkey	USA	27.3.67	1	Banes	São Paulo	21 May 94
5.91 WR		Thierry	Vigneron	FRA	9.3.60	2	GGala	Roma	31 Aug 84
		(40)							
5.91i		Viktor	Ryzhenkov	UZB	25.8.66	2		San Sebastián	15 Mar 91
5.91A		Riaan	Botha	RSA	8.11.70	1		Pretoria	2 Apr 97
5.91		Malte	Mohr	GER	24.7.86	1		Ingolstadt	?? Jun 12
5.91		Konstadinos	Filippídis ¶	GRE	26.11.86	1	DL	Saint-Denis	4 Jul 15
5.90		Pierre	Quinon	FRA	20.2.62	2	Nik	Nice	16 Jul 85
5.90i		Ferenc	Salbert	HUN/FRA	5.8.60	1	Mast	Grenoble	14 Mar 87
5.90		Miroslaw	Chmara	POL	9.5.64	1	BNP	Villeneuve d'Ascq	27 Jun 88
5.90i		Grigoriy	Yegorov	KAZ	12.1.67	1		Yokohama	11 Mar 90
5.90		Denis	Petushinskiy ¶	RUS	28.6.67	1	Znam	Moskva	13 Jun 93
5.90i		Pyotr	Bochkaryov	RUS	3.11.67	1	EI	Paris (B)	12 Mar 94
		(50)							
5.90		Jacob	Davis	USA	29.4.78	1	TexR	Austin	4 Apr 98
5.90		Viktor	Chistyakov	RUS/AUS	9.2.75	1		Salamanca	15 Jul 99
5.90		Pavel	Gerasimov	RUS	29.5.79	1		Rüdlingen	12 Aug 00
5.90		Nick	Hysong	USA	9.12.71	1	OG	Sydney	29 Sep 00
5.90		Giuseppe	Gibilisco	ITA	5.1.79	1	WCh	Saint-Denis	28 Aug 03
5.90i		Igor	Pavlov	RUS	18.7.79	1	EI	Madrid	5 Mar 05
5.90		Lázaro	Borges	CUB	19.6.86	2	WCh	Daegu	29 Aug 11
5.90i		Dmitriy	Starodubtsev	RUS	3.1.86	1		Chelyabinsk	18 Dec 11
		(58)		100th man 5.82, 200th 5.75, 300th 5.70, 400th 5.63, 500th 560					

Best outdoor marks for athletes with lifetime bests indoors

6.00		Gataullin	1		Tokyo	16 Sep 89	5.93	Ecker	1		Ingolstadt	26 Jul 98
6.00		Hooker	1		Perth	27 Jan 08	5.93	Barber	2	DL	London (OS)	25 Jul 15
5.98		Galfione	1		Amiens	23 Jul 99	5.90	Yegorov	2	WCh	Stuttgart	19 Aug 93

Exhibition or Market Square competitions   **Ancillary jump:** 6.05i Bubka   13 Feb 93

6.00		Jean	Galfione	FRA	9.6.71	1		Besançon	23 May 97
5.95		Viktor	Chistiakov	RUS/AUS	9.2.75	1		Chiari	0 Sep 00
5.90		Pyotr	Bochkaryov	RUS	3.11.67	1		Karlskrona	28 Jun 96

LONG JUMP

Mark	Wind	Name		Nat	Born	Pos	Meet	Venue	Date
8.95 WR	0.3	Mike	Powell	USA	10.11.63	1	WCh	Tokyo	30 Aug 91
8.90A WR	2.0	Bob	Beamon	USA	29.8.46	1	OG	Ciudad de México	18 Oct 68
8.87	-0.2	Carl	Lewis	USA	1.7.61	*	WCh	Tokyo	30 Aug 91
8.86A	1.9	Robert	Emmiyan	ARM	16.2.65	1		Tsakhkadzor	22 May 87
8.79	1.9		Lewis			1	TAC	Indianapolis	19 Jun 83
8.79i	-		Lewis			1		New York	27 Jan 84
8.76	1.0		Lewis			1	USOF	Indianapolis	24 Jul 82
8.76	0.8		Lewis			1	NC/OT	Indianapolis	18 Jul 88
8.75	1.7		Lewis			1	PAm	Indianapolis	16 Aug 87
8.74	1.4	Larry	Myricks ¶	USA	10.3.56	2	NC/OT	Indianapolis	18 Jul 88
8.74A	2.0	Erick	Walder ¶	USA	5.11.71	1		El Paso	2 Apr 94
8.74	1.2	Dwight	Phillips	USA	1.10.77	1	Pre	Eugene	7 Jun 09
8.73	1.2	Irving	Saladino	PAN	23.1.83	1	FBK	Hengelo	24 May 08
8.72	-0.2		Lewis			1	OG	Seoul	26 Sep 88
8.71	-0.4		Lewis			1	Pepsi	Los Angeles (Ww)	13 May 84
8.71	0.1		Lewis			1	OT	Los Angeles	19 Jun 84
8.71	1.9	Iván	Pedroso	CUB	17.12.72	1		Salamanca	18 Jul 95
8.71i		Sebastian	Bayer (10)	GER	11.6.86	1	EI	Torino	8 Mar 09
8.70	0.8		Myricks			1	NC	Houston	17 Jun 89
8.70	0.7		Powell			1		Salamanca	27 Jul 93
8.70	1.6		Pedroso			1	WCh	Göteborg	12 Aug 95
8.68	1.0		Lewis			Q	OG	Barcelona	5 Aug 92
8.68	1.6		Pedroso			1		Lisboa	17 Jun 95
8.68	1.7	Juan Miguel	Echevarría	CUB	11.8.98	1		Bad Langensalza	30 Jun 18
8.67	0.4		Lewis			1	WCh	Roma	5 Sep 87
8.67	-0.7		Lewis			1	OG	Barcelona	6 Aug 92
8.66	0.8		Lewis			*	MSR	Walnut	26 Apr 87
8.66	1.0		Myricks			1		Tokyo	23 Sep 87
8.66	0.9		Powell			1	BNP	Villeneuve d'Ascq	29 Jun 90
8.66A	1.4		Lewis			*		Sestriere	31 Jul 94
8.66	0.3		Pedroso			1		Linz	22 Aug 95
8.66	1.6	Loúis	Tsátoumas	GRE	12.2.82	1		Kalamáta	2 Jun 07
8.66	1.0		Echevarría			1	GS	Ostrava	13 Jun 18
		(33/12)							
8.65A	1.3	Luvo	Manyonga ¶	RSA	18.11.91	1	NC	Potchefstroom	22 Apr 17
8.63	0.5	Kareem	Streete-Thompson	CAY/USA	30.3.73	1	GP II	Linz	4 Jul 94

Mark	Wind	Name		Nat	Born	Pos	Meet	Venue	Date
8.62	0.7	James	Beckford	JAM	9.1.75	1		Orlando	5 Apr 97
8.59i		Miguel	Pate	USA	13.6.79	1	NC	New York	1 Mar 02
8.58	1.8	Jarrion	Lawson	USA	6.5.94	2	NC/OT	Eugene	3 Jul 16
8.56i	-	Yago	Lamela	ESP	24.7.77	2	WI	Maebashi	7 Mar 99
8.56	0.2	Aleksandr	Menkov	RUS	7.12.90	1	WCh	Moskva	16 Aug 13
8.54	0.9	Lutz	Dombrowski	GDR	25.6.59	1	OG	Moskva	28 Jul 80
		(20)							
8.54	1.7	Mitchell	Watt	AUS	25.3.88	1	DNG	Stockholm	29 Jul 11
8.53	1.2	Jaime	Jefferson	CUB	17.1.62	1	Barr	La Habana	12 May 90
8.52	0.7	Savanté	Stringfellow	USA	6.11.78	1	NC	Stanford	21 Jun 02
8.52	1.8	Jeff	Henderson	USA	19.2.89	*	PAm	Toronto	22 Jul 15
8.51	1.7	Roland	McGhee	USA	15.10.71	2		São Paulo	14 May 95
8.51	1.7	Greg	Rutherford	GBR	17.11.86	1		Chula Vista	24 Apr 14
8.50	0.2	Llewellyn	Starks	USA	10.2.67	2		Rhede	7 Jul 91
8.50	1.3	Godfrey Khotso	Mokoena	RSA	6.3.85	2	GP	Madrid	4 Jul 09
8.49	2.0	Melvin	Lister	USA	29.8.77	1	SEC	Baton Rouge	13 May 00
8.49	0.6	Jai	Taurima	AUS	26.6.72	2	OG	Sydney	28 Sep 00
		(30)							
8.49	0.7	Christian	Reif	GER	24.10.84	1		Weinheim	31 May 14
8.49A	-0.8	Ruswahl	Samaai	RSA	25.9.91	2	NC	Potchefstroom	22 Apr 17
8.48	0.8	Joe	Greene	USA	17.2.67	3		São Paulo	14 May 95
8.48	0.6	Mohamed Salim	Al-Khuwalidi	KSA	19.6.81	1		Sotteville-lès-Rouen	2 Jul 06
8.47	1.9	Kevin	Dilworth	USA	14.2.74	1		Abilene	9 May 96
8.47	0.9	John	Moffitt	USA	12.12.80	2	OG	Athína	26 Aug 04
8.47	-0.2	Andrew	Howe	ITA	12.5.85	2	WCh	Osaka	30 Aug 07
8.47	0.0		Li Jinzhe	CHN	1.9.89	1		Bad Langensalza	28 Jun 14
8.47A	0.7		Wang Jianan	CHN	27.8.96	1		Guiyang	16 Jun 18
8.46	1.2	Leonid	Voloshin	RUS	30.3.66	1	NC	Tallinn	5 Jul 88
		(40)							
8.46	1.6	Mike	Conley	USA	5.10.62	2		Springfield	4 May 96
8.46	1.8	Cheikh Tidiane	Touré	SEN/FRA	25.1.70	1		Bad Langensalza	15 Jun 97
8.46	0.3	Ibrahin	Camejo	CUB	28.6.82	1		Bilbao	21 Jun 08
8.46	1.3	Luis	Rivera	MEX	21.6.87	1	WUG	Kazan	12 Jul 13
8.45	2.0	Nenad	Stekic	YUG	7.3.51	1	PO	Montreal	25 Jul 75
8.45	0.8	Marquise	Goodwin	USA	19.11.90	1		Baie Mahault	14 May 16
8.44	1.7	Eric	Metcalf	USA	23.1.68	1	NC	Tampa	17 Jun 88
8.44A	1.8	Michel	Tornéus	SWE	26.5.86	1		Monachil	10 Jul 16
8.43	0.8	Jason	Grimes	USA	10.9.59	*	NC	Indianapolis	16 Jun 85
8.43	1.8	Giovanni	Evangelisti	ITA	11.9.61	1		San Giovanni Valdarno	16 May 87
8.43i	-	Stanislav	Tarasenko	RUS	23.7.66	1		Moskva	26 Jan 94
8.43	0.1	Luis Felipe	Méliz	CUB/ESP	11.8.79	2	OD	Jena	3 Jun 00
8.43	-0.2	Ignisious	Gaisah	GHA/NED	20.6.83	2	GGala	Roma	14 Jul 06
8.43	0.7		Shi Yuhao	CHN	26.9.98	2	DL	Shanghai	12 May 18
		(54)							

100th man 8.34, 200th 8.25, 300th 8.19, 400th 8.14, 500th 8.11

Best at low altitude: 8.62 0.8 Manyonga 1 FBK Hengelo 11 Jun 17 8.61 1.3 Emmiyan 1 GWG Moskva 6 Jul 86
8.58 1.8 Walder 1 Springfield 4 May 86   8.45 -1.2 Samaai 1 AfrC Asaba 2 Aug 18

Wind-assisted marks performances to 8.70, performers to 8.43

Mark	Wind	Name		Nat	Born	Pos	Meet	Venue	Date
8.99A	4.4	Mike	Powell	USA	10.11.63	1		Sestriere	21 Jul 92
8.96A	1.2+	Iván	Pedroso	CUB	17.12.72	1		Sestriere	29 Jul 95
8.95A	3.9		Powell			1		Sestriere	31 Jul 94
8.91	2.9	Carl	Lewis	USA	1.7.61	2	WCh	Tokyo	30 Aug 91
8.90	3.7		Powell			1	S&W	Modesto	16 May 92
8.83	2.1	Juan Miguel	Echevarría	CUB	11.8.98	1	DL	Stockholm	10 Jun 18
8.79	3.0		Pedroso			1	Barr	La Habana	21 May 92
8.78	3.1	Fabrice	Lapierre	AUS	17.10.83	1	NC	Perth	18 Apr 10
8.77	3.9		Lewis			1	Pepsi	Los Angeles (Ww)	18 May 85
8.77	3.4		Lewis			1	MSR	Walnut	26 Apr 87
8.73	4.6		Lewis			Q	NC	Sacramento	19 Jun 81
8.73	3.2		Lewis			Q	NC	Indianapolis	17 Jun 83
8.73A	2.6		Powell			1		Sestriere	31 Jul 91
8.73	4.8		Pedroso			1		Madrid	20 Jun 95
8.72	2.2		Lewis			1	NYG	New York	24 May 92
8.72A	3.9		Lewis			2		Sestriere	31 Jul 94
8.70	2.5		Pedroso			1		Padova	16 Jul 95
8.68	4.9	James	Beckford	JAM	9.1.75	1	JUCO	Odessa, Tx	19 May 95
8.68	3.7	Marquis	Dendy	USA	17.11.92	1	NC	Eugene	25 Jun 15
8.66A	4.0	Joe	Greene	USA	17.2.67	2		Sestriere	21 Jul 92
8.64	3.5	Kareem	Streete-Thompson	CAY/USA	30.3.73	2	NC	Knoxville	18 Jun 94
8.63	3.9	Mike	Conley	USA	5.10.62	2	NC	Eugene	20 Jun 86
8.59	2.9	Jeff	Henderson	USA	19.2.89	1	NC/OT	Eugene	3 Jul 16

MEN All-time

Mark	Wind	Name		Nat	Born	Pos	Meet	Venue	Date
8.57	5.2	Jason	Grimes	USA	10.9.59	1	vFRG,AFR	Durham	27 Jun 82
8.53	4.9	Kevin	Dilworth	USA	14.2.74	1		Fort-de-France	27 Apr 02
8.51	3.7	Ignisious	Gaisah	GHA	20.6.83	1	AfCh	Bambous	9 Aug 06
8.49	2.6	Ralph	Boston	USA	9.5.39	1	OT	Los Angeles	12 Sep 64
8.49	4.5	Stanislav	Tarasenko	RUS	23.7.66	2		Madrid	20 Jun 95
8.48	2.8	Kirill	Sosunov	RUS	1.11.75	1		Oristano	18 Sep 95
8.48	3.4	Peter	Burge	AUS	8.7.74	1		Gold Coast (RB)	10 Sep 00
8.48	2.1	Brian	Johnson	USA	25.3.80	1	Conseil	Fort-de-France	8 May 08
8.48	2.8	Lamont Marcell	Jacobs	ITA	26.9.94	1	NC-23	Bressanone	10 Jun 16
8.46	3.4	Randy	Williams	USA	23.8.53	1		Eugene	18 May 73
8.46		Vernon	George	USA	6.10.64	1		Houston	21 May 89
8.44		Keith	Talley	USA	28.1.64	Q		Odessa, Tx	16 May 85
Exhibition:	8.46	Yuriy	Naumkin	RUS	4.11.68	1		Iglesias	6 Sep 96

Best outdoors
8.56 1.3 Lamela 1 Torino 24 Jun 99 8.49 1.6 Bayer 1 NC Ulm 4 Jul 09
8.46A 0.0 Pate 1 Cd. de México 3 May 03 and 8.45 1.5 2 NC Stanford 21 Jun 02, 8.48w 5.6 1 Fort Worth 21 Apr 01

Ancillary marks – other marks during series (to 8.67/8.70w)

8.84	1.7	Lewis	30 Aug 91	8.89Aw	2.4	Pedroso	29 Jul 95	8.75w 2.1 Lewis	16 Aug 87
8.71	0.6	Lewis	19 Jun 83	8.84Aw	3.8	Powell	21 Jul 92	8.75Aw 3.4 Powell	21 Jul 92
8.68	0.3	Lewis	18 Jul 88	8.83w	2.3	Lewis	30 Aug 91	8.73w 2.4 Lewis	18 May 85
8.68	0.0	Lewis	30 Aug 91	8.80Aw	4.0	Powell	21 Jul 92	8.73w Powell	16 May 92
8.67	-0.2	Lewis	5 Sep 87	8.78Aw		Powell	21 Jul 92	8.71Aw Powell	31 Jul 91

TRIPLE JUMP

Mark	Wind	Name		Nat	Born	Pos	Meet	Venue	Date
18.29	WR 1.3	Jonathan	Edwards	GBR	10.5.66	1	WCh	Göteborg	7 Aug 95
18.21	0.2	Christian	Taylor	USA	18.6.90	1	WCh	Beijing	27 Aug 15
18.11	0.8		Taylor			1	Pre	Eugene	27 May 17
18.09	-0.4	Kenny	Harrison	USA	13.2.65	1	OG	Atlanta	27 Jul 96
18.08	0.0	Pedro Pablo	Pichardo	CUB	30.6.93	1	Barr	La Habana	28 May 15
18.06	0.8		Pichardo			1	DL	Doha	15 May 15
18.06	1.1		Taylor			1	Athl	Lausanne	9 Jul 15
18.04	0.3	Teddy	Tamgho	FRA	15.6.89	1	WCh	Moskva	18 Aug 13
18.04	0.8		Taylor			2	DL	Doha	15 May 15
18.01	0.4		Edwards			1	Bisl	Oslo	9 Jul 98
18.00	1.3		Edwards			1	McD	London (CP)	27 Aug 95
17.99	0.5		Edwards			1	EC	Budapest	23 Aug 98
17.99	1.8		Pichardo			2	Athl	Lausanne	9 Jul 15
17.98	WR 1.8		Edwards			1		Salamanca	18 Jul 95
17.98	1.2		Tamgho			1	DL	New York	12 Jun 10
17.97	WR 1.5	Willie	Banks	USA	11.3.56	1	TAC	Indianapolis	16 Jun 85
17.96	0.1		Taylor			1	WCh	Daegu	4 Sep 11
17.96	-0.4		Pichardo			1	GGala	Roma	4 Jun 15
17.95	0.6		Pichardo			1	DL	Doha	4 May 18
17.94	0.0		Pichardo			1		La Habana	8 May 15
17.93	1.6		Harrison			1	DNG	Stockholm	2 Jul 90
17.92	1.6	Khristo	Markov	BUL	27.1.65	1	WCh	Roma	31 Aug 87
17.92	1.9	James	Beckford	JAM	9.1.75	1	JUCO	Odessa, TX	20 May 95
17.92i	WIR -		Tamgho			1	EI	Paris (Bercy)	6 Mar 11
17.92	0.7		Edwards			1	WCh	Edmonton	6 Aug 01
17.91i	WIR -		Tamgho			1	NC	Aubière	20 Feb 11
17.91	1.4		Tamgho			1	Athl	Lausanne	30 Jun 11
17.91	0.9	Will	Claye	USA	13.6.91	1	NC	Sacramento	23 Jun 17
17.90	1.0	Vladimir	Inozemtsev (10)	UKR	25.5.64	1	PTS	Bratislava	20 Jun 90
17.90	0.4	Jadel	Gregório	BRA	16.9.80	1	GP	Belém	20 May 07
17.90i			Tamgho			1	WI	Doha	14 Mar 10
17.89A	WR 0.0	João Carlos	de Oliveira	BRA	28.5.54	1	PAm	Ciudad de México	15 Oct 75
		(32/12)							
17.87	1.7	Mike	Conley	USA	5.10.62	1	NC	San José	27 Jun 87
17.86	1.3	Charles	Simpkins	USA	19.10.63	1	WUG	Kobe	2 Sep 85
17.85	0.9	Yoelbi	Quesada	CUB	4.8.73	1	WCh	Athína	8 Aug 97
17.83i	WIR -	Aliecer	Urrutia	CUB	22.9.74	1		Sindelfingen	1 Mar 97
17.83i	WIR -	Christian	Olsson	SWE	25.1.80	1	WI	Budapest	7 Mar 04
17.81	1.0	Marian	Oprea	ROU	6.6.82	1	Athl	Lausanne	5 Jul 05
17.81	0.1	Phillips	Idowu	GBR	30.12.78	1	EC	Barcelona	29 Jul 10
17.78	1.0	Nikolay	Musiyenko	UKR	16.12.59	1	Znam	Leningrad	7 Jun 86
		(20)							
17.78	0.6	Lázaro	Betancourt ¶	CUB	18.3.63	1	Barr	La Habana	15 Jun 86
17.78	0.8	Melvin	Lister	USA	29.8.77	1	NC/OT	Sacramento	17 Jul 04
17.77	1.0	Aleksandr	Kovalenko	RUS	8.5.63	1	NC	Bryansk	18 Jul 87
17.77i	-	Leonid	Voloshin	RUS	30.3.66	1		Grenoble	6 Feb 94

Mark	Wind	Name		Nat	Born	Pos	Meet	Venue	Date
17.75	0.3	Oleg	Protsenko	RUS	11.8.63	1	Znam	Moskva	10 Jun 90
17.74	1.4	Nelson	Évora	POR	20.4.84	1	WCh	Osaka	27 Aug 07
17.73i		Walter	Davis	USA	2.7.79	1	WI	Moskva	12 Mar 06
17.73i	-	Fabrizio	Donato	ITA	14.8.76	2	EI	Paris (Bercy)	6 Mar 11
17.72i		Brian	Wellman	BER	8.9.67	1	WI	Barcelona	12 Mar 95
17.72	1.3	Sheryf	El-Sheryf	UKR	2.1.89	1	EU23	Ostrava	17 Jul 11
	(30)		El-Sheryf now Seref Osmanoglou TUR						
17.70i		Daniele	Greco	ITA	1.3.89	1	EI	Göteborg	2 Mar 13
17.69	1.5	Igor	Lapshin	BLR	8.8.63	1		Stayki	31 Jul 88
17.69i		Yoandri	Betanzos	CUB	15.2.82	2	WI	Doha	14 Mar 10
17.68	0.4	Danil	Burkenya	RUS	20.7.78	1	NC	Tula	31 Jul 04
17.68A	1.6	Alexis	Copello	CUB	12.8.85	1		Ávila	17 Jul 11
17.66	1.7	Ralf	Jaros	GER	13.12.65	1	ECp	Frankfurt-am-Main	30 Jun 91
17.65	1.0	Aleksandr	Yakovlev	UKR	8.9.57	1	Znam	Moskva	6 Jun 87
17.65	0.8	Denis	Kapustin	RUS	5.10.70	2	Bisl	Oslo	9 Jul 98
17.64	1.4	Nathan	Douglas	GBR	4.12.82	1	NC	Manchester (SC)	10 Jul 05
17.63	0.9	Kenta	Bell	USA	16.3.77	1c2	MSR	Walnut	21 Apr 02
	(40)								
17.62i	-	Yoel	García	CUB	25.11.73	2		Sindelfingen	1 Mar 97
17.62	-0.2	Arne David	Girat	CUB	26.8.84	3	ALBA	La Habana	25 Apr 09
17.60	0.6	Vladimir	Plekhanov	RUS	11.4.58	2	NC	Leningrad	4 Aug 85
17.59i	-	Pierre	Camara	FRA	10.9.65	1	WI	Toronto	13 Mar 93
17.59	0.3	Vasiliy	Sokov	RUS	7.4.68	1	NC	Moskva	19 Jun 93
17.59	0.8	Charles	Friedek	GER	26.8.71	1		Hamburg	23 Jul 97
17.59	0.9	Leevan	Sands	BAH	16.8.81	3	OG	Beijing	21 Aug 08
17.59	0.0		Li Yanxi	CHN	26.6.84	1	NG	Jinan	26 Oct 09
17.58	1.5	Oleg	Sakirkin	KZK	23.1.66	2	NC	Gorkiy	23 Jul 89
17.58	1.6	Aarik	Wilson	USA	25.10.82	1	LGP	London (CP)	3 Aug 07
17.58	-1.7	Ernesto	Revé	CUB	26.2.92	2		La Habana	7 Feb 14
17.58	-0.2		Dong Bin	CHN	22.11.88	3	OG	Rio de Janeiro	16 Aug 16
	(52)		100th man 17.41, 200th 17.20, 300th 17.04, 400th 16.92, 500th 16.82						

Wind-assisted marks – performances to 17.91, performers to 17.59

18.43	2.4	Jonathan	Edwards	GBR	10.5.66	1	ECp	Villeneuve d'Ascq	25 Jun 95
18.20	5.2	Willie	Banks	USA	11.3.56	1	NC/OT	Indianapolis	16 Jul 88
18.17	2.1	Mike	Conley	USA	5.10.62	1	OG	Barcelona	3 Aug 92
18.08	2.5		Edwards			1	BrGP	Sheffield	23 Jul 95
18.05	2.4		Claye			2	Pre	Eugene	27 May 17
18.03	2.9		Edwards			1	GhG	Gateshead	2 Jul 95
18.01	3.7		Harrison			1	NC	Atlanta	15 Jun 96
17.97	7.5	Yoelbi	Quesada	CUB	4.8.73	1		Madrid	20 Jun 95
17.93	5.2	Charles	Simpkins	USA	19.10.63	2	NC/OT	Indianapolis	16 Jul 88
17.92	3.4	Christian	Olsson	SWE	25.1.80	1	GP	Gateshead	13 Jul 03
17.91	3.2		Simpkins			1	NC	Eugene	21 Jun 86
17.82	2.5	Nelson	Évora	POR	20.4.84	1	NC	Seixal	26 Jul 09
17.81	4.6	Keith	Connor	GBR	16.9.57	1	CG	Brisbane	9 Oct 82
17.76A	2.2	Kenta	Bell	USA	16.3.77	1		El Paso	10 Apr 04
17.75		Gennadiy	Valyukevich	BLR	1.6.58	1		Uzhgorod	27 Apr 86
17.75	7.1	Brian	Wellman	BER	8.9.67	2		Madrid	20 Jun 95
17.73	4.1	Vasiliy	Sokov	RUS	7.4.68	1		Riga	3 Jun 89
17.71	2.4	Marquis	Dendy	USA	17.11.92	1	NCAA	Eugene	12 Jun 15
17.69	3.9	Alexis	Copello	CUB	12.8.85	1	ALBA	La Habana	25 Apr 09
17.63	4.3	Robert	Cannon	USA	9.7.58	3	NC/OT	Indianapolis	16 Jul 88
17.59	2.1	Jerome	Romain	DMA/FRA	12.6.71	3	WCh	Göteborg	7 Aug 95

Best outdoor marks for athletes with indoor bests

17.79	1.4	Olsson	1	OG	Athína	22 Aug 04		17.65	1.4	Betanzos 2	ALBA	La Habana	25 Apr 09
17.75	1.0	Voloshin	2	WCh	Tokyo	26 Aug 91				17.67w	5.4	1	Bilbao	1 Jul 06
17.71	-0.7	Davis	1	NC	Indianapolis	25 Jun 06		17.62A	0.1	Wellman	1	El Paso	15 Apr 95
17.70	1.7	Urrutia	1	GP II	Sevilla	6 Jun 96		17.60	1.9	Donato	1	Milano	7 Jun 00
17.67w	3.4	Greco	1	NC	Bressanone	8 Jul 12				17.63w	2.8	1 EC	Helsinki	30 Jun 12

Low altitude best: 17.65 0.1 Copello 1 Barr La Habana 30 May 09

Ancillary marks – other marks during series (to 17.90)

18.16 WR	1.3	Edwards	7 Aug 95		17.93	0.2	Pichardo	28 May 15		18.06w	4.9	Banks	16 Jul 88
18.02	0.8	Taylor	9 Jul 15		17.92i		Tamgho	6 Mar 11		17.90w	2.5	Edwards	25 Jun 95
17.99	0.1	Harrison	27 Jul 96		18.39w	3.7	Edwards	25 Jun 95					

SHOT

23.12 WR		Randy	Barnes ¶	USA	16.6.66	1		Los Angeles (Ww)	20 May 90
23.10			Barnes			1	Jenner	San José	26 May 90
23.06 WR		Ulf	Timmermann	GDR	1.11.62	1	Veniz	Haniá	22 May 88
22.91 WR		Alessandro	Andrei	ITA	3.1.59	1		Viareggio	12 Aug 87
22.86		Brian	Oldfield	USA	1.6.45	1	ITA	El Paso	10 May 75
22.75		Werner	Günthör	SUI	1.6.61	1		Bern	23 Aug 88

Mark	Wind	Name		Nat	Born	Pos	Meet	Venue	Date
22.67		Kevin	Toth ¶	USA	29.12.67	1	KansR	Lawrence	19 Apr 03
22.67		Tom	Walsh	NZL	1.3.92	1		Auckland	25 Mar 18
22.66i			Barnes			1	Sunkist	Los Angeles	20 Jan 89
22.65		Ryan	Crouser	USA	18.12.92	1	NC	Sacramento	25 Jun 17
22.64	WR	Udo	Beyer	GDR	9.8.55	1		Berlin	20 Aug 86
22.62	WR		Timmermann			1		Berlin	22 Sep 85
22.61			Timmermann			1		Potsdam	8 Sep 88
22.60			Timmermann			1	vURS	Tallinn	21 Jun 86
22.60			Walsh			1	WK	Zürich	30 Aug 18
22.57		Joe	Kovacs (10)	USA	28.6.89	1		Tucson	18 May 17
22.56			Timmermann			1		Berlin	13 Sep 88
22.56			Kovacs			1	Herc	Monaco	17 Jul 15
22.55i			Timmermann			1	NC	Senftenberg	11 Feb 89
22.54		Christian	Cantwell	USA	30.9.80	1	GP II	Gresham	5 Jun 04
22.53			Crouser		2	1	Pre	Eugene	26 May 18
22.52		John	Brenner	USA	4.1.61	1	MSR	Walnut	26 Apr 87
22.52			Crouser			1	OG	Rio de Janeiro	18 Aug 16
22.51			Timmermann			1		Erfurt	1 Jun 86
22.51		Adam	Nelson	USA	7.7.75	1		Gresham	18 May 02
22.47			Timmermann			1		Dresden	17 Aug 86
22.47			Günthör			1	WG	Helsinki	2 Jul 87
22.47			Timmermann			1	OG	Seoul	23 Sep 88
22.47			Crouser			1	DL	Rabat	16 Jul 17
22.45			Oldfield			1	ITA	El Paso	22 May 76
22.45			Cantwell			1	GP	Gateshead	11 Jun 06
22.45			Walsh			Q	CG	Gold Coast	8 Apr 18
		(32/13)							
22.44		Darrell	Hill	USA	17.8.93	1	VD-DLF	Bruxelles	31 Aug 17
22.43		Reese	Hoffa	USA	8.10.77	1	LGP	London (CP)	3 Aug 07
22.28		Ryan	Whiting	USA	24.11.86	1	DL	Doha	10 May 13
22.24		Sergey	Smirnov	RUS	17.9.60	2	vGDR	Tallinn	21 Jun 86
22.21		Dylan	Armstrong	CAN	15.1.81	1	NC	Calgary	25 Jun 11
22.20		John	Godina	USA	31.5.72	1		Carson	22 May 05
22.20		David	Storl	GER	27.7.90	1	Athl	Lausanne	9 Jul 15
		(20)							
22.17i		Tomás	Stanek	CZE	13.6.91	1		Düsseldorf	6 Feb 18
22.10		Sergey	Gavryushin	RUS	27.6.59	1		Tbilisi	31 Aug 86
22.10		Cory	Martin	USA	22.5.85	1		Tucson	22 May 10
22.09		Sergey	Kasnauskas	BLR	20.4.61	1		Stayki	23 Aug 84
22.09i		Mika	Halvari	FIN	13.2.70	1		Tampere	7 Feb 00
22.08		Michal	Haratyk	POL	10.4.92	2	GS	Ostrava	13 Jun 18
22.02i		George	Woods	USA	11.2.43	1	LAT	Inglewood	8 Feb 74
22.02		Dave	Laut	USA	21.12.56	1		Koblenz	25 Aug 82
22.00	WR	Aleksandr	Baryshnikov	RUS	11.11.48	1	vFRA	Colombes	10 Jul 76
22.00i		Konrad	Bukowiecki	POL	17.3.97	1		Torun	15 Feb 18
		(30)							
22.00		Darlan	Romani	BRA	9.4.91	1	NC	Bragança Paulista	15 Sep 18
21.98		Gregg	Tafralis ¶	USA	9.4.58	1		Los Gatos	13 Jun 92
21.97		Janus	Robberts	RSA	10.3.79	1	NCAA	Eugene	2 Jun 01
21.96		Mikhail	Kostin	RUS	10.5.59	1		Vitebsk	20 Jul 86
21.96		O'Dayne	Richards	JAM	14.12.88	2	DL	Rabat	16 Jul 17
21.95		Tomasz	Majewski	POL	30.8.81	1	DNG	Stockholm	30 Jul 09
21.93		Remigius	Machura ¶	CZE	3.7.60	1		Praha	23 Aug 87
21.92		Carl	Myerscough ¶	GBR	21.10.79	1	NCAA	Sacramento	13 Jun 03
21.87		C.J.	Hunter ¶	USA	14.12.68	2	NC	Sacramento	15 Jul 00
21.85	WR	Terry	Albritton	USA	14.1.55	1		Honolulu	21 Feb 76
		(40)							
21.83i		Aleksandr	Bagach ¶	UKR	21.11.66	1		Brovary	21 Feb 99
21.82	WR	Al	Feuerbach	USA	14.1.48	1		San José	5 May 73
21.82		Andy	Bloom	USA	11.8.73	1	GPF	Doha	5 Oct 00
21.81		Yuriy	Bilonog ¶	UKR	9.3.74	1	NC	Kiev	3 Jul 03
21.78	WR	Randy	Matson	USA	5.3.45	1		College Station	22 Apr 67
21.78		Dan	Taylor	USA	12.5.82	1		Tucson	23 May 09
21.77i		Mike	Stulce ¶	USA	21.7.69	1	v GBR	Birmingham	13 Feb 93
21.77		Dragan	Peric	YUG	8.5.64	1		Bar	25 Apr 98
21.76		Michael	Carter	USA	29.10.60	2	NCAA	Eugene	2 Jun 84
21.76		Stephen	Mozia	NGR	16.8.93	1		Ústí nad Labem	19 Jul 16
		(50)							

100th man 21.31, 200th 20.82, 300th 20.52, 400th 20.21, 500th 20.02

Not recognised by GDR authorities: 22.11 Rolf Oesterreich GDR 24.8.49 1 Zschopau 12 Sep 76
Best outdoor mark for athlete with indoor best: 22.01 Stanek 1 Schönebeck 2 Jun 17

Mark	Wind	Name		Nat	Born	Pos	Meet	Venue	Date

Drugs disqualification

Mark	Wind	Name	Nat	Born	Pos	Meet	Venue	Date
22.84		Barnes			1		Malmö	7 Aug 90
22.10	Andrey	Mikhnevich ¶	BLR	12.7.76	1		Minsk	11 Aug 11
21.82	Mike	Stulce ¶	USA	21.7.69	1		Brenham	9 May 90

Ancillary marks – other marks during series (to 22.45)

22.84 WR	Andrei	12 Aug 87	22.72 WR	Andrei	12 Aug 87	22.55	Barnes	20 May 90
22.76	Barnes	20 May 90	22.70	Günthör	23 Aug 88	22.49	Nelson	18 May 02
22.74	Andrei	12 Aug 87	22.58	Beyer	20 Aug 86	22.45	Timmermann	22 May 88

DISCUS

MEN All-time

Mark	Wind	Name		Nat	Born	Pos	Meet	Venue	Date
74.08 WR		Jürgen	Schult	GDR	11.5.60	1		Neubrandenburg	6 Jun 86
73.88		Virgilijus	Alekna	LTU	13.2.72	1	NC	Kaunas	3 Aug 00
73.38		Gerd	Kanter	EST	6.5.79	1		Helsingborg	4 Sep 06
72.02			Kanter			1eA		Salinas	3 May 07
71.88			Kanter			1eA		Salinas	8 May 08
71.86 WR		Yuriy	Dumchev	RUS	5.8.58	1		Moskva	29 May 83
71.84		Piotr	Malachowski	POL	7.6.83	1	FBK	Hengelo	8 Jun 13
71.70		Róbert	Fazekas ¶	HUN	18.8.75	1		Szombathely	14 Jul 02
71.64			Kanter			1		Kohila	25 Jun 09
71.56			Alekna			1		Kaunas	25 Jul 07
71.50		Lars	Riedel	GER	28.6.67	1		Wiesbaden	3 May 97
71.45			Kanter			1		Chula Vista	29 Apr 10
71.32		Ben	Plucknett ¶	USA	13.4.54	1	Pre	Eugene	4 Jun 83
71.29		Daniel	Ståhl	SWE	27.8.92	1		Sollentuna	29 Jun 17
71.26		John	Powell (10)	USA	25.6.47	1	NC	San José	9 Jun 84
71.26		Rickard	Bruch	SWE	2.7.46	1		Malmö	15 Nov 84
71.26		Imrich	Bugár	CZE	14.4.55	1	Jenner	San José	25 May 85
71.25			Fazekas			1	WCp	Madrid (C)	21 Sep 02
71.25			Alekna			1	Danek	Turnov	20 May 08
71.18		Art	Burns	USA	19.7.54	1		San José	19 Jul 83
71.16 WR		Wolfgang	Schmidt	GDR	16.1.54	1		Berlin	9 Aug 78
71.14			Plucknett			1		Berkeley	12 Jun 83
71.14		Anthony	Washington	USA	16.1.66	1eA		Salinas	22 May 96
71.12			Alekna			1	WK	Zürich	11 Aug 00
71.08			Alekna			1		Réthimno	21 Jul 06
71.06		Luis Mariano	Delís ¶	CUB	12.12.57	1	Barr	La Habana	21 May 83
71.06			Riedel			1	WK	Zürich	14 Aug 96
71.00			Bruch			1		Malmö	14 Oct 84
70.99			Alekna			1		Stellenbosch	30 Mar 01
70.98		Mac	Wilkins	USA	15.11.50	1	WG	Helsinki	9 Jul 80
70.98			Burns			1	Pre	Eugene	21 Jul 84
		(31/17)							
70.82		Aleksander	Tammert	EST	2.2.73	1		Denton	15 Apr 06
70.66		Robert	Harting	GER	18.10.84	1	Danek	Turnov	22 May 12
70.54		Dmitriy	Shevchenko ¶	RUS	13.5.68	1		Krasnodar	7 May 02
		(20)							
70.38 WRU		Jay	Silvester	USA	27.8.37	1		Lancaster	16 May 71
70.32		Frantz	Kruger	RSA/FIN	22.5.75	1		Salon-de-Provence	26 May 02
70.06		Romas	Ubartas ¶	LTU	26.5.60	1		Smalininkay	8 May 88
70.00		Juan	Martínez ¶	CUB	17.5.58	2	Barr	La Habana	21 May 83
69.95		Zoltán	Kővágó ¶	HUN	10.4.79	1		Salon-de-Provence	25 May 06
69.91		John	Godina	USA	31.5.72	1		Salinas	19 May 98
69.90		Jason	Young ¶	USA	27.5.81	1		Lubbock	26 Mar 10
69.70		Géjza	Valent	CZE	3.10.53	2		Nitra	26 Aug 84
69.67		Fedrick	Dacres	JAM	28.2.94	1	DL	Stockholm	10 Jun 18
69.62		Knut	Hjeltnes ¶	NOR	8.12.51	2	Jen	San José	25 May 85
		(30)							
69.62		Timo	Tompuri	FIN	9.6.69	1		Helsingborg	8 Jul 01
69.59		Andrius	Gudzius	LTU	14.2.91	2	DL	Stockholm	10 Jun 18
69.50		Mario	Pestano	ESP	8.4.78	1	NC	Santa Cruz de Tenerife	27 Jul 08
69.46		Al	Oerter	USA	19.9.36	1	TFA	Wichita	31 May 80
69.44		Georgiy	Kolnootchenko	BLR	7.5.59	1	vUSA	Indianapolis	3 Jul 82
69.40		Art	Swarts ¶	USA	14.2.45	1		Scotch Plains	8 Dec 79
69.36		Mike	Buncic	USA	25.7.62	1		Fresno	6 Apr 91
69.32		Ehsan	Hadadi	IRI	21.1.85	1		Tallinn	3 Jun 08
69.28		Vladimir	Dubrovshchik	BLR	7.1.72	1	NC	Staiki	3 Jun 00
69.26		Ken	Stadel	USA	19.2.52	2	AAU	Walnut	16 Jun 79
		(40)							
68.98		Lukas	Weisshaidinger	AUT	20.2.92	1		Rehlingen	20 May 18
68.94		Adam	Setliff	USA	15.12.69	1		Atascadero	25 Jul 01

Mark	Wind	Name		Nat	Born	Pos	Meet	Venue	Date
68.91		Ian	Waltz	USA	15.4.77	1		Salinas	24 May 06
68.90		Jean-Claude	Retel	FRA	11.2.68	1		Salon-de-Provence	17 Jul 02
68.88		Vladimir	Zinchenko	UKR	25.7.59	1		Dnepropetrovsk	16 Jul 88
68.88		Fedrick	Dacres	JAM	28.2.94	1		Kingston	11 Feb 17
68.76		Jarred	Rome	USA	21.12.76	2cA		Chula Vista	6 Aug 11
68.64		Dmitriy	Kovtsun ¶	UKR	29.9.55	1		Riga	6 Jul 84
68.58		Attila	Horváth	HUN	28.7.67	1		Budapest	24 Jun 04
68.52		Igor	Duginyets	UKR	20.5.56	1	NC	Kyiv	21 Aug 82
(50)			100th man 67.26, 200th 65.53, 300th 64.53, 400th 63.46, 500th 62.46						

Subsequent to or at drugs disqualification   ! recognised as US record

72.34!		Ben	Plucknett ¶	USA	13.4.54	(1)	DNG	Stockholm	7 Jul 81
71.20			Plucknett			(1)	CalR	Modesto	16 May 81
70.84		Kamy	Keshmiri ¶	USA	23.1.69	(1)		Salinas	27 May 92

Sloping ground

72.08		John	Powell	USA	25.6.47	1		Klagshamn	11 Sep 87
69.80		Stefan	Fernholm	SWE	2.7.59	1		Klagshamn	13 Aug 87
69.44		Adam	Setliff	USA	15.12.69	1		La Jolla	21 Jul 01

Light implement: 69.83 Fedrick Dacres   JAM   28.2.94   1   Kingston   10 Feb 18

Ancillary marks – other marks during series (to 70.98)

72.35 Alekna 3 Aug 00   72.30 Kanter 4 Sep 06   71.08 Plucknett 4 Jun 83

HAMMER

Mark	Wind	Name		Nat	Born	Pos	Meet	Venue	Date
86.74 WR		Yuriy	Sedykh	RUS	11.6.55	1	EC	Stuttgart	30 Aug 86
86.66 WR			Sedykh			1	vGDR	Tallinn	22 Jun 86
86.34 WR			Sedykh			1		Cork	3 Jul 84
86.04		Sergey	Litvinov	RUS	23.1.58	1	OD	Dresden	3 Jul 86
85.74			Litvinov			2	EC	Stuttgart	30 Aug 86
85.68			Sedykh			1	BGP	Budapest	11 Aug 86
85.60			Sedykh			1	PTG	London (CP)	13 Jul 84
85.60			Sedykh			1	Drz	Moskva	17 Aug 84
85.20			Litvinov			2		Cork	3 Jul 84
85.14			Litvinov			1	PTG	London	11 Jul 86
85.14			Sedykh			1	Kuts	Moskva	4 Sep 88
85.02			Sedykh			1	BGP	Budapest	20 Aug 84
84.92			Sedykh			2	OD	Dresden	3 Jul 86
84.90		Vadim	Devyatovskiy ¶	BLR	20.3.77	1		Staiki	21 Jul 05
84.88			Litvinov			1	GP-GG	Roma	10 Sep 86
84.86		Koji	Murofushi	JPN	8.10.74	1	Odlozil	Praha	29 Jun 03
84.80			Litvinov			1	OG	Seoul	26 Sep 88
84.72			Sedykh			1	GWG	Moskva	9 Jul 86
84.64			Litvinov			2	GWG	Moskva	9 Jul 86
84.62		Igor	Astapkovich	BLR	4.1.63	1	Expo	Sevilla	6 Jun 92
84.60			Sedykh			1	8-N	Tokyo	14 Sep 84
84.58			Sedykh			1	Znam	Leningrad	8 Jun 86
84.51		Ivan	Tikhon ¶	BLR	24.7.76	1	NC	Grodno	9 Jul 08
84.48		Igor	Nikulin	RUS	14.8.60	1	Athl	Lausanne	12 Jul 90
84.46			Sedykh			1		Vladivostok	14 Sep 88
84.46			Tikhon			1		Minsk	7 May 04
84.40		Jüri	Tamm	EST	5.2.57	1		Banská Bystrica	9 Sep 84
84.36			Litvinov			2	vGDR	Tallinn	22 Jun 86
84.32			Tikhon			1		Staiki	8 Aug 03
84.26			Sedykh			1	Nik	Nice	15 Jul 80
(30/8)									
84.19		Adrián	Annus ¶	HUN	28.6.73	1		Szombathely	10 Aug 03
83.93		Pawel	Fajdek	POL	4.6.89	1	Kuso	Szczecin	9 Jul 15
(10)									
83.68		Tibor	Gécsek ¶	HUN	22.9.64	1		Zalaegerszeg	19 Sep 98
83.46		Andrey	Abduvaliyev	TJK/UZB	30.6.66	1		Adler	26 May 90
83.43		Aleksey	Zagornyi	RUS	31.5.78	1		Adler	10 Feb 02
83.40 @		Ralf	Haber	GDR	18.8.62	1		Athína	16 May 88
	82.54					1		Potsdam	9 Sep 88
83.38		Szymon	Ziółkowski	POL	1.7.76	1	WCh	Edmonton	5 Aug 01
83.30		Olli-Pekka	Karjalainen	FIN	7.3.80	1		Lahti	14 Jul 04
83.04		Heinz	Weis	GER	14.7.63	1	NC	Frankfurt	29 Jun 97
83.00		Balázs	Kiss	HUN	21.3.72	1	GP II	Saint-Denis	4 Jun 98
82.78		Karsten	Kobs	GER	16.9.71	1		Dortmund	26 Jun 99
82.69		Krisztián	Pars	HUN	18.2.82	1	EC	Zürich	16 Aug 14
(20)									

@ *competitive meeting but unsanctioned by GDR federation*

82.64		Günther	Rodehau	GDR	6.7.59	1		Dresden	3 Aug 85
82.62		Sergey	Kirmasov ¶	RUS	25.3.70	1		Bryansk	30 May 98

Mark	Wind	Name		Nat	Born	Pos	Meet	Venue	Date
82.62		Andrey	Skvaruk	UKR	9.3.67	1		Koncha-Zaspa	27 Apr 02
82.58		Primoz	Kozmus	SLO	30.9.79	1		Celje	2 Sep 09
82.54		Vasiliy	Sidorenko	RUS	1.5.61	1		Krasnodar	13 May 92
82.52		Lance	Deal	USA	21.8.61	1	GPF	Milano	7 Sep 96
82.40		Plamen	Minev	BUL	28.4.65	1	NM	Plovdiv	1 Jun 91
82.38		Gilles	Dupray	FRA	2.1.70	1		Chelles	21 Jun 00
82.28		Ilya	Konovalov ¶	RUS	4.3.71	1	NC	Tula	10 Aug 03
82.24		Benjaminas	Viluckis	LIT	20.3.61	1		Klaipeda	24 Aug 86
		(30)							
82.24		Vyacheslav	Korovin	RUS	8.9.62	1		Chelyabinsk	20 Jun 87
82.23		Vladislav	Piskunov ¶	UKR	7.6.78	2		Koncha-Zaspa	27 Apr 02
82.22		Holger	Klose	GER	5.12.72	1		Dortmund	2 May 98
82.16		Vitaliy	Alisevich	BLR	15.6.67	1		Parnu	13 Jul 88
82.08		Ivan	Tanev	BUL	1.5.57	1	NC	Sofia	3 Sep 88
82.00		Sergey	Alay ¶	BLR	11.6.65	1		Stayki	12 May 92
81.85		Wojciech	Nowicki	POL	22.2.89	1	Gyulai	Székesfehérvár	2 Jul 18
81.88		Jud	Logan ¶	USA	19.7.59	1		State College	22 Apr 88
81.81		Libor	Charfreitag	SVK	11.9.77	3	Odlozil	Praha	29 Jun 03
81.79		Christophe	Épalle	FRA	23.1.69	1		Clermont-Ferrand	30 Jun 00
		(40)							
81.78		Christoph	Sahner	FRG	23.9.63	1		Wemmetsweiler	11 Sep 88
81.70		Aleksandr	Seleznyov	RUS	25.1.63	2		Sochi	22 May 93
81.66		Aleksandr	Krykun	UKR	1.3.68	1		Kiev	29 May 04
81.64		Enrico	Sgrulletti	ITA	24.4.65	1		Ostia	9 Mar 97
81.56		Sergey	Gavrilov	RUS	22.5.70	1	Army	Rostov	16 Jun 96
81.56		Zsolt	Németh	HUN	9.11.71	1		Veszprém	14 Aug 99
81.52		Juha	Tiainen	FIN	5.12.55	1		Tampere	11 Jun 84
81.49		Valeriy	Svyatokho	BLR	20.7.81	1	NCp	Brest	27 May 06
81.45		Esref	Apak ¶	TUR	3.1.82	1	Cezmi	Istanbul	4 Jun 05
81.44		Yuriy	Tarasyuk	BLR	11.4.57	1		Minsk	10 Aug 84
		(50)		100th man 80.14, 200th 77.80, 300th 76.02, 400th 7474, 500th 7367					

Drugs disqualification: 86.73   Ivan Tikhon ¶   BLR   24.7.76 (1)   NC   Brest   3 Jul 05

Ancillary marks – other marks during series (to 84.85)

86.68	Sedykh	30 Aug 86	85.82	Sedykh	22 Jun 86	85.42	Sedykh	11 Aug 86	85.20	Sedykh	3 Jul 84

86.68 Sedykh 30 Aug 86 | 85.82 Sedykh 22 Jun 86 | 85.42 Sedykh 11 Aug 86 | 85.20 Sedykh 3 Jul 84
86.62 Sedykh 30 Aug 86 | 85.52 Sedykh 13 Jul 84 | 85.28 Sedykh 30 Aug 86 | 85.04 Sedykh 13 Jul 84
86.00 Sedykh 3 Jul 84 | 85.46 Sedykh 30 Aug 86 | 85.26 Sedykh 11 Aug 86 | 84.98 Sedykh 4 Sep 88
86.00 Sedykh 22 Jun 86 | 85.42 Litvinov 3 Jul 86 | 85.24 Sedykh 11 Aug 86 | 84.92 Litvinov 3 Jul 86

JAVELIN

Mark		Name		Nat	Born	Pos	Meet	Venue	Date
98.48 WR		Jan	Zelezny	CZE	16.6.66	1		Jena	25 May 96
95.66 WR			Zelezny			1	McD	Sheffield	29 Aug 93
95.54A WR			Zelezny			1		Pietersburg	6 Apr 93
94.64			Zelezny			1	GS	Ostrava	31 May 96
94.44		Johannes	Vetter	GER	26.3.93	1		Luzern	11 Jul 17
94.02			Zelezny			1		Stellenbosch	26 Mar 97
93.90		Thomas	Röhler	GER	30.9.91	1	DL	Doha	5 May 17
93.88			Vetter			1		Thum	18 Aug 17
93.09		Aki	Parviainen	FIN	26.10.74	1		Kuortane	26 Jun 99
92.80			Zelezny			1	WCh	Edmonton	12 Aug 01
92.72		Julius	Yego	KEN	4.1.89	1	WCh	Beijing	26 Aug 15
92.70			Vetter			1	ECp-w	Leiria	11 Mar 18
92.61		Sergey	Makarov	RUS	19.3.73	1		Sheffield	30 Jun 02
92.60		Raymond	Hecht	GER	11.11.68	1	Bisl	Oslo	21 Jul 95
92.42			Zelezny			1	GS	Ostrava	28 May 97
92.41			Parviainen			1	ECp-1A	Vaasa	24 Jun 01
92.28			Zelezny			1	GPF	Monaco	9 Sep 95
92.28			Hecht			1	WK	Zürich	14 Aug 96
92.12			Zelezny			1	McD	London (CP)	27 Aug 95
92.12			Zelezny			1	TOTO	Tokyo	15 Sep 95
92.06		Andreas	Hofmann	GER	16.12.91	1		Offenburg	2 Jun 18
91.82			Zelezny			1	McD	Sheffield	4 Sep 94
91.78			Röhler			1	DL	Doha	4 May 18
91.69		Kostadínos	Gatsioúdis	GRE	17.12.73	1		Kuortane	24 Jun 00
91.68			Zelezny			1	GP	Gateshead	1 Jul 94
91.59		Andreas	Thorkildsen (10)	NOR	1.4.82	1	Bisl	Oslo	2 Jun 06
91.56			Vetter			2	DL	Doha	4 May 18
91.53		Tero	Pitkämäki	FIN	19.12.82	1		Kuortane	26 Jun 05
91.53			Röhler			1	GS	Ostrava	28 Jun 17
91.50			Zelezny			1	Kuso	Lublin	4 Jun 94
91.50A			Zelezny			1		Pretoria	8 Apr 96

Mark	Wind	Name		Nat	Born	Pos	Meet	Venue	Date
91.50			Hecht			1		Gengenbach	1 Sep 96
	(32/11)								
91.46	WR	Steve	Backley	GBR	12.2.69	1		Auckland (NS)	25 Jan 92
91.36			Cheng Chao-Tsun	TPE	17.10.93	1	WUG	Taipei	26 Aug 17
91.29		Breaux	Greer	USA	19.10.76	1	NC	Indianapolis	21 Jun 07
90.73		Vadims	Vasilevskis	LAT	5.1.82	1		Tallinn	?? Jul 07
90.60		Seppo	Räty	FIN	27.4.62	1		Nurmijärvi	20 Jul 92
90.44		Boris	Henry	GER	14.12.73	1	Gugl	Linz	9 Jul 97
90.16		Keshorn	Walcott	TTO	2.4.93	1	Athl	Lausanne	9 Jul 15
89.75		Magnus	Kirt	EST	10.4.90	1	DL	Rabat	13 Jul 18
89.73		Jakub	Vadlejch	CZE	10.10.90	2	WCh	London (OS)	12 Aug 17
	(20)								
89.21		Ihab	Abdelrahman ¶	EGY	1.5.89	1	DL	Shanghai	18 May 14
89.16A		Tom	Petranoff	USA	8.4.58	1		Potchefstroom	1 Mar 91
89.15			Zhao Qinggang	CHN	24.7.85	1	AsiG	Incheon	2 Oct 14
89.10	WR	Patrik	Bodén	SWE	30.6.67	1		Austin	24 Mar 90
89.02		Jarrod	Bannister ¶	AUS	3.10.84	1	NC	Brisbane	29 Feb 08
88.98		Antti	Ruuskanen	FIN	21.2.84	1	NC	Pori	2 Aug 15
88.90		Aleksandr	Ivanov	RUS	25.5.82	1	Znam	Tula	7 Jun 03
88.84		Dmitriy	Tarabin	RUS	29.10.91	1	NC	Moskva	24 Jul 13
88.75		Marius	Corbett	RSA	26.9.75	1	CG	Kuala Lumpur	21 Sep 98
88.70		Peter	Blank	GER	10.4.62	1	NC	Stuttgart	30 Jun 01
	(30)								
88.36		Matthias	de Zordo	GER	21.2.88	1	VD	Bruxelles	16 Sep 11
88.34		Vitezslav	Vesely	CZE	27.2.83	Q	OG	London (OS)	8 Aug 12
88.32		Petr	Frydrych	CZE	13.1.88	3	WCh	London (OS)	12 Aug 17
88.29		Julian	Weber	GER	29.8.94	2	ISTAF	Berlin	3 Sep 16
88.24		Matti	Närhi	FIN	17.8.75	1		Soini	27 Jul 97
88.22		Juha	Laukkanen	FIN	6.1.69	1		Kuortane	20 Jun 92
88.20		Gavin	Lovegrove	NZl	21.10.67	1	Bisl	Oslo	6 Jul 06
88.09		Marcin	Krukowski	POL	14.6.92	1	NC	Bialystok	21 Jul 17
88.06		Neeraj	Chopra	IND	24.12.97	1	AsiG	Jakarta	27 Aug 18
88.02		Oliver	Helander	FIN	1.1.97	1		Pietarsaari	7 Jul 18
	(40)								
88.01		Ioánnis	Kiriazis	GRE	19.1.96	1	TexR	Austin	31 Mar 17
88.00		Vladimir	Ovchinnikov	RUS	2.8.70	1		Tolyatti	14 May 95
87.83		Andrus	Värnik	EST	27.9.77	1		Valga	19 Aug 03
87.82		Harri	Hakkarainen	FIN	16.10.69	1		Kuortane	24 Jun 95
87.60		Kazuhiro	Mizoguchi	JPN	18.3.62	1	Jenner	San José	27 May 89
87.40		Vladimir	Sasimovich ¶	BLR	14.9.68	2		Kuortane	24 Jun 95
87.34		Andrey	Moruyev	RUS	6.5.70	1	ECp	Birmingham	25 Jun 94
87.23		Teemu	Wirkkala	FIN	14.1.84	1		Joensuu	22 Jul 09
87.20		Viktor	Zaytsev	UZB	6.6.66	1	OT	Moskva	23 Jun 92
87.20		Peter	Esenwein	GER	7.12.67	1		Rehlingen	31 May 04
87.20A		Guillermo	Martínez	CUB	28.6.81	1	PAm	Guadalajara	28 Oct 11
	(51)	100th man 85.01, 200th 82.70, 300th 80.76, 400th 79.68, 500th 78.64							

Ancillary marks – other marks during series (to 91.48)   new javelin introduced in 1986

95.34	Zelezny	29 Aug 93	92.88	Zelezny		25 May 96	92.26	Zelezny	26 Mar 97
93.06	Vetter	11 Jul 17	92.30	Zelezny		26 Mar 97	91.88	Zelezny	27 Aug 95
							91.67	Vetter	18 Aug 17

Javelins with roughened tails, now banned by the IAAF

96.96	WR	Seppo	Räty	FIN	27.4.62	1		Punkalaidun	2 Jun 91
94.74	Irreg		Zelezny			1	Bisl	Oslo	4 Jul 92
91.98	wn		Räty			1	Super	Shizuoka	8 May 91
90.82		Kimmo	Kinnunen	FIN	31.3.68	1	WCh	Tokyo	26 Aug 91

DECATHLON

9126		Kevin	Mayer	FRA	10.2.92	1		Talence	16 Sep 18
		10.55/0.3	7.80/1.2	16.00	2.05	48.42	13.75/-1.1	50.54 5.45 71.90	4:36.11
9045	WR	Ashton	Eaton	USA	21.1.88	1	WCh	Beijing	29 Aug 15
		10.23/-0.4	7.88/0.0	14.52	2.01	45.00	13.69/-0.2	43.34 5.20 63.63	4:17.52
9039	WR		Eaton			1	NC/OT	Eugene	23 Jun 12
		10.21/0.4	8.23/0.8	14.20	2.05	46.70	13.70/-0.8	42.81 5.30 58.87	4:14.48
9026	WR	Roman	Sebrle	CZE	26.11.74	1		Götzis	27 May 01
		10.64/0.0	8.11/1.9	15.33	2.12	47.79	13.92/-0.2	47.92 4.80 70.16	4:21.98
8994	WR	Tomás	Dvorák	CZE	11.5.72	1	ECp	Praha	4 Jul 99
		10.54/-0.1	7.90/1.1	16.78	2.04	48.08	13.73/0.0	48.33 4.90 72.32	4:37.20
8902			Dvorák			1	WCh	Edmonton	7 Aug 01
		10.62/1.5	8.07/0.9	16.57	2.00	47.74	13.80/-0.4	45.51 5.00 68.53	4:35.13
8900			Dvorák			1		Götzis	4 Jun 00
		10.54/1.3	8.03/0.0	16.68	2.09	48.36	13.89/-1.0	47.89 4.85 67.21	4:42.33

Mark	Wind	Name	Nat	Born	Pos	Meet	Venue	Date
8893		Sebrle			1	OG	Athína	24 Aug 04
	10.85/1.5 7.84/0.3 16.36	2.12 48.36	14.05/1.5 48.72 5.00 70.52 4:40.01					
8893		Eaton			1	OG	Rio de Janeiro	18 Aug 16
	10.46/-0.1 7.94/1.7 14.73	2.01 46.07	13.80/0.7 45.49 5.20 59.77 4:23.33					
8891 WR	Dan	O'Brien	USA	18.7.66	1		Talence	5 Sep 92
	10.43w/2.1 8.08/1.8 16.69	2.07 48.51	13.98/-0.5 48.56 5.00 62.58 4:42.10					
8869		Eaton			1	OG	London (OS)	9 Aug 12
	10.35/0.4 8.03/0.8 14.66	2.05 46.90	13.56/0.1 42.53 5.20 61.96 4:33.59					
8847 WR	Daley	Thompson	GBR	30.7.58	1	OG	Los Angeles	9 Aug 84
	10.44/-1.0 8.01/0.4 15.72	2.03 46.97	14.33/-1.1 46.56 5.00 65.24 4:35.00					
8844w		O'Brien			1	TAC	New York	13 Jun 91
	10.23 7.96 16.06	2.08 47.70	13.95W/4.2 48.08 5.10 57.40 4:45.54					
8842		Sebrle			1		Götzis	30 May 04
	10.92/0.5 7.86w/3.3 16.22	2.09 48.59	14.15/0.3 47.44 5.00 71.10 4:34.09					
8837		Dvorák			1	WCh	Athína	6 Aug 97
	10.60/0.8 7.64/-0.7 16.32	2.00 47.56	13.61/0.8 45.16 5.00 70.34 4:35.40					
8834		Mayer			2	OG	Rio de Janeiro	18 Aug 16
	10.81/-0.4 7.60/0.1 15.76	2.04 48.28	14.02/0.7 46.78 5.40 65.04 4:25.49					
8832 WR	Jürgen	Hingsen	FRG	25.1.58	1	OT	Mannheim	9 Jun 84
	10.70w/2.9 7.76/-1.6 16.42	2.07 48.05	14.07/0.2 49.36 4.90 59.86 4:19.75					
8832	Bryan	Clay	USA	3.1.80	1	NC/OT	Eugene	30 Jun 08
	10.39/-0.4 7.39/-1.6 15.17	2.08 48.41	13.75/1.9 52.74 5.00 70.55 4:50.97					
8825 WR		Hingsen			1		Bernhausen	5 Jun 83
	10.92/0.0 7.74 15.94	2.15 47.89	14.10 46.80 4.70 67.26 4:19.74					
8824		O'Brien			1	OG	Atlanta	1 Aug 96
	10.50/0.7 7.57/1.4 15.66	2.07 46.82	13.87/0.3 48.78 5.00 66.90 4:45.89					
8820		Clay			2	OG	Athína	24 Aug 04
	10.44w/2.2 7.96/0.2 15.23	2.06 49.19	14.13/1.5 50.11 4.90 69.71 4:41.65					
8817		O'Brien			1	WCh	Stuttgart	20 Aug 93
	10.57/0.9 7.99/0.4 15.41	2.03 47.46	14.08/0.0 47.92 5.20 62.56 4:40.08					
8815	Erki	Nool	EST	25.6.70	2	WCh	Edmonton	7 Aug 01
	10.60/1.5 7.63/2.0 14.90	2.03 46.23	14.40/0.0 43.40 5.40 67.01 4:29.58					
8812		O'Brien			1	WCh	Tokyo	30 Aug 91
	10.41/-1.6 7.90/0.8 16.24	1.91 46.53	13.94/-1.2 47.20 5.20 60.66 4:37.50					
8811		Thompson			1	EC	Stuttgart	28 Aug 86
	10.26/2.0 7.72/1.0 15.73	2.00 47.02	14.04/-0.3 43.38 5.10 62.78 4:26.16					
8809		Eaton			1	WCh	Moskva	11 Aug 13
	10.35/-0.5 7.73/0.3 14.39	1.93 46.02	13.72/0.4 45.00 5.20 64.83 4:29.80					
8807		Sebrle			1		Götzis	1 Jun 03
	10.78/-0.2 7.86/1.2 15.41	2.12 47.83	13.96/0.0 43.42 4.90 69.22 4:28.63					
8800		Sebrle			1		Götzis	2 Jun 02
	10.95/0.5 7.79/1.8 15.50	2.12 48.35	13.89/1.6 48.02 5.00 68.97 4:38.16					
8800		Sebrle			1	EC	München	8 Aug 02
	10.83/1.3 7.92/0.8 15.41	2.12 48.48	14.04/0.0 46.88 5.10 68.51 4:42.94					
8795	Damian	Warner (10)	CAN	4.11.89	1	Hypo	Götzis	27 May 18
	10.31/0.6 7.81/0.5 14.83	2.03 47.72	13.56/0.0 47.32 4.80 61.94 4:26.59					
8792	Uwe	Freimuth	GDR	10.9.61	1	OD	Potsdam	21 Jul 84
	11.06/0.4 7.79/1.2 16.30 (30/11)	2.03 48.43	14.66/1.9 46.58 5.15 72.42 4:25.19					
8790	Trey	Hardee	USA	7.2.84	1	WCh	Berlin	20 Aug 09
	10.45/0.2 7.83/1.9 15.33	1.99 48.13	13.86/0.3 48.08 5.20 68.00 4:48.91					
8784	Tom	Pappas	USA	6.9.76	1	NC	Stanford	22 Jun 03
	10.78/0.2 7.96/1.4 16.28	2.17 48.22	14.13/1.7 45.84 5.20 60.77 4:48.12					
8762	Siegfried	Wentz	FRG	7.3.60	2		Bernhausen	5 Jun 83
	10.89 7.49/ 15.35	2.09 47.38	14.00 46.90 4.80 70.68 4:24.90					
8735	Eduard	Hämäläinen	FIN/BLR	21.1.69	1		Götzis	29 May 94
	10.50w/2.1 7.26/1.0 16.05	2.11 47.63	13.82/-3.0 49.70 4.90 60.32 4:35.09					
8727	Dave	Johnson	USA	7.4.63	1		Azusa	24 Apr 92
	10.96/0.4 7.52w/4.5 14.61	2.04 48.19	14.17/0.3 49.88 5.28 66.96 4:29.38					
8725	Dmitriy	Karpov	KAZ	23.7.81	3	OG	Athína	24 Aug 04
	10.50w/2.2 7.81/-0.9 15.93	2.09 46.81	13.97/1.5 51.65 4.60 55.54 4:38.11					
8709	Aleksandr	Apaychev	UKR	6.5.61	1	vGDR	Neubrandenburg	3 Jun 84
	10.96/ 7.57/ 16.00	1.97 48.72	13.93/ 48.00 4.90 72.24 4:26.51					
8706	Frank	Busemann	GER	26.2.75	2	OG	Atlanta	1 Aug 96
	10.60/0.7 8.07/0.8 13.60	2.04 48.34	13.47/0.3 45.04 4.80 66.86 4:31.41					
8698	Grigoriy	Degtyaryov	RUS	16.8.58	1	NC	Kiyev	22 Jun 84
	10.87/0.7 7.42/0.1 16.03 (20)	2.10 49.75	14.53/0.3 51.20 4.90 67.08 4:23.09					
8694	Chris	Huffins	USA	15.4.70	1	NC	New Orleans	20 Jun 98
	10.31w/3.5 7.76w/2.5 15.43	2.18 49.02	14.02/1.0 53.22 4.60 61.59 4:59.43					

Mark	Wind	Name	Nat	Born	Pos	Meet	Venue	Date
8680		Torsten Voss	GDR	24.3.63	1	WCh	Roma	4 Sep 87
		10.69/-0.3 7.88/1.2 14.98	2.10	47.96		14.13/0.1	43.96 5.10 58.02	4:25.93
8670		Michael Schrader	GER	1.7.87	2	WCh	Moskva	11 Aug 13
		10.73/-0.5 7.85/0.2 14.56	1.99	47.66		14.29/0.4	46.44 5.00 65.67	4:25.38
8667 WR		Guido Kratschmer	FRG	10.1.53	1		Bernhausen	14 Jun 80
		10.58w/2.4 7.80/ 15.47	2.00	48.04		13.92/	45.52 4.60 66.50	4:24.15
8663		Rico Freimuth	GER	14.3.88	1		Ratingen	25 Jun 17
		10.44w/3.3 7.60/1.5 14.87	2.01	48.76		13.87/0.7	51.56 4.90 62.33	4:37.04
8654		Leonel Suárez	CUB	1.9.87	1	CAC	La Habana	4 Jul 09
		11.07/0.7 7.42/0.8 14.39	2.09	47.65		14.15/-0.6	46.07 4.70 77.47	4:27.29
8644		Steve Fritz	USA	1.11.67	4	OG	Atlanta	1 Aug 96
		10.90/0.8 7.77/0.9 15.31	2.04	50.13		13.97/0.3	49.84 5.10 65.70	4:38.26
8644		Maurice Smith	JAM	28.9.80	2	WCh	Osaka	1 Sep 07
		10.62/0.7 7.50/0.0 17.32	1.97	47.48		13.91/-0.2	52.36 4.80 53.61	4:33.52
8634 WR		Bruce Jenner	USA	28.10.49	1	OG	Montreal	30 Jul 76
		10.94/0.0 7.22/0.0 15.35	2.03	47.51		14.84/0.0	50.04 4.80 68.52	4:12.61
8627		Robert Zmelik	CZE	18.4.69	1		Götzis	31 May 92
		10.62w/2.1 8.02/0.2 13.93	2.05	48.73		13.84/1.2	44.44 4.90 61.26	4:24.83
(30)								
8626		Michael Smith	CAN	16.9.67	1		Götzis	26 May 96
		11.23/-0.6 7.72/0.6 16.94	1.97	48.69		14.77/-2.4	52.90 4.90 71.22	4:41.95
8617		Andrey Kravchenko	BLR	4.1.86	1		Götzis	27 May 07
		10.86/0.2 7.90/0.9 13.89	2.15	47.46		14.05/-0.1	39.63 5.00 64.35	4:29.10
8605		Arthur Abele	GER	30.7.86	1		Ratingen	26 Jun 16
		10.95/-0.6 748/0.4 1579	198	49.43		14.07/-0.94620	490 7189	4:24.12
8603		Dean Macey	GBR	12.12.77	3	WCh	Edmonton	7 Aug 01
		10.72/-0.7 7.59/0.4 15.41	2.15	46.21		14.34/0.0	46.96 4.70 54.61	4:29.05
8601		Ilya Shkurenyov	RUS	11.1.91	1	NC	Smolensk	10 Jun 17
		10.89/0.7 7.58/0.9 14.15	2.12	49.00		13.95/1.4	44.91 5.30 60.29	4:28.35
8583w		Jón Arnar Magnússon	ISL	28.7.69	1	ECp-?	Reykiavik	5 Jul 98
		10.68/2.0 7.63/2.0 15.57	2.07	47.78		14.33W/5.2	44.53 5.00 64.16	4:41.60
8573					3		Götzis	31 May 98
		10.74/0.5 7.60/-0.2 16.03	2.03	47.66		14.24/0.7	47.82 5.10 59.77	4:46.43
8580		Kai Kazmirek	GER	28.1.91	4	OG	Rio de Janeiro	18 Aug 16
		10.78/-0.1 7.69/-1.0 14.20	2.10	46.75		14.62/0.7	43.25 5.00 64.60	4:31.25
8574		Christian Plaziat	FRA	28.10.63	1	EC	Split	29 Aug 90
		10.72/-0.6 7.77/1.1 14.19	2.10	47.10		13.98/0.4	44.36 5.00 54.72	4:27.83
8574		Aleksandr Yurkov	UKR	21.7.75	4		Götzis	4 Jun 00
		10.69/0.9 7.93/1.8 15.26	2.03	49.74		14.56/-0.9	47.85 5.15 58.92	4:32.49
8571		Lev Lobodin	RUS	1.4.69	3	EC	Budapest	20 Aug 98
		10.66w/2.2 7.42/0.2 15.67	2.03	48.65		13.97/0.9	46.55 5.20 56.55	4:30.27
(40)								
8566		Sebastian Chmara	POL	21.11.71	1		Alhama de Murcia	17 May 98
		10.97w/2.9 7.56/1.2 16.03	2.10	48.27		14.32/1.8	44.39 5.20 57.25	4:29.66
8558		Pascal Behrenbruch	GER	19.1.85	1	EC	Helsinki	28 Jun 12
		10.93/0.8 7.15/-0.8 16.89	1.97	48.54		14.16/0.2	48.24 5.00 67.45	4:34.02
8554		Attila Zsivoczky	HUN	29.4.77	5		Götzis	4 Jun 00
		10.64w/2.1 7.24/-1.0 15.72	2.18	48.13		14.87/-0.9	45.64 4.65 63.57	4:23.13
8548		Paul Meier	GER	27.7.71	3	WCh	Stuttgart	20 Aug 93
		10.57/0.9 7.57/1.1 15.45	2.15	47.73		14.63/0.0	45.72 4.60 61.22	4:32.05
8547		Igor Sobolevskiy	UKR	4.5.62	2	NC	Kiyev	22 Jun 84
		10.64/0.7 7.71/0.2 15.93	2.01	48.24		14.82/0.3	50.54 4.40 67.40	4:32.84
8539(w)		Lindon Victor	GRN	28.2.93	1	SEC	Columbia. SC	12 May 17
		10.64w/3.6 7.35w/2.1 15.18	2.05	48.74		14.45/1.8	55.22 4.70 68.97	4:55.91
8539		Eelco Sintnicolaas	NED	7.4.87	2		Götzis	28 May 17
		10.57/0.5 7.61/0.6 14.62	1.91	48.37		14.16/-1.2	43.52 5.40 62.13	4:30.32
8534		Siegfried Stark	GDR	12.6.55	1	OT	Halle	4 May 80
		11.10w 7.64 15.81	2.03	49.53		14.86w	47.20 5.00 68.70	4:27.7
8534w/8478		Antonio Peñalver	ESP	1.12.68	1		Alhama de Murcia	24 May 92
		(7.19w/4.0) 10.76w/3.9 7.42W/6.2 16.50	2.12	49.50		14.32/0.8	47.38 5.00 59.32	4:39.94
8526		Francisco Javier Benet	ESP	25.3.68	2		Alhama de Murcia	17 May 98
		10.72w/2.9 7.45/-1.2 14.57	1.92	48.10		13.83/1.8	46.12 5.00 65.37	4:26.81
(50)		100th man 8350, 200th 8203, 300th 8101, 400th 8007, 500th 7930						
Drugs dq 8528		Aleksandr Pogorelov ¶	RUS	10.1.80	(3)	WCh	Berlin	20 Aug 09
		10.95/-0.3 7.49/-0.4 16.65	2.08	50.27		14.19/0.3	48.46 5.10 63.95	4:48.70

4 x 100 METRES RELAY

Mark		Name		Meet	Venue	Date
36.84 WR	JAM	N Carter 10.1, Frater 8.9, Blake 9.0, Bolt 8.8	1	OG	London (OS)	11 Aug 12
37.04 WR	JAM	N Carter, Frater, Blake, Bolt	1	WCh	Daegu	4 Sep 11
37.27	JAM	Powell, Blake, Ashmeade, Bolt	1	OG	Rio de Janeiro	19 Aug 16
37.31	JAM	Mullings, Frater, Bolt, Powell	1	WCh	Berlin	22 Aug 09

Mark	Wind	Name	Nat	Born	Pos	Meet	Venue	Date
37.36		JAM Carter, Bailey Cole, Ashmeade, Bolt			1	WCh	Moskva	18 Aug 13
37.36		JAM Carter, Powell, Ashmeade, Bolt			1	WCh	Beijing	29 Aug 15
37.38		USA Demps, Patton, Kimmons, Gatlin			1h2	OG	London (OS)	10 Aug 12
37.38		USA Rodgers, Gatlin, Gay, R.Bailey			1	W.Rly	Nassau	2 May 15
37.39		JAM Carter, Frater, Blake, Bailey-Cole			1h1	OG	London (OS)	10 Aug 12
37.40	WR	USA Marsh, Burrell, Mitchell, C Lewis			1	OG	Barcelona	8 Aug 92
37.40	WR	USA Drummond, Cason, D Mitchell, L Burrell			1s1	WCh	Stuttgart	21 Aug 93
37.41		JAM Carter, Powell, Dwyer, Ashmeade			1h2	WCh	Beijing	29 Aug 15
37.45		USA Kimmons, Spearmon, Gay, Rodgers			1	WK	Zürich	19 Aug 10
37.47		GBR Ujah, Gemili, Talbot, Mitchell-Blake			1	WCh	London (OS)	12 Aug 17
37.48		USA Drummond, Cason, D Mitchell, L Burrell			1	WCh	Stuttgart	22 Aug 93
37.50	WR	USA Cason, Burrell, Mitchell, C Lewis			1	WCh	Tokyo	1 Sep 91
37.52		USA Rodgers, Gatlin, Bacon, Coleman			2	WCh	London (OS)	12 Aug 17
37.58		USA 'Red' Silmon, Rodgers, Salaam, Gatlin			1	Herc	Monaco	19 Jul 13
37.58		JAM Livermore, Bailey-Cole, Ashmeade, Bolt			1	CG	Glasgow	2 Aug 14
37.59		USA Drummond, Montgomery, B Lewis, Greene			1	WCh	Sevilla	29 Aug 99
37.59		USA Conwright, Spearmon, Gay, Smoots			1	WCp	Athína	16 Sep 06
37.60		JPN Yamagata, Iizuka, Kiryu, Cambridge			2	OG	Rio de Janeiro	19 Aug 16
37.61		USA Drummond, Williams, B Lewis, Greene			1	OG	Sydney	30 Sep 00
37.61		USA Kimmons, Gatlin, Gay, Bailey			1	Herc	Monaco	20 Jul 12
37.61		GBR Ujah, Hughes, Gemili, Mitchell-Blake			1	DL	London (OS)	22 Jul 18
37.62		TTO Brown, Burns, Callander, Thompson			2	WCh	Berlin	22 Aug 09
37.64		CAN Haynes, A.Brown, Rodney, DeGrasse			3	OG	Rio de Janeiro	19 Aug 16
37.65		USA Drummond, Williams, C Johnson, Greene			1	ISTAF	Berlin	1 Sep 00
37.65		USA Rodgers, Coleman, Gay, Lawson			1h1	OG	Rio de Janeiro	18 Aug 16
37.66		USA Silmon, Rodgers, Salaam, Gatlin			2	WCh	Moskva	18 Aug 13
		(30 performances by teams from 6 nations) Further bests by nations:						
37.79	WR	FRA Morinière, Sangouma 8.90, Trouabal, Marie-Rose			1	EC	Split	1 Sep 90
37.82		CHN Tang, Xie, Su, Zhang			2h1	OG	Rio de Janeiro	18 Aug 16
37.90		BRA de Lima, Ribeiro, A da Silva, Cl da Silva			2	OG	Sydney	30 Sep 00
37.94		NGR O Ezinwa, Adeniken, Obikwelu, D Ezinwa			1s2	WCh	Athína	9 Aug 97
		(10)						
37.98		TUR Barnes, Harvey, Hekimoglu, Guliyev			2	EC	Berlin	12 Aug 18
38.00		CUB Simón, Lamela, Isasi, Aguilera			3	OG	Barcelona	8 Aug 92
38.01		ANT Walsh, D.Bailey, Jarvis, Church			4h2	WCh	Beijing	29 Aug 15
38.02		URS Yevgenyev, Bryzgin, Muravyov, Krylov			2	WCh	Roma	6 Sep 87
38.02		GER Reus, Unger, Kosenkow, Jakubczyk			1		Weinheim	27 Jul 12
38.03		NED Garia, Martina, Paulina, Burnet			3	EC	Berlin	12 Aug 18
38.12		GHA Duah, Nkansah, Zakari, Tuffour			1s1	WCh	Athína	9 Aug 97
38.17		AUS Henderson, Jackson, Brimacombe, Marsh			1s2	WCh	Göteborg	12 Aug 95
38.17		ITA Donati, Collio, Di Gregorio, Checcucci			2	EC	Barcelona	1 Aug 10
38.24		RSA Bruintjies, Erasmus, Jobodwana, Simbine (20)			2	CG	Gold Coast	14 Apr 18
38.31		POL Masztak, Kuc, Kubaczyk, Krynski			6h2	OG	London (OS)	10 Aug 12
38.41		SKN Lestrod, Rogers, Adams, Lawrence			6h1	OG	London (OS)	10 Aug 12
38.41		BAR S.Brathwaite, Burke, B.Ellis, Hoyte			1	CAG	Barranquilla	2 Aug 18
38.45		AHO Goeloe, Raffaela, Duzant, Martina			6	WCh	Helsinki	13 Aug 05
38.46		URS/RUS Zharov, Krylov, Fatun, Goremykin			4	EC	Split	1 Sep 90
38.46		ESP Viles, Ruiz, Hortelano, Rodríguez			4h1	WCh	Moskva	18 Aug 13
38.47		HKG Tang Yik Chun, Lai Chun Ho, Ng Ka Fung, Tsui Chi Ho			1		Taipei	26 May 12
38.52		BAH Griffith, Fraser, Hart, T.Smith			3h1	CG	Glasgow	1 Aug 14
38.52		DOM De Oloe, Andujar, Del Carmen, Martinez			1	IbAm	Rio de Janeiro	16 May 16
38.53		UKR Rurak, Osovich, Kramarenko, Dologodin (30)			1	ECp	Madrid	1 Jun 96

Multi-nation team

| 37.46 | | Racers TC Bailey/ANT, Blake JAM, Forsythe JAM, Bolt JAM | | | 1 | LGP | London (CP) | 25 Jul 09 |

Hand timed

| 38.3 A | | UKR Kravtsov, Smelyk, Suprun, Ibrahimov | | | 2 | | Erzurum | 10 Jun 17 |

One man disqualified for drugs

37.04		USA Kimmons 10.1, Gatlin 8.9, Gay ¶ 9.0, Bailey 9.0			(2)	OG	London (OS)	11 Aug 12
37.10	(WR)	JAM N Carter ¶, Frater, Bolt, Powell			(1)	OG	Beijing	22 Aug 08
37.91		NGR Asonze ¶, Obikwelu, Effiong, Aliu			(3)	WCh	Sevilla	29 Aug 99

4 x 200 METRES RELAY

1:18.63	WR	JAM Ashmeade 20.5, Weir 19.2, J Brown 19.6, Y Blake 19.4			1	WRly	Nassau	24 May 14
1:18.68	WR	USA - Santa Monica Track Cluc						
		Marsh 20.0, Burrell 19.6, Heard 19.7, C Lewis 19.4			1	MSR	Walnut	17 Apr 94
1:19.10		World All-Stars			2	MSR	Walnut	17 Apr 94
		Drummond USA 20.4, Mitchell USA 19.3, Bridgewater USA 20.3, Regis GBR 19.1						
1:19.11	WR	Santa Monica TC/USA M.Marsh, L Burrell, Heard, C Lewis			1	Penn	Philadelphia	25 Apr 92
1:19.16		USA Red Team Crawford, Clay, Patton, Gatlin			1	PennR	Philadelphia	26 Apr 03
1:19.20		CAN Smellie, Rodney, DeGrasse, A.Brown			1	FlaR	Gainesville	2 Apr 16

MEN All-time

Mark	Wind	Name	Nat	Born	Pos	Meet	Venue	Date
1:19.38	WR	Santa Monica TC/USA Everett, Burrell, Heard, C Lewis			1	R-W	Koblenz	23 Aug 89
1:19.39		USA Blue Drummond, Crawford, B Williams, Greene			1	PennR	Philadelphia	28 Apr 01
1:19.42		CAN Smellie, Rodney, De Grasse, Brown			1	W.Rly	Nassau	23 Apr 17
1:19.45		Santa Monica TC/USA DeLoach, Burrell, C.Lewis, Heard			1	Penn	Philadelphia	27 Apr 91

Best non-US nations

Mark	Wind	Name	Nat	Born	Pos	Meet	Venue	Date
1:20.51		SKN A Adams, L Roland, BJ Lawrence, A Clarke			2	WRly	Nassau	24 May 14
1:20.66		FRA Lemaitre, Fonsat, Bassaw, Romain			3	WRly	Nassau	25 May 14
1:21.10		ITA Tilli, Simionato, Bongiorno, Mennea			1		Cagliari	29 Sep 83
1:21.22		POL Tulin, Balcerzak, Pilarczyk, Urbas			2		Gdansk	14 Jul 01
1:21.29		GBR Adam, Mafe, Christie, Regis			1	vURS	Birmingham	23 Jun 89

4 x 400 METRES RELAY

Mark	Wind	Name	Nat	Born	Pos	Meet	Venue	Date
2:54.29	WR	USA Valmon 44.5, Watts 43.6, Reynolds 43.23, Johnson 42.94			1	WCh	Stuttgart	22 Aug 93
2:55.39		USA Merritt 44.4, Taylor 43.7, Neville 44.16, Wariner 43.18			1	OG	Beijing	23 Aug 08
2:55.56		USA Merritt 44.4, Taylor 43.7, Williamson 44.32, Wariner 43.10			1	WCh	Osaka	2 Sep 07
2:55.74	WR	USA Valmon 44.6, Watts 43.00, M Johnson 44.73, S Lewis 43.41			1	OG	Barcelona	8 Aug 92
2:55.91		USA O Harris 44.5, Brew 43.6, Wariner 43.98, Williamson 43.83			1	OG	Athína	28 Aug 04
2:55.99		USA L Smith 44.62, A Harrison 43.84, Mills 43.66, Maybank 43.87			1	OG	Atlanta	3 Aug 96
2:56.16A	WR	USA Matthews 45.0, Freeman 43.2, James 43.9, Evans 44.1			1	OG	Ciud. México	20 Oct 68
2:56.16	WR	USA Everett 43.79, S Lewis 43.69, Robinzine 44.74, Reynolds 43.94			1	OG	Seoul	1 Oct 88
2:56.60		GBR I Thomas 44.92, Baulch 44.19, Richardson 43.62, Black 43.87			2	OG	Atlanta	3 Aug 96
2:56.65		GBR Thomas 44.8, Black 44.2, Baulch 44.08, Richardson 43.57			2	WCh	Athína	10 Aug 97
2:56.72		BAH Brown 44.9, Pinder 43.5, Mathieu 44.25, Miller 44.01			1	OG	London (OS)	10 Aug 12
2:56.75		JAM McDonald 44.9, Haughton 44.4, McFarlane 44.37, Clarke 43.51			3	WCh	Athína	10 Aug 97
2:56.91		USA Rock 44.7, Brew 44.3, Williamson 44.40, Wariner 43.49			1	WCh	Helsinki	14 Aug 05
2:57.05		USA Nellum 45.2, Mance 43.5, McQuay 43.41, Taylor 44.85			2	OG	London (OS)	10 Aug 12
2:57.25		USA Verburg 44.8, McQuay 44.1, C Taylor 44.6, L Merritt 43.8			1	WRly	Nassau	25 May 14
2:57.29		USA Everett 45.1, Haley 44.0, McKay 44.20, Reynolds 44.00			1	WCh	Roma	6 Sep 87
2:57.30		USA Hall 45.3, McQuay 43.2, Roberts 44.79, Merritt 43.97			1	OG	Rio de Janeiro	20 Aug 16
2:57.32		USA Ramsey 44.9, Mills 44.6, Reynolds 43.74, Johnson 44.11			1	WCh	Göteborg	13 Aug 95
2:57.32		BAH McKinney 44.9, Moncur 44.6, A Williams 44.43, Brown 43.42			2	WCh	Helsinki	14 Aug 05
2:57.53		GBR Black 44.7, Redmond 44.0, Regis 44.22, Akabusi 44.59			1	WCh	Tokyo	1 Sep 91
2:57.57		USA Valmon 44.9, Watts 43.4, D.Everett 44.31, Pettigrew 44.93			2	WCh	Tokyo	1 Sep 91
2:57.59		BAH L Williams 45.0, Pinder 43.8, C Brown 44.2, Mathieu 44.6			2	WRly	Nassau	25 May 14
2:57.82		USA Verburg 44.8, McQuay 44.3, Nellum 44.38, Merritt 44.18			1	WCh	Beijing	30 Aug 15
2:57.86		USA Taylor 45.4, Wariner 43.6, Clement 44.72, Merritt 44.16			1	WCh	Berlin	23 Aug 09
2:57.87		USA L Smith 44.59, Rouser 44.33, Mills 44.32, Maybank 44.63			1s2	OG	Atlanta	2 Aug 96
2:57.91		USA Nix 45.0, Armstead 43.97, Babers 43.75, McKay 44.60			1	OG	Los Angeles	11 Aug 84
2:57.97		JAM McDonald, Haughton McFarlane, D Clarke			1	PAm	Winnipeg	30 Jul 99
2:58.00		POL Rysiukiewicz 45.6, Czubak 44.2, Haczek 44.0, Mackowiak 44.2			2	GWG	Uniondale, NY	22 Jul 98
2:58.03		BAH Bain 45.9, Mathieu 44.1, A Williams 44.02, Brown 44.05			2	OG	Beijing	23 Aug 08
2:58.07		JAM Ayre 44.9, Simpson 44.48, Spence 44.48, Clarke 43.81			3	WCh	Helsinki	14 Aug 05
		(30/5) plus 7 times for teams that contained an athlete who was subsequently banned for drugs abuse						
2:58.12		TTO Solomon 46.1, Richards 43.4, Cedenio 44.41, L. Gordon 44.08			1	WCh	London (OS)	13 Aug 17
2:58.52		BEL Watrin 46.0, J.Borlée 44.1, D.Borlée 44.71, K.Borlée 43.67			4	OG	Rio de Janeiro	20 Aug 16
2:58.56		BRA Cl. da Silva 44.6, A dos Santos 45.1, de Araújo 45.0, Parrela 43.9			2	PAm	Winnipeg	30 Jul 99
2:58.68		NGR Chukwu 45.18, Monye 44.49, Bada 44.70, Udo-Obong 44.31			1	OG	Sydney	30 Sep 00
2:58.96		FRA Djhone 45.4, Keita 44.7, Diagana 44.69, Raquil 44.15			2	WCh	Saint-Denis	31 Aug 03
		(10)						
2:59.06		BOT Makwala 44.9, Sibanda 43.9, Nkobolo 44.94, Maotoanong 45.28			5	OG	Rio de Janeiro	20 Aug 16
2:59.13		CUB Martínez 45.6, Herrera 44.38, Tellez 44.81, Hernández 44.34			1h2	OG	Barcelona	7 Aug 92
2:60.21		RSA Piotoriuo 45.58, Mogawano 43.07, do Boor 44.46, Victor 46.20			3h1	WCh	Daegu	1 Sep 11
2:59.45		RUS Denmukhametov 46.0, Trenikin 44.5, Kudryavtsev 44.63, Ivashko 44.29			4h1	WCh	Beijing	29 Aug 15
2:59.63		KEN D Kitur 45.4, S Kitur 45.13, Kipkemboi 44.76, Kemboi 44.34			3h2	OG	Barcelona	7 Aug 92
2:59.70		AUS Frayne 45.38, Clark 43.86, Minihan 45.07, Mitchell 45.39			4	OG	Los Angeles	11 Aug 84
2:59.86		GDR Möller 45.8, Schersing 44.8, Carlowitz 45.3, Schönlebe 44.1			1	vURS	Erfurt	23 Jun 85
2:59.95		YUG Jovkovic, Djurovic, Macev, Brankovic 44.3			2h3	WCh	Tokyo	31 Aug 91
2:59.96		FRG Dobeleit 45.7, Henrich 44.3, Itt 45.12, Schmid 44.93			4	WCh	Roma	6 Sep 87
3:00.15		DOM Cuesta 45.4, Soriano 43.8, J.Santos 46.58, L.Santos 44.36			6h2	WCh	Beijing	29 Aug 15
		(20)						
3:00.56		QAT Samba 44.6, M.Abbas 45.2, Mohamed 46.43, Haroun 44.41			1	AsiG	Jakarta	30 Aug 18
3:00.64		SEN Diarra 46.53, Dia 44.94, Ndiaye 44.70, Faye 44.47			4	OG	Atlanta	3 Aug 96
3:00.65		ESP Husillos 45.4, Búa 45.3, Echeverry 45.26, García 44.75			5	WCh	London (OS)	13 Aug 17
3:00.76		JPN Karube 45.88, Ito 44.86, Osakada 45.08, Omori 44.94			5	OG	Atlanta	3 Aug 96
3:00.79		ZIM Chiwira 46.2, Mukomana 44.6, Ngidhi 45.79, Harnden 44.20			2h3	WCh	Athína	9 Aug 97
3:00.82A		VEN A Ramírez 45.7, Aguilar 45.3, Acevedo 44.7, Longart 45.2			3	PAm	Guadalajara	28 Oct 11
3:00.91		IND Kunhu, Anas, Dharun, Rajiv			1		Bengaluru	10 Jun 16
3:01.12		FIN Lönnqvist 46.7, Salin 45.1, Karttunen 44.8, Kukkoaho 44.5			6	OG	München	10 Sep 72
3:01.16 A		COL Zambrano, Lemos, Palomeque, Perlaza			1		Medellín	10 Jul 16
3:01.26		IRL Gregan 46.1, Murphy 45.2, Barr 45.05, English 44.96 (30)			8h2	WCh	Beijing	29 Aug 15

Mark	Wind	Name	Nat	Born	Pos	Meet	Venue	Date

Including subsequently banned athlete

2:54.20(WR) USA Young 44.3, Pettigrew ¶ 43.2, Washington 43.5, Johnson 43.2 (1) GWG   Uniondale, NY 22 Jul 98
2:56.35   USA A Harrison 44.36, Pettigrew 44.17, C Harrison 43.53, Johnson 44.29 (1) OG Sydney   30 Sep 00
2:56.45   USA J Davis 45.2, Pettigrew 43.9, Taylor 43.92, M Johnson 43.49 (1) WCh   Sevilla   29 Aug 99
2:56.47   USA Young 44.6, Pettigrew 43.1, Jones 44.80, Washington 44.80 (1) WCh   Athína   10 Aug 97
2:56.60   USA Red Taylor 45.0, Pettigrew 44.2, Washington 43.7, Johnson 43.7 (1) PennR Philadelphia 29 Apr 00
2:57.54   USA Byrd 45.9, Pettigrew 43.9, Brew 44.03, Taylor 43.71   1 WCh   Edmonton   12 Aug 01
2:58.06   RUS Dyldin 45.5, Frolov 44.6, Kokorin 44.34, Alekseyev ¶ 43.56 3 OG Beijing   23 Aug 08

4 x 800 METRES RELAY

7:02.43   KEN Mutua 1:46.73, Yiampoy 1:44.38, Kombich 1:45.92, Bungei 1:45.40   1 VD Bruxelles 25 Aug 06
7:02.82   USA   2 VD Bruxelles 25 Aug 06
            J Harris 1:47.05, Robinson 1:44.03, Burley 1:46.05, Krummenacker 1:45.69
7:03.89 WR GBR Elliott 1:49.14, Cook 1:46.20, Cram 1:44.54, Coe 1:44.01   1   London (CP) 30 Aug 82
7:04.70   RSA van Oudtshoorn 1:46.9, Sepeng 1:45.2, Kotze 1:48.3, J Botha 1:44.3 1 Stuttgart   6 Jun 99
7:06.66   QAT Sultan 1:45.81, Al-Badri 1:46.71, Suleiman 1:45.89, Ali Kamal 1:48.25 4 VD Bruxelles 25 Aug 06
7:07.40   URS Masunov, Kostetskiy, Matvetev, Kalinkin   1   Moskva   5 Aug 84
7:08.5 WR   FRG Kinder 1:46.9, Adams 1:47.5, Bogatzki 1:47.9, Kemper 1:46.2   1   Wiesbaden   13 Aug 66
7:08.89   POL Konieczny 1:48.9, Krawczyk 1:49.1, Lewandowski 1:45.9, Kszczot 1:44.8 2 WRly Nassau 24 May 14

4 x 1500 METRES RELAY

14:22.22 WR KEN Cheboi 3:38.5, S Kiplagat 3:32.4, Magut 3:39.0, A Kiprop 3:32.3   1 WRly Nassau 25 May 14
14:36.23 WR KEN W Biwott 3:38.5, Gathimba 3:39.5, G Rono 3:41.4, Choge 3:36.9   1 VD Bruxelles 4 Sep 09
14:38.8 WR FRG Wessinghage 3:38.8, Hudak 3:39.1, Lederer 3:44.6, Fleschen 3:36.3   1   Köln   16 Aug 77
14:40.4 WR NZL Polhill 3:42.9, Walker 3:40.4, Dixon 3:41.2, Quax 3:35.9   1   Oslo   22 Aug 73
14:40.80   USA Casey 3:38.2, Torrence 3:36.6, Leer 3:39.3, Manzano 3:46.7   2 WRly Nassau 25 May 14
14:41.22   ETH Gebremedhin 3:39.9, Fida 3:37.5, Z Alemayehu 3:46.5, Wote 3:37.3   3 WRly Nassau 25 May 14
14:45.63   URS Kalutskiy, Yakovlev, Legeda, Lotarev   1   Leningrad 4 Aug 85
14:46.04   AUS Gregson 3:39.1, McEntee 3:44.9, Birmingham 3:38.3, Williamsz 3:43.7   4 WRly Nassau 25 May 14
14:46.16   Larios, ESP Jiménez 3:40.9, Pancorbo 3:41.2, A García 3:43.9, Viciosa 3:40.2 1 Madrid 5 Sep 97
14:48.2   FRA Bégouin 3:44.5, Lequement 3:44.3, Philippe 3:42.2, Dien 3:37.2   2   Bourges 23 Jun 79
Mixed Team: 14:44.31 Ali BRN, Birgen KEN, N Kemboi KEN, Campbell IRL   2 VD Bruxelles 4 Sep 09

4 x 1 MILE RELAY

15:49.08 IRL Coghlan 4:00.2, O'Sullivan 3:55.3, O'Mara 3:56.6, Flynn 3:56.98   1   Dublin   17 Aug 85
15:59.57 NZL Rogers 3:57.2, Bowden 4:02.5, Gilchrist 4:02.8, Walker 3:57.07   1   Auckland 2 Mar 83

4 x 110m/120y HURDLES

52.94 USA Blue Richardson, Harris, Merritt, Oliver   1   DrakeR Des Moines 25 Apr 15
53.08 All Stars Riley JAM, R Brathwaite BAR, Parchment JAM, Swift BAR 2 DrakeR Des Moines 25 Apr 15
53.31y USA Red Oliver, Herring, Brown, Merritt   1   PennR Philadelphia 25 Apr 08
53.36 USA Bramlett, Moore, Payne, Merritt   1   DNG Stockholm 7 Aug 07

3000 METRES TRACK WALK

10:43.84	Tom	Bosworth	GBR	17.1.90	1	Anniv	London (OS)	21 Jul 18
10:47.08	Lebogang	Shange	RSA	1.8.90	2	Anniv	London (OS)	21 Jul 18
10:47.11	Giovanni	De Benedictis	ITA	8.1.68	1		S.Giovanni Valdarno	19 May 90
10:52.44+	Yohann	Diniz	FRA	1.1.78	1	in 5k	Villeneuve d'Ascq	27 Jun 08
10:54.70	Dane	Bird-Smith	AUS	15.7.92	1		Brisbane	11 Feb 17
10:56.22	Andrew	Jachno	AUS	13.4.62	1		Melbourne	7 Feb 91
10:56.34+	Roman	Mrázek	SVK	21.1.62	1	in 5k	Bratislava	14 Jun 89
10:56.98	Dawid	Tomala	POL	27.8.89	1	PTS	Samorín	29 Jun 18

Indoors

10:30.28	Tom	Bosworth	GBR	17.1.90	1	GP	Glasgow	25 Feb 18
10:31.42	Andreas	Erm	GER	12.3.76	1		Halle	4 Feb 01
10:49.33	Christopher	Linke	GER	24.10.88	1		Erfurt	9 Feb 18
10:50.0	Denis	Nizhegorodov	RUS	26.7.80	1		Saransk	4 Dec 06
10:52.15	Nils	Brembach	GER	23.2.93	2		Erfurt	9 Feb 18
10:52.77	Callum	Wilkinson	GBR	14.3.97	2	GP	Glasgow	25 Feb 18
10:53+	Mikhail	Shchennikov	RUS	24.12.67	1	in 5k	Moskva	14 Feb 95
10:53.3	Igor	Yerokhin	RUS	4.9.85	2		Saransk	4 Dec 06
10:54.61	Carlo	Mattioli	ITA	23.10.54	1		Milano	6 Feb 80
10:56.30	Marius	Ziukas	LTU	29.6.85	3	GP	Glasgow	25 Feb 18
10:56.77+	Ivano	Brugnetti	ITA	1.9.76	1	in 5k	Torino	21 Feb 09

5000 METRES TRACK WALK

18:05.49	Hatem	Ghoula	TUN	7.6.73	1		Tunis	1 May 97
18:17.22	Robert	Korzeniowski	POL	30.7.68	1		Reims	3 Jul 92
18:18.01	Yohann	Diniz	FRA	1.1.78	1		Villeneuve d'Ascq	27 Jun 08
18:27.34	Francisco Javier	Fernández ¶	ESP	6.3.77	1		Villeneuve d'Ascq	8 Jun 07
18:28.80	Roman	Mrázek	SVK	21.1.62	1	PTS	Bratislava	14 Jun 89
18:30.43	Maurizio	Damilano	ITA	6.4.57	1		Caserta	11 Jun 92

MEN All-time

Mark	Wind	Name		Nat	Born	Pos	Meet	Venue	Date

Indoors

Mark	Wind	Name		Nat	Born	Pos	Meet	Venue	Date
18:07.08		Mikhail	Shchennikov	RUS	24.12.67	1		Moskva	14 Feb 95
18:08.86		Ivano	Brugnetti	ITA	1.9.76	1	NC	Ancona	17 Feb 07
18:11.41		Ronald	Weigel	GDR	8.8.59	1mx		Wien	13 Feb 88
18:11.8		Valeriy	Borchin ¶	RUS	11.9.86	1		Saransk	30 Dec 10
18:15.25		Grigoriy	Kornev	RUS	14.3.61	1		Moskva	7 Feb 92
18:15.54		Andrey	Ruzavin	RUS	28.3.86	1		Samara	30 Jan 14
18:16.54 ?		Frants	Kostyukevich	BLR	4.4.63	2	NC	Gomel	4 Feb 89
18:16.76		Yohann	Diniz	FRA	1.1.78	1		Reims	7 Dec 14
18:19.97		Giovanni	De Benedictis	ITA	8.1.68	1	EI	Genova	28 Feb 92
18:21.76		Ruslan	Dmytrenko	UKR	22.3.86	2		Samara	30 Jan 14
18:22.25		Andreas	Erm	GER	12.3.76	1	NC	Dortmund	25 Feb 01
18:23.18		Rishat	Shafikov	RUS	23.1.70	1		Samara	1 Mar 97
18:24.13		Francisco Javier	Fernández ¶	ESP	6.3.77	1		Belfast	17 Feb 07
18:27.15		Alessandro	Gandellini	ITA	30.4.73	1	NC	Genova	12 Feb 00
18:27.80		Jozef	Pribilinec	SVK	6.7.60	2	WI	Indianapolis	7 Mar 87
18:27.95		Stefan	Johansson	SWE	11.4.67	3	EI	Genova	28 Feb 92
18:28.54		Igor	Yerokhin	RUS	4.9.85	1		Samara	31 Jan 13
18:28.70		Tom	Bosworth	GBR	17.1.90	1	NC	Birmingham	18 Feb 18
Drugs dq: 18:17.13 Vladimir			Kanaykin ¶	RUS	21.3.85	(2)	Winter	Moskva	5 Feb 12
18:26.82		Sergey	Bakulin ¶	RUS	13.11.86	(3)	Winter	Moskva	5 Feb 12

10,000 METRES TRACK WALK

Mark	Wind	Name		Nat	Born	Pos	Meet	Venue	Date
37:53.09		Francisco Javier	Fernández ¶	ESP	6.3.77	1	NC	Santa Cruz de Tenerife	27 Jul 08
37:58.08		Daisuke	Matsunaga	JPN	24.3.95	1		Kitami	7 Jul 18
37:58.6		Ivano	Brugnetti	ITA	1.9.76	1		Sesto San Gioavnni	23 Jul 05
38:01.49		Eiki	Takahashi	JPN	19.11.92	1		Isahaya	13 Dec 15
38:02.60		Jozef	Pribilinec	SVK	6.7.60	1		Banská Bystrica	30 Aug 85
38:06.6		David	Smith	AUS	24.7.55	1		Sydney	25 Sep 86
38:06.28		Miguel Ángel	López	ESP	3.7.88	1	NC	Gijón	24 Jul 16
38:08.13		Yohann	Diniz	FRA	1.1.78	1	NC	Reims	12 Jul 14
38:10.23		Yusuke	Suzuki	JPN	2.1.88	1		Abashiri	16 Jul 15
38:12.13		Ronald	Weigel (10)	GDR	8.8.59	1		Potsdam	10 May 86
38:18.0+		Valdas	Kazlauskas	LTU	23.2.58	1		Moskva	18 Sep 83
38:20.0		Moacir	Zimmermann	BRA	30.12.83	1		Blumenau	7 Jun 08
38:23.73			Wang Zhen	CHN	24.8.91	1		Genova	8 Feb 15
38:24 0+		Bernardo	Segura	MEX	11.2.70	1	SGP	Fana	7 May 94
38:24.23		Dane	Bird-Smith	AUS	15.7.92	1	NC	Sydney	31 Mar 17
38:24.31		Hatem	Ghoula	TUN	7.6.73	1		Tunis	30 May 98
38:26.4		Daniel	García	MEX	28.10.71	1		Sdr Omme	17 May 97
38:26.53		Robert	Korzeniowski	POL	30.7.68	1		Riga	31 May 02
38:27.57		Robert	Heffernan	IRL	20.2.78	1	NC	Dublin	20 Jul 08
38:32.0		Erik	Tysse (20)	NOR	4.12.80	1	NC	Bergen (Fana)	13 Jun 08
Indoors: 38:31.4 Werner			Heyer	GDR	14.11.56	1		Berlin	12 Jan 80

20 KILOMETRES WALK

Mark	Wind	Name		Nat	Born	Pos	Meet	Venue	Date
1:16:36 WR		Yusuke	Suzuki	JPN	2.1.88	1	AsiC	Nomi	15 Mar 15
1:16:43		Sergey	Morozov ¶	RUS	21.3.88	1	NC	Saransk	8 Jun 08
1:17:02		Yohann	Diniz	FRA	1.1.78	1	NC	Arles	8 Mar 15
1:17:16 WR		Vladimir	Kanaykin ¶	RUS	21.3.85	1	RWC	Saransk	29 Sep 07
1:17:21 WR		Jefferson	Pérez	ECU	1.7.74	1	WCh	Saint-Denis	23 Aug 03
1:17:22 WR		Francisco Javier	Fernández ¶	ESP	6.3.77	1		Turku	28 Apr 02
1:17:23		Vladimir	Stankin	RUS	2.1.74	1	NC w	Adler	8 Feb 04
1:17:24			Diniz			1		Lugano	15 Mar 15
1:17:25		Sergey	Shirobokov	RUS	16.2.99	1	NC	Cheboksary	9 Jun 18
1:17:25.6t		Bernardo	Segura	MEX	11.2.70	1	SGP	Bergen (Fana)	7 May 94
1:17:26		Eiki	Takahashi (10)	JPN	19.11.92	1	NC	Kobe	18 Feb 18
1:17:33		Nathan	Deakes	AUS	17.8.77	1		Cixi	23 Apr 05
1:17:36			Kanaykin			1	NC	Cheboksary	17 Jun 07
1:17:36			Wang Zhen	CHN	24.8.91	1		Taicang	30 Mar 12
1:17:38		Valeriy	Borchin ¶	RUS	11.9.86	1	NC-w	Adler	28 Feb 09
1:17:40			Chen Ding	CHN	5.8.92	2		Taicang	30 Mar 12
1:17:41			Zhu Hongjun	CHN	18.8.83	2		Cixi	23 Apr 05
1:17:41		Toshikazu	Yamanishi	JPN	15.2.96	2	NC	Kobe	18 Feb 18
1:17:43			Diniz			1		Lugano	18 Mar 12
1:17:46		Julio	Martínez	GUA	27.9.73	1		Eisenhüttenstadt	8 May 99
1:17:46		Roman	Rasskazov	RUS	28.4.79	1	NC	Moskva	19 May 00
1:17:46		Daisuke	Matsunaga	JPN	24.3.95	3	NC	Kobe	18 Feb 18
1:17:52			Fernández			1		La Coruña	4 Jun 05
1:17:53			Cui Zhide (20)	CHN	11.1.83	3		Cixi	23 Apr 05

Mark	Wind	Name		Nat	Born	Pos	Meet	Venue	Date
1:17:54			Wang Kaihua	CHN	16.2.94	1		Huangshan	4 Mar 17
1:17:55			Borchin			1	NC-w	Adler	23 Feb 08
1:17:56		Alejandro	López	MEX	9.2.75	2		Eisenhüttenstadt	8 May 99
1:18:00			Fernández			2	WCh	Saint-Denis	23 Aug 03
1:18:00			Wang Zhen			1		La Coruña	6 Jun 15
1:18:03			Takahashi			1	NC	Kobe	15 Feb 15
		(30/22)							
1:18:03.3twR			Bo Lingtang	CHN	12.8.70	1	NC	Beijing	7 Apr 94
1:18:05		Dmitriy	Yesipchuk	RUS	17.11.74	1	NC-w	Adler	4 Mar 01
1:18:06		Viktor	Burayev ¶	RUS	23.8.82	2	NC-w	Adler	4 Mar 01
1:18:06		Vladimir	Parvatkin	RUS	10.10.84	1	NC-w	Adler	12 Mar 05
1:18:07			Li Gaobo	CHN	4.5.89	4		Cixi	23 Apr 05
1:18:12		Artur	Meleshkevich	BLR	11.4.75	1		Brest	10 Mar 01
1:18:13 wR		Pavol	Blazek	SVK	9.7.58	1		Hildesheim	16 Sep 90
1:18:13			Wang Hao	CHN	16.8.89	1	NG	Jinan	22 Oct 09
		(30)							
1:18:14		Mikhail	Khmelnitskiy	BLR	24.7.69	1	NC	Soligorsk	13 May 00
1:18:14		Noé	Hernández	MEX	15.3.78	4	WCh	Saint-Denis	23 Aug 03
1:18:16		Vladimir	Andreyev	RUS	7.9.66	2	NC	Moskva	19 May 00
1:18:17		Ilya	Markov	RUS	19.6.72	2	NC-w	Adler	12 Mar 05
1:18:18		Yevgeniy	Misyulya	BLR	13.3.64	1		Eisenhüttenstadt	11 May 96
1:18:18		Sergey	Bakulin ¶	RUS	13.11.86	2	NC-w	Adler	23 Feb 08
1:18:20 wR		Andrey	Perlov	RUS	12.12.61	1	NC	Moskva	26 May 90
1:18:20		Denis	Nizhegorodov	RUS	26.7.80	3	NC-w	Adler	4 Mar 01
1:18:22		Robert	Korzeniowski	POL	30.7.68	1		Hildesheim	9 Jul 00
1:18:23		Andrey	Makarov	BLR	2.1.71	2	NC	Soligorsk	13 May 00
		(40)							
1:18:23		Isamu	Fujisawa	JPN	12.10.87	2	NC	Kobe	19 Feb 17
1:18:24		Alex	Schwazer ¶	ITA	26.12.84	1		Lugano	14 Mar 10
1:18:25		Erick	Barrondo	GUA	14.6.91	3		Lugano	18 Mar 12
1:18:27		Daniel	García	MEX	28.10.71	2	WCp	Podebrady	19 Apr 97
1:18:27			Xing Shucai	CHN	4.8.84	5		Cixi	23 Apr 05
1:18:30			Yu Chaohong	CHN	12.12.76	6		Cixi	23 Apr 05
1:18:31			Han Yucheng	CHN	16.12.78	7		Cixi	23 Apr 05
1:18:32			Li Zewen	CHN	5.12.73	4	WCp	Podebrady	19 Apr 97
1:18:33			Liu Yunfeng ¶	CHN	3.8.79	8		Cixi	23 Apr 05
1:18:34		Eder	Sánchez	MEX	21.5.86	3	WCp	Cheboksary	10 May 08
		(50)							

Probable short course: 1:18:33 Mikhail Shchennikov RUs 24.12.67 1 4-N Livorno 10 Jul 93
100th man 1:19:18, 200th 1:20:12, 300th 1:20:54, 400th 1:21:35, 500th 1:22:00

Drugs disqualification

Mark	Wind	Name		Nat	Born	Pos	Meet	Venue	Date
1:16:53		Vladimir	Kanaykin ¶	RUS	21.3.85	(2)	NC	Saransk	8 Jun 08
1:17:30		Alex	Schwazer ¶	ITA	26.12.84	(1)		Lugano	18 Mar 12
1:17:47		Andrey	Ruzavin ¶	RUS	28.3.86	(1)	NC-w	Sochi	18 Feb 12
1:17:52			Morozov ¶			(2)	NC-w	Sochi	18 Feb 12
1:18:25		Andrey	Krivov ¶	RUS	14.11.85	(3)	NC-w	Sochi	18 Feb 12
1:18:28		Pyotr	Trofimov ¶	RUS	28.11.83	1	NC-w	Sochi	23 Feb 13
1:18:29		Stanislav	Yemelyanov ¶	RUS	23.10.90	(4)	NC-w	Sochi	18 Feb 12

30 KILOMETRES WALK

Mark	Wind	Name		Nat	Born	Pos	Meet	Venue	Date
2:01:13+		Vladimir	Kanaykin ¶	RUS	21.3.85	1	in 35k	Adler	19 Feb 06
2:01:44.1t		Maurizio	Damilano	ITA	6.4.57	1		Cuneo	3 Oct 92
2:01:47+			Kanaykin			1	in 35k	Adler	13 Mar 05
2:02:27+			Kanaykin			1	in 35k	Adler	8 Feb 04
2:02:41		Andrey	Perlov	RUS	12.12.61	1	NC-w	Sochi	19 Feb 89
2:02:45		Yevgeniy	Misyulya	BLR	13.3.64	1		Mogilyov	28 Apr 91
2:03:06		Daniel	Bautista	MEX	4.8.52	1		Cherkassy	27 Apr 80
2:03:50+		Vladimir	Parvatkin	RUS	10.10.84	2	in 35k	Adler	19 Feb 06
2:03:56.5t		Thierry	Toutain	FRA	14.2.62	1		Héricourt	24 Mar 91
2:04:00		Aleksandr	Potashov	BLR	12.3.62	1		Adler	14 Feb 93
2:04:24		Valeriy	Spitsyn	RUS	5.12.65	1	NC-w	Sochi	22 Feb 92
2:04:30		Vitaliy	Matsko (10)	RUS	8.6.60	2	NC-w	Sochi	19 Feb 89
2:04:48		Sergey	Bakulin ¶	RUS	13.11.86	1	NC-w	Sochi	19 Feb 18
2:04:49+		Semyon	Lovkin	RUS	14.7.77	1=	in 35k	Adler	1 Mar 03
2:04:49+		Stepan	Yudin	RUS	3.4.80	1=	in 35k	Adler	1 Mar 03
2:04:50+		Sergey	Kirdyapkin ¶	RUS	16.1.80	2	in 35k	Adler	13 Mar 05
2:04:55.5t		Guillaume	Leblanc	CAN	14.4.62	1		Sept-Iles	16 Jun 90
2:05:01		Sergey	Katureyev	RUS	29.9.67	2	NC-w	Sochi	22 Feb 92
2:05:05		Pyotr	Pochenchuk	UKR	26.7.54	2		Cherkassy	27 Apr 80
2:05:06		Nathan	Deakes	AUS	17.8.77	1	NC	Hobart	27 Aug 06
2:05:08+		Denis	Nizhegorodov	RUS	26.7.80	3	in 35k	Adler	19 Feb 06
2:05:09		Mikhail	Shchennikov (20)	RUS	24.12.67	1	NC-w	Adler	11 Feb 96

MEN All-time

Mark	Wind	Name		Nat	Born	Pos	Meet	Venue	Date

35 KILOMETRES WALK

Mark	Wind	Name		Nat	Born	Pos	Meet	Venue	Date
2:21:31		Vladimir	Kanaykin ¶	RUS	21.3.85	1	NC-w	Adler	19 Feb 06
2:23:17			Kanaykin			1	NC-w	Adler	8 Feb 04
2:23:17			Kanaykin			1	NC-w	Adler	13 Mar 05
2:24:25		Semyon	Lovkin	RUS	14.7.77	1	NC-w	Adler	1 Mar 03
2:24:26		Sergey	Bakulin ¶	RUS	10.11.00	1	NC-w	Adler	1 Mar 09
2:24:50		Denis	Nizhegorodov	RUS	26.7.80	2	NC-w	Adler	19 Feb 06
2:24:53			Bakulin			1	NC-w	Sochi	19 Feb 18
2:24:56			Nizhegorodov			2	NC-w	Adler	1 Mar 09
2:25:19		Andrey	Ruzavin ¶	RUS	28.3.86	3	NC-w	Adler	1 Mar 09
2:25:38		Stepan	Yudin	RUS	3.4.80	2	NC-w	Adler	1 Mar 03
2:25:54		Mikhail	Ryzhov	RUS	17.12.91	1	NC-w	Sochi	27 Feb 15
2:25:58		German	Skurygin ¶	RUS	15.9.63	1	NC-w	Adler	20 Feb 98
2:26:16		Alex	Schwazer ¶	ITA	26.12.84	1		Montalto Di Castro	24 Jan 10
2:26:25		Aleksey	Voyevodin ¶ (10)	RUS	9.8.70	2	NC-w	Adler	8 Feb 04
2:26:29		Yuriy	Andronov	RUS	6.11.71	4	NC-w	Adler	1 Mar 09
2:26:33		Ivan	Noskov	RUS	16.7.88	2	NC-w	Sochi	18 Feb 12
2:26:36		Igor	Yerokhin ¶	RUS	4.9.85	1	NC-w	Sochi	26 Feb 11
2:26:46		Oleg	Ishutkin	RUS	22.7.75	1	NC-w	Adler	9 Feb 97
2:27:02		Yevgeniy	Shmalyuk	RUS	14.1.76	1	NC-w	Adler	20 Feb 00
2:27:07		Dmitriy	Dolnikov	RUS	19.11.72	2	NC-w	Adler	20 Feb 98
2:27:07		Sergey	Sharipov	RUS	14.4.92	1	NC-w	Sochi	18 Feb 17
2:27:21		Pavel	Nikolayev	RUS	18.12.77	3	NC-w	Adler	20 Feb 98
DQ: 2:25:42		Sergey	Kirdyapkin ¶	RUS	18.6.80	(1)	NC-w	Sochi	18 Feb 12

50 KILOMETRES WALK

Mark	Wind	Name		Nat	Born	Pos	Meet	Venue	Date
3:32:33 WR		Yohann	Diniz	FRA	1.1.78	1	EC	Zürich	15 Aug 14
3:33:12			Diniz			1	WCh	London	13 Aug 17
3:34:14 WR		Denis	Nizhegorodov	RUS	26.7.80	1	WCp	Cheboksary	11 May 08
3:34:38		Matej	Tóth	SVK	10.2.83	1		Dudince	21 Mar 15
3:35:27.2t WR			Diniz			1		Reims	12 Mar 11
3:35:29			Nizhegorodov			1	NC	Cheboksary	13 Jun 04
3:35:47		Nathan	Deakes	AUS	17.8.77	1	NC	Geelong	2 Dec 06
3:36:03 WR		Robert	Korzeniowski	POL	30.7.68	1	WCh	Saint-Denis	27 Aug 03
3:36:04		Alex	Schwazer ¶	ITA	26.12.84	1	NC	Rosignano Solvay	11 Feb 07
3:36:06			Yu Chaohong	CHN	12.12.76	1	NG	Nanjing	22 Oct 05
3:36:13			Zhao Chengliang	CHN	1.6.84	2	NG	Nanjing	22 Oct 05
3:36:20			Han Yucheng	CHN	16.12.78	1	NC	Nanning	27 Feb 05
3:36:21			Tóth			2	EC	Zürich	15 Aug 14
3:36:39 WR			Korzeniowski			1	EC	München	8 Aug 02
3:36:42		German	Skurygin ¶ (10)	RUS	15.9.63	2	WCh	Saint-Denis	27 Aug 03
3:36:53		Jared	Tallent	AUS	17.10.84	1	OG	London	11 Aug 12
3:37:04			Schwazer			2	WCp	Cheboksary	11 May 08
3:37:09			Schwazer			1	OG	Beijing	22 Aug 08
3:37:16			Si Tianfeng	CHN	17.6.84	2	OG	London	11 Aug 12
3:37:26 WR		Valeriy	Spitsyn	RUS	5.12.65	1	NC	Moskva	21 May 00
3:37:41 WR		Andrey	Perlov	RUS	12.12.61	1	NC	Leningrad	5 Aug 89
3:37:41		Ivan	Noskov ¶	RUS	16.7.88	3	EC	Zürich	15 Aug 14
3:37:46		Andreas	Erm	GER	12.3.76	3	WCh	Saint-Denis	27 Aug 03
3:37:48			Diniz			1	NC	St.Sebastien-sur-Loire	13 Mar 16
3:37:54		Robert	Heffernan	IRL	20.2.78	3	OG	London	11 Aug 12
3:37:56			Heffernan			1	WCh	Moskva	14 Aug 13
3:37:58			Xing Shucai	CHN	4.8.84	2	NC	Nanning	27 Feb 05
3:38:01		Aleksey	Voyevodin ¶	RUS	9.8.70	4	WCh	Saint-Denis	27 Aug 03
3:38:02			Nizhegorodov			1	WCp	La Coruña	14 May 06
3:38:08		Sergey	Kirdyapkin ¶ (20)	RUS	16.1.80	1	WCh	Helsinki	12 Aug 05
3:38:08		Igor	Yerokhin ¶	RUS	4.9.85	1	NC	Saransk	8 Jun 08
3:38:08			Kirdyapkin			1	WCp	Saransk	13 May 12
		(31/21)							
3:38:17 WR		Ronald	Weigel	GDR	8.8.59	1	IM	Potsdam	25 May 86
3:38:29		Vyacheslav	Ivanenko	RUS	3.3.61	1	OG	Seoul	30 Sep 88
3:38:43		Valentí	Massana	ESP	5.7.70	1	NC	Orense	20 Mar 94
3:38:58		Mikhail	Ryzhov ¶	RUS	17.12.91	2	WCh	Moskva	14 Aug 13
3:39:01			Li Jianbo	CHN	14.11.86	4	OG	London	11 Aug 12
3:39:17			Dong Jimin	CHN	10.10.83	4	NC	Nanning	27 Feb 05
3:39:21		Vladimir	Potemin	RUS	15.1.80	2	NC	Moskva	21 May 00
3:39:22		Sergey	Korepanov	KAZ	9.5.64	1	WCp	Mézidon-Canon	2 May 99
3:39:34		Valentin	Kononen	FIN	7.3.69	1		Dudince	25 Mar 00
		(30)							

Mark	Wind	Name		Nat	Born	Pos	Meet	Venue	Date
3:39:45		Hartwig	Gauder	GDR	10.11.54	3	OG	Seoul	30 Sep 88
3:39:47		Tomohiro	Noda	JPN	24.1.96	1	NC	Takahata	28 Oct 18
3:39:54		Jesús Angel	García	ESP	17.10.69	1	WCp	Podebrady	20 Apr 97
3:40:02		Aleksandr	Potashov	BLR	12.3.62	1	NC	Moskva	27 May 90
3:40:07		Andrey	Plotnikov	RUS	12.8.67	2	NC	Moskva	27 May 90
3:40:08		Tomasz	Lipiec ¶	POL	10.5.71	2	WCp	Mézidon-Canon	2 May 99
3:40:12		Oleg	Ishutkin	RUS	22.7.75	2	WCp	Podebrady	20 Apr 97
3:40:12		Yuki	Yamazaki	JPN	16.1.84	1		Wajima	12 Apr 09
3:40:13		Nikolay	Matyukhin	RUS	13.12.68	3	WCp	Mézidon-Canon	2 May 99
3:40:19		Takayuki	Tanii	JPN	14.2.83	2	AsiG	Incheon	1 Oct 14
		(40)							
3:40:20		Hirooki	Arai	JPN	18.5.88	1	NC	Wajima	19 Apr 15
3:40:23			Gadasu Alatan	CHN	27.1.84	3	NG	Nanjing	22 Oct 05
3:40:39		Igor	Hlavan	UKR	25.9.90	4	WCh	Moskva	14 Aug 13
3:40:40		Vladimir	Kanaykin ¶	RUS	21.3.85	1	NC	Saransk	12 Jun 05
3:40:46	WR	José	Marin	ESP	21.1.50	1	NC	Valencia	13 Mar 83
3:40:46		Yuriy	Andronov ¶	RUS	6.11.71	1		Moskva	11 Jun 12
3:40:57.9t		Thierry	Toutain	FRA	14.2.62	1		Héricourt	29 Sep 96
3:41:02		Francisco Javier	Fernández ¶	ESP	6.3.77	1	NC	San Pedro del Pinatar	1 Mar 09
3:41:02			Wang Zhendong	CHN	11.1.91	1		Huangshan	6 Mar 16
3:41:09		Érick	Barrondo	GUA	14.6.91	1		Dudince	23 Mar 13
		(50)	100th man 3:43:57, 200th 3:48:08, 300th 3:51:32, 400th 3:53:49, 500th 3:56:01						
Drugs disqualification									
3:35:59		Sergey	Kirdyapkin ¶	RUS	16.1.80	(1)	OG	London	11 Aug 12
3:36:55		Vladimir	Kanaykin ¶	RUS	21.3.85	(2)	WCp	Cheboksary	11 May 08
3:37:54		Igor	Yerokhin ¶	RUS	4.9.85	(5)	OG	London	11 Aug 12
3:38:46		Sergey	Bakulin ¶	RUS	13.11.86	(1)	NC	Saransk	12 Jun 11

MEN All-time

100 KILOMETRES WALK

Mark	Wind	Name		Nat	Born	Pos	Meet	Venue	Date
8:38.07		Viktor	Ginko	BLR	7.12.65	1		Scanzorosciate	27 Oct 02
8:43:30			Ginko			1		Scanzorosciate	29 Oct 00
8:44:28			Ginko			1		Scanzorosciate	19 Oct 03
8:48:28		Modris	Liepins	LAT	30.8.66	1		Scanzorosciate	28 Oct 01
8:54:35		Aleksey	Rodionov	RUS	5.3.57	1		Scanzorosciate	15 Nov 98
8:55:12		Pascal	Kieffer	FRA	6.5.61	1		Besançon	18 Oct 92

WOMEN'S ALL-TIME WORLD LISTS

100 METRES

Mark	Wind	Name		Nat	Born	Pos	Meet	Venue	Date
10.49 WR	0.0	Florence	Griffith Joyner	USA	21.12.59	1q1	NC/OT	Indianapolis	16 Jul 88
	@ Probably strongly wind-assisted, but recognised as a US and world record								
10.61	1.2		Griffith Joyner			1	NC/OT	Indianapolis	17 Jul 88
10.62	1.0		Griffith Joyner			1q3	OG	Seoul	24 Sep 88
10.64	1.2	Carmelita	Jeter	USA	24.11.79	1		Shanghai	20 Sep 09
10.65A	1.1	Marion	Jones ¶	USA	12.10.75	1	WCp	Johannesburg	12 Sep 98
10.67	-0.1		Jeter			1	WAF	Thessaloníki	13 Sep 09
10.70 (WR)	1.6		Griffith Joyner			1s1	NC/OT	Indianapolis	17 Jul 88
10.70	-0.1		Jones			1	WCh	Sevilla	22 Aug 99
10.70	2.0		Jeter			1	Pre	Eugene	4 Jun 11
10.70	0.6	Shelly-Ann	Fraser-Pryce	JAM	27.12.86	1	NC	Kingston	29 Jun 12
10.70	0.3	Elaine	Thompson	JAM	28.6.92	1	NC	Kingston	1 Jul 16
10.71	0.1		Jones			1		Chengdu	12 May 98
10.71	2.0		Jones			1s2	NC	New Orleans	19 Jun 98
10.71	-0.3		Fraser-Pryce			1	WCh	Moskva	12 Aug 13
10.71	0.5		Thompson			1	OG	Rio de Janeiro	13 Aug 16
10.71	0.8		Thompson			1	NC	Kingston	23 Jun 17
10.72	2.0		Jones			1	NC	New Orleans	20 Jun 98
10.72	0.0		Jones			1	Herc	Monaco	8 Aug 98
10.72	0.0		Jones			1	Athl	Lausanne	25 Aug 98
10.72	-0.3		Fraser-Pryce			1	VD	Bruxelles	6 Sep 13
10.73	2.0	Christine	Arron	FRA	13.9.73	1	EC	Budapest	19 Aug 98
10.73	0.1		Fraser-Pryce			1	WCh	Berlin	17 Aug 09
10.74	1.3	Merlene	Ottey	JAM/SLO	10.5.60	1	GPF	Milano	7 Sep 96
10.74	0.2		Fraser-Pryce			1	DL	Saint-Denis	4 Jul 15
10.74	1.0	English	Gardner	USA	22.4.92	1	NC	Eugene	3 Jul 16
10.75	0.6		Jones			1	GGala	Roma	14 Jul 98
10.75	0.4	Kerron	Stewart	JAM	16.4.84	1	GGala	Roma	10 Jul 09
10.75	0.1		Stewart			2	WCh	Berlin	17 Aug 09
10.75	1.5		Fraser-Pryce			1	OG	London (OS)	4 Aug 12
10.76	WR 1.7	Evelyn	Ashford (10)	USA	15.4.57	1	WK	Zürich	22 Aug 84

Mark	Wind		Name	Nat	Born	Pos	Meet	Venue	Date
10.76	0.9		Jones			1	VD	Bruxelles	22 Aug 97
10.76	0.3		Jones			1q4	WCh	Sevilla	21 Aug 99
10.76	1.1	Veronica	Campbell-Brown	JAM	15.5.82	1	GS	Ostrava	31 May 11
10.76	-0.3		Fraser-Pryce			1	WCh	Beijing	24 Aug 15
		(33 performances by 11 athletes)							
10.77	0.9	Irina	Privalova	RUS	22.11.68	1rA	Athl	Lausanne	6 Jul 94
10.77	0.7	Ivet	Lalova-Collio	BUL	18.5.84	1	ECp-1A	Plovdiv	19 Jun 04
10.78A	1.0	Dawn	Sowell	USA	27.3.66	1	NCAA	Provo	3 Jun 89
10.78	1.8	Torri	Edwards ¶	USA	31.1.77	1s2	OT	Eugene	28 Jun 08
10.78	1.6	Murielle	Ahouré	CIV	23.8.87	1		Montverde	11 Jun 16
10.78	1.0	Tianna	Bartoletta '	USA	30.8.85	2	NC	Eugene	3 Jul 16
10.78	1.0	Tori	Bowie	USA	27.8.90	3	NC	Eugene	3 Jul 16
10.79	0.0		Li Xuemei	CHN	5.1.77	1	NG	Shanghai	18 Oct 97
10.79	-0.1	Inger	Miller	USA	12.6.72	2	WCh	Sevilla	22 Aug 99
		(20)							
10.79	1.1	Blessing	Okagbare	NGR	9.10.88	1	DL	London (OS)	27 Jul 13
10.81	wr 1.7	Marlies	Göhr'	GDR	21.3.58	1	OD	Berlin	8 Jun 83
10.81	-0.3	Dafne	Schippers	NED	15.6.92	2	WCh	Beijing	24 Aug 15
10.82	-1.0	Gail	Devers	USA	19.11.66	1	OG	Barcelona	1 Aug 92
10.82	0.4	Gwen	Torrence	USA	12.6.65	2	GPF	Paris	3 Sep 94
10.82	-0.3	Zhanna	Pintusevich-Block ¶	UKR	6.7.72	1	WCh	Edmonton	6 Aug 01
10.82	-0.7	Sherone	Simpson	JAM	12.8.84	1	NC	Kingston	24 Jun 06
10.82	0.9	Michelle-Lee	Ahye	TTO	10.4.92	1	NC	Port of Spain	24 Jun 17
10.83	1.7	Marita	Koch	GDR	18.2.57	2	OD	Berlin	8 Jun 83
10.83	-1.0	Juliet	Cuthbert	JAM	9.4.64	2	OG	Barcelona	1 Aug 92
		(30)							
10.83	0.1	Ekateríni	Thánou ¶	GRE	1.2.75	2s1	WCh	Sevilla	22 Aug 99
10.84	1.3	Chioma	Ajunwa ¶	NGR	25.12.70	1		Lagos	11 Apr 92
10.84	1.9	Chandra	Sturrup	BAH	12.9.71	1	Athl	Lausanne	5 Jul 05
10.84	1.8	Kelly-Ann	Baptiste ¶	TTO	14.10.86	1		Clermont	6 Jun 10
10.85	2.0	Anelia	Nuneva	BUL	30.6.62	1h1	NC	Sofia	2 Sep 88
10.85	1.0	Muna	Lee	USA	30.10.81	1	OT	Eugene	28 Jun 08
10.85	2.0	Barbara	Pierre	HAI/USA	28.4.87	1s1	NC	Des Moines	21 Jun 13
10.85	2.0	Aleia	Hobbs	USA	24.2.96	1		Baton Rouge	29 Apr 17
10.85	1.5	Marie Josée	Ta Lou	CIV	18.11.88	1	DL	Doha	4 May 18
10.85	0.0	Dina	Asher-Smith	GBR	4.12.95	1	EC	Berlin	7 Aug 18
		(40)							
10.86	0.6	Silke	Gladisch'	GDR	20.6.64	1	NC	Potsdam	20 Aug 87
10.86	1.2	Chryste	Gaines ¶	USA	14.9.70	1	WAF	Monaco	14 Sep 03
10.86	2.0	Marshevet	Hooker/Myers	USA	25.9.84	2	Pre	Eugene	4 Jun 11
10.87	1.8	Octavious	Freeman	USA	20.4.92	2	NC	Des Moines	21 Jun 13
10.88	0.4	Lauryn	Williams	USA	11.9.83	2	WK	Zürich	19 Aug 05
10.89	1.8	Katrin	Krabbe ¶	GDR	22.11.69	1		Berlin	20 Jul 88
10.89	0.0		Liu Xiaomei	CHN	11.1.72	2	NG	Shanghai	18 Oct 97
10.89	1.5	Allyson	Felix	USA	18.11.85	5	OG	London (OS)	4 Aug 12
10.90	1.4	Glory	Alozie	NGR/ESP	30.12.77	1		La Laguna	5 Jun 99
10.90	1.8	Shalonda	Solomon	USA	19.12.85	2		Clermont	5 Jun 10
		(50)	100th women 10.99, 200th 11.09, 300th 11.15, 400th 11.20, 500th 11.24						

Doubtful wind reading

Mark	Wind		Name	Nat	Born	Pos	Meet	Venue	Date
10.83	0.0	Sheila	Echols	USA	2.10.64	1q2	NC/OT	Indianapolis	16 Jul 88
10.86	0.0	Diane	Williams	USA	14.12.60	2q1	NC/OT	Indianapolis	16 Jul 88

Probably semi-automatic timing: 10.87 1.9 LyudmilaKondratyeva RUS 14.4.58 1 Leningrad 3 Jun 80
Low altitude best: 10.91 1.6 Sowell 1 NC Houston 16 Jun 89

Wind-assisted performances to 10.74 and performers to 10.88

Mark	Wind		Name	Nat	Born	Pos	Meet	Venue	Date
10.54	3.0		Griffith Joyner			1	OG	Seoul	25 Sep 88
10.60	3.2		Griffith Joyner			1h1	NC/OT	Indianapolis	16 Jul 88
10.68	2.2		Jones			1	DNG	Stockholm	1 Aug 00
10.70	2.6		Griffith Joyner			1s2	OG	Seoul	25 Sep 88
10.71	2.2		Fraser-Pryce			1	Pre	Eugene	1 Jun 13
10.71	2.4		Thompson			1		Kingston	7 May 16
10.72	3.0		Jeter			1s1	NC	Eugene	26 Jun 09
10.72	3.2	Tori	Bowie	USA	27.8.90	1s2	NC	Eugene	26 Jun 15
10.72	4.5	Tawanna	Meadows	USA	4.8.86	1		Lubbock	6 May 17
10.72	2.7	Blessing	Okagbare	NGR	9.10.88	1	TexasR	Austin	31 Mar 18
10.74	2.7		Jeter			1	NC	Eugene	24 Jun 11
10.74	3.1		Bowie			1s1	NC	Eugene	3 Jul 16
10.74	2.5		Gardner			1s3	NC	Eugene	3 Jul 16
10.76	3.4	Marshevet	Hooker/Myers	USA	25.9.84	1q1	NC/OT	Eugene	27 Jun 08
10.77	2.3	Gail	Devers	USA	19.11.66	1	Jen	San José	28 May 94
10.77	2.3	Ekateríni	Thánou ¶	GRE	1.2.75	1		Rethymno	28 May 99
10.78	5.0	Gwen	Torrence	USA	12.6.65	1q3	NC/OT	Indianapolis	16 Jul 88

Mark	Wind	Name		Nat	Born	Pos	Meet	Venue	Date
10.78	3.3	Muna	Lee'	USA	30.10.81	2	NC	Eugene	26 Jun 09
10.79	3.3	Marlies	Göhr'	GDR	21.3.58	1	NC	Cottbus	16 Jul 80
10.80	2.9	Pam	Marshall	USA	16.8.60	1	NC	Eugene	20 Jun 86
10.80	2.8	Heike	Drechsler'	GDR	16.12.64	1	Bisl	Oslo	5 Jul 86
10.81	3.6	Jenna	Prandini	USA	20.11.92	1h4	NC	Eugene	2 Jul 16
10.82	2.2	Silke	Gladisch/Möller	GDR	20.6.64	1s1	WCh	Roma	30 Aug 87
10.83	3.9	Sheila	Echols	USA	2.10.84	1h2	NC/OT	Indianapolis	16 Jul 88
10.83	4.5	Candyce	McGrone	USA	24.3.89	2		Lubbock	6 May 17
10.84	2.9	Alice	Brown	USA	20.9.60	2	NC	Eugene	20 Jun 86
10.86	3.4	Lauryn	Williams	USA	11.9.83	2q1	NC/OT	Eugene	27 Jun 08
10.86	3.2	Jasmine	Todd	USA	23.12.93	3s2	NC	Eugene	26 Jun 15
10.87	3.0	Me'Lisa	Barber	USA	4.10.80	1s1	NC	Carson	25 Jun 05
10.88	5.9	Alexandria	Anderson	USA	28.1.87	1		Austin	14 Apr 12
Hand timing: 10.6 0.1 Zhanna Pintusevich ¶				UKR	6.7.72	1		Kiev	12 Jun 97
Drugs disqualification									
10.75	-0.4		Jones			(1)	OG	Sydney	23 Sep 00
10.78	0.1		Jones			(1)	ISTAF	Berlin	1 Sep 00
10.83	1.6	Kelly-Ann	Baptiste ¶	TTO	14.10.86	1	NC	Port of Spain	22 Jun 13
10.85	0.9	Kelli	White ¶	USA	1.4.77	(1)	WCh	Saint-Denis	24 Aug 03
10.79w	2.3	Kelli	White ¶	USA	1.4.77	(1)		Carson	1 Jun 03

200 METRES

Mark	Wind	Name		Nat	Born	Pos	Meet	Venue	Date
21.34wr	1.3	Florence	Griffith Joyner	USA	21.12.59	1	OG	Seoul	29 Sep 88
21.56wr	1.7		Griffith Joyner			1s1	OG	Seoul	29 Sep 88
21.62A	-0.6	Marion	Jones ¶	USA	12.10.75	1	WCp	Johannesburg	11 Sep 98
21.63	0.2	Dafne	Schippers	NED	15.6.92	1	WCh	Beijing	28 Aug 15
21.64	0.8	Merlene	Ottey	JAM	10.5.60	1	VD	Bruxelles	13 Sep 91
21.66	-1.0		Ottey			1	WK	Zürich	15 Aug 90
21.66	0.2	Elaine	Thompson	JAM	28.6.92	2	WCh	Beijing	28 Aug 15
21.69	1.0	Allyson	Felix	USA	18.11.85	1	NC/OT	Eugene	30 Jun 12
21.71wr	0.7	Marita	Koch	GDR	18.2.57	1	v CAN	Karl-Marx-Stadt	10 Jun 79
21.71wr	0.3		Koch			1	OD	Potsdam	21 Jul 84
21.71wr	1.2	Heike	Drechsler'	GDR	16.12.64	1	NC	Jena	29 Jun 86
21.71wr	-0.8		Drechsler			1	EC	Stuttgart	29 Aug 86
21.72	1.3	Grace	Jackson	JAM	14.6.61	2	OG	Seoul	29 Sep 88
21.72	-0.1	Gwen	Torrence (10)	USA	12.6.65	1s2	OG	Barcelona	5 Aug 92
21.74	0.4	Marlies	Göhr'	GDR	21.3.58	1	NC	Erfurt	3 Jun 84
21.74	1.2	Silke	Gladisch'	GDR	20.6.64	1	WCh	Roma	3 Sep 87
21.74	0.6	Veronica	Campbell-Brown	JAM	15.5.82	1	OG	Beijing	21 Aug 08
21.75	-0.1	Juliet	Cuthbert	JAM	9.4.64	2s2	OG	Barcelona	5 Aug 92
21.76	0.3		Koch			1	NC	Dresden	3 Jul 82
21.76	0.7		Griffith Joyner			1q1	OG	Seoul	28 Sep 88
21.76	-0.8		Jones			1	WK	Zürich	13 Aug 97
21.77	-0.1		Griffith Joyner			1q2	NC/OT	Indianapolis	22 Jul 88
21.77	1.0		Ottey			1	Herc	Monaco	7 Aug 93
21.77	-0.3		Torrence			1	ASV	Köln	18 Aug 95
21.77	0.6	Inger	Miller	USA	12.6.72	1	WCh	Sevilla	27 Aug 99
21.77	1.5	Tori	Bowie	USA	27.8.90	1	Pre	Eugene	27 May 17
21.78	-1.3		Koch			1	NC	Leipzig	11 Aug 85
21.78	-0.1		Thompson			1	OG	Rio de Janeiro	17 Aug 16
21.79	1.7		Gladisch			1	NC	Potsdam	22 Aug 87
21.80	-1.1		Ottey			1	Nik	Nice	10 Jul 90
21.80	0.4		Jones			1	GWG	Uniondale, NY	20 Jul 98
		(31/16)							
21.81	-0.1	Valerie	Brisco-Hooks	USA	6.7.60	1	OG	Los Angeles	9 Aug 84
21.83	-0.2	Evelyn	Ashford	USA	15.4.57	1	WCp	Montreal	24 Aug 79
21.85	0.3	Bärbel	Wöckel'	GDR	21.3.55	2	OD	Potsdam	21 Jul 84
21.87	0.0	Irina	Privalova	RUS	22.11.68	2	Herc	Monaco	25 Jul 95
		(20)							
21.88	0.1	Shaunae	Miller-Uibo	BAH	15.4.94	1	WK-DLF	Zürich	24 Aug 17
21.89	0.2	Dina	Asher-Smith	GBR	4.12.95	1	EC	Berlin	11 Aug 18
21.93	1.3	Pam	Marshall	USA	16.8.60	2	NC/OT	Indianapolis	23 Jul 88
21.95	0.3	Katrin	Krabbe ¶	GDR	22.11.69	1	EC	Split	30 Aug 90
21.97	1.9	Jarmila	Kratochvílová	CZE	26.1.51	1	PTS	Bratislava	6 Jun 81
21.99	0.9	Chandra	Cheeseborough	USA	10.1.59	2	NC	Indianapolis	19 Jun 83
21.99	1.1	Marie-José	Pérec	FRA	9.5.68	1	BNP	Villeneuve d'Ascq	2 Jul 93
21.99	1.1	Kerron	Stewart	JAM	16.4.84	2	NC	Kingston	29 Jun 08
22.00	1.3	Sherone	Simpson	JAM	12.8.84	1	NC	Kingston	25 Jun 06
22.01	-0.5	Anelia	Nuneva'	BUL	30.6.62	1	NC	Sofia	16 Aug 87
		(30)							

WOMEN All-time

Mark	Wind	Name		Nat	Born	Pos	Meet	Venue	Date
22.01	0.0		Li Xuemei	CHN	5.1.77	1	NG	Shanghai	22 Oct 97
22.01	0.6	Muna	Lee	USA	30.10.81	4	OG	Beijing	21 Aug 08
22.01	0.2	Candyce	McGrone	USA	24.3.89	4	WCh	Beijing	28 Aug 15
22.02	1.1	Kyra	Jefferson	USA	23.9.94	1	NCAA	Eugene	10 Jun 17
22.04A	0.7	Dawn	Sowell	USA	27.3.66	1	NCAA	Provo	2 Jun 89
22.04	0.5	Blessing	Okagbare	NGR	9.10.88	1		Abilene	24 Mar 18
22.05	1.1	Shericka	Jackson	JAM	16.7.94	1	DL	Paris (c)	30 Jun 18
22.06A	0.7	Evette	de Klerk'	RSA	21.8.65	1		Pietersburg	8 Apr 89
22.07	-0.1	Mary	Onyali	NGR	3.2.68	1	WK	Zürich	14 Aug 96
22.08	0.8	Marie Josée (40)	Ta Lou	CIV	18.11.88	2	WCh	London (OS)	11 Aug 17
22.09	-0.3	Sanya	Richards-Ross	USA	26.2.85	1	DL	New York	9 Jun 12
22.09	-0.2	Shelly-Ann	Fraser-Pryce	JAM	27.12.86	2	OG	London (OS)	8 Aug 12
22.09	1.5	Deajah	Stevens	USA	19.5.95	1	Pac 12	Eugene	14 May 17
22.10	-0.1	Kathy	Cook'	GBR	3.5.60	4	OG	Los Angeles	9 Aug 84
22.11	1.0	Carmelita	Jeter	USA	24.11.79	2	NC/OT	Eugene	30 Jun 12
22.11	0.1	Myriam	Soumaré	FRA	29.10.86	2	VD	Bruxelles	5 Sep 14
22.13	1.2	Ewa	Kasprzyk	POL	7.9.57	2	GWG	Moskva	8 Jul 86
22.14	-0.6	Carlette	Guidry	USA	4.9.68	1	NC	Atlanta	23 Jun 96
22.15	1.0	Shalonda	Solomon	USA	19.12.85	1	NC	Eugene	26 Jun 11
22.16	0.9	Jenna (50)	Prandini	USA	20.11.92	1	DL	London (OS)	22 Jul 18

100th woman 22.32, 200th 22.53, 300th 22.68, 400th 22.78, 500th 22.86

Wind-assisted			*Performers listed to 22.15*						
21.80	3.2	Kimberlyn	Duncan	USA	2.8.91	1	NC	Des Moines	23 Jun 13
21.82	3.1	Irina	Privalova	RUS	22.11.68	1	Athl	Lausanne	6 Jul 94
21.91	2.8	Muna	Lee	USA	30.10.81	1		Fort-de-France	10 May 08
21.97	5.3	Shania	Collins	USA	14.11.96	1h5	NCAA-E	Tampa	25 May 18
22.01	2.9	Michelle-Lee	Ahye	TTO	10.4.92	1		San Marcos	25 Apr 15
22.06	3.8	Jeneba	Tarmoh	USA	27.9.89	1	NC	Sacramento	29 Jun 14
22.06	2.1	Lynna	Irby	USA	6.10.99	1h6	NCAA-E	Tampa	26 May 18
Hand timing									
21.9	-0.1	Svetlana	Goncharenko	RUS	28.5.71	1		Rostov-na-Donu	31 May 98
21.6w	2.5	Pam	Marshall	USA	16.8.60	1	NC	San José	26 Jun 87
Drugs disqualification									
22.05	-0.3	Kelli	White ¶	USA	1.4.77	1	WCh	Saint-Denis	28 Aug 03

300 METRES

Times in 300m races only

35.30A	Ana Gabriela	Guevara	MEX	4.3.77	1		Ciudad de México	3 May 03
35.46	Kathy	Cook'	GBR	3.5.60	1	Nike	London (CP)	18 Aug 84
35.46	Chandra	Cheeseborough	USA	10.1.59	2	Nike	London (CP)	18 Aug 84
Indoors								
35.45	Irina	Privalova	RUS	22.11.68	1		Moskva	17 Jan 93
35.45	Shaunae	Miller-Uibo	BAH	15.4.94	1	Millrose	New York (Arm)	3 Feb 18
35.48 #	Svetlana	Goncharenko	RUS	28.5.71	1		Tampere	4 Feb 98

400 METRES

Mark		Name		Nat	Born	Pos	Meet	Venue	Date
47.60 WR		Marita	Koch	GDR	18.2.57	1	WCp	Canberra	6 Oct 85
47.99 WR		Jarmila	Kratochvílová	CZE	26.1.51	1	WCh	Helsinki	10 Aug 83
48.16 WR			Koch			1	EC	Athína	8 Sep 82
48.16			Koch			1	Drz	Praha	16 Aug 84
48.22			Koch			1	EC	Stuttgart	28 Aug 86
48.25		Marie-José	Pérec	FRA	9.5.68	1	OG	Atlanta	29 Jul 96
48.26			Koch			1	GO	Dresden	27 Jul 84
48.27		Olga	Vladykina'	UKR	30.6.63	2	WCp	Canberra	6 Oct 85
48.45			Kratochvílová			1	NC	Praha	23 Jul 83
48.59		Tatána	Kocembová'	CZE	2.5.62	2	WCh	Helsinki	10 Aug 83
48.60 WR			Koch			1	ECp	Torino	4 Aug 79
48.60			Vladykina			1	ECp	Moskva	17 Aug 85
48.61			Kratochvílová			1	WCp	Roma	6 Sep 81
48.63		Cathy	Freeman	AUS	16.2.73	2	OG	Atlanta	29 Jul 96
48.65			Bryzgina'			1	OG	Seoul	26 Sep 88
48.70		Sanya	Richards	USA	26.2.85	1	WCp	Athína	16 Sep 06
48.73			Kocembová			2	Drz	Praha	16 Aug 84
48.77			Koch			1	v USA	Karl-Marx-Stadt	9 Jul 82
48.82			Kratochvílová			1	Ros	Praha	23 Jun 83
48.83		Valerie	Brisco	USA	6.7.60	1	OG	Los Angeles	6 Aug 84
48.83			Pérec			1	OG	Barcelona	5 Aug 92
48.83			Richards			1	VD	Bruxelles	4 Sep 09
48.85			Kratochvílová			2	EC	Athína	8 Sep 82
48.86			Kratochvílová			1	WK	Zürich	18 Aug 82

Mark	Wind	Name		Nat	Born	Pos	Meet	Venue	Date
48.86			Koch			1	NC	Erfurt	2 Jun 84
48.87			Koch			1	VD	Bruxelles	27 Aug 82
48.88			Koch			1	OG	Moskva	28 Jul 80
48.89	WR		Koch			1		Potsdam	29 Jul 79
48.89			Koch			1		Berlin	15 Jul 84
48.89		Ana Gabriela	Guevara	MEX	4.3.77	1	WCh	Saint-Denis	27 Aug 03
		(30/9)							
48.97		Shaunae (10)	Miller-Uibo	BAH	15.4.94	1	Herc	Monaco	20 Jul 18
49.05		Chandra	Cheeseborough	USA	10.1.59	2	OG	Los Angeles	6 Aug 84
49.07		Tonique	Williams-Darling	BAH	17.1.76	1	ISTAF	Berlin	12 Sep 04
49.08		Salwa Eid	Naser	BRN	23.5.98	2	Herc	Monaco	20 Jul 18
49.10		Falilat	Ogunkoya	NGR	12.5.68	3	OG	Atlanta	29 Jul 96
49.11		Olga	Nazarova ¶	RUS	1.6.65	1s1	OG	Seoul	25 Sep 88
49.16		Antonina	Krivoshapka ¶	RUS	21.7.87	1	NC	Cheboksary	5 Jul 12
49.19		Mariya	Pinigina'	UKR	9.2.58	3	WCh	Helsinki	10 Aug 83
49.24		Sabine	Busch	GDR	21.11.62	2	NC	Erfurt	2 Jun 84
49.26		Allyson	Felix	USA	18.11.85	1	WCh	Beijing	27 Aug 15
49.28	WR	Irena	Szewinska'	POL	24.5.46	1	OG	Montreal	29 Jul 76
		(20)							
49.28		Pauline	Davis-Thompson	BAH	9.7.66	4	OG	Atlanta	29 Jul 96
49.28		Yuliya	Gushchina	RUS	4.3.83	2	NC	Cheboksary	5 Jul 12
49.29		Charity	Opara ¶	NGR	20.5.72	1	GGala	Roma	14 Jul 98
49.30		Petra	Müller'	GDR	18.7.65	1		Jena	3 Jun 88
49.30		Lorraine	Fenton'	JAM	8.9.73	2	Herc	Monaco	19 Jul 02
49.32		Shericka	Williams	JAM	17.9.85	2	WCh	Berlin	18 Aug 09
49.33		Amantle	Montsho ¶	BOT	4.7.83	1	Herc	Monaco	19 Jul 13
49.40		Jearl	Miles-Clark	USA	4.9.66	1	NC	Indianapolis	14 Jun 97
49.41		Christine	Ohuruogu	GBR	17.5.84	1	WCh	Moskva	12 Aug 13
49.42		Grit	Breuer ¶	GER	16.2.72	2	WCh	Tokyo	27 Aug 91
		(30)							
49.43		Kathy	Cook'	GBR	3.5.60	3	OG	Los Angeles	6 Aug 84
49.43A		Fatima	Yusuf	NGR	2.5.71	1	AfG	Harare	15 Sep 95
49.47		Aelita	Yurchenko	UKR	1.1.65	2	Kuts	Moskva	4 Sep 88
49.48		Francena	McCorory	USA	20.10.88	1	NC	Sacramento	28 Jun 14
49.49		Olga	Zaytseva	RUS	10.11.84	1	NCp	Tula	16 Jul 06
49.52		Shakima	Wimbley	USA	23.4.95	1	NC	Des Moines	23 Jun 18
49.53		Vanya	Stambolova ¶	BUL	28.11.83	1	GP	Rieti	27 Aug 06
49.56		Bärbel	Wöckel'	GDR	21.3.55	1		Erfurt	30 May 82
49.56		Monique	Hennagan	USA	26.5.76	1	NC/OT	Sacramento	17 Jul 04
49.57		Grace	Jackson	JAM	14.6.61	1	Nik	Nice	10 Jul 88
		(40)							
49.58		Dagmar	Rübsam'	GDR	3.6.62	3	NC	Erfurt	2 Jun 84
49.59		Marion	Jones ¶	USA	12.10.75	1r6	MSR	Walnut	16 Apr 00
49.59		Katharine	Merry	GBR	21.9.74	1	GP	Athína	11 Jun 01
49.61		Ana Fidelia	Quirot	CUB	23.3.63	1	PAm	La Habana	5 Aug 91
49.63		Novlene	Williams-Mills	JAM	26.4.82	1		Shanghai	23 Sep 06
49.64		Gwen	Torrence	USA	12.6.65	2	Nik	Nice	15 Jul 92
49.64		Ximena	Restrepo	COL	10.3.69	3	OG	Barcelona	5 Aug 92
49.64		Deedee	Trotter	USA	8.12.82	1	NC	Indianapolis	23 Jun 07
49.64		Debbie	Dunn ¶	USA	26.3.78	1	NC	Des Moines	26 Jun 10
		(50)							

Hand timing 100th woman 50.11, 200th 50.71, 300th 51.08, 400th 51.28, 500th 51.48

Hand timing

48.9		Olga	Nazarova ¶	RUS	1.6.65	1	NP	Vladivostok	13 Sep 88
49.2A		Ana Fidelia	Quirot	CUB	23.3.63	1	AmCp	Bogotá	13 Aug 89

Drugs disqualification

49.35		Anastasiya	Kapachinskaya ¶	RUS	21.11.79	(1)	NC	Cheboksary	22 Jul 11

600 METRES

1:22.63		Ana Fidelia	Quirot	CUB	23.3.63	1		Guadalajara, ESP	25 Jul 97
1:22.87		Maria Lurdes	Mutola	MOZ	27.10.72	1		Liège (NX)	27 Aug 02
1:23.35		Pamela	Jelimo	KEN	5.12.89	1		Liège (NX)	5 Jul 12
1:23.5A		Doina	Melinte	ROU	27.12.56	1		Poiana Brasov	27 Jul 86

800 METRES

1:53.28	WR	Jarmila	Kratochvílová	CZE	26.1.51	1		München	26 Jul 83
1:53.43	WR	Nadezhda	Olizarenko'	UKR	28.11.53	1	OG	Moskva	27 Jul 80
1:54.01		Pamela	Jelimo	KEN	5.12.89	1	WK	Zürich	29 Aug 08
1:54.25		Caster	Semenya	RSA	7.1.91	1	DL	Paris (C)	30 Jun 18
1:54.44		Ana Fidelia	Quirot	CUB	23.3.63	1	WCp	Barcelona	9 Sep 89
1:54.60			Semenya			1	Herc	Monaco	20 Jul 18
1:54.68			Kratochvílová			1	WCh	Helsinki	9 Aug 83

WOMEN All-time

Mark	Wind	Name		Nat	Born	Pos	Meet	Venue	Date
1:54.77			Semenya			1	C.Cup	Ostrava	9 Sep 18
1:54.81		Olga	Mineyeva	RUS	1.9.52	2	OG	Moskva	27 Jul 80
1:54.82			Quirot			1	ASV	Köln	24 Aug 97
1:54.85	WR		Olizarenko			1	Prav	Moskva	12 Jun 80
1:54.87			Jelimo			1	OG	Beijing	18 Aug 08
1:54.94	WR	Tatyana	Kazankina ¶	RUS	17.12.51	1	OG	Montreal	26 Jul 76
1:54.97			Jelimo			1	Gaz	Saint-Denis	18 Jul 08
1:54.99			Jelimo			1	ISTAF	Berlin	1 Jun 08
1:55.04			Kratochvílová			1	OsloG	Oslo	23 Aug 83
1:55.05		Doina	Melinte	ROU	27.12.56	1	NC	Bucuresti	1 Aug 82
1:55.1 '			Mineyeva			1	Znam	Moskva	6 Jul 80
1:55.16			Jelimo			1	VD	Bruxelles	5 Sep 08
1:55.16		Caster	Semenya	RSA	7.1.91	1	WCh	London (OS)	13 Aug 17
1:55.19		Maria Lurdes	Mutola	MOZ	27.10.72	1	WK	Zürich	17 Aug 94
1:55.19		Jolanda	Ceplak ¶ (10)	SLO	12.9.76	1rA	NA	Heusden	20 Jul 02
1:55.26		Sigrun	Wodars/Grau	GDR	7.11.65	1	WCh	Roma	31 Aug 87
1:55.27			Semenya			1	Herc	Monaco	21 Jul 17
1:55.27			Semenya			1	WK	Zürich	30 Aug 18
1:55.28			Semenya	RSA	7.1.91	1	OG	Rio de Janeiro	20 Aug 16
1:55.29			Mutola			2	ASV	Köln	24 Aug 97
1:55.32		Christine	Wachtel	GDR	6.1.65	2	WCh	Roma	31 Aug 87
1:55.33			Semenya			1	Herc	Monaco	15 Jul 16
1:55.41			Mineyeva			1	EC	Athína	8 Sep 82
1:55.41			Jelimo			1	Bisl	Oslo	6 Jun 08
		(31/12)							
1:55.42		Nikolina	Shtereva	BUL	25.1.55	2	OG	Montreal	26 Jul 76
1:55.46		Tatyana	Providokhina	RUS	26.3.53	3	OG	Moskva	27 Jul 80
1:55.47		Francine	Niyonsaba	BDI	5.5.93	2	Herc	Monaco	21 Jul 17
1:55.54		Ellen	van Langen	NED	9.2.66	1	OG	Barcelona	3 Aug 92
1:55.54			Liu Dong	CHN	24.12.73	1	NG	Beijing	9 Sep 93
1:55.56		Lyubov	Gurina	RUS	6.8.57	3	WCh	Roma	31 Aug 87
1:55.60		Elfi	Zinn	GDR	24.8.53	3	OG	Montreal	26 Jul 76
1:55.61		Ajee'	Wilson	USA	8.5.94	3	Herc	Monaco	21 Jul 17
		(20)							
1:55.68		Ella	Kovacs	ROU	11.12.64	1	RomIC	Bucuresti	2 Jun 85
1:55.69		Irina	Podyalovskaya	RUS	19.10.59	1	Izv	Kyiv	22 Jun 84
1:55.74		Anita	Weiss'	GDR	16.7.55	4	OG	Montreal	26 Jul 76
1:55.87		Svetlana	Masterkova	RUS	17.1.68	1	Kuts	Moskva	18 Jun 99
1:55.96		Lyudmila	Veselkova	RUS	25.10.50	2	EC	Athína	8 Sep 82
1:55.96		Yekaterina	Podkopayeva'	RUS	11.6.52	1		Leningrad	27 Jul 83
1:55.99		Liliya	Nurutdinova ¶	RUS	15.12.63	2	OG	Barcelona	3 Aug 92
1:56.00		Tatyana	Andrianova	RUS	10.12.79	1	NC	Kazan	18 Jul 08
1:56.0	WR	Valentina	Gerasimova	KAZ	15.5.48	1	NC	Kyiv	12 Jun 76
1:56.0		Inna	Yevseyeva	UKR	14.8.64	1		Kyiv	25 Jun 88
		(30)							
1:56.04		Janeth	Jepkosgei	KEN	13.12.83	1	WCh	Osaka	28 Aug 07
1:56.09		Zulia	Calatayud	CUB	9.11.79	1	Herc	Monaco	19 Jul 02
1:56.1		Ravilya	Agletdinova'	BLR	10.2.60	2	Kuts	Podolsk	21 Aug 82
1:56.15		Natoya	Goule	JAM	30.3.91	3	Herc	Monaco	20 Jul 18
1:56.2 '		Totka	Petrova ¶	BUL	17.12.56	1		Paris (C)	6 Jul 79
1:56.2		Tatyana	Mishkel	UKR	10.6.52	3	Kuts	Podolsk	21 Aug 82
1:56.21		Martina	Kämpfert'	GDR	11.11.59	4	OG	Moskva	27 Jul 80
1:56.21		Zamira	Zaytseva	UZB	16.2.53	2		Leningrad	27 Jul 83
1:56.21		Kelly	Holmes	GBR	19.4.70	2	GPF	Monaco	9 Sep 95
1:56.24			Qu Yunxia	CHN	8.12.72	2	NG	Beijing	9 Sep 93
		(40)							
1:56.40		Jearl	Miles-Clark	USA	4.9.66	3	WK	Zürich	11 Aug 99
1:56.42		Paula	Ivan	ROU	20.7.63	1	Balk	Ankara	16 Jul 88
1:56.43		Hasna	Benhassi	MAR	1.6.78	2	OG	Athína	23 Aug 04
1:56.44		Svetlana	Styrkina	RUS	1.1.49	5	OG	Montreal	26 Jul 76
1:56.51		Slobodanka	Colovic	YUG	10.1.65	1		Beograd	17 Jun 87
1:56.53		Patricia	Djaté	FRA	3.1.71	3	GPF	Monaco	9 Sep 95
1:56.56		Ludmila	Formanová	CZE	2.1.74	4	WK	Zürich	11 Aug 99
1:56.57		Zoya	Rigel	RUS	15.10.52	3	EC	Praha	31 Aug 78
1:56.59		Natalya	Khrushchelyova	RUS	30.5.73	2	NC	Tula	31 Jul 04
1:56.60		Natalya	Tsyganova	RUS	7.2.71	1	NC	Tula	25 Jul 00
1:56.6		Tamara	Sorokina'	RUS	15.8.50	5	Kuts	Podolsk	21 Aug 82
		(51)		100th woman 1:57.38, 200th 1:58.39, 300th 1:59.17, 400th 1:59.3, 500th 2:00.08					

Indoors

| 1:55.85 | | Stephanie | Graf | AUT | 26.4.73 | 2 | EI | Wien | 3 Mar 02 |

Mark	Wind		Name	Nat	Born	Pos	Meet	Venue	Date
Drugs disqualification									
1:54.85		Yelena	Soboleva ¶	RUS	3.10.82	(1)	NC	Kazan	18 Jul 08
1:55.87		Mariya	Savinova ¶	RUS	13.8.85	1	WCh	Daegu	4 Sep 11

1000 METRES

Mark	Wind		Name	Nat	Born	Pos	Meet	Venue	Date
2:28.98	WR	Svetlana	Masterkova	RUS	17.1.68	1	VD	Bruxelles	23 Aug 96
2:29.34	WR	Maria Lurdes	Mutola	MOZ	27.10.72	1	VD	Bruxelles	25 Aug 95
2:30.6	WR	Tatyana	Providokhina	RUS	26.3.53	1		Podolsk	20 Aug 78
2:30.67	WR	Christine	Wachtel	GDR	6.1.65	1	ISTAF	Berlin	17 Aug 90
2:30.70		Caster	Semenya	RSA	7.1.91	1	ISTAF	Berlin	2 Sep 18
2:30.85		Martina	Kämpfert'	GDR	11.11.59	1		Berlin	9 Jul 80
2:31.50		Natalya	Artyomova ¶	RUS	5.1.63	1	ISTAF	Berlin	10 Sep 91
2:31.5	A	Maricica	Puica	ROU	29.7.50	1		Poiana Brasov	1 Jun 86
2:31.51		Sandra	Gasser ¶	SUI	27.7.62	1		Jerez de la Frontera	13 Sep 89
2:31.6	'	Beate	Liebich	GDR	21.2.58	2		Berlin	9 Jul 80

1500 METRES

Mark	Wind		Name	Nat	Born	Pos	Meet	Venue	Date
3:50.07	WR	Genzebe	Dibaba	ETH	8.2.91	1	Herc	Monaco	17 Jul 15
3:50.46	WR		Qu Yunxia	CHN	8.12.72	1	NG	Beijing	11 Sep 93
3:50.98			Jiang Bo	CHN	13.3.77	1	NG	Shanghai	18 Oct 97
3:51.34			Lang Yinglai	CHN	22.8.79	2	NG	Shanghai	18 Oct 97
3:51.92			Wang Junxia	CHN	9.1.73	2	NG	Beijing	11 Sep 93
3:52.47	WR	Tatyana	Kazankina ¶	RUS	17.12.51	1	WK	Zürich	13 Aug 80
3:53.91			Yin Lili ¶	CHN	11.11.79	3	NG	Shanghai	18 Oct 97
3:53.96		Paula	Ivan'	ROU	20.7.63	1	OG	Seoul	1 Oct 88
3:53.97			Lan Lixin	CHN	14.2.79	4	NG	Shanghai	18 Oct 97
3:54.11			Dibaba			1		Barcelona	8 Jul 15
3:54.23		Olga	Dvirna (10)	RUS	11.2.53	1	NC	Kyiv	27 Jul 82
3:54.52			Zhang Ling	CHN	13.4.80	5	NG	Shanghai	18 Oct 97
3:55.0	' WR		Kazankina ¶			1	Znam	Moskva	6 Jul 80
3:55.01			Lan Lixin			1h2	NG	Shanghai	17 Oct 97
3:55.07			Dong Yanmei	CHN	16.2.77	6	NG	Shanghai	18 Oct 97
3:55.22		Laura	Muir	GBR	9.5.93	1	DL	Saint-Denis	27 Aug 16
3:55.30		Hassiba	Boulmerka	ALG	10.7.68	1	OG	Barcelona	8 Aug 92
3:55.33		Süreyya	Ayhan ¶	TUR	6.9.78	1	VD	Bruxelles	5 Sep 03
3:55.38			Qu Yunxia			2h2	NG	Shanghai	17 Oct 97
3:55.47			Zhang Ling			3h2	NG	Shanghai	17 Oct 97
3:55.60			Ayhan			1	WK	Zürich	15 Aug 03
3:55.68		Yuliya	Chizhenko ¶	RUS	30.8.79	1	Gaz	Saint-Denis	8 Jul 06
3:55.82			Dong Yanmei			4h2	NG	Shanghai	17 Oct 97
3:56.0	WR		Kazankina ¶			1		Podolsk	28 Jun 76
3:56.05		Sifan	Hassan	ETH/NED	.93	2	Herc	Monaco	17 Jul 15
3:56.14		Zamira	Zaytseva	UZB	16.2.53	2	NC	Kyiv	27 Jul 82
3:56.14			Hassan			1	FBK	Hengelo	11 Jun 17
3:56.18		Maryam	Jamal	BRN	16.9.84	1	GP	Rieti	27 Aug 06
3:56.22			Ivan			1	WK	Zürich	17 Aug 88
3:56.22			Hassan			1	GGala	Roma	8 Jun 17
3:56.29		Shannon	Rowbury	USA	19.9.84	3	Herc	Monaco	17 Jul 15
		(31/20)							
3:56.31			Liu Dong	CHN	24.12.73	5h2	NG	Shanghai	17 Oct 97
3:56.41		Faith	Kipyegon	KEN	10.1.94	1	Pre	Eugene	28 May 16
3:56.43		Yelena	Soboleva ¶	RUS	3.10.82	2	Gaz	Saint-Denis	8 Jul 06
3:56.50		Tatyana	Pozdnyakova	RUS	4.3.56	3	NC	Kyiv	27 Jul 82
3:56.54		Abeba	Aregawi	ETH/SWE	5.7.90	1	GGala	Roma	31 May 12
3:56.63		Nadezhda	Ralldugina	UKR	15.11.57	1	Drz	Praha	18 Aug 84
3:56.65		Yekaterina	Podkopayeva'	RUS	11.6.52	1		Rieti	2 Sep 84
3:56.7	'	Lyubov	Smolka	UKR	29.11.52	2	Znam	Moskva	6 Jul 80
3:56.7		Doina	Melinte	ROU	27.12.56	1		Bucuresti	12 Jul 86
3:56.77	+	Svetlana	Masterkova	RUS	17.1.68	1	WK	Zürich	14 Aug 96
		(30)							
3:56.8	'	Nadezhda	Olizarenko'	UKR	28.11.53	3	Znam	Moskva	6 Jul 80
3:56.91		Lyudmila	Rogachova	RUS	30.10.66	2	OG	Barcelona	8 Aug 92
3:56.91		Tatyana	Tomashova ¶	RUS	1.7.75	1	EC	Göteborg	13 Aug 06
3:56.97		Gabriela	Szabo	ROU	14.11.75	1	Herc	Monaco	8 Aug 98
3:57.03			Liu Jing	CHN	3.2.71	6h2	NG	Shanghai	17 Oct 97
3:57.05		Svetlana	Guskova	MDA	19.8.59	4	NC	Kyiv	27 Jul 82
3:57.05		Hellen	Obiri	KEN	13.12.89	1	Pre	Eugene	31 May 14
3:57.12		Mary	Decker/Slaney	USA	4.8.58	1	vNord	Stockholm	26 Jul 83
3:57.22		Maricica	Puica	ROU	29.7.50	1		Bucuresti	1 Jul 84
3:57.22		Jennifer	Simpson	USA	23.8.86	2	DL	Saint-Denis	5 Jul 14
		(40)							

WOMEN All-time

Mark	Wind	Name		Nat	Born	Pos	Meet	Venue	Date
3:57.34		Shelby	Houlihan	USA	8.2.93	1	Athl	Lausanne	5 Jul 18
3:57.40		Suzy	Favor Hamilton	USA	8.8.68	1	Bisl	Oslo	28 Jul 00
3:57.4 '		Totka	Petrova ¶	BUL	17.12.56	1	Balk	Athína	11 Aug 79
3:57.41		Jackline	Maranga	KEN	16.12.77	3	Herc	Monaco	8 Aug 98
3:57.46			Zhang Linli	CHN	6.3.73	3	NG	Beijing	11 Sep 93
3:57.64		Gudaf	Tsegay	ETH	23.1.97	1	DL	Stockholm	10 Jun 18
3:57.71		Christiane	Wartenberg'	GDR	27.10.56	2	OG	Moskva	1 Aug 80
3:57.71		Carla	Sacramento	POR	10.12.71	4	Herc	Monaco	8 Aug 98
3:57.72		Galina	Zakharova	RUS	7.9.56	1	NP	Baku	14 Sep 84
3:57.73		Natalya	Yevdokimova ¶	RUS	17.3.78	2	GP	Rieti	28 Aug 05
(50)									

100th woman 3:59.81, 200th 4:02.10, 300th 4:03.9, 400th 4:05.314 500th 4:06.14

Indoors: 3:55.17 WIR   G Dibaba   1   Karlsruhe   1 Feb 14
Drugs disqualification: 3:56.15 Mariem Alaoui Selsouli ¶ MAR 8.4.84 (1)   DL   Saint-Denis   6 Jul 12

| 3:56.62 | | Asli | Çakir Alptekin ¶ | TUR | 20.8.85 | (2) | DL | Saint-Denis | 6 Jul 12 |
| 3:57.65 | | Anna | Alminova ¶ | RUS | 17.1.85 | (1) | DL | Saint-Denis | 16 Jul 10 |

1 MILE

4:12.56 WR		Svetlana	Masterkova	RUS	17.1.68	1	WK	Zürich	14 Aug 96
4:14.30		Genzebe	Dibaba	ETH	8.2.91	1		Rovereto	6 Sep 16
4:14.71		Sifan	Hassan	NED	1.1.93	1	DL	London (OS)	22 Jul 18
4:15.61 WR		Paula	Ivan'	ROU	20.7.63	1	Nik	Nice	10 Jul 89
4:15.8		Natalya	Artyomova ¶	RUS	5.1.63	1		Leningrad	5 Aug 84
4:16.14		Gudaf	Tsegay	ETH	23.1.97	2	DL	London (OS)	22 Jul 18
4:16.15		Hellen	Obiri	KEN	13.12.89	3	DL	London (OS)	22 Jul 18
4:16.71 WR		Mary	Slaney (Decker)	USA	4.8.58	1	WK	Zürich	21 Aug 85
4:16.71		Faith	Kipyegon	KEN	10.1.94	1	VD	Bruxelles	11 Sep 15
4:17.25		Sonia	O'Sullivan	IRL	28.11.69	1	Bisl	Oslo	22 Jul 94

Indoors
4:13.31 WIR		Genzebe	Dibaba	ETH	8.2.91	1	Globen	Stockholm	17 Feb 16
4:17.14 WIR		Doina	Melinte	ROU	27.12.56	1		East Rutherford	9 Feb 90

Drugs dq: 4:15.63 Yelena Soboleva ¶ RUS 3.10.82 1   Moskva   29 Jun 07

2000 METRES

5:25.36 WR		Sonia	O'Sullivan	IRL	28.11.69	1	TSB	Edinburgh	8 Jul 94
5:26.93		Yvonne	Murray	GBR	4.10.64	2	TSB	Edinburgh	8 Jul 94
5:27.50		Genzebe	Dibaba	ETH	8.2.91	1	GS	Ostrava	17 Jun 14
5:28.69 WR		Maricica	Puica	ROU	29.7.50	1	PTG	London (CP)	11 Jul 86
5:28.72 WR		Tatyana	Kazankina ¶	RUS	17.12.51	1		Moskva	4 Aug 84
5:29.43+			Wang Junxia	CHN	9.1.73	1h2	NG	Beijing	12 Sep 93
5:29.64		Tatyana	Pozdnyakova	UKR	4.3.56	2		Moskva	4 Aug 84
5:30.19		Zola	Budd'	GBR	26.5.66	3	PTG	London (CP)	11 Jul 86
5:30.19		Gelete	Burka	ETH	15.2.86	1	VD	Bruxelles	4 Sep 09
5:30.92		Galina	Zakharova	RUS	7.9.56	3		Moskva	4 Aug 84

Indoors:
5:23.75		Genzebe	Dibaba	ETH	8.2.91	1		Sabadell	7 Feb 17
5:30.53		Gabriela	Szabo	ROU	14.11.75	1		Sindelfingen	8 Mar 98

3000 METRES

8:06.11 WR			Wang Junxia	CHN	9.1.73	1	NG	Beijing	13 Sep 93
8:12.18			Qu Yunxia	CHN	8.12.72	2	NG	Beijing	13 Sep 93
8:12.19 WR			Wang Junxia	CHN		1h2	NG	Beijing	12 Sep 93
8:12.27			Qu Yunxia	CHN		2h2	NG	Beijing	12 Sep 93
8:16.50			Zhang Linli	CHN	6.3.73	3	NG	Beijing	13 Sep 93
8:19.78		Ma Liyan	CHN	6.9.68	3h2	NG	Beijing	12 Sep 93
8:20.68		Hellen	Obiri	KEN	13.12.89	1	DL	Doha	9 May 14
8:21.14		Mercy	Cherono	KEN	7.5.91	2	DL	Doha	9 May 14
8:21.26			Ma Liyan	CHN		4	NG	Beijing	13 Sep 93
8:21.42		Gabriela	Szabo	ROU	14.11.75	1	Herc	Monaco	19 Jul 02
8:21.64		Sonia	O'Sullivan	IRL	28.11.69	1	TSB	London (CP)	15 Jul 94
8:21.84			Zhang Lirong	CHN	3.3.73	5	NG	Beijing	13 Sep 93
8:22.06 WR			Zhang Linli	CHN		1h1	NG	Beijing	12 Sep 93
8:22.20		Paula	Radcliffe (10)	GBR	17.12.73	2	Herc	Monaco	19 Jul 02
8:22.22		Almaz	Ayana	ETH	21.11.91	1		Rabat	14 Jun 15
8:22.34			Ayana			1	WK	Zürich	3 Sep 15
8:22.44			Zhang Lirong	CHN		2h1	NG	Beijing	12 Sep 93
8:22.62 WR		Tatyana	Kazankina ¶	RUS	17.12.51	1		Leningrad	26 Aug 84
8:23.11			Ayana			1	DL	Doha	6 May 16
8:23.14			Obiri			1	Herc	Monaco	21 Jul 17
8:23.23		Edith	Masai	KEN	4.4.67	3	Herc	Monaco	19 Jul 02
8:23.26		Olga	Yegorova ¶	RUS	28.3.72	1	WK	Zürich	17 Aug 01

Mark	Wind	Name		Nat	Born	Pos	Meet	Venue	Date
8:23.55		Faith	Kipyegon	KEN	10.1.94	3	DL	Doha	9 May 14
8:23.75			Yegorova			1	GP	Saint-Denis	6 Jul 01
8:23.96			Yegorova			1	GGala	Roma	29 Jun 01
8:24.19			Szabo			2	WK	Zürich	17 Aug 01
8:24.27			Obiri			1	Herc	Monaco	15 Jul 16
8:24.31			Szabo			1	GP	Paris (C)	29 Jul 98
8:24.41		Viola	Kibiwot	KEN	22.12.83	4	DL	Doha	9 May 14
8:24.51+		Meseret	Defar	ETH	19.11.83	1	in 2M	Bruxelles	14 Sep 07
		(30/17)							
8:25.40		Yelena	Zadorozhnaya	RUS	3.12.77	2	GGala	Roma	29 Jun 01
8:25.56		Tatyana	Tomashova ¶	RUS	1.7.75	3	GGala	Roma	29 Jun 01
8:25.62		Berhane	Adere (20)	ETH	21.7.73	3	WK	Zürich	17 Aug 01
8:25.83		Mary	Slaney	USA	4.8.58	1	GGala	Roma	7 Sep 85
8:25.92		Gelete	Burka	ETH	15.2.86	2	DNG	Stockholm	25 Jul 06
8:26.21		Genzebe	Dibaba	ETH	8.2.91	6	DL	Doha	9 May 14
8:26.48		Zahra	Ouaziz	MAR	20.12.69	2	WK	Zürich	11 Aug 99
8:26.53		Tatyana	Samolenko' ¶	UKR	12.8.61	1	OG	Seoul	25 Sep 88
8:26.78 WR		Svetlana	Ulmasova	UZB	4.2.53	1	NC	Kyiv	25 Jul 82
8:27.12 WR		Lyudmila	Bragina	RUS	24.7.43	1	v USA	College Park	7 Aug 76
8:27.15		Paula	Ivan'	ROU	20.7.63	2	OG	Seoul	25 Sep 88
8:27.50		Sifan	Hassan	NED	1.1.93	1	C.Cup	Ostrava	8 Sep 18
8:27.62		Getenesh	Wami	ETH	11.12.74	4	WK	Zürich	17 Aug 01
		(30)							
8:27.83		Maricica	Puica	ROU	29.7.50	2	GGala	Roma	7 Sep 85
8:28.33		Janet	Kisa	KEN	5.3.92	3	Herc	Monaco	15 Jul 16
8:28.41		Sentayehu	Ejigu	ETH	21.6.85	1	Herc	Monaco	22 Jul 10
8:28.51		Irene	Jelagat	KEN	10.12.88	7	DL	Doha	9 May 14
8:28.66		Vivian	Cheruiyot	KEN	11.9.83	2	WAF	Stuttgart	23 Sep 07
8:28.66		Beatrice	Chepkoech	KEN	6.7.91	2	Herc	Monaco	21 Jul 17
8:28.80		Marta	Domínguez	ESP	3.11.75	3	WK	Zürich	11 Aug 00
8:28.83		Zola	Budd'	GBR	26.5.66	3	GGala	Roma	7 Sep 85
8:28.87		Maryam	Jamal	BRN	16.9.84	1	Bisl	Oslo	29 Jul 05
8:29.02		Yvonne	Murray	GBR	4.10.64	3	OG	Seoul	25 Sep 88
		(40)							
8:29.05		Caroline	Kipkirui	KEN	26.5.94	1	DL	Doha	4 May 18
8:29.06		Priscah	Cherono	KEN	27.6.80	3	WAF	Stuttgart	23 Sep 07
8:29.09		Agnes	Tirop	KEN	23.10.95	2	DL	Doha	4 May 18
8:29.14		Lydia	Cheromei ¶	KEN	11.5.77	5	WK	Zürich	11 Aug 00
8:29.36		Svetlana	Guskova	MDA	19.8.59	2	NC	Kyiv	25 Jul 82
8:29.52		Mariem Alaoui	Selsouli ¶	MAR	8.4.84	1	Herc	Monaco	25 Jul 07
8:29.55		Tirunesh	Dibaba	ETH	1.10.85	1	LGP	London (CP)	28 Jul 06
8:29.58		Jennifer	Simpson'	USA	23.8.86	4	VD	Bruxelles	5 Sep 14
8:29.89		Konstanze	Klosterhalfen	GER	18.2.97	2	DL	Birmingham	20 Aug 17
8:29.93		Shannon	Rowbury	USA	19.9.84	5	VD	Bruxelles	5 Sep 14
		(50)	100th woman 8:34.85, 200th 8:41.69, 300th 8:45.73, 400th 8:48.8						
Indoors:									
8:16.60 WIR		Genzebe	Dibaba	ETH	8.2.91	1		Stockholm	6 Feb 14
8:23.72 WIR		Meseret	Defar	ETH	19.11.83	1	Spark	Stuttgart	3 Feb 07
8:23.74		Meselech	Melkamu	ETH	27.4.85	2	Spark	Stuttgart	3 Feb 07
8:25.27		Sentayehu	Ejigu	ETH	21.6.85	2	Spark	Stuttgart	6 Feb 10
8:26.41		Laura	Muir	GBR	9.5.93	1		Karlsruhe	4 Feb 17
8:27.86 WIR		Liliya	Shobukhova ¶	RUS	13.11.77	1	NC	Moskva	17 Feb 06
8:28.49		Anna	Alminova ¶	RUS	17.1.85	2	Spark	Stuttgart	7 Feb 09
8:29.00		Olesya	Syreva ¶	RUS	25.11.83	2	NC	Moskva	17 Feb 06

5000 METRES

Mark	Wind	Name		Nat	Born	Pos	Meet	Venue	Date
14:11.15 WR		Tirunesh	Dibaba	ETH	1.10.85	1	Bisl	Oslo	6 Jun 08
14:12.59		Almaz	Ayana	ETH	21.11.91	1	GGala	Roma	2 Jun 16
14:12.88		Meseret	Defar	ETH	19.11.83	1	DNG	Stockholm	22 Jul 08
14:14.32			Ayana			1	DL	Shanghai	17 May 15
14:15.41		Genzebe	Dibaba	ETH	8.2.91	1	DL	Saint-Denis	4 Jul 15
14:16.31			Ayana			1		Rabat	22 May 16
14:16.63 WR			Defar			1	Bisl	Oslo	15 Jun 07
14:18.37		Hellen	Obiri	KEN	13.12.89	1	GGala	Roma	8 Jun 17
14:18.89			Ayana			1	VD	Bruxelles	9 Sep 16
14:19.76			G Dibaba			1	Pre	Eugene	30 May 15
14:20.87		Vivian	Cheruiyot	KEN	11.9.83	1	DNG	Stockholm	29 Jul 11
14:21.29			G Dibaba			1	Bisl	Oslo	11 Jun 15
14:21.75			Obiri			1	DL	Rabat	13 Jul 18
14:21.97			Ayana			2	DL	Saint-Denis	4 Jul 15

Mark	Wind	Name		Nat	Born	Pos	Meet	Venue	Date
14:22.34		Sifan	Hassan	NED	1.1.93	2	DL	Rabat	13 Jul 18 14:22.47
		Obiri				1	DL	Shanghai	13 May 17
14:22.51			Cheruiyot			2		Oslo	15 Jun 07
14:23.14		Letesenbet	Gidey	ETH	20.3.98	3	DL	Rabat	13 Jul 18
14:23.33		Senbere	Teferi	ETH	3.5.95	4	DL	Rabat	13 Jul 18
14:23.46			T Dibaba			1	GP	Rieti	7 Sep 08
14:23.68			T Dibaba			1	DL	Saint-Denis	6 Jul 13
14:23.75		Liliya	Shobukhova ¶ (10)	RUS	13.11.77	1	NC	Kazan	19 Jul 08
14:24.24		Agnes	Tirop	KEN	23.10.95	5	DL	Rabat	13 Jul 18
14:24.53	WR		Defar			1		New York (RI)	3 Jun 06
14:24.68	WR	Elvan	Abeylegesse ¶	TUR	11.9.82	1	Bisl	Bergen (Fana)	11 Jun 04
14:25.22			G Dibaba			1	Pre	Eugene	26 May 17
14:25.43			Cheruiyot			1	VD	Bruxelles	5 Sep 08
14:25.52			Defar			2	VD	Bruxelles	5 Sep 08
14:25.78			Obiri			2	VD	Bruxelles	9 Sep 16
14:25.84			Ayana			2	DL	Saint-Denis	6 Jul 13
		(30/12)							
14:27.55		Caroline	Kipkirui	KEN	26.5.94	2	VD-DLF	Bruxelles	1 Sep 17
14:28.09	WR		Jiang Bo	CHN	13.3.77	1	NG	Shanghai	23 Oct 97
14:28.39		Sentayehu	Ejigu	ETH	21.6.85	2	DL	Saint-Denis	16 Jul 10
14:29.11		Paula	Radcliffe	GBR	17.12.73	1	ECpS	Bydgoszcz	20 Jun 04
14:29.32		Olga	Yegorova ¶	RUS	28.3.72	1	ISTAF	Berlin	31 Aug 01
14:29.32		Berhane	Adere	ETH	21.7.73	1	Bisl	Oslo	27 Jun 03
14:29.50		Viola	Kibiwot	KEN	22.12.83	2		Rabat	22 May 16
14:29.82			Dong Yanmei	CHN	16.2.77	2	NG	Shanghai	23 Oct 97
		(20)							
14:30.42		Sally	Kipyego	KEN	19.12.85	2	WK	Zürich	8 Sep 11
14:30.88		Getenesh	Wami	ETH	11.12.74	1	NA	Heusden-Zolder	5 Aug 00
14:31.14		Linet	Masai	KEN	5.12.89	2	DL	Shanghai	23 May 10
14:31.20		Gelete	Burka	ETH	15.2.86	2	GS	Ostrava	27 Jun 07
14:31.48		Gabriela	Szabo	ROU	14.11.75	1	ISTAF	Berlin	1 Sep 98
14:31.91		Meselech	Melkamu	ETH	27.4.85	3	DL	Shanghai	23 May 10
14:31.91		Sylvia	Kibet	KEN	28.3.84	4	DL	Shanghai	23 May 10
14:31.95		Faith	Kipyegon	KEN	10.1.94	2	Pre	Eugene	30 May 15
14:32.08		Zahra	Ouaziz	MAR	20.12.69	2	ISTAF	Berlin	1 Sep 98
14:32.33			Liu Shixiang ¶	CHN	13.1.71	3h1	NG	Shanghai	21 Oct 97
		(30)							
14:32.74		Ejagayehu	Dibaba	ETH	25.6.82	3	Bisl	Bergen (Fana)	11 Jun 04
14:32.82		Margaret	Kipkemboi	KEN	9.2.93	4	VD-DLF	Bruxelles	1 Sep 17
14:33.04		Werknesh	Kidane	ETH	21.11.81	2	Bisl	Oslo	27 Jun 03
14:33.13		Gulnara	Galkina'	RUS	9.7.78	2	NC	Kazan	19 Jul 08
14:33.30		Etenesh	Diro	ETH	10.5.91	4	VD	Bruxelles	9 Sep 16
14:33.49		Lucy Wangui	Kabuu	KEN	24.3.84	2	Bisl	Oslo	6 Jun 08
14:33.84		Edith	Masai	KEN	4.4.67	3	Bisl	Oslo	2 Jun 06
14:33.95		Mercy	Cherono	KEN	7.5.91	2	GGala	Roma	2 Jun 16
14:34.45		Shelby	Houlihan	USA	8.2.93	1	NA	Heusden-Zolder	21 Jul 18
14:35.30		Priscah	Jepleting/Cherono	KEN	27.6.80	4	Bisl	Oslo	2 Jun 06
		(40)							
14:36.45	WR	Fernanda	Ribeiro	POR	23.6.69	1		Hechtel	22 Jul 95
14:36.52		Mariem Alaoui	Selsouli ¶	MAR	8.4.84	1	G Gala	Roma	13 Jul 07
14:36.80		Lilian	Rengeruk	KEN	3.5.97	2	Pre	Eugene	26 May 17
14:36.82		Yasemin	Can	TUR	11.12.96	4	GGala	Roma	8 Jun 17
14:37.07		Jéssica	Augusto	POR	8.11.81	5	DL	Saint-Denis	16 Jul 10
14:37.33	WR	Ingrid	Kristiansen'	NOR	21.3.56	1		Stockholm	5 Aug 86
14:38.09		Mariya	Konovalova ¶	RUS	14.8.74	3	NC	Kazan	19 Jul 08
14:38.21		Isabella	Ochichi	KEN	28.10.79	4	VD	Bruxelles	26 Aug 05
14:38.44		Wude	Ayalew	ETH	4.7.87	5	Bisl	Oslo	3 Jul 09
14:38.70		Janet	Kisa	KEN	5.3.92	4		Rabat	22 May 16
		(50)	100th woman 14:47.12, 200th 15:02.28, 300th 15:08.36, 400th 15:14.15, 500th 15:19.0						

Indoors:

14:18.06			G Dibaba			1	XL-G	Stockholm	19 Feb 15
14:24.37	WIR		Defar			1		Stockholm	18 Feb 09
14:24.79			Defar			1	GE Galan	Stockholm	10 Feb 10
14:27.42	WIR		T Dibaba			1	BIG	Boston (R)	27 Jan 07

Drugs disqualification

14:36.79		Alemitu	Bekele ¶	TUR	17.9.77	4	VD	Bruxelles	27 Aug 10

10,000 METRES

29:17.45	WR	Almaz	Ayana	ETH	21.11.91	1	OG	Rio de Janeiro	12 Aug 16
29:31.78	WR		Wang Junxia	CHN	9.1.73	1	NG	Beijing	8 Sep 93
29:32.53		Vivian	Cheruiyot	KEN	11.9.83	2	OG	Rio de Janeiro	12 Aug 16

Mark	Wind	Name		Nat	Born	Pos	Meet	Venue	Date
29:42.56		Tirunesh	Dibaba	ETH	1.10.85	3	OG	Rio de Janeiro	12 Aug 16
29:53.51		Alice Aprot	Nawowuna	KEN	2.1.94	4	OG	Rio de Janeiro	12 Aug 16
29:53.80		Meselech	Melkamu	ETH	27.4.85	1		Utrecht	14 Jun 09
29:54.66			T Dibaba			1	OG	Beijing	15 Aug 08
29:59.20		Meseret	Defar	ETH	19.11.83	1	NC	Birmingham	11 Jul 09
30:01.09		Paula	Radcliffe	GBR	17.12.73	1	EC	München	6 Aug 02
30:04.18		Berhane	Adere (10)	ETH	21.7.73	1	WCh	Saint-Denis	23 Aug 03
30:07.00			Ayana			1	OT	Hengelo	29 Jun 16
30:07.15		Werknesh	Kidane	ETH	21.11.81	2	WCh	Saint-Denis	23 Aug 03
30:07.20			Sun Yingjie ¶	CHN	3.10.77	3	WCh	Saint-Denis	23 Aug 03
30:07.78		Betsy	Saina	KEN	30.6.88	5	OG	Rio de Janeiro	12 Aug 16
30:08.06			Defar			1		Sollentuna	27 Jun 13
30:11.53		Florence	Kiplagat	KEN	27.2.87	2		Utrecht	14 Jun 09
30:11.87		Wude	Ayalew	ETH	4.7.87	3		Utrecht	14 Jun 09
30:12.53		Lornah	Kiplagat (KEN)	NED	1.5.74	4	WCh	Saint-Denis	23 Aug 03
30:13.17		Molly	Huddle	USA	31.8.84	6	OG	Rio de Janeiro	12 Aug 16
30:13.37			Zhong Huandi	CHN	28.6.67	2	NG	Beijing	8 Sep 93
30:13.74	WR	Ingrid	Kristiansen'	NOR	21.3.56	1	Bisl	Oslo	5 Jul 86
30:15.67			T Dibaba			1		Sollentuna	28 Jun 05
30:16.32			Ayana			1	WCh	London (OS)	5 Aug 17
30:17.15			Radcliffe			1	GP	Gateshead	27 Jun 04
30:17.49		Derartu	Tulu	ETH	21.3.72	1	OG	Sydney	30 Sep 00
30:18.39		Ejegayehu	Dibaba (20)	ETH	25.6.82	2		Sollentuna	28 Jun 05
30:19.39			Kidane			1	GP II	Stanford	29 May 05
30:20.75			T Dibaba			1	OG	London (OS)	3 Aug 12
30:21.67		Elvan	Abeylegesse ¶	TUR	11.9.82	1	ECp	Antalya	15 Apr 06
30:22.22		Shalane	Flanagan	USA	8.7.81	2	OG	Beijing	15 Aug 08
30:22.48		Getenesh (31/24)	Wami	ETH	11.12.74	2	OG	Sydney	30 Sep 00
30:22.88		Fernanda	Ribeiro (20)	POR	23.6.69	3	OG	Sydney	30 Sep 00
30:23.07		Alla	Zhilyayeva	RUS	5.2.69	5	WCh	Saint-Denis	23 Aug 03
30:24.36			Xing Huina	CHN	25.2.84	1	OG	Athína	27 Aug 04
30:26.20		Galina	Bogomolova	RUS	15.10.77	6	WCh	Saint-Denis	23 Aug 03
30:26.37		Sally	Kipyego	KEN	19.12.85	2	OG	London (OS)	3 Aug 12
30:26.41		Yasemin	Can	TUR	11.12.96	7	OG	Rio de Janeiro	12 Aug 16
30:26.50		Linet (30)	Masai	KEN	5.12.89	3	OG	Beijing	15 Aug 08
30:26.66		Gelete	Burka	ETH	23.1.86	8	OG	Rio de Janeiro	12 Aug 16
30:26.70		Belaynesh	Oljira	ETH	26.6.90	3	Pre	Eugene	1 Jun 12
30:29.21	mx	Philes	Ongori	KEN	19.7.86	1mx		Yokohama	23 Nov 08
30:29.23		Gladys	Cherono	KEN	12.5.83	2	GS	Ostrava	27 Jun 13
30:29.36		Liliya	Shobukhova ¶	RUS	13.11.77	1	NC	Cheboksary	23 Jul 09
30:30.26		Edith	Masai	KEN	4.4.67	5	WCh	Helsinki	6 Aug 05
30:31.03		Mariya	Konovalova ¶	RUS	14.8.74	2	NC	Cheboksary	23 Jul 09
30:31.42		Inga	Abitova ¶	RUS	6.3.82	1	EC	Göteborg	7 Aug 06
30:32.03		Tegla	Loroupe	KEN	9.5.73	3	WCh	Sevilla	26 Aug 99
30:32.36		Susanne (40)	Wigene	NOR	12.2.78	2	EC	Göteborg	7 Aug 06
30:32.72		Lidiya	Grigoryeva ¶	RUS	21.1.74	3	EC	Göteborg	7 Aug 06
30:35.54		Kimberley	Smith	NZL	19.11.81	2		Stanford	4 May 08
30:35.91		Birhane	Ababel	ETH	10.6.90	4	GS	Ostrava	27 Jun 13
30:36.75		Netsanet	Gudeta	ETH	12.2.91	4	OT	Hengelo	29 Jun 16
30:37.38		Genet	Yalew	ETH	31.12.92	5	OT	Hengelo	29 Jun 16
30:37.68		Benita	Johnson	AUS	6.5.79	8	WCh	Saint-Denis	23 Aug 03
30:38.09			Dong Yanmei	CHN	16.2.77	1	NG	Shanghai	19 Oct 97
30:38.33		Mestawat	Tufa	ETH	14.9.83	1		Nijmegen	25 Jun 08
30:38.78		Jelena	Prokopcuka	LAT	21.9.76	6	EC	Göteborg	7 Aug 06
30:39.41			Lan Lixin	CHN	14.2.79	2	NG	Shanghai	19 Oct 97
		(50)	100th woman 31:07.88, 200th 31:27.99, 300th 31:41.47, 400th 31:52.42, 500th 31:59.94						
Drugs dq: 29:56.34		Elvan	Abeylegesse ¶	TUR	11.9.82	(2)	OG	Beijing	15 Aug 08

HALF MARATHON

Slightly downhill courses included: Newcastle-South Shields 30.5m, Tokyo 33m (to 1998), Lisboa (Spring to 2008) 69m

64:51		Joyciline	Jepkosgei	KEN	8.12.93	1		Valencia	22 Oct 17
64:52			Jepkosgei			1		Praha	1 Apr 17
64:52		Fancy	Chemutai	KEN	20.3.95	1	RAK	Ras Al Khaimah	9 Feb 18
64:55		Mary	Keitany	KEN	18.1.82	2	RAK	Ras Al Khaimah	9 Feb 18
65:04		Joan	Chelimo	KEN	10.11.90	1		Praha	7 Apr 18
65:06		Peres	Jepchirchir	KEN	27.9.93	1	RAK	Ra's Al-Khaymah	10 Feb 17
65:07		Caroline	Kipkirui	KEN	26.5.94	3	RAK	Ras Al Khaimah	9 Feb 18

WOMEN All-time

Mark	Wind	Name		Nat	Born	Pos	Meet	Venue	Date
65:09	WR	Florence	Kiplagat	KEN	27.2.87	1		Barcelona	15 Feb 15
65:12	WR		F Kiplagat			1		Barcelona	16 Feb 14
65:13			Keitany			2	RAK	Ra's Al-Khaymah	10 Feb 17
65:15		Sifan	Hassan	NED	1.1.93	1		København	16 Sep 18
65:22		Violah	Jepchumba #	BRN	23.10.90	2		Praha	1 Apr 17
65:36			Chemutai			2		Valencia	22 Oct 17
65:37			J Chelimo			4	RAK	Ras Al Khaimah	9 Feb 18
65:39	dh		Keitany			1	GNR	South Shields	7 Sep 14
65:40	dh	Paula	Radcliffe (10)	GBR	17.12.73	1	GNR	South Shields	21 Sep 03
65:44	dh	Susan	Chepkemei	KEN	25.6.75	1		Lisboa (60m dh)	1 Apr 01
65:45	dh	Priscah	Jeptoo	KEN	26.6.84	1	GNR	South Shields	15 Sep 13
65:46		Yeshaneh	Ababel	ETH	10.6.90	2		København	16 Sep 18
65:50	WR		Keitany			1		Ra's Al Khaymah	18 Feb 11
65:51			Jepchumba			1		Praha	2 Apr 16
65:52		Edith	Chelimo	KEN	16.7.86	1		Cardiff	1 Oct 17
65:59	dh		Keitany			1	GNR	South Shields	10 Sep 17
66:02			Keitany			1		Ra's Al-Khaymah	13 Feb 15
66:04		Cynthia	Limo	KEN	18.12.89	1		Ra's Al-Khaymah	12 Feb 16
66:07		Gladys	Cherono	KEN	12.5.83	2		Ra's Al-Khaymah	12 Feb 16
66:08			Jepkosgei			3	RAK	Ra's Al-Khaymah	10 Feb 17
66:09		Lucy Wangui	Kabuu	KEN	24.3.84	1		Ra's Al-Khaymah	15 Feb 13
66:09	dh	Meseret	Defar	ETH	19.11.83	2	GNR	South Shields	15 Sep 13
66:09			Kipkirui			2		Praha	7 Apr 18
		(30/18)		* uncertain course measurement					
66:11			P Jeptoo			2		Ra's Al-Khaymah	15 Feb 13
66:11		Eunice	Chumba	BRN	23.5.93	1		København	17 Sep 17
66:11		Netsanet	Gudeta (20)	ETH	12.2.91	1	WCh	Valencia	24 Mar 18
66:11		Gelete	Burka	ETH	23.1.86	1		Valencia	28 Oct 18
66:13		Alia Mohamed	Saeed	UAE	18.5.91	2		Valencia	28 Oct 18
66:14		Worknesh	Degefa	ETH	28.10.90	2		Praha	2 Apr 16
66:19		Joyce	Chepkirui	KEN	20.8.88	1		Praha	5 Apr 14
66:19		Ruth	Chepngetich	KEN	8.8.94	1		Istanbul	30 Apr 17
66:21		Zeineba	Yimer	ETH	17.6.98	4		København	16 Sep 18
66:25		Lornah	Kiplagat	NED	1.5.74	1	WCh	Udine	14 Oct 07
66:26		Genet	Yalew	ETH	31.12.92	3		Ra's Al-Khaymah	12 Feb 16
66:27		Rita	Jeptoo ¶	KEN	15.2.81	3		Ra's Al-Khaymah	15 Feb 13
66:28		Mamitu	Daska	ETH	16.10.83	2		Ra's Al-Khaymah	13 Feb 15
		(30)							
66:29		Mercy Wacera	Ngugi	KEN	17.12.88	1		Houston	17 Jan 16
66:31		Pauline	Korikwiang	KEN	1.3.88	4		Valencia	28 Oct 18
66:35		Brigid	Kosgei	KEN	20.2.94	3		København	17 Sep 17
66:39		Ruti	Aga	ETH	16.1.94	1		Houston	14 Jan 18
66:40	*	Ingrid	Kristiansen	NOR	21.3.56	1	NC	Sandnes	5 Apr 87
66:43	dh	Masako	Chiba	JPN	18.7.76	1		Tokyo	19 Jan 97
66:43		Jemima	Sumgong ¶?	KEN	21.12.84	4	RAK	Ra's Al-Khaymah	10 Feb 17
66:44		Elana	Meyer	RSA	10.10.66	1		Tokyo	15 Jan 99
66:46		Eunice	Jepkirui	BRN	20.5.84	2		Istanbul	30 Apr 17
66:47		Degitu	Azimeraw	ETH	24.1.99	6	RAK	Ras Al Khaimah	9 Feb 18
		(40)							
66:49		Esther	Wanjiru	KEN	27.3.77	2		Tokyo	15 Jan 99
66:50		Tirunesh	Dibaba	ETH	1.10.85	5	RAK	Ra's Al-Khaymah	10 Feb 17
66:50		Buze	Diriba	ETH	9.2.94	4		Houston	14 Jan 18
66:50		Tsehay	Gemechu	ETH	20.5.98	1		New Delhi	21 Oct 18
66:56		Meseret	Hailu	ETH	12.9.90	4		Ra's Al-Khaymah	15 Feb 13
66:56		Pauline	Kamulu	KEN	30.12.94	3	WCh	Valencia	24 Mar 18
66:57	dh	Kara	Goucher	USA	9.7.78	1	GNR	South Shields	30 Sep 07
66:57		Gladys	Chesire	KEN	20.2.93	5		Ra's Al-Khaymah	12 Feb 16
67:00		Roza	Dereje	ETH	6.5.97	2		Istanbul	8 Apr 18
67:03	dh	Derartu	Tulu	ETH	21.3.72	3		Lisboa	1 Apr 01
67:03		Bekelech	Gudeta	ETH	10.10.97	6		København	16 Sep 18
		(51)		100th woman 67:50, 200th 68:43, 300th 69:20, 400th 69:43, 500th 70:07					
Drugs dq:	66:06		Jepchumba			(1)		Ústí nad Labem	16 Sep 17

MARATHON

P = point-to-point or start and finish more than 30% apart, 2nd column

2:15:25	WR	Paula	Radcliffe	GBR	17.12.73	1		London	13 Apr 03
2:17:01		Mary	Keitany	KEN	18.1.82	1		London	23 Apr 17
2:17:18	WR		Radcliffe			1		Chicago	13 Oct 02
2:17:42			Radcliffe			1		London	17 Apr 05

Mark	Wind	Name		Nat	Born	Pos	Meet	Venue	Date
2:17:56		Tirunesh	Dibaba	ETH	1.10.85	2		London	23 Apr 17
2:18:11		Gladys	Cherono	KEN	12.5.83	1		Berlin	16 Sep 18
2:18:31			Dibaba			1		Chicago	8 Oct 17
2:18:31		Vivian	Cheruiyot	KEN	11.9.83	1		London	22 Apr 18
2:18:34		Ruti	Aga	ETH	16.1.94	2		Berlin	16 Sep 18
2:18:35		Brigid	Kosgei	KEN	20.2.94	1		Chicago	7 Oct 18
2:18:35		Ruth	Chepngetich	KEN	8.8.94	1		Istanbul	11 Nov 18
2:18:37			Keitany			1		London	22 Apr 12
2:18:47 WR		Catherine	Ndereba	KEN	21.7.72	1		Chicago	7 Oct 01
2:18:55			T Dibaba			3		Berlin	16 Sep 18
2:18:56			Radcliffe			1		London	14 Apr 02
2:18:58		Tiki	Gelana (10)	ETH	22.10.87	1		Rotterdam	15 Apr 12
2:19:12		Mizuki	Noguchi	JPN	3.7.78	1		Berlin	25 Sep 05
2:19:17		Roza	Dereje	ETH	6.5.97	1		Dubai	26 Jan 18
2:19:19		Irina	Mikitenko	GER	23.8.72	1		Berlin	28 Sep 08
2:19:19			Keitany			1		London	17 Apr 11
2:19:25			G Cherono			1		Berlin	27 Sep 15
2:19:26			Ndereba			2		Chicago	13 Oct 02
2:19:30		Feyse	Tadese	ETH	19.11.88	2		Dubai	26 Jan 18
2:19:31		Aselefech	Mergia	ETH	23.1.85	1		Dubai	27 Jan 12
2:19:34		Lucy Wangui	Kabuu	KEN	24.3.84	2		Dubai	27 Jan 12
2:19:36		Deena	Kastor	USA	14.2.73	1		London	23 Apr 06
2:19:36		Yebrgual	Melese	ETH	18.4.90	3		Dubai	26 Jan 18
2:19:39			Sun Yingjie ¶	CHN	3.10.77	1		Beijing	19 Oct 03
2:19:41		Yoko	Shibui (20)	JPN	14.3.79	1		Berlin	26 Sep 04
2:19:41		Tirfi	Tsegaye	ETH	25.11.84	1		Dubai	22 Jan 16
		(30/21)							
2:19:44		Florence	Kiplagat	KEN	27.2.87	1		Berlin	25 Sep 11
2:19:46 WR		Naoko	Takahashi	JPN	6.5.72	1		Berlin	30 Sep 01
2:19:47		Sarah	Chepchirchir	KEN	27.7.84	1		Tokyo	26 Feb 17
2:19:50		Edna	Kiplagat	KEN	15.11.79	2		London	22 Apr 12
2:19:51			Zhou Chunxiu	CHN	15.11.78	1	Dong-A	Seoul	12 Mar 06
2:19:51		Birhane	Dibaba	ETH	11.9.93	1		Tokyo	25 Feb 18
2:19:52		Mare	Dibaba	ETH	20.10.89	3		Dubai	27 Jan 12
2:19:53		Worknesh	Degefa	ETH	28.10.90	4		Dubai	26 Jan 18
2:19:57		Rita	Jeptoo ¶	KEN	15.2.81	1		Chicago	13 Oct 13
		(30)							
2:20:13		Haftamnesh	Tesfay	ETH	28.4.94	5		Dubai	26 Jan 18
2:20:14		Priscah	Jeptoo	KEN	26.6.84	3		London	22 Apr 12
2:20:30		Bezunesh	Bekele	ETH	29.1.83	4		Dubai	27 Jan 12
2:20:30		Aberu	Kebede	ETH	12.9.89	1		Berlin	30 Sep 12
2:20:36		Meskerem	Assefa	ETH	20.9.85	1		Frankfurt	28 Oct 18
2:20:42		Berhane	Adere	ETH	21.7.73	1		Chicago	22 Oct 06
2:20:43 WR		Tegla	Loroupe	KEN	9.5.73	1		Berlin	26 Sep 99
2:20:45		Gelete	Burka	ETH	23.1.86	6		Dubai	26 Jan 18
2:20:47		Galina	Bogomolova	RUS	15.10.77	2		Chicago	22 Oct 06
2:20:48		Jemima Jelagat	Sumgong ¶	KEN	21.12.84	2		Chicago	13 Oct 13
		(40)							
2:20:48		Amane	Beriso	ETH	13.10.91	2		Dubai	22 Jan 16
2:20:53		Valary	Aiyabei	KEN	8.6.91	3		Berlin	24 Sep 17
2:20:55		Purity	Rionoripo	KEN	10.6.93	1		Paris	9 Apr 17
2:20:57		Jordan	Hasay	USA	21.9.91	3		Chicago	8 Oct 17
2:20:59		Shure	Demise	ETH	21.1.96	4		Dubai	23 Jan 15
2:20:59		Agnes	Barsosio	KEN	5.8.82	2		Paris	9 Apr 17
2:21:01		Meselech	Melkamu	ETH	27.4.85	1		Frankfurt	28 Oct 12
2:21:06 WR		Ingrid	Kristiansen	NOR	21.3.56	1		London	21 Apr 85
2:21:09		Meseret	Hailu	ETH	12.9.90	1		Amsterdam	21 Oct 12
2:21:14		Shalane	Flanagan	USA	8.7.81	3		Berlin	28 Sep 14
2:21:14		Ashete	Bekele	ETH	17.4.88	1		Valencia	2 Dec 18
		(51)							

100th woman 2:22:56, 200th 2:24:29, 300th 2:25:53, 400th 226:47, 500th 2:27:35

Downhill point-to-point course – Boston marathon is downhill overall (139m) and sometimes strongly wind-aided.

2:19:59	D	Buzunesh	Deba	ETH	8.9.87	2		Boston	21 Apr 14
2:20:41	D	Jemima Jelagat	Sumgong	KEN	21.12.84	4		Boston	21 Apr 14
2:20:43	D	Margaret	Okayo	KEN	30.5.76	1		Boston	15 Apr 02

Possibly short

2:20:16		Yeshaneh	Ababel	ETH	10.6.90	1		Abu Dhabi	7 Dec 18
2:20:54		Eunice	Chumba	BRN	23.5.93	2		Abu Dhabi	7 Dec 18

Drugs disqualification

2:18:20		Liliya	Shobukhova ¶	RUS	13.11.77	1		Chicago	9 Oct 11
2:20:23			Wei Yanan ¶	CHN	6.12.81	1		Beijing	20 Oct 02

WOMEN All-time

Mark	Wind	Name		Nat	Born	Pos	Meet	Venue	Date
2:18:57	D	Rita	Jeptoo ¶	KEN	15.2.81	1		Boston	21 Apr 14
2:21:29	D	Aleksandra	Duliba ¶	BLR	9.1.88	6		Boston	21 Apr 14

2000 METRES STEEPLECHASE

Mark		Name		Nat	Born	Pos	Meet	Venue	Date
6:02.16		Virginia	Nyambura	KEN	20.7.93	1	ISTAF	Berlin	6 Sep 15
6:02.47		Beatrice	Chepkoech	KEN	6.7.91	2	ISTAF	Berlin	6 Sep 15
6:03.38		Wioletta	Janowska	POL	9.6.77	1		Gdansk	15 Jul 06
6:04.20		Gesa-Felicitas	Krause	GER	3.8.92	3	ISTAF	Berlin	6 Sep 15
6:04.46		Dorcus	Inzikuru	UGA	2.2.82	1	GP II	Milano	1 Jun 05
6:10.82		Magdalene	Masai	KEN	4.4.93	4	ISTAF	Berlin	6 Sep 15

3000 METRES STEEPLECHASE

Mark		Name		Nat	Born	Pos	Meet	Venue	Date
8:44.32	WR	Beatrice	Chepkoech	KEN	6.7.91	1	Herc	Monaco	20 Jul 18
8:52.78	WR	Ruth	Jebet	KEN/BRN	17.11.96	1	DL	Saint-Denis	27 Aug 16
8:55.10			Chepkoech			1	VD	Bruxelles	31 Aug 18
8:55.29			Jebet			1	WK-DLF	Zürich	24 Aug 17
8:58.78		Celliphine	Chespol	KEN	23.3.99	1	Pre	Eugene	26 May 17
8:58.81	WR	Gulnara	Samitova/Galkina	RUS	9.7.78	1	OG	Beijing	17 Aug 08
8:59.36			Chepkoech			1	DL	Paris (C)	30 Jun 18
8:59.62		Norah	Tanui	KEN	2.10.95	2	VD	Bruxelles	31 Aug 18
8:59.75			Jebet			1	OG	Rio de Janeiro	15 Aug 16
8:59.84			Chepkoech			2	WK-DLF	Zürich	24 Aug 17
8:59.88			Chepkoech			1	AfrC	Asaba	5 Aug 18
8:59.97			Jebet			2	DL	Shanghai	14 May 16
9:00.01		Hyvin	Jepkemoi	KEN	13.1.92	2	Pre	Eugene	28 May 16
9:00.12			Jepkemoi			1	DL	Doha	5 May 17
9:00.70			Chepkoech			2	Pre	Eugene	26 May 17
9:00.85		Courtney	Frerichs	USA	18.1.93	2	Herc	Monaco	20 Jul 18
9:01.57			Chepkoech			2	DL	Doha	5 May 17
9:01.59	WR		Samitova/Galkina			1		Iraklio	4 Jul 04
9:01.60			Jepkemoi			3	VD	Bruxelles	31 Aug 18
9:01.69			Chepkoech			1	DL	Paris (C)	1 Jul 17
9:01.82			Chespol			2	DL	Paris (C)	30 Jun 18
9:01.96			Jepkemoi			2	DL	Saint-Denis	27 Aug 16
9:01.99			Jebet			3	DL	Doha	5 May 17
9:02.58		Emma	Coburn	USA	19.10.90	1	WCh	London (OS)	11 Aug 17
9:03.52			Jebet			3	Pre	Eugene	26 May 17
9:03.70			Tanui			1	ISTAF	Berlin	27 Aug 17
9:03.77			Frerichs			2	WCh	London (OS)	11 Aug 17
9:03.86			Jepkemoi			3	DL	Paris (C)	30 Jun 18
9:04.03			Jepkemoi			3	WCh	London (OS)	11 Aug 17
9:04.17			Tanui			4	DL	Paris (C)	30 Jun 18
		(30/8)							
9:05.36		Habiba	Ghribi	TUN	9.4.84	1	VD	Bruxelles	11 Sep 15
9:06.57		Yekaterina	Volkova ¶ (10)	RUS	16.2.78	1	WCh	Osaka	27 Aug 07
9:07.06		Sofia	Assefa	ETH	14.11.87	1	FBK	Hengelo	11 Jun 17
9:07.14		Milcah	Chemos Cheywa	KEN	24.2.86	1	Bisl	Oslo	7 Jun 12
9:07.41		Eunice	Jepkorir	KEN	17.2.82	2	OG	Beijing	17 Aug 08
9:07.94		Peruth	Chemutai	UGA	10.7.99	6	Herc	Monaco	20 Jul 18
9:08.23		Roseline	Chepngetich	KEN	17.6.97	7	Herc	Monaco	20 Jul 18
9:08.39		Yuliya	Zaripova' ¶	RUS	26.4.86	2	WCh	Berlin	17 Aug 09
9:09.19		Tatyana	Petrova	RUS	8.4.83	2	WCh	Osaka	27 Aug 07
9:09.39		Marta	Dominguez ¶	ESP	3.11.75	1		Barcelona	25 Jul 09
9:09.61		Hiwot	Ayalew	ETH	6.3.90	3	Bisl	Oslo	7 Jun 12
9:10.27		Colleen	Quigley	USA	20.11.92	1	ISTAF	Berlin	2 Sep 18
		(20)							
9:10.71		Daisy	Jepkemei	KEN	13.2.96	8	Herc	Monaco	20 Jul 18
9:10.74		Winfred	Yavi	BRN	31.12.99	9	Herc	Monaco	20 Jul 18
9:11.85		Gesa-Felicitas	Krause	GER	3.8.92	2	ISTAF	Berlin	27 Aug 17
9:12.50		Jennifer	Simpson'	USA	23.8.86	5	WCh	Berlin	17 Aug 09
9:12.55		Lydia	Chepkurui	KEN	23.8.84	2	WCh	Moskva	13 Aug 13
9:13.16		Ruth	Bisibori	KEN	2.1.88	7	WCh	Berlin	17 Aug 09
9:13.22		Gladys	Kipkemboi	KEN	15.10.86	2	GGala	Roma	10 Jun 10
9:13.25		Etenesh	Diro	ETH	10.5.91	6	DL	Paris (C)	1 Jul 17
9:13.35		Karoline Bjerkeli	Grøvdal	NOR	14.6.90	1	NC	Sandnes	26 Aug 17
9:13.53		Gülcan	Mingir	TUR	21.5.89	1	Pavlov	Sofia	9 Jun 12
		(30)							
9:13.85		Virginia	Nyambura	KEN	20.7.93	3	Herc	Monaco	17 Jul 15
9:14.09		Aisha	Praught Leer	JAM	14.12.89	8	VD	Bruxelles	31 Aug 18
9:14.28		Genevieve	LaCaze/Gregson	AUS	4.8.89	6	DL	Saint-Denis	27 Aug 16

Mark	Wind	Name		Nat	Born	Pos	Meet	Venue	Date
9:15.04		Dorcus	Inzikuru	UGA	2.2.82	1	SGP	Athína	14 Jun 05
9:16.51	WR	Alesya	Turova	BLR	6.12.79	1		Gdansk	27 Jul 02
9:16.68		Yekaterina	Ivonina	RUS	14.6.94	1	NC	Kazan	20 Jul 18
9:16.85		Cristina	Casandra	ROU	21.10.77	4	OG	Beijing	17 Aug 08
9:16.94		Mercy	Njoroge	KEN	10.6.86	2	DL	Doha	6 May 11
9:17.15		Wioletta	Frankiewicz/Janowska	POL	9.6.77	1	SGP	Athína	3 Jul 06
9:17.74		Purity	Kirui	KEN	13.8.91	5	VD	Bruxelles	11 Sep 15
		(40)							
9:17.85		Zemzem	Ahmed	ETH	27.12.84	7	OG	Beijing	17 Aug 08
9:18.03		Lydia	Rotich	KEN	8.8.88	3	Bisl	Oslo	4 Jun 10
9:18.35		Donna	MacFarlane	AUS	18.6.77	3	Bisl	Oslo	6 Jun 08
9:18.54		Antje	Möldner-Schmidt	GER	13.6.84	9	WCh	Berlin	17 Aug 09
9:18.54		Jéssica	Augusto	POR	8.11.81	1		Huelva	9 Jun 10
9:18.85		Leah	O'Connor	USA	30.8.92	6	Pre	Eugene	28 May 16
9:19.48		Stephanie	Garcia	USA	3.5.88	8	DL	Saint-Denis	27 Aug 16
9:19.76		Lalita	Babar	IND	2.6.89	4h2	OG	Rio de Janeiro	13 Aug 16
9:20.22		Joan	Chepkemoi	KEN	24.11.93	3	Hanz	Zagreb	29 Aug 17
9:20.23		Mekdes	Bekele	ETH	20.1.87	2		Huelva	13 Jun 08
		(50)		100th woman 9:28.61, 200th 9:39.48, 300th 9:46.76, 400th 9:52.25, 500th 9:56.87					
Drugs disqualification									
9:05.02		Yuliya	Zaripova	RUS	26.4.86	(1)	DNG	Stockholm	17 Aug 12
9:07.32		Marta	Dominguez ¶	ESP	3.11.75	(1)	WCh	Berlin	17 Aug 09

100 METRES HURDLES

Mark	Wind	Name		Nat	Born	Pos	Meet	Venue	Date
12.20	WR 0.3	Kendra	Harrison	USA	18.9.92	1	DL	London (OS)	22 Jul 16
12.21	WR 0.7	Yordanka	Donkova	BUL	28.9.61	1		Stara Zagora	20 Aug 88
12.24	0.9		Donkova			1h		Stara Zagora	28 Aug 88
12.24	0.5		K Harrison			1	Pre	Eugene	28 May 16
12.25	WR 1.4	Ginka	Zagorcheva	BUL	12.4.58	1	v TCH,GRE	Drama	8 Aug 87
12.26	WR 1.5		Donkova			1	Balk	Ljubljana	7 Sep 86
12.26	1.7	Lyudmila	Narozhilenko ¶	RUS	21.4.64	1rB		Sevilla	6 Jun 92
		(later Ludmila Engquist SWE)							
12.26	1.2	Brianna	Rollins/McNeal	USA	18.8.91	1	NC	Des Moines	22 Jun 13
12.27	-1.2		Donkova			1		Stara Zagora	28 Aug 88
12.28	1.8		Narozhilenko			1	NC	Kyiv	11 Jul 91
12.28	0.9		Narozhilenko			1rA		Sevilla	6 Jun 92
12.28	1.1	Sally	Pearson'	AUS	19.9.86	1	WCh	Daegu	3 Sep 11
12.28	0.1		K Harrison			1	Gyulai	Székesfehérvár	4 Jul 17
12.29	WR-0.4		Donkova			1	ASV	Köln	17 Aug 86
12.32	1.6		Narozhilenko			1		Saint-Denis	4 Jun 92
12.33	1.4		Donkova			1		Fürth	14 Jun 87
12.33	-0.3	Gail	Devers	USA	19.11.66	1	NC	Sacramento	23 Jul 00
12.34	-0.5		Zagorcheva			1	WCh	Roma	4 Sep 87
12.34	1.9	Sharika	Nelvis	USA	10.5.90	1h3	NC	Eugene	26 Jun 15
12.34	1.2		Rollins			1	NC	Eugene	8 Jul 16
12.35	WR 0.1		Donkova			1h2	ASV	Köln	17 Aug 86
12.35	-0.2		Pearson			1	OG	London (OS)	7 Aug 12
12.35	0.9	Jasmin	Stowers	USA	23.9.91	1	DL	Doha	15 May 15
12.36	WR 1.9	Grazyna	Rabsztyn (10)	POL	20.9.52	1	Kuso	Warszawa	13 Jun 80
12.36	WR-0.6		Donkova			1	NC	Sofia	13 Aug 86
12.36	1.1		Donkova			1		Schwechat	15 Jun 88
12.36	0.3		Pearson			1s2	WCh	Daegu	3 Sep 11
12.36	1.4		K Harrison			1	Towns	Athens GA	8 Apr 16
12.36	0.6		K Harrison			1	DL	London (OS)	22 Jul 18
12.37	1.4		Donkova			1	ISTAF	Berlin	15 Aug 86
12.37	0.7		Devers			1	WCh	Sevilla	28 Aug 99
12.37	1.5	Joanna	Hayes	USA	23.12.76	1		Athína	24 Aug 04
12.37	-0.2	Dawn	Harper Nelson	USA	13.5.84	2	OG	London (OS)	7 Aug 12
12.37	2.0		Nelvis			1s1	NC	Eugene	27 Jun 15
		(34/12)							
12.39	1.5	Vera	Komisova'	RUS	11.6.53	1	GGala	Roma	5 Aug 80
12.39	1.8	Natalya	Grigoryeva ¶	UKR	3.12.62	2	NC	Kyiv	11 Jul 91
12.40	1.2	Jasmine	Camacho-Quinn	PUR	21.8.96	1	SEC	Knoxville	13 May 18
12.41	0.5	Alina	Talay	BLR	14.5.89	1		St. Pölten	31 May 18
12.42	1.8	Bettine	Jahn	GDR	3.8.58	1	OD	Berlin	8 Jun 83
12.42	2.0	Anjanette	Kirkland	USA	24.2.74	1	WCh	Edmonton	11 Aug 01
12.43	-0.9	Lucyna	Kalek (Langer)	POL	9.1.56	1		Hannover	19 Aug 84
12.43	-0.3	Michelle	Perry (20)	USA	1.5.79	1s1	NC	Carson	26 Jun 05
12.43	0.2	Lolo	Jones	USA	5.8.82	1s1	OG	Beijing	18 Aug 08
12.43	1.2	Queen	Harrison	USA	10.9.88	2	NC	Des Moines	22 Jun 13

Mark	Wind	Name		Nat	Born	Pos	Meet	Venue	Date
12.44	-0.5	Gloria	Uibel (-Siebert)	GDR	13.1.64	2	WCh	Roma	4 Sep 87
12.44	-0.8	Olga	Shishigina ¶	KAZ	23.12.68	1	Spitzen	Luzern	27 Jun 95
12.44	0.4	Glory	Alozie	NGR/ESP	30.12.77	1	Herc	Monaco	8 Aug 98
12.44	0.6	Damu	Cherry ¶	USA	29.11.77	2rA	Athl	Lausanne	11 Jul 06
12.45	1.3	Cornelia	Oschkenat'	GDR	29.10.61	1		Neubrandenburg	11 Jun 87
12.45	1.4	Brigitte	Foster-Hylton	JAM	7.11.74	1	Pre	Eugene	24 May 03
12.45	1.5	Olena	Krasovska	UKR	17.8.76	2	OG	Athína	24 Aug 04
12.45	1.4	Virginia	Powell/Crawford	USA	7.9.83	1	GP	New York	2 Jun 07
		(30)							
12.46	0.7	Perdita	Felicien	CAN	29.8.80	1	Pre	Eugene	19 Jun 04
12.47	1.1	Marina	Azyabina	RUS	15.6.63	1s2	NC	Moskva	19 Jun 93
12.47	1.1	Danielle	Carruthers	USA	22.12.79	2	WCh	Daegu	3 Sep 11
12.48	-0.2	Kellie	Wells	USA	16.7.82	3	OG	London (OS)	7 Aug 12
12.48	1.2	Nia	Ali	USA	23.10.88	3	NC	Des Moines	22 Jun 13
12.48	1.3	Danielle	Williams	JAM	14.9.92	2	DL	Stockholm	10 Jun 18
12.49	0.9	Susanna	Kallur	SWE	16.2.81	1	ISTAF	Berlin	16 Sep 07
12.49	1.0	Priscilla	Lopes-Schliep	CAN	26.8.82	2	VD	Bruxelles	4 Sep 09
12.50	0.0	Vera	Akimova'	RUS	5.6.59	1		Sochi	19 May 84
12.50	-0.1	Delloreen	Ennis-London	JAM	5.3.75	3	WCh	Osaka	29 Aug 07
		(40)							
12.50	0.8	Josephine	Onyia ¶	NGR/ESP	15.7.86	1	ISTAF	Berlin	1 Jun 08
12.50	1.2	Kristi	Castlin	USA	7.7.88	2	NC	Eugene	8 Jul 16
12.51	1.4	Miesha	McKelvy	USA	26.7.76	2	Pre	Eugene	24 May 03
12.51	0.7	Tiffany	Porter'	USA/GBR	13.11.87	2	C.Cup	Marrakech	14 Sep 14
12.52	-0.4	Michelle	Freeman	JAM	5.5.69	1s1	WCh	Athína	10 Aug 97
12.53	0.2	Tatyana	Reshetnikova	RUS	14.10.66	1rA	GP II	Linz	4 Jul 94
12.53	-0.4	Svetla	Dimitrova ¶	BUL	27.1.70	1	Herc	Stara Zagora	16 Jul 94
12.53	1.0	Melissa	Morrison	USA	9.7.71	1	DNG	Stockholm	5 Aug 98
12.54	0.4	Kerstin	Knabe	GDR	7.7.59	3	EC	Athína	9 Sep 82
12.54	0.9	Sabine	Paetz/John'	GDR	16.10.57	1		Berlin	15 Jul 84
12.54	1.7	Nichole	Denby	USA	10.10.82	2s2	OT	Eugene	6 Jul 08
12.54	1.3	Jessica	Ennis	GBR	28.1.86	1H5	OG	London (OS)	3 Aug 12
12.54	1.4	Christina	Manning	USA	29.5.90	1	ISTAF	Berlin	27 Aug 17
		(53)							

100th woman 12.66, 200th 12.81, 300th 12.89, 400th 12.98, 500th 13.08

Wind assisted performances to 12.36, performers to 12.52

12.28	2.7	Cornelia	Oschkenat'	GDR	29.10.61	1		Berlin	25 Aug 87
12.29	3.5		Donkova			1	Athl	Lausanne	24 Jun 88
12.29	2.7	Gail	Devers	USA	19.11.66	1	Pre	Eugene	26 May 02
12.29	3.8	Lolo	Jones	USA	5.8.82	1	NC/OT	Eugene	6 Jul 08
12.30	2.8		Rollins			1s1	NC	Des Moines	22 Jun 13
12.33	2.3		Rollins			1h3	NC	Des Moines	21 Jun 13
12.35	2.4	Bettine	Jahn	GDR	3.8.58	1	WCh	Helsinki	13 Aug 83
12.35	3.7	Kellie	Wells	USA	16.7.82	1		Gainesville	16 Apr 11
12.36	2.2	Dawn	Harper Nelson	USA	13.5.84	1	NC	Eugene	28 Jun 09
12.37	2.7	Gloria	Uibel/Siebert'	GDR	13.1.64	2		Berlin	25 Aug 87
12.37	3.4	Danielle	Carruthers	USA	22.12.79	1s1	NC	Eugene	26 Jun 11
12.40	2.1	Michelle	Freeman	JAM	5.5.69	1	GPF	Fukuoka	13 Sep 97
12.41	2.2	Olga	Shishigina ¶	KAZ	23.12.68	1rA	Athl	Lausanne	5 Jul 95
12.42	2.4	Kerstin	Knabe	GDR	7.7.59	2	WCh	Helsinki	13 Aug 83
12.43	2.7	Yvette	Lewis	USA/PAN	16.3.85	1	MSR	Walnut	20 Apr 13
12.44	2.6	Melissa	Morrison	USA	9.7.71	1		Carson	22 May 04
12.45	2.1	Perdita	Felicien	CAN	29.8.80	1	NC	Victoria	10 Jul 04
12.47	3.0	Tiffany	Porter	USA/GBR	13.11.87	1		Gainesville	21 Apr 12
12.48	3.8	Kristi	Castlin	USA	7.7.88	1		Clermont	2 Jun 12
12.50	2.7	Svetla	Dimitrova ¶	BUL	27.1.70	1		Saint-Denis	10 Jun 94
12.51	3.2	Johanna	Klier'	GDR	13.9.52	1	NC	Cottbus	17 Jul 80
12.51	3.6	Sabine	Paetz/John'	GDR	16.10.57	1		Dresden	27 Jul 84
12.51A	3.3	Yuliya	Graudyn	RUS	13.11.70	1		Sestriere	31 Jul 94
12.52	3.1	Angela	Whyte	CAN	22.5.80	2		Edmonton	29 Jun 13

Probably hand timed Officially 12.36, but subsequent investigations showed this unlikely to have been auto-timed

12.4	0.7	Svetla	Dimitrova ¶	BUL	27.1.70	1		Stara Zagora	9 Jul 97

Hand timed

12.3 WR	1.5	Anneliese	Ehrhardt	GDR	18.6.50	1	NC	Dresden	22 Jul 73
12.3		Marina	Azyabina	RUS	15.6.63	1		Yekaterinburg	30 May 93
12.0w	2.1	Yordanka	Donkova	BUL	28.9.61	1		Sofia	3 Aug 86
12.1w	2.1	Ginka	Zagorcheva	BUL	12.4.58	2		Sofia	3 Aug 86

400 METRES HURDLES

52.34 WR		Yuliya	Nosova-Pechonkina'	RUS	21.4.78	1	NC	Tula	8 Aug 03
52.42		Melaine	Walker	JAM	1.1.83	1	WCh	Berlin	20 Aug 09

Mark	Wind	Name		Nat	Born	Pos	Meet	Venue	Date
52.47		Lashinda	Demus	USA	10.3.83	1	WCh	Daegu	1 Sep 11
52.61	WR	Kim	Batten	USA	29.3.69	1	WCh	Göteborg	11 Aug 95
52.62		Tonja	Buford-Bailey	USA	13.12.70	2	WCh	Göteborg	11 Aug 95
52.63			Demus			1	Herc	Monaco	28 Jul 09
52.64			Walker			1	OG	Beijing	20 Aug 08
52.64		Dalilah	Muhammad	USA	7.2.90	1	NC	Sacramento	25 Jun 17
52.70		Natalya	Antyukh	RUS	26.6.81	1	OG	London (OS)	8 Aug 12
52.73			Walker			2	WCh	Daegu	1 Sep 11
52.74	WR	Sally	Gunnell	GBR	29.7.66	1	WCh	Stuttgart	19 Aug 93
52.74			Batten			1	Herc	Monaco	8 Aug 98
52.75		Shamier	Little	USA	20.3.95	2	NC	Sacramento	25 Jun 17
52.75		Sydney	McLaughlin (10)	USA	7.8.99	1	SEC	Knoxville	13 May 18
52.77		Faní	Halkiá ¶	GRE	2.2.79	1s2	OG	Athína	22 Aug 04
52.77			Demus			2	OG	London (OS)	8 Aug 12
52.79		Sandra	Farmer-Patrick	USA	18.8.62	2	WCh	Stuttgart	19 Aug 93
52.79		Kaliese	Spencer	JAM	6.5.87	1	LGP	London (CP)	5 Aug 11
52.82		Deon	Hemmings	JAM	9.10.68	1	OG	Atlanta	31 Jul 96
52.82			Halkiá			1	OG	Athína	25 Aug 04
52.82			Demus			1	GGala	Roma	10 Jun 10
52.83		Zuzana	Hejnová	CZE	19.12.86	1	WCh	Moskva	15 Aug 13
52.84			Batten			1	WK	Zürich	12 Aug 98
52.88			Muhammad			1	NC	Eugene	10 Jul 16
52.89		Daimí	Pernía	CUB	27.12.76	1	WCh	Sevilla	25 Aug 99
52.90			Buford			1	WK	Zürich	16 Aug 95
52.90		Nezha	Bidouane	MAR	18.9.69	2	WCh	Sevilla	25 Aug 99
52.90			Pechonkina			1	WCh	Helsinki	13 Aug 05
52.92			Antyukh			1	EC	Barcelona	30 Jul 10
52.94	WR	Marina (30/198)	Styepanova'	RUS	1.5.50	1s	Spart	Tashkent	17 Sep 86
52.95		Sheena	Johnson/Tosta	USA	1.10.82	1	NC/OT	Sacramento	11 Jul 04
52.95		Kori	Carter (20)	USA	3.6.92	3	NC	Sacramento	25 Jun 17
53.02		Irina	Privalova	RUS	22.11.68	1	OG	Sydney	27 Sep 00
53.11		Tatyana	Ledovskaya	BLR	21.5.66	1	WCh	Tokyo	29 Aug 91
53.11		Ashley	Spencer	USA	8.6.93	4	NC	Sacramento	25 Jun 17
53.14		Georganne	Moline	USA	6.3.90	5	NC	Sacramento	25 Jun 17
53.17		Debbie	Flintoff-King	AUS	20.4.60	1	OG	Seoul	28 Sep 88
53.20		Josanne	Lucas	TTO	14.5.84	3	WCh	Berlin	20 Aug 09
53.21		Marie-José	Pérec	FRA	9.5.68	2	WK	Zürich	16 Aug 95
53.22		Jana	Pittman/Rawlinson	AUS	9.11.82	1	WCh	Saint-Denis	28 Aug 03
53.24		Sabine	Busch	GDR	21.11.62	1	NC	Potsdam	21 Aug 87
53.25		Ionela (30)	Târlea-Manolache	ROU	9.2.76	2	GGala	Roma	7 Jul 99
53.28		Tiffany	Ross-Williams	USA	5.2.83	1	NC	Indianapolis	24 Jun 07
53.32		Sandra	Glover	USA	30.12.68	3	WCh	Helsinki	13 Aug 05
53.36		Andrea	Blackett	BAR	24.1.76	4	WCh	Sevilla	25 Aug 99
53.36		Brenda	Taylor	USA	9.2.79	2	NC/OT	Sacramento	11 Jul 04
53.37		Tetyana	Tereshchuk	UKR	11.10.69	3s2	OG	Athína	22 Aug 04
53.46		Janieve	Russell	JAM	14.11.93	2	Athl	Lausanne	5 Jul 18
53.47		Janeene	Vickers	USA	3.10.68	3	WCh	Tokyo	29 Aug 91
53.48		Margarita	Ponomaryova'	RUS	19.6.63	3	WCh	Stuttgart	19 Aug 93
53.55		Sara Slott	Petersen	DEN	9.4.87	2	OG	Rio de Janeiro	18 Aug 16
53.58		Cornelia (40)	Ullrich'	GDR	26.4.63	2	NC	Potsdam	21 Aug 87
53.63		Ellen	Fiedler'	GDR	26.11.58	3	OG	Seoul	28 Sep 88
53.65A	mx	Myrtle	Bothma'	RSA	18.2.64	mx		Pretoria	12 Mar 90
53.74A						1		Johannesburg	18 Apr 86
53.67		Perri	Shakes-Drayton	GBR	21.12.88	2	DL	London (OS)	26 Jul 13
53.68		Vania	Stambolova ¶	BUL	28.11.83	1		Rabat	5 Jun 11
53.72		Yekaterina	Bikert	RUS	13.5.80	2	NC	Tula	30 Jul 04
53.74		Ristananna	Tracey	JAM	9.5.92	3	WCh	London (OS)	10 Aug 17
53.77		Irina	Davydova	RUS	27.5.88	1	EC	Helsinki	29 Jun 12
53.84		Natasha	Danvers	GBR	19.9.77	3	OG	Beijing	20 Aug 08
53.85		Angela	Morosanu	ROU	26.7.86	2	DL	Shanghai	18 May 13
53.86		Anna (50)	Jesien	POL	10.12.78	1s3	WCh	Osaka	28 Aug 07
		100th woman 54.45, 200th 55.25, 300th 55.70, 400th 56.04, 500th 56.34							
Drugs disqualification: 53.38		Jiang Limei ¶	CHN	.3.70	(1)			Shanghai	22 Oct 97

HIGH JUMP

Mark	Wind	Name		Nat	Born	Pos	Meet	Venue	Date
2.09	WR	Stefka	Kostadinova	BUL	25.3.65	1	WCh	Roma	30 Aug 87
2.08	WR		Kostadinova			1	NM	Sofia	31 May 86

Mark	Wind	Name		Nat	Born	Pos	Meet	Venue	Date
2.08i		Kajsa	Bergqvist	SWE	12.10.76	1		Arnstadt	4 Feb 06
2.08		Blanka	Vlasic	CRO	8.11.83	1	Hanz	Zagreb	31 Aug 09
2.07 WR		Lyudmila	Andonova ¶	BUL	6.5.60	1	OD	Berlin	20 Jul 84
2.07 WR			Kostadinova			1		Sofia	25 May 86
2.07			Kostadinova			1		Cagliari	16 Sep 87
2.07			Kostadinova			1	NC	Sofia	3 Sep 88
2.07i		Heike	Henkel'	GER	5.5.64	1	NC	Karlsruhe	8 Feb 92
2.07			Vlasic			1	DNG	Stockholm	7 Aug 07
2.07		Anna	Chicherova ¶	RUS	22.7.82	1	NC	Cheboksary	22 Jul 11
2.06			Kostadinova			1	ECp	Moskva	18 Aug 85
2.06			Kostadinova			1		Fürth	15 Jun 86
2.06			Kostadinova			1		Cagliari	14 Sep 86
2.06			Kostadinova			1		Wörrstadt	6 Jun 87
2.06			Kostadinova			1		Rieti	8 Sep 87
2.06i			Kostadinova			1		Pireás	20 Feb 88
2.06			Bergqvist			1		Eberstadt	26 Jul 03
2.06		Hestrie	Cloete	RSA	26.8.78	1	WCh	Saint-Denis	31 Aug 03
2.06		Yelena	Slesarenko	RUS	28.2.82	1	OG	Athína	28 Aug 04
2.06			Vlasic			1		Thessaloníki	30 Jul 07
2.06			Vlasic			1	ECp-1B	Istanbul	22 Jun 08
2.06			Vlasic			1	GP	Madrid	5 Jul 08
2.06		Ariane	Friedrich	GER	10.1.84	1	ISTAF	Berlin	14 Jun 09
2.06i			Vlasic			1		Arnstadt	6 Feb 10
2.06i			Chicherova			1		Arnstadt	4 Feb 12
2.06		Mariya	Lasitskene' (10)	RUS	14.1.93	1	Athl	Lausanne	6 Jul 17
2.05 WR		Tamara	Bykova	RUS	21.12.58	1	Izv	Kyiv	22 Jun 84
2.05		Inga	Babakova	UKR	27.6.67	1		Tokyo	15 Sep 95
2.05i		Tia	Hellebaut	BEL	16.2.78	1	EI	Birmingham	3 Mar 07
2.05		Chaunté	Lowe'	USA	12.1.84	1	NC	Des Moines	20 Jun 10

(60/14) with Further 2.05 performances: Kostadinova 10, Vlasic 10, Bergqvist, Chicherova 2, Hellebaut, Henkel, Cloete, Friedrich, Lasikskene 1

2.04		Silvia	Costa	CUB	4.5.64	1	WCp	Barcelona	9 Sep 89
2.04i		Alina	Astafei	GER	7.6.69	1		Berlin	3 Mar 95
2.04		Venelina	Veneva ¶	BUL	13.6.74	1		Kalamáta	2 Jun 01
2.04i		Antonietta	Di Martino	ITA	1.6.78	1		Banská Bystrica	9 Feb 11
2.04		Irina	Gordeyeva	RUS	9.10.86	1		Eberstadt	19 Aug 12
2.04		Brigetta (20)	Barrett	USA	24.12.90	1	NC	Des Moines	22 Jun 13
2.03 WR		Ulrike	Meyfarth	FRG	4.5.56	1	ECp	London (CP)	21 Aug 83
2.03		Louise	Ritter	USA	18.2.58	1		Austin	8 Jul 88
2.03		Tatyana	Motkova	RUS	23.11.68	2		Bratislava	30 May 95
2.03		Níki	Bakoyiánni	GRE	9.6.68	2	OG	Atlanta	3 Aug 96
2.03i		Monica	Iagar/Dinescu	ROU	2.4.73	1		Bucuresti	23 Jan 99
2.03i		Marina	Kuptsova	RUS	22.12.81	1	EI	Wien	2 Mar 02
2.03		Svetlana	Shkolina	RUS	9.3.86	3	OG	London (OS)	11 Aug 12
2.02i		Susanne	Beyer'	GDR	24.6.61	2	WI	Indianapolis	8 Mar 87
2.02		Yelena	Yelesina	RUS	4.4.70	1	GWG	Seattle	23 Jul 90
2.02		Viktoriya (30)	Styopina	UKR	21.2.76	3	OG	Athína	28 Aug 04
2.02		Ruth	Beitia	ESP	1.4.79	1	NC	San Sebastián	4 Aug 07
2.02i		Kamila	Licwinko'	POL	22.3.86	1	NC	Torun	21 Feb 15
2.02		Elena	Vallortigara	ITA	21.9.91	2	DL	London (OS)	22 Jul 18
2.01 WR		Sara	Simeoni	ITA	19.4.53	1	v Pol	Brescia	4 Aug 78
2.01		Olga	Turchak	UKR	5.3.67	2	GWG	Moskva	7 Jul 86
2.01A		Desiré	du Plessis	RSA	20.5.65	1		Johannesburg	16 Sep 86
2.01i		Gabriele	Günz	GDR	8.9.61	2		Stuttgart	31 Jan 88
2.01		Heike	Balck	GDR	19.8.70	1	vUSSR-j	Karl-Marx-Stadt	18 Jun 89
2.01i		Ioamnet	Quintero	CUB	8.9.72	1		Berlin	5 Mar 93
2.01		Hanne (40)	Haugland	NOR	14.12.67	1	WK	Zürich	13 Aug 97
2.01i		Tisha	Waller	USA	1.12.70	1	NC	Atlanta	28 Feb 98
2.01		Yelena	Gulyayeva ¶	RUS	14.8.67	2		Kalamáta	23 May 98
2.01		Vita	Palamar	UKR	12.10.77	2=	WK	Zürich	15 Aug 03
2.01		Amy	Acuff	USA	14.7.75	4	WK	Zürich	15 Aug 03
2.01		Iryna	Myhalchenko	UKR	20.1.72	1		Eberstadt	18 Jul 04
2.01		Emma	Green Tregaro	SWE	8.12.84	2	EC	Barcelona	1 Aug 10
2.01i		Airine	Palsyte	LTU	13.7.92	1	EI	Beograd	4 Mar 17
2.01		Yuliya	Levchenko	UKR	28.11.97	2	WCh	London (OS)	12 Aug 17
2.01		Nafissatou (49)	Thiam	BEL	19.8.94	1H	Hypo	Götzis	26 May 18

100th woman 1.98, 200th 1.95, 300th 1.93, 400th 1.92, 500th 1.905

Mark	Wind	Name	Nat	Born	Pos	Meet	Venue	Date

Best outdoor marks

Mark		Name						
2.05	Henkel	1	WCh	Tokyo	31 Aug 91			
2.05	Hellebaut	1	OG	Beijing	23 Aug 08			
2.03	Di Martino	1	ECp-1B	Milano	24 Jun 07			
2.02	Iagar/Dinescu	1		Budapest	6 Jun 98			

2.02	Kuptsova	1	FBK	Hengelo	1 Jun 03
2.01	Astafei	2		Wörrstadt	27 May 95
2.00	Kositsyna, Quintero, Bilac, Waller				

Ancillary jumps: 2.06 Kostadinova 30 Aug 87, 2.05i Henkel 8 Feb 92, 2.05i Bergqvist 4 Feb 06, 2.05 Vlasic 31 Aug 09

POLE VAULT

WOMEN All-time

Mark		Name	Nat	Born	Pos	Meet	Venue	Date
5.06 WR	Yelena	Isinbayeva	RUS	3.6.82	1	WK	Zürich	28 Aug 09
5.05 WR		Isinbayeva			1	OG	Beijing	18 Aug 08
5.04 WR		Isinbayeva			1	Herc	Monaco	29 Jul 08
5.03 WR		Isinbayeva			1	GGala	Roma	11 Jul 08
5.03i WIR	Jennifer	Suhr	USA	5.2.82	1		Brockport	30 Jan 16
5.02Ai WIR		Suhr			1	NC	Albuquerque	2 Mar 13
5.01 WR		Isinbayeva			1	WCh	Helsinki	12 Aug 05
5.01i WIR		Isinbayeva			1	XL Galan	Stockholm	23 Feb 12
5.01i		Suhr			1		Fredonia	1 Oct 16
5.00 WR		Isinbayeva			1	LGP	London (CP)	22 Jul 05
5.00i		Isinbayeva			1		Donetsk	15 Feb 09
5.00	Sandi	Morris	USA	8.7.92	1	VD	Bruxelles	9 Sep 16
4.95 WR		Isinbayeva			1	GP	Madrid	16 Jul 05
4.95i		Isinbayeva			1		Donetsk	16 Feb 08
4.95i		Morris			1	NC	Portland	12 Mar 16
4.95i		Morris			1	WI	Birmingham	3 Mar 18
4.95		Morris			1		Greenville	27 Jul 18
4.94	Eliza	McCartney	NZL	11.12.96	1		Jockgrim	17 Jul 18
4.93 WR		Isinbayeva			1	Athl	Lausanne	5 Jul 05
4.93		Isinbayeva			1	VD	Bruxelles	26 Aug 05
4.93i		Isinbayeva			1		Donetsk	10 Feb 07
4.93		Isinbayeva			1	LGP	London (CP)	25 Jul 08
4.93		Morris			1		Houston	23 Jul 16
4.93		Suhr			1		Austin	14 Apr 18
4.92 WR		Isinbayeva			1	VD	Bruxelles	3 Sep 04
4.92		Stuczynski/Suhr			1	NC/OT	Eugene	6 Jul 08
4.92		McCartney			1		Mannheim	23 Jun 18
4.91 WR		Isinbayeva (this jump on 25 Aug)			1	OG	Athína	25 Aug 04
4.91i		Isinbayeva			1		Donetsk	12 Feb 06
4.91		Isinbayeva			1	LGP	London (CP)	28 Jul 06
4.91		Isinbayeva			1	Gaz	Saint-Denis	6 Jul 07
4.91		Suhr			1		Rochester, NY	26 Jul 11
4.91		Suhr			1		Lyndonville	14 Jun 13
4.91	Yarisley	Silva	CUB	1.6.87	1		Beckum	2 Aug 15
4.91i		Suhr			1		Kent	16 Jan 16
4.91	Ekateríni	Stefanídi	GRE	4.2.90	1	WCh	London (OS)	6 Aug 17
4.91iA	Katie	Nageotte	USA	30.6.91	1	NC	Albuquerque	18 Feb 18
	(37/7)							
4.90i	Demi	Payne	USA	30.9.91	2	Mill	New York (A)	20 Feb 16
4.90i	Anzhelika	Sidorova	RUS	28.6.91	2	WI	Birmingham	3 Mar 18
4.88 WR	Svetlana	Feofanova	RUS	16.7.80	1		Iráklio	4 Jul 04
	(10)							
4.87i	Holly	Bleasdale/Bradshaw	GBR	2.11.91	1		Villeurbanne	20 Jan 12
4.87	Fabiana	Murer	BRA	16.3.81	1	NC	São Bernardo do Campo	3 Jul 16
4.85i	Anna	Rogowska	POL	21.5.81	1	EI	Paris (Bercy)	6 Mar 11
4.83	Stacy	Dragila	USA	25.3.71	1	GS	Ostrava	8 Jun 04
4.83	Nikoléta	Kiriakopoúlou	GRE	21.3.86	1	DL	Saint-Denis	4 Jul 15
4.82	Monika	Pyrek	POL	11.8.80	2	WAF	Stuttgart	22 Sep 07
4.82	Silke	Spiegelburg	GER	17.3.86	1	Herc	Monaco	20 Jul 12
4.81	Alana	Boyd	AUS	10.5.84	1		Sippy Downs	2 Jul 16
4.80	Martina	Strutz	GER	4.11.81	2	WCh	Daegu	30 Aug 11
4.80i	Nicole	Büchler	SUI	17.12.83	4	WI	Portland	17 Mar 16
	(20)							
4.78	Tatyana	Polnova	RUS	20.4.79	2	WAF	Monaco	19 Sep 04
4.77	Annika	Becker	GER	12.11.81	1	NC	Wattenscheid	7 Jul 02
4.76	Jirina	Ptácníková'	CZE	20.5.86	1		Plzen	4 Sep 13
4.75	Katerina	Badurová	CZE	18.12.82	2	WCh	Osaka	28 Aug 07
4.75i	Yuliya	Golubchikova	RUS	27.3.83	1		Athína (P)	13 Feb 08
4.75Ai	Kylie	Hutson	USA	27.11.87	2	NC	Albuquerque	2 Mar 13
4.75i	Lisa	Ryzih	GER	27.9.88	2	EI	Beograd	4 Mar 17
4.75	Alysha	Newman	CAN	29.6.94	2		Beckum	27 Aug 17

Mark	Wind	Name		Nat	Born	Pos	Meet	Venue	Date
4.75		Ninon	Guillon-Romarin	FRA	15.4.95	8	Herc	Monaco	20 Jul 18
4.73		Chelsea	Johnson	USA	20.12.83	1		Los Gatos	26 Jun 08
(30)									
4.73		Anastasiya	Savchenko	RUS	15.11.89	1	NCp	Yerino	15 Jun 13
4.73		Angelica	Bengtsson	SWE	8.7.93	1		Karlstad	25 Jul 18
4.72i		Kym	Howe	AUS	12.6.80	2		Donetsk	10 Feb 07
4.72i		Jillian	Schwartz	USA/ISR	19.9.79	1		Jonesboro	15 Jun 08
4.72		Carolin	Hingst	GER	18.9.80	1		Biberach	9 Jul 10
4.71i		Tina	Sutej	SLO	7.11.88	1		Moskva	2 Feb 14
4.71Ai		Mary	Saxer Sibears	USA	21.6.87	1	NC	Albuquerque	23 Feb 14
4.71i		Marion	Fiack	FRA	13.10.92	1		Aubière	10 Jan 15
4.71i		Wilma	Murto	FIN	11.6.98	1		Zweibrücken	31 Jan 16
4.71		Michaela	Meijer	SWE	30.7.93	1		Göteborg	2 Jul 17
(40)									
4.71		Nina	Kennedy	AUS	5.4.97	1		Perth	9 Feb 18
4.70		Yvonne	Buschbaum	GER	14.7.80	1	NC	Ulm	29 Jun 03
4.70		Vanessa	Boslak	FRA	11.6.82	2	ECp-S	Málaga	28 Jun 06
4.70		Angelina	Zhuk/Krasnova	RUS	7.2.91	1	EU23	Tampere	13 Jul 13
4.70i			Li Ling	CHN	6.7.89	1	AsC	Doha	19 Feb 16
4.70		Kristen	Brown	USA	26.5.92	1		Chula Vista	26 Jun 16
4.70		Lexi	Weeks	USA	20.11.96	3	NC	Eugene	10 Jul 16
4.70A		Rosbeilys	Peinado	VEN	26.11.97	1	SAmG	Cochabamba	7 Jun 18
4.68		Anna	Battke	GER	3.1.85	5	ISTAF	Berlin	14 Jun 09
4.67i		Kellie	Suttle	USA	9.5.73	1		Jonesboro	16 Jun 04
4.67		Olga	Mullina	RUS	1.8.92	1		Kuortane	17 Jun 17
4.67i		Olivia	Gruver	USA	29.7.97	1	SEC	College Station	24 Feb 18
4.67		Iryna	Zhuk	BLR	26.1.93	1		Székesfehérvár	30 Jun 18
(53)									

100th woman 4.57, 200th 4.45, 300th 4.35, 400th 4.30, 500th 4.25

Outdoor bests

4.85	Sidorova	2	NC	Cheboksary	21 Jun 16	4.75	Golubchikova	4	OG	Beijing	18 Aug 08
4.83	Rogowska	2	VD	Bruxelles	26 Aug 05	4.73	Ryzih	3		Rottach-Egern	15 Jul 17
4.81	Bradshaw	1		Rottach-Egern	15 Jul 17	4.71	Payne	1		Hammond	8 May 15
4.80	Nageotte	1		Beckum	26 Aug 18	4.70	Hutson	1		Terre Haute	15 Jun 13
4.78	Büchler	2	DL	Doha	6 May 16	4.70	Saxer	1		Chula Vista	6 Jun 13

Ancillary jumps: Isinbayeva: 4.97 15 Feb 09, 4.96 WR 22 Jul 05, 4.95 18 Aug 08, 4.93 29 Jul 08, 4.92i 23 Feb 12

Exhibition: 4.72 Anastasiya Shvedova RUS 3.5.79 1 Aosta 5 Jul 08

LONG JUMP

Mark	Wind	Name		Nat	Born	Pos	Meet	Venue	Date
7.52 WR	1.4	Galina	Chistyakova	RUS	26.7.62	1	Znam	Leningrad	11 Jun 88
7.49	1.3	Jackie	Joyner-Kersee	USA	3.3.62	1	NYG	New York	22 May 94
7.49A	1.7		Joyner-Kersee			1		Sestriere	31 Jul 94
7.48	1.2	Heike	Drechsler	GER	16.12.64	1	v ITA	Neubrandenburg	9 Jul 88
7.48	0.4		Drechsler			1	Athl	Lausanne	8 Jul 92
7.45 WR	0.9		Drechsler'			1	v USSR	Tallinn	21 Jun 86
7.45 WR	1.1		Drechsler			1	OD	Dresden	3 Jul 86
7.45 WR	0.6		Joyner-Kersee			1	PAm	Indianapolis	13 Aug 87
7.45	1.6		Chistyakova			1	BGP	Budapest	12 Aug 88
7.44 WR	2.0		Drechsler			1		Berlin	22 Sep 85
7.43 WR	1.4	Anisoara	Cusmir/Stanciu	ROU	28.6.62	1	RomIC	Bucuresti	4 Jun 83
7.42	2.0	Tatyana	Kotova ¶	RUS	11.12.76	1	ECp-S	Annecy	23 Jun 02
7.40	1.8		Daute' (Drechsler)			1		Dresden	26 Jul 84
7.40	0.7		Drechsler			1	NC	Potsdam	21 Aug 87
7.40	0.9		Joyner-Kersee			1	OG	Seoul	29 Sep 88
7.39	0.3		Drechsler			1	WK	Zürich	21 Aug 85
7.39	0.5	Yelena	Byelevskaya'	BLR	11.10.63	1	NC	Bryansk	18 Jul 87
7.39			Joyner-Kersee			1		San Diego	25 Jun 88
7.37i	-		Drechsler			1	v2N	Wien	13 Feb 88
7.37A	1.8		Drechsler			1		Sestriere	31 Jul 91
7.37		Inessa	Kravets ¶	UKR	5.10.66	1		Kyiv	13 Jun 92
7.36	0.4		Joyner			1	WCh	Roma	4 Sep 87
7.36	1.8		Byelevskaya			2	Znam	Leningrad	11 Jun 88
7.36	1.8		Drechsler			1		Jena	28 May 92
7.35	1.9		Chistyakova			1	GPB	Bratislava	20 Jun 90
7.34	1.6		Daute'			1		Dresden	19 May 84
7.34	1.4		Chistyakova			2	v GDR	Tallinn	21 Jun 86
7.34			Byelevskaya			1		Sukhumi	17 May 87
7.34	0.7		Drechsler			1	v USSR	Karl-Marx-Stadt	20 Jun 87
7.33	0.4		Drechsler			1	v USSR	Erfurt	22 Jun 85
7.33	2.0		Drechsler			1		Dresden	2 Aug 85
7.33	-0.3		Drechsler			1	Herc	Monaco	11 Aug 92

Mark	Wind	Name		Nat	Born	Pos	Meet	Venue	Date
7.33	0.4	Tatyana	Lebedeva	RUS	21.7.76	1	NC	Tula	31 Jul 04
		(33/8)							
7.31	1.5	Yelena	Kokonova'	UKR	4.8.63	1	NP	Alma-Ata	12 Sep 85
7.31	1.9	Marion	Jones ¶	USA	12.10.75	1	Pre	Eugene	31 May 98
		(10)							
7.31	1.7	Brittney	Reese	USA	9.9.86	1	NC	Eugene	2 Jul 16
7.27	-0.4	Irina	Simagina/Meleshina	RUS	25.5.82	2	NC	Tula	31 Jul 04
7.26A	1.8	Maurren	Maggi ¶	BRA	25.6.76	1	SACh	Bogotá	26 Jun 99
7.24	1.0	Larisa	Berezhnaya	UKR	28.2.61	1		Granada	25 May 91
7.24i		Ivana	Spanovic	SRB	10.5.90	1	EI	Beograd	5 Mar 17
7.21	1.6	Helga	Radtke	GDR	16.5.62	2		Dresden	26 Jul 84
7.21	1.9	Lyudmila	Kolchanova	RUS	1.10.79	1		Sochi	27 May 07
7.20 WR	-0.5	Valy	Ionescu	ROU	31.8.60	1	NC	Bucuresti	1 Aug 82
7.20	2.0	Irena	Ozhenko'	LTU	13.11.62	1		Budapest	12 Sep 86
7.20	0.8	Yelena	Sinchukova'	RUS	23.1.61	1	BGP	Budapest	20 Jun 91
		(20)							
7.20	0.7	Irina	Mushayilova	RUS	6.1.67	1	NC	Sankt-Peterburg	14 Jul 94
7.17	1.8	Irina	Valyukevich	BLR	19.11.59	2	NC	Bryansk	18 Jul 87
7.17	0.6	Tianna	Bartoletta'	USA	30.8.85	1	OG	Rio de Janeiro	17 Aug 16
7.16		Iolanda	Chen	RUS	26.7.61	1		Moskva	30 Jul 88
7.16A	-0.1	Elva	Goulbourne	JAM	21.1.80	1		Ciudad de México	22 May 04
7.16	1.6	Sosthene	Moguenara	GER	17.10.89	1		Weinheim	28 May 16
7.14	1.8	Nijole	Medvedeva ¶	LTU	20.10.60	1		Riga	4 Jun 88
7.14	1.2	Mirela	Dulgheru	ROU	5.10.66	1	Balk G	Sofia	5 Jul 92
7.13	2.0	Olga	Kucherenko ¶	RUS	5.11.85	1		Sochi	27 May 10
7.12	1.6	Sabine	Paetz/John'	GDR	16.10.57	2		Dresden	19 May 84
		(30)							
7.12	0.9	Chioma	Ajunwa ¶	NGR	25.12.70	1	OG	Atlanta	2 Aug 96
7.12	1.3	Naide	Gomes	CPV/POR	10.11.79	1	Herc	Monaco	29 Jul 08
7.11	0.8	Fiona	May	GBR/ITA	12.12.69	2	EC	Budapest	22 Aug 98
7.11	1.3	Anna	Nazarova	RUS	3.2.86	1	Mosc Ch	Moskva	20 Jun 12
7.10	1.6	Chelsea	Hayes	USA	9.2.88	2	NC/OT	Eugene	1 Jul 12
7.09 WR	0.0	Vilhelmina	Bardauskiené	LTU	15.6.53	Q	EC	Praha	29 Jul 78
7.09	1.5	Ljudmila	Ninova	AUT	25.6.60	1	GP II	Sevilla	5 Jun 94
7.08	0.5	Marieta	Ilcu ¶	ROU	16.10.62	1	RumIC	Pitesti	25 Jun 89
7.08	1.9	Anastasiya	Mironchik-Ivanova	BLR	13.4.89	1		Minsk	12 Jun 12
7.07	0.0	Svetlana	Zorina	RUS	2.2.60	1		Krasnodar	15 Aug 87
		(40)							
7.07	0.5	Yelena	Sokolova	RUS	23.7.86	2	OG	London (OS)	8 Aug 12
7.07	0.4	Shara	Proctor	AIA/GBR	16.9.88	2	WCh	Beijing	28 Aug 15
7.06	0.4	Tatyana	Kolpakova	KGZ	18.10.59	1	OG	Moskva	31 Jul 80
7.06	-0.1	Niurka	Montalvo	CUB/ESP	4.6.68	1	WCh	Sevilla	23 Aug 99
7.06		Tatyana	Ter-Mesrobyan	RUS	12.5.68	1		Sankt Peterburg	22 May 02
7.05	0.6	Lyudmila	Galkina	RUS	20.1.72	1	WCh	Athína	9 Aug 97
7.05	-0.4	Eunice	Barber	FRA	17.11.74	1	WAF	Monaco	14 Sep 03
7.05	1.1	Darya	Klishina	RUS	15.1.91	1	EU23	Ostrava	17 Jul 11
7.05	2.0	Brooke	Stratton	AUS	12.7.93	1		Perth	12 Mar 16
7.05	1.2	Lorraine	Ugen	GBR	22.8.91	1	NC	Birmingham	1 Jul 18
		(50)							

Wind assisted   *Performances to 7.35, performers to 7.07*

100th woman 6.93, 200th 6.82, 300th 6.76, 400th 6.71, 500th 6.65

7.63A	2.1	Heike	Drechsler	GER	16.12.64	1		Sestriere	21 Jul 92
7.45	2.6		Joyner-Kersee			1	NC/OT	Indianapolis	23 Jul 88
7.39	2.6		Drechsler			1		Padova	15 Sep 91
7.39	2.9		Drechsler			1	Expo	Sevilla	6 Jun 92
7.39A	3.3		Drechsler			2		Sestriere	31 Jul 94
7.36	2.2		Chistyakova			1	Znam	Volgograd	11 Jun 89
7.35	3.4		Drechsler			1	NC	Jena	29 Jun 86
7.23A	4.3	Fiona	May	ITA	12.12.69	1		Sestriere	29 Jul 95
7.22	4.3	Anastasiya	Mironchik-Ivanova	BLR	13.4.89	1	NC	Grodno	6 Jul 12
7.19A	3.7	Susen	Tiedtke ¶	GER	23.1.69	1		Sestriere	28 Jul 93
7.17	3.6	Eva	Murková	SVK	29.5.62	1		Nitra	26 Aug 84
7.15	2.8	Janay	DeLoach-Soukup	USA	12.10.85	Q	NC/OT	Eugene	29 Jun 12
7.14A	4.5	Marieke	Veltman	USA	18.9.71	2		Sestriere	29 Jul 95
7.14	2.2	Blessing	Okagbare	NGR	9.10.88	2	DL	Doha	10 May 13
7.12A	5.8	Níki	Xánthou	GRE	11.10.73	3		Sestriere	29 Jul 95
7.12A	4.3	Nicole	Boegman	AUS	5.3.67	4		Sestriere	29 Jul 95
7.09	2.9	Renata	Nielsen	DEN	18.5.66	2		Sevilla	5 Jun 94
7.08	2.2	Lyudmila	Galkina	RUS	20.1.72	1		Thessaloniki	23 Jun 99
7.07A	5.6	Valentina	Uccheddu	ITA	26.10.66	5		Sestriere	29 Jul 95
7.07A	2.7	Sharon	Couch	USA	13.9.67	1		El Paso	12 Apr 97
7.07A	w	Erica	Johansson	SWE	5.2.74	1		Vygieskraal	15 Jan 00

WOMEN All-time

Mark	Wind	Name		Nat	Born	Pos	Meet	Venue	Date

Best outdoors: 7.10 0.3   Spanovic 1 Beograd 11 Sep 16
Best at low altitude:

| 7.06 | 0.8 | Maggi ¶ | 1 | Milano | 3 Jun 03 | | 7.12w | 3.4 | May | 1 | NC | Bologna | 25 May 96 |

7.17w 2.6   1   São Paulo 13 Apr 02

Ancillary marks – other marks during series (to 7.34/7.36w)

| 7.45 | 1.0 | Chistyakova | 11 Jun 88 | 7.47Aw | 3.1 Drechsler | 21 Jul 92 | 7.38w | 2.2 Chistyakova 11 Jun 88 |
| 7.37 | | Drechsler | 9 Jul 88 | 7.39Aw | 3.1 Drechsler | 21 Jul 92 | 7.36w | Joyner-Kersee 31 Jul 94 |

TRIPLE JUMP

Mark	Wind	Name		Nat	Born	Pos	Meet	Venue	Date
15.50 WR	0.9	Inessa	Kravets ¶	UKR	5.10.66	1	WCh	Göteborg	10 Aug 95
15.39	0.5	Françoise	Mbango	CMR	14.4.76	1	OG	Beijing	17 Aug 08
15.36i		Tatyana	Lebedeva ¶	RUS	21.7.76	1	WI	Budapest	6 Mar 04
15.34	-0.5		Lebedeva			1		Iráklio	4 Jul 04
15.33	-0.1		Kravets			1	OG	Atlanta	31 Jul 96
15.33	1.2		Lebedeva			1	Athl	Lausanne	6 Jul 04
15.32	0.5		Lebedeva			1	Super	Yokohama	9 Sep 00
15.32	0.9	Hrisopiyi	Devetzi ¶	GRE	2.1.76	Q	OG	Athína	21 Aug 04
15.31	0.0	Caterine	Ibargüen	COL	12.2.84	1	Herc	Monaco	18 Jul 14
15.30	0.6		Mbango			1	OG	Athína	23 Aug 04
15.29	0.3	Yamilé	Aldama	CUB/SUD/GBR	14.8.72	1	GGala	Roma	11 Jul 03
15.28	0.3		Aldama			1	GP	Linz	2 Aug 04
15.28	0.9	Yargelis	Savigne	CUB	13.11.84	1	WCh	Osaka	31 Aug 07
15.27	1.3		Aldama			1	GP	London (CP)	8 Aug 03
15.25	-0.8		Lebedeva			1	WCh	Edmonton	10 Aug 01
15.25	-0.1		Devetzí			2	OG	Athína	23 Aug 04
15.25	1.7	Olga	Rypakova	KAZ	30.11.84	1	C.Cup	Split	4 Sep 10
15.23	0.8		Lebedeva			1		Réthimno	23 Jun 04
15.23	0.6		Lebedeva			1	Tsik	Athína	3 Jul 06
15.21	1.2		Aldama			2		Réthimno	23 Jun 04
15.20	0.0	Sarka	Kaspárková	CZE	20.5.71	1	WCh	Athína	4 Aug 97
15.20	-0.3	Tereza	Marinova (10)	BUL	5.9.77	1	OG	Sydney	24 Sep 00
15.20	1.3		Savigne			1	Vard	Réthimno	14 Jul 08
15.19	0.5		Lebedeva			1	Athl	Lausanne	11 Jul 06
15.18	0.3	Iva	Prandzheva ¶	BUL	15.2.72	2	WCh	Göteborg	10 Aug 95
15.18	-0.2		Lebedeva			1	WCh	Saint-Denis	26 Aug 03
15.17	0.4		Ibargüen			1	OG	Rio de Janeiro	14 Aug 16
15.16	0.1	Rodica	Mateescu ¶	ROU	13.3.71	2	WCh	Athína	4 Aug 97
15.16i WIR	-	Ashia	Hansen	GBR	5.12.71	1	EI	Valencia	28 Feb 98
15.16	0.7	Trecia	Smith (30/14)	JAM	5.11.75	2	GP	Linz	2 Aug 04
15.14	1.9	Nadezhda	Alekhina	RUS	22.9.78	1	NC	Cheboksary	26 Jul 09
15.09 WR	0.5	Anna	Biryukova	RUS	27.9.67	1	WCh	Stuttgart	21 Aug 93
15.09	-0.5	Inna	Lasovskaya	RUS	17.12.69	1	ECCp-A	Valencia	31 May 97
15.08i		Marija	Sestak	SLO	17.4.79	1		Athína (P)	13 Feb 08
15.07	-0.6	Paraskeví	Tsiamíta	GRE	10.3.72	Q	WCh	Sevilla	22 Aug 99
15.04	1.7	Yekaterina	Koneva (20)	RUS	25.9.88	2	Pre	Eugene	30 May 15
15.03i		Iolanda	Chen	RUS	26.7.61	1	WI	Barcelona	11 Mar 95
15.03	1.9	Magdelin	Martinez	ITA	10.2.76	1		Roma	26 Jun 04
15.02	0.9	Anna	Pyatykh ¶	RUS	4.4.81	3	EC	Göteborg	8 Sep 06
15.02	-0.4	Yulimar	Rojas	VEN	21.10.95	1		Madrid	23 Jun 16
15.00	1.2	Kène	Ndoye	SEN	20.11.78	2		Iráklio	4 Jul 04
14.99	0.2	Olha	Saladukha	UKR	4.6.83	1	EC	Helsinki	29 Jun 12
14.98	1.8	Sofia	Bozhanova ¶	BUL	4.10.67	1		Stara Zagora	16 Jul 94
14.98	0.2	Baya	Rahouli	ALG	27.7.79	1	MedG	Almeria	1 Jul 05
14.96	0.7	Yelena	Hovorova	UKR	18.9.73	4	OG	Sydney	24 Sep 00
14.94i	–	Cristina	Nicolau (30)	ROU	9.8.77	1	NC	Bucuresti	5 Feb 00
14.94i		Oksana	Udmurtova	RUS	1.2.82	1		Tartu	20 Feb 08
14.90	1.0		Xie Limei	CHN	27.6.86	1		Urumqi	20 Sep 07
14.85	1.2	Viktoriya	Gurova' ¶	RUS	22.5.82	3	NC	Kazan	19 Jul 08
14.84	0.0	Tori	Franklin	USA	7.10.92	1		Baie-Mahault	12 May 18
14.83i	-	Yelena	Lebedenko	RUS	16.1.71	1		Samara	1 Feb 01
14.83	0.5	Yelena	Oleynikova	RUS	9.12.76	1	Odlozil	Praha	17 Jun 02
14.79	1.7	Irina	Mushayilova	RUS	6.1.67	1	DNG	Stockholm	5 Jul 93
14.78i		Adelina	Gavrila	ROU	26.11.78	1		Bucuresti	3 Feb 08
14.78	-0.1	Hanna	Minenko	UKR/ISR	25.9.89	2	WCh	Beijing	24 Aug 15
14.76	0.9	Galina	Chistyakova (40)	RUS	26.7.62	1	Spitzen	Luzern	27 Jun 95
14.76	1.1	Gundega	Sproge ¶	LAT	12.12.72	3		Sheffield	29 Jun 97

Mark	Wind	Name		Nat	Born	Pos	Meet	Venue	Date
14.76	0.4	Kseniya	Detsuk	BLR	23.4.86	*	NCp	Brest	26 May 12
14.73	-1.3	Paraskeví	Papahrístou	GRE	17.4.89	1		Athína (F)	8 Jun 16
14.72	1.8		Huang Qiuyan	CHN	25.1.80	1	NG	Guangzhou	22 Nov 01
14.71	1.4	Athanasía	Pérra	GRE	2.2.83	1	NC	Athína	16 Jun 12
14.71	0.0	Keturah	Orji	USA	5.3.96	4	OG	Rio de Janeiro	14 Aug 16
14.70i		Oksana	Rogova	RUS	7.10.78	1		Volgograd	6 Feb 02
14.69	1.2	Anja	Valant	SLO	8.9.77	3		Kalamáta	4 Jun 00
14.69	1.2	Simona	La Mantia	ITA	14.4.83	1		Palermo	22 May 05
14.69	2.0	Teresa	N'zola Meso	ANG/FRA	30.11.83	1	ECp-S	München	23 Jun 07
14.69	1.3	Núbia	Soares	BRA	26.3.96	1		Sotteville-lès-Rouen	17 Jul 18
	(51)		100th woman 14.46, 200th 14.17, 300th 14.01, 400th 13.86, 500th 13.71						

Wind assisted   *Performances to 15.14, performers to 14.75*

Mark	Wind	Name		Nat	Born	Pos	Meet	Venue	Date
15.24A	4.2	Magdelín	Martínez	ITA	10.2.76	1		Sestriere	1 Aug 04
15.18	2.1		Ibargüen			1	Pre	Eugene	30 May 15
15.17	2.4	Anna	Pyatykh ¶	RUS	4.4.81	2	SGP	Athína	3 Jul 06
15.10	2.7	Keila	Costa	BRA	6.2.83	1		Uberlandia	6 May 07
15.06	2.6	Olga	Saladukha	UKR	4.6.83	1	DNG	Stockholm	29 Jul 11
14.99	6.8	Yelena	Hovorova	UKR	18.9.73	1	WUG	Palma de Mallorca	11 Jul 99
14.85	2.5	Gabriela	Petrova	BUL	29.6.92	1	ET-2	Stara Zagora	20 Jun 15
14.84	4.1	Galina	Chistyakova	RUS	26.7.62	1		Innsbruck	28 Jun 95
14.83	8.3		Ren Ruiping	CHN	1.2.76	1	NC	Taiyuan	21 May 95
14.83	2.2	Heli	Koivula-Kruger	FIN	27.6.75	2	EC	München	10 Aug 02
14.81	2.4	Kseniya	Detsuk	BLR	23.4.86	1	NCp	Brest	26 May 12
14.78	2.7	Kimberly	Williams	JAM	3.11.88	3	Pre	Eugene	1 Jun 13
14.77	2.3	Paraskeví	Papahrístou	GRE	17.4.89	1		Ankara	5 Jun 12
14.75	4.2	Jelena	Blazevica	LAT	11.5.70	1	v2N	Kaunas	23 Aug 97

Best outdoor mark for athlete with all-time best indoors

Mark	Wind		Name			Date		Wind		Pos	Meet	Venue	Date
15.15	1.7	Hansen	1	GPF	Fukuoka	13 Sep 97	14.85	1.4	Udmurtova	1		Padova	31 Aug 08
15.03	1.1	Sestak	6	OG	Beijing	17 Aug 08	14.75	1.1	Gavrila	3	GP II	Rieti	7 Sep 03
14.97WR	0.9	Chen	1	NC	Moskva	18 Jun 93	14.70	1.3	Nicolau	1	EU23	Göteborg	1 Aug 99

Ancillary marks – other marks during series (to 15.19)

15.30	0.5	Mbango	23 Aug 04	15.28	-0.3	Ledebeva	4 Jul 04	15.25i		Ledebeva	6 Mar 04
15.21	-0.2	Mbango	23 Aug 04	15.19	1.0	Lebedeva	3 Jul 06	15.19	1.3	Mbango	17 Aug 08

Drugs disqualification

Mark	Wind		Name			Pos	Meet	Venue	Date
15.32	0.5		Lebedeva			2	OG	Beijing	17 Aug 08
15.23	1.6		Devetzí ¶			3	OG	Beijing	17 Aug 08
15.22	1.5		Devetzí ¶			1		Thessaloníki	9 Jul 08

SHOT

Mark	Wind	Name		Nat	Born	Pos	Meet	Venue	Date
22.63 WR		Natalya	Lisovskaya	RUS	16.7.62	1	Znam	Moskva	7 Jun 87
22.55			Lisovskaya			1	NC	Tallinn	5 Jul 88
22.53 WR			Lisovskaya			1		Sochi	27 May 84
22.53			Lisovskaya			1		Kyiv	14 Aug 88
22.50i		Helena	Fibingerová	CZE	13.7.49	1		Jablonec	19 Feb 77
22.45 WR		Ilona	Slupianek' ¶	GDR	24.9.56	1		Potsdam	11 May 80
22.41			Slupianek			1	OG	Moskva	24 Jul 80
22.40			Slupianek			1		Berlin	3 Jun 83
22.38			Slupianek			1		Karl-Marx-Stadt	25 May 80
22.36 WR			Slupianek			1		Celje	2 May 80
22.34			Slupianek			1		Berlin	7 May 80
22.34			Slupianek			1	NC	Cottbus	18 Jul 80
22.32 WR			Fibingerová			1		Nitra	20 Aug 77
22.24			Lisovskaya			1	OG	Seoul	1 Oct 88
22.22			Slupianek			1		Potsdam	13 Jul 80
22.19		Claudia	Losch	FRG	10.1.60	1		Hainfeld	23 Aug 87
22.14i			Lisovskaya			1	NC	Penza	7 Feb 87
22.13			Slupianek			1		Split	29 Apr 80
22.06			Slupianek			1		Berlin	15 Aug 78
22.06			Lisovskaya			1		Moskva	6 Aug 88
22.05			Slupianek			1	OD	Berlin	28 May 80
22.05			Slupianek			1		Potsdam	31 May 80
22.04			Slupianek			1		Potsdam	4 Jul 79
22.04			Slupianek			1		Potsdam	29 Jul 79
21.99 WR			Fibingerová			1		Opava	26 Sep 76
21.98			Slupianek			1		Berlin	17 Jul 79
21.96			Fibingerová			1	GS	Ostrava	8 Jun 77
21.96			Lisovskaya			1	Drz	Praha	16 Aug 84
21.96			Lisovskaya			1		Vilnius	28 Aug 88
21.95	(30/4)		Lisovskaya			1	IAC	Edinburgh	29 Jul 88

WOMEN All-time

Mark	Wind	Name		Nat	Born	Pos	Meet	Venue	Date
21.89	WR	Ivanka	Khristova	BUL	19.11.41	1		Belmeken	4 Jul 76
21.86		Marianne	Adam	GDR	19.9.51	1	v URS	Leipzig	23 Jun 79
21.76			Li Meisu	CHN	17.4.59	1		Shijiazhuang	23 Apr 88
21.73		Natalya	Akhrimenko	RUS	12.5.55	1		Leselidze	21 May 88
21.69		Viktoriya	Pavlysh ¶	UKR	15.1.69	1	EC	Budapest	20 Aug 98
21.66			Sui Xinmei ¶	CHN	29.1.65	1		Beijing	9 Jun 90
		(10)							
21.61		Verzhinia	Veselinova	BUL	18.11.57	1		Sofia	21 Aug 82
21.60i		Valentina	Fedyushina	UKR	18.2.65	1		Simferopol	28 Dec 91
21.58		Margitta	Droese/Pufe	GDR	10.9.52	1		Erfurt	28 May 78
21.57	@	Ines	Müller'	GDR	2.1.59	1		Athína	16 May 88
21.45						1		Schwerin	4 Jun 86
21.53		Nunu	Abashidze ¶	UKR	27.3.55	2	Izv	Kyiv	20 Jun 84
21.52			Huang Zhihong	CHN	7.5.65	1	NC	Beijing	27 Jun 90
21.46		Larisa	Peleshenko ¶	RUS	29.2.64	1	Kuts	Moskva	26 Aug 00
21.45	WR	Nadezhda	Chizhova	RUS	29.9.45	1		Varna	29 Sep 73
21.43		Eva	Wilms	FRG	28.7.52	2	HB	München	17 Jun 77
21.42		Svetlana	Krachevskaya'	RUS	23.11.44	2	OG	Moskva	24 Jul 80
		(20)	@ competitive meeting, but unsanctioned by GDR federation						
21.31	@	Heike	Hartwig'	GDR	30.12.62	2		Athína	16 May 88
21.27						1		Haniá	22 May 88
21.27		Liane	Schmuhl	GDR	29.6.61	1		Cottbus	26 Jun 82
21.24		Valerie	Adams	NZL	6.10.84	1	WCh	Daegu	29 Aug 11
21.22		Astrid	Kumbernuss	GDR/GER	5.2.70	1	WCh	Göteborg	5 Aug 95
21.21		Kathrin	Neimke	GDR	18.7.66	2	WCh	Roma	5 Sep 87
21.19		Helma	Knorscheidt	GDR	31.12.56	1		Berlin	24 May 84
21.15i		Irina	Korzhanenko ¶	RUS	16.5.74	1	NC	Moskva	18 Feb 99
21.10		Heidi	Krieger	GDR	20.7.65	1	EC	Stuttgart	26 Aug 86
21.09		Nadezhda	Ostapchuk ¶	BLR	12.10.80	1		Minsk	21 Jul 05
21.06		Svetlana	Krivelyova ¶	RUS	13.6.69	1	OG	Barcelona	7 Aug 92
		(30)							
21.05		Zdenka	Silhavá' ¶	CZE	15.6.54	2	NC	Praha	23 Jul 83
21.01		Ivanka	Petrova-Stoycheva	BUL	3.2.51	1	NC	Sofia	28 Jul 79
21.00		Mihaela	Loghin	ROU	1.6.52	1		Formia	30 Jun 84
21.00		Cordula	Schulze	GDR	11.9.59	4	OD	Potsdam	21 Jul 84
20.96		Belsy	Laza	CUB	5.6.67	1		Ciudad de México	2 May 92
20.95		Elena	Stoyanova ¶	BUL	23.1.52	2	Balk	Sofia	14 Jun 80
20.91		Svetla	Mitkova	BUL	17.6.64	1		Sofia	24 May 87
20.80		Sona	Vasícková	CZE	14.3.62	1		Praha	2 Jun 88
20.77		Christina	Schwanitz	GER	24.12.85	1		Beijing	20 May 15
20.72		Grit	Haupt/Hammer	GDR	4.6.66	3		Neubrandenburg	11 Jun 87
		(40)							
20.70		Natalya	Mikhnevich' ¶	BLR	25.5.82	2	NC	Grodno	8 Jul 08
20.63		Michelle	Carter	USA	12.10.85	1	OG	Rio de Janeiro	12 Aug 16
20.61		María Elena	Sarría	CUB	14.9.54	1		La Habana	22 Jul 82
20.61		Yanina	Korolchik' ¶	BLR	26.12.76	1	WCh	Edmonton	5 Aug 01
20.60		Marina	Antonyuk	RUS	12.5.62	1		Chelyabinsk	10 Aug 86
20.54			Zhang Liuhong	CHN	16.1.69	1	NC	Beijing	5 Jun 94
20.53		Iris	Plotzitzka	FRG	7.1.66	1	ASV	Köln	21 Aug 88
20.50i		Christa	Wiese	GDR	25.12.67	2	NC	Senftenberg	12 Feb 89
20.47		Nina	Isayeva	RUS	6.7.50	1		Bryansk	28 Aug 82
20.47			Cong Yuzhen	CHN	22.1.63	2	IntC	Tianjin	3 Sep 88
		(50)	100th woman 19.73, 200th 18.95, 300th 18.33, 400th 17.91, 500th 17.58						

Best outdoor marks

21.58	Ostapchuk ¶	1		Minsk	18 Jul 12	20.82	Korzhanenko ¶	1	Rostov na Donu	30 May 98
21.08	Fedyushina	1		Leselidze	15 May 88		21.06 drugs dq	(1) OG	Athína	18 Aug 04

Ancillary marks – other marks during series (to 22.09)

22.60	Lisovskaya (WR)	7 Jun 87	22.33	Slupianek	2 May 80	22.12	Slupianek	13 Jul 80
22.40	Lisovskaya	14 Aug 88	22.20	Slupianek	13 Jul 80	22.11	Slupianek	7 May 80
22.34	Slupianek	11 May 80	22.19	Lisovskaya	5 Jul 88	22.10	Slupianek	25 May 80
			22.14	Slupianek	25 May 80	22.09	Slupianek	7 May 80
			22.14	Slupianek	13 Jul 80			

Drugs disqualification

21.70i	Nadezhda	Ostapchuk ¶	BLR	12.10.80	(1)	NC	Mogilyov	12 Feb 10

DISCUS

Mark	Wind	Name		Nat	Born	Pos	Meet	Venue	Date
76.80	WR	Gabriele	Reinsch	GDR	23.9.63	1	v ITA	Neubrandenburg	9 Jul 88
74.56	WR	Zdenka	Silhavá' ¶	CZE	15.6.54	1		Nitra	26 Aug 84
74.56		Ilke	Wyludda	GDR	28.3.69	1	NC	Neubrandenburg	23 Jul 89
74.44			Reinsch			1		Berlin	13 Sep 88
74.40			Wyludda			2		Berlin	13 Sep 88

Mark	Wind	Name		Nat	Born	Pos	Meet	Venue	Date
74.08		Diana	Gansky'	GDR	14.12.63	1	v USSR	Karl-Marx-Stadt	20 Jun 87
73.90			Gansky			1	ECp	Praha	27 Jun 87
73.84		Daniela	Costian ¶	ROU	30.4.65	1		Bucuresti	30 Apr 88
73.78			Costian			1		Bucuresti	24 Apr 88
73.42			Reinsch			1		Karl-Marx-Stadt	12 Jun 88
73.36 WR		Irina	Meszynski	GDR	24.3.62	1	Drz	Praha	17 Aug 84
73.32			Gansky			1		Neubrandenburg	11 Jun 87
73.28		Galina	Savinkova'	RUS	15.7.53	1	NC	Donetsk	8 Sep 84
73.26 WR			Savinkova			1		Leselidze	21 May 83
73.26			Sachse/Gansky			1		Neubrandenburg	6 Jun 86
73.24			Gansky			1		Leipzig	29 May 87
73.22		Tsvetanka	Khristova ¶	BUL	14.3.62	1		Kazanlak	19 Apr 87
73.10		Gisela	Beyer	GDR	16.7.60	1	OD	Berlin	20 Jul 84
73.04			Gansky			1		Potsdam	6 Jun 87
73.04			Wyludda			1	ECp	Gateshead	5 Aug 89
72.96			Savinkova			1	v GDR	Erfurt	23 Jun 85
72.94			Gansky			2	v ITA	Neubrandenburg	9 Jul 88
72.92		Martina	Opitz/Hellmann	GDR	12.12.60	1	NC	Potsdam	20 Aug 87
72.90			Costian			1		Bucuresti	14 May 88
72.78			Hellmann			2		Neubrandenburg	11 Jun 87
72.78			Reinsch			1	OD	Berlin	29 Jun 88
72.72			Wyludda			1		Neubrandenburg	23 Jun 89
72.70			Wyludda			1	NC-j	Karl-Marx-Stadt	15 Jul 88
72.54			Gansky			1	NC	Rostock	25 Jun 88
72.52			Hellmann			1		Frohburg	15 Jun 86
72.52			Khristova			1	BGP	Budapest	11 Aug 86
		(31/10)							
72.14		Galina	Murashova	LTU	22.12.55	2	Drz	Praha	17 Aug 84
71.80 WR		Maria	Vergova/Petkova	BUL	3.11.50	1	NC	Sofia	13 Jul 80
71.68			Xiao Yanling ¶	CHN	27.3.68	1		Beijing	14 Mar 92
71.58		Ellina	Zvereva' ¶	BLR	16.11.60	1	Znam	Leningrad	12 Jun 88
71.50 WR		Evelin	Schlaak/Jahl	GDR	28.3.56	1		Potsdam	10 May 80
71.41		Sandra	Perkovic	CRO	21.6.90	1		Bellinzona	18 Jul 17
71.30		Larisa	Korotkevich	RUS	3.1.67	1	RusCp	Sochi	29 May 92
71.22		Ria	Stalman	NED	11.12.51	1		Walnut	15 Jul 84
		Disallowed as Dutch record in 2016 after Stalman admitted drugs use							
70.88		Hilda Elia	Ramos ¶	CUB	1.9.64	1		La Habana	8 May 92
70.80		Larisa	Mikhalchenko	UKR	16.5.63	1		Kharkov	18 Jun 88
		(20)							
70.68		Maritza	Martén	CUB	16.8.63	1	Ib Am	Sevilla	18 Jul 92
70.65		Denia	Caballero	CUB	13.1.90	1		Bilbao	20 Jun 15
70.50 WR		Faina	Melnik	RUS	9.6.45	1	Znam	Sochi	24 Apr 76
70.34 @		Silvia	Madetzky	GDR	24.6.62	3		Athína	16 May 88
69.34						1		Halle	26 Jun 87
70.02		Natalya	Sadova ¶	RUS	15.7.72	1		Thessaloniki	23 Jun 99
69.86		Valentina	Kharchenko	RUS	.49	1		Feodosiya	16 May 81
69.72		Svetla	Mitkova	BUL	17.6.64	2	NC	Sofia	15 Aug 87
69.68		Mette	Bergmann	NOR	9.11.62	1		Florø	27 May 95
69.64		Dani	Stevens	AUS	26.5.88	2	WCh	London (OS)	13 Aug 17
69.51		Franka	Dietzsch	GER	22.1.68	1		Wiesbaden	8 May 99
		(30)							
69.50		Florenta	Craciunescu'	ROU	7.5.55	1	Balk	Stara Zagora	2 Aug 85
69.19		Yaimé	Pérez	CUB	29.5.91	1		Sotteville-lès-Rouen	7 Jul 17
69.17		Gia	Lewis-Smallwood	USA	1.4.79	1	Déca	Angers	30 Aug 14
69.14		Irina	Yatchenko ¶	BLR	31.10.65	1		Staiki	31 Jul 04
69.08		Carmen	Romero	CUB	6.10.50	1	NC	La Habana	17 Apr 76
69.08		Mariana	Ionescu/Lengyel	ROU	14.4.53	1		Constanta	19 Apr 86
68.92		Sabine	Engel	GDR	21.4.54	1	v URS,POL	Karl-Marx-Stadt	25 Jun 77
68.89		Nadine	Müller	GER	21.11.85	1	ECp-w	Bar	18 Mar 12
68.80A		Nicoleta	Grasu	ROU	11.9.71	1		Poiana Brasov	7 Aug 99
68.64		Margitta	Pufe'	GDR	10.9.52	1	ISTAF	Berlin	17 Aug 79
		(40)							
68.62			Yu Hourun	CHN	9.7.64	1		Beijing	6 May 88
68.62			Hou Xuemei	CHN	27.2.62	1	IntC	Tianjin	4 Sep 88
68.60		Nadezhda	Kugayevskikh	RUS	19.4.60	1		Oryol	30 Aug 83
68.58		Lyubov	Zverkova	RUS	14.6.55	1	Izv	Kyiv	22 Jun 84
68.52		Beatrice	Faumuiná	NZL	23.10.74	1	Bisl	Oslo	4 Jul 97
68.49		Julia	Fischer/Harting	GER	1.4.90	1	Werfer	Halle	21 May 16
68.38		Olga	Burova'	RUS	17.9.63	2	RusCp	Sochi	29 May 92
68.18		Tatyana	Lesovaya	KAZ	24.4.56	1		Alma-Ata	23 Sep 82

Mark	Wind	Name		Nat	Born	Pos	Meet	Venue	Date
68.18		Irina	Khval	RUS	17.5.62	1		Moskva	8 Jul 88
68.18		Barbara	Hechevarría	CUB	6.8.66	2		La Habana	17 Feb 89
	(50)								

Unofficial meeting: Berlin 6 Sep 88: 1. Martina Hellmann 78.14, 2. Ilke Wyludda 75.36
100th woman 65.97, 200th 63.90, 300th 62.00, 400th 60.43, 500th 59.26
Downhill: 69.44 Suzy Powell USA 3.9.76 1 La Jolla 27 Apr 02
Drugs disqualification: 70.69 Darya Pishchalnikova ¶ RUS 19.7.85 (1) NC Cheboksary 5 Jul 12
Ancillary marks – other marks during series (to 72.92)

73.32	Reinsch	13 Sep 88	73.28	Gansky	27 Jun 87	73.10	Reinsch	9 Jul 88
73.28	Gansky	11 Jun 87	73.16	Wyludda	13 Sep 88	73.06	Gansky	27 Jun 87
						72.92	Hellmann	20 Aug 87

HAMMER

Mark		Name		Nat	Born	Pos	Meet	Venue	Date
82.98	WR	Anita	Wlodarczyk	POL	8.8.85	1	Skol	Warszawa	28 Aug 16
82.87			Wlodarczyk			1	Skol	Cetniewo	29 Jul 17
82.29	WR		Wlodarczyk			1	OG	Rio de Janeiro	14 Aug 16
81.08			Wlodarczyk			1	Skol	Cetniewo	1 Aug 15
80.85			Wlodarczyk			1	WCh	Beijing	27 Aug 15
80.79			Wlodarczyk			1	NC	Bialystok	23 Jul 17
80.26			Wlodarczyk			1		Cetniewo	12 Jul 16
79.80			Wlodarczyk			1	Skol	Warszawa	15 Aug 17
79.73			Wlodarczyk			1	DL	Doha	6 May 17
79.72			Wlodarczyk			1	GS	Ostrava	27 Jun 17
79.61			Wlodarczyk			1	Kuso	Szczecin	18 Jun 16
79.59			Wlodarczyk			1	NC	Lublin	22 Jul 18
79.58	WR		Wlodarczyk			1	ISTAF	Berlin	31 Aug 14
79.48			Wlodarczyk			1	Werfer	Halle	21 May 16
79.45			Wlodarczyk			1		Forbach	29 May 16
79.42	WR	Betty	Heidler	GER	14.10.83	1		Halle	21 May 11
78.94			Wlodarczyk			1	EC	Berlin	12 Aug 18
78.80		Tatyana	Lysenko ¶	RUS	9.10.83	1	WCh	Moskva	16 Aug 13
78.76			Wlodarczyk			1	EC	Zürich	15 Aug 14
78.74			Wlodarczyk			1	AWC	London (OS)	14 Jul 18
78.69			Wlodarczyk			1	NC	Bydgoszcz	26 Jun 16
78.54			Wlodarczyk			1	GS	Ostrava	19 May 16
78.51			Lysenko			1	NC	Cheboksary	5 Jul 12
78.46			Wlodarczyk			2	WCh	Moskva	16 Aug 13
78.30	WR		Wlodarczyk			1	EAF	Bydgoszcz	6 Jun 10
78.28			Wlodarczyk			1	ET	Cheboksary	21 Jun 15
78.24			Wlodarczyk			1	NC	Kraków	21 Jul 15
78.22			Wlodarczyk			1		Dubnica nad Vahom	21 Aug 13
78.18			Lysenko			1	OG	London (OS)	10 Aug 12
78.17			Wlodarczyk			1		Cetniewo	26 Jul 14
	(30/3)								
78.12		DeAnna	Price	USA	8.6.93	1	NC	Des Moines	23 Jun 18
77.78		Gwen	Berry	USA	29.6.89	1	Kuso	Chorzów	8 Jun 18
77.68			Wang Zheng	CHN	14.12.87	1		Chengdu	29 Mar 14
77.33			Zhang Wenxiu ¶	CHN	22.3.86	1	AsiG	Incheon	28 Sep 14
77.32		Oksana	Menkova ¶	BLR	28.3.82	1		Staiki	29 Jun 08
77.26	WR	Gulfiya	Khanafeyeva ¶	RUS	4.6.82	1	NC	Tula	12 Jun 06
77.13		Oksana	Kondratyeva	RUS	22.11.85	1	Znam	Zhukovskiy	30 Jun 13
	(10)								
76.90		Martina	Hrasnová ¶	SVK	21.3.83	1		Trnava	16 May 09
76.85		Malwina	Kopron	POL	16.11.94	1	WUG	Taipei	26 Aug 17
76.83		Kamila	Skolimowska	POL	4.11.82	1	SGP	Doha	11 May 07
76.72		Mariya	Bespalova ¶	RUS	21.5.86	2		Zhukovskiy	23 Jun 12
76.66		Olga	Tsander	BLR	18.5.76	1		Staiki	21 Jul 05
76.63		Yekaterina	Khoroshikh ¶	RUS	21.1.83	2	Znam	Moskva	24 Jun 06
76.62		Yipsi	Moreno	CUB	19.11.80	1	GP	Zagreb	9 Sep 08
76.56		Alena	Matoshko	BLR	23.6.82	2		Minsk	12 Jun 12
76.33		Darya	Pchelnik ¶	BLR	20.12.81	2		Staiki	29 Jun 08
76.26		Hanna	Malyshik	BLR	4.2.94	1		Brest	27 Apr 18
	(20)								
76.21		Yelena	Konevtsova	RUS	11.3.81	3		Sochi	26 May 07
76.17		Anna	Bulgakova ¶	RUS	17.1.88	2	NC	Moskva	24 Jul 13
76.07	WR	Mihaela	Melinte ¶	ROU	27.3.75	1		Rüdlingen	29 Aug 99
76.05		Kathrin	Klaas	GER	6.2.84	5	OG	London (OS)	10 Aug 12
75.73		Amanda	Bingson	USA	20.2.90	1	NC	Des Moines	22 Jun 13
75.73		Sultana	Frizell	CAN	24.10.84	1		Tucson	22 May 14
75.68		Olga	Kuzenkova ¶	RUS	4.10.70	1	NCp	Tula	4 Jun 00
75.29		Hanna	Skydan	UKR/AZE	14.5.92	1	Isl.Sol	Baku	16 May 17
75.09		Yelena	Rigert'	RUS	2.12.83	1	Kuts	Moskva	15 Jul 13

Mark	Wind	Name		Nat	Born	Pos	Meet	Venue	Date
75.09		Joanna	Fiodorow	POL	4.3.89	2	Skol	Cetniewo	29 Jul 17
		(30)							
75.08		Ivana	Brkljacic	CRO	25.1.83	2	Kuso	Waszawa	17 Jun 07
75.02			Luo Na	CHN	8.10.93	1	WWerf	Halle	26 May 18
74.78		Alexandra	Tavernier	FRA	13.12.93	2	EC	Berlin	12 Aug 18
74.77		Jeneva	McCall/Stevens	USA	28.10.89	2		Dubnica nad Vahom	21 Aug 13
74.66		Manuèla	Montebrun	FRA	13.11.79	1	GP II	Zagreb	11 Jul 05
74.65		Mariya	Smolyachkova	BLR	10.2.85	2		Staiki	19 Jul 08
74.56		Maggie	Ewen	USA	23.9.94	2	NC	Sacramento	25 Jun 17
74.54		Sophie	Hitchon	GBR	11.7.91	3	OG	Rio de Janeiro	15 Aug 16
74.52		Iryna	Sekachyova	UKR	21.7.76	1	NC	Kyiv	2 Jul 08
74.21		Zalina	Petrivskaya' ¶	MDA	5.2.88	1	NC-w	Chisinau	6 Feb 16
		(40)							
74.20		Jessica	Cosby Toruga	USA	31.5.82	3		Tucson	22 May 14
74.20		Brooke	Andersen	USA	23.8.95	1		Tucson	28 Apr 18
74.17		Tuğçe	Sahutoglu ¶	TUR	1.5.88	1		Izmir	19 May 12
74.10		Iryna	Novozhylova	UKR	7.1.86	1		Kyiv	19 May 12
74.03		Amber	Campbell	USA	5.6.81	1	NC	Eugene	6 Jul 16
73.90		Arasay	Thondike	CUB	28.5.86	1		La Habana	18 Jun 09
73.87		Erin	Gilreath	USA	11.10.80	1	NC	Carson	25 Jun 05
73.74		Jennifer	Dahlgren	ARG	21.4.84	1		Buenos Aires	10 Apr 10
73.64		Rosa	Rodríguez	VEN	2.7.86	1		Barquisimeto	16 May 13
73.59		Ester	Balassini	ITA	20.10.77	1	NC	Bressanone	25 Jun 05
		(50)	100th woman 70.73, 200th 67.79, 300th 65.84, 400th 64.38, 500th 63.27						

Downhill: 75.20 Manuéla   Montebrun   FRA   13.11.79 1   Vineuil   18 May 03

Ancillary marks – other marks during series to 78.80 – all by Wlodarczyk

81.77	28 Aug 16	80.73	29 Jul 17	80.31	28 Aug 16	79.67	12 Jul 16	79.39	12 Jul 16
81.74	14 Aug 16	80.69	29 Jul 17	80.27	27 Aug 15	79.62	12 Jul 16	79.31	27 Aug 15
81.63	29 Jul 17	80.42	29 Jul 17	79.68	28 Aug 16	79.60	14 Aug 16	79.27	27 Jun 17
81.27	28 Aug 16	80.40	14 Aug 16	79.68	27 Jun 17	79.58	12 Jul 16	79.23	15 Aug 17

Drugs disqualification

78.69		Oksana	Menkova ¶	BLR	28.3.82	(1)		Minsk	18 Jul 12
78.61			Lysenko			(1)		Sochi	26 May 07
78.19			Menkova			(1)		Brest	28 Apr 12
78.19			Menkova			(1)		Minsk	12 Jun 12
77.36		Gulfiya	Khanafeyeva ¶	RUS	4.6.82	(2)		Sochi	26 May 07
74.47		Zalina	Marghieva ¶	MDA	5.2.88	(1)	Univ Ch	Chisinau	7 May 12

JAVELIN

72.28 wr		Barbora	Spotáková	CZE	30.6.81	1	WAF	Stuttgart	13 Sep 08
71.70 wr		Osleidys	Menéndez	CUB	14.11.79	1	WCh	Helsinki	14 Aug 05
71.58			Spotáková			2	WCh	Daegu	2 Sep 11
71.54 wr			Menéndez			1		Réthimno	1 Jul 01
71.53			Menéndez			1	OG	Athína	27 Aug 04
71.42			Spotáková			1	OG	Beijing	21 Aug 08
70.53		Mariya	Abakumova ¶	RUS	15.1.86	1	ISTAF	Berlin	1 Sep 13
70.20		Christina	Obergföll	GER	22.8.81	1	ECp-S	München	23 Jun 07
70.03			Obergföll			2	WCh	Helsinki	14 Aug 05
69.82			Menéndez			1	WUG	Beijing	29 Aug 01
69.81			Obergföll			1		Berlin (Elstal)	31 Aug 08
69.75			Abakumova			1		Berlin (Elstal)	25 Aug 13
69.57			Obergföll			1	WK	Zürich	8 Sep 11
69.55			Spotáková			1	OG	London (OS)	9 Aug 12
69.53			Menéndez			1	WCh	Edmonton	7 Aug 01
69.48 wr		Trine	Hattestad	NOR	18.4.66	1	Bisl	Oslo	28 Jul 00
69.45			Spotáková			1	Herc	Monaco	22 Jul 11
69.35		Sunette	Viljoen	RSA	6.1.83	1	DL	New York	9 Jun 12
69.34			Abakumova			1	ECp-w	Castellón	16 Mar 13
69.15			Spotáková			1		Zaragoza	31 May 08
69.09			Abakumova			Q	WCh	Moskva	16 Aug 13
69.05			Obergföll			1	WCh	Moskva	18 Aug 13
68.94			Abakumova			1	WK	Zürich	29 Aug 13
68.92		Kathryn	Mitchell	AUS	10.7.82	1	CG	Gold Coast	11 Apr 18
68.91			Hattestad			1	OG	Sydney	30 Sep 00
68.86			Obergföll			1	NC	Kassel	24 Jul 11
68.81			Spotáková			1	Odlozil	Praha	16 Jun 08
68.76			Obergföll			Q	WCh	Daegu	1 Sep 11
68.73			Spotáková			2	DL	New York	9 Jun 12
68.66			Spotáková			1	GGala	Roma	10 Jun 10
		(30/7)							

Mark	Wind	Name		Nat	Born	Pos	Meet	Venue	Date
68.43		Sara	Kolak	CRO	22.6.95	1	Athl	Lausanne	6 Jul 17
68.34		Steffi	Nerius	GER	1.7.72	2		Berlin (Elstal)	31 Aug 08
67.90		Christin	Hussong	GER	17.3.94	1	EC	Berlin	10 Aug 18
		(10)							
67.69		Katharina	Molitor	GER	8.11.83	1	WCh	Beijing	30 Aug 15
67.69			Lu Huihui ¶	CHN	26.6.89	1	WWerf	Halle	26 May 18
67.67		Sonia	Bisset	CUB	1.4.71	1		Salamanca	6 Jul 05
67.51		Miréla	Manjani/Tzelíli	GRE	21.12.76	2	OG	Sydney	30 Sep 00
67.47		Tatyana	Kholodovich	BLR	21.6.91	1	Bisl	Oslo	7 Jun 18
67.32		Linda	Stahl	GER	2.10.85	1	adidas	New York	14 Jun 14
67.30		Vera	Rebrik	RUS	25.2.89	1	NC-w	Adler	19 Feb 16
67.29		Hanna	Hatsko-Fedusova	UKR	3.10.90	1	NC	Kirovohrad	26 Jul 14
67.21		Eda	Tugsuz	TUR	27.3.97	1	Isl.Sol	Baku	18 May 17
67.20		Tatyana	Shikolenko	RUS	10.5.68	1	Herc	Monaco	18 Aug 00
		(20)							
67.16		Martina	Ratej	SLO	2.11.81	2	DL	Doha	14 May 10
67.12			Liu Shiying	CHN	24.9.93	1		Osaka	20 May 18
67.11		Maria	Andrejczyk	POL	9.3.96	Q	OG	Rio de Janeiro	16 Aug 16
66.91		Tanja	Damaske	GER	16.11.71	1	NC	Erfurt	4 Jul 99
66.83		Kimberley	Mickle	AUS	28.12.84	1		Melbourne	22 Mar 14
66.80		Louise	McPaul/Currey	AUS	24.1.69	1		Gold Coast (RB)	5 Aug 00
66.67		Kara	Patterson/Winger	USA	10.4.86	1	NC	Des Moines	25 Jun 10
66.53		Marcelina	Witek	POL	2.6.95	1		Białogard	5 May 18
66.25			Li Lingwei	CHN	26.1.89	2	WCh	London (OS)	9 Aug 17
66.18		Madara	Palameika	LAT	18.6.87	1	VD	Bruxelles	9 Sep 16
		(30)							
66.17		Goldie	Sayers	GBR	16.7.82	1	LGP	London (CP)	14 Jul 12
65.91		Nikola	Brejchová'	CZE	25.6.74	1	GP	Linz	2 Aug 04
65.61A		Nikola	Ogrodníková	CZE	18.8.90	1		Potchefstroom	12 Apr 18
65.17			Zhang Li	CHN	17.1.00	1	AsiG	Inchon	1 Oct 11
65.30		Claudia	Coslovich	ITA	26.4.72	1		Ljubljana	10 Jun 00
65.29		Xiomara	Rivero	CUB	22.11.68	1		Santiago de Cuba	17 Mar 01
65.17		Karen	Forkel	GER	24.9.70	2	NC	Erfurt	4 Jul 99
65.08		Ana Mirela	Termure ¶	ROU	13.1.75	1	NC	Bucuresti	10 Jun 01
64.90		Paula	Huhtaniemi'	FIN	17.2.73	1	NC	Helsinki	10 Aug 03
64.89		Yekaterina	Ivakina	RUS	4.12.64	4	Bisl	Oslo	28 Jul 00
		(40)							
64.87		Kelly	Morgan	GBR	17.6.80	1	NC	Birmingham	14 Jul 02
64.83		Christina	Scherwin	DEN	11.7.76	3	WAF	Stuttgart	9 Sep 06
64.83		Liz	Gleadle	CAN	5.12.88	1		Kawasaki	10 May 15
64.75		Brittany	Borman	USA	1.7.89	2		Kawasaki	10 May 15
64.62		Joanna	Stone	AUS	4.10.72	2		Gold Coast (RB)	5 Aug 00
64.62		Nikolett	Szabó	HUN	3.3.80	1		Pátra	22 Jul 01
64.61		Oksana	Makarova	RUS	21.7.71	2	ECp	Paris (C)	19 Jun 99
64.57		Kelsey-Lee	Barber	AUS	21.9.91	1		Brisbane (Nathan)	28 Mar 18
64.56		Margaryta	Dorozhon	UKR/ISR	4.9.87	1	Bisl	Oslo	11 Jun 15
64.51		Monica	Stoian	ROU	25.8.82	4	WCh	Berlin	18 Aug 09
		(50)	100th woman 62.23, 200th 59.23, 300th 57.36						

Drugs dq:

71.99		Mariya	Abakumova ¶	RUS	15.1.86	1	WCh	Daegu	2 Sep 11

Also Abakumova: 70.78 2 OG Beijing 21 Aug 08, 68.92 Q WCh Berlin 16 Aug 09, 68.89 1 DL Doha 14 May 10

Ancillary marks – other marks during series (to 68.90)

71.25	Abakumova	2 Sep 11	69.32	Abakumova	21 Aug 08	68.95	Obergföll	8 Sep 11
69.42	Menéndez	7 Aug 01	69.22	Spotáková	21 Aug 08	Spec. changed from 1 May 1999.		
69.35	Abakumova	25 Aug 13	69.08	Abakumova	21 Aug 08			

HEPTATHLON

7291 WR	Jackie	Joyner-Kersee	USA	3.3.62	1	OG	Seoul	24 Sep 88
	12.69/0.5	1.86	15.80	22.56/1.6	7.27/0.7	45.66	2:08.51	
7215 WR		Joyner-Kersee			1	NC/OT	Indianapolis	16 Jul 88
	12.71/-0.9	1.93	15.65	22.30/ 0.0	7.00/-1.3	50.08	2:20.70	
7158 WR		Joyner-Kersee			1	USOF	Houston	2 Aug 86
	13.18/-0.5	1.88	15.20	22.85/1.2	7.03w/2.9	50.12	2:09.69	
7148 WR		Joyner-Kersee			1	GWG	Moskva	7 Jul 86
	12.85/0.2	1.88	14.76	23.00/0.3	7.01/-0.5	49.86	2:10.02	
7128		Joyner-Kersee			1	WCh	Roma	1 Sep 87
	12.91/0.2	1.90	16.00	22.95/1.2	7.14/0.9	45.68	2:16.29	
7044		Joyner-Kersee			1	OG	Barcelona	2 Aug 92
	12.85/-0.9	1.91	14.13	23.12/0.7	7.10/1.3	44.98	2:11.78	
7032	Carolina	Klüft	SWE	2.2.83	1	WCh	Osaka	26 Aug 07
	13.15/0.1	1.95	14.81	23.38/0.3	6.85/1.0	47.98	2:12.56	

Mark	Wind	Name	Nat	Born	Pos	Meet	Venue	Date
7013	Nafissatou	Thiam	BEL	19.8.94	1	Hypo	Götzis	28 May 17
	13.34/-0.7	1.98 14.51		24.40/-1.6	6.56/0.8	59.32	2:15.24	
7007	Larisa	Nikitina ¶	RUS	29.4.65	1	NC	Bryansk	11 Jun 89
	13.40/1.4	1.89 16.45		23.97/1.1	6.73w/4.0	53.94	2:15.31	
7001		Klüft			1	WCh	Saint-Denis	24 Aug 03
	13.18/-0.4	1.94 14.19		22.98/1.1	6.68/1.0	49.90	2:12.12	
6985	Sabine	Braun	GER	19.6.65	1		Götzis	31 May 92
	13.11/-0.4	1.93 14.84		23.65/2.0	6.63w/2.9	51.62	2:12.67	
6979		Joyner-Kersee			1	NC	San José	24 Jun 87
	12.90/2.0	1.85 15.17		23.02/0.4	7.25/2.3	40.24	2:13.07	
6955	Jessica	Ennis-Hill	GBR	28.1.86	1	OG	London (OS)	4 Aug 12
	12.54/1.3	1.86 14.28		22.83/-0.3	6.48/-0.6	47.49	2:08.65	
6952		Klüft			1	OG	Athína	21 Aug 04
	13.21/0.2	1.91 14.77		23.27/-0.1	6.78/0.4	48.89	2:14.15	
6946 WR	Sabine	Paetz'	GDR	16.10.57	1	NC	Potsdam	6 May 84
	12.64/0.3	1.80 15.37		23.37/0.7	6.86/-0.2	44.62	2:08.93	
6942	Ghada	Shouaa	SYR	10.9.72	1		Götzis	26 May 96
	13.78/0.3	1.87 15.64		23.78/0.6	6.77/0.6	54.74	2:13.61	
6935 WR	Ramona	Neubert	GDR	26.7.58	1	v USSR	Moskva	19 Jun 83
	13.42/1.7	1.82 15.25		23.49/0.5	6.79/0.7	49.94	2:07.51	
6910		Joyner			1	MSR	Walnut	25 Apr 86
	12.9/0.0	1.86 14.75		23.24w/2.8	6.85/2.1	48.30	2:14.11	
6906		Ennis			1		Götzis	27 May 12
	12.81/0.0	1.85 14.51		22.88/1.9	6.51/0.8	47.11	2:09.00	
6897		John'			2	wOG	Seoul	24 Sep 88
	12.85/0.5	1.80 16.23		23.65/1.6	6.71/ 0.0	42.56	2:06.14	
6889	Eunice	Barber (10)	FRA	17.11.74	1		Arles	5 Jun 05
	12.62w/2.9	1.91 12.61		24.12/1.2	6.78w/3.4	53.07	2:14.66	
6887		Klüft			1	WCh	Helsinki	7 Aug 05
	13.19/-0.4	1.82 15.02		23.70/-2.5	6.87/0.2	47.20	2:08.89	
6878		Joyner-Kersee			1	NC	New York	13 Jun 91
	12.77	1.89 15.62		23.42	6.97/0.4	43.28	2:22.12	
6875		Nikitina			1	ECp-A	Helmond	16 Jul 89
	13.55/-2.1	1.84 15.99		24.29/-2.1	6.75/-2.5	56.78	2:18.67	
6861		Barber			1	WCh	Sevilla	22 Aug 99
	12.89/-0.5	1.93 12.37		23.57/0.5	6.86/-0.3	49.88	2:15.65	
6859	Natalya	Shubenkova	RUS	25.9.57	1	NC	Kyiv	21 Jun 84
	12.93/1.0	1.83 13.66		23.57/-0.3	6.73/0.4	46.26	2:04.60	
6858	Anke	Vater/Behmer	GDR	5.6.61	3	OG	Seoul	24 Sep 88
	13.20/0.5	1.83 14.20		23.10/1.6	6.68/0.1	44.54	2:04.20	
6847		Nikitina			1	WUG	Duisburg	29 Aug 89
	13.47	1.81 16.12		24.12	6.66	59.28	2:22.07	
6845 WR		Neubert			1	v URS	Halle	20 Jun 82
	13.58/1.8	1.83 15.10		23.14/1.4	6.84w/2.3	42.54	2:06.16	
6845	Irina	Belova ¶	RUS	27.3.68	2	OG	Barcelona	2 Aug 92
	13.25/-0.1	1.88 13.77		23.34/0.2	6.82/0.0	41.90	2:05.08	
	(30/13)								
6836	Carolin	Schäfer	GER	5.12.91	2	Hypo	Götzis	28 May 17
	13.09/1.0	1.86 14.76		23.36/0.7	6.57/0.9	49.80	2:14.73	
6832	Lyudmila	Blonska ¶	UKR	9.11.77	2	WCh	Osaka	26 Aug 07
	13.25/0.1	1.92 14.44		24.09/0.3	6.88/1.0	47.77	2:16.68	
6831	Denise	Lewis	GBR	27.8.72	1		Talence	30 Jul 00
	13.13/1.0	1.84 15.07		24.01w/3.6	6.69/-0.4	49.42	2:12.20	
6815	Laura	Ikauniece-Admidina	LAT	31.5.92	3	Hypo	Götzis	28 May 17
	13.10/1.0	1.77 13.53		23.92/-2.9	6.64/0.8	56.17	2:11.76	
6808	Brianne	Theisen-Eaton	CAN	18.12.88	1	Hypo	Götzis	31 May 15
	13.05/-0.2	1.89 13.73		23.34/1.4	6.72/0.9	42.96	2:09.37	
6803	Jane	Frederick	USA	7.4.52	1		Talence	16 Sep 84
	13.27/1.2	1.87 15.49		24.15/1.6	6.43/0.2	51.74	2:13.55	
6778	Nataliya	Dobrynska	UKR	29.5.82	2	EC	Barcelona	31 Jul 10
	13.59/-1.6	1.86 15.88		24.23/-0.2	6.56/0.3	49.25	2:12.06	
	(20)								
6768w	Tatyana	Chernova ¶	RUS	29.1.88	1		Arles	3 Jun 07
	13.04w/6.1	1.82 13.57		23.59w/5.2	6.61/1.2	53.43	2:15.05	
6765	Yelena	Prokhorova	RUS	16.4.78	1	NC	Tula	23 Jul 00
	13.54/-2.8	1.82 14.30		23.37/-0.2	6.72/1.0	43.40	2:04.27	
6759	Katarina	Johnson-Thompson	GBR	9.1.93	2	EC	Berlin	10 Aug 18
	13.34/0.4	1.91 13.09		22.88/1.5	6.68/-0.1	42.16	2:09.84	
6750		Ma Miaolan	CHN	18.1.70	1	NG	Beijing	12 Sep 93
	13.28/1.5	1.89 14.98		23.86/	6.64/	45.82	2:15.33	

Mark	Wind	Name		Nat	Born	Pos	Meet	Venue		Date
6742		Yorgelis	Rodríguez	CUB	25.1.95	2	Hypo	Götzis		27 May 18
	13.48/0.3	1.86	14.95		23.96/-0.6		6.58w/2.3	48.65	2:12.73	
6741		Heike	Drechsler	GER	16.12.64	1		Talence		11 Sep 94
	13.34/-0.3	1.84	13.58		22.84/-1.1		6.95/1.0	40.64	2:11.53	
6735(w)		Hyleas	Fountain	USA	14.1.81	1	NC	Des Moines		26 Jun 10
	12.93w/2.6	1.90	13.73		23.28w/3.3		6.79w/2.7	42.26	2:17.80	
6725		Erica	Bougard	USA	26.7.93	3	Hypo	Götzis		27 May 18
	12.80/1.5	1.86	13.02		23.31/0.4		6.62/1.1	41.97	2:08.42	
6703		Tatyana	Blokhina	RUS	12.3.70	1		Talence		11 Sep 93
	13.69/-0.6	1.91	14.94		23.95/-0.4		5.99/-0.3	52.16	2:09.65	
6702		Chantal	Beaugeant ¶	FRA	16.2.61	2		Götzis		19 Jun 88
	13.10/1.6	1.78	13.74		23.96w/3.5		6.45/0.2	50.96	2:07.09	
	(30)									
6695		Jane	Flemming	AUS	14.4.65	1	CG	Auckland		28 Jan 90
	13.21/1.4	1.82	13.76		23.62w/2.4		6.57/1.6	49.28	2:12.53	
6683		Jennifer	Oeser	GER	29.11.83	3	EC	Barcelona		31 Jul 10
	13.37/-1.0	1.83	13.82		24.07/-0.3		6.68/-0.3	49.17	2:12.28	
6681		Kristina	Savitskaya	RUS	10.6.91	1	NC	Cheboksary		3 Jun 12
	13.52/0.0	1.88	15.27		24.61/0.0		6.65/0.0	46.83	2:14.73	
6660		Ines	Schulz	GDR	10.7.65	3		Götzis		19 Jun 88
	13.56/0.4	1.84	13.95		23.93w/2.8		6.70/0.7	42.82	2:06.31	
6658		Svetla	Dimitrova ¶	BUL	27.1.70	2		Götzis		31 May 92
	13.41/-0.7	1.75	14.72		23.06w/2.4		6.64/1.9	43.84	2:09.60	
6649		Lilli	Schwarzkopf	GER	28.8.83	2	OG	London (OS)		4 Aug 12
	13.26/0.9	1.83	14.77		24.77/0.9		6.30/-0.7	51.73	2:10.50	
6646		Natalya	Grachova	UKR	21.2.52	1	NC	Moskva		2 Aug 82
	13.80	1.80	16.18		23.86		6.65w/3.5	39.42	2:06.59	
6636		Anouk	Vetter	NED	4.2.93	3	WCh	London (OS)		6 Aug 17
	13.31/0.0	1.77	15.09		24.36/-0.4		6.32/-1.0	58.41	2:19.43	
6635		Oljylle	Thlele	ODN	0.0.05	2	OWO	Moskva		7 Jul 00
	13.14/0.6	1.76	16.00		24.18		6.62/1.0	45.74	2:15.30	
6635		Svetlana	Buraga	BLR	4.9.65	3	WCh	Stuttgart		17 Aug 93
	12.95/0.1	1.84	14.55		23.69/0.0		6.58/-0.2	41.04	2:13.65	
	(40)									
6633		Natalya	Roshchupkina	RUS	13.1.78	2	NC	Tula		23 Jul 00
	14.05/-2.8	1.88	14.28		23.47/-0.2		6.45/0.4	44.34	2:07.93	
6623		Judy	Simpson'	GBR	14.11.60	3	EC	Stuttgart		30 Aug 86
	13.05/0.8	1.92	14.73		25.09/0.0		6.56w/2.5	40.92	2:11.70	
6619		Liliana	Nastase	ROU	1.8.62	4	OG	Barcelona		2 Aug 92
	12.86/-0.9	1.82	14.34		23.70/0.2		6.49/-0.3	41.30	2:11.22	
6616		Malgorzata	Nowak'	POL	9.2.59	1	WUG	Kobe		31 Aug 85
	13.27w/4.0	1.95	15.35		24.20/0.0		6.37w/3.9	43.36	2:20.39	
6604		Remigija	Nazaroviene'	LTU	2.6.67	2	URSCh	Bryansk		11 Jun 89
	13.26/1.4	1.86	14.27		24.12/0.7		6.58/0.9	40.94	2:09.98	
6604		Irina	Tyukhay	RUS	14.1.67	3		Götzis		28 May 95
	13.20/-0.7	1.84	14.97		24.33/1.7		6.71/0.5	43.84	2:17.64	
6599A		Jessica	Zelinka	CAN	3.9.81	1	NC	Calgary		28 Jun 12
	12.76/-0.6	1.77	14.74		23.42w/2.1		5.98w/2.9	46.60	2:08.95	
6599		Austra	Skujyté	LTU	12.8.79	33	OG	London (OS)		4 Aug 12
	14.00/0.7	1.92	17.31		25.43/0.9		6.25/-0.6	51.13	2:20.59	
6598		Svetlana	Moskalets	RUS	22.1.69	1	NC	Vladimir		17 Jun 94
	13.20/0.8	1.82	13.78		23.56/0.1		6.74/0.8	42.48	2:14.54	
6591		Svetlana	Sokolova	RUS	0.1.81	1	NC	Tula		23 Jun 04
	13.56/1.1	1.82	15.09		24.02/0.6		6.26/0.3	45.07	2:07.23	
	(50)		100th woman 6424, 200th 6230, 300th 6118, 400th 6027, 500th 5956								

Drugs disqualification

Mark	Wind	Name		Nat	Born	Pos	Meet	Venue		Date
6880		Tatyana	Chernova ¶	RUS	29.1.88	(1)	WCh	Daegu		30 Aug 11
	13.32/0.9	1.83	14.17		23.50/-1.5		6.61/-0.7	52.95	2:08.04	
6618		Lyudmyla	Yosypenko ¶	UKR	24.9.84	4	OG	London (OS)		4 Aug 12
	13.25/0.9	1.83	13.90		23.68/0.6		6.31/-0.6	49.63	2:13.28	

DECATHLON

Mark		Name		Nat	Born	Pos		Venue		Date
8358 WR		Austra	Skujyte	LTU	12.8.79	1		Columbia, MO		15 Apr 05
	12.49/1.6	46.19	3.10	48.78	57.19	14.22w/2.4	6.12/1.6	16.42	1.78	5:15.86
8150		Marie	Collonvillé	FRA	23.11.73	1		Talence		26 Sep 04
	12.48/0.4	34.69	3.50	47.19	56.15	13.96/0.4	6.18/1.0	11.90	1.80	5:06.09

4 x 100 METRES RELAY

				Pos	Meet	Venue	Date
40.82 WR	USA	Madison (-Bartoletta), Felix, Knight, Jeter		1	OG	London (OS)	10 Aug 12
41.01	USA	Bartoletta, Felix, Gardner, Bowie		1	OG	Rio de Janeiro	19 Aug 16
41.07	JAM	Campbell-Brown, Morrison, Thompson, Fraser-Pryce		1	WCh	Beijing	29 Aug 15
41.29	JAM	Russell, Stewart, Calvert, Fraser-Pryce		1	WCh	Moskva	18 Aug 13

Mark	Wind	Name	Nat	Born	Pos	Meet	Venue	Date
41.36		C.Williams, Thompson, Campbell-Brown, Fraser-Pryce	JAM		2	OG	Rio de Janeiro	19 Aug 16
41.37	WR	Gladisch, Rieger, Auerswald, Göhr	GDR		1	WCp	Canberra	6 Oct 85
41.41		Fraser-Pryce, Simpson, Campbell-Brown, Stewart	JAM		2	OG	London (OS)	10 Aug 12
41.47		Gaines, Jones, Miller, Devers	USA		1	WCh	Athína	9 Aug 97
41.49		Bogoslovskaya, Malchugina, Voronova, Privalova	RUS		1	WCh	Stuttgart	22 Aug 93
41.49		Finn, Torrence, Vereen, Devers	USA		2	WCh	Stuttgart	22 Aug 93
41.52		Gaines, Jones, Miller, Devers	USA		1h1	WCh	Athína	8 Aug 97
41.53	WR	Gladisch, Koch, Auerswald, Göhr	GDR		1		Berlin	31 Jul 83
41.55		Brown, Williams, Griffith, Marshall	USA		1	ISTAF	Berlin	21 Aug 87
41.56		B Knight, Felix, Myers, Jeter	USA		1	WCh	Daegu	4 Sep 11
41.58		Brown, Williams, Griffith, Marshall	USA		1	WCh	Roma	6 Sep 87
41.58		L.Williams, Felix, Lee, Jeter	USA		1		Cottbus	8 Aug 09
41.60	WR	Müller, Wöckel, Auerswald, Göhr	GDR		1	OG	Moskva	1 Aug 80
41.60		Simpson, Morrison, Thompson, Fraser-Pryce	JAM		1	WK	Zürich	3 Sep 15
41.61A		Brown, Williams, Cheeseborough, Ashford	USA		1	USOF	USAF Academy	3 Jul 83
41.62		Pinto, Mayer, Lückenkemper, Haase	GER		1		Mannheim	29 Jul 16
41.63		Brown, Williams, Cheeseborough, Ashford	USA		1	v GDR	Los Angeles	25 Jun 83
41.64		Madison, Tarmoh, Knight, L Williams	USA		1h1	OG	London (OS)	9 Aug 12
41.65		Brown, Bolden, Cheeseborough, Ashford	USA		1	OG	Los Angeles	11 Aug 84
41.65		Gladisch, Koch, Auerswald, Göhr	GDR		1	ECp	Moskva	17 Aug 85
41.65		C.Williams, Thompson, Facey, Campbell-Brown	JAM		1	WK	Zürich	1 Sep 16

(25 performances by 4 nations) from here just best by nation

Mark	Wind	Name	Nat	Born	Pos	Meet	Venue	Date
41.77		Philip, Henry, Asher-Smith, Neita	GBR		3	OG	Rio de Janeiro	19 Aug 16
41.78		Girard, Hurtis, Félix, Arron	FRA		1	WCh	Saint-Denis	30 Aug 03
41.92		Fynes, Sturrup, Davis-Thompson, Ferguson	BAH		1	WCh	Sevilla	29 Aug 99
42.03		Baptiste, Ahye, Thomas, Hackett	TTO		3	WCh	Beijing	29 Aug 15
42.04		Povh, Stuy, Ryemyen, Bryzgina	UKR		3	OG	London (OS)	10 Aug 12
42.04		Samuel, Schippers, van Schagen, Sedney (10)	NED		1	EC	Amsterdam	10 Jul 16
42.08mx		Pavlova, Nuneva, Georgieva, Ivanova	BUL		mx		Sofia	8 Aug 84
		42.29 Pencheva, Nuneva, Georgieva, Donkova					Sofia	26 Jun 88
42.23		(Sichuan) Xiao Lin, Li Yali, Liu Xiaomei, Li Xuemei	CHN		1	NG	Shanghai	23 Oct 97
42.29		E dos Santos, Silva, Krasucki, R Santos	BRA		2h3	WCh	Moskva	18 Aug 13
42.29		Del Ponte, Atcho, Kambundji, Kora	SUI		1	Athl	Lausanne	5 Jul 18
42.39		Utondu, Idehen, Opara-Thompson, Onyali	NGR		2h2	OG	Barcelona	7 Aug 92
42.54		Borlée, Mariën, Ouédraogo, Gevaert	BEL		2	OG	Beijing	22 Aug 08
42.56		Nesterenko, Sologub, Nevmerzhitskaya, Dragun	BLR		3	WCh	Helsinki	13 Aug 05
42.59		Possekel, Helten, Richter, Kroniger	FRG		2	OG	Montreal	31 Jul 76
42.60		Emmanuel, Hyacinthe, Fofanah, Bingham	CAN		3h1	WCh	Beijing	29 Aug 15
42.67		Owusu-Agyapong, Acheampong, Gyaman, Amponsah	GHA		1		Cape Coast	8 Jul 16

(20)

Mark	Wind	Name	Nat	Born	Pos	Meet	Venue	Date
42.68		Popowicz, Korczynska, Jeschke, Wedler	POL		3	EC	Barcelona	1 Aug 10
42.73		Jassim, Odiong, Al-Khaldi, Naser	BRN		1	AsiG	Jakarta	30 Aug 18
42.89		Ferrer, López, Duporty, Allen	CUB		6	WCh	Stuttgart	22 Aug 93
42.92		Kashafutdinova, Zyabkina, Rakhmanova, Safronova	KAZ		1		Almaty	4 Jul 16
42.98		Sokolová, Soborová, Kocembová, Kratochvílová	CZE/TCH		1	WK	Zürich	18 Aug 82
42.99A		Massey, Broadrick, Lambert, Gainsford-Taylor	AUS		1		Pietersburg	18 Mar 00
43.03A		M.Murillo, Palacios, Obregón, D Murillo	COL		2	SAm-r	Bogotá	10 Jul 04
43.04		Pistone, Calí, Arcioni, Alloh	ITA		3	ECp-S	Annecy	21 Jun 08
43.07		Tsóni, Kóffa, Vasarmídou, Thánou	GRE		2	MedG	Bari	18 Jun 97
43.25A		Hartman, Moropane, Holtshausen, Seyerling	RSA		2		Pietersburg	18 Mar 00

(30)

Best at low altitude

Mark	Wind	Name	Nat	Born	Pos	Meet	Venue	Date
43.03		M.Murillo, Palacios, Obregón, N.González	COL		3h2	WCh	Helsinki	12 Aug 05
43.18		Wilson, Wells, Robertson, Boyle	AUS		5	OG	Montreal	31 Jul 76

4 x 200 METRES RELAY

Mark		Name			Pos	Meet	Venue	Date
1:27.46	WR	USA Blue Jenkins, Colander-Richardson, Perry, M Jones			1	PennR	Philadelphia	29 Apr 00
1:28.15	WR	GDR Göhr, R.Müller, Wöckel, Koch			1		Jena	9 Aug 80
1:28.77		Tumbleweed, TC Henry GBR, Onuora GBR, Bartoletta USA, Schippers NED			1	FlaR	Gainesville	1 Apr 17
1:28.77	PURE	Athletics Baptiste TTO, Wimbley USA, Bowie USA, Henry-Robinson JAM			1	FlaR	Gainesville	31 Mar 18
1:28.78		Un of Oregon USA Dunmore, Cunliffe, Stevens, Washington			2	FlaR	Gainesville	1 Apr 17
1:29.04		JAM Levy, Jackson, Forbes, Thompson			1	W.Rly	Nassau	22 Apr 17
1:29.42		Texas A & M (USA) Tarmoh, Mayo, Beard, Lucas			1	Penn R	Philadelphia	24 Apr 10
1:29.45		USA Solomon, Meadows, Knight, K Duncan			1	WRly	Nassau	25 May 14
1:29.61		GBR Henry, A Onuora, B Williams, A Philip			2	WRly	Nassau	25 May 14

Drugs dq: 1:29.40 USA Red Colander, Gaines, Miller, M Jones ¶   1   Penn   Philadelphia   24 Apr 04

4 x 400 METRES RELAY

Mark					Pos	Meet	Venue	Date
3:15.17	WR	URS			1	OG	Seoul	1 Oct 88

Ledovskaya 50.12, O.Nazarova 47.82, Pinigina 49.43, Bryzgina 47.80

WOMEN All-time

Mark	Wind	Name	Nat	Born	Pos	Meet	Venue	Date
3:15.51		USA			2	OG	Seoul	1 Oct 88
		D.Howard 49.82, Dixon 49.17, Brisco 48.44, Griffith Joyner 48.08						
3:15.92	WR	GDR G.Walther 49.8, Busch 48.9, Rübsam 49.4, Koch 47.8			1	NC	Erfurt	3 Jun 84
3:16.71		USA Torrence 49.0, Malone 49.4, Kaiser-Brown 49.48, Miles 48.78			1	WCh	Stuttgart	22 Aug 93
3:16.87		GDR Emmelmann 50.9, Busch 48.8, Müller 48.9, Koch 48.21			1	EC	Stuttgart	31 Aug 86
3:16.87		USA Trotter 50.3, Felix 48.1, McCorory 49.39, Richards-Ross 49.10			1	OG	London (OS)	11 Aug 12
3:17.83		USA Dunn 50.5, Felix 48.8, Demus 50.14, Richards 48.44			1	WCh	Berlin	23 Aug 09
3:18.09		USA Richards-Ross 49.3, Felix 49.4, Beard 49.84, McCorory 49.521			1	WCh	Daegu	3 Sep 11
3:18.29		USA			1	OG	Los Angeles	11 Aug 84
		Leatherwood 50.50, S.Howard 48.83, Brisco-Hooks 49.23, Cheeseborough 49.73						
3:18.29		GDR Neubauer 50.58, Emmelmann 49.89, Busch 48.81, Müller 48.99			3	OG	Seoul	1 Oct 88
3:18.38		RUS			2	WCh	Stuttgart	22 Aug 93
		Ruzina 50.8, Alekseyeva 49.3, Ponomaryova 49.78, Privalova 48.47						
3:18.43		URS Ledovskaya 51.7, Dzhigalova 49.2, Nazarova 48.67, Bryzgina 48.67			1	WCh	Tokyo	1 Sep 91
3:18.54		USA Wineberg 51.0, Felix 48.6, Henderson 50.06, Richards 48.93			1	OG	Beijing	23 Aug 08
3:18.55		USA Trotter 51.2, Felix 48.0, Wineberg 50.24, Richards 49.07			1	WCh	Osaka	2 Sep 07
3:18.58		URS I.Nazarova, Olizarenko, Pinigina, Vladykina			1	ECp	Moskva	18 Aug 85
3:18.63		GDR Neubauer 51.4, Emmelmann 49.1, Müller 48.64, Busch 49.48			1	WCh	Roma	6 Sep 87
3:18.71		JAM Whyte 50.0, Prendergast 49.6, Williams-Mills 49.84, Williams 49.22			2	WCh	Daegu	3 Sep 11
3:19.01		USA Trotter 49.8, Henderson 49.7, Richards 49.81, Hennagan 49.73			(1)	OG	Athína	28 Aug 04
		Note team was disqualified as Crystal Cox (subject of retrospective drugs ban) ran for them in the heat						
3.19.02		USA Hayes 50.4, Felix 48.7, Wimbley 49.58, Francis 50.28			1	WCh	London (OS)	13 Aug 17
3:19.04	WR	GDR Siemon' 51.0, Busch 50.0, Rübsam 50.2, Koch 47.9			1	EC	Athína	11 Sep 82
3.19.02		USA Hayes 50.4, Felix 48.7, Wimbley 49.58, Francis 50.28			1	WCh	London (OS)	13 Aug 17
3:19.06		USA Okolo 50.3, Hastings 49.2, Francis 49.82, Felix 49.66			1	OG	Rio de Janeiro	20 Aug 16
3:19.12		URS Baskakova, I.Nazarova, Pinigina, Vladykina			1	Drz	Praha	18 Aug 84
3:19.23	WR	GDR Maletzki 50.05, Rohde 49.00, Streidt 49.51, Brehmer 49.79			1	OG	Montreal	31 Jul 76
3:19.49		GDR Emmelmann, Busch, Neubauer, Koch 47.9			1	WCp	Canberra	4 Oct 85
		(25/3 with USSR and Russia counted separately)						
3:20.04		GBR Ohuruogu 50.6, Okoro 50.9, McConnell 49.79, Sanders 48.76			3	WCh	Osaka	2 Sep 07
3:20.32		CZE/TCH			2	WCh	Helsinki	14 Aug 83
		Kocembová 48.93, Matejkovicová 52.13, Moravcíková 51.51, Kratochvílová 47.75						
3:21.04		NGR Afolabi 51.13, Yusuf 49.72, Opara 51.29, Ogunkoya 48.90			2	OG	Atlanta	3 Aug 96
3:21.21		CAN Crooks 50.30, Richardson 50.22, Killingbeck ¶ 50.62, Payne 50.07			2	OG	Los Angeles	11 Aug 84
3:21.88		BLR Yushchenko 51.40, Khlyustova 50.7, I Usovich 49.97, S Usovich 49.78			5	WCh	Osaka	2 Sep 07
		(10)						
3:21.94		UKR Dzhigalova, Olizarenko, Pinigina, Vladykina			1	URS Ch	Kyiv	17 Jul 86
3:22.34		FRA Landre 51.3, Dorsile 51.1, Elien 50.54, Pérec 49.36			1	EC	Helsinki	14 Aug 94
3:22.49		FRG Thimm 50.81, Arendt 49.95, Thomas 51.50, Abt 50.23			4	OG	Seoul	1 Oct 88
3:23.21		CUB Díaz 51.1, Calatayud 51.2, Clement 50.47, Terrero 50.46			6	OG	Beijing	23 Aug 08
3:23.81		AUS Peris-K 51.71, Lewis 51.69, Gainsford-T 51.06, Freeman 49.35			4	OG	Sydney	30 Sep 00
3:24.28		CHN (Hebei) An X, Bai X, Cao C, Ma Y			1	NG	Beijing	13 Sep 93
3:24.49		POL Guzowska 52.2, Bejnar 50.2, Prokopek 50.47, Jesien 51.59			4	WCh	Helsinki	14 Aug 05
3:25.16		ITA Chigbolu 52.1, Spacca 51.3, Folorunso 51.44, Grenot 50.18			4h2	OG	Rio de Janeiro	19 Aug 16
3:25.68		ROU Ruicu 52.69, Rîpanu 51.09, Barbu 52.64, Tirlea 49.26			2	ECp	Paris (C)	20 Jun 99
3:25.7a		FIN Eklund 53.6, Pursiainen 50.6, Wilmi 51.6, Salin 49.9			2	EC	Roma	8 Sep 74
		(20)						
3:25.81		BUL Ilieva, Stamenova, Penkova, Damyanova			1	v Hun,Pol	Sofia	24 Jul 83
3:26.33		GRE Kaidantzi 53.2, Goudenoúdi 51.6, Boudá 51.76, Halkiá 49.75			3	ECpS	Bydgoszcz	20 Jun 04
3:26.36		BAH L Clarke 52.4, Strachan 51.9, Cox 50.91, Amertil 51.07			6h2	OG	Rio de Janeiro	19 Aug 16
3:26.68		BRA (Bovespa) Coutinho, de Oliveira, Sousa, de Lima			1	NC	São Paulo	7 Aug 11
0:26.06		BOT Moroko 50.3, Dotlogetswe 50.9, Matlhaku 53.00, Montsho 40.50			3	CG	Gold Coast	14 Apr 18
3:26.89		IND R Kaur 53.1, Beenamol 51.4, Soman 52.51, M Kaur 49.85			3h2	OG	Athína	27 Aug 04
3:26.98		NED			6h1	OG	Rio de Janeiro	19 Aug 16
		Ghafoor 52.4, Lisanne de Witte 51.0, van Leuveren 50.99, Laura de Witte 52.49						
3:27.08		CMR Nguimgo 51.7, Kaboud 52.1, Atangana 51.98, Béwouda 51.35			7	WCh	Saint-Denis	31 Aug 03
3:27.14		MEX Rodríguez 53.3, Medina 51.2, Vela 52.94, Guevara 49.70			4h2	WCh	Osaka	1 Sep 07
3:27.48		IRL Andrews 53.4, Cuddihy 49.9, Bergin 52.60, Carey 51.54			(30) 4h3	WCh	Daegu	2 Sep 11

Drugs disqualification

Mark	Wind	Name	Nat	Born	Pos	Meet	Venue	Date
3:18.82		RUS Gushchina 50.6, Litvinova 49.2, Firova 49.20, Kapachinskaya 49.82			(2)	OG	Beijing	23 Aug 08
3:19.36		RUS			(3)	WCh	Daegu	3 Sep 11
		Krivoshapka 50.3, Antyukh 50.0, Litvinova 49.96, Kapachinskaya ¶ 49.22						
3:21.85		BLR Kozak 52.0, Khlyustova 50.3, I Usovich 49.85, S Usovich 49.69			(4)	OG	Beijing	23 Aug 08

4 x 800 METRES RELAY

Mark	Wind	Name	Nat	Born	Pos	Meet	Venue	Date
7:50.17	WR	USSR Olizarenko, Gurina, Borisova, Podyalovskaya			1		Moskva	5 Aug 84
7:51.62		USSR II Ruchayeva, Agletdinova, Zvagintseva, Zhukova			2		Moskva	5 Aug 84
7:52.24		USSR Podkopayeva, Zvyagintseva, Olizarenko, Agletdinova			1		Leningrad	4 Aug 85
7:52.3	WR	USSR			1		Podolsk	16 Aug 76
		Providokhina 1:58.4, Gerasimova 1:59.2, Styrkina 1:57.3, Kazankina ¶ 1:57.4						

Mark	Wind	Name		Nat	Born	Pos	Meet	Venue	Date
7:54.10 WR	GDR	Zinn, Hoffmeister, Weiss, Klapezynski				1	NC	Karl-Marx-Stadt	6 Aug 76
8:00.62	USA	Price 2:01.30, Vessey 2:00.92, Ludlow 1:59.50, Montaño 1:58.90				1	WRly	Nassau	3 May 15

4 x 1500 METRES RELAY

Mark	Wind	Name		Nat	Born	Pos	Meet	Venue	Date
16:33.58 WR	KEN	M Cherono 4:07.5, Kipyegon 4:08.5, Jelagat 4:10.5, Obiri 4:07.1				1	WRly	Nassau	24 May 14
16:55.33	USA	Kampf 4:09.2, Mackey, Grace, Martinez 4:10.2				2	WRly	Nassau	24 May 14
17:08.65	AUS	Buckman 4:08.1, Delaney 4:15.5, McGowan, Duncan 4:16.0				3	WRly	Nassau	25 May 14

5000 METRES WALK (TRACK)

Mark	Wind	Name		Nat	Born	Pos	Meet	Venue	Date
20:01.80 WR		Eleonora	Giorgi	ITA	14.9.89	1		Misterbianco	18 May 14
20:02.60 WR		Gillian	O'Sullivan	IRL	21.8.76	1	NC	Dublin (S)	13 Jul 02
20:03.0 WR		Kerry	Saxby-Junna	AUS	2.6.61	1		Sydney	11 Feb 96
20:07.52 WR		Beate	Anders/Gummelt	GDR	4.2.68	1	vURS	Rostock	23 Jun 90
20:11.45		Sabine	Zimmer/Krantz	GER	6.2.81	1	NC	Wattenscheid	2 Jul 05
20:12.41		Elisabetta	Perrone	ITA	9.7.68	1	NC	Rieti	2 Aug 03
20:15.71		Lyudmyla	Olyanovska ¶	UKR	20.2.93	1		Kyiv	4 Jun 14
20:18.87		Melanie	Seeger	GER	8.1.77	1	NC	Braunschweig	10 Jul 04
20:21.69		Annarita	Sidoti	ITA	25.7.69	1	NC	Cesenatico	1 Jul 95
20:27.59 WR		Ileana	Salvador	ITA	16.1.62	1		Trento	3 Jun 89

10 KILOMETRES WALK

Mark	Wind	Name		Nat	Born	Pos	Meet	Venue	Date
41:04 WR		Yelena	Nikolayeva	RUS	1.2.66	1	NC	Sochi	20 Apr 96
41:16			Wang Yan	CHN	3.5.71	1		Eisenhüttenstadt	8 May 99
41:16		Kjersti	Plätzer (Tysse)	NOR	18.1.72	1	NC	Os	11 May 02
41:17		Irina	Stankina	RUS	25.3.77	1	NC-w	Adler	9 Feb 97
41:24		Olimpiada	Ivanova ¶	RUS	26.8.70	2	NC-w	Adler	9 Feb 97
41:29 WR		Larisa	Ramazanova	RUS	23.9.71	1	NC	Izhevsk	4 Jun 95
41:30 WR		Kerry	Saxby-Junna	AUS	2.6.61	1	NC	Canberra	27 Aug 88
41:30			O Ivanova			2	NC	Izhevsk	4 Jun 95
41:31		Yelena	Gruzinova	RUS	24.12.67	1	NC	Sochi	20 Apr 96
41:37.9t			Gao Hongmiao	CHN	17.3.74	1	NC	Beijing	7 Apr 94
41:38		Rossella	Giordano (10)	ITA	1.12.72	1		Naumburg	25 May 97
41:41			Nikolayeva			2		Naumburg	25 May 97
41:41			Tysse Plätzer			1		Kraków	30 May 09
41:42		Olga	Kaniskina ¶	RUS	19.1.85	2		Kraków	30 May 09
41:42.5t		Lyudmyla	Olyanovska ¶	UKR	20.2.93	1		Mukachevo	1 Nov 14
41:45			Liu Hongyu	CHN	11.1.75	2		Eisenhüttenstadt	8 May 99
41:46		Annarita	Sidoti	ITA	25.7.69	1		Livorno	12 Jun 94
41:46			O Ivanova			1	NC/w	Adler	11 Feb 96
41:47			Saxby-Junna			1		Eisenhüttenstadt	11 May 96
41:48		(20/15)	Li Chunxiu	CHN	13.8.69	1	NG	Beijing	8 Sep 93
41:48	+	Yelena	Lashmanova	RUS	9.4.92	1	in 20k	Cheboksary	9 Jun 18
41:50		Yelena	Arshintseva	RUS	5.4.71	1	NC-w	Adler	11 Feb 95
41:51		Beate	Anders/Gummelt	GER	4.2.68	2		Eisenhüttenstadt	11 May 96
41:52		Tatyana	Mineyeva ¶	RUS	10.8.90	1	NCp-j	Penza	5 Sep 09
41:52		Tatyana	Korotkova	RUS	24.4.80	1		Buy	19 Sep 10
		(20)							
41:53		Tatyana	Sibileva	RUS	17.5.80	1	RWC-F	Beijing	18 Sep 10
41:56		Yelena	Sayko	RUS	24.12.67	2	NC/w	Adler	11 Feb 96
41:56.23t		Nadezhda	Ryashkina	RUS	22.1.67	1	GWG	Seattle	24 Jul 90
41:57.29t		Antonella	Palmisano	ITA	6.8.91	1		Orvieto	23 Apr 17
41:59		Marina	Pandakova	RUS	1.3.89	1		Podolsk	8 May 16
42:01		Tamara	Kovalenko	RUS	5.6.64	3	NC-w	Adler	11 Feb 95
42:01		Olga	Panfyorova	RUS	21.8.77	1	NC-23	Izhevsk	16 May 98
42:02.99t		Sandra	Arenas	COL	17.9.93	1	IbAm	Trujillo	26 Aug 18
42:03		Lina	Bikulova	RUS	1.10.88	1		Bui	13 Sep 14
42:04+		Vera	Sokolova ¶	RUS	8.6.87	1=	in 20k	Sochi	26 Feb 11
		(30)							
42:04+		Anisya	Kirdyapkina ¶	RUS	23.10.89	1=	in 20k	Sochi	26 Feb 11
42:04+		Tatyana	Shemyakina	RUS	3.9.87	1=	in 20k	Sochi	26 Feb 11
42:05+		Margarita	Turova	BLR	28.12.80	1+	in 20k	Adler	12 Mar 05
42:06		Valentina	Tsybulskaya	BLR	19.2.68	4		Eisenhüttenstadt	8 May 99
42:07		Ileana	Salvador	ITA	16.1.62	1		Sesto San Giovanni	1 May 92
42:09		Elisabetta	Perrone	ITA	9.7.68	4		Eisenhüttenstadt	11 May 96
42:11		Nina	Alyushenko	RUS	29.5.68	3	NC	Izhevsk	4 Jun 95
42:12+		Elmira	Alembekova ¶	RUS	30.6.90	1	in 20k	Sochi	27 Feb 15
42:12+		Svetlana	Vasilyeva	RUS	24.7.92	3	in 20k	Sochi	27 Feb 15
42:13		Natalya	Misyulya	BLR	16.4.66	5		Eisenhüttenstadt	8 May 99
42:13.7t		Madelein	Svensson	SWE	20.7.69	2	SGP	Fana	15 May 92
		(41)	50th woman 42:20, 100th 42:59, 200th 43:50, 300th 44:26, 400th 44:49.84						

WOMEN All-time

Mark	Wind	Name		Nat	Born	Pos	Meet	Venue	Date
Best track times									
41:57.22		Kerry	Saxby-Junna	AUS	2.6.61	2	GWG	Seattle	24 Jul 90
42:11.5		Beate	Anders/Gummelt	GER	4.2.68	1	SGP	Fana	15 May 92

20 KILOMETRES WALK

Mark	Wind	Name		Nat	Born	Pos	Meet	Venue	Date
1:23:39		Yelena	Lashmanova	RUS	9.4.92	1	NC	Cheboksary	9 Jun 18
1:24:38	WR		Liu Hong	CHN	12.5.87	1		La Coruña	6 Jun 15
1:24:47		Elmira	Alembekova ¶	RUS	30.6.90	1	NC-w	Sochi	27 Feb 15
1:24:50		Olimpiada	Ivanova ¶	RUS	26.8.70	1	NC-w	Adler	4 Mar 01
1:24:56		Olga	Kaniskina ¶	RUS	19.1.85	1	NC-w	Adler	28 Feb 09
1:24:58			Lashmanova			1	NC	Cheboksary	25 Jun 16
1:25:02	WR		Lashmanova			1	OG	London	11 Aug 12
1:25:03		Marina	Pandakova	RUS	1.3.89	2	NC-w	Sochi	27 Feb 15
1:25:04		Svetlana	Vasilyeva	RUS	24.7.92	3	NC-w	Sochi	27 Feb 15
1:25:08	WR	Vera	Sokolova	RUS	8.6.87	1	NC-w	Sochi	26 Feb 11
1:25:09		Anisya	Kirdyapkina ¶	RUS	23.10.80	2	NC-w	Sochi	26 Feb 11
1:25:11			Kaniskina			1	NC-w	Adler	23 Feb 08
1:25:11			Kirdyapkina			1	NC-w	Sochi	20 Feb 10
1:25:12			Lu Xiuzhi (10)	CHN	26.10.93	1	WCT	Beijing	20 Mar 15
1:25:16			Qieyang Shenjie	CHN	11.11.90	2	OG	London	11 Aug 12
1:25:18		Tatyana	Gudkova	RUS	23.1.78	1	NC	Moskva	19 May 00
1:25:18			Lashmanova			1	NC-w	Sochi	18 Feb 17
1:25:20		Olga	Polyakova	RUS	23.9.80	2	NC	Moskva	19 May 00
1:25:22		Yekaterina	Medvedyeva	RUS	29.3.94	2	NC-w	Sochi	18 Feb 17
1:25:26			Sokolova			2	NC-w	Adler	28 Feb 09
1:25:26			Kirdyapkina			3	NC-w	Adler	28 Feb 09
1:25:27			Alembekova			1	NC-w	Sochi	18 Feb 12
1:25:29		Irina	Stankina	RUS	25.3.77	3	NC	Moskva	19 May 00
1:25:30			Kirdyapkina			2	NC-w	Adler	23 Feb 08
1:25:32		Yelena	Shumkina ¶	RUS	24.1.88	4	NC-w	Adler	28 Feb 09
1:25:35			Sokolova			2	NC-w	Sochi	20 Feb 10
1:25:38			Sokolova			4	NC-w	Sochi	27 Feb 15
1:25:41	WR		Ivanova			1	WCh	Helsinki	7 Aug 05
1:25:42			Kaniskina			1	WCp	Cheboksary	11 May 08
1:25:46		Tatyana	Shemyakina	RUS	3.9.87	3	NC-w	Adler	23 Feb 08
1:25:46			Liu Hong			1		Taicang	30 Mar 12
		(31/17)							
1:25:52		Larisa	Yemelyanova	RUS	6.1.80	5	NC-w	Adler	28 Feb 09
1:25:52		Tatyana	Sibileva	RUS	17.5.80	3	NC-w	Sochi	20 Feb 10
1:25:59		Tamara	Kovalenko	RUS	5.6.64	4	NC	Moskva	19 May 00
		(20)							
1:26:11		Margarita	Turova	BLR	28.12.80	1	NC	Nesvizh	15 Apr 06
1:26:14		Irina	Petrova	RUS	26.5.85	2	NC-w	Adler	19 Feb 06
1:26:16		Lyudmila	Arkhipova	RUS	25.11.78	5	NC-w	Adler	23 Feb 08
1:26:17		Eleonora	Giorgi	ITA	14.9.89	2	ECp	Murcia	17 May 15
1:26:17		María Guadalupe	González	MEX	9.1.89	1	WCp	Roma	7 May 16
1:26:18			Yang Jiayu	CHN	18.2.96	1	WCh	London	13 Aug 17
1:26:22	WR		Wang Yan	CHN	3.5.71	1	NG	Guangzhou	19 Nov 01
1:26:22	WR	Yelena	Nikolayeva	RUS	1.2.66	1	ECp	Cheboksary	18 May 03
1:26:23			Wang Liping	CHN	8.7.76	2	NG	Guangzhou	19 Nov 01
1:26:27		Sofiya	Brodatskaya	RUS	4.10.95	3	NC-w	Sochi	18 Feb 17
		(30)							
1:26:28		Iraida	Pudovkina	RUS	2.11.80	1	NC-w	Adler	12 Mar 05
1:26:29			Wang Na	CHN	29.5.95	2	NGP	Huangshan	4 Mar 17
1:26:34		Tatyana	Kalmykova	RUS	10.1.90	1	NC	Saransk	8 Jun 08
1:26:35			Liu Hongyu	CHN	11.1.75	3	NG	Guangzhou	19 Nov 01
1:26:36		Antonella	Palmisano	ITA	6.8.91	3	WCh	London	13 Aug 17
1:26:36		María	Pérez	ESP	29.4.96	1	EC	Berlin	11 Aug 18
1:26:46			Song Hongjuan	CHN	4.7.84	1	NC	Guangzhou	20 Mar 04
1:26:46		Mariya	Ponomaryova	RUS	18.6.95	3	NC	Cheboksary	25 Jun 16
1:26:47		Irina	Yumanova ¶	RUS	6.11.90	3	NC-w	Sochi	18 Feb 12
1:26:47		Klavdiya	Afanasyeva	RUS	15.1.96	4	NC	Cheboksary	25 Jun 16
		(40)							
1:26:50		Natalya	Fedoskina	RUS	25.6.80	2	ECp	Dudince	19 May 01
1:26:53		Anezka	Drahotová	CZE	22.7.95	4	ECp	Murcia	17 May 15
1:26:57		Lyudmila	Yefimkina	RUS	22.8.81	3	NC-w	Adler	19 Feb 06
1:26:59		Erica	de Sena	BRA	3.5.85	4	WCh	London	13 Aug 17
1:27:07		Kjersti	Tysse Plätzer	NOR	18.1.72	2	OG	Beijing	21 Aug 08
1:27:09		Elisabetta	Perrone	ITA	9.7.68	3	ECp	Dudince	19 May 01
1:27:09		Lyudmyla	Olyanovska ¶	UKR	20.2.93	7	ECp	Murcia	17 May 15

Mark	Wind		Name	Nat	Born	Pos	Meet	Venue	Date
1:27:12		Elisa	Rigaudo	ITA	17.6.80	3	OG	Beijing	21 Aug 08
1:27:14		Antonina	Petrova	RUS	1.5.77	1	NC-w	Adler	1 Mar 03
1:27:18		Alena	Nartova	RUS	1.1.82	6	NC-w	Adler	23 Feb 08
	(50)		100th best woman 1:28:24, 200th 1:30:20, 300th 1:31:37, 400th 1:33:09, 500th 1:34:07						
Drugs dq:	1:25:09		Kaniskina			(2)	OG	London	11 Aug 12
1:27:08	Anna		Lukyanova ¶	RUS	23.4.91	(5)	NC-w	Sochi	18 Feb 12

30/35 KILOMETRES WALK

Mark			Name	Nat	Born	Pos	Meet	Venue	Date
2:19:43		Eleonora	Giorgi	ITA	14.9.89	1		Catania	31 Jan 16
2:22:47	2:45:51	Inês	Henriques	POR	1.5.80	1		Porto de Mos	7 Jan 18
2:24:33	2:48:13	Olga	Shargina	RUS	24.7.96	1	NC-w	Sochi	19 Mar 18
	2:49:23		Liang Rui	CHN	18.6.94	1		Huangshan	4 Mar 18
2:25:18+	2:49:52e	Inês	Henriques			1	in 50k	Berlin	7 Aug 18
	2:50:14		Yin Hang	CHN	7.2.97	2		Huangshan	4 Mar 18
2:26:35	2:50:52		Henriques			1	WCh	London	13 Aug 17
2:26:10	2:50:09		Henriques			1		Porto de Mós	15 Jan 17
	2:50:31		Zhou Kang	CHN	24.12.89	3		Huangshan	4 Mar 18
2:26:39	2:51:42		Yin Hang			2	WCh	London	13 Aug 17

50 KILOMETRES WALK

Mark			Name	Nat	Born	Pos	Meet	Venue	Date
4:04:36			Liang Rui	CHN	18.6.94	1	WTC	Taicang	5 May 18
4:05:56		Inês	Henriques	POR	1.5.80	1	WCh	London	13 Aug 17
4:08:26			Henriques			1		Porto de Mós	15 Jan 17
4:08:58			Yin Hang	CHN	7.2.97	2	WCh	London	13 Aug 17
4:09:09			Yin Hang			2	WTC	Taicang	5 May 18
4:09:21			Henriques			1	EC	Berlin	7 Aug 18
4:09:33		Claire	Tallent	AUS	6.7.81	3	WTC	Taicang	5 May 18
4:10:59		Monica	Svensson	SWE	26.12.78	1		Scanzorosciate	21 Oct 07
4:12:16		Yelena	Ginko	BLR	30.7.76	1		Scanzorosciate	17 Oct 04
4:12:26			Liang Rui			1	NC	Weinan	8 Sep 18
4:12:44		Alina	Tsviliy	UKR	18.9.94	2	EC	Berlin	7 Aug 18
4:12:56		Paola	Pérez	ECU	21.12.89	4	WTC	Taicang	5 May 18
4:13:04		Julia	Takacs	ESP	29.6.89	1	NC	Burjassot	25 Feb 18
4:13:04			Li Maocuo (10)	CHN	20.10.92	1	NGP	Chifeng	3 Jul 18
4:13:28			Ma Faying	CHN	30.8.93	5	WTC	Taicang	5 May 18
4:14:25		Mária	Czaková	SVK	2.10.88	1		Dudince	24 Mar 18
4:14:27			Svensson			1		Scanzorosciate	18 Oct 09
4:14:28		Johana	Ordóñez	ECU	12.12.87	6	WTC	Taicang	5 May 18
4:14:46		Klavdiya	Afanasyeva	RUS	15.1.96	1	NC	Cheboksary	9 Jun 18
4:14:47			Li Maocuo			7	WTC	Taicang	5 May 18
	(20/14)								
4:15:42		Mayra Carolina	Herrera	GUA	20.12.88	1		Owego	9 Sep 17
4:16:27		Jolanta	Dukure	LAT	20.9.79	1		Paralepa	9 Sep 06
4:18:00		Anastasiya	Yatsevich	BLR	18.1.85	9	WTC	Taicang	5 May 18
4:18:31		Nadezhda	Dorozhuk	BLR	23.1.90	10	WTC	Taicang	5 May 18
4:18:50		Valentyna	Myronchuk	UKR	10.8.94	1		Ivano-Frankivsk	20 Oct 18
4:18:56		Ainhoa	Pinedo	ESP	17.2.83	2	NC	Burjassot	25 Feb 18
	(20)								
4:19:04		Magaly	Bonilla	ECU	8.2.92	11	WTC	Taicang	5 May 18
4:20:36		Erika	Morales	MEX	10.12.86	1		Hauppage	24 Oct 18
4:20:46		Khrystyna	Yudkina	UKR	4.12.84	4	EC	Berlin	7 Aug 18
4:20:49			Yang Shuqing	CHN	30.8.96	3	WCh	London	13 Aug 17
4:21:51		Kathleen	Burnett	USA	10.7.88	4	WCh	London	13 Aug 17
4:22:36		Aleksandra	Bushkova	RUS	13.1.97	2	NC	Cheboksary	9 Jun 18
4:23:15		Vasylyna	Vitovshchyk	UKR	30.4.90	5	EC	Berlin	7 Aug 18
4:25:22		Brigita	Virbalyte-Dimsiene	LTU	1.2.85	1		Villa di Serio	17 Oct 10
4:27:13		Olga	Shargina	RUS	24.7.96	3	NC	Cheboksary	9 Jun 18
4:28:13		Evaggelía	Xinoú	GRE	22.11.81	2		Scanzorosciate	17 Oct 04
	(30)								
4:28:53		Neringa	Aidietyté	LTU	5.6.83	1		Ivano-Frankivsk	1 Oct 06
4:28:58		Mar	Juárez	ESP	27.9.93	8	EC	Berlin	7 Aug 18
4:28:59		Kora	Boufflért	FRA	23.4.66	1		Charly-sur-Marne	18 Feb 07
4:29:33		Erin	Talcott'	USA	21.5.78	2	NC	Santee	28 Jan 17
4:29:45		Serena	Sonoda	JPN	10.9.96	1		Takahata	28 Oct 18
4:29:56		Natalia	Bruniko	ITA	23.2.73	2		Scanzorosciate	27 Oct 02
4:30:43		Dusica	Topic	SRB	11.1.82	9	EC	Berlin	7 Aug 18
4:31:41		Mariavittoria	Becchetti	ITA	12.12.94	10	EC	Berlin	7 Aug 18
4:32:14			Jiang Shanshan	CHN	28.2.97	3	NGP	Huangshan	5 Mar 17
4:32:25		Lyudmyla	Shelest	UKR	4.10.74	3		Scanzorosciate	18 Oct 09
	(40)								

WOMEN All-time

Mark	Wind	Name		Nat	Born	Pos	Meet	Venue	Date

JUNIOR MEN'S ALL-TIME LISTS

100 METRES

Mark	Wind	Name		Nat	Born	Pos	Meet	Venue	Date
9.97	1.8	Trayvon	Bromell	USA	10.7.95	1	NCAA	Eugene	13 Jun 14
10.00	1.6	Trentavis	Friday	USA	5.6.95	1h1	NC-j	Eugene	5 Jul 14
10.01	0.0	Darrel	Brown	TTO	11.10.84	1q3	WCh	Saint-Denis	24 Aug 03
10.01	1.6	Jeffery	Demps	USA	8.1.90	2q1	NC/OT	Eugene	28 Jun 08
10.01	0.9	Yoshihide	Kiryu	JPN	15.12.95	1h3	Oda	Hiroshima	29 Apr 13
10.03	0.7	Marcus	Rowland	USA	11.3.90	1	PAm-J	Port of Spain	31 Jul 09
10.04	1.7	DeAngelo	Cherry	USA	1.8.90	1h4	NCAA	Fayetteville	10 Jun 09
10.04	0.2	Christoph	Lemaitre	FRA	11.6.90	1	EJ	Novi Sad	24 Jul 09
10.04	1.9	Abdullah Abkar	Mohammed	KSA	.97	1	MSR	Norwalk	15 Apr 16
10.05		Davidson	Ezinwa	NGR	22.11.71	1		Bauchi	4 Jan 90
10.05	0.1	Adam	Gemili	GBR	6.10.93	1	WJ	Barcelona	11 Jul 12
10.05	0.6	Abdul Hakim	Sani Brown	JPN	6.3.99	1	NC	Osaka	24 Jun 17

Wind assisted to 10.02

Mark	Wind	Name		Nat	Born	Pos	Meet	Venue	Date
9.77	4.2	Trayvon	Bromell	USA	10.7.95	1	Big 12	Lubbock	18 May 14
9.83	7.1	Leonard	Scott	USA	19.1.80	1		Knoxville	9 Apr 99
9.96	4.5	Walter	Dix	USA	31.1.86	1rA	TexR	Austin	9 Apr 05
9.96	5.0	André	De Grasse	CAN	10.11.94	1	JUCO	Hutchinson, KS	18 May 13
9.97	??	Mark	Lewis-Francis	GBR	4.9.82	1q3	WCh	Edmonton	4 Aug 01
9.98	5.0	Tyreek	Hill	USA	1.3.94	2	JUCO	Hutchinson, KS	18 May 13
10.02	2.8	DeAngelo	Cherry	USA	1.8.90	1h2	NC-j	Eugene	26 Jun 09
10.02	2.4	Marcus	Rowland	USA	11.3.90	1	NC-j	Eugene	26 Jun 09

200 METRES

Mark	Wind	Name		Nat	Born	Pos	Meet	Venue	Date
19.93	1.4	Usain	Bolt	JAM	21.8.86	1		Hamilton, BER	11 Apr 04
20.04	0.1	Ramil	Guliyev	AZE	29.5.90	1	WUG	Beograd	10 Jul 09
20.07	1.5	Lorenzo	Daniel	USA	23.3.66	1	SEC	Starkville	18 May 85
20.09	1.6	Noah	Lyles	USA	18.7.97	4	NC/OT	Eugene	9 Jul 16
20.10A	1.7	Clarence	Munyai	RSA	20.2.98	2		Pretoria	1 Mar 17
20.13	1.7	Roy	Martin	USA	25.12.66	1		Austin	11 May 85
20.14	1.8	Tyreek	Hill	USA	1.3.94	1		Orlando	26 May 12
20.14	1.6	Michael	Norman	USA	3.12.97	5	NC/OT	Eugene	9 Jul 16
20.16A	-0.2	Riaan	Dempers	RSA	4.3.77	1	NC-j	Germiston	7 Apr 95
20.18	1.0	Walter	Dix	USA	31.1.86	1s2	NCAA	Sacramento	9 Jun 05
20.20A	0.5	Tlotliso Gift	Leotlela	RSA	12.5.98	3	NC	Potchefstroom	22 Apr 17
20.21A	1.4	Baboloki	Thebe	BOT	18.3.97	1	NC-j	Gaborone	22 May 16

Wind assisted to 20.14

Mark	Wind	Name		Nat	Born	Pos	Meet	Venue	Date
19.86	4.0	Justin	Gatlin	USA	10.2.82	1h2	NCAA	Eugene	30 May 01
20.01	2.5	Derald	Harris	USA	5.4.58	1		San José	9 Apr 77
20.02	2.7	Khance	Meyers	USA	11.1.99	1	JUCO	El Dorado	19 May 18
20.03	2.9	Trentavis	Friday	USA	5.6.95	1	NC-j	Eugene	6 Jul 14
20.04	3.3	Noah	Lyles	USA	18.7.97	1h1	NC/OT	Eugene	7 Jul 16
20.06	2.8	Michael	Norman	USA	3.12.97	1h4	NC/OT	Eugene	7 Jul 16
20.07	3.4	Maxwell	Willis	USA	2.9.98	1h1	Big 12	Lawrence	13 May 17
20.08	9.2	Leonard	Scott	USA	19.1.80	2r2		Knoxville	9 Apr 99
20.10	4.6	Stanley	Kerr	USA	19.6.67	2r2	SWC	Houston	18 May 86

400 METRES

Mark	Wind	Name		Nat	Born	Pos	Meet	Venue	Date
43.87		Steve	Lewis	USA	16.5.69	1	OG	Seoul	28 Sep 88
44.22A		Baboloki	Thebe	BOT	18.3.97	1	NC-j	Gaborone	21 May 16
44.25		Karabo	Sibanda	BOT	2.7.98	5	OG	Rio de Janeiro	14 Aug 16
44.27		Abdelilah	Haroun	QAT	1.1.97	2		La Chaux-de-Fonds	5 Jul 15
44.36		Kirani	James	GRN	1.9.92	1	WK	Zürich	8 Sep 11
44.66		Hamdam Odha	Al-Bishi	KSA	5.5.81	1	WJ	Santiago de Chile	20 Oct 00
44.66		LaShawn	Merritt	USA	27.6.86	1		Kingston	7 May 05
44.69		Darrell	Robinson	USA	23.12.63	2	USOF	Indianapolis	24 Jul 82
44.71A		Luguelín	Santos	DOM	12.11.93	2	PAm	Guadalajara	26 Oct 11
44.73A		James	Rolle	USA	2.2.64	1	USOF	USAF Academy	2 Jul 83
44.75		Darren	Clark	AUS	6.9.65	4	OG	Los Angeles	8 Aug 84
44.75		Deon	Minor	USA	22.1.73	1s1	NCAA	Austin	5 Jun 92

800 METRES

Mark	Wind	Name		Nat	Born	Pos	Meet	Venue	Date
1:41.73		Nijel	Amos	BOT	15.3.94	2	OG	London (OS)	9 Aug 12
1:42.37		Mohammed	Aman	ETH	10.1.94	1	VD	Bruxelles	6 Sep 13
1:42.53		Timothy	Kitum	KEN	20.11.94	3	OG	London (OS)	9 Aug 12
1:42.69		Abubaker	Kaki	SUD	21.6.89	1	Bisl	Oslo	6 Jun 08
1:43.13		Abraham Kipchirchir	Rotich	KEN	26.6.93	1	Herc	Monaco	20 Jul 12
1:43.40		Leonard	Kosencha	KEN	21.8.94	2	Herc	Monaco	20 Jul 12
1:43.55		Donavan	Brazier	USA	15.4.97	1	NCAA	Eugene	10 Jun 16

Mark	Wind	Name		Nat	Born	Pos	Meet	Venue	Date
1:43.56		Robert	Biwott	KEN	28.1.96	2		Barcelona	8 Jul 15
1:43.64		Japheth	Kimutai	KEN	20.12.78	3rB	WK	Zürich	13 Aug 97
1:43.76		Kipyegon	Bett	KEN	2.1.98	2	ISTAF	Berlin	3 Sep 16
1:43.81		Edwin	Melly	KEN	24.3.94	2		Rieti	9 Sep 12

1000 METRES

Mark	Wind	Name		Nat	Born	Pos	Meet	Venue	Date
2:13.93		Abubaker	Kaki	SUD	21.6.89	1	DNG	Stockholm	22 Jul 08
2:15.00		Benjamin	Kipkurui	KEN	28.12.80	5	Nik	Nice	17 Jul 99
2:16.84		Ali	Hakimi	TUN	24.4.76	1		Lindau	28 Jul 95

1500 METRES

Mark	Wind	Name		Nat	Born	Pos	Meet	Venue	Date
3:28.81		Ronald	Kwemoi	KEN	19.9.95	3	Herc	Monaco	18 Jul 14
3:30.10		Robert	Biwott	KEN	28.1.96	7	Herc	Monaco	17 JUl 15
3:30.24		Cornelius	Chirchir	KEN	5.6.83	4	Herc	Monaco	19 Jul 02
3:31.18		Jakob	Ingebrigtsen	NOR	19.9.00	4	Herc	Monaco	20 Jul 18
3:31.13		Mulugueta	Wondimu	ETH	28.2.85	2rA	NA	Heusden	31 Jul 04
3:31.42		Alex	Kipchirchir	KEN	26.11.84	5	VD	Bruxelles	5 Sep 03
3:31.54		Isaac	Songok	KEN	25.4.84	1	NA	Heusden	2 Aug 03
3:31.63		Samuel	Tefera	ETH	23.10.99	2	DL	Shanghai	12 May 18
3:31.64		Asbel	Kiprop	KEN	30.6.89	1	GGala	Roma	11 Jul 08
3:31.70		William	Biwott	KEN	5.3.90	3	GGala	Roma	10 Jul 09
3:32.02		Caleb	Ndiku	KEN	9.10.92	4	FBK	Hengelo	29 May 11
3:32.48		Augustine	Choge	KEN	21.1.87	1	ISTAF	Berlin	3 Sep 06

1 MILE

Mark	Wind	Name		Nat	Born	Pos	Meet	Venue	Date
3:49.29		William	Biwott	KEN	5.3.90	2	Bisl	Oslo	3 Jul 09
3:49.77		Caleb	Ndiku	KEN	9.10.92	5	Pre	Eugene	4 Jun 11
3:50.25		Alex	Kipchirchir	KEN	26.11.84	2	GP II	Rieti	7 Sep 03
3:50.39		James	Kwalia	KEN	12.6.84	1	FBK	Hengelo	1 Jun 03
3:50.41		Noah	Ngeny	KEN	2.11.78	2	Nik	Nice	16 Jul 97
3:50.69		Cornelius	Chirchir	KEN	5.6.83	5	GGala	Roma	12 Jul 02
3:50.83		Nicholas	Kemboi	KEN	18.12.89	6	Bisl	Oslo	6 Jun 08

2000 METRES

Mark	Wind	Name		Nat	Born	Pos	Meet	Venue	Date
4:56.25		Tesfaye	Cheru	ETH	2.3.93	1		Reims	5 Jul 11
4:56.86		Isaac	Songok	KEN	25.4.84	6	ISTAF	Berlin	31 Aug 01
4:58.18		Soresa	Fida	ETH	27.5.93	4		Reims	5 Jul 11
4:58.76		Jairus	Kipchoge	KEN	15.12.92	7		Reims	5 Jul 11

3000 METRES

Mark	Wind	Name		Nat	Born	Pos	Meet	Venue	Date
7:28.19		Yomif	Kejelcha	ETH	1.8.97	1	DL	Saint-Denis	27 Aug 16
7:28.78		Augustine	Choge	KEN	21.1.87	2	SGP	Doha	13 May 05
7:29.71		Tariku	Bekele	ETH	21.1.87	2	GP	Rieti	27 Aug 06
7:30.36		Hagos	Gebrhiwet	ETH	11.5.94	1	DL	Doha	10 May 13
7:30.43		Isiah	Koech	KEN	19.12.93	1	DNG	Stockholm	17 Aug 12
7:30.67		Kenenisa	Bekele	ETH	13.6.82	2	VD	Bruxelles	24 Aug 01
7:30.91		Eliud	Kipchoge	KEN	5.11.84	2	VD	Bruxelles	5 Sep 03
7:32.37		Abreham	Cherkos	ETH	23.9.89	2	Athl	Lausanne	11 Jul 06
7:32.72		John	Kipkoech	KEN	29.12.91	4		Rieti	29 Aug 10
7:33.00		Hailu	Mekonnen	ETH	4.4.80	2		Stuttgart	6 Jun 99
7:33.01		Levy	Matebo	KEN	3.11.89	2	GP	Rieti	7 Sep 08

5000 METRES

Mark	Wind	Name		Nat	Born	Pos	Meet	Venue	Date
12:43.02		Selemon	Barega	ETH	20.1.00	1	VD	Bruxelles	31 Aug 18
12:47.53		Hagos	Gebrhiwet	ETH	11.5.94	2	DL	Saint-Denis	6 Jul 12
12:48.64		Isiah	Koech	KEN	19.12.93	3	DL	Saint-Denis	6 Jul 12
12:52.61		Eliud	Kipchoge	KEN	5.11.84	3	Bisl	Oslo	27 Jun 03
12:53.66		Augustine	Choge	KEN	21.1.87	4	GGala	Roma	8 Jul 05
12:53.72		Philip	Mosima	KEN	2.1.77	2	GGala	Roma	5 Jun 96
12:53.81		Tariku	Bekele	ETH	21.1.87	4	GGala	Roma	14 Jul 06
12:53.98		Yomif	Kejelcha	ETH	1.8.97	1	VD	Bruxelles	11 Sep 15
12:54.07		Sammy	Kipketer	KEN	29.9.81	2	GGala	Roma	30 Jun 00
12:54.19		Abreham	Cherkos	ETH	23.9.89	5	GGala	Roma	14 Jul 06
12:54.58		James	Kwalia	KEN	12.6.84	5	Bisl	Oslo	27 Jun 03
12:56.15		Daniel	Komen	KEN	17.5.76	2	GG	Roma	8 Jun 95

10,000 METRES

Mark	Wind	Name		Nat	Born	Pos	Meet	Venue	Date
26:41.75		Samuel	Wanjiru	KEN	10.11.86	3	VD	Bruxelles	26 Aug 05
26:55.73		Geoffrey	Kirui	KEN	16.2.93	6	VD	Bruxelles	16 Sep 11
26:57.56		Yigrem	Demelash	ETH	28.1.94	4	VD	Bruxelles	7 Sep 12
27:02.81		Ibrahim	Jeylan	ETH	12.6.89	4	VD	Bruxelles	25 Aug 06

Jnr MEN All-time

Mark	Wind	Name		Nat	Born	Pos	Meet	Venue	Date
27:04.00		Boniface	Kiprop	UGA	12.10.85	5	VD	Bruxelles	3 Sep 04
27:04.45		Bernard	Kipyego	KEN	16.7.86	4	FBK	Hengelo	29 May 05
27:06.35		Geoffrey	Kipsang	KEN	28.11.92	10	Pre	Eugene	3 Jun 11
27:06.47		Habtanu	Fikadu	ETH	13.3.88	8	FBK	Hengelo	26 May 07
27:07.29		Moses	Masai	KEN	1.6.86	7	VD	Bruxelles	3 Sep 04
27:08.94		Andamlak	Belihu	ETH	20.11.98	10	WCh	London(OS)	4 Aug 17
27:09.92		Aron	Kifle	ERI	20.2.98	11	WCh	London (OS)	4 Aug 17
27:11.18		Richard	Chelimo	KEN	21.4.72	1	APM	Hengelo	25 Jun 91

HALF MARATHON

Mark	Wind	Name		Nat	Born	Pos	Meet	Venue	Date
59:16		Samuel	Wanjiru	KEN	10.11.86	1		Rotterdam	11 Sep 05
59:21		Stephen	Kiprop	KEN	8.9.99	5		Valencia	28 Oct 18
59:22		Amdework	Walelegn	ETH	11.3.99	2		New Delhi	21 Oct 18
59:31		Geoffrey	Kipsang	KEN	28.11.92	2		New Delhi	27 Nov 11
59:36		Tilahun	Regassa	ETH	18.1.90	1		Lille	6 Sep 08
59.38		Faustin	Baha	TAN	30.5.82	4		Lisboa	26 Mar 00
59:51		Andamlak	Belihu	ETH	20.11.98	2		New Delhi	19 Nov 17
59:57		Eric	Ndiema	KEN	28.12.92	4		Den Haag	14 Mar 10
60:09		Ghirmay	Ghebrselassie	ERI	14.11.95	1		Paderborn	30 Mar 13
60:10		Jonathan	Maiyo	KEN	5.5.88	5		Rotterdam	9 Sep 07

MARATHON

Mark	Wind	Name		Nat	Born	Pos	Meet	Venue	Date
2:04:32		Tsegaye	Mekonnen	ETH	15.6.95	1		Dubai	24 Jan 14
2:06:07		Eric	Ndiema	KEN	28.12.92	3		Amsterdam	16 Oct 11
2:06:15		Bazu	Worku	ETH	15.9.90	2		Paris	5 Apr 09
2:08:17		Edwin	Kibet	KEN	7.7.96	5		Eindhoven	11 Oct 15
2:08:51		Berhanu	Shiferaw	ETH	31.5.93	1		Taiyuan	2 Sep 12
2:08:53		Tola	Shira	ETH	9.6.96	3		Shanghai	8 Nov 15
2:09:08		Ghirmay	Gebrselassie	ERI	14.11.95	6		Chicago	12 Oct 14
2:09:12		Feyisa	Lilesa	ETH	1.2.90	1		Dublin	26 Oct 09
2:10:00		Samuel	Rutto	KEN	?.95	1		Torino	16 Nov 14
2:10:01		Ernest	Ngeno	KEN	20.5.95	2		Torino	16 Nov 14

3000 METRES STEEPLECHASE

Mark	Wind	Name		Nat	Born	Pos	Meet	Venue	Date
7:58.66		Stephen	Cherono	KEN	15.10.82	3	VD	Bruxelles	24 Aug 01
8:01.16		Conseslus	Kipruto	KEN	8.12.94	1	DL	Shanghai	18 May 13
8:03.74		Raymond	Yator	KEN	7.4.81	3	Herc	Monaco	18 Aug 00
8:05.52		Brimin	Kipruto	KEN	31.7.85	1	FBK	Hengelo	31 May 04
8:06.96		Gilbert	Kirui	KEN	22.1.94	2	DL	London (OS)	27 Jul 13
8:07.18		Moussa	Omar Obaid	QAT	18.4.85	4	OG	Athína	24 Aug 04
8:07.69		Paul	Kosgei	KEN	22.4.78	5	DNG	Stockholm	7 Jul 97
8:07.71		Hillary	Yego	KEN	2.4.92	3	DL	Shanghai	15 May 11
8:08.37		Amos	Kirui	KEN	9.2.98	4	GGala	Roma	8 Jun 17
8:09.37		Abel	Cheruiyot/Yugut	KEN	26.12.84	2	NA	Heusden	2 Aug 03
8:11.22		Yemane	Haileselassie	ERI	21.2.98	5	GGala	Roma	8 Jun 17
8:11.31		Jairus	Birech	KEN	15.12.92	5	DL	Saint Denis	8 Jul 11

110 METRES HURDLES (106cm)

Mark	Wind	Name		Nat	Born	Pos	Meet	Venue	Date
13.12	1.6		Liu Xiang	CHN	13.7.83	1rB	Athl	Lausanne	2 Jul 02
13.23	0.0	Renaldo	Nehemiah	USA	24.3.59	1r2	WK	Zürich	16 Aug 78
13.32	0.7	Dejour	Russell	JAM	1.4.00	4	NC	Kingston	24 Jun 17
13.40	-1.0		Shi Dongpeng	CHN	6.1.84	1	NC	Shanghai	14 Sep 03
13.44	-0.0	Colin	Jackson	GBR	18.2.67	1	WJ	Athína	19 Jul 86
13.44	-0.8	Damion	Thomas	JAM	29.6.99	2s3	NCAA-W	Eugene	6 Jun 18
13.46	1.8	Jon	Ridgeon	GBR	14.2.67	1	EJ	Cottbus	23 Aug 85
13.46	-1.6	Dayron	Robles	CUB	19.11.86	1	PAm-J	Windsor	29 Jul 05
13.47	1.9	Holger	Pohland	GDR	5.4.63	2	vUSA	Karl-Marx-Stadt	10 Jul 82
13.47	1.2	Aries	Merritt	USA	24.7.85	4	NCAA	Austin	12 Jun 04
13.47	0.2		Xie Wenjun	CHN	11.7.90	2	GP	Shanghai	20 Sep 08
Wind assisted									
13.39	2.3	Damion	Thomas	JAM	29.6.99	2h2	SEC	Knoxville	12 May 18
13.41	2.6	Dayron	Robles	CUB	19.11.86	1	CAC	Nassau	10 Jul 05
13.42	4.5	Colin	Jackson	GBR	18.2.67	2	CG	Edinburgh	27 Jul 86
13.42	2.6	Antwon	Hicks	USA	12.3.83	1	WJ	Kingston	21 Jul 02
13.47	2.1	Frank	Busemann	GER	26.2.75	1	WJ	Lisboa	22 Jul 94
99 cm Hurdles									
12.99	0.5	Wilhem	Belocian	FRA	22.6.95	1	WJ	Eugene	24 Jul 14
13.06	0.5	Tyler	Mason	JAM	15.1.95	2	WJ	Eugene	24 Jul 14
13.08	2.0	Wayne	Davis	USA	2.7.90	1	PAm-J	Port of Spain	31 Jul 09
13.14	1.6	Eddie	Lovett	USA	25.6.92	1	PAm-J	Miramar	23 Jul 11
13.17	-0.7	David	Omoregie	GBR	1.11.95	1	NC-j	Bedford	22 Jun 14

Mark	Wind	Name		Nat	Born	Pos	Meet	Venue	Date
13.18	1.0	Yordan	O'Farrill	CUB	9.2.93	1	WJ	Barcelona	12 Jul 12
13.20	0.6	Dejour	Russell	JAM	1.4.00	1s3	WJ	Bydgoszcz	20 Jul 16
13.21	1.5	Misana	Viltz	USA	21.2.96	1	NC-j	Eugene	25 Jun 15
Wind assisted to 13.20									
13.03	2.9	Eddie	Lovett	USA	25.6.92	1h1	PAm-J	Miramar	23 Jul 11
13.15	2.7	Brendan	Ames	USA	6.10.88	1	NC-j	Indianapolis	21 Jun 07
13.18		Arthur	Blake	USA	19.8.66	1	GWest	Sacramento	9 Jun 84
13.19	3.8	Chad	Zallow	USA	25.4.97	1		Greensboro	20 Jun 15
Hand timed: 12.9y Renaldo			Nehemiah	USA	24.3.59	1		Jamaica, NY	30 May 77

400 METRES HURDLES

48.02		Danny	Harris	USA	7.9.65	2s1	OT	Los Angeles	17 Jun 84
48.26		Jehue	Gordon	TTO	15.12.91	4	WCh	Berlin	18 Aug 09
48.51		Kerron	Clement	USA	31.10.85	1	WJ	Grosseto	16 Jul 04
48.52		Johnny	Dutch	USA	20.1.89	5	NC/OT	Eugene	29 Jun 08
48.62		Brandon	Johnson	USA	6.3.85	2	WJ	Grosseto	16 Jul 04
48.68		Bayano	Kamani	USA	17.4.80	1	NCAA	Boise	4 Jun 99
48.68		Jeshua	Anderson	USA	22.6.89	1	WJ	Bydgoszcz	11 Jul 08
48.72		Angelo	Taylor	USA	29.12.78	2	NCAA	Bloomington	6 Jun 97
48.74		Vladimir	Budko	BLR	4.2.65	2	DRZ	Moskva	18 Aug 84
48.76A		Llewellyn	Herbert	RSA	21.7.77	1		Pretoria	7 Apr 96
48.79		Kenneth	Ferguson	USA	22.3.84	1	SEC	Knoxville	18 May 03

HIGH JUMP

2.37		Dragutin	Topic	YUG	12.3.71	1	WJ	Plovdiv	12 Aug 90
2.37		Steve	Smith	GBR	29.3.73	1	WJ	Seoul	20 Sep 92
2.36		Javier	Sotomayor	CUB	13.10.67	1		Santiago de Cuba	23 Feb 86
2.35i		Vladimir	Yashchenko	UKR	12.1.59	1	EI	Milano	12 Mar 78
	2.34					1	Prv	Tbilisi	16 Jun 78
2.35		Dietmar	Mögenburg	FRG	15.8.61	1		Rehlingen	26 May 80
2.34		Tim	Forsyth	AUS	17.8.73	1	BisI	Oslo	4 Jul 92
2.33			Zhu Jianhua	CHN	29.5.63	1	AsiG	New Delhi	1 Dec 82
2.33		Patrik	Sjöberg	SWE	5.1.65	1	OsloG	Oslo	9 Jul 83
2.33		Maksim	Nedosekov	BLR	21.1.98	1	EJ	Grosseto	22 Jul 17
2.32i		Jaroslav	Bába	CZE	2.9.84	3		Arnstadt	8 Feb 03
2.32			Huang Haiqiang	CHN	8.2.88	1	WJ	Beijing	17 Aug 06

POLE VAULT

6.05		Armand	Duplantis	SWE	10.11.99	1	EC	Berlin	12 Aug 18
5.80		Maksim	Tarasov	RUS	2.12.70	1	vGDR-j	Bryansk	14 Jul 89
5.80		Raphael	Holzdeppe	GER	28.9.89	2		Biberach	28 Jun 08
5.80i		Emmanouíl	Karalís	GRE	20.10.99	5=	WI	Birmingham	4 Mar 18
5.75		Konstadínos	Filippídis	GRE	26.11.86	2	WUG	Izmir	18 Aug 05
5.75		Chris	Nilsen	USA	13.1.98	3	NC	Sacramento	24 Jun 17
5.72		Andrew	Irwin	USA	23.1.93	1	SEC	Baton Rouge	13 May 12
5.71		Lawrence	Johnson	USA	7.5.74	1		Knoxville	12 Jun 93
5.71		Germán	Chiaraviglio	ARG	16.4.87	1	WJ	Beijing	19 Aug 06
5.71		Shawnacy	Barber	CAN	27.5.94	2	TexR	Austin	29 Mar 13

LONG JUMP

8.35	1.1	Sergey	Morgunov	RUS	9.2.93	1	NC-j	Cheboksary	19 Jun 12
8.34	0.0	Randy	Williams	USA	23.8.53	Q	OG	München	8 Sep 72
8.33	2.0	Maykel	Massó	CUB	8.5.99	1		Madrid	14 Jul 17
8.31	0.8		Shi Yuhao	CHN	26.9.98	1		Beijing	25 Jun 17
8.30	1.8	Miltiádis	Tentóglou	GRE	18.3.98	1	NC	Pátra	18 Jun 17
8.28	0.8	Luis Alberto	Bueno	CUB	22.5.69	1		La Habana	16 Jul 88
8.28	0.8	Juan Miguel	Echevarría	CUB	11.8.98	2		Madrid	14 Jul 17
8.27	1.7	Eusebio	Cáceres	ESP	10.9.91	Q	EC	Barcelona	30 Jul 10
8.25	0.9		Wang Jianan	CHN	27.8.96	3	DL	Shanghai	17 May 15
8.24	0.2	Eric	Metcalf	USA	23.1.68	1	NCAA	Indianapolis	6 Jun 86
8.24	1.8	Vladimir	Ochkan	UKR	13.1.68	1	vGDR-j	Leningrad	21 Jun 87
Wind assisted									
8.40	3.2	Kareem	Streete-Thompson	CAY	30.3.73	1		Houston	5 May 91
8.35	2.2	Carl	Lewis	USA	1.7.61	1	NCAA	Austin	6 Jun 80
8.34	2.3	Juan Miguel	Echevarría	CUB	11.8.98	1		Padova	16 Jul 17
8.29	2.3	James	Beckford	JAM	9.1.75	1		Tempe	2 Apr 94

TRIPLE JUMP

17.50	0.4	Volker	Mai	GDR	3.5.66	1	vURS	Erfurt	23 Jun 85
17.42	1.3	Khristo	Markov	BUL	27.1.65	1	Nar	Sofiya	19 May 84
17.41	1.0	Jordan	Díaz	CUB	23.2.01	1		La Habana	8 Jun 18

Mark	Wind	Name		Nat	Born	Pos	Meet	Venue	Date
17.40A	0.4	Pedro	Pérez	CUB	23.2.52	1	PAm	Cali	5 Aug 71
17.40	0.8	Ernesto	Revé	CUB	26.2.92	1		La Habana	10 Jun 11
17.31	-0.2	David	Girat Jr.	CUB	26.8.84	Q	WCh	Saint-Denis	23 Aug 03
17.29	1.3	James	Beckford	JAM	9.1.75	1		Tempe	2 Apr 94
17.27		Aliecer	Urrutia	CUB	22.9.74	1		Artemisa	23 Apr 93
17.27	1.6	Cristian	Nápoles	CUB	27.11.98	2	NC	La Habana	17 Mar 17
17.24	0.7	Lázaro	Martínez	CUB	3.11.97	2		La Habana	1 Feb 14
17.23	0.2	Yoelbi	Quesada	CUB	4.8.73	1	NC	La Habana	13 May 92
Wind assisted									
17.33	2.1	Teddy	Tamgho	FRA	15.6.89	1	WJ	Bydgoszcz	11 Jul 08
17.24	2.5	Will	Claye	USA	13.6.91	1	NCAA	Fayetteville	13 Jun 09

SHOT

Mark		Name		Nat	Born	Pos	Meet	Venue	Date
21.14		Konrad	Bukowiecki #	POL	17.3.97	2	Bisl	Oslo	9 Jun 16
21.05i		Terry	Albritton	USA	14.1.55	1	AAU	New York	22 Feb 74
20.38						2	MSR	Walnut	27 Apr 74
20.83i		Jordan	Geist	USA	21.7.98	1		Greensburg	22 Dec 16
20.62						1		Tucson	9 Dec 17
20.65		Mike	Carter	USA	29.10.60	1	vSU-j	Boston	4 Jul 79
20.43		David	Storl	GER	27.7.90	2		Gerlingen	6 Jul 09
20.41		Adrian	Piperi	USA	20.1.99	1q	NCAA-W	Sacramento	26 May 18
20.39		Janus	Robberts	RSA	10.3.79	1	NC	Germiston	7 Mar 98
20.38		Jacko	Gill	NZL	10.12.94	1		Auckland (NS)	5 Dec 11
20.20		Randy	Matson	USA	5.3.45	2	OG	Tokyo	17 Oct 64
20.20		Udo	Beyer	GDR	9.8.55	2	NC	Leipzig	6 Jul 74
Drugs dq:	20.54	Andrei	Toader ¶	ROU	26.5.97	(1)	ROU IC	Pitesti	4 Jun 16
6 kg Shot									
23.00		Jacko	Gill	NZL	10.12.94	1		Auckland	18 Aug 13
22.94		Konrad	Bukowiecki	POL	17.3.97	1	NC-j	Suwalki	3 Jul 16
23.34 drugs dq						(1)	WJ	Bydgoszcz	19 Jul 16
22.73		David	Storl	GER	27.7.90	1		Osterode	14 Jul 09
22.30 dq?		Andrei	Toader	ROU	26.5.97	2	WJ	Bydgoszcz	19 Jul 16
22.07		Kyle	Blignaut	RSA	9.11.99	1	WJ	Tampere	10 Jul 18
22.06		Adrian	Piperi	USA	20.1.99	2	WJ	Tampere	10 Jul 18
22.02		Jordan	Geist	USA	21.7.98	1	PAm-J	Trujillo	23 Jul 17
21.96		Edis	Elkasevic	CRO	18.2.83	1	NC-j	Zagreb	29 Jun 02
21.90		John	Maurins	USA	3.8.96	1	NC-j	Eugene	25 Jun 15
23.34 dq		Konrad	Bukowiecki	POL	17.3.97	1	WJ	Bydgoszcz	19 Jul 16

DISCUS

Mark		Name		Nat	Born	Pos	Meet	Venue	Date
65.62		Werner	Reiterer	AUS	27.1.68	1		Melbourne	15 Dec 87
65.31		Mykyta	Nesterenko	UKR	15.4.91	3		Tallinn	3 Jun 08
63.64		Werner	Hartmann	FRG	20.4.59	1	vFRA	Strasbourg	25 Jun 78
63.26		Sergey	Pachin	UKR	24.5.68	2		Moskva	25 Jul 87
63.22		Brian	Milne	USA	7.1.73	1		State College	28 Mar 92
62.58		Matthew	Denny	AUS	2.6.96	2	WUG	Gwangju	11 Jul 15
62.52		John	Nichols	USA	23.8.69	1		Baton Rouge	23 Apr 88
62.43		Martin	Markovic	CRO	13.1.96	1	NC-w	Split	8 Mar 15
62.36		Tulake	Nuermaimaiti	CHN	8.3.82	2	NG	Guangzhou	21 Nov 01
62.16		Zoltán	Kövágó	HUN	10.4.79	1		Budapest	9 May 97
1.75kg Discus									
70.13		Mykyta	Nesterenko	UKR	15.4.91	1		Halle	24 May 08
68.48		Martin	Markovic	CRO	13.1.96	1	NC-j	Varazdin	28 Jun 15
68.02		Bartlomiej	Stój	POL	15.5.98	1	EJ	Eskilstuna	19 Jul 15
67.32		Margus	Hunt	EST	14.7.87	1	WJ	Beijing	16 Aug 06
66.88		Traves	Smikle	JAM	7.5.92	1		Kingston	31 Mar 11
66.81		Matthew	Denny	AUS	2.6.96	1		Brisbane	23 Nov 14
66.47		Moaaz Mohamed	Ibrahim	QAT	8.2.99	1		Cape Town	3 Feb 18
66.45		Gordon	Wolf	GER	17.1.90	1		Halle	23 May 09
66.41		Roje	Stona	JAM	26.2.99	1	Carifta	Willemstad	15 Apr 17
66.27		Clemens	Prüfer	GER	13.8.97	1		Wiesbaden	15 May 16

HAMMER

Mark		Name		Nat	Born	Pos	Meet	Venue	Date
78.33		Olli-Pekka	Karjalainen	FIN	7.3.80	1	NC	Seinäjoki	5 Aug 99
78.14		Roland	Steuk	GDR	5.3.59	1	NC	Leipzig	30 Jun 78
78.00		Sergey	Dorozhon	UKR	17.2.64	1		Moskva	7 Aug 83
76.54		Valeriy	Gubkin	BLR	3.9.67	2		Minsk	27 Nov 86
76.42		Ruslan	Dikiy	TJK	18.1.72	1		Togliatti	7 Sep 91
76.37		Ashraf Amjad	El-Seify	QAT	20.2.95	1		Doha	10 Apr 13
75.52		Sergey	Kirmasov	RUS	25.3.70	1		Kharkov	4 Jun 89
75.42		Szymon	Ziolkowski	POL	1.7.76	1	EJ	Nyíregyház	30 Jul 95

Mark	Wind	Name		Nat	Born	Pos	Meet	Venue	Date
75.24		Christoph	Sahner	FRG	23.9.63	1	vPOL-j	Göttingen	26 Jun 82

6kg Hammer

Mark	Wind	Name		Nat	Born	Pos	Meet	Venue	Date
85.57		Ashraf Amjad	El-Seify	QAT-Y	20.2.95	1	WJ	Barcelona	14 Jul 12
82.97		Javier	Cienfuegos	ESP	15.7.90	1		Madrid	17 Jun 09
82.84		Quentin	Bigot	FRA	1.12.92	1		Bondoufle	16 Oct 11
82.64		Bence	Halász	HUN	4.8.97	1	NC-j	Szombathely	25 Jun 16
82.62		Yevgeniy	Aydamirov	RUS	11.5.87	1	NC-j	Tula	22 Jul 06
81.75		Hlib	Piskunov	UKR	25.11.98	1	EJ	Grosseto	21 Jul 17
81.73		Aleksandr	Shimanovich	BLR	9.2.98	1		Brest	28 Apr 17
81.34		Krisztián	Pars	HUN	18.2.82	1		Szombathely	2 Sep 01
81.32		Hristos	Frantzeskákis	GRE	26.4.00	1		Tripolí	5 May 18
81.16		Özkan	Baltaci	TUR	13.2.94	1		Ankara	31 Jul 13

JAVELIN

Mark	Wind	Name		Nat	Born	Pos	Meet	Venue	Date
86.48		Neeraj	Chopra	IND	24.12.97	1	WJ	Bydgoszcz	23 Jul 16
84.69		Zigismunds	Sirmais	LAT	6.5.92	2		Bauska	22 Jun 11
84.58		Keshorn	Walcott	TTO	2.4.93	1	OG	London (OS)	11 Aug 12
83.87		Andreas	Thorkildsen	NOR	1.4.82	1		Fana	7 Jun 01
83.55		Aleksandr	Ivanov	RUS	25.5.82	2	NC	Tula	14 Jul 01
83.07		Robert	Oosthuizen	RSA	23.1.87	1	WJ	Beijing	19 Aug 06
82.52		Harri	Haatainen	FIN	5.1.78	4		Leppävirta	25 May 96
82.52		Till	Wöschler	GER	9.6.91	1	WJ	Moncton	23 Jul 10
81.95		Jakub	Vadlejch	CZE	10.10.90	1		Domazlice	26 Sep 09
81.91		Patriks	Gailums	LAT	10.5.98	1		Valmiera	12 Jul 17
81.80		Sergey	Voynov	UZB	26.2.77	1		Tashkent	6 Jun 96

DECATHLON

Mark				Nat	Born	Pos	Meet	Venue	Date
8397	Torsten	Voss		GDR	24.3.63	1	NC	Erfurt	7 Jul 82
	10.76	7.66	14.41	2.09	48.37		14.37	41.76 4.80 62.90	4:34.04
8257	Yordani	García		CUB	21.11.88	8	WCh	Osaka	1 Sep 07
	10.73/0.7	7.15/0.2	14.94	2.09	49.25		14.08/-0.2	42.91 4.70 68.74	4:55.42
8114	Michael	Kohnle		FRG	3.5.70	1	EJ	Varazdin	26 Aug 89
	10.95	7.09/0.1	15.27	2.02	49.91		14.40	45.82 4.90 60.82	4:49.43
8104	Valter	Külvet		EST	19.2.64	1		Viimsi	23 Aug 81
	10.7	7.26	13.86	2.09	48.5		14.8	47.92 4.50 60.34	4:37.8
8082	Daley	Thompson		GBR	30.7.58	1	ECp/s	Sittard	31 Jul 77
	10.70/0.8	7.54/0.7	13.84	2.01	47.31		15.26/2.0	41.70 4.70 54.48	4:30.4
8041		Qi Haifeng		CHN	7.8.83	1	AsiG	Busan	10 Oct 02
	11.09/0.2	7.22/0.0	13.05	2.06	49.09		14.54/0.0	43.16 4.80 61.04	4:35.17
8036	Christian	Schenk		GDR	9.2.65	5		Potsdam	21 Jul 84
	11.54	7.18	14.26	2.16	49.23		15.06	44.74 4.20 65.98	4:24.11
7992	Kevin	Mayer		FRA	10.2.92	8		Kladno	16 Jun 11
	11.23/0.1	7.34/0.2	12.44	2.01	48.66		14.74/-2.0	38.64 4.90 60.96	4:19.79
7938	Frank	Busemann		GER	26.2.75	1		Zeven	2 Oct 94
	10.68/1.6	7.37/1.1	13.08	2.03	50.41		14.34/-1.1	39.84 4.40 63.00	4:37.31

IAAF Junior specification with 99cm 110mh, 6kg shot, 1.75kg Discus

Mark				Nat	Born	Pos	Meet	Venue	Date
8435	Niklas	Kaul		GER	11.2.98	1	EJ	Grosseto	23 Jul 17
	11.48/-1.3	7.20/1.6	15.37	2.05	48.42		14.55/-0.2	48.49 4.70 68.05	4:15.51
8190	Ashley	Moloney		AUS	13.3.00	1	WJ	Tampere	11 Jul 18
	10.51/-0.3	7.06/1.1	12.83	2.10	46.86		14.13/-0.3	47.39 4.60 53.67	4:42.65
8141	Johannes	Erm		EST	26.3.98	2	EJ	Grosseto	23 Jul 17
	11.06/0.7	7.42/-0.3	13.44	1.92	48.17		14.66/0.9	43.61 4.50 54.19	4:28.96
8135	Jiri	Sykora		CZE	20.1.95	1	WJ	Eugene	23 Jul 14
	10.92/0.5	7.35/2.0	15.50	1.94	49.00		14.23/-0.1	48.55 4.40 60.56	4:42.10
8131	Arkadiy	Vasilyev		RUS	19.1.87	1		Sochi	27 May 06
	11.28/-0.8	7.70/2.0	14.59	2.00	49.17		14.67/0.6	46.30 4.70 56.96	4:32.10
8126	Andrey	Kravchenko		BLR	4.1.86	1	WJ	Grosseto	15 Jul 04
	11.09/-0.5	7.46-0.2	14.51	2.16	48.98		14.55*/0.4	43.41 4.50 52.84	4:28.46
8124	Kévin	Mayer		FRA	10.2.92	1	EJ	Tallin	24 Jul 11
	11.40/-1.7	7.52/1.5	14.65	2.04	49.41		14.09/0.7	41.00 4.80 56.60	4:25.23

10,000 METRES WALK

Mark		Name		Nat	Born	Pos	Meet	Venue	Date
38:46.4		Viktor	Burayev	RUS	23.8.82	1	NC-j	Moskva	20 May 00
38:54.75		Ralf	Kowalsky	GDR	22.3.62	1		Cottbus	24 Jun 81
38:58.21		Vasiliy	Mizinov	RUS	29.12.97	1	NC-j	Cheboksary	25 Jun 16
39:08.23		Daisuke	Matsunaga	JPN	24.3.95	1		Tama	14 Dec 13
39:28.63		Toshizaku	Yamanishi	JPN	15.2.96	2		Osaka	13 Sep 15
39:28.45		Andrey	Ruzavin	RUS	28.3.86	1	EJ	Kaunas	23 Jul 05
39:30.15		Yuga	Yamashita	JPN	6.2.96	1		Tama	12 Dec 15
39:35.01		Stanislav	Yemelyanov	RUS	23.10.90	1	WJ	Bydgoszcz	11 Jul 08

Jnr MEN All-time

Mark	Wind	Name		Nat	Born	Pos	Meet	Venue	Date

20 KILOMETRES WALK

Mark	Wind	Name		Nat	Born	Pos	Meet	Venue	Date
1:17:25		Sergey	Shirobokov	RUS	16.2.99	1	NC	Chgeboksary	9 Jun 18
1:18:06		Viktor	Burayev	RUS	23.8.82	2	NC-w	Adler	4 Mar 01
1:18:07			Li Gaobo	CHN	23.7.89	4		Cixi	23 Apr 05
1:18.44			Chu Yafei	CHN	5.9.88	5		Yangzhou	22 Apr 06
1:18:52			Chen Ding	CHN	5.8.92	3		Taicang	22 Apr 11
1:18:57			Bai Xuejin	CHN	6.6.87	7		Yangzhou	22 Apr 06
1:19:02		Éder	Sánchez	MEX	21.5.86	11		Cixi	23 Apr 05
1:19:14			Xu Xingde	CHN	12.6.84	3	NC	Yangzhou	12 Apr 03
1:19:34			Li Jianbo	CHN	14.11.86	16		Cixi	23 Apr 05

4 x 100 METRES RELAY

Mark	Wind	Name	Nat	Pos	Meet	Venue	Date
38.66	USA	Kimmons, Omole, I Williams, L Merritt		1	WJ	Grosseto	18 Jun 04
38.96	JAM	Nairne, C Taylor, Matherson, Stephens		2	WJ	Tampere	124 Jul 18
39.01	JPN	Oseto, Hashimoto, Cambridge, Kanamori		1h1	WJ	Barcelona	13 Jul 12
39.05	GBR	Edgar, Grant, Benjamin, Lewis-Francis		1	WJ	Santiago de Chile	22 Oct 00
39.13	GER	Gurski, Vartel, Giese, Eitel		3	WJ	Bydgoszcz	23 Jul 16
39.17	TTO	Simpson, Burns, Holder, Brown		3	WJ	Kingston	21 Jul 02
39.29	BRA	de Araújo, Monteiro, R dos Santos Jnr, Rocha		2h1	WJ	Barcelona	13 Jul 12
39.31	POL	Bijowski, Slowikowski, Zalewski, Jabłonski		3h1	WJ	Barcelona	13 Jul 12

4 x 400 METRES RELAY

Mark	Nat	Name	Pos	Meet	Venue	Date
3:00.33	USA	Herron 45.1, Shinnick 45.1, Hooper 44.73, J Lyles 45.36	1	PAm-J	Trujillo	23 Jul 17
3:02.81	BOT	Poo, Thebe, Sibanda, Talane	2	WJ	Bydgoszcz	24 Jul 16
3:03.77	JAM	Chambers, Carpenter, James, C Taylor	2	PAm-J	Trujillo	23 Jul 17
3:03.80	GBR	Grindley, Patrick, Winrow, Richardson	2	WJ	Plovdiv	12 Aug 90
3:04.05	ITA	Gjetja 47.1, Romano 45.6, Sibilio 46.06, Scotti 45.31	1	WJ	Tampere	15 Jul 18
3:04.11	JPN	Walsh, Yui, Kitagawa, Kato	2	WJ	Eugene	27 Jul 14
3:04.22	CUB	Cadogan, Mordoche, González, Hernández	2	WJ	Athína	20 Jul 86
3:04.50	RSA	le Roux, Gebhardt, Julius, van Zyl	2	WJ	Grosseto	18 Jul 04

JUNIOR WOMEN'S ALL-TIME LISTS

100 METRES

Mark	Wind	Name		Nat	Born	Pos	Meet	Venue	Date
10.88	2.0	Marlies	Oelsner	GDR	21.3.58	1	NC	Dresden	1 Jul 77
10.89	1.8	Katrin	Krabbe	GDR	22.11.69	1rB		Berlin	20 Jul 88
10.98	2.0	Candace	Hill	USA	11.2.99	1		Shoreline	20 Jun 15
10.99	0.9	Angela	Tenorio	ECU	27.1.96	2	PAm	Toronto	22 Jul 15
10.99	1.7	Twanisha	Terry	USA	24.1.99	1	MSR	Torrance	21 Apr 18
11.02	1.5	Tamara	Clark	USA	9.1.99	3	SEC	Knoxville	13 May 18
11.03	1.7	Silke	Gladisch	GDR	20.6.64	3	OD	Berlin	8 Jun 83
11.03	0.6	English	Gardner	USA	22.4.92	1	Pac10	Tucson	14 May 11
11.04	1.4	Angela	Williams	USA	30.1.80	1	NCAA	Boise	5 Jun 99
11.06	0.9	Khalifa	St. Fort	TTO	13.2.98	3	NC	Port of Spain	24 Jun 17
11.07	0.7	Bianca	Knight	USA	2.1.89	4q2	NC/OT	Eugene	27 Jun 08

Wind assisted to 11.04

Mark	Wind	Name		Nat	Born	Pos	Meet	Venue	Date
10.96	3.7	Angela	Williams	USA	30.1.80	1		Las Vegas	3 Apr 99
10.96	2.6	Twanisha	Terry	USA	24.1.99	1	Pac-12	Stanford	13 May 18
10.97	3.3	Gesine	Walther	GDR	6.10.62	4	NC	Cottbus	16 Jul 80
11.01	5.4	Kaylin	Whitney	USA	9.3.98	3	Athl	Lausanne	9 Jul 15
11.02	2.1	Nikole	Mitchell	JAM	5.6.74	1	Mutual	Kingston	1 May 93
11.03	2.2	Dina	Asher-Smith	GBR	4.12.95	1		Mannheim	5 Jul 14
11.04	5.6	Kelly-Ann	Baptiste	TTO	14.10.86	1rB	TexR	Austin	9 Apr 05
11.04	3.1	Desiree	Henry	GBR	26.8.95	1		Clermont	26 Apr 14

200 METRES

Mark	Wind	Name		Nat	Born	Pos	Meet	Venue	Date
22.11A	-0.5	Allyson	Felix	USA	18.11.85	1		Ciudad de México	3 May 03
22.18			0.8			2	OG	Athína	25 Aug 04
22.19	1.5	Natalya	Bochina	RUS	4.1.62	2	OG	Moskva	30 Jul 80
22.37	1.3	Sabine	Rieger	GDR	6.11.63	2	vURS	Cottbus	26 Jun 82
22.39	1.5	Sydney	McLaughlin	USA	7.8.99	1	FlaR	Gainesville	29 Mar 18
22.42	0.4	Gesine	Walther	GDR	6.10.62	1		Potsdam	29 Aug 81
22.43	0.8	Bianca	Knight	USA	2.1.89	1	Reebok	New York (RI)	31 May 08
22.43A	-0.7	Candace	Hill	USA	11.2.99	1	WY	Cali	19 Jul 15
22.45	0.5	Grit	Breuer	GER	16.2.72	2	ASV	Köln	8 Sep 91
22.45	0.9	Shaunae	Miller	BAH	15.4.94	2	NC	Freeport	22 Jun 13
22.47	0.4	Kaylin	Whitney	USA	9.3.98	4	NC	Eugene	28 Jun 15
22.48	1.9	Tamari	Davis	USA	15.2.03	1		Jacksonville	5 May 18

Indoors

Mark		Name		Nat	Born	Pos	Meet	Venue	Date
22.40		Bianca	Knight	USA	2.1.89	1r2	NCAA	Fayetteville	15 Mar 08
22.49		Sanya	Richards	USA	26.2.85	2rA	NCAA	Fayetteville	12 Mar 04

Mark	Wind	Name		Nat	Born	Pos	Meet	Venue	Date
Wind assisted									
22.25	5.6	Bianca	Knight	USA	2.1.89	5	NC/OT	Eugene	6 Jul 08
22.34	2.3	Katrin	Krabbe	GDR	22.11.69	1	WJ	Sudbury	30 Jul 88
22.38	2.1	Candace	Hill	USA	11.2.99	1		Montverde	11 Jun 16
22.41	3.1	Shaunae	Miller	BAH	15.4.94	1		Athens, GA	13 Apr 13
22.41	2.6	Gina	Lückenkemper	GER	21.11.96	1	EJ	Eskilstuna	18 Jul 15
22.44	2.5	Lauren Rain	Williams	USA	25.7.99	1		Norwalk	21 May 16

400 METRES

Mark	Wind	Name		Nat	Born	Pos	Meet	Venue	Date
49.42		Grit	Breuer	GER	16.2.72	2	WCh	Tokyo	27 Aug 91
49.77		Christina	Brehmer	GDR	28.2.58	1		Dresden	9 May 76
49.89		Sanya	Richards	USA	26.2.85	2	NC/OT	Sacramento	17 Jul 04
50.01			Li Jing	CHN	14.2.80	1	NG	Shanghai	18 Oct 97
50.07		Sydney	McLaughlin	USA	7.8.99	1	FlaR	Gainesville	30 Mar 18
50.19		Marita	Koch	GDR	18.2.57	3	OD	Berlin	10 Jul 76
50.46		Kendall	Baisden	USA	5.3.95	2	Big 12	Lubbock	18 May 14
50.50		Ashley	Spencer	USA	8.6.93	1	WJ	Barcelona	13 Jul 12
50.59		Fatima	Yusuf	NGR	2.5.71	1	HGP	Budapest	5 Aug 90
50.70		Shaunae	Miller	BAH	15.4.94	2	NCAA	Eugene	7 Jun 13
50.74		Monique	Henderson	USA	18.2.83	1		Norwalk	3 Jun 00

800 METRES

Mark	Wind	Name		Nat	Born	Pos	Meet	Venue	Date
1:54.01		Pamela	Jelimo	KEN	5.12.89	1	WK	Zürich	29 Aug 08
1:55.45		Caster	Semenya	RSA	7.1.91	1	WCh	Berlin	19 Aug 09
1:56.59		Francine	Niyonsaba	BDI	5.5.93	1	VD	Bruxelles	7 Sep 12
1:57.18			Wang Yuan	CHN	8.4.76	2h2		Beijing	8 Sep 93
1:57.45		Hildegard	Ullrich	GDR	20.12.59	5	EC	Praha	31 Aug 78
1:57.62			Lang Yinglai	CHN	22.8.79	1	NG	Shanghai	22 Oct 97
1:57.63		Maria	Mutola	MOZ	27.10.72	4	WCh	Tokyo	26 Aug 91
1:57.74		Sahily	Diago	CUB	26.8.95	1	Barr	La Habana	25 Jul 14
1:57.77			Lu Yi	CHN	10.4.74	4	NG	Beijing	9 Sep 93
1:57.86		Katrin	Wühn	GDR	19.11.65	1		Celje	5 May 84
1:58.16			Lin Na	CHN	18.1.80	3	NG	Shanghai	22 Oct 97

1000 METRES

Mark	Wind	Name		Nat	Born	Pos	Meet	Venue	Date
2:35.4		Irina	Nikitina	RUS	16.6.61	5	Kuts	Podolsk	5 Aug 79
2:35.4		Katrin	Wühn	GDR	19.11.65	3		Potsdam	12 Jul 84

1500 METRES

Mark	Wind	Name		Nat	Born	Pos	Meet	Venue	Date
3:51.34			Lang Yinglai	CHN	22.8.79	2	NG	Shanghai	18 Oct 97
3:53.91			Yin Lili	CHN	11.11.79	3	NG	Shanghai	18 Oct 97
3:53.97			Lan Lixin	CHN	14.2.79	4	NG	Shanghai	18 Oct 97
3:54.52			Zhang Ling	CHN	13.4.80	5	NG	Shanghai	18 Oct 97
3:56.98		Faith	Kipyegon	KEN	10.1.94	2	DL	Doha	10 May 13
3:59.53		Dawit	Seyaum	ETH	27.7.96	1		Marrakech	8 Jun 14
3:59.60		Gelete	Burka	ETH	15.2.86	5	GP	Rieti	28 Aug 05
3:59.81			Wang Yuan	CHN	8.4.76	7	NG	Beijing	11 Sep 93
3:59.96		Zola	Budd	GBR	26.5.66	3	VD	Bruxelles	30 Aug 85
4:00.05			Lu Yi	CHN	10.4.74	8	NG	Beijing	11 Sep 93
4:00.18		Gudaf	Tsegay	ETH	23.1.97	3	Pre	Eugene	28 May 16

3000 METRES

Mark	Wind	Name		Nat	Born	Pos	Meet	Venue	Date
8:28.83		Zola	Budd	GBR	26.5.66	3	GG	Roma	7 Sep 85
8:33.63		Meskerem	Mamo	ETH	13.4.99	7	DL	Doha	4 May 18
8:35.76		Beyenu	Degefu	ETH	12.7.99	8	DL	Doha	4 May 18
8:35.89		Sally	Barsosio	KEN	21.3.78	2	Herc	Monaco	16 Aug 97
8:36.45			Ma Ningning	CHN	1.6.76	4	NC	Jinan	6 Jun 93
8:36.87		Alemitu	Haroye	ETH	9.5.95	14	VD	Bruxelles	5 Sep 14
8:38.61		Kalkedan	Gezahegn	ETH	8.5.91	5	WAF	Thessaloníki	13 Sep 09
8:38.97		Linet	Masai	KEN	5.12.89	5	GP	Rieti	9 Sep 07
8:39.13		Agnes	Tirop	KEN	23.10.95	3		Rieti	8 Sep 13
8:39.65		Buze	Diriba	ETH	9.2.94	3	Herc	Monaco	20 Jul 12
8:39.90		Gelete	Burka	ETH	15.2.86	3	SGP	Doha	13 May 05

5000 METRES

Mark	Wind	Name		Nat	Born	Pos	Meet	Venue	Date
14:30.88		Tirunesh	Dibaba	ETH	1.10.85	2	Bisl	Bergen (Fana)	11 Jun 04
14:33.32		Letesenbet	Gidey	ETH	20.3.98	3	GGala	Roma	8 Jun 17
14:35.18		Sentayehu	Ejigu	ETH	21.6.85	4	Bisl	Bergen (Fana)	11 Jun 04
14:39.96			Yin Lili	CHN	11.11.79	4	NG	Shanghai	23 Oct 97
14:43.29		Emebet	Anteneh	ETH	13.1.92	5	Bisl	Oslo	9 Jun 11
14:45.33			Lan Lixin	CHN	14.2.79	2h2	NG	Shanghai	21 Oct 97
14:45.71			Song Liqing	CHN	20.1.80	3h2	NG	Shanghai	21 Oct 97

Jnr WOMEN All-time

Mark	Wind	Name		Nat	Born	Pos	Meet	Venue	Date
14:45.90			Jiang Bo	CHN	13.3.77	1		Nanjing	24 Oct 95
14:45.98		Pauline	Korikwiang	KEN	1.3.88	7	Bisl	Oslo	2 Jun 06
14:46.71		Sally	Barsosio	KEN	21.3.78	3	VD	Bruxelles	22 Aug 97
14:47.13		Mercy	Cherono	KEN	7.5.91	7	DL	Shanghai	23 May 10

10,000 METRES

Mark	Wind	Name		Nat	Born	Pos	Meet	Venue	Date
30:26.50		Linet	Masai	KEN	5.12.89	4	OG	Beijing	15 Aug 08
30:31.55			Xing Huina	CHN	25.2.84	7	WCh	Saint-Denis	23 Aug 03
30:39.41			Lan Lixin	CHN	14.2.79	2	NG	Shanghai	19 Oct 97
30:39.98			Yin Lili	CHN	11.11.79	3	NG	Shanghai	19 Oct 97
30:59.92		Merima	Hashim	ETH	.81	3	NA	Heusden-Zolder	5 Aug 00
31:06.20		Lucy	Wangui	KEN	24.3.84	1rA		Okayama	27 Sep 03
31:11.26			Song Liqing	CHN	20.1.80	7	NG	Shanghai	19 Oct 97
31:15.38		Sally	Barsosio	KEN	21.3.78	3	WCh	Stuttgart	21 Aug 93
31:16.50		Evelyne	Kimwei	KEN	25.8.87	1		Kobe	21 Oct 06
31:17.30			Zhang Yingying	CHN	4.1.90	1		Wuhan	2 Nov 07
31:20.38		Tigist	Kiros	ETH	8.6.92	4	GS	Ostrava	31 May 11

HALF MARATHON

Mark	Wind	Name		Nat	Born	Pos	Meet	Venue	Date
66:47		Degitu	Azimeraw	ETH	24.1.99	6	RAK	Ras Al Khaimah	9 Feb 18
67:51		Meseret	Belete	ETH	16.9.99	8		København	16 Sep 18
67:57		Gelana	Abebe	ETH	18.1.90	4		Ras Al Khaimah	20 Feb 09
68:21		Valentine	Kipketer	KEN	5.1.93	1		Lille	3 Sep 11
68:36		Merima	Mohamed	ETH	10.6.92	2		New Delhi	21 Nov 10
68:41		Evelyne	Kimwei	KEN	25.8.87	1		Kobe	19 Nov 06
68:53		Shure	Demise	ETH	21.1.96	4		Ostia	2 Mar 14
69:05		Delillah	Asiago	KEN	24.2.72	1	GWR	Exeter	5 May 91
69:10		Muliye	Dekebo	ETH	13.3.98	5		Ostia	12 Mar 17
69:21		Ann	Wamuchi	KEN	29.9.78	5		Tokyo	19 Jan 97

MARATHON

Mark	Wind	Name		Nat	Born	Pos	Meet	Venue	Date
2:20:59		Shure	Demise	ETH	21.1.96	4		Dubai	23 Jan 15
2:21:32		Bedatu	Hirpa	ETH	28.4.99	3		Frankfurt	28 Oct 18
2:22:38			Zhang Yingying	CHN	4.1.90	1	NC	Xiamen	5 Jan 08
2:23:06		Merima	Mohamed	ETH	10.6.92	3		Toronto	26 Sep 10
2:23:37			Liu Min	CHN	29.11.83	1		Beijing	14 Oct 01
2:23:57			Zhu Xiaolin	CHN	20.4.84	4		Beijing	20 Oct 02
2:25:23		Azmera	Abreha	ETH	.98	3		Amsterdam	15 Oct 17
2:25:48			Jin Li	CHN	29.5.83	6		Beijing	14 Oct 01
2:26:34			Wei Yanan	CHN	6.12.81	1		Beijing	15 Oct 00

3000 METRES STEEPLECHASE

Mark	Wind	Name		Nat	Born	Pos	Meet	Venue	Date
8:58.78		Celliphine	Chespol	KEN	23.3.99	1	Pre	Eugene	26 May 17]
9:07.94		Peruth	Chemutai	UGA	10.7.99	6	Herc	Monaco	20 Jul 18
9:10.74		Winfred	Yavi	BRN	31.12.99	9	Herc	Monaco	20 Jul 18
9:20.37		Birtukan	Adamu	ETH	29.4.92	4		Roma	26 May 11
9:20.55		Ruth	Chebet	KEN/BRN	17.11.96	4	WK	Zürich	28 Aug 14
9:20.65		Tigist	Mekonen	BRN	7.7.97	8	Herc	Monaco	17 Jul 15
9:22.51		Almaz	Ayana	ETH	21.11.91	3	VD	Bruxelles	27 Aug 10
9:23.4A		Mercy	Wanjiru	KEN	2.3.99	1		Nairobi	6 Jun 18
9:23.92		Fancy	Cherono	KEN	2.8.01	3	AfrC	Asaba	5 Aug 18
9:24.51		Ruth	Bisibori	KEN	2.1.88	1		Daegu	3 Oct 07
9:25.91		Roseline	Chepngetich	KEN	17.6.97	3h2	WCh	Beijing	24 Aug 15

100 METRES HURDLES

Mark	Wind	Name		Nat	Born	Pos	Meet	Venue	Date
12.74	1.7	Dior	Hall	USA	2.1.96	3	NCAA	Eugene	13 Jun 15
12.75	1.7	Chanel	Brissett	USA	10.8.99	1	Pac-12	Stanford	13 May 18
12.83A	0.4	Tobi	Amusan	NGR	23.4.97	1		El Paso	30 Apr 16
12.84	1.5	Aliuska	López	CUB	29.8.69	2	WUG	Zagreb	16 Jul 87
12.84	1.2	Tia	Jones	USA	8.9.00	1h1	NC-j	Clovis	25 Jun 16
12.85	2.0	Elvira	German	BLR	19.6.97	1	WJ	Bydgoszcz	24 Jul 16
12.86	1.4	Cortney	Jones	USA	18.6.99	2s2	NCAA	Eugene	7 Jun 18
12.87	2.0	Kendell	Williams	USA	14.6.95	1	NC-j	Eugene	6 Jul 14
12.87	2.0	Rushelle	Burton	JAM	4.12.97	2	WJ	Bydgoszcz	24 Jul 16
12.88	1.5	Yelena	Ovcharova	UKR	17.6.76	2	ECp	Villeneuve d'Ascq	25 Jun 95
12.89	1.3	Anay	Tejeda	CUB	3.4.83	1		Padova	1 Sep 02
Wind assisted									
12.79	3.8	Tobi	Amusan	NGR	23.4.97	2	NCAA	Eugene	11 Jun 16
12.81	3.4	Anay	Tejeda	CUB	3.4.83	1	WJ	Kingston	21 Jul 02
12.82	2.1	Kristina	Castlin	USA	7.7.88	1		College Park	21 Apr 07
12.83	3.7	Tara	Davis	USA	20.5.99	1		Clovis	3 Jun 17

Mark	Wind	Name		Nat	Born	Pos	Meet	Venue	Date

400 METRES HURDLES

Mark	Wind	Name		Nat	Born	Pos	Meet	Venue	Date
52.75		Sydney	McLaughlin	USA	7.8.99	1	SEC	Knoxville	13 May 18
54.40			Wang Xing	CHN	30.11.86	2	NG	Nanjing	21 Oct 05
54.58		Ristananna	Tracey	JAM	5.9.92	2	NC	Kingston	24 Jun 11
54.70		Lashinda	Demus	USA	10.3.83	1	WJ	Kingston	19 Jul 02
54.93			Li Rui	CHN	22.11.79	1	NG	Shanghai	22 Oct 97
55.05A		Zeney	van der Walt	RSA	22.5.00	2	NC	Pretoria	17 Mar 18
55.07		Shamier	Little	USA	20.3.95	1	NCAA	Eugene	13 Jun 14
55.11		Kaliese	Spencer	JAM	6.4.87	1	WJ	Beijing	17 Aug 06
55.15			Huang Xiaoxiao	CHN	3.3.83	2	NG	Guangzhou	22 Nov 01
55.20		Lesley	Maxie	USA	4.1.67	2	TAC	San Jose	9 Jun 84
55.20A		Jana	Pittman	AUS	9.11.82	1		Pietersburg	18 Mar 00
55.20		Anna	Cockrell	USA	28.8.97	1	WJ	Bydgoszcz	22 Jul 16

Drugs disqualification: 54.54 Peng Yinghua ¶ CHN 21.2.79 (2) NG Shanghai 22 Oct 97

HIGH JUMP

Mark	Name		Nat	Born	Pos	Meet	Venue	Date
2.01	Olga	Turchak	UKR	5.3.67	2	GWG	Moskva	7 Jul 86
2.01	Heike	Balck	GDR	19.8.70	1	vURS-j	Karl-Marx-Stadt	18 Jun 89
2.00	Stefka	Kostadinova	BUL	25.3.65	1		Sofia	25 Aug 84
2.00	Alina	Astafei	ROU	7.6.69	1	WJ	Sudbury	29 Jul 88
1.99i	Vashti	Cunningham	USA	18.1.98	1	NC	Portland	12 Mar 16
1.99					1	NC	Sacramento	23 Jun 17
1.98	Silvia	Costa	CUB	4.5.64	2	WUG	Edmonton	11 Jul 83
1.98	Yelena	Yelesina	RUS	5.4.70	1	Druzh	Nyiregyháza	13 Aug 88
1.97	Svetlana	Isaeva	BUL	18.3.67	2		Sofia	25 May 86
1.97i	Mariya	Kuchina	RUS	14.1.93	1		Trinec	26 Jan 11

1.96 Charmaine Gale RSA 27.2.64 4 Apr 81(A), Desislava Aleksandrova BUL 27.10.75 12 Mar 94(i), Marina Kuptsova RUS 22.12.81 26 Jul 00, Blanka Vlasic CRO 8.11.83 20 Jul 02, Airine Palsyte LTU 13.7.92 21 Aug 11, Eleanor Patterson AUS 22.5.96 7 Dec 13, Yaroslava Mayuchikh UKR 19.9.01 22 Dec 18 (i)

POLE VAULT

Mark	Name		Nat	Born	Pos	Meet	Venue	Date
4.71i	Wilma	Murto	FIN	11.6.98	1		Zweibrücken	31 Jan 16
4.52					2	PNG	Turku	29 Jun 16
4.64	Eliza	McCartney	NZL	11.12.96	1		Auckland	19 Dec 15
4.63i	Angelica	Bengtsson	SWE	8.7.93	2		Stockholm	22 Feb 11
4.58					1		Sollentuna	5 Jul 12
4.61	Alyona	Lutkovskaya	RUS	15.3.96	1		Irkutsk	21 May 15
4.60i	Hanna	Shelekh	UKR	14.7.93	3		Donetsk	11 Feb 12
4.60i	Roberta	Bruni	ITA	8.3.94	1	NC	Ancona	17 Feb 13
4.60	Robeilys	Peinado	VEN	26.11.97	1		Barquisimeto	20 May 15
4.60	Lisa	Gunnarsson	SWE	20.8.99	2	TexasR	Austin	31 Mar 18
4.59	Nina	Kennedy	AUS	5.4.97	1		Perth	14 Feb 15
4.57	Angelica	Moser	SUI	9.10.97	1		Frauenkappelen	1 Aug 16
4.55i	Aksana	Gataullina	RUS	17.7.00	1		Sankt Peterburg	23 Feb 18
4.55					2	NC	Kazan	20 Jul 18

LONG JUMP

Mark	Wind	Name		Nat	Born	Pos	Meet	Venue	Date
7.14	1.1	Heike	Daute	GDR	16.12.64	1	PTS	Bratislava	4 Jun 83
7.03	1.3	Darya	Klishina	RUS	15.1.91	1	Znam	Zhukovskiy	26 Jun 10
7.00	-0.2	Birgit	Grosshennig	GDR	21.2.65	2		Berlin	9 Jun 84
6.94	-0.5	Magdalena	Khristova	BUL	25.2.77	2		Kalamáta	22 Jun 96
6.91	0.0	Anisoara	Cusmir	ROU	28.6.62	1		Bucuresti	23 May 81
6.90	1.4	Beverly	Kinch	GBR	14.1.64	*	WCh	Helsinki	14 Aug 83
6.88	0.6	Natalya	Shevchenko	RUS	28.12.66	2		Sochi	26 May 84
6.84		Larisa	Baluta	UKR	13.8.65	2		Krasnodar	6 Aug 83
6.83	1.7	Kate	Hall	USA	12.1.97	1		Greensboro NC	21 Jun 15
6.82	1.8	Fiona	May	GBR	12.12.69	*	WJ	Sudbury	30 Jul 88
6.81	1.6	Carol	Lewis	USA	8.8.63	1	TAC	Knoxville	20 Jun 82
6.81	1.4	Yelena	Davydova	KZK	16.11.67	1	NC-j	Krasnodar	17 Jul 85

Wind assisted to 6.82

Mark	Wind	Name		Nat	Born	Pos	Meet	Venue	Date
7.27	2.2	Heike	Daute	GDR	16.12.64	1	WCh	Helsinki	14 Aug 83
6.93	4.6	Beverly	Kinch	GBR	14.1.64	5	WCh	Helsinki	14 Aug 83
6.88	2.1	Fiona	May	GBR	12.12.69	1	WJ	Sudbury	30 Jul 88
6.84	2.8	Anu	Kaljurand	EST	16.4.69	2		Riga	4 Jun 88

TRIPLE JUMP

Mark	Wind	Name		Nat	Born	Pos	Meet	Venue	Date
14.62	1.0	Tereza	Marinova	BUL	5.9.77	1	WC	Sydney	25 Aug 96
14.57	0.2		Huang Qiuyan	CHN	25.1.80	1	NG	Shanghai	19 Oct 97
14.52	0.6	Anastasiya	Ilyina	RUS	16.1.82	q	WJ	Santiago de Chile	20 Oct 00
14.46	1.0		Peng Fengmei	CHN	2.7.79	1		Chengdu	18 Apr 98
14.43	0.6	Kaire	Leibak	EST	21.5.88	1	WJ	Beijing	17 Aug 06

Mark	Wind	Name		Nat	Born	Pos	Meet	Venue	Date
14.38	-0.7		Xie Limei	CHN	27.6.86	1	AsiC	Inchon	1 Sep 05
14.37i	-		Ren Ruiping	CHN	1.2.76	3	WI	Barcelona	11 Mar 95
	14.36		0.0			1	NC	Beijing	1 Jun 94
14.36	0.0	Dailenys	Alcántara	CUB	10.8.91	3	Barr/NC	La Habana	29 May 09
14.35		Yana	Borodina	RUS	21.4.92	1J	Mosc Ch	Moskva	15 Jun 11
14.32	-0.1	Yelena	Lysak ¶	RUS	19.10.75	1		Voronezh	18 Jun 94
14.29	1.2	Mabel	Gay	CUB	5.5.83	1		La Habana	5 Apr 02
14.28	0.9	Valeriya	Kanatova	UZB	29.8.92	3	NCp	Toshkent	12 Jun 11
Wind assisted									
14.83	8.3		Ren Ruiping	CHN	1.2.76	1	NC	Taiyuan	21 May 95
14.55	3.7	Dailenis	Alcántara	CUB	10.8.91	1	Barr/NC	La Habana	21 Mar 10
14.43	2.7	Yelena	Lysak ¶	RUS	19.10.75	1	WJ	Lisboa	21 Jul 94

SHOT

Mark	Wind	Name		Nat	Born	Pos	Meet	Venue	Date
20.54		Astrid	Kumbernuss	GDR	5.2.70	1	vFIN-j	Orimattila	1 Jul 89
20.51i		Heidi	Krieger	GDR	20.7.65	2		Budapest	8 Feb 84
	20.24					5		Split	30 Apr 84
20.23		Ilke	Wyludda	GDR	28.3.69	1	NC-j	Karl-Marx-Stadt	16 Jul 88
20.12		Ilona	Schoknecht	GDR	24.9.56	2	NC	Erfurt	23 Aug 75
20.02			Cheng Xiaoyan	CHN	30.11.75	3	NC	Beijing	5 Jun 94
19.90		Stephanie	Storp	FRG	28.11.68	1		Hamburg	16 Aug 87
19.63			Wang Yawen	CHN	23.8.73	1		Shijiazhuang	25 Apr 92
19.57		Grit	Haupt	GDR	4.6.66	1		Gera	7 Jul 84
19.48		Ines	Wittich	GDR	14.11.69	5		Leipzig	29 Jul 87
19.46			Gong Lijiao	CHN	24.1.89	Q	OG	Beijing	16 Aug 08
19.42		Simone	Michel	GDR	18.12.60	3	vSU	Leipzig	23 Jun 79
19.23			Zhang Zhiying	CHN	19.7.73	1	NC-j	Hangzhou	8 May 92

DISCUS

Mark	Wind	Name		Nat	Born	Pos	Meet	Venue	Date
74.40		Ilke	Wyludda	GDR	28.3.69	2		Berlin	13 Sep 88
	75.36	unofficial meeting				?		Berlin	6 Sep 88
67.38		Irina	Meszynski	GDR	24.3.62	1		Berlin	14 Aug 81
67.00		Jana	Günther	GDR	7.1.68	6	NC	Potsdam	20 Aug 87
66.80		Svetla	Mitkova	BUL	17.6.64	1		Sofia	2 Aug 83
66.60		Astrid	Kumbernuss	GDR	5.2.70	1		Berlin	20 Jul 88
66.34		Franka	Dietzsch	GDR	22.1.68	2		Saint-Denis	11 Jun 87
66.30		Jana	Lauren	GDR	28.6.70	1	vURS-j	Karl-Marx-Stadt	18 Jun 89
66.08			Cao Qi	CHN	15.1.74	1	NG	Beijing	12 Sep 93
65.96		Grit	Haupt	GDR	4.6.66	3		Leipzig	13 Jul 84
65.22		Daniela	Costian	ROU	30.4.65	3		Nitra	26 Aug 84
65.20			Liu Fengying	CHN	26.1.79	Q	NC	Chengdu	1 Jun 97
64.52		Martina	Opitz	GDR	12.12.60	3	NC	Karl-Marx-Stadt	12 Aug 79

HAMMER

Mark	Wind	Name		Nat	Born	Pos	Meet	Venue	Date
73.24			Zhang Wenxiu	CHN	22.3.86	1	NC	Changsha	24 Jun 05
71.71		Kamila	Skolimowska	POL	4.11.82	1	GPF	Melbourne	9 Sep 01
70.62		Alexandra	Tavernier	FRA	13.12.93	1	WJ	Barcelona	14 Jul 12
70.39		Mariya	Smolyachkova	BLR	10.2.85	1		Staiki	26 Jun 04
70.39		Réka	Gyurátz	HUN	31.5.96	1		Budapest	23 May 15
69.73		Natalya	Zolotukhina	UKR	4.1.85	1		Kyiv	24 Jul 04
69.63		Bianca	Perie	ROU	1.6.90	1	NC-j	Bucuresti	14 Aug 09
69.32		Sofiya	Palkina	RUS	9.6.98	2		Zhukovskiy	16 Jun 17
69.25		Audrey	Ciotani	FRA	13.3.96	1		Gagny	10 May 15
68.98		Ayamey	Medina	CUB	01.2.98	2	Barr	La Habana	27 May 16
68.74		Arasay	Thondike	CUB	28.5.86	2	Barr	La Habana	2 May 05
68.50		Martina	Danisová	SVK	21.3.83	1		Kladno	16 Jun 01

JAVELIN

Mark	Wind	Name		Nat	Born	Pos	Meet	Venue	Date
63.86		Yulenmis	Aguilar	CUB	3.8.96	1	PAm-J	Edmonton	2 Aug 15
63.01		Vira	Rebryk (now RUS)	UKR	25.2.89	1	WJ	Bydgoszcz	10 Jul 08
62.93			Xue Juan	CHN	10.2.86	1	NG	Changsha	27 Oct 03
62.11		Maria	Andrejczyk	POL	9.3.96	1	Skol	Cetniewo	1 Aug 15
62.09			Zhang Li	CHN	17.1.89	1		Beijing	25 May 08
61.99			Wang Yaning	CHN	4.1.80	1	NC	Huizhou	14 Oct 99
61.96		Sofi	Flink	SWE	8.7.95	Q	WCh	Moskva	16 Aug 13
61.79		Nikolett	Szabó	HUN	3.3.80	1		Schwechat	23 May 99
61.61			Chang Chunfeng	CHN	4.5.88	1	NC-j	Chengdu	4 Jun 07
61.49			Liang Lili	CHN	16.11.83	1	NC	Benxi	1 Jun 02
61.38		Annika	Suthe	GER	15.10.85	1-j		Halle	23 May 04
61.38		Haruka	Kitaguchi	JPN	16.3.98	3		Kawasaki	8 May 16

Mark	Wind	Name		Nat	Born	Pos	Meet	Venue	Date

HEPTATHLON

6768w Tatyana Chernova RUS 29.1.88 1 Arles 3 Jun 07
  13.04w/6.1 1.82 13.57 23.59w/5.2 6.61/1.2 53.43 2:15.05
6227   1 WJ Beijing 19 Aug 06
  13.70/1.6 1.80 12.18 24.05/0.3 6.35/-0.4 50.51 2:25.49

6542 Carolina Klüft SWE 2.2.83 1 EC München 10 Aug 02
  13.33/-0.3 1.89 13.16 23.71/-0.3 6.36/1.1 47.61 2:17.99

6465 Sibylle Thiele GDR 6.3.65 1 EJ Schwechat 28 Aug 83
  13.49 1.90 14.63 24.07 6.65 36.22 2:18.36

6436 Sabine Braun FRG 19.6.65 1 vBUL Mannheim 9 Jun 84
  13.68 1.78 13.09 23.88 6.03 52.14 2:09.41

6428 Svetla Dimitrova ¶ BUL 27.1.70 1 NC Sofia 18 Jun 89
  13.49/-0.7 1.77 13.98 23.59/-0.2 6.49/0.7 40.10 2:11.10

6403 Emilia Dimitrova BUL 13.11.67 6 GWG Moskva 7 Jul 86
  13.73 1.76 13.46 23.17 6.29 43.30 2:09.85

6381 Alina Shukh UKR 12.2.99 1 EJ Grosseto 21 Jul 17
  14.46/-1.7 1.87 13.87 25.97/0.3 6.33w/3.2 54.51 2:13.52

6357 Géraldine Ruckstuhl SUI 24.2.98 2 EJ Grosseto 21 Jul 17
  13.98/-1.5 1.81 13.54 24.74/0.1 5.97/1.1 54.32 2:12.56

6298 Nafissatou Thiam BEL 19.8.94 1 EJ Rieti 19 Jul 13
  13.87/1.2 1.89 14.26 25.15/-0.6 6.37/0.1 46.94 2:24.89

6276 Larisa Nikitina RUS 29.4.65 8 URS Ch Kiyev 21 Jun 84
  13.87/1.6 1.86 14.04 25.26/-0.7 6.31/0.1 48.62 2:22.76

6267 Katarina Johnson-Thompson GBR 9.1.93 15 OG London (OS) 4 Aug 12
  13.48/0.9 1.89 11.32 23.73/-0.3 6.19/-0.4 38.37 2:10.76

6253 Niamh Emerson GBR 22.4.99 1 WJ Tampere 13 Jul 18
  13.76/0.5 1.89 12.27 24.80/0.0 6.31w/2.6 39.02 2:09.74

Drugs disqualification: 6534 Svetla Dimitrova BUL 27.1.70 (3) ECp Helmond 16 Jul 89
  13.30/1.0 1.84 14.35 23.33/-2.2 6.47/-1.4 39.20 2:13.56

10 KILOMETRES WALK

Mark		Name		Nat	Born	Pos	Meet	Venue	Date
41:52		Tatyana	Mineyeva	RUS	10.8.90	1	NCp-j	Penza	5 Sep 09
41:55		Irina	Stankina	RUS	25.3.77	1	NC-wj	Adler	11 Feb 95
41:57			Gao Hongmiao	CHN	17.3.74	2	NG	Beijing	8 Sep 93
42:15+		Anisya	Kirdyapkina	RUS	23.10.89	1=	in 20k	Adler	23 Feb 08
42:20		Elvira	Khasanova	RUS	10.1.00	1	NC	Cheboksary	10 Jun 18
42:29		Tatyana	Kalmykova	RUS	10.1.90	1	NC-wj	Adler	23 Feb 08
42:31		Irina	Yumanova	RUS	17.6.90	2	NC-wj	Adler	23 Feb 08
42:43.0	t	Svetlana	Vasilyeva	RUS	24.7.92	1	NC-wj	Sochi	27 Feb 11

20 KILOMETRES WALK

Mark	Name		Nat	Born	Pos	Meet	Venue	Date
1:25:30	Anisya	Kirdyapkina	RUS	23.10.89	2	NC-w	Adler	23 Feb 08
1:26:36	Tatyana	Kalmykova	RUS	10.1.90	1	NC	Saransk	8 Jun 08
1:27:01		Lu Xiuzhi	CHN	26.10.93	2		Taicang	30 Mar 12
1:27:16		Song Hongjuan	CHN	4.7.84	1	NC	Yangzhou	14 Apr 03
1:27:34		Jiang Jing	CHN	23.10.85	2	WCp	Naumburg	2 May 04
1:27:35	Natalya	Fedoskina	RUS	25.6.80	2	WCp	Mézidon-Canon	2 May 99
1:28:08	Anezka	Drahotová	CZE	22.7.95	3	EC	Zürich	14 Aug 14
1:28:23		Song Xiaoling	CHN	21.12.87	2		Yangzhou	22 Apr 06

4 X 100 METRES RELAY

Mark	Nat	Name	Pos	Meet	Venue	Date
43.27	GER	Fehm, Kwadwo, Junk, Montag	1h3	EJ	Grosseto	23 Jul 17
43.29	USA (Blue)	Knight, Tarmoh, Olear, Mayo	1		Eugene	8 Aug 06
43.40	JAM	Simpson, Stewart, McLaughlin, Facey	1	WJ	Kingston	20 Jul 02
43.44A	NGR	Utondu, Iheagwam, Onyali, Ogunkoya	1	AfrG	Nairobi	9 Aug 87
43.68	FRA	Vouaux, Jacques-Sebastien, Kamga, Banco	3	WJ	Grosseto	18 Jul 04
43.81	GBR	Miller, Asher-Smith, S Wilson, Henry	1	EJ	Rieti	21 Jul 13
43.87	URS	Lapshina, Doronina, Bulatova, Kovalyova	1	vGDR-j	Leningrad	20 Jun 87
43.90	IRL	Scott, Moses, Neville. Mumbo-Gula	2	WJ	Tampere	14 Jul 18
43.98	BRA	Silva, Leoncio, Krasucki, Santos	2	PAm-J	São Paulo	7 Jul 07

4 X 400 METRES RELAY

Mark	Nat	Name	Pos	Meet	Venue	Date
3:27.60	USA	Anderson, Kidd, Smith, Hastings	1	WJ	Grosseto	18 Jul 04
3:28.39	GDR	Derr, Fabert, Wöhlk, Breuer	1	WJ	Sudbury	31 Jul 88
3:29.66	JAM	Stewart, Morgan, Walker, Hall	1	PennR	Philadelphia	28 Apr 01
3:30.03	RUS	Talko, Shapayeva, Soldatova, Kostetskaya	2	WJ	Grosseto	18 Jul 04
3:30.38	AUS	Scamps, R Poetschka, Hanigan, Andrews	1	WJ	Plovdiv	12 Aug 90
3:30.46	GBR	Wall, Spencer, James, Miller	2	WJ	Kingston	21 Jul 02
3:30.72	BUL	Kireva, Angelova, Rashova, Dimitrova	3	v2N	Sofia	24 Jul 83
3:30.84	NGR	Abugan, Odumosu, Eze, Adesanya	2	WJ	Beijing	20 Aug 06
3:31.57	ROU	Petrea, Florea, Tîrlea, Nedelcu	1	WJ	Seoul	20 Sep 92

Jnr WOMEN All-time

MEN'S WORLD LISTS 2018

60 METRES INDOORS

Mark	Name		Nat	Born	Pos	Meet	Venue	Date
6.34A	Christian	Coleman	USA	6.3.96	1	NC	Albuquerque	18 Feb
0.07		Coleman			1		Clemson	19 Jan
6.37		Coleman			1	WI	Birmingham	3 Mar
6.40A	Ronnie	Baker	USA	15.10.93	2	NC	Albuquerque	18 Feb
6.42A		Coleman			1s2	NC	Albuquerque	18 Feb
6.42		Su Bingtian	CHN	29.8.89	2	WI	Birmingham	3 Mar
6.43		Su Bingtian			1		Düsseldorf	6 Feb
6.43		Baker			3	WI	Birmingham	3 Mar
6.45A		Baker			1s1	NC	Albuquerque	18 Feb
6.45		Coleman			1s2	WI	Birmingham	3 Mar
6.46		Coleman			1	GP	Boston (R)	10 Feb
6.46A		Coleman			1s2	NC	Albuquerque	17 Feb
6.47		Coleman			1h1		Clemson	19 Jan
6.47		Su Bingtian			1		Karlsruhe	3 Feb
6.47A		Baker			1h1	NC	Albuquerque	17 Feb
6.48		Baker			1	Millrose	New York (A)	3 Feb
6.48		Xu Zhouzheng	CHN	26.12.95	1	NGPF	Beijing	23 Mar
6.50A	Mike	Rodgers	USA	24.4.85	3	NC	Albuquerque	18 Feb
6.51A	Hassan	Taftian	IRI	4.5.93	1	AsiC	Tehran	1 Feb
6.51A	Bryce	Robinson	USA	13.11.93	2h1	NC	Albuquerque	17 Feb
6.52	Andre	Ewers	USA	7.6.95	1		Iowa City	20 Jan
6.52	Yunier	Pérez	ESP	16.2.85	2		Düsseldorf	6 Feb
6.52A	Blake	Smith	USA	28.5.93	2h3	NC	Albuquerque	17 Feb
	(10)							
6.52		Xie Zhenye	CHN	17.8.93	4	WI	Birmingham	3 Mar
6.52	Elijah	Hall	USA	22.8.94	1	NCAA	College Station	10 Mar
6.53	Chijindu	Ujah	GBR	5.3.94	1r4		London (NH)	7 Feb
6.53	Raheem	Chambers	JAM	6.10.97	2	NCAA	College Station	10 Mar
6.54A	Kirk	Wilson	USA	27.5.91	1		Flagstaff	3 Feb
6.54	Everton	Clarke	JAM	24.12.92	2		Karlsruhe	3 Feb
6.54A	Brandon	Carnes	USA	6.3.95	2h2	NC	Albuquerque	17 Feb
6.54A	Jeff	Demps	USA	8.1.90	3s1	NC	Albuquerque	18 Feb
6.55	Jeryl	Brazil	USA	28.3.94	1		Baton Rouge	2 Feb
6.55	Ben Youssef	Meité	CIV	11.11.86	1h3		Metz	11 Feb
	(20)							
6.55	Emre Zafer	Barnes	TUR	7.11.88	1		Istanbul	18 Feb
6.55	Demek	Kemp	USA	26.4.96	3	NCAA	College Station	10 Mar
6.56	Ojie	Edoburun	GBR	2.6.96	4	GP	Glasgow	25 Feb
6.57	Tevin	Hester	USA	10.1.94	2		Clemson	19 Jan
6.57	Arthur Gue	Cissé	CIV	29.12.96	1r4		Reims	31 Jan
6.57	Christophe	Lemaitre	FRA	11.6.90	1h3		Mondeville	3 Feb
6.57	Noah	Lyles	USA	18.7.97	3	GP	Boston (R)	10 Feb
6.57	Ján	Volko	SVK	2.11.96	1		Torun	15 Feb
6.58	Divine	Oduduru	NGR	7.10.96	1		Lubbock	3 Feb
6.59	Kenzo	Cotton	USA	13.5.96	2		Fayetteville	9 Feb
	(30)							
6.59	Kimmari	Roach	JAM	21.9.90	1		Metz	11 Feb
6.59	Andrew	Fisher	BRN	15.12.91	2		Torun	15 Feb
6.59	Adam	Gemili	GBR	6.10.93	6	GP	Glasgow	25 Feb
6.59	Sean	Safo-Antwi	GHA	31.10.90	2s1	WI	Birmingham	3 Mar
6.59	Jaylen	Mitchell	USA	29.7.98	2h1	NCAA	College Station	9 Mar
6.59	Anthony	Schwartz	USA-J	5.9.00	1	HS Nat	New York (Arm)	11 Mar
6.59		Quan Yingrui	CHN	18.11.97	2	NGPF	Beijing	23 Mar
6.60	John	Otugade	GBR	24.1.95	1		London (LV)	13 Jan
6.60A	Tre	James	USA	1.1.96	1		Flagstaff	19 Jan
6.60	Abdullah Abkar	Mohammed	KSA	1.6.97	4	Millrose	New York (Arm)	3 Feb
	(40)							
6.60	Kim	Collins	SKN	5.4.76	5		Karlsruhe	3 Feb
6.60	Julian	Reus	GER	29.4.88	1		Erfurt	9 Feb
6.60	Zdenek	Stromsík	CZE	25.11.94	1	Gugl	Linz	10 Feb
6.60	Emeilo	Ferguson	JAM	16.4.93	1		Lubbock	10 Feb
6.60	Jalen	Miller	USA	17.6.95	2		Lubbock	10 Feb
6.60A	John	Teeters	USA	19.5.93	6s2	NC	Albuquerque	18 Feb
6.60A	Desmond	Lawrence	USA	19.12.91	6s2	NC	Albuquerque	18 Feb
6.60	Jaylen	Bacon	USA	5.8.96	1h3		Birmingham AL	19 Feb
6.60	Derrius	Rodgers	USA	15.10.97	1h3		Cedar Falls	25 Feb
6.60	Bolade	Ajomale	CAN	31.8.95	1h1	NCAA-II	Pittsburg KS	9 Mar
	(50)							

Mark	Wind	Name		Nat	Born	Pos	Meet	Venue	Date
6.60			Liang Jinsheng	CHN	12.1.96	1rB	NGP	Xianlin	11 Mar
6.61		Dominik	Záleský	CZE	23.8.95	1r2		Praha	9 Jan
6.61		Peter	Emelieze	GER	19.4.88	1		Dortmund	21 Jan
6.61		Pavel	Vruchinskiy	RUS	7.4.92	1	Mosc Ch	Moskva	24 Jan
6.61		Kendal	Williams	USA	23.9.95	1		Clemson	10 Feb
6.61		Alexander	Barnum	USA	17.8.97	2		Clemson	10 Feb
6.61		Andrew	Hudson	USA	14.12.96	1h3		Lubbock	10 Feb
6.61		Reece	Prescod	GBR	29.2.96	7	GP	Glasgow	25 Feb
6.61		Cejhae	Greene	ANT	6.10.95	3h1	NCAA	College Station	9 Mar
6.61		Jonte	Baker (60)	USA	23.5.97	2	NCAA-II	Pittsburg KS	10 Mar

Mark	Wind	Name		Nat	Born	Date	Mark	Wind	Name		Nat	Date
6.62	Wilfried	Koffi		CIV	12.10.87	25 Jan	6.62	Emmanuel	Yeboah		GHA	10.8.97	16 Feb
6.62	Filippo	Tortu		ITA	15.6.98	26 Jan	6.62	Andrew	Robertson		GBR	17.12.90	17 Feb
6.62	Ángel David	Rodríguez		ESP	25.4.80	3 Feb	6.62A	Devion	Clayton		USA	1.1.98	17 Feb
6.62	Jimmy	Vicaut		FRA	27.2.92	3 Feb	6.62	Kevin	Kranz		GER	20.6.98	16 Dec
6.62	Marvin	René		FRA	11.4.95	11 Feb	6.63 12 men						

Low altitude bests

Mark		Name		Venue		Date	Mark		Name			Venue		Date
6.52		Rodgers	3	Düsseldorf		6 Feb	6.53		Taftian	5	WI	Birmingham		3 Mar

100 YARDS: In 100m at Ostrava 13 Jun: (0.7) Gatlin 9.26, Simbine & Rodgers 9.36, Gemeli & Smellie 9.45

100 METRES

Mark	Wind	Name		Nat	Born	Pos	Meet	Venue	Date
9.79	-0.3	Christian	Coleman	USA	6.3.96	1	VD	Bruxelles	31 Aug
9.87	-0.1	Ronnie	Baker	USA	15.10.93	1	Skol	Chorzów	22 Aug
9.88	1.1	Noah	Lyles	USA	18.7.97	1	NC	Des Moines	22 Jun
9.88	0.8		Baker			1	DL	Paris (C)	30 Jun
9.89	1.4	Michael	Rodgers	USA	24.4.85	1h3	NC	Des Moines	21 Jun
9.89	0.7		Lyles			1s2	NC	Des Moines	22 Jun
9.90	1.1		Baker			2	NC	Des Moines	22 Jun
9.90	0.2		Baker			1h2	DL	London (OS)	21 Jul
9.90	0.1		Baker			1	DL	London (OS)	21 Jul
9.91	0.4	Zharnel	Hughes	GBR	13.7.95	1rA		Kingston	9 Jun
9.91	0.2		Su Bingtian	CHN	29.8.89	1		Madrid	22 Jun
9.91	0.8	Jimmy	Vicaut	FRA	27.2.92	2	DL	Paris (C)	30 Jun
9.91	0.8		Su Bingtian			3	DL	Paris (C)	30 Jun
9.92	1.7		Rodgers			1	Odlozil	Praha	4 Jun
9.92	0.7	Isiah	Young	USA	5.1.90	1r2		Montverde	9 Jun
9.92	0.3		Vicaut			1		Marseille	16 Jun
9.92	0.4		Rodgers			1		Bellinzona	18 Jul
9.92	0.8		Su Bingtian			1	AsiG	Jakarta	26 Aug
9.93	-0.4		Baker			1	G Gala	Roma	31 May
9.93	0.4		Lyles			2rA		Kingston	9 Jun
9.93	1.9		Young			1h2	NC	Des Moines	21 Jun
9.93	1.4	Cameron	Burrell	USA	11.9.94	2h3	NC	Des Moines	21 Jun
9.93	0.1		Hughes			2	DL	London (OS)	21 Jul
9.93	0.2	Akani	Simbine (10)	RSA	21.9.93	2h2	DL	London (OS)	21 Jul
9.93	-0.3		Baker			2	VD	Bruxelles	31 Aug
9.94	-0.2	Arthur Gue	Cissé	CIV	29.12.96	1		Leverkusen	16 Jun
9.94	1.2		Baker			1s1	NC	Des Moines	22 Jun
9.94	0.8		Simbine			4	DL	Paris (C)	30 Jun
9.94	0.3		Rodgers			1h1		Bellinzona	18 Jul
9.94	0.1		Simbine			3	DL	London (OS)	21 Jul
9.94	-0.5		Coleman			1	DL	Birmingham	18 Aug
9.94	-0.5	Reece	Prescod	GBR	29.2.96	2	DL	Birmingham	18 Aug
9.94	-0.3	Yohan	Blake	JAM	26.12.89	3	VD	Bruxelles	31 Aug
			(33/13)						
9.96	0.2	Tyquendo	Tracey	JAM	10.6.93	4h2	DL	London (OS)	21 Jul
9.97	0.9	Jaylen	Bacon	USA	5.8.96	1q3	NCAA-W	Sacramento	25 May
9.97	0.9		Xie Zhenye	CHN	17.8.93	1		Montreuil	19 Jun
9.97	1.7	Barakat	Al-Harthi	OMA	15.6.88	1	W.Asian	Amman	9 Jul
9.98	1.9	Andre	Ewers	JAM	7.6.95	1q3	NCAA-E	Tampa	25 May
9.99	1.1	Kendal	Williams	USA	23.9.95	1	SEC	Knoxville	13 May
9.99	0.2	Filippo	Tortu	ITA	15.6.98	2		Madrid	22 Jun
			(20)						
9.99	0.4	Jak Ali	Harvey	TUR	5.4.89	2		Bellinzona	18 Jul
10.00	0.5	Cejhae	Greene	ANT	6.10.95	1s2	CAG	Barranjilla	29 Jul
10.00	0.8	Tosin	Ogunode	QAT	2.3.94	2	AsiG	Jakarta	26 Aug
10.00	0.8	Ryota	Yamagata	JPN	10.6.92	3	AsiG	Jakarta	26 Aug
10.01	1.4	Gavin	Smellie	CAN	26.6.86	1		Windsor	19 May
10.01A	-0.7	Alonso	Edward	PAN	8.12.89	1	SAmG	Cochabamba	6 Jun
10.01	0.2	Emile	Erasmus	RSA	3.4.92	2h1		La Chaux-de-Fonds	1 Jul
10.02	1.9	Jeff	Demps	USA	8.1.90	2h2	NC	Des Moines	21 Jun

MEN 2018

Mark	Wind	Name		Nat	Born	Pos	Meet	Venue	Date	
10.02	-0.6	Paulo André	de Oliveira	BRA	20.8.98	1	NC	Bragança Paulista	14	Sep
10.03	-0.7	Justin	Gatlin	USA	10.2.82	1	GS	Ostrava	13	Jun
		(30)								
10.03	1.2	Abdallah Akbar	Mohammed	KSA	1.6.97	1rB	DL	Paris (C)	30	Jun
10.03	1.2	Hassan	Taftian	IRI	4.5.93	2rB	DL	Paris (C)	30	Jun
10.03	0.5	Mario	Burke	BAR	18.3.97	2s2	CAG	Barranquilla	29	Jul
10.04	1.7	Ojie	Edoburun	GBR	2.0.96	2	Odlozil	Praha	4	Jun
10.05	0.5	Jason	Rogers	SKN	31.8.91	3s2	CAG	Barranquilla	29	Jul
10.06A	1.7	Roscoe	Engel	RSA	6.3.89	1s3	NC	Pretoria	15	Mar
10.06	1.1	Sydney	Siame	ZAM	7.10.97	1	PTS	Samorín	29	Jun
10.06	0.0	Chijindu	Ujah	GBR	5.3.94	4	EC	Berlin	7	Aug
10.07A	-1.3	Simon	Magakwe	RSA	25.5.85	1	NC	Pretoria	16	Mar
10.07	1.0	Bryce	Robinson	USA	13.11.93	1rA	MSR	Torrance	21	Apr
		(40)								
10.07	1.9	McKinely	West	USA	26.6.96	2q3	NCAA-E	Tampa	25	May
10.07	1.1	Amaury	Golitin	FRA	28.1.97	1	Med G-23	Jesolo	9	Jun
10.07	1.2	Ameer	Webb	USA	19.3.91	1		Ninove	28	Jul
10.07	1.7	Nesta	Carter	JAM	11.10.85	1	CAG	Barranquila	30	Jul
10.08	2.0	Nethaneel	Mitchell-Blake	GBR	2.4.94	1		Baton Rouge	21	Apr
10.08	0.7	Lamont Marcell	Jacobs	ITA	26.9.94	2		Savona	23	May
10.08	1.7	Emre Zafer	Barnes	TUR	7.11.88	3	Odlozil	Praha	4	Jun
10.08	0.5	Javoy	Tucker	JAM	13.5.97	4s2	CAG	Barranquilla	29	Jul
10.08	0.3	Jorge Henrique	Vides	BRA	24.11.92	1		São Bernardo do Campo	18	Aug
10.09	1.9	Darryl	Haraway	USA	19.3.97	3q3	NCAA-E	Tampa	25	May
		(50)								
10.09A	0.9	Anthony	Schwartz	USA-J	5.9.00	1		Albuquerque	2	Jun
10.09A	-0.7	Alex	Quiñónez	ECU	11.8.89	2	SAmG	Cochabamba	6	Jun
10.09	1.4	Aleixo-Platini	Menga	GER	29.9.87	1		Weinheim	6	Jul
10.10	0.4	Trae	Williams	AUS	5.5.97	1	NC	Gold Coast	16	Feb
10.10A	1.9	Clarence	Munyai	RSA	20.2.98	1s1		Pretoria	24	Feb
10.10A	-0.2	Henricho	Bruintjies	RSA	16.7.93	1s1	NC	Pretoria	16	Mar
10.10	0.3	Kemar	Hyman	CAY	11.10.89	1s3	CG	Gold Coast	8	Apr
10.10	1.4	Divine	Oduduru	NGR	7.10.96	1		Waco	21	Apr
10.10	1.2	Waseem	Williams	JAM	8.1.97	1	Big 10	Bloomington	13	May
10.10	1.1	Raheem	Chambers	JAM	6.10.97	2	SEC	Knoxville	13	May
		(60)								
10.10	1.1	Ramil	Guliyev	TUR	29.5.90	1		Mersin	19	May
10.10	-0.9	Elijah	Hall	USA	22.8.94	2s1	NCAA	Eugene	6	Jun
10.10	0.1	Jevaughn	Minzie	JAM	20.7.95	1rB		Kingston	9	Jun
10.10	0.2	Derick	Silva	BRA	23.4.98	1		Guadalajara, ESP	5	Jul
10.10	0.4	Yoshihide	Kiryu	JPN	15.12.95	3		Bellinzona	18	Jul
10.11A	1.7	Thando	Dlodlo	RSA-J	22.4.99	2s3	NC	Pretoria	15	Mar
10.11	-0.3	Adam	Gemili	GBR	6.10.93	2s1	CG	Gold Coast	8	Apr
10.11	1.9	Tyson	Gay	USA	9.8.82	2r1		Clermont	12	May
10.11	0.7	Tevin	Hester	USA	10.1.94	2r2		Montverde	9	Jun
10.11	0.2		Yang Chun-Han	TPE	1.1.97	1		Hiratsuka	16	Jun
		(70)								
10.11	0.1	Kenroy	Anderson	JAM	27.6.87	1h1	NC	Kingston	21	Jun
10.11	0.0	Julian	Forte	JAM	7.1.93	1h2	NC	Kingston	21	Jun
10.11	1.1	Christopher	Taylor	JAM-J	29.9.99	1		Kingston	30	Jun
10.12	0.9	Keitavious	Walter	USA	16.4.96	1		Gainesville	13	Apr
10.12	1.0	Devin	Quinn	USA	8.6.96	2rA	MSR	Torrance	21	Apr
10.12	0.0	Aaron	Brown	CAN	27.5.92	1h1		Clermont	28	Apr
10.12	-0.3	Micah	Larkins	USA	8.12.94	1		San Antonio	6	May
10.12	1.8	Julius	Morris	MNT	14.4.94	1h2		Houston	12	May
10.12	1.3	Maxwell	Willis	USA	2.9.98	1h2	Big 12	Waco	12	May
10.12	1.1	Mustaqeem	Williams	USA	24.8.95	3	SEC	Knoxville	13	May
		(80)								
10.12	1.3	Cravon	Gillespie	USA	31.7.96	2h3	NCAA-W	Sacramento	24	May
10.12	0.9	Aska	Cambridge	JPN	31.5.93	1h1		Tottori	3	Jun
10.12A	-0.7	Vitor Hugo	dos Santos	BRA	1.2.96	3	SAmG	Cochabamba	6	Jun
10.12	1.9	Chris	Jefferson	USA	25.3.96	3h1	NC	Des Moines	21	Jun
10.12	0.2	Kemar	Bailey-Cole	JAM	10.1.92	2		Guadalajara, ESP	5	Jul
10.13	1.1	Reynier	Mena	CUB	21.11.96	1	Fortún	Camagüey	14	Mar
10.13	0.4	Senoj-Jay	Givans	JAM	30.12.93	4rA		Kingston	9	Jun
10.13	1.0	Carlos	Nascimento	POR	12.10.94	1		Braga	20	Jun
10.13	1.9	Cordero	Gray	USA	9.5.89	4h1	NC	Des Moines	21	Jun
10.13	1.9	Remontay	McClain	USA	21.9.92	5h1	NC	Des Moines	21	Jun
		(90)								
10.13	1.4	Kenzo	Cotton	USA	13.5.96	3h3	NC	Des Moines	21	Jun
10.13	1.1	Ján	Volko	SVK	2.11.96	2	PTS	Samorín	29	Jun

Mark	Wind	Name		Nat	Born	Pos	Meet	Venue	Date	
10.13	1.1	Mouhamadou	Fall	FRA	25.2.92	2h2	NC	Albi	6	Jul
10.14	1.9	Bismark	Boateng	CAN	15.3.92	1		Baton Rouge	28	Apr
10.14	0.3	Ben Youssef	Meité	CIV	11.11.86	2		Marseille	16	Jun
10.14	1.0	Rodrigo	do Nascimento	BRA	26.9.94	2		Braga	20	Jun
10.14	1.4	Riak	Reese	USA	23.11.94	4h3	NC	Des Moines	21	Jun
10.14	1.1	Alex	Wilson	SUI	19.9.90	1	NC	Zofingen	13	Jul
10.14	1.5	Takuya	Nagata	JPN	14.6.94	1		Hiratsuka	21	Jul
10.15	1.9	Andre	De Grasse	CAN	10.11.94	4	Drake R	Des Moines	28	Apr
		(100)								
10.15	1.5	Jake	Doran	AUS-J	17.11.00	1		Jämsä	1	Jul
10.15	1.4	Julian	Reus	GER	29.4.88	2		Weinheim	6	Jul
10.15	0.7	Brandon	Carnes	USA	6.3.95	4rB	Spitzen	Luzern	9	Jul

Mark	Wind	Name		Nat	Born	Date	
10.16	0.8	Warren	Fraser	BAH	8.7.91	5	May
10.16	1.7	Ryan	Clark	USA	14.9.96	25	May
10.16	0.7	Keston	Bledman	TTO	8.3.88	9	Jun
10.16	1.3	Mickaël-Meba	Zézé	FRA	19.5.94	6	Jul
10.16	0.9	Marvin	René	FRA	11.4.95	6	Jul
10.16	1.7	Zdenek	Stromsik	CZE	25.11.94	18	Jul
10.16	1.8	Sergiy	Smelyk	UKR	19.4.87	19	Jul
10.16	1.9	Aitor	Ekobo	ESP	3.1.97	21	Jul
10.16	1.9	Patrick Chinedu	Ike	ESP	26.4.84	21	Jul
10.16	0.0	Churandy	Martina	NED	3.7.84	7	Aug
10.17	1.1	Ncincihli	Titi	RSA	15.12.93	13	May
10.17	1.7	Thando	Roto	RSA	26.9.95	4	Jun
10.17	0.9	Christophe	Lemaitre	FRA	11.6.90	19	Jun
10.17	1.6	Yuki	Koike	JPN	13.5.95	23	Jun
10.17	1.1	Silvan	Wicki	SUI	13.2.95	13	Jul
10.17	1.8	Oleksandr	Sokolov	UKR	6.12.97	19	Jul
10.17	1.9	Ángel David	Rodríguez	ESP	25.4.80	21	Jul
10.18	1.1	Roberto	Skyers	CUB	12.11.91	14	Mar
10.18A	-0.6	Thembo	Monareng	RSA-J	14.2.99	28	Apr
10.18A	-0.6	Chederick	van Wyk	RSA	18.2.95	28	Apr
10.18	-0.7	Mobolade	Ajomale	CAN	31.8.95	26	May
10.18	1.7	Harry	Aikines-Aryeetey	GBR	29.8.88	1	Jun
10.18A	-1.1	Jhonny	Rentería	COL	26.3.97	6	Jun
10.18	1.6	Likoúrgos-Stéfanos	Tsákonas	GRE	8.3.90	29	Jun
10.18	1.2	Lala Muhammad	Zohri	INA-J	1.7.00	11	Jul
10.19	-1.4	Enoch	Adegoke	NGR-J	8.3.00	8	Apr
10.19	0.8	Seye	Ogunlewe	NGR	30.8.91	9	May
10.19		Travis	Collins	USA	26.2.96	5	May
10.19	1.4	Emmanuel	Yeboah	GHA	10.8.97	5	May
10.19	1.5	Josh	Davis	USA	13.10.95	6	May
10.19	1.9	Justin	Walker	USA	30.11.90	12	May
10.19	1.3	T.J. (Tarrick)	Brock	USA	3.2.98	24	May
10.19	-0.2	Egwero	Ogho-Oghene	NGR	26.11.88	16	Jun
10.19	1.4	Demek	Kemp	USA	26.4.96	21	Jun
10.19	-0.1	Taymir	Burnet	NED	1.10.92	1	Jul
10.19	1.8	Diego	Palomeque	COL	5.12.93	7	Jul
10.20	0.4	Rohan	Browning	AUS	31.12.97	16	Jan
10.20	2.0	Sachin	Dennis	JAM-Y	2.8.02	23	Mar
10.20	1.1	Joseph	Amoah	GHA	12.1.97	5	May
10.20	0.0	Kim Kuk-young		KOR	19.4.91	26	Jun
10.20	1.8	Bernardo	Baloyes	COL	6.1.94	7	Jul
10.21A	-0.7	Anaso	Jobodwana	RSA	30.7.92	15	Mar
10.21A	1.7	Samkelo	Sabela	RSA	4.4.95	15	Mar
10.21		Tyreke	Wilson	JAM-J	10.1.00	23	Mar
10.21	0.2	Xu Zhouzheng		CHN	26.12.95	10	Apr
10.21	-0.3	Cravont	Charleston	USA	2.1.98	12	May
10.21	1.3	Zack	Bazile	USA	7.1.96	24	May
10.21	1.7	Karson	Kowalchuk	CAN	30.12.98	25	May
10.21	-0.7	Shota	Iizuka	JPN	25.6.91	3	Jun
10.21	0.4	Kyle	Greaux	TTO	26.4.88	23	Jun
10.21	1.1	Remigiusz	Olszewski	POL	20.9.92	29	Jun
10.21	1.7	Deji	Tobais	GBR	31.10.91	7	Jul
10.21	1.7	Shuhei	Tada	JPN	24.6.96	11	Aug
10.22	0.6	Emanuel	Archibald	GUY	9.9.94	10	Feb
10.22	1.6	Retshidiitswe	Mlenga	RSA-J	27.2.00	5	Apr
10.22	1.6	Malesela	Senona	RSA-J	7.3.99	5	Apr
10.22	1.9	Rodney	Rowe	USA	17.3.97	28	Apr
10.22	1.1	Marcus	Parker	USA	9.10.97	5	May
10.22	0.4	KeSean	Carter	USA-J	15.8.00	12	May
10.22	1.2	Duan	Asemota	CAN	29.8.96	13	May
10.22	-0.7	NaRon	Rollins	USA	18.7.94	26	May
10.22	0.0	Michael	Pohl	GER	18.11.89	3	Jun
10.22	1.5	Jiang Hengnan		CHN	6.10.95	15	Jun
10.22	0.2	Jonathan	Quarcoo	NOR	13.10.96	5	Jul
10.22	2.0	Patrick	Domogala	GER	14.3.93	6	Jul
10.22	1.4	Henrik	Larsson	SWE-J	30.9.99	11	Jul
10.22	1.4	Michael	Stephens	JAM-J	19.8.00	11	Jul
10.22	1.2	Eric	Harrison	USA-J	18.2.99	11	Jul
10.22	1.9	António César	Rodrigues	BRA	12.1.93	14	Jul
10.22	-0.1	Sean	McLean	USA	23.3.92	19	Jul
10.22	-0.4	Cristofer	Valdez	DOM	1.11.94	29	Jul
10.22	0.6	Yazaldes	Nascimento	POR	17.4.86	7	Aug
10.23	0.4	Jack	Hale	AUS	22.5.90	19	Jan
10.23	w?	Oshane	Bailey	JAM	9.8.89	10	Feb
10.23	0.5	Damarcus	Simpson	USA	14.7.93	21	Apr
10.23	-0.3	Cliff	Resias	BAH	8.11.96	6	May
10.23	1.9	Sam	Effah	CAN	29.12.88	12	May
10.23A	1.3	Ngoni	Makusha	ZIM	22.6.94	26	May
10.23	1.8	Przemyslaw	Slowikowski	POL	20.11.93	10	Jun
10.23	1.9	Jarrion	Lawson	USA	6.5.94	21	Jun
10.23	0.1	Jerome	Blake	CAN	18.8.95	6	Jul
10.24	1.1	Nigel	Ellis	JAM	8.8.97	17	Feb
10.24	1.4	Shivnarine	Smalling	JAM	28.9.96	5	May
10.24	1.7	Walter	Dix	USA	31.1.86	12	May
10.24	0.2	Lucas	Jakubczyk	GER	28.4.85	3	Jun
10.24	1.9	Chris	Royster	USA	26.1.92	21	Jun
10.24	1.6	Kevin	Kranz	GER	20.6.98	30	Jun
10.24	0.2	Aldemir	Gomes da Silva	BRA	8.6.92	5	Jul
10.24	1.7	Andrew	Fisher	BRN	15.12.91	9	Jul
10.24	1.8	Rasheed	Dwyer	JAM	29.1.89	16	Jul
10.24	-0.3	Andrew	Ford-Azonwanna	CAN	29.11.95	29	Jul
10.24	-0.1	Asafa	Powell	JAM	23.11.82	22	Aug
10.25	1.1	Harlyn	Pérez	CUB	2.6.95	14	Mar
10.25A	1.3	Jeremy	Dodson	SAM	30.8.87	24	Mar
10.25	1.1	Tommy	Ramdhan	GBR	28.11.96	28	Apr
10.25	1.1	Terrell	Smith	USA	10.10.94	12	May
10.25	1.7	Amir	James	USA	7.12.95	25	May
		(200)					
10.25	0.9	Stuart	Dutamby	FRA	24.4.94	19	Jun
10.25	1.9	Reza	Ghasemi	IRI	24.7.87	29	Jun
10.25	1.1	Ryan	Zézé	FRA	29.1.98	6	Jul
10.25	1.2	Dominic	Ashwell	GBR-J	13.6.99	11	Jul

Wind assisted

Mark	Wind	Name		Nat	Born	Pos	Meet	Venue	Date	
9.78	2.4	Ronnie	Baker	USA	15.10.93	1	Pre	Eugene	26	May
9.84	2.4		Coleman			2	Pre	Eugene	26	May
9.86	4.1	Noah	Lyles	USA	18.7.97	1rF		Gainesville	13	Apr
9.88	2.4	Reece	Prescod	GBR	29.2.96	3	Pre	Eugene	26	May
9.90	2.4		Su Bingtian	CHN	29.8.89	4	Pre	Eugene	26	May
9.91	3.0	Jak Ali	Harvey	TUR	5.4.89	1		Bursa	15	Aug
9.92	4.1	Isiah	Young	USA	5.1.90	2rF		Gainesville	13	Apr
9.92	3.4		Lyles			1h4	NC	Des Moines	21	Jun
9.92	2.1	Nesta	Carter	JAM	11.10.85	1s1	CAG	Barranquila	29	Jul
9.94	2.4		Young			5	Pre	Eugene	26	May
9.98	3.0	Ramil	Guliyev	TUR	29.5.90	2		Bursa	15	Aug
10.00	3.6	Christian	Lyon	USA	19.1.98	1rB	Texas R	Austin	31	Mar
10.00	3.9	Jaylen	Mitchell	USA	29.7.98	1h1		Greensboro	14	Apr

MEN 2018

Mark	Wind	Name		Nat	Born	Pos	Meet	Venue	Date
10.02	3.6	Micah	Larkins	USA	8.12.94	2rB	Texas R	Austin	31 Mar
10.02	2.3	Cravon	Gillespie	USA	31.7.96	2s3	NCAA	Eugene	6 Jun
10.03	6.9	Marqueze	Washington	USA	29.9.93	1		Fayetteville	13 Apr
10.04	3.2	Kalon	Barnes	USA-J	16.12.99	1		Austin	12 May
10.04	3.0	Lamont Marcell	Jacobs	ITA	26.9.94	1h1		Savona	23 May
10.05	2.3	Raheem	Chambers	JAM	6.10.97	4s3	NCAA	Eugene	6 Jun
10.05	2.8	Brandon	Carnes	USA	6.3.95	1h2	PTS	Samorín	29 Jun
10.06	2.3	Waseem	Williams	JAM	8.1.97	5s3	NCAA	Eugene	6 Jun
10.06	5.6	Andrew	Robertson	GBR	17.12.90	1		Manchester	28 Jul
10.06	2.1	Reynier	Mena	CUB	21.11.96	2s1	CAG	Barranquilla	29 Jul
10.07A	3.3	Anaso	Jobodwana	RSA	30.7.92	1		Pretoria	23 Feb
10.07	4.1	Cordero	Gray	USA	9.5.89	2rA	Texas R	Austin	31 Mar
10.07	2.5	Anthony	Schwartz	USA-J	5.9.00	1		Jacksonville	5 May
10.07	3.0	Emmanuel	Yeboah	GHA	10.8.97	1	JUCO	El Dorado	19 May
10.07	3.0	Jaquone	Hoyte	BAR	4.2.98	2	JUCO	El Dorado	19 May
10.07	2.8	Ján	Volko	SVK	2.11.96	2h2	PTS	Samorín	29 Jun
10.08	3.6	Chris	Jefferson	USA	25.3.90	4rB	Texas R	Austin	31 Mar
10.09	3.6	Travis	Collins	USA	26.2.96	5rB	Texas R	Austin	31 Mar
10.09	2.7	Tevin	Hester	USA	10.1.94	1rC	Texas R	Austin	31 Mar
10.09	2.2	NaRon	Rollins	USA	18.7.94	1		San Angelo	8 Apr
10.09	2.1	Cristofer	Valdez	DOM	1.11.94	3s1	CAG	Barranquilla	29 Jul
10.10	2.1	Jack	Hale	AUS	22.5.98	1		Perth	13 Jan
10.10	4.1	Cravont	Charleston	USA	2.1.98	4rF		Gainesville	13 Apr
10.10	2.1	Burkheart	Ellis	BAR	18.9.92	4s1	CAG	Barranquilla	29 Jul
10.11	4.1	Blake	Smith	USA	28.5.93	3rA	Texas R	Austin	31 Mar
10.11	4.6	Kareem	Fair	USA	27.2.94	1		Daytona Beach	7 Apr
10.11	3.4	Devin	Quinn	USA	8.6.96	1		Champaign	14 Apr
10.11	5.0	Ryan	Girk	USA	27.4.96	1		Lawrence	12 May
10.11	3.2	Daisuke	Miyamoto	JPN-J	17.4.99	1		Sagamihara	25 May
10.11	3.0	Zdenek	Stromsik	CZE	25.11.94	1		Brno	18 Jun
10.12	2.6	Kenzo	Cotton	USA	13.5.96	1		Fayetteville	24 Mar
10.12	3.6	Amir	James	USA	7.12.95	6rB	Texas R	Austin	31 Mar
10.12	3.6	Remontay	McClain	USA	21.9.92	1		Redlands, CA	17 May
10.12	3.0	Khance	Meyers	USA-J	11.1.99	4	JUCO	El Dorado	19 May

Mark	Wind			Nat	Born		Date	Mark	Wind			Nat	Born		Date
10.13	3.5	John	Lewis	USA	2.9.96	24 Mar		10.19	2.5	Oraine	Palmer	JAM	31.8.95	4 May
10.13	2.2	Andre	Edwards	JAM-J	20.9.99	8 Apr		10.19	4.5	Tre	James	USA	27.6.98	11 May
10.13	3.7	Jason	Crow	USA	8.3.93	12 May		10.19	3.0	Terence	Ware	USA	.97	19 May
10.13	2.4	Ben Youssef	Meité	CIV	11.11.86	26 May		10.20	2.7	Emmanuel	Tait	USA	25.11.97	6 Apr
10.13	2.3	T.J. (Tarrick)	Brock	USA	3.2.98	6 Jun		10.20	6.1	Jonte	Baker	USA	23.5.97	4 May
10.13	3.6	Raphael	Müller	GER	31.7.94	9 Jun		10.20	3.0	Kasuan	James	USA	22.12.97	19 May
10.13	3.0	Mickaël-Meba	Zézé	FRA	19.5.94	6 Jul		10.20	3.2	Kirara	Shiraishi	JPN	31.5.96	25 May
10.14	6.9	Roy	Ejiakuekwu	GBR	2.2.95	14 Apr		10.20	4.6	Jonathan	Quarcoo	NOR	13.10.96	2 Jun
10.14	2.9	Damarcus	Simpson	USA	14.7.93	13 May		10.20	2.3	Kim	Collins	SKN	5.4.76	17 Jul
10.14	3.6	Samuel	Gordon	GBR	5.10.94	15 Aug		10.20	3.6	Tommy	Ramdhan	GBR	28.11.96	15 Aug
10.14	4.8	Henrik	Larsson	SWE-J	30.9.99	24 Aug		10.20	4.8	Dennis	Leal	SWE	29.10.94	24 Aug
10.15	5.0	Kadrin	Williams	USA	17.2.98	15 Mar		10.21	4.5	Jonathan	Farinha	TTO	16.5.96	17 Feb
10.15	2.9	Demek	Kemp	USA	26.4.96	21 Apr		10.21	2.7	Winston	George	GUY	19.5.87	5 May
10.15	4.8	Erik	Hagberg	SWE	11.4.95	24 Aug		10.21	2.4	Justin	Thomas	USA	6.11.95	5 May
10.15	3.4	Luke	Davids	RSA-Y	17.7.01	15 Oct		10.21	3.5	Makoto	Takiuchi	JPN	14.5.96	10 May
10.16	4.1	Justin	Walker	USA	30.11.90	13 Apr		10.21	3.6	Kevin	Ally	USA	22.8.91	17 May
10.16	2.4	Walter	Dix	USA	31.1.86	14 Apr		10.22	4.4	Akanni	Hislop	TTO	1.6.98	16 Mar
10.16	2.9	Ncincihli	Titi	RSA	15.12.93	21 Apr		10.22A	3.2	Tatenda	Tsumba	ZIM	12.11.91	28 Apr
10.16	6.1	Reggie	Thomas	USA	.96	4 May		10.22	3.1	Samson	Colbrooke	BAH	10.5.97	5 May
10.16	3.7	Roberto	Smith	JAM	20.7.94	6 May		10.22	4.5	Emmanuel	Callender	TTO	5.5.84	17 Feb
10.16	3.2	Kotaro	Iwasaki	JPN	14.6.96	25 May		10.22	2.3	Yu	Onabuta	JPN	6.2.94	19 May
10.17	?	Ngoni	Makusha	ZIM	22.6.94	7 Jul		10.22	1	Sibusiso	Matsenjwa	SWZ	£.5.88	7 Jul
10.17	3.6	Marcus	Parker	USA	9.10.97	31 Mar		10.23	3.0	Joseph	Millar	NZL	24.9.92	6 Jan
10.17	3.6		Kim Tae-hyo	KOR	28.1.93	11 Apr		10.23		Jais	Smith	USA-J	1.9.99	11 Apr
10.17	2.7		Kim Kuk-young	KOR	19.4.91	29 Apr		10.23	3.9	Desmond	Lawrence	USA	19.12.91	14 Apr
10.17	3.2	Ippei	Takeda	JPN	13.3.97	25 May		10.23	2.6	Guy-Elphège	Anouman	FRA	13.6.94	6 May
10.17	2.1	Emanuel	Archibald	GUY	9.9.94	29 Jul		10.23	2.5	Keishawn	Everly	USA-J	8.4.00	11 May
10.18	2.1	Jerome	Blake	CAN	18.8.95	3 Jun		10.23	2.8	Jan	Veleba	CZE	6.12.86	29 Jun
10.18	2.8	Remigiusz	Olszewski	POL	20.9.92	29 Jun		10.23	3.0	Adam	Harris	GUY	21.7.87	14 Jul
10.19	5.0	Tyrone	Thornton	USA	.96	15 Mar		10.23	6.7	James	Williams	GBR	1.10.91	28 Jul
10.19	2.1	Abdul Hakim	Sani Brown	JPN-J	6.3.99	13 Apr								

Low altitude bests

Mark	Wind					Date	Mark	Wind					Date
10.02	0.7	Edward	1rB	Spitz	Luzern	9 Jul	10.13	2.0	Schwartz	1		Fort Lauderdale	25 Apr
10.11	0.3	Magakwe	2	AWC	London (OS)	15 Jul	10.19	0.2	Quiñónez		22 Jun		
10.11	1.7	Bruintjies	4	Odlozil	Praha	4 Jun	10.23	0.3	Monareng		1	Jul	
10.13	0.4	V H dos Santos	1	São Bernardo do C		7 Apr	10.25	1.8	Rentería		7	Jul	

Hand timing

Mark	Wind	Name		Nat	Born	Pos	Meet	Venue	Date
9.9	0.0	Reynier	Mena	CUB	21.11.96	1h2	Fortún	Camagüey	14 Mar
10.0	0.6	Roberto	Skyers	CUB	12.11.91	2		Camagüey	18 May
9.9w	2.6	Roberto	Skyers	CUB	12.11.91	1h		Camagüey	18 May

Mark	Wind	Name		Nat	Born	Pos	Meet	Venue	Date

JUNIORS

See main list for top 4 juniors. 11 performances by 6 men to 10.18. Additional marks and further juniors:

Mark	Wind	Name		Nat	Born	Pos	Meet	Venue	Date
Schwartz	10.13	2.0	1		Fort Lauderdale	25 Apr	10.18	2.0 1h4 FlaR Gainesville	29 Mar
	10.16	1.7	1	FlaR	Gainesville	29 Mar	10.13w	2.1 1 Miami	2 Mar
Dlodlo	10.15A	0.7	2h1	NC	Pretoria	15 Mar	10.15A	-1.3 2 NC Pretoria	15 Mar
10.18A	-0.6	Thembo	Monareng	RSA	14.2.99	1		Sasolburg	28 Apr
10.18	1.2	Lala Muhammad	Zohri	INA-	1.7.00	1	WJ	Tampere	11 Jul
10.19	-1.4	Enoch	Adegoke	NGR	8.3.00	1h4	CG	Gold Coast	8 Apr
10.20	2.0	Sachin	Dennis	JAM-Y	2.8.02	1		Kingston	23 Mar
10.21		Tyreke	Wilson	JAM	10.1.00	1		Kingston	23 Mar
10.22	1.6	Retshiditswe	Mlenga (10)	RSA	27.2.00	1		Paarl	5 Apr
10.22	1.6	Malesela	Senona	RSA	7.3.99	2		Paarl	5 Apr
10.22	0.4	KeSean	Carter	USA	15.8.00	1		Austin	12 May
10.22	1.4	Henrik	Larsson	SWEJ	30.9.99	1s2	WJ	Tampere	11 Jul
10.22	1.4	Michael	Stephens	JAM	19.8.00	2s2	WJ	Tampere	11 Jul
10.22	1.2	Eric	Harrison	USA	18.2.99	3	WJ	Tampere	11 Jul
10.25	1.2	Dominic	Ashwell	GBR	13.6.99	5	WJ	Tampere	11 Jul
10.26	1.8	Daisuke	Miyamoto	JPN-	17.4.99	2h2	Oda	Hiroshima	29 Apr
10.26	0.1	Asani	Hampton	USA	.99	1		Yucaipa	2 May
10.26A	0.9	Taylor	Banks	USA	10.10.00	2		Albuquerque	2 Jun
10.28	-0.2	Tinotenda	Matiyenga (20)	ZIM	9.7.99	2		Fort Worth	17 Mar
10.28		Rylem	Robertson	JAM-Y	23.5.01	2		Kingston	23 Mar

Wind assisted

See main list for top 4 juniors. 8 performances by 7 men to 10.15w. Further juniors:

Mark	Wind	Name		Nat	Born	Pos	Meet	Venue	Date
10.13	2.2	Andre	Edwards	JAM	20.9.99	2		San Angelo	8 Apr
10.14	4.8	Henrik	Larsson	SWE	30.9.99	1	NC	Eskilstuna	24 Aug
10.15	3.4	Luke	Davids	RSA-Y	17.7.01	1	YOG	Buenos Aires	15 Oct
10.19	2.1	Abdul Hakim	Sani Brown	JPN-	6.3.99	2rB		Gainesville	13 Apr
10.23		Jais	Smith	USA	1.9.99	1h2		Lancaster	11 Apr
10.23	2.5	Keishawn	Everly	USA	8.4.00	1		Austin	11 May
10.24	2.2	Raymond	Evekwo	NGR	.99	1		Tulsa	31 Mar
10.24	3.4	Akintola	Alaba	NGR-Y	14.9.01	2	YOG	Buenos Aires	15 Oct

150 METRES

Pretoria 8 Mar: (-0.3) 1. Anaso Jobodwana 30.7.92 15.08, 2. Roscoe Engel 6.3.89 15.17. 3. Luxolo Adams 1.8.96 15.18
Boston 20 May: (+0.2) 1. Noah Lyles USA 18.7.97 18.90; 2. Nethaneel Mitchell-Blake GBR 2.4.94 14.81
Gateshead GNC 8 Sep: (+0.6) 1. Reece Prescod GBR 29.2.96 14.87

200 METRES

Mark	Wind	Name		Nat	Born	Pos	Meet	Venue	Date
9.65	0.9	Noah	Lyles	USA	18.7.97	1	Herc	Monaco	20 Jul
19.67	-0.2		Lyles			1	WK	Zürich	30 Aug
19.69A	-0.5	Clarence	Munyai	RSA	20.2.98	1s1	NC	Pretoria	16 Mar
19.69	2.0		Lyles			1	Pre	Eugene	26 May
19.69	0.4		Lyles			1	Athl	Lausanne	5 Jul
19.75	0.3	Steven	Gardiner	BAH	12.9.95	1		Coral Gables	7 Apr
19.76	0.7	Ramil	Guliyev	TUR	29.5.90	1	EC	Berlin	9 Aug
19.81	0.1	Akeem	Bloomfield	JAM	10.11.97	1	DL	London (OS)	22 Jul
19.83	1.3		Lyles			1	DL	Doha	4 May
19.84	-0.6	Michael	Norman	USA	3.12.97	1	DL	Paris (C)	30 Jun
19.88	0.4		Norman			2	Athl	Lausanne	5 Jul
19.90	1.0		Guliyev			1	Bisl	Oslo	7 Jun
19.90	0.9	Alonso	Edward	PAN	8.12.89	1rA	Spitzen	Luzern	9 Jul
19.92	0.9		Guliyev			1	DL	Stockholm	10 Jun
19.93A	-0.5	Alex	Quiñónez	ECU	11.8.89	1	SAmG	Cochabamba	7 Jun
19.93	1.5	Isiah	Young	USA	5.1.90	1		Montverde	9 Jun
19.96	0.9	Isaac	Makwala (10)	BOT	24.9.85	1		Osaka	20 May
19.96	0.4		Edward			1s2	CAG	Barranquilla	31 Jul
19.97	0.4	Kyle	Greaux	TTO	26.4.88	2s2	CAG	Barranquilla	31 Jul
19.98	1.0	Aaron	Brown	CAN	27.5.92	2	Bisl	Oslo	7 Jun
19.98	-0.2		Guliyev			2	WK	Zürich	30 Aug
19.99	1.3	Jereem	Richards	TTO	13.1.94	2	DL	Doha	4 May
19.99	-0.6	Rai	Benjamin	ANT/USA	27.7.97	2	DL	Paris (C)	30 Jun
19.99	0.9		Guliyev			2	Herc	Monaco	20 Jul
20.00	1.9	Ncincihli	Titi	RSA	15.12.93	1		Columbia, SC	21 Apr
20.00	0.9		Bloomfield			2rA	Spitzen	Luzern	9 Jul
20.00	0.3	Bernardo	Baloyes	COL	6.1.94	1s1	CAG	Barranquilla	31 Jul
20.01	1.9	Luxolo	Adams	RSA	1.8.96	1		Paarl	22 Mar
20.01	0.1		Edward			2	DL	London (OS)	22 Jul
20.03	0.9		Quiñónez			3	Herc	Monaco	20 Jul
		(30/17)							

MEN 2018

Mark	Wind	Name		Nat	Born	Pos	Meet	Venue	Date	
20.04	0.8	Bruno	Hortelano	ESP	18.9.91	1s2	NC	Getafe	22	Jul
20.04	0.7	Nethaneel	Mitchell-Blake	GBR	2.4.94	2	EC	Berlin	9	Aug
20.04	0.7	Alex	Wilson	SUI	19.9.90	3	EC	Berlin	9	Aug
		(20)								
20.07	1.9	Anaso	Jobodwana	RSA	30.7.92	2		Paarl	22	Mar
20.10	0.7	Adam	Gemili	GBR	6.10.93	5	EC	Berlin	9	Aug
20.11	1.6	Elijah	Hall	USA	22.8.94	1	Texas R	Austin	31	Mar
20.13	1.3	Divine	Oduduru	NGR	7.10.96	1	Big 12	Waco	13	May
20.13	1.5	Ameer	Webb	USA	19.3.91	1s1	NC	Des Moines	24	Jun
20.13	0.7	Eseosa	Desalu	ITA	19.2.94	6	EC	Berlin	9	Aug
20.15	0.8	Kendal	Williams	USA	23.9.95	1	SEC	Knoxville	13	May
20.16	0.9		Xie Zhenye	CHN	17.8.93	2		Osaka	20	May
20.18	0.9	Sydney	Siame	ZAM	7.10.97	1		Cork	16	Jul
20.19	-0.9	Christophe	Lemaitre	FRA	11.6.90	4	GS	Ostrava	13	Jun
		(30)								
20.19	0.3	Rasheed	Dwyer	JAM	29.1.89	2s1	CAG	Barranquilla	31	Jul
20.21A	-0.5	Vitor Hugo	dos Santos	BRA	1.2.96	2	SAmG	Cochabamba	7	Jun
20.21	0.2	Jahnoy	Thompson	JAM	16.2.96	1	NC	Kingston	24	Jun
20.23	-1.6	Zharnel	Hughes	GBR	13.7.95	1		Brisbane (Nathan)	28	Mar
20.23	1.6	Derick	Silva	BRA	23.4.98	1		Auburn	21	Apr
20.23	1.0	Mustaqeem	Williams	USA	24.8.95	1s2	NCAA	Eugene	6	Jun
20.23A	0.7	Aldemir	Gomes da Silva	BRA	8.6.92	1h2	SAmG	Cochabamba	7	Jun
20.23	0.7	Yuki	Koike	JPN	13.5.95	1	AsiG	Jakarta	29	Aug
20.23	0.7		Yang Chun-Han	TPE	1.1.97	2	AsiG	Jakarta	29	Aug
20.24	1.2	Ján	Volko	SVK	2.11.96	1	NC	Trnava	8	Jul
		(40)								
20.25	1.5	Jaylen	Bacon	USA	5.8.96	1		San Marcos	13	May
20.26	0.1	Rodney	Rowe	USA	17.3.97	1q1	NCAA-E	Tampa	26	May
20.26	1.1	Jaron	Flournoy	USA	24.11.96	2s1	NCAA	Eugene	6	Jun
20.26	0.4	Reynier	Mena	CUB	21.11.96	4s2	CAG	Barranquilla	31	Jul
20.27	1.6	Dedric	Dukes	USA	2.4.92	2	Texas R	Austin	31	Mar
20.27	1.4	Leon	Reid	IRL	26.7.94	1h2	UK Ch	Birmingham	1	Jul
20.28	1.8	Andre	Ewers	JAM	7.6.95	1h4	NCAA-E	Tampa	25	May
20.28	0.7	Churandy	Martina	NED	3.7.84	1rA		Kortrijk	14	Jul
20.30	1.0	McKinely	West	USA	26.6.96	1h6	NCAA-E	Tampa	25	May
20.32	0.1	Julius	Morris	MNT	14.4.94	1		Houston	13	May
		(50)								
20.33	1.6	Paulo André	de Oliveira	BRA	20.8.98	2		Auburn	21	Apr
20.33	0.8	Keitavious	Walter	USA	16.4.96	3	SEC	Knoxville	13	May
20.34	0.8	Shota	Iizuka	JPN	25.6.91	1	NC	Yamaguchi	24	Jun
20.34	1.4	Sergiy	Smelyk	UKR	19.4.87	1		Kropyvnytskyi	26	Jun
20.34	0.1	Jorge Henrique	Vides	BRA	24.11.92	1	IbAmC	Trujillo	26	Aug
20.35	0.0	Christopher	Taylor	JAM-J	29.9.99	1		Kingston	24	Mar
20.36A	2.0	Marcus	Parker	USA	9.10.97	1		Amarillo	22	Apr
20.36	-0.2	Nigel	Ellis	JAM	8.8.97	1		Kingston	9	Jun
20.37	0.1	Chris	Jefferson	USA	25.3.96	1		San Antonio	6	May
20.37	1.2	Aleixo-Platini	Menga	GER	29.9.87	1r2		Mannheim	24	Jun
		(60)								
20.38	1.1	Kenzo	Cotton	USA	13.5.96	4s1	NCAA	Eugene	6	Jun
20.38	-0.2	Bryce	Robinson	USA	13.11.93	2		Kingston	9	Jun
20.38	-0.2	Gavin	Smellie	CAN	26.6.86	1		Toronto	19	Jun
20.38	1.5	Andrew	Hudson	USA	14.12.96	2s1	NC	Des Moines	24	Jun
20.38	1.4	Miguel	Francis	GBR	28.2.95	2h2	NC	Birmingham	1	Jul
20.38	1.7	Jerome	Blake	CAN	18.8.95	2	NC	Ottawa	7	Jul
20.39	-0.3	Eric	Harrison	USA-J	18.2.99	1	Big 10	Bloomington	13	May
20.39	1.0	Akanni	Hislop	TTO	1.6.98	3h6	NCAA-E	Tampa	25	May
20.39	0.3		Bie Ge	CHN	2.8.92	1rA		Claremont	2	Jun
20.39	0.7	Solomon	Bockarie	NED	18.5.87	8	EC	Berlin	9	Aug
		(70)								
20.40	0.3		Park Tae-geon	KOR	8.5.91	1	NC	Jeongseon	28	Jun
20.40	0.9	Marcus	Lawler	IRL	28.2.95	2		Cork	16	Jul
20.40	1.1	Brendon	Rodney	CAN	9.4.92	2		Nové Mesto nad Metuji	21	Jul
20.41	0.6	Fred	Kerley	USA	7.5.95	1		Tempe	17	Mar
20.41A	1.8	Thando	Dlodlo	RSA-J	22.4.99	2	NC	Pretoria	17	Mar
20.41	0.9	Terrance	Laird	USA	12.10.98	2	Fla R	Gainesville	30	Mar
20.41	1.8	Amir	James	USA	7.12.95	2h4	NCAA-E	Tampa	25	May
20.41	0.0	Stuart	Dutamby	FRA	24.4.94	2		Genève	9	Jun
20.42	1.0	Terrell	Smith	USA	10.10.94	2		Lubbock	27	Apr
20.43	0.9	Riak	Reese	USA	23.11.94	3	Fla R	Gainesville	30	Mar
		(80)								
20.43	1.0	Edmond	Amaning	GBR	27.10.93	1rC		Clermont	12	May

Mark	Wind	Name		Nat	Born	Pos	Meet	Venue	Date
20.43	1.0	Ryan	Clark	USA	14.9.96	4h6	NCAA-E	Tampa	25 May
20.43	1.0	Renard	Howell	JAM	3.3.95	5h6	NCAA-E	Tampa	25 May
20.43	0.4	Kenneth	Bednarek	USA	14.10.98	1h2		La Crosse	1 Jun
20.43	-0.3	Robin	Vanderbemden	BEL	10.2.94	1		Ninove	28 Jul
20.44A	1.8	Roscoe	Engel	RSA	6.3.89	3	NC	Pretoria	17 Mar
20.45A	1.8	Chederick	van Wyk	RSA	18.2.95	4	NC	Pretoria	17 Mar
20.45	1.5	Devin	Quinn	USA	8.6.96	1		Oxford, MS	31 Mar
20.45	-0.9	Mobolade	Ajomale	CAN	31.8.95	1	NCAA-II	Charlotte	26 May
20.46	1.3	Andre	De Grasse	CAN	10.11.94	6	DL	Doha	4 May
		(90)							
0.46	0.1	Cliff	Resias	BAH	8.11.96	2		San Antonio	6 May
20.46	1.1	Teray	Smith	BAH	28.9.94	2rB		Clermont	12 May
20.46	0.8	Jun	Yamashita	JPN	23.8.97	3	NC	Yamaguchi	24 Jun
20.46	0.6	Steven	Müller	GER	15.9.90	1rB		Mannheim	24 Jun
20.46	0.2	Nathon	Allen	JAM	28.10.95	1rB	Spitzen	Luzern	9 Jul
20.46	1.8	Liemarvin	Bonevacia	NED	5.4.89	1rB		Kortrijk	14 Jul
20.46	0.7	Winston	George	GUY	19.5.87	3h3	CAG	Barranquilla	31 Jul
20.46	1.9	António César	Rodrigues	BRA	12.1.93	2	NC	Bragança Paulista	16 Sep
20.47	1.3	Anthony	Schwartz	USA-J	5.9.00	1		Miami	3 Mar
20.47	-0.3	Rodrigo	do Nascimento	BRA	26.9.94	2		Bern	16 Jun
		(100)							
20.47	1.5	Marqueze	Washington	USA	29.9.93	4s1	NC	Des Moines	24 Jun
20.47	0.2	Delano	Williams	GBR	23.12.93	4	NC	Birmingham	1 Jul
20.47	1.0	Andrew	Howe	ITA	12.5.85	1		Rieti	8 Jul
20.47	1.8	Jak Ali	Harvey	TUR	5.4.89	2		Bursa	16 Aug

Mark	Wind	Name		Nat	Born	Pos		Mark	Wind	Name		Nat		Date
20.48	0.3	LaShawn	Merritt	USA	27.6.86	13 Apr		20.59	1.2	Deon	Lendore	TTO	28.10.92	20 May
20.48A	0.5	Sibusiso	Matsenjwa	SWZ	2.5.88	10 Feb		20.59	0.5	Yoshinobu	Imoto	JPN-J	31.7.99	26 May
20.48	-0.4	Mario	Burke	BAR	18.3.97	13 May		20.59	0.8	Jean-Yann	De Grace	MRI	19.5.95	26 May
20.48	-0.4	Kahmari	Montgomery	USA	16.8.97	13 May		20.59	-0.9	NaRon	Rollins	USA	18.7.94	26 May
20.48	-0.9	Likoúrgos-Stéfanos Tsákonas		GRE	8.3.90	13 Jun		20.59A	-0.7	Ngoni	Makusha	ZIM	22.6.94	27 May
20.48	-0.7	Emile	Erasmus	RSA	3.4.92	1 Jul		20.59	0.0	Tommy	Ramdhan	GBR	28.11.96	9 Jun
20.48	-0.1	Jona	Efoloko	GBR-J	23.9.99	13 Jul		20.59	1.3	Daniel	Rodriguez	ESP	26.1.95	28 Jun
20.49	2.0	Omar	McLeod	JAM	25.4.94	29 Mar		20.59	0.9	Dominik	Kopec	POL	5.3.95	15 Aug
20.49	0.8	Ahmed	Ali	SUD	15.11.93	12 May		20.60	-2.1	Joseph	Millar	NZL	24.9.92	18 Feb
20.49	1.5	Justin	Walker	USA	30.11.90	9 Jun		20.60	-0.4	Warren	Weir	JAM	31.10.89	10 Apr
20.49	0.3	Mickaël-Meba	Zézé	FRA	19.5.94	8 Aug		20.60	1.4	Silvan	Wicki	SUI	13.2.95	2 Jun
20.50	2.0	Yancarlos	Martínez	DOM	8.7.92	29 Mar		20.60	0.3	Remontay	McClain	USA	21.9.92	2 Jun
20.51	0.8	Asa	Guevara	TTO	20.12.95	28 Apr		20.60	-1.8	Jeffrey	John	FRA	6.6.92	1 Jul
20.51	1.1	Tevin	Hester	USA	10.1.94	5 May		20.60	2.0	Masafumi	Naoki	JPN	19.11.93	8 Jul
20.51	0.0	Davide	Manenti	ITA	16.4.89	27 May		20.61A	-0.6	Trentavis	Friday	USA	5.6.95	1 Mar
20.51	0.2	Tyquendo	Tracey	JAM	10.6.93	24 Jun		20.61	0.2	Lamont Marcell Jacobs		ITA	26.9.94	6 May
20.51	0.3		Kim Kuk-young	KOR	19.4.91	28 Jun		20.61	0.8	Walter	Dix	USA	31.1.86	12 May
20.52	0.9	Javon	Francis	JAM	14.12.94	27 Jan		20.61	1.9	Maxwell	Willis	USA	2.9.98	12 May
20.52	0.8	Obie	Igbokwe	USA	28.1.97	13 May		20.61	0.9	Kenji	Fujimitsu	JPN	1.5.86	20 May
20.52	1.3	Correion	Mosby	USA	31.1.96	25 May		20.61	0.5	Cravon	Gillespie	USA	31.7.96	25 May
20.52	-0.7	Taymir	Burnet	NED	1.10.92	1 Jul		20.61	0.2	Shane	Brathwaite	BAR	8.2.90	9 Jul
20.52	0.2	Devon	Allen	USA	12.12.94	9 Jul		20.62	2.0	Waseem	Williams	JAM	8.1.97	14 Apr
20.52	1.8	Fode	Sissoko	MLI	9.10.96	14 Jul		20.62	0.5	Khance	Meyers	USA-J	11.1.99	18 May
20.53	0.1	Micah	Larkins	USA	8.12.94	6 May		20.62		Jack	Hale	AUS	22.5.98	22 Dec
20.53	-0.6	Charles	Dobson	GBR-J	20.10.99	12 Jul		20.63	0.3	John	Lundy	USA	15.3.92	23 Jun
20.55	1.6	Ronnie	Baker	USA	15.10.93	31 Mar		20.63	0.9	Robin	Erewa	GER	24.6.91	22 Jul
20.55	1.4	Demek	Kemp	USA	26.4.96	21 Apr		20.63	0.8	Thomas	Somers	GBR	28.4.97	25 Jul
20.55	1.4	Anderson	Devonish	BAR	12.3.94	13 May		20.63	1.5	Y. Muhammed Anas		IND	17.9.94	15 Aug
20.55	-0.3	Nick	Gray	USA	2.6.97	13 May		20.64	1.6	Micaiah	Harris	USA	19.12.98	31 Mar
20.55	2.0	Karol	Zalewski	POL	7.8.93	10 Jun		20.64	0.3	Wallace	Spearmon	USA	24.12.84	13 Apr
20.55	0.7	Mohamed	Yacoub Salem	BRN	1.3.96	29 Aug		20.64	1.4	Abdul Hakim Sani Brown		JPN-J	6.3.99	27 Apr
20.56	1.6	Kwantreyl	McConico	USA	22.8.97	29 Mar		20.64	0.8	Yoshihiro	Someya	JPN	14.7.88	22 May
20.56	1.5	Oraine	Palmer	JAM	.95	4 May		20.64	1.9	Jonatan Chaves Rodrigues		BRA	15.2.95	16 Sep
20.56	1.3	Brandon	Carnes	USA	6.3.95	4 May		20.65	1.0	Alonzo	Russell	BAH	8.9.92	23 Mar
20.56	0.1	Phemelo	Matlhabe	RSA	31.5.97	5 May		20.65	-0.3	Antonio	Infantino	ITA	22.3.91	28 Apr
20.57	-2.1	Alex	Hartmann	AUS	7.3.93	18 Feb		20.65	-0.3	Wataru	Inuzuka	JPN	8.7.97	3 May
20.57	0.6	Anthony	Carpenter	JAM-J	23.1.99	22 Mar		20.65	-0.3	Malik	Moffett	USA	11.4.94	13 May
20.57	0.4	Tyrell	Richard	USA	4.8.97	5 May		20.65	0.9	Shota	Hara	JPN	18.7.92	20 May
20.57	2.0	Tre	James	USA	27.6.98	11 May		20.65A		Peter	Mwai	KEN	30.6.90	23 Jun
20.57	0.5	Dontavius	Wright	USA	3.1.94	2 Jun		20.65	1.8	Jordan	Broome	GBR	4.12.96	1 Jul
20.58	1.0	Zachary	Shinnick	USA-J	8.2.99	24 Mar		20.65	0.7	Aldrich	Bailey	USA	6.2.94	4 Aug
20.58	1.0	Virjilio	Griggs	PAN	15.6.94	12 May		20.66	1.4	Demish	Gaye	JAM	20.1.93	17 Feb
20.58	0.1	Joseph	Amoah	GHA	12.1.97	26 May		20.66	1.4	Dylan	Peebles	USA	2.2.98	7 Apr
20.58	-1.0	Jaquone	Hoyte	BAR	4.2.98	10 Jun		20.66	1.2	Alexander	Gladitz	GER	19.12.94	24 Jun
20.58	1.2	Michael	Bryan	GER	9.6.91	24 Jun		20.66	1.5	Arokia	Rajiv	IND	22.5.91	15 Aug
20.59	1.8	Jared	Hayes	USA-J	19.1.99	13 May		20.66	0.5	Jonathan	Quarcoo (196)	NOR	13.10.96	26 Aug

Disqualified for obstruction: 20.12 0.9 Zharnel Hughes GBR 13.7.95 (1) CG Gold Coast 12 Apr

Indoors

20.02		Elijah	Hall	USA	22.8.94	1	NCAA	College Station	10 Mar
20.45		Nick	Gray	USA	2.6.97	1	Big 10	Geneva OH	24 May

Mark	Wind	Name		Nat	Born	Pos	Meet	Venue	Date

Wind assisted

Mark	Wind	Name		Nat	Born	Pos	Meet	Venue	Date
19.84	2.8		Norman			1	Pac-12	Stanford	13 May
19.98	2.3	Andre	Ewers	JAM	7.6.95	1	ACC	Coral Gables	12 May
20.02	2.7	Khance	Meyers	USA-J	11.1.99	1	JUCO	El Dorado	19 May
20.11	3.6	Mustaqeem	Williams	USA	24.8.95	1h2	NCAA-E	Tampa	25 May
20.23	3.5	Jaron	Flournoy	USA	24.11.96	1		Baton Rouge	28 Apr
20.24	4.1	Marqueze	Washington	USA	29.9.93	1		Fayetteville	13 Apr
20.25	2.7	Kasuan	James	USA	22.12.97	2	JUCO	El Dorado	19 May
20.26	2.8	Cravon	Gillespie	USA	31.7.96	2	Pac-12	Stanford	13 May
20.27	3.6	Eric	Harrison	USA-J	18.2.99	2h2	NCAA-E	Tampa	25 May
20.28A	3.5	Tatenda	Tsumba	ZIM	12.11.91	1		Provo	28 Apr
20.31	6.7	Jun	Yamashita	JPN	23.8.97	1		Sagamihara	27 May
20.33	3.2	Mickaël-Meba	Zézé	FRA	19.5.94	1	NC	Albi	8 Jul
20.37	2.8	Edmond	Amaning	GBR	27.10.93	1rC		Gainesville	13 Apr
20.38	4.2	Virjilio	Griggs	PAN	15.6.94	1		San Antonio	17 Mar
20.38	2.7	Phemelo	Matlhabe	RSA	31.5.97	3	JUCO	El Dorado	19 May
20.38	2.6	Joseph	Amoah	GHA	12.1.97	2h3	NCAA-E	Tampa	25 May
20.39	2.8	Gabriel	Constantino	BRA	9.2.95	2rC		Gainesville	13 Apr
20.39	2.1	Nathon	Allen	JAM	28.10.95	1		Auburn	14 Apr
20.39	2.6	Riak	Reese	USA	23.11.94	3h3	NCAA-E	Tampa	25 May
20.40	2.1	Robin	Vanderbemden	BEL	10.2.94	1		Liège (NX)	19 May
20.41	3.5	Ahmed	Ali	SUD	15.11.93	2		Baton Rouge	28 Apr
20.41	2.8	Anthony	Schwartz	USA-J	5.9.00	1		Jacksonville	5 May
20.42	3.1	Tevin	Hester	USA	10.1.94	1rC		Baton Rouge	21 Apr
20.42	6.7	Yoshinobu	Imoto	JPN-J	31.7.99	2		Sagamihara	27 May
20.43	3.1	John	Gikas	AUS-J	7.10.99	1		Sydney	6 Jan
20.44	3.1	Alex	Hartmann	AUS	7.3.93	2		Sydney	6 Jan

Mark	Wind	Name		Nat	Born	Date		Mark	Wind	Name		Nat	Born	Date
20.46	3.1	Dylan	Peebles	USA	2.2.98	13 Apr		20.55A	2.1	Óscar	Husillos	ESP	18.7.93	16 Jun
20.48	2.3	Brandon	Carnes	USA	6.3.95	12 Apr		20.56	6.4	Jan	Jirka	CZE	5.10.93	26 Aug
20.49	3.1	Vernon	Norwood	USA	10.4.92	21 Apr		20.56	3.2	Jeffrey	John	FRA	6.6.92	8 Jul
20.49	2.7	Christian	Lyon	USA	19.1.98	5 May		20.57	3.8	Chris	Belcher	USA	29.1.94	14 Apr
20.51	3.3	Ryan	Girk	USA	27.4.96	12 May		20.58	5.0	Myles	Pringle	USA	5.9.97	4 May
20.51	3.6	Nick	Gray	USA	2.6.97	25 May		20.59	4.0	Andrew	Robertson	GBR	17.12.90	29 Jul
20.51	2.8	Antonio	Tarantino	USA-J	18.8.00	17 Jun		20.61	2.4	Antonio	Woodard	USA	17.1.97	17 Mar
20.52	4.0	Antonio	Infantino	ITA	22.3.91	29 Jul		20.61	2.3	Dwight	St Hilaire	TTO	5.12.97	29 Mar
20.53	2.6	Tyrell	Richard	USA	4.8.97	5 May		20.61		Ireon	Brown	USA-Y	24.10.01	19 Apr
20.53	3.6	Mohamed	Yacoub Salem	BRN	1.3.96	11 Jul		20.62	2.9	Micaiah	Harris	USA	19.12.98	12 May
20.54	2.3	Shannon	Patterson	USA	3.5.96	12 May		20.62	2.5	Panayiótis	Trivizás	GRE	22.11.87	12 May
20.54	3.4	Jonathan	Quarcoo	NOR	13.10.96	2 Jun		20.62	6.7	Kirara	Shiraishi	JPN	31.5.96	27 May
20.54	2.8	Tomoya	Tamura	JPN	20.8.92	2 Sep		20.63	2.8	Chidi	Okezie	NGR	8.8.93	20 Apr
20.55	2.8	Kalon	Barnes	USA-J	6.12.99	12 May		20.63	2.7	Samson	Colbrooke	BAH	10.5.97	5 May
20.55	3.1	Karson	Kowalchuk	CAN	30.12.98	25 May		20.63A	2.6	Samuel	García	ESP	4.12.91	19 May
								20.63	3.6	Jared	Hayes	USA-J	19.1.99	25 May

Hand timing

Mark	Wind	Name		Nat	Born	Pos	Meet	Venue	Date
19.9	0.0	Reynier	Mena	CUB	21.11.96	1	Fortún	Camagüey	17 Feb
20.4	0.1	Roberto	Skyers	CUB	12.11.91	2		Camagüey	19 May

Low altitude bests

20.36	0.0	Munyai	2s1	CG	Gold Coast	11 Apr		20.38	1.8	A G da Silva	1		NC	Brag.Paulista	16 Sep
20.54	-0.9	Parker		26 May		20.63	1.9	Makusha		22 Mar		20.65	-0.3	Mwai			4 Aug
												20.66	0.7	V H dos Santos			18 Mar

200m Straight Track:
May 20, Boston +0.3. Gardiner 19.88, 2. Edward 20.03, 3, Richards 20.03, 4. Josephus Lyles USA 22.7.98 20.36

JUNIORS

See main list for top 4 juniors. 10 performances by 5 men to 20.52. Additional marks and further juniors:

Mark	Wind	Name		Nat	Born	Pos	Meet	Venue	Date
Taylor	20.38	1 1 1	Carifta Nassau		2 Aug		20.50	0.0	1s0		Kingston		10 May
	20.49	0.0 1	Kingston		19 May		20.42w	3.7	I		Kingston		4 Mar
Harrison	20.44	0.5 1	NC-j	Bloomington	17 Jun		20.46	-0.2	1h4	NC-j	Bloomington		16 Jun
20.48	-0.1	Jona	Efoloko	GBR	23.9.99	1	WJ	Tampere	13 Jul
20.53	-0.6	Charles	Dobson	GBR	20.10.99	1s1	WJ	Tampere	12 Jul
20.57	0.6	Anthony	Carpenter	JAM	23.1.99	1s1		Kingston	22 Mar
20.58	1.0	Zachary	Shinnick	USA	8.2.99	2		Los Angeles	24 Mar
20.59	1.5	Jared	Hayes	USA	19.1.99	2		San Marcos	13 May
20.59	0.5	Yoshinobu	Imoto (10)	JPN-	31.7.99	1h5		Sagamihara	26 May
20.62	0.5	Khance	Meyers	USA	11.1.99	1h3	JUCO	El Dorado	18 May
20.64	1.4	Abdul Hakim	Sani Brown	JPN-	6.3.99	1		Fayetteville	27 Apr
20.68	1.5	Zane	Branco	AUS	4.1.00	1	NC-j	Sydney	18 Mar
20.68	0.1	Abdulaziz	Mohamed	QAT-Y	20.10.01	1r6		Buenos Aires	16 Oct
20.69	0.9	Joe	Fahnbulleh	USA-Y	11.9.01	1	Jnr Oly	Greensboro	28 Jul
20.70A	1.8	Riben	Els	RSA	11.1.00	5	NC	Pretoria	17 Mar
20.72	0.8	Tsebo	Matsoso	RSA	27.5.99	2		Sasolburg	29 Apr
20.73	-1.2	Tyrese	Cooper	USA	21.3.00	1	Jnr Oly	Des Moines	4 Aug
20.74	0.4	Austin	Kratz	USA	20.8.99	1		Arcadia	7 Apr
20.75	1.7	Tylin	Jackson (20)	USA	11.12.99	1		Lancaster	13 Apr

Mark	Wind	Name		Nat	Born	Pos	Meet	Venue	Date	

Wind assisted
See main list for top 5 juniors. 7 performances by 6 men to 20.49w. Additional marks to 20.74

	Schwartz	20.49	3.0 1			Fort Lauderdale	25 Apr			
20.51	2.8	Antonio	Tarantino	USA	18.8.00	1h4	N.Sch	Greensboro	17	Jun
20.55	2.8	Kalon	Barnes	USA	6.12.99	1		Austin	12	May
20.61		Ireon	Brown	USA-Y	24.10.01	1		Mont Belvieu	19	Apr
20.63	3.6	Jared	Hayes	USA	19.1.99	4h2	NCAA-E	Tampa	25	May
20.65		Jacory	Patterson	USA	2.2.00	1		Irmo	17	Mar
20.68	3.1	Edward	Sumler	USA	6.7.00	1		Austin	12	May
20.68	3.7	Chad	Miller	GBR	31.3.00	1		Cardiff	16	May
20.70		Jordan	Booker	USA	17.9.99	2		Mont Belvieu	19	Apr

300 METRES

31.77A		Isaac	Makwala	BOT	24.9.85	1		Pretoria	8	Mar	
32.08A		Clarence	Munyai	RSA	20.2.98	1		Johannesburg	9	Feb	
32.44	Robin	Vanderbemden	BEL	10.2.94	18 Jul	32.68A	Ofentse	Mogawane	RSA	20.2.82	8 Mar
32.57A	Thapelo	Phora	RSA	21.11.91	8 Mar	32.69	Karsten	Warholm	NOR	28.2.96	22 Aug

Intermediate times at Eugene Jun 8: Akeem Bloomfield 31.8, Nathon Allen & Michael Norman 31.9, Kahmari Montgomery 32.3, Mar'yea Harris 32.4

Indoors

32.10		Jereem	Richards	TTO	13.1.94	1	GP	Boston (R)	10	Feb	
32.39	Óscar	Husillos	ESP	18.7.93	20 Jan	32.60	Karol	Zalewski	POL	7.8.93	25 Jan
32.50	Bralon	Taplin	GRN	8.5.92	10 Feb	32.64	Brian	Herron	USA-J	24.11.00	19 Jan
32.51	Steven	Gardiner	BAH	12.9.95	12 Jan	**Hand timing:**					
32.52	Pavel	Maslák	CZE	21.2.91	25 Jan	32.6	Ian	Halpin	AUS	20.4.93	18 Oct

400 METRES

Mark	Name		Nat	Born	Pos	Meet	Venue	Date	
43.61	Michael	Norman	USA	3.12.97	1	NCAA	Eugene	8	Jun
43.87	Steven	Gardiner	BAH	12.9.95	1	DL	Doha	4	May
43.94	Akeem	Bloomfield	JAM	10.11.97	2	NCAA	Eugene	8	Jun
43.99		Gardiner			1	DL	Shanghai	12	May
44.07	Abdelilah	Haroun	QAT	.97	1	DL	London (OS)	21	Jul
44.13	Nathon	Allen	JAM	28.10.95	3	NCAA	Eugene	8	Jun
44.21A	Emmanuel	Korir	KEN	15.6.95	1	NC	Nairobi	23	Jun
44.23	Isaac	Makwala	BOT	24.9.85	2	DL	Shanghai	12	May
44.28		Allen			1	SEC	Knoxville	13	May
44.33	Fred	Kerley	USA	7.5.95	1	G Gala	Roma	31	May
44.33		Bloomfield			1	DL	Rabat	13	Jul
44.34	Nathan	Strother	USA	6.9.95	2	SEC	Knoxville	13	May
44.35		Makwala			1	CG	Gold Coast	10	Apr
44.35		Haroun			1	FBK	Hengelo	3	Jun
44.35	Kirani	James (10)	GRN	1.9.92	1		Kingston	9	Jun
44.36		Kerley			2		Kingston	9	Jun
44.37		Haroun			2	G Gala	Roma	31	May
44.40		Norman			1	Pac-12	Stanford	13	May
44.43	Paul	Dedewo	USA	5.6.91	2	DL	London (OS)	21	Jul
44.43		Gardiner			1	Skol	Chorzów	22	Aug
44.48		Dedewo			1	AWC	London (OS)	15	Jul
44.50		Haroun			2	DL	Doha	4	May
44.50		Dedewo			2	FBK	Hengelo	3	Jun
44.50		James			3	DL	London	21	Jul
44.51		Haroun			3	DL	Shanghai	12	May
44.52		Korir			1		Lignano Sabbiadoro	11	Jul
44.53		Norman			1	MSR	Torrance	21	Apr
44.54	Baboloki	Thebe	BOT	18.3.97	4	DL	London (OS)	21	Jul
44.55	Dwight	St Hillaire	TTO	5.12.97	1q1	NCAA-E	Tampa	25	May
44.56		Dedewo			1	Kuso	Chorzów	8	Jun
	(30/13)								
44.58	Kahmari	Montgomery	USA	16.8.97	1	NC	Des Moines	23	Jun
44.59	Luguelín	Santos	DOM	12.11.92	1	CAG	Barranquilla	1	Aug
44.60	Quincy	Hall	USA	31.7.98	1		Tempe	7	Apr
44.62	Abderrahman	Samba	QAT	5.9.95	5	DL	London (OS)	21	Jul
44.63	Matthew	Hudson-Smith	GBR	26.10.94	6	DL	London (OS)	21	Jul
44.67	Bralon	Taplin	GRN	8.5.92	1		Bragança Paulista	8	Jul
44.69	Bruno	Hortelano	ESP	18.9.91	2		Madrid	22	Jun
	(20)								
44.70	Tyrell	Richard	USA	4.8.97	2s1	NCAA	Eugene	6	Jun
44.73	Wil	London	USA	17.8.97	1		Waco	21	Apr
44.73	Óscar	Husillos	ESP	18.7.93	3		Madrid	22	Jun

MEN 2018

Mark	Name		Nat	Born	Pos	Meet	Venue	Date	
44.74	Rai	Benjamin	ANT/USA	27.7.97	2	MSR	Torrance	21	Apr
44.81	Deon	Lendore	TTO	28.10.92	1r2		Montverde	9	Jun
44.85	Michael	Cherry	USA	23.3.95	3	NC	Des Moines	23	Jun
44.86	Jhon	Perlaza	COL	26.8.94	1		High Point, NC	11	May
44.87	Jonathan	Borlée	BEL	22.2.88	2s1	EC	Berlin	8	Aug
44.88	Christopher	Taylor	JAM-J	29.9.99	1	NC	Kingston	24	Jun
44.91	Karsten	Warholm	NOR	28.2.96	1s3	EC	Berlin	8	Aug
	(30)								
44.93	Luka	Janezic	SLO	14.11.95	2s3	EC	Berlin	8	Aug
44.94	Obie	Igbokwe	USA	28.1.97	2s3	NCAA	Eugene	6	Jun
44.94	Mar'yea	Harris	USA	24.11.97	3s1	NCAA	Eugene	6	Jun
45.00	Nery	Brenes	CRC	25.9.85	4=		Madrid	22	Jun
45.02	Derrick	Mokaleng	RSA	18.6.97	1h1	Big 12	Waco	12	May
45.03	Liemarvin	Bonevacia	NED	5.4.89	1		La Chaux-de-Fonds	1	Jul
45.03	Jonathan	Sacoor	BEL-J	1.9.99	1	WJ	Tampere	13	Jul
45.07	Christian	Taylor	USA	18.6.90	4	FBK	Hengelo	3	Jun
45.07	Kévin	Borlée	BEL	22.2.88	3s3	EC	Berlin	8	Aug
45.08	Demish	Gaye	JAM	20.1.93	1		Kingston	19	May
	(40)								
45.09	Dashawn	Morris	JAM-J	28.2.99	1		Kingston	24	Mar
45.09	Josephus	Lyles	USA	22.7.98	2		Clermont	12	May
45.11	Javon	Francis	JAM	14.12.94	3	CG	Gold Coast	10	Apr
45.11	Karol	Zalewski	POL	7.8.93	1s2	EC	Berlin	8	Aug
45.13A	Jared	Momanyi	KEN	5.5.90	2	NC	Nairobi	23	Jun
45.14	Thapelo	Phora	RSA	21.11.91	2	AfrC	Asaba	3	Aug
45.14	Vitor Ricardo	Santos	POR	18.12.94	3s1	EC	Berlin	8	Aug
45.15	Mohammad Nasser	Abbas	QAT	28.10.96	1rB		Madrid	22	Jun
45.17	Matteo	Galvan	ITA	24.8.88	4s1	EC	Berlin	8	Aug
45.19A	Anthony	Zambrano	COL	17.1.98	1	SAmC-23	Cuenca	29	Sep
	(50)								
45.22	Devin	Dixon	USA	22.9.97	2		Waco	21	Apr
45.22	Gil	Roberts	USA	15.3.89	4	DL	Doha	4	May
45.22	Brycen	Spratling	USA	10.3.92	2		Hamilton	11	May
45.24	Sean	Bailey	JAM	15.7.97	1		Lubbock	5	May
45.24	Y. Muhammed	Anas	IND	17.9.94	1		Nové Mesto nad Metuji	21	Jul
45.24	Chidi	Okezie	NGR	8.8.93	2		Nevis	22	Jul
45.25	Lucas	Búa	ESP	12.1.94	1		Huelva	8	Jun
45.25	Ludvy	Vaillant	FRA	15.3.95	1		Fort-de-France	9	Jun
45.26	Quintaveon	Poole	USA	11.10.96	3		Waco	21	Apr
45.26	Asa	Guevara	TTO	20.12.95	1		Houston	13	May
	(60)								
45.26	Davide	Re	ITA	16.3.93	1	Med G	Tarragona	28	Jun
45.28	Emmanuel	Bamidele	NGR-J	6.7.99	1	CGT	Abuja	16	Feb
45.28	Trevor	Stewart	USA	20.5.97	1h5	NCAA-E	Tampa	24	May
45.28	Alonzo	Russell	BAH	8.2.92	2r2		Montverde	9	Jun
45.30	Steven	Solomon	AUS	16.5.93	4s1	NCAA	Eugene	6	Jun
45.30	Rabah	Yousif	GBR	11.12.86	3s2	EC	Berlin	8	Aug
45.35	Myles	Pringle	USA	5.9.97	1	NCAA-2	Charlotte	26	May
45.38	Yoandys	Lescay	CUB	5.1.94	2	CAG	Barranquilla	1	Aug
45.40	Chantz	Sawyers	JAM-J	6.6.99	4q2	NCAA-E	Tampa	25	May
45.42	Jamal	Walton	CAY	25.11.98	1		Coral Gables	16	Mar
	(70)								
45.42A	Michael	Saruni	KEN	18.6.95	1		Albuquerque	7	Apr
45.45	Dwayne	Cowan	GBR	1.1.85	5s1	EC	Berlin	8	Aug
45.47	Anthony	Carpenter	JAM-J	23.1.99	2		Kingston	24	Mar
45.47	Vernon	Norwood	USA	10.4.92	2h1	NC	Des Moines	21	Jun
45.48	Samuel	García	ESP	4.12.91	3	NC	Getafe	22	Jul
45.49A	Pieter	Conradie	RSA	20.10.94	1		Potchefstroom	20	Feb
45.49	Donald	Blair-Sanford	ISR	5.2.87	2		Genève	9	Jun
45.50	Marcus	Chambers	USA	3.11.94	1		Claremont	2	Jun
45.50	Trey	Fields	USA-J	25.1.99	1	NC-j	Bloomington	17	Jun
45.50	Mikhail	Litvin	KAZ	5.1.96	1		Almaty	29	Jun
	(80)								
45.53	Janis	Leitis	LAT	13.4.89	5s2	EC	Berlin	8	Aug
45.54	Rashard	Clark	USA	4.11.94	1		San Angelo	5	May
45.55	Calvin	Smith	USA	10.12.87	1r1		Montverde	9	Jun
45.55	Mohamed Fares	Jelassi	TUN	29.7.97	1	Med G-23	Jesolo	10	Jun
45.55	Dylan	Borlée	BEL	20.9.92	2	NC	Bruxelles	8	Jul
45.55	Lucas	Carvalho	BRA	16.7.93	1	NC	Bragança Paulista	15	Sep
45.58A	Karabo	Sibanda	BOT	2.7.98	1		Lobatse	10	Feb
45.59	Pavel	Maslák	CZE	21.2.91	7s1	EC	Berlin	8	Aug

Mark	Name		Nat	Born	Pos	Meet	Venue	Date
45.59	Abbas	Abubaker	BRN	17.5.96	1s1	AsiG	Jakarta	25 Aug
45.60	Taj	Burgess	USA-J	15.4.99	2	Big 10	Bloomington	13 May
(90)								
45.63A	Zakithi	Nene	RSA	2.4.98	2	NC	Pretoria	17 Mar
45.63	Julian Jrummi	Walsh	JPN	18.9.96	1		Osaka	20 May
45.63	Youssef Mohamed	Dagher	KUW	15.7.93	1		Guadalajara/ESP	5 Jul
45.64A	Yilmar Andrés	Herrera	COL	29.4.96	2	SAmG	Cochabamba	6 Jun
45.65A	Alphas	Kishoyan	KEN	12.10.94	3	NC	Nairobi	23 Jun
45.67A	Winston	George	GUY	19.5.87	3	SAmG	Cochabamba	6 Jun
45.68	Machel	Cedenio	TTO	6.9.95	1h1	CG	Gold Coast	8 Apr
45.68	Kunle	Fasasi	NGR	23.6.96	2h4	NCAA-E	Tampa	24 May
45.69	Onkabetse	Nkobolo	BOT	22.7.93	2		La Chaux-de-Fonds	1 Jul
45.70	Johannes	Trefz	GER	7.6.92	1	NC	Nürnberg	22 Jul
(100)								
45.70	Rusheen	McDonald	JAM	17.8.92	4	CAG	Barranquilla	1 Aug
45.70	Abdulrahman Khamis	Abbas	BRN	28.1.93	3	AsiG	Jakarta	26 Aug

Mark	Name		Nat	Born	Date
45.71	Bryce	Deadmon	USA	26.3.97	13 May
45.71	Champion	Allison	USA	5.11.98	13 May
45.72	Michael	Berry	USA	10.12.91	9 Jun
45.72	Alexander	Russo	BRA	26.7.94	10 Jun
45.73	Philip	Osei	CAN	30.10.90	23 Jun
45.73	Martyn	Rooney	GBR	3.4.87	8 Aug
45.74	Sean	Burrell	USA-Y	23.2.02	5 May
45.74	Hugo Balduino	de Sousa	BRA	5.3.87	8 Jul
45.75	Jordan	Williams	USA	29.8.98	25 May
45.75	Cameron	Chalmers	GBR	6.2.97	9 Jun
45.76	Warren	Hazel	SKN	10.1.96	25 May
45.76	Fitzroy	Dunkley	JAM	20.5.93	11 Aug
45.76A	Kennedy	Luchembe	ZAM-Y	8.7.01	13 Dec
45.78	Brandon	Valentine-Parris	VIN	17.4.95	26 May
45.78	Arokia	Rajiv	IND	22.5.91	29 Jun
45.78	Lukasz	Krawczuk	POL	15.6.89	8 Aug
45.78	Aruna	Darshana	SRI-J	19.1.99	31 Oct
45.79	Daniele	Corsa	ITA	1.10.96	10 Jun
45.79	Rikuya	Ito	JPN	10.11.98	8 Sep
45.80A	Tyler	Koss	USA	17.2.96	14 Apr
45.81	Kota	Wakabayashi	JPN	23.10.97	6 May
45.82	Yoshinobu	Imoto	JPN-J	31.7.99	3 May
45.82	Nijel	Amos	BOT	15.3.94	11 Jul
45.82	Patrick	Schneider	GER	30.11.92	22 Jul
45.82	Lidio	Feliz	DOM	24.6.97	30 Jul
45.82	Vitaliy	Butrym	UKR	10.1.91	7 Aug
45.84	Alfred	Shirley	USA	19.10.98	25 May
45.84	Yavuz	Can	TUR	23.2.87	2 Jun
45.84	Robert	Parge	ROU	25.4.97	5 Jul
45.84	Edoardo	Scotti	ITA-J	9.5.00	12 Jul
45.85	Ali	Khadivar	IRI	11.11.89	1 Aug
45.86	Zazini	Sokwakhana	RSA-J	23.1.00	7 Apr
45.87	Ricky	Morgan	USA	12.9.95	29 Apr
45.87	Kymari	Gates	USA	2.5.97	12 May
45.87	Gilles-Anthony	Afoumba	CGO	14.6.96	27 May
45.88	Steven	Gayle	JAM	19.3.94	13 Apr
45.88	Jonathan	Webb	USA	28.1.97	13 May
45.91	Raymond	Kibet	KEN	4.2.96	24 May
45.91	Alex	Wesley	USA	27.10.95	6 Jun
45.92	Micaiah	Harris	USA	19.12.98	12 May
45.93A	Leungo	Scotch	BOT	28.2.96	29 Apr
45.93	Teddy	Atine-Venel	FRA	16.3.85	25 Jul
45.94	Fabian	Dammermann	GER	19.10.97	22 Jul
45.95	Marvin	Schlegel	GER	2.1.98	22 Jul
45.96A	Valente	Mendoza	MEX	17.1.97	30 Mar
45.96	Slimane	Moula	ALG-J	25.2.99	10 Jun
45.96	Umajesty	Williams	USA-J	13.4.99	17 Jun
45.96	Mitsoki	Kawauchi	JPN	2.6.97	8 Sep
45.96	Noah	Nirmal Tom	IND	13.11.94	19 Sep
45.97	Anderson	Devonish	BAR	12.3.94	25 May
45.97A	Alison Alves	dos Santos	BRA-J	3.6.00	29 Sep
45.98	Naoki	Kitadani	JPN	12.11.98	3 May
45.98A	Thomas	Staines	GBR	22.2.98	4 May
45.98	Khamal	Stewart-Baynes	CAN-J	22.9.99	23 Jun
45.99	Carlos	Salcido	USA	15.6.97	24 May
45.99	Myles	Misener-Daley	CAN-Y	1.3.01	8 Jun
45.99	H.K.Kalinga	Kumarage	SRI	25.9.92	25 Aug
46.00A	Boniface	Mweresa	KEN	13.11.93	17 Feb
46.00	Demar	Murray	JAM	31.8.91	7 Apr
46.00	Sadam	Koumi	SUD	6.4.94	20 May
46.00	Elija	Godwin	USA-J	1.7.99	17 Jun
46.00	Mikhail	Filatov	RUS	1.7.94	20 Jul
46.01	Trenton	Beram	PHI	1.4.96	25 May
46.01	Justin	Brooks	USA	9.8.96	26 May
46.01A	Leonard	Opiny	UGA	12.12.91	13 Jul
46.01	Maksim	Fedyayev	RUS	1.2.97	20 Jul
46.02	Taichi	Suzuki	JPN	3.5.96	21 Jul
46.02	Tyrese	Cooper	USA-J	21.3.00	4 Aug
46.03	Chevannie	Hanson	JAM	22.9.98	24 Mar
46.03	Aboubacar	Tetndap	CMR	3.9.95	23 Jun
46.04	Luis	Aviles	MEX-Y	3.3.02	30 Mar
46.04	Karayme	Bartley	JAM		12 Apr
46.04A		Guo Zhongze	CHN	7.8.96	16 Jun
46.05	Cordell	Lamb	USA	29.7.96	12 May
46.05	Jonathan	Jones	BAR-J	6.2.99	11 Jul
46.06	Jakub	Krzewina	POL	10.10.89	8 Jun
46.06	Rudolf	Verkhovykh	RUS	3.9.98	7 Jul
46.06	Dariusz	Kowaluk	POL	16.4.96	21 Jul
46.06	Khallifah	Rosser	USA	13.7.95	22 Jul
46.07	A.J.	Digby	USA	30.9.97	26 May
46.07	Rajay	Hamilton	JAM	25.8.95	26 May
46.08	Jun	Kimura	JPN	26.5.91	6 May
46.09	Ojay	Ferguson	BAH	17.10.93	17 Mar
46.09	Rafal	Omelko	POL	16.1.89	20 Jun
46.09	Robin	Vanderbemden	BEL	10.2.94	8 Jul
46.09	Mamadou	Hanne	FRA	6.3.88	25 Jul
46.09	Kaio	Bastos	BRA	11.8.93	15 Sep
46.09A	Daniel	Mbewe	ZAM	30.12.98	13 Dec
(190)					

Hand timing

46.0A	Abdurahman	Abdo	ETH-J	25.9.99	24 May

Low altitude bests

44.52	E Korir	1	Lignano Sabbiadoro	11 Jul
45.98	Conradie	26 May		

46.05 Litvin   29 Jul   46.08 Kishoyan   3 Aug

Indoors

Mark	Name		Nat	Born	Pos	Meet	Venue	Date
44.52		Norman			1	NCAA	College Station	10 Mar
45.16	My'Lik	Kerley	USA	6.6.96	2	NCAA	College Station	10 Mar
45.24	Marqueze	Washington	USA	29.9.93	1rE		Fayetteville	9 Feb
45.47	Pavel	Maslák	CZE	21.2.91	1	WI	Birmingham	3 Mar
45.50A	Dontavius	Wright	USA	3.1.94	1		Albuquerque	10 Feb
45.59A	Aldrich	Bailey	USA	6.2.94	1rB	NC	Albuquerque	18 Feb

Mark	Name		Nat	Born	Date
45.81	Zachary	Shinnick	USA-J	8.2.99	10 Mar
45.82	Jeffrey	Green	USA	18.8.95	24 Feb
45.84	Robert	Grant	USA	31.1.96	24 Feb
45.93	Kenny	Bednarek	USA	14.10.98	8 Dec
45.97	Steven	Champlin	USA	16.2.96	10 Feb
46.04	Cordell	Lamb	USA	29.7.96	24 Feb
46.08	Rhayko	Schwartz	USA	3.3.97	16 Feb

MEN 2018

Mark	Name	Nat	Born	Pos Meet	Venue	Date

JUNIORS

See main list for top 8 juniors. 12 performances by 7 men to 45.50. Additional marks and further juniors:

Mark	Name		Nat	Born	Pos	Meet	Venue	Date
Taylor	45.24	1	Georgetown		2 Jun	45.38	2 WJ Tampere	13 Jul
Bamidele	45.36	6	Madrid		22 Jun			
Sawyers	45.40	3s3	NCAA Eugene		6 Jun			
45.74	Sean	Burrell	USA-Y	23.2.02	1		Baton Rouge	5 May
45.76A	Kennedy	Luchembe	(10)	ZAM-Y	8.7.01	1	Gaborone	13 Dec
45.78	Aruna	Darshana	SRI	19.1.99	1		Colombo	31 Oct
45.82	Yoshinobu	Imoto	JPN	31.7.99	1r2		Fukuroi	3 May
45.84	Edoardo	Scotti	ITA	9.5.00	1s2	WJ	Tampere	12 Jul
45.86	Zazini	Sokwakhana	RSA	23.1.00	1		Paarl	7 Apr
45.96	Slimane	Moula	ALG	25.2.99	3		Jesolo	10 Jun
45.96	Umajesty	Williams	USA	13.4.99	2	NC-j	Bloomington	17 Jun
45.97A	Alison Alves	dos Santos	BRA	3.6.00	2	SAmC-23	Cuenca	29 Sep
45.98	Khamal	Stewart-Baynes	CAN	22.9.99	2		Toronto	23 Jun
45.99	Myles	Misener-Daley	CAN-Y	1.3.01	1		Toronto	8 Jun
46.00	Elija	Godwin	(20)	USA	1.7.99	3	NC-j	Bloomington	17 Jun
45.81i	Zachary	Shinnick	USA	8.2.99	4rB	NCAA	College Station	10 Mar

600 METRES

Mark	Name			Nat	Born	Pos Meet	Venue	Date
1:15.36	Chris		Giesting	USA	10.12.92	1	Nashville	1 Jun
1:15.45+	Nijel		Amos	BOT	15.3.94	1 in 800m	Monaco	20 Jul
1:15.8+	Harun		Abda	USA	1.1.90	2 in 800m	Monaco	20 Jul
1:15.9+	Jonathan	Kitilit	KEN	24.4.94	20 Jul	1:16.08	Tony	van Diepen	NED	17.4.96	13 May
1:15.91	Casimir	Loxsom	USA	17.3.91	1 Jun	1:16.2+	Brandon	McBride	CAN	15.6.94	20 Jul
1:15.94	Jesús	López	MEX	2.8.97	16 Mar	1:16.26	Drew	Piazza	USA	28.1.95	1 Jun
1:16.03A	Pieter	Conradie	RSA	20.10.94	30 Jan	1:16.34	César	Larrosa	ESP	28.4.97	30 May

Indoors

1:14.79A	Michael	Saruni	KEN	18.6.95	1		Albuquerque	20 Jan
1:16.38	Daniel	Kuhn	USA	11.8.95	24 Feb	1:16.40	Erik	Sowinski	USA	21.12.89	20 Jan

800 METRES

Mark	Name		Nat	Born	Pos	Meet	Venue	Date
1:42.05	Emmanuel	Korir	KEN	15.6.95	1	DL	London (OS)	22 Jul
1:42.14	Nijel	Amos	BOT	15.3.94	1	Herc	Monaco	20 Jul
1:42.79		Korir			1	DL	Birmingham	18 Aug
1:43.12	Clayton	Murphy	USA	26.2.95	2	DL	London (OS)	22 Jul
1:43.12	Wycliffe	Kinyamal	KEN	2.7.97	3	DL	London (OS)	22 Jul
1:43.20	Brandon	McBride	CAN	15.6.94	2	Herc	Monaco	20 Jul
1:43.25	Michael	Saruni	KEN	18.6.95	1		Tucson	28 Apr
1:43.29		Amos			4	DL	London (OS)	22 Jul
1:43.46A	Jonathan	Kitilit	KEN	24.4.94	1	NC	Nairobi	23 Jun
1:43.53		Kitilit			2	DL	Birmingham	18 Aug
1:43.65	Saúl	Ordóñez	ESP	10.4.94	3	Herc	Monaco	20 Jul
1:43.73	Ferguson	Cheruiyot	KEN	30.11.89	1	DL	Paris (C)	30 Jun
1:43.77		Kitilit			1	FBK	Hengelo	3 Jun
1:43.82	Cornelius	Tuwei (10)	KEN	24.5.93	4	Herc	Monaco	20 Jul
1:43.83		Kitilit			2	DL	Paris (C)	30 Jun
1:43.91		Kinyamal			1	DL	Shanghai	12 May
1:43.91		Kitilit			5	Herc	Monaco	20 Jul
1:43.95		Kitilit			2	DL	Shanghai	12 May
1:44.08		Cheruiyot			1	Gyulai	Székesfehérvár	2 Jul
1:44.08		Amos			2	Hanz	Zagreb	4 Sep
1:44.15	Elijah	Manangoi	KEN	5.1.93	3	DL	Birmingham	18 Aug
1:44.18		Amos			2	Gyulai	Székesfehérvár	2 Jul
1:44.20	Pierre-Ambroise	Bosse	FRA	11.5.92	6	Herc	Monaco	20 Jul
1:44.21	Joseph	Deng	AUS	7.7.98	7	Herc	Monaco	20 Jul
1:44.26A		Cheruiyot			2	NC	Nairobi	23 Jun
1:44.28	Alfred	Kipketer	KEN	26.12.96	1		Tomblaine	27 Jun
1:44.32	Marcin	Lewandowski	POL	13.6.87	8	Herc	Monaco	20 Jul
1:44.36		Ordóñez			3	DL	Paris (C)	30 Jun
1:44.38		Kitilit			1		Bellinzona	18 Jul
1:44.42	Isaiah	Harris	USA	18.10.96	4	DL	Paris (C)	30 Jun
	(30/16)							
1:44.56	Peter	Bol	AUS	22.2.94	1	DL	Stockholm	10 Jun
1:44.59	Adam	Kszczot	POL	2.9.89	1	EC	Berlin	11 Aug
1:44.61	Jake	Wightman	GBR	11.7.94	5	DL	London (OS)	22 Jul
1:44.73A	Jackson	Kivuva	KEN	11.8.88	3	NC	Nairobi	23 Jun
	(20)							
1:44.73	Guy	Learmonth	GBR	20.4.92	7	DL	London (OS)	22 Jul
1:44.74A	Timothy	Cheruiyot	KEN	20.11.95	1	Prisons	Nairobi	16 Jun

Mark	Name		Nat	Born	Pos	Meet	Venue	Date	
1:44.90	Mostafa	Smaïli	MAR	9.1.97	5	Hanz	Zagreb	4	Sep
1:44.97	Daniel	Rowden	GBR	9.9.97	8	DL	London (OS)	22	Jul
1:44.99	Álvaro	de Arriba	ESP	2.6.94	2		Huelva	8	Jun
1:45.03	Andreas	Kramer	SWE	13.4.97	1		Karlstad	25	Jul
1:45.04	Jesús	López	MEX	2.8.97	1		Mount Pleasant	14	Jul
1:45.04	Elliot	Giles	GBR	26.5.94	9	DL	London (OS)	22	Jul
1:45.07	Erik	Sowinski	USA	21.12.89	3	FBK	Hengelo	3	Jun
1:45.09	Andrew	Osagie	GBR	19.2.88	4	FBK	Hengelo	3	Jun
	(30)								
1:45.10	Thiago	André	BRA	4.8.95	5	FBK	Hengelo	3	Jun
1:45.14	Antoine	Gakémé	BDI	24.12.91	1		Guadalajara, ESP	5	Jul
1:45.15	Rynhardt	van Rensburg	RSA	23.3.92	6	FBK	Hengelo	3	Jun
1:45.16	Kyle	Langford	GBR	2.2.96	2	CG	Gold Coast	12	Apr
1:45.22A	Boaz	Kiprugut	KEN	18.5.98	4	NC	Nairobi	23	Jun
1:45.25	Marco	Arop	CAN	20.9.98	2	NCAA	Eugene	8	Jun
1:45.32	Michal	Rozmys	POL	13.3.95	4	EC	Berlin	11	Aug
1:45.42	Marc	Reuther	GER	23.6.96	8	FBK	Hengelo	3	Jun
1:45.42	Mateusz	Borkowski	POL	2.4.97	5	EC	Berlin	11	Aug
1:45.56	Tolesa	Bodena	ETH-J	18.2.00	3		Huelva	8	Jun
	(40)								
1:45.56	Filip	Snejdr	CZE	16.4.95	4		Tomblaine	27	Jun
1:45.57	Thomas	Staines	GBR	22.2.98	1		Nashville	2	Jun
1:45.60	Luke	Mathews	AUS	21.6.95	3	CG	Gold Coast	12	Apr
1:45.62	Devin	Dixon	USA	22.9.97	1		Baton Rouge	28	Apr
1:45.62A	Moses	Kipkemboi Kibet	KEN	20.11.94	6	NC	Nairobi	23	Jun
1:45.65	Jinson	Johnson	IND	15.3.91	1	I-State	Guwahati	27	Jun
1:45.67	Bryce	Hoppel	USA	5.9.97	4	NCAA	Eugene	8	Jun
1:45.67	Jamal	Al-Hayrani	QAT	26.5.93	1		Nivelles	23	Jun
1:45.68	Amel	Tuka	BIH	9.1.91	5	G Gala	Roma	31	Ma
1:45.69	Edose	Ibadin	NGR	27.2.93	2		Nashville	2	Jun
	(50)								
1:45.70	Ayanleh	Souleiman	DJI	3.12.92	1		Djibouti	30	Mar
1:45.72	Boris	Berian	USA	19.12.92	1	Morton	Dublin (S)	19	Jul
1:45.73	Jamie	Webb	GBR	1.6.94	1		Oordegem	2	Jun
1:45.73	Ryan	Sánchez	PUR	22.6.98	1		Cork	16	Jul
1:45.75	Thomas Arne	Roth	NOR	11.2.91	1	Bisl	Oslo	7	Jun
1:45.81	Alex	Amankwah	USA/GHA	2.3.92	2		Baton Rouge	28	Apr
1:45.83	Drew	Piazza	USA	28.1.95	3		Nashville	2	Jun
1:45.84	Job	Kinyor	KEN	2.9.90	5		Tomblaine	27	Jun
1:45.85	Brandon	Lasater	USA	9.10.92	1		Marietta, GA	19	May
1:45.89A	Edwin	Melly	KEN	23.4.94	3s2	NC	Nairobi	22	Jun
	(60)								
1:45.92	Andreas	Bube	DEN	13.7.87	6	EC	Berlin	11	Aug
1:45.94	Mohamed	Belbachir	ALG	11.1.94	1		Montbéliard	1	Jun
1:46.00	Tadesse	Lemi	ETH-J	20.1.99	2		Djibouti	30	Mar
1:46.00	Solomon	Lekuta	KEN-J	3.10.99	2		Göteborg	18	Aug
1:46.0A	Bernard	Kipyegon	KEN	19.12.90	3		Nairobi	6	Jun
1:46.02	Abubaker Haydar	Abdalla	QAT	10.1.98	2		Nivelles	23	Jun
1:46.04A	Tshepo	Tshite	RSA	15.1.97	1	NC	Pretoria	17	Mar
1:46.05	Abraham	Rotich	BRN	26.6.93	1		Goleniów	20	Jun
1:46.06	Daniel	Kuhn	USA	11.8.95	2	Big 10	Bloomington	13	May
1:46.06	Cooper	Williams	USA	9.3.98	3	Big 10	Bloomington	13	May
	(70)								
1:46.07	Brad	Mathas	NZL	24.6.93	5	CG	Gold Coast	12	Apr
1:46.07	Edward	Kemboi	KEN	12.12.91	4		Nashville	2	Jun
1:46.09	Colby	Alexander	USA	13.6.91	1		Kortrijk	14	Jul
1:46.11	Christoph	Kessler	GER	28.4.95	1		Regensburg	3	Jun
1:46.15	Manjit	Singh	IND	1.9.89	1	AsiG	Jakarta	28	Aug
1:46.17	Jesse	Garn	USA	4.6.93	3		Marietta, GA	19	May
1:46.19	Yassine	Hathat	ALG	30.7.91	1rB		Madrid	22	Jun
1:46.20A	Kabelo	Mohlosi	RSA	20.1.93	1s1	NC	Pretoria	16	Mar
1:46.20	Abdessalem	Ayouni	TUN	16.5.94	3		Montbéliard	1	Jun
1:46.20	Sam	Ellison	USA	5.12.92	2		Mount Pleasant	14	Jul
	(80)								
1:46.20	Abedin	Mujezinovic	BIH	2.6.93	3		Cles	25	Aug
1:46.21	Sammy	Kirongo	KEN	4.2.94	1	FRA Ch	Albi	8	Jul
1:46.23	Jonah	Koech	KEN	12.12.96	6	NCAA	Eugene	8	Jun
1:46.24	Ayoub	Sniba	MAR	5.4.97	3		Oordegem	2	Jun
1:46.24A	Jeremiah	Mutai	KEN	27.12.92	2	Police	Nairobi	13	Jun
1:46.28	Riad	El Chenini	TUN	25.3.97	4		Tübingen	16	Jun
1:46.29	Kumari	Taki	KEN-J	6.5.99	1	FBK	Hengelo	3	Jun

MEN 2018

Mark	Name	Nat	Born	Pos	Meet	Venue	Date
1:46.30	Quamel Prince	USA	20.4.94	5		Nashville	2 Jun
1:46.31	Vincent Crisp	USA	17.8.97	1		Tempe	7 Apr
1:46.31	Benedikt Huber	GER	13.10.89	3		Goleniów	20 Jun
(90)							
1:46.32	Badr El Jalaoui	MAR	28.1.93	3		Dubai	11 May
1:46.35	Jeff Riseley	AUS	11.11.86	2		Canberra	27 Jan
1:46.35	Gabriel Tual	FRA	9.4.98	1rB		Oordegem	26 May
1:46.38	Mouad Zahafi	MAR	9.5.98	1		Ninove	28 Jul
1:46.40	Daniel Andújar	ESP	14.5.94	2		Guadalajara, ESP	5 Jul
1:46.41	Cosmin Trofin	ROU	9.1.96	2		Dessau	8 Jun
1:46.43	Robert Ford	USA	8.3.96	2h4	NC	Des Moines	21 Jun
1:46.44A	Boitumelo Masilo	BOT	5.8.95	1		Gaborone	29 Apr
1:46.45	Ngeno Kipngetich	KEN-J	17.8.00	2	WJ	Tampere	15 Jul
1:46.47	Mohamed Amine Belferrar	ALG	6.2.91	1		Bilda	10 Apr
(100)							
1:46.47	Wesley Vázquez	PUR	27.3.94	3		Rovereto	23 Aug

Mark	Name	Nat	Born	Pos/Date
1:46.50	Harun Abda	USA	1.1.90	16 Jul
1:46.50	Lukás Hodbod	CZE	2.3.96	9 Aug
1:46.52	Benjamin Robert	FRA	4.11.98	26 May
1:46.55	Joshua Ralph	AUS	27.10.91	22 Aug
1:46.55	Amir Moradi	IRI	10.4.90	28 Aug
1:46.56	Yevhen Hutsol	UKR	13.5.90	26 Jun
1:46.59	Norbert Kolombos	KEN-J	.00	7 Jun
1:46.6	Jorge Félix Liranzo	CUB	3.2.94	17 Feb
1:46.62	Saïd Aden Saïd	QAT	.93	14 Jul
1:46.63	Kalle Berglund	SWE	11.3.96	25 Jul
1:46.66	Abubakr Abdalla	SUD	10.1.98	27 Jun
1:46.67	Dean Cronin	IRL	23.5.93	2 Jun
1:46.7A	Ahmed Hasen	ETH-Y	8.6.01	19 Apr
1:46.70	Carlos Villarreal	MEX	10.5.97	28 Apr
1:46.73	Sergey Dubrovskiy	RUS	20.1.95	1 Jul
1:46.74	Timo Benitz	GER	01.10.91	9 Jun
1:46.74	Mohammed Aman	ETH	10.1.94	21 Jul
1:46.75	Sam Prakel	USA	29.10.94	14 Jul
1:46.76	Jorge Montes	MEX	20.12.93	3 Jun
1:46.76	Alexis Miellet	FRA	5.5.95	11 Jul
1:46.78	Jabulane Ncamane	RSA	7.6.94	22 Mar
1:46.79	Mohammed Afsal	IND	3.2.96	27 Jun
1:46.8A	Addisu Girma	ETH-J	10.12.99	3 Feb
1:46.84	Ehab Chiad Hashim	IRQ	30.3.93	11 May
1:46.84	Elliott Crestan	BEL-J	22.2.99	14 Jul
1:46.88	Abdellatif El Guesse	MAR	27.2.93	1 Jun
1:46.88	Zak Curran	IRL	17.12.93	7 Jun
1:46.88	Drew Windle	USA	22.7.92	11 Jul
1:46.88	Chris Giesting	USA	10.12.92	11 Jul
1:46.88	Johan Rogestedt	SWE	27.1.93	28 Jul
1:46.89	Aaron Botterman	BEL	1.5.94	8 Jul
1:46.89	Aymeric Lusine	FRA	13.9.95	19 Jul
1:46.91A	Duran Faro	RSA	5.2.94	27 Mar
1:46.92	Beant Singh	IND-J	10.1.99	27 Jun
1:46.93	Enrico Brazzale	ITA	3.8.95	2 Sep
1:46.94	Adrian Ben	ESP	4.8.98	22 Jun
1:46.94	Ramzi Abdenouz	ALG	23.5.93	5 Jul
1:46.95	Carter Lilly	USA	19.10.95	22 Jun
1:46.97	Zan Rudolf	SLO	9.5.93	4 Sep
1:47.0A	Collins Kipruto	KEN		19 May
1:47.01	Takumi Murashima	JPN	1.10.95	3 May
1:47.03	Alex Rowe	AUS	8.7.92	15 Feb
1:47.04	Dylan Stenson	AUS	30.9.88	15 Feb
1:47.04	Konstantin Kholmogorov	RUS	7.2.96	1 Jul
1:47.05	Andrés Arroyo	PUR	7.6.95	21 Apr
1:47.05	Derek Thomas	USA	9.4.91	22 Jun
1:47.09	Ryan Gregson	AUS	26.4.90	19 Jul
1:47.10	Matheus Pessoa	BRA	9.4.96	1 Sep
1:47.1A	Tasew Yada	ETH-Y	3.10.01	19 Apr
1:47.12	Canaan Solomon	GBR	17.9.98	21 Jul
1:47.13A	Indunil Herath	SRI	27.3.93	16 Jun
1:47.14	Paris Simmons	USA	3.6.91	2 Jun
1:47.14	Robert Heppenstall	CAN	28.2.97	8 Jun
1:47.16A	Theuns Ehlers	RSA	3.12.98	16 Mar
1:47.16	Sho Kawamoto	JPN	1.3.93	8 Jun
1:47.16	Saúl Martinez	ESP	12.2.94	8 Jun
1:47.16	Robert Farken	GER	20.9.97	18 Jul
1:47.17	Pieter Claus	BEL	1.3.93	2 Jun
1:47.19	Matthew Scott	AUS	2.5.97	17 Mar
1:47.19	Christos Demetriou	CYP	22.9.93	26 May
1:47.20A	George Manangoi	KEN-J	29.11.00	8 Mar
1:47.20	Hugo Houyez	FRA	16.12.95	2 Jun
1:47.0A	Omar Amano	ETH-J	3.3.99	9 Dec
1:47.21	Joseph White	USA	16.11.95	21 Apr
1:47.22A	Geoffrey Rutto	UGA	.95	3 Mar
1:47.23	Robert Lister	AUS	6.1.93	15 Feb
1:47.23	Leonard Kosencha	KEN	21.8.94	15 Aug
1:47.24	Joe McAsey	USA	1.6.93	2 Jun
1:47.25	Charles Jones	USA	1.11.95	7 Apr
1:47.26	Ryan Martin	USA	23.3.89	3 May
1:47.28	Ignacio Díaz-Cano	ESP	11.1.94	8 Jun
1:47.29A	Rashid Etiau	UGA		3 Mar
1:47.29	Waleed Suliman	USA	22.9.98	14 Apr
1:47.29	Baptiste Mischler	FRA	23.11.97	27 Jun
1:47.30	Alejandro Estevez	ESP	21.1.92	8 Jun
1:47.3	Anthonio Mascoll	BAR	17.1.93	30 Jul
1:47.33	Michael Rimmer	GBR	3.2.86	19 Jul
1:47.35	Simone Barontini	ITA-J	5.1.99	14 Jul
1:47.35	Jordan Williamsz	AUS	21.8.92	19 Jul
1:47.36	Clay Lambourne	USA	27.11.95	25 May
1:47.36	Max Burgin	GBR-Y	20.5.02	8 Jul
1:47.36	Oussama Cherad	ALG-J	6.3.00	14 Jul
1:47.37	Clement Dhainaut	FRA	22.1.97	16 Jun
1:47.38	Abdirahman Hassan	QAT	13.4.97	21 Jul
1:47.39	Hamid Oualich	FRA	26.4.88	1 Jun
1:47.40	Craig Engels	USA	1.5.94	17 May
1:47.43	Alexander Lomong	SSD	30.9.97	13 May
1:47.43	Dorek Holdsworth	UGA	12.2.90	2 Jun
1:47.44	Mamush Lencho	ETH	24.3.96	21 Jul
1:47.45	Mason Cohen	AUS	19.9.96	17 Feb
1:47.46	Abraham Alvarado	USA	4.8.95	21 Jun
1:47.47	Brannon Kidder	USA	18.11.93	3 May
1:47.48	Willy Tarbei	KEN	30.5.98	19 May
(191)				

Disqualified: 1:47.09 Oussama Cherad ALG-J 6.3.00 15 Jul

Indoors

Mark	Name	Nat	Born	Pos	Meet	Venue	Date
1:44.21	Korir			1	Millrose	New York (Arm)	3 Feb
1:45.10A	Donavan Brazier	USA	15.4.97	1	NC	Albuquerque	18 Feb
1:45.52	Drew Windle	USA	22.7.92	3h1	WI	Birmingham	2 Mar
1:46.83	Christian Harrison	USA	27.9.93				25 Feb
1:46.88	Robert Heppenstall	CAN	28.2.97				10 Mar
1:46.99	Russell Dinkins	USA	27.6.89				10 Feb
1:47.04	Neil Gourley	GBR	7.2.95				24 Feb
1:47.14	John Lewis	USA	18.1.97				24 Feb
1:47.33	Marius Probst	GER	20.8.95				9 Feb
1:47.43	Jan Kubista	CZE	23.9.90				11 Feb
1:47.43	Kevin López	ESP	12.6.90				21 Feb
1:47.47	Patrick Joseph	USA	7.9.95				24 Feb
1:47.48	Mark English	IRL	18.3.93				21 Feb

Drugs disqualification

Mark	Name	Nat	Born	Pos	Venue	Date
1:45.20	Nicholas Kipkoech ¶	KEN	22.10.92	(2)	Tomblaine	27 Jun
1:46.27	Kipyegon Bett ¶	KEN	2.1.98	(3)	Chorzów	8 Jun

Mark	Name		Nat	Born	Pos	Meet	Venue	Date

JUNIORS

See main list for top 5 juniors. 10 performances by 4 men to 1:46.35. Additional marks and further juniors:

Mark	Name		Nat	Born	Pos	Meet	Venue	Date
1:45.63	Bodena			Dubai	11 May	1:46.2A	1	NC	Addis Ababa	19 Apr
1:46.1A	Lemi			Addis Ababa	3 Feb					
1:46.16A	Lekuta	4	CGT	Nairobi	17 Feb	1:46.35	1	WJ	Tampere	15 Jul
1:46.21A		1	KEN-jT	Nairobi	17 Jun					
1:46.59	Norbert	Kolombos	KEN	.00	2		Praha	7 Jun
1:46.7A	Ahmed	Hasen	ETH-Y	8.6.01	3	NC	Addis Ababa	19 Apr
1:46.8A	Addisu	Girma	ETH	10.12.99	3		Addis Ababa	3 Feb
1:46.84	Elliott	Crestan	BEL	22.2.99	2s2	WJ	Tampere	14 Jul
1:46.92	Beant	Singh (10)	IND	10.1.99	4	I-State	Guwahati	27 Jun
1:47.1A	Tasew	Yada	ETH-Y	3.10.01	4	NC	Addis Ababa	19 Apr
1:47.20A	George	Manangoi	KEN	29.11.00	1		Pretoria	8 Mar
1:47.2A	Omer	Amano	ETH	3.5.99	1		Assela	9 Dec
1:47.35	Simone	Barontini	ITA	5.1.99	3s2	WJ	Tampere	14 Jul
1:47.36	Max	Burgin	GBR-Y	20.5.02	1	EY	Györ	8 Jul
1:47.36	Oussama	Cherad	ALG	6.3.00	4s2	WJ	Tampere	14 Jul
1:47.51	Sven	Cepus	CRO	9.12.99	1	BalkC	Stara Zagora	21 Jul
1:47.51	Arlon Tatsunami	Clay	JPN-Y	25.3.02	1		Niigata	14 Oct
1:47.56	Eduardo	Romero	ESP	27.1.99	10		Huelva	10 Jun
1:47.73	Markhim	Lonsdale (20)	GBR	9.1.99	5s2	WJ	Tampere	14 Jul
1:47.67i	Josh	Huey	USA	1.11.99	2		Boston (A)	25 Feb

1000 METRES

Mark	Name		Nat	Born	Pos	Meet	Venue	Date
2:14.88	Ferguson	Cheruiyot	KEN	30.11.89	1	DL	Stockholm	10 Jun
2:16.08	Ayanleh	Souleiman	DJI	3.12.92	1	Gyulai	Székesfehérvár	2 Jul
2:16.09	Sadik	Mikhou	BRN	25.7.90	2	DL	Stockholm	10 Jun
2:16.27	Jake	Wightman	GBR	11.7.94	3	DL	Stockholm	10 Jun
2:16.27	Jonathan	Kitilit	KEN	24.4.94	2	Gyulai	Székesfehérvár	2 Jul
2:16.58	Adam	Kszczot	POL	2.9.89	4	DL	Stockholm	10 Jun
2:16.59	Yassine	Hathat	ALG	30.7.91	3	Gyulai	Székesfehérvár	2 Jul
2:16.79	Jackson	Kivuva	KEN	11.8.88	4	Gyulai	Székesfehérvár	2 Jul
2:16.85	Antoine	Gakémé	BDI	24.12.91	5	DL	Stockholm	10 Jun
2:16.89	Cornelius	Tuwei	KEN	24.5.93	5	Gyulai	Székesfehérvár	2 Jul
2:17.13	Fouad	El Kaam	MAR	27.5.88	15 Aug	2:18.23	Baptiste	Mischler	FRA	23.11.97	20 Jul
2:17.18	Andrew	Osagie	GBR	19.2.88	10 Jun	2:18.30	Andreas	Kramer	SWE	13.4.97	10 Jun
2:17.19	Tamás	Kazi	HUN	16.5.85	2 Jul	2:18.40	Johan	Rogestedt	SWE	27.1.93	2 Jul
2:17.24	Marcin	Lewandowski	POL	13.6.87	15 Aug	2:18.67	Thiago	André	BRA	4.8.95	20 Jul
2:17.40	Alfred	Kipketer	KEN	26.12.96	10 Jun	2:18.87	Tolesa	Bodena	ETH-J	18.2.00	10 Jun
2:17.42	Solomon	Lekuta	KEN-J	3.10.99	20 Jul	2:18.88	Mateusz	Borkowski	POL	2.4.97	15 Aug
2:18.07	George	Manangoi	KEN-J	29.11.00	20 Jul	2:18.92	Ismael	Debjani	BEL	25.9.90	29 Jul
2:18.09	Michal	Rozmys	POL	13.3.95	15 Aug	Indoors					
						2:18.94i	Thomas	Kupers	NED	4.10.91	27 Jan

Drugs disqualification

| 2:16.17 | Nicholas | Kipkoech ¶ | KEN | 22.10.92 | (2) | Gyulai | Székesfehérvár | 2 Jul |
| 2:16.98 | Kipyegon | Bett ¶ | KEN | 2.1.98 | (6) | DL | Stockholm | 10 Jun |

JUNIORS

2:17.42	Solomon	Lekuta	KEN	3.10.99	1	Herc	Monaco	20 Jul
2:18.07	George	Manangoi	KEN	29.11.00	2	Herc	Monaco	20 Jul
2:18.87	Tolesa	Bodena	ETH	18.2.00	9	DL	Stockholm	10 Jun

1500 METRES

3:28.41	Timothy	Cheruiyot	KEN	20.11.95	1	Herc	Monaco	20 Jul
3:29.64	Elijah	Manangoi	KEN	5.1.93	2	Herc	Monaco	20 Jul
3:29.71		Cheruiyot			1	DL	Paris (C)	30 Jun
3:30.01	Filip	Ingebrigtsen	NOR	20.4.93	3	Herc	Monaco	20 Jul
3:30.27		Cheruiyot			1	WK	Zürich	30 Aug
3:31.16		Manangoi			2	WK	Zürich	30 Aug
3:31.18	Jakob	Ingebrigtsen	NOR-J	19.9.00	4	Herc	Monaco	20 Jul
3:31.19	Ayanleh	Souleiman	DJI	3.12.92	5	Herc	Monaco	20 Jul
3:31.22		Cheruiyot			1	G Gala	Roma	31 May
3:31.24		Souleiman			3	WK	Zürich	30 Aug
3:31.48		Cheruiyot			1	DL	Shanghai	12 May
3:31.59	Abdelaati	Iguider	MAR	25.3.87	4	WK	Zürich	30 Aug
3:31.62	Brahim	Kaazouzi	MAR	15.6.90	6	Herc	Monaco	20 Jul
3:31.63	Samuel	Tefera	ETH-J	23.10.99	2	DL	Shanghai	12 May
3:31.77		Souleiman			2	DL	Paris (C)	30 Jun
3:31.77	Matthew	Centrowitz	USA	18.10.89	7	Herc	Monaco	20 Jul
3:31.90	Aman	Wote (10)	ETH	18.4.84	8	Herc	Monaco	20 Jul
3:32.11	Chris	O'Hare	GBR	23.11.90	9	Herc	Monaco	20 Jul
3:32.37		Cheruiyot			1	ISTAF	Berlin	2 Sep

MEN 2018

Mark	Name		Nat	Born	Pos	Meet	Venue	Date	
3:32.49	Jakub	Holusa	CZE	20.2.88	10	Herc	Monaco	20	Jul
3:32.52		Manangoi			1	Hanz	Zagreb	4	Sep
3:32.59	Yomif	Kejelcha	ETH	1.8.97	2	Hanz	Zagreb	4	Sep
3:32.61	Charles	Simotwo	KEN	6.5.95	3	DL	Paris (C)	30	Jun
3:32.72		Iguider			3	DL	Shanghai	12	May
3:32.77		Simotwo			11	Herc	Monaco	20	Jul
3:32.81		Wote			4	DL	Paris (C)	30	Jun
3:32.85		Holusa			5	DL	Paris (C)	30	Jun
3:32.87		F Ingebrigtsen			6	DL	Paris (C)	30	Jun
3:33.21	Ferguson	Cheruiyot	KEN	30.11.89	2	ISTAF	Berlin	2	Sep
3:33.22		Kaazouzi			1	DL	Rabat	13	Jul
	(30/15)								
3:33.96	Jake	Wightman	GBR	11.7.94	12	Herc	Monaco	20	Jul
3:34.20	Charlie Da'Vall	Grice	GBR	7.11.93	5	DL	Rabat	13	Jul
3:34.27	Bethwel	Birgen	KEN	6.8.88	7	DL	Paris (C)	30	Jun
3:34.33	Justus	Soget	KEN-J	22.10.99	5	DL	Shanghai	12	May
3:34.38	Ryan	Gregson	AUS	26.4.90	6	DL	Rabat	13	Jul
	(20)								
3:34.40	Ismael	Debjani	BEL	25.9.90	3	ISTAF	Berlin	2	Sep
3:34.55	Sadik	Mikhou	BRN	25.7.90	8	DL	Paris (C)	30	Jun
3:34.82	Stewart	McSweyn	AUS	1.6.95	1		Tübingen	16	Jun
3:35.01	Josh	Kerr	GBR	8.10.97	1		Azusa	20	Apr
3:35.06	Marcin	Lewandowski	POL	13.6.87	9	DL	Rabat	13	Jul
3:35.07	Taresa	Tolosa	ETH	15.6.98	1	DL	Doha	4	May
3:35.25	Nick	Willis	NZL	25.4.83	7	ISTAF	Berlin	2	Sep
3:35.33	Ronald	Musagala	UGA	16.12.92	1		Tomblaine	27	Jun
3:35.35	Hicham	Oueladha	MAR	31.1.95	11	DL	Rabat	13	Jul
3:35.40	Thiago	André	BRA	4.8.95	7	DL	Shanghai	12	May
	(30)								
3:35.53	George	Manangoi	KEN-J	30.11.00	2	DL	Doha	1	May
3:35.61	Henrik	Ingebrigtsen	NOR	24.2.91	4	DL	London (OS)	22	Jul
3:35.72	Cornelius	Tuwei	KEN	24.5.93	8	ISTAF	Berlin	2	Sep
3:35.74	Youssouf Hiss	Bachir	DJI	.87	5	DL	London (OS)	22	Jul
3:35.81	Brimin	Kiprotich	KEN-J	20.8.99	2		Tomblaine	27	Jun
3:35.83A	Kumari	Taki	KEN-J	6.5.99	3	CGT	Nairobi	17	Feb
3:35.85	Vladimir	Nikitin	RUS	5.8.92	1	NC	Kazan	22	Jul
3:35.90	Drew	Hunter	USA	5.9.97	7	DL	London (OS)	22	Jul
3:35.98	Neil	Gourley	GBR	7.2.95	8	DL	London (OS)	22	Jul
3:36.03	Homiyu	Tesfaye	GER	23.6.93	3		Tomblaine	27	Jun
	(40)								
3:36.05	Robby	Andrews	USA	29.3.91	2	Bisl	Oslo	7	Jun
3:36.07	Justyn	Knight	CAN	19.7.96	2		Azusa	20	Apr
3:36.12	Vincent	Kibet	KEN	6.5.91	9	DL	London (OS)	22	Jul
3:36.13	Rabie	Doukkana	MAR	6.12.87	1		Ninove	28	Jul
3:36.28	Younès	Essalhi	MAR	20.2.93	12	DL	Rabat	13	Jul
3:36.30	Jordan	Williamsz	AUS	21.8.92	2		Padova	2	Sep
3:36.33	Robert	Domanic	USA	10.3.95	3		Azusa	20	Apr
3:36.33	Michael	Kibet	KEN-J	3.9.99	4		Tomblaine	27	Jun
3:36.41	Eric	Avila	USA	3.10.89	1rA	NA	Heusden-Zolder	21	Jul
3:36.49	Melese	Nberet	ETH-Y	29.1.01	2		Montreuil	19	Jun
	(50)								
3:36.51	Isaac	Kimeli	BEL	9.3.94	2		Marseille	16	Jun
3:36.51	Kalle	Berglund	SWE	11.3.96	10	Hanz	Zagreb	4	Sep
3:36.54	Mohad Abdikadar	Sheikh Ali	ITA	12.6.93	10	G Gala	Roma	31	May
3:36.59	James	West	GBR	30.1.96	10	DL	London (OS)	22	Jul
3:36.60	Fouad	El Kaam	MAR	27.5.88	3		Ninove	28	Jul
3:36.61	Sean	McGorty	USA	8.3.95	1		Kortrijk	14	Jul
3:36.81	Izaic	Yorks	USA	17.4.94	12	DL	London (OS)	22	Jul
3:36.84	Sam	Prakel	USA	29.10.94	4		Azusa	20	Apr
3:36.88	Simon	Denissel	FRA	22.5.90	12	DL	Paris (C)	30	Jun
3:36.89	Craig	Engels	USA	1.5.94	2rA	NA	Heusden-Zolder	21	Jul
	(60)								
3:36.90	Jake	Heyward	GBR-J	26.4.99	13	DL	London (OS)	22	Jul
3:36.93	Hicham	Akankam	MAR	4.4.98	2		Tübingen	16	Jun
3:36.95	John	Gregorek	USA	7.12.91	1		Los Angeles (ER)	17	May
3:36.98A	Jeremiah	Kiptanui	KEN-J	.00	3	NC	Nairobi	23	Jul
3:37.0A	Kebede	Endale	ETH-J	22.6.00	1		Assela	9	Dec
3:37.02	Mohamed Ismail	Ibrahim	DJI	1.7.97	2		Barcelona	11	Jul
3:37.06	Patrick	Casey	USA	23.5.90	5	Bisl	Oslo	7	Jun
3:37.07	Marius	Probst	GER	20.8.95	1		Oordegem	26	May
3:37.08	Michal	Rozmys	POL	13.3.95	3		Padova	2	Sep

Mark	Name		Nat	Born	Pos	Meet	Venue	Date
3:37.11	Peter	Callahan	BEL	1.6.91	5		Azusa	20 Apr
	(70)							
3:37.11	Colby	Alexander	USA	13.6.91	4		Lignano Sabbiadoro	11 Jul
3:37.16	Luke	Mathews	AUS	21.6.95	1		Brisbane (N)	28 Mar
3:37.17	Baptiste	Mischler	FRA	23.11.97	13	DL	Paris (C)	30 Jun
3:37.21	Charles	Philibert-Thiboutot	CAN	31.12.90	3rA	NA	Heusden-Zolder	21 Jul
3:37.23	Hillary	Ngetich	KEN	15.9.95	3		Rehlingen	20 May
3:37.35	David	Ribich	USA	27.12.95	6		Azusa	20 Apr
3:37.35	Abdessalem	Ayouni	TUN	16.5.94	2	Med G	Tarragona	29 Jun
3:37.36	Alexandre	Saddedine	FRA	29.9.94	14	DL	Paris (C)	30 Jun
3:37.37A	Laban	Kiplimo	KEN		4	NC	Nairobi	23 Jun
3:37.4A	Tadesse	Lemi	ETH-J	20.1.99	2		Assela	9 Dec
	(80)							
3:37.49	Kyle	Merber	USA	19.11.90	2		Brisbane (N)	28 Mar
3:37.52	Jordan	Gusman	AUS	30.1.94	2		Los Angeles (ER)	17 May
3:37.52	Vincent	Letting	KEN	16.6.93	3		Tübingen	16 Jun
3:37.56	Alexis	Miellet	FRA	5.5.95	4		Montreuil	19 Jun
3:37.74	Timo	Benitz	GER	24.12.91	4		Marseille	16 Jun
3:37.79	Elzan	Bibic	SRB-J	8.1.99	13	Hanz	Zagreb	4 Sep
3:37.81	Boaz	Kiprugut	KEN	18.5.98	4		Rehlingen	20 May
3:37.83	Collins	Cheboi	KEN	25.9.87	8	DL	Doha	4 May
3:37.84	Oliver	Hoare	AUS	29.1.97	8		Azusa	20 Apr
3:37.86	Jinson	Johnson	IND	15.3.91	5	CG	Gold Coast	14 Apr
	(90)							
3:37.91	Mekonnen	Gebremedhin	ETH	11.10.88	4		Sollentuna	28 Jun
3:38.03	Rob	Napolitano	USA	3.11.94	4		Ninove	28 Jul
3:38.05	João	Bussotti Neves	ITA	10.5.93	4		Padova	2 Sep
3:38.18	Llorenç	Sales	ESP	14.7.88	1		Barcelona (S)	1 Jul
3:38.18	Sam	Parsons	USA	18.6.94	5		Lignano Sabbiadoro	11 Jul
3:38.19	Hamish	Carson	NZL	1.11.88	5		Padova	2 Sep
3:38.22	Yemaneberhan	Crippa	ITA	15.10.96	11	G Gala	Roma	31 May
3:38.23	Carlos Martín	Díaz	CHI	9.7.93	2		Oordegem	26 May
3:38.24	Adel	Mechaal	ESP	5.12.90	6		Barcelona (S)	11 Jul
3:38.28	Carlos	Villarreal	MEX	10.5.97	1rB		Azusa	20 Apr
	(100)							
3:38.28A	Lawi	Kosgei	KEN-J	14.1.99	5	NC	Nairobi	23 Jun
3:38.28	Pieter-Jan	Hannes	BEL	30.10.92	6rA	NA	Heusden-Zolder	21 Jul

Mark	Name		Nat	Born	Pos		Mark	Name		Nat	Born	Pos
3:38.29	Tarik	Moukrime	BEL	3.3.92	26 May		3:39.42	Ayoub	Sniba	MAR	5.4.97	26 May
3:38.32	Hassan	Mead	USA	28.6.89	17 May		3:39.45	Daniel	Herrera	MEX	29.11.92	17 May
3:38.44	Johan	Rogestedt	SWE	27.1.93	28 Jun		3:39.50	Fernando Daniel	Martínez	MEX	27.2.90	20 Apr
3:38.48	Sammy	Kirongo	KEN	4.2.94	14 Jul		3:39.51	William	Paulson	GBR	17.11.94	14 May
3:38.58	Andrew	Bayer	USA	3.2.90	22 Jul		3:39.51	Charel	Grethen	LUX	22.6.92	4 Jun
3:38.63	Jesús	Gómez	ESP	24.4.91	26 May		3:39.55	Volodymyr	Kyts	UKR	15.1.87	8 Jul
3:38.63	Jonathan	Sawe	KEN	22.5.95	11 Jul		3:39.56	Reed	Brown	USA	6.8.98	20 Apr
3:38.64	Ferdinand Kvan	Edman	NOR	12.2.93	21 Jul		3:39.56	Amine	Khadiri	CYP	20.11.88	8 Jun
3:38.65	Shoma	Funatsu	JPN	25.9.97	20 Apr		3:39.60	Vincent	Ciattei	USA	21.1.95	15 Jun
3:38.67	Graham	Crawford	USA	29.12.92	17 May		3:39.6A	Birhanu	Sorsa	ETH-J	11.4.00	26 May
3:38.68	Ilham Tanui	Özbilen	TUR	5.3.90	20 May		3:39.6A	Omer	Amano	ETH-J	3.5.99	9 Dec
3:38.69	Jeff	Riseley	AUS	11.11.86	17 Mar		3:39.62	Ryan	Hill	USA	31.1.90	20 Apr
3:38.71	Pieter	Claus	BEL	1.3.93	26 May		3:39.64	Amos	Bartelsmayer	USA	25.7.94	14 Jul
3:38.73	Jan	Hochstrasser	SUI	23.10.88	1 Jan		3:39.65	Mohammed Ayoub	Tiouali	BRN	26.5.91	20 May
3:38.81	Sam	McEntee	AUS	3.2.92	14 May		3:39.68	David	Timlin	USA	10.6.94	14 May
3:38.90	James	Hansen	AUS	27.11.93	17 Mar		3:39.72	Amon	Kemboi	KEN	16.1.87	11 May
3:38.93 +	Clayton	Murphy	USA	26.2.95	26 May		3:39.73	Martin	Casse	FRA	23.6.90	26 May
3:38.95	Salim	Keddar	ALG	23.11.93	19 Jun		3:39.75	Elmar	Engholm	SWE	2.10.92	21 Jul
3:39.01	Simas	Bertasius	LTU	31.10.93	29 Jun		3:39.76	Waleed	Suliman	USA	22.9.98	20 Apr
3:39.05	Samir	Dahmani	FRA	31.3.94	30 Jun		3:39.77	Gonzalo	García	ESP	26.1.95	27 Jun
3:39.07	Blake	Haney	USA	29.3.96	17 May		3:39.81	Ford	Palmer	USA	6.10.90	13 Jul
3:39.09	David	Palacio	ESP	8.6.88	7 Jul		3:39.82	Mick	Stanovsek	AUS	16.1.97	20 Apr
3:39.11	Robin	Hendrix	BEL	14.1.95	28 Jul		3:39.85	Takieddine	Hedeilli	ALG	6.6.96	17 May
3:39.14	Morgan	McDonald	AUS	23.4.96	20 Jan		3:39.86	Jack	Bruce	AUS	31.8.94	20 Apr
3:39.17	Alfredo	Santana	PUR	8.4.91	14 May		3:39.96	Brannon	Kidder	USA	18.11.93	17 May
3:39.17	Jerry	Motsau	RSA	12.3.90	26 May		3:39.97A	Evans	Kipchumba	KEN	.94	17 Feb
3:39.2A	Nibret	Melak	ETH-J	9.10.99	22 Apr		3:40.00	Sam	Worley	USA	10.11.98	20 Apr
3:39.20	Ali	Hamdi	BEL	2.11.89	26 May		3:40.00	Marvin	Heinrich	GER	29.1.97	8 Jun
3:39.22	Tamás	Kazi	HUN	16.5.85	28 Jun		3:40.0	Valentin	Smirnov	RUS	13.2.86	30 Jun
3:39.27	Quentin	Tison	FRA	16.4.96	27 Jun		3:40.03	Marc	Reuther	GER	23.6.96	2 Sep
3:39.30	Djilali	Bedrani	FRA	1.10.93	16 Jun		3:40.04	Garrett	O'Toole	USA	22.3.96	14 May
3:39.31	Ossama	Meslek	ITA	8.1.97	2 Sep		3:40.06	Richard	Douma	NED	17.4.93	14 Jul
3:39.36	Mohamed	Moustaoui	MAR	2.4.85	20 May		3:40.07	Mohamed-Amine	El Bouajaji	FRA	26.7.97	26 May
3:39.37	Robbie	Fitzgibbon	GBR	23.3.96	16 Jun		3:40.10	Corey	Bellmore	CAN	1.12.94	16 Jun
3:39.40	Joshua	Johnson	AUS	6.3.92	17 Mar		3:40.1	Sergey	Dubrovskiy	RUS	20.1.95	30 Jun
3:39.40	Adrián	Ben	ESP	4.8.98	26 Jun		3:40.11	Matthew	Ramsden	AUS	23.7.97	28 Jul
3:39.40 +	Lopez	Lomong	USA	1.1.85	3 Aug		3:40.12	Rorey	Hunter	AUS	2.2.93	18 Feb
3:39.42	Julian	Oakley	NZL	23.6.93	14 May		3:40.14	Jamal	Al-Hayrani	QAT	26.5.93	8 Jun

Mark	Name		Nat	Born	Pos	Meet	Venue	Date
3:40.14	Andréas	Dimitrákis	GRE	8.9.90	8	Jun		
3:40.16	Paul	Chelimo	USA	27.10.90	3	May		
3:40.17 +	Ben	Blankenship	USA	15.12.88	26	May		
3:40.23	Charlie	Marquardt	USA	9.7.94	14	May		
3:40.23	Sampson	Laari	GHA	3.3.93	2	Jun		
3:40.24	Christopher	Sandoval	MEX	29.10.91	20	Apr		
3:40.25	Thomas	Riva	CAN	31.1.02	27	Jun		
3:40.28	Eric	Jenkins	USA	24.11.91	3	May		
3:40.30	Welde	Tufa	ETH-J	29.3.99	1	Jun		
3:40.30	Mike	Foppen	NED	29.11.96	21	Jul		

Mark	Name		Nat	Born	Pos	Meet	Venue	Date
3:40.31	Willie	Fink	USA	7.3.94	15	Jun		
3:40.31	Valentijn	Weinans	NED	29.12.95	16	Jun		
3:40.42	Michael	Wilsmore	GBR	8.6.85	21	Jul		
3:40.44A	Ryan	Mphahlele	RSA	20.6.98	27	Mar		
3:40.44	Abderrahmane	Anou	ALG	29.1.91	26	May		
3:40.46	Chakib	Lachgar	MAR	21.3.89	26	May		
3:40.46	Jimmy	Gressier	FRA	4.5.97	10	Jun		
3:40.49A	Nkosinathi	Sibiya	RSA	1.1.94	27	Mar		
3:40.49	Alex	Rogers	USA	26.6.97	20	Apr		
3:40.49	Ryoji (198)	Tatezawa	JPN	16.5.97	20	May		

Indoors

Mark	Name		Nat	Born	Pos	Meet	Venue	Date
3:33.76+	Edward	Cheserek	KEN	2.2.94	1		Boston (A)	9 Feb
3:39.17+	Brannon	Kidder	USA	18.11.93	10	Feb		
3:39.19+	Ben	Blankenship	USA	15.12.89	3	Feb		
3:39.27	Valentin	Smirnov	RUS	13.2.86	14	Feb		

Mark	Name		Nat	Born	Pos	Meet	Venue	Date
3:39.45	Marc	Alcalá	ESP	7.11.94	13	Feb		
3:39.98	Filip	Sasínek	CZE	8.1.96	15	Feb		
3:40.42	Grzegorz	Kalinowski	POL	22.9.90	15	Feb		

JUNIORS

See main lists for top 13 juniors. 14 performances (inc. 1 indoors) by 6 men to 3:36.1. Additional marks & further juniors:

J Ingebrigtsen	3:36.06	3	Bisl	Oslo			7 Jun		
Tefera	3:34.84	3	GGala	Roma			31 May	3:36.1A	1	NC	Addis Ababa	22 Apr
	3:35.39+	2	in 1M	Eigene			26 May	3:36.05i	1		Vel-de-Reuil	27 Jan
Soget	3:35.28	1		Padova			2 Sep	3:35.71	3	DL	Doha	4 May
	3:35.56	3	DL	London (OS)			22 Jul		

3:39.2A	Nibret	Melak	ETH	9.10.99	3	NC	Addis Ababa	22 Apr
3:39.6A	Birhanu	Sorsa	ETH	11.4.00	1		Assela	26 May
3:39.6A	Omer	Amano	ETH	3.5.99	3		Assela	9 Dec
3:40.30	Welde	Tufa	ETH	29.3.99	7		Montbéliard	1 Jun
3:40.68	Weretew	Eshete	ETH	.99	5		Dessau	8 Jun
3:41.04	Samuel	Abate	ETH	,99	4		Djibouti	30 Mar
3:41.21	Luis	Grijalva (20)	GUA	10.4.99	10rB		Azusa	20 Apr

1 MILE

Mark	Name		Nat	Born	Pos	Meet	Venue	Date
3:49.87	Timothy	Cheruiyot	KEN	20.11.95	1	Pre	Eugene	26 May
3:51.26	Samuel	Tefera	ETH-J	23.10.99	2	Pre	Eugene	26 May
3:52.18	Elijah	Manangoi	KEN	5.1.93	3	Pre	Eugene	26 May
3:52.28	Jakob	Ingebrigtsen	NOR-J	19.9.00	4	Pre	Eugene	26 May
3:53.40	Clayton	Murphy	USA	26.2.95	5	Pre	Eugene	26 May
3:53.61	Matthew	Centrowitz	USA	18.10.89	6	Pre	Eugene	26 May
3:53.86	Lopez	Lomong	USA	1.1.85	1		Raleigh	3 Aug
3:54.53	John	Gregorek	USA	7.12.91	2		Raleigh	3 Aug
3:54.60	Bethwel	Birgen	KEN	6.8.88	7	Pre	Eugene	26 May
3:54.60	Stewart (10)	McSweyn	AUS	1.6.95	1	DL	Birmingham	18 Aug
3:54.64	Sam	Prakel	USA	29.10.94	3		Raleigh	3 Aug
3:54.66	Patrick	Casey	USA	23.5.90	4		Raleigh	3 Aug
3:54.88	Ben	Blankenship	USA	15.12.88	5		Raleigh	3 Aug
3:55.10	Ryan	Gregson	AUS	26.4.90	2	DL	Birmingham	18 Aug
3:55.12	Craig	Engels	USA	1.5.94	6		Raleigh	3 Aug
3:55.21	Sean	McGorty	USA	8.3.95	7		Raleigh	3 Aug
3:55.43	Eric	Avila	USA	3.10.89	1		Memphis	25 Aug
3:55.48	Ryan	Hill	USA	31.1.90	2		Memphis	25 Aug
3:55.53	Chris	O'Hare	GBR	23.11.90	1		Bay Shore	5 Sep
3:55.81	Colby (12)	Alexander	USA	13.6.91	1		West Long Branch	31 Jul
3:55.87	Ayanleh	Souleiman	DJI	3.12.92	8	Pre	Eugene	26 May
3:55.91	Hassan	Mead	USA	28.6.89	8		Raleigh	3 Aug
3:55.96	Paul	Chelimo	USA	27.10.90	3	DL	Birmingham	18 Aug
3:55.97	Charlie	Marquardt	USA	9.7.94	9		Raleigh	3 Aug

3:56.02	Tripp	Hurt	USA	30.10.92	25 Aug		3:56.97	Charlie Da'Vall	Grice	GBR	7.11.93	18 Aug
3:56.03	Thiago	André	BRA	4.8.95	26 May		3:57.02	Luke	Mathews	AUS	21.6.95	26 May
3:56.17	Vincent	Kibet	KEN	6.5.91	18 Aug		3:57.05	Sam	McEntee	AUS	3.2.92	16 Jul
3:56.21	Cristian	Soratos	USA	26.9.92	14 Jul		3:57.06	Hamish	Carson	NZL	1.11.88	16 Jul
3:56.23	Riley	Masters	USA	5.4.90	25 Aug		3:57.07	Jacob	Thomson	USA	29.11.94	3 Aug
3:56.42	Graham	Crawford	USA	29.12.92	25 Aug		3:57.10	Sadik	Mikhou	BRN	25.7.90	7 Jun
3:56.49	Aman	Wote	ETH	18.4.84	26 May		3:57.11	Neil	Gourley	GBR	7.2.95	18 Aug
3:56.62	Charles Philibert-Thiboutot		CAN	31.12.90	5 Sep		3:57.33	Ismael	Debjani	BEL	25.9.90	18 Aug
3:56.66	Robert	Domanic	USA	10.3.95	3 Aug		3:57.34	John	Travers	IRL	16.3.91	19 Jul
3:56.72	Drew	Hunter	USA	5.9.97	19 May		3:57.35	Leonel	Manzano	USA	12.9.84	7 Jun
3:56.74	Rabie	Doukkana	MAR	6.12.87	12 Jul		3:57.42	Corey	Bellmore	CAN	1.12.94	16 Jul
3:56.77	Nick	Willis	NZL	25.4.83	18 Aug		3:57.44	Julian	Oakley	NZL	23.6.93	9 Aug
3:56.86	Drew	Piazza	USA	28.1.95	7 Jun		3:57.48	Rob	Napolitano	USA	3.11.94	31 Jul
3:56.86	Henry	Wynne	USA	18.4.95	19 Jul		3:57.61	Daniel	Herrera	MEX	29.11.92	25 Aug
3:56.90	Mick	Stanovsek	USA	16.1.97	19 Jul		3:57.69	David	Timlin	USA	10.6.92	7 Jun
3:56.92	Jordan	Williamsz	AUS	21.8.92	18 Aug		3:57.69	Willie	Fink	USA	7.3.94	14 Jul

Mark	Name		Nat	Born		Pos	Meet	Venue	Date	
3:57.74	Kyle	Merber	USA	19.11.90	13 Apr	3:57.92	Fernando Daniel Martínez	MEX	27.2.90	13 Apr
3:57.75	Ben	Flanagan	CAN	11.1.95	5 Sep	3:57.92	Taresa	Tolosa	ETH 15.6.98	7 Jun
3:57.83	Ben	True	USA	29.12.85	16 Jul	3:57.97	Filip	Ingebrigtsen	NOR 20.4.93	7 Jun
						(62)				

Indoors

Mark	Name		Nat	Born	Pos	Meet	Venue	Date
3:49.44	Edward	Cheserek	KEN	2.2.94	1		Boston (A)	9 Feb
3:53.40	Izaic	Yorks	USA	17.4.94	1		Boston (A)	25 Feb
3:53.93	Craig	Engels	USA	1.5.94	1		Boston (A)	10 Feb
3:54.14	Chris	O'Hare	GBR	23.11.90	1	Millrose	New York (Arm)	3 Feb
3:54.72	Josh	Kerr	GBR	8.10.97	2	Millrose	New York (Arm)	3 Feb
3:54.77	Ben	Blankenship	USA	15.12.88	3	Millrose	New York (Arm)	3 Feb
3:55.10	Julian	Oakley	NZL	23.6.93	2		Boston (A)	10 Feb
3:55.23	Henry	Wynne	USA	18.4.95	2		Boston (A)	25 Feb
3:55.52	Shadrack	Kipchirchir	USA	22.2.89	1		Boston (A)	27 Jan
3:55.77	Peter	Callahan	BEL	1.6.91	3		Boston (A)	25 Feb
3:55.82	Justyn	Knight	CAN	19.7.96	2		Boston (A)	27 Jan

Mark	Name		Nat	Born		Pos				
3:56.06	Valentin	Smirnov	RUS	13.2.86	4 Feb	3:57.23	Reed	Brown	USA	6.8.98 10 Feb
3:56.06	Brannon	Kidder	USA	18.11.93	25 Feb	3:57.43	Ryoji	Tatezawa	JPN	16.5.97 25 Feb
3:56.44	Vladimir	Nikitin	RUS	5.8.92	4 Feb	3:57.53	Amos	Bartelsmayer	USA	25.7.94 10 Feb
3:56.47	Charlie Da'Vall	Grice	GBR	7.11.93	3 Feb	3:57.64	Carlos	Villarreal	MEX	10.5.97 10 Feb
3:56.95	Yomif	Kejelcha	ETH	1.8.97	27 Jan	3:57.86	Kirubel	Erassa	USA	17.6.93 27 Jan
3:57.20	Corey	Bellmore	CAN	1.12.94	27 Jan					

JUNIORS

See main lists for top 2 juniors. 2 performances by 2 men to 3:56.0. Further juniors:

Mark	Name		Nat	Born	Pos	Meet	Venue	Date
3:59.20	Kumari	Taki	KEN	6.5.99	10	Bisl	Oslo	7 Jun
3:59.43	Brimin	Kiprotich	KEN	20.8.99	4		Cambridge, MA	19 May
3:59.29i	Cooper	Teare	USA	18.8.99	4rB		New York (Arm)	27 Jan

3000 METRES

Mark	Name		Nat	Born	Pos	Meet	Venue	Date
7:28.00	Yomif	Kejelcha	ETH	1.8.97	1		Göteborg	18 Aug
7:32.93		Kejelcha			1	DL	Rabat	13 Jul
7:34.26	Birhanu	Yemataw	BRN	27.2.96	2	DL	Rabat	13 Jul
7:34.79	Stewart	McSweyn	AUS	1.6.95	3	DL	Rabat	13 Jul
7:34.83	Paul	Chelimo	USA	27.10.90	4	DL	Rabat	13 Jul
7:36.13	Muktar	Edris	ETH	14.1.94	5	DL	Rabat	13 Jul
7:36.49	Hagos	Gebrhiwet	ETH	11.5.94	6	DL	Rabat	13 Jul
7:36.81	Ryan	Hill	USA	31.1.90	7	DL	Rabat	13 Jul
7:37.53	Selemon	Barega	ETH-J	20.1.00	1	GS	Ostrava	13 Jun
7:38.19	Eric	Jenkins	USA	24.11.91	8	DL	Rabat	13 Jul
7:38.25		Yemataw			2	GS	Ostrava	13 Jun
7:38.55	Tilahun	Haile (10)	ETH-J	13.5.99	3	GS	Ostrava	13 Jun
7:38.78	Regasa	Chala	ETH	30.4.97	4	GS	Ostrava	13 Jun
7:39.10	Abadi	Hadis	ETH	6.11.97	5	GS	Ostrava	13 Jun
7:39.42	Soufiyan	Bouqantar	MAR	30.8.93	9	DL	Rabat	13 Jul
	(15/13)							
7:41.04	Thierry	Ndikumwenayo	BDI	26.3.97	6	GS	Ostrava	13 Jun
7:41.86	Ben	True	USA	29.12.85	8	GS	Ostrava	13 Jun
7:42.12	Berihu	Aregawi	ETH-Y	28.2.01	2		Göteborg	18 Aug
7:42.53	Cyrus	Rutto	KEN	21.4.92	10	DL	Rabat	13 Jul
7:42.72	Bethwel	Birgen	KEN	6.8.88	11	DL	Rabat	13 Jul
7:42.72	Henrik	Ingebrigtsen	NOR	24.2.91	1		Bergen (Fana)	22 Aug
7:43.13	James	Kibet	KEN	10.11.88	3		Bellinzona	18 Jul
	(20)							
7:43.20	Younès	Essalhi	MAR	20.2.93	4		Bellinzona	18 Jul
7:43.30	Yemaneberhan	Crippa	ITA	15.10.96	9	GS	Ostrava	13 Jun
7:43.36	Haymanot	Alewe	ETH	11.11.97	10	GS	Ostrava	13 Jun
7:43.98	Davis	Kiplangat	KEN	10.7.98	11	GS	Ostrava	13 Jun
7:44.66	Birhanu	Melesse	ETH-J	12.9.99	12	GS	Ostrava	13 Jun
7:44.78	Ronald	Musagala	UGA	16.12.92	13	GS	Ostrava	13 Jun
7:45.03	Charles	Philibert-Thiboutot	CAN	31.12.90	14	GS	Ostrava	13 Jun
7:45.3+	Stanley	Waithaka	KEN-J	9.4.00	4	in 5000	Bruxelles	31 Aug
7:45.91	Abe	Gashahun	ETH	20.4.98	15	GS	Ostrava	13 Jun
7:46.28	Ryan	Gregson	AUS	26.4.90	16	GS	Ostrava	13 Jun
	(30)							
7:46.9+	Getaneh	Tamire Molla	ETH	10.1.94	8	in 5000	Bruxelles	31 Aug
7:47.3+	Richard	Yator	KEN	6.4.98	9	in 5000	Bruxelles	31 Aug
7:47.58	Dawit	Wolde	ETH	19.5.91	1		Sotteville-lès-Rouen	17 Jul
7:47.59	Leonard	Bett	KEN-J	3.11.00	4		Cambridge, MA	19 May

Mark	Name		Nat	Born	Pos					
7:47.93	Peter	Ndegwa	KEN	11.7.92	17 Jul	7:49.48A	Joshua	Cheptegei	UGA	12.9.96 8 Mar
7:48.08	Rhonex	Kipruto	KEN-J	12.10.99	19 May	7:49.6+	Mohammed	Ahmed	CAN	5.1.91 31 Aug
7:48.55	Douglas	Kipserem	KEN	.87	18 Jul	7:49.9+	Bashir	Abdi	BEL	10.2.89 31 Aug

MEN 2018

Mark	Name		Nat	Born	Pos	Meet	Venue		Date
7:50.35	Julien	Wanders	SUI	18.3.96	18		Liévin		18 Jul
7:50.67	Jairus	Birech	KEN	14.12.92	19				19 May
7:50.83	Michael	Kibet	KEN-J	3.9.99	13				13 May
7:51.09	Antonio	Abadía	ESP	2.7.90	11				11 Jul
7:51.09	Hicham	Akankam	MAR	4.4.98	13				13 Jul
7:51.41	Hassan	Mead	USA	28.6.89	11				11 Jul
7:51.44	Thomas	Curtin	USA	8.8.93					7 Jun
7:51.51	Elzan	Bibic	SRB-J	8.1.99					22 Aug
7:51.55	Mouhcine	Outalha	MAR	15.12.98					13 Jul
7:51.59	Graham	Crawford	USA	29.12.92					11 Jul
7:51.67	Brett	Robinson	AUS	8.5.91					18 Aug
				(51)					

Indoors

Mark	Name		Nat	Born	Pos	Meet	Venue	Date
7:36.64	Selemon	Barega	ETH-J	20.1.00	1		Liévin	13 Feb
7:38.74	Edward	Cheserek	KEN	2.2.94	1		Boston (R)	10 Feb
7:39.09	Justus	Soget	KEN-J	22.10.99	1		Glasgow	25 Feb
7:39.92	Abdelaati	Iguider	MAR	25.3.87	3		Karlsruhe	3 Feb
7:40.12	Davis	Kiplangat	KEN	10.7.98	4		Glasgow	25 Feb
7:40.14	Adel	Mechaal	ESP	5.12.90	4		Karlsruhe	3 Feb
7:40.56	Bethwel	Birgen	KEN	6.8.88	5		Karlsruhe	3 Feb
7:41.39	Sadik	Mikhou	BRN	25.7.90	6		Karlsruhe	3 Feb
7:41.88	Soufiane	El Bakkali	MAR	7.1.96	3		Liévin	13 Feb
7:41.97	Paul	Koech	KEN	.91	4		Liévin	13 Feb
7:42.02	Edwin	Soi	KEN	3.3.86	7		Karlsruhe	3 Feb
7:42.14	Gemechu	Dida	ETH-J	12.9.99	5		Glasgow	25 Feb
7:42.34	Albert	Rop	BRN	17.7.92	5		Liévin	13 Feb
7:42.71	Shadrack	Kipchirchir	USA	22.2.89	1		Boston (A)	26 Jan
7:42.78	Dejen	Gebremeskel	ETH	24.11.89	3		Boston (R)	10 Feb
7:42.82	Vladimir	Nikitin	RUS	5.8.92	1		Yekaterinburg	7 Jan
7:44.58	Mohammed Ayoub	Tiouali	BRN	26.5.91	1		Ostrava	25 Jan
7:44.77	Benjamin	Kigen	KEN	5.7.93	2		Ostrava	25 Jan
7:44.93	Emmanuel	Bor	USA	14.4.88	2		Boston (A)	26 Jan
7:45.86	Justyn	Knight	CAN	19.7.96	2	Millrose	New York (Arm)	3 Feb
7:45.96	Djamal Abdi	Dirieh	DJI	.97	8		Karlsruhe	3 Feb
7:47.19	Woody	Kincaid	USA	21.9.92	4	Millrose	New York (Arm)	3 Feb
7:47.21	Andrew	Butchart	GBR	14.10.91	5	Millrose	New York (Arm)	3 Feb
7:47.22	Hamish	Carson	NZL	1.11.88	6	Millrose	New York (Arm)	3 Feb
7:47.36	Garrett	Heath	USA	3.11.85	7	Millrose	New York (Arm)	3 Feb
7:47.43	Kemoy	Campbell	JAM	14.1.91	8	Millrose	New York (Arm)	3 Feb
7:47.48	Kirubel	Erassa	USA	17.6.93	3		Boston (A)	26 Jan
7:47.54	Andrew	Bayer	USA	3.2.90	9	Millrose	New York (Arm)	3 Feb
7:47.66	Julian	Oakley	NZL	23.6.93	10	Millrose	New York (Arm)	3 Feb
7:48.21	Andy	Trouard	USA	22.4.94				10 Feb
7:48.56	Grant	Fisher	USA	22.4.97				10 Feb
7:48.75	Youssouf Hiss	Bachir	DJI	.87				25 Jan
7:49.01	Clemens	Bleistein	GER	29.9.90				2 Mar
7:49.28	Artyom	Leonenko	RUS	7.4.92				7 Jan
7:49.42	Colby	Gilbert	USA	17.3.95				10 Feb
7:49.78	Cameron	Griffith	AUS	31.8.96				10 Feb
7:49.84	Richard	Ringer	GER	27.2.89				13 Feb
7:49.91	Luis	Vargas	MEX	24.5.93				3 Feb
7:49.92	Jon	Davis	USA	10.10.97				10 Feb
7:50.01	Yegor	Nikolayev	RUS	28.4.88				12 Feb
7:50.10	Cole	Rockhold	USA	11.5.95				10 Feb
7:50.15	Rinas	Akhmadiyev	RUS	25.5.89				12 Feb
7:50.18	Jonathan	Davies	GBR	28.10.94				10 Feb
7:50.65	Yassin	Bouih	ITA	24.11.96				2 Mar
7:50.81	David	Ribich	USA	27.12.95				10 Feb
7:50.85	Kyle	Mau	USA	27.8.96				10 Feb
7:50.90	Yevgeniy	Kunts	RUS	21.4.93				12 Feb
7:50.93	Ben	Saarel	USA	8.3.95				10 Feb
7:51.01	Andrew	Heyes	GBR	22.6.90				25 Feb
7:51.23	James	West	GBR	30.1.96				10 Feb
7:51.32	Riley	Masters	USA	5.4.90				10 Feb
7:51.49	Craig	Nowak	USA	20.4.94				10 Feb
7:51.69	Oliver	Hoare	AUS	21.9.97				10 Feb
7:51.71	Mike	Tate	CAN	1.4.95				10 Feb
7:51.85	Valentin	Smirnov	RUS	13.2.86				7 Jan
7:51.95	Ryuhei	Sakaguchi	JPN	5.4.97				10 Feb
7:51.98	Reid	Buchanan	USA	3.2.93				27 Jan
				(57)				

JUNIORS

See main list for top 6 juniors. 13 performances Inc. 6 indoors) by 9 men to 7:50.0. Further juniors:

Mark	Name		Nat	Born	Pos	Meet	Venue	Date
Barega	7:44.9+				2	in 5000	Bruxelles	31 Aug
	7:48.14i				1h2	WI	Birmingham	2 Mar
Haile	7:42.81				2		Bollinzona	18 Jul
	7:45.34i				3		Ostrava	25 Jan
	7:49.94				1		Marina di Carrara	21 Jul
Melesse	7:47.57i				4		Ostrava	25 Jan
7:48.08	Rhonex	Kipruto	KEN-J	12.10.99	5		Cambridge, MA	19 May
7:50.83	Michael	Kibet	KEN-J	3.9.99	1		Montgeron	13 May
7:51.51	Elzan	Bibic	SRB-J	8.1.99	2		Bergen (Fana)	22 Aug
7:52.33	Gemechu	Dida	ETH	12.9.99	7		Cambridge, MA	19 May
7:53.36+	Jacob	Kiplimo	UGA-J	14.11.00		in 2M	Eugene	26 May
7:53.67	Milkesha	Mengesha	ETH	16.4.00	18	GS	Ostrava	13 Jun
7:54.05	Evans	Keitany	KEN	27.11.99	1		Osaka	20 May
7:55.17	Jake	Heyward	GBR	26.4.99	5		Watford	25 Jul
7:53.66i	Cooper	Teare	USA	18.8.99	10		Seattle	24 Feb
7:57.79i	Albert	Chemutai	UGA	25.11.99	7		Metz	11 Feb

2 MILES

Mark	Name		Nat	Born	Pos	Meet	Venue	Date
8:20.01	Selemon	Barega	ETH-J	20.1.00	1	Pre	Eugene	26 May
8:20.91	Paul	Chelimo	USA	27.10.90	2	Pre	Eugene	26 May
8:21.54	Birhanu	Yemataw	BRN	27.2.96	3	Pre	Eugene	26 May

Mark	Name		Nat	Born	Pos	Meet	Venue	Date
8:22.29	Mohammed	Ahmed	CAN	5.1.91	26 May			
8:22.31	Henrik	Ingebrigtsen	NOR	24.2.91	26 May			
8:22.36	Ryan	Hill	USA	31.1.90	26 May			
8:23.50	Eric	Jenkins	USA	24.11.91	26 May			
8:23.76	Ben	True	USA	29.12.85	26 May			

Mark	Name		Nat	Born	Pos	Meet	Venue	Date
8:23.96	Emmanuel	Bor	USA	14.4.88	26 May			
8:24.09	Hassan	Mead	USA	28.6.89	26 May			
8:25.17	Jacob	Kiplimo	UGA-J	14.11.00	26 May			
8:25.44	Albert	Rop	BRN	17.7.92	26 May			
8:26.11	Muktar	Edris	ETH	14.1.94	26 May			

5000 METRES

Mark	Name		Nat	Born	Pos	Meet	Venue	Date
12:43.02	Selemon	Barega	ETH-J	20.1.00	1	VD	Bruxelles	31 Aug
12:45.82	Hagos	Gebrhiwet	ETH	11.5.94	2	VD	Bruxelles	31 Aug
12:46.79	Yomif	Kejelcha	ETH	1.8.97	3	VD	Bruxelles	31 Aug
12:55.18	Muktar	Edris	ETH	14.1.94	4	VD	Bruxelles	31 Aug
12:56.27	Abadi	Hadis	ETH	6.11.97	5	VD	Bruxelles	31 Aug
12:57.55	Paul	Chelimo	USA	27.10.90	6	VD	Bruxelles	31 Aug
12:59.44	Richard	Yator	KEN	6.4.98	7	VD	Bruxelles	31 Aug
12:59.58	Getaneh	Tamire Molla	ETH	10.1.94	8	VD	Bruxelles	31 Aug
13:01.09	Birhanu	Yemataw	BRN	27.2.96	1	Athl	Lausanne	5 Jul
13:02.67		Barega			2	Athl	Lausanne	5 Jul
13:03.08	Mohammed	Ahmed (10)	CAN	5.1.91	9	VD	Bruxelles	31 Aug
13:03.62		Hadis			3	Athl	Lausanne	5 Jul
13:04.04		Molla			4	Athl	Lausanne	5 Jul
13:04.05		Barega			1	DL	Stockholm	10 Jun
13:04.11	Ben	True	USA	29.12.85	10	VD	Bruxelles	31 Aug
13:04.25		Yemataw			2	DL	Stockholm	10 Jun
13:04.63	Tilahun	Haile	ETH-J	13.5.99	1		Huelva	8 Jun
13:04.91	Bashir	Abdi	BEL	10.2.89	11	VD	Bruxelles	31 Aug
13:04.97		Yator			5	Athl	Lausanne	5 Jul
13:05.23	Stewart	McSweyn	AUS	1.6.95	12	VD	Bruxelles	31 Aug
13:06.24		Edris			6	Athl	Lausanne	5 Jul
13:06.76		Hadis			3	DL	Stockholm	10 Jun
13:06.98	Regasa	Chala	ETH	30.4.97	1rA	NA	Heusden-Zolder	21 Jul
13:07.02		Haile			7	Athl	Lausanne	5 Jul
13:07.27	Nibret	Melak Bogale	ETH-J	9.10.99	2rA	NA	Heusden-Zolder	21 Jul
13:07.59	Aron	Kifle	ERI	20.2.98	8	Athl	Lausanne	5 Jul
13:09.06		Kifle			2		Huelva	8 Jun
13:09.64		Yemataw			1	DL	Shanghai	12 May
13:09.66		Chelimo			2	DL	Shanghai	12 May
13:10.14	Stanley M.	Waithaka	KEN-J	9.4.00	3	DL	Shanghai	12 May
	(30/18)							
13:10.65	Dawit	Wolde	ETH	19.5.91	3rA	NA	Heusden-Zolder	21 Jul
13:10.79	Cyrus	Rutto (20)	KEN	21.4.92	4	DL	Shanghai	12 May
13:10.93	Stephen	Kissa	UGA	1.12.95	9	Athl	Lausanne	5 Jul
13:11.84	Albert	Rop	BRN	17.7.92	1		Montreuil	19 Jun
13:11.86	Japheth	Korir	KEN	30.6.93	4rA	NA	Heusden-Zolder	21 Jul
13:13.36	Biyazen	Alehegn	ETH-J	16.9.99	1		Carquefou	16 Jun
13:13.55	Davis	Kiplangat	KEN	10.7.98	9	DL	Shanghai	12 May
13:13.87	Getnet	Wale	ETH-J	16.7.00	2		Carquefou	16 Jun
13:15.44	Berihu	Aregawi	ETH-Y	28.2.01	2		Rovereto	23 Aug
13:15.59	Rabie	Doukkana	MAR	6.12.87	3		Carquefou	16 Jun
13:15.91	Brett	Robinson	AUS	8.5.91	7rA	NA	Heusden-Zolder	21 Jul
13:16.77	Solomon	Berihu	ETH-J	2.10.99	1rB	NA	Heusden-Zolder	21 Jul
	(30)							
13:16.97	Henrik	Ingebrigtsen	NOR	24.2.91	1	Jordan	Stanford	3 May
13:16.97	Riley	Masters	USA	5.4.90	2	Jordan	Stanford	3 May
13:17.06	Jakob	Ingebrigtsen	NOR-J	19.9.00	1	EC	Berlin	11 Aug
13:17.16	Jonathan	Ndiku	KEN	18.9.91	1		Nobeoka	5 May
13:17.65	Bernard	Kimeli	KEN	10.9.95	2		Nobeoka	5 May
13:17.81	Soufiyan	Bouqantar	MAR	30.8.93	4		Montreuil	19 Jun
13:18.34	Evans	Keitany	KEN-J	27.11.99	3		Nobeoka	5 May
13:18.65	Haymanot	Alewe	ETH	11.11.97	4		Carquefou	16 Jun
13:18.73	James	Wangari	KEN	23.3.94	4		Nobeoka	5 May
13:18.74	Justyn	Knight	CAN	19.7.96	2	Jordan	Stanford	3 May
	(40)							
13:18.83	Yemaneberhan	Crippa	ITA	15.10.96	4	Jordan	Stanford	3 May
13:19.05	Morgan	McDonald	AUS	23.4.96	1	NC	Gold Coast	15 Feb
13:19.14	Mourad	Amdouni	FRA	21.1.88	3	EC	Berlin	11 Aug
13:19.26	Robert	Mwei	KEN	11.4.98	5		Nobeoka	5 May
13:19.51	David	McNeill	AUS	6.10.86	2	NC	Gold Coast	15 Feb
13:19.55	Soufiane	Bouchikhi	BEL	22.3.90	8rA	NA	Heusden-Zolder	21 Jul
13:19.66	Jacob	Kiplimo	UGA-J	14.11.00	6	DL	Stockholm	10 Jun
13:19.74A	Edward	Zakayo	KEN-Y	25.11.01	1	KEN-jT	Nairobi	12 Jun

MEN 2018

Mark	Name		Nat	Born	Pos	Meet	Venue	Date	
13:19.81	Hassan	Mead	USA	28.6.89	9	DL	London (OS)	21	Jul
13:19.86	Ronald	Kwemoi	KEN	19.9.95	1		Yokohama	21	Oct
(50)									
13:20.08	Bethwel	Birgen	KEN	6.8.88	11	DL	London (OS)	21	Jul
13:20.22	John	Maina	KEN	3.8.94	6		Nobeoka	5	May
13:20.28	Shadrack	Kipchirchir	USA	22.2.89	13	DL	London (OS)	21	Jul
13:20.33	Derara	Hurisa	ETH	12.7.97	6		Montreuil	19	Jun
13:20.53	Mahiedine	Mekhissi-Benabbad	FRA	15.3.85	5	Jordan	Stanford	3	May
13:20.66	Emmanuel	Bor	USA	14.4.88	14	DL	London (OS)	21	Jul
13:21.07	Andy	Trouard	USA	22.4.94	6	Jordan	Stanford	3	May
13:21.09	Isaac	Kimeli	BEL	9.3.94	7	Jordan	Stanford	3	May
13:21.41	Eric	Jenkins	USA	24.11.91	1		Portland	10	Jun
13:21.93	Bekele	Shiferaw	ETH	14.10.95	8		Nobeoka	5	May
(60)									
13:21.93	Sean	McGorty	USA	8.3.95	10rA	NA	Heusden-Zolder	21	Jul
13:22.13	Joel	Mwaura	KEN-J	20.1.99	9		Nobeoka	5	May
13:22.38	Abe	Gashahun	ETH	20.4.98	3		Huelva	8	Jun
13:22.48	Richard	Ringer	GER	27.2.89	1		Tübingen	16	Jun
13:22.69	Peter	Langat	KEN	20.10.98	10		Nobeoka	5	May
13:22.89	Mekonnen	Gebremedhin	ETH	11.10.88	2		Tübingen	16	Jun
13:23.01	John	Kariuki	KEN	24.11.97	2		Yokohama	21	Oct
13:23.11	Thomas	Curtin	USA	8.8.93	8	Jordan	Stanford	3	May
13:23.14	Marc	Scott	GBR	21.12.93	5	EC	Berlin	11	Aug
13:23.42	Polat Kemboi	Arikan	TUR	12.12.90	6	EC	Berlin	11	Aug
(70)									
13:23.57	Yevgeniy	Rybakov	RUS	27.2.85	1	NC	Kazan	19	Jul
13:23.73	Kemoy	Campbell	JAM	14.1.91	15	DL	London (OS)	21	Jul
13:23.85	Altobeli	da Silva	BRA	3.12.90	9	Jordan	Stanford	3	May
13:24.09	Lawi	Lalang	KEN	15.6.91	10	Jordan	Stanford	3	May
13:24.18	Antonio	Abadia	ESP	2.7.90	4		Huelva	8	Jun
13:24.27	Evans	Yego	KEN	5.9.95	3		Yokohama	21	Oct
13:24.43	Rinas	Akhmadiyev	RUS	6.3.89	7	EC	Berlin	11	Aug
13:24.58	Patrick	Tiernan	AUS	11.9.94	16	DL	London (OS)	21	Jul
13:24.65	Tulu	Merga	ETH-J	12.9.99	1		Kitakyushu	20	Oct
13:24.75	Wesley	Ledama	KEN-J	2.7.99	4		Yokohama	21	Oct
(80)									
13:24.77	Evan	Jager	USA	8.3.89	1		Azusa	19	Apr
13:24.79	Nicholas	Kosimbei	KEN	10.1.96	11		Nobeoka	5	May
13:24.79	Tesfahun	Akinew	ETH-J	29.4.99	5		Carquefou	16	Jun
13:24.79	Julien	Wanders	SUI	18.3.96	8	EC	Berlin	11	Aug
13:25.11	Chris	Thompson	GBR	17.4.81	9	EC	Berlin	11	Aug
13:25.31	Ben	Connor	GBR	17.10.92	11	EC	Berlin	11	Aug
13:25.46	Ryan	Hill	USA	31.1.90	17	DL	London (OS)	21	Jul
13:25.51	Rodgers	Chumo	KEN	3.3.97	12		Nobeoka	5	May
13:25.89	Josephat	Menjo	KEN	20.8.79	1		Oordegem	26	May
13:25.99	Daniel	Kipkemoi	KEN	5.7.96	13		Nobeoka	5	May
(90)									
13:26.21	Fredrick	Kipkosgei	KEN	13.11.96	11rA	NA	Heusden-Zolder	21	Jul
13:26.25	Anatoliy	Rybakov	RUS	27.2.85	2	NC	Kazan	19	Jul
13:26.46	Peter	Kiprotich	KEN	.98	12rA	NA	Heusden-Zolder	21	Jul
13:26.53	Alfred	Ngeno	KEN	2.5.97	2		Nijmegen	8	Jun
13:26.81	Hillary	Dor	USA	22.11.89	12	Jordan	Stanford	3	May
13:27.37	Bernard	Koech	KEN-J	25.11.99	1		Yokohama	2	Dec
13:27.61	Artyom	Leonenko	RUS	7.4.92	3	NC	Kazan	19	Jul
13:27.76	Florian	Carvalho	FRA	9.3.89	6		Carquefou	16	Jun
13:27.62	Joseph	Ndirangu	KEN	9.9.94	1		Toyota	9	Jun
13:27.94	Luc	Bruchet	CAN	23.2.91	13	Jordan	Stanford	3	May
(100)									

Mark	Name		Nat	Born	Date		Mark	Name		Nat	Born	Date	
13:28.03	Alexander	Mutiso	KEN	10.9.96	15	May	13:29.72	Kiprono	Sitonik	KEN-Y	10.11.01	11	Jun
13:28.30	Juan Antonio	Pérez	ESP	6.11.88	8	Jun	13:29.74	Birhanu	Melesse	ETH-J	12.9.99	16	Jun
13:28.53A	Nicholas	Kimeli	KEN	29.9.98	17	Feb	13:29.84	Samuel	Masai	KEN-Y	20.3.01	29	Sep
13:28.53	Edward	Waweru	KEN	3.10.90	13	May	13:29.89	Moses	Koech	KEN	5.4.97	8	Jun
13:28.57	Jack	Bruce	AUS	31.8.94	3	May	13:29.94	Adel	Mechaal	ESP	5.12.90	19	Jul
13:28.96	Younès	Essalhi	MAR	20.2.93	16	Jun	13:30.02	Dillon	Maggard	USA	16.10.95	3	May
13:29.06	Zouhair	Talbi	MAR	8.4.95	26	May	13:30.39	Joe	Klecker	USA	16.11.96	10	Jun
13:29.11	Suguru	Osako	JPN	23.5.91	19	Apr	13:30.43	Henry	Wynne	USA	18.4.95	3	May
13:29.13	Bernard	Kipkemoi	KEN	.94	8	Jun	13:30.48	Filip	Ingebrigtsen	NOR	20.4.93	21	Jul
13:29.31	Sydney	Gidabuday	USA	21.8.96	19	Apr	13:30.56A	David	Bett	KEN	18.10.92	17	Feb
13:29.53	Sam	Parsons	USA	18.6.94	10	Jun	13:30.89	Vladimir	Nikitin	RUS	5.8.92	19	Jul
13:29.53	Dominic	Langat	KEN	15.5.98	11	Jul	13:31.00	Matt	Baxter	NZL	6.8.94	19	Apr
13:29.57	Robin	Hendrix	BEL	14.1.95	19	Apr	13:31.14	Christopher	Cheruiyot	KEN		21	Oct
13:29.65	Abayneh	Degu	ETH	1.12.98	20	Oct	13:31.58	David	Ngure	KEN	.98	21	Oct

Mark	Name		Nat	Born	Pos	Meet	Venue	Date
13:31.70	Teressa	Nyakora	ETH	26.2.95				5 May
13:31.93	Kevin	Kibet	UGA	10.11.98				8 Jun
13:32.00	Grant	Fisher	USA	22.4.97				15 Feb
13:32.02A	James	Kibet	KEN	10.11.88				17 Feb
13:32.03	David	Njuguna	KEN	6.9.89				20 May
13:32.34	Mohammed	Abid	MAR	18.3.95				16 Jun
13:32.41	Reid	Buchanan	USA	3.2.93				24 Jun
13:32.42	Peter	Kiplangat	KEN	6.9.93				22 Apr
13:32.68A	Vincent	Kibet	KEN-J	19.3.99				12 Jun
13:32.73	Philemon	Kiplagat	KEN-Y	20.9.01				5 May
13:32.93	Felix	Kurui	KEN	.86				21 Oct
13:32.94	Awet	Habte	ERI	29.9.97				8 Jun
13:32.94	Oscar	Chelimo	UGA-Y	12.12.01				23 Aug
13:33.08	Andrew	Lorot	KEN	2.12.97				5 May
13:33.18	Diego	Estrada	USA	12.12.89				21 Jul
13:33.51	Kensuke	Horio	JPN	12.8.96				11 Nov
13:33.74	Bernard	Muia	KEN	26.5.95				5 May
13:33.78	Moses	Kibet	UGA	23.3.91				8 Jun
13:34.03	Florian	Orth	GER	24.7.89				21 Jul
13:34.09	Tesfu	Tewelde	ERI	21.7.97				16 Jun
13:34.12	Alexander	Yee	GBR	18.2.98				21 Jul
13:34.15	Amanal	Petros	GER	17.5.95				26 May
13:34.20A	Vincent	Yegon	KEN-J	5.12.00				12 Jun
13:34.50	Jacob	Thomson	USA	29.11.94				21 Jul
13:35.18	Kisaisa	Ledama	KEN	25.6.98				5 May
13:35.31	Kaan Kigen	Özbilen	TUR	15.1.86				11 Aug
13:35.34	Abiyot	Abinet	ETH	10.5.89				20 May
13:35.44A	Samuel	Chebolei	KEN-Y	.01				12 Jun
13:35.76	Jordan	Gusman	AUS	30.1.94				3 May
13:35.77	Benjamin	de Haan	NED	27.2.93				21 Jul
13:35.83	Vincent	Raimoi	KEN	16.7.96				21 Oct
13:36.12	Jonathan	Mellor	GBR	27.12.86				19 Jul
13:36.30	Arsene	Guillorel	FRA	18.1.94				21 Jul
13:36.66	Benuel	Mogeni	KEN-Y	11.3.01				5 May
13:36.78	Titus	Mogusu	KEN	1.1.98				11 Nov
13:36.82A	Peter	Kariuki	KEN	.91				21 Jun
13:36.92	Ezekiel	Chebotibin	KEN	10.7.92				11 Nov
13:36.97	Paul	Tanui	KEN	22.12.90				20 Oct
13:37.06	Zach	Perrin	USA	25.1.95				20 Apr
13:37.24	Shuho	Dairokuno	JPN	23.12.92				28 Apr
13:37.28	Marcel	Fehr	GER	20.6.92				16 Jun
13:37.41A	John	Muritu	KEN	30.6.96				17 Feb
13:37.48	Amon	Kemboi	KEN	16.1.87				20 Apr
13:37.51	Samuel	Mwangi	KEN	19.9.97				5 May
13:37.51	Vincent	Kipkemoi	KEN-J	.99				5 May
13:37.60	Clayton	Young	USA	14.9.93				3 May
13:37.60	Ronald	Musagala	UGA	16.12.92				19 Jun
13:37.75	Taisei	Hashizume	JPN	21.3.97				7 Jul
13:37.92	Vincent	Kiprop	KEN	28.4.95				20 Apr
13:37.97A	Mang'ata	Ndiwa	KEN	12.12.87				17 Feb
13:37.98	Rory	Linkletter	CAN	12.8.96				20 Apr
(180)								

Indoors

Mark	Name		Nat	Born	Pos	Meet	Venue	Date
13:33.64	Amon	Kemboi	KEN	16.1.87			Kemboi	1 Dec
13:34.78	Galen	Rupp	USA	8.5.86			Rupp	27 Jan
13:35.97	Travis	Mahoney	USA	25.7.90			Mahoney	1 Dec

JUNIORS

See main list for top 17 juniors. 18 performances by 13 men to 13:20.0. Additional marks and further juniors:

Mark	Name		Nat	Born	Pos	Meet	Venue	Date
Melak	13:10.99	6	DL	Shanghai				12 May
Waithera	13:15.06	1		Rovereto				23 Aug
13:29.72	Kiprono	Sitonik	KEN-Y	10.11.01	2		Fukagawa	11 Jul
13:29.74	Birhanu	Melesse	ETH	12.9.99	1J		Tübingen	16 Jun
13:29.84	Samuel	Masai	KEN-Y	20.3.01	1		Tokyo (Setagaya)	29 Sep
13:32.68A	Vincent	Kibet (20)	KEN	19.3.99	3		Nairobi	12 Jun

10,000 METRES

MEN 2018

Mark	Name		Nat	Born	Pos	Meet	Venue	Date
27:13.01	Stanley M.	Waithaka	KEN-J	9.4.00	1		Yokohama	10 Nov
27:14.70	Richard	Yator	KEN	6.4.98	1		Yokohama	20 Oct
27:19.62	Joshua	Cheptegei	UGA	12.9.96	1	CG	Gold Coast	13 Apr
27:20.56	Mohammed	Ahmed	CAN	5.1.91	2	CG	Gold Coast	13 Apr
27:21.08	Rhonex	Kipruto	KEN-J	12.10.99	1	WJ	Tampere	10 Jul
27:25.86	Tulu	Merga	ETH-J	12.9.99	1rA		Machida	24 Nov
27:26.27	Bernard	Kimeli	KEN	10.9.95	2rA		Machida	24 Nov
27:28.27	Jonathan	Ndiku	KEN	18.9.91	2		Yokohama	10 Nov
27:28.66	Rodgers	Chumo	KEN	3.3.97	3	CG	Gold Coast	13 Apr
27:30.25	Jacob	Kiplimo (10)	UGA-J	14.11.00	4	CG	Gold Coast	13 Apr
27:30.47	Daniel	Kipkemoi	KEN	5.7.96	3rA		Machida	24 Nov
27:30.90	Jake	Robertson	NZL	14.11.89	5	CG	Gold Coast	13 Apr
27:31.83	Bernard	Koech	KEN-J	25.11.99	4rA		Machida	24 Nov
27:32.04	Amos	Kurgat	KEN	7.3.92	5rA		Machida	24 Nov
27:32.45		Chumo			1		Kobe	22 Apr
27:32.65		Chumo			1		Tajimi	13 Oct
27:33.55	Joseph	Ndirangu	KEN	9.9.94	2		Tajimi	13 Oct
27:36.45	William	Sitonik	KEN	1.3.94	2		Yokohama	20 Oct
27:36.52	Richard	Ringer	GER	27.2.89	1	ECp	London (PH)	19 May
27:36.80	Mourad	Amdouni	FRA	21.1.88	2	ECp	London (PH)	19 May
27:38.16	Hassan	Chani	BRN	8.10.91	1		Maia	2 Jun
27:39.65	Shadrack	Kipchirchir	USA	22.2.89	1	Jordan	Stanford	3 May
27:40.36	J	Kiplimo			2	WJ	Tampere	10 Jul
27:40.69	Evans	Keitany	KEN-J	27.11.99	3		Tajimi	13 Oct
27:41.12	Wesley	Ledama	KEN-J	2.7.99	6rA		Machida	24 Nov
27:41.20	Soufiane	Bouchikhi	BEL	22.3.90	2	Jordan	Stanford	3 May
27:42.16	Alexander	Mutiso	KEN	10.9.96	3		Yokohama	10 Nov
27:42.52	Kisaisa	Ledama	KEN	25.6.98	7rA		Machida	24 Nov
27:43.65	Biyazen	Alehegn	ETH-J	16.9.99	2		Maia	2 Jun
27:44.21	Yemaneberhan	Crippa	ITA	15.10.96	3	ECp	London (PH)	19 May
	(30/27)							
27:44.27	Dominic	Langat	KEN	15.5.98	8rA		Machida	24 Nov
27:44.58	Stephen	Mokoka	RSA	31.1.85	6	CG	Gold Coast	13 Apr
27:44.72	Teressa	Nyakora (30)	ETH	26.2.95	2		Kobe	22 Apr

Mark	Name		Nat	Born	Pos	Meet	Venue	Date
27:44.92	Abraham	Kipyatich	KEN	10.5.93	9rA		Machida	24 Nov
27:45.31	Joel	Mwaura	KEN	20.1.98	1		Osaka	22 Sep
27:47.19	Daniel	Kitonyi	KEN	12.1.94	1		Yokohama	1 Dec
27:47.35	Timothy	Toroitich	UGA	10.10.91	7	CG	Gold Coast	13 Apr
27:48.35	Awet	Habte	ERI	29.9.97	3		Maia	2 Jun
27:48.41	Berihu	Aregawi	ETH-Y	28.2.01	3	WJ	Tampere	10 Jul
27:48.59	James	Rungaru	KEN	14.1.93	2		Yokohama	1 Dec
27:49.49	Nicholas	Kosimbei	KEN	10.1.96	2		Osaka	22 Sep
27:50.56	Adel	Mechaal	ESP	5.12.90	4	ECp	London (PH)	19 May
27:50.89	Stewart	McSweyn	AUS	1.6.95	1	Zát	Melbourne	13 Dec
	(40)							
27:51.20	Davis	Kiplangat	KEN	10.7.98	4		Maia	2 Jun
27:51.94	Alexander	Yee	GBR	18.2.98	5	ECp/NC	London (PH)	19 May
27:52.32	Andrew	Vernon	GBR	7.1.86	6	ECp/NC	London (PH)	19 May
27:52.39	Andrew	Lorot	KEN	2.12.97	1		Fukagawa	11 Jul
27:52.66	Chris	Thompson	GBR	17.4.81	7	ECp/NC	London (PH)	19 May
27:53.59	Kiprono	Sitonik	KEN-Y	10.11.01	10rA		Machida	24 Nov
27:55.85	Tetsuya	Yoroizaka	JPN	20.3.90	1rB		Machida	24 Nov
27:55.95	François	Barrer	FRA	8.6.93	3	Jordan	Stanford	3 May
27:56.04	Simon	Kariuki	KEN	13.2.92	1		Kobe	21 Apr
27:56.11	Garrett	Heath	USA	3.11.85	4	Jordan	Stanford	3 May
	(50)							
27:56.12	Moses	Kibet	UGA	23.3.91	5		Maia	2 Jun
27:56.27	Hiroto	Inoue	JPN	6.1.93	2rB		Machida	24 Nov
27:56.45	Hiroki	Abe	JPN	19.11.97	3rB		Machida	24 Nov
27:56.53	Polat Kemboi	Arikan	TUR	12.12.90	6		Maia	2 Jun
27:57.14	Robert	Mwei	KEN	11.4.98	11rA		Machida	24 Nov
27:57.44	Solomon	Boit	KEN-J	1.10.99	4	WJ	Tampere	10 Jul
27:58.35	Kazuki	Tamura	JPN	16.7.95	4		Fukagawa	11 Jul
27:58.87	Takuya	Fujikawa	JPN	17.12.92	4rB		Machida	24 Nov
27:59.30	Bekele	Shiferaw	ETH	14.10.95	13rA		Machida	24 Nov
27:59.77	Abayneh	Degu	ETH	1.12.98	14rA		Machida	24 Nov
	(60)							
28:00.49	Shuho	Dairokuno	JPN	23.12.92	1		Nobeoka	5 May
28:00.56	Evans	Yego	KEN	5.9.95	15rA		Machida	24 Nov
28:02.65	Patrick	Mathenge	KEN	2.11.96	2		Kobe	21 Apr
28:03.46	Yuma	Higashi	JPN	29.11.95	5rB		Machida	24 Nov
28:03.96	James	Mwangi	KEN	23.6.84	4		Gifu	12 May
28:04.44	Tyler	Day	USA	18.12.96	5	Jordan	Stanford	3 May
28:04.79	Karemi Jeremiah	Thuku	KEN	7.7.94	1		Kitami	7 Jul
28:05.32	Gen	Hachisuka	JPN	29.11.94	6rB		Machida	24 Nov
28:05.34	Dominic	Kiptarus	KEN	3.8.96	1	Bisl	Oslo	7 Jun
28:06.78	Florian	Carvalho	FRA	9.3.89	8	ECp	London (PH)	19 May
	(70)							
28:07.15	Julien	Wanders	SUI	18.3.96	3	Bisl	Oslo	7 Jun
28:07.88	Noah	Droddy	USA	22.9.90	6	Jordan	Stanford	3 May
28:08.30	Taku	Fujimoto	JPN	11.9.89	8rB		Machida	24 Nov
28:08.52	Daiji	Kawai	JPN	22.9.91	9rB		Machida	24 Nov
28:09.55	Connor	McMillan	USA	15.11.95	7	Jordan	Stanford	3 May
28:10.05	Matt	Baxter	NZL	6.8.94	8	Jordan	Stanford	3 May
28:10.39	Kota	Murayama	JPN	23.2.93	17rA		Machida	24 Nov
28:10.70	Bernard	Muia	KEN	26.5.95	6		Tajimi	13 Oct
28:10.90	John	Murltu	KEN	30.6.90	5		Yokohama	10 Nov
28:11.41	Paul	Tanui	KEN	22.12.90	1		Saga	14 Oct
	(80)							
28:11.55	Yuta	Shitara	JPN	18.12.91	6		Yokohama	20 Oct
28:11.76	Bashir	Abdi	BEL	10.2.89	2	EC	Berlin	7 Aug
28:12.05	José Luis	Ostos	PER	9.12.92	9	Jordan	Stanford	3 May
28:12.07	Jack	Rayner	AUS	19.12.95	2	Zát	Melbourne	13 Dec
28:12.53	Kenta	Murayama	JPN	23.2.93	1rC		Machida	24 Nov
28:13.07	Scott	Fauble	USA	5.11.91	10	Jordan	Stanford	3 May
28:13.38	Paul	Gitonga	KEN	20.8.96	7		Yokohama	20 Oct
28:13.49	José Mauricio	González	COL	14.10.88	1		Hayward	30 Mar
28:14.49	Derese	Workneh	ETH	23.7.95	1		Yokohama	21 Apr
28:14.56	Ben	Connor	GBR	17.10.92	11	Jordan	Stanford	3 May
	(90)							
28:15.27	Kazuki	Onishi	JPN	28.3.87	2rC		Machida	24 Nov
28:15.41	Girmaw	Amare	ISR	26.10.87	9	ECp	London (PH)	19 May
28:16.22	Kazuma	Taira	JPN	5.11.94	7		Yokohama	10 Nov
28:16.35	Titus	Mogusu	KEN	1.1.98	19rA		Machida	24 Nov
28:16.43	Vladimir	Nikitin	RUS	5.8.92	1	Znam	Zhukovskiy	30 Jun

Mark	Name		Nat	Born	Pos	Meet	Venue		Date
28:16.95	Hideto	Yamanaka	JPN	17.3.94	8		Yokohama		20 Oct
28:17.1A	Erick	Kiptanui	KEN	19.4.90	1		Nairobi		6 Jun
28:17.24	Antonio	Abadía	ESP	2.7.90	1		Braga		7 Apr
28:17.24A	Vincent	Rono	KEN	22.12.90	1	NC	Nairobi		22 Jun
28:17.63	Tsuyoshi	Ugachi	JPN	27.4.87	6		Fukagawa		11 Jul
	(100)								

Mark	Name		Nat	Born	Date	Mark	Name		Nat	Born	Date
28:17.68	Yamato	Otsuka	JPN	18.3.96	24 Nov	28:26.94	Ryo	Matsumoto	JPN	19.10.90	24 Nov
28:17.81	Akira	Aizawa	JPN	18.7.97	21 Apr	28:27.04	Shinobu	Kubota	JPN	12.12.91	13 Oct
28:18.22	Charles	Ndungu	KEN	20.2.96	11 Jul	28:27.10	Shuhei	Yamamoto	JPN	24.5.91	11 Jul
28:18.39	Hiroyuki	Yamamoto	JPN	30.4.86	11 Jul	28:27.28	Tsubasa	Hayakawa	JPN	2.7.90	24 Nov
28:19.03	Vincent	Kipkemoi	KEN-J	3.1.99	20 Oct	28:27.31	Gilbert	Kigen	KEN	23.12.94	30 Mar
28:19.07	Vincent	Kiprop	KEN	28.4.95	30 Mar	28:27.40	Keita	Yoshida	JPN	31.8.98	24 Nov
28:19.47	Enyew	Mekonnen	ETH	7.4.94	2 Jun	28:27.48	Clayton	Young	USA	14.9.93	30 Mar
28:19.77	Dominic	Nyairo	KEN	22.8.97	21 Apr	28:27.55A	Kipsang	Temoi	KEN		22 Jun
28:19.94	Iván	González	COL	14.8.87	3 May	28:28.08	Taisei	Hashizume	JPN	21.3.97	24 Nov
28:19.98	Samuel	Mwangi	KEN	19.9.97	24 Nov	28:28.19	Masato	Terauchi	JPN	18.10.93	13 Oct
28:21.19	Josephat	Menjo	KEN	20.8.79	14 Jul	28:28.62	Tatsuhiko	Ito	JPN	23.3.98	24 Nov
28:21.25A	Maxwell	Rotich	UGA	5.8.98	13 Jul	28:28.68	Fernando	Carro	ESP	1.4.92	7 Apr
28:21.26	Ezekiel	Chebotibin	KEN	10.7.92	21 Apr	28:28.73	Naoki	Okamoto	JPN	26.5.84	19 May
28:21.37	Lopez	Lomong	USA	1.1.85	30 Mar	28:29.01	Shohei	Kurata	JPN	5.8.92	24 Nov
28:21.4A	Leonard	Oloitiptip	KEN	.90	6 Jun	28:29.18	Yuki	Muta	JPN	26.5.93	24 Nov
28:21.41	Simon	Letaya	KEN	.88	14 Jul	28:29.52	Yevgeniy	Rybakov	RUS	27.2.85	30 Jun
28:21.46	Muthoni	Muiru	KEN	27.3.98	13 May	28:29.54	Watari	Tochigi	JPN	8.5.95	24 Nov
28:22.23	David	Njuguna	KEN	6.9.89	24 Nov	28:29.67	Keiji	Akutsu	JPN	20.3.87	24 Nov
28:22.28	Brendan	Gregg	USA	15.5.89	3 May	28:29.70	Masaru	Aoki	JPN	16.5.90	13 May
28:22.35	James	Bunuka	KEN	1.11.97	9 Jun	28:29.7A	Andamlak	Belihu	ETH	20.11.98	17 Apr
28:22.39	Bernard	Kimani	KEN	10.9.93	21 Apr	28:29.78	Amanal	Petros	GER	17.5.95	7 Apr
28:22.59	Ken	Nakayama	JPN	24.2.97	21 Apr	28:30.01	Lorenzo	Dini	ITA	2.10.94	19 May
28:22.8A	Emmanuel	Keter	KEN	.80	6 Jun	28:30.10	Shohei	Otsuka	JPN	13.8.94	19 May
28:23.11	Abra	Kokob	ERI-J	13.3.99	12 May	28:30.3A	Jemal	Yimer	ETH	11.9.96	17 Apr
28:23.58	Hiroshi	Ichida	JPN	16.6.92	19 May	28:30.3A	Victor	Korir	KEN-Y	14.8.02	11 Jun
28:24.25	Tatsuya	Oike	JPN	18.5.90	13 Oct	28:30.35	Patrick	Mwaka	KEN	2.11.92	13 Oct
28:24.31	Silas	Nalbei	KEN	29.11.95	24 Nov	28:30.52	Atsuto	Shimanuki	JPN	15.7.97	24 Nov
28:24.39	Takumi	Komatsu	JPN	29.9.94	11 Jul	28:30.55	Peter	Muindi	KEN	.90	13 Oct
28:24.85	Samuel	Barata	POR	19.7.93	3 May	28:30.76	Igor	Maksimov	RUS	26.4.92	5 May
28:24.85A	Josphat	Bett	KEN	12.6.90	22 Jun	28:30.83	Takashi	Ichida	JPN	16.6.92	22 Sep
28:25.32	Simon	Debognies	BEL	16.7.96	3 May	28:30.94	Vincent	Raimoi	KEN	16.7.96	21 Apr
28:25.38	Nicolae	Soare	ROU	25.8.91	19 May	28:30.94	Mitsunori	Asaoka	JPN	11.1.93	24 Nov
28:25.56	Daisuke	Momozawa	JPN	19.1.93	24 Nov	28:31.06	Yusuke	Tamura	JPN	17.2.90	24 Nov
28:25.57	Enoch	Omwamba	KEN	4.4.93	19 May	28:31.31	Juan Antonio	Pérez	ESP	6.11.88	7 Aug
28:26.26	Alex	Chesuru	UGA		13 Jul	28:31.50	Sho	Nagato	JPN	13.1.97	24 Nov
28:26.41	Suguru	Osako	JPN	23.5.91	14 Jul	28:31.73	Zouhair	Talbi	MAR	8.4.95	7 Jun
28:26.7A	Taye	Girma	ETH-J	.00	17 Apr	28:31.85	Charles	Nzioka	KEN-J	21.9.99	19 May
28:26.8A	Stephen	Arita	KEN	26.6.88	6 Jun	28:31.89	Ichitaka	Yamashita	JPN	29.7.97	24 Nov
28:26.94	Kazuya	Shiojiri	JPN	8.11.96	24 May	28:31.91	Takumi	Komatsu (178)	JPN	29.9.94	24 Nov

JUNIORS

See main list for top 11 juniors. 12 performances by 9 men to 27:53.0. Additional marks and further juniors:

Mark	Name		Nat	Born	Pos	Meet	Venue	Date
R Kipruto	27:49.6A		1	KEN-jT	Nairobi		11 Jun	
Kiplimo	27:40.36		2	WJ	Tampere	10 Jul		
	27:51.3A		1		Kampala		24 Feb	
28:19.03	Vincent	Kipkemoi	KEN	3.1.99	9		Yokohama	20 Oct
28:26.7A	Taye	Girma	ETH	.00	1	NC	Addis Ababa	17 Apr
28:23.11	Abra	Kokob	ERI	13.3.99	1	ITA Ch	Ferrara	12 May
28:30.3A	Victor	Korir	KEN-Y	14.8.02	3		Nairobi	11 Jun
28:31.85	Charles	Nzioka	KEN	21.9.99	10		Kitakyushu	19 May
28:33.26	Peter	Mwangi	KEN	27.7.99	4		Yokohama	21 Apr
28:34.88	Daichi	Endo	JPN	4.4.99	8		Yokohama	24 Nov
28:37.2A	Kelvin	Kibiwott	KEN	2.6.00	4	KEN-jT	Nairobi	11 Jun
28:38.67	Olika	Adugna (20)	ETH	12.9.99	5	WJ	Tampere	10 Jul

10 KILOMETRES ROAD

Mark	Name		Nat	Born	Pos	Meet	Venue	Date
26:46	Rhonex	Kipruto	KEN-J	12.10.99	1		Praha	8 Sep
27:08		Kipruto			1		New York	29 Apr
27:16	Joshua	Cheptegei	UGA	12.9.96	1		Durban	14 Oct
27:18	Gilbert	Koech	KEN	28.8.93	2		Praha	8 Sep
27:19	Mathew	Kimeli	KEN	4.1.98	2		New York	29 Apr
27:21	Vincent	Kibet	KEN-J	19.3.99	1		Berlin	14 Oct
27:22	Maxwell	Rotich	UGA	5.8.98	1		Santos	20 May
27:24	Davis	Kiplangat	KEN	10.7.98	1		Utrecht	7 Oct
27:25	Julien	Wanders	SUI	18.3.96	1		Houilles	30 Dec
27:26	Emmanuel	Kiprono	KEN	13.6.93	1		Paderborn	31 Mar
27:26		Kimeli			3		Praha	8 Sep
27:28	Jake	Robertson	NZL	14.11.89	1		New Orleans	31 Mar
27:32+	Erick	Kiptanui	KEN	19.4.90	1=	in HMar	Berlin	8 Apr
27:32+	Daniel Kipchumba	Chebii	KEN	12.12.97	1=	in HMar	Berlin	8 Apr

Mark	Name		Nat	Born	Pos	Meet	Venue	Date	
27:32		Wanders			2		Durban	14	Oct
Where better than 10,000m track times									
27:36	Berhanu	Wendimu	ETH-J	.99	2		Houilles	30	Dec
27:37	Amdework	Walelegn	ETH-J	11.3.99	1		Laredo	17	Mar
27:37	Emanuel	Gniki	TAN	18.5.88	2		Utrecht	7	Oct
27:38	Abraham	Kipyatich	KEN	10.5.93	4		Praha	8	Sep
27:40	Josphat Kiptoo	Boit	KEN	25.11.95	1	in 15k	Valencia	2	Jun
27:40	Benard	Lagat	KEN	15.12.94	5		Praha	8	Sep
27:40	Isaac	Temoi	KEN-J	.99	3		Utrecht	7	Oct
27:44	Simon	Cheprot	KEN	2.7.93	2		Oelde	9	Jun
27:44	Peter	Ndorobo	KEN	11.8.93	6		Praha	8	Sep
27:44	Albert	Rop	BRN	17.7.92	4		Utrecht	7	Oct
27:45	Benard	Ngeno	KEN	10.8.96	1		Mobile	24	Mar
27:46	Hicham	Amghar	MAR	15.5.94	7		Praha	8	Sep
27:46	Moses	Koech	KEN	5.4.97	3		Durban	14	Oct
27:47	Stephen	Kissa	UGA	1.12.95	4		Durban	14	Oct
27:48+	Morris	Munene Gachaga	KEN	7.4.95		in HMar	Ras Al Khaimah	9	Feb
27:48+	Jorum	Okumbo	KEN	10.12.97		in HMar	Ras Al Khaimah	9	Feb
27:48+	Alex	Kibet	KEN	20.10.90		in HMar	Ras Al Khaimah	9	Feb
27:48+	James	Mwangi	KEN	29.3.94		in HMar	Ras Al Khaimah	9	Feb
27:48+	Edwin Kiprop	Kiptoo	KEN	14.8.93		in HMar	Ras Al Khaimah	9	Feb
27:48	Antonio	Abadía	ESP	2.7.90	2		Laredo	17	Mar
27:48	Andamlak	Belihu	ETH	20.11.98	1		Ottawa	26	May
27:49+	Wilfred	Kimitei	KEN	11.3.85		in HMar	Ras Al Khaimah	9	Feb
27:49+	Timothy	Rono	KEN	18.9.97		in HMar	Ras Al Khaimah	9	Feb
27:49+	Jemal	Yimer	ETH	11.9.96		in HMar	Ras Al Khaimah	9	Feb
27:49+	Lelisa	Desisa	ETH	14.1.90		in HMar	Ras Al Khaimah	9	Feb
27:49+	Geoffrey	Yegon	KEN	28.8.88		in HMar	Ras Al Khaimah	9	Feb
27:49+	Mang'ata	Ndiwa	KEN	12.12.87		in HMar	Stresa	15	Apr
27:50+	Richard	Mengich	KEN	3.4.89		in HMar	Berlin	8	Apr
27:50+	Ambrose	Bore	KEN	8.8.95		in HMar	Berlin	8	Apr
27:50+	Gilbert	Masai	KEN	16.12.89		in HMar	Berlin	8	Apr
27:50	Benard	Kimeli	KEN	10.9.95	8		Praha	8	Sep
27:50	Abderrahmane	Kachir	MAR	25.9.92	1		Casablanca	16	Sep
27:52	Timothy	Rono	KEN	.97	3		Laredo	17	Mar
27:52	Peter Langat	Cheptot	KEN		4		Laredo	17	Mar
27:53	Albert	Chemutai	UGA-J	25.11.99	3		Houilles	30	Dec
27:54	Mustapha	El Aziz	MAR	24.12.85	2		Casablanca	16	Sep
27:57	Vedic	Cheruiyot	KEN	5.3.96	10		Praha	8	Sep
27:57	Filmon	Ande	ERI	10.2.98	4		Houilles	30	Dec
27:58	Josphat	Chumo	KEN	15.7.96	11		Praha	8	Sep
28:00+	Shadrack Korir	Kimining	KEN	10.2.96		in HMar	Ras Al Khaimah	9	Feb
28:01+	Edward	Waweru	KEN	3.10.90		in HMar	Marugame	4	Feb
28:01	Mande	Bushendich	UGA	7.4.97	5		Durban	14	Oct
28:02+	Kenta	Murayama	JPN	23.2.93		in HMar	Marugame	4	Feb
28:02+	Yuta	Shitara	JPN	18.12.91		in HMar	Marugame	4	Feb
28:02+	Josphat	Tanui	KEN	4.2.94		in HMar	Ras Al Khaimah	9	Feb
28:02+	Aron	Kifle	ERI	20.2.98		in HMar	New Delhi	21	Oct
28:02+	Leonard	Korir	USA	10.12.86		in HMar	New Delhi	21	Oct
28:02+	Abdallah	Mande	UGA	10.5.95		in HMar	New Delhi	21	Oct
28:02+	Abraham	Kiptum	KEN	15.9.89		in HMar	Valencia	28	Oct
28:02+	Abel	Kipchumba	KEN	.94		in HMar	Valencia	28	Oct
28:02+	Stephen	Kiprop	KEN	0.9.99		in HMar	Valencia	28	Oct
28:03+	Leonard	Komon	KEN	10.1.88		in HMar	Valencia	28	Oct
28:03+	Emmanuel Kipkemei	Bett	KEN	29.3.85		in HMar	New Delhi	21	Oct
28:03+	Betesfa	Getahun	ETH	25.9.98		in HMar	New Delhi	21	Oct
28:03+	El Hassan	El Abbassi	BRN	13.4.84		in HMar	Valencia	28	Oct
28:03+	Teshome	Mekonen	ETH	5.8.95		in HMar	Valencia	28	Oct
28:03+	Rhonzas	Kilimo	KEN	5.9.96		in HMar	Valencia	28	Oct
28:03+	Aziz	Lahbabi	MAR	3.2.91		in HMar	Valencia	28	Oct
28:04	Abdennacer	Fathi	MAR	25.1.87	3		Casablanca	16	Sep
28:04+	Abadi	Hadis	ETH	6.11.97		in HMar	Valencia	28	Oct
28:04+	Bernard	Ngeno	KEN	10.8.96		in HMar	Valencia	28	Oct
28:05+	Solomon Kirwa	Yego	KEN	10.5.87		in HMar	Valencia	28	Oct
28:06	Taye	Girma	ETH-J	.00	2		Valencia	14	Jan
28:06+	Noah	Kigen	KEN	12.6.89		in HMar	Berlin	8	Apr
28:06	Hicham	Laqouahi	MAR	13.6.89	4		Casablanca	16	Sep
28:07 A	Marius	Kimutai	KEN	17.5.88	1		Kapsabet	22	Sep
28:08+	Shadrack	Kiplagat	KEN	9.12.77		in HMar	Napoli	4	Feb
28:09	Yohanes	Gebregergish	ERI	1.1.89	3		Valencia	14	Jan
28:09+	Dominic	Nyairo	KEN	22.8.97		in HMar	Marugame	4	Feb

Mark	Name	Nat	Born	Pos Meet	Venue	Date
28:09+ pp	Justus Kangogo	KEN	.95	in HMar	Ostia	11 Mar
28:09+ pp	Moses Kemei	KEN	3.9.93	in HMar	Ostia	11 Mar
28:09 +pp	Galen Rupp	USA	8.5.86	in HMar	Ostia	11 Mar
28:10	Leonard Langat	KEN	7.8.90			8 Apr
28:10	Haftu Teklu	ETH	.90			30 Dec
28:10	Cornelius Kangogo	KEN	31.12.93			30 Dec
28:11+	Evans Kipkorir Cheruiyot	KEN	24.9.91			8 Apr
28:11+	Kaan Kigen Özbilen	TUR	15.1.86			8 Apr
28:11+	Yomif Kejelcha	ETH	1.8.97			16 Sep
28:11+	Felix Kibitok	KEN	.91			16 Sep
28:11+	Asefa Mengistu	ETH	18.1.85			16 Sep
28:11+	Tola Shura Kitata	ETH	9.6.96			16 Sep
28:11	Vincent Yegon	KEN-J	5.12.00			11 Nov
28:12	Amos Kirui	KEN	9.2.98			14 Jan
28:12+	Japheth Korir	KEN	30.6.93			16 Se
28:13+	Asefa Tefera	ETH	14.3.97			8 Apr
28:13	Jimmy Gressier	FRA	4.5.97			30 Dec
28:14	John Muritu	KEN	30.6.96			31 Mar
28:14	Mathew Kisorio	KEN	16.5.89			22 Sep
28:14	Elvis Cheboi	KEN	29.9.95			11 Nov
28:15+	Abrar Osman	ERI	24.6.94			18 Nov
28:16+	Meshack Koech	KEN	27.7.89			16 Sep
28:17	Donald Mitei	KEN	2.4.96			7 Apr
28:18+	Stephen Kibet	KEN	9.11.86			11 Mar
28:18	Edwin Soi	KEN	3.3.86			31 Mar
28:18+	Evans Kigen Kurui	KEN	8.1.93			8 Apr
28:18	Geoffrey Kamworor	KEN	22.11.92			27 May
28:18A	Getaneh Tamire Molla	ETH	10.1.94			28 May
28:19	Douglas Kipserem	KEN	.87			31 Mar
28:19	Paul Kipkorir	KEN	.82			20 May
28:20+	Kazuya Shiojiri	JPN	8.11.96			4 Feb
28:20+	Homiyu Tesfaye	GER	23.6.93			11 Mar
28:21	Alex Oleitiptip Korio	KEN	20.12.90			24 Jun
28:21	Richard Kimunyan	KEN				7 Dec
28:22+	Nobert Kipkoech Kigen	KEN	24.1.93			4 Feb
28:22+	Hillary Kimaiyo	KEN	.94			11 Mar
28:23+	Abiyot Abinet	ETH	10.5.89			4 Feb
28:23+	Kei Katanishi	JPN	18.3.97			4 Feb
28:23	Mohamed El Aaraby	MAR	12.11.89			26 May
28:23	Mohamed Ziani	MAR	.93			26 May
28:24	Gabriel Geay	TAN	10.9.96			24 Jun
28:24	Taha Belkorchi	MAR	-.90			22 Dec
28:25+	Silas Too	KEN	,88			4 Feb
28:25	Gezahagn Mengistu	ETH	.93			9 Jun
28:26+	Takashi Ichida	JPN	16.6.92			4 Feb
28:26+	Yohei Suzuki	JPN	12.2.84			4 Feb
28:26	Moses Kibet	KEN	4.2.97			16 Jun
28:27	Mo Farah	GBR	23.3.83			20 May
28:27	Yismaw Ayenu	ETH	.98			16 Jun
28:27	Berhane Tesfaye	ERI				16 Jun
28:27 pp	Stephen Sambu	KEN	7.7.88			4 Aug
28:27+	Zane Robertson	NZL	141189			23 Sep
28:27+	Muktar Edris	ETH	14.1.94			18 Nov
28:28+	Charles Nzioka	KEN-J	21.9.99			4 Feb
28:28+	Albert Kangogo	KEN	16.8.87			9 Feb
28:28	Hassan Ghachoui	MAR	1.1.95			18 Feb
28:28	James Kibet	UGA	5.6.86			2 Apr
28:28	Moses Kipsiro	UGA	2.9.86			20 May
28:28+	Geoffrey Korir	KEN	2.5.96			2 Jun
28:28	Gizachew Hailu	ETH	18.4.98			16 Jun
28:28	William Wanjiku	KEN	7.5.95			16 Jun
28:29+	Mitsunori Asaoka	JPN	11.1.93			4 Feb
28:29	Hassan Ouazzine	MAR				18 Feb
28:29+	Nguse Amsolom	ERI	10.11.86			4 Aug
28:29 pp	Ben True	USA	29.12.85			4 Aug
28:29	Soufiane Bouchikhi	BEL	22.3.90			8 Sep
28:30	Ashenafi Moges	ETH	97			29 Apr
28:30	Felix Kipkoech	KEN				12 Aug

Downhill 55m: Madrid 31 Dec: 1. Jacob Kiplimo UGA-J 14.11.00 26:41, 2. Abadi Hadis ETH 6.11.97 26:54, 3. Mande Bushendich UGA 7.4.97 27:24, 4. Abrar Osman ERI 24.6.94 27:38. 6. Juan Antonio Pérez ESP 6.11.88 28:16

See also in 10M and Half Marathon lists

15/20 KILOMETRES ROAD

MEN 2018

20k	15k	Name	Nat	Born	Pos Meet	Venue	Date
	41:05	Joshua Cheptegei	UGA	12.9.96	1	Nijmegen	18 Nov
56:25	41:52+	Josphat Kiptoo Boit	KEN	25.11.95	in HMar	Valencia	28 Oct
56:39	41:54+	Edwin Kiprop Kiptoo	KEN	14.8.93	in HMar	Ras Al Khaimah	9 Feb
57:06	42:10+	Lelisa Desisa	ETH	14.1.90	in HMar	Ras Al Khaimah	9 Feb
57:06	42:10+	Bernard Kimeli	KEN	10.9.95	in HMar	Ras Al Khaimah	9 Feb
56:51	42:10+	Mang'ata Ndiwa	KEN	12.12.87	in HMar	Valencia	28 Oct
	42:17+	Leonard Langat	KEN	7.8.90	in HMar	Istanbul	8 Apr
57:12	42:17+	Geoffrey Yegon	KEN	28.8.88	in HMar	Ras Al Khaimah	9 Feb
56:45	42:19+	Amdework Walelegn	ETH-J	11.3.99	in HMar	Istanbul	8 Apr
	42:20+	Gilbert Masai	KEN	16.12.89	in HMar	Berlin	8 Apr
	42:20	Haymanot Alewe	ETH	11.11.97	2	Le Puy-en-Velay	1 May
57:34	42:22+	James Mwangi	KEN	23.3.94	in HMar	Ras Al Khaimah	9 Feb
57:18	42:23+	Hicham Amghar	MAR	15.10.94	in HMar	Valencia	28 Oct
	42:25+	Polat Kemboi Arikan	TUR	12.12.90	in HMar	Istanbul	8 Apr
	42:33+	Josphat Tanui	KEN	4.2.94	in HMar	Praha	7 Apr
	42:34	Abrar Osman	ERI	24.6.94	2	Nijmegen	18 Nov
	42:45+	Abdallah Mande	UGA	10.5.95	in HMar	New Delhi	21 Oct
56:58	42:50+	Jake Robertson	NZL	14.11.89	in HMar	Houston	14 Jan
	42:51 +	Tola Shura Kitata	ETH	9.6.96	in HMar	Houston	14 Jan
	42:53	Emmanuel Kiprono	KEN	13.6.93	3	Le Puy-en-Velay	1 May
	42:55	Muktar Edris	ETH	14.1.94	3	Nijmegen	18 Nov
	42:59	Geoffrey Korir	KEN	2.5.96	3	Valencia	2 Jun
	43:03	Geoffrey Kusuro (28:20+ 10k)	UGA	12.2.89	4	Valencia	2 Jun
	43:06+	Dawit Fikadu (28:03+ 10k)	BRN	29.12.95	in HMar	Valencia	28 Oct
57:07	43:07+	Victor Chumo	KEN	.87	in HMar	Venlo	25 Mar
	43:07+	Emmanuel Kiprono Kipsang (28:09)	KEN	13.6.91	in HMar	Ostia	11 Mar
	43:08	Albert Chemutai	UGA	25.11.99	3	Istanbul	11 Nov
57:14+		Erick Kiptanui	KEN	19.4.90	in HMar	Lisboa	11 Mar
57:35	42:36	Andrew Mangata	KEN-Y	15.6.02?	16	København	16 Sep
57:39	42:51	Haron Lagat	KEN	15.8.83	in HMar	Houston	14 Jan
57:50	42:51	Abayneh Degu	ETH	1.12.98	in HMar	København	16 Sep

+ intermediate time in longer race, A made at an altitude of 1000m or higher, D made in a decathlon, h made in a heat, qf quarter-final, sf semi-final, i indoors, Q qualifying round, r race number, -J juniors, -Y youths (b. 2001 or later)

Mark			Name		Nat	Born	Pos	Meet	Venue	Date

10 MILES ROAD

10M	15k	10k								
44:46+		27:48	Bedan	Karoki	KEN	21.8.90	1	in HMar	Ras Al Khaimah	9 Feb
45:15	42:13	27:50	Joshua	Cheptegei	UGA	12.9.96	1		Zaandam	23 Sep
45:23	42:15	27:52	Rodgers	Chumo	KEN	3.3.97	1		Tilburg	2 Sep
	42:22	27:48+	James	Mwangi	KEN	29.3.94		in HMar	Ras Al Khaimah	9 Feb
45:41	42:27	28:15	Alfred	Ngeno	KEN	2.5.97	2		Zaandam	23 Sep
45:47	42:37	27:51	Noah	Kipkemboi	KEN	2.7.93	2		Tilburg	2 Sep
45:56			John	Muritu	KEN	30.6.96	1		Kosa	2 Dec
45:57			Taku	Fujimoto	JPN	11.9.89	2		Kosa	2 Dec
45:58			Cyrus	Kingori	KEN	5.1.97	3		Kosa	2 Dec
46:04	42:27	28:30	Berhane	Afewerki	ERI	6.5.96	3		Zaandam	23 Sep
46:05			Jeremiah	Thuku	KEN	7.7.94	4		Kosa	2 Dec
46:06			Kazuya	Shiojiri	JPN	8.11.96	5		Kosa	2 Dec
46:08	43:03		Bashir	Abdi	BEL	10.2.89	4		Zaandam	23 Sep
Downhill										
45:44			Daniel	Kemboi	KEN	.86	1		Philadelphia	6 May

HALF MARATHON

GNR – slighly downhill race: 30.5m Newcastle to South Shields

	20k	15k								
58:18	55:18	41:37	Abraham	Kiptum	KEN	15.9.89	1		Valencia	28 Oct
58:33	55:31	41:41	Jemal	Yimer	ETH	11.9.96	2		Valencia	28 Oct
58:42	55:55	41:44	Bedan	Karoki	KEN	21.8.90	1		Ras Al Khaimah	9 Feb
58:42		41:38	Erick	Kiptanui	KEN	19.4.90	1		Berlin	8 Apr
58:44	55:41	41:43	Abadi	Hadis	ETH	6.11.97	3		Valencia	28 Oct
59:00	55:56	41:44		Yimer			2		Ras Al Khaimah	9 Feb
59:06	55:58	41:43	Alex	Kibet	KEN	20.10.90	3		Ras Al Khaimah	9 Feb
59:06			Daniel KipchumbaChebii		KEN	28.5.85	1		Stresa	15 Apr
59:06	56:07	42:02		Chebii			1		København	10 Sep
59:07			Mang'ata	Ndiwa	KEN	12.12.87	2		Stresa	15 Apr
59:09	56:07	42:02		Kiptum			2		København	16 Sep
59:14	56:08	42:02		Yimer			3		København	16 Sep
59:17			Tola	Shura Kitata	ETH	9.6.96	1		Philadelphia	16 Sep
59:17	56:10	42:02	Yomif	Kejelcha (10)	ETH	1.8.97	4		København	16 Sep
59:18			Andamlak	Belihu	ETH	20.11.98	1		New Delhi	21 Oct
59:19			Josphat Kiptoo	Boit	KEN	25.11.95	3		Stresa	15 Apr
59:19	56:17	41:44		Belihu			4		Valencia	28 Oct
59:21	56:12	42:02	Felix	Kibitok	KEN	.91	5		København	16 Sep
59:21	56:16	42:03	Stephen	Kiprop	KEN-J	8.9.99	5		Valencia	28 Oct
59:22			Amdework	Walelegn	ETH-J	11.3.99	2		New Delhi	21 Oct
59:22	56:17	42:03	Bernard Kipkorir	Ngeno	KEN	10.8.96	6		Valencia	28 Oct
59:27dh	56:00	42:14	Mohamed	Farah	GBR	23.3.83	1	GNR	South Shields	9 Sep
59:27	56:17	41:53	El Hassan	El Abbassi	BRN	13.4.84	7		Valencia	28 Oct
59:28	56:17	42:01	Edwin Kiprop	Kiptoo	KEN	14.8.93	6		København	16 Sep
59:28	56:20	41:55	Simon	Cheprot	KEN	2.7.93	8		Valencia	28 Oct
59:29	56:24	42:10	Abel	Kipchumba	KEN	3.2.94	9		Valencia	28 Oct
59:36	56:27	41:44	Jorum	Okumbo	KEN	10.12.97	4		Ras Al Khaimah	9 Feb
59:36	56:27	41:54	Morris	Munene Gachaga	KEN	7.4.95	5		Ras Al Khaimah	9 Feb
59:38	56:38	42:30	James	Rungaru	KEN	14.1.93	1		Den Haag	11 Mar
59:40	56:38	42:02	Wilfred (30/25)	Kimitei	KEN	11.3.85	6		Ras Al Khaimah	9 Feb
59:41	56:38	42:29	Leonard	Langat	KEN	7.8.90	2		Den Haag	11 Mar
59:44	56:48	42:47	Mule	Wasihun	ETH	20.10.93	1		Barcelona	11 Feb
59:47		42:44	Galen	Rupp	USA	8.5.86	1		Ostia	11 Mar
59:47	56:46	42:32	Bernard	Kimeli	KEN	10.9.95	1		Praha	7 Apr
59:48			Mosinet (30)	Geremew	ETH	12.2.92	1		Buenos Aires	26 Aug
59:51		42:42	Aron	Kifle	ERI	20.2.98	4		New Delhi	21 Oct
59:52	56:48	42:19	Lelisa	Desisa	ETH	14.1.90	7		København	16 Sep
59:55	56:48	42:18	Dominic	Kiptarus	KEN	3.8.96	8		København	16 Sep
59:56	56:49	42:33	Geoffrey	Yegon	KEN	28.8.88	2		Praha	7 Apr
59:58	56:48	42:33	Peter	Ndorobo	KEN	11.8.93	3		Praha	7 Apr
59:58	dh	42:14	Jake	Robertson	NZL	14.11.89	2	GNR	South Shields	9 Sep
60:01	56:50	42:09	Asefa	Mengistu	ETH	18.1.85	9		København	16 Sep
60:02	57:14		Geoffrey	Kamworor	KEN	22.11.92	1	WCh	Valencia	24 Mar
60:02	56:51	42:10	Teshome	Mekonen	ETH	5.8.95	12		Valencia	28 Oct
60:03			Victor (40)	Chumo	KEN	.87	1		Lille	1 Sep
60:04	57:15		Hizkel	Tewelde	ERI	15.9.86	2		Lille	1 Sep

Mark			Name		Nat	Born	Pos	Meet	Venue		Date
60:06	56:54	42:33	Shadrack	Kiplagat	KEN	12.12.90	5		Praha		7 Apr
60:06	57:14		Cosmas	Kipchoge	KEN	21.3.86	4		Lille		1 Sep
60:07	56:54	42:19	Asefa	Tefera	ETH	14.3.97	2		Istanbul		8 Apr
60:08	56:55	42:33	Abraham	Kipyatich	KEN	10.5.93	6		Praha		7 Apr
60:08	56:58	42:18	Kaan Kigen	Özbilen	TUR	15.1.86	3		Istanbul		8 Apr
60:09	57:07	42:47	Julien	Wanders	SUI	18.3.96	2		Barcelona		11 Feb
60:09	57:06	42:35	Japheth	Korir	KEN	30.6.93	4		Den Haag		11 Mar
60:09		42:46	Aweke	Ayalew	BRN	23.2.93	5		New Delhi		21 Oct
60:10	57:08	42:49	Moses	Kurong	UGA	7.7.94	3		Barcelona		11 Feb
			(50)								
60:11	57:01	42:18	Alexander	Mutiso	KEN	10.9.96	10		København		16 Sep
60:12		42:43	Leonard	Korir	USA	10.12.86	6		New Delhi		21 Oct
60:14	57:09		Abdallah	Mande	UGA	10.5.95	3		Venlo		25 Mar
60:15	57:08	42:50	Guye	Adola	ETH	20.10.90	2		Houston		14 Jan
60:16	57:25		Yohanes	Gebregergish	ERI	11.1.94	2		Lisboa		11 Mar
60:16	57:07		Gilbert	Masai	KEN	16.12.89	4		Venlo		25 Mar
60:16			Mustapha	El Aziz	MAR	24.12.85	1		Lisboa		14 Oct
60:20	57:12	42:51	Feyisa	Lilesa	ETH	1.2.90	3		Houston		14 Jan
60:20	57:17		Eric	Tirop	KEN	19.5.87	5		Lille		1 Sep
60:21	57:25		Nicholas	Kosimbei	KEN	10.1.96	4		Lisboa		11 Mar
			(60)								
60:21			Geoffrey	Ronoh	KEN	29.11.82	1		Krems		23 Sep
60:22	57:28		Abreham	Cheroben	BRN	10.11.92	2	WCh	Valencia		24 Mar
60:23			Hicham	Amghar	MAR	15.10.94	1		Marrakech		28 Jan
60:24	57:07	42:17	Vincent Kipsang	Rono	KEN	11.11.90	9		Ras Al Khaimah		9 Feb
60:24	57:16	43:07	John	Langat	KEN	31.12.96	5		Venlo		25 Mar
60:24	57:07	42:32	Justus	Kangogo	KEN	10.10.95	7		Praha		7 Apr
60:25		42:42	Barselius	Kipyego	KEN	23.7.93	2		Ústí nad Labem		15 Sep
60:26	57:10	42:17	Evans Kipkorir	Cheruiyot	KEN	24.9.91	5		Istanbul		8 Apr
60:26	57:01	42:04	Betesfa	Getahun	ETH	25.9.98	11		København		16 Sep
60:28	57:30		Atsedu	Tsegay	ETH	17.12.91	5		Lisboa		11 Mar
			(70)								
60:29	57:15	42:50	Clement	Langat	KEN	18.12.91	5		Houston		14 Jan
60:29	57:28		Zersenay	Tadese	ERI	8.2.82	6		Lisboa		11 Mar
60:29		42:22	Emmanuel Kiprono	Bett	KEN	14.7.95	2		Berlin		8 Apr
60:29			Philimon	Maritim	KEN	18.1.88	2		Krems		23 Sep
60:31	57:15	42:28	Edward	Waweru	KEN	3.10.90	1		Marugame		4 Feb
60:36		42:26	Richard	Mengich	KEN	3.4.89	3		Berlin		8 Apr
60:37	57:22	42:51	Samuel	Chelanga	USA	23.2.85	6		Houston		14 Jan
60:38			Mohamed	El Aaraby	MAR	12.11.89	2		Marrakech		28 Jan
60:39	57:28	42:47	Stephen	Kibet	KEN	9.11.86	5		Den Haag		11 Mar
60:40		42:56	Mogos	Shumay	ERI	.97	2		Milano		25 Mar
			(80)								
60:41	57:27	42:51	Stephen	Sambu	KEN	7.7.88	7		Houston		14 Jan
60:41			Abdiwak	Tura	ETH	.95	2		Lisboa		14 Oct
60:42			Paul	Mwangi	KEN	2.1.93	3		Milano		25 Mar
60:42	dh	42:27	Bashir	Abdi	BEL	10.2.89	3	GNR	South Shields		9 Sep
60:42		42:56	Samuel	Mwangi	KEN	19.9.97	3		Krems		23 Sep
60:43	57:40		Patrick	Siele	KEN	27.7.96	6		Lille		1 Sep
60:44		42:44	Moses	Kemei	KEN	3.9.93	2		Ostia		11 Mar
60:44	57:30	42:52	Kisaisa	Ledama	KEN	28.6.98	1		Tachikawa		13 Oct
60:45			Amanuel	Mesel	ERI	29.12.90	3		Lisboa		14 Oct
60:47			Getaneh	Tamire Molla	ETH	10.1.94	5	WCh	Valencia		24 Mar
			(90)								
60:47			Ismael	Kalalei	KEN	25.5.95	4		Lisboa		14 Oct
60:48	57:38	43:08	Philip	Tarbei	KEN	13.2.94	6		Venlo		25 Mar
60:48		42:47	Emmanuel Kipkemei	Bett	KEN	29.3.85	9		New Delhi		21 Oct
60:48	57:34	42:37	Aziz	Lahbabi	MAR	3.2.91	14		Valencia		28 Oct
60:49	57:27	42:50	Alex	Oleitiptip	KEN	20.12.90	8		Houston		14 Jan
60:49			James	Wangari	KEN	23.3.94	8		Lisboa		11 Mar
60:49	57:34	42:38	Rhonzas	Lokitam	KEN	5.9.96	15		Valencia		28 Oct
60:50	57:32	42:51	Tsegay	Tuemay	ERI	20.12.95	9		Houston		14 Jan
60:52			Noah	Kipkemboi	KEN	2.7.93	9		Lisboa		11 Mar
60:52	57:38	43:08	Edwin	Kiptoo	KEN	28.12.87	7		Venlo		25 Mar
			(100)								
60:52	57:36	42:37	Leonard	Komon	KEN	10.1.88	16		Valencia		28 Oct

60:53	Birhan	Neberew	ETH	14.8.94	11 Mar	60:56	William	Wanjiku	KEN	7.5.95	7 Oct
60:53	Mike Kiptum	Boit	KEN		16 Sep	60:57	Shadrack Korir Kimining (42:50)		KEN	10.2.96	9 Feb
60:54	Berhane	Tesfaye	ERI	9.1.87	7 Oct	60:57	Edwin	Koech	KEN	15.5.83	11 Mar
60:55	Taye	Girma	ETH-J	.00	18 Nov	60:59	Terefa	Debela	ETH	20.4.98	7 Oct
60:56	Kipkemboi	Kiprono	KEN	.95	11 Mar	60:59	Khalil	Lemciyeh	MAR	10.12.86	28 Oct

MEN 2018

Mark	Name		Nat	Born	Pos Meet	Venue	Date
61:00+	Eliud	Kipchoge	KEN	5.11.84	22 Apr		
61:00	Evans Kiprop	Cheruiyot	KEN	10.5.82	23 Jun		
61:00	Callum	Hawkins	GBR	22.6.92	28 Oct		
61:01	Haron	Lagat	KEN	15.8.83	14 Jan		
61:01+	Kenenisa	Bekele	ETH	13.6.82	22 Apr		
61:01+	Abel	Kirui	KEN	4.6.82	22 Apr		
61:01+	Daniel	Wanjiru	KEN	25.5.92	22 Apr		
61:01	Suguru	Osako	JPN	23.5.91	3 Sep		
61:01	Abayneh	Degu	ETH	1.12.98	16 Sep		
61:01	Jack	Rayner	AUS	19.12.95	7 Oct		
61:02	Noah	Kigen (42:54)	KEN	12.6.89	8 Apr		
61:02	Titus	Ekiru	KEN	2.1.92	3 Jun		
61:02	Josphat	Tanui	KEN	4.2.94	18 Nov		
61:03	Polat Kemboi	Arikan	TUR	12.12.90	11 Mar		
61:03	Ambrose	Bore (42:54)	KEN	8.8.95	8 Apr		
61:04	Mark Kosgei	Kiptoo	KEN	21.6.76	24 Mar		
61:04	Emmanuel	Kipsang	KEN	13.6.91	15 Apr		
61:05	Meshack	Koech (42:50)	KEN	27.7.89	11 Feb		
61:05	Patrick	Kipkorir	KEN	.96	13 May		
61:06	Philip	Langat (42:51)	KEN	23.4.90	14 Jan		
61:06	Amos	Mitei	KEN	24.6.94	15 Apr		
61:07	Leul	Gebrselassie	ETH	20.9.93	24 Mar		
61:08	Fred	Musobo	UGA	12.8.96	7 Oct		
61:10	Azmeraw	Mengistu	ETH	15.9.92	11 Feb		
61:10	Bernard	Kimani	KEN	10.9.93	11 Mar		
61:11	Stephen	Arita	KEN	26.6.88	24 Mar		
61:11	Evans	Mayaka	KEN	20.12.87	1 Sep		
61:11	Belay	Tilahun	ETH	.95	25 Nov		
61:12	Ben	Connor	GBR	17.10.92	11 Feb		
61:12	Evans	Korir	KEN	.87	18 Feb		
61:12	Sammy	Kitwara	KEN	26.11.86	11 Mar		
61:13	Yuta	Shitara	JPN	18.12.91	4 Feb		
61:14	Leonard	Barsoton	KEN	21.10.94	24 Mar		
61:14	Andrew	Murigutu	KEN Y	18.6.02?	16 Sep		
61:15	Antonio	Abadía	ESP	2.7.90	28 Oct		
61:16	Gilbert	Bii	KEN	10.5.93	7 Oct		
61:17	Mohamed	Ahmami	MAR	12.2.84	28 Jan		
61:17	Precious	Mashele	RSA	13.10.90	18 Nov		
61:18	Timothy	Torotich	UGA	10.10.91	7 Oct		
61:19	Edmond	Kipngetich	KEN	30.4.94	7 Apr		
61:19	Roncer Kipkorir	Konga	KEN	16.12.94	13 May		
61:19	Abraham	Kasongor	KEN	.93	16 Sep		
61:19	Vincent	Laimoi	KEN	16.7.96	17 Nov		
61:20	Homiyu	Tesfaye	GER	23.6.93	11 Mar		
61:20	Solomon	Yego (42:56)	KEN	10.5.87	28 Oct		
61:21	Tadu	Abate	ETH	11.9.97	11 Mar		
61:21	Albert	Rop	BRN	17.7.92	24 Mar		
61:22	Philemon	Lokedi	KEN	4.7.92	25 Mar		
61:22	Kalipus	Lomwai	KEN	10.10.95	1 Jul		
61:22	Kazuya	Shiojiri	JPN	8.11.96	13 Oct		
61:23	Samuel Kiplimo	Kosgei	KEN	20.1.86	24 Mar		
61:24	Isaac	Mwangi (42:51)	KEN	25.8.87	14 Jan		
61:24	Youssef	Benhadi	MAR		28 Jan		
61:25	John	Loitang	KEN	18.3.91	7 Oct		
61:26	Stephen	Mokoka	RSA	31.1.85	24 Mar		
61:28+	Ghirmay	Ghebreslassie	ERI	14.11.95	22 Apr		
61:28	Amos	Kurgat (42:57)	KEN	7.3.92	15 Sep		
61:31	Hillary	Kimaiyo	KEN	.94	11 Mar		
61:32	Ken	Nakayama	JPN	24.2.97	17 Nov		
61:33	Joel	Maina	KEN	3.6.85	25 Mar		
61:33	Timothy	Rono	KEN	18.9.97	27 May		
61:33	Stephen	Kiprotich	UGA	27.2.89	26 Aug		
61:34	Nquse	Amsolom	ERI	10.11.86	24 Mar		
61:34+	Lawrence	Cherono	KEN	7.8.88	22 Apr		
61:35+	Bernard	Kipyego	KEN	16.7.86	26 Jan		
61:35	Festus	Talam	KEN	20.10.94	23 Jun		
61:36	Josephat	Menjo	KEN	20.8.79	24 Mar		
61:37+	Benson	Kipruto	KEN	.91	26 Jan		
61:37	Berhane	Aferwerki	ERI	6.5.96	24 Mar		
61:37	Ezrah	Sang	KEN	8.6.94	25 Mar		
61:38+	Birhanu	Teshome	ETH	.96	26 Jan		
61:38+	Yenew	Alamirew	ETH	27.5.90	26 Jan		
61:38+	Tamirat	Tola	ETH	11.8.91	26 Jan		
61:38	Javier	Guerra	ESP	10.11.83	4 Feb		
61:39+	Ronald	Korir	KEN	.91	26 Jan		
61:39+	Berhanu	Legesse	ETH	11.9.94	26 Jan		
61:39	Mehari	Tsegay	ERI-J	12.2.99	24 Mar		
61:40+	Sisay	Lemma	ETH	12.12.90	26 Jan		
61:40	Yunia	Halton	JPN	13.11.93	16 Sep		
61:40	Henry	Rono	KEN	12.12.96	7 Oct		
61:41	Joseph	Kiptum	KEN	25.9.87	24 Mar		
61:41	Felix	Chemonges	UGA	10.10.95	7 Oct		
61:42	Kenta	Murayama	JPN	23.2.93	4 Feb		
61:42	Koen	Naert	BEL	3.9.89	4 Mar		
61:42	Vitalis	Kwemoi	UGA	.90	7 Oct		
61:43	Bayelign	Teshager	ETH-J	9.2.00	4 Feb		
61:43	Nobert	Kigen	KEN	24.1.93	4 Feb		
61:43	Olika	Adegna	ETH-J	12.9.99	18 Nov		
61:44	Dawit	Fikadu	BRN	29.12.95	28 Jan		
(200)							
61:44	Kenneth	Kipkemoi	KEN	2.8.84	11 Nov		

Downhill course: 60:47   Charles Kamau Karanja   KEN   5.8.97   1   Torino   7 Oct

Drugs disqualification
60:48   Mousaab   Hadout ¶   MAR   11.3.88   (7)   Venlo   25 Mar

JUNIORS

See main list for top 2 juniors. 10 performances by 5 men to 61:40. Additional marks and further juniors:

Kiprop	59:41	1		Ústí nad Labem	15 Sep	60:15	1	Iomouc	23 Jun
	59:44	1		Venlo	25 Mar				
Walelegn	59:50	1		Iastanbul	8 Apr	60:37	13	København	16 Sep
60:55	Taye	Girma	ETH	.00	1		Boulogne-Billancourt	18 Nov	
61:14	Andrew	Mangata	KEN-Y	15.6.02?	16		København	16 Sep	
61:39	Mehari	Tsegay	ERI-	12.2.99	5		Azkoitia	24 Mar	
61:43	Bayelign	Teshager	ETH	9.2.00	5		Marugame	4 Feb	
61:43	Olika	Adegna	ETH	12.9.99	4		Boulogne-Billancourt	18 Nov	
61:50	Joel	Mwaura	KEN	20.1.99	7		Marugame	4 Feb	
62:20	Isaac	Temoi	KEN	.99	10		Den Haag	11 Mar	
62:50	Antenayehu	Danachew	ETH		10		Lille	1 Sep	

25/30 KILOMETRES ROAD

25k	30k							
		In addition to those shown in Marathon listing						
	1:27:24+	Bedan	Karoki	KEN	21.8.90	in Mar	London	22 Apr
1:12:36	1:27:31+	Mohamed	Farah	GBR	23.3.83	in Mar	London	22 Apr
	1:27:33+	Felix	Kibitok	KEN	.91	in Mar	Dubai	26 Jan
1:12:37	1:27:44+	Bedan	Karoki	KEN	21.8.90	in Mar	London	22 Apr
1:12:57	1:27:58	Yenew	Alamirew	ETH	27.5.90	in Mar	Dubai	26 Jan
1:12:38	1:28:30	Kenenisa	Bekele	ETH	13.6.82	in Mar	London	22 Apr
1:12:39	1:28:13+	Daniel	Wanjiru	KEN	25.5.92	in Mar	London	22 Apr
1:12:56+		Felix	Kibitok	KEN	.91	in Mar	Dubai	26 Jan
1:12:56+		Barselius	Kipyego	KEN	23.7.93	in Mar	Dubai	26 Jan
1:13:13	1:29:05+	Birhanu	Teshome	ETH	.96	in Mar	Dubai	26 Jan

Mark		Name		Nat	Born	Pos Meet	Venue	Date
1:13:13	1:29:20+	Benson	Kipruto	KEN	.91	in Mar	Dubai	26 Jan
1:13:50	1:29:03+	Laban	Korir	KEN	30.12.85	in Mar	Amsterdam	21 Oct
1:13:54+		Ronald	Korir	KEN	.91	in Mar	Dubai	26 Jan
1:13:55+		Solomon Kirwa	Yego	KEN	10.5.87	in Mar	Berlin	16 Sep
	1:29:20+	Tsegaye	Mekonnen	ETH	15.6.95	in Mar	Tokyo	25 Feb
1:13:56	1:29:20+	Richard	Mengich	KEN	3.4.89	in Mar	Berlin	16 Sep
1:13:56	1:29:20+	Noah	Kigen	KEN	12.6.89	in Mar	Berlin	16 Sep
1:13:58+		Simon	Cheprot	KEN	2.7.93	in Mar	Berlin	16 Sep
	1:29:21+	Yohanes	Gebregergish	ERI	1.1.89	in Mar	Valencia	2 Dec
	1:29:23+	Vincent	Yator	KEN	11.7.89	in Mar	Frankfurt	28 Oct
	1:29:45 +	Galen	Rupp	USA	8.5.86	in Mar	Chicago	7 Oct
	1:29:47	Keisuke	Hayashi	JPN	24.12.96	1	Kumamoto	18 Feb
	1:29:48	Yuki	Oshikawa	JPN	2.6.90	2	Kumamoto	18 Feb
	1:29:56	Gen	Hachisuka	JPN	29.11.94	3	Kumamoto	18 Feb

Drugs disqualification: 1:29:57 + Samuel Kalalei KEN 13.11.94 in Mar Rotterdam 8 Apr

MARATHON

Mark	25k	30k	Name		Nat	Born	Pos	Venue	Date
2:01:39	1:12:24	1:26:45	Eliud	Kipchoge	KEN	5.11.84	1	Berlin	16 Sep
2:04:00	1:12:57	1:27:38	Mosinet	Geremew	ETH	12.2.92	1	Dubai	26 Jan
2:04:02	1:12:57	1:27:37	Leul	Gebrselassie	ETH	20.9.93	2	Dubai	26 Jan
2:04:06	1:12:56	1:27:38	Tamirat	Tola	ETH	11.8.91	3	Dubai	26 Jan
2:04:06	1:12:57	1:27:37	Asefa	Mengistu	ETH	18.1.85	4	Dubai	26 Jan
2:04:06	1:13:49	1:28:58	Lawrence	Cherono	KEN	7.8.88	1	Amsterdam	21 Oct
2:04:08	1:12:58	1:27:38	Sisay	Lemma	ETH	12.12.90	5	Dubai	26 Jan
2:04:15	1:12:57	1:27:37	Berhanu	Legesse	ETH	11.9.94	6	Dubai	26 Jan
2:04:17	1:12:36	1:27:24		Kipchoge			1	London	22 Apr
2:04:31	1:14:14	1:29:04		Gebrselassie			1	Valencia	2 Dec
2:04:37	1:13:49	1:28:58	Mule	Wasihun	ETH	20.10.93	2	Amsterdam	21 Oct
2:04:40	1:13:49	1:28:58	Solomon	Deksisa (10)	ETH	11.3.94	3	Amsterdam	21 Oct
2:04:43	1:14:15	1:29:07	El Hassan	El Abbassi	BRN	13.4.84	2	Valencia	2 Dec
2:04:44	1:12:57	1:27:37	Abdiwak	Tura	ETH	19.6.97	7	Dubai	26 Jan
2:04:49	1:12:36	1:27:24	Tola	Shura Kitata	ETH	9.6.96	2	London	22 Apr
2:04:53	1:14:14	1:29:04	Mathew	Kisorio	KEN	16.5.89	3	Valencia	2 Dec
2:04:58		1:28:32		Lemma			1	Ljubljana	28 Oct
2:05:11	1:15:20	1:29:46	Mohamed	Farah	GBR	23.3.83	1	Chicago	7 Oct
2:05:21		1:29:38	Emmanuel	Saina	KEN	6.9.92	1	Buenos Aires	23 Sep
2:05:21	1:14:14	1:29:05	Tsegaye	Kebede	ETH	15.1.87	4	Valencia	2 Dec
2:05:22	1:14:14	1:29:08	Nobert	Kigen	KEN	24.1.93	5	Valencia	2 Dec
2:05:24				Geremew			2	Chicago	7 Oct
2:05:26	1:14:14	1:29:05	El Mahjoub	Dazza	MAR	3.3.91	6	Valencia	2 Dec
2:05:30	1:14:24	1:29:20	Dickson	Chumba	KEN	27.10.86	1	Tokyo	25 Feb
2:05:44	1:14:20	1:29:17	Kenneth	Kipkemoi	KEN	2.8.84	1	Rotterdam	8 Apr
2:05:50	1:14:20	1:29:17	Abera	Kuma	ETH	31.8.90	2	Rotterdam	8 Apr
2:05:50		1:29:46	Suguru	Osako	JPN	23.5.91	3	Chicago	7 Oct
2:05:56	1:14:19	1:29:16	Kelkile	Gezahegn	ETH	1.10.96	3	Rotterdam	8 Apr
2:05:57		1:29:46		Kipkemoi			4	Chicago	7 Oct
2:05:58	1:14:19	1:29:17	Laban	Korir	KEN	30.12.85	4	Rotterdam	8 Apr
2:05:59			Lelisa	Desisa	ETH	14.1.90	1	New York	4 Nov
				(31/26)					
2:06:07			Galen	Rupp	USA	8.5.86	1	Praha	6 May
2:06:11		1:29:20	Yuta	Shitara	JPN	18.12.91	2	Tokyo	25 Feb
2:06:15	1:13:48	1:28:58	Gideon	Kipketer	KEN	10.11.92	4	Amsterdam	21 Oct
2:06:21	1:14:14	1:29:04	Sammy	Kitwara	KEN	26.11.86	7	Valencia	2 Dec
				(30)					
2:06:23	1:13:55	1:28:41	Amos	Kipruto	KEN	19.9.92	2	Berlin	16 Sep
2:06:24	1:13:39	1:28:59	Kaan Kigen	Özbilen	TUR	15.1.86	5	Amsterdam	21 Oct
2:06:24	1:14:14	1:29:07	Solomon Kirwa	Yego	KEN	10.5.87	8	Valencia	2 Dec
2:06:25			Paul	Lonyangata	KEN	12.12.92	1	Paris	8 Apr
2:06:26			Geoffrey	Kamworor	KEN	22.11.92	3	New York	4 Nov
2:06:29			Abraham	Kiptum	KEN	15.9.89	1	Daegu	1 Apr
2:06:35			Evans	Korir	KEN	.87	2	Daegu	1 Apr
2:06:41			Ernest	Ngeno	KEN	20.5.95	3	Paris	8 Apr
2:06:41	1:14:18	1:29:23	Martin	Kosgei	KEN	21.3.89	2	Frankfurt	28 Oct
2:06:45		1:29:43	Geoffrey	Kirui	KEN	16.2.93	6	Chicago	7 Oct
				(40)					
2:06:47	1:14:08	1:29:06	Tadu	Abate	ETH	11.9.97	7	Amsterdam	21 Oct
2:06:48	1:13:56	1:29:20	Wilson	Kipsang	KEN	15.3.82	3	Berlin	16 Sep
2:06:49			Peter	Some	KEN	5.6.90	3	Daegu	1 Apr

MEN 2018

Mark			Name		Nat	Born	Pos	Meet	Venue	Date
2:06:51	1:13:48	1:28:58	Jonathan	Kipleting	KEN	20.11.86	8		Amsterdam	21 Oct
2:06:54		1:29:20	Hiroto	Inoue	JPN	6.1.93	5		Tokyo	25 Feb
2:06:57			Wilson	Loyanae	KEN	20.11.88	5		Seoul	18 Mar
2:07:00			Yitayal	Atnafu	ETH	20.1.93	4		Paris	8 Apr
2:07:03		1:28:57	Mark	Korir	KEN	10.1.85	2		Seoul	18 Mar
2:07:07	1:12:42	1:28:00	Abel	Kirui	KEN	4.6.82	4		London	22 Apr
2:07:09		1:29:23	Alex	Kibet	KEN	20.10.90	3		Frankfurt	28 Oct
(50)										
2:07:11			Benson	Kipruto	KEN	.91	3		Seoul	18 Mar
2:07:19			Ayele	Abshero	ETH	28.12.90	3		Hamburg	29 Apr
2:07:20	1:13:49	1:28:58	Hillary	Kipsambu	KEN	4.2.85	9		Amsterdam	21 Oct
2:07:22	1:14:19	1:29:17	Marius	Kipserem	KEN	17.5.88	5		Rotterdam	8 Apr
2:07:26			Abrha	Milaw	ETH	3.1.88	1		Cannes	4 Nov
2:07:27			Yuma	Hattori	JPN	13.11.93	1		Fukuoka	2 Dec
2:07:28	1:14:18	1:29:24	Amos	Mitei	KEN	24.6.94	4		Frankfurt	28 Oct
2:07:30		1:29:20	Feyisa	Lilesa	ETH	1.2.90	6		Tokyo	25 Feb
2:07:32			Elisha	Kipchirchir Rotich	KEN	12.4.90	1		Eindhoven	14 Oct
2:07:33	1:14:14	1:29:11	Deribe	Robi	ETH	20.9.90	9		Valencia	2 Dec
(60)										
2:07:34	1:14:18	1:29:23	Kenneth	Keter	KEN	4.8.96	5		Frankfurt	28 Oct
2:07:37	1:14:14	1:29:10	Benson	Seurei	BRN	27.3.84	10		Valencia	2 Dec
2:07:38			Laban	Mutai	KEN	15.1.88	2		Eindhoven	14 Oct
2:07:45			Marius	Kimutai	KEN	.89	4		Seoul	18 Mar
2:07:46			Augustino	Sulle	TAN	13.10.97	2		Toronto	21 Oct
2:07:50			Vincent	Rono	KEN	22.12.90	3		Eindhoven	14 Oct
2:07:50	1:14:18	1:29:24	Mark Kosgei	Kiptoo	KEN	21.6.76	6		Frankfurt	28 Oct
2:07:53			Joseph	Ndirangu	KEN	9.9.94	1		Otsu	4 Mar
2:07:57			Felix	Kiprotich	KEN	.88	5		Seoul	18 Mar
2:07:57			Stephen	Kiprotich	UGA	27.2.89	5		Hamburg	29 Apr
(70)										
2:07:57		1:29:58	Taku	Fujimoto	JPN	11.9.89	8		Chicago	7 Oct
2:07:59			Bedan	Karoki	KEN	21.8.90	9		Chicago	7 Oct
2:08:03			Cosmas	Kipchoge	KEN	21.3.86	1		Roma	8 Apr
2:08:08			Ryo	Kiname	JPN	22.1.91	7		Tokyo	25 Feb
2:08:08			Anthony	Maritim	KEN	12.11.86	1		Barcelona	11 Mar
2:08:11			Raymond	Choge	KEN	2.1.88	1		Kosice	7 Oct
2:08:15			Aychew	Bantie	ETH	12.9.95	2		Kosice	7 Oct
2:08:16			Shogo	Nakamura	JPN	16.9.92	4		Berlin	16 Sep
2:08:17			Albert	Korir	KEN	2.3.94	2		Otsu	4 Mar
2:08:19			Tariku	Kebede	ETH	.96	2		Seoul	4 Nov
(80)										
2:08:20			Eliud	Kiptanui	KEN	6.6.89	5		Paris	8 Apr
2:08:20	1:14:14	1:29:05	Samuel	Tsegay	ERI	24.2.88	11		Valencia	2 Dec
2:08:22			Dickson	Tuwei	KEN	31.10.92	1		Sevilla	25 Feb
2:08:26			Jake	Robertson	NZL	14.11.89	3		Otsu	4 Mar
2:08:26			Silas	Too	KEN	.89	2		Barcelona	11 Mar
2:08:26			Kenneth	Kiprop Chebobor	KEN	2.8.84	1		Gyeongju	21 Oct
2:08:30			Bazu	Worku	ETH	15.9.90	1		Houston	14 Jan
2:08:30			Felix	Kandie	KEN	10.4.87	3		Toronto	21 Oct
2:08:31			Stephen	Mokoka	RSA	31.1.85	1	NC	Cape Town	23 Sep
2:08:32			Andrew	Kimutai	KEN	12.8.89	3		Sevilla	25 Feb
(90)										
2:08:32			Abdi Ibrahim	Abdo	BRN	24.4.97	2		Roma	8 Apr
2:08:32			Abdela	Godana	ETH		3		Seoul	4 Nov
2:08:34	1:14:18	1:29:24	Asefa	Tefera	ETH	14.3.97	7		Frankfurt	28 Oct
2:08:36			Javier	Guerra	ESP	10.11.83	4	1 NC	Sevilla	25 Feb
2:08:36			Gebretsadik	Adhana	ETH	16.7.92	2		Ljubljana	28 Oct
2:08:43			Douglas	Chebii	KEN	1.11.93	5		Sevilla	25 Feb
2:08:43			Saïd	Aït-Addi	MAR	29.6.82	6		Seoul	18 Mar
2:08:45			Chihiro	Miyawaki	JPN	28.8.91	8		Tokyo	25 Feb
2:08:46			Zersenay	Tadese	ERI	8.2.82	5		Berlin	16 Sep
2:08:47			Barselius	Kipyego	KEN	23.7.93	4		Seoul	4 Nov
(100)										

Mark	Name		Nat	Born	Date		Mark	Name		Nat	Born	Date
2:08:48	Kenji	Yamamoto	JPN	17.11.89	25 Feb		2:08:55	Thomas	Kiplagat	KEN	.87	8 Apr
2:08:48	Kiprotich	Kirui	KEN	22.12.84	8 Apr		2:08:56	Yenew	Alamirew	ETH	27.5.90	26 Jan
2:08:49	Hizkel	Tewelde	ERI	15.9.86	28 Oct		2:08:58	Yuki	Sato	JPN	26.11.86	25 Feb
2:08:50	Shumet	Mengistu	ETH	.88	7 Oct		2:09:01	Titus	Ekiru	KEN	2.1.92	9 Dec
2:08:50	Shifera	Tamru	ETH-J	.99	28 Oct		2:09:04	Fred	Musobo	UGA	12.8.96	4 Nov
2:08:51	Lemi	Berhanu	ETH	13.9.94	29 Sep		2:09:05	Robert	Chemonges	UGA	15.10.97	4 Nov
2:08:52	Yemane	Adhane	ETH	29.2.96	27 May		2:09:06	Asbel	Kipsang	KEN	10.9.93	8 Apr
2:08:53	Paul	Kipkorir	KEN	31.5.82	18 Mar		2:09:07	Samuel Kiplimo	Kosgei	KEN	20.1.86	21 Oct
2:08:53	Kenenisa	Bekele	ETH	13.6.82	22 Apr		2:09:13	Philemon	Kacherlan	KEN	4.7.92	23 Sep

Mark	Name	Nat	Born	Pos	Meet	Venue	Date
2:09:14	John Kipkosgei Korir	KEN	2.12.96				27 May
2:09:14	Herpasa Negassa	ETH	.93				29 Sep
2:09:16	Mohamed El Aaraby (1:29:22)	MAR	12.11.89				7 Oct
2:09:16	Zelalem Bacha	BRN	10.1.88				4 Nov
2:09:18	Tsegaye Mekonnen	ETH	15.6.95				18 Nov
2:09:19	Barnabas Kiptum	KEN	8.10.86				23 Sep
2:09:20	Mekuant Ayenew	ETH	.91				26 Jan
2:09:20	Paul Kangogo	KEN	.89				8 Apr
2:09:21	Michael Githae	KEN	26.8.94				4 Mar
2:09:21	Kipkemoi Kipsang	KEN	10.10.90				23 Sep
2:09:23	Reuben Kerio	KEN	2.6.94				7 Oct
2:09:24	Robert K. Kipkemboi	KEN	19.6.88				21 Oct
2:09:24	Tsegay Getachew	ETH	30.11.96				18 Nov
2:09:24	Abdi Fufa	ETH	27.9.95				18 Nov
2:09:25	Cam Levins	CAN	28.3.89				21 Oct
2:09:26	Tsedat Abege	ETH	18.2.96				11 Mar
2:09:26	Adugna Takele	ETH	26.2.89				27 May
2:09:27	Solomon Mutai	UGA	22.10.92				18 Nov
2:09:28	Justus Kiprotich	KEN	17.7.96				9 Sep
2:09:29	Salaheddine Bounasser	MAR	27.9.90				22 Apr
2:09:30	Tariku Bekele	ETH	21.1.87				4 Nov
2:09:31	Desmond Mokgobu	RSA	23.11.88				4 Feb
2:09:32	Elisha Barno	KEN	22.6.85				14 Jan
2:09:34	Hayato Sonoda	JPN	5.4.89				4 Feb
2:09:34	Mike Kiptum Boit	KEN					21 Oct
2:09:36	Kohei Ogino	JPN	8.12.89				25 Feb
2:09:42	Stephen Chemlany	KEN	9.8.82				6 May
2:09:43	Tadashi Isshiki	JPN	5.6.94				25 Feb
2:09:44	Seboka Nigusse	ETH	.84				8 Apr
2:09:44	Edwin Koech	KEN	25.3.92				13 May
2:09:45	Amanuel Mesel	ERI	29.12.90				2 Dec
2:09:47	Akinobu Murasawa	JPN	28.3.91				25 Feb
2:09:48	Olivier Irabaruta	BDI	25.8.90				4 Nov
2:09:49	Kenneth Mungara	KEN	7.9.73				1 Jul
2:09:49	Dominic Ruto	KEN	.90				29 Sep
2:09:50	Kenta Murayama	JPN	23.2.93				1 Jul
2:09:51	Koen Naert	BEL	3.9.89				12 Aug
2:09:52	Jo Fukuda	JPN	31.12.90				1 Jul
2:09:56	Okbay Tsegay	ERI	.86				16 Sep
2:09:57	Felix Kimutai	KEN	12.2.89				11 Nov
2:09:59	Birhanu Teshome	ETH	.96				8 Apr
2:10:00	Simon Kariuki (1:29:20)	KEN	13.2.92				25 Feb
2:10:00	Justus Kimutai	KEN	2.3.93				8 Apr
2:10:03	Ishmael Busendich	KEN	7.7.91				22 Apr
2:10:04	Robert Kipkorir Kwambai	KEN	22.11.85				8 Apr
2:10:06	Hicham Laqouahi	MAR	13.6.89				8 Apr
2:10:06	Daniel Mesfun	ERI	.88				21 Oct
2:10:08	Jacob Kendagor	KEN	19.9.84				1 Apr
2:10:12	Shohei Otsuka	JPN	13.8.94				4 Feb
2:10:12	Oleksandr Sitkovskyy	UKR	9.6.78				18 Mar
2:10:12	Kenneth Limo	KEN	14.8.90				16 Dec
2:10:13	Asuka Tanaka	JPN	5.11.89				25 Feb
2:10:14	Hiroki Yamagishi	JPN	6.9.91				25 Feb
2:10:15	Eliud Barngetuny	KEN	23.2.87				22 Apr
2:10:15	Takuya Noguchi	JPN	2.7.88				1 Jul
2:10:16	Bernard Kipyego	KEN	16.7.86				18 Mar
2:10:16	Michael Njenga Kunyuga	KEN	27.7.87				8 Apr
2:10:18	Daichi Kamino	JPN	13.9.93				25 Feb
2:10:19	Duncan Koech	KEN	28.12.81				8 Apr
2:10:21	Kengo Suzuki	JPN	11.6.95				25 Feb
2:10:21	Daniel Wanjiru	KEN	25.5.92				4 Nov
2:10:21	Hamid Ben Daoud	MAR	19.2.96				2 Dec
2:10:22	Julius Tuwei	KEN	26.6.93				2 Dec
2:10:24	Richard Mengich	KEN	3.4.89				21 Oct
2:10:30	Joshua Kipkorir	KEN	10.3.94				21 Jan
2:10:31	Vincent Kipruto	KEN	13.9.87				29 Apr
2:10:31	Willy Ngelel	KEN	24.5.96				13 Ma
2:10:32	Motlokoa Nkhabutlane	LES	16.11.84				8 Apr
2:10:32	Alfonce Kigen	KEN	.93				22 Apr
2:10:33	Stephen Chebogut	KEN	9.1.85				29 Apr
2:10:39	Weldu Negash	ERI	12.11.86				1 Apr
2:10:41	Nixson Kurgat	KEN	7.11.87				4 Nov
2:10:41	Fikadu Kebede	ETH	18.10.96				4 Nov
2:10:43	Hilary Kipchumba	KEN	25.11.92				16 Dec
2:10:44	Mohamed Ziani	MAR	.93				9 Dec
2:10:44	Gadisa Berhanu	ETH	.92				9 Dec
2:10:45	Daniele Meucci	ITA	7.10.85				4 Mar
2:10:46	Bashir Abdi	BEL	10.2.89				8 Apr
2:10:49	Leonard Langat	KEN	7.8.90				11 Nov
2:10:53	Geoffrey Kusuro	UGA	12.2.89				28 Oct
2:10:54	Josphat Letting	KEN	1.1.88				4 Feb
2:10:55	Juan Luis Barrios	MEX	24.6.83				25 Feb
	(200)						
2:10:55	Abraham Kiprotich	FRA	17.8.85				11 Nov
2:10:55	Tsegay Tuemay	ERI	20.12.95				9 Dec
2:10:56	Brimin Misoi	KEN	.89				11 Nov
2:10:57	Birhanu Gebru	ETI l	27.1.07				8 Apr

Uncertain distance

Mark	Name	Nat	Born	Pos	Meet	Venue	Date
2:04:04	Marius Kipserem	KEN	17.5.88	1		Abu Dhabi	7 Dec
2:04:16	Abraham Kiptum	KEN	5.9.89	2		Abu Dhabi	7 Dec
2:07:06	Dejene Debela	ETH	.95	3		Abu Dhabi	7 Dec
2:07:12	Thomas Kiplagat	KEN	.87	4		Abu Dhabi	7 Dec
2:09:18	Stanley Biwott	KEN	21.4.86	5		Abu Dhabi	7 Dec

Downhill course

Mark	Name	Nat	Born	Pos	Meet	Venue	Date
2:08:30	Lawi Kiptui	KEN	.93	1		Rennes	28 Oct
2:09:15	Chala Dechase	ETH	13.6.84				28 Oct
2:09:30	Dominic Letting	KEN	10.11.94				28 Oct
2:09:42	Duncan Maiyo	KEN	5.8.90				28 Oct
2:09:54	Birhane Teshome	ETH	.96				28 Oct

Short course

Mark	Name	Nat	Born	Pos	Meet	Venue	Date
2:07:34	Limenih Getachew	ETH	30.4.90	1		Lisboa	14 Oct
2:07:51	Samuel Ndungu	KEN	4.4.88	2		Lisboa	14 Oct
2:07:58	Justus Kimutai	KEN		3		Lisboa	14 Oct
2:08:18	Ishmael Busendich	KEN	7.7.91	4		Lisboa	14 Oct
2:08:22	Nicholas Kirwa	KEN		5		Lisboa	14 Oct
2:08:27	Hicham Laqouahi	MAR	13.6.89	6		Lisboa	14 Oct
2:09:24	Birhan Neberew	ETH	14.8.94				14 Oct
2:09:44	Alfred Kering	KEN	20.11.80				14 Oct
2:10:08	Jonah Chesum	KEN	5.5.89				14 Oct

Drugs disqualification

Mark	Name	Nat	Born	Pos	Meet	Venue	Date
2:10:44	Samuel Kalalei ¶	KEN	13.11.94				8 Apr

JUNIORS

Mark	Name	Nat	Born	Pos	Meet	Venue	Date
2:12:39	Hiribo Shano	ETH	.99	4		Beirut	11 Nov

100 KILOMETRES

Mark	Name	Nat	Born	Pos	Meet	Venue	Date
6:28:05	Hideaki Yamauchi	JPN	16.12.85	1		Grkavscak	8 Sep
6:32:51	Takehiko Gyoba	JPN	23.5.85	2	WCh	Grkavscak	8 Sep
6:33:47	Bongmusa Mthembu	RSA	27.6.83	3	WCh	Grkavscak	8 Sep
6:36:05	Koji Hayasaka	JPN	5.12.83	4	WCh	Grkavscak	8 Sep
6:42:30	Nao Kazami	JPN	9.4.83	5	WCh	Grkavscak	8 Sep
6:42:30	Geoffrey Burns	USA	8.3.90	6	WCh	Grkavscak	8 Sep
6:42:35	Giorgio Calcaterra	ITA	11.2.72	7	WCh	Grkavscak	8 Sep
6:43:22	Anthony Clark	GBR	2.8.77	8	WCh	Grkavscak	8 Sep

MEN 2018

Mark	Name		Nat	Born	Pos	Meet	Venue		Date
6:44:53	Fritjof	Fagerlund	SWE	27.6.74	9	WCh	Grkavescak		8 Sep
6:46:03	Elov	Olsson	SWE	26.7.89	10	WCh	Grkavescak		8 Sep
6:46:45	Si Guosong	CHN	15.12.80	26 Oct	6:52:10	Anthony	Kunkel	USA	7.4.92	7 Apr
6:47:47	Vsevolod	Khudyakov	RUS	8.2.89	9 Sep	6:52:15	Ryo	Obayashi	JPN	30.1.85	21 Oct
6:49:39	Wouter	Decock	BEL	23.9.83	8 Sep	6:52:57	Alexander	Dautel	GER	7.9.88	8 Sep

Wind assisted

Mark	Name		Nat	Born	Pos	Meet	Venue	Date
6:09:14	Nao	Kazami	JPN	9.4.83	1		Yubetsu	24 Jun
6:20:49	Koji	Hayasaka	JPN	5.12.83	2		Yubetsu	24 Jun
6:22:55	Takehiko	Gyoba	JPN	23.5.85	3		Yubetsu	24 Jun
6:23:49	Hideaki	Yamauchi	JPN	16.12.85	4		Yubetsu	24 Jun
6:28:35	Yoshiki	Kawauchi	JPN	8.11.90	5		Yubetsu	24 Jun
6:40:40	Shunpei	Oda	JPN	23.12.96	6		Yubetsu	24 Jun
6:40:46	Tatsuya	Itagaki	JPN	4.1.88	7		Yubetsu	24 Jun
6:41:20	Shunsuke	Hisamoto	JPN	.90	8		Yubetsu	24 Jun
6:41:47	Yoshiki	Takada	JPN	18.7.83	9		Yubetsu	24 Jun
6:48:59	Ryo	Obayashi	JPN	30.1.85	10		Yubetsu	24 Jun

24 HOURS

Mark	Name		Nat	Born	Pos	Meet	Venue	Date
273.674t	Iván	Penalba López	ESP	6.10.91	1		Stadtoldendorf	16 Jun
268.783	Nobuyuki	Takahashi	JPN	1.2.83	1		Tokyo	10 Nov
265.419	Andrzej	Radzikowski	POL	1.4.81	1	EC	Timisoara	26 May
263.540	Stéphane	Ruel	FRA	21.1.66	2	EC	Timisoara	26 May
260.991	Aleksandr	Sorokin	LTU	30.9.81	3	EC	Timisoara	26 May
260.043	Shingo	Inoue	JPN	27.9.80	2		Tokyo	10 Nov
260.016	Felix	Weber	GER	24.3.87	1		Adelaide	15 Jul
259.201	Olivier	Leblond	USA	30.4.72	1		Cleveland	22 Sep
258.890t		Penalba López			1	Asi/Oce	Taipei	1 Dec
257.745	Nicolas	de las Heras	ESP	26.12.64	4	EC	Timisoara	26 May
255.279	Shuhei	Odani	JPN	25.8.88	3		Tokyo	10 Nov
254.264	Erik	Clavery	FRA	7.6.80	1		Albi	20 Oct

Mark	Name		Nat	Born	Pos		Name		Nat	Born	Pos
253.614t	Jacob	Jackson	USA	3.6.77	8 Dec	247.144	Johan	Steene	SWE	25.12.73	27 May
253.432	Dan	Lawson	GBR	13.2.73	26 May	247.089t	Paul	Maskell	GBR	31.5.78	22 Sep
253.420t	Yoshihiko	Ishikawa	JPN	25.4.88	1 Dec	247.018t	Harvey	Lewis	USA	13.4.76	20 Jan
251.725	Raphael	Gerardin	FRA	12.12.73	20 Oct	246.753t	Toshiro	Naraki	JPN	10.8.76	1 Dec
251.373t	Grant	MacDonald	GBR	18.1.79	15 Dec	246.526	Kengo	Takahashi	JPN	.82	11 Nov
251.199	Radek	Brunner	CZE	5.12.74	26 May	246.524	Ludovic	Dilmi	FRA	11.4.65	26 May
250.800	Valentin	Costa	FRA	27.8.66	20 Oct	245.689	Ryo	Abiko	JPN	16.1.75	10 Nov
250.371t	Ullas	Narayana	IND	22.2.80	1 Dec	245.566t	Stephen	Redfern	AUS	15.1.72	2 Jun
249.750	Bjørn Tore	Taranger	NOR	13.4.79	26 May	245.602	John David	Yoon	AUS	19.5.71	14 Jul
249.618t	Greg	Armstrong	USA	29.10.73	8 Dec	**Best track time**					
249.506t	Nicholas	Coury	USA	1.10.87	8 Dec	252.301t	Nobuyuki	Takahashi	JPN	1.2.83	1 Dec
249.150t	Michael	Stocks	GBR	4.4.69	22 Sep	**Indoors**					
247.921t	Bob	Hearn	USA	10.10.65	8 Dec	250.743t	Dan	Välitalo	SWE	19.3.71	24 Nov

2000 METRES STEEPLECHASE

Mark	Name		Nat	Born	Pos	Meet	Venue	Date
5:29.65	Mohamed Ismail	Ibrahim	DJI	1.7.97	1		Goleniów	20 Jun
5:29.94	Krystian	Zalewski	POL	11.4.89	2		Goleniów	20 Jun

3000 METRES STEEPLECHASE

Mark	Name		Nat	Born	Pos	Meet	Venue	Date
7:58.15	Soufiane	El Bakkali	MAR	7.1.96	1	Herc	Monaco	20 Jul
8:01.02	Evan	Jager	USA	8.3.89	2	Herc	Monaco	20 Jul
8:06.19	Benjamin	Kigen	KEN	5.7.93	1	DL	Rabat	13 Jul
8:07.27	Chala	Boyo	ETH	18.1.06	2	DL	Rabat	13 Jul
8:08.40	Conseslus	Kipruto	KEN	8.12.94	1	G Gala	Roma	31 May
8:09.07		Kigen			1	Pre	Eugene	26 May
8:09.58		El Bakkali			3	DL	Rabat	13 Jul
8:09.78		Kipruto			3	Herc	Monaco	20 Jul
8:09.98		Kigen			4	Herc	Monaco	20 Jul
8:10.01		Kigen			2	G Gala	Roma	31 May
8:10.08		Kipruto			1	CG	Gold Coast	13 Apr
8:10.15		Kipruto			1	WK	Zürich	30 Aug
8:10.19		El Bakkali			2	WK	Zürich	30 Aug
8:10.48		Kigen			1	Gyulai	Székesfehérvár	2 Jul
8:10.62	Abraham	Kibiwot	KEN	6.4.96	2	CG	Gold Coast	13 Apr
8:11.22		Beyo			3	G Gala	Roma	31 May
8:11.71		Kipruto			2	Pre	Eugene	26 May
8:11.71		Jager			3	Pre	Eugene	26 May
8:12.20	Hillary	Bor	USA	22.11.89	4	DL	Rabat	13 Jul
8:12.24	Amos	Kirui	KEN	9.2.98	3	CG	Gold Coast	13 Apr
8:12.33	Matt	Hughes	CAN	3.8.89	4	CG	Gold Coast	13 Apr
8:13.13		Hughes			5	DL	Rabat	13 Jul

Mark	Name		Nat	Born	Pos	Meet	Venue	Date	
8:13.18	Nicholas	Bett (10)	KEN	20.12.96	1		Dessau	8	Jun
8:13.22		Jager			3	WK	Zürich	30	Aug
8:13.71		Beyo			1	DL	Doha	4	May
8:14.21		Bor			5	Herc	Monaco	20	Jult
8:14.33		Kipruto			1	DL	Birmingham	18	Aug
8:14.35		Kibiwot			6	DL	Rabat	13	Jult
8:14.61		Beyo			2	DL	Birmingham	18	Aug
8:14.62	Ibrahim	Ezzaydouny	MAR	28.4.91	7	DL	Rabat	13	Jul
	(30/11)								
8:15.07	Lawrence	Kemboi	KEN	15.6.93	2	DL	Doha	4	May
8:16.24	Emmanuel	Bett	KEN	14.7.95	3	DL	Doha	4	May
8:16.97	Mahiedine	Mekhissi-Benabbad	FRA	15.3.85	5	G Gala	Roma	31	May
8:16.97	Leonard	Bett	KEN-J	3.11.00	4	DL	Birmingham	18	Aug
8:17.08	Barnabas	Kipyego	KEN	12.6.95	1		Tomblaine	27	Jun
8:17.17	Albert	Chemutai	UGA-J	25.11.99	6	G Gala	Roma	31	May
8:17.51	Tesfaye	Diriba	ETH	11.9.98	5	DL	Doha	4	May
8:18.04	Kennedy	Njiru	KEN	.86	7	Herc	Monaco	20	Jul
8:18.76	Jairus	Birech	KEN	14.12.92	6	Pre	Eugene	26	May
	(20)								
8:19.30	Fernando	Carro	ESP	1.4.92	9	DL	Rabat	13	Jul
8:19.51	Hicham	Sigueni	MAR	30.1.93	3		Tomblaine	27	Jun
8:19.51	Justus	Lagat	KEN	20.5.96	4		Tomblaine	27	Jun
8:19.61	Yemane	Haileselassie	ERI	21.2.98	2		Huelva	8	Jun
8:20.30	Mohammed	Tindouft	MAR	12.3.93	7	G Gala	Roma	31	May
8:20.55	Djilali	Bedrani	FRA	1.10.93	5		Tomblaine	27	Jun
8:21.08	Abdelkarim	Ben Zahra	MAR	27.10.98	3		Huelva	8	Jun
8:21.21	Hailemariyam	Amare	ETH	22.2.97	7	DL	Doha	4	May
8:21.34	Tafese	Soboka	ETH	29.9.93	1		Montbéliard	1	Jun
8:22.00	John Kibet	Koech	BRN	23.8.95	8	G Gala	Roma	31	May
	(30)								
8:22.40	Maksim	Yakushev	RUS	15.3.92	1	NC	Kazan	20	Jul
8:22.55	Wilberforce	Koros	KEN	.93	2		Liège (NX)	18	Jul
8:22.68	Getnet	Wale	ETH-J	20.7.99	9	Herc	Monaco	20	Jul
8:22.79	Hossein	Keyhani	IRI	26.4.90	1	AsiG	Jakarta	27	Aug
8:23.22	Paul Kipsiele	Koech	KEN	10.11.81	8	Pre	Eugene	26	May
8:23.54	Napoleon	Solomon	SWE	14.2.94	11	G Gala	Roma	31	May
8:23.65	Mohamed Ismail	Ibrahim	DJI	1.7.97	8		Tomblaine	27	Jun
8:23.79	Jigisa	Tolosa Nurgi	ETH	29.3.94	4		Montbéliard	1	Jun
8:24.66	Andrew	Bayer	USA	3.2.90	3	NC	Des Moines	24	Jun
8:25.30	Hillary	Yego	KEN	2.4.92	2		Sollentuna	28	Jun
	(40)								
:25.35	Takele	Nigate	ETH-J	2.10.99	1	WJ	Tampere	15	Jul
8:25.38	Isaac	Updike	USA	21.3.92	1		Kortrijk	14	Jul
8:25.49	Clement	Kemboi	KEN	1.2.92	7		Huelva	8	Jun
8:26.02	Ahmed	Abdelwahed	ITA	26.5.96	2		Kortrijk	14	Jul
8:26.14	Amor	Benyahia	TUN	1.7.85	2	Med G	Tarragona	27	Jun
8:26.18	Martin	Grau	GER	26.3.92	5		Dessau	8	Jun
8:26.24	Joash	Kiplimo	KEN	.91	8		Huelva	8	Jun
8:26.51	Zak	Seddon	GBR	28.6.94	2		Rehlingen	20	May
8:26.52A	Philemon	Ruto	KEN-Y	20.9.01	2		Nairobi	12	Jun
8:26.91	Sebastián	Martos	ESP	20.6.89	9		Huelva	8	Jun
	(50)								
8:27.08	Yoann	Kowal	FRA	28.5.87	5		Montbéliard	1	Jun
8:27.17A	Benjamin	Kiplagat	UGA	4.3.89	1	NC	Kampala	14	Jul
8:27.2	Mounaime	Sassaoui	MAR	20.3.95	1		Rabat	23	May
8:27.25	Jonathan	Romeo	ESP	13.8.94	9		Tomblaine	27	Jun
8:27.46	Hichem	Bouchicha	ALG	19.5.89	3		Rehlingen	20	May
8:27.57	Cleophas	Kandie	KEN-J	14.8.00	13	DL	Rabat	13	Jul
8:27.71	Daniel	Arce	ESP	22.4.92	1		Oordegem	26	May
8:27.72	Krystian	Zalewski	POL	11.4.89	10		Tomblaine	27	Jun
8:27.72	Abdoullah	Bamoussa	ITA	2.6.86	3		Kortrijk	14	Jul
8:28.10	Yohannes	Chiappinelli	ITA	18.8.97	15	G Gala	Roma	31	May
	(60)								
8:28.18	Eric	Peñalver	ESP	23.9.93	2		Oordegem	26	May
8:28.21	Yaser Salem	Bagharab	QAT	1.1.98	2	AsiG	Jakarta	27	Aug
8:28.23	Osama	Zoghlami	ITA	19.6.94	4		Rehlingen	20	May
8:28.39	Stanley	Kebenei	USA	6.11.89	4	NC	Des Moines	24	Jun
8:28.48	Topi	Raitanen	FIN	7.2.96	1h1	EC	Berlin	7	Aug
8:28.55	Jordan	Mann	USA	12.1.93	5	NC	Des Moines	24	Jun
8:28.62	MJ (Michael)	Erb	USA	2.2.94	4h1	NC	Des Moines	22	Jun
8:28.70	Ildar	Nadyrov	RUS	22.4.94	2	NC	Kazan	20	Jul

MEN 2018

Mark	Name		Nat	Born	Pos	Meet	Venue	Date	
8:28.74	Travis	Mahoney	USA	25.7.90	5h1	NC	Des Moines	22	Jun
8:28.78	Mitko	Tsenov	BUL	13.6.93	6	Gyulai	Székesferhérvár	2	Jul
(70)									
8:28.84	Kaur	Kivistik	EST	29.4.91	5h2	EC	Berlin	7	Aug
8:28.88	Haron	Lagat	USA	15.8.83	6	NC	Des Moines	24	Jun
8:29.04	Altobeli	da Silva	BRA	3.12.90	4		Sollentuna	28	Jun
8:29.11	Brian	Shrader	USA	22.7.91	3		Liège (NX)	18	Jul
8:29.14	Kazuya	Shiojiri	JPN	8.11.96	1	NC	Yamaguchi	24	Jun
8:29.31	Abdelhamid	Zerrifi	ALG/FRA	20.6.86	11		Tomblaine	27	Jun
8:29.41	Tom Erling	Kårbø	NOR	4.2.89	1		Leiden	9	Jun
8:29.42	Yuriy	Kloptsov	RUS	22.12.89	3	NC	Kazan	20	Jul
8:29.77	Mason	Ferlic	USA	5.8.93	4		Liège (NX)	18	Jul
8:29.80	Avinash	Sable	IND	13.9.94	1	NC	Bhubaneswar	28	Sep
(80)									
8:29.95	Andrey	Farnosov	RUS	9.7.80	4	NC	Kazan	20	Jul
8:30.10	Aidan	Tooker	USA	26.6.98	6h1	NC	Des Moines	22	Jun
8:30.16	Ieuan	Thomas	GBR	17.7.89	2		Leiden	9	Jun
8:30.29	Joshua	Thompson	USA	9.5.93	5		Kortrijk	14	Jul
8:30.44	Ole	Hesselbjerg	DEN	23.4.90	8h2	EC	Berlin	7	Aug
8:30.52	Jonathan	Hopkins	GBR	3.6.92	3		Oordegem	26	May
8:30.69	Tripp	Hurt	USA	30.10.92	6		Kortrijk	14	Jul
8:30.75	Jonathan	Ndiku	KEN	18.9.91	1		Osaka	22	Sep
8:30.98	Kosei	Yamaguchi	JPN	19.8.91	6		Liège (NX)	18	Jul
8:31.26	Isaac	Yego	KEN	.89	13		Huelva	8	Jun
(90)									
8:31.41	Abdelaziz	Merzougui	ESP	30.8.91	14		Huelva	8	Jun
8:31.43	Dylan	Blankenbaker	USA	6.1.94	3	Jordan	Stanford	3	May
8:31.45A	Ezekiel	Kemboi	KEN	25.5.82	4h2	NC	Nairobi	21	Jun
8:31.61	Donn	Cabral	USA	12.12.89	7h1	NC	Des Moines	22	Jun
8:31.81	Patrick	Karl	GER	3.5.96	2		Pfungstadt	11	Jul
8:31.86A	Festus	Kiprono	KEN	29.12.95	5h2	NC	Nairobi	21	Jun
8:31.91	Jamaine	Coleman	GBR	22.9.95	8		Liège (NX)	18	Jul
8:32.08A	Wesley	Langat	KEN		6h2	NC	Nairobi	21	Jun
8:32.2	Ivan	Lukyanov	RUS	31.1.81	3	Znam	Zhukovskiy	30	Jun
8:32.23	Obsa	Ali	USA	17.2.96	1	NCAA	Eugene	8	Jun
(100)									

8:32.37A	Daniel	Kipchumba	KEN	12.12.97	17 Feb		8:36.96	Bilal	Tabti	ALG	7.6.93	13 May
8:32.59A	Gilbert	Mutai	KEN-Y	26.11.01	21 Jun		8:37.11A	Moses	Kibet	KEN	4.2.97	21 Jun
8:33.12	Johannes	Motschmann	GER	3.8.94	11 Jul		8:37.28A	Titus	Kosgei	KEN		21 Jun
8:33.14	Evans	Chematot	BRN	19.3.96	20 May		8:37.41	Titus	Kibiego	KEN	3.5.96	1 Jun
8:33.28	Víctor	Ruiz	ESP	24.6.93	8 Jun		8:37.50	Vincent	Kipyegon	KEN	31.12.98	20 May
8:33.28	Brandon	Doughty	USA	14.5.93	22 Jun		8:37.89	Konstantin	Plokhotnikov	RUS	24.3.97	7 Jul
8:33.5A	Phenus	Kipleting	KEN	.89	6 Jun		8:37.92	Ryuhei	Sakaguchi	JPN	5.4.97	10 Jun
8:33.58	David	Goodman	USA	21.12.88	3 May		8:37.95	Mohamed Ali	Jelloul	ESP	30.6.94	8 Jun
8:34.13	Tim	Stegemann	GER	4.8.92	27 Jun		8:38.12	Taisei	Ogino	JPN	7.11.97	18 Jul
8:34.17	Leonardo	Feletto	ITA	26.6.95	9 Sep		8:38.24	Yuma	Higashi	JPN	29.11.95	24 Jun
8:34.52	Steven	Fahy	USA	12.6.96	8 Jun		8:38.27	Yasutaka	Ishibashi	JPN	24.8.94	22 Sep
8:34.56	Anthony	Rotich	KEN	1.1.92	2 Jun		8:38.29	Ali Ahmad	Al-Amri	KSA	28.12.87	27 Aug
8:34.80	Ibrahim	Chakir	ESP	4.9.94	7 Jul		8:38.32	Yusuke	Uchikoshi	JPN	11.8.94	30 Mar
8:34.83	Kyle	Medina	USA	8.4.95	22 Jun		8:38.4A	Geoffrey	Ngeno	KEN	11.1.94	6 Jun
8:35.14	Craig	Nowak	USA	20.4.94	3 May		8:38.51	Tarik Langat	Akdag	TUR	16.6.88	26 May
8:35.26	Wogene	Sebisibe	ETH	23.6.98	8 Jun		8:38.60	Igor	Bougnot	FRA	1.9.92	1 Jun
8:35.40	Hashim Salah Abbas		QAT	15.4.94	27 Aug		8:38.70	Tesfaye	Girma	ETH	24.1.97	4 May
8:35.47	Phil	Norman	GBR	20.10.89	8 Jun		8:38.94	Seiya	Shigeno	JPN	23.12.96	22 Apr
8:35.63	Fabian	Clarkson	GER	13.12.90	8 Jun		8:39.03	Jean-Simon	Desgagnés	CAN	26.7.98	10 Jun
8:35.66	Abderraouf	Boubaker	TUN	21.10.88	27 Jun		8:39.19	André	Pereira	POR	10.8.95	2 Jun
8:35.89	José Gregorio Peña		VEN	12.1.87	3 May		8:39.23	Luis Miguel	Borges	POR	4.10.94	8 Jun
8:36.0A	Festus	Kiprotich	KEN-J	27.4.99	6 Jun		8:39.25	Michael	Leet	USA	6.7.95	2 Jun
8:36.02	Andrew	Gardner	USA	20.2.95	22 Jun		8:39.30	Max	Stevens	AUS	16.11.94	4 Feb
8:36.20	Aleksandr	Olkov	RUS	24.9.95	29 May		8:39.30	Jake	Heslington	USA	18.10.94	22 Jun
8:36.57	Mohamed Amine Jihnaoui		TUN	2.4.97	26 May		8:39.34	Noah	Schutte	NED	15.5.95	10 Jun
8:36.7	Mohamed	Er Rachdi	MAR-J	28.2.99	23 May		8:39.34	Ala	Zoghlami	ITA	19.6.94	9 Sep
8:36.71	Alexis	Phelut	FRA	31.3.98	26 May		8:39.4A	Hillary	Mosop	KEN-J	16.12.99	11 Jun
8:36.76	Matthew	Owens	USA	16.8.96	25 May		8:39.50	Frankline	Tonui	KEN	2.8.93	3 May
8:36.76	Clayson	Shumway	USA	.96	25 May		(159)					
8:36.84	Emil	Blomberg	SWE	9.4.92	9 Jun		**Drugs disqualification**					
8:36.88	Justinas	Berzanskis	LTU	12.1.89	7 Aug		8:39.42	Naveen	Kumar ¶	IND	20.1.88	(28 Jun

JUNIORS

See main list for top 6 juniors. 11 performances by 5 men to 8:27.0. Additional marks and further juniors:

L Bett		8:21.40A	1	KEN-jT Nairobi		12 Jun		8:25.39	2	WJ	Tampere	15 Jul
Chenutai		8:18.80	6	DL	Doha	4 May		8:22.31	1		Madrid	22 Jun
		8:19.80	5	CG	Gold Coast	13 Apr						
8:32.59A	Gilbert		Mutai	KEN-Y	26.11.01	7h2	NC			Nairobi	21 Jun
8:36.0A	Festus		Kiprotich	KEN	27.4.99	4				Nairobi	6 Jun

Mark	Name		Nat	Born	Pos	Meet	Venue	Date
8:36.7	Mohamed	Er Rachdi	MAR	28.2.99	1		Rabat	23 May
8:39.4A	Hillary	Mosop (10)	KEN	16.12.99	4h3		Nairobi	11 Jun
8:40.36	Noah	Affolder	USA	11.2.99	1s2	NCAA	Eugene	6 Jun
8:41.35A	Abel	Kiplimo	KEN-Y	20.6.01	5	KEN-jT	Nairobi	12 Jun
8:43.3A	Amsalu	Belaye	ETH		2		Addis Ababa	3 Feb
8:44.12	Mehari	Tsegay	ERI	12.2.99	8	AfCh	Asaba	3 Aug
8:46.0A	Alemu	Kitessa	ETH		4		Assela	26 May
8:46.15A	Lawi	Kosgei	KEN	14.1.99	6	KEN-jT	Nairobi	12 Jun
8:46.3A	Lemecha	Girma	ETH		5		Assela	26 May
8:46.56	Ryuji	Miura	JPN-Y	.02	1		Nara	14 Sep
8:47.07A	Alex	Cherono	KEN	30.12.00	7	KEN-jT	Nairobi	12 Jun
8:49.4A	Belachew	Bitew	ETH		6		Assela	26 Ma

60 METRES HURDLES INDOORS

Mark	Name		Nat	Born	Pos	Meet	Venue	Date
7.42	Grant	Holloway	USA	19.11.97	1		Clemson	10 Feb
7.43A	Jarret	Eaton	USA	24.6.89	1	NC	Albuquerque	18 Feb
7.46	Omar	McLeod	JAM	25.4.94	1h2		Clemson	10 Feb
7.46A	Aries	Merritt	USA	24.7.85	2	NC	Albuquerque	18 Feb
7.46	Andy	Pozzi	GBR	15.5.92	1s2	WI	Birmingham	4 Mar
7.46		Pozzi			1	WI	Birmingham	4 Mar
7.47		Eaton			1		Reims	31 Jan
7.47		Eaton			2	WI	Birmingham	4 Mar
7.47		Holloway			1	NCAA	College Station	10 Mar
7.49		Holloway			1		Clemson	19 Jan
7.49A	Devon	Allen	USA	12.12.94	3	NC	Albuquerque	18 Feb
7.49	Ronald	Levy	JAM	30.10.92	1	GP	Glasgow	25 Feb
	(12/7)							
7.51	Petr	Svoboda	CZE	10.10.84	1		Jablonec	20 Jan
7.51	Milan	Trajkovic	CYP	17.3.92	1s3	WI	Birmingham	4 Mar
7.52	Pascal (10)	Martinot-Lagarde	FRA	22.9.91	2s3	WI	Birmingham	4 Mar
7.53	Aurel	Manga	FRA	24.7.92	1	NC	Liévin	17 Feb
7.57	Ahmad	Al-Moualed	KSA	16.2.88	1h1		Mondeville	3 Feb
7.57A	Brendan	Ames	USA	6.10.88	4	NC	Albuquerque	18 Feb
7.58	Roger	Iribarne	CUB	2.1.96	2s2	WI	Birmingham	4 Mar
7.60	Aleec	Harris	USA	31.10.90	3		Clemson	10 Feb
7.60	Erik	Balnuweit	GER	21.9.88	1 h2		Chemnitz	10 Feb
7.60	Balázs	Baji	HUN	9.6.89	2		Torun	15 Feb
7.60	Gabriel	Constantino	BRA	9.2.95	1		São Caetano do Sul	17 Feb
7.60	Antoine	Lloyd	USA	10.6.96	2	NCAA	College Station	10 Mar
7.61	Ruebin	Walters	TTO	2.4.95	4		Clemson	10 Feb
	(20)							
7.62	Johnathan	Cabral	CAN	31.12.92	2		Mondeville	3 Feb
7.63	Simon	Krauss	FRA	12.2.92	1r2		Reims	31 Jan
7.63	David	King	GBR	13.6.94	3		Metz	11 Feb
7.63	Ashtyn	Davis	USA	10.10.96	3	NCAA	College Station	10 Mar
7.64A	Josh	Thompson	USA	16.1.93	2h2	NC	Albuquerque	17 Feb
7.64	Jaylan	McConico	USA	17.8.98	1		Cedar Falls	25 Feb
7.64	Jovaine	Atkinson	JAM	6.12.95	2h1	NCAA	College Station	9 Mar
7.65	Freddie	Crittenden	USA	3.8.94	1		Staten Island	13 Jan
7.65	Koen	Smet	NED	9.8.92	1		Magglingen	3 Feb
7.65	Konstantin	Shabanov	RUS	17.11.89	1	NC	Moskva	13 Feb
	(30)							
7.65		Zeng Jianhang	CHN	17.9.98	1	NGPF	Beijing	24 Mar
7.66	Ludovic	Payen	FRA	18.2.95	1		Liévin	13 Feb
7.66	Hassane	Fofana	ITA	28.4.92	1	NC	Ancona	17 Feb
7.66A	Aaron	Mallett	USA	26.9.94	2s1	NC	Albuquerque	18 Feb
7.66	Konstadínos	Douvalídis	GRE	10.3.87	3h4	WI	Birmingham	3 Mar
7.65	Chad	Zallow	USA	25.4.97	1h1		Youngstown	23 Feb
7.67	Damian	Warner	CAN	4.11.89	1H	WI	Birmingham	3 Mar
7.68	Paolo	Dal Molin	ITA	31.7.87	1		Ancona	28 Jan
7.68	Benjamin	Sedecias	FRA	18.1.95	3h2		Metz	11 Feb
7.68	Yidiel	Contreras	ESP	27.11.92	3h3	WI	Birmingham	3 Mar
	(40)							
7.69	Angelo	Goss	USA	17.10.92	2		Staten Island	13 Jan
7.69	Mohamed	Koussi	MAR	15.3.94	2r2		Reims	31 Jan
7.69	Abdulaziz	Al-Mandeel	KUW	22.5.89	7s2	WI	Birmingham	4 Mar
7.70	Damian	Czykier	POL	10.8.92	3		Ostrava	25 Jan
7.70	Vitaliy	Parakhonka	BLR	18.8.93	1	NC	Mogilyov	17 Feb
7.70	Trey	Cunningham	USA	26.8.98	1		Clemson	24 Feb
7.70	Artem	Makarenko	RUS	23.4.97	1		Omsk	22 Dec

MEN 2018

Mark		Name	Nat	Born	Pos	Meet	Venue	Date	
7.71		Loïc	Desbonnes	FRA	26.7.91	1h1	NC	Liévin	17	Feb
7.71			Xie Wenjun	CHN	11.7.90	5h4	WI	Birmingham	3	Mar
7.72		Yanick	Hart	JAM	1.10.93	3h2		Clemson	10	Feb
		(50)								
7.73		Greggmar	Swift	BAR	16.2.91	1		Columbus	5	Jan
7.73		Max	Hairston	USA	8.5.94	3		Iowa City	20	Jan
7.73		Eddie	Lovett	ISV	25.6.92	1h1		University Park	26	Jan
7.73		Valdimir	Vukicevic	NOR	6.5.91	3		Liévin	13	Feb
7.73		Jonathas	Brito	BRA	30.11.92	2		São Caetano do Sul	17	Feb
7.73			Pan Zijie	CHN	7.11.95	2		Xianlin	12	Mar
7.74		Lorenzo	Perini	ITA	22.7.94	1h1		Magglingen	3	Feb
7.74		Matt	Moore	USA	23.3.98	2	ACC	Clemson	24	Feb
Low altitude bests										
7.50		Allen	1	Millrose New York (Arm)	3 Feb		7.70	Mallett	2	Iowa City	20 Jan
7.53		Merritt	3	Millrose New York (Arm)	3 Feb						

110 METRES HURDLES

Mark			Name	Nat	Born	Pos	Meet	Venue	Date	
12.92	0.6	Sergey	Shubenkov	RUS	4.10.90	1	Gyulai	Székesfehérvár	2	Jul
12.95	0.6		Shubenkov			1	Athl	Lausanne	5	Jul
12.97	-0.1		Shubenkov			1	DL	Bruxelles	31	Aug
12.99	0.5		Shubenkov			1		Montreuil	19	Jun
13.03	0.9		Shubenkov			1	C.Cup	Ostrava	9	Sep
13.05	0.7		Shubenkov			1h1	DL	Paris (C)	30	Jun
13.07	-0.2		Shubenkov			1	Herc	Monaco	20	Jul
13.08	1.3	Orlando	Ortega	ESP	29.7.91	1	DL	Birmingham	18	Aug
13.09	1.7		Shubenkov			1		Padova	2	Sep
13.10	-0.1		Ortega			2	VD	Bruxelles	31	Aug
13.12	0.9	Ronald	Levy	JAM	30.10.92	2	C.Cup	Ostrava	9	Sep
13.13	0.2		Levy			1	DL	London (OS)	22	Jul
13.15	0.9	Grant	Holloway	USA	19.11.97	1	SEC	Knoxville	13	May
13.15	0.9		Ortega			1	ISTAF	Berlin	2	Sep
13.16	1.9		Holloway			1		Gainesville	13	Apr
13.16	0.2	Omar	McLeod	JAM	25.4.94	1	DL	Shanghai	12	May
13.16	-0.5		Levy			1	NC	Kingston	24	Jun
13.17	0.2		Ortega			2	DL	Shanghai	12	May
13.17	0.0	Pascal	Martinot Lagarde	FRA	22.9.91	1	EC	Berlin	10	Aug
13.17	0.0		Shubenkov			2	EC	Berlin	10	Aug
13.18	-0.1		Shubenkov			1	PNG	Turku	5	Jun
13.18	1.5		Levy			1	DL	Paris (C)	30	Jun
13.18	-0.2		Ortega			2	Herc	Monaco	20	Jul
13.19	-0.3		Levy			1	CG	Gold Coast	10	Apr
13.19	-0.3		Ortega			1h2	DL	Paris (C)	30	Jun
13.20	-0.2		Martinot Lagarde			3	Herc	Monaco	20	Jul
13.21	-0.2	Hansle	Parchment	JAM	17.6.90	4	Herc	Monaco	20	Jul
13.21	0.8		Ortega			1s2	EC	Berlin	10	Aug
13.22	-0.3		Parchment			2	CG	Gold Coast	10	Apr
13.22	1.5		Parchment			2	DL	Paris (C)	30	Jun
13.22	1.0		Martinot Lagarde			1	AWC	London (OS)	14	Jul
13.22	1.3		Levy			2	DL	Birmingham	18	Aug
		(32/7)								
13.23	0.5	Gabriel	Constantino	BRA	9.2.95	2		Montreuil	19	Jun
13.23	1.5	Devon	Allen	USA	12.12.94	3	DL	Paris (C)	30	Jun
13.26	0.0	Gregor	Traber (10)	GER	2.12.92	2s1	EC	Berlin	10	Aug
13.27	0.9	Daniel	Roberts	USA	13.4.98	2	SEC	Knoxville	13	May
13.27	0.6	Balázs	Baji	HUN	9.6.89	2	Gyulai	Székesfehérvár	2	Jul
13.27	1.3	Freddie	Crittenden	USA	3.8.94	4	DL	Birmingham	18	Aug
13.28	0.8	Andrew	Pozzi	GBR	15.5.92	2s2	EC	Berlin	10	Aug
13.31	1.9	Ruebin	Walters	TTO	2.4.95	2		Gainesville	13	Apr
13.31	0.7	Aurel	Manga	FRA	24.7.92	3h1	DL	Paris (C)	30	Jun
13.31	-0.3	Antonio	Alkana	RSA	12.4.90	3h2	DL	Paris (C)	30	Jun
13.33	0.7	Jarret	Eaton	USA	24.6.89	4h1	DL	Paris (C)	30	Jun
13.34	0.9	Johnathan	Cabral	CAN	31.12.92	2		Bellinzona	18	Jul
13.34	0.0		Xie Wenjun	CHN	11.7.90	1	AsiG	Jakarta	28	Aug
		(20)								
13.35	1.8	Ryan	Fontenot	USA	4.5.86	1h1		Montverde	9	Jun
13.36	2.0	Milan	Trajkovic	CYP	17.3.92	3h2	CG	Gold Coast	9	Apr
13.36	0.9	Ahmad	Al-Moualed	KSA	16.2.88	1	Odlozil	Praha	4	Jun
13.36	0.7	Taio	Kanai	JPN	28.9.95	1	NC	Yamaguchi	24	Jun
13.37	0.6	Aries	Merritt	USA	24.7.85	4	Gyulai	Székesfehérvár	2	Jul
13.37	0.9	Aleec	Harris	USA	31.10.90	3		Bellinzona	18	Jul

Mark	Wind	Name		Nat	Born	Pos	Meet	Venue	Date	
13.37	1.1	Damian	Czykier	POL	10.8.92	1	NC	Lublin	22	Jul
13.38	-0.3	Nick	Hough	AUS	20.10.93	3	CG	Gold Coast	10	Apr
13.38	1.1	Ludovic	Payen	FRA	18.2.95	1		Bonneuil-sur-Marne	20	Jun
13.38	1.4	Shane	Brathwaite	BAR	8.2.90	1	CAG	Barranquilla	31	Jul
		(30)								
13.39	0.7	Jason	Joseph	SUI	11.10.98	1s1	NC	Zofingen	14	Jul
13.39	0.0		Chen Kuei-Ju	TPE	22.9.93	2	AsiG	Jakarta	28	Aug
13.40	1.0	David	Kendziera	USA	9.9.94	1q1	NCAA-W	Sacramento	26	May
13.40	-1.0	Vitaliy	Parakhonko	BLR	18.8.93	1	NC	Minsk	20	Jul
13.40	1.8	Paolo	Dal Molin	ITA	31.7.87	1h1	EC	Berlin	9	Aug
13.41	0.6	Konstadínos	Douvalídis	GRE	10.3.87	1		Dráma	28	Apr
13.44A	0.5	Eduardo	de Deus	BRA	8.10.95	1	SAmG	Cochabamba	6	Jun
13.44	-0.8	Damion	Thomas	JAM-J	29.6.99	2s3	NCAA-W	Eugene	6	Jun
13.44	-1.0	Yidiel Islay	Contreras	ESP	27.11.92	4		Madrid	22	Jun
13.44	1.4	Alexander	John	GER	3.5.86	1		Weinheim	6	Jul
		(40)								
13.45	0.7	Shun-ya	Takayama	JPN	3.9.94	2	NC	Yamaguchi	24	Jun
13.45	1.7	Garfield	Darien	FRA	22.12.87	1		Sotteville-lès-Rouen	17	Jul
13.46	-0.1	Antoine	Lloyd	USA	10.6.96	3s1	NC	Des Moines	24	Jun
13.47	1.7	Andrew	Riley	JAM	6.9.88	2		Sotteville-lès-Rouen	17	Jul
13.48	-0.7	Roger	Iribarne	CUB	2.1.96	2h1		Guadalajara, ESP	5	Jul
13.48	1.0	Damian	Warner	CAN	4.11.89	2	NC	Ottawa	7	Jul
13.49	-0.6	Lorenzo	Perini	ITA	22.7.94	1	Med G	Tarragona	30	Jun
13.50	1.8	Hassane	Fofana	ITA	28.4.92	2h1	EC	Berlin	9	Aug
13.50	1.2	Genta	Masuno	JPN	24.5.93	2		Fukui	8	Oct
13.52	-0.1	Erik	Balnuweit	GER	21.9.88	2	NC	Nürnberg	21	Jul
		(50)								
13.53	-0.1	Milan	Ristic	SRB	8.8.91	1		St.George's	21	Apr
13.53	0.7	Koen	Smet	NED	9.8.92	1		Oordegem	26	May
13.53	0.6	Konstantin	Shabanov	RUS	17.11.89	1	NC	Kazan	19	Jul
13.53	1.3	David	King	GBR	13.6.94	8	DL	Birmingham	18	Aug
13.54	1.0	Michael	Dickson	USA	25.1.97	1h1		Greensboro	4	May
13.54	0.9	Petr	Svoboda	CZE	10.10.84	3	Odlozil	Praha	4	Jun
13.55	1.3	Aaron	Mallett	USA	26.9.94	1		Iowa City	12	Apr
13.55	0.8	Deuce	Carter	JAM	28.9.90	1		Kessel-Lo	4	Aug
13.56	0.0	Eddie	Lovett	ISV	25.6.92	1		Leonora	30	Jun
13.56	-0.8	Devon	Hill	USA	26.10.89	3		La Chaux-de-Fonds	1	Jul
		(60)								
13.56	1.1	Artur	Noga	POL	2.5.88	2	NC	Lublin	22	Jul
13.57	1.9	Tremayne	Banks	USA	29.7.92	5		Gainesville	13	Apr
13.57	0.6	Trey	Cunningham	USA	26.8.98	1		Tallahassee	4	May
13.57	2.0	William	Session	USA	22.2.97	2	Big 10	Bloomington	13	May
13.57	1.7	Benjamin	Sedecias	FRA	18.1.95	5		Sotteville-lès-Rouen	17	Jul
13.57			Kim Byung-jun	KOR	15.8.91	5	AsiG	Jakarta	28	Aug
13.58	0.9	Vladimir	Vukicevic	NOR	6.5.91	1		Ninove	28	Jul
13.60A	-0.5	Fanor Andrés	Escobar	COL	17.12.97	1		Medellín	28	Apr
13.60	1.7	Amere	Lattin	USA	17.2.97	1h5	NCAA-W	Sacramento	25	May
13.60	0.8	Elmo	Lakka	FIN	10.4.93	5s2	EC	Berlin	10	Aug
		(70)								
13.60	0.1	Jonathas	Brito	BRA	30.11.92	2h1	NC	Bragança Paulista	14	Sep
13.61A	1.6	Mason	Weh	LBR	14.4.98	1		Amarillo	22	Apr
13.61	0.4	Takumu	Furuya	JPN	12.3.97	4		Osaka	20	May
13.61	1.8	John	Burt	USA	10.2.97	1q2	NCAA-W	Sacramento	26	May
13.62	-0.5	Phillip	Lemonius	JAM	12.12.98	4	NC	Kingston	24	Jun
13.63A	1.4	Ruan	de Vries	RSA	1.2.86	1		Pretoria	24	Feb
13.63A	-0.5	Juan Carlos	Moreno	COL	13.1.94	2		Medellín	28	Apr
13.63	1.5	Mohamed	Koussi	MAR	15.3.94	1		Franconville	6	May
13.63	0.4	Jeffrey	Julmis	HAI	6.1.87	4	NACAC	Toronto	11	Aug
13.64A	0.0	Genaro	Rodríguez	MEX	10.10.90	1		Ciudad de México	30	Mar
		(80)								
13.64	0.7	Dejour	Russell	JAM-J	1.4.00	4h1	CG	Gold Coast	9	Apr
13.64	2.0	DaJuan	Seward	USA	15.8.96	3	Big 10	Bloomington	13	May
13.64	-0.5	Anthony Tyrell	Kuriki	JPN	17.9.96	5		Osaka	20	May
13.64	0.7	Aaron	Lewis	TTO	23.1.96	1h1	NCAA-E	Tampa	25	May
13.64	1.8	Nick	Anderson	USA	28.4.95	4h1		Montverde	9	Jun
13.64	0.7	Shin-ya	Tanaka	JPN	23.6.93	2s1	NC	Yamaguchi	23	Jun
13.64	0.2	Akihiro	Ogata	JPN	8.6.94	2		Hiratsuka	21	Jul
13.65	1.0	Ro'Derick	Spears	USA	14.8.94	3h1	SEC	Knoxville	12	May
13.65	0.6	Jaylan	McConico	USA	17.8.98	1		Terre Haute	13	May
13.65A	-0.3		Zeng Jianhang	CHN	17.9.98	1		Guiyang	17	Jun
		(90)								

MEN 2018

Mark	Wind	Name	Nat	Born	Pos	Meet	Venue	Date
13.65	0.2	Tyler Mason	JAM	15.1.95	1rB		Kortrijk	14 Jul
13.66	1.7	Masahiro Kagimoto	JPN	29.9.95	1		Kyoto	11 May
13.67	0.0	Wellington Zaza	LBR	20.1.95	2		Leonora	30 Jun
13.68	0.9	Cory Poole	USA-J	29.7.99	4	SEC	Knoxville	13 May
13.68	2.0	Justin Veteto	USA	24.3.96	4	Big 10	Bloomington	13 May
13.68	1.3	Simon Krauss	FRA	12.2.92	2h2	NC	Albi	8 Jul
13.69	1.1	Yang Wei-Ting	TPE	22.9.94	1		Zhaoqing	12 Apr
13.69	1.2	Francisco Javier López	ESP	29.12.89	1		San Angelo	5 May
13.70	2.0	Ben Reynolds	IRL	26.9.90	4h2	CG	Gold Coast	9 Apr
13.70A	0.5	Éder António de Souza	BRA	15.10.86	4	SAmG	Cochabamba	6 Jun
(100)								
13.70	1.0	Joseph Daniels	CAN	12.10.98	3	NC	Ottawa	7 Jul

Mark	Wind	Name	Nat	Born	Date
13.71	1.8	Josh Thompson	USA	16.1.93	7 Apr
13.71	1.9	Yanick Hart	JAM	1.10.93	13 Apr
13.71	-0.1	Kevin Mayer	FRA	10.2.92	30 Jun
13.72	0.6	Todd Townsend	USA	24.9.94	13 Apr
13.72	0.1	Yordan O'Farrill	CUB	9.2.93	14 Mar
13.72	0.3	Chad Zallow	USA	25.4.97	28 Apr
13.72	1.6	Hiroyuki Sato	JPN	6.8.90	6 May
13.72	-0.6	Angelo Goss	USA	17.10.92	12 May
13.72	2.0	Luke Siedhoff	USA	21.3.97	13 May
13.73	1.7	Isaiah Moore	USA	12.6.96	7 Apr
13.73	0.6	Dayo Akindele	USA	18.9.96	6 Jun
13.73	0.7	Hiroki Fudaba	JPN	4.2.94	23 Jun
13.73	-0.9	Anastas Eliopoulos	CAN-J	4.3.99	26 Jun
13.73	1.4	Maximilian Bayer	GER	5.12.90	6 Jul
13.73	1.4	Wataru Yazawa	JPN	2.7.91	13 Oct
13.74	1.1	Misana Viltz	USA	21.2.96	7 Apr
13.74	-0.1	Chan Chung Wang	HKG	10.6.91	25 May
13.74	0.7	Job Beintema	NED	24.5.95	26 May
13.74	0.7	Brahian Peña	SUI	3.4.94	14 Jul
13.74	1.2	Shuhei Ishikawa	JPN	29.5.95	8 Oct
13.75	0.7	Patrick Prince	USA	29.5.97	13 May
13.75	1.0	Braxton Canady	USA	13.1.98	26 May
13.75	-0.4	Thingalaya Siddhanth	IND	3.1.91	2 Jun
13.75A	0.5	Javier McFarlane	PER	21.10.91	6 Jun
13.75	0.5	Dimitri Bascou	FRA	20.7.87	19 Jun
13.75	1.8	Filipp Shabanov	RUS	15.8.91	19 Jul
13.75	0.9	Michael Obasuyi	BEL-J	12.8.99	28 Jul
13.75	-1.1	Shunsuke Izumiya	JPN-J	26.1.00	9 Sep
13.75	0.2	Silvio Henrique de Souza	BRA	21.7.93	14 Sep
13.76	1.0	Max Hairston	USA	8.5.94	13 Apr
13.76	-0.6	Pan Zijie	CHN	7.11.95	18 Apr
13.76	0.0	Jonatha Mendes	BRA	14.4.90	9 Jun
13.76A	1.2	Rafael Campos Pereira	BRA	8.4.97	29 Sep
13.78	0.6	Artem Makarenko	RUS	23.4.97	27 Jul
13.79	1.2	Shakiel Chattoo	JAM	22.1.96	30 Mar
13.79	1.0	Jovaine Atkinson	JAM	6.12.95	30 Mar
13.79	1.3	Ivan Mach Di Palmstein	ITA	2.1.92	27 May
13.79	0.9	Kiril Kireyev	RUS	28.8.97	6 Jun
13.79	1.7	David Omoregie	GBR	1.11.95	14 Jun
13.79	1.1	Dominik Bochenek	POL	14.5.87	22 Jul
13.80	1.2	Michael Nicholls	BAR	6.4.97	30 Mar
13.80	1.7	Lafranz Campbell	JAM	19.10.97	4 May
13.80	-0.4	Hideki Omuro	JPN	25.7.90	13 May
13.80	0.5	Artem Shamatryn	UKR	15.6.91	18 Jul
13.81	0.1	Yoan Vila	CUB	31.1.98	14 Mar
13.81A	-0.5	Yeison Rivas	COL	24.9.87	28 Apr
13.81	0.0	Marvin Pistol	FRA	31.7.96	6 May
13.81	1.6	Cameron Hall	USA	12.5.93	12 May
13.81	-0.9	Khai Riley-La Borde	GBR	8.11.95	29 May
13.81	1.4	Dylan Caty	FRA	11.1.97	15 Jul
13.81	1.2	Ryuta Fujii	JPN	29.7.96	8 Oct
13.82	0.1	Caleb Parker	USA	26.6.98	23 Mar
13.82	1.6	William Watson	USA	.98	5 May
13.82	0.9	Wayne Newman	USA	17.1.97	12 May
13.82	0.9	Liam van der Schaaf	NED	8.10.98	19 May
13.82		Mohamed Saad Al-Khafaji	IRQ	17.1.97	25 May
13.82	1.4	Toru Kokubu	JPN	25.8.84	23 Jun
13.82	-0.2	Sergey Solodov	RUS	3.1.96	6 Jul
13.82	-0.2	João Vitor de Oliveira	BRA	15.5.92	8 Jul
13.83	2.0	Xavier Coakley	BAH	1.10.96	14 Apr
13.83	1.9	Juan Scott	USA	27.5.97	27 Apr
13.83	1.7	Keane Bland	USA	25.8.94	4 May
13.83	1.6	Daiki Takeyoski	JPN	1.11.94	6 May
13.83	1.7	Ashtyn Davis	USA	10.10.96	26 May
13.84	0.0	Shusei Nomoto	JPN	25.10.95	12 Apr
13.84	-0.6	Matt Moore	USA	23.3.98	12 May
13.84	1.5	Darien Tennon	USA	27.10.94	12 May
13.84	0.6	Jake Porter	GBR	13.11.93	3 Jun
13.84	-0.1	Martin Vogel	GER	16.3.92	21 Jul
13.84	0.9	Oyeniyi Abejoye	NGR	16.1.93	9 Sep
13.84	0.2	Paulo Henrique da Silva	BRA	29.6.95	14 Sep
13.85	1.6	Ronald Forbes	CAY	5.4.85	12 May
13.85	0.0	Junior Effa Effa	GAB	3.3.96	20 May
13.85	-0.5	Josh Lamers	USA	9.6.96	26 May
13.85A	-0.9	Zhang Tao	CHN	30.9.97	16 Jun
13.85		Lyès Mokdel	ALG	20.6.90	12 Jul
13.85	1.7	Max Hrelja	SWE	30.1.98	11 Aug
13.85	1.5	Tomasu Higashi	JPN	14.4.97	26 Aug
13.86	1.1	Cedric Dubler	AUS	13.1.95	13 Jan
13.86	0.5	Rayzam Shah Wan Sofian	MAS	11.1.88	9 Jul
13.86	0.5	Javier Colomo	ESP	26.3.94	5 Jul
13.86	1.3	Elie Agot	FRA	9.4.91	8 Jul
13.86	-1.1	Arthur Abele	GER	30.7.86	16 Sep
13.86	1.2	Yutaro Furukawa (185)	JPN	3.6.85	8 Oct

Wind assisted

Mark	Wind	Name	Nat	Born	Pos	Meet	Venue	Date
13.01	3.0	Omar McLeod	JAM	25.4.94	1	Pre	Eugene	26 May
13.08	3.0	Shubenkov			2	Pre	Eugene	26 May
13.13	3.0	Devon Allen	USA	12.12.94	3	Pre	Eugene	26 May
13.17	3.0	Ortega			4	Pre	Eugene	26 May
13.27	3.0	Aries Merritt	USA	24.7.85	6	Pre	Eugene	26 May
13.28	2.3	Ruebin Walters	TTO	2.4.95	1h2	SEC	Knoxville	12 May
13.35	2.4	Garfield Darien	FRA	22.12.87	2	NC	Albi	8 Jul
13.38	2.2	Jason Joseph	SUI	11.10.98	2	NC	Zofingen	14 Jul
13.39	2.3	Damion Thomas	JAM-J	29.6.99	2h2	SEC	Knoxville	12 May
13.45	3.5	Takumu Furuya	JPN	12.3.97	1r1		Sagamihara	24 May
13.46	2.2	John Burt	USA	10.2.97	2s1	NCAA	Eugene	6 Jun
13.57	3.6	Francisco Javier López	ESP	29.12.89	2	Texas R	Austin	31 Mar
13.57	2.6	Hideki Omuro	JPN	25.7.90	3	Oda	Hiroshima	29 Apr
13.57	2.4	Nick Anderson	USA	28.4.95	1		Clermont	13 May
13.57	3.5	Braxton Canady	USA	13.1.98	1		Stanford	13 May
13.57	3.4	Anthony Tyrell Kuriki	JPN	17.9.96	1r2		Sagamihara	24 May
13.58	4.1	Tomasu Higashi	JPN	14.4.97	1		Katsuura	28 Oct
13.62	3.6	Charlie Forbes	USA	19.3.95	3	Texas R	Austin	31 Mar
13.62	3.6	Michael Nicholls	BAR	6.4.97	4	Texas R	Austin	31 Mar
13.67	2.9	Justin Veteto	USA	24.3.96	1		Louisville	14 Apr

Mark	Wind	Name		Nat	Born	Pos	Meet	Venue	Date
13.67	4.1	Loic	Desbonnes	FRA	26.7.91	2		Pontoise	20 May
13.68	2.2	Brahian	Peña	SUI	3.4.94	2	NC	Zofingen	14 Jul
13.68	5.0	Jake	Porter	GBR	13.11.93	1		Manchester	29 Jul
13.69	3.4	Chad	Zallow	USA	25.4.97				5 May
13.70	2.4	Shuhei	Ishikawa	JPN	29.5.95				8 Oct
13.71	2.4	Marcus	Maxey	USA	9.10.90				27 Apr
13.71	2.4	Cameron	Hall	USA	12.5.93				12 May
13.71	2.6	Dayo	Akindele	USA	18.9.96				25 May
13.71	2.2	Luke	Siedhoff	USA	21.3.97				6 Jun
13.73	2.4	Elie	Agot	FRA	9.4.91				8 Jul
13.74	2.2	Khai	Riley-La Borde	GBR	8.11.95				7 Jul
13.74A	2.6	Joan	Chaverra	COL	21.3.95				14 Jul
13.74	3.0	Michael	Obasuyi	BEL-J	12.8.99				28 Jul
13.75	4.5	Israel	Nelson	USA	.95				14 Apr
13.76	2.4	Ronald	Forbes	CAY	5.4.85				12 May
13.76	2.2	Chris	Douglas	USA	10.2.97				6 Jun
13.77	2.2	Jovaine	Atkinson	JAM	6.12.95				31 Mar
13.77	2.4	Ryuta	Fujii	JPN	29.7.96				8 Oct
13.78	2.8	Jonathan	Ross	USA	20.9.95				21 Apr
13.78	2.2	Fredrick	Ekholm	SWE	15.6.94				25 Aug
13.80	3.7	Sergey	Solodov	RUS	3.1.96				22 Jun
13.82	4.0	Marvin	Williams	JAM	13.6.96				14 Apr
13.82	2.8	Valdó	Szücs	HUN	29.6.95				13 May
13.82	3.4	Takafumi	Iguchi	JPN	17.5.96				24 May

Low altitude best

Mark	Wind	Name	Nat			Venue		Date
13.49	1.3	de Deus	BRA	1h1		La Chaux-de-Fonds	1	Jul
13.65		Zeng Jianhang	CHN	6	AsiG	Jakarta	28	Aug
13.71	2.0	Moreno	COL				7	Jul
13.88	0.2	Pereira	BRA				14	Sep

Hand timing

Mark	Wind	Name		Nat	Born	Pos	Venue	Date
13.3	0.7	Yordan	O'Farrill	CUB	9.2.93	1	Camagüey	18 May

JUNIORS

See main list for top 3 juniors. 8 performances by 3 men to 13.70. Additional marks and further juniors:

Mark	Wind	Pos	Meet	Venue	Date	Mark	Wind	Pos	Meet	Venue	Date
Thomas	13.45	-1.1	3	NCAA	Eugene	8 Jun	13.65	1.8	1		Baton Rouge	7 Apr
	13.58	1.9	2		Baton Rouge	21 Apr	13.68	1.9	1h4	TexR	Austin	30 Mar
	13.64	0.9	3	SEC	Knoxville	13 May	13.443w	3.6	1	TexR	Austin	31 Mar

Mark	Wind	Name		Nat	Born	Pos	Meet	Venue	Date
13.73	-0.9	Anastas	Eliopoulos	CAN	4.3.99	3	Jerome	Burnaby	26 Jun
13.75	0.9	Michael	Obasuyi	BEL	12.8.99	4		Ninove	28 Jul
13.75	-1.1	Shunsuke	Izumiya	JPN	26.1.00	1		Kawasaki	9 Sep
13.88	1.4	Enrique	Llopis	ESP	15.10.00	1h4	NC	Getafe	21 Jul
13.94	0.1	Pedro	Gutiérrez	CUB	25.4.00	4h1		Camagüey	14 Mar
13.94	-0.9	Luis	Mendy	SEN	2.3.99	5	AfCh	Asaba	4 Aug
13.98	0.1	Tyricke	Dickens (10)	USA	23.3.99	5		Tallahassee	23 Mar
13.99	1.1	Guo Zhongjie		CHN-Y	16.2.01	2		Dalian	4 Aug

Wind assisted

see main list for 1 man – 2 performances by Damian Thomas to 13.70

Mark	Wind	Name		Nat	Born	Pos	Venue	Date
13.74	3.0	Michael	Obasuyi	BEL-J	12.8.99	3h2	Ninove	28 Jul
13.91	2.6	Tyricke	Dickens	USA	23.3.99	3h6	Tampa	25 May
13.96	3.5	Joseph	Anderson	USA	30.8.99	3	Stanford	13 May

110 Metres Hurdles – 99 cm hurdles

Mark	Wind	Name		Nat	Born	Pos	Meet	Venue	Date
12.99	0.3	Damion	Thomas	JAM	29.6.99	1		Kingston	23 Jun
	13.16	0.3		1		WJ	Tampere	12 Feb	
13.00	0.3	Orlando	Bennett	JAM	12.10.99	2		Kingston	23 Jun
	13.30	-0.8		2			Kingston	24 Mar	13.33 0.3 2 WJ Tampere 12 Jul
13.10	-0.8	Dejour	Russell	JAM	1.4.00	1		Kingston	24 Mar
	13.26	0.3		3			Kingston	23 Jun	11 performances by 7 men to 13.33
13.19	-0.6	Shunsuke	Izumiya	JPN	26.1.00	1	NC-j	Nagoya	19 Oct
13.31	1.0	Luis	Salort	ESP	26.7.99	1		Gandia	9 Jun
13.31	1.5	Asahi	Tawada	JPN-Y	.01	1		Fukui	7 Oct
13.32	1.4	Jason	Nicholson	GBR	10.5.99	1s3	WJ	Tampere	11 Jul
13.34	-0.6	Cary	Poole	USA	29.7.99	1	NC-j	Bloomington	15 Jun
13.38	0.0	Michael	Obasuyi	BEL	12.8.99	1		Mannheim	23 Jun
13.39	1.8	Anastas	Eliopoulos (10)	CAN	4.3.99	1		Vancouver	30 May
13.43	-0.8	Rasheed	Broadbelt	JAM	13.8.00	3		Kingston	24 Mar
13.46	0.7	Kentaro	Hiraga	JPN	28.4.99	1		Hiratsuka	15 Jun
13.47	1.1	Enrique	Llopis	ESP	15.10.00	1h7	WJ	Tampere	11 Jul
13.49	1.8	Mattia	Montini	ITA	7.5.99	1h1	NC-j	Agropoli	2 Jun
13.49	0.0	Joshua	Zeller	GBR	19.10.00	2h3		Mannheim	23 Jun
13.52	0.9	Cameron	Murray	USA	12.12.99	1		Greensboro	29 Jul
13.53	1.6	Tre'Bien	Gilbert	USA	18.12.99	1		Austin	12 May
13.54	-0.1	Tade	Ojura	GBR	14.10.99	1h1	N.Sch	Birmingham	14 Jul
13.55	1.2	Just	Kwaou-Mathey	FRA	4.12.99	1		Caen	8 Jul
13.55	-0.6	Rikuto	Higuchi (20)	JPN	19.8.99	2	NC-j	Nagoya	19 Oct

Wind assisted

Mark	Wind	Name		Nat	Born	Pos	Meet	Venue	Date
13.44	3.1	Matheo	Bernat	FRA	27.6.99	1	NC-j	Bondoufle	21 Jul
13.48	4.2	Robert	Teer	USA	6.4.00	1		Austin	11 May
13.52	3.0	Jeanice	Laviolette	fRA	25.1.00	2	Caifta	Nassau	2 Apr

200 METRES HURDLES STRAIGHT

Mark	Wind	Name		Nat	Born	Pos	Venue	Date
22.55	0.3	Eric	Futch	USA	25.4.93	1	Boston	20 May
22.56	2.0	Bershawn	Jackson	USA	8.5.83	1	Manchester	18 May
22.62	0.3	Byron	Robinson	USA	16.2.95	2	Boston	20 May

MEN 2018

Mark	Wind	Name		Nat	Born	Pos	Meet	Venue	Date	

300 METRES HURDLES

Mark	Name		Nat	Born	Pos	Venue	Date	
34.76	Annsert	Whyte	JAM	10.4.87	1	Cheb	4	Sep
35.32	José	Bencosme de Leon	ITA	16.5.92	1	Formia	28	Apr
35.51	Mario	Lambrughi	ITA	5.2.92	2	Formia	28	Apr
35.71	Mattia	Contini	ITA	27.10.94	3	Formia	28	Apr
06.04	Tibor	Koroknai	HUN	24.1.90	2	Cheb	4	Sep
36.05	Martin	Kucera	SVK	10.5.90	3	Cheb	4	Sep

400 METRES HURDLES

Mark	Name		Nat	Born	Pos	Meet	Venue	Date	
46.98	Abderrahman	Samba	QAT	5.9.95	1	DL	Paris (C)	30	Jun
47.02	Rai	Benjamin	ANT/USA	27.7.97	1	NCAA	Eugene	8	Jun
47.37		Samba			1	C.Cup	Ostrava	8	Sep
47.41		Samba			1	DL	Stockholm	10	Jun
47.42		Samba			1	Athl	Lausanne	5	Jul
47.48		Samba			1	G Gala	Roma	31	May
47.54	Kyron	McMaster	IVB	3.1.97	3	DL	Paris (C)	30	Jun
47.57		Samba			1	DL	Doha	4	May
47.60		Samba			1	Bisl	Oslo	7	Jun
47.60		McMaster			1	CAG	Barranquilla	31	Jul
47.64	Karsten	Warholm	NOR	28.2.96	1	EC	Berlin	9	Aug
47.65		Warholm			1	DL	London (OS)	21	Jul
47.66		Samba			1	AsiG	Jakarta	27	Aug
47.81		Warholm			2	DL	Stockholm	10	Jun
47.81	Yasmani	Copello	TUR	15.4.87	2	EC	Berlin	9	Aug
47.82		Warholm			2	G Gala	Roma	31	May
47.90A		Samba			1		Potchefstroom	19	Apr
47.94		Warholm			2	Athl	Lausanne	5	Jul
47.98		Benjamin			1q2	NCAA-W	Sacramento	25	May
48.06		Warholm			3	DL	Paris (C)	30	Jun
48.08		McMaster			1	WK	Zürich	30	Aug
48.10		Warholm			2	WK	Zürich	30	Aug
48.12	Kenny	Selmon	USA	27.8.96	2	NCAA	Eugene	8	Jun
48.18		McMaster			1	NACAC	Toronto	12	Aug
48.21		Selmon			1	NC	Des Moines	23	Jun
48.22		Warholm			2	Bisl	Oslo	7	Jun
48.25		McMaster			1	CG	Gold Coast	12	Apr
48.29	Andre	Clarke	JAM	6.6.92	1		Montverde	9	Jun
48.30	Timothy TJ	Holmes	USA	2.7.95	4	DL	Paris (C)	30	Jun
48.31		Copello			1		Mersin	19	May
48.31	Thomas (31/9)	Barr	IRL	24.7.92	3	EC	Berlin	9	Aug
48.42	David	Kendziera (10)	USA	9.9.94	3	NCAA	Eugene	8	Jun
48.42	Ludvy	Vaillant	FRA	15.3.95	4	EC	Berlin	9	Aug
48.46	Annsert	Whyte	JAM	10.4.87	2	C.Cup	Ostrava	8	Sep
48.47	Abdelmalik	Lahoulou	ALG	7.5.92	1	AfrC	Asaba	3	Aug
48.59	Patryk	Dobek	POL	13.2.94	5	EC	Berlin	9	Aug
48.60	Rasmus	Mägi	EST	4.5.92	1		Antalya	11	Sep
48.65	Khallifah	Rosser	USA	13.7.95	3	NC	Des Moines	23	Jun
48.68	Takatoshi	Abe	JPN	12.11.91	1		Fukuroi	3	May
48.70	Márcio	Teles	BRA	27.1.94	1		Bragança Paulista	16	Sep
48.77	Juander	Santos	DOM	7.5.95	3	CAG	Barranquilla	01	Jul
48.83	Kemar (20)	Mowatt	JAM	12.3.95	4	NCAA	Eugene	8	Jun
48.83	Kerron	Clement	USA	31.10.85	5	DL	Paris (C)	30	Jun
48.88A	Nicholas	Bett	KEN	27.1.90	1		Pretoria	8	Mar
48.89	Timofey	Chalyy	RUS	7.4.94	3s2	EC	Berlin	7	Aug
48.96	Ayyasamy	Dharun	IND	31.12.96	2	AsiG	Jakarta	27	Aug
48.98	Jeffery	Gibson	BAH	15.8.90	1	NA	Heusden-Zolder	21	Jul
48.98	Sergio	Fernández	ESP	1.4.93	7	EC	Berlin	9	Aug
48.99	Mario	Lambrughi	ITA	5.2.92	1		Rieti	13	May
49.00	Quincy	Downing	USA	16.1.93	1		Huelva	8	Jun
49.04	Shawn	Rowe	JAM	7.12.92	2	NC	Kingston	22	Jun
49.04	Byron (30)	Robinson	USA	16.2.95	2s2	NC	Des Moines	22	Jun
49.08	Bershawn	Jackson	USA	8.5.83	2	DL	Doha	4	May
49.10A	Leandro	Zamora	CUB	11.3.96	1		Querétaro	29	Apr
49.10	Taylor	McLaughlin	USA	3.8.97	3s2	NC	Des Moines	22	Jun
49.13	Zied	Azizi	TUN	11.6.91	3	Med G	Tarragona	29	Jun
49.14	Jaheel	Hyde	JAM	2.2.97	1h2	CG	Gold Coast	10	Apr

Mark	Wind	Name		Nat	Born	Pos	Meet	Venue	Date	
49.14		Luke	Campbell	GER	22.11.94	2		La Chaux-de-Fonds	1	Jul
49.17A		Lindsay	Hanekom	RSA	15.5.93	1	NC	Pretoria	17	Mar
49.18		Jack	Green	GBR	6.10.91	4	CG	Gold Coast	12	Apr
49.18		Artur	Langowski	BRA	8.5.91	2	NC	Bragança Paulista	16	Sep
49.22A		Le Roux	Hamman	RSA	6.1.92	2		Pretoria	8	Mar
		(40)								
49.24		Michael	Stigler	USA	5.4.92	2	Drake R	Des Moines	28	Apr
49.24		Tibor	Koroknai	HUN	24.1.90	5s2	EC	Berlin	7	Aug
49.28		Haron	Koech	KEN	27.1.90	3h2	CG	Gold Coast	10	Apr
49.28A		Guillermo	Ruggeri	ARG	26.3.92	1	SAmG	Cochabamba	7	Jun
49.30		Takayuki	Kishimoto	JPN	6.5.90	1	NC	Yamaguchi	23	Jun
49.30		Cornel	Fredericks	RSA	3.3.90	2	Gyulai	Székesfehérvár	2	Jul
49.32A		Zazini	Sokwakhana	RSA-J	23.1.00	2	NC	Pretoria	17	Mar
49.32		Omar	Cisneros	CUB	19.11.89	3		Huelva	8	Jun
49.33		Cameron	French	NZL	17.5.92	1		Canberra	27	Jan
49.34		Victor	Coroller	FRA	21.9.97	4s1	EC	Berlin	7	Aug
		(50)								
49.37		Lorenzo	Vergani	ITA	4.9.93	1		Genève	9	Jun
49.38A		David 'Dai'	Greene	GBR	11.4.86	1		Johannesburg	1	Mar
49.38		Norman	Grimes	USA	6.1.98	1	Big 12	Waco	13	May
49.39		Jordin	Andrade	CPV	5.5.92	4		Huelva	8	Jun
49.40		Craig CJ	Allen	USA	14.2.95	4	NA	Heusden-Zolder	21	Jul
49.41		Muhammad Abdalla	Kounta	FRA	27.10.94	2	NC	Albi	8	Jul
49.45A		Louis 'L.J'	van Zyl	RSA	20.7.85	3		Pretoria	8	Mar
49.46		Infinite	Tucker	USA	22.5.98	2	SEC	Knoxville	13	May
49.46		Mickaël	François	FRA	12.3.88	4		La Chaux-de-Fonds	1	Jul
49.46		Ryo	Kajiki	JPN	8.12.95	1		Hiratsuka	21	Jul
		(60)								
49.47		Eric	Futch	USA	25.4.93	4		Baie-Mahault	12	May
49.48		Romel	Lewis	JAM	28.1.88	3		Montverde	9	Jun
49.48		Hederson	Estefani	BRA	11.9.91	3	NC	Bragança Paulista	16	Sep
49.49		Rilwan	Alowonle	NGR	12.12.93	4h2	CG	Gold Coast	10	Apr
49.50		Mamadou Kassé	Hann	FRA	10.10.86	7	Bisl	Oslo	7	Jun
49.50		Yutaro	Mano	JPN	17.12.96	2h3	NC	Yamaguchi	22	Jun
49.52		José	Bencosme de Leon	ITA	16.5.92	1	NC	Pescara	9	Sep
49.54		Kakeru	Inoue	JPN	19.3.96	1r3		Fukuroi	3	May
49.56		Kurt	Couto	MOZ	14.5.85	3h1	CG	Gold Coast	10	Apr
49.58		Mark	Ujakpor	ESP	18.1.87	6		Huelva	8	Jun
		(70)								
49.59		Bassem	Hemeida	QAT-J	28.9.00	2	WJ	Tampere	14	Jul
49.60		Marvin	Williams	JAM	13.6.96	1	JUCO	El Dorado	19	May
49.62		Mattia	Contini	ITA	27.10.94	2		Rieti	13	May
49.62A		Alfredo	Sepúlveda	CHI	3.8.93	2	SAmG	Cochabamba	7	Jun
49.62			Chen Chieh	TPE	8.5.92	4	AsiG	Jakarta	27	Aug
49.65		Quincy	Hall	USA	31.7.98	1		Stanford	30	Mar
49.66		T. Santhosh	Kumar	IND	1.1.98	5	AsiG	Jakarta	27	Aug
49.67		Landon	Huslig	USA	14.4.95	1	NCAA-2	Charlotte	26	May
49.68		Eric	Cray	PHI	6.11.88	1		Osaka	6	May
49.68		Michael	Tinsley	USA	21.4.84	5		Baie Mahault	12	May
		(80)								
49.69			Feng Zhiqiang	CHN	14.4.98	1		Zhuzhou	17	Apr
49.69		Tatsuhiro	Yamamoto	JPN	23.4.97	2h4	NC	Yamaguchi	22	Jun
49.70		Amere	Lattin	USA	12.7.97	2q3	NCAA-W	Sacramento	25	May
49.71		Constant	Pretorius	RSA	26.1.94	4h1	CG	Gold Coast	10	Apr
49.71		Cory	Poole	USA-J	29.7.99	1	NC-J	Bloomington	16	Jun
49.72		Chad	Miller	JAM	.96	2	NCAA-2	Charlotte	26	May
49.74		Sebastian	Rodger	GBR	29.6.91	2		Oordegem	26	May
49.75		Masayuki	Obayashi	JPN	6.2.96	2		Osaka	6	May
49.77		Maté	Koroknai	HUN	13.1.93	5s3	EC	Berlin	7	Aug
49.78		Mikael Antonio	de Jesus	BRA	19.8.97	1	NC-23	Porto Alegre	29	Apr
		(90)								
49.78		Alison	dos Santos	BRA-J	3.6.00	3	WJ	Tampere	14	Jul
49.80		Ian	Dewhurst	AUS	13.11.90	1	NC	Gold Coast	18	Feb
49.80		Gerald	Drummond	CRC	5.9.94	2	IbAmC	Trujillo	26	Aug
49.81		Javan	Gallimore	JAM	7.8.93	4	NC	Kingston	22	Jun
49.82		Yuki	Matsushita	JPN	9.9.91	3		Osaka	6	May
49.82		Ned	Azemia	SEY	21.8.97	2	JUCO	El Dorado	19	May
49.82A		Sergio	Esquivel	MEX-J	4.5.99	1		Querétaro	26	May
49.83A		Hardus	Maritz	NAM	10.5.90	6		Pretoria	8	Mar
49.85		Fernando	Vega	MEX	19.2.98	5	CAG	Barranquilla	31	Jul
49.86		Jeshua	Anderson	USA	22.6.89	1		Tucson	16	Mar
		(100)								

MEN 2018

Mark	Name		Nat	Born	Pos	Meet	Venue	Date
49.86	Keisuke	Maeno	JPN	10.5.91	3	NC	Yamaguchi	23 Jun
49.88	William	Wynne	USA	30.1.90	13			May
49.88	Takafumi	Iwasaki	JPN	8.12.97	27			May
49.89	Jehue	Gordon	TTO	15.12.91	29			Jul
49.90	Jacob	Paul	GBR	6.2.95	11			Jul
49.91	Javier	Culson	PUR	25.7.84	29			Mar
49.93	Leonardo	Ledgister	JAM-J	27.4.99	11			Jul
49.94	Rovane	Williams	JAM-J	18.5.00	23			Mar
49.94	Ramfis	Vega	PUR	7.1.94	26			Aug
49.96	Pablo Andrés	Ibáñez	ESA	28.10.98	31			Jul
49.97	Jaelen	Williams	USA	7.7.98	24			May
49.97	Ricardo	Cunningham	JAM	3.10.80	22			Jun
49.97	Alain-Hervé	Mfomkpa	SUI	4.6.96	1			Jul
49.98A	Stéphane	Yato	FRA	11.9.92	27			Feb
49.99	Aleksandr	Skorobogatko	RUS	7.8.94	20			Jul
50.00	Ilolo	Izu	USA	28.5.97	30			Mar
50.02	M.P.	Jabir	IND	8.6.96	28			Sep
50.03	Malik	James-King	JAM-J	28.6.99	23			Mar
50.03	Niall	Flannery	GBR	26.4.91	9			Jun
50.03	Yoshihiro	Watanabe	JPN	7.1.97	22			Jun
50.04	Greg	Chiles	USA	2.4.96	25			May
50.05	Jaak-Heinrich	Jagor	EST	11.5.90	13			Jun
50.07	Jauvaney	James	JAM	21.12.98	23			Mar
50.07	Austin	Corley	USA	10.10.96	13			May
50.08	Ryo	Yamamoto	JPN	21.10.95	6			May
50.11	Saber	Boukemouche	ALG	20.4.92	26			May
50.11	Alastair	Chalmers	GBR-J	31.3.00	13			Jul
50.11	Mehboob	Ali	PAK	10.4.90	17			Nov
50.12	Fabian	Norgrove	BAR	6.2.90	24			Jun
50.13	Jacob	Smith	USA	7.10.97	25			May
50.14	Emmanuel Niño	Villalta	CRC	14.2.95	10			Aug
50.15A	Scott	Mecham	USA	31.3.94	28			Apr
50.15	Vijay	Singh Malik	IND	10.1.93	19			Sep
50.16	Malik	Metivier	CAN	-.10.98	24			May
50.16	Michal	Brož	CZE	16.6.92	29			Jul
50.17	José Luis	Gaspar	CUB	25.8.95	8			Jun
50.17	Jakub	Mordyl	POL	15.1.96	8			Jul
50.17	Masaya	Oda	JPN	11.5.95	14			Jul
50.18	Mitsuru	Sugai	JPN	7.1.94	3			May
50.18	Eric	Fogitanz	USA	13.3.97	13			May
50.18	Kotaro	Miyao	JPN	12.7.91	22			Sep
50.19	Vít	Müller	CZE	31.8.96	30			Aug
50.20	Carl	Bengtström	SWE-J	13.1.00	2			Jun
50.21	Quivell	Jordan	USA-J	8.8.99	16			Jun
50.22		Han Se-hyun	KOR	28.7.94	27			Jun
50.25	Demar	Murray	JAM	31.8.91	7			Apr
50.25	Jashanjot	Singh	IND	7.2.95	28			Sep
50.26	Yusuke	Ishida	JPN	25.5.95	6			May
50.26	Emmanuel	Niño	CRC	14.2.95	29			Jul
50.26	Denys	Nechyporenko	UKR	7.1.90	6			Aug
50.27	Yuta	Konishi	JPN	31.7.90	8			Oct
50.28	Deron	Gordon	USA	20.8.96	25			May
50.29	Jayson	Baldridge	USA-J	1.6.99	27			Apr
50.29	Cameron	Samuel	USA-J	27.9.99	13			May
50.29A	Andrés	Silva	URU	27.3.86	7			Jun
50.30	Martin	Kucera	SVK	10.5.90	7			Jul
50.31	Christian	Boyd	USA	14.11.95	25			May
50.31	William	Mutunga	KEN	17.9.93	2			Aug
50.33	Kazunari	Takada	JPN	27.11.97	22			Jul
50.33	Gerber	Blanco	QUA	0.9.93	29			Jul
50.33	Maksims	Sincukovs	LAT	26.6.98	7			Aug
50.34	Leigh	Bennett	AUS	20.4.86	27			Jan
50.35	Kalmon	Stokes	USA	2.12.93	29			Mar
50.35	Eusebio	Haliti	ITA	1.1.91	9			Sep
50.36	Kenroy	Williams	JAM	15.10.95	19			May
50.36	Charles	Brockman	USA-J	31.8.99	25			May
50.36	Michael	Bertil	FRA	2.1.94	8			Jul
50.36	Chris	McAlister	GBR	3.12.95	15			Aug
50.37	Angus	Proudfoot	AUS	2.3.98	18			Feb
50.37		Yu Chia-Hsuan	TPE	22.1.95	26			May
50.37	Yuki	Shinjo	JPN	1 1 97	19			Aug
50.38	Keito	Nonaka	JPN	10.8.96	29			Jun
50.39	Peter	Girardi	USA	12.2.96	21			Jun
50.39A	Diogo	Mestre	POR	20.5.95	22			Jun
50.41	Naoya	Nakano	JPN	3.7.94	22			Jun
50.42	Martin	Tucek	CZE	5.12.95	4			Jun
50.42	Jack	Lawrie	GBR	21.2.96	15			Aug
50.44	Andre	Colebrook	BAH	8.3.94	21			Apr
50.44	Masaki	Toyoda	JPN	17.1.98	3			May
50.44	Chris	Douglas	USA	10.2.97	11			May
50.44	Ivan	Loginov	RUS	19.6.97	7			Jul
50.45	Miloud	Rahmani	ALG	13.12.83	8			Jul
50.46	Emil	Bekric	SRB	14.3.91	6			Aug
50.47	Hugo Balduíno	de Sousa	BRA	5.3.87	18			Mar
50.47	Hirotaka	Tomita	JPN	14.6.96	6			May
50.47	Tatsuya	Tateno	JPN	5.8.91	22			Jul
50.50	Caleb	Corpew	USA	11.2.96	25			May
50.51	Isaiah	Levingston	USA	24.8.98	13			May
50.52	Wilson	Bello	VEN	20.6.95	5			May
50.52	Yuta	Miyakoshi	JPN	.96	19			May
50.52	Yusuke	Shirao	JPN-J	7.9.99	10			Jun
50.52	Matteo	Beria	ITA	20.6.96	10			Jun
50.52	Tomoharu	Kino	JPN	4.8.89	13			Jul
50.54	Shinosuka	Hase	JPN	11.6.96	6			May
50.54	Keisuke	Nozawa	JPN	7.6.91	20			May
50.54	Aleix	Porras	ESP-J	11.9.99	22			Jul
50.54	Jan	Tesar	CZE	26.3.90	29			Jul
50.54		Gong Debin	CHN	9.9.97	16			Sep
50.55	Mahau	Suguimati	BRA	13.11.84	16			Sep
50.56	Antwuan	Musgrove	USA	3.10.96	13			May
(200)								
50.57	Alex	Knibbs	GBR-J	26.4.99	24			Jun
50.57	Danylo	Danylenko	UKR	10.10.94	21			Jul
50.58	Louwtjie	Steenkamp	RSA-J	18.3.99	5			Apr
50.58	Isak	Andersson	SWE	29.1.96	28			Jul
50.58	Hrvoje	Cukman	CRO	28.5.98	29			Jul
50.58	Dmitriy	Koblov	KAZ	30.11.92	26			Aug

Low altitude best

49.08	Bett	2	Mersin	19 May	49.51	Zamora	1	Santo Domingo	6 Jul
49.35	Hamman	3	La Chaux-de-Fonds	1 Jul	49.4h		1	Camagüey	17 Feb
49.42	Sokwakhana	1 W.I	Tampere	14 Jul	49.90	Esquivel J	2	Monterrey	3 Jun
49.48	Greene	3 AWC	London (O8)	15 Jul					
50.41	Maritz	10 Apr	50.44 van Zyl	22 Mar	50.54	Ruggeri			26 Aug

JUNIORS

See main list for top 5 juniors. 11 performances by 5 men to 49.86. Additional marks and further juniors:

Sokwakhana	49.36A	1				Potchefstroom	24 Mar	49.56	4	Odlozil Praha	4 Jun
	49.42	1	WJ			Tampere	14 Jul	49.82A	5	Pretoria	8 Mar
	49.43	1s3	WJ			Tampere	14 Jul	49.86A	1h1	Pretoria	23 Feb
49.93	Leonardo	Ledgister	JAM	27.4.99	4	WJ	Tampere				14 Jul
49.94	Rovane	Williams	JAM	18.5.00	1		Kingston				23 Mar
50.03	Malik	James-King	JAM	28.6.99	2		Kingston				23 Mar
50.11	Alastair	Chalmers	GBR	31.3.00	2s3	WJ	Tampere				13 Jul
50.20	Carl	Bengtström (10)	SWE	13.1.00	1		Göteborg				2 Jun
50.21	Quivell	Jordan	USA-	8.8.99	2	NC-j	Bloomington				16 Jun
50.29	Jayson	Baldridge	USA	1.6.99	3		Fayetteville				27 Apr
50.29	Cameron	Samuel	USA	27.9.99	2	Pac-12	Stanfotd				13 May
50.36	Charles	Brockman	USA	31.8.99	2q2	NCAA-E	Tampa				25 May
50.52	Yusuke	Shirao	JPN-J	7.9.99	1		Gifu				10 Jun
50.54	Aleix	Porras	ESP	11.9.99	2	NC	Getafe				22 Jul
50.57	Alex	Knibbs	GBR	26.4.99	1		Mannheim				24 Jun

Mark	Name		Nat	Born	Pos	Meet	Venue	Date
50.58	Louwtjie	Steenkamp	RSA	18.3.99	2		Paarl	5 Apr
50.62A	Mehdi	Pirjahan	IRI	23.9.99	1		Tehran	27 Sep
50.73	Alessandro	Sibilio (20)	ITA	27.4.99	4s3	WJ	Tampere	14 Jul

HIGH JUMP

Mark			Name				Nat	Born	Pos	Meet	Venue	Date
2.40			Mutaz Essa		Barshim		QAT	24.6.91	1	DL	Doha	4 May
			2.20/1 2.24/1 2.27/1 2.30/1 2.33/2 2.36/1 2.40/1 2.42/xxx									
	2.40	1	Gyulai	Székesfehérvár	2	Jul		2.22/1 2.26/1 2.30/1 2.34/1 2.40/3 2.46/xxx				
	2.38Ai	1	AsiC-I	Tehran	1	Feb		2.15/1 2.20/1 2.25/1 2.30/2 2.33/1 2.36/1 2.38/1 2.40/xxx				
	2.38	1	GS	Ostrava	13	Jun		2.20/1 2.25/1 2.28/1 2.31/1 2.34/x 2.36/x 2.38/1				
	2.36	1	Pre	Eugene	26	May		2.26/1 2.29/1 2.32/1 2.36/3 2.42/xxx				
	2.36	1	Bisl	Oslo	7	Jun		2.20/1 2.25/1 2.30/2 2.33/2 2.36/1 2.40/xxx				
	2.35i	1		Malmö	10	Feb		2.15/1 2.20/1 2.25/1 2.30/2 2.33/2 2.35/2 2.38/xxx				
	2.33i	1	WI	Birmingham	1	Mar		2.20/1 2.25/1 2.29/1 2.33/1 2.36/xxx				
2.40			Danil		Lysenko		RUS	19.5.97	1	Herc	Monaco	20 Jul
			2.20/1 2.24/1 2.27/1 2.30/1 2.33/1 2.40/1									
	2.37i	1		Hustopece	27	Jan		2.15/1 2.20/1 2.25/1 2.28/1 2.31/1 2.33/2 2.37/1 2.39/xxx				
	2.37	1	Athl	Lausanne	5	Jul		2.20/1 2.25/1 2.29/1 2.33/1 2.37/1				
	2.36i	1		Moskva	21	Jan		2.13/1 2.18/1 2.23/1 2.26/2 2.29/2 2.33/1 2.36/1 2.40/xxx				
	2.36i	1	WI	Birmingham	1	Mar		2.15/1 2.20/1 2.25/1 2.29/1 2.33/1 2.36/3				
	2.36	2	GS	Ostrava	13	Jun		2.20/1 2.25/1 2.28/2 2.31/1 2.34/1 2.36/2 2.38/xxx				
	2.35i	1		Yekaterinburg	7	Jan		2.15/1 2.20/1 2.24/1 2.28/1 2.35/1				
	2.35i	1		Trinec	30	Jab		2.15/1 2.20/1 2.24/1 2.27/1 2.30/1 2.33/2 2.35/3 2.40/xxx				
	2.33i	1	NC	Moskva	13	Feb		2.15/1 2.20/1 2.24/1 2.28/1 2.31/1 2.33/1				
	2.33	2	Bisl	Oslo	7	Jun		2.20/1 2.25/1 2.30/1 2.33/1 2.36/xxx				
2.36			Dmitriy		Nabokov		BLR	20.1.96	1		Brest	25 May
			2.15/1 2.20/1 2.24/1 2.28/1- 2.30/1 2.32/1- 2.34/2 2.36/1 2.40/x									
2.36			Brandon		Starc		AUS	24.11.93	1		Eberstadt	26 Aug
			2.20/2 2.24/1 2.27/3 2.30/2 2.33/x 2.36/2 2.40/x									
	2.33	1	DL	Birmingham	18	Aug		2.16/1 2.20/1 2.24/1 2.27/2 2.30/x 2.33/2 2.37/xxx				
	2.33	1	VD	Bruxelles	31	Aug		2.20/2 2.23/1 2.26/3 2.29/1 2.31/2 2.33/2 2.35/xxx				
2.35i			Ivan		Ukhov		RUS	29.3.86	1		Moskva	31 Jan
			2.15/1 2.20/1 2.24/1 2.28/2 2.32/1 2.35/1 2.38/xx									
	2.34	1		Smolensk	29	May		2.15/1 2.22/1 2.28/2 2.34/1 2.37/xxx				
2.35			Bryan		McBride		USA	10.12.91	1		Chula Vista	9 Jun
			2.09/1 2.14/1 2.19/1 2.24/1 2.29/2 2.32/1 2.35/2 2.37/xxx									
2.35			Mateusz		Przybylko		GER	9.3.92	1	EC	Berlin	11 Aug
			2.19/1 2.24/1 2.28/1 2.31/1 2.33/1 2.35/1 2.38/xpp									
	2.33	2	VD	Bruxelles	31	Aug		2.15/1 2.20/1 2.23/2 2.26/2 2.29/1 2.31/2 2.33/3 2.35/xxx				
2.33i			Trey		Culver		USA	18.7.96	1		Lubbock	13 Jan
			2.06/1 2.11/2 2.16/1- 2.21/1 2.24/1 2.27/1 2.30/1 2.33/1 2.36/xxx									
2.33i			Sylwester		Bednarek		POL	28.4.89	2		Trinec	30 Jan
			2.10/1 2.15/1 2.20/1 2.24/2 2.27/1 2.30/1 2.33/3 2.35/xxx									
2.33i			Vernon		Turner (10)		USA	21.8.98	1		Fayetteville	10 Feb
			2.12/1 2.17/1 2.22/3 2.33/1 2.35/xxx									
2.33			Majed El Dein		Ghazal		SYR	21.4.87	2	DL	Doha	4 May
			2.20/2 2.24/1 2.27/2 2.30/2 2.33/1 2.36/xxx									
2.33			Fabian		Delryd		SWE	15.10.96	1		Täby	19 May
			2.11/1 2.17/1 2.22/1 2.27/1 2.30/2 2.33/1 2.36/xxx									
2.33			Maksim		Nedosekov		BLR	21.1.98	2	EC	Berlin	11 Aug
			2.19/1 2.24/1 2.28/xx		2.31/1 2.33/1 2.35/xx	2.37/x						
2.33			Gianmarco		Tamberi		ITA	1.6.92	2		Eberstadt	26 Aug
		(34/14)	2.15/1 2.20/3 2.24/1 2.30/3 2.33/1								
2.32			Michael		Mason		CAN	30.9.86	1		Victoria	12 May
2.32					Wang Yu		CHN	18.8.91	3	Pre	Eugene	26 May
2.32			Ricky		Robertson		USA	19.9.90	2		Chula Vista	9 Jun
2.32			Donald		Thomas		BAH	1.7.84	4	Gyulai	Székesfehérvár	2 Jul
2.32			Naoto		Tobe		JPN	31.3.92	1		Lignano Sabbiadoro	11 Jul
2.31i			Eric		Kynard		USA	3.2.91	1		Manhattan, KS	3 Feb
		(20)										
2.31i			Jamal		Wilson		BAH	1.9.88	1		Birmingham, AL	9 Feb
2.31i			Ilya		Ivanyuk		RUS	9.3.93	3	NC	Moskva	13 Feb
2.31			Jeron		Robinson		USA	30.4.91	1	Texas R	Austin	31 Mar
2.31			Konstadínos		Baniótis		GRE	6.11.86	1		Thessaloníki	27 May
2.31			Andriy		Protsenko		UKR	20.5.88	4	VD	Bruxelles	31 Aug
2.30i			Robbie		Grabarz		GBR	3.10.87	1		Birmingham	7 Jan
2.30i			Matús		Bubeník		SVK	14.11.89	1e2		Hustopece	27 Jan
2.30			Django		Lovett		CAN	6.7.92	3	CG	Gold Coast	11 Apr
2.30			Alperen		Acet		TUR	2.4.98	1		Cluj-Napoca	3 Jun
2.30A			Matthew		Sawe		KEN	2.7.88	1		Nairobi	6 Jun6
		(30)										

MEN 2018

Mark	Name		Nat	Born	Pos	Meet	Venue	Date	
2.30		Woo Sang-hyuk	KOR	23.4.96	1		Boeun	10	Aug
2.29i	Randall	Cunningham	USA	4.1.96	1	NCAA	College Station	10	Mar
2.29i	Shelby	McEwen	USA	6.4.96	1	NCAA	College Station	10	Mar
2.29	Tejaswin	Shankar	IND	21.12.98	1		Lubbock	27	Apr
2.28		Lee Hup Wei	MAS	5.5.87	1		Canberra	27	Jan
2.28i	Edgar	Rivera	MEX	13.2.91	6		Hustopece	27	Jan
2.28i	Tihomir	Ivanov	BUL	11.7.94	1		Sofia	4	Feb
2.28i	Semyen	Pozdnyakov	RUS	28.11.92	4	NC	Moskva	13	Feb
2.28	Takashi	Eto	JPN	5.2.91	1		Gifu	12	May
2.28	Yevgeniy	Korshunov	RUS	11.4.86	2		Smolensk	29	May
	(40)								
2.28A	Eure	Yáñez	VEN	20.5.93	1	SAmG	Cochabamba	6	Jun
2.28	Jermaine	Francis	SKN	9.3.98	3	CAG	Barranquilla	1	Aug
2.28	Luis Joel	Castro	PUR	28.1.91	4	CAG	Barranquilla	1	Aug
2.27i	Keenon	Laine	USA	12.6.97	1		Clemson	6	Jan
2.27i	Viktor	Lonskyy	UKR	27.10.95	1		Hirson	27	Jan
2.27	Allan	Smith	GBR	6.11.92	5	CG	Gold Coast	11	Apr
2.27	Tobias	Potye	GER	16.3.95	1		Regensburg	3	Jun
2.27	Maciej	Grynienko	POL	30.3.98	2	Kuso	Chorzów	8	Jun
2.27	Hamdi Mahamat	Alamine	QAT	15.4.97	1		Karlstad	25	Jul
2.27	Trevor	Barry	BAH	14.6.83	1	Skol	Chorzów	22	Aug
	(50)								
2.27	Eike	Onnen	GER	3.8.82	5=		Eberstadt	26	Aug
2.26i	Douwe	Amels	NED	16.9.91	1		Leverkusen	20	Jan
2.26i	Aleksey	Dmitrik	RUS	12.4.84	3		Moskva	21	Jan
2.26i	Talles	Silva	BRA	20.8.91	1		São Bernardo do Campo	3	Feb
2.26i	Andrey	Skobeyko	BLR	11.6.95	2		Gomel	3	Feb
2.26	Matthew	Campbell	JAM	20.10.96	1	Fla R	Gainesville	30	Mar
2.26A	Roberto	Vilches	MEX-J	21.5.99	1		Querétaro	29	Apr
2.26	Jonathan	Wells	USA	18.4.96	1	Big 10	Bloomington	13	May
2.26	Jonas Kløjgaard	Jensen	DEN	29.2.96	1		Skive	19	May
2.26	Adrijus	Glebauskas	LTU	20.11.94	1		Jerusalem	6	Jun
	(60)								
2.26	Norbert	Kobielski	POL	28.1.97	1		Opole	17	Jun
2.26	Chris	Moleya	RSA	27.1.97	3		Madrid	22	Jun
2,26	Tomohiro	Shinno	JPN	17.8.96	1		Okinawa	30	Jun
2.26	Chris	Baker	GBR	2.2.91	1	NC	Birmingham	1	Jul
2.26	David	Smith	GBR	14.7.91	2	NC	Birmingham	1	Jul
2.26	Bram	Ghuys	BEL	14.2.93	1		Nieuwpoort	15	Jul
2.26	Dmytro	Demyanyuk	UKR	30.6.83	2	NC	Lutsk	20	Jul
2.26	Dmitriy	Kroyter	ISR	18.2.93	1		Schliffange	29	Jul
2.25i	Dmitriy	Semyonov	RUS	2.8.92	4		Chelyabinsk	11	Jan
2.25i	Marco	Fassinotti	ITA	29.4.89	7=		Banská Bystrica	6	Feb
	(70)								
2.25i	Dmitriy	Melsitov	UZB	19.3.96	1	NC	Tashkent	16	Feb
2.25	Siddharth	Yadav	IND	30.1.93	2		Patiala	7	Mar
2.25	Clayton	Brown	JAM	8.12.96	2	SEC	Knoxville	13	May
2.25	Mikhail	Veryovkin	RUS	28.6.91	3		Smolensk	29	May
2.25A	Fernando	Ferreira	BRA	13.12.94	2	SAmG	Cochabamba	6	Jun
2.25A	Carlos	Layoy	ARG	26.2.91	3	SAmG	Cochabamba	6	Jun
2.25	Daniyil	Tsyplakov	RUS	29.7.92	1		Zhukovskiy	13	Jun
2.25	Mikhail	Akimenko	RUS	6.12.95	2		Zhukovskiy	13	Jun
2.25	Balasubramanya	Chethan	IND	18.8.92	1	I State	Guwahati	28	Jun
2.25	Anton	Bodnar	KAZ	4.12.92	1		Almaty	9	Jul
	(80)								
2.25i	Jordan	Wesner	USA	10.6.97	1		Nashville	1	Dec
2.25	Hamish	Kerr	NZL	17.8.96	1		Christchurch	8	Dec
2.24i	Bradley	Adkins	USA	30.12.93	2		Lubbock	13	Jan
2.24	Manjula Kumara	Wijesekara	SRI	30.1.84	1		Diyagama	27	Jan
2.24	Nauraj Singh	Randhawa	MAS	27.1.92	2		Sydney	4	Feb
2.24i	Jakobe	Ford	USA	4.9.98	1		Seattle	11	Feb
2.24i	Nikita	Anishchenkov	RUS	25.7.92	6	NC	Moskva	13	Feb
2.24i	Stefano	Sottile	ITA	26.1.98	1	NC	Ancona	16	Feb
2.24i	Eugenio	Rossi	SMR	6.3.92	2	ITA Ch	Ancona	16	Feb
2.24i	Silvano	Chesani	ITA	17.7.88	4	NC	Ancona	16	Feb
	(90)								
2.24i	Barry	Pender	IRL	2.4.90	1	NC	Dublin	18	Feb
2.24i	Darius	Carbin	USA	4.3.98	2		College Station	24	Feb
2.24i		Yang Lubang	CHN	18.6.97	2		Beijing	24	Mar
2.24	Samuel	Shoultz	USA	.96	1		Charlottesville	6	Apr
2.24	Deante	Kemper	USA	27.3.93	1		Tempe	7	Apr

Mark	Name		Nat	Born	Pos	Meet	Venue	Date
2.24	Demar	Robinson ¶	JAM	13.8.93	1		Coral Gables	10 May
2.24	Ushan	Perera	SRI	22.1.98	1		Colombo	12 May
2.24		Pai Long	CHN	8.10.89	1		Huaian	17 May
2.24	Pavel	Seliverstov	BLR	2.9.96	3		Bialystok	20 May
2.24	Loïc	Gasch	SUI	13.8.94	2		Genève	9 Jun
	(100)							
2.24		Chen Ji	CHN	27.1.90	1	NC	Taiyuan	15 Sep
2.24	Sarvesh Anil	Kushare	IND	17.6.95	1		Bhubaneshwar	26 Sep
2.235	Nate	Patterson	USA-J	21.12.99	2			Jun
2.23i	Landon	Bartel	USA	17.2.96	20			Jan
2.23i	Javen	Reeves	USA	4.12.95	27			Jan
2.23i	David	Smith	PUR	2.5.92	3			Feb
2.23	Luis Joel	Zayas	CUB	7.6.97	4			Feb
2.23i	Guilherme	Cobbo	BRA	1.10.87	17			Feb
2.23i	Mihai	Donisan	ROU	24.7.88	24			Feb
2.23	Falk	Wendrich	GER	12.6.95	13			May
2.23	Mihai	Anastasiu	ROU	11.3.93	19			May
2.23	Tom	Gale	GBR	18.12.98	1			Jul
2.23	Chris	Kandu	GBR	10.9.95	1			Jul
2.23	Adónios	Mérlos	GRE-J	4.4.99	14			Jul
2.23	Breyton	Poole	RSA-J	23.3.00	14			Jul
2.23	JuVaughn	Blake	USA-J	30.4.99	14			Jul
2.23	Andriy	Kovalyov	UKR	11.6.92	20			Jul
2.23	Keitaro	Fujita	JPN	2.10.97	22			Jul
2.23		Vu Duc Anh	VIE	6.2.98	30			Nov
2.22i	Avion	Jones	USA	31.1.94	20			Jan
2.22i	Jeremy	Taiwo	USA	15.1.90	26			Jan
2.22	Jah-Mhai	Perinchief	BER	31.12.97	16			Feb
2.22i	Aleksey	Yefanov	RUS	6.10.97	21			Feb
2.22i	Dominic	Ogbechie	GBR-Y	15.5.02	24			Feb
2.22	Bryant	O'Georgia	USA	11.6.96	24			Mar
2.22	Ryo	Sato	JPN	21.7.94	21			Apr
2.22	James	Harris	USA	18.9.91	4			May
2.22		Hsiang Chun-Hsien	TPE	4.9.93	17			Jun
2.22	Nicolas	De Luca	ITA	7.4.93	5			Jul
2.22		Lee Kwang-tai	KOR	29.1.91	12			Jul
2.22	Kazuhiro	Ota	JPN	11.6.95	21			Jul
2.22	Rai	Mizutani	JPN	12.1.97	5			Aug
2.22	Naoto	Hasegawa	JPN	15.11.96	26			Aug
2.22	Hiromi	Takahari	JPN	13.11.87	7			Oct
2.22		Chen Long	CHN-Y	13.11.02	14			Oct
2.22	Oscar	Miers	AUS-Y	21.11.01	14			Oct
2.21i	Kris	Kornegay-Gober	USA	6.10.91	7			Jan
2.21	Nik	Bojic	AUS	18.1.92	2			Feb
2.21i	Mike	Edwards	GBR/NGR	11.7.90	3			Feb
2.21i	Nikita	Vurbanov	RUS-J	13.4.99	7			Feb
2.21i	Ryan	Lockard	USA	30.8.95	10			Feb
2.21	Joel	Baden	AUS	1.2.96	17			Feb
2.21i	Roman	Loshkaryev	KAZ	28.10.96	20			Feb
2.21i	Tequan	Claitt	USA	18.7.97	23			Feb
2.21	Sean	Lee	USA-J	12.1.00	24			Feb
2.21	Caleb	Parker	USA	26.6.98	30			Mar
2.21	Jake	Grimsman	USA-J	28.1.00	31			Mar
2.21	Tyler	Cronk	USA-J	.99	14			Apr
2.21	Rahman	Minor	USA	28.11.98	14			Apr
2.21i	Grant	Anderson	USA	5.5.95	5			May
2.21	Corion	Knight	USA	18.8.96	10			May
2.21	Jerin	Allen	USA	20.11.95	10			May
2.21	Richard	Newman	USA-J	22.5.99	18			May
2.21	Alexander	Bowen	PAN	3.4.93	9			Jun
2.21	Kyle	Landon	USA	16.10.94	9			Jun
2.21	Vincent	Bharathi	IND	20.5.94	28			Jun
2.21	Luca	Meinke	GER-J	7.6.99	14			Jul
2.21	Raul	Spank	GER	13.7.88	24			Aug
2.21	Ryoichi	Akamatsu	JPN	2.5.95	13			Oct
2.21i	Daniel	Armstrong	USA	24.2.98	7			Dec
2.20i	Arseniy	Rasov	RUS	20.6.92	7			Jan
2.20i	Yuriy	Krymarenko	UKR	11.8.83	10			Jan
2.20Ai	Mohammad Reza	Vazifehdoost	IRI	13.10.93	11			Jan
2.20i	Tyler	Adams	USA	11.2.96	12			Jan
2.20i	Tye	Williams	USA	17.8.96	13			Jan
2.20i	Jaroslav	Bába	CZE	2.9.84	18			Jan
2.20i	Miguel Ángel	Sancho	ESP	24.4.90	19			Jan
2.20i	Samuli	Eriksson	FIN	9.11.95	19			Jan
2.20i	Bastian	Rudolf	GER	1.6.95	20			Jan
2.20i	Vasilios	Constantinou	CYP	13.9.92	27			Jan
2.20i	Aleksandr	Mrykhin	RUS	4.9.96	31			Jan
2.20i	Dan	Lazarica	ROU	11.5.92	3			Feb
2.20i	Abdulkadar	Nuh	QAT-J	6.4.99	6			Feb
2.20i	Lukás	Beer	SVK	23.8.89	6			Feb
2.20	Arturo Joaquín	Abascal	MEX	19.6.95	17			Feb
2.20i	Péter	Bakosi	HUN	23.6.93	17			Feb
2.20i	Thiago Júlio	Alfano Moura	BRA	27.11.95	17			Feb
2.20i	Joel	Khan	GBR-J	30.9.99	25			Feb
2.20A	Mpho	Links	RSA	20.6.96	1			Mar
2.20i	Milton	Harrell	USA	22.1.98	2			Mar
2.20	Enrique	Esquer	MEX	2.12.91	3			Mar
2.20A	Bwalya	Humphrey	ZAM	,99	4			Mar
2.20i		Zhang Guowei	CHN	4.6.91	7			Mar
2.20i	Stefan	Duvivier	USA	10.9.96	10			Mar
2.20i	Lushane	Wilson	JAM	11.9.98	24			Mar
2.20i		Sun Zhao	CHN	8.2.90	24			Mar
2.20		Li Jialun	CHN	16.4.95	16			Apr
2.20	Benjamin	Milligan	USA	29.5.97	28			Apr
2.20	Ryan	Webb	GBR	19.10.97	13			May
2.20	Ernie	Sears	USA	4.12.98	13			May
2.20	Andrey	Churylo	BLR	15.9.93	20			May
2.20	Aleksandr	Kiselyov	BLR-J	28.3.99	25			May
2.20	Martin	Günther	GER	8.10.86	30			May
2.20	Andrey	Rybakov	BLR	14.12.96	7			Jun
2.20	Jean Carlos	Ramírez	CUB	2.1.96	8			Jun
2.20	Keyvan	Ghanbarzadeh	IRI	26.5.90	8			Jun
2.20A		Ding Shuo	CHN	8.4.98	16			Jun
2.20A		Cheng Kaiwei	CHN	22.9.95	16			Jun
2.20	Aleksandr	Asanov	RUS	30.3.96	22			Jun
2.20	Christian	Falocchi (200)	ITA	30.1.97	22			Jun
2.20	Vadym	Kravchuk	UKR	28.10.96	25			Jun
2.20	Simón	Siverio	ESP	2.8.88	29			Jun
2.20	Yuriy	Dergachev	KAZ	13.11.94	9			Jul
2.20	Carlos	Rojas	ESP	10.4.95	14			Jul
2.20		Kang Sung-mo	KOR	22.4.88	25			Jul
2.20	Charles	McBride	USA-Y	16.4.01	29			Jul
2.20	Josué	da Costa	BRA	15.3.93	19			Aug
2.20		Yu Shisuo	CHN	20.2.90	15			Sep
2.20i	Isaiah	Kyle	USA	25.5.97	2			Dec
2.20	Tawan	Kaeodem (210)	THA-J	30.9.99	16			Dec

Best outdoor marks

Mark	Name	Pos	Meet	Venue	Date
2.31	Ivanyuk	3	EC	Berlin	11 Aug
2.30	Wilson	2	CG	Gold Coast	11 Apr
2.29	Kynard	4	Pre	Eugene	26 May
2.28	Turner	1	Big 12	Waco	12 May
2.28	Culver	3	NC	Des Moines	24 Jun
2.27	Bednarek	1	Kuso	Chorzów	8 Jun
2.26	Silva	1		Concepción del Uruguay	23 Mar
2.26	Laine	1		Athens	7 Apr
2.26	Amels	2		Garbsen	13 May
2.26	Rivera	1		Bühl	22 Jun
2.26	Pozdnyakov	3	NC	Kazan	21 Jul
2.25	McEwen	2		Auburn	21 Apr
2.25	Fassinotti	5	Bisl	Oslo	7 Jun
2.25	Skobeyko	2		Hérouville	14 Jun

Mark	Name	Date	Mark	Name	Date
2.23	Bubeník	29 Jun	2.21	Carbin	7 Apr
2.23	Lonskyy	20 Jul	2.21	Grabarz	9 Apr
2.23	Anishchenkov	21 Jul	2.20	Moura	9 Apr
2.23	Cobbo	16 Sep	2.20	Yang Lubang	16 Apr
2.22	Jones	24 Jun	2.20	Rossi	6 May
2.20	Sottile	13 May	2.20	Donisan	19 May
2.20	Bartel	13 May	2.20	Chesani	17 Jun
2.20	Zhang Guowei	17 May	2.20	Constantinou	29 Jun
2.20	Sun Zhao	17 May	2.20	Krymarenko	20 Jul
2.20	Beer	19 May	2.20	Melsitov	27 Aug

Symbols/Abbreviations

+ intermediate time in longer race, A made at an altitude of 1000m or higher, D made in a decathlon, h made in a heat, qf quarter-final, sf semi-final, i indoors, Q qualifying round, r race number, -J juniors, -Y youths (b. 2001 or later)

MEN 2018

Mark	Name			Nat	Born	Pos	Meet	Venue	Date
JUNIORS									
9 performances by 5 men to 2.23									
2.26A	Roberto		Vilches	MEX-J	21.5.99	1		Querétaro	29 Apr
2.25	1		Monterrey	2	Jun		2.24A	1	Ciudad de México	16 Jun
2.24A	1		Ciudad de México	30	Jun		2.23	1	WJ	Tampere	14 Jul
2.235	Nate		Patterson	USA-J	21.12.99	1		Blomington	2 Jun
2.23	Adónios		Mérlos	GRE-J	4.4.99	1=	WJ	Tampere	14 Jul
2.23	Breyton		Poole	RSA-J	23.3.00	3=	WJ	Tampere	14 Jul
2.23	JuVaughn		Blake	USA-J	30.4.99	3=	WJ	Tampere	14 Jul
2.22i	Dominic		Ogbechie	GBR-Y	15.5.02	1		Sheffield	24 Feb
2.22			Chen Long	CHN-Y	13.11.02	1	YOG	Buenos Aires	14 Oct
2.22	Oscar		Miers	AUS-Y	21.11.01	2	YOG	Buenos Aires	14 Oct
2.21i	Nikita		Vurbanov	RUS-J	13.4.99	1	NC-j	Volgograd	7 Feb
2.21	Sean		Lee (10)	USA-J	12.1.00	1		Mission Viejo	24 Feb
2.21	Jake		Grimsman	USA-J	28.1.00	1		Stanford	31 Mar
2.21	Tyler		Cronk	USA-J	.99	1		Pasco	11 Apr
2.21	Richard		Newman	USA-J	22.5.99	1	JUCO	El Dorado	18 May
2.21	Luca		Meinke	GER-J	7.6.99	5	WJ	Tampere	14 Jul
2.20i	Abdulkadar		Nuh	QAT-J	6.4.99	1		Banská Bystrica	6 Feb
2.20i	Joel		Khan	GBR-J	30.9.99	1		Sheffield	25 Feb
2.20	Aleksandr		Kiselyov	BLR-J	28.3.99	4		Brest	25 May
2.20	Charles		McBride	USA-Y	16.4.01	1		Greensboro	29 Jul
2.20	Tawan		Kaeodem	THA-J	30.9.99	1		Nay Pyi Taw	16 Dec
2.19	seven men								

POLE VAULT

Mark	Name			Nat	Born	Pos	Meet	Venue	Date
6.05	Armand		Duplantis	SWE-J	10.11.99	1	EC	Berlin	12 Aug
			5.50/1 5.65/1 5.80/2 5.85/1 5.90/1 5.95/1 6.00/1 6.05/1						
5.93	1		Baton Rouge	5	May		5.45/2 5.82/1 5.93/1		
5.92	3	TexR	Austin	31	Mar		5.47/1 5.72/1 5.92/3 6.02/xxx		
5.91	1		Montreuil	19	Jun		5.61/1 5.81/1 5.91/1 5.96/xxx		
5.90	2	DL	Paris (C)	30	Jun		5.60/1 5.77/2 5.84/2 5.90/3 5.96/xx 6.01/x		
5.88i	5		Clermont-Ferrand	25	Feb		5.43/1 5.60/1 5.73/2 5.81/1 5.88/3 5.93/xxx		
6.00	Timur		Morgunov	RUS	12.10.96	2	EC	Berlin	12 Aug
			5.50/1 5.65/1 5.75/1 5.85/1 5.90/1 5.95/x 6.00/1 6.05/xxx						
5.93	1	VD	Bruxelles	31	Aug		5.53/1 5.68/1 5.78/1 5.83/2 5.88/3 5.93/1		
5.92	1	Znam	Zhukovskiy	30	Jun		5.45/2 5.55/1 5.65/2 5.80/1 5.92/2 6.02/xxx		
5.91i	1	WK	Zürich	29	Aug		5.56/1 5.71/1 5.81/1 5.86/1 5.91/3		
5.96	Sam		Kendricks	USA	7.9.92	1	DL	Paris (C)	30 Jun
			5.45/1 5.60/1 5.70/1 5.77/1 5.84/1 5.90/1 5.96/2 6.05/xxx						
5.93i	1		Clermont-Ferrand	25	Feb		5.43/1 5.60/1 5.73/1 5.81/3 5.88/1 5.93/1 5.98/xxx		
5.92	1	DL	London (OS)	21	Jul		5.46/1 5.61/1 5.71/2 5.80/3 5.86/2 5.92/1 5.97/x 6.05/xx		
5.88	2	VD	Bruxelles	31	Aug		5.53/1 5.63/2 5.68/1 5.73/1 5.78/1 5.83/2 5.88/3 5.93/xxx		
5.95	Renaud		Lavillenie	FRA	18.9.86	1		Austin	14 Apr
			5.60/1 5.75/1 5.85/1 5.95/3 6.01/xxx						
5.95	3	EC	Berlin	12	Aug		5.65/1 5.80/xx 5.85/1 5.95/1 6.00/x 6.05/xx		
5.93i	2		Clermont-Ferrand	25	Feb		5.73/1 5.81/1 5.88/1 5.93/3 5.98/xxx		
5.92	1	TexR	Austin	31	Mar		5.62/1 5.72/1 5.82/1 5.92/1 6.02/xxx		
5.91	1	Kuso	Chorzów	8	Jun		5.61/3 5.81/1 5.91/2 6.01/xxx		
5.91	1	Athl	Lausanne	4	Jul		5.60/1 5.77/3 5.84/1 5.91/2 6.00/xxx		
5.90i	1=		Rouen	10	Feb		5.60/1 5.70/1 5.78/2 5.84/2 5.90/1 5.95/xx 6.00/x		
5.00i	1	WI	Birmingham	4	Mar		5.70/1 5.85/1 5.90/2 6.00/xxx		
5.94	Piotr		Lisek	POL	16.8.92	1		Wittenberg	1 Aug
			5.40/1 5.60/1 5.70/1 5.80/1 5.90/1 5.94/1						
5.88i	6		Clermont-Ferrand	25	Feb		5.60/1 5.73/1 5.81/3 5.88/3 5.93/xxx		
5.92	Shawnacy		Barber	CAN	27.5.94	2	Texas R	Austin	31 Mar
			5.47/1 5.62/1 5.72/1 5.92/3 6.02/xxx						
5.90i	Thiago		Braz da Silva	BRA	16.12.93	1=		Rouen	10 Feb
			5.50/x 5.60/1 5.70/2 5.84/1 5.90/1 6.00/xxx						
5.88i	Raphael		Holzdeppe	GER	28.9.89	1		Karlsruhe	3 Feb
			5.60/1 5.70/1 5.78/1 5.83/2 5.88/3 5.95/xxx						
5.88i	Pawel		Wojciechowski	POL	6.6.89	3		Clermont-Ferrand	25 Feb
			5.43/1 5.60/1 5.73/1 5.81/xx 5.88/1 5.93/xxx						
5.88i	Axel		Chapelle (10)	FRA	24.4.95	4		Clermont-Ferrand	25 Feb
			5.43/2 5.60/2 5.73/2 5.81/1 5.88/2 5.93/xxx						
5.88i	Kévin		Menaldo	FRA	12.7.92	7		Clermont-Ferrand	25 Feb
	(34/11)						5.43/3 5.60/3 5.73/2 5.81/2 5.88/3 5.93/xxx		
5.87i	Andrew		Irwin	USA	23.1.93	1		Black Springs	26 May
5.86	Chris		Nilsen	USA	13.1.98	1		Sioux Falls	5 May
5.86i	Kurtis		Marschall	AUS	25.4.97	3	WK	Zürich	29 Aug

Mark	Name		Nat	Born	Pos	Meet	Venue	Date	
5.85i	Konstadinos	Filippídis	GRE	26.11.86	1		Madrid	8	Feb
5.83Ai	Scott	Houston	USA	11.6.90	1	NC	Albuquerque	17	Feb
5.80i	Dmitry	Zhelyabin	RUS	20.5.90	1		Moskva	25	Jan
5.80i	Emmanouíl	Karalís	GRE-J	20.10.99	5=	WI	Birmingham	4	Mar
5.80	Devin	King	USA	12.3.96	2c2	Texas R	Austin	31	Mar
5.78i	Melker	Svärd Jacobsson	SWE	8.1.94	1	4-N	Uppsala	11	Feb
	(20)								
5.78Ai	Mike	Arnold	USA	13.8.90	3	NC	Albuquerque	17	Feb
5.75i		Xue Changrui	CHN	31.5.91	1		Liévin	13	Feb
5.75	Cole	Walsh	USA	14.6.95	3	NC	Des Moines	23	Jun
5.75	Sondre	Guttormsen	NOR-J	1.6.99	6=	EC	Berlin	12	Aug
5.74 dh?	Arnaud	Art	BEL	28.1.93	1		Recklinghausen	1	Jun
5.72					2		Liège (NX)	19	Jul
5.72i	Valentin	Lavillenie	FRA	16.7.91	2	NC	Liévin	18	Feb
5.72	Stanley	Joseph	FRA	24.10.91	1		Paris (C)	23	Jun
5.71	Matthew	Ludwig	USA	5.7.96	1		Long Beach	21	Apr
5.71	Ivan	Horvat	CRO	17.8.93	1	NC	Zagreb	29	Jul
5.70i	Menno	Vloon	NED	11.5.94	4		Düsseldorf	6	Feb
	(30)								
5.70i	Hussain Asim	Al-Hizam	KSA	4.1.98	1	NCAA	College Station	9	Mar
5.70	Nate	Richartz	USA	2.11.94	1		Coral Gables	11	May
5.70	Alioune	Sène	FRA	3.2.96	1		Aix-les-Bains	20	May
5.70		Zhang Wei	CHN	22.3.94	1		Beijing	27	May
5.70	Rutger	Koppelaar	NED	1.5.93	1		Leiden	9	Jun
5.70	Seito	Yamamoto	JPN	11.3.92	1	NC	Yamaguchi	23	Jun
5.70	Georgiy	Gorokhov	RUS	20.4.93	1	Kuts	Moskva	30	Jul
5.70		Huang Bokai	CHN	26.9.96	1	NC	Taiyuan	14	Sep
5.67i	Claudio Michel	Stecchi	ITA	23.11.91	2		Linz	12	Sep
5.67		Jin Min-sub	KOR	2.9.92	1		Yecheon	20	Jul
	(40)								
5.66	Tray	Oates	USA	14.3.95	1	Fla R	Gainesville	31	Mar
5.66	Diogo	Ferreira	POR	30.7.90	1		Madrid	22	Jun
5.66	Austin	Miller	USA	1.6.94	1		Charlotte	13	Jul
5.66	Germán	Chiaraviglio	ARG	16.4.87	1		Buenos Aires	15	Sep
5.65	Tobias	Scherbarth	GER	17.8.85	1		Hastings	27	Jan
5.65i	Adam	Hague	GBR	29.8.97	1	NC	Birmingham	18	Feb
5.65i	Ben	Broeders	BEL	21.6.95	1		Bad Oeynhausen	22	Feb
5.65i	Ilya	Mudrov	RUS	17.11.91	2=		Sankt Peterburg	23	Feb
5.65	Yevgeniy	Lukyanenko	RUS	23.1.85	1	NC	Kazan	21	Jul
5.62i		Yao Jie	CHN	21.9.90	1		Rennes	27	Jan
	(50)								
5.61i	Adrián	Vallés	ESP	16.3.95	1		Notre Dame, IN	20	Jan
5.61i	Gordon	Porsch	GER	11.3.95	1		Sindelfingen	11	Feb
5.61	K.C.	Lightfoot	USA-J	11.11.99	1		Nixa (75mm pegs)	12	May
5.61	Daniel	Clemens	GER	28.4.92	4		Zweibrücken	16	Jun
5.61	Karsten	Dilla	GER	17.7.89	2		Madrid	22	Jun
5.61	Didac	Salas	ESP	19.5.93	1		Zaragoza	4	Jul
5.60i	Vladyslav	Malykhin	UKR	15.1.98	1		Kyiv	9	Jan
5.60i	Bo Kanda	Lita Baehre	GER-J	29.4.99	1		Leverkusen	20	Jan
5.60i	Tim	Ehrhardt	USA	16.3.95	2		Akron	3	Feb
5.60Ai	Garrett	Starkey	USA	7.10.93	1		Albuquerque	10	Feb
	(60)								
5.60i	Jacob	Wooten	USA	22.4.97	1		Clemson	10	Feb
5.60i	Kevin	Mayer	FRA	10.2.92	4		Rouen	10	Feb
5.60i	Deakin	Volz	USA	12.1.97	3	NCAA	College Station	9	Mar
5.60	Audie	Wyatt	USA	30.4.96	3c2	Texas R	Austin	31	Mar
5.60	Drew	Volz	USA	20.11.92	4c2	Texas R	Austin	31	Mar
5.60	Jake	Albright	USA	22.12.93	1		Manhattan, KS	5	May
5.60	Luke	Winder	USA	2.8.95	1		Naperville	10	May
5.60	Torben	Laidig	GER	13.3.94	2		Coral Gables	11	May
5.60	Kosei	Takekawa	JPN	16.12.97	1		Sagamihara	26	May
5.60	Dylan	Bell	USA	21.7.93	1		Aurora	2	Jun
	(70)								
5.60	Nariharu Jina	Matsuzawa	JPN	6.1.92	1		Toyota	9	Jun
5.60	Charlie	Myers	GBR	12.6.97	1		Hexham	8	Jul
5.60	Daichi	Sawano	JPN	16.9.80	1		Sapporo	8	Jul
5.60	Edi	Maia	POR	10.11.87	1		Lisboa (I)	11	Jul
5.58	Ethan	Bray	USA	18.5.97	2		Tulsa	12	May
5.57	Branson	Ellis	USA-J	19.7.00	1		Austin	12	May
5.56i	Anton	Ivakin	RUS	3.2.91	3		Moskva	17	Jan
5.56i	Eirik Greibrokk	Dolve	NOR	5.5.95	1		Tartu	24	Jan

MEN 2018

Mark	Name		Nat	Born	Pos	Meet	Venue	Date
5.55	Declan	Carruthers	AUS	7.9.97	2		Hastings	27 Jan
5.55i	Tommi	Holttinen	FIN	3.5.97	2		Uppsala	11 Feb
	(80)							
5.55i	Aleksandr	Gripich	RUS	21.9.86	3	NC	Moskva	13 Feb
5.55i	Dominik	Alberto	SUI	28.4.92	1	NC	Magglingen	17 Feb
5.55i	Mareks	Arents	LAT	6.8.86	3		Bad Oeynhausen	22 Feb
5.55i	Tomas	Wecksten	FIN	2.11.96	5		Bad Oeynhausen	22 Feb
5.55i	Rasmus	Jørgensen	DEN	23.1.89	6		Bad Oeynhausen	22 Feb
5.55	Pau Gaspar	Tonnesen	ESP	24.10.92	2		Tempe	7 Apr
5.55	Vladislav	Chemarmazovich	BLR	18.4.95	1		Ust-Kamenogorsk	2 Jun
5.55	Urho	Kujanpää	FIN	18.5.97	1		Virrat	3 Jun
5.55	Robert	Sobera	POL	19.1.91	1		Wroclaw	13 Jun
5.55	Zachery	Bradford	USA-J	29.11.99	1	NC-j	Bloomington	15 Jun
	(90)							
5.55	Alessandro	Sinno	ITA	17.7.94	1		Foggia	27 Jun
5.55	Jan	Kudlicka	CZE	29.4.88	1		Praha	5 Jul
5.55	Masaki	Ejima	JPN-J	6.3.99	3	WJ	Tampere	14 Jul
5.55	Phassapong	Unsum-Ang	THA	2.10.97	1		Chiangrai	21 Nov
5.53Ai	Logan	Cunningham	USA	30.5.91	6=	NC	Albuquerque	17 Feb
5.52	Angus	Armstrong	AUS	17.3.97	1		Sydney	6 Jan
5.52	Baptiste	Boirie	FRA	26.12.92	2=		Paris	23 Jun
5.52	Jules	Cypres	FRA	9.8.97	2=		Paris	23 Jun
5.52	Joel	Leon Benitez	GBR	31.8.98	3		Liège (NX)	18 Jul
5.51i	Chase	Smith	USA	1.4.97	1		Seattle	11 Feb
	(100)							
5.51i	Scott	Marshall	USA	30.6.95	1		Nampa	24 Feb
5.51i	Alexandre	Feger	FRA	22.1.90	3		Clermont-Ferrand	24 Feb
5.51	Cole	Riddle	USA-J	9.4.99	2		Chula Vista	9 Jun
5.51	Ernest John	Obiena	PHI	17.11.95	7		Zweibrücken	16 Jun
5.50i	Chase	Brannon	USA	8.2.91	20	Jan	5.42	Ethan	Cormont	FRA-J	29.9.00	30 May
5.50i	Michal	Balner	CZE	12.9.82	31	Jan	5.42	Torben	Blech	GER	12.2.95	29 Jun
5.50Ai	Adam	Bragg	USA	18.4.93	9	Feb	5.41i	Eelco	Sintnicolaas	NED	7.4.87	4 Feb
5.50i	Brandon	Bray	USA	24.4.97	10	Feb	5.41i	Nick	Meyer	USA	5.2.95	9 Feb
5.50i	Karol	Pawlik	POL	17.3.94	15	Feb	5.41i	Pierre	Cottin	FRA	26.1.98	24 Feb
5.50i	Nikita	Filippov	KAZ	7.10.91	16	Feb	5.41	Jacob	Köhler-Baumann	GER	28.11.93	9 Jun
5.50i	Drew	McMichael	USA	25.5.96	16	Feb	5.41	Igor	Bychkov	ESP	7.3.87	4 Jul
5.50i	Antonio	Ruiz	MEX	4.11.96	21	Feb	5.40Ai	August	Kiles	USA	10.11.95	13 Jan
5.50	Michael	Carr	USA	18.9.96	24	Mar	5.40i	Émile	Denecker	FRA	28.3.92	13 Feb
5.50	Cole	Gorski	USA	16.10.95	7	Apr	5.40A	Valco	van Wyk	RSA-J	26.7.00	15 Mar
5.50	Sean	Collins	USA	29.8.97	14	Apr	5.40	Niel	Giliomee	RSA	5.7.96	6 Apr
5.50	Hiroki	Ogita	JPN	30.12.87	29	Apr	5.40	Bruno	Spinelli	BRA	6.4.97	7 Apr
5.50	Chris	Pillow	USA	8.7.93	5	May	5.40	Keon	Howe	USA	8.12.96	14 Apr
5.50	Sean	Clarke	USA	31.3.98	13	May	5.40	Nick	Maestretti	USA	24.7.93	21 Apr
5.50A	Jorge	Luna	MEX	8.6.96	27	May	5.40A	Victor	Weirich	USA	25.10.87	28 Apr
5.50A	Augusto	Dutra de Oliveira	BRA	16.7.90	8	Jun	5.40	Theódorós-Panayióti Hrisanthópoulos				
5.50	Shunta	Itsumi	JPN	13.4.93	9	Jun				GRE	21.6.93	12 May
5.50	Malte	Mohr	GER	24.7.86	7	Jul	5.40	Han Do-hyun		KOR	28.7.94	19 May
5.50	Mathieu	Collet	FRA	15.3.95	8	Jul	5.40	Nikandros	Stylianou	CYP	22.8.89	20 May
5.50	Danyil	Kotov	RUS	6.2.95	13	Jul	5.40	Dan	Evers	USA	6.11.95	26 May
5.50	Shingo	Sawa	JPN	28.9.96	21	Jul	5.40	Kota	Suzuki	JPN	18.12.95	27 May
5.50		Ding Bangchao	CHN	11.10.96	14	Sep	5.40	Harry	Coppell	GBR	11.7.96	9 Jun
5.48	Barrett	Poth	USA	18.4.96	13	May	5.40	Ilya	Prosvirin	RUS	28.2.95	12 Jun
5.46i	Pål Haugen	Lillefosse	NOR-Y	4.6.01	6	Jan	5.40	Aleix	Pi	ESP	27.1.96	20 Jun
5.46A	Spencer	Allen	CAN	27.9.93	27	May	5.40	Sergey	Grigoryev	KAZ	24.6.92	29 Jun
5.46	Ruben	Miranda	POR	10.6.93	20	Jun	5.40	Florian	Gaul	GER	21.9.91	1 Jul
5.45i	Médhi Amar	Houana	FRA	30.3.94	13	Jan	5.40	Gauvain	Guillon-Romarin	FRA	8.3.98	16 Jul
5.45i	Ivan	Gertleyn	RUS	25.9.87	4	Feb	5.40	Matthias	Orban	FRA-J	21.1.00	22 Jul
5.45i	Dmitriy	Lyubushkin	RUS	21.3.94	8	Feb	5.40	Lamin	Krubally	GER	13.2.95	8 Sep
5.45i	Matteo C.	Capello	ITA	22.4.97	17	Feb	5.40	Abel	Curtinove	BRA	12.5.91	16 Sep
5.45	Luke	Cutts	GBR	13.2.88	12	Apr	5.39	Sander	Moldau	EST		20 Apr
5.45	Adam	Coulon	USA	14.10.97	6	Jun	5.38A	Jake	Blankenship	USA	15.3.94	12 Jun
5.45	Marc	Toney	USA	24.2.95	6	Jun	5.37	Cole	Courtois	USA	6.8.98	12 May
5.45	Thibaut	Collet	FRA-J	17.6.99	23	Jun	5.37	Muntaher Faleh Abdelwahid	IRQ	1.2.98	26 May
5.43i	Mike	Vani	USA	20.6.91	16	Feb	5.36i	i=	Jeffrey	Coover	USA	1.12.87	3 Mar
5.43i	Koen	van der Wijst	NED	7.8.97	18	Feb	5.36	David	Bell	USA	3.10.96	14 Mar
5.43	Paulo	Benavides	USA	27.7.97	4	Aug	5.36	Julian	Otchere	GER	25.4.98	16 Jun
5.42i	Deryk	Theodore	CAN	18.8.89	10	Feb	5.36	Lázaro	Borges	CUB	19.6.86	30 Jun
5.42i	Coty	Cobb	USA	24.7.97	16	Feb	5.36A	Gonzalo	Santamaria (181)	ESP	20.4.96	7 Jul

Best outdoor marks

5.84	Wojciechowski	2	Athl	Lausanne	4 Jul	5.70	Houston	3	DrakeR	Des Moines	27 Apr
5.81	Holzdeppe	1		Zweibrücken	16 Jun	5.70	Chapelle	1		Françonville	6 May
5.80	Marschall	1		Perth	20 Jan	5.70	Svärd Jacobsson	1		Leverkusen	16 Jun
5.75	Filippídis	6=	EC	Berlin	12 Aug	5.70	Braz da Silva	1		Sotteville-lès-Rouen	17 Jul
5.72	Irwin	1		Rottach-Egern	8 Jul	5.65	Zhelyabin	1		Moskva	10 May
5.71	Xue Changrui	3	DL	Shanghai	12 May	5.65	Hague	10	EC	Berlin	12 Aug

Mark	Name			Nat	Born	Pos Meet		Venue	Date
5.63	Al-Hizam	1	Big 12 Waco						13 May
5.61	Yao Jie	5	DL Shanghai						12 May
5.60	Deakin Volz	3	Coral Gables						11 May
5.60	Baehre	1	Soest						10 Jun
5.60	Broeders	3	Leverkusen						16 Jun
5.60	Malykhin	1	Chiari						4 Sep
5.56	Vloon	2	Köln						14 Jul

Mark	Name	Pos	Meet	Venue	Date
5.55	Wooten	4	NCAA	Eugene	6 Jun
5.55	Mudrov	4	GS	Ostrava	13 Jun
5.55	Vallés	1		Zaragoza	20 Jun
5.55	Gripich	3	NC	Kazan	21 Jul
5.52	Stecchi	4		Liège (NX)	18 Jul
5.51	Arents	2		Sopot	2 Jun
5.51	Holttinen	3=q	EC	Berlin	10 Aug

Mark	Name	Date		Mark	Name	Date		Mark	Name	Date
5.50	Ruiz	31 Mar		5.47	Menaldo	31 Mar		5.40	Denecker	6 Jul
5.50	Arnold	25 Apr		5.46	Lillefosse	8 Jul		5.40	Lyubushkin	8 Jul
5.50	Filippov	19 May		5.45	Pawlik	18 May		5.40	Cottin	15 Jul
5.50	Wecksten	24 Jun		5.45	Balner	4 Jun		5.39	Theodore	31 Jul
5.47	Cunningham	31 Mar		5.45	Starkey	23 Jun		5.38	B Bray	13 May
				5.45	Ivakin	21 Jul		5.38	McMichael	13 May
				5.45	Dolve	17 Aug				
				5.45	Mayer	26 Sep				
				5.41	Ehrhardt	13 May				
				5.40	Rouana	20 May				

JUNIORS

See main list for top 9 juniors. 21 performances (inc. 8 indoors) by 3 men to 5.70. Additional marks and further juniors:

Duplantis 6+	5.86	1	DL	Stockholm	10 Jun	5.80	1		Jockgrim	17 Jul
	5.86	3	DL	London (OS)	21 Jul	5.80	1		Karlstad	25 Jul
	5.83Ai	1		Reno	12 Jan	5.73i				9 Feb
	5.82	1	WJ	Tampere	14 Jul	5.71	2	Pre	Eigene	25 May
	5.81	1		Hammond	12 Apr	5.70		two indoors, 1 out		
Karalís	5.78i	1	NC		11 Feb	5.71i				10 Feb

Mark		Name		Nat	Born	Pos Meet		Venue	Date
5.46i	Pål Haugen	Lillefosse (10)		NOR-Y	4.6.01	1		Satra	6 Jan
5.46						1	EY	Györ	8 Jul
5.45	Thibaut	Collet		FRA	17.6.99	1		Blois	23 Jun
5.42	Ethan	Cormont		FRA	29.9.00	1		Créteil	30 May
5.40A	Valco	van Wyk		RSA	26.7.00	1	NC	Pretoria	15 Mar
5.40	Matthias	Orban		FRA	21.1.00	1		Bondoufle	22 Jul
5.34	Colton	Crum		USA	4.2.00	1		Bloomington	2 Jun
5.32	Baptiste	Thiery		FRA-Y	29.6.01	1	YOG	Buenos Aires	16 Oct
5.31	Riccardo	Klotz		AUT	15.1.99	1	NC-23	Linz	24 Jun
5.30A	Tate	Curran		USA	20.3.99	5		Albuquerque	10 Feb
5.30	Dmitroy	Kachanov (20)		RUS-Y	8.1.01	1		Moskva	10 May
5.30	Viktor	Pintusov		RUS	7.2.00	1		Moskva	13 Jun
5.30	Illya	Kravchenko		UKR	8.8.00	1		Kropyvntskyi	26 Jun
5.30	Idan Fauzan	Richsan		INA	11.1.00	1		Kuala Lumpur	24 Jul
5.30	Kazuya	Ishibashi		JPN	26.1.99	2		Sagamihara	16 Sep

LONG JUMP

MEN 2018

8.68 1.7 Juan Miguel Echevarría CUB 11.8.98 1 Bad Langensalza 30 Jun
   8.08 8.20 x 8.68 p x
8.66 1.0 1 GS Ostrava 13 Jun 8.40/-1.0 8.54/0.3 8.66 p 8.54/-1.6 x
8.53 0.5 2 G Gala Roma 31 May x 8.53 x x 8.43/-0.6 x
8.50 0.2 * DL Stockholm 10 Jun 8.03 x 8.29 8.50 p 8.83w
8.46i 1 WI Birmingham 2 Mar 8.19 8.28 x 8.36 8.46 7.86
8.40 1.5 1 Fortún Camagüey 16 Mar x 8.18 p x 8.40 x
8.37 -0.4 1 Guadalajara, ESP 5 Jul 8.37 8.23 p x x x
8.58 0.0 Luvo Manyonga RSA 8.1.91 1 G Gala Roma 31 May
   7.93 8.58 x p x 8.41/0.2
8.58 0.2 1 DL London (OS) 22 Jul 8.16 8.51/0.5 8.53/0.4 8.58 8.43/0.6 8.43/-0.5
8.56 0.2 1 DL Shanghai 12 May x x 8.11 8.43/0.2 x 8.56
8.53 1.5 1 DL Birmingham 18 Aug 8.42/0.6 x x 8.53 7.19 8.47/-0.9
8.51 0.0 1 AWC London (OS) 15 Jul 8.51 8.48/-0.2 8.50/0.3 8.50/0.5
8.46 -0.3 1 Hanz Zagreb 4 Sep 8.46 8.25 8.45/0.2 8.30/-0.3 x p
8.44i 2 WI Birmingham 2 Mar x x 8.33 8.44 x x
8.43 1.2 2 AfrC Asaba 2 Aug 7.93 8.20 8.25 8.43 8.42/1.3 8.36/1.9
8.42 -1.2 2 Bad Langensalza 30 Jun x 8.23 6.66 8.42/-1.2 x 8.42/0.7
8.41 0.6 1 CG Gold Coast 11 Apr 8.24 8.21 x 8.35/0.5 x 8.41
8.40i 1 Metz 11 Feb x x 8.12 8.22 8.27 8.40
8.38 0.1 * Taipei 26 May 8.12 8.40w x 8.18 p 8.38
8.36 0.3 1 WK Zürich 30 Aug 8.32/0.3 8.17 8.25 p 8.13 8.36
8.47A 0.7 Wang Jianan CHN 27.8.96 1 Guiyang 16 Jun
   8.06 8.28 8.47 p p p
8.45 -1.2 Ruswahl Samaai RSA 25.9.91 1 AfrC Asaba 2 Aug
   8.05 8.27 8.31/1.8 8.45 8.44/1.0 8.27
8.37 -0.4 Echevarría 1 Guadalajara, ESP 5 Jul
   8.37 8.23 p x x x
8.44A 0.5 Jeff Henderson USA 19.2.89 1 Provo 28 Apr
   7.97 8.18 8.14w x 8.27w 8.44
8.43 0.7 Shi Yuhao CHN 26.9.98 2 DL Shanghai 12 May
   7.93 8.43 8.02 x 8.21 x
8.42i Marquis Dendy USA 17.11.92 3 WI Birmingham 2 Mar
   7.92 8.02 x 7.86 8.42 8.18

Mark	Wind	Name		Nat	Born	Pos	Meet	Venue	Date
8.41	2.0	Aleksandr	Menkov	RUS	7.12.90	1	Znam	Zhukovskiy	1 Jul
		x	8.02	x				7.74 x	8.41
8.40	1.1	Zarck	Visser	RSA	15.9.89	4		Bad Langensalza	30 Jun
		7.98	8.40	7.67				p 7.95	p
8.38Ai		Jarrion	Lawson (10)	USA	6.5.94	1	NC	Albuquerque	17 Feb
		8.14	8.06	7.91				8.12 8.38	p
8.37	1.9	Zack	Bazile	USA	7.1.96	1	NCAA	Eugene	6 Jun
		(32/11)			8.17	8.37	8.02	7.91 x	8.18
8.34	1.1	Henry	Frayne	AUS	14.4.90	Q	CG	Gold Coast	10 Apr
8.29A	0.4		Zhang Yaoguang	CHN	21.6.93	2		Guiyang	16 Jun
8.27	0.8	Jarvis	Gotch	USA	25.3.92	1	MSR	Torrance	21 Apr
8.27	1.2	Radek	Juska	CZE	8.3.93	1	Danek	Turnov	29 May
8.26A	0.7	Emiliano	Lasa	URU	25.1.90	1	SAmG	Cochabamba	5 Jun
8.25	-0.3	Miltiádis	Tentóglou	GRE	18.3.98	1	EC	Berlin	8 Aug
8.24	-0.3	Tajay	Gayle	JAM	2.8.96	2	NACAC	Toronto	12 Aug
8.23	1.5	Andwuelle	Wright	TTO	8.8.97	1	NC	Port of Spain	23 Jun
8.23	1.0	Sergiy	Nykyforov	UKR	6.2.94	1	NC	Lutsk	19 Jul
		(20)							
8.20	0.5	Stephan	Hartmann	GER	13.1.94	1		Weinheim	26 May
8.20	0.3	Julian	Howard	GER	3.4.89	2		Weinheim	26 May
8.20	0.0	Murali	Sreeshankar	IND-J	27.3.99	1	NC	Bhubaneswar	27 Sep
8.19i		Will	Williams	USA	31.1.95	1	NCAA	College Station	9 Mar
8.19i			Huang Changzhou	CHN	20.8.94	1		Xianlin	11 Mar
8.19	1.9	Aleksandro	Melo	BRA	29.9.95	1	NC	Bragança Paulista	16 Sep
8.18Ai		Mike	Hartfield	USA	29.3.90	3	NC	Albuquerque	17 Feb
8.18	1.6	Terrell	McClain	USA	10.11.95	2		Long Beach	21 Apr
8.18	1.9	Corey	Crawford	USA	12.12.91	1		Chula Vista	9 Jun
8.17	0.6	Grant	Holloway	USA	19.11.97	*	SEC	Knoxville	12 May
		(30)							
8.16	0.5	Dan	Bramble	GBR	14.10.90	Q	DL	London (OS)	22 Jul
8.14	1.1	Jared	Kerr	CAN	25.6.95	1		Cincinnati	12 May
8.14	1.8	D.A.G. Prasad	Wimalasiri	SRI	8.9.92	1	NC	Colombo	5 Aug
8.13	0.8	Kafétien	Gomis	FRA	23.3.80	1	NC	Albi	8 Jul
8.13	0.2	Ramone	Bailey	JAM	31.10.91	3	AWC	London (OS)	15 Jul
8.13	-0.2	Fabian	Heinle	GER	14.5.94	2	EC	Berlin	8 Aug
8.12i		Paulo Sérgio	Oliveira	BRA	1.6.93	1		São Caetano do Sul	17 Feb
8.12i		Charles	Brown	USA	28.5.97	3	NCAA	College Station	9 Mar
8.12	-0.7	Cheswill	Johnson	RSA	30.9.97	2		Paarl	22 Mar
8.12	0.8	Damarcus	Simpson	USA	14.7.93	*		Stanford	12 May
		(40)							
8.12	0.0	Maykel	Vidal	CUB-J	6.1.00	1		La Habana	8 Jun
8.10	1.6	Fabian	Edoki	NGR	30.3.98	1		Abilene	24 Mar
8.10		Yahya	Berrabah	MAR	13.10.81	1		Benguerir	29 Apr
8.10	1.0	Tomasz	Jaszczuk	POL	9.3.92	1	NC	Lublin	22 Jul
8.10	0.1	Thobias	Nilsson Montler	SWE	15.2.96	4	EC	Berlin	8 Aug
8.09i		Cristian	Staicu	ROU	30.7.93	1	NC	Bucuresti	4 Feb
8.09		Mohcine	Khoua	MAR	26.7.98	2		Benguerir	29 Apr
8.09A	1.3		Jie Lei	CHN	8.5.89	4		Guiyang	16 Jun
8.09	1.2	Yuki	Hashioka	JPN-J	23.1.99	1	NC	Yamaguchi	23 Jun
8.09	0.0		Sapwaturrahman	INA	13.5.94	3	AsiG	Jakarta	26 Aug
		(50)							
8.07i		Damar	Forbes	JAM	18.9.90	1		Iowa City	20 Jan
8.07	0.0	Lester	Lescay	CUB	16.10.01	2		La Habana	8 Jun
8.07	1.3	Vladyslav	Mazur	UKR	21.11.96	2	NC	Lutsk	19 Jul
8.07	0.2	Emanuel	Archibald	GUY	9.9.94	1		Leonora	21 Jul
8.06	1.8	Ifeanyi	Otuonye	TKS	27.6.94	3		Chula Vista	9 Jun
8.06	1.5		Ju Eun-jae	KOR	12.6.93	*		Chula Vista	9 Jun
8.06		M	Silambarasan	IND	27.12.92	1		Jalahalli	18 Sep
8.05	1.3		Lin Tzu-Chi	TPE	3.11.97	2		Taipei	26 Ma
8.05	2.0	Feron	Sayers	GBR	15.10.94	1		Genève	9 Jun
8.05A	0.8		Gao Xinglong	CHN	12.3.94	5		Guiyang	16 Jun
		(60)							
8.03	1.6	Lutalo	Boyce	USA	11.8.91	2		Abilene	24 Mar
8.03	0.0	Tim	Duckworth	GBR	18.6.96	1D		Athens, GA	6 Apr
8.03	0.2	Tyrone	Smith	BER	7.8.86	2	CAG	Barranquilla	31 Jul
8.02i		Corion	Knight	USA	18.8.96	1		Fayetteville	9 Feb
8.02i		Artyom	Primak	RUS	14.1.93	2	NC	Moskva	14 Feb
8.02	1.8	Jordan	Latimer	USA	4.3.94	2	NCAA	Eugene	6 Jun
8.01	1.0	Christian	Mitrevski	AUS	12.7.96	*	NC	Gold Coast	18 Feb
8.01	0.6	Ituah	Enahoro	NGR/GER	15.12.97	3		Weinheim	26 Ma
8.01	0.1	Anatoliy	Ryapolov	RUS	31.1.97	1		Maykop	6 Jun

Mark	Wind	Name		Nat	Born	Pos	Meet	Venue	Date	
8.01	1.0	Yann	Randrianasolo	FRA	3.2.94	1	NC	Albi	23	Jun
		(70)								
8.01	0.9	Yasser	Triki	ALG	24.3.97	2	MedG	Tarragona	30	Jun
8.01	0.0	Hibiki	Tsuha	JPN	21.1.98	1		Yokohama	22	Jul
8.01	0.1	Jean Marie	Okutu	ESP	4.8.88	1	NC	Getafe	22	Jul
8.01		W.P.Amila	Jayasiri	SRI	24.1.94	*	NC	Colombo	5	Aug
8.00i		Max	Hess	GER	13.7.96	1		Chemnitz	20	Jan
8.00	0.0	Benjamin	Gföhler	SUI	27.1.94	4		Weinheim	26	Ma
8.00	1.7	Guillaume	Victorin	FRA	26.5.90	2	NC	Albi	8	Jul
8.00	1.6	Tenju	Togawa	JPN	8.1.97	1		Katsuura	23	Sep
7.99i		Adam	McMullen	IRL	5.7.90	1	NC	Abbotstown	18	Feb
7.99		Wayne	Pinnock	JAM-J	24.10.00	1		Kingston	10	Mar
		(80)								
7.99	1.1	Sandaruwan	Piyarathne	SRI	14.4.94	1		Colombo	27	Apr
7.99	0.9	Desmond	Mobley	USA	15.8.95	1		Houston	12	Ma
7.99	1.6	Higor	Alves	BRA	23.2.94	3	NC	Bragança Paulista	16	Sep
7.98	-0.7	Brian	Huber	USA	12.6.95	1	NCAA-2	Charlotte	24	Ma
7.98	0.6	Johannes	Erm	EST	26.3.98	2D	NCAA	Eugene	6	Jun
7.98	1.5	Maksim	Yunyakin	RUS	13.2.96	2		Zhukovskiy	23	Jun
7.98	1.1	Strahinja	Jovancevic	SRB	28.2.93	1		Berane	14	Jul
7.98	1.6	Corentin	Campener	BEL	5.10.90	1		Castres	25	Jul
7.98	0.4	Shotaro	Shiroyama	JPN	6.3.95	5	AsiG	Jakarta	26	Aug
7.97i		Ja'Mari	Ward	USA	21.3.98	1		Columbia, MO	16	Feb
		(90)								
7.97i		Eusebio	Cáceres	ESP	10.9.91	1	NC	Valencia	17	Feb
7.97	-2.6	Kyle	Darrow	USA	12.4.95	1		Storrs	14	Apr
7.97	1.4	Pavel	Shalin	RUS	15.4.87	2	NC	Kazan	20	Jul
7.96i		Jordan	Downs	USA	7.3.96	1		Marion, IN	10	Feb
7.96i		Steffin	McCarter	USA	19.1.97	1	Big 12	Ames	23	Feb
7.96	0.5	Maximilian	Entholzner	GER	18.8.94	2		Oberteuringen	9	Jun
7.96		Sobhan	Taherkhani	IRI	21.9.92	1	NC	Mashad	16	Jun
7.95	1.3	Daiki	Oda	JPN	15.1.96	3	NC	Yamaguchi	23	Jun
7.95	1.9	Denis	Bogdanov	RUS	2.4.91	2	Znam	Zhukovskiy	1	Jul
7.95	-1.1	V.O.	Jinesh	IND	10.4.92	2		Bhubaneswar	27	Sep
		(100)								
7.95Ai		Isaac	Grimes	USA	7.2.98	1		Golden	6	Dec

Mark	Wind	Name		Nat	Born	Pos	Date		Mark	Wind	Name		Nat	Born	Pos	Date	
7.94i		Alper	Kulaksiz	TUR	6.4.92	18	Jan		7.88i		Antonino	Trio	ITA	4.6.93	17	Feb
7.94	1.7	Shown-D	Thompson	JAM	20.1.97	24	Feb		7.88	-3.0	Jonathan	Wells	USA	18.4.96	20	Apr
7.94	1.8	Rodney	Ruffin	USA	17.3.97	13	Apr		7.88	1.0	Charles	Greaves	BAR	31.7.94	24	May
7.94	-0.7	Kevin	Ojiaku	ITA	20.4.89	23	May		7.88		Milad	Darisavi	IRI	7.4.92	16	Jun
7.94	-0.2	Lucas Marcelino dos Santos		BRA	4.1.95	1	Jul		7.88	0.5	Arttu	Pajulahti	FIN	25.9.91	30	Jun
7.93i		Scotty	Newton	USA	19.9.96	23	Feb		7.88	0.0	Yaroslav	Isachenkov	UKR	2.3.95	19	Jul
7.93	-0.1	Ignisious	Gaisah	NED	20.6.83	30	Jun		7.88	1.8	Tiago	da Silva	BRA	23.10.93	18	Aug
7.93	0.0	Kristian	Bäck	FIN	18.7.96	20	Jul		7.87i		Laquarn	Nairn	BAH	31.7.96	27	Jan
7.92	1.8	Ryan	Brown	JAM	10.11.98	24	Feb		7.87i		Bachana	Khorava	GEO	15.3.93	11	Feb
7.92	2.0	Odaine	Lewis	JAM	13.12.96	27	Apr		7.87	1.1	Ronald	Taylor	USA	13.8.90	19	May
7.92	1.3	Kemonie	Briggs	USA	21.5.96	11	May		7.87	1.5	Benjamin	Gabrielsen	DEN	13.6.95	7	Jun
7.92	-0.8	Maykel	Massó	CUB-J	8.5.99	31	May		7.87	0.0	José Luis	Mandros	PER	12.11.98	25	Aug
7.92	0.9	Natsuki	Yamakawa	JPN	24.7.95	23	Jun		7.86i		Treyton	Harris	USA	15.6.97	9	Feb
7.92	-0.1	Mihaíl Mertzanídis-Despotéris		GRE	21.8.87	18	Jul		7.86i		Vitaliy	Muravyov	RUS	1.10.93	14	Feb
7.91	1.7	Daniel	Pineda	CHI	19.9.85	14	Apr		7.86	1.4	Marcus	Jegede	USA	6.11.95	14	Apr
7.91	0.9	Kristian	Pulli	FIN	2.9.94	26	May		7.86	-1.8	Ta'riq	Thomas	USA	19.9.95	5	May
7.91	1.7	Adrian	Riley	JAM	22.1.94	6	Jun		7.85	0.7	Antonmarco	Musso	ITA	30.1.91	8	Jun
7.91	1.1	Benjamin	Arinze	NGR-J	.00	14	Jun		7.85	1.5		Zhu Keqi	CHN-J	4.2.99	11	Jul
7.91	1.2	Denis	Eradiri	BUL	24.10.83	23	Jun		7.85	1.2	Abdul Latif	Romly	MAS	31.3.97	5	Aug
7.91	0.6	Filip	Pravdica	CRO	28.7.95	28	Jul		7.84	1.0	Marcel	Mayack	CMR	17.11.90	10	Apr
7.91	-1.2	Michel	Tornéus	SWE	26.5.86	6	Aug		7.84A	1.4	Peter	Makgato	RSA	21.5.96	28	Apr
7.90i		Andre	Dorsey	USA	11.3.93	19	Jan		7.84	-1.8	Julian	Harvey	USA	17.6.95	11	May
7.90i		Filippo	Randazzo	ITA	27.4.96	3	Feb		7.84	1.3	JuVaughn	Blake/Harrison	USA-J	30.4.99	24	May
7.90i		KeAndre	Bates	USA	24.5.96	9	Mar		7.84	-0.3		Wen Hua-Yu	TPE-Y	9.3.01	26	May
7.90	0.9	Greshan	Dhananjaya	SRI	7.6.97	4	May		7.84	0.0	Taishi	Endo	JPN	3.9.97	23	Jun
7.90	1.7	Barden	Adams	USA	21.9.96	12	May		7.84	1.0		Zhang Jingqiang	CHN	8.5.96	19	Jul
7.90	0.6	Izmir	Smajlaj	ALB	23.9.93	9	Jun		7.84	0.7	Mizuki	Matsubara	JPN	9.9.92	22	Sep
7.90A	-1.0	Bethwel	Langat	KEN	20.11.96	21	Jun		7.83	2.0	Jared	Belardo	USA	29.12.96	13	May
7.90	1.2	Augustin	Bey	FRA	6.6.95	27	Jun		7.83A	0.2		Li Zhipeng	CHN	1.5.95	16	Jun
7.90A	1.8	Héctor	Santos	ESP	6.1.98	8	Jul		7.83	1.1	Dino	Pervan	CRO	12.1.91	20	Jun
7.89	0.5		Lin Hung-Min	TPE	7.9.90	12	Feb		7.83	1.5	Shin-ichiro	Shimono	JPN	10.10.90	2	Sep
7.89i		Greg	Rutherford	GBR	17.11.86	25	Feb		7.82		Luqman Hakim Ramlan		MAS	8.3.95	18	Mar
7.89	1.8	Khotso	Mokoena	RSA	6.3.85	22	Mar		7.82	1.8	Samory	Fraga Bandeira	BRA	29.11.96	12	Apr
7.89	1.8	Kota	Minemura	JPN	22.12.92	28	Mar		7.82	1.2	Bryan	McBride	USA	10.12.91	21	Apr
7.89	1.0	Jacob	Fincham-Dukes	GBR	12.1.97	31	Mar		7.82	0.0	Minato	Ishikura	JPN	12.5.96	1	May
7.89	0.9	Denzel	Harper	USA	5.4.98	12	May		7.82	2.0	Anastásios	Galazoúlas	GRE	2.10.92	26	May
7.89A	1.0	Ivo	Tavares	POR	31.1.96	22	Jun		7.82	2.0	Gabriele	Chilà	ITA	17.9.97	9	Jun
7.89	0.4		Kim Duk-hyung	KOR	8.12.85	27	Jun		7.82	-0.7	Gianluca	Puglisi	GER	10.4.96	9	Jun
7.89	0.9	Sanjin	Šimic	CRO	4.6.92	30	Jun		7.82	0.4	Kamal	Fuller	JAM	20.1.91	23	Jun

MEN 2018

Mark	Wind	Name		Nat	Born	Pos	Meet	Venue	Date
7.82	nwi	Mohammed	Abubakar	GHA	5.3.91	28	Jul		
7.82	1.5	Josh	Cowley	AUS-Y	13.3.01	15	Oct		
7.82		J.H.G.	Sampath	SRI		31	Oct		
7.82	?	Darcy	Roper	AUS	31.3.98	29	Nov		
7.81i		Jean-Pierre	Bertrand	FRA	5.11.92	7	Jan		
7.81i		Kenneth	Fisher	USA	28.2.95	9	Feb		
7.81	1.3	Tom	Soliman	AUS	20.11.93	17	Feb		
7.81	0.7	Liam	Adcock	AUS	21.6.96	18	Feb		
7.81i		Andreas	Otterling	SWE	25.5.86	25	Feb		
7.81i		Martin	Roe	NOR	1.4.92	3	Mar		
7.81	0.0	Zhong Peifeng		CHN	3.3.97	11	Apr		
7.81	0.9	Lourival	Neto	BRA	21.1.91	14	Apr		
7.81	0.5	Damian	Warner	CAN	4.11.89	26	May		

Mark	Wind	Name		Nat	Born	Pos	Meet	Venue	Date
7.81	1.0	Daniel	Solis	ESP	5.11.96	9	Jun		
7.81A		Isaac	Yego	KEN	23.11.94	21	Jun		
7.81	1.5	Raihau	Maiau	FRA	1.8.92	1	Jul		
7.81	0.0	Sahil	Mahabali	IND	27.12.97	27	Sep		
7.80Ai		Eric	Sloan	USA	20.6.94	19	Jan		
7.80		John	Warren	USA	2.3.96	12	May		
7.80	1.1	Darius	Clark	USA	24.11.98	17	May		
7.80		Rail	Kutuyev	RUS	6.8.96	13	Jun		
		(200)							
7.80	-0.4	Mateusz	Rózanski	POL	11.8.98	8	Jul		
7.80	1.3	Piotr	Tarkowski	POL-J	10.8.99	22	Jul		
7.80	1.2	Kevin	Mayer	FRA	10.2.92	15	Sep		
7.80	1.3		Bui Van Dong	THA	23.3.95	13	Dec		

Wind assisted

Mark	Wind	Name		Nat	Born	Pos	Meet	Venue	Date
8.83	2.1	Juan Miguel	Echevarría	CUB	11.8.98	1	DL	Stockholm	10 Jun
8.41A	2.1		Manyonga			1	NC	Pretoria	17 Mar
8.40	2.7		Manyonga			1		Taipei	26 May
8.39	3.4		Henderson			2	DL	Stockholm	10 Jun
				7.79	7.91	8.01w	8.11w	8.39w	8.27w
8.33	3.0	Damarcus	Simpson	USA	14.7.93	1		Stanford	12 May
8.32	2.9	Grant	Holloway	USA	19.11.97	1	SEC	Knoxville	12 May
8.31	4.7	Yugo	Sakai	JPN-J	1.5.99	1		Sagimihara	25 May
8.30	3.4	Yuki	Hashioka	JPN-J	23.1.99	2		Sagimihara	25 May
8.25	3.8	Will	Williams	USA	31.1.95	2	SEC	Knoxville	12 May
8.19	2.5	Tim	Duckworth	GBR	18.6.96	3	SEC	Knoxville	12 May
8.16	2.6	Charles	Brown	USA	28.5.97	2	Texas R	Austin	31 Mar
8.14	2.3	Yahya	Berrabah	MAR	13.10.81	3	AfrC	Asaba	2 Aug
8.12	4.1	J.H.G.	Sampath	SRI		2	NC	Colombo	5 Aug
8.10	3.0	Rodney	Ruffin	USA	17.3.97	1		Hammond, LA	23 Mar
8.09	2.1	Christian	Mitrevski	AUS	12.7.96	1	NC	Gold Coast	18 Feb
8.08	2.1	Odaine	Lewis	JAM	13.12.96	1		Abilene	24 Mar
8.07	2.8		Ju Eun-jae	KOR	12.6.93	2		Chula Vista	9 Jun
8.06	3.3	Corion	Knight	USA	18.8.96	1		Coral Gables	11 May
8.04	2.7	Tazuma	Kawashima	JPN	16.8.96	1		Mito	5 May
8.03	6.9	Shin-ichiro	Shimono	JPN	10.10.90	1		Fukuoka	7 Apr
8.03	4.7	Hibiki	Tsuha	JPN	21.1.98	4		Sagimihara	25 May
8.02	2.6	W.P.Amila	Jayasiri	SRI	24.1.94	3	NC	Colombo	5 Aug
8.01	4.6	Andreas	Otterling	SWE	25.5.86	1		Torremolinos	11 Jul
8.00	2.7	Santiago	Cova	VEN	10.8.96	1		Granada	3 Jun
8.00	3.5	KeAndre	Bates	USA	24.5.96	4	SEC	Knoxville	12 May
7.99		Joseph	Ramie	JAM	14.12.90	1		Montego Bay	10 Feb
7.97		Romeo	N'Tia	BEN	25.2.95	1		Porto Novo	15 Jul
7.97	3.0	Henri	Väyrinen	FIN	16.10.91	1		Tampere	24 Aug

Mark	Wind	Name		Nat	Born	Pos	Date
7.96	5.7	Bryant	Courter	USA	6.10.97	11	May
7.96	2.4	Jean-Pierre	Bertrand	FRA	5.11.92	8	Jul
7.96	3.1	Rayvon	Grey	USA	2.12.97	6	Jun
7.94	6.8	Harrison	Schrage	USA	14.10.97	13	Apr
7.94	6.3	Kenji	Nakamura	JPN	13.8.97	25	May
7.93A		Marcel	Mayack	CMR	17.11.90	3	Mar
7.92	3.6	George	Alexandris	USA	20.2.95	24	May
7.91	3.4	Shun-ya	Fujiwara	JPN	3.12.94	30	Jun
7.91	2.2	Lourival	Neto	BRA	21.1.91	16	Sep
7.90	2.2	Charles	Greaves	BAR	31.7.94	8	Apr
7.90	2.4	Kota	Minemura	JPN	22.12.92	5	May
7.87	2.3	Taishi	Endo	JPN	3.9.97	12	May

Mark	Wind	Name		Nat	Born	Pos	Date
7.87	2.4	Reynold	Banigo	GBR	13.8.98	29	Jul
7.87	2.5	Aleksandr	Petrov	RUS	9.8.86	1	Jul
7.85	4.2	Marcus	Flannigan	USA	20.6.95	12	May
7.85	3.3	Jared	Belardo	USA	29.12.96	12	May
7.84	2.7	Abubakar	Mohammed	GHA	5.3.91	27	Apr
7.84	2.3	Henry	Smith	AUS	19.12.95	13	Dec
7.83	2.6	Albert	MacArthur	USA	24.9.97	12	May
7.83	4.4	Samuele	Cerro	ITA	21.3.95	20	May
7.82	2.4	Roni	Ollikainen	FIN	27.8.90	3	Jun
7.82	3.3		Lin Chia-Hsing	TPE-J	13.7.99	20	Oct
7.81	2.7	Piotr	Tarkowski	POL-J	10.8.99	23	Jun
7.81	2.1	László	Szabó	HUN	22.11.91	1	Jul
7.81	3.0	Takumi	Kurata	JPN	.97	21	Jul

Best outdoor marks

Mark	Wind	Name	Pos	Meet	Venue	Date
8.29	-0.4	Dendy	1	NACAC	Toronto	12 Aug
8.25	0.1	Lawson	3	DL	London (OS)	22 Jul
8.19A	1.0	Huang Ch.	3		Guiyang	16 Jun
8.12A	0.7	Oliveira	2	SAmG	Cochabamba	5 Jun
8.05	0.9	Williams	*	SEC	Knoxville	12 May
8.02	0.9	Hartfield	1		St.George's	21 Apr
7.99	1.1	Forbes	7	DL	Shanghai	12 May
7.97	-0.9	Brown	5	NC	Des Moines	24 Jun

Mark	Wind	Name	Date		Mark	Wind	Name	Date
7.88	1.1	Randazzo	9 Jun		7.87	1.8	Bates	27 Apr
7.88		McMullen	24 Jun		7.86	0.8	Rutherford	2 Jun
					7.86	0.2	Staicu	27 Jul
7.85	0.4	Knight	20 Apr					
7.84	-0.1	Muravyov	6 Jun					
7.80	-0.3	Otterling	26 May					

Low altitude best

Mark	Wind	Name	Pos	Meet	Venue	Date
8.24	0.7	Wang Jianan	1	AsiG	Jakarta	26 Aug
8.20	-0.8	Henderson	5	DL	London (OS)	22 Jul
8.16		Huang Changzhou	1		Nanjing	22 Sep
7.83	1.9	Santos	1		Pamplona	19 May
8.15	0.0	Zhang Yaoguang	2	AsiG	Jakarta	26 Aug
8.00	0.5	Gao Xinglong	6	DL	Shanghai	12 May
7.98	0.3	Oliveira	1		Campinas	5 May
7.81	1.3	Tavares	1		Maia	4 Jul
7.82w	2.9	Tavares	2		Ávila	10 Jul

Unconfirmed: 8.08A Carlos Enrique Valenia COL 4.1.97 1 Bogotá 26 Aug

JUNIORS

See main list for top 5 juniors. 11 performances by 5 men to 7.99. Additional marks and further juniors:

Name	Mark	Wind	Pos	Meet	Venue	Date				
Sreeshankar	7.99	0.4	1	Fed Cp	Patiala		6 Mar			
Vidal	8.01	0.0	1	NC-j	Camagüey		27 Jun	7.99	0.9 2 WJ	Tampere	11 Jul

Mark	Wind	Name		Nat	Born	Pos	Meet	Venue	Date
Hashioka	8.05	0.0 4	AsiG Jakarta	26 Aug	8.03	0.0 q	AsiG Jakarta		25 Aug
	8.03	0.9 1	WJ Tampere	11 Jul					
7.92	-0.8	Maykel	Massó	CUB	8.5.99	8	G Gala	Roma	31 May
7.91	1.1	Benjamin	Arinze	NGR	.00	1		Lagos	14 Jun
7.85	1.5		Zhu Keqi	CHN	4.2.99	4	WJ	Tampere	11 Jul
7.84	1.3	JuVaughn	Blake/Harrison	USA	30.4.99	2q	NCAA-E	Tampa	24 May
7.84	-0.3		Wen Hua-Yu (10)	TPE-Y	9.3.01	4		Taipei	26 May
7.82	1.5	Josh	Cowley	AUS-Y	13.3.01	2	YOG	Buenos Aires	15 Oct
7.79	1.7	Yugo	Sakai	JPN	1.5.99	5	WJ	Tampere	11 Jul
7.78	-0.9	Marko	Ceko	CRO	3.8.00	1		Zagreb	23 May
7.78	1.7	Shandell	Taylor	GBR	16.12.99	1	N.Sch	Birmingham	13 Jul
7.78	0.5		Lin Yu-Tang	TPE	11.5.00	1		Taipei	29 Sep
7.77	1.5	Daiki	Kobayashi	JPN	.99	1		Sagamihara	16 Sep
7.75	1.8	Koki	Kaihoko	JPN	10.4.00	1		Chiba	17 May
7.75	0.1	Benjamin	Schmidtchen	AUS	9.2.00	2		Jämsä	30 Jun
7.75	1.9	Hiroki	Kanbe	JPN	.99	2		Sagamihara	16 Sep
7.75A	1.2	Sifiso	Miya (20)	RSA-Y	1.6.01	1		Gaborone	11 Dec
Wind assisted		see main lists for top 2 juniors							
7.82	3.3		Lin Chia-Hsing	TPE	13.7.99	1		Kaohsiung	20 Oct
7.81	2.7	Piotr	Tarkowski	POL	10.8.99	1	NC-j	Wloclawek	23 Jun
7.77A	3.3	Sifiso	Miya	RSA-Y	1.6.01	1		Boksburg	28 Apr

TRIPLE JUMP

Mark	Wind	Name		Nat	Born	Pos	Meet	Venue	Date
17.95	0.6	Pedro Pablo	Pichardo	POR	30.6.93	1	DL	Doha	4 May
	16.90	17.44/0.5	17.95		17.58/0.8	p	17.53/-0.1		
	17.61	1.8 2 Athl	Lausanne	5 Jul	16.89	17.61	x	17.24 16.98	16.64
	17.60	0.9 * Herc	Monaco	20 Jul	17.28	17.60	17.67w	16.72 p	x
	17.49	0.5 1 VD	Bruxelles	31 Aug	17.31/0.6 x	x	17.49	p	x
	17.40	0.0 3	Baie Mahault	12 May	16.67	16.83	17.40	17.13 16.79	16.70
	17.30	1 ECCp	Birmingham	27 May	17.07	17.30	p	p	
17.81	0.6	Christian	Taylor	USA	18.6.90	2	DL	Doha	4 May
	x	17.32/0.6	17.81		17.57/1.6 16.65	17.69/0.5			
	17.73	-1.3 1 Pre	Eugene	26 May	17.04	16.65	17.24	17.32w/3.5 17.38/0.7	17.73
	17.66	1.8 * Herc	Monaco	20 Jul	17.60/1.8 17.86w	17.50/2.0	17.66/2.0	p	17.66/1.9
	17.62	0.7 1 Athl	Lausanne	5 Jul	17.21	x	17.62	17.55/1.0 17.60/0.8	17.40/0.5
	17.59	-1.9 1 C.Cup	Ostrava	9 Sep	17.59	17.04	p	17.41	17.31
	17.36	1.4 * Gyulai	Székesferhérvár	2 Jul	17.34/1.9 17.31/2.0	p	p	17.36	17.64w
	17.31	0.0 2 VD	Bruxelles	31 Aug	x	17.07	17.22	17.31 17.13	x
17.53	0.3	Almir	dos Santos	BRA	4.9.93	1		Baie Mahault	12 May
	16.97	x	17.53		17.19	x	x		
	17.41i	2 WI	Birmingham	3 Mar	16.70	17.22	16.97	x	17.41	x
	17.37i	1	Liévin	13 Feb	17.05	16.66	17.27	17.37	x	x
	17.35i	1	Madrid	8 Feb	16.96	14.93	17.35	17.19	p	15.45
	17.35	1.1 3 Pre	Eugene	26 May	x	17.35	17.12	17.12 17.20w	14.51
17.44	1.1	Will	Claye	USA	13.6.91	*	Pre	Eugene	26 May
	17.10	16.99	17.24		17.44 17.46w	17.10			
	17.43i	1 WI	Birmingham	3 Ma	16.89	16.86	16.76	17.43 17.35	17.31
	17.40	0.0 2	Baie Mahault	12 Ma	17.02	x	17.40/0.0 17.40/0.0	x	17.00
17.41	1.0	Jordan	Díaz	CUB-Y	23.2.01	1		La Habana	8 Jun
	17.41	x	x		p	p	p		
	17.32	0.5 1	La Habana	17 Feb	x	17.32	x	x	16.42	p
17.40i		Nelson	Évora	POR	20.4.84	3	WI	Birmingham	3 Mar
	17.14	x	17.40		17.25	x	16.71		
	17.30i	2	Madrid	8 Feb	17.02	17.30	x	x	x	x
17.40	0.8	Omar	Craddock	USA	26.4.91	1		Chula Vista	9 Jun
	17.16	17.40	p		p	p	p		
	17.37	0.5 3 Herc	Monaco	20 Jul	17.37	17.20	x	x	p	p
17.40	0.6	Chris	Benard	USA	4.4.90	2		Chula Vista	9 Jun
	17.40	x	x-		p	p	p		
	17.32	0.9 2 NC	Des Moines	22 Jun	16.57	17.32	17.03	16.81	x	x
17.37	0.9	Donald	Scott	USA	23.2.92	1	NC	Des Moines	22 Jun
	x	x	16.69		17.24	x	17.37		
17.34	1.7	Cristian	Nápoles	CUB	27.11.98	1	CAG	Barranquilla	2 Aug
		(31/10)			17.34	17.08w	17.08	16.76	p	15.50
17.28	0.0	Lázaro	Martínez	CUB	3.11.97	1		Camagüey	4 Feb
17.24	1.6	Alexis	Copello	AZE	12.8.85	4	Pre	Eugene	26 May
17.23i		Fabrice	Zango	BUR	25.6.93	1		Val-de-Reuil	27 Jan
17.22	1.8		Dong Bin	CHN	22.11.88	5	Pre	Eugene	26 May
17.20Ai		Chris	Carter	USA	11.3.89	2	NC	Albuquerque	18 Feb
17.16	1.0	KeAndre	Bates	USA	24.5.96	3	NC	Des Moines	22 Jun
17.15	-0.7	Aleksandr	Yurchenko	RUS	30.7.92	1		Zhukovskiy	12 Jul

MEN 2018

Mark	Wind	Name		Nat	Born	Pos	Meet	Venue	Date	
17.11A	-0.5		Zhu Yaming	CHN	4.5.94	1		Guiyang	17	Jun
17.09	0.0	Arpinder	Singh	IND	30.12.92	1	I-State	Guwahati	29	Jun
17.05	1.2	Harold	Corréa	FRA	26.6.88	1	NC	Albi	8	Jul
(20)										
17.02	0.0	Henry	Rosique	CUB	4.1.97	2		La Habana	17	Feb
16.98	1.4	Pablo	Torrijos	ESP	12.5.92	*	NC	Getafe	21	Jul
16.96 dm?		Lasha	Gulelauri	GEO	26.5.93	1		Tbilisi	20	May
16.63			0.2			2		Almaty	30	Jun
16.96	1.3	Miguel	van Assen	SUR	30.7.97	3	CAG	Barranquilla	2	Aug
16.95	1.8	Max	Hess	GER	13.7.96	6	Pre	Eugene	26	May
16.95	1.0	Jean Marc	Pontvianne	FRA	6.8.94	1		Marseille	16	Jun
16.94i		Fabrizio	Donato	ITA	14.8.76	1	NC	Ancona	18	Feb
16.92	1.3	Khotso	Mokoena	RSA	6.3.85	6	DL	Doha	4	May
16.91	0.6	Yasser	Triki	ALG	24.3.97	1	SEC	Knoxville	13	May
16.89i		Martin	Lamou	FRA-J	13.5.99	1	NC	Liévin	18	Feb
(30)										
16.89	-0.4	Nazim	Babayev	AZE	8.10.97	1	UKR Ch	Lutsk	20	Jul
16.89	-0.1		Wu Ruiting	CHN	29.11.95	1	NC	Taiyuan	17	Sep
16.88	0.5	Troy	Doris	GUY	12.4.89	1	CG	Gold Coast	14	Apr
16.87i		Dmitriy	Chizhikov	RUS	6.12.93	1	NC	Moskva	13	Feb
16.86	-2.3	Yordanys	Durañona	DMA	16.6.88	2	CG	Gold Coast	14	Apr
16.84	1.8	Simo	Lipsanen	FIN	13.9.95	3		Marseille	16	Jun
16.83	1.2	Matthew	O'Neal	USA	10.6.94	5	NC	Des Moines	22	Jun
16.82i		O'Brien	Wasome	JAM	24.1.97	1	NCAA	College Station	10	Mar
16.82	0.8	Aleksandro	Melo	BRA	26.9.95	1		Campinas	5	May
16.82	1.3	Kevin	Luron	FRA	8.11.91	2		Montreuil	19	Jun
(40)										
16.82	0.4	Jordan	Scott	JAM	29.6.97	4	CAG	Barranquilla	2	Aug
16.81	1.2	Marcos	Ruiz	ESP	10.3.95	1		Valencia	30	May
16.81	1.8	Denis	Obyortyshev	RUS	16.2.97	1		Chelyabinsk	29	Jul
16.80	-0.4	Marcel	Mayack	CMR	17.11.90	3	CG	Gold Coast	14	Apr
16.80A	-0.8		Cao Shuo	CHN	8.10.91	2		Guiyang	17	Jun
16.78	0.1	Dimítrios	Tsiámis	GRE	12.1.82	3	EC	Berlin	12	Aug
16.78i		Vitaliy	Pavlov	RUS	12.1.97	1	NC-23	Sankt Peterburg	22	Feb
16.77i		Nathan	Douglas	GBR	4.12.82	1	NC	Birmingham	18	Feb
16.77	2.0	Jean-Noël	Cretinoir	FRA	28.12.94	1		Aix-les-Bains	20	May
16.77	0.4	Can	Özüpek	TUR	2.2.96	1	NC	Bursa	8	Jul
(50)										
16.76A	0.5	Mateus Daniel	de Sá	BRA	21.11.95	2	SAmG	Cochabamba	7	Jun
16.76	1.4	Aleksey	Fyodorov	RUS	25.5.91	2	NC	Kazan	22	Jul
16.76	1.4	Dmitriy	Sorokin	RUS	27.9.92	3	NC	Kazan	22	Jul
16.74	-0.2	Karol	Hoffmann	POL	1.6.89	1	AWC	London (OS)	14	Jul
16.73	1.7	Simone	Forte	ITA	20.1.96	1	NC-23	Agropoli	3	Jun
16.73	0.6	Odaine	Lewis	JAM	13.12.96	2	NCAA	Eugene	8	Jun
16.72	1.6	Quentin	Mouyabi	FRA	8.10.98	1	Med-23	Jesolo	10	Jun
16.71i		Clive	Pullen	JAM	18.10.94	2		Fayetteville	10	Feb
16.70	1.0	Ruslan	Kurbanov	UZB	10.2.93	1		Almaty	30	Jun
16.69i		Momchil	Karailiev	BUL	21.5.82	1	NC	Sofia	4	Feb
(60)										
16.69	-0.8	Kaual Kamal	Bento	BRA	10.1.93	1		São Paulo	26	May
16.68	1.6	Yoann	Rapinier	FRA	29.9.89	*	NC	Albi	8	Jul
16.68	0.9	Elvijs	Misans	LAT	8.4.89	1	NC	Riga	28	Jul
16.67	1.9	Ilya	Glazunov	RUS	20.4.04	2		Smolonok	30	May
16.66i			Xu Xiaolong	CHN	20.12.92	1		Xi'an	12	Mar
16.65A	1.2	Reneilwe	Aphane	RSA	24.8.90	1		Pretoria	10	Feb
16.65	0.4	Levon	Aghasyan	ARM	19.1.95	1	NC	Artashat	20	May
16.64	0.8	John	Warren	USA	2.3.96	7	NC	Des Moines	22	Jun
16.63i		Scotty	Newton	USA	19.9.96	1	Big 12	Ames	24	Feb
16.63	0.0	K.V.Rakesh	Babu	IND	20.3.90	2	I-State	Guwahati	29	Jun
(70)										
16.63	2.0	Necati	Er	TUR	24.2.97	2	PTS	Šamorin	29	Jun
16.62	1.0	Tomás	Veszelka	SVK	9.7.95	1		Riga	29	May
16.61	1.8	Jonathan	Drack	MRI	6.11.88	3		Montgeron	13	May
16.61		Muhammad Hakimi	Ismail	MAS	8.4.91	1		Tashkent	10	Jun
16.60i		Marian	Oprea	ROU	6.6.82	1		Bucuresti	20	Jan
16.60	0.9	Fabrizio	Schembri	ITA	27.1.81	1	NC	Pescara	9	Sep
16.59	-0.3	Edislay	Hodelin	CUB-J	31.10.99	4		Camagüey	4	Feb
16.59	1.2	Barden	Adams	USA	21.9.96	2		Fayetteville	28	Apr
16.59	1.0	Kohei	Yamashita	JPN	6.9.94	1	NC	Yamaguchi	24	Jun
16.59	0.7	Ryoma	Yamamoto	JPN	14.7.95	1		Osaka	23	Sep
(80)										

Mark	Wind	Name		Nat	Born	Pos	Meet	Venue	Date
16.57	0.7	Georgi	Tsonov	BUL	2.5.93	2		Riga	29 May
16.57	-2.0	Julian	Reid	GBR	23.9.88	*	NC	Birmingham	30 Jun
16.56i		Maksim	Nesterenko	BLR	1.9.92	1		Mogilyov	17 Jan
16.56	0.0	Tiago	Pereira	POR	19.9.93	1		Salamanca	9 Jun
16.55i		Dmitriy	Plotnitskiy	BLR	26.8.88	1	NC	Mogilyov	16 Feb
16.55	1.3	Alphonso	Jordan	USA	1.11.87	8	NC	Des Moines	22 Jun
16.53	-0.5	Latario	Collie-Minns	BAH	10.3.94	1	NC	Nassau	22 Jun
16.53	1.8	Dimítrios	Monópolis	GRE	4.3.98	1	NC-23	Lárisa	28 Jul
16.53	1.6	Kohei	Nakayama	JPN	8.7.94	1		Kawasaki	9 Sep
16.52	0.0	Andy	Díaz	CUB	25.12.95	4		La Habana	8 Jun
		(90)							
16.52	-0.1	Kaiwan	Culmer	BAH	10.10.96	2	NC	Nassau	22 Jun
16.52	1.9	Pávlos	Bóftsis	GRE	17.9.92	*		Kavála	18 Jul
16.52		Supot	Boonnun	THA	10.7.96	1		Ho Chi Minh	27 Jul
16.52	-0.2		Liu Mingxuan	CHN	16.5.97	2		Yaiyuan	17 Sep
16.51		Renjith	Maheswary	IND	30.1.86	2		Patiala	8 Mar
16.50	1.7	Vicente	Docavo	ESP	13.2.92	3	NC	Getafe	21 Jul
16.49Ai		Brandon	Roulhac	USA	13.12.83	7	NC	Albuqueque	18 Feb
16.49A	-1.0	Menzi	Mthembu	RSA	7.2.95	1		Pretoria	2 Mar
16.49		Deivendran	Arivuselvan	IND	28.5.91	3		Patiala	8 Mar
16.49	1.2	Ivan	Denisov	UZB	22.1.96	3		Almaty	30 Jun
		(100)							

Mark	Wind	Name		Nat	Born	Date
16.48	1.0	Carlos	Veiga	POR	22.2.89	10 Jul
16.47	1.6	Nikólaos	Andrikópoulos	GRE	17.4.97	28 Jul
16.46i		Sergey	Laptev	RUS	7.2.91	3 Feb
16.45A	0.5	Elijah	Kimitei	KEN	25.12.86	17 Feb
16.45A	0.4	Roger	Haitengi	NAM	12.9.83	24 Feb
16.45	1.7		Kim Duk-hyung	KOR	8.12.85	17 Oct
16.44	1.2	Armani	Wallace	USA	11.2.97	26 May
16.44	1.0	Mamadou Chérif	Dia	MLI	13.3.85	4 Aug
16.43	0.0	Pratchaya	Tepparak	THA	1.9.93	29 Aug
16.42	0.9	Shem	James	AUS	12.7.97	28 Jan
16.42	0.0	Clayton	Brown	JAM	8.12.96	13 May
16.42	0.5	Chengetayi	Mapaya	ZIM	19.12.98	8 Jun
16.41	-0.1		Fang Yaoqing	CHN	20.4.96	18 Apr
16.41	1.5	Michael	Puplampu	GBR	11.1.90	12 May
16.40	0.5	Yevgeniy	Ektov	KAZ	1.9.86	30 Jun
16.39i		Benjamin	Compaoré	FRA	5.8.87	18 Feb
16.39i		Jeremiah	Green	USA	9.2.94	24 Feb
16.39A		Isaac	Yego	KEN	23.11.94	21 Jun
16.38i		Andrea	Dallavalle	ITA-J	31.8.99	4 Feb
16.37i		Cristi	Boboc	ROU	5.12.94	3 Feb
16.37	0.3		Wei Xinyu	CHN	28.7.96	18 Apr
16.37	1.5	Tosin	Oke	NGR	1.10.80	12 May
16.37	0.2	Chris	Edwards	USA-J	23.3.99	8 Jun
16.37	0.2	Daniele	Cavazzani	ITA	4.12.92	9 Sep
16.36i		Adrian	Swiderski	POL	26.9.86	15 Feb
16.36	0.0	Arturo	Rodríguez	CUB-J	28.4.99	29 Jun
16.36	0.0	Eldhose	Paul	IND	7.11.96	20 Jul
16.36		Jay Shah	Pradeep	IND	11.10.97	26 Nov
16.35	0.0	Oleksandr	Malosilov	UKR	6.6.97	21 Jul
16.34	0.2	Andy	Hechavarría	CUB-J	14.9.00	4 Feb
16.34i			Fu Haitao	CHN	1.11.93	8 Mar
16.34	1.0	Sanjaya	Jayasinghe	SRI	20.4.82	28 Apr
16.33i		Eric	Sloan	USA	20.6.94	27 Jan
16.33i		Tuomas	Kaukolahti	FIN	6.5.94	10 Mar
16.32	0.0	Mohammed	Salahuddin	IND	24.3.94	29 Jun
16.32	1.1	Yuta	Takenouchi	JPN	23.4.98	27 Oct
16.31	0.6	Bruno	de Souza	BRA	29.9.95	3 Feb
16.30i		Artyom	Bondarenko	BLR	19.6.91	3 Feb
16.30i		Charles	Brown	USA	28.5.97	10 Feb
16.29	0.0	Julio César	Carbonell	CUB-J	16.5.99	29 Jun
16.29	0.9	Samuele	Cerro	ITA	21.3.95	26 May
16.28i		Edoardo	Accetta	ITA	28.3.94	18 Feb
16.28	0.6	Tobia	Bocchi	ITA	7.4.97	23 May
16.28	1.6	Jonathan	Ilori	GBR	14.8.93	10 Jun
16.28		Abdulla	Aboobacker	IND	17.1.96	20 Sep
16.27	0.4	Jean	Rosa	BRA	1.2.90	3 Feb
16.27			Nguyen Van Hung	VIE	4.3.89	30 Nov
16.26	0.0	Emmanuel	Fakiye	AUS	27.11.97	28 Jan
16.26Ai		Khaled	Al-Subaie	KUW	1.3.96	3 Feb
16.26	1.0	John	Lemke	USA	20.12.94	6 May
16.25i		Devontae	Steele	USA	4.1.96	10 Mar
16.25	0.4	Olu	Olamigoke	NGR	19.9.90	20 Apr
16.25	1.5		Li Kuei-Lung	TPE	16.9.92	25 May
16.25	0.4	Kirill	Kovalenko	RUS	20.1.94	7 Jun
16.25A	0.5		Lu Zhiwei	CHN	4.4.96	17 Jun
16.24i		Bryce	Williams	USA	11.6.96	13 Jan
16.24		Unnikrishnan	Karthik	IND	3.6.93	8 Mar
16.24	-0.6	Igor	Syunin	EST	4.12.90	28 Jul

Wind assisted

Mark	Wind	Name		Nat	Born	Pos	Meet	Venue	Date
17.86	2.1	Christian	Taylor	USA	18.6.90	1	Herc	Monaco	20 Jul
17.67	2.4		Pichardo			2	Herc	Monaco	20 Jul
17.64	2.1		Taylor			1	Gyulai	Székesfehérvár	2 Jul
17.46	3.0	Will	Claye	USA	13.6.91	2	Pre	Eugene	26 May
17.31	2.9		Scott			1		Knoxville	14 Apr
			16.57w 16.73w	17.07w	17.24w	17.31w	17.14w		
17.28	2.2	Chris	Carter	USA	11.3.87	1		Houston	4 May
17.23	2.2	Pablo	Torrijos	ESP	12.5.92	1	NC	Getafe	21 Jul
17.09A	2.7	Khotso	Mokoena	RSA	6.3.85	1	NC	Pretoria	16 Mar
16.97	2.2	Kevin	Luron	FRA	8.11.91	2	NC	Albi	8 Jul
16.86	2.2	Tomás	Veszelka	SVK	9.7.95	1		Košice	8 May
16.86	2.1	Jean-Noël	Cretinoir	FRA	28.12.94	1		Montreuil	19 Jun
16.85	2.1	Scotty	Newton	USA	19.9.96	1	Big 12	Waco	13 May
16.83	2.5	Nathan	Douglas	GBR	4.12.82	1	NC	Birmingham	30 Jun
16.83	3.0	Vitaliy	Pavlov	RUS	12.1.97	1	NC-23	Chelyabinsk	8 Jul
16.74	3.9	Yoann	Rapinier	FRA	29.9.89	4	NC	Albi	8 Jul
16.74	2.2	Ryoma	Yamamoto	JPN	14.7.95	1		Fukui	7 Oct
16.70	2.3	Julian	Reid	GBR	23.9.88	2	NC	Birmingham	30 Jun
16.68	2.2	Pávlos	Bóftsis	GRE	17.9.92	1		Kavála	18 Jul
16.63	2.9	Arturo	Rodríguez	CUB-J	28.4.99	3		Camagüey	4 Feb
16.50	2.4	Clayton	Brown	JAM	8.12.96	4		Fayetteville	28 Apr

Mark	Wind	Name		Nat	Born	Pos	Meet	Venue	Date
16.47	2.2	Josh	Honeycutt	USA	7.3.89				21 Apr
16.43	3.0	Jean Cassimiro	Rosa	BRA	1.2.90				25 Mar
16.43	3.6	Tony	Carodine	USA	18.6.94				21 Apr
16.39	2.4	Leevan	Sands	BAH	16.8.81				14 Apr
16.39	2.1	Samuele	Cerro	ITA	21.3.95				26 May
16.35	4.0	MaximilianoDíaz		ARG	15.11.88				25 Mar

Mark	Wind	Name		Nat	Born	Pos	Meet	Venue	Date
16.35	2.3	Artem	Molotkov	RUS	1.7.97	8			Jul
16.34	2.3	Emmanuel	Ineh	NGR-Y	17.3.01	13			Oct
16.28	3.4	Atheetha N.Karunasinghe		SRI	30.11.95	12			May
16.26Anwi		Thalosang	Tshireletso	BOT	14.5.91	27			Jan
16.24	3.0	Tazuma	Kawashima	JPN	16.8.96	27			May

Best outdoor marks

Mark	Wind	Name	Pos	Meet	Venue	Date
17.18	1.6	Carter	1		Houston	17 Mar
17.11	0.0	Zango	1	AfrC	Asaba	4 Aug
17.10	-0.1	Évora	1	EC	Berlin	12 Aug
16.76	1.5	Lamou	1		Montgeron	13 May

Mark	Wind	Name	Pos	Meet	Venue	Date
16.71	0.0	Douglas	6	EC	Berlin	12 Aug
16.65	0.1	Xu Xiaolong	3		Zhaoqing	12 Apr
16.62	0.1	Donato	5		Madrid	22 Jun
16.57	1.2	Newton	3		Fayetteville	28 Apr
16.56	0.4	Karailiev	2	Balk	Stara Zagora	21 Jul

Mark	Wind	Name	Date		Mark	Wind	Name	Pos	Meet	Venue	Date
16.44	2.0	Roulhac	21 Apr		16.47w	3.5	Oprea	30 Jun			
16.40	0.4	Pavlov	30 May		16.28	0.4	Accetta	17 Jun		16.23	Al-Subaie	10 Jul
16.32	0.0	Oprea	26 Jul		16.25	1.5	Pullen	24 Mar		16.23	0.5 Dallavalle	9 Sep

Low altitude best

Mark	Wind	Name	Pos	Venue	Date
16.79	0.2	Zhu Yaming	1	Jakarta	7 Mar

Mark	Wind	Name	Pos	Venue	Date
16.65	0.0	Cao Shuo	2	Zhaoqing	12 Apr
16.58	-1.0	de Sá	3	Bragança Paulista	8 Jul

JUNIORS

See main list for top 3 juniors. 15 performances (and 1 wa) by 2 men to 16.70. Additional marks and further juniors:

Mark	Wind		Name		Nat	Born	Pos	Meet	Venue	Date
J Díaz 2+	17.28	0.0 1							Camagüey	1 Jun
	17.27	1.3 *	CAG						Barranquilla	30 Jun
	17.15	-0.4 1	WJ						Tampere	14 Jul
	17.14	-0.3 1							Camagüey	26 May
	17.14	-0.8 1							La Chaux-de-Fonds	1 Jul
	17.14	1.9 1	YOG						Buenos Aires	13 Oct
	17.09	0.7 q	WJ						Tampere	14 Jul
	17.04	1.9	YOG						Buenos Aires	16 Oct
	17.03	-0.4 2							Camagüey	4 Feb
	16.95	-1.3 2							La Habana	23 Feb
	16.83	-0.1 1	NACAC						Toronto	10 Aug
	17.29w	1	CAG						Barranquilla	30 Jun
Raffin 2+	17.04i	1							Aubière	17 Jun
	16.92i	5	El						Beograd	5 Mar
16.38i	Andrea		Dallavalle		ITA	31.8.99	1	NC-j	Ancona	4 Feb
16.23	0.5						5	NC	Pescara	9 Sep
16.37	0.2	Chris	Edwards		USA	23.3.99	6	NCAA	Eugene	8 Jun
16.36	0.0	Arturo	Rodríguez		CUB	28.4.99	1	NC-j	Camagüey	29 Jun
16.34	0.2	Andy	Hechavarría		CUB	14.9.00	5		Camagüey	4 Feb
16.29	0.0	Julio César	Carbonell		CUB	16.5.99	2		Camagüey	29 Jun
16.23A		Adire	Gur		ETH	23.3.00	1		Addis Ababa	2 Feb
16.23Ai		Kanagaraj	Kamal Raj (10)		IND	3.10.99	2	AsiC-I	Tehran	3 Feb
16.23	1.8		Yu Kyu-min		KOR-Y	22.4.01	1-HS		Iksan	16 Oct
16.22		Chithirvel	Praveen		IND-Y	5.6.01	1		Tirunelveli	9 Jun
16.22	2.0	Florin	Visan		ROU	3.4.99	1		Pitesti	30 Jun
16.22	2.0	Emmanuel	Ineh		NGR-Y	17.3.01	1	Af-Y	Algers	26 Jul
16.18A		Musyoka	Mwema		KEN	28.2.00	1	KEN-jT	Nairobi	10 Jun
16.18	1.9	Jonathan	Seremes		FRA	3.9.00	3	WJ	Tampere	14 Jul
16.16	0.7	Jusniel	Jorrín		CUB-Y	2.2.01	6		Camagüey	4 Feb
16.04	1.9	Hajeem	Araki		JPN	6.9.00	1		Fukui	5 Oct
16.03			Lin Qinwei		CHN	11.7.99	5		Xianlin	8 Mar

Wind assisted

Mark	Wind	Name		Nat	Born	Pos	Meet	Venue	Date
16.34	2.3	Emmanuel	Ineh	NGR-Y	17.3.01	2c1	YOG	Buenos Aires	13 Oct
16.10	2.1	Ravzan	Greco	ROU	23.12.99	2		Cluj-Napoca	3 Jun

SHOT

Mark		Pos	Meet	Name		Nat	Born	Pos	Meet	Venue	Date
22.67				Tom	Walsh	NZL	1.3.92	1		Auckland	25 Mar

21.34 22.67 21.45 21.42 x 21.00

Mark		Pos	Meet	Name	Venue	Date					
	22.60	1	WK	Zürich					30 Aug		

21.06 22.60 21.39 21.87 x 20.55

22.45 Q CG Gold Coast 8 Apr — 22.45

22.31i 1 WI Birmingham 3 Mar — 22.13 x 22.13 x x 22.31

22.29 1 Bisl Oslo 7 Jun — 21.91 21.35 21.79 21.88 21.72 22.29

22.16 1 GS Ostrava 13 Jun — 20.62 21.54 22.16 21.36 21.80 x

22.06 1 Timaru 14 Mar — 21.35 22.06 x 21.13 21.20 x

21.92 1 Athl Lausanne 5 Jul — x x 20.73 20.80 21.92 x

21.87 Hamilton 10 Feb — 20.99 21.87 20.77 21.44 x 21.33

21.84 4 Pre Eugene 26 May — 21.65 21.84 21.33 x x x

21.82 2 DrakeR Des Moines 28 Apr — 21.11 21.82 21.58 21.60 21.77 21.43

22.53 Ryan Crouser USA 18.12.92 1 Pre Eugene 26 May

21.98 21.82 x 22.12 22.53 21.94

22.31 1 Odlozil Praha 4 Jun — x 21.28 x 22.31 22.28 22.09

22.27 1 Kuso Chorzów 8 Jun — x 21.46 x x 22.27 x

22.21 1 Chula Vista 14 May — 22.00 22.21 21.97 22.10 21.58 21.69

22.21 2 Bisl Oslo 7 Jun — x 21.45 21.71 21.54 22.21 x

22.18 3 WK Zürich 30 Aug — 22.11 x 21.56 22.18 21.77 x

22.09 1 Hanz Zagreb 3 Sep — 20.41 21.28 21.24 22.09 x 21.84

22.05 1 Herc Monaco 19 Jul — x 21.30 x 22.05 x x

22.01 1 DrakeR Des Moines 28 Apr — 22.01 x x x x x

22.40 Darrell Hill USA 17.8.93 2 WK Zürich 30 Aug

22.03 22.23 22.40 x 22.08 x

Mark	Wind		Name		Nat	Born	Pos	Meet	Venue	Date
22.17i			Tomás	Stanek	CZE	13.6.91	1		Düsseldorf	6 Feb
						21.57	21.98	22.17	p	x	p
	21.87	5 WK	Zürich		30 Aug	21.33	21.28	21.87	x	x	20.96
	21.83i	2	Torun		15 Feb	x	21.60	21.69	21.65	21.83	21.25
22.08			Michal	Haratyk	POL	10.4.92	2	GS	Ostrava	13 Jun
						x	21.82	22.08	x	x	x
	21.97	2 Pre	Eugene		26 May	21.09	21.50	21.35	20.69	x	21.97
	21.95	1 AWC	London (OS)		14 Jul	21.39	21.77	21.95	21.57		
	21.85	1 NC	Lublin		22 Jul	21.49	x		21.85	21.43	21.82	x
22.00i			Konrad	Bukowiecki	POL	17.3.97	1		Torun	15 Feb
						20.83	22.00	x	x	x	x
22.00			Darlan	Romani	BRA	9.4.91	1	NC	Bragança Paulista	15 Sep
						21.46	x	22.00	21.91	21.61	21.98
	21.95	3 Pre	Eugene		26 May	x	21.62	21.54	20.72	21.95	x
	21.94	1	Bialystok		20 May	x	20.09	21.84	21.75	x	21.94
	21.94	4 WK	Zürich		30 Aug	21.94	x	21.84	21.85	21.65	21.70
	21.89	1 C.Cup	Ostrava		8 Sep	21.24	21.89	21.29	21.07	21.68	
		(34/7)									
21.63			Curtis	Jensen	USA	1.11.90	1		Bragança Paulista	8 Jul
21.62			David	Storl	GER	27.7.90	1		Biberach	9 Jul
21.58			Aleksandr	Lesnoy (10)	RUS	28.7.88	1	NC	Kazan	20 Jul
21.45i			Jordan	Geist	USA	21.7.98	1		Seattle	27 Jan
21.39i			Maksim	Afonin	RUS	6.1.92	1	NC	Moskva	13 Feb
21.36			Stipe	Zunic	CRO	13.12.90	1		Split	16 Jun
21.33i			Josh	Awotunde	NGR/USA	12.6.95	1	SEC	College Station	25 Feb
21.33			Filip	Mihaljevic	CRO	31.7.94	1		Zenica	6 Jun
21.31i			Payton	Otterdahl	USA	2.4.96	1		Fargo	8 Dec
21.27i			Tsanko	Arnaudov	POR	14.3.92	1		Pombal	18 Feb
21.22			Chukwuebuka	Enekwechi	NGR	28.1.93	1		Charlottesville	5 May
21.15i			Mesud	Pezer	BIH	27.8.94	5	WI	Birmingham	3 Mar
21.03i			Ryan	Whiting	USA	24.11.86	7	WI	Birmingham	3 Mar
		(20)								
21.02			Joe	Kovacs	USA	28.6.89	6	GS	Ostrava	13 Jun
21.02			O'Dayne	Richards	JAM	14.12.88	1	CAG	Barranquilla	30 Jul
21.02			Tim	Nedow	CAN	16.10.90	2	NACAC	Toronto	10 Aug
21.00			Bob	Bertemes	LUX	24.5.93	6	EC	Berlin	7 Aug
20.93			Ashinia	Miller	JAM	6.6.93	1		Hamilton	11 May
20.88			Denzel	Comenentia	NED	25.11.95	1	SEC	Knoxville	12 May
20.86i			Mustafa Ahmed	Hassan	EGY	16.12.95	1	NCAA	College Station	9 Mar
20.86			Francisco	Belo	POR	27.3.91	2		Szczecin	15 Aug
20.81			Frank	Elemba	CGO	21.7.90	1		Kenitra	24 Jul
20.77			Damien	Birkinhead	AUS	8.4.93	5	CG	Gold Coast	9 Apr
		(30)								
20.75			Tejinder Pal	Singh	IND	13.11.94	1	AsiG	Jakarta	25 Aug
20.71			Orazio	Cremona	RSA	1.7.89	1	NC	Pretoria	16 Mar
20.68i			Nick	Vena	USA	16.4.93	1		West Long Branch	27 Jan
20.68			Jakub	Szyszkowski	POL	21.8.91	4	Odlozil	Praha	4 Jun
20.65			Jonathan	Jones	USA	23.4.91	3		Tucson	19 May
20.63			Andrzej	Gudro	POL	8.4.94	1		Biala Podlaska	26 May
20.63			Eldred	Henry	IVB	18.9.94	5	NACAC	Toronto	10 Aug
20.60i			Andrei	Gag	ROU	7.4.91	1		Istanbul	18 Feb
20.48			Asmir	Kolasinac	SRB	15.10.84	1		Sarajevo	10 Jun
20.45			Hamza	Alic	BIH	20.1.79	3		Zenica	6 Jun
		(40)								
20.43			Aleksey	Nichipor	BLR	10.4.93	1		Brest	25 May
20.42			Josh	Freeman	USA	22.8.94	6	NC	Des Moines	23 Jun
20.41			Garrett	Appier	USA	15.10.92	2		Hamilton	11 May
20.41			Adrian	Piperi	USA-J	20.1.99	1q	NCAA-W	Sacramento	26 May
20.39			Jared	Kern	USA	10.6.95	1		Terre Haute	13 May
20.37			David	Pless	USA	19.11.90	2		San Diego	14 Apr
20.36i			Frédéric	Dagée	FRA	11.12.92	1		Nice	12 Jan
20.34			Fedrick	Dacres	JAM	28.2.94	2		Kingston	5 May
20.32			Austin	Droogsma	USA	4.3.95	1	Fla R	Gainesville	31 Mar
20.28			Andrew	Liskowitz	USA	22.5.97	1		Fayetteville	28 Apr
		(50)								
20.28			Oghenakpobo	Efekoro	NGR	15.7.96	6	NCAA	Eugene	6 Jun
20.27i			Borja	Vivas	ESP	26.5.84	1	NC	Valencia	17 Feb
20.26			Osman Can	Özdevici	TUR	23.8.95	1		Mersin	20 May
20.24i			Nick	Demaline	USA	1.3.96	1		Geneva, OH	24 Feb
20.24			Nikólaos	Skarvélis	GRE	2.2.93	Q	EC	Berlin	6 Aug
20.22			Willie	Morrison	USA	23.11.96	1	Big 10	Bloomington	13 May

MEN 2018

Mark	Name		Nat	Born	Pos	Meet	Venue	Date	
20.15i	Brett	Neelly	USA	22.11.96	1		Manhattan, KS	8	Dec
20.14i	Patrick	Müller	GER	4.2.96	1		Neubrandenburg	20	Jan
20.14	Ihor	Musiyenko	UKR	22.8.93	1		Kamianets Podilskyi	27	Apr
20.13	Mikhail	Abramchuk	BLR	15.11.92	2	NC	Minsk	20	Jul
		(60)							
20.13	Kristo	Galeta	EST	0.4.83	1		Lihula	4	Aug
20.12i	Carlos	Tobalina	ESP	2.8.85	1		Valencia	27	Jan
20.07	Leonardo	Fabbri	ITA	15.5.97	3		Leiria	14	Jul
20.06i	Kord	Ferguson	USA	16.9.95	2	SEC	College Station	25	Feb
20.04	Konstantin	Lyadusov	RUS	2.3.88	3	NC	Kazan	20	Jul
20.01	Nikita	Zhidkov	RUS	29.2.88	1		Moskva	21	Jun
19.99	Kemal	Mesic	BIH	4.8.85	1		Plievlja	1	Jul
19.95	Shahin	Mehrdelan	IRI	21.6.95	1		Tehran	1	Aug
19.94	Giorgi	Mujaridze	GEO	22.3.98	1		Tbilisi	20	May
19.94	Biaz	Zupancic	SLO	6.4.95	1		Ljubljana	25	Jul
		(70)							
19.93	Tomas	Djurovic	MNE	14.2.94	3		Bar	1	May
19.91	Simon	Bayer	GER	23.11.95	1		Erding	24	Jun
19.90i	Arttu	Kangas	FIN	13.7.93	1	NC	Helsinki	18	Feb
19.90	Jordan	Young	CAN	21.6.93	2		Charlottesville	5	May
19.89	J.C.	Murasky	USA	6.2.93	1		Chula Vista	9	Jun
19.87	Uziel	Muñoz	MEX	8.9.95	4	CAG	Barranquilla	30	Jul
19.85	Wellington	Morais	BRA	6.9.96	1	SAmC-23	Cuenca	29	Sep
19.82	Marcus	Thomsen	NOR	7.1.98	1	NC	Byrkjelo	19	Aug
19.81i	Ivan	Ivanov	KAZ	3.1.92	1		Ust-Kamenogorsk	11	Jan
19.80	McKay	Johnson	USA	15.4.98	2		Stanford	31	Mar
		(80)							
19.80	Patrick	Cronie	NED	5.11.89	2	NA	Heusden-Zolder	21	Jul
19.79	Coy	Blair	USA	10.6.94	2		Ashland, OH	28	Apr
19.79	T'Mond	Johnson	USA	28.7.97	1		San Marcos	12	May
19.79	Jordan	West	USA-J	27.6.99	3	SEC	Knoxville	12	May
19.73	Mohamed	Hamza	EGY	30.8.96	1	NC	El Maadi	13	Apr
19.73	Tobias	Dahm	GER	23.5.87	1		Rechberghausen	3	Jun
19.71	Sebastiano	Bianchetti	ITA	20.1.96	4	Med G	Tarragona	27	Jun
19.70	Viktor	Samolyuk	UKR	5.9.86	2		Kamianets Podilskyi	27	Apr
19.66	Noah	Castle	USA	19.9.96	6q	NCAA-E	Tampa	26	May
19.64	Dennis	Lewke	GER	23.7.93	4		Halle	26	May
		(90)							
19.62i	Nick	Ponzio	USA	4.1.95	1		Seattle	24	Feb
19.62	Jan Josef	Jeuschede	GER	23.4.93	7		Thum	17	Aug
19.61	Marius	Musteata	ROU	11.1.97	2		Cluj Napoca	2	Jun
19.61	Grant	Cartwright	USA	19.11.94	11	NCAA	Eugene	6	Jun
19.61	Willian	Douado	BRA	6.1.94	2	NC	Bragança Paulista	15	Sep
19.59i	Kiriáko	Zótos	GRE	17.1.96	2		Pireás	10	Feb
19.57	Naveen	Chhikara	IND	14.12.96	2		Patiala	6	Mar
19.56i	Martin	Novák	CZE	5.10.92	2	NC	Praha	18	Feb
19.56	Sourabh	Vij	IND	14.6.87	1		Kochi	15	May
19.55	Demyan	Seskin	RUS	4.8.97	1		Sankt Peterburg	21	Jun
		(100)							

Mark	Name		Nat	Born	Date		Mark	Name		Nat	Born	Date	
19.54	Mario	Cota	MEX	11.9.90	31	Mar	19.27	Richard	Cervantes	USA	16.6.95	21	Apr
19.52		Liu Yang	CHN	29.10.86	25	Aug	19.27	Ladislav	Prásil	CZE	17.5.90	19	May
19.49i	Nate	Esparza	USA	24.4.98	20	Jan	19.26	Bo	Farrow	USA	3.12.93	11	May
19.47i	Jack	Lembcke	USA	9.3.96	10	Feb	19.26	Jalil	Brewer	USA	21.5.98	13	May
19.46	Odisséas	Mouzenídis	GRE-J	30.6.99	28	Jul	19.25i	Sergey	Dementyev	UZB	1.6.90	25	Jan
19.45	Frántsi-Anastásios	Latiflári	GRE	8.8.96	28	Jul	19.25i	Leif	Arrhenius	SWE	15.7.86	25	Jan
19.44	Dillon	Simon	DMA	5.3.92	8	Apr	19.24i	Brian	Williams	USA	18.12.94	10	Feb
19.44	Wictor	Petersson	SWE	1.5.98	20	Apr	19.24	Scott	Lincoln	GBR	7.5.93	14	Jul
19.43	Leonid	Ekimov	GER	19.12.89	23	Jun	19.20	Maris	Urtans	LAT	9.2.81	20	May
19.42i	Ali	Samari	IRI	7.1.93	2	Feb	19.19i	Andrzej	Naszko	POL	9.5.94	15	Feb
19.42	William	Braido	BRA	18.3.92	24	Mar	19.19	Kayle	Blignaut	RSA-J	9.11.99	1	Mar
19.42	Jacob	Mahin	USA	30.5.93	11	May	19.18	Connor	Bandel	USA	21.10.97	12	May
19.42	Maksim	Sidorov	RUS	13.5.86	11	Jul	19.15i	Bodo	Göder	GER	27.6.93	7	Feb
19.40i	Alex	Renner	USA	28.12.93	18	Feb	19.15		Jung Il-woo	KOR	28.3.86	25	Aug
19.40	Georgi	Ivanov	BUL	13.3.85	6	Aug	19.14i	Adam	Kessler	USA	9.1.97	25	Feb
19.37i	Ayomidotun	Ogundeji	USA	24.2.96	20	Jan	19.14	Roger	Steen	USA	17.5.92	14	Apr
19.37	Cedric	Trinemeier	GER	21.11.97	18	May	19.14	Lukas	Dennis	GER	15.2.94	10	May
19.36i	Itamir	Levi	ISR	11.11.91	27	Jan	19.14	Mykola	Bahach	UKR	24.6.93	22	May
19.35	Péter	Simon	HUN	18.9.94	28	Apr	19.13i	Matt	Katnik	USA	10.10.96	20	Jan
19.35	Sarunas	Banevicius	LTU	20.11.91	27	Jul	19.13	Timo	Kööpikkä	FIN	10.5.94	20	Jul
19.33	Jan	Parol	POL	11.11.95	20	May	19.12	Akeem	Stewart	TTO	4.7.92	8	Apr
19.30i	Nicolai	Ceban	MDA	4.2.95	24	Feb	19.12	Charles	Lenford	USA	17.3.98	28	Apr
19.29i		Tian Zhizhong	CHN	15.12.92	24	Mar	19.12	Roman	Kokoshko	UKR	16.8.96	19	May
19.28i	Reno	Tuufuli	USA	15.2.96	23	Feb	19.12i	Dmitriy	Karpuk	BLR-J	5.11.99	21	Dec

Mark	Name	Nat	Born	Pos Meet	Venue	Date
19.11	Li Jun	CHN	2.1.93			17 Jun
19.10	Marco Fortes	POR	26.9.82			21 Jul
19.09i	Josh McDonald	USA	18.8.94			23 Feb
19.05i	Wu Jiaxing	CHN	29.3.90			24 Mar
19.05	Shahin Jaafari	IRI	15.5.96			25 Oct
19.04	Alex Wellington	USA	2.3.95			26 May
19.04	Ivan Emilianov	MDA	19.2.77			27 May
19.03i	Kristoffer Thomsen	DEN	21.2.96			25 Feb
19.02	Burger Lambrechts	RSA	6.8.98			27 Apr
19.01i	Lucas Warning	USA	3.2.95			20 Jan
18.99i	Duke Kicinski	USA	14.3.96			13 Jan
18.99	Jasdeep Singh	IND	6.10.90			27 Jun
18.98	Chang Ming-Huang	TPE	7.8.82			25 Aug
18.95	Jason van Rooyen	RSA	4.2.97			1 Mar
18.95	Mohamed Eskandari	IRI	27.7.90			25 Oct
18.93i	Corey Murphy	USA	3.11.96			18 Feb
18.93	Armin Sinancevic	SRB	14.8.96			12 Jul
18.90	José Angel Pinedo	ESP	30.7.90			2 Jun
18.89	Luke Vaughn	USA	24.8.94			13 May
18.88	Christian Zimmermann	GER	9.7.94			19 May
18.85	Joseph Maxwell	CAN	3.4.98			12 May
18.85	Daichi Nakamura	JPN	15.1.93			20 May
18.85	Nik Huffman	USA	18.7.94			26 May
18.83i	Silas Ristl	GER	1.4.95			27 Jan
18.83	Morteza Nazimi	IRI	24.12.88			20 May
18.82	Daniel Pardo	ESP	8.3.96			22 Jul
18.81	Rimantas Martisauskas	LTU	18.9.86			11 May
18.80i	Gaëtan Bucki	FRA	9.5.80			17 Feb
18.79	Onwuka Kalo Eke	NGR	1.1.95			2 Aug
18.78	Daniel Ståhl	SWE	27.8.92			25 Aug
18.77	Jaco Engelbrecht	RSA	8.3.87			11 Feb
18.77	Christopher Reed	USA	22.7.92			23 Mar
18.77	Artyom Podolskiy	RUS	21.7.93			11 Jul
18.76i	Szymon Mazur	POL	2.9.98			18 Feb
18.76	Aaron Castle	USA	7.10.93			17 Mar
18.76	Praveen Singh	IND	10.10.93			26 Sep
18.75	Nikolas Curtiss	USA	25.8.97			26 May
18.75	Oleg Tomashevich	BLR-J	31.5.00			20 Jul
18.74i	Antoine Duponchel	FRA	7.1.96			16 Dec
18.73i	Ricky Hurley	USA	17.7.97			16 Feb
18.73	Eric Favors	USA	16.11.96			24 Mar
18.72i	Eric Jackson	USA	17.12.96			10 Mar
18.72	Isaac Odugbesan	NGR	22.4.98			21 Apr
18.72	Murat Gündüz	TUR	1.3.93			22 Apr
18.71	Sun Shuai	CHN	20.1.96			14 Sep
18.70i	David Schall	USA	1.10.96			6 Jan
18.70i	Tristen Newman	USA	30.1.96			13 Jan
18.70	Felipe Valencia	MEX	6.3.95			13 May

(196)

Best outdoor marks

Mark	Name			Pos Meet	Venue	Date
21.66	Bukowiecki	2	EC		Berlin	7 Aug
21.52	Stanek	1	NC		Kladno	29 Jul
20.99	Whiting	2			Auckland	25 Mar
20.96	Otterdahl	1			Tulsa	12 May
20.80	Afonin	2			Moskva	11 Jun
20.79	Pezer	1			Bottnaryd	16 Jun
20.77	Awotunde	2	SEC		Knoxville	12 May
20.65	Arnaudov	1			Schifflange	29 Jul
20.44	Hassan	3	NCAA		Eugene	6 Jun
20.41	Geist	1			Tucson	28 Apr
20.19	Gag	1	Balk C		Stara Zagora	21 Jul
20.18	Demaline	8	NCAA		Eugene	6 Jun
20.12	Tobalina	1			Granollers	14 Jul
20.04	Dagée	4			Montreuil	19 Jun
20.03	Vivas	1			Málaga	27 Jan
19.86	Ferguson	4q	NCAAE		Tampa	26 May
19.59	Neelly	1			Lubbock	27 Apr
19.57	Kangas	4	Sule		Tartu	3 Jun
19.56	Vena	1			Bethlehem, PA	14 Apr

Mark	Name	Date		Mark	Name	Date
19.49	Müller	21 Jul		19.10	Novák	29 May
19.40	Renner	4 May		19.04	Wu Jiaxing	18 May
19.40	Ivanov	25 Aug		19.03	Levi	4 Jul
19.32	Ponzio	29 Apr		19.01	Dementyev	2 Jun
19.17	Tuufuli	26 May		19.00	Göder	9 Jun
18.98	Naszko	1 May		18.94	Thomsen	2 Jun
18.98	Samari	20 May		18.90	Murphy	17 May
18.97	Warning	19 May		18.85	Williams	12 May
18.94	Zótos	17 Mar		18.75	Katnik	2 Jun
18.94	Tian Zhizhong	18 Apr		18.70	Karpuk	28 Apr

JUNIORS

See main list for top 2 juniors. 5 performances by 2 men to 19.70. Additional marks and further juniors:

Mark	Name		Nat	Born	Pos Meet	Venue	Date				
Piperi	20.41	4	NCAA			Eugene	6 Jun	20.19	1	Waco	12 May
West	19.70	2				Fayetteville	28 Apr				
19.46	Odisséas	Mouzenídis	GRE	30.6.99	1 NC-23	Lárisa	28 Jul				
19.19	Kayle	Blignaut	RSA	9.11.99	1	Johannesburg	1 Mar				
19.12i	Dmitriy	Karpuk	BLR	5.11.99	1	Minsk	21 Dec				
18.70					2	Brest	28 Apr				
18.75	Oleg	Tomashevich	BLR	31.5.00	3 NC	Minsk	20 Jul				
18.26	Jeff	Duensing	USA	8.6.01	1	La Mirada	15 Dec				
18.11	Eero	Ahola	FIN	15.1.99	2	Loimaa	18 Aug				
18.04	Cooper	Campbell	USA	3.2.99	3	Waco	12 May				

6 kg Shot

Mark	Name		Nat	Born	Pos Meet	Venue	Date				
22.07	Kyle	Blignaut	RSA	9.11.99	1 WJ	Tampere	10 Jul				
21.65					1	Boksburg	28 Apr	20.90	1	Gaborone	12 Dec
22.06	Adrian	Piperi	USA	20.1.99	2 WJ	Tampere	10 Jul				
21.50					1 NC-j	Bloomington	16 Jun	32.42	q WJ	Tampere	10 Jul
21.44	Dmitriy	Karpuk	BLR	5.11.99	1	Brest	28 Apr				
21.26					1	Tel Aviv	13 May				
21.16	Jordan	West	USA	27.6.99	2 NC-j	Bloomington	16 Jun				
21.09	Eero	Ahola	FIN	15.1.99	1 Nordic-j	Hvidovre	12 Aug				
21.07	Odisséas	Mouzenídis	GRE	30.6.99	3 WJ	Tampere	10 Jul				
20.74	Valentin	Moll	GER	21.6.99	1 Wefer	Halle	26 May				
20.37	Oleg	Tomashevich	BLR	31.5.00	5 WJ	Tampere	10 Jul				
20.14	John	Meyer	USA	1.12.99	3 NC-j	Bloomington	16 Jun				
19.92	Ryan	Ballantyne (10)	NZL	8.1.99	1	Sydney	16 Mar				
19.85	Aiden	Harvey	AUS	16.9.99	7 WJ	Tampere	10 Jul				
19.80	Moazz Mohamed	Ibrahim	QAT	8.2.99	1 ArabC	Amman	19 Apr				
19.80	Arttu	Korkesalo	FIN	4.2.00	1	Ikaalinen	22 Jun				
19.74	Alexander	Kolesnikoff	AUS	30.9.00	1	Mannheim	23 Jun				
19.60	Jacob	Wilson	USA	2.2.99	4 NC-j	Bloomington	16 Jun				
19.60	Nerman	Stitkovac	BIH	14.9.00	1	Zenica	22 Sep				
19.57i	Bogdan	Zdravkovic	SRB	27.3.99	1 NC-j	Beograd	27 Jan				

MEN 2018

Mark		Name		Nat	Born	Pos	Meet	Venue		Date
19.49		I'¢ason	Mahéras	GRE	17.11.00	2	NC-j	Tríkala		17 Ju
19.45		Triston	Gibbons	BAR	1.1.99	1		St. Michael		24 Jun
19.28i		Timo	Northoff (20)	GER	18.1.00	2		Halle		24 Feb
19.28i		Artem	Levchenko	UKR	3.9.99	2		Minsk		25 Feb

DISCUS

Mark			Name		Nat	Born	Pos	Meet	Venue		Date
69.72			Daniel	Ståhl	SWE	27.8.92	1	NC	Eskilstuna		26 Aug
						64.91	x	67.48	65.88	69.72	x
	69.11	1		Karlstad	25 Jul	x	x	66.31	69.11	x	x
	68.23	2	EC	Berlin	8 Aug	x	x	64.20	68.23	x	x
	68.12	1		Helsingborg	6 Jul	65.26	66.74	68.12	x	65.68	64.12
	68.03	2		Chula Vista	12 Apr	64.43	64.24	x	59.62	68.03	x
	68.00	1	vFIN	Tampere	1 Sep	68.00	62.70	x	65.92	65.86	x
69.67			Fedrick	Dacres	JAM	28.2.94	1	DL	Stockholm		10 Jun
						68.15	69.67	x	66.01	x	x
	68.84	1		Mona	8 Mar						
	68.67	1	VD	Bruxelles	31 Aug	68.67	67.34	x	x	67.24	x
	68.51	1	G Gala	Roma	31 May	66.69	68.51	65.68	64.99	66.37	67.01
	68.47	1	NACAC	Toronto	12 Aug	65.89	67.39	64.19	x	66.46	68.47
	68.35	1	Danek	Turnov	29 May	66.59	x	x	63.68	67.03	68.35
	68.20	1	CG	Gold Coast	13 Apr	65.55	66.09	68.20	67.14	67.51	65.00
	68.17	1	Hanz	Zagreb	4 Sep	64.33	x	65.11	65.21	x	68.17
	68.12	1	Sule	Tartu	3 Jun	67.72	x	68.12			
	68.08	1		Kingston	20 Jan	63.28	65+	67.31	?	68.08	x
	67.97	1	C.Cup	Ostrava	8 Sep	58.38	x	66.64	63.86	67.97	
69.59			Andrius	Gudzius	LTU	14.2.91	2	DL	Stockholm		10 Jun
						67.64	69.49	66.54	67.08	x	67.77
	69.30	1	Kuso	Chorzów	8 Jun	65.58	66.34	63.75	66.29	66.92	69.30
	69.13	1		Tartu	19 May	x	x	68.08	65.87	65.44	69.13
	69.04	1	Bisl	Oslo	7 Jun	x	67.41	69.04	x	69.00	65.04
	68.98	1		Vilnius	24 Apr	62.15	67.09	68.98	x	x	66.96
	68.98	1		Utena	2 Jun	67.77	68.07	x	67.15	x	68.98
	68.46	1	EC	Berlin	8 Aug	63.75	62.89	67.19	67.66	x	68.46
	68.17	2	G Gala	Roma	31 May	68.17	65.03	x	67.38	66.98	67.51
	67.82	1	ECCp	Birmingham	26 May	67.42	x	x	67.82		
68.98			Lukas	Weisshaidinger	AUT	20.2.92	1		Rehlingen		20 May
						x	58.29	68.57	x	68.98	x
	68.21	1		Santa Cruz de Tenerife	15 Apr	68.21	64.75	64.30	62.34	65.63	65.13
68.85			Ehsan	Hadadi	IRI	20.1.85	1		Chula Vista		12 Apr
						59.40	67.99	68.85	66.27	68.67	67.08
68.61			Reggie	Jagers	USA	13.8.94	1	NC	Des Moines		24 Jun
			(30/6)			63.54	61.70	66.92	x	68.61	x
67.72			Traves	Smikle	JAM	7.5.92	2		Kingston		20 Jan
						65.87	?	66.52	?	67.72	x
67.59			Christoph	Harting	GER	10.4.90	1		Schönebeck		18 May
						x	66.35	65.41	x	x	67.59
67.06			Mason	Finley	USA	7.10.90	2	NC	Des Moines		24 Jun
66.98			Martin	Wierig (10)	GER	10.6.87	2		Schönebeck		18 May
66.59			Daniel	Jasinski	GER	5.8.89	2	Danek	Turnov		29 May
66.51			Philip	Milanov	BEL	6.7.91	4	DL	Stockholm		10 Jun
66.51			Lois Maikel	Martínez	ESP	3.6.81	1		Castellón		4 Jul
66.32			Sam	Mattis	USA	10.3.94	1		Tucson		17 May
00.30			Mauricio	Ortega	COL	4.8.94	1	CAG	Barranquilla		29 Jul
66.22			Alin Alexandru	Firfirica	ROU	3.11.95	1		Zenica		6 Jun
66.05			Andrew	Evans	USA	25.1.91	1		Rathdrum		1 Jun
65.98			David	Wrobel	GER	13.2.91	3		Schönebeck		18 May
65.84			Simon	Pettersson	SWE	3.1.94	1		Malmö		20 Jun
65.78			Piotr	Malachowski	POL	7.6.83	1	NC	Lublin		21 Jul
			(20)								
65.66			Zoltán	Kövágó	HUN	10.4.79	1		Szombathely		26 Jul
65.53			Gudni Valur	Gudnason	ISL	11.10.95	1		Hafnarfjördur		9 Jul
65.48			Jason	Harrell	USA	10.1.91	1		Chula Vista		9 Jun
65.47			Chad	Wright	JAM	25.3.91	1		Schliffange		29 Jul
65.34			Rodney	Brown	USA	21.5.93	2		Rathdrum		1 Jun
65.27			Jorge	Fernández	CUB	2.10.87	2	CAG	Barranquilla		29 Jul
65.20			Victor	Hogan	RSA	25.7.89	1		Marseille		16 Jun
65.15			Robert	Urbanek	POL	29.4.87	1		Radom		27 May
65.13			Robert	Harting	GER	18.10.84	3	Kuso	Chorzów		8 Jun
64.75			Aleksey	Khudyakov	RUS	31.3.95	1		Sochi		7 Feb
			(30)								

Mark	Name		Nat	Born	Pos	Meet	Venue	Date	
64.67	Matthew	Denny	AUS	2.6.96	Q	CG	Gold Coast	12	Apr
64.46	Gerd	Kanter	EST	6.5.79	1	Skol	Cetniewo	8	Jul
64.37	Róbert	Szikszai	HUN	30.9.94	2		Szombathely	19	May
64.19	Giovanni	Faloci	ITA	13.10.85	1		Tarquinia	13	Jun
64.05	Lolassonn	Djouhan	FRA	18.5.91	1		Angoulème	1	Jun
63.99	Jared	Schuurmans	USA	20.8.87	5	NC	Des Moines	24	Jun
63.72	Martin	Kupper	EST	31.5.89	1		Tallinn	23	Jun
63.63	Jakob	Gardenkrans	SWE	15.8.97	3		Chula Vista	12	Apr
63.62	Nazzareno	Di Marco	ITA	30.4.85	2		Tarquinia	13	Jun
63.62	Apostolos	Parellis	CYP	24.7.85	8	EC	Berlin	8	Aug
	(40)								
63.56	Benn	Harradine	AUS	14.10.82	2	NC	Gold Coast	16	Feb
63.56	Erik	Cadée	NED	15.2.84	1		Leiden	9	Jun
63.55	Hannes	Kirchler	ITA	22.12.78	3		Tarquinia	13	Jun
63.55	Martin	Maric	CRO	19.4.84	1		Split	17	Jul
63.50	Henning	Prüfer	GER	7.3.96	1		Potsdam	13	Jun
63.45	János	Huszák	HUN	5.2.92	3	ECp-w	Leiria	10	Mar
63.34	Mykyta	Nesterenko	UKR	15.4.91	Q	EC	Berlin	7	Aug
63.30	Ola Stunes	Isene	NOR	29.1.95	1		Albufeira	5	Apr
63.28	Danijel	Furtula	MNE	31.7.92	2		Split	17	Jul
63.24	Martin	Markovic	CRO	13.1.96	1	ECp-w23	Leiria	10	Mar
	(50)								
63.23	Viktor	Butenko	RUS	10.3.93	1		Lisboa	25	Feb
63.17	Axel	Härstedt	SWE	28.2.87	2		Malmö	20	Jun
63.17	Nick	Percy	GBR	5.12.94	1		Bedford	7	Jul
63.13	Luke	Vaughn	USA	24.8.94	6	NC	Des Moines	24	Jun
62.97	Michael	Ohakwe	USA	20.7.92	4		Chula Vista	12	Apr
62.91	Ashmon	Lucas	USA	15.2.97	1		La Jolla	14	Apr
62.76	Federico	Apolloni	ITA	14.3.87	4		Tarquinia	13	Jun
62.36	Sven Martin	Skagestad	NOR	13.1.95	1		Hornnes	28	Jul
62.16	Masateru	Yugami	JPN	14.4.93	1	NC	Yamaguchi	24	Jun
62.04	Bartlomiej	Stój	POL	15.5.96	1	NC-23	Sieradz	1	Jul
	(60)								
62.03	Kristian	Ceh	SLO-J	17.2.99	2	Med G	Tarquinia	29	Jun
61.94	Brett	Morse	GBR	11.2.89	2		Manchester	15	Aug
61.82A	Behnam	Shiri	IRI	21.3.93	1		Tehran	18	Apr
61.72	Niklas	Arrhenius	SWE	10.9.82	5		Bottnaryd	16	Jun
61.68	Phillip	Jagers	USA	12.8.95	7	NC	Des Moines	24	Jun
61.54	Brian	Williams	USA	18.12.94	1		Baton Rouge	28	Apr
61.48	Domantas	Poska	LTU	10.1.96	2		Vilnius	24	Apr
61.42	Gleb	Sidorchenko	RUS	15.5.86	2	Znam	Zhukovskiy	30	Jun
61.34A	Mohammed	Samimi	IRI	29.3.87	1		Tehran	20	May
61.30	Ahmed Mohamed	Dheeb	QAT	29.9.85	1		Paarl	23	Jan
	(70)								
61.29	Greg	Thompson	GBR	5.5.94	1	Penn R	Philadelphia	28	Apr
61.15	Nikolay	Sedyuk	RUS	29.4.88	3	NC	Kazan	21	Jul
61.13	Marek	Bárta	CZE	8.12.92	1	Fla R	Gainesville	30	Mar
60.97	David	Lucas	USA	6.6.96	2	Penn R	Philadelphia	28	Apr
60.96	Julian	Wruck	AUS	6.7.91	3	NC	Gold Coast	16	Feb
60.91	Aleksandr	Dobrenshkiy	RUS	11.3.94	4	NC	Kazan	21	Jul
60.87	Reno	Tuufuli	USA	15.2.96	2	Big 10	Bloomington	13	May
60.83	Edujose	Lima	POR	2.3.96	2		Leiria	14	Jul
60.79	Mario	Cota	MEX	11.9.90	4	CAG	Barranquilla	29	Jul
60.77	Muhd Irfan	Shamsuddin	MAS	16.8.95	2		Merksem	1	Jul
	(80)								
60.76	Josh	Syrotchen	USA	19.4.94	1		St.Charles, MO	31	Mar
60.70	Aleksandr	Kirya	RUS	23.3.92	5	NC	Kazan	21	Jul
60.68	Torben	Brandt	GER	19.5.95	7		Schönebeck	18	May
60.67	Jordan	Young	CAN	21.6.93	1		Charlottesville	5	May
60.66	Tomás	Vonavka	CZE	4.6.90	1		Kladno	14	Jul
60.61	Wojciech	Praczyk	POL	10.1.93	1		Wiechlice	14	Apr
60.59	Roland	Varga	CRO	22.10.77	2		St Pölten	31	May
60.58	Jerimiah	Evans	USA	16.9.98	3	Big 10	Bloomington	13	May
60.57	Juan José	Caicedo	ECU	20.7.92	1		León	28	Jul
60.40	Mitch	Cooper	AUS	2.6.95	5	CG	Gold Coast	13	Apr
	(90)								
60.40	Clemens	Prüfer	GER	13.8.97	2	NC-23	Heilbronn	30	Jun
60.30A	Leif	Arrhenius	SWE	15.7.86	1		Provo	22	Sep
60.29	Viktor	Trus	BLR	11.11.96	1	NC	Minsk	20	Jul
60.26	Basil	Bingham	JAM	1.9.94	5	CAG	Barranquilla	29	Jul
60.19	Kord	Ferguson	USA	19.6.95	1		Auburn	21	Apr

MEN 2018

Mark	Name		Nat	Born	Pos	Meet	Venue	Date
60.11	Pyry	Niskala	FIN	6.11.90	1		Laihia	4 Jun
60.09	Francisco	Belo	POR	27.3.91	2		Leiria	15 Jul
60.09	Kadhem	Dagher	IRQ	29.11.95	2	AsiG	Jakarta	29 Aug
60.05	Kole	Weldon	USA	25.3.92	1		Lubbock	5 May
60.04	Filip	Mihaljevic	CRO	31.7.94	8	Hanz	Zagreb	4 Sep
(100)								

Mark	Name		Nat	Born	Date
60.00	Pawel	Pasinski	POL	6.3.93	12 May
59.95	Stephen	Mozia	NGR	16.8.93	12 Apr
59.93	Frank	Casañas	ESP	18.10.78	26 May
59.89	Ben	Hammer	USA	25.10.96	11 May
59.83	Giulio	Anesa	ITA	7.7.96	2 Jun
59.80	Yeóryios	Trémos	GRE	21.3.89	17 Jun
59.74	Frantz	Kruger	FIN	22.5.75	4 Jun
59.74	George	Armstrong	GBR	8.12.97	15 Aug
59.67	Jason	Morgan	JAM	6.10.82	28 Apr
59.66	Alex	Rose	SAM	7.11.91	21 Apr
59.64	Duke	Kicinski	USA	14.3.96	24 Mar
59.56	Dharamraj	Yadav	IND	26.1.91	26 Sep
59.45	Payton	Otterdahl	USA	2.4.96	19 Apr
59.44	Essa Mohammed	Al-Zankawi	KUW	14.10.92	29 Aug
59.42	Mesud	Pezer	BIH	27.8.94	12 Apr
59.41	Douglas	dos Reis	BRA	9.12.95	8 Jul
59.37	Maximilian	Klaus	GER	7.2.96	21 Jul
59.33	Marshall	Hall	NZL	7.10.88	4 Mar
59.32	Jan	Marcell	CZE	4.6.85	20 Jun
59.27	Irfan	Yildirim	TUR	26.7.88	15 Aug
59.21	Brett	Olsen	USA	30.8.92	5 May
59.15	John	Kolb	USA	9.12.97	12 May
59.15	Damian	Kaminski	POL	15.12.93	1 Jul
59.14	Aleksey	Sysoyev	RUS	8.8.85	21 Jul
59.02	János	Káplár	HUN	8.2.94	28 Jun
58.99	Raphaïl	Antoniou	CYP	4.8.95	9 Jun
59.04	Claudio	Romero	CHI-J	10.7.00	16 Nov
58.81	Denzel	Comenentia	NED	25.11.95	5 May
58.80	Tadej	Hribar	SLO-J	1.2.87	6 Jun
58.73	Richard	Cervantes	USA	16.6.95	30 Mar
58.69	Noah	Kennedy-White	USA	18.5.95	13 Apr
58.67	George	Evans	GBR	21.1.98	13 May
58.66	Kyle	Douglass	USA	3.11.95	11 May
58.65	Sebastian	Scheffel	GER	17.11.93	27 Jan
58.56	Georgios	Koniarakis	CYP-J	7.2.99	10 Jun
58.55	Ryan	Camp	USA	25.11.97	7 Apr
58.49A	Omid	Eivaz	IRI		20 May
59.92	Caspar	Hattink	NED	1.6.93	23 Jun
58.41	Moaaz Mohamed	Ibrahim	QAT-J	8.2.99	3 Mar
58.40	Hleb	Zhuk	BLR	24.3.98	5 Apr
58.40	Sam	Elsner	USA	20.12.94	24 May
58.39	Jordan	Guehaseim	FRA	16.6.97	13 Jun
58.37	Christian	Zimmermann	GER	9.7.94	24 Jun
58.33	Gian Piero	Ragonesi	ITA	19.4.95	23 Mar
58.30	Rafel	Vallery	GER	8.10.95	28 Apr
58.28	Kai	Schmidt	GER	11.2.93	13? May
58.27	El Bachir	Mbarki	MAR	9.3.96	2 May
58.23	Benedikt	Stienen	GER	12.1.92	8 Jul
58.22	Werner	Visser	RSA	27.2.98	2 Aug
58.20	Akeem	Stewart	TTO	4.7.92	18 Feb
58.18	Sergiu	Ursu	ROU	26.4.80	13 Jun
58.15	Ruslan	Valitov	UKR	24.2.97	26 Apr
58.15	Terrell	Adams	USA	19.3.98	28 Apr
58.15	Bryan	Burns	USA	21.2.95	6 May
58.15	Dennis	Valliulin	ISR	29.7.89	11 Jun
60.00	Justin	Ramirez	USA	3.11.93	15 Apr
(156)					

Drugs disqualification

58.10	Baljinder	Singh ¶	IND	23.7.89	28 Jun

Light implement

Mark	Name		Nat	Born	Pos		Venue	Date
69.83	Fedrick	Dacres	JAM	28.2.94	1		Kingston	10 Feb
				65.78	66.37	67.00	68.46 68.08 69.83	
58.75	Glendford	Watson	JAM	11.7.95	5		Kingston	10 Feb

JUNIORS

Mark	Name		Nat	Born	Pos	Meet	Venue	Date
62.03	Kristian	Ceh	SLO	17.2.99	2	Med G	Tarquinia	29 Jun
	61.98	q	Med G	Tarquinia	27 Jun	59.84	1	Zagreb	5 May
	61.11	4	BalkC	Stara Zagora	20 Jul	59.25	1	Ljubljana	24 Jun
58.94	Claudio	Romero	CHI	10.7.00	1		Santiago de Chile	16 Nov
58.80	Tadej	Hribar	SLO	1.2.87	3		Zenica	6 Jun
58.56	Georgios	Koniarakis	CYP	7.2.99	1		Jesolo	10 Jun
58.41	Moaaz Mohamed	Ibrahim	QAT	8.2.99	2		Split	3 Mar
57.96	Roje	Stona	JAM	26.2.99	5		Kingston	20 Jan
57.74	Yevgeniy	Bogutskiy	BLR	7.9.22	2		Talinn	25 Aug
57.66	Kai	Chang	JAM	29.1.00	2		Kingston	2 Jun
56.84	Gabriel	Oladipo	USA	17.4.99	2		Waco	21 Apr
56.69	Hossein	Rassouli	IRI	22.12.99	2		Tehran	10 Oct
56.50	Turner	Washington	USA	10.2.99	1		Tuscon	28 Apr
56.19	Sam	Welsh	USA	30.1.00	1		Manchester CT	21 Jul
56.11	Elijah	Mason	USA	19.1.99	2		Bellingham	00 Apr
55.81	Mario	Díaz	CUB	8.12.99	1		Las Tunas	9 Feb

1.75KG DISCUS

Mark	Name		Nat	Born	Pos	Meet	Venue	Date
66.47	Moaaz Mohamed	Ibrahim	QAT	8.2.99	1		Cape Town	3 Feb
	64.24	1		Al-Kuwait	6 Apr	64.19	2	Slovenska Bistrica	26 May
66.06	Kristjan	Ceh	SLO	17.2.99	1		Vyskov	16 Jun
	65.86	1		Leibnitz	6 May	63.91	1	Novo Mesto	4 Jul
	64.47	1		Slovenska Bistrica	26 May				
65.90	Georgios	Koniarakis	CYP	7.2.99	1		Tel Aviv	13 May
	63.94	1		Brest	28 Apr	10 performances by 4 men over 63.80			
64.76	Yevgeniy	Bogutskiy	BLR	7.9.22	2		Tel Aviv	13 Ma
63.77	Roje	Stona	JAM	26.2.99	1	Carifta	Nassau	31 Mar
62.87	Emanuel	Sousa	POR	4.4.99	1		Mannheim	23 Jun
62.66A	Hossein	Rassouli	IRI	22.12.99	1		Tehran	26 Apr
62.37	Mario	Díaz	CUB	8.12.99	1		La Habana	9 Jun
62.36	Kai	Chang	JAM	29.1.00	1	WJ	Tampere	15 Jul
61.78	Dabirac Miuguel	Pérez (10)	CUB	8.9.00	1		La Habana	19 May
61.15	Gabriel	Oladipo	USA	17.4.99	1	NC-j	Bloomington	17 Jun

Mark	Name		Nat	Born	Pos	Meet	Venue	Date
60.81	Claudio	Romero	CHI	10.7.00	3	WJ	Tampere	15 Jul
60.79	Elijah	Mason	USA	19.1.99	2	NC-j	Bloomington	17 Jun
60.41	Jakub	Lewoszewski	POL	7.2.00	1		Warszawa	1 Jul
60.38		Wang Yuhan	CHN	15.5.99	q	WJ	Tampere	14 Jul
60.34	Tim	Ader	GER	29.1.99	1		Neubrandenburg	12 May
60.10	Turner	Washington	USA	10.2.99	3	NC-j	Bloomington	17 Jun
59.49	Jakub	Forejt	CZE	13.7.00	1		Hradec Kralové	15 Sep
59.40A	Ignatius	Marais	RSA	4.3.99	1		Boksburg	27 Apr
59.31	Ángel	Álverez	CUB	25.2.00	3		Camagüey	27 Jun
59.25	Caspar	Jørgensen	DEN	11.4.99	1		København	26 Jun

1.62kg Discus

Mark	Name		Nat	Born	Pos	Meet	Venue	Date
64.62	Sam	Welsh	USA	30.1.00	1		Bowdoin	19 May

HAMMER

Mark	Name		Nat	Born	Pos	Meet	Venue	Date					
81.85	Wojciech	Nowicki	POL	22.2.89	1	Gyulai	Székesfehérvár	2 Jul					
				78.57	80.29	81.81-	78.44	x	81.85				
81.45	1		Gliwice	10 Jun	75.24	78.60	79.43	81.14	81.45	80.96			
80.63	1	Kuso	Chorzów	8 Jun	76.08	x	78.55	80.63	80.63	x			
80.26	1	NC	Lublin	20 Jul	x	77.93	79.59	79.34	80.26	77.16			
80.13	2	Skol	Cetniewo	8 Jul	x	80.07	78.72	80.13	79.14	78.92			
80.12	1	EC	Berlin	7 Aug	77.19	80.00	80.12	79.00	x	78.81			
79.41	1	PNG	Turku	5 Jun	76.89	79.41	x	77.66	x	x			
78.80	2		Forbach	27 May	x	78.28	x	78.80	x	78.22			
81.14	Pawel	Fajdek	POL	4.6.89	2	Gyulai	Székesfehérvár	2 Jul					
				4.6.89	x	80.41	78.97	x	76.82	81.14			
80.70	1		Halle	26 May	78.65	76.14	x	78.16	x	80.70			
80.57	1	Skol	Cetniewo	8 Jul	80.57	80.32	79.43	78.44	x	x			
80.14	2	NC	Lublin	20 Jul	x	72.68	x	x	x	80.14			
80.04	2	Kuso	Chorzów	8 Jun	x	x	- 78.92	x	80.04	78.66			
79.79	2		Gliwice	10 Jun	x	79.01	x	79.79	78.16	x			
79.71	1		Kielce	12 May	x	79.71	x	x	78.58	78.19			
79.57	1		Forbach	27 May	79.57	78.06	78.91	77.17	78.00	78.87			
79.44	1	Skol	Chorzów	22 Aug	x	75.42	76.70	77.05	78.63	79.44			
79.43	1		Coral Gables	7 Apr	76.86	x	78.10	79.43	77.45	79.08			
78.86	2	PNG	Turku	5 Jun	x	78.86	x	x	76.45	77.06			
78.69	2	EC	Berlin	7 Aug	78.69	x	x	x	78.34	76.02			
78.51	1		Osaka	20 May	x	74.89	88.51	77.98	77.72	x			
80.26	Nick	Miller	GBR	1.5.93	1	CG	Gold Coast	8 Apr					
				1.5.93	63.60	x	76.48	80.26	79.75	x			
78.29	1		Stanford	30 Mar	76.77	76.86	78.29	76.36	x	x			
79.57	Bence	Halász	HUN	4.8.97	1		Budapest	2 Jun					
				4.8.97	74.98	x	77.14	x	x	79.57			
78.66	2		Halle	26 May	78.66	75.58	76.58	77.17	x	78.61			
78.57	3	Gyulai	Székesfehérvár	2 Jul	76.99	78.08	76.75	78.57	75.66	78.32			
78.22	1	NC	Székesfehérvár	23 Jun	75.90	78.22	x	x	x	75.06			
78.59	Esref	Apak	TUR	3.1.82	1		Mersin	20 May					
				3.1.82	77.20	78.52	78.59	77.51					
78.39	1		Bursa	21 Apr	76.07	78.27	77.63	78.17	78.39	77.93			
78.18	Dilshod	Nazarov	TJK	6.5.82	3	Kuso	Chorzów	8 Jun					
	(30/6)												

Mark	Name		Nat	Born	Pos	Meet	Venue	Date
78.13	Sergey	Kolomoyets	BLR	11.8.89	1		Minsk	14 Apr
78.04	Gleb	Dudarov	BLR	17.10.96	1	Kans R	Lawrence	20 Apr
77.71	Mostafa	Al-Gamal	EGY	1.10.88	1	NC	El Maadi	11 Apr
77.37	Pavel	Boreysha (10)	BLR	16.2.91	1	4-N	Minsk	22 Jun
77.29	Yevgeniy	Korotovskiy	RUS	21.6.92	1		Adler	24 Feb
77.04	Ashraf Amjad	El-Seify	QAT	20.2.95	3	PNG	Turku	5 Jun
77.02	Denis	Lukyanov	RUS	14.7.89	1		Adler	14 Feb
77.00	Marcel	Lomnicky	SVK	6.7.87	4	Kuso	Chorzów	8 Jun
76.98	Quentin	Bigot	FRA	1.12.92	1		Metz	28 Jun
76.96	Sean	Donnelly	USA	1.4.93	1		Tucson	17 May
76.87	Humberto	Mansilla	CHI	22.5.96	1	SAmC-23	Cuenca	29 Sep
76.86	Eivind	Henriksen	NOR	14.9.90	5	EC	Berlin	7 Aug
76.84	Özkan	Baltaci	TUR	13.2.94	2		Mersin	20 May
76.81	Serghei	Marghiev (20)	MDA	6.11.92	1	NC	Chisinau	26 May
76.53	Mihaíl	Anastasákis	GRE	3.12.94	2		Nikíti	20 Jun
76.41	Denzel	Comenentia	NED	25.11.95	1	NCAA	Eugene	6 Jun
76.14	Alex	Young	USA	1.9.94	1	MSR	Torrance	19 Apr
76.13	Sergey	Litvinov	RUS	27.1.86	1		Adler	14 May
76.10	Javier	Cienfuegos	ESP	15.7.90	1	NC	Getafe	21 Jul

MEN 2018

Mark	Name		Nat	Born	Pos	Meet	Venue	Date	
75.96	Joaquin	Gómez	ARG	14.10.96	2	SAmC-23	Cuenca	29	Sep
75.86	Diego	del Real	MEX	6.3.94	4	C.Cup	Ostrava	9	Sep
75.79	Ivan	Tikhon	BLR	24.7.76	6	EC	Berlin	7	Aug
75.61	Aleksey	Sokirskiy	RUS	16.3.85	2		Adler	14	Feb
75.54	Nejc	Plesko	SLO	9.10.92	1		Zagreb	30	Jun
	(30)								
75.50	Hlib	Piskunov	UKR	25.11.98	1		Kyiv	4	Jul
75.47	Henri	Liipola	FIN	24.4.94	1		Kaustinen	30	Jun
75.11	Chris	Bennett	GBR	17.12.89	1		Brisbane (Nathan)	22	Mar
74.88	Matthew	Denny	AUS	2.6.96	2	CG	Gold Coast	8	Apr
74.88	Zakhar	Makhrosenko	BLR	10.10.91	2		Brest	8	Jun
74.79	Daniel	Roberts	USA	11.12.94	1		Ashland	28	Apr
74.75	Reinier	Mejías	CUB	22.9.90	1		La Habana	2	Jun
74.74	Oleg	Dubitskiy	BLR	14.10.90	1	NC	Minsk	21	Jul
74.71	Marco	Lingua	ITA	4.6.78	4		Nikíti	20	Jun
74.56	Wágner	Domingos	BRA	23.6.83	1		Slovenska Bistrica	26	May
	(40)								
74.55	Simone	Falloni	ITA	26.9.91	1		Lucca	28	Apr
74.51	Andrey	Romanov	RUS	19.9.94	3		Smolensk	29	May
74.46	Yuriy	Shayunov	BLR	22.10.87	2		Brest	27	Apr
74.43	Volodomyr	Myslyvchuk	UKR	25.4.96	1-u23		Nova Kakhovka	31	Mar
74.42	Serhiy	Reheda	UKR	6.2.94	1		Nova Kakhovka	31	Mar
74.33	Pedro José	Martin	ESP	12.8.92	2		Soria	16	Jun
74.31	Gabriel Enrique	Kehr	CHI	3.9.96	3	SAmC-23	Cuenca	29	Sep
74.19	Anders	Eriksson	SWE	22.3.94	1	SEC	Knoxville	11	May
74.06	Sukhrob	Khodjayev	UZB	21.5.93	3	AsiG	Jakarta	26	Aug
74.02	Roberto	Janet	CUB	29.8.86	1		La Habana	17	Feb
	(50)								
74.01	Bence	Pásztor	HUN	5.2.95	1		Székesfehérvár	7	Jun
73.90	Nikolay	Bashan	RUS	18.11.93	4		Adler	14	May
73.85	Rudy	Winkler	USA	6.12.94	1	Big 10	Bloomington	13	May
73.80	Joseph	Ellis	GBR	10.4.96	1		Ashland	5	Jun
73.71	Alaa El-Din	El-Ashry	EGY	6.1.91	2	NC-w	El Maadi	7	Sep
73.50	Daniel	Haugh	USA	3.5.95	1		Baton Rouge	28	Apr
73.48	Mergen	Mammedov	TKM	24.12.90	1		Almaty	30	Jun
73.46	David	Söderberg	FIN	11.8.79	1		Helsinki	29	Jul
73.45	Allan	Wolski	BRA	18.1.90	3		Slovenska Bistrica	26	May
73.26	António Vital e	Silva	POR	23.1.88	3	ECCp	Birmingham	27	May
	(60)								
73.24	Jake	Norris	GBR-J	30.6.99	3	NCAA	Eugene	6	Jun
73.16	Roberto	Sawyers	CRC	17.10.86	3	IbAmC	Trujillo	24	Aug
73.12	Mark	Dry	GBR	11.10.87	3	CG	Gold Coast	8	Apr
73.02	Alberto	González	ESP	1.6.98	1	NC-w	Montijo	3	Mar
73.01	Hassan Mohamed	Mahmoud	EGY	10.2.84	2	NC	El Maadi	11	Apr
72.98	Conor	McCullough	USA	31.1.91	5	NC	Des Moines	22	Jun
72.91	Ákos	Hudi	HUN	10.8.91	1		Szombathely	28	Jun
72.86	Matija	Greguric	CRO	17.9.96	1		Split	5	Mar
72.84	A.G.	Kruger	USA	18.2.79	1		Sioux Falls	5	May
72.81	Thomas	Mardal	NOR	16.4.97	1		Gävle	10	Aug
	(70)								
72.72	Adam	Keenan	CAN	26.3.93	3	NACAC	Toronto	12	Aug
72.65	Ilya	Terentyev	RUS	25.1.95	5		Adler	14	May
72.47	Morgan	Shigo	USA	1.2.96	6	NCAA	Eugene	6	Jun
72.37		Lee Yun-chul	KOR	28.3.82	1	NC	Jeongseon	26	Jun
72.31	Taylor	Campbell	GBR	30.6.96	2		Loughborough	20	May
72.29	Igor	Yevseyev	RUS	27.3.96	1	NC-w23	Adler	24	Feb
72.21	Abou	Serri Mohamed	EGY	20.2.91	3	NC	Cairo	27	Apr
72.16	Nikólaos	Gavriilídis	GRE	15.3.95	1		Kavála	18	Jul
72.11	Tuomas	Seppänen	FIN	16.5.86	1		Kurikka	15	Sep
72.09	Aaron	Kangas	FIN	3.7.97	2		Somero	25	May
	(80)								
72.08	Colin	Dunbar	USA	27.6.88	2		Long Beach	20	Apr
71.92	Adam	Kelly	USA	6.7.97	2		Princeton	6	Apr
71.67	Johannes	Bichler	GER	3.7.90	1	NC	Nürnberg	22	Jul
71.62	Osian	Jones	GBR	23.6.93	2		Brisbane (Nathan)	28	Mar
71.60	Hilmar Örn	Jónsson	ISL	6.5.96	1		Coral Gables	10	May
71.49		Wang Shizhu	CHN	20.2.89	10		Halle	26	May
71.34	Yasmani	Fernández	CUB	7.4.95	3		La Habana	17	Feb
71.34	Oscar	Vestlund	SWE	27.4.93	1		Arvika	29	Jul
71.33	Giacomo	Proserpio	ITA	22.4.97	1		Saronno	8	Jul

Mark	Name		Nat	Born	Pos	Meet	Venue	Date
71.29	AJ	McFarland	USA	17.3.96	8	NCAA	Eugene	6 Jun
	(90)							
71.22	Aleksandr	Shimanovich	BLR	9.2.98	1		Brest	25 May
70.88	Tristan	Schwandke	GER	23.5.92	2	NC	Nürnberg	22 Jul
70.87	Tommi	Remes	FIN	20.1.94	1		Joensuu	4 Jun
70.86	Roman	Zholudyev	BLR	8.1.96	2		Minsk	11 Jul
70.73	Arkadiusz	Rogowski	POL	30.3.93	1		Warszawa	3 Jun
70.72	Konstadínos	Kostoglídis	GRE	10.8.90	1		Thessaloníki	9 Jun
70.64	Kevin	Arreaga	ESP	23.10.95	3		Charlottesville	21 Apr
70.63	Kunihiro	Sumi	JPN	27.2.94	1	NC	Yamaguchi	22 Jun
70.62	Chris	Harmse	RSA	31.5.73	1	NC	Pretoria	16 Mar
70.47	Craig	Murch	GBR	27.6.93	4		Loughborough	25 Jul
	(100)							

70.36	Tshepang	Makhethe	RSA	19.2.96	3 May		68.95	Callum	Brown	GBR	20.7.94	12 May
70.32	Eslam	Mosaad	EGY	23.7.94	4 Aug		68.90	Balázs	Varga	HUN	30.1.98	28 Jun
70.24	Dempsey	McGuigan	IRL	30.8.93	2 Jul		68.90	Alexej	Mikhailov	GER	12.4.96	22 Jul
70.20	Miroslav	Pavlícek	CZE	31.3.87	26 Jun		68.82	Yushiro	Hosaka	JPN	16.10.91	15 Jul
70.15	Lukás	Melich	CZE	16.9.80	5 May		68.81	Ragnar	Carlsson	SWE-J	16.11.00	31 Aug
70.13	Yann	Chaussinand	FRA	11.5.98	25 Jul		68.80	Viorel Cristian	Ravar	ESP	3.10.95	24 May
70.12	Roope	Auvinen	FIN	17.2.98	22 Jun		68.79	Carel	Haasbroek	RSA	27.2.98	16 Mar
70.10	Peyman	Ghalenouei	IRI	29.1.92	18 Apr		68.77	Danyil	Danilov	RUS	5.1.98	6 Jun
70.06	Alisher	Eshbekov	TJK/RUS	31.5.90	24 Feb		68.76	Hristos	Frantzeskákis	GRE-J	26.4.00	28 Jul
70.06	Serhiy	Perevoznikov	UKR	7.4.95	10 Nov		68.75	Andriy	Martynyuk	UKR	25.9.90	26 May
70.02	Myhaylo	Kokhan	UKR-J	22.1.01	16 Feb		68.73	Frédéric	Pouzy	FRA	18.2.83	4 Jul
69.94	Igors	Sokolovs	LAT	17.8.74	12 May		68.70	Yeóryios	Korakídis	GRE	16.11.98	22 Jul
69.94	Ryota	Kashimura	JPN	13.8.91	22 Sep		68.69	Dário	Manso	POR	1.7.82	4 Jul
69.86	Jordan	Crayon	USA	15.8.94	5 Jun		68.68	Marco	Bortolato	ITA	11.2.94	27 Jan
69.73	Iván	Menglebéi	GRE	25.1.95	5 May		68.67	Renaldo	Frechou	RSA	4.3.92	19 Apr
69.73	Reza	Moghaddam	IRI	17.11.88	25 Oct		68.62	Igor	Vinichenko ¶	RUS	11.4.84	6 Jun
69.58	Yudai	Kimura	JPN	19.10.96	18 May		68.57	Kaveh	Mousavi	IRI	27.5.85	20 May
69.58	Petro	Vivcharuk	UKR	9.7.94	26 May		68.54	Ahmed Amgad	El-Seify	QAT	1.10.96	10 Mar
69.58	Ivan	Aksyonov	RUS	16.8.95	2 Jun		68.53	Grant	Cartwright	USA	19.11.94	22 Jun
69.58	Gary	Randolph	USA	2.5.93	6 Jun		68.52	Steffan	Stroh	USA	8.12.94	4 May
69.57	Brock	Eager	USA	26.5.96	31 Mar		68.51	Tom	Posterna	USA	17.7.03	4 May
69.52	Gleb	Volik	RUS	17.12.96	24 Feb		68.50	Markus	Kokkonen	FIN	17.5.95	8 Sep
69.52	Andreas	Sahner	GER	27.1.85	23 Jun		68.47	Pyotr	Nekiportes	RUS	6.5.97	24 Feb
69.46	Alexandros	Poursanides	CYP	23.1.93	5 May		68.44		Gong Shixian	CHN	24.8.96	1 Apr
69.45	Naoki	Uematsu	JPN	13.11.94	15 Sep		68.33	Igor	Buryi	RUS	8.4.93	14 Feb
69.39	Mattias	Lindberg	SWE	2.1.90	17 Jun		68.28	Jack	Dalton	AUS	20.5.94	8 Apr
69.32	Alan	Cumming	RSA	21.3.96	20 Feb		68.25	Erick	Loomis	USA	18.2.96	14 Apr
69.32	Michael	Shanahan	USA	5.12.94	14 Apr		68.23	Jac Lloyd	Palmer	GBR	13.3.96	2 Jun
69.19	Joe	Frye	USA	20.7.88	6 Apr		68.16	Paul	Hützen	GER	7.3.91	22 Jul
69.10		Qi Dakai	CHN	23.5.87	1 Apr		68.04	Maksim	Mikhalap	BLR	12.1.94	11 Feb
69.05	Erik	Escobedo	USA	12.4.96	11 May		68.04	Maksim	Mitskov	BLR	1.12.95	8 Jun
69.03	Nikolay	Bryl	BLR	30.11.97	25 May		68.04	Ryan	McCullough	IRL	21.4.89	25 Jun
69.00	Yevgeniy	Ivanov	BLR	11.6.92	11 Feb			(166)				

JUNIORS

73.24	Jake	Norris	GBR	30.6.99	3	NCAA		Eugene	6 Jun
	72.70	1			Tempe		23 Mar	70.98	1	Lafayette	16 Mar
	72.64	2			Baton Rouge		28 Apr	70.04	1	Baton Rouge	7 Apr
	71.72	1			Baton Rouge		21 Apr	69.07	4	SEC	Knoxville	11 May
	71.06	2			Austin		29 Mar	10 performances by 2 men over 69.50			
70.02	Myhaylo	Kokhan	UKR-Y	22.1.01	12	NC-w23		Mukachevo	16 Feb
68.81	Ragnar	Carlsson	SWE	16.11.00	5	vFIN		Tampere	31 Aug
68.76	Hristos	Frantzeskákis	GRE	26.4.00	1	NC-23		Lárisa	28 Jul
67.64	Ashish	Jakhar	IND	5.1.99	1			Patiala	8 Mar
67.09	Miguel Alberto	Zamora	CUB	25.1.99	3			Las Tunas	10 Feb
67.00	Donát	Varga	HUN	8.4.00	4			Szombathely	19 May
65.74	Alencar	Pereira	BRA	18.2.99	4	NC		Bragança Paulista	14 Sep
65.73	Myhaylo	Havrylyuk	UKR	19.10.99	4	NC-w23		Mukachevo	16 Feb
65.67	Georgio	Olivieri (10)	ITA	5.11.00	4	NC		Pescara	9 Sep
65.08	Lasha	Gurgenidze	GEO	5.10.99	2			Tbilisi	20 May

6 KG HAMMER

81.32	Hristos	Frantzeskákis	GRE	26.4.00	1			Tripolí		5 May
	80.05	1			Halle		26 May	10 performances by 4 men over 77.70		
80.65	Jake	Norris	GBR	30.6.99	1	WJ		Tampere		13 Jul
	80.45	1	NC-j	Bedford		16 Jun	79.15	1	Eton	1 Jul
	80.28	1		Mannheim		23 Jun	78.91	1	Manchester	15 Aug
	79.55	1		Baton Rouge		7 Apr	10 performances by 4 men over 78.50		
79.68	Myhaylo	Kokhan	UKR-Y	22.1.01	2	WJ		Tampere		13 Jul
78.76	Miguel	Zamora	CUB	25.1.99	1			La Habana		9 Jun
77.71	Myhaylo	Havrylyuk	UKR	19.10.99	3	WJ		Tampere		13 Jul
77.62	Ragnar	Carlsson	SWE	16.11.00	4	WJ		Tampere		13 Jul

MEN 2018

HAMMER

Mark	Name	Nat	Born	Pos	Meet	Venue	Date
77.21	Georgio Olivieri	ITA	5.11.00	1		San Benedetto del Tronto	16 Sep
76.86	Ashish Jakhar	IND	5.1.99	1	Asi-J	Gifu	7 Jun
75.99	Hugo Tavernier	FRA	1.12.99	5	WJ	Tampere	13 Jul
75.43	Donát Varga (10)	HUN	8.4.00	1		Miskolc	10 Jun
74.54	Julio Nóbile	ARG-Y	5.11.01	1		Buenos Aires	8 Dec
74.34	Fabio Hessling	GER	17.9.99	1		Rostock	28 Jul
74.08	Damneet Singh	IND	10.3.00	2	Asi-J	Gifu	7 Jun
73.75	Bayley Campbell	GBR	24.6.00	1		Loughborough	22 Apr
73.64	Valentin Andreyev	BUL-Y	19.1.02	2	Balk-J	Istanbul	21 Jun
73.35	Earwyn Abdou	FRA	30.6.99	1		Salon-de-Provence	13 Jun
73.06	Denis Shabasov	BLR	27.3.00	1		Novopolotsk	23 Nov
72.50	Mihaita Micu	ROU	27.9.99	1	NC-wj	Bucuresti	21 Mar
72.30	Kostadínos Záltos	GRE	5.2.00	2J		Trípoli	5 May
72.00	Lasha Gurgenidze (20)	GEO	5.10.99	1		Tbilisi	6 May
71.90	Sergey Zverev	RUS-Y	13.4.01	1		Maykop	21 May

12 lb (5.44kg) Hammer

Mark	Name	Nat	Born	Pos	Meet	Venue	Date
73.97	Michael Feldman	USA	22.11.99	1		Princeton	16 Jul
72.77	Jordan Geist	USA	21.7.98	1	N.Sch	Greensboro	17 Jun

JAVELIN

Mark	Name	Nat	Born	Pos	Meet	Venue	Date	Series
92.70	Johannes Vetter	GER	26.3.93	1	ECp-w	Leiria	11 Mar	x 85.57 88.28 84.29 92.70 82.80
91.56				2	DL	Doha	4 May	91.56 89.74 x 83.97 84.78 84.24
91.22A				1		Potchefstroom	27 Feb	84.38 87.11 p 85.17 91.22 83.13
89.34				2	Pre	Eugene	25 May	x 88.37 89.34 80.74 x x
87.83				3	NC	Nürnberg	22 Jul	84.69 x x x 87.83 x
92.06	Andreas Hofmann	GER	16.12.91	1		Offenburg	2 Jun	89.70 85.31 92.06 87.49 87.23 87.92
91.44				1		Rehlingen	20 May	91.44 86.60 86.20 x x 83.10
91.44				1	WK	Zürich	30 Aug	81.10 85.96 91.44 x p 85.95
90.08				3	DL	Doha	4 May	78.61 87.14 90.08 84.54 87.34 x
89.82				1	DL	Birmingham	18 Aug	85.10 89.82 85.51 p p 80.94
89.55				1	NC	Nürnberg	22 Jul	89.55-84.54 85.76 82.71 82.74 84.41
88.58				2	DL	Rabat	13 Jul	87.11 88.58 x x 79.17 x
88.48				1		Jena	30 Jun	88.48 x 81.94 x 80.36 82.06
87.60				2	EC	Berlin	9 Aug	85.61 87.60 x x x 85.48
91.78	Thomas Röhler	GER	30.9.91	1	DL	Doha	4 May	80.64 91.78 x 84.18 x 85.70
90.75				1		Dessau	8 Jun	82.57 x 86.08 82.11 86.81 90.75
89.88				1	Pre	Eugene	25 May	x 84.82 x 89.88 x x
89.47				1	EC	Berlin	9 Aug	x 88.02 89.47 87.58 p 87.90
88.09				2	NC	Nürnberg	22 Jul	x 80.14 83.97 x x 88.09
89.75	Magnus Kirt	EST	10.4.90	1	DL	Rabat	13 Jul	84.80 83.50 83.47 84.46 x 89.75
88.73				1	PNG	Turku	5 Jun	x 88.73 x 80.67 x 85.90
88.45				1	Sule	Tartu	3 Jun	88.45 78.45 p p p x
88.43				1		Kohila	7 Sep	88.43 78.15 85.90 82.89 80.75 85.58
88.28				1	NC	Tallinn	28 Jul	82.17 88.28 79.65 79.93 84.57 x
89.02	Jakub Vadlejch	CZE	10.10.90	1	Odlozil	Praha	4 Jun	85.20 89.02 x 86.06 84.58 x
88.94				1	PTS	Šamorin	29 Jun	x 83.30 88.94 x 83.07 x
88.76				2		Rehlingen	20 May	88.76 x 83.42 x x x
88.36				1	GS	Ostrava	13 Jun	x 88.30 83.80 87.09 84.15 81.98
88.06	Neeraj Chopra	IND	24.12.97	1	AsiG	Jakarta	27 Aug	83.46 x 88.06 83.25 86.36 X
88.02	Oliver Helander (30/7)	FIN	1.1.97	1		Pietersaari	7 Jul	88.02 p p p p p
86.63	Julian Weber	GER	29.8.94	2	DL	Birmingham	18 Aug	
86.37	Alexandru Novac	ROU	24.3.97	1		Nembro	5 Jul	
85.46	Paraskevás Batzávalis (10)	GRE/CYP	25.11.94	1		Trípoli	5 May	
85.38	Dmitriy Tarabin	RUS	29.10.91	1		Zhukovskiy	13 Jun	
85.32	Marcin Krukowski	POL	14.6.92	5	WK	Zürich	30 Aug	
85.17	Bernhard Seifert	GER	15.2.93	3		Offenburg	2 Jun	
84.96	Keshorn Walcott	TTO	2.4.93	1	NC	Port of Spain	23 Jun	
84.80	Rolands Strobinders	LAT	14.4.92	1		Ventspils	2 Jun	
84.60	Cheng Chao-Tsun	TPE	17.10.93	1		Karlstad	21 Jul	
84.43	Adrian Mardare	MDA	20.6.95	2	Odlozil	Praha	4 Jun	
83.89	Gatis Cakss	LAT	13.6.95	1		Riga	29 May	
83.85	Petr Frydrych	CZE	13.1.88	1	NC	Kladno	29 Jul	
83.85	Cyprian Mrzyglód (20)	POL	2.2.98	Q	EC	Berlin	8 Aug	

Mark	Name		Nat	Born	Pos	Meet	Venue	Date
83.71	Ahmed Bader	Magour	QAT	3.3.96	7	DL	Doha	4 May
83.63	Hamish	Peacock	AUS	15.10.90	1		Hobart	5 Jan
82.82	Anderson	Peters	GRN	21.10.97	1	NCAA	Eugene	6 Jun
82.67	Edis	Matusevicius	LTU	30.6.96	3		Ogre	15 Jun
82.64	Tero	Pitkämaki	FIN	19.12.82	2		Vantää	26 May
82.59	Antti	Ruuskanen	FIN	21.2.84	2		Joensuu	4 Jul
82.46A		Ma Qun	CHN	8.2.94	1		Guiyang	15 Jun
82.36	Tanel	Laanmäe	EST	29.9.89	1		Kladno	14 Jul
82.30	Vitezslav	Vesely	CZE	27.2.83	2		Radom	27 May
82.28	Shivpal	Singh	IND	6.7.95	1	I-State	Guwahati	28 Jun
	(30)							
82.22		Liu Qizhen	CHN	17.9.95	2	AsiG	Jakarta	27 Aug
82.05	Pavel	Meleshko	BLR	24.11.92	4		Rehlingen	20 May
81.45	David	Carreón	MEX	23.3.94	1		Tucson	17 May
81.44	Jaroslav	Jílek	CZE	22.10.89	3	Odlozil	Praha	4 Jun
81.40A	Arley	Ibargüen	COL	4.12.82	1		Cali	14 Apr
81.22	D.G.Sampath	Ranasinghe	SRI	1.9.88	1		Diyagama	27 Jan
81.06	Bartosz	Osewski	POL	20.3.91	2		Warszawa	14 Jul
80.91A	Julius	Yego	KEN	4.1.89	1	NC	Nairobi	21 Jun
80.91	Sindri Hrafn	Gudmundsson	ISL	21.11.95	4		Jena	30 Jun
80.83	Ryohei	Arai	JPN	23.6.91	1	3-N	Sapporo	8 Jul
	(40)							
80.75	Arshad	Nadeem	PAK	2.1.97	3	AsiG	Jakarta	27 Aug
80.64	Odel	Jainaga	ESP	14.10.97	1		Castellón	17 Feb
80.64	Dawid	Kosciów	POL	5.6.90	3	NC	Lublin	20 Jul
80.63	Rajender	Singh	IND	5.4.86	2	I-State	Guwahati	28 Jun
80.55	Yuriy	Kushniruk	UKR	6.12.94	1	NC	Lutsk	19 Jul
80.44	Vedran	Samac	SRB	22.1.90	1		Sremska Mitrovica	17 Jun
80.33	Ioánnis	Kiriazis	GRE	19.1.96	2	SEC	Knoxville	11 May
80.26	Norbert	Rivasz-Tóth	HUN	6.5.96	2	ECp-w23	Leiria	11 Mar
80.25A	Johannes	Grobler	RSA	6.8.97	1		Pretoria	2 Mar
80.24	Roberto	Bertolini	ITA	9.10.85	1		Trieste	14 Jul
	(50)							
80.21	Nicolás	Quijera	ESP	24.6.96	2	NCAA	Eugene	6 Jun
80.18	Takuto	Kominami	JPN	26.7.95	1		Osaka	23 Sep
80.04	Vipin	Kasana	IND	4.8.89	2		Patiala	27 Feb
79.93		Huang Shih-Feng	TPE	2.3.92	3		Osaka	20 May
79.92	Mart	ten Berge	NED	27.4.91	3	ECp-w	Leiria	11 Mar
79.90	Shakiel	Waithe	TTO	10.6.95	1		Port of Spain	18 Feb
79.89	Jiannis	Smaliós	SWE	17.2.87	1		Bålsta	12 May
79.83	Phil-Mar	van Rensburg	RSA	23.6.89	4	CG	Gold Coast	14 Apr
79.73	Carlos	Armenta	MEX	5.9.87	2		Tucson	17 May
79.56	Skirmantas	Simoliunas	LTU	13.3.94	5		Ogre	15 Jun
	(60)							
79.46A		Zhu Kai	CHN	24.8.98	3		Guiyang	15 Jun
79.44	Ayumu	Ishiyama	JPN	2.6.96	1		Kitakyushu	27 Oct
79.42	Lukasz	Grzeszczuk	POL	3.3.90	5		Riga	29 May
79.42	Gen	Naganuma	JPN	31.3.98	1		Tama	27 Oct
79.41	Tim	Herman	BEL	19.10.90	1		Sint-Niklaas	20 Oct
79.16	Amit	Kumar	IND	18.9.92	2		Patiala	6 Mar
79.15	Emin	Öncel	TUR	1.5.97	1		Mersin	6 May
79.15	Vladislav	Panasenkov	RUS	22.5.96	1		Smolensk	7 Jun
79.07	Capers	Williamson	USA	13.10.92	5		Jena	30 Jun
78.89	R.M.Sumedha	Ranasinghe	SRI	10.2.91	1		Colombo	29 Oct
	(70)							
78.86	Toni	Keränen	FIN	16.6.98	2	NC	Jyväskylä	22 Jul
78.77	Takuma	Nakanishi	JPN	8.4.94	1		Ise	8 Jul
78.65A	Leslain	Baird	GUY	5.5.87	2	SAmG	Cochabamba	6 Jun
78.57A	Braian	Toledo	ARG	8.9.93	3	SAmG	Cochabamba	6 Jun
78.53	George	Zaharia	ROU	3.8.95	1		Poiana Brasov	9 Jun
78.52	Michael	Shuey	USA	2.2.94	3		Tucson	17 May
78.45	Toni	Kuusela	FIN	21.1.94	4		Lappeenranta	23 Aug
78.44	Piotr	Lebioda	POL	28.5.92	3		Warszawa	19 May
78.44	Jami	Kinnunen	FIN	31.3.95	2		Espoo	13 Jun
78.38	Lassi	Etelätalo	FIN	30.4.88	3		Vantää	26 May
	(80)							
78.30	Rafal	Gierek	POL	24.2.96	3		Kladno	14 Jun
78.25	Patrik	Zenúch	SVK	30.12.90	3	PTS	Šamorin	29 Jun
78.20	Benjamin	Langton-Burnell	NZL	10.7.92	2		Gold Coast	18 Feb
78.20	Valeriy	Izotov	BLR	12.4.97	3	4-N	Minsk	22 Jun
78.19	Hubert	Chmielak	POL	19.6.89	1		Bialogard	2 Jun

Mark	Name		Nat	Born	Pos	Meet	Venue	Date
78.10	Albert	Reynolds	LCA	28.3.88	Q	CG	Gold Coast	13 Apr
78.10	Patriks	Gailums	LAT	10.5.98	14q	EC	Berlin	8 Aug
78.07	Markim	Felix	GRN	8.10.97	3	TTO Ch	Port of Spain	23 Jun
78.04	Lars	Timmermann	NED	19.4.91	1		Amsterdam	12 May
77.94	Ansis	Bruns	LAT	30.3.89	3		Ventspils	2 Jun
	(90)							
77.88	Janis Svens	Griva	LAT	23.4.93	2		Jelgava	17 Jun
77.84	Mauro	Fraresso	ITA	13.1.93	1		Rieti	25 Feb
77.64	Kenji	Ogura	JPN	8.6.95	2	Oda	Hiroshima	29 Apr
77.59	Anro	van Eeden	RSA-J	19.5.99	1		Paarl	6 Apr
77.52	Shoji	Toyota	JPN	13.1.98	1		Nagoya	14 Jul
77.49	Aaron	True	USA	7.11.95	1		Cincinnati	13 May
77.44	Cruz	Hogan	AUS	22.2.94	2		Sydney	17 Mar
77.43	Luke	Cann	AUS	17.7.94	Q	CG	Gold Coast	13 Apr
77.41		Bae You-il	KOR	16.6.94	1		Iksan	16 Oct
77.33	Tatsuya	Sakamoto	JPN	4.5.96	2	NC	Yamaguchi	23 Jun
	(100)							
77.33	Dmytro	Sheremet	UKR	19.11.92	2	NC	Lutsk	19 Jul

Mark	Name		Nat	Born	Date
77.27	Valeriy	Iordan	RUS	14.2.92	30 May
77.21	Joshua	Robinson	AUS	4.10.85	18 Feb
77.13	Kim	Amb	SWE	31.7.90	25 Aug
77.08A	Tobie	Holtzhausen	RSA	25.5.87	23 Feb
77.02	Kazunori	Yagi	JPN	31.1.94	26 Aug
76.94	Teo	Takala	FIN	6.6.94	22 Jul
76.91	Matviy	Krutiyenko	UKR	25.11.96	19 Jul
76.91A	Francisco	Muse	CHI	9.4.96	30 Sep
76.67	Yoshihiro	Nakajima	JPN	12.3.93	22 Jun
76.59	Osmani	Laffita	CUB	14.8.94	9 Jun
76.48	Nils	Fischer	GER	18.10.97	5 May
76.48A	Alex	Kiprotich	KEN	10.10.94	21 Jun
76.42	Abhishek	Singh	IND	20.5.95	28 Sep
76.34	Erki	Leppik	EST	18.3.88	14 Jul
76.33	Genki	Dean	JPN	30.12.91	23 Sep
76.32	Bobur	Shokirjanov	UZB	5.12.90	2 Jun
76.32A	Pedro Luiz	Barros	BRA	16.7.97	30 Sep
76.25	Roman	Klem	GER	17.8.96	22 Jul
76.19	Dagbjartur Dadi	Jónsson	ISL	13.11.97	29 Jun
76.16		Zhi Qiang	CHN	20.2.94	15 Sep
76.06A	Jaime Dayron	Márquez	COL	11.6.83	14 Apr
76.05	Unmet	Degirmenci	TUR	23.7.98	13 May
76.02	Curtis	Thompson	USA	8.2.96	11 Aug
76.02		Park Won-kil	KOR	24.2.90	17 Oct
75.99	Andrey	Doroshev	RUS	17.3.95	20 Jul
75.96	Atsushi	Kawano	JPN	6.1.97	16 Sep
75.92	Jani	Karvinen	FIN	7.2.94	19 Aug
75.92	Jaako	Hauta-aho	FIN	10.1.97	6 Sep
75.90	Teemu	Narvi	FIN-J	2.7.00	6 Sep
75.89	Stephen	Rice	IRL	11.1.96	19 Jul
75.87	Davinder	Singh	IND	18.12.88	11 Feb
75.83A		Hu Haoran	CHN	28.9.98	15 Jun
75.81	Anand	Haveri	IND	19.2.89	19 Sep
75.78	Aleksey	Kotkovets	BLR	7.6.98	21 Jul
75.76	Maximilian	Slezák	SVK	2.7.96	29 Jun
75.73	Ravinder	Singh Khaira	IND	19.3.86	19 Jul
75.72	Isak	Oskarsson	SWE	2.3.96	3 Aug
75.69	Samuel Kure	Adams	NGR	12.8.94	5 Aug
75.60	Pradeep	Lakmal	SRI	16.5.94	15 Sep
75.66		Long Zexuan	CHN	8.9.94	15 Sep
75.63	Bilal	Nouali	MAR	26.9.94	6 May
75.61	Yuta	Sakiyama	JPN	5.4.96	7 Apr
75.52	Dejan	Mileusnic	BIH	16.11.91	30 Mar
75.49	Krystian	Bondarenko	POL	22.10.91	20 Jul
75.46	David	Ocampo	MEX	14.2.92	14 Apr

Mark	Name		Nat	Born	Date
75.43	Niu Heqing		CHN	16.4.97	15 Sep
75.41	Daan	Meijer	NED	17.2.83	24 Jun
75.41	Manu	Quijera	ESP	13.1.98	21 Jul
75.39	Kensei	Hanada	JPN	14.4.96	15 Jun
75.38	Sahil	Silwal	IND-J	17.12.00	28 Sep
75.36	Branko	Paukovic	SRB	28.5.91	7 Apr
75.35	Shu	Mori	JPN	14.11.96	29 Apr
75.35	Mateusz	Kwasniewski	POL	16.7.95	20 Jul
75.31	Nash	Lowis	AUS-J	6.11.99	14 Jul
75.27	Ismet	Pekbak	TUR-J	10.6.99	27 May
75.27	James	Whiteaker	GBR	8.10.98	18 Aug
75.20	Rocco	van Rooyen	RSA	23.12.92	22 Mar
75.20A	Erich	Wiese	RSA	1.6.97	27 Apr
75.16	Rhys	Stein	AUS	15.5.96	18 Sep
75.14	Jonas	Bonewit	GER	30.7.95	3 Feb
75.10	Riley	Dolezal	USA	16.11.85	23 Jun
75.08	Ivan	Filippov	RUS	28.8.96	7 Jun
75.07	William	White	AUS	27.11.95	18 Feb
75.04	Matija	Kranjc	SLO	12.6.84	21 Jul
75.00	Liam	O'Brien	AUS	13.4.96	14 Dec
74.98	Yarovis	Contreras	CUB-J	25.8.00	16 Mar
74.96	Tadahiro	Nishiyama	JPN	.96	23 Aug
74.95	Akito	Aragaki	JPN	28.7.91	23 Jan
74.80	Masaaki	Michiue	JPN	17.12.94	17 Mar
74.76	Mark	Slavov	BUL	17.3.94	4 Aug
74.63	Chris	Carper	USA	19.4.92	1 Jul
74.61	Vladislav	Polyunin	UZB	4.12.98	19 May
74.47	Simon	Litzell	SWE	11.2.97	25 Aug
74.40	Jani	Kiiskilä	FIN	28.12.89	22 Jul
74.39	Aleksandr	Kozlowski	BLR	6.2.95	7 Jun
74.34	Ivan	Zaytsev	UZB	7.11.88	29 Sep
74.32	Nikolay	Orlov	RUS-J	7.1.99	6 Feb
74.29	Hernu	van Vuuren	RSA	15.4.98	27 Apr
74.29	Abhishek	Drall	IND	11.5.98	27 Nov
74.28	Taneli	Juutinen	FIN	25.10.94	4 Jul
74.26	Taran	Taylor	USA-J	1.2.99	13 May
74.25	Boris	Bezdolniy	RUS	1.4.97	7 Jul
74.22	Waruna Lakshan	Dayarathne	SRI	14.5.88	5 Aug
74.18	Mykola	Kalyush	UKR	12.8.87	11 Mar
74.18	Edgar	Jara	PAR	8.1.93	17 Mar
74.16	Majid Mohsen Ali	Al-Badri	EGY	29.9.95	27 Apr
74.17	Antonio	Fent	ITA	31.1.88	8 Sep
74.14	Ilya	Shapovalov	RUS	16.1.94	6 Feb
74.11	Joe	Harris	GBR	23.5.97	11 Mar
	(190)				

JUNIORS

Mark	Name		Nat	Born	Pos	Meet	Venue	Date
77.59	Anro	van Eeden	RSA	19.5.99	1		Paarl	6 Apr
75.90	Teemu	Narvi	FIN	2.7.00	2		Kuortane	6 Sep
75.15		1	Pihtipudas	28 Jun	74.64	1	Nordic-j Hvidovre	12 Aug
74.95		6	Lappeenranta	23 Aug				
75.38	Sahil	Silwal	IND	17.12.00	3	NC	Bhubaneswar	28 Sep
74.88		8	Kuortane	23 Jun	10 performances by 6 men over 74.50			
75.31	Nash	Lowis	AUS	6.11.99	1	WJ	Tampere	14 Jul
75.27	Ismet	Pekbak	TUR	10.6.99	1		Ekisehir	27 May
74.98	Yarovis	Contreras	CUB	25.8.00	1	Fortún	Camagüey	16 Mar
74.32	Nikolay	Orlov	RUS	7.1.99	1		Sochi	6 Feb
74.26	Taran	Taylor	USA	1.2.99	2		Cincinnati	13 May

Mark	Name		Nat	Born	Pos	Meet	Venue	Date
73.93	Kristjan	Jaunpujens	LAT	6.6.99	1q	WJ	Tampere	13 Jul
73.76	Tzuriel	Pedigo (10)	USA	9.1.00	2	WJ	Tampere	14 Jul
73.61	Leandro	Ramos	POR	21.9.00	1		Vagos	24 Feb
73.44	Maurice	Voigt	GER	8.9.00	3	WJ	Tampere	14 Jul
73.30	Tim	Egbers	NED	11.11.99	1		Vught	2 Apr
73.02	Pedro	Rodrigues	BRA	18.6.99	1		Bragança Paulista	22 Jun
72.73		Liu Zhekai	CHN	18.8.00	5		Zhuzhou	18 Apr
72.47	Domítrios	Tsítsos	GRE	27.9.00	1		Thessaloníki	17 Mar
72.07	Kirill	Fomenko	RUS	6.1.99	2	NC-j	Chelyabinsk	23 Jun
71.62	Krisjanis	Suntazs	LAT	19.12.00	1		Saldus	21 Jun
71.57		Song Qingshu	CHN	23.12.00	7		Zhuzhou	18 Apr
71.47	Arshdeep	Singh (20)	IND	5.4.99	1		Colombo	5 May

INDOOR HEPTATHLON

Mark	Name		Nat	Born	Pos	Meet	Venue	Date
6348	Kevin	Mayer	FRA	10.2.92	1	WI	Birmingham	3 Mar
	6.85	7.55	15.67	2.02	7.83	5.00	2:39.64	
6343	Damian	Warner	CAN	4.11.89	2	WI	Birmingham	3 Mar
	6.74	7.39	14.90	2.02	7.67	4.90	2:37.12	
6265	Maicel	Uibo	EST	27.12.92	3	WI	Birmingham	3 Mar
	7.20	7.41	14.30	2.17	8.19	5.30	2:38.51	
6238	Kai	Kazmirek	GER	28.1.91	4	WI	Birmingham	3 Mar
	7.15	7.68	14.55	2.05	7.95	5.20	2:42.15	
6188	Tim	Duckworth	GBR	18.6.96	1	NCAA	College Station	10 Mar
	6.84	7.74	13.59	2.17	8.23	5.16	2:56.23	
6090	Hunter	Veith	USA	14.1.95	2	NCAA	College Station	10 Mar
	6.90	7.54	13.39	2.08	7.99	4.76	2:43.33	
6081	Tyler	Adams	USA	11.2.96	3	NCAA	College Station	10 Mar
	6.99	7.38	12.12	2.20	7.97	4.56	2:36.14	
6043	Zach	Ziemek	USA	23.2.93	1		Lincoln NE	3 Feb
	6.89	7.10	14.02	2.03	8.08	5.27	2:49.95	
6021	Jan	Dolezal	CZE	6.6.96	1	NC	Praha (Strom)	11 Feb
	7.01 (10)	7.59	14.31	1.99	7.96	4.90	2:49.42	
6016	Oleksiy	Kasyanov	UKR	26.8.85	1		Aubière	14 Jan
	6.92	7.45	13.78	2.02	7.80	4.66	2:46.22	
6014	Ruben	Gado	FRA	13.12.93	1	v4Nat	Madrid	28 Jan
	6.99	7.33	12.91	2.00	8.32	5.30	2:40.96	
5997	Eelco	Sintnicolaas	NED	7.4.87	5	WI	Birmingham	3 Mar
	6.96	7.15	14.09	1.90	7.97	5.30	2:45.93	
5988	Johannes	Erm	EST	26.3.98	4	NCAA	College Station	10 Mar
	7.11	7.64	13.77	1.99	8.38	4.96	2:39.45	
5980	Samuel	Remédios	POR	24.2.92	1	NC	Pombal	11 Feb
	6.92	7.52	13.70	2.03	7.98	5.00	2:57.33	
5979	Jorge	Ureña	ESP	8.10.93	1		Valencia	22 Dec
	6.99	7.31	14.13	2.01	7.99	4.80	2:44.57	
5973	Dominik	Distelberger	AUT	16.3.90	1	NC	Wien	4 Feb
	6.93	7.40	12.84	1.95	7.96	4.90	2:40.42	
5951	Adam Sebastian	Helcelet	CZE	27.10.91	2	NC	Praha (Strom)	11 Feb
	7.05	7.41	14.65	2.05	7.97	4.60	2:48.98	
5951	Martin	Roe	NOR	1.4.92	1		Sandnes	4 Mar
	6.92	7.81	15.71	1.90	8.43	4.80	2:51.03	
5935A	Jeremy	Taiwo	USA	15.1.90	1	NC	Albuquerque	17 Feb
	7.15 (20)	7.10	12.75	2.10	8.19	5.05	2:41.36	
5934	T.J.	Lawson	USA	25.1.97	5	NCAA	College Station	10 Mar
	7.09	7.40	14.46	2.02	8.36	4.76	2:40.89	
5923A	Wolf	Mahler	USA	26.9.94	2	NC	Albuquerque	17 Feb
	6.99	7.24	13.07	1.92	8.18	5.15	2:40.43	
5908	Fredrik	Samuelsson	SWE	16.2.95	1	NC	Norrköping	11 Feb
	7.09	7.28	13.43	2.08	8.14	4.85	2:47.44	
5906	Tim	Nowak	GER	13.8.95	2		Aubière	14 Jan
	7.23	6.96	14.30	2.02	7.80	4.66	2:46.22	
5904	Artem	Makarenko	RUS	23.4.97	1	NC	Smolensk	15 Feb
	6.91	7.05	13.85	2.02	7.81	4.60	2:46.53	
5874	Gabriel	Moore	USA	10.1.96	6	NCAA	College Station	10 Mar
	6.94	7.33	14.38	1.99	8.11	4.46	2:44.01	
5871	Yuriy	Yeremich	BLR	24.10.95	1		Siaulai	24 Dec
	7.07	7.41	13.02	2.01	8.14	5.00	2:51.95	
5866	Karl Robert	Saluri	EST	6.8.93	1		Fayetteville	27 Jan
	6.90	7.38	14.04	1.90	8.43	4.70	2:37.42	

MEN 2018

Mark	Name		Nat	Born	Pos	Meet	Venue	Date
5866	Marcus	Nilsson	SWE	3.5.91	2	NC	Norrköping	11 Feb

7.23   6.84   15.43   1.96   8.28   5.05   2:40.40

5864	Maxence	Pecatte	FRA	9.1.97	17 Feb
5842A	Devon	Williams	USA	17.1.94	17 Feb
5825	Romain	Martin	FRA	12.7.88	28 Jan
5824	Marek	Lukás	CZE	16.7.91	11 Feb
5010	Dastien	Auzell	FRA	22.10.89	17 Feb
5810	Trent	Nytes	USA	21.12.95	24 Feb
5807	Manuel	Eitel	GER	28.1.97	14 Jan
5804	Hans-Christian	Hausenberg	EST	18.9.98	3 Feb
5797	Yevgeniy	Likhanov	RUS	10.1.95	15 Feb
5789	Karel	Tilga	EST	5.2.98	3 Feb

5784	Sergey	Timshin	RUS	25.11.92	15 Feb
5783	Pavel	Rudnev	RUS	26.10.92	15 Feb
5762	Taavi	Tsernjavski	EST	4.3.95	3 Feb
5758	Nick	Guerrant	USA	23.9.97	24 Feb
5730	Nathaniel	Mechler	CAN	31.3.97	10 Mar
5730	Joe	Delgado	USA	8.1.95	10 Mar
5725	Scott	Filip	USA	28.1.95	18 Feb
5717	Teddy	Frid	USA	22.10.96	10 Mar
5714	Nikita	Kulik	RUS	10.8.97	15 Feb
5713	Gaël	Quérin	FRA	26.6.87	17 Feb
5709	Jonay	Jordán	ESP	12.5.91	18 Feb

DECATHLON

9126 Kevin Mayer FRA 10.2.92 1 Talence 16 Sep
10.55/0.3 7.80/1.2 16.00 2.05 48.42 13.75/-1.1 50.54 5.45 71.90 4:36.11

8795 Damian Warner CAN 4.11.89 1 Hypo Götzis 27 May
10.31/0.6 7.81/0.5 14.83 2.03 47.72 13.56/0.0 47.32 4.80 61.94 4:26.59

8514 Maicel Uibo EST 27.12.92 2 Hypo Götzis 27 May
11.04/-0.6 7.57/2.0 14.78 2.12 50.32 14.66/-2.4 46.58 5.30 61.75 4:27.54

8481 Arthur Abele GER 30.7.86 1 Ratingen 17 Jun
10.85/1.0 7.28/-0.1 15.93 1.89 48.40 14.01/0.9 44.77 4.90 67.61 4:22.22

8431 Abele 1 EC Berlin 8 Aug
10.86/0.3 7.42/0.1 15.64 1.93 48.01 13.94/0.3 45.42 4.60 68.10 4:30.84

8407 Uibo 1 Athens, Ga 7 Apr
11.12/1.0 7.42/-0.2 14.71 2.13 50.29 14.97/0.3 47.83 5.17 64.42 4:34.63

8342 Pieter Braun NED 21.1.93 3 Hypo Götzis 27 May
11.12/0.4 7.62/0.5 15.28 2.00 49.25 14.40/0.2 45.52 4.90 58.77 4:24.29

8336 Tim Duckworth GBR 18.6.96 1 NCAA Eugene 7 Jun
10.57/0.5 8.01/0.8 13.15 2.13 48.78 14.37/-0.7 42.76 5.11 57.27 5:01.27

8329 Kai Kazmirek GER 28.1.91 4 Hypo Götzis 27 May
10.99/0.5 7.56/1.4 14.03 2.06 47.27 14.42/0.2 43.76 4.70 61.53 4:30.75

8321 Ilya Shkurenyov RUS 11.1.91 2 EC Berlin 8 Aug
11.12/-0.2 7.55/1.7 13.43 2.02 48.95 14.44/0.1 46.53 5.30 59.13 4:31.38

8310 Abele 2 Talence 16 Sep
10.84/0.3 7.19/1.1 15.20 1.93 48.48 13.86/-1.1 44.67 4.75 65.35 4:33.78

8304 Mathias Brugger GER 6.8.92 5 Hypo Götzis 27 May
10.98/0.4 7.32w/2.3 15.11 2.00 48.02 14.24/0.0 46.04 5.00 51.72 4:23.93

8303 Lindon Victor (10) GRN 28.2.93 1 CG Gold Coast 10 Apr
10.70/-0.1 7.24/0.2 15.79 2.01 49.48 14.87/0.3 52.32 4.60 71.10 5:04.75

8294 Zach Ziemek USA 23.2.93 1 NC Des Moines 22 Jun
10.65/1.4 7.23/-0.2 13.92 2.02 49.99 14.63/0.9 50.90 5.35 56.54 4:47.38

8290 Vitaliy Zhuk BLR 10.9.96 3 EC Berlin 8 Aug
11.12/-0.2 7.05/1.5 15.65 1.99 48.41 14.66/0.1 45.46 4.90 66.19 4:30.81

8229 Cedric Dubler AUS 13.1.95 1 NC Gold Coast 17 Feb
10.63/1.7 7.58/0.1 13.01 2.10 49.01 14.21/-1.4 41.03 5.20 56.37 4:50.53

8229 Tim Nowak GER 13.8.95 3 Talence 16 Sep
11.19/-0.3 7.56w/2.3 14.50 1.96 49.29 14.72/-0.9 45.31 4.85 64.00 4:26.80

8228 Martin Roe NOR 1.4.92 1 Firenze 28 Apr
10.82/-0.9 7.53/0.6 15.46 1.92 49.78 15.15/-0.4 48.26 4.75 66.64 4:40.97

8220 Niklas Kaul GER 11.2.98 4 EC Berlin 8 Aug
11.36/-0.2 7.20/0.2 13.85 2.08 49.28 14.78/0.1 46.30 4.70 67.72 4:23.67

8205 Kaul 6 Hypo Götzis 27 May
11.29/0.3 7.29/1.3 14.20 2.09 48.41 14.77/-1.9 42.01 4.70 68.76 4:31.44

8182 Shkurenyov 7 Hypo Götzis 27 May
11.09/0.4 7.53/1.6 13.98 2.00 49.40 14.44/0.0 42.56 5.20 56.56 4:31.66

8181 Ziemek 1 MSR Azusa 19 Apr
10.72/1.3 7.34w/2.8 13.68 2.07 50.03 14.53/1.2 48.54 5.20 51.14 4:45.28

8171 Pierce Lepage CAN 22.1.96 2 CG Gold Coast 10 Apr
10.62/0.0 7.44/0.0 13.98 2.07 47.81 14.71/-0.8 43.90 4.90 58.24 4:58.00

8165 Fredrik Samuelsson SWE 16.2.95 8 Hypo Götzis 27 May
10.90/0.4 7.49/1.2 14.18 2.06 49.96 14.38/0.0 42.64 4.90 59.33 4:39.36

8162 Zhuk 9 Hypo Götzis 27 May
11.07/0.3 7.11/0.5 15.29 1.97 49.18 14.81/-2.6 45.91 4.80 63.45 4:30.36

8160 Duckworth 5 EC Berlin 8 Aug
10.65/0.3 7.57w/2.5 13.61 2.17 49.87 14.55/0.3 41.94 5.10 54.78 4:58.26

8145 Duckworth 2 Athens, Ga 7 Apr
10.40/1.0 8.03/0.0 13.71 2.13 48.92 14.59/0.3 44.12 4.67 54.60 5:17.98

8137 Karl Robert Saluri EST 6.8.93 2 NCAA Eugene 7 Jun
10.50/0.5 7.70w/2.7 14.41 1.83 48.14 15.25/-0.7 42.95 4.81 56.91 4:24.49

Mark	Name		Nat	Born	Pos	Meet	Venue			Date
8131		Roe			6	EC	Berlin			8 Aug
	10.86/0.3	7.61/0.8	15.48	1.96	49.42		15.31/0.1	42.22	4.80	64.53	4:41.40
8126(w)	Ruben	Gado	FRA	13.12.93	1	NC	Albi			7 Jul
	10.77w/2.9	7.55w/2.5	13.63	1.91	48.58		14.88/1.2	39.87	5.10	56.41	4:20.86
	{30/20)									
8121	Manuel	Eitel	GER	28.1.97	2		Ratingen			17 Jun
	10.47/1.0	7.37/1.0	14.31	1.92	49.09		14.68/0.7	43.14	4.80	61.67	4:41.56
8120	Marcus	Nilsson	SWE	3.5.91	3		Ratingen			17 Jun
	11.25/1.0	6.95/0.7	14.91	1.98	50.52		14.58/1.3	45.07	5.00	63.68	4:24.62
8101	Karel	Tilga	EST	5.2.98	11	Hypo	Götzis			27 May
	11.04/0.3	7.33/1.0	15.32	2.09	49.82		15.25/-2.4	40.72	4.70	69.25	4:46.34
8099	Larbi	Bouraada	ALG	10.5.88	1	AfrC	Asaba			3 Aug
	10.93/-0.2	7.41w/2.2	12.81	2.06	48.38		14.70/	40.27	4.70	66.87	4:38.42
8067	Jan	Dolezal	CZE	6.6.96	8	EC	Berlin			8 Aug
	11.08/0.1	7.12/0.1	14.03	2.02	49.42		14.58/0.3	45.81	4.80	62.67	4:41.27
8048	Geormi	Jaramillo	VEN	6.3.89	1	NC	Barquisimeto			5 May
	10.86/-0.5	7.59/1.3	16.10	1.83	48.56		14.10/-1.8	44.86	4.50	61.60	5:00.05
8048	Ituah	Enahoro	GER/NGR	15.12.97	5		Ratingen			17 Jun
	10.63/1.0	7.45/-0.7	14.19	1.86	47.91		14.35/0.9	47.56	4.40	52.94	4:31.29
8046	Hunter	Veith	USA	14.1.95	1	Texas R	Austin			29 Mar
	10.72/0.9	7.78/0.9	13.47	2.10	48.66		14.77w/2.1	37.47	4.90	55.76	4:52.63
8046	Johannes	Erm	EST	26.3.98	3	NCAA	Eugene			7 Jun
	10.86w/2.3	7.98/0.6	13.46	1.98	48.34		14.88/-0.7	44.21	4.81	55.21	4:54.46
8044	Tim	Ehrhardt	USA	16.3.95	1		Charlottesville			21 Apr
	10.67/1.0	7.29/1.9	14.49	1.93	47.57		15.80/-0.3	41.40	5.20	53.08	4:30.04
	(30)									
8036	Romain	Martin	FRA	12.7.88	1		Hexham			22 Jul
	11.07/-1.3	7.08/0.8	14.42	2.08	49.87		14.39/-0.7	39.57	5.01	59.05	4:38.86
8032	Dennis	Hutterer	GER	4.5.96	1		Darmstadt			13 May
	11.10/0.0	7.27/0.0	14.18	2.08	50.53		15.10/-0.9	48.41	4.90	53.26	4:34.13
8026	Leonel	Suárez	CUB	1.9.87	1	CAG	Barranquila			30 Jul
	11.17w/2.1	7.14/1.9	13.84	2.05	50.53		14.57/1.9	44.72	4.70	64.00	4:34.21
8019	Solomon	Simmons	USA	26.9.93	2	NC	Des Moines			22 Jun
	10.67/1.4	7.25/-0.2	14.30	1.87	49.22		14.32/0.9	45.78	4.65	60.94	4:44.54
8015	Artem	Lukyanenko	RUS	30.1.90	1		Kazan			17 Aug
	11.35/0.3	7.84/-1.6	14.43	2.00	49.71		14.52/0.6	43.56	5.10	58.35	4:40.88
8012	Florian	Obst	GER	24.2.93	6		Ratingen			17 Jun
	10.76/1.0	7.28/1.3	15.54	1.86	48.81		14.78/0.9	50.97	4.70	55.31	4:54.87
8007	Thomas	Van Der Plaetsen	BEL	24.12.90	13	Hypo	Götzis			27 May
	11.14/-0.6	7.67/0.2	14.00	2.06	50.26		14.78/-2.6	44.46	5.20	59.41	5:14.93
7985	Yuriy	Yeremich	BLR	24.10.95	2		Firenze			28 Apr
	10.96/-0.9	7.62/-0.6	12.98	2.07	51.14		14.36/0.6	39.49	5.15	59.30	4:55.53
7980	Steve	Bastien	USA	4.3.94	1	vGER	Knoxville			28 Jul
	10.61/1.5	7.28/1.5	12.92	1.96	47.78		14.61/0.3	38.21	4.91	56.45	4:35.67
7954	Luiz Alberto	de Araújo	BRA	27.9.87	2		Kladno			16 Jun
	10.92/1.6	7.12/1.2	14.22	1.93	49.88		14.50/0.2	46.41	4.80	56.45	4:38.37
	(40)									
7949	Simone	Cairoli	ITA	12.9.90	10	EC	Berlin			8 Aug
	10.94/0.3	7.49/1.3	13.25	2.05	48.77		14.66/0.1	35.30	4.60	59.62	4:28.30
7948	Keisuke	Ushiro	JPN	24.7.86	14	Hypo	Götzis			27 May
	11.27/-0.6	7.09/1.5	14.26	2.00	49.98		15.08/-2.4	46.77	4.90	60.96	4:40.95
7934	Jorge	Ureña	ESP	8.10.93	15	Hypo	Götzis			27 May
	11.05/0.4	7.06/0.8	13.80	2.00	49.61		14.49/0.0	38.53	4.90	59.68	4:30.10
7925	Harrison	Williams	USA	7.3.96	1		Stanfotd			6 May
	11.06/1.5	7.23/-0.3	13.71	1.96	48.67		14.44/0.4	43.01	5.25	45.92	4:37.91
7925	Bastien	Auzeil	FRA	22.10.89	16	Hypo	Götzis			27 May
	11.26/-0.6	7.06/-1.6	15.43	2.00	50.35		14.89/-1.9	44.24	4.70	61.57	4:39.91
7925	Artem	Makarenko	RUS	23.4.97	1	NC	Smolensk			5 Jul
	10.78/-0.2	7.03/0.0	14.35	1.95	48.20		13.83/0.8	38.83	4.80	54.19	4:45.03
7921	Pawel	Wiesiolek	POL	13.8.91	1	NC	Suwalki			2 Jun
	11.10/-2.1	7.39/1.9	13.35	1.96	49.58		14.77/0.8	44.87	4.90	56.87	4:41.31
7913	José Gregorio	Lemos	COL	4.6.91	2	CAG	Barranquilla			30 Jul
	11.12w/2.1	7.03/0.9	16.60	1.87	51.14		14.58/1.9	55.12	4.10	65.80	4:58.00
7901	Gabriel	Moore	USA	10.1.96	2	SEC	Knoxville			11 May
	10.69/1.1	7.20w/2.2	14.23	1.91	49.33		14.69	48.28	4.50	57.66	4:51.18
7886	Felipe Vinicius	dos Santos	BRA	30.7.94	1		São Bernardo do Campo			8 Apr
	10.64/1.4	7.55/-0.3	12.94	1.95	49.61		14.20	42.16	4.68	57.21	4:57.36
	(50)									
7876	Scott	Filip	USA	28.1.95	3	Texas R	Austin			29 Mar
	10.71/0.9	7.47/0.6	13.33	2.04	48.07		14.81w/2.3	39.30	4.40	55.33	4:42.04

Mark	Name		Nat	Born	Pos Meet	Venue	Date
7873	Taavi	Tsernjavski	EST	4.3.95	3	Firenze	28 Apr
	11.29/-0.5	7.15/0.4 14.29	1.95	49.70	14.98/0.6	44.94 4.85 57.75	4:35.79
7863	Maksim	Andraloits	BLR	17.6.97	4	Firenze	28 Apr
	10.92/-0.9	7.17/-0.1 15.06	2.01	49.25	14.69/0.0	44.17 4.65 50.65	4:46.95
7858(w)	Briander	Rivero	CUB	23.4.91	3 CAG	Barranquilla	30 Jul
	10.94w/2.1	7.41w/2.3 13.55	2.05	49.44	14 46/1 9	44.61 4.20 66.80	4:43.86
7853	Rik	Taam	NED	17.1.97	1	Amstelveen	21 May
	10.87/0.3	7.07/0.0 13.94	2.09	48.54	14.78/-0.4	40.55 4.45 52.51	4:34.67
7852	Joe	Delgado	USA	8.1.95	4 NCAA	Eugene	7 Jun
	10.88w/2.3	7.20/1.4 13.79	1.95	48.41	15.13/-1.5	40.20 4.61 54.01	4:22.36
7849	Akihiko	Nakamura	JPN	23.10.90	2 NC	Nagano	17 Jun
	10.79/1.4	7.30w/3.1 12.26	1.93	49.17	14.20/0.2	37.39 4.70 54.52	4:21.16
7819	Marek	Lukás	CZE	16.7.91	1	Pacov	19 Jul
	11.09/1.6	6.97/2.0 14.58	1.90	51.38	14.75/-0.7	42.59 4.80 64.66	4:39.72
7809	Sutthisak	Singkhon	THA	5.10.96	2 AsiG	Jakarta	26 Aug
	10.85/1.5	7.54/-0.2 13.71	2.00	48.49	14.88/-0.8	36.84 4.80 51.35	4:24.75
7786	Kyle	Cranston	AUS	3.9.92	2 NC	Gold Coast	17 Feb
	10.96/1.7	7.26/0.6 13.66	1.92	50.65	14.82/-1.4	43.99 4.50 60.89	4:38.72
(60)							
7764A	Friedrich	Pretorius	RSA	4.8.95	1 NC	Pretoria	6 Mar
	10.92w/2.4	7.50w/2.7 12.45	2.04	50.09	14.52/-1.1	40.77 4.80 50.64	4:47.72
7763	Felix	Hepperle	GER	23.11.89	5 vUSA	Knoxville	28 Jul
	10.93/1.5	7.47/1.9 12.48	1.93	49.01	15.44/0.8	40.13 5.01 53.25	4:35.54
7756	Kurt	Felix	GRN	4.7.88	4 CG	Gold Coast	10 Apr
	11.20/-0.1	7.26/-0.4 15.24	1.95	50.49	15.25/0.3	48.04 4.20 67.47	5:04.32
7752	Yuma	Maruyama	JPN	3.6.98	3 NC	Nagano	17 Jun
	10.80/1.4	7.59w/2.9 12.80	1.99	50.27	17.08/0.2	38.71 4.20 59.93	4:48.83
7739	Rody	de Wolff	NED	9.4.97	2	Amstelveen	21 May
	11.21/0.3	7.13/0.0 14.28	1.94	48.78	14.67/-0.4	43.49 4.35 58.50	4:43.73
7724(w)	T,l	Lawson	USA	26.1.07	1	Knoxville	13 Apr
	10.92/1.8	7.38/1.6 14.02	2.04	49.80	14.92w/2.9	39.87 4.60 51.39	4:48.61
7723	Nathan	Hite	USA	14.5.96	3 SEC	Knoxville	11 May
	10.66/1.1	7.12w/2.6 14.32	1.91	49.66	15.04	43.70 4.40 57.89	4:49.75
7722	Nathaniel	Mechler	CAN	31.3.97	2 MSR	Azusa	19 Apr
	10.73/1.3	7.64w/2.1 12.86	1.98	48.59	14.83/-1.5	35.23 4.50 48.54	4:30.67
7722	Markus	Ballengee	USA	8.1.98	7 NCAA	Eugene	7 Jun
	11.24w/2.2	6.60w/2.2 13.24	2.01	49.72	14.72/-0.7	43.48 4.81 54.56	4:30.17
7718	Jérémy	Lelièvre	FRA	8.2.91	7	Ratingen	17 Jun
	11.02/1.0	7.21/0.5 14.60	1.83	49.52	14.89/1.3	42.35 4.50 53.05	4:25.58
(70)							
7708	Vasyl	Ivanytskyy	UKR	29.1.91	1 NC	Kropyvnytskyi	26 Jun
	11.29/-0.5	6.98/1.0 12.82	2.08	50.04	15.14/0.0	43.02 4.65 58.64	4:40.78
7708	Yevgeniy	Likhanov	RUS	10.1.95	3 NC	Smolensk	5 Jul
	11.27/-0.2	7.27/0.0 14.22	1.98	50.40	14.36/0.8	46.17 4.40 56.65	4:58.72
7702	Dan	Golubovic	USA	29.11.93	4 NC	Des Moines	22 Jun
	11.26/0.1	6.65/-0.2 13.65	1.87	50.20	14.62/0.9	43.39 4.95 59.99	4:36.30
7695	Kevin	Nielsen	USA	12.1.93	8 NCAA	Eugene	7 Jun
	10.93w/2.2	7.42/1.2 12.75	2.01	49.30	15.11/-0.7	37.41 4.61 50.63	4:28.70
7683	Trent	Nytes	USA	21.12.95	3 MSR	Azusa	19 Apr
	11.08/1.6	7.31/0.8 13.93	2.19	49.79	15.28/0.4	39.68 4.30 50.88	4:45.89
7683(w)	Axel	Hubert	FRA	16.2.96	2 NC	Albi	7 Jul
	11.05w/2.9	7.17w/3.0 14.25	1.88	50.02	14.50/1.8	40.10 4.70 61.86	4:59.61
7673	William	Dougherty	USA	9.6.95	5	Azusa	20 Apr
	11.02/1.6	7.06w/2.9 14.28	2.01	50.50	15.28/-1.5	39.81 4.80 51.93	4:37.55
7671	Gong	Kewei	CHN	29.6.94	4 Asi G	Jakarta	26 Aug
	10.85/1.6	7.70/0.8 11.60	1.91	49.25	14.39/0.0	35.36 4.60 53.46	4:35.06
7658	Darko	Pesic	MNE	30.11.92	1 Balk C	Stara Zagora	21 Jul
	11.38/0.7	6.88/-0.4 15.18	1.93	51.16	14.92/-0.1	45.09 4.40 56.68	4:29.99
7655	Elmo	Savola	FIN	10.3.95	15 EC	Berlin	8 Aug
	11.05/0.1	6.93/1.0 13.41	1.99	49.54	14.87/0.1	42.92 4.60 57.12	5:01.22
(80)							
7619	Nick	Guerrant	USA	23.9.97	10 NCAA	Eugene	7 Jun
	10.90w/2.3	7.16/0.7 12.56	1.98	49.67	15.11/-1.5	43.29 4.41 55.48	4:43.80
7607	Santiago	Ford	CUB	25.8.97	2 Fortún	Camagüey	16 Mar
	11.21/0.4	6.56w/2.6 13.23	2.07	50.77	14.86/0.9	46.42 4.10 64.28	4:45.79
7602	Luca	Bernaschina	SUI	30.6.95	1	Tenero	16 Jun
	11.17/0.3	7.33/0.3 14.15	1.89	50.16	14.83/0.0	39.34 4.70 51.19	4:38.41
7600	Lars Vikan	Rise	NOR	23.11.88	6	Firenze	28 Apr
	11.52/-0.5	7.26/0.2 14.84	1.98	51.40	15.67/0.1	44.61 4.65 52.67	4:37.07
7598	Pablo	Trescoli	ESP	4.3.95	1	Málaga	6 May
	11.11/1.4	7.11/-3.1 13.32	1.97	50.25	14.44/1.5	41.02 4.40 49.75	4:31.20

Mark	Name		Nat	Born	Pos	Meet	Venue			Date
7588w	Steele	Wasik	USA	8.12.95	1	Big 12	Waco			11 May
	10.81w/3.1	7.07w/4.1 13.75	1.96	51.49		14.44w/3.4	40.29	4.38	60.50	4:58.16
7582	Ben	Gregory	GBR	21.11.90	4		Kladno			16 Jun
	11.45/-0.6	7.03/1.7 13.34	1.90	49.84		14.76/0.2	39.84	4.80	54.52	4:32.46
7576	Adrian	Riley	JAM	22.1.94	2		Houston			10 May
	10.97/0.5	7.66/0.1 12.77	1.95	49.80		15.45/-0.1	44.97	4.35	55.46	5:01.56
7573	Damien	Berthenet	FRA	3.9.96	3	NC	Albi			7 Jul
	11.13/-0.5	7.17w/4.2 12.64	2.00	51.46		14.68/1.8	39.66	4.60	55.88	4:40.44
7559	Eduard	Mikhan	BLR	7.6.89	2		Brest			16 Jun
	11.02/0.4	6.98/0.7 14.16	1.88	50.33		15.23/0.3	45.82	4.60	53.67	4:49.38
	(90)									
7555	Derek	Jacobus	USA	23.7.95	4	SEC	Knoxville			11 May
	10.88/1.1	7.35/2.0 12.96	1.91	50.20		15.76	37.44	4.60	55.01	4:29.13
7550	Lennard	Biere	GER	3.2.97	8	vUSA	Knoxville			28 Jul
	11.27/1.4	7.40/1.3 15.37	1.93	51.98		15.05/0.8	43.60	4.61	58.89	5:16.93
7547	Marvin	Bollinger	GER	7.10.96	1		Püttlingen			27 May
	11.17/0.8	7.19/0.9 13.55	2.04	52.15		15.15/0.2	39.92	4.70	55.87	4:50.33
7545	John	Lane	GBR	29.1.89	5		Kladno			16 Jun
	10.89/1.6	7.28/0.5 13.41	1.96	48.93		14.68/-0.7	40.80	4.80	52.88	5:28.77
7524	Rauno	Liitmäe	EST	24.1.94	5	SEC	Knoxville			11 May
	11.33/1.1	6.80/1.1 14.27	1.97	51.60		15.19	39.15	4.50	67.00	4:48.54
7522	Andri	Oberholzer	SUI	24.7.96	1		Amriswil			8 Jul
	11.23/0.2	7.08/0.0 14.66	2.03	51.03		14.95/0.0	38.98	5.01	47.01	5:01.03
7519	Reinis	Kregers	LAT	22.1.92	1	LTU Ch	Palanga			28 Jul
	11.17w/2.7	7.06/0.6 14.02	1.98	51.10		15.50/1.3	43.61	4.20	59.20	4:43.05
7518	Bae	Sang-hwa	KOR	21.7.90	1		Iksan			16 Oct
	11.10/0.7	6.97/0.4 13.11	1.97	51.14		14.83/1.7	37.54	4.50	57.9	4:35.61
7517	Vadym	Adamchuk	UKR	30.5.94	1		Náxos			3 Jun
	11.19/0.6	7.46/1.7 14.55	1.87	50.56		15.50/2.0	39.56	4.50	52.97	4:37.59
7512	Juuso	Hassi	FIN	4.4.93	1	NC	Jyväskylä			22 Jul
	10.97/0.0	6.99/-0.1 14.05	1.84	49.28		15.11/0.7	40.63	4.50	56.41	4:46.94
	(100)									

Mark		Name		Nat	Born	Date			Name		Nat	Born	Date
7508(w)	Aaron	Booth		NZL	12.9.96	11 May	7464	Chong	Dong-hwi		KOR	15.12.98	16 Oct
7505(w)	Valentin	Charles		FRA	10.8.97	7 Jul	7463	Niklas	Ransiek		GER	22.4.96	28 Jul
7500(w)	Atsu	Nyamadi		GHA	1.6.94	7 Jul	7448	Risto	Lillemets		EST	20.11.97	16 Aug
7496(w) 7477	Harry	Maslen		GBR	2.9.96	8 Apr	7442	Mohd	Al Mannai		QAT	12.9.92	26 Aug
7496	Sawyer	Smith		USA	6.10.94	13 May	7438	Aleksandr	Tabala		RUS	23.5.86	21 May
7496	Luca	Dieckmann		GER	11.1.98	17 Jun	7436	Jakob	Samuelsson		SWE	19.2.98	17 Jun
7495	Mitch	Modin		USA	12.4.95	4 Jul	7435A	Andy	Preciado		ECU	12.10.97	25 Mar
7491	Benjamin	Ose		USA	10.12.96	6 May	7435	Alex	Bloom		USA	19.2.96	3 Jun
7481	Gaël	Quérin		FRA	26.6.87	13 May	7427	Pavel	Rudnev		RUS	26.10.92	5 Jul
7480	Mario	Arancón		ESP	29.3.94	22 Jul	7424	Gerzon	Izaguirre		VEN	3.8.95	5 May
7472	Keisuke	Okuda		JPN	23.10.96	17 Jun	7412	Yevgeniy	Chernov		RUS	9.11.91	21 May
7472	Rafal	Abramowski		POL	23.2.95	22 Jul	7412	Kimihito	Morimoto		JPN	21.4.93	17 Jun
7471	Ludovic	Besson		FRA	27.1.98	24 Jun	7412	Yaroslav	Novitskiy		RUS	4.4.88	16 Aug
7470	Jean Baptiste	Nutte		BEL	19.11.98	22 Jul	7402	Teddy	Frid		USA	.97	13 May
7467	Tim	Wunderlich		USA	2.4.87	28 Jul		(131)					
7467	Jefferson	Santos		BRA	30.8.95	15 Sep	**Best with legal wind**						
7465	Alec	Diamond		AUS	9.8.97	14 Jan	7484	Steele	Wasik		USA	8.12.95	19 Apr

Best at low altitude

7730	Friedrich	Pretorius	RSA	4.8.95	2	AfCh	Asaba			2 Aug
	11.27/-0.2	7.51/1.6 13.81	2.00	51.22		14.97/	39.88	4.60	59.84	4:41.16

JUNIORS

7203	Finley	Gaio	SUI	15.4.99	4		Aubagne			29 Jul
	10.95/0.5	7.27/-0.3 12.64	1.76	49.87		14.36/-1.2	31.48	4.50	53.04	4:57.01

IAAF junior specification – with 99cm 110mh, 6kg SP, 1.75kg DT

8190	Ashley	Moloney	AUS	13.3.00	1	WJ	Tampere			11 Jul
	10.51/-0.3	7.06/1.1 12.83	2.10	46.86		14.13/-0.3	47.39	4.60	53.67	4:42.65
7817	Stepan	Kekin	RUS	13.11.00	1	NCp	Adler			21 May
	10.83/0.4	7.26/0.2 14.33	1.85	50.27 / 14.31/-1.2			44.20	4.80	57.10	4:54.35
7798	Gary	Haasbroek	AUS	15.3.99	2	WJ	Tampere			11 Jul
	10.92/-0.3	7.26/0.3 13.28	2.01	49.20 / 14.26/-0.3			40.54	4.30	55.25	4:35.48
	7740	Moloney (1), 7723 Haasbroek (2) Melbourne 4 Mar								
7717	Finley	Gaio	SUI	15.4.99	1		Landquart			20 May
	10.81/1.4	7.52/3.0 14.86	1.86	49.31 / 13.94/-0.6			38.79	4.40	48.04	4:44.28
7697	Makenson	Gletty	FRA	2.4.99	1		Oyonnax			24 Jun
	10.85/-0.3	6.87/1.6 16.13	2.03	49.88 / 14.35/0.0			43.54	4.20	46.40	4:47.48
7642	Simon	Ehammer	SUI	7.2.00	3	WJ	Tampere			11 Jul
	11.14/-0.3	7.45/0.0 13.44	2.01	50.15 / 14.13/-0.3			36.22	4.70	49.09	4:47.3
7562	Kyle	Garland	USA	28.5.00	1	NC-j	Bloomington IN			16 Jun
	0.95/-0.1	6.83/-0.5 15.55	2.03	50.57 / 13.80/1.1			43.21	3.75	53.04	5:00.16

MEN 2018

Mark	Name		Nat	Born	Pos	Meet	Venue			Date
7552	Manuel	Wagner	GER	8.3.99	4	WJ	Tampere			11 Jul
	11.08/-0.3	6.81/-1.0 12.01	1.83	49.72 / 14.72/0.5			44.74	4.50	57.43	4:29.45
7524	Andreas	Bechmann	GER	28.9.99	1		Bernhausen			2 Jun
	11.54/-1.5	6.91/-0.1 14.48	1.98	50.79 / 15.15/0.1			43.78	4.60	51.57	4:38.30
7455	Steven	Fauvel-Clinch	(10) FRA	10.4.00	2		Oyonnax			24 Jun
	11.09/-0.3	7.07/-0.2 12.88	2.00	49.17 / 14.48/0.0			34.18	4.40	47.52	4:33.06
7454	Leon	Okafor	AUT	24.12.99	6	WJ	Tampere			11 Jul
	11.41/-0.3	6.62/2.5 14.03	1.92	50.27 / 14.98/0.5			44.63	4.50	56.44	4:46.50
7430	Maximilian	Kluth	GER	18.7.00	1	NC	Wesel			24 Aug
	11.20/1.4	6.84/0.6 14.91	1.92	49.74 / 15.04/0.9			42.69	3.90	51.96	4:33.39
7392	Tom-Lucas	Greiner	GER	6.12.99	2	NC	Wesel			24 Aug
	11.31/1.4	6.86/-0.4 13.75	1.89	50.31 / 14.65/0.9			41.48	4.20	53.49	4:36.85
7365	José	Santana	BRA	27.3.99	1		Bragança Paulista			23 Jun
	11.22/-0.1	6.91/0.8 13.07	1.94	50.18 / 14.26/0.3			33.37	4.20	58.98	4:42.31
7354	Ayden	Owens	PUR	28.5.00	1		Medford			24 Jun
	10.68/1.2	6.71/1.8 12.43	1.93	48.94 / 13.92/0.9			39.38	4.28	43.79	4:51.83
7333	Jules	Couzin	FRA	26.4.99	3		Oyonnax			24 Jun
	11.22/-0.3	6.84/1.5 12.68	1.82	49.09 / 14.73/0.0			39.00	4.50	47.66	4:28.23
7270	Lauri	Hulleman	NED	18.2.99	1		Den Haag			3 Jun
	11.59/-1.5	7.11/2.4 12.79	1.86	50.22 / 15.59/-0.7			37.31	4.45	56.58	4:31.27
7262	Leo	Neugebauer	GER	19.6.00	4		Bernhausen			2 Jun
	11.45/-1.1	6.81/-0.7 14.27	2.07	51.51 / 15.02/0.1			44.95	4.50	43.61	5:10.02
7257	Nicolas	Gerome	FRA	7.11.99	4		Oyonnax			24 Jun
	11.47/1.3	6.96/1.7 12.59	1.94	50.57 / 15.27/0.0			37.38	4.40	51.06	4:29.22
7256	Manuel	Dias (20)	POR	28.2.99	1		Arona			3 Jun
	11.18/0.1	7.06/2.2 13.26	1.75	50.06 / 15.15/0.9			38.78	4.55	46.22	4:29.48

4 X 100 METRES RELAY

Mark	Nat	Team	Pos	Meet	Venue	Date
37.61	GBR	Ujah, Hughes, Gemili, Mitchell-Blake	1	DL	London (OS)	22 Jul
37.00	GBR	Ujah, Hughes, Gemili, Aikines-Aryeetey	1	EC	Berlin	12 Aug
37.84	GBR	Ujah, Hughes, Gemili, Mitchell-Blake	1h1	EC	Berlin	12 Aug
37.85	JPN	R Yamagata, Iizuka, Kiryu, Cambridge	1	DL	Osaka	20 May
37.98	TUR	Barnes, Harvey, Hekimoglu, Guliyev	2	EC	Berlin	12 Aug
38.03	NED	Garia, Martina, Paulina, Burnet	3	EC	Berlin	12 Aug
38.08	USA- ATPS	Coleman, Gatlin, Baker, Rogers	1		Knoxville	14 Apr
38.09	JPN	Koike, Iizuka, Kiryu, Cambridge	2	DL	London (OS)	22 Jul
38.13	GBR-ENG	Arthur, Hughes, Kilty, Aikines-Aryeetey	1	CG	Gold Coast	14 Apr
38.15	GBR-ENG	Arthur, Hughes, Kilty, Aikines-Aryeetey	1h2	CG	Gold Coast	13 Apr
38.16	JPN	Yamagata, Tada, Kiryu, Cambridge	1	AsiG	Jakarta	30 Aug
38.20	JPN	Yamagata, Tada, Kiryu, Cambridge	1h1	AsiG	Jakarta	29 Aug
38.21	NED	Garia, Martina, Paulina, Burnet	3	DL	London (OS)	22 Jul
38.24	RSA	Bruintjies, Erasmus, Jobodwana, Simbine	2	CG	Gold Coast	14 Apr
38.25	RSA	Simbine, Magakwe, Erasmus, Bruintjies	1	AfrC	Asaba	3 Aug
38.30	NED	Garia, Martina, Paulina, Burnet	2h1	EC	Berlin	12 Aug
38.30	TUR	Barnes, Harvey, Hekimoglu, Guliyev	3h1	EC	Berlin	12 Aug
38.31	GBR-ENG	Kilty, Hughes, Gemili, Aikines-Aryeetey	1		Brisbane (N)	28 Mar
38.33	BRA- E.C.Pinheiros	Constantino, Vides, D. Silva, P. de Oliveira	1	NC	Bragança Paulista	15 Sep
38.35	JAM	E.Clarke, O.Bailey, Weir, Blake	3	CG	Gold Coast	14 Apr
38.39	USA	L.Collins, Gatlin, Hester, Jus.Warner	1	PennR	Philadelphia	28 Apr
		(21 performances by teams from 8 nations)				
38.41	BAR	S.Brathwaite, Burke, B.Ellis, Hoyte	1	CAG	Barranquilla	2 Aug
38.42	CAN	Brown, Smellie, Aiomale, De Grasse (10)	1	Jerome	Burnaby	27 Jun
38.49	ITA	Cattaneo, Desalu, Manenti, Tortu	1	Med G	Tarragona	30 Jun
38.51	FRA	Zeze, Rene, Dutamby, Fall	4	EC	Berlin	12 Aug
38.52	NGR	Adegoke, Itsekiri, Ogho-Ogene, Ogunlewe	2h2		Gold Coast	13 Apr
38.56	GER	Bryan, Domogala, Schmidt, Menga	4	AWC	London (OS)	14 Jul
38.58	AUS	T.Williams, Browning, Hale, J.Clarke	4	CG	Gold Coast	14 Apr
38.71	DOM	Valdez, Andújar, del Carmen, Y.Martínez	2	CAG	Barranquilla	2 Aug
38.71	UKR	Sokolov, Ibrahimov, Suprun, Smelyk	5	EC	Berlin	12 Aug
38.72	CHN	Su, Liang, Bie, Xu	3	DL	Osaka	20 May
38.77	POL	Grzeskowiak, Olszewski, Kope, Slowikowski	1		Goleniów	20 Jun
38.77	INA	Fadlin, Zohri, Rimbawan, Kertanegara	1	AsiG	Jakarta	30 Aug
		(20)				
38.89	TTO	N.Farinha, J.Farinha, Purcell, Greaux	3	NACAC	Toronto	12 Aug
38.92	CIV	T Konan, Koffi, Cissé, Meite	3	AfrC	Asaba	3 Aug
38.92	FIN	Rantala, Ahlfors, Lehtonen, Purola	6	EC	Berlin	12 Aug
38.94	CZE	Stromšik, Veleba, Jirka, Maslák	4h1	EC	Berlin	12 Aug
38.97A	COL	Rentería, Palomeque, Chará, Baloyes	1	SAmG	Cochabamba	7 Jun
38.98	TPE	Wei Yiching, Yang, Wei Taicheng, Wang	4	AsiG	Jakarta	30 Aug

Mark		Name	Nat	Born	Pos	Meet	Venue		Date
39.03A	VEN	Aguilar, Vásquez, Nieves, Ramírez			2	SAmG	Cochabamba		7 Jun
39.03	CUB	H.Pérez, Skyers, Mena, Iribane			5	CAG	Barranquilla		2 Aug
39.07	POR	Lopes, Antunes, Curvelo, C Nascimento			7	EC	Berlin		12 Aug
39.08	SRI	Eashan, Ambepitiya, Ashroff, De Silva			6	CG	Gold Coast		14 Apr
		(20)							

39.10	KOR	30 Aug	39.29	THA	30 Aug	39.49	GRE	12 Aug	39.71A ISR	14 Jul	**Best at low altitude**	
39.12	ESP	12 Aug	39.37	MAS	14 Apr	39.59	PHI	29 Aug	**Hand timing**		39.17 COL	2 Aug
39.13	SUI	12 Aug	39.37	ZIM	3 Aug	39.67	BRN	29 Aug	39.0	SEN	2 Jun	39.48 ROU	20 Jul
39.18A	ROU	14 Jul	39.44	HKG	26 May						39.63 VEN	2 Aug

Mixed nationalities

38.05		Americas - USA/JAM Rogers, Lyles, Blake/JAM, Tracey/JAM			1	C.Cup	Ostrava		8 Sep
38.17		USA/BAR – Un. Houston Lewis, Hall, Burke/BAR, Burrell			1	NCAA	Eugene		8 Jun
38.36		JAM/GBR – Racers TC Minzie, Hughes/GBR, K.Anderson, Blake			1		Kingston		24 Feb

JUNIORS

38.88	USA	Harrison, Schwartz, Kratz, M Williams			1	WJ	Tampere		14 Jul
38.96	JAM	Nairne, C Taylor, Matherson, Stephens			2	WJ	Tampere		14 Jul
39.13	GER	Ansah-Peprah, Schulte, Skupin-Alfa, Brandner			1h2	WJ	Tampere		13 Jul
39.18	JPN	Fukushima, Miyamoto, Ueyama, Yasuda			1h3	WJ	Tampere		13 Jul
39.33A	RSA				1		Boksburg		28 Apr
39.49	GBR	Asdhwell, Miller, Olse, Dobson			6	DL	London (OS)		22 Jul
39.67	TTO	Benjamin, Hosten, Pierce, Edwards			3h3	WJ	Tampere		13 Jul
39.72	TPE	Lin Yu-Tang, Wei Tai-Sheng, Hao-Hua Lu, Yeh Shou-Po			2	Asi-J	Gifu		9 Jun
39.75	ITA	Libera, Paissan, Marchei, Patta			1h1	WJ	Tampere		13 Jul
39.75	CZE	Jíra, Hampl, Krsek, Vejrazka			5	WJ	Tampere		14 Jul

4 X 200 METRES RELAY

1:21.10		USA White Younh, Walker, Friday, Belcher			2	FlaR	Gainesville		31 Mar
1:21.19		Un. of Houston Burke BAR, Burrell, Montgomery, Hall			1		Prairie View		24 Mar
1:21.20		Un. of Houston Lattin, Burrell, Montgomery, Hall			1	TexR	Austin		31 Mar

Mixed nationalities

1:20.79		PURE Athletics Edward PAN, M Lyles, J Lyles, Harvey TUR			I	FlaR	Gainesville		31 Mar

4 X 400 METRES RELAY

2:59.47	BEL	D.Borlée 46.1, J.Borlée 44.8, Sacoor 44.70, K.Borlée 43.91			1	EC	Berlin		11 Aug
2:59.78	USA	Strother 45.2, Ibokwe 44.6, Dedewo 44.77, Montgomery 45.13			1	AWC	London (OS)		15 Jul
2:59.91		USA- Texas A&M Deadmon 45.5, K.Johnson 45.1, Izu 45.42, D.Dixon 43.92			2	NCAA	Eugene		8 Jun
3:00.36	GBR	Yousif 46.1, Cowan 45.3, Hudson-Smith 44.77, Rooney 44.24			2	EC	Berlin		11 Aug
3:00.56	QAT	Samba 44.6, M.Abbas 45.2, Mohamed 46.43, Haroun 44.41			1	AsiG	Jakarta		30 Aug
3:00.60	USA	Strother, Igbokwe, Cherry 45.19, Montgomery 44.48			1	NACAC	Toronto		12 Aug
3:00.78	ESP	Husillos 45.8,B úa 44.7, S.García 44.80, Hortelano 45.56			3	EC	Berlin		11 Aug
3:00.92	KEN	Momanyi 46.5, Kishoyan 45.7, H.Koech 45.1, E.Korir 43.6			1	AfrC	Asaba		5 Aug
3:01.13		USA- Texas A&M Deadmon 45.6, K.Johnson 45.5, Izu 45.13, D.Dixon 44.45			1s1	NCAA	Eugene		6 Jun
3:01.17		USA- Texas A&M Rose 46.3, Deadmon 45.1, Izu 45.4, D.Dixon 44.4			1	SEC	Knoxville		13 May
3:01.23		USA- Texas A&M Deadmon, K.Johnson, Izu 45.39, D.Dixon 44.13			2h2	NCAA-W	Sacramento		26 May
3:01.31	USA	M.Washington 46.4, Cherry 44.5, Chambers 44.84, Berry 45.57			1	Penn R	Philadelphia		28 Apr
3:01.62	GBR	Chalmers 46.9, Cowan 44.9, Yousif 45.08, Rooney 44.80			1h1	EC	Berlin		10 Aug
3:01.67	FRA	Anne 46.5, Hanne 45.1, Afine 45.24, Jordier 44.91			2h1	EC	Berlin		10 Aug
3:01.78	BOT	Maotoanong 46.5, Thebe 44.3, Nkobolo 46.38, Makwala 44.54			1	CG	Gold Coast		14 Apr
		15 performances from 8 nations!							
3:01.85	IND	Kunhu Muhammed 46.1, Dharun 45.7, Anas 45.7, Rajiv 44.4			2	AsiG	Jakarta		30 Aug
3:01.92	BAH	Ferguson 46.0, T.Smith 46.0, Newbold 45.31, Russell 44.52			2	CG	Gold Coast		14 Apr
3:01.94	JPN	Walsh 45.5, Koike 46.1, Abe 46.0, Iizuka 44.3 (10)			3	AsiG	Jakarta		30 Aug
3:01.97	JAM	Gayle 46.2, Gaye 44.8, Rose 46.40, Francis 44.54			3	CG	Gold Coast		14 Apr
3:02.11	ITA	Corsa 46.40, Tricca 45.53, Aceti 45.31, Re 44.87			1		Bern		16 Jun
3:02.27	POL	Zalewski 46.0, Omelko 45.5, Krawczuk 45.06, Duszynski 45.72			5	EC	Berlin		11 Aug
3:02.52	CZE	Sorm 47.1, Desensky 45.1, Müller 45.71, Maslák 44.59			3h1	EC	Berlin		10 Aug
3:02.74	SRI	Dharshana 45.8, Premakumara 46.6, Kodikara 45.9, Kumarage 44.4			4	AsiG	Jakarta		30 Aug
3:02.85	TTO	Lendore 45.80, Richards 44.64, Quow 46.70, Cedenio 45.71			4	CG	Gold Coast		14 Apr
3:03.16	GER	Trefz 46.9, Cowan 45.1, Dammermann 46.13, Schneider 45.09			3	AWC	London (OS)		15 Jul
3:03.50	RSA	Nene 46.6, Fredericks 46.2, Conradie 46.4, Phora 44.3			2	AfrC	Asaba		5 Aug
3:03.51	NED	van Diepen, Bonevacia, Agard, Dobber			3		Bern		16 Jun
3:03.87	CUB	Zamora, Chacón, Rojas, Lescay			1	CAG	Barranquilla		2 Aug
		(20)							
3:03.92	DOM	L.Santos, J.Santos, Charles, Bonon			2	CAG	Barranquilla		2 Aug
3:03.97	BRN	Isah 45.8, Ali Khamis 46.2, Ab.Khamis 46.8, Abbas 45.2			5	AsiG	Jakarta		30 Aug
3:04.32	BRA	EC Pinheiros Constantino, Estefani, Alves dos Santos, A G da Silva			1		Bragança Paulista		16 Sep
3:04.35	COL	Palomeque, R.Rodríguez, Y.Herrera, Perlaza			3	CAG	Barranquilla		2 Aug
3:04.74	CAN	Harper, Cole, Osei, George 44.67			5	NACAC	Toronto		12 Aug
3:04.88		RUS- Sankt Peterburg Rafilovich, Rudenko, Kukharenko, Filatov			1	NC	Kazan		22 Jul

Mark		Name	Nat	Born	Pos	Meet	Venue		Date
3:04.88	NGR	Erayokan 45.6, Alowonle 47.4, Salihu 46.3, Okezie 45.6			3	AfrC	Asaba		5 Aug
3:04.98	ZAM	Kafunda (?) 48.4, Siame 44.3, Hazemba 46.9, Mbewe 45.4			4	AfrC	Asaba		5 Aug
3:05.27	ALG	Moula 47.1, Belbachir 45.8, Hathat 46.4,Lahoulou 46.0			5	AfrC	Asaba		5 Aug
3:05.28	TUR	Altinas, Copello, Ören, Can			4	Med G	Tarragona		30 Jun
	(30)								

| 3:05.75A | VEN | 8 Jun | 3:05.97 | BAR | 12 Aug | 3:06.92 | IRQ | 29 Aug | 3:07.69 | TPF | 14 Feb | 3:08.02 | SUI | 16 Jun |
| 3:05.93 | UKR | 10 Aug | 3:06.55 | IRL | 10 Aug | 3:06.98 | CHN | 29 Aug | 3:07.80 | CRO | 20 Aug | 3:08.15 | IRL | 16 Jun |

Disqualified

| 3:01.79 | RSA | Phora 45.2, Conradie 46.0, Nene 45.49, Mokaleng 44.96 | | | (2) | AWC | London (OS) | | 15 Jul |
| 3:04.22 | AUS | Goodwin 46.8, Mowen 46.1, Ralph 46.54, Solomon 44.55 | | | (3h2) | CG | Gold Coast | | 13 Apr |

Mixed nationalities (USA and others)

2:59.00	UUSC	Morgan 45.9, Benjamin/ANT 43.6, Shinnick 45.85, Norman 43.62			1	NCAA	Eugene		8 Jun
3:00.56	LSU	J.Thompson/JAM 46.2, Mosby 45.1, Howell/JAM 45.20, Flournoy 44.05			3	NCAA	Eugene		8 Jun
3:01.00	Florida	Fasasi/NGR 46.4, Holloway 44.6, Sawyers/JAM 45.29, Vedel/DEN 44.74			1	Fla R	Gainesville		31 Mar
3:01.11	USC	Benjamin/ANT, Shinnick, Ford 46.92, Norman 43.06			1h2	NCAA-W	Sacramento		26 May
3:01.30	USC	Morgan 46.3, Benjamin/ANT 44.1, Shinnick 45.67, Norman 45.18			2s1	NCAA	Eugene		6 Jun
3:01.61	Florida	Fasasi/NGR 45.0, Sawyers/JAM 44.5, Vedel/DEN 45.96, Holloway 45.35			3s1	NCAA	Eugene		6 Jun

Indoors

3:00.77	USA/ANT – USC	Shinnick 46.24, Benjamin/ANT 44.35, Morgan 45.67, Norman 44.52			1	NCAA	College Station		10 Mar
3:01.39	USA	Texas A&M Izu 46.57, Grant 44.84, Dixon 45.48, M Kerley 44.52			2	NCAA	College Station		10 Mar
3:01.43	Florida	Fasasi NGR 46.42, Holloway 44.91, Sawyers JAM 45.36, Vedel DEN 44.75			3	NCAA	Coll. Station		10 Mar
3:01.77	POL	Zalewski 45.73, Omelko 45.17, Krawczuk 45.87, Krzewina 45.00			1	WI	Birmingham		4 Mar
3:02.52	TTO	Lendore 46.57, Richards 45.02, Guevara 45.66, L Gordon 45.27			4	WI	Birmingham		4 Mar

JUNIORS

3:04.05	ITA	Gjetja 47.1, Romano 45.6, Sibilio 46.06, Scotti 45.31			1	WJ	Tampere		15 Jul
3:05.26	USA	Godwin 46.2, Ramey 48.6, Robinson 45.28, Fields 45.21			2	WJ	Tampere		15 Jul
3:05.64	GBR	Haydock-Wilson 46.7, Brier 46.4, Chalmers 46.75, Knibbs 45.87			3	WJ	Tampere		15 Jul
3:06.37	Calabar High School, JAM				1		Kingston		10 Mar
3:06.65	FRA	Saidy 47.4, Andant 46.1, Leblois 47.00, Mbaye 46.21			4	WJ	Tampere		15 Jul
3:07.05	BEL	van den Bergh 47.8, Sacoor 44.7, Mazebo 47.78, R Borlée 46.86			5	WJ	Tampere		15 Jul
3:07.45	BOT	Ndori, Phokedi, Nzamani, Eppie			1		Gaborone		15 Dec
3:07.80	GER	Ringel 48.4, Bretschneider 46.6, Leppelsack 46.72, Bredau 46.17			6	WJ	Tampere		15 Jul
3:08.07A	RSA				1		Boksburg		28 Apr
3:08.31	BAR	Hoyte-Small, Griffith, Bishop, J Jones			2	Carifta	Nassau		2 Apr
3:08.53	AUS	Kopp 48.2, Davis 46.3, Murrant 45.65, Moloney 48.41			2h2	WJ	Tampere		14 Jul
3:08.70	SRI	Niku, Ravisha, Indrajith, Darshana			1	Asi-J	Gifu		10 Jun

4 X 800 METRES RELAY

At Boston (Allston) 25 Feb: 1, 7:11.30i Hoka NJNYTC McAsey 1:49.03, Merber 1:47.11, Giesting 1:47.43, Garn 1:47.73
2. 7:11.84i   Atlanta TC Hazouri 1:49.84, Peterson 1:48.73, E Kemboi KEN 1:45.55, Lasater 1:47.72
3. 7:12.25   DistrictTC Henderson 1:49.16, Livingston 1:47.19, Ibadin NGR 1:46.92, Centrowitz 1:48.98

3000 METRES TRACK WALK

10:43.84	Tom	Bosworth	GBR	17.1.90	1	Anniv	London (OS)		21 Jul
10:47.08	Lebogang	Shange	RSA	1.8.90	2	Anniv	London (OS)		21 Jul
10:56.06	Dane	Bird-Smith	AUS	15.7.92	1		Brisbane (Nathan)		28 Mar
10:56.98	Dawid	Tomala	POL	27.8.89	1	PTS	Samorín		29 Jun
11:02.9	Dementiy	Cheparev	RUS	28.10.92	1		Saransk		28 Oct
11:03.32		Shange			2	PTS	Samorín		29 Jun
11:04.1	Sergey	Rakov	RUS-J	13.6.99	2		Saransk		28 Oct
11:12.7	Aleksey	Kudashkin	RUS	1.2.97	3		Saransk		28 Oct
11:13i	Daisuke	Matsunaga	JPN	24.3.95	1	in 5k	Abashiri		4 Jul
11:13.77	Callum	Wilkinson	GBR	14.3.97	3	Anniv	London (OS)		21 Jul
11:23.0	Sergey	Kozhevnikov	RUS-Y	9.5.01	4		Saransk		28 Oct
11:26.22	Mirosla	Úradník	SVK	24.3.96	3	PTS	Samorín		29 Jun
11:28.41	Evan	Dunfee	CAN	28.9.90	28 Mar	11:32.2	Aleksandr	Garin	RUS-J 28.12.99	28 Oct
11:28.9	Roman	Yevstifeyev	RUS	19.9.92	28 Oct	11:33.42	Nick	Christie	USA 29.9.91	21 Jul
11:31.3	Sergey	Sharipov	RUS	14.4.92	28 Oct	11:39.43	Dominik	Cerny	SVK 1.11.97	29 Jun

Indoors

10:30.28	Tom	Bosworth	GBR	17.1.90	1	GP	Glasgow		25 Feb
10:49.33	Christopher	Linke	GER	24.10.88	1		Erfurt		9 Feb
10:52.15	Nils	Brembach	GER	23.2.93	2		Erfurt		9 Feb
10:52.77	Callum	Wilkinson	GBR	14.3.97	2	GP	Glasgow		25 Feb
10:56.30	Marius	Ziukas	LTU	29.6.85	3	GP	Glasgow		25 Feb
10:58.89		Tomala			4	GP	Glasgow		25 Feb
11:06.57	Diego	García	ESP	19.1.96	5	GP	Glasgow		25 Feb
11:13.47	Karl	Junghannß	GER	6.4.96	3		Erfurt		9 Feb
11:17.35	Leo	Köpp	GER	23.5.98	4		Erfurt		9 Feb
11:38.25	Giorgio	Rubino	ITA	15.4.86	6	GP	Glasgow		25 Feb

Mark	Name		Nat	Born	Pos	Meet	Venue	Date	

5000 METRES TRACK WALK

Mark	Name		Nat	Born	Pos	Meet	Venue	Date	
18:37.84	Daisuke	Matsunaga	JPN	24.3.95	1		Abashiri	4	Jul
18:43.17	Veli-Matti	Partanen	FIN	28.10.91	1		Espoo	13	Jun
18:51.86	Masatora	Kawano	JPN	23.10.98	2		Abashiri	4	Jul
18:54.21	Fumitaka	Oikawa	JPN	5.4.95	1		Uozu	20	May
18:57.13	Yohann	Diniz	FRA	1.1.78	1		Reims	20	May
18:59.83		Partanen			1		Lappeenranta	27	Aug
19:01.20	Tom	Bosworth	GBR	17.1.90	1	NC	Birmingham	1	Jul
19:02.28	Yuta	Koga	JPN-J	15.7.99	1		Ageo	10	Nov
19:03.04	Gabriel	Bordier	FRA	8.10.97	1		Nantes	19	May
19:05.92		Diniz			1		Remims	29	Apr
19:08.91	Yuga	Yamashita	JPN	6.2.96	2		Uozu	20	May
19:10.14	Eiki	Takahashi	JPN	19.11.92	1		Kumagaya	20	May
19:15.09	Miguel Ángel	López	ESP	3.7.88	1		Murcia	6	Jun
19:17.41	Callum	Wilkinson	GBR	14.3.97	2	NC	Birmingham	1	Jul
19:17.78	Viktor	Shumik	UKR	21.5.98	1		Kropyvnytskyi	25	Jun
19:18.32	Álvaro	Martín	ESP	18.6.94	1		Palencia	27	Jun
19:23.78	Gianluca	Picchiottino	ITA	22.8.96	114	Jul	19:27.10 Tomohiro Noda JPN 24.1.96 4 Jul
19:24.13	Koki	Ikeda	JPN	3.5.98	4	Jul	19:32.68 Eduard Zabuzhenko UKR 18.4.98 25 Jun
19:25.51	Alex	Wright	IRL	19.12.90	27	May	19:32.80 Luis Alberto Amezcua ESP 1.5.92 14 Jul
19:26.00	Serhiy	Budza	UKR	6.12.84	25	Jun	19:35.73 Manuel Bermudez ESP 12.12.97 6 Jun
							19:36.61 Evan Dunfee CAN 28.9.90 28 Jan
Indoors									
18:28.70	Tom	Bosworth	GBR	17.1.90	1	NC	Birmingham	18	Feb
18:45.7	Sergey	Shiroborokov	RUS-J	16.2.99	1		Saransk	30	Dec
18:52.94	Ruslan	Dmytrenko	UKR	22.3.86	1		Kyiv	9	Jan
18:55.26	Francesco	Fortunato	ITA	13.12.94	1	NC	Ancona	17	Feb
18:58.0	Aleksey	Kudashkin	RUS	1.2.97	2		Saransk	30	Dec
18:58.27	Marius	Ziukas	LTU	29.6.85	1	NC	Klaipeda	17	Feb
18:59.62	Alex	Wright	IRL	19.12.90	1	NC	Dublin	17	Feb
19:01.08	Sergey	Rakov	RUS-J	13.6.99	3		Saransk	30	Dec
19:02.59	Ivan	Losev	UKR	26.1.86	2		Kyiv	9	Jan
19:09.1	Salavat	Ilkayev	RUS-J	14.9.00	1J		Saransk	30	Dec
19:10.13	Nils	Brembach	GER	23.2.93	1		Erfurt	2	Mar
19:15.97	Aleksandr	Lyakhovich	BLR	4.7.89	1	NC	Mogilyov	17	Feb
19:23.59	Erick	Barrondo	GUA	14.6.91	1	BW	Bratislava	28	Jan

JUNIORS

Mark	Name		Nat	Born	Pos	Meet	Venue	Date	
19:34.14	David	Kuster	FRA-J	25.3.99	1		Liévin	22	Dec
19:35.5	Sergey	Kozhevnikov	RUS-Y	9.5.01	2J		Saransk	30	Dec
19:38.81	Declan	Tingay	AUS	6.2.99	2		Canberra	28	Jan

10,000 METRES TRACK WALK

Mark	Name		Nat	Born	Pos	Meet	Venue	Date	
37:58.08	Daisuke	Matsunaga	JPN	24.3.95	1		Kitami	7	Jul
38:39.28	Perseus	Karlström	SWE	2.5.90	1	vFIN	Tampere	1	Sep
38:40.04	Koki	Ikeda	JPN	3.5.98	2		Kitami	7	Jul
38:44.13	Veli-Matti	Partanen	FIN	28.10.91	1	vSWE	Tampere	1	Sep
38:50.37	Masatora	Kawano	JPN	23.10.98	3		Kitami	7	Jul
39:01.20	Fumitaka	Oikawa	JPN	5.4.95	4		Kitami	7	Jul
39:05.19	Yusuke	Suzuki	JPN	2.1.88	1		Osaka	22	Sep
39:05.44		Ikeda			1		Fukui	7	Oct
39:22.41		Karlström			1		Canberra	14	Jun
39:23.23		Matsunaga			2		Osaka	22	Sep
39:24.49		Suzuki			5		Kitami	7	Jul
39:27.04	Toshikazu	Yamanishi	JPN	15.2.96	3		Osaka	22	Sep
	(12/8)								
39:31.72	Álvaro	Martín	ESP	18.6.94	1	NC	Getafe	22	Jul
39:33.7	Moacir	Zimmermann (10)	BRA	30.12.83	1		Blumenáu	18	Aug
39:38.27	Gianluca	Picchiottino	ITA	22.8.96	1		Livorno	22	Apr
39:40.28	Katsuji	Suzuki	JPN	31.7.98	1		Tama	15	Dec
39:44.59	Kohei	Toyama	JPN	.98	2		Tama	15	Dec
39:50.44		Wang Rui	CHN-J	1.9.99	1		Torino	26	May
39:50.85	Luis Alberto	Amezcua	ESP	1.5.92	2	NC	Getafe	22	Jul
39:54.6	César	Rodríguez	PER	25.6.97	1	NCp	Lima	20	Jul
39:55.75	Tatsuhiko	Nagayama	JPN-J	24.12.99	3		Tama	15	Dec
40:00.13		Wang Qin	CHN	8.5.94	2		Torino	26	May
40:00.95	Yutaro	Koga	JPN-J	15.7.99	4		Fukui	7	Oct
40:02.51	Federico	Tontodonati (20)	ITA	30.10.89	3		Torino	26	May
40:04.3	Luis	Campos	PER	10.11.95	2	NCp	Lima	20	Jul
40:11.80	Evan	Dunfee	CAN	28.9.90	14	Jun	40:17.62 Dawid Tomola POL 27.8.89 20 Jul
40:16.16	Tomohiro	Noda	JPN	24.1.96	22	Sep	40:17.82 Sho Sakazaki JPN-J 22.2.99 21 Jan
40:17.08	Miguel Ángel López		ESP	3.7.88	22	Jul	40:20.07 Kai Kobayashi JPN 28.2.93 22 Sep

MEN 2018

Mark	Name	Nat	Born	Pos	Meet	Venue	Date
40:20.57	Zhang Jun	CHN	20.7.98				26 May
40:20.59	Artur Brzozowski	POL	29.3.85				20 Jul
40:21.56	Isamu Fujisawa	JPN	12.10.87				22 Sep
40:22.96	Hiroto Jusho	JPN-J	11.1.00				21 Jan
40:23.05	Tatsuhiko Nagayama	JPN-J	24.12.99				7 Oct
40:24.6	Salavat Ilkayev	RUS-J	14.9.00				18 Feb
40:24.99	Ato Ibañez	SWE	14.11.85				1 Sep
Indoor: 40:21.88	Dmitriy Dyubin	BLR	12.7.90				16 Feb

JUNIORS - SEE MAIN LIST FOR TOP THREE JUNIORS AND:

Mark	Name	Nat	Born	Pos	Meet	Venue	Date
40:17.82	Sho Sakazaki	JPN	22.2.99	1		Wakayama	21 Jan
40:22.90	Hiroto Jusho	JPN	11.1.00	1J		Wakayama	21 Jan
40:24.6	Salavat Ilkayev	RUS	14.9.00	1	NC-wj	Sochi	18 Feb
40:32.06	David Hurtado	ECU	21.4.99	2	WJ	Tampere	14 Jul
40:41.0	Sergey Rakov	RUS	13.6.99	2	NC-wj	Sochi	18 Feb
40:45.26	José Ortiz	GUA	8.3.00	3	WJ	Tampere	14 Jul
40:47.78	Akshdeep Singh	IND	12.7.00	1	NC-j	Ranchi	3 Nov
40:49.72	Declan Tingay	AUS	6.2.99	4	WJ	Tampere	14 Jul
40:56.16	Juned Khan	IND	10.5.99	2	NC-j	Ranchi	3 Nov
41:04.22	Wang Zhaozhao	CHN	1.9.99	5	WJ	Tampere	14 Jul
41:18.85	Kim Ming-yu	KOR	28.2.99	2		Youngju	29 Sep
41:13.31	Takumi Suzuki	JPN	14.1.99	12		Tama	1 Dec
41:19.21	Motofumi Suwa	JPN	22.10.99	9		Osaka	22 Sep
41:23.81	Yu Takeuchi	JPN	19.10.99	9		Sagamihara	26 May

10 KILOMETRES ROAD WALK

Where superior to track times. See also intermediate times in 20k list

Mark	Name	Nat	Born	Pos	Meet	Venue	Date
39:19	Massimo Stano	ITA	27.2.92	1	NC	Pescara	7 Sep
39:26	Gianluca Picchiottino	ITA	22.8.96	2	NC	Pescara	7 Sep
39:57	Cui Lihong	CHN-J	13.5.99	1	NC-j	Weinan	7 Sep
40:01	Aleksey Golovin	RUS	24.12.88	1		Mis	6 May
40:03	Francesco Fortunato	ITA	13.12.94	3	NC	Pescara	7 Sep
40:04+	José Luis Doctor	MEX	14.6.96	in 20k		La Coruña	2 Jun
40:06	Li Xiaobin	CHN-J	10.10.99	2	NC-j	Weinan	7 Sep
40:07	Zheng Yao	CHN-J	11.0.00	1	WTC-J	Taicang	5 May

Mark	Name	Nat	Born	Date		Mark	Name	Nat	Born	Date
40:12	Wang Zhaozhao	CHN-J	1.9.99	5 May		40:21	Takumi Suzuki	JPN-J	14.1.99	18 Feb
40:14	Hiroto Jusho	JPN-J	11.1.00	18 Feb		40:24	Salavat Ilkayev	RUS	14.9.00	18 Feb
40:17	José Ortiz	GUA	8.3.00	5 May		40:24	Sun Shuai	CHN-J	15.9.99	5 May
40:18	Federico Tontodonati	ITA	30.10.89	7 Sep						

Doubtful distance: Thika (A) 19 May: 1. Samuel Gathimba KEN 39:27.8, 2. Stephen Mutuku KEN 39:44.2

MORE JUNIORS

Mark	Name	Nat	Born	Pos	Meet	Venue	Date
40:12	Wang Zhaozhao	CHN	1.9.99	2	WTC-J	Taicang	5 May
40:14	Hiroto Jusho	JPN	11.1.00	1	NC-j	Kobe	18 Feb
40:21	Takumi Suzuki	JPN	14.1.99	2	NC-j	Kobe	18 Feb
40:24	Salavat Ilkayev	RUS	14.9.00	1	NC-wj	Sochi	18 Feb
40:24	Sun Shuai	CHN	15.9.99	4	WTC-J	Taicang	5 May
40:25	Wen Yongjie	CHN	28.9.99	4	NC-j	Weinan	7 Sep
40:26	Zhu Xiaoqiang	CHN	21.4.00	5	NC-j	Weinan	7 Sep
40:30	Sho Sakazaki	JPN	22.2.99	1		Wajima	14 Apr
40:32	Tatsuhiko Nagayama	JPN	24.12.99	2		Wajima	14 Apr
40:33	Shi Xiukun	CHN	24.6.99	6	NC-j	Weinan	7 Sep
40:35	Xu Hao	CHN	6.2.99	7	NC-j	Weinan	7 Sep
40:38	Zhang Jiaxu	CHN	4.1.00	8	NC-j	Weinan	7 Sep
40:39	Mikita Kalyada	BLR	15.7.00	1		Gomel	4 Apr
40:40	Yuta Koga	JPN	15.7.99	3		Takahata	28 Oct
40:41	Sergey Rakov	RUS	13.6.99	2	NC-wj	Sochi	18 Feb
40:46	Motofumi Suwa	JPN	22.10.99	3		Wajima	14 Apr
40:56	Yohanis Algaw	ETH	14.8.99	6	WTC-J	Taicang	5 May

20 KILOMETRES WALK

20k	10k	Name	Nat	Born	Pos	Meet	Venue	Date
1:17:25	38:25	Sergey Shirobokov	RUS-J	16.2.99	1	NC	Cheboksary	9 Jun
1:17:26	39:00	Eiki Takahashi	JPN	19.11.92	1	NC	Kobe	18 Feb
1:17:41	39:00	Toshikazu Yamanishi	JPN	15.2.96	2	NC	Kobe	18 Feb
1:17:46	39:00	Daisuke Matsunaga	JPN	24.3.95	3	NC	Kobe	18 Feb
1:18:53	39:20	Shirobokov			1	NC-w	Sochi	19 Feb
1:18:54	39:23	Vasiliy Mizinov	RUS	29.12.97	2	NC-w	Sochi	19 Feb
1:19:04A		Samuel Gathimba	KEN	26.10.87	1	CGT	Nairobi	17 Feb
1:19:06A		Simon Wachira	KEN	6.5.84	2	CGT	Nairobi	17 Feb
1:19:13	39:46	Koki Ikeda	JPN	3.5.98	4	NC	Kobe	18 Feb
1:19:14	40:05	Eider Arévalo	COL	9.3.93	1		La Coruña	2 Jun
1:19:15	39:00	Isamu Fujisawa (10)	JPN	12.10.87	5	NC	Kobe	18 Feb
1:19:17	39:46	Fumitaka Oikawa	JPN	5.4.95	6	NC	Kobe	18 Feb
1:19:18	39:58	Diego García	ESP	19.1.96	2		La Coruña	2 Jun

Mark		Name		Nat	Born	Pos	Meet	Venue	Date	
1:19:19	39:45	Hirooki	Arai	JPN	18.5.88	7	NC	Kobe	18	Feb
1:19:34	39:58	Dane	Bird-Smith	AUS	15.7.92	1	CG	Gold Coast	8	Apr
1:19:38	39:57	Tom	Bosworth	GBR	17.1.90	2	CG	Gold Coast	8	Apr
1:19:45			Wang Kaihua	CHN	16.2.94	1		Huangshan	3	Mar
1:19:49	40:19	Kirill	Frolov	RUS	29.9.93	3	NC-w	Sochi	19	Feb
1:19:49	40:04	Tomohiro	Noda	JPN	24.1.96	3		La Coruña	2	Jun
1:19:51	39:58		Gathimba			3	CG	Gold Coast	8	Apr
1:19:52	39:46	Masatora	Kawano	JPN	23.10.98	8	NC	Kobe	18	Feb
1:20:11	40:05		Kawano			4		La Coruña	2	Jun
1:20:12			Matsunaga			1		Tokyo	1	Jan
1:20:21	40:30	Roman	Yevstifeyev (20)	RUS	19.9.92	4	NC-w	Sochi	19	Feb
1:20:24	39:45		Noda			9	NC	Kobe	18	Feb
1:20:24	40:05		Jin Xiangqian	CHN	18.3.97	5		La Coruña	2	Jun
1:20:30		Perseus	Karlström	SWE	2.5.90	1		Adelaide	11	Feb
1:20:31		Marius	Ziukas	LTU	29.6.85	2		Adelaide	11	Feb
1:20:31			Gao Yingchao	CHN	18.1.98	2		Huangshan	3	Mar
1:20:36			Matsunaga			1		Takahata	28	Oct
1:20:38			Cai Zelin	CHN	11.4.91	3		Huangshan	3	Mar
1:20:40		Christopher	Linke	GER	24.10.88	1		Naumburg	14	Apr
1:20:42		Álvaro	Martín	ESP	18.6.94	1	EC	Berlin	11	Aug
1:20:46	39:57		Martín			6		La Coruña	2	Jun
		(34/27)								
1:20:49	39:58	Benjamin	Thorne	CAN	19.3.93	3	CG	Gold Coast	8	Apr
1:20:51		Massimo	Stano	ITA	27.2.92	4	EC	Berlin	11	Aug
1:20:53		Ivan	Losev	UKR	26.1.86	1	NC-w	Lutsk	10	Mar
		(30)								
1:20:54	40:05	Miguel Ángel	López	ESP	3.7.88	7		La Coruña	2	Jun
1:21:00			Niu Wenchao	CHN	20.4.98	5		Huangshan	3	Mar
1:21:02	40:27	Aleksey	Shevchuk	RUS	10.8.97	5	NC-w	Sochi	19	Feb
1:21:10	39:46	Satoshi	Maruo	JPN	28.11.91	10	NC	Kobe	18	Feb
1:21:10			Zhang Jun	CHN	20.7.98	1		Taicang	7	May
1:21:12			Bian Tongda	CHN	1.4.91	6		Huangshan	3	Mar
1:21:12		Ruslan	Dmytrenko	UKR	22.3.86	2	NC-w	Lutsk	10	Mar
1:21:13	40:05	Manuel	Soto ¶	COL	28.1.94	9		La Coruña	2	Jun
1:21:14	40:06	Yusuke	Suzuki	JPN	2.1.88	2		Takahata	28	Oct
1:21:23			Yin Jiaxing	CHN	16.3.94	7		Huangshan	3	Mar
		(40)								
1:21:25		Ivan	Banzeruk	UKR	9.2.90	3	NC-w	Lutsk	10	Mar
1:21:25		Nils	Brembach	GER	23.2.93	5	EC	Berlin	11	Aug
1:21:28	40:30	Aleksey	Golovin	RUS	24.12.88	6	NC-w	Sochi	19	Feb
1:21:29	39:49	Kai	Kobayashi	JPN	28.2.93	11	NC	Kobe	18	Feb
1:21:30	40:27	Andrey	Tryapkin	RUS	1.12.97	7	NC-w	Sochi	19	Feb
1:21:30		José Leyver	Ojeda	MEX	12.11.85	2		Naumburg	14	Apr
1:21:31		Yerko	Araya	CHI	14.2.86	3		Adelaide	11	Feb
1:21:32		Kolothum Thodi	Irfan	IND	8.2.90	1	NC	New Delhi	18	Feb
1:21:32		Manish	Singh	IND	5.5.91	2	NC	New Delhi	18	Feb
1:21:35		Hagen	Pohle	GER	5.3.92	8	EC	Berlin	11	Aug
		(50)								
1:21:40		Neeraj	Singh	IND	15.8.94	3	NC	New Delhi	18	Feb
1:21:46		Stefano	Chiesa	ITA	25.5.96	4		Lugano	11	Mar
1:21:47	39:57	Takayuki	Tanii	JPN	14.2.83	12	NC	Kobe	18	Feb
1:21:47	40:25	Quentin	Rew	NZL	16.7.84	5	CG	Gold Coast	8	Apr
1:21:48			Chen Rui	CHN	11.8.96	8		Huangshan	3	Mar
1:21:52		Federico	Tontodonati	ITA	30.10.89	2		Roma	4	Mar
1:21:52			Kim Hyun-sub	KOR	31.5.85	3		Nomi	18	Mar
1:21:52		Kevin	Campion	FRA	23.5.88	9	EC	Berlin	11	Aug
1:21:53		Sunil	Singh	IND	28.11.97	4	NC	New Delhi	18	Feb
1:21:53		Aleksandr	Lyakhovich	BLR	4.7.89	1		Gomel	4	Apr
		(60)								
1:21:54		Yutaro	Koga	JPN-J	15.7.99	3		Takahata	28	Oct
1:21:55		Eknath Sambhaji	Turambekar	IND	18.1.98	5	NC	New Delhi	18	Feb
1:21:55	40:06	Noel Ali	Chama	MEX	15.9.97	10		La Coruña	2	Jun
1:21:57		Isaac	Palma	MEX	26.10.90	5		Lugano	11	Mar
1:21:57		Georgiy	Sheyko	KAZ	24.8.89	4		Nomi	18	Mar
1:22:06		João	Vieira	POR	20.2.76	11		La Coruña	2	Jun
1:22:10		Kulwant	Singh	IND	20.3.90	6	NC	New Delhi	18	Feb
1:22:10		Richard	Vargas	VEN	28.12.94	1		Warszawa	23	Jun
1:22:13		Horacio	Nava	MEX	20.1.82	2		Podébrady	7	Apr
1:22:15		Gabriel	Bordier	FRA	8.10.97	12		La Coruña	2	Jun
		(70)								

Mark	Name		Nat	Born	Pos	Meet	Venue	Date
1:22:18	Alex	Wright	IRL	19.12.90	10	EC	Berlin	11 Aug
1:22:18.16t	Mauricio	Arteaga	ECU	8.8.88	1	IbAmC	Trujillo	26 Aug
1:22:19	Artur	Brzozowski	POL	29.3.85	1	NC	Warszawa	23 Jun
1:22:19		Sun Song	CHN	15.12.96	2	NC	Weinan	7 Sep
1:22:21	Brian	Pintado	ECU	29.7.95	5	WTC	Taicang	6 May
1:22:23	Takumi	Saito	JPN	23.3.93	6		Nomi	18 Mar
1:22:23	Eder	Sanchez	MEX	21.5.86	4		Naumburg	14 Apr
1:22:24	Andrés	Chocho	ECU	4.11.83	4		Rio Maior	7 Apr
1:22:24	Viktor	Shumik	UKR	21.5.98	11	EC	Berlin	11 Aug
1:22:27		Choi Byung-kwang	KOR	7.4.91	1		Iksan	16 Oct
(80)								
1:22:28	Ricardo	Ortiz	MEX	7.2.95	3		Podébrady	7 Apr
1:22:31		Wei Xubao	CHN	1.2.93	3		Taicang	7 May
1:22:34	José Luis	Doctor	MEX	14.6.96	5		Rio Maior	7 Apr
1:22:34		Joo Hyun-myong	KOR	31.5.97	2		Iksan	16 Oct
1:22:35	Callum	Wilkinson	GBR	14.3.97	7	CG	Gold Coast	8 Apr
1:22:39	Vikas	Singh	IND	6.7.96	3	NC	New Delhi	18 Feb
1:22:44	Dawid	Tomala	POL	27.8.89	2	NC	Warszawa	23 Jun
1:22:45		Zhaxi Yangben	CHN	15.4.96	3	NC	Weinan	7 Sep
1:22:46		Gao Wenkui	CHN	28.7.95	4		Taicang	7 May
1:22:48	Gianluca	Picchiottino	ITA	22.8.96	3	2 NC23	Roma	4 Mar
(90)								
1:22:48	Aléxandros	Papamihaíl	GRE	18.9.88	6		Rio Maior	7 Apr
1:22:50		Lu Xiaotong	CHN	24.7.97	4	NC	Weinan	7 Sep
1:22:51	Karl	Junghannß	GER	6.4.96	3		Naumburg	14 Apr
1:22:52	Luis Alberto	Amezcua	ESP	1.5.92	3		Castellón	18 Mar
1:22:53		Peng Chen	CHN	8.7.97	1		Shangrao	14 Apr
1:22:56		Lu Ning	CHN-J	12.2.99	5		Taicang	7 May
1:22:58	Takuma	Toyama	JPN	8.1.96	4		Takahata	28 Oct
1:23:01	Sergey	Sharipov	RUS	14.4.92	4	NC	Cheboksary	9 Jun
1:23:04	Francesco	Fortunato	ITA	13.12.94	16	EC	Berlin	11 Aug
1:23:06	Satya	Narayan	IND-J	10.6.00	8	NC	New Delhi	18 Feb
(100)								

Mark	Name		Nat	Born		Date		Mark	Name		Nat	Born		Date
1:23:07	Jordy	Jiménez	ECU	11.2.94	2	Jun		1:23:58	Rafal	Sikora	POL	17.2.87	23	Jun
1:23:10	Michael	Hosking	AUS	16.10.85	11	Feb		1:24:00A	Peter	Theuri	KEN		17	Feb
1:23:10		Sun Shuai	CHN-J	15.9.99	7	Sep		1:24:01A	José Leonardo	Montaña	COL	21.3.92	18	Feb
1:23:11	Ryosuke	Kawagishi	JPN	15.6.96	18	Feb		1:24:02	Máté	Helebrandt	HUN	12.1.89	22	Apr
1:23:14	Eduard	Zabuzhenko	UKR	18.4.98	10	Mar		1:24:02		Zhu Guowen	CHN	20.8.97	7	Sep
1:23:14		Zhong Heng	CHN	7.11.95	7	Sep		1:24:02		Cao Wenlong	CHN	4.3.98	7	Sep
1:23:15		Li Liangyong	CHN	28.5.96	14	Apr		1:24:03	Serhiy	Budza	UKR	6.12.84	10	Mar
1:23:19	Michele	Antonelli	ITA	23.5.94	4	Mar		1:24:03	Giorgio	Rubino	ITA	15.4.86	6	May
1:23:20	Jai	Bhagwan	IND	26.4.87	18	Feb		1:24:03		Ma Youshan	CHN	21.9.95	7	Sep
1:23:20	Lebogang	Shange	RSA	1.8.90	24	Sep		1:24:03		Zhang Wanxin	CHN	25.10.96	7	Sep
1:23:23	Koichiro	Morioka	JPN	2.4.85	18	Feb		1:24:06		Cha Jinhong	CHN	27.5.97	7	May
1:23:23	José Alessandro	Bagio	BRA	16.4.81	7	Apr		1:24:07	Manuel	Bermúdez	ESP	12.12.97	18	Mar
1:23:22.96t	César Augusto	Rodríguez	PER	26.6.97	26	Aug		1:24:09	Miroslav	Úradník	SVK	24.3.96	23	Jun
1:23:25	José Alejandro	Barrondo	GUA	16.9.96	7	Apr		1:24:09	Katsuji	Suzuki	JPN	31.7.98	28	Oct
1:23:26	Yuki	Ito	JPN	12.4.92	18	Feb		1:24:10	Ankit	Kumar	IND	16.6.92	18	Feb
1:23:26	Juan Manuel	Cano	ARG	12.12.87	7	Apr		1:24:12	Akito	Mochida	JPN	.97	18	Feb
1:23:26	Evan	Dunfee	CAN	28.9.90	8	Apr		1:24:14	Leonardo	Dei Tos	ITA	27.4.92	8	Jun
1:23:27	Oleksiy	Kazanin	UKR	22.5.82	16	Jun		1:24:15	Bence	Venyercsán	HUN	8.1.96	22	Apr
1:23:28		Liu Xu	CHN	11.12.94	3	Mar		1:24:20	Hitoshi	Warita	JPN	26.9.91	18	Feb
1:23:31	Hayato	Katsuki	JPN	28.11.90	18	Feb		1:24:23	Rafal	Fedaczynski	POL	3.12.80	11	Feb
1:23:31	Miguel	Carvalho	POR	2.9.94	7	Apr		1:24:24	Rydian	Cowley	AUS	4.1.91	2	Dec
1:23:33		Zeng Qingcun	CHN	3.4.95	3	Mar		1:24:29		Kim Dae-ho	KOR	30.4.88	18	Mar
1:23:33		Zhou Yangjun	CHN	17.10.96	3	Mar		1:24:29	Omar	Sierra	COL	10.9.88	7	Apr
1:23:33		Wang Zhaozhao	CHN-J	1.9.99	7	Sep		1:24:29	Jakub	Jelonek	POL	7.7.85	7	Apr
1:23:41	Kyohei	Dairaku	JPN	30.8.96	18	Feb		1:24:30	Motofumi	Suwa	JPN-J	22.10.99	28	Oct
1:23:43	Yutaro	Murayama	JPN	29.9.98	18	Feb		1:24:33		Li Peng	CHN	10.11.94	7	Sep
1:23:45	Kazuki	Takahashi	JPN	17.6.96	1	Jan		1:24:34		Xin Zhaoyang	CHN	30.6.98	14	Apr
1:23:45	Andrés	Olivas	MEX	27.5.98	7	Apr		1:24:35	José María	Raymundo	GUA	1.9.93	7	Apr
1:23:49	Ever	Palma	MEX	18.3.92	18	Mar		1:24:36	Yuhsuke	Naka	JPN	.98	18	Feb
1:23:50	Ryosuke	Kondo	JPN	25.12.97	28	Oct		1:24:36	Cian	McManamon	IRL	11.10.91	11	Mar
1:23:53	Rafal	Augustyn	POL	14.5.84	11	Feb		1:24:39		Wu Bing	CHN	8.7.98	7	Sep
1:23:53	Hayato	Sakakibara	JPN	4.12.98	18	Feb		1:24:40	Brandon	Segura	MEX	30.4.96	2	Jun
1:23:53		Zhang Hongliang	CHN-J	1.1.99	7	May		1:24:41	Damian	Blocki (169)	POL	28.4.89	11	Feb
1:23:55		Xu Hao	CHN-J	6.2.99	7	May		**Best track time**						
1:23:57	Baljinder	Singh	IND	18.9.86	18	Feb		1:24:07.00t	Juan Manuel	Cano	ARG	12.12.87	26	Aug
1:23:57	Carl	Dohmann	GER	18.5.90	14	Apr								

JUNIORS

See main list for top 4 juniors, 10 performances by 8 men to 1:24:00. Additional marks and further juniors:

Lu Ning	1:23:20	8	NC	Weinan			7 Sep	
1:23:10		Sun Shuai	CHN-J	15.9.99	6	NC	Weinan	7 Sep
1:23:33		Wang Zhaozhao	CHN	1.9.99	11	NC	Weinan	7 Sep

Mark		Name	Nat	Born	Pos	Meet	Venue	Date
1:23:53		Zhang Hongliang	CHN	1.1.99	8		Taicang	7 May
1:23:55		Xu Hao	CHN	6.2.99	9		Taicang	7 May
1:24:30	Motofumi	Suwa	JPN	22.10.99	7		Takahata	28 Oct
1:24:56	Tatsuhiki	Nagayama (10)	JPN	24.12.99	11		Nomi	14 Mar
1:25:32		Zhou Xiaojun	CHN	9.9.99	17		Taicang	7 May
1:25:45		Zhang Jiaxu	CHN	4.1.00	19		Taicang	7 May
1:26:16	Yohanis	Algaw	ETH	14.8.99	1	NC	Addis Ababa	20 Apr
1:26:20		Liu Zhi	CHN	22.3.00	25		Taicang	7 May
1:26:34		Wen Yongjie	CHN	28.9.99	29		Taicang	7 May
1:26:49	Yu	Takeuchi	JPN	19.10.99	14		Takahata	28 Oct
1:26:52		Wang Zhending	CHN	7.9.99	18		Xi'an	7 Sep
1:26:54		Zhang Hongliang	CHN	.99	19?		Xi'an	7 Sep

30-35 KILOMETRES WALK

30k	35k		Name	Nat	Born	Pos	Meet	Venue	Date
2:04:48	2:24:53	Sergey	Bakulin	RUS	13.11.86	1	NC-w	Sochi	19 Feb
2:07:04		Veli-Matti	Partanen	FIN	28.10.91	1	NC	Espoo	17 Jun
2:07:00	2:28:58	Dementiy	Cheparev	RUS	28.10.92	2	NC-w	Sochi	19 Feb
2:06:57	2:29:32	Sergey	Sharipov	RUS	14.4.92	3	NC-w	Sochi	19 Feb
2:08:06	2:30:13	Aleksey	Kudashkin	RUS	1.2.97	4	NC-w	Sochi	19 Feb
	2:30:51	Giorgio	Rubino	ITA	15.4.86	1		Grosseto	28 Jan
2:11:06	2:32:31+	Tomohiro	Noda	JPN	24.1.96	1	in 50k	Takahata	28 Oct
	2:32:37	Federico	Tontodonati	ITA	30.10.89	2		Grosseto	28 Jan
	2:33:11		Han Jijiang	CHN	20.7.93	1		Huangshan	4 Mar
	2:33:18		Wang Qin	CHN	8.5.94	2		Huangshan	4 Mar
	2:33:19+	Marco	De Luca	ITA	12.5.81	3		Grosseto	28 Jan
	2:33:38		Wang Rui	CHN	6.1.96	3		Huangshan	4 Mar
2:11:45	2:33:40+	Kai	Kobayashi	JPN	28.2.93	2	in 50k	Takahata	28 Oct
2:11:59+			Bakulin			1=	in 50k	Cheboksary	9 Jun
2:11:59+			Cheparev			1=	in 50k	Cheboksary	9 Jun
	2:33:55		Ceng Qingsheng	CHN	3.4.95	4		Huangshan	4 Mar
	2:34:20		Shan Rongjiang	CHN	26.10.96	5		Huangshan	4 Mar
2:12:16	2:36:00+	Isamu	Fujisawa	JPN	12.10.87		in 50k	Takahata	28 Oct
2:13:02	2:34:28	Valeriy	Litanyuk	UKR	2.4.94	1	NC-w	Lutsk	11 Mar
	2:34:41		Yang Liang	CHN	25.4.93	6		Huangshan	4 Mar
2:13:10			Kudashkin			3	in 50k	Cheboksary	9 Jun
2:13:10	2:35:26	Maryan	Zakalnytskyy	UKR	19.8.94	2	NC-w	Lutsk	11 Mar
2:13:27		Jarkko	Kinnunen	FIN	19.1.84	2	NC	Espoo	17 Jun
2:13:50			Lu Ning	CHN-J	12.9.99	1J		Huangshan	4 Mar
	2:35:57		Zhong Heng	CHN	7.11.95	7		Huangshan	4 Mar
2:13:50	2:35:57+	Matej	Tóth	SVK	10.2.83	1	in 50k	Dudince	24 Mar
	2:36:01		Meng Zhongkai	CHN	15.12.97	8		Huangshan	4 Mar
Doubtful mark									
	2:29:26	Sergey	Rakov	RUS-J	13.6.99	1		Kostroma	9 Sep

50 KILOMETRES WALK

Mark		Name	Nat	Born	Pos	Meet	Venue	Date
3:39:47	Tomohiro	Noda	JPN	24.1.96	1	NC	Takahata	28 Oct
3:42:20	Sergey	Bakulin	RUS	13.11.86	1	NC	Cheboksary	9 Jun
3:42:46	Matej	Tóth	SVK	10.2.83	1		Dudince	24 Mar
3:44:25	Hirooki	Arai	JPN	18.5.88	1	WTC	Taicang	5 May
3:44:31	Hayato	Katsuki	JPN	28.11.90	2	WTC	Taicang	5 May
3:44:43	Veli-Matti	Partanen	FIN	28.10.91	2		Dudince	24 Mar
3:44:52	Satoshi	Maruo	JPN	28.11.91	3	WTC	Taicang	5 May
3:44:59	Maryan	Zakalnytskyy	UKR	19.8.94	4	WTC	Taicang	5 May
3:45:29		Wang Qin	CHN	8.5.94	5	WTC	Taicang	5 May
3:45:56		Noda			1	NC	Wajima	15 Apr
3:46:26	Kai	Kobayashi (10)	JPN	28.2.93	2	NC	Takahata	28 Oct
3:46:32		Zakalnytskyy			1	EC	Berlin	7 Aug
3:47:27		Tóth			2	EC	Berlin	7 Aug
3:47:30	Masatora	Kawano	JPN	23.10.98	3	NC	Takahata	28 Oct
3:47:59	Dmitriy	Dyubin	BLR	12.7.90	3	EC	Berlin	7 Aug
3:48:01		Wang Rui	CHN	6.1.96	6	WTC	Taicang	5 May
3:48:22	Rafal	Augustyn	POL	14.5.84	7	WTC	Taicang	5 May
3:48:35	Håvard	Haukenes	NOR	22.4.90	4	EC	Berlin	7 Aug
3:48:54	Perseus	Karlström	SWE	2.5.90	8	WTC	Taicang	5 May
3:48:58	Quentin	Rew	NZL	16.7.84	9	WTC	Taicang	5 May
3:49:17	Ivan	Banzeruk	UKR	9.2.90	10	WTC	Taicang	5 May
3:49:54	Rafal	Sikora	POL	17.2.87	11	WTC	Taicang	5 May
3:50:18	Evan	Dunfee (20)	CAN	28.9.90	12	WTC	Taicang	5 May

MEN 2018

Mark	Name		Nat	Born	Pos	Meet	Venue	Date	
3:50:27	Andrés	Chocho	ECU	4.11.83	1		Monterrey	25	Feb
3:50:27	Carl	Dohmann	GER	18.5.90	5	EC	Berlin	7	Aug
3:51:22	Jonathan	Hilbert	GER	24.1.95	1	NC	Aschersleben	14	Oct
3:51:37		Augustyn			6	EC	Berlin	7	Aug
3:51:54	Takayuki	Tanii	JPN	14.2.83	4	NC	Takahata	28	Oct
3:52:17	Shuto	Goto	JPN	26.2.94	5	NC	Takahata	28	Oct
3:52:25		Dyubin			13	WTC	Taicang	5	May
	(30/25)								
3:52:40	Jarkko	Kinnunen	FIN	19.1.84	2	GER Ch	Aschersleben	14	Oct
3:53:00	Michele	Antonelli	ITA	23.5.94	14	WTC	Taicang	5	May
3:53:05	Valeriy	Litanyuk	UKR	2.4.94	15	WTC	Taicang	5	May
3:53:10	Bernardo	Barrondo	GUA	5.6.93	16	WTC	Taicang	5	May
3:53:32	Brendan	Boyce	IRL	15.10.86	17	WTC	Taicang	5	May
	(30)								
3:53:37	José Leyver	Ojeda	MEX	12.11.85	2		Monterrey	25	Feb
3:53:48	Jesús Ángel	García	ESP	17.10.69	18	WTC	Taicang	5	May
3:54:08	Nathaniel	Seiler	GER	6.4.96	8	EC	Berlin	7	Aug
3:54:20	Dementiy	Cheparev	RUS	28.10.92	2	NC	Cheboksary	9	Jun
3:54:31	Adrian	Blocki	POL	11.4.90	19	WTC	Taicang	5	May
3:54:57	Dmytro	Sobchuk	UKR	7.11.95	1	NC	Ivano-Frankivsk	20	Oct
3:55:04	Claudio	Villanueva	ECU	3.8.88	21	WTC	Taicang	5	May
3:55:09	Andrea	Agrusti	ITA	30.8.95	22	WTC	Taicang	5	May
3:55:24	Caio	Bonfim	BRA	19.3.91	1	AUS Ch	Melbourne	2	Dec
3:55:28	José Ignacio	Díaz	ESP	22.11.79	9	EC	Berlin	7	Aug
	(40)								
3:55:47	Marco	De Luca	ITA	12.5.81	10	EC	Berlin	7	Aug
3:55:48	José Leonardo	Montaña	COL	21.3.92	4		Dudince	24	Mar
3:56:05	Marc	Tur	ESP	30.11.94	1	NC	Burjassot	25	Feb
3:56:37	Benjamin	Sánchez	ESP	10.3.85	25	WTC	Taicang	5	May
3:56:40	Candeep	Kumar	IND	10.12.00	1	NO	New Delhi	17	Feb
3:57:05	Aurélien	Quinion	FRA	27.1.93	3	GER Ch	Aschersleben	14	Oct
3:57:25		Luo Dongpo	CHN	23.6.95	1	NC	Weinan	8	Sep
3:57:31	Omar	Zepeda	MEX	8.7.77	3		Monterrey	25	Feb
3:57:33		Han Jijiang	CHN	20.7.93	26	WTC	Taicang	5	May
3:58:17		Bian Tongda	CHN	1.4.91	2	NC	Weinan	8	Sep
	(50)								
3:58:25	Bence	Venyercsán	HUN	8.1.96	13	EC	Berlin	7	Aug
3:58:29	Artur	Mastianica	LTU	30.7.92	14	EC	Berlin	7	Aug
3:58:49	Isamu	Fujisawa	JPN	12.10.87	6	NC	Takahata	28	Oct
3:58:56	Jitender	Singh	IND	20.3.89	2	NC	New Delhi	17	Feb
3:59:07	Serhiy	Budza	UKR	6.12.84	2	NC	Ivano-Frankivsk	20	Oct
3:59:14	Aleksey	Terentyev	RUS	19.7.91	3	NC	Cheboksary	9	Jun
3:59:21	Dusan	Majdán	SVK	8.9.87	15	EC	Berlin	7	Aug
3:59:23A	Luis	Campos	PER	10.11.95	2	SAmG	Cochabamba	5	Jun
3:59:32	Andrey	Hrechkovskyy	UKR	30.8.93	28	WTC	Taicang	5	May
3:59:47		Niu Wenbin	CHN	20.1.91	3	NC	Weinan	8	Sep
	(60)								
3:59:48	Leonardo	Dei Tos	ITA	27.4.92	1	NC	Reggio Emilia	21	Oct
4:00:06	Arnis	Rumbenieks	LAT	4.4.88	5		Dudince	24	Mar
4:00:35	Dhamen	Singh	IND	15.10.89	3	NC	New Delhi	17	Feb
4:00:40	Tadas	Suskevicius	LTU	22.5.85	6		Dudince	24	Mar
4:00:45	Cristian	Berdeja	MEX	21.6.81	4		Monterrey	25	Feb
4:00:59	Chandan	Singh	IND	0.0.07	4	NO	New Delhi	17	Feb
4:01:17	Gregorio	Angelini	ITA	24.6.96	2	NC	Reggio Emilia	21	Oct
4:01:24	Luis	Bustamante	MEX	10.6.84	5		Monterrey	25	Feb
4:01:51	Dominik	Cerny	SVK	1.11.97	3	ITA Ch	Reggio Emilia	21	Oct
4:02:01		Wang Hao	CHN	16.8.89	2		Chifeng	3	Jul
	(70)								
4:02:15		Luo Yadong	CHN	15.1.92	4	NC	Weinan	8	Sep
4:02:28	Horacio	Nava	MEX	20.1.82	6		Monterrey	25	Feb
4:02:36	Karl	Junghannß	GER	6.4.96	31	WTC	Taicang	5	May
4:02:38		Joo Hyun-myong	KOR	31.5.97	32	WTC	Taicang	5	May
4:02:41		Wang Chao	CHN	2.5.96	5	NC	Weinan	8	Sep
4:03:09	Yuki	Yamazaki	JPN	16.1.84	4		Wajima	15	Apr
4:03:09		Meng Zhongkai	CHN	15.12.97	6	NC	Weinan	8	Sep
4:03:19	Michal	Morvay	SVK	19.8.96	4	ITA Ch	Reggio Emilia	21	Oct
4:03:39	Lukás	Gdula	CZE	6.12.91	8		Dudince	24	Mar
4:03:42	James	Rendón	COL	7.7.85	1	SAmC	Sucúa	10	Mar
	(80)								
4:03:42	Yuya	Suganami	JPN	23.10.95	7	NC	Takahata	28	Oct

Mark	Name		Nat	Born	Pos	Meet	Venue	Date
4:03:43		Wei Xubao	CHN	1.2.93	7	NC	Weinan	8 Sep
4:03:53		Xiong Denghua	CHN	29.5.95	4		Chifeng	3 Jul
4:03:53	Anatole	Ibáñez	SWE	14.11.85	20	EC	Berlin	7 Aug
4:03:55	Sergiy	Susyk	UKR	21.7.93	3	NC	Ivano-Frankivsk	20 Oct
4:04:19		Peng Shiyi	CHN	16.9.98	8	NC	Weinan	8 Sep
4:04:35		Liu Wenxing	CHN	5.12.96	9	NC	Weinan	8 Sep
4:04:48	Diego	Pinzón	COL	12.2.85	1		Owego, NY	30 Sep
4:04:51		Luo Jiayu	CHN	3.4.98	10	NC	Weinan	8 Sep
4:04:53	Anton	Radko	UKR	2.6.95	4	NC	Ivano-Frankivsk	20 Oct
(90)								
4:05:02	Mathieu	Bilodeau	CAN	27.11.83	34	WTC	Taicang	5 May
4:05:05A	Ronal	Quispe	BOL	5.3.89	3	SAmG	Cochabamba	5 Jun
4:05:15	Hugo	Andrieu	FRA	16.10.92	35	WTC	Taicang	5 May
4:05:28	Jorge	Ruiz	COL	17.5.89	2	CAG	Barranquilla	1 Aug
4:05:28	Jakub	Jelonek	POL	7.7.85	1	NC	Wien	6 Oct
4:05:41	Katsuya	Ishii	JPN	25.10.97	8	NC	Takahata	28 Oct
4:05:43	Pablo	Oliva	ESP	15.10.96	5	NC	Burjassot	25 Feb
4:06:20	Yuki	Ito	JPN	12.4.92	36	WTC	Taicang	5 May
4:06:32	Tomofumi	Kanno	JPN	25.4.93	6		Wajima	15 Apr
4:06:34	Dominic	King	GBR	30.5.83	10		Dudince	24 Mar
(100)								

Mark	Name		Nat	Born	Pos/Date		Mark	Name		Nat	Born	Pos/Date
4:06:50	Ihor	Saharuk	UKR	3.6.88	5 May		4:09:07	Marc	Mundell	RSA	7.7.83	24 Oct
4:07:27	Hitoshi	Warita	JPN	26.9.91	28 Oct		4:09:12	Aleksey	Kudashkin	RUS	1.2.97	9 Jun
4:07:40		Zhang Mingkai	CHN	30.9.98	3 Jul		4:09:32	Nick	Christie	USA	29.9.91	20 Jan
4:07:47	David	Velásquez	ECU	26.4.94	10 Mar		4:09:43	Jyoti	Tawtiya	IND	16.6.86	17 Feb
4:07:57	Tatsuya	Tanaka	JPN	.90	28 Oct		4:09:53	Oleksiy	Shelest	UKR	27.3.73	20 Oct
4:08:16	Daniel	King	GBR	30.5.83	24 Mar		(112)					
4:08:41	Florin Alin	Stirbu	ROU	21.4.92	27 Oct							

WOMEN'S WORLD LISTS 2018

60 METRES INDOORS

Mark	Name		Nat	Born	Pos	Meet	Venue	Date
6.97	Murielle	Ahouré	CIV	23.8.87	1	WI	Birmingham	2 Mar
7.01		Ahouré			1s1	WI	Birmingham	2 Mar
7.02A	Javianne	Oliver	USA	26.12.94	1	NC	Albuquerque	18 Feb
7.03	Mujinga	Kambundji	SUI	17.6.92	1	NC	Magglingen	17 Feb
7.05	Marie Josée	Ta Lou	CIV	18.11.88	2	WI	Birmingham	2 Mar
7.05		Kambundji			3	WI	Birmingham	2 Mar
7.06	Tatjana	Pinto	GER	2.7.92	1	NC	Dortmund	17 Feb
7.07		Ahouré			1		Hpouston	27 Jan
7.07		Ta Lou			1		Metz	11 Feb
7.07		Ta Lou			1	GP	Glasgow	25 Feb
7.07	Elaine	Thompson	JAM	28.6.92	2s1	WI	Birmingham	2 Mar
7.07	Aleia	Hobbs	USA	24.2.96	1	NCAA	College Station	10 Mar
(								
7.08A	Mikiah	Brisco	USA	14.7.96	1		Albuquerque	3 Feb
7.08	Dina	Asher-Smith	GBR	4.12.95	1h1	GP	Glasgow	25 Feb
7.09	Carina	Horn (10)	RSA	9.3.89	2		Metz	11 Feb
7.09	Dafne	Schippers	NED	15.6.92	1	NC	Apeldoorn	17 Feb
7.11	Gina	Lückenkemper	GER	21.11.96	1		Dortmund	21 Jan
7.11	Carolle	Zahi	FRA	12.6.94	1h4	WI	Birmingham	2 Mar
7.12	Lisa	Mayer	GER	2.5.96	2		Karlsruhe	3 Feb
7.12	Asha	Philip	GBR	25.10.90	3		Karlsruhe	3 Feb
7.12	Natalliah	Whyte	JAM	9.8.97	3	NCAA	College Station	10 Mar
7.13	Remona	Burchell	JAM	15.9.91	1		Mondeville	3 Feb
7.13	Michelle-Lee	Ahye	TTO	10.4.92	6	WI	Birmingham	2 Mar
7.14	Tori	Bowie	USA	27.8.90	2	Millrose	New York (Arm)	3 Feb
7.14	Christania	Williams	JAM	17.10.94	4	GP	Glasgow	25 Feb
(20)								
7.15	Jonielle	Smith	JAM	30.1.96	1h1	NCAA	College Station	9 Mar
7.17	Ezinne	Okparaebo	NOR	3.3.88	5		Karlsruhe	3 Feb
7.17	Jamile	Samuel	NED	24.4.92	2	NC	Apeldoorn	17 Feb
7.17	Kate	Hall	USA	12.1.97	2h1	NCAA	College Station	9 Mar
7.18	Kortnei	Johnson	USA	11.8.97	1		Fayetteville	27 Jan
7.18	Morolake	Akinuson	USA	17.5.94	1h1		Lubbock	27 Jan
7.18A	Makenzie	Dunmore	USA	7.10.97	1		Albuquerque	10 Feb
7.18	Ewa	Swoboda	POL	26.7.97	3		Torun	15 Feb
7.19A	Ashley	Henderson	USA	4.12.95	2		Albuquerque	10 Feb
7.19A	Destiny	Carter	USA	9.10.92	2	NC	Albuquerque	18 Feb
(30)								

MEN 2018

Mark	Wind	Name		Nat	Born	Pos	Meet	Venue	Date
7.20A			Liang Xiaojing	CHN	7.4.97	1	AsiC	Tehran	2 Feb
7.20		Rosângela	Santos	BRA	20.12.90	1		Liévin	13 Feb
7.20		Quanesha	Burks	USA	15.3.95	2h2	GP	Glasgow	25 Feb
7.21		Imani	Lansiquot	GBR	17.12.97	5		Torun	15 Feb
7.21		Kelly-Ann	Baptiste	TTO	14.10.86	6s1	WI	Birmingham	2 Mar
7.21		Cassondra	Hall	USA	23.9.97	3h2	NCAA	College Station	9 Mar
7.21			Wei Yongli	CHN	11.10.91	1	NGP	Xi'an	11 Mar
7.22		Orlann	Ombissa-Dzangue	FRA	26.5.91	2r5		Reims	31 Jan
7.22		Jada	Baylark	USA	17.10.97	3		Fayetteville	9 Feb
7.22		Simone	Facey	JAM	7.5.85	6		Torun	15 Feb
(40)									
7.22		Naomi	Sedney	NED	17.12.94	3	NC	Apeldoorn	17 Feb
7.22A		Teahna	Daniels	USA	27.3.97	3	NC	Albuquerque	18 Feb
7.22		Twanisha	Terry	USA-J	24.1.99	5h2	NCAA	College Station	9 Mar
7.23		Anna	Kiełbasinska	POL	26.6.90	1h2		Spała	4 Feb
7.23		Rebekka	Haase	GER	2.1.93	1h1		Chemnitz	10 Feb
7.23		Klára	Seidlová	CZE	10.3.94	1	NC	Praha	17 Feb
7.24		Deajah	Stevens	USA	19.5.95	1		New York (Arm)	26 Jan
7.24		Barbara	Pierre	USA	28.4.87	4h1		Karlsruhe	3 Feb
7.24		Daryll	Neita	GBR	29.8.96	1s1	NC	Birmingham	17 Feb
7.24		Ajla	Del Ponte	SUI	15.7.96	2	NC	Magglingen	17 Feb
(50)									
7.24		Jayla	Kirkland	USA-J	13.2.99	1		Clemson	24 Feb
7.24		Ka'tia	Seymour	USA	3.10.97	2		Clemson	24 Feb
7.24		Anna	Bongiorni	ITA	15.9.93	4h6	WI	Birmingham	2 Mar
7.25		Kristina	Timanovskaya	BLR	19.11.96	1		Mogilev	17 Jan
7.25		Gayon	Evans	JAM	15.1.90	4		Düsseldorf	6 Feb
7.25		Ky	Westbrook	USA	25.2.96	2		Clemson	10 Feb
7.25		Celera	Barnes	USA	2.12.98	3		Clemson	10 Feb
7.25		Gabrielle	Thomas	USA	7.12.96	1h2		Hanover NH	24 Feb
7.25			Yuan Qiqi	CHN	26.10.95	1	NGP	Xianlin	7 Mar
7.25		Tamari	Davis	USA-Y	15.2.03	1	HS Nat	New York (Arm)	11 Mar
(60)									

Mark	Name		Nat	Born	Date
7.26	Shavine	Hodges	JAM	22.10.91	19 Jan
7.26	Rebakah	Smith	USA	1.1.98	19 Jan
7.26	Schillonie	Calvert-Powell	JAM	27.7.88	20 Jan
7.26	Bianca	Williams	GBR	18.12.93	17 Feb
7.26	Crystal	Emmanuel	CAN	27.11.91	2 Mar
7.26	Dianna	Johnson	JAM	12.11.95	10 Mar
7.26A	Marybeth	Sant	USA	6.4.95	7 Dec
7.27	Hrystyna	Stuy	UKR	3.2.88	18 Jan
7.27	Torie	Robinson	USA	11.6.96	27 Jan
7.27	Lorène	Bazolo	POR	4.5.83	3 Feb
7.27	Salomé	Kora	SUI	8.6.94	17 Feb
7.27	Rachel	Miller	GBR	29.1.90	17 Feb
7.27	Vitória Cristina	Rosa	BRA	12.1.96	17 Feb
7.27	Amy	Foster	IRL	2.10.88	18 Feb
7.27A	Jerayah	Davis	USA	15.4.96	23 Feb
7.27	Kiara	Parker	USA	28.10.96	24 Feb
7.28	Jura	Levy	JAM	4.11.90	20 Jan
7.28	Dezerea	Bryant	USA	27.4.93	3 Feb
7.28	Kristina	Sivkova	RUS	28.2.97	4 Feb
7.28	Shauna	Helps	JAM	23.10.96	24 Feb
7.29	Leya	Buchanan	CAN	17.8.96	12 Jan
7.29	Brianna	Duncan	USA	6.10.98	13 Jan
7.29	Kerron	Stewart	JAM	16.4.84	28 Jan
7.29	Isidora	Jiménez	CHI	10.8.93	3 Feb
7.29	Rafailía	Spanoudáki-Hatziríga	GRE	7.6.94	10 Feb
7.29	Stephanie	Kalu	NGR	5.8.93	17 Feb
7.29	Tamara	Clark	USA-J	9.1.99	24 Feb

Best at low altitude

7.10	Oliver	4s1	WI	Birmingham	2 Mar	7.10	Brisco	1	SEC	College Station	25 Feb

100 METRES

Mark	Wind	Name		Nat	Born	Pos	Meet	Venue	Date
10.85	1.5	Marie Josée	Ta Lou	CIV	18.11.88	1	DL	Doha	4 May
10.85	0.0	Dina	Asher-Smith	GBR	4.12.95	1	EC	Berlin	7 Aug
10.88	1.9		Ta Lou			1	Pre	Eugene	26 May
10.89	0.1		Ta Lou			1	Herc	Monaco	20 Jul
10.90	1.5	Blessing	Okagbare	NGR	9.10.88	2	DL	Doha	4 May
10.90	1.9	Aleia	Hobbs	USA	24.2.96	1q3	NCAA-E	Tampa	25 May
10.90	1.9	Murielle	Ahouré	CIV	23.8.87	2	Pre	Eugene	26 May
10.90	1.3		Ta Lou			1	Athl	Lausanne	5 Jul
10.91	1.6		Ahouré			1	Bisl	Oslo	7 Jun
10.91	0.0		Hobbs			1s3	NCAA	Eugene	7 Jun
10.91	0.6		Hobbs			1	NC	Des Moines	22 Jun
10.92	1.5		Hobbs			1	SEC	Knoxville	13 May
10.92	1.6		Asher-Smith			2	Bisl	Oslo	7 Jun
10.93	1.5	Elaine	Thompson	JAM	28.6.92	3	DL	Doha	4 May
10.93	0.4		Hobbs			1h4	SEC	Knoxville	12 May
10.93	-0.1		Asher-Smith			1	DL	Stockholm	10 Jun
10.93	0.2		Asher-Smith			1s1	EC	Berlin	7 Aug
10.95	1.1		Ta Lou			1		Montreuil	19 Jun
10.95	1.1	Mujinga	Kambundji	SUI	17.6.92	1	NC	Zofingen	13 Jul
10.96	1.5		Ahouré			4	DL	Doha	4 May

Mark	Wind	Name		Nat	Born	Pos	Meet	Venue	Date
10.96	0.6	Ashley	Henderson	USA	4.12.95	2	NC	Des Moines	22 Jun
10.96	0.9	Jenna	Prandini	USA	20.11.92	1	NACAC	Toronto	11 Aug
10.97	1.7		Hobbs			1h1	NC	Des Moines	21 Jun
10.97	-0.5		Asher-Smith			1	NC	Birmingham	30 Jun
10.98	0.3		Henderson			1		Tucson	28 Apr
10.98	1.5	Carina	Horn (10)	RSA	9.3.89	5	DL	Doha	4 May
10.98	1.8		Hobbs			1h2	NCAA-E	Tampa	24 May
10.98	1.9		Thompson			3	Pre	Eugene	26 May
10.98	1.5	Shania	Collins	USA	14.11.96	1s1	NCAA	Eugene	7 Jun
10.98	0.6		Prandini			3	NC	Des Moines	22 Jun
10.98	0.1	Shelly-Ann	Fraser-Pryce	JAM	27.12.86	1	DL	London (OS)	21 Jul
10.98	0.2	Gina	Lückenkemper	GER	21.11.96	2s1	EC	Berlin	7 Aug
10.98	0.0		Lückenkemper			2	EC	Berlin	7 Aug
			(33/13)						
10.99	1.7	Twanisha	Terry	USA-J	24.1.99	1	MSR	Torrance	21 Apr
10.99	1.8	Dezerea	Bryant	USA	27.4.93	1h2	NC	Des Moines	21 Jun
10.99	1.2		Wei Yongli	CHN	11.10.91	1h1		La Chaux-de-Fonds	1 Jul
10.99	0.0	Dafne	Schippers	NED	15.6.92	3	EC	Berlin	7 Aug
11.01A	-1.5	Ángela	Tenorio	ECU	27.1.96	1h1	SAmG	Cochabamba	6 Jun
11.01	1.5	Carolle	Zahi	FRA	12.6.94	1	NC	Albi	7 Jul
11.02	1.5	Tamara	Clark	USA-J	9.1.99	3	SEC	Knoxville	13 May
			(20)						
11.02	0.9	English	Gardner	USA	22.4.92	1	Quercia	Rovereto	23 Aug
11.03	1.9	Tori	Bowie	USA	27.8.90	5	Pre	Eugene	26 May
11.03	0.3	Vitória Cristina	Rosa	BRA	12.1.96	1		Guadalajara, ESP	5 Jul
11.04	1.5	Natalliah	Whyte	JAM	9.8.97	4	SEC	Knoxville	13 May
11.04	1.1	Jada	Baylark	USA	17.10.97	1q2	NCAA-W	Sacramento	25 May
11.04	-0.1	Kristina	Timanovskaya	BLR	19.11.96	1		Minsk	11 Jul
11.05	0.4	Mikiah	Brisco	USA	14.7.96	1q2	NCAA-E	Tampa	25 May
11.06	1.6	Michelle-Lee	Ahye	TTO	10.4.92	3	Bisl	Oslo	7 Jun
11.06	1.5	Orlann	Ombissa-Dzangue	FRA	26.5.91	2	NC	Albi	7 Jul
11.07	1.6	Semoy	Hackett	TTO	27.11.88	1		Montverde	9 Jun
			(30)						
11.07	0.1	Jonielle	Smith	JAM	30.1.96	3	DL	London (OS)	21 Jul
11.08	1.5	Ariana	Washington	USA	27.8.96	2s1	NCAA	Eugene	7 Jun
11.10	1.7	Kortnei	Johnson	USA	11.8.97	1h1	NCAA-E	Tampa	24 May
11.10	1.9	Javianne	Oliver	USA	26.12.94	8	Pre	Eugene	26 May
11.10	0.3	Jamile	Samuel	NED	24.4.92	2s3	EC	Berlin	7 Aug
11.11	0.9	Teahna	Daniels	USA	27.3.97	1		Waco	13 May
11.11	-0.1	Tatjana	Pinto	GER	2.7.92	1h1		Regensburg	3 Jun
11.11	0.1	Imani	Lansiquot	GBR	17.12.97	5	DL	London (OS)	21 Jul
11.11	0.9	Crystal	Emmanuel	CAN	27.11.91	3	NACAC	Toronto	11 Aug
11.12A	-1.2	Narcisa	Landázuri	ECU	25.11.92	1h2	SAmG	Cochabamba	6 Jun
			(40)						
11.13	1.7	Briana	Williams	JAM-Y	21.3.02	1		Jacksonville	17 Mar
11.13	1.4	Taylor	Bennett	USA	15.1.97	1h2		Waco	12 May
11.13	1.5	Kiara	Parker	USA	28.10.96	7	SEC	Knoxville	13 May
11.13	1.7	Ka'Tia	Seymour	USA	3.10.97	2h1	NCAA-E	Tampa	24 May
11.13	1.6	Tamari	Davis	USA-Y	15.2.03	3		Montverde	9 Jun
11.13	0.6	Aaliyah	Brown	USA	6.1.95	5	NC	Des Moines	22 Jun
11.13	0.4	Shericka	Jackson	JAM	16.7.94	3		Kingston	22 Jun
11.15	0.8	Lekeisha	Lawson	USA	3.6.87	1		Chula Vista	9 Jun
11.15	1.5	Orphée	Neola	FRA	1.2.91	2s3	NC	Albi	6 Jul
11.16	0.9	Kevona	Davis	JAM-Y	20.12.01	1		Kingston	23 Mar
			(50)						
11.16	0.4	Celera	Barnes	USA	2.12.98	3q2	NCAA-E	Tampa	25 May
11.16	-0.1	Kristal	Awuah	GBR-J	7.8.99	1rB	ISTAF	Berlin	2 Sep
11.17	0.9	Leya	Buchanan	CAN	17.8.96	2		Waco	13 May
11.17	1.6	Hajar Saad	Al-Khaldi	BRN	17.3.95	1	W.Asian	Amman	9 Jul
11.18	1.2	Kianna	Gray	USA	30.12.96	2h6	NCAA-E	Tampa	24 May
11.18	1.1	Ivet	Lalova-Collio	BUL	18.5.84	3		Montreuil	19 Jun
11.18	1.8	Deajah	Stevens	USA	19.5.95	3h2	NC	Des Moines	21 Jun
11.18	0.0	Barbara	Pierre	USA	28.4.87	2		Bragança Paulista	8 Jul
11.19	-0.4	Quanesha	Burks	USA	15.3.95	2		Baton Rouge	28 Apr
11.19	1.9	Gabrielle	Thomas	USA	7.12.96	2h4	NCAA-E	Tampa	24 May
			(60)						
11.19A	-1.2	Isidora	Jiménez	CHI	10.8.93	2h2	SAmG	Cochabamba	6 Jun
11.19	-0.5	Daryll	Neita	GBR	29.8.96	2	NC	Birmingham	30 Jun
11.19	0.4	Jeneba	Tarmoh	USA	27.9.89	1rB		Bellinzona	18 Jul
11.20	0.0	Brianne	Bethel	BAH	5.7.98	1		Cincinnati	13 May
11.20	0.3	Viktoriya	Zyabkina	KAZ	4.9.92	1		Almaty	29 Jun

WOMEN 2018

Mark	Wind	Name		Nat	Born	Pos	Meet	Venue	Date
11.20	-0.5	Bianca	Williams	GBR	18.12.93	3	NC	Birmingham	30 Jun
11.20	1.4	Sarah	Atcho	SUI	1.6.95	1s2	NC	Zofingen	13 Jul
11.20	1.7	Hrystyna	Stuy	UKR	3.2.88	1	NC	Lutsk	19 Jul
11.21	0.5	Asha	Philip	GBR	25.10.90	1s1	CG	Gold Coast	8 Apr
11.21	1.0	Christania	Williams	JAM	17.10.94	2	CG	Gold Coast	9 Apr
(70)									
11.21	0.9	Cassondra	Hall	USA	23.9.97	1		Coral Gables	14 Apr
11.21	0.9	Rachel	Misher	USA	4.2.97	2		Coral Gables	14 Apr
11.21	0.8	Kayla	White	USA	24.9.96	1h2		Greensboro	14 Apr
11.21	1.5	Deanna	Hill	USA	13.4.96	2q1	NCAA-W	Sacramento	25 May
11.21	1.6	Janet	Amponsah	GHA	12.4.93	4		Montverde	9 Jun
11.21	1.1	Irene	Siragusa	ITA	23.6.93	1		Orvieto	17 Jun
11.21	1.8	Gabriele	Cunningham	USA	22.2.98	4h2	NC	Des Moines	21 Jun
11.21	1.4	Zakiya	Denoon	TTO	23.1.95	1s1		Port of Spain	23 Jun
11.21	1.2	Ajla	Del Ponte	SUI	15.7.96	2h1		La Chaux-de-Fonds	1 Jul
11.22	1.0	Gayon	Evans	JAM	15.1.90	3	CG	Gold Coast	9 Apr
(80)									
11.22	0.6	Devynne	Charlton	BAH	26.11.95	1		Bloomington	13 May
11.22	1.9	Rebekah	Smith	USA	1.5.98	4q3	NCAA-E	Tampa	25 May
11.22	0.5	Jura	Levy	JAM	4.11.90	3h2		Kingston	22 Jun
11.23	0.7	Kelly-Ann	Baptiste	TTO	14.10.86	3		Clermont	28 Apr
11.23	1.5	Jasmin	Reed	USA-J	21.2.00	2q3	NCAA-W	Sacramento	25 May
11.23	0.7	Khalifa	St. Fort	TTO	13.2.98	2		Port of Spain	23 Jun
11.23	0.0	Rosângela	Santos	BRA	20.12.90	3		Bragança Paulista	8 Jul
11.23mx	1.4	Rachel	Miller	GBR	29.1.90	1mx		London (LV)	1 Aug
11.23	-0.1	Ewa	Swoboda	POL	26.7.97	1	Skol	Chorzów	22 Aug
11.24	0.2	Naomi	Sedney	NED	17.12.94	3		Gainesville	13 Apr
(90)									
11.24	1.0	Charminique	Hackney	USA	20.1.98	1		Prairie View	6 May
11.24	1.6	Ezinne	Okparaebo	NOR	3.3.88	7	Bisl	Oslo	7 Jun
11.24	1.2	Andrea	Purica	VEN	21.11.95	1h2	CAG	Barranquilla	29 Jul
11.25	0.3	Makenzie	Dunmore	USA	7.10.97	2		Tucson	28 Apr
11.25	-0.3	Kerron	Stewart	JAM	16.4.84	2		Kingston	19 May
11.25	0.4	Maia	McCoy	USA	9.12.96	6q2	NCAA-E	Tampa	25 May
11.25	1.5	Angie	Annelus	USA	10.1.97	3q3	NCAA-W	Sacramento	25 May
11.25	1.1	Salomé	Kora	SUI	8.6.94	3	NC	Zofingen	13 Jul
11.26	-0.3	Natasha	Morrison	JAM	17.11.92	3		Kingston	19 May
11.26	1.9	Shauna	Helps	JAM	23.10.96	5q3	NCAA-E	Tampa	25 May
(100)									
11.26	1.1	Laura	Müller	GER	11.12.95	1h2		Weinheim	6 Jul

Mark	Wind	Name	Nat	Born	Date
11.27A	1.7	Tebogo Mamathu	RSA	27.5.95	16 Mar
11.27	1.7	Destinee Brown	USA	6.7.94	21 Apr
11.27	2.0	Brianna Duncan	USA	6.10.98	28 Apr
11.27	1.4	Raven Grant	USA	.97	12 May
11.27	1.8	Rafailía Spanoudáki-Hatziríga	GRE	7.6.94	26 May
11.27	1.6	Tawanna Meadows	USA	4.8.86	9 Jun
11.28	0.1	Brittany Brown	USA	18.4.95	21 Apr
11.28	0.7	Bethany White	USA	.96	5 May
11.28	0.6	Felicia Brown	USA	27.10.93	5 May
11.28	1.8	Stella Akakpo	FRA	28.2.94	6 May
11.28	2.0	Phil Healy	IRL	19.11.94	6 Jun
11.29	1.2	Kasheika Cameron	JAM	22.10.98	23 Mar
11.29	1.6	Destiny Smith Barnott	USA	26.7.06	20 Apr
11.29	0.3	Lauren Rain Williams	USA-J	23.7.99	28 Apr
11.29	1.9	Lisa-Marie Kwayie	GER	27.10.96	28 Apr
11.29	1.6	Tiffany Townsend	USA	14.6.89	12 May
11.29	2.0	Caitland Smith	USA	24.3.96	13 May
11.29	1.2	Alfreda Steele	USA	19.12.97	24 May
11.29	1.1	Sindija Buksa	LAT	14.12.97	29 May
11.29	0.5	Dutee Chand	IND	3.2.96	29 Jun
11.29	0.5	Marije van Hunenstijn	NED	2.3.95	1 Jul
11.29	-0.4	Kristina Sivkova	RUS	28.2.97	27 Jul
11.30	0.5	Kate Hall	USA	12.1.97	12 May
11.30	0.0	Allyson Felix	USA	18.11.85	12 May
11.30	1.4	Estela García	ESP	20.3.89	21 Jul
11.30	0.3	Ofonime Odiong	BRN	13.3.97	26 Aug
11.31A	1.7	Cassidy Williamson	RSA	24.10.98	16 Mar
11.31A	0.6	Tobi Amusan	NGR	23.4.97	24 Mar
11.31	0.4	Yunisleidy García	CUB-J	11.8.99	27 Jun
11.32	1.2	Candyce McGrone	USA	24.3.89	21 Apr
11.32	0.5	Torie Robinson	USA	11.6.96	28 Apr
11.32	1.4	Rushelle Burton	JAM	4.12.97	12 May
11.32	1.6	Kai Selvon	TTO	13.4.92	9 Jun
11.32	0.1	Shashalee Forbes	JAM	10.5.96	22 Jun
11.32	0.5	Jodean Williams	JAM	11.11.93	22 Jun
11.32	-0.5	Lorraine Ugen	GBR	22.8.91	30 Jun
11.32	0.0	Franciela Krasucki	BRA	26.4.88	8 Jul
11.33	1.9	Shavine Hodges	JAM	22.10.91	28 Apr
11.33	1.8	Jennifer Montag	GER	11.2.98	30 Jun
11.33	1.7	Maria Isabel Pérez	ESP	1.3.93	21 Jul
11.33	0.7	Lorène Dorcas Bazolo	POR	4.5.83	29 Jul
11.34	1.6	Janeek Brown	JAM	14.5.98	27 Apr
11.34	0.6	Jayla Kirkland	USA-J	13.2.99	24 May
11.34	1.5	Brenessa Thompson	GUY	22.7.96	25 May
11.34A	1.3	Kong Lingwei	CHN	28.7.95	15 Jun
11.34	-1.1	Daija Lampkin	USA-J	11.7.99	15 Jun
11.35	1.2	Phyllis Francis	USA	4.5.92	21 Apr
11.35	1.7	Kynnedy Flannel	USA-J	12.7.00	13 May
11.35	1.4	Rebekka Haase	GER	2.1.93	26 May
11.35	1.4	Inna Eftimova	BUL	19.6.88	2 Jun
11.35	0.4	Keshia Kwadwo	GER-J	10.7.99	3 Jun
11.35		Shenel Crooke	SKN	12.10.93	17 Jun
11.35	0.1	Sherone Simpson	JAM	12.8.84	22 Jun
11.35	-0.1	Liang Xiaojing	CHN	7.4.97	14 Sep
11.36	0.4	Reyare Thomas	TTO	23.11.87	8 Apr
11.36	0.0	LaTessa Johnson	USA	13.4.97	13 May
11.37	-0.7	Gladys Igbinosun	NGR	23.7.93	14 Feb
11.37	1.4	De'Shalyn Jones	USA	5.1.96	21 Apr
11.37	1.7	Diamond Spaulding	USA	29.9.96	21 Apr
11.37	0.7	India Brown	USA	29.1.96	5 May
11.37	0.6	Ashton Purvis	USA	12.7.92	2 Jun
11.37	0.4	Jessica-Bianca Wessolly	GER	11.12.96	3 Jun
11.37	1.7	Mikele Barber	USA	4.10.80	9 Jun
11.37	1.7	Kaylin Whitney	USA	9.3.98	21 Jun
11.37	1.3	Joanna Atkins	USA	6.1.89	16 Jul
11.38	0.1	Abby Steiner	USA-J	24.11.99	2 Jun
11.38	0.2	Diana Vaisman	ISR	23.7.98	4 Jul
11.38	1.9	Anastasiya Grigoryeva	RUS	7.11.93	19 Jul
11.38	-0.4	Ashleigh Nelson	GBR	20.2.91	21 Jul

Mark	Wind	Name	Nat	Born	Pos	Meet	Venue	Date
11.39	1.2	Michae Harriott	JAM-J	1.6.00				31 Mar
11.39	0.6	Savannah Roberson	USA	15.1.96				13 May
11.39	0.1	Kendra Harrison	USA	18.9.92				20 May
11.39	0.4	Adriana Rodríguez	CUB-J	12.7.99				27 Jun
11.39	-0.7	Anna Bongiorni	ITA	15.9.93				20 Jul
11.39	1.5	Marileidy Paulino	DOM	25.10.96				29 Jul
11.40A	1.4	Victoria Woodward	ARG	30.11.91				13 May
11.40	1.7	Shannon Ray	USA	31.12.95				24 May
11.40	1.1	Joy Udo-Gabriel	NGR-J	2.6.99				18 Jul
11.40		Le Tu Chinh	VIE	4.7.97				27 Nov
11.41A	1.6	Tamzin Thomas	RSA	6.10.97				15 Mar
11.41	1.0	Euricka Hardy	USA	21.3.95				6 May
11.41	0.7	Paula Sevilla	ESP	28.6.97				9 Jun
11.41	0.5	Kimberlyn Duncan	USA	2.8.91				9 Jul
11.41	1.3	Corinne Humphreys	GBR	7.11.91				16 Jul
11.42	1.6	Chelsea Francis	USA	14.10.96				24 Mar
11.42	0.5	Hannah Cunliffe	USA	9.1.96				21 Apr
11.42	1.3	Chisato Fukushima	JPN	27.6.88				29 Apr
11.42	0.8	Madiea Ghafoor	NED	9.9.92				26 May
11.42	-1.1	Thelma Davies	USA-J	8.5.00				15 Jun
11.42		Shanice Elliott	SKN-J	.99				17 Jun
11.42	1.2	Krisztina Khorosheva	RUS	5.4.93				19 Jul
11.42	0.6	Cristina Lara	ESP	5.8.95				21 Jul
11.42	-0.5	Olga Safronova	KAZ	5.11.91				26 Aug
11.42	0.1	K. Ranga	IND	24.4.95				10 Dec
11.43		ten women						

Wind assisted

Mark	Wind	Name	Nat	Born	Pos	Meet	Venue	Date
10.72	2.7	Blessing Okagbare	NGR	9.10.88	1	TexasR	Austin	31 Mar
10.86	3.7	Aleia Hobbs	USA	24.2.96	1	TexasR	Austin	31 Mar
10.89	2.2	Hobbs			1s2	NC	Des Moines	22 Jun
10.91	3.0	Ashley Henderson	USA	4.12.95	1h4	NC	Des Moines	21 Jun
10.91	2.4	Ahouré			1		Sotteville-lès-Rouen	17 Jul
10.93	2.2	Hobbs			1h1	TexasR	Austin	30 Mar
10.95	3.0	Jenna Prandini	USA	20.11.92	2h4	NC	Des Moines	21 Jun
10.96	2.6	Twanisha Terry	USA-J	24.1.99	1	Pac-12	Stanford	13 May
10.97	3.5	Terry			1		Los Angeles	24 Mar
10.97	3.4	Kortnei Johnson	USA	11.8.97	1h3	TexasR	Austin	30 Mar
10.98	3.5	Deanna Hill	USA	13.4.96	2		Los Angeles	24 Mar
10.98	3.7	Johnson			2	TexasR	Austin	31 Mar
10.99	2.7	Mikiah Brisco	USA	14.7.96	2	TexasR	Austin	31 Mar
10.99	2.8	Gabrielle Thomas	USA	7.12.96	1q1	NCAA-E	Tampa	25 May
11.02	5.8	Jada Baylark	USA	17.10.97	1		Fayetteville	14 Apr
11.02	2.8	Kianna Gray	USA	30.12.96	2q1	NCAA-E	Tampa	25 May
11.04	3.5	Javianne Oliver	USA	26.12.94	1		Knoxville	14 Apr
11.04	2.3	Jonielle Smith	JAM	30.1.96	1	CAG	Barranquilla	30 Jul
11.07	3.5	Sydney McLaughlin	USA-J	7.8.99	2		Knoxville	14 Apr
11.12	3.6	Sha'Carri Richardson	USA-J	25.3.00	1		Austin	13 May
11.12	2.7	Ewa Swoboda	POL	26.7.97	1	NC	Lublin	20 Jul
11.15	2.3	Khalifa St. Fort	TTO	13.2.98	2	CAG	Barranquilla	30 Jul
11.16	3.7	Torie Robinson	USA	11.6.96	5	TexasR	Austin	31 Mar
11.16	3.7	Brenessa Thompson	GUY	22.7.96	6	TexasR	Austin	31 Mar
11.16	3.0	Phil Healy	IRL	19.11.94	1		Waterford	5 May
11.17	3.8	Maria Isabel Pérez	ESP	1.3.93	1	NC	Getafe	21 Jul
11.17	3.3	Rosemary Chukwuma	NGR-Y	5.12.01	1r2	YOG	Buenos Aires	15 Oct
11.19	3.1	Tawanna Meadows	USA	4.8.86	1		Austin	14 Apr
11.19	5.8	Janeek Brown	JAM	14.5.98	3		Fayetteville	14 Apr
11.19	3.1	Cassondra Hall	USA	23.9.97	4s2	NCAA	Eugene	7 Jun
11.20A	3.3	Dianna Johnson	JAM	12.11.95	1		Golden	29 Apr
11.20	3.8	Cristina Lara	ESP	5.8.95	2	NC	Getafe	21 Jul
11.21	3.8	Reyare Thomas	TTO	23.11.87	1		Port of Spain	17 Feb
11.21	2.7	Kerron Stewart	JAM	16.4.84	1		Auburn	14 Apr
11.21	3.0	Candyce McGrone	USA	24.3.89	4h4	NC	Des Moines	21 Jun
11.22	3.4	Savannah Roberson	USA	15.1.96	1		Louisville	14 Apr
11.22	2.3	Chelsea Francis	USA	14.10.96	1		San Marcos	28 Apr
11.23	2.7	Anna Kielbasinska	POL	26.6.90	2	NC	Lublin	20 Jul
11.23	3.3	Julien Alfred	LCA-Y	10.6.01	2r2	YOG	Buenos Aires	15 Oct
11.24	3.5	Jasmine Camacho-Quinn	PUR	21.8.96	3		Knoxville	14 Apr
11.24	2.8	Jayla Kirkland	USA-J	13.2.99	4q1	NCAA-E	Tampa	25 May
11.24	2.1	Mercy Ntia-Obong	NGR		1		Lagos	14 Jun
11.25	3.5	Shannon Ray	USA	31.12.95	3		Los Angeles	24 Mar
11.25	3.7	LaTessa Johnson	USA	13.4.97	8	TexasR	Austin	31 Mar
11.25	4.0	Destiny Smith-Barnett	USA	26.7.96	1h2		Clovis	11 May
11.25	3.1	Aniekeme Alphonsus	NGR	25.12.98	1		Tulsa	12 May
11.25	4.5	Shian Hyde	JAM		1	JUCO	El Dorado	19 May

Mark	Wind	Name	Nat	Born	Date
11.26	4.5	Robyn Byrd	USA		19 May
11.27	2.2	Marileidy Paulino	DOM	25.10.96	29 Jul
11.28	2.4	Inna Eftimova	BUL	19.6.88	26 Jun
11.29	3.3	Gabriela Anahí Suárez	ECU-Y		19 May
11.30	2.5	Courtne' Davis	USA	29.6.96	21 Apr
11.30	3.2	Simone Glenn	USA	16.5.96	11 May
11.30	3.2	Venessa D'arpino	USA	13.12.95	12 May
11.30	3.7	Klára Seidlová	CZE	10.3.94	18 Jul
11.32	6.0	Hanna-Maari Latvala	FIN	30.10.87	1 Jul
11.33	3.5	Anavia Battle	USA-J	28.3.99	24 Mar
11.33	2.6	Rene Medley	JAM	21.8.96	6 May
11.33	4.5	Keosha Saunders	USA		19 May
11.33	2.2	Magdalena Stefanowicz	POL-J	21.9.00	23 Jun
11.34	4.0	Rochene Smith	JAM	19.4.95	11 May
11.34	4.5	Nercely Soto	VEN	23.8.90	19 May
11.34	2.5	Helene Rønningen	NOR	4.9.98	7 Jun
11.34	3.0	Kimberlyn Duncan	USA	2.8.91	19 May
11.34	2.2	Martyna Kotwila	POL-J	13.1.99	23 Jun
11.35	5.8	Lakayla Harris	USA	29.1.97	14 Apr
11.35	4.9	Katara Nelson	USA	7.3.95	12 May
11.35	7.0	Kimbely Baptiste	GBR	27.12.92	28 Jul
11.37	3.3	Aiyanna Stiverne	CAN	20.2.95	7 Apr
11.37	3.2	Kaysha Love	USA	24.9.97	11 May
11.37	3.3	Melanise Chapman	USA	28.4.91	17 May
11.37	4.9	Sarah Richard-Mingas	FRA	2.4.98	6 Jul
11.38A	2.9	Arria Minor	USA-Y	9.2.01	7 Apr

WOMEN 2018

Mark	Wind	Name		Nat	Born	Pos	Meet	Venue	Date
11.38	2.4	Simone	Facey	JAM	7.5.85	17 Jul			
11.39	3.3	Symone	Mason	USA-J	31.8.99	7 Apr			
11.39	2.1	Tiffani	Johnson	USA		27 Apr			
11.41	2.1	Jessica	Peris	AUS	7.1.90	7 Jan			

11.41	3.4	Amber	Ivy	USA	2.11.97	30 Mar
11.41	3.7	Wadeline	Jonathas	HAI	19.2.98	5 May
11.42	2.5	Persis	Williams-Mensah	GHA	15.6.96	11 May
11.42	4.6	Ornella	Livingston	JAM	19.5.91	13 May
11.42	7.0	Hannah	Brier	GBR	3.2.98	28 Jul

Best at low altitude

11.13	0.3	Tenorio	2	Guadalajara, ESP	5 Jul
11.23	1.1	Landázuri	2h1	Guadalajara, ESP	5 Jul
11.30	1.2	Mamathu		1	Jul

11.35	0.3	Jiménez		4 May
			11.27w 2.2	21 Jul
11.41	0.1	T Thomas		20 Jun

Hand timed

11.1	0.1	Lorraine	Martins	BRA-J	4.4.00	2h1		São Paulo	26 May
11.2	-2.0	Inna	Eftimova	BUL	19.6.88	1h2		Stara Zagora	20 Jul
10.7mxw		Marie Josée	Ta Lou	CIV	18.11.88	1mx		Abidjan	29 Apr

JUNIORS

See main list for top 7 juniors. 10 performances by 6 women to 11.16 (and 4 wa by 3) Additional marks and further juniors:

Terry		11.03	0.4	1s1	WJ	Tampere	12 Jul
		11.08	1.5	3s1	NCAA	Eugene	7 Jun

		11.12	1.5	1q1	NCAA	W Sacramento	25 May
		10.97w	2.6	1		Stanford	24 Mar

B Williams		11.16	0.0	1	WJ	Tampere	12 Jul

11.29	0.3	Lauren Rain	Williams	USA	25.7.99	3		Tucson	28 Apr
11.31	0.4	Yunisleidy	García	CUB	11.8.99	1		Camagüey	27 Jun
11.34	0.6	Jayla	Kirkland (10)	USA	13.2.99	4h3	NCAA-E	Tampa	24 May
11.34	-1.1	Daija	Lampkin	USA	11.7.99	2	NC-j	Bloomington	15 Jun
11.35	1.7	Kynnedy	Flannel	USA	12.7.00	1		Austin	13 May
11.35	0.4	Keshia	Kwadwo	GER	10.7.99	1h3		Regensburg	3 Jun
11.38	0.1	Abby	Steiner	USA	24.11.99	1		Columbus	2 Jun
11.39	1.2	Michae	Harriott	JAM	1.6.00	1-19	CariftaG	Nassau	31 Mar
11.39	0.4	Adriana	Rodríguez	CUB	12.7.99	2		Camagüey	27 Jun
11.40	1.1	Joy	Udo-Gabriel	NGR	2.6.99	1		Asaba	18 Jul
11.42	-1.1	Thelma	Davies	USA	8.5.00	5	NC-j	Bloomington	15 Jun
11.42		Shanice	Elliott	SKN	.99	2h1	NC	Basseterre	17 Jun
11.43	0.4	Candace	Hill (20)	USA	11.2.99	4rB		Bellinzona	18 Jul

Wind assisted see main list for top 5 juniors

11.29	3.3	Gabriela Anahí	Suárez	ECU-Y	2.2.01	3r2	YOG	Buenos Aires	15 Oct
11.33	3.5	Anavia	Battle	USA	28.3.99	4		Los Angeles	24 Mar
11.33	2.2	Magdalena	Stefanowicz	POL	21.9.00	1	NC-j	Wloclawek	23 Jun
11.34	2.2	Martyna	Kotwila	POL	13.1.99	2	NC-j	Wloclawek	23 Jun
11.38A	2.9	Arria	Minor	USA-Y	9.2.01	1		Denver	7 Apr
11.39	3.3	Symone	Mason	USA	31.8.99	4		Coral Gables	7 Apr

150 METRES STRAIGHT

16.23	0.7	Shaunae	Miller-Uibo	BAH	15.4.94	1		Boston	20 May
16.57	0.7	Michelle-Lee	Ahye	TTO	10.4.92	2		Boston	20 May
16.60	1.6	Marie Josée	Ta Lou	CIV	18.11.88	1		Manchester	18 May
16.49w	2.6	Michelle-Lee	Ahye	TTO	10.4.92	1		Gateshead	8 Sep

16.72	1.6	Allyson	Felix	USA	18.11.85	18 May
16.75	0.7	Shashalee	Forbes	JAM	10.5.96	20 May

16.95	0.7	Hannah	Cunliffe	USA	9.1.96	20 May
16.80w	2.6	Daryll	Neita	GBR	29.8.96	8 Sep
16.97w	2.6	Jodie	Williams	GBR	28.9.93	8 Sep

200 METRES

21.89	0.2	Dina	Asher-Smith	GBR	4.12.95	1	EC	Berlin	11 Aug
22.04	0.5	Blessing	Okagbare	NGR	9.10.88	1		Abilene	24 Mar
22.05	1.1	Shericka	Jackson	JAM	16.7.94	1	DL	Paris (c)	30 Jun
22.06	-0.4	Shaunae	Miller-Uibo	BAH	15.4.94	1	DL	Shanghai	12 May
22.09	0.9		Miller-Uibo			1	CG	Gold Coast	12 Apr
22.11	0.1		Miller-Uibo			1		Kingston	9 Jun
22.12	0.1		Miller-Uibo			1	VD	Bruxelles	31 Aug
22.14	0.2	Dafne	Schippers	NED	15.6.92	2	EC	Berlin	11 Aug
22.15	0.4		Miller-Uibo			1	DL	Birmingham	18 Aug
22.16	0.9	Jenna	Prandini	USA	20.11.92	1	DL	London (OS)	22 Jul
22.16	0.1		Miller-Uibo			1	C.Cup	Ostrava	9 Sep
22.18	0.9		Jackson			2	CG	Gold Coast	12 Apr
22.19	0.9	Gabrielle	Thomas	USA	7.12.96	2	DL	London (OS)	22 Jul
22.22	-0.2		Prandini			1s2	NC	Des Moines	24 Jun
22.22	0.9		Jackson			3	DL	London (OS)	22 Jul
22.25	0.6	Lynna	Irby	USA	6.12.98	1	SEC	Knoxville	13 May
22.25	0.9		Asher-Smith			4	DL	London (OS)	22 Jul
22.28	0.1		Jackson			1s1	CG	Gold Coast	11 Apr
22.28	0.4		Jackson			1		Kingston	24 Jun
22.28	0.1		Schippers			2	C.Cup	Ostrava	9 Sep
22.29	0.9		Asher-Smith			3	CG	Gold Coast	12 Apr
22.29	-0.5		Miller-Uibo			1	DL	Rabat	13 Jul

Mark	Wind	Name		Nat	Born	Pos	Meet	Venue	Date	
22.30	0.9	Elaine	Thompson	JAM	28.6.92	4	CG	Gold Coast	12	Apr
22.30	1.1		Prandini			2	DL	Paris (c)	30	Jun
22.31	0.4		Asher-Smith			2	DL	Birmingham	18	Aug
22.32	0.6		Thomas			1		Coral Gables	7	Apr
22.33	1.1		Asher-Smith			1s1	EC	Berlin	10	Aug
22.34	1.7	Shakima	Wimbley (10)	USA	23.4.95	1		Clermont	28	Apr
22.34	-0.4		Schippers			2	DL	Shanghai	12	May
22.34	0.9	Marie Josée (30/11)	Ta Lou	CIV	18.11.88	5	DL	London (OS)	22	Jul
22.35	0.2		Jackson			1	AWC	London (OS)	15	Jul
22.37	0.9	Jamile	Samuel	NED	24.4.92	6	DL	London (OS)	22	Jul
22.39	1.5	Sydney	McLaughlin	USA-J	7.8.99	1	FlaR	Gainesville	29	Mar
22.42	2.0	Brittany	Brown	USA	18.4.95	1s1	NC	Des Moines	24	Jun
22.42	2.0	Phyllis	Francis	USA	4.5.92	2s1	NC	Des Moines	24	Jun
22.45	0.2	Mujinga	Kambundji	SUI	17.6.92	4	EC	Berlin	11	Aug
22.46	2.0	Jeneba	Tarmoh	USA	27.9.89	3s1	NC	Des Moines	24	Jun
22.47	0.6	Shania	Collins	USA	14.11.96	2	SEC	Knoxville	13	May
22.48	1.9	Tamari	Davis	USA-Y	15.2.03	1		Jacksonville	5	May
22.48	-0.2	Kyra (20)	Jefferson	USA	23.9.94	2s2	NC	Des Moines	24	Jun
22.49	-0.3	Ashley	Henderson	USA	4.12.95	2s3	NCAA	Eugene	7	Jun
22.50	-0.1	Briana	Williams	JAM-Y	21.3.02	1	WJ	Tampere	14	Jul
22.51	1.9	Lauren Rain	Williams	USA-J	25.7.99	1		Tucson	28	Apr
22.53	1.4	Makenzie	Dunmore	USA	7.10.97	1h2		Stanford	12	May
22.53	0.9	Tamara	Clark	USA-J	9.1.99	1h1	NCAA-E	Tampa	25	May
22.54	2.0	Ariana	Washington	USA	27.8.96	4s1	NC	Des Moines	24	Jun
22.55	0.9	Natalliah	Whyte	JAM	9.8.97	1		Auburn	21	Apr
22.56	0.5	Kortnei	Johnson	USA	11.8.97	1q3	NCAA-E	Tampa	26	May
22.59	0.5	Mikiah	Brisco	USA	14.7.96	2q2	NCAA-E	Tampa	26	May
22.59	-1.3	Beth (30)	Dobbin	GBR	7.6.94	1	NC	Birmingham	1	Jul
22.60	-0.8	Murielle	Ahouré	CIV	23.8.87	2		Ostrava	13	Jun
22.60	-1.3	Bianca	Williams	GBR	18.12.93	2	NC	Birmingham	1	Jul
22.62	1.7	Joanna	Atkins	USA	31.1.89	2		Clermont	28	Apr
22.62	0.1	Ofonime	Odiong	BRN	13.3.97	5	C.Cup	Ostrava	9	Sep
22.63	-0.2	Ivet	Lalova-Collio	BUL	18.5.84	1	DL	Stockholm	10	Jun
22.63	-0.2	Kimberlyn	Duncan	USA	2.8.91	4s2	NC	Des Moines	24	Jun
22.64	1.4	Angie	Annelus	USA	10.1.97	2h2		Stanford	12	May
22.64	1.7	Semoy	Hackett	TTO	27.11.88	1		Port of Spain	24	Jun
22.67	0.9	Janet	Amponsah	GHA	12.4.93	2		Auburn	21	Apr
22.67	1.1	Deanna (40)	Hill	USA	13.4.96	1q2	NCAA-W	Sacramento	26	May
22.67	-0.3	Crystal	Emmanuel	CAN	27.11.91	2	NACAC	Toronto	12	Aug
22.69	1.6	Jasmine	Camacho-Quinn	PUR	21.8.96	2		Fayetteville	27	Apr
22.71	1.4	Kendall	Ellis	USA	8.3.96	3h2		Stanford	12	May
22.72	0.8	Kevona	Davis	JAM-Y	20.12.01	1		Kingston	24	Mar
22.73	0.3	Abby	Steiner	USA-J	24.11.99	1		Columbus	2	Jun
22.73	1.5	Viktoriya	Zyabkina	KAZ	4.9.92	1		Almaty	30	Jun
22.73	1.9	Vitória Cristina	Rosa	BRA	12.1.96	1h1	NC	Bragança Paulista	15	Sep
22.74	0.6	Jessica	Beard	USA	8.1.89	2		Coral Gables	7	Apr
22.74	-0.1	Brianne	Bethel	BAH	5.7.98	1		Cincinnati	13	May
22.74	1.4	Twanisha (50)	Terry	USA-J	24.1.99	1q1	NCAA-W	Sacramento	26	May
22.74	-0.3	Ka'Tia	Seymour	USA	3.10.97	3s3	NCAA	Eugene	7	Jun
22.74	1.7	Kayelle	Clarke	TTO	28.2.96	2		Port of Spain	24	Jun
22.75	0.1	Tori	Bowie	USA	27.8.90	1		St. Georges	21	Apr
22.75	2.0	Jodie	Williams	GBR	28.9.93	1		Genève	9	Jun
22.76	0.6	Aiyanna	Stiverne	CAN	20.2.95	3		Coral Gables	7	Apr
22.77	-0.1	LaTessa	Johnson	USA	13.4.97	2		Cincinnati	13	May
22.78	-1.3	Shannon	Hylton	GBR	19.12.96	4	NC	Birmingham	1	Jul
22.80	1.6	Jaide	Stepter	USA	25.9.94	1		Prairie View	24	Mar
22.80	0.4	Sarah	Atcho	SUI	1.6.95	1		La Chaux-de-Fonds	1	Jul
22.80	0.6	Shashalee (60)	Forbes	JAM	10.5.96	1	CAG	Barranquilla	1	Aug
22.81	1.5	Kendra	Harrison	USA	18.9.92	3	FlaR	Gainesville	29	Mar
22.81	-0.8	Deajah	Stevens	USA	19.5.95	2h2	NC	Des Moines	23	Jun
22.82	1.1	Ashton	Purvis	USA	12.7.92	3		Claremont	2	Jun
22.83A	0.9	Justine	Palframan	RSA	4.11.93	1		Sasolburg	29	Apr
22.84	0.1	Tatjana	Pinto	GER	2.7.92	1		Weinheim	26	May
22.85	1.1	Felicia	Brown	USA	27.10.93	1		Clermont	12	May
22.87		Taylor	Bennett	USA	15.1.97	1		Waco	13	May

WOMEN 2018

Mark	Wind	Name		Nat	Born	Pos	Meet	Venue	Date	
22.87	0.3	Marileidy	Paulino	DOM	25.10.96	1h3	CAG	Barranquilla	31	Jul
22.87	1.1	Laura	Müller	GER	11.12.95	4s1	EC	Berlin	10	Aug
22.88	0.5	Kianna	Gray	USA	30.12.96	3q3	NCAA-E	Tampa	26	May
(70)										
22.88	0.0	Jodean	Williams	JAM	11.11.93	1s1	CAG	Barranquilla	31	Jul
22.88	1.5	Katarina	Johnson-Thompson	GBR	9.1.93	1H4	EC	Berlin	9	Aug
22.89A	1.9	Arria	Minor	USA-Y	9.2.01	1h2		Lakewood	17	May
22.89	-0.6	Jessica-Bianca	Wessolly	GER	11.12.96	1	NC	Nürnberg	22	Jul
22.90	1.4	Jasmin	Reed	USA-J	21.2.00	2q1	NCAA-W	Sacramento	26	May
22.92	0.7	Diamond	Spaulding	USA	29.9.96	1		Los Angeles	14	Apr
22.92	-0.2		Kong Lingwei	CHN	28.7.95	1h4	NGP	Huaian	17	May
22.92	0.5	Kristina	Timanovskaya	BLR	19.11.96	1		Szczecin	15	Aug
22.93	-1.7	Riley	Day	AUS-J	30.3.00	1	NC	Gold Coast	18	Feb
22.93	-0.4	Dezerea	Bryant	USA	27.4.93	3rB		Gainesville	13	Apr
(80)										
22.93	0.8	Aleia	Hobbs	USA	24.2.96	1rB		Coral Gables	14	Apr
22.93	1.7	Ángela	Tenorio	ECU	27.1.96	4		Clermont	28	Apr
22.93	1.5	Kaylin	Whitney	USA	9.3.98	1rB		Clermont	12	May
22.93	0.7	Jayla	Kirkland	USA-J	13.2.99	1h2	NC-j	Bloomington	16	Jun
22.94	0.5	Brianna	McNeal	USA	18.8.91	1		Long Beach	19	Apr
22.94	-0.5	Anavia	Battle	USA-J	28.3.99	2		Bloomington	13	May
22.94	0.5	Ashleigh	Nelson	GBR	20.2.91	1rB		Genève	9	Jun
22.94	1.2	Gunta	Vaicule	LAT	9.3.95	1		Ogre	16	Jun
22.95	1.7	Tramesha	Hardy	USA	24.3.96	1		San Marcos	13	May
22.95	-1.3	Finette	Agyapong	GBR	1.2.97	5	NC	Birmingham	1	Jul
(90)										
22.96	1.8	Zakiya	Denoon	TTO	23.1.95	3h3	NCAA-E	Tampa	25	May
22.97	1.7	Shauna	Helps	JAM	23.10.96	2		Tallahassee	23	Mar
22.97	1.6		Wei Yongli	CHN	11.10.91	1rB		Madrid	22	Jun
22.98	-0.1	María	Bolibonáki	GRE	10.6.01	1	NC	Pátra	16	Jul
22.99	0.6	Taylor	Washington	USA	6.5.93	4		Coral Gables	7	Apr
22.99	-0.5	Brionna	Thomas	USA	21.3.96	3		Bloomington	13	May
22.99	1.3	Agne	Serksniene	LTU	18.2.88	1	NC	Zofingen	14	Jul
22.99	0.3	Phil	Healy	IRL	19.11.94	3		Cork	16	Jul
22.99	2.0	Martyna	Kotwila	POL-J	13.1.99	1	NC	Lublin	22	Jul
23.00	-0.6	Jada	Baylark	USA	17.10.97	2		Baton Rouge	21	Apr
(100)										
23.00	0.1	Dutee	Chand	IND	3.2.96	1s1	AsiG	Jakarta	28	Aug

Mark	Wind	Name		Nat	Born	Date		Mark	Wind	Name		Nat	Born	Date	
23.01	0.6	Nercely	Soto	VEN	23.8.90	7	Apr	23.14	0.4	Candyce	McGrone	USA	24.3.89	19	May
23.01	0.4	Symone	Mason	USA-J	31.8.99	12	May	23.14	0.9	Nadine	Gonska	GER	23.1.90	26	May
23.01	0.8	Kiana	Horton	USA	29.1.97	12	May	23.15	1.2	Floria	Guei	FRA	2.5.90	6	May
23.02	0.3	Stephenie Ann	McPherson	JAM	25.11.88	5	May	23.15	0.4	Rebekah	Smith	USA	1.5.98	12	May
23.02	1.6	NaAsha	Robinson	USA	23.1.97	12	May	23.15	1.0	Polina	Miller	RUS-J	9.6.00	22	May
23.02	0.9	Sindija	Buksa	LAT	14.12.97	29	May	23.15	0.5	Cassondra	Hall	USA	23.9.97	26	May
23.02	0.5	Carolle	Zahi	FRA	12.6.94	29	Jun	23.15	0.1	Katrin	Fehm	GER	16.4.98	26	May
23.03	1.5	Tiffany	Townsend	USA	14.6.89	12	May	23.15	1.1		Ge Manqi	CHN	13.10.97	2	Jun
23.03	1.7	Caitland	Smith	USA	24.3.96	13	May	23.16	0.9	Daija	Lampkin	USA-J	11.7.99	25	May
23.03	1.8	Brianna	Duncan	USA	6.10.98	25	May	23.16	-0.9	Madiea	Ghafoor	NED	9.9.92	16	Jun
23.03	1.4	Krisztina	Khorosheva	RUS	5.4.93	21	Jul	23.17	-0.5	Chloe	Abbott	USA	25.7.98	13	May
23.04	2.0	Brenessa	Thompson	GUY	22.7.96	24	Mar	23.17		Germaine	Abessolo Bivina	CMR	9.5.90	8	Jul
23.04	1.4	Katara	Nelson	USA	7.3.95	31	Mar	23.18	-1.8	Kynnedy	Flannel	USA-J	12.7.00	17	Jun
23.04	2.0	De'Shalyn	Jones	USA	5.1.96	14	Apr	23.19	-0.6	Hannah	Jackson	USA	28.2.97	21	Apr
23.04	0.4	Gabriele	Cunningham	USA	22.2.98	12	May	23.19	1.9	Kiara	Parker	USA	28.10.96	11	May
23.04	0.6	Anna	Kielbasinska	POL	26.0.90	21	Jul	23.19	1.7	Reyare	Thomas	TTO	23.11.87	24	Jun
20.00	-1.7	Maddie	Coates	AUS	27.9.97	18	Feb	23.20	0.0	Aniekeme	Alphonsus	NGR	25.12.98	31	Mar
23.06	0.2	Irene	Siragusa	ITA	23.6.93	27	May	23.20	0.9	Jura	Levy	JAM	4.11.90	21	Apr
23.07	1.9	Alaysha	Johnson	USA	20.7.96	28	Apr	23.20	1.1		Huang Guifen	CHN	20.8.97	2	Jun
23.07	0.4	Ajla	Del Ponte	SUI	15.7.96	1	Jul	23.21	1.9	Venessa	D'arpino	USA	13.12.95	28	Apr
23.09	0.5	Gloria	Hooper	ITA	3.3.92	29	Jun	23.21	0.0	Jennifer	Galais	FRA	7.3.92	22	Jun
23.10	-0.2	Rachel	Misher	USA	4.2.97	24	Mar	23.21	1.7	Leya	Buchanan	CAN	17.8.96	7	Jul
23.10	0.2	Thelma	Davies	USA-J	8.5.00	16	Jun	23.21	2.0	Line	Kloster	NOR	27.2.90	7	Jul
23.10	0.0	Hima	Das	IND-J	9.1.00	27	Jun	23.22	0.5	Alfreda	Steele	USA	19.12.97	30	Mar
23.10	1.5	Louisa	Grauvogel	GER	28.9.96	9	Aug	23.22	-0.6	Jada	Martin	USA	8.6.95	21	Apr
23.11	1.6	Tynia	Gaither	BAH	16.3.93	24	Mar	23.22	1.9	Amber	Ivy	USA	2.11.97	28	Apr
23.11	0.5	Maia	McCoy	USA	9.12.96	26	May	23.22	1.3	Kanika	Beckles	GRN	3.10.91	20	May
23.11	0.5	Estela	García	ESP	20.3.89	29	Jun	23.22	-0.3	Rene	Medley	JAM	21.8.96	26	May
23.11	-1.0	Inna	Eftimova	BUL	19.6.88	21	Jul	23.22		Yunisleidy	García	CUB-J	11.8.99	3	Jun
23.12A	1.7	Tamzin	Thomas	RSA	6.10.97	17	Mar	23.23A	0.4	Narcisa	Landázuri	ECU	25.11.92	25	Mar
23.12	1.6	Shamier	Little	USA	20.3.95	24	Mar	23.23	1.5	Kori	Carter	USA	3.6.92	29	Mar
23.12	1.3	Cornelia	Halbheer	SUI	16.8.92	14	Jul	23.23	0.0	Cierra	White	USA	29.4.93	5	May
23.12	-0.6	Rebekka	Haase	GER	2.1.93	22	Jul	23.24	-0.1	Gina	Bass	GAM	3.5.95	10	Apr
23.13A	1.0	Isidora	Jiménez	CHI	10.8.93	7	Jun	23.24	2.0	A'Keyla	Mitchell	USA	25.11.95	14	Apr
23.14	0.2	Kai	Selvon	TTO	13.4.92	17	Mar	23.24	1.2	Rafailía	Spanoudáki-Hatzirígi	GRE	7.6.94	2	Jun
23.14	0.6	Amarachi	Pipi	GBR	26.11.95	24	Mar	23.24	0.3	Caisja	Chandler	USA-J	18.6.00	2	Jun
23.14	0.5	Christine	Botlogetswe	BOT	1.10.95	29	Apr	23.24	0.0	Estelle	Raffai	FRA	6.2.98	22	Jun

Mark	Wind	Name		Nat	Born	Pos	Meet	Venue	Date
23.26A	0.1	Mariely	Sánchez	DOM	30.12.88				28 Apr
23.26	-0.5	Savannah	Roberson	USA	15.1.96				13 May
23.26	1.2	Haisha	Bisiolu	NGR	16.5.97				25 May
23.27	-1.7	Larissa	Pasternatsky	AUS	11.12.91				18 Feb
23.27	1.3	Sada	Williams	BAR	1.12.97				18 Feb
23.27	0.4	Maggie	Barrie	SLE	29.5.96				21 Apr
23.27	1.9	Mauricia	Prieto	TTO	20.11.95				12 May
23.27	1.8	Jenae	Ambrose	BAH	29.12.97				25 May
23.27	1.2	Helene	Rønningen	NOR	4.9.98				7 Jun
23.28	1.7	Libania	Grenot	ITA	12.7.83				28 Apr
23.28	-0.1	Lenysse	Dyer	USA	6.3.97				5 May
23.29	0.8	Wadeline	Jonathas	HAI	19.2.98				17 Mar
23.29	0.7	Brigitte	Ntiamoah	FRA	5.3.94				3 Jun
23.29	2.0	Schillonie	Calvert-Powell	JAM	27.7.88				13 Jun
23.29	1.7	Phylicia	George	CAN	16.11.87				7 Jul
(189)									

Indoors

Mark	Wind	Name		Nat	Born	Pos	Meet	Venue	Date
22.41		Ashley	Henderson	USA	4.12.95	1r2	NCAA	College Station	10 Mar
22.88		Léa	Sprunger	SUI	5.3.90	1	NC	Magglingen	18 Feb
22.99		Payton	Chadwick	USA	29.11.95	1rB		Fayetteville	26 Jan
23.02		Quanera	Hayes	USA	7.3.92				12 Jan
23.03		Daija	Lampkin	USA-J	11.7.99				24 Feb
23.07		Danyel	White	USA	10.2.98				9 Mar
23.14		Hannah	Jackson	USA	28.2.97				25 Feb
23.16		Anna	Cockrell	USA	28.8.97				27 Jan
23.21		Amber	Ivy	USA	2.11.97				24 Feb
23.23		Georganne	Moline	USA	6.3.90				10 Feb
23.26		Briana	Guillory	USA	21.11.97				3 Feb
23.29		Ashley	Spencer	USA	8.6.93				20 Jan

Wind assisted

Mark	Wind	Name		Nat	Born	Pos	Meet	Venue	Date
21.97	5.3	Shania	Collins	USA	14.11.96	1h5	NCAA-E	Tampa	25 May
22.06	2.4	Lynna	Irby	USA	6.12.98	1h6	NCAA-E	Tampa	25 May
22.13	4.6	Gabrielle	Thomas	USA	7.12.96	1	TexasR	Austin	31 Mar
22.21	4.8	Jasmine	Camacho-Quinn	PUR	21.8.96	1h4	NCAA-E	Tampa	25 May
22.37	2.9	Makenzie	Dunmore	USA	7.10.97	1	Pac-12	Stanford	13 May
22.43	5.3	Maia	McCoy	USA	9.12.96	2h5	NCAA-E	Tampa	25 May
22.49	2.9	Deanna	Hill	USA	13.4.96	2	Pac-12	Stanford	13 May
22.52	3.6	Kortnei	Johnson	USA	11.8.97	1		Baton Rouge	7 Apr
22.52	2.2	Angie	Annelus	USA	10.1.97	2s1	NCAA	Eugene	7 Jun
22.57	4.8	Ka'Tia	Seymour	USA	3.10.97	2h4	NCAA-E	Tampa	25 May
22.64	2.4	Cassondra	Hall	USA	23.9.97	2h6	NCAA-E	Tampa	25 May
22.65	5.3	Kianna	Gray	USA	30.12.96	3h5	NCAA-E	Tampa	25 May
22.75	2.2	Natasha	Hastings	USA	23.7.86	1		Austin	14 Apr
22.81	4.8	Savannah	Roberson	USA	15.1.96	3h4	NCAA-E	Tampa	25 May
22.89	5.3	Gabriele	Cunningham	USA	22.2.98	4h5	NCAA-E	Tampa	25 May
22.91	5.0	Jada	Baylark	USA	17.10.97	1		Fayetteville	14 Apr
22.91	2.3	Jayla	Kirkland	USA-J	13.2.99	2	NC-j	Bloomington	17 Jun
22.92	3.6	Carolle	Zahi	FRA	12.6.94	1	NC	Albi	8 Jul
22.93	3.6	Rachel	Misher	USA	4.2.97	3		Baton Rouge	7 Apr
22.95	3.4	Kynnedy	Flannel	USA-J	12.7.00	1r1		Austin	13 May

Mark	Wind	Name		Nat	Born	Date
22.97	3.6	Hannah	Jackson	USA	28.2.97	7 Apr
22.98	2.6	Javianne	Oliver	USA	26.12.94	14 Apr
22.98	2.9	Kayla	White	USA	24.9.96	5 May
22.98	2.7	Sindija	Buksa	LAT	14.12.97	28 Jun
22.99	2.4	Daziah	Green	USA		25 May
23.02	3.6	Sha'Carri	Richardson	USA-J	25.3.00	13 May
23.03	4.8	Symone	Darius	USA	1.3.98	25 May
23.04	3.1	Chelsea	Francis	USA	14.10.96	28 Apr
23.06	3.1	Lenysse	Dyer	USA	6.3.97	11 May
23.09	4.0	India	Brown	USA	29.1.96	14 Apr
23.09	3.0	Hajar Saad	Al-Khaldi	BRN	17.3.95	11 Jul
23.10	2.4	Gina	Bass	GAM	3.5.95	18 Jul
23.11	2.4	Daija	Lampkin	USA-J	11.7.99	11 May
23.11	5.3	Kristina	Knott	PHI	25.9.95	25 May
23.12	5.3	Chloe	Abbott	USA	25.7.98	14 Apr
23.13	3.4	Jessica	Peris	AUS	7.1.90	7 Jan
23.13	3.6	Amandine	Brossier	FRA	15.8.95	8 Jul
23.14	4.1	Wadeline	Jonathas	HAI	19.2.98	5 May
23.15	2.6	Lakayla	Harris	USA	29.1.97	5 May
23.16	3.0	Naomi	Sedney	NED	17.12.94	29 Mar
23.16	5.3	Stephanie	Osuji	NGR	6.1.97	25 May
23.17	3.5	Shafiqua	Maloney	VIN-J	27.2.99	13 May
23.17	2.4	Kanika	Beckles	GRN	3.10.91	9 Jun
23.18	4.8	Jade	Harrison	USA		25 May
23.19	2.3	Najia	Hudspeth	USA	25.10.96	6 Apr
23.20	3.1	Maggie	Barrie	SLE	29.5.96	27 Apr
23.20	2.1	Madeline	Price	CAN	11.9.95	10 May
23.20	2.4	Jasmine	Jones	USA-Y	30.11.01	25 May
23.21A	3.0	Gabriela Anahí	Suárez	ECU-Y	2.2.01	19 Aug
23.22	3.6	Sara	Limp	USA		21 Apr
23.23	3.7	Simone	Glenn	USA	16.5.96	11 May
23.23	2.4	Lisa-Anne	Barrow	BAR	13.12.96	11 May
23.23	2.1	Robyn	Byrd	USA		19 May
23.24	4.2	Travia	Jones	CAN	12.7.95	6 Apr
23.24		Kimbely	Baptiste	GBR	27.12.92	8 Jul
23.25	3.4	Yana	Kachur	UKR	13.1.97	3 Jun
23.28	3.6	Alexandra	Bezeková	SVK	13.8.92	8 Jul
23.29	2.7	Shavine	Hodges	JAM	22.10.91	21 Apr
23.29	3.6	Juanita	Mainoo	USA	11.8.96	21 May
23.29	2.4	Kamaria	Durant	TTO	24.2.91	27 May

Best at low altitude

Mark	Wind	Name		Nat	Born	Date
23.21	1.1	Isidora	Jiménez	CHI	10.8.93	23 Jul

Doubtful: 23.24 S. Dhanalakshmi IND 5.6.98 28 Nov

Hand timing

Mark	Wind	Name		Nat	Born	Pos	Meet	Venue	Date
23.1h	0.0	Adriana	Rodríguez	CUB-J	12.7.99	1h3	Fortún	Camagüey	17 Feb
22.2mxw		Marie Josée	Ta Lou	CIV	18.11.88	1mx		Abidjan	29 Apr

JUNIORS

See main list for top 14 juniors (& 4 wa). 12 performances (1 indoor) by 7 to 22.74. Additional marks and further juniors:

Name	Mark	Wind	Pos	Meet	Venue	Date
McLaughlin	22.68i			NCAA	College Station	2 Mar
T Davis	22.55	1.4	1		Greensboro	28 Jul
Clark	22.57	-0.7	1		Gainesville	13 Apr
	22.73	0.5	2q1	NCAA E	Tampa	26 May
	22.64	0.6	3	SEC	Knoxville	13 May

Mark	Wind	Name		Nat	Born	Pos	Meet	Venue	Date
23.01	0.4	Symone	Mason	USA	31.8.99	1		Coral Gables	12 May
23.10	0.2	Thelma	Davies	USA	8.5.00	2h1	NC-j	Bloomington	16 Jun
23.10	0.0	Hima	Das	IND-	9.1.00	1	I-State	Guwahati	27 Jun
23.15	1.0	Polina	Miller	RUS	9.6.00	1		Maykop	22 May
23.16	0.9	Daija	Lampkin	USA	11.7.99	3h1	NCAA-E	Tampa	25 May
	23.03i					1h8	SEC	College Station	24 Feb

Mark	Wind	Name		Nat	Born	Pos	Meet	Venue	Date
23.18	-1.8	Kynnedy	Flannel (20)	USA	12.7.00	2	N.Sch	Greensboro	17 Jun
Wind assisted see main list for top 2 juniors									
23.02	3.6	Sha'Carri	Richardson	USA	25.3.00	1r2		Austin	13 May
23.11	2.4	Daija	Lampkin	USA	11.7.99	3h6	SEC	Knoxville	11 May
23.17	3.5	Shafiqua	Maloney	VIN	27.2.99	1		Terre Haute	13 May

200 METRES STRAIGHT

Mark	Wind	Name		Nat	Born	Pos	Meet	Venue	Date
22.16	0.9	Anastasia	Le-Roy	JAM	11.9.87	1		Boston	20 May
22.31	0.9	Joanna	Atkins	USA	31.1.89	2		Boston	20 May
22.86	0.9	Tynia	Gaither	BAH	16.3.93	3		Boston	20 May

300 METRES

36.74		Agne	Serksniene	LTU	18.2.88	1			Basel		12 May
37.07	Iga	Baumgart-Witan	POL	11.4.89	19 May		37.29	Anna	Kiełbasinska	POL	26.6.90	19 May
37.10	Tetyana	Melnyk	UKR	2.4.95	19 Aug		37.30	Estela	García	ESP	20.3.89	11 Jul
37.13	Laura	de Witte	NED	7.0.95	20 Aug		37.31	Line	Kloster	NOR	27.2.90	10 Jun
37.21	Maria Benedicta Chigbolu		ITA	27.7.89	24 Apr		37.32	Agata	Zupin	SLO	17.3.98	26 May

Indoors

35.45		Shaunae	Miller-Uibo	BAH	15.4.94	1	Millrose	New York (Arm)		3 Feb
36.73		Lynna	Irby	USA	6.12.98	1		Clemson		6 Jan
36.85		Phyllis	Francis	USA	4.5.92	1		College Station		3 Feb
36.89	Sarah	Atcho	SUI	1.6.95	11 Feb	37.23	Jaide	Stepter	USA	25.4.94	3 Feb
36.96	Gunta	Latiseva-Cudare	LAT	9.3.95	13 Feb	37.28	Courtney	Okolo	USA	15.3.94	3 Feb
36.98	Shamier	Little	USA	20.3.95	3 Feb	37.34	Anita	Horvat	SLO	7.9.96	25 Jan
37.01	Floria	Guei	FRA	2.5.90	11 Feb	37.34	Alexis	Holmes	USA		8 Dec
37.02	Anna	Kiełbasinska	POL	26.6.90	13 Feb	37.35	Jessica	Beard	USA	8.1.89	12 Jan
37.08	Sage	Watson	CAN	20.6.94	3 Feb	37.39	Justyna	Swiety-Ersetic	POL	3.12.92	10 Feb
37.19	Travia	Jones	CAN	12.7.95	20 Jan	37.43	Ashley	Spencer	USA	8.6.93	3 Feb

400 METRES

Mark		Name		Nat	Born	Pos	Meet	Venue	Date
48.97		Shaunae	Miller-Uibo	BAH	15.4.94	1	Herc	Monaco	20 Jul
49.08		Salwa Eid	Naser	BRN	23.5.98	2	Herc	Monaco	20 Jul
49.32			Naser			1	C.Cup	Ostrava	8 Sep
49.33			Naser			1	VD	Bruxelles	31 Aug
49.52			Miller-Uibo			1	Pre	Eugene	26 May
49.52		Shakima	Wimbley	USA	23.4.95	1	NC	Des Moines	23 Jun
49.53			Miller-Uibo			1	Gyulai	Székesfehérvár	2 Jul
49.55			Naser			1	DL	Paris (C)	30 Jun
49.62		Caster	Semenya	RSA	7.1.91	2	C.Cup	Ostrava	8 Sep
49.78			Naser			1	Athl	Lausanne	5 Jul
49.80		Lynna	Irby	USA	6.12.98	1	NCAA	Eugene	9 Jun
49.84			Naser			1	DL	Stockholm	10 Jun
49.96			Semenya			1	AfrC	Asaba	3 Aug
49.98			Naser			1	Bisl	Oslo	7 Jun
49.99		Kendall	Ellis	USA	8.3.96	1	Pac-12	Stanford	13 May
50.06			Semenya			1	Skol	Chorzów	22 Aug
50.07		Sydney	McLaughlin	USA-J	7.8.99	1	FlaR	Gainesville	30 Mar
50.07		Phyllis	Francis	USA	4.5.92	2	DL	Stockholm	10 Jun
50.08		Jessica	Beard	USA	8.1.89	2	NC	Des Moines	23 Jun
50.09			Naser			1	AsiG	Jakarta	26 Aug
50.11			Irby			1s3	NCAA	Eugene	7 Jun
50.15		Amantle	Montsho (10)	BOT	4.7.83	1	CG	Gold Coast	11 Apr
50.18			Wimbley			1		Gainesville	13 Apr
50.19			Ellis			2	NCAA	Eugene	9 Jun
50.31		Stephenie Ann	McPherson	JAM	25.11.88	1	DL	London (OS)	22 Jul
50.37			Ellis			3	NC	Des Moines	23 Jun
50.39			Beard			2	DL	Paris (C)	30 Jun
50.40			Beard			2	Athl	Lausanne	5 Jul
50.41		Justyna	Swiety-Ersetic	POL	3.12.92	1	EC	Berlin	11 Aug
50.44			Irby			1q1	NCAA-E	Tampa	25 May
		(30/12)							
50.45		María	Belibasáki	GRE	19.6.91	2	EC	Berlin	11 Aug
50.52		Léa	Sprunger	SUI	5.3.90	1		La Chaux-de-Fonds	1 Jul
50.57		Anastasia	Le-Roy	JAM	11.9.87	2	CG	Gold Coast	11 Apr
50.63		Makenzie	Dunmore	USA	7.10.97	2	Pac-12	Stanford	13 May
50.63		Jaide	Stepter	USA	25.9.94	4	Athl	Lausanne	5 Jul
50.65		Courtney	Okolo	USA	15.3.94	4	NC	Des Moines	23 Jun
50.69		Sharrika	Barnett	JAM	16.4.97	1	SEC	Knoxville	13 May
50.69		Amina	Seyni	NIG	24.10.96	1		Rovereto	23 Aug
		(20)							

Mark	Name		Nat	Born	Pos	Meet	Venue	Date	
50.77	Lisanne	de Witte	NED	10.9.92	3	EC	Berlin	11	Aug
50.78	Brionna	Thomas	USA	21.3.96	3	NCAA	Eugene	9	Jun
50.79	Hima	Das	IND-J	9.1.00	2	AsiG	Jakarta	26	Aug
50.82	Shamier	Little	USA	20.3.95	4	DL	Stockholm	10	Jul
50.89	Christine	Botlogetswe	BOT	1.10.95	1		Genève	9	Jun
50.99	Agne	Serksniene	LTU	18.2.88	3		La Chaux-de-Fonds	1	Jul
51.12	Madiea	Ghafoor	NED	9.9.92	1		Bellinzona	18	Jul
51.13	Anyika	Onuora	GBR	28.10.84	5	DL	London (OS)	22	Jul
51.14	Eleni	Artymata	CYP	16.5.86	2		Bellinzona	18	Jul
51.18	Malgorzata	Holub-Kowalik	POL	30.10.92	1	NC	Lublin	21	Jul
	(30)								
51.21	Chrisann	Gordon	JAM	18.9.94	1		Clermont	12	May
51.21	Alexis	Holmes	USA-J	28.1.00	1	N.Sch	Greensboro	17	Jun
51.21	Laviai	Nielsen	GBR	13.3.96	1s1	EC	Berlin	9	Aug
51.22	Yinka	Ajayi	NGR	11.8.97	1		Abuja	17	Mar
51.22	Kiana	Horton	USA	29.1.97	1		Waco	13	May
51.22	Anita	Horvat	SLO	7.9.96	5	Herc	Monaco	20	Jul
51.24	Iga	Baumgart-Witan	POL	11.4.89	5	EC	Berlin	11	Aug
51.25	Nirmala	Sheoran drugs dq?	IND	15.7.95	2	I-State	Guwahati	29	Jun
51.29	Daina	Harper	USA	26.5.95	2		Osaka	20	May
51.30	Briana	Guillory	USA	21.11.97	6	NC	Des Moines	23	Jun
	(40)								
51.31A	Justine	Palframan	RSA	4.11.93	1	NC	Pretoria	17	Mar
51.32	Maximilia	Imali	KEN	8.12.96	5	CG	Gold Coast	11	Apr
51.32	Libania	Grenot	ITA	12.7.83	2	MedG	Tarragona	28	Jun
51.33	Kaelin	Roberts	USA-J	6.1.99	3	Pac-12	Stanford	13	May
51.35	Allyson	Felix	USA	18.11.85	2	Kuso	Chorzów	8	Jul
51.36	Maggie	Barrie	SLE	29.5.96	2		Bloomington	13	May
51.36	Amy	Allcock	GBR	24.8.93	6	DL	London (OS)	22	Jul
51.36	Zoey	Clark	GBR	25.10.94	7	DL	London (OS)	22	Jul
51.40	Patience	George	NGR	25.11.91	1		Abuja	16	Feb
51.40	Titania	Markland	JAM	1.2.94	3		Bloomington	13	May
	(50)								
51.41	Christine	Day	JAM	23.8.86	2		Kingston	24	Jun
51.46	Jasmine	Blocker	USA	9.6.92	3s1	NC	Des Moines	22	Jun
51.49	Camille	Laus	BEL	23.5.93	4		La Chaux-de-Fonds	1	Jul
51.50	Floria	Guei	FRA	2.5.90	4s1	EC	Berlin	9	Aug
51.51	Anneliese	Rubie-Renshaw	AUS	22.4.92	3s3	CG	Gold Coast	10	Apr
51.53	Symone	Mason	USA-J	31.8.99	1		Coral Gables	12	May
51.57	Chloe	Abbott	USA	25.7.98	1q3	NCAA-E	Tampa	25	May
51.58	Yekaterina	Renzhina	RUS	18.10.94	1		Zhukovskiy	23	Jun
51.60	Rachel	Misher	USA	4.2.97	2	SEC	Knoxville	13	May
51.60	Gunta	Vaicule	LAT	9.3.95	4s3	EC	Berlin	9	Aug
	(60)								
51.62	Sage	Watson	CAN	20.6.94	1		Tucson	17	Mar
51.65	Polina	Miller	RUS-J	9.6.00	5s3	EC	Berlin	9	Aug
51.67	Felecia	Majors	USA	12.2.95	3	SEC	Knoxville	13	May
51.69	Cynthia	Bolingo Mbongo	BEL	12.1.93	1h2	EC	Berlin	8	Aug
51.74	Taylor	Manson	USA-J	29.9.99	1	NC-j	Bloomington	17	Jun
51.76	Taylor	Washington	USA	6.5.93	3		Gainesville	13	Apr
51.76	Hannah	Waller	USA	22.6.98	2q1	NCAA-W	Sacramento	25	May
51.76	Maria Benedicta	Chigbolu	ITA	27.7.89	1h3	EC	Berlin	8	Aug
51.79	Anjali	Devi	IND	15.9.98	1		Bhubaneswar	26	Sep
51.80	Joanna	Atkins	USA	31.1.89	4		Gainesville	13	Apr
	(70)								
51.82	Emerald	Egwim	NGR	27.11.95	1h1		Bloomington	13	May
51.82	Akua	Obeng-Akrofi	GHA	26.6.96	4q1	NCAA-E	Tampa	25	May
51.84	Cátia	Azevedo	POR	9.3.94	2h1	EC	Berlin	8	Aug
51.86	Lisa-Anne	Barrow	BAR	13.12.96	1q2	NCAA-W	Sacramento	25	May
51.86	Aiyanna	Stiverne	CAN	20.2.95	1	NC	Ottawa	7	Jul
51.87	Patrycja	Wyciszkiewicz	POL	8.1.94	4	Kuso	Chorzów	8	Jun
51.87	Emily	Diamond	GBR	11.6.91	3		Genève	9	Jun
51.87	Eilidh	Doyle	GBR	20.2.87	1rB	Skol	Chorzów	22	Aug
51.89	Tatum	Waggoner	USA	6.9.95	4	Pac-12	Stanford	13	May
51.90	Briyahna	DesRosiers	USA	11.3.96	5	Pac-12	Stanford	13	May
	(80)								
51.91	Serenity	Douglas	USA	25.4.98	2		Waco	13	May
51.92A	Arria	Minor	USA-Y	9.2.01	1h2		Lakewood	17	May
51.94	Bendere	Oboya	AUS-J	17.4.00	2	NC	Gold Coast	17	Feb
51.95	Roxana	Gómez	CUB-J	7.1.99	1		Camagüey	2	Jun
51.97	Perri	Shakes-Drayton	GBR	21.12.88	2		Marseille	16	Jun

WOMEN 2018

Mark	Name	Nat	Born	Pos	Meet	Venue	Date
51.98	Katara Nelson	USA	7.3.95	1		Tucson	28 Apr
51.99	Amalie Hammild Iuel	NOR	17.4.94	9	DL	London (OS)	22 Jul
52.00	Nadine Gonska	GER	23.1.90	1		Mannheim	24 Jun
52.04	Quincy Malekani	ZAM	15.3.95	2		Gaborone	29 Apr
52.04	Aliyah Abrams	GUY	3.4.97	4q2	NCAA-E	Tampa	25 May
(90)							
52.05	Shiann Salmon	JAM-J	31.3.99	1		Kingston	24 Mar
52.05	Shannon Kalawan	JAM	25.11.97	1	NCAA-II	Charlotte	26 May
52.06	Raevyn Rogers	USA	7.9.96	1		Eugene	4 May
52.07	Andrea Miklos	ROU-J	17.4.99	2	WJ	Tampere	12 Jul
52.08	Glory Nathaniel Onome	NGR	23.1.96	3		Abuja	17 Mar
52.08	Deborah Sananés	FRA	26.10.95	5		Genève	9 Jun
52.09	Sarah Moore	USA	23.5.97	5q2	NCAA-E	Tampa	25 May
52.11	Tiffany James	JAM	31.1.97	4		Kingston	24 Jun
52.12	Martyna Dabrowska	POL	5.4.94	1rB	Kuso	Chorzów	8 Jun
52.12A	Leni Shida	UGA	22.5.94	1		Kampala	21 Jul
(100)							

Mark	Name	Nat	Born	Date
52.13	Travia Jones	CAN	12.7.95	28 Apr
52.14	Janieve Russell	JAM	14.11.93	17 Feb
52.14	Lenysse Dyer	USA	6.3.97	13 May
52.14A	Yenifer Padilla	COL	1.1.90	6 Jun
52.14	Anna Kielbasinska	POL	26.6.90	27 Jul
52.14	Laura Bueno	ESP	25.5.93	8 Aug
52.15	Alena Mamina	RUS	30.5.90	23 Jun
52.16	Laura de Witte	NED	7.8.95	1 Jul
52.17	Geisa Coutinho	BRA	1.6.80	15 Sep
52.19	Zola Golden	USA	20.6.97	12 May
52.19	Phil Healy	IRL	19.11.94	9 Jun
52.19	Bianca Razor	ROU	8.8.94	8 Aug
52.20	Tetyana Melnyk	UKR	2.4.95	9 Aug
52.24	Laura Müller	GER	11.12.95	27 Jun
52.25	Ayomide Folorunso	ITA	17.10.96	5 May
52.25	Yanique Haye-Smith	JAM	22.3.90	
52.25	Margo Van Puyvelde	BEL	21.12.95	14 Jul
52.26	Amarachi Pipi	GBR	26.11.95	12 May
52.26	Tamara Salaski	SRB	16.10.88	20 Jul
52.27	Uche Nwogwugwu	USA	26.9.98	25 May
52.27	Elea Mariama Diarra	FRA	8.3.90	8 Jul
52.27	Quach Thi Lan	VIE	18.10.95	28 Nov
52.28	NaAsha Robinson	USA	23.1.97	25 May
52.29	Asaine Hall	JAM	29.3.95	27 Apr
52.30	Madeline Price	CAN	11.9.95	12 May
52.30	Junelle Bromfield	JAM	8.2.98	23 Jun
52.32	Sara Limp	USA		13 May
52.33	Kimberly Harris	USA-Y	11.7.02	27 May
52.36	Imaobong Nse Uko	NGR-Y	20.2.04	13 Dec
52.37	Jahneya Mitchell	USA		13 May
52.37	Tierra Robinson-Jones	USA-J	22.11.99	2 Jun
52.38	Robin Reynolds	USA	22.2.94	29 Mar
52.38	Raphaela Boaheng Lukudo	ITA	29.7.94	8 Sep
52.38	Gabriella O'Grady	AUS	18.2.97	1 Dec
52.39	Anna Jefferson	USA	29.4.98	12 May
52.40	Cierra Dunston	USA	1.8.96	12 May
52.40	Nicky van Leuveren	NED	25.5.90	26 May
52.40	Kaliese Spencer	JAM	6.5.87	23 Jun
52.41	Iveta Putalová	SVK	24.3.88	1 Jul
52.42	Rhonda Whyte	JAM	6.11.90	10 Mar
52.42	Julia Madubuike	USA-J	16.4.00	17 Jun
52.44	Anna Ryzhykova	UKR	24.11.89	18 Jul
52.45	Derri-Ann Hill	JAM	17.11.95	24 Jun
52.45	Athing Mu	USA-Y	8.6.02	14 Jul
52.46	Alexandra Bezeková	SVK	13.8.92	1 Jul
52.46	Kseniya Aksyonova	RUS	14.1.88	20 Jul
52.48	Morgan Mitchell	AUS	3.10.94	26 Jan
52.48	Abike Egbeniyi	NGR	23.10.94	21 Apr
52.48	Yuliya Spiridonova	RUS	6.3.93	9 Jun
52.49	Praise Idamadudu Oghenefejiro	NGR	18.12.98	17 Mar
52.49	Karrington Winters	USA	14.4.97	13 May
52.50	Hannah Williams	GBR	23.4.98	9 Jun
52.51A	Zurian Hechavarría	CUB	10.8.95	29 Apr
52.51	Alesha Kelly	JAM	17.9.97	23 Jun
52.52	Kennedy Simon	USA-J	12.2.00	12 May
52.52	Jan'Taijah Ford	USA-Y	5.3.01	17 Jun
52.54	Natalia Kaczmarek	POL	17.1.98	21 Jul
52.55	Shae Anderson	USA-J	7.4.99	13 May
52.56	Taylor Sharpe	CAN	2.12.96	24 May
52.58	Tovea Jenkins	JAM	27.10.92	9 Apr
52.58	Kyra Constantine	CAN	1.8.98	25 May
52.58	Alina Lohvynenko	UKR	18.7.90	18 Jul
52.59A	Megan Hunter	USA-Y	31.5.01	28 Apr
52.60A	Wenda Nel	RSA	30.7.88	1 Mar
52.60	Agnes Raharolahy	FRA	7.11.92	27 May
52.60A	Martina Weil	CHI-J	12.7.99	29 Sep
52.61	Jasmine Malone	USA	19.9.96	7 Apr
52.62	Sparkle McKnight	TTO	21.12.91	4 May
52.62A	Tong Zenghuan	CHN	29.11.95	16 Jun
52.63	Kanika Beckles	GRN	3.10.91	9 Jun
52.63	Giancarla Dimich Trevisan	ITA	17.2.93	23 Jun
52.63	Viktoriya Tkachuk	UKR	8.11.94	25 Jun
52.63	Elina Mikhina	KAZ	16.7.94	26 Jun
52.65	Kendra Clarke	CAN	16.11.96	12 May
52.65	Brigitte Ntiamoah	FRA	5.3.94	9 Jun
52.66	Natalie Price	USA	5.8.98	13 May
52.66	Shadae Hylton	JAM	29.1.95	26 May
52.66	Barbora Malíková	CZE-Y	30.12.01	7 Jul
52.67	Modesta Morauskaite	LTU	2.10.95	2 Jun
52.68	Matilda Hellqvist	SWE	28.7.93	8 Aug
52.70	Veronica Mutua	KEN	2.2.92	9 Apr
52.71	Stacey-Ann Williams	JAM-J	8.3.99	10 Jul
52.72	Dalilah Muhammad	USA	7.2.90	30 Mar
52.72	Flordaliza Cofil	DOM-J	27.10.00	1 Aug
52.73	Bailey Lear	USA-Y	17.3.01	17 Jun
52.74	Aleksandra Gaworska	POL	7.11.95	29 May
52.74	Mary Abichi	GBR	19.11.90	1 Jul
52.75	Dominique Blake	JAM	15.2.87	27 May
52.76	D'Airien Jackson	USA	3.3.97	24 May
52.78	Jolie Carbo	USA	23.9.95	24 May
52.78	Venessa D'arpino	USA	13.12.95	24 May
52.78	Ella Connolly	AUS-J	13.7.00	11 Jul
52.79	Caitlin Jones	AUS	14.6.92	17 Feb
52.79	Victoria Powell	USA	28.5.98	13 May
52.79	Anastasiya Bryzgina	UKR	9.1.98	31 May
52.79	Irina Davydova	RUS	27.5.88	21 Jun
(196)				

Indoors

Mark	Name	Nat	Born	Pos	Meet	Venue	Date
50.34	Ellis			1	NCAA	College Station	10 Mar
50.36	McLaughlin			2	NCAA	College Station	10 Mar
50.55	Courtney Okolo	USA	15.3.94	1	WI	Birmingham	3 Mar
51.39	Georganne Moline	USA	6.3.90	1		Lubbock	10 Feb
51.46A	Quanera Hayes	USA	7.3.92	3rB	NC	Albuquerque	18 Feb
51.82				1		Fayetteville	8 Feb
51.60	Eilidh Doyle	GBR	20.2.87	3	WI	Birmingham	3 Mar
52.07	Amarachi Pipi	GBR	26.11.95	3h4	NCAA	College Station	9 Mar
52.08	Phil Healy	IRL	19.11.94	1		Wien	27 Jan
52.11A	Natasha Hastings	USA	23.7.86	2h1	NC	Albuquerque	17 Feb

Mark	Name		Nat	Born	Pos	Meet	Venue	Date
52.12	Tovea	Jenkins	JAM	27.10.92	2		Clemson	10 Feb

Mark	Name		Nat	Born	Pos	Meet	Venue	Date
52.20	Morgan	Burks-Magee	USA-J	6.3.99	24 Feb			
52.35	Carly	Muscaro	USA	18.5.95	27 Jan			
52.39A	Jasmine	Malone	USA	19.9.96	24 Feb			
52.53	Elina	Mikhina	KAZ	16.7.94	16 Feb			
52.63	Aleksandra	Gaworska	POL	7.11.95	18 Feb			
52.64	Kelsey	Balkwill	CAN	19.9.92	9 Feb			

52.67	Ashley	Spencer	USA	8.6.93	9 Feb
52.76	Svetlana	Golendova	KAZ	25.7.93	16 Feb
52.78	Maja	Ciric	SRB	7.11.89	20 Jan

Best at low altitufde

52.25	Minor	17	Jun
52.42	Shida	2	Aug

JUNIORS

See main list for top 12 juniors. 15 performances (3 indoor) by 7 women to 51.74. Additional marks and further juniors:

McLaughlin	50.52i	1	SEC	College Station	25 Feb	51.34i	1h4	NCAA	College Staaion	9 Mar
	50.97i	1h3	SEC	College Station	24 Feb					
Das	51.00	2h1	AsiG	Jakarta	25 Aug	51.46	1	WJ	Tampere	12 Jul
	51.13	1		Guwahati	29 Jun	51.53	3s1	CG	Gold Coast	10 Apr
	51.32	6	CG	Gold Coast	11 Apr					

Mark	Name		Nat	Born	Pos	Meet	Venue	Date
52.33	Kimberly	Harris	USA-Y	11.7.02	1		Douglasville	27 May
52.36	Imaobong Nse	Uko	NGR-Y	20.2.04	1		Abuja	13 Dec
52.37	Tierra	Robinson-Jones	USA	22.11.99	1		Clovis	2 Jun
52.42	Julia	Madubuike	USA	16.4.99	4	NC-j	Bloomington	17 Jun
52.45	Athing	Mu	USA-Y	8.6.02	1		Kissimmee	14 Jul
52.52	Kennedy	Simon	USA	12.2.00	1		Berry	12 May
52.52	Jan'Taijah	Ford	USA-Y	5.3.01	5	NC-j	Bloomington	17 Jun
52.55	Shae	Anderson	USA	7.4.99	6	Pac-12	Stanford	13 May
52.20i	Morgan	Burks-Magee	USA-J	6.3.99	2h3	SEC	College Station	24 Feb

500 METRES

Mark	Name		Nat	Born	Pos	Meet	Venue	Date
1:08.65	Aleksandra	Gaworska	POL	7.11.95	1		Kraków	6 May
1:09.72i	Olga	Kosichenko	USA		1		Boston (Allston)	10 Feb

600 METRES

Mark	Name		Nat	Born	Pos	Meet	Venue	Date
1:25.37+	Caster	Semenya	RSA	7.1.91	1	in 800	Paris (C)	30 Jun
1:25.8+	Francine	Niyonsaba	BDI	5.5.93	2	in 800	Paris (C)	30 Jun
1:26.14	Ajee'	Wilson	USA	8.5.94	1		Cheb	4 Sep
1:26.21	:aura	Bueno	ESP	25.5.93	1		Barcelona (S)	11 Jul

800 METRES

Mark	Name		Nat	Born	Pos	Meet	Venue	Date
1:54.25	Caster	Semenya	RSA	7.1.91	1	DL	Paris (C)	30 Jun
1:54.60		Semenya			1	Herc	Monaco	20 Jul
1:54.77		Semenya			1	C.Cup	Ostrava	9 Sep
1:55.27		Semenya			1	WK	Zürich	30 Aug
1:55.86	Francine	Niyonsaba	BDI	5.5.93	2	DL	Paris (C)	30 Jun
1:55.92		Semenya			1	Pre	Eugene	26 May
1:55.96		Niyonsaba			2	Herc	Monaco	20 Jul
1:56.06		Semenya			1	AfrC	Asaba	5 Aug
1:56.15	Natoya	Goule	JAM	30.3.91	3	Herc	Monaco	20 Jul
1:56.45	Ajee'	Wilson	USA	8.5.94	4	Herc	Monaco	20 Jul
1:56.68		Semenya			1	CG	Gold Coast	13 Apr
1:56.71	Habitam	Alemu	ETH	9.7.97	5	Herc	Monaco	20 Jul
1:56.86		Wilson			2	Pre	Eugene	26 May
1:56.88		Niyonsaba			3	Pre	Eugene	26 May
1:57.11		Wilson			3	DL	Paris (C)	30 Jun
1:57.16		Wilson			2	C.Cup	Ostrava	9 Sep
1:57.17		Alemu			4	DL	Paris (C)	30 Jun
1:57.25		Semenya			1	Bisl	Oslo	7 Jun
1:57.36		Goule			3	C.Cup	Ostrava	9 Sep
1:57.47	Rabab	Arrafi	MAR	12.1.91	6	Herc	Monaco	20 Jul
1:57.52		Wilson			1	NACAC	Toronto	11 Aug
1:57.69		Goule			5	DL	Paris (C)	30 Jun
1:57.69	Raevyn	Rogers	USA	7.9.96	7	Herc	Monaco	20 Jul
1:57.78		Alemu			4	Pre	Eugene	26 May
1:57.80A		Semenya			1	NC	Pretoria	17 Mar
1:57.80		Niyonsaba			1	Athl	Lausanne	5 Jul
1:57.86		Wilson			2	WK	Zürich	30 Aug
1:57.90		Niyonsaba			1	DL	Rabat	13 Jul
1:57.95		Goule			2	NACAC	Toronto	11 Aug
1:57.97		Niyonsaba			2	AfrC	Asaba	5 Aug
	(30/7)							
1:58.01	Ce'Aira	Brown	USA	4.11.93	1		Karlstad	25 Jul
1:58.04	Emily	Jerotich	KEN	13.5.86	1		Tomblaine	27 Jun
1:58.05	Charlene	Lipsey (10)	USA	16.7.91	6	DL	Paris (C)	30 Jun

WOMEN 2018

Mark	Name		Nat	Born	Pos	Meet	Venue	Date	
1:58.07	Margaret	Wambui	KEN	15.9.95	2	CG	Gold Coast	13	Apr
1:58.39	Halimah	Nakaayi	UGA	16.10.94	2		Tomblaine	27	Jun
1:58.83	Renelle	Lamote	FRA	26.12.93	9	Herc	Monaco	20	Jul
1:58.96	Nelly	Jepkosgei	KEN	14.7.91	4	Bisl	Oslo	7	Jun
1:59.09	Laura	Muir	GBR	9.5.93	5	Bisl	Oslo	7	Jun
1:59.25	Eunice	Sum	KEN	2.9.88	9	DL	Paris (C)	30	Jun
1:59.27	Malika	Akkaoui	MAR	25.12.87	6	DL	Rabat	13	Jul
1:59.34	Lynsey	Sharp	GBR	11.7.90	3	DL	London (OS)	22	Jul
1:59.35	Sifan	Hassan	NED	1.1.93	10	DL	Paris (C)	30	Jun
1:59.41	Winnie	Nanyondo	UGA	23.8.93	5	AfrC	Asaba	5	Aug
	(20)								
1:59.58	Nataliya	Pryshchepa	UKR	11.9.94	4	C.Cup	Ostrava	9	Sep
1:59.68	Kaela	Edwards	USA	8.12.93	4	NC	Des Moines	24	Jun
1:59.74	Diribe	Welteji	ETH-Y	13.5.02	1	WJ	Tampere	12	Jul
1:59.84	Mahelet	Mulugeta	ETH	20.3.95	3		Tomblaine	27	Jun
1:59.85	Sanne	Wolters-Verstegen	NED	10.11.85	1		Bruxelles	30	Jun
1:59.86	Adelle	Tracey	GBR	27.5.93	2s2	EC	Berlin	8	Aug
1:59.87	Aleksandra	Gulyayeva	RUS	30.4.94	1		Zhukovskiy	23	Jun
1:59.93	Alexandra	Bell	GBR	4.11.92	1		Watford	26	May
2:00.02A	Dorcus	Ajok	UGA	12.7.94	1		Kampala	3	Mar
2:00.06	Noëlie	Yarigo	BEN	26.12.85	2		Heusden-Zolder	21	Jul
	(30)								
2:00.08	Olivia	Baker	USA	12.6.96	6	NC	Des Moines	24	Jun
2:00.09	Hanna	Green	USA	16.10.94	7	NC	Des Moines	24	Jun
2:00.09	Marta	Pen	POR	31.7.93	5		Tomblaine	27	Jun
2:00.13	Georgia	Griffith	AUS	5.12.96	1		Portland	15	Jun
2:00.15	Rose Mary	Almanza	CUB	13.7.92	3	NACAC	Toronto	11	Aug
2:00.2A	Tola	Kore	ETH	16.1.97	1	NC	Addis Ababa	19	Apr
2:00.24	Brittany	McGowan	AUS	24.4.91	1	NC	Gold Coast	18	Feb
2:00.26	Olha	Lyakhova	UKR	18.3.92	1h1	EC	Berlin	7	Aug
2:00.28	Eglay	Nalyanya	KEN	28.5.96	3h1	CG	Gold Coast	12	Apr
2:00.32	Anna	Sabat	POL	9.11.93	3s2	EC	Berlin	8	Aug
	(40)								
2:00.35	Charline	Mathias	LUX	23.5.92	3		Heusden-Zolder	21	Jul
2:00.39	Shelayna	Oskan-Clarke	GBR	20.1.90	4s2	EC	Berlin	8	Aug
2:00.42	Selina	Büchel	SUI	26.7.91	3h1	EC	Berlin	7	Aug
2:00.45	Laura	Roesler	USA	19.12.91	4	DL	London (OS)	22	Jul
2:00.47	Claudia	Saunders	FRA	19.5.94	11	DL	Paris (C)	30	Jun
2:00.48	Christina	Hering	GER	9.10.94	1		Tübingen	16	Jun
2:00.52	Hanna	Hermansson	SWE	18.5.89	6s2	EC	Berlin	8	Aug
2:00.59	Simoya	Campbell	JAM	1.3.94	2		Kingston	22	Jun
2:00.60	Cynthia	Anais	FRA	18.1.88	2	NC	Albi	7	Jul
2:00.62	Angie	Petty	NZL	16.8.91	5h1	CG	Gold Coast	12	Apr
	(50)								
2:00.67	Emily	Richards	USA	21.7.95	1		Nashville	2	Jun
2:00.72	Sabrina	Southerland	USA	18.12.95	1q3	NCAA-W	Sacramento	25	May
2:00.74	Brenda	Martinez	USA	8.9.87	6	Bisl	Oslo	7	Jun
2:00.75	Liga	Velvere	LAT	10.2.90	5		Rovereto	23	Aug
2:00.77	Agnes	Abu	GHA	1.5.92	3		Nashville	2	Jun
2:00.80	Mary	Kuria	KEN	29.11.87	2		Guadalajara	5	Jul
2:00.80	Yekaterina	Zavyalova	RUS	1.3.91	1	NC	Kazan	20	Jul
2:00.81	Keely	Small	AUS-J	9.6.01	6h1	CG	Gold Coast	12	Apr
2:00.81	Lindsey	Butterworth	CAN	27.9.92	5	NACAC	Toronto	11	Aug
2:00.85	Caitlin	Collier	USA-J	5.8.99	4		Nashville	2	Jun
	(60)								
2:00.87	Lauren	Johnson	USA	4.5.87	2		Lignano	11	Jul
2:00.88	Madeline	Kopp	USA	4.4.95	5		Nashville	2	Jun
2:00.88	Sarah	McDonald	GBR	2.8.93	1A		Watford	8	Aug
2:00.92	Renée	Eykens	BEL	8.6.96	1		Rehlingen	20	May
2:00.92	Kate	Grace	USA	24.10.88	6		Rovereto	23	Aug
2:00.95	Yusneysi	Santiusti	ITA	24.12.84	7	DL	London (OS)	22	Jul
2:01.00	Yekaterina	Kupina	RUS	2.2.86	2		Zhukovskiy	23	Jun
2:01.01	Angelika	Cichocka	POL	15.3.88	4h1	EC	Berlin	7	Aug
2:01.05	Aníta	Hinriksdóttir	ISL	13.1.96	3		Tübingen	16	Jun
2:01.13	Carley	Thomas	AUS-J	26.12.00	2	WJ	Tampere	12	Jul
	(70)								
2:01.14	Avi	Wilson-Perteete	USA-J	13.5.99	2q3	NCAA-W	Sacramento	25	May
2:01.18	Jazmine	Fray	JAM	6.6.97	1		Los Angeles	14	Apr
2:01.2A	Hirut	Meshesha	ETH-Y	20.1.01	2		Assela	24	May
2:01.25	Maitë	Bouchard	CAN	24.8.95	1		Heusden-Zolder	21	Jul
2:01.26	Darroneshia	Lott	USA	9.3.93	6		Nashville	2	Jun

Mark	Name		Nat	Born	Pos	Meet	Venue	Date
2:01.29	Delia	Sclabas	SUI-J	8.11.00	3	WJ	Tampere	12 Jul
2:01.36	Diana	Mezuliáníková	CZE	10.4.92	4		Szczecin	15 Aug
2:01.4A	Fireweyni	Haile	ETH--Y	12.2.01	3		Assela	24 May
2:01.46	Hedda	Hynne	NOR	13.3.90	8	Bisl	Oslo	7 Jun
2:01.46	Samantha	Watson	USA-J	10.11.99	1	NC-j	Bloomington	16 Jun
(80)								
2:01.51	Genzebe	Dibaba	ETH	8.2.91	4		Ostrava	13 Jun
2:01.54	Esther	Guerrero	ESP	7.2.90	3		Barcelona (S)	11 Jul
2:01.58	Lydia	Cheruto	KEN-J	23.11.00	4		Padova	2 Sep
2:01.60mx	Katie	Snowden	GBR	9.3.94	1		London (Eltham)	18 Jul
2:01.77					1		London (Eltham)	7 Jul
2:01.60mx	Anzhela	Shevchenko	RUS	29.10.87	2	NC	Kazan	20 Jul
2:01.61	Cory	McGee	USA	29.5.92	2rB		Concord	7 Jun
2:01.61	Jenna	Westaway	CAN	19.6.94	2	NC	Ottawa	8 Jul
2:01.61	Claire	Mooney	IRL	21.6.92	2		Heusden-Zolder	21 Jul
2:01.62	Justine	Fedronic	FRA	11.5.91	3		Heusden-Zolder	21 Jul
2:01.65	Yngvild	Elvemo	NOR	28.5.90	9	Bisl	Oslo	7 Jun
(90)								
2:01.67	Lore	Hoffmann	SUI	25.7.96	7s2	EC	Berlin	8 Aug
2:01.71	Stephanie	Brown	USA	29.7.91	3	MSR	Torrance	21 Apr
2:01.72	Marina	Pospelova	RUS	23.7.90	3	NC	Kazan	20 Jul
2:01.73	Meg	Manley	USA	3.6.93	4		Heusden-Zolder	21 Jul
2:01.75	Danaïd	Prinsen	NED	20.8.97	4		Guadalajara	5 Jul
2:01.77	Natalia	Evangelidou	CYP	10.3.91	7h1	CG	Gold Coast	12 Apr
2:01.78	Revee	Walcott-Nolan	GBR	6.3.95	1		London (Eltham)	20 Jun
2:01.80		Wang Chunyu	CHN	17.1.95	1	AsiG	Jakarta	28 Aug
2:01.81	Alena	Brooks	TTO	14.11.91	5h3	CG	Gold Coast	12 Apr
2:01.82	Marta	Pérez	ESP	19.4.93	5		Guadalajara	5 Jul
(100)								

Mark	Name		Nat	Born	Date
2:01.85	Lovisa	Lindh	SWE	9.7.91	18 Aug
2:01.87	Yelena	Murashova	RUS	5.10.87	19 Jul
2:01.90	Gabriela	Gajanová	SVK-J	12.10.99	12 Jul
2:01.98	Rachel	Schneider	USA	18.7.91	7 Apr
2:02.02	Ellie	Baker	GBR	3.6.98	8 Jun
2:02.04	Sofia	Ennaoui	POL	30.8.95	1 Jun
2:02.04	Sarah	Schmidt	GER	4.10.96	14 Jul
2:02.07	Julianne	Labach	CAN	14.11.96	8 Jul
2:02.08	Svetlana	Uloga	RUS	23.11.86	20 Jul
2:02.11mx	Laura	Weightman	GBR	1.7.91	18 Jun
2:02.13	Ciara	Mageean	IRL	12.3.92	19 Jul
2:02.14	Sara	Kuivisto	FIN	18.8.91	22 Jul
2:02.18	Kendra	Chambers	USA	11.9.90	31 May
2:02.18	Egle	Balciunaite	LTU	31.10.88	7 Aug
2:02.21	Kristiina	Mäki	CZE	22.9.91	15 Aug
2:02.23	Manal	Bahraoui	BRN	6.1.94	21 May
2:02.24	Kimberley	Ficenec	USA	23.7.94	2 Jun
2:02.26	Tanja	Spill	GER	16.12.95	8 Jun
2:02.28	Elena	Bellò	ITA	18.1.97	26 May
2:02.35mx	Hanna	Klein	GER	6.4.93	28 Apr
2:02.38	Sadi	Henderson	USA	12.4.96	25 May
2:02.40	Dina	Aleksandrova	RUS	9.8.92	23 Jun
2:02.40	Margarita	Mukasheva	KAZ	4.1.86	28 Aug
2:02.41	Aaliyah	Miller	USA	28.8.98	13 May
2:02.41	Dana	Mecke	USA	20.9.87	21 Jun
2:02.42	Abbey	de la Motte	AUS	24.2.94	18 Jan
2:02.44	Carly	Muscaro	USA	18.5.95	25 May
2:02.45	Chrishuna	Williams	USA	31.3.93	13 Jun
2:02.45	Meraf	Bahta	SWE	24.6.89	13 Jun
2:02.47	Skylyn	Webb	USA	25.1.95	26 May
2:02.47	Irene	Baldessari	ITA	21.1.93	8 Sep
2:02.52	Hannah	Segrave	GBR	14.4.95	2 Jun
2:02.53	Angelika	Sarna	POL	1.10.97	10 Jun
2:02.54	Yume	Kitamura	JPN	23.12.95	24 Jun
2:02.55	Leila	Boufaarirane	FRA	2.10.91	26 May
2:02.62	Jemma	Reekie	GBR	6.3.98	1 Jun
2:02.63	Natalia	Romero	ESP	17.11.88	3 Jun
2:02.63	Síofra	Cléirigh Büttner	IRL	21.7.95	19 Jul
2:02.64	Elizabeth	Whelan	CAN	5.10.93	24 Jun
2:02.64	Mari	Smith	GBR	14.11.96	11 Jul
2:02.65	Katharina	Trost	GER	28.6.95	8 Jun
2:02.71	Ayaka	Kawata	JPN-J	22.8.99	3 May
2:02.71	Susan	Aneno	UGA	27.7.96	25 May
2:02.72	Clarisse	Moh	FRA	6.12.86	8 Jun
2:02.73	Ayano	Shiomi	JPN-J	26.11.99	20 May
2:02.73	Alexa	Efraimson	USA	20.2.97	18 Jul
2:02.76	Sarah	Healy	IRL-Y	13.2.01	26 Jun
2:02.76	Cecilia	Barowski	USA	7.12.92	11 Jul
2:02.78	Angel	Piccirillo	USA	8.1.94	31 May
2:02.88	Danae	Rivers	USA	3.2.98	22 Jun
2:02.89	Weronika	Wyka	POL	7.1.94	10 Jun
2:02.89	Hannah	England	GBR	6.3.87	18 Aug
2:02.92	Madeleine	Kelly	CAN	28.12.95	24 Jun
2:02.98	Hannah	Fields	USA	4.2.93	14 Jul
2:02.99	Déborah	Rodríguez	URU	2.12.92	11 Mar
2:02.99	Ashley	Taylor	CAN	12.5.95	24 Jun
2:02.99	Simona	Vrzalová	CZE	7.4.88	29 Jun
2:03.00	Emily	Lipari	USA	19.11.92	14 Jul
2:03.02	Laurence	Côté	CAN	9.2.91	8 Jul
2:03.04	Kayla	Johnson	USA-J	1.5.99	14 Apr
2:03.04	Charlotte	Mouchet	FRA	5.6.96	26 May
2:03.04	Paulina	Mikiewicz-Lapinska	POL	13.7.92	26 Jun
2:03.06	Mhairi	Hendry	GBR	31.3.96	26 May
2:03.07	Solange Andreia	Pereira	ESP	12.12.89	22 Jun
2:03.08	Mariela Luisa	Real	MEX	22.3.93	21 Apr
2:03.08	Alethia	Marrero	PUR	13.5.95	13 May
2:03.13	Adanech	Anbesa	ETH	23.1.98	28 Jun
2:03.13	Sonia	Gaskin	BAR	4.10.94	30 Jul
2:03.15	Fellan	Ferguson	JAM	15.3.94	25 May
2:03.18	Abike	Egbeniyi	NGR	23.10.94	7 Jun
2:03.20	Katie-Ann	McDonald	GBR-J	1.6.00	11 Jul
2:03.22	Katrina	Anderson	NZL	22.3.92	18 Feb
2:03.29	Kristen	Metcalfe	CAN	30.3.96	2 Jun
2:03.30	Corane	Gazeau	FRA	23.10.96	14 Jul
2:03.32	Leah	Barrow	GBR	21.1.93	26 May
2:03.34	Yekaterina	Alekseyeva	RUS	22.5.98	7 Jul
2:03.36	Rachel	Pocratsky	USA	23.1.97	12 May
2:03.36	Darya	Borisevich	BLR	6.4.90	20 May
2:03.40	Claudia	Bobocea	ROU	11.6.92	11 Jul
2:03.41	Inessa	Gusarova	RUS	29.10.95	12 Jul
2:03.44	Jackline	Wambui	KEN-J	8.2.00	11 Jul
2:03.44	Alena	Shukhtuyeva	RUS	7.12.93	19 Jul
2:03.44	Bianka	Kéri	HUN	19.4.94	7 Aug
2:03.45	Heather	MacLean	USA	31.8.95	28 Apr
2:03.47	Khadija	Benkassem	MAR	20.4.98	2 Jun
2:03.48	Catriona	Bissett	AUS	1.3.94	8 Mar
2:03.48	Siham	Hilali	MAR	2.5.86	28 Jun
2:03.49	Zoya	Naumov	ESP	17.7.95	11 Jul
2:03.50	Eleonora	Vandi (189)	ITA	15.3.96	8 Sep

Indoors

Mark	Name		Nat	Born	Pos	Meet	Venue	Date
1:59.81	Shelayna	Oskan-Clarke	GBR	20.1.90	3	WI	Birmingham	4 Mar
2:00.70	Angelika	Cichocka	POL	15.3.88	3		Liévin	13 Feb

WOMEN 2018

Mark	Name		Nat	Born	Pos	Meet	Venue		Date
2:01.22	Jenna	Westaway	CAN	19.6.94	1	GP	Boston (R)		10 Feb
2:01.30	Mhairi	Hendry	GBR	31.3.96	2	NC	Birmingham		18 Feb
2:01.61	Cecilia	Barowski	USA	7.12.92	2		Boston (Allston)		25 Feb
2:02.46	Síofra Cléirigh Büttner	IRL	21.7.95	10 Mar		2:02.92	Olga Kosichenko	USA	9 Feb
2:02.61	Hannah	Fields	USA	4.2.93	25 Feb		2:02.95	Elizabeth Whelan	CAN 5.10.93	9 Feb
2:02.70	Tatyana	Vinogradova	RUS	9.12.88	4 Feb		2:03.17	Rachel Pocratsky	USA 23.1.97	24 Feb
2:02.86	Santa	Tkhakur	RUS	23.4.93	4 Feb		2:03.38	Shannon Osika	USA 15.6.93	3 Feb

Drugs disqualification

2:00.0A	Chaltu	Shume	ETH	23.12.96	(1)	NC	Addis Ababa	19 Apr

JUNIORS

See main list for top 10 juniors. 12 performances by 10 women to 2:01.6. Additional mark and further juniors:

Welteji	2:00.6A	1	NC	Addis Abada	18 Feb		2:00.9A	1	Assela	24 May
2:01.90	Gabriela	Gajanová	SVK	12.10.99	4	WJ	Tampere		12 Jul
2:02.71	Ayaka	Kawata	JPN	22.8.99	1		Fukuroi		3 May
2:02.73	Ayano	Shiomi	JPN	26.11.99	4		Osaka		20 May
2:02.76	Sarah	Healy	IRL-Y	13.2.01	2		Belfast		26 Jun
2:03.04	Kayla	Johnson	USA	1.5.99	1		Coral Gables		14 Apr
2:03.20	Katie-Ann	McDonald	GBR	1.6.00	2s2	WJ	Tampere		11 Jul
2:03.44	Jackline	Wambui	KEN	8.2.00	3s1	WJ	Tampere		11 Jul
2:03.51	Barbora	Malóková	CZE	30.12.01	1	NC-y	Praja		24 Jun
2:03.73	Camryn	McIntish	USA	24.6.99	6s2	NCAA	Eugene		7 Jun
2:04.00	Isabelle	Boffey (20)	GBR	13.4.00	4	LI	Loughborough		20 May

1000 METRES

Mark	Name		Nat	Born	Pos	Meet	Venue		Date
2:30.70	Caster	Semenya	RSA	7.1.91	1	ISTAF	Berlin		2 Sep
2:31.01		Semenya			1	DL	Rabat		13 Jul
2:33.92	Laura	Muir	GBR	9.5.93	1	DL	Birmingham		18 Aug
2:34.48	Renelle	Lamote	FRA	26.12.93	2	DL	Birmingham		18 Aug
2:34.59	Adelle	Tracey	GBR	27.5.93	3	DL	Birmingham		18 Aug
2:34.88	Halimah	Nakaayi	UGA	16.10.94	2	ISTAF	Berlin		2 Sep
2:35.30	Nelly	Jepkosgei	KEN	14.7.91	3	ISTAF	Berlin		2 Sep
2:35.43A		Semenya			1		Pretoria		8 Mar
2:35.54	Katie	Snowden	GBR	9.3.94	4	DL	Birmingham		18 Aug
2:35.85	Ce'Aira	Brown	USA	4.11.93	2	DL	Rabat		13 Jul
2:36.13	Kaela	Edwards	USA	8.12.93	3	DL	Rabat		13 Jul
2:36.13	Winnie	Nanyondo	UGA	23.8.93	4	DL	Rabat		13 Jul
2:36.53	Colleen	Quigley	USA	20.11.92	5	DL	Birmingham		18 Aug
2:36.79	Jemma	Reekie	GBR	6.3.98	6	DL	Birmingham		18 Aug
2:37.46	Olha	Lyakhova	UKR	18.3.92	5	ISTAF	Berlin		2 Sep
2:37.49	Sanne	Wolters-Verstegen	NED	10.11.85	6	DL	Rabat		13 Jul
2:37.56	Laura	Weightman	GBR	1.7.91	6	ISTAF	Berlin		2 Sep
2:37.80	Brittany	McGowan	AUS	24.4.91	7	DL	Birmingham		18 Aug
2:37.82	Winny	Chebet	KEN	20.12.90	7	DL	Rabat		13 Jul
2:37.85	Esther	Guerrero	ESP	7.2.90	8	DL	Rabat		13 Jul
2:38.20	Simona	Vrzalová	CZE	7.4.88	18 Aug		2:40.09	Charline Mathias	LUX 23.5.92	13 May
2:38.61	Noëlie	Yarigo	BEN	26.12.85	2 Sep		2:40.80	Katharina Trost	GER 28.6.95	13 Aug
2:38.70	Stephanie	Brown	USA	29.7.91	2 Sep		2:40.81	Sara Kuivisto	FIN 18.8.91	19 Aug
2:38.87	Angie	Petty	NZL	16.8.91	18 Aug		**Indoors**			
2:39.85	Christina	Hering	GER	9.10.94	13 May		2:40.11	Aleksandra Gulyayeva	RUS 30.4.94	20 Jan
							2:40.15	Anastasiya Makarova	RUS 6.3.92	20 Jan

1500 METRES

Mark	Name		Nat	Born	Pos	Meet	Venue		Date
3:56.68	Genzebe	Dibaba	ETH	8.2.91	1	Kuso	Chorzów		8 Jun
3:57.34	Shelby	Houlihan	USA	8.2.93	1	Athl	Lausanne		5 Jul
3:57.41+	Sifan	Hassan	NED	.93	1	in 1M	London (OS)		22 Jul
3:57.64	Gudaf	Tsegay	ETH	23.1.97	1	DL	Stockholm		10 Jun
3:58.18	Laura	Muir	GBR	9.5.93	2	Athl	Lausanne		5 Jul
3:58.39		Hassan			3	Athl	Lausanne		5 Jul
3:58.49		Muir			1	VD	Bruxelles		31 Aug
3:58.53		Muir			2	DL	Stockholm		10 Jun
3:58.88+	Hellen	Obiri	KEN	13.12.89	2	in 1M	London (OS)		22 Jul
3:58.94		Houlihan			2	VD	Bruxelles		31 Aug
3:59.06		Houlihan			1	Pre	Eugene		26 May
3:59.07		Tsegay			4	Athl	Lausanne		5 Jul
3:59.09+		Tsegay			3	in 1M	London (OS)		22 Jul
3:59.15	Rabab	Arrafi	MAR	12.1.91	5	Athl	Lausanne		5 Jul
3:59.30		Muir			2	Pre	Eugene		26 May
3:59.37	Jenny	Simpson	USA	23.8.86	3	Pre	Eugene		26 May
3:59.41		Hassan			3	VD	Bruxelles		31 Aug
3:59.51		Arrafi			4	Pre	Eugene		26 May
3:59.60		Tsegay			1		Madrid		22 Jun

Mark	Name		Nat	Born	Pos	Meet	Venue	Date	
3:59.68		Tsegay			4	VD	Bruxelles	31	Aug
3:59.92	Caster	Semenya	RSA	7.1.91	1	DL	Doha	4	May
4:00.01+		Simpson			4	in 1M	London (OS)	22	Jul
4:00.28		Arrafi			3	DL	Stockholm	10	Jun
4:00.34		Simpson			4	DL	Stockholm	10	Jun
4:00.44		Semenya			6	Athl	Lausanne	5	Jul
4:00.60	Winny	Chebet (10)	KEN	20.12.90	5	Pre	Eugene	26	May
4:00.60		Hassan			1	DL	Birmingham	18	Aug
4:00.68+		Muir			5	in 1M	London (OS)	22	Jul
4:00.71		Semenya			1	CG	Gold Coast	10	Apr
4:00.86	Linden (30/11)	Hall	AUS	29.6.91	6	Pre	Eugene	26	May
4:00.99	Nelly	Jepkosgei	KEN	14.7.91	2	DL	Doha	4	May
4:01.41	Habitam	Alemu	ETH	9.7.97	3	DL	Doha	4	May
4:01.75	Besu	Sado	ETH	12.1.96	4	DL	Doha	4	May
4:01.76	Laura	Weightman	GBR	1.7.91	7	Athl	Lausanne	5	Jul
4:01.78	Alemaz	Teshale	ETH-J	5.7.99	5	DL	Doha	4	May
4:01.98	Eilish	McColgan	GBR	25.11.90	8	Athl	Lausanne	5	Jul
4:02.06	Sofia	Ennaoui	POL	30.8.95	3	DL	Birmingham	18	Aug
4:02.31	Meraf	Bahta	SWE	24.6.89	6	DL	Stockholm	10	Jun
4:02.44	Axumawit (20)	Embaye	ETH	18.10.94	4	DL	Birmingham	18	Aug
4:02.65	Brenda	Martinez	USA	8.9.87	7	Pre	Eugene	26	May
4:02.81	Dawit	Seyaum	ETH	27.7.96	8	Pre	Eugene	26	May
4:03.02	Colleen	Quigley	USA	20.11.92	1	Skol	Chorzów	22	Aug
4:03.09	Beatrice	Chepkoech	KEN	6.7.91	2	CG	Gold Coast	10	Apr
4:03.17	Sarah	McDonald	GBR	2.8.93	5	DL	Birmingham	18	Aug
4:03.44	Melissa	Courtney	GBR	30.8.93	3	CG	Gold Coast	10	Apr
4:03.87	Judy	Kiyeng	KEN	10.12.94	8	DL	Doha	4	May
4:03.99	Marta	Pen	POR	31.7.93	7	DL	Birmingham	18	Aug
4:04.05+	Kate	Grace	USA	24.10.88	8	in 1M	London (OS)	22	Jul
4:04.13	Ciara (30)	Mageean	IRL	12.3.92	1		Barcelona	11	Jul
4:04.17	Georgia	Griffith	AUS	5.12.96	5	CG	Gold Coast	10	Apr
4:04.76	Aleksandra	Gulyayeva	RUS	30.4.94	1	Znam	Zhukovskiy	30	Jun
4:04.80	Simona	Vrzalová	CZE	7.4.88	3		Ostrava	13	Jun
4:04.88	Marta	Pérez	ESP	19.4.93	5		Madrid	22	Jun
4:04.98	Charlene	Lipsey	USA	16.7.91	2		Cambridge	19	May
4:05.12	Maureen	Koster	NED	3.7.92	6		Madrid	22	Jun
4:05.18	Ajee'	Wilson	USA	8.5.94	1		Swarthmore	14	May
4:05.38	Eunice	Sum	KEN	2.9.88	9	DL	Doha	4	May
4:05.56	Stephanie	Twell	GBR	17.8.89	7	CG	Gold Coast	10	Apr
4:05.57	Karoline Bjerkeli (40)	Grøvdal	NOR	14.6.90	10	DL	Stockholm	10	Jun
4:05.68	Emily	Lipari	USA	19.11.92	1		Heusden-Zolder	21	Jul
4:05.75	Elise	Vanderelst	BEL	27.1.98	11	VD	Bruxelles	31	Aug
4:05.83	Gabriela	Stafford	CAN	13.9.95	2		Nashville	2	Jun
4:05.88	Mary	Kuria	KEN	29.11.87	9	CG	Gold Coast	10	Apr
4:05.88	Sara	Vaughn	USA	16.5.86	4		Barcelona	11	Jul
4:05.95	Diana	Sujew	GER	2.11.90	3	Kuso	Chorzów	8	Jun
4:06.01	Fantu	Worku	ETH-J	29.3.99	6		Ostrava	13	Jun
4:06.04	Helen	Schlachtenhaufen	USA	14.3.95	1r2		Heusden-Zolder	21	Jul
4:06.05	Winnie	Nanyondo	UGA	23.8.93	10	CG	Gold Coast	10	Apr
4:06.11+	Jemma (50)	Reekie	GBR	6.3.98	13	DL	London (OS)	22	Jul
4:06.12	Diana	Mezuliáníková	CZE	10.4.92	7		Ostrava	13	Jun
4:06.26	Cory	McGee	USA	29.5.92	5		Barcelona	11	Jul
4:06.34	Konstanze	Klosterhalfen	GER	18.2.97	1	NC	Nürnberg	22	Jul
4:06.46	Hanna	Klein	GER	6.4.93	2		Tübingen	16	Jun
4:06.51	Elena	Burkard	GER	10.2.92	2	NC	Nürnberg	22	Jul
4:06.55	Katie	Snowden	GBR	9.3.94	11	CG	Gold Coast	10	Apr
4:06.71	Stephanie	Brown	USA	29.7.91	1		Portland	10	Jun
4:06.71	Kristiina	Mäki	CZE	22.9.91	5	Skol	Chorzów	22	Aug
4:06.75	Darya	Borisevich	BLR	6.4.90	5		Tübingen	16	Jun
4:06.76	Zoe (60)	Buckman	AUS	21.12.88	12	CG	Gold Coast	10	Apr
4:06.77	Karissa	Schweizer	USA	4.5.96	1		Kortrijk	14	Jul
4:06.80	Shannon	Osika	USA	15.6.93	1		Memphis	25	Aug
4:07.06	Alexa	Efraimson	USA	20.2.97	3		Heusden-Zolder	21	Jul
4:07.08	Malika	Akkaoui	MAR	25.12.87	12	DL	Lausanne	5	Jul
4:07.16	Hanna	Hermansson	SWE	18.5.89	7	EC	Berlin	12	Aug

WOMEN 2018

Mark	Name		Nat	Born	Pos	Meet	Venue	Date
4:07.20	Dominique	Scott Efurd	RSA	24.6.92	4		Cambridge	19 May
4:07.32	Nicole	Sifuentes	CAN	30.6.86	3		Nashville	2 Jun
4:07.33	Danielle	Jones	USA	21.8.96	3		Portland	10 Jun
4:07.45	Yelena	Korobkina	RUS	25.11.90	2	NC	Kazan	22 Jul
4:07.50	Jessica	Judd	GBR	7.1.95	1		Manchester (Str)	18 Aug
	(70)							
4:07.50	Winfredah	Nzisa	KEN	30.5.97	2		Huelva	8 Jun
4:07.69	Rosie	Clarke	GBR	17.11.91	7		Tübingen	16 Jun
4:07.79	Elinor	Purrier	USA	20.2.95	1		Lignano	11 Jul
4:07.87	Inessa	Gusarova	RUS	29.10.95	3	NC	Kazan	22 Jul
4:07.88	Margherita	Magnani	ITA	26.2.87	3		Huelva	8 Jun
4:07.88	Kalkidan	Gezahegne	BRN	8.5.91	1	AsiG	Jakarta	30 Aug
4:07.90	Esther	Guerrero	ESP	7.2.90	4		Huelva	8 Jun
4:08.03	Yekaterina	Storozheva	RUS	22.1.93	4	NC	Kazan	22 Jul
4:08.04	Rachel	Schneider	USA	18.7.91	2	AWC	London (OS)	14 Jul
4:08.12	Caterina	Granz	GER	14.3.94	9		Tübingen	16 Jun
	(80)							
4:08.21	Lauren	Johnson	USA	4.5.87	2h1	NC	Des Moines	21 Jun
4:08.52	Solange Andreia	Pereira	ESP	12.12.89	5		Huelva	8 Jun
4:08.62	Dana	Giordano	USA	30.12.93	5h1	NC	Des Moines	21 Jun
4:08.75	Jessica	Hull	AUS	22.10.96	1	NCAA	Eugene	9 Jun
4:08.77	Josephine	Chelangat	KEN	10.10.98	10		Tübingen	16 Jun
4:08.78	Yelena	Murashova	RUS	5.10.87	5	NC	Kazan	22 Jul
4:08.92	Lucia	Stafford	CAN	17.8.98	1	AWC	Ninove	28 Jul
4:08.96	Sara	Kuivisto	FIN	18.8.91	8		Barcelona	11 Jul
4:09.02	Helen	Lobun	KEN-J	18.3.99	1	AWC	Kobe	22 Apr
4:09.03	Danielle	Aragon	USA	1.7.94	3		Lignano	11 Jul
	(90)							
4:09.10	Katie	Mackey	USA	12.11.87	6		Portland	10 Jun
4:09.12	Tigist	Gashaw	BRN	25.12.96	2	AsiG	Jakarta	30 Aug
4:09.14	Nikki	Hiltz	USA	23.10.94	2	NCAA	Eugene	9 Jun
4:09.25	Sarah	Healy	IRL-Y	13.2.01	1y		Tübingen	16 Jun
4:09.26	Sarah	MacPherson	CAN	8.5.91	6		Heusden-Zolder	21 Jul
4:09.34	Cristina	Espejo	ESP	13.10.94	4	Morton	Dublin (S)	19 Jul
4:09.44	Ce'Aira	Brown	USA	4.11.93	1	FlaR	Gainesville	30 Mar
4:09.49	Elise	Cranny	USA	8.5.96	3	NCAA	Eugene	9 Jun
4:09.50	Siham	Hilali	MAR	2.5.86	1		Halluin	27 Jun
4:09.52	Nicole	Tully	USA	30.10.86	1		New York	14 Jun
	(100)							

Mark	Name		Nat	Born	Pos	Date		Mark	Name		Nat	Born	Pos	Date
4:09.59	Christina	Aragon	USA	17.6.97	9	Jun		4:11.00A	Edina	Jebitok	KEN-Y	10.11.01	12	Jun
4:09.68	Dinke	Ferdesa	ETH-J	28.5.99	1	Jun		4:11.03	Anzhela	Shevchenko	RUS	29.10.87	21	Jul
4:09.71	Amy	Griffiths	GBR	22.3.96	18	Aug		4:11.07	Grace	Barnett	USA	29.6.95	7	Jun
4:09.74	Vanessa	Fraser	USA	27.7.95	14	Jul		4:11.08	Anna Emilie	Møller	DEN	28.7.97	2	Aug
4:09.74	Katelyn	Ayers	CAN	9.2.95	14	Jul		4:11.12	Chloe	Tighe	AUS	28.9.90	17	Feb
4:09.81	Beyenu	Degefu	ETH-J	12.7.99	1	Jun		4:11.19	Mel	Lawrence	USA	29.8.89	10	Jun
4:09.81	Megan	Mansy	USA	27.3.94	11	Jul		4:11.23	Anna	Silvander	SWE	22.6.93	28	Jul
4:09.83	Sarah	Brown	USA	15.10.86	14	Jun		4:11.25mx	Esther	Chebet	UGA	10.9.97	31	Aug
4:09.95mx	Paulina	Kaczynska	POL	24.7.91	26	May		4:11.3A	Celliphine	Chespol	KEN-J	23.3.99	16	Jun
	4:10.03				8	Jun		4:11.31	Sofie	Van Accom	BEL	7.6.89	16	Jun
4:10.01	Anastasiya	Kalina	RUS	16.2.94	22	Jul		4:11.31	Madeline	Hills	AUS	15.5.87	14	Jul
4:10.03	Rachel	Pocratsky	USA	23.1.97	12	May		4:11.33	Renée	Eykens	BEL	8.6.96	26	May
4:10.04	Angelika	Cichocka	POL	15.3.88	10	Aug		4:11.36	Ophélie Claude-Boxberger		FRA	18.10.88	1	Jun
4:10.05	Gloria	Kite	KEN	29.12.98	11	Jul		4:11.37	Taryn	Rawlings	USA	17.4.96	9	Jun
4:10.10	Delia	Sclabas	SUI-J	8.11.00	5	Jul		4:11.48	Jamie	Morrissey	USA	14.9.95	21	Apr
4:10.11	Linn	Nilsson	SWE	15.10.90	21	Jul		4:11.55	Dana	Mecke	USA	20.9.87	17	May
4:10.12	Stephanie	Garcia	USA	3.5.88	2	Jun		4:11.55	P.Unnikrishnan Chithra		IND	9.6.95	29	Jun
4:10.14	Renata	Plis	POL	5.2.85	22	Aug		4:11.55	Eglay	Nalyanya	KEN	28.5.96	4	Jul
4:10.22	Amela	Terzic	SRB	2.1.93	8	Jun		4:11.57	Sinclaire	Johnson	USA	13.4.98	26	May
4:10.31	Rhianwedd	Price-Weimer	GBR	11.8.94	30	Mar		4:11.60	Natalya	Aristarkhova	RUS	31.10.89	6	Jun
4:10.42	Feyisa	Adanech	ETH	23.1.98	1	Jun		4:11.65	Bone	Cheluke	ETH	11.11.98	11	Jul
4:10.43	Mirriam	Cherop	KEN-J	25.6.99	19	May		4:11.65	Geneviève	Lalonde	CAN	5.9.91	14	Jul
4:10.53	Dorcus	Ajok	UGA	12.7.94	8	Jun		4:11.69	Lonah Chemtai Salpeter		ISR	12.12.88	4	Jul
4:10.54	Mariah	Kelly	CAN	19.8.91	21	Jul		4:11.83	Courtney	Hufsmith	CAN	.98	27	Jun
4:10.66	Jessica	O'Connell	CAN	10.2.89	27	Jun		4:11.97	Jenny	Blundell	AUS	9.5.94	17	Feb
4:10.68	Marina	Pospelova	RUS	23.7.90	21	Jul		4:12.07	Katrina	Coogan	USA	15.11.93	28	Jul
4:10.70	Anna	Kupayeva	RUS	24.11.90	21	Jul		4:12.10	Brittany	McGowan	AUS	24.4.91	28	Mar
4:10.71	Katharina	Trost	GER	28.6.95	16	Jun		4:12.21	Sasha	Gollish	CAN	27.12.81	27	Jun
4:10.78	Hannah	England	GBR	6.3.87	16	Jun		4:12.26	Molly	Sughroue	USA	2.9.95	7	Jun
4:10.82	Danae	Rivers	USA	3.2.98	30	Mar		4:12.29	Elodie	Normand	FRA	6.10.88	26	May
4:10.83	Janelle	Noe	USA	23.3.95	7	Jul		4:12.29	Yekaterina	Sokolova	RUS	16.12.95	21	Jul
4:10.95	Lindsey	Butterworth	CAN	27.9.92	20	Apr		4:12.31	Elena	Bellò	ITA	18.1.97	11	Jul
4:10.98	Natalia	Evangelidou	CYP	10.3.91	9	Apr		4:12.36	Anna	Shields	USA	21.2.91	14	Jun
4:10.98	Rebecca	Addison	USA	28.5.91	2	Jun		4:12.36	Oumaima	Saoud	MAR	5.8.96	14	Jul
4:10.98+	Kate	Van Buskirk	CAN	9.6.87	3	Aug		4:12.38	Claudia	Saunders	FRA	19.5.94	3	May
4:10.99	Regan	Yee	CAN	4.7.95	21	Jul		4:12.39	Denise	Krebs	GER	27.6.87	26	May

Mark	Name		Nat	Born	Pos	Meet	Venue	Date
4:12.44	Monika	Choudhary	IND	28.6.94				29 Jun
4:12.46	Eleanor	Fulton	USA	17.5.93				27 Jun
4:12.48	Aurélie	Dubé-Lavoie	CAN	6.3.96				27 Jun
4:12.50	Caroline	Högardh	SWE	16.11.92				21 Jul
4:12.52	Olivia	Burdon	NZL	26.1.98				20 Apr
4:12.53	Yekaterina	Ivonina	RUS	14.6.94				13 Jun
4:12.56	Alexis	Fuller	USA	7.5.97				20 Apr
4:12.63	Dina	Aleksandrova	RUS	9.8.92				29 May
4:12.72	Yolanda	Ngarambe	SWE	14.9.91				28 Jul
4:12.82	Manal	Bahraoui	BRN	6.1.94				1 Jun
4:12.84	Jhuma	Khatun drugs dq?	IND	28.8.88				29 Jun
4:12.96	Jessica	Harris	USA	14.3.96				7 Jun
4:13.12	Lili	Das	IND	18.3.98				29 Jun
4:13.16A	Lydia	Cheruto	KEN-J	23.11.00				17 Feb
4:13.21	Caroline	Kipkirui	KEN	26.5.94				29 Jun
4:13.31	Mariana	Machado	POR-J	12.11.00				8 Jun
4:13.35	Alex	Wilson	USA	16.6.93				14 Jul
4:13.44	Olga	Vovk	RUS	13.2.93				29 May
	(189)							

Indoors

Mark	Name		Nat	Born	Pos	Meet	Venue	Date
3:57.45		Dibaba			1		Karlsruhe	3 Feb
4:02.21	Beatrice	Chepkoech	KEN	6.7.91	1	GP	Glasgow	25 Feb
4:04.00	Konstanze	Klosterhalfen	GER	18.2.97	2		Karlsruhe	3 Feb
4:04.95	Aisha	Praught Leer	JAM	14.12.89	2	GP	Boston (R)	10 Feb
4:06.35	Angelika	Cichocka	POL	15.3.88	2		Düsseldorf	6 Feb
4:07.71	Linn	Nilsson	SWE	15.10.90	7		Torun	15 Feb
4:09.42	Kate	Van Buskirk	CAN	9.6.87	3h2	WI	Birmingham	2 Mar
4:09.54	Aníta	Hinriksdóttir	ISL	13.1.96				6 Feb
4:10.05	Stacey	Smith	GBR	4.2.90				25 Feb
4:10.36	Luiza	Gega	ALB	5.11.88				18 Feb
4:10.37	Claudia	Bobocea	ROU	11.6.92				6 Feb
4:10.85	Gesa-Felicitas	Krause	GER	3.8.92				25 Feb
4:13.35	Sanne	Wolters-Verstegen	NED	10.11.85				13 Feb

JUNIORS

See main list for top 4 juniors. 12 performances (2 indoors) by 8 women to 4:10.5. Additional marks and further juniors:

Mark	Name		Nat	Born	Pos	Meet	Venue	Date
Teshale	4:05.36i	4			Torun		15 Feb	
	4:07.47	10	DL		Birmingham		18 Aug	
4:09.68	Dinke	Ferdesa	ETH	28.5.99	1		Andújar	1 Jun
4:09.81	Beyenu	Degefu	ETH	12.7.99	2		Andújar	1 Jun
4:10.10	Delia	Sclabas	SUI	8.11.00	15	Athl	Lausanne	5 Jul
4:10.43	Mirriam	Cherop	KEN	25.6.99	6		Cambridge	19 May
4:11.00A	Edina	Jebitok	KEN-Y	10.11.01	1		Nairobi	12 Jun
4:11.3A	Celliphine	Chespol (10)	KEN	23.3.99	1		Nairobi	16 Jun
4:13.16A	Lydia	Cheruto	KEN	23.11.00	8		Nairobi	17 Feb
4:13.31	Mariana	Machado	POR	12.11.00	9		Huelva	8 Jun
4:13.31	Nozomi	Tanaka	JPN	4.9.99	1		Toyota	15 Sep
4:14.05	Katrina	Robinson	NZL	8.8.00	5	AUS Ch	Gold Coast	17 Feb
4:14.11	Sarah	Eckel	AUS	27.5.99	7	NC	Gold Coast	17 Feb
4:14.45	Katelyn	Tuohy	USA-Y	18.3.02	1		Cicero	8 Jun
4:14.46	Bibi	Abera	ETH	29.4.00	1		Nijmegen	8 Jun
4:14.80	Erin	Wallace	GBR	18.5.00	4		Watford	26 May
4:15.48	Cynthia	Baire	KEN-Y	.02	1		Satsumasendai	11 Jun
4:16.3A	Werknesh	Mulatu (20)	ETH		4		Assela	26 May

The junior continuation lines for Teshale: 4:08.68i 1 Gent 10 Feb; 4:09.67 1 WJ Tampere 15 Jul.

1 MILE

Mark	Name		Nat	Born	Pos	Meet	Venue	Date
4:14.71	Sifan	Hassan	NED	1.1.93	1	DL	London (OS)	22 Jul
4:16.14	Gudaf	Tsegay	ETH	23.1.97	2	DL	London (OS)	22 Jul
4:16.15	Hellen	Obiri	KEN	13.12.89	3	DL	London (OS)	22 Jul
4:17.30	Jenny	Simpson	USA	23.8.86	4	DL	London (OS)	22 Jul
4:19.28	Laura	Muir	GBR	9.5.93	5	DL	London (OS)	22 Jul
4:20.49	Laura	Weightman	GBR	1.7.91	6	DL	London (OS)	22 Jul
4:20.51	Winny	Chebet	KEN	20.12.90	7	DL	London (OS)	22 Jul
4:20.51	Genzebe	Dibaba	ETH	8.2.91	1		Padova	2 Sep
4:20.70	Kate	Grace	USA	24.10.88	8	DL	London (OS)	22 Jul
4:20.85	Sarah	McDonald (10)	GBR	2.8.93	9	DL	London (OS)	22 Jul
4:21.40	Linden	Hall	AUS	29.6.91	10	DL	London (OS)	22 Jul
4:21.54	Simona	Vrzalová	CZE	7.4.88	11	DL	London (OS)	22 Jul
4:22.45	Marta	Pen	POR	31.7.93	1	ISTAF	Berlin	2 Sep
4:23.34	Sofia	Ennaoui	POL	30.8.95	12	DL	London (OS)	22 Jul
4:24.27	Konstanze	Klosterhalfen	GER	18.2.97	3	ISTAF	Berlin	2 Sep
4:24.82	Alexa	Efraimson	USA	20.2.97	4	ISTAF	Berlin	2 Sep
4:25.07	Eilish	McColgan	GBR	25.11.90	5	ISTAF	Berlin	2 Sep
4:25.47	Shannon	Osika	USA	15.6.93	1		Memphis	25 Aug
4:25.99	Besu	Sado	ETH	12.1.96	2	FBK	Hengelo	3 Jun
4:26.05	Stephanie	Twell (20)	GBR	17.8.89	6	ISTAF	Berlin	2 Sep
4:26.63	Dominique	Scott Efurd	RSA	24.6.92	2		Concord MA	7 Jun
4:26.75	Ciara	Mageean	IRL	12.3.92	7	ISTAF	Berlin	2 Sep
4:27.03	Meraf	Bahta	SWE	24.6.89	3	FBK	Hengelo	3 Jun
4:27.09	Helen	Schlachtenhaufen	USA	14.3.95	3		Concord	7 Jun
4:27.16	Jemma	Reekie	GBR	6.3.98	13	DL	London (OS)	22 Jul
4:27.23	Rachel	Schneider	USA	18.7.91	1		Falmouth	18 Aug
4:27.28	Charlene	Lipsey	USA	16.7.91	1		Raleigh	3 Aug

WOMEN 2018

Mark	Name		Nat	Born	Pos	Meet	Venue	Date
4:27.29	Melissa	Courtney	GBR	30.8.93	5	FBK	Hengelo	3 Jun
4:27.31	Sara	Vaughn	USA	16.5.86	2		Raleigh	3 Aug
4:27.32	Judy	Kiyeng	KEN	10.12.94	6	FBK	Hengelo	3 Jun
	(30)							
4:27.78	Cory	McGee	USA	29.5.92	3		Raleigh	3 Aug
4:27.81	Nicole	Sifuentes	CAN	30.6.86	4		Raleigh	3 Aug
4:28.10	Winnie	Nanyondo	UGA	23.8.93	7	FBK	Hengelo	3 Jun
4:28.16	Lauren	Johnson	USA	4.5.87	4		Concord MA	7 Jun
4:28.25	Marta	Pérez	ESP	19.4.93	8	FBK	Hengelo	3 Jun
4:28.36	Renata	Plis	POL	5.2.85	8	ISTAF	Berlin	2 Sep
4:28.38	Diana	Sujew	GER	2.11.90	9	FBK	Hengelo	3 Jun
4:28.62	Emily	Lipari	USA	19.11.92	1		West Chester	9 Aug
4:28.67	Kate	Van Buskirk	CAN	9.6.87	5		Raleigh	3 Aug
4:29.11	Sanne	Wolters-Verstegen	NED	10.11.85	10	FBK	Hengelo	3 Jun
	(40)							
4:29.20	Aníta	Hinriksdóttir	ISL	13.1.96	11	FBK	Hengelo	3 Jun
4:29.56	Katie	Snowden	GBR	9.3.94	12	FBK	Hengelo	3 Jun
Indoors								
4:26.55	Elinor	Purrier	USA	20.2.95	1		Boston (Allston)	9 Feb
4:26.92	Kate	Van Buskirk	CAN	9.6.87	1		New York (Arm)	27 Jan
4:27.44	Gabriela	Stafford	CAN	13.9.95	2		Boston (Allston)	9 Feb
4:27.54	Karissa	Schweizer	USA	4.5.96	3		New York (Arm)	27 Jan
4:27.69	Nicole	Sifuentes	CAN	30.6.86	1		Ann Arbor	13 Jan

4:30.05	Colleen	Quigley	USA	20.11.92	3 Feb	4:31.98	Millie	Paladino	USA	18.10.95	9 Feb
4:31.09	Becca	Addison	USA	28.5.91	25 Feb	4:32.30	Olivia	Burdon	NZL	26.1.98	24 Feb
4:31.29	Elise	Cranny	USA	8.5.96	24 Feb	4:32.67	Natalija	Piliusina	LTU	22.10.90	27 Jan
4:31.66	Lucia	Stafford	CAN	17.8.98	27 Jan	4:33.00	Rhianwedd	Price-Weimer	GBR	11.8.94	10 Mar
4:31.76	Jessica	Hull	AUS	22.10.96	24 Feb	4:33.40	Kellyn	Taylor	USA	22.7.86	27 Jan
4:31.82	Danielle	Jones	USA	21.8.96	10 Mar	4:33.98	Kaela	Edwards	USA	8.12.93	3 Feb

JUNIORS

Mark	Name		Nat	Born	Pos	Meet	Venue	Date
4:29.74	Biri	Abera	ETH-J	29.4.00	13	FBK	Hengelo	3 Jun
4:33.87	Katelyn	Tuohy	USA-Y	18.3.02	1	NBNO	Greensboro	16 Jun

2000 METRES

Mark	Name		Nat	Born	Pos	Meet	Venue	Date
5:27.73	Genzebe	Dibaba	ETH	8.2.91	1		Montreuil	19 Jun
5:37.12	Meraf	Bahta	SWE	24.6.89	2		Montreuil	19 Jun
5:38.19	Beyenu	Degefu	ETH-J	12.7.99	3		Montreuil	19 Jun
5:40.65	Gloria	Kite	KEN	29.12.98	4		Montreuil	19 Jun
5:41.04	Karoline Bjerkeli	Grøvdal	NOR	14.6.90	1		Florø	2 Jun

5:42.67+	Agnes	Tirop	KEN	23.10.95	4 May	5:43.1+	Caroline	Kipkirui	KEN	26.5.94	4 May
5:42.9+	Lilian	Rengeruk	KEN	3.5.97	4 May	5:43.2+	Jenny	Simpson	USA	23.8.86	4 May
5:43.0+	Letesenbet	Gidey	ETH	20.3.98	4 May	5:43.2+	Hyvin	Jepkemoi	KEN	13.1.92	4 May
5:43.0+	Yasemin	Can	TUR	11.12.96	4 May	5:43.4+	Hellen	Obiri	KEN	13.12.89	4 May
						5:43.5+	Meskerem	Mamo	ETH-J	13.4.99	4 May

Indoors								
5:41.10i	Yelena	Korobkina	RUS	25.11.90	1		Yekaterinburg	7 Jan
5:42.12i	Aleksandra	Gulyayeva	RUS	30.4.94	7 Jan	c.5:43.2i+ mx Laura	Muir	GBR	9.5.93	7 Jan

3000 METRES

Mark	Name		Nat	Born	Pos	Meet	Venue	Date
8:27.50	Sifan	Hassan	NED	1.1.93	1	C.Cup	Ostrava	8 Sep
8:29.05	Caroline	Kipkirui	KEN	26.5.94	1	DL	Doha	4 May
8:29.09	Agnes	Tirop	KEN	23.10.95	2	DL	Doha	4 May
8:30.51	Hyvin	Jepkemoi	KEN	13.1.92	3	DL	Doha	4 May
8:30.83	Jenny	Simpson	USA	23.8.86	4	DL	Doha	4 May
8:30.96	Letesenbet	Gidey	ETH	20.3.98	5	DL	Doha	4 May
8:32.21		Tirop			1	DL	Birmingham	18 Aug
8:32.49	Senbere	Teferi	ETH	3.5.95	2	C.Cup	Ostrava	8 Sep
8:33.13	Lilian	Rengeruk	KEN	3.5.97	6	DL	Doha	4 May
8:33.37		Rengeruk			1	Hanz	Zagreb	4 Sep
8:33.43		Rengeruk			2	DL	Birmingham	18 Aug
8:33.61	Norah	Tanui	KEN	2.10.95	2	Hanz	Zagreb	4 Sep
8:33.63	Meskerem	Mamo (10)	ETH-J	13.4.99	7	DL	Doha	4 May
8:33.78	Gudaf	Tsegay	ETH	23.1.97	3	Hanz	Zagreb	4 Sep
8:34.65	Kalkidan	Gezahegne	BRN	8.5.91	4	Hanz	Zagreb	4 Sep
8:35.76	Beyenu	Degefu	ETH-J	12.7.99	8	DL	Doha	4 May
8:36.20	Hellen	Obiri	KEN	13.12.89	3	C.Cup	Ostrava	8 Sep
8:36.24	Yasemin	Can	TUR	11.12.96	9	DL	Doha	4 May
8:36.26		Obiri			3	DL	Birmingham	18 Aug
8:37.09		Tanui			10	DL	Doha	4 May
	(20/15)							
8:37.21	Susan	Krumins	NED	8.7.86	5	Hanz	Zagreb	4 Sep

Mark	Name		Nat	Born	Pos	Meet	Venue	Date
8:37.68	Alemaz	Teshale	ETH-J	5.7.99	6	Hanz	Zagreb	4 Sep
8:38.04	Konstanze	Klosterhalfen	GER	18.2.97	4	C.Cup	Ostrava	8 Sep
8:38.49	Eilish	McColgan	GBR	25.11.90	4	DL	Birmingham	18 Aug
8:39.07	Gloria	Kite	KEN	29.12.98	3	PNG	Turku	5 Jun
(20)								
8:39.20	Melissa	Courtney	GBR	30.8.93	5	DL	Birmingham	18 Aug
8:41.69	Eva	Cherono	KEN	15.8.96	5	PNG	Turku	5 Jun
8:41.9+	Genzebe	Dibaba	ETH	8.2.91	4	in 5000	Rabat	13 Jul
8:42.88	Lonah Chemtai	Salpeter	ISR	12.12.88	7	DL	Birmingham	18 Aug
8:43.00	Loice	Chemnung	KEN	22.2.97	2		Rovereto	23 Aug
8:43.83	Axumawit	Embaye	ETH	18.10.94	7	Hanz	Zagreb	4 Sep
8:44.13	Ejgayehu	Taye	ETH-J	10.2.00	8	DL	Birmingham	18 Aug
8:44.24	Rosemary	Wanjiru	KEN	9.12.94	1		Yokohama	10 Nov
8:44.47	Katie	Mackey	USA	12.11.87	3	DL	London (OS)	21 Jul
8:45.43	Elena	Burkard	GER	10.2.92	9	DL	Birmingham	18 Aug
(30)								
8:45.67	Gabriela	Stafford	CAN	13.9.95	4	DL	London (OS)	21 Jul
8:45.97	Camille	Buscomb	NZL	11.7.90	1		Cork	16 Jul
8:46.43	Elinor	Purrier	USA	20.2.95	2		Cork	16 Jul
8:46.79	Stephanie	Twell	GBR	17.8.89	11	DL	Birmingham	18 Aug
8:46.86	Jessica	O'Connell	CAN	10.2.89	3		Cork	16 Jul
8:47.24	Shuru	Bulo	ETH	27.6.98	1		Osaka	20 May
8:47.73	Fotyen	Tesfay	ETH	17.2.98	11	DL	Doha	4 May
8:48.21	Rina	Nabeshima	JPN	16.12.93	8	DL	London (OS)	21 Jul
8:48.65	Lauren	Paquette	USA	27.6.86	9	DL	London (OS)	21 Jul
8:48.69	Helen	Lobun	KEN-J	18.3.99	2		Osaka	20 May
(40)								
8:49.38	Genevieve	LaCaze/Gregson	AUS	4.8.89	11	Hanz	Zagreb	4 Sep
8:49.61	Emily	Sisson	USA	12.10.91	4		Cork	16 Jul
8:50.11	Cynthia	Baire	KEN-Y	.02	1		Oita	13 Oct
8:50.58	Ann	Mwangi	KEN	8.12.88	3		Osaka	20 May
8:51.11	Martha	Mokaya	KEN-J	1.3.00	1		Fukui	8 Oct
8:51.93	Aberash	Minsewo	ETH-Y	22.2.01	13	DL	Doha	4 May
8:52.33	Zoe	Buckman	AUS	21.12.88	5		Osaka	20 May
8:52.41	Tabitha	Kamau	KEN-J	3.7.00	2		Fukui	8 Oct
8:52.53	Alexa	Efraimson	USA	20.2.97	3		Rovereto	23 Aug
8:52.73	Anna Emilie	Møller	DEN	28.7.97	1		Bergen	22 Aug
(50)								
8:53.27	Linden	Hall	AUS	29.6.91	1		Sydney	17 Mar
8:53.29	Jessica	Judd	GBR	7.1.95	11	DL	London (OS)	21 Jul
8:53.41	Andrea	Seccafien	CAN	27.8.90	2		Lapinlahti	28 Jul
8:54.01	Nozomi	Tanaka	JPN-J	4.9.99	1	WJ	Tampere	11 Jul
8:54.2+	Dominique	Scott Efurd	RSA	24.6.92	9	in 5000	Rabat	13 Jul
8:54.71	Agnes	Mukari	KEN-Y	15.12.02	2		Ise	6 Aug
8:54.91+	Margaret	Kipkemboi	KEN	9.2.93	6	in 5000	Eugene	26 May
8:55.14	Tomoka	Kimura	JPN	12.11.94	1		Kitami	7 Jul
8:55.14	Dana	Giordano	USA	30.12.93	12	DL	London (OS)	21 Jul
8:55.19	Sheila	Chelangat	KEN	11.4.98	13	DL	London (OS)	21 Jul
(60)								
8:55.34	Claudia	Bobocea	ROU	11.6.92	6		Osaka	20 May
8:55.81	Jip	Vastenburg	NED	21.3.94	1		Utrecht	1 Jun
8:56.39	Meselu	Berhe	ETH-J	29.5.00	2	WJ	Tampere	11 Jul
8:56.53	Sarah	Pagano	USA	23.7.91	6		Cork	16 Jul
8:56.75+	Rachel	Schneider	USA	18.7.91	2	in 5000	Des Moines	27 Apr

Mark	Name		Nat	Born	Date	Mark	Name		Nat	Born	Date
8:57.02	Minami	Yamanouchi	JPN	21.12.92	7 Jul	8:59.20	Tsige	Gebreselama	ETH-J	30.9.00	11 Jul
8:57.09+	Stephanie	Garcia	USA	3.5.88	27 Apr	8:59.72	Beatrice	Chebet	KEN-J	5.3.00	18 Aug
8:57.11	Sandra	Eriksson	FIN	4.6.89	5 Jun	9:00.45	Yelena	Korobkina	RUS	25.11.90	13 Jun
8:57.30+	Brenda	Martinez	USA	8.9.87	27 Apr	9:00.46	Paulina	Kaczynska	POL	24.7.91	5 Jun
8:57.37	Melissa	Duncan	AUS	30.1.90	28 Jul	9:00.50	Yuna	Wada	JPN-J	7.8.99	11 Jul
8:57.38	Grace	Kimanzi	KEN	1.3.92	7 Jul	9:00.7A	Alemitu	Tariku	ETH-J	28.9.00	9 Dec
8:57.61	Meraf	Bahta	SWE	24.6.89	28 Jun	9:00.76	Zena	Jemutai	KEN-J	2.12.00	11 Jul
8:57.73	Teresa	Musso	KEN-Y	.02	24 Nov	9:01.27mx	Emily	Brichacek	AUS	7.7.90	3 Mar
8:57.78	Ririka	Hironaka	JPN-J	24.11.00	8 Oct	9:01.76mx	Paige	Campbell	AUS	27.6.96	3 Nov
8:57.89	Linn	Nilsson	SWE	15.10.90	28 Jun	9:02.77+	Alice	Nawowuna	KEN	2.1.94	26 May
8:58.04	Sandra	Tuei	KEN	20.1.98	4 May	9:03.06mx	Emily	Hosker Thornhill	GBR	27.10.92	1 Aug
8:58.63	Tomomi	Musembi Takamatsu	JPN-J	23.2.00	20 May	9:03.16	Viktória	Gyürkés	HUN	15.10.92	18 Aug
8:58.66	Mao	Ichiyama	JPN	29.5.97	20 May	9:03.25	Margherita	Magnani	ITA	26.2.87	5 Jun
8:58.97	Muwangi	Lebekka ?	KEN-Y	15.6.01	11 Aug	9:03.77	Harumi	Okamoto	JPN	7.2.98	15 Oct
8:59.09	Naomi	Muthoni	KEN	.98	12 May	9:03.84	Katrina	Robinson	NZL-J	8.8.00	17 Mar
8:59.17	Charlotta	Fougberg	SWE	19.6.85	18 Aug	9:03.84	Camilla	Richardsson	FIN	14.9.93	5 Jun
						9:03.96	Marta	Pérez	ESP	19.4.93	23 Aug

Indoors

Mark	Name		Nat	Born	Pos	Meet	Venue	Date
8:31.23	Genzebe	Dibaba	ETH	8.2.91	1		Sabadell	13 Feb

Mark	Name		Nat	Born	Pos	Meet	Venue	Date	
8:34.45		Hassan			1		Seattle	27	Jan
8:36.01	Shelby	Houlihan	USA	8.2.93	1		Boston (Allston)	3	Feb
8:36.01	Konstanze	Klosterhalfen	GER	18.2.97	1	NC	Dortmund	18	Feb
8:37.21mx	Laura	Muir	GBR	9.5.93	1		Glasgow	7	Jan
8:45.78		Muir			1	GP	Birmingham	1	Mar
8:39.15	Beatrice	Chepkoech	KEN	6.7.91	2		Ostrava	25	Jan
0:09.55	Fantu	Worku	ETH-J	29.3.99	3		Ostrava	25	Jan
8:40.20	Marielle	Hall	USA	28.1.92	2		Boston (Allston)	3	Feb
8:41.08	Fotyen	Tesfay	ETH	17.2.98	2	GP	Boston (R)	10	Feb
8:41.10	Aisha	Praught Leer	JAM	14.12.89	1	Millrose	New York (Arm)	3	Feb
8:41.16	Emma	Coburn	USA	19.10.90	2	Millrose	New York (Arm)	3	Feb
8:41.18	Dominique	Scott Efurd	RSA	24.6.92	3	Millrose	New York (Arm)	3	Feb
8:41.60	Karissa	Schweizer	USA	4.5.96	4	Millrose	New York (Arm)	3	Feb
8:41.94	Stephanie	Twell	GBR	17.8.89	3	GP	Boston (R)	10	Feb
8:42.46	Meraf	Bahta	SWE	24.6.89	1		Madrid	8	Feb
8:43.15	Katie	Mackey	USA	12.11.87	5	Millrose	New York (Arm)	3	Feb
8:43.28	Shalane	Flanagan	USA	8.7.81	2		Seattle	27	Jan
8:47.30	Rosie	Clarke	GBR	17.11.91	4		Madrid	8	Feb
8:47.81	Lauren	Paquette	USA	27.6.86	6	Millrose	New York (Arm)	3	Feb
8:48.99	Ruth	Jebet ¶?	BRN	17.11.96	5		Ostrava	25	Jan
8:49.02	Kate	Van Buskirk	CAN	9.6.87	7	Millrose	New York (Arm)	3	Feb
8:49.78	Geneviève	Lalonde	CAN	5.9.91	5	GP	Boston (R)	10	Feb
8:50.80	Hawi	Feysa	ETH-J	1.2.99	5		Madrid	8	Feb
8:50.96	Mel	Lawrence	USA	29.8.89	8	Millrose	New York (Arm)	3	Feb
8:51.07	Emily	Lipari	USA	19.11.92	9	Millrose	New York (Arm)	3	Feb
8:51.90	Yelena	Korobkina	RUS	25.11.90	1	NC	Moskva	12	Feb
8:53.63	Sofia	Ennaoui	POL	30.8.95	7		Ostrava	25	Jan
8:53.97	Claudia	Bobocea	ROU	11.6.92	8		Ostrava	25	Jan
8:54.08	Gesa-Felicitas	Krause	GER	3.8.92	2	NC	Dortmund	18	Feb
8:54.35	Allie	Ostrander	USA	24.12.96	2	NCAA	College Station	10	Mar
8:54.56	Margherita	Magnani	ITA	26.2.87	9		Ostrava	25	Jan
8:56.29	Caterina	Granz	GER	14.3.94	3	NC	Dortmund	18	Feb
8:56.34	Yekaterina	Ivonina	RUS	14.6.94	2	NC	Moskva	12	Feb

Mark	Name		Nat	Born	Date		Mark	Name		Nat	Born	Date	
8:57.07	Simona	Vrzalová	CZE	7.4.88	25	Jan	9:00.67	Luiza	Gega	ALB	5.11.88	17	Feb
8:57.15	Yelena	Sedova	RUS	1.3.90	12	Feb	9:01.27	Natalya	Koloskova	RUS	19.7.88	12	Feb
8:57.47	Ednah	Kurgat	KEN	15.6.91	10	Feb	9:01.30	Erin	Teschuk	CAN	25.10.94	20	Jan
8:58.29	Regan	Yee	CAN	4.7.95	27	Jan	9:01.53	Olga	Kungina	RUS	13.5.86	12	Feb
8:58.50	Jessica	Hull	AUS	22.10.96	10	Feb	9:01.62	Gina	Sereno	USA	16.6.95	10	Feb
8:58.69	Erin	Finn	USA	19.11.94	20	Jan	9:01.86	Christina	Aragon	USA	17.6.97	10	Feb
8:59.18	Olivia	Burdon	NZL	26.1.98	10	Feb	9:01.96	Amy-Eloise	Neale	GBR	5.8.95	13	Jan
8:59.23	Vanessa	Fraser	USA	27.7.95	10	Feb	9:02.42	Alina	Reh	GER	23.5.97	18	Feb
8:59.69	Sharon	Lokedi	KEN	10.3.94	10	Feb	9:03.18	Marta	Pen	POR	31.7.93	3	Feb
							9:03.51	Weini	Kelati	ERI	1.12.96	10	Mar

JUNIORS

See main list for top 12 juniors + 2 indoors. 12 performances (2 indoors) by 7 women to 8:51.0 and further juniors:

Mamo	8:38.651	PNG	Turku		5	Jun	8:43.56i3		Madrid	8 Feb
	8:42.191		Rovereto		23	Aug	8:43.87i4		Ostrava	25 Jan
Degefu	8:39.464	PNG	Turku		5	Jun				
8:57.73	Teresa	Musso	KEN-Y	.02	1			Okayama	24	Nov
8:57.78	Ririka	Hironaka	JPN	24.11.00	3			Fukui	8	Oct
8:57.89	Linn	Nilsson	SWE	15.10.90	2			Sollentuna	28	Jun
8:58.04	Sandra	Tuei	KEN	20.1.98	15	DL		Doha	4	May
8:58.63	Tomomi	Musembi Takamatsu	JPN	23.2.00	8			Osaka	20	May
8:58.97	Muwangi	Lebekka ?	KEN-Y	15.0.01	1			Takamatsu	11	Aug
8:59.20	Tsige	Gebreselama	ETH	30.9.00	3	WJ		Tampere	11	Jul
8:59.72	Beatrice	Chebet	KEN	5.3.00	15	DL		Birmingham	18	Aug
9:00.50	Yuna	Wada	JPN	7.8.99	4	WJ		Tampere	11	Jul
9:00.7A	Alemitu	Tariku	ETH	28.9.00	1			Assela	9	Dec
9:00.76	Zena	Jemutai (20)	KEN	2.12.00	5	WJ		Tampere	11	Jul

Indoors

8:50.80	Hawi	Feysa	ETH	1.2.99	5		Madrid	8	Feb
9:05.26i	Katelyn	Tuohy	USA-Y	18.3.02	1		Staten Island	6	Jan

2 MILES

9:16.78	Jenny	Simpson	USA	23.8.86	1	DrakeR	Des Moines	27	Apr
9:31.89	Rachel	Schneider	USA	18.7.91	2	DrakeR	Des Moines	27	Apr
9:32.82	Brenda	Martinez	USA	8.9.87	3	DrakeR	Des Moines	27	Apr
9:37.86	Stephanie	Garcia	USA	3.5.88	4	DrakeR	Des Moines	27	Apr

+ intermediate time in longer race, A made at altitude of 1000m or higher, H made in a heptathlon, h made in a heat, qf quarter-final, sf semi-final, i Indoors, Q qualifying round, r race number, -J U20, -Y youths (born 2001 or later)

Mark	Name		Nat	Born	Pos	Meet	Venue	Date	

5000 METRES

Mark	Name		Nat	Born	Pos	Meet	Venue	Date	
14:21.75	Hellen	Obiri	KEN	13.12.89	1	DL	Rabat	13	Jul
14:22.34	Sifan	Hassan	NED	1.1.93	2	DL	Rabat	13	Jul
14:23.14	Letesenbet	Gidey	ETH	20.3.98	3	DL	Rabat	13	Jul
14:23.33	Senbere	Teferi	ETH	3.5.95	4	DL	Rabat	13	Jul
14:24.24	Agnes	Tirop	KEN	23.10.95	5	DL	Rabat	13	Jul
14:26.89	Genzebe	Dibaba	ETH	8.2.91	1	Pre	Eugene	26	May
14:30.29		Gidey			2	Pre	Eugene	26	May
14:34.45	Shelby	Houlihan	USA	8.2.93	1	NA	Heusden-Zolder	21	Jul
14:35.03		Obiri			3	Pre	Eugene	26	May
14:36.13		Tirop			1		Bellinzona	18	Jul
14:38.39		Obiri			1	WK	Zürich	30	Aug
14:38.77		Hassan			2	WK	Zürich	30	Aug
14:40.97		Teferi			3	WK	Zürich	30	Aug
14:42.98		G Dibaba			6	DL	Rabat	13	Jul
14:43.96	Caroline	Kipkirui	KEN	26.5.94	4	WK	Zürich	30	Aug
14:44.24		Tirop			5	WK	Zürich	30	Aug
14:46.12		Hassan			1	EC	Berlin	12	Aug
14:48.5A		Obiri			1		Nairobi	6	Jun
14:50.24		G Dibaba			6	WK	Zürich	30	Aug
14:51.30	Gudaf	Tsegay	ETH	23.1.97	4	Pre	Eugene	26	May
14:52.83	Eilish	McColgan (10)	GBR	25.11.90	7	DL	Rabat	13	Jul
14:53.05		McColgan			2	EC	Berlin	12	Aug
14:53.14	Loice	Chemnung	KEN	22.2.97	2		Bellinzona	18	Jul
14:55.63		Kipkirui			8	DL	Rabat	13	Jul
14:57.52		Gidey			7	WK	Zürich	30	Aug
14:57.63	Yasemin	Can	TUR	11.12.96	3	EC	Berlin	12	Aug
15:01.15	Lilian	Rengeruk	KEN	3.5.97	5	Pre	Eugene	26	May
15:01.44	Molly	Huddle	USA	31.8.84	2	NA	Heusden-Zolder	21	Jul
15:01.98	Margaret	Kipkemboi	KEN	9.2.93	6	Pre	Eugene	26	May
15:02.44	Karissa	Schweizer (30/16)	USA	4.5.96	3	NA	Heusden-Zolder	21	Jul
15:03.73	Konstanze	Klosterhalfen	GER	18.2.97	4	EC	Berlin	12	Aug
15:04.14	Dominique	Scott Efurd	RSA	24.6.92	4	NA	Heusden-Zolder	21	Jul
15:04.75	Melissa	Courtney	GBR	30.8.93	5	EC	Berlin	12	Aug
15:05.21	Meskerem	Mamo (20)	ETH-J	13.4.99	1		Tübingen	16	Jun
15:06.19	Madeline	Hills	AUS	15.5.87	5	NA	Heusden-Zolder	21	Jul
15:06.84	Gloria	Kite	KEN	29.12.98	2		Tübingen	16	Jun
15:07.90	Aberash	Minsewo	ETH-Y	22.2.01	3		Tübingen	16	Jun
15:08.08	Kalkidan	Gezahegne	BRN	8.5.91	1	AsiG	Jakarta	28	Aug
15:08.17	Meraf	Bahta	SWE	24.6.89	10	WK	Zürich	30	Aug
15:08.20	Marielle	Hall	USA	28.1.92	6	NA	Heusden-Zolder	21	Jul
15:08.61	Rosemary	Wanjiru	KEN	9.12.94	1	Oda	Hiroshima	28	Apr
15:09.42	Eva	Cherono	KEN	15.8.96	4		Tübingen	16	Jun
15:09.62	Vanessa	Fraser	USA	27.7.95	7	NA	Heusden-Zolder	21	Jul
15:09.65	Susan	Krumins (30)	NED	8.7.86	6	EC	Berlin	12	Aug
15:10.91	Rina	Nabeshima	JPN	16.12.93	9	Pre	Eugene	26	May
15:11.00	Alice Aprot	Nawowuna	KEN	2.1.94	10	Pre	Eugene	26	May
15:11.27	Sarah	Pagano	USA	23.7.91	8	NA	Heusden-Zolder	21	Jul
15:12.17	Elena	Burkard	GER	10.2.92	5		Tübingen	16	Jun
15:13.66	Emily	Sisson	USA	12.10.91	9	NA	Heusden-Zolder	21	Jul
15:13.89	Teresa	Musso	KEN-Y	.02	1		Oita	20	Oct
15:15.23	Lauren	Paquette	USA	27.6.86	11	Pre	Eugene	26	May
15:15.34A	Beatrice	Chepkoech	KEN	6.7.91	3	NC	Nairobi	23	Jun
15:15.35	Andrea	Seccafien	CAN	27.8.90	6		Tübingen	16	Jun
15:15.35	Cynthia	Baire (40)	KEN-Y	.02	2		Oita	20	Oct
15:15.65	Grace	Kimanzi	KEN	1.3.92	2	Oda	Hiroshima	28	Apr
15:15.77	Jip	Vastenburg	NED	21.3.94	10	NA	Heusden-Zolder	21	Jul
15:15.80	Nozomi	Tanaka	JPN-J	4.9.99	1		Niigata	14	Oct
15:15.88	Rachel	Schneider	USA	18.7.91	2	Jordan	Stanford	3	May
15:15.89	Martha	Mokaya	KEN-J	1.3.00	3		Oita	20	Oct
15:16.13	Ancuta	Bobocel	ROU	3.10.87	7	EC	Berlin	12	Aug
15:16.34	Kate	Van Buskirk	CAN	9.6.87	3	Jordan	Stanford	3	May
15:16.53	Helen	Lobun	KEN-Y	18.3.99	1		Nobeoka	5	May
15:17.47	Hanna	Klein	GER	6.4.93	1	NC	Nürnberg	22	Jul
15:17.81	Lonah Chemtai	Salpeter (50)	ISR	12.12.88	1		Kortrijk	14	Jul

WOMEN 2018

Mark	Name		Nat	Born	Pos	Meet	Venue	Date	
15:17.83	Joyline	Cherotich	KEN	22.3.98	3		Nijmegen	8	Jun
15:18.14	Linn	Nilsson	SWE	15.10.90	4	Jordan	Stanford	3	May
15:18.36	Jessica	O'Connell	CAN	10.2.89	2		Portland	10	Jun
15:18.43	Melissa	Duncan	AUS	30.1.90	4		Nijmegen	8	Jun
15:18.77	Linden	Hall	AUS	29.6.91	1		Newcastle	20	Jan
15:18.77	Stephanie	Twell	GBR	17.8.89	5		Nijmegen	8	Jun
15:18.88	Katie	Mackey	USA	12.11.87	3	Jordan	Stanford	3	May
15:19.11	Yelena	Korobkina	RUS	25.11.90	1	NC	Kazan	19	Jul
15:19.61	Maureen	Koster	NED	3.7.92	6	Jordan	Stanford	3	May
15:20.06	Ednah	Kurgat	KEN	15.6.91	7	Jordan	Stanford	3	May
(60)									
15:20.08	Yui	Fukuda	JPN	1.6.95	8	Jordan	Stanford	3	May
15:20.14	Naomi	Muthoni	KEN	.98	1r2	Oda	Hiroshima	28	Apr
15:20.24	Ann	Mwangi	KEN	8.12.88	3	Oda	Hiroshima	28	Apr
15:20.52	Tabitha	Kamau	KEN-J	3.7.00	4		Oita	20	Oct
15:20.56	Harumi	Okamoto	JPN	7.2.98	2		Yokohama	1	Dec
15:20.66	Rachel	Cliff	CAN	1.4.88	2		Los Angeles	17	May
15:21.31	Minami	Yamanouchi	JPN	21.12.92	4	Oda	Hiroshima	28	Apr
15:22.71	Weini	Kelati	ERI	1.12.96	10	Jordan	Stanford	3	May
15:23.44	Fabienne	Schlumpf	SUI	17.11.90	5		Bellinzona	18	Jul
15:23.65	Sinead	Diver	AUS	17.2.77	1		Geelong	22	Dec
(70)									
15:23.71	Stephanie	Garcia	USA	3.5.88	12	Jordan	Stanford	3	May
15:23.80	Charlotta	Fougberg	SWE	19.6.85	12	NA	Heusden-Zolder	21	Jul
15:24.01	Hitomi	Niiya	JPN	26.2.88	2		Niigata	14	Oct
15:24.09	Yekaterina	Ishova	RUS	17.1.89	2	NC	Kazan	19	Jul
15:24.16	Amy-Eloise	Neale	GBR	5.8.95	13	Jordan	Stanford	3	May
15:24.68	Camille	Buscomb	NZL	11.7.90	7		Nijmegen	8	Jun
15:24.70	Keiko	Nogami	JPN	6.12.85	4		Nobeoka	5	May
15:25.30	Alina	Reh	GER	23.5.97	2	NC	Nürnberg	22	Jul
15:25.44	Margherita	Magnani	ITA	26.2.87	14	Jordan	Stanford	3	May
15:25.84	Laura	Weightman	GBR	1.7.91	3	CG	Gold Coast	14	Apr
(80)									
15:26.58	Denise	Krebs	GER	27.6.87	3	NC	Nürnberg	22	Jul
15:26.64	Yelena	Sedova	RUS	1.3.90	3	NC	Kazan	19	Jul
15:26.76	Tomomi	Musembi Takamatsu	JPN-J	23.2.00	6		Yokohama	1	Dec
15:27.09	Sharon	Lokedi	KEN	10.3.94	3h1	NCAA-W	Sacramento	26	May
15:27.46	Allie	Ostrander	USA	24.12.96	2h2	NCAA-W	Sacramento	26	May
15:27.82	Nicole	Sifuentes	CAN	30.6.86	15	Jordan	Stanford	3	May
15:28.64	Darya	Maslova	KGZ	6.5.95	1		Bishkek	17	Jun
15:29.00	Mariam	Waithera	KEN	23.12.96	4		Osaka	23	Sep
15:29.25	Sarah	Chelangat	UGA-Y	5.6.01	8		Nijmegen	8	Jun
15:29.44	Natasha	Wodak	CAN	17.12.81	4		Portland	10	Jun
(90)									
15:29.67	Paulina	Kaczynska	POL	24.7.91	7		Tübingen	16	Jun
15:30.17	Juliet	Chekwel	UGA	25.5.90	4	CG	Gold Coast	14	Apr
15:30.39	Fantu	Worku	ETH-J	29.3.99	1		Marseille	16	Jun
15:30.59	Emelia	Gorecka	GBR	29.1.94	16	Jordan	Stanford	3	May
15:30.59	Erin	Clark	USA	28.12.94	5h1	NCAA-W	Sacramento	26	May
15:30.70	Katrina	Coogan	USA	15.11.93	17	Jordan	Stanford	3	May
15:30.74	Naruha	Sato	JPN	2.10.97	7		Yokohama	1	Dec
15:30.77	Beatrice	Chebet	KEN-J	5.3.00	1	WJ	Tampere	10	Jul
15:30.87	Ejgayehu	Taye	ETH-J	10.2.00	2	WJ	Tamporo	10	Jul
15:31.21	Bontu	Edao Rebitu	BRN	12.12.97	2		Marseille	16	Jun
(100)									

15:31.49	Shuru	Bulo	ETH	27.6.98	5	May		15:34.43	Kaori	Morita	JPN	19.9.95	28	Apr
15:31.5A	Hawi	Feysa	ETH-J	1.2.99	22	Apr		15:34.44	Olivia	Burdon	NZL	26.1.98	26	May
15:31.63	Riko	Matsuzaki	JPN	24.12.92	10	Jun		15:34.44	Fiona	O'Keeffe	USA	24.5.98	10	Jun
15:31.71	Miku	Moribayashi	JPN-J	5.9.99	5	May		15:35.78	Chelsea	Blaase	USA	10.4.94	10	Jun
15:31.74	Pauline	Kamulu	KEN	30.12.94	20	May		15:35.96	Svetlana	Simakova	RUS	12.6.87	19	Jul
15:32.26A	Pascalia	Kipkoech	KEN	22.12.88	23	Jun		15:35.96mx	Muwani	Lebakka ?	KEN-Y	15.6.01	8	Sep
15:32.40	Meselu	Berhe Kahsay	ETH-J	29.5.00	21	Jul		15:36.02	Mai	Shoji	JPN	9.12.93	5	May
15:32.74	Selah	Busienei	KEN	27.12.91	16	Jun		15:36.11	Mao	Ichiyama	JPN	29.5.97	14	Jul
15:32.93	Beyenu	Degefu	ETH-J	12.7.99	16	Jun		15:36.30	Regan	Yee	CAN	4.7.95	17	May
15:32.95	Marie	Bouchard	FRA	7.12.93	20	Apr		15:36.3A	Desta	Burka	ETH-J	1.2.99	22	Apr
15:33.15	Erin	Finn	USA	19.11.94	20	Apr		15:36.33	Miyuki	Uehara	JPN	22.11.95	24	Jun
15:33.17	Sheila	Chelangat	KEN	11.4.98	18	Jul		15:37.06	Rika	Kaseda	JPN-J	2.3.99	5	May
15:33.22	Cally	Macumber	USA	19.8.90	10	Jun		15:37.17	Nanami	Watanabe	JPN	24.12.98	24	Jun
15:33.25	Louise	Carton	BEL	16.4.94	21	Jul		15:37.17	Nelly	Ngeiywo	KEN	10.1.92	6	Jul
15:33.41	Ririka	Hironaka	JPN-J	24.11.00	5	May		15:37.20A	Margaret	Muriuki	KEN	21.3.86	23	Jun
15:33.65	Tomoka	Kimura	JPN	12.11.94	23	Sep		15:37.23	Jessica	Judd	GBR	7.1.95	11	Aug
15:34.01	Girmawit	Gebrzihair	ETH-Y	21.11.01	10	Jul		15:37.26	Lyudmila	Lebedeva	RUS	23.5.90	19	Jul
15:34.42	Celia	Sullohern	AUS	5.7.92	16	Feb		15:37.27	Danielle	Shanahan	USA	13.8.94	17	May

Mark	Name	Nat	Born	Pos Meet	Venue	Date
15:37.31	Katarzyna Rutkowska	POL	14.1.94	14 Jul		
15:37.47	Eloise Wellings	AUS	9.11.82	16 Feb		
15:37.51	Yuka Hori	JPN	13.6.96	14 Jul		
15:37.56	Saori Noda	JPN	30.3.93	5 May		
15:37.71	Yuka Suzuki	JPN-J	14.9.99	1 Dec		
15:38.16	Honami Maeda	JPN	17.7.96	14 Jul		
15:38.21A	Delvin Meringor	KEN	1.8.92	23 Jun		
15:38.29	Misaki Kato	JPN	15.6.91	23 Sep		
15:38.32	Alicia Monson	USA	13.5.98	26 May		
15:38.40	Shiori Yano	JPN	11.2.95	1 Dec		
15:38.57	Jessica Drop	USA	7.10.98	20 Apr		
15:38.78	Sanjivani Jadhav drugs dq?	IND	12.7.96	26 Jun		
15:39.17	Allie Buchalski	USA	12.1.95	21 Apr		
15:39.18	Loganathan Suriya	IND	7.7.90	13 Feb		
15:39.30	Mikuni Yada	JPN-J	29.10.99	5 May		
15:39.68	Claire Duck	GBR	29.8.85	12 May		
15:39.87	Zeyituna Husan	ETH-J	12.1.99	7 Apr		
15:40.47	Natsuki Sekiya	JPN	16.5.97	28 Apr		
15:40.56	Sakiho Tsutsui	JPN	19.1.96	20 Oct		
15:40.61	Nada Ina Pauer	AUT	11.11.86	16 Jun		
15:40.75mx	Emily Brichacek	AUS	7.7.90	10 Feb		
15:40.88	Makena Morley	USA	21.11.96	20 Apr		
15:41.01	Yukari Ishizawa	JPN	16.4.88	28 Apr		
15:41.09	Charlotte Taylor	GBR	17.1.94	26 May		
15:41.11	Stevie Stockton	GBR	23.8.89	12 May		
15:41.21	Caroline Kurgat	KEN	20.4.93	3 May		
15:41.26	Paige Stoner	USA	31.1.96	3 May		
15:41.47	Caroline Chepkemoi	KEN	1.3.93	16 Jun		
15:41.62	Samantha Nadel	USA	5.6.94	26 May		
15:41.66	Nozomi Musen Takamatsu	JPN	31.8.97	5 May		
15:42.04	Natalya Koloskova	RUS	19.7.88	12 Jul		
15:42.15	Sandra Eriksson	FIN	4.6.89	31 Aug		
15:42.35	Olivia Pratt	USA	21.1.94	17 May		
15:42.49	Maho Shimizu	JPN	7.5.95	7 Jul		
15:42.76	Ashley Maton	USA	20.11.93	20 Apr		
15:42.87	Svetlana Kudzelich	BLR	7.5.87	7 Jun		
(172)						

Indoors

Mark	Name	Nat	Born	Pos	Venue	Date
15:14.78	Ednah Kurgat	KEN	15.6.91	1	Boston (A)	1 Dec
15:15.24	Weini Kelati	KEN	1.12.96	2	Boston (A)	1 Dec
15:15.47	Sharon Lokedi	KEN	10.3.94	3	Boston (A)	1 Dec
15:15.52	Emily Infeld	USA	21.3.90	1	Seattle	10 Feb
15:15.64	Gwen Jorgensen	USA	25.4.86	2	Seattle	10 Feb
15:16.38	Allie Ostrander	USA	24.12.96	4	Boston (A)	1 Dec
15:24.32	Elise Cranny	USA	8.5.96	5	Boston (A)	1 Dec
15:25.35	Dorcas Wasike	KEN	2.7.96	6	Boston (A)	1 Dec
15:26.01	Charlotte Prouse	CAN	9.2.97	7	Boston (A)	1 Dec
15:28.07	Jaci Smith	USA	5.1.97	8	Boston (A)	1 Dec
15:32.38	Aubrey Roberts	USA	30.1.98	1		1 Dec
15:33.20	Lauren LaRocco	USA	15.2.96	1		1 Dec
15:34.76	Jessica Pascoe	AUS	26.2.97	1		1 Dec
15:37.12	Katelyn Tuohy	USA-Y	18.3.02	20		20 Jan
15:39.24	Olga Kungina	RUS	13.5.86	1		14 Feb
15:41.63	Elly Henes	USA	13.10.98	1		2 Dec
15:42.50	Rachel Johnson	USA	30.4.93	1		10 Feb
15:42.60	Clare O'Brien	AUS-J	13.1.99	1		10 Feb

Disqualified for cutting in after the start: 15:01.00 Salpeter EC Berlin 12 Aug

JUNIORS

See main list for top 11 juniors. 13 performances by 9 women to 15:28.0. Additional marks and further juniors:

Name	Mark	Pos	Meet	Venue	Date				
Mamo	15:20.56	12	WK	Zürich	30 Aug				
Mokaya	15:20.27	1		Yokohama	1 Dec	15:23.07	2	Nobeoka	5 May
Lobun	15:19.59	1		Yokohama	20 Oct				

Mark	Name	Nat	Born	Pos Meet	Venue	Date
15:31.5A	Hawi Feysa	ETH	1.2.99	1 NC	Addis Ababa	22 Apr
15:31.71	Miku Moribayashi	JPN	5.9.99	6	Nobeoka	5 May
15:32.40	Meselu Berhe Kahsay	ETH	29.5.00	15 NA	Heusden-Zolder	21 Jul
15:32.93	Beyenu Degefu	ETH	12.7.99	3	Marseille	16 Jun
15:33.41	Ririka Hironaka	JPN	24.11.00	7	Nobeoka	5 May
15:34.01	Girmawit Gebrzihair	ETH-Y	21.11.01	3 WJ	Tampere	10 Jul
15:35.96mx	Muwani Lebakka ?	KEN-Y	15.6.01	1mx	Takamatsu	8 Sep
15:36.3A	Desta Burka	ETH	1.2.99	3 NC	Addis Ababa	22 Apr
15:37.06	Rika Kaseda (20)	JPN	2.3.99	9	Nobeoka	5 May

10,000 METRES

Mark	Name	Nat	Born	Pos Meet	Venue	Date
30:41.85	Pauline Kamulu	KEN	30.12.94	1	Fukagawa	11 Jul
30:56.94	Kamulu			1	Osaka	21 Sep
31:16.48	Minami Yamanouchi	JPN	21.12.92	1	Yamaguchi	8 Dec
31:17.28	Grace Kimanzi	KEN	1.3.92	2	Yamaguchi	8 Dec
31:28.20	Harumi Okamoto	JPN	7.2.98	3	Yamaguchi	8 Dec
31:28.81	Rina Nabeshima	JPN	16.12.93	4	Yamaguchi	8 Dec
31:31.17	Stacy Ndiwa	KEN	6.12.92	1 AfrC	Asaba	4 Aug
31:32.50	Hitomi Niiya	JPN	26.2.88	1 Zátopek	Melbourne	13 Dec
31:33.03	Lonah Chemtai Salpeter	ISR	12.12.88	1 ECp	London (PH)	19 May
31:36.12	Alice Nawowuna	KEN	2.1.94	2 AfrC	Asaba	4 Aug
31:38.4A	Mercyline Chelangat (10)	UGA	17.12.97	1	Kampala	3 Mar
31:39.0A	Stella Chesang	UGA	1.12.96	2	Kampala	3 Mar
31:39.63	Salpeter			1	Tel Aviv	26 Apr
31:41.47	Gloria Kite	KEN	29.12.98	1	Maia	2 Jun
31:43.12	Ancuta Bobocel	ROU	3.10.87	2 ECp	London (PH)	19 May
31:43.29	Salpeter			1 EC	Berlin	8 Aug
31:44.13	Shiori Yano	JPN	11.2.95	1	Yamaguchi	8 Dec
31:45.30	Chesang			1 CG	Gold Coast	9 Apr
31:45.32	Gete Alemayehu	ETH	27.8.98	2	Maia	2 Jun
31:46.36	Ndiwa			2 CG	Gold Coast	9 Apr

WOMEN 2018

Mark	Name		Nat	Born	Pos	Meet	Venue	Date	
31:48.41		Chelangat			3	CG	Gold Coast	9	Apr
31:48.93	Yuka	Hori	JPN	13.6.96	6		Yamaguchi	8	Dec
31:49.81	Beatrice	Mutai	KEN	19.4.87	4	CG	Gold Coast	9	Apr
31:50.17	Natsuki	Sekiya	JPN	16.5.97	7		Yamaguchi	8	Dec
31:50.18	Natasha	Wodak	CAN	17.12.81	5	CG	Gold Coast	9	Apr
31:50.75	Celia	Sullohern (20)	AUS	5.7.92	6	CG	Gold Coast	9	Apr
01:50.90	Sinead	Diver	AUS	17.2.77	2	Zátopek	Melbourne	13	Dec
31:51.1A	Pauline	Korikwiang	KEN	1.3.88	1	NC	Nairobi	22	Jun
31:52.32	Molly	Huddle	USA	31.8.84	1	NC	Des Moines	21	Jun
31:52.42	Mizuki	Matsuda	JPN	31.5.95	1	NC	Yamaguchi	22	Jun
	(30/24)								
31:52.55	Susan	Krumins	NED	8.7.86	2	EC	Berlin	8	Aug
31:54.83	Jessica	Tonn	USA	15.2.92	1	Jordan	Stanford	3	May
31:55.68	Gwen	Jorgensen	USA	25.4.86	1		Stanford	30	Mar
31:56.43	Sarah	Pagano	USA	23.7.91	2	Jordan	Stanford	3	May
31:56.68	Marielle	Hall	USA	28.1.92	2	NC	Des Moines	21	Jun
31:56.86	Rachel	Cliff	CAN	1.4.88	3	Jordan	Stanford	3	May
	(30)								
31:57.56	Chelsea	Blaase	USA	10.4.94	4	Jordan	Stanford	3	May
31:57.66	Rosemary	Wanjiru	KEN	9.12.94	1		Kumagaya	19	May
31:57.82	Ayuko	Suzuki	JPN	8.10.91	2	NC	Yamaguchi	22	Jun
31:57.85	Carrie	Dimoff	USA	31.5.83	2		Stanford	30	Mar
31:57.91	Mao	Ichiyama	JPN	29.5.97	5	Jordan	Stanford	3	May
31:57.95	Kaori	Morita	JPN	19.9.95	8		Yamaguchi	8	Dec
31:57.97	Juliet	Chekwel	UGA	25.5.90	7	CG	Gold Coast	9	Apr
32:00.55	Karissa	Schweizer	USA	4.5.96	3		Stanford	30	Mar
32:01.04	Madeline	Hills	AUS	15.5.87	8	CG	Gold Coast	9	Apr
32:05.05	Stephanie	Bruce	USA	14.1.84	3	NC	Des Moines	21	Jun
	(40)								
32:06.31	Emily	Sisson	USA	12.10.91	4	NC	Des Moines	21	Jun
32:07.23	Darya	Maslova	KGZ	6.5.95	1	AsiG	Jakarta	25	Aug
32:07.70	Keiko	Nogami	JPN	6.12.85	1		Kitakyushu	19	May
32:09.20	Sharon	Lokedi	KEN	10.3.94	1	NCAA	Eugene	7	Jun
32:10.50	Sara	Moreira	POR	17.10.85	1		Braga	7	Apr
32:11.12	Eunice	Chumba	BRN	23.5.93	2	AsiG	Jakarta	25	Aug
32:11.81	Dorcas	Wasike	KEN	2.7.96	2	NCAA	Eugene	7	Jun
32:11.92	Sandra	Tuei	KEN	20.1.98	10	CG	Gold Coast	9	Apr
32:12.53	Ayumi	Hagiwara	JPN	1.6.92	5		Osaka	21	Sep
32:12.78		Zhang Deshun	CHN	21.2.96	3	AsiG	Jakarta	25	Aug
	(50)								
32:13.74	Salomé	Nyirarukundo	RWA	20.12.97	11	CG	Gold Coast	9	Apr
32:13.79	Yukari	Abe	JPN	21.8.89	1		Kobe	22	Apr
32:13.87	Honami	Maeda	JPN	17.7.96	2		Fukagawa	11	Jul
32:15.71	Charlotte	Arter	GBR	18.6.91	3	ECp	London (PH)	19	May
32:15.73	Alice	Wright	GBR	3.11.94	4		Stanford	30	Mar
32:17.0A	Joyciline	Jepkosgei	KEN	8.12.93	2		Nairobi	6	Jun
32:17.17	Alina	Reh	GER	23.5.97	1		Regensburg	23	Jun
32:17.81	Ellie	Pashley	AUS	10.12.88	3	Zátopek	Melbourne	13	Dec
32:17.95	Charlotte	Taylor	GBR	17.1.94	5	NCAA	Eugene	7	Jun
32:18.32	Alia Mohamed	Saeed	UAE	18.5.91	4	AsiG	Jakarta	25	Aug
	(60)								
32:18.35	Rochelle	Kanuho	USA	4.7.90	1		Portland	9	Jun
32:18.59	Yuka	Takashima	JPN	12.5.88	6	NC	Yamaguchi	22	Jun
32:18.70	Sakiho	Isutsui	JPN	19.1.96	7	NC	Yamaguchi	22	Jun
32:19.34	Meraf	Bahta	SWE	24.6.89	3	EC	Berlin	8	Aug
32:19.59	Kasumi	Nishihara	JPN	1.3.89	4		Kobe	22	Apr
32:20.37	Anna	Gehring	GER	15.11.96	2		Regensburg	23	Jun
32:20.72	Inês	Monteiro	POR	18.5.80	3		Maia	2	Jun
32:21.11	Ai	Hosoda	JPN	27.11.95	10		Yamaguchi	8	Dec
32:21.19	Catarina	Ribeiro	POR	31.5.90	4		Maia	2	Jun
32:22.09	Failuna Abdi	Matanga	TAN	28.10.92	12	CG	Gold Coast	9	Apr
	(70)								
32:22.38	Emily	Brichacek	AUS	7.7.90	4	Zátopek	Melbourne	13	Dec
32:22.82	Mai	Shoji	JPN	9.12.93	11		Yamaguchi	8	Dec
32:23.38	Paige	Stoner	USA	31.1.96	6		Stanford	30	Mar
32:23.56	Loganathan	Suriya	IND	7.7.90	13	CG	Gold Coast	9	Apr
32:23.91	Camille	Buscomb	NZL	11.7.90	14	CG	Gold Coast	9	Apr
32:24.27	Natsuki	Omori	JPN	22.6.94	4		Fukagawa	11	Jul
32:24.57	Misaki	Kato	JPN	15.6.91	6		Osaka	21	Sep
32:24.78	Molly	Seidel	USA	12.7.94	8	NC	Des Moines	21	Jun
32:25.86	Chuna	Takano	JPN	30.10.97	6		Kobe	22	Apr

Mark	Name		Nat	Born	Pos	Meet	Venue	Date
32:26.24	Anna	Rohrer	USA	27.2.97	6	NCAA	Eugene	7 Jun
(80)								
32:26.65	Misaki	Hayashida	JPN	31.1.96	13		Yamaguchi	8 Dec
32:27.35	Anna	Matsuda	JPN	18.4.94	7		Kobe	22 Apr
32:28.15	Jaci	Smith	USA	5.1.97	5h1	NCAA-W	Sacramento	24 May
32:28.58	Makena	Morley	USA	21.11.96	6h1	NCAA-W	Sacramento	24 May
32:28.88	Erin	Clark	USA	28.12.94	7h1	NCAA-W	Sacramento	24 May
32:29.35	Carolina	Tabares	COL	18.7.86	6	Jordan	Stanford	3 May
32:30.24	Shitaye	Eshete	BRN	21.5.90	5	AsiG	Jakarta	25 Aug
32:30.97	Roxana	Bârca	ROU	22.6.88	1rB	ECp	London (PH)	19 May
32:31.40	Katarzyna	Rutkowska	POL	14.1.94	4	ECp	London (PH)	19 May
32:31.55	Ednah	Kurgat	KEN	15.6.91	1		Clovis	10 May
(90)								
32:32.84	Rachel	Johnson	USA	30.4.93	7	Jordan	Stanford	3 May
32:33.10	Philippa	Bowden	GBR	29.3.95	5	ECp	London (PH)	19 May
32:33.24	Caroline	Kurgat	KEN	20.4.93	7		Stanford	30 Mar
32:33.38	Kinsey	Middleton	CAN	22.11.92	3		Portland	9 Jun
32:33.61		Ahn Seul-ki	KOR	29.5.92	6		Fukagawa	11 Jul
32:33.76	Mizuki	Tanimoto	JPN	18.12.94	7		Fukagawa	11 Jul
32:34.03	Eva	Cherono	KEN	15.8.96	1		Leiden	9 Jun
32:34.07	Sophie	Duarte	FRA	31.7.81	6	ECp	London (PH)	19 May
32:34.34	Yasemin	Can	TUR	11.12.96	5	EC	Berlin	8 Aug
32:34.37	Yuki	Munehisa	JPN	15.12.97	8		Fukagawa	11 Jul
(100)								

Mark	Name		Nat	Born	Pos	Meet	Venue	Date
32:34.47	Charlotta	Fougberg	SWE	19.6.85	1 Sep			
32:34.73	Louise	Small	GBR	27.3.92	19 May			
32:35.26	Stevie	Stockton	GBR	23.8.89	19 May			
32:36.15	Natalie	Tanner	GER	3.9.95	30 Mar			
32:36.32	Kayoko	Fukushi	JPN	25.3.82	8 Dec			
32:36.76	Yelena	Korobkina	RUS	25.11.90	5 May			
32:37.54	Yuka	Suzuki	JPN-J	14.9.99	24 Nov			
32:37.80	Katrina	Wootton	GBR	2.9.85	19 May			
32:37.89	Weronika	Pyzik	POL	14.5.96	24 May			
32:38.22	Sabrina	Mockenhaupt	GER	6.12.80	9 Jun			
32:38.45	Jennifer	Nesbitt	GBR	24.1.95	19 May			
32:39.01	Camilla	Richardsson	FIN	14.9.93	19 Apr			
32:39.16	Paige	Campbell	AUS	27.6.96	13 Dec			
32:39.30	Clare	O'Brien	AUS-J	13.1.99	24 May			
32:39.37	Emelia	Gorecka	GBR	29.1.94	19 May			
32:40.58	Miriam	Dattke	GER	24.6.98	19 May			
32:41.67	Honoka	Tanaike	JPN	21.3.97	8 Dec			
32:41.92	Weini	Kelati	ERI	1.12.96	10 May			
32:42.10	Yuka	Ando	JPN	16.3.94	22 Apr			
32:42.43A	Perine	Nengampi	KEN	.89	22 Jun			
32:44.49	Gladys	Tejeda	PER	30.9.85	19 Apr			
32:44.78	Mikako	Nishida	JPN	7.8.91	8 Dec			
32:44.81	Wakana	Itsuki	JPN	7.4.94	19 May			
32:44.93	Naruha	Sato	JPN	2.10.97	24 Nov			
32:45.05	Kaitlyn	Benner	USA	25.9.96	24 May			
32:45.51	Erin	Finn	USA	19.11.94	13 May			
32:45.94	Yelena	Sedova	RUS	1.3.90	30 Jun			
32:46.10	Rino	Goshima	JPN	29.10.97	24 Nov			
32:46.10	Nanami	Aoki	JPN	6.1.95	8 Dec			
32:46.29	Ayano	Ikemitsu	JPN	18.4.91	19 May			
32:46.34	Svetlana	Kudzelich	BLR	7.5.87	8 Aug			
32:47.83	Elaina	Tabb	USA	17.12.91	19 Apr			
32:48.54	Olena	Serdyuk	UKR	4.11.81	19 Jul			
32:49.91	Emma	Mitchell	IRL	2.9.93	9 Apr			
32:50.25	Ayano	Ikeuchi	JPN	29.10.94	8 Dec			
32:50.30	Maitane	Melero	ESP	20.2.83	19 May			
32:51.47	Eloise	Wellings	AUS	9.11.82	9 Apr			
32:51.53	Rie	Fujita	JPN	18.10.94	22 Apr			
32:51.71	Hiroko	Miyauchi	JPN	19.6.83	11 Jul			
32:51.98	Rika	Kaseda	JPN-J	2.3.99	8 Dec			
32:52.85	Claire	Duck	GBR	29.8.85	19 May			
32:52.89	Nuria	Lugueros	ESP	9.4.88	7 Apr			
32:53.96	Misora	Daido	JPN	24.11.98	11 Jul			
32:54.90	Kanami	Sagayama	JPN	9.7.98	8 Dec			
32:55.04	Danielle	Shanahan	USA	13.8.94	30 Mar			
32:55.10	Madoka	Nakano	JPN	14.8.91	8 Dec			
32:55.13	Sayaka	Sato	JPN	27.5.94	4 Jul			
32:55.29	Yukari	Wada	JPN	20.7.95	11 Jul			
32:56.01	Yomogi	Akasaka	JPN	.95	8 Dec			
32:56.91	Nana	Sato	JPN	24.9.89	11 Jul			
32:57.11	Lyudmila	Lebedeva	RUS	23.5.90	30 Jun			
32:57.31	Yuliya	Shmatenko	UKR	10.10.91	19 May			
32:57.61	Eri	Utsunomiya	JPN	17.6.93	4 Jul			
32:57.88	Anne Marie	Blaney	USA	9.9.93	3 May			
32:57.89	Ikumi	Fukura	JPN	11.8.97	11 Jul			
32:58.05	Lauren	LaRocco	USA	15.2.96	24 May			
32:58.17	Riko	Matsuzaki	JPN	24.12.92	8 Dec			
32:58.50	Airu	Kouchi	JPN-J	.99	24 Nov			
32:59.05A	Glenrose	Xaba	RSA	31.12.94	23 Feb			
32:59.07	Misato	Kagayama	JPN	11.11.96	24 Nov			
32:59.51	Molly	Grabill	USA	31.8.92	9 Jun			
32:59.58	Yevheniya	Prokofyeva	UKR	5.6.95	19 Jul			
32:59.75	Emily	Durgin	USA	15.5.94	3 May			
(163)								

JUNIORS

Mark	Name		Nat	Born	Pos	Meet	Venue	Date
32:37.54	Yuka	Suzuki	JPN	14.9.99	1		Yokohama	24 Nov
32:39.30	Clare	O'Brien	AUS	13.1.99	9h1	NCAA-W	Sacramento	24 May
32:51.98	Rika	Kaseda	JPN	2.3.99	16		Yamaguchi	8 Dec
		33:29.20	1	Yokohama	6 Sep	11 performances by 10 women to 33:30.0		
32:58.50	Airu	Kouchi	JPN	.99	4		Yokohama	24 Nov
33:05.48	Tomoki	Tagawa	JPN	.99			Yamaguchi	8 Dec
33:15.51	Shiori	Yoshizono	JPN	2.6.99	8		Yokohama	24 Nov
33:21.55	Shino	Hasegawa	JPN	1.8.99	1		Kyoto	15 Dec
33:21.74	Miyu	Ichise	JPN	23.6.99	10		Yokohama	24 Nov
33:21.88	Miku	Moribayashi	JPN	5.9.99	2		Gifu	12 May
33:24.99	Yuki	Shibahara (10)	JPN	6.4.99	12		Yokohama	24 Nov
33:27.72	Mana	Taniguchi	JPN	29.5.99	2		Kyoto	15 Dec
33:27.83	Mikuni	Yada	JPN	29.10.99	3		Gifu	12 May
33:31.51	Junna	Suzuki	JPN	18.3.00	3rB		Fukagawa	11 Jul

10 KILOMETRES ROAD

Mark	Name		Nat	Born	Pos	Meet	Venue	Date
30:14+	Joan	Chelimo	KEN	10.11.90	1	in HMar	Praha	7 Apr

WOMEN 2018

Mark	Name		Nat	Born	Pos	Meet	Venue	Date
30:19	Caroline	Kipkirui	KEN	26.5.94	1		Praha	8 Sep
30:22	Fancy	Chemutai	KEN	20.3.94	2		Praha	8 Sep
30:23	Diana	Kipyokei	KEN	.94	3		Praha	8 Sep
30:28+		Kipkirui			2	in HMar	Praha	7 Apr
30:34+		Chemutai				in HMar	Ras Al Khaimah	9 Feb
30:34+	Joyciline	Jepkosgei	KEN	8.12.93		in HMar	Ras Al Khaimah	9 Feb
30:36+	Mary	Keitany	KEN	18.1.82		in HMar	Ras Al Khaimah	9 Feb
30:36+		Kipkirui				in HMar	Ras Al Khaimah	9 Feb
30:36+		J Chelimo				in HMar	København	16 Se
30:37+	Sifan	Hassan	NED	1.1.93		in HMar	København	16 Sep
30:50	Agnes	Tirop	KEN	23.10.95	1		Tilburg	2 Sep
30:57	Sandra	Tuei	KEN	20.1.98	1		Valencia	14 Jan
30:57+	Yeshaneh	Ababel	ETH	10.6.90		in HMar	København	16 Sep
30:57+	Zeineba	Yimer	ETH	17.6.98		in HMar	København	16 Sep
31:00	Dorcas	Tuitoek	KEN	31.1.98	1		Paderborn	31 Mar
31:07	Tsehay	Gemechu	ETH	20.5.98	2		Tilburg	2 Sep
31:08	Tirunesh	Dibaba	ETH	1.10.85	1		Manchester	20 May
31:10+	Ruth	Chepngetich	KEN	8.8.94		in HMar	København	16 Sep
31:12	Gete	Alemayehu	ETH	27.8.98	1		Houilles	30 Dec
31:13	Helen	Tola	ETH	21.11.94	2		Houilles	30 Dec
31:14	Stella	Chesang	UGA	1.12.96	1		Durban	14 Oct
31:17	Norah	Tanui	KEN	2.10.95	2		Valencia	14 Jan
31:17+		J Chelimo				in HMar	Ras Al Khaimah	9 Feb
31:17+	Helen	Tola	ETH	21.11.94		in HMar	Ras Al Khaimah	9 Feb
31:17+	Naomi	Rotich	KEN	.94		in HMar	Ras Al Khaimah	9 Feb
31:17		Tuitoek			4		Praha	8 Sep
31:17	Eva	Cherono	KEN	15.8.96	1		Utrecht	7 Oct
31:18+	Brigid	Kosgei	KEN	20.2.94		in HMar	Ras Al Khaimah	9 Feb
31:18+	Gladys	Cherono	KEN	12.5.83		in HMar	Ras Al Khaimah	9 Feb
31:18+	Degitu	Azimeraw	ETH-J	24.1.99		in HMar	Ras Al Khaimah	9 Feb
31:18+	Lucy	Cheruiyot	KEN	4.1.97		in HMar	Ras Al Khaimah	9 Feb
31:19		Tirop			1		Bengaluru	27 May
31:20+	Hiwot	Gebrekidan	ETH	11.5.95		in HMar	København	16 Sep
31:20	Clémence	Calvin	FRA	17.5.90	1		Languex	16 Jun
Where better than 10,000m track times								
31:21+	Meseret	Belete	ETH-J	16.9.99		in HMar	København	16 Sep
31:21+	Bekelech	Gudeta	ETH	10.10.97		in HMar	København	16 Sep
31:22	Senbere	Teferi	ETH	3.5.95	2		Bengaluru	27 May
31:23	Alina	Reh	GER	23.5.97	1		Berlin	14 Oct
31:25	Perine	Nengampi	KEN	.89	5		Praha	8 Sep
31:26	Ababel	Yeshaneh	ETH	10.6.90	2		Cape Elizabeth	4 Aug
31:33+	Ruti	Aga	ETH	16.1.94	1	in HMar	Houston	14 Jan
31:33	Mercyline	Chelangat	UGA	17.12.97	2		Durban	14 Oct
31:34	Mary	Munanu	KEN	12.12.94	3		Valencia	14 Jan
31:34	Rosemary	Wanjiru	KEN	9.12.94	6		Praha	8 Sep
31:35	Dibaba	Kuma	ETH	14.9.96	4		Valencia	14 Jan
31:35	Kaltoum	Bouaasayriya	MAR	23.8.82	1		Meknès	18 Feb
31:36	Alia Mohamed	Saeed	UAE	18.5.91	1		Ottawa	26 May
31:36+	Edith	Chelimo	KEN	16.7.86		in HMar	Valencia	28 Oct
31:36+	Pauline	Korikwiang	KEN	1.3.88		in HMar	Valencia	28 Oct
31:36+	Diana	Kipyokei	KEN	.94		in HMar	Valencia	28 Oct
31:36+	Yeshi	Chekole	ERI	12.7.97		in HMar	Valencia	28 Oct
31:37	Dorcas	Kimeli	KEN	5.7.97	1		Casablanca	25 Feb
31:37+	Gelete	Burka	ETH	23.1.86		in HMar	Valencia	28 Oct
31:38+	Eunice	Chumba	BRN	23.5.93		in HMar	Ras Al Khaimah	9 Feb
31:38+	Netsanet	Gudeta	ETH	12.2.91	4	in HMar	Valencia	24 Mar
31:38	Caroline	Chepkemoi	KEN	1.3.93	1		Valenciennes	15 Apr
31:38+	Nancy	Kiprop	KEN	7.7.79		in HMar	Ústí Nad Labem	15 Sep
31:38	Meraf	Bahta	SWE	24.6.89	1		Hole	20 Oct
31:40	Molly	Huddle	USA	31.8.84	3		Cape Elizabeth	4 Aug
31:41+	Yisak	Melat	ETH	.92		in HMar	Venlo	25 Mar
31:41+	Parendis	Lekapana	KEN	4.8.91		in HMar	Venlo	25 Mar
31:42	Silenat	Yismaw	ETH	19.3.97	1		Agadir	11 Nov
31:43	Karoline Bjerkeli	Grøvdal	NOR	14.6.90	2		Hole	20 Oct
31:45+	Susan	Krumins	NED	8.7.86		in 10M	Zaandam	23 Sep
31:46	Gladys	Kimaina	KEN	1.3.93	2		Berlin	14 Oct
31:47	Edith	Chelimo	KEN	16.7.86	2		Ottawa	26 May
31:48	Mary	Waithera	KEN	12.12.74	1		Laredo	17 Mar
31:48+	Joy	Loyce	KEN	3.3.88		in HMar	Venlo	25 Mar
31:48	Lucy	Macharia	KEN	7.12.87	1		Roanne	8 Apr

Mark	Name	Nat	Born	Pos	Meet	Venue	Date
31:50+	Worknesh Degefa	ETH	28.10.90	3	in HMar	Praha	7 Apr
31:50	Loice Chemnung	KEN	22.2.97	7		Praha	8 Sep
31:52+	Kejeta Melat	ETH	.92	1	in HMar	Berlin	8 Apr
31:53	Eilish McColgan	GBR	25.11.90	1		Doha	12 Jan
31:55	Mary Ngugi	KEN	17.12.88	1		Boston	24 Jun
31:57	Joyciline Jepkosgei	KEN	8.12.93	2		Manchester	20 May
31:57	Caroline Rotich	KEN	13.5.84	2		Boston	24 Jun
31:59	Susan Jeptoo	KEN	7.3.87	2		Languex	16 Jun
31:59	Mamitu Daska	ETH	16.10.83	3		Boston	24 Jun
32:00+	Evaline Chirchir	KEN	.98	3	in HMar	Valencia	2 Jun
32:01+	Desi Jisa Mokonin	BRN	12.7.97		in HMar	Valencia	24 Mar
32:01+	Shitaye Eshete	BRN	21.5.90		in HMar	Valencia	24 M
32:01	Fabienne Schlumpf	SUI	17.11.90	3		Berlin	14 Oct
32:03	Abreha Tsige	ETH-J	21.9.00	1		Valencia	2 Dec
32:04	Buze Diriba	ETH	9.2.94	1		New York	29 Apr
32:04	Ellie Pashley	AUS	10.12.88	2		Launceston	3 Jun
32:05	Monicah Ngige	KEN	7.11.93	1		New Orleans	31 Mar
32:05	Daisy Jepkemei	KEN	13.2.96	2		Astana	16 Sep
32:06	Kalkidan Gezahegne	BRN	8.5.91	5		Valencia	14 Jan
32:06	Aselefech Mergia	ETH	23.1.85	2		New York	29 Apr
32:06	Irvette van Zyl	RSA	5.7.87	3		Durban	14 Oct
32:07	Beth Potter	GBR	27.12.91	1		Clitheroe	30 Dec
32:08	Aliphine Tuliamuk	USA	5.4.89	2		New York	9 Jun
32:09	Yui Fukuda	JPN	1.6.95	1		Yamaguchi	11 Feb
32:09	Fatiha Asmid	MAR	.92	2		Meknès	18 Feb
32:10	Fatima Ezzahra Gardadi	MAR	20.3.92	3		Meknès	18 Feb
32:11+	Dera Dida	ETH	26.10.96		in HMar	Ústí Nad Labem	15 Sep
32:12	Pascalia Kipkoech	KEN	22.12.88	1		Kapsabet	22 Sep
32:12	Soukaina Atanane	MAR	28.6.94	3		Valencia	2 Dec
32:13	Naomi Vaati	KEN		1		Stadskanaal	2 Apr
32:13+	Martina Strähl	SUI	7.5.87	2	in HMar	Berlin	8 Apr
32:14	Karolina Nadolska	POL	6.9.81	4		Berlin	14 Oct
32:15	Maureen Koster	NED	3.7.92	1		Brunssum	18 Mar
32:17	Joyce Chepkemoi	KEN	.93	1		Saint-Denis	21 Oct
32:19	Goytatom Gebreselassie	ETH	15.1.95	1		Charleston	7 Apr
32:19	Rkia El Moukim	MAR	22.2.88	2		Agadir	11 Nov
32:20	Laura Thweatt	USA	17.12.88	4		Ottawa	26 May
32:20	Valentine Chepkwemoi	KEN	6.9.96	2		Utrecht	7 Oct
32:21+	Antonina Kwambai	KEN	.92				7 Apr
32:21	Hiwot Ayalew	ETH	6.3.90				7 Apr
32:22	Jessica O'Connell	CAN	10.2.89				4 Feb
32:22	Joyce Kandie	KEN	30.5.79				22 Sep
32:23	Sarah van der Wielen	SWE	18.2.95				8 Sep
32:25	Betsy Saina	KEN	30.6.88				20 May
32:25	Meskerem Amare	ETH	1.10.97				16 Jun
32:26	Ivine Chepkemoi	KEN	20.8.97				3 Feb
32:27	Maeregu Shegae	ETH	.98				16 Jun
32:28+	Risper Chebet	KEN	6.6.92				7 Apr
32:31	Risper Gesabwa	KEN	10.2.89				3 Feb
32:31	Birhane Dibaba	ETH	11.9.93				20 May
32:34	Kellyn Taylor	USA	22.7.86				4 Feb
32:34	Vicoty Chepngeno	KEN	.93				24 Mar
32:34	Stephanie Twell	GBR	17.8.89				28 May
32:34+	Meskerem Assefa	ETH	20.9.85				16 Sep
32:34+	Belaynesh Oljira	ETH	26.6.90				16 Sep
32:34+	Rahma Tusa	ETH	14.9.93				16 Sep
32:34+	Mary Wacera Ngugi	KEN	17.12.88				16 Sep
32:35	Liv Westphal	FRA	22.12.93				14 Jan
32:35	Brilliant Jepkorir	KEN	9.3.95				21 Oct
32:37	Tomoka Kimura	JPN	12.11.94				11 Feb
32:39+	Filomena Chepchirchir	KEN	1.12.81				7 Apr
32:39	Leonida Mosop	KEN	10.10.91				21 Oct
32:40	Lilian Jelagat	KEN	23.1.89				31 Mar
32:40	Abeba Ejigu	ETH-J					7 Dec
32:41	Lisa Weightman	AUS	16.1.79				18 Feb
32:41	Agnes Keino	KEN	.88				9 Sep
32:42	Betty Lembus	KEN	.96				22 Sep
32:42	Jessica Judd	GBR	7.1.95				30 Dec
32:44	Mercyline Cherono	KEN	4.1.92				16 Jun
32:45	Yekaterina Korneyenko	BLR	17.3.88				30 Dec
32:46	Birtukan Fento	ETH	18.6.89				9 Jun
32:47	Zeineba Yimer	ETH	17.6.98				27 May
32:47	Tabitha Wambui	KEN	29.12.83				26 Aug
32:48	Bornes Kitur	KEN	.88				22 Sep
32:48	Cavaline Nahimana	BDI	14.1.97				2 Dec
32:49	Yuko Kikuchi	JPN	8.6.92				18 Mar
32:49	Diane Nukuri	BDI	1.12.84				9 Jun
32:50	Ophélie Claude-Boxberger	FRA	18.10.88				30 Dec
32:51+	Perine Nengampi	KEN	1.1.89				15 Sep
32:52	Jess Piasecki	GBR	18.4.90				2 Sep
32:52+	Visiline Jepkesho	KEN	30.12.89				16 Sep
32:53	Etagegne Woldu	ETH	10.5.96				28 May
32:53	Berhane Gebrekidan	ETH-J?	.99				16 Jun
32:54	Emily Hosker Thornhill	GBR	27.10.92				9 Dec
32:56	Sinke Dessie	ETH	11.10..94				29 Apr
32:57	Mekdes Woldu	ETH	20.10.92				25 Mar
33:00	Gemma Steel	GBR	12.11.85				28 May
33:00	Ingvill Måkestad Bovim	NOR	7.8.81				20 Oct

Downhill

Mark	Name	Nat	Born	Pos	Venue	Date
29:54	Brigid Kosgei	KEN	20.2.94	1	Madrid (55m)	31 Dec
29:59	Hellen Obiri	KEN	13.12.89	2	Madrid (55m)	31 Dec
30:40	Tirunesh Dibaba	ETH	1.10.85	3	Madrid (55m)	31 Dec
31:17A	Tirop			1	Ziwa (70m)	1 Dec
31:40	Trihas Gebre	ESP	29.4.90	4	Madrid (55m)	31 Dec
31:42	Valary Jemeli	KEN	8.6.91	3	Ziwa (70m)	1 Dec
31:43	Catarina Ribeiro	POR	31.5.90	5	Madrid (55m)	31 Dec
31:53	Esther Chebet	UGA	10.9.97	6	Madrid (55m)	31 Dec
32:08	Chaltu Dida	ETH	20.9.92	1	Morlaix (86m)	4 Nov
32:36	Emma Bates	USA	8.7.92			22 Apr
32:40	Deborah Samum	KEN	.95			1 Dec

WOMEN 2018

Mark		Name		Nat	Born	Pos	Meet	Venue		Date
32:41	Sara	Hall		USA	15.4.83	4	Jul	32:52 Allie Kieffer USA 16.9.87		4 Jul

15 KILOMETRES ROAD

See also below in Half Marathon lists

Mark	Name		Nat	Born	Pos	Meet	Venue	Date
47:07+	Diana	Kipyokei	KEN	5.5.94		in HMar	Istanbul	8 Apr
47:19	Stella	Chesang	UGA	1.12.96	1		Nijmegen	18 Nov
47:35	Eveline	Chirchir	KEN	-.92	2		Nijmegen	18 Nov
47:41	Susan	Krumins	NED	8.7.86	3		Nijmegen	18 Nov
48:18	Yasemin	Can	TUR	11.12.96	1		Istanbul	11 Nov
48:29	Kidsan	Alema	ETH	.95	4		Nijmegen	18 Nov
48:36	Delvin	Meringor	KEN	1.8.92	1		Mersin	16 Dec
48:53	Dorcas	Tuitoek	KEN	31.1.98	1		Le Puy-en-Velay	1 May
49:01	Daisy	Kimeli	KEN	28.11.94	3		Istanbul	11 Nov
49:01	Florence	Kiplagat	KEN	27.2.87	5		Nijmegen	18 Nov
49:04	Maureen	Koster	NED	3.7.92	6		Nijmegen	18 Nov
49:20	Molly	Seidel	USA	120794	3		Jacksonville	10 Mar
49:20 +	Sarah	van der Wielen	SWE	18.2.95		in 10M	Zaandam	23 Sep
49:30	Rika	Kaseda	JPN-J	2.3.99	7		Nijmegen	18 Nov

10 MILES ROAD

15k	10M	Name		Nat	Born	Pos	Meet	Venue	Date
	49:29	Caroline	Kipkirui	KEN	26.5.94		in HMar	Ras Al Khaimah	9 Feb
	49:30+	Fancy	Chemutai	KEN	20.3.94		in HMar	Ras Al Khaimah	9 Feb
	49:30+	Mary	Keitany	KEN	18.1.82		in HMar	Ras Al Khaimah	9 Feb
47:29	50:45	Lonah Chemtai	Salpeter	ISR	12.12.88	1		Zaandam	23 Sep
47:30	50:46	Dibaba	Kuma	ETH	14.9.96	2		Zaandam	23 Sep
	51:16+	Mare	Dibaba	ETH	20.10.89		in Mar	London	22 Apr
47:55	51:30	Susan	Krumins	NED	8.7.86	3		Zaandam	23 Sep
	52:07	Monicah	Ngige	KEN	7.11.93	1		Pittsburgh	5 Nov
48:28	52:08	Mercyline	Chelangat	UGA	17.12.97	4		Zaandam	23 Sep

20 KILOMETRES ROAD

20k	15k	Name		Nat	Born	Pos	Meet	Venue	Date
63:33	47:28+	Eunice	Chumba	BRN	23.5.93		in HMar	Houston	14 Jan
64:13+		Nancy	Kiprop	KEN	7.7.79		in HMar	Venlo	25 Mar
65:32+	49:25	Lonah Chemtai	Salpeter	ISR	12.12.88		in HMar	Valencia	24 Mar
65:54	48:14+	Zerfie	Limeneh	ETH	10.2.97		in HMar	Istanbul	8 Apr

Also see below in Half Marathon lists

20k	15k	Name		Nat	Born	Pos					Name		Nat	Born	Date
66:16+	49:21	Antonina	Kwambai	KEN	.92	7 Apr	66:21 +	49:48	Betsy	Saina	KEN	30.6.88	28 Oct
66:16 +		Perendis	Lekapana	KEN	4.8.91	22 Apr	66:22+	48:37	Parendis	Lekapana	KEN	4.8.91	25 Mar
66:17+		Sinead	Diver	AUS	17.2.77	1 Jul	66:23+	49:27	Kaori	Morita	JPN	19.9.95	4 Feb
66:18 +	49:47	Mare	Dibaba	ETH	20.10.89	28 Oct	66:25+		Lucy	Cheruiyot	KEN	4.1.97	9 Feb
66:19 +		Dera	Dida	ETH	26.10.96	28 Oct	66:25+	49:29	Valary	Aiyabei	KEN	8.6.91	22 Apr
66:19 +		Haftamnesh	Tesfay	ETH	28.4.94	28 Oct	66:45+		Aselefech	Mergia	ETH	23.1.85	26 Jan
66:21 +		Antonina	Kwambai	KEN	1.4.92	1 Sep	66:58+	48:57	Visiline	Jepkesho	KEN	30.12.89	16 Sep

HALF MARATHON

Slightly downhill course: GNR: Newcastle to South Shields 30.5m

Mark	20k	15k	Name		Nat	Born	Pos	Meet	Venue	Date
64:52	61:35	46:07	Fancy	Chemutai	KEN	20.3.94	1	RAK	Ras Al Khaimah	9 Feb
64:55	61:34	46:08	Mary	Keitany	KEN	18.1.82	2	RAK	Ras Al Khaimah	9 Feb
65:04	61:44	45:54	Joan	Chelimo	KEN	10.11.90	1		Praha	7 Apr
65:07	61:40	46:08	Caroline	Kipkirui	KEN	26.5.94	3	RAK	Ras Al Khaimah	9 Feb
65:15	61:56	46:09	Sifan	Hassan	NED	1.1.93	1		København	16 Sep
65:37	62:14	46:48		J Chelimo			4	RAK	Ras Al Khaimah	9 Feb
65:46	62:24	46:48	Yeshaneh	Ababel	ETH	10.6.90	2		København	16 Sep
66:09	62:37	46:26		Kipkirui			2		Praha	7 Apr
66:11	62:53	47:30	Netsanet	Gudeta	ETH	12.2.91	1	WCh	Valencia	24 Mar
66:11	62:55	47:21	Gelete	Burka	ETH	23.1.86	1		Valencia	28 Oct
66:13	62:56	47:21	Alia Mohamed	Saeed	UAE	18.5.91	2		Valencia	28 Oct
66:15	62:12	46:09		J Chelimo			3		København	16 Sep
66:18	62:57	47:21	Edith	Chelimo (10)	KEN	16.7.86	3		Valencia	28 Oct
66:21	62:55	46:49	Zeineba	Yimer	ETH	17.6.98	4		København	16 Sep
66:22	62:54	47:00		Ababel			1		Istanbul	8 Apr
66:31	63:05	47:21	Pauline	Korikwiang	KEN	1.3.88	4		Valencia	28 Oct
66:39	63:13	47:28	Ruti	Aga	ETH	16.1.94	1		Houston	14 Jan
66:46	63:04	46:25	Joyciline	Jepkosgei	KEN	8.12.93	5	RAK	Ras Al Khaimah	9 Feb
66:47	63:26	47:15	Degitu	Azimeraw	ETH-J	24.1.99	6	RAK	Ras Al Khaimah	9 Feb
66:48				Kipkirui			2		Houston	14 Jan
66:49	63:26	47:15	Brigid	Kosgei	KEN	20.2.94	7	RAK	Ras Al Khaimah	9 Feb
66:50	63:24	47:29	Mary Wacera	Ngugi	KEN	17.12.88	3		Houston	14 Jan
66:50	63:24	47:29	Buze	Diriba	ETH	9.2.94	4		Houston	14 Jan
66:50		47:51	Tsehay	Gemechu	ETH	20.5.98	1		New Delhi	21 Oct

Mark			Name		Nat	Born	Pos	Meet	Venue	Date
66:54	63:33	47:38		Jepkosgei			2	WCh	Valencia	24 Mar
66:56	63:33	47:34	Pauline	Kamulu (20)	KEN	30.12.94	3	WCh	Valencia	24 Mar
66:56				Jepkosgei			2		New Delhi	21 Oct
66:59				Yimer			3		New Delhi	21 Oct
67:00	63:28	47:00	Roza	Dereje	ETH	6.5.97	2		Istanbul	8 Apr
67:02	63:35	47:13	Ruth	Chepngetich	KEN	8.8.94	5		København	16 Sep
			(30/22)							
67:03	63:34	47:13	Bekelech	Gudeta	ETH	11.10.97	6		København	16 Sep
67:07	63:43	47:23	Diana	Kipyokei	KEN	5.5.94	5		Valencia	28 Oct
67:13	63:34	47:15	Gladys	Cherono	KEN	12.5.83	8	RAK	Ras Al Khaimah	9 Feb
67:16		47:52	Stacy	Ndiwa	KEN	6.12.92	4		New Delhi	21 Oct
67:17	63:45	47:45	Eunice	Chumba	BRN	23.5.93	4	WCh	Valencia	24 Mar
67:18			Yebrgual	Melese	ETH	18.4.90	1		Lisboa	14 Oct
67:25	63:48	47:29	Molly	Huddle	USA	31.8.84	7		Houston	14 Jan
67:32		47:24	Nancy	Kiprop	KEN	7.7.79	2		Ústí Nad Labem	15 Sep
			(30)							
67:36	64:04	47:20	Hiwot	Gebrekidan	ETH	11.5.95	7		København	16 Sep
67:39+	64:05	47:46	Tirunesh	Dibaba	ETH	1.10.85	1	in Mar	London	22 Apr
67:43dh		48:35	Vivian	Cheruiyot	KEN	11.9.83	1	GNR	South Shields	9 Sep
67:47	64:08	47:29	Helen	Tola	ETH	21.11.94	9	RAK	Ras Al Khaimah	9 Feb
67:51	64:15	47:48	Meseret	Belete	ETH-J	16.9.99	8		København	16 Sep
67:54		48:36	Sutume	Asefa	ETH	11.12.94	1	Stra	Milano	25 Mar
67:55			Lonah Chemtai	Salpeter	ISR	12.12.88	2		Lisboa	14 Oct
67:58	64:21	47:34	Yeshi	Chekole	ERI	12.7.97	7		Valencia	28 Oct
68:07			Antonina	Kwambai	KEN	1.4.92	1		Paris	4 Mar
68:10			Zerfie	Limeneh	ETH	10.2.97	2		Paris	4 Mar
			(40)							
68:10	64:55	48:43	Desi Jisa	Mokonin	BRN	12.7.97	7	WCh	Valencia	24 Mar
68:10	64:38	48:20	Worknesh	Degefa	ETH	28.10.90	3		Praha	7 Apr
68:11dh		48:35	Linet	Masai	KEN	5.12.89	4	GNR	South Shields	9 Sep
68:12	64:53	48:44	Dalilah Abdelkadir Gosa		BRN	27.6.98	9	WCh	Valencia	24 Mar
68:20			Pauline	Njeru	KEN	12.12.88	3		Paris	4 Mar
68:22	64:45	47:59	Naomi	Rotich	KEN	.94	10	RAK	Ras Al Khaimah	9 Feb
68:22			Sharon	Cherop	KEN	16.3.84	4		Paris	4 Mar
68:25	64:56	48:44	Shitaye	Eshete	BRN	21.5.90	10	WCh	Valencia	24 Mar
68:30	64:59	48:43	Zinash	Mekonnen	ETH	11.9.96	11	WCh	Valencia	24 Mar
68:34	65:13	48:50	Meskerem	Assefa	ETH	20.9.85	9		København	16 Sep
			(50)							
68:35			Celestine	Chepchirchir	KEN	.90	5		Paris	4 Mar
68:36	65:17	49:06	Tejitu	Daba	BRN	16.6.91	1		Barcelona	11 Feb
68:36	65:13	48:51	Belaynesh	Oljira	ETH	26.6.90	10		København	16 Sep
68:37	65:17		Dibaba	Kuma	ETH	14.9.96	2		Barcelona	11 Feb
68:38	65:01	48:20	Jordan	Hasay	USA	21.9.91	8		Houston	14 Jan
68:38	65:13	48:51	Monicah	Ngige	KEN	7.11.93	11		København	16 Sep
68:41	65:01	48:07	Yisak	Melat	ETH	.92	2		Venlo	25 Mar
68:48	66:01	49:06	Salomé	Nyirarukundo	RWA	20.12.97	3		Barcelona	11 Feb
68:59			Daisy	Kimeli	KEN	28.11.94	2		Adana	7 Jan
69:01			Delvin	Meringor	KEN	1.8.92	3		Adana	7 Jan
			(60)							
69:02		49:37	Haftamnesh	Tesfay	ETH	28.4.94	1		Ostia	11 Mar
69:02	65:16	48:23	Joy	Loyce	KEN	3.3.88	3		Venlo	25 Mar
69:07			Tabitha	Wambui	KEN	29.12.83	1		Dronten	16 Dec
69:10			Vivian	Kiplagat	KEN	.88	1		Buenos Aires	26 Aug
69:11+	65:36	49:12	Edna	Kiplagat	KEN	15.11.79		in Mar	Berlin	16 Sep
69:12	65:44	49:17	Honami	Maeda	JPN	17.7.96	1		Okayama	23 Dec
69:15			Mare	Dibaba	ETH	20.10.89	1		Glasgow	30 Sep
69:17	65:42	48:57	Veronica	Maina	KEN	8.8.89	9		Houston	14 Jan
69:17	65:35	48:51	Betsy	Saina	KEN	30.6.88	1		Marugame	4 Feb
69:18	65:39	48:05	Joyce	Chepkirui	KEN	20.8.88	4		Istanbul	8 Apr
			(70)							
69:20			Sinead	Diver	AUS	17.2.77	1	NC	Sunshine Coast	19 Aug
69:20	65:51	49:28	Ellie	Pashley	AUS	10.12.88	2		Okayama	23 Dec
69:21		49:27	Dera	Dida	ETH	26.10.96	2		Ostia	11 Mar
69:21			Joyce	Chepkemoi	KEN	3.3.95	1		Trento	7 Oct
69:22	65:40	48:07	Etagegne	Woldu	ETH	10.5.96	5		Istanbul	8 Apr
69:23	65:54	49:32	Pascalia	Kipkoech	KEN	22.12.88	3		Yangzhou	22 Apr
69:23			Parendis	Lekapana	KEN	4.8.91	1		Krems	23 Sep
69:25	65:51	49:22	Risper	Chebet	KEN	6.6.92	4		Praha	7 Apr
69:26	66:01	49:13	Mimi	Belete	BRN	9.6.88	4		Barcelona	11 Feb
69:27	65:56		Sara	Hall	USA	15.4.83	1		Gold Coast	1 Jul
			(80)							

WOMEN 2018

Mark			Name		Nat	Born	Pos	Meet	Venue	Date
69:29		48:54	Martina	Strähl	SUI	7.5.87	2		Berlin	8 Apr
69:31			Alina	Reh	GER	23.5.97	1		Köln	7 Oct
69:32	65:58	49:32	Birhane	Dibaba	ETH	11.9.93	4		Yangzhou	22 Apr
69:34			Wude	Ayalew	ETH	4.7.87	1		Xiameng	25 Nov
69:35+			Lydia	Cheromei	KEN	11.5.77		in Mar	Valencia	2 Dec
69:36	66:01	49:06	Failuna Abdi	Matanga	TAN	28.10.92	5		Barcelona	11 Feb
00:00	05.50	48.31	Helah	Kiprop	KEN	7.4.85	10		Houston	14 Jan
69:39			Goytatom	Gebreselassie	ETH	15.1.95	2		Boston	7 Oct
69:44	65:54	48:14	Peninah	Kandie	KEN	22.6.92	7		Istanbul	8 Apr
69:44			Daisy	Cherotich	KEN	.97	1		Verbania	15 Apr
			(90)							
69:45		49:35	Aselefech	Mergia	ETH	23.1.85	2		Olomouc	23 Jun
69:45			Juliet	Chekwel	UGA	25.5.90	1		Cardiff	7 Oct
69:45+	66:03	49:15	Margaret	Agai	KEN	10.6.88		in Mar	Istanbul	11 Nov
69:47+			Tadelech	Bekele	ETH	11.4.91		in Mar	London	22 Apr
69:49			Betty	Lembus	KEN	9.7.91	3		Lisboa	14 Oct
69:50			Mamitu	Daska	ETH	16.10.83	4		Boston	7 Oct
69:51		49:34	Trihas	Gebre	ESP	29.4.90	3		Olomouc	23 Jun
69:52	66:12	49:26	Filomena	Chepchirchir	KEN	1.12.81	6		Praha	7 Apr
69:52		49:41	Clémence	Calvin	FRA	17.5.90	4		Olomouc	23 Jun
69:52		48:22	Lucy	Cheruiyot	KEN	4.1.97	3		Ústí Nad Labem	15 Sep
			(100)							
69:55+	66:19	49:46	Bedatu	Hirpa	ETH-J	28.4.99		in Mar	Frankfurt	28 Oct
69:55+	66:19	49:47	Worknesh	Alemu	ETH	.90		in Mar	Frankfurt	28 Oct
69:55+	66:20	49:46	Abebech	Afework	ETH	11.12.90		in Mar	Frankfurt	28 Oct
69:56+	66:21	49:48	Stella	Barsosio	KEN	-.93		in Mar	Frankfurt	28 Oct
69:56+	66:19	49:47	Sentayehu	Lewetegn	ETH	9.5.96		in Mar	Frankfurt	28 Oct
70:04			Aliphine	Bolton	USA	5.4.89	1	NC	Pittsburgh	6 May
70:07			Rose	Chelimo	BRN	12.7.89	2		Glasgow	30 Sep
70:08+	66:27	49:49	Feyse	Tadese	ETH	19.11.88		in Mar	Dubai	26 Jan
70:08+	66:27	49:50	Sehbere	Teferi	ETH	3.5.95		in Mar	Dubai	26 Jan
70:08			Rachel	Cliff	CAN	1.4.88	1		The Woodlands	3 Mar
70:09+	66:27	49:50	Muliye	Dekebo	ETH	13.3.98		in Mar	Dubai	26 Jan
70:09+	66:27	49:50	Genet	Yalew	ETH	31.12.92		in Mar	Dubai	26 Jan
70:09+	66:27	49:50	Azmera	Abreha	ETH	.98		in Mar	Dubai	26 Jan
70:09+			Visiline	Jepkesho	KEN	30.12.89		in Mar	Rotterdam	8 Apr
70:10	66:23	49:27	Kaori	Morita	JPN	19.9.95	2		Marugame	4 Feb

Mark		Name		Nat	Born	Pos	Meet	Date
70:10	Sara	Dossena		ITA	22.11.84	23 Sep		
70:10+	Shure	Demise		ETH	21.1.96	7 Oct		
70:10+	Florence	Kiplagat		KEN	27.2.87	7 Oct		
70:11 49:29	Valary	Aiyabei		KEN	8.6.91	22 Apr		
70:11 49:25	Perine	Nengampi		KEN	.89	15 Sep		
70:13	Gladys	Kipkoech		KEN	24.8.96	1 Jul		
70:13	Margaret	Muriuki		KEN	21.3.86	7 Oct		
70:14+49:45	Shasho	Insermu		ETH	16.9.93	21 Oct		
70:15 49:21	Ruth	Waithera		KEN	.90	25 Mar		
70:16+	Meseret	Gola		ETH	30.12.97	21 Oct		
70:16	Kellyn	Taylor		USA	22.7.86	11 Nov		
70:17	Laura	Thweatt (66:38)		USA	17.12.88	1 Jul		
70:18	Nancy	Jelagat		KEN	24.12.87	1 Jul		
70:18	Vicoty	Chepngeno		KEN	93	18 Nov		
70:20+	Amy	Cragg		USA	21.1.84	25 Feb		
70:21	Ancuta	Bobocel		ROU	3.10.87	24 Mar		
70:24	Hawi	Magersa		ETH-J	19.11.00	24 Mar		
70:26	Dezunesh	Getachew		ETH	-.97	7 Jan		
70:26	Berhane	Gebrekidan		ETH-J	13.3.99	25 Mar		
71:02	Mao	Ichiyama		JPN	29.5.97	24 Mar		
71:02+	Biruktayit	Eshetu		ETH	29.9.90	8 Apr		
71:02	Mizuki	Tanimoto		JPN	18.12.94	23 Dec		
71:03	Lilian	Jelagat		KEN	23.1.89	25 Mar		
71:04 49:36	Rebecca	Kangogo		KEN	.92	11 Mar		
71:04	Chaltu	Negasa		ETH	20.9.92	18 Mar		
71:04	Anne Mari	Hyrryläinen		FIN	15.8.78	8 Apr		
71:04	Celia	Sullohern		AUS	5.7.92	7 Oct		
71:05	Yuka	Hori		JPN	13.6.96	11 Feb		
71:06	Lily	Partridge		GBR	9.3.91	4 Mar		
71:06	Susan	Jeptoo		KEN	7.3.87	16 Sep		
71:07	Sanae	El Otmani		MAR	20.12.86	28 Jan		
71:09	Dolshi	Tesfu		ERI-J	17.6.99	24 Mar		
71:09	Catarina	Ribeiro		POR	31.5.90	7 Oct		
71:10	Doreen	Chesang		UGA	12.8.90	7 Oct		
71:11	Birtukan	Fente		ETH	18.6.89	18 Nov		
71:12+	Veronica	Nyaruai		KEN	29.10.89	7 Oct		
71:15	Rebekah	Wade		USA	9.2.89	14 Jan		
	(200)							
71:15	Cynthia	Kosgei		KEN	.93	8 Apr		
71:15	Lucy	Karimi		KEN	6.10.86	15 Sep		

Excessively downhill

Mark	Name		Nat	Born	Pos	Venue	Date
68:26	Meseret	Defar	ETH	19.11.83	1	San Diego (86.5m)	3 Jun
69:43	Caroline	Rotich	KEN	13.5.84	1	Santa Fe (400m)	16 Sep
71:05A	Filomena	Cheyech	KEN	5.7.82	2	Eldoret	7 Oct

JUNIORS

See main list for top 2 juniors. 9 performances by 7 women to 72:30. Additional marks and further juniors:

	Mark		Pos		Venue		Date			
Azimeraw	69:53		1		Gifu		22 Apr			
Belete	68:09		6	WCh	Valencia		24 Mar	70:35A	2 NC	Sendafa	28 Jan
	69:06		1		Göteborg		19 May			
T Abreha	70:45 ??		1		Laayoune		4 Nov			

Mark	Name		Nat	Born	Pos	Meet	Venue	Date
70:24	Hawi	Magersa	ETH	19.11.00	1		Azkoitia	24 Mar
70:26	Berhane	Gebrekidan	ETH	13.3.99	2		Warszawa	25 Mar
70:40	Tsige	Abreha	ETH	21.9.00	1		Tamesna	11 Nov
71:59	Irene	Kimais	KEN	.00	6		Eldoret	7 Oct
72:19	Luula	Weledgebriel	ETH	17.3.99	39	WCh	Valencia	24 Mar

Mark	Name		Nat	Born	Pos	Meet	Venue	Date
72:41	Hikaru	Sudo	JPN	.99	5		Matsue	18 Mar
73:20		Choe Il-gyong	PRK-Y	.01	1		Pyongyang	8 Apr

In addition to those shown in Marathon listing

25/30 KILOMETRES ROAD

25k	30k	Name		Nat	Born	Pos	Meet	Venue	Date
1:20:24	1:37:03	Mary	Keitany	KEN	18.1.82	1	in Mar	London	22 Apr
1:20:53	1:37:55	Tirunesh	Dibaba	ETH	1.10.85	2	in Mar	London	22 Apr
1:22:54	1:39:30	Betsy	Saina	KEN	30.6.88		in Mar	Frankfurt	28 Oct
1:22:54	1:39:30	Abebech	Afework	ETH	11.12.90		in Mar	Frankfurt	28 Oct
1:22:54	1:39:30	Dera	Dida	ETH	26.10.96		in Mar	Frankfurt	28 Oct
1:23:04	1:40:27	Stella	Barsosio	KEN	-.93		in Mar	Frankfurt	28 Oct
1:23:04	1:40:35+	Margaret	Agai	KEN	10.6.88		in Mar	Istanbul	11 Nov
1:23:10	1:40:03	Desi	Jisa Mokonin	BRN	12.7.97		in Mar	Dubai	26 Jan
1:23:10	1:40:04+	Netsanet	Gudeta	ETH	12.2.91		in Mar	Dubai	26 Jan
1:23:17	1:39:52+	Birhane	Dibaba	ETH	11.9.93		in Mar	Tokyo	25 Feb
1:23:20		Yeshaneh	Ababel	ETH	10.6.90		in Mar	Dubai	26 Jan
1:23:24	1:40:33	Visiline	Jepkesho	KEN	30.12.89		in Mar	Rotterdam	8 Apr
	1:41:29	Celestine	Chepchirchir	KEN	.90		in Mar	Wien	22 Apr
1:23:35	1:42:05	Azmera	Abreha	ETH-J	21.9.00		in Mar	Dubai	26 Jan
1:23:36	1:41:39 +	Meseret	Gola	ETH	30.12.97		in Mar	Amsterdam	21 Oct
1:23:59	1:43:09+	Marta	Lema	ETH	30.12.90		in Mar	Paris	8 Apr
1:24:35	1:41:40+	Meseret	Defar	ETH	19.11.83		I Mar	Amsterdam	21 Oct
1:24:13	1:42:48	Sutume	Asefa	ETH	11.12.94		in Mar	Ljubljana	28 Oct
1:24:17	1:42:25	Genet	Yalew	ETH	31.12.92		in Mar	Dubai	26 Jan
1:24:34+		Biruktayit	Eshetu	ETH	29.9.90		in Mar	Rotterdam	8 Apr
1:24:36	1:41:49	Honami	Maeda	JPN	17.7.96		in Mar	Berlin	16 Sep
1:24:37	1:41:58	Merima	Mohammed	BRN	10.6.92		in Mar	Nagoya	11 Mar
1:24:40	1:42:01	Dalilah	Abdelkadir Gosa	BRN	27.6.98		in Mar	Roma	8 Apr
1:24:40	1:42:07	Amane	Gobena	ETH	1.9.82		in Mar	Praha	6 May
1:24:43+	1:43:27	Meseret	Gebre	ETH	17.2.93		in Mar	Valencia	2 Dec
1:24:45	1:43:01	Helah	Kiprop	KEN	7.4.85		in Mar	Tokyo	25 Feb
1:24:55	1:42:30	Veronica	Nyaruai	KEN	29.10.89		in Mar	Chicago	7 Oct
1:25:00	1:42:50	Rei	Ohara	JPN	10.8.90		in Mar	Nagoya	11 Mar
1:25:00	1:43:23	Filomena	Cheyech	KEN	5.7.82		in Mar	Nagoya	11 Mar
1:25:20	1:42:45	Yuka	Ando	JPN	16.3.94		in Mar	Osaka	28 Jan
	1:42:53+	Jessica	Trengove	AUS	15.8.87		in Mar	Gold Coast	1 Jul
	1:43:19+	Zinash	Debebe	ETH	12.10.96		in Mar	Sevilla	25 Feb

MARATHON

	25k	30k	Name		Nat	Born	Pos	Venue	Date
2:18:11	1:21:52	1:38:04	Gladys	Cherono	KEN	12.5.83	1	Berlin	16 Sep
2:18:31	1:21:56	1:38:19	Vivian	Cheruiyot	KEN	11.9.83	1	London	22 Apr
2:18:34	1:21:54	1:38:04	Ruti	Aga	ETH	16.1.94	2	Berlin	16 Sep
2:18:35	1:23:29		Brigid	Kosgei	KEN	20.2.94	1	Chicago	7 Oct
2:18:35	1:21:25	1:37:43	Ruth	Chepngetich	KEN	8.8.94	1	Istanbul	11 Nov
2:18:55	1:21:55	1:38:24	Tirunesh	Dibaba	ETH	1.10.85	3	Berlin	16 Sep
2:19:17	1:23:09	1:39:41	Roza	Dereje	ETH	6.5.97	1	Dubai	26 Jan
2:19:30	1:23:09	1:39:42	Feyse	Tadese	ETH	19.11.88	2	Dubai	26 Jan
2:19:36	1:23:10	1:39:41	Yebrgual	Melese	ETH	18.4.90	3	Dubai	26 Jan
2:19:51	1:23:17	1:39:52	Birhane	Dibaba (10)	ETH	11.9.93	1	Tokyo	25 Feb
2:19:53	1:23:09	1:39:41	Worknesh	Degefa	ETH	28.10.90	4	Dubai	26 Jan
2:20:13	1:23:10	1:39:43	Haftamnesh	Tesfay	ETH	28.4.94	5	Dubai	26 Jan
2:20:13	1:21:56	1:38:19		Kosgei			2	London	22 Apr
2:20:36	1:22:55	1:39:30	Meskerem	Assefa	ETH	20.9.85	1	Frankfurt	28 Oct
2:20:36	1:23:35			Melese			2	Shanghai	18 Nov
2:20:45	1:23:10	1:39:42	Gelete	Burka	ETH	23.1.86	6	Dubai	26 Jan
2:20:47	1:22:54	1:39:30		Tesfay			2	Frankfurt	28 Oct
2:21:14	1:23:58	1:40:42	Ashete	Bekele	ETH	17.4.88	1	Valencia	2 Dec
2:21:18	1:21:58	1:38:23	Edna	Kiplagat	KEN	15.11.79	4	Berlin	16 Sep
2:21:18				Dereje			2	Chicago	7 Oct
2:21:19				Aga			2	Tokyo	25 Feb
2:21:32	1:22:55	1:39:31	Bedatu	Hirpa	ETH-J	28.4.99	3	Frankfurt	28 Oct
2:21:38			Valary	Aiyabei	KEN	8.6.91	1	Beijing	16 Sep
2:21:40	1:23:04	1:40:02	Tadelech	Bekele	ETH	11.4.91	3	London	22 Apr
2:21:42	1:23:17	1:39:53	Amy	Cragg (20)	USA	21.1.84	3	Tokyo	25 Feb
2:21:45	1:23:10	1:39:42	Dera	Dida	ETH	26.10.96	7	Dubai	26 Jan
2:21:45	1:24:37	1:41:09		Assefa			1	Nagoya	11 Mar
2:21:51			Azmera	Abreha	ETH-J	21.9.00	2	Shanghai	18 Nov
2:21:53	1:22:54	1:39:30	Belaynesh	Oljira	ETH	26.6.90	4	Frankfurt	28 Oct

WOMEN 2018

Mark			Name		Nat	Born	Pos	Venue	Date
2:22:07	1:23:17	1:39:59	Shure	Demise	ETH	21.1.96	4	Tokyo	25 Feb
2:22:11	1:22:47	1:40:01	Lydia	Cheromei	KEN	11.5.77	2	Valencia	2 Dec
2:22:15				Demise			3	Chicago	7 Oct
2:22:17				Burka			1	Ottawa	27 May
2:22:23	1:24:37	1:41:22	Mizuki	Matsuda	JPN	31.5.95	5	Berlin	16 Sep
2:22:29		1:40:32	Mimi	Belete	BRN	9.6.88	1	Toronto	21 Oct
2:22:35		1:40:31	Marta	Lema	ETH	30.12.90	2	Toronto	21 Oct
2:22:39	1:22:54	1:39:30		Dida			5	Frankfurt	28 Oct
2:22:44	1:25:20	1:42:05		M Matsuda			1	Osaka	28 Jan
2:22:45	1:22:55	1:39:31	Sintayehu	Lewetegn	ETH	9.5.96	6	Frankfurt	28 Oct
2:22:46	1:22:55	1:39:32	Nancy	Kiprop (30)	KEN	7.7.79	7	Frankfurt	28 Oct
2:22:48	1:24:37	1:40:52		Aiyabei			2	Nagoya	11 Mar
2:22:48	1:22:04	1:39:28	Helen	Tola	ETH	21.11.94	6	Berlin	16 Sep
2:22:48			Mary	Keitany (43/32)	KEN	18.1.82	1	New York	4 Nov
2:22:56	1:23:59	1:41:38	Betsy	Saina	KEN	30.6.88	1	Paris	8 Apr
2:22:58	1:24:13	1:41:11	Visiline	Jepkesho	KEN	30.12.89	1	Ljubljana	28 Oct
2:23:06	1:23:59	1:41:38	Gulume	Tollesa	ETH	11.9.92	3	Paris	8 Apr
2:23:07	1:24:37	1:41:33	Hanami	Sekine	JPN	26.2.96	3	Nagoya	11 Mar
2:23:15	1:24:13	1:41:10	Selly	Chepyego	KEN	3.10.85	2	Ljubljana	28 Oct
2:23:28	1:23:11	1:40:02	Shasho	Insermu	ETH	16.9.93	2	Amsterdam	21 Oct
2:23:29		1:41:14	Ruth	Chebitok	KEN	26.12.90	3	Toronto	21 Oct
2:23:31	1:25:16	1:42:35	Azmera	Gebru (40)	ETH	5.5.92	3	Amsterdam	21 Oct
2:23:34	1:24:13	1:41:10	Dibaba	Kuma	ETH	14.9.96	3	Ljubljana	28 Oct
2:23:37	1:23:58	1:40:53	Tinbit	Weldegebril	ETH	17.9.89	3	Valencia	2 Dec
2:23:39	1:24:22	1:41:37	Desi	Jisa Mokonin	BRN	12.7.97	4	Amsterdam	21 Oct
2:23:40			Betty	Lembus	KEN	9.7.91	3	Shanghai	18 Nov
2:23:43	1:23:59	1:41:38	Stella	Barsosio	KEN	.93	5	Paris	8 Apr
2:23:46	1:24:42	1:42:01	Rahma	Tusa	ETH	14.9.93	1	Roma	8 Apr
2:23:46	1:25:15	1:42:36	Linet	Masai	KEN	5.12.89	5	Amsterdam	21 Oct
2:23:48	1:25:20	1:42:01	Honami	Maeda	JPN	17.7.96	2	Osaka	28 Jan
2:23:54			Afera	Godfay	ETH	25.9.91	4	Shanghai	18 Nov
2:24:08		1:42:13	Hirut	Tibebu (50)	ETH	13.12.94	1	Seoul	18 Mar
2:24:11	1:23:10	1:39:43	Senbere	Teferi	ETH	3.5.95	9	Dubai	26 Jan
2:24:17		1:43:16	Lonah Chemtai	Salpeter	ISR	12.12.88	1	Firenze	25 Nov
2:24:19		1:42:19	Bornes	Kitur	KEN	.88	1	Praha	6 May
2:24:29			Kellyn	Taylor	USA	22.7.86	1	Duluth	16 Jun
2:24:30			Margaret	Agai	KEN	10.6.88	2	Seoul	18 Mar
2:24:31		1:42:13	Monica	Jepkoech	KEN	.85	3	Seoul	18 Mar
2:24:35	1:23:58	1:40:53	Aberu	Mekuria	ETH	24.12.83	4	Valencia	2 Dec
2:24:38		1:42:35	Jackline	Chepngeno	KEN	16.1.93	6	Amsterdam	21 Oct
2:24:47			Letebrhan	Gebreslasea	ETH	29.10.90	1	Dongying	5 May
2:24:51			Biruktayit	Degefa (60)	ETH	29.9.90	1	Houston	14 Jan
2:24:51			Shitaye	Eshete	BRN	21.5.90	1	Hamburg	29 Apr
2:25:01		1:42:13	Mulu	Seboka	ETH	24.9.84	4	Seoul	18 Mar
2:25:02	1:24:00	1:41:39	Abebech	Afework	ETH	11.12.90	7	Paris	8 Apr
2:25:02	1:24:14	1:41:37	Sharon	Cherop	KEN	16.3.84	4	Ljubljana	28 Oct
2:25:19			Sinead	Diver	AUS	17.2.77	1	Melbourne	14 Oct
2:25:24	1:22:54	1:39:30	Mare	Dibaba	ETH	20.10.89	11	Frankfurt	28 Oct
2:25:24	1:25:18	1:43:28	Dulce	Félix	POR	23.10.82	6	Valencia	2 Dec
2:25:25			Olga	Mazuronak	BLR	14.4.89	1	Düsseldorf	29 Apr
2:25:27			Carla Salomé	Rocha	POR	25.4.90	8	Berlin	16 Sep
2:25:28			Debele	Beyene (70)	ETH		2	Hamburg	29 Apr
2:25:35		1:42:44	Kaoutar	Boulaïd	MAR	10.10.89	1	Sevilla	25 Feb
2:25:35			Dalilah	Abdelkadir Gosa	BRN	27.6.98	1	Saitama	9 Dec
2:25:41		1:43:38		Kim Do-yeon	KOR	2.9.93	5	Seoul	18 Mar
2:25:46			Miyuki	Uehara	JPN	22.11.95	9	Berlin	16 Sep
2:25:48			Muluhabt	Tsega	ETH	11.9.89	5	Shanghai	18 Nov
2:25:49			Amane	Gobena	ETH	1.9.82	1	Mumbai	21 Jan
2:25:51		1:43:11	Haimanot	Alemayehu	ETH	17.6.90	2	Sevilla	25 Feb
2:25:55	1:23:17	1:40:18	Zinash	Mekonnen	ETH	11.9.96	7	Amsterdam	21 Oct
2:25:57			Waganesh	Mekasha	ETH	16.1.92	1	Hengshui	29 Sep
2:25:59			Jessica	Trengove (80)	AUS	15.8.87	4	Toronto	21 Oct
2:26:03	1:24:54	1:42:48	Rose	Chelimo	BRN	12.7.89	6	London	22 Apr
2:26:08	1:23:30	1:40:05	Florence	Kiplagat	KEN	27.2.87	4	Chicago	7 Oct
2:26:10	1:24:35	1:42:20	Shuko	Genemo	ETH	.95	5	Ljubljana	28 Oct
2:26:11			Hiwot	Gebrekidan	ETH	11.5.95	2	Ottawa	27 May

Mark			Name		Nat	Born	Pos	Meet	Venue	Date
2:26:13	1:24:04	1:41:39	Yuka	Takashima	JPN	12.5.88	8		Paris	8 Apr
2:26:20			Sara	Hall	USA	15.4.83	3		Ottawa	27 May
2:26:22			Shalane	Flanagan	USA	8.7.81	3		New York	4 Nov
2:26:28	1:24:40	1:42:14	Reina	Iwade	JPN	8.12.94	4		Nagoya	11 Mar
2:26:28			Clémence	Calvin	FRA	17.5.90	2	EC	Berlin	12 Aug
2:26:28			Workenesh	Edesa	ETH	11.9.92	2		Hengshui	29 Sep
	(90)									
2:26:31			Eva	Vrabcová-Nyvltová	CZE	6.2.86	3	EC	Berlin	12 Aug
2:26:33	1:25:54	1:43:36	Keiko	Nogami	JPN	6.12.85	5		Nagoya	11 Mar
2:26:41			Fatuma	Sado	ETH	11.10.91	1		Xiamen	7 Jan
2:26:44			Molly	Huddle	USA	31.8.84	4		New York	4 Nov
2:26:44			Tigist	Girma	ETH	.93	1		Guangzhou	9 Dec
2:26:50	1:22:55	1:39:35	Worknesh	Alemu	ETH	.90	12		Frankfurt	28 Oct
2:26:52	1:23:10	1:39:44	Muliye	Dekebo	ETH	13.3.98	10		Dubai	26 Jan
2:26:54			Gebeyanesh	Ayele	ETH	1.5.95	3		Hengshui	29 Sep
2:26:56			Eunice	Chumba	BRN	23.5.93	2		Beijing	16 Sep
2:26:58		1:41:49	Celestine	Chepchirchir	KEN	.90	5		Toronto	21 Oct
	(100)									
2:27:06		1:43:17	Mercy	Kibarus	KEN	25.2.84	6		Seoul	18 Mar

Mark	Split	Name	Nat	Born	Date
2:27:08		Belaynesh Tsegaye	ETH	.97	11 Mar
2:27:08		Vivian Kiplagat	KEN	.88	8 Apr
2:27:12		Maurine Chepkemoi	KEN	24.5.98	29 Sep
2:27:15		Zinash Debebe	ETH	12.10.96	9 Dec
2:27:16		Milliam Ebongon	KEN	10.2.92	7 Oct
2:27:21		Melesech Tsegaye	ETH	26.1.94	14 Jan
2:27:25		Meseret Defar	ETH	19.11.83	21 Oct
2:27:29		Rei Ohara	JPN	10.8.90	16 Sep
2:27:31		Kim Hye-gyong	PRK	9.3.93	8 Apr
2:27:32		Gladys Chepchirchir	KEN	21.3.86	14 Jan
2:27:35		Tsehay Desalegn	ETH	28.10.91	4 Nov
2:27:37		Yuka Ando	JPN	16.3.94	28 Jan
2:27:40		Hanae Tanaka	JPN	12.2.90	11 Mar
2:27:41		Merima Mohammed	BRN	10.6.92	11 Mar
2:27:42		Jo Un-ok	PRK	29.8.92	8 Apr
2:27:44		Maryna Damantsevich	BLR	6.6.85	12 Aug
2:27:46		Genet Yalew	ETH	31.12.92	26 Jan
2:27:46	1:42:34	Agnes Barsosio	KEN	5.8.82	1 Jul
2:27:49		Anastasiya Ivanova	BLR	4.11.82	12 Aug
2:27:51		Desiree Linden	USA	26.7.83	4 Nov
2:27:53	1:42:13	Guteni Shone	ETH	17.11.91	18 Mar
2:27:53		Sara Dossena	ITA	22.11.84	21 Aug
2:27:55		Ri Kwang-ok	PRK		8 Apr
2:28:01		Janet Rono	KEN	8.12.88	1 Apr
2:28:02		Salomé Nyirarukundo	RWA	20.12.97	23 Sep
2:28:07		Martina Strähl	SUI	7.5.87	12 Aug
2:28:08		Kebede Megertu	ETH		18 Nov
2:28:11		Truphena Chepchirchir	KEN	21.6.90	28 Jan
2:28:12		Allie Kieffer	USA	16.9.87	4 Nov
2:28:17		Ahn Seul-ki	KOR	29.5.92	1 Apr
2:28:19		Alice Kibor	KEN	14.5.86	8 Apr
2:28:22		Georgina Rono	KEN	19.5.84	20 May
2:28:22		Magdalene Masai	KEN	4.4.93	11 Nov
2:28:26		Lilia Fiscovici	MDA	29.3.89	28 Oct
2:28:27		Peris Cherono Lagat	KEN	.88	5 May
2:28:31		Sardana Trofimova	RUS	28.3.88	13 May
2:28:32		Ayuko Suzuki	JPN	8.10.91	26 Aug
2:28:35		Meskerem Abera	ETH	6.12.87	15 Apr
2:28:38		Sylvia Kibet	KEN	28.3.84	9 Dec
2:28:39		Racheal Mutgaa	KEN	.88	11 Nov
2:28:41		Nurit Yimam	ETH	.95	28 Jan
2:28:45		Pamela Rotich	KEN	25.12.84	1 Apr
2:28:49		Winnie Jepkorir	KEN	10.6.90	1 Apr
2:28:50		Tejitu Daba	BRN	15.6.91	16 Sep
2:28:53		Anne Mari Hyryläinen	FIN	15.8.78	26 Jan
2:28:53		Rachel Cliff	CAN	1.4.88	16 Sep
2:28:56		Meseret Legesse	ETH	28.8.87	25 Mar
2:28:56	1:40:30	Amane Beriso	ETH	13.10.91	21 Oct
2:28:58		Helah Kiprop	KEN	7.4.85	25 Feb
2:28:58		Mao Kiyota	JPN	12.9.93	11 Mar
2:29:05		Aberash Fayesa	ETH	.95	11 Nov
2:29:11		Lisa Weightman	AUS	16.1.79	4 Nov
2:29:21	1:43:10	Sechale Delasa	ETH	20.9.91	25 Feb
2:29:22		Misaki Kato	JPN	15.6.91	11 Mar
2:29:24		Lily Partridge	GBR	9.3.91	22 Apr
2:29:25		Lindsay Flanagan	USA	24.1.91	28 Oct
2:29:26		Sheila Chepkoech	KEN	.90	8 Apr
2:29:28		Helaria Johannes	NAM	13.8.80	23 Sep
2:29:29		Anja Scherl	GER	12.4.86	28 Jan
2:29:31		Madina Deme Armino	ETH	22.10.97	11 Nov
2:29:32	1:43:15	Risper Chebet	KEN	6.6.92	6 May
2:29:35		Marie Imada	JPN	18.1.90	9 Dec
2:29:38		Miharu Shimokado	JPN	24.4.90	1 Jul
2:29:40		Sheila Jerotich	KEN	6.6.89	7 Oct
2:29:41		Giovanna Epis	ITA	11.10.88	25 Feb
2:29:45		Sutume Asefa	ETH	11.12.94	28 Oct
2:29:48		Nazret Weldu	ERI	1.1.90	11 Nov
2:29:49		Yurie Doi	JPN	8.12.88	11 Mar
2:29:50		Doris Changeiywo	KEN	12.12.84	8 Apr
2:29:53		Kaori Yoshida	JPN	4.8.81	28 Jan
2:29:55		Katharina Heinig	GER	22.8.89	28 Oct
2:29:57		Tigist Teshome	ETH	11.3.87	18 Feb
2:29:59		Tsehay Alemu Maru	ETH	.94	9 Dec
2:30:00		Failuna Abdi Matanga	TAN	28.10.92	23 Sep
2:30:03		Mari Ozaki	JPN	16.7.75	28 Jan
2:30:06		Catherine Bertone	ITA	6.5.72	12 Aug
2:30:07		Michi Numata	JPN	6.5.89	11 Mar
2:30:09		Hirut Alemayehu	ETH	19.12.93	7 Jan
2:30:09		Hiroko Yoshitomi	JPN	26.12.83	11 Nov
2:30:10		Fantu Jimma	ETH	11.9.87	21 Jan
2:30:13		Abeba Gebremeskel	ETH	18.1.89	4 Nov
2:30:14		Jane Jelagat	KEN	25.11.83	18 Mar
2:30:14		Stephanie Twell	GBR	17.8.89	2 Dec
2:30:15		Meseret Mengistu	ETH	6.3.90	7 Jan
2:30:18		Askale Maracchi	ETH	.87	16 Jun
2:30:19		Celia Sullohern	AUS	5.7.92	1 Jul
2:30:20		Li Dan	CHN	1.5.95	15 Apr
2:30:20		Li Wei	CHN	2.12.92	18 Nov
2:30:24		Ednah Mukwana	KEN	.85	25 Mar
2:30:24		Alina Prokopyeva	RUS	16.8.85	30 Apr
2:30:24		Nina Lauwaert	BEL	6.8.88	14 Oct
2:30:25		Ayantu Abera	ETH	12.9.95	18 Nov
2:30:26		Valeria Straneo	ITA	5.4.76	2 Dec
2:30:28		Kumeshi Sichala	ETH	.95	29 Sep
2:30:29		Aynalem Kasahun	ETH	28.11.93	8 Apr
2:30:30		He Yinli	CHN	20.9.88	18 Nov
	(197)				

Excessively downhill Sacramento 2 Dec & Rennes 26 Oct

Mark	Name	Nat	Born	Pos	Date
2:28:19	Emma Bates	USA	8.7.92	2	Dec
2:29:20	Stephanie Bruce	USA	14.1.84	2	Dec
2:29:40	Almaz Negede	ETH	19.2.87	28	Oct
2:30:25	Sam Roecker	USA	15.10.91	2	Dec

Possibly short

Mark	Name		Nat	Born	Pos	Venue	Date
2:20:16	Yeshaneh	Ababel	ETH	10.6.90	1	Abu Dhabi	7 Dec
2:20:54	Eunice	Chumba	BRN	23.5.93	2	Abu Dhabi	7 Dec
2:25:09	Chaltu	Waka	ETH	25.9.85	4	Abu Dhabi	7 Dec
2:29:14	Caroline	Kilel	KEN	21.3.81	5	Abu Dhabi	7 Dec

WOMEN 2018

Mark	Name		Nat	Born	Pos	Meet	Venue	Date

Short course Lisboa 14 Oct: 2:24:56 Kuftu Dadiso ETH (1), 2:28:35 Tigist Mamuye ETH 27.9.90 (3)

Drugs disqualification

2:27:02 Lucy   Kabuu ¶   KEN 24.3.84   8Apr │ 2:28:27 Ruth   Wanjiru ¶   KEN 11.9.81 28Jan
2:27:31   Kim Hye-song ¶ PRK 9.3.93   8Apr │

JUNIORS

See main list for top 2 juniors. 7 performances by 6 women to 72:30. Additional marks and further juniors:

Hirpa	2:25:54	3		Sevilla		25 Feb			
2:32:56	Bekelu		Beji		ETH	21.8.99	1	Changsha	21 Oct
	2:33:02	2		Taipei		9 Dec			

100 KILOMETRES

Mark	Name		Nat	Born	Pos	Meet	Venue	Date
7:20:34	Nikolina	Sustic	CRO	24.7.87	1	WCh	Grkavescak	8 Sep
7:22:16	Radka	Churanová	CZE	3.6.77	1		Plzen	24 Mar
7:22:41	Nele	Alder-Baerens	GER	1.4.78	2	WCh	Grkavescak	8 Sep
7:33:15		Alder-Baerens			1		Rheine	10 Mar
7:35:44	Irono	Kinnegim	NED	8.1.75	1		Amiens	13 Oct
7:37:56	Mai	Fujisawa	JPN	21.9.74	1		Yubetsu	24 Jun
7:39:07		Fujisawa			3	WCh	Grkavescak	8 Sep
7:39:45	Mikiko	Ota	JPN	28.4.75	4	WCh	Grkavescak	8 Sep
7:44:01		Ota			2		Yubetsu	24 Jun
7:44:50	Nadezhda	Gogoleva	RUS	6.8.84	1		Sankt Peterburg	9 Sep
7:44:58	Aiko	Kanematsu	JPN	18.5.80	5	WCh	Grkavescak	8 Sep
7:45:41	Dina	Zakharchenko	RUS	10.9.83	1		Sankt Peterburg	9 Sep
7:47:07	Itsuka	Azumi (10)	JPN	.89	3		Yubetsu	24 Jun
7:49:18		Kanematsu			4		Yubetsu	24 Jun
7:49:33	Yuko	Kusunose	JPN	29.5.79	6	WCh	Grkavescak	8 Sep
	(15/11)							
7:51:13	Salome	Cooper	RSA	26.7.75	7	WCh	Grkavescak	8 Sep
7:52:04	Katarina	Honkala Noora	FIN	1.7.92	8	WCh	Grkavescak	8 Sep
7:52:39	Kajsa	Berg	SWE	16.1.79	9	WCh	Grkavescak	8 Sep
7:53:57	Samantha	Amend	GBR	25.5.79	1	NC	Redwick	31 Mar
7:54:55	Leonie	Ton	NED	14.1.75	10	WCh	Grkavescak	8 Sep
7:55:05	Nadezhda	Shikhanova	RUS	14.5.84	2		Sankt Peterburg	9 Sep
7:57:35	Caroline	Boller	USA	10.12.74	11	WCh	Grkavescak	8 Sep
7:58:11	Julie	Hamulecki	CAN	21.11.80	12	WCh	Grkavescak	8 Sep
7:58:50	Alicia	Pérez	ESP	28.2.90	13	WCh	Grkavescak	8 Sep
7:59:12	Susanne	Kraus	GER	.80	3		Rheine	10 Mar
7:59:17	Fikile	Mbuthuma	RSA	23.12.80	14	WCh	Grkavescak	8 Sep
8:00:34	Hinke	Schokker	NED	26.9.83	1		Winschoten	8 Sep

8:01:20	Tomomi	Nakajima	JPN	.90	24 Jun	8:06:46	Nadezhda	Shaposhnikova	RUS	13.12.91	9 Sep
8:03:11	Emily	Harrison	USA	13.2.86	8 Sep	8:07:05	Radka	Churanova	RUS	3.6.77	26 Oct
8:03:49	Tereza	Zuzanková	CZE	18.9.86	24 Mar	8:07:54	Wioletta	Paduszynska	POL	18.7.85	8 Sep
8:05:38	Malgorzata	Pazda-Pozorska	POL	16.2.82	10 Nov	8:07:59	Liza	Howard	USA	1.2.72	7 Apr
8:05:39	Valeria	Sesto	ARG	17.12.72	8 Sep	8:08:37	Miho	Nakata	JPN	.89	21 Oct
8:05:57	Veronika	Jurisic	CRO	6.4.77	8 Sep	8:10:31	Patrycja	Bereznowska	POL	17.10.75	10 Nov
8:06:14	Lisa	Collett	RSA	3.7.77	8Sep.	8:10:56	Anna	Karasiuk	RUS	13.9.97	9 Sep

Note - Women running within the main pack of slower male runners at Yubetsu benefitted far less from the strong wind assistance.

24 HOURS

Mark	Name		Nat	Born	Pos	Meet	Venue	Date
262.192t	Camille	Herron	USA	25.12.81	1		Phoenix	8 Dec
243.355	Patrycja	Bereznowska	POL	17.10.75	1	EO	Timisoara	26 May
241.921	Stine	Rex	DEN	8.6.79	2	EC	Timisoara	26 May
240.697	Malgorzata	Pazda-Pozorska	POL	16.2.82	3	EC	Timisoara	26 May
236.401	Monika	Biegasiewicz	POL	25.5.76	4	EC	Timisoara	26 May
236.364t	Megan	Alvarado	USA	29.8.88	1		Palatka	20 Jan
232.930t	Viktorija	Tomaseviciene	LTU	15.5.80	1		Barcelona	15 Dec
232.702	Anke	Libuda	GER	3.4.79	1		Bottrop	1 Sep
232.390		Bereznowska			1		Lyse	8 Sep
229.981	Nadezhda	Gudareva	RUS	15.9.95	1	NC	Moskva	13 May
228.848t	Julia	Fatton (10)	GER	24.4.72	1		Barcelona	15 Dec
228.643	Anna	Grundahl	SWE	6.4.76	5	EC	Timisoara	26 May
228.399	Aneta	Rajda	POL	6.5.76	2		Lyse	8 Sep
228.389	Nadezhda	Shikhanova	RUS	14.5.84	2	NC	Moskva	13 May
227.263		Rajda			6	EC	Timisoara	26 May
226.225		Alvarado			1		Cleveland	22 Sep
225.428	Szvetlana	Zétényi	HUN	10.7.76	1		Velence	15 Sep
225.312t	Micah	Morgan	USA	20.1.83	2		Phoenix	8 Dec
	(18/15)							
224.619	Tracy	Dean	GBR	22.9.71	7	EC	Timisoara	26 May

Mark	Name		Nat	Born	Pos	Meet	Venue		Date
221.993	Yuko	Kusunose	JPN	29.5.79	1		Tokyo		10 Nov
221.146	Milena	Grabska-Grzegorczyk	POL	18.6.78	9	EC	Timisoara		26 May
220.858	Amy	Masner	IRL	22.11.73	10	EC	Timisoara		27 May
220.249	Samantha	Amend	GBR	25.5.79	1		Belfast		23 Jun
219.112t	Yuri	Matsumoto	JPN	27.2.78					1 Dec
218.177t	Tia	Jones	AUS	5.9.65					1 Dec
217.217t	Antje	Krause	GER	1.5.72					27 Oct
216.528	Aya	Doi	JPN	9.11.81					10 Nov
216.117t	Wendy	Shaw	GBR	5.10.77					15 Dec
215.384	Stephanie	Gicquel	FRA	9.7.82					20 Oct
214.559	Viktoria	Makai	HUN	1.7.80					27 May
214.465	Alison	Young	GBR	26.11.73					27 May
213.120t	Sarah	Morwood	GBR	22.3.83					22 Sep
213.013	Christelle	Bourreau	FRA	10.1.67					20 Oct
212.700t	Aiko	Kanematsu	JPN	18.5.80					1 Dec
212.536	Mara	Guler-Cionca	ROU	4.1.77					26 May
210.417t	Michaela	Dimitriadu	CZE	23.12.73					27 Oct
210.132	Mariana	Nenu	ROU	18.7.74					29 Jun

Indoors

Mark	Name		Nat	Born	Pos	Meet	Venue	Date
228.079t	Simone	Durry	GER	24.3.75	1		Oslo	24 Nov
221.413	Mizuki	Aotani	JPN	5.12.13	1		Espoo	24 Feb

2000 METRES STEEPLECHASE

Mark	Name		Nat	Born	Pos	Meet	Venue		Date
6:15.46	Viktória	Gyürkës	HUN	15.10.92	1		Györ		19 May
6:16.60	Ophélie	Claude-Boxberger	FRA	18.10.88	1		Pliezhausen		13 May
6:17.68	Fancy	Cherono	KEN-Y	2.8.01	1-17	Afr-Y	Alger		27 Jul
6:20.82	Elena	Burkard	GER	10.2.92	2		Pliezhausen		13 May
6:26.86	Mekides	Abebe	ETH-Y	29.7.01	2-17	Afr-Y	Alger		27 Jul
6:27.25	Antje	Möldner-Schmidt	GER	13.6.84					13 May
6:27.60	Zita	Kácser	HUN	2.10.88					19 May
6:28.76	Kriszta	Kószás		HUN	26.8.94				19 May

3000 METRES STEEPLECHASE

Mark	Name		Nat	Born	Pos	Meet	Venue	Date
8:44.32	Beatrice	Chepkoech	KEN	6.7.91	1	Herc	Monaco	20 Jul
8:55.10		Chepkoech			1	VD	Bruxelles	31 Aug
8:59.36		Chepkoech			1	DL	Paris (C)	30 Jun
8:59.62	Norah	Tanui	KEN	2.10.95	2	VD	Bruxelles	31 Aug
8:59.88		Chepkoech			1	AfrC	Asaba	5 Aug
9:00.85	Courtney	Frerichs	USA	18.1.93	2	Herc	Monaco	20 Jul
9:01.60	Hyvin	Jepkemoi	KEN	13.1.92	3	VD	Bruxelles	31 Aug
9:01.82	Celliphine	Chespol	KEN-J	23.3.99	2	DL	Paris (C)	30 Jun
9:03.86		Jepkemoi			3	DL	Paris (C)	30 Jun
9:04.17		Tanui			4	DL	Paris (C)	30 Jun
9:04.41		Jepkemoi			3	Herc	Monaco	20 Jul
9:04.96		Jepkemoi			1	GGala	Roma	31 May
9:05.06	Emma	Coburn	USA	19.10.90	4	Herc	Monaco	20 Jul
9:05.14		Chespol			2	GGala	Roma	31 May
9:06.51		Coburn			4	VD	Bruxelles	31 Aug
9:06.75		Chespol			5	VD	Bruxelles	31 Aug
9:07.07		Frerichs			6	VD	Bruxelles	31 Aug
9:07.17		Tanui			3	GGala	Roma	31 May
9:07.20		Tanui			5	Herc	Monaco	20 Jul
9:07.27		Chepkoech			1	DL	Shanghai	12 May
9:07.92		Chepkoech			1	C.Cup	Ostrava	9 Sep
9:07.94	Peruth	Chemutai	UGA-J	10.7.99	6	Herc	Monaco	20 Jul
9:08.13		Coburn			4	GGala	Roma	31 May
9:08.23	Roseline	Chepngetich	KEN	17.6.97	7	Herc	Monaco	20 Jul
9:09.30		Tanui			2	DL	Shanghai	12 May
9:09.61		Chespol			2	AfrC	Asaba	5 Aug
9:09.63		Jepkemoi			1	Bisl	Oslo	7 Jun
9:09.70		Coburn			2	Bisl	Oslo	7 Jun
9:10.27	Colleen	Quigley	USA	20.11.92	1	ISTAF	Berlin	2 Sep
9:10.71	Daisy	Jepkemei	KEN	13.2.96	8	Herc	Monaco	20 Jul
	(30/10)							
9:10.74	Winfred	Yavi	BRN-J	31.12.99	9	Herc	Monaco	20 Jul
9:14.09	Aisha	Praught Leer	JAM	14.12.89	8	VD	Bruxelles	31 Aug
9:16.68	Yekaterina	Ivonina	RUS	14.6.94	1	NC	Kazan	20 Jul
9:18.36	Karoline Bjerkeli	Grøvdal	NOR	14.6.90	11	Herc	Monaco	20 Jul
9:19.80	Gesa-Felicitas	Krause	GER	3.8.92	1	EC	Berlin	12 Aug
9:21.34	Purity	Kirui	KEN	13.8.91	5	DL	Shanghai	12 May
9:22.00	Luiza	Gega	ALB	5.11.88	9	GGala	Roma	31 May
9:22.29	Fabienne	Schlumpf	SUI	17.11.90	2	EC	Berlin	12 Aug
9:22.85	Joan	Chepkemoi	KEN	24.11.93	6	DL	Shanghai	12 May
9:23.4A	Mercy	Wanjiru	KEN-J	2.3.99	1		Nairobi	6 Jun
	(20)							
9:23.69	Genevieve	LaCaze/Gregson	AUS	4.8.89	3	ISTAF	Berlin	2 Sep
9:23.92	Fancy	Cherono	KEN-Y	2.8.01	3	AfrC	Asaba	5 Aug
9:27.03	Woynshet	Ansa	ETH	9.4.96	4	AfrC	Asaba	5 Aug
9:28.61	Marusa	Mismas	SLO	24.10.94	4	ISTAF	Berlin	2 Sep

Mark	Name		Nat	Born	Pos	Meet	Venue	Date	
9:29.42A	Mercy	Chepkurui	KEN-J	16.9.00	2		Nairobi	11	Jun
9:29.74	Adva	Cohen	ISR	24.3.96	5	EC	Berlin	12	Aug
9:29.76	Elena	Burkard	GER	10.2.92	6	EC	Berlin	12	Aug
9:30.62	Caroline	Tuigong	KEN	12.3.90	4		Ostrava	13	Jun
9:31.36	Habiba	Ghribi	TUN	9.4.84	10	GGala	Roma	31	May
9:31.66	Anna Emilie (30)	Møller	DEN	28.7.97	7	EC	Berlin	12	Aug
9:31.84	Irene	Sánchez-Escribano	ESP	25.9.92	8	EC	Berlin	12	Aug
9:31.84	Ophëlie	Claude-Boxberger	FRA	18.10.88	9	EC	Berlin	12	Aug
9:32.08	Rosie	Clarke	GBR	17.11.91	12	GGala	Roma	31	May
9:32.3A	Naomi	Chepkemoi	KEN-J	2.3.99	2		Nairobi	6	Jun
9:32.68	Mel	Lawrence	USA	29.8.89	2		Liège (NX)	18	Jul
9:34.02	Isabel	Mattuzzi	ITA	23.4.95	5h2	EC	Berlin	10	Aug
9:35.19	Geneviève	Lalonde	CAN	5.9.91	3		Liège (NX)	18	Jul
9:35.42	Viktória	Gyürkës	HUN	15.10.92	7	ISTAF	Berlin	2	Sep
9:35.47	Ozlem	Kaya	TUR	20.4.90	8	ISTAF	Berlin	2	Sep
9:36.15	Emma (40)	Oudiou	FRA	2.1.95	8h2	EC	Berlin	10	Aug
9:36.26	Jana	Sussmann	GER	12.10.90	9	ISTAF	Berlin	2	Sep
9:36.6A	Elizabeth	Mueni	KEN	28.12.91	3		Nairobi	6	Jun
9:37.28	Nataliya	Strebkova	UKR	6.3.95	6h1	EC	Berlin	10	Aug
9:37.31	Regan	Yee	CAN	4.7.95	1	AWC	Ninove	28	Jul
9:37.91	Katarzyna	Kowalska	POL	7.4.85	1		Goleniów	20	Jun
9:38.57	Allie	Ostrander	USA	24.12.96	1		Stanford	30	Mar
9:39.07	Natalya	Koloskova	RUS	19.7.88	2	NC	Kazan	20	Jul
9:39.25	Antje	Möldner-Schmidt	GER	13.6.84	3		Goleniów	20	Jun
9:39.59	Sudha	Singh	IND	25.6.86	1	I-State	Guwahati	28	Jun
9:39.68	Tugba (50)	Güvenç	TUR	9.7.94	15	GGala	Roma	31	May
9:41.05	Martina	Merlo	ITA	19.2.93	8h1	EC	Berlin	10	Aug
9:41.1A	Deborah	Samum	KEN	.95	4		Nairobi	6	Jun
9:41.16	Alicja	Konieczek	POL	2.11.94	9h1	EC	Berlin	10	Aug
9:41.24	Shalaya	Kipp	USA	19.8.90	4	NC	Des Moines	23	Jun
9:41.32	Marie	Bouchard	FRA	7.12.93	1	Jordan	Stanford	3	May
9:41.70	Janica	Rauma	FIN	24.6.86	10h2	EC	Berlin	10	Aug
9:41.73	Matylda	Kowal	POL	11.1.89	5		Goleniów	20	Jun
9:42.14	Charlotta	Fougberg	SWE	19.6.85	1	NC	Eskilstuna	25	Aug
9:42.30	Camilla	Richardsson	FIN	14.9.93	3	Gyulai	Székesfehërvár	1	Jul
9:42.94	Yekaterina (60)	Sokolenko	RUS	13.9.92	1	NCp	Smolensk	29	May
9:43.1A	Joyline	Chemutai	KEN		5		Nairobi	6	Jun
9:43.48	María Josë	Pérez	ESP	12.6.92	16	GGala	Roma	31	May
9:43.70	María Teresa	Urbina	ESP	20.3.85	2		Huelva	8	Jun
9:43.83		Nguyen Thi Oanh II	VIE	15.8.95	3	AsiG	Jakarta	27	Aug
9:44.59	Chiara	Scherrer	SUI	24.1.96	4		Huelva	8	Jun
9:44.75	Emily	Oren	USA	20.9.93	5	NC	Des Moines	23	Jun
9:44.79	Agrie	Belachew	ETH-J	20.1.99	5	WJ	Tampere	13	Jul
9:44.82	Maya	Rehberg	GER	28.4.94	13		Ostrava	13	Jun
9:44.92	Rima	Chenah	ALG	11.2.96	3		Los Angeles	17	May
9:44.92	Francesca (70)	Bertoni	ITA	29.12.93	5		Huelva	8	Jun
9:45.37	Victoria	Mitchell	AUS	25.4.82	1	NC	Gold Coast	18	Feb
9:45.45	Charlotte	Prouse	CAN	9.2.97	2	NCAA	Eugene	9	Jun
9:45.79	Jessica	Furlan	CAN	15.3.90	2	AWC	Ninove	28	Jul
9:46.10	Fadwa	Sidi Madane	MAR	20.11.94	18	GGala	Roma	31	May
9:46.19	Michele	Finn	IRL	16.12.89	1	NC	Dublin	29	Jul
9:46.30		Zhang Xinyan	CHN	9.2.94	4	AsiG	Jakarta	27	Aug
9:46.58	Caren	Chebet	KEN-J	24.5.00	9	DL	Shanghai	12	May
9:46.76	U.K.Nilani	Rathnayake	SRI	8.8.90	1	NC	Colombo	3	Aug
9:46.83	Rosie	Donegan	AUS	1.7.93	4		Los Angeles	17	May
9:46.98	Paige (80)	Stoner	USA	31.1.96	3	NCAA	Eugene	9	Jun
9:47.14	Lucie	Sekanová	CZE	5.8.89	11	ISTAF	Berlin	2	Sep
9:47.42		Xu Shuangshuang	CHN	6.4.96	5	AsiG	Jakarta	27	Aug
9:47.71	Ann	Gathoni	KEN	5.3.98	11	DL	Shanghai	12	May
9:47.89	Svetlana	Kudzelich	BLR	7.5.87	11h1	EC	Berlin	10	Aug
9:47.97	Val	Constien	USA	21.3.96	1h2	NCAA-W	Sacramento	25	May
9:48.33	Claire	Borchers	USA	20.4.96	4	NCAA	Eugene	9	Jun
9:48.37	Alex	Wilson	USA	16.6.93	3h2	NC	Des Moines	21	Jun
9:48.38	Birtukan	Adamu	ETH	29.4.92	12	DL	Shanghai	12	May
9:48.40	Tatiane Raquel	da Silva	BRA	10.6.90	1	IbAmC	Trujillo	25	Aug

Mark	Name		Nat	Born	Pos	Meet	Venue	Date
9:48.57	Grayson	Murphy	USA	28.6.95	1s1	NCAA	Eugene	7 Jun
(20)								
9:48.89	Tori	Gerlach	USA	2.6.94	5h2	NC	Des Moines	21 Jun
9:49.00	Paige	Campbell	AUS	27.6.96	2	NC	Gold Coast	18 Feb
9:49.04	Courtney	Coppinger	USA	17.1.95	7	NCAA	Eugene	9 Jun
9:49.33	Cierra	Simmons	USA	.95	8	NCAA	Eugene	9 Jun
9:50.17	Aimee	Pratt	GBR	3.10.97	1	IFAM	Oordegem	26 May
9:50.19	Natalya	Leontyeva	RUS	5.7.87	3	NC	Kazan	20 Jul
9:50.4A	Mercy	Njoroge	KEN	10.6.86	6		Nairobi	6 Jun
9:50.53A	Joan	Rotich	KEN	27.11.93	4		Nairobi	17 Feb
9:50.68	Megan	Rolland	USA	30.8.88	2		Nashville	2 Jun
9:50.94	Jessica	Kamilos	USA	3.8.93	6h2	NC	Des Moines	21 Jun
(100)								
9:50.94	Caroline	Högardh	SWE	16.11.92	3	AWC	Ninove	28 Jul

Mark	Name		Nat	Born	Date
9:50.96	Etalemahu	Sintayehu	ETH-Y	23.2.01	13 Jul
9:51.29	Alsu	Gabdullina	RUS	12.5.94	25 May
9:51.49	Madeline	Strandemo	USA	12.7.95	25 May
9:51.79	Irene	van der Reijken	NED	13.8.93	18 Jul
9:52.71	Kristlin	Gear	USA-J	20.7.99	25 May
9:53.00	Kerry	O'Flaherty	IRL	15.7.81	26 May
9:53.02	Laura	Dalla Montà	ITA	6.10.93	9 Sep
9:53.06	Devin	Clark	USA	10.6.97	25 May
9:53.18	Anna	Tropina	RUS	3.11.98	20 Jul
9:53.22	Yukari	Ishizawa	JPN	16.4.88	23 Jun
9:53.36	Zita	Kácser	HUN	2.10.88	10 Aug
9:53.59	Elizabeth	Bird	GBR	4.10.94	3 May
9:53.75	Blanca	Fernández	ESP	1.4.92	7 Jul
9:54.01	Taylor	Austin	USA	26.3.94	30 Mar
9:54.55	Nell	Crosby	USA	.96	25 May
9:55.41	Chinta	Yadav	IND	26.3.93	28 Jun
9:55.53	Charlotte	Wilson	AUS	2.10.92	20 Jan
9:55.76	Katy	Kunc	USA	18.10.95	21 Jun
9:55.84	Carolina	Robles	ESP	4.12.91	8 Jun
9:56.0A	Nancy	Sang	KEN	.94	6 Jun
9:56.17	Sarah	Scott	USA	16.8.96	9 Jun
9:56.19	Sümeyye	Erol	TUR	15.6.97	20 May
9:56.26	Morgan	Wedekind	USA	15.5.95	25 May
9:56.3A	Purity	Cheromei	KEN		6 Jun
9:56.34	Viktoriya	Ivanova	RUS	21.11.91	20 Jul
9:56.53	Sarah	Pease	USA	9.11.87	4 May
9:56.73	Chavi	Yadav	IND	15.8.92	28 Jun
9:56.77	Bri	Ilarda	AUS	19.2.96	5 Jan
9:56.80	Leah	Hanle	GER	3.3.97	22 Jul
9:56.95	Nana	Sato	JPN	24.9.89	23 Jun
9:57.04	Alice	Hill	USA-J	6.8.99	13 Jul
9:57.25	Erin	Teschuk	CAN	25.10.94	28 Jul
9:57.28	Sage	Hurta	USA	23.6.98	12 May
9:57.36	Agnes Thurid	Gers	GER	4.8.97	22 Jul
9:57.45	Lisa	Oed	GER-J	2.1.99	13 Jul
9:57.66	Oumaima	Saoud	MAR	5.8.96	28 Jun
9:57.75	Rachel	King	USA		25 May
9:57.82	Catherone	Beauchemin	CAN	31.8.98	22 Jul
9:58.32	Khushbu	Gupta	IND	7.11.98	13 Dec
9:58.45	Susan	Tanui	USA	28.3.87	2 Jun
9:58.61	Alycia	Butterworth	CAN	1.10.92	18 Jul
9:58.75	Amy	Cashin	AUS	28.7.94	7 Jun
9:58.89	Yui	Yabuta	JPN	4.3.96	23 Jun
9:58.92	Iona	Lake	GBR	15.1.93	11 Apr
9:58.98	Shelby	Brown	USA	9.12.95	20 Apr
9:59.33	Emily	de La Bruyere	USA/FRA	31.3.93	10 Jun
9:59.37	Jessy	Lacourse	CAN	5.2.97	5 Jul
9:59.67	Montanna	McAvoy	AUS-J	21.7.00	10 Jul
9:59.73	Soyoka	Segawa	JPN	28.7.94	23 Jun
9:59.94	Hannah	Steelman	USA-J	9.6.99	7 Jul
10:00.01	Ana Cristina	Narváez	MEX	12.8.91	2 Aug
10:00.35	Emily	Hamlin	USA		25 May
10:00.49	Manami	Nishiyama	JPN-J	9.12.99	13 Jul
10:00.63	Stella	Radford	AUS	25.6.95	3 Feb
10:00.78	Katelyn	Ayers	CAN	9.2.95	5 Jul
10:00.81	Eilish	Flanagan	IRL	2.5.97	25 May
10:00.96	Colett	Rampf	GER	23.7.91	25 May
10:01.02	Aneta	Konieczek	POL	8.6.97	25 May
10:01.71	Mariola	Slusarczyk	POL	4.1.90	1 Jun
10:01.88	Julia	Howley	CAN	8.8.96	10 Jun
10:01.95	Grace	Fetherstonhaugh	CAN-J	13.10.00	10 Jun
10:02.04	Kako	Okada	JPN	12.2.98	9 Sep
10:02.20	Kristina	Hendel	CRO	13.5.96	26 May
10:02.33	Linda	Wrede	GER	9.10.93	26 May
10:02.67	Gabrielle	Jennings	USA	15.9.98	25 May
10:02.8A	Meswat	Amare	FTH		25 Dec
10:03.11	Sandra	Eriksson	FIN	4.6.89	25 Jul
10:03.18	Bridget	Blake	USA	9.5.95	25 May
10:03.22	Anne-Sophie	Vittet	FRA	24.12.88	26 May
10:03.46	Derya	Kunur	TUR-J	1.9.99	13 Jul
10:04.37	Erin	Clark	USA	28.12.94	28 Apr
10:04.37	Julie	Friend	USA	22.6.95	25 May
10:04.52	Anna	McDonald	USA	28.2.95	25 May
10:04.66	Lisa	Tertsch	GER	1.12.98	2 Jun
10:04.7		Ro Hyo-gyong	PRK-J	9.1.99	1? Oct
10:04.8		Ju Ok-byol	PRK	20.5.97	1? Oct
(178)					

JUNIORS

See main list for top 9 juniors. 15 performances by 3 women to 9:22.0. Additional marks and further juniors:

Name	Mark	Pos	Meet	Venue	Date	Mark	Pos	Meet	Venue	Date
Chespol 4+	9:12.05	10	Herc	Monaco	20 Jul	9:12.78	1	WJ	Tampere	13 Jul
Chemutai	9:13.58	7	VD	Bruxelles	31 Aug	9:18.87	2	WJ	Tampere	13 Jul
	9:16.89	1	GS	Ostrava	13 Jun					
Yavi	9:12.74	5	DL	Paris (C)	30 Jun	9:16.38	6	GGala	Roma	31 May
	9:14.52	9	VD	Bruxelles	31 Aug	9:17.86	3	C.Cup	Ostrava	9 Sep

Mark	Name		Nat	Born	Pos	Meet	Venue	Date
9:50.96	Etalemahu	Sintayehu (10)	ETH-Y	23.2.01	6	WJ	Tampere	13 Jul
9:52.71	Kristlin	Gear	USA	20.7.99	3h2	NCAA-E	Tampa	25 May
9:57.04	Alice	Hill	USA	6.8.99	7	WJ	Tampere	13 Jul
9:57.45	Lisa	Oed	GER	2.1.99	8	WJ	Tampere	13 Jul
9:59.67	Montanna	McAvoy	AUS	21.7.00	2h1	WJ	Tampere	10 Jul
9:59.94	Hannah	Steelman	USA	9.6.99	8s1	NCAA	Eugene	7 Jun
10:00.49	Manami	Nishiyama	JPN	9.12.99	9	WJ	Tampere	13 Jul
10:01.95	Grace	Fetherstonhaugh	CAN	13.10.00	8		Portland	10 Jun
10:03.46	Derya	Kunur	TUR	1.9.99	12	WJ	Tampere	13 Jul
10:04.7		Ro Hyo-gyong	PRK	9.1.99	1	NC	Pyongyang	1? Oct
10:05.61	Maritu	Ketema (20)	ETH	21.2.00	14	DL	Shanghai	12 May

60 METRES HURDLES INDOORS

Mark	Name		Nat	Born	Pos	Meet	Venue	Date
7.70A	Sharika	Nelvis	USA	10.5.90	1	NC	Albuquerque	18 Feb
7.70	Kendra	Harrison	USA	18.9.92	1	WI	Birmingham	3 Mar

Mark	Name		Nat	Born	Pos	Meet	Venue	Date	
7.72		Harrison			1		Celmson	11	Feb
7.72A		Harrison			2	NC	Albuquerque	18	Feb
7.73A	Christina	Manning	USA	29.5.90	3	NC	Albuquerque	18	Feb
7.77		Manning			1		Düsseldorf	6	Feb
7.77A		Harrison			1s2	NC	Albuquerque	18	Feb
7.77		Harrison			1h4	WI	Birmingham	2	Mar
7.79		Manning			1	GP	Glasgow	25	Feb
7.79		Harrison			1s2	WI	Birmingham	3	Mar
7.79		Manning			2	WI	Birmingham	3	Mar
7.80		Nelvis			1		Karlsruhe	3	Feb
7.80		Nelvis			2		Düsseldorf	6	Feb
7.80A		Maning			1s1	NC	Albuquerque	18	Feb
	(14/3)								
7.83	Pamela	Dutkiewicz	GER	28.9.91	3		Düsseldorf	6	Feb
7.83	Nadine	Visser	NED	9.2.95	1s3	WI	Birmingham	3	Mar
7.84	Cindy	Roleder	GER	21.8.89	3		Karlsruhe	3	Feb
7.86	Isabelle	Pedersen	NOR	27.1.92	3s3	WI	Birmingham	3	Mar
7.88	Alina	Talay	BLR	14.5.89	4		Karlsruhe	3	Feb
7.88A	Jasmin	Stowers	USA	23.9.91	3s2	NC	Albuquerque	18	Feb
7.89A	Tobi	Amusan	NGR	23.4.97	1s3		Albuquerque	20	Jan
	(10)								
7.89	Devynne	Charlton	BAH	26.11.95	2s1	WI	Birmingham	3	Mar
7.91A	Queen	Harrison	USA	10.9.88	5	NC	Albuquerque	18	Feb
7.92	Sally	Pearson	AUS	19.9.86	3s2	WI	Birmingham	3	Mar
7.93	Payton	Chadwick	USA	29.11.95	1h2	NCAA	College Station	9	Mar
7.93	Anna	Cockrell	USA	28.8.97	2	NCAA	College Station	10	Mar
7.94A	Dior	Hall	USA	2.1.96	1s2		Albuquerque	20	Jan
7.94A	Kristi	Castlin	USA	7.7.88	2h3	NC	Albuquerque	17	Feb
7.94A	Bridgette	Owens	USA	14.3.92	7	NC	Albuquerque	18	Feb
7.95	Jasmine	Camacho-Quinn	PUR	21.8.96	2		Clemson	10	Feb
7.98A	Erica	Bougard	USA	26.7.93	1P	NC	Albuquerque	16	Feb
	(20)								
7.98	Tara	Davis	USA-J	20.5.99	1h1	NCAA	College Station	9	Mar
7.99	Nadine	Hildebrand	GER	20.9.87	7		Karlsruhe	3	Feb
8.00A	Kori	Carter	USA	3.6.92	3h3	NC	Albuquerque	17	Feb
8.00A	Tiffani	McReynolds	USA	4.12.91	4s2	NC	Albuquerque	18	Feb
8.01	Hanna	Plotitsyna	UKR	1.1.87	3		Torun	15	Feb
8.02	Jeanine	Williams	JAM	28.1.97	2		Clemson	19	Jan
8.02	Stephanie	Bendrat	AUT	5.3.91	1	NC	Linz	18	Feb
8.02	Cortney	Jones	USA-J	18.6.99	4	NCAA	College Station	10	Mar
8.03	Nooralotta	Neziri	FIN	9.11.92	1		Metz	11	Feb
8.03	Alaysha	Johnson	USA	20.7.96	2		Seattle	24	Feb
	(30)								
8.04	Tonea	Marshall	USA	17.12.98	1		Fayetteville	9	Feb
8.04A	Jade	Barber	USA	4.4.93	5s1	NC	Albuquerque	18	Feb
8.04	Lindsay	Lindley	NGR	6.10.89	1		Athlone	21	Feb
8.04	Janeek	Brown	JAM	14.5.98	2	SEC	College Station	25	Feb
8.05	Gabriele	Cunningham	USA	22.2.98	4		Clemson	10	Feb
8.05	Eline	Berings	BEL	28.5.86	1h1		Gent	10	Feb
8.05	Elvira	Herman	BLR	9.1.97	2	NC	Mogilyov	17	Feb
8.05	Taliyah	Brooks	USA	8.2.95	P	NCAA	College Station	10	Mar
8.05	Tia	Jones	USA-J	8.9.00	1	HS Nat	New York (Arm)	11	Mar
8.05	Grace	Stark	USA-Y	6.5.01	2	HS Nat	New York (Arm)	11	Mar
	(40)								
8.06	Kayla	White	USA	24.9.96	5	NCAA	College Station	10	Mar
8.07A	Emily	Sloan	USA-J	26.5.00	5h3	NC	Albuquerque	17	Feb
8.07	Gréta	Kerekes	HUN	9.10.92	1	NC	Budapest	18	Feb
8.07	Andrea	Ivancevic	CRO	21.8.84	4s3	WI	Birmingham	3	Mar
8.08	Amber	Hughes	USA	23.8.94	1		Clemson	6	Jan
8.08	Ricarda	Lobe	GER	13.4.94	7		Düsseldorf	6	Feb
8.08	Kendell	Williams	USA	14.6.95	2P2	WI	Birmingham	2	Mar
8.09	Luca	Kozák	HUN	1.6.96	1		Val-de-Reuil	27	Jan
8.09	Monique	Morgan	JAM	14.10.85	4	Millrose	New York (Arm)	3	Feb
8.09	Pedrya	Seymour	BAH	29.5.95	2		Fayetteville	9	Feb
	(50)								
8.09	Chanel	Brissett	USA-J	10.8.99	5		Clemson	10	Feb
8.09	Brittley	Humphrey	USA	6.3.98	2h2	SEC	College Station	24	Feb
8.10A*	Lorenda	Holston	USA	15.8.95	1		Colorado Springs	8	Dec
8.10	Eefje	Boons	NED	18.7.94	2		Athlone	21	Feb
8.11	Elisávet	Pesirídou	GRE	12.2.92	1	NC	Pireás	11	Feb
8.12	Solène	Ndama	FRA	23.9.98	3		Eaubonne	9	Feb

Mark	Wind	Name	Nat	Born	Pos	Meet	Venue	Date
8.12		Reetta Hurske	FIN	15.5.95	2	NC	Helsinki	18 Feb
8.13		Marylyn Nwawulor	GBR	20.9.92	3		Gent	10 Feb
8.13		Nnenya Hailey	USA	23.2.94	1h2	NC	Montréal	10 Feb
8.13		Beate Schrott	AUT	15.4.88	2	NC	Linz	18 Feb
		(60)						
8.13		Rushelle Burton	JAM	4.12.97	2	Big 12	Ames	24 Feb
8.14		Mikiah Brisco	USA	14.7.96				27 Jan
8.14		Ivana Loncarek	CRO	8.4.91				27 Jan
8.14		Mariya Aglitskaya	RUS	20.6.91				8 Feb
8.14		Khaddi Sagnia	SWE	20.4.94				11 Feb
8.14		Laura Valette	FRA	16.2.97				18 Feb
8.15		Daeshon Gordon	JAM	8.11.96				9 Feb
8.15		Jacklyn Howell	USA	3.10.96				10 Feb
8.15		Franziska Hofmann	GER	27.3.94				17 Feb
8.15		Jasmine Jones	USA	30.11.01				11 Mar
8.16		Tiffany Porter	GBR	13.11.87				26 Jan
8.16		Karolina Kołeczek	POL	15.1.93				15 Feb
8.16		Megan Marrs	GBR	25.9.97				17 Feb
8.16A		Evonne Britton	USA	10.10.91				17 Feb
8.17		Kaylor Harris	USA	31.10.98				19 Jan
8.17		Lotta Harala	FIN	26.3.92				23 Jan
8.17		Yasmin Miller	GBR	24.5.95				3 Feb
8.17		Anamaria Nesteriuc	ROU	29.11.93				17 Feb
8.17		Katerina Cachová	CZE	26.2.90				17 Feb
8.17		Tiara McMinn	USA	23.2.99				24 Feb
8.18		Karel Elodie Ziketh	CIV	23.9.91				19 Jan
8.18		Nina Morozova	RUS	15.9.89				30 Jan
8.18		Dawn Harper Nelson	USA	13.5.84				3 Feb
8.18		Vanessa Clerveaux	HAI	17.6.94				7 Feb
8.18		Sarah Hammond	CAN	1.1.96				23 Feb
8.18		Jessica Lee	USA					24 Feb
8.19		Faith Ross	USA	7.3.98				3 Feb
8.19		Andrea Carolina Vargas	CRC	28.5.96				10 Feb
8.19		Veronica Borsi	ITA	13.6.87				17 Feb
8.19		Monika Zapalska	GER	24.5.94				17 Feb
8.19		Wu Shuijiao ¶	CHN	19.6.91				8 Mar

Best at low altitude

Mark	Wind	Name			Venue	Date
7.98	Hall	4			Fayetteville	27 Jan
7.98	Stowers	3	GP		Boston (R)	10 Feb
7.90	Amusan	1	Millrose		New York (Arm)	3 Feb
8.00	Q Harrison	4	GP		Boston (R)	10 Feb
8.00	Castlin	5	GP		Boston (R)	10 Feb
8.06	Owens	1			Seattle	27 Jan
8.07	Bougard	1P2	WI		Birmingham	2 Mar

100 METRES HURDLES

Mark	Wind	Name	Nat	Born	Pos	Meet	Venue	Date
12.36	0.6	Kendra Harrison	USA	18.9.92	1	DL	London (OS)	22 Jul
12.38	1.3	Brianna McNeal	USA	18.8.91	1	DL	Stockholm	10 Jun
12.40	1.2	Jasmine Camacho-Quinn	PUR	21.8.96	1	SEC	Knoxville	13 May
12.41	0.5	Alina Talay	BLR	14.5.89	1		St. Pölten	31 May
12.41	0.2	McNeal			1h2	DL	London (OS)	22 Jul
12.43	1.5	McNeal			1	MSR	Torrance	21 Apr
12.44	0.9	McNeal			1	Spitzen	Luzern	9 Jul
12.46	0.8	K Harrison			1h1	NC	Des Moines	22 Jun
12.46	-1.4	K Harrison			1	NC	Des Moines	23 Jun
12.47	0.6	McNeal			2	DL	London (OS)	22 Jul
12.48	1.3	Danielle Williams	JAM	14.9.92	2	DL	Stockholm	10 Jun
12.49	-0.1	Williams			1	C.Cup	Ostrava	8 Sep
12.50	0.9	McNeal			1	DL	Shanghai	12 May
12.50	1.0	Talay			1	v3N	Minsk	22 Jun
12.50	-0.5	K Harrison			1h1	DL	London (OS)	22 Jul
12.51	0.1	McNeal			1	DL	Rabat	13 Jul
12.51	0.6	Sharika Nelvis	USA	10.5.90	3	DL	London (OS)	22 Jul
12.52	0.9	Nelvis			2	DL	Shanghai	12 May
12.52	-0.1	K Harrison			2	C.Cup	Ostrava	8 Sep
12.53	0.5	K Harrison			1	DL	Doha	4 May
12.54	2.0	Camacho-Quinn			1s1	NCAA	Eugene	7 Jun
12.55	1.3	Talay			3	DL	Stockholm	10 Jun
12.55	0.7	Nelvis			1	Gyulai	Székesfehérvár	2 Jul
12.55	0.6	Williams			4	DL	London (OS)	22 Jul
12.55	0.9	K Harrison			1	NACAC	Toronto	11 Aug
12.56	0.9	K Harrison			3	DL	Shanghai	12 May
12.56	0.2	Christina Manning	USA	29.5.90	2h2	DL	London (OS)	22 Jul
12.57	0.6	Manning			5	DL	London (OS)	22 Jul
12.58	0.5	McNeal			2	DL	Doha	4 May
12.58	1.6	Camacho-Quinn			1h3	SEC	Knoxville	12 May
12.58	0.7	K Harrison			2	Gyulai	Székesfehérvár	2 Jul
12.58	0.1	Nelvis			2	DL	Rabat	13 Jul
		(32/7)						
12.63	0.6	Queen Harrison	USA	10.9.88	6	DL	London (OS)	22 Jul
12.64	1.4	Elvira German	BLR	9.1.97	1	PTS	Samorín	29 Jun
12.65	0.2	Rushelle Burton (10)	JAM	4.12.97	1		Waco	13 May
12.67	0.9	Pamela Dutkiewicz	GER	28.9.91	2	Spitzen	Luzern	9 Jul
12.68	-1.3	Sally Pearson	AUS	19.9.86	1h1		Brisbane (N)	4 Feb
12.68	0.2	Tobi Amusan	NGR	23.4.97	1	CG	Gold Coast	13 Apr
12.70	1.6	Devynne Charlton	BAH	26.11.95	1		Baton Rouge	7 Apr
12.70	2.0	Alaysha Johnson	USA	20.7.96	2s1	NCAA	Eugene	7 Jun
12.71	0.9	Jasmin Stowers	USA	23.9.91	4	DL	Shanghai	12 May
12.71	1.3	Nadine Visser	NED	9.2.95	4	DL	Stockholm	10 Jun
12.72	0.2	Pedrya Seymour	BAH	29.5.95	2		Waco	13 May

WOMEN 2018

Mark	Wind	Name		Nat	Born	Pos	Meet	Venue	Date	
12.72	0.6	Eline	Berings	BEL	28.5.86	1		Liège (NX)	18	Jul
12.72	0.2	Isabelle	Pedersen	NOR	27.1.92	4h2	DL	London (OS)	22	Jul
		(20)								
12.74	1.1	Yanique	Thompson	JAM	12.3.96	2h1		Kingston	24	Jun
12.75	1.7	Chanel	Brissett	USA-J	10.8.99	1	Pac-12	Stanford	13	May
12.75	0.7	Dawn	Harper Nelson	USA	13.5.84	4	Gyulai	Székesfehérvár	2	Jul
12.77	0.2	Solène	Ndama	FRA	23.9.98	2s2	EC	Berlin	9	Aug
12.77	-0.5	Cindy	Roleder	GER	21.8.89	3	EC	Berlin	9	Aug
12.78	1.8	Kori	Carter	USA	3.6.92	1h3	NC	Des Moines	22	Jun
12.79	1.5	Bridgette	Owens	USA	14.3.92	2	MSR	Torrance	21	Apr
12.79	1.2	Alexis	Duncan	USA	16.8.98	2	SEC	Knoxville	13	May
12.79	0.7	Jeanine	Williams	JAM	28.1.97	1h2		Kingston	24	Jun
12.80	1.5	Erica	Bougard	USA	26.7.93	1H5	Hypo	Götzis	26	May
		(30)								
12.80	1.7	Janeek	Brown	JAM	14.5.98	2s3	NCAA	Eugene	7	Jun
12.81	-0.6	Rikenette	Steenkamp	RSA	16.10.92	1		La Chaux-de-Fonds	1	Jul
12.83	1.7	Dior	Hall	USA	2.1.96	2	Pac-12	Stanford	13	May
12.84	0.0	Evonne	Britton	USA	10.10.91	2		Bellinzona	18	Jul
12.85	0.1	Andrea	Ivancevic	CRO	21.8.84	4	Hanz	Zagreb	4	Sep
12.86	-0.2	Ebony	Morrison	USA	28.12.94	1		Coral Gables	14	Apr
12.86	1.4	Cortney	Jones	USA-J	18.6.99	2s2	NCAA	Eugene	7	Jun
12.86	1.9	Luca	Kozák	HUN	1.6.96	1	NC	Székesfehérvár	23	Jun
12.86	0.7	Nooralotta	Neziri	FIN	9.11.92	1r2		Joensuu	4	Jul
12.86	1.7	Eefje	Boons	NED	18.7.94	1		Guadalajara	5	Jul
		(40)								
12.88	1.7	Anna	Cockrell	USA	28.8.97	3	Pac-12	Stanford	13	May
12.88	2.0	Tonea	Marshall	USA	17.12.98	3s1	NCAA	Eugene	7	Jun
12.89	-0.5	Tia	Jones	USA-J	8.9.00	1	NC-j	Bloomington	16	Jun
12.90	1.5	Andrea Carolina	Vargas	CRC	28.5.96	1	CAG	Barranquilla	31	Jul
12.90	0.2	Ricarda	Lobe	GER	13.4.94	3s2	EC	Berlin	9	Aug
12.91	1.0	Brianna	McGhee	USA	8.11.93	2		Claremont	2	Jun
12.92	1.7	Kayla	White	USA	24.9.96	1		Greensboro	14	Apr
12.93	1.6	Jacklyn	Howell	USA	3.10.96	2h3	SEC	Knoxville	12	May
12.93	0.7	Nickiesha	Wilson	JAM	28.7.86	2h2		Kingston	24	Jun
12.93	1.3	Karolina	Koleczek	POL	15.1.93	1		Inowrocław	1	Sep
		(50)								
12.94	1.2	Taliyah	Brooks	USA	8.2.95	4	SEC	Knoxville	13	May
12.94	1.7	Klaudia	Siciarz	POL	15.3.98	1	v3N-23	Kraków	8	Jul
12.94	0.8	Stephanie	Bendrat	AUT	5.3.91	1	NC	Klagenfurt	22	Jul
12.95	2.0	Louisa	Grauvogel	GER	28.9.96	1H	NCAA	Eugene	9	Jun
12.95	1.9	Gréta	Kerekes	HUN	9.10.92	2	NC	Székesfehérvár	23	Jun
12.96	0.4	Jade	Barber	USA	4.4.93	3h2	NC	Des Moines	22	Jun
12.96	0.0	Kristi	Castlin	USA	7.7.88	1		Tomblaine	27	Jun
12.97	0.4	Nadine	Hildebrand	GER	20.9.87	6	ISTAF	Berlin	2	Sep
12.98	1.9	Kendell	Williams	USA	14.6.95	3		Claremont	2	Jun
12.98	2.0	Mecca	McGlaston	USA	23.7.98	5s1	NCAA	Eugene	7	Jun
		(60)								
12.99	0.8	Tiffany	Porter	GBR	13.11.87	3h2	CG	Gold Coast	12	Apr
12.99	0.8	Michelle	Jenneke	AUS	23.6.93	4h2	CG	Gold Coast	12	Apr
12.99	1.0	Luminosa	Bogliolo	ITA	3.7.95	1		Savona	23	May
13.00	1.9	Cyrena	Samba-Mayela	FRA-J	31.10.00	1		Grenoble	20	May
13.00	0.1	Franziska	Hofmann	GER	27.3.94	1		Regensburg	3	Jun
13.00	0.2	Elisávet	Pesirídou	GRE	12.2.92	3s1	EC	Berlin	9	Aug
13.01	1.0	Maribel	Caicedo	ECU	1.4.98	1		Clermont	12	May
13.01	-1.0	Brittany	Anderson	JAM-Y	31.1.01	2	WJ	Tampere	15	Jul
13.02	1.4	Brianna	Beahan	AUS	1.11.91	2		Perth	13	Jan
13.02	1.1	Tiffani	McReynolds	USA	4.12.91	1		Waco	21	Apr
		(70)								
13.02	1.7	Jessica	Duckett	USA	22.1.97	1		Cincinnati	13	May
13.02	1.2	Brittley	Humphrey	USA	6.3.98	5	SEC	Knoxville	13	May
13.03	1.7	Génesis	Romero	VEN	6.11.95	2		Guadalajara, ESP	5	Jul
13.03	0.6	Veronika	Chervinskaya	RUS	24.8.98	1		Chelyabinsk	27	Jul
13.04	1.8	Raven	Clay	USA	5.10.90	1		Gainesville	13	Apr
13.04	1.3	Laura	Valette	FRA	16.2.97	2		Sotteville-lès-Rouen	17	Jul
13.05	0.3	Michelle	Atherley	USA	9.12.95	1H		Coral Gables	10	May
13.05	0.6	Shimayra	Williams	JAM	2.12.95	5		Kingston	24	Jun
13.05	1.7	Vanessa	Clerveaux	HAI	17.6.94	1s2	CAG	Barranquilla	30	Jul
13.06	0.1	Beate	Schrott	AUT	15.4.88	2h3	EC	Berlin	8	Aug
		(80)								
13.07	0.4	Emma	Spagnola	USA	18.3.96	1h6	NCAA-W	Sacramento	25	May
13.07	1.7	MacKenzie	Hill	USA	5.1.86	4h1		Chula Vista	9	Jun

Mark	Wind	Name		Nat	Born	Pos	Meet	Venue	Date
13.07	1.4	Fanny	Quénot	FRA	2.10.90	1		Castres	25 Jul
13.08	0.9		Wu Shuijiao ¶	CHN	19.6.91	9	DL	Shanghai	12 May
13.09	2.0	Tara	Davis	USA-J	20.5.99	6s1	NCAA	Eugene	7 Jun
13.09	0.9	Amoi	Brown	JAM-J	11.1.99	1		Kingston	23 Jun
13.10	1.9	Dara	Perry	USA	29.8.97	1		Buffalo	12 May
13.10	1.3	Caitlyn	Little	USA-J	1.2.99	2h1	SEC	Knoxville	12 May
13.10	1.0	Jasmyne	Graham	USA	6.5.97	1		Clovis	12 May
13.11	0.7	Ivana	Loncarek	CRO	8.4.91	1		Slovenska Bistrica	26 May
	((0)								
13.11	0.6		Jung Hye-lim	KOR	1.7.87	1		Tottori	3 Jun
13.11	0.0	Awa	Sène	FRA	24.7.94	1		Pontoise	22 Jun
13.11	0.7	Reetta	Hurske	FIN	15.5.95	3r2		Joensuu	4 Jul
13.12	0.7	Amber	Hughes	USA	23.8.94	2h1		Clermont	12 May
13.12	-0.5	Tiara	McMinn	USA-J	23.2.99	4	NC-j	Bloomington	16 Jun
13.13	1.3	Anamaria	Nesteriuc	ROU	29.11.93	2		Haniá	19 May
13.13	-0.1	Carolin	Schäfer	GER	5.12.91	2H3		Ratingen	16 Jun
13.13	1.5	Ayako	Kimura	JPN	11.6.88	1s1	NC	Yamaguchi	23 Jun
13.13	1.7	Hanna	Plotitsyna	UKR	1.1.87	1		Padova	2 Sep
13.14	0.6	Daeshon	Gordon	JAM	8.11.96	1		San Antonio	6 May
	(100)								
13.14	2.0	Annimari	Korte	FIN	8.4.88	1		Valencia	30 Jun
13.14	?	Cindy	Billaud	FRA	11.3.86	1h1	NC	Albi	6 Jul

Mark	Wind	Name		Nat	Born	Date		Mark	Wind	Name		Nat	Born	Date
13.15	1.7	Kyra	Atkins	USA	1.9.92	7 Jun		13.25	1.7	Rayane	Santos	BRA	9.1.96	14 Jul
13.15	1.8	Lotta	Harala	FIN	26.3.92	28 Jun		13.26	0.3	Ciara	Leonard	USA	7.12.97	25 May
13.15	0.6	Anne	Zagré	BEL	13.3.90	8 Jul		13.26	0.7	Kristina	Churylo	BLR	26.10.91	11 Jul
13.16	1.9	Selina	Von Jackowski	SUI	10.12.97	12 May		13.26	0.2	Cindy	Ofili	GBR	5.8.94	22 Jul
13.16	-0.2	Savannah	Roberson	USA	15.1.96	13 May		13.27	1.7	Milan	Young	USA-J	22.6.99	21 Apr
13.16	1.7	Grace	Stark	USA-Y	6.5.01	2 Jun		13.27	1.6	Chanice	Taylor-Chase	CAN	6.8.93	28 Apr
13.16	0.0	Coralie	Comte	FRA	15.10.95	22 Jun		13.27	1.7	Jenea	McCammon	GUY	9.6.91	30 Jul
13.16	1.7	Elin	Westerlund	SWE	4.2.90	28 Jun		13.28	0.2	Ariel	Jones	USA	18.7.95	13 May
13.17	0.4	Megan	Simmonds	JAM	18.3.94	12 Apr		13.28	-0.9	Dominique	Turner	USA	9.10.97	25 May
13.17	0.9	Chantel	Ray	USA	3.1.96	13 May		13.28	1.4	Michelle	Harrison	CAN	6.12.92	23 Jun
13.17	1.7	Hitomi	Shimura	JPN	8.11.90	23 Jun		13.28	1.4	Klaudia	Sorok	HUN	21.2.98	29 Jun
13.17	1.1	Masumi	Aoki	JPN	16.4.94	24 Jun		13.28	0.3	Nina	Morozova	RUS	15.9.89	11 Jul
13.17	-0.2		Wu Yanni	CHN	28.7.97	16 Sep		13.28	0.5	Sevval	Ayaz	TUR-J	25.9.00	14 Jul
13.18	1.5	Camri	Austin	USA	22.9.98	26 May		13.28	1.7	Eliecit	Palacios	COL	15.8.87	30 Jul
13.19	1.1	Kierre	Beckles	BAR	21.5.90	24 Mar		13.28	1.7	Nicole	Setterington	CAN	18.4.9	54 Aug
13.19	0.4	Alicia	Barrett	GBR	21.5.98	12 Apr		13.29A	-0.4		Chen Jiamin	CHN	1.5.96	17 Jun
13.19	0.6	Celeste	Mucci	AUS-J	11.8.99	12 Apr		13.30	0.3	Chisato	Kiyoyama	JPN	24.7.91	14 Apr
13.19	1.7	Madeleine	Akobundu	USA	24.4.98	14 Apr		13.30	1.0	Angelika	Wegierska	ITA	12.4.94	23 May
13.19	0.0	Esther	Turpin	FRA	29.4.96	20 May		13.30	1.0	Lucie	Koudelová	CZE	6.7.9	44 Jun
13.19	-0.2	Sarah	Missinne	BEL	16.5.95	2 Jun		13.30	0.0	Anastasiya	Nikolayeva	RUS	24.9.95	30 Jun
13.19	1.4	Christie	Moerman	CAN	5.10.86	23 Jun		13.31	0.2	Alexis	Woodley	USA	6.5.98	28 Apr
13.19	0.0	Caridad	Jerez	ESP	23.1.91	8 Aug		13.31	0.8	Chinyere	Njoku	USA	24.2.97	12 May
13.20A	2.0	Alyssa	Monteverde-Dalton	USA	15.1.93	28 Apr		13.31	1.7	Mako	Fukube	JPN	28.10.9	53 Jun
13.20	1.0	Gabriele	Cunningham	USA	22.2.98	28 Apr		13.31	1.7	Keira	Christie-Galloway	CAN-J	3.12.99	14 Jun
13.20	-0.6	Monique	Morgan	JAM	14.10.85	20 May		13.31A	-0.4		Wang Dou	CHN	18.5.93	17 Jun
13.20	0.8	Kaila	Barber	USA	4.4.93	14 Jun		13.31	1.0	Julia	Rzadzinska	POL	30.5.92	28 Jun
13.21	1.8	Brandeé	Johnson	USA	3.4.98	13 Apr		13.31	1.4	Farah	Jacques	CAN	8.2.90	25 Jul
13.21	1.2	Tyra	Gittens	TTO	6.6.98	11 May		13.31	1.6	Grit	Sadeiko	EST	29.7.89	15 Sep
13.21	1.0	Destinee	Rocker	USA-J	10.9.99	12 May		13.31A	-1.4	Micaela	de Mello	BRA-J	7.3.00	29 Sep
13.21	1.7	Elisa Maria	Di Lazzaro	ITA	5.6.98	5 Jul		13.32	0.4	Elisa	Girard-Mondoloni	FRA	13.6.95	22 Jun
13.21	0.9	Yekaterina	Galitskaya	RUS	24.2.87	19 Jul		13.32	-0.1	Megan	Marrs	GBR	25.9.97	26 Jun
13.21	1.4	Rosvitha	Okou	CIV	5.9.86	25 Jul		13.32	1.8	Edith	Doekoe	FRA	16.9.92	6 Jul
13.22	0.7	Megan	Tapper	JAM		24 Jun		13.33	1.1	Hope	Bender	USA	2.1.97	25 May
13.23	1.7	Breana	Norman	USA	14.9.92	14 Apr		13.33	-0.6	Danielle	Kohlwey	USA	3.8.97	25 May
13.23	1.0	Janelle	Perry	USA	29.8.97	28 Apr		13.33	-1.3	Yasmin	Miller	GBR	24.5.95	26 May
13.23	2.0	Jocselyn	Powell	USA	24.10.95	12 May		13.33	1.7	Kendra	Leger	CAN-J	12.2.99	14 Jun
13.23	1.5	Alex	Gochenour	USA	17.2.93	26 May		13.33	0.3	Nataliya	Ruchkivska	UKR	28.5.96	17 Jun
13.23	1.7	Katerina	Cachová	CZE	26.2.90	15 Sep		13.33	0.9	Jessica	Hunter	GBR	4.12.96	17 Jun
13.24	1.0	Milan	Parks	USA	5.11.96	28 Apr		13.33	1.6	Alia	Armstrong	USA-J	28.12.00	18 Jul
13.24	1.6	Cha'mia	Rothwell	USA	18.4.98	6 May		13.33	0.2	Emilia	Nova	INA	20.8.95	26 Aug
13.24	0.6	Jerica	Love	USA	24.9.97	6 May		13.34	-0.4	Joni Tomicic	Prezelj	SLO	25.8.93	20 Jun
13.24	1.7	Kaylah	Robinson	USA-J	27.6.99	13 May		13.34	0.4	Nicla	Mosetti	ITA	24.8.97	14 Jul
13.24	1.3	Jada	Hicks	USA-J	9.2.0	01 Jun		13.34	-1.0	Sacha	Alessandrini	FRA-J	7.6.99	15 Jul
13.24	1.5	Briggite	Merlano	COL	29.4.82	31 Jul		13.34	0.0	Hanna	Chubkovtsova	UKR	20.4.94	18 Jul
13.25	-0.8	Marthe Yasmine	Koala	BUR	8.3.9	48 Jul		13.34	-0.3	Ayumi	Kobayashi	JPN-Y	25.3.01	2 Aug
13.25	1.7	Shermaine	Williams	JAM	4.2.90	13 Jun		13.34	0.4	Katarina	Johnson-Thompson	GBR	9.1.93	9 Aug
									(194)					

Hand timing

13.1	0.0	Adriana	Rodríguez	CUB-J	12.7.99	1h1	Fortún	Camagüey	16 Feb

Wind assisted

12.37	2.5		K Harrison			1	DrakeR	Des Moines	28 Apr
12.40	3.1		K Harrison			1		Knoxville	14 Apr
12.53	2.6		Camacho-Quinn			1		Fayetteville	27 Apr
12.61	2.5	Tobi	Amusan	NGR	23.4.97	2	DrakeR	Des Moines	28 Apr
12.64	3.3	Rushelle	Burton	JAM	4.12.97	1	TexasR	Austin	31 Mar

WOMEN 2018

Mark		Name		Nat	Born	Pos	Meet	Venue	Date
12.67	2.7	Sally	Pearson	AUS	19.9.86	1		Brisbane (N)	4 Feb
12.70	2.2	Rikenette	Steenkamp	RSA	16.10.92	1h1		La Chaux-de-Fonds	1 Jul
12.73	3.3	Tonea	Marshall	USA	17.12.98	2	TexasR	Austin	31 Mar
12.73	2.6	Janeek	Brown	JAM	14.5.95	2		Fayetteville	27 Apr
12.74	2.5	Jeanine	Williams	JAM	28.1.97	1h5	NCAA-E	Tampa	25 May
12.74	2.3	Klaudia	Siciarz	POL	15.3.98	1		Lublin	22 Jul
12.75	2.8	Andrea Carolina	Vargas	CRC	20.5.90	1s1	CAG	Barranquilla	30 Jul
12.79	2.4	Anna	Cockrell	USA	28.8.97	1h1		Stanford	12 May
12.81	2.4	Tiffani	McReynolds	USA	4.12.91	2h2	PTS	Samorín	29 Jun
12.82	2.6	Taliyah	Brooks	USA	8.2.95	4		Fayetteville	27 Apr
12.90	4.0	Karolina	Koleczek	POL	15.1.93	1		Radom	27 May
12.91	2.3	Kayla	White	USA	24.9.96	1		Greensboro	5 May
12.92	2.9	Raven	Clay	USA	5.10.90	1h1		Gainesville	13 Apr
12.96	3.5	Savannah	Roberson	USA	15.1.96	2		Louisville	14 Apr
12.97	3.0	Emma	Spagnola	USA	18.3.96	1		Louisville	28 Apr
13.04	3.2	Tara	Davis	USA-J	20.5.99	1	TexasR	Austin	31 Mar
13.04	2.5	Daeshon	Gordon	JAM	20.8.96	2h5	NCAA-E	Tampa	25 May
13.04	2.1	Awa	Sène	FRA	24.7.94	1	NC	Albi	7 Jul
13.07	2.4	Reetta	Hurske	FIN	15.5.95	3r2		Kuortane	23 Jun
13.09	2.1	Tiara	McMinn	USA-J	23.2.99	1h6	NCAA-E	Tampa	25 May
13.11	3.1	Chantel	Ray	USA	14.1.96	5		Knoxville	14 Apr

Mark		Name		Nat	Born	Date
13.13	2.3	Madeleine	Akobundu	USA	22.4.98	5 May
13.13	2.7	Ciara	Leonard	USA	7.12.97	12 May
13.13	2.5	Ayumi	Kobayashi	JPN-J	25.3.01	8 Oct
13.14	3.5	Jasmine	Barge	USA	2.1.97	14 Apr
13.14	3.6	Chisato	Kiyoyama	JPN	24.7.91	29 Apr
13.15	3.6	Jocselyn	Powell	USA	24.10.95	7 Apr
13.15	4.9	Mako	Fukube	JPN	28.10.95	19 May
13.15	2.8	Sacha	Alessandrini	FRA-J	7.6.99	23 Jun
13.16	3.6	Hitomi	Shimura	JPN	8.11.90	29 Apr
13.17	4.8	Hikari	Tanaka	JPN	29.6.98	25 May
13.17	2.1	Brandeé	Johnson	USA	3.4.98	25 May
13.17	2.5	Jabreuna	Brimlett	USA	14.7.97	25 May
13.17	2.5	Summer	Thorpe	USA	20.6.98	25 May
13.18	3.3	Mariam	Abdul-Rashid	USA	21.9.97	31 Mar
13.18	3.1	Domonique	Turner	USA	9.10.97	14 Apr
13.20	4.8	Yuri	Okubo	JPN	4.3.97	25 May
13.20	2.1	Rosvitha	Okou	CIV	5.9.86	7 Jul

Mark		Name		Nat	Born	Date
13.20	2.8	Briggite	Merlano	COL	29.4.82	30 Jul
13.21	2.3	Kaylah	Robinson	USA-J	27.6.99	12 May
13.23	3.5	Morgan	Lewis	USA-J	25.7.99	11 May
13.23	4.0	Megan	Marrs	GBR	25.9.97	27 May
13.23	2.5	Hanna	Chubkovtsova	UKR	20.4.94	18 Jul
13.25	3.6	Nina	Morozova	RUS	3.4.89	11 Jul
13.26	3.3	Milan	Young	USA-J	22.6.99	31 Mar
13.26	2.2	Nicla	Mosetti	ITA	24.8.97	9 Jun
13.26	2.7	Klaudia	Sorok	HUN	21.2.98	29 Jun
13.27	2.3	Jessica	Lee	USA		14 Apr
13.27	2.7	Karel Elodie	Ziketh	CIV	23.9.91	20 Apr
13.27	2.7	Anastasiya	Nikolayeva	RUS	24.9.95	11 Jul
13.28	2.4	Brittney	Trought	GBR	15.10.96	12 May
13.30	4.9	Jessica	Hunter	GBR	4.12.96	29 Jul
13.30	2.9	Sayaka	Kobayashi	JPN	17.5.96	26 Aug
13.31	3.3	Stanislava	Lajčáková	SVK	20.4.96	7 Jul
13.31	2.5	Manaka	Shibata	JPN-Y	2.3.01	8 Oct

JUNIORS

See main list for top 8 juniors. 12 performances (+1 wa) by 4 women to 13.03. Additional marks and further juniors:

Brissett 12.86 1.5 2q1 NCAA-W Sacramento 26 May 12.95 -0.5 3 NC-j Bloomington 16 Jun
12.94 1.9 1rB MSR Torrance 21 Apr 13.02 1.4 4s2 NCAA Eugene 7 Jun
C Jones 12.91 -0.5 2 NC-j Bloomington 16 Jun 12.93w 2.7 2 Coral Gables 13 May
T Jones 13.01 -1.0 1 WJ Tampere 15 Jul 13.03 1.8 1 Powder Springs 28 Apr

Mark		Name		Nat	Born	Pos	Meet	Venue	Date
13.16	1.7	Grace	Stark	USA-Y	6.5.01	1		Kentwood	2 Jun
13.19	0.6	Celeste	Mucci	AUS-J	11.8.99	1H2	CG	Gold Coast	12 Apr
13.21	1.0	Destinee	Rocker	USA-J	10.9.99	2		Clovis	12 May
13.24	1.7	Kaylah	Robinson	USA-J	27.6.99	6	Pac-12	Stanford	13 May
13.24	1.3	Jada	Hicks	USA-J	9.2.00	1h1		Clovis	1 Jun
13.27	1.7	Milan	Young	USA-J	22.6.99	2r2		Baton Rouge	21 Apr
13.28	0.5	Sevval	Ayaz	TUR-J	25.9.00	2s3	WJ	Tampere	14 Jul
13.31	1.7	Keira	Christie-Galloway	CAN-J	3.12.99	2		Guelph	14 Jun
13.31A	-1.4	Micaela	de Mello	BRA-J	7.3.00	1	SAm-23	Cuenca	29 Sep
13.33	1.7	Kendra	Leger	CAN-J	12.2.99	3		Guelph	14 Jun
13.33	1.6	Alia	Armstrong	USA	28.12.00	1s1	N.Sch	Greensboro	18 Jul
13.34	-1.0	Sacha	Alessandrini (20)	FRA	7.6.99	4	WJ	Tampere	15 Jul
13.34	-0.3	Ayumi	Kobayashi	JPN-Y	25.3.01	1		Ise	2 Aug

Wind assiated see main list for top 2 juniors

Mark		Name		Nat	Born	Pos	Meet	Venue	Date
13.13	2.5	Ayumi	Kobayashi	JPN	25.3.01	1		Fukui	8 Oct
13.15	2.8	Sacha	Alessandrini	FRA	7.6.99	1		Blois	23 Jun
13.21	1.7	Kaylah	Robinson	USA	27.6.99	2		Stanford	12 May
13.23	3.5	Morgan	Lewis	USA	25.7.99	1h1		Clovis	11 May
13.26	3.3	Milan	Young	USA-J	22.6.99	7	TexasR	Austin	31 Mar
13.31	2.5	Manaka	Shibata	JPN-Y	2.3.01	2		Fukui	8 Oct

200 METRES HURDLES

Mark		Name		Nat	Born	Pos	Venue	Date
25.20	-1.0	Dalilah	Muhammad	USA	7.2.90	1	Northridge	10 Mar
25.93	-0.8	Ayomide	Folorunso	ITA	17.10.96	1	Milano	15 Sep
26.79	0.9	Olena	Yanovska	UKR	15.2.90	1	Vinnytsia	19 May
26.96	0.9	Mariya	Mykolenko	UKR	4.4.94	2	Vinnytsia	19 May

Straight: Boston 20 May: +0.6 1. Ebony Morrison USA 28.12.94 25.80; 2. Shamier Little USA 20.3.95 25.90, 3. Cassandra Tate USA 11.9.90 26.15; 4. Rhonda Whyte JAM 6.11.90 26.19, 5. Kierre Beckles BAR 21.5.90 26.78

Mark	Name		Nat	Born	Pos	Meet	Venue	Date	

300 METRES HURDLES

Mark	Name		Nat	Born	Pos	Meet	Venue	Date	
38.97	Line	Kloster	NOR	27.2.90	1		Lillestrøm	27	May
39.03	Ayomide	Folorunso	ITA	17.10.96	1		La Spezia	21	Apr
39.28	Robine	Schürmann	SUI	31.1.89	1		Zöfingen	19	May
39.35	Amalie Hammild	Juel	NOR	17.4.94	2		Lillestrøm	27	May
39.82	Léa	Sprunger	SUI	5.3.90	1		Langenthal	10	May

400 METRES HURDLES

Mark	Name		Nat	Born	Pos	Meet	Venue	Date	
52.75	Sydney	McLaughlin	USA-J	7.8.99	1	SEC	Knoxville	13	May
53.32	Shamier	Little	USA	20.3.95	1	NACAC	Toronto	12	Aug
53.41		Little			1	Athl	Lausanne	5	Jul
53.46	Janieve	Russell	JAM	14.11.93	2	Athl	Lausanne	5	Jul
53.60		McLaughlin			1		Fayetteville	27	Apr
53.61		Little			1	NC	Des Moines	24	Jun
53.62		Russell			1	C.Cup	Ostrava	9	Sep
53.63		Russell			1	Spitzen	Luzern	9	Jul
53.65	Dalilah	Muhammad	USA	7.2.90	1	Bisl	Oslo	7	Jun
53.77		Muhammad			1	DL	Shanghai	12	May
53.78		Russell			2	DL	Shanghai	12	May
53.79		Muhammad			2	Spitzen	Luzern	9	Jul
53.81		Russell			2	NACAC	Toronto	12	Aug
53.86		Little			2	C.Cup	Ostrava	9	Sep
53.88		Muhammad			1	WK	Zürich	30	Aug
53.90	Georganne	Moline	USA	6.3.90	3	Athl	Lausanne	5	Jul
53.94		Little			2	Bisl	Oslo	7	Jun
53.95		Little			1	DL	London (OS)	21	Jul
53.96		McLaughlin			1	NCAA	Eugene	9	Jun
53.96		Russell			2	DL	London (OS)	21	Jul
53.97		Moline			1	GGala	Roma	31	May
54.01		Russell			1h2	CG	Gold Coast	10	Apr
54.04		Moline			1	Odlozil	Praha	4	Jun
54.06		Russell			1	Pre	Eugene	26	May
54.08		Russell			2	GGala	Roma	31	May
54.09		Muhammad			2	Pre	Eugene	26	May
54.12		Moline			2	NC	Des Moines	24	Jun
54.15		McLaughlin			1s3	NCAA	Eugene	7	Jun
54.16		Russell			1	Gyulai	Székesfehérvár	2	Jul
54.18		Russell			1		Kingston	22	Jun
	(30/5)								
54.33	Léa	Sprunger	SUI	5.3.90	1	EC	Berlin	10	Aug
54.47	Anna	Ryzhykova	UKR	24.11.89	3	C.Cup	Ostrava	9	Sep
54.48	Kemi	Adekoya	BRN	16.1.93	1	AsiG	Jakarta	27	Aug
54.55	Sage	Watson	CAN	20.6.94	3	Bisl	Oslo	7	Jun
54.61	Wenda	Nel	RSA	30.7.88	2h2	CG	Gold Coast	10	Apr
	(10)								
54.66	Ashley	Spencer	USA	8.6.93	3	Spitzen	Luzern	9	Jul
54.67	Leah	Nugent	JAM	23.11.92	1		Kingston	9	Jun
54.80	Eilidh	Doyle	GBR	20.2.87	1h1	CG	Gold Coast	10	Apr
54.90	Rhonda	Whyte	JAM	6.11.90	3		Kingston	22	Jun
54.94	Cassandra	Tate	USA	11.9.90	2	Odlozil	Praha	4	Jun
54.98	Yadisleidy	Pedroso	ITA	28.1.87	1		Genève	9	Jun
55.01	Glory	Nathaniel Onome	NGR	23.1.96	3h2	CG	Gold Coast	10	Apr
55.05A	Zeney	van der Walt	RSA-J	22.5.00	2	NC	Pretoria	17	Mar
55.08	Rushell	Clayton	JAM	18.10.92	4		Kingston	22	Jun
55.11	Zudikey	Rodríguez	MEX	14.3.87	2	CAG	Barranquilla	31	Jul
	(20)								
55.13	Zurian	Hechavarría	CUB	10.8.95	3	CAG	Barranquilla	31	Jul
55.15	Sparkle	McKnight	TTO	21.12.91	2h1	CG	Gold Coast	10	Apr
55.16	Ayomide	Folorunso	ITA	17.10.96	4	GGala	Roma	31	May
55.16	Zuzana	Hejnová	CZE	19.12.86	5	Bisl	Oslo	7	Jun
55.20	Hanne	Claes	BEL	4.8.91	1	NC	Bruxelles	8	Jul
55.21	Meghan	Beesley	GBR	15.11.89	3s3	EC	Berlin	8	Aug
55.23	Irina	Kolesnichenko	RUS	27.5.88	1	Znam	Zhukovskiy	1	Jul
55.24	Vera	Rudakova	RUS	20.3.92	4s3	EC	Berlin	8	Aug
55.26	Amalie Hammild	Iuel	NOR	17.4.94	6	Bisl	Oslo	7	Jun
55.28	Viktoriya	Tkachuk	UKR	8.11.94	1		Szczecin	15	Aug
	(30)								
55.30		Quach Thi Lan	VIE	18.10.95	2	AsiG	Jakarta	27	Aug
55.38	Ristananna	Tracey	JAM	9.5.92	2		George Town	2	Jun

WOMEN 2018

Mark	Name		Nat	Born	Pos	Meet	Venue	Date	
55.41	Nikita	Tracey	JAM	18.9.90	3h1		Kingston	21	Jun
55.48	Sara Slott	Petersen	DEN	9.4.87	1		København	26	Jun
55.49	Line	Kloster	NOR	27.2.90	1		La Chaux-de-Fonds	1	Jul
55.53	Robine	Schürmann	SUI	31.1.89	1		Basel	21	May
55.54	Aminat	Odeyemi	BRN	27.6.97	2		Goleniów	20	Jun
55.54	Kymber	Payne	USA	4.6.96	4	NC	Des Moines	24	Jun
55.60	Gianna	Woodruff	PAN	18.11.93	6	CAG	Barranquilla	31	Jul
55.69	Katrina	Seymour	BAH	7.1.93	5h1	CG	Gold Coast	10	Apr
	(40)								
55.71	Anna	Cockrell	USA	28.8.97	2	NCAA	Eugene	9	Jun
55.73	Lauren	Wells	AUS	3.8.88	5h2	CG	Gold Coast	10	Apr
55.74	Yanique	Haye-Smith	JAM	22.3.90	3		George Town	2	Jun
55.78	Shiann	Salmon	JAM-J	31.3.99	1		Kingston	23	Mar
55.84	Joanna	Linkiewicz	POL	2.5.90	5	DL	Shanghai	12	May
55.88	Fiorella	Chiappe	ARG	1.1.96	2	BEL Ch	Bruxelles	8	Jul
55.95	Margo	Van Puyvelde	BEL	21.12.95	1		Heusden-Zolder	21	Jul
56.04	Valeriya	Khramova	RUS	13.8.92	2	NC	Kazan	20	Jul
56.06	Ranae	McKenzie	JAM	28.10.96	1		Waco	13	May
56.14	Melissa	González	COL	24.6.94	3		Baton Rouge	28	Apr
	(50)								
56.16	Symone	Black	USA	26.10.95	1		Bloomington	13	May
56.19	Aurélie	Chaboudez	FRA	9.5.93	6s2	EC	Berlin	8	Aug
56.22	Janeil	Bellille	TTO	18.6.89	4		Leonora	30	Jun
56.23	Noelle	Montcalm	CAN	3.4.88	4		Baton Rouge	28	Apr
56.23	Kiah	Seymour	USA	11.1.94	3h1	NC	Des Moines	23	Jun
56.25	Mariya	Mykolenko	UKR	4.4.94	2	NC	Lutsk	21	Jul
56.30	Grace	Claxton	PUR	19.8.93	1rB	FlaR	Gainesville	29	Mar
56.31	Justien	Grillet	BEL	18.7.94	4	NC	Bruxelles	8	Jul
56.34	Kelsey	Balkwill	CAN	19.9.92	1rD		Ninove	28	Jul
56.48	Kirsten	McAslan	GBR	1.9.93	2	NC	Birmingham	1	Jul
	(60)								
56.51	Emma	Spagnola	USA	18.3.96	1q1	NCAA-W	Sacramento	25	May
56.52	Justyna	Saganiak	POL	1.12.95	2	NC	Lublin	21	Jul
56.53	Jessica	Turner	GBR	8.8.95	1		Tarare	23	Jun
56.54	Djamila	Böhm	GER	15.7.94	1		Rhede	16	Jun
56.55	Tia Adana	Belle	BAR	16.6.96	7h1	CG	Gold Coast	10	Apr
56.56	Danielle	Dowie	JAM	5.5.92	5h1		Kingston	21	Jun
56.59	Daniela	Roman	AUS	7.1.96	2	NC	Gold Coast	18	Feb
56.64	Deonca	Bookman	USA	29.10.95	4h2	NC	Des Moines	23	Jun
56.66	Kaila	Barber	USA	4.4.93	5h2	NC	Des Moines	23	Jun
56.66	Lamiae	Lhabze	MAR	19.5.84	2	AfrC	Asaba	5	Aug
	(70)								
56.68	Sanda	Belgyan	ROU	17.12.92	2h2	EC	Berlin	7	Aug
56.69	Xahria	Santiago	CAN-J	9.10.99	2		Bloomington	13	May
56.70	Emilia	Ankiewicz	POL	22.11.90	1rB		Rovereto	23	Aug
56.74	Abasiono	Akpan	NGR-J	15.12.00	1		Asaba	18	Jul
56.77	Samantha	Gonzalez	USA	14.11.96	1		Coral Gables	12	May
56.77	Anu	Raghavan	IND	20.4.93	3h2	AsiG	Jakarta	26	Aug
56.81	Yasmin	Giger	SUI-J	6.11.99	6s3	EC	Berlin	8	Aug
56.84	Eri	Utsunomiya	JPN	11.4.93	1		Osaka	6	May
56.84	Portia	Bing	NZL	17.4.93	2	NC	Albi	8	Jul
56.86	Agata	Zupin	SLO	17.3.98	5	Odlozil	Praha	4	Jun
	(80)								
56.87	Sarah	Carli	AUS	5.9.94	3	NC	Gold Coast	18	Feb
56.89	Ariel	Jones	USA	18.7.95	3s1	NCAA	Eugene	7	Jun
56.94	Andrenette	Knight	JAM	19.11.96	2q2	NCAA-E	Tampa	25	May
56.94	Olena	Kolesnychenko	UKR	3.6.93	4	NC	Lutsk	21	Jul
56.95	Christine	Salterberg	GER	9.6.94	2		Rhede	16	Jun
56.95	Anaïs	Lufutucu	FRA	24.4.92	3	NC	Albi	8	Jul
56.99	Shannon	Kalawan	JAM	25.11.97	1rB	FlaR	Gainesville	29	Mar
56.99	Kaliese	Spencer	JAM	6.5.87	3		St. Georges	21	Apr
57.01	Brandeé	Johnson	USA	3.4.98	2q1	NCAA-E	Tampa	25	May
57.02	Jauna	Murmu	IND	16.8.90	1	I-State	Guwahati	26	Jun
	(90)								
57.04	Anna Sjoukje	Runia	NED	19.2.95	3q1	NCAA-E	Tampa	25	May
57.04	Saritaben	Gayakwad	IND	1.6.94	1		Jablonec	15	Aug
57.10	Natalia	Wosztyl	POL-J	28.8.99	3	NC	Lublin	21	Jul
57.11	Markeeta	Thomas	USA	29.7.97	3q2	NCAA-E	Tampa	25	May
57.11	Sara	Gallego	ESP-J	21.10.00	4	WJ	Tampere	13	Jul
57.18	Brenna	Porter	USA	.94	1q2	NCAA-W	Sacramento	25	May
57.19	Sanique	Walker	JAM-J	8.4.00	1		Kingston	4	Mar

Mark	Name		Nat	Born	Pos	Meet	Venue	Date	
57.19	Lina	Nielsen	GBR	13.3.96	3	LEAP	Loughborough	25	Jul
57.21	Nicole	Stephens	USA	14.10.98	4q2	NCAA-E	Tampa	25	May
57.22	Yelizaveta	Anikiyenko	RUS	30.6.94	2		Zhukovskiy	23	Jun
	(100)								
57.22	Linda	Olivieri	ITA	14.7.98	3		La Chaux-de-Fonds	1	Jul
57.22	Emma	Zapletalová	SVK-J	24.3.00	1s3	WJ	Tampere	12	Jul

Mark	Name		Nat	Born	Pos	Meet	Date		Mark	Name		Nat	Born		Date	
57.23	Lakeisha	Warner	IVB	15.9.97			12	May	57.63	Anju	Rani	IND	25.9.92		28	Sep
57.25	Aisha	Naibe-Wey	SLE	3.8.93			15	Jun	57.65	Masai	Russell	USA-J	17.6.00		16	Jun
57.26	Viivi	Lehikoinen	FIN-J	27.8.99			22	Jul	57.67	Ariel	Terrell	USA	4.5.96		13	May
57.27	Maureen	Maiyo	KEN	28.5.85			5	Aug	57.71	Rachel	Schow	USA	3.5.97		13	May
57.28	Jocselyn	Powell	USA	24.10.95			29	Mar	57.71	Hayley	McLean	GBR	9.9.94		1	Jul
57.29		Huang Yan	CHN	12.1.96			17	May	57.72	Kaitlin	Walker	USA	24.10.95		28	Apr
57.30	Shamaria	Lovett	USA	3.12.96			25	May	57.74	María	Matos	DOM-J	20.4.99		12	Jul
57.30	Jessica	Duckett	USA	22.1.97			25	Aug	57.74	Valeria	Cabezas	COL-Y	16.10.01		25	Aug
57.30	Irina	Takuntseva	RUS	14.11.90			1	Jul	57.77	Vanessa	Watson	USA-Y	28.10.01		16	Jun
57.30	Valentina	Cavalleri	ITA	8.12.95			1	Jul	57.78	Candice	McLeod	JAM	15.11.96		26	Apr
57.31	Manami	Kira	JPN	23.10.91			20	May	57.78	Hilla	Uusimäki	FIN	12.6.96		22	Jul
57.32	Lauren	Thompson	GBR	12.2.92			10	Jun	57.80	Kana	Koyama	JPN	16.12.98		6	May
57.36	Faith	Ross	USA	7.3.98			24	Jun	57.81	Gontse	Morake	RSA-Y	16.6.01		5	Apr
57.40	Mariam	Abdul-Rashid	CAN	21.9.97			29	Mar	57.81	De'Andreah	Young	USA	16.1.98		28	Apr
57.42	Brenna	Detra	USA	.96			25	May	57.81	Satsuki	Umehara	JPN	22.5.94		6	May
57.43	M.	Arpitha	IND	11.2.93			8	Mar	57.81	Daniela	Ledecká	SVK	4.11.96		7	Aug
57.43	Rebecca	Sartori	ITA	22.5.97			10	Jun	57.81	Nea	Mattila	FIN-J	24.11.99		1	Sep
57.44	Elif	Gören	TUR	11.2.90			6	May	57.82A	Amanda	Jaynes	USA	24.6.96		28	Apr
57.44	Aleksandra	Gaworska	POL	7.11.95			16	Jun	57.83	Sára	Mátó	HUN-J	23.12.00		12	Jul
57.48	Maeva	Contion	FRA	31.5.92			8	Jul	57.84	Jess	Gulli-Nance	AUS	19.3.88		18	Feb
57.50	Rita	Ossai	NGR	21.10.95			15	Feb	57.84	Yekaterina	Belanovich	BLR	14.1.91		21	Jul
57.51	Elisabeth	Slettum	NOR	31.8.86			18	Jul	57.86	Alissa	Brooks-Johnson	USA	1.8.95		31	Mar
57.48	Sarah	Wells	CAN	10.11.89			2	Jun	57.86		Mo Jiadie	CHN-J	6.1.00		16	Jun
57.53	Jurnee	Woodward	USA-J	21.11.99			16	Jun	57.88	Karolina	Pahlitzsch	GER	5.4.94		7	Apr
57.53	Axelle	Dauwens	BEL	1.12.90			28	Jul	57.88	Ilaria	Verderio	ITA	22.4.98		6	May
57.53	Daniela	Rojas	CRC	26.11.97			25	Aug	57.92	Hanna	Palmqvist	SWE	20.1.96		9	Jun
57.55	Johanna	Holmén Svensson	SWE	7.3.95			13	Jun	57.93	Medinah	Spencer	USA			24	May
57.55	Alessandra	Silva	BRA	2.7.91			16	Sep	57.95	Jasmine	Barge	USA	2.1.97		13	May
57.56	Birexus	Hawkins	USA	18.7.98			13	May	57.95	Nora	Ritzen	NED	3.7.93		2	Jun
57.55	Sayaka	Aoki	JPN	15.12.86			21	Jul	57.95	Britton	Wilson	USA-J	13.11.00		16	Jun
57.57	Brooke	Jaworski	USA-Y	16.1.01			12	Jul	57.95	Wanessa	Zavolski	BRA	6.3.89		16	Sep
57.60	Kiana	Hawn	USA	5.12.95			29	Mar	57.97	Lucie	Kudela	FRA	28.6.97		15	Jul
57.63	Kimona	Smikle	JAM				26	May	58.00	Farah	Clerc (168)	FRA	31.7.90		1	Jun

Best at low altitude: 55.34   Zeney   van der Walt   RSA-J   22.5.00   1   WJ   Tampere   13   Jul

JUNIORS

See main list for top 10 juniors. 11 performances by 3 women to 56.00. Additional marks and further juniors:

	Name		Nat	Born	Pos	Meet	Venue	Date	
McLaughlin	54.78		1h3	NCAA-E	Tampa			24	May	55.50	1q3	NCAA-E	Tampa		24	May

McLaughlin   54.78   1h3 NCAA-E Tampa   24 May   55.50   1q3 NCAA-E Tampa   24 May
  4+   54.85   1h1 SEC   Knoxville   12 May
van der Walt   55.34   1   WJ   Tampere   13 Jul   55.42   1   Celle Ligure   3 Jul

Mark	Name		Nat	Born	Pos	Meet	Venue	Date	
57.26	Viivi	Lehikoinen	FIN	27.8.99	1	NC	Jyväskylä	22	Jul
57.53	Jurnee	Woodward	USA	21.11.99	1	NC-j	Bloomington	16	Jun
57.57	Brooke	Jaworski	USA-Y	16.1.01	3s3	WJ	Tampere	12	Jul
57.65	Masai	Russell	USA	17.6.00	3	NC-j	Bloomington	16	Jun
57.74	María	Matos	DOM	20.4.99	4s1	WJ	Tampere	12	Jul
57.74	Valeria	Cabezas	COL-Y	16.10.01	3	IbAmC	Trujillo	25	Aug
57.77	Vanessa	Watson	USA-Y	28.10.01	4	NC-j	Bloomington	16	Jun
57.81	Gontse	Morake	RSA-Y	16.6.01	5		Apr		
57.81	Nea	Mattila	FIN	24.11.99	1	vSWE	Tampere	1	Sep
57.83	Sára	Mátó (230)	HUN	23.12.00	5s1	WJ	Tampere	12	Jul

HIGH JUMP

Mark	Name		Nat	Born	Pos	Meet	Venue	Date							
2.04i	Mariya	Lasitskene	RUS	14.1.93	1		Volgograd	27	Jan						
							1.85/1 1.91/2. 1.96/2 2.01/2 2.04/1 2.07/xxx									
2.04	1	DL	Paris (C)	30 Jun			1.85/1 1.90/1 1.94/1 1.97/1 2.00/2 2.04/1 2.08/xxx								
2.04	1	DL	London (OS)	22 Jul			1.87/1 1.91/1 1.95/1 2.00/2 2.02/2 2.04/1 2.08/xxx								
2.03	1	FBK	Hengelo	3 Jun			1.85/1 1.88/1 1.91/1 1.94/2 1.97/1 2.03/2 2.05/xxx								
2.02i	1		Banská Bystrica	6 Feb			1.84/1 1.88/1 1.91/3 1.94/2 1.97/3 2.02/2 2.06/xx								
2.02	1	GGala	Roma	31 May			1.84/1 1.88/1 1.91/2 1.94/1 1.97/1 2.01/2 2.04/xxx								
2.01i	1		Moskva	17 Jan			1.86/1 1.90/1 1.97/2 2.01/1 2.04/xxx								
2.01i	1	WI	Birmingham	1 Mar			1.84/1 1.89/1 1.93/1 1.96/1 2.01/2 2.07/xxx								
2.01	1		Zhukovskiy	23 Jun			1.85/1 1/91/1. 1.96/2 2.01/2 2.04/xxx								
2.00i	1		Madrid	8 Feb			1.85/1 1.90/1 1.95/2 2.00/2 2.07/xxx								
2.00i	1		Torun	15 Feb			1.85/1 1.90/1 1.93/1 1.95/1 2.00/1 2.05/xxx								
2.00	1	DL	Stockholm	10 Jun			1.85/1 1.90/1 1.94/1 1.97/2 2.00/1 2.02/xxx								
2.00	1	NC	Kazan	19 Jul			1.85/1 1.90/1 1.94/1 1.96/1 2.00/1 2,05/xxx								
2.00	1	EC	Berlin	10 Aug			1.87/1 1.91/1 1.94/1 1.96/1 1.98/1 2.00/2 2.04/xxx								
2.00	1	C.Cup	Ostrava	9 Sep			1.82/1 1.87/1 1.91/1 1.93/1 1.95/1 1.97/3 2.00/1 2.05/xxx								

Mark	Name			Nat	Born	Pos	Meet	Venue	Date
	2.00i	1	Minsk		22 Dec	1.84/1 1.90/1 1.92/1 1.94/1 1.96/x 1.98/1 2.00/2 2.07/xxx			
	1.99i	1	Moskva		21 Jan	1.85/2 1.90/1 1.95/1 1.99/1 2.02/xxx			
	1.97	1 DL	Shanghai		12 May	1.80/1 1.85/2 1.88/1 1.91/2 1.94/2 1.97/1 2.00/xxx			
	1.97	1	Göteborg		18 Aug	1.84/1 1.88/1 1.91/1 1.97/3 2.01/xxx			
	1.97	1 WK	Zürich		30 Aug	1.85/1 1.90/1 1.94/1 1.97/2 2.00/xxx			
2.02	Elena		Vallortigara	ITA	21.9.91	2	DL	London (QS)	?? Jul
					1.79/1 1.83/1 1.87/1 1.91/1 1.95/2 2.00/3 2.02/3 2.04/xx				
2.01	Nafissatou		Thiam	BEL	19.8.94	1H	Hypo	Götzis	26 May
					1.83/1 1.86/1 1.89/1 1.92/1 1/95/1 1.98/? 2.01/2				
	1.97	2 DL	Paris (C)		30 Jun	1.85/1 1.90/2 1.94/3 1.97/2 2.00/xxx			
2.00	Mirela		Demireva	BUL	28.9.89	2	DL	Stockholm	10 Jun
					1.85/3 1.90/1 1.94/2 2.00/3 2.02/xxx				
	2.00	2 EC	Berlin		10 Aug	1.87/1 1.91/1 1.94/2 2.00/3 2.04/xxx			
1.98	Anna		Chicherova	RUS	22.7.82	1		Moskva	30 Jul
					1.82/1 1.85/1 1.91/1 1.94/3 1.98/1 2.00/xxx				
1.98i	Kateryna		Tabashnyk	UKR	15.6.94	2		Minsk	22 Dec
					1.80/1 1.84/1 1.88/3 1.90/1 1.92/1 1.94/1 1.96/1 1.98/1 2.00/xxx				
1.98i	Yuliya		Levchenko	UKR	28.11.97	3		Minsk	22 Dec
					1.80/1 1.84/1 1.88/1 1.90/1 1.92/1 1.94/2 1.96/2 1.98/3 2.00/xxx				
	1.97i	1	Kyiv		10 Jan	1.80/1 1.83/1 1.86/1 1.89/1 1.92/1 1.94/1 1.97/3			
	1.97i	1	Cottbus		31 Jan	1.80/1 1.85/1 1.88/1 1.91/1 1.94/1 1.97/1 2.00/xxx			
	1.97	3 DL	Paris (C)		30 Jun	1.80/1 1.85/1 1.90/1 1.94/1 1.97/3 2.00/xxx			
1.97iA	Vashti		Cunningham	USA	18.1.98	1	NC	Albuquerque	18 Feb
					1.82/1 1.85/1 1.88/1 1.91/2 1.94/3 1.97/1 2.01/xx				
1.97	Morgan		Lake	GBR	12.5.97	1	NC	Birmingham	30 Jun
					1.79/2 1.83/1 1.87/2 1.90/3 1.93/1 1.97/2 2.00/xxx				
1.96	Levern		Spencer	LCA	23.6.84	1	Filothei	Athína (F)	13 Jun
	(33/10)								
1.96	Marie-Laurence	Jungfleisch	GER	7.10.90	1		Bühl	22 Jun
1.96	Airine	Palsyte	LTU	13.7.92	4	EC	Berlin	10 Aug
1.96	Svetlana	Radzivil	UZB	17.1.87	1	AsiG	Jakarta	29 Aug
1.96i	Yaroslava	Mahuchikh	UKR-Y	19.9.01	4		Minsk	22 Dec
1.94	Yuliya	Chumachenko	UKR	2.10.94	1		Mykolaiv	18 May
1.94	Erika	Kinsey	SWE	10.3.88	2		Zoetermeer	6 Jun
1.94	Oksana	Okuneva	UKR	14.3.90	3	NC	Lutsk	19 Jul
1.94	Nadezhda	Dusanova	UZB	17.11.87	2	AsiG	Jakarta	29 Aug
1.93i	Iryna	Herashchenko	UKR	10.3.95	1		Ostrava	25 Jan
1.93i	Michaela	Hrubá	CZE	21.2.98	2		Ostrava	25 Jan
	(20)								
1.93i	Katarina	Johnson-Thompson	GBR	9.1.93	1		Eaubonne	9 Feb
1.93i	Alessia	Trost	ITA	8.3.93	3	WI	Birmingham	1 Mar
1.93	Imke	Onnen	GER	17.8.94	1		Garbsen	13 May
1.93	Sofie	Skoog	SWE	7.6.90	1		Sollentuna	28 Jun
1.92i	Logan	Boss	USA	4.8.97	1		Cambridge MA	2 Feb
1.92i	Ana	Simic	CRO	5.5.90	1	BalkC	Istanbul	17 Feb
1.92	Bianca	Salming	SWE	22.11.98	1H		Pärnu	16 Jun
1.92	Inika	McPherson	USA	29.9.86	2	NC	Des Moines	23 Jun
1.92	Ella	Junnila	FIN	6.12.98	2		Joensuu	4 Jul
1.92	Karina	Taranda	BLR-J	10.2.99	1	WJ	Tampere	15 Jul
	(30)								
1.91Ai	Liz	Patterson	USA	9.6.88	1		Air Force Academy	27 Jan
1.91	Nicola	McDermott	AUS	28.12.96	3	CG	Gold Coast	14 Apr
1.91	Alyx	Treadore	CAN	15.5.92	4	CG	Gold Coast	14 Apr
1.91A	Ximena	Esquivel	MEX	22.8.97	1		Querétaro	29 Apr
1.91	Tonje	Angelsen	NOR	17.1.90	3		Sollentuna	28 Jun
1.91	Claire	Orcel	BEL	2.12.97	1	NC	Bruxelles	8 Jul
1.90i	Serena	Capponcelli	ITA	24.1.89	1		Gent	6 Jan
1.90i	Marija	Vukovic	MNE	21.1.92	2		Brno	7 Feb
1.90i	Nikki	Manson	GBR	15.10.94	1	Univ Ch	Glasgow	10 Feb
1.90		Wang Yang	CHN	14.2.89	1		Jakarta	14 Feb
	(40)								
1.90A	María Fernanda	Murillo	COL-J	21.1.99	1		Medellín	28 Apr
1.90	Lada	Pejchalová	CZE	15.11.98	1		Praha	19 May
1.90	Viktoria	Gottlieb	GER	14.3.95	1		Weinheim	26 May
1.90A	Desirée	Rossit	ITA	19.3.94	1		Ávila	10 Jul
1.90	Sommer	Lecky	IRL-J	14.6.00	2	WJ	Tampere	15 Jul
1.90	Tatyana	Odineva	RUS	25.5.83	3	NC	Kazan	19 Jul
1.90	Daniela	Stanciu	ROU	15.10.87	1	NC	Pitesti	26 Jul
1.89i	Zarriea	Willis	USA	14.11.96	1		Lubbock	10 Feb
1.89i	Maja	Nilsson	SWE-J	8.12.99	2	v3N	Uppsala	11 Feb
1.89iA	Erica	Bougard	USA	26.7.93	1P	NC	Albuquerque	16 Feb
	(50)								

Mark	Name		Nat	Born	Pos	Meet	Venue	Date
1.89	Jeannelle	Scheper	LCA	21.11.94	1		Athens, GA	5 May
1.89	Hanna	Gorodskaya	BLR	31.1.93	1		Brest	25 May
1.89	Niamh	Emerson	GBR-J	22.4.99	1H	WJ	Tampere	12 Jul
1.89	Tatyana	Yermachenkova	RUS	9.9.98	1		Chelyabinsk	28 Jul
1.88i	Nicole	Greene	USA	2.5.97	1		Chapel Hill	13 Jan
1.88i	Yevgeniya	Kononova	RUS	28.9.89	1		Moskva	4 Feb
1.88i	Doreen	Amata	NGR	6.5.88	2	GP	Boston (R)	10 Feb
1.88i	Chelsie	Decoud	USA	28.6.96	1		Birmingham AL	19 Feb
1.88i	Yorgelis	Rodríguez	CUB	25.1.95	2P	WI	Birmingham	2 Mar
1.88i		Hu Linpeng	CHN	29.12.95	1	NGP	Dalian	8 Mar
	(260)							
1.88	Eleanor	Patterson	AUS	22.5.96	2		Sydney	17 Mar
1.88	Tatiána	Goúsin	GRE	26.1.94	3	MSR	Torrance	21 Apr
1.88	Loretta	Blaut	USA	22.3.96	1		Cincinnati	13 May
1.88i		Lu Jiawen	CHN-Y	19.8.02	1		Jinzhou	17 May
1.88	Yekaterina	Stepanova	RUS	24.7.94	2	NCp	Smolensk	30 May
1.88	Natalya	Aksenova	RUS	6.6.97	1	NC-23	Chelyabinsk	7 Jul
1.88	Eleriin	Haas	EST	4.7.92	1	FIN Ch	Jyväskylä	22 Jul
1.88	Elina	Kakko	FIN	12.1.97	1	Nord-23	Gävle	11 Aug
1.87i	Marine	Vallet	FRA	9.9.93	1	NC	Liévin	17 Feb
1.87	Isis	Guerra	CUB-J	11.11.99	1	Fortún	Camagüey	14 Mar
	(70)							
1.87	Alysha	Burnett	AUS	4.1.97	2H	CG	Gold Coast	12 Apr
1.87	Priscilla	Frederick	ANT	14.2.89	5	CG	Gold Coast	14 Apr
1.87	Alexus	Henry	USA	14.12.96	1H		Azusa	18 Apr
1.87	Abigail	Kwarteng	GHA		1		Lubbock	5 May
1.87	Marusa	Cernjul	SLO	30.6.92	1		Ljubljana	27 Jun
1.87	Mariya	Kochanova	RUS-Y	30.5.02	5	WJ	Tampere	15 Jul
1.87	Urte	Baikstyte	LTU-J	8.5.99	6	WJ	Tampere	15 Jul
1.87	Jessica	Kähärä	FIN-Y	1.8.01	1	NC-y	Espoo	11 Aug
1.87		Pham Thi Diem	VIE	24.1.90	1		Hanoi	30 Nov
1.86i	Prisca	Duvernay	FRA	26.5.91	1		Nantes	20 Jan
	(80)							
1.86i	Amina	Smith	USA	10.1.92	1		New York (Arm)	27 Jan
1.86i	Erika	Furlani	ITA	2.1.96	1	NC-23	Ancona	4 Feb
1.86i	Liliya	Klintsova	UKR	12.7.97	5	NC	Sumy	10 Feb
1.86i	Maryia	Shulgina	BLR	14.8.89	2	NC	Mogilyov	17 Feb
1.86	Cassie	Purdon	AUS	24.10.96	1	NC	Gold Coast	18 Feb
1.86	Hannah	Joye	AUS	4.1.96	1		Brisbane	3 Mar
1.86	Susan	Jackson	USA	26.7.89	1	TexasR	Austin	31 Mar
1.86	Tynita	Butts	USA	10.6.90	1=		Tempe	7 Apr
1.86	Tyra	Gittens	TTO	6.6.98	1H	SEC	Knoxville	11 May
1.86	Margarita	Korneychuk	RUS	21.2.95	H	NCp	Adler	20 May
	(90)							
1.86	Taisya	Roslova	BLR	7.2.92	3		Brest	25 May
1.86	Saleta	Fernández	ESP	15.7.97	1		Los Corrales de Buelna	2 Jun
1.86	Kadriye	Aydin	TUR	2.7.95	1		Istanbul	10 Jun
1.86	Lovisa	Östervall	SWE	9.3.97	2H	v2N	Pärnu	16 Jun
1.86	Natalya	Spiridonova	RUS-Y	31.7.02	1	NC-y	Kaluga	16 Jun
1.86	Paulina	Borys	POL	14.5.98	1	NC-23	Sieradz	30 Jun
1.86	Iale	Eden	GER	25.3.98	2		Hamburg	7 Jul
1.86	Elina	Smolander	FIN	11.10.89	4	NC	Jyväskylä	22 Jul
1.86	Louise	Ekman	SWE	10.4.97	2	Nord-23	Gävle	11 Aug
1.86	Safina	Sadullayeva	UZB	4.3.98	1		Tashkent	29 Sep
	(100)							
1.86i	Solène	Gicquel	FRA	1.12.94	1		Mayenne	23 Dec
1.855	Katie	Isenbarger	USA-J	20.5.99	1		Indianapolis	3 May

Mark	Name		Nat	Born		Mark	Name		Nat	Born	
1.85i	Madeline	Fagan	USA	4.6.96	20 Jan	1.85A	Andrea	Stapleton-Johnson	USA	.96	28 Apr
1.85i	Jordan	Fields	USA	30.7.98	20 Jan	1.85	Sofiya	Voronina	RUS	22.10.97	30 May
1.85iA	Shelley	Spires	USA	19.3.96	27 Jan	1.85	Katarina	Mögenburg	NOR	16.6.91	9 Jun
1.85iA	Petra	Luterán	HUN	15.6.97	27 Jan	1.85	Jossie	Graumann	GER	18.3.94	9 Jun
1.85i	Kimberly	Williamson	JAM	2.10.93	3 Feb	1.85	Teresa Maria	Rossi	ITA	12.4.92	10 Jun
1.85i	Alina	Shukh	UKR-J	12.2.99	9 Feb	1.85	Shelby	Tyler	USA-Y	28.3.01	16 Jun
1.85i	Rimma	Hordiyenko	UKR	30.12.95	9 Feb	1.85	Sanaa	Barnes	USA-J	10.8.00	16 Jun
1.85i	Stacey	Destin	USA	7.11.96	10 Feb	1.85	Alisa	Presnyakova	RUS	7.3.98	7 Jul
1.85i	Aleksandra	Nowakowska	POL	23.4.98	15 Feb	1.85	Moe	Sasegbon	NGR	16.9.91	8 Jul
1.85i	Quamecha	Morrison	USA	22.11.96	17 Feb	1.85	Nadezhda	Dubovitskaya	KAZ	12.3.98	9 Jul
1.85i	Hanne	Van Hessche	BEL	5.7.91	17 Feb	1.85	Sophie	Weißenborn	GER	24.9.97	27 Jul
1.85i	Nina	Schultz	CAN	12.11.98	24 Feb	1.85	Katerina	Cachová	CZE	26.2.90	9 Aug
1.85i	Lissa	Labiche	SEY	18.2.93	25 Feb	1.85		Duong Thi Viet Anh	VIE	30.12.90	30 Nov
1.85	Lamara	Distin	JAM-J	3.3.00	2 Apr	1.84i	Nikola	Strachová	CZE	13.5.94	7 Jan
1.85	Valdiléia	Martins	BRA	19.9.89	8 Apr	1.84i	Emily	Borthwick	GBR	2.9.97	14 Jan
1.85	Clarissa	Cutliff	USA		14 Apr	1.84i	Mariya	Zhodzik	BLR	19.8.97	27 Jan

Mark	Name		Nat	Born	Pos	Meet	Venue			Date
1.84i	Bethan	Partridge	GBR	11.7.90	27 Jan	1.84		Liu Sang	CHN	23.12.96	24 May
1.84i	Haleigh	Knapp	USA	22.8.96	27 Jan	1.84	Khadiya	Hollingsworth	USA	29.10.96	25 May
1.84i	Jelena	Rowe	USA-J	1.8.99	3 Feb	1.84	Anabela	Neto	POR	25.3.91	2 Jun
1.84i	Ligia-Damaris	Bara	ROU	26.1.94	4 Feb	1.84	Esmanur	Alkaç	TUR	15.9.96	2 Jun
1.84i	Claire	Kieffer-Wright	USA	27.9.95	10 Feb	1.84	Abby	Ward	GBR-J	19.4.99	10 Jun
1.84i	Eliska	Klucinová	CZE	14.4.88	11 Feb	1.84	Nadezhda	Andryukhina	RUS-Y	3.7.01	16 Jun
1.84i	Linda	Sandblom	FIN	18.10.89	18 Feb	1.84	Alina	Yablokova	UZB-J	29.9.00	17 Jun
1.84i	Taliyah	Brooks	UOA	8.2.95	9 Mar	1.84	Vilena	Komarova	RUS-Y	26.12.01	5 Jul
1.84i		Deng Siyi	CHN	21.8.97	12 Mar	1.84	Martyna	Lewandowska	POL-J	26.10.00	13 Jul
1.84A	Autumn	Gardner	USA	6.2.95	14 Apr	1.84	Lavinja	Jürgens	GER-J	13.1.00	13 Jul
1.84		Wang Xueyi	CHN	3.8.91	18 Apr	1.84	Rümeysa	Ökdem	TUR-J	2.7.00	20 Jul
1.84	Erinn	Beattie	USA	8.4.97	18 Apr	1.84	Yana	Maksimova	BLR	9.1.89	20 Jul
1.84	Amanda	Vergara	VEN	29.8.97	4 May	1.84	Michalina	Kwasniewska	POL	22.10.91	21 Jul
1.84	Lily	Lowe	USA	16.9.98	12 May	1.84	Laura	Rautanen	FIN	13.2.88	22 Jul
1.84	Sepideh	Tavakoli	IRI	2.3.89	21 May		(163)				

Best outdoors

1.96	Tabashnyk	1		Kropyvnytskyi	25 Jun	1.88	Herashchenko	6= FBK		Hengelo	3 Jun
1.96	Cunningham	1	AWC	London (OS)	15 Jul	1.87	Vukovic	5		Sollentuna	28 Jun
1.95	Mahuchikh	1c2	YOG	Buenos Aires	15 Oct	1.87	Manson	3	NC	Birmingham	30 Jun
1.91	Simic	1		Slovenska Bistrica	26 May	1.87	Nilsson	7	WJ	Tampere	15 Jul
1.91	L Patterson	1	Morton	Dublin (S)	19 Jul	1.86	Willis	1		Tempe	7 Apr
1.91	Trost	5=	DL	London (OS)	22 Jul	1.86	Y Rodríguez	2H	Hypo	Götzis	26 May
1.91	Johnson-Thompson	9	DL	London (OS)	22 Jul	1.86	Bougard	3H	Hypo	Götzis	26 May
1.91	Hrubá	6	EC	Berlin	10 Aug	1.86	Furlani	1	Med-23	Jesolo	10 Jun
1.85	A Smith	27 Apr	1.85	Klintsova	7 Jul	1.84	Partridge	14 Apr	1.84	Hu Linpeng	24 May
1.85	Kononova	30 May	1.84	Bara	2 Jun	1.84	Rowe	5 May	1.84	Sandblom	19 Aug
1.85	Duvernay	17 Jun	1.84	Schultz	12 Apr	1.84	Strachová	19 May			

JUNIORS

See main list for top 13 juniors. 13 performances (inc. 2 indoor) by 4 to 1.90. Additional marks and further juniors:

Mahuchikh 2+	1.94	1	EY	Györ	8 Jul	1.92	1c1	YOG	Buenos Aires	12 Oct
	1.93	1	NC-y	Lutsk	16 Jun	1.90i	1	NC-y	Sumy	1 Feb
	1.93	2		Schifflange	29 Jul					
Taranda	1.90	1		Brest	7 Jun					
Murillo	1.90A	1	SAmG	Cochabamba	5 Jun	1.90	3	WJ	Tampere	15 Jul
1.85i	Alina	Shukh		UKR	12.2.99	1=P	NC	Sumy	9 Feb
1.85	Lamara	Distin		JAM	3.3.00	1	CariftaG	Nassau	2 Apr
1.85	Shelby	Tyler		USA-Y	28.3.01	1	NC-j	Bloomington	16 Jun
1.85	Sanaa	Barnes		USA	10.8.00	2	NC-j	Bloomington	16 Jun
1.84i	Jelena	Rowe		USA	1.8.99	2		College Station	3 Feb
	1.84					2		Lubbock	5 May
1.84	Abby	Ward		GBR	19.4.99	1		Manchester	10 Jun
1.84	Nadezhda	Andryukhina (20)		RUS-Y	3.7.01	2	NC-y	Kaluga	16 Jun
1.84	Alina	Yablokova		UZB	29.9.00	1		Bishkek	17 Jun
1.84	Vilena	Komarova		RUS-Y	26.12.01	1H	EY	Györ	5 Jul
1.84	Martyna	Lewandowska		POL	26.10.00	Q	WJ	Tampere	13 Jul
1.84	Lavinja	Jürgens		GER	13.1.00	Q	WJ	Tampere	13 Jul
1.84	Rümeysa	Ökdem		TUR	2.7.00	3	BalkC	Stara Zagora	20 Jul

POLE VAULT

4.95i	Sandi		Morris		USA	8.7.92	1	WI	Birmingham	3 Mar
					4.50/1 4.60/1 4.70/2 4.75/1 4.80/3 4.85/x 4.90/2 4.95/3 5.04/xxx					
	4.95	1	Greenville	27 Jul	4.45/1 4.55/1 4.65/1 4.75/1 4.85/3 4.95/2 5.07/xxx					
	4.90iA	1	Reno	12 Jan	4.51/1 4.61/1 4.71/2 4.80/3 4.90/3					
	4.88	1	Drake Des Moines	28 Apr	4.50/1 4.60/2 4.70/1 4.80/3 4.88/1 5.01/xxx					
	4.00iA	2	NC Albuquerque	18 Feb	4.51/1 4.61/2 4.71/1 4.76/1 4.81/xx 4.86/1 4.91/xx					
	4.86	1	DL Stockholm	10 Jun	4.55/1 4.65/1 4.75/1 4.86/3 4.94/xxx					
	4.85	3	C.Cup Ostrava	8 Sep	4.45/1 4.55/1 4.65/1 4.70/3 4.75/2 4.80/1 4.85/2 4.90/xxx					
	4.84	1	DL Doha	4 May	4.54/1 4.64/1 4.74/3 4.84/3 5.01/xx					
	4.82	2	WK Zürich	30 Aug	4.42/1 4.57/1 4.67/2 4.77/2 4.82/1 4.87/x 4.92/xx					
4.94			Eliza	McCartney	NZL	11.12.96	1		Jockgrim	17 Jul
					4.60/1 4.70,1 4.80/2 4.87/2 4.94/3 5.01/x					
	4.92	1	Mannheim	23 Jun	4.50/1 4.70/1 4.86/1 4.92/2 5.00/xxx					
	4.85	2	Pre Eugene	26 May	4.50/3 4.60/1 4.70/2 4.80/3 4.85/1 4.90/xxx					
4.93			Jenn	Suhr	USA	5.2.82	1		Austin	14 Apr
					4.61/1 4.71/1 4.93/1 5.01/xxx					
	4.87	2	Jockgrim	17 Jul	4.60/1 4.70/1 4.80/1 4.87/2 4.94/x					
	4.85	1	Pre Eugene	26 May	4.60/1 4.70/1 4.80/3 4.85/1 4.90/xxx					
	4.83	1	TexR Austin	31 Mar	4.60/1 4.70/1 4.83/2 5.01/xxx					
	4.82	1	Fort Worth	17 Mar	4.56/1 4.72/1 4.82/1					
	4.82	2	Athl Lausanne	5 Jul	4.62/1 4.72/2 4.82/2 4.88/xxx					
4.91iA			Katie	Nageotte	USA	30.6.91	1	NC	Albuquerque	18 Feb
					4.41/1 4.51/1 4.61/1 4.71/1 4.76/1 4.81/1 4.86/1 4.91/1 5.04/xxx					

Mark	Name		Nat	Born	Pos	Meet	Venue	Date
	4.86i	1		Clermont-Ferrand	25 Feb			

4.86i 1 Clermont-Ferrand 25 Feb 4.50/1 4.62/1 4.72/1 4.80/1 4.86/2 4.92/xxx
4.90i Anzhelika Sidorova RUS 28.6.91 2 WI Birmingham 3 Mar
　　4.60/1 4.70/1 4.80/1 4.85/1 4.90/3 4.95/xxx
　4.87i 1 NC Moskva 12 Feb 4.55/1 4.65/1 4.76/1 4.87/2
　4.86i 1 Moskva 4 Feb 4.55/1 4.66/1 4.81/2 4.86/1
　4.86i 2 Clermont-Ferrand 25 Feb 4.50/1 4.62/1 4.72/1 4.80/1 4.86/3 4.92/xxx
　4.85 1 Herc Monaco 20 Jul 4.60/2 4.75/1 4.80/1 4.85/2 4.90/xx
　4.85 1 C.Cup Ostrava 8 Sep 4.45/1 4.65/1 4.70/1 4.75/1 4.80/x 4.85/2 4.90/xxx
　4.82 3 Athl Lausanne 5 Jul 4.52/1 4.72/2 4.82/3 4.88/xxx
　4.82 3 WK Zürich 30 Aug 4.42/1 4.57/1 4.67/1 4.77/2 4.82/3 4.87/xxx
4.87 Ekateríni Stefanídi GRE 4.2.90 1 WK Zürich 30 Aug
　　4.67/1 4.77/2 4.82/1 4.87/1 4.92/xxx
　4.85 1 EC Berlin 9 Aug 4.65/1 4.75/1 4.80/1 4.85/3 4.96/xxx
　4.85 2 C.Cup Ostrava 8 Sep 4.65/1 4.75/3 4.80/1 4.85/2 4.90/xxx
　4.83i 1 Liévin 13 Feb 4.62/2 4.72/3 4.83/2 4.91/xxx
　4.82i 1 Rouen 10 Feb 4.60/1 4.72/1 4.82/1 4.92/xxx
　4.82 1 Athl Lausanne 5 Jul 4.62/1 4.72/1 4.82/2 4.88/xxx
　　(34/6)

Mark	Name		Nat	Born	Pos	Meet	Venue		Date
4.80	Holly	Bradshaw	GBR	2.11.91	3		Jockgrim		17 Jul
4.80	Yarisley	Silva	CUB	1.6.87	2=	Herc	Monaco		20 Jul
4.80	Nikoléta	Kiriakopoúlou	GRE	21.3.86	2	EC	Berlin		9 Aug
4.75	Alysha	Newman (10)	CAN	29.6.94	1	CG	Gold Coast		13 Apr
4.75	Ninon	Guillon-Romarin	FRA	15.4.95	8	Herc	Monaco		20 Jul
4.73	Angelica	Bengtsson	SWE	8.7.93	1		Karlstad		25 Jul
4.71	Nina	Kennedy	AUS	5.4.97	1		Perth		9 Feb
4.70A	Rosbeilys	Peinado	VEN	26.11.97	1	SAmG	Cochabamba		7 Jun
4.67i	Olivia	Gruver	USA	29.7.97	1	SEC	College Station		24 Feb
4.67	Iryna	Zhuk	BLR	26.1.93	1		Székesfehérvár		30 Jun
4.66i	Lexi	Jacobus	USA	20.11.96	1	NCAA	College Station		10 Mar
4.65	Olga	Mullina	RUS	1.8.92	1	NC	Kazan		20 Jul
4.62i	Kristen	Hixson/Leland	USA	1.7.92	1		Notre Dame		3 Feb
4.62i	Maryna	Kylypko	UKR	10.11.95	4		Clermont-Ferrand		25 Feb
		(20)							
4.62i	Lisa	Ryzih	GER	27.9.88	6		Clermont-Ferrand		25 Feb
4.61iA	Morgann	LeLeux	USA	14.11.92	4	NC	Albuquerque		18 Feb
4.61i	Tori	Hoggard	USA	20.11.96	2	NCAA	College Station		10 Mar
4.61	Emily	Grove	USA	22.5.93	2		Chula Vista		19 May
4.61	Megan	Clark	USA	10.6.94	1		Chula Vista		9 Jun
4.60iA	Anicka	Newell	CAN	5.8.93	1		Albuquerque		10 Feb
4.60	Lisa	Gunnarsson	SWE-J	20.8.99	2	TexasR	Austin		31 Mar
4.60	Angelina	Krasnova	RUS	7.2.91	2		Cheboksary		12 Jun
4.60	Jacqueline	Otchere	GER	5.5.96	4	AWC	London (OS)		14 Jul
4.60		Li Ling	CHN	6.7.89	5	AWC	London (OS)		14 Jul
		(30)							
4.60	Wilma	Murto	FIN	11.6.98	1	NC	Jyväskylä		20 Jul
4.56	Juliana	Campos	BRA	17.10.96	1		Castellón		26 Jun
4.56i	Annie	Rhodes-Johnigan	USA	13.5.95	1		Belton		29 Dec
4.55i	Jirina	Ptácníková	CZE	20.5.86	1		Praha		13 Feb
4.55i	Aksana	Gataullina	RUS-J	17.7.00	1		Sankt Peterburg		23 Feb
4.53	Molly	Caudery	GBR-J	17.3.00	1		Mannheim		23 Jun
4.52i	Katharina	Bauer	GER	12.6.90	1		Dortmund		21 Jan
4.51i	Friedelinde	Petershofen	GER	19.8.95	3		Potsdam		19 Jan
4.51iA	Kristen	Brown	USA	26.5.92	5	NC	Albuquerque		18 Feb
4.51	Amálie	Svábíková	CZE-J	22.11.99	1	WJ	Tampere		12 Jul
		(40)							
4.50i	Anjuli	Knäsche	GER	18.10.93	1		Hamburg		4 Feb
4.50i	Polina	Knoroz	RUS-J	20.7.99	1	NC-j	Volgograd		7 Feb
4.50	Kortney	Ross	USA	26.7.92	6	DrakeR	Des Moines		28 Apr
4.50	Lene	Retzius	NOR	4.1.96	1		Oslo		30 May
4.50	Marion	Lotout	FRA	19.11.89	1		Pézenas		9 Jun
4.50	Tina	Sutej	SLO	7.11.88	1		Ried		15 Jun
4.50	Justyna	Smietanka	POL	24.9.94	1	NC	Lublin		21 Jul
4.47i	Lucy	Bryan	GBR	22.5.95	1		Akron		3 Feb
4.46	Bridget	Guy	USA	18.3.96	1		Charlottesville		20 Apr
4.46	Eléni-Klaoúdia	Pólak	GRE	9.9.96	5		Athína		22 Jun
		(50)							
4.45i	Michaela	Meijer	SWE	30.7.93	1		Malmö		27 Jan
4.45i	Tatyana	Shvydkina	RUS	8.5.90	3		Moskva		4 Feb
4.45i	Alyona	Lutkovskaya	RUS	15.3.96	4		Moskva		4 Feb
4.45i	Minna	Nikkanen	FIN	9.4.88	1	v3N	Uppsala		11 Feb
4.45i	Femke	Pluim	NED	10.5.94	1	NC	Apeldoorn		17 Feb

WOMEN 2018

Mark	Wind	Name		Nat	Born	Pos	Meet	Venue	Date
4.45		Lakan	Taylor	USA	21.6.95	7	TexasR	Austin	31 Mar
4.45		Madison	Heath	USA	3.11.95	8	TexasR	Austin	31 Mar
4.45		Yelizaveta	Bondarenko	RUS-J	1.7.99	1	NC-j	Chelyabinsk	22 Jun
4.45		Sydney	Walter	USA	15.11.93	6	NC	Des Moines	24 Jun
4.45		Carolin	Hingst	GER	18.9.80	1		Erding	7 Jul
	(60)								
4.45		Irina	Ivanova	RUS	19.4.96	4	NC	Kazan	20 Jul
4.45		Stefanie	Dauber	GER	31.7.87	2	NC	Nürnberg	22 Jul
4.45		Mónica	Clemente	ESP	20.5.96	1	NC	Getafe	22 Jul
4.45		Maialen	Axpe	ESP	4.5.93	2	NC	Getafe	22 Jul
4.45		Angelica	Moser	SUI	9.10.97	2		Schaan	8 Sep
4.45		Olivia	McTaggart	NZL-J	9.1.00	1		Auckland	17 Nov
4.42i		Romana	Malácová	CZE	15.5.87	1		Ostrava	25 Jan
4.42		Alice	Moindrot	FRA-J	20.8.99	1cC		Aubière	16 Jun
4.42		Rachel	Baxter	USA-J	5.4.99	1	NC-j	Bloomington	17 Jun
4.42		Bonnie	Draxler	USA	13.10.95	1		San Diego	8 Dec
	(70)								
4.41i		Marion	Fiack	FRA	13.10.92	3		Orléans	13 Jan
4.41i		Martina	Schultze	GER	12.9.90	5		Potsdam	19 Jan
4.41i		Desiree	Freier	USA	24.7.96	5	NCAA	College Station	10 Mar
4.41		Madeline	Gardner	USA	24.9.95	2		Charlottesville	20 Apr
4.40i		Regine	Kramer	GER	5.4.93	4		Dortmund	21 Jan
4.40i		Saga	Andersson	FIN-J	30.3.00	1	SM	Helsinki	17 Feb
4.40i			Chen Qiaoling	CHN-J	22.11.99	1	NGP	Xianlin	7 Mar
4.40		Liz	Parnova	AUS	9.5.94	2		Perth	9 Feb
4.40		Marion	Buisson	FRA	19.2.88	3	NC	Albi	7 Jul
4.40		Carolina	Moll	USA	28.4.94	1		Charlotte	13 Jul
	(80)								
4.40		Roberta	Bruni	ITA	8.3.94	1		Rieti	29 Aug
4.40i		Lyudmila	Petrova	RUS	15.12.93	1		Omsk	22 Dec
4.38i		Laura	Taylor	USA	22.4.96	2		Lexington	3 Feb
4.37i		Thiziri	Daci	FRA	15.12.97	1		Clermont-Ferrand	24 Feb
4.36		Kally	Long	USA	28.8.95	4		Fayetteville	28 Apr
4.36		Taylor	Amann	USA	6.5.96	1		Bloomington	13 May
4.36		Sonia	Malavisi	ITA	31.10.94	7		Athína	22 Jun
4.36		Reena	Koll	EST	15.11.96	1		Tartu	25 Jul
4.36i		Dailis	Caballero	CUB	6.3.88	2		Belton	29 Dec
4.35i		Elisa	Molinarolo	ITA	29.1.94	1		Padova	20 Jan
	(90)								
4.35		Lindsey	Murray	USA	22.7.96	3	SEC	Knoxville	13 May
4.35		Kamila	Przybyla	POL	3.5.96	4	EAF	Bydgoszcz	29 May
4.35		Stélla-Iró	Ledáki	GRE	18.7.88	3		Athína (F)	13 Jun
4.35		Malen	Ruiz de Azua	ESP	17.11.95	1		Valladolid	16 Jun
4.35		Lea	Bachmann	SUI	25.6.96	1		Winterthur	27 Jun
4.35		Mallaury	Sautereau	FRA	1.8.96	1	NC-23	Niort	14 Jul
4.35		Miren	Bartolomé	ESP	2.1.98	3=	NC	Getafe	22 Jul
4.35		Jill	Marois	USA	8.6.94	7		Greenville	27 Jul
4.35		Buse	Arikazan	TUR	8.7.94	1	Club	Bursa	15 Aug
4.34		Andrea	Willis	USA	26.7.98	2		Waco	12 May
	(100)								

Mark	Name		Nat	Born	Pos	Date		Mark	Name		Nat	Born	Pos	Date
4.33i	Demet	Parlak	TUR	26.7.96	3	3 Feb		4.30	Silke	Spiegelburg	GER	17.3.86	3	3 Jun
4.33	Solène	Guiloineau	FRA	17.3.92	14	14 Jul		4.30	Helen	Falda	ITA	13.2.96	7	7 Jun
4.31i		Xu Huiqin	CHN	4.9.93	6	6 Jan		4.30	Jade	Vigneron	FRA	6.6.01	0	0 Jun
4.31i	MoKenzie	Johnson	USA	26.9.94	10	10 Feb		4.30	Natalia	Uy	USANPII	6.3.94	16	16 Jun
4.31i	Martina	Strutz	GER	4.11.81	11	11 Feb		4.30A		Yang Yang	CHN	23.12.95	17	17 Jun
4.31	Katherine	Pitman	USA	21.11.94	24	24 Apr		4.30A		She Chenyao	CHN-J	21.8.00	17	17 Jun
4.31	Alex	Pevtsova	USA	29.9.93	9	9 Jun		4.30	Anastasiya	Surova	RUS	26.9.96	6	6 Jul
4.31	Marta	Onofre	POR	28.1.91	8	8 Jul		4.30	Anastasia	Popov	FRA	29.7.96	7	7 Jul
4.30i	Erica	Ellis	USA-J	17.6.01	6	6 Jan		4.30	Sophie	Gutermuth	USA	2.11.92	29	29 Jul
4.30i	Annika	Roloff	GER	10.3.91	7	7 Jan		4.30	Chayanisa	Chomchuendee	THA	9.9.88	28	28 Aug
4.30i	Anastasiya	Sadovnikova	RUS	22.6.95	11	11 Jan		4.30	Joana	Ribeiro Costa	BRA	15.8.81	16	16 Sep
4.30i	Yana	Hladiychuk	UKR	21.5.93	27	27 Jan		4.28i	Karlie	Place	USA	9.11.95	27	27 Jan
4.30i	Aurélie	De Ryck	BEL	17.12.92	28	28 Jan		4.28iA	Kathryn	Tomczak	USA	17.7.97	27	27 Jan
4.30i	Fanny	Smets	BEL	21.4.86	13	13 Feb		4.28	Kaitlyn	Merritt	USA	27.3.97	3	3 May
4.30i	Lauren	Martinez	USA	16.10.96	24	24 Feb		4.28	Killiana	Heymans	NED	24.1.97	21	21 Jul
4.30i	Maria-leonore	Tavares	POR	24.9.85	3	3 Mar		4.28	Robin	Wingbermühle	NED	20.5.92	21	21 Jul
4.30A	Alisandra	Negrete	MEX	4.10.92	30	30 Mar		4.27i	Emily	Presley	USA	22.1.97	13	13 Jan
4.30	Alina	McDonald	USA	26.2.97	7	7 Apr		4.27	Eboni	Hall	USA	25.7.97	5	5 May
4.30	Sally	Peake	GBR	8.2.86	13	13 Apr		4.27	Nastassja	Campbell	USA-J	19.7.00	30	30 Mar
4.30	Kristen	Denk	USA	15.2.97	14	14 Apr		4.27	Mackenzie	Hayward	USA-J	4.7.00	30	30 Mar
4.30	Marissa	Kalsey	USA	23.3.94	14	14 Apr		4.27	Chloe	Cunliffe	USA-J	10.5.00	7	7 Jul
4.30		Song Tingting	CHN	23.3.94	14	14 Apr		4.26i	Brooke	Catherine	USA	22.7.97	10	10 Feb
4.30		Niu Chunge	CHN-J	14.2.00	23	23 May		4.26iA	Jacqueline	Williams	USA	13.11.94	18	18 Feb
4.30	Diamara	Planell	PUR	16.2.93	3	3 Jun		4.26	Carla	Franch	ESP	25.10.89	4	4 Jul

Mark	Wind	Name		Nat	Born	Date
4.26		Leni Freyja	Wildgrube	GER-Y	15.8.01	7 Jul
4.25		Lisa	Campbell	AUS	26.8.92	13 Jan
4.25i		Charlotte	Gaudy	FRA	6.11.96	13 Jan
4.25i		Agnieszka	Kaszuba	POL	31.8.98	4 Feb
4.25i		Jade	Ive	GBR	22.1.92	17 Feb
4.25i		Laura	Marty	USA	29.12.97	23 Feb
4.25i		Gabriela	Leon	USA	17.6.99	23 Feb
4.25i		Rivka 'Becky'	Arbiv	USA	8.11.98	23 Feb
4.25		Shay	Petty	USA	1.1.96	30 Mar
4.25		Jenna	Frantz	USA-J	7.6.99	30 Mar
4.25		Ellen	Olsson	SWE	9.3.97	29 May
4.25		Zuzana	Prazáková	CZE	26.4.97	4 Jun
4.25		Hanna	Jansson	SWE	5.3.95	9 Jun
4.25		Mariya	Zakharutkina	RUS	14.8.96	14 Jun
4.25		Julia	Fixsen	USA-J	13.11.00	17 Jun
4.25		Sophia	Franklin	USA-J	28.4.99	17 Jun
4.25		Pascale	Stöcklin	SUI	5.2.97	27 Jun
4.25		Carmelita	Correa	MEX	5.12.88	28 Jun
4.25		Sophie	Cook	GBR	12.9.94	30 Jun
4.25		Ria	Möllers	GER	5.3.96	30 Jun
4.25		Andrea	San José	ESP	4.10.97	22 Jul
4.25		Elina	Lampela	FIN	18.2.98	31 Jul
4.24i		Lauren	Chorny	USA	22.6.93	27 Jan
4.24i		Hulda	Thorsteinsdóttir	ISL	10.6.91	11 Feb
4.22i		Chloé	Henry	BEL	5.3.87	22 Feb
4.22		Erika	Malaspina	USA	4.2.98	12 May
4.22		Rachael	Wolfs	CAN	13.9.95	27 May
4.21Ai		Reagann	Leleux	USA-J	31.10.99	13 Jan
4.21i		Zsófia	Siskó	HUN	8.10.94	27 Jan
4.21i		Karla	da Silva	BRA	12.11.84	17 Feb
4.21		Makiah	Hunt	CAN	24.1.98	12 May
4.21		Laura	Weyrowitz	GER	28.9.94	23 May
4.20i		Tatiane	Carne	ITA	18.4.90	14 Jan
4.20i		Aneta	Morysková	CZE	19.9.92	27 Jan
4.20i		Tomomi	Abiko	JPN	17.3.88	4 Feb
4.20i		Ekateríni	Vayená	GRE	21.6.95	13 Feb
4.20i		Nikol	Jiroutová	CZE	30.3.92	13 Feb
4.20i		Sierra	Hansen	USA	19.9.95	23 Feb
4.20		Jessie	Johnson	USA	21.11.93	24 Mar
4.20		Imogen	Ayris	NZL-J	12.12.00	25 Mar
4.20		Patrícia	dos Santos	BRA	13.6.84	25 Mar
4.20		Hannah	McWilliams	USA	.93	14 Apr
4.20		Kyley	Foster	USA		20 Apr
4.20		Brysun	Stately	USA	22.11.86	21 Apr
4.20		Hailey	Sweatman	USA	17.12.97	21 Apr
4.20		Sophie	Gutermuth	USA	2.11.92	28 Apr
4.20		Sara	Stevens	USA	16.4.96	28 Apr
4.20			Wu Chia-Ju	TPE-J	17.12.99	6 May
4.20			Wu Zuocheng	CHN-J	26.5.99	11 May
4.20		Kimberly	Peterson	USA	2.10.95	12 May
4.20		Charlotte	Iva	FRA-J	11.2.99	20 May
4.20		Nikola	Pöschlová	CZE	10.9.98	26 May
4.20		Victoria	von Eynatten	GER	6.10.91	2 Jun
4.20		Mariya	Temnikova	RUS	9.7.95	3 Jun
4.20		Marijke	Wijnmaalen	NED	12.6.98	9 Jun
4.20		Sommer	Knight	USA-J	2.4.99	17 Jun
4.20		Cátia	Pereira	POR	5.7.89	20 Jun
4.20		Anna	Airault	FRA-J	30.9.00	23 Jun
4.20		Lisa	Salomon	CUB	7.4.98	23 Jun
4.20		Elien	Vekemans	BEL-Y	30.4.01	24 Jun
4.20		Desiree	Singh	GER	17.8.94	6 Jul
4.20		Yekaterina	Kalmykova	RUS	7.10.90	13 Jul
4.20		Nina	Klyuzheva	RUS	23.11.97	4 Aug
4.20		Katherine	Ibarbo	COL	14.2.96	25 Aug
4.20		Stefany	Castillo	COL	12.2.96	25 Aug
4.20		(214)	Lim Eun-ji	KOR	2.4.89	28 Aug

Best outdoors

Mark	Name	Pos	Meet	Venue	Date
4.80	Nageotte	1		Beckum	26 Aug
4.65	Jacobus	1	SEC	Knoxville	13 May
4.61	Hixson/Leland	1		Osaka	20 May
4.60	LeLeux	1		Hammond	13 Apr
4.55	Gruver	1	NCAA	Eugene	7 Jun
4.55	Johnigan	5	NC	Des Moines	24 Jun
4.55	Gataullina	2	NC	Kazan	20 Jul
4.51	Hoggard	2		Fayetteville	28 Apr
4.51	Newell	2		Osaka	20 May
4.50	Kylypko	1	NC	Lutsk	20 Jul
4.45	Brown	1		Long Beach	19 Apr
4.45	Knäsche	1		Engen	6 May
4.45	Shvydkina	2	Znam	Zhukovskiy	30 Jun
4.39	Andersson	1		Somero	1 Jul
4.35	Laura Taylor	9=	TexR	Austin	31 Mar
4.35	Bryan	9=	TexR	Austin	31 Mar
4.35	Petershofen	1		Soest	10 Jun
4.35	Nikkanen	2	NC	Jyväskylä	20 Jul

4.30 Chen Qiaoling 17 Apr	4.30 Strutz 9 Jun	4.25 Xu Huiqin 28 Jun	4.20 Tomczak 19 Apr
4.30 Hladiychuk 4 May	4.30 Tavares 23 Jun	4.25 Knoroz 20 Jul	4.20 Molinarolo 29 Apr
4.30 Pluim 6 May	4.30 Daci 14 Jul	4.25 Ive 8 Sep	4.20 Chorny 9 May
4.30 Kramer 27 May	4.30 Bauer 17 Jul	4.22 Fiack 23 Jun	4.20 Gaudy 20 May
4.30 Sadovnikova 29 May	4.28 De Ryck 21 Jul	4.21 Catherine 12 May	4.20 Siskó 3 Jun
4.30 Petrova 3 Jun	4.26 Presley 11 May	4.21 Thorsteinsdóttir 25 Jun	4.20 Henry 16 Jun
4.30 Martinez 7 Jun	4.25 Place 2 May	4.20 Marty 14 Apr	4.20 Vayená 14 Jul

Extra Trial: 4.57i Annie Rhodes-Johnigan USA 13.5.95 1   Lucas 20 Jan
Exhibition: 4.45 Angelica Moser SUI 9.10.97 1   Langenthal 31 Aug
Irregular
4.50 dh? Sydney Walter USA 15.11.93 1   Louisville 29 Jul
4.30 dh? Sophie Gutermuth USA 2.11.92   29 Jul
4.22 Charlotte Iva FRA-J 11.2.99   18 Dec

JUNIORS

See main list for top 10 juniors. 10 performances (inc. 5 indoors) by 5 to 4.46. Additional marks and further juniors:

Gunnarsson 4.53 1 Castres 25 Jul   4.46i 1 Clemson 26 Jan
Gataullina 2+ 4.50i 1 Moskva 9 Jan
Knoroz 4.50i 1 Sankt-Peterburg 23 Feb

Mark	Name		Nat	Born	Pos	Meet	Venue	Date
4.30i	Erica	Ellis	USA	17.6.01	1c2		Akron	6 Jan
Best out: 4.30	Chen Qiaoling		CHN-J	22.11.99	2	NGP	Zhuzhou	17 Apr
4.30		Niu Chunge	CHN	14.2.00	1	NGP	Chongqing	23 May
4.30A		She Chenyao	CHN	21.8.00	3	NGPF	Guiyang	17 Jun
4.27	Nastassja	Campbell	USA	19.7.00	1-HS	TexasR	Austin	30 Mar
4.27	Mackenzie	Hayward	USA	4.7.00	2-HS	TexasR	Austin	30 Mar
4.27	Chloe	Cunliffe	USA	10.5.00			Bend (75mm pegs)	7 Jul
4.26	Leni Freyja	Wildgrube	GER-Y	15.8.01	1	EY	Györ	7 Jul
4.25	Jenna	Frantz	USA	7.6.99	3	TexasR	Austin	30 Mar
4.25	Julia	Fixsen	USA	13.11.00	2	NC-j	Bloomington	17 Jun
4.25	Sophia	Franklin (20)	USA	28.4.99	3	NC-j	Bloomington	17 Jun
Best out: 4.25	Polina	Knoroz	RUS	20.7.99	7	NC	Kazan	20 Jul

WOMEN 2018

LONG JUMP

Mark	Wind	Name	Nat	Born	Pos	Meet	Venue	Date	Series
7.05	1.2	Lorraine Ugen	GBR	22.8.91	1	NC	Birmingham	1 Jul	6.60/0.0 7.05 x x p p
6.88	1.2				2	DL	London (OS)	21 Jul	6.68 x x x x 6.88
6.86	0.1				1	AWC	London (OS)	14 Jul	6.35 6.86 6.43 x
6.85	1.7				1	DL	Stockholm	10 Jun	6.85/1.7 x x 0.70 0.85/1.3 6.35w
6.99	0.6	Malaika Mihambo	GER	3.2.94	1		Weinheim	26 May	6.24 6.78 6.56 6.63 6.76 6.99
6.96	1.5				1	DL	Birmingham	18 Aug	6.49 x 6.60 6.82/-0.3 6.65 6.96
6.90	1.3				1	Athl	Lausanne	5 Jul	x x 6.49 x 6.70 6.90
6.86	0.1				2	C.Cup	Ostrava	9 Sep	6.65 6.86 6.77 6.58
6.85	1.8				2	DL	Stockholm	10 Jun	6.63w 6.67 6.63 6.85 p p
6.84,6.99	1.8	Ivana Spanovic	SRB	10.5.90	*	MedG	Tarragona	27 Jun	7.04w 6.99*/1.8 6.95/1.3 6.79/1.5 x p
6.96i					1	WI	Birmingham	4 Mar	6.89 6.74 x 6.96 p p
6.93i					1		Beograd	21 Feb	6.64 6.85 6.93 6.72 6.67 p
6.92	2.0				*		Athína	26 May	x x 6.66 6.71 6.98w 6.92/2.0
6.90	0.8				2	Athl	Lausanne	5 Jul	6.90 6.57 6.58 6.67 6.32 6.62
6.84	0.5				Q	EC	Berlin	9 Aug	x 6.56 6.84
6.93	0.8	Caterine Ibargüen	COL	12.2.84	1	C.Cup	Ostrava	9 Sep	6.68 6.76 x 6.85/-0.2 6.93
6.87	0.5				1		Marseille	16 Jun	6.58 6.76 6.87 x 6.72 6.78
6.92i		Khaddi Sagnia	SWE	20.4.94	1	GP	Glasgow	25 Feb	6.92 x p 5.37 p p
6.85i					1	NC	Gävle	17 Feb	6.67 x 6.85 p 6.46
6.92	1.8	Christabel Nettey	CAN	2.6.91	1		Brisbane (Nathan)	28 Mar	6.85/2.0 6.92 6.82/2.0 6.79 6.73 p
6.88	0.6				1	Kuso	Chorzów	8 Jun	6.31 6.88 6.56 6.52 6.05 p
6.84	0.2				1	CG	Gold Coast	12 Apr	6.84 6.79/-0.3 6.64 6.68 6.65 2.77
6.91	0.2	Shara Proctor	GBR	16.9.88	1	DL	London (OS)	21 Jul	6.82/0.5 6.80/0.7 6.87/0.5 6.91 6.83/0.4 6.64
6.89	0.0				Q	CG	Gold Coast	11 Apr	6.89
6.89i		Brittney Reese	USA	9.9.86	2	WI	Birmingham	4 Mar	6.76 6.61 6.77 6.89 6.72 6.64
6.88Ai					1	NC	Albuquerque	18 Feb	6.74 6.66 6.88 x 6.88 x
6.87	0.7				2	Kuso	Chorzów	8 Jun	6.69 6.78/0.3 6.68 6.62 6.87
6.88	1.9	Brooke Stratton	AUS	12.7.93	2		Brisbane (Nathan)	28 Mar	6.60 6.88 6.63w 6.65 6.76 6.88w/2.1
6.86	0.2	Jazmin Sawyers (10)	GBR	21.5.94	2	NC	Birmingham	1 Jul	x 6.69 6.72 6.68 6.78w 6.86
6.85i		Sosthene Moguenara	GER	17.10.89	3	WI	Birmingham	4 Mar	6.59 6.85 x 6.31 6.23 6.30
6.84	1.6				2		Weinheim	26 May	6.41 6.84 5.52 x x 6.73

(31/11)

Mark	Wind	Name	Nat	Born	Pos	Meet	Venue	Date
6.83	0.5	Ese Brume	NGR	20.1.96	1	AfrC	Asaba	3 Aug
6.81i		Quanesha Burks	USA	15.3.95	4	WI	Birmingham	4 Mar
6.81	0.8	Keturah Orji	USA	5.3.96	1	SEC	Knoxville	13 May
6.81	0.5	Krystyna Hryshutyna	UKR	21.3.92	2	NC	Lutsk	19 Jul
6.80	1.2	Éloyse Lesueur-Aymonin	FRA	15.7.88	2		Marseille	16 Jun
6.80	1.3	Juliet Itoya	ESP	17.8.86	1	NC	Getafe	21 Jul
6.78	1.2	Taliyah Brooks	USA	8.2.95	1		Fayetteville	24 Mar
6.77	2.0	Kylie Price	USA	1.10.93	3		Chula Vista	19 May
6.77	-0.1	Sha'Keela Saunders (20)	USA	10.12.93	1	Gyulai	Székesfehérvár	2 Jul
6.77	0.6	Anastasiya Mironchik-Ivanova	BLR	13.4.89	1	NC	Minsk	21 Jul
6.75	0.0	Chanice Porter	JAM	25.5.94	1		Athens, GA	5 May
6.74	0.1	Bianca Stuart	BAH	17.5.88	1		Douglasville	27 May
6.74	0.1	Tianna Bartoletta	USA	30.8.85	1		Padova	8 Jun
6.73i		Kate Hall	USA	12.1.97	1	NCAA	College Station	9 Mar
6.73	-0.1	Maryna Bekh	UKR	18.7.95	2	EC	Berlin	11 Aug
6.72	1.7	Nektaria Panagi	CYP	20.3.90	1		Árgos Orestikó	4 Jul
6.72	1.3	Alina Rotaru	ROU	5.6.93	1	NC	Pitesti	27 Jul
6.71i		Katarina Johnson-Thompson	GBR	9.1.93	1	NC	Birmingham	17 Feb
6.71	-0.7	Tara Davis (30)	USA-J	20.5.99	1	NC-j	Bloomington	16 Jun
6.70	0.4	Nadja Käther	GER	29.9.88	3		Weinheim	26 May
6.70	2.0	Yelena Sokolova	RUS	23.7.86	1	Znam	Zhukovskiy	1 Jul
6.69A	0.8	Eliane Martins	BRA	26.5.86	1		Medellín	28 Apr
6.69	-0.5	Florentina Iusco	ROU	8.4.96	1		Bucuresti	13 May
6.69	1.9	Kendell Williams	USA	14.6.95	*		Chula Vista	19 May

Mark	Wind	Name		Nat	Born	Pos	Meet	Venue	Date
6.69	1.5	Malaina	Payton	USA	16.10.91	2		Chula Vista	9 Jun
6.69	1.8	Jahisha	Thomas	GBR	22.11.94	4	NC	Birmingham	1 Jul
6.69	0.9	Alexandra	Wester	GER	21.3.94	2	NC	Nürnberg	22 Jul
6.68	1.9	Fátima	Diame	ESP	22.9.96	3	MedG	Tarragona	27 Jun
6.68	0.0	Julia	Gerter	GER	13.7.94	3	NC	Nürnberg	22 Jul
		(40)							
6.67	0.7	Yanis	David	FRA	12.12.97	2	SEC	Knoxville	13 May
6.67	0.6	Yekaterina	Koneva	RUS	25.9.88	1		Maykop	6 Jun
6.66	1.3	Naa	Anang	AUS	10.3.95	2		Gold Coast	18 Feb
6.66A	1.5	Paola	Mautino	PER	1.6.90	1	SAmG	Cochabamba	6 Jun
6.66	1.3	Melanie	Bauschke	GER	14.7.88	1		Oberteuringen	9 Jun
6.65A		Joëlle	Mbumi Nkouindjin	CMR	25.5.86	1		Bafoussam	3 Mar
6.65i			Wang Qingling	CHN	14.1.93	1	NGP	Xianlin	11 Mar
6.65A	1.3	Karin	Melis Mey	TUR	31.5.84	1		Potchefstroom	12 Apr
6.65	1.3	Darrielle	McQueen	USA	29.5.96	3	SEC	Knoxville	13 May
6.64		Jessica	Noble	JAM	5.2.97	2		Kingston	10 Mar
		(50)							
6.64A	0.2		Xu Xiaoling	CHN	13.5.92	1	NGPF	Guiyang	15 Jun
6.64	1.5	Marthe Yasmine	Koala	BUR	8.3.94	1H		Kladno	16 Jun
6.64	-0.9	Milica	Gardasevic	SRB	28.9.98	1		Berane	14 Jul
6.63i		Ksenija	Balta	EST	1.11.86	1	NC	Tallinn	18 Feb
6.63	2.0	Lauma	Griva	LAT	27.10.84	1		Riga	29 Jul
6.62	0.6	Nafissatou	Thiam	BEL	19.8.94	1H	Hypo	Götzis	27 May
6.62	1.1	Erica	Bougard	USA	26.7.93	2H	Hypo	Götzis	27 May
6.62	0.2	Laura	Strati	ITA	3.10.90	1		Nembro	5 Jul
6.61	1.3	Tissanna	Hickling	JAM	7.1.98	2		Kingston	7 Apr
6.61	1.8	Yelena	Mashinistova	RUS	29.3.94	1		Moskva	21 Jun
		(60)							
6.61	2.0	Evelise	Veiga	POR	3.3.96	5	MedG	Tarragona	27 Jun
6.60i		Lanae-Tava	Thomas	USA-Y	28.1.01	1		Houghton	20 Jan
6.60A	0.8	Natalie	Aranda	PAN	22.2.95	3	SAmG	Cochabamba	6 Jun
6.60	1.2	Abigail	Irozuru	GBR	3.1.90	5		Marseille	16 Jun
6.58i		Yariagnis	Argüelles	CUB	18.4.84	1		Dortmund	21 Jan
6.58	0.0	Paula Beatriz	Álvarez	CUB	11.9.95	1		La Habana	8 Jun
6.57	1.2	Rougui	Sow	FRA	7.6.95	4	SEC	Knoxville	13 May
6.56A	-0.3	Jéssica Carolina	dos Reis	BRA	17.3.93	4	SAmG	Cochabamba	6 Jun
6.56	0.0	Paraskeví	Papahrístou	GRE	17.4.89	1	NC	Pátra	15 Jul
6.55	1.8	Háido	Alexoúli	GRE	29.3.91	*		Athína (K)	26 May
		(70)							
6.55			Bui Thi Thu Thao	VIE	29.4.92	1		Ho Chi Minh	26 Jul
6.55	-0.1	Angela	Morosanu	ROU	26.7.86	14q	EC	Berlin	9 Aug
6.54	1.5	Aries	Sánchez	VEN	1.3.96	1		Ponce	7 Apr
6.54	0.0	Sarea	Alexander	USA	15.2.96	1		San Antonio	6 May
6.54	1.9	Sydney	Conley	USA	11.12.93	3		Chula Vista	9 Jun
6.54	1.1	Yekaterina	Kropivko	RUS	13.6.97	1	NC-23	Chelyabinsk	7 Jul
6.53	0.7	Melanie	Winters	USA	11.11.93	1		Akron	5 May
6.53	2.0	Mara	Griva	LAT	4.8.89	1		Riga	29 May
6.53A	1.3	Macarena	Reyes	CHI	30.3.84	5	SAmG	Cochabamba	6 Jun
6.53A	-0.2		Lu Minjia	CHN	29.12.90	2	NGPF	Guiyang	15 Jun
		(80)							
6.52i		Tania	Vicenzino	ITA	1.4.86	1	NC	Ancona	17 Feb
6.52	-0.8	Maria Natalia	Londa	INA	29.10.90	1		Los Angeles	14 Apr
6.52	1.4	Chantel	Malone	IVB	2.12.91	2	CAG	Barranquilla	30 Jul
6.51	-0.7	Nayana	James	IND	18.10.95	1	Fed Cup	Patiala	6 Mar
6.51	1.8	Irisdaymi	Herrera	CUB	18.4.92	1	Fortún	Camagüey	15 Mar
6.51	1.1	Hanne	Maudens	BEL	12.3.97	2	NC	Bruxelles	8 Jul
6.51	0.4	Lea-Jasmin	Riecke	GER-J	25.4.00	1	WJ	Tampere	13 Jul
6.51	0.0	Narayanan V.	Pinto	IND	2.5.91	2	AsiG	Jakarta	27 Aug
6.50		Baileh	Simms	USA	26.4.95	*		Tulsa	31 Mar
6.50	1.8	Neja	Filipic	SLO	22.4.95	4	Gyulai	Székesfehérvár	2 Jul
		(90)							
6.49	0.1	Lauren	Wells	AUS	3.8.88	3	NC	Gold Coast	18 Feb
6.49	0.6	Tristine	Johnson	USA	28.9.92	1		Charlottesville	28 Apr
6.48	0.0	Jessamyn	Sauceda	MEX	22.5.89	2	MSR	Torrance	21 Apr
6.48	0.2	Yekaterina	Khalyutina	RUS	16.1.91	2		Zhukovskiy	11 Jul
6.48	1.3	Adéla	Záhorová	CZE-J	13.11.99	*		Tábor	18 Jul
6.48	-1.1	Gabriela	Petrova	BUL	29.6.92	2	BalkC	Stara Zagora	20 Jul
6.47iA		Jessie	Gaines	USA	12.8.90	3	NC	Albuquerque	18 Feb
6.47	1.7	Chelsea	Hayes	USA	9.2.88	2		Baton Rouge	21 Apr
6.47	1.3	Lynique	Beneke	RSA	30.3.91	1		Sasolburg	29 Apr
6.47	0.0	Tyra	Gittens	TTO	6.6.98	5	SEC	Knoxville	13 May
		(100)							

WOMEN 2018

Mark	Wind	Name		Nat	Born	Pos	Meet	Venue	Date
6.47	1.2	Anna	Jagaciak Michalska	POL	10.2.90	1	NC	Lublin	22 Jul
6.46	0.3	Courtney	Corrin	USA	12.12.97				20 Apr
6.46	0.3	Michelle	Fokam	USA	8.6.98				12 May
6.46	2.0	Alice	Hopkins	GBR	30.12.98				16 Jun
6.46	1.2	Malin	Marmbrandt	SWE	29.4.85				6 Jul
6.45i		Milena	Mitkova	BUL	26.1.90				17 Feb
6.45	0.0	Taishia	Pryce	JAM	14.7.97				24 Mar
6.45	1.5	Adriana	Rodríguez	CUB-J	12.7.99				27 May
6.44	0.8	Ayaka	Kora	JPN-Y	22.3.01				9 Jun
6.44	0.4		Zhong Jiawei	CHN-J	7.2.99				9 Jun
6.44	1.4	Daniella	Sacama-Isidore	FRA	8.3.90				9 Jun
6.44	-0.4	Jasmine	Todd	USA	23.12.93				23 Jun
6.44A	1.8	Cora	Salas	ESP	27.9.95				10 Jul
6.44	1.4	Erica	Jarder	SWE	2.4.86				15 Jul
6.43	0.0	Precious	Okoronkwo	NGR	19.10.96				15 Feb
6.43i		Jhoanmy	Luque	VEN	20.12.95				23 Feb
6.43A	0.2	Krystal	Liburd	SKN	22.8.97				14 Apr
6.43	1.4	Hitomi	Nakano	JPN	23.11.90				22 Apr
6.43	0.7	Jana	Veldáková	SVK	3.6.81				19 May
6.43	1.3	Anasztázia	Nguyen	HUN	9.1.93				2 Jul
6.42i		Marie-José	Ebwea Bile	FRA	7.2.97				3 Feb
6.42	2.0	Madisen	Richards	USA	15.11.96				7 Jun
6.42	0.4	Kira	Kytölä	FIN	25.6.93				20 Jul
6.41i		Polina	Lukyanenkova	RUS	15.7.98				30 Jan
6.41i		Olga	Sudareva	BLR	22.2.84				3 Feb
6.41i		Petra	Farkas	HUN-J	30.4.99				11 Feb
6.41	0.7	Parinya	Chuaimaroeng	THA	16.12.97				4 May
6.41	1.6	Niamh	Emerson	GBR-J	22.4.99				1 Jul
6.41			Nguyen Thi Truc Mai	VIE	20.3.97				26 Jul
6.40i		Savannah	Carson	USA	30.3.95				13 Jan
6.40i		Ivona	Dadic	AUT	29.12.93				2 Mar
6.40A		Susana	Hernández	MEX-J	18.1.99				24 Apr
6.40A	0.8	Alysbeth	Félix	PUR	7.3.93				28 Apr
6.39i		Nina	Schultz	CAN	10.11.00				5 Feb
6.39	1.8	Todea-Kay	Willis	JAM	23.11.88				2 Jun
6.39	0.1	Jasmine	Moore	USA-Y	1.5.01				16 Jun
6.39	1.4	Lucy	Hadaway	GBR-J	11.6.00				28 Jul
6.39	1.2	Annik	Kälin	SUI-J	27.4.00				16 Sep
6.38	0.9	Jessica	Penney	AUS	21.12.87				14 Jan
6.38	1.5	Tay-Leih	Clark	AUS	8.2.98				18 Feb
6.38i		Merle	Homeier	GER-J	27.8.99				25 Feb
6.00	0.0	Keila	Costa	BRA	6.2.83				5 May
6.38	0.7	Dominique	Bullock	USA	14.5.96				24 May
6.38	1.0	Diána	Lesti	HUN	30.3.98				7 Jun
6.38	0.7	Larissa	Iapichino	ITA-Y	18.7.02				16 Jun
6.38	0.0	Josie	Oliarnyk	GBR-J	27.3.00				1 Jul
6.38	0.3	Aleksandra	Yevstyunina	RUS	8.7.93				11 Jul
6.38	1.6	Hafdís	Sigurdardóttir	ISL	12.2.87				21 Jul
6.38	0.0		Chen Shuiqing	CHN-J	12.4.00				14 Sep
6.37iA		Shanice	McPherson	JAM	12.3.94				3 Feb
6.37	1.6	Andrea	Thompson	AUS	2.10.98				16 Feb
6.37	0.9	Madeline	Holmberg	USA	26.10.96				13 May
6.37	1.8	María	Vicente	ESP-Y	28.3.01				0 Jul
6.37	-0.2	Yekaterina	Solovyova	RUS	23.11.95				11 Jul
6.36i		Birte	Damerius	GER	13.12.91				3 Feb
6.36i		Tähti	Alver	EST	4.12.94				18 Feb
6.36A	1.2	Flor	Álvarez	DOM	18.10.90				28 Apr
6.36	0.4	Hilary	Kpatcha	FRA	5.5.98				23 Jun
6.36	1.8	Carlijn	Ter Laak	NED	16.2.97				24 Jun
6.36	1.8	Sophie	Weißenberg	GER	24.9.97				30 Jun
6.36A	0.4	Thelma Nohemí	Fuentes	GUA	20.8.92				14 Jul
6.36	1.3		Chen Ting	CHN	28.8.97				18 Jul
6.36	1.5	Katerina	Cachová	CZE	26.2.90				21 Jul
6.35	-0.9	De'Von	Johnson	USA	.94				7 Apr
6.35	0.8	Shylia	Riley	USA	26.7.96				27 Apr
6.35	1.5	Alyssa	Thompson	USA	25.9.94				6 May
6.35	0.5	Kiara	Williams	USA	15.9.96				13 May
6.35	1.6	Angelika	Faka	POL	15.1.96				27 May
6.35	0.2		Gong Luying	CHN-J	22.2.00				15 Jun
6.35	1.9	Efthimía	Kolokithá	GRE	9.7.87				4 Jul
6.35	1.8	Zhanna	Zelikova	RUS	22.2.95				20 Jul

(171)

Wind assisted

Mark	Wind	Name		Nat	Born	Pos	Meet	Venue	Date
7.19	3.1	Brittney	Reese	USA	9.9.86	1		Chula Vista	19 May
		x 7.19w 7.00w/4.5 6.82w/2.4 x 6.77w							
7.04	2.2	Ivana	Spanovic	SRB	10.5.90	1	MedG	Tarragona	27 Jun
		7.04w 6.99*/1.8 6.95/1.3 6.79/1.5 x p							
6.98	2.5		Spanovic			1		Athína	26 May
		x x 6.66 6.71 6.98w 6.92/2.0							
6.91	3.6	Kendell	Williams	USA	14.6.95	2		Chula Vista	19 May
		x x 6.35 6.72w 6.69 6.91w							
6.89	2.3		Williams			1		Chula Vista	9 Jun
		x x 6.77w 6.39w 6.89w x							
6.88A	2.4	Juliet	Itoya	ESP	17.8.86	1		Ávila	10 Jul
		6.23 6.88w 6.30 x x 6.58w							
6.88	2.3	Sha'Keela	Saunders	USA	18.12.93	1		Kortrijk	14 Jul
		6.51 6.46 6.46 6.58 6.62 6.88w							
6.86	2.2	Maryna	Bekh	UKR	18.7.95	1	NC	Lutsk	19 Jul
		x x 6.70 x x 6.86w							
6.84	2.3		Proctor			3		Brisbane (Nathan)	28 Mar
		x 6.18 6.41 6.36 6.46 6.84w							
6.77	5.7	Nektaria	Panagi	CYP	20.3.90	1	NC	Paralimni	17 Jun
6.73	4.1	Tissanna	Hickling	JAM	7.1.98	1		Kingston	10 Mar
6.69	2.3	Yanis	David	FRA	12.12.97	1		Gainesville	13 Apr
6.69	3.0	Jéssica Carolina	dos Reis	BRA	17.3.93	1		Campinas	5 May
6.65	2.9	Háido	Alexoúli	GRE	29.3.91	2		Athína (K)	26 May
6.64	3.7	Abigail	Irozuru	GBR	3.1.90	5	NC	Birmingham	1 Jul
6.63	2.7	Jasmine	Todd	USA	23.12.93	1		Prairie View	24 Mar
6.61	2.3	Gabrielle	Thomas	USA	7.12.96	1		Philadelphia	6 May
6.61	5.5	Malin	Marmbrandt	SWE	29.4.85	1		Málaga	15 Jul
6.60	3.2	Aries	Sánchez	VEN	1.3.96	1		Gurabo	16 Mar
6.58	2.3	Yorgelis	Rodríguez	CUB	25.1.95	3H	Hypo	Götzis	27 May
6.56	2.6	Baileh	Simms	USA	26.4.95	1		Tulsa	31 Mar
6.53	2.3	Erica	Jarder	SWE	2.4.86	8	DL	Stockholm	10 Jun
6.51	3.1	Todea-Kay	Willis	JAM	23.11.88	2		Kingston	14 Apr
6.51	4.4	Sumire	Hata	JPN	4.5.96	1		Okinawa	30 Jun
6.51	4.1	Adéla	Záhorová	CZE-J	13.11.99	1		Tábor	18 Jul
6.50	2.8	Mercy Uyoyo	Abire	NGR	20.7.97	1		Tulsa	12 May
6.50	3.0	Courtney	Corrin	USA	12.12.97	1		Stanford	12 May
6.49	5.2	Jhoanmy	Luque	VEN	20.12.95	1		Waco	12 May
6.47	3.4	Madisen	Richards	USA	15.11.96	2		Stanford	12 May

Mark	Wind	Name		Nat	Born	Pos	Meet	Venue		Date

6.47	2.2	Evelis	Aguilar	COL	3.1.93	2H	CAG	Barranquilla		1 Aug
6.47	3.4	Madisen	Richards	USA	15.11.96	12 May				
6.47	2.2	Evelis	Aguilar	COL	3.1.93	1 Aug				
6.45	3.1	Samara	Spencer	JAM	30.10.96	12 May				
6.45	3.1	Irène	Pusterla	SUI	21.6.88	14 Jul				
6.45	2.2	Alysbeth	Félix	PUR	7.3.93	30 Jul				
6.44	5.2	Keishorea	Armstrong	USA		26 Apr				
6.43	3.0	Savannah	Carson	USA	30.3.95	7 Jun				
6.41	nwi	Jasmine	Moore	USA-J	1.5.01	11 Apr				
6.40	nwi	Kynnedy	Flannel	USA-J	12.7.00	3 Mar				

			Nat	Born	Pos	Meet	Venue		Date
6.39	2.5	Yana	Nikulina	RUS	2.7.90	29 May
6.39	2.3	Hafdís	Sigurdardóttir	ISL	12.2.87	21 Jul
6.38	3.9	Fatim	Affessi	SUI	8.7.93	7 Jul
6.37	3.2	Katerina	Cachová	CZE	26.2.90	27 May
6.37	2.9	Sophie	Weißenberg	GER	24.9.97	30 Jun
6.37A	3.5	Maya	Evans	USA-J	12.6.99	2 Jun
6.37	2.9	Hanna	Minenko	ISR	25.9.89	5 Jul
6.36	2.3	Alyssa	Thompson	USA	25.9.94	6 May
6.36	3.2	Tebecca	Chapman	GBR	27.9.92	10 Jun

Best outdoors

6.87	0.7	Reese	2	Kuso	Chorzów	8 Jun
6.84	1.6	Moguenara	2		Weinheim	26 May
6.71	1.9	Sagnia	1	NC	Eskilstuna	26 Aug
6.46A	-0.1	Wang Qingling		15 Jun	6.42	1.4	Mitkova
6.44	0.3	Vicenzino		27 May	6.38	0.0	Luque
6.44	0.4	Argüelles		29 Jun	6.38	1.4	Carson

Best at low altitude

6.67	1.1	Martins	4		Marseille	16 Jun
6.68w	2.8	Martins	1	NC	Bragança P.	16 Sep
6.44	1.9	Melis Mey		27 Jun	6.40	1.3	Félix
6.43	1.4	Aranda		8 Jul	6.38	1.9	Mautino
6.40	1.8	Reyes		31 Mar			

6.70	0.9	Johnson-Thompson 5	DL	London (OS)	21 Jul
6.63	1.2	Hall	3		Athens, GA	5 May
6.63	0.4	Balta	Q	EC	Berlin	9 Aug
6.59	1.1	Burks	6	DL	Stockholm	10 Jun
			20	Jul	6.38	-0.5	Sudareva	8 Jun
			27	Apr	6.38	1.7	Farkas	9 Sep
			13	May	6.35	0.1	Dadic	10 Aug
6.50	0.1	Xu Xiaoling	1	AsiG	Jakarta	27 Aug
6.50	-0.4	Lu Minjia	4	AsiG	Jakarta	27 Aug
6.48	-0.4	dos Reis	1		São Bernardo	27 Jan
			30	Jul	6.49w	3.8	Mautino	24 Aug
			24	Aug	6.35w	2.4	Fuentes	22 Jun

JUNIORS

See main list for top 4 juniors. 11 performances (inc. 4 indoors) by 5 women to 6.45. Additional marks and further juniors:

T Davis		6.63	-2.1	2		Athens, GA	6 Apr		6.47i		5	SEC	College Station	24 Feb
		6.63	1.9	1	NSR	Torrance	21 Apr		6.45	0.4	*	NCAA	Eugene	7 Jun
		6.50i		3		NCAA College Station	9 Mar		6.48w	2.1	5	NCAA	Eugene	7 Jun
Thomas		6.58i		1		Rochester	17 Feb							
6.45	1.5	Adriana		Rodríguez	CUB	12.7.99	4H	Hypo	Götzis	27 May
6.44	0.8	Ayaka		Kora	JPN-Y	22.3.01	1	AsC-J	Gifu	9 Jun
6.44	0.4			Zhong Jiawei	CHN	7.2.99	2	AsC-J	Gifu	9 Jun
6.41i		Petra		Farkas	HUN	30.4.99	1		Budapest	11 Feb
6.41	1.6	Niamh		Emerson	GBR	22.4.99	6	NC	Birmingham	1 Jul
6.40A		Susana		Hernández (10)	MEX	18.1.99	1		Toluca	24 Apr
6.39	0.1	Jasmine		Moore	USA-Y	1.5.01	2	NC-j	Bloomington	16 Jun
6.39	1.4	Lucy		Hadaway	GBR	11.6.00	1		Manchester	28 Jul
6.39	1.2	Annik		Kälin	SUI	27.4.00	1		Bregenz	16 Sep
6.38i		Merle		Homeier	GER	27.8.99	1		Halle	25 Feb
6.38	0.7	Larissa		Iapichino	ITA-Y	18.7.02	1	NC-17	Rieti	16 Jun
6.38	0.0	Josie		Oliarnyk	GBR	27.3.00	7	NC	Birmingham	1 Jul
6.38	0.0			Chen Shuiqing	CHN	12.4.00	1	NC	Taiyuan	14 Sep
6.37	1.8	María		Vicente	ESP-Y	28.3.01	1H	EY	Györ	6 Jul
6.35A	0.2			Gong Luying	CHN	22.2.00	5	NGPF	Guiyang	15 Jun
6.34i		Ananda		Hansson (20)	SWE	19.10.99	1	v3N	Uppsala	11 Feb
6.34	1.2	Maelly		Dalmat	FRA-Y	1.10.01	1		Blois	23 Jun

Wind assisted   2 performances by 2 women to 6.45

6.41	nwi	Jasmine	Moore	USA	1.5.01	1		Lancaster	11 Apr
6.40	nwi	Kynnedy	Flannel	USA	12.7.00	1		Dickinson	3 Mar
6.37A	3.5	Maya	Evans	USA	12.6.99	1		Albuquerque	2 Jun

Doubtful mark: 6.42 Rimpi Buragohain IND-J 10.12.99 1 Patna 15 Sep

TRIPLE JUMP

14.96	0.1	Caterine		Ibargüen	COL	12.2.84	1	DL	Rabat	13 Jul
						14.70/0.0 14.71/-0.7 14.53/0.5 14.40/-0.3 14.96 14.91/0.0					
	14.92	1.2	1	CAG	Barranquilla	1 Aug	14.66w/2.2 14.74w/4.9 14.79/1.2 14.76w/3.9 14.92 x			
	14.56	-0.3	1	WK	Zürich	30 Aug	14.08 14.56 14.34 14.37 14.43/-0.3 x			
	14.54A	0.6	1		Medellín	28 Apr	14.02 14.22 x x 14.54			
14.84	0.0	Tori		Franklin	USA	7.10.92	1		Baie-Mahault	12 May
						14.54/0.0 14.84 14.78/0.0 14.57/0.0 x 14.54/0.5					
	14.57	0.2	2	Bisl	Oslo	7 Jun	14.13 14.52/0.9 14.21 x x 14.57			
14.69	1.3	Núbia		Soares	BRA	26.3.96	1		Sotteville-lès-Rouen	17 Jul
						14.19 14.69 14.26w p x x p					
	14.59A	0.2	1	SAmG	Cochabamba	7 Jun	x 14.38/0.6 14.59 14.59/0.8 x x p			
14.67	0.3	Yekaterina		Koneva	RUS	25.9.88	1		Maykop	7 Jun
						14.10 14.31 11.97 x 14.67 x					
	14.66	2.0	*	NC	Kazan	22 Jul	14.79w 14.62/1.5 p 14.66/2.0 x 14.64/1.4			
	14.50	1.8	1		Zhukovskiy	13 Jun	13.99 14.50 x x p x			
14.64	0.7	Kimberly		Williams	JAM	3.11.88	1	CG	Gold Coast	10 Apr
						x 14.34/0.6 x 14.37/1.2 x 14.64					
	14.56	0.7	2	DL	Paris (C)	30 Jun	13.35 14.56/0.7 14.40 14.38 14.56/0.9 14.43			

WOMEN 2018

Mark	Wind	Name		Nat	Born	Pos	Meet	Venue		Date
	14.50	-0.6 3 Bisl	Oslo		7 Jun	14.14	14.39w	14.50	14.25 14.46/0.9	14.38
14.63i		Yulimar	Rojas	VEN	21.10.95	1	WI	Birmingham		3 Mar
						14.24	14.07 14.27	14.36 14.63		x
14.62	1.5	Keturah	Orji	USA	5.3.96	1	SEC	Knoxville		13 May
						14.49w/2.1 x	x	x	14.51w/2.4	14.62
	14.60	0.6 2 AWC	London (OS)		15 Jul	14.21	14.51/-0.2	14.60	14.40	
	14.59	1.9 1 NC	Des Moines		21 Jun	14.34	x	14.59	x 14.10w	x
	14.53i	1	Clemson		20 Jan	14.53	14.28 14.04	p	p	p
14.61	0.8	Shanieka	Ricketts	JAM	2.2.92	1	AWC	London (OS)		15 Jul
						14.29	14.29 14.61	14.57/1.1		
	14.55	0.0 2 DL	Shanghai		12 May	14.20	x	x	14.25 14.55	x
	14.55	-0.8 2 WK	Zürich		30 Aug	14.19	14.52/0.0	x	14.42 14.55	14.45/0.0
	14.52	1.0 2 CG	Gold Coast		10 Apr	14.52/1.0 x	14.33	14.16 14.39		x
14.60	1.7	Paraskeví	Papahrístou	GRE	17.4.89	*	BalkC	Stara Zagora		20 Jul
						14.74w	14.60/1.7	p	p p	p
	14.60	-0.1 1 EC	Berlin		10 Aug	x	14.60	x	x x	14.32/0.1
14.55	-0.2	Ana	Peleteiro (10)	ESP	2.12.95	1	NC	Getafe		22 Jul
	(30/10)					14.39/1.4	14.54w/2.7	14.55 13.73	x	x
14.47	1.4	Elena	Panturoiu	ROU	24.2.95	1		Montreuil		19 Jun
14.47	1.6	Yosiry	Urrutia	COL	26.6.86	*	CAG	Barranquilla		1 Aug
14.45	-0.5	Kristin	Gierisch	GER	20.8.90	2	EC	Berlin		10 Aug
14.44i		Viktoriya	Prokopenko	RUS	17.4.91	1		Moskva		3 Feb
14.43	0.4	Jeanine	Assani Issouf	FRA	17.8.92	1	NC	Albi		8 Jul
14.41	-0.9	Hanna	Minenko	ISR	25.9.89	Q	EC	Berlin		8 Aug
14.40	0.8	Gabriela	Petrova	BUL	29.6.92	1		Plovdiv		19 May
14.33	-0.4	Neele	Eckhardt	GER	2.7.92	Q	EC	Berlin		8 Aug
14.31	0.3	Kristiina	Mäkelä	FIN	20.11.92	1	NC	Jyväskylä		21 Jul
14.31	-0.1	Rouguy	Diallo	FRA	5.2.95	Q	EC	Berlin		8 Aug
	(20)									
14.30i		Irina	Vaskovskaya	BLR	2.4.91	1	NCp	Gomel		3 Feb
14.30	-0.5	Liadagmis	Povea	CUB	6.2.96	1		Bragança Paulista		8 Jul
14.26	0.0	Olga	Rypakova	KAZ	30.11.84	1	AsiG	Jakarta		30 Aug
14.24	1.3	Anna	Jagaciak Michalska	POL	10.2.90	1	NC	Lublin		20 Jul
14.22	-0.8	Ana José	Tima	DOM	10.10.89	2		Kingston		9 Jun
14.20	1.4	Olha	Saladukha	UKR	4.6.83	1	Veniz	Haniá		2 Jun
14.20	-2.9	Darya	Nidbaykina	RUS	26.12.94	2		Zhukovskiy		13 Jun
14.19	1.9	Patrícia	Mamona	POR	21.11.88	3		Sotteville-lès-Rouen		17 Jul
14.18	1.6	Aleksandra	Nacheva	BUL-Y	20.8.01	1	WJ	Tampere		15 Jul
14.17	1.0	Parinya	Chuaimaroeng	THA	16.12.97	1		Taipei		25 May
	(30)									
14.17	-1.5	Susana	Costa	POR	22.9.84	Q	EC	Berlin		8 Aug
14.15	0.4	Yanis	David	FRA	12.12.97	1	MedG	Tarragona		29 Jun
14.15	0.2	Hanna	Krasutska	UKR	20.7.95	2	NC	Lutsk		21 Jul
14.15	-1.6	Naomi	Ogbeta	GBR	18.4.98	Q	EC	Berlin		8 Aug
14.14	0.5	Valentina	Kosolapova	RUS	11.7.97	1	NC-23	Chelyabinsk		8 Jul
14.13i		Dovile	Dzindzaletaite	LTU	14.7.93	3		Madrid		8 Feb
14.08i		Thea	LaFond	DMA	5.4.94	1		University Park		17 Feb
14.08	1.4	Patricia	Sarrapio	ESP	16.11.82	1		Castellón		16 Jun
14.07i		Ilionis	Guillaume	FRA	13.1.98	1	NC	Liévin		17 Feb
14.07	0.2	Irina	Ektova	KAZ	8.1.87	1		Almaty		30 Jun
	(40)									
14.05	0.4	Ottavia	Cestonaro	ITA	12.1.95	2	MedG	Tarragona		29 Jun
14.05A	1.2	Dariya	Derkach	ITA	27.3.93	1		Ávila		10 Jul
14.05	0.9	Tähti	Alver	EST	4.12.94	1	NC	Tallinn		28 Jul
14.02i		Anna	Krylova	RUS	3.10.85	3		Moskva		3 Feb
14.02i		Natalya	Yevdokimova	RUS	7.9.93	4		Moskva		3 Feb
14.02A	1.9	Ivonne	Rangel	MEX	24.8.93	1		Querétaro		29 Apr
14.02	0.2	Grace	Anigbata	NGR	16.9.98	1	AfrC	Asaba		5 Aug
14.00	1.1	Marie-José	Ebwea Bile	FRA	7.2.97	2		Fayetteville		28 Apr
13.95	2.0	Violetta	Skvortsova	BLR	15.4.98	1		Brest		25 May
13.95	1.1	María	Vicente	ESP-Y	28.3.01	1	EY	Györ		8 Jul
	(50)									
13.95	-0.4	Jessie	Maduka	GER	23.4.96	5	AWC	London (OS)		15 Jul
13.93	0.0		Vu Thi Men	VIE	10.7.90	3	AsiG	Jakarta		30 Aug
13.92	0.3	Davisleidis L.	Velazco	CUB-J	4.9.99	1		La Habana		23 Feb
13.92	0.3	Fátima	Diame	ESP	22.9.96	3	MedG	Tarragona		29 Jun
13.91	1.7	Sandisha	Antoine	LCA	5.11.91	5	CAG	Barranquilla		1 Aug
13.90	-0.2	Keila	Costa	BRA	6.2.83	3		Bragança Paulista		8 Jul
13.90	1.1	Lecabela	Quaresma	POR	26.12.89	*		Sotteville-lès-Rouen		17 Jul
13.89	1.2	Chaquinn	Cook	USA	10.7.97	3	MSR	Torrance		21 Apr
13.87	0.5	Jenny	Elbe	GER	18.4.90	3		Garbsen		13 May

Mark	Wind	Name		Nat	Born	Pos	Meet	Venue	Date	
13.87	1.8	Merilyn	Uudmäe	EST	26.3.91	2		Tallinn	7	Jul
		(60)								
13.87	0.0	Sokhna	Galle	FRA	23.4.94	4	NC	Albi	8	Jul
13.86	0.9	Olha	Korsun	UKR	11.11.96	3	NC	Lutsk	21	Jul
13.85i			Rao Fan	CHN	1.1.96	1	NGP	Xianlin	8	Mar
13.84	1.6	Imani	Oliver	USA	7.3.93	1		Auburn	14	Apr
13.82		Ruslana	Tsyhotska	UKR	23.3.86	1		New York	22	Jul
13.81A		Liuba M.	Zaldívar	CUB	5.4.93	1		Cuenca	24	Mar
13.81	1.7	Sanna	Nygård	FIN	22.3.88	1		Torremolinos	11	Jul
13.81	1.5	Mirieli	Santos	BRA-J	1.4.99	2	WJ	Tampere	15	Jul
13.79A	-0.6		Chen Ting	CHN	28.8.97	1	NGPF	Guiyang	16	Jun
13.78iA		Andrea	Geubelle	USA	21.6.91	2	NC	Albuquerque	17	Feb
		(70)								
13.78i			Wang Rong	CHN	1.7.96	2	NGP	Xianlin	12	Mar
13.78A	1.8	Patience	Ntshingila	RSA	26.8.89	1	NC	Pretoria	16	Mar
13.77	1.5	Dana	Veldáková	SVK	3.6.81	1		Tábor	18	Jul
13.76A	0.2	Giselly Andrea	Landázuri	COL	8.8.92	3		Medellín	28	Apr
13.76	1.6	Yelyzaveta	Babii	UKR	24.7.97	4	NC	Lutsk	21	Jul
13.76	0.2		Wang Wupin	CHN	18.1.91	1	NGP	Dalian	7	Aug
13.75	1.2	Nadia	Eke	GHA	11.1.93	1		Columbia	24	Mar
13.75	-1.1	Laura	Samuel	GBR	19.2.91	2	NC	Birmingham	30	Jun
13.75	0.0	Tamara	Myers	BAH	27.7.93	2		Leonora	30	Jun
13.74	1.6	Diana	Zagainova	LTU	20.6.97	2		Ogre	15	Jun
		(80)								
13.72	0.0	Thelma Nohemí	Fuentes	GUA	20.8.92	1	NC	San Salvador	23	Jun
13.69i			Chen Jie	CHN	2.3.98	2	NGP	Xianlin	8	Mar
13.69	1.2	Jhoanmy	Luque	VEN	20.12.95	1	DrakeR	Des Moines	28	Apr
13.68	1.0	Eva	Pepelnak	SLO-J	4.10.00	4	WJ	Tampere	15	Jul
13.68	0.9		Li Xiaohong	CHN	8.1.95	2	NGP	Dalian	7	Aug
13.67	1.8	Danellys	Dutil	CUB	12.2.95	2		Camagüey	4	Feb
13.67	0.3	Olesya	Ivanenko	RUS	6.10.82	2		Maykop	7	Jun
13.67	1.0	Oda Utsi	Onstad	NOR	12.5.90	1		Nadderud	17	Jun
13.67	1.3	Janne	Nielsen	DEN	8.6.93	*		Sotteville-lès-Rouen	17	Jul
13.66	1.4		Fu Luna	CHN	3.5.95	1	NGP	Zhuzhou	17	Apr
		(90)								
13.66	-0.1		Pan Youqi	CHN-J	10.7.00	1	NC	Taiyuan	16	Sep
13.65	0.0	Zinzi	Chanbangu	RSA	28.9.96	1		Sasolburg	27	Apr
13.65	0.3	Evelise	Veiga	POR	3.3.96	2	Med-23	Jesolo	10	Jun
13.64		Biljana	Topic	SRB	17.10.77	1		Dimitrovgrad	15	Jul
13.64	0.4		Li Ying	CHN	29.3.94	2	NC	Taiyuan	16	Sep
13.63	-1.5	Caroline	Ehrhardt	CAN	6.2.92	4	NACAC	Toronto	12	Aug
13.63	0.5		Renu	IND	21.12.98	1		Bhubaneswar	25	Sep
13.62	1.2	Kristína	Alvertsián	GRE	4.7.90	3		Athína (K)	26	May
13.62	0.6	Mara	Griva	LAT	4.8.89	4		Ogre	15	Jun
13.61i		Sabina	Allen	JAM		5	NCAA	College Station	10	Mar
		(100)								
13.61	1.0	LaChyna	Roe	USA	29.7.97	4	SEC	Knoxville	13	May
13.61	1.1	Kira	Kytölä	FIN	25.6.93	2	NC	Jyväskylä	21	Jul

Mark	Wind	Name		Nat	Born	Pos		Mark	Wind	Name		Nat	Born	Pos
13.60	0.2	Ayanna	Alexander	TTO	20.7.82	28 Apr		13.45	-0.2	Beyza	Tilki	TUR	3.3.94	21 Jul
13.60	-0.5	H.D.Vidusha Lakshani		SRI	28.12.96	5 Aug		13.44	1.5	Meggan	O'Riley	AUS	18.3.89	16 Feb
13.59i			Li Yu	CHN	28.1.00	8 Mar		13.44	-0.5	Eva	Mustar	SLO	30.9.96	20 Jul
13.58	0.0	Blessing	Ibrahim	NGR	4.4.90	14 Feb		13.43	1.9	Paetyn	Revell	USA	24.2.95	24 Mar
13.58	-1.1	LaJarvia	Brown	USA	14.2.98	14 Apr		13.43	1.5	Jasmine	Moore	USA-Y	1.5.01	31 Mar
13.57	0.6	Lerato	Schele	LES	10.3.94	10 Apr		13.43	1.9	Jakayla	Hand	USA	29.4.96	20 Apr
13.57	0.5		Bae Chan-mi	KOR	24.3.91	16 Jun		13.43	1.9	Claudine	de Jesus	BRA	9.9.94	5 May
13.56A	0.2	Silvana	Segura	PER	6.11.90	7 Jun		13.43	1.1	Michelle	Fokam	USA	8.6.98	13 May
13.55	-0.3	Paola	Borovic	CRO	26.6.95	20 Jul		13.43	1.6	Esra	Yilmaz	TUR-J	5.1.00	4 Jun
13.54	-0.6	Lynnika	Pitts	USA	19.5.92	28 Apr		13.43	2.0	Eszter	Bajnok	HUN	26.4.97	29 Jun
13.54	0.6	Ruta	Lasmane	LAT-J	17.12.00	15 Jul		13.43	1.4	Yelena	Drozhilina	RUS	21.1.98	8 Jul
13.53i		Cristina	Bujin	ROU	22.11.94	20 Jan		13.42	1.3	Ruth Marie	Ndoumbe	ESP	1.1.87	22 Jul
13.53	1.0	Nathalie	Marie-Nély	FRA	24.11.86	29 Apr		13.40		Hashini Praboda Balasooriya		SRI	10.7.98	13 Sep
13.52	0.2	Ana Margarida Oliveira		POR	18.7.95	26 Jul		13.39i		Mariya	Ovchinnikova	KAZ	19.10.98	11 Jan
13.51i		Irina	Gumenyuk	RUS	6.1.88	8 Feb		13.39	2.0	Adrianna	Szóstak	POL	2.3.96	8 Jul
13.51i		Birte	Damerius	GER	13.12.91	10 Feb		13.39	0.2	Tânia Ferreira da Silva		BRA	17.12.86	15 Sep
13.51	0.5		Li Yanmei	CHN	6.2.90	24 May		13.38	1.9	Aina	Griksaite	LTU	23.11.94	3 Jun
13.49	-0.5	Fatim	Affessi	SUI	8.7.93	1 Jul		13.38	0.0	Nellickal Varkey Sheena		IND	22.11.92	28 Jun
13.49	1.6	Olga	Velmyakina	RUS	3.8.92	22 Jul		13.38	1.4	Emma	Pullola	FIN	18.12.96	30 Jun
13.48	1.9	Ja'la	Henderson	USA	13.3.97	26 May		13.38	0.8	Yekaterina	Kropivko	RUS	13.6.97	8 Jul
13.47i		Kateryna	Popova	UKR	7.8.96	11 Feb		13.37i		Carmen	Toma	ROU	28.3.89	3 Feb
13.46	1.1	Jahisha	Thomas	GBR	22.11.94	26 May		13.37A	0.2	Valeria	Quispe	BOL	2.9.97	7 Jun
13.46	0.7	Georgiana	Anitei	ROU-J	26.3.99	2 Jun		13.37	0.6	Shaina	Mags	POR	11.4.92	22 Jul
13.45i			Zhou Minjuan	CHN	22.4.96	24 Mar		13.36i			Yang Yang	CHN-Y	23.8.01	24 Mar
13.45	0.7	Joëlle Mbumi Nkouindjin		CMR	25.5.86	10 Apr		13.36	1.7	Leyanis	Pérez	CUB-Y	10.1.02	4 Feb
13.45	1.9	Diana	Adasko	RUS-J	18.1.99	24 Jun		13.36	1.3	Natricia	Hooper	GUY	24.11.98	10 Apr

WOMEN 2018

Mark	Wind	Name		Nat	Born	Pos	Meet	Venue	Date
13.36			Tran Huy Hoa	VIE	8.8.91				12 Apr
13.36	1.0	Anastasiya	Abasheyeva	RUS	11.12.97				8 Jul
13.35i			Zeng Rui	CHN	6.2.98				8 Mar
13.35	1.5	Jehvania	Whyte	JAM					21 Apr
13.35		Jamaa	Chnaïk	MAR	28.7.84				6 May
13.35	0.8		Cai Linxia	CHN	6.10.98				24 May
13.35	1.6	Aliaksandra	Malafeyeva	BLR	12.9.98				25 May
13.35	1.6	Darya	Dyachenko	UKR	15.2.96				26 Jun
13.34iA		Viershanie	Latham	USA				1.8.95	17 Feb
13.33	0.0	K.M.	Sonam	IND				15.5.98	28 Jun
13.33	1.1		Duan Yuxuan	CHN				18.5.96	19 Jul
13.32		Angela	Barrett	GBR				25.12.85	23 Jun
13.31	0.1	Yargelis	Savigne	CUB				13.11.84	26 May
13.30	1.0	Hanifah	Abdulqadir	JAM					13 May
13.30	0.2	Ashley	Anderson	USA				12.11.96	26 May
(169)									

Wind assisted

Mark	Wind	Name		Nat	Born	Pos	Meet	Venue	Date
14.89	2.5		Ibargüen			1	Bisl	Oslo	7 Jun

14.89w/0.2 14.68w/2.3 14.69/1.5 14.83/0.7 x

| 14.79 | 2.3 | Yekaterina | Koneva | RUS | 25.9.88 | 1 | NC | Kazan | 22 Jul |

14.79w 14.62/1.5 p 14.66/2.0 x 14.64/1.4

| 14.74 | 2.1 | Paraskeví | Papahrístou | GRE | 17.4.89 | 1 | BalkC | Stara Zagora | 20 Jul |

14.74w 14.60/1.7 p p p p

| 14.57 | 2.3 | Hanna | Minenko | ISR | 25.9.89 | 1 | | Jerusalem | 6 Jun |

14.57w x x x x x

| 14.52 | 3.8 | | Franklin | | | 2 | NC | Des Moines | 21 Jun |

14.48/0.4 14.20w 14.12w x 13.57w 14.52w

| 14.52 | 3.2 | | Koneva | | | 1 | Znam | Zhukovskiy | 30 Jun |

14.16 14.52w p p p p

14.48	4.4	Gabriela	Petrova	BUL	29.6.92	1		Ruen	13 May
14.48	2.9	Yosiry	Urrutia	COL	26.6.86	2	CAG	Barranquilla	1 Aug
14.44	2.1	Liadagmis	Povea	CUB	6.2.96	3	CAG	Barranquilla	1 Aug
14.25	2.3	Olha	Saladukha	UKR	4.6.83	1		Kropyvnytskyi	26 Jun
14.22	2.8	Imani	Oliver	USA	7.3.93	3	NC	Des Moines	21 Jun
14.21	3.9	Hanna	Krasutska	UKR	20.7.95	2		Kropyvnytskyi	26 Jun
14.19	2.6	Lecabela	Quaresma	POR	26.12.89	2		Sotteville-lès-Rouen	17 Jul
14.06	3.2	Ottavia	Cestonaro	ITA	12.1.95	1		Modena	23 Jun
14.03	5.1	Dana	Veldáková	SVK	3.6.81	1	PTS	Samorín	29 Jun
13.83	3.8	Jasmine	Moore	USA-Y	1.5.01	1		Austin	11 May
13.83	3.0	Caroline	Ehrhardt	CAN	6.2.92	1		London, ON	3 Aug
13.76	3.3	Janne	Nielsen	DEN	8.6.93	5		Sotteville-lès-Rouen	17 Jul
13.65	3.8	Eszter	Bajnok	HUN	26.4.97	2	PTS	Samorín	29 Jun
13.60	3.7	Paetyn	Revell	USA	24.2.95				13 May
13.60	2.8	Nathalie	Marie-Nély	FRA	24.11.86				22 Jun
13.59	3.7	Lynnika	Pitts	USA	19.5.92				21 Jun
13.58	2.3	Irina	Gumenyuk	RUS	6.1.88				2 Jun
13.58	2.4	Georgiana	Anitei	ROU-J	26.3.99				30 Jun
13.53	2.8	Tugba	Aydin	TUR	25.8.94				7 Jul
13.51	2.1	Sinead	Gutzmore	GBR	9.10.86				30 Jun
13.50	2.1	Ja'la	Henderson	USA	13.3.97				26 May
13.49	3.2	Darya	Dyachenko	UKR	15.2.96				26 Jun
13.48	2.4	Krisztina	Hoffer	HUN	6.8.90				23 Jun
13.42	2.1	Jehvania	Whyte	JAM					24.8.96 21 Apr
13.41	3.3	Adrianna	Szóstak	POL					2.3.96 20 May
13.41	6.9	Zara	Asante	GBR					7.7.92 29 Jul
13.39	2.4	Emma	Pullola	FIN					18.12.06 8 Jul
13.38	2.5	Toni	Smith	USA					13.10.84 24 Mar
13.37	2.4	Amber	Hughes	USA					23.8.94 21 Apr
13.37	2.5	Darrielle	McQueen	USA					29.5.96 28 Apr
13.37	2.2	Natricia	Hooper	GUY					24.11.98 19 May
13.32	2.4	Danylle	Kurywchak	USA					15.7.94 19 May
13.31	4.6	Diana	Cauldwell	JAM					6 May

Best outdoors

Mark	Wind	Name	Pos	Meet/Venue	Date
14.01	0.0	LaFond	3	Baie-Mahault	12 May
13.97	1.6	Dzindzaletaite	4	Sotteville	17 Jul
13.93	-0.1	Prokopenko	6	DL Shanghai	12 May
13.51	-0.7	Gumenyuk			30 May
13.45	-0.1	Wang Rong			17 Apr

13.45	1.4	Geubelle				
13.44	1.7	Zhou Minjuan				
13.43	1.5	Rao Fan				

13.93	1.4	Vaskovskaya	1		Brest	7 Jun
13.92	1.0	Yevdokimova	3	NC	Kazan	22 Jul
13.67	2.0	Krylova	4	NCp	Smolensk	30 May
13.64	1.6	Guillaume	5	NC	Albi	8 Jul

21 Jun	13.39	0.6	Chen Jie	7 Aug
17 Apr	13.37	0.5	Popova	21 Jul
17 Apr	13.32	0.0	Zeng Rui	11 Apr

Best at low altitude

13.86	0.6	Derkach	1		Orvieto	17 Jun
13.69	0.0	Chen Ting	4	AsiG	Jakarta	30 Aug
10.00	0.2	Zaldívar				8 Jul

13.67	0.7	Rangel	*	CAG	Barranquilla	1 Aug
13.80w 2.6			6	CAG	Barranquilla	1 Aug
13.54	1.7	Landázuri				7 Jul
13.16	0.0	Ougura				25 Aug

JUNIORS

See main list for top 6 juniors. 10 performances (and 1 wa) by 4 women to 13.78. Additional marks and further juniors:

Name	Mark	Wind	Pos	Meet	Venue	Date	Mark	Wind	Pos	Meet	Venue	Date
Nacheva	14.00	-0.6	1	NC-j	Sofia	17 Jun	13.80	0.6	2		Athína	26 May
	13.88	0.7	2	EY	Györ	8 Jul	13.88w	2.5	3		Rouen	13 May
Velazco	13.86	0.0	2		La Habana	3 Mar	13.78	1.4	3	WJ	Tampere	15 Jul

Mark	Wind	Name		Nat	Born	Pos	Meet	Venue	Date
13.54	0.6	Ruta	Lasmane	LAT	17.12.00	5	WJ	Tampere	15 Jul
13.46	0.7	Georgiana	Anitei	ROU	26.3.99	2		Cluj-Napoca	2 Jun
13.45	1.9	Diana	Adasko	RUS	18.1.99	1	NC-j	Chelyabinsk	24 Jun
13.43	1.5	Jasmine	Moore (10)	USA-Y	1.5.01	1-HS	TexasR	Austin	31 Mar
13.43	1.6	Esra	Yilmaz	TUR	5.1.00	1	NC-j	Istanbul	4 Jun
13.36i			Yang Yang	CHN-Y	23.8.01	4	NGPF	Beijing	24 Mar
13.36	1.7	Leyanis	Pérez	CUB-Y	10.1.02	3		Camagüey	4 Feb
13.29	1.8	Jessica	Kähärä	FIN-Y	1.8.01	3	EY	Györ	8 Jul
13.27	0.7	Spiriroúla	Karíadi	GRE-Y	30.1.01	4	EY	Györ	8 Jul
13.26	0.7		Chen Shuiqing	CHN	12.4.00	7		Chongqing	24 May
13.26	1.8	Camilla	Vigato	ITA	5.9.00	1	NC-j	Agropoli	3 Jun
13.23	-2.4	Tessy	Ebosele	NGR-Y	28.7.02	1	ESP-y	Gijón	23 Jun
13.21	0.5	Roksan	Khudoyarova	UZB-Y	30.1.01	1		Bangkok	4 Jul

Mark		Name		Nat	Born	Pos	Meet	Venue		Date
13.19	1.4	Nerisnelia	Sousa (20)	BRA	24.2.01	1		Cuiaba		18 Mar
best out:	13.25 0.3		Yang Yang	CHN-Y	23.8.01	7	NC	Taiyuan		16 Sep
Wind assisted										
13.58	2.4	Georgiana	Anitei	ROU-J	26.3.99	1-		Pitesti		30 Jun
13.22	3.2		Vu Thi Ngoc Ha	VIR	21.5.00	1	Asi-J	Gifu		7 Jun

SHOT

Mark	Name		Nat	Born	Pos	Meet	Venue		Date
20.38		Gong Lijiao	CHN	24.1.89	1	NGPF	Guiyang		17 Jun
		19.45	19.63	19.75	19.26	19.79	20.38		
20.31	1 Herc	Monaco	19 Jul	19.44	19.89	20.02	19.90	20.06	20.31
19.99	1 DL	Shanghai	12 May	19.27	19.99	19.87	x	x	19.85
19.90	1 AWC	London (OS)	15 Jul	18.92	19.53	19.35	19.90		
19.83	1 VD	Bruxelles	30 Aug	18.70	19.39	19.56	19.61	19.83	19.56
19.66	1 AsiG	Jakarta	26 Aug	19.09	19.43	19.19	x	19.26	19.66
19.63	3 C.Cup	Ostrava	9 Sep	19.17	19.58	19.44	19.63	19.25	
19.53i	1 NGPF	Beijing	24 Mar	18.96	19.03	18.87	18.89	19.29	19.53
19.51	1 NGP	Zhaoqing	12 Apr	18.90	19.12	18.92	18.91	19.05	19.51
19.30	1 NGP	Huaian	18 May	18.57	19.14	18.84	18.88	19.18	19.30
20.06	Christina	Schwanitz	GER	24.12.85	1	NC	Nürnberg		20 Jul
		19.55	x	x	18.05	20.06	x		
19.78	1	Biberach	9 Jul	19.78	x	19.36	x	19.08	x
19.73	2 C.Cup	Ostrava	9 Sep	18.88	19.73	19.21	19.07		
19.51	3 Herc	Monaco	19 Jul	19.17	19.08	19.51	19.06	x	18.96
19.50	1	Gelenau	21 May	18.73	19.34	19.01	19.50	18.97	x
19.50	3 VD	Bruxelles	30 Aug	18.68	19.01	19.50	x	18.89	18.94
19.40	1 DL	Rabat	13 Jul	19.40	19.11	19.27	19.29	x	x
19.39	1	Halle	12 May	19.39	19.12	18.92	x	x	18.76
19.74	Raven	Saunders	USA	15.5.96	1	C.Cup	Ostrava		9 Sep
		x	18.38	19.74	19.27	18.39			
19.67	2 Herc	Monaco	19 Jul	18.23	19.25	x	x	19.67	x
19.64	2 VD	Bruxelles	30 Aug	x	17.88	19.64	x	x	x
19.56	1	Auburn	21 Apr	19.09	19.56	19.42	19.08	19.27	x
19.51	1	Baton Rouge	28 Apr	x	19.51	19.05,	x	x	x
19.62i	Anita	Márton	HUN	15.1.89	1	WI	Birmingham		2 Mar
		18.29	18.30	19.48	x	18.96	19.62		
19.46	Maggie	Ewen	USA	23.9.94	1		Tucson		28 Apr
		x	18.46	18.45	x	18.46	19.46		
19.29	1 NC	Des Moines	24 Jun	17.94	19.09	x	18.58	19.29	18.74
19.38	Paulina	Guba	POL	14.5.91	1	Skol	Cetniewo		8 Jul
		18.40	18.45	19.38	19.35	18.69	x		
19.33	1 EC	Berlin	8 Aug	18.77	18.77	x	18.49	19.02	19.33
19.29	2 AWC	London (OS)	15 Jul	18.30	18.60	19.29	18.82		
19.36	Danniel	Thomas-Dodd	JAM	11.11.92	1	CG	Gold Coast		13 Apr
		18.36	18.70	18.57	18.44	19.36,			
19.31	Valerie	Adams	NZL	6.10.84	4	Herc	Monaco		19 Jul
	(31/8)								
19.23	Jessica	Ramsey	USA	26.7.91	2	NC	Des Moines		24 Jun
19.21	Alyona	Dubitskaya (10)	BLR	25.1.90	2	DL	Rabat		13 Jul
18.97	Natalia	Ducó	CHI	31.1.89	1		Fort Lauderdale		18 May
	Ducó: Pending doping case; positive in a control in Chile on 19 April								
18.95	Radoslava	Mavrodieva	BUL	13.3.87	1	BalkC	Stara Zagora		20 Jul
18.77i		Gao Yang	CHN	1.3.93	4	WI	Birmingham		2 Mar
18.70	Monique	Riddick	USA	8.11.89	1		West Point		10 May
18.68	Fanny	Roos	SWE	2.1.95	1		La Jolla		14 Apr
18.68	Jessica	Woodard	USA	4.2.95	2	NCAA	Eugene		7 Jun
18.63	Melissa	Boekelman	NED	11.5.89	1		Vught		15 Sep
18.60	Cleopatra	Borel	TTO	10.3.79	1		Santiago de Chile		7 Feb
18.60	Brittany	Crew	CAN	6.3.94	3		Madrid		22 Jun
18.58	Yaniuvis	López	CUB	1.2.86	1		Bragança Paulista		8 Jul
	(20)								
18.55i	Jeneva	Stevens	USA	28.10.89	1	NC	Montréal		10 Feb
18.52	Alyona	Bugakova	RUS	24.4.97	1		Moskva		13 Jun
18.52	Sarah	Mitton	CAN	20.6.96	1		Collegeville		10 Aug
18.48	Klaudia	Kardasz	POL	2.5.96	4	EC	Berlin		8 Aug
18.45	Dimitriana	Surdu	MDA	12.5.94	3	ECp-w	Leiria		10 Mar
18.43	Sara	Gambetta	GER	18.2.93	1	ISTAF	Berlin		2 Sep
18.42	Yuliya	Leontyuk	BLR	31.1.84	4	DL	Shanghai		12 May
18.35	Viktoryia	Kolb	BLR	26.10.93	1		Brest		29 Jun
18.28i	Irina	Tarasova	RUS	15.4.87	1		Moskva		4 Feb
18.27	Erin	Farmer	USA	11.8.95	1		Los Angeles		31 Mar
	(30)								

WOMEN 2018

Mark	Name		Nat	Born	Pos	Meet	Venue	Date	
18.21	Alina	Kenzel	GER	10.8.97	1		Rechberghausen	3	Jun
18.18i	Dani	Hill	USA	16.5.91	1		Allendale	9	Feb
18.16	Michelle	Carter	USA	12.10.85	5		Kingston	9	Jun
18.15		Bian Ka	CHN	5.1.93	3	Werfer	Halle	26	May
18.14i	Emmonnie	Henderson	USA	5.11.94	1		Clemson	24	Feb
18.12	Emel	Dereli	TUR	25.2.96	1	Med-23	Jesolo	10	Jun
18.11	Alena	Abramchuk	BLR	14.2.88	2	NC	Minsk	20	Jul
18.10	Geisa	Arcanjo	BRA	19.9.91	1	IbAmC	Trujillo	26	Aug
18.09	Lena	Giger	USA	7.6.96	2		La Jolla	14	Apr
18.09	Ahymara	Espinoza	VEN	28.5.85	2	SAmG	Cochabamba	7	Jun
	(40)								
18.04	María Fernanda	Orozco	MEX	25.1.98	1		Querétaro	26	May
18.03	Janeah	Stewart	USA	21.7.96	5	NC	Des Moines	24	Jun
17.94	Alena	Pasechnik	BLR	17.4.95	1		Minsk	11	Jul
17.89	Rachel	Fatherly	USA	20.4.94	2		Tucson	17	May
17.83i		Guo Tianqian	CHN	1.6.95	1	NGP	Dalian	8	Mar
17.81i	McKenzie	Warren	USA	3.12.93	1		Seattle	27	Jan
17.78	Chase	Ealey	USA	20.7.94	3		Tucson	17	May
17.78	Anna	Avdeyeva	RUS	6.4.85	1	Znam	Zhukovskiy	30	Jun
17.76	Sophie	McKinna	GBR	31.8.94	5	CG	Gold Coast	13	Apr
17.73	Ashlie	Blake	USA	7.6.96	2		Los Angeles	31	Mar
	(50)								
17.68	Yevgeniya	Solovyova	RUS	28.6.86	2	NCp	Smolensk	30	May
17.68		Song Jiayuan	CHN	15.9.97	1		Guangzhou	30	Dec
17.67i	Felisha	Johnson	USA	24.7.89	1		Anderson	3	Feb
17.66	Lloydricia	Cameron	USA	8.4.96	2		Gainesville	13	Apr
17.57	Breana	Jemison	USA	11.12.93	1		La Jolla	31	Mar
17.56	Ischke	Senekal	RSA	8.1.93	1		Sasolburg	28	Apr
17.52	Aliyah	Gustafson	USA	3.5.95	1		Buffalo	11	May
17.49	Keely	Medeiros	BRA	30.4.87	4		Bragança Paulista	9	Jul
17.40	Rachel	Wallader	GBR	1.9.89	6	CG	Gold Coast	13	Apr
17.46	Katharina	Maisch	GER	12.6.97	1		Neubrandenburg	12	May
	(60)								
17.46	Jessica	Inchude	GBS	25.3.96	1		Almada	31	May
17.45	Sarah	Schmidt	GER	9.7.97	5		Osterode	1	Jun
17.41	Olha	Holodna	UKR	14.11.91	1		Kyiv	15	Jun
17.37	Divine	Oladipo	GBR	5.10.98	4q	NCAA-E	Tampa	24	May
17.35	Portious	Warren	TTO	2.3.96	2	SEC	Knoxville	12	May
17.34i	Sade	Olatoye	USA	25.1.97	1		Columbus	5	Jan
17.34	Laulauga	Tausaga-Collins	USA	22.5.98	4	NCAA	Eugene	7	Jun
17.33		Zhang Linru	CHN-J	23.9.99	1	NC-j	Nanchang	11	May
17.32	Jess	St. John	ANT	15.12.95	7	CG	Gold Coast	13	Apr
17.32	Noora Salem	Jassem	BRN	27.11.96	1	NC	Getafe	21	Jul
	(70)								
17.31	Samantha	Noennig	USA	28.7.98	2		Tucson	28	Apr
17.31	Amelia	Strickler	GBR	24.1.94	Q	EC	Berlin	7	Aug
17.30i	Chiara	Rosa	ITA	28.1.83	1		Padova	3	Feb
17.30i	Alyssa	Wilson	USA-J	20.2.99	3		Albuquerque	10	Feb
17.28	Jorinde	van Klinken	NED-J	2.2.00	1		Emmeloord	16	Jun
17.24i	Gleneve	Grange	JAM	6.7.95	1		Notre Dame	17	Feb
17.24		Geng Shuang	CHN	9.7.93	2	NC	Taiyuan	17	Sep
17.23	Stamatía	Skarvéli	GRE	17.8.95	3	SEC	Knoxville	12	May
17.22	Tia	Brooks-Wannemacher	USA	2.8.90	5		Tucson	19	May
17.17i	Taryn	Suttie	CAN	7.12.90	4	NC	Montréal	10	Feb
	(80)								
17.16i	Kiley	Sabin	USA	28.4.96	5	NCAA	College Station	9	Mar
17.15i	Christina	Hillman	USA	6.10.93	6	NC	Albuquerque	17	Feb
17.12	Yelena	Smolyanova	UZB	16.2.86	1		Bishkek	17	Jun
17.11	Lindsay	Baker	USA-J	10.4.99	1		Columbus	21	Apr
17.11	Banke	Oginni	USA	8.5.96	3q	NCAA-W	Sacramento	24	May
17.11	Frida	Åkerström	SWE	29.11.90	2	vFIN	Tampere	1	Sep
17.09	Maddison-Lee	Wesche	NZL-J	13.6.99	1	WJ	Tampere	11	Jul
17.08	Ányela	Rivas	COL	13.8.89	1	NC	Barranquilla	8	Jul
17.08	Assunta	Legnante	ITA	14.5.78	1		Ascoli Piceno	28	Jul
17.06	Úrsula	Ruiz	ESP	11.8.83	13q	EC	Berlin	7	Aug
	(90)								
17.05	Tochi	Nlemchi	USA	26.3.95	1		Cincinnati	13	May
17.05	Markéta	Cervenková	CZE	20.8.91	1		Kladno	14	Jul
17.03	Jessica	Cérival	FRA	20.1.82	1		St-Louis	2	Jun
17.02	Galissia	Cause	USA	5.10.95	2		Cincinnati	13	May

Mark	Name		Nat	Born	Pos	Meet	Venue	Date
17.01	Torie	Owers	NZL	6.3.94	3		Auckland	25 Mar
17.00	Julia	Ritter	GER	13.5.98	6	NC	Nürnberg	20 Jul
16.97	Ashley	Davis	USA	10.3.97	1		Baton Rouge	21 Apr
16.97	Lena	Urbaniak	GER	31.10.92	2		Bad Boll	1 May
16.95	Senja	Mäkitörmä	FIN	31.5.94	1	NC	Jyväskylä	21 Jul
	(100)							

Mark	Name		Nat	Born	Date
16.94	Khayla	Dawson	USA	18.3.98	13 Apr
16.94	Valeriya	Zyryanova	RUS	12.8.90	15 May
16.94	Evaggelía	Sofáni	GRE	28.1.85	10 Jun
16.94i	Bailey	Retzlaff	USA	22.4.97	7 Dec
16.93	Josephine	Terlecki	GER	17.2.86	28 Jun
16.86	Crystal	Onwukaife	USA	25.3.98	5 May
16.83		Lee Mi-young	KOR	19.8.79	14 Oct
16.82	Brenn	Flint	USA	9.6.97	17 Mar
16.81i	Jessica	Maroszek	USA	26.2.92	26 Jan
16.80	Sophia	Rivera	USA	17.10.98	4 May
16.80	Benthe	König	NED	7.4.98	7 Jul
16.78i	Elena	Bruckner	USA	14.4.98	3 Feb
16.78i	Lauren	Evans	USA	.95	8 Dec
16.77		Chen Xiarong	CHN	21.12.98	17 Jun
16.77	Ivana	Gallardo	CHI	20.3.93	22 Sep
16.75	Selina	Dantzler	GER-J	12.3.00	26 May
16.75		Lin Chia-Ying	TPE	5.11.82	25 Jul
16.74i	Elizabeth	Iversen	USA	7.11.94	9 Feb
16.72i	Michaela	Dendinger	USA	9.5.95	3 Feb
16.69i	Yekaterina	Burmistrova	RUS	18.8.90	13 Feb
16.69	Brittany	Smith	USA	25.3.91	25 Mar
16.69	Alexis	Chiles	USA	.95	24 May
16.67	Anna	Rüh	GER	17.6.93	18 May
16.65	Viktoriya	Klochko	UKR	2.9.92	22 Jun
16.64	Alexandra	Emilianov	MDA-J	19.9.99	28 Apr
16.63	Magdalena	Żebrowska	POL	11.1.91	12 May
16.63		Jiang Yue	CHN	6.10.98	18 May
16.63	Eliana	Bandeira	POR	1.7.96	20 Jun
16.61i	Toni	Tupper	USA	3.11.95	23 Feb
16.61i	Micaela	Hazlewood	USA	18.6.95	23 Feb
16.61	Brittany	Cox	USA	18.4.88	27 Apr
16.60	Yuliya	Bayrak	UKR	9.2.98	7 Jun
16.58	Mackenna	Howard	USA	25.1.96	28 Apr
16.58	Ieva	Zarankaite	LTU	23.11.94	11 May
16.54	Courtney	Pasiowitz	USA	.95	12 May
16.53	Meia	Gordon	USA	12.3.98	20 Apr
16.53	Olivia	Moriconi	CAN	27.4.96	21 Apr
16.52	Nia	Britt	USA	12.2.97	13 May
16.52	Zada	Swoopes	USA-J	24.3.99	26 May
16.51	Anastasiya	Popova	RUS	18.9.96	30 Jun
16.50i	Annette	Echikunwoke	USA	29.7.96	24 Feb
16.50	Yemisi	Ogunleye	GER	3.10.98	26 May
16.49	María Belén	Toimil	ESP	5.5.94	28 Apr
16.49	Cherisse	Murray	TTO	13.9.93	19 May
16.46	Latavia	Maines	USA		19 May
16.45	Navjeet	Kaur	IND	6.3.95	8 Mar
16.44	Yelena	Bezruchenko	RUS	23.7.96	28 Jul
16.42	Haley	Teel	USA	20.6.96	28 Apr
16.00	Aya	Ota (198)	JPN	13.4.95	19 Aug
16.42	Anna	Niedbala	POL	10.7.98	22 Jul
16.37	Devia	Brown	JAM	21.3.98	14 Apr
16.36i	Vera	Kunova	RUS	2.4.90	13 Feb
16.34	Rosario	Sánchez	MEX	3.4.88	14 Apr
16.31	Katelyn	Daniels	USA	11.4.95	24 May
16.31	Snezhana	Trofimets	RUS-J	1.7.99	6 Jul
16.29	Caroline	Metayer	FRA	22.11.92	8 Jul
16.28	Dianelis	Delís	CUB-J	21.4.99	2 Jun
16.27i	Senja	Mäkitörmä	FIN	31.5.94	17 Feb
16.26	Yiliena	Otamendi	CUB	12.4.96	10 Feb
16.26i	Sunflower	Greene	USA	.96	10 Mar
16.26		Yu Tianxiao	CHN-Y	6.6.01	1 Apr
16.26	Brianna	Cueva	USA	6.6.95	14 Apr
16.25i	Sydney	Giampietro	ITA-J	27.1.99	3 Mar
16.24i	Nayoka	Clunis	JAM	7.10.95	6 Jan
16.22	Debbie	Ajagbe	USA	2.11.98	11 May
16.22	Irina	Kirichenko	RUS	18.5.87	6 Jun
16.21i	Shelby	Gunnells	USA	1.1.97	8 Dec
16.20	Ambar	Sánchez	VEN	10.4.92	5 May
16.20	Trine	Mulbjerg	DEN	23.4.90	12 May
16.19		He Bing	CHN	31.5.98	5 Apr
16.19	Victoria	McKinley	USA	15.10.98	24 May
16.14i	Rose Sharon	Pierre-Louis	FRA	7.9.94	17 Feb
16.14	Nora	Monie	USA	4.6.97	28 Apr
16.14		Lee Su-kyung	KOR	15.2.93	3 May
16.13	Tamia	Crockett	USA		12 May
16.13	Agnieszka	Maluskiewicz	POL	18.3.89	26 Aug
16.12	Eden	Francis	GBR	19.10.88	1 Jul
16.11i		Sun Yue	CHN-Y	19.6.01	12 Mar
16.11	Jena	Black	USA	10.9.96	11 May
16.11	Kaisa	Kymäläinen	FIN	11.10.94	21 Jul
16.11	Nanaka	Kori	JPN	2.5.97	28 Oct
16.09i	Nicole	Fautsch	USA	17.1.98	3 Feb
16.09	Jasmine	Smith	USA	2.6.95	26 May
16.09	Brittany	Jones	USA-J	15.5.99	17 Jun
16.08	Meike	Strydom	RSA-J	25.8.00	15 May
16.08	Lea	Riedel	GER-J	19.5.99	29 Jul
16.05	Saily	Viart	CUB	10.9.95	10 Feb
16.05	Layselys R.	Jiménez	CUB--Y	18.2.01	10 Feb
16.05	Christine	Bohan	USA		4 May
16.05	Cassaundra	Roper	USA	25.6.96	24 May
16.05	Kathleen	Young	USA-J	31.7.99	17 Jun
16.05	Maura	Kimmel	USA	1.3.98	23 Jun
16.03i	Jessica	Schilder	NED-J	19.3.99	17 Feb
16.01	Claudia	Ababio	GHA	15.10.96	24 May
16.01	Kätlin	Piirimäe	EST	8.11.95	7 Jul
16.00	Brandy	Williams	USA	15.7.97	24 Mar
16.00	Brandy	Thomas	USA	1.8.97	21 Apr
16.00	Abigale	Wilson	USA	28.1.97	11 May

Best outdoors

19.12	Márton	1	ECp-w	Leiria		10 Mar
18.36	Gao Yang	2		Osterode		1 Jun
18.33	Stevens	4		Kingston		9 Jun
18.09	Tarasova	1		Moskva		11 Jun
18.02	Hill	1		Rathdrum		2 Jun
17.76	Guo Tianqian	3	NGP	Zhaoqing		12 Apr
17.26	M Warren	1		Gresham		10 Mar
17.21	Alyssa Wilson	6	NCAA	Eugene		7 Jun
17.08	Rosa	1	NC	Pescara		9 Sep

16.99	Suttie	2			16.73	Olatoye	21 Apr
Timaru 14				Mar	16.57	Burmistrova	20 Jul
16.89	Sabin		28 Apr		16.55	Dendinger	12 May
16.89	Grange		11 May		16.54	Bruckner	21 Apr
16.05	Sun Yue		5 Apr				
16.04	Clunis		28 Apr				
16.53	Tupper		13 May		16.10	Echikunwoke	31 Mar
16.45	Retzlaff		12 May		16.10	Greene	26 May
16.41	Evans		24 May		16.10	Pierre-Louis	2 Jun
16.11	Kunova		20 Jul		16.09	Iversen	24 May

WOMEN 2018

JUNIORS

See main list for top 5 juniors. 12 performances (2 indoor) by 5 women to 17.77. Additional marks and further juniors:

Zhang L	17.15	2cB	Werf	Halle	26 May		17.05	2	WJ	Tampere	11 Jul
Wilson 2+	17.02	Q	WJ	Tampere	11 Jul					
van Klinken	17.05i	1	NC-j	Apeldoorn	11 Feb		17.05	3	WJ	Tampere	11 Jul
Wesche	17.00	1		Manheim	23 Jun					

16.75	Selina	Dantzler	GER	12.3.00	1J	Werfer	Halle	26 May
16.64	Alexandra	Emilianov	MDA	19.9.99	3		Fayetteville	28 Apr
16.52	Zada	Swoopes	USA	24.3.99	1	NCAA-II	Charlotte	26 May

Mark		Name		Nat	Born	Pos	Meet	Venue		Date
16.31		Snezhana	Trofimets	RUS	1.7.99	3	NC-23	Chelyabinsk		6 Jul
16.28		Dianelis	Delís (10)	CUB	21.4.99	3		La Habana		2 Jun
16.26			Yu Tianxiao	CHN-Y	6.6.01	4	NGP	Chengdu		1 Apr
16.25i		Sydney	Giampietro	ITA-J	27.1.99	1	v2N-J	Nantes		3 Mar
	15.97					2		Jesolo		10 Jun
16.11i			Sun Yue	CHN-Y	19.6.01	3	NGP	Xianlin		12 Mar
16.09		Brittany	Jones	USA	15.5.99	3	NC-j	Bloomington		17 Jun
16.08		Meike	Strydom	RSA	25.8.00	2	NC	Pretoria		15 Mar
16.08		Lea	Riedel	GER	19.5.99	1	NC-j	Rostock		29 Jul
16.05		Kathleen	Young	USA	31.7.99	4	NC-j	Bloomington		17 Jun
16.03i		Jessica	Schilder	NED	19.3.99	3	NC	Apeldoorn		17 Feb
15.99		Hanna	Meinikmann	GER	28.3.99	2	Werf	Halle		26 May
15.85i		Josefine	Klisch (20)	GER-Y	19.7.01	1		Hannover		27 Jan
15.85		Essence	Henderson	USA	11.3.99	18q	NCAA-W	Sacramento		24 May

DISCUS

Mark		Name		Nat	Born	Pos	Meet	Venue		Date
71.38		Sandra	Perkovic	CRO	21.6.90	1	DL	Doha		4 May
					66.78	67.41	71.38	66.34	x	66.98
	69.13	1	Split		5 Mar	x	67.49	65.89	x	69.13 66.44
	68.93	1 GGala	Roma		31 May	64.13	x	65.11	x	68.93 x
	68.92	1	Bellinzona		18 Jul	68.92	68.04	65.47	x	x x
	68.60	1 DL	Paris (C)		30 Jun	47.51	68.60	x	65.63	x 67.85
	68.44	1 NC-w	Split		3 Mar	?	?	68.44	only other valid throw 67.35
	68.44	1 C.Cup	Ostrava		8 Sep	68.44	x	64.92	65.57	x
	67.62	1 EC	Berlin		11 Aug	x	59.09	59.97,	x	67.62 x
	67.60	1 Hanz	Zagreb		4 Sep	x	66.10	67.60	x	65.80 64.43
	67.24	1 DL	London (OS)		22 Jul	67.24	x	x	x	x x
	66.46	1 MedG	Tarragona		28 Jun	66.46	x	x	x	x x
	66.22	1 PNG	Turku		5 Jun	66.22	x	x	x	x x
69.06		Dani	Stevens	AUS	26.5.88	1	CG	Gold Coast		12 Apr
					61.39	64.51	65.43	68.26	65.10	x
	66.09	1	Sydney		17 Mar	63.68	x	66.09	x	65.67 x
	66.02	1	Sydney		2 Feb	65.64	60.76	60.55	61.23	66.02 x
	65.30	1 NC	Gold Coast		18 Feb	65.30	63.53	x	62.59	x 63.50
67.82		Yaimé	Pérez	CUB	29.5.91	1		Las Tunas		10 Feb
					65.18	65.40	67.82	x	63.52	65.07
	66.82	2 DL	Doha		4 May	65.33	66.82	63.75	64.82	63.62 65.68
	66.62	2 GGala	Roma		31 May	58.68	66.62	65.42	x	65.31 64.44
	66.55	2 DL	Paris (C)		30 Jun	61.66	x	66.55	61.42	65.35 64.18
	66.00	1 CAG	Barranquilla		31 Jul	63.76	66.00	65.87	64.35	63.36 64.47
	65.42	1	Guadalajara, ESP		5 Jul	60.83	64.99	65.42	62.00	62.59 61.08
	65.30	2 C.Cup	Ostrava		8 Sep	62.27	65.00	63.02	64.01	65.30
66.09		Denia	Caballero	CUB	13.1.90	2		Las Tunas		10 Feb
					x	64.78	66.09	x	x	61.31
	65.10	2 CAG	Barranquilla		31 Jul	64.99	65.10	62.32	61.18	x x
67.03			Chen Yang	CHN	10.7.91	1		Osterode		2 Jun
					63.66	64.50	64.29	64.53	64.03	67.03
	66.56	1 WWerf	Halle		26 May	59.16	63.20	62.79	66.56	66.11 63.98
	65.42A	1 NGPF	Guiyang		15 Jun	62.60	x	64.26	64.46	x 65.42
	65.12	1 AsiG	Jakarta		30 Aug	59.61	64.4	63.57	64.20	64.89 65.12
65.15		Claudine	Vita	GER	19.9.96	2	WWerf	Halle		26 May
					58.33	65.15	61.87	x	63.96	x
65.10		Andressa	de Morais	BRA	21.12.90	1		Bragança Paulista		8 Jul
	(31/7)					64.03	63.30	64.49	65.10	
64.66		Fernanda	Borges	BRA	26.7.88	2	NC	Bragança Paulista		15 Sep
64.58			Feng Bin	CHN	3.4.94	3	WWerf	Halle		26 May
63.92		Yelena	Panova (10)	RUS	2.3.87	1	Rus Cup	Smolensk		29 May
63.73			Su Xinyue	CHN	8.11.91	4	WWerf	Halle		26 May
63.55		Valarie	Allman	USA	23.2.95	1	NC	Des Moines		21 Jun
63.00		Nadine	Müller	GER	21.11.85	2	EC	Berlin		11 Aug
62.91		Shanice	Craft	GER	15.5.93	1	NC	Nürnberg		22 Jul
62.66		Anna	Rüh	GER	17.6.93	5	WWerf	Halle		26 May
62.47		Maggie	Ewen	USA	23.9.94	2		Chula Vista		12 Apr
62.41		Yuliya	Maltseva	RUS	30.11.90	1		Sochi		7 Feb
62.37		Irina	Rodrigues	POR	5.2.91	1		Vagos		24 Feb
62.26		Seema	Punia	IND	27.7.83	3	AsiG	Jakarta		30 Aug
62.10		Shadae	Lawrence	JAM	31.12.95	1q	NCAA-w	Sacramento		25 May
	(20)									
61.97		Subenrat	Insaeng	THA	10.2.94	1		Kolín		19 Jul
61.63		Julia	Harting	GER	1.4.90	5	NC	Nürnberg		22 Jul

Mark	Name		Nat	Born	Pos	Meet	Venue	Date	
61.47	Alex	Collatz	USA	25.5.93	1		Claremont	2	Jun
61.16	Rachel	Dincoff	USA	24.12.93	1		Tucson	19	May
61.11	Kristin	Pudenz	GER	9.2.93	6	NC	Nürnberg	22	Jul
61.10	Whitney	Ashley	USA	18.2.89	1		Long Beach	21	Apr
61.09	Gia	Lewis-Smallwood	USA	1.4.79	5	DL	London (OS)	22	Jul
61.04	Kamalpreet	Kaur	IND	3.4.96	1		Lucknow	17	Aug
61.02	Liliana	Cá	POR	5.11.86	1		Lisboa	25	Feb
60.97	Summer	Pierson	USA	3.9.78	2		Rathdrum	1	Jun
	(30)								
60.78	Dragana	Tomasevic	SRB	4.6.82	1		Sremska Mitrovica	23	Jun
60.74	Tara-Sue	Barnett	JAM	9.10.93	1		Lawrence	12	May
60.65	Laulauga	Tausaga-Collins	USA	22.5.98	3	NC	Des Moines	21	Jun
60.54	Siositina	Hakeai	NZL	1.3.94	1		Auckland	7	Mar
60.44	Kelsey	Card	USA	20.8.92	1		Tucson	17	May
60.39	Serena	Brown	BAH	15.9.98	1	TexasR	Austin	31	Mar
60.24	Alexandra	Emilianov	MDA-J	19.9.99	1		Waco	12	May
60.16	Gabi	Jacobs	USA	20.8.96	5	NC	Des Moines	21	Jun
60.02	Corinne	Nugter	NED	28.3.92	1		Heerhugowaard	17	May
59.83	Jade	Lally	GBR	30.3.87	1		St. Clement	30	Aug
	(40)								
59.72	Daisy	Osakue	ITA	16.1.96	1		San Angelo	8	Apr
59.57	Daria	Zabawska	POL	16.4.95	1		Lódⓧ	19	May
59.56		Lu Xiaoxin	CHN	22.2.89	4		Osterode	2	Jun
59.45	Veronika	Domjan	SLO	3.9.96	1		Zagreb	23	May
59.42	Hrisoúla	Anagnostopoúlou	GRE	27.8.91	1		Trípoli	5	May
59.18	Navjeet	Kaur	IND	6.3.95	1		Patiala	27	Feb
59.15i	Chioma	Onyekwere	NGR	28.6.94	1		Allendale	22	Dec
	58.09				1	AfrC	Asaba	3	Aug
59.12	Valentina	Aniballi	ITA	19.4.84	1		Tarquinia	13	Jun
59.02	Jorinde	van Klinken	NED-J	2.2.00	1	WWerf 23	Halle	27	May
58.95	Taryn	Gollshewsky	AUS	18.5.93	1c2		Leiria	15	Jul
	(50)								
58.91	Kellion	Knibb	JAM	25.12.93	1		Gainesville	13	Apr
58.85	Izabela	da Silva	BRA	2.8.95	3		Bragança Paulista	8	Jul
58.63	Yekaterina	Strokova	RUS	17.12.89	2	Znam	Zhukovskiy	30	Jun
58.41	Sandeep	Kumari drugs dq?	IND	10.12.92	1	I-State	Guwahati	26	Jun
58.40	Shanice	Love	JAM	9.6.97	3	CAG	Barranquilla	31	Jul
58.36	Salla	Sipponen	FIN	13.3.95	1		Lapinlahti	28	Jul
58.35	Sabina	Asenjo	ESP	3.8.86	1		Castellón	16	Jun
58.31	Eliska	Stanková	CZE	11.11.84	2		Praha	7	Jun
58.19	Julia	Ritter	GER	13.5.98	5		Chula Vista	12	Apr
58.14	Jessica	Woodard	USA	4.2.95	3	TexasR	Austin	31	Mar
	(60)								
58.09	Pauline	Pousse	FRA	17.9.87	1	NC	Albi	7	Jul
58.05	Marike	Steinacker	GER	4.3.92	5		Schönebeck	18	May
58.05	Isheka	Binns	JAM	9.1.96	1		Kingston	2	Jun
58.03		Xie Yuchen	CHN	12.5.96	3	NGP	Zhaoqing	11	Apr
57.98	Agnes	Esser	CAN	22.8.95	4		Long Beach	21	Apr
57.94	Natalya	Shirobokova	RUS	18.1.94	3		Zhukovskiy	23	Jun
57.90	Marija	Tolj	CRO-J	29.11.99	1	NC-j	Split	3	Mar
57.88	Anita	Márton	HUN	15.1.89	1		Senta	19	May
57.75	Katelyn	Daniels	USA	11.4.95	2		Bloomington	13	May
57.48	Karolina	Urban	POL	18.10.98	1		Sopot	26	May
	(70)								
57.40	Viktoriya	Klochko	UKR	2.9.92	1		Dnipro	8	Jun
57.38	Stefania	Strumillo	ITA	14.10.89	2		Tarquinia	13	Jun
57.37	Chinwe	Okoro	NGR	20.6.89	2	AfrC	Asaba	3	Aug
57.34	Micaela	Hazlewood	USA	18.6.95	1	DrakeR	Des Moines	27	Apr
57.15	Ieva	Zarankaite	LTU	23.11.94	3	MSR	Torrance	21	Apr
57.04	Vanessa	Kamga	SWE	19.11.98	2=	WWerf 23	Halle	27	May
57.03	Mélanie	Pingeon	FRA	4.11.86	1		Aix-les-Bains	20	May
56.98	Pamela	Amaechi	USA-J	12.3.99	1	NC-j	Bloomington	15	Jun
56.97	Lidia	Augustyniak	POL	14.5.94	1		Goleniów	20	Jun
56.96	Sanna	Kämäräinen	FIN	8.2.86	1	NC	Jyväskylä	22	Jul
	(80)								
56.88	Nadezhda	Derkach	RUS	18.4.96	1-23		Sochi	7	Feb
56.82	Rachel	Andres	CAN	21.4.87	1	NC	Ottawa	6	Jul
56.80	Helena	Leveelahti	FIN-J	30.9.99	2	WJ	Tampere	12	Jul
56.79	Melany	Matheus	CUB-Y	19.1.01	1j		Camagüey	29	Jun
56.69A	Ischke	Senekal	RSA	8.1.93	1		Pretoria	2	Mar
56.62	Abigale	Wilson	USA	28.1.97	7		Long Beach	21	Apr

WOMEN 2018

Mark	Name		Nat	Born	Pos	Meet	Venue	Date	
56.61	Karen	Gallardo	CHI	6.3.84	1		Santiago de Chile	21	Apr
56.60	Giada	Andreutti	ITA	16.2.95	1	NC-w	Rieti	24	Feb
56.49	Eden	Francis	GBR	19.10.88	3c2		Leiria	15	Jul
56.48	Alison	Szykowny	USA	17.8.93	2		Columbia	21	Apr
	(90)								
56.41	Stamatía	Skarvéli	GRE	17.8.95	1		Los Angeles	24	Mar
56.39	Te Rina	Keenan	NZL	29.9.90	3	NC	Gold Coast	18	Feb
56.37	Kirsty	Law	GBR	11.10.86	4c2		Leiria	15	Jul
56.29	Kristina	Rakocevic	MNE	13.6.98	1		Bar	14	Feb
56.24	Kätlin	Töllasson	EST	4.6.93			Tallinn	5	Jun
56.07	Irene	Donzelot	FRA	8.12.88	1		Vénissieux	11	Jul
56.05	Rosalina	Álvarez	CUB	3.1.97	3		La Habana	24	Feb
55.98	June	Kintana	ESP	12.4.95	2	NC	Getafe	22	Jul
55.93	Lidiane Milena	Cansian	BRA	8.1.92	4	NC	Bragança Paulista	15	Sep
55.88	Kimberley	Mulhall	AUS	9.1.91	1		Melbourne	11	Mar
	(100)								

Mark	Name		Nat	Born	Date		Mark	Name		Nat	Born	Date	
55.84	Djeneba	Touré	AUT	8.4.96	27 May		54.72	Karyna	Cherednychenko	UKR	18.6.96	26 Jun
55.79	Fanny	Roos	SWE	2.1.95	31 Aug		54.72	Mariya	Telushkina	KAZ	3.4.94	30 Jun
55.74	Melissa	Ausman	USA	26.4.95	13 Apr		54.70	Meia	Gordon	USA	12.3.98	12 May
55.73	Kayla	Hopkins	USA	23.4.96	28 Apr		54.69	Thelma Lind	Kristjánsdóttir	ISL	25.9.97	19 Jul
55.68	Zakiya	Rashid	USA	1.2.97	24 Mar		54.67	Calea	Carr	USA	.96	9 Jun
55.67	Mariya	Ogritsko	RUS	1.3.94	10 May		54.59	Seasons	Usual	USA-J	24.3.99	24 Mar
55.67	Anastasiya	Vityugova	RUS	13.3.97	29 Jul		54.56	Violetta	Ignatyeva	RUS-Y	16.1.02	8 Jul
55.58	Makenli	Forrest	USA-J	2.12.99	12 May		54.48	Rachel	Varner	USA	20.7.83	1 Aug
55.51	Kayla	Melgar	USA	22.6.96	16 Mar		54.45	Veronika	Watzek	AUT	13.8.85	29 Apr
55.48	Amy	Holder	GBR	4.8.96	10 Jun		54.45	Leia	Braunagel	GER-J	5.10.00	4 Aug
55.37	Silinda	Morales	CUB-J	30.8.00	12 Jul		54.44	Alena	Belyakova	RUS	21.12.98	6 Jun
55.24	Lisa Brix	Pedersen	DEN	16.8.96	14 Jul		54.44A		Liang Yan	CHN	2.1.95	15 Jun
55.21	Katrine	Bebe	DEN	27.1.91	12 Jun		54.40		Yang Huanhuan	CHN-J	3.1.00	13 May
55.15	Sarah	Thornton	USA	29.8.86	21 Apr		54.40A	Ailén	Armada	ARG	3.10.98	29 Sep
55.11	Alyssa	Wilson	USA-J	20.2.99	29 Apr		54.30	Yekaterina	Burmistrova	RUS	18.8.90	12 Jul
55.10	Mónika	Nowak	POL	11.7.95	27 Jul		54.26	Alma	Pollorena	MEX	17.9.98	13 Apr
55.07	Debbie	Ajagbe	USA	2.11.98	24 Mar		54.23	Divine	Oladipo	GBR	5.10.98	26 Apr
55.05	Lloydricia	Cameron	USA	8.4.96	13 May		54.23	Phoebe	Dowson	GBR	17.4.94	28 May
55.04	Katarzyna	Moß	POL	20.12.94	10 Jun		54.16	Aleksandra	Grubba	POL	19.6.96	19 May
55.01	Dóra	Kerekes	HUN	19.4.94	21 Apr		54.11	Andrea	Alarcón	ESP	3.12.94	16 Jun
55.00	Brianna	Cueva	USA	6.6.95	6 Apr		54.02	Svetlana	Serova	BLR	28.8.86	11 Jul
55.00	Ashley	Anumba	USA-J	11.6.99	6 May		54.00	Madison	Pollard	USA	22.10.98	21 Apr
54.95	Fiona	Richards	JAM	20.11.98	20 Jan		53.98	Erin	Reese	USA	14.1.85	31 Mar
54.93	Natalina	Capoferri	ITA	6.11.92	13 Jun		53.97	Aixa	Middleton	PAN	6.2.88	31 Jul
54.91	Nataliya	Semenova	UKR	7.7.82	18 Feb		53.94	Katarzyna	Hnatiuk	POL	2.4.96	10 May
54.91	Janeah	Stewart	USA	21.7.96	13 May		53.93		Cui Ran	CHN	7.2.94	17 May
54.89	Jessica	Maroszek	USA	26.2.92	21 Apr		53.84	Jeia	Gilliam	USA	30.10.95	14 Apr
54.88	Alexandra	Morgan	ASA	19.5.91	21 Jun		53.83	Maura	Kimmel	USA	1.3.98	30 Mar
54.79	Marie-Francine Mvoto Abeng		FRA	3.1.87	7 Jul		53.83	Alexa	Evans	USA	27.11.93	2 Jun
54.75	Alex	Meyer	USA	8.4.96	5 May		53.82	Molli	Detloff	USA	15.1.96	21 Apr
54.74	Shelby	Moran	USA-J	3.4.00	9 May		53.82	Yolandi	Stander	RSA	27.11.98	29 Apr
54.74	Nanaka	Kori	JPN	2.5.97	2 Nov		53.70	Miranda	Daucher	USA	31.5.95	15 Apr
53.68	Ivana	Gallardo	CHI	20.3.93	20 Oct		53.68	Courtney	Massengale	USA	.96	5 May
53.66	Alida	van Daalen (168)	NED-Y	12.4.02	13 May		53.68	Portious	Warren	TTO	2.3.96	25 May

JUNIORS

See main list for top 6 juniors. 11 performances by 3 women to 57.15. Additional marks and further juniors:

Emilianov	58.83	Q	EC	Berlin	9 Aug	58.10	8	EC	Berlin	11 Aug
	58.26	1	Balk-j	Istanbul	21 Jun	57.89	1	WJ	Tampere	12 Jul
van Klinken	58.14	1		Emmeloord	17 Jun	57.10	2	NC	Utrecht	23 Jun
Tolj	57.86	2	NC	Zagreb	29 Jul	57.10	7	Hanz	Zagreb	4 Sep

Mark	Name		Nat	Born	Pos	Meet	Venue	Date	
55.58	Makenli	Forrest	USA	2.12.99	2		Coral Gables	12	May
55.37	Silinda	Morales	CUB	30.8.00	3	WJ	Tampere	12	Jul
55.11	Alyssa	Wilson	USA	20.2.99	1		Westwood	29	Apr
55.00	Ashley	Anumba (10)	USA	11.6.99	1		Philadelphia	6	May
54.74	Shelby	Moran	USA	3.4.00	1		Newberg	9	May
54.59	Seasons	Usual	USA	24.3.99	1		Abilene	24	Mar
54.56	Violetta	Ignatyeva	RUS-Y	16.1.02	1	EY	Győr	8	Jul
54.45	Leia	Braunagel	GER	5.10.00	1		Walldorf	4	Aug
54.40		Yang Huanhuan	CHN	3.1.00	1	NC-j	Nanchang	13	May
53.66	Alida	van Daalen	NED-Y	12.4.02			Breda	13	May
53.59	Veronica	Fraley	USA	27.5.00	1	PennR	Philadelphia	26	Apr
53.27	Amanda	Ngandu-Ntumba	FRA	24.6.00	1		Dijon	30	May
53.26	Lauren	Jones	USA	14.4.99	2	PennR	Philadelphia	26	Apr
53.26	Erica	Grotegeer (20)	USA	27.6.00	1		Clovis	2	Jun

HAMMER

| 79.59 | Anita | Włodarczyk | POL | 8.8.85 | 1 | NC | Lublin | 22 | Jul |

Mark	Name		Nat	Born	Pos	Meet	Venue		Date
				x	66.43	76.57	77.05	79.59	x
78.94	1 EC	Berlin	12 Aug	69.35	76.50	77.82	78.94	78.55	x
78.74	1 AWC	London (OS)	14 Jul	72.78	75.77	78.74	76.61		
77.77	1	Stalowa Wola	28 Jul	64.61	77.77	77.07	x	77.01	x
76.43	1 GS	Ostrava	12 Jun	68.88	70.65	74.55	76.38	76.43	x
76.17	1	Madrid	22 Jun	71.72	76.17	70.99	x	75.28	69.51
76.17	1	Madrid	22 Jun	71.72	76.17	70.99	x	75.28	69.51
75.52	2 Kuso	Chorzów	8 Jun	69.66	75.52	x	74.37	75.48	75.31
75.10	Q EC	Berlin	10 Aug	69.81	75.10				
74.63	1 Gyulai	Székesfehérvár	1 Jul	70.85	73.31	x	72.89	74.05	74.63
78.12	DeAnna	Price	USA	8.6.93	1 NC	Des Moines			23 Jun
				73.81	x	x	76.35	78.12	77.01
77.65	1	Rathdrum	2 Jun	x	77.65	75.44	75.07	74.64	77.11
76.27	1	Kingston	19 May	73.54	75.96	76.27	76.08		
75.96	1	Bloomington	4 May	72.89	x	75.96	72.50	73.43	71.05
75.46	1 C.Cup	Ostrava	8 Sep	72.64	x	75.13	74.97	75.46	
74.60	1 NACAC	Toronto	10 Aug	73.92	74.60	74.14	x	x	
x									
77.78	Gwen	Berry	USA	29.6.89	1	Kuso	Chorzów	8	Jun
				77.78	73.02	75.91	77.19	73.01	x
74.21	2 GS	Ostrava	12 Jun	72.45	72.36	73.62	x	x	74.21
76.26	Hanna	Malyshik	BLR	4.2.94	1		Brest		27 Apr
				67.32	x	72.96	76.26	p	p
74.35	1 NC	Minsk	21 Jul	x	65.50	71.91	x	74.35	x
75.02		Luo Na	CHN	8.10.93	1 WWerf	Halle			26 May
				72.86	74.24	74.01	75.02	73.69	x
74.78	Alexandra	Tavernier	FRA	13.12.93	2 EC	Berlin			12 Aug
				74.78	69.49	70.74	68.35	73.92	74.20
74.09	4 Kuso	Chorzów	8 Jun	72.63	72.81	72.33	73.09	74.07	74.09
74.53	Maggie	Ewen	USA	23.9.94	1		Tempe		6 Apr
				72.86	x	73.61	x	74.53	73.89
74.38	1	Stanford	12 May	63.82	69.49	4	74.38	x	x
74.39	Joanna	Fiodorow	POL	4.3.89	1 Skol	Chorzów			22 Aug
				71.80	72.00	x	72.23	74.39	73.54
74.25	2 NC	Lublin	22 Jul	71.99	74.25	x	72.56	71.71	71.24
74.18	3 Kuso	Chorzów	8 Jun	73.44	73.38	74.18	72.80	70.98	71.97
74.00	3 EC	Berlin	12 Aug	69.55	71.41	74.00	73.72	71.70	x
74.20	Brooke	Andersen	USA	23.8.95	1		Tucson		28 Apr
				72.00,	x	66.46	74.20	71.35	73.33
74.02	Hanna	Skydan	AZE	14.5.92	Q EC	Berlin			10 Aug
				74.02		only throw			
	(30/10)								
73.73		Wang Zheng	CHN	14.12.87	4 GS	Ostrava			12 Jun
73.48	Sophie	Hitchon	GBR	11.7.91	2 AWC	London (OS)			14 Jul
73.25	Martina	Hrasnová	SVK	21.3.83	1	Banská Bystrica			2 Jun
73.22	Yelizaveta	Tsareva	RUS	26.3.93	1 Znam	Zhukovskiy			30 Jun
72.92	Janeah	Stewart	USA	21.7.96	1 NCAA	Eugene			7 Jun
72.92	Malwina	Kopron	POL	16.11.94	2	Stalowa Wola			28 Jul
72.70	Zalina	Petrivskaya	MDA	5.2.88	1 NC	Chisinau			26 May
72.63	Iryna	Klymets	UKR	4.10.94	1	Kyiv			15 Jun
72.52	Réka	Gyurátz	HUN	31.5.96	1	Szombathely			26 Jul
72.24		Liu Tingting	CHN	29.1.90	2 WWerf	Halle			26 May
	(20)								
71.96	Jillian	Weir	CAN	9.2.93	2 NACAC	Toronto			10 Aug
71.66	Kıvılcım	Salman	TUR	27.3.92	1 NC	Bursa			8 Jul
71.50	Kathrin	Klaas	GER	6.2.84	7 EC	Berlin			12 Aug
70.98A	Jenny	Dahlgren	ARG	27.8.84	1 SAmG	Cochabamba			5 Jun
70.96	Bianca	Ghelber	ROU	1.6.90	2	Cluj-Napoca			2 Jun
70.93A	Rosa	Rodríguez	VEN	2.7.86	2 SAmG	Cochabamba			5 Jun
70.92	Barbara	Spiler	SLO	2.1.92	1	Cakovec			30 Sep
70.62	Ida	Storm	SWE	26.12.91	1	Bottnaryd			17 Jun
70.41	Jessica	Ramsey	USA	26.7.91	5 NC	Des Moines			23 Jun
70.05	Jeneva	Stevens	USA	28.10.89	1	Oxford, MS			13 Apr
	(30)								
69.99	Heavin	Warner	USA	4.3.93	2	Rathdrum			2 Jun
69.94	Julia	Ratcliffe	NZL	14.7.93	1 CG	Gold Coast			10 Apr
69.89	Amanda	Bingson	USA	20.2.90	3	Kingston			19 May
69.86	Sofiya	Palkina	RUS	9.6.98	1	Pärnu			19 Aug
69.80	Marina	Nikisenko	MDA	28.6.86	2 NC	Chisinau			26 May
69.72	Alyona	Shamotina	UKR	27.12.95	1	Dnipro			7 Jun
69.68	Anna Maria	Orel	EST	11.12.96	1	Oslo			30 May

WOMEN 2018

Mark	Name		Nat	Born	Pos	Meet	Venue	Date	
69.60	Camille	Sainte Luce	FRA	18.4.96	3	MedG	Tarragona	27	Jun
69.48	Anastasiya	Maslova	BLR	16.10.97	2	NC	Minsk	21	Jul
69.42	Krista	Tervo	FIN	15.11.97	1		Jyväskylä	9	Jun
	(40)								
69.35	Iryna	Novozhylova	UKR	7.1.86	2		Nova Kakhovka	31	Mar
69.34	Charlene	Woitha	GER	21.8.03	1oD	WWerf	Halle	26	May
69.16	Anamari	Kozul	CRO	20.1.96	2		Zenica	6	Jun
69.10	Stamatía	Skarvéli	GRE	17.8.95	3	NCAA	Eugene	7	Jun
69.10	Natalya	Polyakova	RUS	9.12.90	1		Moskva	22	Jun
69.01	Katerina	Safránková	CZE	8.6.89	1		Ostrava	1	Jul
68.82	Berta	Castells	ESP	24.1.84	1		Manresa	17	Jul
68.79	Inga	Linna	FIN	21.2.95	1		Helsinki	29	Jul
68.57	Audrey	Ciofani	FRA	13.3.96	2	NC	Albi	8	Jul
68.41	Katarzyna	Furmanek	POL	19.2.96	4	NC	Lublin	22	Jul
	(50)								
68.38	Zeliha	Uzunbilek	TUR	10.6.91	1		Mersin	13	May
68.32	Anastasiya	Kolomoyets	BLR	15.7.94	2		Novopolotsk	23	Nov
68.28	Soukaina	Zakkour	MAR	13.10.93	1	AfrC	Asaba	2	Aug
68.21	Janee'	Kassanavoid	USA	19.1.95	1		Waco	11	May
68.20	Alex	Hulley	AUS	24.7.97	2	CG	Gold Coast	10	Apr
68.14	Éva	Orbán	HUN	29.11.84	1		Székesfehérvár	7	Jun
67.75	Laura	Igaune	LAT	2.10.88	1		Charlottesville	28	Apr
67.63	Vanessa	Sterckendries	BEL	15.9.95	1		Saint-Mard	6	Oct
67.61	Tuğçe	Sahutoglu	TUR	1.5.88	2		Mersin	17	Feb
67.47	Nikola	Lomnická	SVK	16.9.88	2		Banská Bystrica	2	Jun
	(60)								
67.45	Temi	Ogunrinde	NGR	29.2.96	2	MSR	Torrance	19	Apr
67.42	Nicole	Zihlmann	SUI	30.7.86	2	Spitzen	Luzern	9	Jul
67.34	Marinda	Petersson	SWE	3.2.95	6		Fränkisch-Crumbach	20	May
67.17	Greta	Ahlberg	SWE	29.3.98	1	NC	Eskilstuna	26	Aug
67.06	Tracey	Andersson	SWE	5.12.84	3		Bottnaryd	17	Jun
66.99	Alyssa	Wilson	USA-J	20.2.99	4	NCAA	Eugene	7	Jun
66.93	Mariana Grasielly	Marcelino	BRA	16.7.92	1	NC	Zagreb	28	Jul
66.90		Yan Ni	CHN	7.2.93	4	NGP	Chengdu	1	Apr
66.90	Molli	Detloff	USA	15.1.96	2		Long Beach	20	Apr
66.89	Alina	Shayunova	BLR	2.3.90	3		Brest	27	Apr
	(70)								
66.87	Bianca	Lazar	ROU	24.2.93	1		Bucuresti	23	Jun
66.87	Pavla	Kuklová	CZE	1.11.96	2		Ostrava	1	Jul
66.86	Queen	Obisesan	NGR	15.9.82	1		Abuja	15	Feb
66.86		Zhou Mengyuan	CHN-J	3.9.99	2	NGPF	Guiyang	17	Jun
66.80	Beatrice Nedberge	Llano	NOR	14.12.97	4		Bottnaryd	17	Jun
66.77	Valeria	Chiliquinga	ECU	27.2.91	3	SAmG	Cochabamba	5	Jun
66.75	Kati	Ojaloo	EST	31.1.90	2		Oslo	30	May
66.67	Ashley	Bryant	USA	15.7.95	1		Norman	20	Apr
66.67	Lauren	Stuart	CAN	16.11.91	2	NC	Ottawa	6	Jul
66.65	Merja	Korpela	FIN	15.5.81	2		Saarijärvi	24	Jun
	(80)								
66.63	Destiney	Coward	USA	26.5.96	1		Storrs	14	Apr
66.62	Alena	Lysenko	RUS	3.2.88	2		Sochi	6	Feb
66.57	Ayamey	Medina	CUB	21.2.98	1		La Habana	17	Feb
66.56	Yrlena	Sobaleva	BLR	11.5.93	3	NC	Minsk	21	Jul
66.49	Maddy	Nilton	USA	3.3.87	1		Eugene	7	Jun
66.46	Elianne	Despaigne	CUB	11.1.97	5	IbAmC	Trujillo	25	Aug
66.43	Jennifer	Batu	CGO	24.10.93	3	AfrC	Asaba	2	Aug
66.32	Cintia	Gergelics	HUN	16.11.91	3		Szombathely	26	Jul
66.07	Nicole	Bradley	NZL	23.4.92	1		Hastings	27	Jan
66.06	Sara	Fantini	ITA	16.9.97	1		Modena	23	Jun
	(90)								
65.92	Carolin	Paesler	GER	16.12.90	5	Spitzen	Luzern	9	Jul
65.84		Zong Dan	CHN	19.1.95	3	NGPF	Guiyang	17	Jun
65.81	Carly	Fehringer	USA	9.11.91	1		Kearney	12	Apr
65.72	Lara	Nielsen	AUS	19.12.92	1		Brisbane (N)	4	Feb
65.61	Camryn	Rogers	CAN-J	7.6.99	2		Berkeley	28	Apr
65.61	Sophie	Gimmler	GER	18.3.96	1	NC-23	Heilbronn	1	Jul
65.58	Veronika	Kanuchová	SVK	19.4.93	3		Trnava	7	Jul
65.42	Susen	Küster	GER	27.7.94	5cB	WWerf	Halle	26	May
65.36	Claudia	Stravs	SLO	11.2.94	1	NC	Celje	15	Jul
	(100)								
65.35		Xu Xinying	CHN	17.2.97	4	NGPF	Guiyang	17	Jun
65.34	Wendy	Koolhaas	NED	2.1.80	9	Jun			
65.32	Hitomi	Katsuyama	JPN	21.5.94	3	Jun			

Mark	Name	Nat	Born	Date
65.31	Aleksandra Kokowska	POL	28.4.95	12 May
65.24	Akane Watanabe	JPN	13.8.91	3 May
65.16	Erin Reese	USA	14.1.85	13 May
65.15	Lara Boman	USA	16.2.96	12 May
65.13	Iryna Sekachyova	UKR	21.7.76	15 Jun
65.00	Makenli Forrest	USA-J	2.12.99	27 Apr
64.96	Aleksandra Smiech	POL	2.10.97	8 Jul
64.91	Anastasiaa Mazurina	BLR	21.2.93	18 Jan
64.89	Valeriya Ivanenko	UKR-Y	16.8.01	23 Jun
64.85	Emma Thor	SWE	20.11.97	19 Apr
64.80	Natalya Pospelova	RUS	28.6.96	29 Jul
64.78	Yaritza Martínez	CUB-J	3.2.00	3 Mar
64.77	Helene Sofie Ingvaldsen	NOR	22.6.96	7 Jun
64.70	Michaela Dendinger	USA	9.5.95	24 May
64.67	Amanda Armendáris	CUB-J	19.11.00	3 Mar
64.64A	Johana Moreno	COL	15.4.85	5 Jun
64.64	Tereza Králová	CZE	22.10.89	29 Jul
64.61	Trude Raad	NOR	27.4.90	30 May
64.57	Michaela Walsh	IRL	17.12.98	30 Jun
64.54	Hana Feilzer	USA	8.8.96	4 May
64.52	Katerna Skypalová	CZE-J	20.2.99	15 May
64.50	Sade Olatoye	USA	25.1.97	20 Apr
64.49	Zouina Bouzebra	ALG	3.10.90	2 Aug
64.40	Osarumen Odeh	ESP	15.11.95	19 May
64.40	Yuliya Kysylyova	UKR	6.5.97	8 Jul
64.26	Nayoka Clunis	JAM	7.10.95	20 Apr
64.19	Nycia Ford	USA		13 May
64.16	Jillian Shippee	USA-J	19.4.99	16 Jun
64.05	Laura Redondo	ESP	3.7.88	26 May
64.01	Anastasiya Borodulina	RUS	7.11.98	14 May
63.98	Whitney Simmons	USA		4 May
63.94	Sultana Frizell	CAN	24.10.84	10 Apr
63.89	Kaylee Antill	USA	28.8.96	26 May
63.89	Huang Weilu	CHN-J	1.9.99	17 Jun
63.87	Rebecca Keating	GBR	31.8.97	17 Mar
63.82	Tiffany Okieme	USA	8.1.94	17 Mar
63.82	Yelena Krechik	BLR	20.7.87	21 Jul
63.81	Katerna Chlupová	CZE	22.10.86	29 Jul
63.80	Sarita Prakash Singh	IND	26.10.89	5 Mar
63.69	Aisiah Tuiasosopo	USA	.94	11 May
63.66	Olga Shishimorova	RUS	14.9.95	24 Feb
63.65	Vânia Silva	POR	8.6.80	6 May
63.65	Valarie Allman	USA	23.2.95	12 May
63.62	Agnes Esser	CAN	22.8.95	20 Apr
63.61	Ana Stanciu	ROU-J	13.6.00	22 Jun
63.57	Kelcey Bedard	USA	10.4.96	11 May
63.53	Sara Killinen	FIN-Y	9.4.01	30 Jun
63.49	Celina Julin	DEN	12.8.94	12 May
63.47	Annette Echikunwoke	USA	29.7.96	5 Jun
63.21	Adéla Korecková	CZE	5.7.97	1 Jul
63.17	Mariana García	CHI-J	19.3.99	3 Mar
63.16	Lucia Prinetti Anzalapaya	ITA	3.11.97	11 Feb
63.14	Sarah Pate	USA	.94	20 Apr
63.05	Alegna Osorio	CUB-Y	5.2.02	9 Feb
63.04	Tatyana Ramanovich	BLR-J	26.3.00	15 Jun
63.02	Viktoriya Sakhno	UKR	18.12.97	17 Feb
63.02	Lorelei Taillandier	FRA	8.8.91	6 May
62.99	Agata Zienkowicz	POL	17.12.95	12 May
62.98	Samantha Borutta	GER-J	7.8.00	19 May
62.96	Chrystalla Kyriakou	CYP	4.10.96	19 May
62.95	Gabby Figueroa	USA	20.2.96	20 Apr
62.95	Natasha Akbarizadeh	CAN	8.4.96	20 Apr
62.94	Dasiana Larson	USA	4.4.96	11 May
62.90	Laëtitia Bambara	BUR	30.3.84	27 May
62.89	Leia Mistowski	USA	8.11.96	12 May
62.89	Jessica Mayho	GBR	14.6.93	4 Aug
62.79	Kajsa Wennberg	SWE	17.10.96	22 Aug
62.70	Johanna Witka	FIN	21.12.98	22 Jun
62.66	Rymma Filimoshkina	UKR	15.4.86	17 Feb
62.63	Frida Bååth	SWE	5.7.97	27 May
62.62	Daniela Gómez	ARG	24.8.93	18 Aug
62.53	Phillipa Wingate	GBR	12.5.93	21 Apr
62.51	Emily Bassett	USA		26 May
62.49	Mingkamon Koomphon	THA	4.1.98	19 Jul
62.48	Terrisa Russell	USA		11 May
62.45	Tamami Saeki	JPN	5.8.93	23 Sep
62.42	Lauren Bruce	NZL	23.3.97	27 Jan
62.42	Christina MacDonald	USA	2.8.95	24 May
62.39	Anna Paula Pereira	BRA	7.8.86	8 Apr
62.37	Taylor Scaife	USA	25.12.96	14 Apr
62.35	Ksenia Safonova	EST	6.11.93	12 May
62.30	Viktoriya Golda	UKR	5.2.97	27 May
62.29	Ilse Kaaja	FIN	7.8.92	22 Jun
62.29	Sina Mai Holthuijsen	NED	17.7.96	1 Jul
62.23	Marika Kaczmarek	POL	25.4.96	22 Jul
62.12	Alice Delmer	FRA	30.12.93	9 Jun
62.10A	Mayra Gaviria	COL	22.5.97	30 Sep
62.09	De'Ondra Young	USA	26.4.96	20 Apr
62.05	Zhao Fan	CHN	26.3.97	4 Apr
62.02	Michelle Döpke	GER	21.7.97	9 Jul
62.01	Galina Mityaeva	CAN	29.4.91	23 May

(193)

JUNIORS

See main list for top 3 juniors. 10 performances by 4 woman to 65.00. Additional marks and further juniors:

Name	Mark	Pos	Venue	Date	Mark	Pos	Meet	Venue	Date
Wilson	66.63	2	Stanford	12 May	66.33	1	NC-j	Bloomington	16 Jun
Zhou M	66.57	5	Chengdu	1 Apr	65.18	5		Chengdu	5 Apr
Rogers	65.28	1	Berkeley	7 Apr	65.02	2		Tempe	24 Mar

Mark	Name		Nat	Born	Pos	Meet	Venue	Date
65.00	Makenli	Forrest	USA	2.12.99	2		Louisville	27 Apr
64.89	Valeriya	Ivanenko	UKR-Y	16.8.01	1	NC-j	Kropyvnytskyi	23 Jun
64.78	Yaritza	Martínez	CUB	3.2.00	2		La Habana	3 Mar
64.67	Amanda	Armendáris	CUB	19.11.00	3		La Habana	3 Mar
64.52	Katełina	Skypalová	CZE	20.2.99	1		Susice	15 May
64.16	Jillian	Shippee	USA-	19.4.99	2	NC-j	Bloomington	16 Jun
63.89		Huang Weilu (10)	CHN	1.9.99	6	NGPF	Guiyang	17 Jun
63.61	Ana	Stanciu	ROU	13.6.00	1	Balk-j	Istanbul	22 Jun
63.53	Sara	Killinen	FIN-Y	9.4.01	5		Kaustinen	30 Jun
63.17	Mariana	García	CHI	19.3.99	1		Temuco	3 Mar
63.05	Alegna	Osorio	CUB-Y	5.2.02	1j		Las Tunas	9 Feb
63.04	Tatyana	Ramanovich	BLR	26.3.00	1	NC-J	Brest	15 Jun
62.98	Samantha	Borutta	GER	7.8.00	1J		Fränkisch-Crumbach	19 May
61.84	Ximena	Zorrilla	PER	2.11.00	2	SAmCh	Cuemca	30 Sep
61.75		Ji Li	CHN	14.12.00	7		Guiyang	17 Sep
61.75	Kiira	Väänänen	FIN	6.1.99	6		Kaustinen	30 Jun
61.65	Nino	Tsikvadze (20)	GEO	14.2.99	1	NC	Tbilisi	20 May

JAVELIN

Mark		Name	Nat	Born	Pos	Meet	Venue			Date
68.92		Kathryn Mitchell	AUS	10.7.82	1	CG	Gold Coast			11 Apr
					68.92	x	x	62.40	68.14	x
68.57	1	Melbourne		3 Mar	65.97	x	66.13	68.57	62.89	x
67.58	1	Melbourne		11 Feb	x	67.58	65.89	x	65.56	64.47

WOMEN 2018

Mark	Pos	Meet	Name	Nat	Born	Venue	Date	Series
66.73	1					Melbourne	21 Jan	66.73 x 62.01 63.45 61.80 65.58
65.51	1	NC				Gold Coast	17 Feb	64.77 65.51 63.79 64.39 61.89 60.65
64.84	1					Sydney	17 Mar	57.11 64.84 58.67 p p p
67.90	1	EC	Christin Hussong	GER	17.3.94	Berlin	10 Aug	67.90 62.53 x x x 59.15
67.29	Q	EC				Berlin	9 Aug	67.29 only throw
66.36	2	WWerf				Halle	26 May	66.36 63.29 59.54 x 60.17 x
65.07	1					Thum	17 Aug	62.34 64.03 63.82 65.07 64.12 60.94
67.69	1	WWerf	Lu Huihui	CHN	26.6.89	Halle	26 May	x 65.92 x 62.20 x 67.69
66.90A	1	NGPF				Guiyang	16 Jun	66.38 64.04 65.39 65.05 66.90 61.91
66.85	1	DL				Shanghai	12 May	64.39 65.88 66.85 60.83 64.73 66.26
65.66	1	NGP				Zhaoqing	11 Apr	64.72 64.07 x 65.66 62.24 63.30
65.63	1	NGP				Chengdu	5 Apr	64.00 64.73 63.05 63.97 65.63 64.50
65.54	1	DL				London (OS)	21 Jul	64.97 65.54 61.89 63.40 63.40 62.52
65.45	1	NC				Taiyuan	14 Sep	63.84 64.61 63.81 63.28 65.45 64.75
65.11	2	Bisl				Oslo	7 Jun	65.11 64.09 64.27 60.08 62.74 64.36
67.47	1	Bisl	Tatyana Kholodovich	BLR	21.6.91	Oslo	7 Jun	x 56.21 58.71 60.77 61.33 67.47
66.99	1	WK				Zürich	30 Aug	x 64.29 63.96 62.41 62.85 66.99
66.59	1					Lappeenranta	23 Aug	x 66.59 61.69 x 64.34 64.69
64.77	1	NC				Minsk	21 Jul	61.53 64.77 x 61.63 62.86 60.85
67.12	1		Liu Shiying	CHN	24.9.93	Osaka	20 May	67.12 x x x x 62.96
66.09	1	AsiG				Jakarta	28 Aug	66.09 65.15 65.39 65.23 64.13 p
66.00	2	WK				Zürich	30 Aug	61.39 64.53 66.00 p p 63.10
66.53	1		Marcelina Witek	POL	2.6.95	Białogard	5 May	62.23 66.53 p p p p
66.10	1	NC	Martina Ratej	SLO	2.11.81	Celje	14 Jul	63.20 64.52 x 66.10 61.00 p
65.61A	1		Nikola Ogrodníková	CZE	18.8.90	Potchefstroom	12 Apr	
65.36	2	DL				London (OS)	21 Jul	58.20 65.36 x p p p
65.02	1	Athl				Lausanne	5 Jul	57.94 54.40 65.02 54.53 57.58 x
65.20	1		Eda Tugsuz	TUR	27.3.97	Mersin	18 Feb	59.98 65.20 p p p p
64.75	3	WK	Kara Winger	USA	10.4.86	Zürich	30 Aug	62.60 61.94 64.75 60.23 60.69 61.95
			(32/10)					
64.57	1		Kelsey-Lee Barber	AUS	21.9.91	Brisbane (Nathan)	28 Mar	
63.18	1	NC	Lina Muze	LAT	4.12.92	Riga	28 Jul	
62.98	1		Madara Palameika	LAT	18.6.87	Riga	29 May	
62.58	2		Anete Kocina	LAT	5.2.96	Riga	29 May	
62.46A	1		Sunette Viljoen	RSA	6.1.83	Sasolburg	27 Mar	
62.42	1	ECp-w	Sigrid Borge	NOR	3.12.95	Leiria	10 Mar	
62.39	1	NC	Laila Domingos	BRA	30.7.82	Zagreb	29 Jul	
62.21	1		Sinta Sprudzane	LAT	26.2.88	Ogre	15 Jun	
61.91	4	Spitzen	Katharina Molitor	GER	8.11.83	Luzern	9 Jul	
61.61	2		Liveta Jasiunaite	LTU	26.7.94	Ogre	15 Jun	
			(20)					
61.53	5	DL	Liz Gleadle	CAN	5.12.88	Shanghai	12 May	
61.25	1	NC	Lidia Parada	ESP	11.6.93	Getafe	21 Jul	
61.21	2	NC	Su Lingdan	CHN	12.1.97	Taiyuan	14 Sep	
60.91	1		Yekaterina Starygina	RUS	26.8.95	Krasnodar	25 Feb	
60.79	1	NC	Marina Saito	JPN	15.10.95	Yamaguchi	23 Jun	
60.71	4		Risa Miyashita	JPN	26.4.84	Osaka	20 May	
60.60	5	Spitzen	Dana Bergrath	GER	24.4.94	Luzern	9 Jul	
60.60	1	BalkC	Marija Vucenovic	SRB	3.4.93	Stara Zagora	21 Jul	
60.59	2		Alexie Alais	FRA	9.10.94	Aix-les-Bains	20 May	
60.59	1		Sofi Flink	SWE	8.7.95	Joensuu	4 Jul	
			(30)					
60.51A	1		Irena Sedivá	CZE	19.1.92	Potchefstroom	19 Apr	
60.48	1		Haruka Kitaguchi	JPN	16.3.98	Kawasaki	8 Sep	
60.36	1	NCAA	Mackenzie Little	AUS	22.12.96	Eugene	7 Jun	
60.34	2		Ásdís Hjálmsdóttir	ISL	28.10.85	Joensuu	4 Jul	
60.29	1		Yulenmis Aguilar	CUB	3.8.96	La Habana	9 Jun	
60.24	1		Vera Rebrik	RUS	25.2.89	Adler	15 May	
60.21	3		Hanna Hatsko-Fedusova	UKR	3.10.90	Riga	29 May	
59.98	1-23	WWerf	Yu Yuzhen	CHN	5.3.98	Halle	27 May	
59.96	Q	EC	Jenni Kangas	FIN	3.7.92	Berlin	9 Aug	
59.72A	1		María Lucelly Murillo	COL	5.5.91	Medellín	28 Apr	
			(40)					

Mark	Name		Nat	Born	Pos	Meet	Venue	Date	
59.69	Arantxa	Moreno	ESP	16.1.95	1		Castellón	11	Jul
59.59	Ariana	Ince	USA	14.3.89	1	NACAC	Toronto	12	Aug
59.55	Coralys	Ortiz	PUR	16.4.85	1		Gurabo	19	May
59.44		Zhu Dandan	CHN	1.3.94	2	NGP	Zhuzhou	17	Apr
59.36A		Zhang Li	CHN	17.1.89	4	NGPF	Guiyang	16	Jun
59.32	Svetlana	Pechnikova	RUS	6.9.94	2		Adler	15	May
59.18	Yuka	Mori	JPN	21.7.92	2	NC	Yamaguchi	23	Jun
59.01	Liina	Laasma	EST	13.1.92	3		Ogre	15	Jun
58.80	Mariya	Safonova	RUS	28.10.94	2		Zhukovskiy	13	Jun
58.50	Eloah Caetano	Scramin	BRA	8.6.96	1		São Bernardo do Campo	7	Apr
(50)									
58.41	H.L.Dilhani	Lekamge	SRI	14.1.87	1		Diyagama	27	Jan
58.40	Indre	Jakubaityte	LTU	24.1.76	3		Talsi	28	Jun
58.36	Alyssa	Olin	USA	14.7.96	1		Tempe	17	Mar
58.32	Matilde	Andraud	FRA	28.4.89	1		Rheinau-Freistett	1	Jul
58.32	Mikako	Yamashita	JPN	3.5.97	1		Kitakyushu	2	Nov
58.29	Kiho	Kuze	JPN	28.3.95	4	Oda	Hiroshima	29	Apr
58.27	Zahra	Bani	ITA	31.12.79	1		Conegliano	15	Jun
58.19	Sara	Jemai	ITA	12.4.92	1	NC	Pescara	9	Sep
58.17	Annu	Rani	IND	29.8.92	1		Lucknow	19	Aug
58.00	Tatsiana	Korzh	BLR	17.3.93	2		Florø	2	Jun
(60)									
57.93	Carolina	Visca	ITA-J	31.5.00	3	NC	Pescara	9	Sep
57.92	Jucilene	de Lima	BRA	14.9.90	2		Campinas	5	May
57.91	Nafissatou	Thiam	BEL	19.8.94	1H	EC	Berlin	10	Aug
57.75	Suvi	Kemppainen	FIN	25.1.98	1		Pudasjärvi	21	Jun
57.55	Heidi	Nokelainen	FIN	30.9.90	4		Lappeenranta	23	Aug
57.50	Sofía	Ifantídou	GRE	5.1.85	1		Thessaloníki	28	Apr
57.48	Anna	Wessman	SWE	9.10.89	8		Jena	30	Jun
57.41	Paola	Padovan	ITA	4.12.95	1		Isernia	19	May
57.38	Lisanne	Schol	NED	22.6.91	1		Zoetermeer	9	Sep
57.29	Jenna	Gray	USA	28.2.98	2	NCAA	Eugene	7	Jun
(70)									
57.11		Ge Lijuan	CHN	17.7.97	3	NC	Taiyuan	14	Sep
57.09	Kateryna	Derun	UKR	24.9.93	1	NC	Lutsk	19	Jul
57.00	Tori	Peeters	NZL	17.5.94	1		Dunedin	28	Jan
56.96	Kelechi	Nwanaga	NGR	24.12.97	1	AfrC	Asaba	4	Aug
56.87	Viktoriya	Yermakova	BLR	18.1.95	2	NC	Minsk	21	Jul
56.86	Tomoka	Kuwazoe	JPN-J	1.2.99	1		Hiratsuka	15	Jun
56.84		Kim Kyung-ae	KOR	5.3.88	1	NC	Jeongseon	28	Jun
56.66	Saara	Lipsanen	FIN	13.9.95	2	NC	Jyväskylä	21	Jul
56.59	Annika	Fuchs	GER	29.4.97	1	NC-23	Heilbronn	30	Jun
56.57	Orie	Ushiro	JPN	24.8.90	3		Brisbane (Nathan)	28	Mar
(80)									
56.54	Avione	Allgood	USA	14.12.93	2	NC	Des Moines	21	Jun
56.51	Rafaela	Gonçalves	BRA	27.11.91	2		Bragança Paulista	9	Jun
56.50		Li Huei-Chun	TPE-J	12.5.99	2		Taipei	25	May
56.48	Anna	Tarasyuk	BLR	30.10.97	2	ECp-w23	Leiria	10	Mar
56.31	Klaudia	Maruszewska	POL	28.8.97	3	EAF	Bydgoszcz	29	May
56.31	Géraldine	Ruckstuhl	SUI	24.2.98	2H	EC	Berlin	10	Aug
56.22	Gundega	Griva	LAT	8.4.91	4	NC	Riga	28	Jul
56.22	Kaja Mørch	Pettersen	NOR-Y	6.11.01	1		Larvik	26	Sep
56.21	Maura	Fiamoncini	USA-J	23.6.99	1		Selinsgrove	31	Mar
56.20	Kristen	Clark	USA	8.4.96	1		Baton Rouge	28	Apr
(90)									
56.17	Nicolle	Murphy	USA	19.10.94	1		Oxford	31	Mar
56.15		Lo Thi Hoang	VIE	6.10.97	1		Hanoi	1	Dec
56.14	Hirono	Nakata	JPN	2.10.97	1		Nagoya	12	May
56.13	Bernarda	Letnar	SLO	26.12.89	2		Palmanova	1	May
56.04	Jelena	Jaakkola	FIN	7.3.89	2cA		Pihtipudas	1	Jul
55.95	Daniela	Nisimura	BRA	26.3.94	2		São Bernardo do Campo	17	Mar
55.95	Alina	Shukh	UKR-J	12.2.99	1j	WJ	Tampere	11	Jul
55.81	Petra	Andrejsková	CZE	25.6.92	1		Meziborí	9	Sep
55.79	Angéla	Moravcsik	HUN	13.5.96	1		Zalaegerszeg	19	May
55.66	Haruna	Kaneko	JPN	18.1.97	1		Okinawa	29	Jun
(100)									

Mark	Name			Nat	Born	Pos	Date	Mark	Name		Nat	Born	Pos	Date
55.65	Haley	Crouser		USA	11.2.94	11 May		55.50	Esthefany	Chacón	VEN	1.11.97	7 Apr	
55.59A	Laura	Paredes		PAR	30.8.96	29 Sep		55.50	Christine	Winkler	GER	4.5.95	2 Jun	
55.57A		Sun Xiaomei		CHN	2.12.96	16 Jun		55.50	Hitomi	Sukenaga	JPN	4.5.88	2 Sep	
55.55	Laura	Whittingham		GBR	6.6.86	1 Jul		55.49	Stella	Weinberg	NOR	21.10.98	16 Jun	
55.53	Alexia	Kogut Kubiak		FRA	22.1.88	24 Feb		55.46		Dai Qianqian	CHN-J	23.8.00	1 Apr	

Mark	Name		Nat	Born	Pos Meet	Venue	Date
55.43		Chen Chen	CHN	19.1.96	14 Sep		
55.39	Mailen	Brooks	CUB-J	26.1.00	9 Jun		
55.33	Kanaki	Asano	JPN	7.11.96	24 Aug		
55.27		Wang Ying	CHN-Y	5.6.01	5 Apr		
55.16	Evelina	Mendes	FRA	2.1.98	16 Sep		
55.11	Dana	Baker	USA-J	7.10.99	29 Jun		
55.06	Margaux	Nicollin	FRA	1.5.95	24 Feb		
54.95A	Yuleixy Anahí	Angulo	ECU-Y	2.1.01	29 Sep		
54.94	María Paz	Ríos	CHI	13.10.89	18 Feb		
54.85	Callie	Jones	USA	26.12.98	23 Mar		
54.85	Mirell	Luik	EST	3.1.97	29 May		
54.85	Sharmila	Kumari	IND	2.3.95	25 Sep		
54.83	Kseniya	Zybina	RUS	1.2.89	15 May		
54.82A	Jo-Ané	van Dyk	RSA	3.10.97	8 Mar		
54.78	Kylee	Carter	USA	10.6.97	26 Apr		
54.76	Riko	Nishimura	JPN	1.11.93	19 May		
54.75	Ai	Yamauchi	JPN	6.12.94	3 Jun		
54.71	Bethany	Drake	USA	10.10.93	12 Aug		
54.70	Shiori	Toma	JPN	7.2.90	28 Jul		
54.69	Jatta Mari	Jääskeläinen	FIN	27.2.94	20 Jul		
54.69		Bui Thi Xuan	VIE	29.12.89	1 Dec		
54.67	Luz Mariana	Castro	MEX	23.1.97	17 May		
54.63	Desirée	Schwarz	GER	24.4.92	7 Apr		
54.57	Mayu	Oshiro	JPN	.96	8 Apr		
54.55	Ashley	Pryke	CAN	7.7.97	17 Mar		
54.54		Jin Pingping	CHN	23.8.93	14 Sep		
54.51A	Flor Dennis	Ruiz	COL	24.1.91	4 Mar		
54.49	Emilie	Ingerø	NOR	28.9.95	30 Jun		
54.45	Christina	Kiffe	GER	2.5.92	21 Jul		
54.35	Laura	Pesola	FIN	12.5.96	24 Jun		
54.34	Nadine	Broersen	NED	29.4.90	24 Jun		
54.33	Roosa	Ylönen	FIN-J	29.4.99	20 Jul		
54.24	Maria	Andrejczyk	POL	9.3.96	4 Jul		
54.22		Hu Hyo-jung	KOR	19.12.94	30 Jun		
54.20	Svetlana	Parfyonova	BLR	30.10.87	11 Feb		
54.18		Chen Jiajia	CHN	14.10.98	1 Apr		
54.16	Sae	Takemoto	JPN-J	23.11.99	8 Jun		
54.11A	Janette	Lepistö	FIN	20.10.93	6 Mar		
54.08	Emma	Hamplett	GBR	27.7.98	17 Jun		
54.05A	Merly	Cabrera	COL	29.8.96	14 Sep		
54.04	Haruka	Matoba	JPN	24.4.87	11 Apr		
54.00	Rebekah	Wales	USA	2.10.95	28 Apr		
53.99	Sara	Zabarino	ITA-J	8.8.99	10 Jul		
53.96	Skylar	Ciccolini	USA-Y	23.7.01	2 Jun		
53.95	Ane	Dahlen	NOR	6.6.94	22 Aug		
53.87	Gabrielle	Kearney	USA	7.10.96	11 May		
53.84	Reina	Kimura	JPN-Y	.01	20 May		
53.82	Florina	Necsoiu	ROU	19.4.97	3 Jun		
53.80A	Lucy	Aber	UGA	14.1.84	2 Jun		
53.75	Carolin	Näslund	SWE	23.1.98	24 Aug		
53.73	Carolin	Schäfer	GER	5.12.91	10 Aug		
53.70	Pushpa	Jakhar	IND	29.11.97	7 Mar		
53.60	Tatjana	Mirkovic	SRB	10.8.90	26 May		
53.60	Elisabeth	Lithell	SWE	19.2.90	28 Jun		
53.59		Liao Yu	CHN-J	18.5.00	11 May		
53.56	Mari	Klaup-McColl	EST	27.2.90	17 Jun		
53.52		Yu Ying	CHN-Y	23.7.01	5 Apr		
53.48	Réka	Szilágyi	HUN	19.1.96	7 Apr		
53.42	Danielle	Collier	USA	16.12.96	20 Apr		
53.42	Rupinder	Kaur	IND	8.11.88	13 Dec		
53.40	Sophia	Rivera	USA	17.10.98	31 Mar		
53.40	Nadeeka	Lakmali	SRI	18.9.81	30 Oct		
53.39		Han Hyo-hee	KOR	3.6.86	13 Apr		
53.39	Laura	Ikauniece-Admidina	LAT	31.5.92	28 Jul		
53.38	Mirann	Naraoka	JPN-Y	4.3.01	7 Oct		
53.36	Atina	Kamasi	SRB	30.10.97	28 Apr		
53.32	Nuttha	Nacharn	THA	4.6.90	28 Aug		
		(177)					

JUNIORS

See main list for top 6 juniors. 10 performances by 7 women to 55.40. Additional marks and further juniors:

Mark	Name		Nat	Born	Pos	Meet	Venue	Date
Visca	56.79	1				Firenze		27 Apr
Kuwazoe	55.66	2	WJ			Tampere		11 Jul
Pettersen	55.48	1	Nordic-j			Hvidovre		12 Aug
55.46		Dai Qianqian	CHN	23.8.00	5	NGP	Chengdu	1 Apr
55.39	Mailen	Brooks	CUB	26.1.00	9			Jun	La Habana	9 Jun
55.27		Wang Ying	CHN-Y	5.6.01	2	NGP	Chengdu	5 Apr
55.11	Dana	Baker (10)	USA	7.10.99	1		East Stroudsburg	29 Jun
54.95A	Yuleixy Anahí	Angulo	ECU-Y	2.1.01	2	SAm-23	Cuenca	29 Sep
54.33	Roosa	Ylönen	FIN	29.4.99	Q	NC	Jyväskylä	20 Jul
54.16	Sae	Takemoto	JPN	23.11.99	2	AsiC-J	Gifu	8 Jun
53.99	Sara	Zabarino	ITA	8.8.99	Q	WJ	Tampere	10 Jul
53.96	Skylar	Ciccolini	USA-Y	23.7.01	1		Freeport	2 Jun
53.84	Reina	Kimura	JPN-Y	.01	1		Otsu	20 May
53.59		Liao Yu	CHN	18.5.00	2	NC-j	Nanchang	11 May
53.52		Yu Ying	CHN-Y	23.7.01	5		Chengdu	5 Apr
53.38	Mirann	Naraoka	JPN-Y	4.3.01	1Y		Fukui	7 Oct
53.28	Oleksandra	Zarytska (20)	UKR	21.7.99	2	NC-j	Kropyvnytskyi	21 Jun

INDOOR PENTATHLON

Mark	Name		Nat	Born	Pos	Meet	Venue	Date
4700A	Erica	Bougard	USA	26.7.93	1	NC	Albuquerque	16 Feb
	7.98 1.89 12.76 6.20 2:13.77							
4750	Katarina	Johnson-Thompson	GBR	9.1.93	1	WI	Birmingham	2 Mar
	8.36 1.91 12.68 6.50 2:16.63							
4700	Ivona	Dadic	AUT	29.12.93	2	WI	Birmingham	2 Mar
	8.32 1.82 14.27 6.40 2:17.82							
4663	Eliska	Klucinová	CZE	14.4.88	1	NC	Praha (Strom)	11 Feb
	8.51 1.84 14.52 6.26 2:17.34							
4637	Yorgelis	Rodríguez	CUB	25.1.95	3	WI	Birmingham	2 Mar
	8.57 1.88 14.15 6.15 2:17.70							
4583	Xénia	Krizsán	HUN	13.1.93	1	NC	Budapest	10 Feb
	8.39 1.79 14.21 6.14 2:16.2							
4572	Taliyah	Brooks	USA	8.2.95	1	NCAA	College Station	9 Mar
	8.05 1.84 12.16 6.36 2:22.44							
4508A	Kendell	Williams	USA	14.6.95	2	NC	Albuquerque	16 Feb
	8.11 1.74 12.55 6.38 2:19.22							
4502	Nina	Schultz	CAN	12.11.98	1		Lubbock	9 Feb
	8.28 1.82 11.61 6.39 2:19.79							

Mark	Name		Nat	Born	Pos	Meet	Venue	Date
4472	Alina	Shukh	UKR	12.2.99	1	NC	Sumy	9 Feb
	8.88	1.85 13.48 6.05 2:16.47						
	(10)							
4464	Katerina	Cachová	CZE	26.2.90	2	NC	Praha (Strom)	11 Feb
	8.34	1.75 12.20 6.31 2:16.21						
4456	Antoinette	Nana Djimou	FRA	2.8.85	2	v4N	Madrid	28 Jan
	8.30	1.72 14.88 6.19 2:25.15						
4455	Géraldine	Ruckstuhl	SUI	24.2.98	1		Magglingen	4 Feb
	8.64	1.81 13.74 5.93 2:16.50						
4446	Noor	Vidts	BEL	30.5.96	1	NC	Gent	4 Feb
	8.54	1.76 13.87 6.18 2:20.25						
4440	Caroline	Agnou	SUI	26.5.96	2		Magglingen	4 Feb
	8.55	1.69 14.48 6.34 2:21.03						
4424	Lecabela	Quaresma	POR	26.12.89	8	WI	Birmingham	2 Mar
	8.51	1.76 14.12 6.01 2:19.85						
4405A	Alex	Gochenour	USA	17.2.93	3	NC	Albuquerque	16 Feb
	8.35	1.71 13.91 6.01 2:18.27						
4385	Adrianna	Sułek	POL	3.4.99	1	NC	Torun	17 Feb
	8.52	1.83 12.26 5.98 2:19.14						
4381	Georgia	Ellenwood	CAN	5.8.95	3	NCAA	College Station	9 Mar
	8.55	1.78 12.31 5.96 2:14.28						
4377	Solène	Ndama	FRA	23.9.98	1		Lyon	3 Feb
	8.15	1.74 12.82 5.82 2:16.66						
	(20)							
4365	Jaclyn	Siefring	USA	30.9.95	4	NCAA	College Station	9 Mar
	8.67	1.69 12.72 6.19 2:14.64						
4364	Esther	Turpin	FRA	29.4.96	1	NC	Liévin	17 Feb
	8.35	1.69 13.22 6.09 2:17.88						
4353	Yana	Maksimova	BLR	9.1.89	1	NCp	Gomel	3 Feb
	8.77	1.80 14.14 5.68 2:17.32						
4335	Yelizaveta	Aksyonova	RUS	10.7.96	1	NC	Smolensk	14 Feb
	8.64	1.78 13.25 5.83 2:17.87						
4328	Györgyi	Zsivoczky-Farkas	HUN	13.2.85	2	NC	Budapest	10 Feb
	8.58	1.82 13.76 5.65 2:21.52						
4323	Rimma	Hordiyenko	UKR	30.12.95	2	NC	Sumy	9 Feb
	8.55	1.85 13.17 5.96 2:29.42						
4320	Lucia	Vadlejch	SVK	8.11.88	3	NC	Praha (Strom)	11 Feb
	8.61	1.75 12.04 6.09 2:16.65						
4319	Sarah	Lagger	AUT	3.9.99	2	NC	Wien	4 Feb
	8.81	1.76 13.73 5.70 2:14.05						
4318	Louisa	Grauvogel	GER	28.9.96	5	NCAA	College Station	9 Mar
	8.23	1.75 12.29 5.93 2:20.51						
4303	Bianca	Salming	SWE	22.11.98	1	NC	Norrköping	11 Feb
	9.02	1.84 13.21 5.67 2:16.12						
	(30)							
4300	Karin	Strametz	AUT	18.4.98	3	NC	Wien	4 Feb
	8.43	1.70 11.93 6.17 2:17.72						

4291	Joanne	Rowland	GBR	29.12.89	28 Jan	4198*	Jordan	Gray	USA	22.4.93 8 Dec
4269	Niki	Oudenaarden	CAN	14.1.94	19 Jan	4198	Erika	Wärff	SWE	16.7.00 11 Feb
4264	Aleksandra	Butvina	RUS	14.2.86	14 Feb	4197	Tyra	Gittens	TTO	6.6.98 9 Mar
4260A	Emilyn	Dearman	USA	1.1.95	16 Feb	4193	Meriem	Sahnoune	FRA	5.6.94 17 Feb
4257	Michelle	Atherley	USA	9.12.95	9 Mar	4190	Alissa	Brooks-Johnson	USA	1.8.95 9 Mar
4246	Margarita	Korneychuk	RUS	21.2.95	14 Feb	4180	Carmen	Ramos	ESP	18.6.98 28 Jan
4235	Mareike	Arndt	GER	29.1.92	3 Feb	4176	Cassandre	Aguessy Thomas	FRA	1.9.97 14 Jan
4218		Wang Qingling	CHN	14.1.93	8 Mar	4175	Holly	Hankenson	USA	4.6.95 22 Feb
4216	Madeline	Holmberg	USA	26.10.96	9 Mar	4160	Yelena	Yermolina	RUS	2.2.89 14 Feb
4208	Anaëlle	Nyabeu Djapa	FRA	15.9.92	17 Feb	4151	Rachael	McIntosh	CAN	17.1.91 19 Jan
4205	Hanne	Maudens	BEL	12.3.97	4 Feb	4150	Kate	O'Connor	IRL	12.12.00 3 Feb
4199	Amanda Marie Grefstad Frøynes		NOR	13.9.98	20 Jan					

HEPTATHLON

Mark	Name		Nat	Born	Pos	Meet	Venue	Date
6816	Nafissatou	Thiam	BEL	19.8.94	1	EC	Berlin	10 Aug
	13.69/0.4	1.91 15.35 24.81/0.4		6.60/1.1	57.91		2:19.35	
6806	Thiam				1	Hypo	Götzis	27 May
	13.45/0.1	2.01 15.29 24.61/1.2		6.62/0.6	47.20		2:18.62	
6759	Katarina	Johnson-Thompson	GBR	9.1.93	2	EC	Berlin	10 Aug
	13.34/0.4	1.91 13.09 22.88/1.5		6.68/-0.1	42.16		2:09.84	
6742	Yorgelis	Rodríguez	CUB	25.1.95	2	Hypo	Götzis	27 May
	13.48/0.3	1.86 14.95 23.96/-0.6		6.58w/2.3	48.65		2:12.73	
6725	Erica	Bougard	USA	26.7.93	3	Hypo	Götzis	27 May
	12.80/1.5	1.86 13.02 23.31/0.4		6.62/1.1	41.97		2:08.42	
6602	Carolin	Schäfer	GER	5.12.91	3	EC	Berlin	10 Aug
	13.33/0.4	1.79 14.12 23.75/1.5		6.24/0.9	53.73		2:14.65	

WOMEN 2018

Mark	Name		Nat	Born	Pos	Meet	Venue	Date
6552	Ivona	Dadic	AUT	29.12.93	4	EC	Berlin	10 Aug
	13.66/0.0	1.82 14.06	23.61/1.5	6.35/0.1		47.42	2:11.87	
6549		Schäfer			1		Ratingen	
	13.13/-0.1	1.78 13.53	23.73/0.6	6.19/-0.2		53.69	2:15.87	
6457		Schäfer			1	Deca	Talence	
	13.34/1.6	1.80 13.64	24.08/0.5	6.10/0.7		51.58	2:15.10	
6436		Rodríguez			1	CAC-g	Barranquilla	
	13.60w/2.3	1.83 14.23	24.56/0.1	6.23/1.9		48.96	2:15.50	
6426	Anouk	Vetter	NED	4.2.93	4	Hypo	Götzis	27 May
	13.46/0.1	1.71 15.91	23.89/0.4	6.25/0.9		51.27	2:23.41	
6414		Vetter			5	EC	Berlin	10 Aug
	13.55/0.4	1.76 14.79	23.97/1.5	6.30/1.7		51.25	2:22.84	
6413		Dadic			2		Ratingen	17 Jun
	13.56/-0.1	1.72 14.86	23.76/0.6	6.09/2.0		49.19	2:13.35	
6400	Katerina	Cachová	CZE	26.2.90	6	EC	Berlin	10 Aug
	13.29/0.4	1.85 12.71	24.25/0.4	6.36/-0.5		44.64	2:14.91	
6391	Géraldine	Ruckstuhl	SUI	24.2.98	2	Deca	Talence	16 Sep
	13.85/0.1	1.83 13.82	24.96/0.7	5.96/0.5		55.11	2:13.98	
6381		Cachova			3	Deca	Talence	16 Sep
	13.23/1.6	1.80 13.32	24.44/0.5	6.28/1.0		46.39	2:14.61	
6367	Xénia	Krizsán (10)	HUN	13.1.93	7	EC	Berlin	10 Aug
	13.64/0.0	1.79 13.99	25.05/-0.8	6.24/0.7		45.45	2:07.61	
6347		Bougard			1	NC	Des Moines	24 Jun
	12.96/0.5	1.84 12.49	23.67/-0.5	6.03/0.7		40.31	2:11.08	
6337	Verena	Preiner	AUT	1.2.95	8	EC	Berlin	10 Aug
	13.58/0.0	1.73 13.76	24.12/1.5	6.09/0.8		48.79	2:11.29	
6327		Bougard			1		Firenze	28 Apr
	13.26/0.4	1.84 11.76	23.62/2.0	6.12/-1.6		42.63	2:11.35	
6308		Preiner			5	Hypo	Götzis	27 May
	10.60/0.0	1.71 14.19	24.07/1.2	6.08/0.6		44.37	2:08.62	
6285	Evelis	Aguilar	COL	3.1.93	2	CAC-g	Barranquilla	2 Aug
	13.92w/2.3	1.77 13.64	23.95/0.1	6.47w/2.2		43.01	2:16.18	
6260		Ruckstuhl			9	EC	Berlin	10 Aug
	13.90/1.4	1.79 12.96	25.04/-0.8	5.90/-0.8		56.31	2:15.13	
6255		Johnson-Thompson			1	CG	Gold Coast	13 Apr
	13.54/0.6	1.87 11.54	23.56/-0.4	6.50/0.3		40.46	2:21.24	
6253	Niamh	Emerson	GBR-J	22.4.99	1	WJ	Tampere	13 Jul
	13.76/0.5	1.89 12.27	24.80/0.0	6.31w/2.6		39.02	2:09.74	
6252	Hanne	Maudens	BEL	12.3.97	6	Hypo	Götzis	27 May
	14.00/-0.3	1.80 13.28	24.28/1.2	6.36/0.1		40.96	2:11.14	
6244		Cachova			7	Hypo	Götzis	27 May
	13.29/1.5	1.77 12.69	24.46/-0.6	6.37w/3.2		42.51	2:14.69	
6244		Krizsán			4	Deca	Talence	16 Sep
	13.76/0.1	1.80 13.91	25.44/0.7	6.07/1.2		48.44	2:13.26	
6230	Esther	Turpin	FRA	29.4.96	8	Hypo	Götzis	27 May
	13.26/0.3	1.74 13.21	24.59/1.2	6.32/1.3		42.82	2:14.12	
6225	Sarah	Lagger	AUT-J	3.9.99	2	WJ	Tampere	13 Jul
	14.21/0.5	1.77 14.38	24.86/-0.1	6.15/0.3		45.76	2:11.53	
	(30/16)							
6179	Grit	Sadeiko	EST	29.7.89	5	Deca	Talence	16 Sep
	13.31/1.6	1.80 12.34	24.83/-0.2	5.93/1.4		47.70	2:14.98	
6177	Alina	Shukh	UKR J	12.2.99	9	Hypo	Götzis	27 May
	14.33/ 0.3	1.77 14.14	25.88/1.8	5.95/1.8		52.46	2:10.93	
6173	Georgia	Ellenwood	CAN	5.8.95	1	Big10	Bloomington	12 May
	13.76/1.1	1.78 12.69	24.21w/2.1	6.11/1.2		45.94	2:16.37	
6169	Mareike	Arndt	GER	29.1.92	3		Ratingen	17 Jun
	13.44/-0.1	1.63 15.06	23.70/0.6	5.96w/2.9		43.84	2:15.48	
	(20)							
6165	Sophie	Weißenberg	GER	24.9.97	1	vUSA	Knoxville	28 Jul
	13.95/1.9	1.85 13.01	24.26/-1.5	6.16/0.0		43.76	2:20.52	
6162	Louisa	Grauvogel	GER	28.9.96	4		Ratingen	17 Jun
	13.13/-0.1	1.69 13.22	23.36/0.6	5.85/2.0		44.14	2:15.95	
6144	Allison	Reaser	USA	9.9.92	11	Hypo	Götzis	27 May
	13.45/0.1	1.65 12.98	23.82/-0.6	6.07/0.5		44.54	2:11.61	
6137	Chari	Hawkins	USA	21.5.91	1	ENG Ch	Bedford	27 May
	13.56/0.5	1.80 12.78	24.44/-1.7	6.07w/2.8		43.71	2:17.64	
6136	Marthe Y	Koala	BUR	8.3.94	1		Kladno	16 Jun
	13.56/0.9	1.75 12.73	24.24/0.1	6.64/1.5		44.90	2:29.65	
6133	Nina	Schultz	CAN	12.11.98	2	CG	Gold Coast	13 Apr
	13.47/0.6	1.84 12.13	25.02/-0.3	6.19/0.3		43.11	2:17.40	

Mark	Name		Nat	Born	Pos	Meet	Venue	Date
6116	Anna	Maiwald	GER	21.7.90	5		Ratingen	17 Jun
	13.77/-0.1	1.72 14.40 24.23/1.1		5.97w/3.6	42.84		2:15.61	
6111	Alex	Gochenour	USA	17.2.93	13	Hypo	Götzis	27 May
	13.23/1.5	1.68 14.25 24.40/-0.6		6.10/0.7	40.94		2:16.48	
6104	Daryna	Sloboda	UKR	19.6.95	1	NC	Kropyvnytskyi	26 Jun
	14.49/0.3	1.82 13.69 25.33/-0.8		6.20/0.0	41.17		2:10.39	
6094	Adriana	Rodríguez	CUB-J	12.7.99	14	Hypo	Götzis	27 May
	13.51/0.1	1.77 13.29 23.72/0.4		6.45/1.5	35.15		2:23.01	
(30)								
6081A	Giovana	Cavaleti	BRA	13.1.89	1	SAmC	Cochabamba	8 Jun
	13.80/0.1	1.80 13.00 24.09/-0.5		6.10/0.2	40.12		2:18.26	
6074	Tyra	Gittens	TTO	6.9.98	1	SEC	Knoxville	12 May
	13.21/1.2	1.86 12.82 24.01/1.6		6.37/1.0	36.71		2:32.41	
6057	Lucia	Vadlejch	SVK	8.11.88	15	Hypo	Götzis	27 May
	14.04/-1.0	1.74 12.17 24.67/-1.2		6.33/1.9	42.58		2:12.97	
6050	Lindsay	Schwartz	USA	23.4.90	2	vGER	Knoxville	28 Jul
	13.65/1.9	1.70 13.82 24.63/-1.5		6.02/-1.2	41.42		2:13.55	
6050	Celina	Leffler	GER	9.4.96	1	NC-23	Wesel	25 Aug
	13.64/0.9	1.74 13.18 24.15/0.7		6.17/-0.9	42.36		2:21.93	
6036	Rimma	Hordiyenko	UKR	30.12.95	2	NC	Kropyvnytskyi	26 Jun
	13.50/0.3	1.82 13.15 25.15/-0.8		6.16/0.2	42.17		2:24.38	
6026	Swapma	Barman	IND	29.10.96	1	AsiG	Jakarta	29 Aug
	13.98/-0.1	1.82 12.69 26.08/-0.1		6.05/0.0	50.63		2:21.13	
6015	Diane	Marie-Hardy	FRA	19.2.96	2	NC	Albi	7 Jul
	13.94/1.2	1.66 13.02 24.57/1.8		6.09/1.9	42.47		2:09.38	
6011	Mari	Klaup-McColl	EST	27.2.90	1		Pärnu	17 Jun
	14.13/0.7	1.83 12.92 25.98/1.7		5.96/1.0	53.56		2:25.67	
5999	Odile	Ahouanwanou	BEN	5.1.91	1	AfrC	Asaba	5 Aug
	13.71	1.77 14.10 24.76		5.94/0.6	44.80		2:26.50	
(40)								
5986	Yana	Maksimova	BLR	9.1.89	16	Hypo	Götzis	27 May
	14.71/-0.3	1.83 14.39 26.12/1.6		5.81/1.1	46.51		2:14.60	
5985	Bianca	Salming	SWE	22.11.88	2	3N	Pärnu	17 Jun
	14.80/1.5	1.92 13.32 26.48/1.7		5.78/1.3	45.82		2:13.21	
5977	Alissa	Brooks-Johnson	USA	1.8.95	1	Pac12	Stanford	6 May
	13.68/0.8	1.74 12.55 24.40w/2.2		5.89/1.5	41.60		2:14.81	
5976	Madeline	Holmberg	USA	26.10.96	2	Big10	Bloomington	12 May
	13.95/1.1	1.60 13.20 23.79w/2.1		6.37/0.9	43.35		2:20.55	
5954		Wang Qingling	CHN	14.1.93	2	AsiG	Jakarta	29 Aug
	13.49/1.2	1.73 11.97 24.74/-0.5		6.44/0.0	39.33		2:21.79	
5950	Lecabela	Quaresma	POR	26.12.89	16	EC	Berlin	10 Aug
	14.19/0.0	1.79 13.64 25.61/0.2		6.10/0.5	39.27		2:14.70	
5946	Taliyah	Brooks	USA	8.2.95	1	TexR	Austin	1 Mar
	13.28/1.6	1.72 11.72 23.99/0.9		6.30/0.0	36.91		2:21.17	
5939	Adrianna	Sulek	POL-J	3.4.99	3	WJ	Tampere	13 Jul
	13.80/0.3	1.62 13.21 24.02/0.0		6.06/0.6	39.35		2:12.38	
5939	Vanessa	Spinola	BRA	5.5.90	2	NC	Bragança Paulista	16 Sep
	14.22/1.6	1.76 13.28 24.51/0.4		5.97/0.9	41.56		2:18.15	
5932	Solène	Ndama	FRA	23.9.98	17	Hypo	Götzis	27 May
	13.34/1.5	1.74 13.12 24.48/1.6		6.02w/2.6	33.88		2:15.96	
(50)								
5925	Mariya	Pavlova	RUS	21.5.96	1		Kazan	17 Aug
	13.86/0.0	1.83 12.83 25.36/0.2		6.04/1.4	40.70		2:21.92	
5923	Viktoriya	Vaseykina	RUS	19.3.97	1		Adler	21 May
	14.34/-1.1	1.80 12.63 25.33/0.0		6.18/-0.1	43.72		2:21.03	
5915	Celeste	Mucci	AUS-J	11.8.99	4	CG	Gold Coast	13 Apr
	13.19/0.6	1.75 12.22 24.59/-0.4		6.10/-0.5	43.03		2:29.73	
5905A	Carmen	Ramos	ESP	18.6.98	1	NC-23	Soria	8 Jul
	14.03/0.7	1.72 12.28 24.73/1.0		6.00/0.0	42.68		2:15.13	
5898	Angela	Whyte	CAN	22.5.80	5	CG	Gold Coast	13 Apr
	13.35/0.6	1.72 11.48 25.36/-0.4		6.07/-0.9	44.58		2:18.79	
5898	Purnima	Hembram	IND	10.7.93	1	I-State	Guwahati	29 Jun
	13.78/0.0	1.75 11.81 24.90		5.93	44.15		2:17.95	
5886	Kendall	Gustafson	USA	30.3.95	2	Pac12	Stanford	6 May
	14.08/0.8	1.80 13.08 25.02w/2.2		5.72/1.0	46.56		2:24.49	
5881	Annie	Kunz	USA	16.2.93	5	NC	Des Moines	24 Jun
	13.84/0.1	1.72 14.64 24.94/-2.0		5.75/0.1	39.06		2:19.04	
5879	Ana Camila	Pirelli	PAR	30.1.89	1	IbAm	Trujillo	26 Aug
	14.08/-0.6	1.66 13.78 25.32/-0.5		5.67/0.9	47.12		2:13.40	
5878	Niki (60)	Oudenaarden	CAN	14.1.94	6	CG	Gold Coast	13 Apr
	14.64/0.3	1.69 13.85 25.03/-0.4		5.84/-0.4	45.42		2:14.10	

Mark	Name		Nat	Born	Pos	Meet	Venue	Date
5877	Lisa	Linnell	SWE	30.4.91	6		Ratingen	17 Jun
	14.13/1.2	1.75 12.29 25.23/0.9		5.94/1.8		41.40	2:12.37	
5873	Yuki	Yamasaki	JPN	6.6.95	3	AsiG	Jakarta	29 Aug
	14.02/1.2	1.70 12.13 24.75/-0.5		5.89/0.0		46.48	2:17.75	
5872(w)	Jaclyn	Siefring	USA	30.9.95	2A		Azusa	19 Apr
	14.12w/3.4	1.69 12.32 24.80/1.0		6.15/1.8		38.97	2:11.81	
5864	Karin	Strametz	AUT	18.4.98	8		Ratingen	17 Jun
	13.49/1.2	1.63 11.94 24.88/1.1		6.10/0.4		44.02	2:17.24	
5862	Rachael	McIntosh	CAN	17.1.91	3A		Azusa	19 Apr
	14.19w/3.4	1.72 12.48 25.25/1.5		5.92/0.7		42.61	2:12.22	
5858	Maria	Huntington	FIN	13.3.97	1	NC	Jyväskylä	20 Jul
	13.56/0.5	1.68 12.24 25.06/-0.5		6.23/0.5		43.58	2:23.87	
5853	Ashtin	Zamzow	USA	13.8.96	6	NC	Des Moines	24 Jun
	13.91/0.1	1.72 12.35 24.93/-2.0		5.67/0.2		50.60	2:22.95	
5848	Luisaris	Toledo	VEN	29.12.92	3	CAC-g	Barranquilla	2 Aug
	14.40w/2.3	1.62 12.37 24.63/0.1		6.12w/2.1		43.77	2:12.27	
5845	Paulina	Ligarska	POL	9.4.96	1	NC	Suwałki	2 Jun
	14.54/-1.6	1.82 13.48 25.33/-2.1		5.81/1.1		41.31	2:18.86	
5844	Annik	Kälin	SUI-J	27.4.00	18	Hypo	Götzis	27 May
	13.88/-1.0	1.77 12.18 24.67/1.6		6.10/-0.5		37.60	2:20.46	
	(70)							
5839	Emma	Oosterwegel	NED	29.6.98	9		Ratingen	17 Jun
	13.78/1.2	1.69 12.50 25.06/1.6		5.70/-1.9		48.06	2:19.52	
5837	Cassandre	Aguessy Thomas	FRA	1.9.97	3	NC	Albi	7 Jul
	13.74/1.2	1.75 12.84 24.61/1.8		6.10/1.6		36.47	2:22.80	
5826	Yekaterina	Voronina	UZB	16.2.92	5	AsiG	Jakarta	29 Aug
	14.72/1.2	1.76 12.59 25.68/-0.5		5.64/0.0		49.91	2:14.81	
5825	Riley	Cooks	USA	6.12.93	8	NC	Des Moines	24 Jun
	13.47/0.5	1.69 13.23 24.35/0.1		5.89/-0.5		42.31	2:28.61	
5821	Eri	Utsunomiya	JPN	11.4.93	1		Tokyo	22 Apr
	13.92/-2.4	1.66 11.15 24.79/-0.4		5.90/0.5		42.12	2:09.80	
5821	Ayesha	Champagnie	JAM	10.3.96	3	Big10	Bloomington	12 May
	14.31/1.1	1.66 14.79 24.78w/2.1		5.63/-0.5		49.53	2:26.50	
5818	Claudia	Conte	ESP-J	14.11.99	1	v5N-J	Aubagne	29 Jul
	14.47/-0.8	1.78 12.08 25.43/0.8		5.83/0.0		43.79	2:14.51	
5818A	Martha Valeria	Araujo	COL	12.5.96	1	SAm-23	Cuenca	30 Sep
	13.84/0.7	1.69 12.21 24.94/1.7		6.15/0.3		46.19	2:27.36	
5816	Michelle	Atherley	USA	9.12.95	4A		Azusa	19 Apr
	13.28/1.4	1.72 12.41 23.96w/2.1		5.84/1.8		29.89	2:14.16	
5815	Elizabeth	Morland	IRL	3.3.98	2		Arona	3 Jun
	13.63w/2.1	1.70 11.49 24.99/0.0		6.12/0.0		43.49	2:22.23	
	(80)							
5812	Alysbeth	Félix	PUR	7.3.93	21	Hypo	Götzis	27 May
	13.91/0.3	1.74 11.12 24.93/-1.2		6.11/-0.9		41.04	2:17.92	
5810	Miia	Sillman	FIN	3.6.95	2	NC	Jyväskylä	20 Jul
	14.03/0.5	1.83 12.81 25.50/-0.5		5.99/-0.6		40.99	2:26.93	
5798A	Anna	Hall	USA-Y	23.3.01	1		Albuquerque	1 Jun
	14.03/0.5	1.82 10.66 24.56/-3.0		6.06/0.0		35.96	2:17.18	
5794	Amanda Marie	Frøynes	NOR	13.9.98	5	NCAA	Eugene	9 Jun
	14.27/0.9	1.75 12.21 25.60/0.8		5.77/-1.7		44.63	2:14.98	
5793	Tori	West	AUS	14.10.95	1		Brisbane (St. Lucia)	7 Jan
	14.43/-0.4	1.77 12.46 24.27/1.0		5.88/1.0		44.50	2:27.85	
5793w	Kaylee	Hinton	USA	19.4.97	1	Big12	Waco	12 May
	13.49/w3.5	1.79 10.10 23.85w/6.5		5.95w/2.7		35.20	2:19.19	
5791	Vanessa	Grimm	GER	22.4.97	10		Ratingen	17 Jun
	14.14/0.5	1.69 13.70 24.78/1.1		5.83/1.9		40.35	2:19.02	
5788(w)	Juanita	Webster-Freeman	USA	13.11.96	1		Azusa	11 May
	13.60w/3.2	1.80 12.47 25.71w/2.2		5.91/0.7		38.50	2:21.89	
5788	Annaelle	Nyabeu Djapa	FRA	15.9.92	4	NC	Albi	7 Jul
	13.54/1.2	1.72 13.22 25.55/1.8		6.09/1.3		36.43	2:21.03	
5787	Hertta	Heikkinen	FIN	27.10.94	3	NC	Jyväskylä	20 Jul
	14.09/0.5	1.71 12.72 24.70/-0.5		5.85/-0.4		40.34	2:17.91	
	(90)							
5782	Patricia	Ortega	ESP	18.4.94	1B		Azusa	19 Apr
	13.66/1.0	1.78 11.25 24.82/2.4		5.84/0.3		33.53	2:11.53	
5771	Jutta	Heikkinen	FIN	27.10.94	4	NC	Jyväskylä	20 Jul
	13.83/0.5	1.71 12.84 25.49/-0.5		5.68/-0.1		46.34	2:21.72	
5766	Meg	Hemphill	JPN	23.5.96	2		Nagano	17 Jun
	13.68/1.6	1.68 11.22 25.20/2.2		6.16/1.6		42.79	2:20.81	
5761	Alyssa	Thompson	USA	25.9.94	3	Pac12	Stanford	6 Ma
	14.26/0.0	1.62 11.16 24.59/2.2		6.36w/2.3		41.14	2:16.04	

Mark	Name		Nat	Born	Pos	Meet	Venue	Date
5759	Emilyn	Dearman	USA	1.1.95	10	NC	Des Moines	24 Jun
	13.57/0.5	1.69 12.97 25.13/0.1		5.74/-0.8 37.10 2:14.93				
5754	Lovisa	Östervall	SWE	9.3.97	3	3N	Pärnu	17 Jun
	14.20/0.7	1.86 11.27 25.34/2.2		5.80/-0.8 40.95 2:21.26				
5743	Shaina	Burns	USA	21.3.96	2	SEC	Knoxville	12 Ma
	13.91/2.0	1.74 14.06 25.89/1.6		5.55/0.0 42.54 2:20.76				
5742	Kiara	Reddingius	AUS	2.1.92	2	NC	Gold Coast	6 Feb
	14.32/-1.8	1.72 12.11 24.48/1.1		5.68w/2.9 44.49 2:20.31				
5725	Hope	Bender	USA	2.1.97	2B		Azusa	19 Apr
	13.59/0.0	1.60 11.90 23.97/2.5		5.78/-0.6 35.72 2:11.30				
5719	Lyndsey	Lopes	USA	23.8.97	4	Pac12	Stanford	6 Ma
	13.63/0.8 (100)	1.74 10.86 24.31/2.2		5.86w/2.8 38.14 2:21.04				
5719	Aleksandra	Butvina	RUS	14.2.86	1		Smolensk	6 Jul
	14.86/-0.3	1.74 13.69 25.43/0.3		5.86/0.1 40.41 2:17.84				

Mark	Name		Nat	Born	Date		Mark	Name		Nat	Born	Date
5717	Janika	Baarck	GER-J	1.9.99	25 Aug		5523	Jenny	Kimbro	USA	17.4.98	19 Apr
5699	Alysha	Burnett	AUS	4.1.97	16 Feb		5523	Lucia	Mokrásová	SVK	27.3.94	12 May
5695	Katherine	O'Connor	IRL-J	12.12.00	13 Apr		5523	Sharlota	Paehlitse	BLR	20.11.98	16 Jun
5686	Nada	Chroudi	TUN	20.11.87	28 Apr		5523	Sterling	Lester	USA-J	13.11.00	17 Jun
5686	Crystiane	Barroso	BRA	26.8.88	16 Sep		5522(w)	Peyton	Wade	USA	12.2.96	12 May
5678	Ida	Eikeng	NOR-J	25.6.99	10 Jun		5519	Kristella	Jurkatamm	EST	9.4.96	17 Jun
5677	Iryna	Rofe-Beketova	UKR	18.9.98	26 Jun		5519		Shen Muhan	CHN	5.1.97	29 Aug
5672	Sofia	Ifantidou	GRE	5.1.85	8 Jul		5514	Valvanuz	Cañizo	ESP	29.12.96	29 Jul
5660	Jade	O'Dowda	GBR-J	9.9.99	13 Jul		5511(w)	Jestena	Mattson	USA	17.3.97	12 May
5651	Yelena	Yermolina	RUS	2.2.89	21 May		5509(w)	Carly	Paul	USA	5.8.96	14 Apr
5650(w)	Maya	Neal	LBR	22.12.96	12 May		5501	Priscillia	Fonds	FRA	3.7.96	29 Jul
5649	Yekaterina	Netsvetayeva	BLR	26.6.89	16 Jun		5499	Elisa	Pineau	FRA	26.10.98	3 Jun
5649	Barbara	Hernando	ESP	12.8.88	22 Jul		5494	Marijke	Esselink	NED-J	22.6.99	3 Jun
5638(w)	Ida	Thunberg	SWE-J	16.7.99	10 Jun		5491w	Lauren	Taubert	USA	20.3.98	12 May
5632(w)	Emilie	Berge	NOR	7.12.97	12 May		5487	Katie	Garland	GBR	27.1.97	27 May
5632w	Ariel	Okorie	USA	11.9.98	12 May		5487	Camryn	Newton-Smith	AUS-J	27.4.00	13 Jul
5630	Andrea	Obetzhofer	AUT-J	15.2.99	10 Jun		5475	Myke	van de Wiel	NED	4.6.97	24 Jun
5619	Andrea	Thompson	AUS	2.10.98	16 Feb		5474	Nicole	Warwick	USA	31.8.98	19 Apr
5619	Grace	McKenzie	IRL	4.12.96	5 May		5474	Ottilianí	Tsilumoúla	GRE	3.1.92	3 Jun
5614	Margarita	Korneychuk	RUS	21.2.95	6 Jul		5468	Anna	Kerbachová	CZE	5.3.00	3 Jun
5611	Casidhe	Simmons	AUS	6.2.95	7 Jan		5465	Marina	Pshichkina	RUS	8.5.97	28 Jul
5606	Mathilde	Rey	SUI-J	29.3.00	3 Jun		5462	Jaida	Lemmons	USA	25.8.98	11 May
5603	Jenifer Nicole	Norberto	BRA	4.10.96	16 Sep		5458	Erinn	Beattie	USA	8.4.97	5 May
5598	Noor	Vidts	BEL	30.5.96	10 Aug		5454	Alexus	Henry	USA	14.12.96	19 Apr
5597	Nikki	Larch-Miller	USA	13.8.94	24 Jun		5451	Laura	Voss	GER	29.1.94	26 Aug
5593	Barbora	Zatloukalová	CZE	3.6.97	29 Jul		5443	Liksy	Joseph	IND	17.2.90	28 Apr
5590	Aliyah	Whisby	USA	23.2.98	19 Apr		5441	Emma	Stenlöf	SWE	25.6.96	17 Jun
5590	Jessica	Taylor-Jemmett	GBR	27.6.88	16 Jun		5437	Migle Liepa	Muraskaite	LTU	16.6.98	5 May
5584	Sára	Mátó	HUN-J	23.12.00	20 May		5437	Kseniya	Trubinova	RUS-J	21.4.00	24 Jun
5579(w)	Celia	Perron	FRA	18.4.97	7 Jul		5437		Chu Chia-Ling	TPE	11.1.91	29 Aug
5574	Rose	Jackson	USA	12.5.95	3 Jun		5435	Riko	Nishimura	JPN	1.11.93	17 Jun
5574	Christina	Kiffe	GER	2.5.92	26 Aug		5433	Maja	Wichhart-Donzo	USA	6.3.97	19 Apr
5566	Lisa	Maihöfer	GER	28.10.98	17 Jun		5433	Jessica	Rautelin	FIN	16.1.97	20 Jul
5564	Katerina	Dvoráková	CZE	10.5.97	28 Apr		5431(w)	Teddi	Maslowski	USA	6.8.93	11 May
5563	Hoda	Hagras	EGY	11.5.95	7 Jul		5431	Lucy	Turner	GBR	14.2.97	5 Aug
5559	Emma	Nwofor	GBR	22.8.96	27 May		5430	Rachel	Limburg	AUS	7.7.97	14 Jan
5556(w)	Erika	Wärff	SWE-J	16.7.00	20 May		5424	Akiko	Ito	JPN	25.5.95	3 Aug
5556	Izabela	Mikolajczyk	POL	4.9.90	2 Jun		5423	Eleonora	Ferrero	ITA	29.12.94	28 Apr
5547	Isabel	Posch	AUT-J	28.2.00	10 Jun		5411	Johanna	Siebler	GER-J	28.6.00	6 May
5545	Michelle	Weitzel	GER	18.6.87	17 Jun		5404(w)	Urte	Bacianskaite	LTU-J	17.9.00	10 Jun
5541	Aaron	Howell	USA	3.10.95	19 Apr		5404	Dariya	Dikhanova	UKR-J	23.3.00	29 Jul
5536	Chie	Kiriyama	JPN	2.8.91	17 Jun		5403	Elisa	Kirvesniemi	FIN	18.12.85	20 Jul
5533(w)	Meriem	Sahnoune	FRA	5.6.94	7 Jul		5402	Kolbi	Sims	USA	16.6.97	12 May
5529	Ellen	Barber	GBR	5.12.97	27 May		5402	Lydia	Boll	SUI-J	1.12.99	29 Jul
5529	Jana	Novotna	CZE-J	26.1.99	3 Jun		5401	Irma	Gunnarsdottir	ISL	4.2.98	10 Jun
5527	Lisa	Steinlage	GER	22.6.93	17 Jun		5400	Elise	Lovell	GBR	9.5.92	28 Apr
5526	Holly	Hankenson	USA	4.6.95	11 May		**Best non wind-assisted**					
5524	Céline	Albisser	SUI	5.5.96	29 Jul		5585		Hinton	USA		7 Apr
							5429		Okorie	USA		7 Apr

Best at low altitude

5958		Cavalati	BRA		1	NC	Bragança Paulista	16 Sep
	13.78/1.6	1.70 13.83 24.61/0.4		6.21/1.4 37.10 2:17.37				

5744 Araujo COL 2 Aug   5660 A Hall USA 17 Jun   5630 Ramos ESP 3 Jun

JUNIORS

See main list for top 9 juniors. 10 performances by 6 women to 5915. Additional marks and further juniors:

Emerson	6043		3	CG	Gold Coast	13 Apr
	14.08/0.6	1.84 12.13 24.83/-0.3		6.06/-1.1 40.34 2:12.18		
Shukh	5985		15	EC	Berlin	10 Aug
	14.42/0.0	1.76 14.43 26.57/0.2		5.81/-1.2 51.20 2:15.09		
Lagger	6156		10	Hypo	Götzis	27 May
	14.24/-0.3	1.77 13.33 24.57/1.6		6.01w/2.6 46.92 2:11.70		

WOMEN 2018

Mark	Name		Nat	Born	Pos	Meet	Venue	Date
Lagger	6058	13 EC Berlin		10 Aug				
	14.46/0.0	1.76 13.54	25.16/-0.8		6.14/1.1	45.30	2:13.14	
5717	Janika	Baarck (10)	GER	1.9.99	1	NC-j	Wesel	25 Aug
	14.33/0.9	1.59 13.70	24.90/0.2		6.06/0.6	39.83	2:17.43	
5695	Katherine	O'Connor	IRL	12.12.00	8	CG	Gold Coast	13 Apr
	14.99/0.3	1.78 11.97	25.26/-0.4		5.64/0.1	46.34	2:18.30	
5678	Ida	Eikong	NOR	25.8.99	1	Nord-j	Jessheim	10 Jun
	13.56/1.7	1.67 13.07	23.98/3.8		5.84w/2.4	45.94	2:44.65	
5660	Jade	O'Dowda	GBR	9.9.99	7	WJ	Tampere	13 Jul
	14.04/0.5	1.71 12.33	25.03/0.1		6.10/0.1	35.05	2:21.74	
5638(w)	Ida	Thunberg	SWE	16.7.99	2	Nord-j	Jessheim	10 Jun
	13.58/1.7	1.58 12.87	25.26/3.8		5.74w/3.6	47.77	2:28.07	
5630	Andrea	Obetzhofer	AUT	15.2.99	1		Lustenau	10 Jun
	14.59/0.1	1.65 14.18	24.96/0.4		5.70/-0.9	42.28	2:23.81	
5606	Mathilde	Rey	SUI	29.3.00	1		Bernhausen	3 Jun
	14.60/0.1	1.71 12.66	25.03/1.0		5.49/1.0	42.62	2:18.82	
5584	Sára	Mátó	HUN	23.12.00	1	NC	Györ	20 May
	14.60/0.4	1.72 9.87	24.70/0.2		5.67w/2.1	39.40	2:09.79	
5556(w)	Erika	Wärff	SWE	16.7.00	1		Landquart	20 May
	14.70/0.1	1.75 12.58	25.68w/3.0		5.75w/3.1	43.81	2:27.98	
5547	Isabel	Posch	AUT	28.2.00	2		Lustenau	10 Jun
	13.85/1.2	1.68 10.85	24.52/1.2		5.78/0.6	40.60	2:26.35	
5529	Jana	Novotna (20)	CZE	26.1.99	1	NC-j	Kolin	3 Jun
	14.23/0.2	1.72 11.26	25.77/0.0		6.05/0.7	37.86	2:22.93	

4 X 100 METRES RELAY

Mark		Name		Pos	Meet	Venue	Date
41.88	GBR	Philip, Lansiquot, B Williams, Asher-Smith		1	EC	Berlin	12 Aug
42.05	LSU, US	Brisco, K Johnson, Misher, Hobbs		1	SEC	Knoxville	13 May
42.09	LSU, USA	Brisco, K Johnson, Misher, Hobbs		1s1	NCAA	Eugene	7 Jun
42.15	NED	Schippers, van Hunenstijn, Samuel, Sedney		2	EC	Berlin	12 Aug
42.19	GBR	Philip, Lansiquot, B Williams, Neita		1h1	EC	Berlin	12 Aug
42.23	GER	Kwayie, Lückenkemper, Pinto, Haase		3	EC	Berlin	12 Aug
42.24	GER	Haase, Kwadwo, Pinto, Lückenkemper		1		Regensburg	3 Jun
42.25	LSU, USA	Brisco, K Johnson, Misher, Hobbs		1	NCAA	Eugene	9 Jun
42.28	GBR	Philip, Lansiquot, B Williams, Asher-Smith		1	WK	Zürich	30 Aug
42.29	SUI	Del Ponte, Atcho, Kambundji, Kora		1	Athl	Lausanne	5 Jul
42.30	SUI	Del Ponte, Atcho, Kambundji, Kora		4	EC	Berlin	12 Aug
42.34	GER	Kwayie, Lückenkemper, Pinto, Haase		1h2	EC	Berlin	12 Aug
42.36	GBR	Philip, Lansiquot, B Williams, Neita		1	Anniv	London (OS)	22 Jul
42.42	LSU, USA	Brisco, K Johnson, Misher, Hobbs		1h3	NCAA-E	Tampa	26 May
42.46	England, GBR	Philip, Asher-Smith, B Williams, Ugen		1	CG	Gold Coast	14 Apr
42.49	LSU, USA	Brisco, K Johnson, Misher, Hobbs		1		Baton Rouge	28 Apr
42.49	GER	Kwayie, Kwadwo, Lückenkemper, Haase		2	Athl	Lausanne	5 Jul
42.49	SUI	Del Ponte, Atcho, Kambundji, Kora		2	WK	Zürich	30 Aug
42.50	LSU, USA	Brisco, K Johnson, Misher, Hobbs		1		Baton Rouge	7 Apr
42.50	USA Red	Parker, S Collins, Bryant, Prandini		1	NACAC	Toronto	12 Aug
		(20 performances by teams from 5 nations)					
42.52	JAM	C Williams, Morrison, Evans, Thompson		2	CG	Gold Coast	14 Apr
42.59	CHN	Liang Xiaojing, Wei Yongli, Ge Manqi, Yuan Qiqi		2	Anniv	London (OS)	22 Jul
42.73	BRN	Jassim, Odiong, Al-Khaldi, Naser		1	AsiG	Jakarta	30 Aug
42.75	NGR	Udo-Gabriel, Okagbare, Amusan, Chukwuma		3	CG	Gold Coast	14 Apr
43.06	FRA (10)	Ombissa-Dzangue, Akakpo, Galais, Zahi		3h1	EC	Berlin	12 Aug
43.20	POL	Ciba, Kielbasinska, Kotwila, Swoboda		4h1	EC	Berlin	12 Aug
43.31	ESP	M I Pérez, E García, Sevilla, Lara		2	MedG	Tarragona	30 Jun
43.42	ITA	Abreu, Hooper, Siragusa, Alloh		7	EC	Berlin	12 Aug
43.50	TTO	St.Fort, Hackett, R Thomas, Selvon		4	CG	Gold Coast	14 Apr
43.50	CAN	Harrison, Emmanuiel, P George, Westney		3	NACAC	Toronto	12 Aug
43.64	GHA	Owusu-Agyapong, Acheampong, Halutie, Amponsah		5	CG	Gold Coast	14 Apr
43.68	RSA	Steenkamp, Mamathu, T Thomas, Horn		6	AWC	London (OS)	15 Jul
43.68	DOM	M Sánchez, Paulino, Medina, De Aza		3	CAG	Barranquilla	2 Aug
43.73	BRA	Orcampi Unimed Rayane Santos, Azevedo, V dos Santos, Rosa		1	NC	Bragança Paulista	15 Sep
43.76	AUS (20)	Pearson, Coates, Day, Breen		2		Brisbane (Nathan)	28 Mar
43.80	IRL	J Healy, P Healy, Neville, Akpe-Moses		4h2	EC	Berlin	12 Aug
43.82	KAZ	Zyabkina, Mikhina, Golendova, Safronova		3	AsiG	Jakarta	30 Aug
43.90	UKR	Plotitsyna, Kalistratova, Kachur, Holyenyeva		5h2	EC	Berlin	12 Aug
44.03	HUN	Nguyen, Kaptur, Kozák, Sorok		3		Genève	9 Jun
44.09	DEN	Østergård, Karstoft, Graversgaard, Kramer		6h2	EC	Berlin	12 Aug
44.11	JPN	Fukushima, Ichikawa, Saito, Maeyama		2		Osaka	20 May

Mark		Name	Nat	Born	Pos	Meet	Venue		Date
44.12	CZE	Domská, Pírková, Slaninová, Seidlová			7h2	EC	Berlin		12 Aug
44.18A	ECU	Chillambo, Tenorio, Poroso, Suárez			1	SAmC	Cuenca		29 Sep
44.19	COL	A González, Obregón, Rivera, Palacios			4	CAG	Barranquilla		2 Aug
44.37	CUB	Montes, A Rodríguez, Alfonso, Y García			1		La Habana		8 Jun

(30)

44.40	CIV	3 Aug	44.51	SWE	12 Aug	44.69	RUS	29 May	44.72	CYP	30 Jun	45.00	FIN	31 Aug
44.48	GRE	12 Aug	44.56	THA	30 Aug	44.71A	VEN	7 Jun	44.91	POR	5 May	45.14	BAH	1 Apr

Mixed Nationalities USA and others shown

42.11		Americas Tenorio ECU, Miller-Uibo BAH, Prandini USA, Rosa BRA			1	C.Cp	Ostrava	8 Sep
42.30		Un. Kentucky Barnes, Camacho-Quinn PUR, K Clarke, K Gray			2	SEC	Knoxville	13 May
42.49		Kentucky Barnes, Camacho-Quinn PUR, K Clark TTO, Gray			2h1	NCAAE	Tampa	26 May

JUNIORS

43.80	GER	Dönicke, Kwadwo, Junk, Schwab			1h1	WJ	Tampere	13 Jul
43.90	IRL	Scott, Akpe-Moses, Neville, Jumbo-Gula			2	WJ	Tampere	14 Jul
44.05	GBR	Awuah, Rees, Adam, Carr			3	WJ	Tampere	14 Jul
44.24	FRA	Atatou, Alessandrini, Mignon, Marcelin			4	WJ	Tampere	14 Jul
44.61	POL	Skrzyszowska, Stefanowicz, Potasznik, Kotwiła			5	WJ	Tampere	14 Jul
44.64		Holmwood Tech, JAM			1		Kingston	24 Mar
44.65	SUI	Goll, Lemmens, Vancardo, Gutschmidt			6	WJ	Tampere	14 Jul
44.78	AUS	Owusu-Afriyie, Edwards, Johnson, Gross			7	WJ	Tampere	14 Jul
45.06	CHN	Lin Yuwei, Zhu Cuiwei, Tao Yanan, Feng Lulu			1	Asi-J	Gifu	9 Jun
45.14	BAH	Cartwright, Parker, Kinteh, S Wells			2	Carifta	Nassau	1 Apr

4 X 200 METRES RELAY

1:28.77		PURE Athletics Baptiste TTO, Wimbley USA, Bowie USA, Henry-Robinson JAM	1	FlaR	Gainesville	31 Mar
1:30.76		Un. Kentucky	1		Knoxville	14 Apr

4 X 400 METRES RELAY

3:24.00	JAM	Day 52.0, Le-Roy 50.9, Russell 50.62, McPherson 50.45	1	CG	Gold Coast	14 Apr
3:24.28	USA	B Thomas 51.6, Blocker 50.7, Horton 51.44, Okolo 50.45	1	AWC	London (OS)	14 Jul
3:24.29	JAM	Day 51.8, Russell 50.4, James 52.27, McPherson 49.70	2	AWC	London (OS)	14 Jul
3:25.29	NGR	P George 51.7, Onome 52.0, Oghenefejiro 51.25, Ajayi 50.29	2	CG	Gold Coast	14 Apr
3:25.91	FRA	Diarra 52.4, Sananes 51.8, Anais 51.57, Guei 50.14	3	AWC	London (OS)	14 Jul
3:26.08	USA Red	Guillory, Blocker, Horton, Okolo 49.78	1	NACAC	Toronto	12 Aug
3:26.16	USA Red	Little, Hayes, A Spencer 52.24, Okolo 50.44	1	TexR	Austin	31 Mar
3:26.17	POL	Hołub 51.5, Wyciszkiewicz 52.0, Dabrowska 51.48, Baumgart 51.12	4	AWC	London (OS)	14 Jul
3:26.48	GBR	Clark 52.1, Allcock 51.3, Agyapong 51.69, Diamond 51.34	5	AWC	London (OS)	14 Jul
3:26.59	POL		1	EC	Berlin	11 Aug
		Hołub-Kowalik 52.3, Baumgart-Witan 51.4, Wyciszkiewicz 51.20, Swiety-Ersetic 51.71				
3:26.71		Purdue, USA Abbott, B Thomas, S Black, J Mitchell	1h1	NCAA-E	Tampa	26 May
3:26.73	USA Red	Stepter 51.1, Blocker 51.1, Chambers 53.10, D Harper 51.38	1	PennR	Philadelphia	28 Apr
3:26.86	BOT	Moroko 53.3, Botlogetswe 50.9, Matlhaku 53.00, Montsho 49.59	3	CG	Gold Coast	14 Apr
3:27.07	USA Red	Jefferson, Beard, Wimbley, Washington	1	FlaR	Gainesville	31 Mar
3:27.13		Purdue Un, USA Abbott, B Thomas, S Black, J Mitchell	2	NCAA	Eugene	9 Jun
3:27.17	FRA	Diarra 52.6, Sananes 51.8, Raharolahy 51.18, Guei 51.59	2	EC	Berlin	11 Aug
3:27.21		England GBR	4	CG	Gold Coast	14 Apr
		Onuora 52.2, Agyapong 51.5, Shakes-Drayton 52.33, Diamond 51.07				
3:27.25	JAM	McPherson, James, Le-Roy 51.57, Day 52.12	2	NACAC	Toronto	12 Aug
3:27.40	GBR	Clark 52.5, Onuora 52.0, Allcock 51.48, Doyle 51.50	3	EC	Berlin	11 Aug
3:27.43	AUS	Rubie 51.60, Sargent-Jones 52.07, Wells 52.73, Mitchell 51.03	5	CG	Gold Coast	14 Apr
		(20 performances by teams from 8 nations)				
3:27.63	ITA	Chigbolu 52.6, Folorunso 51.3, Lukudo 51.34, Grenot 52.38	1h1	EC	Berlin	10 Aug
3:27.69	BEL	Bolingo Mbongo 53.0, Claes 51.1, Grillet 52.49, Laus 51.10	4	EC	Berlin	11 Aug

(10)

3:28.04	CAN	Powell, Stiverne, Jones, A Brown	3	NACAC	Toronto	12 Aug
3:28.72	IND	Das, Poovamma, Gayakwad, Vismaya	1	AsiG	Jakarta	30 Aug
3:29.46	SUI	Halbheer, Schürmann, Atcho, L Sprunger	3		Bern	16 Jun
3:29.48	CUB	Hechavarría, Almanza, Casanova, Gómez	1	CAG	Barranquilla	2 Aug
3:30.33	GER	Gonska 53.0, Müller 51.6, Pahlitzsch 52.58, Mergenthaler 53.14	6	EC	Berlin	11 Aug
3:30.57	NED	Ghafoor, Lisanne de Witte, Dopheide, Laura de Witte	4		Bern	16 Jun
3:30.61	BRN	Odeyemi, Jassim, Odiong, Naser	2	AsiG	Jakarta	30 Aug
3:31.54	ESP	Bueno, Parra, C Sánchez, Bokesa	3	MedG	Tarragona	30 Jun
3:31.87A	COL	Chávez, Escobar, M González, Padilla	1	SAmG	Cochabamba	8 Jun
3:31.95	ROU	Miklos 54.0, Balan 54.4, Belgyan 52.17, Razor 51.44	4h2	EC	Berlin	10 Aug

(20)

3:32.11	SVK	Zapletalová, Putalová, Ledecká, Bezeková	4h1	EC	Berlin	10 Aug
3:32.61	SWE	Hellqvist 53.7, Hjelmer 52.5, Magnusson 53.88, Duffy 52.55	5h2	EC	Berlin	10 Aug
3:33.03	LTU	Misiunaite, Balciunaite, Morauskaite, Serksniene	1		Vilnius	29 Jun
3:33.23	VIE	Nguyen Thi Oanh, Nguyen Thi Hang, Hoang Thi Ngoc, Quach Thi Lan	3	AsiG	Jakarta	30 Aug

WOMEN 2018

Mark		Name	Nat	Born	Pos	Meet	Venue		Date
3:33.35	POR	Mentai 54.2i, Monteiro 54.4, Azevedo 52.29, Évora 52.53			7h1	EC	Berlin		10 Aug
3:33.42A	CHI	Weil, Jiménez, Echeverría, Mackenna			2	SAmG	Cochabamba		8 Jun
3:33.64	DOM	Cofil, Medina, Durán, E Del Carmen			4	CAG	Barranquilla		2 Aug
3:33.65	PUR	Claxton, Marrero, Scott, Garcia			5	CAG	Barranquilla		2 Aug
3:33.72	CHN	Liang Nuo, Cheng Chong, Pan Gaoqin, Huang Guifen			4	AsiG	Jakarta		30 Aug
3:33.89	GRE	Karkalátou, Mourtá, Zigóri, Á Vasilíou			2	BalkC	Stara Zagora		21 Jul
		(30)							

3:33.91	MAR	30 Jun	3:34.64	SRB	21 Jul	3:35.74	HUN	21 Jul	3:38.14	FIN	1 Sep	3:38.9A	ETH	22 Apr
3:34.14	JPN	30 Aug	3:34.88A	KEN	21 Jun	3:35.96A	ARG	8 Jun	3:38.18	ZAM	5 Aug	3:39.11	SRI	15 Sep
3:34.18	RUS	22 Jul	3:35.03	UGA	14 Apr	3:35.96	IRL	10 Aug	3:38.41	LAT	16 Jun	3:39.58	CZE	8 Jul
3:34.55	BRA	15 Jul	3:35.56	MEX	3 Jun	3:36.73	KAZ	30 Aug	3:38.98	BLR	16 Jun			

Mixed Nationalities

Mark		Name		Pos	Meet	Venue	Date
3:25.99	Un. Kentucky	Ross, Camacho-Quinn PUR, McLaughlin, Clarke TTO		1	SEC	Knoxville	13 May
3:26.92	Un. Kentucky	Ross, Camacho-Quinn, McLaughlin, K Clarke		1	FlaR	Gainesville	31 Mar
3:27.06	USC, USA	Constantine CAN, Cockrell, D Hill, Ellis		1	NCAA	Eugene	9 Jun
3:27.30	Florida Un, USA	Manson, Barnett, Stephens, Sharpe CAN		2	SEC	Knoxville	13 May
3:27.32	USA Blue	Stepter, D Harper, Blake JAM, Blocker		2	TexR	Austin	31 Mar

Indoors

3:23.85	USA	Q Hayes 51.51, Moline 50.87, Wimbley 51.29, C Okolo 50.18		1	WI	Birmingham	4 Mar
3:26.09	POL			2	WI	Birmingham	4 Mar
		Swiety-Ersetic 52.18, Wyciszkiewicz 50.97, Gaworska 51.31, Hołub-Kowalik 51.63					
3:31.32	UKR	Melnyk 53.04, Klymiuk 54.50, Ryzhykova 51.53, Bryzhina 52.25	4		WI	Birmingham	4 Mar
3:34.90	CZE	Hofmanová 54.44, Pírková 53.64, Petrzilková 54.19, Vondrová 52.63		4h2	WI	Birmingham	4 Mar

Disqualified

3:24.16	JAM	Jenkins 51.94, Russell 50.51, Le-Roy 51.34, McPherson 50.37	dq	WI	Birmingham	4 Mar

Best at low altitude

3:32.61	COL	Chávez, Escobar, M González, Padilla		3	CAG	Barranquilla	2 Aug
3:35.45	KEN	5 Aug	3:36.99	ARG	26 Aug		

JUNIORS

3:28.74	USA	Mason 51.4, Anderson 51.5, Madubuike 54.31, Manson 51.59	1	WJ	Tampere	15 Jul
3:31.36	AUS	Connolly 52.2, Jardine 50.6, Russell 54.27, Thomas 51.47	2	WJ	Tampere	15 Jul
3:31.90	JAM	Josephs 53.6, S-A Williams 52.9, Salmon 50.80, Taylor 54.64	3	WJ	Tampere	15 Jul
3:31.93	CAN	Santiago 52.5, Rynda 53.9, Best 52.55, Samuel 53.03	4	WJ	Tampere	15 Jul
3:32.84	GER	Hofmann 54.9, Hartmann 52.4, Kaufmann 53.22, Schwab 52.32	5	WJ	Tampere	15 Jul
3:34.00	ITA	Pitzalis 54.9, Coiro 52.9, Gherardi 54.04, Vandi 52.17	6	WJ	Tampere	15 Jul
3:34.09	DOM	Durán 53.4, Reyes 54.6, Matos 53.14, Cofil 52.9	7	WJ	Tampere	15 Jul
3:34.55	BRA	M Santos 55.2, T Silva 51.8, C da Silva 53.50, Lima 54.09	8	WJ	Tampere	15 Jul
3:36.70	JPN	Shiom 54.2i, Aono 55.0, Sekimoto 54.56, Kawata 52.95	3h2	WJ	Tampere	14 Jul
3:38.23	POL	Widawska 55.6, Wosztyl 53.6, Bartnowska 55.80, Łozowska 53.28	4h1	WJ	Tampere	14 Jul
3:38.49	HUN	Molnár 55.1, Répássy 54.7, Köszegi 55.84, Mátó 52.90	5h1	WJ	Tampere	14 Jul

4 X 800 METRES RELAY INDOORS

8:05.89	USA	Williams 2:05.10, Rogers 2:00.45, Lipsey 2:01.98, Wilson 1:58.37	1	Millrose	New York (Arm)	3 Feb
8:11.45		New York All-Stars	2	Millrose	New York (Arm)	3 Feb
		Barowski 2:03.94, Sharp GBR 2:03.18, C Brown 2:00.45, Chambers 2:03.90				
8:17.75	JAM	Ferguson 2:05.32, Campbell 2:02.13, McDonald 2:07.04, Goule 2:03.27	3	Mill	New York (Arm)	3 Feb

4 X 100 METRES HURDLES RELAY

53.16	Georgia Tech Un USA	J Williams JAM, Collins, Stewart, Bauman	1	FlaR	Gainesville	31 Mar

3000 METRES TRACK WALK

Mark	Name		Surname	Nat	Born	Pos	Meet	Venue			Date
12:00.87	María		Pérez	ESP	29.4.96	1		Huelva			8 Jun
12:06.72	Brigita		Virbalyte-Dimsiene	LTU	1.2.85	1		Utena			2 Jun
12:08.3	Elvira		Khasanova	RUS-J	10.1.00	1		Saransk			28 Nov
12:23.93	Laura		García Caro	ESP	16.4.95	2		Huelva			8 Jun
12:30:58	Zivile		Vaiciukeviciute	LTU	3.4.96	2		Utena			2 Jun
12:34.29	Mária	Czaková		SVK	2.10.88	29 Jun	12:36.89	Émilie	Menuet	FRA 27.11.91	20 May

Indoors

11:55.30	Antonella		Palmisano	ITA	6.8.91	1	NC	Ancona			17 Feb
12:19.15			Virbalyte-Dimsiene			1	NC	Klaipeda			17 Feb
12:29.77	Zivile		Vaiciukeviciute	LTU	3.4.96	2	NC	Klaipeda			17 Feb
12:34.54	Mária	Czaková		SVK	2.10.88	28 Jan	12:39.02	Anezka	Drahotová	CZE 22.7.95	21 Feb
12:37.11	Eleonora	Dominici		ITA	22.2.96	17 Feb	12:39.39	Ana	Cabecinha	POR 29.4.84	10 Feb

5000 METRES TRACK

20:38.16	María		Pérez	ESP	29.4.96	1		Granollers		14 Jul
20:48.75	Anezka		Drahotová	CZE	22.7.95	1		Uherské Hradiste		26 Aug
20:59.79			Pérez			1		Castellón		16 Jun
21:00.15			Qieyang Shenjie	CHN	11.11.90	1		Torino		26 May
21:08.97	Kumiko		Okada	JPN	17.10.91	1	NSF	Fukui		8 Oct

Mark	Name	Nat	Born	Pos	Meet	Venue	Date
21:14.20	Raquel González	ESP	16.11.89	2		Granollers	14 Jul
21:18.22	González			1		Barcelona	1 Jul
21:20.98	Julia Takacs	ESP	29.6.89	2		Castellón	16 Jun
21:23.51	Valentina Trapletti	ITA	12.7.85	1		Modena	23 Jun
21:24.40	Nanako Fujii	JPN-J	7.5.99	2	NSF	Fukui	8 Oct
21:26.45	Lu Xiuzhi	CHN	26.10.93	2		Torino	26 May
21:26.93	Lidia Sánchez-Puebla	ESP	17.7.96	1		Palencia	27 Jun
21:28.84	Tamara Havrylyuk	UKR	14.12.95	1		Kropyvnytskyi	25 Jun
21:32.68mx	Jemima Montag	AUS	15.2.98				4 Mar
21:35.00	Ana Cabecinha	POR	29.4.84				26 May
21:39.68	Eleonora Giorgi	ITA	14.9.89				18 Apr
21:40.27	Wang Yingliu	CHN	1.3.92				17 Jul
21:42.20	Inna Kashyna	UKR	27.9.91				16 Jun
21:46.95	Inês Henriques	POR	1.5.80				23 Jun
21:48.09	Maria Michta Coffey	USA	23.6.86				28 Apr
21:53.33	Ma Zhenxia	CHN	1.8.98				26 May
21:53.90	Chahineze Nasri	TUN	3.6.96				23 Jun

Indoors

Mark	Name	Nat	Born	Pos	Meet	Venue	Date
20:39.9	Yelena Lashmanova	RUS	9.4.92	1		Saransk	30 Dec
20:55.3	Elvira Khasanova	RUS-J	10.1.00	2		Saransk	30 Dec
21:25.37	Bethan Davies	GBR	7.11.90	1	NC	Birmingham	18 Feb
21:30.9	Klavdiya Afanasyeva	RUS	15.1.96	3		Saransk	30 Dec

JUNIORS

Mark	Name	Nat	Born	Pos	Meet	Venue	Date
22:23.26	Xi Ricuo	CHN-Y	9.8.01	1	YOG	Buenos Aires	12 Oct
22:29.52	Sofia Ramos	MEX-Y	25.8.02	2	YOG	Buenos Aires	12 Oct
21:54.25i	Meryem Bekmez	TUR	31.7.00	1		Istanbul	13 Jan

See also 20km list for many intermediate 10k times.

10 KILOMETRES WALK

Mark	Name	Nat	Born	Pos	Meet	Venue	Date
42:02.99t	Sandra Arenas	COL	17.9.93	1	IbAm	Trujillo	26 Aug
42:20	Elvira Khasanova	RUS-J	10.1.00	1	NC-j	Cheboksary	10 Jun
42:56.97t	Kimberley García	PER	19.10.93	2	IbAm	Trujillo	26 Aug
43:01	Brigita Virbalyte Dimsiene	LTU	1.2.85	1		Gdansk	15 Aug
43:02	Virbalyte			1		Druskininkai	8 Sep
43:05.8t	Khasanova			1	NC-wj	Sochi	18 Feb
43:18.31	Inês Henriques	POR	1.5.80	1	NC	Leiria	7 Jul
43:37.95t	Raquel González	ESP	16.11.89	1	NC	Getafe	21 Jul
43:47	Nadiya Borovska	UKR	25.2.81	1		Lutsk	1 Jul
43:50.25t	Laura García Caro	ESP	16.4.95	2	NC	Getafe	21 Jul
43:51.8t	Ana Cabecinha	POR	29.4.84	2	NC	Leiria	7 Jul
43:55.22t	Kumiko Okada	JPN	17.10.91	1		Osaka	22 Sep
44:07+	Eleonora Giorgi	ITA	14.9.89		in 20k	Berlin	11 Aug
44:09	Inna Kashyna	UKR	27.9.91	7	EC	Berlin	11 Aug
44:12.75t	Gloria Morejón	ECU-J	30.5.00	3	IbAm	Trujillo	26 Aug
44:13.37t	Nanako Fujii	JPN-J	7.5.99	2		Osaka	22 Sep
44:13.88t	Alegna González	MEX-J	2.1.99	1	WJ	Tampere	14 Jul
44:15	Ma Li	CHN-J	15.1.00	1		Huangshan	3 Mar
44:17.69t	Meryem Bekmez	TUR-J	31.7.00	2	WJ	Tampere	14 Jul
44:29.96t	Kaori Kawazoe	JPN	30.5.95	3		Osaka	22 Sep
44:33.19t	Janeth Guamán	ECU	15.1.88	4	IbAm	Trujillo	26 Aug
44:36+	Wang Yingliu	CHN	1.3.92		in20k	Rio Maior	7 Apr
44:41+	Wang Na	CHN	29.5.95		in20k	Taicang	5 May
44:46	Li Wenxiu	CHN-J	11.12.00	2		Huangshan	3 Mar
44:46+	Jemima Montag	AUS	15.2.98		in 20K	Taicang	5 May
44:53.65t	Magaly Bonilla	ECU	8.2.92	5	IbAm	Trujillo	26 Aug
44:56.63t	Anastasiya Taushkanova	RUS	25.3.96	1		Chelyabinsk	29 Jul
44:59	Tamara Havrylyuk	UKR	14.12.95	2		Lutsk	1 Jul
45:02	Shi Yuxia	CHN-J	1.1.99	1		Shangrao	14 Apr
45:05	Lidia Sánchez-Puebla	ESP	17.7.96	1		Móstoles	4 Feb
45:06+	Yang Liujing	CHN	22.8.98		in20k	Taicang	5 May
45:08+	Viktoryia Roshchupkina	BLR	23.5.95		in 20k	Berlin	11 Aug
45:10.42t	Katie Hayward	AUS-J	23.7.00	5	WJ	Tampere	14 Jul
45:11+	Ma Zhenxia	CHN	1.8.98		in 20k	La Coruña	2 Jun
45:18	Liu Yajing	CHN-J	25.2.00	2		Shangrao	14 Apr
45:18	Yang Weiwei	CHN-J	3.8.99	1	NC-j	Weinan	8 Sep
45:23	Bai Xueying	CHN-J	26.4.00	3		Shangrao	14 Apr
45:23.05t	Rachelle de Orbeta	PUR-J	27.3.00	7	WJ	Tampere	14 Jul
45:27	Mariya Filyuk	UKR	14.10.95	3		Lutsk	1 Jul
45:28.72t	Ai Michiguchi	JPN	3.6.88	1		Kitami	7 Jul

Mark	Name	Nat	Born	Date		Mark	Name	Nat	Born	Date
45:32.2t	Yuliya Lipanova	RUS-J	24.6.99	18 Feb		45:47	Amanda Cano	ESP	19.8.94	27 Jan
45:33	Valentina Trapletti	ITA	12.7.85	7 Sep		45:49.43t	Ayse Tekdal	TUR-J	3.4.99	14 Jul
45:41	Andrea Martínez	MEX	4.5.88	25 Aug		45:51.58t	Noelia Vargas	CRC-J	17.4.00	14 Jul
45:42	Monika Vaiciukeviciute	LTU	3.4.96	28 Apr		45:55.58t	Edna Barros	POR	18.12.96	17 Mar
45:45.62t	Maria Michta Coffey	USA	23.6.86	3 Jun		45:56.45t	Bekki Smith	AUS	25.11.86	14 Jan
45:46.37t	Olga Shargina	RUS	24.7.96	29 Jul		45:57+	Yehualeye Beletew	ETH	31.7.98	5 May
45:46.93t	Jessica Ching Siu Nga	HKG	11.2.87	7 Jul		45:57.81t	Taylor Ewert	USA-Y	21.11.01	14 Jul

WOMEN 2018

Mark	Name		Nat	Born	Pos	Meet	Venue	Date
46:01+	Claire	Tallent	AUS	6.7.81				8 Apr
46:02.17t	Margarita	Nikiforova	RUS	19.8.98				29 Jul
46:03	Mirna	Ortiz	GUA	28.2.87				3 Feb
46:03+	Eleonora	Dominici	ITA	22.2.96				5 May
46:03+	Baby	Soumya	IND	20.4.90				5 May
46:05		Lu Xiuzhi	CHN	26.10.93				4 Feb
46:07.32t	Chiaki	Asada	JPN	21.1.91				15 Dec
46:17.3t	Evelin	Inga	PER	16.4.98				21 Jul
46:18.1t	Leidy	Guerra	PER	27.9.98				21 Jul
46:22	Rena	Goto	JPN	6.9.95				15 Apr
46:24+	Nami	Kumagai	JPN	9.7.96				1 Jan
46:25.03t	Mar	Juárez	ESP	27.9.93				21 Jul
46:26.18t	Barbara	Kovács	HUN	26.7.93				26 Aug

Track bests

Mark	Name		Nat	Born	Pos	Meet	Venue	Date
44:33.03	María	Pérez	ESP	29.4.96	3	NC	Getafe	21 Jul
45:13.73	Lidia	Sánchez-Puebla	ESP	17.7.96	1	Med-23	Jesolo	9 Jun
45:15.69	Julia	Takacs	ESP	29.6.89	6	IbAm	Trujillo	26 Aug
45:20.59		Ma Li	CHN-J	15.1.00	1	Asi-J	Gifu	7 Jun
45:21.39t		Shi Yuxia	CHN-J	1.1.99	6	WJ	Tampere	14 Jul
45:27.50	Mária	Czaková	SVK	2.10.88	1		Monthey	21 Apr

JUNIORS

See main list for top 13 juniors. 10 performances by 7 women to 45:00. Additional performances:

Morejón   44:19.40t   3   WJ   Tampere   14 Jul   44:58   1   Súcua   27 Jan
Su Wenxiu   44:36   4   Huangshan   4 Mar

Mark	Name		Nat	Born	Pos	Meet	Venue	Date
45:32.2t	Yuliya	Lipanova	RUS	24.6.99	3	NC-wj	Sochi	18 Feb
45:49.43t	Ayse	Tekdal	TUR	3.4.99	8	WJ	Tampere	14 Jul
45:51.58t	Noelia	Vargas	CRC	17.4.00	9	WJ	Tampere	14 Jul
45:57.81t	Taylor	Ewert	USA-Y	21.11.01	10	WJ	Tampere	14 Jul

20 KILOMETRES WALK

10 kilometre times in second column

Mark	10k	Name		Nat	Born	Pos	Meet	Venue	Date
1:23:39	41:48	Yelena	Lashmanova	RUS	9.4.92	1	NC	Cheboksary	9 Jun
1:26:23	44:09		Lashmanova			1	NC w	Sochi	19 Feb
1:26:28	43:10		Qieyang Shenjie	CHN	11.11.90	1		La Coruña	2 Jun
1:26:36	44:07	María	Pérez	ESP	29.4.96	1	EC	Berlin	11 Aug
1:26:38	44:40	María Guadalupe	González	MEX	9.1.89	1	WTC	Taicang	5 May
1:27:03	44:07	Anežka	Drahotová	CZE	22.7.95	2	EC	Berlin	11 Aug
1:27:06	44:40		Qieyang Shenjie			2	WTC	Taicang	5 May
1:27:11	44:09	Mariya	Ponomaryova	RUS	18.6.95	2	NC w	Sochi	19 Feb
1:27:22	44:41		Yang Jiayu	CHN	18.2.96	3	WTC	Taicang	5 May
1:27:30	44:07	Antonella	Palmisano	ITA	6.8.91	3	EC	Berlin	11 Aug
1:27:36			Qieyang Shenjie			1		Huangshan	3 Mar
1:27:36			Yang Jiayu			2		Huangshan	3 Mar
1:27:42	43:31	Sofiya	Brodatskaya	RUS	4.10.95	2	NC	Cheboksary	9 Jun
1:27:46			González			1		Monterrey	24 Feb
1:27:57	44:09		Brodatskaya			3	NC w	Sochi	19 Feb
1:27:58	44:11	Julia	Takacs (10)	ESP	29.6.89	2		La Coruña	2 Jun
1:27:59	44:11	Brigita	Virbalyte Dimsiene	LTU	1.2.85	4	EC	Berlin	11 Aug
1:28:04	44:26		Qieyang Shenjie			1		Rio Maior	7 Apr
1:28:07	43:59	Zivile	Vaiciukeviciute	LTU	3.4.96	5	EC	Berlin	11 Aug
1:28:11	44:41	Érica	de Sena	BRA	3.5.85	4	WTC	Taicang	5 May
1:28:15	44:07	Laura	García Caro	ESP	16.4.95	6	EC	Berlin	11 Aug
1:28:31	44:41	Eleonora	Giorgi	ITA	14.9.89	5	WTC	Taicang	5 May
1:28:37			Wang Yingliu	CHN	1.3.92	3		Huangshan	3 Mar
1:28:40	44:41		Drahotová			6	WTC	Taicang	5 May
1:28:41	44:35		Palmisano			2		Rio Maior	7 Apr
1:28:48	44:30	Sandra	Arenas	COL	17.9.93	1		Dudince	24 Mar
1:28:49	44:26		Giorgi			1		Poděbrady	8 Apr
1:28:50	44:47		Pérez			7	WTC	Taicang	5 May
1:28:56	44:41	Kimberley	García	PER	19.10.93	8	WTC	Taicang	5 May
1:28:58	44:46	Inna	Kashyna	UKR	27.9.91	9	WTC	Taicang	5 May
	(30/19)								
1:29:06			Lu Xiuzhi (20)	CHN	26.10.93	1	NC	Weinan	7 Sep
1:29:08	44:09	Yekaterina	Ryzhova	RUS	29.3.94	4	NC w	Sochi	19 Feb
1:29:15			Wang Na	CHN	29.5.95	4		Huangshan	3 Mar
1:29:15	44:35	Inês	Henriques	POR	1.5.80	3		Rio Maior	7 Apr
1:29:22	44:11	Nadiya	Borovska	UKR	25.2.81	1	NC w	Lutsk	11 Mar
1:29:28			Ma Zhenxia	CHN	1.8.98	2	NC	Weinan	7 Sep
1:29:31			Yang Liujing	CHN	22.8.98	3	NC	Weinan	7 Sep
1:29:32			Ma Li	CHN-J	15.1.00	4	NC	Weinan	7 Sep
1:29:41	44:29	Ana	Cabecinha	POR	29.4.84	3		La Coruña	2 Jun
1:29:46			Su Wenxiu	CHN	28.6.98	5	NC	Weinan	7 Sep
1:29:50	44:11	Reykhan	Kagramanova	RUS	1.6.97	3		Cheboksary	9 Jun
	(30)								
1:29:57	44:37	Valentina	Trapletti	ITA	12.7.85	9	EC	Berlin	11 Aug
1:30:15	44:53	Raquel	González	ESP	16.11.89	4		La Coruña	2 Jun
1:30:15			Li Maocuo	CHN	20.10.92	2		Suzhou	24 Sep

Mark		Name		Nat	Born	Pos	Meet	Venue	Date	
1:30:29			Gesang Zhuoma	CHN	16.7.98	6	NC	Weinan	7	Sep
1:30:37		Paola	Pérez	ECU	21.12.89	2	SAmC	Sucúa	10	Mar
1:30:40A		Grace	Njue Wanjiru	KEN	10.1.79	1		Nairobi	6	Jun
1:30:49	45:27	Olga	Yeliseyeva	RUS	6.9.98	6	NC w	Sochi	19	Feb
1:31:00	44:24	Meryem	Bekmez	TUR-J	31.7.00	11	EC	Berlin	11	Aug
1:31:03	45:21	Mária	Czaková	SVK	2.10.88	20	WTC	Taicang	5	May
1:31:07			Zhao Wenli	CHN	11.12.96	8		Huangshan	3	Mar
		(40)								
1:31:15	44:34	Marina	Novikova	RUS	1.3.89	4	NC	Cheboksary	9	Jun
1:31:17			Qiji Zhuoma	CHN	27.5.98	9		Huangshan	3	Mar
1:31:21	45:11	Lidia	Sánchez-Puebla	ESP	17.7.96	6		La Coruña	2	Jun
1:31:22	45:20	Viktoryia	Roshchupkina	BLR	23.5.95	21	WTC	Taicang	5	May
1:31:23		Bekki	Smith	AUS	25.11.86	1	OCE Ch	Adelaide	11	Feb
1:31:26		Jemima	Montag	AUS	15.2.98	2	OCE Ch	Adelaide	11	Feb
1:31:29		Claire	Tallent	AUS	6.7.81	3	OCE Ch	Adelaide	11	Feb
1:31:29		Baby	Soumya	IND	20.4.90	1	NC	New Delhi	17	Feb
1:31:29	44:57	Kumiko	Okada	JPN	17.10.91	22	WTC	Taicang	5	May
1:31:32	45:06	Alana	Barber	NZL	8.7.87	23	WTC	Taicang	5	May
		(50)								
1:31:47		Yehualeye	Beletew	ETH	31.7.98	1	AfrC	Asaba	5	Aug
1:31:53	45:50	Bethan	Davies	GBR	7.11.90	3		Lugano	11	Mar
1:31:57	45:40	Yana	Smerdova	RUS	7.2.98	7	NC w	Sochi	19	Feb
1:31:57	45:38	Margarita	Nikiforova	RUS	19.8.98	5	NC	Cheboksary	9	Jun
1:32:08			Ni Yuanyuan	CHN	6.4.95	9	NC	Weinan	7	Sep
1:32:09		Maria	Michta Coffey	USA	23.6.86	1		Philadelphia	8	Apr
1:32:12.5A		Leidy	Guerra	PER	27.9.98	1	SAm-23	Cuenca	29	Sep
1:32:14			Duan Dandan	CHN	23.5.95	10	NC	Weinan	7	Sep
1:32:16	44:50	Antigóni	Drisbióti	GRE	21.3.84	13	EC	Berlin	11	Aug
1:32:17		Khushbir	Kaur	IND	9.7.93	2	NC	New Delhi	17	Feb
		(60)								
1:32:20	45:21	Chahineze	Nasri	TUN	3.6.96	24	WTC	Taicang	5	May
1:32:28		Anastasiya	Tauslikanova	RUS	26.0.00	6	NC	Cheboksary	9	Jun
1:32:29	45:34	Valeria	Ortuño	MEX	27.5.98	6		Podébrady	7	Apr
1:32:36	45:39	Emilia	Lehmeyer	GER	11.4.97	14	EC	Berlin	11	Aug
1:32:38	45:45	Valentyna	Myronchuk	UKR	10.8.94	3	NC w	Lutsk	11	Mar
1:32:44	46:27	Khrystyna	Yudkina	UKR	4.12.84	4	NC w	Lutsk	11	Mar
1:32:48			Yang Fuyao	CHN	6.12.96	11		Huangshan	3	Mar
1:32:49	45:14	Émilie	Menuet	FRA	27.11.91	15	EC	Berlin	11	Aug
1:32:50	46:31	Katarzyna	Zdziebło	POL	28.11.96	1		Zaniemysl	14	Apr
1:32:51			Jiang Shanshan	CHN	28.2.97	12		Huangshan	3	Mar
		(70)								
1:32:53			Tang Caihong	CHN	29.4.96	13		Huangshan	3	Mar
1:32:57	46:09	Saskia	Feige	GER	13.8.97	16	EC	Berlin	11	Aug
1:32:58			Wang Qiong	CHN	1.1.98	2		Shangrao	14	Apr
1:33:06	46:03	Janeth	Guamán	ECU	15.1.88	30	WTC	Taicang	5	May
1:33:11	46:03	Sandra	Galvis	COL	28.6.86	31	WTC	Taicang	5	May
1:33:17			Xiao Xianghua	CHN	19.2.97	14		Huangshan	3	Mar
1:33:27		Nanako	Fujii	JPN-J	7.5.99	1		Takahata	28	Oct
1:33:30		Teresa	Zurek	GER	29.7.98	2 U23		Naumburg	14	Apr
1:33:33	46:12	Yuliya	Turova	RUS	9.6.97	9	NC w	Sochi	19	Feb
1:33:33		Eleonora	Dominici	ITA	22.2.96	2	NC	Roma	4	Mar
		(80)								
1:33:34	46:25	Mariya	Filyuk	UKR	14.10.95	18	EC	Berlin	11	Aug
1:33:39	46:24	Ana Veronica	Rodean	ROU	23.6.84	19	EC	Berlin	11	Aug
1:33:40		Regan	Lamble	AUS	14.10.91	5	OCE Ch	Adelaide	11	Feb
1:33:41			Shi Yuxia	CHN-J	1.1.99	11	NC	Weinan	7	Sep
1:33:42	46:03	Ai	Michiguchi	JPN	3.6.88	34	WTC	Taicang	5	May
1:33:43	46:12	Alegna	González	MEX-J	2.1.99	7		Podébrady	7	Apr
1:33:44	45:56	Kaori	Kawazoe	JPN	30.5.95	2	NC	Kobe	18	Feb
1:33:44			Ma Yiming	CHN	10.9.97	5		Taicang	7	May
1:33:45	46:29	Annabel	Orjuela	COL	24.7.88	36	WTC	Taicang	5	May
1:33:46	46:11	Yeseida	Carrillo	COL	22.10.93	8		Podébrady	7	Apr
		(90)								
1:33:55		Ángela	Castro	BOL	21.2.93	4	SAmC	Sucúa	10	Mar
1:33:56A		Emily	Ngii	KEN	13.8.86	2		Nairobi	6	Jun
1:33:58		Miranda	Melville	USA	20.3.89	2		Philadelphia	8	Apr
1:33:59	46:06	Andreea	Arsine	ROU	14.9.88	38	WTC	Taicang	5	May
1:34:00	45:00	Darya	Melenteva	RUS	7.4.98	10	NC w	Sochi	19	Feb
1:34:05			Wang Lixue	CHN	15.12.96	6		Taicang	7	May
1:34:09		Karamjit	Kaur	IND	5.2.91	3	NC	New Delhi	17	Feb

WOMEN 2018

Mark	Name	Nat	Born	Pos	Meet	Venue	Date
1:34:13	Li Leilei	CHN	18.8.89	16		Huangshan	3 Mar
1:34:13 46:03	Mirna Ortiz	GUA	28.2.87	39	WTC	Taicang	5 May
1:34:20	Kseniya Buldygina	RUS	20.9.98	11	NC w	Sochi	19 Feb
	(100)						
1:34:20	Tamara Havrylyuk	UKR	14.12.95	2	NC	Sumy	16 Jun
1:34:22	Anastasiya Yatsevich	BLR	18.1.85				27 Jun
1:34:23	Lana Ryazanova	RUS	11.9.99				10 Feb
1:34:23	Li Qiuye	CHN	2.12.93				7 May
1:34:26	Robyn Stevens	USA	24.4.83				8 Apr
1:34:28	Vasylyna Vitovshchyk	UKR	30.4.90				21 Oct
1:34:31	Xue Ke	CHN	14.3.98				3 Mar
1:34:33	Nicole Colombi	ITA	29.12.95				5 May
1:34:33	Cun Hailu	CHN	15.8.97				7 Sep
1:34:40	Mayra Carolina Herrera	GUA	20.12.88				7 Apr
1:34:44	Jeon Yang-eun	KOR	24.5.88				5 May
1:34:44	Liu Yu	CHN	18.3.98				7 Sep
1:34:45	Jessica Ching Siu Nga	HKG	11.2.87				16 Dec
1:34:52	Liao Wenqing	CHN-J	9.1.99				7 Sep
1:34:57	Shanti Kumari	IND	15.8.94				17 Feb
1:35:03	Violaine Averous	FRA	15.3.85				18 Mar
1:35:03	Edna Barros	POR	18.12.96				5 May
1:35:18	Rachel Tallent	AUS	20.2.93				11 Feb
1:35:20	Liang Rui	CHN	18.6.94				24 Sep
1:35:27	Yin Hang	CHN	7.2.97				7 Sep
1:35:28	Lee Jeong-eun	KOR	13.9.94				16 Jun
1:35:32	Zhang Lifang	CHN	6.12.97				14 Apr
1:35:35	Ravina	IND	21.5.97				18 Mar
1:35:35	Monika Vaiciukeviciute	LTU	3.4.96				5 May
1:35:36	Paulina Buziak	POL	16.12.86				23 Jun
1:35:37	Mar Juárez	ESP	27.9.93				18 Mar
1:35:37	Yang Shuqing	CHN	30.8.96				7 May
1:35:38	Anastasiya Kalashnikova	RUS	29.6.97				9 Sep
1:35:43	Gemma Bridge	GBR	17.5.93				5 May
1:35:43 1A	Karin Jaramillo	ECU	21.1.87				25 Sep
1:35:44	Marine Quennehen	FRA	1.8.91				5 May
1:35:50	Clemence Beretta	FRA	22.12.97				18 Mar
1:35:52	Yuki Yoshizumi	JPN	7.1.96				18 Mar
1:35:52	Diana Aydosova	KAZ	5.5.95				5 May
1:35:53	Chen Minjing	CHN	23.10.96				7 Sep
1:35:59	Bai Tiantian	CHN	14.8.98				14 Apr
1:36:01	Amanda Cano	ESP	19.8.94				18 Mar
1:36:05	Nami Kumagai	JPN	9.7.96				18 Feb
1:36:14	Heather Lewis	GBR	25.10.93				11 Mar
1:36:20	Noelia Vargas	CRC-J	17.4.00				24 Oct
1:36:23	Chen Yumin	CHN	8.2.97				14 Apr
1:36:25	Ilse Guerrero	MEX	24.3.93				7 Apr
1:36:25	María Pérez	MEX	20.8.88				2 Jun
1:36:29	Kristina Saltanovic	LTU	20.2.75				4 Feb
1:36:29	María Guadalupe Sánchez	MEX	4.8.95				2 Jun
1:36:33	Viviane Lyra	BRA	29.7.93				7 Apr
1:36:36	Yukiho Mizoguchi	JPN	6.12.97				18 Feb
1:36:36	Kristina Mavletova	RUS	28.9.98				19 Dec
1:36:39	Zhao Fenyan	CHN	21.7.96				14 Apr
1:36:40	Chiaki Asada	JPN	21.1.91				18 Mar
1:36:41	Ma Faying	CHN	30.8.93				7 Sep
1:36:42	Wang Jiahui	CHN	1.1.98				14 Apr
1:36:45	Serena Sonoda	JPN	10.9.96				18 Feb
1:36:45	Amandine Marcou	FRA	26.4.92				5 May
1:37:04A	Ingrid Hernández	COL	29.11.88				18 Feb
1:37:04.0At	Nadia González	MEX	21.3.97				24 Apr
1:37:08	Olga Niedziałek	POL	30.6.97				23 Jun
1:37:10	Lei Fei	CHN	8.8.07				14 Apr
1:37:12	Elisa Neuvonen	FIN	19.3.91				11 Aug
1:37:13	Jessica Pickles	AUS	6.2.94				11 Feb
1:37:13	Maritza Rafaela Poncio	GUA	3.12.94				24 Mar
1:37:13	Joanna Bemowska	POL	27.6.94				23 Jun
1:37:15	Ayman Ratova	KAZ	23.4.91				24 Jul
1:37:15	Ivana Renic	CRO	8.12.92				8 Dec
1:37:16	Xiong Cuihong	CHN	1.5.98				3 Mar
1:37:16	Corinne Baudoin	FRA	22.2.80				18 Mar
1:37:19	Barbara Kovács	HUN	26.7.93				22 Apr
1:37:23	Rebeca Enríquez	MEX	10.12.97				24 Feb
1:37:23	Masumi Fuchise	JPN	2.9.86				28 Oct
1:37:24	Kelly Ruddick	AUS	19.4.73				11 Feb
1:37:24	Jiang Pengqin	CHN	5.9.95				14 Apr
1:37:24	Kathleen Burnett	USA	7.10.88				24 Apr
1:37:25	Maria Larios	ESP	29.10.92				18 Mar
1:37:27	Hanna Shevchuk	UKR	18.7.96				21 Oct
1:37:28	Priyanka Goswami	IND	10.3.96				17 Feb
1:37:30	Alejandra Ortega	MEX	8.7.94				24 Feb
1:37:31	Dalia Oliveras	PUR	13.7.98				8 Apr
1:37:31	Natalya Nikitina	RUS	7.10.98				9 Jun
1:37:35	Elianay Pereira	BRA	11.5.84				2 Jun
1:37:37	Maika Yagi	JPN-J	21.1.99				28 Oct
1:37:41	Olena Mizernyuk	UKR	23.11.95				21 Oct
1:37:47	Agnese Pastare	LAT	22.10.88				24 Mar
1:37:50	Mara Ribeiro	POR	11.5.95				7 Apr
1:37:54	Kate Veale	IRL	5.1.94				8 Dec
1:37:57	(165) Zhu Kunyu	CHN	14.5.96				14 Apr

Track bests

Mark	Name	Nat	Born	Date
1:35:21.6	Maria Michta Coffey	USA	23.6.86	22 Jun
1:37:56.0t	Kathleen Burnett	USA	10.7.88	22 Jun

JUNIORS

See main list for top 5 juniors. 9 performances by 8 women to 1:36:00. Additional performance:

Bekmez 1:36:08 4 Alytus 8 Jun

Mark	Name	Nat	Born	Pos	Meet	Venue	Date
1:34:52	Liao Wenqing	CHN-J	9.1.99	14	NC	Weinan	7 Sep
1:36:20	Noelia Vargas	CRC-J	17.4.00	1		Hauppage	24 Oct
1:37:37	Maika Yagi	JPN-J	21.1.99	5		Takahata	28 Oct
1:38:28	Kristina Ivanova	RUS	19.1.99	16	NC w	Sochi	19 Feb
1:39:07	Zhong Yuan (10)	CHN	25.5.99	21		Shangrao	14 Apr
1:39:15	Marina Peña	ESP	19.3.99	12		La Coruña	2 Jun

30-35 KILOMETRES WALK

30k	35k	Name	Nat	Born	Pos	Meet	Venue	Date
2:22:47	2:45:51	Inês Henriques	POR	1.5.80	1		Porto de Mos	7 Jan
2:24:33	2:48:13	Olga Shargina	RUS	24.7.96	1	NC-w	Sochi	19 Mar
	2:49:23	Liang Rui	CHN	18.6.94	1		Huangshan	4 Mar
	2:50:14	Yin Hang	CHN	7.2.97	2		Huangshan	4 Mar
	2:50:31	Zhou Kang	CHN	24.12.89	3		Huangshan	4 Mar
	2:51:58	Anastasiya Yatsevich	BLR	18.1.85	1	NCp	Gomel	4 Apr
	2:52:05	Ma Faying	CHN	30.8.93	4		Huangshan	4 Mar
	2:52:17	Li Maocuo	CHN	20.10.92	5		Huangshan	4 Mar
2:28:07	2:53:35	Nadezhda Mokeyeva	RUS	10.1.95	2	NC-w	Sochi	19 Mar
	2:53:43	Ainhoa Pinedo	ESP	17.2.83	1		Algeciras	3 Feb
	2:54:23	Xiao Han	CHN	12.11.98	6		Huangshan	4 Mar
	2:56:03	Bai Tiantian	CHN	14.8.98	7		Huangshan	4 Mar
	2:56:07	Zhao Huimin	CHN	12.10.93	8		Huangshan	4 Mar
	2:56:35	Nadezhda Dorozhuk	BLR	23.1.90	2	NCp	Gomel	4 Apr

Mark			Name		Nat	Born	Pos	Meet	Venue	Date
	2:57:50			Li Ping	CHN	7.1.94	9		Huangshan	4 Mar
2:32:46	2:58:18		Aleksandra	Bushkova	RUS	13.1.97	3	NC-w	Sochi	19 Mar
	2:58:20			Chen Yumin	CHN	8.2.97	10		Huangshan	4 Mar
	2:58:55			Ji Yefang	CHN	4.3.96	11		Huangshan	4 Mar

50 KILOMETRES WALK

Mark			Name		Nat	Born	Pos	Meet	Venue	Date
4:04:36	2:28:17	2:52:53		Liang Rui	CHN	18.6.94	1	WTC	Taicang	5 May
4:09:09	2:28:17	2:52:54		Yin Hang	CHN	7.2.97	2	WTC	Taicang	5 May
4:09:21	2:25:18	2:49:52e	Inês	Henriques	POR	1.5.80	1	EC	Berlin	7
4:09:33	2:28:18	2:53:34	Claire	Tallent	AUS	6.7.81	3	WTC	Taicang	5 May
4:12:26				Liang Rui			1	NC	Weinan	8 Sep
4:12:44	2:30:13	2:55:02e	Alina	Tsviliy	UKR	18.9.94	2	EC	Berlin	7 Aug
4:12:56	2:30:05	2:54:40	Paola	Pérez	ECU	21.12.89	4	WTC	Taicang	5 May
4:13:04	2:31:53	2:56:59	Julia	Takacs	ESP	29.6.89	1	NC	Burjassot	25 Feb
4:13:04				Li Maocuo	CHN	20.10.92	1	NGP	Chifeng	3 Jul
4:13:28	2:29:11	2:54:21		Ma Faying	CHN	30.8.93	5	WTC	Taicang	5 May
4:14:25	2:34:53	3:00:48	Mária	Czaková (10)	SVK	2.10.88	1		Dudince	24 Mar
4:14:28	2:32:57	2:58:18	Johana	Ordóñez	ECU	12.12.87	6	WTC	Taicang	5 May
4:14:46	2:27:44		Klavdiya	Afanasyeva	RUS	15.1.96	1	NC	Cheboksary	9 Jun
4:14:47	2:28:17	2:52:54		Li Maocuo			7	WTC	Taicang	5 May
4:15:22	2:34:18	2:58:23e		Takacs			3	EC	Berlin	7 Aug
4:15:51				Li Maocuo			2	NC	Weinan	8 Sep
4:16:37	2:33:07	2:58:46		Takacs			8	WTC	Taicang	5 May
4:18:00	2:34:52	2:59:58	Anastasiya	Yatsevich	BLR	18.1.85	9	WTC	Taicang	5 May
4:18:31	2:35:06	3:00:19	Nadezhda	Dorozhuk	BLR	23.1.90	10	WTC	Taicang	5 May
4:18:50			Valentyna	Myronchuk	UKR	10.8.94	1		Ivano-Frankivsk	20 Oct
4:18:56			Ainhoa	Pinedo	ESP	17.2.83	2	NC	Burjassot	25 Feb
4:19:04	2:32:57	2:58:24	Magaly	Bonilla	ECU	8.2.92	11	WTC	Taicang	5 May
4:19:43				Bonilla			1	SAmC	Sucúa	10 Mar
4:20:36			Erika	Morales	MEX	10.12.86	1		Hauppage	24 Oct
4:20:46	2:34:18		Khrystyna	Yudkina	UKR	4.12.84	4	EC	Berlin	7 Aug
4:22:15				Yudkina			12	WTC	Taicang	5 May
4:22:36	2:35:46		Aleksandra	Bushkova (20)	RUS	13.1.97	2	NC	Cheboksary	9 Jun
4:23:15	2:31:17	2:58:12e	Vasylyna	Vitovshchyk	UKR	30.4.90	5	EC	Berlin	7 Aug
4:24:08				Vitovshchyk			13	WTC	Taicang	5 May
4:24:59	2:34:57			Czaková			6	EC	Berlin	7 Aug
		(30/21)								
4:27:13	2:30:52		Olga	Shargina	RUS	24.7.96	3	NC	Cheboksary	9 Jun
4:28:30			Mayra Carolina	Herrera	GUA	20.12.88	14	WTC	Taicang	5 May
4:28:58			Mar	Juárez	ESP	27.9.93	8	EC	Berlin	7 Aug
4:29:45			Serena	Sonoda	JPN	10.9.96	1		Takahata	28 Oct
4:30:43			Dusica	Topic	SRB	11.1.82	9	EC	Berlin	7 Aug
4:31:41			Mariavittoria	Becchetti	ITA	12.12.94	10	EC	Berlin	7 Aug
4:32:43			Tiia	Kuikka	FIN	30.11.94	18	WTC	Taicang	5 May
4:32:47			Agnieszka	Ellward	POL	26.3.89	2	1 NC	Dudince	24 Mar
4:32:47				Bai Tiantian	CHN	14.8.98	2	NGP	Chifeng	3 Jul
		(30)								
4:34:16				Li Qiuye	CHN	2.12.93	3	NGP	Chifeng	3 Jul
4:35:39			Ivana	Renic	CRO	21.8.96	12	EC	Berlin	7 Aug
4:37:43			Maria	Larios	ESP	29.10.92	19	WTC	Taicang	5 May
4:37:43			Lyudmyla	Shelest	UKR	4.10.74	20	WTC	Taicang	5 May
4:38:23			Kseniya	Radko	UKR	18.8.94	21	WTC	Taicang	5 May
4:38:48			Nair	da Rosa	BRA	22.3.80	3	SAmC	Sucúa	10 Mar
4:39:01			Nami	Kumagai	JPN	9.7.96	2		Wajima	15 Apr
4:40:00			Aleksandra	Ovsyannikova	RUS	16.6.93	4	NC	Cheboksary	9 Jun
4:41:39			Viviane	Lyra	BRA	29.7.93	1	NC	Bragança Paulista	15 Sep
4:41:44			Nikolítsa	Andreopoúlou	GRE	26.3.83	3		Dudince	24 Mar
		(40)								
4:42:17				Chi Meijiao	CHN	28.6.96	3	NC	Weinan	8 Sep
4:42:37			Yoci	Caballero	PER	2.2.93	4	SAmC	Sucúa	10 Mar
4:42:58			Bianka	Dittrich	GER	6.7.93	1		Aschersleben	14 Oct
4:43:03			Yuki	Yoshizumi	JPN	7.1.96	3		Takahata	28 Oct
4:43:26				Xia Kaili	CHN	16.3.96	4	NC	Weinan	8 Sep
4:43:46			Inès	Pastorino	FRA	20.10.92	2		Aschersleben	14 Oct
4:43:48			Joanna	Bemowska	POL	27.6.94	4		Dudince	24 Mar
4:43:48				Xiao Han	CHN	12.11.98	4	NGP	Chifeng	3 Jul
4:45:51				Jiang Pengqin	CHN	5.9.95	5	NGP	Chifeng	3 Jul
4:46:12			Mariela	Sánchez	MEX	25.8.91	1		Santee	20 Jan
		(50)								

WOMEN 2018

Mark	Name		Nat		Born	Pos	Meet	Venue		Date
4:46:33	Maeva	Casale	FRA	5.3.97	14 Oct		Erin	Talcott	USA	21.5.78	25 Feb
4:47:50	Kathleen	Burnett	USA	10.7.88	20 Jan		Miriam	Gutiérrez	ECU	8.7.81	10 Mar
4:48:00	Natalie	le Roux	RSA	10.6.82	5 May		Aggeliki	Makrí	GRE	25.9.78	14 Jan
4:48:08	Lucie	Champalou	FRA	29.4.90	5 May			Zhang Yan	CHN	3.1.97	8 Sep
4:48:46	Chiaki	Yamato	JPN	20.11.90	15 Apr		Mylène	Ortiz	FRA	15.2.79	14 Oct
4:49:33	Nadezhda	Mokeyeva	RUS	10.1.96	9 Jun			Zhu Ruonan	CHN	14.3.98	8 Sep
4:52:07	Beatrice	Foresti	ITA	29.10.98	21 Oct		Lizbeth	Silva	MEX	00.9.09	25 Feb
4:50:08		Yang Shuqing	CHN	30.8.96	3 Jul		Cécile	Naze	FRA	27.11.95	14 Oct
4:53:38	María Dolores	Marcos	ESP	18.8.79	25 Feb		Jeanne	Billa	FRA	21.2.96	14 Oct
4:53:50	Akane	Tamaki	JPN-Y	2.1.01	15 Apr		Liliya	Stepanova	RUS	13.11.96	9 Jun
4:54:31	Kelly	Ruddick	AUS	19.4.73	2 Dec		Anett	Torma	HUN	2.9.84	20 Jan

TOKYO 2020 OLYMPIC QUALIFICATION

THE IAAF COUNCIL has approved the qualification system and entry standards for the 2020 Olympic Games in Tokyo. Athletes will have more opportunities to achieve the Olympic entry standards under the new system, which extends the qualification window by two months for most events. This will start on 1 May 2019 (instead of 1 July 2019), to include more international competitions such as the IAAF Diamond League, and end on 29 June 2020. The qualification period for the marathon and 50k walk will extend from 1 Jan 2019 to 31 May 2020 to give the qualified athletes more time to prepare specifically for the Games. The period for 10,000m, 20k walk and combined events: 1 Jan 2019 to 29 June 2020. The deadline for entries to be submitted to Tokyo is 6 July 2020.

After extensive consultation with key stakeholders, the Council has decided to introduce a dual qualification system, combining both the entry standards and the new World Ranking System, to determine which athletes are eligible for Olympic selection in 2020. Under this new qualification process, an athlete can qualify for the 2020 Olympics in one of two ways:
• Achieve the entry standard within the respective qualification period
• Qualify by virtue of his/her IAAF World Ranking position in the selected event at the end of the respective qualification period.

The process is designed to achieve about 50% of the target numbers for each event through entry standards and the remaining 50% through the IAAF world ranking system.

The IAAF consulted with the Competition, Athletes' and Coaches' Commissions prior to this decision and will continue working with the Athletes' Commission, the Athletes Representatives (ARs) and the Member Federations (MFs) to ensure the qualification system is well understood. Workshops will be scheduled with athletes, ARs and MFs during this year.

The Entry Standards for Tokyo

Standards for men & women; entry numbers per event in brackets.

100 (56): 10.05/11.15; 200 (56): 20.24/22.80; 400 (48): 44.90/51.35; 800 (48): 1:45.20/1:59.50; 1500 (45): 3:35.00/4:04.20; 5000 (42): 13:13.50/15:10.00; 10,000 (27): 27:28.00/31:25.00; Mar (80): 2:11:30/2:29:30; 3000SC (45): 8:22.00/9:30.00; 110/100H (40): 13.32/12.84; 400H (40): 48.90/55.40; HJ (32): 2.33/1.96; PV (32): 5.80/4.70; LJ (32): 8.22/6.82; TJ (32): 17.14/14.32; SP (32): 21.10/18.50; DT (32): 66.00/63.50; HT (32): 77.50/72.50; JT (32): 85.00/64.00; Dec/Hep (24): 8350/6420; 20kW (60): 1:21:00/1:31:00; 50kW (60; men only): 3:50:00; Mixed 4x400 (16).

Marathons: The first 10 at the Doha World Champs, the top 5 finishers at IAAF Gold Label Marathons & top 10 finishers at Tokyo, Boston, London, Berlin, Chicago & New York held during the qualification period will also be considered as having achieved the entry standard.

Indoor performances for all field events and for races of 200m and longer will be accepted except for performances at 200m and over (including combined events) achieved on oversized tracks.

Relays: Maximum of 16 teams per event. The first 8 in Doha automatically qualify, the remaining 8 teams being selected according to IAAF World Lists at 29 June 2020. Qualification period: 1 May 2019 to 29 June 2020.

Further details of the qualification process are on the IAAF website iaaf.org

AS THE SERIES heads into its 10th year, the IAAF **Diamond League** Board and Meeting Directors, together with the IAAF, have been reviewing the future of the Diamond League from 2020 onwards. Major changes approved by the IAAF Council are that the longest track event will be 3000m, the number of scoring disciplines will be reduced from 32 to 24 (12 male and 12 female), each meeting will be televised globally in a faster-paced 90 minute format (down from two hours), and the number of meetings, held on a weekly basis, will be reduced from 14 to 12, leading to a single final at the end of the season.

Name		Nat	Born	Ht/Wt	Event	2018 Mark	Pre-2018 Best

MEN'S INDEX 2018

Athletes included are those ranked in the top 100s at standard (World Championships) events (plus shorter lists for 1000m, 1M, 2000m and 3000m). Those with detailed biographical profiles are indicated in first column by:
* in this year's Annual, ^ featured in a previous year's Annual.

	Name	First	Nat	Born	Ht/Wt	Event	2018 Mark	Pre-2018 Best
	Abadía	Antonio	ESP	2.7.90	181/70	5000	13:24.18	13:12.68- 16
						10k	28:17.24	28:07.14- 16
	Abate	Tadu	ETH	11.9.97	168/55	Mar	2:06:47	-0-
	Abbas	Abdulrahman Khamis	BRN	28.1.93		400	45.70	
	Abbas	Mohammad Nasser	QAT	28.10.96	183/70	400	45.15	45.59A- 16
	Abdallah	Abubaker Haydar	QAT	10.1.98	181/68	800	1:46.02	
	Abdelwahed	Ahmed	ITA	26.5.96	186/73	3kSt	8:26.02	8:36.73- 17
	Abdi	Bashir	BEL	10.2.89	188/59	5000	13:04.91	13:06.10- 15
	10k	28:11.76		27:36.40- 14		HMar	60:42dh	61:50- 17
	Abdo	Abdi Ibrahim	BRN	24.4.97		Mar	2:08:32	2:12:00- 17
	Abe	Hiroki	JPN	19.11.97	171/57	10k	27:56.45	28:40.51- 17
	Abe	Takatoshi	JPN	12.11.91	189/82	400h	48.68	48.94- 17
*	Abele	Arthur	GER	30.7.86	184/80	Dec	8481	8605- 16
	Abramchuk	Mikhail	BLR	15.11.92	192/110	SP	20.13	20.18i- 16, 20.16- 17
	Abshero	Ayele	ETH	28.12.90	167/52	Mar	2:07:19	2:04:23- 12
	Abubaker	Abbas	BRN	17.5.96	175/64	400	45.59	45.15- 15
	Acet	Alperen	TUR	2.4.98	193/79	HJ	2.30	2.22- 17
	Adamchuk	Vadym	UKR	30.5.94	188/80	Dec	7517	7021- 16
	Adams	Barden	USA	21.9.96	190/75	TJ	16.59	16.29, 16.38w- 17
	Adams	Luxolo	RSA	1.8.96	184/73	200	20.01	20.51A- 17
	Adhana	Gebretsadik	ETH	16.7.92	158/50	Mar	2:08:36	2:06:21- 12
	Adkins	Bradley	USA	30.12.93	190/79	HJ	2.24i	2.29i- 15, 2.26- 16
*	Adola	Guye	ETH	20.10.90	175/54	HMar	60:15	59:06- 14
	Afonin	Maksim	RUS	6.1.92	184/115	SP	21.39i, 20.80	21.09i, 21.07- 17
	Aghasyan	Levon	ARM	19.1.95	191/76	TJ	16.65	16.85A, 16.59i, 16.57- 17
	Agrusti	Andrea	ITA	30.8.95	180/65	50kW	3:55:09	3:56:17- 16
*	Ahmed	Mohammed	CAN	5.1.91	175/61	5000	13:03.08	13:01.74- 16
						10k	27:20.56	27:02.35- 17
	Aït-Addi	Saïd	MAR	29.6.82		Mar	2:08:43	2:08:11- 17
	Ajomale	Mobolade	CAN	31.8.95	180/64	200	20.45	20.59- 16
	Akankam	Hicham	MAR	4.4.98	170/59	1500	3:36.93	3:40.21- 17
	Akhmadiyev	Rinas	RUS	6.3.89	180/640	5000	13:24.43	13:35.75- 15
	Akimenko	Mikhail	RUS	6.12.95	196/86	HJ	2.25	2.24- 14
	Akinew	Tesfahun	ETH-J	29.4.99		5000	13:24.79	13:52.91A-17
	Al-Gamal	Mostafa	EGY	1.10.88	191/105	HT	77.71	81.27- 14
	Al-Harthi	Barakat	OMA	15.6.88	172/64	100	9.97	10.05- 16
	Al-Hayrani	Jamal	QAT	26.5.93	175/61	800	1:45.67	1:46.16- 15
	Al-Hizam	Hussain Asim	KSA	4.1.98	180/73	PV	5.70i, 5.63	5.60- 17
	Al-Moualed	Ahmad	KSA	16.2.88	180/66	110h	13.36	13.57A, 13.60- 11
	Alamine	Hamdi Mahamat	QAT	15.4.97	193/75	HJ	2.27	2.26- 17
	Alberto	Dominik	SUI	28.4.92	182/80	PV	5.55i	5.55- 16
	Albright	Jake	USA	22.12.93	183/75	PV	5.60	5.60- 17
	Alehegn	Biyazen	ETH-J	16.9.99	176/61	5000	13:13.36	13:23.51- 17
						10k	27:43.65	27:32.51- 17
	Alewe	Haymanot	ETH	11.11.97	167/52	3000	7:43.36	-0-
						5000	13:18.65	
	Alexander	Colby	USA	13.6.91	183/64	800	1:46.09	1:47.00- 17
	1500	3:37.11		3:34.88- 16		1M	3:55.81	3:54.94- 16
	Ali	Ahmed	SUD	15.11.93	180/80	200	20.49, 20.41w	20.16- 16
	Ali	Obsa	USA	17.2.96	173/57	3kSt	8:32.23	8:45.55- 17
	Alic	Hamza	BIH	20.1.79	186/127	SP	20.45	20.82- 17
	Alkana	Antonio	RSA	12.4.90	185/77	110h	13.31	13.11- 17
	Allen	Craig CJ	USA	14.2.95	178/75	400h	49.40	49.40- 17
*	Allen	Devon	USA	12.12.94	183/82	110h	13.23, 13.13w	13.03- 16
*	Allen	Nathon	JAM	28.10.95	178/68	200	20.46, 20.39w	20.70- 16
						400	44.13	44.19- 17
	Alowonle	Rilwan	NGR	12.12.93	175/66	400h	49.49	50.02- 15
	Alves	Higor	BRA	23.2.94	181/75	LJ	7.99	8.19- 16
	Amaning	Edmond	GBR	27.10.93	183/75	200	20.43, 20.37w	20.86, 20.52w- 17
	Amankwah	Alex	USA/GHA	2.3.92	179/61	800	1:45.81	1:44.80- 17
	Amare	Girmaw	ISR	26.10.87	172/60	10k	28:15.41	28:10.32- 15
	Amare	Hailemariyam	ETH	22.2.97	165/50	3kSt	8:21.21	8:13.39- 17
*	Amdouni	Mourad	FRA	21.1.88	175/60	5000	13:19.14	13:14.19- 09. 13:11.18i- 17
						10k	27:36.80	-0-
	Amels	Douwe	NED	16.9.91	193/68	HJ	2.26i, 2.26	2.28- 13
	Amezcua	Luis Alberto	ESP	1.5.92	183/67	20kW	1:22:52	1:19:46- 17

Name		Nat	Born	Ht/Wt	Event	2018 Mark	Pre-2018 Best
Amghar	Hicham	MAR	15.10.94	167/52	HMar	60:23	62:21- 17
Amoah	Joseph	GHA	12.1.97	180/68	200	20.458, 20.38w	20.82, 20.48w- 17
* Amos	Nijel	BOT	15.3.94	179/60	800	1:42.14	1:41.73- 12
Anas	Y. Muhammed	IND	17.9.94	176/64	400	45.24	45.32- 17
Anastasákis	Mihaíl	GRE	3.12.94	183/103	HT	76.53	77.72- 17
Anderson	Jeshua	USA	22.6.89	187/84	400h	49.86	47.00- 11
Anderson	Kenroy	JAM	27.6.87	178/75	100	10.11	10.16- 13, 10.15w- 11
Anderson	Nick	USA	28.4.95	186/77	110h	13.64, 13.57w	13.49- 17
Andrade	Jordin	CPV	5.5.92	183/73	400h	49.39	49.24- 15
Andraloits	Maksim	BLR	17.6.97	189/83	Dec	7863	7858- 17
André	Thiago	BRA	4.8.95	177/62	800	1:45.10	1:44.81- 17
					1500	3:35.40	3:35.28- 17
^ Andrews	Robby	USA	29.3.91	177/68	1500	3:36.05	3:34.78- 12
Andrieu	Hugo	FRA	16.10.92	182/62	50kW	4:05:15	4:06:42- 17
Andújar	Daniel	ESP	14.5.94	183/78	800	1:46.40	1:45.17- 17
Angelini	Gregorio	ITA	24.6.96		50kW	4:01:17	4:08:22- 17
Anishchonkov	Nikita	RUS	25.7.92	188/80	HJ	2.24i, 2.23	2.30- 11
Antonelli	Michele	ITA	23.5.94	177/64	50kW	3:53:00	3:49:07- 17
* Apak	Esref	TUR	3.1.82	186/105	HT	78.59	81.45- 05
Aphane	Reneilwe	RSA	24.8.90	175/73	TJ	16.65A	16.75A- 17, 16.02- 15
Apolloni	Federico	ITA	14.3.87	187/90	DT	62.76	61.78- 15
Appier	Garrett	USA	15.10.92	197/114	SP	20.41	20.79- 16
* Arai	Hirooki	JPN	18.5.88	180/62	20kW	1:19:19	1:19:25- 17
					50kW	3:44:25	3:40:20- 15
^ Arai	Ryohei	JPN	23.6.91	183/96	JT	80.83	86.83- 14
Araya	Yerko	CHI	14.2.86	174/59	20kW	1:21:31	1:20:47.2t- 11
Arce	Daniel	ESP	22.4.92	190/72	3kSt	8:27.71	8:29.24- 17
Archibald	Emanuel	GUY	9.9.94	178/75	LJ	8.07	7.71, 7.88w- 17
Aregawi	Berihu	ETH-Y	28.2.01	173/55	3000	7:42.12	
5000	13:15.44				10k	27:18.11	
Arents	Mareks	LAT	6.8.86	190/90	PV	5.55i, 5.51	5.70- 16
* Arévalo	Eider	COL	9.3.93	165/58	20kW	1:19:14	1:18:53- 17
* Arikan	Polat Kemboi	TUR	12.12.90	173/62	5000	13:23.42	13:05.98- 11
					10k	27:56.53	27:35.50- 16
Arivuselvan	Deivendran	IND	28.5.91	178/73	TJ	16.49	16.20- 15
Armenta	Carlos	MEX	5.9.87	190/90	JT	79.73	75.52A-13
Armstrong	Angus	AUS	17.3.97	191/80	PV	5.52	5.50- 17
Arnaudov	Tsanko	POR	14.3.92	192/118	SP	21.27i, 20.65	21.56- 17
de Araújo	Luiz Alberto	BRA	27.9.87	190/90	Dec	7954	8315- 16
Arnold	Mike	USA	13.8.90	190/84	PV	5.78Ai, 5.50	5.77Ai- 16, 5.72A- 15, 5.70- 13
Arop	Marco	CAN	20.9.98	194/82	800	1:45.25	1:47.08- 17
Arreaga	Kevin	ESP	23.10.95	182/107	HT	70.64	69.28- 16
Arrhenius	Leif	SWE	15.7.86	192/120	DT	60.30A	64.46- 11
Arrhenius	Niklas	SWE	10.9.82	192/125	DT	61.72	66.22- 11
Art	Arnaud	BEL	28.1.93	185/83	PV	5.74dh?, 5.72	5.71- 17
Arteaga	Mauricio	ECU	8.8.88	173/65	20kW	1:22:18.16t	1:21:08- 16
Atnafu	Yitayal	ETH	20.1.93	172/55	Mar	2:07:00	2:07:21- 17
* Augustyn	Rafal	POL	14.5.84	178/71	50kW	3:48:22	3:43:22- 16
Auzeil	Bastien	FRA	22.10.89	190/82	Dec	7925	8191- 16
Avila	Eric	USA	3.10.89	176/64	1500	3:36.41	3:36.37- 16
					1M	3:55.43	3:56.50- 16
Awotunde	Josh	NGR/USA	12.6.95	188/107	SP	21,33i, 20.77	20.11- 16
Ayalew	Aweke	BRN	23.2.93	182/64	HMar	60:09	63.01- 14
Ayouni	Abdessalem	TUN	16.5.94	187/79	800	1:46.20	1:45.63- 17
					1500	3:37.35	3:41.99- 15
Azemia	Ned	SEY	21.8.97	178/65	400h	49.82	50.74- 16
Azizi	Zied	TUN	11.6.91	184/75	400h	49.13	50.05- 17
* Babayev	Nazim	AZE	8.10.97	185/70	TJ	16.89	17.18- 17
Babu	K.V.Rakesh	IND	20.3.90	180/70	TJ	16.63	16.52- 17
Bachir	Youssouf Hiss	DJI	.87	178/70	1500	3:35.74	3:36.96- 15
Bacon	Jaylen	USA	5.8.96	183/75	100	9.97	10.00, 9.97w- 17
					200	20.25	20.18- 17
Bae Sang-hwa		KOR	21.7.90	180/70	Dec	7518	7448- 14
Bae You-il		KOR	16.6.94		JT	77.41	78.21- 17
Bagharab	Yaser Salem	QAT	1.1.98	170/57	3kSt	8:28.21	8:35.10- 17
Bailey	Aldrich	USA	6.2.94	183/70	400	45.59Ai	45.19- 12
Bailey	Ramone	JAM	31.10.91	179/77	LJ	8.13	8.16- 17
Bailey	Sean	JAM	15.7.97	183/73	400	45.24	45.59i, 45.76- 17
* Bailey-Cole	Kemar	JAM	10.1.92	195/86	100	10.12	9.92- 15
Baird	Leslain	GUY	5.5.87	184/84	JT	78.65A	73.56- 17
* Baji	Balázs	HUN	9.6.89	192/84	110h	13.27	13.15- 17

Name		Nat	Born	Ht/Wt	Event	2018 Mark	Pre-2018 Best
Baker	Chris	GBR	2.2.91	197/84	HJ	2.26	2.36i, 2.29- 16
Baker	Ronnie	USA	15.10.93	178/80	100	9.87, 9.78w	9.98, 9.86w- 17
* Bakulin	Sergey	RUS	13.11.86	169/58	50kW	3:42:20	3:43:26- 10
Ballengee	Markus	USA	8.1.98	196/91	Dec	7722	6779- 17
Balnuweit	Erik	GER	21.9.88	189/75	110h	13.52	13.44, 13.32w-13
Baloyes	Bernardo	COL	6.1.94	177/66	200	20.00	20.43- 14, 20.11A, 20.36w- 17
Baltaci	Özkan	TUR	13.2.94	187/111	HT	76.84	76.61- 17
Bamidele	Emmanuel	NGR-J	6.7.99	191/75	400	45.28	46.48- 17
Bamoussa	Abdoullah	ITA	2.6.86	170/59	3kSt	8:27.72	8:22.00- 17
^ Baniótis	Konstadínos	GRE	6.11.86	202/80	HJ	2.31	2.34- 13
Banks	Tremayne	USA	29.7.92	178/70	110h	13.57	13.62- 15, 13.56w- 17
Bantie	Aychew	ETH	12.9.95		Mar	2:08:15	
^ Banzeruk	Ivan	UKR	9.2.90	180/71	20kW	1:21:25	1:22:08- 15
					50kW	3:49:17	3:44:49- 14
* Barber	Shawnacy	CAN	27.5.94	190/82	PV	5.92	6.00Ai- 16, 5.93- 15
* Barega	Selemon	ETH-J	20.1.00	173/59	3000	7:37.53, 7:36.64i	7:38.90- 17
2M	8:20.01				5000	12:43.02	12:55.58- 17
Barnes	Emre Zafer	TUR	7.11.88	178/73	100	10.08	10.12- 16, 10.02Aw- 17
Barnes	Kalon	USA-J	16.12.99	183/78	100	10.04w	10.22- 17
* Barr	Thomas	IRL	24.7.92	183/73	400h	48.31	47.97- 16
Barrer	François	FRA	8.6.93	182/57	10k	27:55.95	-0-
Barrondo	Bernardo	GUA	5.6.93		50kW	3:53:10	-0-
^ Barry	Trevor	BAH	14.6.83	190/77	HJ	2.27	2.32- 11
* Barshim	Mutaz Essa	QAT	24.6.91	192/70	HJ	2.40	2.43- 14
Bárta	Marek	CZE	8.12.92	194/110	DT	61.13	61.38- 16
Bashan	Nikolay	RUS	18.11.92	182/95	HT	73.90	75.00- 17
Bastien	Steve	USA	4.3.94	183/76	Dec	7980	8015- 17
Bates	KeAndre	USA	24.5.96	181/75	LJ	7.90i, 8.00w	8.11, 8.32w- 16
					TJ	17.16	16.81i, 16.75. 16.76w- 17
Batzávalis	Paraskevás	GRE/CYP	25.11.94	185/85	JT	85.46	85.95- 16
Baxter	Matt	NZL	6.8.94	175/59	10k	28:10.05	28:48.02- 17
Bayer	Andrew	USA	3.2.90	180/60	1500	3:38.58	3:34.47- 13
3000	7:47.54i		7:38.90- 17		3kSt	8:24.66	8:14.46- 17
Bayer	Simon	GER	23.11.95	189/105	SP	19.91	19.30- 17
* Bazile	Zack	USA	7.1.96	178/79	LJ	8.37	7.97- 17
Bednarek	Kenneth	USA	14.10.98	185/84	200	20.43	
* Bednarek	Sylwester	POL	28.4.89	198/75	HJ	2.33i, 2.27	2.33i- 17, 2.32- 09
Bedrani	Djilali	FRA	1.10.93	179/59	3kSt	8:20.55	8:28.34- 16
Belbachir	Mohamed	ALG	11.1.94	175/64	800	1:45.94	1:46.35- 17
Belferrar	Mohamed Amine	ALG	6.2.91	180/69	800	1:46.47	1:45.01- 16
Belihu	Andamlak	ETH	20.11.98	181/62	HMar	59:18	59:51- 17
Bell	Dylan	USA	21.7.93	195/85	PV	5.60	5.70A- 16
Belo	Francisco	POR	27.3.91	193/120	SP	20.86	20.86- 17
					DT	60.09	62.01- 17
Ben Zahra	Abdelkarim	MAR	27.10.98	182/64	3kSt	8:21.08	8:30.76- 17
* Benard	Chris	USA	4.4.90	190/79	TJ	17.40	17.48- 17
Bencosme de Leon	José	ITA	16.5.92	187/77	400h	49.52	49.22- 17
Benitz	Timo	GER	24.12.91	170/56	1500	3:37.74	3:34.87- 17
* Benjamin	Rai	ANT/USA	27.7.97	191/77	200	19.99	20.64- 17
400	44.74		45.72- 17		400h	47.02	48.33- 17
Bennett	Chris	GBR	17.12.89	188/115	HT	75.11	76.45- 16
Bento	Kaual Kamal	BRA	10.1.93	189/75	TJ	16.69	16.89- 14
Benyahia	Amor	TUN	1.7.85	176/54	3kSt	8:26.14	8:14.05- 13
Berdeja	Cristian	MEX	21.6.81	169/58	50kW	4:00:45	3:50:19- 15
Berglund	Kalle	SWE	11.3.96	179/62	1500	3:36.51	3:36.60- 17
Berian	Boris	USA	19.12.92	180/73	800	1:45.72	1:43.34- 15
Berihu	Solomon	ETH-J	2.10.99	172/55	5000	13:16.77	13:12.67- 16
Bernaschina	Luca	SUI	30.6.95	191/87	Dec	7602	7396- 17
^ Berrabah	Yahya	MAR	13.10.81	186/75	LJ	8.10, 8.14w	8.40- 09
Bertemes	Bob	LUX	24.5.93	187/118	SP	21.00	20.63i- 17, 20.14- 16
Berthenet	Damien	FRA	3.9.96	193/75	Dec	7573	7292- 17
Bertolini	Roberto	ITA	9.10.85	187/100	JT	80.24	81.68- 17
Bertrand	Jean-Pierre	FRA	5.11.92	180/71	LJ	7.81i, 7.96w	8.08i- 17, 8.03- 16
Bett	Emmanuel	KEN	14.7.95	170/55	3kSt	8:16.24	8:23.2A- 17
^ Bett	Emmanuel Kipkemei	KEN	30.3.83	170/55	HMar	60:48	60:08- 15
Bett	Emmanuel Kiprono	KEN	14.7.95	160/48	HMar	60:29	65:17- 17
Bett	Leonard	KEN-J	3.11.00	173/57	3000	7:47.59	-0-
					3kSt	8:16.97	
^ Bett	Nicholas	KEN	27.1.90	186/77	400h	48.88A, 49.08	47.79- 15
* Bett	Nicholas	KEN	20.12.96	172/52	3kSt	8:13.18	8:10.07- 16

Name		Nat	Born	Ht/Wt	Event	2018 Mark	Pre-2018 Best
Bett ¶	Kipyegon	KEN	2.1.98	182/70	800	1:46.27dq	1:43.76- 16
					1000	2:16.98dq	-0-
* Beyo	Chala	ETH	18.1.96	174/57	3kSt	8:07.27	8:13.24- 17
Bian Tongda		CHN	1.4.91	170/58	20kW	1:21:12	1:19:34- 13
					50kW	3:58:17	3:48:41- 17
Bianchetti	Sebastiano	ITA	20.1.96	188/125	SP	19.71	10.78 16
Bibic	Łzan	SRB-J	8.1.99	197/70	1500	3:37.79	3:47.40- 16
Bichler	Johannes	GER	3.7.90	186/95	HT	71.67	71.70- 17
Bie Ge		CHN	2.8.92	184/75	200	20.39	20.64- 17
Biere	Lennard	GER	3.2.97		Dec	7550	7539- 16
* Bigot	Quentin	FRA	1.12.92	179/95	HT	76.98	78.58- 14
Bilodeau	Mathieu	CAN	27.11.83	185/73	50kW	4:05:02	3:53:56- 16
Bingham	Basil	JAM	1.9.94	185/102	DT	60.26	60.77- 17
* Bird-Smith	Dane	AUS	15.7.92	178/66	20kW	1:19:34	1:19:28- 17
* Birech	Jairus	KEN	14.12.92	170/56	3kSt	8:18.76	7:58.41- 14
* Birgen	Bethwel	KEN	6.8.88	178/64	1500	3:34.27	3:30.77- 13
1M	3:54.60	3:50.42- 13			3000	7:42.72, 7:40.56i	7:32.48- 16	5000	13:20.08	13:04.66- 16
Birkinhead	Damien	AUS	8.4.93	190/130	SP	20.77	21.35- 17
Blair	Coy	USA	10.6.94	190/130	SP	19.79	20.14- 17
Blair-Sanford	Donald	ISR	5.2.87	193/84	400	45.49	45.04- 15
Blake	Jerome	CAN	18.8.95	181/75	200	20.38	20.87- 17
* Blake	Yohan	JAM	26.12.89	181/79	100	9.94	9.69- 12
Blankenbaker	Dylan	USA	6.1.94	183/64	3kSt	8:31.43	8:31.17- 17
Blankenship	Ben	USA	15.12.88	173/61	1M	3:54.88, 3:54.77i	3:53.04- 17
Blocki	Adrian	POL	11.4.90	173/63	50kW	3:54:31	3:47:16- 16
* Bloomfield	Akeem	JAM	10.11.97	188/77	200	19.81	20.66- 16, 20.29w- 17
					400	43.94	44.74- 17
Boateng	Bismark	CAN	15.3.92	178/73	100	10.14	10.32, 10.21w- 16
Bockarie	Solomon	NED	18.5.87	170/64	200	20.39	20.37- 16, 20.21w- 17
Bodena	Tolesa	ETH-J	18.2.00	177/61	800	1:46.66	1:47.10A- 17
Bodnar	Anton	KAZ	4.12.92	187/69	HJ	2.25	2.24i- 16, 2.21- 13
Bóftsis	Pávlos	GRE	17.9.92	177/72	TJ	16.52, 16.68w	16.23 -17, 16.28w- 13
Bogdanov	Denis	RUS	2.4.91	180/73	LJ	7.95	8.04- 14
Boirie	Baptiste	FRA	26.12.92	171/65	PV	5.52	5.65- 17
Boit	Josphat Kiptoo	KEN	25.11.95	173/52	HMar	59:19	-0-
Boit	Solomon	KEN-J	1.10.99	170/55	10k	27:57.44	29:16.5A- 17
Bol	Peter	AUS	22.2.94	168/57	800	1:44.56	1:45.21- 17
Bollinger	Marvin	GER	7.10.96	187/82	Dec	7547	7735- 17
Bonevacia	Liemarvin	NED	5.4.89	180/81	200	20.46	20.62- 15
					400	45.03	44.72- 15
* Bonfim	Caio	BRA	19.3.91	170/58	50kW	3:55:24	3:47:02- 16
Boonnun	Supot	THA	10.7.96	177/68	TJ	16.52	15.87i- 17, 15.81- 15
Bor	Emmanuel	USA	14.4.88	167/52	3000	7:44.93i	7:56.09i- 11
					5000	13:20.66	13:28.79- 17
* Bor	Hillary	USA	22.11.89	168/57	5000	13:26.81	14:03.45- 08
					3kSt	8:12.20	8:11.82- 17
Bordier	Gabriel	FRA	8.10.97	183/70	20kW	1:22:15	1:23:03- 17
* Boreysha	Pavel	BLR	16.2.91	193/120	HT	77.37	78.60- 16
Borkowski	Mateusz	POL	2.4.97	168/65	800	1:45.42	1:47.11i- 17, 1:47.62- 16
Borlée	Dylan	BEL	20.9.92	190/77	400	45.55	45.57- 15
* Borlée	Jonathan	BEL	22.2.88	180/70	400	44.87	44.43- 12
* Borlée	Kévin	BEL	22.2.88	180/71	400	45.07	44.56- 12
* Bosse	Pierre-Ambroise	FRA	11.5.92	185/68	800	1:44.20	1:42.53- 14
* Bosworth	Tom	GBR	17.1.90	184/64	20kW	1:19:38	1:20:13- 16
Bouchicha	Hichem	ALG	19.5.89	183/70	3kSt	8:27.46	8:20.11- 13
Bouchikhi	Soufiane	BEL	22.3.90	171/54	5000	13:19.55	13:22.18- 17
					10k	27:41.20	28:07.15- 17
Bouqantar	Soufiyan	MAR	30.8.93	173/54	3000	7:39.42	7:38.65- 17
					5000	13:17.81	13:14.06- 17
^ Bouraada	Larbi	ALG	10.5.88	187/84	Dec	8099	8521- 16
Boyce	Brendan	IRL	15.10.86	183/76	50kW	3:53:32	3:48:55- 15
Boyce	Lutalo	USA	11.8.91	178/75	LJ	8.03	7.87- 15, 7.91i, 7.95w- 16
Bradford	Zachery	USA-J	29.11.99	184/77	PV	5.55	5.28- 17
Bramble	Dan	GBR	14.10.90	178/76	LJ	8.15	8.21- 15
Brandt	Torben	GER	19.5.95	190/105	DT	60.68	62.09- 17
^ Brathwaite	Shane	BAR	8.2.90	185/75	110h	13.38	13.21- 15
* Braun	Pieter	NED	21.1.93	182/80	Dec	8342	8334- 16
Bray	Ethan	USA	18.5.97	185/79	PV	5.58	5.31- 17
* Braz da Silva	Thiago	BRA	16.12.93	193/84	PV	5.90i	6.03- 16
* Brazier	Donavan	USA	15.4.97	188/73	800	1:45.10Ai	1:43.55- 16
Brembach	Nils	GER	23.2.93	184/68	20kW	1:21:25	1:20:42- 17

Name		Nat	Born	Ht/Wt	Event	2018 Mark	Pre-2018 Best
Brenes	Nery	CRC	25.9.85	174/62	400	45.00	44.60- 16
Brito	Jonathas	BRA	30.11.92	187/75	110h	13.60	13.63, 13.60w- 17
Broeders	Ben	BEL	21.6.95	178/75	PV	5.65i, 5.60	5.61- 16
* Brown	Aaron	CAN	27.5.92	185/79	100	10.12	9.96, 9.95w- 16
					200	19.98	20.00- 16
Brown	Charles	USA	28.5.97	185/73	LJ	8.12i, 7.97, 8.16w	8.14, 8.30w- 17
Brown	Clayton	JAM	8.12.96	184/77	HJ	2.25	2.25i, 2.21- 17
					TJ	16.42, 16.50w	16.58i- 17, 16.17- 15
Brown	Rodney	USA	21.5.93	183/109	DT	65.34	66.00- 16
Bruchet	Luc	CAN	23.2.91	175/60	5000	13:27.94	13:24.10- 16
Brugger	Mathias	GER	6.8.92	189/90	Dec	8304	8294- 17
Bruintjies	Henricho	RSA	16.7.93	178/70	100	10.10A, 10.11	9.97- 15, 9.89w- 16
Bruns	Ansis	LAT	30.3.89	182/93	JT	77.94	82.00- 17
Brzozowski	Artur	POL	29.3.85	173/67	20kW	1:22:19	1:20:33- 17
Búa	Lucas	ESP	12.1.94	185/70	400	45.25	45.50A, 45.90- 17
Bube	Andreas	DEN	13.7.87	178/65	800	1:45.92	1:44.89- 12
Bubeník	Matús	SVK	14.11.89	197/78	HJ	2.30i, 2.23	2.31i, 2.29- 15
Budza	Serhiy	UKR	6.12.84	181/75	50kW	3:59:07	3:47:36- 13
* Bukowiecki	Konrad	POL	17.3.97	191/140	SP	22.00i, 21.66	21.97i, 21.59- 17
Burgess	Taj	USA-J	15.4.99	175/61	400	45.60	47.42- 16
Burke	Mario	BAR	18.3.97	175/64	100	10.03	10.17, 10.14w- 17
Burrell	Cameron	USA	11.9.94	173/68	100	9.93	9.93, 9.90w- 17
Burt	John	USA	10.2.97	190/79	110h	13.61, 13.48w	13.85, 13.75w- 17
Bussotti Neves	João	ITA	10.5.93	180/62	1500	3:38.05	3:37.12- 17
Bustamante	Luis	MEX	10.6.84		50kW	4:01:24	3:48:45- 17
* Butchart	Andrew	GBR	14.10.91	175/64	3000	7:47.21i	7:37.56- 17
Butenko	Viktor	RUS	10.3.93	196/116	DT	63.23	65.97- 13
Cabral	Donn	USA	12.12.89	175/60	3kSt	8:31.61	8:13.37- 15
Cabral	Johnathan	CAN	31.12.92	193/82	110h	13.34	13.35- 16, 13.22w- 15
^ Cáceres	Eusebio	ESP	10.9.91	175/68	LJ	7.97i	8.37- 13
^ Caùée	Erikc	NED	15.2.84	201/120	DT	63.56	67.30- 12
* Cai Zelin		CHN	11.4.91	172/55	20kW	1:20:38	1:18:47- 12
Caicedo	Juan José	ECU	20.7.92	185/82	DT	60.57	57.99- 17
Cairoli	Simone	ITA	12.9.90	183/77	Dec	7949	7875- 17
Cakss	Gatis	LAT	13.6.95	184/93	JT	83.89	80.06- 15
Callahan	Peter	BEL	1.6.91	183/68	1500	3:37.11	3:37.57- 17
Cambridge	Aska	JPN	31.5.93	180/76	100	10.12	10.08, 9.98w- 17
Campbell	Kemoy	JAM	14.1.91	165/57	3000	7:47.43i	7:40.79i- 16, 7:41.87- 17
					5000	13:23.73	13:20.39- 15, 13:14.45i- 17
Campbell	Luke	GER	22.11.94	189/79	400h	49.14	49.40- 17
Campbell	Matthew	JAM	20.10.96	188/90	HJ	2.26	2.20i- 17, 2.19- 16
Campbell	Taylor	GBR	30.6.96	191/100	HT	72.31	73.40- 17
Campener	Corentin	BEL	5.10.90	175/64	LJ	7.98	7.94, 8.05w- 16
Campion	Kevin	FRA	23.5.88	183/63	20kW	1:21:52	1:20:28- 17
Campos	Luis	PER	10.11.95	171/66	50kW	3:59:23A	4:05:47- 16
Canady	Braxton	USA	13.1.98	182/73	110h	13.75, 13.57w	13.93, 13.89w- 17
Cann	Luke	AUS	17.7.94	183/90	JT	77.43	81.07- 17
* Cao Shuo		CHN	8.10.91	183/69	TJ	16.80A, 16,65	17.35- 12
Carbin	Darius	USA	4.3.98	198/82	HJ	2.24i, 2.21	2.25- 16
Carnes	Brandon	USA	6.3.95	175/73	100	10.15, 10.05w	10.06, 9.97w- 17
Carpenter	Anthony	JAM-J	23.1.99	184/75	400	45.47	46.53- 17
Carreón	David	MEX	23.3.94	183/95	JT	81.45	77.58- 17
Carro	Fernando	ESP	1.4.92	175/67	3kSt	8:19.30	8:21.78- 15
Carruthers	Declan	AUS	7.9.97	188/84	PV	5.55	5.40- 16
Carson	Hamish	NZL	1.11.88	181/66	1500	3:38.19	3:36.25- 16
					3000	7:47.22i	7:49.24- 11
* Carter	Chris	USA	11.3.89	186/80	TJ	17.20Ai, 17.18, 17.28w	17.18- 16
Carter	Deuce	JAM	28.9.90	182/75	110h	13.55	13.20- 16
Carter	Nesta	JAM	11.10.85	178/70	100	10.07, 9.92w	9.78- 10
Cartwright	Grant	USA	19.11.94	193/114	SP	19.61	19.17- 16
Carvalho	Florian	FRA	9.3.89	183/70	5000	13:27.76	13:32.00- 17
					10k	28:06.78	-0-
Carvalho	Lucas	BRA	16.7.93	183/73	400	45.55	45.37- 17
Casey	Patrick	USA	23.5.90	175/60	1500	3:37.06	3:35.32 -14
					1M	3:54.66	3:52.62- 14
Castle	Noah	USA	19.9.96	196/118	SP	19.66	18.06- 17
Castro	Luis Joel	PUR	28.1.91	195/72	HJ	2.28	2.29- 16
* Cedenio	Machel	TTO	6.9.95	183/70	400	45.68	44.01- 16
Ceh	Kristian	SLO-J	17.2.99	205/115	DT	62.03	52.22- 17
* Centrowitz	Matthew	USA	18.10.89	175/61	1500	3:31.77	3:30.40- 15
					1M	3:53.61	3:50.53- 14

Name		Nat	Born	Ht/Wt	Event	2018 Mark		Pre-2018 Best
Cerny	Dominik	SVK	1.11.97		50kW	4:01:51		-0-
Chala	Regasa	ETH	30.4.97	170/60	3000	7:38.78		-0-
					5000	13:06.98		-0-
Chalyy	Timofey	RUS	7.4.94	190/79	400h	48.89		48.57- 16
Chama	Noel Ali	MEX	15.9.97		20kW	1:21:55		1:23:47- 17
Chambers	Marcus	USA	3.11.94	178/75	400	45.50		44.92 17
Chambers	Raheem	JAM	6.10.97	177/73	100	10.10, 10.05w		10.20- 17
Chani	Hassan	BRN	8.10.91	171/55	10k	27:38.16		27:56.48- 16
* Chapelle	Axel	FRA	24.4.95	182/77	PV	5.88i, 5.70		5.80i, 5.72- 17
Charleston	Cravont	USA	2.1.98	180/73	100	10.21, 10.10w		10.35, 10.07w- 17
Chebii	Douglas	KEN	1.11.93		Mar	2:08:43		2:09:48- 17
^ Cheboi	Collins	KEN	25.9.87	175/64	1500	3:37.83		3:30.34- 15
Chelanga	Samuel	USA	23.2.85	168/57	HMar	60:37		61:04- 13
* Chelimo	Paul	USA	27.10.90	171/57	1M	3:55.96		4:02.80i- 12
3000	7:34.83	7:31.57- 17			2M	8:20.91	8:28.53Ai- 17	5000 12:57.55 13:03.90- 16
Chemarmazovich	Vladislav	BLR	18.4.95		PV	5.55		5.30i- 16, 5.30- 17
Chemutai	Albert	UGA-J	25.11.99	185/65	3kSt	8:17.17		8:23.18- 17
Chen Chieh		TPE	8.5.92	183/68	400h	49.62		49.05- 15
Chen Ji		CHN	27.1.90	189/64	HJ	2.24		2.24- 10
Chen Kuei-Ju		TPE	22.9.93	188/79	110h	13.39		13.55- 17
Chen Rui		CHN	11.8.96		20kW	1:21:48		1:23:07- 16
* Cheng Chao-Tsun		TPE	17.10.93	182/88	JT	84.60		91.36- 17
Cheparev	Dementiy	RUS	28.10.92		50kW	3:54:20		3:43:05- 17
Cheprot	Simon	KEN	2.7.93	183/62	HMar	59:28		59:20- 13
* Cheptegei	Joshua	UGA	12.9.96	179/61	10k	27:19.62		26:49.94- 17
* Cheroben	Abreham	BRN	10.11.92	174/58	HMar	60:22		58:48- 14
* Cherono	Lawrence	KEN	7.8.88	178/61	Mar	2:04:06		2:05:09- 17
* Cherry	Michael	USA	23.3.95	186/75	400	44.85		44.66- 17
* Cheruiyot	Evans Kipkorir	KEN	24.9.91	175/55	HMar	60:26		61:09- 17
* Cheruiyot	Ferguson	KEN	30.11.89	183/73	800	1:43.73		1:42.04- 14
1000	2:14.88		2:16.88- 14		1500	3:33.21		3:49.0A- 14
* Cheruiyot	Timothy	KEN	20.11.95	178/64	800	1:44.74A		1:45.92A- 14
1500	3:28.41		3:29.10- 17		1M	3:49.87		3:49.64- 17
Chesani	Silvano	ITA	17.7.88	190/75	HJ	2.24i		2.33i, 2.31 -13
* Cheserek	Edward	KEN	2.2.94	168/57	1500	3:33.76+i		3:36.50- 14
1M	3:49.44i	3:52.01i- 17, 4:03.29- 11			3000	7:38.74i		7:40.51i- 16
Chethan	Balasubramanya	IND	18.8.92	184/64	HJ	2.25		2.20- 16
Chhikara	Naveen	IND	14.12.96		SP	19.57		19.18- 17
Chiappinelli	Yohannes	ITA	18.8.97	171/55	3kSt	8:28.10		8:27.34- 17
Chiaraviglio	Germán	ARG	16.4.87	192/77	PV	5.66		5.75- 15
Chiesa	Stefano	ITA	25.5.96	186/73	20kW	1:21:46		1:25:21- 17
Chizhikov	Dmitriy	RUS	6.12.93	194/85	TJ	16.87i		17.20- 15
Chmielak	Hubert	POL	19.6.89	188/88	JT	78.19		82.58- 14
* Chocho	Andrés	ECU	4.11.83	167/67	20kW	1:22:24		1:20:07- 16
					50kW	3:50:27		3:42:57A- 16
Choge	Raymond	KEN	2.1.88		Mar	2:08:11		2:08:39- 16
Choi Byung-kwang		KOR	7.4.91	185/70	20kW	1:22:27		1:21:20- 14
* Chopra	Neeraj	IND	24.12.97	184/80	JT	88.06		86.48- 16
* Chumba	Dickson	KEN	27.10.86	167/50	Mar	2:05:30		2:04:32- 14
* Chumo	Rodgers	KEN	3.3.97	165/49	5000	13:25.51		13:18.98- 16
					10k	27:28.66		27:25.23- 16
Chumo	Victor	KEN	.87	175/59	HMar	60:03		62:07- 16
Cionfuegos	Javier	ESP	15.7.90	193/134	HT	76.10		76.71- 13
^ Cisneros	Omar	CUB	19.11.89	186/80	400h	49.32		47.93- 13
Cissé	Arthur Gue	CIV	29.12.96	174/64	100	9.94		10.19- 17
Clark	Rashard	USA	4.11.94	186/77	400	45.54		46.14- 14
Clark	Ryan	USA	14.9.96	185/77	200	20.43		20.46- 15
Clarke	Andre	JAM	6.6.92	190/79	400h	48.29		49.19- 17
* Claye	Will	USA	13.6.91	180/68	TJ	17.44, 17.46w		17.91, 18.05w- 17
Clemens	Daniel	GER	28.4.92	181/74	PV	5.61		5.60- 13
^ Clement	Kerron	USA	31.10.85	188/84	400h	48.83		47.24- 05
* Coleman	Christian	USA	6.3.96	175/75	100	9.79		9.82- 17
Coleman	Jamaine	GBR	22.9.95	175/61	3kSt	8:31.91		8:34.19- 15
Collie-Minns	Latario	BAH	10.3.94	173/64	TJ	16.53		17.18, 17.25w- 15
Collins	Travis	USA	26.2.96	178/68	100	10.19, 10.09w		10.45- 16
Comenentia	Denzel	NED	25.11.95	186/114	SP	20.88		20.33- 17
DT	58.81		58.00- 17		HT	76.41		71.75- 17
Connor	Ben	GBR	17.10.92	183/64	5000	13:25.31		13:29.90- 17
					10k	28:14.56		28:23.58- 17
Conradie	Pieter	RSA	20.10.94	182/73	400	45.49A, 45.98		45.15A, 45.58- 17

Name		Nat	Born	Ht/Wt	Event	2018 Mark	Pre-2018 Best
* Constantino	Gabriel	BRA	9.2.95	186/77	200	20.67, 20.39w	20.82- 15
					110h	13.23	13.50- 16
Contini	Mattia	ITA	27.10.94	189/72	400h	49.62	49.94- 16
Contreras	Yidiel Islay	ESP	27.11.92	185/78	110h	13.44	13.35- 15
Cooper	Mitch	AUS	2.6.95	196/115	DT	60.40	63.98- 17
* Copello	Alexis	AZE	12.8.85	185/80	TJ	17.24	17.68A- 11, 17.65, 17.69w- 09
* Copello	Yasmani	TUR	15.4.87	196/86	400h	47.81	47.92- 16
Coroller	Victor	FRA	21.9.97	181/65	400h	49.34	49.30- 17
Corréa	Harold	FRA	26.6.88	190/78	TJ	17.05	17.08, 17.11w- 16
Cota	Mario	MEX	11.9.90	188/115	DT	60.79	63.35- 16
Cotton	Kenzo	USA	13.5.96	185/87	100	10.13, 10.12w	10.07- 16, 9.96w- 17
					200	20.38	20.35- 16, 20.20w- 17
Courter	Bryant	USA	6.10.97	180/73	LJ	7.96w	7.50- 17
Couto	Kurt	MOZ	14.5.85	180/67	400h	49.56	49.02- 12
Cova	Santiago	VEN	10.8.96	175/70	LJ	8.00w	7.89- 17
Cowan	Dwayne	GBR	1.1.85	188/82	400	45.45	45.34- 17
* Craddock	Omar	USA	26.4.91	178/79	TJ	17.40	17.53- 15
Cranston	Kyle	AUS	3.9.92	186/83	Dec	7786	7703- 16
Crawford	Corey	USA	12.12.91	190/86	LJ	8.18	8.22i- 14, 8.12- 17
Cray	Eric	PHI	6.11.88	176/73	400h	49.68	48.98- 16
Cremona	Orazio	RSA	1.7.89	192/130	SP	20.71	21.12- 17
Cretinoir	Jean-Noël	FRA	28.12.94	178/64	TJ	16.77, 16.86w	16.51- 14
Crippa	Yemaneberhan	ITA	15.10.96	174/53	1500	3:38.22	3:38.37- 16
3000	7:43.30	7:55.31- 17		5000	13:18.83	13:36.65- 16, 13:23.99i- 17	10k 27:44.21	-0-
Crisp	Vincent	USA	17.8.97	175/64	800	1:46.31	1:46.97- 16
Crittenden	Freddie	USA	3.8.94	183/73	110h	13.27	13.42- 17
Cronie	Patrick	NED	5.11.89	188/108	SP	19.80	19.55- 16
* Crouser	Ryan	USA	18.12.92	201/135	SP	22.53	22.65- 17
Culmer	Kaiwan	BAH	10.10.96	178/75	TJ	16.52	16.08, 16.12w- 17
Culver	Trey	USA	18.7.96	193/75	HJ	2.33i, 2.28	2.26- 16
Cunningham	Logan	USA	30.5.91	183/80	PV	5.53Ai, 5.47	5.75- 17, 5.80dh- 16
Cunningham	Randall	USA	4.1.96	196/84	HJ	2.29i	2.27i- 17, 2.26 16
Cunningham	Trey	USA	26.8.98	182/75	110h	13.57	-0-
Curtin	Thomas	USA	8.8.93	173/61	5000	13:23.11	13:26.55- 17
Cypres	Jules	FRA	9.8.97	177/71	PV	5.52	5.45- 17
Czykier	Damian	POL	10.8.92	186/73	110h	13.37	13.28- 17
da Silva	Altobeli	BRA	3.12.90	181/60	5000	13:23.85	13:41.17- 15
					3kSt	8:29.04	8:23.67- 17
* Dacres	Fedrick	JAM	28.2.94	194/115	SP	20.34	20.46- 17
					DT	69.67, 69.83lt	68.88- 17
Dagée	Frédéric	FRA	11.12.92	192/108	SP	20.36i, 20.04	20.04- 17
Dagher	Kadhem	IRQ	29.11.95	194/110	DT	60.09	60.89- 17
Dagher	Youssef Mohamed	KUW	15.7.93	180/75	400	45.63	46.27- 15
Dahm	Tobias	GER	23.5.87	203/117	SP	19.73	20.56i, 20.42- 16
Dairokuno	Shuho	JPN	23.12.92	168/51	10k	28:00.49	27:46.55- 15
Dal Molin	Paolo	ITA	31.7.87	182/76	110h	13.40	13.47- 14
Daniels	Joseph	CAN	12.10.98	181/70	110h	13.70	13.94, 13.88w- 17
* Darien	Garfield	FRA	22.12.87	187/76	110h	13.45, 13.35w	13.09- 17
Darrow	Kyle	USA	12.4.95	183/75	LJ	7.97	7.72- 15
Day	Tyler	USA	18.12.96	178/61	10k	28:04.44	28:46.07- 17
Dazza	El Mahjoub	MAR	3.3.91	167/52	Mar	2:05:26	-0-
de Arriba	Álvaro	ESP	2.6.94	180/65	800	1:44.99	1:45.06- 17
* De Grasse	Andre	CAN	10.11.94	180/73	100	10.15	9.91- 16, 9.69w- 17
					200	20.46	19.80- 16, 19.58w- 15
* De Luca	Marco	ITA	12.5.81	188/69	50kW	3:55:47	3:44:47- 16
de Wolff	Rody	NED	9.4.97	200/93	Dec	7739	7527- 17
Debela	Dejene	ETH	9.1.95	180/62	Mar	2:07:06?	2:07:10- 17
Debjani	Ismael	BEL	25.9.90	174/60	1500	3:34.40	3:33.70- 17
* Dedewo	Paul	USA	5.6.91	185/73	400	44.43	45.13- 17
Degu	Abayneh	ETH	1.12.98	176/59	10k	27:59.77	28:13.60- 17
Dei Tos	Leonardo	ITA	27.4.92	180/62	50kW	3:59:48	-0-
Deksisa	Solomon	ETH	11.3.94	170/55	Mar	2:04:40	2:06:22- 16
del Real	Diego	MEX	6.3.94	185/103	HT	75.86	77.49- 16
Delgado	Joe	USA	8.1.95	185/79	Dec	7852	7590- 17
Delryd	Fabian	SWE	15.10.96	205/87	HJ	2.33	2.25i, 2.22- 17
Demaline	Nick	USA	1.3.96	188/127	SP	20.24i, 20.18	20.15- 17
Demps	Jeff	USA	8.1.90	175/77	100	10.02	10.01- 08, 9.90w- 17
^ Demyanyuk	Dmytro	UKR	30.6.83	200/84	HJ	2.26	2.35- 11
* Dendy	Marquis	USA	17.11.92	190/75	LJ	8.42i, 8.29	8.42- 16, 8.68w- 15
Deng	Joseph	AUS	7.7.98	173/61	800	1:44.21	1:46.51- 17
Denisov	Ivan	UZB	22.1.96		TJ	16.49	15.90- 17

Name		Nat	Born	Ht/Wt	Event	2018 Mark	Pre-2018 Best
Denissel	Simon	FRA	22.5.90	181/60	1500	3:36.88	3:34.54- 13
Denny	Matthew	AUS	2.6.96	195/115	DT	64.67	65.37- 16
					HT	74.88	73.37- 17
Desalu	Eseosa	ITA	19.2.94	179/69	200	20.13	20.31- 16
* Desisa	Lelisa	ETH	14.1.90	170/52	HMar	59:52	59:30- 11
					Mar	2:05:59	2:04;45- 13
de Deus	Eduardo	BRA	0.10.95	187/82	110h	13.44A, 13.49	13.51, 13.42w- 17
Dewhurst	Ian	AUS	13.11.90	185/73	400h	49.80	49.52- 14
Dharun	Ayyasamy	IND	31.12.96	177/66	400h	48.96	50.51- 16
Dheeb	Ahmed Mohamed	QAT	29.9.85	195/113	DT	61.30	63.70. 64.56dq- 10
Di Marco	Nazzareno	ITA	30.4.85	196/98	DT	63.62	62.38- 17
* Díaz	Andy	CUB	25.12.95	180/68	TJ	16.52	17.40- 17
Díaz	Carlos Martín	CHI	9.7.93	174/58	1500	3:38.23	3:37.82- 16
* Díaz	Jordan	CUB-Y	23.2.01	192/73	TJ	17.41	17.30A, 16.66- 17
Díaz	José Ignacio	ESP	22.11.79	168/53	50kW	3:55:28	3:48:08- 17
Dickson	Michael	USA	25.1.97	188/75	110h	13.54	13.67- 16
Dida	Gemechu	ETH J	12.0.00	166/50	3000	7:42.14I	-0-
Dilla	Karsten	GER	17.7.89	189/80	PV	5.61	5.73i, 5.72- 11
Diriba	Tesfaye	ETH	11.9.98	185/66	3kSt	8:17.51	8:13.33- 17
Dirieh	Djamal Abdi	DJI	.97	170/60	3000	7:45.96i	-0-
Dixon	Devin	USA	22.9.97	196/82	400	45.22	46.91- 16
					800	1:45.62	1:45.71- 17
Djouhan	Lolassonn	FRA	18.5.91	188/118	DT	64.05	65.10- 17
Djurovic	Tomas	MNE	14.2.94	190/98	SP	19.93	19.85- 17
Dlodlo	Thando	RSA-J	22.4.99	177/64	100	10.11A	10.16A- 17
					200	20.41A	20.78- 17, 20.63A- 16
^ Dmitrik	Aleksey	RUS	12.4.84	191/69	HJ	2.26i	2.40i- 14, 2.36- 11
^ Dmytrenko	Ruslan	UKR	22.3.86	180/67	20kW	1:21:12	1:18:37- 14
do Nascimento	Rodrigo	BRA	26.9.94	181/75	100	10.14	10.21- 16
					200	20.47	20.77- 16, 20.65w- 15
* Dobek	Patryk	POL	13.2.94	183/75	400h	48.59	48.40- 15
Dobrenshkiy	Aleksandr	RUS	11.3.94	195/110	DT	60.91	60.81- 16
Docavo	Vicente	ESP	13.2.92	182/72	TJ	16.50	16.72- 12
Doctor	José Luis	MEX	14.6.96		20kW	1:22:34	1:21:55- 17
Dohmann	Carl	GER	18.5.90	182/62	50kW	3:50:27	3:45:21- 17
Dolezal	Jan	CZE	6.6.96	190/85	Dec	8067	7730- 16
Dolve	Eirik Greibrokk	NOR	5.5.95	185/80	PV	5.56i, 5.45	5.66- 16
Domanic	Robert	USA	10.3.95	186/70	1500	3:36.33	3:38.73+- 17
Domingos	Wágner	BRA	23.6.83	183/126	HT	74.56	78.63- 16
^ Donato	Fabrizio	ITA	14.8.76	189/82	TJ	16.94i, 16.62	17.73i- 11,17.60- 00, 17.63w- 12
* Dong Bin		CHN	22.11.88	179/67	TJ	17.22	17.58- 16
Donnelly	Sean	USA	1.4.93	183/107	HT	76.96	74.35- 16
Doran	Jake	AUS-J	17.11.00	175/70	100	10.15	10.47- 16
Doris	Troy	GUY	12.4.89	174/73	TJ	16.88	17.18- 16
Douado	Willian	BRA	6.1.94	188/114	SP	19.61	20.22- 17
Dougherty	William	USA	8.5.95	185/86	Dec	7673	7471(w)- 17
^ Douglas	Nathan	GBR	4.12.82	183/71	TJ	16.77i, 16.71, 16.83w	17.64- 05
Doukkana	Rabie	MAR	6.12.87	168/57	1500	3:36.13	3:37.81- 14
					5000	13:15.59	-0-
Douvalídis	Konstadínos	GRE	10.3.87	184/78	110h	13.41	13.33- 15
Downing	Quincy	USA	16.1.93	185/75	400h	49.00	48.13- 17
Downs	Jordan	USA	7.3.96		LJ	7.96i	7.30- 17
Drack	Jonathan	MRI	6.11.88	184/77	TJ	16.61	16.96, 17.05w- 15
Droddy	Noah	USA	22.9.90	178/59	10k	28:07.88	28:22.62- 16
Droogsma	Austin	USA	4.3.95	190/132	SP	20.32	19.70- 17
Drummond	Gerald	CRC	5.9.94	178/75	400h	49.80	50.41- 14
Dry	Mark	GBR	11.10.87	184/110	HT	73.12	76.93- 15
Dubitskiy	Oleg	BLR	14.10.90	184/100	HT	74.74	76.67- 15
Dubler	Cedric	AUS	13.1.95	190/82	Dec	8229	8114- 16
* Duckworth	Tim	GBR	18.6.96	185/80	LJ	8.03, 8.19w	7.87- 17
					Dec	8336	7973- 17
Dudarov	Gleb	BLR	17.10.96	196/109	HT	78.04	74.20- 17
* Dukes	Dedric	USA	2.4.92	180/70	200	20.27	19.97- 14, 19.86w- 15
Dunbar	Colin	USA	27.6.88	190/115	HT	72.08	73.56- 15
* Dunfee	Evan	CAN	28.9.90	186/68	50kW	3:50:18	3:41:38- 16
* Duplantis	Armand	SWE-J	10.11.99	181/68	PV	6.05	5.90- 17
Durañona	Yordanys	DMA	16.6.88	188/75	TJ	16.86	17.20A- 14, 17.02, 17.28w- 09
Dutamby	Stuart	FRA	24.4.94	176/74	200	20.41	20.78- 14
* Dwyer	Rasheed	JAM	29.1.89	188/80	200	20.19	19.80- 15
Dyubin	Dmitriy	BLR	12.7.90		50kW	3:47:59	4:03:53- 12
* Eaton	Jarret	USA	24.6.89	183/82	110h	13.33	13.25- 16

Name		Nat	Born	Ht/Wt	Event	2018 Mark	Pre-2018 Best
* Echevarría	Juan Miguel	CUB	11.8.98	186/75	LJ	8.68, 8.83w	8.28, 8.34w- 17
Edoburun	Ojie	GBR	2.6.96	183/77	100	10.04	10.12, 9.93w- 17
Edoki	Fabian	NGR	30.3.98	188/73	LJ	8.10	7.91A, 8.02Aw- 16
* Edris	Muktar	ETH	14.1.94	172/57	3000	7:36.13	7:32.31- 17
					5000	12:55.18	12:54.83- 14
* Edward	Alonso	PAN	8.12.89	183/73	100	10.01A, 10.02	10.02-14. 9.97w- 09
					200	19.90	19.81- 09
Efekoro	Oghenakpobo	NGR	15.7.96	190/138	SP	20.28	20.39- 17
Ehrhardt	Tim	USA	16.3.95	186/90	PV	5.60i, 5.41	5.50i- 17, 5.31- 15
					Dec	8044	7677- 15
Eitel	Manuel	GER	28.1.97	180/80	Dec	8121	7825- 17
Ejima	Masaki	JPN-J	6.3.99	189/75	PV	5.55	5.65- 17
El Aaraby	Mohamed	MAR	12.11.89	164/52	HMar	60:38	61:45- 17
* El Abbassi	El Hassan	BRN	13.4.84	171/54	HMar	59:27	61:09- 13
					Mar	2:04:43	2:10:57- 17
El Aziz	Mustapha	MAR	24.12.85	175/60	HMar	60:16	59:29- 16
* El Bakkali	Soufiane	MAR	7.1.96	188/70	3000	7:41.88i	7:49.68- 16
					3kSt	7:58.15	8:04.83- 17
El Chenini	Riad	TUN	25.3.97	180/66	800	1:46.28	1:46.24- 17
El Jalaoui	Badr	MAR	28.1.93		800	1:46.32	1:47.14- 16
El Kaam	Fouad	MAR	27.5.88	177/62	1500	3:36.60	3:33.71- 13
El-Ashry	Alaa El-Din	EGY	6.1.91	183/95	HT	73.71	75.41- 15
* El-Seify	Ashraf Amjad	QAT	20.2.95	183/100	HT	77.04	78.19- 16
* Elemba	Frank	CGO	21.7.90	200/115	SP	20.81	21.20- 16
Ellis	Branson	USA-J	19.7.00	185/77	PV	5.57	4.99- 17
Ellis	Burkheart	BAR	18.9.92	175/64	100	10.10w	10.17- 16
Ellis	Joseph	GBR	10.4.96	181/102	HT	73.80	70.98- 17
Ellis	Nigel	JAM	8.8.97	186/77	200	20.36	20.40- 16
Ellison	Sam	USA	5.12.92	190/75	800	1:46.20	1:47.46- 16
Enahoro	Ituah	NGR/GER	15.12.97	187/80	LJ	8.01	7.64- 17
					Dec	8048	8028- 17
Endale	Kebede	ETH-J	22.6.00		1500	3:37.0A	
Enekwechi	Chukwuebuka	NGR	28.1.93	181/107	SP	21.22	21.07- 17
Engel	Roscoe	RSA	6.3.89	178/72	100	10.06A	10.19- 11, 10.12w- 15
					200	20.44A	20.51A- 15, 20.60- 16
Engels	Craig	USA	1.5.94	187/73	1500	3:36.89	3:35.95- 17
					1M	3:55.12, 3:53.93i	3:57.67- 17
Entholzner	Maximilian	GER	18.8.94	182/79	LJ	7.96	7.92- 17
Er	Necati	TUR	24.2.97		TJ	16.63	16.34, 16.50w- 17
Erasmus	Emile	RSA	3.4.92	186/84	100	10.01	10.08A, 10.12- 17
Erassa	Kirubel	USA	17.6.93	172/61	3000	7:47.48i	7:49.17i- 13
Erb	MJ (Michael)	USA	2.2.94	184/73	3kSt	8:28.62	8:26.75- 17
Eriksson	Anders	SWE	22.3.94	190/100	HT	74.19	71.76- 17
Erm	Johannes	EST	26.3.98	198/91	LJ	7.98	7.64- 17
					Dec	8046	7593- 16
Escobar	Fanor Andrés	COL	17.12.97	185/70	110h	13.60A	13.71A- 17
Esquivel	Sergio	MEX-J	4.5.99	181/68	400h	49.82A, 49.90	50.19- 17
Essalhi	Younès	MAR	20.2.93	181/68	1500	3:36.28	3:35.52- 13
					3000	7:43.20	7:46.24- 16
Estefani	Hederson	BRA	11.9.91	184/75	400h	49.48	49.13- 17
^ Etelätalo	Lassi	FIN	30.4.88	193/90	JT	78.38	84.98- 14
Eto	Takashi	JPN	5.2.91	183/67	HJ	2.28	2.30- 17
Evans	Andrew	USA	25.1.91	198/110	DT	66.05	66.61- 17
Evans	Jerimiah	USA	16.9.98	190/109	DT	60.58	54.00- 17
* Évora	Nelson	POR	20.4.84	181/70	TJ	17.40i, 17.10	17.74- 07, 17.82w- 09
Ewers	Andre	JAM	7.6.95	173/64	100	9.98	10.13- 17
					200	20.28, 19.98w	20.62, 20.52w- 17
Ezzaydouny	Ibrahim	MAR	28.4.91	181/65	3kSt	8:14.62	8:18.50- 17
Fabbri	Leonardo	ITA	15.5.97	196/105	SP	20.07	19.33- 17
Fair	Kareem	USA	27.2.94	172/64	100	10.26, 10.11w	10.37, 10.28w- 17
* Fajdek	Pawel	POL	4.6.89	186/118	HT	81.14	83.93- 15
Fall	Mouhamadou	FRA	25.2.92	192/87	100	10.13	10.39, 10.27w- 17
Falloni	Simone	ITA	26.9.91	187/110	HT	74.55	75.73- 17
Faloci	Giovanni	ITA	13.10.85	191/115	DT	64.19	64.77- 13
* Farah	Mohamed	GBR	23.3.83	171/58	HMar	59:27dh	59:22dh, 59:32- 15
					Mar	2:05:11	2:08:21- 14
Farnosov	Andrey	RUS	9.7.80	182/66	3kSt	8:29.95	8:21.95- 11
Fasasi	Kunle	NGR	23.6.96	183/75	400	45.68	45.43- 16
^ Fassinotti	Marco	ITA	29.4.89	192/73	HJ	2.25i, 2.25	2.35i- 16, 2.33- 15
Fauble	Scott	USA	5.11.91	175/61	10k	28:13.07	28:00.43- 16
* Felix	Kurt	GRN	4.7.88	190/88	Dec	7756	8509- 17

Name		Nat	Born	Ht/Wt	Event	2018 Mark	Pre-2018 Best
Felix	Markim	GRN	8.10.97	190/91	JT	78.07	78.80- 17
Feng Zhiqiang		CHN	14.4.98	184/73	400h	49.69	49.66- 17
Ferguson	Kord	USA	16.9.95	198/109	SP	20.06i,19.86	19.05- 16
					DT	60.19	61.44- 17
Ferlic	Mason	USA	5.8.93	188/68	3kSt	8:29.77	8:21.57- 16
^ Fernández	Jorge	CUB	2.10.87	190/100	DT	65.27	66.50- 14
Fernández	Oergio	COR	1.4.90	100/70	400h	48.98	48.87- 16
Fernández	Yasmani	CUB	7.4.95	180/85	HT	71.34	70.26- 16
Ferreira	Diogo	POR	30.7.90	175/77	PV	5.66	5.71- 17
Ferreira	Fernando	BRA	13.12.94	188/57	HJ	2.25A	2.30- 17
Fields	Trey	USA-J	25.1.99	175/68	400	45.50	46.45- 17
Filip	Scott	USA	28.1.95	188/85	Dec	7876	7915- 17
* Filippídis	Konstadinos	GRE	26.11.86	188/73	PV	5.85i, 5.75	5.91- 15
* Finley	Mason	USA	7.10.90	203/150	DT	67.06	68.03- 17
Firfirica	Alin Alexandru	ROU	3.11.95	196/108	DT	66.22	65.03- 16
Flournoy	Jaron	USA	24.11.96	183/77	200	20.26, 20.23w	20.24- 17
Fofana	Hassane	ITA	28.4.92	184/78	110h	13.50	13.52- 16
Fontenot	Ryan	USA	4.5.86	188/75	110h	13.35	13.44- 13, 13.39w -12
* Forbes	Damar	JAM	18.9.90	185/77	LJ	8.07i, 7.99	8.29- 17, 8.35w- 13
Ford	Jakobe	USA	4.9.98	196/75	HJ	2.24i	2.23- 17
Ford	Robert	USA	8.3.96	178/64	800	1:46.43	1:47.57- 16
Ford	Santiago	CUB	25.8.97	186/79	Dec	7607	7756- 17
^ Forte	Julian	JAM	7.1.93	186/73	100	10.11	9.91- 17
Forte	Simone	ITA	20.1.96	181/73	TJ	16.73	16.62i- 16, 16.24- 15
Fortunato	Francesco	ITA	13.12.94	178/52	20kW	1:23:04	1:22:01- 17
* Francis	Javon	JAM	14.12.94	183/73	400	45.11	44.50- 15
Francis	Jermaine	SKN	9.3.98	193/86	HJ	2.28	2.22- 17
* Francis	Miguel	GBR	28.2.95	186/75	200	20.38	19.88, 19.67dt- 16
* François	Mickaël	FRA	12.3.88	180/70	400h	49.46	49.35- 13
Fraresso	Mauro	ITA	13.1.93	193/82	JT	77.84	78.28- 17
Frayne	Henry	AUS	14.4.90	187/72	LJ	8.34	8.27- 12
^ Fredericks	Cornel	RSA	3.3.90	178/70	400h	49.30	48.14- 11
Freeman	Josh	USA	22.8.94	193/134	SP	20.42	20.91- 17
French	Cameron	NZL	17.5.92	180/73	400h	49.33	49.72- 15
Frolov	Kirill	RUS	29.9.93		20kW	1:19:49	1:21:11- 15
* Frydrych	Petr	CZE	13.1.88	198/99	JT	83.85	88.32- 17
Fujikawa	Takuya	JPN	17.12.92	161/50	10k	27:58.87	28:20.31- 14
Fujimoto	Taku	JPN	11.9.89	166/52	10k	28:08.30	28:20.96 -14
					Mar	2:07:57	-0-
Fujisawa	Isamu	JPN	12.10.87	165/53	50kW	3:58:49	-0-
Fujisawa	Isamu	JPN	12.10.87	165/53	20kW	1:19:15	1:18:23- 17
Furtula	Danijel	MNE	31.7.92	195/115	DT	63.28	64.60- 13
Furuya	Takumu	JPN	12.3.97	183/77	110h	13.61, 13.45w	13.73- 16, 13.70w- 17
* Futch	Eric	USA	25.4.93	175/70	400h	49.47	48.18- 17
^ Fyodorov	Aleksey	RUS	25.5.91	184/73	TJ	16.76	17.42- 15
Gado	Ruben	FRA	13.12.92	180/73	Dec	8126(w)	7839- 17
^ Gag	Andrei	ROU	7.4.91	195/118	SP	20.60i, 20.19	21.06- 16
Gailums	Patriks	LAT	10.5.98	192/85	JT	78.10	81.91- 17
^ Gakémé	Antoine	BDI	24.12.91	170/57	800	1:45.14	1:44.09- 15
					1000	2:16.85	2:20.25i-16
Galeta	Kristo	EST	9.4.83	190/94	SP	20.13	19.78- 16
Gallimore	Javan	JAM	7.8.93	183/75	400h	49.81	49.76- 13
Galvan	Matteo	ITA	24.8.88	182/70	400	45.17	45.12- 10
Gao Wenkui		CHN	28.7.95		20kW	1:22:46	1:23:15- 15
* Gao Xinglong		CHN	12.3.94	181/65	LJ	8.05A, 8.00	8.34- 15
Gao Yingchao		CHN	18.1.98		20kW	1:20:31	1:28:05- 16
* García	Diego	ESP	19.1.96	174/60	20kW	1:19:18	1:20:34- 17
^ García	Jesús Ángel	ESP	17.10.69	172/64	50kW	3:53:48	3:39:54- 97
García	Samuel	ESP	4.12.91	195/90	400	45.48	45.00A, 45.36- 17
Gardenkrans	Jakob	SWE	15.8.97	207/110	DT	63.63	58.09- 17
* Gardiner	Steven	BAH	12.9.95	188/75	200	19.75	20.63- 16, 20.51w- 15
					400	43.87	43.89- 17
Garn	Jesse	USA	4.6.93	179/61	800	1:46.17	1:45.04- 17
Gasch	Loïc	SUI	13.8.94	192/78	HJ	2.24	2.26- 17
Gashahun	Abe	ETH	20.4.98	165/50	3000	7:45.91	8:03.00- 16
					5000	13:22.38	
Gathimba	Samuel	KEN	26.10.87	165/57	20kW	1:19:04A	1:19:24- 16
* Gatlin	Justin	USA	10.2.82	185/79	100	10.03	9.74- 15
Gavriilídis	Nikólaos	GRE	15.3.95	191/107	HT	72.16	72.02- 16
^ Gay	Tyson	USA	9.8.82	180/73	100	10.11	9.69- 09, 9.68w- 08
Gaye	Demish	JAM	20.1.93	188/77	400	45.08	44.55- 17*

Name		Nat	Born	Ht/Wt	Event	2018 Mark	Pre-2018 Best
* Gayle	Tajay	JAM	2.8.96	183/75	LJ	8.24	8.00- 17
Gdula	Lukás	CZE	6.12.91	178/65	50kW	4:03:39	3:54:29- 16*
Gebregergish	Yohanes	ERI	11.1.94	167/50	HMar	60:16	60:21- 16
^ Gebremedhin	Mekonnen	ETH	11.10.88	180/64	1500	3:37.91	3:31.45- 12
					5000	13:22.89	13:29.37- 17
^ Gebremeskel	Dejen	ETH	24.11.89	178/53	3000	7:42.78i	7:34.14i- 12, 7:45.9- 10
* Gebrhiwet	Hagos	ETH	11.5.94	167/55	3000	7:36.49	7:30.36- 13
					5000	12:45.82	12:47.53- 12
* Gebrselassie	Leul	ETH	20.9.93	170/55	Mar	2:04:02	-0-
Geist	Jordan	USA	21.7.98	184/115	SP	21.45i, 20.41	20.83i- 16, 20.63- 17
* Gemili	Adam	GBR	6.10.93	178/73	100	10.11	9.97- 15
					200	20.10	19.97- 16
George	Winston	GUY	19.5.87	174/66	200	20.46	20.41- 17, 20.4- 14
					400	45.67A	45.16- 17
* Geremew	Mosinet	ETH	12.2.92	174/57	HMar	59:48	59:11- 14
					Mar	2:04:00	2:06:09- 17
Getahun	Betesfa	ETH	25.9.98	165/50	HMar	60:26	62:48- 16
Gezahegn	Kelkile	ETH	1.10.96	169/52	Mar	2:05:56	2:06:56- 17
Gföhler	Benjamin	SUI	27.1.94	178/75	LJ	8.00	8.13- 16
* Ghazal	Majed El Dein	SYR	21.4.87	193/70	HJ	2.33	2.36- 16
Ghuys	Bram	BEL	14.2.93	192/77	HJ	2.26	2.25- 16
^ Gibson	Jeffery	BAH	15.8.90	186/79	400h	48.98	48.17- 15
Gierek	Rafal	POL	24.2.96	193/83	JT	78.30	72.49- 17
Gikas	John	AUS-J	7.10.99	178/75	200	20.43w	
Giles	Elliot	GBR	26.5.94	173/64	800	1:45.04	1:44.99- 17
Gillespie	Cravon	USA	31.7.96	175/66	100	10.12, 10.02w	10.21, 10.04w- 16
					200	20.61, 20.26w	20.20- 16
Girk	Ryan	USA	27.4.96	185/77	100	10.11w	10.49, 10.48w- 17
Gitonga	Paul	KEN			10k	28:13.38	30:03.12- 17
Givans	Senoj-Jay	JAM	30.12.93	178/73	100	10.13	9.96- 16, 9.90w- 14
Glazunov	Ilva	RUS	20.4.94	187/77	TJ	16.67	16.46- 17
Glebauskas	Adrijus	LTU	20.11.94	201/80	HJ	2.26	2.23- 17
Godana	Abdela	ETH			Mar	2:08:32	2:09:45- 17
Golitin	Amaury	FRA	28.1.97	170/63	100	10.07	10.35, 10.32w- 17
Golovin	Aleksey	RUS	24.12.88		20kW	1:21:28	1:22:06- 14
Golubovic	Dan	USA	29.11.93	194/86	Dec	7702	7717- 17
Gomes da Silva	Aldemir	BRA	8.6.92	179/67	200	20.23A, 20.38	20.15- 17
Gómez	Joaquin	ARG	14.10.96	178/95	HT	75.96	74.28- 17
^ Gomis	Kafétien	FRA	23.3.80	183/67	LJ	8.13	8.26- 15
Gong Kewei		CHN	29.6.94	185/80	Dec	7671	7481- 17
González	Alberto	ESP	1.6.98	195/110	HT	73.02	65.82- 17
González	José Mauricio	COL	14.10.88	183/	10k	28:13.49	28:27.69- 17
Gorokhov	Georgiy	RUS	20.4.93	183/75	PV	5.70	5.70i- 16, 5.65- 15
Gotch	Jarvis	USA	25.3.92	185/73	LJ	8.27	8.24- 16, 8.37w- 17
Goto	Shuto	JPN	26.2.94		50kW	3:52:17	3:59:23- 15
Gourley	Neil	GBR	7.2.95	184/68	1500	3:35.98	3:39.92- 16
^ Grabarz	Robbie	GBR	3.10.87	192/87	HJ	2.30i, 2.21	2.37- 12
Grau	Martin	GER	26.3.92	176/64	3kSt	8:26.18	8:24.29- 14
Gray	Cordero	USA	9.5.89	173/68	100	10.13, 10.07w	10.11- 12, 10.03w- 14
Gray	Nick	USA	2.6.97	181/66	200	20.45i	20.38, 19.96w- 17
Greaux	Kyle	TTO	26.4.88	190/80	200	19.97	20.19- 17
Green	Jack	GBR	6.10.91	187/82	400h	49.18	48.60- 12
Greene	Cejhae	ANT	6.10.95	174/68	100	10.00	10.01- 16
^ Greene	David 'Dai'	GBR	11.4.86	183/75	400h	49.38A, 49.48	47.84- 12
Gregorek	John	USA	7.12.91	178/61	1500	3:36.95	3:35.00- 17
					1M	3:54.53	3:55.27- 16, 3:53.15i- 17
Gregory	Ben	GBR	21.11.90	184/82	Dec	7582	7882- 16
* Gregson	Ryan	AUS	26.4.90	184/68	1500	3:34.38	3:31.06- 10
1M	3:55.10		3:52.24- 10		3000	7:46.28	7:42.19- 17
Greguric	Matija	CRO	17.9.96	187/90	HT	72.86	72.35- 17
Grey	Rayvon	USA	2.12.97	183/70	LJ	7.96w	7.93i, 7.74- 16
Grice	Charlie Da'Vall	GBR	7.11.93	182/68	1500	3:34.20	3:33.60- 16
Griggs	Virjilio	PAN	15.6.94	183/82	200	20.38w	20.82- 17
Grimes	Isaac	USA	7.2.98	183/73	LJ	7.95Ai	7.31Ai- 17
Grimes	Norman	USA	6.1.98	188/77	400h	49.38	50.10- 15
Gripich	Aleksandr	RUS	21.9.86	190/80	PV	5.55i, 5.55	5.85i- 15, 5.75- 09
Griva	Janis Svens	LAT	23.4.93	185/90	JT	77.88	79.36- 16
Grobler	Johannes	RSA	6.8.97	176/79	JT	80.25A	80.59- 16
Grynienko	Maciej	POL	30.3.98	201/85	HJ	2.27	2.22- 17
Grzeszczuk	Lukasz	POL	3.3.90	189/95	JT	79.42	84.77- 14
Gudmundsson	Sindri Hrafn	ISL	21.11.95	178/86	JT	80.91	77.28- 14

Name		Nat	Born	Ht/Wt	Event	2018 Mark	Pre-2018 Best
Gudnason	Gudni Valur	ISL	11.10.95	198/115	DT	65.53	63.50- 15
Gudro	Andrzej	POL	8.4.94	187/108	SP	20.63	19.40- 17
* Gudzius	Andrius	LTU	14.2.91	200/130	DT	69.59	69.21- 17
Guerra	Javier	ESP	10.11.83	173/58	Mar	2:08:36	2:09:33- 15
Guerrant	Nick	USA	23.9.97	185/81	Dec	7619	6937- 16
Guevara	Asa	TTO	20.12.95	186/75	400	45.26	46.31- 17
Gulelauri	Lasha	GEO	26.5.93	174/65	TJ	16.87/A16.96 dm/16.63, 16.62i- 16, 16.58- 15	
* Guliyev	Ramil	TUR	29.5.90	187/73	100	10.10, 9.98w	9.97, 9.9 -17
					200	19.76	19.88- 15
Gusman	Jordan	AUS	30.1.94	178/64	1500	3:37.52	3:37.97- 17
Guttormsen	Sondre	NOR-J	1.6.99	183/71	PV	5.75	5.41- 17
Habte	Awet	ERI	29.9.97	172/57	10k	27:48.35	-0-
Hachisuka	Gen	JPN	29.11.94	169/49	10k	28:05.32	28:31.64- 17
* Hadadi	Ehsan	IRI	20.1.85	193/125	DT	68.85	69.32- 08
* Hadis	Abadi	ETH	6.11.97	170/63	3000	7:39.10	-0-
5000	12:56.27		13:02.49- 16		HMar	58:44	60:25- 17
Hague	Adam	GBR	29.8.97	188/73	PV	5.65I, 5.65	5.60- 15
Haile	Tilahun	ETH-J	13.5.99	171/55	3000	7:38.55	-0-
					5000	13:04.63	13:44.9A- 17
Haileselassie	Yemane	ERI	21.2.98	175/57	3kSt	8:19.61	8:11.22- 17
* Halász	Bence	HUN	4.8.97	188/93	HT	79.57	78.85- 17
Hale	Jack	AUS	22.5.98	175/66	100	10.23, 10.10w	10.21- 16, 10.13w- 14
* Hall	Elijah	USA	22.8.94	174/73	100	10.10	10.11, 10.00w- 17
					200	20.11, 20.20i	20.21, 19.96w- 17
Hall	Quincy	USA	31.7.98	185/75	400	44.60	45.12- 17
					400h	49.65	49.02- 17
Hamman	Le Roux	RSA	6.1.92	186/69	400h	49.22A, 49.35	49.24A, 49.60- 16
Hamza	Mohamed	EGY	30.8.96	189/115	SP	19.73	20.32- 16
Han Jijiang		CHN	20.7.93		50kW	3:57:33	4:00:28- 17
Hanekom	Lindsay	RSA	15.5.93	176/65	400h	49.17A	49.03A, 49.81- 16
Hann	Mamadou Kassé	FRA	10.10.86	189/79	400h	49.50	48.40- 17
Hannes	Pieter-Jan	BEL	30.10.92	186/72	1500	3:38.28	3:34.49- 14
* Haratyk	Michal	POL	10.4.92	194/136	SP	22.08	21.88- 17
Haraway	Darryl	USA	19.3.97	170/64	100	10.09	10.20- 14
Harmse	Chris	RSA	31.5.73	184/118	HT	70.62	80.63- 05
* Haroun	Abdelilah	QAT	.97	178/73	400	44.07	44.27- 15
^ Harradine	Benn	AUS	14.10.82	198/115	DT	63.56	68.20- 13
Harrell	Jason	USA	10.1.91	188/109	DT	65.48	62.28- 17
* Harris	Aleec	USA	31.10.90	185/77	110h	13.37	13.11- 15
Harris	Isaiah	USA	18.10.96	182/70	800	1:44.42	1:44.53- 17
Harris	Mar'yea	USA	24.11.97	174/66	400	44.94	45.45- 17
Harrison	Eric	USA-J	18.2.99	174/68	200	20.39, 20-.27w	21.55- 16
Härstedt	Axel	SWE	28.2.87	197/130	DT	63.17	66.03- 16
* Hartfield	Mike	USA	29.3.90	190/77	LJ	8.18Ai, 8.02	8.34- 16, 8.42w- 15
* Harting	Christoph	GER	10.4.90	207/120	DT	67.59	68.37- 16
^ Harting	Robert	GER	18.10.84	201/127	DT	65.13	70.66- 12
Hartmann	Alex	AUS	7.3.93	188/80	200	20.57, 20.44w	20.45- 16
Hartmann	Stephan	GER	13.1.94	185/84	LJ	8.20	7.93- 16
* Harvey	Jak Ali	TUR	5.4.89	182/73	100	9.99, 9.91w	9.92A- 16, 10.01- 15
					200	20.47	20.38- 15
Hashioka	Yuki	JPN-J	23.1.99	176/64	LJ	8.09, 8.30w	8.05, 8.07w- 17
Hassan	Mustafa Ahmed	EGY	16.12.95	193/118	SP	20.86i, 20.44	21.31- 17
Hassi	Juuso	FIN	4.4.93	185/79	Dec	7512	7734- 16
Hattat	Yassine	ALG	30.7.91	180/63	800	1:46.15	1:44.61- 16
					1000	2:16.59	2:16.76- 14
Hattori	Yuma	JPN	13.11.93	176/60	Mar	2:07:27	2:09:46dh-17
Haugh	Daniel	USA	3.5.95	184/105	HT	73.50	67.31- 17
* Haukenes	Håvard	NOR	22.4.90	180/68	50kW	3:48:35	3:43:40- 17
Heath	Garrett	USA	3.11.85	178/65	3000	7:47.36i	7:37.40i- 14, 7:37.97- 15
					10k	27:56.11	-0-
Heinle	Fabian	GER	14.5.94	189/73	LJ	8.13	8.25- 13
Helander	Oliver	FIN	1.1.97	195/85	JT	88.02	80.25- 17
Hemeida	Bassem	QAT-J	28.9.00	184/75	400h	49.59	-0-
* Henderson	Jeff	USA	19.2.89	178/82	LJ	8.44A, 8.20	8.52- 15, 8.59w- 16
Henriksen	Eivind	NOR	14.9.90	191/116	HT	76.86	75.57- 12
Henry	Eldred	IVB	18.9.94	196/159	SP	20.63	20.00- 15
Hepperle	Felix	GER	23.11.89	191/85	Dec	7763	7699- 17
Herman	Tim	BEL	19.10.90	179/75	JT	79.41	78.98- 12
Herrera	Yilmar Andrés	COL	29.4.96	175/65	400	45.64A	45.48A, 46.02- 17
* Hess	Max	GER	13.7.96	186/79	LJ	8.00i	8.03i- 16
					TJ	16.95	17.52i- 17, 17.20- 16, 17.24w-17

	Name		Nat	Born	Ht/Wt	Event	2018 Mark	Pre-2018 Best
	Hesselbjerg	Ole	DEN	23.4.90	183/70	3kSt	8:30.44	8:27.86- 17
	Hester	Tevin	USA	10.1.94	170/66	100	10.11, 10.09w	10.05, 9.87w- 15
						200	20.51, 20.42w	20.13- 16
	Heyward	Jake	GBR-J	26.4.99	183/68	1500	3:36.90	3:42.12- 17
	Higashi	Tomasu	JPN	14.4.97		110h	13.85, 13.58w	14.16- 17
	Higashi	Yuma	JPN	29.11.95	175/57	10k	28:03.46	29:14.78- 16
	Hilbert	Jonathan	GER	24.1.95	175/62	50kW	3:51:22	4:05:49- 17
*	Hill	Darrell	USA	17.8.93	192/150	SP	22.40	22.44- 17
	Hill	Devon	USA	26.10.89	185/75	110h	13.56	13.35- 12, 13.32w- 13
*	Hill	Ryan	USA	31.1.90	176/60	1M	3:55.48	3:54.89i- 13, 3:56.78- 12
	3000	7:36.81		7:30.93- 16		5000	13:25.46	13:05.69- 15
	Hislop	Akanni	TTO	1.6.98	175/66	200	20.39	20.84- 17
	Hite	Nathan	USA	14.5.96	192/91	Dec	7723	6274- 15
	Hoare	Oliver	AUS	29.1.97	188/73	1500	3:37.84	3:43.48- 17
	Hodelin	Edislay	CUB-J	31.10.99		TJ	16.59	16.10- 17
	Hoffmann	Karol	POL	1.6.89	197/80	TJ	16.74	17.16- 16
*	Hofmann	Andreas	GER	16.12.91	195/108	JT	92.06	91.07- 17
	Hogan	Cruz	AUS	22.2.94	186/86	JT	77.44	75.15- 16
^	Hogan	Victor	RSA	25.7.89	198/108	DT	65.20	65.33- 13, 67.62dq- 16
*	Holloway	Grant	USA	19.11.97	188/82	110h	13.15	13.39- 17
						LJ	8.17, 8.32w	8.05i, 8.04- 17
*	Holmes	Timothy TJ	USA	2.7.95	182/73	400h	48.30	48.44- 17
	Holttinen	Tommi	FIN	3.5.97	188/68	PV	5.55i, 5.51	5.40- 17
*	Holusa	Jakub	CZE	20.2.88	183/72	1500	3:32.49	3:33.36- 16
*	Holzdeppe	Raphael	GER	28.9.89	181/78	PV	5.88i, 5.81	5.94- 15
	Hopkins	Jonathan	GBR	3.6.92	184/70	3kSt	8:30.52	8:34.03- 17
	Hoppel	Bryce	USA	5.9.97	179/68	800	1:45.67	1:48.52- 17
	Hortelano	Bruno	ESP	18.9.91	181/72	200	20.04	20.12- 16
						400	44.69	46.22- 15
	Horvat	Ivan	CRO	17.8.93	188/77	PV	5.71	5.76i- 17, 5.70- 15
	I lough	Nick	AUS	20.10.93	191/86	110h	13.38	13.42- 15
	Houston	Scott	USA	11.6.90	193/79	PV	5.83Ai, 5.70	5.78- 17
	Howard	Julian	GER	3.4.89	178/75	LJ	8.20	8.15- 17
^	Howe	Andrew	ITA	12.5.85	184/73	200	20.47	20.28- 04
	Howell	Renard	JAM	3.3.95	188/82	200	20.43	20.15- 16
	Hoyte	Jaquone	BAR	4.2.98	175/66	100	10.07w	10.38, 10.14w- 17
	Hrechkovskyy	Andrey	UKR	30.8.93	174/54	50kW	3:59:32	3:49:06- 14
	Huang Bokai		CHN	26.9.96	183/75	PV	5.70	5.75i- 16, 5.55- 17
*	Huang Changzhou		CHN	20.8.94	183/75	LJ	8.19i, 8.19A, 8.16	8.28- 17
	Huang Shih-Feng		TPE	2.3.92	178/88	JT	79.93	86.64- 17
	Huber	Benedikt	GER	13.10.89	182/72	800	1:46.31	1:46.57- 16
	Huber	Brian	USA	12.6.95	186/77	LJ	7.98	
	Hubert	Axel	FRA	16.2.96	185/91	Dec	7683(w)	7526- 17
	Hudi	Ákos	HUN	10.8.91	185/95	HT	72.91	76.93- 13
	Hudson	Andrew	USA	14.12.96	180/73	200	20.38	20.43- 17
*	Hudson-Smith	Matthew	GBR	26.10.94	194/78	400	44.63	44.48- 16
*	Hughes	Matt	CAN	3.8.89	180/64	3kSt	8:12.33	8:11.64- 13
*	Hughes	Zharnel	GBR	13.7.95	190/79	100	9.91	10.10- 16, 10.08w- 17
						200	20.23, 20.12dq	20.02- 15
	Hunter	Drew	USA	5.9.97	175/61	1500	3:35.90	3:36.77- 17
	Hurisa	Derara	ETH	12.7.97	172/57	5000	13:20.33	14:31.77- 14
	Hurt	Tripp	USA	30.10.92	178/64	3kSt	8:30.69	8:37.92- 17
	Husillos	Óscar	ESP	18.7.93	180/66	400	44.73	45.16- 17
	Huslig	Landon	USA	14.4.95	185/75	400h	49.67	50.99- 17
	Huszák	János	HUN	5.2.92	197/118	DT	63.45	64.89- 16
	Hutterer	Dennis	GER	4.5.96	193/89	Dec	8032	7780- 17
*	Hyde	Jaheel	JAM	2.2.97	180/73	400h	49.14	48.52- 17
	Hyman	Kemar	CAY	11.10.89	178/74	100	10.10	9.95- 12, 9.85Aw- 15
	Ibadin	Edose	NGR	27.2.93	172/64	800	1:45.69	1:45.87- 17
	Ibáñez	Anatole	SWE	14.11.85	177/69	50kW	4:03:53	3:48:42- 14
	Ibargüen	Arley	COL	4.12.82	182/85	JT	81.40A	81.23A- 16, 81.07- 09
	Ibrahim	Mohamed Ismail	DJI	1.7.97	171/60	1500	3:37.02	3:36.98- 17
						3kSt	8:23.65	8:23.77- 16
	Igbokwe	Obie	USA	28.1.97	181/73	400	44.94	45.54- 17
*	Iguider	Abdelaati	MAR	25.3.87	170/52	1500	3:31.59	3:28.79- 15
						3000	7:39.92i	7:30.09- 16
	Iizuka	Shota	JPN	25.6.91	185/80	200	20.34	20.11- 16
*	Ikeda	Koki	JPN	3.5.98	168/53	20kW	1:19:13	1:20:48- 17
	Imoto	Yoshinobu	JPN-J	31.7.99	168/55	200	20.59, 20.42w	21.09- 17
*	Ingebrigtsen	Filip	NOR	20.4.93	187/75	1500	3:30.01	3:32.43- 16

Name		Nat	Born	Ht/Wt	Event	2018 Mark	Pre-2018 Best
* Ingebrigtsen	Henrik	NOR	24.2.91	180/69	1500	3:35.61	3:31.46- 14
3000	7:42.72		7:42.19- 13		5000	13:16.97	13:27.10- 15
* Ingebrigtsen	Jakob	NOR-J	19.9.00	181/65	1500	3:31.18	3:39.92- 17
1M	3:52.28		3:56.29- 17		5000	13:17.06	13:35.84- 17
Inoue	Hiroto	JPN	6.1.93	164/53	10k	27:56.27	28:08.04- 17
					Mar	2:06:54	2:08:22- 17
Inoue	Kakeru	JPN	19.3.96	171/57	400h	49.54	50.31- 17
Irfan	Kolothum Thodi	IND	8.2.90	184/59	20kW	1:21:32	1:20:21- 12
Iribarne	Roger	CUB	2.1.96	183/68	110h	13.48	13.39- 17
Irwin	Andrew	USA	23.1.93	190/84	PV	5.87i, 5.72	5.75i- 15, 5.75- 17
Isene	Ola Stunes	NOR	29.1.95	193/106	DT	63.30	61.36- 16
Ishii	Katsuya	JPN	25.10.97		50kW	4:05:41	-0-
Ishiyama	Ayumu	JPN	2.6.96	179/91	JT	79.44	77.91- 17
Ismail	Muhammad Hakimi	MAS	8.4.91	188/80	TJ	16.61	16.77- 17
Ito	Yuki	JPN	12.4.92		50kW	4:06:20	3:55:54- 15
Ivakin	Anton	RUS	3.2.91	178/73	PV	5.56i	5.70i- 15, 5.65- 14
Ivanov	Ivan	KAZ	3.1.92	202/144	SP	19.81i, 19.40	20.51i-dm- 16, 20.00- 17
Ivanov	Tihomir	BUL	11.7.94	198/77	HJ	2.28i	2.31- 17
Ivanytskyy	Vasyl	UKR	29.1.91	186/80	Dec	7708	7801- 17
Ivanyuk	Ilya	RUS	9.3.93	183/75	HJ	2.31i, 2.31	2.31i- 17, 2.30- 15
Izotov	Valeriy	BLR	12.4.97	186/86	JT	78.20	76.50- 17
* Jackson	Bershawn	USA	8.5.83	173/69	400h	49.08	47.30- 05
Jacobs	Lamont Marcell	ITA	26.9.94	188/79	100	10.08, 10.04w	10.23- 16
Jacobus	Derek	USA	23.7.95	185/86	Dec	7555	7635- 17
* Jager	Evan	USA	8.3.89	186/66	5000	13:24.77	13:02.40- 13
					3kSt	8:01.02	8:00.45- 15
Jagers	Phillip	USA	12.8.95	183/95	DT	61.68	62.71- 16
* Jagers	Reggie	USA	13.8.94	188/118	DT	68.61	62.51- 17
Jainaga	Odel	ESP	14.10.97	193/80	JT	80.64	77.66A- 17
James	Amir	USA	7.12.95	175/79	100	10.12w	10.36, 10.19w- 16
					200	20.41	20.63, 20.56w- 17
James	Kasuan	USA	22.12.97	175/68	200	20.69, 20.25w	
* James	Kirani	GRN	1.9.92	185/74	400	44.35	43.74- 14
^ Janet	Roberto	CUB	29.8.86	187/106	HT	74.02	78.02- 15
Janezic	Luka	SLO	14.11.95	192/83	400	44.93	44.84- 17
Jaramillo	Geormi	VEN	6.3.89	185/80	Dec	8048	8126w, 8039- 17
* Jasinski	Daniel	GER	5.8.89	207/125	DT	66.59	67.16- 16
Jaszczuk	Tomasz	POL	9.3.92	195/83	LJ	8.10	8.18- 17
Jayasiri	W.P.Amila	SRI	24.1.94	173/63	LJ	8.01, 8.02w	8.15- 16
Jefferson	Chris	USA	25.3.96	180/74	100	10.12, 10.08w	10.31, 10.08w- 17
					200	20.37	20.61- 17
Jelassi	Mohamed Fares	TUN	29.7.97	182/75	400	45.55	48.59i-17
Jelonek	Jakub	POL	7.7.85	184/71	50kW	4:05:28	-0-
Jenkins	Eric	USA	24.11.91	170/61	3000	7:38.19	7:39.43i- 16, 7:40.36- 17
					5000	13:21.41	13:07.33- 15, 13:05.85i- 17
Jensen	Curtis	USA	1.11.90	193/130	SP	21.63	20.69- 17
Jensen	Jonas Kløjgaard	DEN	29.2.96	197/77	HJ	2.26	2.23- 15
de Jesus	Mikael Antonio	BRA	19.8.97	183/70	400h	49.78	49.62- 16
Jeuschede	Jan Josef	GER	23.4.93	187/110	SP	19.62	19.49- 17
Jie Lei		CHN	8.5.89		LJ	8.09A	8.07- 14
Jilek	Jaroslav	CZE	22.10.89	183/85	JT	81.44	83.19- 16
Jin Min-sub		KOR	2.9.92	185/77	PV	5.67	5.65- 14
Jin Xiangqian		CHN	18.3.97	175/60	20kW	1:20:24	1:10:12- 17
Jinesh	V.O.	IND	10.4.92		LJ	7.95	7.69- 17
* Jobodwana	Anaso	RSA	30.7.92	187/71	100	10.07Aw	10.10 -13
					200	20.07	19.87- 15
John	Alexander	GER	3.5.86	185/77	110h	13.44	13.35- 09
Johnson	Cheswill	RSA	30.9.97	175/64	LJ	8.12	7.81A, 7.90Aw- 17
Johnson	Jinson	IND	15.3.91	180/68	800	1:45.65	1:45.98 -16
					1500	3:37.86	3:44.9- 16
Johnson	McKay	USA	15.4.98	180/105	SP	19.80	18.71- 17
Johnson	T'Mond	USA	29.7.97	181/136	SP	19.79	19.03- 17
Jones	Jonathan	USA	23.4.91	183/127	SP	20.65	20.93- 17
Jones	Osian	GBR	23.6.93	185/102	HT	71.62	70.00- 17
Jónsson	Hilmar Örn	ISL	6.5.96	183/107	HT	71.60	72.38- 17
Joo Hyun-myong		KOR	31.5.97	172/64	20kW	1:22:34	1:25:51- 17
					50kW	4:02:38	-0-
Jordan	Alphonso	USA	1.11.87	190/75	TJ	16.55	16.89- 15
Jørgensen	Rasmus	DEN	23.1.89	180/75	PV	5.55i	5.65- 13
Joseph	Jason	SUI	11.10.98	188/75	110h	13.39, 13.38w	13.93- 17
Joseph	Stanley	FRA	24.10.91	181/71	PV	5.72	5.75- 16

Name		Nat	Born	Ht/Wt	Event	2018 Mark	Pre-2018 Best
Jovancevic	Strahinja	SRB	28.2.93	187/74	LJ	7.98	7.92- 16
Ju Eun-jae		KOR	12.6.93	190/78	LJ	8.06, 8.07w	7.83, 7.86w- 17
Julmis	Jeffrey	HAI	6.1.87	183/80	110h	13.63	13.47- 16, 13.38w- 11
Junghannss	Karl	GER	6.4.96	179/57	20kW	1:22:51	1:22:08- 17
					50kW	4:02:36	3:47:01- 17
* Juska	Radek	CZE	8.3.93	195/82	LJ	8.27	8.31- 17
Kaazouzi	Brahim	MAR	15.6.90	175/62	1500	3:31.62	3:34.46- 17
Kagimoto	Masahiro	JPN	29.9.95	182/71	110h	13.66	13.72- 16
Kajiki	Ryo	JPN	8.12.95	176/62	400h	49.46	49.33- 17
Kalalei	Ismael	KEN	25.5.95		HMar	60:47	62:13- 16
* Kamworor	Geoffrey	KEN	22.11.92	168/54	HMar	60:02	58:54- 13
					Mar	2:06:26	2:06:12- 12
Kanai	Taio	JPN	28.9.95	179/65	110h	13.36	13.53, 13.46w- 17
Kandie	Cleophas	KEN-J	14.8.00	161/48	3kSt	8:27.57	8:30.9A- 17
* Kandie	Felix	KEN	10.4.87	178/62	Mar	2:08:30	2:06:03- 17
Kangas	Aaron	FIN	3.7.97	180/90	HT	72.09	70.30- 17
Kangas	Arttu	FIN	13.7.93	186/108	SP	19.90i, 19.57	20.30- 16
Kangogo	Justus	KEN	10.10.95	173/55	HMar	60:24	59:31- 17
Kanno	Tomofumi	JPN	25.4.93		50kW	4:06:32	3:54:24- 15
* Kanter	Gerd	EST	6.5.79	196/125	DT	64.46	73.38- 06
^ Karailiev	Momchil	BUL	21.5.82	188/75	TJ	16.69i, 16.56	17.41- 09
* Karalís	Emmanouíl	GRE-J	20.10.99	183/75	PV	5.80i	5.70i, 5.63- 17
Kårbø	Tom Erling	NOR	4.2.89	188/75	3kSt	8:29.41	8:34.19- 17
Kariuki	John	KEN	24.11.97	166/50	5000	13:23.01	13:32.87- 17
Kariuki	Simon	KEN	13.2.92	171/54	10k	27:56.04	27:53.50- 16
Karl	Patrick	GER	3.5.96	190/74	3kSt	8:31.81	8:35.93- 16
* Karlström	Perseus	SWE	2.5.90	184/73	20kW	1:20:30	1:19:11- 16
					50kW	3:48:54	3:44:35- 17
* Karoki	Bedan	KEN	21.8.90	169/53	HMar	58:42	59:10- 17
					Mar	2:07:59	2:07:41- 17
Kasana	Vipin	IND	4.8.89	180/79	JT	80.04	78.08- 04
Katsuki	Hayato	JPN	28.11.90	168/58	50kW	3:44:31	3:48:36- 17
Kaul	Niklas	GER	11.2.98	192/84	Dec	8220	-0-
Kawai	Daiji	JPN	22.9.91	174/53	10k	28:08.52	28:44.27- 16
Kawano	Masatora	JPN	23.10.98		20kW	1:19:52	1:23:51- 17
					50kW	3:47:30	
Kawashima	Tazuma	JPN	16.8.96		LJ	8.04w	7.92, 7.97w- 16
* Kazmirek	Kai	GER	28.1.91	189/91	Dec	8329	8580- 16
* Kebede	Tariku	ETH	.96		Mar	2:08:19	2:07:48- 17
* Kebede	Tsegaye	ETH	15.1.87	158/50	Mar	2:05:21	2:04:38- 12
* Kebenei	Stanley	USA	6.11.89	174/61	3kSt	8:28.39	8:08.30- 17
Keenan	Adam	CAN	26.3.93	180/102	HT	72.72	72.57- 17
Kehr	Gabriel Enrique	CHI	3.9.96	190/114	HT	74.31	71.33- 16
Keitany	Evans	KEN-J	27.11.99	181/65	5000	13:18.34	13:21.72- 17
					10k	27:40.69	-0-
* Kejelcha	Yomif	ETH	1.8.97	186/58	1500	3:32.59	3:32.94- 17
3000	7:28.00	7:28.19- 16		5000	12:46.79	12:53.98- 15	HMar	59:17	-0-
Kelly	Adam	USA	6.7.97	186/104	HT	71.92	68.96- 17
Kemboi	Clement	KEN	1.2.92	180/65	3kSt	8:25.49	8:10.65- 16
Kemboi	Edward	KEN	12.12.91	170/57	800	1:46.07	1:44.77- 17
^ Kemboi	Ezekiel	KEN	25.5.82	175/62	3kSt	8:31.45A	7:55.76- 11
Kemboi	Lawrence	KEN	15.6.93	170/57	3kSt	8:15.07	8:17.79- 16
Kemei	Moses	KEN	3.9.93	163/50	HMar	60:44	
Kemper	Deante	USA	27.3.93	181/70	HJ	2.24	2.27Ai- 16, 2.24- 17
Kipsambu	Hilary	KEN	4.2.85	163/52	Mar	2:07:20	2:09:28- 17
Kipserem	Marius	KLEN	17.5.88	172/57	Mar	2:07:22	2:06:11- 16
* Kendricks	Sam	USA	7.9.92	189/79	PV	5.96	6.00- 17
Kendziera	David	USA	9.9.94	190/84	110h	13.40	13.39- 17
					400h	48.42	49.00- 17
Keränen	Toni	FIN	16.6.98	185/85	JT	78.86	72.43- 17
* Kerley	Fred	USA	7.5.95	188/86	200	20.41	20.24- 17
					400	44.33	43.70- 17
Kerley	My'Lik	USA	6.6.96	193/75	400	45.16i	44.85- 17
Kern	Jared	USA	10.6.95	185/125	SP	20.39	20.47i, 19.65- 17
Kerr	Hamish	NZL	17.8.96	197/80	HJ	2.25	2.17- 17
Kerr	Jared	CAN	25.6.95	173/63	LJ	8.14	7.85- 14
Kerr	Josh	GBR	8.10.97	186/73	1500	3:35.01	3:35.99- 17
					1M	3:54.72i	3:59.90i- 17
Kessler	Christoph	GER	28.4.95	190/74	800	1:46.11	1:46.71- 17
Keter	Kenneth	KEN	4.8.96	165/50	Mar	2:07:34	
Keyhani	Hossein	IRI	26.4.90	175/63	3kSt	8:22.79	8:33.76- 17

Name		Nat	Born	Ht/Wt	Event	2018 Mark	Pre-2018 Best
Khodjayev	Sukhrob	UZB	21.5.93	186/105	HT	74.06	78.22- 15
Khoua	Mohcine	MAR	26.7.98	191/80	LJ	8.09	7.91- 17, 7.97w- 16
Khudyakov	Aleksey	RUS	31.3.95	191/107	DT	64.75	63.38- 17
Kibet	Alex	KEN	20.10.90	172/52	HMar	59:06	59:32- 17
					Mar	2:07:09	-0-
Kibet	James	KEN	10.11.88	172/57	3000	7:43.13	
Kibet	Michael	KEN-J	3.9.99	172/57	1500	3:36.33	
Kibet	Moses	UGA	23.3.91	165/55	10k	27:56.12	28:05.71- 14
Kibet	Stephen	KEN	9.11.86	172/55	HMar	60:39	58:54- 12
* Kibet	Vincent	KEN	6.5.91	173/57	1500	3:36.12	3:31.96 -14
Kibitok	Felix	KEN	.91	172/55	HMar	59:21	63:26A-17
* Kibiwot	Abraham	KEN	6.4.96	175/55	3kSt	8:10.62	8:09.25- 16
* Kifle	Aron	ERI	20.2.98	167/52	5000	13:07.59	13:13.31- 17
					HMar	59:51	-0-
* Kigen	Benjamin	KEN	5.7.93	173/57	3000	7:44.77i	
					3kSt	8:06.19	8:11.38- 17
Kigen	Nobert	KEN	24.1.93	165/52	Mar	2:05:22	2:05:13- 17
Kim Byung-jun		KOR	15.8.91	190/80	110h	13.57	13.39- 17
^ Kim Hyun-sub		KOR	31.5.85	175/53	20kW	1:21:52	1:19:13- 15
Kimeli	Bernard	KEN	10.9.95	172/55	5000	13:17.65	-0-
10k	27:26.27		28:09.46- 17		HMar	59:47	-0-
Kimeli	Isaac	BEL	9.3.94	175/59	1500	3:36.51	3:37.66- 17
					5000	13:21.09	13:34.48- 14
Kimitei	Wilfred	KEN	11.3.85	172/57	HMar	59:40	60:12- 17
Kimutai	Andrew	KEN	12.8.89		Mar	2:08:32	2:10:22- 17
Kimutai	Marius	KEN	.89	167/57	Mar	2:07:45	2:05:47- 16
Kiname	Ryo	JPN	22.1.91	168/53	Mar	2:08:08	2:10:30- 17
Kincaid	Woody	USA	21.9.92	173/55	3000	7:47.19i	7:48.89i-16
King	David	GBR	13.6.94	186/77	110h	13.53	13.48- 17, 13.4- 16
King	Devin	USA	12.3.96	185/75	PV	5.80	5.70- 16
King	Dominic	GBR	30.5.83	179/60	50kW	4:06:34	3:55:48- 16
Kinnunen	Jami	FIN	31.3.95	184/78	JT	78.44	78.12- 16
Kinnunen	Jarkko	FIN	19.1.84	187/69	50kW	3:52:40	3:46:25- 12
* Kinyamal	Wycliffe	KEN	2.7.97	186/75	800	1:43.12	1:43.94- 17
Kinyor	Job	KEN	2.9.90	176/68	800	1:45.84	1:43.76- 12
Kipchirchir	Shadrack	USA	22.2.89	175/60	1M	3:55.52i	4:07.13i- 11
3000	7:42.71i 7:56.20i-13		5000	13:20.28		13:18.52- 16 10k 27:39.65	27:07.55- 17
Kipchirchir Rotich	Elisha	KEN	12.4.90	170/55	Mar	2:07:32	2:08:58- 17
Kipchoge	Cosmas	KEN	21.3.86	176/63	HMar	60:06	60:23- 15
					Mar	2:08:03	2:08:45- 17
* Kipchoge	Eliud	KEN	5.11.84	167/52	Mar	2:01:39	2:03:05- 16, 2:00:25irr- 17
Kipchumba	Abel	KEN	3.2.94	166/52	HMar	59:29	63:10- 17
Kipchumba	Daniel	KEN	12.12.97	172/57	HMar	59:06	
Kipkemboi	Noah	KEN	2.7.93		HMar	60:52	
Kipkemboi Kibet	Moses	KEN	20.11.94	177/60	800	1:45.62A	1:45.7A- 17
Kipkemoi	Daniel	KEN	5.7.96	170/52	5000	13:25.99	13:26.38- 17
					10k	27:30.47	27:45.46- 17
* Kipkemoi	Kenneth	KEN	2.8.84	165/54	Mar	2:05:44	2:17:41A-13
* Kipketer	Alfred	KEN	26.12.96	169/61	800	1:44.28	1:42.87- 16
* Kipketer	Gideon	KEN	10.11.92	178/57	Mar	2:06:15	2:05:51- 17
^ Kipkoech ¶	Nicholas	KEN	22.10.92	168/57	800	1:45.20dq	1:43.37A-16
					1000	2:16.17dq	2:16.68- 16
Kipkosgei	Fredrick	KEN	13.11.96	170/57	5000	13:26.21	13:13.16- 17
Kiplagat	Benjamin	UGA	4.3.89	186/61	3kSt	8:27.17A	8:03.81- 10
Kiplagat	Shadrack	KEN	12.12.90	172/57	HMar	60:06	
Kiplagat	Thomas	KEN	.87		Mar	2:07:12?	2:07:52- 14
Kiplangat	Davis	KEN	10.7.98	167/52	3000	7:43.98, 7:40.12i	7:38.33- 17
5000	13:13.55		13:16.35- 16		10k	27:51.20	28:53.28A-16
Kipleting	Jonathan	KEN	20.11.86	171/55	Mar	2:06:51	2:17:40A-17
* Kiplimo	Jacob	UGA-J	14.11.00	170/55	5000	13:19.66	13:13.64- 17
					10k	27:30.25	27:26.68- 16
Kiplimo	Joash	KEN	.91	184/65	3kSt	8:26.24	8:24.26A- 15
Kiplimo	Laban	KEN		183/65	1500	3:37.37A	
Kipngetich	Ngeno	KEN-J	17.8.00	171/57	800	1:46.45	1:48.65A- 17
Kiprono	Festus	KEN	29.12.95	175/57	3kSt	8:31.86A	8:26.24- 15
* Kiprop	Stephen	KEN-J	8.9.99	173/52	HMar	59:21	-0-
Kiprop Chebobor	Kenneth	KEN	2.8.84	165/54	Mar	2:08:26	2:09:44- 17
Kiprotich	Brimin	KEN-J	20.8.99	174/57	1500	3:35.81	3:41.85A-15
Kiprotich	Felix	KEN	.88		Mar	2:07:57	2:06:54- 17
Kiprotich	Peter	KEN	.98		5000	13:26.46	-0-
* Kiprotich	Stephen	UGA	27.2.89	172/56	Mar	2:07:57	2:06:33- 15

Name		Nat	Born	Ht/Wt	Event	2018 Mark	Pre-2018 Best
Kiprugut	Boaz	KEN	18.5.98	173/61	800	1:45.22A	1:44.64A- 16
					1500	3:37.81	3:36.47- 17
* Kipruto	Amos	KEN	19.9.92	165/50	Mar	2:06:23	2:05:43- 17
Kipruto	Benson	KEN	.91	167/52	Mar	2:07:11	2:07:21- 17
* Kipruto	Conseslus	KEN	8.12.94	171/55	3kSt	8:08.40	8:00.12- 16
* Kipruto	Rhonex	KEN-J	12.10.99	172/57	10k	27:21.08	28:56.5A- 17
* Kipsang	Wilson	KEN	15.3.82	178/59	Mar	2:06:48	2:03:13- 16
Kipserem	Marius	KEN	17.5.88		Mar	2:04:04?, 2:07:22	2:06:11- 16
^ Kiptanui	Eliud	KEN	6.6.89	169/55	Mar	2:08:20	2:05:21- 15
Kiptanui	Erick	KEN	19.4.90	173/62	10k	28:17.1A	
					HMar	58:42	-0-
Kiptanui	Jeremiah	KEN-J	.00	167/54	1500	3:36.98A	
Kiptarus	Dominic	KEN	3.8.96	168/52	10k	28:05.34	-0-
					HMar	59:55	60:53- 17
Kiptoo	Edwin Kiprop	KEN	14.8.93	181/60	HMar	59:28	59:26- 15
Kiptoo	Ewin	KEN	28.12.87		HMar	60:52	60:06- 17
^ Kiptoo	Mark Kosgei	KEN	21.6.76	175/64	Mar	2:07:50	2:06:00- 15
* Kiptum	Abraham	KEN	15.9.89	175/57	HMar	58:18	59:36- 16
					Mar	2:06:29, 2:04:16?	2:05:26- 17
Kipyatich	Abraham	KEN	10.5.93	171/50	10k	27:44.92	28:03.92- 17
					HMar	60:08	60:03- 15
Kipyego	Barnabas	KEN	12.6.95	176/57	3kSt	8:17.08	8:09.13- 16
Kipyego	Barselius	KEN	23.7.93	174/55	HMar	60:25	59:14- 17
					Mar	2:08:47	2:13:06- 17
Kipyegon	Bernard	KEN	19.12.90	181/65	800	1:46.0A	1:45.21A- 17
Kirchler	Hannes	ITA	22.12.78	191/113	DT	63.55	65.01- 07
* Kiriazis	Ioánnis	GRE	19.1.96	194/98	JT	80.33	88.01- 17
Kirongo	Sammy	KEN	4.2.94	176/62	800	1:46.21	1:45.3A, 1:45.38 -14
* Kirt	Magnus	EST	10.4.90	192/89	JT	89.75	86.65- 15
* Kirui	Abel	KEN	4.6.82	177/62	Mar	2:07:07	2:05:04- 09
* Kirui	Amos	KEN	9.2.98	169/54	3kSt	8:12.24	8:08.37- 17
* Kirui	Geoffrey	KEN	16.2.93	170/54	Mar	2:06:45	2:06:27- 16
Kirya	Aleksandr	RUS	23.3.92	187/102	DT	60.70	62.22- 17
Kiryu	Yoshihide	JPN	15.12.95	175/69	100	10.10	9.98- 17, 9.87w- 15
Kishimoto	Takayuki	JPN	6.5.90	171/61	400h	49.30	48.41- 12
Kishoyan	Alphas	KEN	12.10.94	164/60	400	45.65A	44.75A, 45.81- 15
^ Kisorio	Mathew	KEN	16.5.89	178/62	Mar	2:04:53	2:06:33- 15
Kissa	Stephen	UGA	1.12.95	174/61	5000	13:10.93	13:13.00- 17
* Kitilit	Jonathan	KEN	24.4.94	171/61	800	1:43.46A	1:43.05- 16
					1000	2:16.27	2:13.95- 16
Kitonyi	Daniel	KEN	12.1.94	163/51	10k	27:47.19	27:49.89- 16
^ Kitwara	Sammy	KEN	26.11.86	177/54	Mar	2:06:21	2:04:28- 14
Kivistik	Kaur	EST	29.4.91	179/68	3kSt	8:28.84	8:32.23- 15
^ Kivuva	Jackson	KEN	11.8.88	172/59	800	1:44.73A	1:43.72- 10
					1000	2:16.79	2:17.47- 08
Kloptsov	Yuriy	RUS	22.12.89	176/64	3kSt	8:29.42	8:28.03- 14
Knight	Corion	USA	18.8.96	193/84	LJ	8.02i, 8.06w	7.66- 16
1500	3:36.07			3:39.23- 16	3000	7:45.86i	7:47.82i- 17
Knight	Justyn	CAN	19.7.96	171/59	5000	13:18.74	13:17.51- 17
* Kobayashi	Kai	JPN	28.2.93	165/53	20kW	1:21:29	1:19:12- 15
					3		
					50kW	3:46:26	3:41:19- 17
Kobielski	Norbert	POL	28.1.97	202/80	HJ	2.26	2.26- 17
Koech	Bernard	KEN-J	25.11.99	173/57	5000	13:27.37	
					10k	27:31.83	-0-
^ Koech	Haron	KEN	27.1.90	188/79	400h	49.28	48.49- 16
Koech	John Kibet	BRN	23.8.95	174/59	3kSt	8:22.00	8:09.62- 16
Koech	Jonah	KEN	12.12.96	175/61	800	1:46.23	1:46.53- 16
Koech	Paul	KEN	.91	167/52	3000	7:41.97i	
^ Koech	Paul Kipsiele	KEN	10.11.81	168/57	3kSt	8:23.22	7:54.31- 12
Koga	Yutaro	JPN-J	15.7.99	176/57	20kW	1:21:54	1:26:23- 17
Koike	Yuki	JPN	13.5.95	178/72	200	20.23	20.58- 17, 20.34w- 14
* Kolasinac	Asmir	SRB	15.10.84	186/137	SP	20.48	21.58- 15
Kolomoyets	Sergey	BLR	11.8.89	191/110	HT	78.13	77.52- 11
Kominami	Takuto	JPN	26.7.95	172/80	JT	80.18	79.17- 17
^ Komon	Leonard	KEN	10.1.88	175/52	HMar	60:52	59:14- 14
Koppelaar	Rutger	NED	1.5.93	187/73	PV	5.70	5.65i. 5.60- 17
Korir	Albert	KEN	2.3.94	184/62	Mar	2:08:17	2:08:40- 17
* Korir	Emmanuel	KEN	15.6.95	177/64	400	44.21A, 44.52	44.53A- 17
					800	1:42.05	1:43.10- 17
Korir	Evans	KEN	.87	168/54	Mar	2:06:35	2:09:42- 17

Name		Nat	Born	Ht/Wt	Event	2018 Mark	Pre-2018 Best
^ Korir	Japheth	KEN	30.6.93	168/55	5000	13:11.86	13:11.44i- 12, 13:14.56- 17
					HMar	60:09	60:08- 17
Korir	Laban	KEN	30.12.85	162/50	Mar	2:05:58	2:05:54- 16
* Korir	Leonard	USA	10.12.86	173/61	HMar	60:12	59:52- 17
Korir	Mark	KEN	10.1.85	175/59	Mar	2:07:03	2:05:49- 15
Koroknai	Maté	HUN	13.1.93	191/79	400h	49.77	50.33- 14
Koroknai	Tibor	HUN	24.1.90	190/77	400h	49.24	49.74- 17
Koros	Wilberforce	KEN	.93		3kSt	8:22.55	8:29.8A- 17
Korotovskiy	Yevgeniy	RUS	21.6.92	184/102	HT	77.29	74.46- 16
Korshunov	Yevgeniy	RUS	11.4.86	193/84	HJ	2.28	2.29i- 14, 2.26- 15
Kosciów	Dawid	POL	5.6.90	193/95	JT	80.64	78.80- 17
Kosgei	Lawi	KEN-J	14.1.99	171/57	1500	3:38.28A	3:40.77- 15
Kosgei	Martin	KEN	21.3.89		Mar	2:06:41	2:07:22- 16
Kosimbei	Nicholas	KEN	10.1.96	175/59	5000	13:24.79	13:17.08- 16
10k	27:49.49		27:02.59- 16		HMar	60:21	-0-
Kostoglídis	Konstadínos	GRE	10.8.90	181/101	HT	70.72	75.10- 16
Kounta	Muhammad Abdalla	FRA	27.10.94	184/70	400h	49.41	50.84- 17
Koussi	Mohamed	MAR	15.3.94	182/77	110h	13.63	13.69- 16
* Kovacs	Joe	USA	28.6.89	181/132	SP	21.02	22.57- 17
* Kövágó	Zoltán	HUN	10.4.79	204/127	DT	65.66	69.95- 06
^ Kowal	Yoann	FRA	28.5.87	174/58	3kSt	8:27.08	8:12.53- 13
Kramer	Andreas	SWE	13.4.97	190/73	800	1:45.03	1:45.13- 17
Krauss	Simon	FRA	12.2.92	182/77	110h	13.68	13.50- 14, 13.41w- 13
Kregers	Reinis	LAT	22.1.92	188/82	Dec	7519	7618-14
Kroyter	Dmitriy	ISR	18.2.93	189/71	HJ	2.26	2.29- 15
Kruger	A.G.	USA	18.2.79	193/118	HT	72.84	79.26- 04
* Krukowski	Marcin	POL	14.6.92	182/92	JT	85.32	88.09- 17
* Kszczot	Adam	POL	2.9.89	178/64	800	1:44.59	1:43.30- 11
					1000	2:16.58	2:15.72- 14
^ Kudlicka	Jan	CZE	29.4.88	184/76	PV	5.55	5.83- 16
Kuhn	Daniel	USA	11.8.95	183/68	800	1:46.06	1:46.69- 16
Kujanpää	Urho	FIN	18.5.97	188/80	PV	5.55	5.55i, 5.45- 17
* Kuma	Abera	ETH	31.8.90	160/50	Mar	2:05:50	2:05:56- 14
Kumar	Amit	IND	18.9.92	182/88	JT	79.16	79.14- 16
Kumar	Sandeep	IND	16.12.86	183/68	50kW	3:56:40	3:56:00- 17
Kumar	T. Santhosh	IND	1.1.98	176/64	400h	49.66	50.16- 17
^ Kupper	Martin	EST	31.5.89	195/108	DT	63.72	66.67- 15
Kurbanov	Ruslan	UZB	10.2.93	180/73	TJ	16.70	16.40, 16.87dm- 16
Kurgat	Amos	KEN	7.3.92	160/48	10k	27:32.04	
Kuriki	Anthony Tyrell	JPN	17.9.96	187/75	110h	13.64, 13.57w	13.60- 17
Kurong	Moses	UGA	7.7.94	165/52	HMar	60:10	59:50- 17
Kushare	Sarvesh Anil	IND	17.6.95		HJ	2.24	2.21- 17
Kushniruk	Yuriy	UKR	6.12.94	181/92	JT	80.55	78.40- 17
Kuusela	Toni	FIN	21.1.94	183/82	JT	78.45	75.63- 13
* Kwemoi	Ronald	KEN	19.9.95	180/68	5000	13:19.86	13:16.14- 15
* Kynard	Eric	USA	3.2.91	193/86	HJ	2.31i, 2.29	2.37- 13
Laanmäe	Tanel	EST	29.9.89	183/94	JT	82.36	85.04- 16
Lagat	Haron	USA	15.8.83	185/72	3kSt	8:28.88	8:15.80- 11
Lagat	Justus	KEN	20.5.96	168/55	3kSt	8:19.51	8:18.46- 17
Lahbabi	Aziz	MAR	3.2.91	169/55	HMar	60:48	59:14- 14
Lahoulou	Abdelmalik	ALG	7.5.92	180/70	400h	48.47	48.62- 16
Laidig	Torben	GER	13.3.94	187/82	PV	5.60	5.70- 17
Laine	Keenon	USA	12.6.97	193/79	HJ	2.27i, 2.26	2.25- 17
Laird	Terrance	USA	12.10.98	175/64	200	20.41	21.27- 16
Lakka	Elmo	FIN	10.4.93	183/83	110h	13.60	13.69- 17
Lalang	Lawi	KEN	15.6.91	170/58	5000	13:24.09	13:00.95- 13
Lambrughi	Mario	ITA	5.2.92	184/74	400h	48.99	49.35- 16
Lamou	Martin	FRA-J	13.5.99	182/70	TJ	16.89i, 16.76	16.97- 17
Lane	John	GBR	29.1.89	186/88	Dec	7545	7965- 17
Langat	Clement	KEN	18.12.91	180/65	HMar	60:29	64:01- 16
Langat	Dominic	KEN	15.5.98	177/59	10k	27:44.27	-0-
Langat	John	KEN	31.12.96	170/63	HMar	60:24	60:41- 17
Langat	Leonard	KEN	7.8.90	170/55	HMar	59:41	59:18- 16
Langat	Peter	KEN	20.10.98	169/55	5000	13:22.69	13:37.34A-16
Langat	Wesley	KEN			3kSt	8:32.08A	
Langford	Kyle	GBR	2.2.96	183/66	800	1:45.16	1:45.25- 17
Langowski	Artur	BRA	8.5.91	183/77	400h	49.18	49.73- 15
Langton-Burnell	Benjamin	NZL	10.7.92	183/82	JT	78.20	82.44- 17
Larkins	Micah	USA	8.12.94	173/75	100	10.12, 10.02w	10.26- 17, 10.15w- 16
Lasa	Emiliano	URU	25.1.90	180/75	LJ	8.26A	8.19- 17
Lasater	Brandon	USA	9.10.92	184/73	800	1:45.85	1:47.09- 17

Name		Nat	Born	Ht/Wt	Event	2018 Mark	Pre-2018 Best
Latimer	Jordan	USA	4.3.94	190/82	LJ	8.02	7.81- 15
Lattin	Amere	USA	17.2.97	188/79	110h	13.60	13.59- 16
					400h	49.70	50.59- 17
* Lavillenie	Renaud	FRA	18.9.86	177/71	PV	5.95	6.16i- 14, 6.05- 15
Lavillenie	Valentin	FRA	16.7.91	170/66	PV	5.72i	5.80i- 15, 5.71- 16
Lawler	Marcus	IRL	28.2.95	185/77	200	20.40	20.71, 20.43w- 17
Lawson	TJ	USA	25.1.97	193/84	Dec	7724(w)	7725- 17
* Lawson	Jarrion	USA	6.5.94	188/75	LJ	8.38Ai, 8/25	8.58- 16
Layoy	Carlos	ARG	26.2.91	184/66	HJ	2.25A	2.24- 12
Learmonth	Guy	GBR	20.4.92	184/73	800	1:44.73	1:45.10- 17
Lebioda	Piotr	POL	28.5.92	187/85	JT	78.44	78.56- 16
Ledama	Kisaisa	KEN	25.6.98	168/52	10k	27:43.52	28:14.79- 17
					HMar	60:44	-0-
Ledama	Wesley	KEN-J	2.7.99	173/57	5000	13:24.75	13:19.12- 17
					10k	27:41.12	28:14.79- 17
Lee Hup Wei		MAS	5.5.87	178/62	HJ	2.28	2.27 -08
Lee Yun-chul		KOR	28.3.82	188/110	HT	72.37	73.77- 17
Legesse	Berhanu	ETH	11.9.94	168/55	Mar	2:04:15	-0-
Leitis	Janis	LAT	13.4.89	188/70	400	45.53	45.60- 17
Lekuta	Solomon	KEN-J	3.10.99	178/61	800	1:46.00	1:45.4A- 17
Lelièvre	Jérémy	FRA	8.2.91	193/82	Dec	7718	7911- 12
* Lemaitre	Christophe	FRA	11.6.90	189/74	200	20.19	19.80- 11
Lemi	Tadesse	ETH-J	20.1.99		800	1:46.00	1:46.54- 17
					1500	3:37.4A	
* Lemma	Sisay	ETH	12.12.90	170/57	Mar	2:04:08	2:05:16- 16
Lemonius	Phillip	JAM	12.12.98	181/73	110h	13.62	-0-
Lemos	José Gregorio	COL	4.6.91	191/93	Dec	7913	7762- 17
Lendore	Deon	TTO	28.10.92	179/75	400	44.81	44.36- 14
Leon Benitez	Joel	GBR	31.8.98	183/79	PV	5.52	5.51- 17
Leonenko	Artyom	RUS	7.4.92	185/64	5000	13:27.61	13:43.23- 17
Lepage	Pierce	CAN	22.1.96	201/91	Dec	8171	8027- 16
Lescay	Lester	CUB-Y15.10.01	182/68	LJ	8.07	7.79A- 17	
Lescay	Yoandys	CUB	5.1.94	181/77	400	45.38	45.00- 16
* Lesnoy	Aleksandr	RUS	28.7.88	194/116	SP	21.58	21.40- 14
Letting	Vincent	KEN	16.6.93	171/60	1500	3:37.52	3:35.12- 16
* Levy	Ronald	JAM	30.10.92	184/77	110h	13.12	13.05- 17
* Lewandowski	Marcin	POL	13.6.87	180/64	800	1:44.32	1:43.72- 15
1000	2:17.24		2:14.30- 16		1500	3:35.06	3:34.04- 17
Lewis	Aaron	TTO	23.1.96	184/73	110h	13.64	14.11- 17
Lewis	Odaine	JAM	13.12.96	170/70	LJ	7.92, 8.08w	7.69, 7.71w- 17
					TJ	16.73	15.86- 14
Lewis	Romel	JAM	28.1.88	178/75	400h	49.48	49.32- 16
Lewke	Dennis	GER	23.7.93	193/118	SP	19.64	19.68- 17
Lightfoot	K.C.	USA-J11.11.99	188/75	PV	5.61	5.40A- 17	
Liipola	Henri	FIN	24.4.94	188/105	HT	75.47	75.31- 17
Liitmäe	Rauno	EST	24.1.94		Dec	7524	7509- 15
Likhanov	Yevgeniy	RUS	10.1.95	187/82	Dec	7708	7869- 15
* Lilesa	Feyisa	ETH	1.2.90	158/50	HMar	60:20	59:22- 12
					Mar	2:07:30	2:04:52- 12
Lima	Edujose	POR	2.3.96	184/95	DT	60.83	55.86- 17
Lin Tzu-Chi		TPE	3.11.97	170/65	LJ	8.05	7.76- 17
^ Lingua	Marco	ITA	4.6.78	176/118	HT	74.71	79.97- 08
* Linke	Christopher	GER	24.10.88	191/66	20kW	1:20:40	1:18:59- 17
Lipsanen	Simo	FIN	13.9.95	191/72	TJ	16.84	17.14- 17
* Lisek	Piotr	POL	16.8.92	194/96	PV	5.94	6.00i, 5.99- 17
Liskowitz	Andrew	USA	22.5.97	188/120	SP	20.28	19.15- 17
Lita Baehre	Bo Kanda	GER-J	29.4.99	193/87	PV	5.60i, 5.60	5.61- 17
Litanyuk	Valeriy	UKR	2.4.94	175/75	50kW	3:53:05	3:58.33- 16
Litvin	Mikhail	KAZ	5.1.96	182/72	400	45.50	46.08A-15
* Litvinov	Sergey	RUS	27.1.86	185/110	HT	76.13	80.98- 12
Liu Mingxuan		CHN	16.5.97		TJ	16.52	16.64- 17
Liu Qizhen		CHN	17.9.95	182/95	JT	82.22	81.15A- 17
Liu Wenxing		CHN	5.12.96		50kW	4:04:35	-0-
Lloyd	Antoine	USA	10.6.96	188/75	110h	13.46	13.69- 16, 13.52w- 17
Lokitam	Rhonzas	KEN	5.9.96		HMar	60:49	62:44A-17
* Lomnicky	Marcel	SVK	6.7.87	177/106	HT	77.00	79.16- 14
Lomong	Lopez	USA	1.1.85	178/67	1M	3:53.86	3:51.21i, 3:51.45- 13
* London	Wil	USA	17.8.97	183/68	400	44.73	44.47- 17
Lonskyy	Viktor	UKR	27.10.95	184/67	HJ	2.27i, 2.23	2.28- 17
Lonyangata	Paul	KEN	12.12.92	170/55	Mar	2:06:25	2:06:10- 17
López	Francisco Javier	ESP	29.12.89	181/70	110h	13.69, 13.57w	13.62- 15, 13.56w- 16

Name		Nat	Born	Ht/Wt	Event	2018 Mark	Pre-2018 Best
López	Jesús	MEX	2.8.97	182/66	800	1:45.04	1:45.51- 17
* López	Miguel Ángel	ESP	3.7.88	181/70	20kW	1:20:54	1:19:14- 15
Lorot	Andrew	KEN	2.12.97	168/55	10k	27:52.39	28:13.13- 17
Losev	Ivan	UKR	26.1.86	170/77	20kW	1:20:53	1:19:33- 14
Lovett	Django	CAN	6.7.92	193/72	HJ	2.30	2.27- 17
Lovett	Eddie	ISV	25.6.92	181/73	110h	13.56	13.31A- 15, 13.39, 13.29w- 13
^ Loyanae	Wilson	KEN	20.11.00		Mar	2:06.57	2:05:13- 16
Lu Ning		CHN-J	12.2.99		20kW	1:22:56	-0-
Lu Xiaotong		CHN	24.7.97		20kW	1:22:50	1:22:55- 17
Lucas	Ashmon	USA	15.2.97	193/111	DT	62.91	47.77- 16
Lucas	David	USA	6.6.96	188/105	DT	60.97	61.43- 17
Ludwig	Matthew	USA	5.7.96	177/82	PV	5.71	5.70- 17
Lukáš	Marek	CZE	16.7.91	180/75	Dec	7819	7903- 16, 7997w- 17
Lukyanenko	Artem	RUS	30.1.90	193/84	Dec	8015	8177- 13
^ Lukyanenko	Yevgeniy	RUS	23.1.85	190/79	PV	5.65	6.01- 08
Lukyanov	Denis	RUS	14.7.89	190/115	HT	77.02	79.61- 13
Lukyanov	Ivan	RUS	31.1.81	178/67	3kSt	8:32.2	8:18.97- 08
Luo Dongpo		CHN	23.6.95		50kW	3:57:25	3:50:38- 17
Luo Jiayu		CHN	3.4.98		50kW	4:04:51	-0-
Luo Yadong		CHN	15.1.92		50kW	4:02:15	3:48:48- 15
Luron	Kevin	FRA	8.11.91	184/80	TJ	16.82, 16.97w	16.85- 17, 16.89w- 16
Lyadusov	Konstantin	RUS	2.3.88	190/125	SP	20.04	20.88i, 20.62- 16
Lyakhovich	Aleksandr	BLR	4.7.89	171/65	20kW	1:21:53	1:21:12- 17
Lyles	Josephus	USA	22.7.98	184/73	400	45.09	45.30- 17
* Lyles	Noah	USA	18.7.97	180/70	100	9.88, 9.86w	10.14- 15, 9.9- 16, 9.95w- 18
					200	19.65	19.90- 17
Lyon	Christian	USA	19.1.98	165/57	100	10.00w	10.43, 10.33w- 17
* Lysenko	Danil	RUS	19.5.97	192/73	HJ	2.40	2.38- 17
Ma Qun		CHN	8.2.94	183/88	JT	82.46A	79.91- 17
Maeno	Keisuke	JPN	10.5.91	180/67	400h	49.86	49.06- 17
Magakwe	Simon	RSA	25.5.85	177/73	100	10.07A, 10.11	9.98A- 14, 10.11- 12
* Mägi	Rasmus	EST	4.5.92	188/74	400h	48.60	48.40- 16
* Magour	Ahmed Bader	QAT	3.3.96	190/90	JT	83.71	85.23- 17
Maheswary	Renjith	IND	30.1.86	177/72	TJ	16.51	17.30- 16
Mahmoud	Hassan Mohamed	EGY	10.2.84	188/110	HT	73.01	78.39- 16
Mahoney	Travis	USA	25.7.90	175/61	3kSt	8:28.74	8:25.44- 16
Maia	Edi	POR	10.11.87	176/75	PV	5.60	5.70- 13
Maina	John	KEN	3.8.94	179/53	5000	13:20.22	13:16.82- 16
Majdán	Dusan	SVK	8.9.87	180/67	50kW	3:59:21	3:53:26- 14
Makarenko	Artem	RUS	23.4.97	183/79	Dec	7925	8112- 17
Makhrosenko	Zakhar	BLR	10.10.91	182/105	HT	74.88	77.41- 16
* Makwala	Isaac	BOT	24.9.85	183/79	200	19.96	19.77- 17, 19.7A- 14
					400	44.23	43.72- 15
* Malachowski	Piotr	POL	7.6.83	194/135	DT	65.78	71.84- 13
Mallett	Aaron	USA	26.9.94	188/79	110h	13.55	13.37, 13.24w- 17
Malykhin	Vladyslav	UKR	15.1.98	184/76	PV	5.60i, 5.60	5.70- 17
Mammedov	Mergen	TKM	24.12.90	187/108	HT	73.48	74.01- 13
* Manangoi	Elijah	KEN	5.1.93	181/65	800	1:44.15	1:44.8A- 17
	1500	3:29.64		3:28.80- 17	1M	3:52.18	3:49.08- 17
Manangoi	George	KEN-J	29.11.00	176/59	1500	3:35.53	3:40.1A- 17
Mande	Abdallah	UGA	10.5.95	166/52	HMar	60:14	60:51- 17
Manga	Aurel	FRA	24.7.92	188/75	110h	13.31	13.27- 17, 13.25w- 16
Mann	Jordan	USA	12.1.93	170/64	3kSt	8:28.55	8:36.73- 17
Mano	Yutaro	JPN	17.12.96	176/68	400h	49.50	50.38- 17
Mansilla	Humberto	CHI	22.5.96	180/100	HT	76.87	74.41- 17
* Manyonga	Luvo	RSA	8.1.91	185/65	LJ	8.58	8.65A, 8.62- 17
Mardal	Thomas	NOR	16.4.97	185/105	HT	72.81	68.34- 17
Mardare	Adrian	MDA	20.6.95	193/92	JT	84.43	83.93- 17
* Marghiev	Serghei	MDA	6.11.92	194/99	HT	76.81	78.72- 15
Maric	Martin	CRO	19.4.84	196/115	DT	63.55	67.92- 14
Maritim	Anthony	KEN	12.11.86	173/57	Mar	2:08:08	2:09:13- 17
Maritim	Philimon	KEN	18.1.88	176/59	HMar	60:29	61:56- 17
Maritz	Hardus	NAM	10.5.90	190/79	400h	49.83A, 50.41	49.48- 17
Markovic	Martin	CRO	13.1.96	190/110	DT	63.24	62.43- 15
* Marschall	Kurtis	AUS	25.4.97	188/78	PV	5.86i, 5.80	5.73- 17
Martin	Pedro José	ESP	12.8.92	188/100	HT	74.33	71.65- 13
Martin	Romain	FRA	12.7.88	198/86	Dec	8036	8104 -14
* Martín	Álvaro	ESP	18.6.94	181/62	20kW	1:20:42	1:19:36- 16
^ Martina	Churandy	NED	3.7.84	178/75	200	20.28	19.81- 16
* Martínez	Lázaro	CUB	3.11.97	192/83	TJ	17.28	17.24- 14
Martínez	Lois Maikel	ESP	3.6.81	183/123	DT	66.51	67.45- 05

Name		Nat	Born	Ht/Wt	Event	2018 Mark	Pre-2018 Best
* Martinot Lagarde	Pascal	FRA	22.9.91	190/80	110h	13.17	12.95- 14
Martos	Sebastián	ESP	20.6.89	178/63	3kSt	8:26.91	8:18.31- 14
* Maruo	Satoshi	JPN	28.11.91	175/60	20kW	1:21:10	1:19:42- 15
					50kW	3:44:52	3:43:03- 17
Maruyama	Yuma	JPN	3.6.98	193/83	Dec	7752	7066- 17
Masai	Gilbert	KEN	16.12.89	169/55	HMar	60:16	59:31- 16
Masilo	Boitumelo	BOT	5.8.95	173/64	800	1:46.44A	1:45.87- 16
* Maslák	Pavel	CZE	21.2.91	176/67	400	45.59, 465.47i	44.79- 14
Mason	Michael	CAN	30.9.86	188/67	HJ	2.32	2.33- 15
Mason	Tyler	JAM	15.1.95	183/73	110h	13.65	13.32A, 13.39- 15
Masters	Riley	USA	5.4.90	185/73	5000	13:16.97	13:17.97- 15
Mastianica	Artur	LTU	30.7.92	173/63	50kW	3:58:29	4:01:56- 17
Masuno	Genta	JPN	24.5.93	182/76	110h	13.50	13.40- 17
Mathas	Brad	NZL	24.6.93	186/75	800	1:46.07	1:46.97- 17
Mathenge	Patrick	KEN	2.11.96	169/53	10k	28:02.65	27:49.96- 17
Mathews	Luke	AUS	21.6.95	188/75	800	1:45.60	1:45.16- 16
					1500	3:37.16	3:35.57- 17
Matlhabe	Phemelo	RSA	31.5.97	179/64	200	20.56, 20.38w	20.87A, 20.67Aw- 16
* Matsunaga	Daisuke	JPN	24.3.95	174/60	20kW	1:17:46	1:18:53- 16
Matsushita	Yuki	JPN	9.9.91	176/64	400h	49.82	49.10- 16
Matsuzawa	Nariharu Jina	JPN	6.1.92	167/69	PV	5.60	5.40- 14
Mattis	Sam	USA	19.3.94	185/100	DT	66.32	67.45- 16
Matusevicius	Edis	LTU	30.6.96	184/79	JT	82.67	84.78- 17
Mayack	Marcel	CMR	17.11.90	180/84	TJ	16.80	15.80- 16
* Mayer	Kevin	FRA	10.2.92	186/82	PV	5.60i, 5.41	5.40- 16
110h	13.71				13.75- 17		
					Dec	9126	8834- 16
Mazur	Vladyslav	UKR	21.11.96	173/71	LJ	8.07	8.04, 8.06w- 17
* McBride	Brandon	CAN	15.6.94	195/75	800	1:43.20	1:43.95- 16
McBride	Bryan	USA	10.12.91	188/77	HJ	2.35	2.30- 15
McCarter	Steffin	USA	19.1.97	176/73	LJ	7.96i	7.83i- 17, 7.70- 16
McClain	Remontay	USA	21.9.92	188/85	100	10.13, 10.12w	10.07, 9.82w- 15
McClain	Terrell	USA	10.11.95	196/88	LJ	8.18	7.95- 16
McConico	Jaylan	USA	17.8.98	183/77	110h	13.65	14.19, 13.91w- 17
McCullough	Conor	USA	31.1.91	186/102	HT	72.98	77.20- 14
McDonald	Morgan	AUS	23.4.96	183/66	5000	13:19.05	13:15.83- 17
^ McDonald	Rusheen	JAM	17.8.92	175/73	400	45.70	43.93- 15
McEwen	Shelby	USA	6.4.96	190/77	HJ	2.29i, 2.25	2.23- 17
McFarland	AJ	USA	17.3.96	186/105	HT	71.29	66.09- 17
McGorty	Sean	USA	8.3.95	187/77	1500	3:36.61	3:40.62- 15
1M	3:55.21		3:53.95i- 16, 4:00.35- 14		5000	13:21.93	13:24.25- 16
McLaughlin	Taylor	USA	3.8.97	183/75	400h	49.10	49.45- 16
* McLeod	Omar	JAM	25.4.94	180/73	110h	13.16, 13.10w	12.90- 17
* McMaster	Kyron	IVB	3.1.97	187/79	400h	47.54	47.80- 17
McMillan	Connor	USA	15.11.95	180/59	10k	28:09.55	29:13.87- 15
McMullen	Adam	IRL	5.7.90	197/87	LJ	7.99i, 7.88	7.85, 7.94w- 17
McNeill	David	AUS	6.10.86	175/59	5000	13:19.51	13:18.60- 12
McSweyn	Stewart	AUS	1.6.95	184/65	1500	3:34.82	3:41.31+- 16
1M	3:54.60		3:55.97- 17		3000	7:34.79	7:47.65- 17
5000	13:05.23		13:19.98- 17		10k	27:50.89	28:29.65- 16
Mead	Hassan	USA	28.6.89	174/61	5000	13:19.81	13:02.80- 14
^ Mechaal	Adel	ESP	5.12.90	184/67	1500	3:38.24	3:34.70- 17
3000	7:40.14i		7:35.28- 17		10k	27:50.56	32:09.9- 10
Mechler	Nathaniel	CAN	31.3.97		Dec	7722	7374- 17
Mehrdelan	Shahin	IRI	21.6.95	188/135	SP	19.95	17.69A-16
* Meité	Ben Youssef	CIV	11.11.86	179/70	100	10.14	9.96- 16, 9.84w- 17
Mejías	Reinier	CUB	22.9.90	178/98	HT	74.75	75.98- 13
* Mekhissi-Benabbad	Mahiedine	FRA	15.3.85	190/75	5000	13:20.53	14:32.9- 05
					3kSt	8:16.97	8:00.09- 13
Mekonen	Teshome	ETH	5.8.95	171/55	HMar	60:02	60:27- 15
Melak Bogale	Nibret	ETH-J	9.10.99	170/55	5000	13:07.27	-0-
Meleshko	Pavel	BLR	24.11.92	187/90	JT	82.05	85.01- 17
Melesse	Birhanu	ETH-J	12.9.99	174/56	3000	7:44.66	
Melly	Edwin	KEN	23.4.94	178/60	800	1:45.89A	1:43.81- 12
Melo	Aleksandro	BRA	29.9.95	179/56	LJ	8.19	8.18- 17
					TJ	16.82	16.67- 17
Melsitov	Dmitriy	UZB	19.3.96	187/68	HJ	2.25i, 2.20	2.19- 17
Mena	Reynier	CUB	21.11.96	174/79	100	10.13, 9.9, 10.06w	10.17, 10.08w- 15, 9.9- 17
					200	20.26, 19.9	20.32- 15
^ Menaldo	Kévin	FRA	12.7.92	176/66	PV	5.88i, 5.47	5.83- 17
Meng Zhongkai		CHN	15.12.97		50kW	4:03:09	3:54:35- 17

Name		Nat	Born	Ht/Wt	Event	2018 Mark	Pre-2018 Best
Menga	Aleixo-Platini	GER	29.9.87	187/78	100	10.09	10.15- 16
					200	20.37	20.27- 16
Mengich	Richard	KEN	3.4.89	185/68	HMar	60:36	59:35- 16
Mengistu	Asefa	ETH	18.1.85	166/52	HMar	60:01	59:54- 17
					Mar	2:04:06	2:08:41- 16
Menjo	Josephat	KEN	20.8.79	168/50	5000	13:25.89	12:55.95- 10
* Menkov	Aleksandr	RUS	7.12.90	170/74	LJ	8.41	8.56- 13
Merber	Kyle	USA	19.11.90	180/64	1500	3:37.49	3:34.54- 15
Merga	Tulu	ETH-J	12.9.99	163/50	5000	13:24.65	
					10k	27:25.86	-0-
* Merritt	Aries	USA	24.7.85	182/70	110h	13.37, 13.27w	12.80- 12
Merzougui	Abdelaziz	ESP	30.8.91	177/62	3kSt	8:31.41	8:18.03- 12
Mesel	Amanuel	ERI	29.12.90	175/57	HMar	60:45	60:10- 13
Mesic	Kemal	BIH	4.8.85	196/110	SP	19.99	20.74- 16
Meyers	Khance	USA-J	11.1.99	184/77	100	10.12w	10.43- 17
					200	20.62, 20.02w	20.78- 16
Miellet	Alexis	FRA	5.5.95	181/63	1500	3:37.50	3:39.55- 17
* Mihaljevic	Filip	CRO	31.7.94	201/113	SP	21.33	21.30- 17
					DT	60.04	63.76- 17
Mikhan	Eduard	BLR	7.6.89	194/85	Dec	7559	8152- 11
* Mikhou	Sadik	BRN	25.7.90	174/61	1000	2:16.09	2:22.88- 11
1500	3:34.55					3:31.34- 17	7:39.02- 16
					3000	7:41.39i	
* Milanov	Philip	BEL	6.7.91	191/118	DT	66.51	67.26, 68.44dh- 16
Milaw	Abrha	ETH	3.1.88	160/50	Mar	2:07:26	2:07:46- 14
Miller	Ashinia	JAM	6.6.93	189/100	SP	20.93	20.45- 17
Miller	Austin	USA	1.6.94	190/82	PV	5.66	5.50- 17
Miller	Chad	JAM	.96	183/73	400h	49.72	51.39- 16
* Miller	Nick	GBR	1.5.93	188/112	HT	80.26	77.55- 15
Minzie	Jevaughn	JAM	20.7.95	173/66	100	10.10	10.02- 16
Misans	Elvijs	LAT	8.4.89	182/73	TJ	16.68	17.02i- 17, 16.77- 16
Misahler	Baptiste	FRA	23.11.97	182/62	1500	3:37.17	3:39.58- 16
Mitchell	Jaylen	USA	29.7.98	178/73	100	10.00w	10.54, 10.49w- 17
* Mitchell-Blake	Nethaneel	GBR	2.4.94	188/79	100	10.08	9.99- 17
					200	20.04	19.95-16
Mitei	Amos	KEN	24.6.94	167/54	Mar	2:07:28	-0-
Mitrevski	Christian	AUS	12.7.96	185/77	LJ	8.01, 8.09w	7.97, 8.05w- 17
Miyamoto	Daisuke	JPN-J	17.4.99	170/60	100	10.26, 10.11w	10.23, 10.20w- 17
Miyawaki	Chihiro	JPN	28.8.91	174/55	Mar	2:08:45	2:11:50- 14
* Mizinov	Vasiliy	RUS	29.12.97	167/55	20kW	1:18:54	1:21:48- 17
Mobley	Desmond	USA	15.8.95	183/73	LJ	7.99	7.54- 13, 7.62w- 16
Mogusu	Titus	KEN	1.1.98	176/53	10k	28:16.35	28:28.40- 16
Mohammed	Abdallah Akbar	KSA	1.6.97	178/75	100	10.03	10.04- 16
Mohlosi	Kabelo	RSA	20.1.93	173/57	800	1:46.20A	1:46.45A- 16
Mokaleng	Derrick	RSA	18.6.97	183/74	400	45.02	45.96- 17
* Mokoena	Khotso	RSA	6.3.85	190/73	TJ	16.92, 17.09Aw	17.35- 14
Mokoka	Stephen	RSA	31.1.85	156/50	10k	27:44.58	27:40.73- 12
					Mar	2:08:31	2:07:40- 15
Moleya	Chris	RSA	27.1.97	189/62	HJ	2.26	2.25A- 17
Momanyi	Jared	KEN	5.5.90	181/70	400	45.13A	46.42A-16
Monópolis	Dimítrios	GRE	4.3.98	187/70	TJ	16.53	15.81- 17
Montaña	José Leonardo	COL	21.3.92	168/61	50kW	3:55:48	3:52:48A- 16
Montgomery	Kahmari	USA	16.8.97	175/66	400	44.58	45.13- 16
Moore	Gabriel	USA	10.1.06	190/88	Dec	7901	7699- 17
Morais	Wellington	BRA	6.9.90		SP	19.85	18.68- 17
Moreno	Juan Carlos	COL	24.6.94	176/68	110h	13.63A, 13.71	13.72A, 13.89- 17
* Morgunov	Timur	RUS	12.10.96	188/77	PV	6.00	5.80i- 16, 5.80- 17
Morris	Dashawn	JAM-J	28.2.99	178/68	400	45.09	46.67- 17
Morris	Julius	MNT	14.4.94	178/68	100	10.12	10.15A, 10.28- 17, 10.06Aw- 15
					200	20.32	20.28A, 20.30- 17
Morrison	Willie	USA	23.11.96	184/120	SP	20.22	19.79i, 19.69- 16
Morse	Brett	GBR	11.2.89	191/114	DT	61.94	66.84- 13
Morvay	Michal	SVK	19.8.96		50kW	4:03:19	
Mouyabi	Quentin	FRA	8.10.98	179/69	TJ	16.72	16.40- 17
* Mowatt	Kemar	JAM	12.3.95	188/77	400h	48.83	48.49- 17
Mrzyglód	Cyprian	POL	2.2.98	185/73	JT	83.85	80.52- 17
Mthembu	Menzi	RSA	7.2.95	179/75	TJ	16.49A	16.43A-16
Mudrov	Ilya	RUS	17.11.91	190/79	PV	5.65i, 5.55	5.80- 16
Muia	Bernard	KEN	26.5.95		10k	28:10.70	28:21.71- 17
Mujaridze	Giorgi	GEO	22.3.98		SP	19.94	18.14- 17
Mujezinovic	Abedin	BIH	2.6.93	182/64	800	1:46.20	1:46.38- 17
Müller	Patrick	GER	4.2.96	197/110	SP	20.14i, 19.49	19.25- 16

Name		Nat	Born	Ht/Wt	Event	2018 Mark	Pre-2018 Best
Müller	Steven	GER	15.9.90	178/70	200	20.46	20.80- 17
Munene Gachaga	Morris	KEN	7.4.95	167/54	HMar	59:36	60:35- 16
Muñoz	Uziel	MEX	8.9.95	179/110	SP	19.87	18.35- 17
* Munyai	Clarence	RSA	20.2.98	176/66	100	10.10A	10.20A- 17
					200	19.69A, 20.36	20.10A, 20.31- 17
Murasky	J.C.	USA	6.2.93	203/123	SP	19.89	20.21- 16
Murayama	Kenta	JPN	23.2.93	176/55	10k	28:12.53	27:39.95- 15
Murayama	Kota	JPN	23.2.93	174/53	10k	28:10.39	27:29.69- 16
Murch	Craig	GBR	27.6.93	183/107	HT	70.47	69.79- 16
Muritu	John	KEN	30.6.96		10k	28:10.90	
* Murphy	Clayton	USA	26.2.95	182/68	800	1:43.12	1:42.93- 16
					1M	3:53.40	3:51.99- 17
Musagala	Ronald	UGA	16.12.92	176/61	1500	3:35.33	3:33.65- 17
					3000	7:44.78	-0-
Musiyenko	Ihor	UKR	22.8.93	186/128	SP	20.14	19.51- 17
Musteata	Marius	ROU	11.1.97		SP	19.61	17.85i -16, 17.44- 17
Mutai	Jeremiah	KEN	27.12.92	173/60	800	1:46.24A	1:43.9A- 13
Mutai	Laban	KEN	15.1.88		Mar	2:07:38	2:08:01- 12
Mutiso	Alexander	KEN	10.9.96	171/52	5000	13:28.03	13:21.90- 16
10k	27:42.16		27:39.25- 16		HMar	60:11	60:57- 17
Mwangi	James	KEN	23.6.84	175/58	10k	28:03.96	27:49.27- 09
Mwangi	Paul	KEN	2.1.93		HMar	60:42	61:25- 16
Mwangi	Samuel	KEN	19.9.97	169/51	HMar	60:42	63:45- 17
Mwaura	Joel	KEN	20.1.98	168/50	5000	13:22.13	13:27.52- 17
					10k	27:45.31	27:45.37- 17
Mwei	Robert	KEN	11.4.98	168/55	5000	13:19.26	13:39.6A- 17
					10k	27:57.14	28:46.8A- 17
Myers	Charlie	GBR	12.6.97	188/79	PV	5.60	5.45- 17
Myslyvchuk	Volodomyr	UKR	25.4.96	190/84	HT	74.43	71.45- 17
N'Tia	Romeo	BEN	25.2.95		LJ	7.97w	7.55- 16
Nabokov	Dmitriy	BLR	20.1.96	186/69	HJ	2.36	2.29i- 16, 2.28- 17
Nadeem	Arshad	PAK	2.1.97	187/95	JT	80.75	78.33- 16
Nadyrov	Ildar	RUS	22.4.94	182/68	3kSt	8:28.70	8:34.15- 17
Naganuma	Gen	JPN	31.3.98		JT	79.42	71.45- 17
Nagata	Takuya	JPN	14.6.94	181/70	100	10.14	10.19- 15
Nakamura	Akihiko	JPN	23.10.90	180/73	Dec	7849	8180- 16
Nakamura	Shogo	JPN	16.9.92	172/52	Mar	2:08:16	-0-
Nakanishi	Takuma	JPN	8.4.94	181/88	JT	78.77	77.64- 16
Nakayama	Kohei	JPN	8.7.94	173/70	TJ	16.53	16.03- 16, 16.19w- 17
* Nápoles	Cristian	CUB	27.11.98	181/80	TJ	17.34	17.27- 17
Napolitano	Rob	USA	3.11.94	175/60	1500	3:38.03	3:39.75- 17
Narayan	Satya	IND-J	10.6.00		20kW	1:23:06	-0-
Nascimento	Carlos	POR	12.10.94	171/64	100	10.13	10.33- 16, 10.19w- 12
^ Nava	Horacio	MEX	20.1.82	175/62	20kW	1:22:13	1:20:56- 16
					50kW	4:02:28	3:42:51- 14
* Nazarov	Dilshod	TJK	6.5.82	187/115	HT	78.18	80.71- 13
Nberet	Melese	ETH-Y	29.1.01	177/60	1500	3:36.49	
* Ndiku	Jonathan	KEN	18.9.91	170/55	5000	13:17.16	13:11.99- 09
10k	27:28.27		27:11.23- 16		3kSt	8:30.75	8:07.75- 11
Ndikumwenayo	Thierry	BDI	26.3.97	163/50	3000	7:41.04	7:58.97i-17, 8:06.05- 14
Ndirangu	Joseph	KEN	9.9.94	168/49	5000	13:22.62	13:19.42- 17
10k	27:33.55		27:46.14- 17		Mar	2:07:53	-0-
Ndiwa	Mang'ata	KEN	12.12.87	175/60	HMar	59:07	-0-
Ndorobo Kwemoi	Peter	KEN	11.8.93	168/55	HMar	59:58	60:13- 16
* Nedosekov	Maksim	BLR	21.1.98	188/70	HJ	2.33	2.33- 17
* Nedow	Tim	CAN	16.10.90	198/125	SP	21.02	21.33i- 16, 20.98- 14
Neelly	Brett	USA	22.11.96	198/114	SP	20.15i, 19.59	19.16- 16
Nene	Zakithi	RSA	2.4.98	188/75	400	45.63A	46.41A- 17
Nesterenko	Maksim	BLR	1.9.92	193/82	TJ	16.56i	16.85- 16
Nesterenko	Mykyta	UKR	15.4.91	208/136	DT	63.34	66.23- 16
Newton	Scotty	USA	19.9.96	179/74	TJ	16.63i, 16.57, 16.85w	15.98,16.26i,16.43w- 17
Ngeno	Alfred	KEN	2.5.97	170/52	5000	13:26.53	13:19.38- 16
Ngeno	Bernard Kipkorir	KEN	16.8.96	175/55	HMar	59:22	
Ngeno	Ernest	KEN	20.5.95	166/50	Mar	2:06:41	2:07:49- 16
Ngetich	Hillary	KEN	15.9.95	171/57	1500	3:37.23	3:32.97- 16
Nichipor	Aleksey	BLR	10.4.93	193/115	SP	20.43	20.52- 17
Nicholls	Michael	BAR	6.4.97	183/75	110h	13.80, 13.62w	13.76- 17
Nielsen	Kevin	USA	12.1.93	188/77	Dec	7695	7467A- 15, 7439- 17
Nigate	Takele	ETH-J	2.10.99	183/68	3kSt	8:25.35	8:20.76- 17
Nikitin	Vladimir	RUS	5.8.92	168/60	1500	3:35.85	3:37.14- 17
1M	3:56.44i		3000	7:42.82i		7:44.65i- 17	10k	28:16.43	29:20.20- 15

Name		Nat	Born	Ht/Wt	Event	2018 Mark	Pre-2018 Best
* Nilsen	Chris	USA	13.1.98	196/84	PV	5.86	5.75- 17
Nilsson	Marcus	SWE	3.5.91	185/90	Dec	8120	8104(w)- 13
Nilsson Montler	Thobias	SWE	15.2.96	187/72	LJ	8.10	8.04- 17
Niskala	Pyry	FIN	6.11.90	191/105	DT	60.11	61.66- 17
Niu Wenbin		CHN	20.1.91		50kW	3:59:47	3:46:12- 17
Niu Wenchao		CHN	20.4.98		20kW	1:21:00	1:25:23- 16
Njiru	Kennedy	KEN	.88	177/60	3kSt	8:18.04	8:13.3A- 17
Nkobolo	Onkabetse	BOT	22.7.93	183/74	400	45.69	45.10- 15
* Noda	Tomohiro	JPN	24.1.96	174/58	20kW	1:19:49	1:20:04- 17
					50kW	3:39:47	-0-
^ Noga	Artur	POL	2.5.88	195/82	110h	13.56	13.26- 13, 13.20w- 10
* Norman	Michael	USA	3.12.97	183/73	200	19.84	20.14, 20.06w- 16
					400	43.61	44.60- 17
Norris	Jake	GBR-J	30.6.99	186/102	HT	73.24	68.86- 17
* Norwood	Vernon	USA	10.4.92	187/77	400	45.47	44.44- 15
Novac	Alexandru	ROU	24.3.97	186/84	JT	86.37	82.90- 17
Novák	Martin	CZE	5.10.92	190/115	3P	19.56i, 19.10	19.70- 15
Nowak	Tim	GER	13.8.95	183/78	Dec	8229	7942- 17
* Nowicki	Wojciech	POL	22.2.89	196/112	HT	81.85	80.47- 17
Nyakora	Teressa	ETH	26.2.95	171/54	10k	27:44.72	27:38.93- 15
Nykyforov	Sergiy	UKR	6.2.94	194/85	LJ	8.23	8.18i- 17, 8.11, 8.18w- 16
Nytes	Trent	USA	21.12.95	185/83	Dec	7683	7224- 16
^ O'Farrill	Yordan	CUB	9.2.93	183/72	110h	13.72, 13.3	13.19, 12.9- 14
O'Hare	Chris	GBR	23.11.90	174/60	1500	3:32.11	3:33.61- 17
					1M	3:55.53, 3:54.14i	3:52.91i- 16, 3:53.34- 17
O'Neal	Matthew	USA	10.6.94	185/74	TJ	16.83	17.12, 17.28w- 17
Oakley	Julian	NZL	23.6.93	176/61	1M	3:55.10i, 3:57.44	3:57.22i- 15, 3:58.89- 14
Oates	Tray	USA	14.3.95	186/79	PV	5.66	5.65- 16
Obayashi	Masayuki	JPN	6.2.96		400h	49.75	49.70- 17
Oberholzer	Andri	SUI	24.7.96		Dec	7522	7827- 17
Obst	Florian	GER	24.2.93	188/86	Dec	8012	7576- 17
Obyortyshev	Denis	RUS	16.2.97		TJ	16.81	16.38- 16
Oda	Daiki	JPN	15.1.96	180/73	LJ	7.95	8.04- 17
Oduduru	Divine	NGR	7.10.96	175/70	100	10.10	10.25, 10.0- 16, 10.09w- 17
					200	20.13	20.34- 16, 20.25w- 14
Ogata	Akihiro	JPN	8.6.94	185/73	110h	13.64	13.88, 13.78w- 15
Ogunode	Tosin	QAT	2.3.94	183/77	100	10.00	10.18- 16, 10.17w- 17
Ogura	Kenji	JPN	8.6.95	180/80	JT	77.64	78.32- 17
Ohakwe	Michael	USA	20.7.92	190/107	DT	62.97	61.29- 17
Oikawa	Fumitaka	JPN	5.4.95	168/54	20kW	1:19:17	1:20:45- 17
Ojeda	José Leyver	MEX	12.11.85	164/52	20kW	1:21:30	1:22:30- 11
					50kW	3:53:37	3:45:09- 17
Okezie	Chidi	NGR	8.8.93	196/79	400	45.24	45.76- 16
Okumbo	Jorum	KEN	10.12.97	170/55	HMar	59:36	58:48- 17
Okutu	Jean Marie	ESP	4.8.88	179/68	LJ	8.01	8.17A- 16, 8.01- 14, 8.05w- 12
Oleitiptip	Alex	KEN	20.12.90	176/58	HMar	60:49	58:51- 17
Oliva	Pablo	ESP	15.10.96	169/55	50kW	4:05:43	4:00:31- 16
de Oliveira	Paulo André	BRA	20.8.98	183/75	100	10.02	10.18, 10.08w- 17
					200	20.33	20.58, 20.31w- 17
Oliveira	Paulo Sérgio	BRA	1.6.93	185/65	LJ	8.12i, 8.12A, 7.98	8.13- 14
Omuro	Hideki	JPN	25.7.90	180/67	110h	13.80, 13.57w	13.48- 17, 13.47w- 16
Öncel	Emin	TUR	1.5.97	186/100	JT	79.15	80.20- 17
Onishi	Kazuki	JPN	28.3.87		10k	28:15.27	28:27.53- 17
* Onnen	Eike	GER	3.8.82	194/83	HJ	2.27	2.34- 07
^ Oprea	Marian	ROU	6.6.82	191/80	TJ	16.60i, 16.32, 16.47w	17.81- 05
* Ordóñez	Saúl	ESP	10.4.94	178/63	800	1:43.65	1:45.28- 11
Ortega	Mauricio	COL	4.8.94	184/102	DT	66.30	65.84, 67.45dh- 16
* Ortega	Orlando	ESP	29.7.91	185/70	110h	13.08	12.94- 15
Ortiz	Ricardo	MEX	7.2.95		20kW	1:22:28	1:21:45- 16
^ Osagie	Andrew	GBR	19.2.88	189/72	800	1:45.09	1:43.77- 12
* Osako	Suguru	JPN	23.5.91	170/53	Mar	2:05:50	2:07:19- 17
Osewski	Bartosz	POL	20.3.91	194/104	JT	81.06	83.89- 12
Ostos	José Luis	PER	9.12.92	160/50	10k	28:12.05	27:53.58- 17
* Otterdahl	Payton	USA	2.4.96	193/120	SP	21.31i, 20.96	18.62- 17
Otterling	Andreas	SWE	25.5.86	183/80	LJ	7.81i, 8.01w	8.12i- 16, 8.06, 8.13w- 15
Otuonye	Ifeanyi	TKS	27.6.94	184/73	LJ	8.06	7.88- 16, 7.98w- 15
Oueladha	Hicham	MAR	31.1.95	175/60	1500	3:35.35	3:36.61- 17
* Özbilen	Kaan Kigen	TUR	15.1.86	170/54	HMar	60:08	59:58- 11
					Mar	2:06:24	2:06:10- 16
Özdevici	Osman Can	TUR	23.8.95	191/110	SP	20.26	19.88- 17
Özüpek	Can	TUR	2.2.96	184/72	TJ	16.77	16.10- 17

Name		Nat	Born	Ht/Wt	Event	2018 Mark	Pre-2018 Best
Pai Long		CHN	8.10.89		HJ	2.24	2.28- 12
Palma	Isaac	MEX	26.10.90	174/59	20kW	1:21:57	1:20:54- 16
Panasenkov	Vladislav	RUS	22.5.96	190/95	JT	79.15	79.93- 17
Papamihaíl	Aléxandros	GRE	18.9.88	178/63	20kW	1:22:48	1:21:12- 12
Parakhonko	Vitaliy	BLR	18.8.93	190/78	110h	13.40	13.66- 17
* Parchment	Hansle	JAM	17.6.90	196/90	110h	13.21	12.94- 14
* Parellis	Apostolos	CYP	24.7.85	186/110	DT	63.62	65.69- 16
Park Tae-geon		KOR	8.5.91	181/64	200	20.40	20.65- 16
Parker	Marcus	USA	9.10.97	175/70	200	20.36A, 20.54	20.77- 17
Parsons	Sam	USA	18.6.94	182/64	1500	3:38.18	3:44.52- 17
Partanen	Veli-Matti	FIN	28.10.91	178/62	50kW	3:44:43	3:49:00- 17
Pásztor	Bence	HUN	5.2.95	186/95	HT	74.01	75.74- 15
Pavlov	Vitaliy	RUS	12.1.97	177/73	TJ	16.78i, 16.40, 16.83w	16.26i- 17, 16.06- 15
Payen	Ludovic	FRA	18.2.95	185/80	110h	13.38	13.49- 17
Peacock	Hamish	AUS	15.10.90	186/96	JT	83.63	84.39- 16
Peñalver	Eric	ESP	23.9.93	173/58	3kSt	8:28.18	8:36.16- 17
Pender	Barry	IRL	2.4.90	192/75	HJ	2.24i	2.26i, 2.20- 16
Peng Chen		CHN	8.7.97		20kW	1:22:53	1:21:59- 17
Peng Shiyi		CHN	16.9.98		50kW	4:04:19	
Percy	Nick	GBR	5.12.94	190/105	DT	63.17	63.38- 16
Pereira	Tiago	POR	19.9.93	185/66	TJ	16.56	16.05- 14
Perera	Ushan	SRI	22.1.98		HJ	2.24	2.15- 17
Perini	Lorenzo	ITA	22.7.94	186/76	110h	13.49	13.62, 13.54w- 17
Perlaza	Jhon	COL	26.8.94	180/60	400	44.86	45.45A- 16, 45.77- 17
Pesic	Darko	MNE	30.11.92	189/89	Dec	7658	7846- 17
Peters	Anderson	GRN	21.10.97	187/84	JT	82.82	84.81- 17
* Pettersson	Simon	SWE	3.1.94	198/105	DT	65.84	64.88- 17
* Pezer	Mesud	BIH	27.8.94	198/120	SP	21.15i, 20.79	21.40- 17
Philibert-Thiboutot	Charles	CAN	31.12.90	178/62	1500	3:37.21	3:34.23- 15
1M	3:56.62				3:54.52- 15	3000	7:45.03	7:46.22i- 17
Phera	Thapelo	RSA	21.11.91	183/77	400	45.14	45.39A- 17, 46.50- 16
Piazza	Drew	USA	28.1.95	185/73	800	1:48.83	1:45.69- 17
Picchiottino	Gianluca	ITA	22.8.96		20kW	1:22:48	1:23:46- 17
* Pichardo	Pedro Pablo	POR	30.6.93	185/71	TJ	17.95	18.08- 15
Pinnock	Wayne	JAM-J	24.10.00	178/63	LJ	7.99	7.27A- 17
Pintado	Brian	ECU	29.7.95	168/57	20kW	1:22:21	1:21:17- 17
Pinzón	Diego	COL	12.2.85		50kW	4:04:48	
Piperi	Adrian	USA-J	20.1.99	188/130	SP	20.41	-0-
Piskunov	Hlib	UKR	25.11.98	182/96	HT	75.50	73.52- 17
* Pitkämäki	Tero	FIN	19.12.82	195/92	JT	82.64	91.53- 05
Piyarathne	Sandaruwan	SRI	14.4.94		LJ	7.99	7.43- 16, 7.84w- 17
Plesko	Nejc	SLO	9.10.92	186/97	HT	75.54	74.30- 17
Pless	David	USA	19.11.90	191/109	SP	20.37	20.37- 16
Plotnitskiy	Dmitriy	BLR	26.8.88	189/80	TJ	16.55i	16.91- 10
Pohle	Hagen	GER	5.3.92	178/63	20kW	1:21:35	1:19:58- 16
Pontvianne	Jean Marc	FRA	6.8.94	170/60	TJ	16.95	17.13- 17
Ponzio	Nick	USA	4.1.95	183/132	SP	19.62i, 19.32	19.53- 15
Poole	Cory	USA-J	29.7.99	185/70	110h	13.68	
					400h	49.71	49.88- 17
Poole	Quintaveon	USA	11.10.96	173/66	400	45.26	46.50- 15
Porsch	Gordon	GER	11.3.95	183/77	PV	5.61i	5.35- 17
Poska	Domantas	LTU	10.1.96	199/107	DT	61.48	62.47- 16
Potye	Tobias	GER	16.3.95	198/72	HJ	2.27	2.25- 17
Pozdnyakov	Semyen	RUS	28.11.92	194/80	HJ	2.28i, 2.26	2.23i, 2.21- 11
* Pozzi	Andrew	GBR	15.5.92	186/79	110h	13.28	13.14, 13.13w- 17
Praczyk	Wojciech	POL	10.1.93	192/108	DT	60.61	60.87- 14
Prakel	Sam	USA	29.10.94	176/61	1500	3:36.84	3:37.79- 17
					1M	3:54.64	3:55.89- 17
* Prescod	Reece	GBR	29.2.96	193/75	100	9.94, 9.88w	10.03- 17
Pretorius	Constant	RSA	26.1.94	184/80	400h	49.71	49.28A, 49.69- 17
Pretorius	Friedrich	RSA	4.8.95	187/84	Dec	7764A, 7730	8002A- 17, 7780- 16
Primak	Artyom	RUS	14.1.93	190/77	LJ	8.02i	8.22- 17
Prince	Quamel	USA	20.4.94	173/64	800	1:46.30	1:46.76- 17
Pringle	Myles	USA	5.9.97	183/70	400	45.35	45.77- 17
Probst	Marius	GER	20.8.95	183/65	1500	3:37.07	3:38.54- 17
Proserpio	Giacomo	ITA	22.4.97	182/93	HT	71.33	67.99- 17
Protsenko	Andriy	UKR	20.5.88	194/80	HJ	2.31	2.40- 14
Prüfer	Clemens	GER	13.8.97	198/113	DT	60.40	62.48- 17
Prüfer	Henning	GER	7.3.96	201/125	DT	63.50	60.93- 17
* Przybylko	Mateusz	GER	9.3.92	195/79	HJ	2.35	2.35- 17
Pullen	Clive	JAM	18.10.94	175/73	TJ	16.71i, 16.25	17.19i- 17, 16.90- 16

Name		Nat	Born	Ht/Wt	Event	2018 Mark	Pre-2018 Best
Quijera	Nicolás	ESP	24.6.96	188/85	JT	80.21	76.77- 17
Quinion	Aurélien	FRA	27.1.93	178/62	50kW	3:57:05	-0-
Quinn	Devin	USA	8.6.96	183/75	100	10.12, 10.11w	10.20- 17
					200	20.45	20.80, 20.49w- 17
* Quiñónez	Alex	ECU	11.8.89	176/65	100	10.09A, 10.19	10.09A- 13, 10.13- 17
					200	19.93A	20.27- 17
Quispe	Ronal	DOL	5.3.89	164/57	50kW	4:05:05A	4:02:00- 16
Radko	Anton	UKR	2.6.95	175/56	50kW	4:04:53	
Raitanen	Topi	FIN	7.2.96	185/74	3kSt	8:28.48	8:37.42- 17
Ramie	Joseph	JAM	14.12.90		LJ	7.99w	7.60, 7.62w- 13
Ranasinghe	D.G.Sampath	SRI	1.9.88	178/87	JT	81.22	78.70- 17
Ranasinghe	R.M.Sumedha	SRI	10.2.91	182/82	JT	78.89	83.04- 15
Randhawa	Nauraj Singh	MAS	27.1.92	193/68	HJ	2.24	2.29- 16
Randrianasolo	Yann	FRA	3.2.94	184/83	LJ	8.01	7.82i- 16, 7.81- 17
^ Rapinier	Yoann	FRA	29.9.89	182/70	TJ	16.68, 16.74w	17.45- 13
Rayner	Jack	AUS	12.12.95	175/59	10k	28:12.07	28:59.24- 17
Re	Davide	ITA	16.3.93	183/75	400	45.26	45.40A, 45.56- 17
Reese	Riak	USA	23.11.94	180/68	100	10.14	10.21, 10.13w- 17
					200	20.43, 20.39w	20.43- 17
Reheda	Serhiy	UKR	6.2.94	190/100	HT	74.42	76.92- 17
Reid	Julian	GBR	23.9.88	186/77	TJ	16.57, 16.70w	16.98, 17.10w- 09
Reid	Leon	IRL	26.7.94	173/66	200	20.27	20.38- 17
Remes	Tommi	FIN	20.1.94	183/98	HT	70.87	72.55- 16
Rendón	James	COL	7.7.85	155/55	50kW	4:03:42	3:47:41- 14
Resias	Cliff	BAH	8.11.96	175/66	200	20.46	21.09- 17
Reus	Julian	GER	29.4.88	177/73	100	10.15	10.01- 16, 9.99w- 17
Reuther	Marc	GER	23.6.96	193/77	800	1:45.42	1:45.22- 17
Rew	Quentin	NZL	16.7.84	175/63	20kW	1:21:47	1:21:12- 17
					50kW	3:48:58	3:46:29- 17
Reynolds	Albert	LCA	28.3.88	178/87	JT	78.10	79.44- 17
Reynolds	Ben	IRL	26.9.90	188/77	110h	13.70	13.48- 15
Ribich	David	USA	27.12.95	183/64	1500	3:37.35	3:39.56- 17
Richard	Tyrell	USA	4.8.97	188/77	400	44.70	46.41- 17
* Richards	Jereem	TTO	13.1.94	183/66	200	19.99	19.97- 17
* Richards	O'Dayne	JAM	14.12.88	177/120	SP	21.02	21.96- 17
Richartz	Nate	USA	2.11.94	186/77	PV	5.70	5.51- 17
Riley	Adrian	JAM	22.1.94	183/85	Dec	7576	7398A-17
^ Riley	Andrew	JAM	6.9.88	188/80	110h	13.47	13.14- 13
Ringer	Richard	GER	27.2.89	182/63	5000	13:22.48	13:10.94- 15
					10k	27:36.52	28:05.96- 17
Rise	Lars Vikan	NOR	23.11.88	184/86	Dec	7600	7942- 11
Riseley	Jeff	AUS	11.11.86	192/74	800	1:46.35	1:44.48- 12
Ristic	Milan	SRB	8.8.91	186/72	110h	13.53	13.39- 16
Rivasz-Tóth	Norbert	HUN	6.5.96	182/86	JT	80.26	83.08- 17
Rivera	Edgar	MEX	13.2.91	191/80	HJ	2.28i, 2.26	2.30i, 2.29- 16
Rivero	Briander	CUB	23.4.91	189/91	Dec	7858(w)	7719- 17
Roberts	Daniel	USA	13.4.98	186/77	110h	13.27	13.82, 13.75w- 17
Roberts	Daniel	USA	11.12.94	183/107	HT	74.79	69.84- 17
* Roberts	Gil	USA	15.3.89	188/81	400	45.22	44.22 -17
Robertson	Andrew	GBR	17.12.90	174/72	100	10.06w	10.10 -14
Robertson	Jake	NZL	14.11.89	180/65	10k	27:30.90	27:45.46- 14
	HMar	59:58dh			60:01- 17	Mar	2:08:26	-0-
Robertson	Ricky	USA	19.9.90	178/70	HJ	2.32	2.32- 12
Robi	Doribe	ETH	20.9.90	165/50	Mar	2:07:33	2:05:58- 15
Robinson	Brett	AUS	8.5.91	173/57	5000	13:15.91	13:18.96- 13
Robinson	Bryce	USA	13.11.93	178/75	100	10.07	9.99, 9.96w- 15
					200	20.38	20.30, 20.29w- 15
Robinson	Byron	USA	16.2.95	175/73	400h	49.04	48.50- 17
* Robinson	Jeron	USA	30.4.91	193/73	HJ	2.31	2.31- 15
Robinson ¶	Demar	JAM	13.8.93	190/70	HJ	2.24	2.22i-dq. 2.20- 17
Rodger	Sebastian	GBR	29.6.91	188/75	400h	49.74	49.19- 13
* Rodgers	Michael	USA	24.4.85	178/73	100	9.89	9.85- 11, 9.80w- 14
Rodney	Brendon	CAN	9.4.92	190/84	200	20.40	19.96- 16
Rodrigues	António César	BRA	12.1.93	183/68	200	20.46	20.53- 15
Rodríguez	Arturo	CUB-J	28.4.99	192/78	TJ	16.63w	16.43- 17
Rodríguez	Genaro	MEX	10.10.90	185/77	110h	13.64A	13.72A- 14, 13.79- 17
Roe	Martin	NOR	1.4.92	187/86	Dec	8228	8144- 17
Rogers	Jason	SKN	31.8.91	173/66	100	10.05	10.01- 13, 9.98Aw- 15, 10.0- 16
Rogowski	Arkadiusz	POL	30.3.93	182/100	HT	70.73	73.10- 15
* Röhler	Thomas	GER	30.9.91	192/92	JT	91.78	93.90- 17
Rollins	NaRon	USA	18.7.94	190/82	100	10.22, 10.09w	

Name		Nat	Born	Ht/Wt	Event	2018 Mark	Pre-2018 Best
* Romani	Darlan	BRA	9.4.91	188/140	SP	22.00	21.82- 17
Romanov	Andrey	RUS	19.9.94	180/90	HT	74.51	74.60- 16
Romeo	Jonathan	ESP	13.8.94	174/59	3kSt	8:27.25	8:31.36- 17
Rono	Vincent	KEN	22.12.90	165/55	10k	28:17.24A	27:52.19- 11
					Mar	2:07:50	2:10:23- 17
Rono	Vincent Kipsang	KEN	11.11.90	165/55	HMar	60:24	59:27- 17
Ronoh	Geoffrey	KEN	29.11.82	182/62	HMar	60:21	59:45- 14
* Rop	Albert	BRN	17.7.92	176/55	3000	7:42.34i	7:32.02- 16
					5000	13:11.84	12:51.96- 13
Rosique	Henry	CUB	4.1.97		TJ	17.02	
Rosser	Khallifah	USA	13.7.95	190/75	400h	48.65	49.04- 16
Rossi	Eugenio	SMR	6.3.92	192/72	HJ	2.24i	2.27- 15
Roth	Thomas Arne	NOR	11.2.91	183/68	800	1:45.75	1:46.15- 14
Rotich	Abraham	BRN	26.6.93	183/64	800	1:46.05	1:43.13- 12
^ Roulhac	Brandon	USA	13.12.83	188/73	TJ	16.49Ai, 16.44	17.26, 17.44w- 09
Rowden	Daniel	GBR	9.9.97	177/61	800	1:44.97	1:46.64- 17
Rowe	Rodney	USA	17.3.97	180/77	200	20.26	20.79, 20.61w- 17
Rowe	Shawn	JAM	7.12.92	193/84	400h	49.04	49.36- 17
Rozmys	Michal	POL	13.3.95	187/72	800	1:45.32	1:45.70- 17
					1500	3:37.08	3:36.37- 17
Ruffin	Rodney	USA	17.3.97	173/70	LJ	7.94, 8.10w	7.62i- 17
Ruggeri	Guillermo	ARG	26.3.92	183/77	400h	49.28A	49.69- 17
Ruiz	Jorge	COL	17.5.89	167/57	50kW	4:05:28	3:50:37- 17
Ruiz	Marcos	ESP	10.3.95	183/69	TJ	16.81	16.44- 17
Rumbenieks	Arnis	LAT	4.4.88	173/63	50kW	4:00:06	3:58:35- 08
Rungaru	James	KEN	14.1.93	174/58	10k	27:48.59	27:22.53- 11
					HMar	59:38	60:12- 15
* Rupp	Galen	USA	8.5.86	180/62	HMar	59:47	60:30- 11
					Mar	2:06:07	2:09:20- 17
Russell	Alonzo	BAH	8.2.92	183/75	400	45.28	45.25- 16
Russell	Dejour	JAM-J	1.4.00	185/79	110h	13.64	13.32- 17
Ruto	Philemon	KEN-Y	20.9.01		3kSt	8:26.52A	8:21.30- 17
Rutto	Cyrus	KEN	21.4.92	173/52	3000	7:42.53	7:37.57- 13
					5000	13:10.79	13:03.44- 17
* Ruuskanen	Antti	FIN	21.2.84	189/86	JT	82.59	88.98- 15
Ryapolov	Anatoliy	RUS	31.1.97	183/65	LJ	8.01	7.96- 15
Rybakov	Anatoliy	RUS	27.2.85	160/51	5000	13:26.25	13:30.24- 17
Rybakov	Yevgeniy	RUS	27.2.85	160/51	5000	13:23.57	13:30.12- 17
de Sá	Mateus Daniel	BRA	21.11.95	184/82	TJ	16.76A, 16.58	16.87- 17
Sable	Avinash	IND	13.9.94	171/60	3kSt	8:29.80	8:39.81- 17
Sacoor	Jonathan	BEL-J	1.9.99	188/73	400	45.03	46.21- 17
Saddedine	Alexandre	FRA	29.9.94	179/61	1500	3:37.36	3:38.86- 16
Saina	Emmanuel	KEN	6.9.92	174/55	Mar	2:05:21	-0-
Saito	Takumi	JPN	23.3.93	178/61	20kW	1:22:23	1:19:44- 16
Sakai	Yugo	JPN-J	1.5.99	184/64	LJ	7.79, 8.31w	7.68- 17
Sakamoto	Tatsuya	JPN	4.5.96	183/86	JT	77.33	75.58- 17
Salas	Didac	ESP	19.5.93	187/75	PV	5.61	5.60- 14
Sales	Llorenç	ESP	14.7.88	179/67	1500	3:38.18	3:37.21- 17
Saluri	Karl Robert	EST	6.8.93	178/75	Dec	8137	8108- 16
* Samaai	Ruswahl	RSA	25.9.91	178/73	LJ	8.45	8.49A- 17, 8.38, 8.40w- 16
Samac	Vedran	SRB	22.1.90	183/90	JT	80.44	80.90- 15
* Samba	Abderrahman	QAT	5.9.95	187/75	400	44.62	46.04A- 16
					400h	46.98	48.31A, 48.44- 17
Sambu	Stephen	KEN	7.7.88	169/55	HMar	60:41	60:41- 13
Samimi	Mohammed	IRI	29.3.87	188/104	DT	61.34A	65.46- 14
Samolyuk	Viktor	UKR	5.9.86	184/120	SP	19.70	19.44- 10
Sampath	J.H.G.	SRI			LJ	7.82, 8.12w	
Samuelsson	Fredrik	SWE	16.2.95	187/83	Dec	8165	8172- 17
Sánchez	Benjamin	ESP	10.3.85	185/72	50kW	3:56:37	3:55:45- 15
^ Sánchez	Eder	MEX	21.5.86	176/67	20kW	1:22:23	1:18:34- 08
Sánchez	Ryan	PUR	22.6.98	179/64	800	1:45.73	1:45.58- 17
dos Santos	Alison	BRA-J	3.6.00	190/75	400h	49.78	53.82- 17
* dos Santos	Almir	BRA	4.9.93	191/80	TJ	17.53	16.86- 17
dos Santos	Felipe Vinicius	BRA	30.7.94	181/80	Dec	7886	8019- 15
Santos	Juander	DOM	7.5.95	188/79	400h	48.77	48.59- 17
* Santos	Luguelín	DOM	12.11.92	173/61	400	44.59	44.11- 15
dos Santos	Vitor Hugo	BRA	1.2.96	185/75	100	10.12A, 10.13	10.11- 16
					200	20.21A, 20.66	20.50- 17
Santos	Vitor Ricardo	POR	18.12.94	182/73	400	45.14	45.74- 14
Sapwaturrahman		INA	13.5.94	177/71	LJ	8.09	7.90- 17

Name		Nat	Born	Ht/Wt	Event	2018 Mark	Pre-2018 Best
* Saruni	Michael	KEN	18.6.95	180/78	400	45.42A	45.69A- 17
					800	1:43.25	1:44.61A- 17
Sassaoui	Mounaime	MAR	20.3.95	183/68	3kSt	8:27.2	8:34.66- 16
Savola	Elmo	FIN	10.3.95	189/77	Dec	7655	7956- 17
^ Sawano	Daichi	JPN	16.9.80	183/75	PV	5.60	5.83- 05
Sawe	Matthew	KEN	2.7.88	193/66	HJ	2.30A	2.25A, 2.20- 15, 2.22i- 16
Sawyers	Chantz	JAM-J	0.0.99	185/77	400	45.40	46.31- 17
Sawyers	Roberto	CRC	17.10.86	189/107	HT	73.16	77.15- 16
Sayers	Feron	GBR	15.10.94	186/77	LJ	8.05	7.89, 7.95w- 17
Schembri	Fabrizio	ITA	27.1.81	183/73	TJ	16.60	17.27- 09
^ Scherbarth	Tobias	GER	17.8.85	195/84	PV	5.65	5.76i- 09, 5.75- 16
Schuurmans	Jared	USA	20.8.87	198/118	DT	63.99	66.10- 15
Schwandke	Tristan	GER	23.5.92	184/93	HT	70.88	70.42- 15
Schwartz	Anthony	USA-J	5.9.00	183/78	100	10.09A, 10.13, 10.07w	10.15 -17
					200	20.47, 20.41w	20.66- 17
* Scott	Donald	USA	23.2.92	183/84	TJ	17.37	17.25- 17
Scott	Jordan	JAM	29.6.97	175/73	TJ	16.82	16.44- 17, 16.61w- 16
Scott	Marc	GBR	21.12.93	177/62	5000	13:23.14	13:22.37- 17
Seddon	Zak	GBR	28.6.94	179/61	3kSt	8:26.51	8:30.17- 17
Sedecias	Benjamin	FRA	18.1.95	177/78	110h	13.57	13.41- 17
Sedyuk	Nikolay	RUS	29.4.88	198/115	DT	61.15	64.72- 08
Seifert	Bernhard	GER	15.2.93	190/88	JT	85.17	84.62- 17
Seiler	Nathaniel	GER	6.4.96	175/65	50kW	3:54:08	3:55:13- 17
Seliverstov	Pavel	BLR	2.9.96	197/77	HJ	2.24	2.32i- 17, 2.30- 16
Selmon	Kenny	USA	27.8.96	188/82	400h	48.12	48.60- 17
Semyonov	Dmitriy	RUS	2.8.92	195/77	HJ	2.25i	2.31i- 15, 2.28- 14
Sène	Alioune	FRA	3.2.96	186/78	PV	5.70	5.60- 16
Seppänen	Tuomas	FIN	16.5.86	180/107	HT	72.11	76.20- 16
Sepúlveda	Alfredo	CHI	3.8.93	182/73	400h	49.62A	49.86- 16
Serri Mohamed	Abou	EGY	20.2.91		HT	72.21	
Seslin	Demyan	RUS	4.8.97		SP	19.55	17.87- 17
Session	William	USA	22.2.97	186/82	110h	13.57	13.91- 17
Seurei	Benson	BRN	27.3.84	172/62	Mar	2:07:37	2:16:25A-17
Seward	DaJuan	USA	15.8.96	190/77	110h	13.64	14.06- 17
Shabanov	Konstantin	RUS	17.11.89	184/75	110h	13.53	13.35- 11
Shalin	Pavel	RUS	15.4.87	175/73	LJ	7.97	8.25- 10, 8.33w- 11
Shamsuddin	Muhd Irfan	MAS	16.8.95	189/102	DT	60.77	62.55- 17
Shankar	Tejaswin	IND	21.12.98	193/80	HJ	2.29	2.26- 16
Sharipov	Sergey	RUS	14.4.92		20kW	1:23:01	1:23:10- 15
^ Shayunov	Yuriy	BLR	22.10.87	189/120	HT	74.46	80.72- 09
Sheikh Ali	Mohad Abdikadar	ITA	12.6.93	175/63	1500	3:36.54	3:38.53- 15
Sheremet	Dmytro	UKR	19.11.92	182/82	JT	77.33	77.16- 16
Shevchuk	Aleksey	RUS	10.8.97		20kW	1:21:02	1:20:57- 17
Sheyko	Georgiy	KAZ	24.8.89	183/70	20kW	1:21:57	1:20:47- 17
* Shi Yuhao		CHN	26.9.98	178/61	LJ	8.43	8.31- 17
Shiferaw	Bekele	ETH	14.10.95	171/54	5k	13:21.93	13:26.19- 17
					10k	27:59.30	28:10.54- 16
Shigo	Morgan	USA	1.2.96	186/111	HT	72.47	67.94- 17
Shimanovich	Aleksandr	BLR	9.2.98	190/100	HT	71.22	68.70- 16
Shimono	Shin-ichiro	JPN	10.10.90	177/64	LJ	8.03w	8.11- 15
Shinno	Tomohiro	JPN	17.8.96		HJ	2.26	2.21- 16
Shiojiri	Kazuya	JPN	8.11.96	170/54	3kSt	8:29.14	8:31.89- 16
Shiri	Behnam	IRI	21.9.00	190/110	DT	61.03A	60.48- 16
* Chirobohov	Sergey	RUS-J	16.2.99	168/57	20kW	1:17:25	1:18:26- 17
Shiroyama	Shotaro	JPN	6.3.95	178/64	LJ	7.98	8.01- 16
Shitara	Yuta	JPN	18.12.91	170/48	10k	28:11.55	27:41.97- 17
					Mar	2:06:11	2:09:03- 17
* Shkurenyov	Ilya	RUS	11.1.91	191/82	Dec	8321	8601- 17
Shoultz	Samuel	USA	.96	188/73	HJ	2.24	2.18A- 16
Shrader	Brian	USA	22.7.91	180/64	3kSt	8:29.11	8:32.94- 17
* Shubenkov	Sergey	RUS	4.10.90	190/75	110h	12.92	12.98- 15, 12.7- 16
Shuey	Michael	USA	2.2.94	196/93	JT	78.52	79.91- 17
Shumay	Mogos	ERI	.97	170/54	HMar	60:40	61:09- 15
Shumik	Viktor	UKR	21.5.98	180/75	20kW	1:22:24	1:28:44- 17
* Shura Kitata	Tola	ETH	9.6.96	165/50	HMar	59:17	60:10- 17
					Mar	2:04:49	2:05:50- 17
Siame	Sydney	ZAM	7.10.97	178/70	100	10.06	10.22, 10.06w, 9.88A-dt- 17
					200	20.18	20.29- 17
* Sibanda	Karabo	BOT	2.7.98	192/79	400	45.58A	44.25- 16
Sidorchenko	Gleb	RUS	15.5.86	197/110	DT	61.42	62.55- 13
Siele	Patrick	KEN	27.7.96		HMar	60:43	

Name		Nat	Born	Ht/Wt	Event	2018 Mark	Pre-2018 Best
Sigueni	Hicham	MAR	30.1.93	175/55	3kSt	8:19.51	8:16.54- 15
Sikora	Rafal	POL	17.2.87	187/76	50kW	3:49:54	3:46:16- 11
Silambarasan	M	IND	27.12.92		LJ	8.06	7.73- 13
Silva	António Vital e	POR	23.1.88	183/110	HT	73.26	71.48- 17
Silva	Derick	BRA	23.4.98	181/68	100	10.10	10.33, 10.26w- 16
					200	20.23	20.61- 17
Silva	Talles	BRA	20.8.91	190/78	HJ	2.26i, 2.26	2.30- 17
* Simbine	Akani	RSA	21.9.93	176/74	100	9.93	9.89 -16
Simmons	Solomon	USA	26.9.93	196/91	Dec	8019	7936- 16
Simoliunas	Skirmantas	LTU	13.3.94	200/95	JT	79.56	77.10- 17
* Simotwo	Charles	KEN	6.5.95	178/60	1500	3:32.61	3:32.59- 17
Simpson	Damarcus	USA	14.7.93	175/68	LJ	8.12, 8.33w	8.12- 16, 8.36w- 17
Singh	Arpinder	IND	30.12.92	188/80	TJ	17.09	17.17- 14
Singh	Chandan	IND	8.6.87		50kW	4:00:58	4:04:19- 17
Singh	Dhamen	IND	15.10.89		50kW	4:00:35	4:09:40- 17
Singh	Jitender	IND	20.3.89		50kW	3:58:56	4:02:12- 17
Singh	Kulwant	IND	20.3.90		20kW	1:22:10	-0-
Singh	Manish	IND	5.5.91	174/65	20kW	1:21:32	1:20:26- 16
Singh	Manjit	IND	1.9.89	176/68	800	1:46.15	1:48.04- 17
Singh	Neeraj	IND	15.8.94		20kW	1:21:40	1:27:25- 14
Singh	Rajender	IND	5.4.86	175/89	JT	80.63	82.23- 15
Singh	Shivpal	IND	6.7.95	181/90	JT	82.28	79.77- 16
Singh	Sunil	IND	28.11.97		20kW	1:21:53	1:27:50- 17
Singh	Tejinder Pal	IND	13.11.94	193/120	SP	20.75	20.40- 17
Singh	Vikas	IND	6.7.96		20kW	1:22:39	1:30:56- 16
Singkhon	Sutthisak	THA	5.10.96	189/78	Dec	7809	7732- 17
Sinno	Alessandro	ITA	17.7.94	187/79	PV	5.55	5.45i- 16, 5.45- 17
Sitonik	Kiprono	KEN-Y	10.11.01	167/52	10k	27:53.59	-0-
* Sitonik	William	KEN	1.3.94	165/52	10k	27:36.45	26:54.66- 16
Skagestad	Sven Martin	NOR	13.1.95	201/130	DT	62.36	65.20- 16
Skrou̯úlis	Nikólaos	GRE	2.2.93	185/121	SP	20.24	20.61- 16
Skobeyko	Andrey	BLR	11.6.95	188/73	HJ	2.26i, 2.23	0.00 14
Skyers	Roberto	CUB	12.11.91	187/83	100	10.18, 10.0, 9.9w	10.11,9.9- 16, 10.06w- 17
Smaïli	Mostafa	MAR	9.1.97	172/61	800	1:44.90	1:45.05- 16
Smaliós	Jiannis	SWE	17.2.87	191/92	JT	79.89	81.89- 16
Smellie	Gavin	CAN	26.6.86	180/75	100	10.01	10.09- 15, 9.97w- 17
					200	20.38	20.38- 17, 20.16w- 15
Smelyk	Sergiy	UKR	19.4.87	178/74	200	20.34	20.30- 14
Smet	Koen	NED	9.8.92	186/74	110h	13.53	13.58, 13.52w- 13
* Smikle	Traves	JAM	7.5.92	193/120	DT	67.72	67.12- 12
Smith	Allan	GBR	6.11.92	198/84	HJ	2.27	2.29i- 15, 2.26- 13
Smith	Blake	USA	28.5.93	183/75	100	10.11w	10.25, 10.11w- 15
Smith	Calvin	USA	10.12.87	180/75	400	45.55	44.81- 10
Smith	David	GBR	14.7.91	188/77	HJ	2.26	2.26i- 15, 2.25- 14
Smith	Teray	BAH	28.9.94	185/77	200	20.46	20.25- 17
Smith	Terrell	USA	10.10.94	182/75	200	20.42	20.51- 15, 20.44w- 16
Smith	Tyrone	BER	7.8.86	183/70	LJ	8.03	8.34- 17
Snejdr	Filip	CZE	16.4.95	181/71	800	1:45.56	1:47.08- 17
Sniba	Ayoub	MAR	5.4.97	183/66	800	1:46.24	1:47.27- 15
Sobchuk	Dmytro	UKR	7.11.95	180/64	50kW	3:54:57	3:58:49- 16
^ Sobera	Robert	POL	19.1.91	190/77	PV	5.55	5.81i- 15, 5.70. 5.80ex- 14
Soboka	Tafese	ETH	29.9.93	176/60	3kSt	8:21.34	8:13:22- 17
^ Söderberg	David	FIN	11.8.79	185/100	HT	73.46	78.83- 03
Soget	Justus	KEN-J	22.10.99	178/61	1500	3:34.33	3:32.97A- 17
					3000	7:39.09i	
* Soi	Edwin	KEN	3.3.86	172/55	3000	7:42.02i	7:27.55- 11
Sokirskiy	Aleksey	RUS	16.3.85	185/108	HT	75.61	78.91- 12
Sokwakhana	Zazini	RSA-J	23.1.00	175/64	400h	49.32A, 49.42	
Solomon	Napoleon	SWE	14.2.94	165/54	3kSt	8:23.54	8:28.86- 17
^ Solomon	Steven	AUS	16.5.93	186/73	400	45.30	44.97- 12
Some	Peter	KEN	5.6.90	162/50	Mar	2:06:49	2:05:38- 13
Sorokin	Dmitriy	RUS	27.9.92	176/73	TJ	16.76	17.29- 15
Soto ¶	Manuel	COL	28.1.94	174/60	20kW	1:21:13	1:20:36- 16
Sottile	Stefano	ITA	26.1.98	182/70	HJ	2.24i, 2.20	2.22- 16
* Souleiman	Ayanleh	DJI	3.12.92	177/60	800	1:45.70	1:42.97- 15
	1000	2:16.08	2:13.49- 16		1500	3:31.19	3:29.58 -14 1M 3:55.87 3:47.32- 14
de Souza	Éder António	BRA	15.10.86	189/85	110h	13.70A	13.46- 15
Sowinski	Erik	USA	21.12.89	186/70	800	1:45.07	1:44.58- 14
Spears	Ro'Derick	USA	14.8.94	188/77	110h	13.65	13.77, 13.45w- 15
Spratling	Brycen	USA	10.3.92	175/68	400	45.22	45.09- 14
Sreeshankar	Murali	IND-J	27.3.99	174/61	LJ	8.20	7.72- 17

Name		Nat	Born	Ht/Wt	Event	2018 Mark	Pre-2018 Best
St Hillaire	Dwight	TTO	5.12.97	188/80	400	44.55	46.30- 17
* Ståhl	Daniel	SWE	27.8.92	200/150	DT	69.72	71.29- 17
Staicu	Cristian	ROU	30.7.93	180/65	LJ	8.09i, 7.86	7.87- 16
Staines	Thomas	GBR	22.2.98	184/73	800	1:45.57	1:50.39A-17
* Stanek	Tomás	CZE	13.6.91	190/127	SP	22.17i, 21.52	22.01- 17
* Stano	Massimo	ITA	27.2.92	179/63	20kW	1:20:51	1:22:16- 15
* Starc	Brandon	AUS	24.11.93	188/73	HJ	2.36	2.31- 15
Starkey	Garrett	USA	7.10.93	175/73	PV	5.60Ai, 5.45	5.50- 17
Stecchi	Claudio Michel	ITA	23.11.91	186/77	PV	5.67i, 5.52	5.60- 12
Stewart	Trevor	USA	20.5.97	178/70	400	45.28	46.44- 16
* Stigler	Michael	USA	5.4.92	178/70	400h	49.24	48.26- 17 '
Stój	Bartlomiej	POL	15.5.96	193/115	DT	62.04	64.64- 16
* Storl	David	GER	27.7.90	199/122	SP	21.62	22.20- 15
Strobinders	Rolands	LAT	14.4.92	189/106	JT	84.80	85.07- 17
Stromsik	Zdenek	CZE	25.11.94	175/80	100	10.16, 10.11w	10.29- 17
* Strother	Nathan	USA	6.9.95	183/70	400	44.34	45.07- 16
* Su Bingtian		CHN	29.8.09	172/04	100	9.91, 9.00w	9.99- 15, 9.92w- 17
* Suárez	Leonel	CUB	1.9.87	181/76	Dec	8026	8654- 09
Suganami	Yuya	JPN	23.10.95		50kW	4:03:42	-0-
Sulle	Augustino	TAN	13.10.97		Mar	2:07:46	2:10:01- 17
Sumi	Kunihiro	JPN	27.2.94	173/112	HT	70.63	70.05- 17
Sun Song		CHN	15.12.96		20kW	1:22:19	1:20:25- 17
Suskevicius	Tadas	LTU	22.5.85	175/65	50kW	4:00:40	3:51:58- 14
Susyk	Sergiy	UKR	21.7.93	178/68	50kW	4:03:55	4:25:52- 17
Suzuki	Yusuke	JPN	2.1.88	171/58	20kW	1:21:14	1:16:36- 15
* Svärd Jacobsson	Melker	SWE	8.1.94	188/78	PV	5.78i, 5.70	5.70- 16
Svoboda	Petr	CZE	10.10.84	195/83	110h	13.54	13.27- 10
Syrotchen	Josh	USA	19.4.94	188/107	DT	60.76	60.56- 16
Szikszai	Róbert	HUN	30.9.94	200/118	DT	64.37	63.20- 14
Szyszkowski	Jakub	POL	21.8.91	193/145	SP	20.68	20.02- 17
Taam	Nili	NLD	17.1.97	190/82	Dec	7853	7412- 17
^ Tadese	Zersenay	ERI	8.2.82	158/52	HMar	60:29	58:23- 10
					Mar	2:08:46	2:10:41- 12
Taftian	Hassan	IRI	4.5.93	178/75	100	10.03	10.04- 16
Taherkhani	Sobhan	IRI	21.9.92	175/73	LJ	7.96	7.90- 16
Taira	Kazuma	JPN	5.11.94	177/57	10k	28:16.22	28:30.23- 17
* Takahashi	Eiki	JPN	19.11.92	175/56	20kW	1:17:26	1:18:03- 15
Takayama	Shun-ya	JPN	3.9.94	183/71	110h	13.45	13.44- 17
Takekawa	Kosei	JPN	16.12.97	174/62	PV	5.60	5.30- 16
Taki	Kumari	KEN-J	6.5.99	172/59	800	1:46.29	1:46.2A- 15
					1500	3:35.83A	3:36.07- 17
* Tamberi	Gianmarco	ITA	1.6.92	189/71	HJ	2.33	2.39- 16
* Tamire Molla	Getaneh	ETH	10.1.94	171/55	3000	7:46.9+	7:52.54+- 17
5000	12:59.58		13:05.59- 16		HMar	60:47	60:34- 17
Tamura	Kazuki	JPN	16.7.95	167/50	10k	27:58.35	28:18.31- 16
Tanaka	Shin-ya	JPN	23.6.93	183/73	110h	13.64	13.64- 17
^ Tanii	Takayuki	JPN	14.2.83	167/57	20kW	1:21:47	1:20:39- 04
					50kW	3:51:54	3:40:19- 14
* Tanui	Paul	KEN	22.12.90	172/54	10k	28:11.41	26:50.60- 17
* Taplin	Bralon	GRN	8.5.92	180/73	400	44.67	44.38- 16
* Tarabin	Dmitriy	RUS	29.10.91	176/85	JT	85.38	88.84- 13
Tarbei	Philip	KEN	13.2.94		HMar	60:48	60:13- 17
* Taylor	Christian	USA	18.6.90	190/75	400	45.07	45.17- 11
					TJ	17.81, 17.86w	18.21- 15
Taylor	Christopher	JAM-J	29.9.99	178/70	100	10.11	10.44- 16
200	20.35		20.38- 17		400	44.88	45.27A- 15, 45.41- 17
Tefera	Asefa	ETH	14.3.97	166/50	HMar	60:07	61:50- 17
					Mar	2:08:34	
* Tefera	Samuel	ETH-J	23.10.99	171/52	1500	3:31.63	3:33.78- 17
					1M	3:51.26	-0-
Teles	Márcio	BRA	27.1.94	180/68	400h	48.70	48.94- 17
ten Berge	Mart	NED	27.4.91	186/86	JT	79.92	78.46- 17
* Tentóglou	Miltiádis	GRE	18.3.98	187/70	LJ	8.25	8.30- 17
Terentyev	Aleksey	RUS	19.7.91		50kW	3:59:14	4:05:14- 17
Terentyev	Ilya	RUS	25.1.95	184/100	HT	72.65	71.88- 17
^ Tesfaye	Homiyu	GER	23.6.93	183/66	1500	3:36.03	3:31.98- 14
Tewelde	Hizkel	ERI	15.9.86	173/57	HMar	60:04	60:29- 15
* Thebe	Baboloki	BOT	18.3.97	178/68	400	44.54	44.02- 17
Thomas	Damion	JAM-J	29.6.99	186/77	110h	13.44, 13.39w	-0-
* Thomas	Donald	BAH	1.7.84	190/75	HJ	2.32	2.37- 16
Thomas	Ieuan	GBR	17.7.89	180/65	3kSt	8:30.16	8:33.59- 17

Name		Nat	Born	Ht/Wt	Event	2018 Mark	Pre-2018 Best
Thompson	Chris	GBR	17.4.81	180/70	5000	13:25.11	13:11.51- 10
					10k	27:52.56	27:27.36- 11
Thompson	Greg	GBR	5.5.94	188/110	DT	61.29	60.28- 17
Thompson	Jahnoy	JAM	16.2.96	188/77	200	20.21	20.90- 17
Thompson	Joshua	USA	9.5.93	181/75	3kSt	8:30.29	8:32.90- 17
Thomsen	Marcus	NOR	7.1.98	185/115	SP	19.82	19.40- 17
^ Thorne	Benjamin	CAN	19.3.93	180/57	20kW	1:20:49	1:19:55- 16
Thuku	Karemi Jeremiah	KEN	7.7.94	176/62	10k	28:04.79	27:28.27- 14
Tiernan	Patrick	AUS	11.9.94	183/68	5000	13:24.58	13:13.44- 17
^ Tikhon	Ivan	BLR	24.7.76	186/110	HT	75.79	84.51- 08, 86.73dq- 05
Tilga	Karel	EST	5.2.98	198/90	Dec	8101	7489- 17
Timmermann	Lars	NED	19.4.91	180/84	JT	78.04	79.59- 10
Tindouft	Mohammed	MAR	12.3.93	175/60	3kSt	8:20.30	8:20.28- 17
* Tinsley	Michael	USA	21.4.84	185/74	400h	49.68	47.70- 13
Tiouali	Mohammed Ayoub	BRN	26.5.91	175/60	3000	7:44.58i	-0-
Tirop	Eric	KEN	19.5.87	170/55	HMar	60:20	62:20- 15
Titi	Ncincihli	RSA	15.12.93 Apr		167/61	20.00	200,20.14- 17
Tobalina	Carlos	ESP	2.8.85	187/127	SP	20.12i, 20.12	20.57- 17
* Tobe	Naoto	JPN	31.3.92	194/74	HJ	2.32	2.31- 14
Togawa	Tenju	JPN	8.1.97		LJ	8.00	7.70, 7.88w- 15
* Tola	Tamirat	ETH	11.8.91	181/59	Mar	2:04:06	2:04:11- 17
Toledo	Braian	ARG	8.9.93	187/100	JT	78.57A	83.32- 15
Tolosa	Taresa	ETH	15.6.98	181/64	1500	3:35.07	3:34.47- 17
Tolosa Nurgi	Jigisa	ETH	29.3.94	188/70	3kSt	8:23.79	8:21.33- 16
Tomala	Dawid	POL	27.8.89	182/65	20kW	1:22:44	1:20:30- 13
Tonnesen	Pau Gaspar	ESP	24.10.92	196/89	PV	5.55	5.53i- 16, 5.40- 17
Tontodonati	Federico	ITA	30.10.89	169/55	20kW	1:21:52	1:21:56- 16
Too	Silas	KEN	.89	169/55	Mar	2:08:26	2:15:19A-17
Tooker	Aidan	USA	26.6.98	171/57	3kSt	8:30.10	8:39.34- 17
Toroitich	Timothy	UGA	10.10.91	169/57	10k	27:47.35	27:21.09- 17
Torrijos	Pablo	ESP	12.6.92	187/78	TJ	16.98, 17.23w	17.04i- 15, 16.96- 17
Tortu	Filippo	ITA	15.6.98	187/75	100	9.99	10.15- 17
* Tóth	Matej	SVK	10.2.83	185/72	50kW	3:42:46	3:34:38- 15
Toyama	Takuma	JPN	8.1.96		20kW	1:22:58	
Toyota	Shoji	JPN	13.1.98		JT	77.52	
Traber	Gregor	GER	2.12.92	189/77	110h	13.26	13.21- 16
Tracey	Tyquendo	JAM	10.6.93	179/75	100	9.96	10.12- 17
* Trajkovic	Milan	CYP	17.3.92	187/72	110h	13.36	13.25- 17
Trefz	Johannes	GER	7.6.92	200/94	400	45.70	45.81- 17
Trescoli	Pablo	ESP	4.3.95	197/85	Dec	7598	7634- 17
Triki	Yasser	ALG	24.3.97	188/80	LJ	8.01	8.03- 17
					TJ	16.91	16.85- 17
Trofin	Cosmin	ROU	9.1.96	180/68	800	1:46.41	1:47.90- 17
Trouard	Andy	USA	22.4.94	178/62	5000	13:21.07	13:36.43- 17
True	Aaron	USA	7.11.95		JT	77.49	69.88- 17
* True	Ben	USA	29.12.85	183/70	3000	7:41.86	7:35.53- 17
					5000	13:04.11	13:02.74- 14
Trus	Viktor	BLR	11.11.96	197/110	DT	60.29	62.17- 17
Tryapkin	Andrey	RUS	1.12.97		20kW	1:21:30	1:25:24- 17
Tsegay	Atsedu	ETH	17.12.91	164/50	HMar	60:28	58:47- 12
Tsegay	Samuel	ERI	24.02.88	176/55	Mar	2:08:20	2:07:28- 11
Tsenov	Mitko	BUL	13.6.93	185/64	3kSt	8:28.78	8:20.87- 14
Tsernjavski	Taavi	EST	4.3.95	196/86	Dec	7873	7802- 17
Tshite	Tshepo	RSA	15.1.97	165/55	800	1:46.04A	1:47.11A- 17
Tsiámis	Dimítrios	GRE	12.1.82	178/67	TJ	16.78	17.55- 06
Tsonov	Georgi	BUL	2.5.93	172/66	TJ	16.57	17.03, 17.11w- 15
Tsuha	Hibiki	JPN	21.1.98	168/65	LJ	8.01, 8.03w	8.09- 17
Tsumba	Tatenda	ZIM	12.11.91	175/73	200	20.67A, 20.68, 20.28Aw	20.44- 16, 20.42w- 17
^ Tsyplakov	Daniyil	RUS	29.7.92	190/75	HJ	2.25	2.34i, 2.33- 14
Tual	Gabriel	FRA	9.4.98	182/68	800	1:46.35	1:48.02- 17
Tucker	Infinite	USA	22.5.98	196/90	400h	49.46	50.70- 16
Tucker	Javoy	JAM	13.5.97	178/77	100	10.08	10.49- 17
Tuemay	Tsegay	ERI	20.12.95	172/55	HMar	60:50	61:38dh- 17, 61:39- 15
^ Tuka	Amel	BIH	9.1.91	187/77	800	1:45.68	1:42.51- 15
Tur	Marc	ESP	30.11.94	190/70	50kW	3:56:05	-0-
Tura	Abdiwak	ETH	.95	176/59	HMar	60:41	62:58- 17
					Mar	2:04:44	2:09:26- 17
Turambekar	Eknath Sambhaji	IND	18.1.98		20kW	1:21:55	1:24:36- 17
Turner	Vernon	USA	21.8.98	188/77	HJ	2.33i, 2.28	2.28- 17
Tuufuli	Reno	USA	15.2.96	190/120	DT	60.87	62.06- 17

Name		Nat	Born	Ht/Wt	Event	2018 Mark	Pre-2018 Best
Tuwei	Cornelius	KEN	24.5.93	179/64	1000	2:16.89	-0-
					1500	3:35.72	
Tuwei	Dickson	KEN	31.10.92	180/64	Mar	2:08:22	2:09:27- 16
Tuwei	Cornelius	KEN	24.5.93	179/64	800	1:43.82	1:45.3A- 17
Ugachi	Tsuyoshi	JPN	27.4.87	163/49	10k	28:17.63	27:40.69- 11
* Uibo	Maicel	EST	27.12.92	188/86	Dec	8514	8356- 15
* Ijah	Ohijindu	GBR	5.3.94	180/75	100	10.06	9.96- 14, 9.95w- 17
Ujakpor	Mark	ESP	18.1.87	192/80	400h	49.58	49.65- 16
* Ukhov	Ivan	RUS	29.3.86	192/83	HJ	2.35i, 2.34	2.42i, 2.41- 14
Unsum-Ang	Phassapong	THA	2.10.97	169/64	PV	5.55	5.40- 17
Updike	Isaac	USA	21.3.92	180/64	3kSt	8:25.38	8:31.42- 16
* Urbanek	Robert	POL	29.4.87	200/120	DT	65.15	66.93- 12
* Ureña	Jorge	ESP	8.10.93	178/82	Dec	7934	8125- 17
Ushiro	Keisuke	JPN	24.7.86	196/95	Dec	7948	8308- 17
* Vadlejch	Jakub	CZE	10.10.90	190/93	JT	89.02	89.73- 17
Vaillant	Ludvy	FRA	15.3.95	180/64	400	45.25	45.92- 17
					400h	48.42	49.31- 17
Valdez	Cristofer	DOM	1.11.94	175/64	100	10.22, 10.09w	10.23, 10.20w- 17
Vallés	Adrián	ESP	16.3.95	190/76	PV	5.61i, 5.55	5.70- 17
van Assen	Miguel	SUR	30.7.97	186/84	TJ	16.96	16.94- 17
* Van Der Plaetsen	Thomas	BEL	24.12.90	188/82	Dec	8007	8332- 16
van Eeden	Anro	RSA-J	19.5.99		JT	77.59	77.78- 17
van Rensburg	Phil-Mar	RSA	23.6.89	188/92	JT	79.83	80.49A- 17
van Rensburg	Rynhardt	RSA	23.3.92	184/70	800	1:45.15	1:45.33- 16
van Wyk	Chederick	RSA	18.2.95	183/73	200	20.45A	21.14A- 16
^ van Zyl	Louis 'L.J'	RSA	20.7.85	186/75	400h	49.45A, 50.44	47.66- 11
Vanderbemden	Robin	BEL	10.2.94	183/72	200	20.43, 20.40w	20.45- 17
^ Varga	Roland	CRO	22.10.77	196/125	DT	60.59	67.38- 02
Vargas	Richard	VEN	28.12.94	178/70	20kW	1:22:10	1:22:10- 16
Vaughn	Luke	USA	24.8.94	201/120	DT	60.13	58.25- 17
Väyrinen	Henri	FIN	16.10.91	185/75	LJ	7.97w	8.07A- 16, 7 93-15, 8.05w- 17
Vázquez	Wesley	PUR	27.3.94	184/73	800	1:46.47	1:44.64- 14
Vega	Fernando	MEX	19.2.98	178/62	400h	49.85	49.96-17
Veith	Hunter	USA	14.1.95	185/79	Dec	8046	7866- 17
Vena	Nick	USA	16.4.93	194/120	SP	20.68i, 19.56	20.42- 17
Venyercsán	Bence	HUN	8.1.96	173/56	50kW	3:58:25	4:02:35- 16
Vergani	Lorenzo	ITA	4.9.93	188/78	400h	49.37	49.36- 17
Vernon	Andrew	GBR	7.1.86	178/65	10k	27:52.32	27:42.62- 15
Veryovkin	Mikhail	RUS	28.6.91		HJ	2.25	2.29i- 15, 2.23- 14
* Vesely	Vitezslav	CZE	27.2.83	186/94	JT	82.30	88.34- 12
Vestlund	Oscar	SWE	27.4.93	189/110	HT	71.34	73.34- 17
Veszelka	Tomás	SVK	9.7.95	183/79	TJ	16.62, 16.86w	16.63- 17
Veteto	Justin	USA	24.3.96	188/70	110h	13.68	13.85, 13.77w- 17
Vetter	Johannes	GER	26.3.93	188/105	JT	92.70	94.44- 17
* Vicaut	Jimmy	FRA	27.2.92	188/83	100	9.91	9.86- 15
Victor	Lindon	GRN	28.2.93	191/90	Dec	8303	8539(w)- 17
Victorin	Guillaume	FRA	26.5.90	184/78	LJ	8.00	7.91i- 14, 7.86- 11
Vidal	Maykel	CUB-J	6.1.00	175/64	LJ	8.12	7.88A, 7.85- 17
Vides	Jorge Henrique	BRA	24.11.92	190/77	100	10.08	10.26, 10.22w- 16
					200	20.34	20.38- 14
^ Vieira	João	POR	20.2.76	174/58	20kW	1:22:06	1:20:09- 06
Vij	Sourabh	IND	14.6.87	180/105	SP	19.56	19.15- 10, 19.80dq- 12
Vilches	Roberto	MEX-J	21.5.99	193/84	HJ	2.26A	2.25A, 2.21- 17
Villanueva	Claudio	ECU	3.8.88	168/55	50kW	3:55:04	3:49:27- 17
Villarreal	Carlos	MEX	10.5.97	173/61	1500	3:38.28	3:41.75- 17
* Visser	Zarck	RSA	15.9.89	178/70	LJ	8.40	8.41- 15
^ Vivas	Borja	ESP	26.5.84	203/140	SP	20.27i, 20.03	21.07- 14
Vloon	Menno	NED	11.5.94	177/77	PV	5.70i, 5.56	5.85- 17
Volko	Ján	SVK	2.11.96	179/75	100	10.13, 10-.07w	10.15- 17
					200	20.24	20.33- 17
Volz	Deakin	USA	12.1.97	178/75	PV	5.60i, 5.60	5.66i- 17, 5.65- 16
Volz	Drew	USA	20.11.92	181/75	PV	5.60	5.62i, 5.50- 16
Vonavka	Tomás	CZE	4.6.90	197/109	DT	60.66	63.18- 16
de Vries	Ruan	RSA	1.2.86	187/88	110h	13.63A 13.59A,13.67-13,13.57Aw-15,13.23dt-17	13.54- 16
Vukicevic	Vladimir	NOR	6.5.91	193/83	110h	13.58	13.54- 16
Wachira	Simon	KEN	6.5.84	170/65	20kW	1:19:06A	1:23:26- 16
Waithaka	Stanley M	KEN-J	9.4.00	168/55	3000	7:45.3+	7:50.64- 17
5000	13:10.14		13:57.5 - 17		10k	27:13.01	
Waithe	Shakiel	TTO	10.6.95	201/85	JT	79.90	79.53- 16
* Walcott	Keshorn	TTO	2.4.93	188/90	JT	84.96	90.16- 15
Wale	Getnet	ETH-J	16.7.00	178/60	5000	13:13.87	-0-
					3kSt	8:22.68	8:12.28- 17

Name		Nat	Born	Ht/Wt	Event	2018 Mark	Pre-2018 Best
Walelegn	Amdework	ETH-J	11.3.99	167/52	HMar	59:22	-0-
Walsh	Cole	USA	14.6.95	190/80	PV	5.75	5.50- 17
Walsh	Julian Jrummi	JPN	18.9.96	175/75	400	45.63	45.35- 16
* Walsh	Tom	NZL	1.3.92	186/123	SP	22.67	22.21- 16
Walter	Keitavious	USA	16.4.96	178/77	100	10.12	10.21, 9.98w- 17
					200	20.33	20.43- 17
Walters	Ruebin	TTO	2.4.95	184/70	110h	13.31, 13.28w	13.30- 17
Walton	Jamal	CAY	25.11.98	190/77	400	45.42	44.99- 17
* Wanders	Julien	SUI	18.3.96	175/60	5000	13:24.79	13:37.48- 17
10k	28:07.15		28:06.17- 17		HMar	60:09	61:43- 17
Wang Chao		CHN	2.5.96		50kW	4:02:41	4:07:51- 16
Wang Hao		CHN	16.8.89	180/65	50kW	4:02:01	3:41:55- 09
* Wang Jianan		CHN	27.8.96	178/61	LJ	8.47A. 8.24	8.29- 17
* Wang Kaihua		CHN	16.2.94	180/65	20kW	1:19:45	1:17:54- 17
* Wang Qin		CHN	8.5.94	178/65	50kW	3:45:29	3:50:16- 16
Wang Rui		CHN	6.1.96	180/65	50kW	3:48:01	-0-
Wang Shizhu		CHN	20.2.89	184/100	HT	71.49	76.12- 17
* Wang Yu		CHN	18.8.91	192/73	HJ	2.32	2.33- 13
Wangari	James	KEN	23.3.94	175/58	5000	13:18.73	13:13.93- 16
					HMar	60:49	59:07- 16
Ward	Ja'Mari	USA	21.3.98	175/68	LJ	7.97i	8.13- 17
* Warholm	Karsten	NOR	28.2.96	187/78	400	44.91	44.87- 17
					400h	47.64	48.22- 17
* Warner	Damian	CAN	4.11.89	185/83	110h	13.48	13.27- 15
					Dec	8795	8695- 15
Warren	John	USA	2.3.96	178/73	TJ	16.64	16.27- 16
Washington	Marqueze	USA	29.9.93	188/84	100	10.03w	10.07- 17
200	20.47, 20.24w		20.32- 17		400	45.24i	45.63i- 17, 45.99- 15
* Wasihun	Mule	ETH	20.10.93	166/52	HMar	59:44	60:08- 14
					Mar	2:04:37	2:05:39- 17
Wasik	Steele	USA	9.12.95	196/86	Dec	7588w, 7484	7715(w)- 17
Wasome	O'Brien	JAM	24.1.97	177/64	TJ	16.82i	16.49i- 17, 16.00 16
Waweru	Edward	KEN	3.10.90	178/58	HMar	60:31	62:08- 14
* Webb	Ameer	USA	19.3.91	175/75	100	10.07	9.94, 9.90w- 16
					200	20.13	19.85- 16
Webb	Jamie	GBR	1.6.94	183/68	800	1:45.73	1:46.59- 16
* Weber	Julian	GER	29.8.94	190/94	JT	86.63	88.29- 16
Wecksten	Tomas	FIN	2.11.96	182/76	PV	5.55i, 5.50	5.51- 17
Weh	Mason	LBR	14.4.98	186/77	110h	13.61A	14.37, 13.94w- 17
Wei Xubao		CHN	1.2.93		20kW	1:22:31	1:21:46- 16
					50kW	4:03:43	4:09:36- 13
* Weisshaidinger	Lukas	AUT	20.2.92	196/136	DT	68.98	67.24- 15
Weldon	Kole	USA	25.3.92	193/114	DT	60.05	62.48- 16
Wells	Jonathan	USA	18.4.96	188/82	HJ	2.26	2.20i, 2.17- 15
Wesner	Jordan	USA	10.6.97	193/84	HJ	2.25i	2.23- 17
West	James	GBR	30.1.96	172/59	1500	3:36.59	3:39.65- 17
West	Jordan	USA-J	27.6.99	183/118	SP	19.79	-0-
West	McKinely	USA	26.6.96	173/66	100	10.07	10.29, 10.05w- 17
					200	20.30	20.65, 20.49Aw- 17
* Whiting	Ryan	USA	24.11.86	191/134	SP	21.03i, 20.99	22.28- 13
* Whyte	Annsert	JAM	10.4.87	185/75	400h	48.46	48.07- 16
* Wierig	Martin	GER	10.6.87	202/127	DT	66.98	68.33- 12
Wiesiolek	Pawel	POL	13.8.91	194/84	Dec	7921	8140- 15
* Wightman	Jake	GBR	11.7.94	173/60	800	1:44.61	1:45.42- 17
1000	2:16.27		-0-		1500	3:33.96	3:34.17- 17
Wijesekara	Manjula Kumara	SRI	30.1.84	183/73	HJ	2.24	2.27- 04
Wilkinson	Callum	GBR	14.3.97	179/63	20kW	1:22:35	1:22:17- 17
Williams	Brian	USA	18.12.94	188/109	DT	61.54	65.13- 17
Williams	Cooper	USA	9.3.98	188/77	800	1:46.06	1:49.75- 16
Williams	Delano	GBR	23.12.93	183/72	200	20.47	20.27- 13
Williams	Harrison	USA	7.3.96	190/82	Dec	7925	8032- 16
Williams	Kendal	USA	23.9.95	180/73	100	9.99	10.06- 16, 9.98w- 15
					200	20.15	20.26- 15, 20.11w- 16
Williams	Marvin	JAM	13.6.96	181/75	400h	49.60	49.90- 15
Williams	Mustaqeem	USA	24.8.95	175/73	100	10.12	10.31- 13
					200	20.23, 20.11w	20.64- 13, 20.59w- 16
Williams	Trae	AUS	5.5.97	168/66	100	10.10	10.27- 16
Williams	Waseem	JAM	8.1.97	168/64	100	10.10, 10.06w	10.40- 14
Williams	Will	USA	31.1.95	183/79	LJ	8.19i, 8.05, 8.25w	8.03- 15, 8.09w- 17
Williamson	Capers	USA	13.10.92	201/97	JT	79.07	75.15- 17
Williamsz	Jordan	AUS	21.8.92	172/64	1500	3:36.30	3:36.74- 12

Name		Nat	Born	Ht/Wt	Event	2018 Mark	Pre-2018 Best
Willis	Maxwell	USA	2.9.98	170/64	100	10.12	10.18, 10.03w- 17
* Willis	Nick	NZL	25.4.83	183/68	1500	3:35.25	3:29.66- 15
* Wilson	Alex	SUI	19.9.90	182/79	100	10.14	10.11, 10.08w- 17
					200	20.04	20.37- 17
Wilson	Jamal	BAH	1.9.88	188/68	HJ	2.31i, 2.30	2.31i, 2.30- 16
Wimalasiri	D.A.G. Prasad	SRI	8.9.92	173/63	LJ	8.14	7.00- 15, 8.13w- 17
Winder	Luke	USA	2.8.95	185/75	PV	5.60	5.56- 17
Windle	Drew	USA	22.7.92	183/73	800	1:45.52i, 1:46.88	1:44.63- 17
Winkler	Rudy	USA	6.12.94	186/102	HT	73.85	76.76- 16
* Wojciechowski	Pawel	POL	6.6.89	190/81	PV	5.88i, 5.84	5.93- 17
Wolde	Dawit	ETH	19.5.91	177/60	3000	7:47.58	7:41.69i- 16, 7:42.65- 11
					5000	13:10.65	13:10.13- 17
Wolski	Allan	BRA	18.1.90	185/110	HT	73.45	75.22- 17
Woo Sang-hyuk		KOR	23.4.96	187/66	HJ	2.30	2.30- 17
Wooten	Jacob	USA	22.4.97	183/73	PV	5.60i, 5.55	5.46i- 16, 5.45- 17
Workneh	Derese	ETH	23.7.95	169/51	10k	28:14.49	28:19.16- 16
Worku	Bazu	ETH	15.9.90	170/52	Mar	2:08:30	2:05:25- 10
* Wote	Aman	ETH	18.4.84	181/64	1500	3:31.90	3:29.91- 14
Wright	Alex	IRL	19.12.90	173/64	20kW	1:22:18	1:21:17- 17
Wright	Andwuelle	TTO	8.8.97	174/65	LJ	8.23	7.58- 15, 7.60w- 14
Wright	Chad	JAM	25.3.91	188/110	DT	65.47	65.03- 15
Wright	Dontavius	USA	3.1.94	178/68	400	45.50Ai	45.12- 16
Wrobel	David	GER	13.2.91	195/125	DT	65.98	64.66- 17, 64.93dh- 16
^ Wruck	Julian	AUS	6.7.91	198/125	DT	60.96	68.16- 13
Wu Ruiting		CHN	29.11.95		TJ	16.89	17.18- 17
Wyatt	Audie	USA	30.4.96	190/84	PV	5.60	5.70- 17
Wynne	Henry	USA	18.4.95	186/75	1M	3:55.23i. 3:56.86	3:58.74i- 16, 4:05.04- 13
* Xie Wenjun		CHN	11.7.90	188/77	110h	13.34	13.23- 14
Xie Zhenye		CHN	17.8.93	185/80	100	9.97	10.04, 9.91w- 17
					200	20.16	20.20- 17
Xiong Donghua		CHN	29.5.95		50kW	4:03:53	4:06:21- 15
Xu Xiaolong		CHN	20.12.92	185/70	TJ	16.66i, 16.65	16.93- 15
* Xue Changrui		CHN	31.5.91	183/60	PV	5.75i, 5.71	5.82- 17
Yadav	Siddharth	IND	30.1.93	184/68	HJ	2.25	2.23- 17
Yakushev	Maksim	RUS	15.3.92	173/61	3kSt	8:22.40	8:19.19- 17
Yamagata	Ryota	JPN	10.6.92	176/70	100	10.00	10.00- 17
Yamaguchi	Kosei	JPN	19.8.91	171/58	3kSt	8:30.98	8:36.30- 16
Yamamoto	Ryoma	JPN	14.7.95	178/62	TJ	16.59, 16.74w	16.87, 16.91w- 17
Yamamoto	Seito	JPN	11.3.92	181/70	PV	5.70	5.77Ai- 16, 5.75- 13
Yamamoto	Tatsuhiro	JPN	23.4.97	176/65	400h	49.69	49.92- 17
Yamanaka	Hideto	JPN	17.3.94	169/52	10k	28:16.95	28:26.03- 13
* Yamanishi	Toshikazu	JPN	15.2.96	164/51	20kW	1:17:41	1:19:03- 17
Yamashita	Jun	JPN	23.8.97	181/73	200	20.46, 20.31w	20.59- 17
Yamashita	Kohei	JPN	6.9.94	179/69	TJ	16.59	16.06- 15
Yamazaki	Yuki	JPN	16.1.84	179.65	50kW	4:03:09	3:40:12- 09
Yáñez	Eure	VEN	20.5.93	194/77	HJ	2.28A	2.31- 17
Yang Chun-Han		TPE	1.1.97	176/65	100	10.11	10.20- 17
					200	20.23	20.53- 15
Yang Lubang		CHN	18.6.97	193/80	HJ	2.24i	2.20- 17
Yang Wei-Ting		TPE	22.9.94	182/73	110h	13.69	13.57- 17
Yao Jie		CHN	21.9.90	188/85	PV	5.62i, 5.61	5.70- 16
Yator	Richard	KEN	6.4.98	175/57	3000	7;47.3+	7:53.3A- 15
5000	12:59.44		13:22.66- 17		10k	27:14.70	27:52.10- 17
Yeboah	Emmanuel	GHA	10.8.97	177/65	100	10.07w	10.25- 17
Yee	Alexander	GBR	18.2.98	172/55	10k	27:51.94	-0-
Yego	Evans	KEN	5.9.95	171/56	5000	13:24.27	13:38.13- 17
					10k	28:00.56	28:36.57- 17
* Yego	Hillary	KEN	2.4.92	178/60	3kSt	8:25.30	8:03.57- 13
Yego	Isaac	KEN	.89	177/60	3kSt	8:31.26	8:31.4A- 17
* Yego	Julius	KEN	4.1.89	175/90	JT	80.91A	92.72- 15
Yego	Solomon Kirwa	KEN	10.5.87	175/58	Mar	2:06:24	2:07:12- 17
Yegon	Geoffrey	KEN	28.8.88	168/55	HMar	59:56	59:44- 16
* Yemataw	Birhanu	BRN	27.2.96	167/54	3000	7:34.26	7:44.29- 16
2M	8:21.54				5000	13:01.09	13:09.26- 16
Yeremich	Yuriy	BLR	24.10.95	178/75	Dec	7985	7817- 15
Yevseyev	Igor	RUS	27.3.96		HT	72.29	68.80- 16
Yevstifeyev	Roman	RUS	19.9.92		20kW	1:20:21	1:22:21- 15
* Yimer	Jemal	ETH	11.9.96	163/48	HMar	58:33	-0-
Yin Jiaxing		CHN	16.3.94		20kW	1:21:23	1:20:56- 17
Yorks	Izaic	USA	17.4.94	174/64	1500	3:36.81	3:37.74- 16
					1M	3:53.40i	3:53.89i- 16, 3:58.57- 17

Name		Nat	Born	Ht/Wt	Event	2018 Mark	Pre-2018 Best
Yoroizaka	Tetsuya	JPN	20.3.90	166/52	10k	27:55.85	27:29.74- 15
Young	Alex	USA	1.9.94	188/105	HT	76.14	74.39- 17
* Young	Isiah	USA	5.1.90	183/75	100	9.92. 9.92w	9.97- 17, 9.82w- 15
					200	19.93	19.86- 13, 19.75w- 15
Young	Jordan	CAN	21.6.93	190/113	SP	19.90	19.80- 15
					DT	60.67	62.76- 17
Yousif	Rabah	GBR	11.12.86	183/75	400	45.30	44.54- 15
Yugami	Masateru	JPN	14.4.93	183/104	DT	62.16	59.24- 17
Yunyakin	Maksim	RUS	13.2.96	188/75	LJ	7.98	7.90i, 7.77- 16
Yurchenko	Aleksandr	RUS	30.7.92	182/73	TJ	17.15	16.94i, 16.76- 17
Zahafi	Mouad	MAR	9.5.98	183/68	800	1:46.38	1:47.45- 17
Zaharia	George	ROU	3.8.95	191/85	JT	78.53	77.79- 16
* Zakalnytskyy	Maryan	UKR	19.8.94	180/65	50kW	3:44:59	3:53:50- 17
* Zakayo	Edward	KEN-Y	25.11.01	173/57	5000	13:19.74A	
Zalewski	Karol	POL	7.8.93	189/86	400	45.11	45.84- 16
Zalewski	Krystian	POL	11.4.89	187/75	3kSt	8:27.72	8:16.20- 14
Zambrano	Anthony	COL	17.1.98	179/68	400	45.19A	45.81- 16
Zamora	Leandro	CUB	11.3.96	186/75	400h	49.10A, 49.51, 49.4	49.58- 17
* Zango	Fabrice	BUR	25.6.93	180/75	TJ	17.23i, 17.11	16.97- 17
Zaza	Wellington	LBR	20.1.95	175/70	110h	13.67	13.68- 17, 13.59w- 16
Zeng Jianhang		CHN	17.9.98	183/75	110h	13.65A, 13.65	13.86A- 17
Zenúch	Patrik	SVK	30.12.90	184/86	JT	78.25	84.83- 14
Zepeda	Omar	MEX	8.7.77	177/68	50kW	3:57:31	3:45:28A- 16
Zerrifi	Abdelhamid	ALG/FRA	20.6.86	170/57	3kSt	8:29.31	8:25.96- 13
Zézé	Mickaël-Meba	FRA	19.5.94	174/61	200	20.49, 20.33w	20.47- 17
Zhang Jun		CHN	20.7.98		20kW	1:21:10	1:24:11- 17
Zhang Wei		CHN	22.3.94	188/77	PV	5.70	5.65- 15
Zhang Yaoguang		CHN	21.6.93	176/68	LJ	8.29A, 8.15	8.19- 17
Zhaxi Yangben		CHN	15.4.96		20kW	1:22:45	1:23:09- 17
Zhelyabin	Dmitry	RUS	20.5.90	187/75	PV	5.80i, 5.65	5.70i- 17, 5.65- 12
Zhidkov	Nikita	RUS	30.2.88		SP	20.01	19.71- 12
Zholudyev	Roman	BLR	8.1.96		HT	70.86	70.08- 17
Zhu Kai		CHN	24.8.98		JT	79.46A	68.56- 17
Zhu Yaming		CHN	4.5.94	187/74	TJ	17.11A, 16.79	17.23- 17
Zhuk	Vitaliy	BLR	10.9.96	187/86	Dec	8290	7921- 17
* Ziemek	Zach	USA	23.2.93	190/77	Dec	8294	8413- 16
Ziukas	Marius	LTU	29.6.85	185/70	20kW	1:20:31	1:21:27- 17
Zoghlami	Osama	ITA	19.6.94	182/58	3kSt	8:28.23	8:22.94- 17
Zótos	Kiriáko	GRE	17.1.96	187/100	SP	19.59i	19.47- 17
* Zunic	Stipe	CRO	13.12.90	188/115	SP	21.36	21.48- 17
Zupancic	Biaz	SLO	6.4.95	188/114	SP	19.94	18.93- 17

WOMEN'S INDEX 2018

Name		Nat	Born	Ht/Wt	Event	2018 Mark	Pre-2018 Best
Ababel	Yeshaneh	ETH	10.6.90	157/42	HMar	65:46	67:21- 17
					Mar	2:20:16?	2:33:10- 13
Abbott	Chloe	USA	25.7.98	167/54	400	51.57	52.68- 17
Abdelkadir Gosa	Dalilah	BRN	27.6.98		Mar	2:25:35	-0-
Abe	Yukari	JPN	21.8.89	154/48	10000	32:13.79	32:24.61- 17
Abire	Mercy Uyoyo	NGR	20.7.97		LJ	6.50w	6.18- 16
Abramchuk	Alena	BLR	14.2.88	182/95	SP	18.11	19.24- 13
Abrams	Aliyah	GUY	3.4.97	163/53	400	52.04	52.04- 16
Abreha	Azmera	ETH-J	21.9.00	162/45	Mar	2:21:51	2:25:23- 17
Abu	Agnes	GHA	1.5.92	170/65	800	2:00.77	2:02.70- 17
* Adams	Valerie	NZL	6.10.84	193/120	SP	19.31	21.24- 11
Adamu	Birtukan	ETH	29.4.92	164/49	3kSt	9:48.38	9:20.37- 11
* Adekoya	Kemi	BRN	16.1.93	168/57	400h	54.48	54.12- 15
Afanasyeva	Klavdiya	RUS	15.1.96		50kW	4:14:46	-0-
Afework	Abebech	ETH	11.12.90	152/42	Mar	2:25:02	2:23:33- 15
* Aga	Ruti	ETH	16.1.94	159/45	HMar	66:39	68:07- 16
					Mar	2:18:34	2:20:41- 17
Agai	Margaret	KEN	10.6.88	154/44	HMar	69:45+	69:43- 17
					Mar	2:24:30	2:23:28- 13
Aguessy Thomas	Cassandre	FRA	1.9.97	174/60	Hep	5837	5794- 17
Aguilar	Evelis	COL	3.1.93	170/62	Hep	6285	6270A, 6263- 16
Aguilar	Yulenmis	CUB	3.8.96	167/70	JT	60.29	63.86- 15
Agyapong	Finette	GBR	1.2.97	180/70	200	22.95	22.86- 17
Ahlberg	Grete	SWE	29.5.98	176.79	HT	67.17	64.25- 17
Ahn Seul-ki		KOR	29.5.92	161/46	10000	32:33.61	33:23.43- 16
Ahouanwanou	Odile	BEN	5.1.91	178/71	Hep	5999	6131(w)- 17
* Ahouré	Murielle	CIV	23.8.87	167/57	100	10.90	10.78-16
					200	22.60	22.24- 13

Name		Nat	Born	Ht/Wt	Event	2018 Mark	Pre-2018 Best
Ahye	Michelle-Lee	TTO	10.4.92	168/59	100	11.06	10.82- 17
Aiyabei	Valary	KEN	8.6.91	156/42	Mar	2:21:38	2:20:53- 17
Ajayi	Yinka	NGR	11.8.97	163/54	400	51.22	51.30- 17
Ajok	Dorcus	UGA	12.7.94	162/65	800	2:00.02A	2:00.79- 17
Åkerström	Frida	SWE	29.11.90	172/88	SP	17.11	16.72- 14
* Akkaoui	Malika	MAR	25.12.87	160/46	800	1:59.27	1:57.64- 13
					1500	4:07.08	4:03.36- 17
Akpan	Abasiono	NGR-J	15.12.00	168/52	400h	56.74	60.65- 17
Aksenova	Natalya	RUS	6.6.97		HJ	1.88	1.92- 16
Al-Khaldi	Hajar Saad	BRN	17.3.95	160/45	100	11.17	11.42- 16
Alais	Alexie	FRA	9.10.94	168/68	JT	60.59	57.81- 16
Alemayehu	Gete	ETH	27.8.98		10000	31:45.32	
Alemayehu	Haimanot	ETH	17.6.90		Mar	2:25:51	
* Alemu	Habitam	ETH	9.7.97	171/52	800	1:56.71	1:57.05- 17
					1500	4:01.41	4:14.67- 15
Alemu	Worknesh	ETH	.90		Mar	2:26:50	2:30:04- 17
Alexander	Sarea	USA	15.2.96	178/64	LJ	6.54	6.10- 17, 6.21w- 17
Alexoúli	Háido	GRE	29.3.91	179/59	LJ	6.55, 6.65w	6.78- 16
Alfred	Julien	LCA-Y	10.6.01	170/52	100	11.23w	11.53- 17
Allcock	Amy	GBR	24.8.93	167/57	400	51.36	52.83- 14
Allen	Sabina	JAM			TJ	13.61i	13.11- 16
Allgood	Avione	USA	14.12.93	165/	JT	56.54	58.81- 16
Allman	Valarie	USA	23.2.95	183/70	DT	63.55	64.69- 17
* Almanza	Rose Mary	CUB	13.7.92	166/53	800	2:00.15	1:57.70- 15
Álvarez	Paula Beatriz	CUB	11.9.95	164/58	LJ	6.58	6.48- 13, 6.59w- 17
Álvarez	Rosalina	CUB	3.1.97		DT	56.05	55.61- 17
Alver	Tähti	EST	4.12.94	180/64	TJ	14.05	13.50- 17
Alvertsián	Kristína	GRE	4.7.90	175/62	TJ	13.62	13.60- 17
Amaechi	Pamela	USA-J	12.3.99	175/75	DT	60.00	53.94- 17
Amann	Taylor	USA	6.5.96	173/62	PV	4.36	4.20- 17
^ Amata	Doreen	NGR	6.5.88	185/55	HJ	1.88i	1.95- 08
Amponsah	Janet	GHA	12.4.93	167/52	100	11.21	11.29, 11.12w- 15
					200	22.67	22.90A- 17, 22.99- 16
* Amusan	Tobi	NGR	23.4.97	164/52	100h	12.68, 12.16w	12.57- 17
Anagnostopoúlou	Hrisoúla	GRE	27.8.91	176/79	DT	59.42	61.53- 17
Anais	Cynthia	FRA	18.1.88	158/48	800	2:00.60	2:03.73- 17
Anang	Naa	AUS	10.3.95	165/54	LJ	6.66	6.68- 17
Andersen	Brooke	USA	23.8.95	170/84	HT	74.20	68.62- 17
Anderson	Brittany	JAM-Y	31.1.01	165/60	100h	13.01	-0-
Andersson	Saga	FIN-J	30.3.00	168/53	PV	4.40i, 4.39	4.42- 17
Andersson	Tracey	SWE	5.12.84	167/87	HT	67.06	70.99- 16
Andraud	Matilde	FRA	28.4.89	172/68	JT	58.32	63.54- 16
Andrejsková	Petra	CZE	25.6.92	176/64	JT	55.81	57.48- 14
Andreopoúlou	Nikolítsa	GRE	26.3.83		50kW	4:41:44	-0-
Andres	Rachel	CAN	21.4.87		DT	56.82	55.84- 14
Andreutti	Giada	ITA	16.2.95	180/75	DT	56.60	55.70- 17
^ Angelsen	Tonje	NOR	17.1.90	179/62	HJ	1.91	1.97- 12
Aniballi	Valentina	ITA	19.4.84	176/85	DT	59.12	58.55- 15
Anigbata	Grace	NGR	16.9.98		TJ	14.02	12.96- 16
Anikiyenko	Yelizaveta	RUS	30.6.94	170/60	400h	57.22	57.37- 15
Anitei	Georgiana	ROU-J	26.3.99		TJ	13.58	13.49- 15, 13.50w- 15
Ankiewioz	Emilia	POL	22.11.90	178/64	400h	56.70	55.89- 16
Annelus	Angie	USA	10.1.97	168/57	100	11.25	11.43- 16
					200	22.64, 22.52w	23.22- 16
Ansa	Woynshet	ETH	9.4.96	158/42	3kSt	9:27.03	9:30.03- 17
Antoine	Sandisha	LCA	5.11.91	178/61	TJ	13.91	13.50A- 15, 13.47- 16
Aragon	Danielle	USA	1.7.94	161/48	1500	4:09.03	4:12.50- 17
Aranda	Natalie	PAN	22.2.95	175/85	LJ	6.60A, 6.43	6.49A. 6.46- 17
Araujo	Martha Valeria	COL	12.5.96	165/62	Hep	5818A, 5744	5703- 17
Arcanjo	Geisa	BRA	19.9.91	180/92	SP	18.10	19.02- 12
* Arenas	Sandra	COL	17.9.93	160/50	20kW	1:28:48	1:28:10- 17
Argüelles	Yariagnis	CUB	18.4.84	173/55	LJ	6.58i, 6.44	6.70A- 15, 6.66- 09
Arikazan	Buse	TUR	8.7.94	171/55	PV	4.35	4.32i- 17, 4.15- 16
Arndt	Mareike	GER	29.1.92	185/70	Hep	6169	6106- 17
* Arrafi	Rabab	MAR	12.1.91	167/64	800	1:57.47	1:58.55- 15
					1500	3:59.15	4:01.75- 17
Arsine	Andreea	ROU	14.9.88	160/49	20kW	1:33:59	1:33:46- 17
Arter	Charlotte	GBR	18.6.91	168/52	10000	32:15.71	32:37.52- 17
Artymata	Eleni	CYP	16.5.86	178/58	400	51.14	51.61- 17
Asefa	Sutume	ETH	11.12.94	153/42	HMar	67:54	68:40- 17

Name		Nat	Born	Ht/Wt	Event	2018 Mark	Pre-2018 Best
Asenjo	Sabina	ESP	3.8.86	181/95	DT	58.35	61.89- 16
* Asher-Smith	Dina	GBR	4.12.95	165/55	100	10.85	10.99- 15
					200	21.89	22.07- 15
* Ashley	Whitney	USA	18.2.89	183/93	DT	61.10	64.80- 15
Assani Issouf	Jeanine	FRA	17.8.92	169/57	TJ	14.43	14.40- 16, 14.48w- 17
* Assefa	Meskerem	ETH	20.9.85	155/43	HMar	68:34	67:42- 17
					Mar	2:20:36	2:24:18- 17
Atcho	Sarah	SUI	1.6.95	180/63	100	11.20	11.33, 11.23w- 17
					200	22.80	22.90- 17
Atherley	Michelle	USA	9.12.95	173/64	100h	13.05	13.44, 13.42w- 16
					Hep	5816	
* Atkins	Joanna	USA	31.1.89	180/64	200	22.62, 22.31St	22.27, 22.19w- 14
					400	51.80	50.39- 09
Augustyniak	Lidia	POL	14.5.94	187/84	DT	56.97	59.36- 16
Avancini	Lívia	BRA	8.5.92		SP	16.97	17.12- 17
^ Avdeyeva	Anna	RUS	6.4.85		SP	17.78	20.07- 09
Awuah	Kristal	GBR-J	7.8.99	166/55	100	11.16	11.61- 17
Axpe	Maialen	ESP	4.5.93	170/56	PV	4.45	4.30- 17
^ Ayalew	Wude	ETH	4.7.87	150/44	HMar	69:34	67:58- 09
Aydin	Kadriye	TUR	2.7.95	173/57	HJ	1.86	1.80- 12
Ayele	Gebeyanesh	ETH	1.5.95		Mar	2:26:54	2:32:25- 17
Azevedo	Cátia	POR	9.3.94	170/50	400	51.84	51.63- 16
Azimeraw	Degitu	ETH-J	24.1.99	163/48	HMar	66:47	
Babii	Yelyzaveta	UKR	24.7.97	180/67	TJ	13.76	
Bachmann	Lea	SUI	25.6.96		PV	4.35	4.10- 15
* Bahta	Meraf	SWE	24.6.89	177/51	10000	32:19.34	31:13.06- 17
1500	4:02.31	4:00.49- 17	1M	4:27.03		4:25.26- 16	2000 5:37.12 -0-
3000	8:42.46i		8:37.50- 17		5000	15:08.17	14:49.95- 16
Bai Tiantian		CHN	14.8.98		50kW	4:32:47	
Baikstyte	Urte	LTU-J	8.5.99	177/57	HJ	1.87	1.80- 16
Baire	Cynthia	KEN-Y	02	159/44	5000	15:15.35	
Bajnok	Eszter	HUN	26.4.97		TJ	13.43, w13.65	13.27- 17
Baker	Lindsay	USA-J	10.4.99	175/82	SP	17.11	
Baker	Olivia	USA	12.6.96	163/52	800	2:00.08	2:01.02- 16
Balkwill	Kelsey	CAN	19.9.92	175/62	400h	56.34	56.80- 15
^ Balta	Ksenija	EST	1.11.86	168/53	LJ	6.63i, 6.63	6.87i- 09, 6.87- 10
^ Bani	Zahra	ITA	31.12.79	173/71	JT	58.27	62.75- 05
* Baptiste	Kelly-Ann	TTO	14.10.86	160/54	100	11.23	10.84- 10, 10.83dq- 13
Barber	Alana	NZL	8.7.87	163/52	20kW	1:31:32	1:32:23- 17
Barber	Jade	USA	4.4.93	170/64	100h	12.96	12.85, 12.70w- 15
Barber	Kaila	USA	4.4.93	163/54	400h	56.66	55.53- 16
* Barber (Roberts)	Kelsey-Lee	AUS	21.9.91	175/70	JT	64.57	64.53- 17
Bârca	Roxana	ROU	22.6.88	167/46	10000	32:30.97	33:46.65- 17
Barman	Swapma	IND	29.10.96	164/52	Hep	6026	5942- 17
Barnes	Celera	USA	2.12.98	166/52	100	11.16	11.41, 11.35w- 16
Barnett	Sharrika	JAM	16.4.97	168/52	400	50.69	51.67- 17
Barnett	Tara-Sue	JAM	9.10.93	178/81	DT	60.74	61.66- 17
Barowski	Cecilia	USA	7.12.92	170/59	800	2:01.61i, 2:02.76	2:00.90- 17
Barrie	Maggie	SLE	29.5.96	164/54	400	51.36	52.27- 17
Barrow	Lisa-Anne	BAR	13.12.96	168/59	400	51.86	
Barsosio	Stella	KEN	.93		Mar	2:23:43	2:28:14- 17
* Bartoletta	Tianna	USA	30.8.85	168/60	LJ	6.74	7.17- 16
Bartolomé	Miren	ESP	2.1.98	175/61	PV	4.35	4.30- 17
Battle	Anavia	USA-J	28.3.99	171/57	200	22.94	23.55- 17
Batu	Jennifer	CGO	24.10.93	162/72	HT	66.43	62.79- 17
Bauer	Katharina	GER	12.6.90	179/68	PV	4.52i, 4.40	4.65- 15
Baumgart-Witan	Iga	POL	11.4.89	178/57	400	51.24	51.71- 17
Bauschke	Melanie	GER	14.7.88	178/62	LJ	6.66	6.83- 09
Baxter	Rachel	USA-J	5.4.99	163/52	PV	4.42	4.41- 17
Baylark	Jada	USA	17.10.97	168/57	100	11.04, 11.02w	11.38. 11.19w- 17
					200	23.00, 22.91w	23.28, 23.11w- 17
Beahan	Brianna	AUS	1.11.91	168/57	100h	13.02	13.03- 16, 12.96w- 17
* Beard	Jessica	USA	8.1.89	168/57	200	22.74	22.81- 13
					400	50.08	50.56- 09
Becchetti	Mariavittoria	ITA	12.12.94	160/43	50kW	4:31:41	-0-
Beesley	Meghan	GBR	15.11.89	167/63	400h	55.21	54.52- 15
Bekele	Ashete	ETH	17.4.88	169/52	Mar	2:21:14	2:23:43- 15
* Bekele	Tadelech	ETH	11.4.91	154/40	HMar	69:47+	68:38- 13
					Mar	2:21:40	2:21:54- 17
* Bekh-Romanchuk	Maryna	UKR	18.7.95	174/59	LJ	6.73, 6.86w	6.93- 16
Bekmez	Meryem	TUR-J	31.7.00		20kW	1:31:00	

Name		Nat	Born	Ht/Wt	Event	2018 Mark	Pre-2018 Best
Belachew	Agrie	ETH-J	20.1.99	164/48	3kSt	9:44.79	9:37.17- 16
Belete	Meseret	ETH-J	16.9.99	166/52	HMar	67:51	
* Belete	Mimi	BRN	9.6.88	169/55	HMar	69:26	69:15- 17
					Mar	2:22:29	
Beletew	Yehualeye	ETH	31.7.98	165/52	20kW	1:31:47	1:31:58- 16
Belgyan	Sanda	ROU	17.12.92	164/48	400h	56.68	57.96- 16
Belibanáki	Maria	GRE	19.6.91	174/54	200	22.98	23.00- 17
					400	50.45	55.10- 11
Bell	Alexandra	GBR	4.11.92	166/55	800	1:59.93	2:00.53- 16
Belle	Tia Adana	BAR	16.6.96	178/59	400h	56.55	55.42- 17
Bellille	Janeil	TTO	18.6.89	172/60	400h	56.22	55.41- 14
Bemowska	Joanna	POL	27.6.94	169/53	50kW	4:43:48	-0-
Bender	Hope	USA	2.1.97		Hep	5725	5212- 17
Bendrat	Stephanie	AUT	5.3.91	164/52	100h	12.94	13.14- 17, 13.04w- 16
Beneke	Lynique	RSA	30.3.91	165/54	LJ	6.47	6.81- 13
* Bengtsson	Angelica	SWE	8.7.93	163/51	PV	4.73	4.70- 15
Bennett	Taylor	USA	15.1.97	170/59	100	11.13	11.33- 16, 11.19w- 17
					200	22.87	22.71- 16, 22.47w- 17
Bergrath	Dana	GER	24.4.94	168/80	JT	60.60	56.96- 17
Berhe	Meselu	ETH-J	29.5.00		3000	8:56.39	
Berings	Eline	BEL	28.5.86	162/53	100h	12.72	12.87- 14
* Berry	Gwen	USA	29.6.89	176/80	HT	77.78	76.77- 17
Bertoni	Francesca	ITA	29.12.93	176/55	3kSt	9:44.92	9:43.80- 17
Bethel	Brianne	BAH	5.7.98	172/57	100	11.20	11.40, 11.28w- 16
					200	22.74	23.47- 15, 23.12w- 17
Beyene	Debele	ETH			Mar	2:25:28	
Bian Ka		CHN	5.1.93	182/115	SP	18.15	18.71- 15
^ Billaud	Cindy	FRA	11.3.86	165/59	100h	13.14	12.56- 14
Bing	Portia	NZL	17.4.93	179/65	400h	56.84	58.89- 16
* Bingson	Amanda	USA	20.2.90	170/89	HT	69.89	75.73- 13
Binns	Isheka	JAM	9.1.96	175/85	DT	58.05	58.84- 17
Blaase	Chelsea	USA	10.4.94	165/52	10000	31:57.56	32:08.39- 16
Black	Symone	USA	26.10.95	158/50	400h	56.16	56.01- 17
Blake	Ashlie	USA	7.6.96	178/105	SP	17.73	17.49- 17
Blaut	Loretta	USA	22.3.96	188/64	HJ	1.88	1.86i- 16, 1.83- 17
Blocker	Jasmine	USA	9.6.92	170/57	400	51.46	51.66- 16
Bobocea	Claudia	ROU	11.6.92	176/53	3000	8:55.34, 8:53.97i	8:51.58i- 17, 9:11.39- 15
Bobocel	Ancuta	ROU	3.10.87	163/52	5000	15:16.13	15:56.00- 15
					10000	33:43.12	32:18.94- 17
Boekelman	Melissa	NED	11.5.89	177/86	SP	18.63	18.66- 17
Bogliolo	Luminosa	ITA	3.7.95	170/60	100h	12.99	13.44- 17
Böhm	Djamila	GER	15.7.94	175/58	400h	56.54	56.92- 17
Bolingo Mbongo	Cynthia	BEL	12.1.93	165/54	400	51.69	52.60- 15
Bondarenko	Yelizaveta	RUS-J	1.7.99	170/57	PV	4.45	4.40i, 4.30- 16
Bonilla	Magaly	ECU	8.2.92	152/54	50kW	4:19:04	
Bookman	Deonca	USA	29.10.95		400h	56.64	57.84- 17
Boons	Eefje	NED	18.7.94	176/68	100h	12.86	12.98- 17
Borchers	Claire	USA	20.4.96	165/52	3kSt	9:48.33	9:56.57- 17
* Borel	Cleopatra	TTO	10.3.79	168/93	SP	18.60	19.42- 11
Borge	Sigrid	NOR	3.12.95	181/82	JT	62.42	63.28- 17
Borges	Fernanda	BRA	26.7.88	165/65	DT	64.66	64.01- 14
Borisevich	Darya	BLR	6.4.90	170.52	1500	4:06.75	4:07.79- 17
Borovska	Nadiya	UKR	25.2.81	163/50	20kW	1:29:22	1:30:03- 12
Borys	Paulina	POL	14.5.98	181/60	HJ	1.86	1.87i- 16, 1.82- 14
Boss	Logan	USA	4.8.97	173/60	HJ	1.92i	1.90i, 1.89- 17
Botlogetswe	Christine	BOT	1.10.95	172/55	400	50.89	51.82A- 17, 52.37- 16
Bouchard	Maitë	CAN	.95	174/60	800	2:01.25	2:03.49- 17
Bouchard	Marie	FRA	7.12.93	168/53	3kSt	9:41.32	9:45.69- 16
* Bougard	Erica	USA	26.7.93	168/57	100h	12.80	12.93, 12.90w- 17
	HJ	1.89iA	1.92- 17	LJ	6.62		6.59- 17 Hep 6725	6557- 17
Boulaïd	Kaoutar	MAR	10.10.89	159/45	Mar	2:25:35	2:31:26- 16
Bowden	Philippa	GBR	29.3.95	162/49	10000	32:33.10	33:43.24- 17
* Bowie	Tori	USA	27.8.90	175/61	100	11.03	10.78- 16, 10.72w- 15
					200	22.75	21.77- 16
Bradley	Nicole	NZL	23.4.92	176/87	HT	66.07	64.44- 17
* Bradshaw	Holly	GBR	2.11.91	175/68	PV	4.80	4.87i- 12, 4.81- 17
Brichacek	Emily	AUS	7.7.90	166/52	10000	32:22.38	33:02.55- 11
Brisco	Mikiah	USA	14.7.96	165/54	100	11.05, 10.99w	10.96- 17
					200	22.59	23.23- 17
Brissett	Chanel	USA-J	10.8.99	163/52	100h	12.75	12.95- 16
Britton	Evonne	USA	10.10.91	173/59	100h	12.84	12.87- 16, 12.83w- 17

Name		Nat	Born	Ht/Wt	Event	2018 Mark		Pre-2018 Best
Brodatskaya	Sofiya	RUS	4.10.95		20kW	1:27:42		1:26:27- 17
Brooks	Alena	TTO	14.11.91	165/54	800	2:01.81		2:02.70- 17
Brooks	Taliyah	USA	8.2.95	176/60	100h	12.94, 12.82w		13.14- 17, 13.12w- 15
LJ	6.78			6.50- 17	Hep	5946		6099- 17
Brooks-Johnson	Alissa	USA	1.8.95	175/64	Hep	5977		5803- 15
Brooks-Wannemacher	Tia	USA	2.8.90	183/109	SP	17.22		19.73- 16
Brown	Aaliyah	USA	6.1.95	173/60	100	11.13		11.01- 17
Brown	Amoi	JAM-J	11.1.99	171/57	100h	13.09		13.33- 17
Brown	Brittany	USA	18.4.95	164/55	200	22.42		22.55, 22.30w- 17
Brown	Ce'Aira	USA	4.11.93	168/55	800	1:58.01		2:00.84- 17
1000	2:35.85			2:52.49i- 17	1500	4:09.44		4:27.89- 17
Brown	Felicia	USA	27.10.93	168/57	200	22.85		22.19- 16
Brown	Janeek	JAM	14.5.98	165/52	100	11.34, 11.19w		
					100h	12.80, 12.73w		13.16- 17
Brown	Kristen	USA	26.5.92	167/57	PV	4.51iA, 4.45		4.70- 16
Brown	Serena	BAH	15.9.98		DT	60.39		56.84- 17
Brown	Stephanie	USA	29.7.91	163/50	800	2:01.71		2:02.59- 11
					1500	4:06.71		4:07.55- 15
Bruce	Stephanie	USA	14.1.84	165/49	10000	32:05.05		31:59.88- 17
* Brume	Ese	NGR	20.1.96	167/58	LJ	6.83		6.83- 16
Bruni	Roberta	ITA	8.3.94	170/54	PV	4.40		4.60i- 13, 4.45- 14
Bryan	Lucy	GBR	22.5.95	162/48	PV	4.47i, 4.35		4.40- 13
Bryant	Ashley	USA	15.7.95	172/70	HT	66.67		61.94- 16
Bryant	Dezerea	USA	27.4.93	157/50	100	10.99		11.00- 15, 10.96w- 14
					200	22.93		22.18- 15
Buchanan	Leya	CAN	17.8.96	180/65	100	11.17		11.32, 11.15w- 17
* Büchel	Selina	SUI	26.7.91	168/55	800	2:00.42		1:57.95- 15
^ Buckman	Zoe	AUS	21.12.88	172/55	1500	4:06.76		4:03.22- 16
					3000	8:52.33		8:56.29- 15
Bugakova	Alyona	RUS	24.4.97	187/95	SP	18.52		18.06- 17
Bui Thi Thu Thao		VIE	29.4.92	162/53	LJ	6.55		6.68- 17
Buisson	Marion	FRA	19.2.88	176/60	PV	4.40		4.60- 09
Buksa	Sindija	LAT	14.12.97	175/	200	23.02, 22.98w		23.12- 17
Bulo	Shuru	ETH	27.6.98	159/44	3000	8:47.24		8:57.46- 17
* Burka	Gelete	ETH	23.1.86	165/45	HMar	66:11		68:18- 17
					Mar	2:20:45		2:30:40- 13
Burkard	Elena	GER	10.2.92	167/52	1500	4:06.51		4:10.92- 17
3000	8:45.43	9:05.28mx- 17	5000	15:12.17		16:05.84- 14	3kSt	9:29.76	-0-
* Burks	Quanesha	USA	15.3.95	160/55	100	11.19		11.21, 11.18w- 17
					LJ	6.81i, 6.59		6.93A, 6.84, 6.91w- 15
Burnett	Alysha	AUS	4.1.97	182/68	HJ	1.87		1.86- 17
Burns	Shaina	USA	21.3.96		Hep	5743		
Burton	Rushelle	JAM	4.12.97	175/61	100h	12.65, 12.64w		12.65- 17
Buscomb	Camille	NZL	11.7.90	164/51	3000	8:45.97		9:05.24-16
5000	15:24.68			15:19.81- 17	10000	32:33.91		31:45.02- 17
Bushkova	Aleksandra	RUS	13.1.97		50kW	4:22:36		
Butterworth	Lindsey	CAN	27.9.92	175/60	800	2:00.81		2:02.13- 17
Butts	Tynita	USA	10.6.90	179/60	HJ	1.86		1.91- 14
Butvina	Aleksandra	RUS	14.2.86		Hep	5719		
Cá	Liliana	POR	5.11.86	184/93	DT	61.02		59.33- 10
Caballero	Dailis	CUB	6.3.88	166/59	PV	4.36i		4.51- 11
* Caballero	Denia	CUB	13.1.90	175/73	DT	66.09		70.65- 15
Caballero	Yoci	PER	2.2.93		50kW	4:42:37		4:49:45- 17
* Cabecinha	Ana	POR	29.4.84	168/82	20kW	1:29:41		1:27:46- 08
* Cachová	Katerina	CZE	26.2.90	173/63	Hep	6400		6337(w)- 17
Caicedo	Maribel	ECU	1.4.98	168/61	100h	13.01		13.19A, 13.34, 13.04Aw- 17
Calvin	Clémence	FRA	17.5.90	166/55	HMar	69:52		71:17- 16
					Mar	2:26:28		-0-
* Camacho-Quinn	Jasmine	PUR	21.8.96	180/73	100	11.24w		11.61, 11.39w- 16
200	22.69, 22.21w	22.87, 22.70w- 16			100h	12.40		12.69, 12.54w- 16
Cameron	Lloydricia	USA	8.4.96	186/111	SP	17.66		17.47i, 17.39- 17
Campbell	Paige	AUS	27.6.96		3kSt	9:49.00		9:57.78- 17
Campbell	Simoya	JAM	1.3.94	167/54	800	2:00.59		1:59.26- 15
Campos	Juliana	BRA	17.10.96	170/57	PV	4.56		4.10- 17
* Can	Yasemin	TUR	11.12.96	166/49	3000	8:36.24		8:38.5- 17
5000	14:57.63			14:36.82- 17	10000	32:34.34		30:26.41- 16
Cansian	Lidiane Milena	BRA	8.1.92	180/100	DT	55.93		57.66- 17
Capponcelli	Serena	ITA	24.1.89	184/72	HJ	1.90i		1.89i- 17, 1.87- 08
Card	Kelsey	USA	20.8.92	178/116	DT	60.44		63.52- 16
Carli	Sarah	AUS	5.9.94	165/50	400h	56.87		58.05- 11
Carrillo	Yeseida	COL	22.10.93	168/52	20kW	1:33:46		1:31:14- 17

WOMEN'S INDEX

Name		Nat	Born	Ht/Wt	Event	2018 Mark	Pre-2018 Best
* Carter	Kori	USA	3.6.92	165/57	100h	12.78	12.76- 13
* Carter	Michelle	USA	12.10.85	175/107	SP	18.16	20.63- 16
Castells	Berta	ESP	24.1.84	174/79	HT	68.82	70.52- 16
* Castlin	Kristi	USA	7.7.88	170/75	100h	12.96	12.50- 16, 12.48w- 12
Castro	Ángela	BOL	21.2.93	160/54	20kW	1:33:55	1:30:33- 16
Caudery	Molly	GBR-J	17.3.00	180/68	PV	4.53	4.35- 17
Gause	Qalissia	USA	5.10.95		SP	17.02	15.90- 17
Cavaleti	Giovana	BRA	13.1.89	181/70	Hep	6081A, 5958	5808- 16
Cérival	Jessica	FRA	20.1.82	187/120	SP	17.03	17.99i- 11, 17.87- 09
Cernjul	Marusa	SLO	30.6.92	177/56	HJ	1.87	1.93- 16
Cervenková	Markéta	CZE	20.8.91	185/85	SP	17.05	16.86- 16
Cestonaro	Ottavia	ITA	12.1.95	176/68	TJ	14.05, 14.06w	13.76- 15
Chaboudez	Aurélie	FRA	9.5.93	173/60	400h	56.19	55.51- 15
Chadwick	Payton	USA	29.11.95	194/73	200	22.99i	
Champagnie	Ayesha	JAM	10.3.96	180/68	Hep	5821	
Chanbangu	Zinzi	RSA	28.9.96	185/63	TJ	13.65	13.60A, 13.53- 16
Chand	Dutoo	IND	3.2.96	160/50	200	23.00	23.34- 16
Charlton	Devynne	BAH	26.11.95	161/54	100	11.22	11.31, 11.30w- 17
					100h	12.70	12.74, 12.67w- 17
Chebet	Beatrice	KEN-J	5.3.00	160/45	5000	15:30.77	
Chebet	Caren	KEN-J	24.5.00		3kSt	9:46.58	
Chebet	Risper	KEN	6.6.92	176/48	HMar	69:25	70:43- 15
* Chebet	Winny	KEN	20.12.90	165/50	1500	4:00.60	3:59.16- 17
					1M	4:20.51	4:19.55- 17
Chebitok	Ruth	KEN	26.12.90		Mar	2:23:29	
Chekole	Yeshi	ERI	12.7.97		HMar	67:58	69:13- 17
Chekwel	Juliet	UGA	25.5.90	165/52	5000	15:30.17	15:20.15- 16
10000	31:57.97		31:37.99- 16		HMar	69:45	71:46- 17
Chelangat	Josephine	KEN	10.10.98	159/45	1500	4:08.77	
Chelangat	Sarah	UGA-Y	5.6.01	158/42	5000	15:29.25	
Chelangat	Sheila	KEN	11.4.98	158/52	3000	8:55.19	8:59.89- 16
Chelangat	Mercyline	UGA	17.12.97	160/45	10000	31:38.4A	31:40.48- 17
Chelimo	Joan	KEN	10.11.90	168/50	HMar	65:04	66:25- 17
* Chelimo	Rose	BRN	12.7.89	162/45	Mar	2:26:03	2:22:51dh- 17, 2:24:14- 16
Chelimo	Edith	KEN	16.7.86	165/50	HMar	66:18	65:52- 17
Chemnung	Loice	KEN	22.2.97	158/42	3000	8:43.00	9:19.27A- 14
					5000	14:53.14	
* Chemutai	Fancy	KEN	20.3.94	163/52	HMar	64:52	65:36- 17
Chemutai	Joyline	KEN			3kSt	9:43.1A	
* Chemutai	Peruth	UGA-J	10.7.99	165/50	3kSt	9:07.94	9:27.72- 17
Chen Jie		CHN	2.3.98		TJ	13.69i, 13,39	13.47i, 13.46- 17
Chen Qiaoling		CHN-J	22.11.99	175/55	PV	4.40i	4.40- 17
Chen Ting		CHN	28.8.97	168/55	TJ	13.79A, 13.69	13.85- 16
* Chen Yang		CHN	10.7.91	180/97	DT	67.03	63.61- 16
Chenah	Rima	ALG	11.2.96	160/52	3kSt	9:44.92	9:44.42- 17
Chepchirchir	Celestine	KEN	.90		HMar	68:35	
Chepchirchir	Filomena	KEN	1.12.81	165/43	HMar	69:35	68:06- 12
Chepkemoi	Joan	KEN	24.11.93	163/48	3kSt	9:22.85	9:20.22- 17
Chepkemoi	Joyce	KEN	3.3.95		HMar	69:21	
Chepkemoi	Naomi	KEN-J	2.3.99		3kSt	9:32.3A	
^ Chepkirui	Joyce	KEN	20.8.88	152/48	HMar	69:18	66:19- 14
* Chepkoech	Beatrice	KEN	6.7.91	171/57	1500	4:03.09, 4:02.21i	4:03.2A- 17, 4:03.28- 15
3000	8:39.16i	8:20.66- 17	5000	15:15.34A	14:39.33- 17	3kSt	8.44.32	8:59.84- 17
Chopkurui	Mercy	KEN-J	16.9.00		3kSt	9:29.42A	
Chepngeno	Jackline	KEN	16.1.93	164/48	Mar	2:24:38	
Chepngetich	Roseline	KEN	17.6.97	166/55	3kSt	9:08.23	9:25.91- 15
* Chepngetich	Ruth	KEN	8.8.94	160/44	HMar	67:02	66:19- 17
					Mar	2:18:35	2:22:36- 17
Chepyego	Selly	KEN	3.10.85	160/42	Mar	2:23:15	2:36:43- 15
* Cheromei	Lydia	KEN	11.5.77	168/45	HMar	69:35+	67:26- 12
					Mar	2:22:11	2:21:30- 12
Cherono	Eva	KEN	15.8.96	163/48	10000	32:34.03	
3000	8:41.69				5000	15:09.42	
Cherono	Fancy	KEN-Y	2.8.01	165/45	3kSt	9:23.92	
* Cherono	Gladys	KEN	12.5.83	161/45	HMar	67:13	66:07- 16
					Mar	2:18:11	2:19:25- 15
Cherop	Sharon	KEN	16.3.84	157/45	HMar	68:22	67:08- 11
					Mar	2:25:02	2:22:28- 13
Cherotich	Daisy	KEN	.97		HMar	69:44	
Cherotich	Joyline	KEN	22.3.98	156/42	5000	15:17.83	
Cheruiyot	Lucy	KEN	4.1.97		HMar	69:52	67:23- 17

Name		Nat	Born	Ht/Wt	Event	2018 Mark	Pre-2018 Best
* Cheruiyot	Vivian	KEN	11.9.83	155/38	HMar	67:43dh	67:44dh- 17
					Mar	2:18:31	2:23:35- 18
Cheruto	Lydia	KEN-J	23.11.00	162/48	800	2:01.58	2:02.06A- 17
Chervinskaya	Veronika	RUS	24.8.98	171/60	100h	13.03	13.18- 17
* Chesang	Stella	UGA	1.12.96	158/42	10000	31:39.0A	
* Chespol	Celliphine	KEN-J	23.3.99	163/48	3kSt	9:01.82	8:58.78- 17
Chi Meijiao		CHN	28.6.96		50kW	4:42:17	
Chiappe	Fiorella	ARG	1.1.96	174/59	400h	55.88	57.02- 17
* Chicherova	Anna	RUS	22.7.82	180/57	HJ	1.98	2.07- 11
Chigbolu	Maria Benedicta	ITA	27.7.89	172/53	400	51.76	51.67- 15
Chiliquinga	Valeria	ECU	27.2.91	163/66	HT	66.77	62.86- 15
Chuaimaroeng	Parinya	THA	16.12.97	165/50	TJ	14.17	13.63- 17
Chukwuma	Rosemary	NGR-Y	5.12.01	161/54	100	11.17w	11.85, 11.71w- 17
Chumachenko	Yuliya	UKR	2.10.94	185/65	HJ	1.94	1.93i- 16, 1.92- 15
Chumba	Eunice	BRN	23.5.93	160/46	10000	32:11.12	32:22.29- 15
HMar	67:17		66:11- 17		Mar	2:26:56, 2:20:54?	2:24:17- 17
^ Cichocka	Angelika	POL	15.3.88	170/56	800	2:01.01, 2:00.70i	1:58.41- 17
					1500	4:10.04, 4:06.35i	4:01.61- 17
Ciofani	Audrey	FRA	13.3.96	174/70	HT	68.57	69.25- 15
Claes	Hanne	BEL	4.8.91	175/60	400h	55.20	57.30- 14
Clark	Erin	USA	28.12.94	161/47	5000	15:30.59	15:50.96i- 17, 15:57.54- 15
					10000	32:28.88	33:03.22- 17
Clark	Kristen	USA	8.4.96	175/77	JT	56.20	52.31- 17
Clark	Megan	USA	10.6.94	167/57	PV	4.61	4.63- 16
Clark	Tamara	USA-J	9.1.99	167/55	100	11.02	11.46- 17
					200	22.53	23.53- 16
Clark	Zoey	GBR	25.10.94	165/60	400	51.36	51.81- 17
Clarke	Kayelle	TTO	28.2.96	175/59	200	22.74	22.97- 17
Clarke	Rosie	GBR	17.11.91	170/57	1500	4:07.69	4:12.10- 15
3000	8:47.30i		8:51.02- 17		3kSt	9:32.08	9:32.10- 17
Claude-Boxberger	Ophélie	FRA	12.10.88	169/54	3kSt	9:31.84	9:34.96- 16
Claxton	Grace	PUR	19.8.93	167/52	400h	56.30	55.85- 16
Clay	Raven	USA	5.10.90	168/59	100h	13.04, 12.92w	12.93- 16, 12.87w- 17
Clayton	Rushell	JAM	18.10.92	175/61	400h	55.08	56.29- 15
Clemente	Mónica	ESP	20.5.96	173/60	PV	4.45	4.15- 17
Clerveaux	Vanessa	HAI	17.6.94	170/59	100h	13.05	13.13, 13.01w- 17
Cliff	Rachel	CAN	1.4.88	163/47	5000	15:20.66	15:28.5- 16
10000	31:56.86		32:00.03- 17		HMar	70:08	72:07- 17
* Coburn	Emma	USA	19.10.90	173/55	3000	8:41.16i	8:48.60- 17
					3kSt	9:05.06	9:02.58- 17
Cockrell	Anna	USA	28.8.97	178/66	100h	12.88, 12.79w	12.89- 17
					400h	55.71	55.14- 17
Cohen	Adva	ISR	24.3.96	155/41	3kSt	9:29.74	10:07.82- 17
Collatz	Alex	USA	25.5.93	173/77	DT	61.47	57.82- 15
Collier	Caitlin	USA-J	5.8.99	174/60	800	2:00.85	2:03.32- 17
Collins	Shania	USA	14.11.96	171/59	100	10.98	11.34- 17
					200	22.47, 21.97w	22.81- 17
Conley	Sydney	USA	11.12.93	176/60	LJ	6.54	6.66, 6.81w- 17
Constien	Val	USA	21.3.96	175/59	3kSt	9:47.97	10:05.65- 16
Conte	Claudia	ESP-J	14.11.99	170/59	Hep	5818	5281w, 5190- 17
Coogan	Katrina	USA	15.11.93	164/50	5000	15:30.70	15:34.34- 14
Cook	Chaquinn	USA	10.7.97		TJ	13.89	13.51- 17
Cooks	Riley	USA	6.12.93	173/60	Hep	5825	5671- 17
Coppinger	Courtney	USA	17.1.95	179/60	3kSt	9:49.04	10:19.62- 17
Corrin	Courtney	USA	12.12.97		LJ	6.50	6.40- 13, 6.56w- 15
Costa	Keila	BRA	6.2.83	170/62	TJ	13.90	14.58- 13, 15.10w- 07
* Costa	Susana	POR	22.9.84	178/65	TJ	14.17	14.35- 17
* Courtney	Melissa	GBR	30.8.93	170/54	1500	4:03.44	4:05.82- 17
1M	4:27.29 4:23.15- 17		3000	8:43.72mx- 17, 9:13.87- 16	5000	15:04.75 15:28.95- 17	
Coward	Destiney	USA	26.5.96		HT	66.63	62.51- 17
* Craft	Shanice	GER	15.5.93	185/69	DT	62.91	65.88- 14
* Cragg	Amy	USA	21.1.84	163/46	Mar	2:21:42	2:27:03- 14
Cranny	Elise	USA	8.5.96	161/48	1500	4:09.49	4:09.64- 16
					5000	15:24.32i	15:49.27- 16
Crew	Brittany	CAN	6.3.94	176/111	SP	18.60	18.58- 17
Cunningham	Gabriele	USA	22.2.98	165/52	100	11.21	11.26- 17
					200	23.04, 22.89w	23.26- 16
* Cunningham	Vashti	USA	18.1.98	185/66	HJ	1.97iA	1.99i- 15, 1.99- 17
Czaková	Mária	SVK	2.10.88	165/60	20kW	1:31:03	1:32:23- 15
					50kW	4:14:25	-0-
da Rosa	Nair	BRA	22.3.80		50kW	4:38:48	4:39:28- 17

Name		Nat	Born	Ht/Wt	Event	2018 Mark			Pre-2018 Best
da Silva	Izabela	BRA	2.8.95	178/95	DT	58.85			58.81- 15
da Silva	Tatiane Raquel	BRA	10.6.90	162/49	3kSt	9:48.40			9:46.86- 16
Daba	Tejitu	BRN	16.6.91	162/44	HMar	68:36			68:21- 17
Dabrowska	Martyna	POL	5.4.94	175/55	400	52.12			52.01- 17
Daci	Thiziri	FRA	15.12.97	157/53	PV	4.37i, 4.30			4.20i, 4.15- 16
* Dadic	Ivona	AUT	29.12.93	179/65	Hep	6552			0417- 17
^ Dahlgren	Jenny	ARG	27.8.84	180/115	HT	70.98A			73.74- 10
Daniels	Katelyn	USA	11.4.95	178/93	DT	57.75			60.54- 16
Daniels	Teahna	USA	27.3.97	165/55	100	11.11			11.06- 13
Das	Hima	IND-J	9.1.00	1167/52	400	50.79			
^ Daska	Mamitu	ETH	16.10.83	164/45	HMar	69:50			66:28- 15
Dauber	Stefanie	GER	31.7.87	168/61	PV	4.45			4.30- 17
David	Yanis	FRA	12.12.97	169/58	LJ	6.67, 6.69w			6.56- 17
					TJ	14.15			13.93i, 13.78, 13.92w- 17
Davies	Bethan	GBR	7.11.90	170/62	20kW	1:31:53			1:33:04- 17
Davis	Ashley	USA	10.3.97		SP	16.97			16.33 17
Davis	Kevona	JAM-Y	20.12.01	170/60	100	11.16			11.24- 17
					200	22.72			22.97- 17
Davis	Tamari	USA-Y	15.2.03	167/52	100	11.13			11.48, 11.34w- 17
					200	22.48			23.21- 17
Davis	Tara	USA-J	20.5.99	168/59	100h	13.09, 13.04w			12.95- 17
					LJ	6.71			6.73, 6.80w- 17
* Day	Christine	JAM	23.8.86	168/51	400	51.41			50.14- 15
Day	Riley	AUS-J	30.3.00	170/60	200	22.93			23.26- 17
de Witte	Lisanne	NED	10.9.92	175/65	400	50.77			51.71- 17
Dearman	Emilyn	USA	1.1.95	173/62	Hep	5759			5924w, 5625- 17
Decoud	Chelsie	USA	28.6.96	173/59	HJ	1.88i			1.85- 17
* Defar	Meseret	ETH	19.11.83	155/42	HMar	68:26 dh			66:09- 13
Degefa	Biruktayit	ETH	29.9.90	157/40	Mar	2:24:51			2:23:51- 15
* Degefa	Worknesh	ETH	28.10.90	159/42	HMar	69:10			66:14- 16
					Mar	2:19:53			2:22:36- 17
Degefu	Beyenu	ETH-J	12.7.99	165/49	2000	5:38.19			
					3000	8:35.76			8:41.76- 16
Dekebo	Muliye	ETH	13.3.98		Mar	2:26:52			
Del Ponte	Ajla	SUI	15.7.96	168/56	100	11.21			11.42- 17
* Demireva	Mirela	BUL	28.9.89	180/58	HJ	2.00			1.97- 16
* Demise	Shure	ETH	21.1.96	168/54	Mar	2:22:07			2:20:59- 15
Denoon	Zakiya	TTO	23.1.95	178/59	100	11.21			11.31- 17
					200	22.96			23.22- 17
* Dereje	Roza	ETH	6.5.97	168/52	HMar	67:00			67:23- 17
					Mar	2:19:17			2:22:43- 17
Dereli	Emel	TUR	25.2.96	181/110	SP	18.12			18.57- 16
Derkach	Dariya	ITA	27.3.93	167/56	TJ	14.05A, 13.86			14.15- 16
Derkach	Nadezhda	RUS	18.4.96	184/90	DT	56.88			53.50- 17
Derun	Kateryna	UKR	24.9.93	168/71	JT	57.09			62.82- 16
Despaigne	Elianne	CUB	11.1.97	176/83	HT	66.46			61.98- 13
DesRosiers	Briyahna	USA	11.3.96	160/50	400	51.90			52.28- 17
Detloff	Molli	USA	15.1.96	173/79	HT	66.90			64.98- 17
Devi	Anjali	IND	15.9.98		400	51.79			
Diallo	Rouguy	FRA	5.2.95	168/52	TJ	14.31			14.20, 14.44w- 14
Diame	Fátima	ESP	22.9.96	170/52	LJ	6.68			6.48- 17, 6.55w- 15
					TJ	13.92			14.03 17
Diamond	Emily	GBR	11.6.91	173/57	400	51.87			51.23- 16
* Dibaba	Birhane	ETH	11.9.93	159/44	HMar	69:32			67:47- 16
					Mar	2:19:51			2:21:19- 17
* Dibaba	Genzebe	ETH	8.2.91	168/52	800	2:01.51			1:59.37-17
1500	3:56.68	3:50.07- 15		1M	4:20.51	4:13.31i, 4:14.30- 16	2000	5:27.73	5:23.75i- 17,5:27.50- 14
3000	8:41.9+, 8:31.23i	8:16.60i, 8:26.21- 14				5000	14:26.89		14:15.41- 15
* Dibaba	Mare	ETH	20.10.89	152/40	HMar	69:15			67:13- 10
					Mar	2:25:24			2:19:52- 12
* Dibaba	Tirunesh	ETH	1.10.85	155/44	HMar	67:39+			66:50- 17
					Mar	2:18:55			2:17:56- 17
* Dida	Dera	ETH	26.10.96	155/42	HMar	69:21			68:06- 17
					Mar	2:21:45			
Dimoff	Carrie	USA	31.5.83	155/46	10000	31:57.85			32:47.75- 15
Dincoff	Rachel	USA	24.12.93	180/?	DT	61.16			58.48- 17
* Diriba	Buze	ETH	9.2.94	160/43	HMar	66:50			71:49- 16
Dittrich	Bianka	GER	6.7.93		50kW	4:42:58			
Diver	Sinead	AUS	17.2.77	160/44	5000	15:23.65			16:24.46- 12
10000	31:50.98	33:18.41- 17		HMar	69:20		Mar	2:25:19	2:31:37- 15
Dobbin	Beth	GBR	7.6.94	167/59	200	22.59			23.31- 17

Name		Nat	Born	Ht/Wt	Event	2018 Mark	Pre-2018 Best
Domingos	Laila	BRA	30.7.82	180/80	JT	62.39	62.52- 17
Dominici	Eleonora	ITA	22.2.96		20kW	1:33:33	1:33:32- 17
Domjan	Veronika	SLO	3.9.96	178/94	DT	59.45	60.11- 16
Donegan	Rosie	AUS	1.7.93		3kSt	9:46.83	9:49.16- 16
Donzelot	Irene	FRA	8.12.88	170/68	DT	56.07	57.66- 12
Dorozhuk	Nadezhda	BLR	23.1.90		50kW	4:18:31	
Douglas	Serenity	USA	25.4.98	167/55	400	51.91	53.42- 15
Dowie	Danielle	JAM	5.5.92	173/60	400h	56.56	54.94- 13
* Doyle	Eilidh	GBR	20.2.87	172/59	400	51.87, 51.60i	51.45i, 51.83- 13
					400h	54.80	54.09- 16
* Drahotová	Anežka	CZE	22.7.95	183/63	20kW	1:27:03	1:26:53- 15
Draxler	Bonnie	USA	13.10.95	155/48	PV	4.42	4.35- 17
Drisbióti	Antigóni	GRE	21.3.84	162/52	20kW	1:32:16	1:30:56- 16
Duan Dandan		CHN	23.5.95		20kW	1:32:14	1:28:37- 17
^ Duarte	Sophie	FRA	31.7.81	170/54	10000	32:34.07	32:36.32- 14
* Dubitskaya	Alyona	BLR	25.1.90	182/77	SP	19.21	19.03- 14
Duckett	Jessica	USA	22.1.97	161/52	100h	13.02	13.37, 13.18w- 17
Ducó	Natalia	CHI	31.1.89	177/95	SP	18.97 ?drugs suspension	18.80- 12
Duncan	Alexis	USA	16.8.98	159/55	100h	12.79	12.93- 16
* Duncan	Kimberlyn	USA	2.8.91	173/59	200	22.63	22.19- 12, 21.80w- 13
Duncan	Melissa	AUS	30.1.90	170/55	3000	8:57.37	8:58.14- 14
					5000	15:18.43	16:19.58- 17
Dunmore	Makenzie	USA	7.10.97	170/65	100	11.25	11.92, 11.64w- 16
200	22.53, 22.37w			22.90- 17	400	50.63	51.42- 17
Dusanova	Nadezhda	UZB	17.11.87	174/56	HJ	1.94	1.96i, 1.95- 09
Dutil	Danellys	CUB	12.2.95		TJ	13.67	13.77- 15
* Dutkiewicz	Pamela	GER	28.9.91	170/63	100h	12.67	12.61- 17
Duvernay	Prisca	FRA	26.5.91	180/60	HJ	1.86i	1.88i, 1.87- 17
Dzindzaletaite	Dovile	LTU	14.7.93	168/58	TJ	14.13i, 13.97	14.23- 15. 14.26w- 14
Ealey	Chase	USA	20.7.94	178/84	SP	17.78	18.46- 16
Ebwea Bile	Mario José	FRA	7.2.97	178/73	TJ	14.00	13.63i, 13.39, 13.69w- 17
Eckhardt	Neele	GER	2.7.92	168/52	TJ	14.33	14.35- 17
Edao Rebitu	Bontu	BRN	12.12.97	164/50	5000	15:31.21	15:16.70- 17
Eden	Iale	GER	25.3.98		HJ	1.86	1.83i- 16, 1.81- 17
Edesa	Workenesh	ETH	11.9.92		Mar	2:26:28	2:24:04- 16
Edwards	Kaela	USA	8.12.93	165/52	800	1:59.68	2:01.97- 16
					1000	2:36.13	
Efraimson	Alexa	USA	20.2.97	170/57	1500	4:07.06	4:03.39- 15
1M	4:24.82		4:27.39- 16		3000	8:52.53	9:00.16- 14
Egwim	Emerald	NGR	27.11.95	167/55	400	51.82	51.99- 17
Ehrhardt	Caroline	CAN	6.2.92	175/63	TJ	13.63, 13.83w	13.59, 13.83w- 17
Eke	Nadia	GHA	11.1.93	170/59	TJ	13.75	13.93- 17
Ekman	Louise	SWE	10.4.97		HJ	1.86	1.80- 17
Ektova	Irina	KAZ	8.1.87	172/63	TJ	14.07	14.48- 11
Elbe	Jenny	GER	18.4.90	180/62	TJ	13.87	14.28- 16, 14.38w- 15
Ellenwood	Georgia	CAN	5.8.95	170/63	Hep	6173	5935- 16
* Ellis	Kendall	USA	8.3.96	173/59	200	22.71	22.79- 17
					400	49.99	50.00- 17
Ellward	Agnieszka	POL	26.3.89	186/54	50kW	4:32:47	4:41:58- 17
Elvemo	Yngvild	NOR	28.5.90	167/52	800	2:01.65	2:01.77- 16
* Embaye	Axumawit	ETH	18.10.94	160/50	1500	4:02.44	4:02.35- 14
					3000	8:43.83	8:49.52i- 17, 8:51.82- 15
* Emerson	Niamh	GBR-J	22.4.99	179/68	HJ	1.89	1.89- 16
					Hep	6253	6013- 17
Emilianov	Alexandra	MDA-J	19.9.99	183/79	DT	60.24	58.09- 16
Emmanuel	Crystal	CAN	27.11.91	170/59	100	11.11	11.14, 11.06w- 17
					200	22.67	22.50- 17
* Ennaoui	Sofia	POL	30.8.95	158/40	1500	4:02.06	4:01.00- 16
					3000	8:53.63i	8:45.29i- 17, 8:59.44- 14
Eriksson	Sandra	FIN	4.6.89	163/48	3000	8:57.11	8:54.06i- 15, 8:55.13- 14
^ Eshete	Shitaye	BRN	21.5.90	164/51	10000	32:30.24	30:47.25- 12
HMar	68:25		70:10- 17		Mar	2:24:51	2:25:36- 16
Espejo	Cristina	ESP	13.10.94	163/46	1500	4:09.34	4:14.71- 14
Espinoza	Ahymara	VEN	28.5.85	170/60	SP	18.09	18.19- 16
Esquivel	Ximena	MEX	22.8.97	175/57	HJ	1.91A	1.90A- 16
Esser	Agnes	CAN	22.8.95	183/86	DT	57.98	57.02- 17
Evangelidou	Natalia	CYP	10.3.91	170/56	800	2:01.77	2:02.10- 16
Evans	Gayon	JAM	15.1.90	158/50	100	11.22	11.24- 16
* Ewen	Maggie	USA	23.9.94	178/79	SP	19.46	18.12i, 17.72- 17
DT	62.47		60.51- 17		HT	74.53	74.56
Eykens	Renée	BEL	8.6.96	171/56	800	2:00.92	2:00.00- 16

Name		Nat	Born	Ht/Wt	Event	2018 Mark	Pre-2018 Best
Fantini	Sara	ITA	16.9.97	170/72	HT	66.06	68.24- 17
Farmer	Erin	USA	11.8.95	183/107	SP	18.27	18.12- 17
Fatherly	Rachel	USA	20.4.94	180/86	SP	17.89	17.75- 17
Fedronic	Justine	FRA	11.5.91	168/54	800	2:01.62	1:59.86- 16
Fehringer	Carly	USA	9.11.91	168/93	HT	65.81	66.68- 17
Feige	Saskia	GER	13.8.97	167/52	20kW	1:32:57	1:07:14- 17
* Felix	Allyson	USA	18.11.85	168/57	400	51.35	49.26- 15
Félix	Alysbeth	PUR	7.3.93	171/59	Hep	5812	6124A, 6033- 16
Félix	Dulce	POR	23.10.82	165/53	Mar	2:25:24	2:25:15- 15
* Feng Bin		CHN	3.4.94	184/95	DT	64.58	65.14- 16
Fernández	Saleta	ESP	15.7.97	180/61	HJ	1.86	1.83i- 16, 1.83- 17
Feysa	Hawi	ETH-J	1.2.99	162/48	3000	8:50.80i	
Fiack	Marion	FRA	13.10.92	170/60	PV	4.41i, 4.22	4.71i- 15, 4.55- 14
Fiamoncini	Maura	USA-J	23.6.99		JT	56.21	48.79- 16
Filipic	Neja	SLO	22.4.95	172/56	LJ	6.50	6.51- 16
Filyuk	Mariya	UKR	14.10.95	164/49	20kW	1:33:34	1:34:51- 16
Finn	Michele	IRL	16.12.89	160/52	3kSt	9:46.19	9:43.19- 16
* Fiodorow	Joanna	POL	4.3.89	169/89	HT	74.39	75.09- 17
* Flanagan	Shalane	USA	8.7.81	165/50	3000	8:43.28i	8:33.25i, 8:35.34- 07
					Mar	2:26:22	2:21:14- 14
Flannel	Kynnedy	USA-J	12.7.00	173/59	200	23.18, 22.95w	23.34- 17
Flink	Sofi	SWE	8.7.95	168/71	JT	60.59	61.96- 13
Folorunso	Ayomide	ITA	17.10.96	170/55	400h	55.16	55.50- 16
Forbes	Shashalee	JAM	10.5.96	160/55	200	22.80	22.71- 17
^ Fougberg	Charlotta	SWE	19.6.85	165/51	5000	15:23.80	15:55.76- 16
					3kSt	9:42.14	9:23.96- 14
Francis	Chelsea	USA	14.10.96	163/52	100	11.42, 11.22w	11.34- 17
Francis	Eden	GBR	19.10.88	178/85	DT	56.49	59.78- 11
* Francis	Phyllis	USA	4.5.92	178/61	200	22.42	22.50- 16
					400	50.07	49.92- 17
Franklin	Tori	USA	7.10.92	173/55	TJ	14.84	14.03- 17
Fraser	Vanessa	USA	27.7.95	168/52	5000	15:09.62	15:25.48- 17
* Fraser-Pryce	Shelly-Ann	JAM	27.12.86	160/52	100	10.98	10.70- 12
Fray	Jazmine	JAM	6.6.97	165/48	800	2:01.18	2:00.69i- 17, 2:03.25- 16
Frederick	Priscilla	ANT	14.2.89	178/68	HJ	1.87	1.91- 15
Freier	Desiree	USA	24.7.96	152/52	PV	4.41i	4.45- 14
* Frerichs	Courtney	USA	18.1.93	167/52	3kSt	9:00.85	9:03.77- 17
Frøynes	Amanda Marie	NOR	13.9.98	178/64	Hep	5794	5493- 16
Fu Luna		CHN	3.5.95	164/52	TJ	13.66	13.59- 14
Fuchs	Annika	GER	29.4.97		JT	56.59	51.32- 16
Fuentes	Thelma Nohemí	GUA	20.8.92	173/68	TJ	13.72	13.00- 17
Fujii	Nanako	JPN-J	7.5.99		20kW	1:33:27	
Fukuda	Yui	JPN	1.6.95	162/47	5000	15:20.08	15:20.11- 17
Furlan	Jessica	CAN	15.3.90	165/54	3kSt	9:45.79	9:33.45- 14
Furlani	Erika	ITA	2.1.96	174/51	HJ	1.86i, 1.86	1.92- 17
Furmanek	Katarzyna	POL	19.2.96	174/76	HT	68.41	69.60- 17
Gaines	Jessie	USA	12.8.90	164/52	LJ	6.47iA	6.55- 14
Gallardo	Karen	CHI	6.3.84	175/95	DT	56.61	61.10- 15
Galle	Sokhna	FRA	23.4.94	165/50	TJ	13.87	13.61- 17, 13.62w- 11
Gallego	Sara	ESP-J	21.10.00	164/51	400h	57.11	57.88- 17
Galvis	Sandra	COL	28.6.86	165/60	20kW	1:33:11	1:30:00- 17
Gambetta	Sara	GER	18.2.93	183/80	SP	18.43	18.46- 17
* Gao Yang		CHN	1.3.93	178/110	SP	18.77i, 18.36	19.20- 16
* Garcia	Stephanie	USA	3.5.88	168/52	3000	8:57.09+	8:52.74- 17
					5000	15:23.71	15:16.56- 16
* García	Kimberley	PER	19.10.93	167/44	20kW	1:28:56	1:29:13- 17
García Caro	Laura	ESP	16.4.95	165/56	20kW	1:28:15	1:29:29- 17
Gardasevic	Milica	SRB	28.9.98	175/59	LJ	6.64	6.56, 6.62w- 17
* Gardner	English	USA	22.4.92	162/50	100	11.02	10.74- 16
Gardner	Madeline	USA	24.9.95	165/57	PV	4.41	4.15i- 17
Gashaw	Tigist	BRN	25.12.96	172/54	1500	4:09.12	4:05.58- 15
Gataullina	Aksana	RUS-J	17.7.00	177/64	PV	4.55i, 4.55	4.45- 17
Gathoni	Ann	KEN	5.3.98	163/48	3kSt	9:47.71	9:41.40- 15
Gayakwad	Saritaben	IND	1.6.94	168/50	400h	57.04	59.32- 16
Ge Lijuan		CHN	17.7.97		JT	57.11	54.01- 15
Gebre	Trihas	ESP	29.4.90	163/46	HMar	69:51	69:57- 17
Gebrekidan	Hiwot	ETH	11.5.95	156/44	HMar	67:36	68:00- 16
					Mar	2:26:11	2:25:45- 17
Gebreselassie	Goytatom	ETH	15.1.95	152/42	HMar	69:39	
Gebreslasea	Letebrhan	ETH	29.10.90	155/40	Mar	2:24:47	2:25:01- 17
Gebru	Azmera	ETH	5.5.92	160/45	Mar	2:23:31	

Name		Nat	Born	Ht/Wt	Event	2018 Mark	Pre-2018 Best
* Gega	Luiza	ALB	5.11.88	166/56	3kSt	9:22.00	9:26.05- 17
Gehring	Anna	GER	15.11.96		10000	32:20.37	-0-
Gemechu	Tsehay	ETH	20.5.98	160/52	HMar	66:50	
Genemo	Shuko	ETH	.95		Mar	2:26:10	2:24:31- 16
Geng Shuang		CHN	9.7.93		SP	17.24	18.06i, 17.87- 16
George	Patience	NGR	25.11.91	176/61	400	51.40	50.71- 15
Gergelics	Cintia	HUN	16.11.91	170/73	HT	66.32	67.55- 17
Gerlach	Tori	USA	2.6.94	167/50	3kSt	9:48.89	9:46.76- 17
* German	Elvira	BLR	9.1.97	168/54	100h	12.64	12.85- 16
Gerter	Julia	GER	13.7.94	185/60	LJ	6.68	6.35i- 11, 6.35- 12
Gesang Zhuoma		CHN	16.7.98		20kW	1:30:29	
Geubelle	Andrea	USA	21.6.91	165.57	TJ	13.78iA, 13.45	13.85- 16, 13.96w- 17
Gezahegne	Kalkidan	BRN	8.5.91	163/44	1500	4:07.88	4:00.97- 11
3000	8:34.65		8:38.61- 08		5000	15:08.08	15:07.19- 17
Ghafoor	Madiea	NED	9.9.92	169/53	400	51.12	52.27- 17
Ghelber	Bianca	ROU	1.6.90	170/70	HT	70.96	73.52- 10
* Ghribi	Habiba	TUN	9.4.84	170/57	3kSt	9:31.36	9:05.36- 15
Gicquel	Solène	FRA	1.12.94	186/60	HJ	1.86i	1.85- 16
* Gidey	Letesenbet	ETH	20.3.98	163/48	3000	8:30.96	8:41.6- 17
					5000	14:23.14	14:33.31- 17
* Gierisch	Kristin	GER	20.8.90	178/69	TJ	14.45	14.46i, 14.46w- 15, 14.40- 17
Giger	Lena	USA	7.6.96	170/93	SP	18.09	17.00- 17
Giger	Yasmin	SUI-J	6.11.99	180/60	400h	56.81	55.90- 17
Gimmler	Sophie	GER	18.3.96	178/81	HT	65.61	65.75- 17
Giordano	Dana	USA	30.12.93	174/57	1500	4:08.62	4:11.86- 16
					3000	8:55.14	9:07.28i- 15, 9:22.27- 14
* Giorgi	Eleonora	ITA	14.9.89	163/52	20kW	1:28:31	1:26:17- 15
Girma	Tigist	ETH	.93		Mar	2:26:44	2:29:05- 17
Gittens	Tyra	TTO	6.6.98	174/60	HJ	1.86	1.85- 16
LJ	6.47		6.22, 6.39i- 17		Hep	6074	5490w- 17, 5337- 16
^ Gleadlo	Liz	CAN	5.12.88	183/95	JT	61.53	64.83- 15
* Gobena	Amane	ETH	1.9.82	163/48	Mar	2:25:49	2:21:51- 16
Gochenour	Alex	USA	17.2.93	183/70	Hep	6111	6129- 17
Godfay	Afera	ETH	25.9.91	156/42	Mar	2:23:54	2:28:46- 17
Gollshewsky	Taryn	AUS	18.5.93	184/80	DT	58.95	60.27- 16
Gómez	Roxana	CUB-J	7.1.99	169/54	400	51.95	51.46- 17
Gonçalves	Rafaela	BRA	27.11.91	168/70	JT	56.51	57.77- 17
* Gong Lijiao		CHN	24.1.89	174/110	SP	20.38	20.43- 16
Gonska	Nadine	GER	23.1.90	169/57	400	52.00	52.51- 17
Gonzalez	Samantha	USA	14.11.96	170/55	400h	56.77	59.66- 13
González	Alegna	MEX-J	2.1.99		20kW	1:33:43	
* González	María Guadalupe	MEX	9.1.89	162/48	20kW	1:26:38	1:26:17- 16
González	Melissa	COL	24.6.94	168/66	400h	56.14	56.23A, 56.29- 17
González	Raquel	ESP	16.11.89	176/55	20kW	1:30:15	1:28:36- 14
^ Gordon	Chrisann	JAM	18.9.94	164/52	400	51.21	50.13- 17
Gordon	Daeshon	JAM	8.11.96	168/60	100h	13.14, 13.04w	12.97- 15
Gorecka	Emelia	GBR	29.1.94	172/52	5000	15:30.59	15:07.45- 14
Gorodskaya	Hanna	BLR	31.1.93		HJ	1.89	1.90- 15
Gosa	Dalilah Abdelkadir	BRN	27.6.98		HMar	68:12	72:29- 17
Gottlieb	Viktoria	GER	14.3.95	177/57	HJ	1.90	1.82i, 1.80- 16
* Goule	Natoya	JAM	30.3.91	160/50	800	1:56.15	1:59.38- 16
Goúsin	Tatiána	GRE	26.1.94	188/63	HJ	1.88	1.91- 17
* Grace	Kate	USA	24.10.88	173/55	800	2:00.92	1:58.28- 16
1500	4:04.05+		4:03.59- 17		1M	4:20.70	4:22.93i, 4:24.01- 17
Graham	Jasmyne	USA	6.5.97	160/50	100h	13.10	13.17- 15
Grange	Gleneve	JAM	6.7.95	170/75	SP	17.24i, 16.89	17.29- 17
Granz	Caterina	GER	14.3.94	173/53	1500	4:08.12	4:13.22- 16
					3000	8:56.29i	9:06.21i- 17, 9:13.02- 16
Grauvogel	Louisa	GER	28.9.96	173/61	100h	12.95	13.50- 17
					Hep	6162	5747- 15
Gray	Jenna	USA	28.2.98	186/	JT	57.29	50.29- 17
Gray	Kianna	USA	30.12.96	171/57	100	11.18, 11.02w	11.20, 11.12w- 16
					200	22.88, 22.65w	22.79, 22.58w- 16
Green	Hanna	USA	16.10.94	168/59	800	2:00.09	2:01.17- 15
Greene	Nicole	USA	2.5.97	183/64	HJ	1.88i	1.87- 15
Grenot	Libania	ITA	12.7.83	175/61	400	51.32	50.30- 09
Griffith	Georgia	AUS	5.12.96	163/50	800	2:00.13	2:00.90- 17
					1500	4:04.17	4:07.32- 17
Grillet	Justien	BEL	18.7.94	170/57	400h	56.31	58.11- 17
Grimm	Vanessa	GER	22.4.97		Hep	5791	5694- 17
Griva	Gundega	LAT	8.4.91	168/62	JT	56.22	57.32A- 13

Name		Nat	Born	Ht/Wt	Event	2018 Mark	Pre-2018 Best
Griva	Lauma	LAT	27.10.84	181/62	LJ	6.63	6.86- 11
Griva	Mara	LAT	4.8.89	171/57	LJ	6.53	6.59, 6.70w- 11
					TJ	13.62	13.81- 11
* Grøvdal	Karoline Bjerkeli	NOR	14.6.90	167/52	1500	4:05.57	4:07.25- 17
2000	5:41.04				3kSt	9:18.36	9:13.35- 17
Grove	Emily	USA	22.5.93	168/61	PV	4.61	4.60- 11
Gruver	Olivia	USA	29.7.97	170/64	PV	4.67i, 4.55	4.50- 17
Guamán	Janeth	ECU	15.1.88	155/47	20kW	1:33:06	1:31:31- 17
* Guba	Paulina	POL	14.5.91	180/90	SP	19.38	18.63i- 16, 18.24- 17
Gudeta	Bekelech	ETH	11.10.97		HMar	67:03	71:14- 17
* Gudeta	Netsanet	ETH	12.2.91	162/45	HMar	66:11	67:26- 17
* Guei	Floria	FRA	2.5.90	166/53	400	51.50	50.84- 16
Guerra	Isis	CUB-J	11.11.99	174/55	HJ	1.87	1.84- 17
Guerra	Leidy	PER	27.9.98		20kW	1:32:12.5A	1:37:12.0t- 17
Guerrero	Esther	ESP	7.2.90	160/57	800	2:01.54	2:00.77- 17
					1500	4:07.90	4:16.02- 15
Guillaume	Ilionis	FRA	13.1.90	178/64	TJ	14.07i, 13.64	13.66, 13.97w- 17
* Guillon-Romarin	Ninon	FRA	15.4.95	163/53	PV	4.75	4.60- 17
Guillory	Briana	USA	21.11.97	165/57	400	51.30	52.89- 17
Gulyayeva	Aleksandra	RUS	30.4.94	173/59	800	1:59.87	1:58.34- 17
1000	2:40.11i 2:39.76i- 17		1500	4:04.76		4:04.49- 17	2000 5:42.12i 5:44.42i- 17
Gunnarsson	Lisa	SWE-J	20.8.99	171/62	PV	4.60	4.55- 17
Guo Tianqian		CHN	1.6.95	180/110	SP	17.83i, 17.76	18.59- 15
Gusarova	Inessa	RUS	29.10.95	162/52	1500	4:07.87	4:11.72- 16
Gustafson	Aliyah	USA	3.5.95		SP	17.52	16.35i- 17, 16.17- 16
Gustafson	Kendall	USA	30.3.95	178/64	Hep	5886	
Güvenç	Tugba	TUR	9.7.94	166/50	3kSt	9:39.68	9:26.09- 17
Guy	Bridget	USA	18.3.96	165/57	PV	4.46	4.23- 16
Gyurátz	Réka	HUN	31.5.96	175/70	HT	72.52	71.27- 17
Gyürkës	Viktória	HUN	15.10.92	172/61	3kSt	9:35.42	9:10.00 17
Haas	Eleriin	EST	4.7.92	180/60	HJ	1.88	1.94- 14
Hackett	Semoy	TTO	27.11.88	173/70	100	11.07	11.07- 16. 11.04dq- 12, 10.98w- 11
					200	22.64	22.51A- 15, 22.55- 12, 22.14w- 11
Hackney	Charminique	USA	20.1.98	159/48	100	11.24	11.78- 16, 11.76w- 15
Hagiwara	Ayumi	JPN	1.6.92	155/41	10000	32:12.53	31:41.80- 14
Haile	Fireweyni	ETH-Y	12.2.01		800	2:01.4A	
Hakeai	Siositina	NZL	1.3.94	182/105	DT	60.54	59.81- 15
Hall	Anna	USA-Y	23.3.01		Hep	5798A	
Hall	Cassondra	USA	23.9.97	170/59	100	11.21, 11.19w	11.34, 11.22w- 17
					200	22.64	22.92- 17
Hall	Dior	USA	2.1.96	168/55	100h	12.83	12.74- 15
Hall	Kate	USA	12.1.97	173/64	LJ	6.73i, 6.63	6.83- 15
Hall	Linden	AUS	29.6.91	167/51	1500	4:00.86	4:01.78- 16
1M	4:21.40 4:23.96- 17		3000	8:53.27		9:12.00- 15	5000 15:18.77 15:53.96- 16
Hall	Marielle	USA	28.1.92	160/52	3000	8:40.20i	8:54.48- 14
5000	15:08.20 15:06.45- 15				10000	31:56.68	31:37.45- 16
Hall	Sara	USA	15.4.83	163/48	HMar	69:27	69:37- 17
					Mar	2:26:20	2:27:21- 17
Hardy	Tramesha	USA	24.3.96	165/55	200	22.95	23.06, 22.92w- 17
Harper	Daina	USA	26.5.95	178/64	400	51.29	50.64- 17
^ Harper Nelson	Dawn	USA	13.5.84	168/61	100h	12.75	12.37- 12, 12.36w- 09
* Harrison	Kendra	USA	18.9.92	163/52	200	22.81	23.00- 16, 22.85w- 17
					100h	12.36	12.20 16
* Harrison	Queen	USA	10.9.88	170/60	100h	12.63	12.43- 13
* Harting	Julia	GER	1.4.90	190/84	DT	61.63	68.49- 16
* Hasay	Jordan	USA	21.9.91	163/45	HMar	68:38	67:55- 17
* Hassan	Sifan	NED	1.1.93	170/49	800	1:59.35	1:56.81- 17
1500	3:57.41+ 3:56.14- 17		1M	4:14.71		4:18.20- 15	3000 8:27.50 8:28.90- 17
5000	14:22.34 14:41.24- 17				HMar	65:15	77:10- 11
* Hastings	Natasha	USA	23.7.86	173/63	200	22.75w	22.57- 16, 22.55w- 14, 22.50St- 17
					400	52.11A	49.84- 07
Hata	Sumire	JPN	4.5.96		LJ	6.51w	6.08, 6.31w- 17
Hatsko-Fedusova	Hanna	UKR	3.10.90	174/73	JT	60.21	67.29- 14
Hawkins	Chari	USA	21.5.91	170/57	Hep	6137	5956- 16
Hayashida	Misaki	JPN	31.1.96	166/48	10000	32:26.65	32:44.64- 16
Haye-Smith	Yanique	JAM	22.3.90	170/55	400h	55.74	56.10- 17
Hayes	Chelsea	USA	9.2.88	168/55	LJ	6.47	7.10- 12
* Hayes	Quanera	USA	7.3.92	172/59	400	51.46Ai, 51.82i	49.71- 17
Hazlewood	Micaela	USA	18.6.95	175/77	DT	57.34	56.75- 17
Healy	Phil	IRL	19.11.94	165/57	100	11.28, 11.16w	11.49, 11.36w- 14
200	22.99			23.32- 17	400	52.08i, 52.19	53.49i- 17, 53.58- 16

Name		Nat	Born	Ht/Wt	Event	2018 Mark	Pre-2018 Best
Healy	Sarah	IRL-Y	13.2.01	162/50	1500	4:09.25	4:19.85- 17
Heath	Madison	USA	3.11.95	173/59	PV	4.45	4.35- 17
Hechavarría	Zurian	CUB	10.8.95	164/58	400h	55.13	55.97A- 15, 56.02- 17
Heikkinen	Hertta	FIN	27.10.94	170/60	Hep	5787	5597- 17
Heikkinen	Jutta	FIN	27.10.94	171/63	Hep	5771	5747- 17
* Hejnová	Zuzana	CZE	19.12.86	170/55	400h	55.16	52.83- 13
Helps	Shauna	JAM	23.10.96	166/52	200	22.97	23.23.21- 1706- 17
Hembram	Purnima	IND	10.7.93	167/57	Hep	5898	5798- 17
Hemphill	Meg	JPN	23.5.96	167/57	Hep	5766	5907- 17
* Henderson	Ashley	USA	4.12.95	168/59	100	10.96, 10.91w	11.01- 17, 10.96w- 16
					200	22.49, 22.41i 22.54A, 22.35w- 17, 22.64- 16	
Henderson	Emmonnie	USA	5.11.94	188/107	SP	18.14i	17.98- 17
Hendry	Mhairi	GBR	31.3.96		800	2:01.30i	2:03.37- 17
* Henriques	Inês	POR	1.5.80	156/48	20kW	1:29:15	1:29:00- 16
					50kW	4:09:21	4:05:56- 17
Henry	Alexus	USA	14.12.96	168/52	HJ	1.87	1.83- 15
Herashchenko	Iryna	UKR	10.3.95	181/61	HJ	1.93i	1.95i- 14, 1.95- 17
Hering	Christina	GER	9.10.94	185/62	800	2:00.48	1:59.54- 15
Hermansson	Hanna	SWE	18.5.89	171/62	800	2:00.52	2:00.43- 17
					1500	4:07.16	4:18.58- 17
Herrera	Irisdaymi	CUB	18.4.92	167/66	LJ	6.51	6.56- 14
Herrera	Mayra Carolina	GUA	20.12.88	163/54	50kW	4:28:30	4:15:42- 17
Hickling	Tissanna	JAM	7.1.98	168/54	LJ	6.61, 6.73w	6.39- 17, 6.48w- 16
Hilali	Siham	MAR	2.5.86	161/58	1500	4:09.50	4:01.33- 11
Hildebrand	Nadine	GER	20.9.87	158/51	100h	12.97	12.64- 16
* Hill	Dani	USA	16.5.91	178/95	SP	18.18i, 18.02	19.64- 17
Hill	Deanna	USA	13.4.96	168/55	100	11.21, 10.98w	11.17, 11.01w- 17
					200	22.67, 22.49w	22.41, 22.30w- 17
Hill	MacKenzie	USA	5.1.86	166/54	100h	13.07	13.27- 17
Hillman	Christina	USA	6.10.93	178/84	SP	17.15i	18.15i, 17.73- 14
Hills	Madeline	AUS	15.5.87	174/51	5000	15:06.19	15:04.05- 16
					10000	32:01.04	31.41.10- 17
Hiltz	Nikki	USA	23.10.94	162/52	1500	4:09.14	4:10.28- 17
^ Hingst	Carolin	GER	18.9.80	174/60	PV	4.45	4.72- 10
Hinriksdóttir	Aníta	ISL	13.1.96	161/50	800	2:01.05	2:00.05- 17
Hinton	Kaylee	USA	19.4.97	175/64	Hep	5793w, 5585	5869(w)- 17
Hirpa	Bedatu	ETH-J	28.4.99		Mar	2:21:32	2:34:18- 17
* Hitchon	Sophie	GBR	11.7.91	170/74	HT	73.48	74.54- 16
Hixson/Leland	Kristen	USA	1.7.92	170/60	PV	4.62i, 4.61	4.65- 16
Hjálmsdóttir	Ásdís	ISL	28.10.85	175/65	JT	60.34	63.43- 17
* Hobbs	Aleia	USA	24.2.96	172/59	100	10.90, 10.86w	10.85- 17
					200	22.93	23.80- 13
Hoffmann	Lore	SUI	25.7.96	172/54	800	2:01.67	2:03.03- 17
Hofmann	Franziska	GER	27.3.94	175/69	100h	13.00	12.87- 14
Högardh	Caroline	SWE	16.11.92	171/53	3kSt	9:50.94	10:19.00- 12
Hoggard	Tori	USA	20.11.96	167/60	PV	4.61i, 4.51	4.57i, 4.55- 17
Holmberg	Madeline	USA	26.10.96	170/57	Hep	5976	5636- 18
Holmes	Alexis	USA-J	28.1.00	180/68	400	51.21	54.45- 16
Holodna	Olha	UKR	14.11.91	183/95	SP	17.41	18.72- 13
Holub-Kowalik	Malgorzata	POL	30.10.92	168/56	400	51.18	51.67- 16
Hordiyenko	Rimma	UKR	30.12.95	172/63	Hep	6036	5737- 17
Hori	Yuka	JPN	13.6.96	155/40	10000	31:48.93	31:59.80- 17
Horn	Carina	RSA	9.3.89	169/56	100	10.98	11.06- 15, 11.05w- 17
Horton	Kiana	USA	29.1.97	164/54	400	51.22	55.45- 13
Horvat	Anita	SLO	7.9.96	174/56	400	51.22	51.94- 17
Hosoda	Ai	JPN	27.11.95		10000	32:21.11	32:26.99- 17
* Houlihan	Shelby	USA	8.2.93	160/54	1500	3:57.34	4:03.39- 16
3000	8:36.01i			8:37.40- 17	5000	14:34.45	15:00.37- 17
Howell	Jacklyn	USA	3.10.96	160/52	100h	12.93	12.90, 12.87w- 16
* Hrasnová	Martina	SVK	21.3.83	177/88	HT	73.25	76.90- 09
* Hrubá	Michaela	CZE	21.2.98	182/62	HJ	1.93i, 1.91	1.95i- 16, 1.94- 17
Hryshutyna	Krystyna	UKR	21.3.92	176/59	LJ	6.81	6.81- 15
Hu Linpeng		CHN	29.12.95		HJ	1.88i, 1.84	1.84- 16
* Huddle	Molly	USA	31.8.84	163/48	5000	15:01.44	14:42.64- 14
10000	31:52.32	30:13.67- 16		HMar	67:25	67:41- 16 Mar 2:26:44	2:28:13- 16
Hughes	Amber	USA	23.8.94	175/60	100h	13.12	13.27- 15, 13.12w- 17
Hull	Jessica	AUS	22.10.96	167/52	1500	4:08.75	4:13.48- 17
Hulley	Alex	AUS	24.7.97	171/90	HT	68.20	68.66- 17
Humphrey	Brittley	USA	6.3.98	172/57	100h	13.02	13.24- 16
Huntington	Maria	FIN	13.3.97	171/61	Hep	5858	5496- 17
Hurske	Reetta	FIN	15.5.95	168/56	100h	13.11, 13.07w	13.16- 16

Name		Nat	Born	Ht/Wt	Event	2018 Mark	Pre-2018 Best
Hussong	Christin	GER	17.3.94	187/82	JT	67.90	66.41- 16
* Hylton	Shannon	GBR	19.12.96	168/52	200	22.78	22.94, 22.73w- 15
Hynne	Hedda	NOR	13.3.90	172/57	800	2:01.46	1:59.87- 17
* Ibargüen	Caterine	COL	12.2.84	185/70	LJ	6.93	6.73A, 6.87Aw, 6.63, 6.66w- 12
					TJ	14.96	15.31- 14
Ichiyama	Mao	JPN	29.5.97	157/42	10000	31:57.91	31:40.01- 17
Ifantídou	Sofía	GRE	5.1.85	164/53	JT	57.50	59.23- 17
Igaune	Laura	LAT	2.10.88	170/70	HT	67.75	68.94- 12
Imali	Maximilia	KEN	8.12.96	169/59	400	51.32	51.18A- 17
Ince	Ariana	USA	14.3.89	180/75	JT	59.59	61.38- 17
Inchude	Jessica	GBS	25.3.96	175/81	SP	17.46	16.90i, 16.60- 17
* Infeld	Emily	USA	21.3.90	163/48	5000	15:15.52i	14:56.33- 17
Insaeng	Subenrat	THA	10.2.94	183/105	DT	61.97	61.12- 16
Insermu	Shasho	ETH	16.9.93		Mar	2:23:28	2:30:03- 17
* Irby	Lynna	USA	6.12.98	168/55	200	22.25,22.06w	23.58i- 17,23.77- 13,23.53w- 16
					400	49.80	51.39- 16
Irozuru	Abigail	GBR	3.1.90	170/61	LJ	6.60, 6.64w	6.80- 12
Ishova	Yekaterina	RUS	17.1.89	164/52	5000	15:24.09	15:19.94- 11
Itoya	Juliet	ESP	17.8.86	174/63	LJ	6.80, 6.88Aw	6.79- 16
Iuel	Amalie Hammild	NOR	17.4.94	180/59	400	51.99	51.81- 17
					400h	55.26	55.38- 17
Iusco	Florentina	ROU	8.4.96	178/60	LJ	6.69	6.79i, 6.78w- 15, 6.71- 14
Ivancevic	Andrea	CRO	21.8.84	167/59	100h	12.85	12.87- 15
Ivanenko	Olesya	RUS	6.10.82	165/56	TJ	13.67	14.54i- 08, 14.50- 06
Ivanova	Irina	RUS	19.4.96		PV	4.45	4.20- 17
Ivonina	Yekaterina	RUS	14.6.94	164/52	3000	8:56.34i	9:12.69i- 16, 9:32.49- 14
					3kSt	9:16.68	9:24.66- 16
Iwade	Reina	JPN	8.12.94	154/42	Mar	2:26:28	2:24:38- 16
Jaakkola	Jelena	FIN	7.3.89	172/76	JT	56.04	58.89- 08
Jackson	Hannah	USA	28.2.97	155/57	200	23.11i, 23.07w	23.33, 23.00w- 17
Jackson	Shericka	JAM	16.7.94	174/59	100	11.13	11.24- 17
					200	22.05	22.46- 17
Jackson	Susan	USA	26.7.89	186/65	HJ	1.86	1.91- 14
Jacobs	Gabi	USA	20.8.96	173/82	DT	60.16	58.23- 17
Jacobus	Lexi	USA	20.11.96	167/60	PV	4.66i, 4.65	4.70- 16
* Jagaciak Michalska	Anna	POL	10.2.90	178/68	LJ	6.47	6.74- 10
					TJ	14.24	14.33, 14.40w- 16
Jakubaityte	Indre	LTU	24.1.76	177/70	JT	58.40	63.65- 07
James	Nayana	IND	18.10.95	181/72	LJ	6.51	6.55- 17
James	Tiffany	JAM	31.1.97	160/52	400	52.11	51.32- 16
Jarder	Erica	SWE	2.4.86	173/59	LJ	6.44, 6.53w	6.71i- 13, 6.70- 15
Jasiunaite	Liveta	LTU	26.7.94	174/68	JT	61.61	61.32- 16
Jassem	Noora Salem	BRN	27.11.96	175/90	SP	17.32	17.69- 17
Jebet ¶?	Ruth	BRN	17.11.96	165/49	3000	8:48.99i	8:47.24i- 16, 9:09.8A- 13
* Jefferson	Kyra	USA	23.9.94	165/57	200	22.48	22.02- 15
Jemai	Sara	ITA	12.4.92	178/65	JT	58.19	57.20- 15
Jemison	Breana	USA	11.12.93	178/93	SP	17.57	17.36- 16
Jenkins	Tovea	JAM	27.10.92	172/60	400	52.12i, 52.58	51.99- 17
Jenneke	Michelle	AUS	23.6.93	172/63	100h	12.99	12.82- 15
Jepkemei	Daisy	KEN	13.2.96	167/50	3kSt	9:10.71	9:19.68- 17
* Jepkemoi	Hyvin	KEN	13.1.92	156/45	3000	8:30.51	9:00.01St- 16
					3kSt	9:01.60	9:00.01- 16
Jepkesho	Visiline	KEN	30.12.89	160/45	Mar	2:22:58	2:21.37- 17
Jepkoech	Monica	KEN	.85		Mar	2:24:31	2:26:58- 17
* Jepkosgei	Joyciline	KEN	8.12.93	156/52	10000	32:17.0A	31:28.28- 16
					HMar	66:46	64:51- 17
* Jepkosgei	Nelly	KEN	14.7.91	164/53	800	1:58.96	1:59.40- 13
1000	2:35.30		2:35.43- 13		1500	4:00.99	4:02.75- 17
Jerotich	Emily	KEN	13.5.86	155/44	800	1:58.04	2:00.0A- 16
Jiang Shanshan		CHN	28.2.97		20kW	1:32:51	1:33:39- 17
Jiménez	Isidora	CHI	10.8.93	170/54	100	11.19A, 11.35, 11.27w	11.33- 15
Jisa Mokonin	Desi	BRN	12.7.97	163/48	Mar	2:23:39	
Johnson	Alaysha	USA	20.7.96	160/52	100h	12.70	12.69, 12.68w- 17
Johnson	Brandeé	USA	3.4.98	163/52	400h	57.01	56.16- 16
Johnson	Dianna	JAM	12.11.95	165/55	100	11.20A	11.40- 17
Johnson	Felisha	USA	24.7.89	185/105	SP	17.67i	19.26- 16
Johnson	Kortnei	USA	11.8.97	165/52	100	11.10,10.97w	11.09- 17
					200	22.56, 22.52w	22.78- 16, 22.50w- 17
Johnson	LaTessa	USA	13.4.97	165/52	200	22.77	22.80, 22.75w- 16
Johnson	Lauren	USA	4.5.87	170/52	800	2:00.87	2:01.59- 16
1500	4:08.21		4:04.17- 15		1M	4:28.16	4:25.04- 16

Name		Nat	Born	Ht/Wt	Event	2018 Mark		Pre-2018 Best
Johnson	Rachel	USA	30.4.93	165/	10000	32:32.84		33:11.98- 15
Johnson	Tristine	USA	28.9.92	172/57	LJ	6.49		6.24- 16
* Johnson-Thompson	Katarina	GBR	9.1.93	183/70	200	22.88		22.79- 16
	HJ 1.93i 1.98- 16			LJ 6.71i, 6.70 6.93i- 15,	6.92- 14	Hep	6759		6691- 17
Jones	Ariel	USA	18.7.95	165/52	400h	56.89		56.44- 17
Jones	Cortney	USA-J	18.6.99	168/55	100h	12.86		13.06- 17
Jones	Danielle	USA	21.8.96	165/54	1500	4:07.33		4:08.42- 17
Jones	Tia	USA-J	8.9.00	163/52	100h	12.89		12.84- 16
Jorgensen	Gwen	USA	25.4.86	167/52	5000	15:15.64i		15:52.19- 09
					10000	31:55.68		33:38.38- 09
Joye	Hannah	AUS	4.1.96	177/63	HJ	1.86		1.92- 15
Juárez	Mar	ESP	27.9.93	156/47	50kW	4:28:58		-0-
Judd	Jessica	GBR	7.1.95	178/60	1500	4:07.50		4:03.73- 17
					3000	8:53.29		8:43.24mx, 8:59.60- 17
Jung Hye-lim		KOR	1.7.87	167/52	100h	13.11		13.04, 12.86w- 16
* Jungfleisch	Marie-Laurence	GER	7.10.90	181/68	HJ	1.96		2.00- 16
Junnila	Ella	FIN	6.12.98	183/60	HJ	1.92		1.83- 17
Kaczynska	Paulina	POL	24.7.91	176/52	5000	15:29.67		15:33.25- 17
Kagramanova	Reykhan	RUS	1.6.97		20kW	1:29:50		1:35:44- 17
Kähärä	Jessica	FIN-Y	1.8.01	171/54	HJ	1.87		1.80- 17
Kakko	Elina	FIN	12.1.97	177/58	HJ	1.88		1.85i- 14, 1.83- 13
Kalawan	Shannon	JAM	25.11.97	168/52	400	52.05		53.19- 16
					400h	56.99		56.29- 16
Kälin	Annik	SUI-J	27.4.00	168/57	Hep	5844		5664- 17
Kämäräinen	Sanna	FIN	8.2.86	184/86	DT	56.96		61.07- 15
Kamau	Tabitha	KEN-J	3.7.00	151/40	3000	8:52.41		8:58.35- 16
					5000	15:20.52		15:57.80- 17
* Kambundji	Mujinga	SUI	17.6.92	168/59	100	10.95		11.07- 15
					200	22.45		22.42- 17
Kamga	Vanessa	SWE	19.11.98	177/90	DT	57.04		54.91- 17
Kamilos	Jessica	USA	0.0.00	168/48	3kSt	9:50.94		9:41.28- 16
* Kamulu	Pauline	KEN	30.12.94	154/45	5000	15:31.74		14:58.82- 17
	10000 30:41.85			31:47.13- 17	HMar	66:56		68:04- 17
Kandie	Peninah	KEN	22.6.92		HMar	69:44		
Kaneko	Haruna	JPN	18.1.97		JT	55.66		
Kangas	Jenni	FIN	3.7.92	178/74	JT	59.96		60.98- 17
Kanuchová	Veronika	SVK	19.4.93	170/69	HT	65.58		69.48- 16
Kanuho	Rochelle	USA	4.7.90	160/44	10000	32:18.35		32:08.76- 15
Kardasz	Klaudia	POL	2.5.96	179/77	SP	18.48		17.90- 17
Kashyna	Inna	UKR	27.9.91	162/49	20kW	1:28:58		1:30:11- 17
Kassanavoid	Janee'	USA	19.1.95	175/79	HT	68.21		66.97- 17
Käther	Nadja	GER	29.9.88	178/62	LJ	6.70		6.68i- 14, 6.66- 10
Kato	Misaki	JPN	15.6.91	155/40	10000	32:24.57		31:59.72- 16
Kaur	Kamalpreet	IND	3.4.96	186/106	DT	61.04		55.95- 17
Kaur	Karamjit	IND	5.2.91		20kW	1:34:09		1:40:02- 17
Kaur	Khushbir	IND	9.7.93	155/49	20kW	1:32:17		1:31:40- 14
Kaur	Navjeet	IND	6.3.95	178/60	DT	59.18		56.36- 14
Kawazoe	Kaori	JPN	30.5.95	158/48	20kW	1:33:44		1:33:09- 17
Kaya	Ozlem	TUR	20.4.90	160/49	3kSt	9:35.47		9:30.23- 15
Keenan	Te Rina	NZL	29.9.90	180/84	DT	56.39		60.78- 15
* Keitany	Mary	KEN	18.1.82	158/45	HMar	64:55		65:13- 17
					Mar	2:22:48		2:17:01- 17
Kelati	Weini	ERI	1.12.96	159/42	5000	15:22.71, 15:15.24i		15:37.03i- 17
Kemppainen	Suvi	FIN	25.1.98	165/61	JT	57.75		53.00- 17
Kennedy	Nina	AUS	5.4.97	166/57	PV	4.71		4.59- 15
Kenzel	Alina	GER	10.8.97	183/78	SP	18.21		17.68i, 17.61- 17
Kerekes	Gréta	HUN	9.10.92	164/54	100h	12.95		13.10, 12.97w- 17
Khalyutina	Yekaterina	RUS	16.1.91	169/60	LJ	6.48		6.51- 13
* Kholodovich	Tatyana	BLR	21.6.91	181/83	JT	67.47		66.34- 61
Khramova	Valeriya	RUS	13.8.92	170/60	400h	56.04		55.70- 17
Kielbasinska	Anna	POL	26.6.90	170/55	100	11.23w		11.34- 15
Kilel	Caroline	KEN	21.3.81	172/54	Mar	2:29:14		2:22:34- 13
Kim Do-yeon		KOR	2.9.93	163/44	Mar	2:25:41		2:31:24- 17
Kim Kyung-ae		KOR	5.3.88	163/62	JT	56.84		58.77- 15
Kimanzi	Grace	KEN	1.3.92	161/48	3000	8:57.38		9:04.96- 09
	5000 15:15.65			15:16.44- 16	10000	31:17.28		31:57.35- 15
Kimeli	Daisy	KEN	28.11.94		HMar	68:59		
Kimura	Ayako	JPN	11.6.88	168/53	100h	13.13		13.03- 13, 12.99w- 17
Kimura	Tomoka	JPN	12.11.94	154/43	3000	8:55.14		9:04.47- 11
* Kinsey	Erika	SWE	10.3.88	185/68	HJ	1.94		1.97- 15
Kintana	June	ESP	12.4.95	175/74	DT	55.98		56.30- 17

Name		Nat	Born	Ht/Wt	Event	2018 Mark	Pre-2018 Best
* Kipkemboi	Margaret	KEN	9.2.93	162/45	3000	8:54.91+	8:30.11- 17
					5000	15:01.98	14:47.24- 16
* Kipkirui	Caroline	KEN	26.5.94	162/47	3000	8:29.05	8:42.2- 17
5000	14:43.96		14:27.55- 17		HMar	65:07	66:53- 17
Kipkoech	Pascalia	KEN	22.12.88	153/42	HMar	69:23	67:17- 12
* Kiplagat	Edna	KEN	15.11.79	163/47	HMar	60:11	67:41- 12
					Mar	2:21:18	2:19:50- 12
* Kiplagat	Florence	KEN	27.2.87	155/42	Mar	2:26:08	2:19:44- 11
Kiplagat	Vivian	KEN	.88		HMar	69:10	68:21- 11
Kipp	Shalaya	USA	19.8.90	170/58	3kSt	9:41.24	9:28.72- 16
^ Kiprop	Helah	KEN	7.4.85	164/48	HMar	69:38	67:39- 13
Kiprop	Nancy	KEN	7.7.79	164/48	HMar	67:32	67:22- 17
					Mar	2:22:46	2:24:20- 13
Kipyokei	Diana	KEN	5.5.94	160/54	HMar	67:07	68:38- 16
* Kiriakopoúlou	Nikoléta	GRE	21.3.86	167/56	PV	4.80	4.83- 15
Kirkland	Jayla	USA-J	13.2.99	168/52	200	22.93, 22.91w	23.15- 16
* Kirui	Purity	KEN	13.8.91	162/47	3kSt	9:21.34	9:17.74- 15
Kitaguchi	Haruka	JPN	16.3.98	178/80	JT	60.48	61.38- 16
Kite	Gloria	KEN	29.12.98	170/52	2000	5:40.65	
3000	8:39.07		5000	15:06.84			10000	31:41.47
Kitur	Bornes	KEN	.88		Mar	2:24:19	2:29:01- 17
Kiyeng	Judy	KEN	10.12.94	160/45	1500	4:03.87	4:04.4A- 17
					1M	4:27.32	4:29.29- 16
^ Klaas	Kathrin	GER	6.2.84	168/72	HT	71.50	76.05- 12
Klaup-McColl	Mari	EST	27.2.90	180/58	Hep	6011	6023(w)- 15, 6002- 13
Klein	Hanna	GER	6.4.93	172/55	1500	4:06.46	4:04.15- 17
					5000	15:17.47	15:17.14- 17
Klintsova	Liliya	UKR	12.7.97	177/57	HJ	1.86i, 1.85	1.86- 17
Klochko	Viktoriya	UKR	2.9.92	187/115	DT	57.40	58.01- 15
Kloster	Line	NOR	27.2.90	175/60	400h	55.49	56.18- 17
* Klosterhalfen	Konstanze	GER	18.2.97	169/52	1500	4:06.34, 4:04.00i	3:58.92- 17
1M	4:24.27		3000	8:38.04, 8:36.01i	8:29.89- 17	5000	15:03.73	14:51.38- 17
Klymets	Iryna	UKR	4.10.94	169/71	HT	72.63	72.53- 17
Knäsche	Anjuli	GER	18.10.93	169/61	PV	4.50i, 4.45	4.55- 16
Knibb	Kellion	JAM	25.12.93	193/93	DT	58.91	62.73- 17
Knight	Andrenette	JAM	19.11.96	170/54	400h	56.94	56.98- 16
Knoroz	Polina	RUS-J	20.7.99	175/60	PV	4.50i, 4.25	4.50i, 4.45- 17
Koala	Marthe Yasmine	BUR	8.3.94	174/68	LJ	6.64	6.52- 17
					Hep	6136	6230(w)- 17
Kochanova	Mariya	RUS-Y	30.5.02	176/57	HJ	1.87	1.82- 17
Kocina	Anete	LAT	5.2.96	176/65	JT	62.58	64.47- 17
Kolb	Viktoryia	BLR	26.10.93	182/90	SP	18.35	17.71- 17
Koleczek	Karolina	POL	15.1.93	169/49	100h	12.93, 12.90w	12.91, 12.87w- 15
Kolesnichenko	Irina	RUS	27.5.88	170/65	400h	55.23	53.77- 12
Kolesnychenko	Olena	UKR	3.6.93	172/58	400h	56.94	55.48- 16
Koll	Reena	EST	15.11.96		PV	4.36	4.31i- 16, 4.20- 14
Kolomoyets	Anastasiya	BLR	15.7.94		HT	68.32	69.20- 16
Koloskova	Natalya	RUS	19.7.88	164/48	3kSt	9:39.07	9:31.95- 16
* Koneva	Yekaterina	RUS	25.9.88	169/55	LJ	6.67	6.82i- 15, 6.70, 6.80w- 11
					TJ	14.67, 14.79w	15.04- 15
Kong Lingwei		CHN	28.7.95	165/55	200	22.92	23.42- 17
Konieczek	Alicja	POL	2.11.94	159/41	3kSt	9:41.16	9.49.74- 17
Kononova	Yevgeniya	RUS	28.9.89	175/63	HJ	1.00i, 1.85	1.92- 12
Kopp	Madeline	USA	4.4.95	168/56	800	2:00.88	2:03.00- 17
* Kopron	Malwina	POL	16.11.94	169/89	HT	72.92	76.85- 17
Kora	Salomé	SUI	8.6.94	173/66	100	11.25	11.27- 17
Kore	Tola	ETH	16.1.97		800	2:00.2A	2:00.61- 17
* Korikwiang	Pauline	KEN	1.3.88	163/39	10000	31:51.1A	31:06.29- 10
					HMar	66:31	72:03A- 15
Korneychuk	Margarita	RUS	21.2.95		HJ	1.86	1.89- 17
Korobkina	Yelena	RUS	25.11.90	163/47	1500	4:07.45	4:04.90- 17
2000	5:41.10i		3000	8:51.90i, 9:00.45	8:47.61i- 15, 8:51.00- 14	5000	15:19.11	15:14.67- 14
Korpela	Merja	FIN	15.5.81	170/75	HT	66.65	69.56- 09
Korsun	Olha	UKR	11.11.96	174/60	TJ	13.86	13.01- 17
Korte	Annimari	FIN	8.4.88	166/52	100h	13.14	13.46- 12, 13.25w- 17
Korzh	Tatsiana	BLR	17.3.93	175/75	JT	58.00	62.10- 16
* Kosgei	Brigid	KEN	20.2.94	163/46	HMar	66:49	66:35- 17
					Mar	2:18:35	2:20:22- 17
Kosolapova	Valentina	RUS	11.7.97	168/52	TJ	14.14	13.71- 17, 13.74w- 16
^ Koster	Maureen	NED	3.7.92	175/56	1500	4:05.12	3:59.79- 15
					5000	15:19.61	15:07.20- 16

Name		Nat	Born	Ht/Wt	Event	2018 Mark	Pre-2018 Best
Kotwila	Martyna	POL-J	13.1.99	169/55	200	22.99	23.83, 23.61w- 17
Kowal	Matylda	POL	11.1.89	165/54	3kSt	9:41.73	9:35.13- 16
Kowalska	Katarzyna	POL	7.4.85	177/55	3kSt	9:37.91	9:26.93- 09
Kozák	Luca	HUN	1.6.96	166/55	100h	12.86	13.10, 12.99w- 17
Kozul	Anamari	CRO	20.1.96	178/76	HT	69.16	63.88, 64.62irr- 17
Kramer	Regine	GER	5.4.93	168/59	PV	4.40i, 4.30	4.40- 16
^ Krasnova	Angelina	RUS	7.2.91	168/55	PV	4.60	4.70- 13
Krasutska	Hanna	UKR	20.7.95	180/64	TJ	14.15, 14.21w	13.70- 15
* Krause	Gesa-Felicitas	GER	3.8.92	167/55	3000	8:54.08i	8:49.43i- 16, 9:02.04- 15
					3kSt	9:19.80	9:11.85- 17
Krebs	Denise	GER	27.6.87	170/46	5000	15:26.58	-0-
* Krizsán	Xénia	HUN	13.1.93	171/62	Hep	6367	6390- 17
Kropivko	Yekaterina	RUS	13.6.97	166/52	LJ	6.54	6.38- 14
* Krumins	Susan	NED	8.7.86	170/54	3000	8:37.21	8:34.41- 17
	5000	15:09.65		14:51.25- 17	10000	31:52.55	31:20.24- 17
Krylova	Anna	RUS	3.10.85	177/65	TJ	14.02i, 13.67	14.40- 14
Kudzelich	Svetlana	BLR	7.5.87	170/52	3kSt	9:47.89	9:27.95- 14
Kuikka	Tiia	FIN	30.11.94	165/49	50kW	4:32:43	
Kuivisto	Sara	FIN	18.8.91	175/55	1500	4:08.96	4:12.78- 16
Kuklová	Pavla	CZE	1.11.96	172/74	HT	66.87	63.45- 17
Kuma	Dibaba	ETH	14.9.96		HMar	68:37	69:21- 16
					Mar	2:23:34	
Kumagai	Nami	JPN	9.7.96		50kW	4:39:01	
Kumari drugs dq?	Sandeep	IND	10.12.92	180/89	DT	58.41	54.93- 16
Kunz	Annie	USA	16.2.93	183/70	Hep	5881	6038- 16
Kupina	Yekaterina	RUS	2.2.86	172/59	800	2:01.00	1:59.21- 13
Kurahara	Natsumi	JPN	.97		50kW	4:44:45	
Kurgat	Caroline	KEN	20.4.93		10000	32:33.24	33:38.30- 16
Kurgat	Ednah	KEN	15.6.91	169/50	3000	8:57.47i	9:13.47Ai- 17
	5000	15:20.06, 15:14.78i		15:19.03i, 15:26.00- 17	10000	32:31.55	34:38.75- 15
Kuria	Mary	KEN	29.11.87	157/48	800	2:00.80	2:01.67- 13
					1500	4.03.06	4:02.19- 12
Küster	Susen	GER	27.7.94	165/69	HT	65.42	71.25- 17
Kuwazoe	Tomoka	JPN-J	1.2.99	167/60	JT	56.86	54.50- 17
Kuze	Kiho	JPN	28.3.95	165/58	JT	58.29	58.98- 13
Kwambai	Antonina	KEN	1.4.92		HMar	68:07	69:49- 17
Kwarteng	Abigail	GHA			HJ	1.87	1.76- 17
Kylypko	Maryna	UKR	10.11.95	164/60	PV	4.62i, 4.50	4.65- 16
Kytölä	Kira	FIN	25.6.93	178/62	TJ	13.61	12.97, 12.99w- 16
Laasma	Liina	EST	13.1.92	178/77	JT	59.01	63.65- 16
* LaCaze/Gregson	Genevieve	AUS	4.8.89	164/53	3000	8:49.38	8:45.81i- 17, 8:52.28- 16
					3kSt	9:23.69	9:14.28- 16
LaFond	Thea	DMA	5.4.94	173/65	TJ	14.08i, 14.01	14.20- 17
Lagger	Sarah	AUT-J	3.9.99	174/60	Hep	6225	6083- 17
* Lake	Morgan	GBR	12.5.97	178/64	HJ	1.97	1.96- 17
Lally	Jade	GBR	30.3.87	183/81	DT	59.83	65.10- 16
Lalonde	Geneviève	CAN	5.9.91	167/47	3000	8:49.78	9:05.78i- 16, 9:36.77- 08
					3kSt	9:35.19	9:29.99- 17
* Lalova-Collio	Ivet	BUL	18.5.84	168/55	100	11.18	10.77- 04
					200	22.63	22.32- 15
Lamble	Regan	AUS	14.10.91	174/55	20kW	1:33:40	1:29:33- 16
* Lamote	Renelle	FRA	26.12.93	168/57	800	1:58.83	1:58.01- 16
					1000	2:34.48	
Landázuri	Giselly Andrea	COL	8.8.92	174/57	TJ	13.76A, 13.54	13.97A, 13.81- 13
Landázuri	Narcisa	ECU	25.11.92	160/52	100	11.12A, 11.23	11.26A, 11.27- 16
Lansiquot	Imani	GBR	17.12.97	170/59	100	11.11	11.34- 17
Lara	Cristina	ESP	5.8.95	164/49	100	11.42, 11.20w	11.40, 11.36w- 17
Larios	Maria	ESP	29.10.92	164/49	50kW	4:37:43	-0-
* Lashmanova	Yelena	RUS	9.4.92	170/48	20kW	1:23:39	1:24:58- 16
* Lasitskene	Mariya	RUS	14.1.93	182/60	HJ	2.04i	2.06- 17
Laus	Camille	BEL	23.5.93	175/60	400	51.49	54.69- 17
Law	Kirsty	GBR	11.10.86	177/80	DT	56.37	57.79- 12
Lawrence	Mel	USA	29.8.89	167/52	3000	8:50.96	9:03.22i, 9:36.91- 09
					3kSt	9:32.68	9:34.94- 17
Lawrence	Shadae	JAM	31.12.95	173/84	DT	62.10	62.59- 17
Lawson	Lekeisha	USA	3.6.87	168/57	100	11.15	11.06- 15
Lazar	Bianca	ROU	24.2.93	166/74	HT	66.87	65.48- 16
Le-Roy	Anastasia	JAM	11.9.87	172/57	200	22.16St	23.08- 08
					400	50.57	50.84- 14
Lecky	Sommer	IRL-J	14.6.00	180/60	HJ	1.90	1.85- 17
Ledáki	Stélla-Iró	GRE	18.7.88	170/58	PV	4.35	4.50- 12

Name		Nat	Born	Ht/Wt	Event	2018 Mark	Pre-2018 Best
Leffler	Celina	GER	9.4.96	174/61	Hep	6050	6070- 17
^ Legnante	Assunta	ITA	14.5.78	190/125	SP	17.08	19.04- 06
Lehmeyer	Emilia	GER	11.4.97	175/53	20kW	1:32:36	1:34:24- 17
Lekamge	H.L.Dilhani	SRI	14.1.87	167/61	JT	58.41	58.11- 17
Lekapana	Parendis	KEN	4.8.91		HMar	69:23	69:13- 17
LeLeux	Morgann	USA	14.11.92	170/61	PV	4.61iA, 4.60	4.65- 17
Lema	Marta	ETH	00.12.90		Mar	2:22:35	2:24:32- 16
Lembus	Betty	KEN	9.7.91		HMar	69:49	69:25- 17
					Mar	2:23:40	2:29:31- 17
Leontyeva	Natalya	RUS	5.7.87	168/48	3kSt	9:50.19	9:52.36- 17
^ Leontyuk	Yuliya	BLR	31.1.84	185/80	SP	18.42	19.79- 08
^ Lesueur-Aymonin	Éloyse	FRA	15.7.88	181/65	LJ	6.80	6.92- 14, 7.04w- 12
Letnar	Bernarda	SLO	26.12.89	177/72	JT	56.13	57.84- 17
* Levchenko	Yuliya	UKR	28.11.97	179/60	HJ	1.98i	2.01- 17
Leveelahti	Helena	FIN-J	30.9.99	190/95	DT	56.80	54.67- 17
^ Levy	Jura	JAM	4.11.90	157/50	100	11.22	11.06- 17
Lewetegn	Sintayehu	ETH	9.5.96	161/48	Mar	2:22:45	
^ Lewis-Smallwood	Gia	USA	1.4.79	183/93	DT	61.09	69.17- 14
Lhabze	Lamiae	MAR	19.5.84	178/59	400h	56.66	55.51- 13
Li Huei-Chun		TPE-J	12.5.99		JT	56.50	54.39- 17
Li Leilei		CHN	18.8.89	160/46	20kW	1:34:13	1:31:49- 15
* Li Ling		CHN	6.7.89	180/65	PV	4.60	4.70i- 16,4.56- 15
* Li Maocuo		CHN	20.10.92		20kW	1:30:15	1:31:00- 17
					50kW	4:13:04	4:47:28- 16
Li Qiuye		CHN	2.12.93		50kW	4:34:16	4:42:27- 17
Li Xiaohong		CHN	8.1.95	178/87	TJ	13.68	14.20- 15
Li Ying		CHN	29.3.94		TJ	13.64	13.44- 17
* Liang Rui		CHN	18.6.94		50kW	4:04:36	-0-
Ligarska	Paulina	POL	9.4.96	184/64	Hep	5845	5585- 17
de Lima	Jucilene	BRA	14.9.90	174/63	JT	57.92	62.89- 14
Limanah	Zeifie	ETH	10.2.97		HMar	68:10	71:02- 17
Linkiewicz	Joanna	POL	2.5.90	172/55	400h	55.84	55.25- 16
Linna	Inga	FIN	21.2.95	172/72	HT	68.79	68.25- 15
Linnell	Lisa	SWE	30.4.91	176/68	Hep	5877	5890- 17
Lipari	Emily	USA	19.11.92	153/48	1500	4:05.68	4:07.29- 17
					3000	8:51.07i	8:57.24i- 17
Lipsanen	Saara	FIN	13.9.95	178/65	JT	56.66	56.20- 17
* Lipsey	Charlene	USA	16.7.91	168/57	800	1:58.05	1:57.38- 17
1500	4:04.98		4:10.68- 17		1M	4:27.28	4:30.13i- 17
Little	Caitlyn	USA-J	1.2.99	160/54	100h	13.10	13.29- 17
Little	Mackenzie	AUS	22.12.96	179/73	JT	60.36	57.60- 14
* Little	Shamier	USA	20.3.95	163/52	400	50.82	50.40- 17
					400h	53.32	52.75- 17
* Liu Shiying		CHN	24.9.93	179/76	JT	67.12	66.47- 17
Liu Tingting		CHN	29.1.90	178/87	HT	72.24	73.06- 14
Llano	Béatrice Nedberge	NOR	14.12.97	169/90	HT	66.80	67.86- 16
Lo Thi Hoang		VIE	6.10.97		JT	56.15	50.34- 16
Lobe	Ricarda	GER	13.4.94	171/59	100h	12.90	12.91- 17
Lobun	Helen	KEN-J	18.3.99	170/46	1500	4:09.02	4:07.06- 17
3000	8:48.69		8:53.70- 17		5000	15:16.53	15:12.89- 16
Lokedi	Sharon	KEN	10.3.94	168/54	5000	15:27.09, 15:15.47i	15:39.05i, 15:44.51- 17
					10000	32:09.20	32:46.10- 17
Lomnická	Nikola	SVK	16.0.88	160/70	HT	67.47	71.58- 14
Lonsarek	Ivana	CRO	8.4.91	163/54	100h	13.11	13.09- 16
Londa	Maria Natalia	INA	29.10.90	167/59	LJ	6.52	6.70- 15
Long	Kally	USA	28.8.95	180/62	PV	4.36	4.42i, 4.40- 17
Lopes	Lyndsey	USA	23.8.97		Hep	5719	
López	Yaniuvis	CUB	1.2.86	180/71	SP	18.58	18.92- 17
Lotout	Marion	FRA	19.11.89	165/54	PV	4.50	4.60- 13
Lott	Darroneshia	USA	9.3.93	183/61	800	2:01.26	2:06.20- 13
Love	Shanice	JAM	9.6.97	183/82	DT	58.40	54.72- 16
Loyce	Joy	KEN	3.3.88		HMar	69:02	
* Lu Huihui		CHN	26.6.89	171/68	JT	67.69	67.59- 17
Lu Jiawen		CHN-Y	19.8.02		HJ	1.88i	1.71- 17
Lu Minjia		CHN	29.12.90	172/58	LJ	6.53A, 6.50	6.74- 09
Lu Xiaoxin		CHN	22.2.89	184/90	DT	59.56	63.27- 13
* Lu Xiuzhi		CHN	26.10.93	167/52	20kW	1:29:06	1:25:12- 15
* Lückenkemper	Gina	GER	21.11.96	170/58	100	10.98	10.95- 17
Lufutucu	Anaïs	FRA	24.4.92	168/57	400h	56.95	57.49- 15
* Luo Na		CHN	8.10.93	173/75	HT	75.02	72.27- 17

Name		Nat	Born	Ht/Wt	Event	2018 Mark	Pre-2018 Best
Luque	Jhoanmy	VEN	20.12.95	158/52	LJ	6.43i, 6.38, 6.49w	6.58. 6.63w- 17
					TJ	13.69	13.65i, 13.54, 13.80w- 17
Lutkovskaya	Alyona	RUS	15.3.96	164/55	PV	4.45i	4.61- 15
Lyakhova	Olha	UKR	18.3.92	174/57	800	2:00.26	1:58.64- 15
					1000	2:37.46	
Lyra	Viviane	BRA	29.7.93		50kW	4:41:39	
Lysenko	Alena	RUS	3.2.88		HT	66.62	69.01- 14
Ma Faying		CHN	30.8.93		50kW	4:13:28	4:49:54- 16
Ma Li		CHN-J	15.1.00		20kW	1:29:32	
Ma Yiming		CHN	10.9.97		20kW	1:33:44	1:31:32- 17
Ma Zhenxia		CHN	1.8.98		20kW	1:29:28	1:33:16- 17
Mackey	Katie	USA	12.11.87	165/53	1500	4:09.10	4:03.81- 15
3000	8:44.47, 8:43.15i		8:46.58- 16		5000	15:18.88	15:04.74- 14
MacPherson	Sarah	CAN	8.5.91	171/54	1500	4:09.26	4:09.90- 17
Maduka	Jessie	GER	23.4.96	184/70	TJ	13.95	13.61- 17
Maeda	Honami	JPN	17.7.96	166/43	10000	32:13.87	32:43.42- 16
HMar	69:12		70:22- 17		Mar	2:23:48	2:28:48- 17
* Mageean	Ciara	IRL	12.3.92	168/56	1500	4:04.13	4:01.46- 16
					1M	4:26.75	4:22.40- 17
Magnani	Margherita	ITA	26.2.87	161/45	1500	4:07.88	4:06.05- 14
3000	8:54.56i, 9:03.25		8:51.81i, 8:51.82- 14		5000	15:25.44	15:30.91- 17
* Mahuchikh	Yaroslava	UKR-Y	19.9.01	165/45+	HJ	1.96i, 1.95	1.92A- 17
Maina	Veronica	KEN	8.8.89		HMar	69:17	70:20- 17
Maisch	Katharina	GER	12.6.97	177/78	SP	17.46	17.11i, 16.98- 17
Maiwald	Anna	GER	21.7.90	176/62	Hep	6116	6111- 15
Majors	Felecia	USA	12.2.95	168/57	400	51.67	51.29- 16
Mäkelä	Kristiina	FIN	20.11.92	185/67	TJ	14.31	14.24- 16
Mäki	Kristiina	CZE	22.9.91	170/50	1500	4:06.71	4:08.19- 17
Mäkitörmä	Senja	FIN	31.5.94	180/82	SP	16.95	15.30- 17
Maksimova	Yana	BLR	9.1.89	182/70	Hep	5986	6198- 12
Malácová	Romana	CZE	15.5.87	164/57	PV	4.42i	4.62i- 16, 4.61- 17
Malavisi	Sonia	ITA	31.10.94	173/67	PV	4.00	4.51- 16
Malekani	Quincy	ZAM	15.3.95	174/65	400	52.04	
Malone	Chantel	IVB	2.12.91	175/62	LJ	6.52 6.69A- 15, 6.67i, 6.70w- 17, 6.66w- 12
Maltseva	Yuliya	RUS	30.11.90	187/84	DT	62.41	63.48- 15
* Malyshik	Hanna	BLR	4.2.94	175/90	HT	76.26	74.94- 17
Mamathu	Tebogo	RSA	27.5.95		100	11.30	
Mamo	Meskerem	ETH-J	13.4.99	149/40	3000	8:33.63	
					5000	15:05.21	15:18.06- 16
* Mamona	Patrícia	POR	21.11.88	168/53	TJ	14.19	14.65- 16
Manley	Meg	USA	3.6.93	163/52	800	2:01.73	2:03.06- 17
* Manning/Clemons	Christina	USA	29.5.90	163/54	100h	12.56	12.54- 17
Manson	Nikki	GBR	15.10.94	174/65	HJ	1.90i, 1.87	1.86- 17
Manson	Taylor	USA-J	29.9.99	171/57	400	51.74	53.18- 17
Marcelino	Mariana Grasielly	BRA	16.7.92	168/77	HT	66.93	67.02- 17
Marie-Hardy	Diane	FRA	19.2.96	166/59	Hep	6015	5731- 17
Markland	Titania	JAM	1.2.94	168/52	400	51.40	52.86- 15
Marmbrandt	Malin	SWE	29.4.85	166/58	LJ	6.46, 6.61w	6.52A- 17, 6.50, 6.52w- 16
Marois	Jill	USA	8.6.94	175/59	PV	4.35	4.45- 17
Marshall	Tonea	USA	17.12.98	178/75	100h	12.88, 12.73w	13.04- 16
* Martinez	Brenda	USA	8.9.87	163/52	800	2:00.74	1:57.91- 13
1500	4:02.65 4:00.94- 13				3000	8:57.30+	9:17.80i- 08 2M 9:32.82 9:51.91i- 13
Martins	Eliane	BRA	26.5.86	160/49	LJ	6.69A, 6.67, 6.68w	6.72- 16, 6.73w- 15
* Márton	Anita	HUN	15.1.89	171/84	SP	19.62i, 19.12	19.87- 16
					DT	57.88	60.94- 16
Maruszewska	Klaudia	POL	28.8.97	180/72	JT	56.31	57.59- 16
^ Masai	Linet	KEN	5.12.89	170/55	HMar	68:11dh	69:33- 16
					Mar	2:23:46	-0-
Mashinistova	Yelena	RUS	29.3.94	165/52	LJ	6.61	6.67- 15
Maslova	Anastasiya	BLR	16.10.97		HT	69.48	66.38- 16
Maslova	Darya	KGZ	6.5.95	170/50	5000	15:28.64	15:00.42- 17
					10000	32:07.23	31:36.90- 16
Mason	Symone	USA-J	31.8.99	161/55	400	51.53	52.42- 17
Matanga	Failuna Abdi	TAN	28.10.92	148/37	10000	32:22.09	31:47.37- 17
					HMar	69:36	73:34- 15
Matheus	Melany	CUB-Y	19.1.01	172/73	DT	56.79	52.22- 17
Mathias	Charline	LUX	23.5.92	173/61	800	2:00.35	2:01.30- 15
Matsuda	Anna	JPN	18.4.94	159/43	10000	32:27.33	32:07.11- 17
Matsuda	Mizuki	JPN	31.5.95	159/43	10000	31:52.42	32:07.11- 17
					Mar	2:22:23	-0-
Mattuzzi	Isabel	ITA	23.4.95	163/47	3kSt	9:34.02	9:57.68- 17

Name		Nat	Born	Ht/Wt	Event	2018 Mark			Pre-2018 Best
Maudens	Hanne	BEL	12.3.97	178/64	LJ	6.51			6.48- 16
					Hep	6252			6113- 17
Mautino	Paola	PER	1.6.90	175/63	LJ	6.66A, 6.38, 6.49w			6.48, 6.55w- 15
* Mavrodieva	Radoslava	BUL	13.3.87	178/86	SP	18.95			18.67- 13
* Mazuronak	Olga	BLR	14.4.89	176/56	Mar	2:25:25			2:23:54- 16
Mbumi Nkouindjin	Joëlle	CMR	25.5.86	170/63	LJ	6.65A			6.42- 16
McAslan	Kirsten	GBR	1.0.03	100/54	400i	56.48			57.31- 17
* McCartney	Eliza	NZL	11.12.96	179/66	PV	4.94			4.82- 17
* McColgan	Eilish	GBR	25.11.90	176/59	1500	4:01.98			4:01.60- 17
1M	4:25.07	-0		3000	8:38.49		8:31.00- 17	5000	14:52.83	14:48.49- 17
McCoy	Maia	USA	9.12.96	172/57	100	11.25			11.63- 14
					200	23.11, 22.43w			23.58- 17
McDermott	Nicola	AUS	28.12.96	186/63	HJ	1.91			1.90-17
McDonald	Sarah	GBR	2.8.93	158/50	800	2:00.88			2:01.10- 16
1500	4:03.17			4:05.48- 17	1M	4:20.85		4:32.06i- 17, 4:46.38- 13
McGee	Cory	USA	29.5.92	168/52	800	2:01.61			2:01.94- 16
1500	4:06.26			4:06.67- 13	1M	4:27.78		4:27.67i- 17, 4:28.55- 16
McGhee	Brianna	USA	8.11.93	164/55	100h	12.91			12.88- 16
McGlaston	Mecca	USA	23.7.98	175/59	100h	12.98			13.18- 15
McGowan	Brittany	AUS	24.4.91	163/49	800	2:00.24			2:01.26- 14
^ McGrone	Candyce	USA	24.3.89	168/59	100	11.32, 11.21w			11.00- 15, 10.83w- 17
McIntosh	Rachael	CAN	17.1.91	174/62	Hep	5862			5789- 14
McKenzie	Ranae	JAM	28.10.96	167/57	400h	56.06			57.80- 16
McKinna	Sophie	GBR	31.8.94	172/95	SP	17.76			17.14- 16
McKnight	Sparkle	TTO	21.12.91	165/55	400h	55.15			55.41A- 15, 55.46- 17
* McLaughlin	Sydney	USA-J	7.8.99	174/61	100	11.07w			
200	22.39	23.53- 16, 22.96w- 17		400	50.07	51.61i- 17, 51.87- 16		400h	52.75	53.82- 17
McMinn	Tiara	USA-J	23.2.99	170/56	100h	13.12, 13.09w			13.67- 17
* McNeal	Brianna	USA	18.8.91	164/55	200	22.94			23.04, 23.02w- 13
					100h	12.38			12.26- 13
* McPherson	Inika	USA	23.9.86	163/55	HJ	1.92			1.96, 2.00dq- 14
McPherson	Stephenie Ann	JAM	25.11.88	168/55	400	50.31			49.92- 13
McQueen	Darrielle	USA	29.5.96	170/57	LJ	6.65			6.55- 17
McReynolds	Tiffani	USA	4.12.91	153/50	100h	13.02, 12.81w			12.77- 14, 12.70w- 15
McTaggart	Olivia	NZL-J	9.1.00	172/62	PV	4.45			4.40- 17
Meadows	Tawanna	USA	4.8.86	168/55	100	11.27, 11.19w			11.11- 14, 10.72w- 17
Medeiros	Keely	BRA	30.4.87	180/100	SP	17.49			17.58- 14
Medina	Ayamey	CUB	21.2.98	164/73	HT	66.57			68.98- 16
Meijer	Michaela	SWE	30.7.93	172/63	PV	4.45i			4.71- 17
Mekasha	Waganesh	ETH	16.1.92	159/45	Mar	2:25:57			
Mekonnen	Zinash	ETH	11.9.96		HMar	68:30			
					Mar	2:25:55			
Mekuria	Aberu	ETH	24.12.83		Mar	2:24:35			2:25:30- 15
Melat	Yisak	ETH	.92		HMar	68:41			70:27- 12
Melenteva	Darya	RUS	7.4.98		20kW	1:34:00			
* Melese	Yebrgual	ETH	18.4.90	164/55	HMar	67:18			68:21- 15
					Mar	2:19:36			2:22:51- 17
^ Melis Mey	Karin	TUR	31.5.84	173/57	LJ	6.65A, 6.44			6.93- 07
Melville	Miranda	USA	20.3.89	160/54	20kW	1:33:58			1:31:42- 16
Menuet	Émilie	FRA	27.11.91	155/44	20kW	1:32:49			1:31:38- 16
* Mergia	Aselefech	ETH	23.1.85	168/51	HMar	69:45			67:21- 11
Meringor	Delvin	KEN	1.8.92		HMar	69:01			
Merlo	Martina	ITA	19.2.93	165/45	3kSt	9:41.05			10:04.33- 17
Meshesha	Hirut	ETH Y	20.1.01	166/52	800	2:01.2A			2:0..32A- 17
Mezuliáníková	Diana	CZE	10.4.92	169/54	800	2:01.36			2:02.69- 14
					1500	4:06.12			4:11.53i- 17, 4:11.84- 14
Michiguchi	Ai	JPN	3.6.88	159/53	20kW	1:33:42			1:31:51- 16
Michta Coffey	Maria	USA	23.6.86	165/51	20kW	1:32:09			1:30:49- 14
Middleton	Kinsey	CAN	22.11.92		10000	32:33.38			32:34.97- 17
* Mihambo	Malaika	GER	3.2.94	170/55	LJ	6.99			6.95- 16
Miklos	Andrea	ROU-J	17.4.99	165/51	400	52.07			52.31- 17
Miller	Polina	RUS-J	9.6.00	167/52	400	51.65			
Miller	Rachel	GBR	29.1.90	166/55	100	11.23mx			11.45- 17
* Miller-Uibo	Shaunae	BAH	15.4.94	185/69	200	22.06			21.88, 21.76St- 17
					400	48.97			49.44- 16
* Minenko	Hanna	ISR	25.9.89	178/61	TJ	14.41, 14.57w			14.78- 15
Minor	Arria	USA-Y	9.2.01	168/52	200	22.89A			23.51A, 23.87- 17
Minor	Arria	USA-Y	9.2.01	168/52	400	51.92A, 52.25			52.05- 17
Minsewo	Aberash	ETH-Y	22.2.01	160/45	3000	8:51.93			9:24.62A- 17
					5000	15:07.90			
* Mironchik-Ivanova	Anastasiya	BLR	13.4.89	171/54	LJ	6.77			7.08, 7.22w- 12

Name		Nat	Born	Ht/Wt	Event	2018 Mark	Pre-2018 Best
Misher	Rachel	USA	4.2.97	163/54	100	11.21	
200	23.10, 22.93w		23.17, 22.94w- 16		400	51.60	52..07- 17
Mismas	Marusa	SLO	24.10.94	161/50	3kSt	9:28.61	9:35.10- 15
* Mitchell	Kathryn	AUS	10.7.82	168/72	JT	68.92	66.12- 17
Mitchell	Victoria	AUS	25.4.82	164/48	3kSt	9:45.37	9:30.84- 06
Mitton	Sarah	CAN	20.6.96	170/82	SP	18.52	16.53i, 16.32- 17
Miyashita	Risa	JPN	26.4.84	171/71	JT	60.71	60.86- 16
* Moguenara	Sosthene	GER	17.10.89	182/68	LJ	6.85i, 6.84	7.16- 16
Moindrot	Alice	FRA-J	20.8.99	172/65	PV	4.42	4.10- 17
Mokaya	Martha	KEN-J	1.3.00	150/42	3000	8:51.11	8:54.68- 17
					5000	15:15.89	15:13.81- 17
Mokonin	Desi Jisa	BRN	12.7.97	163/48	HMar	68:10	69:07- 17
^ Möldner-Schmidt	Antje	GER	13.6.84	174/55	3kSt	9:39.25	9:18.54- 09
Molinarolo	Elisa	ITA	29.1.94	171/60	PV	4.35i	4.25- 17
* Moline	Georganne	USA	6.3.90	178/59	400	51.39i	51.93- 17
					400h	53.90	53.14- 17
^ Molitor	Katharina	GER	8.11.83	182/76	JT	61.91	67.69- 15
Moll	Carolina	USA	28.4.94	165/52	PV	4.40	4.50- 15
Møller	Anna Emilie	DEN	28.7.97	166/52	3000	8:52.73	8:47.83- 16
					3kSt	9:31.66	9:32.68 16
Montag	Jemima	AUS	15.2.98	159/50	20kW	1:31:26	1:34:18- 17
Montcalm	Noelle	CAN	3.4.88	166/53	400h	56.23	55.81- 14
Monteiro	Inês	POR	18.5.80	158/50	10000	32:20.72	31:13.58- 10
* Montsho	Amantle	BOT	4.7.83	173/57	400	50.15	49.33- 13
Mooney	Claire	IRL	21.6.92	169/53	800	2:01.61	2:04.23- 17
Moore	Jasmine	USA-Y	1.5.01		TJ	13.43, 13.83w	13.29- 17
Moore	Sarah	USA	23.5.97	160/54	400	52.09	53.70- 17
* de Morais	Andressa	BRA	21.12.90	178/100	DT	65.10	64.68- 17
Morales	Erika	MEX	10.12.86		50kW	4:20:36	5:02:33- 17
Moravcsik	Angéla	HUN	13.5.96		JT	55.79	54.47- 15
^ Moreira	Sara	POR	17.10.85	168/51	10000	32:10.50	31:12.93- 15
Moreno	Arantxa	ESP	16.1.95	173/67	JT	59.69	56.89- 17
Mori	Yuka	JPN	21.7.92	164/63	JT	59.18	59.22- 12
Morita	Kaori	JPN	19.9.95	160/44	10000	31:57.95	31:59.94- 11
Morland	Elizabeth	IRL	3.3.98		Hep	5815	5801- 17
Morley	Makena	USA	21.11.96	160/48	10000	32:28.58	33:29.22- 17
^ Morosanu	Angela	ROU	26.7.86	178/57	LJ	6.55	6.66- 17
* Morris	Sandi	USA	8.7.92	172/65	PV	4.95i, 4.95	5.00- 16
Morrison	Ebony	USA	28.12.94	165/57	100h	12.86	12.76- 16
Moser	Angelica	SUI	9.10.97	168/63	PV	4.45	4.61- 17
Mucci	Celeste	AUS-J	11.8.99	174/62	Hep	5915	5870- 17
Mueni	Elizabeth	KEN	28.12.91		3kSt	9:36.6A	9:33.49- 09
* Muhammad	Dalilah	USA	7.2.90	170/62	400h	53.65	52.64- 17
* Muir	Laura	GBR	9.5.93	162/54	800	1:59.09	1:58.69- 17
1000	2:33.92		2:31.93i- 17, 2:40.5e- 16		1500	3:58.18	3:55.22- 16
1M	4:19.28		4:18.03- 17		3000	8:37.21 mx	8:26.41i, 8:30.64- 17
Mukari	Agnes	KEN-Y	15.12.02		3000	8:54.71	
Mulhall	Kimberley	AUS	9.1.91	176/78	DT	55.88	58.53- 16
Müller	Laura	GER	11.12.95	172/57	200	22.87	22.65- 17
* Müller	Nadine	GER	21.11.85	193/90	DT	63.00	68.89- 12
Mullina	Olga	RUS	1.8.92	166/60	PV	4.65	4.67- 17
Mulugeta	Mahelet	ETH	20.3.95	164/52	800	1:59.84	2:00.77- 17
Munehisa	Yuki	JPN	15.12.97		10000	32:34.37	31:58.46- 17
Murashova	Yelena	RUS	5.10.87	163/52	1500	4:08.78	4:07.23- 17
Murillo	María Fernanda	COL-J	21.1.99	173/61	HJ	1.90A	1.85- 16
Murillo	María Lucelly	COL	5.5.91	170/62	JT	59.72A	57.16A- 10
Murmu	Jauna	IND	16.8.90	162/52	400h	57.02	56.58- 10
Murphy	Grayson	USA	28.6.95	161/50	3kSt	9:48.57	9:53.04- 17
Murphy	Nicolle	USA	19.10.94	165/66	JT	56.17	56.35- 16
Murray	Lindsey	USA	22.7.96		PV	4.35	4.34- 16
Murto	Wilma	FIN	11.6.98	182/68	PV	4.60	4.71i, 4.52- 16
Musembi Takamatsu	Tomomi	JPN-J	23.2.00	160/42	5000	15:26.76	
Mutai	Beatrice	KEN	19.4.87	152/38	10000	31:49.81	32:14.0A- 15
Muthoni	Naomi	KEN			5000	15:20.14	
Muthoni	Teresa	KEN			5000	15:13.89	
Muze	Lina	LAT	4.12.92	181/75	JT	63.18	62.09- 16
Mwangi	Ann	KEN	8.12.88	172/51	3000	8:50.58	8:43.54- 09
					5000	15:20.24	15:05.34- 09
Myers	Tamara	BAH	27.7.93	173/55	TJ	13.75	14.03- 17
Mykolenko	Mariya	UKR	4.4.94	170/57	400h	56.25	58.22- 15

Name		Nat	Born	Ht/Wt	Event	2018 Mark		Pre-2018 Best
Myronchuk	Valentyna	UKR	10.8.94	165/53	20kW	1:32:38		1:33:59- 17
					50kW	4:18:50		
Nabeshima	Rina	JPN	16.12.93	160/45	3000	8:48.21		9:03.17- 17
5000	15:10.91		15:11.83- 17		10000	31:28.81		32:19.18- 17
Nacheva	Aleksandra	BUL-Y	20.8.01	170/57	TJ	14.18		13.64- 17
* Nageotte	Katie	USA	30.6.91	168/59	PV	4.01iA, 4.00		4.73- 17
Nakaayi	Halimah	UGA	16.10.94	160/55	800	1:58.39		1:59.78- 16
					1000	2:34.88		
Nakata	Hirono	JPN	2.10.97		JT	56.14		52.74- 17
Nalyanya	Eglay	KEN	28.5.96	166/50	800	2:00.28		2:00.98A- 16
Nanyondo	Winnie	UGA	23.8.93	164/48	800	1:59.41		1:58.63- 14
1000	2:36.13		1500	4:06.05		4:07.93- 17	1M	4:28.16
* Naser	Salwa Eid	BRN	23.5.98	167/50	400	49.08		49.88- 17
Nasri	Chahineze	TUN	3.6.96	168/51	20kW	1:32:20		1:34.35- 16
Nathaniel Onome Glory		NGR	23.1.96	169/60	400	52.08		52.2=- 17
					400h	55.01		55.30- 17
* Nawowuna	Alice Aprot	KEN	2.1.94	174/55	5000	15:11.00		14:39.56- 16
					10000	31:36.12		29:53.51- 16
* Ndama	Solène	FRA	23.9.98	176/66	100h	12.77		13.18- 17
					Hep	5932		5657- 17
* Ndiwa	Stacy	KEN	6.12.92	156/44	10000	31:31.17		34:37.2A- 17
					HMar	67:16		69:09- 17
Neale	Amy-Eloise	GBR	5.8.95	173/57	5000	15:24.16		15:39.30- 17
Neita	Daryll	GBR	29.8.96	172/61	100	11.19		11.14- 17
* Nel	Wenda	RSA	30.7.88	169/52	400h	54.61		54.37- 15
Nelson	Ashleigh	GBR	20.2.91	175/69	200	22.94		22.96- 16
Nelson	Katara	USA	7.3.95	165/57	400	51.98		55.10- 15
* Nelvis	Sharika	USA	10.5.90	178/64	100h	12.51		12.34- 15
Neola	Orphée	FRA	1.2.91	162/46	100	11.15		11.22- 17
Nesteriuc	Anamaria	ROU	29.11.92	160/50	100h	13.13		13.19- 17
* Nettey	Christabel	CAN	2.6.91	182/59	LJ	6.92		6.99- 15
Newell	Anicka	CAN	5.8.93	175/64	PV	4.60iA, 4.51		4.65- 17
* Newman	Alysha	CAN	29.6.94	172/67	PV	4.75		4.75- 17
Neziri	Nooralotta	FIN	9.11.92	174/60	100h	12.86		12.81- 16
Ngige	Monicah	KEN	7.11.93		HMar	68:38		
Ngii	Emily	KEN	13.8.86	152/48	20kW	1:33:56A		1:37:54A- 13
* Ngugi	Mary Wacera	KEN	17.12.88	155/	HMar	66:50		66:29- 16
Nguyen Thi Oanh II		VIE	15.8.95	165/50	3kSt	9:43.83		
Ni Yuanyuan		CHN	6.4.95		20kW	1:32:08		1:29:14- 17
Nidbaykina	Darya	RUS	26.12.94	168/57	TJ	14.20		14.21- 17
Nielsen	Janne	DEN	8.6.93		TJ	13.67, 13.76w		13.34, 13.48w- 17
Nielsen	Lara	AUS	19.12.92	168/80	HT	65.72		66.90- 17
Nielsen	Laviai	GBR	13.3.96	168/54	400	51.21		52.25- 15
Nielsen	Lina	GBR	13.3.96	168/54	400h	57.19		57.87- 17
* Niiya	Hitomi	JPN	26.2.88	164/45	5000	15:24.01		15:10.20- 12
					10000	31:32.50		30:59.19- 12
Nikiforova	Margarita	RUS	19.8.98		20kW	1:31:57		
Nikisenko	Marina	MDA	28.6.86	185/85	HT	69.80		72.53- 15
Nikkanen	Minna	FIN	9.4.88	169/53	PV	4.45i, 4.35		4.61i- 16, 4.60- 15
Nilles	Maddy	USA	3.3.97	184/90	HT	66.49		61.69- 17
Nilsson	Linn	SWE	15.10.90	169/55	1500	4:10.11, 4:07.71i		4:08.47- 17
3000	8:57.89		9:01.50- 17		5000	15:18.14		15:48.46- 16
Nilsson	Maja	SWE-J	8.12.99	183/65	HJ	1.09i, 1.87		1.90- 17
Nishihara	Kasumi	JPN	1.3.89	162/47	10000	32:19.59		31:53.69- 14
Nisimura	Daniela	BRA	26.3.94	174/81	JT	55.95		59.03- 17
* Niyonsaba	Francine	BDI	5.5.93	161/56	800	1:55.86		1:55.47- 17
Njeru	Pauline	KEN	12.12.88		HMar	68:20		70:38- 17
^ Njoroge	Mercy	KEN	10.6.86	158/46	3kSt	9:50.4A		9:16.94- 11
Njue Wanjiru	Grace	KEN	10.1.79	164/45	20kW	1:30:40A		1:30:43- 16
Nlemchi	Tochi	USA	26.3.95	175/91	SP	17.05		16.77- 16
Noble	Jessica	JAM	5.2.97	173/64	LJ	6.64		6.46- 17
Noennig	Samantha	USA	28.7.98	180/85	SP	17.31		16.78- 17
Nogami	Keiko	JPN	6.12.85	160/46	5000	15:24.70		15:28.47- 08
10000	32:07.70		32:14.58- 15		Mar	2:26:33		2:28:19- 15
Nokelainen	Heidi	FIN	30.9.90	170/68	JT	57.55		62.13- 16
Novikova	Marina	RUS	1.3.89		20kW	1:31:15		1:25:03=- 15
Novozhylova	Iryna	UKR	7.1.86	175/90	HT	69.35		74.10- 12
Ntshingila	Patience	RSA	26.8.89	175/65	TJ	13.78A		13.90A- 16, 13.89- 12
* Nugent	Leah	JAM	23.11.92	168/62	400h	54.67		54.45- 16
Nugter	Corinne	NED	28.3.92	182/80	DT	60.02		57.97- 17
Nwanaga	Kelechi	NGR	24.12.97	170/59	JT	56.96		58.15- 17

Name		Nat	Born	Ht/Wt	Event	2018 Mark		Pre-2018 Best
Nyabeu Djapa	Annaelle	FRA	15.9.92	174/63	Hep	5788		5817- 14
Nygård	Sanna	FIN	22.3.88	176/60	TJ	13.81		13.76- 17
Nyirarukundo	Salomé	RWA	20.12.97	157/42	10000	32:13.74		31:45.82- 18
					HMar	68:48		71:30- 17
Nzisa	Winfredah	KEN	30.5.97	158/48	1500	4:07.53		4:04.46- 17
O'Connell	Jessica	CAN	10.2.89	158/48	3000	8:46.86		8:51.37- 15
					5000	15:18.36		15:06.44- 15
Obeng-Akrofi	Akua	GHA	26.6.96	168/70	400	51.82		52.47- 17
* Obiri	Hellen	KEN	13.12.89	160/50	1500	3:58.88+		3:57.05- 14
1M	4:16.15 4:16.56- 17				3000	8:20.88- 14	5000 14:21.75	14:18.37- 17
Obisesan	Queen	NGR	15.9.82	172/90	HT	66.86		63.79- 13
Oboya	Bendere	AUS-J	17.4.00	165/44	400	51.94		52.69- 17
Odeyemi	Aminat	BRN	27.6.97	168/60	400h	55.54		56.08- 17
Odineva	Tatyana	RUS	25.5.83	181/64	HJ	1.90		1.84- 16
Odiong	Ofonime	BRN	13.3.97	168/60	200	22.62		22.74- 16
Ogbeta	Naomi	GBR	18.4.98	180/64	TJ	14.15		13.64, 13.68w- 17
Oginni	Banke	USA	8.5.96		SP	17.11		15.57- 17
* Ogrodníková	Nikola	CZE	18.8.90	175/73	JT	65.61A		62.24- 17
Ogunrinde	Temi	NGR	29.2.96	179/77	HT	67.45		64.01- 17
Ojaloo	Kati	EST	31.1.90	165.72	HT	66.75		67.26- 15
Okada	Kumiko	JPN	17.10.91	158/44	20kW	1:31:29		1:29:40- 16
* Okagbare	Blessing	NGR	9.10.88	180/68	100	10.90, 10.72w		10.79, 10.75w- 13
					200	22.04		22.23- 14
Okamoto	Harumi	JPN	7.2.98	160/44	5000	15:20.56		15:33.08- 16
					10000	31:28.20		32:17.29- 17
* Okolo	Courtney	USA	15.3.94	168/54	400	50.65, 50.55i		49.71- 16
Okoro	Chinwe	NGR	20.6.89	184/84	DT	57.37		61.58- 16
Okparaebo	Ezinne	NOR	3.3.88	164/56	100	11.24		11.10- 12, 11.0- 15
* Okuneva	Oksana	UKR	14.3.90	175/62	HJ	1.94		1.98- 14
Oladipo	Divine	GBR	5.10.98	175/86	SP	17.37		16.64- 17
Olatoye	Sade	USA	25.1.97		SP	17.34i, 16.73		16.71i, 16.69- 17
Olin	Alyssa	USA	14.7.96	168/63	JT	58.36		53.18- 17
Oliver	Imani	USA	7.3.93	165/59	TJ	13.84, 14.22w		14.02- 16
Oliver	Javianne	USA	26.12.94	155/57	100	11.10, 11.04w		11.16- 17
					200	22.98w		23.47, 22.99w- 17
Olivieri	Linda	ITA	14.7.98	173/58	400h	57.22		57.00- 17
* Oljira	Belaynesh	ETH	26.6.90	165/49	HMar	68:36		67:27- 11
					Mar	2:21:53		2:25:01- 13
Ombissa-Dzangue	Orlann	FRA	26.5.91	168/51	100	11.06		11.30- 17
Omori	Natsuki	JPN	22.6.94	162/46	10000	32:24.27		
Onnen	Imke	GER	17.8.94	190/66	HJ	1.93		1.89- 15
Onstad	Oda Utsi	NOR	12.5.90		TJ	13.67		13.35- 14
Onuora	Anyika	GBR	28.10.84	175/69	400	51.13		50.87- 15
Onyekwere	Chioma	NGR	28.6.94	175/95	DT	59.15i, 58.09		54.43- 16
Oosterwegel	Emma	NED	29.6.98		Hep	5839		5525- 16
Orbán	Éva	HUN	29.11.84	173/75	HT	68.14		73.44- 13
Orcel	Claire	BEL	2.12.97	191/68	HJ	1.91		1.88- 17
Ordóñez	Johana	ECU	12.12.87	166/52	50kW	4:14:28		
Orel	Anna Maria	EST	11.12.96	171/70	HT	69.68		68.71- 16
Oren	Emily	USA	20.9.93	175/60	3kSt	9:44.75		9:40.65- 17
Orji	Keturah	USA	5.3.96	166/61	LJ	6.81		6.72i, 6.71w- 17, 6.63- 15
					TJ	14.62		14.71- 16
Orjuela	Annabel	COL	24.7.88	150/43	20kW	1:33:45		1:32:40- 17
Orozco	María Fernanda	MEX	25.1.98	177/105	SP	18.04		17.15- 17
Ortega	Patricia	ESP	18.4.94	170/56	Hep	5782		5451- 15
Ortiz	Coralys	PUR	16.4.85	178/61	JT	59.55		60.37- 16
Ortiz	Mirna	GUA	28.2.87	158/44	20kW	1:34:13		1:28:32- 13
Ortuño	Valeria	MEX	27.5.98		20kW	1:32:29		1:31:48- 17
Osakue	Daisy	ITA	16.1.96	181/84	DT	59.72		58.06- 17
Osika	Shannon	USA	15.6.93	161/48	1500	4:06.80		4:06.17- 17
					1M	4:25.47	4:28.45- 16	
* Oskan-Clarke	Shelayna	GBR	20.1.90	171/60	800	2:00.39, 1:59.81i		1:58.86- 15
Östervall	Lovisa	SWE	9.3.97	173/60	HJ	1.86		1.80- 16
					Hep	5754		5723- 16
Ostrander	Allie	USA	24.12.96	158/45	3000	8:54.35i		8:54.27i- 16
5000	15:27.46, 15:16.38i		15:21.85i, 15:24.74- 16		3kSt	9:38.57		9:41.31- 17
Otchere	Jacqueline	GER	5.5.96	167/56	PV	4.60		4.30- 17
Oudenaarden	Niki	CAN	14.1.94	178/69	Hep	5878		6000- 17
Oudiou	Emma	FRA	2.1.95	172/54	3kSt	9:36.15		9:44.74- 15
Ovsyannikova	Aleksandra	RUS	16.6.93		50kW	4:40:00		
Owens	Bridgette	USA	14.3.92	163/52	100h	12.79		12.71- 12, 12.62w- 14

Name		Nat	Born	Ht/Wt	Event	2018 Mark	Pre-2018 Best
Owers	Torie	NZL	6.3.94	170/80	SP	17.01	17.50- 16
Padovan	Paola	ITA	4.12.95	181/68	JT	57.41	57.21- 17
Paesler	Carolin	GER	16.12.90	167/72	HT	65.92	70.76- 14
Pagano	Sarah	USA	23.7.91	160/47	3000	8:56.53	8:58.91- 17
5000	15:11.27				15:18.57- 17	10000	31:56.43	32:16.03- 16
* Palameika	Madara	LAT	18.6.87	184/76	JT	62.98	66.18- 16
Palframan	Justine	RSA	4.11.93	165/64	200	22.83A	22.84- 17
					400	51.31A	51.27- 15
Palkina	Sofiya	RUS	9.6.98	174/70	HT	69.86	69.32- 17
* Palmisano	Antonella	ITA	6.8.91	166/49	20kW	1:27:30	1:26:36- 17
* Palsyte	Airine	LTU	13.7.92	186/62	HJ	1.96	2.02i- 17, 1.98- 14
Pan Youqi		CHN-J	10.7.00		TJ	13.66	13.11A, 13.07- 17
Panagi	Nektaria	CYP	20.3.90	165/52	LJ	6.72, 6.77w	6.66- 17
Panova	Yelena	RUS	2.3.87	185/95	DT	63.92	63221- 15
* Panturoiu	Elena	ROU	24.2.95	170/57	TJ	14.47	14.43- 17
* Papahrístou	Paraskeví	GRE	17.4.89	170/53	LJ	6.60	6.60- 12
					TJ	14.60, 14.74w	14.73- 16, 14.77w- 12
Paquette	Lauren	USA	27.6.86	163/45	3000	8:48.65, 8:47.81i	8:54.71i, 8:56.99- 17
					5000	15:15.23	15:14.45- 16
Parada	Lidia	ESP	11.6.93	174/70	JT	61.25	59.03- 15
Parker	Kiara	USA	28.10.96	167/57	100	11.13	11.39- 16, 11.19w- 17
Parnova	Liz	AUS	9.5.94	175/57	PV	4.40	4.51- 17
Pasechnik	Alena	BLR	17.4.95		SP	17.94	17.18- 17
Pashley	Ellie	AUS	10.12.88	163/50	10000	32:17.81	34:39.52- 16
					HMar	69:20	
Pastorino	Inès	FRA	20.10.92	158/47	50kW	4:43:46	-0-
Patterson	Eleanor	AUS	22.5.96	182/66	HJ	1.88	1.96- 13
Patterson	Liz	USA	9.6.88	183/65	HJ	1.91Ai, 1.91	1.94- 17
Paulino	Marileidy	DOM	25.10.96	172/60	200	22.87	23.77- 17
Pavlova	Mariya	RUS	21.5.96	174/64	Hep	5925	5905- 17
Payne	Kymber	USA	4.6.96	168/54	400h	55.54	55.50- 17
Payton	Malaina	USA	16.10.91	163/52	LJ	6.69	6.61- 17
* Pearson	Sally	AUS	19.9.86	166/60	100h	12.68, 12.67w	12.28- 11
Pechnikova	Svetlana	RUS	6.9.94		JT	59.32	56.88- 17
Pedersen	Isabelle	NOR	27.1.92	168/54	100h	12.72	12.75- 17
Pedroso	Yadisleidy	ITA	28.1.87	168/51	400h	54.98	54.54- 13
Peeters	Tori	NZL	17.5.94	174/67	JT	57.00	56.84- 17
* Peinado	Rosbeilys	VEN	26.11.97	168/62	PV	4.70A	4.65- 17
Pejchalová	Lada	CZE	15.11.98	181/62	HJ	1.90	1.90- 16
* Peleteiro	Ana	ESP	2.12.95	171/52	TJ	14.55	14.23- 17
Pen	Marta	POR	31.7.93	153/46	800	2:00.09	2:03.42- 14
1500	4:03.99				4:05.71- 17	1M	4:22.45	4:38.21i- 16
Pepelnak	Eva	SLO-J	4.10.00		TJ	13.68	13.06- 17
Pereira	Solange Andreia	ESP	12.12.89	168/49	1500	4:08.52	4:06.39- 17
* Pérez	María	ESP	29.4.96	156/48	20kW	1:26:36	1:29:37- 17
Pérez	Maria Isabel	ESP	1.3.93	160/51	100	11.33, 11.17w	11.53- 17
Pérez	María Josë	ESP	12.6.92	159/48	3kSt	9:43.48	9:40.51- 17
Pérez	Marta	ESP	19.4.93	169/53	800	2:01.82	2:03.31- 17
1500	4:04.88				4:05.82- 17	1M	4:28.25	
Pérez	Paola	ECU	21.12.89	148/55	20kW	1:30:37	1:29:06- 17
					50kW	4:12:56	
* Pérez	Yaimé	CUB	29.5.91	174/79	DT	67.82	69.19- 17
* Perkovic	Sandra	CRO	21.6.90	183/80	DT	71.38	71.41- 17
Perry	Dara	USA	29.8.97	167/57	100h	13.10	13.53- 16
Pesirídou	Elisávet	GRE	12.2.92	174/55	100h	13.00	12.93- 16
* Petersen	Sara Slott	DEN	9.4.87	171/57	400h	55.48	53.55- 16
Petershofen	Friedelinde	GER	19.8.95	181/68	PV	4.51i, 4.35	4.55- 17
Petersson	Marinda	SWE	3.2.95	166/76	HT	67.34	70.01- 17
* Petrivskaya	Zalina	MDA	5.2.88	174/90	HT	72.70	74.21- 16
* Petrova	Gabriela	BUL	29.6.92	167/61	LJ	6.48	6.46- 15
					TJ	14.40, 14.48w	14.66, 14.85w- 15
Petrova	Lyudmila	RUS	15.12.93		PV	4.40i, 4.30	4.30i- 17, 4.10- 15
Pettersen	Kaja Mørch	NOR-Y	6.11.01		JT	56.22	50.38- 17
Petty	Angie	NZL	16.8.91	164/55	800	2:00.62	1:59.06- 15
Pham Thi Diem		VIE	24.1.90	168/52	HJ	1.87	1.91- 13
* Philip	Asha	GBR	25.10.90	163/54	100	11.21	11.10- 15
^ Pierre	Barbara	USA	28.4.87	160/57	100	11.18	10.85- 13
Pierson	Summer	USA	3.9.78	180/84	DT	60.97	61.23- 15, 61.25dh- 09
Pinedo	Ainhoa	ESP	17.2.83	171/60	50kW	4:18:56	-0-
Pingeon	Mélanie	FRA	4.11.86	180/85	DT	57.03	55.87- 14
Pinto	Narayanan V.	IND	2.5.91	168/52	LJ	6.51	6.66- 16

Name		Nat	Born	Ht/Wt	Event	2018 Mark	Pre-2018 Best
Pinto	Tatjana	GER	2.7.92	170/56	100	11.11	11.00, 10.96w- 17
					200	22.84	23.02- 15, 22.53w- 17
Pipi	Amarachi	GBR	26.11.95	166/55	400	52.07i, 62.26	52.96- 17
Pirelli	Ana Camila	PAR	30.1.89	175/70	Hep	5879	5886A, 5748- 16
Plis	Renata	POL	5.2.85	165/51	1M	4:28.36	4:25.32- 15
Plotitsyna	Hanna	UKR	1.1.87	182/68	100h	13.13	12.89, 12.8- 17
Pluim	Femke	NED	10.5.94	180/62	PV	4.45i, 4.30	4.55- 15
Pólak	Eléni-Klaoúdia	GRE	9.9.96	174/61	PV	4.46	4.35- 17
Polyakova	Natalya	RUS	9.12.90	176/75	HT	69.10	70.04- 14
* Ponomaryova	Mariya	RUS	18.6.95		20kW	1:27:11	1:26:46- 16
Porter	Brenna	USA	.94	174/60	400h	57.18	57.65A- 17
Porter	Chanice	JAM	25.5.94	170/57	LJ	6.75	6.67- 17
* Porter	Tiffany	GBR	13.11.87	172/62	100h	12.99	12.51- 14, 12.47w- 12
Pospelova	Marina	RUS	23.7.90	164/53	800	2:01.72	1:59.70- 12
Pousse	Pauline	FRA	17.9.87	184/84	DT	58.09	62.68- 16
* Povea	Liadagmis	CUB	6.2.96	165/61	TJ	14.30, 14.44w	14.56- 16
* Prandini	Jenna	USA	20.11.92	172/59	100	10.96, 10.95w	10.92- 15, 10.81w- 16
					200	22.16	22.20, 22.18w- 15
Pratt	Aimee	GBR	3.10.97		3kSt	9:50.17	9:59.86- 17
* Praught Leer	Aisha	JAM	14.12.89	173/55	1500	4:04.95i	4:05.52- 15
3000	8:41.10		8:53.43- 17		3kSt	9:14.09	9:19.29- 17
Preiner	Verena	AUT	1.2.95	177/64	Hep	6337	6232- 17
* Price	DeAnna	USA	8.6.93	172/109	HT	78.12	74.91- 17
Price	Kylie	USA	1.10.93	178/64	LJ	6.77	6.67- 14
Prinsen	Danaïd	NED	20.8.97	168/52	800	2:01.75	2:03.96- 17
* Proctor	Shara	GBR	16.9.88	174/56	LJ	6.91	7.07- 15
Prokopenko	Viktoriya	RUS	17.4.91	174/60	TJ	14.44i, 13.93	14.28- 16
Prouse	Charlotte	CAN	9.2.97	165/60	5000	15:26.01i	
					3kSt	9:45.45	9:44.62- 16
* Pryshchepa	Nataliya	UKR	11.9.94	163/49	800	1:59.58	1:58.60- 16
Przybyla	Kamila	POL	2.5.96	170/54	PV	4.35	4.40- 17
^ Ptácníková	Jirina	CZE	20.5.86	175/69	PV	4.55i	4.76- 13
Pudenz	Kristin	GER	9.2.93	180/92	DT	61.11	62.89- 17
Punia	Seema	IND	27.7.83	183/85	DT	62.26	64.84- 04
Purdon	Cassie	AUS	24.10.96	176/59	HJ	1.86	1.88- 15
Purica	Andrea	VEN	21.11.95	179/65	100	11.24	11.25, 11.18w- 17
Purrier	Elinor	USA	30.2.95	160/50	1500	4:07.79	4:12.35i, 4:14.48- 17
1M	4:26.55i		4:29.44i- 17, 4:32.05- 17		3000	8:46.43	8:55.68i- 17
Purvis	Ashton	USA	12.7.92	173/60	200	22.82	22.70i- 13, 22.86- 12
* Qieyang Shenjie		CHN	11.11.90	160/50	20kW	1:26:28	1:25:16- 12
Qiji Zhuoma		CHN	27.5.98		20kW	1:31:17	
Quach Thi Lan		VIE	18.10.95	173/54	400h	55.30	56.67- 16
Quaresma	Lecabela	POR	26.12.89	172/67	TJ	13.90, 14.19w	13.31- 11
					Hep	5950	6174- 17
Quénot	Fanny	FRA	2.10.90	164/53	100h	13.07	13.57- 17
* Quigley	Colleen	USA	20.11.92	173/59	1000	2:36.53	
1500	4:03.02		4:03.93- 17		3kSt	9:10.27	9:15.97- 17
Radko	Kseniya	UKR	18.8.94	161/50	50kW	4:38:23	4:34:49- 17
* Radzivil	Svetlana	UZB	17.1.87	184/61	HJ	1.96	1.97- 12
Raghavan	Anu	IND	20.4.93	166/52	400h	56.77	57.21- 17
Rakocevic	Kristina	MNE	13.6.98	189/79	DT	56.29	58.30- 16
Ramos	Carmen	ESP	18.6.98	167/60	Hep	5905A	5550- 17
Ramsey	Jessica	USA	26.7.91	165/85	SP	19.23	18.42- 15
					HT	70.41	69.47- 15
Rangel	Ivonne	MEX	24.8.93	158/52	TJ	14.02A, 13.67,13.80w	13.47A-13, 13.48Aw- 15
Rani	Annu	IND	29.8.92	165/63	JT	58.17	61.86- 17
Rao Fan		CHN	1.1.96	170/59	TJ	13.85i, 13.43	13.93i- 17, 13.56- 15
Ratcliffe	Julia	NZL	14.7.93	171/66	HT	69.94	70.75- 16
* Ratej	Martina	SLO	2.11.81	178/69	JT	66.10	67.16- 10
Rathnayake	U.K.Nilani	SRI	8.8.90	160/59	3kSt	9:46.76	10:03.94- 17
Rauma	Janica	FIN	24.6.86	160/48	3kSt	9:41.70	
Ray	Chantel	USA	14.1.96		100h	13.17, 13.11w	13.32, 13.09w- 17
Reaser	Allison	USA	9.9.92	171/61	Hep	6144	5990- 16
* Rebrik	Vera	RUS	25.2.89	176/65	JT	60.24	67.30- 16
Reddingius	Kiara	AUS	2.1.92		Hep	5742	5537- 16
Reed	Jasmin	USA-J	21.2.00	167/55	100	11.23	11.58, 11.51w- 17
					200	22.90	22.84, 22.64w- 17
Reekie	Jemma	GBR	6.3.98	164/50	1000	2:36.79	
1500	4:06.11+		4:12.28- 17		1M	4:27.16	4:40.55- 17
* Reese	Brittney	USA	9.9.86	170/61	LJ	6.89i, 6.67, 7.19w	7.31- 16

Name		Nat	Born	Ht/Wt	Event	2018 Mark	Pre-2018 Best
Reh	Alina	GER	23.5.97	174/52	5000	15:25.30	15:10.01- 17
10000	32:17.17		-0-		HMar	69:31	71:23- 17
Rehberg	Maya	GER	28.4.94	170/58	3kSt	9:44.82	9:31.98- 16
dos Reis	Jéssica Carolina	BRA	17.3.93	168/59	LJ	6.56A, 6.48, 6.69w	6.69- 16
* Rengeruk	Lilian	KEN	3.5.97	161/44	3000	8:33.13	8:32.73- 17
					5000	15:01.15	14:36.80- 17
Renic	Ivana	CRO	21.8.96	177/64	50kW	4:35:39	
Renu		IND	21.12.98		TJ	13.63	13.45- 17
Renzhina	Yekaterina	RUS	18.10.94	172/57	400	51.58	51.21- 17
Retzius	Lene	NOR	4.1.96	171/60	PV	4.50	4.35- 17
Reyes	Macarena	CHI	30.3.84	167/52	LJ	6.53A, 6.40	6.60- 12
Rhodes-Johnigan	Annie	USA	13.5.95	173/64	PV	4.56i, 4.55, 4.57i et	4.61- 17
Ribeiro	Catarina	POR	31.5.90	167/50	10000	32:21.19	32:27.88- 17
Richards	Emily	USA	21.7.95	170/52	800	2:00.67	2:00.62- 17
Richardson	Sha'Carri	USA-J	25.3.00	168/52	100	11.12w	11.28- 17
Richardsson	Camilla	FIN	14.9.93	174/52	3kSt	9:42.30	9:41.73- 17
* Ricketts	Shanieka	JAM	2.2.92	182/66	TJ	14.61	14.57- 16
Riddick	Monique	USA	8.11.89	168/84	SP	18.70	18.89- 17
Riecke	Lea-Jasmin	GER-J	25.4.00	182/65	LJ	6.51	6.23- 16
Ritter	Julia	GER	13.5.98	180/95	SP	17.00	17.24- 17
					DT	58.19	55.43- 17
Rivas	Ányela	COL	13.8.89	180/82	SP	17.08	17.53- 12
Roberson	Savannah	USA	15.1.96	168/55	100	11.39, 11.22w	11.62- 16
200	23.26, 22.81w	23.26, 22.81w- 17			100h	13.16, 12.96w	13.33, 13.21w- 17
Roberts	Kaelin	USA-J	6.1.99	168/55	400	51.33	52.28- 16
Robinson	Torie	USA	11.6.96	155/55	100	11.32, 11.16w	11.31- 17
Rocha	Carla Salomé	POR	25.4.90	158/48	Mar	2:25:27	2:27:08- 17
Rodean	Ana Veronica	ROU	23.6.84	168/56	20kW	1:33:39	1:34:07- 16
Rodrigues	Irina	POR	5.2.91	181/81	DT	62.37	63.96- 16
Rodríguez	Adriana	CUB-J	12.7.99	172/62	Hep	6094	6006- 10
^ Rodríguez	Rosa	VEN	2.7.86	180/85	HT	70.93A	73.64- 13
* Rodríguez	Yorgelis	CUB	25.1.95	173/66	HJ	1.88i, 1.86	1.95- 17
LJ	6.58w				6.50- 17	Hep	6742	6594- 17
Rodríguez	Zudikey	MEX	14.3.87	168/56	400h	55.11	55.78A- 14. 56.10- 10
Roe	LaChyna	USA	29.7.97		TJ	13.61	12.61- 17
Roesler	Laura	USA	19.12.91	168/54	800	2:00.45	1:59.04- 14
Rogers	Camryn	CAN-J	7.6.99	175/82	HT	65.61	63.42- 17
* Rogers	Raevyn	USA	7.9.96	171/64	400	52.06	52.30- 16
					800	1:57.69	1:57.10- 17
Rohrer	Anna	USA	27.2.97	170/50	10000	32:26.24	31:58.99- 17
* Rojas	Yulimar	VEN	21.10.95	189/75	TJ	14.63i	15.02- 16
* Roleder	Cindy	GER	21.8.89	178/68	100h	12.77	12.59- 15
Rolland	Megan	USA	30.8.88	173/57	3kSt	9:50.68	9:35.31- 16
Roman	Daniela	AUS	7.1.96		400h	56.59	58.70- 17
Romero	Génesis	VEN	6.11.95	170/77	100h	13.03	13.09- 16
Roos	Fanny	SWE	2.1.95	173/79	SP	18.68	18.21- 17
^ Rosa	Chiara	ITA	28.1.83	178/95	SP	17.30i, 17.08	19.15- 07
Rosa	Vitória Cristina	BRA	12.1.96	170/56	100	11.03	11.24- 17
					200	22.73	22.93, 22.67w- 17
Roshchupkina	Viktoriya	BLR	23.5.95		20kW	1:31:22	1:33:16- 17
Roslova	Taisya	BLR	7.2.92		HJ	1.86	1.90i- 15, 1.88- 14
Ross	Kortney	USA	26.7.92	180/64	PV	4.50	4.60Ai, 4.55- 17
Russil	Desirée	ITA	19.3.94	181/53	HJ	1.90A	1.07- 16
^ Rotaru	Alina	ROU	5.6.93	175/54	LJ	6.72	6.78- 17
Rotich	Caroline	KEN	13.5.84	161/45	HMar	69:43 dh	69:15- 17
Rotich	Joan	KEN	27.11.93		3kSt	9:50.53A	9:33.34- 14
Rotich	Naomi	KEN	.94		HMar	68:22	68:44- 17
Rubie-Renshaw	Anneliese	AUS	22.4.92	172/56	400	51.51	51.69- 15
Ruckstuhl	Géraldine	SUI	24.2.98	175/64	JT	56.31	58.31- 17
					Hep	6391	6357- 17
Rudakova	Vera	RUS	20.3.92	175/57	400h	55.24	54.48- 16
* Rüh	Anna	GER	17.6.93	184/74	DT	62.66	66.14- 15
Ruiz	Úrsula	ESP	11.8.83	170/84	SP	17.06	18.28- 17
Ruiz de Azua	Malen	ESP	17.11.95	170/55	PV	4.35	4.26- 16
Runia	Anna Sjoukje	NED	19.2.95	169/55	400h	57.04	57.03- 17
* Russell	Janieve	JAM	14.11.93	175/63	400h	53.46	53.96- 16
Rutkowska	Katarzyna	POL	14.1.94	177/60	10000	32:31.40	33:07.28- 17
* Rypakova	Olga	KAZ	30.11.84	178/53	TJ	14.26	15.25- 10
* Ryzhova	Yekaterina	RUS	29.3.94		20kW	1:29:08	1:25:22- 17
* Ryzhykova	Anna	UKR	24.11.89	177/67	400h	54.47	54.35- 12
Ryzih	Lisa	GER	27.9.88	179/60	PV	4.62i	4.75i- 17, 4.73- 16

Name		Nat	Born	Ht/Wt	Event	2018 Mark	Pre-2018 Best
Sabat	Anna	POL	9.11.93	168/53	800	2:00.32	2:03.36- 16
Sabin	Kiley	USA	28.4.96	181/100	SP	17.16i, 16.89	17.17i, 16.65- 17
Sadeiko	Grit	EST	29.7.89	172/62	Hep	6179	6280- 17
* Sado	Besu	ETH	12.1.96	165/50	1500	4:01.75	3:59.47- 16
					1M	4:25.99	4:39.27i- 17
Sado	Fatuma	ETH	11.10.91	165/48	Mar	2:26:41	2:24:16- 15
Sadullayeva	Safina	UZB	4.3.98	180/57	HJ	1.86	1.85- 17
Saeed	Alia Mohamed	UAE	18.5.91	164/53	10000	32:18.32	31:10.25- 16
					HMar	66:13	-0-
Safonova	Mariya	RUS	28.10.94		JT	58.80	57.45- 16
Safránková	Katerina	CZE	8.6.89	191/105	HT	69.01	72.47- 16
Saganiak	Justyna	POL	1.12.95	163/54	400h	56.52	58.09- 16
* Sagnia	Khaddi	SWE	20.4.94	173/63	LJ	6.92i, 6.71	6.78- 15
Sahutoglu	Tugçe	TUR	1.5.88	180/120	HT	67.61	74.17- 12
* Saina	Betsy	KEN	30.6.88	163/48	HMar	69:17	69:27- 14
					Mar	2:22:56	-0-
Sainte Luce	Camille	FRA	18.4.96	180/84	HT	69.60	67.22- 17
Saito	Marina	JPN	15.10.95	164/64	JT	60.79	62.37- 17
* Saladukha	Olha	UKR	4.6.83	175/55	TJ	14.20, 14.25w	14.99- 12, 15.06w- 11
Salman	Kıvılcım	TUR	27.3.92	167/80	HT	71.66	72.55- 12
Salming	Bianca	SWE	22.11.98	178/67	HJ	1.92	1.90- 17
					Hep	5985	5894- 17
Salmon	Shiann	JAM-J	31.3.99	173/57	400	52.05	55.29- 16
					400h	55.78	57.78- 16
* Salpeter	Lonah Chemtai	ISR	12.12.88	165/52	3000	8:42.88	9:26.44- 17
5000	15:17.81			16:12.51- 17	10000	31:33.03	32:43.89- 17
HMar	67:55			72:48- 17	Mar	2:24:17	2:40:16- 16
Salterberg	Christine	GER	9.6.94	178/59	400h	56.95	56.97- 17
Samba-Mayela	Cyrena	FRA-J	31.10.00	166/57	100h	13.00	13.22- 17
* Samuel	Jamile	NED	24.4.92	168/57	100	11.10	11.12- 14, 11.04w- 17
					200	22.37	22.72- 14
Samuel	Laura	GBR	19.2.91	165/68	TJ	13.75	14.09- 14
Samum	Deborah	KEN	.95		3kSt	9:41.1A	
Sananés	Deborah	FRA	26.10.95	171/52	400	52.08	51.75- 16
Sánchez	Aries	VEN	1.3.96	170/59	LJ	6.54,6.60w	6.24- 15
Sánchez-Escribano	Irene	ESP	25.9.92	173/57	3kSt	9:31.84	9:40.30- 17
Sánchez-Puebla	Lidia	ESP	17.7.96	169/52	20kW	1:31:21	1:30:51- 17
Santiago	Xahria	CAN-J	9.10.99	165/50	400h	56.69	56.79- 15
Santiusti	Yusneysi	ITA	24.12.84	161/48	800	2:00.95	1:58.53- 12
Santos	Mirieli	BRA-J	1.4.99	170/59	TJ	13.81	13.21- 14
* Santos	Rosângela	BRA	20.12.90	165/55	100	11.23	10.91- 17
Sarrapio	Patricia	ESP	16.11.82	168/58	TJ	14.08 14.16A- 16, 14.10- 10, 14.30w- 12	
Sato	Naruha	JPN	2.10.97	156/41	5000	15:30.74	15:43.49- 17
Sauceda	Jessamyn	MEX	22.5.89	173/60	LJ	6.48	6.74A, 6.38- 17
Saunders	Claudia	FRA	19.5.94	159/50	800	2:00.47	2:00.63- 15
* Saunders	Raven	USA	15.5.96	165/125	SP	19.74	19.76- 17
* Saunders	Sha'Keela	USA	18.12.93	168/59	LJ	6.77, 6.88w	6.90i, 6.92w- 17, 6.89- 16
Sautereau	Mallaury	FRA	1.8.96	160/55	PV	4.35	4.31- 17
^ Sawyers	Jazmin	GBR	21.5.94	167/52	LJ	6.86	6.75, 6.86w- 16
* Schäfer	Carolin	GER	5.12.91	176/66	100h	13.13	13.07- 17
					Hep	6602	6836- 17
Scheper	Jeannelle	LCA	21.11.94	175/60	HJ	1.89	1.96- 15
Scherrer	Chiara	SUI	24.1.96		3kSt	9:44.59	10:06.41- 17
* Schippers	Dafne	NED	15.6.92	179/68	100	10.99	10.81- 15
					200	22.14	21.63- 15
Schlachtenhaufen	Helen	USA	14.3.95	163/47	1500	4:06.04	4:11.15- 17
					1M	4:27.09	4:40.79i- 17
* Schlumpf	Fabienne	SUI	17.11.90	183/62	3kSt	9:22.29	9:21.65- 17
					5000	15:23.44	15:47.29- 17
Schmidt	Sarah	GER	9.7.97	182/85	SP	17.45	17.05- 17
Schneider	Rachel	USA	18.7.91	168/52	1500	4:08.04	4:06.90- 15
1M	4:27.23	4:25.62i- 17, 4:31.04- 15			2M	9:31.89	
3000	8:56.75+	8:58.84i- 16, 9:05.08- 15			5000	15:15.88	15:33.06- 17
Schol	Lisanne	NED	22.6.91	176/63	JT	57.38	58.72- 17
Schrott	Beate	AUT	15.4.88	177/68	100h	13.06	12.82- 12
Schultz	Nina	CAN	22.11.98	178/62	Hep	6133	6021- 17
Schultze	Martina	GER	12.9.90	172/62	PV	4.41i	4.50- 13
Schürmann	Robine	SUI	31.1.89	165/56	400h	55.53	56.65- 15
* Schwanitz	Christina	GER	24.12.85	180/103	SP	20.06	20.77- 15
Schwartz	Lindsay	USA	23.4.90	178/64	Hep	6050	6036- 16

Name		Nat	Born	Ht/Wt	Event	2018 Mark			Pre-2018 Best
Schweizer	Karissa	USA	4.5.96	164/50	1500	4:06.77			4:15.77- 17
1M	4:27.54i		4:35.61i- 17		3000	8:41.60i			9:06.60i- 17, 9:35.64- 15
5000	15:02.44		15:17.31i, 15:18.69- 17		10000	32:00.55			-0-
Sclabas	Delia	SUI-J	8.11.00	161/47	800	2:01.29			2:04.30- 17
Scott Efurd	Dominique	RSA	24.6.92	160/50	1500	4:07.20			4:08.04- 17
1M 4:26.63	4;28.47i, 4:30.24- 17				3000 8:41.18i, 8:54.2i	8:41.33 17		5000 15:04.14	15.20.10- 17
Scramin	Eloah Caetano	BRA	8.6.96		JT	58.50			56.91- 17
^ Seboka	Mulu	ETH	24.9.84	158/45	Mar	2:25:01			2:21:56- 15
Seccafien	Andrea	CAN	27.8.90	152/46	3000	8:53.41			9:03.92i- 17
					5000	15:15.35			15:08.59- 17
Sedivá	Irena	CZE	19.1.92	173/70	JT	60.51A			59.89- 15
Sedney	Naomi	NED	17.12.94	170/61	100	11.24			11.25, 11.01w- 17
Sedova	Yelena	RUS	1.3.90	170/55	3000	8:57.15i			9:25.73i- 14, 9:34.10- 09
					5000	15:26.64			15:28.95i- 16, 15:43.63- 13
Seidel	Molly	USA	12.7.94	165/47	10000	32:24.78			33:18.37- 15
Sekanová	Lucie	CZE	5.8.89	170/57	3kSt	9:47.14			0:41.84- 15
Sekine	Hanami	JPN	26.2.96	156/42	Mar	2:23:07			
Sekiya	Natsuki	JPN	16.5.97	166/48	10000	31:50.17			32:47.50- 17
* Semenya	Caster	RSA	7.1.91	170/64	400	49.62			50.40- 16
800	1:54.25	1:55.16- 17			1000	2:30.70		1500 3:59.92	4:01.99- 17
* de Sena	Érica	BRA	3.5.85	168/55	20kW	1:28:11			1:26:59- 17
Sène	Awa	FRA	24.7.94	169/57	100h	13.11, 13.04w			13.30- 16
Senekal	Ischke	RSA	8.1.93	175/110	SP	17.56			16.97- 17
					DT	56.69A			56.86- 16
Serksniene	Agne	LTU	18.2.88	173/60	200	22.99			23.24- 14
					400	50.99			51.62- 14
* Seyaum	Dawit	ETH	27.7.96	158/45	1500	4:02.81			3:58.09- 16
Seymour	Ka'Tia	USA	3.10.97	164/50	100	11.13			11.26A- 16, 11.33- 17
					200	22.74, 22.57w			23.26- 16, 22.89w- 17
Seymour	Katrina	BAH	7.1.93	170/61	400h	55.69			56.32- 17
Seymour	Kiah	USA	11.1.94	178/64	400h	56.23			54.67- 16
^ Seymour	Pedrya	BAH	29.5.95	168/57	100h	12.72			12.64- 16
Seyni	Amina	NIG	24.10.96	167/54	400	50.69			52.17- 17
^ Shakes-Drayton	Perri	GBR	21.12.88	170/67	400	51.97			50.50- 13
Shamotina	Alyona	UKR	27.12.95	178/88	HT	69.72			72.37- 17
Shargina	Olga	RUS	24.7.96		50kW	4:27:13			
* Sharp	Lynsey	GBR	11.7.90	175/60	800	1:59.34			1:57.69- 16
Shayunova	Alina	BLR	2.3.90		HT	66.89			70.31- 12
Shelest	Lyudmyla	UKR	4.10.74	167/56	50kW	4:37:43			4:32:25- 09
Sheoran ¶?	Nirmala	IND	15.7.95	166/52	400	51.25			51.28- 17
Shevchenko	Anzhela	RUS	29.10.87	177/58	800	2:01.60 mx			2:03.34- 11
Shi Yuxia		CHN-J	1.1.99		20kW	1:33:41			
Shida	Leni	UGA	22.5.94	170/65	400	52.12A, 52.42			52.51- 15
Shirobokova	Natalya	RUS	18.1.94	173/79	DT	57.94			60.46- 16
Shoji	Mai	JPN	9.12.93	153/41	10000	32:22.82			32:27.36- 14
* Shukh	Alina	UKR-J	12.2.99	175/60	JT	55.95			56.54- 17
					Hep	6177			6381- 17
Shulgina	Maryia	BLR	14.8.89		HJ	1.86i			1.90i- 14, 1.86- 10
Shume	Chaltu	ETH	23.12.96	162/48	800	2:00.0A dq			2:01.59- 15
Shvydkina	Tatyana	RUS	8.5.90	171/62	PV	4.45i, 4.45			4.50i, 4.45- 15
Siciarz	Klaudia	POL	15.3.98	182/62	100h	12.94, 12.74w			13.27- 17
Sidi Madane	Fadwa	MAR	20.11.94	162/50	3kSt	9:46.10			9:27.07- 15
* Sidorova	Anzhelika	RUS	28.6.91	170/62	PV	4.50i, 4.85			4.85- 16
Siefring	Jaclyn	USA	30.9.95	168/61	Hep	5872(w)			5750- 17
Sifuentes	Nicole	CAN	30.6.86	173/57	1500	4:07.32			4:03.97- 16
1M	4:27.81, 4:27.69i		4:28.51- 17		5000	15:27.82			15:19.15- 15
Sillman	Miia	FIN	3.6.95	178/66	Hep	5810			5540- 15
* Silva	Yarisley	CUB	1.6.87	169/68	PV	4.80			4.91- 15
* Simic	Ana	CRO	5.5.90	177/58	HJ	1.92i, 1.91			1.95- 15
Simmons	Cierra	USA	.95	174/57	3kSt	9:49.33			10:12.52- 17
Simms	Baileh	USA	26.4.95		LJ	6.50, 6.56w			6.33, 6.36i, 6.38w- 17
* Simpson	Jenny	USA	23.8.86	165/50	1500	3:59.37			3:57.22- 14
1M	4:17.30 4:19.98- 17			2M	9:16.78	9:18.35i- 15		3000 8:30.83	8:29.58- 14
Singh	Sudha	IND	25.6.86	163/52	3kSt	9:39.59			9:26.55- 16
Sipponen	Salla	FIN	13.3.95	178/73	DT	58.36			57.39- 17
Siragusa	Irene	ITA	23.6.93	161/49	100	11.21			11.31, 11.26w- 17
* Sisson	Emily	USA	12.10.91	165/47	3000	8:49.61			8:52.60i, 9:09.12- 15
5000	15:13.66		15:02.10i, 15:10.90- 17		10000	32:06.31			31:25.64- 17
Skarvéli	Stamatía	GRE	17.8.95	173/80	SP	17.23			17.77i, 16.76- 17
DT	56.41		54.32- 16		HT	69.10			65.26- 17
* Skoog	Sofie	SWE	7.6.90	181/65	HJ	1.93			1.94- 16

Name		Nat	Born	Ht/Wt	Event	2018 Mark	Pre-2018 Best
Skvortsova	Violetta	BLR	15.4.98	178/58	TJ	13.95	13.94, 14.21w- 17
* Skydan	Hanna	AZE	14.5.92	183/114	HT	74.02	75/29- 17
Sloboda	Daryna	UKR	19.6.95	181/68	Hep	6104	5986- 17
Small	Keely	AUS-Y	9.6.01	158/49	800	2:00.81	2:01.46- 17
Smerdova	Yana	RUS	7.2.98		20kW	1:31:57	
Smietanka	Justyna	POL	24.9.94	178/60	PV	4.50	4.45- 17
Smith	Amina	USA	10.1.92	175/59	HJ	1.86i, 1.85	1.91- 16
Smith	Bekki	AUS	25.11.86	165/46	20kW	1:31:23	1:29:49- 16
Smith	Jaci	USA	5.1.97	161/48	5000	15:28.07i	16:04.68- 17
					10000	32:28.15	33:54.99- 17
Smith	Jonielle	JAM	30.1.96	171/59	100	11.07, 11.04w	11.13, 11.08w- 17
Smith	Rebekah	USA	1.5.98	163/52	100	11.22	11.47- 17
Smolander	Elina	FIN	11.10.89	185/58	HJ	1.86	1.86- 12
Smolyanova	Yelena	UZB	16.2.86	174/85	SP	17.12	17.68- 12
Snowden	Katie	GBR	9.3.94	167/52	800	2:01.60mx, 2:01.77	2:00.92mx-17, 2:01.77- 15
1000	2:35.54				1500	4:06.55	4:05.29- 17
Soares	Núbia	BRA	26.3.96	176/52	TJ	14.69	14.56- 17
Sobaleva	Yrlena	BLR	11.5.93	180/96	HT	66.56	72.86- 15
Sokolenko	Yekaterina	RUS	13.9.92	164/50	3kSt	9:42.94	9:25.77- 15
* Sokolova	Yelena	RUS	23.7.86	170/61	LJ	6.70	7.07- 12
Solovyova	Yevgeniya	RUS	28.6.86	185/90	SP	17.68	18.71i- 12, 18.50- 16
Song Jiayuan		CHN	15.9.97	179/90	SP	17.68	17.93- 17
Sonoda	Serena	JPN	10.9.96		50kW	4:29:45	
Soumya	Baby	IND	20.4.90	175/54	20kW	1:31:29	1:41:04- 17
Southerland	Sabrina	USA	18.12.95	166/52	800	2:00.72	2:03.10i, 2:03.74- 16
Sow	Rougui	FRA	7.6.95	170/58	LJ	6.57	6.72- 17
Spagnola	Emma	USA	18.3.96	176/57	100h	13.07, 12.97w	13.21, 13.02w- 17
					400h	56.51	57.88- 17
* Spanovic	Ivana	SRB	10.5.90	176/65	LJ	6.99, 7.04w	7.24i- 17, 7.10- 16
Spaulding	Diamond	USA	29.9.96	163/57	200	22.92	22.94i- 17, 23.07- 17
* Spencer	Ashley	USA	8.6.93	168/54	400h	54.66	53.11- 17
Spencer	Kaliese	JAM	6.5.87	175/63	400h	56.99	52.79- 11
* Spencer	Levern	LCA	23.6.84	180/54	HJ	1.96	1.98- 10
Spiler	Barbara	SLO	2.1.92	184/79	HT	70.92	71.25- 12
Spinola	Vanessa	BRA	5.5.90	178/68	Hep	5939	6188- 16
Spiridonova	Natalya	RUS-Y	31.7.02		HJ	1.86	
Sprudzane	Sinta	LAT	26.2.88	185/72	JT	62.21	64.38- 13
* Sprunger	Léa	SUI	5.3.90	183/69	200	22.88i	22.38- 16
400	50.52		51.09- 17		400h	54.33	54.29- 17
St. Fort	Khalifa	TTO	13.2.98	164/52	100	11.23, 11.15w	11.06- 17
St. John	Jess	ANT	15.12.95	181/78	SP	17.32	16.27- 16
Stafford (De-Bues)	Gabriela	CAN	13.9.95	165/53	1500	4:05.83	4:03.55- 17
1M	4:27.44i		4:29.07i- 16, 4:32.8- 15		3000	8:45.67	9:13.10- 14
Stafford	Lucia	CAN	17.8.98	162/52	1500	4:08.92	4:16.45- 17
Stanciu	Daniela	ROU	15.10.87	175/57	HJ	1.90	1.94- 14
Stanková	Eliska	CZE	11.11.84	181/82	DT	58.31	60.48- 16
Starygina	Yekaterina	RUS	26.8.95	177/73	JT	60.91	58.59- 13
Steenkamp	Rikenette	RSA	16.10.92	169/55	100h	12.81, 12.70w	12.99, 12.92w- 17
* Stefanídi	Ekateríni	GRE	4.2.90	172/63	PV	4.87	4.91- 17
Steinacker	Marike	GER	4.3.92	184/80	DT	58.05	59.03- 15
Steiner	Abby	USA-J	24.11.99	168/55	200	22.73	23.75- 16
Stepanova	Yekaterina	RUS	24.7.94		HJ	1.88	1.88- 16
Stephens	Nicole	USA	14.10.98	167/52	400h	57.21	
* Stepter	Jaide	USA	25.9.94	173/64	200	22.80	23.23- 16
					400	50.63	50.91- 15
Sterckendries	Vanessa	BEL	15.9.95		HT	67.63	65.46- 16
* Stevens	Dani	AUS	26.5.88	182/82	DT	68.26	69.64- 17
* Stevens	Deajah	USA	19.5.95	172/60	100	11.18	11.00,10.89w- 17
					200	22.81	22.25- 16
* Stevens	Jeneva	USA	28.10.89	178/102	SP	18.55i, 18.33	19.11- 16
					HT	70.05	74.77- 13
Stewart	Janeah	USA	21.7.96	183/102	SP	18.03	17.86- 17
					HT	72.92	64.69- 17
Stewart	Kerron	JAM	16.4.84	175/61	100	11.25, 11.21w	10.75- 09
Stiverne	Aiyanna	CAN	20.2.95	168/55	200	22.76	23.22- 16
					400	51.86	52.00- 17
Stoner	Paige	USA	31.1.96	160/50	10000	32:23.38	33:55.69- 17
					3kSt	9:46.98	10:02.65- 17
Storm	Ida	SWE	26.12.91	190/95	HT	70.62	71.52- 17
Storozheva	Yekaterina	RUS	22.1.93	170/57	1500	4:08.03	4:15.66- 16
* Stowers	Jasmin	USA	23.9.91	175/64	100h	12.71	12.47- 17

Name		Nat	Born	Ht/Wt	Event	2018 Mark	Pre-2018 Best
Strähl	Martina	SUI	7.5.87	168/52	HMar	69:29	71:50- 16
Strametz	Karin	AUT	18.4.98	172/61	Hep	5864	5840- 17
Strati	Laura	ITA	3.10.90	171/58	LJ	6.62	6.72A, 6.63, 6.70w- 17
* Stratton	Brooke	AUS	12.7.93	168/58	LJ	6.88	7.05- 16
Stravs	Claudia	SLO	11.2.94	175/73	HT	65.36	63.96- 17
Strebkova	Nataliya	UKR	6.3.95	167/50	3kSt	9;37,28	9·44.52- 17
Strickler	Amelia	GBR	24.1.94	171/100	SP	17.31	17.13- 17
Strokova	Yekaterina	RUS	17.12.89	184/80	DT	58.63	65.78- 14
Strumillo	Stefania	ITA	14.10.89	182/81	DT	57.38	59.80- 16
Stuart	Bianca	BAH	17.5.88	168/52	LJ	6.74	6.83- 15, 6.91w- 11
Stuart	Lauren	CAN	16.11.91	168/79	HT	66.67	67.56- 15
Stuy	Hrystyna	UKR	3.2.88	168/60	100	11.20	11.24- 14
Su Lingdan		CHN	12.1.97	175/59	JT	61.21	59.21- 17
Su Wenxiu		CHN	28.6.98		20kW	1:29:46	
* Su Xinyue		CHN	8.11.91	179/70	DT	63.73	65.59- 16
* Suhr	Jenn	USA	5.2.82	180/64	PV	4.93	5.03i- 16, 4.92- 08
Sujew	Diana	GER	2.11.90	166/52	1500	4:05.95	4:05.62- 13
					1M	4:28.38	
Sulek	Adrianna	POL-J	3.4.99	173/62	Hep	5939	5784- 17
Sullohern	Celia	AUS	5.7.92	158/45	10000	31:50.75	32:31.22- 17
* Sum	Eunice	KEN	2.9.88	172/53	800	1:59.25	1:56.99- 15
					1500	4:05.38	4:01.54- 14
Surdu	Dimitriana	MDA	12.5.94	174/95	SP	18.45	18.83- 11
Suriya	Loganathan	IND	7.7.90	170/58	10000	32:23.56	32:39.86- 16
Sussmann	Jana	GER	12.10.90	166/47	3kSt	9:36.26	9:39.46- 17
^ Sutej	Tina	SLO	7.11.88	173/59	PV	4.50	4.71i- 14, 4.61- 11
Suttie	Taryn	CAN	7.12.90	182/95	SP	17.17i, 16.99	17.88- 16
Suzuki	Ayuko	JPN	8.10.91	154/38	10000	31:57.82	31:18.16- 16
Svábíková	Amálie	CZE-J	22.11.99	181/64	PV	4.51	4.50- 17
* Swiety-Ersetic	Justyna	POL	3.12.92	167/57	400	50.41	51.15- 17
* Swoboda	Ewa	POL	26.7.97	164/55	100	11.23, 11.12w	11.12, 11.10w- 16
Szykowny	Alison	USA	17.8.93		DT	56.48	55.91- 15
* Ta Lou	Marie Josée	CIV	18.11.88	159/57	100	10.85, 10.7w mx	10.86- 16
					200	22.34	22.21- 16
Tabares	Carolina	COL	18.7.86	162/50	10000	32:29.35	32:24.24- 15
* Tabashnyk	Kateryna	UKR	15.6.94	178/62	HJ	1.98i, 1.96	1.95- 17
* Tadese	Feyse	ETH	19.11.88	167/53	Mar	2:19:30	2:20:27- 14
* Takacs	Julia	ESP	29.6.89	171/55	20kW	1:27:58	1:28:44- 13
					50kW	4:13:04	-0-
Takano	Chuna	JPN	30.10.97	153/41	10000	32:25.86	32:37.21- 17
Takashima	Yuka	JPN	12.5.88	153/42	10000	32:18.59	31:33.33- 17
					Mar	2:26:13	
* Talay	Alina	BLR	14.5.89	164/54	100h	12.41	12.63- 16
Tallent	Claire	AUS	6.7.81	163/50	20kW	1:31:29	1:28:53- 12
					50kW	4:09:33	-0-
Tanaka	Nozomi	JPN-J	4.9.99	153/43	3000	8:54.01	8:54.27- 17
					5000	15:15.80	15:32.34- 17
Tang Caihong		CHN	29.4.96		20kW	1:32:53	1:34:41- 16
Tanimoto	Mizuki	JPN	18.12.94	151/40	10000	32:33.76	32:18.44- 16
* Tanui	Norah	KEN	2.10.95	160/44	3000	8:33.61	9:24.02- 11
					3kSt	8:59.62	9:03.70- 17
Taranda	Karina	BLR-J	10.2.99	181/60	HJ	1.92	1.89-17
^ Tarasova	Irina	RUS	15.4.87	183/110	SP	18.28i, 18.09	10.35- 12
Tarasyuk	Anna	BLR	30.10.97	183/75	JT	56.48	58.00- 17
^ Tarmoh	Jeneba	USA	27.9.89	167/59	100	11.19	10.93- 13
					200	22.46	22.23- 15, 22.06w- 14
* Tate	Cassandra	USA	11.9.90	174/64	400h	54.94	54.01- 15
Tausaga-Collins	Laulauga	USA	22.5.98	188/105	SP	17.34	15.09- 17
					DT	60.65	59.37- 17
Taushkanova	Anastasiya	RUS	25.3.96		20kW	1:32:28	1:36:58- 17
* Tavernier	Alexandra	FRA	13.12.93	170/82	HT	74.78	74.39- 15
Taye	Ejgayehu	ETH-J	10.2.00		3000	8:44.13	
					5000	15:30.87	
Taylor	Charlotte	GBR	17.1.94	159/45	10000	32:17.95	32:11.80- 17
Taylor	Kellyn	USA	22.7.86	167/52	Mar	2:24:29	2:28:40- 15
Taylor	Lakan	USA	21.6.95	160/52	PV	4.45	4.45i, 4.31- 17
Taylor	Laura	USA	22.4.96	173/62	PV	4.38i, 4.35	4.31- 17
* Teferi	Senbere	ETH	3.5.95	159/45	3000	8:32.49	8:34.32- 15
5000	14:23.33		14:29.82- 16		Mar	2:24:11	
Tenorio	Ángela	ECU	27.1.96	167/59	100	11.01A, 11.13	10.99- 15
					200	22.93	22.84A, 22.86, 22.59w- 15

Name		Nat	Born	Ht/Wt	Event	2018 Mark		Pre-2018 Best
Terry	Twanisha	USA-J	24.1.99	168/54	100	10.99, 10.96w		11.37- 17, 11.34w- 15
					200	22.74		23.21- 17
Tervo	Krista	FIN	15.11.97	165/64	HT	69.42		68.27- 17
Tesfay	Fotyen	ETH	17.2.98	160/40	3000	8:47.7, 8:41.08i		8:47.46- 16
Tesfay	Haftamnesh	ETH	28.4.94	162/48	HMar	69:02		
					Mar	2:20:13		
Teshale	Alemaz	ETH-J	5.7.99	163/48	1500	4:01.78		4:04.94- 17
					3000	8:37.68		
* Thiam	Nafissatou	BEL	19.8.94	184/69	HJ	2.01		1.98- 16
LJ	6.62	6.58- 16	JT	57.91		59.32- 17	Hep 6816	7013- 17
Thomas	Brionna	USA	21.3.96	164/55	200	22.99		23.52- 15
					400	50.78		52.22- 17
Thomas	Carley	AUS-J	26.12.00	166/52	800	2:01.13		2:03.66- 17
* Thomas	Gabrielle	USA	7.12.96	170/57	100	11.19, 10.99w		11.24, 11.15w- 17
200	22.19, 22.13w	22.47, 22.37w- 16			LJ	6.61w		6.27- 17
Thomas	Jahisha	GBR	22.11.94	164/55	LJ	6.69		6.39i, 6.32, 6.35w- 17
Thomas	Lanae-Tava	USA-Y	28.1.01	168/55	LJ	6.60i		6.68- 17
Thomas	Markeeta	USA	29.7.97	178/59	400h	57.11		57.36- 17
Thomas	Reyare	TTO	23.11.87	168/60	100	11.36, 11.21w		11.22- 16, 11.16w- 14
* Thomas-Dodd	Danniel	JAM	11.11.92	168/91	SP	19.36		19.15- 17
Thompson	Alyssa	USA	25.9.94		Hep	5761		
Thompson	Brenessa	GUY	22.7.96	163/52	100	11.34, 11.16w		11.14- 16
* Thompson	Elaine	JAM	28.6.92	169/57	100	10.93		10.70- 16
				7	200	22.30		21.66- 15
Thompson	Yanique	JAM	12.3.96	163/55	100h	12.74		12.69- 17
Tibebu	Hirut	ETH	13.12.94		Mar	2:24:08		2:23:35- 17
Tima	Ana José	DOM	10.10.89	168/56	TJ	14.22		14.22- 16
Timanovskaya	Kristina	BLR	19.11.96	167/54	100	11.04		11.28- 17
					200	22.92		23.13, 23.1- 17
* Tirop	Agnes	KEN	23.10.95	165/50	3000	8:29.09		8:35.23- 17
					5000	14:24.24		14:33.09- 17
Tkachuk	Viktoriya	UKR	8.11.94	178/69	400h	55.28		55.32- 16
* Todd	Jasmine	USA	23.12.93	165/55	LJ	6.44, 6.63w		6.84- 15
* Tola	Helen	ETH	21.11.94	166/50	HMar	67:47		69:48- 17
					Mar	2:22:48		2:22:51- 17
Toledo	Luisaris	VEN	29.12.92	175/60	Hep	5848		5785- 17
Tolj	Marija	CRO-J	29.11.99	184/85	DT	57.90		53.95- 17
Tõllasson	Kätlin	EST	4.6.93		DT	56.24		55.68- 17
Tollesa	Gulume	ETH	11.9.92	155/42	Mar	2:23:06		2:23:12- 15
^ Tomasevic	Dragana	SRB	4.6.82	175/80	DT	60.78		63.63- 06
Tonn	Jessica	USA	15.2.92	164/48	10000	31:54.83		34:00.33- 15
^ Topic	Biljana	SRB	17.10.77	180/60	TJ	13.64		14.56- 09
Topic	Dusica	SRB	11.1.82		50kW	4:30:43		4:41:55- 17
Tracey	Adelle	GBR	27.5.93	164/50	800	1:59.86		2:00.04mx- 16, 2:00.24- 17
					1000	2:34.59		
Tracey	Nikita	JAM	18.9.90	173/63	400h	55.41		55.01- 17
* Tracey	Ristananna	JAM	9.5.92	170/61	400h	55.38		53.74- 17
Trapletti	Valentina	ITA	12.7.85	173/53	20kW	1:29:57		1:30:35- 17
Treasure	Alyx	CAN	15.5.92	180/63	HJ	1.91		1.94- 16
Trengove	Jessica	AUS	15.8.87	168/54	Mar	2:25:59		2:27:01- 17
* Trost	Alessia	ITA	8.3.93	188/68	HJ	1.93i		2.00i, 1.98- 13
Tsareva	Yelizaveta	RUS	26.3.93	177/82	HT	73.22		71.73- 17
Tsega	Muluhabt	ETH	11.9.89	165/54	Mar	2:25:48		2:28:08- 17
* Tsegay	Gudaf	ETH	23.1.97	159/45	1500	3:57.64		3:59.55- 17
1M	4:16.14	4:24.98i- 16	3000	8:33.78		8:50.74i- 17	5000 14:51.30	-0-
Tsutsui	Sakiho	JPN	19.1.96	153/38	10000	32:18.70		32:16.44- 17
* Tsviliy	Alina	UKR	18.9.94	155/42	50kW	4:12:44		
Tsyhotska	Ruslana	UKR	23.3.86	165/56	TJ	13.82		14.53- 12
Tuei	Sandra	KEN	20.1.98	160/45	10000	32:11.92		33:23.8A- 17
Tugsuz	Eda	TUR	27.3.97	171/68	JT	65.20		67.21- 17
Tuigong	Caroline	KEN	12.3.90	169/52	3kSt	9:30.62		9:28.81- 16
Tully	Nicole	USA	30.10.86	156/45	1500	4:09.52		4:05.89- 15
Turner	Jessica	GBR	8.8.95	177/59	400h	56.53		56.08- 17
Turova	Yuliya	RUS	9.6.97		20kW	1:33:33		1:32:21- 17
Turpin	Esther	FRA	29.4.96	174/54	Hep	6230		5940- 17
Tusa	Rahma	ETH	14.9.93	162/46	Mar	2:23:46		2:25:12- 17
^ Twell	Stephanie	GBR	17.8.89	168/54	1500	4:05.56		4:02.54- 10
1M	4:26.05	4:25.39- 17	3000	8:46.79, 8:41.94i		8:40.98- 16	5000 15:18.77	14:54.08- 10
Uehara	Miyuki	JPN	22.11.95	154/39	Mar	2:25:46		
* Ugen	Lorraine	GBR	22.8.91	178/64	LJ	7.05		6.97i- 17, 6.92, 6.96w- 15
Urban	Karolina	POL	18.10.98	185/87	DT	57.48		53.88- 17

Name		Nat	Born	Ht/Wt	Event	2018 Mark		Pre-2018 Best
Urbaniak	Lena	GER	31.10.92	175/95	SP	16.97		18.32i, 18.02- 16
Urbina	María Teresa	ESP	20.3.85	177/53	3kSt	9:43.70		9:41.95- 09
* Urrutia	Yosiry	COL	26.6.86	175/61	TJ	14.47, 14.48w		14.58- 14
Ushiro	Orie	JPN	24.8.90	174/68	JT	56.57		55.89- 14
Utsunomiya	Eri	JPN	11.4.93	166/54	400h	56.84		57.22- 17
					Hep	5821		6660 10
Uudmäe	Merilyn	EST	26.3.91	175/61	TJ	13.87		13.55i- 17, 13.51- 16
Uzunbilek	Zeliha	TUR	10.6.91	176/80	HT	68.38		64.26- 12
Vadlejch	Lucia	SVK	8.11.88	178/68	Hep	6057		6103- 17
Vaiciukeviciute	Zivile	LTU	3.4.96	164/54	20kW	1:28:07		1:31:23- 17
Vaicule	Gunta	LAT	9.3.95	179/68	200	22.94		23.15- 17
					400	51.60		51.37- 17
Valette	Laura	FRA	16.2.97	174/60	100h	13.04		13.04- 17
Vallet	Marine	FRA	9.9.93	174/56	HJ	1.87i		1.88- 16
* Vallortigara	Elena	ITA	21.9.91	179/56	HJ	2.02		1.91- 10
Van Buskirk	Kate	CAN	9.6.87	178/60	1500	4:09.42i		4:05.38- 14
1M	4:26.92i 4:28.08- 14				3000	8:49.02i	8:52.08i- 17 5000	15:16.34 15:22.17- 17
van der Walt	Zeney	RSA-J	22.5.00	176/60	400h	55.05A, 55.34		57.94- 17
van Klinken	Jorinde	NED-J	2.2.00	180/85	DT	59.02		51.57- 16
					SP	17.28		16.89- 17
Van Puyvelde	Margo	BEL	21.12.95		400h	55.95		57.05- 17
Vanderelst	Elise	BEL	27.1.98	172/57	1500	4:05.75		4:12.28- 17
Vargas	Andrea Carolina	CRC	28.5.96	168/60	100h	12.90, 12.75w		13.12- 17
Vaseykina	Viktoriya	RUS	19.3.97	177/64	Hep	5923		5501- 17
Vaskovskaya	Irina	BLR	2.4.91	179/65	TJ	14.30i, 13.93		14.23i, 14.19- 16
Vastenburg	Jip	NED	21.3.94	181/59	3000	8:55.81		8:49.50- 15
					5000	15:15.77		15:27.40- 14
Vaughn	Sara	USA	16.5.86	155/48	1500	4:05.88		4:04.56- 17
					1M	4:27.31		4:34.29- 11
Veiga	Evelise	POR	3.3.96	168/55	LJ	6.61		6.51- 16
					TJ	13.65		13.29- 17, 13.41w- 16
Velazco	Davisleidis L.	CUB-J	4.9.99	170/60	TJ	13.92		14.08- 16
^ Veldáková	Dana	SVK	3.6.81	182/68	TJ	13.77, 14.03w		14.51- 08, 14.59w- 10
Velvere	Liga	LAT	10.2.90	171/59	800	2:00.75		2:02.18i- 17, 2:02.71- 16
* Vetter	Anouk	NED	4.2.93	177/62	Hep	6426		6636- 17
Vicente	María	ESP-Y	28.3.01	176/63	TJ	13.95		13.21, 13.72w- 17
Vicenzino	Tania	ITA	1.4.86	167/64	LJ	6.52i, 6.44		6.65- 14
* Viljoen	Sunette	RSA	6.1.83	168/64	JT	62.46A		69.35- 12
* Virbalyte Dimsiene	Brigita	LTU	1.2.85	165/50	20kW	1:27:59		1:30:20- 15
Visca	Carolina	ITA-J	31.5.00	169/65	JT	57.93		56.15- 17
* Visser	Nadine	NED	9.2.95	175/63	100h	12.71		12.78, 12.57w- 17
* Vita	Claudine	GER	19.9.96	179/81	DT	65.15		64.45- 17
Vitovshchyk	Vasylyna	UKR	30.4.90	166/54	50kW	4:23:15		4:37:55- 17
Voronina	Yekaterina	UZB	16.2.92	175/65	Hep	5826		6212- 15
Vrabcová-Nyvltová	Eva	CZE	6.2.86	162/48	Mar	2:26:31		2:29:41- 17
Vrzalová	Simona	CZE	7.4.88	168/52	1500	4:04.80		4:07.08- 17
1M	4:21.54				4:48.9- 16 3000	8:57.07		8:58.30- 17
Vu Thi Men		VIE	10.7.90	170/57	TJ	13.93		14.15- 17
Vucenovic	Marija	SRB	3.4.93	172/70	JT	60.60		58.58- 17
Vukovic	Marija	MNE	21.1.92	194/69	HJ	1.90i		1.95- 16
Waggoner	Tatum	USA	6.9.95	174/61	400	51.89		52.52- 16
Waithera	Mariam	KEN	23.12.96	169/49	5000	15:29.00		15:20.94 16
Waka	Chaltu	ETH	25.9.85		Mar	2:26:00?		2.29.30- 15
Walcott-Nolan	Revee	GBR	6.3.95	176/55	800	2:01.78		2:02.32- 16
Walker	Sanique	JAM-J	8.4.00	173/59	400h	57.19		57.20- 16
Wallader	Rachel	GBR	1.9.89	180/87	SP	17.48		17.53- 16
Waller	Hannah	USA	22.6.98	167/60	400	51.76		52.34- 17
Walter	Sydney	USA	15.11.93	170/58	PV	4.45, 4.50 dh?		4.55- 17
* Wambui	Margaret	KEN	15.9.95	175/66	800	1:58.07		1:56.87- 17
Wambui	Tabitha	KEN	29.12.83	162/62	HMar	69:07		70:08- 17
Wang Chunyu		CHN	17.1.95	175/55	800	2:01.80		1:59.93- 16
Wang Lixue		CHN	15.12.96		20kW	1:34:05		1:35:56- 17
Wang Na		CHN	29.5.95		20kW	1:29:15		1:26:29- 17
Wang Qingling		CHN	14.1.93	170/58	LJ	6.65i, 6.46A		6.45- 17
					Hep	5954		6033- 17
Wang Qiong		CHN	1.1.98		20kW	1:32:58		
Wang Rong		CHN	1.7.96		TJ	13.78i, 13.45		14.09i- 13, 13.98- 14
Wang Wupin		CHN	18.1.91	163/48	TJ	13.76		14.10- 15
Wang Yang		CHN	14.2.89	185/65	HJ	1.90		1.92- 12
Wang Yingliu		CHN	1.3.92		20kW	1:28:37		1:28:15- 17
* Wang Zheng		CHN	14.12.87	174/108	HT	73.73		77.68- 14

Name		Nat	Born	Ht/Wt	Event	2018 Mark	Pre-2018 Best
Wanjiru	Mercy	KEN-J	2.3.99		3kSt	9:23.4A	
Wanjiru	Rosemary	KEN	9.12.94	159/44	10000	31:57.66	31:41.23- 17
3000	8:44.24		8:48.44- 14		5000	15:08.61	15:09.68- 17
Warner	Heavin	USA	4.3.93	180/86	HT	69.99	69.33- 16
Warren	McKenzie	USA	3.12.93	176/105	SP	17.81i, 17.26	17.62i, 17.39- 17
Warren	Portious	TTO	2.3.96	168/96	SP	17.35	16.90- 17
* Washington	Ariana	USA	27.8.96	175/59	100	11.08	11.01- 16, 10.97w- 17
					200	22.54	22.21- 16
Washington	Taylor	USA	6.5.93	175/64	200	22.99	22.48- 16
					400	51.76	50.25- 16
Wasike	Dorcas	KEN	2.7.96	152/40	5000	15:25.35i	
					10000	32:11.81	
* Watson	Sage	CAN	20.6.94	175/62	400	51.62	51.84i- 17, 52.01- 16
					400h	54.55	54.52- 17
Watson	Samantha	USA-J	10.11.99	174/57	800	2:01.46	2:00.65- 17
Webster-Freeman	Juanita	USA	13.11.96		Hep	5788(w)	5607- 17
Wei Yongli		CHN	11.10.91	166/54	100	10.99	11.24- 16
					200	22.97	23.04- 17
* Weightman	Laura	GBR	1.7.91	172/58	1500	4:01.76	4:00.17- 14
1M	4:20.49		4:20.88- 17		5000	15:25.84	15:08.24- 17
Weir	Jillian	CAN	9.2.93	177/78	HT	71.96	72.50- 17
Weißenberg	Sophie	GER	24.9.97	183/65	Hep	6165	5171- 15
Weldegebril	Tinbit	ETH	17.9.89		Mar	2:23:37	2:28:15- 17
Wells	Lauren	AUS	3.8.88	179/86	400h	55.73	55.08- 13
					LJ	6.49	6.52, 6.54w- 17
Welteji	Diribe	ETH-Y	13.5.02	157/45	800	1:59.74	
Wesche	Maddison-Lee	NZL	13.6.99	179/85	SP	17.09	15.62- 17
Wessman	Anna	SWE	9.10.89	164/70	JT	57.48	61.42- 16
Wessolly	Jessica-Bianca	GER	11.12.96	168/56	200	22.89	23.26- 17
West	Tori	AUS	14.10.95		Hep	5793	5570- 17
Westaway	Jenna	CAN	19.6.94	168/52	800	2:01.61, 2:01.22i	2:01.97- 16
^ Wester	Alexandra	GER	21.3.94	180/64	LJ	6.63	6.95i, 6.79, 7.00w- 16
White	Kayla	USA	24.9.96	165/52	100	11.21	11.39- 17
200	22.98w		23.70- 16		100h	12.92, 12.91w	12.94- 17
^ Whitney	Kaylin	USA	9.3.98	167/57	200	22.93	22.47- 15
^ Whyte	Angela	CAN	22.5.80	170/56	Hep	5898	6018- 14
Whyte	Natalliah	JAM	9.8.97	170/55	100	11.04	11.55- 15
					200	22.55	22.77- 17
Whyte	Rhonda	JAM	6.11.90	170/55	400h	54.90	54.29- 17
Williams	Bianca	GBR	18.12.93	167/55	100	11.20	11.17- 14
					200	22.60	22.58- 14
Williams	Briana	JAM-Y	21.3.02	162/52	100	11.13	11.30- 17
					200	22.50	23.57, 23.53w- 17
* Williams	Christania	JAM	17.10.94	157/52	100	11.21	10.96- 16
* Williams	Danielle	JAM	14.9.92	168/59	100h	12.48	12.56- 17
* Williams	Jeanine	JAM	28.1.97	168/57	100h	12.79, 12.74w	12.99- 17
Williams	Jodean	JAM	11.11.93	175/65	200	22.88	22.94- 17
^ Williams	Jodie	GBR	28.9.93	174/65	200	22.75	22.46- 14
* Williams	Kendell	USA	14.6.95	173/64	100h	12.98	12.82- 17
					LJ	6.69, 6.91w	6.54i- 14, 6.49- 17
* Williams	Kimberly	JAM	3.11.88	169/66	TJ	14.64	14.62, 14.78w- 13
Williams	Lauren Rain	USA-J	25.7.99	170/57	200	22.51	22.80, 22.44w- 16
Williams	Shimayra	JAM	2.12.95	170/56	100h	13.05	12.81- 17
Willis	Andrea	USA	26.7.98	163/	PV	4.34	4.19A- 16
Willis	Todea-Kay	JAM	23.11.88		LJ	6.39, 6.51w	6.42, 6.66w- 17
Willis	Zarriea	USA	14.11.96		HJ	1.89i	1.85i, 1.82- 17
Wilson	Abigale	USA	28.1.97		DT	56.62	51.17- 17
* Wilson	Ajee'	USA	8.5.94	169/55	800	1:56.45	1:55.61- 17
					1500	4:05.18	4:12.10- 14
Wilson	Alex	USA	16.6.93	170/55	3kSt	9:48.37	9:40.90- 14
Wilson	Alyssa	USA-J	20.2.99	178/91	SP	17.30i, 17.21	17.70- 17
					HT	66.99	58.28- 16
Wilson	Nickiesha	JAM	28.7.86	174/66	100h	12.93	12.79- 09, 12.63w- 08
Wilson-Perteete	Avi	USA-J	13.5.99	164/48	800	2:01.14	2:09.31- 15
* Wimbley	Shakima	USA	23.4.95	187/61	200	22.34	22.43- 15
					400	49.52	50.36- 17
* Winger	Kara	USA	10.4.86	183/86	JT	64.75	66.67- 10
Winters	Melanie	USA	11.11.93	172/61	LJ	6.53	6.06, 6.07w- 16
Witek	Marcelina	POL	2.6.95	174/67	JT	66.53	63.31- 17
* Włodarczyk	Anita	POL	8.8.85	176/90	HT	79.59	82.98- 16

Name		Nat	Born	Ht/Wt	Event	2018 Mark	Pre-2018 Best
Wodak	Natasha	CAN	17.12.81	160/45	5000	15:29.44	15:37.70- 16
					10000	31:50.18	31:41.59- 15
Woitha	Charlene	GER	21.8.93	178/77	HT	69.34	70.98- 16
Woldu	Etagegne	ETH	10.5.96		HMar	69:22	
Wolters-Verstegen	Sanne	NED	10.11.85	168/53	800	1:59.85	1:59.29- 16
1000	2:37.49				2:38.05- 16	1M	4:29.11
Woodard	Jessica	USA	4.2.95	178/86	SP	18.68	18.36- 17
					DT	58.14	56.64- 17
Woodruff	Gianna	PAN	18.11.93	170/57	400h	55.60	55.76- 17
Worku	Fantu	ETH-J	29.3.99	162/46	1500	4:06.01	4:05.81- 17
3000	8:39.55i				8:50.36i- 17	5000	15:30.39
Wosztyl	Natalia	POL-J	28.8.99	170/57	400h	57.10	58.40- 17
Wright	Alice	GBR	3.11.94	161/48	10000	32:15.73	32:29.28- 17
Wu Shuijiao ¶		CHN	19.6.91	161/53	100h	13.08	12.72- 14
Wyciszkiewicz	Patrycja	POL	8.1.94	173/58	400	51.87	51.31- 15
Xia Kaili		CHN	16.3.96		50kW	4:43:26	
Xiao Han		CHN	12.11.08		50kW	4.43.48	
Xiao Xianghua		CHN	19.2.97		20kW	1:33:17	1:32:16- 17
Xie Yuchen		CHN	12.5.96	197/79	DT	58.03	58.30- 16
Xu Shuangshuang		CHN	6.4.96		3kSt	9:47.42	10:01.68- 16
Xu Xiaoling		CHN	13.5.92	175/64	LJ	6.64A, 6.50	6.66i- 16, 6.63- 12
Xu Xinying		CHN	17.2.97		HT	65.35	63.31- 15
Yamanouchi	Minami	JPN	21.12.92	171/54	3000	8:57.02	
5000	15:21.31				15:49.26- 17	10000	31:16.48
Yamasaki	Yuki	JPN	6.6.95	165/57	Hep	5873	5751- 16
Yamashita	Mikako	JPN	3.5.97	168/70	JT	58.32	59.94- 17
Yan Ni		CHN	7.2.93	176/62	HT	66.90	68.56- 16
Yang Fuyao		CHN	6.12.96		20kW	1:32:48	1:35:07- 17
* Yang Jiayu		CHN	18.2.96	163.48	20kW	1:27:22	1:26:18- 13
Yang Liujing		CHN	22.8.98		20kW	1:29:31	
Yano	Ohori	JPN	11.2.95	151/39	10000	31:44.13	
Yarigo	Noëlie	BEN	26.12.85	165/52	800	2:00.06	1:59.12- 16
Yatsevich	Anastasiya	BLR	18.1.85	158/48	50kW	4:18:00	
* Yavi	Winfred	BRN-J	31.12.99	157/48	3kSt	9:10.74	9:22.67- 17
Yee	Regan	CAN	4.7.95	162/52	3kSt	9:37.31	9:53.99- 16
Yeliseyeva	Olga	RUS	6.9.98		20kW	1:30:49	
Yermachenkova	Tatyana	RUS	9.9.98		HJ	1.89	1.87i, 1.85- 17
Yermakova	Viktoriya	BLR	18.1.95		JT	56.87	59.35- 17
Yevdokimova	Natalya	RUS	7.9.93	164/50	TJ	14.02i, 13.92	13.97- 17
Yimer	Zeineba	ETH	17.6.98	162/48	HMar	66:21	71:31- 17
* Yin Hang		CHN	7.2.97	161/50	50kW	4:09:09	4:08:58- 17
Yoshizumi	Yuki	JPN	7.1.96	167/51	50kW	4:43:03	
Yu Yuzhen		CHN	5.3.98		JT	59.98	56.57- 17
Yudkina	Khrystyna	UKR	4.12.84	169/58	20kW	1:32:44	1:37:31- 17
					50kW	4:20:46	4:32:14- 17
Zabawska	Daria	POL	16.4.95	185/92	DT	59.57	60.23- 15
Zagainova	Diana	LTU	20.6.97	179/62	TJ	13.74	13.64- 17
Zahi	Carolle	FRA	12.6.94	170/66	100	11.01	11.13- 17
					200	23.02, 22.92w	24.14- 15
Záhorová	Adéla	CZE-J	13.11.99	177/68	LJ	6.48, 6.51w	6.15- 17
Zakkour	Soukaina	MAR	13.10.93	178/80	HT	68.28	63.95- 17
Zaldívar	Liuba M.	CUB	5.4.93	161/54	TJ	13.81A, 13.60	14.51A- 16, 14.20- 13
Zamzow	Ashtin	USA	13.8.06	100/57	Hep	5853	5829- 16
Zapletalová	Emma	SVK-J	24.3.00		400h	57.22	60.80- 17
Zarankaite	Ieva	LTU	23.11.94	176/80	DT	57.15	54.62- 17
Zavyalova	Yekaterina	RUS	1.3.91	175/65	800	2:00.80	1:57.53- 12
Zdziebło	Katarzyna	POL	28.11.96	160/49	20kW	1:32:50	1:34:49- 16
Zhang Deshun		CHN	21.2.96	162/47	10000	32:12.78	32:58.17- 15
Zhang Li		CHN	17.1.89	174/65	JT	59.36A	65.47- 14
Zhang Linru		CHN-J	23.9.99	176/82	SP	17.33	16.47- 17
Zhang Xinyan		CHN	9.2.94	170/55	3kSt	9:46.30	9:28.54- 16
Zhao Wenli		CHN	11.12.96		20kW	1:31:07	1:33:16- 17
Zhou Mengyuan		CHN-J	3.9.99	167/64	HT	66.86	63.20- 17
Zhu Dandan		CHN	1.3.94		JT	59.44	59.19- 16
Zhuk	Iryna	BLR	26.1.93	166/60	PV	4.67	4.60- 17
Zihlmann	Nicole	SUI	30.7.86		HT	67.42	64.83- 16
Zong Dan		CHN	19.1.95		HT	65.84	63.86- 17
Zupin	Agata	SLO	17.3.98	176/59	400h	56.86	55.96- 17
Zurek	Teresa	GER	29.7.98		20kW	1:33:30	1:39:14- 16
Zyabkina	Viktoriya	KAZ	4.9.92	170/55	100	11.20	11.19- 15, 11.15dt- 16
					200	22.73	22.66- 16

REFERENCE BOOKS 2018–19

Sydney Wooderson: A Very British Hero by Rob Hadgraft. Published by The Book Guild Ltd. From the author at 77 Old Ferry Road, Wivenhoe, Essex CO7 9SW; price (for UK customers) £12 (inc. postage), or via Amazon or bookguild.co.uk. The detailed story of this great runner is highly recommended.

The Track in the Forest by Bob Burns. Hardback 248 pages. Published by Chicago Review Press at US$ 26.99. Available at £12.88 plus delivery from Amazon in the UK. This fascinating book tells how the 1968 US team came together for a 2-month training camp and the staging of the final Olympic Trials at Echo Summit, California set at almost the identical high altitude of Mexico City and some 1000 feet above the town of South Lake Tahoe. Four world records were set at the Trials and a great US team went on to win 12 gold medals and set six world records at the Games. This is all set against the background of a turbulent year in the USA.

Latvijas Vieglatletikas Vesture 1992-2018. Hardback 240x160m, 536 pages. This magnificent work by Andris Stagis is the third in his series of books detailing, in most comprehensive fashion, the history of Latvian athletics. Well illustrated (including several colour sections) with text in Latvian and plenty of statistics. 25 euro plus 15 euro postage from Andris Stagis, Druvienas 18-80 P.K.62, LV-1079 Riga, Latvia. Previous volumes Part 1 1897-1944 and Part 2 1944-1991. Andris can be contacted at andris.stagis@athletics.lv

The Golden Book of Yugoslav Athletics Lists more than 2500 men and women who were represented former Yugoslavia (1919-2006), with complete lists of result of Yugoslav athletes at international competitions. and year lists leaders in Yugoslavia 1919-2006 including war-years (1941-4).

Hard cover, more than 600 photos!

Progression of Yugoslav National Records in Athletics (1919-2006) Over 3000 records for men and women with compete details and index of record holders. Also Indoor records of Yugoslavia (1939-2006). Hard cover, more than 400 photos.

Each book is **40 EUR** inc. post&packing (cash only) from GAJIĆ LJUBIŠA (ATFS), Vukašina Stefanovića 9, 35000, JAGODINA – SRBIJA (Serbia). akvozd57@gmail.com

ANNUALS

L'athlétisme africain/african athletics 2018. A5, 152 pages. By Yves Pinaud. Published by Éditions Polymédias. The author continued his great service for African athletics with the 37th edition in this splendid series. There are 100 deep men's and women's lists for Africa for 2017, with all-time lists and official continental records. 25 euro, £20 or US $30 including postage from La Mémoire du Sport, 166 rue de Decize, 03000 Moulins, France. Also available: booklist with very extensive list of athletics books and magazines for sale: librairie.polymedias@orange.fr. Very sadly Yves said that this will be the last edition of this Annual.

Anuario Del Atletismo Español 2017-2018 With members of the AEEA, the Spanish Federetion published the latest edition of their massive national Annual. The 1875 pages (!) contain all conceivable results, 2018 and all-time lists, historical material and biographies etc. with many illustrations in colour. Digital version available: http//www.rfea.es/revista/libros.rfea_Anuario2018.htm

Asian athletics 2017 Rankings. A5 114 pages. This, the 29th successive edition of Heinrich Hubbeling's great work in chronicling Asian athletics, was published for the first time as an e-book. Top 30 lists for 2017 for athletes from Asian nations, with continuation lists for countries other than China and Japan (up to 4 best per country), national records set in 2017, and full lists of Asian records. Euro 15 in cash Euro or US$ or by Inter-national Money Order from the author, Haaksbergener Str 25, 48691 Vreden, Germany. Copies also available for 1998, 2004-08, 2011 and 2014-16 and Asian all-time rankings as at 31.12.2000 at €15 each. email hhubbeling@t-online.de.

Athlérama 2017. A5 832pp. The latest edition of the French Annual, edited by Patricia Doilin with a strong team of compilers, was again a superb reference book, packed with information on French athletics – records, profiles of 83 top athletes, results, deep year lists for 2017 for all age groups plus all-time lists and indexes of top performers. Maintaining the sequence, there are French top ten lists and reviews for 1917 (much limited by WW I) and 1967. Profiled athlete of the year was Yohann Diniz. 28 euros from the FFA, 33 avenue Pierre de Coubertin, 7540 Paris Cedex 13, France. email Patricia.Doilin@athle.org. See www.athle.fr.

BRITISH ATHLETICS 2018. A5 442 pages. The 60th NUTS Annual, edited by Tony Miller, Rob Whittingham, and Peter Matthews. Deep year lists for 2017 in all age groups, all-time lists, records, major results, merit rankings, obituaries and index. Now published on Lulu.com: http://www.lulu.com/content/paperback-book/british-athletics-2018/22478482

Fast Annual 2018. The 40th edition of the US Annual, general editor Tom Casacky, was not published in printed form this year, but was prepared as a 608 page pdf with all the usual contents: records, 50-70 deep US lists for 2017 and all-time, with 15-deep junior and college all-time lists. The massive index section included annual progressions and championships details for top American and resident foreign athletes. Contact: tom@interis.com

Israel Athletics Annual 2018/19. 240 x 170mm, 58pp, illustrated. By David Eiger and Arit Cooks for the Israeli Athletic Association. Records, championship results, 2018 top 20s and all-time lists, with profiles of leading Israeli athletes. 8 euro or US $9 from David Eiger, 10 Ezra Hozsofer Str, Herzliya 46 371, Israel. Past editions from 1986 onwards also available at a reduced price.

Latvijas Vieglatletikas Gadagramata 2019. A5 328 pp. An exemplary example of a national annual with its most comprehensive coverage of Latvian athletics for 2018, including a chronology of the year, records, results, athlete profiles and year and all-time lists by ATFS member Andris Stagis. From the Latvian Athletic Association, Augsiela 1, Riga LV-1009, Latvia. email: lvs@lat-athletics.lv

ANNUAIRE FLA 2018. A4 272p. The Luxembourg Annual, edited by Georges Klepper, is as usual a magnificent and extraordinarily comprehensive volume, with reviews, results, 2018 and all-time lists, plus many colour photographs. 25 euros locally, by post €28 in Luxembourg, €33 elsewhere to account no. LU32 1111 0200 0321 0000. See www.fla.lu

Sverige-Bästa 2017. A5 298 pages. Edited by Jonas Hedman. Detailed 2017 Swedish lists for seniors (100 deep), and younger age groups (20 deep).179 Swedish crowns, 18 euros or $20 (plus postage and shipping) from the Swedish Athletic Association: Svenska Friidrottsförbundet, Heliosgatan 3, 120 30 Stockholm, Sweden. Email: info@friidrott.se

Yleisurheilu 2018. A5 672pp. The Finnish Yearbook, published by Suomen Urheilulitto (Finnish Athletics) and compiled by Juhani and Mirko Jalava, contained every conceivable statistic for Finnish athletics (with results and deep year lists) for the past year. There are also world indoor, outdoor and junior lists for the year. 20 euros plus 14 euros for postage and packaging.

Orders by e-mail to juhani@tilastopaja.fi

Ranking Permanente del Atietismo Dominicano by Arisnel Rodriguez Sosa is an electronic book in pdf format that contains the top 30 performances and top 50 performers for each event for the Dominican Republic. Price US $30 via Paypal or in dollars – contact the author at arisnel.r@gmail.com. Details at: https://sites.google.com/site/atletismodominicano/

Combined Events Statistics

Hans van Kuijen is no longer producing his Combined Events Annual in book form – but is providing his comprehensive world data in pdf-file format, so the following (new and previous publications) are available: 2018 Annual Combined Events – €15, Statistics handbook Götzis 2018 – €10, Statistics handbook ECCE 1993-2017 – €15, 100 Olympic handbook Decathlon 1912-2012 – €15. All-time best files – Decathlon performers over 7500 and performances over 8000, Heptathlon performers over 5500 and performances over 6000 – each €5. Orders to: Hans van Kuijen, de Bergen 66, 5706 RZ Helmond, Netherlands. email j.kuijen4@upcmail.nl.

Payments can be made to BIC-code: ABNANL2A, IBAN code: NL79ABNA0523127898

NURMI – Athletics in the 19th Century, A Statistical Review Volume III 1857-1864 by Ari Törmä. A4 116 pages. Published by the Finnish Athletics Archive Association, this has unique lists by event for each year in this period. See www.aritorma.net.

The Ukrainian Federation have published books by Ivan Kachkivskyi and Serhiy Baranov as pdfs on their website – see https://statistics.uaf.org.ua.books

Statistics 2018 – the Ukrainian Annual

National Indoor Competitions 2019 – handbook for the indoor season; includes first three at all events at UKR Indoor Championships senior, U20 and U18 2003-18.

See: https://statistics.uaf.org.ua/books/

TRACK STATS. he NUTS quarterly bulletins, edited by Bob Phillips, are 64-page A5 booklets that feature fasciniting historical articles and statistics. Subscription details from Liz Sissons at lizsissons9@gmail.com

The **Spanish statisticians' group, the AEEA** produces magnificent publications. Membership (four bulletins per year) is 55 euros per year (€61 outside Europe) from AEEA secretary Ignacio Mansilla, C/Encinar del Rey, 18 - 28450 Collado

Mediano, Madrid, Spain. email: imansilla@rfea.es

Lista Española de Todos Los Tiempos. 356 pages. This publication by the AEEA of Spanish all-time lists (as at 31.10.2018) is described by co-author (with Ignacio Mansilla) Miguel Villaseñor as "the hugest ranking in the world". Lists are typically 120-200 deep for both performances and performers for all standard men's and women's events with shorter lists for other events. Available to download from the Spanish Federation. See
http://www.rfea.es/web/noticias/desarrollo.asp?codigo=11384#.XCyfB02WxoI

The **DGLD** – the **German** statistical group, Deutsche Gesellschaft für Leichtathletik-Dokumentation produces three annual bulletins plus an annual German lists book. The annual subscription is 55 euro per year. Contact Manfred Holzhausen, Bergheimer Str.33, 41515 Grevenbroich, Germany; manfred.holzhausen@gmx.de. Website: www.ladgld.de

Also published by the DGLD is the latest in the series of books dealing with the history of 100 years of athletics in Germany, event-by-event – **100 Jahre Leichtathletik in Deutschland** is **200m der Männer** by Harry Themel. This 484 page A5 book contains immense detail about the men's 200m (also 4x200m relay), including results of championships and internationals, annual ranking lists and all-time lists at various dates. 25 euros from Manfred Holzhausen (as above). No cheques from outside Germany.

IAAF Publications

Facts & Figures – IAAF World U20 Championships Tampere 2018, the latest in a series of IAAF statistical reference books, can be downloaded from iaaf.org. The 80 pages include the first three placings in every edition of the championships since 1986 and a country by country record of achievement.

European Athletics Publications

The **Statistics Handbook** for the European Indoor Champs (741 A5 pages), is available on the European Athletics website (european-athletics.org). Contents include complete results (over 200 pages) of every European Indoors since 1970, lists of multiple medallists, country index, athlete index, European all-time lists and national indoor records. It was available to the media as a very heavy book at the event. While the layout was vastly improved from previous handbooks, with a smaller, tidier font and lighter paper the extreme weight and size could have been much reduced.

European Athletics 2018 Statistics Yearbook. 672 A5 pages provides comprehensive lists and records for 2018. Again, see EA website.

The **EA Annual Review 2018** can also be downloaded from its website.

Hall of Fame

In each Annual from 2001 we have included athletes in our Hall of Fame. Every year we select five athletes and this year's selections are:

John Walker (New Zealand) (b. 12 Jan 1952) – World's first sub-3:50 miler, 3:49.4 in 1975, also world record for 2000m, 4:51.4 in 1976 prior to winning Olympic 1500m title. In 1985 became first to run 100 sub four-minute miles. Knighted in 2009.

Gisela Mauermayer (Germany) (1913-95) – Olympic champion in 1936 and European in 1938 (also shot silver) in run of 86 consecutive discus contests 1935-49 with ten world records, seven in 1935 and three in 1936. Also three world records at pentathlon.

Ulrike Meyfarth (FRG/Germany) (b. 4 May 1956) – Olympic high jump champion at 16 years 123 days in Munich 1972 with world record 1.92m, and won again 12 years later in 1984 with 2.02, having set further world records with 2.02 in 1982 (to win European title) and 2.03 in 1983.

Rosa Mota (Portugal) (b. 29 Jun 1958) – Great marathon record with Olympic title in 1988 (3rd in 1984), World 1987 and European 1982 (on debut at distance), 1986 and 1990. Also won most of the big city races and ran world record for 20km in 1986.

Steve Ovett (GBR) – Olympic champion at 800m in 1980 (also bronze at 1500m), European 800m silver at 800m in 1974 and 1978, before winning gold at 1500m. Won 45 successive races at 1500m or 1 mile 1977-80, Three world records at 1500m and two at 1 mile, also world best at 2 miles. 1986 Commonwealth Games champion at 5000m.

WORLD INDOOR LISTS 2019 – MEN

60 METRES
Note: including some marks from December 2018 (*), # Oversized track (over 200m)

Time	First	Last	Nat	DOB	Pos	Meet	Venue	Date
6.47		Su Bingtian	CHN	29.8.89	1		Birmingham	16 Feb
6.50	Grant	Holloway	USA	19.11.97	1	NCAA	Birmingham	9 Mar
6.52	Divine	Oduduru	NGR	7.10.96	1	Big 12	Lubbock	23 Feb
6.53	Reece	Prescod	GBR	29.2.96	1	ISTAF	Berlin	1 Feb
6.53	Arthur Gue	Cissé	CIV	20.12.90	2	ISTAF	Berlin	1 Feb
6.53A	Emmanuel	Wells	USA		1		Albuquerque	9 Feb
6.54	Cravont	Charleston	USA	2.1.98	1		Clemson	8 Feb
6.54	Mike	Rodgers	USA	24.4.85	3		Birmingham	16 Feb
6.54	Takuya	Kawakami	JPN	8.6.95	4		Birmingham	16 Feb
6.54	Abdul Hakim	Sani Brown	JPN	6.3.99	2h2	NCAA	Birmingham	8 Mar
6.55	John	Teeters	USA	19.5.93	1h3		Norman	2 Feb
6.55	Emre Zafer	Barnes	TUR	7.11.88	1		Metz	10 Feb
6.55	Demek	Kemp	USA	26.4.96	1		Columbia	16 Feb
6.55	Kasaun	James	USA	22.12.97	3h2	NCAA	Birmingham	8 Mar
6.55	Mario	Burke	BAR	18.3.97	2	NCAA	Birmingham	9 Mar
6.56	Andrew	Hudson	USA	14.12.96	3		Lubbock	25 Jan
6.56	Kevin	Kranz	GER	20.6.98	1h4	NC	Leipzig	16 Feb
6.57	Shuhei	Tada	JPN	24.6.96	1		College Station	16 Feb
6.57	Bryce	Robinson	USA	13.11.93	2		Düsseldorf	20 Feb
6.57	Cravon	Gillespie	USA	31.7.96	4	NCAA	Birmingham	9 Mar
6.58	Filippo	Tortu	ITA	15.6.98	1h1		Ancona	20 Jan
6.58	Ján	Volko	SVK	2.11.96	2		Madrid	8 Feb
6.58	Emmanuel	Yeboah	GHA	10.8.97	1		Lubbock	15 Feb

Time	First	Last	Nat	DOB	Date		Time	First	Last	Nat	DOB	Date
6.59	Bryand	Rincher	USA		25 Jan		6.60	Micah	Williams	USA	12.11.01	10 Mar
6.59	Javelin	Guidry	USA	6.8.98	26 Jan		6.61	Mustaqeem	Williams	USA	24.8.95	18 Jan
6.59	Anthony	Schwartz	USA	5.9.00	8 Feb		6.61	Davon	DeMoss	USA	20.5.96	19 Jan
6.59	Chijindu	Ujah	GBR	5.3.94	13 Feb		6.61	Brandon	Carnes	USA	6.3.95	8 Feb
6.59	Cordero	Gray	USA	9.5.89	24 Feb		6.61	Nick	Gray	USA	2.6.97	8 Feb
6.60	Cameron	Burrell	USA	11.9.94	26 Jan		6.61	McKinely	West	USA	26.6.96	17 Feb
6.60	Sean	Safo-Antwi	GHA	31.10.90	27 Jan		6.61	Luo Wenyi		CHN	14.4.98	19 Feb
6.60	Henrik	Larsson	SWE	30.9.99	16 Feb		6.61	Derrius	Rodgers	USA	15.10.97	22 Feb
6.60	Brendon	Stewart	USA	29.7.00	23 Feb		6.61	Tavarius	Wright	USA		2 Mar
6.60		Xuan Dajun	CHN	2.1.98	27 Feb		6.61	Ryan	Clark	USA	14.9.96	8 Mar

200 METRES

Time	First	Last	Nat	DOB	Pos	Meet	Venue	Date
20.08	Divine	Oduduru	NGR	7.10.96	1	Big 12	Lubbock	23 Feb
20.30	Kenny	Bednarek	USA	14.10.98	1		Lincoln	2 Feb
20.33	Andrew	Hudson	USA	14.12.96	1h3	Big 12	Lubbock	22 Feb
20.48	Nick	Gray	USA	2.6.97	1	Big 10	Ann Arbor	23 Feb
20.49	Kasaun	James	USA	22.12.97	1		Lubbock	26 Jan
20.55	Elijah	Hall	USA	22.8.94	1		Clemson	9 Feb
20.55	Jaron	Flournoy	USA	24.11.96	1h4	SEC	Fayetteville	22 Feb
20.61	Keitavious	Walter	USA	16.4.96	1h2	NCAA	Birmingham	8 Mar
20.62	Obi	Igbokwe	USA	28.1.97	1h3	NCAA	Birmingham	8 Mar
20.63	Eric	Allen	USA	23.8.99	2		Lubbock	26 Jan
20.63	Kahmari	Montgomery	USA	16.8.97	1		College Station	2 Feb

Time	First	Last	Nat	DOB	Date		Time	First	Last	Nat	DOB	Date
20.65	Mustaqeem	Williams	USA	24.8.95	23 Feb		20.67	Karayme	Bartley	JAM		23 Feb
20.66	McKinely	West	USA	26.6.96	17 Feb		20.69	Grant	Holloway	USA	19.11.97	19 Jan
20.67	Chris	Jefferson	USA	25.3.96	2 Feb		20.69	Dylan	Peebles	USA	2.2.98	22 Feb
							20.69	Ryan	Clark	USA	14.9.96	23 Feb

300 METRES

Time	First	Last	Nat	DOB	Pos	Meet	Venue	Date
32.26	Steven	Gardiner	BAH	12.9.95	1		Columbia	16 Feb
32.49	Jacory	Patterson	USA-J	2.2.00	1		Blacksburg	11 Jan
32.49	Bralon	Taplin	GRN	8.5.92	1		College Station	2 Feb
32.55	Rai	Benjamin	USA	27.7.97	1		Boston (R)	26 Jan

Time	First	Last	Nat	DOB	Date		Time	First	Last	Nat	DOB	Date
32.79	Pavel	Maslák	CZE	21.2.91	12 Feb		32.89	Antonio	Woodard	USA	17.1.97	8 Dec
32.81	Dontavius	Wright	USA	3.1.94	24 Feb		32.89	Austin	Cole	CAN	31.10.98	7 Mar

400 METRES

Time	First	Last	Nat	DOB	Pos	Meet	Venue	Date
44.82	Tyrell	Richard	USA	4.8.97	1	NCAA	Birmingham	9 Mar
45.03	Kahmari	Montgomery	USA	16.8.97	2	NCAA	Birmingham	9 Mar
45.05	Karsten	Warholm	NOR	28.2.96	1	EI	Glasgow	2 Mar
45.16	Wil	London	USA	17.8.97	3	NCAA	Birmingham	9 Mar
45.25	Quincy	Hall	USA	31.7.98	4	NCAA	Birmingham	9 Mar
45.26	Bralon	Taplin	GRN	8.5.92	1		College Station	16 Feb
45.35	Obi	Igbokwe	USA	28.1.97	1		Clemson	8 Feb
45.38	Jonathan	Jones	BAR	6.2.99	1		Lubbock	8 Feb
45.60	Ashton	Hicks	USA	16.2.99	2	Big 12	Lubbock	23 Feb
45.66	Óscar	Husillos	ESP	18.7.93	2	EI	Glasgow	2 Mar
45.67	Derrick	Mokaleng	RSA	18.6.97	2		Lubbock	8 Feb
45.68	Devin	Dixon	USA	22.9.97	2		Clemson	8 Feb
45.82	Bryce	Deadmon	USA	26.3.97	2		Lubbock	25 Jan

45.82	Izaiah	Brown		USA	1.1.97	1	Big 10	Ann Arbor		23 Feb

46.04	Jacory	Patterson	USA	2.2.00	23 Feb	46.12	Myles	Pringle	USA	5.9.97	26	Jan
46.07	Alejandro	Perlaza	COL	26.8.94	9 Mar	46.13	Luka	Janezic	SLO	14.11.95	26	Jan
46.07	Benjamin	Lobo Vedel	DEN	23.9.97	9 Mar	46.13	Tony	van Diepen	NED	17.4.96	2	Mar
46.09	Taj	Burgess	USA	15.4.99	3 Mar	46.15	Arinze	Chance	GUY	20.1.96	19	Jan

Oversized track

45.67	Myles	Pringle		USA	5.9.97	1r1	NCAA-II	Pittsburg	9 Mar

45.93	Kenny	Bednarek	USA	14.10.98	8 Dec	46.02	Mar'yea	Harris	USA	24.11.97	2	Feb
45.96	Rashard	Clark	USA	4.11.94	9 Mar	46.14	Wayne	Lawrence	USA		2	Feb

600 METRES

1:13.77	Donavan	Brazier	USA	15.4.97	1	NC	Staten Island	24 Feb
1:15.20	Sam	Ellison	USA	5.12.92	2	NC	Staten Island	24 Feb
1:15.31A	Thomas	Staines	GBR	22.2.98	1		Albuquerque	1 Feb
1:15.32	Kameron	Jones	USA	12.11.97	3	NC	Staten Island	24 Feb

1:15.67	Chris	Giesting	USA	10.12.92	24 Feb	1:15.95A	Isaiah	Jewett	USA	6.2.97	18	Jan
1:15.78	Tre	Hinds	BAR	8.12.95	15 Feb	1:16.24	Erik	Sowinski	USA	21.12.89	24	Feb
1:15.93	Charles	Jones	USA	1.11.95	15 Feb	1:16.49	Quamel	Prince	USA	20.4.94	8	Feb

800 METRES

1:43.98	Michael	Saruni	KEN	18.6.95	1	Millrose	New York (Armory)	9 Feb
1:44.41	Donavan	Brazier	USA	15.4.97	2	Millrose	New York (Armory)	9 Feb
1:45.27	Devin	Dixon	USA	22.9.97	1		Lubbock	26 Jan
1:45.90	Marco	Arop	CAN	20.9.98	1		Clemson	9 Feb
1:45.92	Clayton	Murphy	USA	26.2.95	1		Winston-Salem	2 Feb
1:46.13	Sam	Ellison	USA	5.12.92	3	Millrose	New York (Armory)	9 Feb
1:46.27#	Thomas	Staines	GBR	22.2.98	1		Allendale	8 Feb
1:46.46	Bryce	Hoppel	USA	5.9.97	1	NCAA	Birmingham	9 Mar
1:46.48	Chris	Giesting	USA	10.12.92	1		Boston (A)	9 Feb
1:46.52	Andreas	Kramer	SWE	13.4.97	1		Karlsruhe	2 Feb
1:46.53	Abraham	Alvarado	USA	4.8.95	2		Boston (A)	9 Feb
1:46.59	Joseph	White	USA	16.11.95	4	Millrose	New York (Armory)	9 Feb
1:46.61	Erik	Sowinski	USA	21.12.89	5	Millrose	New York (Armory)	9 Feb
1:46.62	Saul	Ordóñez	ESP	10.4.94	3		Boston (R)	26 Jan
1:46.63	Álvaro	de Arriba	ESP	2.6.94	1		Düsseldorf	20 Feb
1:46.67	Edose	Ibadin	NGR	27.2.93	1		Boston (A)	24 Feb
1:46.75	Amel	Tuka	BIH	9.1.91	1		Ostrava	12 Feb

1:46.87	Robert	Heppenstall	CAN	28.2.97	23 Feb	1:47.18	Balázs	Vindics	HUN	28.3.94	3	Feb
1:46.91	Isaiah	Jewett	USA	6.2.97	26 Jan	1:47.24#	Cooper	Williams	USA	9.3.98	16	Feb
1:46.92	Mark	English	IRL	18.3.93	13 Feb	1:47.27	Joseph	Deng	AUS	7.7.98	16	Feb
1:46.98	Guy	Learmonth	GBR	20.4.92	26 Jan	1:47.28	Vincent	Crisp	USA	17.8.97	26	Jan
1:46.99	Filip	Snejdr	CZE	16.4.95	12 Feb	1:47.28	Danyil	Peremetov	RUS	18.3.95	3	Feb
1:47.05	Carlton	Orange	USA	11.3.97	26 Jan	1:47.29	Jonah	Koech	KEN	12.12.96	26	Jan
1:47.13	Jamie	Webb	GBR	1.6.94	3 Mar	1:47.29	Michał	Rozmys	POL	13.3.95	2	Feb

1000 METRES

2:18.34#	Yomif	Kejelcha	ETH	1.8.97	1	Seattle	12 Jan
2:18.64#	Clayton	Murphy	USA	26.2.95	2	Seattle	12 Jan
2:18.98	Craig	Engels	USA	1.5.94	1	New York (Armory)	26 Jan
2:19.18#	Brannon	Kidder	USA	18.11.93	3	Seattle	12 Jan
2:19.35	Abraham	Alvarado	USA	4.8.95	1	Boston (A)	26 Jan
2:19.78	Johnny	Gregorek	USA	7.12.91	2	New York (Armory)	26 Jan
2:19.87#	Sam	Prakel	USA	29.10.94	4	Seattle	12 Jan

1500 METRES

3:31.04	Samuel	Tefera	ETH	23.10.99	1		Birmingham	16 Feb
3:31.25+	Yomif	Kejelcha	ETH	1.8.97	1	in 1M	Boston (A)	3 Mar
3:35.10	Stewart	McSweyn	AUS	1.6.95	3		Birmingham	16 Feb
3:35.21+	Johnny	Gregorek	USA	7.12.91	2	in 1M	Boston (A)	3 Mar
3:35.66+	Sam	Prakel	USA	29.10.94	3	in 1M	Boston (A)	3 Mar
3:35.72	Josh	Kerr	GBR	8.10.97	4		Birmingham	16 Feb
3:35.79+	Craig	Engels	USA	1.5.94	4	in 1M	Boston (A)	3 Mar
3:36.02	Jakob	Ingebrigtsen	NOR-J	19.9.00	1		Düsseldorf	20 Feb
3:36.09+	Henry	Wynne	USA	18.4.95	5	in 1M	Boston (A)	3 Mar
3:36.50	Marcin	Lewandowski	POL	13.6.87	2		Torun	6 Feb
3:36.63	Kalle	Berglund	SWE	11.3.96	3		Torun	6 Feb
3:37.14+	Rob	Napolitano	USA	3.11.94	6	in 1M	Boston (A)	3 Mar
3:37.40+	Clayton	Murphy	USA	26.2.95	2	in 1M	New York (Armory)	9 Feb
3:37.42	Chris	O'Hare	GBR	23.11.90	5		Birmingham	16 Feb
3:37.50+	Bethwel	Birgen	KEN	6.8.88	2	in 1M	Boston (R)	26 Jan
3:37.52	Ryan	Gregson	AUS	26.4.90	6		Birmingham	16 Feb
3:37.71+	Edward	Cheserek	KEN	2.2.94	3	in 1M	New York (Armory)	9 Feb
3:37.90+	Jeremy	Hernandez	USA	13.4.96	7	in 1M	Boston (A)	3 Mar
3:38.01	Vincent	Kibet	KEN	6.5.91	7		Birmingham	16 Feb
3:38.32	Neil	Gourley	GBR	7.2.95	8		Birmingham	16 Feb

3:38.53	Michał	Rozmys	POL	13.3.95	4		Torun				6 Feb
3:38.60	Aman	Wote	ETH	18.4.84	6 Feb	3:39.17	Simon	Denissel	FRA	22.5.90	2 Feb
3:38.62	Filip	Ingebrigtsen	NOR	20.4.93	20 Feb	3:39.40	Saul	Ordóñez	ESP	10.4.94	2 Feb
3:39.04	Charlie Da'Vall	Grice	GBR	7.11.93	16 Feb	3:39.50+	Oliver	Hoare	AUS	29.1.97	9 Feb
3:39.16+	Nick	Willis	NZL	25.4.83	9 Feb	3:39.53	Elliot	Giles	GBR	26.5.94	16 Feb

1 MILE

3:47.01	Yomif	Kejelcha	ETH	1.8.97	1		Boston (A)	3 Mar
3:49.98	Johnny	Gregorek	USA	7.12.91	2		Boston (A)	3 Mar
3.50.94	Sam	Prakel	USA	29.10.94	3		Boston (A)	3 Mar
3:51.26	Henry	Wynne	USA	18.4.95	4		Boston (A)	3 Mar
3:53.29	Edward	Cheserek	KEN	2.2.94	2	Millrose	New York (Armory)	9 Feb
3:53.30	Clayton	Murphy	USA	26.2.95	3	Millrose	New York (Armory)	9 Feb
3:53.65	Josh	Kerr	GBR	8.10.97	4	Millrose	New York (Armory)	9 Feb
3:53.89	Craig	Engels	USA	1.5.94	5		Boston (A)	3 Mar
3:54.28	Rob	Napolitano	USA	3.11.94	6		Boston (A)	3 Mar
3:54.77	Vladimir	Nikitin	RUS	5.8.92	1	Winter	Moskva	3 Feb
3:54.80	Nick	Willis	NZL	25.4.83	6	Millrose	New York (Armory)	9 Feb
3:54.82	Bethwel	Birgen	KEN	6.8.88	2		Boston (R)	26 Jan
3:54.83	Oliver	Hoare	AUS	29.1.97	7	Millrose	New York (Armory)	9 Feb
3:55.32#	Amos	Bartelsmeyer	GER	25.7.94	2		Seattle	12 Jan
3:55.66	Jeremy	Hernandez	USA	13.4.96	7		Boston (A)	3 Mar

3:56.41	Marcin	Lewandowski	POL	13.6.87	13 Feb	3:56.78	Waleed	Suliman	USA	22.9.98	9 Feb
3:56.46	Stewart	McSweyn	AUS	1.6.95	13 Feb	3:56.85	Ryan	Gregson	AUS	26.4.90	13 Feb
3:56.60	Nanami	Arai	JPN	26.12.94	24 Feb	3:56.93	Vincent	Kibet	KEN	6.5.91	26 Jan

2000 METRES

5:00.34	Birhanu	Yemataw	BRN	27.2.96	1	Liévin	10 Feb
5:00.55	Soufiane	El Bakkali	MAR	7.1.96	2	Liévin	10 Feb

3000 Metres

7:37.41	Hagos	Gebrhiwet	ETH	11.5.94	1		Boston (R)	26 Jan
7:42.62	Grant	Fisher	USA	22.4.97	1	Millrose	New York (Armory)	9 Feb
7:42.76	Morgan	McDonald	AUS	20.4.96	2	Millrose	New York (Armory)	9 Feb
7:42.93	Edward	Cheserek	KEN	2.2.94	2		Boston (R)	26 Jan
7:44.77	Amon	Kemboi	KEN	16.1.87	3	Millrose	New York (Armory)	9 Feb
7:44.90	Stewart	McSweyn	AUS	1.6.95	1		Metz	10 Feb
7:45.56	Adel	Mechaal	ESP	5.12.90	3		Boston (R)	26 Jan
7:46.00	Birhanu	Yemataw	BRN	27.2.96	1		Mondeville	2 Feb
7:46.45	Vladimir	Nikitin	RUS	5.8.92	1		Yekaterinburg	7 Jan
7:46.50	Andrew	Butchart	GBR	14.10.91	4		Boston (R)	26 Jan
7:47.29	Chala	Beyo	ETH	18.1.96	2		Mondeville	2 Feb
7:47.60	Antonio	Abadía	ESP	2.7.90	1		Valencia	18 Jan

7:47.78	Chris	O'Hare	GBR	23.11.90	26 Jan	7:48.81	Oliver	Hoare	AUS	29.1.97	26 Jan
7:48.03	Eric	Avila	USA	3.10.89	9 Feb	7:49.16	Sam	Parsons	GER	18.6.94	26 Jan
7:48.36	Patrick	Tiernan	AUS	11.9.94	9 Feb	7:49.47#	Amos	Bartelsmeyer	GER	25.7.94	26 Jan
7:48.72	Travis	Mahoney	USA	25.7.90	9 Feb	7:49.73	Filip	Ingebrigtsen	NOR	20.4.93	10 Feb
7:48.76	Jesús	Gómez	ESP	24.4.91	18 Jan	7:49.95	Brian	Barraza	USA	16.5.95	9 Feb
7:48.80	Ben	Flanagan	CAN	11.1.95	26 Jan	7:50.17	Kyle	Mau	USA	27.8.96	26 Jan

5000 METRES

13:08.05	Edward	Cheserek	KEN	2.2.94	1	Boston (A)	24 Feb
13:10.23	Emmanuel	Bor	USA	14.4.88	2	Boston (A)	24 Feb
13:14.96	Hillary	Bor	USA	22.11.89	3	Boston (A)	24 Feb
13:21.35	Sean	McGorty	USA	8.3.95	1	Boston (A)	8 Feb
13:21.97	Marc	Scott	GBR	21.12.93	2	Boston (A)	8 Feb
13:27.81	Hyuga	Endo	JPN	5.8.98	3	Boston (A)	8 Feb

60 METRES HURDLES

7.35	Grant	Holloway	USA	19.11.97	1	NCAA	Birmingham	9 Mar
7.41	Daniel	Roberts	USA	13.4.98	2	NCAA	Birmingham	9 Mar
7.49	Orlando	Ortega	ESP	29.7.91	1		Torun	6 Feb
7.51	Jarret	Eaton	USA	24.6.89	1		Birmingham	16 Feb
7.52	Pascal	Martinot-Lagarde	FRA	22.9.91	1	NC	Miramas	16 Feb
7.52	Milan	Trajkovic	CYP	17.3.92	2		Düsseldorf	20 Feb
7.53	Trey	Cunningham	USA	26.8.98	1		New York (Armory)	25 Jan
7.53	Freddie	Crittenden	USA	3.8.94	2		Birmingham	16 Feb
7.56	Aaron	Mallett	USA	26.9.94	1h1		Iowa City	19 Jan
7.56	Jason	Joseph	SUI	11.10.98	1h3	NC	St. Gallen	17 Feb
7.57	Aurel	Manga	FRA	24.7.92	2	NC	Miramas	16 Feb
7.60	Devon	Allen	USA	12.12.94	1	NC	Staten Island	24 Feb
7.61	Wilhem	Belocian	FRA	22.6.95	2		Metz	10 Feb
7.61	Andy	Pozzi	GBR	15.5.92	2s2	FI	Glasgow	3 Mar
7.02	Konstantin	Shabanov	RUS	17.11.89	1	NC	Moskva	14 Feb
7.62	Gabriel	Constantino	BRA	9.2.95	4		Birmingham	16 Feb

7.62	Gregor	Traber	GER	2.12.92	1 NC	Leipzig	16 Feb
7.62		Zeng Jianhang	CHN	17.9.98	1	Hangzhou	20 Mar
7.63A		Xie Wenjun	CHN	11.7.90	1	Albuquerque	9 Feb
7.63A	Yaqoub	Al-Yoha	KUW	31.1.93	1	Tehran	4 Mar

7.64	Josh	Thompson	USA	16.1.93	19 Jan	7.65	Konstadínos	Douvalídis	GRE	10.3.87	3 Mar
7.64	David	King	GBR	13.6.94	16 Feb	7.66	Damion	Thomas	JAM	29.6.99	18 Jan
7.64	Yidiel	Contreras	ESP	27.11.92	16 Feb	7.66	Chad	Zallow	USA	25.4.97	26 Jan
7.65	Elmo	Lakka	FIN	10.4.93	2 Mar	7.66	Lorenzo	Perini	ITA	22.7.94	2 Mar

HIGH JUMP

2.35	Naoto	Tobe	JPN	31.3.92	1	Karlsruhe	2 Feb
2.34		Wang Yu	CHN	18.8.91	2	Düsseldorf	20 Feb
2.32	Gianmarco	Tamberi	ITA	1.6.92	1 NC	Ancona	16 Feb
2.31	Ivan	Ukhov	RUS	29.3.86	1	Chelyabinsk	17 Jan
2.31	Shelby	McEwen	USA	6.4.96	1	Columbia	2 Feb
2.30	Maksim	Nedosekov	BLR	21.1.98	1	Minsk	22 Dec
2.30	Andrii	Protsenko	UKR	20.5.88	1 NC	Sumy	8 Feb
2.30	Mikhail	Akimenko	RUS	6.12.95	1 NC	Moskva	14 Feb
2.28	Daniyil	Tsyplakov	RUS	29.7.92	1	Moskva	14 Jan
2.28	Tihomir	Ivanov	BUL	11.7.94	1 BalkC	Istanbul	16 Feb
2.28	Semen	Pozdnyakov	RUS	28.11.92	1	Sankt Peterburg	17 Feb
2.28	Aleksandr	Asanov	RUS	30.8.95	2	Sankt Peterburg	17 Feb
2.28	Juvaughn	Harrison	USA	30.4.99	1 SEC	Fayetteville	22 Feb
2.28	Keenon	Laine	USA	12.6.97	2 SEC	Fayetteville	22 Feb
2.28	Tejaswin	Shankar	IND	21.12.98	1 Big 12	Lubbock	23 Feb
2.28	Mateusz	Przybylko	GER	9.3.92	Q EI	Glasgow	1 Mar

2.27	Jeron	Robinson	USA	30.4.91	12 Jan	2.26	Joel	Castro	PUR	28.1.91	23 Jan
2.27A	Ernie	Sears	USA	4.12.98	19 Jan	2.26	Martin	Heindl	CZE	2.6.92	26 Jan
2.27	Ilya	Ivanyuk	RUS	9.3.93	1 Feb	2.26	Sylwester	Bednarek	POL	28.4.89	26 Jan
2.27	Edgar	Rivera	MEX	13.2.91	9 Feb	2.26	Lukás	Beer	SVK	23.8.89	5 Feb
2.27	Konstadínos	Baniótis	GRE	6.11.86	9 Feb	2.26	Darius	Carbin	USA	4.3.98	9 Feb
2.27	Donald	Thomas	BAH	1.7.84	9 Feb	2.26	Alperen	Acet	TUR	2.4.98	16 Feb
2.27	Chris	Baker	GBR	2.2.91	9 Feb	2.26	Falk	Wendrich	GER	12.6.95	17 Feb
2.26	Roberto	Vilches	MEX	21.5.99	11 Jan	2.25	four men				
2.26	Darryl	Sullivan	USA	28.12.97	19 Jan						

POLE VAULT

5.93	Piotr	Lisek	POL	16.8.92	1	Clermont-Ferrand	24 Feb
5.93	Sam	Kendricks	USA	7.9.92	2	Clermont-Ferrand	24 Feb
5.92	Armand	Duplantis	SWE	10.11.99	1 SEC	Fayetteville	22 Feb
5.90	Paweł	Wojciechowski	POL	6.6.89	1 EI	Glasgow	2 Mar
5.88	Andrew	Irwin	USA	24.1.93	1	Fayetteville	8 Feb
5.87	Kurtis	Marschall	AUS	25.4.97	3	Clermont-Ferrand	24 Feb
5.83	Matt	Ludwig	USA	5.7.96	1	Akron	25 Jan
5.82	Renaud	Lavillenie	FRA	18.9.86	1	Tignes	10 Jan
5.82	Melker	Svärd Jacobsson	SWE	8.1.94	1 v3N	Rud	10 Feb
5.80	Thiago	Braz da Silva	BRA	16.12.93	5	Clermont-Ferrand	24 Feb
5.80	Claudio Michel	Stecchi	ITA	23.11.91	6	Clermont-Ferrand	24 Feb
5.75	Emmanouíl	Karalís	GRE	20.10.99	1	Mondeville	2 Feb
5.75	Chris	Nilsen	USA	13.1.98	1	Brookings	22 Feb
5.73A	Sondre	Guttormsen	NOR	1.6.99	1	Albuquerque	8 Feb
5.73	Jacob	Wooten	USA	22.4.97	3 NCAA	Birmingham	8 Mar
5.71	Axel	Chapelle	FRA	24.4.95	1	Orléans	12 Jan
5.71	Alioune	Sène	FRA	3.2.96	2	Orléans	12 Jan
5.71A	Seito	Yamamoto	JPN	11.3.92	2	Reno	18 Jan
5.71	Scott	Houston	USA	11.6.90	1	Blacksburg	2 Feb
5.70	Konstadínos	Filippídis	GRE	26.11.86	4	Cottbus	30 Jan
5.70	Robert	Sobera	POL	19.1.91	3	Lódz	4 Feb
5.70	Bo Kanda	Lita Baehre	GER	29.4.99	1	Chemnitz	10 Feb
5.70	Georgiy	Gorokhov	RUS	20.4.93	Q EI	Glasgow	1 Mar
5.68	KC	Lightfoot	USA	11.11.99	1	Lubbock	15 Feb
5.65	Raphael	Holzdeppe	GER	28.9.89	6	Cottbus	30 Jan
5.63A	Cole	Walsh	USA	14.6.95	1	Flagstaff	2 Feb
5.63	Zachery	Bradford	USA	29.11.99	3	Fayetteville	8 Feb
5.63	Devin	King	USA	12.3.96	4	Fayetteville	8 Feb
5.63A	Audie	Wyatt	USA	30.4.96	2	Albuquerque	8 Feb
5.63	Hussain Asim	Al-Hizam	KSA	4.1.98	2 Big 12	Lubbock	22 Feb
5.63	Clayton	Fritsch	USA		7 NCAA	Birmingham	8 Mar
5.62	Thibaut	Collet	FRA	17.6.99	1=	Clermont-Ferrand	22 Feb
5.62	Ethan	Cormont	FRA-J	29.9.00	1=	Clermont-Ferrand	22 Feb

5.60	Yevgeniy	Lukyanenko	RUS	23.1.85	30 Jan	5.58	Branson	Ellis	USA	19.7.00	8 Mar
5.60		Zhang Wei	CHN	22.3.94	9 Feb	5.57	Pål Haugen	Lillefosse	NOR	4.6.01	16 Feb
5.60	Jake	Albright	USA	22.12.93	15 Feb	5.56	Urho	Kujanpää	FIN	18.5.97	16 Jan
5.60		Ding Bangchao	CHN	11.10.96	3 Mar	5.56	Malte	Mohr	GER	24.7.86	1 Feb
5.58	Drew	McMichael	USA	25.5.96	22 Feb	5.55	eight men				

LONG JUMP

8.38	Miltiádis	Tentóglou	GRE	18.3.98	1	EI	Glasgow		3 Mar
8.30	Aleksandr	Menkov	RUS	7.12.90	1	Winter	Moskva		3 Feb
8.21	Juan Miguel	Echevarría	CUB	11.8.98	1		Birmingham		16 Feb
8.21		Huang Changzhou	CHN	20.8.94	1		Nanjing		19 Feb
8.17	Thobias	Nilsson Montler	SWE	15.2.96	2	EI	Glasgow		3 Mar
8.11		Zhang Yaoguang	CHN	21.6.93	2		Nanjing		19 Feb
8.10	Tajay	Gayle	JAM	2.8.96	2		Birmingham		10 Feb
8.00	Rayvon	Grey	USA	2.12.97	1		Lubbock		18 Jan
8.05	Lamont Marcell	Jacobs	ITA	26.9.94	2		Madrid		8 Feb
8.04	Jean-Pierre	Bertrand	FRA	5.11.92	1	NC	Miramas		16 Feb
8.03	Serhii	Nykyforov	UKR	6.2.94	Q	EI	Glasgow		1 Mar
8.03	Strahinja	Jovancevic	SRB	28.2.93	3	EI	Glasgow		3 Mar
8.02	Grant	Holloway	USA	19.11.97	1		Fayetteville		26 Jan
8.01	Fabian	Edoki	NGR	30.3.98	1		Nashville		19 Jan
8.00		Zhang Jingqiang	CHN	8.5.96	2		Nanjing		23 Feb
7.99	Odaine	Lewis	JAM	3.12.96	1		Lubbock		12 Jan
7.99	Eusebio	Cáceres	ESP	10.9.91	1	NC	Antequera		16 Feb
7.99	Jacob	Fincham-Dukes	GBR	12.1.97	1	Big 12	Lubbock		22 Feb
7.98	Emiliano	Lasa	URU	25.1.90	3		Madrid		8 Feb
7.96	Trumaine	Jefferson	USA	19.11.97	2	NCAA	Birmingham		8 Mar
7.95A	Isaac	Grimes	USA	7.2.98	1		Golden		7 Dec

7.94	Charles	Brown	USA	1.2.88	12	Jan		7.93	Tomasz	Jaszczuk	POL	9.3.92	17	Feb
7.94	Henri	Väyrynen	FIN	16.10.91	26	Jan		7.92	Malik	Moffett	USA	11.4.94	26	Jan
7.94	Damar	Forbes	JAM	11.9.90	15	Feb		7.92		Li Zhipeng	CHN	1.5.95	27	Feb
7.94	Yann	Randrianasolo	FRA	3.2.94	16	Feb		7.91	Michel	Tornéus	SWE	26.5.86	2	Feb
7.93	Jordan	Latimer	USA	4.3.94	2	Feb		7.90	Anatoliy	Ryapolov	RUS	31.1.97	14	Feb
7.93	Héctor	Santos	ESP	6.1.98	16	Feb		7.89	Maximilian	Entholzner	GER	18.8.94	26	Jan

TRIPLE JUMP

17.58	Fabrice	Zango	BUR	25.6.93	1		Paris		27 Jan
17.46	Almir	dos Santos	BRA	4.9.93	1		Kent		9 Feb
17.35		Zhu Yaming	CHN	4.5.94	1		Nanjing		19 Feb
17.32	Pedro Pablo	Pichardo	POR	30.6.93	1		Braga		17 Feb
17.29	Nazim	Babayev	AZE	8.10.97	1	EI	Glasgow		3 Mar
17.18	Chris	Carter	USA	11.3.89	1		Houston		26 Jan
17.12	Yasser	Triki	ALG	24.3.97	1	SEC	Fayetteville		23 Feb
17.11	Nelson	Évora	POR	20.4.84	2	EI	Glasgow		3 Mar
17.10	Max	Heß	GER	13.7.96	3	EI	Glasgow		3 Mar
16.98	Simo	Lipsanen	FIN	13.9.95	2		Liévin		10 Feb
16.95	Yoann	Rapinier	FRA	29.9.89	2		Eaubonne		19 Jan
16.92	Clive	Pullen	JAM	18.10.94	1		Blacksburg		16 Feb
16.90	Jordan	Scott	JAM	29.6.97	2		Clemson		9 Feb
16.85	Donald	Scott	USA	23.2.92	1	NC	Staten Island		24 Feb
16.84	Aleksandr	Yurchenko	RUS	30.7.92	1	NC	Moskva		15 Feb
16.83	Dmitriy	Sorokin	RUS	27.9.92	2	NC	Moskva		15 Feb
16.83	Chengetayi	Mapaya	ZIM	19.12.98	1	Big 12	Lubbock		23 Feb
16.82		Fang Yaoqing	CHN	20.4.96	1		Xi'an		28 Feb
16.81	John	Warren	USA	2.3.96	1		Nashville		19 Jan
16.79	Levon	Aghasyan	ARM	19.1.95	1		Istanbul		20 Feb
16.78	Tomas	Veszelka	SVK	9.7.95	Q	EI	Glasgow		1 Mar
16.77	Jordan A.	Díaz	CUB	23.2.01	1s1		Paris		27 Jan
16.76	Simone	Forte	ITA	20.1.96	1	NC	Ancona		17 Feb
16.75	Jah-Nhai	Perinchief	BER	31.12.97	2	Big 12	Lubbock		23 Feb
16.72	Armani	Wallace	USA	11.2.97	1		Lubbock		26 Jan
16.72	Fabrizio	Donato	ITA	14.8.76	2	NC	Ancona		17 Feb
16.71	Tobia	Bocchi	ITA	7.4.97	3	NC	Ancona		17 Feb
16.69	Odaine	Lewis	JAM	13.12.96	1		Lubbock		9 Feb
16.65		Xu Xiaolong	CHN	20.12.92	2		Xi'an		28 Feb
16.65	Kevin	Luron	FRA	8.11.91	Q	EI	Glasgow		1 Mar

16.62	Can	Özüpek	TUR	2.2.96	3	Feb		16.55	Daniele	Cavazzani	ITA	4.12.92	17	Feb
16.61	Pablo	Torrijos	ESP	12.5.92	17	Feb		16.51	Adrian	Swiderski	POL	27.9.86	27	Jan
16.58	Vitaliy	Pavlov	RUS	12.1.97	25	Jan		16.51		Liu Mingxuan	CHN	16.5.97	24	Feb
16.57	Alexis	Copello	AZE	12.8.85	10	Feb		16.48	Aleksey	Fyodorov	RUS	25.5.91	15	Feb
								16.48	Nathan	Douglas	GBR	4.12.82	1	Mar

SHOT

22.33	Ryan	Crouser	USA	18.12.92	1	Millrose	New York (Armory)		9 Feb
21.81	Payton	Otterdahl	USA	2.4.96	1		Brookings		23 Feb
21.65	Michał	Haratyk	POL	10.4.92	1	EI	Glasgow		1 Mar
21.54	David	Storl	GER	27.7.90	2	EI	Glasgow		1 Mar
21.40	Joe	Kovacs	USA	28.6.89	2	NC	Staten Island		23 Feb
21.25	Tomáš	Staněk	CZE	13.0.91	3	EI	Glasgow		1 Mar
21.15	Jordan	Geist	USA	21.7.98	1		Lubbock		9 Feb
21.09	Chuk	Enekwechi	NGR	28.1.93	1		Notre Dame		16 Feb

21.08	Mesud	Pezer	BIH	27.8.94	Q	EI	Glasgow	1 Mar
21.03	Bob	Bertemes	LUX	24.5.93	1		Potsdam	13 Feb
20.98	Adrian	Piperi	USA	20.1.99	2	NCAA	Birmingham	8 Mar
20.97	Francisco	Belo	POR	27.3.91	4	EI	Glasgow	1 Mar
20.95	Konrad	Bukowiecki	POL	17.3.97	1		Lodz	4 Feb
20.81	Andrei	Gag	ROU	27.4.91	1		Bacau	26 Jan
20.72	Denzel	Comenentia	NED	25.11.95	1		Fayetteville	9 Feb
20.70	Maksim	Afonin	RUS	6.1.92	1	NC	Moskva	14 Feb
20.69	Leonardo	Fabbri	ITA	15.4.97	1	NC	Ancona	17 Feb
20.68A	Tim	Nedow	CAN	16.10.90	1		Ogden	26 Jan
20.68	O'Dayne	Richards	JAM	14.12.88	2		Nehvizdy	1 Feb
20.65	Wictor	Petersson	SWE	1.5.98	1	NC-23	Växjö	24 Feb
20.63	Josh	Awotunde	NGR/USA	12.6.95	3	NC	Staten Island	23 Feb
20.61	Eldred	Henry	IVB	18.9.94	1		Findlay	23 Feb
20.58	Marcus	Thomsen	NOR	7.1.98	1		Rud	5 Jan
20.54	Ashinia	Miller	JAM	6.6.93	3	Millrose	New York (Armory)	9 Feb
20.51	Aleksandr	Lesnoy	RUS	17.7.88	1		Volgograd	19 Jan
20.47	Jakub	Szyszkowski	POL	21.8.91	1		Spała	3 Feb
20.47	McKay	Johnson	USA	15.4.98	2		Seattle	23 Feb
20.39	Carlos	Tobalina	ESP	2.8.85	1	NC	Antequera	16 Feb
20.34	Asmir	Kolasinac	SRB	15.10.84	2		Beograd	20 Feb
20.34	Nikólaos	Skarvélis	GRE	2.2.93	Q	EI	Glasgow	1 Mar
20.33	Daniel	McArthur	USA	17.3.98	4	NCAA	Birmingham	8 Mar
20.32	Stipe	Zunic	CRO	13.12.90	3		Beograd	20 Feb
20.21	Tsanko	Arnaudov	POR	14.3.92	1		Pombal	27 Jan
20.20	Kiriákos	Zótos	GRE	17.1.96	1		Thessaloníki	19 Jan
20.16	Giorgi	Mujaridze	GEO	22.3.98	1	NC	Tbilisi	9 Feb
20.15*	Brett	Neelly	USA	22.11.96	1		Manhattan KS	8 Dec
20.06					1		Fayetteville	26 Jan
20.10	Orazio	Cremona	RSA	1.7.89	3		Sassnitz	9 Feb
20.03	Curtis	Jensen	USA	1.11.90	4	NC	Staten Island	23 Feb
20.00	David	Pless	USA	19.11.90	5	NC	Staten Island	23 Feb

19.99	Frédéric	Dagée	FRA	11.12.92	16 Feb		19.73	Oleg	Tomasevich	BLR	31.5.00	29 Jan
19.94	Coy	Blair	USA	10.6.94	9 Feb		19.69	Matt	Katnik	USA	10.10.96	8 Mar
19.91	Kemal	Mesic	BIH	4.8.85	9 Feb		19.68	Aliksey	Nichipor	BLR	10.4.93	29 Jan
19.91 ?	Zack	Short	HON		22 Feb		19.67A	Uziel	Muñoz	MEX	8.9.95	26 Jan
19.89	Kord	Ferguson	USA	19.6.95	9 Feb		19.67	Andrew	Liskowitz	USA	22.5.97	23 Feb
19.88	Konstantin	Lyadusov	RUS	2.3.88	14 Feb		19.66	Maksim	Sidorov	RUS	13.5.86	14 Feb
19.84	Dotun	Ogundeji	USA	24.2.96	23 Feb		19.66	Corey	Murphy	USA	3.11.96	17 Feb
19.83	David	Kornack	USA		9 Mar		19.65	Nick	Vena	USA	16.4.93	1 Dec
19.80	Armin	Sinancevic	SRB	14.8.96	26 Jan		19.60	Jared	Kern	USA	10.6.95	26 Jan
19.75	Christian	Zimmermann	GER	9.7.94	2 Feb		19.59	Noah	Castle	USA		8 Mar

DISCUS

63.06	Lukas	Weißhaidinger	AUT	20.2.92	1	ISTAF	Berlin	1 Feb
62.55	Martin	Wierig	GER	10.6.87	2	ISTAF	Berlin	1 Feb

WEIGHT (16KG)

24.12	Daniel	Haugh	USA	3.5.95	1	NC	Staten Island	22 Feb
24.11	Payton	Otterdahl	USA	2.4.96	1	NCAA	Birmingham	9 Mar
23.98	Conor	McCullough	USA	31.1.91	2	NC	Staten Island	22 Feb
23.67	Alex	Young	USA	1.9.94	3	NC	Staten Island	22 Feb
23.65	Grant	Cartwright	USA	19.11.94	1		Nashville	8 Feb
23.56	Joe	Ellis	GBR	10.4.96	2		Nashville	8 Feb
23.52	Denzel	Comenentia	NED	25.11.95	2		Birmingham	11 Jan

23.38	Sean	Donnelly	USA	1.4.93	22 Feb		22.95	Colin	Dunbar	USA	27.6.88	22 Feb
23.38	Adam	Kelly	EST	6.7.97	9 Mar		22.59	Thomas	Mardal	NOR	16.4.97	23 Feb
23.35	A.J.	McFarland	USA	17.3.96	23 Feb		22.57	Michael	Shanahan	USA	5.12.94	22 Feb
23.29	Gleb	Dudarov	BLR	17.10.96	22 Feb		22.47	Morgan	Shigo	USA	1.2.96	2 Feb
23.19	Daniel	Roberts	USA	11.12.94	22 Feb		22.47	David	Lucas	USA	6.6.96	16 Feb

HEPTATHLON

6218	Jorge		Ureña	ESP	8.10.93	1	EI	Glasgow	3 Mar
	6.96	7.39	14.68	2.07	7.78	5.00	2:44.27	
6156	Tim		Duckworth	GBR	18.6.96	2	EI	Glasgow	3 Mar
	6.85	7.79	12.97	2.13	8.16	5.00	2:49.44	
6145	Ilya		Shkurenyov	RUS	11.1.91	3	EI	Glasgow	3 Mar
	7.18	7.66	14.30	2.04	8.02	5.20	2:45.35	
6132	Thomas		Van Der Plaetsen	BEL	24.12.90	1	NC	Gent	3 Feb
	7.27	7.67	14.30	2.02	8.22	5.50	2:46.45	
6125	Fredrik		Samuelsson	SWE	16.2.95	4	EI	Glasgow	3 Mar
	7.06	7.66	14.69	2.07	8.20	5.00	2:45.99	
6114	Artem		Makarenko	RUS	23.4.97	1		Moskva	30 Jan
	6.90	7.27	14.47	2.00	7.74	4.90	2:43.93	

6085	Janek	Oiglane	EST	25.4.94	1		Tallinn	3 Feb
	7.07	7.34	15.16	2.01	8.13	5.19	2:46.73	
6042	Harrison	Williams	USA	7.3.96	1	NCAA	Birmingham	9 Mar
	7.05	7.35	13.59	2.03	8.13	5.16	2:43.38	
6025	Basile	Rolnin	FRA	21.1.94	1	NC	Miramas	17 Feb
	7.13	7.45	14.71	2.06	8.09	5.15	2:54.52	
6017	Andreas	Bechmann	GER	28.9.99	1	NC	Halle	27 Jan
	7.05	7.29	14.34	2.06	8.43	5.20	2:45.66	
6006	Jiří	Cykora	CZE	20.1.95	1	NC	Praha (Strom)	10 Feb
	7.02	7.50	14.56	2.01	7.95	4.75	2:47.48	
5996	Johannes	Erm	EST	26.3.98	1	SEC	Fayetteville	23 Feb
	7.12	7.55	14.37	1.95	8.13	4.94	2:41.30	
5975	Gabriel	Moore	USA	10.1.96	2	NCAA	Birmingham	9 Mar
	6.82	7.21	14.86	2.03	8.02	4.56	2:47.06	
5951	Martin	Roe	NOR	1.4.92	7	EI	Glasgow	3 Mar
	7.03	7.53	15.60	1.95	8.36	4.90	2:46.17	
5950	Karl Robert	Saluri	EST	6.8.93	2		Tallinn	3 Feb
	6.77	7.61	14.82	1.86	8.26	4.69	2:43.85	
5949	Gary	Haasbroek	AUS	15.3.99	1		Houston	26 Jan
	7.02	7.65	11.52	2.03	8.14	5.10	2:46.15	
5944	Nick	Guerrant	USA	23.9.97	3	NCAA	Birmingham	9 Mar
	7.00	7.31	13.93	2.06	8.30	4.86	2:45.33	
5907	Jan	Dolezal	CZE	6.6.96	2	NC	Praha (Strom)	10 Feb
	7.06	7.39	14.13	2.01	7.95	4.65	2:47.60	
5905	Manuel	Eitel	GER	28.1.97	3		Tallinn	3 Feb
	6.82	7.31	14.76	1.95	8.09	4.79	2:53.26	
5903	Tim	Nowak	GER	13.8.95	2	NC	Halle	27 Jan
	7.22	7.00	14.79	2.00	8.39	5.10	2:39.74	

5895	Kristjan	Rosenberg	EST	16.5.94	3 Feb		5819	Aaron	Booth	NZL	12.9.96	26 Jan
5871	Yuriy	Yeremich	BLR	24.10.95	14 Dec		5811	Mihail	Dudas	SRB	1.11.89	3 Feb
5868	Tim	Ehrhardt	USA	16.3.95	23 Feb		5809	Ayden	Owens	PUR	28.5.00	9 Mar
5863	Vasyl	Ivanytskyy	UKR	29.1.91	8 Feb		5805	Bastien	Auzeil	FRA	22.10.89	17 Feb
5851	Yevgeniy	Likhanov	RUS	10.1.95	20 Jan		5797	Julien	Ullvås	FRA	11.6.96	27 Jan
5847	Jared	Seay	USA	8.4.97	9 Mar		5797	Mathias	Brugger	GER	6.8.92	27 Jan
5825	Solomon	Simmons	USA	26.9.93	18 Jan		5796	Jérémy	Lelièvre	FRA	8.2.91	17 Feb

3000 Metres Walk: 11:06.69 Alex Wright IRL 19.12.90 1 AAIG Dublin 2 Feb

5000 Metres Walk

18:28.5	Vasiliy	Mizinov	RUS	29.12.97	1		Chelyabinsk		6 Jan
18:33.86	Christopher	Linke	GER	24.10.88	1		Halle		1 Mar
18:45.7*	Sergey	Shirobokov	RUS	16.2.99	1		Saransk		30 Dec
18:47.63	Francesco	Fortunato	ITA	13.12.94	1	NC	Ancona		16 Feb
18:51.73	Gabriel	Bordier	FRA	8.10.97	1		Rennes		2 Feb
18:53.87	Alex	Wright	IRL	19.12.90	1	NC	Dublin		16 Feb
18:58.0*	Aleksey	Kudashkin	RUS	1.2.97	30 Dec	19:08.81	Nils	Brembach	GER	23.2.93	1 Mar
19:01.8*	Sergey	Rakov	RUS	13.6.99	30 Dec	19:09.1*	Salavat	Ilkayev	RUS	14.9.00	30 Dec

WORLD INDOOR LISTS 2019 – WOMEN

60 METRES

7.02	Marie Josée	Ta Lou	CIV	18.11.88	1		Düsseldorf	20 Feb
7.08	Ewa	Swoboda	POL	26.7.97	1h1		Karlsruhe	2 Feb
7.08	Mujinga	Kambundji	SUI	17.6.92	1	NC	St. Gallen	16 Feb
7.10	English	Gardner	USA	22.4.92	1	Millrose	New York (Armory)	9 Feb
7.10		Ge Manqi	CHN	13.10.97	1		Hangzhou	19 Mar
7.12	Asha	Philip	GBR	25.10.90	1		Dortmund	27 Jan
7.13	Aleia	Hobbs	USA	24.2.96	1		Baton Rouge	15 Feb
7.13	Elaine	Thompson	JAM	28.6.92	1		Birmingham	16 Feb
7.14	Kortnei	Johnson	USA	11.8.97	2		Baton Rouge	15 Feb
7.14	Dafne	Schippers	NED	15.6.92	2	EI	Glasgow	2 Mar
7.14	Twanisha	Terry	USA	24.1.99	1	NCAA	Birmingham	9 Mar
7.15	Kiara	Parker	USA	28.10.96	1		Fayetteville	26 Jan
7.15	Orlann	Ombissa-Dzangue	FRA	26.5.91	1h1		Paris	27 Jan
7.15	Michelle-Lee	Ahye	TTO	10.4.92	2	Millrose	New York (Armory)	9 Feb
7.15	Kristina	Sivkova	RUS	28.2.97	1	NC	Moskva	13 Feb
7.15A	Destiny	Smith-Barnett	USA	26.7.96	1h3	MWC	Albuquerque	22 Feb
7.15	Kristal	Awuah	GBR	7.8.99	4	EI	Glasgow	2 Mar
7.16	Shania	Collins	USA	19.11.96	1	NC	Staten Island	24 Feb
7.17	Ajla	Del Ponte	SUI	15.7.96	2	NC	St. Gallen	16 Feb
7.18A	Marybeth	Sant	USA	6.4.95	1		Boulder	12 Jan
7.18A	Kandace	Thomas	USA	6.2.93	1	RMAC	Alamosa	23 Feb
7.19	Javianne	Oliver	USA	26.12.94	3	Millrose	New York (Armory)	9 Feb
7.19	Rachel	Miller	GBR	29.1.90	3h1		Birmingham	16 Feb
7.19	Lisa Marie	Kwayie	GER	27.10.96	1	NC	Leipzig	16 Feb

Mark	First	Last	Nat	DOB	Pos	Meet	Place	Date
7.19	Teahna	Daniels	USA	27.3.97	2	NCAA	Birmingham	9 Mar
7.19	Ka'tia	Seymour	USA	3.10.97	3	NCAA	Birmingham	9 Mar

Mark	First	Last	Nat	DOB	Date		Mark	First	Last	Nat	DOB	Date
7.20	Sha'Carri	Richardson	USA	25.3.00	26 Jan		7.23	Tamara	Clark	USA	9.1.99	26 Jan
7.20	Deajah	Stevens	USA	19.5.95	9 Feb		7.23	Rebekka	Haase	GER	2.1.93	2 Feb
7.20	Remona	Burchell	JAM	15.9.91	16 Feb		7.23	Imani	Lansiquot	GBR	17.12.97	6 Feb
7.21	Kristina	Timanovskaya	BLR	19.11.96	18 Jan		7.23	Kate	Hall	USA	12.1.97	24 Feb
7.21	Maja	Mihalinec	SLO	17.12.89	2 Mar		7.24	Carolle	Zahi	FRA	12.6.94	26 Jan
7.21	Dianna	Johnson	JAM	12.11.95	9 Mar		7.24	Maia	McCoy	USA	9.12.96	8 Feb
7.22	Kiara	Grant	JAM	8.10.00	23 Feb		7.24	Jamile	Samuel	NED	24.4.92	20 Feb
7.23	Gabriele	Cunningham	USA	22.2.98	26 Jan		7.25	six women				

200 METRES

Mark	First	Last	Nat	DOB	Pos	Meet	Place	Date
22.66	Kayla	White	USA	24.9.96	1	NCAA	Birmingham	9 Mar
22.80	Anavia	Battle	USA	28.3.99	1	Big 10	Ann Arbor	23 Feb
22.83	Angie	Annelus	USA	10.1.97	1r2		Lubbock	15 Feb
22.88	Kynnedy	Flannel	USA-J	12.7.00	1		Clemson	19 Jan
22.90	Tamara	Clark	USA	9.1.99	1	SEC	Fayetteville	23 Feb
22.91	Lanae-Tava	Thomas	USA-J	28.1.01	1r1		Lubbock	15 Feb
22.93	Lauren Rain	Williams	USA	25.7.99	2r2		Lubbock	15 Feb
22.97	Abby	Steiner	USA	24.11.99	1		Fayetteville	25 Jan
22.97	Payton	Chadwick	USA	29.11.95	2		Fayetteville	25 Jan
23.00	Jayla	Kirkland	USA	13.2.99	2rB		Lubbock	15 Feb

Mark	First	Last	Nat	DOB	Date		Mark	First	Last	Nat	DOB	Date
23.02	Brenessa	Thompson	GUY	22.7.96	26 Jan		23.10	Kendra	Harrison	USA	18.9.92	9 Feb
23.03	Maia	McCoy	USA	9.12.96	22 Feb		23.12	Ka'tia	Seymour	USA	3.10.97	15 Feb
23.03	Kiana	Horton	USA	29.1.97	22 Feb		23.12	Brianne	Bethel	BAH		15 Feb
23.04	Rebekka	Haase	GER	2.1.93	16 Feb		23.13	Kiara	Parker	USA	28.10.96	22 Feb
23.04	Kortnei	Johnson	USA	11.8.97	8 Mar		23.16	Savyon	Toombs	USA	2.6.98	16 Feb
23.08	Sha'Carri	Richardson	USA-J	25.3.00	9 Feb		23.19	Cambrea	Sturgis	USA	27.3.99	9 Feb

300 METRES

Mark	First	Last	Nat	DOB	Pos	Meet	Place	Date
35.95	Brittany	Brown	USA	18.4.95	1	NC	Staten Island	23 Feb
35.98	Gabby	Thomas	USA	7.12.96	2	NC	Staten Island	23 Feb
36.69	Cynthia	Bolingo Mbongo	BEL	12.1.93	1		Gent	23 Feb

Mark	First	Last	Nat	DOB	Date		Mark	First	Last	Nat	DOB	Date
36.72	Léa	Sprunger	SUI	5.3.90	10 Feb		36.97	Kendall	Ellis	USA	8.3.96	26 Jan
36.75	Jordan	Lavender	USA	23.7.93	19 Jan		37.01	Tamara	Clark	USA	9.1.99	11 Jan

400 METRES

Mark	First	Last	Nat	DOB	Pos	Meet	Place	Date
51.50	Kaelin	Roberts	USA	6.1.99	1	NCAA	Birmingham	9 Mar
51.61	Léa	Sprunger	SUI	5.3.90	1	EI	Glasgow	2 Mar
51.62	Cynthia	Bolingo Mbongo	BEL	12.1.93	2	EI	Glasgow	2 Mar
51.86	Antonina	Krivoshapka	RUS	21.7.87	1	Winter	Moskva	3 Feb
51.91	Iga	Baumgart-Witan	POL	11.4.89	1		Torun	6 Feb
52.02	Lynna	Irby	USA	6.12.98	1	SEC	Fayetteville	23 Feb
52.09	Syaira	Richardson	USA	29.10.98	2	SEC	Fayetteville	23 Feb
52.14	Justyna	Swiety-Ersetic	POL		2		Torun	6 Feb
52.14	Alexis	Holmes	USA-J	28.1.00	1	Big 10	Ann Arbor	23 Feb
52.18	Kiana	Horton	USA	29.1.97	1	Big 12	Lubbock	23 Feb
52.24	Stephenie Ann	McPherson	JAM	25.11.88	1		Birmingham	16 Feb
52.27	Aliyah	Abrams	GUY	3.4.97	2	NCAA	Birmingham	9 Mar
52.31	Phil	Healy	IRL	19.11.94	1		Wien	26 Jan

Mark	First	Last	Nat	DOB	Date		Mark	First	Last	Nat	DOB	Date
52.32	Anna	Kiełbasinska	POL	26.6.90	17 Feb		52.52	Tierra	Robinson-Jones	USA	22.11.99	23 Feb
52.32	Kyra	Constantine	CAN	1.8.98	9 Mar		52.53	Deborah	Sananes	FRA	26.10.95	17 Feb
52.33	Agné	Serksniené	LTU	18.2.88	1 Mar		52.54	Hannah	Waller	USA	22.6.98	26 Jan
52.34	Lisanne	de Witte	NED	10.9.92	2 Mar		52.55	Athing	Mu	USA-Y	8.6.02	23 Feb
52.43	Eilidh	Doyle	GBR	20.2.87	16 Feb		52.57	Ayomide	Folorunso	ITA	17.10.96	2 Feb
52.46	Polina	Miller	RUS-J	9.6.00	1 Mar		52.57	Agnes	Raharolahy	FRA	7.11.92	17 Feb
52.48	Raphaela	Lukudo	ITA	29.7.94	2 Mar		52.60	Kethlin	Campbell	USA	29.4.99	23 Feb
52.51	Sara	Limp	USA		9 Feb		**Oversized track**					
52.51	Sharrika	Barnett	JAM	16.4.97	23 Feb		52.07	Kyra	Constantine	CAN	1.8.98	23 Feb
							52.34	Gabby	Scott	PUR	13.1.97	23 Feb

500 Metres: 1:09.46 Sydney McLaughlin USA 7.8.99 1 Boston (R) 26 Jan

600 METRES

Mark	First	Last	Nat	DOB	Pos	Meet	Place	Date
1:23.57	Athing	Mu	USA-Y	8.6.02	1	NC	Staten Island	24 Feb
1:24.88	Raevyn	Rogers	USA	7.9.96	2	NC	Staten Island	24 Feb
1:25.91	Ajee'	Wilson	USA	8.5.94	1		New York (Armory)	26 Jan
1:26.33	Natoya	Goule	JAM	30.3.91	1		Clemson	19 Jan
1:26.75	Olivia	Baker	USA	12.6.96	2		New York (Armory)	26 Jan

800 METRES

Mark	First	Last	Nat	DOB	Pos	Meet	Place	Date
1:58.60	Ajee'	Wilson	USA	8.5.94	1	Millrose	New York (Armory)	9 Feb
1:59.13	Natoya	Goule	JAM	30.3.91	2	Millrose	New York (Armory)	9 Feb
1:59.37	Aleksandra	Gulyayeva	RUS	30.4.94	1	Winter	Moskva	3 Feb
1:59.49	Habitam	Alemu	ETH	9.7.97	1		Torun	6 Feb
1:59.50	Laura	Muir	GBR	9.5.93	2		Torun	6 Feb

1:59.74	Ce'Aira	Brown	USA	4.11.93	3	Millrose	New York (Armory)	9 Feb
1:59.80	Laura	Roesler	USA	19.12.91	1		Boston (A)	8 Feb
1:59.87	Jenna	Westaway	CAN	19.6.94	1		Boston (A)	24 Feb
2:00.40	Sofia	Ennaoui	POL	30.8.95	3		Torun	6 Feb
2:00.59	Yekaterina	Zavyalova	RUS	1.3.91	1	NC	Moskva	14 Feb
2:00.98	Selina	Büchel	SUI	26.7.91	4		Torun	6 Feb
2:01.08	Claudia	Saunders	FRA	19.5.94	2		Boston (A)	24 Feb
2:01.10	Liga	Velvere	LAT	10.2.90	1		Eaubonne	12 Feb
2:01.10	Shelayna	Oskan-Clarke	GBR	20.1.90	1		Birmingham	16 Feb
2:01.33	Raevyn	Rogers	USA	7.9.96	4	Millrose	New York (Armory)	9 Feb
2:01.46	Esther	Guerrero	ESP	7.2.90	1		Sabadell	6 Feb
2:01.75	Cynthia	Anais	FRA	18.1.88	2		Eaubonne	12 Feb
2:01.83	Svetlana	Uloga	RUS	23.11.86	3	NC	Moskva	14 Feb
2:01.95	Adelle	Tracey	GBR	27.5.93	2		Birmingham	16 Feb
2:02.00	Renelle	Lamote	FRA	26.12.93	5		Torun	6 Feb

2:02.03	Nelly	Jepkosgei	KEN	14.7.91	10 Feb		2:02.64	Diribe	Welteji	ETH-Y	13.5.02	10 Feb
2:02.15	Zoya	Naumov	ESP	17.7.95	6 Feb		2:02.65	Allie	Wilson	USA	31.3.96	8 Feb
2:02.15	Renée	Eykens	BEL	8.6.96	16 Feb		2:02.70	Lovisa	Lindh	SWE	0.7.01	10 Feb
2:02.18	Mahelet	Mulugeta	ETH	20.3.95	6 Feb		2:02.80#	Hanna	Green	USA	16.10.94	15 Feb
2:02.28	Lynsey	Sharp	GBR	11.7.90	16 Feb		2:02.92	Shannon	Osika	USA	15.6.93	2 Feb
2:02.34	Mari	Smith	GBR	14.11.96	16 Feb		2:02.92	Emily	Richards	USA	21.7.95	8 Feb
2:02.50	Diana	Mezuliáníková	CZE	10.4.92	17 Feb		2:02.94	Danae	Rivers	USA	3.2.98	26 Jan
2:02.59	Sanne	Wolters-Verstegen	NED	10.11.85	2 Mar		2:02.94	Simona	Vrzalová	CZE	7.4.88	17 Feb

1000 METRES

2:34.71	Ajee'	Wilson	USA	8.5.94	1	NC	Staten Island	24 Feb
2:35.40	Hanna	Green	USA	16.10.94	2	NC	Staten Island	24 Feb
2:35.62	Ce'Aira	Brown	USA	4.11.93	3	NC	Staten Island	24 Feb
2:36.03	Aleksandra	Gulyayeva	RUS	30.4.94	1		Yekaterinburg	7 Jan
2:36.60	Laura	Roesler	USA	19.12.91	4	NC	Staten Island	24 Feb
2:37.04	Jenna	Westaway	CAN	19.6.94	1		Boston (A)	8 Feb

2:37.40	Genzebe	Dibaba	ETH	8.2.91	10 Feb		2:38.21	Rabab	Arrafi	MAR	12.1.91	10 Feb
2:37.55	Natoya	Goule	JAM	30.3.91	26 Jan		2:38.59	Danae	Rivers	USA	3.2.98	12 Jan
2:37.78	Madeleine	Kelly	CAN	28.12.95	8 Feb		2:38.60	Hannah	Fields	USA	4.2.93	24 Feb
2:37.80	Winnie	Nanyondo	UGA	23.8.93	10 Feb		2:38.95	Claudia	Saunders	FRA	19.5.94	26 Jan

1500 METRES

3:59.08	Genzebe	Dibaba	ETH	8.2.91	1			Sabadell	6 Feb
4:01.84+	Laura	Muir	GBR	9.5.93	1	in 1M		Birmingham	16 Feb
4:02.70+	Konstanze	Klosterhalfen	GER	18.2.97	1	in 1M		New York (Armory)	9 Feb
4:05.22	Sofia	Ennaoui	POL	30.8.95	1			Ostrava	12 Feb
4:05.73	Simona	Vrzalová	CZE	7.4.88	2			Ostrava	12 Feb
4:06.16+	Colleen	Quigley	USA	20.11.92	2	in 1M		New York (Armory)	9 Feb
4:06.55+	Kate	Grace	USA	24.10.88	3	in 1M		New York (Armory)	9 Feb
4:06.76	Ciara	Mageean	IRL	12.3.92	1			Athlone	13 Feb
4:07.05	Claudia	Bobocea	ROU	11.6.92	2			Athlone	13 Feb
4:07.64+	Shannon	Osika	USA	15.6.93	4	in 1M		New York (Armory)	9 Feb
4:08.05	Marta	Pérez	ESP	19.4.93	1h2	EI		Glasgow	1 Mar
4:08.09	Marusa	Mismas	SLO	24.10.94	3			Ostrava	12 Feb
4:08.31	Darya	Borisevich	BLR	6.4.90	4h2	EI		Glasgow	1 Mar
4:08.36+	Gabriela	DeBues-Stafford	CAN	13.9.95	1	in 1M		Boston (R)	26 Jan
4:08.36+	Cory	McGee	USA	29.5.92	5	in 1M		New York (Armory)	9 Feb
4:08.38+	Dawit	Seyaum	ETH	27.7.96	2	in 1M		Boston (R)	26 Jan
4:08.48	Amela	Terzic	SRB	2.1.93	1			Istanbul	17 Feb
4:08.50+	Elinor	Purrier	USA	20.2.95	3	in 1M		Boston (R)	26 Jan
4:08.59+	Katie	Mackey	USA	12.11.87	6	in 1M		New York (Armory)	9 Feb
4:08.00	Hailu	Lemlem	ETH	21.5.01	2			Oubadell	6 Feb
4:09.32	Yekaterina	Korneyenko	BLR	17.3.88	2h1	EI		Glasgow	1 Mar
4:09.58	Luiza	Gega	ALB	5.11.88	3			Istanbul	17 Feb

4:10.13+	Yolanda	Ngarambe	SWE	14.9.91	26 Jan		4:11.24+	Danae	Rivers	USA	3.2.98	12 Feb
4:10.17+	Brenda	Martinez	USA	8.9.87	26 Jan		4:11.36	Renata	Plis	POL	5.2.85	12 Feb
4:10.39	Solange Andreia	Pereira	ESP	12.12.89	18 Jan		4:11.38	Caterina	Granz	GER	14.3.94	9 Feb
4:10.81	Esther	Guerrero	ESP	7.2.90	18 Jan		4:11.55+	Helen	Schlachtenhaufen	USA	14.3.95	9 Feb
4:10.98+	Amanda	Eccleston	USA	18.6.90	9 Feb		4:11.73	Hanna	Klein	GER	6.4.93	27 Jan
4:11.01	Anna	Silvander	SWE	22.6.93	1 Mar		4:11.81	Violah	Lagat	KEN	13.3.89	17 Feb

I MILE

4:18.75	Laura	Muir	GBR	9.5.93	1		Birmingham	16 Feb
4:19.98	Konstanze	Klosterhalfen	GER	18.2.97	1	Millrose	New York (Armory)	9 Feb
4:22.86	Colleen	Quigley	USA	20.11.92	2	Millrose	New York (Armory)	9 Feb
4:24.27	Kate	Grace	USA	24.10.88	3	Millrose	New York (Armory)	9 Feb
4:24.80	Gabriela	DeBues-Stafford	CAN	13.9.95	1		Boston (R)	26 Jan
4:24.88	Elinor	Purrier	USA	20.2.95	2		Boston (R)	26 Jan
4:25.71	Shannon	Osika	USA	15.6.93	4	Millrose	New York (Armory)	9 Feb
4:26.39	Katie	Mackey	USA	12.11.87	5	Millrose	New York (Armory)	9 Feb

4:26.79	Cory	McGee	USA	29.5.92	6	Millrose	New York (Armory)	9 Feb
4:26.84	Dawit	Seyaum	ETH	27.7.96	3		Boston (R)	26 Jan
4:28.12	Ce'Aira	Brown	USA	4.11.93	1		Boston (A)	3 Mar
4:28.30	Yolanda	Ngarambe	SWE	14.9.91	5		Boston (R)	26 Jan
4:28.31	Ciara	Mageean	IRL	12.3.92	6		Boston (R)	26 Jan
4:28.81	Helen	Schlachtenhaufen	USA	14.3.95	7	Millrose	New York (Armory)	9 Feb
4:29.11	Brenda	Martinez	USA	8.9.87	7		Boston (R)	26 Jan
4:29.40	Winnie	Nanyondo	UGA	23.8.93	2		Birmingham	16 Feb
4:29.47	Danae	Rivers	USA	3.2.98	8	Millrose	New York (Armory)	9 Feb
4:29.54	Amanda	Eccleston	USA	18.6.90	9	Millrose	New York (Armory)	9 Feb
4:29.74	Rabab	Arrafi	MAR	12.1.91	3		Birmingham	16 Feb
4:29.74	Heather	MacLean	USA	31.8.95	2		Boston (A)	3 Mar
4:29.92	Shelby	Houlihan	USA	8.2.93	2	NC	Staten Island	23 Feb

4:31.03	Jessica	Hull	AUS	22.10.96	26 Jan	4:31.69	Yekaterina	Storozheva	RUS	22.1.93	3 Feb
4:31.42#	Nikki	Hiltz	USA	23.10.94	8 Feb	4:31.71#	Hannah	Fields	USA	4.2.93	3 Feb
4:31.51	Svetlana	Aplachkina	RUS	28.11.92	3 Feb	4:31.78	Anastasiya	Kalina	RUS	16.2.94	3 Feb
4:31.66	Danielle	Aragon	USA	1.7.94	8 Feb	4:32.08	Aleksandra	Gulyayeva	RUS	30.4.94	17 Feb

3000 METRES

8:30.61	Laura	Muir	GBR	9.5.93	1	EI	Glasgow	1 Mar
8:32.47	Konstanze	Klosterhalfen	GER	18.2.97	1	NC	Leipzig	16 Feb
8:38.22	Melissa	Courtney	GBR	30.8.93	3	EI	Glasgow	1 Mar
8:39.45	Alina	Reh	GER	23.5.97	4	EI	Glasgow	1 Mar
8:43.76	Alemaz	Teshale	ETH	5.7.99	1		Madrid	8 Feb
8:44.68	Karoline Bjerkeli	Grøvdal	NOR	14.6.90	1	v3N	Rud	10 Feb
8:45.97	Alicia	Monson	USA	13.5.98	1	Millrose	New York (Armory)	9 Feb
8:46.27	Gudaf	Tsegay	ETH	23.1.97	3		Karlsruhe	2 Feb
8:46.44	Rachel	Schneider	USA	18.7.91	2	Millrose	New York (Armory)	9 Feb
8:46.50	Jessica	O'Connell	CAN	10.2.89	3	Millrose	New York (Armory)	9 Feb
8:46.60	Aisha	Praught Leer	JAM	14.12.89	4	Millrose	New York (Armory)	9 Feb
8:47.59	Claudia	Bobocea	ROU	11.6.92	2		Madrid	8 Feb
8:47.61	Maureen	Koster	NED	3.7.92	5		Karlsruhe	2 Feb
8:48.92*	Elinor	Purrier	USA	20.2.95	1		Boston (A)	15 Dec
8:49.92	Axumawit	Embaye	ETH	18.10.94	6		Karlsruhe	2 Feb
8:50.57	Hanna	Klein	GER	6.4.93	7		Karlsruhe	2 Feb

8:52.27	Emma	Coburn	USA	19.10.90	9 Feb	8:55.26#	Allie	Ostrander	USA	24.12.96	8 Feb
8:53.91#	Jessica	Hull	AUS	22.10.96	8 Feb	8:55.28	Ejgayehu	Taye	ETH-J	10.2.00	16 Feb
8:53.97	Yolanda	Ngarambe	SWE	14.9.91	8 Feb	8:55.68#	Nicole	Hutchinson	CAN	17.6.97	8 Feb
8:53.98	Tsige	Gebreselama	ETH-J	30.9.00	2 Feb	8:55.97#	Lauren	Gregory	USA	13.4.98	8 Feb
8:53.98	Weini	Kelati	ERI	1.12.96	9 Feb	8:56.04	Luiza	Gega	ALB	5.11.88	16 Feb
8:54.08	Svetlana	Aplachkina	RUS	28.11.92	13 Feb	**2 Miles**					
8:54.58	Vanessa	Fraser	USA	27.7.95	8 Feb	9:31.38	Shelby	Houlihan	USA	8.2.93	24 Feb
8:54.92	Rabab	Arrafi	MAR	12.1.91	12 Feb	9:33.70	Katie	Mackey	USA	12.11.87	24 Feb
8:55.03	Meskerem	Mamo	ETH	13.4.99	16 Feb	9:34.65	Elinor	Purrier	USA	20.2.95	24 Feb

5000 METRES

14:52.02	Laura	Muir	GBR	9.5.93	1		Glasgow	4 Jan
14:57.45	Gabriela	DeBues-Stafford	CAN	13.9.95	2		Glasgow	4 Jan
15:07.17	Marielle	Hall	USA	28.1.92	1		Boston (A)	24 Feb
15:11.56	Karissa	Schweizer	USA	4.5.96	2		Boston (A)	24 Feb
15:12.55	Courtney	Frerichs	USA	18.1.93	3		Boston (A)	24 Feb
15:14.75	Vanessa	Fraser	USA	27.7.95	4		Boston (A)	24 Feb
15:14.78*	Ednah	Kurgat	KEN	15.6.91	1		Boston (A)	1 Dec
15:15.24*	Weini	Kelati	ERI	1.12.96	2		Boston (A)	1 Dec
15:15.47*	Sharon	Lokedi	KEN	10.3.94	3		Boston (A)	1 Dec
15:15.80	Konstanze	Klosterhalfen	GER	18.2.97	1		Boston (R)	26 Jan
15:16.38*	Allie	Ostrander	USA	24.12.96	4		Boston (A)	1 Dec

15:24.32*	Elise	Cranny	USA	8.5.96	1 Dec	15:28.46#	Caroline	Kurgat	KEN	20.4.93	25 Jan
15:25.35*	Dorcas	Wasike	KEN	2.7.96	1 Dec	15:31.26	Alicia	Monson	USA	13.5.98	3 Mar
15:26.01*	Charlotte	Prouse	CAN	9.2.97	1 Dec	15:32.38*	Aubrey	Roberts	USA	30.1.98	1 Dec
15:28.07*	Jaci	Smith	USA	5.1.97	1 Dec	15:32.79	Kim	Conley	USA	14.3.86	24 Feb

60 METRES HURDLES

7.85	Sharika	Nelvis	USA	10.5.90	1	NC	Staten Island	24 Feb
7.86	Evonne	Britton	USA	28.7.91	2	NC	Staten Island	24 Feb
7.87	Nadine	Visser	NED	9.2.95	1	EI	Glasgow	3 Mar
7.89	Pamela	Dutkiewicz	GER	28.9.91	1	ISTAF	Berlin	1 Feb
7.90	Christina	Clemons (Manning)	USA	29.5.90	1		Clemson	26 Jan
7.90	Chanel	Brissett	USA	10.8.99	1		Fayetteville	8 Feb
7.91	Cindy	Roleder	GER	21.8.89	2	ISTAF	Berlin	1 Feb
7.92	Kayla	White	USA	24.9.96	2	NCAA	Birmingham	9 Mar
7.93	Payton	Chadwick	USA	29.11.95	1h1	NCAA	Birmingham	8 Mar
7.95	Janeek	Brown	JAM	14.5.98	2		Fayetteville	8 Feb
7.95	Klaudia	Siciarz	POL	15.3.98	1	NC	Torun	16 Feb
7.95	Tiara	McMinn	USA	23.2.99	1	ACC	Blacksburg	23 Feb
7.96	Alina	Talay	BLR	14.5.89	1	NC	Gent	17 Feb

7.96	Dior	Hall	USA	2.1.96	3h1	NCAA	Birmingham	8 Mar
7.97	Elvira	German	BLR	9.1.97	1	NC	Mogilyov	29 Jan
7.97	Nooralotta	Neziri	FIN	9.11.92	1	NC	Kuopio	17 Feb
7.97	Reetta	Hurske	FIN	15.5.95	2	NC	Kuopio	17 Feb
7.97	Luca	Kozák	HUN	1.6.96	1s1	EI	Glasgow	3 Mar
7.98	Anna	Cockrell	USA	28.8.97	2h2	NCAA	Birmingham	8 Mar
8.00	Mecca	McGlaston	USA	23.7.98	4h1	NCAA	Birmingham	8 Mar
8.01	Naomi	Taylor	USA	9.11.98	4	NCAA	Birmingham	0 Mar
8.02	Sacha	Alessandrini	FRA	7.6.99	1	NC	Miramas	17 Feb
8.02	Gréta	Kerekes	HUN	9.10.92	1	NC	Budapest	17 Feb

8.03	Hanna	Plotitsyna	UKR	1.1.87	4 Feb		8.04	Madeleine	Akobundu	USA	24.4.98	8 Mar
8.03	Tobi	Amusan	NGR	23.4.97	9 Feb		8.05	Mariya	Aglitskaya	RUS	20.6.91	3 Feb
8.03	Solène	Ndama	FRA	23.9.98	9 Feb		8.06	Andrea	Ivancevic	CRO	21.8.84	12 Feb
8.03	Karolina	Kołeczek	POL	15.1.93	16 Feb		8.06	Amber	Hughes	USA	23.9.94	16 Feb
8.04	Tonea	Marshall	USA	17.12.98	8 Feb		8.06	Faith	Ross	USA	7.3.98	22 Feb
8.04	Eline	Berings	BEL	28.5.86	9 Feb		8.06	Cortney	Jones	USA	18.6.99	8 Mar
8.04	Matilda	Bogdanoff	FIN	8.10.90	17 Feb		8.09	three women				

HIGH JUMP

2.04	Mariya	Lasitskene	RUS	14.1.93	1	Winter	Moskva	3 Feb
2.02	Anna	Chicherova	RUS	22.7.82	2	NC	Moskva	15 Feb
2.00	Yuliya	Levchenko	UKR	28.11.97	1		Eaubonne	12 Feb
1.99	Kateryna	Tabashnyk	UKR	15.6.94	1		Hustopece	26 Jan
1.99	Yaroslava	Mahuchikh	UKR-J	19.9.01	2		Hustopece	26 Jan
1.98	Airiné	Palsyté	LTU	13.7.92	2		Cottbus	30 Jan
1.97	Morgan	Lake	GBR	12.5.97	3		Hustopece	26 Jan
1.97	Iryna	Herashchenko	UKR	10.3.95	2	NC	Sumy	7 Feb
1.96	Imke	Onnen	GER	17.8.94	1	NC	Leipzig	17 Feb
1.96	Vashti	Cunningham	USA	18.1.98	1	NC	Staten Island	23 Feb
1.96	Katarina	Johnson-Thompson	GBR	9.1.93	1P	EI	Glasgow	1 Mar
1.94	Svetlana	Radzivil	UZB	17.1.87	4		Hustopece	26 Jan
1.94	Alessia	Trost	ITA	8.3.93	5		Hustopece	26 Jan
1.94	Karina	Taranda	BLR	10.2.99	2		Brno	6 Feb
1.94	Daniela	Stanciu	ROU	15.10.87	1	NC	Bucuresti	7 Feb
1.94	Marie-Laurence	Jungfleisch	GER	7.10.90	1		Weinheim	8 Feb
1.94	Tatiána	Goúsin	GRE	26.1.94	1	NC	Pireás	9 Feb
1.94	Michaela	Hrubá	CZE	21.2.98	6	EI	Glasgow	3 Mar
1.93	Yuliya	Chumachenko	UKR	2.10.94	4	NC	Sumy	7 Feb
1.93	Erika	Kinsey	SWE	10.3.88	Q	EI	Glasgow	1 Mar
1.92	Safina	Sadullayeva	UZB	4.3.98	1		Ust-Kamenogorsk	19 Jan
1.92	Oksana	Okuneva	UKR	14.3.90	3		Sumy	25 Jan
1.92	Nadezhda	Dusanova	UZB	17.11.87	1		Nehvizdy	1 Feb
1.92	Aleksandra	Yaryshkina	RUS	10.6.94	3	NC	Moskva	15 Feb
1.92	Elena	Vallortigara	ITA	21.9.91	1	NC	Ancona	16 Feb
1.92	Marija	Vukovic	MNE	21.1.92	2	BalkC	Istanbul	16 Feb
1.91	Levern	Spencer	LCA	23.6.84	1		Clemson	19 Jan
1.91	Priscilla	Frederick	ANT	14.2.89	7		Hustopece	26 Jan
1.91	Ana	Simic	CRO	5.5.90	8		Hustopece	26 Jan
1.91	Marusa	Cernjul	SLO	30.6.92	10	EI	Glasgow	3 Mar
1.91	Morgan	Smalls	USA-Y	11.5.02	1		New York (Armory)	9 Mar

1.90	Ella	Junnila	FIN	6.12.98	16 Jan		1.90	Tatyana	Yermachenkova	RUS	9.9.98	21 Feb
1.90	Prisca	Duvernay	FRA	26.5.91	26 Jan		1.90	Natalya	Spiridonova	RUS-Y	31.7.02	21 Feb
1.90	Maja	Nilsson	SWE	8.12.99	26 Jan		1.90	Grete	Udras	EST	11.3.88	22 Feb
1.90	Tonje	Angelsen	NOR	17.1.90	3 Feb		1.89	Klára	Krejciriová	CZE	22.4.02	26 Jan
1.90	Salome	Lang	SUI	18.11.97	6 Feb		1.88	Liliya	Klintsova	UKR	12.7.07	15 Jan
1.90	Sofie	Skoog	SWE	7.6.90	9 Feb		1.88	Tatyana	Odinova	RUS	25.5.83	20 Jan
1.90	Jessica	Kähärä	FIN-J	1.8.01	17 Feb		1.88	Manon	Schoop	NED	7.8.99	17 Feb
1.90	Bianca	Salming	SWE	22.11.98	17 Feb		1.88	Ty	Butts/Townsend	USA	10.6.90	23 Feb
1.90	Christina	Honsel	GER	7.7.97	17 Feb		1.88	Amina	Smith	USA	29.8.92	23 Feb
1.90	Claire	Orcel	BEL	2.12.97	17 Feb		1.87	six women				

POLE VAULT

4.91	Anzhelika	Sidorova	RUS	28.6.91	1		Madrid	8 Feb
4.86	Katie	Nageotte	USA	13.6.91	1		Boston (R)	26 Jan
4.81	Holly	Bradshaw	GBR	2.11.91	1		Birmingham	16 Feb
4.81	Nikoléta	Kiriakopoúlou	GRE	21.3.86	3		Birmingham	16 Feb
4.81	Angelica	Bengtsson	SWE	8.7.93	1=		Clermont-Ferrand	24 Feb
4.75	Michaela	Meijer	SWE	30.7.93	1	v3N	Rud	10 Feb
4.74A	Ekateríni	Stefanídi	GRE	4.2.90	1		Reno	18 Jan
4.73	Ninon	Guillon-Romarin	FRA	15.4.95	3=		Clermont-Ferrand	24 Feb
4.73	Alysha	Newman	CAN	29.6.94	3=		Clermont-Ferrand	24 Feb
4.68	Lexi	Jacobus	USA	20.11.96	1	SEC	Fayetteville	23 Feb
4.65	Irina	Zhuk	BLR	26.1.93	5		Clermont-Ferrand	24 Feb
4.65	Angelica	Moser	SUI	9.10.97	4=	EI	Glasgow	3 Mar

4.63	Lisa	Ryzih	GER	27.9.88	5=		Karlsruhe	2 Feb
4.63A	Kortney	Ross	USA	26.7.92	1		Albuquerque	9 Feb
4.63		Li Ling	CHN	6.7.89	2		Szczecin	12 Feb
4.61	Annie	Johnigan	USA	13.5.95	3		Boston (R)	26 Jan
4.60	Tori	Hoggard	USA	20.11.96	2	SEC	Fayetteville	23 Feb
4.59	Morgann	LeLeux	USA	14.11.92	2		Eaubonne	12 Feb
4.58A	Jenn	Suhr	USA	5.2.82	2		Albuquerque	9 Feb
4.56	Tina	Sutej	SLO	7.11.88	1		Zagreb	20 Feb
4.56	Kristen	Leland	USA	1.7.92	3	NC	Staten Island	24 Feb
4.56	Bonnie	Draxler	USA	13.10.95	2	NCAA	Birmingham	9 Mar
4.55	Irina	Ivanova	RUS	19.4.96	1		Chelyabinsk	17 Jan
4.55	Katharina	Bauer	GER	12.6.90	2	NC	Leipzig	16 Feb
4.53	Emily	Grove	USA	22.5.93	1		Fayetteville	9 Feb
4.52	Olivia	Gruver	USA	29.7.97	1		Seattle	26 Jan
4.51	Lisa	Gunnarsson	SWE	20.8.99	3		Fayetteville	25 Jan
4.51	Romana	Malácová	CZE	15.5.87	1		Praha (Strom)	9 Feb

4.50	Dailis	Caballero	CUB	6.3.88	18 Jan		4.45	Lyudmila	Petrova	RUS	15.12.93	3 Feb
4.50		Xu Huiqin	CHN	4.9.93	31 Jan		4.45	Aksana	Gataullina	RUS-J	17.7.00	5 Feb
4.50	Yelizaveta	Bondarenko	RUS	1.7.99	3 Feb		4.43	Lucy	Bryan	GBR	22.5.95	22 Feb
4.50	Maryna	Kylypko	UKR	10.11.95	8 Feb		4.43	Jade	Ive	GBR	22.1.92	10 Mar
4.50	Eléni-Klaoúdia	Pólak	GRE	9.9.96	10 Feb		4.41	Bridget	Guy	USA	18.3.96	9 Mar
4.50	Olga	Mullina	RUS	1.8.92	13 Feb		4.40	Alina	McDonald	USA	26.2.97	19 Jan
4.50	Yarisley	Silva	CUB	1.6.87	16 Feb		4.40	Marion	Lotout	FRA	19.11.89	16 Feb
4.50	Maialen	Axpe	ESP	4.5.93	16 Feb		4.40	Alice	Moindrot	FRA	20.8.99	16 Feb
4.50	Sonia	Malavisi	ITA	31.10.94	17 Feb		4.40	Roberta	Bruni	ITA	8.3.94	17 Feb
4.50	Chloe	Cunliffe	USA-J	10.5.00	17 Mar		4.40	Liz	Parnova	AUS	9.5.94	24 Feb
4.47	Rachel	Baxter	USA	5.4.99	22 Feb		4.40	Amálie	Svábíková	CZE	22.11.99	2 Mar
4.46	Desiree	Freier	USA	24.7.96	9 Mar		4.40		Ren Mengqian	CHN	4.10.93	19 Mar
4.45	Sophie	Gutermuth	USA	2.11.92	26 Jan		4.39	Nastassja	Campbell	USA-J	19.7.00	12 Jan

LONG JUMP

6.99	Malaika	Mihambo	GER	3.2.94	1	ISTAF	Berlin	1 Feb
6.99	Ivana	Spanovic	SRB	10.5.90	1	EI	Glasgow	3 Mar
6.93	Anastasiya	Mironchik-Ivanova	BLR	13.4.89	2	EI	Glasgow	3 Mar
6.85	Maryna	Bekh-Romanchuk	UKR	18.7.95	1	NC	Sumy	8 Feb
6.70	Alina	Rotaru	ROU	5.6.93	1	NC	Bucuresti	7 Feb
6.68	Tania	Vicenzino	ITA	1.4.86	Q	EI	Glasgow	2 Mar
6.64	Khaddi	Sagnia	SWE	20.4.94	1		Sätra	4 Feb
6.63	Yelena	Sokolova	RUS	23.7.86	1	NC	Moskva	14 Feb
6.60	Yekaterina	Koneva	RUS	25.9.88	1		Slavyansk-na-Kubani	6 Jan
6.60	Éloyse	Lesueur-Aymonin	FRA	15.7.88	2		Metz	10 Feb
6.59	Abigail	Irozuru	GBR	3.1.90	2		Birmingham	16 Feb
6.58	Sosthene	Moguenara	GER	17.10.89	2		Dortmund	27 Jan
6.58	Laura	Strati	ITA	3.10.90	3		Metz	10 Feb
6.56	Ksenija	Balta	EST	1.11.86	4	ISTAF	Berlin	1 Feb
6.54	Fatima	Diame	ESP	22.9.96	1		San Sebastián	2 Feb
6.53	Hanne	Maudens	BEL	12.3.97	1	NC	Gent	17 Feb
6.53	Katarina	Johnson-Thompson	GBR	9.1.93	1P	EI	Glasgow	1 Mar

6.52	Milica	Gardasevic	SRB	28.9.98	19 Jan		6.48	Yekaterina	Kropivko	RUS	13.6.97	14 Jan
6.52	Kate	Hall	USA	12.1.97	26 Jan		6.48	Hrystyna	Hrishutina	UKR	21.3.92	18 Jan
6.52	Florentina	Iusco	ROU	8.4.96	2 Feb		6.47	Annika	Gärtz	GER	24.8.94	17 Feb
6.51	Keturah	Orji	USA	5.3.96	8 Feb		6.47	Hilary	Kpatcha	FRA	5.5.98	17 Feb
6.51	Anasztázia	Nguyen	HUN	9.1.93	9 Feb		6.46	Krystyna	Hryshutyna	UKR	21.3.92	11 Jan
6.50	Jahisha	Thomas	GBR	22.11.94	19 Jan		6.46	Kendell	Williams	USA	14.6.95	2 Feb
6.50		Lu Minjia	CHN	29.12.90	23 Feb		6.46	Evelise	Veiga	POR	3.3.96	9 Feb
6.49	Hafdís	Sigurdardóttir	ISL	12.2.87	20 Jan		6.46	Yanis	David	FRA	12.12.97	22 Feb
6.49	Quanesha	Burks	USA	15.3.95	9 Feb		6.46	Jasmyn	Steels	USA		8 Mar
6.49	Rougui	Sow	FRA	7.6.95	22 Feb		6.46	Deborah	Acquah	GHA		8 Mar

TRIPLE JUMP

14.92	Yulimar	Rojas	VEN	21.10.95	1		Madrid	8 Feb
14.81	Yekaterina	Koneva	RUS	25.9.88	1		Moskva	25 Jan
14.73	Ana	Peleteiro	ESP	2.12.95	1	EI	Glasgow	3 Mar
14.59	Kristin	Gierisch	GER	20.8.90	1		Chemnitz	10 Feb
14.57	Tori	Franklin	USA	7.10.92	2		Madrid	8 Feb
14.55	Keturah	Orji	USA	5.3.96	1	NC	Staten Island	24 Feb
14.50	Paraskeví	Papahrístou	GRE	17.4.89	2	EI	Glasgow	3 Mar
14.47	Olha	Saladukha	UKR	4.6.83	3	EI	Glasgow	3 Mar
14.44	Patrícia	Mamona	POR	21.11.88	3		Madrid	8 Feb
14.43	Susana	Costa	POR	22.9.84	5	EI	Glasgow	3 Mar
14.39	Rouguy	Diallo	FRA	5.2.95	4		Madrid	8 Feb
14.38	Kristiina	Mäkelä	FIN	20.11.92	5		Madrid	8 Feb
14.23	Elena	Panțuroiu	ROU	24.2.95	1	NC	Bucuresti	6 Feb
14.11	Darya	Nidbaykina	RUS	26.12.94	1		Moskva	20 Jan
14.05	Naomi	Ogbeta	GBR	18.4.98	1	NC	Birmingham	9 Feb

Mark	First	Last	Nat	DOB	Pos	Meet	City	Date
14.03	Yanis	David	FRA	12.12.97	1	NCAA	Birmingham	9 Mar
14.02	Thea	Lafond	DMA	5.4.94	1		Clemson	9 Feb
14.01	Hanna	Krasutska	UKR	20.7.95	1		Sumy	26 Jan
13.98	Jeanine	Assani Issouf	FRA	17.8.92	2	NC	Miramas	16 Feb
13.97	Diana	Zagainova	LTU	20.6.97	1	NC	Siauliai	15 Feb
13.96	Dovilé	Dzindzaletaité	LTU	14.7.93	2	NC	Siauliai	15 Feb
13.94	Irina	Vaskovskaya	BLR	2.4.91	1	NC	Mogilyov	29 Jan
13.92	Patricia	Sarrapio	ESP	16.11.82	1	NC	Antequera	10 Feb

Mark	First	Last	Nat	DOB	Date		Mark	First	Last	Nat	DOB	Date
13.87	Hanna	Minenko	ISR	25.9.89	8 Feb		13.74	Zeng Rui		CHN	6.2.98	24 Feb
13.83	Chaquinn	Cook	USA	10.7.97	9 Mar		13.71	María	Vicente	ESP-J	28.3.01	8 Feb
13.80	Xu Ting		CHN	23.2.97	24 Feb		13.71	Chen Ting		CHN	28.8.97	19 Mar
13.78	Marie-José	Ebwea Bile	FRA	7.2.97	7 Dec		13.69	Valentina	Kosolapova	RUS	11.7.97	14 Jan
13.76	Jenny	Elbe	GER	18.4.90	16 Feb		13.68	Natalya	Yevdokimova	RUS	7.9.93	20 Jan
13.76	Tan Qiujiao		CHN-J	28.5.00	24 Feb		13.67	Chen Jie		CHN	2.3.98	24 Feb
13.75	Irina	Ektova	KAZ	8.1.87	22 Jan		13.66	Lynnika	Pitts	USA	19.5.92	24 Feb

SHOT

Mark	First	Last	Nat	DOB	Pos	Meet	City	Date
19.54	Christina	Schwanitz	GER	24.12.85	1	NC	Leipzig	16 Feb
19.28	Maggie	Ewen	USA	23.9.94	1		Boston (R)	26 Jan
19.14		Gong Lijiao	CHN	24.1.89	1		Hangzhou	20 Mar
19.12	Radoslava	Mavrodieva	BUL	13.3.87	1	EI	Glasgow	3 Mar
19.00	Anita	Márton	HUN	15.1.89	3	EI	Glasgow	3 Mar
18.94	Alyona	Dubitskaya	BLR	25.1.90	1	NC	Mogilyov	29 Jan
18.84A	Chase	Ealey	USA	20.7.94	1		Albuquerque	9 Feb
18.73	Jessica	Ramsey	USA	26.7.91	3		Torun	6 Feb
18.63	Klaudia	Kardasz	POL	2.5.96	Q	EI	Glasgow	1 Mar
18.61	Fanny	Roos	SWE	2.1.95	1	NC	Norrköping	17 Feb
18.52	Dimitriana	Surdu	MDA	12.4.94	2	BalkC	Istanbul	16 Feb
18.30	Viktoryia	Kolb	BLR	26.10.93	1		Minsk	21 Dec
18.26	Dani	Hill	USA	16.5.91	1		Allendale	25 Jan
18.23		Song Jiayuan	CHN	15.9.97	2		Hangzhou	20 Mar
18.20	Alena	Abramchuk	BLR	14.2.88	2		Minsk	18 Jan
18.20	Alyona	Gordeyeva	RUS	24.4.97	1	NC	Moscow	14 Feb
18.17	Sara	Gambetta	GER	18.2.93	Q	EI	Glasgow	1 Mar
18.10	Paulina	Guba	POL	14.5.91	3		Lodz	4 Feb
18.09	Alina	Kenzel	GER	10.8.97	Q	EI	Glasgow	1 Mar
18.02	Emel	Dereli	TUR	25.2.96	1		Istanbul	17 Feb
17.97	Sophie	McKinna	GBR	31.8.94	1	NC	Birmingham	10 Feb
17.95	Rachel	Fatherly	USA	20.4.94	5	NC	Staten Island	24 Feb
17.91	Samantha	Noennig	USA	28.7.98	1	NCAA	Birmingham	8 Mar
17.90	Jessica	Woodard	USA	4.2.95	1		Fayetteville	9 Feb
17.89	Lena	Giger	USA	7.6.96	2	NCAA	Birmingham	8 Mar
17.88	Sade	Olatoye	USA	25.1.97	1	Big 10	Ann Arbor	23 Feb

Mark	First	Last	Nat	DOB	Date		Mark	First	Last	Nat	DOB	Date
17.79	Laulauga	Tausaga-Collins	USA	22.5.98	23 Feb		17.58	Jess	Woodard	USA	4.2.95	2 Feb
17.77	Katharina	Maisch	GER	12.6.97	9 Feb		17.58	Jeneva	Stevens	USA	28.10.89	2 Feb
17.77	Brittany	Crew	CAN	6.3.94	22 Feb		17.57	Janeah	Stewart	USA	21.7.96	26 Jan
17.76A	Devia	Brown	JAM	21.3.98	15 Feb		17.50	Aliyah	Gustafson	USA	3.5.95	26 Jan
17.76	Monique	Riddick	USA	8.11.89	24 Feb		17.48		Bian Ka	CHN	5.1.93	28 Feb
17.74	Anna	Avdeyeva	RUS	6.4.85	14 Feb		17.47	Kiley	Sabin	USA	28.4.96	16 Feb
17.73A	Alyssa	Wilson	USA	20.2.99	11 Jan		17.42	Khayla	Dawson	USA	18.3.98	2 Feb

DISCUS

Mark	First	Last	Nat	DOB	Pos	Meet	City	Date
63.89	Nadine	Müller	GER	21.11.85	1	ISTAF	Berlin	1 Feb
62.19	Claudine	Vita	GER	19.9.96	2	ISTAF	Berlin	1 Feb
60.23	Shanice	Craft	GER	15.5.93	3	ISTAF	Berlin	1 Feb
59.15*	Chioma	Onyekwere	NGR	25.6.94	1		Grand Valley	22 Dec

WEIGHT   (16KG)

Mark	First	Last	Nat	DOB	Pos	Meet	City	Date
24.82	Janeah	Stewart	USA	21.7.96	1		Nashville	8 Feb
24.57	DeAnna	Price	USA	8.6.93	1		Bloomington	25 Jan
24.46	Sade	Olatoye	USA	25.1.97	1	NCAA	Birmingham	9 Mar
24.11*	Kaitlyn	Long	USA	25.4.96	1		Brookings	30 Nov
24.06	Stamatía	Skarvélis	GRE	17.8.95	1	SEC	Fayetteville	23 Feb
23.53	Ida	Storm	SWE	26.12.91	1	NC	Norrköping	16 Feb
23.49	Annette	Echikunwoke	USA	29.7.96	1		Columbus	15 Feb
23.42	Jeneva	Stevens	USA	28.10.89	2		Nashville	18 Jan
23.33	Janee'	Kasanavoid	USA	19.1.95	1		Manhattan	16 Feb
23.26	Laulauga	Tausaga-Collins	USA	22.5.98	1		Lincoln	1 Feb

Pentathlon

Mark	First	Last	Nat	DOB	Pos	Meet	City	Date
4983	Katarina	Johnson-Thompson	GBR	9.1.93	1	EI	Glasgow	1 Mar
	8.27	1.96	13.15	6.53	2:09.13			
4731	Niamh	Emerson	GBR	22.4.99	2	EI	Glasgow	1 Mar
	8.54	1.07	13.93	6.29	2:12.56			
4723	Solène	Ndama	FRA	23.9.98	3	EI	Glasgow	1 Mar
	8.09	1.78	14.23	6.21	2:11.92			

Score	First	Last	Nat	Date	Rk	Ch	City	Date
4702	Ivona	Dadic	AUT	29.12.93	4	EI	Glasgow	1 Mar
	8.53	1.84	13.33	6.42	2:12.15			
4701	Laura	Ikauniece	LAT	31.5.92	5	EI	Glasgow	1 Mar
	8.29	1.84	13.31	6.33	2:14.01			
4637	Verena	Preiner	AUT	1.2.95	6	EI	Glasgow	1 Mar
	8.38	1.75	14.32	6.15	2:09.91			
4608	Xénia	Krizsán	HUN	13.1.93	7	EI	Glasgow	1 Mar
	8.45	1.78	14.17	6.05	2:10.50			
4581	Alina	Shukh	UKR	12.2.99	1	NC	Sumy	7 Feb
	8.86	1.83	15.08	6.07	2:15.24			
4569	Hanne	Maudens	BEL	12.3.97	1	NC	Gent	3 Feb
	8.68	1.76	13.95	6.37	2:13.98			
4547	Michelle	Atherley	USA	9.12.95	1	NCAA	Birmingham	8 Mar
	8.16	1.78	13.01	6.07	2:14.34			
4496	Kendell	Williams	USA	14.6.95	1	NC	Staten Island	22 Feb
	8.18	1.81	12.34	6.35	2:23.69			
4489	Géraldine	Ruckstuhl	SUI	24.2.98	1	NC	Magglingen	3 Feb
	8.70	1.81	14.55	5.96	2:17.62			
4462	Eliska	Klucinová	CZE	14.4.88	1	NC	Praha (Strom)	9 Feb
	8.67	1.77	14.83	6.18	2:22.77			
4412	María	Vicente	ESP-J	28.3.01	1	NC	Antequera	16 Feb
	8.35	1.78	12.42	6.36	2:24.91			
4412	Jordan	Gray	USA	22.4.93	2	NCAA	Birmingham	8 Mar
	8.70	1.72	14.35	5.81	2:19.55			
4379	Emilyn	Dearman	USA	26.4.95	1		Warrenburg	2 Feb
	8.38	1.74	13.60	5.98	2:20.11			
4372	Aliyah	Whisby	USA		2		Clemson	26 Jan
	8.41	1.81	11.75	6.15	2:21.50			
4372	Sarah	Lagger	AUT	3.9.99	2	NC	Linz	3 Feb
	9.09	1.75	14.01	6.17	2:16.80			
4357	Adrianna	Sułek	POL	3.4.99	1	NC	Torun	16 Feb
	8.56	1.77	12.46	6.08	2:18.32			
4338	Annik	Kälin	SUI-J	27.4.00	1	NC	Magglingen	3 Feb
	8.47	1.72	11.91	6.28	2:18.56			
4332	Mariya	Pavlova	RUS	21.5.96	1	NC	Kirov	13 Feb
	8.51	1.82	13.06	5.78	2:21.73			
4330	Kelsey	Herman	USA	15.6.96	1	SEC	Fayetteville	22 Feb
	8.29	1.73	12.31	6.10	2:20.81			

4320	Esther	Turpin	FRA	29.4.96	17 Feb	4284	Noor	Vidts	BEL	30.5.96	16 Feb
4319	Diane	Marie-Hardy	FRA	19.2.96	17 Feb	4265	Rimma	Buinenko	UKR	30.12.95	7 Feb
4303	Miia	Sillman	FIN	3.6.95	3 Feb	4262	Iryna	Rofe-Beketova	UKR	18.9.98	7 Feb
4302	Anna	Hall	USA-J	23.3.01	22 Feb	4262	Hope	Bender	USA	2.1.97	8 Mar
4294	Ashtin	Zamzow	USA	13.8.96	8 Mar	4255	Juanita	Webster-Freeman	USA	13.11.96	22 Feb
4293	Erinn	Beattie	USA	8.4.97	8 Mar	4250	Aleksandra	Butvina	RUS	14.2.86	13 Feb
4287	Stacey	Destin	USA	7.11.96	8 Mar	4246	Cassandre	Aguessy Thomas	FRA	1.9.97	17 Feb
4285	Paulina	Ligarska	POL	9.4.96	16 Feb	4243	Annie	Kunz	USA	16.2.93	22 Feb

3000 METRES WALK

| 12:13.31 | Brigita | Virbalyté-Dimsiené | LTU | 1.2.85 | 1 | NC | Siauliai | 15 Feb |
| 12:23.15 | Antonella | Palmisano | ITA | 6.8..91 | 1 | NC | Ancona | 16 Feb |

5000 METRES WALK

20:39.9*	Yelena	Lashmanova	RUS	9.4.92	1		Saransk	30 Dec
20:55.3*	Elvira	Kashanova	RUS	10.1.00	2		Saransk	30 Dec
21:05.79	Inna	Kashyna	UKR	27.9.91	1		Kyiv	11 Jan
21:30.9*	Klavdiya	Afanasyeva	RUS	15.1.96	3		Saransk	30 Dec

10,000 METRES WALK

| 45:28.42 | Anastasiya | Yatsevich | BLR | 18.1.85 | 1 | NC | Mogilyov | 29 Jan |

Late additions and corrections

OBITUARY: Elzbieta Krysinska, She competed in European Champs at rowing in 1957.

International Championships Changes. Drugs dqs – move rest up accordingly
2010 World Indoors: W 400/4x400: Firova 2/2R (and from 3/2R at Continental Cup)
2010 European Champs: W 400: 1 Firova, JT: 5 Abakumova
2012 European Champs: WHT: 3 Bulgakova
2016 European Champs: SP: 6 Toader
Anisya Kirdyapkina 20kW: OG: 2012- 4, WCh: 2011 & 2013- 2; WCp: 2012- 5; ECp: 2011- 2, 2013- 1; WUG: 2013- 1

Women's name changes
Olena Mizernyuk   Borchuk

EUROPEAN INDOOR CHAMPIONSHIPS 2019

Glasgow, GBR 1-3 March

A superb double of 1500m and 3000m wins by the Scottish athlete Laura Muir provided the headlines for an excellent championships. This was hugely appreciated by capacity crowds and repeated her 2017 double in Belgrade, providing a perfect ending to the first day as Muir sped away from Konstanze Klosterhalfen, sprinting the last lap in 28.32 and timed for her second 1500m in 4:04.96. Just before that Katarina Johnson-Thompson, assured of the pentathlon gold medal, won the 800m in fine style by winning in a time that took 3.65 secs off her indoor pb and gave her the fourth best pentathlon score of all-time at 4983 points – and Niamh Emerson, who had also excelled throughout the day, held on in a close contest for the silver medal, setting or equalling her indoor best in every event, for a world age-19 best 4731 and a British 1-2. Muir returned two days later to take the 1500m in consummate style.

Karsten Warholm took 0.51 off his Norwegian record for 400m as his 45.05 tied the 31 year-old European record set by Thomas Schönlebe. There was also much attention on his compatriot, the amazing Jakob Ingebrigtsen. The 18 year-old duly won the 3000m with brother Henrik taking the bronze medal. However, even Jakob could not match the last 52.67 for 400m run by Marcin Lewandowski in the 1500m.

As usual at major indoor championships, the field events had more strength in depth than the track. Favourites and world leaders Mariya Lasitskene (HJ 2.01) and Anzhelika Sidorova (PV 4.85) regained titles won in 2015 (as did KJT), but there were also major breakthroughs from the triple jump winners Nazim Babayev

17.29 and Ana Peleteiro 14.73 and long jumper Militiádis Tentóglou, while Ivana Spanoviç tied the 2019 world lead by winning a third consecutive long jump title with 6.99. Tentóglou's 8.38 was a world-leading mark for the indoor season as was KJT's pentathlon, Jorge Ureña's 6218 score in the heptathlon, Léa Sprunger's 51.61 for 400m and Poland's 3:28.77 at 4x400m. There were just two championship bests: Muir's 8:30.61 for 3000m and Warholm's 45.05 for 400m and the standard in some events was modest, although often in exciting contests.

Poland were top of the medal table, as they had been in 2017, with 5 gold medals but Britain won the most overall medals with 12 (4 gold, 10 silver, 2 bronze), beating their previous record of 10 in 2007 and 2017, and easily topped the points table. In all 14 nations won gold medals, including Cyprus (Milan Trajkovic at 60m hurdles) for the first time, But amazingly there were none for France or Germany, although they were 2nd equal and 5th on the points table.

Pawel Wojciechowski beat compatriot Piotr Lisek 5.90 to 5.85 in the pole vault, while Poland's other winners, were Lewandowski, Michal Haratyk, who had a clear shot win with 21.65, Ewa Swoboda, easily the fastest in each round of the women's 60m, and their women's 4x400m team..

There was a record number of competitors in the track events, but the field events, these days, are restricted in numbers with high qualifying standards. This is always a great pity for these are the athletes who most need and enjoy indoor competition and a far higher proportion of the best men and women in these events contest the Championships compared to the track athletes.

MEN

60 Metres (2)
1. Ján Volko SVK		6.60
2. Emre Zafer Barnes TUR		6.61
3. Joris van Gool NED		6.62
4. Richard Kilty GBR		6.66
5. Konstadínos Zíkos GRE		6.67
6. Amaury Golitin FRA		6.67
7. Ojie Edoburun GBR		6.67
8. Kevin Kranz GER		6.73

400 Metres (2)
1. Karsten Warholm NOR	45.05*
2. Óscar Husillos ESP	45.66
3. Tony van Diepen NED	46.13
4. Luka Janezic SLO	46.15
5. Fabrisio Saidy FRA	46.80
6. Lucas Bua ESP	46.92

800 Metres (3)
1. Álvaro de Arriba ESP	1:46.83
2. Jamie Webb GBR	1:47.13
3. Mark English IRL	1:47.39
4. Mariano García ESP	1:47.58
5. Andreas Bube DEN	1:47.67
6. Amel Tuka BIH	1:47.91
7. Andreas Kramer SWE	1:48.06

1500 Metres (3)
1. Marcin Lewandowski POL	3:42.85
2. Jakob Ingebrigtsen NOR-J	3:43.23
3. Jesús Gómez ESP	3:44.39
4. Filip Sasínek CZE	3:45.27
5. Simon Denissel FRA	3:45.50
6. Marius Probst GER	3:45.76
7. Karl Bebendorf GER	3:46.88
8. Robbie Fitzgibbon GBR	3:47.08
dns. Neil Gourley GBR	–

3000 Metres (2)
1. Jakob Ingebrigtsen NOR-	7:56.15
2. Chris O'Hare GBR	7:57.19
3. Henrik Ingebrigtsen NOR	7:57.19
4. Djilali Bedrani FRA	7:58.40
5, Jonas Leanderson SWE	7:59.16
6. Amos Bartelsmeyer GER	7:59.62
7. Jimmy Gressier FRA	8:00.89
8. Sam Atkin GBR	8:01.43
9. Yoann Kowal FRA	8:02.85
10. Andrew Butchart GBR	8:03.11

60 Metres Hurdles (3)
1, Milan Trajkovic CYP		7.60
2. Pascal Martinot-Lagarde FRA		7.61
3. Aurel Manga FRA		7.63
4. Orlando Ortega ESP		7.64
5. Konstadínos Douvalídis GRE		7.65
6. Andy Pozzi GBR		7.68
7. Wilhelm Belocian FRA		7.68
8. Elmo Lakka FIN		7.74

High Jump (2)
1. Gianmarco Tamberi ITA	2.32
2= Konstadínos Baniótis GRE	2.26
2= Andriy Protsenko UKR	2.26
4= Chris Baker GBR	2.22
4= Tihomir Ivanov BUL	2.22
6. Sylwester Bednarek POL	2.22
7. Falk Wendrich GER	2.18
8. Mateusz Przybylko GER	2.18

Pole Vault (2)
1. Pawel Wojciechowski POL	5.90
2. Piotr Lisek POL	5.85
3. Melder Svärd Jacobsson SWE	5.75
4= Emmanouil Karalís GRE	5.65

4= Claudio Michel Stecchi ITA 5.65
6. Sondre Guttormsen NOR 5.55
7. Bo Kanda Lita Baehre GER 5.55
8. Georgiy Gorokhov ANA/RUS 5.55

Long Jump (3)
1. Militiádis Tentóglou GRE 8.38
2. Thobias Nilsson Montler SWE 8.17
3. Strahinja Jovancevic SRB 8.03
4. Eusebio Cáceres ESP 7.98
5. Serhiy Nykyforov UKR 7.89
6. Tomasz Jaszczuk POL 7.80
7. Radek Juska CZE 7.79
8. Vladyslav Mazur UKR 7.75

Triple Jump (3)
1. Nazim Babayev AZE 17.29
2. Nelson Évora POR 17.11
3. Max Hess GER 17.10
4. Yoann Rapinier FRA 16.72
5. Kevin Luron FRA 16.63
6. Tomás Veszelká SVK 16.35
7. Nathan Douglas GBR 16.33
8. Simone Forte ITA 15.54

Shot (1)
1. Michal Haratyk POL 21.65
2. David Storl GER 21.54
3. Tomás Stanek CZE 21.25
4. Francisco Belo POR 20.97
5. Bob Bertemes LUX 20.70
6. Mesud Pezer BIH 20.69
7. Marcus Thomsen NOR 20.22
8. Nikólaos Skarvélis GRE 20.13

Heptathlon (2/3)
1. Jorge Ureña ESP 6218
2. Tim Duckworth GBR 6156
3. Ilya Shkurenyov ANA/RUS 6145
4. Fredrik Samuelsson SWE 6125
5. Andreas Bechmann GER 6001
6. Thomas Van Der Plaetsen BEL
   5989
7. Martin Roe NOR 5951
8. Vitaliy Zhuk BLR 5689

4 x 400 Metres Relay (3)
1. BEL 3:06.27
   Wattrin 46.81, D Borlée 46.52, J
   Borlée 46.75, K Borlée 46.19
2. ESP 3:06.32
   Husillos 46.40, Guijarro 47.22, Bua
   45.74, Erta 46.96
3. FRA 3:07.71 Anne 47.20, Jordier
   46.78, Courbière 46.80, Saidy 47.13
4. POL 3:08.40 5. GBR 3:08.48
6. ITA 3:09.48

Women – 60 Metres (2)
1. Ewa Swoboda POL 7.09
2. Dafne Schippers NED 7.14
3. Asha Philip GBR 7.15
4. Kristal Awuah GBR 7.15
5. Mujinga Kambundji SUI 7.16
6. Maja Mihalinec SLO 7.21
7. Kristina Timanovskaya BLR 7.26
8. Ajla Del Ponte SUI 7.30

400 Metres (1-1-2)
1. Léa Sprunger SUI 51.61
2. Cynthia Bolingo Mbongo BEL
   51.62
3, Lisanne de Witte NED 52.34
4. Agne Serksniene LTU 52.40
5, Raphaela Lukudo ITA 52.48
6. Justyna Swiety-Ersetic POL 52.64

800 Metres (1)
1, Shelayna Oskan-Clarke GBR
   2:02.58
2. Renelle Lamote FRA 2:03.00
3. Olha Lyakhova UKR 2:03.24
4. Renée Eykens BEL 2:03.32
5. Mari Smith GBR 2:03.45
6. Esther Guerrero ESP 2:04.07

1500 Metres (3)
1. Laura Muir GBR 4:05.92
2. Sofia Ennaoui POL 4:09.30
3. Ciara Mageean IRL 4:09.43
4. Yekaterina Korneyenko BLR
   4:11.59
5. Darya Borisevich BLR 4:11.92
6. Simona Vrzalová CZE 4:12.16
7. Claudia Bobocea ROU 4:13.40
8. Marta Pérez ESP 4:13.56
9. Amela Terzic SRB 4:24.20

3000 Metres (1)
1. Laura Muir GBR 8:30.61*
2. Konstanze Klosterhalfen GER
   8:34.06
3. Melissa Courtney GBR 8:38.22
4, Alina Reh GER 8:39.45
5. Karoline Bjerkeli Grøvdal NOR
   8:52.12
6. Maureen Koster NED 8:56.22
7. Eilish McColgan GBR 8:59.71
8. Célia Antón ESP 9:00.57
9. Viktória Gyürkés HUN 9:03.56

60 Metres Hurdles (3)
1. Nadine Visser NED 7.87
2. Cindy Roleder GER 7.97
3. Elvira German BLR 8.00
4. Reeta Hurske FIN 8.02
5. Gréta Kerekes HUN 8.03
6. Nooralotta Neziri FIN 8.09
7. Andrea Ivancevic CRO 8.14
dns. Luca Kozák HUN –

High Jump (3)
1. Mariya Lasitskene ANA/RUS 2.01
2. Yuliya Levchenko UKR 1.99
3. Airiné Palsyté LTU 1.97
4. Kateryna Tabashnyk UKR 1.97
5. Iryna Herashchenko UKR 1.94
6. Michaela Hrubá CZE 1.94
7= Erika Kinsey SWE 1.91
7= Imke Onnen GER 1.91

Pole Vault (3)
1. Anzhelika Sidorova ANA/RUS 4.85
2. Holly Bradshaw GBR 4.75
3. Nikoléta Kiriakopoúlou GRE 4.65
4= Angelica Moser SUI 4.65
4= Ekateríni Stefanídi GRE 4.65
6. Iryna Zhuk BLR 4.65
7. Ninon Guillon-Romarin FRA 4.65
8. Michaela Meijer SWE 4.45

Long Jump (3)
1. Ivana Spanovic SRB 6.99
2. Anastasiya Mironchik-Ivanova
   BLR 6.93
3. Maryna Bekh-Romanchuk UKR
   6.84
4. Malaika Mihambo GER 6.83
5. Alina Rotaru ROU 6.64
6. Tania Vicenzino ITA 6.58
7. Abigail Irozuru GBR 6.50
8. Florentina Iusco ROU 6.49

Triple Jump (3)
1. Ana Peleteiro ESP 14.73
2. Paraskeví Papahrístou GRE 14.50
3. Olha Saladukha UKR 14.47
4. Patricia Mamona POR 14.43
5. Susana Costa POR 14.43
6. Kristiina Mäkelä FIN 14.29
7. Rouguy Dialllo FRA 14.18
8. Hanna Krasutska UKR 13.95

Shot (3)
1. Radoslava Mavrodieva BUL 19.12
2. Christina Schwanitz GER 19.11
3. Anita Márton HUN 19.00
4. Alyona Dubitskaya BLR 18.71
5. Klaudia Kardasz POL 18.23
6. Fanny Roos SWE 18.21
7. Sara Gambetta GER 17.60
8. Alina Kenzel GER 17.55

Pentathlon (1)
1. Katerina Johnson-Thompson GBR
   4983
2. Niamh Emerson GBR 4731
3. Solène Ndama FRA 4723
4, Ivona Dadic AUT 4702
5. Laura Ikauniece LAT 4701
6. Verena Preiner AUT 4637
7. Xénia Krizsán HUN 4608
8. Hanne Maudens BEL 4440

4 x 400 Metres Relay (3)
1. POL 3:28.77 Kielbasinska 52.45,
   Baumgart-Witan 51.41, Holub-
   Kowalik 52.63, Swiety-Ersetic 52.28
2. GBR 3:29.55
   Laviai Nielsen 52.67, Clark 52.34,
   Anning 53.10, Doyle 51.44
3. ITA 3:31.90
   Lukudo 52.85, Folorunso 52.38,
   Bazzoni 53.42, Milani 53.25
4. FRA 3:32.12 5. BEL 3:32.46
6. SUI 3:33.72

Leading Nations – Medals & Points

Nation	G	S	B	Points
GBR	4	6	2	122.5
POL	5	2	-	72
FRA	--	2	3	72
ESP	3	2	1	69
GER	-	4	1	66.5
UKR	-	2	3	48.5
GRE	1	2	1	45.5
NOR	2	1	1	40
NED	1	1	3	36
BLR	-	1	1	33
ITA	1	-	1	29.5
SWE	1	-	1	29.5
BEL	1	1	-	28
SUI	1	-	-	22.5
POR	-	1	-	21
CZE	-	-	1	19
SRB	1	-	1	14
BUL	1	-	-	12.5
IRL	-	-	2	12
HUN	-	-	2	12
FIN	-	-	-	12

SVK (1G), LTU (1B) 11; AZE (1G), CYP
(1G), AUT, SLO 8; TUR, ROU 7; BIH
6, DEN, LAT, LUX 4; CRO 2
ANA/RUS athletes won 2G & 1B,
23 points

WORLD CROSS-COUNTRY CHAMPIONSHIPS 2019

At Aarhus, Denmark 30 March

AT THE PREVIOUS IAAF World Cross Country Champs in Kampala in 2017 the host nation Uganda came away with a gold medal in the U20 men's race courtesy of Jacob Kiplimo plus team bronzes in the senior men's and U20 women's races. The big disappointment was the misjudgement by Joshua Cheptegei in the senior race; he was 11 sec clear at the start of the last lap but blew up to finish 30th. No mistake this time as he and Kiplimo (still a junior) finished one-two well ahead of defending champion Geoffrey Kamworor and led Uganda to team victory over Kenya and holders Ethiopia. There were other successes for Uganda as Oscar Chelimo placed third in the U20 race and helped his team into second place, while the senior women's team finished third. European representation on home ground and on a novel and demanding course was particularly poor and only ten nations finished scoring teams in all four races: 1, ETH 102 total points; 2, KEN 128; 3, UGA 161; 4, GBR 649; 5, AUS 677; 6, JPN 750; 7, USA 799; 8, CAN 878; 9, ESP 934; 10, DEN 1043. East African domination was mainatiened as the only non-African medal went to Japan with bronze in the U20 women's team.

The specially designed course featuerd a welcome return to "true cross-country" with many hills and sections of mud, sand and water.

Senior Men 10.24 km

1. Joshua Cheptegei UGA	31:40
2. Jacob Kiplimo UGA-J	31:44
3. Geoffrey Kamworor KEN	31:55
4. Aron Kifle ERI	32:04
5. Selemon Barega ETH-J	32:16
6. Rhonex Kipruto KEN	32:17
7. Thomas Ayeko UGA	32:25
8. Andamlak Belihu ETH	32:29
9. Thierry Ndikumwenayo BDI	32:29
10. Joel Ayoko UGA	32:32
11. Rodrigue Kwizéra BDI	32:37
12. Albert Chemutai UGA	32:46
13. Ricahrd Yator KEN	32:51
14. Onesphoré Nzikwinkunda BDI	32:56
15. Abdi Fufa ETH	33:01
16. Precious Mashele RSA	33:05
17. Robel Fsiha SWE	33:06
18. Mogos Tuemay ETH	33:06
19. Birhanu Yemataw BRN	33:08
20. Ouassim Oumaiz ESP	33:10
21. Rodgers Chumo KEN	33:11
22. Filmon Ande ERI	33:12
23. Albert Rop BRN	33:15
24. Dawit Fikadu BRN	33:18
25. Enyew Mekonnen ETH	33:23
26. Aras Kaya TUR	33:25

27. Maxwell Rotich UGA	33:28
28. Awet Habte ERI	33:32
29. Yemane Haileselassie ERI	33:33
00. Brett Robinson AUS	33:34

140 of 141 finished

Team 4 to score, 18 teams completed

1. UGA	20	10. TAN	194
2. KEN	43	11. USA	198
3. ETH	46	12. RSA	212
4. ERI	83	13. RWA	222
5. BDI	91	14. JPN	297
6. BRN	99	15. DEN	336
7. ESP	181	16. CAN	347
8. AUS	188	17. NZL	382
9. GBR	190	18. CHN	509

U20 Men 7.728 km

1. Milkesa Mengesha ETH	23:52
2. Tadese Worku ETH-Y	23:54
3. Oscar Chelimo UGA	23:55
4. Leonard Bett KEN	24:02
5. Tsegaye Kidanu ETH	24:07
6. Hosea Kiplangat UGA	24:08
7. Edwin Bett KEN	24:18
8. Samuel Masai KEN	24:19
9. Samuel Kibet UGA	24:29
10. Gebregewergs Teklay ETH	24:34
11. Dinkalme Ayele ETH	24:36
12. Jakob Ingebrigtsen NOR	24:39
13. Yohans Kifle ERI	25:06
14. Mathew Chekwurui UGA	25:07
15. Charles Katul Lokir KEN	25:09

98 of 102 finished

Team 4 to score. 16 teams completed

1. ETH	18	9. AUS	187
2. UGA	32	10. FRA	190
3. KEN	34	11. PER	195
4. MAR	144	12. CAN	207
5. RSA	150	13. DEN	224
6. USA	154	14. ESP	262
7. JPN	154	15. NZL	301
8. GBR	174	16. LBN	382

Senior Women 10.24 km

1. Hellen Obiri KEN	36:14
2. Dera Dida ETH	36:16
3. Letesenbet Gidey ETH	36:24
4. Rachael Chebet UGA	36:47
5. Peruth Chemutai UGA	36:49
6. Tsehay Gemechu ETH	36:56
7. Beatrice Chepkoech KEN	37:12
8. Eva Cherono KEN	37:13
9. Deborah Samum KEN	37:18
10. Zenebu Fikadu ETH	37:24
11. Fotyen Tesfay ETH	37:29
12. Lilian Rengeruk KEN	37:35
13. Juliet Chekwel UGA	37:35
14. Esther Chebet UGA	37:36
15. Anna Emilie Møller DEN	37:51
16. Failuna Matanga TAN	37:56
17. Hawi Feysa ETH	37:59
18. Fionnuala McCormack IRL	37:59
19. Shitaye Eshete BRN	38:08
20. Geneviève Lalonde CAN	38:10
21. Stella Chesang UGA	38:14
22. Liz Westphal FRA	38:18
23. Elena Burkard GER	38:26

24. Darya Mykhaylova UKR	38:41
25. Irene Sánchez-Escribano ESP	38:44
26. Melissa Duncan AUS	38:47
27. Nazret Weldu ERI	38:51
28. Desi Jisa Mokonin BRN	38:51
29. Paige Campbell AUS	38:52
30. Kate Avery GBR	38:55

115 of 118 finished

Team 4 to score. 16 teams completed

1. ETH	21	9. FRA	198
2. KEN	25	10. ESP	210
3. UGA	36	11. TAN	211
4. GBR	132	12. JPN	227
5. AUS	134	13. DEN	229
6. BRN	152	14. PER	278
7. CAN	186	15. CHN	336
8. USA	190	16. LBN	446

U20 Women 5.78 km

1. Beatrice Chebet KEN	20:50
2. Alemitu Tariku ETH	20:50
3. Tsigie Gebreselama ETH	20:50
4. Sarah Chelangat UGA	20:51
5. Girmawit Gebrzihair ETH	20:53
6. Betty Kibet KEN	21:03
7. Mizan Alem ETH	21:09
8. Wede Kefale ETH	21:14
9. Jackline Rotich KEN	21:17
10. Lydia Cheruto KEN	21:44
11. Meselu Kahsay ETH	21:46
12. Mercy Chepkorir KEN	21:49
13. Mercy Jerop KEN-Y	21:54
14. Ayuka Kazama JPN	21:58
15. Ririka Hironaka JPN	22:00

100 of 102 finished

Team 4 to score, 16 teams completed

1. ETH	17	9. MAR	195
2. KEN	26	10. FRA	210
3. JPN	72	11. NZL	232
4. UGA	73	12. CHN	235
5. RSA	132	13. DEN	254
6. CAN	138	14. USA	257
7. GBR	153	15. ESP	281
8. AUS	168	16. PER	346
8. RSA	181	16. ITA	256

Mixed Relay 8.24 km

1. ETH   25:49
(Kebede Endale 6:01, Bone Choluke 6:47, Teddese Lemi 5:51, Fantu Worku 7:10)

2. MAR   26:22
(Soufiane El Bakkali 6:10, Kaoutar Farkoussi 6:51, Abdelaati Iguider 6:02, Rababe Arafi 7:19)

3. KEN   26:29
(Conseslus Kipruto 6:04. Jarinter Mwasya 6:47, Elijah Manangoi 5:50, Winfred Mbithe 7:48)

4. USA	27:01
5. UGA	27:35
6. ESP	27:47
7. CAN	27:57
8. DEN	28:47
9. TAN	28:48
dq. CHN	